Mrs. T

35 … Road,

Apt. 3, RE3-4928

Vancouver 8.

KEY TO FRENCH

I. VOWELS

Key-word No.	Symbol	Final open position		Followed by a LONG consonant		Followed by a SHORT consonant	
1	i	[fi]	fit	[fi:j]	fille	[fis]	fils
2	e	[fe]	fée				
3	ɛ	[fɛ]	(il) fait	[fɛ:t]	fête	[fɛt]	(un) fait
4	a	[fa]	fa	[fa:r]	phare	[fam]	femme
5	ɑ	[bɑ]	bas	[fɑ:z]	phase		
6	ɔ			[fɔ:r]	fort	[fɔl]	folle
7	o	[fo]	faux	[fo:t]	faute		
8	u	[fu]	fou	[fu:r]	four	[ful]	foule
9	y	[fy]	fut	[fy:r]	furent	[fym]	fume
10	ø	[fø]	feu	[fø:tr]	feutre		
11	œ			[œ:r]	heure	[œf]	œuf
12	ə	[fə'zɛ]	faisait				
13	ɛ̃	[fɛ̃]	feint	[fɛ̃:t]	feinte		
14	ɑ̃	[fɑ̃]	fend	[fɑ̃:t]	fente		
15	õ	[fõ]	fond	[fõ:t]	fonte		
16	œ̃	[de'fœ̃]	défunt	[de'fœ̃:t]	défunte		

II. SEMI-VOWELS

		Before vowels		After vowels		Between vowels	
17	j	[pje]	pied	[fi:j]	fille	[kri'je]	crier
18	w	[wi]	oui				
19	ɥ	[ɥit]	huit				

PHONETIC TRANSCRIPTION

III. CONSONANTS

Key-word No.	Symbol	Initial position		Final position	
20	p	[po]	pot	[to:p]	taupe
21	b	[bo]	beau	[o:b]	aube
22	t	[tɑ̃]	tant	[ɑ̃:t]	hante
23	d	[dɑ̃]	dent	[õ:d]	onde
24	k	[kɑ]	cas	[sak]	sac
25	g	[gɑ̃]	gant	[bag]	bague
26	f	[fu]	fou	[tuf]	touffe
27	v	[vu]	vous	[ku:v]	couve
28	s	[sɛl]	sel	[lɛs]	laisse
29	z	[zɛl]	zèle	[lɛ:z]	lèse
30	ʃ	[ʃu]	chou	[buʃ]	bouche
31	ʒ	[ʒu]	joue	[bu:ʒ]	bouge
32	l	[lu]	loup	[ul]	houle
33	m	[mɛ]	mais	[ɛ:m]	aime
34	n	[ny]	nu	[yn]	une
35	ɲ	[(a)ɲo]	agneau	[viɲ]	vigne
36	ṙ	[ru]	roue	[pu:r]	pour

IV. OTHER SYMBOLS

37	h	[la'haʃ]	la hache	The aspirate "h" in Canadian French
38	ʔ	[ləʔo]	le haut	Glottal stop to avoid hiatus
39	*	[le'zɔm]	les *hommes	Shows possibility of "liaison" with preceding syllable
40	'	[sine'ma]	cinéma	Stress mark; shows that *following* syllable is stressed

PRESENTED TO PRÉSENTÉ À

. . J. Hykawy . . . . .

This advance copy of Canada's first bilingual dictionary is presented to you with the compliments of The Royal Bank of Canada to mark the occasion of the Canadian Conference on Education in Montreal, March 4-8, 1962.

Cet exemplaire hors commerce du premier dictionnaire français-anglais rédigé au Canada vous est offert en hommage par La Banque Royale du Canada à l'occasion de la tenue à Montréal de la Conférence canadienne sur l'Education.

ÉDITION ABRÉGÉE

DICTIONNAIRE CANADIEN

FRANÇAIS–ANGLAIS

ANGLAIS–FRANÇAIS

Le présent dictionnaire a été rédigé au
Centre de recherches lexicographiques de l'Université de Montréal,
avec l'approbation du Conseil des Gouverneurs

McCLELLAND AND STEWART LIMITED

CONCISE EDITION

THE CANADIAN DICTIONARY

FRENCH–ENGLISH

ENGLISH–FRENCH

This Dictionary was prepared at the

Lexicographic Research Centre, University of Montreal,

by arrangement with the Board of Governors

⚜ ✿ ⚜ ✿ ⚜ ✿ ⚜ ✿ ⚜ ✿ ⚜ ✿ ⚜ ✿ ⚜ ✿ ⚜ ✿ ⚜ ✿ ⚜

Jean-Paul Vinay, A Q, M.S.R.C.

Pierre Daviault, M.S.R.C.

Henry Alexander, M.A., F.R.S.C.

EDITOR IN CHIEF/RÉDACTEUR EN CHEF

Jean-Paul Vinay, A Q, M.S.R.C.

de la Société Royale du Canada
M.A., *Agrégé de l'Université*
Directeur de la Section de Linguistique
de l'Université de Montréal

EDITORS/RÉDACTEURS

Pierre Daviault

de la Société Royale du Canada
Directeur des Services de Traduction
Gouvernement du Canada
Ottawa

Henry Alexander, M.A., F.R.S.C.

Professor Emeritus of
English Language and Literature
Queen's University
Kingston

GENERAL EDITORS/RÉDACTION

Jean Darbelnet, A Q

Agrégé de l'Université
Professor of French
Bowdoin College
Maine

R. W. Jeanes, B.A.

Docteur de l'Université
Department of French
Victoria College
Toronto

SPECIAL EDITORS/RÉDACTION TECHNIQUE

F. E. L. Priestley, PH.D., F.R.S.C.

Department of English
University College, Toronto
(CANADIAN ENGLISH SPELLING)

Donald E. Hamilton, M.A.

Department of History
Downsview Collegiate Institute
Toronto
(ENGLISH PHONETICS)

Gilles-R. Lefebvre, M.A., PH.D.

Faculté des Lettres
Université de Montréal
(PHONÉTIQUE FRANÇAISE)

Gilles des Marchais, M.A.

Romance Language Department
Mount Allison University
Sackville, N.B.
(CLASSIFICATION DES VERBES FRANÇAIS)

PREFACE

It is a curious fact that as a bilingual country, Canada has until now lacked something that is essential to communication—an authoritative dictionary. This book has been designed to remedy that deficiency by providing a Canadian standard for precise translation, communication and understanding between our two great cultures.

The concise edition of *The Canadian Dictionary* is the first published result of work that began at the University of Montreal in 1954. Shortly afterwards, under the auspices of the Board of Governors of the University and in association with the publishers, the Lexicographic Research Centre was established to study Canada's two official languages.

This dictionary, the result of seven years of intensive research at the Centre, and of many more years of preparation by its editors, represents the combined skills of linguists, editors, and translators from all parts of Canada and indeed of North America. As editor-in-chief I am indebted for their contributions to all those whose names appear in this volume and to many others. To them must go the credit for the merits of this dictionary. The major share of responsibility for its limitations must be mine.

I wish to emphasize that this is not a dialect or regional dictionary. The

PRÉFACE

Il est curieux de constater que le Canada, pays bilingue, ne disposait pas jusqu'ici de l'instrument essentiel à toute communication linguistique: un dictionnaire bilingue spécialement conçu pour ses besoins. Dans l'espoir de remédier à cette situation, nous avons composé le *Dictionnaire canadien*, que nous dédions à tous ceux qui veulent connaître, apprécier et interpréter nos deux grandes cultures nationales.

La présente *Édition abrégée* est le premier résultat concret des travaux en lexicographie commencés à l'Université de Montréal dès 1954. Peu de temps après cette date, le Conseil des Gouverneurs de l'université, ayant passé un accord avec les éditeurs, créa un *Centre de Recherches lexicographiques* chargé d'étudier et de décrire les deux langues officielles du Canada.

Le dictionnaire que nous présentons aujourd'hui, couronnement de sept années de recherches, a bénéficié au premier chef de la longue expérience de mes deux collègues, Pierre Daviault et Henry Alexander. C'est également la synthèse des efforts de nombreux collaborateurs venus de différentes parties du Canada et même des États-Unis. En ma qualité de rédacteur en chef, je tiens à remercier tous ceux dont les noms paraissent aux pages qui suivent, et bien d'autres encore: le mérite de cet ouvrage leur revient, tandis que m'incombent en large part les erreurs qui pourraient s'y trouver.

Qu'il me soit permis de souligner que le présent ouvrage n'est ni un glossaire dialectal, ni un dictionnaire régional. Le lecteur y trouvera toutes les

reader will find in its pages the rules and usage which reflect international standards of French and English, but he will also find direct guidance on the terminology and style which are peculiar to the French and English of Canada.

Many of the existing bilingual dictionaries merely give translations without placing the words in proper context and without indicating the level of use. With this in mind we have wherever possible given patterns of usage which will enable the student to use effectively the treasure-house of words contained in the language.

To obtain the best possible value from this dictionary the reader should devote close study to the preliminary pages in which the editors have set out the rules and principles on which it has been compiled.

On behalf of the University of Montreal, the Publishers and Editorial Board I should like to express thanks to the Biermans Foundation for the donation of funds that made the project possible.

J.-P. V.

règles de morphologie et d'usage qui relèvent de la norme internationale du français et de l'anglais modernes; mais il trouvera également des données précises sur la phonétique, le lexique et les tours propres au français et à l'anglais du Canada.

Trop de dictionnaires bilingues se contentent de donner des équivalents sans replacer les termes dans leur contexte ou sans en indiquer le niveau stylistique. Nous avons voulu éviter ce reproche en facilitant au lecteur, dans toute la mesure du possible, l'utilisation rationnelle des richesses lexicales mises à sa disposition.

Dans ce but, je ne saurais trop recommander la lecture attentive des pages de l'*Introduction*, où les différents collaborateurs de l'ouvrage expliquent les principes suivis au cours de notre commun travail.

Au nom de l'Université de Montréal, au nom des éditeurs et au mien propre, je voudrais, en terminant, remercier la Fondation Biermans de l'aide matérielle qui rendit possible la réalisation de nos travaux.

J.-P. V.

NOTE ON THE ENGLISH SPELLING

There has been in the past no generally accepted standard for Canadian spelling of English—to correspond to the Oxford or Webster dictionaries for British and American—but there has arisen a generally accepted practice reflected in government publications, the products of the principal publishing houses, and many Canadian journals and periodicals. It is this general practice which this dictionary records. For the vast majority of words in the language there is no difference between Canadian, American, and British spelling; the comparative few which do show variation naturally attract most attention.

The chief cases in which usage differs in American and British English, and the generally preferred Canadian usages, are as follows:

	PREFERRED CANADIAN USAGE
1. *-our*, *-or* (honour, labour)	*-our*
2. *-re*, *-er* (centre, theatre)	*-re*
3. *-ize*, *-ise* (recognize, harmonize)	*-ize*
4. *-ae*, *-e* (aesthetic, encyclopaedia)	*-ae*
5. *-ce*, *-se* (defence, licence)	*-ce*
6. *-ll-*, *-l-* (woollen, traveller, levelling)	*-ll*

A number of other words also vary in American and British usage, and in these Canadian usage coincides sometimes with the one, sometimes with the other, and occasionally with neither. Canadians usually call a man who makes a bet a *bettor* (not *better*); they usually spell *cheque* (not *check*), *employee* (not *employe*), *grey* (not *gray*), *jail* (rather than *gaol*), *mould*, *mouldy*, *moult* (rather than *mold*, *moldy*, *molt*), *moustache* (not *mustache*), *pajama* (not *pyjama*), *plough* (rather than *plow*), *premise* (rather than *premiss*), *syrup* (rather than *sirop*), *tire* (not *tyre*), and *wagon* (not *waggon*).

The one aspect of spelling upon which there is no agreement, and which no one has so far successfully systematized, is the treatment of compound words. These are sometimes printed "solid" (*windmill*), sometimes with a hyphen (*wash-out*), and sometimes separately (*hand brake*).

American practice shows a greater tendency than British to eliminate hyphens, but the difference is one of degree, modern usage generally being to limit hyphenated forms as much as possible. An attempt has been made in this dictionary to prescribe a limited use of hyphens.

1. Compounds are printed separately unless the compound offers a special reason for doing otherwise.
2. The compound is printed solid if (a) the separate meanings are largely submerged in the compound (as in *blackboard*, *horsepower*) or if (b) the separate meanings are retained, but their association is so invariable as to need special emphasis for separation (as in *blackbird*, *fireplace*, *wildcat*).
3. Hyphenation is limited to the following cases: (a) compound adjectives (*red-blooded*, *cross-country*); (b) multiple compounds (*man of-war*, *forget-me-not*); (c) with normal compounds to avoid confusion (*de-ice*, *re-form*—as distinct from *reform*); (d) with verb and adverb if printing solid would create confusion through adjacent vowels (*flare-up*, *drive-in*, but *knockout*, *breakdown*); (e) with a prefix and proper name or title (*vice-president*, *post-Hellenic*); (f) with noun and agential noun (*shock-absorber*, *engine-driver*); (g) with agential noun and adverb (*passer-by*, *runner-up*); (h) with verb and noun (*cure-all*, *fly-wheel*).

ENGLISH ABBREVIATIONS

abbr./eviation
absol./ute(ly)
abus./ively
Acct., Accounting
Acous./tics
adj./ective
Adm(in)./istration
adv./erb(ially)
Aero./nautics
Agric./ulture
Alg./ebra
Anat./omy
Anthr./opology
Antiq./uity
approx./imately
Arch./itecture
art./icle
Artil./lery
Astr./onomy
attrib./utive(ly)
Auto./mobilism
aux./iliary
Bact./eriology
Bibl./ical
Biol./ogy
Bot./any
Br./itish
©, Canada, Canadian, Canadianism
card./inal
Chem./istry
Cin./ematography
coll./ective
Com./merce
compar./ative
cond./itional
conj./unction
def./inite
dem./onstrative
Den./tistry
dim./inutive
dir./ect
Econ./omics
e.g., for example
Elect./ricity
Eng./lish
Engr., Engineering
esp./ecially
&c., et cetera
ex./ample
except./ion
exclam./ative
ext., by extension
f., feminine
Fam./iliar
Fig./urative
Fin./ance
Fortif./ications
Fr., French, France
gen./eral(ly)
Geog./raphy
Geol./ogy
Geom./etry
Govt., Government
Gram./mar
Gymn./astics
Her./aldry
Hist./ory
Hyg./iene
i.e., id est, that is
imperat./ive
impers./onal
indef./inite
Ind./ian (Amerindian)
indic./ative
ind./irect
Ind(us)./try
inf./initive
Ins./urance
interj./ection
interrog./ation
intr./ansitive
inv(ar)./iable
Iron./ical
irreg./ular
Journ./alism
Jur./isprudence
Lat./in
Ling./uistics
Lit./erary
Loc./ution
m., masculine
Math./ematics
Meas./ure
Mec./hanics
Med./icine
Metall./urgy
Mil./itary
Mus./ic
Myth./ology
n., noun
Naut./ical
neg./ative
num./eral
obj./ect
Onomat./opeia
Opt./ics
ord./inal
Ornith./ology
o's, one's
o.s., oneself
Parl./iament
Pedag./ogy
Pej./orative
Pers./on(al)
Pharm./acy
Phil./osophy
Phon./etics
Phot./ography
Phys./ics
pl(ur)./al
Poet./ical
Pol./itics
poss./essive
p.p., past participle
pref./ix
prep./osition
pr(es).part., present participle
princ./ipally
Print./ing
pron./oun, pronominal
Prot./estant(ism)
Prov./erb
Psych./ology
Pub./licity
q.v., quod vide, see
Rail./ways
R.C., Roman Catholic
Rel./igion
s(ing)./ular
Sch./ool
Sculp./ture
Sl./ang
s.o., someone
s.o.'s, someone's
Sport./ing
sth., something
subj./ect
subjunc./tive
suff./ix
superl./ative
Surg./ery
syn./onym
Tech./nical
Tel./ephone
Teleg./raph
Thea(t)./re
tr./ansitive
Typ./ography
UN, United Nations
Univ./ersity
US, American
usual./ly
v., verb
Var./iation
Vulg./ar
Zool./ogy

EXPLANATION OF SYMBOLS

(1) , A comma separates an example from its translation. The comma is also used to separate equivalent translations or shades of stylistic difference. Ex: **unique** . . . only, single, the only one. Used in the examples, the comma separates two possible translations on the same semantic level.

(2) ; A semicolon separates two translations of a single word located on different semantic levels. Ex: **abstraction** . . . abstraction *f*; vol *m*. Where the semantic division is more definite, numbers are used.

(3) **1.2.** Boldface numerals define the semantic subdivisions of a single entry when it is useful to emphasize these distinctions.

(4) / A slant sign indicates the possibility of substituting, in an example, one segment of the utterance for another. Ex: *Whose car did you come in?* Dans quelle auto, Dans l'auto de qui/êtes-vous venu? To be read: Dans quelle auto êtes-vous venu? or Dans l'auto de qui êtes-vous venu?

(5) **:** For a given meaning a colon indicates the beginning of the examples, the purpose of which is to define the translations or to show special uses.

(6) ‖ Two vertical lines separate changes in the part of speech occurring within one entry.

(7) + A plus sign indicates that the word (or a part of it) can be followed by a grammatical element: suffix, preposition, verbal endings, &c. Ex: **faire** (+ infin.) refers to forms of the type *faire cuire*. In the table of French verbs, **aim+** shows the stem from which the verb forms *aimons, aimez, &c.*, are constructed.

(8) = An equals sign gives the exact meaning of abbreviations. Ex: *a.m.* [= *ante meridiem*]. It sometimes indicates a synonym to which the reader may refer. Ex: A.B. (=B.A.).

(9) ∼ A curved line replaces the main entry wherever it does not undergo a spelling change: **call,** ∼ *up,* is to be read *call, call up.*

(10) [ ] Brackets enclose explanations which are intended to make clear a meaning or a point of grammar: **baisser** [sight, strength, &c.] to fail, defines the semantic area of **baisser**, but the words in brackets are not to be used in translating. Brackets are likewise used to present a grammatical or stylistic explanation. Ex: **bateau** *n.m.*, boat [for large vessels, use NAVIRE].

(11) - A hyphen in the main entries replaces an unchanged segment of a word to which another segment is added. Ex: **ancien, -ne** is to be read *ancien, ancienne*; **antenna, -s** is to be read *antenna, antennas.*

(12) . . . Three dots replace a word group or a word which can be inserted in an utterance, in a position which must be stated precisely. Ex: *to give . . . to*; *ne . . . guère.* Three dots can also show the incompleteness of an example. Ex: *I told you that . . .*

(13) ☞ A pointing hand draws attention to points of grammar or usage.

(14) → An arrow draws attention to a translation which is not literal and is of special interest for comparative stylistics. Ex: *when* → date à laquelle, époque à laquelle.

(15) × An × draws attention to the presence of a *deceptive cognate*, a word resembling the heading but expressing an entirely different meaning. Ex: **presently** *adv.* [×] dans quelques instants, bientôt; in some cases the corresponding cognate is shown in brackets [× présentement], and for additional information reference may be made to it.

(16) ŒIL CHILD Words printed in small capitals are references to the French or to the English part of the Dictionary; the reader can refer to either for supple-

mentary information, especially on grammar. For certain very common irregular forms, small capitals are used to refer the reader to the main heading: **yeux** cf. ŒIL; **children** cf. CHILD.

(17) © A circled © indicates a Canadianism. This term is used to mean either a word peculiar to Canada, e.g. © *raquetteur*, © *komatik*, or a usage peculiar to Canada, e.g. © *banc de neige*.

(18) [Abus.] In some cases a Canadianism may be termed an abuse of language; such cases are considered to be popular forms contrary to the spirit of the language. The standard international equivalent is usually given with such terms. Ex: **used car**, © [Abus.] char usagé; [Fr.] auto(mobile) d'occasion.

(19) * An asterisk indicates a neologism or a word which is not yet fully accepted in current use. Ex: ***oléoduc.** In French phonetic transcription the asterisk specifies *h* "aspirate."

(20) † A dagger indicates a form or a meaning which is archaic or purely literary.

(21) (*m*) In cases in which an entry or a translation is both *adjective* and *noun*, the gender of the noun is shown in parentheses. Ex: *annexe* (*f*). When a word is both *m.* and *f.* with the same form for both, this is shown as *m*/*f*.

(22) | A single vertical line separates the stem from its endings, both in the spelling in the main entry and in the phonetic transcriptions. The vertical line indicates the point after which the word changes, or the presence of a prefix, e.g. **vénéneu|x, -se** should be read *vénéneux, vénéneuse*; **un|able,** *unable* as opposed to *until.*

NOTES ON THE USE OF THE FRENCH-ENGLISH SECTION

1. ADJECTIVES

The entry is always given in the basic masculine singular form. The feminine form is given whenever this form exists; e.g. **usurpat|eur, -rice** should be read *usurpateur, usurpatrice*. The plural is given only if it is not formed according to the usual rules.

2. COMPARISON: *Adjectives and Adverbs*

The comparative and superlative degrees of comparison are not given when formed according to the usual rules. Adjectives such as *bon,* whose comparative and superlative forms are irregular, show these forms.

3. NOUNS

The entry is always the basic masculine singular, or feminine singular form. Whenever there is both a masculine and a feminine form, both are given, the masculine form being placed first. E.g. **chanteu|r, -se** should be read *chanteur, chanteuse*. The plural form is not given if it is formed according to the usual grammatical rules.

4. COMPOUND NOUNS

The plural of the compound noun is generally given, as there is no regular system for its formation. In general, the meaning of the compound dictates which part is to be pluralized, e.g. *arrière-pensée, arrière-pensées*. But often this logic is ignored.

5. VERBS

All verbs are found under the uninflected infinitive form, and are classified as (a) *transitive*, i.e. requiring an object unless in the absolute sense, e.g. *Il boit de l'eau*, He drinks water, or (abs.) *Il boit*, He drinks; (b) *intransitive*, i.e., used without an object, e.g. *Il boite*, He limps; (c) *pronominal* (reflexive), e.g. *Ma chemise s'use*, My shirt is wearing out. The pronominal (reflexive) verbs are listed immediately after their non-reflexive form, e.g. **user** [y'ze] #3 *v. intr.* . . . ‖ *v. tr.* . . . ‖ **s'user,** *v. pron.*

The active compound tenses of most French verbs are formed with the verb *avoir*. Those exceptional verbs which form their compound tenses with the verb *être* are followed by the notation (conj. ÊTRE). The pronominal (reflexive) verbs form their compound tenses with *être*.

Because of the complex verbal system in French, the reader is referred by a number (#3, #5, &c.) to the Table of French Verbs (see p. xiv). The more irregular forms are given after the main entry, e.g. **voyager, voyageant,** #5; **vivre, vivant, vécu,** #52.

Whenever a conjugated form or a participle differs radically in spelling from the infinitive, this form is given as an entry and the reader is then referred to the infinitive, e.g. **vaille,** &c. cf. VALOIR.

TABLE OF FRENCH VERBS

The table on page xiv gives a treatment of the French verb conjugation in which all so-called irregularities have been reduced to a pattern common to all verbs. The table emphasizes the importance of the verb *stems*, which may undergo variation both phonetically and in spelling. Once the stems are known, they can be used in conjunction with the fixed sets of endings which are common to all tenses of the conjugation, within a given group of verbs. The Dictionary follows the now classical scheme of assigning all French verbs to three groups:

Group I: The infinitive ends in *-er*, the first person singular of the present indicative in *-e*, the present participle in *-ant*. EXAMPLE: *aimer, j'aime, aimant, j'ai aimé* (past participle).

Group II: The infinitive ends in *-ir*, the first person singular of the present indicative in *-is*, the present participle in *-issant*. EXAMPLE: *finir, je finis, finissant, j'ai fini* (past participle).

Group III: Irregular verbs not falling into the two previous groups. The infinitives end in *-oir*, or *-re*, or *-ir* (but without the *-iss-* forms of Group II), and the other tenses are irregular. EXAMPLES: *vouloir, je veux, voulant, j'ai voulu; prendre, je prends, prenant, j'ai pris; dormir, je dors, dormant, j'ai dormi.*

The table lists at the beginning the endings which are common to verbs of all groups: the imperfect indicative, the future, the conditional, the present subjunctive, the imperfect subjunctive, and the present participle.

The present indicative, past definite, and present imperative endings, which vary from one verb group to the other, are listed at the beginning of each verb group. The past participle and present infinitive endings of the Group III verbs, which are unpredictable, are listed separately for each verb.

The numbers at the left side of the table, preceded by a # sign, are the same as those by which any verb in the Dictionary is referred to the model verb in the table. The verb in the Dictionary follows the same conjugation as the given model.

The plus sign, following a stem, is used here to indicate that the endings should follow immediately after it. The numerals following the stem (2, 4, 5, 6, &c.) refer to the persons of the verb for which this stem should be used.

The table does not give compound tenses, which are made up of a given simple tense of an auxiliary followed by the past participle of the verb. The table does, however, list past participles. The auxiliaries, conjugated in all tenses, will be found in any good grammar.

The body of the Dictionary has been so compiled as to aid students who in their reading come upon a difficult, uncommon, or variable verb form. For verbs in Groups II and III, the Dictionary has entries for all forms of the verb which have a stem differing from the infinitive. The entries **cru** and **croyant,** for example, send the reader to **croire,** which is identified as a model #74 verb; **trayant** refers him to **traire,** a model #38 verb. For verbs in Group I, the infinitive only is given. And for verbs which display only regular spelling shifts, as ç from c, or ge from g, the Dictionary does not list as entries all forms which show this shift. Verbs in Group II list with the infinitive the present participle and the past participle, to avoid confusion with Group III verbs which have a similar infinitive ending.

TABLE OF FRENCH VERBS

	I PRESENT INDICATIVE	II PAST DEFINITE	III IMPERFECT INDICATIVE	IV FUTURE	V CONDITIONAL
Endings valid for all conjugation models	SEE BELOW FOR VERBS GROUPS I, II, III		1.+ais 2.+ais 3.+ait 4.+ions 5.+iez 6.+aient	1.+rai 2.+ras 3.+ra 4.+rons 5.+rez 6.+ront	1.+rais 2.+rais 3.+rait 4.+rions 5.+riez 6.+raient
Endings valid for verbs of Group I	1.+e 2.+es 3.+e 4.+ons 5.+ez 6.+ent	1.+ai 2.+as 3.+a 4.+âmes 5.+âtes 6.+èrent	ENDINGS: ABOVE		
GROUP I MODEL #3	aim+	aim+	aim+	aime+	aime+
#4	agac+ 1, 2, 3, 5, 6 agaç+4	agaç+ 1, 2, 3, 4, 5 agac+6	agaç+ 1, 2, 3, 6 agac+4, 5	agace+	agace+
#5	rag+ 1, 2, 3, 5, 6 rage+4	rage+ 1, 2, 3, 4, 5 rag+6	rage+ 1, 2, 3, 6 rag+4, 5	rage+	rage+
#6	rapièc+ 1, 2, 3, 6 rapiéç+4 rapiéc+5	rapiéç+ 1, 2, 3, 4, 5 rapiéc+6	rapiéç+ 1, 2, 3, 6 rapiéc+4, 5	rapiéce+	rapiéce+
#7	sièg+ 1, 2, 3, 6 siége+4 siég+5	siége+ 1, 2, 3, 4, 5 siég+6	siége+ 1, 2, 3, 6 siég+4, 5	siége+	siége+
#8	appell+ 1, 2, 3, 6 appel+4, 5	appel+	appel+	appelle+	appelle+
#9	cèl+ 1, 2, 3, 6 cel+4, 5	cel+	cel+	cèle+	cèle+
#10	cèd+ 1, 2, 3, 6 céd+4, 5	céd+	céd+	céde+	céde+
#11	pai+/pay+ 1, 2, 3, 6 pay+4, 5	pay+	pay+	paie+ paye+	paie+ paye+
#12	broi+ 1, 2, 3, 6 broy+4, 5	broy+	broy+	broie+	broie+
#13	envoi+ 1, 2, 3, 6 envoy+4, 5	envoy+	envoy+	enver+	enver+
#14	v+ais +as +a all+ons +ez v+ont	all+	all+	i+	i+
#15	dépèc+ 1, 2, 3, 6 dépeç+4 dépec+5	dépeç+ 1, 2, 3, 4, 5 dépec+6	dépeç+ 1, 2, 3, 6 dépec+4, 5	dépèce+	dépèce+
#16	grassey+	grassey+	grassey+	grasseye+	grasseye+

VI PRESENT SUBJUNCTIVE	**VII** IMPERFECT SUBJUNCTIVE	**VIII** IMPERATIVE	**IX** PRESENT PARTICIPLE	**X** PAST PARTICIPLE	**XI** INFINITIVE
1.+e 2.+es 3.+e 4.+ions 5.+iez 6.+ent	1.+sse 2.+sses 3.+^t 4.+ssions 5.+ssiez 6.+ssent	SEE BELOW FOR VERBS GROUPS I, II, III	+ant	SEE BELOW FOR VERBS GROUPS I, II, III	
ENDINGS: ABOVE		1.+— 2.+e 3.+— 4.+ons 5.+ez 6.+—		+é ENDING: ABOVE	+er
aim+	aima+	aim+	aim+	aim+	aim+
agac+	agaça+	agac+2, 5 agaç+4	agaç+	agac+	agac+
rag+	ragea+	rag+2, 5 rage+4	rage+	rag+	rag+
rapièc+ 1, 2, 3, 6 rapiéc+4, 5	rapiéça+	rapièc+2 rapiéç+4 rapiéc+5	rapiéç+	rapiéc+	rapiéc+
sièg+ 1, 2, 3, 6 siég+4, 5	siégea+	sièg+2 siége+4 siég+5	siége+	siég+	siég+
appell+ 1, 2, 3, 6 appel+4, 5	appela+	appell+2 appel+4, 5	appel+	appel+	appel+
cèl+ 1, 2, 3, 6 cel+4, 5	cela+	cèl+2, cel+4, 5	cel+	cel+	cel+
cèd+ 1, 2, 3, 6 céd+4, 5	céda+	cèd+2, céd+4, 5	céd+	céd+	céd+
pai+/pay+ 1, 2, 3, 6 pay+4, 5	paya+	pai+, pay+2 pay+4, 5	pay+	pay+	pay+
broi+ 1, 2, 3, 6 broy+4, 5	broya+	broi+2 broy+4, 5	broy+	broy+	broy+
envoi+ 1, 2, 3, 6 envoy+4, 5	envoya+	envoi+2 envoy+4, 5	envoy+	envoy+	envoy+
aill+ 1, 2, 3, 6 all+4, 5	alla+	v+a all+ons +ez	all+	all+	all+
dépèc+ 1, 2, 3, 6 dépec+4 dépec+5	dépeça+	dépèc+2 dépeç+4 dépec+5	dépeç+	dépec+	dépec+
grassey+	grasseya+	grassey+	grassey+	grassey+	grassey+

		I PRESENT INDICATIVE	II PAST DEFINITE	III IMPERFECT INDICATIVE	IV FUTURE	V CONDITIONAL
	Endings valid for verbs of Group **II**	1.+s 2.+s 3.+t 4.+ons 5.+ez 6.+ent	1.+is 2.+is 3.+it 4.+îmes 5.+îtes 6.+irent	ENDINGS: SEE P. XIV		
GROUP II	MODEL #17	fini+1, 2, 3 finiss+ 4, 5, 6	fin+	finiss+	fini+	fini+
GROUP II	#18	haï+ 1, 2, 3 haïss+ 4, 5, 6	haï+s +s +t +mes +tes +rent	haïss+	haï+	haï+
	Endings valid for verbs of Group **III**	1.+s 2.+s 3.+t 4.+ons 5.+ez 6.+ent	1.+s 2.+s 3.+t 4.+^mes 5.+^tes 6.+rent	ENDINGS: SEE P. XIV		
GROUP III	MODEL #19	assaill+ *as* #3	assailli+	assaill+	assailli+	assailli+
GROUP III	#20	cueill+ *as* #3	cueilli+	cueill+	cueille+	cueille+
GROUP III	#21	dor+1, 2, 3 dorm+ 4, 5, 6	dormi+	dorm+	dormi+	dormi+
GROUP III	#22	tienn+1, 2, 3 ten+4, 5 tienn+6	t+ins +ins +înt +înmes +întes +inrent	ten+	tiend+	tiend+
GROUP III	#23	acquier+ 1, 2, 3 acquér+ 4, 5 acquièr+6	acqui+	acquér+	acquer+	acquer+
GROUP III	#24	cour+	couru+	cour+	cour+	cour+
GROUP III	#25	ouvr+ *as* #3	ouvri+	ouvr+	ouvri+	ouvri+
GROUP III	#26	men+1, 2, 3 ment+4, 5, 6	menti+	ment+	menti+	menti+
GROUP III	#27	fui+ 1, 2, 3, 6 fuy+4, 5	fui+	fuy+	fui+	fui+
GROUP III	#28	ser+1, 2, 3 serv+4, 5, 6	servi+	serv+	servi+	servi+
GROUP III	#29	vau+x +x +t val+4, 5, 6	valu+	val+	vaud+	vaud+
GROUP III	#30	assoi+ 1, 2, 3, 6 assoy+4, 5	assi+	assoy+	assoi+	assoi+

VI PRESENT SUBJUNCTIVE	VII IMPERFECT SUBJUNCTIVE	VIII IMPERATIVE	IX PRESENT PARTICIPLE	X PAST PARTICIPLE	XI INFINITIVE
ENDINGS: SEE P. XV		1.+— 2.+s 3.+— 4.+ons 5.+ez 6.+—	ENDING: P. XV	+i	+ir
finiss+	fini+	fini+2 finiss+4, 5	finiss+	fin+	fin+
haïss+	haï+sse +sses +t +ssions +ssiez +ssent	haï+2, haïss+4, 5	haïss+	ha+ï	ha+ïr
ENDINGS: SEE P. XV		1.+— 2.+s 3.+— 4.+ons 5.+ez 6.+—	ENDING: P. XV	COMPLETE FORMS SHOWN BELOW	
assaill+	assailli+	assaill+ as #3	assaill+	assaill+i	assaill+ir
cueill+	cueilli+	cueill+ as #3	cueill+	cueill+i	cueill+ir
dorm+	dormi+	dor+2 dorm+4, 5	dorm+	dorm+i	dorm+ir
tienn+1, 2, 3, 6 ten+4, 5	t+insse +insses +înt +inssions +inssiez +inssent	tien+2 ten+4, 5	ten+	ten+u	ten+ir
acquièr+ 1, 2, 3, 6 acquér+4, 5	acqui+	acquier+2 acquér+ 4, 5	acquér+	acqu+is	acquér+ir
cour+ ouvr+	couru+ ouvri+	cour+ ouvr+ as #3	cour+ ouvr+	cour+u ouv+ert	cour+ir ouvr+ir
ment+	menti+	men+2 ment+4, 5	ment+	ment+i	ment+ir
fui+1, 2, 3, 6 fuy+4, 5	fui+	fui+2 fuy+4, 5	fuy+	fu+i	fu+ir
serv+	servi+	ser+2 serv+4, 5	serv+	serv+i	serv+ir
vaill+ 1, 2, 3, 6 val+4, 5	valu+	vau+x val+4, 5	val+	val+u	val+oir
assoi+ 1, 2, 3, 6 assoy+4, 5	assi+	assoi+2 assoy+4, 5	assoy+	ass+is	ass+eoir

		I PRESENT INDICATIVE	II PAST DEFINITE	III IMPERFECT INDICATIVE	IV FUTURE	V CONDITIONAL
		ENDINGS: SEE P. XVI		ENDINGS: SEE P. XIV		
MODEL	#31	assied+ 1, 2 assied assey+ 4, 5, 6	assi+	assey+	asseye+ assié+	asseye+ assié+
	#32	voi+ 1, 2, 3, 6 voy+4, 5	vi+	voy+	ver+	ver+
	#33	meu+1, 2, 3 mouv+4, 5 meuv+6	mu+	mouv+	mouv+	mouv+
	#34	reçoi+ 1, 2, 3 recev+4, 5 reçoiv+6,	reçu+	recev+	recev+	recev+
	#35	vainc+1, 2 vainc vainqu+ 4, 5, 6	vainqui+	vainqu+	vainc+	vainc+
	#36	crain+1, 2, 3 craign+ 4, 5, 6	craigni+	craign+	craind+	craind+
	#37	fai+1, 2, 3 fais+4 fait+5 f +6	fi+	fais+	fe+	fe+
GROUP III	#38	trai+ 1, 2, 3, 6 tray+4, 5	*(no form)*	tray+	trai+	trai+
	#39	nai+1, 2 naî+t naiss+ 4, 5, 6	naqui+	naiss+	naît+	naît+
	#40	connai+ 1, 2 connaî+t connaiss+ 4, 5, 6	connu+	connaiss+	connaît+	connaît+
	#41	prend+1, 2 prend pren+4, 5 prenn+6	pri+	pren+	prend+	prend+
	#42	fend+1, 2 fend fend +4, 5, 6	fendi+	fend+	fend+	fend+
	#43	bat+1, 2 bat batt+4, 5, 6	batti+	batt+	batt+	batt+
	#44	met+1, 2 met mett+4, 5, 6	mi+	mett+	mett+	mett+
	#45	di+1, 2, 3 dis+4, 6 dit+5	di+	dis+	di+	di+
	#46	médi+1, 2, 3 médis+ 4, 5, 6	médi+	médis+	médi+	médi+
	#47	maudi+ 1, 2, 3 maudiss+ 4, 5, 6	maudi+	maudiss+	maudi+	maudi+

VI PRESENT SUBJUNCTIVE	VII IMPERFECT SUBJUNCTIVE	VIII IMPERATIVE	IX PRESENT PARTICIPLE	X PAST PARTICIPLE	XI INFINITIVE
ENDINGS: SEE P. XV		ENDINGS: P. XVII	ENDING: P. XV	COMPLETE FORMS SHOWN BELOW	
assey+	assi+	assied+2 assey+4, 5	assey+	ass+is	ass+eoir
voi+ 1, 2, 3, 6 voy+4, 5	vi+	voi+2 voy+4, 5	voy+	v+u	v+oir
meuv+ 1, 2, 3, 6 mouv+4, 5	mu+	meu+2 mouv+4, 5	mouv+	m+û	mouv+oir
reçoiv+ 1, 2, 3, 6 recev+4, 5	reçu+	reçoi+2 recev+4, 5	recev+	reç+u	recev+oir
vainqu+	vainqui+	vainc+2 vainqu+4, 5	vainqu+	vainc+u	vainc+re
craign+	craigni+	crain+2 craign+4, 5	craign+	crain+t	craind+re
fass+	fi+	fui+2 fais+ons fait+es	fais+	fai+t	fai+re
trai+ 1, 2, 3, 6 tray+4, 5	(*no form*)	trai+2 tray+4, 5	tray+	trai+t	trai+re
naiss+	naqui+	nai+2 naiss+4, 5	naiss+	n+é	naît+re
connaiss+	connu+	connai+2 connaiss+ 4, 5	connaiss+	conn+u	connaît+re
prenn+1, 2, 3, 6 pren+4, 5	pri+	prend+2 pren+4, 5	pren+	pr+is	prend+re
fend+	fendi+	fend+	fend+	fend+u	fend+re
batt+	batti+	bat+2 batt+4, 5	batt+	batt+u	batt+re
mett+	mi+	met+2 mett+4, 5	mett+	m+is	mett+re
dis+	di+	di+2 dis+4 dit+5	dis+	di+t	di+re
médis+	médi+	médi+2 médis+ 4, 5	médis+	médi+t	médi+re
maudiss+	maudi+	maudi+2 maudiss+ 4, 5	maudiss+	maudi+t	maudi+re

		I PRESENT INDICATIVE	II PAST DEFINITE	III IMPERFECT INDICATIVE	IV FUTURE	V CONDITIONAL
		ENDINGS: SEE P. XVI		ENDINGS: SEE P. XIV		
MODEL	#48	écri+1, 2, 3 écriv+4, 5, 6	écrivi+	écriv+	écri+	écri+
	#49	li+1, 2, 3 lis+4, 5, 6	lu+	lis+	li+	li+
	#50	ri+	ri+	ri+	ri+	ri+
	#51	sui+1, 2, 3 suiv+4, 5, 6	suivi+	suiv+	suiv+	suiv+
	#52	vi+1, 2, 3 viv+4, 5, 6	vécu+	viv+	viv+	viv+
	#52A	romp+	rompi+	romp+	romp+	romp+
	#53	clo+1, 2, 3 (*no form*) (*no form*) clos+ent	(*no form*)	(*no form*)	clo+	clo+
	#54	coud+ 1, 2 coud cous+4, 5, 6	cousi+	cous+	coud+	coud+
	#55	résou+ 1, 2, 3 résolv+ 4, 5, 6	résolu+	résolv+	résoud+	résoud+
	#56	cui+1, 2, 3 cuis+4, 5, 6	cuisi+	cuis+	cui+	cui+
	#57	nui+1, 2, 3 nuis+4, 5, 6	nuisi+	nuis+	nui+	nui+
GROUP III	#58	conclu+	conclu+	conclu+	conclu+	conclu+
	#59	(*no form*) 1, 2, 3 défaill+ 4, 5, 6	défailli+	défaill+	(*no form*)	(*no form*)
	#60	(*no form*)	ou+ïs +ïs +ït +ïmes +ïtes +ïrent	(*no form*)	(*no form*)	(*no form*)
	#61	bou+1, 2, 3 bouill+ 4, 5, 6	bouilli+	bouill+	bouilli+	bouilli+
	#61A	advien+3	adv+int	adven+3	adviend+3	adviend+3
	#62	meur+ 1, 2, 3, 6 mour+4, 5	mouru+	mour+	mour+	mour+
	#63	gi+1, 2 gî+t gis+4, 5, 6	(*no form*)	gis+	(*no form*)	(*no form*)
	#64	déchoi+ 1, 2, 3, 6 déchoy+4, 5,	déchu+	déchoy+	décher+	décher+
	#65	veu+x +x +t voul+4, 5 veul+6	voulu+	voul+	voud+	voud+
	#66	sied+(3) sié+6	(*no form*)	sey+3, 6	sié+3, 6	sié+3, 6
	#66A	(*no form*)	(*no form*)	(*no form*)	(*no form*)	(*no form*)
	#67	messied+ 3(r)	(*no form*)	messey+3	messié+3	messié+3

VI PRESENT SUBJUNCTIVE	VII IMPERFECT SUBJUNCTIVE	VIII IMPERATIVE	IX PRESENT PARTICIPLE	X PAST PARTICIPLE	XI INFINITIVE
ENDINGS: SEE P. XV		ENDINGS: P. XVII	ENDING: P. XV	COMPLETE FORMS SHOWN BELOW	
écriv+	écrivi+	écri+2 écriv+4, 5	écriv+	écri+t	écri+re
lis+	lu+	li+2 lis+4, 5	lis+	l+u	li+re
ri+	ri+	ri+	ri+	r+i	ri+re
suiv+	suivi+	sui+2 suiv+4, 5	suiv+	suiv+i	suiv+re
viv+	vécu+	vi+2 viv+4, 5	viv+	véc+u	viv+re
romp+	rompi+	romp+	romp+	romp+u	romp+re
clos+	(*no form*)	clo+2 (*no form*) clo+4, 5	clos+	clo+s	clo+re
cous+	cousi+	coud+2 cous+4, 5	cous+	cous+u	coud+re
résolv+	résolu+	résou+2 résolv+ 4, 5	résolv+	résou+s résol+u	résoud+re
cuis+	cuisi+	cui+2 cuis+4, 5	cuis+	cui+t	cui+re
nuis+	nuisi+	nui+2 nuis+4, 5	nuis+	nu+i	nui+re
conclu+	conclu+	conclu+	conclu+	concl+u	conclu+re
(*no form*)	défailli+	(*no form*)	défaill+	défaill+i	défaill+ir
(*no form*)	(*no form*)	(*no form*)	(*no form*)	ou+ï	ou+ïr
bouill+	bouilli+	bou+2 bouill+ 4, 5	bouill+	bouill+i	bouill+ir
advienn+3	adv+înt	(*no form*)	adven+	adven+u	adven+ir
meur+ 1, 2, 3, 6 mour+4, 5	mouru+	meur+2 mour+4, 5	mour+	mor+t	mour+ir
(*no form*)	(*no form*)	(*no form*)	gis+	(*no form*)	gés+ir
déchoi+ 1, 2, 3, 6 déchoy+4, 5	déchu+	déchoi+2 déchoy+ 4, 5	(*no form*)	déch+u	déch+oir
veuill+ 1, 2, 3, 6 voul+4, 5	voulu+	veu+x voul+4, 5	voul+	voul+u	voul+oir
sié+3, 6	(*no form*)	(*no form*)	sé+ sey+	(*no form*)	s+eoir
(*no form*)	(*no form*)	(*no form*)	sé+ant	s+is	s+eoir
messié+3	(*no form*)	(*no form*)	(*no form*)	(*no form*)	mess+eoir

		I PRESENT INDICATIVE	II PAST DEFINITE	III IMPERFECT INDICATIVE	IV FUTURE	V CONDITIONAL
		ENDINGS: SEE P. XVI			ENDINGS: SEE P. XIV	
GROUP III	MODEL #68	sursoi+ 1, 2, 3, 6 sursoy+4, 5	sursi+	sursoy+	surseoi+	surseoi+
	#69	sai+1, 2, 3 sav+4, 5, 6	su+	sav+	sau+	sau+
	#69A	pleu+3 pleuv+6	plu+3, 6,	pleuv+3, 6	pleuv+3, 6	pleuv+3, 6
	#70	peu+x pui+s +x +t pouv+4, 5 peuv+6	pu+	pouv+	pour+	pour+
	#71	brai+3, 6	*(no form)*	bray+3, 6	brai+3, 6	*(no form)*
	#72	pai+1, 2 paî+t paiss+ 4, 5, 6	*(no form)*	paiss+	paît+	paît+
	#73	boi+1, 2, 3 buv+4, 5 boiv+6	bu+	buv+	boi+	boi+
	#74	croi+ 1, 2, 3, 6 croy+4, 5	cru+	croy+	croi+	croi+
	#75	croî+1, 2, 3 croiss+ 4, 5, 6	crû+1, 2, 3, 6 +mes +tes	croiss+	croît+	croît+
	#76	moud+1, 2 moud moul+4, 5, 6	moulu+	moul+	moud+	moud+

NOTES ON THE PHONETIC TRANSCRIPTION OF FRENCH

1. THE ALPHABET

The alphabet used for the phonetic transcriptions of French words in this Dictionary is that of the International Phonetic Association (I.P.A.). Apart from its intrinsic qualities of legibility and simplicity, the I.P.A. system has the advantage of being widely used both on this continent and in Europe in grammars, textbooks, and dictionaries. More detailed information about the alphabet may be found in the booklet *The Principles of the I.P.A.*, 1949, A. C. Gimson, University College, London W.C.1.

2. THE TYPE OF TRANSCRIPTION

For every language, speech sounds tend to be limited to a finite number of articulatory "possibilities" called *phonemes*. These are the units which make up words. While linguists differ as to the best way to classify and transcribe phonemes, it is obvious that some minimal list must be established in order to teach the language. The phonemes used in this Dictionary appear on the inside covers, front and back, for both French and English.

3. THE TYPE OF PRONUNCIATION

The type of pronunciation recorded in the Dictionary, shown in brackets after each entry, represents a normalized type of northern French, the "international standard." This conforms in all essentials to the norm taught in schools in Canada and elsewhere,

VI	VII	VIII	IX	X	XI
PRESENT SUBJUNCTIVE	IMPERFECT SUBJUNCTIVE	IMPERATIVE	PRESENT PARTICIPLE	PAST PARTICIPLE	INFINITIVE
ENDINGS: SEE P. XV		ENDINGS: P. XVII	ENDING: P. XV	COMPLETE FORMS SHOWN BELOW	
sursoi+ 1, 2, 3, 6 sursoy+4, 5	sursi+	sursoi+2 sursoy+ 4, 5	sursoy+	surs+is	surs+eoir
sach+	su+	sach+ *as* #3	sach+	s+u	sav+oir
pleuv+3, 6	plû+3, 6	(*no form*)	pleuv+	pl+u	pleuv+oir
puiss+	pu+	(*no form*)	pouv+	p+u	pouv+oir
(*no form*)	(*no form*)	(*no form*)	bray+	brai+t	brai+re
paiss+	(*no form*)	pai+2 paiss+4, 5	paiss+	(*no form*)	paît+re
boiv+ 1, 2, 3, 6 buv+4, 5	bu+	boi+2 buv+4, 5	buv+	b+u	boi+re
croi+ 1, 2, 3, 6 croy+4, 5	cru+	croi+2 croy+4, 5	croy+	cr+u	croi+re
croiss+	cru+	croî+2 croiss+4, 5	croiss+	cr+û	croît+re
moul+	moulu+	moud+2 moul+4, 5	moul+	moul+u	moud+re

and is acceptable in all parts of the French speaking world. It also embodies some important features of the evolution of modern French as spoken in the area which includes Paris, the Atlantic seaboard north of the Loire and the Channel seaboard south of Belgium: for instance, the tendency to use /a/ instead of /ɑ/ in pretonic syllables and the shift towards /e/ in final open position, where preceding generations used /ɛ/. Language changes constantly, and we have endeavoured to give a transcription which reflects the state of present-day pronunciation of French.

In linguistics, the best transcription of a language is that which accounts for the maximum of data with a minimum of symbols. But this type of transcription—sometimes called *broad*—is not always easy to handle in the classroom. We have accordingly chosen here to show a *narrower* type of transcription, including some subphonemic details which students are apt to overlook. Thus *vowel length*, which in French is automatic except for a few dozen words in [ɛ], has been consistently shown by the phonetic sign (ː). Students will thus be reminded of the sharp contrast between short syllables, e.g. *type* [tip], and long ones, e.g. *tire* [tiːr]. In final open position, all vowels are pronounced short, as *thé* [te], *assis* [a'si], *cinéma* [sine'ma].

The possibility of dropping the [ə], called *e muet* in most grammars, has been suggested by parentheses, e.g. *acheter* [aʃ(ə)'te], which is usually pronounced [aʃ'te]. This system makes it possible to show cases where the [ə] is *always* omitted, e.g. *médecin* [met'sɛ̃], or *never* omitted, e.g. *crevette* [krə'vɛt].

The phonetic transcriptions usually show only that part of an entry which differs from the preceding one. This is marked in the main entry by a vertical line (|).

4. CANADIAN FRENCH VARIANTS

The "international standard" transcribed in this Dictionary is taught in Canadian schools and universities, and it is widely used by public speakers, announcers of Radio-Canada, educators, public officials, members of the clergy, journalists, and the like. But the speech of French Canadians often shows a certain admixture of local variants, which have also been given, preceded by the sign ©.

These are of two kinds. Some phonemes of the international standard may show specifically Canadian variants, while others do not; these variants give a distinctive flavour to Canadian French compared with, say, Provençal French or Belgian French. The transcription used in this Dictionary covers Canadian variants insofar as the international standard and Canadian French use the same phoneme.

Furthermore, Canadian French speakers may use one phoneme in places where the international standard uses another; thus many Canadian French speakers use the phoneme /e/ in *mai* where the international standard has /ɛ/. Similarly, in non-final open position, where there is a good deal of fluctuation among speakers, it is usual to hear a close [o] in *Saint-Donat* instead of the open [ɔ]. Conversely, whereas most young speakers of French elsewhere now use only three nasal vowels, and pronounce words in /œ̃/ with the /ɛ̃/ phoneme, thus confusing *brin* and *brun*, this tendency seems exceedingly rare in Canada.

Cases of discrepancy arising from this second type of variants are shown, wherever possible, by adding a second transcription after the first, preceded by the sign ©, thus *mai* [mɛ © me].

NOTES ON THE PHONOLOGY OF CANADIAN FRENCH

The five million speakers of French in Canada and parts of the United States naturally show pronunciation features of their own after two centuries or more of complete separation from France. However, these distinctive features—some newly acquired, a majority left over from an earlier period—are in fact not very numerous if one considers the time of this separation and the physical distance.

Moreover, the traits to be found in *some* degree in French-Canadian speech, are not necessarily always found in one speaker. The influence of radio, TV, and movies, a greater awareness of speech problems at the primary school level, more frequent contacts with the "international standard"—all these tend to eliminate some features, leaving what may be called a middle-of-the-road pronunciation typical of Canada, yet perfectly understandable and acceptable wherever French is spoken.

1. VOWELS

A. *Diphthongization of Long Vowels*

In cases where the international standard has long vowels, Canadian French shows a tendency to diphthongize certain vowels.

	EXAMPLE	INTERNATIONAL STANDARD	CANADIAN FRENCH
/ɛ/	—*reine*	[rɛ:n]	[rɛɪn]
	—*père*	[pɛ:r]	[pɛɪr]
	—*rêve*	[rɛ:v]	[rɛɪv]
	—*maître*	[mɛ:tr]	[mɛɪtr]
/a/	*lavage*	[la'va:ʒ]	[la'vaɑʒ]
/ɑ/	*âme*	[ɑ:m]	[ɑʊm, ɔʊm]
/ø/	*feutre*	[fø:tr]	[føʏtr]
/œ/	*beurre*	[bœ:r]	[bœʏr]
/o/	*rose*	[ro:z]	[roʊz]

B. *Vowel Length and Distribution of Stress*

In standard French, stress normally falls on the last uttered syllable of a stress group; in Canadian French, the distribution of stress is somewhat different, owing to the presence of a rather strong secondary accent. Since vowel length in French is closely

connected with the ictus of stress, it follows that a secondary stress will result in a secondary (or half) length. This occurs in open penult syllables when the vowel of the last syllable is short, for the vowels /ɛ/, /o/, /ɑ/, and /ø/.

EXAMPLE		INTERNATIONAL STANDARD	CANADIAN FRENCH
/ɛ/	*embêter*	[ɑ̃bɛ'te]	[ɑ̃ˌbɛ·'te]
/o/	*arroser*	[aro'ze]	[aˌro·'ze]
/ɑ/	*pâté*	[pɑ'te]	[ˌpɑ·'te]
/ø/	*jeûner*	[ʒø'ne]	[ˌʒø·'ne]

In the same position, nasal vowels show the same tendency, e.g. /ɑ̃/ *entrer*: international standard [ɑ̃'tre], Canadian French [ˌɑ̃·'tre].

In penult syllables followed by /r/, the vowels /i/, /u/ and /y/ show the same tendency.

EXAMPLE		INTERNATIONAL STANDARD	CANADIAN FRENCH
/i/	*tirer*	[ti're]	[ˌti·'re]
/u/	*pourri*	[pu'ri]	[ˌpu·'ri]
/y/	*huron*	[y'rõ]	[ˌy·'rõ]

c. *Lax Vowels in Closed Syllables*

(a) In closed *short* syllables, the international standard vowels /i/, /u/, /y/ are almost always articulated in Canada in a very lax fashion; they open out and tend to be centralized, i.e. obscured. These lax vowels, which can be transcribed by the symbols /ɪ/, /ʊ/, /ʏ/, resemble, at least for the first two, the English vowels in *pit* and *put* [pɪt], [pʊt]; and final /i/ followed by /n/ is often lax and open.

EXAMPLE	INTERNATIONAL STANDARD	CANADIAN FRENCH
rite	[rit]	[rɪt]
rude	[ryd]	[rʏd]
route	[rut]	[rʊt]
lime	[lim]	[lɪm]
lune	[lyn]	[lʏn]

(b) Before a voiceless consonant (/t/, /k/, /s/) the above three vowels (/i/, /u/, /y/) develop a voicelessness which at times completely destroys their timbre; they remain as "ghost" vowels (whispered vowels), and keep their rhythmic value.

EXAMPLE	INTERNATIONAL STANDARD	CANADIAN FRENCH
université	[ynivɛrsi'te]	[ynivɛrs(*i*)'te]
député	[depy'te]	[dep(*y*)'te]
en tout cas	[ɑ̃tu'kɑ]	[ɑ̃t(*u*)'kɑ]

D. *Canadian Variants*

(a) In final stressed position, short /a/ and /ɑ/ of the international standard occur in Canadian French as /ɔ/, a back variety of international French vowel No. 6. The /a/ of *Canada*, in international standard /kana'da/, becomes in Canadian French /kana'dɔ/. The /ɑ/ of *Les États(-Unis)*, in international standard [leze'tɑ], becomes in Canadian French [leze'tɔ]. In closed stressed position, long /ɑ/ of the international standard is often a diphthongized variety of /ɔ/, e.g. *un as*, international standard [œ̃'nɑːs]; Canadian French [œ̃'nɑʊs].

(b) There is a marked tendency in Canadian French for the four *nasal* vowels to show a different articulation from the international standard. Thus *bien*, [bjɛ̃] often becomes [bjẽ], i.e. a closer vowel resembling that of *été* [e'te] is nasalized instead of the open /ɛ/ of *tête* [tɛːt]; the most noticeable difference affects the /ɑ̃/ phoneme, which in Canadian French is usually an open front /a/ nasalized instead of an open back /ɑ/. Examples are *temps*, international standard [tɑ̃]; Canadian French [tã]; and *vent*, international standard [vɑ̃]; Canadian French [vã].

This tendency has the effect of bringing Canadian French /ɑ̃/ very close acoustically speaking to international French /ɛ̃/; thus international French *cinq* [sɛ̃:k], pronounced without the final /k/ as in *cinq dollars* [sɛ̃ dɔ'la:r], may sound at first to a French Canadian ear like *cent dollars*; conversely Canadian French *cent dollars* may be interpreted by a European speaker as *cinq dollars*.

2. CONSONANTS

A. The majority of French Canadians, with the important exception of the Acadians (Gaspé, the Maritime Provinces), pronounce /t/ and /d/ followed by the close vowels /i/ and /y/ with a marked friction, which resembles the clusters /ts/ and /dz/ of the English words *bits* [bɪts] and *adze* [ædz]. In careful speech, one hears usually nothing more than a slight sibilant. This phenomenon also takes place in front of the "lax" variety of /i/ and /y/.

EXAMPLE	INTERNATIONAL STANDARD	CANADIAN FRENCH
tirer	[ti're]	[tsi're]
petit	[pə'ti]	[pə'tsi]
voiture	[vwa'ty:r]	[vwa'tsy:r]
petite	[pə'tit]	[pə'tsɪt]
tuque	[tyk]	[tsyk]

B. *The Two "R's" of French Canada*

In Europe as in French Canada, the phoneme /r/ may represent either of two articulations: (a) a rolled consonant, articulated by the tip of the tongue against the teeth-ridge, represented here by [r]; (b) a rolled or fricative consonant articulated by the back of the tongue against the uvula: this is called rather loosely "le *r* grasseyé," which we represent here by the symbol [ʀ].

The great majority of speakers of the international standard use the uvular [ʀ], and efforts are often exerted in school to teach it. It is usually much simpler to have students articulate a good lingual rolled [r]. In French Canada the two articulations are found side by side, the back uvular [ʀ] and its variants being uppermost in Quebec City and the lower part of the St. Lawrence valley, the lingual [r] in Montreal and generally east of Three Rivers. Thus, *arriver*, in international standard [aʀi've], in Eastern Quebec is spoken as [aʀi've], and in Western Quebec as [ari've].

C. *Other Variants*

The standard fricatives /ʒ/ and to a lesser degree /ʃ/ are sometimes replaced by a voiced [ʜ] and a velar fricative /x/.

EXAMPLE	INTERNATIONAL STANDARD	CANADIAN FRENCH
gentil	[ʒɑ̃'ti]	[ʜɑ̃'tsi]
léger	[le'ʒe]	[le'ʜe]
j'ai cherché	[ʒeʃɛr'ʃe]	[ʜexɛr'ʃe]

This voiced /ʜ/ should not be confused with the phoneme that Canadians pronounce in words written with "h aspirée," a voiceless [h] similar to that used in English in *hat*, *hook*. Thus *la hache*, in international standard [la'aʃ], or [la''ʔaʃ], sometimes becomes in Canadian French [la 'aʃ] or [la 'haʃ].

There is a common tendency throughout the French Canadian linguistic area to sound the *-t* which comes at the end of a word and is preceded by a vowel. A good example is the almost universal articulation of a final *-t* in family names such as *Talbot* [tal'bɔt], *Chabot* [ʃa'bɔt], *Drolet* [drɔ'lɛt]. In some cases the spelling has been changed to reflect this tendency, e.g. *Vinet* spelt *Vinette*. Among common words which retain a final written *-t* in the pronunciation are: *but*, international standard [by], Canadian French [bʏt]; *tout*, international standard [tu], Canadian French [tʊt], especially in group final position. At the popular level, [frɛt] for *froid*, international standard [frwa], and [lɛt] for *laid*, international standard [lɛ], are often heard.

ABRÉVIATIONS FRANÇAISES

abr./éviation
absol./ument
abus./ivement
Acad./émique
Acous./tique
adj./ectif
Adm./inistration
adv./erbe, adverbial
Aéro./nautique
Agric./ulture
Alg./èbre
Anat./omie
Antiq./uité
approx./imatif
Arch./itecture
Archéol./ogie
Arg.ot(ique)
Art, Beaux-arts
art./icle
Artil./lerie
Assur./ance
Astr./onomie
Attrib./ut
Auto./mobilisme
Aviat./ion
aux./iliaire
Bactér./iologie
Banq./ues
Biol./ogie
Bot./anique
Br./itannique
©, Canada, canadien, canadianisme
card./inal
Cath./olique
cf., confer, comparez
ch. de fer, Chemins de fer
Chim./ie
Ciné./ma
coll./ectif
Com./merce
compar./atif
compl./ément
Compt./abilité
cond./itionnel
conj./ugué avec, conjonction
Constr./uction
Cout./ure
Cul./inaire
déf./ini
dém./onstratif
Dent./aire
dim./inutif
dir./ect
Écon./omique
Électr./icité
Enfant./in
&c., et caetera
ÉU, États-Unis
ex./emple
except./ion
exclam./atif
ext., par extension
f., féminin
Fam./ilier
Fig./uratif
Fin./ance
Fr./ançais, France
gén./éral(ement)
Géog./raphie
Géol./ogie
Géom./étrie
Gouv./ernement
Gram./maire
Gymnas./tique
Hér./aldique
Hist./oire
Hort./iculture
Hyg./iène
impérat./if
impers./onnel
Impr./imerie
Ind./ien (Amérindien)
ind./irect
indéf./ini
indic./atif
Indus./trie
inf./infin
interj./ection
interrog./atif
intr./ansitif
Intro./duction
invar./iable
Iron./iquement
irrég./ulier
Journ./alisme
Jur./isprudence
Lat./in
Ling./uistique
Lit./téraire
Loc./ution
m., masculin
Mar./ine, Maritime
Math./ématiques
Méc./anique
Méd./ecine
Métal./lurgie
Mil./itaire
Mus./ique
Mythol./ogie
n., nom
Naut./ique
nég./atif, négation
num./éral
Onomat./opée
ONU, Nations Unies
Opt./ique
ord./inal
Orn./ithologie
Parl./ement
part.pas., p.p., participe passé
part.pr., p.pr., participe présent
pas./sif
Péj./oratif
Pers./onne, personnel
Pharm./acie
Philos./ophie
Phon./étique
Photo./graphie
Phys./ique
pl(ur)./iel
Poét./ique
Polit./ique
Pop./ulaire
poss./essif
préf./ixe
prép./osition, prépositive
prés./ent
prét./érit
princ./ipalement
pr(on)./om, pronominal
Prot./estant
Prov./erbe
Psych./ologie
Pub./licité
qq., quelques
qqch., quelque chose
qqun, quelqu'un
q.v., quod videre, voir
réfl./échi
rel./atif
Rel./igion
s., sing., singulier
Scol./aire
Sculpt./ure
Sp./ort
subj(onc)./tif
suff./ixe
suj./et
superl./atif
syn./onyme
Tech./nique
Tél./écommunications
Text./ile
Théâ./tre
Théol./ogie
Top./onymie
tr./ansitif
TV, Télévision
Typ./ographie
usuel./lement
v., verbe
Vulg./aire
Zool./ogie

EXPLICATION DES SYMBOLES

(1) Une virgule sépare les exemples de leur traduction. La virgule sert également à séparer deux traductions équivalentes ou deux nuances stylistiques. Ex: **absolute** . . . absolu, total. Employée dans les exemples, la virgule sépare deux traductions possibles se situant sur le même plan sémantique.

(2) ; Le point et virgule sépare deux traductions d'un même mot qui se situent dans des parties différentes de l'aire sémantique. Ex: **abstraction** . . . abstraction *f*; vol *m*. Pour indiquer une subdivision sémantique plus marquée, on se sert de chiffres.

(3) **1.2.** Les chiffres gras précisent les subdivisions sémantiques d'un même article, lorsqu'il y a avantage à faire ressortir ces distinctions.

(4) / La barre oblique indique la possibilité de substituer, dans les exemples, un segment de l'énoncé à un autre. Ex: *Whose car did you come in?*, Dans quelle auto, Dans l'auto de qui/êtes-vous venu? Se lit: Dans quelle auto êtes-vous venu? ou Dans l'auto de qui êtes-vous venu?

(5) : Deux points indiquent, pour un sens donné, le commencement des exemples dont le but est de préciser les traductions ou d'indiquer des particularités d'emploi.

(6) || La double barre indique le changement des parties du discours à l'intérieur d'un même article.

(7) + Une croix verticale placée après un mot (ou une partie de ce mot) signifie que ce dernier peut être suivi d'un élément grammatical: suffixe, préposition, régime d'un verbe, &c. Ex: **faire** (+ infin.) renvoie à des formes telles que *faire cuire*; dans le tableau des verbes français, **aim+** indique le radical à partir duquel on doit reconstituer les formes verbales *aimons*, *aimez*, &c.

(8) = Le signe d'égalité précise la valeur des abréviations. Ex: *a.m.* (= *ante meridiem*). Il indique parfois un synonyme auquel le lecteur pourra se reporter. Ex: A.B. (= B.A.).

(9) ~ Une ligne courbée remplace l'article principal toutes les fois qu'il ne subit aucun changement morphologique: **call**, **~ up**, se lit *call*, *call up*.

(10) [ ] Les crochets encadrent des explications destinées à préciser un sens ou un point de grammaire. Ex: **baisser** [sight, strength, &c.], to fail, précise le sens de **baisser**. Les mots entre crochets servent également à présenter une explication grammaticale ou stylistique. Ex: **bateau** *n.m.*, boat [for large vessels, use NAVIRE].

(11) - Le trait d'union est utilisé dans l'en-tête des articles pour remplacer un segment inchangé d'un mot, auquel s'ajoute un autre segment. Ex: **ancien, -ne** se lit *ancien*, *ancienne*; **antenna, -s**, se lit *antenna*, *antennas*.

(12) . . . Les points de suspension remplacent un mot ou un groupe de mots pouvant s'insérer dans un énoncé et dont il importe de préciser la place. Ex: *to give . . . to*; *ne . . . guère*. Les points peuvent également indiquer qu'un exemple n'est pas une phrase complète. Ex: *I told you that* . . .

(13) ☞ Le symbole d'une main attire l'attention sur un point de grammaire ou d'usage.

(14) → La flèche horizontale attire l'attention sur une traduction oblique, présentant un intérêt particulier du point de vue de la stylistique comparée. Ex: *when* → date à laquelle, époque à laquelle.

(15) × La croix de Saint-André attire l'attention sur la présence d'un *faux-ami*, mot qui ressemble à l'article mais dont le sens est tout autre. Ex: **presently** *adv.*, [×] dans quelques instants, bientôt; dans certains cas, le faux-ami correspondant est indiqué entre crochets [× présentement]; on pourra s'y reporter pour un complément d'information.

(16) ŒIL CHILD Les mots imprimés en petites capitales sont des renvois, soit à la partie française, soit à la partie anglaise du Dictionnaire; le lecteur est invité à s'y reporter pour information, particulièrement en ce qui concerne la grammaire. Dans le cas de certaines formes irrégulières très fréquentes,

on se sert des petites capitales pour renvoyer à la rubrique principale: yeux cf. ŒIL; **children** cf. CHILD.

(17) © Le symbole d'un © dans un cercle indique un canadianisme. Par "canadianisme" on entend soit un mot particulier au Canada, p. ex. © *raquetteur*, © *komatik*, soit une acception particulière au Canada, p. ex. © *banc de neige*.

(18) [Abus.] Dans certains cas, un canadianisme peut être déclaré "abusif": on a estimé qu'il s'agissait alors d'une forme populaire contrevenant au génie de la langue. Le terme international correspondant est généralement indiqué. Ex: **used car,** © [Abus.] char usagé, [Fr.] auto(mobile) d'occasion.

(19) * L'astérisque indique un néologisme, ou un mot non encore complètement entré dans l'usage. Ex: ***oléoduc.** Dans la transcription phonétique du français, l'astérisque précise que *h* est "aspiré."

(20) † Le symbole d'un poignard indique une forme ou un sens vieillis, ou exclusivement littéraires.

(21) (*m*) Dans le cas de rubriques qui sont à la fois *adjectif* et *nom*, le genre du nom est indiqué entre parenthèses. Ex: *annexe* (*f*). Lorsqu'un mot peut être à la fois *m.* et *f.* sans changer de forme, cette particularité est indiquée par *m/f*.

(22) | Le trait vertical est utilisé dans les en-têtes orthographiques et phonétiques pour séparer le radical de sa désinence ou un préfixe du radical; en général, ce trait indique l'endroit à partir duquel un dérivé présente des changements. Ex: **vénéneu|x, -se** se lit *vénéneux, vénéneuse*; **un|able** se lit *unable*, par opposition à *until*.

NOTES SUR LA PARTIE ANGLAIS-FRANÇAIS

1. CANADIANISMES

Tous les articles dont la langue de départ est l'anglais reflètent l'usage canadien et nord-américain à moins d'indication contraire. Leur traduction dans la langue d'arrivée reflète l'usage commun au franco-canadien et au français international. Les signes © ou [Fr.] précisent les mots ou expressions d'usage exclusivement canadien ou français (européen). En règle générale, si © précède l'indication grammaticale, il se réfère au mot de la langue de départ; après les indications grammaticales, au mot de la langue d'arrivée.

2. DÉRIVÉS

Les dérivés sont placés normalement suivant l'ordre alphabétique à la suite du mot de base et dans le même article: **urge . . . || urgency . . . || urgent . . . || urgently.** Dans les cas où des dérivés ne peuvent suivre le mot de base, on les trouvera à leur place alphabétique: **gaiety . . . gay; abound . . . abundance . . . || abundant.** Les verbes à postpositions se trouvent, en règle générale, dans le même article que le mot de base.

3. DÉRIVÉS HYPOSTATIQUES

La morphologie très souple de l'anglais permet fréquemment à cette langue d'utiliser une même *forme* pour des *espèces* différentes: *look* peut être un nom aussi bien qu'un verbe; *short* un adjectif aussi bien qu'un adverbe ou un nom. Le passage d'une espèce de ces dérivés hypostatiques à l'autre est indiqué par ||, soit **some,** *adj.* . . . || *adv.*

4. MOTS COMPOSÉS

Ils peuvent se présenter typographiquement (a) en un seul mot, (b) en deux mots réunis par un trait d'union ou (c) sans trait d'union. Les mots composés du type (a) et (b) ont été placés à titre d'article à leur place alphabétique dans la liste des dérivés, sous le premier élément: **watch . . . || watchdog . . . || watch-maker,** &c.

Eu égard à la fréquence de composés du type (c), c'est-à-dire sans trait d'union, et surtout au fait qu'ils demandent en français des traductions particulières qu'il importait de préciser dans un dictionnaire de ce genre, nous les avons cités généralement dans le corps de l'article où apparaît leur premier élément: on trouvera donc *university student* à *university*, *Upper Canada* à *upper*, &c. Étant donné que l'orthographe des composés varie selon les usages canadien, britannique et américain, nous invitons le lecteur à lire la Note on the English Spelling, page ix.

5. VERBES

Tous les verbes anglais sont cités à l'infinitif sans *to* en tête des articles. Les irrégularités orthographiques, telles que le redoublement de la consonne finale de l'infinitif avant la flexion, sont indiquées entre crochets: **wet,** *v. tr.* **[-tt-]**. Le lecteur qui connaît la formation des temps des verbes réguliers anglais lira correctement **wetted, wetted, wetting.** (Voir plus bas, "Note sur les verbes anglais.")

Les verbes de conjugaison irrégulière sont cités à l'infinitif, et suivis de la forme du prétérit, du participe passé et parfois du participe présent, dans le cas d'un redoublement de la consonne finale du radical: **weave, wove, woven; swim, swam, swum, swimming.** Les variations orthographiques régulières ne sont pas indiquées.

6. SUBSTANTIFS

Le pluriel des substantifs anglais n'est donné que s'il est irrégulier: **child,** *pl.* **children.** Les variations orthographiques régulières ne sont pas indiquées (**hero,** *heroes*; **cry,** *cries*; **church,** *churches*, &c.). Les substantifs français ne sont donnés qu'au singulier, sauf dans les exemples. On indique leur genre par *m*, *f*, ou *m/f* s'il s'agit de substantifs possédant les deux genres.

7. EMPLOI DES MAJUSCULES POUR LES NOMS ET ADJECTIFS DE NATIONALITÉ

En anglais, les noms et adjectifs de nationalité prennent toujours une majuscule: *an Italian*, un Italien; *Italian wines*, des vins italiens. Parfois s'ils ont acquis un sens spécialisé, ils ne prennent plus la majuscule: *venetian blinds*, jalousies; *paris green*, vert de Scheele. Les noms et les adjectifs composés anglais prennent toujours une majuscule et sont unis par un trait d'union: *an Italian-American*, un Italo-Américain.

8. ADJECTIFS

En anglais, les formes comparative et superlative des adjectifs sont données lorsqu'elles sont irrégulières: **good, better, best,** à l'exception des adjectifs qui se terminent en *-y*, et qui prennent tous les désinences *-ier*, *-iest*.

NOTE SUR LES VERBES ANGLAIS

1. VERBES RÉGULIERS

Sont considérés comme réguliers les verbes qui, sans changer la voyelle du radical, forment leur prétérit et leur participe passé en ajoutant *-ed* à la forme de l'infinitif: *walk, walked, walked*. Le participe présent s'obtient en ajoutant le suffixe *-ing* à la forme de l'infinitif: *walk, walking*; dans certains cas, la consonne finale du radical est redoublée devant les formes passées et participiales: *wet, wetting*.

2. VERBES IRRÉGULIERS

(a) *Les verbes forts*. Les verbes forts forment leur prétérit et leur participe passé en changeant la voyelle du radical et parfois en ajoutant au participe passé les désinences *-en*, *-n*, ou *-ne*: *write, wrote, written*. Devant une voyelle brève, la consonne finale du radical est redoublée dans l'écriture. Le participe présent est régulier: *writing*.

(b) *Verbes mixtes*. Les verbes mixtes forment le prétérit et le participe passé en changeant la voyelle du radical et en ajoutant un *-t* ou un *-d*. Ex. *keep, kept, kept*; *shoe, shod, shod*. Si le mot se termine déjà par un *-t* ou un *-d*, on n'ajoute rien à la finale, mais on observe le changement de voyelle à l'intérieur du radical: *sit, sat, sat*. Le participe présent est régulier.

(c) *Les verbes monoformes*. Ces verbes n'ont qu'une forme pour l'infinitif, le prétérit et le participe passé. Le suffixe du passé se confond alors avec la consonne finale. Ces verbes se terminent toujours par un *-t* ou un *-d*. Ex. *cut, cut, cut*; *spread, spread,*

FRANÇAIS-ANGLAIS/FRENCH-ENGLISH

A, a [a] *n.m.* [first letter of the alphabet] A, a: *Écrivez trois A,* Write three A's; *un A majuscule,* a capital A; *la lettre A,* the letter A; *Écrivez le A* [no elision] *à gauche,* Write the A on the left; *ne savoir ni A ni B,* not to know one's ABC's; *depuis A jusqu'à Z,* from A to Z.

a, as [a] cf. AVOIR.

à [a] [☞ à le = **au**; à les = **aux**] *prép.* **1.** [sans mouvement] at, in: *passer l'hiver ~ Vancouver,* to spend the winter in V.; *~ l'école,* at school; *~ l'église,* at church; *~ la maison,* at home; *assis ~ sa table,* sitting at his desk; *habiter* (~) *Montréal,* to live in M. **2.** [avec mouvement] to: *tomber ~ terre,* to fall to the ground; *Il va ~ Toronto,* He/goes, is going/to T.; *la première rue ~ droite,* the first street to the right; *atteler un cheval ~ une voiture,* to hitch a horse to a carriage; *au nord de, ~ l'est de . . . ,* north of, east of . . . **3.** [attribution à] to: *Donnez-le ~ Paul,* Give it to P.; *C'est ~ vous de jouer,* → It's your/move, turn to play/; *~ qui est ce livre?,* Whose book is this? *Ce livre est ~ moi,* This book/is mine, belongs to me/, → This is my book. **4.** [origine] from: *Il habite ~ cinq milles d'ici,* He lives five miles from here; *~ dix milles à la ronde,* within ten miles (from), for ten miles; *arracher qqch. ~ qqun,* to wrench sth. from s.o.; *remonter ~ la source,* to trace . . . back to its/source, origin/. **5.** [manière] by, on: *fait ~ la main,* made by hand; *~ la pelle,* with a shovel; *~ la/livre, douzaine/,* by the/pound, dozen/; *~ pied,* on foot; *~ cheval,* on horseback; *parler ~ voix basse,* to speak in a low voice. **6.** [temps]: *~ midi,* at noon; *~ 8 h.,* at 8 (A.M.); *~ ce moment,* at that moment; *~ cette occasion,* on this occasion; *au moment de partir,* on/leaving, starting/; *être ~ l'heure,* to be on time. **7.** [caractérisation]: *tasse f à thé,* tea cup [☞ Different from *tasse de thé,* cup of tea]; *un chapeau ~ la mode,* a fashionable, stylish/ hat; *roulement m ~ billes,* ball bearings; *fil m ~ coudre,* sewing thread; *machine f ~ écrire,* typewriter; *soupe f ~ l'oignon,* onion soup; *plein ~ déborder,* full to/the brim, overflowing/; *L'homme ~ l'oreille cassée,* The man with a broken ear; *L'homme au complet blanc,* The man in a white suit. **8.** [☞ signs on shops, &c.]: *Au lion d'or,* The Golden Lion; [Loc.] *Au secours!,* Help!; *Au voleur!,* Stop thief!; *Au feu!,* Fire! Fire!; *~ quoi bon?,* What's the use?

abaissement [abɛs|'mɑ̃] *n.m.* lowering (falling); humbling. || **abaisser** [-e] #3 *v. tr.* **1.** to lower. **2.** to reduce. **3.** to humble. **4.** [Math.] to bring down (figure); to drop (perpendicular). || **s'abaisser** *v. pron.* **1.** to decline, to fall away (of land). **2.** to stoop (to).

abandon [abɑ̃d|õ] *n.m.* **1.** surrender, giving up. **2.** desertion, neglect: *à l'~,* in a state of neglect. **3.** ease, unrestraint (of attitude). || **abandonné, -e** [-ɔ'ne] || *adj.* abandoned, forsaken, deserted: *un enfant ~,* an abandoned child. || **abandonner** [-ɔ'ne] #3 *v. tr.* **1.** to give up. **2.** to forsake, to desert. **3.** to drop (idea). || **s'abandonner** *v. pron.* to give o.s. up (to, *à*), to give way (to, *à*): *~ au désespoir,* to give way to despair.

abasourdi, -e [abazur'd|i] || *adj.* **1.** deafened. **2.** dumbfounded, bewildered. || **abasourdir** [-i:r] #17 *v. tr.* **1.** to deafen. **2.** to bewilder.

abâtardir [abatar'di:r] #17 *v. tr.* to debase. || **s'abâtardir** *v. pron.* to degenerate.

abat-jour [aba'ʒu:r] *n.m.* [*pl. unchanged*] lampshade. || **abats** [a'ba] *n. mpl.* offals; giblets. || **abattage** [-'ta:ʒ] *n.m.* felling (of trees); slaughtering. || **abattement** [abat'mɑ̃] *n.m.* prostration, despondency, dejection; [impôt] *~ à la base,* personal allowance. || **abattis** [-'ti] *n.m.* felled trees; giblets. || **abattoir** [aba'twa:r] *n.m.* slaughterhouse, abattoir.

abattre [a'bat|r] #43 *v. tr.* to knock down, to overthrow: *~ un arbre,* to fell a tree; *~ un avion,* to shoot down a plane; *~ un cheval,* to kill a horse. || **s'abattre** *v. pron.* to fall on top of, to come down on: *Un orage s'est abattu sur la ville,* A storm broke out over the city; *ne pas se laisser abattre,* to keep one's chin up.

abattu, -e [-y] *adj.* depressed, dejected, downhearted.

abbaye [abɛ'i] *n.f.* abbey, monastery.

abbé [a'be] *n.m.* [R.C.] abbot; father; abbé: *monsieur l'~,* Father; *monsieur l'~ Durand,* Father Durand. || **abbesse** [a'bɛs] *n.f.* [R.C.] abbess.

abcès [ap'sɛ] *n.m.* abscess, gathering; [gencive] gumboil.

abdication [abdik|a'sjõ] *n.f.* abdication. || **abdiquer** [-e] #3 *v. intr.* to abdicate.

abdomen [abdɔ'mɛn] *n.m.* abdomen.

abdominal, -e [abdɔmi'nal] *adj.* abdominal.

abduct|eur, -rice [abdyk|'tœːr, -'tris] *adj. & n.m.* abductor (muscle). || **abduction** [abdyk'sjõ] *n.f.* abduction.

abécédaire [abese'dɛːr] *n.m.* spelling book.

abeille [a'bɛːj] *n.f.* bee.

aberration [abɛra'sjõ] *n.f.* [Tech.] aberration; [Fig.] aberration, mental derangement.

abêtir [abɛ'tiːr] #17 *v. tr.* to make stupid, besot.

abhorrer [abɔ're] #3 *v. tr.* to abhor.

abîme [a'biːm] *n.m.* abyss, chasm, void: *Il y a un ~ entre les deux,* There's a/world/wide gap, between the two.

abîmé, e [abi'me] *adj.* **1.** damaged, spoiled. **2.** *~ dans ses pensées,* deep in thought. || **abîmer** [abi'me] #3 *v. tr.* to spoil, to damage, to ruin. || **s'abîmer** *v. pron.* **1.** to get spoiled, to go bad. **2.** *~ dans ses pensées,* to/sink, founder/in(to) one's thoughts.

Abitibi (l') [labiti'bi] *n.f.* Abitibi.

abject [ab'ʒɛk|t] *adj.* abject, base. || **abjection** [-'sjõ] *n.f.* abjection, abasement.

abjurer [abʒy're] #3 *v. tr.* to abjure, to forswear; to renounce.

ablution [ably'sjõ] *n.f.* ablution: *faire ses ablutions,* to perform one's ablutions.

abnégation [abnega'sjõ] *n.f.* self-denial.

aboi [a'bwa] *n.m.* barking: *être aux abois,* to be at bay. || **aboiement, aboîment** [abwa'mɑ̃] *n.m.* barking (of dogs, &c.). cf. ABOYER.

aboîteau [abwa'to] © *n.m.* aboiteau.

abolir [abɔ'liːr] #17 *v. tr.* to abolish, to discontinue.

abolition [abɔli'sjõ] *n.f.* abolishment; [debt] cancelling; [Jur.] abrogation.

abominable [abɔmi'n|abl] *adj.* abominable, hateful, heinous. || **abomination** [-a'sjõ] *n.f.* abomination, execration: *avoir en ~,* to abominate.

abondamment [abõd|a'mɑ̃] *adv.* plentiful. || **abondance** [-ɑ̃ːs] *n.f.* abundance, great quantity, plenty: *être en ~,* to be plentiful; [Pers.] *parler d' ~,* to ad-lib. || **abondant, -e** [-ɑ̃, -ɑ̃ːt] *adj.* abundant, plentiful; heavy (rain, &c.).

abonder [abõ'de] #3 *v. intr.* to abound (*en,* in/with).

abonné, -e [abɔ'n|e] *n.* subscriber (to periodicals, &c.); consumer (of water, gas, &c.). || **abonnement** [-'mɑ̃] *n.m.* subscription (to periodicals, &c.); season ticket (on railways, &c.). || **abonner** [-e] #3 *v. tr.* to get a subscription for (s.o.): *Il m'a abonné au* Monde, He got me a subscription to the *Monde.* || **s'abonner** *v. pron.* to subscribe (to a paper, *à un journal*), to become a subscriber (to, *à*).

abord [a'bɔːr] *n.m.* **1.** landing © [often used in place names]: *L'Abord à Plouffe,* cf. ABORDER. **2.** approach, manner of receiving: *être d'un ~ /facile, difficile/,* to be /accessible, aloof/. || **d'abord** [da'bɔːr] *inv.* at first; in the first place: *tout d'abord, au premier abord, de prime abord,* in the very first place, at first; *dès l'abord,* from the first.

abordable [abɔr'dabl] *adj.* [place] accessible; [price] reasonable; [Pers.] affable, easy of address.

abordage [abɔr'd|aːʒ] *n.m.* **1.** collision. †**2.** boarding (of enemy ship). || **aborder** [-e] #3 *v. intr.* **1.** to land, to come alongside. **2.** *v. tr.* to collide with; to come up to (a person); to come to (a new topic). || **abords** [a'bɔːr] *n.mpl.* approaches (to property, monument, &c.), outskirts: *les ~ du village,* the outskirts of the village.

aborti|f, -ve [abɔr't|if, -iːv] *adj.* abortive.

aboucher [abu'ʃe] #3 *v. tr.* to bring together; to bring about an interview between. || **s' ~** *v. pron.* to get in touch (with, *avec*).

aboutir [abu't|iːr] #17 *v. intr.* **1.** to lead to, to end at. **2.** to succeed: *Ses démarches n'ont pas abouti,* His efforts were unsuccessful. || **aboutissement** [-is'mɑ̃] *n.m.* result, outcome.

aboyer [abwa'je] #12 *v. intr.* to bark (at s.o., *après qqun*). cf. ABOI.

abrasi|f, -ve [abra'z|if, -iːv] *adj. & n.* (*m.*) abrasive.

abrégé, -e [abre'ʒe] *adj.* short(er) edition of book, article; digest; abstract. || *n.m.* digest, abridgment, précis: *l' ~ du Littré,* the shorter Littré. || **abréger** [abre'ʒe] #7 *v. tr.* to shorten, to cut down (to), to abbreviate; to abridge: *~ un séjour,* to cut short a stay; *~ un mot,* to abbreviate a word; *~ un ouvrage,* to abridge a work.

abreuver [abrœ'v|e] #3 *v. tr.* **1.** to water (animals). **2.** [Fig.] *~ qqun d'injures,* to abuse repeatedly. || **s'abreuver** *v. pron.* [of animals] to drink. || **abreuvoir** [-waːr] *n.m.* watering place, trough.

abréviation [abrevja'sjõ] *n.f.* abbreviation, contraction; curtailment.

abri [a'bri] *n.m.* shelter: *être à l' ~ de,* to be protected from; *se mettre à l' ~ de,* to take shelter from; *mettre à l' ~,* to put out of (the rain, &c.).

abricot [abri'ko] *n.m.* apricot.

abriter [abri'te] #3 *v. tr.* to shelter, to shield, to protect. || **s'abriter** *v. pron.* to get under cover.
abroger [abrɔ'ʒe] #5 *v. tr.* [order] to rescind; [law] to abrogate, repeal.
abrupt, -e [a'brypt] *adj.* steep; [Fig.] sudden, [manières] abrupt.
abruti, -e [abry't|i] *adj.* stupid, dazed. || *n.m.* stupid fellow; blockhead. || **abrutir** [-i:r] #17 *v. tr.* to stupefy, to daze. || **abrutissant** [-i'sɑ̃] *adj.* stupefying, head-splitting, extremely boring: *un travail* ~, drudgery. || **abrutissement** [-is'mɑ̃] *n.m.* **1.** debasement, degradation. **2.** stupidity.
absence [ap's|ɑ̃:s] *n.f.* absence; /want, lack/of; blank (of mind): *avoir des absences*, to be absent-minded [≠ PRÉSENCE D'ESPRIT]; *en l'* ~ *de*, in the absence of; ~ *motivée*, excused absence. || **absent, -e** [-ɑ̃, -ɑ̃:t] **1.** *adj.* absent, away (from home, from school); missing. **2.** *n.* absentee; missing person: *Combien y a-t-il d'absents en classe aujourd'hui?* How many are absent from class today?; *Il y a deux absents*, Two are absent. || **s'absenter** [-ɑ̃te] #3 *v. pron.* to be absent, to go away, to be away: [Fig.] ~ *sans permission*, to take French leave.
abside [ap'sid] *n.f.* apse.
absinthe [ap'sɛ̃:t] *n.f.* absinth; wormwood.
absolu, -e [apsɔ'ly] **1.** *adj.* absolute; unlimited, unrestricted; peremptory, despotic: *la monarchie absolue*, absolute monarchy; *Défense absolue d'entrer*, Positively no admittance. **2.** *n.m.* the Absolute, the Ultimate. || **absolument** [-'mɑ̃] *adv.* absolutely; entirely, completely; peremptorily: *refuser* ~ *de faire qqch.*, to refuse flatly to do sth.; [Loc.] *Absolument!*, Absolutely!
absolution [apsɔly'sjõ] *n.f.* [R.C.] absolution; remission, forgiveness (of sins): *recevoir l'* ~, to receive/absolution, forgiveness/; *donner l'* ~, to absolve, to give absolution, to/give, grant/absolution (for sins).
absorbant, -e [apsɔr|'bɑ̃, -'bɑ̃:t] *adj.* **1.** absorbent: *pouvoir* ~ *(du coton, &c.)*, absorbability, absorbent quality (of cotton, &c.). **2.** [Fig.] engrossing, absorbing (task): *Ce travail est particulièrement* ~, This work is particularly/engrossing, absorbing/. || **absorbé, -e** [-'be] *adj.* [chiefly fig.] busy; engrossed in: ~ *par sa tâche*, engrossed in his work. || **absorber** [-'be] #3 *v. tr.* **1.** to absorb, to imbibe. **2.** to take (medicine). **3.** [Fig.] to take up (time). || **s'absorber** *v. pron.* to be absorbed, to be engrossed in one's work. || **absorption** [-'psjõ] *n.f.* absorption; drinking or eating; taking.
absoudre [ap'sudr] #55 *v. tr.* [R.C.] to absolve, to acquit: *pouvoir d'* ~, power of absolution; to pardon, to forgive: ~ *qqun d'une faute*, To forgive, to pardon/s.o.'s error, mistake/, to acquit s.o. cf. ABSOLUTION. || **L'absoute** [lap'sut] **1.** Formerly a public absolution given on Holy Thursday. **2.** Prayers, with sprinkling and benediction of the casket, said in a funeral ceremony. || **absoute** [ap'sut] *n.f.* absolution.
abstenir (s') de [sapstə'ni:r] #22 *v. pron.* [conj. ÊTRE] to abstain, to refrain/from. || **abstention** [apstɑ̃'sjõ] *n.f.* abstention, abstaining (from voting). || **abstinence** [apsti'n|ɑ̃:s] *n.f.* **1.** abstinence, fasting. **2.** abstemiousness, temperance. || **abstinent, -e** [-ɑ̃(:t)] *adj.* abstemious, temperate.
abstraction [apstrak'sjõ] *n.f.* abstraction: *faire* ~ *de*, to omit, to leave out. || **abstraire** [ap'str|ɛ:r] #38 *v. tr.* [conj. AVOIR] to abstract, to separate. || **s'abstraire (de),** *v. pron.* [conj. ÊTRE] to isolate oneself from. || **abstrait, -e** [-ɛ, -ɛt] *adj.* abstract; abstracted: *un sujet* ~, an abstract subject. ≠ CONCRET. || *n.m.* abstract, obscure: *résoudre un problème dans l'* ~, to solve a problem in the abstract.
absurde [ap'syrd] *adj.* absurd: *faire une démonstration par l'* ~, to demonstrate by reduction to the absurd. || **absurdité** [i'te] *n.f.* nonsense, absurdity.
abus [a'by] *n.m.* **1.** abuse: *réformer les* ~, to redress abuses, to remedy an evil. **2.** misuse; overindulgence in: ~ *de /l'alcool, du tabac*, excessive use of/alcohol, tobacco; ~ *de confiance*, abuse of confidence, breach of trust; [Loc.] *(Il) y a de l'* ~ *!* → That's the limit! || **abuser** [-'ze] #3 *v. intr.* to take advantage of, to abuse: ~ *de la bonté de qqun*, to take advantage of s.o.'s kindness; ~ *d'un privilège*, to abuse a privilege. || *v. tr.* to deceive. || **s'abuser,** *v. pron.* to be mistaken: *Si je ne m'abuse*, If I am not mistaken. || **abusi|f, -ve** [-'zif, -'zi:v] *adj.* excessive. || **abusivement** [-ziv'mɑ̃] *adv.* abusively; excessively.
acabit [aka'bi] *n.m.* sort: *de cet* ~, of that sort; *Ils sont du même* ~, They are tarred with the same brush.
académicien [akademi'sjɛ̃] *n.m.* member of an Academy. || **académie** [akade'mi] *n.f.* **1.** academy: *l'Académie Française*, the French Academy; *être reçu à l'Académie*,

to be admitted to the Academy. **2.** school. **3.** [Fr.] Académie [territorial division of the school and university system]. || **académique** [-k] *adj.* academic.

Acadie (l') [(l)aka'd|i] *n.f.* Acadia. || **Acadien, -ne** [-jɛ̃, -jɛn] *n.* & *adj.* Acadian.

acajou, *pl.* **acajous** [aka'ʒu] *n.m.* mahogany: *noix d'* ~, cashew nut.

acariâtre [aka'rjɑːtr] *adj.* cantankerous.

accablant, -e [akɑ'bl|ɑ̃, -ɑ̃ːt] *adj.* oppressive, overwhelming: *des preuves accablantes,* damning evidence; *par une chaleur accablante,* in an oppressive heat. || **accablé, -e** [-e] *adj.* overwhelmed, overcome: ~ *de fatigue* [Fam.] tired out. || **accablement** [-ə'mɑ̃] *n.m.* dejection, prostration. || **accabler** [-e] #3 *v. tr.* [conj. AVOIR (action), ÊTRE (état)] to overcome; to overwhelm.

accalmie [akal'mi] *n.f.* **1.** [tempête, bataille] lull, calm; [bruit] hush. **2.** [maladie] intermission.

accaparement [akapar|'mɑ̃] *n.m.* [Com.] buying up, cornering; [esprit] monopoly, engrossment. || **accaparer** [-e] #3 *v. tr.* [Com.] to buy up, to corner, to hoard; [esprit] to monopolize, engross.

accéder [akse'de] #10 *v. intr.* **1.** to have access (to, *à*). **2.** to comply (with, *à*), to grant (a request).

accélérateur [akseler|a'tœːr] *n.m.* accelerator: *appuyer sur l'* ~, to step on the gas. || **accélération** [-a'sjɔ̃] *n.f.* acceleration; speeding up (of process). || **accélérer** [-e] #10 *v. tr.* to speed up, to expedite: ~ *l'acheminement du courrier,* to speed up the handling of mail.

accent [ak'sɑ̃] *n.m.* **1.** accent: *Il parle avec un léger* ~, He speaks with a slight accent. **2.** stress: *L'* ~ *(tonique) tombe sur la dernière syllabe,* The stress falls on the last syllable; [Fig.] *mettre l'* ~ *sur,* to stress. **3.** [French spelling] accent: *l'* ~ *aigu,* e acute. || **accentuer** [-'tɥe] #3 *v. tr.* **1.** to stress, to accentuate (a word). **2.** [Fig.] to accentuate (a trend, &c.).

acceptable [aksɛp't|abl] *adj.* acceptable. || **acceptation** [-asjɔ̃] *n.f.* acceptance. || **accepter** [-e] #3 *v. tr.* to accept: *Il a accepté de le faire,* He has agreed to do it; *faire* ~ *(une idée),* to sell (an idea).

acception [aksɛp'sjɔ̃] *n.f.* acceptation, meaning (of a word).

accès [ak'sɛ] *n.m.* [unchanged in pl.] **1.** access, admittance: *avoir* ~ *à,* to have access to; *Accès aux trains,* → To the trains. **2.** fit, attack (of fever, &c.); bout, spurt (of energy); [Loc.] *par* ~, by fits and starts; *dans un* ~ *de colère,* in a fit of anger. || **accessible** [-'sibl] *adj.* accessible, within reach. || **accession** [-'sjɔ̃] *n.f.* accession.

accessoire [aksɛ'swa|ːr] *adj.* accessory, subsidiary. || *n.m.* part, attachment, fixture; [Théât.] prop(erty). || **accessoirement** [-r'mɑ̃] *adv.* accessorily, subsidiarily.

accident [aksi'dɑ̃] *n.m.* **1.** accident: *par* ~, accidentally, by chance. **2.** accident, casualty, mishap: ~ *de la circulation,* traffic accident; *provoquer un* ~, to cause an accident. **3.** ~ *de terrain,* rise (or hollow) in the ground. || **accidenté, -e**[1] [-'te] *adj.* rough, broken (ground). || **accidenté, -e**[2] *n.m.* casualty; one injured in an accident: *les accidentés du travail,* those injured while working. || **accidentel, -le** [-'tɛl] *adj.* accidental, fortuitous. || **accidentellement** [-tɛl'mɑ̃] *adv.* accidentally, by chance.

accise [ak'siːz] *n.f.* excise: *droit d'* ~, excise duty.

acclamation [aklama'sjɔ̃] *n.f.* acclamation, cheer: *par* ~, by acclamation. || **acclamer** [-e] #3 *v. tr.* to cheer, applaud; [Fig.] to acclaim.

acclimatation [aklimat|a'sjɔ̃] *n.f.* acclimatization; *Jardin m d'Acclimatation* (Paris), Zoological garden. || **acclimater** [-e] #3 *v. tr.* to acclimate, to acclimatize. || **s'acclimater** *v. pron.* (à) to become acclimatized (to); [Fig.] to become, get/adapted (to).

accointance [akwɛ̃'tɑ̃ːs] *n.f.* [*usual. pl.*] dealings, connections.

accolade [akɔ'lad] *n.f.* **1.** accolade, embrace [used in conferring decoration]: *donner l'* ~ *(à,* to), → to embrace s.o., to greet s.o.; *une* ~ *fraternelle,* a fraternal, brotherly embrace. **2.** [Mus.] accolade; [Print.] brace: *mettre en* ~, to brace. || **accoler** [akɔ'le] #3 *v. tr.* **1.** to embrace, hug. **2.** to brace.

accommodant, -e [akɔmɔ'd|ɑ̃, -ɑ̃ːt] *adj.* accommodating; easy to get on with, easy to deal with. || **accommodement** [-'mɑ̃] *n.m.* arrangement; compromise. || **accommoder** [-e] #3 *v. tr.* **1.** to accommodate, to adjust. **2.** to prepare (a dish). || **s'accommoder (de)** [(s)-e] *v. pron.* to make shift with, to be content with, to put up with.

accompagnat|eur, -rice [akɔ̃paɲ|a'tœːr, -a'tris] *n.* [Mus.] accompanist. || **accompagnement** [-'mɑ̃] *n.m.* accompaniment. || **accompagner** [-e] #3 *v. tr.* **1.** to accompany, to escort: ~ *un ami à la gare,* to see a friend to the station. **2.** [Mus.] to accompany: ~ *au piano,* to accompany on the piano. || **s'accompagner** *v. pron.* to accompany o.s. (on the piano).

accompli, -e [akõ'pl|i] || *adj.* accomplished; done, performed, perfect: *mettre devant le fait* ~, to present with a fait accompli. || **accomplir** [-i:r] #17 *v. tr.* to accomplish; to complete, to perform: ~ *des prouesses*, to accomplish feats of valour, to do great deeds. || **accomplissement** [-is'mɑ̃] *n.m.* fulfilment.

accord [a'k|ɔ:r] *n.m.* **1.** accord, harmony: *l'* ~ *des différentes parties du tableau*, the unity, harmony of the different parts of the picture; *vivre en parfait* ~, to live in harmony. **2.** agreement: *L'* ~ *s'est fait sur tous les points*, Agreement was reached on all points; *mettre d'* ~, to reconcile; *être d'* ~, to agree; *n'être pas d'* ~, to disagree; *tomber d'* ~, to agree on sth.; [Fam.] *d'* ~, O.K., agreed, granted; *d'un commun* ~, by common consent. **3.** [Mus.] chord; *être d'* ~, to be in tune. || **accordé, -e** [-ɔr'de] *adj.* **1.** granted. **2.** in tune. || **accorder**[1] [-ɔr'de] #3 *v. tr.* **1.** to reconcile, to bring together. **2.** to grant, admit: *Je vous l'accorde*, I'll go along with you on that. **3.** to make (part of speech) agree. || **accorder**[2] #3 *v. tr.* to tune (a violin, &c.). || **s'accorder** *v. pron.* to get along (with, *avec*).

accordéon [akɔrde|'õ] *n.m.* accordion. || **accordéoniste** [-ɔ'nist] *n.* accordion player, accordionist.

accoster [akɔs'te] #3 *v. tr.* **1.** [Naut.] to come alongside: *Le bateau accoste au quai*, The boat/comes, draws/alongside the quay. **2.** [Fig.] to come up to s.o.: *Il m'a accosté dans la rue*, He stopped me in the street, He came up to me in the street.

accotement [akɔt'mɑ̃] *n.m.* side path, shoulder (of road).

accouchement [akuʃ|'mɑ̃] *n.m.* confinement, delivery. || **accoucher** [-e] #3 *v. intr.* to be delivered (of, *de*).

accouder (s') [saku'de] #3 *v. pron.* [conj. ÊTRE] to lean on one's elbow(s). cf. COUDE.

accouplement [akuplə'mɑ̃] *n.m.* coupling; pairing; joining; linking; mating; [Méc.] connection; [Méd.] mating.

accoupler [aku'ple] #3 *v. tr.* to couple; to pair, mate; [bœufs] to yoke; [Tech.] to join, couple up.

accourir [aku'ri:r] #24 *v. intr.* [conj. AVOIR (action), ÊTRE (état)] to come running: *Il est accouru vers moi*, He ran up to me.

accoutrement [akutrə'mɑ̃] *n.m.* costume; [Fam.] get-up.

accoutumance [akuty'mɑ̃:s] *n.f.* custom, practice, use. || **accoutumé, -e** [akuty'm|e] *adj.* accustomed; customary, habitual. || **accoutumer** [-e] #3 *v. tr.* [conj. AVOIR (action), ÊTRE (état)] to accustom; to train; to get used to; to inure. **1.** *Avoir accoutumé de* ~ [used only in the compound tenses], to have the habit of, to be accustomed to: *Je n'ai point accoutumé de dissimuler mes fautes*, I am not in the habit of hiding my/faults, mistakes. **2.** *être accoutumé à qqch.*, to be used to sth. || **s'accoutumer (à)** #3 *v. pron.* to get used to; to be accustomed to.

accréditer [akredi'te] #3 *v. tr.* to accredit; to confirm. || **s'** ~ *v. pron.* to gain credence.

accroc [a'kr|o] *n.m.* **1.** rent, tear (in dress, &c.), cf. ACCROCHER. **2.** [Fig.] stain, blot; liberty (taken with sth.): *faire un* ~ *à la vérité*, to twist facts; *C'est un* ~ *à son honneur*, It is a blot on his escutcheon. || **accrochage** [-ɔ'ʃa:ʒ] *n.m.* **1.** hooking, hitching. **2.** [Mil.] skirmish; [Fig.] run in (with, *avec*). **3.** catch, hitch. || **accrocher** [-ɔ'ʃe] #3 *v. tr.* **1.** to hook, to hang (on a hook). **2.** to catch (clothes on a nail, &c.), to sideswipe (a car): ~ *son habit à un clou*, (1) to hang one's coat on a nail, (2) to catch one's coat on a nail (and tear it). **3.** [Fig.] to get hold of, to nab; [Fam.] to click. || **s'accrocher** *v. pron.* to be caught on; to hang on: *Il s'accroche à une branche*, He/catches on to, hangs on to/a branch; [Fig.] *Il s'accroche au moindre espoir*, He clutches at every straw; ~ *à qqun*, to cling to s.o.

accroire [a'krwa:r] #74 *v. intr.*: *en faire* ~ *à*, to impose upon; *s'en faire* ~, to overestimate o.s.

accroissement [akrwas'mɑ̃] *n.m.* [plante] growth; [Fin.] increase, rise, rising. || **accroître** [a'krwa:tr] #40 *v. tr.* [conj. AVOIR (action), ÊTRE (état)] to increase; to enlarge; to augment. || **s'accroître** *v. pron.* to grow.

accroupir (s') [sakru'pi:r] #17 *v. pron.* to crouch, squat.

accueil [a'k|œ:j] *n.m.* reception, welcome, greeting: *faire bon* ~ *à qqun*, to welcome s.o., to give s.o. a friendly welcome; *recevoir un* ~ *chaleureux*, to receive a warm welcome. || **accueillant, -e** [-œ'jɑ̃(:t)] *adj.* welcoming, pleasing. || **accueillir** [-œ'ji:r] #20 *v. tr.* to receive (well or ill); to welcome, to greet s.o.

acculer [aky'le] #3 *v. tr.* to corner; to bring to bay.

accumulateur [akymyl|atœ:r] *n.m.* [abbr. as **accu**, *pl.* **accus**]; [Auto] battery. || **accumuler** [-e] #3 *v. tr.* to accumulate; to gather (together); to amass; to heap up. || **s'accumuler** *v. pron.* to pile up.

accumulation [akymyla'sjõ] *n.f.* accumulation; [Fin.] hoarding.

accusat|eur, -rice [akyz|a'tœ:r, -a'tris] *n. & adj.* accuser, accusing; [Jur.] prosecutor. || **accusation** [akyza'sjo] *n.f.* accusation, charge; [Jur.] indictment, prosecution: *mettre en* ~, to indict. || **accusé, -e** [akyze] *n.* the/accused, prisoner, defendant; [Com.] ~ *de réception*, acknowledgment (of a letter, &c.). || **accuser** #3 *v. tr.* **1.** ~ *qqun de qqch.*, to accuse s.o. of, to charge s.o. with, sth. **2.** [une baisse, une perte, une différence] to show, indicate. 3. [Loc.] ~ *réception de*, to acknowledge (receipt of). || **s'accuser** *v. pron.*: ~ *d'une faute*, to/confess, admit/a mistake.

acerbe [a'sɛrb] *adj.* [goût] bitter, sour; [parole] biting, sharp.

acéré, -e [ase're] *adj.* steely; [pointe] keen, sharp; [parole] biting, cutting.

achalandage [aʃalɑ̃'da:ʒ] *n.m.* custom, trade.

achalandé, -e [aʃalɑ̃'de] *adj.* [Com., usual. *bien* ~] **1.** well-patronized. **2.** [Abus.] well-stocked.

achaler [aʃa'le] #3 *v. tr.* © [Fam.] to trouble, bother.

acharné, -e [aʃar'n|e] *adj.* tenacious, obstinate; fierce, desperate: *travailleur* ~, a demon for work; *travail* ~, unremitting labour; *des combats acharnés*, severe fighting. || **acharnement** [-ə'mɑ̃] *n.m.* determination, stubbornness: *lutter avec* ~, to fight tooth and nail. || **s'acharner** [-e] #3 *v. pron.* to be bent upon, to pursue relentlessly: ~ *à l'étude, au travail*, to keep one's nose to the grindstone; ~ *contre qqun*, to harass s.o., to keep attacking s.o.

achat [a'ʃa] *n.m.* purchase: *faire des achats*, to go shopping; *pouvoir m d'* ~, purchasing power.

acheminement [aʃmin|'mɑ̃] *n.m.* advance, progression; [lettre, &c.] handling; [merchandise] forwarding, routing. || **acheminer** [-e] #3 *v. tr.* to handle (mail, &c.). || **s'acheminer** *v. pron.* to wend one's way (toward).

acheter [aʃ|'te] #9 *v. tr.* to buy, to purchase; [Fig.] to bribe. || **acheteu|r, -se** [-'tœ:r, -'tø:z] *n.* buyer (≠ CLIENT).

achevé, -e [aʃ|'ve] *adj.* finished; accomplished, perfect. || **achèvement** [-ɛv'mɑ̃] *n.m.* completion; conclusion. || **achever** [-'ve] #9 *v. tr.* to finish; to complete; [Fig.] to do for: ~ *les blessés*, to dispatch the wounded; [☞ souvent rendu par UP]: ~ *de boire*, to drink up.

achigan [aʃi'gɑ̃] © *n.m.* bass: ~ *à grande bouche*, large-mouth bass; ~ *à petite bouche*, small-mouth bass; ~ *de roche*, rock bass (red eye).

acide [a'sid] **1.** *n.m.* acid. **2.** *adj.* acid, sour. || **acidité** [-i'te] *n.f.* acidity. || **acidulé, -e** [asidy'le] *adj.* acidulated: *bonbon* ~, acid drop.

acier [a'sje] *n.m.* steel. || **aciérie** [-'ri] *n.f.* steelworks.

acompte [a'kõ:t] *n.m.* account, cash down, down payment; instalment.

Açores (les) [(lez) a'sɔ:r] *n.fpl.* the Azores.

à-côté (de) [ako'te] *prép.* by, alongside, next to. || **à-côtés** *n.mpl.* (d'une affaire), side issue; [dépense] extra.

à-coup [a'ku] *n.m.* jerk, jolt.

acoustique [akus'tik] *adj.* acoustic. || *n.f.* acoustics.

acquéreur [ake'rœ:r] *n.m.* buyer, purchaser. || **acquérir** [ak|e'ri:r] #23 *v. tr.* **1.** to buy, acquire. **2.** to obtain, get: ~ *de l'influence*, to gain influence. || **acquis, -e** [-i, -i:z] *adj.* **1.** acquired, secured: *mal* ~, ill-gotten; *bien m mal* ~, ill-gotten goods. **2.** devoted (to, *à*): *Il est* ~ *à nos idées*, He shares our convictions. **3.** recognized: *Ce principe est maintenant* ~, This principle has now been recognized; *tenir pour* ~, to take for granted. || *n.m.* experience, cumulative knowledge (of school subject, &c.), background. || **acquisition** [akizi'sjõ] *n.f.* acquisition, purchase: *faire l'* ~ *de*, → to acquire, purchase; [Fig.] *une bonne* ~, a new asset (to a society, group, &c.).

acquit [a'ki] *n.m.* receipt, discharge; [Com.] *Pour* ~, Paid (with thanks). [☞ *See below.*] *Par* ~ *de conscience*, For conscience's sake. || **acquittement** [-t'mɑ̃] *n.m.* [Jur.] acquittal; [Com.] discharge, payment. || **acquitter** #3 [-'te] [Com.] ~ *une dette*, to pay (off) a debt; ~ *une facture*, to pay a bill, to receipt a bill.

acre [a:kr, © ɑ:kr] *n.m.* [measure = 4,840 square yards] acre.

âcre [ɑ:kr] *adj.* acrid, sour; pungent, sharp; [Fig.] bitter, caustic (remarks, &c.). || **âcreté** [ɑkrə'te] *n.f.* [goût] bitterness, acridity; [odeur] pungency.

acrimonie [akrimɔ'ni] *n.f.* acrimony, bitterness.

acrobate [akrɔ'ba|t] *n.m/f* acrobat. || **acrobatie** [-'si] *n.f.* acrobatics, stunt: [air meet] *faire des acroba ies*, to perform stunts. || **acrobatique** [akroba'tik] *adj.* acrobatic.

acte [akt] *n.m.* **1.** action; act: *se livrer à des*

actes de violence, to resort to violence; *faire ~ d'autorité,* → to put one's foot down; *faire ~ d'héritier,* to claim the estate. **2.** (legal) document, certificate, deed; statement: *~ de décès,* death certificate; *~ de naissance,* birth certificate; *rédiger un ~* , to draw up a document; *donner ~ de,* to acknowledge officially. **3.** [Théât.] act. || **act|eur, -rice** [-œːr, -ris] *n.* actor, actress; player.

acti|f, -ve [-if, -iːv] *adj.* active, busy: *l'armée active,* the/active, regular/army [+ *la réserve*]. || **actif** [ak'tif] *n.m.* [Gram.] active voice; [Fin.] assets; [Fig.] asset: *à son ~* , to his credit.

action [ak'sj|õ] *n.f.* **1.** action, operation: *~ de grâces,* thanksgiving. **2.** motion, activity: *L'artillerie entra en ~* , The artillery went into action; [Journ.] *rayon d' ~* , coverage. **3.** deed, feat; [Mil.] engagement, battle: *faire une ~ d'éclat,* to perform a feat; *une bonne ~* , a good deed. **4.** [Com.] stock, share. || **actionnaire** [-ɔ'nɛːr] *n.m.* stockholder. || **actionner** [-ɔ'ne] ♯3 *v. tr.* to set in motion, to drive; [Jur.] to sue, to bring an action against.

activement [aktiv'mã] *adv.* actively, diligently.

activer [akti've] ♯3 *v. tr.* to stir up; to quicken; to activate; to push. || **activité** [aktivi'te] *n.f.* activity, briskness: *rappeler à l' ~* , to call back to military duty; *Le volcan est entré en ~* , The volcano started to erupt.

actrice cf. ACTEUR.

actuaire [ak'tɥɛːr] *n.m.* actuary.

actualité [aktɥali'te] *n.f.* topical subject; current news: *l' ~* , the news, current events; [movie] *les actualités,* the news, the newsreel; *perdre de son ~* , → to become stale. || **actuel, -le** [ak'tɥɛl] *adj.* present; real, effective, [×] cf. ACTUAL. || **actuellement** [-'mã] *adv.* now, at the present time, [×] cf. ACTUALLY.

acuité [akɥi'te] *n.f.* [douleur] sharpness, acuteness; [son] shrillness; [sens] keenness.

adage [a'daːʒ] *n.m.* saying, adage.

adaptation [adapta'sjõ] *n.f.* adaptation; adjustment: *faculté d' ~* , adaptability. || **adapté, -e** [adap't|e] *adj.* suited (to); fitting; adapted, adjusted (to, *à*). || **adapter** [-e] ♯3 *v. tr.* to adapt (to, *à*), to adjust; to fit, to apply (to, *à*). || **s'adapter à,** *v. pron.* to become used to, to become adjusted; to fit: *Les prises de courant européennes ne s'adaptent pas aux appareils canadiens,* European-made plugs do not fit Canadian appliances.

additi|f, -ve [adi|'tif, -'tiːv] *adj.* additive. || *n.m.* additional clause, rider. || **addition** [adisj|õ] *n.f.* addition, sum; thing added; [Com.] check, bill: *L' ~ , s'il vous plaît.* The check, please. || **additionné, -e** *adj. de l'eau additionnée de vinaigre,* → vinegar diluted with water. || **additionnel, -le** [adisjɔ'nɛl] *adj.* additional, extra: *clause ~* , rider. || **additionner** [-ɔ'ne] ♯3 *v. tr.* to add up, to mix (with, *de*), to dilute (with, *de*).

adénoïde [adenɔ'id] *n.* adenoids.

adepte [a'dɛpt] *n. & adj.* adept.

adéquat, -e [ade'kwa(t)] *adj.* adequate (to, *à*); sufficient (for, *à*); equivalent.

adhérence [ade|'rãːs] *n.f.* **1.** adhesion. || **adhér|ent, -e** [-'rã, -'rãːt] *adj. & n.* adherent; follower, member: *membre ~ (d'une société),* associate member. || **adhérer** (à) [-'re] ♯10 *v. tr.* to cling to, to adhere to; [Fig.] to join (a party). || **adhési|f, -ve** [ade'z|if, -iːv] *adj. & n. (m.)* adhesive. || **adhésion** [-zjõ] *n.f.* adherence; agreement, support: *donner son ~ à un projet,* to give one's approval to a project, → to agree on.

adieu, -x [a'djø] *n.m.* **1.** farewell, leave: *faire ses adieux à,* to say goodbye to; to take leave; [Fig.] *dire ~ à,* to kiss goodbye to. **2.** *interj. inv.* Goodbye! Farewell!

adjacent, -e [adʒa's|ã, -ãːt] *adj.* [rooms] adjoining; [properties] contiguous; [angles] adjacent.

adjectif [adʒek'tif] *n.m.* adjective.

adjoindre [adʒ|wɛ̃ːdr] ♯36 *v. tr.* to adjoin, add, associate. || **adjoint, -e** [-wɛ̃(ːt)] *adj.* associate, assistant: *directeur ~* , assistant manager; [industrie privée] executive vice-president. || *n.* associate, assistant, deputy. || **adjonction** [-õk'sjõ] *n.f.* adjunction, addition.

adjudant [adʒy'dã] *n.m.* company sergeant-major; warrant officer; © adjutant.

adjudication [adʒy|dika'sjõ] *n.f.* **1.** adjudication, tender. **2.** giving out of a contract, disposal (of sth.) by auction. || **adjuger** [-'ʒe] ♯5 *v. tr.* to award, adjudicate, grant; [aux enchères] to knock down; [un prix, &c.] to grant, give.

adjurer [adʒy're] ♯3 *v. tr.* to entreat, beseech.

admettre [ad'mɛtr] ♯44 *v. tr.* **1.** to admit, allow. **2.** to let (s.o., sth.) in; to receive (in a house, an association); to pass (an examination). **3.** to concede, to grant: *Admettons un instant que . . . ,* Let's suppose for the sake of argument that . . .; *en admettant que . . . ,* even if . . .

administrat|eur, -rice [administra|'tœːr,

-'tris] *n.* **1.** administrator, manager, executive. **2.** [membre d'un conseil d'administration] director, trustee, regent. || **administrati|f, -ve** [-'tif, -'ti:v] *adj.* administrative: *style* ~, officialese. || **administration** [-a'sjõ] *n.f.* **1.** administration, management, direction: *conseil d'* ~, board of directors, governors. **2.** [coll.] the management (of a company), the administration, the government (of a country): ~ *centrale*, civil government. || **administrer** [-e] #3 *v. tr.* **1.** to govern, manage, control: [Fig.] ~ *une raclée*, to give a good beating. **2.** [R.C.] ~ *un sacrement*, to administer a sacrament.

admirable [admi'r|abl] *adj.* admirable; wonderful. || **admirablement** [-ablə'mɑ̃] *adv.* admirably, perfectly. || **admirat|eur, -rice** [a'tœ:r, -a'tris] *n.* admirer, [Fam.] fan. || **admiration** [-a'sjõ] *n.f.* admiration, wonder. || **admirer** [-e] #3 *v. tr.* to admire; to wonder (at).

admis, -e [ad'mi(:z)] *adj.* admitted, received, accepted: *Ce n'est pas* ~, → This is not done. cf. ADMETTRE. || **admissible** [-'sibl] *adj.* allowable, permissible; eligible (to a post), [Sch.] who has passed the written and may take the oral examination. || **admission** [-'sjõ] *n.f.* [×] admission, [douane] entry.

admonester [admɔnɛs'te] #3 *v. tr.* to admonish; to reprove (a child, &c.).

admonition [admɔni'sjõ] *n.f.* admonition.

adolescence [adɔlɛ'sɑ̃:s] *n.f.* adolescence, youth. || **adolescent, -e** [adolɛ'sɑ̃, -ɑ̃:t] *n. & adj.* youth, teenager, adolescent.

adonner (s') [sadɔ'ne] #3 *v. pron.* to give o.s. up (to, *à*); to take (to, *à*); [Péj.] to be addicted to; © to get along (with).

adopter [adɔp|'te] #3 *v. tr.* **1.** to adopt (child, new product, &c.), to take up (an attitude): ~ *une ligne de conduite*, to take a line. **2.** to pass (a bill, a motion). || **adopti|f, -ve** [-'tif, -'ti:v]: *enfant m* ~, adopted child; *père m* ~, foster father. || **adoption** [-'sjõ] *n.f.* adoption.

adorable [adɔ'r|abl] *adj.* **1.** adorable, venerable. **2.** charming, bewitching, delightful. || **adorat|eur, -rice** [a'tœ:r, -a'tris] *n.m/f* worshipper. || **adoration** [-a'sjõ] *n.f.* worship, adoration. || **adorer** [-e] #3 *v. tr.* to adore, to worship; [Fig.] to dote upon (a child), to idolize.

adosser [ado'se] #3 *v. tr.* to build (*contre*, against a wall, &c.). || **s'adosser** *v. pron.* to lean (against, *à*, *contre*); to lean back.

adoucir [adus|i:r] #17 *v. tr.* to soften, sweeten; [Fig.] to mitigate, alleviate. || **adoucissant, -e** [-i'sɑ̃, -i'sɑ̃:t] *adj.* softening, soothing. || **adoucissement** [-is'mɑ̃] *n.m.* softening; mitigation.

adresse [a'drɛs] *n.f.* **1.** address; direction: *Quelle est votre adresse?* → Where do you live? **2.** © speech. **3.** skill, cleverness. cf. ADROIT. || **adresser** [-e] #3 *v. tr.* **1.** to address (a letter to, *à*); to direct (s.o. to). **2.** ~ *la parole à*, to speak to. || **s'adresser à,** *v. pron.* to apply to; to speak to, to address (an audience): *Prière de* ~ *au guichet à côté*, Next wicket, please; *Un homme s'est adressé à moi dans la rue*, a man spoke to me on the street.

adroit, -e [a'drw/a, -at] *adj.* **1.** skilful, dexterous: *Il est* ~ *de ses mains*, He is clever with his hands. **2.** clever, adroit.

adroitement [adrwat'mɑ̃] *adv.* skilfully, shrewdly.

aduler [ady'le] #3 *v. tr.* to flatter, fawn upon.

adulte [a'dylt] *adj. & n.m/f* adult, grown-up.

adultère [adyl'tɛ:r] *adj.* adulterous. || *n.m.* adultery; [person] adulterer, *f.* adulteress.

advenir [advə'ni:r] #22 *v. intr.* to happen, occur: *advienne que pourra*, come what may.

adverbe [ad'vɛrb] *n.m.* adverb.

adversaire [advɛr'sɛ:r] *n.m.* opponent; [Fig.] competitor. || **adverse** [ad'vɛrs] *adj.* opposite; contrary: *camp* ~, enemy camp; *circonstance* ~, contrary circumstance.

adversité [advɛrsi'te] *n.f.* adversity, misfortune, disaster.

aération [aer|a'sjõ] *n.f.* ventilation, airing. || **aérer** [-e] #10 *v. tr.* to ventilate, air.

aérien, -ne [ae'rj|ɛ̃, -ɛn] *adj.* aerial; [Fig.] light, airy: *métro m* ~, elevated railway; *pont* ~, airlift.

aéro- [aero-] *prefix* [Greek: pertaining to the air, hence] → || **aérodrome** [-'dro:m] *n.m.* airfield, airdrome. || **aérodynamique** [aerodina'mik] *adj.* aerodynamic: *de ligne* ~, streamlined. || *n.f.* aerodynamics. || **aérogare** [-'ga:r] *n.f.* airline terminal. || **aéronautique** [aerono'tik] *adj.* aeronautical. || *n.f.* aeronautics. || **aéronef** [-'nɛf] *n.m.* [Tech.] aircraft. || **aéroplane** [-'plan] *n.m.* airplane; now obs. → AVION. || **aéroport** [-'pɔ:r] *n.m.* airport.

affabilité [afabili'te] *n.f.* affability. || **affable** [a'fɑ:bl] *adj.* courteous, friendly.

affadir [afa'di:r] #17 *v. tr.* to make tasteless, to render insipid.

affaiblir [afɛ'bl|i:r] #17 *v. tr.* to weaken, enfeeble; [Fig.] to lessen, attenuate. cf. FAIBLE. || **affaiblissement** [-is'mɑ̃] *n.m.* weakening, decay; [état] debility.

affaire [a'f|ɛ:r] *n.f.* **1.** affair, business, matter, concern: *avoir ~ à,* to deal with; *avoir ~ avec,* to have business to transact with; *faire son ~ à qqun,* to take care of s.o., to settle s.o.'s hash; *J'en fais mon ~,* I'll take care of it, Leave it to me; *Cela fait mon ~,* It suits me; *C'est son ~,* That's his concern, Let him worry about that; *Il connaît son ~,* He knows his business; *Ce fut l' ~ d'un instant,* It was done in a jiffy; *En voilà une ~,* That's a pretty kettle of fish. **2.** case: *l' ~ Landru,* the Landru case. ‖ *n.fpl.* **1.** business, affairs: *être dans les affaires,* to be in business; *le ministre des Affaires extérieures,* the Secretary of State for External Affairs. **2.** things, belongings: *Range tes ~,* Put your things away. ‖ **affairé, -e** [-ɛ're] *adj.* busy, bustling. ‖ **s'affairer** *v. pron.* to bustle around, to fuss.

affaissement [afɛs'mɑ̃] *n.m.* subsidence; depression; prostration; [Méd.] collapse. ‖ **s'affaisser**[safɛ'se] #3 *v. pron.* to settle, slump.

affamé, -e [afa'me] *adj.* famished, starving; [Fig.] ravenous. ‖ **affamer** [afa'me] #3 *v. tr.* to starve.

affectation [afɛkt|a'sjõ] *n.f.* affectation, pretence; mannerism; appropriation (of funds), assignment (of person) ‖ **affecté, -e** [-e] *adj.* affected, simulated; earmarked, assigned (to, *à*). ‖ **affecter** [-e] #3 *v. tr.* to affect; to pretend (to, *de*); to earmark, to assign. ‖ **s'affecter** *v.pron.* to grieve (over, *de*).

affection [afɛk|'sjõ] *n.f.* **1.** affection, love. **2.** ailment, disease. ‖ **affectueusement** [-tuøz'mɑ̃] *adv.* affectionately, fondly. ‖ **affectueu|x, -se** [-'tɥø, -'tɥø:z] *adj.* affectionate, tender, loving.

afférent, -e [afe'rɑ̃(:t)] *adj.* relevant, applicable, pertaining.

affermer [afɛr'me] #3 *v. tr.* to farm out.

affermir [afɛr'm|i:r] #17 *v. tr.* to strengthen; [pouvoir] consolidate. ‖ **s'affermir** *v. pron.* to harden. ‖ **affermissement** [-is'mɑ̃] *n.m.* strengthening, hardening; [pouvoir] consolidation.

affichage [afiʃa:ʒ] *n.m.* (bill-)posting: *tableau m d' ~,* bulletin board, [Br.] notice-board. ‖ **affiche** [a'fiʃ] *n.f.* bill, poster; sign. ‖ **afficher** [-e] #3 *v. tr.* to post (up) (a bill): *Défense d' ~,* → Post no bills; [Fig.] to make a show of, to parade. ‖ **s'afficher,** *v. pron.* to make a show of o.s.

affiler [afi'le] #3 *v. tr.* to sharpen; to whet.

affiliation [afilj|a'sjõ] *n.f.* affiliation. ‖ **affilier** [-e] #3 *v. tr.* to affiliate (with, *à*). ‖ **s' affilier** *v. pron.* to affiliate o.s. (with, *à*).

affiner [afi'ne] #3 *v. tr.* to refine.

affinité [afini'te] *n.f.* [also Fig.] affinity; relationship (by marriage); [things] connection.

affirmati|f, -ve [afirm|a'tif, -a'ti:v] *adj.* affirmative, positive. ‖ **affirmation** [-a'sjõ] *n.f.* assertion. ‖ **affirmative** [-a'ti:v] *n.f.* affirmative. ‖ **affirmer** [-e] #3 *v. tr.* to affirm, assert. ‖ **s'affirmer** *v. pron.* to assert o.s.

affleurer [aflœ're] #3 *v. tr.* to be flush with. ‖ *v. intr.* [Géol.] to crop out.

affliction [aflik'sjõ] *n.f.* affliction, (deep) sorrow. ‖ **affligé, -e** [afli'ʒe] *adj.* afflicted, grieved, distressed. ‖ **affliger** [afli'ʒe] #5 *v. tr.* [corps] to afflict, distress, pain; [qqun] to grieve.

affluence [afly|'ɑ̃:s] *n.f.* affluence; [Fig.] abundance, wealth; throng, crowd; *heures d' ~,* rush hours. ‖ **affluent** [-ɑ̃] *n.m.* affluent, tributary. ‖ **affluer** [-e] #3 *v. intr.* to flow, run (towards, to, into, *vers, à, dans*); to be abundant.

affolé, -e [afɔ'l|e] *adj.* distracted; panicky. ‖ **affolement** [-'mɑ̃] *n.m.* distraction; panic. ‖ **affoler** [afɔ'le] #3 *v. tr.* to bewilder, disturb; [boussole] to unsettle; [machine] to race. ‖ **s'affoler** *v. pron.* to panic, to become panicky; to dote (*de,* on).

affranchi, -e [afrɑ̃'ʃi] *adj.* [Pers.] emancipated, free(d); [letter] stamped, prepaid. ‖ *n.* freed/-man, -woman/.

affranchir [afrɑ̃'ʃ|i:r] #17 *v. tr.* **1.** to (set) free (a slave); to release. **2.** [Postes] to frank (a letter), to prepay: *enveloppe affranchie,* prepaid, stamped/envelope. ‖ **s'affranchir** *v.pron.* to become emancipated (from, *de*). ‖ **affranchissement** [-ismɑ̃] *n.m.* liberation, emancipation; [Postes] postage; franking, stamping.

affrètement [afrɛt'mɑ̃] *n.m.* chartering, freighting. ‖ **affréter** [afre'te] #10 *v. tr.* to freight, charter: © *~ un avion,* to charter a plane.

affreusement [afrøz'mɑ̃] *adv.* horridly, frightfully. ‖ **affreu|x, -se** [a'fr|ø, -ø:z] *adj.* frightful; hideous; horrible, ghastly.

affront [a'frõ] *n.m.* affront, snub, insult: *faire (un) ~ à qqun,* to snub, to insult s.o. ‖ **affronter** [-'te] #3 *v. tr.* to brave, to stand up against: *~ qqun,* to face, to defy (s.o.).

affubler [afy'ble] #3 *v. tr.* to deck out, rig out (*de,* in).

affût [a'fy] *n.m.* ambush: *chasser à l' ~,* to stalk; *être à l' ~ de qqch.* (des nouvelles,

d'une occasion), to lie in wait for, to watch for, to be on the lookout for.
affûter [afy'te] #3 *v. tr.* to whet; © to taper (off); to whittle.
afin de [+ inf.] [a'fɛ̃d(ə)] *prép.* (in order) to. || **afin que** [-k(ə)] [+ subj.] *conj.* in order that, so that.
africain, -e [afri'k|ɛ̃, -ɛn] *adj. & n.* African. || **Afrique** [a'frik] *n.f.* Africa: *l' ~ du Nord*, North Africa; *l' ~ du Sud*, South Africa, cf. UNION.
agaçant, -e [aga's|ɑ̃, -ɑ̃:t] *adj.* aggravating, annoying. || **agacement** [agas|'mɑ̃] *n.m.* **1.** irritation, annoyance, peevishness. **2.** [des dents, des nerfs] setting on edge. || **agacer** [-e] #4 *v. tr.* to irritate, annoy, © to tease, ogle.
âge [ɑ:ʒ] *n.m.* **1.** age (years): *Quel ~ avez-vous?* How old are you?; *d'un certain ~*, middle-aged; *être d'un ~ à, être en ~ de*, to be old enough to . . . ; *être dans la force de l' ~*, to be in the prime of life; *être en ~ de se marier*, to be of marriage-able age, to be old enough to marry. **2.** period; epoch: *l' ~ de la pierre*, the Stone Age; *le Moyen Age*, the Middle Ages. || **âgé, -e** [a'ʒe] *adj.* aged; old: *~ de dix ans*, ten years old; *plus ~*, older; *le plus ~*, the oldest, eldest.
agence [a'ʒɑ̃:s] *n.f.* agency, bureau; [Bank, &c.] branch: *~ immobilière*, real estate office; *~ de publicité*, advertising agency.
agencement [aʒɑ̃s|'mɑ̃] *n.m.* arrangement, fitting together. || **agencer** [-e] #4 *v. tr.* to arrange, dispose; [avec soin] to adjust; [Méc.] to put together.
agenda [aʒɛ̃'da] date book, engagement book, diary.
agenouiller s' [saʒnu'je] #3 *v. pron.* to kneel down. cf. GENOU.
agent [a'ʒɑ̃] *n.m.* **1.** agent, officer; deputy: *~ de change*, stockbroker; *~ consulaire*, consular agent. **2.** *agent* (*de police*), policeman, constable; patrolman.
agglomération [aglɔmera'sjɔ̃] *n.f.* mass, aggregation; built-up area: *L' ~ parisienne*, Greater Paris.
agglomérer [aglɔme're] #10 *v. tr.* to agglomerate.
aggraver [agra've] #3 *v. tr.* to aggravate; to make worse. || *s' ~ v. pron.* to become aggravated; to worsen.
agile [a'ʒil] *adj.* agile, nimble; active. || **agilité** [-i'te] *n.f.* nimbleness, agility.
agioter [aʒjɔ'te] #3 *v. intr.* to job; to speculate, gamble, play the market.
agir [a'ʒ|i:r] #17 *v. intr.* **1.** to act, take action; to behave: *~ à sa guise, à sa tête*, to do as one pleases. **2.** to operate, have an effect (on, *sur*). **3. s'agir,** *impers.* → *Il s'agit de . . . , De quoi s'agit-il?* What is it about? What's all this about? || **agissant** [-i'sɑ̃, -i'sɑ̃:t] *adj.* active, busy; effective. || **agissements** [-is'mɑ̃] *n.mpl.* doings, goings-on [usual. pej.].
agitation [aʒit|a'sjɔ̃] *n.f.* agitation, disturbance; excitement, restlessness: *~ des esprits*, social unrest. || **agité, -e** [aʒi'te] *adj.* [Pers.] restless, fidgety; [foule] riotous; [époque] unsettled; [mer] choppy, wild; [Méd.] [Pers.] restless, [nuit] sleepless, [sommeil] fitful. || **agiter** [-e] #3 *v. tr.* to agitate; to stir, disturb; to wave (a flag, &c.); [Fig.] *~ une question*, to debate a point. || **s'agiter** *v. pron.* to be agitated, restless, excited; to rush around.
agneau [a'ɲo] *n.m.* lamb.
agnostique [agnɔs'tik] *adj.* agnostic.
agonie [agɔ'ni] *n.f.* death throes; [Fig.] decline (of a regime, &c.): *être à l' ~*, to be at the point of death, dying. || **agonisant, -e** [-'zɑ̃, -'zɑ̃:t] *adj.* dying; in the throes of death; in a dying state. || *n.* a dying person. || **agoniser** [-'ze] #3 *v. intr.* to be dying, at the point of death.
agrafe [a'graf] *n.f.* hook, clasp. || **agrafer** #3 *v. tr.* [-e] to hook (on), to staple. || **agrafeuse** [-ø:z] *n.f.* stapler.
agraire [a'grɛ:r] *adj.* agrarian; → land: *réforme ~*, land reform.
agrandir [agrɑ̃'d|i:r] #17 *v. tr.* to enlarge; to increase, augment; to aggrandize. || **s'agrandir** *v. pron.* to grow, become larger, to expand. || **agrandissement** [-is'mɑ̃] *n.m.* enlargement; expansion.
agrarien, -ne [agra'rj|ɛ̃, -ɛn] *adj.* agrarian.
agréable [agre'abl] *adj.* agreeable, nice; pleasing, pleasant. || **agréablement** [-ə'mɑ̃] *adv.* agreeably, pleasantly.
agréé, -e [agre'e] *adj.* recognized, accepted, chartered: © *comptable agréé*, chartered accountant. || **agréer** [agre'e] #3 *v. tr.* to accept; [être d'accord] to agree to (a proposal, &c.). || *v. intr.* to please, be acceptable (to, *à*).
agrégé, -e [agre'ʒe] *n.*: *professeur ~*, © associate professor, [Fr.] agrégé *m* [on a par with Ph.D.]. || **agréger** [agre'ʒe] #7 *v. tr.* to aggregate, associate (*à*, to). || **s'agréger** *v. pron.*: *~ à*, to join.
agrément [agre'mɑ̃] *n.m.* **1.** assent, approval. **2.** pleasure, charm: *arts d' ~*, accomplishments.
agrès [a'grɛ] *n.mpl.* rigging (of a ship); [Gym.] apparatus.
agresseur [agrɛs|œ:r] *n.m.* aggressor, assailant. || **agressi|f, -ve** [-if, -i:v] *adj.* aggres-

sive. || **agression** [-jõ] *n.f.* aggression; attack.
agricole [agri'k|ɔl] *adj.* agricultural. || **agriculteur** [-yl'tœ:r] *n.m.* farmer [×] FERMIER. || **agriculture** [-yl'ty:r] *n.f.* agriculture; farming.
agripper [agri'pe] #3 *v. tr.* to clutch, grab. || **s'agripper** (à) to clutch, grab (to).
aguerri [agɛ'ri] *adj.* seasoned, hardened, inured.
aguets [a'gɛ] *n.mpl.* watch(ing). [only in phrase]: *être, se tenir aux* ~, to be on the watch, lookout.
ah! [ɑ] *interj.* ah! oh!: *Ah ça!,* Now look!
ahuri, -e [ay'ri] *adj.* bewildered, open-mouthed. || **ahurissement** [-is'mɑ̃] *n.m.* bewilderment, stupefaction.
ai; aie; aient; aies; ait, cf. AVOIR.
aide [ɛ:d] **1.** *n.f.* aid; help; relief: *à l'* ~ *de,* with (the help of); *venir en* ~ *à,* to help. **2.** *n.m.* helper, assistant, aide. || **aider** [ɛ'de] #3 *v. tr.* to help, aid; to assist, relieve (the poor): ~ *qqun à/descendre, monter, passer par-dessus, &c.,* → to help s.o./down, up, over, &c. || **s'aider** (mutuellement, les uns les autres) to help one another. cf. S'ENTR'AIDER.
aïe! [aj] *interj.* ouch!
aïeul, -e [a'j|œl] *n.* grandfather *m.,* grandmother *f.* || **aïeux** [-ø] *n.mpl.* ancestors; forefathers, forebears.
aigle [ɛgl] *n.m.* eagle [is feminine when referring to the female or when used in heraldry].
aiglefin [ɛglə'fɛ̃] *n.m.* haddock.
aigre [ɛgr] *adj.* sour, bitter; [Fig.] harsh, bitter; acrimonious. || **aigreur** [-œ:r] *n.f.* sourness, acidity, heartburn; bitterness, acrimony. || **aigri, -e** [-i] *adj.* [Fig.] embittered, soured. || **aigrir** [-i:r] #17 *v. tr.* to sour, make sour; [Fig.] to embitter. || **s'aigrir** #17 *v. pron.* to turn sour; to grow bitter.
aigu, aiguë [e'gy] *adj.* acute (angle); sharp, pointed; shrill (sound), acute (pain).
aiguille [e'gɥi:j] *n.f.* needle; [horloge] hand; [église] spire; [Rail.] switch.
aiguiller [egɥi'je] #3 *v. tr.* [Tech.] to shunt, to switch; [Fig.]: ~ *sur,* to switch on to.
aiguillon [egɥi'jõ] *n.m.* goad; [dard] sting; [Fig.] [passion] spur; [remords] pricks.
aiguillot [ɛgɥi'jo] © *n.m.* spring dog fish.
aiguiser [egi'ze] #3 *v. tr.* to sharpen; to whet.
ail [a:j] *pl.* **aulx** [o] *n.m.* garlic.
aile [ɛl] *n.f.* wing; [de moulin] sail; [d'hélice] blade; [d'auto] fender: *voler de ses propres ailes,* to stand on one's feet. || **ailé, -e** [-e] *adj.* winged.
aileron [ɛl'rõ] *n.m.* [oiseau] pinion; [pingouin] flipper, [requin] fin; [avion] aileron, wing-flap.
aille, &c., cf. ALLER.
ailleurs [a'jœ:r] *adv.* elsewhere, somewhere else; [Loc.] *d'* ~, besides, moreover; *par* ~, furthermore, incidentally.
aimable [ɛ'mabl] *adj.* friendly, kind, pleasant, amiable.
aimant[1], -e [ɛ'm|ɑ̃, -ɑ̃:t] *adj.* loving, affectionate.
aimant[2] [ɛ'mɑ̃] *n.m.* magnet. || **aimanté** [-'te] *adj.*: *aiguille aimantée* (*de la boussole*), magnetic needle.
aimer [ɛ'me] #3 *v. tr.* **1.** to love, be in love with: *se faire* ~, to endear. **2.** to like, be fond of, delight in: *Aimez-vous la musique?* Are you/fond of music, → a music lover? **3.** *aimer bien,* to like: *Il vous aime bien,* He likes you. **4.** *aimer mieux* [= PRÉFÉRER], to prefer, like better: *J'aime mieux Mozart,* → I had rather have M.; give me M. any time. || **s'aimer,** *v. pron.* to love oneself: *Aimez-vous les uns les autres,* Love one another.
aine [ɛ:n] *n.f.* groin.
aîné, -e [ɛ'ne] *adj.* & *n.* elder, eldest; senior: *le fils* ~, [de deux] the elder son; [de plus de deux] the eldest son.
ainsi [ɛ̃'si] **1.** *adv.* thus, so; in this way, that way: *Ainsi soit-il,* So be it; amen; *s'il en est* ~, if such is the case. **2.** *conj.* thus: ~ *on l'oublia,* Thus he was forgotten; ~ *que,* in the same way as, as well as, as.
air[1] [ɛ:r] *n.m.* air, wind; airing: *courant d'* ~, draught; *en plein* ~, in the open (air); *prendre l'* ~, (1) to take a walk; (2) [avion] to take off, to become air-borne. || © *Air-Canada,* Trans-Canada Airlines, TCA. || **airs** *n.mpl.* the sky: *dans les* ~, in the air; *par la voie des* ~, by air.
air[2] *n.m.* look; appearance: *avoir l'* ~, to look, seem: *Il a l'* ~ *malade,* He looks ill; *un* ~ *de famille,* a family likeness. || **airs** *n.mpl.*: *prendre de grands* ~, to give oneself airs.
air[3] *n.m.* [Mus.] tune: *un* ~ *d'opéra,* an operatic aria.
airain [ɛ'rɛ̃] *n.m.* †brass, bronze.
aire [ɛ:r] *n.f.* **1.** threshing floor. **2.** area, surface, space. **3.** point of the compass. **4.** eyrie.
airelle [ɛ'rɛl] *n.f.,* cf. BLEUET. ~ *du Canada,* blueberry.
aisance [ɛ'zɑ̃:s] *n.f.* **1.** ease, facility; freedom (of movement): *avoir de l'* ~, to

have poise, to have an ease of manner. **2.** comfort, easy circumstances: *être dans l'* ~, to be well off.

aise [ɛ:z] *n.f.* ease; comfort: *à l'* ~, at ease; comfortable; *mal à l'* ~, ill at ease; *à votre* ~, as you like. || *adj.* glad: *je suis/bien, †fort/aise de,* I am very glad to. || **aisé** [ɛ'ze] *adj.* [manières] easy, free; [vêtement] comfortable; [financièrement] well-off, well-to-do. || **aisément** [-'mɑ̃] *adv.* easily, readily. || **aises** *n.fpl.* comfort: *aimer ses* ~, to like to be comfortable; *prendre ses* ~, to make oneself comfortable.

aisselle [ɛ'sɛl] *n.f.* armpit.

aîtres [ɛ:tr] *n.mpl.* the ins-and-outs (of a house).

ajonc [a'ʒɔ̃] *n.m.* furze, gorse.

ajournement [aʒurn|ə'mɑ̃] *n.m.* adjournment; postponement; [Jur.] summons. || **ajourner** [-e] #3 *v. tr.* to adjourn, postpone; [discussion] to table; [candidat] to send back.

ajouter [aʒu'te] #3 *v. tr.* to add, join: *ajouter foi à,* to give credence to.

ajuster [aʒys'te] #3 *v. tr.* to adjust; [vêtement] to fit; [piano] to tune; to aim at (gibier). || **ajusteur** [aʒys'tœ:r] *n.m.* fitter.

alacrité [alakri'te] *n.f.* alacrity.

alambic [alɑ̃'bik] *n.m.* still.

alanguir [-'gi:r] #17 *v. tr.* to weaken, enfeeble. || **s'alanguir** *v. pron.* to languish; [attitude] to droop. || **alanguissement** [alɑ̃|gis'mɑ̃] *n.m.* languor, weakness.

alarmant, -e [alarm|ɑ̃, -ɑ̃:t] *adj.* alarming, causing concern, anxiety. || **alarme** [a'larm] *n.f.* alarm; sudden fear: *Donner l'* ~, To give the alarm. || **alarmer** [-e] #3 *v. tr.* to startle, frighten, alarm. || **s'alarmer** *v. pron.* to take alarm, to alarm o.s.

Alaska [alas'ka] *n.* Alaska: *la route de l'* ~, the Alaska highway.

Albanie [alba'ni] *n.f.* Albania.

albâtre [al'bɑ:tr] *n.m.* alabaster.

albatros [alba'tro:s] *n.m.* albatross.

Alberta, l' [albɛr|'ta] *n.f.* Alberta; *en, dans l'/Alberta,* in, to/A. || **albertain, -e** [-'tɛ̃, -'tɛn] *adj. & n.* Albertan, (of) Alberta.

albinos [albi'no:s] *n.m.* albino.

album [al'bɔm] *n.m.* [timbres] album; [coupures] scrap book; [dessin] sketch book.

albumen [alby'mɛn] *n.m.* albumen.

alcali [alka'li] *n.m.* alkali.

alchimie [alʃi'mi] *n.f.* alchemy.

alcool [al'k|ɔl © = oɔl] *n.m.* alcohol; spirits.

alcôve [al'ko:v] *n.f.* alcove, recess; [dortoir] cubicle.

aléa [ale'a] *n.m.* risk, hazard. || **aléatoire** [-'twa:r] *adj.* risky, precarious.

alène [a'lɛ:n] *n.f.* awl.

alentour (de) [alɑ̃'tu:r] **1.** *adv.* about, around, round about. || *n.pl.* neighbourhood, vicinity (of a town).

Aléoutes [ale'ut] **1.** *n.m.* Aleut (Eskimo); *n.fpl.* Aleutians; *les (îles) Aléoutiennes,* the Aleutian Islands, the Aleutians.

alerte[1] [a'lɛrt] *n.f.* alarm, warning: *sonner l'* ~, to sound the alarm; *se tenir en* ~, to be on the alert. || *interj. Alerte!* Look out! || **alerter** [-e] #3 *v. tr.* ~ *l'opinion publique,* to tell the public, to arouse public opinion.

alerte[2] *adj.* alert (mind, &c.), brisk, agile.

aléser [ale'ze] #10 *v. tr.*: to bore, drill.

alevin [al'vɛ̃] *n.m.* fry, young fish.

algarade [alga'rad] *n.f.* quarrel.

algèbre [al'ʒɛbr] *n.f.* algebra.

Alger [al'ʒe] *n.f.* Algiers. || **Algérie** [-'ri] *n.f.* Algeria. || **algérien, -ne** [-'rjɛ̃, -'rjɛn] *adj. & n.* Algerian. || **algérois, -e** [-'rwa, -'rwa:z] *adj.* (of) Algiers.

Algonquin, -e [algɔ̃'k|ɛ̃, -in] *n.m.* (langue) Algonquian; (homme) Algonquin.

algue [alg] *n.f.* seaweed.

alibi [ali'bi] *n.m.* alibi.

aliénation [aljena'sjɔ̃] *n.f.* alienation, transfer; [Pers.] estrangement: ~ *mentale,* mental derangement.

aliéné, -e [alje'ne] *adj. & n.* insane, insane person: *asile d'aliénés,* mental hospital.

aliéner [alje'ne] #10 *v. tr.* [biens, droits] to alienate, transfer; [Pers.] to alienate, estrange; [esprit] to unbalance.

alignement [aliɲ|'mɑ̃] *n.m.* alignment, line-up: ~ *des roues,* wheel alignment. || **aligner** [-e] #3 *v. tr.* to align, to line up; [Mil.] to draw up, dress. [Fig.] *s'aligner sur (la politique d'un parti),* to toe the line, to fall in line with.

aliment [ali'mɑ̃] *n.m.* food: *apprêter les aliments,* to cook. cf. CUISINE, RÉGIME, NOURRITURE. || **alimentaire** [-'tɛ:r] *adj.* [having to do with food] *régime* ~, diet; *pâtes (alimentaires),* macaroni, spaghetti. || **alimentation** [-ta'sjɔ̃] *n.f.* **1.** feeding. **2.** food; grocery trade: [Fr.] *un magasin d'* ~, a food store. **3.** alimentation, supplies; [Tech.] feed. || **alimenter** [-'te] #3 *v. tr.* to feed; to supply. || **s'alimenter** *v. pron.* to take nourishment, to feed o.s.

alité [ali'te] *adj.* confined to one's bed. || **s'aliter** [sali'te] #3 *v. pron.* to take to one's bed (when ill).

alizé [ali'ze] *n.m.* trade wind.

allaiter [alɛ'te] #3 *v. tr.* to suckle.

allant [a'lɑ̃] *n.m.* initiative, go, dash: *avoir de l'* ~ , *être plein d'* ~ , to be full of /energy, [Fam.] pep/.

allécher [alle'ʃe] #10 *v. tr.* to allure, entice.

allée [a'le] *n.f.* walk; *grande* ~ , drive, driveway; [Loc.] *allées et venues*, coming and going. [×] ALLEY.

alléger [alle'ʒe] #7 *v. tr.* to lighten; [Fig.] to alleviate, relieve (pain, &c.), cf. LÉGER.

allégorie [alegɔ'ri] *n.f.* allegory. || **allégorique** [-k] *adj.* allegorical.

allègre [a'lɛgr] *adj.* lively, cheerful; brisk. || **allégresse** [ale'grɛs] *n.f.* joy, cheerfulness, elation.

alléguer [ale'ge] #10 *v. tr.* **1.** to cite. **2.** to allege, adduce, give (a reason).

Allemagne [al'm|aɲ] *n.f.* Germany. || **allemand, -e** [-ɑ̃, -ɑ̃:d] *adj.* German. || **Allemand, -e** *n.* German.

aller [a'le] #14 *v. intr.* **1.** to go: *s'en* ~ , to go away, to go off; ~ *chercher*, to go get, to fetch. **2.** [of health] to be: *Il va mieux*, He is better. **3.** to be becoming, to suit: *Le bleu lui va bien*, Blue is very becoming to her; *Cela me va*, It suits me. **4.** [Loc.] *Allons!*, Come now!; *Allez-y!*, Go to it!, More power to you!; *Cela va sans dire*, It goes without saying. || **aller** *n.m.* run, (outgoing) trip: *à l'* ~ , on the way/over/out/; *(billet d') aller et retour* [Rail.], round-trip ticket, [Br.] return ticket; ~ *simple*, one-way ticket, [Br.] single (ticket).

allergie [alɛr'ʒi] *n.f.* allergy.

alliage [a'lj|a:ʒ] *n.m.* alloy. || **alliance** [-ɑ̃:s] *n.f.* **1.** alliance, covenant, union **2.** wedding ring. cf. JONC. || **allié, -e** [-e] *adj.* allied, related (by marriage). *n.* ally. || **allier** [-e] #3 *v. tr.* to ally; to unite, blend; [Tech.] to alloy. || **s'allier (à)** *v. pron.* to join forces with to ally o.s. (to, with); to marry (into a family).

alligator [aliga'tɔ:r] *n.m.* alligator.

allô! [a'lo] *interj.* **1.** [Téléphone] hello [☞ often doubled in Fr., allô-allô!]. **2.** © hello! [call of greeting or surprise].

allocation [alɔka'sjõ] *n.f.* allocation; assignment; allotment; allowance: ~ *familiale*, family allowance.

allocution [alɔky'sjõ] *n.f.* address, speech.

allonge [a'lõ:ʒ] *n.f.* © shed, lean-to.

allongement [alõʒ'mɑ̃] *n.m.* lengthening; elongation. || **allonger** [alõ'ʒe] #5 *v. tr.* to lengthen; to stretch (out), elongate: ~ *son tir*, to raise one's sights. || **s'allonger** *v. pron.* to become longer or taller, to stretch out; to lie down.

allouer [a'lwe] #3 *v. tr.* to allow, grant, allocate, award.

allumage [aly'm|a:ʒ] *n.m.* [Auto] ignition. || **allumer** [-e] #3 *v. tr.* **1.** to light (up), kindle (a fire); to set fire to, to set . . . on fire. **2.** [Fig.] to inflame, stir up (passions). **s'allumer** *v. pron.* to kindle, to ignite. || **allumette** [-ɛt] *n.f.* match: *frotter une* ~ , to strike a match.

allumoir [aly'mwa:r] *n.m.* lighter.

allure [a'ly:r] *n.f.* **1.** walk, gait. **2.** pace: *à toute* ~ , at full speed. **3.** conduct, behaviour, manner; *Il a une drôle d'* ~ , He looks odd; © *Ça n'a pas d'* ~ , It doesn't make sense.

allusion [ally'zjõ] *n.f.* allusion, hint: *faire* ~ *à*, to hint (at), to allude (to), to refer (to).

almanach [alma'na(k)] *n.m.* almanac, calendar.

aloi [a'lwa] *n.m.* [only in]: *de bon* ~ , genuine, sterling; *de mauvais* ~ , dubious.

alors [a'lɔ:r] *adv.* **1.** then; at that time: *jusqu'* ~ , up to then. **2.** in that case: [Fam.] *Et alors?*, So what? cf. APRÈS. || **alors que,** whereas; while.

alose [a'lo:z] *n.f.* (common) shad.

alouette [a'lwɛt] *n.f.* lark; © meadowlark; ~ *des champs*, skylark.

alourdir [alur'd|i:r] #17 *v. tr.* to make . . . heavy, to weigh . . . down. || **s'alourdir** *v. pron.* to become heavy, sluggish. || **alourdissant, -e** [-i'sɑ̃, -i'sɑ̃:t] *adj.* heavy, oppressive.

aloyau [alwa'jo] *n.m.* sirloin.

Alpes [alp] *n.fpl.* the Alps: *les* ~ *françaises*, the French Alps. || **alpestre** [-ɛstr] *adj.* (pertaining to the Alps) → Alpine.

alphabet [alfa'b|ɛ] *n.m.* alphabet; reader, speller. || **alphabétique** [-e'tik] *l'ordre* ~ alphabetical order.

alpin, -e [alp|ɛ̃ -in] *adj.* Alpine [Fr.] *chasseur m* ~ , Alpine rifleman. || **alpinisme** [-i'nism] *n.m.* mountaineering. || **alpiniste** [-i'nist] *n.m.* (mountain climber) mountaineer [☞ but a person who lives in the mountains is *un montagnard*].

Alsace [al'zas] *n.f.* Alsace. || **alsacien, -ne,** [-jɛ̃, -jɛn] *adj. & n.* Alsatian.

altération [altera'sjõ] *n.f.* adulteration; deterioration; debasement; change; break (in the voice). || **altéré, -e** [alte'r|e] *adj.* thirsty, thirsting (for, *de*); altered for the worst: *d'une voix altérée par l'émotion*, in a quavering voice. || **altérer** [-e] #10 *v. tr.* to impair, adulterate; to make thirsty. [×] cf. ALTER. || **s'altérer** *v. pron.* to deteriorate, go bad.

alternance [altɛrn|ɑ̃:s] *n.f.* alternation. || **alternati|f, -ve** [-a'tif, -a'ti:v] *adj.* alternate;

alternative, alternating: *courant* ~ , A.C. (current). cf. CONTINU. || **alternative** *n.f.* choice (between two things), option. [×] ALTERNATIVE. || **alternativement** [-ativ'mɑ̃] *adv.* alternately, by turns. || **alterner** [-e] #3 *v. tr.* to alternate; to rotate (crops).

altesse [al'tɛs] *n.f.* highness: *Son Altesse royale,*/His, Her/Royal Highness.

alti|er, -ère [al't|je, -jɛːr] *adj.* haughty, proud. || **altitude** [-i'tyd] altitude: *prendre de l'* ~ , to climb.

alto [al'to] *n.m.* [instrument] viola; [voix] alto.

altruisme [altry'ism] *n.m.* altruism.

aluminium [alymi'njɔm] *n.m.* © [US] aluminum; [Br.] aluminium.

alun [a'lœ̃] *n.m.* alum.

***alunir** [aly'niːr] #17 *v. intr.* to land (on the moon).

alvéole [alve'ɔl] *n.m.* [Tech.] alveolus; cell (in a honeycomb); socket (of a tooth).

amabilité [amabili'te] *n.f.* kindness, friendliness.

amadou [ama'du] *n.m.* amadou, tinder, touchwood.

amadouer [ama'dwe] #3 *v. tr.* to coax.

amaigri, -e [amɛ'gr|i] *adj.* thinner, emaciated. || **amaigrir** [-iːr] #17 *v. tr.* & *intr.* to make (s.o.) look thinner, to have a reducing effect on. || **amaigrissant, -e** [-i'sɑ̃, -i'sɑ̃ːt] *adj.* reducing, emaciating: *régime* ~ , reducing diet. || **amaigrissement** [-is'mɑ̃] *n.m.* reducing; emaciation.

amalgame [amal'gam] *n.m.* conglomeration, amalgam, medley.

amalgamer [amalga'me] #3 *v. tr.* to amalgamate; [Jur.] to consolidate, to merge.

amande [a'mɑ̃ːd] *n.f.* almond; kernel (of some fruits); [Fig.] *en* ~ , almond-shaped.

amant, †amante [ɑ'm|ɑ̃, -ɑ̃ːt] *n.* lover.

amarre [a'maːr] *n.f.* mooring (rope); hawser; cable.

amarrer [ama're] #3 *v. tr.* [navire] to moor; [à quai] to berth; [canot] to secure.

amas [a'mɑ] *n.m.* heap, pile, mound. || **amasser** [-'se] #3 *v. tr.* to accumulate, to heap up; to gather, to hoard (money); to collect (pictures, &c.): *Pierre qui roule n'amasse pas mousse,* A rolling stone gathers no moss. || **s'amasser** *v. pron.* to gather, to pile up.

amateur [ama'tœːr] *n.m.* **1.** lover of a thing; connoisseur: ~ *de hockey,* hockey fan; ~ *de musique,* a music lover. **2.** amateur, non-professional: *travailler à qqch. en* ~ , to do sth. as a hobby.

Amazone, l' [ama'zoːn] *n.* the Amazon (River).

†ambages [ɑ̃'baːʒ] *n.fpl.* [usual. in the neg.]: *sans* ~ , frankly, straight from the shoulder; *Il le lui déclara sans* ~ , He gave it to him straight.

ambassade [ɑ̃ba'sad] *n.f.* embassy: *l'* ~ *du Canada à Paris,* the Canadian Embassy in Paris. || **ambassadeur** [-œːr] *n.m.* ambassador. || **ambassadrice** [-ris] *n.f.* ambassadress [the masc. is also used].

ambiance [ɑ̃'bj|ɑ̃ːs] *n.f.* (intellectual) atmosphere, environment. || **ambiant, -e** [-ɑ̃, -ɑ̃ːt] *adj.* [Tech.] ambient, surrounding: *l'air* ~ , the ambient air.

ambidextre [ɑ̃bi'dɛkstr] *adj.* ambidextrous. || *n.m/f.* ambidexter.

ambigu, -ë [ɑ̃bi'g|y] *adj.* ambiguous. || **ambiguïté** [-ɥi'te] *n.f.* ambiguity.

ambitieusement [-ɑ̃bisjøz'mɑ̃] *adv.* ambitiously. || **ambitieu|x, -se** [ɑ̃bi'sj|ø, -øːz] *adj.* & *n.* ambitious, aspiring. || **ambition** [-õ] *n.f.* ambition. || **ambitionner** [-ɔ'ne] #3 *v. tr.* to aspire to, desire; © to monopolize.

ambivalence [ɑ̃biva'lɑ̃ːs] *n.f.* ambivalence.

ambre [ɑ̃ːbr] *n.m.* amber.

ambulance [ɑ̃by'l|ɑ̃ːs] *n.f.* ambulance; field hospital. || **ambulancier** [-ɑ̃ː'sje] *n.m.* ambulance driver. || **ambulant, -e** [-ɑ̃, -ɑ̃ːt] *adj.* travelling, itinerant: *marchand m* ~ , (street) vendor, peddler, hawker.

âme [ɑːm] *n.f.* **1.** soul, spirit: *Dieu ait son* ~ , God have mercy on/him, her/; *corps et* ~ , body and soul; *de toute son* ~ , heart and soul; *rendre l'* ~ , to give up the ghost. **2.** person: *une ville de dix mille âmes,* a town of ten thousand inhabitants; *une bonne* ~ , a kind soul; *pas* ~ *qui vive,* not a (living) soul.

amélioration [ameljɔr|a'sjõ] *n.f.* improvement: *susceptible d'* ~ , → that can be improved. || **améliorer** [-e] #3 *v. tr.* to improve. || **s'améliorer** *v. pron.* to get better, to improve: *Sa santé s'améliore,* His health is getting better.

amen [a'mɛn] *n.m.* & *interj.* amen.

aménagement [amenaʒ'mɑ̃] *n.m.* arrangement; equipment, fitting.

aménager [amena'ʒe] #5 *v. tr.* [locaux] to fit up; [chute d'eau] to harness; [ville] to plan; [Fin., impôts] to adjust.

amende [ɑ'mɑ̃ːd] *n.f.* fine: *mettre à l'* ~ , *infliger une* ~ *à,* to fine; *faire* ~ *honorable,* to make amends.

amendement [amɑ̃d'mɑ̃] *n.m.* improvement; [Jur.] amendment.

amener [am'ne] #9 *v. tr.* to bring (along); to lead; to induce: *Elle l'a amené à changer* *d'avis*, She induced him to change his mind; *Amenez votre ami*, Bring your friend; *amener/huit, six, douze* (aux dés), to turn up/an eight, a six, a twelve; *~ son pavillon*, to strike one's flag.

aménité [ameni'te] *n.f.* amenity: *sans ~*, roughly, harshly.

amenuiser [amənɥi'ze] #3 *v. tr.* to thin, whittle; to pare. || **s' ~** *v. pron.* to dwindle, thin down.

am|er, -ère [a'm|ɛːr] *adj.* bitter; sad, painful: *un goût ~*, a bitter taste; *rendre ~*, to make bitter. || **amèrement** [-ɛr'mɑ̃] *adv.* bitterly; grievously: *pleurer ~*, to weep bitter tears.

américain, -e [ameri'k|ɛ̃, -ɛn] *adj.* American; → US: *un citoyen ~*, a US citizen; [Fam.] Yankee, Yank: *Il a l'œil ~*, He is pretty sharp; *le dollar ~*, the US dollar. || *n.*: *C'est un Américain*, He is an American; [langue] American (English): *Traduit de l'américain*, From the American original.

américanisme [amerika'nism] *n.m.* americanism.

amérindien, -ne [amerɛ̃'dj|ɛ̃, -ɛn] *adj. & n.* Amerindian (i.e. American Indian), Amerind.

Amérique [ame'rik] *n.f.* America; the United States (of America): *l' ~ du Nord*, North America; *l' ~ latine*, Latin America.

amerrir (ou **amérir**) [ame'riːr] #17 *v. intr.* to alight on the water.

amertume [amɛr'tym] *n.f.* bitterness; grief; affliction.

ameublement [amœblə'mɑ̃] *n.m.* furniture, furnishings.

ameuter [amø'te] #3 *v. tr.* **1.** to train (dogs). **2.** to rouse, excite (the populace). || **s'ameuter** *v. pron.* to get stirred up (against, *contre*).

ami, -e [a'mi] *n.* friend; [Fam.] *un ami*, a boy friend; *une amie*, a girl friend; [Fr.] *une petite amie*, a mistress. || *adj.* friendly (to): *en pays ~*, in a friendly country.

amiante [a'mjɑ̃ːt] *n.f.* asbestos.

amibe [a'mib] *n.f.* amœba.

amical, -e [ami'kal] *adj.* friendly. || **amicalement** [-'mɑ̃] *adv.* in a friendly way.

amidon [ami'd|õ] *n.m.* starch. || **amidonner** [-ɔ'ne] #3 *v. tr.* to starch.

aminci [amɛ̃'s|i] *adj.* slender; slim; [bois] planed down. || **amincir** [-iːr] #17 *v. tr.* to make thinner, to make (s.o.) look slim, slender; to thin down (wood). || **s'amincir** *v. pron.* to become thin(ner). || **amincissant, -e** [-i'sɑ̃, -i'sɑ̃ːt] *adj.* thinning. || **amincissement** [-is'mɑ̃] *n.m.* thinning; thinning down (of wood); growing thin; reduction.

amiral [ami'ral] *n.m.* admiral: *navire ~*, flagship.

amitié *n.f.* [ami'tje] friendship; friendliness: *se lier/se prendre/d' ~ avec qqun*, to become friends with s.o.; *envoyer ses amitiés*, to send one's kind regards.

ammonia|c, -que [amɔ'njak] *adj.* ammoniacal. || **ammoniac** *n.m.* ammonia.

amnésie [amne'zi] *n.f.* amnesia.

amnistie [amnis'ti] *n.f.* amnesty.

amoindrir [amwɛ̃'driːr] #17 *v. tr.* to diminish, lessen; to depreciate, belittle. || **s'amoindrir** *v. pron.* to grow less, to diminish.

amoindrissement [amwɛ̃dris'mɑ̃] *n.m.* lessening, decrease.

amollir [amɔ'l|iːr] #17 *v. tr.* to soften; to enervate. || **s'amollir** *v. pron.* to soften; to weaken.

amonceler [amõs'le] #8 *v. tr.* to heap up, accumulate. || **s'amonceler** *v. pron.* to accumulate, pile up.

amont [a'mõ] *n.m.*: *en ~*, *vers l' ~*, upstream.

amorçage [amɔr'saːʒ] *n.m.* priming.

amorce [a'mɔrs] *n.f.* [poisson, &c.] bait; [fusil, pompe, mine] priming; [Electr.] fuse; [Fig.] lure, allurement; starting, beginning. || **amorcer** [amɔr'se] #4 *v. tr.* [pêche] to bait; [fusil, pompe, mine] to prime; [Fig.] to initiate, begin.

amorphe [a'mɔrf] *adj.* amorphous, shapeless, flabby.

amortir [amɔr't|iːr] #17 *v. tr.* **1.** [coup, choc, &c.] to soften, absorb; [couleur] to tone down; [son] to deaden, muffle; [douleur] to deaden; [passions] to calm. **2.** [dette] to pay off (over a period of time); [immeuble, outillage, &c.] to amortize. || **s'amortir** *v. pron.* [coup, choc] to be absorbed by, softened; [ardeur] to be calmed; [rentes, dettes, &c.] to be paid off. || **amortissement** [-is'mɑ̃] *n.m.* [d'un emprunt, &c.] repayment, redemption; [industriel] amortization; [Fig.] [passions, haines] calming: *caisse, fonds/d' ~*, sinking fund. || **amortisseur** [-i'sœːr] *n.m.* [d'une voiture, &c.] shock-absorber; [d'un son] sound-absorber; [Elect.] damper.

amour [a'm|uːr] *n.m.* [often *f.* when *pl.*] love; passion: © *être/tomber/en amour*, to be/fall/in love; © *Pour l'amour!*, For the love of/Pete, Mike/!, For Heaven's sake! || **amoureu|x, -se** [-u'rø(ːz)] *adj.* in love (with, *de*). || *n.* lover; sweetheart.

amovible [amɔ'vibl] *adj.* removable; revocable; detachable.

ampère [ɑ̃'pɛ,r] *n.m.* ampere.
amphibie [ɑ̃fi'bi] *adj.* amphibious. || *n.m.* amphibian.
amphithéâtre [ɑ̃fite'ɑːtr] *n.m.* amphitheatre; (lecture) theatre.
ample [ɑ̃ːpl] *adj.* [vêtements] loose; [robes] full; [espace] ample; [quantité] ample, copious; [geste] sweeping. || **ampleur** [ɑ̃'plœːr] *n.f.* amplitude, extent. || **amplificateur** [ɑ̃plifika'tœːr] *n.m.* amplifier. || **amplifier** [ɑ̃pli'fje] #3 *v. tr.* to amplify, enlarge on. || **amplitude** [ɑ̃pli'tyd] *n.f.* amplitude.
ampoule [ɑ̃'pul] *n.f.* **1.** blister. **2.** phial; ampoule. **3.** (electric) bulb.
amputation [ɑ̃pyta'sjɔ̃] *n.f.* amputation. || **amputer** [ɑ̃py'te] #3 *v. tr.* to amputate (arm, leg, &c.).
amusant, -e [amy'z|ɑ̃, -ɑ̃ːt] *adj.* funny; amusing; pleasing. || **amusement** [-'mɑ̃] *n.m.* amusement, entertainment. || **amuser** || [-e] *v. tr.* **1.** to amuse, entertain (s.o.). **2.** to deceive, [Fam.] to fool (s.o.). || **s'amuser** *v. pron.* to have a good time; to enjoy o.s.; to be amused (at), to amuse o.s. (by, *à*).
amygdale [ami'dal] *n.f.* tonsil.
an [ɑ̃] *n.m.* year: *jour de l'* ~, New Year's Day; *bon* ~, *mal* ~, year in, year out; *en l'* ~ *de grâce,* in the year of our Lord; *avoir dix ans,* to be ten years old, cf. ANNÉE.
anachronique [anakrɔ'ni|k] *adj.* anachronistic. || **anachronisme** [-sm] *n.m.* anachronism.
analgésie [analʒe'zi] *n.f.* analgesia. || **analgésique** [-k] *adj.* analgesic.
analogie [analɔ'ʒi] *n.f.* analogy. || **analogique** [-k] *adj.* analogical. || **analogue** [ana'lɔg] *adj.* analogous, similar (to, *à*).
analphabète [analfa'bɛt] *adj. & n.* illiterate.
analyse [ana'liːz] *n.f.* anaylsis: *en dernière* ~, in the last analysis. || **analyser** [anali'ze] #3 *v. tr.* to analyse; [Gram.] to parse. || **analytique** [anali'tik] *adj.* analytic(al).
ananas [ana'na] *n.m.* pineapple.
anarchie [anar'ʃi] *n.f.* anarchy, chaos. || **anarchiste** [-st] *n.m.* anarchist.
anatomie [anatɔ'mi] *n.f.* anatomy.
anatomique [anatɔ'mik] *adj.* anatomical.
ancestral [ɑ̃sɛs'tral] *adj.* ancestral. || **ancêtre** [ɑ̃'sɛːtr] *n.m.* ancestor, forefather.
anchois [ɑ̃'ʃwa] *n.m.* anchovy.
ancien, -ne [ɑ̃'sj|ɛ̃, -ɛn] old, ancient, antiquated; former, late, retired: *des meubles anciens,* antique furniture; *un* ~ *étudiant,* a former student.
ancrage [ɑ̃'kraːʒ] *n.m.* anchoring, anchorage.
ancre [ɑ̃ːkr] *n.f.* [Naut.] anchor: *jeter l'* ~, to cast anchor; *lever l'* ~, to weigh anchor. || **ancrer** [ɑ̃'kre] #3 *v. tr. & intr.* to anchor; to secure. || **s'ancrer** [sɑ̃'kre] *v. pron.* **1.** to anchor. **2.** [Fig.] to establish o.s., to dig in.
Andes, les [ɑ̃ːd] *n.fpl.* the Andes.
andouille [ɑ̃'duj] *n.f.* chitterlings [pl.]; [Fig.] fool, ninny.
André [ɑ̃'dre] *n.m.* = Andrew.
âne [ɑːn] *n.m.* ass; donkey; [Fig.] fool: *un* ~ *bâté,* a blockhead.
anéantir [aneɑ̃t|iːr] #17 *v. tr.* to annihilate, destroy; [Fig.] to overwhelm. || **anéantissement** *n.m.* [-is'mɑ̃] annihilation, destruction; [Fig.] prostration.
anecdote [anɛk'dɔt] *n.f.* anecdote.
anémie [ane'm|i] *n.f.* anæmia. || **anémier** [-je] #3 *v. tr.* to render anæmic. || **s'anémier** *v. pron.* to become anæmic. || **anémique** [-ik] *adj.* anæmic.
ânerie [an'ri] *n.f.* gross ignorance; stupidity; asinine remark.
ânesse [ɑ'nɛs] *n.f.* she-ass.
anesthésie [anɛste'zi] *n.f.* anæsthesia.
anfractuosité [ɑ̃fraktɥɔzi'te] *n.f.* anfractuosity; sinuosity; cranny: *les anfractuosités de la côte,* the indentations along the coast.
ange [ɑ̃ːʒ] *n.m.* angel; [Fig., Fam.] a dear, a darling: *être aux anges,* to be blissfully happy. || **angélique** [ɑ̃ʒ|-e'lik] *adj.* angelic(al), pure. *n.* [Bot.] angelica. || **Angélus** [-e'lys] *n.m.* [R.C.] Angelus.
angevin, -e [ɑ̃ʒ'v|ɛ̃, -in] *adj. & n.* native of, pertaining to, Anjou [a French province].
angine [ɑ̃'ʒin] *n.f.* angina; [Fam.] sore throat; [Méd.] tonsillitis; ~ *de poitrine,* angina pectoris.
anglais, -e [ɑ̃'gl|ɛ, -ɛːz] *adj.* **1.** English, British: [Fig.] *filer à l'anglaise,* to take French leave. **2.** © (English-speaking) Canadian: *le Canada* ~, English-speaking Canada. || **Anglais, -e** *n.* Englishman, Englishwoman, © (an English-speaking) Canadian; *les Anglais,* the English, the British, © the (English-speaking) Canadians. || **anglais** *n.m.* English, the English language.
angle [ɑ̃ːgl] *n.m.* angle; corner: *à l'* ~ *d'une rue,* at a street corner; [Fig.] *sous l'* ~ *de,* from the angle of.
Angleterre [ɑ̃gl|ətɛːr] *n.f.* England, [loosely] Britain. || **anglican, -e** [-i'kɑ̃, -i'kan] *adj. & n.* Anglican: *l'Église anglicane du Canada,*

the Church of England in Canada. || **anglicisme** [-i'sism] *n.m.* anglicism. || **anglo-** [-o-] *préf.* Anglo- [Having to do with the English]: ~ *-américain*, Anglo-American; ~ *-canadien*, English-Canadian; *Îles fpl anglo-normandes*, the Channel Islands. ~ *-protestant*, Anglo-Protestant; ~ *-saxon*, Anglo-Saxon.

angoissant, -e [ɑ̃gwa's|ɑ̃, -ɑ̃:t] *adj.* agonizing, anxious. || **angoisse** [ɑ̃'gwa:s] *n.f.* anxiety, agony, anguish.

anguille [ɑ̃'gi:j] *n.f.* eel; [Fig.] *Il y a ~ sous roche*, There is something in the wind.

angulaire [ɑ̃gy'l|ɛ:r] *adj.* angular; [Fig.] *pierre f. ~*, cornerstone. || **anguleu|x, -se** [-ø, -ø:z] *adj.* angular, gaunt, stiff.

animal [ani'mal] *n.m.* animal; brute, beast. || *adj.* animal, brutish.

animateur [anima|'tœ:r, -'tris] *adj.* animating; life-giving. || *n.m.* promoter; prime mover. || **animation** [-'sjõ] *n.f.* animation; liveliness, excitement, bustle. || **animé, -e** [ani'm|e] *adj.* animated; lively, gay. (Ciné.) *dessin ~*, (animated) cartoon. || **animer** [-e] #3 *v. tr.* to animate, to set in motion; to enliven. || **s'animer** *v. pron.* to come to life, to become animated, lively.

animosité [animozi'te] *n.f.* animosity.

anis [a'ni] *n.m.* anise: *graine d'* ~, aniseed.

annales [a'nal] *n.fpl.* annals, historical records.

anneau [a'no] *n.m.* ring; link (of a chain); ringlet (of hair).

année [a'ne] *n.f.* year; *l'* ~ *scolaire*, the school year, the academic session, [US] the college year; *bonne ~ !*, Happy New Year! cf. AN.

annexe [a'nɛks] *n.f.* annex, appendix; addition, supplement, [document] rider. || *adj.* annexed, enclosed. || **annexer** [-e] #3 *v. tr.* to annex; [livre] to append; [dans une lettre] to enclose (documents, &c.). || **annexion** [-jõ] *n.f.* annexation.

annihiler [anii'|le] #3 *v. tr.* to annihilate.

anniversaire [anivɛr'sɛ:r] *n.m.* & *adj.* anniversary; birthday.

annonce [a'n|õ:s] *n.f.* announcement, notification; ad(vertisement); [Jour.] ad.: *petites annonces*, © *annonces classées*, classified ads. || **annoncer** [-õ'se] #4 *v. tr.* **1.** to announce, herald. **2.** to announce, show (a visitor) in. **3.** © to advertise. || **annonceur** [-õ'sœ:r] *n.m.* **1.** advertiser, sponsor. **2.** [Radio] © announcer.

Annonciation [anõsja'sjõ] *n.f.* [jour] Lady Day; [fête] Annunciation.

annoncier [-õ'sje] *n.m.* [Fr.] advertising agent; © advertiser.

annoter [anɔ'te] #3 *v. tr.* to annotate.

annuaire [a'nɥ|ɛ:r] *n.m.* year book: *l'* ~ *du téléphone*, telephone directory. cf. AN. || **annuel, -le** [-ɛl] *adj.* yearly, annual. || **annuité** [-i'te] *n.f.* annuity.

annulaire [any'lɛ:r] *n.m.* the ring finger [the fourth finger]. cf. ANNEAU.

annulation [anyl|a'sjõ] *n.m.* cancellation; [mariage] annulment. [contrat] voidance. || **annuler** [-e] #3 *v. tr.* to cancel, annul, to make void.

anoblir [anɔ'bli:r] #17 *v. tr.* to ennoble; [Br.] to raise to the peerage.

anodin [anɔ'dɛ̃] *adj.* mild, harmless, innocuous.

anomalie [anɔma'li] *n.f.* anomaly.

ânon [ɑ'n|õ] *n.m.* ass's foal; [Fam.] dunce. || **ânonner** [-ɔ'ne] #3 *v. tr.* to drone out, to mumble. || *v. intr.* to hem and haw.

anonymat [anɔni'ma] *n.m.* anonymity.

anonyme [anɔ'nim] *adj.* & *n.* anonymous, nameless: [Com.] *société* ~, limited company.

anormal, -e [anɔr'mal] *adj.* abnormal.

anse [ɑ̃:s] *n.f.* handle (of a pan, basket, &c.); ear (of a pot); [Géog.] cove.

antagonisme [ɑ̃tagɔ'nism] *n.m.* antagonism. || **antagoniste** [ɑ̃tagɔ'nist] *adj.* & *n.* antagoniste.

Antarctique (l') [(l)ɑ̃tark'tik] *n.m.* Antarctica.

antécédent, -e [ɑ̃tese'dɑ̃(:t)] *adj.* antecedent, precedent. || *n.m.* [usual. pl.] background, past history.

antenne [ɑ̃'tɛn] *n.f.* antenna, aerial.

antérieur, -e [ɑ̃te'rj|œ:r] *adj.* [dans le temps] **1.** previous, earlier. **2.** [dans l'espace] forward, anterior. || **antérieurement** [-œr'mɑ̃] *adv.* previously, at an earlier date.

anthologie [ɑ̃tɔlɔ'ʒi] *n.f.* anthology.

anthropologie [ɑ̃trɔpɔlɔ'ʒi] *n.f.* anthropology.

anti- [ɑ̃ti] *préf.* [= opposed to], as in **antiaérien, -ne** *adj.* antiaircraft. || **antibiotique** [-bjɔ'tik] *n.m.* antibiotic [penicillin, &c.]. || **antichambre** [-'ʃɑ̃:br] *n.f.* anteroom. || **antichar** [-'ʃa:r] *adj. inv.* antitank.

anticipation [ɑ̃tisip|a'sjõ] *n.f.* anticipation; *anticipations fpl*, science fiction. || **anticiper** [-e] #3 *v. tr.* to anticipate; to forestall.

anticlérical, -e [ɑ̃tikleri'kal] *adj.* anticlerical.

Anticosti (l'île d') [ɑ̃tikɔs'ti] *n.m.* Anticosti Island.

antidérapant, -e [ɑ̃tidera'pɑ̃(:t)] *adj.* non-skid (tire, &c.).

antidote [ɑ̃ti'dɔt] *n.m.* antidote (*à*, *de*, for, against).

antigel [-'ʒɛl] *n.m.* antifreeze.

antillais, -e [ɑ̃ti'jɛ(:)z] *adj.& n.* West Indian. || **Antilles** [ɑ̃'tij] *n.fpl.* [Géog.] the West Indies, the Antilles: *La mer des* ~ , the Caribbean Sea.

antipathie [ɑ̃tipa'ti] *n.f.* antipathy, aversion: *éprouver de l'* ~ *à l'égard de qqun,* to dislike s.o. || **antipathique** [-k] *adj.* not likable: *Je le trouve* ~ , → I don't like him.

antipode [ɑ̃ti'pɔd] *n.m.* antipode; [Fig.] exact opposite (*de,* of/to); [Australie] *aux antipodes,* down under.

antiquaire [ɑ̃ti'kɛ:r] *n.m.* antique dealer. || **antique** [ɑ̃'tik] *adj.* ancient: *la Grèce* ~, Ancient Greece. || **antiquité** [-i'te] *n.f.* **1.** antiquity. **2.** antique.

antiseptique [ɑ̃tisɛp'tik] *adj.* antiseptic. || *n.m.* antiseptic, germ-killer.

Antoine [ɑ̃'twan] *n.m.* = Anthony.

antre [ɑ̃:tr] *n.m.* cave, den; [animal] lair.

Anvers [ɑ̃'vɛrs] *n.* Antwerp. || **Anversois, -e** [-a(:z)] *adj. & n.* of Antwerp.

anxiété [ɑ̃ksj|e'te] *n.f.* anxiety; uneasiness, deep concern. || **anxieu|x, -se** [-ø(:z)] *adj.* anxious, uneasy.

août [(a)u] *n.m.* August.

apache [a'paʃ] *n.m.* [bandit] thug, apache; [Indien] Apache.

apaisement [apɛz'mɑ̃] *n.m.* appeasement; pacifying (*ou* PACIFICATION); [soif] quenching; [souffrance] alleviation. || *pl.* [Fig.] assurances. || **apaiser** [apɛ'ze] #3 *v. tr.* to appease, calm, pacify; to alleviate (sorrow, pain); to quench (one's thirst); to appease (one's hunger). || **s'apaiser** *v. pron.* to quiet down, cool down, to subside.

Apalaches (Les) [(lez)apa'laʃ] *n.mpl.* Appalachian Mountains.

apathie [apa'ti] *n.f.* apathy. || **apathique [-k]** *adj.* apathetic.

apercevoir [apɛrs|ə'vwa:r], **apercevant** [-ə'vɑ̃], **aperçu** [-y] #34 *v. tr.* **1.** to see [usually in the distance]. **2.** [Fig.] to see. || **s'apercevoir (de)** [sapɛrsə'vwa:r] *v. pron.* to notice, realize: *Il ne s'en est pas aperçu,* He did not realize it. || **aperçu** [apɛr'sy] *n.m.* glimpse, insight; rough estimate, general outline.

apéritif [aperi'tif] *n.m.* aperitif, appetizer.

à peu près [apø'prɛ] *adv.* nearly, about. || **à-peu-près** *n.m.* approximation.

apeuré, -e [apœ're] *adj.* frightened.

apitoiement [apitwa|'mɑ̃] *n.m.* compassion. || **apitoyer** [-'je] #12 *v. tr.* to touch, move, with compassion. || **s'apitoyer** *v. pron.* to be moved to/pity, compassion/: ~ *sur,* to pity, to commiserate with.

aplanir [apla'ni:r] #17 *v. tr.* [bois, &c.] to plane; [route] to level; [Fig.] to smooth (down); [difficulties] to iron out.

aplatir [apla'ti:r] #17 *v. tr.* to flatten (out), beat flat. || **s'** ~ *v. pron.* to flatten out, to lie flat; [Fig.] to crouch.

aplomb [a'plɔ̃] *n.m.* **1.** equilibrium. **2.** [Fig.] self-command, aplomb; [Péj.] cheek, impudence: *Avoir l'* ~ *de faire quelque-chose,* To have the nerve to do something.

apoplexie [apɔplɛk'si] *n.f.* apoplexy.

apostolat [apɔstɔ'l|a] *n.m.* apostolate. || **apostolique** [-ik] apostolic: *nonce* ~ , Papal nuncio.

apostrophe [apɔs'trɔf] *n.f.* apostrophe. || **apostropher** [-e] #3 *v. tr.* to hail; †to apostrophize.

apôtre [a'po:tr] *n.m.* apostle: *le symbole des Apôtres,* the Apostles' creed.

apparaître [apa'r|ɛ:tr], **apparaissant** [-ɛ'sɑ̃], **apparu** [-y] #46 *v. intr.* **1.** to appear, to come to light, to become visible. **2.** to appear, seem, become evident.

appareil [apa'rɛj] *n.m.* apparatus; machine; device; instrument; [photo] camera; [Fr.] mouthpiece (of telephone); *Qui est à l'* ~ *?,* Who is speaking? || **appareillage** [-a:ʒ] *n.m.* **1.** equipment, outfit; [petits appareils] fixtures: ~ *électrique,* fixtures. **2.** [Naut.] sailing.

appareiller [aparɛ'je] #3 *v. tr.* **1.** to match, pair. **2.** [Naut.] to get under way.

apparemment [apara'mɑ̃] *adv.* apparently. || **apparence** [apa'r|ɑ̃:s] *n.f.* appearance; looks: *en* ~ , seemingly, outwardly; *selon toute* ~ , in all probability; *n.fpl.* appearances: *sauver les apparences,* to save face. || **apparent, -e** [-ɑ̃(:t)] *adj.* apparent, visible; conspicuous. || **apparition** [-i'sjɔ̃] *n.f.* apparition; appearance: *faire une* ~ , to put in an appearance.

appartement [apartə'mɑ̃] *n.m.* flat, apartment; [hôtel] suite of rooms; © room.

appartenance [apartə'nɑ̃:s] *n.f.* affiliation: *l'* ~ *à un parti politique,* party affiliation. || **appartenir** [apartə'n|i:r] #22 *v. intr.* **1.** to belong (to, *à*); to pertain. **2.** [Admin.] to concern; to be the privilege of: *Il vous appartiendra de . . . ,* It will be your concern to . . .

appauvrir [apo'vr|i:r] #17 *v. tr.* to impoverish; to weaken. || **s'appauvrir** *v. pron.* to become poor, to grow poorer; [Fig.] to degenerate. || **appauvrissement** [-is'mɑ̃] *n.m.* impoverishment; degeneration.

appel [a'pɛl] *n.m.* **1.** call, roll call: *faire* ~ *à,* to call on, to call in, to have recourse to; *faire un* ~ *téléphonique,* to place a phone call. **2.** appeal: *interjeter un* ~ , to lodge an appeal; *Cour d'* ~, Appellate Court. || **appeler** [a'ple] #8 *v. tr.* **1.** to call; to call for; summon, to send for: *appeler le médecin,* to call for a doctor; *On appela un médecin,* A doctor was sent for. **2.** to name. **3.** to require, to call for. || **s'appeler** *v. pron.* to be called, named: *Comment t'appelles-tu?,* → What's your name?; *Je m'appelle Marie,* → My name is Mary.

appendice [apɑ̃'dis] *n.m.* [Anat.] appendage; [livre] appendix (pl. -ices); [Méd.] appendix (pl. -es). || **appendicite** [-it] *n.f.* appendicitis.

appentis [apɑ̃'ti] *n.m.* lean-to.

appesantir [apəzɑ̃'ti:r] #17 *v. tr.* to weigh down, to make heavy. || **s'appesantir** *v. pron.* to become/heavy, drowsy/; to weigh (sur, *on*); [Fig.] to dwell at length on.

appétissant, -e [apeti'sɑ̃(:t)] *adj.* appetizing. || **appétit** [ape'ti] *n.m.* appetite: *manger de bon* ~, to enjoy one's food.

applaudir [aplo'd|i:r] #17 *v. tr.* to applaud; to praise; to cheer. || *v. intr.* to clap: *On applaudit fort,* There was loud applause. ||**applaudissements** [-is'mɑ̃] *n.mpl.* applause.

applicable [apli'k|abl] *adj.* applicable; appropriate (to, *à*). || **application** [-a'sjõ] *n.f.* **1.** applying: *mettre en* ~, → to implement; [Jur.] enforcement; → to enforce. **2.** assiduous/attention, care/: *(travailler) avec* ~, to work/assiduously, studiously/. || **applique** [a'plik] *n.f.* [broderie] applique; [Electr.] wall bracket. || **appliqué** [apli'ke] *adj.* studious, diligent (pupil); applied (science). || **appliquer** #3 *v. tr.* **1.** to apply, put on, lay on. **2.** to put . . . to use; to carry out, to apply. || **s'appliquer (à)** *v. pron.* to apply oneself to; to do one's very best.

appoint [a'pwɛ̃] *n.m.* **1.** *faire l'* ~, to give the exact change. **2.** help. || **appointements** [-t'mɑ̃] *n.mpl.* salary. || **appointer** [-'te] #3 *v. tr.* to pay a salary to.

apport [a'pɔ:r] *n.m.* contribution; [Fin.] share; [Géol.] deposit. || **apporter** [apɔr'te] #3 *v. tr.* **1.** to bring; [preuves] to adduce, produce. **2.** [Fig.] to bring about, to cause.

apposer [apo'ze] #3 *v. tr.* [affiche] to post, stick up; [sceau] to affix: [signature] to append: [Jur.] ~ *les scellés,* to put . . . under seal.

appréciable [apre'sj|abl] *adj.* appreciable. || **appréciation** [-a'sjõ] *n.f.* appreciation; estimate, estimation: *porter une* ~ *sur,* to judge, appraise. || **apprécier** [-e] #3 *v. tr.* to appreciate, esteem; to value, estimate.

appréhender [apreɑ̃|'de] #3 *v. tr.* **1.** to apprehend, be apprehensive of; to dread. **2.** to arrest (criminals). || **appréhensi|f, -ve** [apreɑ̃'s|if, -i:v] *adj.* apprehensive, anxious. || **appréhension** [-'sjõ] *n.f.* apprehension, dread, fear (*de*, of).

apprenant [aprə'nɑ̃] cf. APPRENDRE.

apprendre [a'pr|ɑ̃:dr], **apprenant** [-ə'nɑ̃], **appris** [-i] #41 *v. tr.* **1.** to learn; to be taught: ~ *par cœur,* to learn by heart; ~ *à lire,* to learn to read. **2.** to hear, learn: *J'ai appris qu'il était malade,* I heard he was sick. **3.** to teach: ~ *qqch. à qqun,* to teach s.o. sth.; *Cela lui apprendra,* That'll teach him; *Vous ne m'apprenez rien,* You're telling me! || **apprenti** [aprɑ̃'ti] *n.m.* apprentice; [Fig.] novice. || **apprentissage** [-'sa:ʒ] *n.m.* apprenticeship.

apprêt [a'prɛ] *n.m.* [usually *pl.*] **1.** preparations (for a trip). **2.** [Fig.] affectation (of manners). || **apprêter** [-'te] #3 *v. tr.* to prepare, get ready; to cook. || **s'apprêter** *v. pron.* to get ready (to, *à*); to be about (to).

appris, -e [a'pri(:z)] cf. APPRENDRE.

apprivoisé, -e [aprivwa'ze] *adj.* tame: *un écureuil* ~, a pet squirrel. || **apprivoiser** #3 *v. tr.* to tame, domesticate (animals).

approbateur [aprɔba|'tœ:r] *adj.* approving. || **approbation** [-'sjõ] *n.f.* approval, approbation: *incliner la tête en signe d'* ~, to nod assent.

approchable [aprɔ'ʃ|abl] *adj.* approachable, accessible. || **approché, -e** [-e] *adj.* approximate. || **approcher** [-e] #3 *v. tr.* to draw near, bring close to, bring up: *approchez une chaise de la table,* bring a chair to the table. || *v. intr.* to come near, approach: *Nous approchons de la mer,* We are getting near the water; *Nous approchons du but,* The end is in sight; *Le printemps approche,* Spring is coming. || **s'approcher** [saprɔ'ʃe] *v. pron.* to come up (to, *de*), to go up to: *Un inconnu s'approcha de lui,* A stranger came up to him.

approfondi, -e [aprɔfõ'd|i] *adj.* thorough, careful. || **approfondir** [-i:r] #17 *v. tr.* **1.** to make deeper, to deepen. **2.** [Fig.] to go deeply into (a topic), to study thoroughly. || **s'approfondir** *v. pron.* to get deeper: *aller en s'approfondissant,* to get deeper and deeper.

appropriation [aprɔprija'sjõ] *n.f.* appropriation; [illicite] embezzlement. || **approprié, -e** [aprɔpri'je] *adj.* appropriate, fitting (*à*, to), suitable (*à*, to/for). || **approprier** [aprɔpri'je] #3 *v. tr.* **1.** to fit, adapt (*à*, to); to make fit (*à*, for). **2.** to clean. || **s'approprier** *v. pron.* to appropriate; to usurp.

approuves [apru've] #3 *v. tr.* **1.** to approve, endorse. **2.** to approve of, agree with: *J'approuve votre manière d'agir,* I approve of your attitude.

approvisionnement [aprɔvizjɔn|'mɑ̃] *n.m.* **1.** supplying. **2.** *pl.* supply, stock, supplies. || **approvisionner** [-e] #3 *v. tr.* to supply (with, *en*), to stock. || **s'approvisionner** *v. pron.* to get, to lay in supplies (of, *en*): *Il s'approvisionne chez X,* He shops at X's.

approximati|f, -ve [aprɔksima't|if, -i:v] *adj.* approximate; rough. || **approximativement** [-iv'mɑ̃] *adv.* approximately, nearly, roughly.

appui [a'pɥi] *n.m.* **1.** support, prop, stay: *point m d'* ~, fulcrum, purchase. **2.** [Fig.] support, help, backing: *sans* ~, friendless, unprotected; *à l'* ~ *de,* in support of. || **appuyer** ['je] #12 *v. tr.* **1.** to prop, lean (on, *sur*). **2.** to support, back up. || **s'appuyer** *v. pron.* **1.** to lean, rest (on, *sur*; against, *contre*). **2.** to rely on.

âpre [ɑ:pr] *adj.* harsh, rough; bitter: ~ *au gain,* greedy, grasping.

âprement [ɑprə'mɑ̃] *adv.* harshly; [amèrement] bitterly; [avidement] greedily.

après [a'prɛ] *prép., adv. & conj.* **1.** after: ~ *tout,* after all; *l'instant d'* ~, the next moment; *d'* ~, according to; *d'* ~ *lui,* according to him; *dessiner d'* ~ *nature,* to draw from life. **2.** afterwards, later: *Et* ~*?,* And so what? **3.** [followed by verb] ~ *avoir lu,* after reading, after he had read; ~ *qu'il eût lu,* after he had read, when he had read. **4.** © *être* ~ *faire qqch.,* to be busy doing sth. || **après-demain** [aprɛ|d'mɛ̃] *adv.* (the) day after tomorrow. || **après-guerre** [-'gɛ:r] *n.m.* post-war period. || **après-midi** [-mi'di] *n.m.* afternoon.

âpreté [aprə'te] *n.f.* harshness, roughness; sharpness, bitterness.

à-propos [aprɔ'po] *n.m.* aptness, suitability, opportuneness.

apte [apt] *adj.* fit, qualified (*à,* to); [Jur.] capable (of, *à*). || **aptitude** [-i'tyd] *n.f.* aptitude, fitness, capacity: *certificat d'* ~ (à l'enseignement), teacher's certificate. || *n.fpl.* abilities, qualifications; gifts (for, *à*).

aquaplane [akwa'plan] *n.m.* surf-board, aquaplane.

aquarium [akwa'rjɔm] *n.m.* aquarium.

aquatique [akwa'tik] *adj.* aquatic; watery.

aqueduc [akə'dyk] *n.m.* aqueduct.

aqueu|x, -se [a'kø(:z)] *adj.* watery; aqueous.

arabe [a'rab] *n.m/f.* **1.** Arab. **2.** *n.m.* [langue] Arabic. || *adj.* **1.** [peuple] Arab: *la Ligue* ~, the Arab League. **2.** [contrée] Arabian. **3.** [langue] Arabic: *chiffres arabes,* Arabic figures. || **Arabie** [-i] *n.f.* Arabia: ~ *Saoudite,* Saudi Arabia; *désert d'* ~, Arabian desert.

arable [a'rabl] *adj.* arable; tillable.

arachide [ara'ʃid] *n.f.* peanut; © *beurre m d'* ~, peanut butter; *huile f d'* ~, peanut oil.

araignée [arɛ'ɲe] *n.f.* spider: *toile d'* ~, spider's web; [poussière] cobweb; [Fig.] *une* ~ *au plafond,* a bee in one's bonnet.

arbitrage [arbi'tr|a:ʒ] *n.m.* arbitration. || **arbitraire** [-ɛ:r] *adj.* arbitrary. || **arbitre** [ar'bitr] *n.m.* **1.** arbitrator; [sport] referee, umpire. **2.** [Phil.] *libre* ~, freewill. || **arbitrer** [-e] #3 *v. tr.* to arbitrate; [Sport] to referee.

arbre [arbr] *n.m.* **1.** tree: ~ *généalogique,* family tree. **2.** [Tech.] shaft; axletree: ~ *moteur,* drive-shaft. || **arbrisseau** [arbri'so] *n.m.* sapling; shrub. || **arbuste** [ar'byst] *n.m.* shrub, bush.

arc [ark] *n.m.* **1.** bow, †long bow: *tir à l'* ~, archery. **2.** [Géom.] arc, curve: ~ *électrique,* electric arc. **3.** [Arch.] arch: ~ *de triomphe,* triumphal arch. || **arc-en-ciel** [-ɑ̃'sjɛl] *pl.* **arcs-en-ciel** *n.m.* rainbow.

archaïque [arka'ik] *adj.* archaic.

archange [ar'kɑ̃:ʒ] *n.m.* archangel.

arche [arʃ] *n.f.* [Arch.] arch; [Bible] Ark: *l'* ~ *de Noé,* Noah's Ark.

archéologie [arkeɔlɔ'ʒi] *n.f.* archeology.

archer [-e] *n.m.* archer, bowman.

archet [ar'ʃɛ] *n.m.* bow (of violin, &c.).

archevêché [arʃəv|ɛ'ʃe] *n.m.* archbishopric, archbishop's palace. || **archevêque** [-ɛ:k] *n.m.* archbishop.

archipel [arʃi'pɛl] *n.m.* archipelago.

architecte [arʃi'tɛkt] *n.m.* architect. || **architecture** [-y:r] *n.f.* architecture.

archives [ar'ʃi:v] *n.fpl.* archives, records; record office.

arctique [ark'tik] *adj. & n.* Arctic: *l'Océan Arctique,* the Arctic Ocean.

ardemment [ard|a'mɑ̃] *adv.* ardently, eagerly. || **ardent, -e** [-ɑ̃(:t)] *adj.* burning; fiery, ardent. || **ardeur** [-œ:r] *n.f.* heat, ardour, passion.

ardoise [ar'dwa:z] *n.f.* slate.

ardu, -e [ar'dy] *adj.* arduous, difficult.

are [a:r] *n.m.* [measure] are [= 100 square metres].

arène [a'rɛ:n] *n.f.* [cirque] ring; [taureaux] bullring; [gladiateurs] arena; © [Sport] arena; rink.

arête [a'rɛ:t] *n.f.* **1.** (fish)bone. **2.** ridge, crest.

argent [ar'ʒɑ̃] *n.m.* **1.** silver. **2.** money:

gagner de l' ~, to make money; ~ *liquide*, cash; ~ *comptant*, cash. **3.** currency: *payable en* ~ *français*, payable in French currency. || **argenterie** [-'tri] *n.f.* silverware; silver (plate). || **argentin,**[1] **-e** [-'tɛ̃, -'tin] *adj.* silvery, silver-toned. || **argentin,**[2] **-e** *n. & adj.* Argentine (also Argentinian).

argile [ar'ʒil] *n.f.* clay: ~ *réfractaire*, fire clay.

argot [ar'g|o] *n.m.* slang; [trade] jargon. || **argotique** [-ɔ'tik] *adj.* slangy.

argument [argy'mɑ̃] *n.m.* argument, reasoning. || **argumenter** [-'te] #3 *v. intr.* to argue.

aride [a'rid] *adj.* arid, dry, barren. || **aridité** [-i'te] *n.f.* aridity, barrenness; [Fig.] dullness.

aristocrate [aristɔ'kra|t] *n.m/f.* aristocrat. || **aristocratie** [-'si] *n.f.* aristocracy. || **aristocratique** [-'tik] *adj.* aristocratic.

arithmétique [aritme'tik] *n.f.* arithmetic.

armateur [arma'tœ:r] *n.m.* ship-owner.

armature [arma'ty:r] *n.f.* brace; frame; [Mus.] key signature; [Electr.] armature.

arme [arm] *n.f.* **1.** weapon, arm: *porter les armes*, to bear arms; *port d'* ~, gun licence; *déposer les armes*, to lay down one's arms. **2.** arm, branch, service: *la cinquième* ~, the air force. || **armé, -e** [-e] *adj.* armed, equipped (with, *de*): *attaque à main armée*, hold up; *les forces armées*, the armed forces. || **armée** [-e] *n.f.* army; force(s): ~ *permanente*, standing army; ~ *de terre*, the Army; ~ *de l'air*, the Air Force; ~ *de mer*, the Navy. || **armement** [-ə'mɑ̃] *n.m.* armament; arming, equipment. || **armer** [-e] #3 *v. tr.* **1.** to arm. **2.** to commission (a ship). **3.** to cock (a rifle), to set (a bomb), || **s'** ~ *v. pron.* to arm o.s. (with, *de*). *s'* ~ *de courage*, to summon o.'s courage. **armistice** [-is'tis] *n.m.* armistice.

armoire [ar'mwa:r] *n.f.* wardrobe: ~ *à glace*, wardrobe with a mirror.

armoiries [armwa'ri] *n.fpl.* coat of arms. || **armure** [ar'm|y:r] *n.f.* armour; suit of armour. || **armurerie** [-yr'ri] *n.f.* [dépôt] armoury; [fabrique] arms factory. || **armurier** [-y'rje] *n.m.* gunsmith; [Mil.] armourer.

aromate [arɔ'mat] *n.m.* spice. || **aromatiser** [-i'ze] #3 *v. tr.* to flavour. || **arôme** [a'ro:m] *n.m.* aroma, flavour.

arpent [ar'pɑ̃] *n.m.* acre. || **arpentage** [-'ta:ʒ] *n.m.* land-surveying. || **arpenter** [-'te] #3 *v. tr.* **1.** to survey (land). **2.** to walk up and down. || **arpenteur** [-'tœ:r] *n.m.* surveyor.

arracher [ara'ʃe] #3 *v. tr.* **1.** to tear out, pull/out, up; to extract, draw (teeth); to uproot, pluck, root out (weeds). **2.** [Fig.] to wring from, obtain. || **s'arracher** (à) *v. pron.* to tear oneself away (from work, &c.); *s'* ~ *les cheveux*, to tear one's hair. || **d'arrache-pied** [daraʃ'pje] *loc. adv.* unremittingly: *travailler* (*ou faire travailler qqun*) ~, to keep one's (or another's) nose to the grindstone.

arrangement [arɑ̃ʒ|'mɑ̃] *n.m.* arrangement; adjustment; agreement, terms: *arriver à un* ~, to compromise. || **arranger** [-e] #5 *v. tr.* **1.** to arrange, adjust, set in order. **2.** to repair, fix. **3.** to settle (one's affairs). || **s'arranger** *v. pron.* **1.** to manage (with, *avec*), to make shift with. **2.** to come to terms, to compromise. **3.** [Loc.] *Ça s'arrangera*, It will work itself out.

arrestation [arɛsta'sjõ] *n.f.* arrest: *opérer une* ~, to make an arrest.

arrêt [a'rɛ] *n.m.* **1.** stop; halt; [Autobus] ~ *obligatoire*, → Buses stop here; ~ *facultatif*, → Buses stop here on request; *marquer un temps d'* ~, to pause. **2.** sentence, judgment, decree: ~ *de mort*, death sentence; *mandat m d'* ~, warrant. || **arrêté, -e** [-'te] *adj.* fixed; decreed, resolved: *avoir des idées bien arrêtées*, to know what one wants. || **arrêté** *n.m.* order, decree, bylaw: ~ *ministériel*, minister's decision. || **arrêter** [-'te] #3 *v. tr.* **1.** to stop, delay, hold in check; to arrest: *se faire* ~, to be arrested, given in charge. **2.** to decide on (a plan); to settle (an account); to hire, engage (a servant). || **s'** ~ *v. pron.* **1.** to stop: *s'* ~ *court*, to stop short. **2.** to decide on, to choose: *Il s'arrêta au second parti*, He chose the second solution.

arrière [a'rjɛ:r] **1.** *n.m.* back (part), rear (end); [Naut.] stern; [Auto.] rear. || *adj. & adv.*: *en* ~, behind; *à l'* ~, aft; *faire machine* ~, to reverse an engine, to go into reverse. || **arrière-goût** [arjɛr|'gu] *pl.* **arrière-goûts** *n.m.* after-taste, faint taste. || **arrière-grand'mère** [-grɑ̃'mɛ:r] *f.* great-grandmother. || **arrière-grand-père** [-grɑ̃'pɛ:r] *n.m.* great-grandfather. || **arrière-pensée** [-pɑ̃'se] *pl.* **arrière-pensées** *n.f.* ulterior motive. || **arrière-petit-fils** [-p(ə)ti'fis] *n.m.* great-grandson. || **arrière-petite-fille** [-p(ə)tit'-'fij] *n.f.* great-granddaughter. || **arrière-petits-enfants** [-p(ə)tizɑ̃'fɑ̃] *mpl.* great-grandchildren. || **arrière-plan** [arjɛr'plɑ̃] *n.m.* background. || **arrière-saison** [-sɛ'zõ] *n.f.* late fall. || **arriéré, -e** [arje're] *n. & adj.* [enfant] backward.

arrivage [ari'va:ʒ] *n.m.* arrival; new consignment. || **arrivant** [ari'v|ɑ̃] *n.m.* arrival, (new)comer. || **arrivée** [-e] *n.f.* arrival;

coming; arriving; advent; [Tech.] intake (of steam): *dès son ~*, immediately upon arriving; *le poteau d' ~*, the winning post. || **arriver** [-e] #3 *v. intr.* **1.** to arrive, come; (airplane) land. **2.** to happen, occur, take place: *Qu'est-il arrivé?*, What happened? *Il lui est arrivé un accident*, → He met with an accident. **3.** *~ à*, to succeed in, to manage to: *Nous en sommes arrivés à ne plus le croire*, We have got to the point where we don't believe him any more.

arriviste [ari'vist] *n.m/f.* climber, go-getter.

arrogance [arɔ'g|ɑ̃:s] *n.f.* arrogance, haughtiness. || **arrogant, -e** [-ɑ̃(:t)] *adj.* arrogant, overbearing.

arroger, s' [sarɔ'ʒe] #5 *v. pron.* to arrogate to o.s.

arrondir [arõ'd|i:r] #17 *v. tr.* to make round, round off, round out. || **s'arrondir** *v. pron.* to become round. || **arrondissement** [-is'mɑ̃] *n.m.* district; [in Paris] ward, postal district.

arrosage [aro'z|a:ʒ] *n.m.* watering, sprinkling; [viande] basting. || **arroser** [-e] #3 *v. tr.* **1.** to water, sprinkle. **2.** to baste (a roast); [Fam.] to celebrate; *Ça s'arrose!*, Let's celebrate! || **arrosoir** [-wa:r] *n.m.* watering can.

arsenal [arsə'nal] *n.m.* [Mil.] arsenal; armoury; [Naut.] dockyard; [Fig.] storehouse.

arsenic [arsə'nik] *n.m.* arsenic.

art [a:r] *n.m.* **1.** art; skill: *avoir l' ~ de*, to have the knack of; *ouvrage m d' ~*, feat of engineering; *œuvre f d' ~*, work of art; *(pl.) les beaux-arts*, the fine arts. **2.** *(pl.)* © arts: *Baccalauréat m ès Arts*, Bachelor of Arts, B.A.

artère [ar't|ɛ:r] *n.f.* [Méd.] artery; [road] thoroughfare. || **artériel, -le** [-e'rjɛl] *adj.* arterial.

arthrite [ar'trit] *n.f.* arthritis.

artichaut [arti'ʃo] *n.m.* artichoke.

article [ar'tikl] *n.m.* **1.** article. **2.** object, item, thing, commodity. **3.** clause (of a contract, deed, &c.).

articulation [artiky|la'sjõ] *n.f.* [doigt] knuckle; [membre] articulation; [Tech.] joint. **articulé, -e** [-'le] *adj.* articulated, hinged. || **articuler** #3 *v. tr.* to articulate; [Tech.] to link, join. || *v. intr.* to enunciate. || **s'articuler** *v. pron.* to be connected, linked to; [Mil.] *~ en largeur*, to spread out.

artifice [arti'fis] *n.m.* artifice, guile, stratagem: *feu m. d' ~*, fireworks. || **artificiel, -le** [-jɛl] *adj.* artificial. || **artificiellement** [-jɛl'mɑ̃] *adv.* artificially.

artillerie [artij|'ri] *n.f.* artillery, ordnance. || **artilleur** [-œ:r] *n.m.* [Mil.] gunner.

artisan [arti'z|ɑ̃] *n.m.* craftsman; [Fig.] builder, maker. || **artisanat** [-a'na] *n.m.* handicraft; cottage industry.

artiste [ar'tist] *n.m/f.* artist; actor, actress, trouper. || **artistique** [-ik] *adj.* artistic.

as[1] [ɑ:s] *n.m.* ace [cards, dice, sports, &c.]: *~ du volant*, racing star.

as[2] [a] cf. AVOIR.

asbeste [az'bɛst] *n.m.* asbestos; cf. AMIANTE.

ascendant, -e [asɑ̃'dɑ̃(:t)] *adj.* rising, climbing, → upward. || *n.m.* ascendency, influence (*sur*, on).

ascenseur [asɑ̃'s|œ:r] *n.m.* elevator, [Br.] lift. || **ascension** [-jõ] *n.f.* ascent, climb: *faire l' ~ d'une montagne*, to climb a mountain; *le jour de l'Ascension*, Ascension Day.

ascète [a'sɛt] *n.m/f.* ascetic.

asiatique [azja'tik] *adj.* Asiatic; Asian. || *n.m/f.* Asiatic.

asile [a'zil] *n.m.* shelter; refuge, home: *chercher ~, trouver ~*, to seek, to find, refuge in . . . ; *~ d'aliénés*, mental hospital.

aspect [as'pɛ] *n.m.* aspect; view; appearance.

asperge [as'pɛrʒ] *n.f.* asparagus.

asperger [aspɛr'ʒe] #5 *v. tr.* to sprinkle, spray (*de*, with).

aspérité [asperi'te] *n.f.* asperity; raggedness, roughness (of surface, &c.); [Fig.] harshness, sharpness (of voice, character).

asphalte [as'falt] *n.m.* asphalt, road metal; [Fig.] sidewalk. || **asphalter** [-e] #3 *v. tr.* to asphalt; to pave (a road): *route asphaltée (macadamisée)*, paved road.

asphyxie [asfik's|i] *n.f.* asphyxiation. || **asphyxier** [-je] #3 *v. tr.* to asphyxiate. || *v. intr.* [Fig.] to choke, to gasp for air.

aspirant [aspi'rɑ̃] *n.m.* candidate, aspirant; [Naut.] midshipman; [Mil.] cadet. || *adj.*: *pompe f. aspirante*, suction pump. || **aspirateur** [aspir|a'tœ:r] *n.m.* vacuum cleaner. || **aspiration** [-a'sjõ] *n.f.* **1.** [Physiol.] inspiration, inhaling (of air); [Ling.] aspiration, puff (of air). **2.** aspiration; ideal, yearning (for, after, *à*). || **aspirer** [-e] #3 *v. tr.* **1.** to breathe in. **2.** to aspire (to, *à*), to hanker (for).

aspirine [aspi'rin] *n.f.* aspirin.

assaillant [asa|'jɑ̃] *n.m.* assailant, attacker. || **assaillir** [-'ji:r] #19 *v. tr.* to assault, attack; [Fig.] to beset (*de*, with).

assainir [asɛ'n|i:r] #17 *v. tr.* to make healthier; to purify, to decontaminate; [Fig.] to reform, purge. || **assainissement**

[-is'mɑ̃] *n.m.* decontamination, sanitation; [Fig.] reform.

assaisonnement [asɛzɔn|'mɑ̃] *n.m.* seasoning, flavouring; [salade] dressing; condiment, relish. || **assaisonner** [-e] #3 *v. tr.* to season.

assassin [asa's|ɛ̃] *n.m.* murderer, *f* murderess: ~ *politique*, assassin. || *adj.* **1.** murderous; [Fig.] killing (glance). **2.** provocative, bewitching (smile). || **assassinat** [-i'na] *n.m.* murder, assassination. || **assassiner** [-i'ne] #3 *v. tr.* to murder, assassinate.

assaut [a'so] *n.m.* **1.** assault, attack, onslaught: *donner l'* ~ *à*, to storm, take by storm. **2.** [escrime, lutte] bout.

assèchement [asɛʃ'mɑ̃] *n.m.* draining. || **assécher** [ase'ʃe] #10 *v. tr.* to dry, drain.

assemblage [asɑ̃'bla:ʒ] *n.m.* [action] assembling, gathering; [de choses, de gens] assemblage, gathering; [Tech.] assembling, joining; [Méc.] coupling, joint; [Electr.] gathering. || **assemblée** [asɑ̃'ble] *n.f.* assembly; gathering; meeting; [Rel.] congregation. || **assembler** #3 *v. tr.* **1.** to assemble, put together [cf. also RASSEMBLER]. **2.** [Tech.] to join; to frame (planks). || **s'assembler** *v. pron.* to assemble, gather.

asséner [ase'ne] #9 *v. tr.* to strike, hit.

assentiment [asɑ̃ti'mɑ̃] *n.m.* assent, consent, approbation: *signe d'* ~ , nod; *donner son* ~ *à*, to approve.

asseoir [a'swa:r] #30 & 31 *v. tr.* to seat, set, place; to establish. || **s'asseoir** [sa'swa:r] *v. pron.* to sit down: *Asseyez-vous, je vous prie*, Please be seated.

assermenter [asɛrmɑ̃'te] #3 *v. tr.* to swear in.

asservir [asɛr'v|i:r] #17 *v. tr.* to enslave, subjugate (*à*, to). || **asservissement** [-is'mɑ̃] *n.m.* enslavement, bondage.

assez [a'se] *adv.* **1.** [+ nom] enough: *Nous avons* ~ *d'essence*, We have enough gas; *Nous en avons* ~ , We have enough. **2.** *adj.* enough: *Il n'est pas* ~ *fort*, He is not strong enough. **3.** *adj.* [Fig.] rather: *C'est* ~ *curieux*, It's rather odd. **4.** [Loc.] *En voilà* ~ *!*, That's enough!, Cut it out!; *J'en ai* ~ , I have had enough, I am fed up. **5.** [= very] so: © *C'est* ~ *beau !*, It is so (very) nice! [= Fr. si, tellement].

assidu, -e [asi|'dy] *adj.* assiduous, steady; painstaking. || **assiduité** [-dɥi'te] *n.f.* assiduity, assiduousness. || **assidûment** [-dy'mɑ̃] *adv.* assiduously.

assieds, &c.; **assiérai, &c.** cf. ASSEOIR.

assiéger [asje'ʒe] #7 *v. tr.* to besiege; [Fig.] to beset, harass (*de*, with).

assiette [a'sjɛt] *n.f.* **1.** plate; dish. **2.** stable position; [impôts] basis: *Il n'est pas dans son* ~ , He is under the weather. || **assiettée** [asje'te] *n.f.* plateful, plate.

assignation [asiɲa'sjõ] *n.f.* [Jur.] subpœna, writ: *remettre une* ~ *à*, to serve a writ on; [Fin.] assignment, allotment.

assigner [asi'ɲe] #3 *v. tr.* **1.** [sum] to earmark (*pour*, for); to ascribe (*à*, to). **2.** [job, &c.] to fix, appoint; [Jur.] to subpœna, to issue a writ against.

assimilation [asimil|a'sjõ] *n.f.* assimilation; [d'immigrants] integration. || **assimiler** [-e] #3 *v. tr.* to assimilate; to rank, compare (*à*, with). || **s'assimiler** *v. pron.* [food, doctrine] to assimilate; [to become alike] to integrate o.s. (*à*, in).

assis, -e [a'si(:z)] *adj.* seated; sitting: *être* ~ , to sit. || **assise** [a'si:z] *n.f.* seating; [Arch.] course, layer; [roche] bed. *assises n.fpl.* foundation, groundwork; [Jur.] assizes.

assistance [asis't|ɑ̃:s] *n.f.* **1.** audience, attendance spectators; [Rel.] congregation. **2.** assistance help, aid, relief (of old people): *prêter* ~ *à*, to come to the rescue of. || **assistant** [-ɑ̃] **1.** *n.m.* bystander, onlooker, spectator, member of the audience. **2.** assistant. || **assister** [-e] #3 *v. tr.* to help, assist. || *v. intr.* (*à*, —) to attend, be present at: ~ *à la réunion*, to attend the meeting.

association [asɔsj|a'sjõ] *n.f.* association; partnership, union. || **associé, -e** [-e] *adj.* associated; in partnership. || *n.* partner. || **associer** [-e] #3 *v. tr.* to associate, unite, join. || **s'associer** (**à**) *v. pron.* **1.** to have a part in, to share. **2.** to go into partnership with.

assoiffé, -e [aswa'fe] *adj.* thirsty, thirsting (for, *de*): ~ *de science*, thirsting for knowledge; ~ *de sang*, bloodthirsty. || **assoiffer** #3 *v. tr.* to make (s.o.) thirsty.

assombrir [asõ'bri:r] #17 *v. tr.* to darken, obscure; [Fig.] to cloud (over). || **s'assombrir** *v. pron.* to darken, become dark; [Fig.] to cloud over.

assommant, -e [asɔ'mɑ̃(:t)] *adj.* stunning; [Fam., Péj.] boring, tiresome.

assommer [asɔ'me] #3 *v. tr.* to fell, knock down; [Fig.] to stun, overpower; [Fam.] to bother, bore.

Assomption [asõp'sjõ] *n.f.* [R.C.] Assumption (of the Blessed Virgin).

assorti, -e [asɔr|'ti] *adj.* **1.** matched, paired. **2.** assorted, mixed. || **assortiment** [-ti'mɑ̃] *n.m.* **1.** match(ing). **2.** assortment. || **assortir** [-'ti:r] #17 *v. tr.* to match, pair (*à*, with); [Fig.] to suit. || *v. intr.* to match, suit. || **s'assortir** *v. pron.* to go (well, badly) together.

assoupir [asu'p|i:r] #17 *v. tr.* to make drowsy, sleepy. || **s'assoupir** *v. pron.* to fall asleep, to doze off, to grow drowsy; [Fig.] to be stilled, quiet down. || **assoupissement** [-is'mɑ̃] *n.m.* drowsiness, dozing.

assouplir [asu'pl|i:r] #17 *v. tr.* to make supple, flexible: *s' ~ les muscles*, to limber up; *La réglementation a été assouplie*, Regulations have been eased. || **s'assouplir** *v. pron.* to become more supple, more tractable. || **assouplissement** [-is'mɑ̃] *n.m.* greater flexibility, greater ease; *exercices d' ~*, physical jerks.

assourdir [asur'd|i:r] #17 *v. tr.* to deafen. || **assourdissant, -e** [-i'sɑ̃(:t)] *adj.* deafening.

assouvir [asu'vi:r] #17 *v. tr.* to satiate; [faim] to satisfy; [soif] to quench; [souvent Péj.] to indulge; to gratify.

assujettir [asyʒɛ't|i:r] #17 *v. tr.* [people] to subdue, subjugate; [Fig., passions] to master; to secure, fasten. || **s'assujettir** (à) *v. pron.* to oblige, to force o.s. (to do sth.). || **assujettissement** [-is'mɑ̃] *n.m.* subjection; [Fig.] mastering, obligation (to, towards, *à*).

assumer [asy'me] #3 *v. tr.* to assume, undertake.

assurance [asy'r|ɑ̃:s] *n.f.* **1.** assurance, (self-) confidence: *avec ~*, with assurance, confidently; *Vous en avez l' ~*, You can count on it. **2.** insurance, assurance: *~ contre les incendies*, fire insurance. || **assuré, -e** [-e] *adj.* **1.** firm, sure. **2.** assured, confident. **3.** [Com.] insured. || **assurer** [-e] #3 *v. tr.* **1.** to assure (of, *de*): *Je vous l'assure*, I can assure you. **2.** to insure: *~ contre un risque*, to cover a risk. || **s'assurer** *v. pron.* **1.** to make certain, to ascertain (que + ind., that); to make sure (*de*, of). **2.** to insure o.s.: *~ sur la vie*, to have one's life insured. || **assureur** [-œ:r] *n.m.* insurer.

asthme [asm] *n.m.* asthma.

astigmatisme [astigma'tism] *n.m.* astigmatism.

astiquer [asti'ke] #3 *v. tr.* to furbish, polish; [Fig., Fam.] *être bien astiqué*, to be well groomed.

astre [astr] *n.m.* star; heavenly body.

astreindre [as'tr|ɛ̃:dr], **astreignant** [-ɛ'ɲɑ̃], **astreint** [-ɛ̃] #36 *v. tr.* to compel, force (to, *à*). || **s'astreindre** (*à*, to) [sas'trɛ̃:dr] *v. pron.* to bind, force (o.s.).

astrologie [astrɔlɔ'ʒi] *n.f.* astrology.

astronome [astrɔ'nɔm] *n.m.* astronomer. || *adj.* astronomic(al). || **astronomie** [-i] *n.f.* astronomy. || **astronomique** [astrɔnɔ'mik] *adj.* astronomical.

astuce [as'tys] *n.f.* astuteness; [Fam.] trick; [jeu de mots] pun, witticism. || **astucieu|x, -se** [asty'sjø(:z)] *adj.* astute, [Péj.] crafty, wily; witty.

atelier [atə'lje] *n.m.* **1.** workshop, shop. **2.** [artiste] studio.

Athabasca (l') [(l)atabas'ka] *n.f.* Athabaska River.

athée [a'te] *n.m/f* atheist. || *adj.* atheistic.

athéisme [ate'ism] *n.m.* atheism.

Athènes [a't|ɛ:n] *n.f.* Athens. || **athénien, -ne** [-e'nj|ɛ̃, -ɛn] *adj. & n.* Athenian.

athlète [a'tlɛt] *n.m.* athlete. || **athlétique** [atle'ti|k] *adj.* athletic. || **athlétisme** [-sm] *n.m.* athletics.

Atlantique (l') [(l)atlɑ̃'tik] *n.m.* the Atlantic (Ocean): © *Les Provinces fpl atlantiques*, The Atlantic Provinces. || *adj.* Atlantic.

atlas [a'tlɑ:s] *n.m.* atias.

atmosphère [atmɔs'f|ɛ:r] *n.f.* atmosphere. || **atmosphérique** [-e'rik] *adj.* atmospherical.

atoca, ataca [atɔ'kɑ] © *n.m.* cranberry.

atome [a'to:m] *n.m.* atom. || **atomique** *adj.* atomic.

atomiser [atɔmi'ze] #3 *v. tr.* [détruire] to atomize; [pulvériser] to atomize, pulverize.

atout [a'tu] *n.m.* **1.** [Cards] trump: *un ~*, a trump card. **2.** [Fig.] asset.

âtre [ɑ:tr] *n.m.* hearth, fireplace.

atroce [a'trɔs] *adj.* excruciating; agonizing. || **atrocité** [-i'te] *n.f.* atrocity.

atrophie [atrɔ'fi] *n.f.* atrophy.

attabler (s') [sata'ble] #3 *v. pron.* to sit down (to table): *Ils étaient attablés*, → They were having (lunch, dinner, &c.).

attachant, -e [ata'ʃɑ̃(:t)] *adj.* engaging (personality), captivating. || **attache** [a'taʃ] *n.f.* fastening: *avoir des attaches avec*, to be connected with. || **attaché, -e** [-e] *adj.* **1.** fastened, tied up. **2.** attached, devoted (to, *à*). *n.m.* [Dipl.] attaché. || **attachement** [-'mɑ̃] *n.m.* attachment. || **attacher** [-e] #3 *v. tr.* **1.** to fasten, tie. **2.** [Fig.] to attach. || **s' ~** *v. pron.* to become attached (to, *à*).

attaquant [ata'kɑ̃] *n.m.* assailant, attacker. || **attaque** [a'tak] *n.f.* **1.** attack. **2.** [Méd.] fit, stroke. || **attaquer** [-e] #3 *v. tr.* **1.** attack, assail. **2.** *~ en justice*, to bring an action against. || **s'attaquer (à)** *v. pron.* to tackle, to take on.

attardé, -e [atar'de] *adj.* late; [Péj.] belated; backward. || **attarder** #3 *v. tr.* to keep late, to delay. || **s'attarder** *v. pron.* to linger; [Péj.] to loiter: *s' ~ à*, to linger over.

atteindre [a'tǀɛ̃:dr] #36 *v. tr.* **1.** to reach, attain. **2.** to hit. ‖ **atteint, -e** [-ɛ̃(:t)] *p.p.* **atteindre.** ‖ **atteinte** [-ɛ̃:t] *n.f.* **1.** reach: *hors d'* ~, beyond reach. **2.** infringement (of, *à*): *porter* ~ *à,* to harm, to be detrimental to.

attelage [a'tlǀa:ʒ] *n.m.* **1.** harnessing; [Tech.] coupling. **2.** team (of horses). ‖ **atteler** [-e] #8 *v. tr.* to harness. ‖ **s'atteler** *v. pron.* [Fig.] buckle (to, *à*).

attendant [atɑ̃'dɑ̃] *adv.*: *en attendant,* in the meantime; ~ *que,* until. ‖ **attendre** [a'tɑ̃:dr] #42 *v. tr.* **1.** to wait for, to await: *Je l'attends depuis une heure,* I've been waiting for him for an hour. **2.** to expect: *Je l'attends demain,* I expect him tomorrow. ‖ **s'attendre** *v. pron.* to expect: *Je m'attends à ce qu'il soit en retard,* I expect him to be late.

attendrir [atɑ̃dri:r] #17 *v. tr.* to touch, move, mollify. ‖ **attendrissant, -e** [a'tɑ̃drǀi'sɑ̃(:t)] *adj.* touching, moving.

attendu (que) [atɑ̃dy(kə)] whereas.

attentat [atɑ̃'ta] *n.m.* criminal attempt (*contre,* against); outrage: ~ *contre la sûreté de l'État,* treason, felony.

attente [a'tɑ̃:t] *n.f.* wait(ing): *salle d'* ~, waiting-room.

attenter (à) [atɑ̃'te] #3 *v. intr.* to make a (criminal) attempt (*à,* on/against/): ~ *à ses jours,* to attempt suicide.

attentiǀf, -ve [atɑ̃ǀ'tif, -'ti:v] *adj.* attentive, considerate. ‖ **attention** [-'sjõ] *n.f.* attention; notice: *faire* ~ *à,* to pay attention (to); *attirer l'* ~ *de qqun sur qqch.,* to call s.o.'s attention to sth.; *porter son* ~ *sur,* to direct one's attention to; *Attention!,* Watch it!; *Attention au train,* Look out for the train; *Attention aux enfants,* Look out for children. ‖ **attentionné, -e** [atɑ̃sjɔ-'ne] *adj.* considerate: *bien* ~, well-meaning.

atténuer [ate'nɥe] #3 *v. tr.* [couleur, son] to subdue, soften; [un jugement] to tone down; [Fam.] to soft-pedal (demands, &c.).

atterrer [atɛ're] #3 *v. tr.* to stun: *être atterré,* to be thunderstruck.

atterrir [atɛǀ'ri:r] #17 *v. intr.* to land; [Naut.] to make a landfall. ‖ **atterrissage** [-ri'sa:ʒ] *n.m.* landing: ~ *forcé,* forced landing.

attester [atɛs'te] #3 *v. tr.* [certifier] to certify; [témoigner] to bear witness to, to testify to; to call to witness.

attiédir [atje'di:r] #17 *v. tr.* [le chaud] to cool, [le froid] to warm; [l'ardeur] to damp. ‖ **s'attiédir** *v. pron.* [Fig.] to cool /off, down/; to become lukewarm.

attirance [ati'rɑ̃:s] *n.f.* attraction (to, *vers*); fascination (for). ‖ **attirant, -e** [ati'rǀɑ̃(:t)] *adj.* attractive, appealing. ‖ **attirer** [-e] #3 *v. tr.* to draw, attract, pull. ‖ **s'attirer** *v. pron.* to bring on o.s.: ~ *des ennuis,* to get into trouble.

attiser [ati'ze] #3 *v. tr.* [le feu] to poke, stir/(the fire); [Fig.] to (a)rouse: ~ *la haine,* to stir up hatred.

attitré, -e [ati'tre] *adj.* appointed, recognized: *fournisseur* ~ *de (la Cour),* by appointment to (the Court).

attitude [ati'tyd] *n.f.* attitude; posture.

attraction [atrak'sjõ] *n.f.* attraction; [spectacle] number, act. ‖ **attrait** [a'trɛ] *n.m.* attraction, appeal: *avoir de l'* ~ *pour,* to be attractive to.

attrape [a'trap] *n.f.* snare, trap; [Fig.] trick, hoax. ‖ **attraper** [atra'pe] #3 *v. tr.* to catch; to take, seize; [au piège] to snare, trap; [maladie] to catch: ~ *au vol,* to catch on the fly; [Loc.] *se faire* ~, (1) to get ticked off, (2) to be had, to be taken in, (3) [Mil.] to get caught.

attrayant, -e [atrɛ'jɑ̃(:t)] *adj.* attractive, engaging.

attribuer [atri'bɥe] #3 *v. tr.* to attribute, to impute (sth. to s.o.); [un privilège] to confer an award. ‖ **s'attribuer** *v. pron.* [privilège] to assume, to take upon o.s.

attribut [atri'by] *n.m.* attribute.

attribution [atriby'sjõ] *n.f.* attribution; allotment, assignment. ‖ *pl.* duties, attributions.

attristé, -e [atris'te] *adj.* sad, sorrowful (face, look). ‖ **s'attrister** #3 *v. pron.* to become, grow/sad; [Fig.] to cloud over.

attroupement [atrupǀ'mɑ̃] *n.m* mob; milling crowd. ‖ **s'attrouper** [-e] #3 *v. pron.* to crowd; to mill around: *Défense de* ~ !, Move on!, Break it up!

au, aux [o] cf. À [= à le, à les].

aubaine [o'bɛn] *n.f.* godsend; opportunity; © [Com.] (good) value; bargain sale.

aube [o:b] *n.f.* dawn; daybreak.

auberge [o'bɛrʒ] *n.f.* inn: ~ *de la jeunesse,* youth hostel.

aubergine [obɛr'ʒin] *n.f.* eggplant.

aucun, -e [o'kǀœ̃, -yn] *adj.* any. ‖ *pron.* anyone: *n'avoir aucun livre français,* not to have any French books; *n'en avoir* ~, not to have any, to have none. ‖ **aucunement** [-yn'mɑ̃] *adv.* in no way, by no means, not at all. ‖ **d'aucuns** [do'kœ] *pron. ind. pl.* some: ~ *penseront que . . . ,* some will think that . . .

audace [o'daǀs] *n.f.* daring, boldness, audacity. ‖ **audacieuǀx, -se** [-'sjø(:z)] *adj.* audacious.

au-dedans [odə'dɑ̃] *adv.* within, inside: ~ *de, loc. prép.* within, inside.
au-dehors [odə'ɔ:r] *adv.* outside. || **au-delà** (de) [odlɑ] *adv.* beyond. || **au-dessous** [od'su] *adv.* below; underneath: ~ *de, prep.* under; beneath. || **au-dessus** [od'sy] *adv.* above; over: *deux étages* ~, two floors above; ~ *de,* above; over. || **au-devant** (de) [odə'vɑ̃] *loc. prep.*: *aller* ~ *qqun,* to go to meet s.o.
audible [o'dibl] *adj.* audible. || **audience** [o'djɑ̃:s] *n.f.* **1.** hearing: *trouver* ~ *auprès de,* to find favour with. **2.** [Jur.] hearing, session, sitting, court: *L'* ~ *est levée,* Court is adjourned. || **audio-visuel** [odjovi'zɥɛl] *adj.* audio-visual: *matériel* ~, audio-visual aids. || **audit|eur, -rice** [odi|'tœ:r, -'tris] *n.m/f* hearer, listener: *les auditeurs,* the audience. || **auditi|f, -ve** [-'tif, -'ti:v] *adj.* auditory. || **audition** [-'sjõ] *n.f.* hearing, audition: *faire passer une* ~, to give an audition. || **auditoire** [-'twa:r] *n.m.* audience. || **auditorium** [oditɔ'rjɔm] *n.m.* auditorium.
auge [o:ʒ] *n.f.* feeding trough: ~ *d'écurie,* manger.
augmentation [ɔgmɑ̃t|a'sjõ] *n.f.* increase; [US] raise, [Br.] rise; enlargement. || **augmenter** [-e] #3 *v. tr. & intr.* **1.** to increase, raise. **2.** to go up, increase: *La vie augmente,* The cost of living is going up.
augure [o'gy:r] *n.m.* augury, omen: *de bon* ~, auspicious; *de mauvais* ~, ominous.
auguste [o'gyst] *adj.* august, imposing, majestic.
aujourd'hui [oʒur'dɥi] *adv.* **1.** [jour] today. **2.** [époque] today, nowadays.
aumône [o'mo:n] *n.f.* alms: *faire l'* ~, to give (to the poor). || **aumônier** [omo'nje] *n.m.* chaplain: ~ *militaire,* army chaplain, padre.
auparavant [opara'vɑ̃] *adv.* before; previously; earlier.
auprès [o'prɛ] *adv.* near; by: ~ *de,* near (to); close to: *trouver bon accueil* ~ *qqun,* to be well received by s.o.; *Ne m'oubliez pas* ~ *de X,* Please remember me to X.
auquel [o'kɛl] *pron. rel.* ou *interrog.* cf. LEQUEL.
aurai [ɔ're] cf. AVOIR.
auréole [ore'ɔl] *n.f.* aura, halo. || **auréolé, -e** [-e] *adj.* haloed.
au revoir [or(ə)'vwa:r] *interj.* goodbye (till we meet again); [Fam.] Be seeing you.
auriculaire [oriky'lɛ:r] *adj.* auricular. || *n.m.* the little finger.
aurore [o'rɔ:r] *n.f.* dawn, daybreak, break of day: ~ *boréale,* northern lights, aurora borealis.
auspice [ɔs'pis] *n.m.* (*usual. pl.*) auspice: *sous les auspices de,* under the auspices of, sponsored by.
aussi[1] [o'si] *adv.* [never used at the beginning of a sentence] also, too, likewise: *Il sait* ~ *l'allemand,* He also knows German; *Je le sais* ~, I know it too. || **aussi**[2] *conj.* **1.** [+ que] as: *Il est aussi las que vous,* He is as weary as you are. **2.** [starting sentence and followed by inversion] therefore: *Aussi ne viendra-t-il pas,* Therefore he will not come.
aussitôt [osi'to] *adv.* immediately; at once. || **aussitôt que** *conj.* as soon as: ~ *dit,* ~ *fait,* no sooner said than done.
austère [ɔs't|ɛ:r] *adj.* austere, severe, stern. || **austérité** [-eri'te] *n.f.* austerity, strictness, sternness.
Australie [ostra'l|i] *n.f.* Australia. || **australien, -ne** [-jɛ̃, -jɛn] *adj. & n.* Australian.
autant (de) [o'tɑ̃] *adv.* as much; as many; as far, &c.: ~ *que,* as much as; in the same way as; *d'* ~ *plus que,* all the more so as.
autel [o'tɛl] *n.m.* altar: *nappe d'* ~, altar cloth: *conduire la fiancée à l'* ~: to give the bride away.
auteur [o'tœ:r] *n.m.* author: *droits d'* ~, royalties.
authenticité [otɑ̃ti|si'te] *n.f.* authenticity; genuineness. || **authentifier, authentiquer** [-'fje, -'ke] #3 *v. tr.* to authenticate; to make valid. || **authentique** [-k] *adj.* authentic, genuine.
auto[1] [o'to] *n.f.* © *m.* (*pl.* **-s**) auto, car. cf. AUTOMOBILE.
auto-[2] [*Prefix* = self(-working)]: **autobiographie** [otobjɔgra'fi] *n.f.* autobiography. || **autobiographique** [-k] *adj.* autobiographic(al). || **autobus** [oto'bys] *n.m.* bus. || **autocar** [oto'ka:r] *n.m.* sightseeing bus. || **autoclave** [otɔ'kla:v] *n.m.* autoclave, sterilizer; pressure cooker. || **autocrate** [otɔ'kra|t] *n.m.* autocrat. || *adj.* autocratic. || **autocratie** [-'si] *n.f.* autocracy. || **autocratique** [-'tik] *adj.* autocratic. || **autodidacte** [otɔdi'dakt] *adj.* self-taught. || *n.m.* autodidact. || **autogène** [otɔ'ʒɛ:n] *adj.* autogenous: *soudure f* ~, welding. || **autographe** [oto'graf] *adj.* autograph (letter). || *n.m.* autograph. || **automate** [oto'mat] *n.m.* automaton. || **automatique** [-'ik] *adj.* automatic: *distributeur* ~, vending machine.
automnal, -e [otɔm'nal] *adj.* autumnal. || **automne** [o'tɔn] *n.f.* fall, autumn.

automobile [ɔtomɔ'bil] *adj.* **1.** self-moving; self-propelling: *canot* ~, speed boat. **2.** cf. AUTO. || **automobilisme** [-ism] *n.m.* motoring.
autonome [ɔtɔ'nɔm] *adj.* autonomous, self-governing. || **autonomie** [ɔtɔnɔ'mi] *n.f.* autonomy, self-government, home rule.
autopsie [otɔp'si] *n.f.* autopsy, post-mortem examination.
autorail [oto'ra:j] *n.m.* railcar.
autorisation [ɔtɔriz|a'sjõ] *n.f.* authorization, authority, permit; licence: *accorder l'* ~, to grant permission. || **autorisé, -e** [-'ze] *adj.* authorized, authoritative: *de source autorisée*, authoritatively. || **autoriser** [-'ze] #3 *v. tr.* to permit, authorize, empower (to, *à*). || **autoritaire** [-'tɛ:r] *adj.* domineering, overbearing; authoritarian. || **autorité** [-'te] *n.f.* authority, power: *les autorités locales*, local authorities.
autoroute [ɔto'rut] *n.f.* turnpike, limited access highway.
auto-stop [ɔto'stɔp] *n.m.* hitch-hiking: *faire de l'* ~, hitch-hike; to thumb a ride. cf. POUCE. || **auto-stoppeur** [-œ:r] *pl.* **auto-stoppeurs,** *n.m.* hitch-hiker. cf. POUCE.
autour, autour de [o'tu:r] *adv. prep.* around; about.
autre [o:tr] *adj.* other: *l'* ~ *livre*, the other book; *les autres livres*, the other books; *un* ~ *livre*, another book; *d'autres livres*, other books; ~ *chose*, something else, one more thing; ~ *part*, elsewhere, somewhere else. || *pron.* other: *l'* ~, the other; *les autres*, the others; *un* ~, another, another one; *d'autres*, others; *quelqu'un d'* ~, someone else; *A d'autres!*, Tell that to the Marines!; *quelque chose d'* ~, something else. || **autrefois** [otrə|'fwa] *adv* formerly. || **autrement** [-'mã] *adv.* otherwise: *Il en va* ~ *de*, It's not the same thing as . . .
Autriche [o'triʃ] *n.f.* Austria. || **autrichien, -ne** [-jɛ̃, -jɛn] *adj.* & *n.* Austrian.
autruche [o'tryʃ] *n.f.* ostrich: *faire l'* ~, to bury one's head in the sand.
autrui [o'trɥi] *indef. pron.* others, other people; one's neighbour.
auvent [o'vã] *n.m.* awning.
aux [o] [= à les] cf. À.
auxiliaire [ɔgzi'ljɛ:r] *adj.* auxiliary (verb &c.). || *n.* auxiliary; assistant, aide.
auxquels, auxquelles [o'kɛl] *pron. rel.* ou *interrog. pl.* cf. LESQUELS, LESQUELLES.
avachi, -e [ava'ʃi] *adj.* [Fam.] **1.** out of shape. **2.** [personne] sprawling, slumped.
avais, avez, avons cf. AVOIR.
aval¹ [a'val] *n.m. pl.* -s [Fin.] endorsement (on bill).
aval² *n.m.* lower part (of river): *en* ~ *de*, downstream from.
avalanche [ava'lɑ̃:ʃ] *n.f.* avalanche; [Fig.] shower.
avaler [ava'le] #3 *v. tr.* **1.** to swallow: ~ *d'un trait*, to gulp down. **2.** [Fig.] to endure, to put up with.
avance [a'vɑ̃:s] *n.f.* **1.** advance, start: *prendre de l'* ~ *sur qqun*, to get ahead of s.o.; *d'* ~, in advance; *en* ~, before time, early. **2.** advance payment. **3.** *pl.* overtures: *faire des avances à qqun*, to make overtures to s.o. || **avancé, -e** [avɑ̃'s|e] *adj.* advanced; forward. || **avancement** [-'mã] *n.m.* **1.** advancing, advancement, progress. **2.** promotion. || **avancer** [-e] #4 *v. tr.* to move forward, to advance: ~ *une chaise*, to draw up a chair; ~ *une montre*, to set a watch forward. || *v. intr.* **1.** to move forward, to advance: ~ *à pas de géants*, to make great strides. **2.** to be promoted. **3.** [montre] to gain: *Ma montre avance de deux minutes par jour*, My watch gains two minutes a day; to be fast: *Ma montre avance de cinq minutes*, My watch is five minutes fast. || **s'avancer** *v. pron.* to/come, go/ forward: ~ *d'un pas*, to take a step forward.
avant¹ [a'vã] *adv. prep.* before: ~ *son arrivée*, before his arrival; ~ *d'arriver*, before arriving; ~ *qu'il arrive*, before he arrives. || *n.m.* front; *en* ~, in front; *en* ~*!* forward!, go ahead!; ~ *tout*, above all.
avant-² [Prefix before nouns & adj. = fore-, front-] || **avant-bras** *n.m.* forearm. || **avant-centre** *n.m.* [Sport.] centre-forward. || **avant-coureur** *adj.* & *n.* forerunner. || **avant-derni|er, -ère** *adj.* & *n.* last but one. || **avant-garde** *n.f.* vanguard. || **avant-goût** *n.m.* foretaste. || **avant-hier** *adv.* the day before yesterday. || **avant-port** *n.m.* outer harbour. || **avant-poste** *n.m.* [Mil.] outpost. || **avant-première** *n.f.* preview. || **avant-projet** *n.m.* pilot project; draught. || **avant-propos** *n.m.* foreword. || **avant-scène** *n.f.* proscenium. || **avant-veille** *n.f.* the day before (that day).
avantage [avɑ̃'t|a:ʒ] *n.m.* advantage, profit: *à son* ~, to one's profit; *avoir l'* ~, to have the edge; *avoir* ~ *à faire qqch.*, to find it profitable to do sth. || **avantageusement** [-øz'mã] *adv.* advantageously. || **avantageu|x, -se** [-a'ʒ|ø(:z)] *adj.* advantageous, profitable.
avare [a'va:r] *adj.* miserly. || *n.m.* miser. || **avarice** [ava'ris] *n.f.* avarice.
avarie [ava'r|i] *n.f.* damage: *avoir une* ~ *de machine*, to break down. || **avarié, -e** [-je] *adj.* damaged, spoiled. || **avarier** [-je] #3

v. tr. to damage. || **s'avarier** *v. pron.* to spoil, to go bad.

avec [a'vɛk] *prép.* **1.** [sens général]: [accompagnement] with: *Venez ~ moi,* Come with me; [Loc.] *Et ~ ça?,* Anything else?; *~ ça,* into the bargain. **2.** [manière] → [gén. rendu par un adverbe]: *Il ferma la porte ~ précaution,* He closed the door /gently, softly/; *~ soin,* carefully; *~ bruit,* noisily; *~ tact,* tactfully; *~ concision,* concisely. **3.** [moyen, matière] with, from: *Ouvrez ~ cette clef,* Open with this key, Use this key; *~ l'aide de Dieu,* with God's help; *fait ~ du pétrole,* derived from petroleum. **4.** [simultanéité ou durée]: *levé ~ le jour,* up with the dawn; *~ l'âge,* with age; *~ le temps,* in time. **5.** [opposition] in spite of: *Et ~ cela, il est malheureux,* In spite of everything, he is not happy; *se battre ~ qqun,* to fight against s.o. **6.** [relation] under: *étudier le piano ~ X,* to study the piano under X. || **d'avec** [da'vɛk] *loc. prép.* [séparation ou différence]: *divorcer ~ sa femme,* to divorce one's wife; *Séparez X ~ Y,* Separate X from Y.

avenant, -e [av'nɑ̃] *adj.* pleasing, comely.

avènement [avɛn'mɑ̃] *n.m.* **1.** advent (of Christ). **2.** accession (to the throne).

avenir [av'ni:r] *n.m.* future; time to come: *à l' ~,* in the future; [×] do not confuse with *à venir,* (yet) to come.

Avent [a'vɑ̃] *n.m.* [Rel.] Advent.

aventure [avɑ̃'t|y:r] *n.f.* adventure, chance: *à l' ~,* at random. || **aventuré, -e** [-y're] *p.p.* AVENTURER. || **aventurer** [-y're] #3 *v. tr.* to risk, to venture, to gamble. || **s'aventurer** *v. pron.* to venture. || **aventuri|er, -ère** [-y'rje, -y'rjɛ:r] *n.* adventurer, swindler.

avenue [av'ny] *n.f.* avenue.

averse [a'vɛrs] *n.f.* [×] shower; downpour; [Fig.] flood, deluge.

aversion [avɛr'sjõ] *n.f.* aversion, dislike: *avoir de l' ~ pour qqun,* to dislike s.o.

averti, -e [avɛr'ti] *adj.* forewarned; informed; experienced.

avertir [avɛr't|i:r] #17 *v. tr.* to warn, caution; to notify. || **avertissant** [-i'sɑ̃] *p.pr.* of AVERTIR. || **avertissement** [-is'mɑ̃] *n.m.* warning, notice. || **avertisseur** [-i'sœ:r] *adj.* warning. || *n.m.* motor horn: *~ d'incendie,* fire alarm.

aveu [a'vø] *n.m.* admission: *faire l' ~ de qqch.,* to confess, to admit sth.

aveuglant, -e [avœ'glɑ̃(:t)] *adj.* blinding. || **aveugle** [a'vœ:gl] *adj.* blind. || *n.m/f* blind man, blind woman. || **aveuglé, -e** [avœ'gl|e] *p.p.* of AVEUGLER. || **aveugler** [-e] #3 *v. tr.* to blind. || **aveuglette** [-ɛt] *n.f.* [only in] *à l' ~,* blindly, groping one's way.

aviat|eur, -rice [avja|'tœ:r, -'tris] *n.* aviator, airman, airwoman. || **aviation** [-'sjõ] *n.f.* aviation: *~ civile,* civil aviation.

avide [a'vid] *adj.* eager (to, *de*), avid; grasping, greedy. || **avidement** [-'mɑ̃] *adv.* eager, avidly. || **avidité** [-i'te] *n.f.* avidity; greed.

avilir [avi'l|i:r] #17 *v. tr.* to debase, degrade; [Com.] to depreciate. || **avilissement** [-is'mɑ̃] *n.m.* debasement, degradation; [Com.] depreciation.

avion [a'vjõ] *n.m.* airplane; plane: *par ~,* air mail; *prendre l' ~,* to fly; *aller à New York en ~,* → to fly to New York.

aviron [avi'rõ] *n.m.* oar (in France, esp. type used to propel river boats) [× RAME]; © [canoe] paddle [PAGAIE].

avis [a'vi] *n.m.* **1.** opinion; advice: *à mon ~,* in my opinion; to my mind: *être de l' ~ de qqun,* to share s.o.'s opinion; *être d' ~ de faire qqch.,* to favour doing sth. **2.** notice, warning. || **avisé, -e** [-'ze] *adj.* shrewd, well-advised. || **aviser** [-'ze] #3 *v. tr.* **1.** to notify, advise. **2.** to see (from a distance), to notice. || *v. intr.* to consider, to take appropriate action: *J'aviserai,* I'll see what should be done. || **s'aviser** *v. pron.* take upon o.s., to take it into one's head (to, *de*).

aviver [avi've] #3 *v. tr.* to revive; [couleur] to touch up; [feu] to stir up; [sentiment] to stimulate; [l'appétit] to whet.

avocat [avɔ'ka] *n.m.* **1.** lawyer; counsel, © advocate: *~ d'assises,* criminal lawyer. **2.** [Fig.] advocate, intercessor.

avoine [a'vwan] *n.f.* oats.

avoir [a'vwa:], **ayant** [ɛ'jɑ̃], **eu** [y] *v. tr.* **1.** [posséder] to have: *En avez-vous?* Do you have any?; *Je n'en ai pas,* I don't have any; *Elle a les yeux bleus,* She has blue eyes, Her eyes are blue. **2.** [se procurer] to get: *Où avez-vous eu cela?,* Where did you get this?; *Je l'ai eu pour un dollar,* I got it for one dollar. **3.** [sensation] → to be: *~ chaud,* to be warm; *~ faim,* to be hungry; *~ soif,* to be thirsty; *~ sommeil,* to be sleepy. **4.** [dimensions] → to be: *Il a presque six pieds,* He is nearly six feet tall; *Le train a une heure de retard,* The train is an hour late. **5.** [Loc.]: *~ une haute opinion de,* to think highly of; *~ de l'importance,* to be important; *~ tort,* to be wrong; *~ lieu,* to take place; *~ lieu de,* to have reason to. **6.** [aux. de temps, de mode, d'aspect]: *Il a fini,* He has finished; *J'ai quelque chose à vous dire,* I have something to tell you; *en ~ pour*, to be through in: *Il n'en a plus pour longtemps*, (1) He will soon be through. (2) He is not long for this world. || *v. impers.*: *y avoir, il y a*, to be. **1.** [espace] there is, there are: *Il n'y a pas de place dans ma valise*, There's no room in my bag; *Il n'y a pas de danger*, There is no danger; *Qu'y a-t-il?*, What is it?, What's the matter?; *Il y a cinq milles jusqu'à l'église*, It is five miles to the church. **2.** [temps—durée] it is: *Il y a deux ans qu'il est parti*, It is two years since he left. [temps—date] ago: *C'est arrivé il y a deux jours*, It happened two days ago.

avoisinant, -e [avwazi'n|ɑ̃(:t)] *adj.* adjoining, next. || **avoisiné, -e** [-e] *p.p.* of AVOISINER. || **avoisiner** [-e] #3 *v. intr.* to be near, to border on.

avorton [avɔr'tõ] *n.m.* [Fam.] undersized child, runt.

avouable [a'vw|abl] *adj.* avowable. || **avoué** [-e] *n.m.* lawyer; solicitor, attorney-at-law. || **avouer** [-e] #3 *v. tr.* to confess, admit. || **s'avouer** *v. pron.*: *~ coupable*, to plead guilty.

avril [a'vril] *n.m.* April: *poisson d' ~*, April fool.

axe [aks] *n.m.* axis; [Tech.] axle, pin.

axiome [ak'sjo:m] *n.m.* axiom.

ayant cf. AVOIR. || **ayant droit** [ejɑ̃'drwa] *pl.* **ayants droit** *n.m.* rightful claimant, beneficiary. || **ayez** [ɛ'je], **ayons** [ɛ'jõ] cf. AVOIR.

azote [a'zɔt] *n.m.* nitrogen.

azur [a'zy:r] *n.m.* azure, blue: *bleu m d' ~*, sky blue.

B

B, b [be] *n.m.* [letter] B, b.

baba [ba'ba] *n.m.* [sponge] cake (with currants and rum syrup). || *adj. inv.* [Fam.]: *en rester ~*, to be flabbergasted.

babil [ba'bil] *n.m.* prattling (of a child). || **babillard, -e** [babi'ja:r(d)] *adj.* [enfant] talkative; [ruisseau] babbling; [oiseau] chattering. || *n.m.* chatterer; © notice board. || **babiller** [babi'je] #3 *v. intr.* to prattle, to babble; [Fig.] to chatter.

babine [ba'bin] *n.f.* hanging lip [of certain animals, e.g. dog], chop: [Fig.] *s'en lécher les babines*, to lick one's chops.

babiole [ba'bjɔl] *n.f.* knick-knack; trinket; toy; [Péj.] trifle.

bâbord [ba'bɔ:r] *n.m.* [Naut.] port, left side (of ships).

babouin [ba'bwɛ̃] *n.m.* baboon.

bac [bak] *n.m.* **1.** ferry(boat). **2.** tank, vat: *~/à fiches, à dossiers/*, file basket. **3.** [Fam.] [= BACCALAURÉAT] preferred in Canada to BACHOT.

baccalauréat [bakalɔre'a] *n.m.* [often abbr. to *bachot*, *bac*] Bachelor's degree: *~ ès/ arts, sciences/*, Bachelor of/Arts, Science/; *obtenir un ~*, to receive a Bachelor's degree.

bâche [bɑ:ʃ] *n.f.* tarpaulin.

bacheli|er, -ère [baʃə|'lje, -'ljɛ:r] *n.* holder of a Bachelor's degree. [× CÉLIBATAIRE.]

bachot [ba'ʃo] *n.m.* **1.** [Fam. & Fr.] [= BACCALAURÉAT]. **2.** dinghy.

bacille [ba'sil] *n.m.* bacillus.

bâcler [bɑ'kle] #3 *v. tr.* [travail] to botch; to go hastily over; [porte] to bar; [Fam.] to block.

bactérie [bakte'ri] *n.f.* bacterium, -a.

badaud [ba'do] *n.m.* loiterer.

badigeon [badi|'ʒõ] *n.m.* whitewash. || **badigeonner** [-ʒɔ'ne] #3 *v. tr.* **1.** to whitewash. **2.** [gorge] to paint.

badin [ba'dɛ̃] *n.m.* †banterer, joker. *adj.* bantering, playful: *humeur badine*, playful mood. || **badinage** [badi|'na:ʒ] *n.m.* banter. || **badiner** [-'ne] #3 *v. intr.* to banter, joke.

bâdrage [bɑ'dra:ʒ] © *n.m.* nuisance, annoyance. || **bâdrer** [bɑ'dre] © *v. tr.* to bother, to annoy.

Baffin [ba'fɛ̃] *n.m.* ©: *la terre de ~*, Baffin Island.

bafouillage [bafu'ja:ʒ] *n.m.* stammering, spluttering. || **bafouiller** [bafu'je] #3 *v. tr. & intr.* to splutter, stammer (an excuse, &c.).

bagage [ba'ga:ʒ] *n.m.* [usual. pl.] **bagages** **1.** [coll.] baggage, piece of baggage: *faire ses bagages,* to pack (up), to pack one's bags; *enregistrer ses bagages,* to check one's bags; ~ *à main,* (a piece of) hand-baggage; *plier* ~ , to get up and go. **2.** [Fig.]: *avec ce léger* ~ *(de connaissances),* with this scanty background.

bagarre [ba'ga:r] *n.f.* scuffle, squabble; (social) disorder, violence: [Fig.] *chercher la* ~ , to spoil for a fight.

bagatelle [baga'tɛl] *n.f.* **1.** trifle, bauble; [Fig.] a trifling sum. **2.** a trifling affair: *s'amuser à des bagatelles,* → to fritter away one's time.

†**bagne** [baɲ] *n.m.* pen(itentiary); © [abus.] hard labour.

bagnole [ba'ɲɔl] *n.f.* [Fam.] car; [old] jalopy, heap.

bagout [ba'gu] *n.m.* glibness: *avoir du* ~ , to have the gift of the gab.

bague [bag] *n.f.* ring: ~ *de fiançailles,* engagement ring; *porter une* ~ , to wear a ring.

baguette [ba'gɛt] *n.f.* rod, stick, switch; (conductor's) baton; [drum] drumstick; [Fr. bread] French stick; [chinoise] chopstick. ~ *magique,* (fairy's, magic) wand; [Fig.] *mener (qqun) à la* ~ , to keep a tight rein on, to be very strict with/s.o.

bah! [bɑ:] *interj.* Nonsense!, Who cares?

Bahamas (les) [baa'ma] *f.* The Bahamas.

bahut [ba'y] *n.m.* chest, cupboard.

bai, -e[1] [bɛ] *adj.* [colour] bay: *une jument baie,* a bay mare.

baie[2] [bɛ, © be] *n.f.* **1.** bay, gulf: *la* ~ *d'Hudson,* Hudson Bay.

baie[3] [bɛ, © be] *n.f.* **1.** berry. **2.** opening (for a door or window); [Naut.] hatch.

baignade [bɛ'ɲad] *n.f.* bath, bathing; [lieu] bathing place; [chevaux] watering.

baigner [bɛ'ɲe] #3 *v. tr.* **1.** [laver] to bathe. **2.** [Fig.] to bathe, wash (the shore); [lumière] to suffuse. || *v. intr.* to be awash (in, *dans*), to be suffused (with, *dans*). || **se baigner** *v. pron.* to go/for a swim, swimming/. || **baigneu|r, -se** [bɛ|'ɲœ:r, -'ɲø:z] *n.* bather, swimmer. || **baignoire** [-ɲwa:r] *n.f.* bathtub; [Fr., Theat.] lower box (seats).

bail [ba:j] *n.m.*, pl. **baux** lease, agreement: *passer, signer/un* ~ , to sign a lease; *louer (une ferme) à qqun,* to lease (a farm)/out to, from/s.o.; *prendre un appartement à* ~ , to lease an apartment.

bâillant, -e [bɑ'jɑ̃(:t)] *adj.* gaping, yawning. || **bâillement** [bɑj'mɑ̃] *n.m.* yawn, yawning. || **bâiller** [bɑ'je] #3 *v. intr.* **1.** to yawn: *J'en baillais d'ennui,* I was bored to tears. **2.** [Fig.] to gape. cf. BÉANT.

†**bailleur** [ba'jœ:r] lessor [i.e. s.o. who leases]; [Fig.] ~ *de fonds,* silent partner; moneylender.

†**bailli** [ba'ji] *n.m.* bailiff, judge.

bâillon [bɑ|'jõ] *n.m.* gag, muzzle; [Fig.] *mettre un* ~ *à qqun,* to silence s.o. || **bâillonné, -e** [-jɔ'ne] *adj.* gagged, [Fig.] silenced. || **bâillonner** #3 *v. tr.* to gag; [Fig.] to silence (the press, s.o.).

bain [bɛ̃] *n.m.* bath; © (bath) tub: ~ *de soleil,* sun bath; *salle de* ~ , bathroom; *prendre un* ~ , to take a bath; [Fig.] *être dans le* ~ , to be in/the soup, a mess/.

baïonnette [bajɔ'nɛt] *n.f.* bayonet: ~ *au canon!,* Fix bayonets!

baiser [bɛ'ze] *n.m.* kiss. || #3 *v. tr.*: ~ *la main d'une dame,* to kiss a lady's hand [otherwise use EMBRASSER, q.v.].

baisse [bɛ:s] *n.f.* [level of water, temperature, &c.] drop, lowering, falling; [tide] ebb, going out; [Fig.] weakening, decline (of influence, authority); [prices] fall, decline: *en* ~ , falling. || **baisser** [bɛ'se] #3 *v. tr.* to lower, let down; [phares] to dim; [chien, cheval] to lay back (the ears); [light, gas] to turn down; [head] to hang; [eyes] to cast down: *se jeter tête baissée dans qqch.,* to rush headlong into sth. || *v. intr.* [eau, lumière, &c.] to subside, to decline; [vue, force] to fail; [température] to fall; [prix] to drop, sag: *faire* ~ , to lower. || **se baisser** *v. pron.* to bend down, to stoop (over): ~ *brusquement,* to duck.

bajoue [ba'ʒu] *n.f.* chap, flabby cheek.

bal [bal] *n.m.* ball, dance.

balade [ba'lad] *n.f.* [Fam.] outing; [à pied] stroll; [en voiture] drive. || **se balader** [-e] #3 *v. pron.* to saunter; to go out for/a stroll, a drive/.

baladeuse [bala'dø:z] *n.f.* trailer; [Electr.] trouble lamp.

balafre [ba'lafr] *n.f.* [cicatrice] scar; [visage] gash, slash.

balai [ba'lɛ] *n.m.* broom; [plus petit] brush, duster; *donner un coup de* ~ , to sweep, to dust.

balance [ba'lɑ̃:s] *n.f.* **1.** balance, (pair of) scales; [Fig.] *faire pencher la* ~ *(en faveur de qqun),* to tip the scales (in s.o.'s favour). **2.** [Fig.] indecision, hesitation: *être en* ~ , to be/doubtful, in suspense/; [Com.] balance: ~ *du commerce,* balance of trade.

balancement [balɑ̃s|'mɑ̃] *n.m.* swinging; [de côté] swaying; [sur une chaise] rocking; [Fig.] wavering. || **balancer** [-e] #4 *v. tr.* [conj. AVOIR (action), ÊTRE (état)]. **1.** to swing (sth.) back and forth, to rock sth. (from side to side). **2.** [Fig.] to weigh (the pros and cons); to waver; to balance (an account). **3.** to toss (sth. out the window); [Fam. & Fig.] to fire (s.o.). || *v. intr.* [Fig.] to hesitate, waver (between two possibilities); [victoire] to hang in the balance. || **se balancer** *v. pron.* to seesaw, to teeter; [balançoire] to swing; [chaise] to rock; [Fam.] *Je m'en balance.* I don't give a hang, To heck with it. || **balançoire** [-wa:r] *n.f.* teeter (-totter), seesaw; [escarpolette] swing.

balancier [balɑ̃'sje] *n.m.* [horloge] pendulum; [montre] balance wheel; [Méc.] beam.

balayage [balɛ'j|a:ʒ] *n.m.* [dust] sweeping up, sweeping out (of a room), dusting off (of a shelf); [TV. screen] scanning. || **balayer** [-e] #11 *v. tr.* **1.** [dust, rubbish, &c.] to sweep up; to sweep (sth.) off (a table, shelf, &c.). **2.** [vent] to sweep (the clouds out of the sky); [mer] to sweep over (a ship, a bridge); [Mil.] to mow down; [obstacles, arguments] to sweep away. || **balayeu|r, -se** [-œ:r, -ø:z] *n.* sweeper, road-, street-/sweeper.

balbutier [balby'sje] #3 *v. tr. & intr.* [enfant] to babble; [d'émotion] to stammer (out).

balcon [bal'kõ] *n.m.* balcony; [Théât.] dress circle.

Bâle [bɑ:l] *n.f.* Basel.

baleine [a'l|ɛ:n] *n.f.* whale; ~ *de corset,* whalebone. || **baleinière** [-ɛ'njɛ:r] *n.f.* whale boat.

balise [ba'l|i:z] *n.f.* [terrain d'aviation] ground beacon; [Naut.]: ~ *flottante,* buoy. || **baliser** [i'ze] #3 *v. tr.* to beacon, buoy: *piste balisée,* flare path.

balistique [balis'tik] *adj.* ballistic. *n.f.* ballistics.

baliverne [bali'vɛrn] *n.f.* twaddle, [Fam.] hooey. *pl.* nonsense, rubbish.

ballade [ba'lad] *n.f.* [poème] ballad.

ballast [ba'last] *n.m.* ballast; [Naut.] water-ballast.

balle [bal] *n.f.* **1.** ball: ~ *de tennis,* tennis ball; *faire rebondir une* ~, to bounce a ball; [Fig.] *renvoyer la* ~ *à qqun,* to turn the tables on s.o.; © ~ *au camp,* baseball. **2.** [revolver, rifle] bullet: *mettre, loger/une* ~ *dans la cible,* to put a bullet in the target. **3.** [cotton, rags, wool] bale: *mettre en* ~, to bale.

ballerine [bal'rin] *n.f.* ballet dancer, ballerina. || **ballet** [ba'lɛ] *n.m.* ballet.

ballon [ba'lõ] *n.m.* **1.** balloon: *monter en* ~, to go up in a balloon. **2.** [basket, foot, socker, &c.] ball; punching bag. || © **ballon-panier** [-pa'nje] *n.m.* basketball.

ballot [ba'lo] *n.m.* package, bundle; [Fam.] fool, sucker. [× BALLOT = bulletin de vote.]

ballotter [balɔ'te] #3 *v. tr. & intr.* to toss about, to shake; *ballotté par les vagues,* tossed by the waves.

balourd, -e [ba'l|u:r, -urd] *adj.* slow-witted, doltish. || *n.m.* lout, blockhead.

Baltique (la) [(la) bal'tik] *n.f.* the Baltic (sea).

balustrade [balys'trad] *n.f.* hand rail, railing.

bambin, -e [bɑ̃'b|ɛ̃, -in] *n.* little child, tot.

bambou [bɑ̃'bu] *n.m.* bamboo: [Fam.] *coup de* ~, sunstroke; the blues.

ban [bɑ̃] *n.m.* **1.** †[Hist.] banishment, sentence of exile: *mettre au* ~ *de la société,* to outlaw; *être au* ~ *de,* to be ostracized by . . . **2.** [*usual. pl.*] solemn proclamation, announcement: *les bans de mariage,* announcement (of bans, marriage).

banal, -e [ba'nal] *adj.* common, commonplace, banal, trivial: *peu* ~, unusual. || **banalité** [-i'te] *n.f.* triviality; truism.

banane [ba'nan] *n.f.* banana: *régime de bananes,* stalk of bananas. || **bananier** [-je] *n.m.* banana tree.

banc [bɑ̃] *n.m.* bench; [école] form; [jury] box; [église] pew: © *Cour du Banc de la Reine,* Queen's Bench; [corail, &c.] reef; [sable] bank, shoal; [de poisson] school (of fish); [huîtres] bed; © [de neige] bank.

bancaire [bɑ̃'kɛ:r] *adj.* banking.

bancal, -e [bɑ̃'kal] *adj.* [jambe] bow-, bandy-legged; [table, &c.] wobbly.

bandage [bɑ̃'da:ʒ] *n.m.* **1.** [Méd.] bandaging; [pansement] bandage. **2.** [Auto.] tire. || **bande** [bɑ̃:d] *n.f.* **1.** band; [terrain, étoffe, film] strip; [roue] tire; [billard] cushion; [papier] wrapper, strip; [territoire] belt; [Radio] band; [mitrailleuse] belt (of shells); [chirurgie] bandage. **2.** [often Pej.] gang, ring (of smugglers, thieves, &c.); band (of people); pack (of wolves): *faire* ~ *à part,* to keep to o.s.; *se mettre en* ~, to band together. || **bandeau** [bɑ̃'d|o] *n.m.* headband; blindfold: *mettre un* ~/*à, sur les yeux de*/ *qqun,* to blindfold s.o.; [Fig.] *avoir un* ~ *sur les yeux,* to be blind to sth. || **bander** [-e] #3 *v. tr.* to bandage, tie up; to bind up (a wound); to band (a wheel);

to string (a bow): ~ *les yeux à qqun*, to blindfold s.o.
banderole [bɑ̃d'rɔl] *n.f.* pennant.
bandit [bɑ̃'di] *n.m.* bandit; gangster; [Fam.] scoundrel, rogue.
bandoulière [bɑ̃du'ljɛ:r] *n.f.* shoulder-belt (for a gun); *porter en* ~, carry across o.'s back.
banjo [bɑ̃n'ʒo] *n.m.* banjo.
banlieue [bɑ̃'ljø] *n.f.* outskirts: *de* ~, suburban; *train m de* ~, suburban train.
banni, -e [ba'ni] *adj.* exiled, outlawed. || *n.* exile, outlaw. || **bannière** [ba'njɛ:r] *n.f.* banner, standard.
bannir [-i:r] #17 *v. tr.* to exile, banish (*de*, from); to outlaw.
banque [bɑ̃:k] *n.f.* bank: © ~ *à charte*, chartered bank; *employé de* ~, bank clerk; [Fig.] ~ *de sang*, blood bank.
banqueroute [bɑ̃k'rut] *n.f.* bankruptcy: *faire* ~, to go bankrupt.
banquet [bɑ̃'kɛ] *n.m.* banquet, public dinner.
banquette [bɑ̃'kɛt] *n.f.* bench; [train, autobus] seat; [golf] bunker.
banquier [bɑ̃'kje] *n.m.* banker.
banquise [bɑ̃'ki:z] *n.f.* ice field, ice pack.
baptême [ba'tɛ:m] *n.m.* baptism, christening: ~ *d'un navire*, christening of a ship; *nom de* ~, given, first, Christian/name. || **baptiser** #3 *v. tr.* [conj. AVOIR (action), ÊTRE (état)] to baptize, christen: [ext.] to name, to dub; [Fam.] (du vin), to water down wine.
baptismal, -e [batis'mal] *adj.* baptismal: *fonts baptismaux*, fonts.
Baptiste [ba'tist] *n.m.* Baptist; *Jean-Baptiste* **1.** John the Baptist. **2.** © [nickname for French Canadians].
baquet [ba'kɛ] *n.m.* bucket, tub; [abreuvoir] trough.
bar [ba:r] *n.m.* bar: [Fr.] ~ *américain*, cocktail bar.
baraque [ba'rak] *n.f.* shack, hovel; shanty; [foire] booth. || **baraquement** [-'mɑ̃] *n.m.* [esp. Mil.] (quonset) huts.
baratte [ba'rat] *n.f.* churn.
barbare [bar'b|a:r] *adj.* barbarous; uncivilized; [Péj.] cruel, barbaric. || *n.m.* barbarian. || **barbarie** [-a'ri] *n.f.* [cruauté] barbarity, cruelty; [absence de culture] barbarism.
barbe [barb] *n.f.* **1.** beard; whiskers: *se raser la* ~, to shave (one's whiskers, beard); *se laisser pousser la* ~, to let one's beard grow, → to grow a beard; [Fig.] *rire dans sa* ~, → to laugh/in, up/one's sleeve; *faire qqch. à la* ~ *de qqun*, to do sth./in, to/s.o.'s face. **2.** [Fam.] bore: *Quelle* ~ *!*, What a bore!; *La* ~ *!*, Dry up!, Drop dead!
barbelé, -e [barbə'le] *adj.* barbed: *fil de fer* ~, barbed wire, cf. BROCHE.
barbiche [bar'biʃ] *n.f.* goatee.
barbier [bar'bje] *n.m.* [obsolescent in Fr.] © barber; © *salon m. de* ~, barber shop [= Fr. salon de coiffeur].
barbiturique [barbity'rik] *adj.* barbituric. || *n.* barbiturate; *pl.* [Fam.] © goof balls.
barboter [bar|bɔ'te] #3 *v. intr.* paddle, splash about. || *v. tr.* [Fam. = dérober] to filch. || **barbote** [-'bɔt] © *n.f.* (illegal) gambling-house.
barbouillage [barbu'ja:ʒ] *n.m.* [peinture] smearing; daubing; [écriture] scribbling, scrawl. || **barbouiller** [barbu'je] #3 *v. tr.* [peinture] to smear, daub; [salir] to smear, begrime; [encre] to smut, blot; [écriture] to scribble; [peinture] to paint poorly, to daub; [Fam.] to upset (one's stomach). || **se barbouiller** *v. pron.* to daub, to smear o.s. (with sth.): [Fig.] *Le ciel se barbouille*, It's clouding /up, over/. || **barbouilleu|r, -se** *n.* [peinture] dauber (of paints); [écrivain] scribbler, hack.
barbu, -e [bar'by] *adj.* bearded, unshaven. || *n.m.* bearded man.
bardeau [bar'do] *n.m.* shingle; [mur] clapboard.
barême [ba'rɛ:m] *n.m.* [impôts] schedule; [prix] price list; [statistiques] graph; ready reckoner.
baril [ba'ri] *n.m.* [en métal] drum, barrel; [en bois] keg, cask.
bariolage [barjɔ'la:ʒ] *n.m.* [gén. Péj.] motley.
bariolé, -e [barjɔ'le] *adj.* **1.** of many colours, many-coloured. **2.** gaudy.
barlot [bar'lo] *n.m.* © sled.
baromètre [barɔ'm|ɛ:tr] *n.m.* barometer; [Fam.] glass. || **barométrique** [-e'trik] *adj.* barometric.
baron, -ne [ba'r|ɔ̃, -ɔn] *n.* baron, baroness.
baroque [ba'rɔk] *adj.* **1.** quaint, odd. **2.** [Arch. style] baroque. || *n.m.* quaintness, oddness; [style] baroque.
barque [bark] *n.f.* [grande] boat, barge; [petite] bark; (fishing) smack: [Fig.] *Bien mener sa* ~, To know how to handle o.s.; *Deux patrons font chavirer la* ~, Too many cooks spoil the broth.
barrage [ba'ra:ʒ] *n.m.* dam; [barrière] barrier, fence; [police] road block; [Fig.] obstruction.
barre [ba:r] *n.f.* **1.** bar, rod; [savon] cake; [or] ingot; [rayure] band, stripe; [du T] cross-stroke. **2.** [Naut.] helm:

l'homme de ~, helmsman; [Jur.] *La* ~ *des témoins*, the witness box; [Fig.] *avoir* ~ *sur qqun*, to have a pull with s.o. || **barré, -e** [ba're] *adj.* [chemin, passage, &c] barred, blocked; © [porte] locked; [écriture] crossed out. || **barreau** [ba'r|o] *n.m.* small/bar, rod/; [échelle] rung; [fenêtre] bar; [Jur.] the Bar: *être reçu au* ~, to be admitted to the Bar. || **barrer** [-e] #3 *v. tr.* [conj. AVOIR (action), ÊTRE (état)] to bar; to obstruct; © to lock (a door); to cross out (an item); to block (up), close (a road); to dam (a river).

barrette[1] [ba'rɛt] *n.f.* [Rel.] biretta.

barrette[2] [ba'rɛt] *n.f.* barrette, clasp.

barricade [bari'kad] *n.f.* barricade. || **barricader** [-e] #3 *v. tr.* to barricade.

barrière [ba'rjɛ:r] *n.f.* barrier; [ouvrante] gate; [course] starting gate; [pour compter les personnes qui passent] turnpike; [Fig.] defence, barrier (*contre*, against).

barrique [ba'rik] *n.f.* large barrel, hogshead.

baryton [bari'tõ] *n. & adj.* [Mus.] baritone.

bas [bɑ] *n.m.* **1.** bottom, foot; lower part (of the face, back, &c.): *au* ~ *de la page*, at the/bottom, foot/of the page; *aller de* ~ *en haut*, to go from the bottom to the top; *le* ~ *d'une/montagne, colline/*, the/foot, bottom/of a/mountain, hill/. **2.** stocking: ~ *de/soie, nylon/*, silk, nylon/stocking.

bas, -se [bɑ(:s)] *adj.* [absolu] low; [rel.] [ville] lower: *le Bas Rhin*, the Lower Rhine; © *le Bas du Fleuve*, the Lower St. Lawrence; [Mus.] low; [Loc.]: *au* ~ *mot*, at the (very) least. || *adv.* [s'incliner, voler, chanter] low: *plus* ~, lower; [creuser] deeper; [étage] down; [écrit] further on; [Fig., le moral, un malade] *être très* ~, to be very low: ~ *les/mains, pattes/*, hands off; (*mettre*) *chapeau* ~ *devant* ..., hats off/before, to/. . . ; *parler tout* ~, to speak in a whisper; *A* ~ *!*, Down with!; *en* ~, below; [maison] downstairs; *en* ~ *de*, [être] at the bottom of, [tomber] off (sth.).

basané, -e [baza'ne] *adj.* tanned, sunburnt, swarthy.

basculant, -e [basky'lɑ̃(:t)] *adj.* tipping: *pont* ~, drawbridge; *siège* ~, reclining seat. || **bascule** [bas'kyl] *n.f.* **1.** rocker; teeter, seesaw. **2.** scales, public scale [for heavy objects]; *fauteuil à* ~, rocking (chair), rocker; *wagon à* ~, dump cart. || **basculer** [-e] #3 *v. tr.* to tip/up, over/. || *v. intr.* to rock, teeter; to tilt: *faire* ~, to upset, to knock over.

base [bɑ:z] *n.f.* **1.** base; [édifice] foundation, base; [argument] basis: *de* ~, basic; [Fig.] *jeter les bases de*, to lay the foundations of. **2.** [Naut.] base; [Aviat.] air base. || **basé, -e** [bɑ'ze] *adj.* based.

baseball [bez'bɑ:l] *n.m.* [Sport.] baseball; *terrain de* ~, baseball diamond.

baser [bɑ'ze] #3 *v. tr.* to found, to base (*sur*, on).

basket(ball) [baskɛt'bɑ:l] *n.m.* basketball.

basque [bask] *n. & adj.* Basque.

basse-cour [bɑs'ku:r] *n.f.* farmyard, poultry yard; barnyard.

bassesse [bɑ'sɛs] *n.f.* baseness; base action.

bassin [ba's|ɛ̃] *n.m.* [fleuve] basin; [fontaine] pool (of a fountain); [cuvette] bowl, basin; [eau] reservoir; [de radoub] dry dock; ~ *houiller*, coal field. || **bassine** [-in] *n.f.* basin; [Cul.] pan.

basson [ba'sõ] *n.m.* [instrument] bassoon; [Pers.] bassoonist.

bastion [bas'tjõ] *n.m.* bastion; [Fig.] stronghold.

bât [bɑ] *n.m.* pack, packsaddle; *cheval de* ~, pack horse; [Fig.] *C'est là que le* ~ *le blesse*, There's the rub.

bataille [ba't|a:j] *n.f.* battle: [navale] naval engagement; [Fig.] quarrel, fight: *cheval de* ~, war horse, [Fig.] favourite subject. || **batailler** #3 *v. intr.* to fight, battle (*contre*, against); [Fig.] to argue heatedly. || **bataillon** [-a'jõ] *n.m.* battalion.

bâtard, -e [ba't|a:r, -ard] *adj.* bastard, [animal] mongrel; [enfant] illegitimate; [race] degenerate. || *n.m.* bastard; [animal] mongrel, crossbreed.

bateau [ba'to] *n.m.* boat: [a medium-sized, or small craft; for large vessels use NAVIRE] ~ *de course*, racing craft; [× ‡*navire de course*, privateer]; ~ *de pêche*, fishing boat, schooner; [Fr.] ~ *mouche*, sightseeing boat; ~ *de plaisance*, yacht; ~ *à voiles*, sail(ing) boat: [Fig.] *monter un* ~ *à qqun*, to pull s.o.'s leg. || **bateau-citerne** [-si'tɛrn] *n.m.* tanker. || **bateau-feu, -phare** [-'fø, -'fa:r] *n.m.* lightship. || **bateau pilote** [pi'lɔt] *n.m.* pilot boat. || **bateau-pompe** [-'põ:p] *n.m.* fire boat. || **bateli|er, -ère** [batə'lj|e, -ɛ:r] *n.* boatman, boatwoman.

bâti, -e [bɑ'ti] *adj.* built: [Fam., Pers.] *bien* ~, well built.

bâtiment [-'mɑ̃] *n.m.* **1.** building; building/trade, industry/: *entrepreneur en* ~, building contractor. **2.** vessel, ship [applied to any type of craft] ~ *de guerre*, man-of-war. **3.** © farm; barn.

bâtir [bɑ't|i:r] #17 *v. tr.* **1.** to build,

erect; [plan] to construct, lay out (a plan). **2**. to baste (a garment). || *v. intr.* to build: *terrain à* ~, building lot. || **se bâtir** *v. pron.* **1.** to be under construction. **2.** to have a house built.

bâtisse [-is] *n.f.* [Fr.] [Péj.] building, © (any) building [use BÂTIMENT].

bâtisseur [bɑti'sœ:r] *n.m.* builder.

batiste [ba'tist] *n.f.* batiste, cambric.

bâton [bɑ't|õ] *n.m.* stick; [long] staff, pole; [gros] cudgel; [de chaise] rung, cross-bar; [d'agent de police] nightstick, [Br.] truncheon; [rouge à lèvres] (lip)stick; © [de chef d'orchestre] baton; [Loc.] *donner des coups de* ~, → to beat (with a stick); *à bâtons rompus*, by fits and starts; *mettre des bâtons dans les roues*, to put a spoke in (s.o.'s) wheel, to throw a wrench in the/gears, works/. || **bâtonner** [-ɔ'ne] #3 *v. tr.* to beat (with a stick); to cudgel. || **bâtonnet** [-ɔ'nɛ] *n.m.* small stick; [chinois] chopstick.

bats; **batte,** &c. cf. BATTRE.

battant [ba't|ɑ̃] *n.m.* clapper (of a bell); swinging door; folding leaf (of a table, counter): [Fig.] *ouvrir les portes à deux battants*, → to fling the doors wide open. || **battant, -e** [-ɑ̃(:t)] *adj.* beating: *le cœur* ~, with throbbing heart; [pluie] driving, pelting; [porte] swinging, self-closing; [Fig.] ~ *neuf*, brand-new; *à l'heure battante*, on the hour, at the stroke of.

battement [bat'mɑ̃] *n.m.* beat(ing); stamp(ing) (of feet); clap(ping) (of hands); beat(ing), flutter(ing) (of wings); flutter(ing) (of eyelashes); beat(ing) (of the heart, pulse, &c.): ☞ *battements de cœur*, heart palpitations.

batterie [bat'ri] *n.f.* **1.** [Mil.] battery; [Fig.] set, collection (of things): ~ *de cuisine*, set of kitchen utensils; battery cf. ACCUMULATEUR: ~ *auxiliaire*, booster battery; [Mus.] percussion section (of an orchestra).

batteur [ba't|œ:r] *n.m.* [blé] thresher; [à œufs] © egg-beater; [Sport.] © batsman.

batteuse [-ø:z] *n.f.* threshing machine; [Fr.] egg-beater.

battoir [-wa:r] *n.m.* bat, beater.

battre [batr], **battant** [ba't|ɑ̃], **battu** [-y] #43 *v. tr.* to beat, [comme plâtre] to thrash; [ennemi, adversaire] to beat, [chercher] scour (the country); [cœur] to throb, to thump; [cartes] to shuffle; [monnaie] to coin, to mint; [beurre] to churn; [crème] to whisk; [le blé] to thresh; [des ailes] to flap, flutter; [Loc.] ~ *sa coulpe*, to regret one's sins; ~ *qqun à plate couture*, to beat s.o. hollow, → to whip s.o.; [Mus.] ~ *la mesure*, to beat (time); [Naut.] ~ *pavillon* (américain, &c.), to fly the (US, &c.) flag; ~ *son plein*, to be at its height. || *v. intr.* [pluie] to beat; [porte] to bang; [horloge] to tick; [Mil.] ~ *en retraite*, to retreat, fall back. || **se battre** [sə'batr] *v. pron.* to fight (*contre*, against; *avec*, with). || **battu, -e** [ba'ty] *adj.* beaten, well worn; [yeux] tired.

batture [ba'ty:r] © *n.f.* strand [Fr. *estran*]; rocky shore; ice foot.

baudet [bo'dɛ] *n.m.* donkey.

baume [bo:m] *n.m.* balm, balsam; [Fig.] balm.

bavard, -e [ba'v|a:r, -ard] *adj.* talkative, chatty; [Péj.] gossipy, gabby. || *n.* chatterbox; [Péj.] gossip(er). || **bavardage** [-ar'da:ʒ] *n.m.* chattering; chatter, chit-chat; [Péj.] gossip(ing), idle talk. || **bavarder** [-ar'de] #3 *v. intr.* **1.** to chat, chatter. **2.** to gossip. || **bavasser** [-a'se] *v. intr.* © [Pop.] to gossip.

bave [ba:v] *n.f.* drivel; [bébé] drool; [animal] slobber; froth; [limace] slime. || **baver** [ba've] #3 *v. intr.* to drivel; to drool, to slobber; to froth. || **bavette** [ba'vɛt] *n.f.* bib: [Fam.] *tailler des bavettes*, to gossip. || **baveu|x, -se** [ba'vø(:z)] *adj.* drooling, [lettre] blurred; [Cul.] juicy.

bavure [ba'vy:r] *n.f.* [encre] smudge; [metal] burr.

bazar [ba'za:r] *n.m.* five-and-ten; general store; © bazaar, charity sale.

bazou [ba'zu] © *n.m.* [Fam.] jalopy, heap. cf. TACOT.

béant, -e [be'ɑ̃(:t)] *adj.* yawning (chasm), gaping (wound): *la bouche béante*, open-mouthed.

béat, -e [be'a(t)] *adj.* [gen. derogatory] smug, complacent: *un air* ~, a smug /air, expression/.

béatifier [beati|'fje] #3 *v. tr.* [Rel.] to beatify. || **béatitude** [-'tyd] *n.f.* [Rel.] beatitude; [Fig.] bliss.

beau, belle [bo, bɛl] *adj.* [☞ Has a second masc. sing. form (*bel*) which is used before nouns beginning with a vowel or a mute *h*, ex. *un bel homme*, a handsome man] [fem.] beautiful, lovely, [masc.] handsome, nice- *ou* good-looking; [chose, animal] beautiful, lovely, [moins fort] nice-, fine-(looking); [temps] fair, nice, fine, good; [talent, intelligence] great; [invention, &c.] wonderful; [pensée, sentiment] noble; [somme d'argent] handsome, large: *avoir* ~ [+ *inf.*] . . . , [inf.] + in vain, vainly; *au* ~ *milieu*, right, exactly/in the middle: *le bel âge*, the carefree years; *un bel âge*, a ripe old age; *de plus belle*, more and more, more, worse, faster, &c./than ever. || *n.m.* **1.** beauty: *l'étude du* ~, the study of beauty; *voir tout en* ~, to look on the bright side. || **beau-fils** [bo|'fis] *pl. beaux-fils n.m.* **1.** stepson; **2.** [gendre] son-in-law. || **beau-frère** [-'frɛ:r] *pl. beaux-frères n.m.* brother-in-law. || **beau-père** [-'pɛ:r] *pl. beaux-pères n.m.* **1.** stepfather. **2.** father-in-law.

beaucoup [bo'ku] *adv.* [before a noun, is always followed by *de*; the noun is not preceded by the def. article] **1.** [nombre] (a great) many. **2.** [quantité] a great deal, a lot, much: *pour* ~ *(de personnes)*, for many (people); *de* ~, by far; [avec un verbe] a great deal, a lot, [au négatif] much: *Je travaille* ~, I work a great deal, a lot; *Je ne travaille pas* ~, I don't do much work; ~ */plus, moins, mieux, trop/*, a great deal, a lot/more, less, better/, too much. [☞ Do not confuse *beaucoup de*, much [+ sing.]; many [+ pl.] and *de beaucoup*, by far.]

beauté [bo'te] *n.f.* beauty, loveliness: *de toute* ~, extremely lovely, splendid.

beaux-arts [bo'za:r] *n.mpl.* fine arts: *l'École des Beaux-Arts*, the School of Fine Arts.

bébé [be'be] *n.m.* baby.

bec [bɛk] *n.m.* **1.** [d'oiseau] beak, bill; [Fam.] mouth, nose (of a person): *coup de* ~, a pick, peck; [Fig.] *clouer le* ~ *à qqun*, to shut s.o. up; *prise f de bec*, squabble, fighting words; [Fam.] *se rincer le* ~, to wet one's whistle; © *un petit* ~, a little kiss. **2.** nib (of a pen); spout (of a pitcher, coffee pot); stem (of a pipe), mouthpiece (of a clarinet); nozzle (of a hose): ~ *de gaz*, gas light, lamp-post.

bécasse [be'kas] *n.f.* woodcock. || **bécassine** [-in] *n.f.* snipe.

bêche [bɛʃ] *n.f.* spade. || **bêcher** [-e] #3 *v. tr. & intr.* to dig (up); [Fig., Fam.] to rib.

bécosses [be'kɔs] © *n.mpl.* [Pop.] the john.

becquée [bɛ'ke] *n.f.* beakful: *donner la* ~, to feed (its young).

bedaine [bə'dɛn] *n.f.* [Fam.] paunch.

bedeau [bə'do, © be'do] *n.m.* beadle; verger.

bedonner [bədɔ'ne] #3 *v. intr.* to grow /paunchy, pot-bellied/, to develop a paunch.

bée [be] *adj.* [*fem.* only]: *rester bouche* ~, to stand/open-mouthed, gaping/.

bégaiement [begɛ|'mɑ̃] *n.m.* stammering, stuttering. || **bégayer** [-'je] #11 *v. intr.* to stammer, to stutter. || *v. tr.* [une excuse] to falter out. || **bègue** [bɛg] *n.m/f.* stammerer, stutterer.

béguin [be'gɛ̃] *n.m.* baby's bonnet; [Fam.] boy, girl/-friend/; infatuation: *avoir le* ~ *pour*, to have a crush on.

behaviorisme [bievjɔ'rism] *n.m.* [Philos.] behaviourism.

beige [bɛ:ʒ] *adj.* beige.

beigne [bɛɲ] © *n.m.*; [Fr.] **beignet** [-ɛ] *n.m.* doughnut, fritter.

bel, belle [bɛl] cf. BEAU.

Belcher, (l'archipel des) [(larʃipɛl dɛ) bɛl'ʃɛ:r] *n.* Belcher Islands.

bêlement [bɛl|'mɑ̃] *n.m.* bleating. || **bêler** [-e] #3 *v. intr.* to bleat.

belette [bə'lɛt] *n.f.* weasel.

belge [bɛlʒ] *adj. & n.* Belgian. || **Belgique** [-ik] *n.f.* Belgium.

bélier [be'lje] *n.m.* ram; [Mil.] battering ram.

belle [bɛl] *n.f.* **1.** beauty, belle: *La Belle au bois dormant*, Sleeping Beauty. **2.** [jeu] deciding game; [tennis] final set. || **belle-mère** [-'mɛ:r] *n.f.* mother-in-law (pl. mothers-in-law); step-mother. || **belle-sœur** [-'sœ:r] *n.f.* sister-in-law (pl. sisters-in law).

belligérant, -e [bɛlliʒe'rɑ̃(:t)] *adj.* belligerent, at war. || *n.m.* belligerent.

belliqueu|x, -se [bɛlli'kø(:z)] *adj.* pugnacious, quarrelsome [used when speaking of a person].

bémol [be'mɔl] *n. & adj.* [Mus.] flat.

ben [bɛ̃] *interj.* [familiar form of *bien*] ~ *oui!*, Why yes!

bénédicité [benedisi'te] *n.m.*: *dire le* ~, to say grace.

Bénédictin, -e [benedik't|ɛ̃, in] *n. & adj.* [Rel.] Benedictine.

bénédiction [benedik'sjõ] *n.f.* blessing; [d'une église] consecration: ~ *nuptiale*, marriage ceremony; [Fam.] godsend, stroke of luck.

bénéfice [bene'fis] *n.m.* [Com.] profit, earnings; [Rel.] benefice; [Jur.] *le* ~ *du doute*, the benefit of doubt; [Théâ.] benefit (performance): ~ */brut, net/*, gross, net/profit. || **bénéficiaire** [-jɛ:r] *n.* beneficiary; [cheque] payee. || *adj.*: *solde* ~, credit balance. || **bénéficier** [-je] #3 *v. intr.* to benefit (from a reduction), to profit (*de*, by), to make a profit (*de*, from): *faire* ~ *qqun d'une réduction*, to allow s.o. a discount.

bénéfique [bene'fik] *adj.* [astrologie] benefic, beneficent.

benêt [bə'nɛ] *adj.m.* silly, stupid. || *n.m.* [Fam.] sap, simpleton.

bénévole [bene'vɔl] *adj.* **1.** gentle, kind. **2.** unpaid, voluntary.

béni, -e [be'n|i] cf. BÉNIR. || *adj.* hallowed, blessed [used only in connection with people]: *Vous êtes bénie entre toutes les femmes*, Blessed art thou among women. || **bénignité** [-iɲi'te] *n.f.* **1.** benignity, benevolence. **2.** [Méd.] mildness. || **bénin, bénigne** [be'n|ɛ̃, -iɲ] *adj.* **1.** [bien-veillant] benign, benignant. **2.** [Méd., léger] non-malignant, benign. || **bénir** [-iːr] #17 *v. tr.* to bless; [par des cérémonies] to consecrate, sanctify: *~ le ciel*, to thank heaven, → to thank one's (lucky) stars. || **bénit, -e** [-i(t)] *adj.* consecrated, holy [when referring to people use *béni*]: *eau bénite*, holy water; *pain ~*, consecrated bread. || **bénitier** [-i'tje] *n.m.* holy-water basin.

benjamin, -e [bɛ̃ʒa'm|ɛ̃, -in] *n. & adj.* junior; youngest (child).

benzine [bɛ̃'zin] *n.f.* benzine.

béquille [be'kiːj] *n.f.* crutch; doorhandle [porte de magasin].

bercail [bɛr'kaːj] *n.m.* sheepfold; [Fig.] fold.

berceau [bɛr's|o] *n.m.* cradle; [tonnelle] arbour; [voûte] barrel: *dès le ~*, from birth; *encore au ~*, still in/one's, its/ infancy. || **bercer** [-e] #4 *v. tr.* **1.** to rock, cradle: *~ un enfant dans les bras*, to rock, cradle a child in one's arms. **2.** [Fig.] to soothe, calm (a pain, hurt, &c.); to cherish (a hope); to stimulate (the imagination). || *v. intr.* to delude (s.o.) (with, *de*) (vain promises, false hopes, illusions, &c.). || **se bercer** *v. pron.* **1.** to rock o.s. (in a hammock, rocking chair, &c.). **2.** [Fig.] to delude o.s. (with false hopes, illusions, &c.) || **berceuse** [-øːz] *n.f.* lullaby, cradle song; hanging cradle; rocking chair.

béret [be'rɛ] *n.m.* beret; [Fam.] © French pancake.

berge [bɛrʒ] *n.f.* [rivière] (steep) bank.

berg|er, -ère [bɛr'ʒ|e, -ɛːr] *n.* shepherd, shepherdess.

Berlin [bɛr'l|ɛ̃] *n.m.* Berlin.

berline [bɛr'lin] *n.f.* [Auto. = 4 portes, 4 glaces] sedan.

berlingot [bɛrlɛ̃'go] *n.m.* caramel (candy).

berlot [bar'lo] © *n.m.* sleigh.

berlue [bɛr'ly] *n.f.* [Fig., Fam.]: *avoir la ~*, to be (grossly) mistaken.

berme [bɛrm] *n.f.* [road, &c.] soft shoulder.

Bermudes, (les) [(le) bɛr'myd] *n.f.* Bermuda.

bernache [bɛr'naʃ] © *n.f.* Canada goose. cf. OUTARDE.

Berthe [bɛrt] *n.f.* Bertha.

besogne [bə'zɔɲ] *n.f.* (piece of) work; job, task: *se mettre à la ~*, to set to work. || **besogner** [-e] #3 *v. intr.* to slave, to work hard. || **besogneu|x, -se** [-ø(ːz)] *adj.* hard-up, needy (person).

besoin [bə'zwɛ̃] *n.m.* **1.** need, want: *avoir ~ de*, to need, to have need of: *au ~*, *en cas de ~*, as the case may be. **2.** needs, want, poverty: *être dans le ~*, to be in need. **3.** craving (*de*, for); yearning (*de*, for).

bestial, -e [bɛs'tj|al] *adj.* brutish, bestial. || **bestialité** [bɛstjali'te] *n.f.* bestiality, brutishness. || **bestiaux** [-o] *n.mpl.* [coll.] livestock, cattle. cf. BÉTAIL.

bestiole [bɛs'tjɔl] *n.f.* tiny creature; insect.

bétail [be'taj] *n.m.* [coll.]; *pl.* *bestiaux*, livestock, cattle: *gros, menu/ ~*, large, small/livestock.

bête [bɛːt] *n.f.* beast; animal; [dumb] creature: *chercher la petite ~*, to look for the smallest mistake, to be over-critical; [Loc.] *petites bêtes*, insects, cf. BIBITE; *~ à cornes*, animal with horns; *~ noire*, pet aversion; *~ féroce*, wild beast; *~ fauve*, deer, [by ext.] big game; *~ de somme*, beast of burden; © *~ à patates*, potato bug. © *~ puante*, skunk; cf. MOUFFETTE. || *adj.* stupid, silly, foolish. || **bêtise** [bɛː'tiːz] *n.f.* blunder; piece of nonsense, foolishness.

béton [be'tõ] *n.m.* concrete: *~ armé*, reinforced concrete.

betterave [bɛ'traːv] *n.f.* beet: *~ sucrière*, sugar beet.

beuglement [bøglə'mɑ̃] *n.m.* [taureau] bellowing; [vache] lowing; [Fam.] bawling. || **beugler** [bø'gl|e] #3 *v. intr.* to bellow, to bawl, to low.

beurre [bœːr] *n.m.* **1.** butter; *beurre/frais, salé/*, unsalted, salted/butter; *~ noir*, browned butter; [Fig.] *avoir un œil au ~ noir*, to have a black eye; *~* [Fr.] *de cacahuète*, © *d'arachide*, peanut butter; *tartine de ~*, slice, piece/of bread and butter. **2.** [Fig.] *faire son ~*, to make one's /pile, pot/; to feather one's nest; *tenir l'assiette au ~*, to be on the gravy train. || **beurrée** [bœ'r|e] *n.f.* [Fam.] slice of bread and butter. || **beurrer** [-e] #3 *v. tr.* to butter; to spread. || **beurrerie** [-'ri] *n.f.* †buttery; creamery, butter factory, butter room. || **beurrier** [-je] *n.m.* butter dish. **beurri|er, -ère** [-je, -jɛːr] *adj.* (of) butter: *l'industrie beurrière*, the butter industry.

bévue [be'vy] *n.f.* a blunder, slip: *commettre une ~*, to make a blunder, [Fam.] to pull a boner.

biais [bjɛ] *n.m.* bias, slant: *de* ~, *en* ~, slantwise, aslant; *regarder de* ~, to look sideways at; [Fig.] shift, expedient: *trouver un* ~, to find a round-about method (of doing . . .).

bibelot [bib'lo] *n.m.* knick-knack, trinket, curio.

biberon [bib'rõ] *n.m.* (baby) bottle: *nourrir un enfant au* ~, to feed, bring up/a baby on the bottle.

bibite, bebite [bi'bit, bɔ'bit] © *n.f.* bug, insect; [Fam.] *être en* ~, to be mad.

Bible [bibl] *n.f.* Bible.

bibliographie [bibliɔgra'fi] *n.f.* bibliography. || **bibliographique** [-k] *adj.* bibliographical. || **bibliothécaire** [bibliɔte'kɛːr] *n.m/f.* librarian. || **bibliothèque** [bibliɔ'tɛk] *n.f.* **1.** library; [salle de lecture] reading-room; [de gare] newsstand; [meuble] bookcase, bookshelves: *Bibliothèque nationale*, National Library; ~ *circulante*, lending library.

biblique [bi'blik] *adj.* biblical.

bicarbonate [bikarbɔ'nat] *n.m.*: ~ *de soude*, bicarbonate of soda, sodium bicarbonate.

biceps [bi'sɛps] *adj. & n.(m.)* biceps.

biche [biʃ] *n.f.* doe, hind.

bicoque [bi'kɔk] *n.f.* [Fam.] shanty.

bicyclette [bisi'klɛt] *n.f.* bicycle; [Fam.] bike: *aller à* ~, to cycle, to ride a bicycle; [Sport.] *faire de la* ~, to cycle.

bidon [bi'dõ] *n.m.* [à essence, à lait] can: [Mil.] canteen.

bielle [bjɛl] *n.f.* rod: ~ *motrice*, driving rod.

bien[1] [bjɛ̃] *adv.* **1.** well: *Elle danse, chante, joue*/ ~, She/dances, sings, plays/well. [☞ Précisez en anglais la qualité décrite par ~]: *Il parle* ~ *anglais*, He speaks good English; ~ *ajusté*, tight-fitting; *viser* ~, to aim carefully; ~ *caché*, securely hidden; ~ *essuyer la vaisselle*, to wipe dishes clean; ~ *frotté*, brightly polished; ~ *balayé*, swept clean; ~ *peigné*, neatly dressed (hair); *livre* ~ *écrit*, well-written book; *homme* ~ *bâti*, well-built man; *une balle* ~ *frappée*, a well-hit ball; *maison* ~ *construite*, well-built house. **2.** [être bien + p.p.]: *être* ~ *écrit(e)(s)*, to be well written; *être* ~ *mérité*, to be well deserved. **3.** [être + bien] [chose] to be nice, lovely; [Pers.] to be nice; [apparence] to be nice looking; [approbation] to be fine, all right, O.K.; [confort] to be comfortable: *Tout est* ~ *qui finit* ~, All's well that ends well. **4.** fine, good: *C'est un homme* ~, He is a fine gentleman. **5.** [Loc.] *être, se mettre*/ ~ *avec qqun*, → to be, to get/on good terms with s.o.; *être* ~ *ensemble*, to get along well together. **6.** [santé] *aller, se porter*/ ~, to be fine; *Vous allez, vous vous portez*/ ~ ?, → How are you (feeling)?; (*Je vais, Je me porte*) ~, *merci*, (I am feeling) fine, thank you. **7.** [augmentatif] very: *Il est* ~ *malade*, He is very sick; *Il est* ~ *mal*, He is dangerously ill; ~ *entendu*, of course, naturally; ~ *loin*, a long way, very far; ~ *mieux*, much better; ~ *sûr*, absolutely, of course. **8.** [Loc.] *aussi* ~, anyhow; in any case; *aussi* ~ *que*, as well as; ~ *du*, ~ *des*, a great many, a lot of: *Vous vous donnez* ~ *du mal*, You're taking a lot of trouble; *Je l'ai vu* ~ *des fois*, I saw him/quite often, many times/; ~ *plus*, What's more; ~ *que*, although. [+ subjunc.]; *si* ~ *que*, so that; *ou* ~, or else. || *interj. Bien!*, Good!; *Très* ~ *!*, Very good! [Pour accepter une proposition] very well; *Eh* ~ *!*, Well!; *Eh* ~ *?*, Well?

bien[2] [bjɛ̃] *n.m.* **1.** good; [s.o.'s, everyone's, the common, the public, the general] welfare; *faire grand* ~ *à, beaucoup de* ~ *à*, to do/a great deal, a lot/of good/ to . . . , → to help/a great deal, a lot/; *dire du* ~ *de qqun*, to speak well of s.o.; *en* ~, favourably. **2.** possessions; [valeur] riches, wealth, [choses] goods; [propriété] property, &c. **3.** [*pl.*] [terre] good things, [ciel] blessings; *les biens de ce monde*, the/riches, good things/of this world; *les biens que Dieu accorde*, the blessings which God gives; [Jur.] *biens mobiliers*, chattels, personal property; *biens immeubles*, real estate.

bien-aimé, -e [bjɛ̃ne'me] *adj. & n.* beloved, darling. || **bien-être** [bjɛ̃'nɛːtr] *n.m.* well-being, welfare, comfort; © welfare: *Ministère de la Santé nationale et du Bien-être social*, Department of National Health and Welfare.

bienfaisance [bjɛ̃fə'z|ɑ̃ːs] *n.f.* charity, benevolence: *œuvre f de* ~, charity; charitable/society, institution/. || **bienfaisant, -e** [-ɑ̃(ːt)] *adj.* charitable; [chose] beneficial. || **bienfait** [bjɛ̃'fɛ] *n.m.* favour, kindness; utility, advantage. || **bienfait|eur, -rice** [-'tœːr, -'tris] *n.* benefactor, benefactress.

bienheureu|x, -se [bjɛ̃nœ'rø(ːz)] *adj.* **1.** blissful, happy. **2.** [Rel.] blessed.

bienséance [bjɛ̃se|'ɑ̃ːs] *n.f.* decency, propriety; decorum. || **bienséant, -e** [-ɑ̃(ːt)] *adj.* decent, proper; decorous.

bientôt [bjɛ̃'to] *adv.* soon, shortly, in a little while: *A ~ !*, See you soon!, Be seeing you!

bienveillance [bjɛ̃vɛ'j|ɑ̃:s] *n.f.* benevolence, kindness: *par ~*, out of kindness; *avec ~*, kindly. || **bienveillant, -e** [-ɑ̃(:t)] *adj.* benevolent, kindly disposed (*envers*, towards).

bienvenu, -e [bjɛ̃v'ny] *adj.* welcome: *être le ~, la bienvenue*, to be welcome; [to a group] *Soyez les bienvenus!*, Welcome!; © *Bienvenu!* [as response to thanks], You're welcome! || *n.f.*: *souhaiter la ~ à qqun*, to welcome s.o. (to . . .); *discours de ~*, speech of welcome.

bière[1] [bjɛ:r] *n.f.* beer, ale; *~ blonde*, lager; *~ à la pression*, draught beer.

bière[2] *n.f.* coffin.

biffer [bi'fe] #3 *v. tr.* to strike out, cross out (a word, &c.).

bifteck [bif'tɛk] *n.m.* [Fr.] beefsteak; [© use *steak*] *~ /bleu, saignant, à point, bien cuit*, very rare, rare, medium, well-done/steak.

bifurcation [bifyrk|a'sjõ] *n.f.* bifurcation; [rivière] embranchment; [tronc d'arbre] branching; [route] branching out, forking; [Rail.] junction; [Electr.] shunt. || **bifurquer** [-e] #3 *v. intr.* to bifurcate, fork, branch off.

bigame [bi'gam] *adj.* bigamous. || *n.m/f.* bigamist. || **bigamie** [-i] *n.f.* bigamy.

bigarré, -e [biga'r|e] *adj.* variegated, motley. || **bigarrer** [-e] #3 *v. tr.* to variegate, mottle. || **bigarrure** [-y:r] *n.f.* variegation; motley.

bigot, -e [bi'g|o, -ɔt] *adj.* priest-ridden, bigoted. || *n.* pietist, bigot.

bigoudi [bigu'di] *n.m.* hair-curler.

bijou, *pl.* **-x** [bi'ʒu] *n.m.* jewel, piece of jewellery: [Fig.] gem, darling. || **bijouterie** [-'tri] *n.f.* **1.** jewel trade. **2.** jeweller's shop. **3.** [coll.] jewels, jewellery. || **bijoutier** [-'tje] *n.m.* jeweller.

bilan [bi'lɑ̃] *n.m.* balance sheet; [compte] balance: *dresser le ~*, to draw up the balance sheet; [liquidation] statement.

bile [bil] *n.f.* bile, gall; [Fig.] *se faire de la ~*, to worry, to fret; *échauffer, remuer la ~ à qqun*, to rile, anger/s.o.

biliaire [bi'lj|ɛ:r] *adj.* [Méd.] biliary: *calcul ~*, gallstone. || **bilieu|x, -se** [-ø(:z)] *adj.* bilious; [teint] jaundiced; [caractère] choleric.

bilingue [bi'l|ɛ̃:g] *adj.* bilingual: *le Canada est un pays ~*, Canada is a bilingual country. || **bilinguisme** [-ɛ̃'gɥism] *n.m.* bilingualism.

billard [bi'ja:r] *n.m.* [jeu] billiards; [salle] billiard room; [salle publique] billiard parlour, pool room; [table] billiard table.

bille[1] [bi:j] *n.f.* [bois] sawlog.

bille[2] *n.f.* [de billard] billiard ball; [d'enfant] marble; [en acier] ball: *roulement à billes*, ball bearing; *stylo à ~*, ball-point pen.

billet [bi'jɛ] *n.m.* **1.** note, (short) letter: *~ doux*, love letter. **2.** [Com.] note, bill: *~ de banque*, bank note; bill; *un ~ de mille dollars*, a thousand-dollar bill. **3.** ticket: [Rail.] *~ d'aller et retour*, round-trip, return/ticket; *~ simple*, one-way ticket. **4.** invitation: *~ de faire part*, announcement.

billevesée [bilvə'ze] *n.f.* [gén. plur.] rubbish; hooey.

billion [bi'ljõ] *n.m.* [Br.] one thousand million; [US] billion.

bimoteur [bimɔ'tœ:r] *n.m.* twin-engine plane.

bine [bın] © *n.f.* [Pop.] bean.

binette [bi'nɛt] *n.f.* [Agric.] hoe; weeder.

†**binocle** [bi'nɔkl] *n.m.* pince-nez, eye-glasses.

biochimie [bjoʃi'mi] *n.f.* biochemistry.

biographe [bjɔ'graf] *n.m.* biographer. || **biographie** [-i] *n.f.* biography. || **biographique** [-ik] *adj.* biographical.

biologie [bjɔlɔ'ʒi] *n.f.* biology. || **biologique** [-k] *adj.* biological. || **biologiste** [-st] *n.m/f.* biologist.

biplace [bi'plas] *n.m.* [Auto., avion] two-seater. || **biplan** [bi'plɑ̃] *n.m.* biplane, two-winged plane.

Birman, -e [bir'm|ɑ̃, an] *n. & adj.* Burmese. **Birmanie** [-a'ni] *n.f.* Burma.

bis,[1] **-e** [bi(:z)] *adj.* (greyish-) brown, brownish(-grey): *pain ~*, whole-wheat, brown/bread.

bis[2] [bis] *adv.* twice; once more. || *interj.* (répétition) repeat. Encore!

biscornu, -e [biskɔr'ny] *adj.* crooked, misshapen; [Fig.] cranky, bizarre.

biscotte [bis'kɔt] *n.f.* rusk; Melba toast.

biscuit [bis'kɥi] *n.m.* biscuit, cracker: *~ de Savoie*, sponge cake.

biscuiterie [biskɥi'tri] *n.f.* biscuit/company, trade/.

bise [bi:z] *n.f.* north wind; [Fig.] cold blast.

biseau [bi'zo] *n.m.* [outil] bevel, chamfer. || **biseauter** [-'te] #3 *v. tr.* to bevel, chamfer.

bison [bi'zõ] *n.m.* bison; buffalo.

bissextile [bisɛks'til] *adj.*: *année ~*, leap year.

bistouri [bistu'ri] *n.m.* [Méd.] lancet.

bistre [bistr] *adj.* dark brown; [teint] swarthy, dark-complexioned.

bistrot [bis'tro] *n.m.* café; [Fam.] pub.

bizarre [bi'z|a:r] *adj.* odd, strange; bizarre, eccentric. || **bizarrerie** [-ar'ri] *n.f.* oddness, quaintness; eccentricity, peculiarity.

blackbouler [blakbu'le] #3 *v. tr.* to blackball, turn down (by vote); [Fam.] to flunk, fail.

blafard, -e [bla'f|a:r, -ard] *adj.* [teint] wan, pallid (colour, complexion, &c.); [lumière] dull, bleak.

blague [blag] *n.f.* **1.** tobacco pouch. **2.** [Fig. & Fam.] tall story; hoax, joke; trick, gag: *(toute) ~ à part,* (all) joking aside; *sans ~ !,* no kidding!; *faire une bonne ~ à qqun,* to play a good trick on s.o. || **blaguer** [e] #3 *v. tr.* [Fam.] to kid (s.o.) to make fun of (s.o., sth.). || *v. intr.* to joke, [Fam.] to kid. || **blagueu|r, -se** [-œ:r, -ø:z] *n.* joker, story-teller, †wag. || *adj.* joking, bantering.

blaireau [blɛ'ro] *n.m.* badger.

blâmable [blɑ'mabl] *adj.* blamable, blameworthy. || **blâme** [blɑ:m] *n.m.* blame; [plus fort] censure: *encourir un ~,* to be reprimanded. || **blâmer** [blɑ'me] #3 *v. tr.* [conj. AVOIR (action), ÊTRE (état)] to blame, to find fault with; [plus fort] to censure.

blanc[1] [blɑ̃], **blanche** [blɑ̃:ʃ] *adj.* **1.** [couleur] white: *blanche comme la neige,* white as snow; *La Maison Blanche,* The White House. **2.** [Fig.] innocent, pure. **3.** blank: *une feuille blanche,* a blank sheet (of paper); *chèque en ~,* blank cheque. **4.** [voix] lifeless; [nuit] sleepless; [coup] futile; [examen] trial; [vers] blank.

blanc[2] [blɑ̃] *n.m.* **1.** whiteness, white; white (paint): *un ~ de perle,* pearly white; *peindre en ~,* to paint white; *le ~ des yeux,* the whites of the eyes; *geler à ~,* to freeze solid; *chauffer à ~,* to heat white-hot; *cartouche chargée à ~,* blank shell; *saigner à ~,* to bleed white; [Fig.] to ruin. **2.** white (meat, wine, of the eyes, of an egg); blank (space); [cible] bull's eye; [linge] linens; [Anthrop.] white man, woman; [Mus.] blanche, half note; [billard] white (ball): *donner dans le ~,* to hit the bull's eye; *de but en ~,* point blank; *exposition f de ~,* white sale; [Fig.] © *se mettre au ~,* to go too far, to stick one's neck out. || **blanc-bec** [-'bɛk] *n.m.* tenderfoot, greenhorn.

blanchâtre [-'ʃɑ:tr] *adj.* whitish. || **blancheur** [-'ʃœ:r] *n.f.* [choses] whiteness: *une ~ éclatante,* a brilliant white; [Fig.] purity, innocence. || **blanchi, -e** [-'ʃi] cf. BLANCHIR.

blanchir [blɑ̃'ʃ|i:r] #17 *v. tr.* to bleach, whiten; [nettoyer] to clean, wash; to blanch (vegetables); [Fig.] to justify: *rien ne peut le ~,* nothing can cleanse him. || *v. intr.* [Pers.] to become pale, to pale (with, *de*): *~ de peur, de colère,* to (grow, become) pale with fear, anger; [cheveux, os, &c.] to become, grow, get/white. || **blanchissage** [-i'sa:ʒ] *n.m.* washing, laundering: *envoyer au ~,* to send to the/wash, laundry/; *la note de ~,* the laundry bill. || **blanchissant, -e** [-i'sɑ̃(:t)] *adj.* [aube] paling; [os] bleaching. || **blanchisserie** [-is'ri] *n.f.* laundry. || **blanchisseu|r, -se** [-i'sœ:r, -i'sø:z] *n.* laundry man, -woman. || **blanc-manger** [blɑ̃mɑ̃'ʒe] *n.m.* blancmange. || **blanc-seing** [blɑ̃'sɛ̃] *n.m.* blank signature; [Fig.] *donner un ~ à qqun,* to give s.o. full powers.

blasé, -e [blɑ'ze] *adj.* blasé, indifferent. || **blaser** #3 *v. tr.* to pall, cloy. || **se blaser** *v. pron.* to become indifferent (*de,* to); to grow weary (*de,* of).

blason [blɑ'zɔ̃] *n.m.* blazon, coat of arms.

blasphème [blas'f|ɛ:m] *n.m.* blasphemy; © (profane) oath, swear word. || **blasphémer** [-e'me] #10 *tr. & intr.* to blaspheme; to profane (sth. holy); © to swear.

blatte [blat] *n.f.* cockroach; black-beetle.

blé [ble] *n.m.* wheat, [Br.] corn: *cultiver du ~,* to grow wheat; *~ noir,* [= sarrasin] buckwheat; © *~ d'Inde,* (Indian) corn, cf. MAÏS.

blême [blɛ:m] *adj.* livid, (sickly) pale; [lumière] bleak. || **blêmir** [blɛ'mi:r] #17 *v. intr.* [Pers.] to turn/pale, livid/, [lumière] to grow/wan, bleak/.

blessant, -e [blɛ's|ɑ̃(:t)] *adj.* [Fig.] offensive, cutting. || **blessé, -e** [-e] *adj.* wounded, injured: *les blessés,* [Coll.] the wounded; *grièvement ~,* seriously injured. || **blesser** [-e] #3 *v. tr.* **1.** to wound; [moins fort] to hurt; [plus général] to injure; [soulier] to pinch; [bât] to rub: *~ à coups de/cornes, couteau, dents, &c/* [☞ se rend par un verbe simple] to gore, stab, bite, &c. **2.** [Fig.] to wound, to hurt (s.o.'s feelings); to offend (s.o.); to break (the standards of good taste, conventions, &c.); to prejudice (s.o.'s interests). || **se blesser** *v. pron.* **1.** to wound o.s.; to hurt o.s.: *Il s'est blessé à la main,* He hurt his hand. **2.** [Fig.] to take offence. || **blessure** [-y:r] *n.f.* wound; [moins fort] hurt; [plus général] injury; [Fig.] wound, injury.

blet, -te [blɛ(t)] *adj.* over-ripe, soft (fruit).

bleu [blø] *n.m.* blue; [lessive] bluing; [blessure] black and blue mark; [dépêche] telegram, wire; [photo] blue print; [combinaisons] overalls, coveralls; [Fam.] raw recruit; [Loc.] © *en voir de bleues*, to have a rough time (of it); © [Pop.] *avoir les bleus*, to have the blues; *n'y voir que du* ~, to be all at sea, not to be able to make head or tail of sth. ‖ *adj.* blue: *conte* ~, a tall tale; *colère bleue*, violent rage; *avoir une peur bleue*, to be frozen with fear.

bleuet[1] [blø'ɛ] *n.m.* © blueberry, cf. AIRELLE.

bleuet[2] *n.m.* [Fr.] cornflower.

bleuir [blø|'i:r] #17 *v. tr.* to tint, to dye blue; [métal] to blue. ‖ *v. intr.* to turn blue: *de froid*, with cold. ‖ **bleuté, -e** [-'te] *adj.* bluish, steel-blue. ‖ **bleuter** [-'te] #3 *v. tr.* to tinge with blue; [linge] to blue.

blindage [blɛ̃'da:ʒ] *n.m.* [Mil.] armour (plate). ‖ **blinder** [blɛ̃'de] #3 *v. tr.* to armour-plate; [Tech.] to sheet.

bloc [blɔk] *n.m.* [taillé] block; [informe] lump, mass; [Pers., idées] group; [de papier] pad: ~ *politique*, a political/ bloc, group/; *en* ~, as a group, together; *faire* ~ */avec, contre/*, to work as a unit/ with, against/; *visser à* ~, to screw [vis] in, [écrou] on tight; *serrer les freins à* ~, to jam on the brakes; [Fam.] *mettre au* ~, to put in the clink. ‖ **blocus** [-ys] *n.m.* [par terre] siege *m*; [par mer] blockade: *forcer le* ~, to run the blockade.

blond, -e [blõ(:d)] *adj.* [cheveux] blond; [teint] fair; [blé] golden; [bière] pale (ale). ‖ *n.m.* [couleur] blond: ~ */platiné, cendré/*, platinum, ash/blond; [homme] blond. ‖ **blonde** [blõ:d] *n.f.* blonde; © sweetheart; [bière] pale (ale). ‖ **blondir** [blõ'di:r] #17 *v. intr.* to turn blond; [Fig.] to become/yellow, golden/.

bloquer [blɔ'ke] #3 *v. tr.* [chemin, couloir, &c.] to close (off); [Sport.] to block, stop (a pass, the ball, an opponent); to besiege (a city); to blockade (a port); to block (s.o.'s way); to freeze (a bank account, s.o.'s credit); © [Fam.] ~ *un examen*, to flunk an exam, cf. COLLER. ‖ **se bloquer** *v. pron.* to jam, catch.

blottir, se [səblɔ'ti:r] #17 *v. pron.* to huddle (up); [dans un fauteuil] to curl up; [dans les bras] to snuggle up to.

blouse [blu:z] *n.f.* smock; [de travail] overall: ~ *blanche*, lab coat; [couture] blouse.

bluet [bly'ɛ] *n.m.* cf. BLEUET.

bobard [bɔ'ba:r] *n.m.* [Fam.] hooey, baloney.

bobine [bɔ'bin] *n.f.* [d'une machine à coudre] bobbin; [fil à coudre, ruban] spool; [film] reel; [Electr.] coil; [Fam.] face, pan.

bœuf, -s [bœf, bø] *n.m.* ox [× *pl.* oxen]; [bovin élevé pour la viande] beef, [castré] steer; [la viande] beef: [Fig. & Fam.] *fort comme un* ~, strong as an ox; ~ *salé*, corned beef; [Loc.] *mettre la charrue avant les bœufs*, to put the cart before the horse.

bohémien, -ne [bɔe'mj|ɛ̃, -ɛn] *n. & adj.* Bohemian; gypsy.

boire [bwa:r] *n.m.* drink: *le* ~ *et le manger*, → food and drink. ‖ *v. tr.* #73 to drink; [soleil] to drink up (the dew); [éponge] to soak up; [buvard] to blot up; [Fig.] to swallow (an insult). ‖ *v. intr.* to drink: ~ */chaud, tiède, frais/*, to drink sth./hot, warm, cool/; ~ *à grands traits*, to drink in long gulps, → to gulp; ~ *à petites gorgées*, → to sip; *faire* ~ *des animaux*, to water animals; ~ *comme un trou*, to drink like a fish. ‖ **se boire** *v. pron.* to be drunk: *la bière se boit froide*, beer is drunk cold. ‖ **bois**[1] &c. cf. BOIRE.

bois[2] [bwa] *n.m.* wood; [de charpente, de construction] lumber; *chantier de* ~, lumber yard; *industrie du* ~, lumbering industry; [sur pied, vif] timber: ~ *rabougri*, stunted timber; *abattre le* ~, to cut timber; © *maison en* ~ *rond*, log house; *un* ~, a wood; [× woods est un générique et en même temps un pl.] *trois* ~, three woods; [mais] *marcher dans le* ~, to walk in the woods; [cerf, orignal, &c.] antlers; [fusil, &c.] stock, butt; [Mus.] woodwinds; [de lit] bedstead; [lance] shaft; [Loc.] ~ */dur, tendre/*, hard, soft/wood; ~ *de chauffage*, firewood; *poêle à* ~, wood stove; *de, en/* ~, wooden; ~ *de pâte*, pulpwood; *temps des* ~, wood-cutting/ time, season/. ‖ **boisé, -e** [bwa'ze] *adj.* wooded; © panelled (room). ‖ *n.m.* © woodlot.

boisseau, -x [bwa'so] *n.m.* bushel: *au* ~, by the bushel; [Fig.] *mettre la lumière sous le* ~, to hide one's light under a bushel.

boisson [bwa'sõ] *n.f.* ~ *alcoolisée*, liquor; ~ *forte*, hard liquor; drink.

boîte [bwa:t] *n.f.* **1.** box; [postale] (postal) box; [aux lettres] mailbox; [crânienne] (brain) pan; [de résistance] rheostat; [en fer-blanc] can, tin; [à ouvrage] (sewing)-basket; [à bijoux] (jewel) box, case. **2.** [contenu] box: ~ *de bonbons* box, of candy; ~ *de petits pois,* can of peas. 3. [Fam.] joint, dive: ~ *de nuit,* night-club, dance hall: *Cet établissement est une* ~, This place is a (real) dive, joint. 4. [Argot] mouth, trap, box.

boiter [bwa'tǀe] #3 *v. intr.* 1. to limp: ~ *du pied/gauche, droit/,* to limp with the /left, right/foot. 2. [meuble] to wobble; [Fig.] [raisonnement] to be defective. ǁ **boiteuǀx, -se** [-ø(:z)] *n.* a lame/man, woman/. ǁ *adj.* [personne et par ext. raison, justice] lame; [paix] makeshift.

bol [bɔl] *n.m.* bowl.

bolchévique [bɔlʃe'vik] *adj.* bolshevik.

Bolivie (la) [(la) bɔli'vi] *n.f.* Bolivia.

bombance [bõ'bɑ̃:s] *n.f.* [Fam.] carouse: *faire* ~, to carouse.

bombardement [bõbardǀə'mɑ̃] *n.m.* [canon] bombardment, shelling; [par avion] bombing. ǁ **bombarder** [-e] #3 *v. tr.* [marine] to bombard, [artillerie] to shell, [aviation] to bomb; [pierres] to pelt; [Fig. & Fam.] to bombard (with requests, telegrams, flowers, &c.). ǁ **bombardier** [-je] *n.m.* [Aviat.] bomber. ǁ **bombe** [bõ:b] *n.f.* 1. bomb: *lâcher, jeter, lancer, laisser tomber/des bombes sur . . .*, to drop bombs on . . . 2. [Fam.] binge, spree: *faire la* ~, to go on a spree. 3. © boiler, kettle. ǁ **bombé, -e** [bõ'be] *adj.* convex.

bomber [bõ'be] #3 *v. tr.* [le dos] to round one's back; [la poitrine] to throw, stick/out one's chest. ǁ *v. intr.* to bulge out.

bon, -ne [bõ, bɔn] *compar.* **meilleur** [mɛ'jœ:r] *superl.* **le meilleur.** *adj.* 1. good, kind, obliging: *un* ~ *père,* a/good, kind/father; *C'est un* ~ *garçon,* He's a good kid; *Vous êtes trop* ~ */pour, envers/moi,* You are too/good, kind/to me; *une bonne action,* a good deed; *être bien* ~, to be very kind. 2. good, capable, clever: ~ *mot,* joke. 3. good, right, correct, proper: *du* ~ *français,* correct French; *employer le* ~ *outil,* to use the/right, correct/tool; *une bonne conduite,* good behaviour, proper conduct; ~ *à manger,* good to eat, edible; *mettre à la bonne place,* to put in the/right, correct, proper/place; *être dans la bonne voie,* to be on the right track. 4. good, useful: *être* ~ *à tout,* to be good [Pers.] at everything, [chose] for anything; *obtenir de bons résultats,* to get good results. 5. good, advantageous, profitable: *une bonne affaire,* a good, profitable business; ~ *rendement,* a good yield; ~ *emploi,* good job; *n'attendre rien de* ~ *de,* to expect nothing good/from, of/; *bonne occasion,* good, excellent opportunity; *prendre les choses du* ~ *côté,* to look at things on the bright side; *Bonne année!,* Happy New Year!; [Loc.] *A quoi* ~ *!*, What's the use! 6. good, agreeable: *du* ~ *vin,* good wine; *un* ~ *repas,* a good meal; *de bons moments,* some good times; *se donner du* ~ *temps,* to take it easy; *Il fait* ~ + inf., *Il est* ~ *de* + inf., It's good to . . . 7. good, faithful: ~ */camarade, mari/,* good, faithful/comrade, husband/. 8. good, full, quite: *une bonne distance,* quite a distance; *cinq bons kilomètres,* a good five kilometres, → at least five kilometres; *attendre une bonne heure,* to wait a good, full hour, → to wait at least an hour; *un* ~ *nombre de,* quite a number of; *un* ~ *bout de temps,* quite a while; *coûter un* ~ *prix,* → to be expensive. ǁ *interj.*: (*C'est*) *bon!,* (That's) fine!; [suffire] I understand; [Fam.] *Bon Dieu!* → My God! [× n'est pas l'équivalent de *Good God!* qui, en anglais, est un juron plus fort]. ǁ *adv.*: *sentir* ~, to smell/nice, good/; *tenir* ~, to hold /tight, fast/; *pour de* ~, [sérieusement] in earnest; [définitivement] for good.

bon [bõ] *n.m.* 1. good: *le* ~ *de l'histoire,* the best part of the story; *les bons et les méchants,* the good and the bad. 2. [Com.] order, voucher; [Fin.] bond, bill: ~ *de caisse,* cash voucher; *bons de la défense,* victory bonds; ~ *d'épargne,* savings certificate.

bonbon [bõ'bǀõ] *n.m.* (piece of) candy; [Br.] sweet, bonbon. ǁ **bonbonnière** [-ɔ'njɛ:r] *n.f.* candy box.

bond [bõ] *n.m.* 1. [homme, animaux] bound, leap, spring; [cheval] jump: *s'élancer d'un* ~, to take off with a bound, → to bound away; *franchir d'un bond,* → to bounce over, to clear in a (single) bound. 2. [corps élastique] bounce: *prendre la balle au* ~, to hit the ball on the (first) bounce, [Fig.] to seize an opportunity; *faire faux* ~, [une balle, &c.] to leave s.o. in the lurch; *faire un* ~, to bounce.

bondé, -e [bõ'de] *adj.* crammed, jammed full.

bondir [bõ'dǀi:r] #17 *v. intr.* 1. [à l'assaut] to spring, rush: ~ *dans* (*la montagne, la forêt, le pré, &c*) to jump, caper about (in the mountains, the forest, the meadow, &c); ~ *sur,* to pounce on. 2. [Fig. une personne, le cœur] to jump (with joy). 3. [corps élastique] to bounce. ǁ **bondissant, -e** [-i'sɑ̃(:t)] *adj.* [animal] capering, frisking; [cœur] pounding. ǁ **bondissement** [-is'mɑ̃] *n.m.* leaping, bounding.

bonheur [bɔ'nœ:r] *n.m.* 1. happiness;

[plus fort] bliss: *faire le ~ de qqun*, (a) to make s.o. happy; (b) → to be s.o.'s pride and joy; *être au comble du ~*, → to be bubbling over with happiness. **2.** good fortune; [Fam.] luck: *avoir le ~ de*, to have the good fortune to; *avoir du ~ (dans une entreprise, &c.)*, to be /fortunate, lucky/(in an undertaking, &c.)/; *~ imprévu, inespéré*, unlooked for, unhoped for (piece of) good fortune, luck; *porter ~*, to bring (good) luck (*à*, to); *par ~*, luckily; *au petit ~*, haphazardly. **3.** felicity (of expression) *s'exprimer avec ~*, to have an apt turn of phrase.

bonhomie [bɔnɔ'mi] *n.f.* good-nature; simplicity.

bonhomme [bɔ'nɔm] *n.m.* **1.** good/fellow, sort, chap/: *faire le ~*, to pretend to be a good/fellow, sort, chap/. **2.** old man, old fellow [fém. bonne femme]. **3.** *mon petit ~*, my little man. **4.** [dessiner] rough pictures (of humans only): *~ de neige*, snowman. || *adj.* good-natured: *prendre un air ~*, to put on a good-natured air; [Péj.] bland countenance.

boniment [bɔni'mɑ̃] *n.m.* (circus barker's) line, come-on; (salesman's) pitch, patter: *débiter des boniments*, to reel off a/line, pitch/.

bonjour [bõ'ʒu:r] *n.m.* **1.** hello, good day; [le matin] good morning; [l'après-midi] good afternoon: *simple comme ~*, (as) easy as pie; *dire ~ à*, to greet s.o. **2.** © [when taking leave] So long, Goodbye.

bonne[1] [bɔn] *n.f.* maid, servant: *~ d'enfant*, nursemaid.

bonne[2] [bɔn] cf. BON. || **Bonne-Espérance** (cap de) [(kap də) bɔnɛspe'rɑ̃:s] *n.m.* the Cape of Good Hope. || **bonne-femme** [-'fam] *n.f.* old woman, cf. BONHOMME.

bonnement [bɔn'mɑ̃] *adv.*: *tout ~*, simply, plainly.

bonnet [bɔ'nɛ] *n.m.* cap; [de femme, d'enfant] bonnet: *~ de nuit*, night cap; *~ d'âne*, dunce cap; [Mil.] *~ de police*, fatigue cap; [Loc. et Prov.] *prendre qqch. sous son ~*, to pull sth. out of one's hat; [autorité] to take it upon o.s.; *avoir la tête près du ~*, to be a sorehead, hothead; *C'est ~ blanc et blanc ~*, It's six of one and half a dozen of the other.

bonneterie [bɔn'tri] *n.f.* hosiery.

bonsoir [bõ'swa:r] *n.m. & interj.* good-evening; [en se quittant le soir] goodbye.

bonté [bõ'te] *n.f.* [nature] kindness, goodness; [bonne disposition] benevolence, kind-heartedness: *Ayez la ~ de ...*, Be so kind as to ... ; kindly [+ Imperative]; *~ divine!*, My goodness!, Good gracious! || *n.fpl.* kindness, favours.

bord [bɔ:r] *n.m.* **1.** [chemin, fossé, table, &c.] edge; [route] (road)side; [tasse, chapeau] brim, edge; [précipice] brink, edge; [bateau] side; [du trottoir] curb; [fleuve] bank, edge; [mer] shore, seashore; *au ~ de la route*, by the roadside; [Naut.] *monter à ~*, to go on board; *moteur hors ~*, outboard motor; *jeter par-dessus ~*, to throw overboard; *un verre rempli jusqu'au ~*, a glass full to the brim. **2.** [Fig.] *au ~ du désastre*, on the/brink, verge/of disaster; *être du même ~ que ...*, to belong to the same party as, to share the same views as ...

bordeaux [bɔr'do] *n.m.* *(vin m de) ~*, Bordeaux: *~ rouge*, claret.

bordée [bɔr'de] *n.f.* **1.** volley; [coups de canon] broadside; © *~ de neige*, heavy snowfall. **2.** [Fig. & Fam.] *tirer une ~*, to go on a spree.

bordel [bɔr'dɛl] *n.m.* brothel.

border [bɔr'de] #3 *v. tr.* [conj. AVOIR (action), ÊTRE (état)] [buis, rochers, fossé, &c.] to border (a road, garden, &c.); [arbres, la foule] to line (a street, road, &c.); to trim, edge (a garment); [bateau] to skirt (the coast); to tuck in (the sheets): *~ qqun dans son lit*, to tuck s.o. into bed.

bordereau [bɔrdə'ro] *n.m.* list, memorandum; [banque] slip; [compte] statement; [expedition] consignment note.

bordure [bɔr'dy:r] *n.f.* border, edge; [bois] skirt(s); [ville] outskirts: *~ de trottoir*, curb (= [Br.] kerb); *en ~ de*, bordering on, on the skirts of.

boréal, -e [bɔre'al] *adj.* boreal: *aurore boréale*, northern lights.

borgne [bɔrɲ] *adj.* one-eyed.

borique [bɔ'rik] *adj.* boric, boracic.

borne [bɔrn] *n.f.* boundary marker; landmark: *~ routière*, milestone; *~ kilométrique*, milepost; *~ fontaine*, street fountain, © [abus.] fire hydrant; [Electr.] terminal post (of a battery). || *n.fpl.* limits, boundaries; *sans bornes*, without limits, → limitless, boundless. || **borné, -e** [-e] *adj.* limited, restricted (view, needs, horizon); [Péj.] narrow-minded (person), narrow (mind). || **borner** [-e] #3 *v. tr.* **1.** to stake out (a field, road, &c); [limiter] to border. **2.** [Fig.] to limit, restrict. **se borner** *v. pron.* [Pers.] to limit, restrict o.s., [chose] to be limited, restricted (*à*, to).

bosquet [bɔs'kɛ] *n.m.* [arbres] grove; [arbuste] thicket, bluff.

bosse [bɔs] *n.f.* **1.** [au dos] hump; [sur le corps] bump, lump; [terrain] mound, hump; [sur une surface] (convexe) bump, © (concave) dent: [Fig.] *avoir la ~ de*, to have a gift for; [beaux-arts] *travailler, relever/en ~*, to emboss; [Fam.] *rouler sa ~*, to knock about. ‖ **bossu, -e** [-y] *n.* hunchback. *adj.* hunchbacked (person), humped (animal).

botanique [bɔta'ni|k] *n.f.* botany. ‖ *adj.* botanical: *Jardin ~*, Botanical Gardens. ‖ **botaniste** [-st] *n.* botanist.

botte[1] [bɔt] *n.f.* (high top) boot: *~ en caoutchouc*, rubber boot; *bottes de pêche*, hip waders; *bottes de pompier*, fireman's boots; [Loc.] *avoir du foin dans ses bottes*, to be well off.

botte[2] *n.f.* [fleurs, carottes, radis] bunch; [feuilles] sheaf; [foin] truss, bundle; [grosse botte] bale.

botté, -e [bɔ'te] *adj.* booted: *Le Chat ~*, Puss-in-Boots.

botteler [bɔt'le] #8 *v. tr.* to tie in bunches; [flowers, carrots, radishes, asparagus, &c.]; to tie in bundles [wheat, oats, rye, &c.] to bale [hay, straw, &c.].

botter [bɔ't|e] #3 *v. tr.* **1.** to put shoes on (s.o. or sth.). **2.** [Fam.] to kick, boot: *~ le derrière à qqun*, to kick, boot/s.o.'s behind; *~ un ballon*, to kick a ball. ‖ **se botter** *v. pron.* to put one's/boots, shoes/ on. ‖ **bottier** [-je] *n.m.* bootmaker. ‖ **bottine** [-in] *n.f.* high shoe; [bébé] bootee: © *de ski*, ski boot; [Fig.] *avoir les deux pieds dans la même ~*, to have one's head screwed on backwards.

bouc [buk] *n.m.* he-goat; [barbiche] billy-goat; goatee; buck: [Fig.] *~ émissaire*, scapegoat; [Fam.] fall guy.

boucan[1] [bu'kɑ̃] *n.m.* [Fam.] racket, row: *faire du ~*, to kick up a row.

boucan[2] [bu'kɑ̃] © *n.m.* smoke-house. ‖ **boucane** [bu'kan] © *n.f.* smoke: *faire de la ~*, to give off smoke. ‖ **boucaner** [-e] *v. tr.* to cure: © *hareng boucané*, cf. SAUR.

bouche [buʃ] *n.f.* **1.** [Pers.] mouth: *mettre l'eau à la ~*, to make s.o.'s mouth water; *faire la petite ~*, → to turn up one's nose (at sth.), to be difficult (to please); *rire à pleine ~*, to laugh out loud; [Fig.] *fermer la ~ à qqun*, to silence s.o.; *demeurer ~ close*, to remain silent. **2.** [Fig.] person, mouth: *avoir six bouches à nourrir*, to have six mouths to feed. **3.** [volcan, caverne, puits, canon, égout, fleuve] mouth; [chaleur] vent; [fusil] muzzle; [métro] (subway) entrance: *~ d'incendie*, fire hydrant.

bouché, -e [bu'ʃe] *adj.* **1.** [trou] plugged; [égout] clogged, plugged; [chemin] blocked; [temps] cloudy; [bouteille] corked, stoppered; [ext.] *du vin ~*, bottled wine. **2.** [Fig.] [esprit] dull; [Pers.] stupid, dense.

bouchée [bu'ʃe] *n.f.* **1.** mouthful, bite: *prendre une ~*, to take a/bite, mouthful/; *Je l'ai/eu, acheté/pour une ~ de pain*, I bought it for a song; *manger une ~*, to eat a/bite, mouthful/. **2.** [Cul.] patty (shell): *~ à la reine*, chicken patty.

boucher[1] [bu'ʃe] #3 *v. tr.* **1.** [ouverture] [petit] to plug, [plus grand] to block up; [chemin, rue, &c.] to block; [bouteille] to cork, to stop; [vue] to block, to obstruct. **2.** [Fig.]: *~ la route de qqun*, to block s.o.'s path, way. ‖ **se boucher** *v. pron.* to become/plugged, clogged/; *~ le nez*, to plug, to hold/one's nose; *~ les oreilles*, to plug one's ears.

boucher[2] *n.m.* butcher. ‖ **bouchère** [bu|'ʃɛːr] *n.f.* butcher's wife. ‖ **boucherie** [buʃ'ri] *n.f.* **1.** butcher's shop; butcher's trade, business; [abattoir] slaughterhouse; meat department. **2.** [Fig.] butchery, slaughter: *envoyer des soldats à la ~*, to send soldiers to the slaughter.

bouchon [bu'ʃõ] *n.m.* **1.** plug; [liège] cork; [caoutchouc, verre] stopper; [d'un tonneau] bung: *faire sauter le ~*, to pop/a, the/cork. **2.** [pêche] float.

boucle [bukl] *n.f.* buckle: *~ de soulier*, shoe buckle; [cheveux] curl, lock; [rivière, ficelle] loop: *~ d'oreille*, earring; [Aéro.] *boucler la ~*, to loop the loop; [Fig. & Fam.] *se serrer la ~*, to tighten one's belt. ‖ **bouclé, -e** [-e] *adj.* buckled; [cheveux] curled; [Fig. & Fam.] locked (up), shut down. ‖ **boucler** [-e] #3 *v. tr.* **1.** to buckle: *~ une courroie*, to buckle a strap. **2.** [dossier] to close; [Fam.] to lock up (a store, a prisoner); to ring (a bull, a pig); [cheveux] to curl; [ficelle] to loop; [une affaire] to wind up. ‖ *v. intr.* [cheveux] to curl.

bouctouche [buk'tuʃ] © *n.f.* (Bouctouche) oyster.

bouder [bu'd|e] #3 *v. intr.* to sulk; to be cool (towards s.o.): *~ à la besogne*, → to be work-shy; *~ dans un coin*, to sulk in a corner. ‖ *v. tr.* to sulk; to pout. ‖ **bouderie** [-'ri] *n.f.* sulking, sulk(iness). ‖ **boudeu|r, -se** [-œːr, -øːz] *n.* sulky person. ‖ *adj.*: *air, visage/~*, sullen, moody/look, face.

boudin [bu'dɛ̃] *n.m.* blood sausage, black pudding.

boudoir [bu'dwaːr] *n.m.* boudoir, powder room.

boue [bu] *n.f.* **1.** mud. **2.** [Fig.] filth, mud: *tirer qqun de la* ~, to drag s.o. through the mire.
bouée [bwe] *n.f.* buoy.
boueur [bu'œ:r] *n.m.* garbageman.
boueu|x, -se [bu'ø(:z)] *adj.* muddy; [sol] spongy. || *n.m.* garbage collector.
bouffant, -e [bu'fɑ̃(:t)] *adj.* full, puff (sleeves); [culotte] baggy; [jupe] full. || *n.m.* [cheveux, manche] puff (on a sleeve); [jupe] flare.
bouffée [bu'fe] *n.f.* **1.** puff, whiff (of air, smoke); breath (of air). **2.** [Fig.] burst, fit (of anger, &c.).
bouffer [bu'fe] #3 *v. intr.* [jupe, manche, &c.; cheveux] to stand out, to puff out; [pâte] to swell (up), to puff up. || *v. tr.* to puff/up, out/(one's cheeks); [Fam.] to eat; to guzzle.
bouffi, -e [bu'f|i] *adj.* [figure] puffy; [yeux] swollen; [Fig.] ~ *de*, puffed up with (vanity), bloated with (rage); *un style* ~, inflated style. || **bouffir** [-i:r] #17 *v. tr. & intr.* to swell, to puff up. || *v. intr.* to become swollen, bloated.
bouffon [bu'fõ] *n.m.* buffoon, jester. || *adj.* droll, ridiculous.
bouge [bu:ʒ] *n.m.* slum, hovel.
bougeoir [bu'ʒwa:r] *n.m.* candlestick [to be carried]. cf. CHANDELIER.
bouger [bu'ʒe] #5 *v. intr.* to move, to stir; [au nég.] to budge: *Ne bougez pas de là*, Don't/budge, move, stir/from there; → stay put. || *v. tr.* [Fam.] to move, shift (furniture about the room, &c.).
bougie [bu'ʒi] *n.f.* **1.** (wax) candle: †*moucher, éteindre une* ~, to snuff out, to put out/a candle. **2.** [Electr.] candlepower: *une lampe de 5 bougies*, a five-candle-power bulb. **3.** [Auto.] sparkplug.
bougon, -ne [bu'g|õ, -ən] *adj.* grouchy, grumpy. || *n.* grumbler, grouser.
bouillant, -e [bu'j|ɑ̃(:t)] *adj.* **1.** [action] boiling, [état] boiling hot: *de l'eau bouillante*, boiling water; *boire qqch. de* ~, to drink sth./boiling, piping/hot. **2.** [Fig.] hot-tempered (person): ~ *de* (*colère, fureur, impatience*), boiling with; ~ *d'*(*énergie, enthousiasme*), bubbling (over) with, bursting with. || **bouilli, -e** [-i] *adj.* [eau, viande] boiled. || *n.m.* boiled/beef, mutton, &c.); © (thin) /beef, mutton/stew. cf. RAGOÛT. || **bouillie** [-i] *n.f.* **1.** [bébé] †pap, gruel; [pâte à papier] pulp. || **bouillir** [-i:r] #61 *v. intr.* to boil: *faire* ~, to boil; *L'eau bout*, The water is boiling; [ext.] *Le chaudron bout*, The/kettle, pot/is boiling, [Fig.] to boil (with anger, exasperation, &c.); to be itching (*de faire qqch.*, to do sth.). || **bouilloire** [-wa:r] *n.f.* (tea-) kettle.
bouillon [bu'j|õ] *n.m.* **1.** bouillon, broth: [Bactér.] ~ (*de culture*), (culture) broth. **2.** bubble [given off by a boiling liquid]: *faire bouillir à gros bouillons*, → to bring to a/quick, fast/boil. || **bouillonnement** [-ɔn'mɑ̃] *n.m.* **1.** seething, [moins fort] bubbling; [de chaleur] boiling; [vagues] foaming. **2.** [Fig.] [âme, cœur] stirring; [sang] seething; [pensées, passions] tumult. || **bouillonner** [-ɔ'ne] #3 *v. intr.* **1.** to seethe, [moins fort] to bubble; [de chaleur] to boil. **2.** [Fig.] ~ *de*, to seethe with (anger, fury). || **bouillotte** [-ɔt] *n.f.* hot-water bottle.
boulanger [bulɑ̃'ʒ|e] *n.m.* baker. || #5 *v. tr.* to knead (bread); to make bread. || **boulangère** [-ɛ:r] *n.f.* baker's wife. || **boulangerie** [-'ri] *n.f.* bakery, baker's shop.
boule [bul] *n.m.* [billard] ball; [quilles] bowl: *jeu de* ~, bowling alley. cf. QUILLE [balustre] knob: ~ *de neige*, snowball; *se rouler en* ~, to roll, curl/up in a ball; *boules de gomme*, gum drops; [Fam.] *perdre la* ~, to go nuts; *être, se mettre/ en* ~, to be, get/cross.
bouleau [bu'lo] *n.m.* birch: *écorce de* ~, birch bark.
bouledogue [bul'dɔg] *n.m.* bulldog: [Iron.] *aimable comme un* ~, friendly as a → bear.
boulet [bu'lɛ] *n.m.* (cannon-)ball; [charbon] ovoids; [Fig.] millstone (round s.o.'s neck); *traîner le* ~, to wear a ball and chain.
boulette [bu'lɛt] *n.f.* [pain, &c.] pellet; [pâte] doughball; [viande] meat ball; [Fig., = erreur] bloomer.
boulevard [bul'va:r] *n.m.* [*abr.* **Boul., Bd**] boulevard, avenue [bordered by trees].
bouleversant, -e [bulvɛr's|ɑ̃(:t)] *adj.* [émotion] upsetting; [nouvelles] staggering (piece of news). || **bouleversé, -e** [-e] *adj.* [terrain, chambre, &c.] (completely) upset, turned (completely) upside down; [Fig.] distressed, upset. || **bouleversement** [-ə'mɑ̃] *n.m.* upset, confusion; [Fig.] upheaval, disruption. || **bouleverser** [-e] #3 *v. tr.* to upset; to disrupt; to turn upside down; [Fig.] to (completely) upset, to throw into confusion.
boulon [bu'l|õ] *n.m.* bolt. || **boulonner** [-ɔ'ne] #3 *v. tr.* to bolt.
boulot [bu'lo] *n.m.* [Fam.] job.
bouquet[1] [bu'kɛ] *n.m.* (large) shrimp, prawn.

bouquet[2] [buk|ɛ] *n.m.* **1.** [fleurs] bunch, bouquet, [feuilles, plumes] cluster. **2.** [goût] aroma (of a cigar); bouquet (of wine, brandy, &c). **3.** climax, grand finale: [Fam.] *Ça, c'est le ~ !* That's the final straw! || **bouquetière** [-tjɛːr] *n.f.* flower/girl, woman/.

bouquin [bu'k|ɛ̃] *n.m.* old book, well-thumbed book; [Fam.] book. || **bouquiner** [-i'ne] #3 *v. tr.* to browse; to go book-hunting. || **bouquiniste** [-i'nist] *n.m.* book-shop, book corner; dealer in second-hand books.

bourbeu|x, -se [bur'bø(ːz)] *adj.* muddy, miry.

bourdonnement [burdɔn|'mɑ̃] *n.m.* [abeille, bourdon] buzz(ing); [plus doux] [moteur en marche, mouche, oiseau qui vole] hum(ming), [dans les oreilles] ringing, singing; [d'une foule] drone; [voix] buzz; [Tél.] ~ *d'appel*, dial tone. || **bourdonner** [-e] #3 *v. intr.* [abeille, bourdon, scie mécanique] to buzz; [plus doux] [moteur, mouche, petit oiseau] to hum; [foule] to hum, to murmur; [oreilles] to hum, to buzz. || *v . intr.* to hum; [oreilles] to ring, sing.

bourgeois, -e [burʒwa|(ːz)] *adv.* [Péj.] bourgeois, common; plain, homely (cooking, clothing). || *n.m.* **1.** [Hist.] †burgess; (citizen) of a borough; [société] middle-class person, bourgeois; [Péj.] common (person); *en* ~, in plain clothes. **2.** [Fam. esp. ©] boss; [Vulg.] *la bourgeoise*, the missus, the wife. || **bourgeoisie** [-'zi] *n.f.* [Péj.] bourgeoisie, middle class: *grande* ~, upper middle class; *petite* ~, lower middle class.

bourgeon [bur'ʒ|õ] *n.m.* **1.** bud; [arbre] shoot. **2.** [Fig.] pimple. || **bourgeonner** [-ɔ'ne] #3 *v. intr.* to bud, sprout, shoot; [Fig.] to break out in pimples.

Bourgogne (la) [(la) bur'g|ɔɲ] *n.f.* [Géog.] Burgundy; *un bourgogne*, a (bottle of) B.

bourgot [bur'go] © *n.m.* moose-caller.

bourguignon, -ne [burgiɲ|õ,| -ɔn] *adj.* of, from/Burgundy, Burgundian.

bourrage [bu'raːʒ] *n.m.* cramming; [trou] filling, padding: ~ *de crâne*, ballyhoo.

bourrasque [bu'rask] *n.f.* [vent] gust; [plus fort, avec pluie] squall; [neige] flurry.

bourreau [bu'ro] *n.m.* executioner, [pendaison] hangman; [Fig.] tormenter, torturer: ~ *de travail*, eager beaver, plugger.

bourreler [bur'l|e] #9 *v. tr.* [de remords] to torment, rack (with). || **bourrelet** [-ɛ] *n.m.* [de chair] bulge; [de graisse] roll; [de fenêtre] weather stripping. || **bourrer** [bu're] #3 *v. tr.* to pack tight (*de*, with); [matelas, pipe, valise] to stuff, with; [le crâne] to stuff, cram/with; [Fig.] ~ *de coups*, to pummel. || **se bourrer** *v. pron.* [Péj.] to stuff o.s. (with food).

bourrique [bu'rik] *n.f.* female donkey; [Fig. & Fam.] ignoramus, dunce, duffer.

bourru, -e [bu'ry] *adj.* [étoffe] rough; coarse; [Fig.] surly, grumpy.

bourse [burs] *n.f.* **1.** †purse, bag. cf. SAC; money, funds: *La ~ ou la vie*, Your money or your life. **2.** [Fig.] bursary, scholarship, grant. **3.** [valeurs] *La Bourse*, Stock Exchange; ~ *du Travail*, Labour Exchange.

boursier [bur'sje] *n.m.* [étudiant] scholar, /scholarship-, fellowship-/holder.

boursoufler [bursu'fl|e] #3 *v. tr.* to puff up; [graisse] to bloat; [Fig.] to inflate. || **se boursoufler** *v. pron.* [pain, peinture] to become/puffed up, bloated/; [peinture] to blister. || **boursouflure** [-yːr] *n.f.* swelling, puffiness; [sol] heave; [peinture] blister.

bousculade [busky'l|ad] *n.f.* a rush (for), a general scurry (for); scramble, scuffle. || **bousculer** [-e] #3 *v.tr.* [*conj.*AVOIR(action), ÊTRE (état)] to jostle, shove/(s.o.); to knock over, upset sth.; [Fig.] to rush, hurry/s.o.: *être bousculé*, to be hurried. || **se bousculer** *v. pron.* to jostle, hustle; to hurry.

boussole [bu'sɔl] *n.f.* compass; [Fig.] *perdre la* ~, to be all at sea.

bout [bu] *n.m.* **1.** end; tip (of the tongue, nose, finger). **2.** bit, piece, fragment; scrap (of paper), chunk (of bread), butt (of a cigar, cigarette); part (of a sermon); [Loc.] *faire un ~ de chemin avec qqun*, to go, walk/a way with s.o.; *Il a marché un ~ de temps*, He walked a while; [Fig.] *répéter qqch. à tout ~ de champ*, to repeat sth./continuously, at every occasion/; *à (au) ~ de*, at the end (of); *joindre les deux bouts*, to make ends (both ends) meet; *tirer à ~ portant*, to fire point-blank; *mener par le ~ du nez*, to lead by the nose; *au ~ du compte*, when all is said and done; *montrer le ~ de son nez*, to show one's face; *tenir le bon* ~, to have the whip hand, to hold the long end of the stick; *savoir sur le ~ des doigts*, to have at one's fingertips; *être à ~ d'efforts*, to be worn out.

boutade [bu'tad] *n.f.* **1.** whim: *par boutades*, by fits and starts. **2.** sally, flash of wit.

bouteille [bu'tɛj] *n.f.* **1.** bottle: *boire à*

la ~ , to drink out of the bottle; *mettre en* ~ , to bottle; ~ */isolante, Thermos,* Thermos bottle. **2.** cylinder: ~ *d'oxygène,* cylinder of oxygen.

boutique [bu'tik] *n.f.* shop, store [souvent Fam. ou Péj. en français] [foire] booth; [atelier] workshop: *tenir* ~ , to run a shop, store; *parler* ~ , to talk shop; [Fig., Fam.] joint.

bouton [bu't|õ] *n.m.* [fleur] bud: [porte, radio] knob; [Electr.] switch; [Méd.] pimple; [vêtement] button; [manchettes] cufflink; [à pression] snap, dome-/fastener; [col] button, stud; ~ *de contact,* ignition switch. || **boutonner** [-ɔ'ne] #3 *v. intr.* [plante] to bud; [visage, peau, &c.] to break out in pimples. || *v. tr.* to button (up) (a coat, &c). || **se boutonner** *v. pron.* to button o.s. up; [vêtement] to button (at the back, front, side, &c).

boutonneu|x, -se [butɔ'nø(:z]) *adj.* pimply.

boxe [bɔks] *n.f.* boxing: *un/match, combat/ de* ~ , a boxing match.

B.P. [= Boîte postale], **P.O.** Box [= Post Office Box].

bracelet [bras'lɛ] *n.m.* bracelet; [cheville] anklet; [cercle] bangle; [en cuir, pour montre] watch-strap; [Méd.] wrist-band. || **bracelet-montre** [braslɛ'mõ:tr] *n.m.* wrist-watch.

braconner [brakɔ'n|e] #3 *v. intr.* to poach. || **braconnier** [-je] *n.m.* poacher.

braillard, -e [brɑ'j|a:r, -ard] *adj.* [Péj.] bawling; noisy; [querelleur] brawling; [enfant] squalling. || *n.m.* bawler, loud talker; brawler. || **brailler** [-e] #3 *v. intr.* to bawl; [enfant] to cry, to squall. || *v. tr.* to bawl out (a song, &c.).

braire [brɛ:r], **brayant** [brɛ'jã], **brait** [brɛ] #71 *v. intr.* to bray.

braise [brɛ:z] *n.f.* **1.** glowing coals, embers; charcoal; [Fig.] *être sur la* ~ , to be on hot coals. **2.** [Fam.] dough, cash.

bran [brã] *n.m.* [bois] © ~ *de scie,* sawdust; [son] bran.

brancard [brã'k|a:r] *n.m.* [voiture] shaft; [civière] stretcher. || **brancardier** [-ar'dje] *n.m.* stretcher-bearer.

branchage [brã'ʃa:ʒ] *n.m.* branches, boughs: *hutte de branchages,* bowery. || **branche** [brã:ʃ] *n.f.* **1.** branch, bough, limb (of a tree); branch (of a husk). **2.** [par analogie] [deer] horn; [artery, &c.] branch; [lustre] arm; [fourche] prong; [lunettes] bow. **3.** branch (of a family); [division] branch, section/(of science, teaching, enterprise); [Com.] line: *Dans quelle* ~ *travaillez-vous?,* What line are you in? || **brancher** [-e] #3 *v. tr.* [tuyau, installation électrique] to connect; [Electr.] to plug in [une fiche]. || **se brancher** *v. pron.* to perch (on a branch); [Tech.] to connect up (*sur,* with).

brandir [brã'di:r] #17 *v. tr.* to brandish; [avec mouvement] to wave, flourish.

branlant, -e [brã'lã(:t)] *adj.* [bâtiment] tumbledown; [meuble] shaky, [table, pas] unsteady; [pierre] rocking; [dent] loose; [Fig.] tottering.

branle [brã:l] *n.m.* **1.** [cloche] swing(ing), [Tech.] oscillation; [tête] shaking; [Fig.] impulse, start: *mettre en* ~ , to set in motion, to start; *se mettre en* ~ , to get under way. || **branler** [brã'le] #3 *v. tr.* to shake (one's head). || *v. intr.* [meuble] to be shaky, wobbly; [tooth, horseshoe] to be loose.

bras [brɑ] *n.m.* **1.** arm: *se promener* ~ *dessus,* ~ *dessous,* to walk arm in arm; *porter/entre, sur, dans les/* ~ , to carry in one's arms; *être en* ~ *de chemise,* to be in (one's) shirtsleeves; *les* ~ *ballants,* with one's arms hanging (at one's sides); [Fig.] *avoir le* ~ *long,* to have a wide influence. **2.** [Fig. main-d'œuvre] man, hand: *manquer de* ~ , to lack/men, hands/. **3.** [par anal.] arm (of an octopus, tree, river, sea, chair, pair of scales); handle (of a stretcher, oar); [Loc.] *à bras,* by hand; *charrette à bras,* handcart; *à tour de bras,* with might and main; *frapper à bras raccourcis,* to hit with all one's might; *à bras le corps,* around the waist.

brasier [brɑ'zje] *n.m.* glowing/fire, coals/; [Fig.] blazing inferno.

brassard [bra'sa:r] *n.m.* armband, arm badge.

brasse [bras] *n.f.* [nage] breast stroke; †[mesure] fathom.

brasser [bra's|e] #3 *v. tr.* [bière] to brew; [agiter] to stir (up), to mix; [Fig., Com.]: ~ *des affaires,* to handle a lot of business, to do a roaring trade. || **brasserie** [-'ri] *n.f.* [fabrique] brewery; [fabrication] brewing, beer-making; [débit] beer parlour, beer garden. || **brasseur** [-œ:r] *n.m.* brewer; [Fig.] ~ *d'affaires,* tycoon.

brassière [bra'sjɛ:r] *n.f.* [×] shoulder strap.

brave [brav] *adj.* brave, bold [when placed after the noun]; honest, good [when placed in front]: ~ *homme,* good man; *homme* ~ , brave man; *Il est bien* ~ , He is really nice. || *n.m.* brave man: *les braves,* the brave. || **bravement** [-'mã] *adv.* bravely, courageously. || **braver** [-e] #3 *v. tr.* **1.** to brave, face bravely: ~ *la colère de qqun,* to face s.o.'s wrath. **2.**

to stand (insolently) up to; to defy, dare (s.o.).

bravo [bra'vo] *n.m.* Bravo! Well done! *pl.* applause: *les ~ de la foule,* the cheers of the crowd.

bravoure [bra'vu:r] *n.f.* bravery, courage; gallantry: *acte m de ~*, deed of valour; courageous action; [style] *morceau m de ~*, purple patch.

brebis [brə'bi] *n.f.* ewe; [Fig.] sheep, lamb: *les ~ perdues d'Israël,* the lost sheep of Israel; *~ galeuse,* black sheep; *un loup déguisé en ~*, a wolf in sheep's clothing.

brèche [brɛʃ] *n.f.* breach; [mur] gap, hole, [blade] notch: *faire ~ à qqch.,* to breach, to make a breach; [Fig.]: *battre en ~*, to disparage s.o., to run s.o. down; *être sur la ~*, to hold the fort, to be hard at it.

bredouiller [brədu'je] #3 *v. tr. & intr.* to mumble, to stammer (out).

br|ef, -ève [brɛ|f, —:v] *adj.* [durée] brief, short; [ton de la voix] sharp, curt. || *adv.* briefly, in short: [parler] curtly. || *n.m.* [papal] brief.

Brésil, (le) [(lə) bre'zil] *n.m.* Brazil: *noix du ~*, Brazil nut. || **brésilien, -ne** [-jɛ̃, -jɛn] *adj. & n.* Brazilian.

Bretagne [brə'taɲ] *n.f.* [Géog.] **1.** Brittany: *la Basse ~*, Lower Brittany. **2.** [Hist.] Britannia, Britain. **3.** *La Grande-Bretagne,* Great Britain, Britain.

bretelle [brə'tɛl] *n.f.* [chemise] shoulder-strap; [fusil] sling. || *pl.* suspenders; braces.

breton, -ne [brə't|ɔ̃, -ɔn] *adj.* Breton [from Brittany]. || *n.* Breton.

breuvage [brœ'va:ʒ] *n.m.* [☞ in Fr. the word is obsolescent. cf. BOISSON] beverage, drink; © [boisson chaude terminant les repas] beverage.

brevet [brə'vɛ] *n.m.* **1.** certificate, diploma; licence: *~ d'enseignement,* teaching certificate; *~ de pilote,* pilot's licence. **2.** [d'invention] patent: *bureau des brevets,* patent office; *prendre un ~*, to take out a patent. || **breveté, -e** [brəv'te] *adj.* certified, licensed: *pilote ~*, licensed pilot; [Schol.] graduate; [spécialiste] qualified. || **breveter** #9 *v. tr.* to patent, to issue a patent; [permis] to license; [Mil.] to commission.

bréviaire [bre'vjɛ:r] *n.m.* breviary.

bribes [brib] *n.fpl.* scraps, bits; [conversation] snatches.

bricolage [brikɔ'l|a:ʒ] *n.m.* do-it-yourself; pottering (about). || **bricoler** [-e] #3 *v. intr.* to do sth. by o.s.; to tinker, potter/(about the house, &c.). || **bricoleur** [-œ:r] *n.m.* potterer, handy-man.

bride [brid] *n.f.* bridle, rein; [couture] strap, bridle; [chapeau] string; [Loc.] *à ~ abattue,* (at) full speed; *lâcher la ~ à,* to give free rein to; *serrer la ~ à,* to curb.

brider [bri'de] #3 *v. tr.* to bridle; [volaille] to truss; [Fig.] to restrain.

brièvement [brijɛv'|mɑ̃] *adv.* briefly, in short. cf. BREF. || **brièveté** [-'te] *n.f.* brevity; terseness.

brigade [bri'gad] *n.f.* [police] squad, force; [Mil.] brigade *f*; [Fr.] *général de ~*, brigadier.

brigand [bri'gɑ̃] *n.m.* †highwayman; brigand, bandit; [Fig.] rascal.

brillamment [brij|a'mɑ̃] *adv.* brilliantly. || **brillant** [-ɑ̃] *n.m.* **1.** [surface lisse] lustre; sheen; [cire, cirage] shine, polish; [couleur] brightness; [esprit] brilliancy; [papier, porcelaine] gloss(iness). **2.** (cut) diamond. || **brillant, -e** [-ɑ̃(:t)] *adj.* brilliant, bright, shining; [couleur] gay, bright; [Fig.] brilliant, talented; [avenir] bright, [conversation] sparkling; [situation] prosperous. || **briller** [-e] #3 *v. intr.* to shine; [étoile] to glitter, sparkle; [phare] to glare; [lumière froide] to gleam; [lumière rouge] to glow; [Fig.] to be conspicuous, to stand out (*par,* for).

brimer [bri'me] #3 *v. tr.* to bully, to haze.

brin [brɛ̃] *n.m.* [pousse] shoot; [herbe] grass; [muguet] spray; [ficelle] strand; [Fig.] a touch of, a shade of. || **brindille** [brɛ'di:j] *n.f.* sprig, twig.

brique [brik] *n.f.* **1.** brick; *maison/en ~, de briques/,* brick house; *ton de ~*, brick-coloured, brick-red. **2.** [savon, glace] cake, bar.

briquet [bri'kɛ] *n.m.* lighter.

bris [bri] *n.m.* breaking: [Jur.] wilful damage; breach.

brise [bri:z] *n.f.* breeze, gentle wind; *forte ~*, stiff breeze.

brisé, -e [bri'z|e] *adj.* broken; [Fig.] tired out: *~ de fatigue,* completely worn out. || **brisées** [-e] *n.fpl.*: [Fig.] *marcher sur les ~ de,* to poach on s.o.'s preserves. || **brise-glace** [-'glas] *n.m. invar.* [Naut.] ice-breaker. || **briser** [-e] #3 *v. tr.* to break [d'un coup sec] to snap; [du verre] to shatter; [avec force] to smash; [des liens] to burst; [Fig., grève] to break; [avenir, santé] to ruin; [projets] to shatter; [une résistance] to overcome, to crush: *La voiture me brise,* Automobile travel tires me; *~ la carrière de qqun,* to ruin s.o.'s career; *~ un entretien,* to end, to break off/an interview/. || **se briser** *v. pron.* to break, to shatter, snap, &c.

[cf. *v. tr.*]: *La porcelaine se brise facilement,* Porcelain breaks easily.

britannique [brita'nik] *adj.* British; [King, Queen] Britannic: *les îles Britanniques,* the British Isles. || *n.* Britisher; [coll.] *les Britanniques,* the British.

broc [bro] *n.m.* pitcher, jug.

brocanteu|r, -se [brɔkɑ̃'t|œ:r, -ø:z] *n.* second-hand dealer, junk dealer.

broche [brɔʃ] *n.f.* peg, pin; [textile] spindle; [Cul.] spit, skewer; [costume] brooch, breastpin, © wire.

brocher [brɔ'ʃe] #3 *v. tr.* [livre] to stitch.

brochet [brɔ'ʃɛ] *n.m.*: ~ *commun,* pike, jack fish.

brocheuse [brɔ'ʃ|ø:z] *n.f.* stapler; [reliure] stitcher. || **brochure** [-y:r] *n.f.* brochure, pamphlet; [reliure] stitching.

broder [brɔ'd|e] #3 *v. tr.* to embroider. || **broderie** [-'ri] *n.f.* embroidery.

bromure [brɔ'my:r] *n.m.* bromide.

broncher [brɔ̃'ʃe] #3 *v. intr.* †to budge; [Fig.] to flinch: *sans* ~, without flinching, unflinching(ly).

bronchial, -e [brɔ̃'kjal] *adj.* bronchial.

bronchite [brɔ̃'ʃit] *n.f.* bronchitis.

bronze [brɔ̃:z] *n.m.* bronze. || **bronzé, -e** [brɔ̃'ze] *adj.* [Fig.] bronzed, tanned. || **se bronzer** [(sə) brɔ̃'ze] #3 *v. pron.* to (sun-) tan, to bronze.

brosse [brɔs] *n.f.* brush: ~ *à habits,* clothes brush; ~ *à dents,* tooth brush; *donner un coup de* ~, to brush; [Argot. ©] *prendre une* ~ [= Fr. prendre une cuite], to get drunk. || **brosser** [-e] #3 *v. tr.* to brush (away, off); [le plancher] to scrub; to paint [with a brush]; [Fig.] to give an outline of, to sketch.

broue [bru] © *n.f.* froth (on beer); [Fig.] *faire de la* ~, to talk big.

brouette [bru'ɛt] *n.f.* wheelbarrow. || **brouetter** [-e] #3 *v. tr.* to cart in a barrow.

brouhaha [brua'a] *n.m.* hubbub.

brouillard [bru'ja:r] *n.m.* **1.** fog; [mouillé] mist: *Il y a du brouillard,* It is foggy; *Le* ~ */tombe, se dissipe/,* Fog is/rolling in, clearing/; *perdu dans le* ~, fog-bound; [Fig., Fam.] *être dans le* ~, to be/hazy (about), in a mist/.

brouille [bruj] *n.f.* quarrel, estrangement. || **brouillé, -e** [-e] *adj.* **1.** blurred; [Cul.] *œufs brouillés,* scrambled eggs. **2.** on bad terms. || **brouiller** [-e] #3 *v. tr.* **1.** to jumble, mix up; [image] to blur; [Radio] to jam; [œufs] to scramble; [Fig.] [idée] to confuse; [Fam.] to sow discord. || **se brouiller** *v. pron.* to become clouded, riled; to fall out with (s.o.).

broussailles [bru's|a:j] *n.fpl.* [sous-bois] undergrowth, underbrush, brushwood; [Fig. sing.] *la barbe en broussaille,* shaggy beard. || **broussailleu|x, -se** [-a'jø(:z)] *adj.* bushy; [Fig.] bushy, shaggy.

brouter [bru'te] #3 *v. tr. & intr.* to graze, to browse.

broyer [brwa'je] #12 *v. tr.* [aliments] to crush, grind; [avec les dents] to crunch; [dans un mortier] to pound; [Fig.] ~ *du noir,* to have the blues.

broyeuse [brwa'jø:z] *n.f.* brake.

bru [bry] *n.f.* daughter-in-law.

bruine [brɥin] *n.f.* drizzle.

bruire [brɥ|i:r] [☞ only used in 3rd pers. present indic. & imperfect; pres. part. **bruissant**] #47 *v. intr.* [feuille] to rustle, [eau] murmur, [vent] sigh, whisper; [barrage] plash; [machines] to hum. || **bruissement** [-is'mɑ̃] *n.m.* hum (of machinery), buzzing (of bus), [continuous soft, muted sound] rustle, murmur, soughing, &c. [see above].

bruit [brɥi] *n.m.* noise; *sans* ~, quietly, noiselessly. [☞ L'anglais possède une gamme très riche de mots dénotant les bruits, correspondant au fr. *un bruit de . . .* ; on en trouvera ci-dessous les principaux, classés selon la qualité du bruit.] **1.** [bruits faibles] [petits pieds, grêle] patter; [glace dans un verre] clink; [grelots] rattle; [pluie sur le toit] pattering; [arbres qui s'égouttent] dripping; [robinet] drip. **2.** [bruits forts] [assourdissant] din; [canon, mer, orage] roar; [canon] boom; [voitures, tonnerre] rumble; [pas lourds] tramp; [marteau] clanking, hammering. **3.** [bruits secs, soudains] [coup de fusil] crack, bang, ping; [coup de fouet] crack; [boite qui se ferme] snap; [branche qui casse] crack, snap; [assiette] clatter; [couteau qui se ferme] click; [bouchon] pop; [déchirure] rip; [pierre dans l'eau] plop; [cristal] tinkle. **4.** [bruits prolongés] [ailes] whirr; [cascade] splash; [barrage] plash; [fouet] swish; [vagues] wash; [friture] sizzle; [balle] whizz; [roues métalliques] rattle; [pneus] whirr; [sirène] hoot(ing); [broiement] crunch. **5.** [bruits confus] [bataille] din; [chute molle] thud; [orage lointain] rumble; [foule] uproar; [voix] sound; buzz, hum. **6.** [bruits métalliques] [chaînes] clank-(ing); [gong] clang(ing); [cloche] clash; [trompette] blare. **7.** [Fig.] stir, disturbance, †ado; [rumeur] noise, rumour: *Le* ~ *court que . . .* , Rumour has it that . . . ; *faire du* ~, to create a sensation.

brûlant, -e [bry'l|ɑ̃(:t)] *adj.* burning; [feu] blazing; [soleil] scorching hot; [Cul.] piping hot, good and hot; [malade] feverish; [Fig.] ardent, eager: ~ *de*, eager to; [question] delicate.

brûlé, -e [-e] *adj.* burnt, [hâlé] sunburnt: *tête brûlée*, dare-devil. || **brûler** [-e] #3 *v. tr.* **1.** to burn, [peau, &c.] to scorch; [eau bouillante] to scald; [cheveux] to singe; [café] to roast; [récoltes] to parch (up), to wilt; [acide] to corrode. **2.** [Fig.] ~ *un feu rouge*, to go through a red light; ~ *les étapes*, to make rapid /progress, strides/; ~ *le pavé*, to burn up the road; ~ *la cervelle à qqun*, to blow s.o.'s brains out; ~ *ses vaisseaux*, to burn one's bridges. || *v. intr.* to burn, [ampoule électrique] to be/on, alight/; [Cul.] to burn; [Fig.] ~ *d'envie de*, to be (simply) dying to . . . || **brûleur** [-œ:r] *n.m.*: ~ *à gaz*, gas-burner; ~ /*à mazout*, © *à huile*, oil-burner; ~ *de café*, roaster. || *n.m.* © **brûlis** [-i] *n.m.* [burnt-up area] brûlée. || **brûlure** [-y:r] *n.f.* burn; [eau bouillante] scald; [Méd.] ~ *d'estomac*, heartburn.

brume [brym] *n.f.* (thick) fog [esp. at sea]: ~ *de chaleur*, haze; *trompe de* ~, foghorn; ~ *artificielle*, smoke screen. || **brumeu|x, -se** [-ø(:z)] *adj.* foggy, misty.

brun, -e [brœ̃, bryn] *adj.* brown; [cheveux] dark (-haired); [bière] dark (stout, &c.). || *n.m.* dark man. || *n.f.* brunette.

brunante [bry'nɑ̃:t] © *n.f.*: *à la* ~, at /dusk, nightfall/.

brune [bry:n] *n.f.* **1.** [Fr.] dusk, nightfall. cf. BRUNANTE. **2.** [×] brunette: *une grande* ~, a tall brunette. || **brunette** [bry'nɛt] *n.f.* a small brunette.

bruni, -e [bry'n|i] *adj.* burnished, polished; [Fig.] sunburnt. || **brunir** [-i:r] #17 *v. tr.* **1.** [metal] to polish, burnish. **2.** to tan, to bronze. || *v. intr.* to become, turn/brown.

brusque [brysk] *adj.* sudden; [ton] sharp, brusque; [caractère] short, gruff; [personnalité] blunt. || **brusquement** [-ə'mɑ̃] *adv.* abruptly, suddenly. || **brusquer** [-e] #3 *v. tr.* [conj. AVOIR (action), ÊTRE (état)] to be/rude, blunt, sharp, impolite/(to s.o.), to treat (s.o.) with scant, little courtesy; [Fig.] to hurry, precipitate (things, matters): ~ *une affaire*, to rush a case. || **brusquerie** [-ə'ri] *n.f.* abruptness, bluntness; suddenness.

brut, -e [bry|(t)] *adj.* **1.** [matière] raw, unrefined; [or] nugget; [pétrole] crude (oil); [diamond] rough, uncut; [bois] lumber. **2.** [Com.] gross (weight, price, profit). **3.** [Fig.,†] brutish, uncouth. || **brutal, -e** [-'tal] *adj.* **1.** [fait, instinct] brutal; [force] brute, rude, brutish; [manières] uncouth, rough; [coup] savage. **2.** [Fig.] direct, plain, unvarnished. || **brutalement** [-tal'mɑ̃] *adv.* brutally, rudely; [avec rudesse] roughly; [avec méchanceté] savagely; [sans ménagements] bluntly: *Je lui ai parlé* ~, → I gave it to him straight from the shoulder. || **brutaliser** [-tali'ze] #3 *v. tr.* to treat in a/brutal, unkind/manner; to bully, to ill-treat. || **brutalité** [-tali'te] *n.f.* brutality, savagery; coarseness, uncouthness; brutal, savage/act. || **brute** [bryt] *n.f.* brute.

Bruxelles [bry'sɛl] *n.f.* Brussels: *chou de* ~, Brussels sprout.

bruyamment [brɥij|a'mɑ̃] *adv.* noisily, loudly, boisterously. || **bruyant, -e** [-ɑ̃(:t)] *adj.* noisy, loud, boisterous. cf. BRUIT.

bruyère [brɥi'jɛ:r] *n.f.* [plante] heather; [terrain] heath; [pipe] French briar: *coq m. de* ~, grouse.

bu, -e [by] cf. BOIRE.

buanderie [bɥɑ̃d|'ri] *n.f.* laundry-room, wash house; © laundry. || **buandi|er, -ère** [-je, -jɛ:r] © laundry|man, -woman.

buccal, -e [by'kal] *adj.* [of the mouth] buccal: [Méd.] *par voie buccale*, taken orally.

bûche [byʃ] *n.f.* (fire) log: *la* ~ *de Noël*, Yule log; [Cul.] jelly roll; [Fig.] [chute] spill, cropper; [personne stupide] blockhead, clod. || **bûcher**[1] [-e] *n.m.* **1.** woodshed; [tas de bois] woodpile; †[funéraire] pyre; [supplice] stake: *Jeanne d'Arc monta sur le* ~, Joan of Arc was burned at the stake. || **bûcher**[2] [-e] © #3 *v. tr.* to cut down, fell/trees. || **bûcher**[3] [-e] *v. intr.* to cram (for exams); to slave (at one's work). || **bûcheron** [-'rõ] *n.m.* lumberjack, woodcutter. || **bûcheu|r, -se** [-œ:r, -ø:z] *n.* plodder, hard worker; crammer; © woodcutter.

bucolique [bukɔ'lik] *adj.* pastoral, bucolic.

budget [byd'ʒ|ɛ] *n.m.* budget; ~ *des dépenses*, estimates; [Fam.] *boucler le* ~, (to manage) to make both ends meet. || **budgétaire** [-e'tɛ:r] *adj.* budgetary; *prévisions fpl. budgétaires*, budget estimates; *exercice m.* ~, fiscal year.

buée [bɥe] *n.f.* steam, haze; [sur une glace] mist, vapour.

buffet [by'fɛ] *n.m.* **1.** sideboard; china cupboard; buffet. **2.** buffet (table), refreshment table; [Rail.] refreshment room, restaurant: ~ *-éclair*, quick lunch, snack bar.

buffle [byfl] *n.m.* (water) buffalo. [The American buffalo, use BISON.]

buggy [bɔ'ge] © *n.m.* buggy, cart.
building [bil'diŋ] *n.m.* [Fr.] (modern) building, block: *le ~ des Nations Unies* (à New-York), the UN building [☞ © use ÉDIFICE in this sense].
buis [bɥi] *n.m.* box (tree); cf. IF; boxwood; [Rel.] ~ *bénit*, palm.
buisson [bɥi's|õ] *n.m.* bush; thicket. || **buissonnière** [-ɔ'njɛ:r] *adj.*: *faire l'école* ~, to play/truant, hooky/.
bulbe [bylb] *n.m.* [Bot.] bulb.
bulbeu|x, -se [byl'bø(:z)] *adj.* bulbous.
bulgare [byl'g|a:r] *adj.* & *n.* *m/f.* Bulgarian, Bulgar. || **Bulgarie** [-a'ri] *n.f.* Bulgaria.
bulle [byl] *n.f.* **1.** bubble: *faire des bulles*, to blow bubbles. **2.** (papal) bull.
bulletin [byl'tɛ̃] *n.m.* **1.** (official) bulletin, report: ~ *de nouvelles*, news bulletin; ~ *météorologique*, weather report; [école] ~ (*trimestriel*), report card. **2.** ~ *de vote*, ballot. **3.** ticket, receipt, certificate; [Com.] ~ *de consigne*, (deposit) cheque; ~ *de commande*, order form; ~ *de bagages*, baggage cheque; ~ *d'expédition*, waybill.
bure [by:r] *n.f.* [étoffe] homespun; [Fig.] sackcloth.
bureau [by'ro] *n.m.* **1.** desk; writing desk. **2.** [salle] office, bureau: ~ *de poste*, post office; ~ *de renseignements*, information bureau; [succursale] branch. **3.** [Adm.] department; board, committee, governing body; [d'une société] the officers (of an association, &c.). **4.** [Fr.] ~ *de tabac*, tobacconist, cigar store; [Mil.] *le Deuxième* ~, (Military) Intelligence. || **bureaucrate** [-'krat] *n.m/f.* bureaucrat. || **bureaucratie** [-kra'si] *n.f.* bureaucracy; [Péj.] red tape. || **bureaucratique** [-kra'tik] *adj.* bureaucratic.
burette [by'rɛt] *n.f.* [Rel.] cruet; ~ *d'huile*, oil can, oiler; [Chim.] burette.
buriner [byri'ne] #3 *v. tr.* to engrave; [Fig.] to mark.
buse [by:z] *n.f.* buzzard; [Fam.] nitwit: ~ *à queue rousse*, red-tailed hawk.
busqué, -e [bys'ke] *adj.* [nez] aquiline, hooked.
buste [byst] *n.m.* bust; chest: *redresser le* ~, to stick out one's chest.
but [by] *n.m.* target, mark; [Sport.] goal; [Fig.] goal, aim: [Loc.] *dans le ~ de*, with a view to, in order to; *être loin du* ~, to be far off the mark; *sans* ~, aimless(ly); *aller droit au* ~, to come to the point; *de ~ en blanc*, point-blank; abruptly; [Sport.]: *envoyer la balle dans le* ~, to score, to make a score; *marquer un* ~, to make/a goal, a basket, a run/; to score; *toucher le* ~, to touch base.
buté, -e [by'te] *adj.* obstinate, stubborn. || **buter** #3 *v. intr.* **1.** to rest, lean against; to abut (*contre*, against). **2.** [se heurter] to stumble (*contre*, over). || **se buter** *v. pron.* **1.** [Fig.] to be obstinate about, to be set on, to insist on. **2.** [Fig.] to come, run up against: ~ *à une difficulté*, to run up against a/snag, difficulty/.
butin [by'tɛ̃] *n.m.* **1.** spoils, booty, loot. **2.** © [Fam.] clothes, [Fam.] duds.
butiner [byti'ne] #3 *v. tr.* to gather; [Péj.] to pilfer. || *v. intr.* [abeilles] to gather honey.
butoir [by'twa:r] *n.m.* (door-)stop, check; [Rail.] buffer.
butor [by'tɔ:r] *n.m.* bittern; [Fam.] churl, lout; ~ (*d'Amérique*), marsh hen.
butte [byt] *n.f.* hillock, mound; [Géog.] butte; [Fig.] butt: *en ~ à*, exposed to, a butt to/criticism, &c.
buvable [by'vabl] *adj.* drinkable, fit for drinking; [Méd.] *ampoule f* ~, to be taken orally.
buvard [by'va:r] *n.m.* **1.** blotter (paper). **2.** (desk) blotter; blotting-pad.
buvette [by'v|ɛt] *n.f.* **1.** bar. **2.** coke bar, soda fountain. || **buveu|r, -se** [-œ:r, -ø:z] *n.* & *adj.* **1.** drinker: ~ *d'eau*, teetotaler. **2.** [habitude] tippler, drunkard.
byzantin, -e [bizɑ̃'t|ɛ̃, -in] *n.* & *adj.* Byzantine.

C, c [se] *n.m.* (the letter) C, c. || **C', c'** cf. CE.
ça [sa] *pron. dém.* [Fam. = CELA]: *Je n'aime pas ça,* I don't like/that, it/.
†**ça** [sa] *adv.*: ~ *et là,* here and there, this way and that. || *interj.* Well!: ~ , *par exemple!,* How do you like that?, What do you know about that?
cabale [ka'bal] *n.f.* [faction] cabal; © [Pol.] (door-to-door) canvassing: *faire une* ~ *en faveur de,* to canvass for. || © **cabaleur** [-œ:r] *n.m.* canvasser.
cabane [ka'ban] *n.f.* hut, cabin; (rabbit-) hutch; © ~ *à sucre,* saphouse.
cabaret [kaba'r|ɛ] *n.m.* **1.** tavern, beer parlour; night club, cabaret. **2.** liquor cabinet; © tray (for cafeteria, &c.). || **cabareti|er, -ère** [-'tje] *n.m.* tavern keeper.
cabas [ka'ba] *n.m.* shopping basket.
cabestan [kabɛs'tɑ̃] *n.m.* [Naut.] windlass, capstan.
cabine [ka'bin] *n.f.* cabin: ~ *téléphonique,* (phone) booth. **2.** cabin, stateroom.
cabinet [kabi'nɛ] *n.m.* **1.** closet: ~ *de toilette,* dressing-room; [usual. pl.] *cabinets (d'aisances),* toilet. **2.** *cabinet (de travail),* study; office (of lawyer); [Law] chambers; ~ *de consultation,* consulting room; practice (of lawyer): *Il a repris son* ~ , He's gone back to legal practice; ~ *de lecture,* lending library. **3.** cabinet (of government): *Le* ~ *a démissionné,* The cabinet has resigned.
câble [kɑ:bl] *n.m.* **1.** cable, rope: ~ *de remorque,* hawser, tow line. **2.** cablegram, cable: *expédier un* ~ , to send a cable. || **câbler** [kɑ'ble] #3 *v. tr.* [telegram] to cable; [Electr.] to wire (up).
caboche [ka'bɔʃ] *n.f.* [clou] hobnail; [Fam. tête] noodle. || **cabochon** [-õ] *n.m.* uncut gem; [clou] brass nail; [Fam. tête] noodle.
Cabot, Détroit de [ka'bɔt] *n.m.* Cabot Strait.
cabotage [kabo'ta:ʒ] *n.m.* coasting trade: *faire du* ~ *(sur la côte du Pacifique),* to coast (along the Pacific Coast).
cabotin, -e [kabo't|ɛ̃, -in] *n.* (poor) actor, barnstormer, ham. || **cabotinage** [-i'na:ʒ] *n.m.* overacting, ranting.
cabrer [kɑ'bre] #3 *v. tr.* [Aéro.] to elevate (plane): *faire* ~ *un cheval,* to make a horse rear. || **se cabrer** *v. pron.* **1.** [horse] to rear, [Br.] to jib; [plane] buck. **2.** [Fig.] to kick over the traces.
cabriole [kabri'jɔl] *n.f.* caper, leap: *faire des cabrioles,* to cut capers.
cabriolet [kabrijɔ'lɛ] *n.m.* †gig; [Auto.] coupé: ~ *décapotable,* convertible.
caca|huète, -houète [kaka|'ɥɛt, -'wɛt] *n.f.* peanut.
cacao [kaka'o] *n.m.* cocoa (bean).
cachalot [kaʃa'lo] *n.m.* cachalot, sperm whale.
cache [kaʃ] *n.f.* hiding place, [usual. replaced by CACHETTE]; [coureur de bois] cache || *n.m.* [Photo., Ciné.] mask, screen. || **cache-cache** [-'kaʃ] *n.m.* hide-and-seek: *jouer à* ~ , to play hide-and-seek. || **cache-col** [-'kɔl] *n.m.* scarf. || **cache-nez** [-'ne] *n.m.* muffler, scarf. || **cacher** [ka'ʃe] #3 *v. tr.* **1.** to hide, conceal; to cover up, put out of sight. **2.** [Fig.] to mask, dissemble (one's feelings, one's intentions). || **se cacher** *v. pron.* to hide o.s. (from, *de*), to withdraw (to a secret place).
cachet [ka'ʃɛ] *n.m.* **1.** seal, stamp (on document): ~ *de la poste,* postmark; [stamp which makes the seal], ring, seal: *apposer un* ~ *sur,* to seal (a document); [Hist.] *lettre de* ~ , warrant of arrest. **2.** fee (of an artist). **3.** [Méd.] cachet, tablet. **4.** [Fig.] mark (of distinctiveness, originality): *avoir un* ~ *d'élégance,* to have an air, a mark/of elegance.
cacheter [kaʃ'te] #8 *v. tr.* to seal up (a bottle), to seal (an envelope).
cachette [ka'ʃɛt] *n.f.* hiding place: *jouer à la* ~ , to play hide-and-seek; *en* ~ , secretly, behind s.o.'s back.
cachot [ka'ʃo] *n.m.* dungeon, (dark) cell; (by extension) prison.
cachotterie [kaʃɔt|'ri] *n.f.* [usual. pl.] secrecy. || **cachotti|er, -ère** [-je, -jɛ:r] *adj. & n.* secretive (person).
cactus [kak'tys] *n.m.* cactus.
cadastre [ka'dastr] *n.m.* **1.** land titles register. **2.** land survey.
cadavérique [kadave'rik] *adj.* cadaverous: *rigidité* ~, rigor mortis. || **cadavre** [ka'da:vr] *n.m.* corpse, dead body: *ensevelir un* ~ , to bury a corpse.
cadeau [ka'do] *n.m.* gift, present: *donner un* ~ , to give a present; *faire* ~ *(de qqch. à qqun),* to make a present (of sth. to s.o.).
cadenas [kad'n|ɑ] *n.m.* padlock: ~ *à chiffres,* combination padlock: © *la loi du* ~ , Padlock Law. || **cadenasser** [a'se] #3 *v. tr.* to padlock.
cadence [ka'dɑ̃:s] *n.f.* **1.** rhythm (of motion, music, verse): *danser en* ~ , to dance in time/in rhythm, with the music/; [Mus.] cadenza. **2.** speed, output (of a worker, factory, machine): ~ *accélérée,* increased speed, speeded-up (production).
cadet, -te [ka'dɛ(t)] *n.* **1.** younger (child);

[Sport.] junior (player); junior: *Elle est ma ~ de trois ans*, She is my junior by three years; [Fig.] *le ~ de mes soucis*, the least of my worries. **2.** [Mil.] cadet. || *adj.* second (child); younger, youngest: *être le fils ~*, to be/the second son, the youngest son; *son ~*, his kid brother.

cadran [ka'drɑ̃] *n.m.* dial: *~ solaire*, sundial; [Fig.] *faire le tour du ~*, to sleep around the clock.

cadre [kaːdr] *n.m.* **1.** [picture, door, car, bicycle, &c.] frame; [Fig.] outline (of a book, of a study): *dans le ~ de ses attributions*, within its terms of reference. **2.** limits, confines, bounds (of an area): *sortir du ~ de ses fonctions*, to overstep one's authority. **3.** [Mil.] staff, cadre: *les cadres*, the management. || **cadrer** [ka'dre] #3 *v. tr.* to tally, agree (with); to fit.

cadu|c, -que [ka'dyk] *adj.* decrepit, frail; [Bot.] deciduous: *arbres à feuilles caduques*, deciduous trees, cf. FEUILLU; [Jur.] *être caduc*, to have lapsed, to be null.

cafard [ka'faːr] *n.m.* [Fam.] **1.** the blues: *avoir le ~*, to have the blues, to be down in the mouth. **2.** (spy) tattle-tale, tale-bearer. **3.** cockroach, cf. BLATTE. || *adj.* hypocritical, bigoted, sanctimonious (air, person).

café [ka'fe] *n.m.* **1.** coffee: *~ noir*, black coffee; *~ au lait*, coffee with milk, coffee and milk, © [égal à café-crème]; *café-crème*, coffee with cream. **2.** [colour] coffee-coloured: *une robe* (*couleur de*) *~*, a coffee-coloured dress. **3.** restaurant: © *~ dansant*, grill, nightclub. || **caféine** [kafe'in] *n.f.* caffeine. || **cafétéria** [kafete'rja] © *n.f.* cafeteria. || **cafetier** [kaf'tje] *n.m.* owner of a café. || **cafetière** [kaf(ə)'tjɛːr] *n.f.* coffee pot.

cage [kaːʒ] *n.f.* cage; frame, shell; [by extension] *~ d'escalier*, stair well; *~ d'ascenseur*, elevator shaft; *~ thoracique*, rib cage; [Fig.] prison, pen.

cagnotte [ka'ɲɔt] *n.f.* kitty, pool.

cagoule [ka'gul] *n.f.* [moine] cowl; [pénitent] hood.

cahier [ka'je] *n.m.* notebook; [Schol.] copybook, exercise book; section (of a book).

cahot [ka'o] *n.m.* jolt, jar, bump (of a vehicle); *pl.* jolting. || **cahotement** [kaɔt|'mɑ̃] *n.m.* bumping, jarring, jolting (of a vehicle). || **cahoter** [-e] #3 *v. tr.* to jolt, jar, shake, bump.

caille [kɑːj] *n.f.* quail.

caillé, -e [kɑ'j|e] *n.m.* curd(s), junket. || *adj.* curdled (milk), clotted (blood). || **cailler** (se) [(sə) kɑ'je] #3 *v. intr. & pron.* [milk] to curdle; [blood] to clot. || **caillot** [-o] *n.m.* clot (of blood).

caillou, *pl.* **-x** [ka'ju] *n.m.* pebble, small stone: *lancer des cailloux*, to throw rocks. || **cailloute|ux, -se** [-'tø(ːz)] *adj.* rocky (road), pebbly (beach). || **cailloutis** [-'ti] *n.m.* rubble.

Caire (le) [lə'kɛːr] *n.m.* Cairo.

caisse [kɛːs] *n.f.* **1.** (packing) case, chest, box, trunk. **2.** [Fin.] cash box, till, (cash) counter; treasury; fund; bank: *~ d'épargne*, savings bank; *argent en ~*, cash on hand; *tenir la ~*, to keep the cash; *faire la ~*, to balance the cash. **3.** [Mus.] *grosse ~*, drum. || **caissi|er, -ère** [kɛ's|je, -'jɛːr] *n.* cashier. || **caisson** [-õ] *n.m.* **1.** powder box, chest; [Mil.] powder wagon. **2.** [hydraulic] caisson; coffer dam. **3.** [Arch.] panelled, coffered ceiling.

cajoler [kaʒɔ'le] #3 *v. tr.* to cajole, coax, wheedle.

calage [ka'laːʒ] *n.m.* [meuble] wedging; [roue] scotching; [Auto.] sta ing; [Aéro.] chocking.

calamité [kalami'te] *n.f.* (public) calamity, disaster; (great) misfortune: *la guerre est une ~*, war is a calamity.

calcaire [kal'kɛːr] *n.m.* limestone. || *adj.* calcareous, chalky.

calcifier (se) [(sə) kalsi'fje] #3 *v. tr. & pron.* to calcify.

calciner [kalsi'ne] #3 *v. tr.* to char, to burn to a cinder. || **se calciner** *v. pron.* to calcine.

calcium [kal'sjɔm] *n.m.* calcium.

calcul [kal'kyl] *n.m.* reckoning, calculation, computation; [Math.] calculus: *règle à ~* (*s*), slide rule; *~ mental*, mental arithmetic, to reckon in one's head; *~ différentiel et intégral*, calculus; [Fig.] *faux ~*, miscalculation; *tromper le ~ de qqun*, to upset s.o.'s calculation. || **calculat|eur, -rice** [-a'tœːr, -a'tris] *adj.* calculating. || *n.m/f.* **1.** computer, calculator. **2.** [Fig.] (level-headed) person, schemer.

calculer [-e] #3 *v. tr.* to calculate, compute, reckon; [Fig.] to plan, scheme. || *v. intr.* to reckon; [Fig.] to be sparing.

cale [kal] *n.f.* **1.** hold (of ship): *vider les cales*, to empty the hold; *~ sèche*, dry dock; *fond de ~*, bilge: *passager de ~*, stowaway; [Fig.] *être à fond de ~*, to be broke. **2.** wedge, chock, block; prop, strut; shim.

calé, -e [ka'le] *adj.* [Méch.] jammed (piston); [auto] stalled; [Fig. & Fam.]

être ~ /sur, en/un sujet, to be well up on a subject, to be well versed in a subject.
calebasse [kal'bɑ:s] *n.f.* calabash; gourd.
†**calèche** [ka'lɛʃ] *n.f.* barouche.
caleçon [kal'sõ] *n.m.* (men's) shorts, tights; [Fam.] long-Johns.
calembour [kalɑ̃'bu:r] *n.m.* pun, play on words.
calendrier [kalɑ̃dri'je] *n.m.* calendar.
calepin [kal'pɛ̃] *n.m.* notebook: *noter qqch. sur son ~*, to enter sth. into one's notebook.
caler [ka'le] #3 *v. tr.* to block (up), to wedge, to level (a piece of furniture), to clamp, to adjust (a microscope), to prop up (a sick person); to stall (a motor). || *v. intr.* (of a motor) to stall: *le moteur a calé*, the motor stalled.
calfater [kalfa'te] #3 *v. tr.* to caulk.
calfeutrage [kalfø'tr|a:ʒ] *n.m.* [weather] stripping (of a window, a door); blocking, plugging (of cracks and holes). || **calfeutrer** [-e] #3 *v. tr.* to weather-strip (a door, a window), to block, plug (holes, cracks).
calibrage [kali'bra:ʒ] *n.m.* calibration; gauging, calipering. || **calibre** [ka'libr] *n.m.* **1.** calibre, bore (of small arms), size (of a bullet). **2.** [Fig.] quality, calibre (of persons). || **calibrer** [-e] #3 *v. tr.* **1.** to caliper; [measure] to gauge, measure. **2.** [donner le calibre] to calibrate.
calice [ka'lis] *n.m.* **1.** [Rel.] chalice; drinking cup: *vider un ~ amer*, to drink a bitter cup. **2.** [Bot.] calyx.
calicot [kali'ko] *n.m.* calico.
Californie [kalifɔr'ni] *n.f.* California.
califourchon [kalifur'ʃõ] *n.m.* [ne s'emploie que dans la locution] *à ~*, astride, astraddle, © bottom, backside.
câlin, -e [kɑl|ɛ̃, -in] *adj.* winning (child, ways), wheedling, loving. || **câliner** [-i'ne] #3 *v. tr.* to fondle, caress. || **câlinerie** [-in'ri] *n.f.* caressing, fondling, coaxing, cajoling.
calleu|x, -se [ka'l|ø(:z)] *adj.* horny, callous (skin, &c.): *des mains calleuses*, horny hands.
calligraphie [kaligra'fi] *n.f.* calligraphy, penmanship.
callosité [-ozi'te] *n.f.* callosity, callus.
calmant [kal'mɑ̃] *n.m.* sedative. || *adj.* soothing, calming. || **calme** [kalm] *n.m. & adj.* calm; still(ness): *avoir du ~, garder (tout) son ~*, to keep cool, composed; *le ~ plat*, dead calm. || **calmer** #3 *v. tr.* to calm, soothe, pacify: *~ la colère de qqun*, to calm, soothe s.o.'s anger; *~ la douleur*, to relieve pain. || **se calmer** *v. pron.* **1.** [chose] to die down, abate, subside. **2.** [personne] to compose, calm o.s., to recover one's composure: *le vent se calme*, the wind is dying down.
calomniat|eur, -rice [kalɔmn|ja'tœ:r, -ja'tris] *adj.* slanderous, libellous. || *n.* calumniator, slanderer. || **calomnie** [-i] *n.f.* calumny, slander, libel. || **calomnier** [-je] #3 *v. tr.* to slander, libel. || **calomnieu|x, -se** [-jø(:z)] *adj.* slanderous, libellous.
calorie [kalɔ'ri] *n.f.* calorie.
calorifère [kalɔri'fɛ:r] *n.m.* register; © radiator; heating system. || *adj.* heat conveying. || **calorifuger** [kalɔrify'ʒe] #5 *v. tr.* to insulate.
calotte [ka'lɔt] *n.f.* **1.** skullcap (usually worn by the clergy and so by extension has the meaning of) [Fr.] [Péj.] the clergy, the priests, the cloth: *la ~ du crâne*, brainpan. **2.** [Fam.] a tap (on the head), a cuff, a box (on the side of the head). || **calotter** [-e] #3 *v. tr.* to box (s.o.'s ears), to cuff (s.o.).
calque [kalk] *n.m.* tracing: *papier ~*, tracing paper; *faire un ~*, to make a tracing; [Ling.] translation loan-word. || **calquer** [-e] #3 *v. tr.* to trace, copy.
calumet [kaly'mɛ] *n.m.* calumet; pipe: [Fig.] *offrir le ~ de paix*, to/offer, smoke/ a peace pipe.
calvaire [kal'vɛ:r] *n.m.* [Rel.] Calvary; Stations of the Cross.
calvinisme [kalvinis|m] *n.m.* Calvinism. || **calviniste** [-t] *adj.* Calvinistic(al) || *n.* Calvinist.
calvitie [kalvi'si] *n.f.* baldness, cf. CHAUVE.
camarade [kama'rad] *n.m. f.* comrade, (class)mate. || **camaraderie** [-'ri] *n.f.* **1.** comradeship, fellowship, intimacy. **2.** set, clique.
camard, -e [ka'm|a:r, -ard] *adj.* snub-nosed. || **camarde (la)** [-ard] *n.f.* [pop.] death.
Cambodge [kɑ̃'bɔdʒ] *n.m.* Cambodia.
cambouis [kɑ̃'bwi] *n.m.* dirty oil, grease.
cambré, -e [kɑ̃'bre] *adj.* [pied] arched; [taille] shapely. || **cambrer** #3 *v. tr.* [pied] to arch: *~ la taille*, to brace o.s. up.
cambriolage [kɑ̃brijɔ'l|a:ʒ] *n.m.* burglary, house-breaking. || **cambrioler** [-e] #3 *v. tr.* to burglarize, to break into (a building), to ransack. || **cambrioleur** [-œ:r] *n.m.* burglar.
cambrure [kɑ̃'bry:r] *n.f.* arch; instep (of the foot); curve (of back); camber (of wood).
cambuse [kɑ̃'by:z] *n.f.* [chantier] canteen; [Naut.] storeroom; [Fam.] hovel.

came [kam] *n.f.* cam: *arbre à* ~, camshaft.
camée [ka'me] *n.m.* cameo.
caméléon [kamele'õ] *n.m.* chameleon.
camélia [kame'lja] *n.m.* camellia.
camelot [kam'lo] *n.m.* cheap (woollen) cloth; [ext.] seller (of cheap goods), huckster; newsboy, newspaper vendor.
camelote [kam'lɔt] *n.f.* junk, trash, cheap goods; (poorly constructed) house.
caméra [kame'ra] *n.f.* cine- or T.V.-camera [×] cf. APPAREIL.
camion [ka'mj|õ] *n.m.* [avec moteur] truck; [Br.] lorry; ~ *à chevaux*, wagon. || **camionnage** [-ɔ'na:ʒ] *n.m.* **1.** [entreprise] trucking trade, business; cartage and hauling. **2.** trucking/cartage, freight/ charges. || **camionnette** [-ɔ'nɛt] *n.f.* light truck, delivery van. || **camionneur** [-ɔ'nœ:r] *n.m.* truck-driver; teamster; truck(ing) contractor: *Syndicat des Camionneurs*, Teamster(s') Union.
camisole [kami'zɔl] *n.f.* bedjacket; © undershirt: ~ *de force*, straitjacket.
camomille [kamɔ'mi:j] *n.f.* camomile; [tisane] camomile tea.
camouflage [kamu'fl|a:ʒ] *n.m.* camouflage, disguising. || **camoufler** [-e] #3 *v. tr.* to disguise, camouflage.
camp [kã] *n.m.* camp (site): *asseoir, planter/le* ~, to pitch camp; *lever le* ~, to/strike, break/camp; © ~ *d'été*, summer cottage; [Fam.] *ficher le* ~, to scram.
campagnard, -e [kãpaɲ|a:r, -ard] *n.* countryman, -woman, hillbilly, rustic, peasant. || *adj.* backwoods, rustic. || **campagne** [kã'paɲ] *n.f.* **1.** country; field: *à la* ~, in the country; *de* ~, from the country, rural; *en rase* ~, out in the open; *battre la* ~, to scour the country (for). **2.** [Fig.] campaign: ~ *électorale*, election campaign.
campagnol [kãpa'ɲɔl] *n.m.* field mouse.
campanule [kãpa'nyl] *n.f.* bluebell.
campement [kãp|'mã] *n.m.* camping; encampment; camp ground. || **camper** [-e] #3 *v. intr.* to camp; to set up, pitch camp. *v. tr.* [Fam.] to fix, to place firmly: ~ *son chapeau sur sa tête*, to jam one's hat on one's head. || **se camper** *v. pron.* to plant o.s. || **campeu|r, -se** [-œ:r, -ø:z] *n.* camper.
camphre [kã:fr] *n.m.* camphor.
camping [kã'piŋ] *n.m.* [Fr.] camping; camp ground: *faire du* ~, to go camping.
campus [kã'pys] © *n.m.* campus,* domaine *m* universitaire.
camus, -e [ka'my(:z)] *adj.* snub(-nosed), pug(-nosed).

Canada [kana'd|a] *n.m.* **1.** Canada [personnalisé au feminin en anglais]: Canada will have her hands full . . ., le Canada aura de quoi s'occuper. **2.** Canadian: *pommes du* ~, Canadian apples; *le consul du* ~, the Canadian consul; [Hist.] *au* ~ [†*en* ~], in Canada; *le Bas-* ~, Lower Canada; *le Haut-* ~, Upper Canada; *Le premier gouverneur général du* ~, Canada's first Governor General; *le* ~ */français, anglais/*, French, English/ (speaking) Canada. || **canadien, -ne** [kanad|-jɛ̃, -jɛn] *n.* Canadian, © French-Canadian; *les Canadiens français*, the French Canadians. || *n.f.* [Fr.] storm coat; station wagon; (birch bark) canoe. || *adj.* Canadian: *ma femme est canadienne*, → my wife is a Canadian; *du (fromage)/* ~, *doux/*, mild Canadian (cheese).
canaille [ka'nɑ:j] *n.f.* [coll.] rabble, riffraff, mob; [une personne seulement] rascal, rogue, villain.
can|al, -aux [ka'n|al, -o] *n.m.* **1.** canal, channel; © TV channel: *le* ~ *Welland*, the Welland canal. **2.** pipe, conduit, tube. **3.** [Fig.] channel, means. || **canalisation** [-aliza'sjõ] *n.f.* canalization (of a river): ~ *du gaz naturel*, laying the mains for natural gas. || **canaliser** [-ali'ze] #3 *v. tr.* **1.** to canalize; [Fig.] to guide in a single direction. **2.** to transport (by pipe, &c.): ~ *du pétrole*, to/pipe, ship/oil by pipe line. **3.** [Fig.] to/direct, channel/(people): ~ *des spectateurs*, to direct the spectators.
canapé [kana'pe] *n.m.* sofa, settee; [Culin.] canapé.
canard [ka'n|a:r] *n.m.* **1.** duck; [male] drake. **2.** [Fam.] false news; hoax: *lancer un* ~, to spread false news. || **canardière** [-ar'djɛ:r] *n.f.* duck pond; [la chasse] (duck) blind; shotgun (for shooting ducks).
canari [kana'ri] *n.m.* canary. || **Canarie** [kana'ri] *n.f.* Canary: *les (Iles) Canaries*, the Canary Islands, the Canaries.
Canayen, -ne [kana'j|ɛ̃, -ɛn] © *adj.* [Fam.] Canuck.
cancan [kã'kã] *n.m.* gossip; tittle-tattle. || **cancaner** [kãka'ne] #3 *v. intr.* to gossip; to dance the cancan.
cancer [kã'sɛ:r] *n.m.* cancer: *avoir un* ~, to have cancer; *souffrir du* ~, to suffer from cancer.
cancre [kã:kr] *n.m.* [Fam.] dunce, good-for-nothing.
candeur [kã'dœ:r] *n.f.* candour, ingenuousness; artlessness, guilelessness, purity.
candidat [kãdi'da] *n.m.* candidate: *choisir*,

élire/un ~, to/choose, elect/a candidate; *être* ~ *à*, to be a candidate for. ‖ **candidature** [-'ty:r] *n.f.* candidacy: *poser sa* ~ *à un poste*, → to/apply, make application/ for a position; *poser sa* ~ *au poste de . . .*, → to apply for . . . ; *faire acte de* ~, to become a candidate.

candide [kɑ̃'did] *adj.* ingenuous, candid; artless, guileless, pure. ‖ **candidement** [-'mɑ̃] *adv.* candidly, openly, frankly; artlessly, guilelessly.

cane [kan] *n.f.* (female) duck. ‖ **caneton** [-'tɔ̃] *n.m.* duckling.

canette [ka'nɛt] *n.f.* [machine à coudre] spool; beer bottle; © ~ *de bière*, can of beer.

canevas [kan'vɑ] *n.m.* **1.** backing cloth (for rugs, tapestry, &c.). **2.** plan, sketch, outline (of a literary work).

caniche [ka'niʃ] *n.m.* poodle.

canicule [kani'kyl] *n.f.* canicule; dogdays.

canif [ka'nif] *n.m.* penknife, pocket knife.

canine [ka'nin] *n.f.* canine (tooth). ‖ *adj.* canine, of dogs: *exposition* ~, dog show.

canne [kan] *n.f.* cane, walking stick; reed, cane: ~ *à sucre*, sugar cane; ~ *à pêche*, fishing rod.

cannelle [ka'nɛl] *n.f.* **1.** cinnamon. **2.** spigot, spout.

cannelure [kan'ly:r] *n.f.* groove, slot, channel; [Arch.] flute, fluting.

cannibale [kani'bal] *adj.* [peuplade] cannibal; man-eating; cannibalistic. ‖ *n.m.* cannibal. ‖ **cannibalisme** [-ism] *n.m.* cannibalism.

canoë [kanɔ'e] © [ka'no] *n.m.* [Fr.] canoe [in Canada use CANOT].

canon[1] [ka'no] *n.m.* **1.** [Artil.] cannon. **2.** barrel (of gun), cylinder (of a key, lock). **3.** (small) glass (of wine): *boire un* ~, to drink a glass of wine. **4.** [Zool.] cannon bone (of horses, &c.).

canon[2] [ka'nõ] *n.m.* [Rel.] canon: *droit* ~, canon law. ‖ **canonique** [kanɔ'ni|k] *adj.* canonical. ‖ **canoniser** [-'ze] #3 *v. tr.* to canonize (a saint).

canonnade [kanɔ'n|ad] *n.f.* gunfire, cannonade. ‖ **canonner** [-e] #3 *v. tr.* to cannonade, to shell. ‖ **canonnier** [-je] *n.m.* gunner. ‖ **canonnière** [-jɛ:r] *n.f.* gunboat.

canot [ka'n|o] *n.m.* [Naut.] boat; © canoe: © ~ *de maître*, Montreal canoe, freighter canoe; © ~ *d'York*, York boat; ~ *de sauvetage*, lifeboat; ~ *pneumatique*, rubber liferaft, lifeboat. ‖ **canotage** [-ɔ'ta:ʒ] *n.m.* boating, rowing, © canoeing: *faire du* ~, to go boating.

cantaloup [kɑ̃ta'lup] *n.m.* cantaloup.

cantate [kɑ̃'tat] *n.f.* cantata.

cantatrice [kɑ̃ta'tris] *n.f.* (professional) singer.

cantine [kɑ̃'tin] *n.f.* [Mil.] canteen; officer's chest, kitbag.

cantique [kɑ̃'tik] *n.m.* hymn, (sacred) song.

canton [kɑ̃'t|õ] *n.m.* canton, district; © township: *les Cantons de l'Est*, the Eastern Townships. ‖ **cantonal, -e** [-ɔ'nal] *adj.* district. ‖ **cantonnement** [-ɔn'mɑ̃] *n.m.* **1.** billeting, quartering (of troops); billets, quarters. ‖ **cantonner** [-ɔ'ne] #3 *v. tr.* to billet [soldiers]. ‖ **se cantonner** *v. pron.* [Fig.] to confine o.s. to (*à*), to limit o.s. to. ‖ **cantonnier** [kɑ̃tɔ'nje] *n.m.* roadman, roadmender; [Rail.] section man.

caoutchouc [kaut'ʃu] *n.m.* rubber; rubber goods: *bottes de* ~, rubber, gum/boots; *imperméable en* ~, rubber raincoat; *caoutchoucs, mpl.*, rubbers, cf. PARDESSUS. ‖ **caoutchouter** [-'te] #3 *v. tr.* to rubberize.

cap [kap] *n.m.* **1.** cape, headland: *le* ~ *Breton*, Cape Breton; *île du Cap-Breton*, Cape Breton Island; *franchir, doubler/ un* ~, to round a cape; [Fig.] *le* ~ *de la quarantaine*, the age of forty. **2.** head, course: *mettre le* ~ *sur*, to head, steer/ for; *mettre le* ~ *au large*, to head out to sea. **3.** *armé de pied en* ~, armed from head to toe.

capable [ka'pabl] *adj.* **1.** able, capable; qualified, competent; © skilled: *un homme très* ~, a very able man. **2.** [© ☞ often used instead of POUVOIR, SAVOIR]: *Je ne suis pas* ~ = *Je ne peux pas*; *Je ne sais pas*, I can't; I don't know how. ‖ **capacité** [kapasi'te] *n.f.* **1.** capacity [battery; vase, measure, &c.]: *Ce récipient a une* ~ *d'un gallon*, This container holds one gallon. **2.** aptitude, capacity, talent.

cape [kap] *n.f.* **1.** cape, (hooded) cloak: *sous* ~, secretly, in secret; *rire sous* ~, to laugh up one's sleeve; *film de* ~ *et d'épée*, cloak-and-dagger/film, show/.

capillaire [kapi'l|ɛ:r] *adj.* capillary. ‖ **capillarité** [-ari'te] *n.f.* capillarity.

capitaine [kapi'tɛn] *n.m.* captain; [Naut., Fam.] skipper.

capital [kapi'tal] *n.m.* assets, capital, principal: ~ *et intérêt*, principal and interest; *s'établir avec de minces capitaux*, to start out on a shoestring. ‖ *adj.* essential, chief, principal, fundamental, basic: *un fait* ~, a very important fact, an essential point; *d'une importance capitale*, of paramount importance; *la peine capitale*, death penalty.

capitale [kapi'tal] *n.f.* **1.** capital (city). **2.** [Print.] capital (letter) [☞ for handwriting use MAJUSCULE]. || **capitaliser** [-i'ze] #3 *v. tr.* to capitalize; to save (money). || **capitalisme** [-ism] *n.m.* capitalism.

capiteu|x, -se [kapi'tø(:z)] *adj.* [vin] heady; [Fig.] sensuous, exciting.

capitonner [kapitɔ'ne] #3 *v. tr.* to pad; to quilt, upholster (chairs, &c.).

capitulation [kapityl|a'sjõ] *n.f.* capitulation, surrender (on certain terms): ~ *sans conditions*, unconditional surrender. || **capituler** [-e] #3 *v. intr.* to capitulate, surrender.

caporal [kapɔ'r|al, -o] *n.m.* [Mil.] corporal; (coarse) tobacco, shag: *Le Petit Caporal* [nickname given to Napoleon], the Little Corporal.

capot [ka'po] *n.m.* [Auto.] hood, [Br.] bonnet; [Naut.] tarpaulin; cowling (of airplane); © ~ *de chat*, (man's) greatcoat, coonskin coat.

capote [ka'pɔt] *n.f.* [esp. Mil.] greatcoat; [Auto.] top, [Br.] hood.

capoter [kapɔ'te] #3 *v. intr.* to capsize, overturn.

caprice [ka'pris] *n.m.* caprice, fancy, whim: *céder aux caprices d'un enfant*, to give in to the/whims, fancies/of a child. || **capricieu|x, -se** [-jø(:z)] *adj.* capricious, moody.

capsule [kap'syl] *n.f.* **1.** cap, seal (of bottle). **2.** [Méd.] capsule. **3.** [Mil.] primer, (percussion) cap.

capter [kap'te] #3 *v. tr.* **1.** to receive, to pick up, to intercept: ~ *l'image*, to pick up, receive/a picture; ~ *un son à la radio*, to pick up a sound over the radio. **2.** to dam up, to harness: ~ *une rivière*, to harness a river. **3.** [Fig.] to obtain (by undue influence), to win (s.o.) over.

captieu|x, -se [kap'sjø(:z)] *adj.* captious, specious.

capti|f, -ve [kap't|if, -i:v] *adj.* captive: *tenir* ~ , to keep s.o. in captivity. || *n. m/f.* captive, prisoner. || **captivant, -e** [-i'vɑ̃(:t)] *adj.* thrilling, (very) interesting, engrossing: *une lecture captivante*, an interesting/book, article, &c./. || **captiver** [-i've] #3 *v. tr.* to captivate, to hold the interest: ~ *un auditoire*, to hold an audience's interest. || **captivité** [-ivi'te] *n.f.* captivity, †bondage.

capture [kap't|y:r] *n.f.* capture, seizure; [the thing seized] prize. || **capturer** [-y're] #3 *v. tr.* to capture; [person] to arrest.

capuchon [kapy'ʃõ] *n.m.* hood (of coat, parka); cap (of a pen).

capucin [kapy'sɛ̃] *n.m.* [Rel.] Capuchin (friar).

capucine [kapy'sin] *n.f.* nasturtium.

caquet [ka'k|ɛ] *n.m.* cackle, cackling (of hens), chatter (of magpies); [persons] chatter: gift of the gab; [Loc.] *rabattre le* ~ *à qqun*, to take a person down a notch. || **caquetage** [kak'ta:ʒ] *n.m.* [hens] cackling; [Pers.] chatter. || **caqueter** [-'te] #8 *v. intr.* to cackle (of hens); [Fig.] to chatter noisily, to gossip.

car[1] [ka:r] *conj.* [☞ Always at the beginning of sentence or clause] for, because; as.

car[2] [ka:r] [Fr.] *n.m.* [= *autocar*] (intercity) bus; (sight-seeing) bus [for a city bus, use AUTOBUS].

carabin [kara'bɛ̃] © *n.m.* [Fam.] university student; college boy [the feminine form is *poutchinette*]; [Fr.] medical student, medic.

carabine [kara'bin] *n.f.* carbine, rifle: ~ *à air comprimé*, air gun, air rifle.

carabiné, -e [karabi'ne] *adj.* [Fam.] strong, stiff (drink); violent (fever).

caracoler [karakɔ'le] #3 *v. intr.* [cheval] to prance.

caractère [karak't|ɛ:r] *n.m.* **1.** [Impr.] character, letter, symbol; [movable] type. **2.** characteristic, feature, stamp: *Les caractères dominants de la race humaine*, The dominant features of the human race; [☞ Utilisez le nom abstrait] *le* ~ *français de . . .*, Frenchness. **3.** nature, disposition, character: *sortir de son* ~ , [Fam.] to go off one's rocker; *avoir un* ~ *entier*, to be categorical; *avoir de la force de* ~ , to have strength of character; *le* ~ *facile d'une personne*, the good humour, good-naturedness of a person; *avoir un bon* ~ , to be good-natured. **4.** title, official capacity: *en* ~ *de*, in the capacity of. || **caractériser** [-eri'ze] #3 *v. tr.* to characterize, distinguish, mark, be peculiar to (sth., s.o.). || **se caractériser** *v. pron.* to take on, assume/a character; to be/distinguishable, distinguished/by. || **caractéristique** [-eris'tik] *n.f.* distinguishing, salient, typical/feature.

carafe [ka'raf] *n.f.* decanter, [glass] water bottle. || **carafon** [-õ] *n.m.* (small) decanter for wine.

Caraïbes (mer des) [(mɛr de) kara'ib] *n.* the Caribbean Sea. cf. ANTILLES.

caramel [kara'mɛl] *n.m.* caramel, burnt sugar: ~ *au beurre*, butterscotch.

carapace [kara'pas] *n.f.* [tortoise, &c.] shell.

caravane [kara'van] *n.f.* caravan; party (of

conducted tourists); convoy; [Fr.] [camping] trailer.

carbonate [karbɔ'nat] *n.m.* carbonate.

carbone [kar'bɔn] *n.m.* carbon: *papier* ~, carbon paper. || **carbonique** [-ik] *adj. acide* ~, carbonic acid. || **carboniser** [-i'ze] #3 *v. tr.* to carbonize (bones), to char (wood); to burn.

carburant [karby'rɑ̃] *n.m.* fuel (for motors).

carburateur [karbyra'tœ:r] *n.m.* carburettor.

carcajou [karka'ʒu] *n.m.* © wolverine, glutton cf. GLOUTON [= blaireau *m* du Labrador].

carcasse [kar'kas] *n.f.* **1.** carcass. **2.** framework (of sth.), shell, skeleton, body.

cardage [kar'd|a:ʒ] *n.m.* carding. || **carder** [-e] #3 *v. tr.* to card, comb out.

cardiaque [kar'djak] *adj.* & *n.* cardiac: *crise* ~, heart attack.

cardinal, -e [kardi'n|al, -o] *adj.* cardinal, chief: *nombres cardinaux*, cardinal numbers; *vertus cardinales*, cardinal virtues; *points cardinaux*, cardinal points. || *n.m.* [Rel.] cardinal.

cardiographe [kardjɔ'graf] *n.m.* cardiograph. || **cardiologie** [kardjɔlɔ'ʒi] *n.f.* cardiology.

carême [ka'rɛ:m] *n.m.* [Rel.] Lent; (Lenten) fast: *faire son* ~, to keep Lent; [Fig.] *face, figure/de* ~, long, mournful/face.

carence [ka'rɑ̃:s] *n.f.* **1.** insolvency; [Fig.] shirking (of one's responsibilities), neglect (of children by parents). **2.** [Méd.] deficiency: *maladie par* ~, deficiency disease.

carène [ka'rɛn] *n.f.* [Naut.] keel.

caressant, -e [karɛ'sɑ̃(:)t] *adj.* caressing: *enfant* ~, affectionate, loving/child. || **caresse** [ka'rɛs] *n.f.* caress, pat: *faire des caresses à un chien*, to pat, fondle a dog. || **caresser** [-e] #3 *v. tr.* to pat, caress; to fondle, stroke (an animal): [Fig.] ~ *qqun du regard*, to look fondly at s.o.; ~ *une idée*, to entertain an idea.

cargaison [karg|ɛ'zɔ̃] *n.f.* cargo; freight: *embarquer la* ~, to load the cargo; ~ *mixte*, general cargo. || **cargo** [-o] *n.m.* [×] cargo boat, freighter; tramp (steamer).

caribou [kari'bu] *n.m.* © caribou: [Fam.] © *du petit* ~, "moose-milk," white biddy.

caricature [karika't|y:r] *n.f.* caricature. || **caricaturer** [-y're] #3 *v. tr.* to caricature, ridicule. || **caricaturiste** [-y'rist] *n.m.* caricaturist.

carie [ka'r|i] *n.f.* decay, caries (of teeth); blight (of plants): ~ *dentaire*, dental caries. || **carié, -e** [-je] *adj.* bad, carious, decayed (teeth); blighted (plant).

carillon [kari'j|ɔ̃] *n.m.* chime, carillon; pealing, chiming (of bells, carillon). || **carillonner** [-ɔ'ne] #3 *v. intr.* to ring, play/the chimes; [Fam.] to ring (a bell) loudly: ~ *à la porte*, to lean on the doorbell. || *v. tr.* to announce (with a peal of bells). || **carillonneur** [-ɔ'nœ:r] *n.m.* bellringer.

carlingue [kar'lɛ̃:g] *n.f.* cockpit.

carme, *nf.* **carmélite** [karm(e'lit)] *n.m.* [Rel.] carmelite.

carmin [kar'mɛ̃] *n.m.* carmine, crimson: *laque f carminée*, carmine.

carnage [kar'na:ʒ] *n.m.* carnage, massacre, slaughter.

carnassi|er, -ère [karna'sj|e, ɛ:r] *adj.* carnivorous, flesh-eating (animal). || *n.mpl.* carnivorous animals, carnivora. || **carnassière** [karna'sjɛ:r] *n.f.* game-bag.

carnation [karna'sjɔ̃] *n.f.* flesh/tint, colour/.

carnaval [karna'v|al] *pl.* **carnavals** [-al] *n.m.* carnival.

carnet [kar'nɛ] *n.m.* notebook; book (of tickets): ~ *de banque*, bank book; ~ *de chèques*, cheque book; ~ *de commandes*, order book; ~ *de bord*, log book.

carnivore [karni'vɔ:r] *adj.* carnivorous. || *n.m.* carnivore.

Carole [ka'rɔl] *n.f.* Carol.

Caroline du Nord, du Sud, la *n.f.* North, South/Carolina.

carotte [ka'rɔt] *n.f.* carrot; [Fig.] *tirer une* ~ *à qqun*, to trick s.o. out of his money. || *adj. inv.* red, carrotty: *avoir les cheveux* ~, [Fam.] to be carrots. || **carotte-à-Moreau** © *n.f.* musquash root, cowbane.

carpe [karp] *n.f.* **1.** [poisson] carp; © ~ *à cochons*, sucker; *faire un saut de* ~, to turn a somersault. **2.** [Méd.] wrist, carpus.

carpette [kar'pɛt] *n.f.* (throw)rug. [× for carpet, use TAPIS.]

carquois [kar'kwa] *n.m.* quiver.

carré, -e [ka're, © kɑ're] *adj.* **1.** square, square-built, squared: *épaules carrées*, square, broad/shoulders; © *danse carrée*, square dance. **2.** downright: ~ *en affaires*, straightforward, direct in business. **3.** [Math.] square: *racine carrée*, square root; *pied* ~, square foot. || *n.m.* **1.** square: *le* ~ *d'un nombre*, the square of a number. **2.** landing (of a staircase). cf. PALIER. **3.** [Naut.] officers' mess, quarters. **4.** patch: ~ *de choux*, cabbage patch; © square [in a town].

carreau [ka'ro, © kɑ'ro] *n.m.* **1.** tile, flag: ~ *en pierre*, flagstone. **2.** windowpane, glass. **3.** checks: *une étoffe à carreaux*, a checked cloth [© = *carreauté*]. **4.** [cards] diamonds. **5.** mine head. **6.** floor (of a room, &c.): *~ des halles*, market square; *coucher sur le ~*, to sleep on the floor; [Fam.] *demeurer sur le ~*, to be killed on the spot.

carrefour [kar'fu:r] *n.m.* crossroads; traffic circle; intersection; [Fig.] *être au ~*, to be at a parting of the ways. || **carrefours** *n.mpl.* forum, symposium.

carrelage [kar'l|a:ʒ] *n.m.* tiling, (tiled) flooring. || **carreler** [-e] #8 *v. tr.* to lay tiles, flagstones (to make a floor).

carrément [kare'mɑ̃] *adv.* squarely; [Fig.] firmly, directly, bluntly, in a straightforward manner: *couper qqch. ~*, to cut sth. on the square, squarely; *répondre ~*, to reply frankly, directly; bluntly.

carrer [ka're] #3 *v. tr.* to square (a number, a board). || **se carrer** *v. pron.* to plunk o.s. down (in a chair); to ensconce o.s.

carrière[1] [ka'rjɛ:r] *n.f.* **1.** career, profession; course: *embrasser la ~ de médecin*, to choose medicine as a profession. **2.** free rein: *donner ~ à un cheval*, to give a horse a free rein; *donner libre ~ à son imagination*, to give one's fancy a free rein; *se donner ~*, to let o.s. go.

carrière[2] [ka'rjɛ:r] *n.m.* (stone) quarry.

carriole [kɑ'rjɔl] *n.f.* light cart; carryall, carriole; © sled.

carrossable [karɔ'sabl] *adj.*: *route ~*, carriage road. || **carrosse** [ka'rɔs] *n.m.* statecoach, coach; © pram, baby-carriage. || **carrosserie** [-'ri] *n.f.* body [esp. auto body].

carrure [ka'ry:r] *n.f.* breadth (of shoulders): *homme d'une belle ~*, well-built, broad-shouldered/man.

cartable [kar'tabl] *n.m.* [d'écolier] satchel.

carte [kart] *n.f.* **1.** card: *~ de crédit*, credit card; *~ d'identité*, identity card; *~ de visite*, visiting card; *~ postale*, postcard. **2.** [jeu de société] card: *jouer aux cartes*, *faire une partie de cartes*, to play cards; [Fig.] *cartes sur table*, aboveboard; *abattre ses cartes*, to show one's hand; *tirer les cartes*, to tell fortunes. **3.** menu: *à la ~*, à la carte; *Puis-je voir la ~ ?*, May I see the menu?; *~ des vins*, wine list. **4.** map, chart: *dresser la ~ d'une région*, to map/an area, a region/; *~ marine*, chart.

cartel [kar'tɛl] *n.m.* cartel, trust; monopoly.

cartilage [karti'la:ʒ] *n.m.* cartilage; gristle.

cartographie [kartɔgra'fi] *n.f.* cartography, map making.

carton [kar'tõ] *n.m.* **1.** cardboard; cardboard box: *~ à chapeau*, hatbox; [Art] *~ à dessin*, portfolio. **2.** sketch (for a larger work). **3.** target (of cardboard): *faire un ~*, to fill a target.

cartouche [kar'tuʃ] *n.f.* shell, round (of ammunition), cartridge: *~ à blanc*, blank cartridge. || *n.m.* inset.

cas [kɑ] *n.m.* **1.** case, occasion, situation, circumstance, instance: *~ semblable*, similar/case, situation/; *le ~ échéant*, should the occasion arise, in case of need; *en ce ~*, in/this, that/case; *C'est le ~ ou jamais*, It's now or never; *C'est bien le ~ de le dire*, You said it; *être dans le ~ de*, to be likely to; *en ~ d'alarme*, at a time of emergency; *au ~ contraire*, if not, otherwise; *En cas de non-distribution, prière de retourner à . . .*, If not delivered, please return to . . . **2.** [Jur.] case, crime, process: *se mettre dans un mauvais ~*, to get mixed up in an illegal affair. **3.** [Méd.] case: *plusieurs ~ de poliomyélite*, several cases of poliomyelitis. **4.** [Gram.] case. **5.** question: *~ de conscience*, moral, religious/question. **6.** [Loc.] *faire ~ de qqch.*, to appreciate, value/sth., to take sth. into account; *faire grand ~ de*, to place a lot of/value, importance/ on . . . ; *faire peu de ~ de*, to place little/value, importance/on . . . ; *se faire un ~ de conscience de faire qqch.*, to make it a matter of honour to do sth. **7.** [Loc. adv.] *en tout cas*, in any case; *en ~ que*, *au ~ où*, in case that, if that is the case; *dans, pour/le ~ où*, in the event of.

casani|er, -ère [kaza'nj|e, -ɛ:r] *adj.* stay-at-home.

cascade [kas'kad] *n.f.* cascade, waterfall. [× smaller than CHUTE].

case [ka:z] *n.f.* **1.** hut, cabin, shanty, small house: *la ~ de l'Oncle Tom*, Uncle Tom's Cabin. **2.** square (of a chequerboard); (mail) box; pigeonhole, section (of a shelf), blank square (on a paper); [Fig.] *Il lui manque une ~*, He has a screw loose.

caser [kɑ'ze] #3 *v. tr.* **1.** to put away (in a drawer), to store away: *~ du linge*, to put away the linen. **2.** [Fig.] to place; to find work for; [Fam.] *Elle a trois filles à ~*, She has three daughters to marry off. || **se caser** *v. pron.* to settle down, to find a home.

caserne [ka'zɛrn] *n.f.* barracks, station. || **caserner** [-e] #3 *v. tr.* to accommodate in barracks.

casier [ka'zje] © [kɑ'zje] *n.m.* [piece of furniture made up of pigeonholes]: *~ à* *bouteilles*, bottle rack; *casiers d'une malle*, trays of a trunk; ~ *à homards*, lobster pot; [Jur.] ~ *judiciaire*, police record.

casino [kazi'no] *n.m.* casino, gambling house.

Caspienne (la mer) [kas'pjɛn] *n.f.* The Caspian Sea.

casque [kask] *n.m.* helmet; © fur cap; [Fam.] ~ *à mèche*, night cap. || **casquette** [-ɛt] *n.f.* cap.

cassable [kɑ'sabl] *adj.* breakable.

cassant, -e [kɑ'sɑ̃] *adj.* **1.** brittle (china). **2.** [Fig.] curt, abrupt (tone). || **casse** [kɑ:s] *n.f.* breakage, damage; break, sharp splinters: *payer la* ~ , to pay the breakage; *faire de la* ~ , to damage, break (a lot of things). **3.** [Typ.] case: *haut de* ~ , upper case, *bas de* ~ , lower case. || **cassé, -e** [kɑ'se] *adj.* weak, trembling, infirm: *voix cassée*, weak, trembling voice; *vieillard tout* ~ , broken old man; © [*abus.*] broke, without money.

casse-cou [kɑs'ku] *n.m. inv.* deathtrap, dangerous place, corner.

casse-croûte [kɑs'krut] *n.m. inv.* lunch, snack, sandwich; © snack bar.

casser [kɑ'se] #3 *v. tr.* **1.** to break, to shatter, crush: [Fig. & Fam.] ~ *la croûte*, to have, grab/a snack, bite; ~ *la figure, le cou/à qqun*, to beat s.o. up; [Fig.] ~ *sa pipe*, to die. **2.** [Jur.] to break: ~ *un testament*, to break a will; [Mil.] to break (s.o. in rank); © ~ *le français*, to speak broken French. || **se casser** *v. pron.* to break, to give way, to snap: [Fig. & Fam.] ~ *la tête*, to rack one's brain; ~ *la voix*, to ruin one's voice.

casserole [kas'rɔl] *n.f.* casserole, saucepan.

casse-tête [kɑs'tɛ:t] *n.m. inv.* **1.** war-club. **2.** [Fig.] difficult problem, headache; © crossword puzzle: *C'est un* ~ *chinois*, It's all Greek (to me).

cassette [ka'sɛt] *n.f.* casket, case; money-box: ~ *à bijoux*, jewel case.

cassis [ka'si(s)] *n.m. inv.* **1.** black currant (bush). **2.** [on Fr. roads] bump.

cassonade [kasɔ'nad] *n.f.* brown sugar.

cassot [kɑ'so] *n.m.* © [cornet d'écorce] cornet; screw (of bark).

cassure [kɑ'sy:r] *n.f.* crack, break; [Tech.] fracture, fissure; [Fig.] rupture, break-up: ~ *dans une amitié*, a rupture in a friendship.

castagnettes [kasta'ɲɛt] *n.fpl.* castanets.

caste [kast] *n.f.* caste.

castor [kas'tɔ:r] *n.m.* beaver: *digue f de* ~ , beaver dam; © [Hist.] beaver [a coin].

casuel, -le [ka'zɥɛl] *adj.* casual, contingent. || *n.m.* casual, contingent (income).

cataclysme [kata'klism] *n.m.* cataclysm, disaster.

catalogue [kata'lɔg] *n.m.* catalogue [for college or university catalogues, use *annuaire m*, or *programme m*]: *Demandez notre* ~ , → Write for, Phone for/our catalogue. || **cataloguer** [-e] #3 *v. tr.* to catalogue, list.

cataplasme [kata'plasm] *n.m.* poultice.

catapulte [kata'pylt] *n.m.* catapult.

cataracte [kata'rakt] *n.f.* **1.** cataract, falls: *les* ~ *du Nil*, the Cataracts of the Nile. **2.** [Méd.] cataract (of the eyes).

catarrhe [ka'ta:r] *n.m.* catarrh.

catastrophe [katas'trɔf] *n.f.* catastrophe, calamity, cataclysm.

catéchiser [kateʃi|'ze] #3 *v. tr.* [Rel.] to catechize; [Fig.] to try to convince, to reason with. || **catéchisme** [-sm] *n.m.* catechism.

catéchumène [kateky'mɛn] *n.* [Rel.] catechumen.

catégorie [kategɔ'ri] *n.f.* category, class. || **catégorique** [-k] *adj.* categorical: *opposer un refus* ~ *(à)*, to counter with a flat refusal.

caténaire [kate'nɛ:r] *adj.* connected (in a series): *réaction* ~ , chain reaction.

cathédrale [kate'dral] *n.f.* cathedral.

catherinette [katri'nɛt] © *n.f.* blackberry.

cathode [ka'tɔd] *n.f.* cathode. || **cathodique** [-ik] *adj.* cathodic: *rayons cathodiques*, cathode rays.

catholicisme [katoli'si|sm] *n.m.* Catholicism. || **catholicité** [-'te] *n.f.* catholicity, Catholicism. || **catholique** [katɔ'lik] *adj.* & *n.* Catholic, Roman Catholic, R.C.; [Fam.] *Ce n'est pas* ~ , It doesn't/look, sound/right.

Caucase (le) [ko'ka:z] *n.m.* Caucasus.

cauchemar [koʃ'mɑ:r] *n.m.* nightmare.

caucus [ko'kys] *n.m.* © caucus.

causal, -e [ko'zal] *adj.* causal, causative. || **causalité** [-i'te] *n.f.* causality: *principe de* ~ , law of cause and effect.

causant, -e [ko'zɑ̃(:t)] *adj.* talkative, chatty.

cause [ko:z] *n.f.* **1.** cause, motive, interest: *agir sans* ~ , to act without reason, motive; *à* ~ *de*, on account of, because of, owing to; *et pour* ~ , for a very good reason, with good reason; *questions hors de* ~ , questions (which are) beside the point, irrelevant questions. **2.** [Jur.] lawsuit, case, action: *faire* ~ *commune avec qqun*, to stand by s.o., to make common cause with s.o.; *avoir gain de* ~ , to win a case; *mettre qqun en* ~ , to implicate s.o.

causer [ko'z|e] #3 *v. tr.* **1.** to cause. **2.** to

chat, to converse: *On en cause,* People are talking. || **causerie** [-'ri] *n.f.* (informal) talk, lecture: *souper-~*, dinner-meeting. || **causette**[-ɛt] [Fam.] *n.f.* little chat, conversation: *faire la ~ avec qqun*, to pass the time of day with s.o. || **causeu|r, -se** [-œ:r, -ø:z] *adj.* talkative, chatty. || *n.*: *un brillant ~*, a brilliant speaker. || *n.f. causeuse,* sofa, small settee.

caustique [kos'tik] *adj.* [Méd.] caustic, corrosive; [Fig.] cutting, biting.

cauteleu|x, -se [kot'lø(:z)] *adj.* wily, cunning; wary: *esprit ~*, cunning mind.

cautériser [koteri'ze] #3 *v. tr.* to cauterize, to sear (a wound).

caution [ko'sj|õ] *n.f.* [Jur.] bail, guarantee; [Fin.] security, collateral: *être ~ de qqun,* to vouch for s.o.; *se porter ~ pour: qqun,* to go bail for s.o.; *sujet à ~*, unreliable. || **cautionnement** [-ɔn'mã] *n.m.* [Com.] caution money; [Jur.] surety bond, guaranty.

cavalcade [kaval'kad] *n.f.* cavalcade, procession.

cavalerie [kava|l'ri] *n.f.* cavalry. || **cavalier** [-'lje] *n.m.* †cavalier; horseman; [Mil.] cavalryman; [Fam.] © boy friend; [danse] partner.

cave [ka:v] *n.f.* cellar; wine cellar; © [cards] stake: *perdre sa ~*, to lose one's stake. || *adj.* hollow, sunken. || **caveau** [ka'vo] *n.m.* burial vault.

caverne [ka'vɛrn] *n.f.* cave, cavern: *homme m des cavernes,* cave man. || **caverneu|x, -se** [-ø(:z)] *adj.* **1.** cavernous. **2.** [voix] hollow, deep.

caviar [ka'vja:r] *n.m.* caviar.

cavité [kavi'te] *n.f.* cavity, hollow.

Cayes (Les) de (la) Floride [kaj] *n.fpl.* (The) Florida Keys.

ce[1] [sə]; **c'** + vowels. **(A)** *pron. dém.* **1.** [choses] this, that; these, those: *C'est ma maison,* This is my house; *Ce sont des érables,* Those are maples. **2.** [personnes] this, &c. [or → personal pronoun subjects]: *C'est mon frère,* This is my brother, He is my brother; *Ce sont eux!,* Here they are!; *C'est une Anglaise,* She is an English /girl, woman/; *Ce sont des Canadiens,* They are Canadians. **3.** [abstractions; adjectifs]: *C'est bien,* That's nice; *C'est parfait, merveilleux, &c.,* It's/perfect, wonderful, &c./; *C'est/cela, ça/,* That's /it, right/; *C'est faux!,* It isn't true!; *C'est assez,* That's enough; *Est-ce à vous?,* Is this/Are these/yours? **4.** [réponses] *Qui est là?, C'est moi!;* Who's here? It's me!; *Qui est-ce qui a fait cela? C'est moi!,* Who did that? I did; *A qui est ce livre?, C'est à moi,* Whose book is this? It's mine. **(B)** [ce en combinaison avec QUI, QUE, QUOI] **1.** *Qu'est-ce que c'est?,* What's this? What is it?; *Qu'est-ce que c'est que ça?,* What's/this, that/? †*Qu'est-ce à dire?,* What does this mean?; *c'est pourquoi,* that's why. **2.** *C'est moi qui le lui ai donné, I* gave it to him; *C'est à lui de jouer,* It's *his* turn to play; It's *his* move; *C'est lui le patron, He*'s the boss; *C'est la première fois que je le vois,* This is the first time I have seen him; *C'est à vous que je parlais tout à l'heure?,* Was it you I was speaking to a moment ago? **3.** *C'est bien cela qui est arrivé, C'est précisément ce qui est arrivé,* This is precisely what happened; *Tout ce qui brille n'est pas or;* All that glitters is not gold; [Fam.] *Ce que c'est ennuyeux!,* How boring! **4.** [Loc.] *Je ne m'attendais pas à ce qu'il vint,* I didn't expect he would come; *pour ce qui est de moi,* as for me . . . ; *Ce qui est fait est fait,* It's no use crying over spilt milk.

ce[2] [sə]; before words beginning with vowels and 'mute *h*': **cet** [sɛt] *m*; **cette** [sɛt] *f*; *pl.* **ces** [sɛ, se] *adj.* **1.** this, that; these, those [☞ often coupled with . . . **ci,** . . . **là** to emphasize the distinction between *this* and *that*]: *ce garçon, ce garçon-ci,* this boy [here]; *ce garçon, ce garçon-là,* that boy [there]; *ces gens-là qui . . . ,* those (people) who . . . ; *~ soir,* tonight; *~ matin,* this morning; *~ jour-là,* that day; *un de ces jours,* one of these days. **2.** [exclam.] *Cette idée!,* The idea!; *Ah, ces enfants!* → Those children are the limit!; [interrog.; Fam.] *Ce dictionnaire, il est bientôt fini?,* How about the dictionary? Isn't it completed yet?

ceci [sə'si] *pr. dém.* [losing ground before CELA] this here.

cécité [sesi'te] *n.f.* blindness: *être atteint de ~*, to be blind.

céder [se'de] #10 *v. tr.* to cede, to yield, to give in, to resign: *~ sa place,* to give up one's place; *~ (son fonds de commerce),* to sell; [Fig.] *le ~ à qqun,* to be inferior to s.o.; *~ à la force,* to yield, submit/to force; *~ le pas,* to give way. || *v. intr.* to yield, to cede, to bend, to break: *La porte a cédé sous les coups,* The door gave way under the blows.

cédille [se'di:j] *n.f.* cedilla.

cèdre [sɛ:dr] *n.m.* cedar (-tree); cedar (-wood).

cédule [se'dyl] *n.f.* [Jur.] notification; schedule (of taxes).

ceindre [sɛ̃:dr] **ceignant** [sɛ'ɲɑ̃], **ceint** [sɛ̃] #36 *v. tr.* to surround, encircle; †to gird: ~ *une ville de murailles,* to wall a town; † ~ *l'épée,* to gird on the sword, to go to war;†~*la couronne,* to mount the throne, to take the crown.

†**ceint, -e** [sɛ̃(:t)] *adj.* girt with, cf. CEINDRE.

ceinture [sɛ̃'t|y:r] *n.f.* belt, sash; [Anat.] waist; © ~ *fléchée,* arrow sash; [Fig.] *se serrer la* ~ , to tighten one's belt. || **ceinturer** [-y're] #3 *v. tr.* to girdle; [Fig.] to encircle, compass.

cela [s(ə)'la] [Fam.] **ça** [sa] *pr. dém.* **1.** as opposed to *ceci*; *comme ceci . . . comme cela,* like this . . . like that. **2.** [sans préciser d'opposition] that: *c'est ça?,* is that it? [= is it correct?]; that's it!; *ça va?,* How are things? How are you?

célébrant [sele'brɑ̃] *n.m.* [R.C., officiating priest] celebrant.

célèbre [se'lɛbr] *adj.* celebrated, famous, renowned, illustrious.

célébrer [sele'bre] #10 *v. tr.* [× Do not use in absolute sense of "having a gay time."] to celebrate (a hero), to solemnize (an event); [Rel.] ~ *la messe,* to say mass.

célébrité [selebri'te] *n.f.* **1.** celebrity, fame. **2.** star, well-known figure.

†**celer** [sə'le] #9 *v. tr.* to conceal.

céleri [sɛl'ri] *n.m.* celery: *pied de* ~ , head of celery; *morceau m de* ~ , stick of celery.

céleste [se'lɛst] *adj.* heavenly, [Astr.] celestial: *Père* ~ , God, Heavenly Father; *bleu* ~ , sky-blue.

célibat [seli'ba] *n.m.* celibacy. || **célibataire** [-'tɛ:r] *adj.* & *n.* unmarried person: *n.m.* bachelor; *n.f.* spinster.

celle, celles [sɛl] cf. CELUI.

cellophane [sɛlɔ'fan] *n.f.* cellophane.

cellule [sɛ'lyl] *n.f.* cell: ~ *photoélectrique,* photoelectric cell.

celluloïde [sɛlylɔ'id] *n.m.* celluloid.

cellulose [sɛly'lo:z] *n.f.* cellulose: *ruban de* ~ , Scotch tape.

celtique [sɛl'tik] *adj. & n.m.* Celt, Celtic.

celui [sə'lɥi] *pl.* **ceux** [sø] *pr. dém.* **1.** [+ DE] that of, [or possessive case]: *c'est* ~ *de mon frère,* it is that of my brother, it is my brother's; *celles que j'ai achetées,* the ones I bought. **2.** [+ QUI, QUE]: [personne] he who, she who, the one; [chose] the one (that), that which, which: ~ *que je préfère,* the one I like best; *Quel est* ~ *qui l'a fait?,* Who did it? || *pl.* those who; those which; the one which: *celles qui n'ont pas de livres,* Those who are without books . . . ; *tous ceux qui sont ici,* all those who are here; *voici ceux que j'ai achetés,* here are the ones I bought. **3.** [composé avec -ci, -là]: **celui-ci,** this one (here), this . . .; *celui-là,* that one (over there) that . . . [☞ Forms in -là are becoming more frequent]; *donnez-moi ceux-là,* give me those (down here).

cendre [sɑ̃:dr] *n.f.* **1.** ashes *n.* (*pl.*), cinders (*pl.*): *cendre(s) volcanique(s),* volcanic ash(es); *les cendres d'un feu,* cinders. **2.** ash: *cendre(s) de cigarette,* cigarette ash; *Mercredi des Cendres,* Ash Wednesday. **3.** [Fig., *pl.*] [mortal] remains. || **cendrier** [sɑ̃dri'je] *n.m.* ashtray.

cenellier [snɛ'lje] © *n.m.* hawthorn, cf. AUBÉPINE.

cénotaphe [senɔ'taf] *n.m.* cenotaph.

cens [sɑ̃:s] *n.m.* census; property qualification.

censé, -e [sɑ̃'s|e] [× Do not confuse with SENSÉ] *adj.* supposed, considered, reputed: *Je ne suis pas* ~ *le savoir,* I am not supposed to know it; *Nul n'est* ~ *ignorer la loi,* Ignorance of the law is no defence. || **censeur** [-œ:r] censor, critic; [in French *lycées*] vice-principal.

censure [sɑ̃'s|y:r] *n.f.* censorship; censure, blame: *s'exposer à la* ~ *du public,* to expose o.s. to public blame, censure. || **censurer** [-y're] #3 *v. tr.* [criticize] to censure, blame; [censorship] to censor.

cent[1] [sɛnt, © sɛn] *n.m.* [☞ the colloquial form is fem.] cent. [cf. SOU.]

cent[2] [sɑ̃, sɑ̃t + vowel or *h* mute, except cent un, cent onze] *adj.* [☞ agrees in plural: *deux cents,* except when followed by another number: *deux cent trois*] (one) hundred, a hundred. *deux cents,* two hundred; 10 *pour cent,* 10%, ten per cent. || *n.m.*: *un* ~ *d'œufs,* one hundred eggs. cf. CENTAINE. || **centaine** [sɑ̃t'|ɛn] *n.f.* (about) a hundred: *par centaines,* by the hundred, hundreds of . . . || **centenaire** [-t'nɛ:r] *n.m.* = 100th anniversary] centennial, centenary. || *adj.* & *n.m.* a hundred years old; centenarian. || **centième** [-'tjɛm] *adj.* hundredth, 100th. || *n.m.* (one-)hundredth. || **centigrade** [-ti'grad] *adj.* centesimal; centigrade; [Fam.] *thermomètre* ~ , = centigrade thermometer. || **centime** [-'tim] *n.m.* centime [1/100 of a franc]. || **centimètre, cm** [-ti'mɛ:tr] *n.m.* [1/100 of a metre] centimetre. || © **centin** [-'tɛ̃] *n.m.* cent [☞ rarely used. cf. CENT.]

central, -e [sɑ̃'tral] *adj.* central; chief, head, principal: *chauffage* ~ , central heating; *bureau* ~ *de la poste,* Postal

Head Office. || *n.m.* exchange: ~ *téléphonique*, telephone exchange. || **centrale** [sɑ̃'tral] *n.f.* [Electr.] powerhouse. || **centralisation** [-iza'sjõ] *n.f.* centralization. || **centraliser** [-i'ze] #3 *v. tr.* to centralize. || **centre** [sɑ̃:tr] *n.m.* centre, middle: ~ *de villégiature*, holiday resort; © ~ *social des étudiants*, Student Union Building; ~ *commercial*, shopping centre; ~ *de la ville*, downtown district; [Fr.] *Centre national de la Recherche scientifique* [CNRS], National Research Board. || **centrifuge** [sɑ̃tri'fy~ʒ] *adj.* centrifugal.

cependant [səpɑ̃'dɑ̃] *adv.* in the meantime, meanwhile, however.

céramique [sera'mik] *n.f.* [art] ceramics.

cercle [sɛrkl] *n.m.* circle: ~ *polaire*, Arctic Circle; [Fig.] club: *aller au* ~, to go to the club; ~ *français*, French Club.

cercueil [sɛr'kœ:j] *n.m.* coffin.

céréale [sere'al] *m.f.* cereal: © breakfast food: *plantes céréales*, cereals.

cérébral, -e [sere'bral] *adj.*: *paralysie cérébrale*, cerebral palsy.

cérémonie [seremɔ'n|i] *n.f.* **1.** ceremony. **2.** politeness, duty: *visite de* ~, duty call, visit; *sans* ~, unceremoniously, informal (gathering); *Ne faites pas de cérémonies*, Don't stand on ceremony. || **cérémonieu|x, -se** [-jø(:z)] *adj.* ceremonious, formal.

cerf [sɛ:r] *n.m.* stag, deer (in general); ~ *du Canada*, wapiti, elk; ~ *de Virginie*, deer [© usual. called *chevreuil*]. || **cerf-volant** [sɛrvɔ'lɑ̃] *n.m.* kite.

cerise [s(ə)'r|i:z] *n.f.* cherry. || *adj.* cherry-red: *des tentures rouge* ~, cherry-red drapes. || **cerisier** [-i'zje] *n.m.* cherry tree.

cerne [sɛrn] *n.m.* ring, circle [esp. around eyes]. || **cerné, -e** [-e] *adj.* [Mil.] encircled; [Fig.]: *avoir les yeux cernés*, to have rings under the eyes. || **cerner** #3 *v. tr.* to surround, encircle; to close in upon, corner/s.o.

certain, -e [sɛr't|ɛ̃, -ɛn] *adj.* **1.** [follows noun] certain, positive, sure: *un fait* ~, a positive fact; *indice m* ~, a sure indication; *sûr et* ~, undoubtedly; *C'est chose certaine*, This is an undoubted fact. **2.** [precedes noun] certain, some: *homme d'un* ~ *âge*, middle-aged man; *certaines choses*, some, certain/things; *depuis un* ~ *temps*, for some time, for quite a while. || *pron. ind.* some (people): *certains pensent que . . .*, some (people) think (that . . .). || *adv.* © [Fam.] sure: *Il viendra* ~, He'll come for sure [☞ Fr. CERTAINEMENT]. || **certainement** [-ɛn'mɑ̃] *adv.* certainly, surely, for sure. || **certes** [sɛrt] *adv.* & *interj.* certainly; surely; *Certes!*, Indeed!, How true!

certificat [sɛrtif|i'ka] *n.m.* [Sch.] certificate, diploma; testimonial: *établir un* ~, to make out a certificate; *se présenter au* ~, to/take, write/one's Junior High School exams. || **certifier** [-je] #3 *v. tr.* to certify, attest; to vouch (for).

cerveau [sɛr'v|o] *n.m.* **1.** brain [the organ], cf. CERVELLE: *rhume m de* ~, head cold; ~ *électronique*, electronic brain. **2.** [Fig.] brains, intelligence, judgment. || **cervelle** [-ɛl] *n.f.* **1.** brain [as material]: ~ *de mouton*, sheep's brain; *brûler la* ~ *à qqun*, to blow s.o.'s brains out; *tête sans* ~, empty-headed person, brainless [= écervelé]. **2.** [Fig. & Fam.] brain, intelligence: *se creuser la* ~, to rack one's brain.

ces [sɛ] *pron. dém. m/f.pl.* these, those.

cesse [sɛ:s] *n.f.* ceasing, respite: *n'avoir de* ~ *que . . .*, not to rest till . . . ; *sans* ~, *loc. adv.* unceasingly, without (a) letup; *parler sans* ~, to keep on chattering, to chatter away. || **cesser** [sɛ'se] #3 *v. tr.* to stop, cease: ~ *le travail*, to stop work(ing): *Notre commerce avec l'étranger n'a cessé de s'améliorer*, → Our foreign trade has improved steadily. || *v. intr.* to come to an end, to finish, to stop: *La pluie a cessé*, The rain has/ended, stopped/; *Cessez de pleurer*, Stop crying.

cession [sɛ'sjõ] *n.f.* transfer; [Jur.] assignment. cf. CÉDER.

c'est-à-dire [sɛta'di:r] *Loc. conj.* [abr. c.-à-d.] that is to say [abbr. i.e.].

cet, cette [sɛt] *pron. dém.* this. cf. CE.

ceux (-ci, -là) [sø('si, -'la)] *pron. dém. mpl.* these, those; they.

Ceylan [se'lɑ̃] [☞ Do not use def. article] *n.m.* Ceylon.

chacal [ʃa'kal] *pl.* **-s** *n.m.* jackal: ~ *d'Amérique*, coyote.

chacun, -e [ʃa'k|œ̃, -yn] *pr. ind.* **1.** each, each one: *Je les ai vus chacun séparément*, I saw them each/in turn, one after the other/. **2.** every one, everybody: ~ *sait* (*que*), everybody knows (that); ~ *à son goût*, every man to his taste; [Fam.] ~ *sa chacune*, every Jack his Jill; ~ *pour soi*, every man for himself.

chagrin, -e [ʃa'gr|ɛ̃] *adj.* sad, troubled. || *n.m.* grief, sorrow, regret, trouble: *avoir du* ~, to be sad; *mourir de* ~, to die of/heartbreak, a broken heart/. || **chagriner** [-i'ne] #3 *v. tr.* to grieve, afflict.

chahut [ʃa'y] *n.m.* horseplay, row, racket: *faire/du, un grand/* ~, to kick up a row.

chaîne [ʃɛ:n] *n.f.* **1.** chain; [prison] chains,

fetters; [collier] necklace; [de montagnes] (mountain) range. **2.** [Fig.] chain, sequence (of events); series: *réaction en* ~, chain reaction; *travail à la* ~, assembly line. || **chaînon** [ʃɛ'nõ] *n.m.* link.

chair [ʃɛ:r] *n.f.* flesh; [peau] skin; [viande] meat; [fruit] pulp; [Loc.] ~ *de poule*, gooseflesh.

chaire [ʃɛ:r] *n.f.* chair (at a university); [Rel.] pulpit: *avoir la* ~ *de français*, to hold the chair of French.

chaise [ʃɛ:z] *n.f.* chair [× not used in Fig. sense: *the chair*, cf. PRÉSIDENT] ~ *d'enfant*, high chair; ~ *berceuse*, rocking chair; ~ *électrique*, electric chair; ~ *-longue*, reclining seat, chaise longue: *être assis entre deux chaises*, to be between the devil and the deep blue sea.

chaland [ʃa'lã] *n.m.* barge, scow.

châle [ʃɑ:l] *n.m.* shawl.

chalet [ʃa'lɛ] *n.m.* chalet, © country cottage, camp: ~ *de nécessité*, public lavatory.

chaleur [ʃa'lœ|:r] *n.f.* heat, warmth: *les chaleurs*, the hot season; © *la baie des Chaleurs*, Chaleur Bay; [Fig.] passion, *avec* ~, passionately. || **chaleureusement** [-røz'mã] *adv.* warmly, cordially. || **chaleureu|x, -se** [-'rø(:z)] *adj.* warm; cordial: *applaudissements* ~, hearty, warm/applause.

chaloupe [ʃa'lup] *n.f.* launch, long-boat; © boat, rowboat [☞ in this meaning, Fr. uses CANOT].

chalumeau [ʃaly'mo] *n.m.* [Mus.] tube, pipe; flute; [Tech.] blow torch.

chamailler (se) [ʃamɑ'je] #3 *v. pron.* to quarrel, wrangle (*à propos de*, about).

chamarrer [ʃama're] #3 *v. tr.* to decorate (a uniform, &c), to trim: *la poitrine chamarrée*, → beribboned.

chambranle [ʃã'brã:l] *n.m.* mantelpiece; [door, window] frame.

chambre [ʃã:br] *n.f.* **1.** room [☞ Mostly used as short form of *chambre à coucher*, bedroom: © = any room], bedroom; *femme f de* ~, chambermaid; *la* ~ *des machines*, engine room; ~ *à louer*, room to/let, rent/; ~ *noire*, darkroom; ~ *d'ami*, guest room, spare bedroom; [Auto.] ~ *à air*, tube (of a tire); *retenir, commander/une* ~, to reserve a room. **2.** assembly; congress; house; © *Chambre des communes*, the House of Commons, the Commons; [Fr.] †*Chambre des députés*, †*la Chambre*, Chamber of Deputies. **3.** Board; organization: *Chambre f de Commerce*, Board of Trade. [N.B. In *Montreal*, there are two parallel organizations, *La Chambre de Commerce du district de Montréal* and the *Montreal Board of Trade*; each name is kept untranslated.] *Chambre de Commerce internationale* (C.C.I.), International Chamber of Commerce (I.C.C.); [Fin.] *Chambre de compensation*, Clearing House; *Chambre des Notaires*, Board of Notaries. || **chambré** [ʃã'br|e] *adj.* [wine] at room temperature. || **chambreur** [-œ:r] © [*abus.*] *n.m.* roomer, lodger.

chameau [ʃa'mo] *n.m.* camel.

chamois [ʃa'mwa] *n.m.* [animal] chamois: *peau f de* ~, shammy. || *adj.* [couleur] fawn-coloured, chamois.

champ [ʃã] *n.m.* field, [pl.] open country: ~ *de blé*, wheat field; *sur-le-* ~, *adv.* immediately: *Il est mort au champ d'honneur*, He died on the field of battle; ~ *de Mars*, drill ground; *fleurs des champs*, wild flowers; ~ *de bataille*, battlefield; ~ *de course*, race track; ~ *du repos*, graveyard; [Fig.] ~ *d'expérience*, field; ~ *d'application*, applicability; ~/ *magnétique, électrique*/, magnetic, electric/field; ~ *de force*, field of force; ~ *opératoire*, operating theatre; ~ *d'une médaille*, background of a medal; *avoir le* ~ *libre*, to have a clear field; [Loc.] *à tout bout de* ~, on every corner, at every opportunity.

champagne [ʃã'paɲ] *n.m.* champagne.

champêtre [ʃã'pɛ:tr] *adj.* rural, rustic, of the fields: *travaux champêtres*, work in the fields.

champignon [ʃãpi'ɲõ] *n.m.* [☞ Fr. does not distinguish between *mushroom* and *toadstool*. cf. VÉNÉNEUX] mushroom: *omelette aux champignons*, mushroom omelette; *pousser comme un* ~, to mushroom; *ville* ~, fast-growing city.

champion [ʃã'pj|õ] *n.m.* champion. || **championnat** [-ɔ'na] *n.m.* championship: *disputer un* ~, to play for the championship; © *le* ~ *mondial*, World Series [US].

chance [ʃã:s] *n.f.* chance, luck: *la* ~ *de sa vie*, chance of a lifetime; *avoir de la* ~, to be lucky; *Il a toutes les chances pour lui*, All the odds are in his favour; *Je vais courir la* ~, I'll take the chance; *Bonne* ~ *!*, Good luck!; *avoir des chances de*, to stand a good chance of; *avoir la* ~ *de faire qqch.*, to be/lucky, fortunate/to be able to do sth.

chanceler [ʃãs'le] #8 *v. intr.* **1.** to sway, stagger [de vieillesse] to totter: *Il entra en chancelant*, → He staggered into (the room). **2.** [Fig.] to waver: ~ *dans sa résolution,* to waver (in one's resolution).

chancelier [ʃɑ̃sə'lje] *n.m.* chancellor; secretary: *grand* ~ , Lord Chancellor.

chanceu|x, -se [ʃɑ̃'sø(:z)] *adj.* **1.** [= qui a de la chance] lucky [☞ in this sense, much used in ©; for Fr., use → *avoir de la chance*]. **2.** [= qui s'en remet au hasard] hazardous, risky.

chandail [ʃɑ̃'d|a:j] *pl.* **-s** [-a:j] *n.m.* sweater.

chandelier [ʃɑ̃d|ə'lje] *n.m.* candlestick; †candle-maker. ‖ **chandelle** [-ɛl] *n.f.* [†cf. BOUGIE; Rel. CIERGE] (tallow) candle; [Loc. Fig.] (*en*) *voir trente-six chandelles,* to see stars; *brûler la* ~ *par les deux bouts,* to burn the candle at both ends; *monter en* ~ , to rocket; *devoir une* (*fière*) ~ *à qqun,* to owe more than one can repay.

change [ʃɑ̃:ʒ] *n.m.* [Com. [×] = opération bancaire] change, exchange: *agent de* ~ , stockbroker; *le cours du* ~ , the rate of exchange; [Fig.] *donner le* ~ *à qqun,* to lead s.o. astray. © [*abus.*] change, cf. MONNAIE.

changeant, -e [ʃɑ̃'ʒ|ɑ̃(:t)] *adj.* changing, fickle; [temps] unsettled. ‖ **changement** [-'mɑ̃] *n.m.* change, shift; alteration; *sans* ~ , without change, unchanged: ~ *de vitesse,* gearshift; *apporter un* ~ (*à*), to make a change (in), to alter sth.

changer [-e] #5 *v. tr.* [conj. AVOIR (action) et ÊTRE (état).] **1.** to change, exchange: changer (une chose pour une autre) to change for; *Ça change tout,* That changes everything; *se* ~ *les idées,* to get away from routine; ~ *son fusil d'épaule,* to change one's mind. [followed by *de*] ~ *de vêtements,* to change. **2.** to alter; to change [gears] *changer* (*de vitesse*), [money] *changer de l'argent* (*à la banque*); ~ *de place* (*avec*), to change places (with); ~ *de train,* to change trains. ‖ *v. intr.* to alter; to change: *Le temps va* ~ , We are going to have a change in the weather; *Il est très changé,* He's altered a lot. ‖ se **changer** *v. pron.* to change (one's clothes); ~ *en,* to turn into (eau, &c.). ‖ **changeur** [-œ:r] *n.m.* (money-)changer.

chanoine [ʃa'nwan] *n.m.* Canon.

chanson [ʃɑ̃'s|õ] *n.f.* song: *L'air ne fait pas la* ~ , A tune does not make a song; *C'est toujours la même* ~ , It's always the same old story; *la Chanson de Roland,* the Song of Roland. ‖ **chansonni|er, -ère** [-ɔ'nj|e, -ɛ:r] *n.* song-writer; song book.

chant [ʃɑ̃] *n.m.* song, singing: *le* ~ *du cygne,* swan song; *plain-* ~, plainsong. ‖ **chanter** [-'te] #3 *v. tr.* to sing; [coq] to crow; [Fam.] *Qu'est-ce que vous me chantez?,* What sort of story are you giving me?; *Je le ferai si ça me chante,* I'll do it if it happens to suit me; *faire* ~ (*qqun*), to blackmail. ‖ **chanteu|r, -se** [-'tœ:r, -'tø:z] *n.* singer: *maître* ~ , blackmailer.

chantier [ʃɑ̃'tje] *n.m.* **1.** lumberyard, timberyard; [naval] shipyard; [construction] works; work area: [Fig.] *mettre en* ~ , to start work on, [Naut.] to lay down. **2.** © lumber camp; shanty. © *faire* ~ , to lumber, log, go out logging; *aller aux chantiers,* to go out into the bush, to go /lumbering, logging/; © *le temps des chantiers,* logging season.

chantonner [ʃɑ̃tɔ'ne] #3 *v. tr.* to hum.

chanvre [ʃɑ̃:vr] *n.m.* hemp.

chaos [ka|'o] *n.m.* [ne pas confondre avec *cahot*] chaos, confusion. ‖ **chaotique** [-ɔ'tik] *adj.* chaotic, confused.

chaparder [ʃapar'de] #3 *v. tr.* [Fam.] to steal, to pinch, to snatch.

chapeau, -x [ʃa'po] *n.m.* hat; [roue] (hub) cap: *ôter* (*enlever*) *son* ~ , to take one's hat off; [Fam.] *travailler du* ~ , to have a bee in one's bonnet; ~ *de cardinal,* cardinal's red hat; ~ *bas,* hat in hand.

chapelain [ʃa'plɛ̃] *n.m.* chaplain.

chapelet [ʃap'lɛ] *n.m.* beads, rosary: *réciter, dire/son* ~ , to/recite, count/ one's beads; [Fig.] string (of onions, &c): *un* ~ *d'injures,* a string of abuse.

chapelle [ʃa'pɛl] *n.f.* chapel: *maître de* ~ , musical director, choir master.

chaperon [ʃap'rõ] *n.m.* **1.** †hood: *le Petit Chaperon rouge,* Little Red Riding Hood. **2.** person: [no fem. form] chaperon.

chapitre [ʃa'pitr] *n.m.* chapter (of a book); item (of a budget); [Rel.] chapter house; [Fig.] *avoir, ne pas avoir/voix au* ~ , to have/a say, no say/in the matter.

chaque [ʃak] *adj. indéf.* [☞ requires a singular verb] **1.** each, every: ~ *jour,* every day; ~ *fois que je le vois,* each time I see him. **2.** [Fam.] each: $2 *each.* cf. CHACUN.

char [ʃa:r] *n.m.* **1.** chariot, wagon; [parade] float: ~ /*de combat, d'assaut*/, tank. **2.** © [going out of fashion] automobile; *petit* ~ , street car; † *les gros chars,* train.

charabia [ʃara'bja] *n.m.* gibberish, jargon.

charade [ʃa'rad] *n.f.* charade.

charbon [ʃar'b|õ] *n.m.* coal; ~ *de bois,* charcoal; [Fig.] *être sur des charbons ardents,* to be/on tenterhooks, in a stew/; [Méd.] carbuncle. ‖ **charbonnage** [-ɔ'na:ʒ] *n.m.* coal-mining; colliery. ‖ **charbonner**

[-ɔ'ne] *v.tr.* to char, burn. || *v. intr.* to coal. || **charbonnier** [-ɔ'nje] *n.m.* coal man, coal dealer; [Naut.] collier, coal boat.

charcuterie [ʃarkyt|'ri] *n.f.* **1.** delicatessen, pork-butcher's shop. **2.** [the food itself] delicatessen(s). || **charcuti|er, -ère** [-je, -jɛ:r] *n.* pork butcher.

chardon [ʃar'dõ] *n.m.* thistle.

chardonneret [ʃardɔn'rɛ] *n.m.* goldfinch: ~ *des pins,* pine siskin.

charge [ʃarʒ] *n.f.* **1.** load, burden: ~ /*négative, positive*/, negative, positive/ charge. **2.** [Mil.] charge: ~ *de cavalerie,* cavalry charge; *Il est revenu à la* ~, He tried again. **3.** position, charge, care: *Il est à ma* ~, He is in my care, I am supporting him; *les devoirs de ma* ~, the duties of my position; © *entrer en* ~, to take up one's duties; *avoir* ~ *de qqch,* to be in charge of sth.; *donner* ~ *à qqun de faire qqch.,* to give s.o. the responsibility of doing sth. **4.** utilities and extras: *Le loyer est de 100 dollars plus les charges,* The rent is 100 dollars plus the utilities; *avoir* ~ *d'âmes,* to be responsible for others. || **chargé, -e** [-e] *adj.* [appareil photo] full; [fusil] loaded; [d'un poids] laden (with), overloaded (with); [Fig.] ~ *de faire qqch.,* to be entrusted with. || **chargé** *m* **d'affaires** chargé d'affaires, envoy. || **chargement** [-ə'mã] *n.m.* load, cargo; lading [of ship], loading (of gun); charging (of battery). || **charger** [-e] #5 *v. tr.* [conj. AVOIR (action), ÊTRE (état)]. **1.** to load: ~ *un navire,* to load a boat; ~ *un appareil de photo,* to load a camera; ~ *une arme à feu,* to load a gun; ~ *une table de mets,* to load a table with food. **2.** [Mil.] to attack. **3.** to give a responsibility to; to entrust with: *Je vous charge de me remplacer,* I am giving you the responsibility of replacing me; *chargé d'une position,* (to be) given the responsibility of a position. **4.** overload, exaggerate: ~ *un récit,* to exaggerate a story. || **se charger** (de) *v. pron.* to undertake, to take upon o.s.: *Je m'en charge,* I'll look after it, I'll take care of it.

chariot [ʃa'rjo] *n.m.* wagon; baby walker; go-cart; carriage (of a typewriter).

charitable [ʃari't|abl] *adj.* charitable (*envers qqun,* towards s.o.). || **charité** [-e] *n.f.* charity: *acte de* ~, act of charity, love; alms: *faire la* ~ *à qqun,* to give charity to s.o.; *dame de* ~, district visitor; *Œuvres de* ~, Welfare agency.

charlatan [ʃarla'tã] *n.m.* charlatan, quack.

charmant, -e [ʃar'mã(:t)] *adj.* charming, delightful: *le Prince Charmant,* Prince Charming. || **charme** [ʃarm] *n.m.* charm, spell: [Fig.] *se porter comme un* ~, to be fit as a fiddle; *le* ~ *de la poésie,* the beauty of poetry; *Rien ne résiste à ses charmes,* Nothing can resist her/charms, beauty/; *chanteur de* ~, crooner. || **charmer** [-e] #3 *v. tr.* [conj. AVOIR (action), ÊTRE (état)] to charm, bewitch: ~ *les serpents,* to charm snakes; [Fig.] to delight, please: (*Je suis*) *charmé de vous voir,* (I am) delighted to see you. || **charmeur** [-œ:r] *n.m.* charmer.

charnel, -le [ʃar'nɛl] *adj.* carnal, sensual.

charnière [ʃar'njɛ:r] *n.f.* hinge.

charnu, -e [ʃar'ny] *adj.* fleshy, plump; [fruit] pulpy.

charogne [ʃa'rɔɲ] *n.f.* carrion.

charpente [ʃar'pã:t] *n,f.* frame. || **charpenté, -e** *adj.* [ʃarpã't|e] built, framed: *solidement* ~, well-built [man, &c], well-constructed (plot, &c.). || **charpentier** [-je] *n.m.* carpenter; [de navire] shipwright.

charrette [ʃa'rɛt] *n.f.* cart.

charrier [ʃa'rje] #3 *v. tr.* to cart, carry (down), transport: *Le fleuve charrie du sable,* The river carries down sand. || **charroi** [ʃa'rwa] *n.m.* cartage.

charron [ʃa'rõ] *n.m.* cart-maker; wheelwright.

charroyer [ʃarwa'je] #12 *v. tr.* to cart, to transport (by cart or wagon).

charrue [ʃa'ry] *n.f.* plough; [Fig.] *mettre la* ~ *devant les bœufs,* to put the cart before the horse.

charte [ʃart] *n.f.* charter: [Hist.] (*la*) *Grande Charte,* Magna Carta.

chas [ʃɑ] *n.m.* eye (of a needle).

chasse [ʃas] *n.f.* **1.** chase, hunt, hunting: *aller à la* ~, to go hunting; ~ *au cerf,* deer hunting; [Fig.] *donner la* ~ *à un voleur,* to chase, pursue/a thief. **2.** game (killed in hunting). || **chasser** [-e] #3 *v. tr. & intr.* **1.** to hunt. **2.** to chase, to drive: ~ *l'ennemi de ses positions,* to chase, to drive the enemy from his position; ~ *un troupeau devant soi,* to drive a flock in front of o.s.; ~ *un clou,* to drive a nail in; *chassé-croisé,* chassé-croisé (a dance step). **3.** to discharge: ~ *un domestique,* to fire a servant. || **chasseur** [-œ:r] *n.m.* hunter; [hôtel] bellboy; [aviation] fighter (plane).

châssis [ʃɑ'si] *n.m.* frame, chassis; [Auto.] (auto)body, chassis; [fenêtre] sash.

chaste [ʃast] *adj.* chaste. || **chasteté** [-ə'te] *n.f.* chastity.

chat, -te [ʃa(t)] *n.* cat [le mâle est appelé *tomcat*]; *petit* ~, kitten. cf. CHATON; ©

~ -*sauvage*, raccoon. cf. RATON LAVEUR: [Loc.] *A bon ~ bon rat*, Tit for tat; *acheter ~ en poche*, to buy a pig in a poke; *Il ne faut pas réveiller le ~ qui dort*, Let sleeping dogs lie; [Fam.] *J'ai d'autres chats à fouetter*, I've other fish to fry; *~ échaudé craint l'eau froide*, Once bitten twice shy.

châtaigne [ʃɑ'tɛɲ] *n.f.* chestnut. ‖ **châtaignier** [-je] *n.m.*: chestnut (-tree, -wood).

châtain, -e [ʃɑ't|ɛ̃, -ɛn] *adj.* light brown, chestnut: *cheveux châtains*, light brown hair.

château [ʃɑ'to] *n.m.* castle, country house: *~ d'eau*, water reservoir, water tower; *un ~ de cartes*, a house of cards; *bâtir des châteaux en Espagne*, to build castles in the air.

châtier [ʃɑ't|je] #3 *v. tr.* to punish, chastise. ‖ **châtiment** [-i'mɑ̃] *n.m.* punishment.

chatoiement [ʃatwa'mɑ̃] *n.m.* shimmer; [pierre précieuse] glistening; [étoffe] sheen.

chaton [ʃa'tõ] *n.m.* kitten.

chatouillement [ʃatuj|'mɑ̃] *n.m.* tickling. ‖ **chatouiller** [-e] #3 *v. tr.* to tickle. ‖ **chatouilleu|x, -se** [-ø(:z)] *adj.* ticklish; [Fig.] touchy.

chatoyant, -e [ʃatwa'j|ɑ̃(:t)] *adj.* changing, varying. ‖ **chatoyer** [-e] #12 *v. intr.* [pierres précieuses] to glisten; [étoffes] to shimmer; to change colour.

chaud, -e [ʃo(:d)] *adj.* **1.** warm, hot: *avoir ~*, to be, feel/hot; *Il fait ~*, It is hot; [Fig.] *J'ai eu ~!*, It was a close shave, touch and go. **2.** [Fig.] lively, animated, heated, ardent: *une chaude dispute*, a/heated, lively/dispute. **3.** [Fam.] recent: *une nouvelle toute chaude*, news just off the press. ‖ *n.m.* heat, warmth: *Cela ne (me) fait ni chaud ni froid*, It is completely indifferent (to me); *Tenir au ~*, Keep in a warm place. ‖ **chaudement** [ʃod'mɑ̃] *adv.* warmly; [Fig.] warmly, eagerly: *Il fut ~ félicité*, He was warmly congratulated.

chaudière [ʃo'djɛ:r] *n.f.* boiler, furnace [cf. © FOURNAISE]; © [seau en fer] bucket, pail; *la Chaudière*, the Chaudière River.

chaudron [ʃo'drõ] *n.m.* cauldron.

chauffage [ʃo'fa:ʒ] *n.m.* heating: *~ central*, central heating: *~ automatique*, stoker; *entrepreneur en ~*, heating contractor; *unité de ~*, heater unit; *~/à l'eau, à air chaud, à la vapeur/*, hot water, steam, hot air/heating. ‖ **chauffe** [ʃo:f] *n.f.* heating; stoking furnace: *~ -bain m*, *~ -eau m* heater, [Br.] geyser. ‖ **chauffer** [ʃo'f|e] #3 *v. tr.* to heat, warm (up): *faire ~ le moteur*, to warm up the engine; © [abus.] to drive (a car, bus, &c.); [Fig.] to cram (for an exam). ‖ *v. intr.* to become warm, get hot: *Le moteur chauffe*, The engine is getting hot; *Le café chauffe*, The coffee is warming up; [Fam.] *Ça chauffe!*, Things are getting warm! ‖ **se chauffer** *v. pron.* to warm o.s., get warm (by the fire, *au feu*). ‖ **chaufferette** [-'rɛt] *n.f.* space heater.

chauffeur [-œ:r] *n.m.* [Auto.] chauffeur, driver; locomotive, (navire) stoker.

chaume [ʃo:m] *n.m.* straw; stubble, stubble field.

chaumière [ʃo'mjɛ:r] *n.f.* thatched-roofed cottage.

chaussée [ʃo'se] *n.f.* **1.** causeway; embankment: *~ de castors*, beaver dam. **2.** (the middle of the)/street, road/: *Ne marchez pas sur la ~*, Do not walk in the street; *~ glissante par temps humide*, (road) slippery when wet; [Fr.] *rez-de-~*, ground floor.

chausser [ʃo's|e] #3 *v. tr.* **1.** to put/shoes, slippers, stockings/on (s.o., sth.): *~ ses bottines*, to put on one's boots. **2.** to supply with footwear. ‖ *v. tr. & intr.* to fit the foot: *Ces souliers le chaussent parfaitement*, These shoes fit him perfectly; *(Du) combien chaussez-vous?*, What size do you wear? ‖ **chaussette(s)** [-ɛt] *n.f.* socks; © *pl.* slippers. ‖ **chausson(s)** [-õ] *n.m.* slippers, © socks. ‖ **chaussure** [-y:r] *n.f.* [☞ The most comprehensive form to designate any type of footwear] shoe; [Com.] footwear: *Je ne sais pas la pointure de mes chaussures*, I do not know the size of my shoes; *trouver ~ à son pied*, to get suited; *brosser les ~*, to brush, polish/one's shoes.

chauve [ʃo:v] *adj.* bald, bare. ‖ *n.* bald head.

chauve-souris [ʃovsu'ri] *n.f.* bat.

chauvin, -e [ʃo'v|ɛ̃, -in] *n. & adj.* chauvinist(ic), jingoist(ic). ‖ **chauvinisme** [-i'nism] *n.m.* chauvinism, jingoism.

chaux [ʃo] *n.f.* lime.

chavirer [ʃavi're] #3 *v. intr.* [bateau] to capsize; [Fig.] être chaviré, to be upset.

chef [ʃɛf] *n.m.* **1.** head: *le ~ de l'État*, the head of the State; *~ de famille*, head of the family; *~ -lieu*, county seat, chief town. **2.** chief, leader: *~ d'état-major*, chief of staff; *~ de file*, leader; *en ~*. chief, e.g. *ingénieur en ~*, chief engineer: [d'équipe] foreman; [Sport.] captain (of a team); [Mus.] *~ d'orchestre*, conductor; [Rail.] *~ de train*, train conductor; *~ de gare*, stationmaster;

[Scout.] ~ *de troupe*, scoutmaster. **3.** [restaurant] chef. **4.** [Loc.] *de mon propre* ~, on my own authority, off my own bat.

chef-d'œuvre [ʃɛ'dœ:vr] *pl.* **-s-** *n.m.* masterpiece.

†**chelin** [ʃlɛ̃] *n.m.* cf. SHILLING.

chemin [ʃə'mɛ̃] *n.m.* way; route; road: *voleur de grand* ~, highwayman; *Ce* ~ *va à Paris*, This road leads to Paris; *se frayer un* ~, to shoulder, push/ one's way through (a crowd); *ne pas y aller par quatre chemins*, not to mince matters; *trouver son* ~ *par la ville*, to find one's way about, around the/city, town/; *faire du* ~, to progress, to make progress; *rentrer dans le droit* ~, to turn over a new leaf; *être sur le bon* ~, to be on the right road. || **chemin de fer** [ʃmɛ̃d'fɛ:r] railway, railroad: *Chemins de fer nationaux du Canada*, Canadian National Railways (CN); *Chemin de fer du Pacifique-Canadien*, Canadian Pacific Railways (CPR) [☞ For the track itself, cf. VOIE]. || **chemineau** [ʃəmi'no] *n.m.* tramp, hobo.

cheminée [ʃəmi'ne] *n.f.* [extérieure] chimney; [intérieure] flue; [âtre] fireplace, mantelpiece: ~ *d'appel*, air shaft, ventilating shaft; [de navire] funnel; [d'usine] smoke stack.

cheminer [ʃəm|i'ne] #3 *v. intr.* to walk (along), to proceed slowly.

cheminot [ʃəmi'no] *n.m.* railwayman, railroad employee, railroader.

chemise [ʃə'm|i:z] *n.f.* **1.** [hommes] shirt; [femmes] chemise: ~ *de nuit*, night dress, night shirt; *en/bras, manches/de* ~, in shirt sleeves; © *pommes de terre en* ~, baked potatoes. **2.** folder, jacket (for filing); dust jacket (of a book). || **chemiserie** [-iz'ri] *n.f.* manufacturing of, trade in/shirts; shop, store/in which this is done; haberdashery. || **chemisier** [-i'zje] *n.m.* shirtmaker; haberdasher; [corsage] blouse.

chenal [ʃə'nal] *n.m.* channel; fairway © snye: © *petits poissons mpl de schenaux*, smelt.

chêne [ʃɛ:n] *n.m.* oak.

chenil [ʃə'nil] *n.m.* kennel.

chenille [ʃə'ni:j] *n.f.* caterpillar; tread (of caterpillar tractor); [textiles] chenille (-spread).

chèque [ʃɛk] *n.m.* cheque; (bank) cheque: ~ *endossé*, endorsed cheque; *endosser un* ~, to endorse a cheque; *encaisser, toucher/un* ~, to cash a cheque; *payer par* ~, to pay by cheque; *faire, établir/un* ~, to write a cheque; *libeller un* ~ *à l'ordre de*, to make a cheque to the order of; *tirer un* ~ *sur la banque X*, to draw a cheque on X bank; *refuser un* ~, to reject a cheque; ~ *sans provision*, cheque without sufficient funds (N.S.F.); ~ *en duplicata*, duplicate cheque; ~ *au porteur*, bearer cheque; *carnet de chèques* [chéquier], cheque book; ~ *en blanc*, blank cheque; ~ *barré* (*Fr.*), crossed cheque; ~ *refusé*, rejected cheque; ~ *visé* ©, certified cheque; ~ *de voyage*, traveller's cheque.

ch|er, -ère [ʃɛ:r] *adj.* **1.** dear, beloved: *un ami très* ~, a very dear friend; ~ *monsieur*, Dear Mr. Smith [☞ rather informal], ~ *ami*, Dear (+ prénom), ~ *collègue*, Dear (Professor X ou autre titre). **2.** expensive, costly: *La vie ici n'est pas chère*, It is not expensive to live here; *pas* ~, cheap.

chercher [ʃɛr'ʃe] #3 *v. tr.* **1.** to look for, search for, seek: *Que cherchez-vous?*, What are you looking for? **2.** [chercher à] try to; [aller chercher] to go (and) get: *Il est allé* ~ *du secours*, He has gone to get help; *envoyer* ~ *le médecin*, to send for a doctor; ~ *à se sauver*, to try to escape; ~ *noise à qqun*, to pick on s.o., to try to pick a fight with s.o.

chère[1] [ʃɛ:r] cf. CHER.

chère[2] *n.f.* fare: *faire bonne* ~, to live well.

chèrement [ʃɛr'mɑ̃] *adv.* **1.** dearly, lovingly. **2.** at a high price, dearly: *défendre, vendre/* ~ *sa vie*, to sell one's life dearly.

chéri, -e [ʃe'r|i] *adj.* cherished, beloved. || *n.* darling, beloved. || **chérir** [-i:r] #17 *v. tr.* to love tenderly, dearly; to cherish: ~ *sa mère*, to love one's mother dearly.

chéti|f, -ve [ʃe't|if, -i:v] *adj.* [santé] weak, sickly; [taille] puny; [plante] stunted.

cheval [ʃə'val] *n.m.* **1.** horse: ~ *de selle*, saddle horse; ~ *de course*, race horse; *à* ~, on horseback, astride; *aller, monter/à* ~, to ride, to go horseback riding; cf. JUMENT; [Fig.] *être à* ~ *sur* (*les principes*), to be a stickler for. **2.** [motor, car] *cheval-vapeur m, pl. chevaux-vapeur* [abr. CV], horse-power [HP]. **3.** ~ *marin*, walrus. cf. MORSE.

chevaleresque [ʃəval|'rɛsk] *adj.* chivalrous. || **chevalerie** [-'ri] *n.f.* chivalry; knighthood. || **chevalier** [-je] *n.m.* knight; [Fig.] ~ *d'industrie*, soldier of fortune. || **chevalin, -e** [-ɛ̃, -in] *adj.* equine: *boucherie f chevaline*, horse butcher; [Fig.] *profil* ~, horse-face.

chevauchée [ʃəvo'ʃe] *n.f.* ride. || **chevauche-**

ment [-'mɑ̃] *n.m.* **1.** riding. **2.** overlapping. || **chevaucher** [-e] #3 *v. intr.* **1.** to ride (on a horse). **2.** [Fig.] to overlap; to straddle, span.

chevelu, -e [ʃə'vl|y] *adj.* hairy, long-haired: *cuir* ~, scalp. || **chevelure** [-y:r] *n.f.* hair (of the head); [Astr.] tail (of a comet).

chevet [ʃə'vɛ] *n.m.*: *table de* ~, bedside table; [Fig.] *C'est mon livre de* ~, It's my Bible.

cheveu [ʃə'vø] *n.m.* hair; *pl.* (the) hair [☞ reste au sing.]: *se faire couper les cheveux,* to get a haircut; *arriver comme un* ~ *sur la soupe,* to arrive very inappropriately; *à un* ~ *de,* to be a hair's breadth from; *à faire dresser les cheveux sur la tête,* terrifying, to make one's hair stand on end; *se faire des cheveux* (*blancs*), to worry o.s. grey.

cheville [ʃə'vi:j] *n.f.* **1.** ankle. **2.** peg, bolt (of a hinge); [Fig.] ~ *ouvrière,* kingbolt, backbone (of a group, &c.).

chèvre [ʃɛ:vr] *n.f.* (she-) goat; © ~ *des Rocheuses,* Rocky Mountain goat. || **chevreau** [ʃə'vro] *n.m.* kid, young goat.

chèvrefeuille [ʃɛvrə'fœ:j] *n.m.* honeysuckle.

chevrette [ʃə'vrɛt] *n.f.* kid, young goat [female].

chevreuil [ʃə'vrœ:j] *n.m.* roebuck. cf. CERF; © deer.

chevron [ʃə'vrõ] *n.m.* **1.** rafter (of a building). **2.** [Mil.] chevron.

chevronné, -e [ʃəvrɔ'ne] *adj.* [Fig.] experienced: *soldat* ~, seasoned soldier.

chevroter [ʃəvrɔ'te] #3 *v. intr.* [chèvre] to bleat: [Fig.] *d'une voix chevrotante,* in a quaver(ing voice).

chez [ʃe] *prép.* **1.** at (the home of), at s.o.'s place: *Il est* ~ *son père,* He is at his father's house; ~ *Pierre,* at Pierre's (house); [☞ chez + pron.]: ~*/moi, toi, lui, elle, nous, vous, eux, elles/,* [without movement] at home; [with movement] home: *M. Dupont n'est pas* ~ *lui,* Mr. D. is not at home; *Mr. D. rentre* ~ *lui,* Mr. D. is going home. **2.** in (+ name of country), among: ~ *les Canadiens,* in Canada, among Canadians; in (+ name of author) ~ *Homère,* in the poems of Homer. **3.** with (the Smiths, &c.): *Il habite* ~ *les X,* He lives with the X's; *C'est une habitude* ~ *lui de . . .,* It's a habit with him to . . . || **chez-moi, chez-soi, chez-nous** [-'mwa, -'swa, -'nu] *n.m.* [varies according to speaker(s)] home: *avoir un chez-soi,* to have a home.

chic [ʃik] *n.m.* skill, knack; style: *avoir le* ~ *pour faire qqch.,* to have a knack for doing sth.; *avoir du* ~, to have style. || *adj. inv.* stylish: *les robes chic,* stylish dresses; decent: *se montrer* ~, to be decent; *un* ~ *type,* a good guy.

chicane [ʃi'kan] *n.f.* [Jur.] chicanery; [Fig.] quarrel, dispute. || **chicaner** [-e] #3 *v. intr*: to quibble (*sur,* over). || **chicanerie** [-'ri] *n.f.* quibbling, dispute. || **chicaneur** [-œ:r] *n.m.* quibbler.

chiche! [ʃiʃ] *interj.* [Fam.] I dare you!; ~ *que . . .,* (I) bet you that . . .

chien, -ne [ʃjɛ̃, ʃjɛn] *n.m.* **1.** dog, bitch [☞ L'emploi de *bitch* au figuré est vulgaire]: ~ *de berger,* sheep dog; ~ *de chasse,* hound; © ~ *esquimau,* husky, huskie; ~ *de garde,* watch dog; © ~ *des prairies,* prairie dog. **2.** [Loc. Fig.] *malade comme un* ~, sick as a dog; *un temps de* ~, terrible weather; *mener une vie de* ~, to lead a dog's life; *comme un* ~ *dans un jeu de quilles,* like a bull in a china shop. **2.** [of a gun] cock.

chiffon [ʃi'f|õ] *n.m.* rag, scrap (of paper); [Fam.] frills (on women's dresses). || **chiffonner** [-ɔ'ne] #3 *v. tr.* to crumple, wrinkle: ~ *une robe,* to wrinkle a dress; [Fig.] to ruffle, vex, bother: *Cette affaire me* ~, That business bothers me.

chiffre [ʃifr] *n.m.* **1.** number, figure [On écrit au sing.: *en chiffre rond,* in round numbers]: *Les chiffres ne concordent pas,* The figures don't/agree, add up/; [Com.] ~ *d'affaires,* turnover. **2.** cipher: *message /en* ~, *chiffré/,* coded message, in cipher. || **chiffrer** [-e] #3 *v. intr.* to calculate. || *v. tr.* to number (pages); to encode (a message); to reckon (a sum). [☞ Usual. in *pron.* form]: *Ces dépenses se chiffrent à . . .,* The expenses add up to . . .

chignon [ʃi'ɲõ] *n.m.* chignon, [hair] bun.

Chili (le) [ʃi'li] *n.m.* Chile.

chimère [ʃi'm|ɛ:r] *n.f.* chimera, idle fancy. || **chimérique** [-e'rik] *adj.* chimeric, unreal.

chimie [ʃi'mi] *n.f.* chemistry. || **chimique** [-k] *adj.* chemical. || **chimiste** [-st] *n.m.* chemist.

chimpanzé [ʃɛ̃pɑ̃'ʒe] *n.m.* chimpanzee.

Chine (la) [ʃin] *n.f.* China: *la mer de* ~, the China Sea; *encre de* ~, India ink. || **chinois, -e** [ʃi'nwa(:z)] *adj. & n.* Chinese: [language] *le chinois,* Chinese; [inhabitants] *les Chinois mpl,* the Chinese, *un Chinois,* a Chinese, a Chinaman [ce dernier mot tend à être péj.].

chinook [ʃi'nuk] *n.m.* © **1.** [warm wind of Western Canada] chinook. **2.** [fish] spring, chinook/salmon.

chipoter [ʃipɔ'te] #3 *v. tr.* to pick (at o.'s food); [price, argument] to haggle.

chiquer [ʃi'ke] #3 *v. tr. & intr.* to chew tobacco.

chiropraticien [kiroprati'sjɛ̃] *n.m.* © chiropractor.

chirurgical, -e [ʃiryrʒ|i'kal] *adj.* surgical: *intervention ~* , operation. ‖ **chirurgie** [-i] *n.f.* surgery. ‖ **chirurgien, -ne** [-jɛ̃, -jɛn] *n.* surgeon.

chlore [klɔːr] *n.m.* chlorine.

chloroforme [klɔrɔ'fɔrm] *n.m.* chloroforme.

choc [ʃɔk] *n.m.* **1.** [blow received] blow, shock; [on object] impact. **2.** [☞ s'accompagnant de bruit: dépend du bruit]: *~ sourd*, thump; *~ mou*, thud; *~ métallique*, clatter; *~ violent*, crash. **3.** [Fig.] conflict (of ideas); [mental] shock: *troupes fpl de ~* , shock troops; *idée f, phrase f/de ~* , slogan, punch line.

chocolat [ʃoko'lɑ] *n.m.* chocolate: *une tablette de ~* , a chocolate bar; *une glace au ~* , chocolate ice cream; *boire un ~* , to have, drink/a cup of chocolate. ‖ *adj.* chocolate-coloured, dark brown.

chœur [kœːr] [× Do not confuse with CŒUR] *n.* **1.** [Mus.] choir, chorus: *chanter en ~* , to sing in chorus. **2.** [Arch.] chancel [of a church]. *enfant m de ~* , altar boy.

choisi, -e [ʃwa'z|i] *adj.* selected, chosen: *morceaux choisis*, selected works [of an author]. ‖ **choisir** [-iːr] #17 *v. tr.* to choose, select (from, *parmi, dans*): *de deux maux ~ le moindre*, to choose the lesser of two evils. ‖ **choix** [ʃwa] *n.m.* **1.** selection, choice: *faire un ~ parmi . . .* , to select from; *au ~* , by choice; [Com.] *un dollar au ~* , all priced at one dollar; *questions au ~* , optional questions. **2.** *de ~* , choice, first class: *de tout premier ~* , of the best quality.

chômage [ʃo'm|aːʒ] *n.m.* stoppage, shutdown [of a factory]; unemployment [of workmen]: *être en ~* , to be unemployed; *assurance-~* , unemployment insurance. ‖ **chômer** [-e] #3 *v. intr.* **1.** to be idle, out of work: *. . . ne chôme pas*, . . . is kept busy. **2.** to keep (a holiday): *le 1er juillet est une fête chômée*, July 1st is a holiday. ‖ **chômeur** [-œːr] *n.m.* unemployed worker; *les chômeurs*, the unemployed.

chopine [ʃɔ'pin] *n.f.* © pint.

choquant, -e [ʃɔ'k|ɑ̃(ːt)] *adj.* shocking, disagreeable; offensive. ‖ **choquer** [-e] #3 *v. tr.* **1.** to shock, offend (s.o.). **2.** (s'entre)-choquer, to clink [glasses], to bump (against each other). ‖ **se choquer (de qqch.)** *v. pron.* to take offence (at sth.); to be shocked, offended (by sth.).

chorégraphie [kɔregra'fi] *n.f.* choreography.

chose [ʃoːz] *n.f.* **1.** thing, object, cf. AUTRE, QUELQUE. **2.** matter, affair: *peu de ~* , *une ~ sans importance*, a trifle, a trifling matter; *~ curieuse . . .* , strangely enough; *ce n'est pas ~ facile*, it is not an easy matter, → this is a ticklish problem. **3.** [générique] property; matter, affair: *être la ~ de qqun*, to be a mere tool in the hands of s.o.; †*la ~ publique*, the common weal; [Fam.] thingummy, doings. ‖ **choses** *fpl.* things, affairs; matter: *aller au fond des ~* , to go to the heart of the matter; *un état de ~* , a state of affairs; *faire bien les ~* , to spare no expense; [Fam.] *dites bien des ~ à (votre femme, &c.)*, my regards to (your wife, &c.).

chou [ʃu] *n.m.* cabbage: *~ de Bruxelles*, Brussels sprouts; *chou(x)-fleur(s)*, cauliflower; *une soupe aux choux*, cabbage soup; *~ à la crème*, cream puff; [Fig.] dearest: *Bonjour, mon petit ~* , Hello, honey. ‖ **choucroute** [-'krut] *n.f.* sauerkraut.

chouette [ʃwet] *n.f.* owl: *~ épervière*, hawk owl.

choyer [ʃwa'je] #12 *v. tr.* to pet, coddle: [Fig.] *~ une idée*, to/hang on to, cherish/ an idea.

chrétien, -ne [kre'tj|ɛ̃, -ɛn] *adj. & n.* Christian. ‖ **chrétienté** [kretjɛ̃'te] *n.f.* Christendom. cf. CHRISTIANISME.

Christ (le) [krist] *n.m.* **1.** (Jesus) Christ. **2.** [☞ with indef. art.] crucifix. ‖ **christianisme** [-ja'nism] *n.m.* Christianity [the religion itself] × cf. CHRÉTIENTÉ.

chrome [kroːm] *n.m.* chrome, chromium. ‖ **chromé, -e** [kro'me] *adj.* chrome-plated.

chromosome [kromo'zoːm] *n.m.* chromosome.

chronique [krɔ'nik] *adj.* [Méd.] chronic. ‖ *n.f.* [news report] chronicle, news: *~ financière*, financial news.

chronologie [krɔnɔlɔ'ʒi] *n.f.* chronology.

chrysanthème [krizɑ̃'tɛm] *n.m.* chrysanthemum.

chuchotement [ʃyʃɔt'mɑ̃] *n.m.* whisper, whsipering. ‖ **chuchoter** [ʃyʃɔ'te] #3 *v. tr.* to whisper.

chut! [ʃyt] *interj.* hush!, hsst!, ssh!

chute [ʃyt] *n.f.* fall: *faire une ~* , to fall; *~ d'eau*, waterfall: *les chutes du Niagara*, Niagara Falls; *la ~ du jour*, sundown, dusk; [Fig.] downfall, decline; [of a play] failure.

Chypre (l'île de) [ʃipr] *f.* Cyprus.

-ci[1] [si] *adv.* [☞ is joined to nouns which are preceded by *ce, cet, cette, ces* and to the dem. pron. *celle, celui, ceux*: e.g. *cet homme-ci, celui-ci*] here: *ci-gît*, here lies. || *loc. adv. par-ci, par-là*, here and there; *ci-après*, thereafter; *Ci-joint vous trouverez ma lettre*, Enclosed (herewith) you will find my letter; *voir/ci-dessus, dessous/*, see/above, below/; *voir ci-contre*, see opposite page. || *pron. dém.* this, this here: *comme ci, comme ça*, so-so.

ci-[2] [si] [☞ precedes the prep.] *loc. adv.* here- [or separate word, see below; these adv. follow the nouns, but see CI-INCLUS] [tous les équivalents anglais suivent le nom, sauf ABOVE qui peut le précéder.] || **ci-après** [-a'prɛ] below.

ci-contre [-'kõ:tr] *adv.* opposite: *la page* ~ , the opposite page. || **ci-dessous** [-də'su] *adv.* below. || **ci-dessus** [-də'sy] above(-mentioned) cf. CI-JOINT, CI-INCLUS. || **ci-gît** [-'ʒi] [found only on tombstones]: ~ *X. Y.*, Here lies X.Y.

cible [sibl] *n.f.* target; [Fig.] *être la* ~ (*des critiques, &c.*), to be a butt to (criticism, &c.).

ciboulette [sibu'lɛt] *n.f.* chives.

cicatrice [sika'tri|s] *n.f.* scar. || **(se) cicatriser** [-'ze] ♯3 *v. tr. & pron.* to heal up, to scar.

cidre [sidr] *n.m.* cider.

ciel [sjɛl] *n.m.* **1.** [*pl.* **cieux**] [sjø] sky: *Le* ~ *se couvre*, It's getting cloudy, It's clouding up; *à* ~ *ouvert*, open. **2.** [*pl.* **ciels**] [sjɛl] sky [in paintings, or in the meaning of *canopy*], the heavens: *Ce peintre fait bien les ciels*, This painter does his skies well; *Des ciels comme tu n'en vois qu'ici*, Skies such as you have never seen anywhere else; [climate] *les ciels brûlants des tropiques*, the burning tropical skies; [Aéro.] *Air France dans tous les ciels*, Air France in every sky; *ciel de lit*, canopy of a bed. **3.** [Rel.] heaven: *bénir le* ~ , to thank one's (lucky) stars; *prendre le* ~ *à témoin*, as Heaven is my witness; *Cette idée m'est tombée du* ~ , The idea came to me out of the blue; *remuer* ~ *et terre*, to move heaven and earth; *Aide-toi, le* ~ *t'aidera*, God helps those who help themselves; *Que le* ~ *m'en préserve*, Heaven forbid.

cierge [sjɛrʒ] *n.m.* (wax) candle, taper.

cigale [si'gal] *n.f.* cicada.

cigare [si'g|a:r] *n.m.* cigar: *fumer le* ~ , to smoke cigars; *fumer un* ~ , to smoke a cigar. || **cigarette** [-a'rɛt] *n.f.* cigarette.

cigogne [si'gɔɲ] *n.f.* stork.

ciguë [si'gy] *n.f.* hemlock.

cil [sil] *n.m.* eyelash.

cime [sim] *n.f.* [mountain] summit; [tree] top; [Fig.] highest (honours, &c.).

ciment [si'mɑ̃] *n.m.* cement (≠ concrete); glue: ~ *armé*, cf. BÉTON. || **cimenter** [-'te] ♯3 *v. tr.* to cement.

cimetière [sim(ə)'tjɛ:r] *n.m.* cemetery, graveyard.

cinéaste [sine'ast] *n.m.* movie producer; scenario writer.

cinéma [sine'm|ɑ] *n.m.* cinema; movie (theatre): *aller au* ~ , to go to the movies; *faire du* ~ , to be a movie actor; ~ *en plein air*, drive-in (theatre). || **cinémathèque** [-a'tɛk] *n.f.* film library.

cingler [sɛ̃'gle] ♯3 *v. intr.* to steer a course; [Naut.] to sail (on, *vers, sur*). || *v. tr.* to sting, lash; [Fig.] to sting, cut (with remarks): *une riposte cinglante*, a stinging retort.

cinq [sɛ̃:k], often [sɛ̃] in compound forms, e.g. *cinq cents* [sɛ̃'sɑ̃]; [sɛ̃] is also used in © when *cinq* is followed by consonant, e.g. *cinq piastres* [sɛ̃'pjastr] *adj.* five: *le* ~ , number five; [date] fifth; *le 5 juin*, the 5th of June; [money] ~ *cents*, a nickel; [time] *moins* ~ , five to (the hour); [Loc.] *Il était moins* ~ *!*, It was a close/thing, shave/. || **cinquantaine** [sɛ̃kɑ̃'tɛ:n] *n.f.*: *une* ~ *de* . . . , about fifty . . . ; *un homme dans la* ~ , a man in his fifties. || **cinquante** [sɛ̃'k|ɑ̃:t] *adj. num.* fifty: © ~ *sous*, half dollar, four bits. || **cinquantième** [-ɑ̃'tjɛm] *n.m. & adj. num.* (the) fiftieth. || **cinquième** [sɛ̃'kjɛm] *n.m. & adj. num.* (the) fifth: *Il habite au* ~ , He lives on the fifth floor [© sixth floor].

cintre [sɛ̃:tr] *n.m.* **1.** curvature; curve (of an arch): *plein* ~ , round arch. **2.** coat-hanger. || **cintrer** [sɛ̃'tre] ♯3 *v. tr.* to bend; [Arch.] to arch.

cirage [si'ra:ʒ] *n.m.* [action] waxing; (shoe) polish: ~ *d'un plancher*, waxing of a floor.

circoncire [sirkõ|'si:r] *v. tr.* to circumcise. || **circoncision** [-si'zjõ] *n.f.* circumcision.

circonférence [sirkõfe'rɑ̃:s] *n.f.* circumference; perimeter.

circonflexe [sirkõ'flɛks] *adj.*: *accent* ~ [^], the, a/circumflex.

circonscription [sirkõskrip'sjõ] *n.f.*: ~ *électorale*, electoral district, constituency

circonscrire [sirkõs'kri:r] ♯48 *v. tr.* to circumscribe; [Fig.] to limit (*à*, to). || **se circonscrire** *v. pron.* to limit o.s. (*à*, to).

circonspect, -e [sirkõ'spɛk|t] *adj.* wary, circumspect. || **circonspection** [-sjõ] *n.f.* circumspection.

circonstance [sirkõs'tǀɑ̃:s] *n.f.* circumstance, occasion: [Mus., &c.] *de* ~, special (music, &c.); *pour la* ~, for the occasion; *mesure f de* ~, emergency measure; *orateur m de* ~, guest speaker. ǁ **circonstancié, -e** [-ɑ̃'sje] *adj.* detailed.

circonvenir [sirkõv(ə)'ni:r] #22 *v. tr.* to circumvent.

circuit [sir'kɥi] *n.m.* **1.** circuit, tour: *faire le* ~ *en 5 minutes*, to make the round in 5 minutes; *le* ~ *des lacs suisses*, a tour of the Swiss lakes; (*course*) *en* ~ *fermé*, a circular track; [Sport.] © *coup de* ~, home run. **2.** [Electr.] *un court* ~, a short circuit.

circulaire [sirky'lɛ:r] *adj.* circular. ǁ *n.f.* circular (letter).

circulation [sirkylǀa'sjõ] *n.f.* **1.** [blood, &c.] circulation: *retirer de la* ~, to call in. **2.** [voirie] traffic: *feux mpl de* ~, traffic lights; ~ *interdite*, no thoroughfare. ǁ **circuler** [-e] #3 *v. tr.* to circulate, pass (from hand to hand); [Fig.] to spread: *faire* ~ *une nouvelle*, to spread a piece of news. *v. intr.* to move (about): *Circulez!*, Move along!

cire [si:r] *n.f.* wax, floorwax. ǁ **ciré, -e** [si're] *adj.* waxed, polished: *toile* ~, oilcloth. ǁ *n.m.* raincoat, oilskins; mackintosh. ǁ **cirer** [si'rǀe] #3 *v. tr.* to wax, polish. ǁ **cireuse** [-ø:z] *n.f.* floor-waxer.

cirque [sirk] *n.m.* circus.

ciseau [si'zǀo] *n.m.* chisel. ǁ **ciseaux** [-o] *n.mpl.* scissors; [de tailleur, &c.] shears. ǁ **ciseler** [-'le] #8 *v. tr.* to engrave, [métal] to chisel; [Fig.] to work (sth.) over carefully.

citadelle [sita'dɛl] *n.f.* citadel.

citadin, -e [sita'dǀɛ̃, -in] *n.* city dweller.

citation [sita'sjõ] *n.f.* quotation; citation; [Jur.] summons.

cité [si'te] *n.f.* [×] city: ~ *ouvrière*, low rent development (for workmen); ~ *universitaire*, university residences, *avoir droit de* ~, to be acceptable; *Le port des shorts n'a pas droit de* ~ *à Montréal*, Wearing shorts is not acceptable in Montreal.

citelle [si'tɛl] *n.m.*: © ~ *du Canada* (ou *écureuil de terre*), gopher.

citer [si'te] #3 *v. tr.* **1.** to mention, quote: ~ *Homère*, to quote Homer; *Il a été cité à l'ordre du jour*, He was cited for bravery; ~ *en exemple*, to quote (s.o.) as an example. **2.** [Jur.] to summon: ~ *en justice*, to summon.

citerne [si'tɛrn] *n.f.* (underground) cistern; tank; [Mar.] *navire* ~, tanker.

citoyen, -ne [sitwa'jǀɛ̃, -ɛn] *n.* citizen. ǁ **citoyenneté** [-ɛn'te] *n.f.* citizenship.

citron [si'trǀõ] *n.m.* lemon. ǁ *adj. invar.* lemon (-coloured). ǁ **citronnade** [-ɔ'nad] *n.f.* lemonade, lemon squash [also: *citron pressé*].

citrouille [si'tru:j] *n.f.* pumpkin.

civière [si'vjɛ:r] *n.f.* stretcher.

civil, -e [si'vil] *adj.* civil (≠ military): *guerre civile*, civil war; *état* ~, marital status; *Bureau de l'état* ~, Bureau of Vital Statistics; *dans le* ~, in civil life: *un agent en* ~, plainclothes policeman; [Fig.] courteous, civil: *des manières fort civiles*, very polite manners. ǁ **civilement** [-'mɑ̃] *adv.* **1.** civilly: *se marier* ~, to have a civil marriage. **2.** †politely, courteously.

civilisation [sivilizǀa'sjõ] *n.f.* civilization. ǁ **civiliser** [-e] #3 *v. tr.* to civilize. ǁ **se civiliser** *v. pron.* to become civilized.

civilité [sivili'te] *n.f.* politeness, courtesy.

civique [si'viǀk] *adj.* civic: *droits civiques*, civic rights. ǁ **civisme** [-sm] *n.m.* public-spiritedness.

clair, -e [klɛ:r] *adj.* **1.** [lumière] bright; [salle, temps, voix] clear. **2.** [colour] light: *rouge* ~, light red. **3.** thin: *potage* ~, clear soup; *sauce claire*, thin gravy. **4.** [Fig.] clear, obvious: *C'est* ~ (*comme le jour*) *que* ..., It's clear (as day) that ...; *C'est* ~ *comme de l'eau de roche*, It's as clear as crystal. ǁ *adv.* plainly, clearly: *voir* ~, to see clearly, to have good eyesight; [Fig.] to understand; *parler* ~ to speak/plainly, clearly/. ǁ *n.m.* [moon, &c.] light: ~ *de lune*, moonlight; *au* ~ *de la lune*, by moonlight; [Fig.] *tirer une affaire au* ~, to clear up an affair.

clairière [klɛ'rjɛ:r] *n.f.* clearing, glade.

claironner [klɛrɔ'ne] #3 *v. tr.* to trumpet, to clarion forth.

clairsemé, -e [klɛrsə'me] *adj.* [cheveux] thin, sparse; [population] scattered.

clairvoyance [klɛrvwa'jǀɑ̃:s] *n.f.* [seconde vue] clairvoyance; [Fig.] clearsightedness. ǁ **clairvoyant, -e** [-ɑ̃(:t)] *adj.* clairvoyant; [Fig.] clearsighted.

clameur [kla'mœ:r] *n.f.* clamour, uproar.

clan [klɑ̃] *n.m.* clan; [Fig., Péj.] clique.

clandestin, -e [klɑ̃dɛs'tǀɛ̃, -in] *adj.* clandestine, secret. ǁ **clandestinité** [-ini'te] *n.f.* underground movement.

clapotement [klapɔtǀ'mɑ̃] *n.m.* lapping, splash(ing) of waves. ǁ **clapoter** [-e] #3 *v. intr.* to lap, splash.

claque [klak] *n.f.* **1.** slap, smack: *donner une* ~, to slap (s.o.'s face). **2.** © rubber.

claqué, -e [kla'ke] *adj.* [Fam.] tired, worn out: *être* ~, to be dog-tired.

claquement [klak|'mɑ̃] *n.m.* crack (of a whip); slap, smash, clapping (of the hand); slam (of a door). || **claquer** [-e] #3 *v. tr.* [des mains] to clap; [de la langue] to smack; [une porte] to slam: *je claque des dents,* my teeth are chattering; [Fig.. Vulg.] to croak, die.

clarifier [klari'fje] #3 *v. tr.* to clarify, to purify.

clarinette [klari'nɛt] *n.f.* clarinet; clarinet player.

clarté [klar'te] *n.f.* **1.** light, brightness: *la ~ du jour,* the light of day. **2.** clearness, transparency; [Fig.] clarity (of style); *pl. les premières clartés du soleil,* the first rays of sunlight.

classe [klɑːs] *n.f.* **1.** class, category: *la ~ ouvrière,* the working class; [Rail.] *voyager en première* (~), to travel first class; [Com.] *de grande ~*, first class, foremost; top quality; *un enregistrement, une automobile/de grande ~*, a high-fidelity, top-quality recording; a first-class, top-quality car; [Naut.] *un navire de la ~ Dunkerque,* a ship of the Dunkerque class; [Fam.] *avoir de la ~*, to have/class, style/; *un pianiste de grande ~*, an outstanding, a first-class/ pianist. **2.** class; classroom; grade, form: *les petites classes,* the lower grades, *les grandes classes,* the higher grades; [Fam.] *aller en classe* (= aller à l'école), to go to school; *être premier de ~*, to be the first in the class; *la rentrée des classes,* school opening; *~ mixte,* mixed class; *suivre la ~ de X. au Conservatoire,* to take Mr. X's class in the Conservatory. || **classé, -e** [klɑ's|e] *adj.* sorted, filed; [Com.] classified; © *annonces classées* (de la presse), classified ads; [Jur.] *une affaire classée,* a closed case. || **classement** [-'mɑ̃] *n.m.* classification; filing: *~ des fiches,* filing of/cards, slips/. || **classer** [-e] #3 *v. tr.* **1.** to classify, file: *~ par ordre alphabétique,* to file in alphabetical order; *~ des livres, des papiers,* to arrange (file) books, papers; *~ . . . par ordre de grandeur,* to arrange/in order of size, by size/. **2.** *~ une affaire,* to shelve a question. || **classeur** [-œːr] *n.m.* filing cabinet; file.

classicisme [klasi'sism] *n.m.* classicism, → classical character (of).

classification [klasif|ika'sjɔ̃] *n.f.* (établissement de classes) classification. || **classifier** [-je] #3 *v. tr.* to classify, to sort out.

classique [kla'sik] *adj.* classical; © *cours m, collège m/ ~*, classical college; *n.mpl. les classiques* (*et les modernes*), the classics, the classical/authors, writers/ (and the/modern, contemporary/writers, &c.).

clause [kloːz] *n.f.* [Jur.] clause; [contrat] stipulation, provision.

clavecin [klav'sɛ̃] *n.m.* harpsichord.

clavicule [klavi'kyl] *n.f.* clavicle.

clavier [kla'vje] *n.m.* keyboard (of piano, typewriter).

clef, clé [kle] *n.f.* **1.** key: *fermer à ~*, to lock [cf. BARRER]; *mettre sous ~*, to put under lock and key, to lock up; [Fig.] *prendre la ~ des champs,* to set . . . free; *la ~ du bonheur,* → passport to happiness; *poste-clef m,* a key job. **2.** [outil] wrench, spanner: *~ anglaise,* monkey wrench.

clémence [kle'm|ɑ̃ːs] *n.f.* clemency, leniency. || **clément, -e** [-ɑ̃(ːt)] *adj.* lenient.

cleptomane [klɛptɔ'man] *n.m/f.* kleptomaniac.

clerc [klɛːr] *n.m.* **1.** cleric, clergyman. **2.** [Jur.] clerk: [Fam.] *faire un pas de ~*, to make a blunder.

clergé [klɛr'ʒe] *n.m.* clergy. || **clérical, -e** [kleri'kal] *adj.* [×] clerical [= of the clergy; for the meaning "clerical error," see ERREUR].

cliché [kli'ʃe] *n.m.* [Typo.] plate, cut; [Photo.] exposure; negative; [style] cliché.

client, -e [kli'j|ɑ̃(ːt)] *n.* [avocat, &c.] client; [Com.] customer; [Méd.] patient. || **clientèle** [-ɑ̃'tɛl] *n.f.* [Com.] customers; [Com.] goodwill; *~ d'avocat, de médecin,* practice.

cligner [kli'ɲe] #3 *v. intr.*: *~ /du regard, des yeux/*, to blink.

clignotant [kliɲɔ't|ɑ̃] *n.m.* [Auto.] signal light; directional light; [traffic light] blinker. || **clignoter** [-e] #3 *v. intr.* [eye] to blink; [stars] to twinkle; [light, flame] to flicker.

climat [kli'ma] *n.m.* climate; [Fig.] mood, atmosphere: [Fig.] *un ~ de sympathie régnait dans la salle,* In the hall a harmonious atmosphere prevailed.

clin [klɛ̃] *n.m.* wink: *faire un ~ d'œil à qqun,* to wink at s.o.; *clins d'yeux* [deux yeux] blink; *en un ~ d'œil,* very quickly, in the wink of an eye, in a jiffy. cf. ŒIL.

clinique [kli'nik] *n.f.* clinic, nursing home. || *adj.* clinic(al).

clique [klik] *n.f.* [Péj.] clique; [Fam.]: *toute la ~*, all the rest of it; *prendre ses cliques et ses claques,* to clear off bag and baggage.

cliquetis [klik'ti] *n.m.* [glasses] clinking;

[ice in a glass, bell] tinkling; [chains] rattling; [keys] jingling.

cloche [klɔʃ] *n.f.* × [for detailed rendering of *bell*, see under BELL] bell: *sonner la* ~, to ring the bell: [by ext. is applied to numerous bell-shaped things] dish cover; [Méd.] blister. || **clocher** [-e] *n.m.* steeple; [Fig.] parish. || #3 *v. intr.* to limp; [Fig.] *Il y a qqch. qui cloche,* There's something wrong there. || **clochette** [-ɛt] *n.f.* (hand-) bell; [Bot.] bell-flower.

cloison [klwa'zõ] *n.f.* partition; [Naut.] bulkhead; [Fig.] division: *la* ~ *entre les classes sociales,* the barrier between social classes.

cloître [klwa:tr] *n.m.* cloister.

clore [klɔ:r], **closant** [klo'zã], **clos** [klo] #53 *v. tr.* [☞ has gen. been replaced by FERMER] to block (up) (a passage), to close, shut (up); to enclose (a park); to end (a discussion); to close (out) an account.

clos, -e cf. CLORE.

clos, -e [klo(:z)] *adj.* closed, shut (up fast): *à la nuit* ~, in the dark of the night; fastened: *volets* ~, closed shutters; *à huis* ~, in camera, behind closed doors; *les yeux* ~, blindfold; *demeurer bouche close,* to keep silent; [Fig.] *lettre close,* a sealed book. || **clos** [klo] *n.m.* [enclosed cultivated field] enclosure, close; [Fr.] vineyard, ~ *Vougeot* [and the wine from that vineyard], Vougeot vineyard, Clos Vougeot vintage.

clôture [klo't|y:r] *n.f.* enclosure, fence: ~ *de fer,* iron railing, fence; [Fig.] closing. || **clôturer** [-y're] #3 *v. tr.* to enclose, fence in; [Fig.] to bring to an end, wind up.

clou [klu] *n.m.* **1.** nail: ~ *de girofle,* clove; [Fig.] *river son* ~ *à qqun,* to shut s.o. up. **2.** [Méd.] boil; [Fig. & Fam.] **1.** old broken-down car, bicycle, &c., rattle-trap. **2.** feature attraction (on a program). || **clouer** [-'e] #3 *v. tr.* to nail; [Fig.] to immobilize, rivet: ~ *le bec à qqun,* to shut s.o.'s mouth; *être cloué au lit,* to be bedridden.

clouter [-'te] #3 *v. tr.* to stud: [Fr.] *passage clouté,* pedestrian/crossing, crosswalk/.

club [klœb © klyb] *n.m.* club.

coaguler (se) [(sə) kɔagy'le] #3 *v. tr. & pron.* to coagulate, to congeal.

coalition [kɔali'sjõ] *n.f.* coalition, alliance.

cocaïne [kɔka'in] *n.f.* cocaine.

cocher [kɔ'ʃe] *n.m.* driver, coachman; *porte cochère,* carriage entrance, main entrance. || #3 *v. tr.* to notch, nick.

cochon [kɔ'ʃ|õ] *n.m.* **1.** pig, hog: ~ *d'Inde,* guinea pig; ~ *de lait,* suckling pig. **2.** [meat; in this sense, Fam.] pork. || *adj.* filthy; [Fam.] dirty. || **cochonnerie** [-ɔn'ri] *n.f.* [Fam.] dirty/trick, talk.

cocorico [kɔkɔri'ko] *n.m.* cock-a-doodle-do.

code [kɔd] *n.m.* [collection of laws] code; [the laws themselves] law; [signals]: *écrire en* ~, to send a coded message; ~ *de la route,* traffic regulations; ~ *de la politesse,* the rules of polite society.

codéine [kɔde'in] *n.f.* codeine.

codifier [kɔdi'fje] #3 *v. tr.* to codify.

cœur [kœ:r] *n.m.* **1.** heart; stomach; breast; bosom: *maladie de* ~, heart disease; *avoir mal au* ~, to feel/(sea-)sick, nauseated/; *serrer qqun sur son* ~, to clasp s.o. to one's/heart, breast/; *Cela me réchauffe le* ~, It warms the cockles of my heart; [R.C.] *le Sacré-Cœur,* the Sacred Heart. **2.** centre, core, heart: *le* ~ *de la ville,* the/heart, centre/of the town; *le* ~ *de l'été,* the height of summer; *le* ~ *de l'hiver,* the depth of winter. **3.** [Fig.] heart, conscience; courage, [Fam.] "guts": *de bon* ~, *de grand* ~, willingly, heartily; *avoir le* ~ *à,* to be in the mood for [+ ing], to feel like [+ ing]: *prendre qqch. à* ~, to take sth. to heart; *avoir du* ~ *au ventre,* to have guts. **4.** heart, kindness; love: *affaire de* ~, love affair; [Journ.] *Courrier m du* ~, Advice to the lovelorn; *avoir du* ~, to be kind-hearted; *avoir un* ~ *d'or,* to have a heart of gold; *avoir le* ~ *sur la main,* to wear one's heart on one's sleeve; *de tout mon* ~, with all my heart; *sans* ~, heartless, cruel. || **cœurs-saignants** [-sɛ'ɲã] © *n.m.pl.* [Bot.] bleeding hearts.

coexistence [kɔɛgzis'tã:s] *n.f.* coexistence: ~ *pacifique,* peaceful coexistence.

coffre [kɔfr] *n.m.* chest; [Auto.] trunk; [jewels] box; © ~ *de sûreté,* safe. || **coffre-fort** [-ə'fɔ:r] *n.m.* safe, strong-box. || **coffrer** [-e] #3 *v. tr.* [Fam.] to jug. || **coffret** [-ɛ] *n.m.* small box, gift box; © safety deposit box.

cognac [kɔ'ɲak] *n.m.* brandy, cognac.

†**cognée** [kɔ'ɲe] *n.f.* woodsman's axe.

cogner [kɔ'ɲe] #3 *v. tr. & intr.* to bang, hit; to hammer: ~ *sur la porte,* to bang on the door; *Le moteur cogne,* The motor knocks; ~ *dur,* to hit hard. || **se cogner** *v. pron.* to bump (up) against (*à, contre*).

cohabiter [kɔabi'te] #3 *v. intr.* to cohabit.

cohérent, -e [kɔe'rã(:t)] *adj.* coherent.

cohési|f, -ve [kɔe'z|if, -i:v] *adj.* cohesive.

cohue [kɔ'y] *n.f.* crowd, mob; disorder, tumult.

†**coi, -te** [kwa(:t)] *adj.*: *se tenir* ~ , to lie low, to keep quiet.
coiffe [kwa:f] *n.f.* (lady's) coif, headgear. || **coiffé, -e** [kwa'f|e] *adj.* [head] covered; wearing a hat; [Fig.] infatuated; lucky: *être né* ~ , to be born lucky; [Fig.] ~ *de neige*, snow-capped. || **coiffer** [-e] #3 *v. tr.* **1.** to cover s.o.'s head. **2.** to do s.o.'s hair. || **se coiffer** *v. pron.* to put on one's hat, to cover o.s.; to do one's hair; [Fig.] (de qqun) to become infatuated (with s.o.). || **coiffeu|r, -se** [-œ:r, -ø:z] *n. n.m/f* barber; hairdresser: *salon m de coiffure*, barber shop. || *n.f.* [lady's] dressing table. || **coiffure** [-y:r] *n.f.* headgear, head style.
coin [kwɛ̃] *n.m.* **1.** corner, angle: *au* ~ *de la rue*, on the corner; *regarder du* ~ *de l'œil*, to look out of the corner of one's eye; *tous les* ~ *et recoins de qqch.*, every nook and corner; *connaître une affaire dans tous les coins*, to know all the ins and outs (of an affair); [dans un magasin] *le* ~ *des petits*, kiddies' corner. **2.** wedge. **3.** stamp (for coins, medals, &c.).
coincer [kwɛ̃'se] #4 *v. tr.* **1.** to wedge, to check. **2.** to corner (s.o.). **3.** [Fig. & Fam.] to pinch, arrest s.o.
coïncidence [kɔɛ̃si'd|ɑ̃:s] *n.f.* coincidence. || **coïncider** [-e] #3 *v. intr.* to coincide (with, *avec*).
coke [kɔk] © [ko:k] *n.m.* [charbon] coke.
col [kɔl] *n.m.* **1.** collar; neck: *le* ~ *d'une bouteille*, the neck of a bottle; [shirt] *un* ~ */souple, raide/*, a/soft, hard/collar; ~ *Claudine*, Peter Pan collar; cf. FAUX-COL. **2.** (mountain) pass. **3.** © necktie.
colère [kɔ'l|ɛ:r] *n.f.* anger; wrath: *se mettre en* ~ *contre qqun*, to get angry at s.o.; *être en* ~ , to be angry; *avec* ~ , angrily; [Fig.] violence, fury: *la* ~ *des vents*, the violence of the winds. || *adj. inv.* irritable, easily angered: *Il est bien* ~ , He is really touchy. || **coléreu|x, -se** [-e'rø(:z)] *adj.* irritable, irascible, easily angered. || **colérique** [-e'rik] *adj.* choleric.
colibri [kɔli'bri] *n.m.* [ou *oiseau-mouche*] humming bird.
colimaçon [kɔlima'sõ] *n.m.* snail; [Fig.] *escalier m en* ~ , winding staircase.
colis [kɔ'li] *n.m.* sack, parcel: *envoyer par* ~ *postal*, to send (by) parcel post. cf. PAQUET.
collaborat|eur, -rice [kɔlabɔr|a'tœ:r] *n.* collaborator; colleague, associate: ~ *d'une revue*, contributor. || **collaboration** [-a'sjõ] *n.f.* collaboration; contribution; cooperation. || **collaborer** [-e] #3 *v. intr.* to collaborate (in, *à*; with, *avec*).
collant, -e [kɔ'lɑ̃(:t)] *adj.* sticky; [Fig.] *une personne collante*, a person hard to get rid of. || *n.m.* tights; leotards. || **collant** [kɔ'lɑ̃] *n.m.* [Théât.] tights.
collatéral, -e [kɔlate'ral] *adj.* collateral. || *n.m.* collateral.
collation [kɔla'sj|õ] *n.f.* **1.** granting [of degree, diploma, &c.]: ~ *des diplômes*, commencement (exercise), graduation. **2.** snack, light meal: *prendre, faire/une* ~ , to have a light meal. || **collationner** [-ɔ'ne] #3 *v. tr.* to collate, compare; †to have a snack.
colle [kɔl] *n.f.* glue, paste; [Fam.] difficult problem, "poser"; [Sch. Sl.] detention; oral test.
collecte [kɔ'lɛk|t] *n.f.* [Rel.] collection; [Rel.] collect; [vieux papiers, &c.] collecting. || **collecteur** [-'tœ:r] *n.m.* tax collector. || *adj.*: *égout/conduit/* ~ , main sewer, conduit. || **collecti|f, -ve** [-'tif, -'ti:v] *adj.* collective, joint: [Gram.] *nom.* ~ , collective noun. || *n.m.* [Gram.] collective (noun). || **collection** [-'sjõ] *n.f.* [philatélie, &c.] collection; [Fig., of several things] set. || **collectionner** [-sjɔ'ne] #3 *v. tr.* to collect, gather; to accumulate. || **collectionneur** [-sjɔ'nœ:r] *n.m.* [stamp, &c.] collector (de timbres-poste, &c.). || **collectivité** [-tivi'te] *n.f.* community.
collège [kɔ'lɛ:ʒ] *n.m.* **1.** [group of people having the same authority, or position] college, examining board; © *le* ~ *des Médecins et Chirurgiens*, the College of Physicians and Surgeons; ~ *électoral*, electoral college. **2.** †[Fr.] secondary school, high school; [Br.] grammar school. [☞ restricted to private schools, e.g. *le Collège Stanislas*]. **3.** © ~ *classique*, classical college [granting B.A. in Quebec]. **4.** †[Fr.] institute, school/of higher studies: *le Collège de France* [do not translate]. || **collegial, -e** [kɔle|'ʒjal] *adj.* collegiate: © *enseignement* ~ , college course. || **collégien, -ne** [-'ʒjɛ̃, -'ʒjɛn] *n.* **1.** †[Fr.] schoolboy, schoolgirl. **2.** © high-school, college/student [use ÉTUDIANT/E].
collègue [kɔ'lɛg] *n. m/f.* colleague; [Fam.] fellow member, fellow teacher, &c.: *Monsieur et cher* ~, My dear (Mr. Smith).
coller [kɔ'le] #3 *v. tr.* to stick, glue, paste: [Fig.] ~ *son front à la vitre*, to press one's forehead against the glass. || *v. intr.* to stick: *Ce papier colle mal*, This paper doesn't stick very well; [Fam., Fr.] *Ça colle!*, O.K.! [Sch.] ~ *à un examen*, to flunk (an exam); © *Ça colle*, It's hot and

sticky. || **se coller** *v. pron.* (ensemble), to stick together.

collet [kɔ'lɛ] *n.m.* **1.** collar [☞ only in set phrases; otherwise use COL]: *saisir qqun au* ~, to grab s.o. by the collar; © *collet blanc*, white collar (worker). **2.** snare: *attraper des lapins au* ~, to snare rabbits. **3.** [Fig.] ~ *monté*, prudish, strait-laced/person.

collier [kɔ'lje] *n.m.* **1.** necklace. **2.** [de chien, de cheval] dog collar, horse collar.

colline [kɔ'lin] *n.f.* hill, © *La colline parlementaire*, Parliament Hill [Ottawa].

collision [kɔli'zjõ] *n.f.* collision; [Fig.] clash, conflict: *entrer en* ~ *avec . . .*, to collide with . . .

colloque [kɔl'lɔk] *n.m.* symposium, discussion group.

colombe [kɔ'lɔ̃:b] *n.f.* dove.

Colombie (la) [(la) kɔlõ'bi] *n.f.* [South America] Colombia; *la Colombie Britannique*, British Columbia.

colon [kɔ'lõ] *n.m.* colonist, farmer; colonial.

colonel [kɔlɔ'nɛl] *n.m.* colonel; [aviation] group captain.

colonial [kɔlɔ'njal] *adj.* colonial. || *n.m.* colonial: [Fr.] *la Coloniale*, Colonial infantry, the Marines. || **colonialisme** [-ism] *n.m.* imperialism, colonialism. || **colonie** [kɔlɔ'ni] *n.f.* colony, settlement: ~ *de la Couronne*, Crown colony; ~ *de vacances*, summer, holiday/camp; [group] *la* ~ *française* (*d'Edmonton*), the French (Canadian) colony (in E.). || **colonisat|eur, -rice** [-za'tœ:r, -za'tris] *adj.* colonizing. || **colonisation** [-za'sjõ] *n.f.* colonization, settling. || **coloniser** [-'ze] *v. tr.* to colonize, settle.

colonne [kɔ'lɔn] *n.f.* column; [Arch.] pillar: *les colonnes d'un journal*, the columns of a newspaper; ~ *vertébrale*, spine, spinal column.

colorant [kɔlɔ'r|ɑ̃] *n.m.* dye, stainer. || **coloration** [-a'sjõ] *n.f.* [action] colouring; [teinte] colouration, shade. || **coloré, -e** [-e] *adj.* coloured; ruddy; *teint* ~, ruddy, florid/complexion; *style* ~, colourful style. || **colorer** [-e] *v. tr. & intr.* **1.** to colour: ~ *qqch. en vert*, to colour sth. green. **2.** [Fig.] to modify, influence (feelings, behaviour). || **colorier** [-je] #3 *v. intr.* to paint, colour [generally used in the sense of adding colour to sth.]. || **coloris** [-i] *n.m.* colour(ing), hue: ~ *du style*, richness, brilliance/ of style; *d'un* ~ *sombre*, of a sombre hue.

colossal, -e [kɔlɔ'sal] *adj.* colossal, gigantic.

colporter [kɔlpɔr't|e] #3 *v. tr.* to peddle, hawk; [nouvelles] to spread. || **colporteur** [-œ:r] *n.m.* peddler, hawker; [de nouvelles] newsmonger.

combat [kõ'ba] *n.m.* fight, struggle; [Mil.] battle, fighting; [Aviat.] combat: *livrer* ~ *à qqun*, to give battle to s.o., to fight s.o.; *engager le* ~, to go into action; ~ *singulier*, single combat; *hors de* ~, disabled. || **combati|f, -ve** [-'tif, -'ti:v] *adj.* pugnacious; competitive. || **combattant, -e** [-'tɑ̃(:t)] *adj.* fighting. || *n.m.* fighter, combatant: *anciens combattants*, veterans. || **combattre** [-tr] #43 *v. tr.* to fight (with); to struggle (against); [Fig.] to war against (abuses); to fight against (sleep); to contend against (a political opponent). || *v. intr.* to fight, strive, struggle: ~ *jusqu'à la mort*, to fight to the death.

combien (de) [kõ'bjɛ̃] *adv. interrog. partitif*, how/much, many, far, long/: *C'est* ~ *?*, How much is it?, *Je vous dois* ~ *?*, How much do I owe you?; *Le* ~ *sommes-nous?*, What's the date (today)?; ~ *mesure-t-il?*, How tall is he?; ~ *a-t-on payé?*, How much did we pay? || *n.m. inv.* [Pop.] *Il passe tous les* ~ *?*, How often does he come?

combinaison [kõbinɛ'zõ] *n.f.* **1.** combination, grouping, arrangement: ~ *de couleurs*, colour scheme. **2.** [de mécanicien] overalls; [de femme] slip, underwear.

combine [kõ'bin] *n.f.* [Fam.] racket, scheme.

combiné [-e] *n.m.* French telephone, hand phone. || **combiner** [-e] #3 *v. tr.* to unite, combine; [Fig.] to devise, contrive: ~ *un plan*, to plan. || **se combiner** *v. pron.* to unite, combine (*avec*, with).

comble [kõ:bl] *n.m.* **1.** †[Arch.] attic, roof: *de fond en* ~, from top to bottom. **2.** heaped measure; [Fig.] the limit [☞ dépend du contexte: the height (of folly), the depth (of despair), &c.]; the degree: *Ça c'est le* ~, That takes the cake; *pour* ~ *de malheur*, to crown everything; *mettre le* ~ *à*, to cap. || *adj.* heaping, overflowing; packed: *la salle est* ~, It's a full house, The house is packed; [Fig.] *La mesure est* ~, That's the last straw. || **combler** [kõ'ble] #3 *v. tr.* **1.** to heap (up), to overload. **2.** ~ *un fossé*, to fill up a ditch; ~ *d'honneurs*, to shower honours on; [déficit] to make up; [désirs], to gratify; [lacune] to fill.

combustible [kõbys't|ibl] *adj.* combustible. *n.m.* fuel. || **combustion** [-jõ] *n.f.* combustion.

comédie [kɔme'd|i] *n.f.* [genre] comedy; [pièce] play; [Fig.] *Cessez cette ~ !,* Cut out, stop/the acting. || **comédien, -ne** [-jɛ̃, -jɛn] *n.* comedian, actor; [Fig.] shammer.

comestible [kɔmɛs'tibl] *adj.* edible, eatable: *champignon ~* , mushrooms. || *n.mpl.* foodstuffs, cf. VIVRES.

comète [kɔ'mɛt] *n.f.* comet.

cométique [kɔme'tik] © *n.m.* [= traîneau à chiens], komatik.

comique [kɔ'mik] *adj.* comic(al), funny; [Théât.] comic. || *n.m.* comedian, humorist.

comité [kɔmi'te] *n.m.* committee [× smaller group than COMMISSION]: *~ d'accueil,* reception committee; [Fig.] *en petit ~* , a friendly gathering, an informal meeting.

commandant [kɔmɑ̃'dɑ̃] *n.m.* commanding officer; [grade] major; [Aviat.] squadron-leader; [Naut.] captain: *Oui, mon ~ !,* Yes, Sir! || **commande** [kɔ'm|ɑ̃:d] *n.f.* **1.** order: *sur ~* , (made) to order; *passer, faire/une ~* , to place an order; *~ postale,* mail order. **2.** control: *~ à distance,* remote control; *organes de ~* , controls; [Fig.] *sourire de ~* , forced smile. || **commandement** [-ɑ̃d'mɑ̃] *n.m.* **1.** command, order; *~ verbal,* verbal order; *Les commandements de Dieu,* God's commandments. **2.** command: *avoir le ~ d'une armée,* to be in/charge, command/of an army. || **commander** [-ɑ̃'de] #3 *v. tr.* to command, order: *~ le respect,* to command respect; *~ un repas,* to order a meal. || *v. intr.* to master: *~ à ses passions,* to master one's desires. || **se commander** *v. pron.* **1.** to control o.s. **2.** to communicate: *Ces salles se commandent,* These are connecting rooms.

commanditaire [kɔmɑ̃di'tɛ:r] *n.m.* sponsor, backer.

comme [kɔm] *conj.* **1.** [comparison] like, as: *fort ~ un bœuf,* strong as a bull; *agir ~ un enfant,* to act like a child; *C'est tout ~* , It's six of one and half a dozen of the other, It's as broad as it is long. **2.** [manner] like, as: *Cela n'est pas arrivé ~ je m'y attendais,* It did not turn out as I expected. **3.** [cause] because, as: *~ j'avais faim, je mangeais,* As I was hungry, I ate. **4.** [time] as, when: *~ j'allais sortir, il est venu,* As I was about to leave, he arrived. || *adv.* **1.** [exclam.] how, to what point: *~ il fait beau!,* How beautiful it is!; Isn't it beautiful!; *~ c'est pénible!,* How painful it is!, It is really painful! **2.** [manner] how: *Vous voyez ~ il agit,* You see how he acts; [Fam.] *~ ci, ~ ça,* so, so; *~ tout,* like everything; *tout ~* , just like.

commençant, -e [kɔmɑ̃'s|ɑ̃(:t)] *adj.* beginning. || *n.* beginner, tyro. || **commencement** [-'mɑ̃] *n.m.* beginning, commencement: *au ~,* in the beginning; *dès le ~* , from the beginning, at the outset. || **commencer** [-e] #4 *v. tr.* [conj. AVOIR (action), ÊTRE (état)] to begin; to start, to commence. || *v. intr.* to begin: *pour ~* , to begin with, first of all; *~ à,* to begin, start to: *Commencez par le commencement,* Begin at the beginning.

comment [kɔ'mɑ̃] *adv.* **1.** How? In what way?: *~ allez-vous?,* How are you?; *~ est-il venu?,* How did he come?; *~ faire?,* What is to be done?; *Comment?,* What (did you say)?; *~ donc?* [sense varies with the intonation] How come? || *interj.* [surprise, indignation] What?: *Mais ~ donc!,* By all means!; *~ ! Vous êtes toujours là?,* What! Are you still here? || *n.m.*: *savoir le pourquoi et le ~ d'une chose,* to know the why and wherefore of a thing.

commentaire [kɔmɑ̃'t|ɛ:r] *n.m.* (news) commentary; (literary) criticism; (critical) comment: *Cela se passe de commentaires,* That speaks for itself; *pas de commentaires,* no comments; *faire des commentaires sur autrui,* to criticize others. || **commenter** [-e] #3 *v. tr.* to comment (on); to criticize.

commérage [kɔme'ra:ʒ] *n.m.* gossip(ing).

commerçant, -e [kɔmɛr'sɑ̃(:t)] *adj.* commercial, business: *rue f commerçante,* shopping street; *quartier m ~* , business district; *les quartiers commerçants,* downtown; *nation f commerçante,* mercantile nation. || *n.m.* tradesman: *~ en gros,* merchant, wholesale dealer. || *pl.* tradespeople.

commerce [kɔ'mɛrs] *n.m.* **1.** commerce, trade, business (cf. AFFAIRES, NÉGOCE): *~ /en gros, en détail/,* wholesale, retail, trade; *faire le ~ de,* to deal in; *faire le ~ /en gros, de détail/,* to wholesale, to retail; *former une société de ~* , to set up a commercial firm, business; *Chambre de Commerce des Jeunes* (de la Province de Québec), Junior Chamber of Commerce. **2.** dealings, connections (with): *avoir, lier/ ~ avec qqun,* to have dealings with s.o.; *être en/ ~ , relation/avec qqun,* to be connected with s.o.; *avoir un ~ douteux avec qqun,* to have shady dealings with s.o.; *être d'un ~ agréable,* to be easy to get along with; *rompre tout ~* [avec qqun], to break off all/relations, dealings/. || **commercer** [-e] #4 *v. tr.* to trade. || **commercial, -e** [-jal] *adj.* commercial: *système* ~, commercial system. || *n.m.* © [TV] commercial.

commère [kɔ'mɛ:r] *n.f.* **1.** gossip, tattler. **2.** © godmother.

commettre [kɔ'm|ɛtr], **commettant** [-ɛ'tɑ̃], **commis** [-i] #44 *v. tr.* **1.** to commit: ~ *une erreur,* to commit an error, to make a mistake; ~ *une bévue,* to make a blunder. **2.** compromise: ~ *sa réputation,* to compromise one's reputation.

commis [kɔ'mi] *n.m.* [aux écritures] clerk; [à la vente] salesman; employee: ~ *voyageur,* commercial traveller, travelling salesman.

commisération [kɔmizera'sjõ] *n.f.* commiseration.

commissaire [kɔmi's|ɛ:r] *n.m.* commissary, commissioner: ~ *de police,* police commissioner; ~ *-priseur,* auctioneer; appraiser, valuer; © ~ *d'écoles,* school commissioner. || **commissariat** [-a'rja] *n.m.* the office of the commissioner: ~ *de police,* police station.

commission [-jõ] *n.f.* **1.** commission, committee, board: ~ *d'enquête,* board of enquiry; ~ *d'examen,* board of examiners; ~ *d'assurance-chômage,* Unemployment Insurance Commission; ~ *royale,* Royal Commission. **2.** message, errand: *faire une* ~, to run an errand. **3.** commission: *travailler à* ~, to work on commission; ~ *de 2 pour cent,* 2 per cent commission. || **commissionnaire** [-jɔ'nɛ:r] *n.m.* **1.** commission agent. **2.** messenger: *petit* ~, errand boy.

commode [kɔ'mɔd] *adj.* **1.** convenient; comfortable; [Pers.] easygoing. **2.** *n.f.* dresser; chest of drawers, [US] bureau. || **commodément** [-e'mɑ̃] *adv.* conveniently, comfortably. || **commodité** [-i'te] *n.f.* convenience, comfort: *pour la* ~ *des clients,* to accommodate the customers. || *n.fpl.* rest rooms.

commodore [kɔmɔ'dɔ:r] *n.m.* [Naut.] commodore.

commotion [kɔmɔ'sjõ] *n,f.* commotion; [brain] concussion.

commun, -e [kɔ'm|œ̃, -yn] *adj.* common; usual: *amis communs,* mutual friends; *avoir des intérêts communs,* to have common interests; *d'un* ~ *accord,* with one accord; *aller contre le sens* ~, to go against common sense; *nom* ~, common noun; *expression peu commune,* unusual expression; *des gens communs,* common people; *en* ~, in common. || *n.m.* common people: *le* ~ *des hommes,* the common run of people.

communal, -e [kɔmy'nal] *adj.* communal: *école* ~, public, elementary/school.

communautaire [kɔmyno't|ɛ:r] *adj.* communal. || **communauté** [-e] *n.f.* **1.** community (of ideas, &c.). **2.** corporation, society, order: ~ *de biens* [entre mari et femme], co-ownership; ~ *de frères,* Society of Brothers; ~ *française,* French community.

commune [kɔ'myn] *n.f.* commune [smallest political territorial division of France]; [New England] town; municipal district, township, municipality: *la Chambre des communes,* the House of Commons; *les Communes,* the Commons.

communiant, -e [kɔmy'njɑ̃] *n.* communicant.

communicati|f, -ve [kɔmynika|'tif, -'ti:v] *adj.* communicative, talkative; infectious (laughter). || **communication** [-'sjõ] *n.f.* communication: ~ *téléphonique,* telephone call; *donner* ~ *de qqch. à qqun,* to inform s.o. of sth.; *donner qqch. en* ~ *à qqun,* to communicate sth. to s.o.; *entrer, être/en* ~ *avec qqun,* to/get, be/ in touch with s.o.; *mettre en* ~, to connect; *obtenir* ~ *d'un document,* to be shown a document upon request.

communier [kɔmy'nj|e] #3 *v. intr.* to communicate, to take the Sacrament. || **communion** [-õ] *n.f.* **1.**: *recevoir la* ~, to receive Holy Communion, to take the Sacrament. **2.** religious body.

communiqué [kɔmyni'ke] *n.m.* communiqué, press release. || **communiquer** #3 *v.tr.* **1.** to communicate, to pass on, to impart: *Il m'a communiqué votre invitation,* He gave me your invitation. **2.** [Fig.] to share: ~ *sa joie,* to share one's /happiness, joy/. || *v. intr.* to communicate, to join: *chambres qui communiquent,* connecting rooms; *faire* ~, to connect; ~ *avec qqun,* to be in touch with s.o.

commutateur [kɔmyta'tœ:r] *n.m.* switch.

compact, -e [kõ'pak(t)] *adj.* compact.

compagne [kõ'paɲ] *n.f.* cf. COMPAGNON. || **compagnie** [-i] *n.f.* **1.** company: *tenir* ~ *à qqun,* to keep s.o. company; *fausser* ~ *à qqun,* to give s.o. the slip; *la bonne* ~, polite society. **2.** company [*Co.*, Cie.]; covey (of partridges); company (of soldiers); *la* ~ *de Téléphone Bell,* the Bell Telephone Company; ~ *d'aviation,* airline company; *la* ~ *de Jésus,* the Society of Jesus; *la* ~ *de la Baie d'Hudson,* Hudson's Bay Company [HBC]. || **compagnon** [-õ] *n.m.* companion, partner: *~ de travail,* fellow worker; *un joyeux ~*, a good fellow.

comparable [kõpa'r|abl] *adj.* comparable (with, to, *à*). ‖ **comparaison** [-ɛ'zõ] *n.f.* comparison: *établir une ~ entre deux choses,* to draw a parallel between two things; *en ~ de, par ~ avec,* compared with, by comparison with; *sans ~*, beyond compare.

comparaître [kõpa'r|ɛ:tr], **comparaissant** [-ɛ'sɑ̃], **comparu** [-y] #40 *v. intr.* to appear: *~ devant le juge,* to appear before the judge.

comparati|f, -ve [kõpar|a'tif, -a'ti:v] *adj. & n.m.* comparative. ‖ **comparativement** [-ativ'mɑ̃] *adv.* comparatively. ‖ **comparer** [-e] #3 *v. tr.* to compare: *Littérature comparée,* → Comparative literature.

†**comparoir** [kõpa'rwa:r] *v. intr.* [Only the inf. and the pres. part. are used] to appear; cf. COMPARAÎTRE.

compartiment [kõparti'mɑ̃] *n.m.* compartment: *~ de wagon-lit,* roomette; *~ pour fumeurs,* smoking compartment.

comparu [kõpa'ry] cf. COMPARAÎTRE. ‖ **comparution** [-'sjõ] *n.f.* [Jur.] appearance: *non ~*, default.

compas [kõ'pɑ] *n.m.* **1.** compasses, dividers. **2.** [Naut.] compass: [Fig.] *avoir le ~ dans l'œil,* to have a/good, accurate/eye.

compassion [kõpa'sjõ] *n.f.* compassion, pity: *avoir ~ de,* to have pity on.

compatible [kõpa'tibl] *adj.* compatible.

compatir [kõpa't|i:r] #17 *v. tr.* to sympathize with. ‖ **compatissant, -e** [-i'sɑ̃(:t)] *adj.* compassionate, sympathizing.

compatriote [kõpatri'jɔt] *n. m/f.* compatriot, fellow country/man, -woman/.

compensation [kõpɑ̃s|a'sjõ] *n.f.* compensation: *offrir une ~*, to make up (for, *pour*); *en ~ de,* to compensate for; [Fin.] *Chambre f de ~*, clearing-house. ‖ **compenser** [-e] #3 *v. tr.* to compensate for, make up for; to offset [favorablement].

compère [kõ'pɛ:r] *n.m.* [Péj.] accomplice, associate; © godfather.

compétence [kõpe't|ɑ̃:s] *n.f.* **1.** jurisdiction: *Ce n'est pas de ma ~*, That's not in my line. **2.** competence, skill. **compétent, -e** [-ɑ̃(:t)] *adj.* competent, efficient.

compétit|eur, -rice [kõpeti't|œ:r, -ris] *n.* competitor.

compiler [kõpi'le] #3 *v. tr.* to compile.

complaire [kõ'pl|ɛ:r], **complaisant** [-ɛ'zɑ̃], **complu** [-y] #49 *v. intr.* to please, to humour: *~ à qqun,* to humour s.o. ‖ **se complaire (à)** *v. pron.* to take delight in, to derive pleasure from. ‖ **complaisamment** [-ɛza'mɑ̃] *adv.* obligingly, willingly. ‖ **complaisance** [-ɛ'zɑ̃:s] *n.f.* **1.** compliance, kindness: *Auriez-vous la ~ de ...,* Would you be so kind as to ...; *faire qqch. par pure ~*, to do sth. out of pure kindness. **2.** complacence, self-satisfaction: *se regarder avec ~*, to be self-satisfied. ‖ **complaisant, -e** [-ɛ'zɑ̃(:t)] *adj.* **1.** obliging, willing. **2.** self-satisfied. **3.** flatterer: *Vous êtes (par) trop ~*, You are too kind.

complément [kõple'mɑ̃] *n.m.* complement: *~ du verbe,* object.

compl|et, -ète [kõ'pl|ɛ(t)] *adj.* complete; full: *trousseau ~*, complete trousseau; *autobus ~*, loaded bus; *salle complète,* full house; *La famille était au grand ~*, The whole family was there. ‖ *n.m.* [vêtement] suit, lounge suit. ‖ **complètement** [-ɛt'mɑ̃] *adv.* completely; fully. ‖ **compléter** [-e'te] #10 *v. tr.* [×] to complete, to finish; to supplement: *Complétez les phrases suivantes,* Complete the following sentences.

complication [kõplika'sjõ] *n.f.* complication.

complice [kõ'plis] *adj. & n.m/f.* accomplice, a party to. ‖ **complicité** [-i'te] *n.f.* complicity.

complies [kõ'pli] *n.fpl.* [Rel.] compline.

compliment [kõpli'mɑ̃] *n.m.* compliment: *un ~/peu flatteur, douteux/,* a/left-handed, back-handed/compliment. *pl.* congratulations; regards: *présenter ses compliments,* to present o.'s compliments; *compliments à/Monsieur X, la firme Y,* (my) compliments to Mr. X, to the firm of Y; kind regards to Mr. X, the company Y.

compliquer [kõpli'ke] #3 *v. tr.* to complicate. ‖ **se compliquer** *v. pron.* to become complicated; to worsen: *sa maladie se complique,* his, her/illness is getting worse.

complot [kõ'plo] *n.m.* plot, conspiracy: [Fig.] *tremper dans le ~*, to have a finger in the pie.

complu [kõ'ply] [*p.p.* de COMPLAIRE] *invar.*: *Ces femmes se sont toujours complu dans l'exercice de la charité,* These women have always found pleasure in being charitable.

componction [kõpõk'sjõ] *n.f.* compunction.

comportement [kõpɔrt|ə'mɑ̃] *n.m.* behaviour. ‖ **comporter** [-e] #3 *v. tr.* to include, to admit of; to allow: *Cette règle comporte des exceptions,* → There are exceptions to this rule. ‖ **se comporter** *v. pron.* to behave, to conduct o.s.

composant, -e [kõpo'z|ɑ̃(:t)] *adj.* & *n.f.* component (part). ‖ **composé, -e** [-e] *adj.* compound; composed (of, *de*); *mot* ~, compound word; ~ *chimique*, chemical compound; *intérêts composés*, accrued, compound/interest. ‖ *n.m.* compound. ‖ **composer** [-e] #3 *v. tr.* to compose (a poem); to compound, to make up (a prescription); to dial (a number). ‖ *v. intr.* to settle with, to come to an arrangement: ~ *avec ses créanciers*, to settle with one's creditors. ‖ **se composer (de)** *v. pron.* to be/made up, composed/of, to consist of: *Ce livre se compose de . . .*, This book is made up of . . . ; *se composant de*, being composed of. ‖ **composition** [-i'sjõ] *n.f.* **1.** [action] composition. **2.** essay. **3.** agreement, settlement: *entrer en* ~ *avec qqun*, to reach an agreement with s.o.

compote [kõ'pɔt] *n.f.* compote, stewed fruit. [☞ Le compl. de ce mot s'écrit gén. au plur.]: *une* ~ */de poires, de pommes, d'abricots, de cerises/*, stewed /pears, apples, apricots, cherries/; *en* ~, stewed; [Fig.] crushed to a pulp.

compréhensible [kõpreɑ̃'sibl] *adj.* comprehensible, understandable. ‖ **comprendre** [kõ'prɑ̃:dr] #41 *v. tr.* **1.** to comprise, to include: *Paris comprend 20 arrondissements*, Paris is made up of 20 municipal districts. **2.** to understand, grasp; to make sense of: *Je n'y comprends rien*, I can't make head or tail of it; *C'est à n'y rien* ~, It's beyond me, I can't understand it; *faire* ~ *à qqun*, to make it clear to s.o.; *faire* ~, to hint at; *se faire (bien)* ~, to make o.s. clear. ‖ **se comprendre** *v. pron.* **1.** to understand one another, [Fig.] to get on well with. **2.** *cela se comprend*, that goes without saying.

compresse [kõ'pr|ɛs] *n.f.* compress. ‖ **compresseur** [-ɛ'sœ:r] *n.m.* compressor. ‖ *adj.* compressing: *rouleau-* ~, steamroller.

compressible [kõprɛ'sibl] *adj.* compressible. ‖ **comprimer** [kõpri'me] #3 *v. tr.* to compress; to check, to restrain.

compris, -e [kõ'pri(:z)] *adj.* included: *y* ~, including; *non* ~, not including. [☞ Sans aux. et placées devant le compl., ces expressions sont invar.]: *Tous frais payés/y* ~ *les réparations, les réparations y comprises/*, All expenses paid, including repairs; *Il a $5,000 de revenus,/non* ~ *la maison où il loge, la maison où il loge non comprise/*, He has an income of $5,000, not including the house he lives in; *Tout (est)* ~, Everything (is) included.

compromettant, -e [kõprɔm|ɛ'tɑ̃(:t)] *adj.* dangerous, incriminating: *action compromettante*, incriminating action. ‖ **compromettre** [-ɛtr], **compromettant** [-ɛ'tɑ̃], **compromis** [-i] #44 *v. tr.* to compromise; to endanger: ~ *sa santé*, to endanger one's health. ‖ **se compromettre** *v. pron.* to become compromised; to get involved in. ‖ **compromis** [-i(:z)] *n.m.* compromise.

comptabilité [kõtabili'te] *n.f.* **1.** bookkeeping, accounting. **2.** accounts; accounting department: *la* ~ *d'une compagnie*, the accounts of a firm. ‖ **comptable** [kõ'tabl] *n.* accountant, bookkeeper: © ~ *agréé*, chartered accountant; *machine f comptable*, accounting machine. ‖ *adj.* accountable, responsible.

comptant [kõ'tɑ̃] *adj.* ready (money, &c.): *paiement* ~, cash payment. ‖ *n.m.* cash. ‖ *adv.*: *payer* ~, to pay cash down.

compte [kõ:t] *n.m.* **1.** [calcul] count, reckoning: *un* ~ *rond*, in round numbers; *faire le* ~ *de*, to reckon up, add up; [Fig.] *tenir* ~ *de*, to take . . . into account; *ne tenir aucun* ~ *de*, → to ignore. **2.** profit, advantage: *trouver son* ~ *à . . .*, to find it advantageous to . . . ; *J'y trouve mon* ~, It pays me (to . . .). **3.** [banque] account: *ouvrir, fermer/un* ~, to open, close/an account; ~ *courant*, current account. **4.** [comptabilité; pl.] accounts: *tenir ses comptes*, to keep one's accounts; *rendre* ~ *de*, to report on; [livre] to review; [Fig.] *demander* ~ *à qqun*, to bring s.o. to account (for sth.). **5.** [Fig.] account, behalf: *(faire qqch.) pour le* ~ *de*, (to do . . .) on s.o.'s behalf; *pour mon* ~, as far as I am concerned. **6.** [Loc.] *à bon* ~, cheap; *en fin de* ~, *au bout du* ~, in the long run, in the end, after all; *ne pas se rendre* ~ *de qqch.*, not to/realize, understand/sth.; not to take sth. into account; *tout* ~ *fait*, everything considered; [Fig.] *en prendre pour son* ~, to get it in the neck; *être laissé pour* ~, to be left high and dry; *régler son* ~ *à qqun*, to square accounts with s.o.

compte rendu [kõt|rɑ̃'dy] *n.m.* report, rundown, account; [de livre] review: *faire le* ~ *de*, to report; to review. ‖ **compte-gouttes** [-'gut] *n.m. inv.* dropper. ‖ **compte-tours** [-'tu:r] *n.m. inv.* [Auto, &c.] tachometer.

compter [kõ'te] #3 *v. tr.* **1.** to count, reckon; [dénombrer] to number, †tell: *tout compté*, all told. **2.** to charge; [trop cher] to overcharge (for sth.). **3.** [Fig.] to count: *~ au nombre de . . .*, to count among; to expect, to intend: *Je compte venir demain,* I intend/to come, coming/ tomorrow; [Loc.] *sans ~* [+ to say nothing of], exclusive of; *sans ~ que,* without mentioning that. || *v. intr.* **1.** to count, reckon: *dépenser sans ~*, to squander; *à ~ du 15 octobre*, as from October 15. **2.** to count, rely/(on, *sur*): *Je compte sur vous,* I depend upon you; to reckon (with, *avec*). **3.** to be counted: *ça ne compte pas*, that does not count.

comptoir [kõ'twa:r] *n.m.* **1.** counter, bar: *café ~*, coffee/bar, counter/. **2.** agency, branch: *notre ~ d'Angleterre*, our British agency. **3.** bank: *~ d'escompte*, discount bank; © *~ postal*, mail-order house.

compulser [kõpyl'se] #3 *v. tr.* to examine (documents).

comte [kõ:t] *n.m.* count; [Br.] earl.

comté [kõ'te] *n.m.* [Pol.] county: *~ de Joliette*, Joliette county.

comtesse [kõ'tɛs] *n.f.* countess.

concasser [kõkɑ'se] #3 *v. tr.* to pound, grind.

concave [kõ'kav] *adj.* concave.

concéder [kõse'de] #10 *v. tr.* to concede, to grant.

conception [kosɛp'sjõ] *n.f.* **1.** conception, conceiving: [R.C.] *l'Immaculée ~*, the Immaculate Conception. **2.** [Fig.] conception, understanding: *avoir la ~ d'une chose*, to understand sth.

concernant [kõsɛr'n|ɑ̃] *prép.* concerning, relating to. || **concerner** [-e] #3 *v. tr.* to concern, to relate to: *Cela ne me concerne pas,* That's no business of mine; *en ce qui me concerne*, as far as I am concerned.

concert [kõ'sɛ:r] *n.m.* concert, harmony: *aller au ~*, to go to the concert; [Fig.] *agir de ~ avec qqun*, to work/with s.o., together/. [☞ Do not confuse *de concert* avec *de conserve.*]

concerter [kõsɛr'te] #3 *v. tr.* to plan. || **se concerter** *v. pron.* to consult, plan together.

concerto [kõsɛr'to] *n.m.* concerto.

concession [kõsɛ'sjõ] *n.f.* concession; grant (of land): *faire une ~*, to make a concession, to stretch, strain/a point. || *n.f.* © [terme de colonisation] concession, grant (of land); homestead; back country.

concevable [kõs'vabl] *adj.* conceivable.

concevoir [kõs|ə'vwa:r], **concevant** [-ə'vɑ̃], **conçu** [-y] #34 *v. tr.* **1.** to conceive. **2.** [Fig.] to conceive, to invent, to imagine: *~ un plan*, to conceive, devise/a plan; *Je ne peux pas ~ une telle idée,* I cannot conceive of such an idea.

concierge [kõsjɛrʒ] *n. m/f.* janitor, caretaker. || **conciergerie** [-(ə)'ri] *n.f.* janitor's quarters; © [abus.] apartment house: *La Conciergerie*, The Conciergerie [a prison in Paris, famous during the Revolution].

conciliabule [kõsilja'byl] *n.m.* secret conference; whispered conversation.

concilier [kõsi'lje] #3 *v. tr.* to reconcile, conciliate: *~ des adversaires*, to reconcile adversaries. || **se concilier** *v. pron.* to agree with s.o.: *~ qqun*, to ingratiate o.s. with s.o.

concis, -e [kõ'si(:z)] *adj.* [style] concise; [récit] brief, terse.

concision [kõsi'zjõ] *n.f.* conciseness, brevity: *avec ~*, concisely.

concitoyen, -ne [kõsitwa'j|ɛ̃, -ɛn] *n.* fellow citizen, townsman.

conclu, -e [kõ'kl|y] *adj.* concluded. || **concluant, -e** [-yɑ̃(:t)] *adj.* conclusive: *peu, non/ ~*, inconclusive. || **conclure** [-y:r] #58 *v. tr.* to conclude: *~ la paix*, to conclude peace; *~ une chose d'une autre,* to/infer, deduce/one thing from another. || *v. intr.* **1.** to conclude, end. **2.** to decide, agree: *~ à*, to come to the conclusion that . . . ; *Il a conclu à la validité de l'expérience,* He found the experiment was valid; *Il refuse de ~*, He refuses to agree. || **conclusion** [-y'zjõ] *n.f.* conclusion; inference; *pl.* [Jur.] motion, plea: *en arriver à une ~*, to arrive at, to come to/ a conclusion; *tirer une ~*, to draw a conclusion, to make an inference; *en tirer ses propres conclusions*, to draw one's own conclusions; to put two and two together.

concombre [kõ'kõ:br] *n.m.* cucumber.

concorde [kõ'kɔrd] *n.f.* harmony. || **concorder** [-e] #3 *v. intr.* to agree (*avec*, with).

concourir [kõku'ri:r] #24 *v. intr.* **1.** to conduce (*à*, to). **2.** [examen] to compete (*avec*, with; *pour*, for).

concours [kõ'ku:r] *n.m.* **1.** concourse, meeting. **2.** assistance, help: *prêter son ~ à qqun*, to help s.o., to collaborate with s.o.; *par le ~ de*, with the help of. **3.** competition, match, examination: *~ de natation*, swimming meet; *~ hippique*, horse show; *~ d'admission*, entrance examination; *hors ~*, in a class/by itself, of acknowledged excellence/.

concr|et, -ète [kõ'krɛ(t)] *adj.* [cas] actual; [nombre] concrete; [substance] concrete, solid.

conçu, -e [kõ′sy] cf. CONCEVOIR.
concurrence [kõky′r|ɑ:s] *n.f.* competition, rivalry: *faire ~ à*, to compete with; *en ~*, in competition; *jusqu'à ~ de*, up to. || **concurrent, -e** [-ɑ̃(:t)] *n.* competitor, rival; candidate: *un ~ que l'on ne croyait pas dangereux*, a dark horse; *être élu sans ~*, to be elected by acclamation. || *adj.* competitive, rival.
condamnation [kõdan|a′sjõ] *n.f.* condemnation; sentence: *passer ~ sur qqch.*, to admit o.s. to be in the wrong. || **condamné, -e** [-e] *n.* condemned prisoner, convict: *~ à mort*, prisoner/under sentence of death, condemned to death/. || **condamner** [-e] #3 *v. tr.* **1.** to condemn, to sentence: *~ au silence*, to silence; *~ un malade*, to give up a sick person (as beyond recovery). **2.** to blame, to condemn; [ext.] to forbid: *~ la vente de qqch.*, to forbid the sale of sth. **3.** to wall, block up: *~ une porte*, to wall up a door.
condensateur [kõdɑ̃sa|′tœ:r] *n.m.* condenser. || **condensation** [-′sjõ] *n.f.* condensation. **(se) condenser** [(sɔ) kõdɑ̃′se] #3 *v. tr. & pron.* to condense.
condescendance [kõdɛsɑ̃′d|ɑ:s] *n.f.* condescension. || **condescendant, -e** [-ɑ̃(:t)] *adj.* condescending. || **condescendre** [kõdɛ′sɑ̃:dr] #42 *v. intr.* to condescend (*à*, to).
condisciple [kõdi′sipl] *n. m/f.* classmate.
condition [kõdi′sj|õ] *n.f.* condition, circumstance: *à ~ que*, provided that; *dans ces conditions*, under these/conditions, circumstances/; *conditions raisonnables*, reasonable conditions; *se rendre sans ~*, to surrender unconditionally; *à ces conditions*, on these terms; *sous ~*, conditionally. || **conditionnel, -le** [-ɔ′nɛl] *adj.* & [Gram.] *n.m.* conditional. || **conditionner** [-ɔ′ne] #3 *v. tr.* **1.** to condition; to season. **2.** to package, to prepare/goods for market.
condoléance(s) [kõdɔle′ɑ:s] *n.f. usual. pl.* condolence, sympathy: *exprimer, offrir, présenter/à qqun ses ~*, to express, offer/one's sympathy to s.o.; *lettre de ~*, letter of condolence.
conduct|eur, -rice [kõdyk′t|œ:r, -ris] *n.* **1.** driver; [Fig.] conductor, leader. **2.** conductor (of heat, electricity, &c.). || *adj.* driving; [Electr.] conducting. || *n.m.* director: *~ des ponts et chaussées*, public works engineer. || **conduire** [kõ′d|ɥi:r], **conduisant** [-ɥi′zɑ̃], **conduit** [-ɥi] #56 *v. tr.* to conduct, lead, guide; to drive: *~ une armée*, to lead an army; *~ qqun chez soi*, to escort s.o. home; *Il conduit bien sa barque*, He manages his affairs well; *permis de ~*, driving licence; *savoir ~*, to know how to drive; *Le cuivre conduit l'électricité*, Copper conducts electricity. || **se conduire** *v. pron.* to conduct o.s., to behave: *se mal conduire, se conduire mal*, to misbehave.
conduit [kõ′dɥi] *n.m.* tube, conduit; passage, channel: *~ souterrain*, underground drain; *~ auditif*, auditory duct; *sauf-~*, safe-conduct.
conduite [kõ′dɥit] *n.f.* **1.** conduct, behaviour: *changer de ~*, to mend one's ways. **2.** command, management, driving: *la ~ d'une auto*, the driving of a car; *~ intérieure*, sedan. **3.** tube, pipe: *~ d'eau*, water pipe. **4.** *faire la ~ à qqun*, to accompany s.o.
cône [ko:n] *n.m.* cone: *en forme de ~*, conical.
confection [kõfɛk′sjõ] *n.f.* construction, making: *la ~ d'une machine*, the construction of a machine; ready-made clothes: *maison de ~*, dressmaking firm; *acheter une robe de ~*, to buy a ready-made dress.
confédération [kõfedera′sjõ] *n.f.*: confederation © *Les Pères de la Confédération*, the Fathers of Confederation.
conférence [kõfe′r|ɑ:s] *n.f.* **1.** conference, meeting, convention: © *La ~ des Universités du Commonwealth*, Conference of Commonwealth Universities. **2.** lecture, talk: *faire une ~*, to give a lecture; *~ de presse*, press conference; *~ au sommet*, summit conference; *~ sur un pied d'entière égalité*, a round-table conference. || **conférenci|er, -ère** [-ɑ̃′sj|e, -ɛ:r] *n.* lecturer, speaker.
confesse [kõ′fɛ|s] *n.f.* [Rel.] confession: *aller à ~*, to go to confession. || **confesser** [-′se] #3 *v. tr.* **1.** to confess, to acknowledge: *~ sa foi*, to profess, to proclaim/one's faith. **2.** to hear s.o.'s confession; [Fig.] *~ qqun*, to make s.o. own up to sth. || **se confesser** *v. pron.* to confess o.s. || **confession** [-′sjõ] *n.* **1.** confession. **2.** denomination: *De quelle ~ êtes-vous?*, To what denomination do you belong? || **confessionnal** [-sjɔ′nal] *n.m.* confessional; grandfather chair. || **confessionnel, -le** [-sjɔ′nɛl] *adj.* denominational.
confiance [kõ′fj|ɑ:s] *n.f.* **1.** confidence, trust: *avoir ~ en qqun*, → to trust s.o.; *avoir ~ dans la parole de qqun*, → to trust s.o.'s word; *faire ~ à qqun*, → to trust s.o.; *abus m de ~*, breach of trust, embezzlement. **2.** confidence, reliance:

~ *en soi*, self-confidence; *homme de* ~, → trustworthy, reliable/person. || **confiant, -e** [-ɑ̃(:t)] *adj.* confiding, trusting (*dans*, in); self-confident.
confidence [kɔ̃fi'd|ɑ̃:s] *n.f.* secret, confidence: *faire une* ~, to tell a secret; *faire* ~ *de qqch. à qqun*, to confide sth. to s.o. || **confident -e** [-ɑ̃(:t)] *n.* confidant. || **confidentiel, -le** [-ɑ̃'sjɛl] *adj.* confidential.
confié, -e [kɔ̃'fje] *adj.* confided (in), entrusted (to); placed in charge (of): *être* ~ *à qqun*, to be s.o.'s charge. || **confier** #3 *v. tr.* to trust, to entrust; to confide. || **se confier** *v. pron.* ~ /*à, dans, en*/, to confide (in), to rely (on).
configuration [kɔ̃figyra'sjɔ̃] *n.f.* configuration.
confiné, -e [kɔ̃fi'ne] *adj.* confined: *air* ~, stale air. || **confiner** #3 *v. intr.* to border (on): *Le Canada confine aux États-Unis*, Canada borders on the United States. || *v. tr.* to confine, imprison.
confire [kɔ̃'fi:r] #46 *v. tr.* [cornichons] to pickle; [fruits] to preserve.
confirmation [kɔ̃fir|ma'sjɔ̃] *n.f.* confirmation, corroboration; ratification; [Théol.] confirmation. || **confirmer** [-'me] #3 *v. tr.* [conj. AVOIR (action), ÊTRE (état)] to confirm, corroborate: ~ *une nouvelle*, to confirm a piece of news; [Théol.] to confirm.
confiscation [kɔ̃fiska'sjɔ̃] *n.f.* confiscation.
confiserie [kɔ̃fiz'ri] *n.f.* confectionery trade.
confisquer [kɔ̃fis'ke] #3 *v. tr.* to take away; [Jur.] to confiscate, seize.
confiture [kɔ̃fi'ty:r] *n.f.* [☞ Le compl. de ce mot s'écrit gén. au plur.] preserve, jam: *de la* ~ *de fraises*, strawberry jam.
conflagration [kɔ̃flagra'sjɔ̃] *n.f.* conflagration.
conflit [kɔ̃'fli] *n.m.* conflict: *entrer en* ~ *avec*, to conflict with; *en* ~, → conflicting (opinions, &c.).
confluent [kɔ̃fly'ɑ̃] *n.m.* confluent, meeting (of two streams of water); [Fig.] meeting, junction.
confondre [kɔ̃'fɔ̃:dr] #42 *v. tr.* **1.** to confuse; [mêler] to confound; [se tromper] to mistake . . . for: ~ *deux personnes*, to/confuse, mix up/two people. **2.** to merge, to blend: *L'Outaouais et le St-Laurent confondent leurs eaux*, The Ottawa and the St. Lawrence rivers blend their waters. **3.** [stupéfier] to astound, dumbfound. || **se confondre** *v. pron.* to be confused, to blend (with); to be lost (in): *se* ~ *en excuses*, to apologize profusely. || **confondu** [kɔ̃fɔ̃'dy] *adj.* disconcerted, confused: ~ *de* (*reconnaissance*), overwhelmed by (gratitude).
conforme [kɔ̃'fɔrm] *adj.*: ~ *à*, consistent (with), true (to), identical (with); [Jur.] *pour copie* ~, certified true copy. || **conformément** (à) [-emɑ̃(ta)] *adv.* in accordance (with), according to. || **conformer** [-e] #3 *v. tr.* to shape, to form; [Fig.] to conform: *Il faut* ~ *sa conduite à ses paroles*, You have to practise what you preach. || **se conformer à** *v. pron.* to conform o.s. to, to comply (with): *se* ~ *au mot d'ordre*, to toe the/line, mark/. || **conformiste** [kɔ̃fɔr'mist] *n.m.* conformist. || **conformité** [-i'te] *n.f.* conformity, similarity (*avec*, with); accordance: *en* ~ *de*, in accordance with.
confort [kɔ̃'f|ɔ:r] *n.m.* comfort, ease: *le* ~ *moderne*, modern convenience; *pneu* ~, balloon tire. || **confortable** [-ɔr'tabl] *adj.* comfortable; [fauteuil] easy; [pièce] cosy. || **confortablement** [-ə'mɑ̃] *adv.* comfortably.
confrère [kɔ̃'fr|ɛ:r] *n.m.* colleague; [d'une société] fellow member. || **confrérie** [-e'ri] *n.f.* brotherhood, sisterhood; [société] guild, club.
confronter [kɔ̃frɔ̃'te] #3 *v. tr.* [Pers.] to confront; [choses] to compare (*à*, with).
confus, -e [kɔ̃'f|y(:z)] *adj.* **1.** confused, mixed up; [souvenir] vague; [style] obscure; [bruit] faint, indistinct. **2.** embarrassed, disconcerted; overwhelmed (by kindness, &c.): *Je suis tout* ~, I am terribly sorry. || **confusément** [-yze'mɑ̃] *adv.* confusedly, vaguely, faintly. || **confusion** [-y'zjɔ̃] *n.f.* **1.** confusion; [erreur] mistake; [désordre] disorder. **2.** shame, embarrassment: *remplir* (*qqun*) *de* ~, → to confuse (s.o.).
congé [kɔ̃'ʒe] *n.m.* **1.** holiday: *congés payés*, holidays with pay. **2.** leave of absence: ~ *de maladie*, sick leave. **3.** dismissal, discharge: *donner* ~ *à un ouvrier*, to dismiss, lay off/a workman; *donner, signifier son* ~ *à*, to give notice to; *prendre* ~ *de*, to take leave of. **4.** [douane, &c.] clearance; permit. || **congédier** [kɔ̃ʒe'dje] #3 *v. tr.* [domestique] to discharge, dismiss; [ouvriers] to lay off; [visiteur] to send away.
congélation [kɔ̃ʒela'sjɔ̃] *n.f.* congelation, icing; [aliments] freezing: ~ *à basse température*, deep freezing. || **(se) congeler** [(sə) kɔ̃ʒ'le] #9 *v. tr. & pron.* to congeal, freeze.
congénital, -e [kɔ̃ʒeni'tal] *adj.* congenital.
congestion [kɔ̃ʒɛs'tj|ɔ̃] *n.f.* congestion: ~ *cérébrale*, stroke; ~ *pulmonaire*,

pneumonia. || **congestionné, -e** [-ɔ'ne] *adj.* flushed. || **congestionner** [-ɔ'ne] #3 *v. tr.* to congest; [visage] to flush; [Fig.] to block, congest (a road, &c.).

Congo (le) [(lə) kõ'go] *n.m.* the Congo (river); the Congo.

congrégation [kõgrega'sjõ] *n.f.* congregation: [Rel.] *la Congrégation de la Sainte-Vierge,* the Sodality of Our Lady.

congrès [kõ'grɛ] *n.m.* congress, convention; [US] *le Congrès,* the Congress; *membre m du* ~, Congressman. || **congressiste** [-'sist] *n. m/f.* Congress member.

conifère [kɔni'fɛ:r] *adj.* evergreen, coniferous. || *n.m.* evergreen.

conique [kɔ'nik] *adj.* conical; [Math.] conic.

conjecture [kõʒɛk'ty:r] *n.f.* conjecture, surmise: *faire, se livrer à/des conjectures,* to surmise, indulge in speculation.

conjoint, -e [kõ'ʒw|ɛ̃(:t)] *adj.* joint: *commission conjointe,* joint committee; [marié] married. || *n.* spouse: *les conjoints,* husband and wife; *les futurs conjoints,* the bride and bridegroom. || **conjointement** [-ɛ̃t'mɑ̃] *adv.* jointly.

conjonction [kõʒõk'sjõ] *n.f.* conjunction, union; [Gram.] conjunction.

conjoncture [kõʒõk'ty:r] *n.f.* conjuncture, connection: *dans cette* ~, in this /juncture, connection/.

conjugaison [kõʒygɛ'zõ] *n.f.* [Gram.] conjugation.

conjugal, -e [kõʒy'gal] *adj.* conjugal: *le domicile* ~, home; *la vie conjugale,* married life.

conjuguer [kõʒy'ge] #3 *v. tr.* to conjugate; [Fig.] to combine.

conjuration [kõʒyr|a'sjõ] *n.f.* conspiracy, plot. || **conjuré** [-e] *n.m.* conspirator. || **conjurer** [-e] #3 *v. tr.* **1.** to conspire, plot (against). **2.** to conjure, exorcise (a demon). **3.** to ward off, avert (a disaster).

connaissance [kɔnɛ's|ɑ:s] *n.f.* **1.** knowledge; [approfondie] command: *avoir* ~ *de qqch.,* to know sth.; *prendre* ~ *de qqch.,* to learn of sth.; *une* ~ *approfondie,* a thorough knowledge; *faire qqch. en* ~ *de cause,* to do sth./knowingly, with full knowledge of the facts; *avoir une parfaite* ~ *du français,* to have a perfect command of French; [*pl.*] knowledge, learning: *acquérir des connaissances,* to acquire knowledge. **2.** acquaintance: *faire la* ~ *de qqun,* to meet s.o., to become acquainted with s.o.; *amis et connaissances,* friends and acquaintances; *être en pays de* ~, to be on familiar ground, to be with old friends; (*Je suis*) *très heureux d'avoir fait votre* ~, (I am) very glad to have met you; *C'est une vieille* ~, He's an old/friend, acquaintance/. **3.** consciousness: *perdre* ~, to lose consciousness, to faint; *sans* ~, → unconscious; *reprendre* ~, to come to.

connaissant [-ɑ̃] cf. CONNAÎTRE.

connaisseu|r, -se [-œ:r] *n.* expert; connoisseur.

connaître [kɔ'nɛ:tr], **connaissant** [kɔnɛ'sɑ̃], **connu** [kɔ'ny] #40 *v. tr.* **1.** to know, to be acquainted with: *Je le connais de vue,* I know him by sight; *se faire* ~, to make o.s. known; [Fig.] to make a name for o.s. **2.** to understand, to have a general knowledge of (sth.): ~ *les règles du jeu,* to know, understand/the rules of the game; ~ *le latin,* to know Latin. **3.** to be experienced in; to experience: ~ *la misère,* to know what poverty is. || *v. tr. ind.* to be competent to judge: *Le comité n'a pas à* ~ *de cela,* That is not within the terms of/reference, competence/of the committee. || **se connaître** *v. pron.* **1.** to know o.s., one another: *Ils se sont connus en 1940,* They/met, became acquainted/in 1940; *Ils se connaissaient déjà,* They already knew each other. **2.** to know one's way about, to be experienced; to be a good judge of: ~ *en chevaux,* to be a good judge of horses; *Il s'y connaît,* He knows what he is doing.

connivence [kɔni'vɑ̃:s] *n.f.* connivance: *agir, être/de* ~ *avec qqun,* to connive with s.o.

connu, -e [kɔ'ny] *adj.*: *bien* ~, well-known, noted: *un auteur bien* ~, a well-known author; ~ *sous le nom de,* going by the name of . . .

conquérant, -e [kõke'r|ɑ̃(:t)] *adj.* conquering. || *n.m.* conqueror. || **conquérir** [-i:r] **conquérant** [-ɑ̃], **conquis** [kõ'ki] #23 *v. tr.* to conquer; [Fig., l'estime, l'affection] to win. || **conquête** [kõ'kɛ:t] *n.f.* conquest; [Fig.] *faire la* ~ *de qqun,* to win s.o.'s heart. || **conquis, -e** [kõ'ki(:z)] cf. CONQUÉRIR.

consacré, -e [kõsa'kre] *adj.* accepted, recognized; [par l'usage] established; [Rel.] consecrated (*à,* to); [Fig.] devoted (*à,* to). || **consacrer** #3 *v. tr.* **1.** [Rel.] to consecrate: ~ *une église,* to dedicate a church; [Fig.] ~ *sa vie,* to devote one's life (*à,* to). **2.** [réputation] to establish; [erreur] to sanction; [droit] to confirm.

consciemment [kõsja'mɑ̃] *adv.* consciously; knowingly.

conscience [kõ'sjɑ̃:s] *n.f.* [sens moral]

conscience; [scrupule] conscientiousness: *se faire ~ de,* to make it a matter of conscience to; *~ nette,* clear conscience; *cas de ~*, matter of conscience; *par acquit de ~*, for conscience's sake; *travailler avec ~*, to work conscientiously; *en ~*, conscientiously; †[sens physique] consciousness [☞ use CONNAISSANCE]: *prendre ~ de,* → to realize; *prise f de ~*, awareness; *avoir ~ de,* to be conscious of. || **consciencieu|x, -se** [kõsjɑ̃'sjø(:z)] *adj.* conscientious.

conscient, -e [kõ'sjɑ̃(:t)] *adj.* conscious; aware (of).

consécuti|f, -ve [kõseky't|if, -i:v] *adj.* consecutive.

conseil [kõ's|ɛ:j] *n.m.* **1.** [piece of] advice, counsel: *donner un ~*, to give a piece of advice; *prendre ~ de qqun,* to ask s.o.'s advice; *faire qqch. sur le ~ de qqun,* to do sth. on the advice of s.o.; *La nuit porte ~*, I'll sleep on it; *demander ~ à qqun,* to ask s.o.'s advice. **2.** counsellor: *ingénieur-~*, consulting engineer; *~ /de la Reine, du Roi/,* Queen's, King's/ counsel; *C.R.,* Q.C., K.C. **3.** court, council: *~ municipal,* municipal, city/ council. || *n.m.*: *~ de l'Europe,* Council of Europe; *Conseil de recherches pour la défense,* Defence Research Board; *Conseil national de recherches,* National Research Council; © *~ Privé,* Privy Council; © *~ du Trésor,* Treasury Board; © *~ législatif,* Legislative Council; *~ des ministres,* Cabinet; *~ de Sécurité,* Security Council. **4.** [Mil.] *~ de guerre,* court-martial: *passer en ~ de guerre,* to be court-martialled; *~ de révision,* [US] draft board. || **conseill|er¹, -ère** [-ɛ'je, -ɛ'jɛ:r] *n.* [qui conseille] counsellor; [membre d'un conseil] councillor, adviser; *~ municipal,* town, city/councillor; alderman; *~ juridique,* legal adviser. || **conseiller²** [-ɛ'je] #3 *v. tr.* to counsel; to advise, to give advice to: *~ à qqun de faire qqch.*, to advise s.o. to do sth.; *~ qqch. à qqun,* to recommend sth. to s.o.

consentement [kõsɑ̃t|'mɑ̃] *n.m.* consent, assent: *du ~ de tous,* by general consensus. || **consentir** [-i:r] #26 *v. intr.* to consent, agree (*à,* to ☞ or use *~ que* + subj.): *Je consens que vous le fassiez,* I consent to your doing it. || *v. tr.*: *~ un prêt,* to grant a loan.

conséquence [kõse|'kɑ̃:s] *n.f.* consequence, result: (*fait*) *lourd de conséquences,* (fact) of great importance; *sans ~*, unimportant; *ne pas tirer à ~*, to be of no consequence.

|| **conséquent (par)** [par kõse'kɑ̃] *adv.* consequently, accordingly, as a result. || **conséquent, -e** [-'kɑ̃(:t)] *adj.* rational (action, &c.); consistent: *être ~ avec soi-même,* to be consistent with o.s.

conservat|eur, -rice [kõsɛrva|'tœ:r, -'tris] *adj.* conservative [Pol.] Conservative: = © *le parti progressiste-conservateur,* the Progressive-Conservative party. || *n.m.* curator, keeper; [bibliothèque] librarian; [Pol.] conservative. || **conservation** [-'sjõ] *n.f.* **1.** conservation, preservation: *instinct de ~*, self-defence. **2.** [conserves] preserving, canning. || **conserve** [kõ'sɛrv] *n.f.* **1.** preserves; canned, bottled/food: *conserves de légumes,* canned vegetables; *~ au vinaigre,* pickles; *boîte f de conserve,* can of food; *mettre en ~*, to bottle, can, preserve. || *n.fpl.* dark glasses. **2.** company: *naviguer de ~*, to sail in company; *aller de ~*, to go together. || **conserver** [-e] #3 *v. tr.* to preserve, maintain: *~ sa santé,* to preserve one's health; *~ ses amis,* to keep one's friends; [Cul.] to preserve, can, bottle/food. || **se conserver** *v. pron.* to keep: *articles qui ne se conservent pas,* perishable goods.

considérable [kõside'rabl] *adj.* considerable; important: *homme ~*, man of importance.

considération [kõside|ra'sjõ] *n.f.* consideration, regard; motive: *en ~ de,* in recognition of; *prendre en ~*, to take into consideration; [style] *agréez l'assurance de ma ~ distinguée,* → yours truly. || **considérer** [-'re] #10 *v. tr.* **1.** to consider, examine: *Il faut ~ que,* It must be borne in mind that. **2.** [Fig.] to esteem, to look up to: *être très considéré,* to be highly thought of.

consigne [kõ'siɲ] *n.f.* **1.** orders: *manquer à la ~*, to disobey orders; *ne connaître que la ~*, Orders are orders; *être de ~*, to be on duty. **2.** [Mil.]: *consigné,* confined (to barracks). **3.** baggage, check/ room: *mettre qqch. à la ~*, to check sth. **4.** [on an article] deposit.

consistance [kõsis'tɑ̃:s] *n.f.* consistency; [Fig.] strength (of mind, character).

consister [kõsis'te] #3 *v. intr.* to consist (*dans, en,* of); to be composed (of): *En quoi cela consiste-t-il?,* What does /that, it/consist of?

consolant, -e [kõsɔ'l|ɑ̃(:t)] *adj.* consoling, comforting: *Ce n'est guère ~*, → That is cold comfort. || **consolat|eur, -rice** [-a'tœ:r, -a'tris] *n.* comforter. || *adj.* comforting, consoling. || **consolation** [-a'sjõ] *n.f.*

consolation, comfort. ‖ **consoler** [-e] #3 *v. tr.* to console, comfort. ‖ **se consoler** *v. pron.* to be comforted, consoled (*de*, for); to get over.

consolidation [kõsɔlid|a'sjõ] *n.f.* consolidation, strengthening; [construction] bracing. ‖ **consolider** [-e] #3 *v. tr.* to strengthen; [Tech.] to brace; [Fig.] to consolidate.

consommat|eur, -rice [kõsɔm|a'tœ:r, -a'tris] *n.* consumer; [dans un café] customer. ‖ **consommation** [-a'sjõ] *n.f.* **1.** consumption, use: *la ~ de l'électricité*, electrical, power/consumption; *denrées de ~*, consumer goods. **2.** drink (in a café): *payer les consommations*, to pay for the drinks. **3.** accomplishment; [marriage] consummation. ‖ **consommé, -e** [-e] *adj.* **1.** consummate; skilled: *technicien ~*, skilled technician. **2.** consumed, used (up). ‖ *n.m.* [Cul.] clear soup, consomme. ‖ **consommer** [-e] #3 *v. tr.* **1.** to consume, to use (up): *Ce moteur consomme beaucoup d'essence*, This motor uses a lot of gas. **2.** to complete, consummate. ‖ *v. intr.* to have a drink [in a café]. ‖ **se consommer** *v. pron.* [food] to be consumed; [products] to be used; [crime, &c.] to be perpetrated; [ceremony] to be consummated.

consonance [kõsɔ'nɑ̃:s] *n.f.*: consonance; (*parler*) *aux consonances étrangères*, foreign-sounding.

consonne [kõ'sɔn] *n.f.* [Ling.] consonant.

conspirat|eur, -rice [kõspir|a'tœ:r, -a'tris] *n.* conspirator. ‖ **conspiration** [-a'sjõ] *n.f.* conspiracy; plot. ‖ **conspirer** [-e] #3 *v. tr.* to conspire, plot (*contre*, against): *~ à la ruine de qqun*, to plot to ruin s.o. ‖ *v. intr.* to contribute, concur (*à*, to).

constamment [kõst|a'mɑ̃] *adv.* constantly, continually. ‖ **constance** [-ɑ̃:s] *n.f.* constancy, perseverance, steadfastness: *avec ~*, → steadfastly. ‖ **constant, -e** [-ɑ̃(:t)] *adj.* constant, firm, steady; [persévérant] unremitting; [durable] lasting; †[patent] certain, established. ‖ *n.f.* [Math.] constant.

constatation [kõstat|a'sjõ] *n.f.* ascertainment: *faire une ~*, → to note; [police] investigation; [Jur.] verification; [de décès] proof: *les constatations d'usage*, (police) inquiry. ‖ **constater** [-e] #3 *v. tr.* **1.** to establish, to note. **2.** to record, certify: *~ un décès*, to certify a death. **3.** to ascertain, to find; to verify: *Vous pouvez le ~ vous-même*, You can see for yourself.

constellation [kõstɛla'sjõ] *n.f.* constellation.

consternation [kõstɛrn|a'sjõ] *n.f.* consternation, dismay. ‖ **consterné, -e** [-e] *adj.* staggered, dismayed (*de*, at); [Fam.] *être ~ par qqch.*, to be/staggered, floored/ by sth. ‖ **consterner** [-e] #3 *v. tr.* to dismay; to be astonished: *nouvelle qui consterne le pays*, news which stunned the nation.

constipation [kõstipa'sjõ] *n.f.* constipation.

constituant, -e [kõsti'tɥ|ɑ̃(:t)] *adj.* constituent; component, integral part/of; [Hist.] *Assemblée Constituante*, Constituent Assembly. ‖ **constitué, -e** [-e] *adj.* constituted (*par*, by), formed (*par*, by); [Fig.] *bien ~*, healthy, of sound constitution. ‖ **constituer** [-e] #3 *v. tr.* **1.** to constitute, set up; to form, make up: *~ une commission*, to set up a committee; [dot] to settle (a dowry) on s.o.; *~ une société*, to form a/corporation, society/. ‖ **se constituer** *v. pron.* to form (*en*, in): *~ prisonnier*, to give o.s. up.

constitution [kõstity'sjõ] *n.f.* **1.** constitution, formation, forming; [de société] incorporation; [Chim.] composition: *~ de l'eau*, composition of water; [Méd.]: *avoir une ~ robuste*, to have a robust constitution; [Pol.] constitution (of a country).

constructeur [kõstryk|'tœ:r] *n.m.* manufacturer; [bâtiments] builder; contractor. ‖ **construction** [-'sjõ] *n.f.* **1.** [action] construction, building: *matériaux de ~*, building materials; *bois de ~*, timber; *auto f de ~ américaine*, US-built car; *~ de logements*, housing project. **2.** [édifice] structure, building: *une ~ de trois étages*, a three-storey building. ‖ **construire** [kõs'trɥi:r], **construisant, construit** #56 *v. tr.* to construct, to build: *~ une maison*, to build a house; *~ une auto*, to make a car; *se faire ~ une maison*, to have a house built; [Fig.] to compose, write. ‖ **se construire** *v. pron.* [état] to be being/built, erected; [résultat] to be built; [pour soi] to have a house built; [Gram.] *~ avec le génitif*, to be construed with the genitive.

consul [kõ'syl] *n.m.* consul; *~ général*, consul general: *le ~ de France à Toronto*, the French Consul in Toronto. ‖ **consulat** [-a] *n.m.* consulate: *le ~ général de France*, the French Consulate General.

consultant, -e [kõsyl't|ɑ̃(:t)] *adj. & n.* consultant; consulting: *avocat ~*, consulting attorney. ‖ **consultati|f, -ve** [-a'tif, -a'ti:v] *adj.* advisory: *à titre ~*, in an advisory capacity. ‖ **consultation** [-a'sjõ] *n.f.* consultation; [d'avocat] opinion; [Méd.] clinic; ~ *externe*, out-patients/clinic, department/; *heures de* ~ [on the door of a doctor's or a lawyer's office] office hours; [Pol.] ~ *populaire*, poll, referendum. || **consulter** [-e] #3 *v. tr.* [médecin, dictionnaire] to consult; [qqun] to seek s.o.'s advice, to take the advice of s.o.; [Fig.] ~ *sa raison*, to let one's reason be one's guide. || **se consulter** *v. pron.* to consider; to reflect (*au sujet de*, upon).

consumé, -e [kõsy'me] *adj.* [× CONSOMMÉ] consumed; [Fig.] ~ *par* (*un violent désir de*), burnt up by, consumed with. || **consumer** #3 *v. tr.* to consume, burn up, destroy: *Le feu peut* ~ *une maison en quelques minutes*, Fire can destroy a house in a matter of minutes; [Fig.] to consume, eat up. || **se consumer** *v. pron.* [fuel] to burn out; [Fig.] to be consumed; to/waste, pine/away.

contact [kõ'takt] *n.m.* contact, touch: [Fig.] *prendre* ~ *avec qqun*, to get in touch with s.o.; [Electr.] switch: *mettre, couper/le* ~, to turn/on, off/, to switch /on, off/.

contagieu|x, -se [kõta'ʒj|ø(:z)] *adj.* contagious; catching. || *n.* contagious person. || **contagion** [-õ] *n.f.* contagion.

conte [kõ:t] *n.m.* tale, story; [Péj.] yarn: ~ *de fées*, fairy tale; ~ *à dormir debout*, a tall story, [Fam.] baloney.

contemplati|f, -ve [kõtɑ̃pl|a'tif, -a'ti:v] *adj.* contemplative. || **contemplation** [-a'sjõ] *n.f.* contemplation; meditation. || **contempler** [-e] #3 *v. tr.* [méditer] to contemplate; to meditate upon; [regarder] to behold.

contemporain, -e [kõtɑ̃pɔ'r|ɛ̃, -ɛn] *adj.* **1.** [de même époque] contemporary (*de*, with). **2.** [actuel] contemporary, present-day. || *n.* contemporary.

contenance [kõt'nɑ̃:s] *n.f.* [bouteille] capacity; [champ] area; [Fig.] countenance, composure: *faire bonne* ~, to put on a bold front, to keep a stiff upper lip; *perdre* ~, to lose one's composure.

contenant [kõt'n|ɑ̃] *n.m.* container. || *adj.* containing. || **contenir** [-i:r] #22 *v. tr.* **1.** to contain, hold; [livre] to contain, include. **2.** [sa colère, &c.] to restrain, control. || **se contenir** *v. pron.* to restrain, control/o.s.

content, -e [kõ't|ɑ̃(:t)] *adj.* **1.** content, satisfied (*de*, with). **2.** pleased, glad: *Il est trop* ~ *de lui-même*, → He's too /smug, self-complacent/. || *n.m.*: *avoir son* ~ *de*, to have one's fill of; *manger tout son* ~, to eat one's fill. || **contentement** [-ɑ̃t'mɑ̃] *n.m.* content, satisfaction: ~ *de soi*, self-complacency. || **contenter** [-ɑ̃'te] #3 *v. tr.* to satisfy, gratify. || **se contenter** *v. pron.* to be satisfied (*de*, with): ~ *de peu*, to be easily satisfied; ~ *de* [+ inf.], merely to [+ verb].

contentieux [kõtɑ̃'sjø] *n.m.* [Com.]: *service du* ~, claims, legal/law branch. department. || *adj.* [Jur.] contentious.

contenu, -e [kõt'ny] *adj.* restrained; [caractère] reserved; [rire] stifled. || *n.m.* contents.

conter [kõ'te] #3 *v. tr.* to relate, to tell: *en* ~ *de belles sur*, to tell tall stories about; *en* ~ *à* . . . , to take . . . in.

contestable [kõtɛs't|abl] *adj.* questionable, debatable. || **contestation** [-a'sjõ] *n.f.* dispute, argument: *en* ~ *avec*, at variance with; *sans* ~, without opposition. cf. CONTESTE. || **conteste** [kõ'tɛst] *n.m.*: *sans* ~, unquestionable, indubitable. || **contester** [-e] #3 *v. tr.* [un testament] to contest; [une affirmation] to question, challenge. || *v. intr.* to dispute: *aimer à* ~, to like to argue.

conteu|r, -se [kõ't|œ:r, -ø:z] *n.* narrator, story-teller.

contigu, -ë [kõti'gy] *adj.* contiguous, adjoining (*à*, to).

continent[1], -e [kõti'nɑ̃(:t)] *adj.* continent, chaste.

continent[2] [kõti'nɑ̃] *n.m.* continent; mainland: *le Nouveau* ~, the New World. cf. MONDE. || **continental, -e** [-'tal] *adj.* [×] continental.

continu, -e [kõti'n|y] *adj.* continuous; [space, time] unbroken, unceasing; [Electr.] *courant* ~, direct current, D.C. current. || *n.* [Philos.] continuum. || **continuel, -le** [-ɥɛl] *adj.* [esp. used for duration in time] continual, ceaseless. || **continuellement** [-ɥɛl'mɑ̃] *adv.* continually, ceaselessly. || **continuer** [-e] #3 *v. tr.* **1.** to continue [☞ utilisez un composé avec ON] ~ *son travail*, to keep on working; ~ *son voyage*, to journey on; ~ *son vol*, to fly on. **2.** [ligne de chemin de fer, &c.] to extend, prolong. || *v. intr.* to continue, go on, keep on [see above]: ~ *à chanter*, to sing on, &c. || **se continuer** *v. pron.* to continue; to extend (*jusqu'à*, as far as).

contour [kõ'tu:r] *n.m.* contour.

contractant, -e [kõtrak't|ɑ̃(:t)] *adj.*: *les parties contractantes*, the contracting parties. || **contracté, -e** [-e] *adj.* [de douleur] contorted, distorted; [mâchoires] set; [Gram.] contracted. || **con-**

tracter[1] [-e] #3 *v. tr.* to enter into/an agreement, a contract/; [habitude] to acquire; [obligation] to incur; [dette] to contract; [rhume] to catch. **contracter**[2] [-e] #3 *v. tr.* [froid; Gram.] to contract. || **se contracter** *v. pron.* to contract; to shrink.

contracteur [kõtrak'toɛ:r] © *n.m.* [abus.] cf. ENTREPRENEUR. || **contractuel, -le** [kõtrak't|ɥɛl] *adj.* by, on/ contract.

contradiction [kõtradik|'sjõ] *n.f.* **1.** contradiction: *avoir l'esprit de* ~, to oppose on principle, [Fam.] to be contrary. **2.** inconsistency: *en* ~ *avec*, inconsistent with. || **contradictoire** [-'twa:r] *adj.* contradictory, opposing: *conférence f* ~, debate, forum; [Jur.] *examen* ~, cross-examination.

contraindre [kõ'tr|ɛ̃:dr], **contraignant** [-ɛ'ɲɑ̃], **contraint** [-ɛ̃] #36 *v. tr.* **1.** to compel, force (*à*, to): ~ *à/reculer, avancer/*, → to force/back, on, &c.). || **2.** to restrain, curb: ~ *ses goûts*, to control, restrain/ one's appetites. || **se contraindre** *v. pron.* to restrain o.s. || **contraint, -e** [-ɛ̃(:t)] *adj.* [Pers.] forced, compelled (*de*, to); [sourire] forced; [attitude] stiff, constrained. || **contrainte** [-ɛ̃:t] *n.f.* **1.** constraint, compulsion; [Jur.] distraint, warrant: ~ *par corps*, arrest. **2.** restraint: *parler sans* ~, → to speak frankly.

contraire [kõ'tr|ɛ:r] *adj.* **1.** contrary, opposite: *être d'un avis* ~, to be of the opposite opinion; *sauf avis* ~, unless you hear/to the contrary, otherwise/; *en sens* ~, in the opposite direction. **2.** [Fig.] harmful, adverse: *Le tabac vous est* ~, Tobacco is bad for you; *Ce climat vous est* ~, This climate does not agree with you. || *n.m.* contrary: *au* ~, on the contrary; *au* ~ *de*, unlike. || **contrairement** [-ɛr'mɑ̃] *adv.* contrarily, contrary to: ~ *à ce que je disais*, contrary to what I said. || **contrarié, -e** [-a'rje] *adj.* annoyed, vexed. || **contrarier** [-a'rje] #3 *v. tr.* **1.** to vex, provoke: *Voilà qui me contrarie*, That really annoys me. **2.** to oppose, hinder. **3.** to contrast (colours).

contraste [kõ'trast] *n.m.* contrast.

contrat [kõ'tra] *n.m.* contract, deed; agreement.

contravention [kõtravɑ̃'sjõ] *n.f.* (minor) infraction, police offence; [Fam.] *recevoir une* ~, to get a ticket.

contre [kõ:tr] *prép*, against: *dresser une échelle* ~ *un mur*, to lean a ladder against a wall; *agir* ~ *son gré*, to act against one's will; *Les Canadiens jouent* ~ *les Leafs*, The Canadiens are playing against the Leafs; *S'assurer* ~ *l'incendie*, To insure against fire; ~ *toute attente*, contrary to all expectations; *se fâcher* ~ *qqun*, to get angry with s.o.; *livraison* ~ *remboursement*, C.O.D. || *adv.* near, against: *se tenir* ~ *qqun*, to stand near to s.o.; *voter* ~ *qqch.*, to vote against sth.; *ci-*~, on the opposite/page, side/; *par* ~, on the other hand, however. || *n.m.*: *Le pour et le* ~ *d'une question*, The pros and cons of a question. || **contre-bas** [kõtrə'bɑ] *loc. adv.* lower level: *regarder en* ~, to look down on, over. || **contre-cœur** (à) [akõtrə'kœ:r] *loc. adv.* reluctantly, unwillingly. || **contre-coup** [kõtrə|ku] *n.m.* rebound; [Fig.] consequence, repercussion. || **contre-jour** [-'ʒu:r] *n.m.* back lighting; unfavourable, false/light; *assis à* ~, to be sitting with one's back to the light. || **contre-pied** [-'pje] *n.m.* [Fig.] opposite, contrary: *prendre le* ~ *d'une opinion*, to take the opposite side of an opinion; [Sport.] *à* ~, on the wrong foot; *lancer le ballon à* ~, to shoot on the wrong foot. || **contre-plaquer** [-pla'ke] *v. tr.* to make plywood, to laminate (wood). || **contre-plaqué** [kõtrəpla'ke] *n.m.* plywood, veneer.

contrebande [kõtrə'bɑ̃:d] *n.f.* contraband. || **contrebandier** [kõtrəbɑ̃'dje] *n.m.* smuggler.

contrebasse [kõtrə'bɑ:s] *n.f.* double bass; [Fam.] bass fiddle.

contredire [kõtrə'd|i:r] #46 *v. tr.* **1.** to contradict (s.o.); to gainsay, contradict (an opinion). **2.** to be/contrary to, inconsistent with/. || **se contredire** *v. pron.* to contradict/o.s., one another/. || **contredit** [-i]: *sans* ~, unquestionably, without doubt.

contrefaçon [kõtrəf|a'sõ] *n.f.* [action] counterfeiting; forging; [objet] counterfeit, forgery. || **contrefaire** [-ɛ:r] #37 *v. tr.* to counterfeit (money), to forge (a signature); to copy (a picture); to mimic (a person), to simulate (illness, &c.). || **contrefait, -e** [-ɛ(t)] *adj.* forged, counterfeit; feigned (illness); deformed (person).

contremaître [kõtrə'mɛ:tr] *n.m.* foreman, overseer.

contrepoids [kõtrə'pwɑ] *n.m.* counterweight: [Fig.] *servir de* ~ *à*, to counterbalance.

contrepoison [kõtrəpwa'zõ] *n.m.* antidote.

contre remboursement [kõtrərɑ̃bursə'mɑ̃] *m.* C.O.D., C.O.D. order.

contretemps [kõtrə'tɑ̃] *n.m.* inconvenience, upset; [music] syncopation: *à contre-*

temps, inopportunely; *agir à* ~ , to act at the wrong moment.

contrevent [kõtrə'vɑ̃] *n.m.* **1.** shutter. **2.** bracing (in the frame of a building).

contribuable [kõtri'b|ɥabl] *n.m.* ratepayer, taxpayer. || *adj.* taxable. || **contribuer** [-ɥe] #3 *v. tr.* to contribute: ~ *à une dépense*, to help pay an expense; ~ *au succès d'une entreprise*, to contribute to the success of an undertaking. || **contribution** [-y'sjõ] *n.f.* **1.** contribution: *apporter une précieuse* ~ , to give invaluable assistance. **2.** tax, duty; excise: *payer une* ~ , to pay a tax.

contrition [kõtri'sjõ] *n.f.* contrition: *acte de* ~ , act of contrition.

contrôle [kõ'tr|o:l] *n.m.* **1.** [Mil.] roll. **2.** check point, inspection point; box-office (theatre): *passer au* ~, to go through a check point. **3.** inspection, checking; suspension: *le* ~ *des billets de théâtre*, the taking of theatre tickets; ~ *postal*, postal inspection; *être chargé du* ~ *de qqun*, to be placed in charge of s.o. **4.** control: *perdre le* ~ *sur soi-même*, to lose control of o.s. **5.** hallmark, government stamp. || **contrôler** [-o'le] *v. tr.* **1.** to check, inspect; to verify. **2.** to hall-mark (silver, &c.). **3.** [Fig.] to correct (sth.), to supervise (s.o.). || **contrôleu|r, -se** [-o'l|œ:r, -ø:z] *n.* **1.** inspector, controller. **2.** supervisor. **3.** ticket collector, conductor (on a train), driver (on a city bus); ~ *du Trésor*, Comptroller of the Treasury.

controverse [kõtrɔ'vɛrs] *n.f.* controversy, dispute.

contusion [kõty'zj|õ] *n.f.* contusion, bruise. || **contusionné, -e** [-ɔ'ne] *adj.* bruised. || **contusionner** [-ɔ'ne] #3 *v. tr.* to bruise.

convaincant [-ɛ̃'kɑ̃(:t)] *adj.* convincing: *argument* ~ , convincing argument.

convaincre [kõ'v|ɛ̃:kr] #35 *v. tr.* **1.** to convince. **2.** (always followed by *de*, of) to convict: ~ *d'un mensonge*, to catch telling a lie. || **convaincu, -e** [-ɛ̃'ky] *adj.* **1.** convinced, earnest: *Il en est* ~ , He is sure of it, He is convinced; *parler d'un ton* ~, to speak with conviction. **2.** convicted: ~ *de trahison*, convicted of treason.

convalescence [kõvalɛ's|ɑ:s] *n.f.* convalescence: *entrer en* ~ , to be on the road to recovery. || **convalescent, -e** [-ɑ̃(:t)] *adj. & n.* convalescent.

convenable [kõv'nabl] *adj.* proper, suitable, decent: *mariage* ~ , proper, suitable/marriage; *recevoir un salaire* ~ , to be paid a suitable wage; *choisir un moment* ~ , to choose a convenient /moment, time/; *Cela n'est pas* ~ , that is not/done, nice/; *n'avoir rien de* ~ *à se mettre*, to have nothing suitable to wear. || **convenablement** [-ə'mɑ̃] *adv.* suitably, properly, decently: *faire qqch.* ~ , to do sth. properly. || **convenir** [kõv|'ni:r] *v. tr.* **1.** [with *avoir*] to be appropriate: *Cette position ne m'a pas convenu*, That position did not suit me. **2.** to agree (upon): *être convenu de*, to come to an agreement: *C'est convenu*, It's/agreed, settled/; *arriver à l'heure convenue*, to arrive at the /appointed, agreed/time; *prix convenu*, price agreed on. **3.** to admit, recognize: ~ *qu'on a eu tort*, to admit that one was wrong. **4.** *v. impers.* to be right, proper, convenient: *Il convient de faire mon travail*, It is/right, fitting/that I do my work. || **convenu, -e** [-'ny] *adj.* ordinary, conventional, banal: *langage* ~ , ordinary language.

convention [kõvɑ̃'sjõ] *n.f.* **1.** agreement, pact: ~ *verbale*, verbal agreement. **2.** © [abus.]: *la* ~ *des libéraux*, the Liberal Convention. **3.** *pl.* conventions, standards: *les* ~ *sociales*, social conventions. **4.** clauses (of an agreement), terms. || **de convention** *loc. adv.* conventional, accepted: *language* ~ , accepted speech.

conventionnel, -le [kõvɑ̃sjɔ'nɛl] *adj.* conventional.

converger [kõvɛr'ʒe] #5 *v. intr.* to converge.

conversation [kõvɛrs|a'sjõ] *n.f.* conversation; talk, chat: *entamer une* ~, *entrer en* ~, *nouer* ~ /*avec qqun*, to/start a, enter into/conversation with s.o.; *prendre part à une* ~ , to join in a conversation; *soutenir la* ~ , to keep the conversation going; *amener la* ~ *sur qqch.*, to/bring, steer/the conversation around to sth. || **converser** [-e] #3 *v. intr.* to talk [*causer* is preferable], to converse.

conversion [kõvɛr'sjõ] *n.f.* conversion, change: [Mil.] wheeling: ~ *à droite*, to right wheel; *échelle de* ~ , conversion table.

converti, -e [kõvɛr't|i] *adj.* converted. || *n.* convert. || **convertible** [-ibl] *adj.* [Fin.] convertible (*en*, into). || **convertir** [-i:r] #17 *v. tr.* to convert, bring over (*à*, to). || **se convertir** *v. pron.* to become converted (*à*, to); [Fig.] to reform. || **convertissable** [-i'sabl] *adj.* convertible.

convertisseur [kõvɛrti'sœ:r] *n.m.*: converter.

convexe [kõ'vɛks] *adj.* convex.

conviction [kõvik'sjõ] *n.f.* conviction: [Jur.] *pièce à* ~, exhibit; *avoir l'intime*

~ *que* . . . , to be deeply convinced that . . .

convoi [kɔ̃'vwa] *n.m.* (funeral) procession; convoy (of ships, vehicles, people); train: *le ~ était très long*, the train was very long; ~ *de voyageurs*, passenger train.

convoiter [kɔ̃vwa't|e] #3 *v. tr.* to covet: ~ *les biens de qqun*, to covet s.o.'s possessions. || **convoitise** [-i:z] *n.f.* covetousness.

convulsi|f, -ve [kɔ̃vyl's|if, -i:v] *adj.* convulsive. || **convulsion** [kɔ̃vyl'sjɔ̃] *n.f.* convulsion.

coopérat|eur, -rice [koɔpera|'tœ:r, -'tris] *n.* cooperator. || **coopérati|f, -ve** [-'tif, -'ti:v] *adj.* cooperative. || *n.f.* cooperative. || **coopération** [-'sjɔ̃] *n.f.* cooperation. || **coopérer** [koɔpe're] #10 *v. intr.* to cooperate (with, *avec*).

coordination [koɔrd|ina'sjɔ̃] *n.f.* coordination. || **coordonner** [-ɔ'ne] *v. tr.* to coordinate.

cop|ain, -ine [kɔ'p|ɛ̃, -in] *n.* [Fam.] pal, buddy, chum.

copeau [kɔ'po] *n.m.* [bois] shaving, chips; [métal] cutting, turning.

Copenhague [kɔpɛ'nag] *n.f.* Copenhagen.

copiage [kɔ'pja:ʒ] *n.m.* copying, plagiarism. || **copie** [kɔ'p|i] *n.f.* [×] **1.** copy, carbon copy; reproduction: *dessin d'après ~*, a reproduction (from a picture); [Photo.] print. **2.** [Scol.] paper, written exercise (which is handed in). || **copier** [-je] #3 *v. tr.* to copy: ~ *qqun*, to imitate s.o.; [Scol.] ~ *le devoir de qqun*, to crib from s.o.'s assignment.

copieu|x, -se [kɔ'pjø(:z)] *adj.* copious.

copiste [kɔ'pist] *n.m./f.* copyist; [imitateur] copier: *faute de ~*, clerical error.

coq [kɔk] *n.m.* rooster, cock: *rouge comme un ~*, red as a beet; [la boxe] *poids ~*, bantamweight; *être comme un ~ en pâte*, to be/sitting pretty, in clover/.

coque [kɔk] *n.f.* **1.** shell; [d'œuf] eggshell: *œuf à la ~*, boiled egg. **2.** [Naut.] hull; [Auto.] body shell.

coquelicot [kɔkli'ko] *n.m.* poppy.

coqueluche [kɔk'lyʃ] *n.f.* whooping-cough; [Fig., Fam.] *être la ~ de*, to be the idol of.

coquet, -te [kɔ'kɛ(t)] *adj.* **1.** coquettish, flirtatious. **2.** [maison, costume] smart, stylish; [jardin] trim. **3.** fairly large; generous: *somme coquette*, tidy sum.

coquetier [kɔk'tj|e] *n.m.* eggcup. || **coquetière** [-ɛ:r] *n.f.* egg-boiler, poacher.

coquette [kɔ'kɛt] *n.f.* coquette, flirt. || **coquettement** [-'mɑ̃] *adv.* stylishly, smartly. || **coquetterie** [-'ri] *n.f.* **1.** coquetry. **2.** stylishness, smartness, elegance.

coquillage [kɔki'ja:ʒ] *n.m.* **1.** shellfish. **2.** shell. cf. COQUILLE. || **coquille** [kɔ'ki:j] *n.f.* [œuf, noix, mollusque] shell: *coquilles Saint-Jacques*, scallops; [Tech.] misprint, typographical error.

coquin, -e [kɔ'k|ɛ̃, -in] *n.* scoundrel, rogue; [Fam.] rascal. || *adj.* roguish.

cor [kɔ:r] *n.m.* **1.** points (on the antlers of a deer, &c.). **2.** [Mus.] [instrument] horn; [musicien] horn-player; ~ *d'harmonie*, French horn; ~ *anglais*, English horn. **3.** [au pied] corn. **4.** [Loc.] [clamour] *à ~ et à cri*, hue and cry; *demander à ~ et à cri*, to clamour for.

corail [kɔ'ra:j] *n.m.* coral. || *adj.* coral-red.

Coran [kɔ'rɑ̃] *n.m.* [Rel.] Koran.

corbeau [kɔr'bo] *n.m.* raven; [applied also to the smaller, more common bird] crow.

corbeille [kɔr'bɛ:j] *n.f.* **1.** basket: ~ *à papier*, waste(-paper) basket. **2.** [jardin] flower bed. **3.** [Théât.] dress circle. **4.** [Fig.]: ~ *de mariage*, (groom's) wedding gifts (to the bride).

corbillard [kɔrbija:r] *n.m.* hearse.

cordage [kɔr'da:ʒ] *n.m.* **1.** [nom générique] cordage; [d'un navire] rigging; [de chanvre, jute, &c.] rope. **2.** [Tech.] stringing [d'une raquette]; cording [de bois].

corde [kɔrd] *n.f.* **1.** rope, cord; [à linge] (clothes) line: *cordes vocales*, vocal cords; ~ *à sauter*, skipping rope; [Fig.] *être au bout de sa ~*, to be at the end of one's/rope, tether/; *avoir plus d'une ~ à son arc*, to have several strings to one's bow; *être usé jusqu'à la ~*, to be threadbare. **2.** [racing] rail: *tenir la ~*, to be on the rail. || **cordeau** [-o] *n.m.* [arpenteur] tracing line [refers only to the string used by carpenters, gardeners, &c. to make a straight line]: *tirée au ~*, in a straight line, carefully laid out. || **cordelette** [-də'lɛt] *n.f.* small rope. || **corder** [kɔr'de] #3 *v. tr.* **1.** [un paquet, une malle, &c.] to tie up, to cord. **2.** to cord.

cordial, -e [kɔr'djal] *adj.* cordial, hearty; warm. || *n.m.* [Méd.] cordial, stimulant. || **cordialement** [-'mɑ̃] *adv.* cordially, warmly. || **cordialité** [-i'te] *n.f.* cordiality, heartiness.

Cordillère (la) [kɔrdi'jɛ:r] *n.f.* the Cordillera.

cordon [kɔr'dɔ̃] *n.m.* **1.** cord, string, twist: ~ *de sonnette*, bell-pull; [Fig.] *délier les cordons de sa bourse*, to undo one's purse strings. **2.** ribbon, decoration: *le ~ de la Légion d'Honneur*, the ribbon of the Legion of Honour. **3.** [Mil.]: *~ de police,* police cordon. || **cordon-bleu** [-'blø] *n.m.* expert cook.

cordonnerie [kɔrdɔn|'ri] *n.f.* [lieu] shoemaker's (shop); [profession] shoemaking. || **cordonnier** [-je] *n.m.* shoemaker, cobbler.

Corée (la) [(la) kɔ're] *n.f.* Korea. || **coréen, -ne** [kɔre|'ɛ̃, -ɛn] *adj. & n.* Korean.

corne [kɔrn] *n.f.* **1.** [sur la tête des animaux] horn: *bêtes à cornes,* cattle; *prendre le taureau par les cornes,* to take the bull by the horns. **2.** [substance] horn; [du sabot] hoof; [de livre] dog-ear.

cornée [kɔr'ne] *n.f.* [Anat.] cornea.

corneille [kɔr'nɛːj] *n.f.* crow.

cornemuse [kɔrnə'myːz] *n.f.* bagpipe.

corner [kɔr'ne] #3 *v. intr.* [Auto.] to blow a horn; to honk; [Fig.] to ring (in the ears): *Les oreilles me cornent,* My ears are ringing; *Cornez!,* Honk! || *v. tr.* **1.** to fold, dog-ear (the page of a book). **2.** [Fig., Fam.] to trumpet (news) about.

cornet [kɔr'nɛ] *n.m.* **1.** *~ de glace,* ice-cream cone; *~ acoustique,* ear trumpet; *~ à dés,* dice-box; [Tél.] telephone receiver. **2.** [Mus.] *~ à pistons,* cornet.

cornette [kɔr'nɛt] *n.f.* nun's cornet, coif.

cornichon [kɔrni'ʃõ] *n.m.* gherkin; [après l'avoir fait confire] pickles; [Fam.] stupid, dope.

cornu, -e[1] [kɔr'ny] *adj.* horned; [Fig.] absurd (reasoning, &c.).

cornue[2] [kɔr'ny] *n.f.* [Chim.] retort.

corollaire [kɔrɔ'lɛːr] *n.m.* [Math.] corollary; [ext.] deduction, inference.

coronaire [kɔrɔ'nɛːr] *adj.* coronary.

corporati|f, -ve [kɔrpɔra|'tif, -tiːv] *adj.* corporate; [guild, &c.] corporative. || **corporation** [-'sjõ] *n.f.* [×] guild; [Jur.] corporation.

corporel, -le [kɔrpɔ'rɛl] *adj.* **1.** [material] corporeal. **2.** [physical] corporal, bodily.

corps [kɔːr] *n.m.* **1.** body, matter: *~ simple,* element; *~ céleste,* heavenly body; [Naut.] *~ mort,* (fixed) anchor. **2.** [vivant] body: *le ~ humain,* the human body, [mort] body, corpse; *combat ~ à ~,* hand-to-hand fighting; *se jeter à ~ perdu dans qqch.,* to throw o.s. recklessly into sth.; *garde du ~,* bodyguard; *à mi- ~,* up to the waist; *à son ~ défendant,* in self-defence, reluctantly; *~ et âme,* body and soul; *perdu ~ et biens,* lost with all hands. **3.** main part, body of sth.: hull (of a ship); cylinder (of a pump); body, shell (of a car); body, hollow shell (of a musical instrument); frame (of a building); trunk (of a tree); *prendre ~,* to take/form, shape/. **4.** group, body (of people or things); [Mil.] corps: *le ~ enseignant,* the Faculty; *~ diplomatique,* diplomatic corps; *esprit de ~,* group spirit, loyalty, morale. **5.** consistence, body (of materials): *étoffe avec du ~,* cloth with body.

corpulence [kɔrpyl|ɑ̃ːs] *n.f.* corpulence, stoutness. || **corpulent, -e** [-ɑ̃(ːt)] *adj.* corpulent, stout.

corpuscule [kɔrpys'kyl] *n.m.* corpuscle.

corral [kɔ'ral] *n.m.* corral.

correct, -e [kɔ'rɛk|t] *adj.* [Pers.] correct, [emploi] proper; [récit] exact, accurate. || **correct|eur, -rice** [-'tœːr, -'tris] *n.* corrector, [Imp.] proof-reader. || **correcti|f, -ve** [-'tif, -'tiːv] *adj.* corrective. || **correction** [-'sjõ] *n.f.* **1.** punishment, correction: *administrer une ~ à qqun,* to punish s.o.; *maison de ~,* reformatory; *appareil de ~ auditive,* hearing aid. **2.** correction (of an exercise, &c.): *sauf ~,* subject to correction. || **correctionnel, -le** [-sjɔ'nɛl] *adj.*: *tribunal ~,* /police, magistrate's/ court.

corrélation [kɔrela'sjõ] *n.f.* correlation: *mettre en ~,* → to correlate with.

correspondance [kɔrɛspõ'd|ɑ̃ːs] *n.f.* **1.** correspondence, concordance: *~ d'idées,* agreement of ideas, thinking alike. **2.** mail, correspondence: *ouvrir, dépouiller/ sa ~,* to open one's mail; *être en ~ avec qqun,* to be writing to s.o. **3.** transfer, connection: [Rail.] transfer point: *trains en ~,* trains which make connection. || **correspondant, -e** [-ɑ̃(ːt)] *adj.* corresponding; agreeing: *angles ~,* corresponding angles. || *n.* **1.** correspondent: *~ de guerre,* war correspondent; *~ à l'étranger* foreign correspondent. **2.** guardian. || **correspondre** [kɔrɛs'põːdr] #42 *v. intr.* **1.** to tally, to agree: *théorie qui ne correspond pas aux faits,* theory which does not agree with the facts; [ch. de fer] to connect (*avec,* with). **2.** to correspond (with), to write to (s.o.). **3.** to adjoin: *deux chambres qui correspondent,* adjoining rooms.

corridor [kɔri'dɔːr] *n.m.* corridor, hall, passage.

corrigé [kɔri'ʒe] *adj.* corrected. || *n.m.* corrected copy, key. || **corriger** #5 *v. tr.* **1.** to correct (an exercise, an error); [épreuves] to read, to correct. **2.** to punish: *~ un enfant,* to punish a child. || **se corriger** *v. pron.* to improve, to correct o.s.; [d'une habitude] to break o.s. of.

corroborant [kɔrɔbɔ|'rɑ̃] *adj.* corroborating, confirming. ‖ **corroboration** [-ra'sjõ] *n.f.* corroboration, confirmation. ‖ **corroborer** [-re] #3 *v. tr.* to corroborate, confirm.

corrodant, -e [kɔrɔ|'dɑ̃(:t)] *adj.* [action] corroding, corrosive. ‖ *n.m.* corrosive. ‖ **corroder** [-'de] #3 *v. tr.* to corrode.

corrompre [kɔ'rõ:pr], **corrompant** [kɔrõ|'pɑ̃], **corrompu** [-'py] #52A *v. tr.* **1.** to corrupt; to bribe (with money): ~ *les mœurs de qqun*, to corrupt s.o.'s morals; ~ *un juge*, to bribe a judge. **2.** to spoil, to taint; [l'eau] to pollute: *La chaleur corrompt la viande*, Heat spoils meat. ‖ **corrompu, -e** [-'py] *adj.* **1.** corrupt, bribed (morals, &c.). **2.** spoiled, tainted; [l'eau] polluted.

corrosi|f, -ve [kɔrɔ'z|if, -i:v] *adj.* corrosive.

corruption [kɔryp'sjõ] *n.f.* **1.** decay, decomposition (of organic material). **2.** [action] corrupting; corruption; [donner de l'argent à qqun] bribing (a witness, &c.); [gén.] graft.

corsage [kɔr'sa:ʒ] *n.m.* blouse; bodice (of a dress).

corsaire [kɔr'sɛ:r] *n.m.* privateer; captain (of a privateer); [Fig.] shark.

Corse (la) [kɔrs] *n.f.* Corsica. ‖ *adj. & n.* Corsican.

corsé, -e [kɔr'se] *adj.* [vin] full-bodied, strong; [drap] heavy, solid; [sauce] spicy, strong; [repas] rich, heavy; [Fig.] [histoire] spicy, racy; [affaire] complicated (intrigue). ‖ **corser** #3 *v. tr.* [Fam.] to spike (wine, &c.); [Fam.] to beef up (a meal); [Fig.] to spice up (a story, a play, &c.): *L'affaire se corse*, Complications have set in.

corset [kɔr'sɛ] *n.m.* corset.

cortège [kɔr'tɛ:ʒ] *n.m.* procession, train: ~ *funèbre*, funeral procession.

corvée [kɔr've] *n.f.* forced labour; chore, drudgery; [Mil.] fatigue party: *Quelle ~ !*, What a chore!

corvette [kɔr'vɛt] *n.f.* corvette.

cosmétique [kɔsme'tik] *adj.* cosmetic. ‖ *n.m.* cosmetic; [pour les cheveux] hair oil.

cosmique [kɔs'mik] *adj.* cosmic.

cosmopolite [kɔsmɔpɔ'lit] *adj. & n.m.* cosmopolitan. ‖ **cosmopolitisme** [-ism] *n.m.* cosmopolitanism.

cosse [kɔs] *n.f.* [des légumes] pod, hull; [blé d'Inde] husk.

cossu, -e [kɔ'sy] *adj.* with a heavy/pod, shell/; [Fig.] rich, monied; substantial.

costume [kɔs'tym] *n.m.* [d'un pays, &c.] costume, dress; [complet] suit: ~ *d'homme*, man's suit; ~ *tailleur*, (lady's) tailored suit; ~ *trois pièces*, three-piece suit; ~ *sur mesures*, made-to-measure suit. ‖ **se costumer** [-e] *v. pron.* [en] to dress up (as): *bal costumé*, /fancy dress, costume/ball.

cote [kɔt] *n.f.* [note] letter, number; [book] call-mark; [d'une monnaie, d'une valeur] quotation; [T.V.] rating; racing (quoted) odds; [sur une carte, &c.] altitude (above sea level); [Fig., Fam.] *avoir la* ~, to be highly thought of.

côte [ko:t] *n.f.* **1.** [Anat.] rib; side: ~ *à* ~, side by side; ~ *de porc*, pork chop: *se tenir les côtes de rire*, to hold one's sides from laughing. **2.** [rivage] coast, shore: [Fr.] *la Côte d'Azur*, the Riviera; © *la Côte nord*, the North Shore of the St. Lawrence; [ext.] coastal waters; [Naut.] *se mettre à la* ~, to run aground. **3.** [pente] slope: *à mi-côte*, halfway/up, down/(a mountain). **4.** road [which runs up a slope]; © road [running at right angle from a "rang"]. ‖ **Côte-de-l'Or** [kot də 'lɔ:r] *n.f.* Gold Coast [now Ghana].

côté [ko'te] *n.m.* **1.** side: *de ce* ~ /*-ci, -là*/, on/this, that/side; *de* ~, sideways; [regard] sidelong; *le* ~ *faible de qqun*, s.o.'s weak spot; *prendre les choses par le bon* ~, to look on the bright side of things; *de tous côtés*, from all sides; *mettre de l'argent de* ~, to put some money aside; *à* ~ *de*, beside; *répondre à* ~, to miss the point; *marcher de* ~, to walk sideways; *courir de* ~ *et d'autre*, to run back and forth; *regarder des deux côtés*, to look both ways; *du* ~ *du père*, on the father's side; *Il laisse son travail de* ~, He neglects his work; *mettre (de l'argent) de* ~, to lay, put/ money by; [opposition de deux arguments] *d'un* ~ . . . , *de l'autre, d'un autre* ~, on the one hand . . . on the other (hand); *par certains côtés*, in some ways.

coteau [ko'to] *n.m.* small hill, low hillside.

côtelette [kot'lɛt] *n.f.* [veau] cutlet, [mouton, porc] chop.

coter [kɔ'te] #3 *v. tr.* [numéroter] to number (a chapter, article, &c.); [indiquer le cours d'une valeur, &c.] to quote, to give a quotation on; [imposer une cotisation] to assess; [une carte géographique] to mark the elevations on; [un employé, un devoir] to rate; [Fig.] *bien coté*, in high esteem; [Géog.] *point m coté*, landmark.

côti|er, -ère [ko'tj|e, -ɛ:r] *adj.* (of the) shore; [marine de guerre] coastal; [marine marchande] coasting. cf. CABOTAGE.

cotisation [kɔtiz|a'sjõ] *n.f.* [impôt] assessment; share (of a common expense): *~ de l'Association des étudiants,* Student Union fees; [société] dues: *verser une ~*, to send in one's subscription. || **cotiser** [-e] #3 *v. intr.* to assess; [société] to subscribe. || **se cotiser** *v. pron.* to take up a collection; [Fam.] to pass the hat (to buy a present for s.o.).

coton [kɔ't|õ] *n.m.* cotton: *~ hydrophile,* (absorbent) cotton wool; *filer un mauvais ~*, to be/in a bad way, in poor health/. || **cotonnade** [-ɔ'nad] *n.f.* cotton cloth, calico. || **cotonneu|x, -se** [-ɔ'nø(:z)] *adj.* fleecy, downy.

côtoyer [kotwa'je] #12 *v. tr.* to skirt; to go along the edge of (a forest, a river, &c.); [arbres] to hug (a river's edge); [Naut.] to coast, to sail along the coast; [Fig.] to rub elbows with.

cou [ku] *n.m.* **1.** neck (of man, animals, &c.): *se casser le ~*, to break one's neck; *jusqu'au ~ dans le travail,* up to one's ears in work; *sauter, se jeter/au ~ de qqun,* to welcome s.o. with open arms; *prendre ses jambes à son ~*, to take to one's heels.

couard, -e [kw|a:r, -ard] *adj.* cowardly, cf. POLTRON. || *n.m.* coward. || **couardise** [-ar'di:z] *n.f.* cowardice: *faire preuve de ~*, to show cowardice.

couchage [ku'ʃ|a:ʒ] *n.m.* [action] bedding down; [literie] bedding: *sac de ~*, sleeping bag. || **couchant, -e** [-ɑ̃(:t)] *adj. soleil ~*, setting sun; *chien ~*, setter. || *n.m.* sunset; [par opposition au levant] the west; [Fig.] *le ~ de la vie,* the declining years of life. || **couche** [kuʃ] *n.f.* **1.** bed, couch. **2.** diaper; [Br.] napkin. **3.** [biologie] layer, stratum; [peinture] coat(ing): *~ arable,* topsoil; *par ~*, in layers; [société] generation. **4.** *n.fpl.* confinement, childbirth. || **couché, -e** [-e] *adj.* in bed; [écriture] slanting; [position] recumbent. || **coucher** [-e] #3 *v. tr.* **1.** to put to bed: *~ un enfant,* to put a child to bed; *envoyer ~ les enfants,* to send the children to bed. **2.** to bend over, to flatten down: *la neige a couché le blé,* the snow flattened the wheat. **3.** [Fig.] *~ qqun en joue,* to aim (a gun) at s.o.; *~ qqch. par écrit,* to write sth. down; *~ qqun dans son testament,* to mention s.o. in one's will. || *v. intr.* to spend the night: *~ à la belle étoile,* to sleep under the stars; *chambre à ~*, bedroom. || **se coucher** *v. pron.* to go to bed; to lie down; [soleil] to set: *Allez vous ~ !,* Go away!, Go lie down!; *heure de se ~*, bedtime; *se ~ sur le dos,* to lie, sleep/on one's back; *Je me suis couché à six heures,* I went to bed at six o'clock. || *n.m.* **1.** going to bed: *C'est l'heure du ~ !,* Time to go to bed. **2.** setting (of the sun): *~ de soleil,* sunset, sundown. || **couchette** [-ɛt] *n.f.* cot, crib; [ch. de fer] berth; [Naut.] bunk.

coucou [ku'ku] *n.m.* cuckoo; [pendule] cuckoo clock.

coude [kud] *n.m.* elbow; [route] (sharp) turn; [rivière] bend; [Tech.] knee: *un coup de ~*, a dig with the elbow; *donner un coup de ~ à qqun,* to nudge s.o.; *~ à ~*, side by side; *jouer des coudes,* to elbow. || **coudé, -e** [-e] *adj.* [Tech.] bent, cranked. || *n.f.* **1.** [mesure] cubit: [Fig.] *à cent coudées au-dessus de,* way ahead of, immensely superior to; *avoir ses coudées franches,* to have a free hand. || **couder** [-e] *v. tr.* to bend, crank.

cou-de-pied [kud'pje] *n.m.* instep.

coudoiement [-wa'mɑ̃] *n.m.* jostling, elbowing. || **coudoyer** [-wa'je] #12 *v. tr.* [être en contact avec] to rub elbows with.

coudre [kudr], **cousant** [ku'zɑ̃], **cousu** [ku'zy] #54 *v. tr. & intr.* to sew (on, up): *~ un bouton,* to sew on a button; *machine à ~*, sewing machine.

couenne [kwan] *n.f.* (pork-)rind, crackling: [Fam.] *Quelle ~ !,* What a dope!

couette [kwɛt] *n.f.* © pigtail.

coulage [ku'l|a:ʒ] *n.m.* [liquide] leaking; [dans un moule] casting; [d'un bateau] sinking; [sabordage] scuttling; [Fam.] waste. || **coulant, -e** [-ɑ̃(:t)] *adj.* sliding, free; [style] flowing; [Péj.] accommodating; [langue] flowing, fluent. || *n.m.* sliding ring. || **coulée** [-e] *n.f.* [de lave] outflow, outpouring; [metal] tapping, casting; [écriture] cursive writing; [piste] run (of wild animals). || **couler** [-e] #3 *v. intr.* **1.** to run, to flow; [temps] to slip by: *Le Fraser coule vers l'ouest,* The Fraser /flows, runs/west. **2.** to leak: *stylo qui coule,* leaky pen. **3.** [Naut.] to sink; [par ext.] to slide down (from sth.): *Le navire a coulé à pic,* The ship went down like a rock; *se laisser ~ au bas d'un arbre,* to slide down (from) a tree. || *v. tr.* **1.** [Mus.] to slur (notes); to pour, to cast (metals, glass, &c.): *~ une statue,* to cast a statue; *faire ~ de l'eau,* to turn on the water, to let the water run; *faire ~ les larmes de qqun,* to bring tears to s.o.'s eyes. **2.** to sink (a boat): *faire ~ un navire,* to sink a boat. **3.** to ruin, spoil (an affair); to discredit (s.o.); [Fam.] © to fail (a student). || **se couler** *v. pron.* to slip, glide (through a crowd, &c.): *se* *couler le long d'une corde*, to slide down a rope; [Fam.] *se la couler douce*, to take it easy.

couleur [ku'lœ:r] *n.f.* **1.** colour; [diffus] hue, tint; (*homme*) *de* ~, coloured (man); ~ /*claire, foncée*/, light, dark/ colour; [pl.] complexion, colour: *Il a des couleurs*, His colour is good. **2.** colour, paint: *couleurs à l'huile*, oil paints; [Fr.] *marchand de couleurs* (also *droguiste*), paint dealer, hardware dealer. **3.** [pl.] colours, flag: *hisser, amener*/*les couleurs*, to hoist, strike/the colours: *film en* ~, colour/film, picture/. **4.** [Fig.]: *sous* ~ *de*, under pretence of; ~ *locale*, local colour; *en faire voir* (*à qqun*) *de toutes les couleurs*, to play all sorts of tricks (on s.o.).

couleuvre [ku'lœ:vr] *n.f.* grass-snake.

coulisse [ku'lis] *n.f.* **1.** groove (in a piece of wood, &c.): *une porte à* ~, a sliding door; *trombone à* ~, slide trombone. **2.** [Théât.] wing; [Fin.] curb exchange; [Polit.] lobby: [Fig.] *se tenir dans la* ~, to remain behind the scene.

couloir[1] [ku'lwa:r] *n.m.* [étroit et long] corridor; [autobus] gangway; [bateau] passageway; [vestibule] lobby: *intrigues de* ~, behind-the-scene intrigues, lobbying.

couloir[2] [ku'lwa:r] © *n.m.* strainer.

coulpe [kulp] *n.f.* *battre sa* ~, to repent of one's sins.

coup [ku] *n.m.* [☞ Appears in many contexts where English has separate word, e.g. *blow, kick, slap*, &c. Meanings have been grouped under (1) *blows* and their effects, (2) *actions* and Fig. senses.] [**A. Heurts**] **1.** [avec un instrument]: blow: ~ *de bâton*, blow, whack; ~ *d'épée*, cut, thrust; ~ *de fouet*, lash; ~ *de hache*, chop, ~ *de marteau*, stroke; ~ *de poignard*, stab; ~ *de sabre*, slash; [☞ verbes]: *donner*/*un* ~ *de bâton*/, to hit with a stick, to cudgel; /*un* ~ *de canne*/, to cane; /*un* ~ *de fouet*/, to whip; /*un* ~ *de règle*/, to rap; /*un* ~ *de poignard*/, to stab; *enfoncer à coups de marteau*, to hammer (a nail) in. **2.** [parties du corps]: ~ *de pied*, kick; ~ *de poing*, blow, cuff; ~ *d'aile*, (wing-) flap; ~ *de bec*, peck; ~ *de coude*, nudge; [Fig.] ~ *d'œil*, glance, glimpse; [☞ verbes] *donner*/*un* ~ *de pied*/*à qqun*, → to kick s.o.; /*un* ~ *de poing*/, to punch s.o. (on the nose, &c.); /*un* ~ *de coude*/, to nudge s.o.; /*un* ~ *de dent*/, to bite s.o.; /*un* ~ *d'œil à*/, to glance at. **3.** [résultat] bruise: *Il était meurtri de coups*, He was covered with bruises; *Il a reçu un* ~ *de pied*, He was kicked; *un* ~ *de poing sur l'œil*, a punch in the eye; *se donner un* ~ *sur le genou*, to knock o.'s knee; *tué sur le* ~, killed outright; *être blessé d'un* ~ *de feu*, to be wounded by gunshot; to be shot [☞ peut signifier aussi: "être tué d'un coup de feu"]; cf. *Il a été blessé d'une balle à la jambe*, He was shot in the leg; [Fig.] ~ *de sang*, stroke; ~ *de froid*, chill; ~ *de soleil*, sunburn; [plus grave] sunstroke. **4.** [arme à feu] shot: ~ *de canon*, gunshot; ~ *de fusil*, rifleshot, gunshot; *recevoir un* ~ *de fusil*, to be wounded by gunshot. cf. §3. **5.** [projectile] round (of ammunition) [Fam.] ammo; *un fusil à deux coups*, double-barrelled gun. **6.** [bruit du coup: brusque] ~ *sec*, snap; crack; ~ *à la porte* [violent] rap; [ordinaire] knock; [discret] tap; ~ *de tonnerre* [brusque] clap (of thunder); ~ *de feu*, (rifle-)shot; report. cf. BRUIT. **7.** [bruit prolongé] ~ *de sonnette*, ring; ~ *de cloche*, peal; ~ *de sifflet*, whistle; ~ *de téléphone*, ring; [action] call; ~ *de tonnerre* [roulement] peal (of thunder); ~ *de fouet*, [bruit] crack; [mouvement] lash. cf. BRUIT. [**B. Actions**] **1.** [gestes] ~ *de balai*, sweep of the broom, ~ *de brosse*, brush-up; ~ *de*/*crayon, pinceau*/, stroke; ~ *d'archet*, bowing; [☞ verbes]: *donner*/*un* ~ *de fer*/*à* . . . , to press, iron . . . ; /*un* ~ *de balai à*/, to sweep; /*un* ~ *de brosse à*/, to brush; /*un* ~ *de pinceau à*/, to touch up [with paint]. **2.** [jeux, sports]: [dames, échecs] move; [dés] throw; [football] kick; [tennis] stroke; [golf] shot, stroke; [pêche] ~ *de filet*, haul. **3.** [tentative]: ~ *d'essai*, first go; *un* ~ *de maître*, a masterful stroke; ~ *de hasard*, stroke of luck, fluke; [Fam.] ~ *dur*, staggering blow, [Fam.] stunner; ~ *du sort*, stroke of bad luck; ~ *d'État*, coup; *risquer le* ~, to take one's chance; *réussir son* ~, to bring it off, to pull off a coup. **4.** [éléments]: ~ *de mer*, lurch; ~ *de roulis*, roll; ~ *de tangage*, pitch; ~ *de vent*, gust (of wind); ~ *de tempête*, gale; ~ *de tonnerre*, thunderclap; [Fig.] *entrer en* ~ *de vent*, to burst into. **5.** [occasion d'agir; cf. FOIS] *à coups de* . . . , by . . . , with the help of . . . ; *à* ~ *sûr*, with absolute certainty, [Fam.] dead sure; *après* ~, when it is too late, after it's over; *à tout* ~, *à tous les coups*, every time; ~ *sur* ~, in/close, rapid/succession; *d'un seul* ~, at once, at one go; *du premier* ~, at first/blow, go/; *pour le* ~, this time; *tout à* ~, all of a sudden, suddenly. **6.** [boisson] *boire un* ~ , to have a drink; *prendre un* (*petit*) ~ , to have a (quick) one; [Fam.] *un* ~ *de /blanc, rouge/*, [Fam.] a shot of white wine, red wine; *boire à petits coups* to sip. **C.** [☞ Many of these expressions are also used figuratively; some of them are repeated below]: ~ *de massue*, floorer; ~ *de tête*, rash impulse; ~ *d'œil* [spectacle] sight; *donner le* ~ *de grâce*, to give the finishing blow (*à*, to); *donner un* ~ *de main à*, to lend s.o. a helping hand; *donner un* ~ *de téléphone*, to call up s.o. on the phone; *passer un* ~ *de fil*, to give s.o. a (phone) call; *faire un* ~ *de tête*, to act rashly; *faire un sale* ~ *à*, to do the dirty on s.o.; *jeter un* ~ *d'œil à*, to glance at; [travail] to give . . . the once-over; [livre] to glance through ; *Cela m'a /donné, fait/un* ~ , It came as/a blow, a shock/; *porter un* ~ , to deal a heavy blow (*à*, to); *Tenez le* ~ *!*, (Keep your) chin up!; *tomber sous le* ~ *d'une loi*, to come under (the provisions of) a law.

coupable [ku'pabl] *adj.* guilty: *se rendre* ~ *de*, to be guilty of. || *n.m.* guilty person, culprit.

coupant [ku'pɑ̃] *adj.* **1.** cutting, sharp (tools, &c.). **2.** [Fig.] cutting, biting: *un ton* ~ , a cutting tone. || *n.m.* edge (of a blade).

coupe[1] [kup] *n.f.* cup, goblet, glass: *une* ~ *à champagne*, champagne glass; ~ *de champagne*, a glass of champagne; [Sport] cup.

coupe[2] [kup] *n.f.* [action] cutting; cut (of a suit, dress): *une* ~ *de cheveux*, a hair cut; *la* ~ *des cartes*, cutting of the cards; [Fig.] *être sous la* ~ *de qqun*, to be under s.o.'s/thumb, rule/; pause [between lines of a poem, in a sentence]; cross section; outline: ~ *horizontale*, horizontal cross section. || **coupe-circuit** [kup|sir'kɥi] *n.m. inv.* circuit-breaker, cut-out. || **coupe-feu** [-'fø] *n.m. inv.* fire-break. || **coupe-file** [-'fil] *n.m.* (police) pass. || **coupe-gorge** [-'gɔrʒ] *n.m. inv.* death trap; den of thieves. || **coupe-jarret** [-ʒa'rɛ] *n.m.* cut-throat. || **coupe-papier** [-pa'pje] *n.m. inv.* paper knife. || **coupe-vent** [-'vɑ̃] *n.m.* © windbreaker.

coupé, -e [ku'pe] *adj.* broken, cut; [liquide] diluted. || *n.m.* coupé.

couper [ku'pe] #3 *v. tr.* **1.** to cut; [arbre] to cut down; ~ *en morceaux*, to cut up; ~ *un habit*, to cut out a suit; [Fig.] *froid qui coupe*, biting cold; ~ *le gaz*, to turn off the gas. **2.** to interrupt: *Il m'a coupé la parole*, He interrupted me. **3.** to mix, dilute (liquids): ~ *le vin* (*avec de l'eau*), to dilute wine (with water). || *v. intr.* to cut: ~ *à travers champs*, to cut across (a field); ~ *au plus court*, to take a short cut; [Fig.] ~ *court à*, to cut short; [Fam.] ~ *à* (*une corvée*), to dodge (a chore). || **se couper** *v. pron.* to cut o.s.; [lines] to cross; [Fam.] to contradict o.s.

couperet [kup'rɛ] *n.m.* chopper, cleaver; blade (of the guillotine).

couperosé, -e [kupro'ze] *adj.* pimpled, blotchy.

couple [kupl] *n.f.* a couple (*de*, of), †brace; two or three. || *n.m.* [male and female] couple, pair. || **coupler** [-e] #3 *v. tr.* to couple, attach together.

couplet [ku'plɛ] *n.m.* verse.

coupon [ku'pɔ̃] *n.m.* **1.** remnant [of yard goods]. **2.** coupon; ticket.

coupure [ku'py:r] *n.f.* **1.** [fait par un instrument tranchant] cut: *se faire une* ~ , to cut o.s.; [dans une pièce de théâtre, &c.] cut, deletion; [de journal, &c.] clipping; [de courant] break. **2.** [billet de banque] denomination.

cour [ku:r] *n.f.* **1.** yard, courtyard: ~ *de récréation*, play(ing)ground; *basse-* ~ , farmyard; © ~ *de bois*, lumber yard. **2.** [royale] (the) Court; [Jur.] Court: ~ *d'appel*, court of appeal; ~ *martiale*, court-martial. **3.** courtship: *faire la* ~ *à qqun*, to court s.o.; to curry favour with s.o.

courage [ku'r|a:ʒ] *n.m.* courage; [Fig.] heart, valiance; [Fam.] go, guts: *travailler avec* ~ , to work hard; *se sentir le* ~ *de . . .*, to feel up to (doing) . . . ; *faire preuve de* ~ , to show courage; *reprendre* ~ , to take heart. || **courageusement** [-a'ʒøz'mɑ̃] *adv.* courageously. || **courageu|x, -se** [-a'ʒø(:z)] *adj.* courageous, valiant; [alliés] gallant; [au travail] hard-working.

couramment [kur|a'mɑ̃] *adv.* [parler] fluently; [lire] easily; [d'habitude] generally, commonly: (*qui*) *s'emploie* ~ , commonly used. || **courant, -e** [-ɑ̃(:t)] *adj.* **1.** running: *eau courante*, running water; *chien* ~ , hound. **2.** current; present: *le mois* ~ , the current month; *dépenses courantes*, current expenses; *le prix* ~ , present price, list price. **3.** general, common: [banque] *compte* ~ , current account; *monnaie courante*, legal tender. || *n.m.* **1.** [rivière] current, stream (of water); [mer] tide, race; [air] draught; [Electr.] ~ *continu*, D.C. current; ~

alternatif, A.C. current. **2.** [Fig.] movement, current: *un ~ d'opinion,* a wave of (public) opinion; [temps] *dans le ~ de,* in the course of (the week, the month). || **au courant** (de) [okurã (də)] *loc. adv.*: *être ~*, to be well-informed, to be conversant with; *se tenir ~ des événements,* to keep/abreast of, up with/ the times; *mettre qqun ~ de,* to inform, tell/s.o. about; [Fam.] to keep s.o. posted (on).

courbature [kurba'tǀy:r] *n.f.* stiffness, ache; [cheval] foundering. || **courbaturer** [-y're] #3 *v. tr.* to cause to ache, to tire/out, all over/.

courbe [kurb] *adj.* curved. || *n.f.* curve; [rivière] bend; [graphique] graph, curve: *~ de niveau,* contour line. || **courbé, -e** [-e] *adj.* curved, crooked, bent: *~ en deux,* bent double. || **courber** [-e] #3 *v. tr.* to bend; to bow (down): *~ la tête,* to bow one's head. || *v. intr.* to bend, sag: *toit qui courbe sous le poids de la neige,* roof sagging under the weight of the snow. || **se courber** *v. pron.* **1.** to bow o.s., to stoop; to bend. **2.** [Fig.] to humble o.s. (*devant,* to).

courbure [kur'by:r] *n.f.* curvature; [tuyau] bend, curve.

coureu|r, -se [ku'r|œ:r, -ø:z] *n.* **1.** [Sport.] runner, racer: © *~ de bois,* coureur de bois; *~ cycliste,* bicycle racer. **2.** [Péj.] gadabout, vagabond; libertine.

courge [kurʒ] *n.f.* gourd, pumpkin.

courir [ku'ri:r] *v. intr.* **1.** to run, to move rapidly: *~ ça et là,* to run about; *~ à bride abattue,* to run at breakneck speed; [Fig.] *le bruit court que . . .*, there is a rumour that . . . ; [Fig.] *par le temps qui court,* nowadays; *sente qui court entre les arbres,* a trail which winds among the trees; [Fam.] *Tu peux toujours ~*, You can whistle for it; *~ après,* to run after; *~ au plus pressé,* to do the most important thing first. || *v. tr.* **1.** to chase, to hunt; to run about: *~ un animal,* to hunt, run/ an animal; *~ le monde,* to roam the world; *faire ~ un bruit,* to spread a rumour; *faire ~ un cheval,* to race a horse.

couronne [ku'rɔn] *n.f.* **1.** [de roi] crown, [de fleurs] wreath; [Pol.] *la Couronne,* the Crown: *les diamants de la ~*, the Crown jewels; *avocat de la ~*, Crown attorney. || **couronné, -e** [-e] *adj.* crowned; [littérature] *~ par l'Académie française,* awarded a prize by the French Academy; *roman ~*, prize(-winning) novel. || **couronnement** [-'mã] *n.m.* **1.** coronation (of a sovereign); [Arch.] top, cap. **2.** [Fig.] crowning; perfection: *~ d'une œuvre,* the finishing touch on a piece of work. || **couronner** [-e] #3 *v. tr.* **1.** to crown (a sovereign, &c.); [le haut d'un édifice] to cope; [de feuilles] to wreathe. **2.** [Fig.] to reward; to award a prize: *Le succès a couronné ses efforts,* Success crowned his efforts. || **se couronner** *v. pron.* to cut o.'s knee.

courrier [ku'rje] *n.m.* **1.** mail, letters: *faire son ~*, to write one's letters; *par retour du ~*, by return mail; *dépouiller son ~*, to open one's mail. **2.** messenger, courier. **3.** [column in newspaper] *~ mondain,* social column; *~ du cœur,* Advice to the lovelorn.

courroie [ku'rwa] *n.f.* strap; belt (of machine).

courroucer [kuru'se] #4 *v. tr.* to anger, to provoke.

cours [ku:r] *n.m.* **1.** course, flow: *le ~ du sang dans les veines,* the flow of blood in the veins; [Fig.] *donner libre ~ à son imagination,* to give free rein to one's imagination. **2.** course, path; length; [maladie, &c.] course: *voyage au long ~*, ocean trip, lengthy voyage; *en ~ de route,* on the way; *les ~ d'eau,* rivers. **3.** course, class: *~ d'histoire,* history course; *suivre des ~*, to take classes, courses; *donner des ~*, to teach courses, classes; *étudier en ~ /privés, particuliers/,* to study at home, to have a private tutor; *salle de ~*, lecture room, class room; *le programme des ~*, curriculum; *~ spécialisé,* honours course; *~ d'application,* demonstration course; *~ du soir,* night, evening/class. **4.** circulation (of merchandise); (current) price, rate: *le ~ du marché,* market price; *pièce qui n'a plus ~*, coin which is no longer legal tender, out of circulation; [ext.] *idées qui n'ont plus ~*, outdated ideas.

course [kurs] *n.f.* **1.** race; run: *participer à une ~*, to compete, take part/in a race; *~ de chevaux,* horse race. **2.** course [a distance covered]; stroke (of a piston): *faire une longue ~ en campagne,* to take a long/walk, ride, drive/in the country; *faire des courses,* to go shopping; *garçon de courses,* errand boy. || **coursier** [-je] *n.m.* **1.** [cheval] charger. **2.** [moulin] millrace.

court[1], **-e** [ku:r, kurt] *adj.* short, brief: [insuffisant] limited, insufficient: *avoir la vue courte,* to be short-sighted. || *n.*:

prendre, couper/au plus ~ , to take a short cut. || *adv.* short: *couper* ~ *à qqch.*, to cut sth. short; *être à* ~ *de qqch.*, to be short of sth.; *pris de* ~ , taken unaware; *rester* ~ , to stop short; *tout* ~ , that's all, just that.

court[2] [ku:r] *n.m.* [tennis] court.

courtage [kur'ta:ʒ] *n.m.* brokerage; [commission] brokerage fee, commission.

courtaud, -e [kur'to(:d)] *adj.* thickset, stocky.

court-circuit [kursir'kɥi] *n.m.* short circuit.

courtier [kur'tje] *n.m.* [actions] broker; [représentant, assurance, douane] salesman, agent.

courtisan [kurti'z|ɑ̃] *n.m.* courtier; [Fig.] flatterer. || **courtisane** [-an] *n.f.* courtesan. || **courtiser** [-e] #3 *v. tr.* to court, to woo; [Péj.] to flatter, to apple-polish.

courtois, -e [kurtw|a(:z)] *adj.* courteous, polite. || **courtoisie** [-'zi] *n.f.* courtesy, politeness.

couru, -e [ku'ry] *adj.* popular (show, actor, &c.); [conférencier] sought after: [Fam.] *C'est* ~ , That's for sure. cf. COURIR.

cousin[1], **-e** [ku'z|ɛ̃, -in] *n.* cousin: ~ *germain*, first cousin.

cousin[2] [ku'zɛ̃] *n.m.* gnat.

coussin [ku's|ɛ̃] *n.m.* cushion. || **coussinet** [-i'nɛ] *n.m.* **1.** small cushion, pad. **2.** bearing; bushing.

cousu, -e [ku'zy] *adj.* sewed; sewn; [Fig.] *être tout* ~ *d'or*, to be rolling in money; ~ *de fil blanc*, obvious, easily seen through. cf. COUDRE.

coût [ku] *n.m.* [de production, d'une marchandise, d'un service, &c.] cost; *indice du* ~ *de la vie*, cost of living index. || **coûtant, -e** [-'tɑ̃(:t)] *adj.* cost, costing: *au prix* ~ , at cost price.

couteau [ku't|o] *n.m.* knife: ~ *de poche*, pocket knife; ~ *à découper*, carving knife; [Tech.] blade; [Fig.] *être à couteaux tirés avec qqun*, to be at daggers drawn with s.o. || **coutellerie** [-ɛl'ri] *n.f.* [collection] cutlery; [lieu] cutlery store.

coûter [ku|'te] #3 *v. intr.* **1.** to cost: [Fam.] *Cela m'a coûté les yeux de la tête*, That cost me a small fortune; *Ceci coûte très cher*, This is very expensive. **2.** to be painful, difficult: *Tout effort me coûte*, Every effort is painful; *Il n'y a que le premier pas qui coûte*, The first step is always the worst. || *v. tr.* to cost: ~ *la vie*, to cost one's life; *coûte que coûte*, cost what it may. || **coûteu|x, -se** [-'tø(:z)] *adj.* costly, expensive.

coutume [ku'tym] *n.f.* custom, habit: *avoir* ~ *de* (+ *infin.*), to be accustomed to, to be in the habit of sth. (+ ing); *comme de* ~ , as usual. || **coutumi|er, -ère** [-je, -jɛ:r] *adj.* customary, usual: *être* ~ *de* (*mentir*), to be in the habit of (lying); *être* ~ *du fait*, to be an old hand (at it); *droit* ~ , common law.

couture [ku't|y:r] *n.f.* [action] sewing; [résultat] seam; needlework; [cicatrice] scar; *maison de* ~ , dressmaking establishment; *la haute* ~ , fashion dressmaking, haute couture; *sans* ~ , seamless; [Fig.] *battre qqun à plate-* ~ , to beat s.o. hollow, to win easily. || **couturier** [-y'rje] *n.m.* couturier, dressmaker. || **couturière** [-y'rjɛ:r] *n.f.* seamstress, dressmaker.

couvée [ku've] *n.f.* [œufs] sitting; [poussins] brood, hatch; [Fig.] brood.

couvent [ku'vɑ̃] *n.m.* **1.** [Rel.] convent, monastery: ~ *de femmes*, nunnery. **2.** convent, boarding school.

couver [ku've] #3 *v. tr.* **1.** to brood; to sit (on eggs). **2.** [Fig.] to hatch (a plot), to prepare; [Fam.] ~ *qqun des yeux*, to gaze at s.o.; ~ *qqun*, to pamper s.o. || *v. intr.* to smoulder: *feu, passion/qui couve*, smouldering/fire, passion/.

couvercle [ku'vɛrkl] *n.m.* lid, cover.

couvert [ku'vɛ:r] *n.m.* **1.** [table] setting, cover: *mettre deux couverts*, to set the table for two; *mettre le* ~ , to set the table; *ôter le* ~ , to clear the table; [Rest.] cover charge; *le vivre et le* ~ board and lodging. **2.** cover, shelter: *à* ~ , under cover, in a safe place; *se mettre à* ~ , to take shelter; [Fig.] *mettre sa fortune à* ~ , to safeguard one's fortune; [Fig.] *sous le* ~ *du ministre de l'éducation*, under the signature of the Minister of Education; *sous le* ~ *de l'amitié*, under a pretence of friendship. || *adj.* covered (*de*, with): ~ *d'herbes*, overgrown with grass; [toit] roofed; [tête] with one's hat on: *Restez* ~ , Keep your hat on; [ciel] clouded; [Fig.] obscure: *à mots couverts*, covertly; ~ *de neige*, snow-covered, snow-clad.

couverture [kuvɛr'ty:r] *n.f.* cover, covering; [Const.] roofing: ~ *de lit*, bedspread; ~ *de livre*, cover, wrapper; ~ *de laine*, woollen blanket; ~ *de voyage*, plaid, car blanket.

couveuse [ku'vø:z] *n.f.* [poule] setting hen; [appareils] incubator.

couvre [ku:vr] cf. COUVRIR. || **couvre-feu** [kuvrə|'fø] *n.m.* curfew. || **couvre-lit** [-'li] *n.m.* bedspread. || **couvre-pied(s)**

[-'pje] *n.m.* (fancy) quilt. ‖ **couvreur** [ku'vrœ:r] *n.m.* [Pers.] roofer; [entrepreneur] roofing contractor.

couvrir [ku'vri:r] #25 *v. tr.* **1.** to cover; [Constr.] to roof; [Fig.] *Le bruit couvrait mes paroles,* The noise drowned out my words; ~ *de (fleurs),* to cover with (flowers); [Fig.] ~ *une distance,* to cover a distance; ~ *de honte,* to cover with shame. **2.** [Fig.] to clothe. **3.** [Fig.] to conceal; to safeguard. ‖ **se couvrir** *v. pron.* to cover (o.s.); [ciel] to cloud over; [arbres, &c.] to leaf out; [la tête] to put on one's hat.

coyote [kɔ'jɔt] *n.m.* coyote.

C.R. [= Conseiller *m*/du Roi, de la Reine] K.C., Q.C. [= King's Counsel, Queen's Counsel].

crachat [kra'ʃ|a] *n.m.* spit; †spittle. ‖ **craché, -e** [-e] *adj.* spit; [Fig.] exact: *C'est son père tout* ~, He's the spitting image of his father. ‖ **cracher** [-e] #3 *v. tr.* to spit; [Fig.] to spit, spew out: *Défense de* ~, No spitting. ‖ **crachoir** [-wa:r] *n.m.* spittoon.

craie [krɛ] *n.f.* chalk.

craindre [krɛ̃:dr], **craignant** [krɛ'ɲɑ̃], **craint** [krɛ̃] #36 *v. tr.* **1.** to fear: *ne* ~ *personne,* to be afraid of no one; ~ *pour,* to be anxious about. **2.** ~ *que* + *subj.* [☞ When the sentence is affirmative, the expletive *ne* is usual. placed before the subordinate verb]: *Je crains qu'il ne vienne,* I am afraid that he may come. [☞ However, it is important to notice that the subordinate verb may be truly negative even though the governing verb is affirmative]. *Je crains qu'il ne vienne pas,* I am afraid that he/may not come, is not coming/. **3.** ~ *de (mourir, échouer),* to be afraid of dying, failing. ‖ **crainte** [krɛ̃:t] *n.f.* fear: *N'ayez* ~, Have no fear; *sans* ~, fearless; *Ne dormez pas de* ~ *qu'il (ne) vienne,* Keep your eyes open/lest, in case/he comes; *Soyez prêt de* ~ *qu'il ne vienne pas,* Be ready, in case he doesn't come. ‖ **crainti|f, -ve** [krɛ̃'t|if, -i:v] *adj.* timid, [qui manifeste de la peur] fearful.

cramoisi, -e [kramwa'zi] *adj.* crimson.

crampe [krɑ̃:p] *n.f.* cramp.

crampon [krɑ̃'p|ɔ̃] *n.m.* **1.** cramp, clamp. **2.** spike; caulk (of a horseshoe); [en U] staple. **3.** [Fig. & Fam.] bore. ‖ **cramponner** [-ɔ'ne] #3 *v. tr.* to clamp; [Fam.] to pester, to buttonhole (s.o.). ‖ **se cramponner** (à) *v. pron.* to cling (to): ~ *désespérément à . . .*, to hang on/like grim death, for dear life/to.

cran [krɑ̃] *n.m.* **1.** notch, nick; [ceinture] hole: [Fig.] *baisser, monter/d'un* ~, to drop down, go up/a notch; ~ *de sûreté,* safety catch; [Fig.] *Il est à* ~, He is ready to explode. **2.** [Fam.] courage, grit, pluck; [front] audacity, energy: *Il a du* ~, He has a lot of (courage, audacity, energy).

crâne [kra:n] *n.m.* skull, cranium: *fracture du* ~, skull fracture: *se bourrer le* ~ *(de),* to cram one's head (with). ‖ *adj.* plucky, courageous. ‖ **crâner** [kra'ne] #3 *v. intr.* to swagger, swank.

crapaud [kra'po] *n.m.* toad; [fauteuil] low armchair; [piano] baby grand.

crapet [kra'pɛ] © *n.m.*: ~ *soleil,* sunfish; ~ *calicot,* calico bass; ~ *gris,* rock bass, rockfish.

crapule [kra'pyl] *n.f.* debauchery; [Pers.] scoundrel. ‖ **crapuleu|x, -se** [-ø(:z)] *adj.* dissolute; filthy.

craquement [krak|'mɑ̃] *n.m.* cracking, creaking. ‖ **craquer** [-e] #3 *v. intr.* **1.** to crack, [itératif] to crackle; [déchirer] to split: *faire* ~ *ses doigts,* to crack one's fingers; *avoir les poches pleines à* ~, to have one's pockets jammed full; *La neige craque sous les pieds,* The snow crunches under foot. **2.** [Fig., Fam.] to be cracking up: *Affaire qui craque,* Business which is cracking up.

crasse[1] [kras] *adj.* [ignorance] gross, crass.

crasse[2] [kras] *n.f.* **1.** dirt, filth; [métal] slag, scum. **2.** [Fig.] stinginess; misery; [Fam.] *faire une* ~ *à qqun,* to play a dirty trick on s.o. ‖ **crasseu|x, -se** [-ø(:z)] *adj.* filthy, dirty.

cratère [kra'tɛ:r] *n.m.* crater.

cravache [kra'vaʃ] *n.f.* riding/-whip, -crop/. ‖ **cravacher** [-e] #3 *v. tr.* to flog, horsewhip.

cravate [kra'vat] *n.f.* (neck) tie: *nouer, dénouer/sa* ~, to tie, undo/one's tie.

crayeu|x, -se [krɛ'jø(:z)] *adj.* chalky.

crayon [krɛ'j|ɔ̃] *n.m.* pencil; (a pencil) sketch: ~ *de couleur,* crayon. ‖ **crayonnage** [-ɔ'na:ʒ] *n.m.* pencil sketch. ‖ **crayonner** [-ɔ'ne] #3 *v. tr.* to sketch; to draw in pencil.

créance [kre'ɑ̃:s] *n.f.* **1.** trust, belief: *lettres de* ~, credentials; *ajouter* ~ *à qqch.,* to have faith in sth. **2.** claim, debt: *lettre de* ~, letter of credit; *avoir* ~ *sur qqun,* to have a claim on s.o.; ~ *hypothécaire,* mortgage. ‖ **créanci|er, -ère** [kreɑ̃'sj|e, -ɛ:r] *n.* creditor.

créateur, -rice [krea|'tœ:r, -'tris] *n.* creator; inventor [d'une société, &c.] founder. ‖ *adj.* creative. ‖ **création** [-'sjɔ̃] *n.f.*

creation: ~ *littéraire*, creative writing. || **créature** [-'ty:r] *n.f.* creature; © woman.
crèche [krɛʃ] *n.f.* [Lit.] crib; [institution] crèche, day nursery; manger.
crédibilité [kredibili'te] *n.f.* credibility.
crédit [kre'di] *n.m.* **1.** credit; [par extension] reputation: *acheter, vendre/à* ~, to buy, sell/on credit; *faire* ~ *à qqun*, to give s.o. credit; ~ *foncier*, loan society; *ouvrir un* ~, to open an account. **2.** sum (voted for a certain purpose); appropriation. **3.** © ~ *scolaire*, school credit. || **créditer** [-'te] #3 *v. tr.* to credit (with, *de*). || **créditeu|r, -se** [-'tœ:r, -'tø:z] *n.* creditor.
crédule [kre'dyl] *adj.* credulous. || **crédulité** [-i'te] *n.f.* credulity.
créer [kre'e] #3 *v. tr.* to create; [commencer] to start, found (a business, a city, &c.); [des ennuis à qqun] to cause.
crémaillère [krema'jɛ:r] *n.f.* **1.** pothook; [Fig. & Fam.] *pendre la* ~, to have a house warming. **2.** [Tech.] rack.
crème [krɛm] *n.f.* **1.** cream; custard; [couleur] cream: ~ *glacée*, ice cream; ~ *de beauté*, skin, beauty/cream. **2.** [Fig.] pick, cream, best; © ~ *à la glace*, ice cream. || **crémerie** [krem|'ri] *n.f.* dairy (products); [petit restaurant] dairy bar; luncheonette. || **crémeu|x, -se** [-ø(:z)] *adj.* creamy. || **crémier, -ère** [-je, -jɛ:r] *n.* dairyman, dairywoman; dairymaid.
crénelé [kren'le] *adj.* notched: *tour crénelée*, tower with battlements. || **créneler** #8 *v. tr.* to notch; to cut cogs in (wheels); to mill (a coin).
créole [kre'ɔl] *n.* [personne] Creole. || *n.m.* [langue] Creole. || *adj.* Creole.
crêpe [krɛ:p] *n.m.* [tissue] crêpe; [en signe de deuil] mourning band; *semelles de* ~, crêpe soles. || *n.f.* pancake: *faire sauter une* ~, to flip a pancake.
crépitement [krepit|'mɑ̃] *n.m.* crackling (of fire); pattering (of rain). || **crépiter** [-e] #3 *v. intr.* [feu] to crackle; [pluie] to patter.
crépu, -e [kre'py] *adj.* [cheveux] frizzly, kinky; [feuille] crinkled, crinkly.
crépuscule [krepys'kyl] *n.m.* twilight, dusk.
cresson [krɛ'sõ] *n.m.* (water-) cress.
crête [krɛ:t] *n.f.* crest, ridge; summit; comb (of a rooster, &c.): ~ *d'une vague*, the crest of a wave; *une fois arrivé à la* ~, once they had reached the summit.
Crète (île de) [(il də) 'krɛ:t] *n.f.* Crete.
crétin, -e [kre't|ɛ̃, -in] *n.* idiot, blockhead, numskull.
cretons (& gretons) [krə'tõ, grə'tõ] © *n. mpl.* [= Fr. rillettes *fpl*] greaves, potted mince.
creusage [krø'z|a:ʒ] *n.m.* [dans le sol] excavation, digging; hollowing (out), grooving (of wood, &c.); digging (of hole, &c.); sinking (of well, &c.). || **creusé, -e** [-e] *adj.* [par endroits] hollowed out; [visage] lined (with, *de*); [dans le sol] dug; [sur une colonne] cut into. || **creuser** [-e] #3 *v. tr.* **1.** [construction] to excavate; to hollow, scoop/out; to dig (a hole, a mine, a well, &c.); to make one's (eyes, cheeks, &c.) hollow; [un sillon] to plough. **2.** [Fig.] to study (a question, &c.) thoroughly. **3.** to make hungry: *La marche creuse l'estomac*, Walking makes one hungry. || **se creuser** *v. pron.* to hollow out; [Fig.] *se creuser la tête*, to rack one's brains.
creuset [krø'zɛ] *n.m.* crucible.
creu|x, -se [krø(:z)] *adj.* hollow; deep (hole); empty (stomach): *avoir des yeux* ~, to be hollow-eyed; [Fig.] *esprit* ~, vacant mind; *heures creuses*, slack hours. || *n.m.* hollow; deep (voice); trough (of a wave): *avoir un bon* ~, to have a fine bass voice; *avoir un* ~ *dans l'estomac*, to have an empty stomach.
crevaison [krəvɛ'zõ] *n.f.* flat (tire).
crevasse [krə'vas] *n.f.* crack, crevice.
crève-cœur [krɛv'kœ:r] *n.m. inv.* heartbreak; keen disappointment.
crevé, -e [krə've] *adj.* [ballon, balle, pneu, &c.] punctured; [yeux] put out; [mort] dead; [très fatigué] worn out. || **crever** [krə've] #9 *v. tr.* to burst, to break (out); to put out (the eyes); to puncture (a tire); [Sl.] to die: ~ *une digue*, to burst a dam; [Fig.] *Cela vous crève les yeux*, It's staring you in the face; ~ *le cœur*, to break one's heart. || *v. intr.* **1.** to burst, break: *Le nuage creva*, The cloud burst, There was a cloudburst; *rouler un an sans* ~, to drive a year without a flat. **2.** [of animals and, in slang, of persons] to die: ~ *de faim*, to die of starvation; ~ *d'orgueil*, to burst with pride.
crevette [krə'vɛt] *n.f.* shrimp; [plus grand] prawn.
cri [kri] *n.m.* cry (of persons and animals): *pousser, jeter/un* ~, to shout, to cry out; *un* ~ *aigu*, a scream; *un* ~ *déchirant*, a shriek; *un* ~ *de gonds*, a squeaking of hinges; [Fig.] *le dernier* ~, the latest style. || **criailler** [-ɑ'je] #3 *v. intr.* [protester] to grumble; [US, Fam.] to beef: ~ *après qqun*, to scold s.o. || **criant, -e** [-'jɑ̃(:t)] *adj.* [injustice] crying, shocking; [Fig.] [couleurs] loud, shocking; [preuve]

glaring, evident. || **criard, -e** [-'ja:r, -'jard] *adj.* [voix] shrill; [dettes] pressing; [couleurs] loud, shocking.

crible [kribl] *n.m.* sieve, sifter: *passer au ~*, to screen, sift; [Fig.] to examine carefully. || **cribler** [-e] #3 *v. tr.* **1.** to sift, screen. **2.** [Fig.] to riddle (with holes); to cover (with blows); *être criblé de dettes*, to be up to one's ears in debt.

cric [krik] *n.m.* lever, jack.

cricri (cri-cri) [kri'kri] *n.m.* [Fam.] cricket; [le cri du grillon] chirping.

criée [kri'j|e] *n.f.* auction: *vente à la ~*, public auction.

crier [-e] #3 *v. intr.* to shout, to cry (out): *~ après qqun*, to scold s.o.; *Les gonds crient*, The hinges squeak; *~ à tue-tête*, to shout (at the top of one's lungs). || *v. tr.* to shout: *~ des injures à qqun*, to shout insults at s.o.; [Fig.] *~ misère*, to complain of poverty; *sans ~ gare*, without a word of warning; [Fig.] *~ son innocence*, to proclaim one's innocence. || **crieu|r, -se** [-œ:r, -ø:z] *n.* crier; [marchand ambulant] hawker; *un ~ de journaux*, newsboy, [Fam.] newsie.

crime [krim] *n.m.* crime. || **criminel, -le** [-i'nɛl] *adj. & n.* criminal.

crin [krɛ̃] *n.* hair; [de cheval] horsehair; [végétal] fibre.

crinière [kri'njɛ:r] *n.f.* mane (of horse and lion), plume (on a helmet); [Fig.] (wild) mop (of hair).

crique [krik] *n.f.* creek, cove. || *n.m.* © creek, stream.

criquet [kri'kɛ] *n.m.* cricket.

crise [kri:z] *n.f.* **1.** turning point (in a sickness); attack; fit: *~ cardiaque*, heart attack; *~ de colère*, fit of anger; *~ nerveuse*, nervous breakdown; *~ de nerfs*, a fit of hysterics. **2.** [Fig.] crisis; emergency: *~ politique*, political crisis; *~ économique*, depression.

crispant, -e [kris'p|ɑ̃(:t)] *adj.* aggravating; irritating (mannerisms). || **crispation** [-a'sjɔ̃] *n.f.* contraction. || **crisper** [-e] #3 *v. tr.* **1.** to shrivel; to clench (one's fists); to contort (one's face). **2.** [Fig.] to put (s.o., s.o.'s nerves) on edge; to irritate. || **se crisper** *v. pron.* [chose] to shrivel up; [Pers.] to wince, to become tense; [se fâcher] to become irritated.

crissement [kris|'mɑ̃] *n.m.* grating, grinding (of teeth, &c.); crunching (of gravel). || **crisser** [-e] #3 *v. intr.* [dents] to grind; [gravier] to crunch.

cristal [kris'tal] *n.m.* crystal; cut glass. || **cristallin, -e** [-ɛ̃, -in] *adj.* crystalline, crystal-clear. || **cristalliser** [-i'ze] #3 *v. tr. & intr.* to crystallize.

critère [kri'tɛ:r] *n.m.* criterion [pl. criteria]; [Sport.] trial.

critique [kri'tik] *adj.* critical, crucial; [qui détermine] determining: *situation f ~*, emergency. || *n.f.* [article] criticism; review: *faire la ~ d'une pièce*, to write a review of a play, to review a play. || *n.m.* [Pers.] critic, judge. || **critiqué, -e** [-e] *adj.* criticized, blamed. || **critiquer** [-e] #3 *v. tr.* to criticize, find fault with.

croassement [kroas|'mɑ̃] *n.m.* [corbeau] caw; [grenouille] croaking. || **croasser** [-e] #3 *v. tr.* to caw, croak.

croc [kro] *n.m.* hook (on a wall, &c.); boat hook; [loup, chien, &c.] fang; [sanglier, &c.] tusk; canine tooth (of man). || **croc-en-jambe** [krɔkɑ̃'ʒɑ̃:b] *n.m.* pl. **crocs-en-jambe** *n.m.* trip: *donner un ~ à qqun*, to trip s.o. (up).

croche [krɔʃ] © *adj.* bent, twisted, curved; [Fig.] crooked [affair, &c.]. || *n.f.* [Mus.] quaver, eighth note: *double ~*, semiquaver, sixteenth note.

crocher [krɔ'ʃe] #3 *v. tr.* to hook; © [Fam.] [un ami par le bras, &c.] to grab.

crochet [krɔ'ʃ|ɛ] *n.m.* (small) hook; skeleton key; [Impr.] square brackets; [Cout.] crochet hook, crocheting; [boxe] hook; (pl.) fangs (of serpents); © [de cheveux] kisscurl; [Fig.] *faire un ~*, [route] to make a detour; [Pers.] to go out of o.'s way: *aux crochets de qqun*, at s.o.'s expense. || **crocheter** [-'te] #3 *v. tr.* to pick (a lock); [Cout.] to crochet.

crochu, -e [krɔ'ʃy] *adj.* hooked; [doigts] crooked: [Fig.] *avoir les mains crochues*, to have sticky fingers, to be a thief.

crocodile [krɔkɔ'dil] *n.m.* crocodile: *des larmes de ~*, crocodile tears.

croire [krwa:r], **croyant** [krwa'jɑ̃], **cru** [kry] #74 *v. tr.* **1.** to believe, think: *à l'en ~*, from what he says, if he is to be believed; *Je n'en crois pas mes yeux*, I can't believe my eyes; *Je crois que oui*, I/think, believe/so; *Je vous crois!*, I should say so!; *Croyez-le bien*, Depend on it. **2.** [à qqun, qqch.] to believe in (s.o., sth.); [en qqun] to have confidence in s.o.; *On peut croire ce qu'il dit*, You can bank on what he says. || **se croire** *v. pron.* to think o.s. (sth.): *~ très malin*, to think o.s. very clever.

croisade [krwa'zad] *n.f.* crusade.

croisé, -e [krwa'ze] *adj.* twilled (cloth); alternate (rhyme); cross (fire); cross (breed); folded (arms); crossed (legs):

mots croisés, crossword puzzle. || *n.m.* [Pers.] crusader; [Text.] twill.

croisée [krwa'z|e] *n.f.* **1.** crossing, intersection: *à la ~ des chemins*, at the crossroads. **2.** casement window. || **croisement** [-'mã] *n.m.* crossing; folding (of the arms), cross-breeding; crossroads, intersection: *~ dangereux*, dangerous intersection. || **croiser** [-e] #3 *v. tr.* to cross; to fold (the arms); [Auto.] to pass (when going in the opposite direction); [Zool.] to cross-breed (animals, &c.). || *v. intr.* [Naut.] to cruise. || **se croiser** *v. pron.* to pass one another, each other (going in the opposite direction); to fold (one's arms, &c.). || **croiseur** [-œ:r] *n.m.* cruiser. || **croisière** [-jɛ:r] *n.f.* cruise: *faire une ~*, to go for a cruise.

croissance [krwa's|ã:s] *n.f.* growth; [Fig.] increase.

croissant, -e [-ã(:t)] *adj.* growing, increasing; crescent. || *n.m.* (crescent-shaped) bun; [instrument] bill hook.

croître [krwa:tr], **croissant** [krwa'sã], **crû** [kry] #75 *v. intr.* to grow; [jours] to lengthen, get longer; [lune] to wax; [crue] to rise: [Fam.] *~ et embellir*, [en mieux] to get better and better; [Péj.] to go from bad to worse.

croix [krwa] *n.f.* cross: *en ~*, crosswise; *Croix-Rouge*, Red Cross; *~ de guerre*, Military Cross; *signer son nom d'une ~*, to make one's X; *faire une ~*, to put a check mark [√] (before a list of objects, &c.).

croquant, -e [krɔ'kã(:t)] *adj.* crisp; [Fam.] crunchy. || *n.m.* †boor, wretch.

croque-mort [krɔk'mɔ:r] *n.m.* [Fr.] (undertaker's) helper, assistant.

croquer [krɔ'ke] #3 *v. intr.* to crunch: *Le sucre croque sous la dent*, Sugar crunches when you chew it. || *v. tr.* to munch; [très vite] to gulp, to bolt; [Fig.] to dissipate (wealth); to waste; [Fam.] *croquer le marmot*, to cool one's heels; [Fig.] to sketch; to take a snapshot: *~ sur le vif*, to sketch from a model.

croquis [krɔ'ki] *n.m.* sketch; [littérature] plan, outline: *faire un ~ de*, → to sketch.

crosse [krɔs] *n.f.* (bishop's) crozier; (hockey) stick, (golf) club; butt (of a rifle), grip (of a pistol); [Sport.] lacrosse.

crotte [krɔt] *n.f.* [Vulg.] mud, dirt; dung. || **crotté, -e** [-e] *adj.* dirty, spattered (with mud, slush, &c.). || **crotter** [-e] #3 *v. tr.* to dirty. || **se crotter** *v. pron.* to get dirty, soiled.

croulant, -e [kru'l|ã(:t)] *adj.* tottering, crumbling; [Fig.] ramshackle. || **crouler** [-e] #3 *v. intr.* to collapse, to fall (down, in); to crumble; [Fig.]: *faire ~ la salle (sous les applaudissements)*, to bring down the house (with applause).

croupe [krup] *n.f.* [cheval] croup, crupper; [Fig.] rump: *monter en ~*, to ride behind (the saddle).

croupetons (à) [akrup'tõ] *loc. adv.* on o.'s haunches: *assis ~*, squatting, sitting on o.'s haunches.

croupi, -e [kru'p|i] *adj.* [eau] stagnant, foul. || **croupir** [-i:r] #17 *v. intr.* [eau] to stagnate, to grow foul; [Fig.] to stagnate, to wallow (*dans*, in). || **croupissant, -e** [-i'sã(:t)] *adj.* stagnating; growing foul.

croustelle [krus'tɛl] © *n.f.* potato chips.

croustillant, -e [krusti'jã(:t)] *adj.* crisp (biscuit, &c.); [Fam.] spicy (story).

croûte [krut] *n.f.* **1.** crust (of bread, &c.); patty shell; rind (of cheese); scab (on a sore); [Fam.] *casser la ~*, to have a snack. **2.** [Art, Fam.] daub. || **croûton** [-õ] *n.m.* crust (of bread); chunk (of bread).

croyable [krwa'j|abl] *adj.* believable, credible. || **croyance** [-ã:s] *n.f.* belief; [Rel.] creed, faith. || **croyant, -e** [-ã(:t)] *adj.* believing. || *n.* believer: *les croyants*, the faithful.

cru[1] [kry] cf. CROIRE.

cru[2] [kry] *adj.* **1.** [matériaux] raw, crude; [viande] uncooked, [brique] unburnt. **2.** [lumière] harsh; [couleurs] raw; [paroles] crude, rough: *monter à ~*, to ride bareback.

cru[3] [kry] *n.m.* vintage; [region] wine region: *vin m du ~*, local wine; [Fig.] *de mon propre ~*, of my own/creation, making/.

crû [kry] cf. CROÎTRE.

cruauté [kryo'te] *n.f.* cruelty, act of cruelty.

cruche [kryʃ] *n.f.* **1.** jug, pitcher. **2.** [Fig., Fam.] fool, blockhead. || **cruchon** [-õ] *n.m.* small jug, pitcher; pot (of cider).

crucial, -e [kry'sjal] *adj.* **1.** cross-shaped. **2.** [Fig.] crucial, paramount (importance, &c.).

crucifier [krusi'f|je] #3 *v. tr.* to crucify. || **crucifix** [-i] *n.m.* crucifix.

crudité [krydi'te] *n.f.* rawness (of food): *manger des crudités*, to eat raw fruit, vegetables; [Fig.] harshness (of light); [vulgarité] crudeness: *dire des crudités*, to say indecent things.

crue [kry] *n.f.* [montée] rising (of a river, &c.); [périodique] overflowing, flooding.

cruel, -le [kry'ɛl] *adj.* cruel, harsh. || **cruellement** [-'mã] *adv.* cruelly.

crustacé [krysta'se] *n.m.* shellfish; [pl. coll.] crustacea.

Cuba [ky'ba] *n.* Cuba.

cubage [ky'ba:ʒ] *n.m.*cubic/content, volume/. ‖ **cube** [kyb] *n.m.* cube; [play] building blocks. ‖ *adj.* cubic: *mètre* ~ , cubic metre. ‖ **cuber** [-e] #3 *v. tr.* to cube. ‖ **cubique** [-ik] *adj.* cubic(al); [Math.] *racine f* ~ , cube root. ‖ **cubisme** [ky'bism] *n.m.* cubism.

cueillette [kœ'j|ɛt] *n.f.* [action] gathering, picking (of flowers, fruit, &c.); [saison] harvest time. ‖ **cueillir** [-i:r] #20 *v. tr.* to pick, gather (flowers, fruit); [Fam.] ~ *un voleur*, to nab a thief.

cuiller or **cuillère** [kɥi'j|ɛ:r] *n.f.* spoon: ~ *à thé*, teaspoon; ~ *à/bouche, soupe/*, tablespoon. ‖ **cuillerée** [-e're] *n.f.* spoonful: *une grande* ~ , a heaping spoonful.

cuir [kɥi:r] *n.m.* leather, hide; skin: ~ *chevelu*, scalp; ~ *repoussé*, tooled leather.

cuirasse [kɥi'ras] *n.f.* breastplate; [navire, &c.] armour plate. ‖ **cuirassé, -e** [-e] *adj.* armour-plated, armoured. ‖ *n.m.* [Naut.] armoured ship, battleship. ‖ **cuirasser** [-e] #3 *v. tr.* to armour plate.

cuire [kɥi:r], **cuisant, cuit** #56 *v. tr.* to cook, [au four] to bake; [à l'eau] to boil; [à la casserole] to stew; [porcelaine, &c.] to fire: ~ *le pain*, to bake bread; ~ *à petit feu*, to simmer; ~ *des briques*, to fire bricks; *faire* ~ *qqch.*, to cook sth. ‖ *v. intr.* **1.** to cook, be cooking: *La viande cuit dans son jus*, The meat is cooking in its juice. **2.** [Fig.] to smart, to burn: *Les yeux me cuisent*, My eyes are /smarting, burning/; *Il vous en cuira*, You will be sorry for it. ‖ **cuisant, -e** [kɥi'zɑ̃(:t)] *adj.* [blessure] painful; [piment, poivre] hot, [saveur] biting, [froid] biting, [Fig.] [désir] burning; [défaite] stinging; [déception] painful; [remarque, réflexion] stinging.

cuiseur [kɥi'zœ:r] *n.m.* pressure cooker.

cuisine [kɥi'zin] *n.f.* **1.** [lieu] kitchen: *petite* ~ , kitchenette. **2.** cooking, cuisine: *recettes de* ~ , recipes; *la* ~ *française*, French/cooking, cuisine/; *savoir faire la* ~ , to know how to cook; *livre de* ~ , cook(ery) book; *faire la* ~ , to do the cooking, to cook. ‖ **cuisini|er, -ère** [-je, -jɛ:r] *n.* [Pers.] cook; [object] cook stove, kitchen range.

cuisse [kɥis] *n.f.* thigh: *cuisses de grenouille*, frog's legs. ‖ **cuisseau** [-o] *n.m.* leg (of lamb, &c.). ‖ **cuisson** [kɥi'sõ] *n.f.* cooking; [au four] baking; [d'un liquide] boiling; [Tech.] firing (of bricks, pottery, &c.); [Méd.] burning sensation: . . . *demande une* ~ *prolongée*, → must be cooked for a long time.

cuit, -e [kɥi(t)] *adj.* cooked, baked; fired [of bricks]: *trop* ~ , overdone, overcooked; ~ *à point*, well/cooked, done.

cuite [kɥit] *n.f.* drinking spree, drunk: *prendre une* ~ , to go on a/(drinking) spree, drunk/. cf. © BROSSE.

cuivre [kɥi:vr] *n.m.* copper; [Mus.] brass (instruments); [Naut., pl.] brasswork; ~ *jaune*, brass (cf. LAITON). ‖ **cuivré, -e** [kɥi'vre] *adj.* [couvert de cuivre] coppered, [couleur de cuivre] copper-coloured; metallic (sound); *voix* ~ , resounding, vibrant/voice.

cul [ky] *n.m.* [vulgar except when used in compound words] backside, bottom. ‖ **cul-de-jatte** [-d'ʒat] *n.m.* legless cripple. ‖ **cul-de-sac** [-d'sak] *n.m.* blind alley.

culasse [ky'las] *n.f.* [fusil, canon] breech; [Auto.] cylinder head.

culbute [kyl'byt] *n.f.* [Gymnas.] somersault; [chute] tumble, heavy fall: *faire la* ~ , to turn a somersault; [Fig., ministère] to fall; [Com.] to fail. ‖ **culbuter** [-e] #3 *v. tr.* to overthrow, upset; *être culbuté par une voiture*, to be knocked down by a car. ‖ *v. intr.* to turn a somersault; to fall head over heels.

culinaire [kyli'nɛ:r] *adj.* culinary.

culminant, -e [kylmi'n|ɑ̃(:t)] *adj.* culminating: *point* ~ , highest point (of a mountain); climax, zenith (of power). ‖ **culminer** [-e] #3 *v. intr.* to reach the highest point; to culminate.

culot [ky'lo] *n.m.* **1.** bottom, base [of church lamps, spark plug, shell case, &c.]. **2.** [Fam.] cheek, nerve: *Il ne manque pas de* ~ , → He has plenty of nerve.

culotte [ky'lɔt] *n.f.* [d'homme] pants; knee-breeches; [d'enfant] knee pants; [de femme] panties: ~ *de cheval*, riding breeches; ~ *de sport*, short pants, shorts; [pl., Fam.] pants: *une paire de culottes*, a pair of pants. cf. PANTALON. ‖ **culotté, -e** [-e] *adj.* [Fam.] cheeky: *Il est* ~ , He's got a nerve. ‖ **culotter** [-e] #3 *v. tr.* to put pants on s.o.; to break in (a pipe). **se culotter** *v. pron.* to put one's pants on; [pipe] to season, mellow.

culpabilité [kylpabili'te] *n.f.* guilt.

culte [kylt] *n.m.* **1.** worship: *le* ~ *du soleil*, sun worship. **2.** creed, religion, (religious) service: *le* ~ *protestant*, the Protestant service. **3.** [Fig.] worship, adoration: *avoir le* ~ *des livres*, to adore books.

cultivable [kylti'v|abl] *adj.* fit for cultivation, tillable. ‖ **cultivat|eur, -rice** [-a'tœ:r, -a'tris] *n.* farmer. ‖ **cultivé, -e** [-e] *adj.* cultivated (land); cultured (mind); well read (man). ‖ **cultiver** [-e] #3 *v. tr.* **1.**

to cultivate; [la terre] to till, to farm. **2.** to raise, grow: ~ *du maïs*, to raise corn. **3.** [Fig.] to cultivate, educate: ~ *son esprit*, to improve one's mind. || **culture** [kyl'ty:r] *n.f.* **1.** [de la terre] agriculture, farming; [des plantes] cultivation, growing: *la* ~ *des pommes*, apple growing; [des abeilles] breeding. **2.** [pl.] crops; [terres] cultivated lands. **3.** [Fig.] culture: ~ *générale*, background; *la* ~ *grecque*, Greek civilization. || **culturel, -le** [kylty'rɛl] *adj.* cultural.

cupide [ky'pid] *adj.* greedy, covetous. || **cupidité** [-i'te] *n.f.* greed(iness); cupidity.

curable [ky'rabl] *adj.* curable. || **curati|f, -ve** [kyra't|if, -i:v] *adj.* curative. || **cure**[1] [ky:r] *n.f.* **1.** cure, (course of) treatment. **2.** [Fig.] *n'en avoir* ~, to take no notice of (sth.).

cure[2] [ky:r] *n.f.* [Rel., fonction] charge, vicarship; [résidence] vicarage, rectory; [R.C.] presbytery. || **curé** [ky're] *n.m.* [R.C.] parish priest, curé; [Prot.] vicar, rector, pastor.

curer [ky're] #3 *v. tr.* to clean out (a ditch, pipe); to clean, pick (one's nails, teeth); to dredge (a river).

curieusement [kyrj|øz'mɑ̃] *adv.* curiously; [étrange] oddly, quaintly. || **curieu|x, -se** [-ø(:z)] *adj.* **1.** inquisitive, [Péj.] prying; inquiring: *un esprit* ~, an inquiring mind. **2.** [étrange] curious, odd, peculiar: *chose curieuse*, curiously enough, → strange to say. || *n.m.* **1.** curious person; [badaud] sightseer, bystander: *un attroupement de* ~, a crowd of (interested) spectators. **2.** odd, curious/thing, event/: *le* ~ *de l'affaire*, the odd part of it. || **curiosité** [-ɔzi'te] *n.f.* curiosity: *avoir, manifester/de la* ~, to be curious, to show curiosity; *par* ~, out of curiosity. || *n.fpl.* oddities, rare things, curios: *visiter les* ~ *de Québec*, to visit the sights of Quebec.

cutané, -e [kyta'ne] *adj.* cutaneous.

cuve [ky:v] *n.f.* vat, tub; [Photo.] tank.

cuvée [ky've] *n.f.* vintage.

cuver [ky've] #3 *v. intr. & tr.* [wine] to ferment, to work: [Fam.] ~ *son vin*, to sleep it off.

cuvette [ky'vɛt] *n.f.* washbasin; shallow pan; ~ (*d'aisance*), toilet bowl.

cycle [sikl] *n.m.* cycle. || **cyclique** [-ik] *adj.* cyclic(al). || **cyclisme** [-ism] *n.m.* cycling. || **cycliste** [-ist] *n. m/f.* cyclist.

cyclone [si'klo:n] *n.m.* cyclone.

cygne [siɲ] *n.m.* swan: [Fig.] *le chant du* ~, the swan song.

cylindre [si'l|ɛ̃:dr] *n.m.* [Géom., Tech.] cylinder; voirie (steam)roller. || **cylindrique** [-ɛ̃'drik] *adj.* cylindrical.

cynique [si'nik] *adj.* cynical; [Péj.] cynical, impudent. || *n.m.* cynic.

cyprès [si'prɛ] *n.m.* cypress: ~ *jaune*, yellow cedar.

D

D, d [de] [letter] D, d. cf. A. || **d'** cf. DE.

d'accord [da'kɔ:r] *inv.* agreed; [Fam.] O.K. = *d'ac!*: *être* ~, to agree (on, *sur*); *être* ~ *avec qqun*, to agree with s.o. cf. ACCORD §2.

dactylo(graphe) [daktilɔ'graf] *n.m/f.* typist. || *n.m.* © typewriter. || **dactylographie** [-i] *n.f.* typing, typewriting. || **dactylographier** [-je] #3 *v. tr.* to type(write).

dada [da'da] [Fam.] *n.m.* hobby horse; *enfourcher son* ~, to ride one's hobby horse.

dague [da:g] *n.f.* **1.** dagger. **2.** [wild boar] tusks. cf. CROC.

dahlia [da'lja] *n.m.* dahlia.

daigner [dɛ'ɲe] #3 *v. tr.* to deign, to condescend.

daim [dɛ̃] *n.m.* deer; buckskin, suede; *chaussures de* ~, suede shoes. || **daine** [dɛn] *n.f.* doe, female deer.

dais [dɛ] *n.m.* canopy.

Dakota du Nord (le) [dakɔ'ta] *n.m.* North Dakota. || **Dakota du Sud** *n.m.* South Dakota.

dallage [da'la:ʒ] *n.m.* **1.** flagstones. **2.** paving with flagstones. || **dalle** [dal] *n.f.* flagstone. || **daller** [-e] #3 *v. tr.* to pave with flagstones.

Damas [da'mɑːs] *n.m.* Damascus.
dame [dam] *n.f.* **1.** lady. **2.** married woman. **3.** [*pl.*] women (in general): *vêtements de dames,* women's clothes. **4.** [cartes, échecs] queen; [jeu de dames] king: *jeu de dames,* checkers, [Br.] draughts.
damier [-je] *n.m.* checkerboard, [Br.] draught-board.
damnation [dɑn|a'sjõ] *n.f.* damnation. || **damné, -e** [-e] *adj.* damned: *C'est l'âme damnée de . . . ,* He is a mere tool in the hands of . . . || **damner** #3 *v. tr.* to damn. || **se damner** *v. pron.* to incur damnation.
dandiner, se [sədɑ̃di'ne] #3 *v. pron.* [en marchant] to waddle; [sans marcher] to shift from one foot to the other.
Danemark [dan'mark] *n.m.* Denmark.
danger [dɑ̃'ʒ|e] *n.m.* danger: *être à l'abri du ~,* to be safe; *être en ~ de mort,* to be in mortal danger; *courir un ~,* to run a risk; *mettre en ~,* to endanger; [Fam.] *pas de ~,* no fear, not likely. || **dangereusement** [-røz'mɑ̃] *adv.* dangerously. || **dangereu|x, -se** [-'rø(:z)] *adj.* dangerous.
Daniel [da'njɛl] *n.m.* = Daniel. || **Danielle** *n.f.* = Danielle.
danois, -e [da'nwa(:z)] *adj.* Danish. || **Danois, -e** *n.* Dane; [chien] *danois,* Great Dane.
dans [dɑ̃] *prép.* **1.** [lieu, sans mouvement] in; on, among, from, out of: *Il est ~ son bureau,* He is in his study; *~ la rue,* on the street; *~ la foule,* in the crowd; *boire ~ le creux de sa main,* to drink out of one's cupped hand; *passer ses vacances ~ les Laurentides,* to spend one's vacation in the Laurentians. **2.** [lieu où l'on va] in, into: *Mettez-le ~ le tiroir,* Put it in the drawer; *Il entra ~ la pièce,* He entered (into) the room. **3.** [limite, délai] within, in: *~ le courant de l'année,* in the course of the year; *~ un rayon de cinq milles,* within five miles of; *~ une semaine,* within a week; a week from now; *~ l'après-midi,* in the afternoon. **4.** [état, manière] in, under: *~ ces conditions,* under the circumstances; *être ~ l'embarras,* to be in a fix; *~ ce cas,* in this case; *~ le doute . . . ,* when in doubt. **5.** [approximation] about: *Cela vaut ~ les cent dollars,* It is worth about one hundred dollars.
dansant, -e [dɑ̃'sɑ̃(:t)] *adj.* dancing, dance: *soirée, matinée/dansante,* dance; *thé ~,* tea dance. || **danse** [dɑ̃:s] *n.f.* dance, dancing: *la prochaine ~,* the next dance; *Il aime la ~,* He likes dancing; *la ~ de Saint-Guy,* St. Vitus's dance. || **danser** [dɑ̃'s|e] #3 *v. intr.* to dance: [Fig.] *ne savoir sur quel pied ~,* not to know which way to turn. || *v. tr.* to dance (a waltz, &c.); [Fig.] *faire ~ qqun,* to dance with s.o. || **danseu|r, -se** [-œ:r, -ø:z] *n.* dancer.
dard [da:r] *n.m.* [arme] spear; [insecte] sting. || **darder** [dar'de] #3 *v. tr.* to dart: *Le soleil darde ses rayons,* The sun is beating down.
date [dat] *n.f.* date: *portant la ~ du 26 mai 1960,* dated May 26, 1960; *en ~ de,* dated; *amitié de vieille ~,* longstanding friendship; *prendre ~,* to make/a date, an appointment/; *fixer une ~,* to set a date. || **dater** [-e] #3 *v. tr.* to date. || *v. intr.* to date (from, *de*): *à ~ d'aujourd'hui,* from now on; [Fig.] *~ de loin,* to go far back.
datte [dat] *n.f.* date [the fruit]. || **dattier** [-je] *n.m.* date palm.
dauphin [do'fɛ̃] *n.m.* **1.** dolphin. **2.** Dauphin, French crown prince.
davantage [davɑ̃'ta:ʒ] *adv.* more; longer: *ne pas en dire ~,* to say no more; *Je ne peux pas rester ~,* I cannot stay any longer; *bien ~,* much more.
Davis (le détroit de) ['dejvis] *n.m.* Davis Strait.
de[1] [də] before vowels or "mute" *h,* **d'** [d]; ☞ before *le,* use **du** [dy]; before *les,* use **des** [de] *prép.* **A.** [Rapports sémantiques] ☞ In this section will be found equivalents of *de* grouped according to meaning. **1.** [contenu]: *un essaim d'abeilles,* a swarm of bees; *un paquet ~ cigarettes,* a package of cigarettes; *une tasse ~ thé,* a cup of tea [☞ but *une tasse à thé* = a tea cup]; *un verre ~ vin,* a glass of wine; *un livre d'histoires,* a story book; *exposition f d'horticulture,* flower show. **2.** [matière] in, [→ adjectives]: *un vase ~ cuivre,* a copper pot; *table ~ bois,* wooden table; *mur ~ pierre(s),* stone wall; *bas ~ soie,* silk stocking(s). **3.** [destination, direction] *Entrée ~ la gare,* → To the station; *la route ~ Québec,* the road to Q.; *le train ~ Toronto,* the train for T., the T. train [But see §4]; *couteau m ~ cuisine,* kitchen knife; *robe f ~ chambre,* bathrobe, dressing gown; *balle f ~ tennis,* tennis ball; *robe ~ soirée,* evening dress. **4.** [provenance] from, out of: *Il vient de Québec,* He comes from Q.; *D'où sortez-vous?,* Where do you come from?; *le train ~ Toronto,* the train from T. [But see §3]; *Il sortit $5 de sa poche,* He took (a) $5 (bill) out of his pocket. **5.** [même sens,

avec étoffement]: *De la part* ~ . . . , From . . . ; *du haut* ~ . . . , from (the hill, &c.); *à partir* ~ . . . , from; *au bout* ~ , at the end of, after; *dans un délai* ~ , within. 6. [quantité, grandeur, distance]: *une maison* ~ *trois étages*, a three-storied house; *haut* ~ *10 pieds*, ten feet high; *large* ~ *5 pieds*, 5 feet/wide, in width/; *un billet* ~ *dix dollars*, a ten-dollar bill; *une auto de deux mille dollars*, a $2,000 car; *à cinq milles* ~ *là*, five miles farther; *peu* ~ *temps après*, some time later, a few days, months/later. 7. [qualité]: *un homme d'esprit*, a witty man; *chef m d'orchestre*, conductor; *vinaigre m* ~ *vin*, wine vinegar; *bleu* ~ *Prusse*, Prussian blue; *un drôle* ~ *type*, a queer fellow. **8.** [moyen, agent]: *voyager de/jour, nuit/*, to travel by/day, night/; *vivre* ~ *légumes*, to live on vegetables; *couvert* ~ *neige*, covered with snow, → snow covered; *Je le brisai* ~ *mon couteau*, I broke it with my knife; *armé d'un bâton*, armed with a stick; *aimé* ~ *ses enfants*, loved by one's children; *d'un bond*, at a leap; *d'un seul coup*, at one blow; *un tableau* ~ *Turner*, a picture by T. **9.** [cause]: *pleurer* ~ *joie*, to weep for joy; *tomber* ~ *fatigue*, to be (utterly) exhausted; *mourir* ~ */soif, faim/*, to die of /thirst, hunger/. **B.** [Rapports grammaticaux: ☞ Many types of relations are expressed in Fr. by *de*, which thus corresponds to a variety of prepositions in Eng.; some of the following examples have been covered in the previous paragraphs under A, but are quoted again in a different perspective]: **1.** [marque de possession] of, 's [☞ 's s'emploie surtout avec des noms d'êtres animés et dans certaines locutions]: *la maison* ~ *mon père*, the house of my father, my father's house; *les œuvres* ~ *Shakespeare*, S.'s works; *le fil du rasoir*, the razor's edge; *à bout* ~ *ressources*, at one's wits' end; *un ami* ~ *mon père*, a friend of my father's. **2.** [complément du nom] of [or → compound forms]: *le sommet* ~ *la montagne*, the top of the mountain; *le livre* ~ *Job*, the Book of Job; *le régime des pluies*, the rainfall; *bateau m* ~ *guerre*, warship; *lampe f.* ~ *poche*, flashlight; *semaine f de quarante heures*, forty-hour week. **3.** [caractérisation[1]: ☞ use adjectives in Eng.]: *le journal d'hier*, yesterday's paper; *l'ambassadeur du Canada*, the Canadian ambassador; *un livre* ~ *français*, a French book; *asile m. d'aliénés*, mental hospital; *une église* ~ *campagne*, a rural church; *un Canadien* ~ *naissance*, a native Canadian; *à la fin d'octobre*, in late October; *un regard* ~ *compassion*, a compassionate look. **4.** [caractérisation[2]: ☞ other equivalents]: *d'une manière bourrue*, gruffly; *d'une façon inattendue*, unexpectedly; *un tronc d'arbre*, a tree trunk; *un bruit* ~ *pas*, footfall, cf. BRUIT; *un coup* ~ *feu*, a shot, cf. COUP. **5.** [grammaticalisation]: *un roman* ~ *Dickens*, a novel by D.; *la Turquie d'Europe*, Turkey in Europe; *la chambre du second*, the room on the second floor; *une faute* ~ *grammaire*, a mistake in grammar; *un guide* ~ *Québec*, a guide-book to Q. **6.** [explétif] *deux* ~ *plus*, two more; *et tous* ~ *rire*, everyone burst out laughing; [Fam.] *espèce d'imbécile*, silly ass.

de[2] [d(ə)], **du** [dy], **de l'** [dəl], **de la** [dəla]; *pl.* **des** [de] *art. partitif* [☞ in affirmative sentences; denotes "certain quantity of" as against totality] some, any: *Voulez-vous/du pain, de l'eau, de la crème, des légumes/?*, Would you like some/bread, water, cream, vegetables/?; *Avez-vous des amis ici?*, Do you have any friends here?

de[3] [də], **d'** [☞ to be used in negative sentences & after adv. of quantity]: *Je ne veux pas/de pain, d'eau, de crème, de légumes/*, I don't want any/bread, water, cream, vegetables/; *Je n'ai pas de pain*, I have no bread; *J'ai besoin/de pain, d'eau, de crème, de légumes/*, I need some/bread, water, cream, vegetables/; *Je n'ai pas d'amis ici*, I don't have any friends here, I have no friends here; *beaucoup* ~ *gens*, many people.

dé [de] *n.m.* thimble; [*pl.*] dice: *un coup de dés*, a gamble.

dé [a prefix indicating *the opposite of, the contrary of*: cf. Eng. *un-*, *dis-*; only the more important examples are given here. Note that the "opposite" often does not exist as a separate word, e.g. *dégourdir*, to stretch (one's legs), is not the "opposite" of *gourdir*, but of *gourd*, adj. stiff, numb.]

déambuler [deɑ̃by'le] #3 *v. intr.* to walk along.

débâcle [de'bɑ:kl] *n.f.* **1.** break-up (of ice on a river). **2.** downfall, disaster, collapse.

déballage [deba'l|a:ʒ] *n.m.* unpacking; display (of goods). ‖ **déballer** [-e] #3 *v. tr.* **1.** to unpack. **2.** [colporteur] to spread out one's merchandise.

débandade [debɑ̃'d|ad] *n.f.* scattering (of a crowd); routing (of an army); helter-skelter flight, stampede; *à la* ~ , in confusion. ‖ **débander** [-e] #3 *v. tr.* **1.** to take the bandage off (a cut). **2.** to unstring (a bow). || **se débander** *v. pron.* [Mil.] to break, to disperse in confusion.

débarbouiller [debarbu'j|e] #3 *v. tr.* to wash the face of (child). || **se débarbouiller** *v. pron.* to wash. || **débarbouillette** [-ɛt] © *n.f.* facecloth; washrag.

débarcadère [debarka'dɛːr] *n.m.* **1.** landing stage, pier. **2.** [Rail.] arrival platform.

débardeur [debar'dœːr] *n.m.* stevedore, longshoreman.

débarquement [debark|ə'mɑ̃] *n.m.* [marchandises] unloading; [passagers] landing, disembarkation. || **débarquer** [-e] #3 *v. intr.* to land (from a boat); © to get off (a bus or a train). || *v. tr.* to unload (freight).

débarras [deba'r|ɑ] *n.m.* **1.** [Fam.] riddance: *Bon* ~ , Good riddance. **2.** storeroom. **3.** © clearing. || **débarrasser** [-a'se] #3 *v. tr.* to relieve, to rid; to clear (a table, &c.). || **se débarrasser** *v. pron.* to get rid of, to shake off.

débat [de'ba] *n.m.* debate, dispute: *soulever, vider/un* ~ , to raise, settle a question; [Jur.] *suivre les débats*, to follow the hearings of a trial. || **débattre** [-tr] #43 *v. tr.* to debate, to discuss. || **se débattre** *v. pron.* to struggle.

débauche [de'boːʃ] *n.f.* **1.** debauch(ery). **2.** [Fig.] [excessive use of sth.] riot (of colours), orgy. || **débauché, -e** [debo'ʃe] *adj.* profligate, dissolute. || **débaucher** #3 *v. tr.* **1.** to seduce away from work, to incite to strike. **2.** to lay off workers. **3.** to debauch, to corrupt.

débile [de'bil] *adj.* weak, feeble. || **débilité** [-i'te] *n.f.* weakness, feebleness. || **débiliter** [-i'te] #3 *v. tr.* to weaken, to debilitate. *climat débilitant*, enervating climate.

débit [de'bi] *n.m.* **1.** sawing up, cutting up (of wood). **2.** flow, delivery, output: *le* ~ *d'un fleuve*, the rate of discharge of a river; *avoir un* ~ *facile*, to have a fluent delivery; *le* ~ *d'une mine*, the output of a mine. **3.** retailing (of an article): *article d'un bon* ~ , fast-moving article. **4.** retail store, esp. tobacconist's shop, wine shop. **5.** [Auto.] debit. || **débitant** [-'tɑ̃] *n.m.* **1.** retailer. **2.** [Fr.] liquor store keeper. || **débiter** [-'te] #3 *v. tr.* **1.** to cut up; to saw up (wood, stone): ~ *un bœuf*, to cut up a steer. **2.** to turn out, produce (a certain quantity in a certain time): *Cette usine débite quatre mille voitures par mois*, This plant produces four thousand cars a month. **3.** to retail: ~ *de la viande*, to retail meat. **4.** [Fig.] to recite, to recount: ~ *tout ce qu'on sait*, to spill all one knows; [Péj.] ~ *un discours*, to recite a (poor) speech. **5.** [Com.] to sell, to make out a (sales) check for. || **débiteur** [-'tœːr] *n.m.* debtor.

déblaiement [deblɛ|'mɑ̃] *n.m.* clearing-away; removal: ~ *de la neige*, snow removal. || **déblayer** [-'je] #11 *v. tr.* **1.** to clear (away), to remove: ~ *une cour*, to clear a yard; ~ *la neige*, to remove the snow. **2.** [Fig.] ~ *le terrain*, to clear the way.

déboire [de'bwaːr] *n.m.* disappointment.

déboisé, -e [debwa'z|e] *adj.* deforested. || **déboisement** [-'mɑ̃] *n.m.* deforestation. || **déboiser** [-e] #3 *v. tr. & intr.* to clear (of trees), to deforest.

déboîter [debwɑ'te] #3 *v. tr.* to pull out of joint, to dislocate.

débonnaire [debɔ'nɛːr] *adj.* good-natured, meek.

débordant, -e [debɔr'd|ɑ̃(ːt)] *adj.* overflowing: ~ *de santé*, overflowing with health; *avoir une joie* ~ , to be bubbling over with joy. || **débordé, -e** [-e] *adj.* swamped (with work); [Mil.] outflanked. || **déborder** [-e] #3 *v. intr.* to overflow, to overrun: *rivière qui déborde*, flooding river; *salle pleine à* ~ , room full to overflowing; ~ *de vie*, to be full of vitality. || *v. tr.* **1.** to jut out; to outflank (an army); to extend beyond, to be out of line; *pierre qui déborde le mur*, stone sticking out from the wall. **2.** [Naut.] to shove off.

débouché, -e [debu'ʃe] *n.m.* outlet, opening. || **déboucher** #3 *v. tr.* to clean out (a pipe, &c.); to clear (a passageway), to uncork (a bottle). || *v. intr.* to emerge/into, on to; to come out/into, on to: *Le camion a débouché sur la route*, The truck entered the highway.

déboulonner [debulɔ'ne] #3 *v. tr.* to unbolt, [Fig.] to tear apart.

débourrer [debu're] #3 *v. tr.* to unplug; to unstop; to knock out (a pipe).

débours [de'buːr] *n.m.* disbursements. || **débourser** [debur'se] #3 *v. tr.* to disburse, to pay.

debout [də'bu] *adv.* **1.** standing: *être* ~ , to stand; *se mettre* ~ , to stand up; *mettre* ~ , to set upright. **2.** up, out of bed: *Debout!*, Get up!; *Il dormait* ~ , He was asleep on his feet. **3.** [Loc.] *Cela ne tient pas* ~ , It does not make sense; *une histoire à dormir* ~ , a long-winded, tiresome story.

déboutonné, -e [debutɔ'ne] *adj.* unbuttoned. || **déboutonner** #3 *v. tr.* to unbutton. || **se déboutonner** *v. pron.* to come unbuttoned; to unbutton one's clothes.

débraillé, -e [debrɑ'je] *adj.* dishevelled,

sloppily dressed, slovenly; [Fig.] loose, slovenly, unbuttoned.
débrayage [debrɛ'j|a:ʒ] *n.m.* throwing out of gear: *pédale f. de* ~, clutch; work stoppage. || **débrayé, -e** [-e] *adj.* out of gear. || **débrayer** [-e] #11 *v. tr.* **1.** to throw out of gear, to put into neutral. **2.** to stop work.
débrider [debri'de] #3 *v. tr.* **1.** to unbridle: [Fig.] *sans* ~, without a break. **2.** [Méd.] to incise a wound.
débris [de'bri] *n.mpl.* fragments, remains; [Géol.] debris: ~ *d'un repas*, the remains of a meal; ~ *d'un naufrage*, wreckage.
débrouillard, -e [debru'j|a:r, -ard] *adj.* resourceful: *Il est très* ~, He gets around. || **débrouiller** [-e] #3 *v. tr.* **1.** to unravel, to disentangle: ~ *les comptes de qqun*, to straighten out s.o.'s accounts. **2.** [Fig. & Fam.] to teach s.o. the ropes. || **se débrouiller** *v. pron.* to manage, to get along; to shift for o.s.: *Il sait* ~, He knows how to take care of himself.
début [de'by] *n.m.* **1.** beginning. **2.** debut, first appearance: *une œuvre de* ~, a first work. **3.** first move, lead (at game). || **débutant, -e** [-'tɑ̃(:t)] *n.* beginner, tyro, novice. || **débuter** [-'te] #3 *v. intr.* **1.** to begin, to start out: *Il a débuté à vingt-cinq dollars par semaine*, He began at twenty-five dollars a week. **2.** to move first, to lead.
deçà [də'sa] *adv.* here, on this side: ~ *et delà*, ~ *delà*, here and there; *La maison est en* ~ *de la route*, The house is (on) this side of the road; *L'obus tomba en deçà*, The shell fell short.
décacheter [dekaʃ'te] #8 *v. tr.* to unseal, to (break) open.
décadence [deka'd|ɑ̃:s] *n.f.* decay, decline, decadence. || **décadent, -e** [-ɑ̃(:t)] *adj.* declining, decadent.
décalage [deka|'la:ʒ] *n.m.* staggering, shifting; lag shift. || **décaler** [-'le] #3 *v. tr.* to set/back, forward/, to stagger.
décalitre [deka'litr] *n.m.* decalitre [about 10 quarts].
décalquer [dekal'ke] #3 *v. tr.* to trace.
décamper [dekɑ̃'pe] #3 *v. intr.* to decamp, to clear out, to take off.
décanter [dekɑ̃'te] #3 *v. tr.* to decant (a liquid): *faire, laisser/* ~ *un liquide*, to allow a liquid to settle.
décaper [deka'pe] #3 *v. tr.* to scrape, to scour.
décapiter [dekapi'te] #3 *v. tr.* to decapitate, to behead.
décapotable [dekapɔ'tabl] *adj.* convertible: *cabriolet* ~, convertible.
décédé, -e [dese'de] *adj.* deceased. || **décéder** #10 *v. intr.* to die.
déceler [des'le] #9 *v. tr.* **1.** to detect, to sense. **2.** to disclose; to reveal.
décembre [de'sɑ̃:br] *n.m.* December.
décemment [des|a'mɑ̃] *adv.* decently, properly, in a becoming manner. || **décence** [-ɑ̃:s] *n.f.* decency, modesty. || **décent, -e** [-ɑ̃(:t)] *adj.* decent, modest, proper.
décentraliser [desɑ̃trali'ze] #3 *v. tr. & intr.* to decentralize.
déception [desɛp'sjõ] *n.f.* disappointment. [×] cf. DECEPTION.
décerner [desɛr'ne] #3 *v. tr.* to award.
décès [de'sɛ] *n.m.* decease, cf. DÉCÉDER.
décevant, -e [des'v|ɑ̃(:t)] *adj.* deceptive, misleading; disappointing. || **décevoir** [-wa:r], **décevant**, [-ɑ̃], **déçu** [de'sy] #34 conj. AVOIR [action], ÊTRE [état] to deceive; to disappoint.
déchaîné, -e [deʃɛn|e] *adj.* running wild, gone mad, broken loose: *Il est* ~, Nothing will stop him. || **déchaînement** [-mɑ̃] *n.m.* outburst, unleashing. || **déchaîner** [-e] #3 *v. tr.* †**1.** to unchain, to turn loose: ~ *les chiens*, to unleash the dogs. **2.** [Fig.] to let loose: *Son inconduite déchaîna ma colère*, His bad conduct roused my anger. || **se déchaîner** *v. pron.* to run riot, to break loose; [a storm] to break: ~ *contre qqch.*, to rage against sth.
déchanter [deʃɑ̃'te] #3 *v. intr.* to sing small, to come down a peg or two.
décharge [de'ʃarʒ] *n.f.* **1.** [arme] firing; [Electr.] discharge; [accumulateur] discharging; [barrage] overflow; [paiement] receipt. **2.** dumping ground, storeroom. **3.** [Jur.] *témoin à* ~, witness for the defence. || **décharger** [-e] #5 *v. tr.* **1.** to unload: ~ *un navire, des marchandises*, to unload a ship, freight; ~ *un fusil*, to fire a rifle, to unload a rifle (without firing). **2.** discharge: ~ *des accumulateurs*, to discharge a battery. **3.** to relieve: ~ *qqun de sa valise*, to relieve s.o. of his suitcase; ~ *sa conscience*, to relieve one's conscience; ~ *sa colère*, to vent one's anger. || *v. intr.* to unload. || **se décharger** *v. pron.* to discharge, to go off; to free o.s.: *Il s'en décharge sur moi*, He relies on me for that.
décharné, -e [deʃar'ne] *adj.* very thin, gaunt, skinny.
déchaussé, -e [deʃo'se] *adj.* with one's shoes off, barefoot. || **déchausser** [deʃo'se] #3 *v. tr.* **1.** to take off [person's] shoes. **2.** to bare (the roots of a tree): ~ *les dents*, to cause gums to recede. || **se déchausser** *v. pron.* **1.** to take off one's shoes. **2.** [dents]

to be loosened (from recession of the gums).

déchéance [deʃe'ɑ̃:s] *n.f.* downfall, loss of crown or rights, losing caste.

déchet [de'ʃɛ] *n.m.* refuse, waste.

déchiffrer [deʃi'fre] #3 *v. tr.* **1.** to decipher, to make out; to read music by sight. **2.** [Fig.] to figure out, to understand: ~ *une énigme*, to figure out a riddle.

déchiqueté, -e [deʃik'te] *adj.* jagged (mountain, rock); indented (coast), tattered (flag). || **déchiqueter** #8 *v. tr.* to cut up into shreds, pieces, bits; to slash, to hack.

déchirant, -e [deʃi'r|ɑ(:t)] *adj.* piercing (cry); heart-breaking (farewell, &c.). || **déchiré, -e** [-e] *adj.* torn (clothing, flesh, &c.). || **déchirement** [-'mɑ̃] *n.m.* **1.** tearing, ripping; rending. **2.** [Fig.] heartbreak. **3.** [Pol.] strife. || **déchirer** [-e] #3 *v. tr.* **1.** to tear, to rip: ~ *une étoffe*, to tear, rip/a cloth; ~ *une feuille de papier en deux*, to tear a piece of paper in two; *Elle a déchiré sa robe*, She tore her dress; *déchirer une lettre*, to tear up a letter. **2.** [Fig.] to rend (a country into two parts); to pierce (the ear); to break (the heart). || **déchirure** [-y:r] *n.f.* tear, rent.

déchoir [de'ʃ|wa:r] #64 *v. intr.* to lose caste, to come down in the world. || **déchu, -e** [-y] *p.p. of* DÉCHOIR. || *adj.* fallen, deprived of one's status or rights.

décidé, -e [desi'd|e] *adj.* determined, resolved; decided. || **décidément** [-e'mɑ̃] *adv.* decidedly. || **décider** [-e] #3 *v. tr.* to decide (sth.), to persuade (s.o.): *On a fini par le* ~, He was finally persuaded. || *v. intr.* to decide (to, *de*): ~ *en dernier ressort*, to make the final decision. || **se décider** *v. pron.* to decide, to arrive at a decision: *Il s'est décidé à partir*, He (finally) decided to go; ~ *pour qqch.*, to decide in favour of sth.

décigramme [desi'gram] *n.m.* decigram. || **décilitre** [desi'litr] *n.m.* decilitre. || **décimal, -e** [desi'm|al] *adj.* decimal: *fraction décimale*, decimal fraction.

décimer [-e] #3 *v. tr.* to decimate.

décimètre [desi'mɛ:tr] *n.m.* decimetre.

décisi|f, -ve [desi'z|if, -i:v] *adj.* decisive (tone); positive (man); crucial (moment); conclusive (argument). || **décision** [-jõ] *n.f.* decision; resolution; [Jur.] ruling: *prendre une* ~ , to make, to come to/a decision; *revenir sur une* ~ , to change one's mind; *montrer de la* ~ , to show determination.

déclamation [deklam|a'sjõ] *n.f.* elocution, oratory: *discours plein de* ~ , bombastic, flowery/speech. || **déclamatoire** [-a'twa:r] *adj.* declamatory, high-flown. || **déclamer** [-e] #3 *v. tr.* **1.** to declaim, recite. **2.** [Péj.] to spout, rant.

déclaration [deklar|a'sjõ] *n.f.* declaration; [Jur.] affidavit: ~ *en douane*, customs declaration; ~ *de revenu*, income-tax return. || **déclaré, -e** [-e] *adj.* declared open. || **déclarer** [-e] #3 *v. tr.* to declare; to proclaim: *Avez-vous qqch. à* ~ ?, Do you have anything to declare?; ~ *ses intentions*, to make one's intentions known; ~ *la guerre* (à un pays), to declare war (on a country). || **se déclarer** *v. pron.* **1.** to break out: *L'incendie se déclara au troisième étage*, The fire broke out on the third floor. **2.** to come out for, to declare o.s.: ~ *pour, contre/un candidat*, to come out/for, against/a candidate.

déclassé, -e [dekla'se] *adj.* **1.** who has lost class. **2.** obsolete, struck off the records. || *n.* social outcast. || **déclasser** #3 *v. tr.* **1.** to do away with a classification. **2.** to move to a lower class or category: ~ *une forteresse*, to declare a fortress obsolete.

déclencher [deklɑ̃'ʃe] *v. tr.* #3. **1.** to release, to unlatch, to unleash. **2.** to set in motion, to start, to trigger.

déclic [de'klik] *n.m.* [bruit] click; [mécanisme] trigger.

déclin [de'kl|ɛ̃] *n.m.* decline: *être à son* ~ , to be declining, to be on the wane.

déclinaison [-inɛ'zõ] *n.f.* **1.** [Astr.] declination. **2.** [Gram.] declension.

déclinant, -e [dekli'n|ɑ̃(:t)] *adj.* declining: *puissance déclinante*, declining power. || **décliner** [-e] #3 *v. intr.* **1.** to decline, to go down; [moon] to wane: *Le jour décline*, The day is drawing to a close; *Ses forces déclinent avec l'âge*, His strength is declining with age. **2.** [boussole] to deviate (from the geographic North). || *v. tr.* **1.** to refuse, to decline (an offer, honour, responsibility). **2.** [Gram.] to decline (a noun, &c.). 3. [Fig.] ~ *son identité*, to state one's name.

décocher [dekɔ'ʃe] #3 *v. tr.* to shoot (an arrow).

décoiffer [dekwa'fe] #3 *v. tr.* **1.** to put s.o.'s hair out of order. **2.** to take off hat or cap. || **se décoiffer** *v. pron.* **1.** to undo one's hair. **2.** to take off one's hat.

déçois, &c., déçoive, &c. cf. DÉCEVOIR.

décollage [dekɔ'l|a:ʒ] *n.m.* [d'une chose collée] unsticking, ungluing; [avion] take-off. || **décoller** [-e] #3 *v. tr.* to unstick; to loosen, to remove. || *v. intr.* [Aéro.] to take off. || **se décoller** *v. pron.* to come unstuck.

décolleté, -e [dekɔl'te] *adj.* low-necked.

|| **se décolleter** [sə dekɔl'te] #8 *v. pron.* to wear a low-necked dress.
décolorant, -e [dekɔlɔ'r|ɑ̃(:t)] *adj.* bleaching (properties, agent). || *n.m.* bleach. || **décoloration** [-a'sjõ] *n.f.* discolouration, fading. || **décoloré, -e** [-e] *adj.* discoloured, bleached; faded, colourless. || **décolorer** [-e] #3 *v. tr.* to discolour, to bleach. || **se décolorer** *v. pron.* to fade, to lose colour.
décombres [de'kõ:br] *n.mpl.* rubble, debris.
décommander [dekɔmɑ̃'de] #3 *v. tr.* to cancel, countermand.
décomposé, -e [dekõpo'z|e] *adj.* **1.** decomposed. **2.** [visage] discomposed, distorted (by grief or fear). || **décomposer** [-e] #3 *v. tr.* **1.** to decompose, to separate (into its elements); [Fig.] ~ *une phrase,* to break down a sentence. cf. ANALYSER: ~ *un pas de danse,* to break down a dance step (into its parts). **2.** to decay, to rot: *La chaleur décompose les matières animales,* Heat/decays, rots/animal matter. **3.** to discompose, to distort: *La souffrance a décomposé les traits de son visage,* Suffering distorted his features. || **se décomposer** *v. pron.* **1.** to be decomposed, to be broken down (into, *en*). **2.** to decay. || **décomposition** [-i'sjõ] *n.f.* **1.** decomposition, breaking down (into the component parts). **2.** decomposition, decaying, rotting.
décompte [de'k|õ:t] *n.m.* **1.** deduction: *venir en* ~, to be subtracted. **2.** detail (of account), breakdown. || **décompter** [-õ'te] #3 *v. tr.* to subtract (from a sum).
déconcertant, -e [dekõsɛr't|ɑ̃(:t)] *adj.* disconcerting, upsetting. || **déconcerter** [-e] #3 *v. tr.* to disconcert, to baffle: *nullement déconcerté,* unabashed.
déconfit, -e [dekõ'f|i(t)] *adj.* discomfited, crestfallen. || **déconfiture** [-i'ty:r] *n.f.* discomfiture.
déconseiller [dekõsɛ'je] #3 *v. tr.* to advise against: *Je le lui ai déconseillé,* I advised him against it.
déconsidérer [dekõside're] #10 *v. tr.* to bring into disrepute. || **se déconsidérer** *v. pron.* to appear in a bad light.
décontenancé, -e [dekõtnɑ̃'se] *adj.* confused, taken aback, nonplussed. || **décontenancer** #4 *v. tr.* [Fam.] to rattle, to put out of countenance.
déconvenue [dekõv'ny] *n.f.* disappointment.
décor [de'kɔ:r] *n.m.* **1.** setting, scene, scenery: *changement de* ~, change of scene. **2.** show. || **décorat|eur, -rice** [dekɔra|'tœ:r, -'tris] *n.* (interior) decorator. || **décorati|f, -ve** [-'tif, -'ti:v] *adj.* decorative, ornamental: *Il est très* ~, He is very handsome. || **décoration** [-'sjõ] *n.f.* **1.** decoration: *effectuer la* ~ *d'un appartement,* to decorate an apartment. **2.** medal, decoration: *recevoir une* ~, to receive a decoration. || **décorer** [dekɔ're] #3 *v. tr.* **1.** to decorate, ornament. **2.** to confer an honour on (s.o.): *On l'a décoré de la Légion d'Honneur,* He was awarded the Legion of Honour.
décortiquer [dekɔrti'ke] #3 *v. tr.* to husk, to shell.
décorum [dekɔ'rɔm] *n.m.* decorum, propriety.
découcher [deku'ʃe] #3 *v. intr.* to sleep out.
découler [deku'le] #3 *v. intr.* to stem, to result (from, *de*).
découpe-biscuits [dekup|bis'kɥi] © *n.m.* cookie-cutter. || **découper** [-e] #3 *v. tr.* **1.** to cut out, to cut up: ~ *des images,* to cut out pictures; ~ *un article,* to clip an article. **2.** to carve (meat). || **se découper** *v. pron.* to stand out (against, *sur*).
découplé, -e [deku'ple] *adj.*: *bien* ~, well set up, strapping. || **découpler** #3 *v. tr.* to uncouple, unleash.
décourageant, -e [dekura'ʒ|ɑ̃(:t)] *adj.* discouraging. || **découragé, -e** [-e] *adj.* discouraged. || **découragement** [-'mɑ̃] *n.m.* discouragement: *se laisser aller au* ~, to lose heart. || **décourager** [-e] #5 *v. tr.* conj. AVOIR [action], ÊTRE [état] to discourage: ~ *qqun de faire qqch.,* to discourage s.o. from doing sth. || **se décourager** *v. pron.* to become discouraged, to lose heart.
décousu, -e [deku'zy] *adj.* **1.** unsewn. **2.** [Fig.] disconnected.
découvert, -e [deku'v|ɛ:r, -ɛrt] *adj.* uncovered, open (ground); overdrawn (account). || *n.m.* overdraught; open ground. || **découverte** [-ɛrt] *n.f.* discovery, detection: *aller à la* ~, to explore.
découvrir [deku'vr|i:r], **découvrant** [-ɑ̃], **découvert** [-ɛ:r] #25 *v. tr.* **1.** to uncover: ~ *un plat,* to uncover a dish. **2.** to lay bare, to expose: ~ *son cœur,* to open one's heart to s.o.; [Mil.] ~ *un flanc à l'ennemi,* to expose a flank to the enemy. **3.** to discover, to find (out); to detect: ~ *du pétrole,* to strike oil; ~ *un vaccin,* to discover a vaccine; ~ *une faute,* to detect an error. **4.** [Fig.] to reveal, to tell: ~ *un secret,* to reveal a secret. || **se découvrir** *v. pron.* **1.** to take off one's hat. **2.** [temps] to clear up. **3.** to expose o.s. (to blows, &c.); to leave o.s. open. **4.** to be found out; to become visible: *La mer se découvrait peu à peu,* Little by little the sea became visible.

décrasser [dekra'se] #3 *v. tr.* to clean, to scrub, to scour.

décrépit, -e [dekre'pi|(t)] *adj.* decrepit, dilapidated. || **décrépitude** [-'tyd] *n.f.* decrepitude, decay.

décret [de'kr|ɛ] *n.m.* decree, order: ~ *-loi*, order-in-council. || **décréter** [-e'te] #10 *v. tr.* to decree; [Jur.] to issue (a writ against).

décrier [dekri'je] #3 *v. tr.* to decry, to disparage, to discredit.

décrire [de'kr|i:r], **décrivant** [-i'vɑ̃], **décrit** [-it] #48 *v. tr.* **1.** to describe, to depict. **2.** to form, describe (a curve, a circle).

décrocher [dekrɔ'ʃe] #3 *v. tr.* **1.** to unhook, take down, get down (a coat from a hook, &c.); to lift (a telephone receiver); to unsling (a hammock); to uncouple, disconnect (a locomotive, coach); to dislocate (one's jaw); to undo (a clasp): [Fig.] *bâiller à se ~ la mâchoire*, → to yawn one's head off. **2.** [Fig.] to manage to get: ~ *la timbale*, to carry off the prize; ~ *le grand succès*, to make a big hit; © [profits] ~ *les quatre chiffres*, to touch four figures. **3.** [Fig.] to get one's watch out of pawn. || *v. intr.* [Mil.] to lose touch. || **se décrocher** *v. pron.* to be, become/unhooked, unfastened.

décroître [de'krwa:tr], **décroissant, décru** #40 *v. intr.* to decrease, to diminish, to drop.

décrotter [dekrɔ't|e] #3 *v. tr.* to scrape clean. || **décrotteur** [-œ:r] *n.m.* shoeshine (boy). || **décrottoir** [-wa:r] *n.m.* scraper.

décrue [de'kry] *n.f.* [étiage, &c.] decrease, drop, cf. DÉCROÎTRE.

déçu, -e [de'sy] *adj* disappointed, cf. DÉCEVOIR.

dédaigner [dedɛ'ɲ|e] #3 *v. tr.* to disdain, to look down on: *Ce n'est pas à ~*, It's not to be sneezed at. || **dédaigneu|x, -se** [-ø(:z)] *adj.* disdainful, stand-offish. || **dédain** [de'dɛ̃] *n.m.* disdain, scorn: *traiter qqun avec ~*, to treat s.o. with disdain.

dedans [də'dɑ̃] *adv.* inside, within; *au ~*, inside; *au, en ~*, inside, within; *fourrer ~*, to mislead, to deceive; *se mettre ~*, to blunder, [Fam.] to goof. || *n.m.* the inside.

dédicace [dedi'kas] *n.f.* autograph. || **dédicacer** [-e] #4 *v. tr.* to autograph.

dédier [de'dje] #3 *v. tr.* **1.** to inscribe. **2.** to dedicate (*à*, to).

dédire, se [sə de'di:r] #46 *v. pron.* to go back (on statement): *Je ne m'en dédis pas*, I don't take it back. || **dédit** [de'di] *n.m.* **1.** forfeit. **2.** retractation.

dédommagement [dedɔmaʒ|'mɑ̃] *n.m.* compensation, indemnity. || **dédommager** [-e], **dédommageant** [-ɑ̃] #5 *v. tr.* **1.** to indemnify (for, *de*). **2.** [Fig.] to compensate: *La réussite l'a dédommagé de ses efforts*, The result was worth the effort.

dédouaner [dedwa'ne] #3 *v. tr.* to clear through the customs.

dédoublement [dedubl|ə'mɑ̃] *n.m.* division into two; duplication, splitting (in two). || **dédoubler** [-e] #3 *v. tr.* to divide in(to) two: [Scol.] ~ *une classe*, to split a class.

déduction [dedyk'sjõ] *n.f.* deduction; [raisonnement] inference. || **déduire** [de'dɥ|i:r], **déduisant** [-i'zɑ̃], **déduit** [-i] #56 *v. tr.* **1.** to deduct: ~ *ses frais*, to deduct one's expenses (from, *de*). **2.** to deduce, infer.

défaillance [defa'j|ɑ̃:s] *n.f.* **1.** swoon, fainting spell. **2.** [Fig.] momentary moral weakness: *Chacun a ses moments de ~*, Everyone has/his, her/moments of weakness. **3.** [Fig.] failing, failure; lapse: ~ *de mémoire*, a lapse of memory. || **défaillant, -e** [-ɑ̃(:t)] *adj.* failing, faltering: *mémoire défaillante*, failing memory. || **défaillir** [-i:r], **défaillant** [-ɑ̃], **défailli** [-i] #59 *v. intr.* [☞ *Not* used in the sing. of the present, the simple future, conditional present, the subj. and the imperat.] to faint; to grow weak (when speaking of moral or physical strength): *Ses forces commencent à ~*, His strength is beginning to fail; *sans ~*, without flinching; *prêt à ~*, feeling faint.

défaire [de'f|ɛ:r] #37 *v. tr.* **1.** to undo, to unfasten. **2.** to defeat. || **se défaire** *v. pron.* **1.** to come undone. **2.** to get rid (of, *de*). || **défait, -e** [-ɛ(t)] *adj.* worn, drawn (face); unmade (bed); disarranged (hair); undone, loose (screw, button): *Le lit n'avait pas été ~*, The bed had not been slept in. || **défaite** [-ɛt] *n.f.* defeat: *essuyer une ~*, to suffer a defeat; [Fig.] excuse, shift.

défaut [de'fo] *n.m.* **1.** lack, absence: *à ~ de*, for want of, in place of; *faire ~*, to be lacking; *Sa mémoire lui fait souvent ~*, His memory often fails him; *Le temps lui a fait ~*, He lacked the time. **2.** (physical) defect, blemish; (moral) fault; weakness: *sans ~*, faultless, without a blemish; *C'est là son moindre ~*, That is the least of/his, her/faults. **3.** [Jur.] default: *faire ~*, to default. **4.** [Fig.] *mettre en ~*, to baffle: *le ~ de la cuirasse*, the chink in one's armour; *prendre qqun en ~*, to catch s.o./in the wrong, napping/.

défavorable [defavɔ'rabl] *adj.* unfavourable.

défecti|f, -ve [defɛk't|if, -i:v] *adj.* [Used

mostly as an adj. of the word *verbe*]: *verbe* ~, defective verb.

défection [defɛk'sjõ] *n.f.* defection, desertion.

défectueu|x, -se [defɛk'tɥ|ø(:z)] *adj.* faulty, defective. || **défectuosité** [-ozi'te] *n.f.* defect, flaw. cf. DÉFAUT.

défend, défendais, &c. cf. DÉFENDRE. || **défendable** [defɑ̃'d|abl] *adj.* [Mil.] defensible; [Fig., argument] tenable. || **défend|eur, -eresse** [-œ:r, -rɛs] *n.* [Jur.] defendant. || **défendre** [de'fɑ̃:dr] *p.p.* **défendu,** #42 *v. tr.* **1.** to defend, to defend one's country; *Les habits nous défendent du froid,* Clothes protect us from the cold. **2.** to forbid, to prohibit: *Je vous le défends bien,* I forbid you to do it; ~ *formellement,* to forbid strictly. || **se défendre** *v. pron.* **1.** to defend o.s.; to protect o.s.: *savoir* ~, to know how to take care of o.s. **2.** to forbid o.s.; [usual. neg.]: *Il ne put* ~ *d'y penser,* He could not help thinking about it. **3.** to deny: *Il s'est défendu de l'avoir fait,* He denied doing it; ~ *(d'une prétention),* to disclaim. || **défendu, -e** [defɑ̃'dy] *adj.* **1.** forbidden: *C'est défendu,* That's not allowed, It's forbidden; *Il est (strictement)* → *formellement* ~ *de . . . , . . .* is (positively) forbidden. [☞ On public notices, use *Défense de . . .*] **2.** defended, protected: *L'endroit est bien* ~, The place is well protected.

défense [de'f|ɑ̃:s] *n.f.* **1.** defence, protection: *prendre la* ~ *de qqun,* to come to s.o.'s defence; [Jur.] *une* ~ *brillante,* a brilliant defence; ~ *légitime,* self-defence; ~ *passive,* civil defence. **2.** fortifications, defences. **3.** prohibition: *Défense de stationner,* No parking; *Défense d'afficher,* Post no bills; *Défense (absolue) d'entrer,* (Positively) no admittance: *faire* ~ *à qqun de,* to forbid s.o. to. **4.** [Jur.] counsel (for the defence). **5.** tusk (of certain animals): *les défenses d'un éléphant,* the tusks of an elephant. || **défenseur** [-ɑ̃'sœ:r] *n.m.* **1.** defender: ~ *du peuple,* defender of the people. **2.** [Jur.] counsel for the defence. || **défensi|f, -ve** [-ɑ̃'s|if, -i:v] *adj.* defensive: *armée* ~, defensive army. || **défensive** [-i:v] *n.f.*: *être, se tenir/sur la* ~, to be on the defensive.

déférence [defe'rɑ̃:s] *n.f.* deference, respect (*envers, à l'égard de,* towards).

déferler [defɛr'le] #3 *v. intr.* [vagues] to break (upon, *sur*); to unfurl.

défi [de'fi] *n.m.* **1.** challenge: *jeter un* ~ *à qqun,* to challenge s.o.; *mettre qqun au* ~ *de faire qqch.,* to dare, defy/s.o. to do sth.; *relever un* ~, to take up a challenge. **2.** defiance: *en* ~ *de qqch.* in defiance of sth.; ~ *à l'autorité,* defiance of authority.

défiance [de'fj|ɑ:s] *n.f.* **1.** distrust, suspicion: *sans* ~, trusting, unsuspecting. || **défiant, -e** [-ɑ̃(:t)] *adj.* distrustful, wary, cautious. || **défier** [-e] #3 *v. tr.* to challenge, to dare: *Je vous défie de le faire,* I dare you to do it, I bet you can't do it. **2.** to defy. || **se défier (de)** *v. pron.* to be diffident (about); not to trust.

défigurer [defigy're] #3 *v. tr.* **1.** to disfigure, to spoil, to ruin. **2.** [Fig.] to distort (facts).

défilé [defi'le] *n.m.* **1.** defile, gorge, mountain pass. **2.** march past, parade: ~ *de troupes,* procession, parade of troops; ~ *de modes,* fashion show. || **défiler** #3 *v. tr.* **1.** to unstring, to unthread (a needle). **2.** [Mil.] to put (troops, guns, &c.) under cover. || *v. intr.* **1.** to walk in a line: ~ *en file indienne,* to walk in Indian file. **2.** [Mil.] to march past, to parade; [ext.] to file by, past; [Fig.] *Le paysage défile aux fenêtres du train,* The countryside flies by the train windows. || **se défiler** *v. pron.* **1.** to get under cover. **2.** [Fam.] to slink off, not to make a stand.

défini, -e [defi'n|i] *adj.* defined, definite, fixed: *passé* ~, past historic, past perfect, preterite; *article* ~, definite article; *mot mal* ~, poorly defined word. || **définir** [-i:r] #17 *v. tr.* to define (sth.); to describe (s.o.). || **définissable** [-i'sabl] *adj.* definable. || **définiti|f, -ve** [-i|'tif, -'ti:v] *adj.* definitive, final, standard (edition, &c.): *résultats définitifs (d'un examen),* final results (of an exam); *à titre* ~, permanently; *en définitive loc. adv.* in short; finally, after all. || **définition** [-'sjõ] *n.f.* definition. || **définitivement** [-tiv'mɑ̃] *adv.* positively; finally.

défoncé, -e [defõ'se] *adj.* **1.** broken, bashed in: *Il avait le crâne* ~, His skull was bashed in. **2.** torn up: *La route était défoncée,* The road was torn up. || **défoncer** #4 *v. tr.* to knock the bottom out of (a box), to stave in (a barrel), to break, tear/up (a road).

déformer [defɔr'me] #3 *v. tr.* **1.** to deform, to put out of shape. **2.** [Fig.] to distort (the truth, facts, thoughts). || **se déformer** *v. pron.* to get out of shape; [bois] to warp.

défraîchi [defrɛ'ʃi] *adj.* faded; [Com.] shopworn.

défraie, défraierai, &c. cf. DÉFRAYER. || **défrayer** [defrɛ'je] #11 *v. tr.* **1.** to defray (s.o.'s expenses): *défrayé de tout,* with all expenses paid. **2.** [Fig.] to carry (a conversation); to be the subject of (the conversation).

défricher [defri'ʃe] #3 ***v. tr.*** to clear, reclaim (land). cf. FRICHE.

défunt, -e [de'fœ̃(:t)] *adj.* deceased. ‖ *n.* the deceased, the late (Mr. X.).

dégagé, -e [dega'ʒ|e] *adj.* easy, free; redeemed. ‖ **dégagement** [-'mɑ̃] *n.m.* [chaleur] release; release (from a promise); clearing (from obstacle); widening (of street or approach to building). ‖ **dégager** [-e] ††5 *v. tr.* **1.** to redeem (from a pawnshop, &c.); to clear (of a mortgage). **2.** to clear (place), to free (one's hand, &c. from sth.); [Fig. & Fam.] *Allons, dégagez!*, Get a move on! 3. [Fig.] to release, free (s.o. from a promise, obligation): *Je l'ai dégagé de sa parole*, I released him from his promise. **4.** [Fig.] to bring out: ~ *l'idée essentielle*, to bring out the important idea. **5.** [Fig.] to give off (an odour, vapour): *Cette fleur dégage un parfum délicieux*, This flower gives off a delightful perfume. ‖ **se dégager** *v. pron.* to free o.s., to break loose: ~ *d'une promesse*, to get out of, to take back/a promise; *Enfin, la vérité se dégage*, At last the truth is coming out.

dégarni, -e [degar'n|i] *adj.* [salle] empty; [lit] stripped: *avoir le front* ~, to have a receding hairline. ‖ **dégarnir** [-i:r] #17 *v. tr.* to dismantle, to unfurnish (a room), to strip (a bed). ‖ **se dégarnir** *v. pron.* [salle] to empty; to lose one's hair; [arbre] to lose its leaves.

dégât(s) [de'ga] *n.m.(pl.)* damage; *dégâts matériels*, property damage.

dégel [de'ʒ|ɛl] *n.m.* thaw. ‖ **dégeler** [-'le] #9 *v. tr.* to thaw (out): ~ *une conduite d'eau*, to thaw out a water pipe. ‖ **dégeler** [-'le] #8 *v. intr.* to thaw: *Le lac dégèle*, The lake is thawing out. ‖ *v. impers. Il dégèle*, It's thawing.

dégénérer [deʒene're] #10 *v. intr.* conj. AVOIR [action], ÊTRE [état] to degenerate, to deteriorate: *dispute qui dégénère en rixe*, argument which turns into a scuffle.

dégivrage [deʒi'vr|a:ʒ] *n.m.* defrosting. ‖ **dégivreur** [-œ:r] *n.m.* defroster.

dégonflé, -e [degɔ̃'fle] *adj.* [pneu, &c.] deflated; [Pop.] coward. ‖ **dégonfler** #3 *v. tr.* to deflate (a tire, balloon, &c.); [swelling] to reduce; [Fam.] to debunk (a hero, &c.). ‖ **se dégonfler** *v. pron.* **1.** to go down; to subside, [tire] to deflate. **2.** [Pop.] to back/down, out/ (at the last minute).

dégorger [degɔr'ʒe] #5 *v. tr.* **1.** to disgorge, to spew (out). **2.** to clear, free (a canal, pipe). ‖ *v. intr.* to overflow; to discharge (into, *dans*).

dégourdi, -e [degur'd|i] *adj.* **1.** limbered (fingers, &c.). **2.** warmed (water). **3.** [Fig.] lively, smart, sharp (person). ‖ **dégourdir** [-i:r] #17 *v. tr.* conj. AVOIR [action], ÊTRE [état] **1.** to stretch (one's limbs, &c.). **2.** to warm, to take the chill off (water). **3.** [Fig.] to smarten (s.o.) up. ‖ **se dégourdir** *v. pron.* to get smart; to get, become/ warm.

dégoût [de'gu] *n.m.* **1.** distaste, aversion, dislike (for certain foods): *prendre en* ~, to take a dislike to. **2.** [Fig.] loathing, aversion (for sth. or s.o.). ‖ **dégoûtant, -e** [-'tɑ̃(:t)] *adj.* disgusting, distasteful; [Fam.] sickening. ‖ **dégoûté, -e** [-'te] *adj. & n.* **1.** disgusted. **2.** [Fig.] fastidious, squeamish (person): *faire le* ~, to be difficult to please. ‖ **dégoûter** [-'te] #3 *v. tr.* **1.** to disgust, to cause to lose one's appetite, taste (for sth.). **2.** to disgust, to be loathsome to: *être dégoûté de qqch.*, to loath sth. **3.** to take away one's desire (for sth.), to make one lose interest in.

dégouttant, -e [degu't|ɑ̃(:t)] *adj.* dripping, dropping [liquids]. ‖ **dégoutter** [-e] #3 *v. intr.* to drip, to drop.

dégradation [degrad|a'sjɔ̃] *n.f.* **1.** damage. **2.** [Mil., Jur.] degradation. ‖ **dégradé, -e** [-e] *adj.* defaced; shaded. ‖ *n.* shading (off). ‖ **dégrader** [-e] #3 *v. tr.* **1.** [Mil.] to reduce to the ranks; [Fam.] to break (s.o.). **2.** to deface (a wall). **3.** to shade off. **4.** to debase, to demean.

dégraissage [degrɛ's|a:ʒ] *n.m.* **1.** scouring, clearing; skimming (of milk). cf. ÉCRÉMER. **2.** French cleaning, the removing of grease spots (from clothes). ‖ **dégraisser** [-e] #3 *v. tr.* to scour (pans), to clean (clothes); to skim (milk).

degré [də'gre] *n.m.* **1.** step (of a stair). **2.** [Fig.] degree (of relationship); division (of a measuring instrument); step (in the social scale); [Math.] degree (of an angle); [Géog.] degree (of latitude and longitude); stage (of an illness, of advancement). ‖ **par degrés** [pardə'gre] *loc. adv.* by degrees, gradually.

dégringoler [degrɛ̃gɔ'le] #3 *v. tr. & intr.* **1.** [Fam.] to roll, to tumble (down); to go clattering down: ~ *l'escalier*, to come, go/clattering down the stairs. **2.** [Fig.] [entreprise] to go downhill: *Les prix dégringolent*, Prices are dropping fast.

dégrossir [degro'si:r] #17 *v. tr.* to rough out.

déguenillé, -e [degəni'je] *adj.* tattered, ragged. || *n.* ragged person, beggar.

déguerpir [degɛr'pi:r] #17 *v. intr.* [Fam.] to beat it, clear out.

déguisement [degiz|'mɑ̃] *n.m.* **1.** disguising; disguise. **2.** [Fig.] dissimulation, disguise: *sans* ~, plainly. || **déguiser** [-e] #3 *v. tr.* to disguise.

déguster [degys'te] #3 *v. tr.* **1.** to taste. **2.** [Fig.] to savour; to sip (a drink); to eat (sth.) with relish.

dehors [də'ɔ:r] *adv.* out, outside: *dîner* ~, to dine out; *Il est* ~, He is outside; *mettre* ~, to turn out; [à la porte] to sack. || *interj.*: *Dehors!*, Out (with you)!, Get out! || *Loc. adv. au* ~, outside; *de* ~, from outside: *regarder du* ~, looking in from outside; *en* ~, outside; *en* ~ *de*, beside, outside of; beyond. || *n.* outside (of a house); [Fig.] appearances.

déité [dei'te] *n.f.* deity.

déjà [de'ʒa] *adv.* **1.** already: *Il était* ~ *là*, He was already there. **2.** previously, before: *Je l'ai* ~ *vu*, I have seen him before. **3.** as early as: *Il y était* ~ *en 1940*, He was there as early as 1940. **4.** [Fam., for intensifying]: *Comment vous appelez-vous* ~ ?, What did you say the name was?, *Ce n'est* ~ *pas si mal*, It's not at all bad.

déjeuner [deʒœ'ne] *n.m.* [le matin] breakfast; [Fr.] [à midi] lunch (= © dîner); [Fr.] *petit* ~ (= © déjeuner) breakfast: *prendre le* ~, to have lunch, © breakfast. || **déjeuner** #3 *v. intr.* © to breakfast, to have breakfast; [Fr.] to breakfast, to lunch.

déjouer [de'ʒwe] #3 *v. tr.* to foil, outwit.

delà [də'la] **(au** ~, **par** ~**)** [od(ə)'la, pardə'la] *adv. & prép.* (of place) beyond, on the other side (of). [☞ always preceded by *par* ~, *au* ~, †*en* ~]: *au-delà des frontières*, beyond the borders; *par delà la mer*, beyond the sea; *On peut vous prêter un million et au-delà*, We can lend you a million and more; *au-delà des nuages*, above the clouds. || **au-delà** [od(ə)'la] *n.m.* the world beyond, the hereafter.

délabré, -e [delɑ'bre] *adj.* dilapidated, in ruins; [Fig.] shattered (health).

délacer [delɑ'se] #4 *v. tr.* to undo (one's shoestrings); to unlace.

délai [de'lɛ] *n.m.* **1.** delay: *agir sans* ~, to act without delay; *dernier* ~, deadline. **2.** period of time (allowed for sth.): *dans le plus bref* ~, as soon as possible; *dans un* ~ *de quatre semaines*, within four weeks.

délaisser [delɛ'se] #3 *v. tr.* to forsake, to desert, to abandon: *être délaissé de ses parents*, to be/deserted, abandoned/by one's parents; ~ *un travail difficile*, to quit a difficult job.

délassement [delɑs|'mɑ̃] *n.m.* rest, relaxation: ~ *préféré*, favourite pastime. || **délasser** [-e] #3 *v. tr.* conj. AVOIR [action], ÊTRE [état] to refresh, to relax. || **se délasser** *v. pron.* to relax, to take it easy.

délayer [delɛ'je] #11 *v. tr.* to dilute; to temper (colours); [Fig.] to spin out (a speech).

délectable [delɛk't|abl] *adj.* delicious; [Fig.] delightful. || **se délecter** [-e] #3 *v. pron.* to take delight (in, *à*).

délégation [deleg|a'sjõ] *n.f.* delegation (of authority); [personnes] delegation. || **délégué** [-e] *n.m.* [convention, assembly] delegate: *le* ~ *du Canada*, the Canadian delegate. || **déléguer** [-e] #10 *v. tr.* to delegate (people); to assign (a task).

délester [delɛs'te] #3 *v. tr.* [bateau] to unballast; to lighten; [Fig.] to relieve.

délibération [deliber|asjõ] *n.f.* deliberation. || **délibéré, -e** [-e] *adj.* deliberate. || **délibérer** #10 *v. tr.* to deliberate.

délicat, -e [deli'k|a(t)] *adj.* **1.** delicate (health, situation); dainty, fastidious. **2.** tricky, thorny, difficult. **3.** according to good taste: *procédé peu* ~, unscrupulous behaviour. || *n.m.* finicky, fastidious/ person: *faire le* ~, to be finicky, difficult. || **délicatement** [-at'mɑ̃] *adv.* delicately, daintily; tastefully, tactfully. || **délicatesse** [-a'tɛs] *n.f.* **1.** delicacy (of a food, of a work, of a flavour, of a perfume, of a situation); refinement (of features, of a thought, &c.); fineness, daintiness (of colouring, &c.); fastidiousness (of conscience): *être en* ~ *avec qqun*, to be at odds with s.o. **2.** weakness, fragility: *la* ~ *de ses poumons*, the weakness of/his, her/lungs.

délice [de'lis] *n.m.* (in the sing.) et *f.* (in the pl.) pleasure(s), delight(s): *faire ses délices de*, to take delight in. || **délicieusement** [-jøz'mɑ̃] *adv.* delightfully. || **délicieu|x, -se** [-jø(:z)] *adj.* delightful, charming; [au goût] delicious.

délictueu|x, -se [delik'tɥø(:z)] *adj.* unlawful, punishable: *acte* ~, offence, misdemeanour.

délié, -e [de'lje] *adj.* **1.** slim, thin, slender. **2.** quick, penetrating, nimble (mind); [Fam.] *avoir la langue bien* ~, to be very talkative. || **délier** #3 *v. tr.* **1.** to untie: *sans bourse* ~, without spending a cent. **2.** [Fig.] to free, to release; [Rel.] to absolve: ~ *qqun d'un serment,* to release s.o. from an oath; ~ *la langue de qqun,* to loosen s.o.'s tongue.

délimitation [delimit|a'sjõ] *n.f.* fixing (of boundaries); defining (of powers). || **délimiter** [-e] #3 *v. tr.* to fix (boundaries); to define (powers).

délinquant, -e [delɛ̃'kɑ̃(:t)] *n.* delinquent: ~ *primaire,* first offender.

délirant, -e [deli'rɑ̃(:t)] *adj.* **1.** delirious; frantic, frenzied. **2.** [Fig.] rapturous, ecstatic [joy, &c.]. || **délire** [de'l|i:r] *n.m.* **1.** delirium: *accès de* ~, attack of delirium; *être en* ~, to be delirious. **2.** [Fig.] frenzy. || **délirer** [-i're] #3 *v. intr.* to be delirious, to rave.

délit [de'li] *n.m.* misdemeanour, offence, crime: *être pris en flagrant* ~, to be caught in the act.

délivrance [deli'vr|ɑ̃:s] *n.f.* **1.** release, setting free, deliverance. **2.** issue (of tickets, a certificate). || **délivrer** [-e] #3 *v. tr.* **1.** to release (s.o. from sth.), to free. **2.** to deliver (sth.); to issue (tickets, a certificate, &c.).

déloger [delɔ'ʒe] #5 *v. intr.* to turn out (of a lodging); to move (from a lodging): [Fig.] ~ *sans tambour ni trompette,* to steal quietly away. || *v. tr.* to dislodge, to oust (s.o. or sth.).

déloyal, -e [delwa'j|al] *adj.* dishonest, crooked. || **déloyauté** [-o'te] *n.f.* dishonesty.

déluge [de'ly:ʒ] *n.m.* deluge, flood.

déluré, -e [dely're] *adj.* wide-awake, sharp.

démailler [dema'je] #3 *v. tr.* to undo the meshes (of a net, &c.). || **se démailler** *v. pron.* [bas, &c.] © to run, [Br.] to ladder.

demain [də'mɛ̃] *adv.* tomorrow: *A* ~ *!,* See you tomorrow! *de* ~ *en huit,* a week from tomorrow.

démancher [demɑ̃'ʃe] #3 *v. tr.* to remove the handle; © to take to pieces; to put out of order.

demande [də'm|ɑ̃:d] *n.f.* request, application: *faire sa* ~, to send in a request, to apply; *sur* ~, on request, on application. || **demander** [-ɑ̃'de] #3 *v. tr.* **1.** to ask (for): *On vous demande au téléphone,* You are wanted on the phone; *Je vous demande pardon,* I beg your pardon; ~ *à qqun,* to ask s.o.; ~ *qqun,* to ask for s.o.; *Votre frère est venu vous* ~, Your brother called for you. **2.** to require: *Cela demande du temps,* It requires time. || **se demander** *v. pron.* to wonder (whether, *si*). || **demande|ur, -resse** [-ɑ̃'d|œ:r, -rɛs] *n.* plaintiff.

démangeaison [demɑ̃ʒ|ɛ'zõ] *n.f.* itch, itching. || **démanger** [-e] #5 *v. intr.* to itch: [Fig.] *La langue lui démange,* He is itching to say sth.

démanteler [demɑ̃'tle] #9 *v. tr.* to dismantle (a fortress).

démarcation [demarka'sjõ] *n.f.* demarcation.

démarchage [demar'ʃa:ʒ] *n.m.* canvassing.

démarche [de'marʃ] *n.f.* **1.** step, gait, walk: *Je le reconnais à sa* ~, I know him by his walk, gait, step. **2.** [Fig.] step, errand: *faire une* ~ *auprès de qqun,* to go and see s.o. (about, *au sujet de*); *Il a fait les démarches nécessaires,* He took the necessary steps. || **démarcheur** [-œ:r] *n.m.* canvasser.

démarquer [demar'ke] #3 *v. tr.* **1.** [du linge] to take off the label from; [un livre, de l'argenterie, &c.] to take off all marks; [Com.] to mark down (the prices). **2.** [une œuvre littéraire, &c.] to plagiarize with slight changes.

démarrage [dema'r|a:ʒ] *n.m.* starting (of a car); unmooring (of a ship): ~ *rapide,* quick get-away. || **démarrer** [-e] #3 *v. tr.* to unmoor (a ship); to cast off the mooring lines (of a ship). || *v. intr.* [bateau] **1.** to leave port, to cast off: *Le bateau démarre à deux heures,* The ship leaves (the dock) at two o'clock. **2.** [Auto] to start, to drive off: *Le moteur ne veut pas* ~, The motor won't start. **3.** [Fig.] to get under way: *une entreprise qui a du mal à* ~, a business which has difficulty in getting under way, started. **4.** [Fig. & nég.] *Il ne démarre pas de là,* He won't budge from that. || **démarreur** [-œ:r] *n.m.* [manivelle] crank; [électrique] starter.

démasquer [demas'ke] #3 *v. tr.* **1.** to unmask. **2.** [Fig.] to show up, unmask, expose.

démêlé [demɛ'le] *n.m.* dispute, quarrel; difficulty: *avoir des démêlés avec,* to be at cross purposes with. || **démêler** #3 *v. tr.* **1.** to untangle, unravel (string, &c.); to comb out (hair); to card (wool). **2.** to discern, to make (s.o.) out (in the gloom, dark): ~ *la vérité/du, d'avec le/ mensonge,* to distinguish truth from falsehood. **3.** © to mix: ~ *un gâteau, du ciment,* to mix a cake, (a batch of) cement.

démembrer [demɑ̃'bre] #3 *v. tr.* to dismember.

déménagement [demenaʒ|'mɑ̃] *n.m.* removal, moving: *voiture de* ~, /moving, furniture/van. || **déménager** [-e] #5 *v. tr.* to move (one's furniture to another house). || *v. intr.* **1.** to move house, change (one's) address. **2.** [Fig. & Fam.] to go off one's head. || **déménageur** [-œːr] *n.m.* (furniture) mover.

démence [de'mɑ̃ːs] *n.f.* insanity, madness.

démener, se [se dem'ne] #9 *v. pron.* to exert o.s.

dément, -e [de'mɑ̃(ːt)] *adj.* [personne] insane.

démenti [demɑ̃'t|i] *n.m.* **1.** denial, contradiction, refutation: *donner le* ~ *à qqch.*, to deny, refute sth. **2.** shame; failure. || **démentir** [-iːr] #26 *v. tr.* **1.** to contradict, refute: ~ *un témoin*, to refute a witness. **2.** to deny, belie: *ses actions démentent ses paroles*, his actions belie his words. || **se démentir** *v. pron.* to contradict o.s.; [qualité d'un ouvrage, &c.] to fall off; [efforts] to flag.

démesuré [deməzy're] *adj.* huge; excessive, inordinate, immeasurable. || **démesurément** [-'mɑ̃] *adv.* excessively, inordinately, enormously.

démettre [de'mɛtr] #44 *v. tr.* to dislocate, to put (sth.) out of joint; [Jur.] to dismiss (a case). || **se** ~ *v. pron.* **1.** to be put out of joint. **2.** to resign: ~ *de ses fonctions*, to resign one's position.

demeure [də'm|œːr] *n.f.* **1.** residence, dwelling, †abode: *dernière* ~, the last resting place. **2.** delay, deferring: *Il n'y a pas péril en la* ~, There is no harm in waiting; *mise en* ~ *(de faire qqch.)*, formal notice, summons (to do sth.). || **demeurer** [-œ're] #3 *v. intr.* **1.** to stop, remain, stay: ~ *à son poste*, to stay at one's post; ~ *chez soi*, to stay (at) home; *en* ~ *là*, to stop here. **2.** to live, dwell: *Il demeure à Montréal*, He lives in Montreal.

demi[1] [də'mi] *n.m.* **1.** half (of sth.). **2.** glass (of beer) [about half a litre]. **3.** [Sport] half, halfback.

demi[2] [də'mi] *adj.* half, semi-, half-. ☞ When placed before the noun, *demi* is invariable and is joined to the noun by a hyphen: *demi-douzaine*, half-dozen; *un* ~ *-verre d'eau*, half a glass of water; *demi-fixe*, semi-portable; *une demi-heure d'attente*, a half-hour wait; *à* ~ *mort*, half dead. || **demi-cercle** [-'sɛrkl] *n.m.* semi-circle. || **demi-clos** [-'klo] *adj. inv.* half-closed. || **demi-finale** [-fi'nal] *n.f.* semi-final. || **demi-frère, demi-frères** [-'frɛːr] *n.m.* half brother. || **demi-heure, demi-heures** [-'œːr] *n.f.* half hour. || **demi-jour, demi-jours** [-'ʒuːr] *n.m.* half light (of dawn), twilight; dusk. || **demi-journée** [-ʒur'ne] *n.f.* half day: *avoir un emploi à la* ~, to have a half-day job, to work half days. || **demi-mesure** [-mə'zyːr] *n.f.* half measure. || **demi-pension** [-pɑ̃'sjõ], **demi-pensions** *n.f.* partial board (noon meal only). || **demi-pensionnaire** [-pɑ̃sjɔ-'nɛːr] *n.m/f.* day boarder (noon meal only). || **demi-place** [-'plas], **demi-places** *n.f.* [moyens de transport] half fare, [spectacles] half price. || **demi-sœur** [-'sœːr] *n.f.* half sister.

demie [də'mi] *n.f.* half hour: *L'horloge sonne la* ~, The clock strikes the half hour.

démission [demi'sj|õ] *n.f.* resignation: *donner sa* ~, to resign; *offrir sa* ~, to hand in one's resignation; *remettre sa* ~, to tender one's resignation. || **démissionner** [-ɔ'ne] #3 *v. intr.* to resign.

démobilisation [demɔbiliz|a'sjõ] *n.f.* demobilization. || **démobiliser** [-e] #3 *v. tr.* to demobilize.

démocrate [demɔ'kra|t] *n.m/f.* democrat. || **démocratie** [-'si] *n.f.* democracy. || **démocratique** [-'tik] *adj.* democratic.

démodé, -e [demɔ'de] *adj.* out of style, old-fashioned.

demoiselle[1] [dəmwa'zɛl] *n.f.* young lady, miss; single woman: ~ *d'honneur*, bridesmaid.

demoiselle[2] *n.f.* dragonfly.

démolir [demɔ'l|iːr] #17 *v. tr.* **1.** to demolish, to tear down. **2.** to ruin, to tear apart, to knock out. || **démolition** [-i'sjõ] *n.f.* demolition; wrecking: *équipe de* ~, wrecking crew.

démon [de'mõ] *n.m.* **1.** demon, devil. **2.** [enfant] imp, rascal.

démonétiser [demɔneti'ze] #3 *v. tr.* [argent] to call in, withdraw from circulation.

démonstrat|eur, -rice [demõstra|'tœːr, -'tris] *n.* [Pers.] demonstrator. || **démonstrati|f, -ve** [-'tif, -'tiːv] *adj.* demonstrative: *adjectif* ~, demonstrative adjective. || **démonstration** [-'sjõ] *n.f.* demonstration: *faire une* ~, to give a demonstration, to demonstrate.

démontable [demõ't|abl] *adj.* collapsible. || **démonté, -e** [-e] *adj.* **1.** dismounted, dismantled. **2.** taken aback. **3.** [mer] raging. || **démonter** [-e] #3 *v. tr.* **1.** to unseat, unhorse (a rider). **2.** to take (sth.) to pieces; to strip, to dismantle. **3.** [Fig.] to nonplus, to disconcert, [Fam.] to faze. || **se démonter** *v. pron.* **1.** to come apart. **2.** [Fig.] to get upset, [Fam.] rattled; to lose one's poise: *ne pas* ~ *facilement*, not to get upset easily.

démontrer [demõ'tre] #3 *v. tr.* to prove; to show, to demonstrate: ~ *un théorème*, to prove a theorem; ~ *sa gentillesse*, to show one's kindness; ~ *la fausseté d'une affirmation*, to prove the falseness of a declaration.

démoraliser [demɔrali'ze] #3 *v. tr.* to demoralize.

démordre (de) [de'mɔrdr] #42 *v. intr.* [Fig.] to give/in, up/: *Il n'en démordra pas*, He'll never change on that.

démuni, -e [demy'n|i] *adj.* short (of money); stripped (of troops). ‖ **démunir** [-i:r] #17 *v. tr.* [une place forte, une machine, &c.] to strip. ‖ **se démunir** *v. pron.* to deprive o.s. of; to part with.

dénaturé, -e [denaty're] *adj.* **1.** unnatural. **2.** perverted, depraved: *un goût* ~, a perverted taste. ‖ **dénaturer** #3 *v. tr.* **1.** to adulterate (food). **2.** [Fig.] to twist, distort, to misrepresent (statement), to pervert (s.o.'s taste, character).

dénégation [denega'sjõ] *n.f.* denial: *faire un signe de* ~, to shake one's head. ‖ **déni** [de'ni] *n.m.* denial, refusal (to carry out one's duty): ~ *de justice*, miscarriage of justice.

dénicher [deni'ʃe] #3 *v. tr.* **1.** to take (birds, eggs) from a nest: *aller* ~ *les oiseaux*, to go bird's nesting. **2.** to find, to ferret out. ‖ *v. intr.* to leave the nest, to fly the coop.

denier [də'nje] *n.m.* **1.** farthing, †mite (ancient coins); small coin: *Denier de Saint-Pierre*, Peter's pence. **2.** [Indus.] denier: *des bas de 30 deniers*, 30-denier stockings. **3.** *plur.* funds, money: *de ses propres deniers*, out of his own pocket; *les* ~ *publics*, public funds.

dénier [de'nje] #3 *v. tr.* to deny: ~ *qqch. à qqun*, to deny s.o. sth.; [responsabilité] to disclaim.

dénigrer [deni'gre] #3 *v. tr.* to disparage, to speak ill of.

Denis [də'ni] *n.m.* = Dennis.

dénombrer [denõ'bre] #3 *v. tr.* to count, to enumerate.

dénomination [denɔm|ina'sjõ] *n.f.* name, denomination. ‖ **dénommer** [-e] #3 *v. tr.* to name.

dénoncer [denõ's|e] #4 *v. tr.* **1.** to denounce, to inform against: ~ *un espion*, to denounce a spy. **2.** [Fig.] to reveal, indicate: *Ses manières dénonçaient un homme cultivé*, His manners revealed a cultured man. ‖ **dénonciat|eur, -rice** [-ja|'tœ:r, -'tris] *n.* informer. ‖ **dénonciation** [-'sjõ] *n.f.* **1.** denunciation. **2.** [Com. & Jur.] notice of termination (of an agreement, partnership, treaty).

dénoter [denɔ'te] #3 *v. tr.* to denote, indicate, show.

dénouement [den|u'mã] *n.m.* outcome; [Théât.]denouement; [d'une destinée, &c.] unfolding. ‖ **dénouer** [-we] #3 *v. tr.* **1.** to untie, undo (a knot). **2.** to unravel, solve (a mystery); to untangle (a plot). ‖ **se dénouer** *v. pron.* [lacet, &c.] to come untied; [intrigue, complications] to unfold.

denrée [dã're] *n.f.* commodity, produce: *denrées alimentaires*, foodstuffs.

dense [dã:s] *adj.* thick; [Fig.] compact (style); substantial. ‖ **densité** [dãsi'te] *n.f.* density.

dent [dã] *n.f.* **1.** tooth (*pl.* teeth): ~ *branlante*, loose tooth; *avoir mal aux dents*, to have (a) toothache; *faire ses dents*, to cut one's teeth; *arracher une* ~ *à qqun*, to pull s.o.'s tooth; *brosse à dents*, toothbrush; *coup de* ~, bite; *grincer des dents*, to grind one's teeth; *serrer les dents*, to grit one's teeth. **2.** [Fig.] *armé jusqu'aux dents*, armed to the teeth; *n'avoir rien à se mettre sous la* ~, not to have a bite to eat; *avoir une* ~ *contre qqun*, to have a grudge against s.o.; *avoir la* ~ *dure*, to be a harsh critic; *coup de* ~, disparaging remark; *déchirer qqun à belles dents*, to tear s.o.'s reputation to pieces; *ne pas desserrer les dents*, not to open one's mouth; *être sur les dents*, to be bone tired; *manger du bout des dents*, to nibble; *parler entre les dents*, to/speak, mutter/ through one's teeth; *rire à belles dents*, to laugh heartily; *rire du bout des dents*, to give a forced laugh. ‖ **dentaire** [-'tɛ:r] *adj.* dental: *art* ~, dentistry. ‖ **dental, -e** [-'tal] *adj.* dental (consonants, &c.). ‖ **denté, -e** [-'te] *adj.* toothed, notched, indented: *roue dentée*, cogwheel. ‖ **dentelé, -e** [-t'le] *adj.* indented, notched, jagged; serrated (leaf); scalloped (design). ‖ **denteler** [-t'le] #8 *v. tr.* to notch, to indent, to serrate, to scallop.

dentelle [dã'tɛl] *n.f.* lace, lace work. ‖ **dentelure** [dãt|'ly:r] *n.f.* [côte] indentations; [montagne] jagged outline; [feuille] serrations; [timbre] perforations.

dentier [dã'tje] *n.m.* (set of) false teeth, denture; [Fam.] plate. ‖ **dentifrice** [-i'fris] *n.m.* tooth paste, dentifrice. ‖ **dentiste** [-ist] *n.m.* dentist: *chirurgien* ~, dental surgeon. ‖ **dentition** [-i'sjõ] *n.f.* **1.** teething. **2.** set of teeth. ‖ **denture** [-y:r] *n.f.* set of teeth [natural].

dénuder [deny'de] #3 *v. tr.* to bare, lay bare.

dénué, -e [de'nɥe] *adj.* destitute, devoid (of, *de*); completely lacking (in, *de*). ‖ **dénuement** [deny'mã] *n.m.* (extreme) poverty: *être dans un grand* ~, to be in great poverty.

dépannage [depa′n|a:ʒ] *n.m.* repairs, [action] fixing, repairing: *équipe de* ∼, wrecking crew. || **dépanner** [-e] #3 *v. tr.* **1.** to make emergency repairs (to a stalled car, &c.). **2.** [Fig.] to get (s.o.) out of difficulty. || **dépanneur** [-œ:r] *n.m.* wrecker.

dépareillé, -e [deparɛ′je] *adj.* unmatched: *exemplaire* ∼, odd number (of periodical). © [= sans pareil] outstanding, priceless.

départ [de′pa:r] *n.m.* departure: *être sur son* ∼, to be on the point of leaving; [Fig.] *point de* ∼, starting point; *l'heure de* ∼ *du train*, train time; *prendre un mauvais* ∼, to get off on the wrong foot.

département [departə′mɑ̃] *n.m.* **1.** [US, ©] county; [Fr.] department. **2.** department, [Br.] ministry [less used than MINISTÈRE]; *Département des Archives Publiques*, Department of Public Archives.

départir [depar′ti:r] #17 *v. tr.* to allot. || **se départir (de qqch.)** *v. pron.* to give up, to renounce (sth.); ∼ *d'un droit*, to renounce a/right, claim/.

dépasser [depɑ′se] #3 *v. tr.* **1.** to go beyond, to extend beyond: *Il me dépasse d'une tête*, He is a head taller than I. **2.** to show; to stick out. **3.** to exceed: *Cela dépasse mes moyens*, It's beyond my means. **4.** to overtake, to pass (a car).

dépaysé, -e [depei′ze] *adj.* feeling strange, out of place. || **dépayser** #3 *v. tr.* to make (s.o.) feel (strange, out of place).

dépecer [depə′se] #15 *v. tr.* [boucher, &c.] to cut up (a beef, &c.); [lion, &c.] to tear apart (its prey); to break up (a boat, &c.); [Fig.] to partition, cut, break/up (a territory).

dépêche [de′pɛ:ʃ] *n.f.* [less used than NOTE] **1.** dispatch, note: ∼ *diplomatique*, diplomatic dispatch. **2.** telegram: *envoyer une* ∼, to send a telegram. || **dépêcher** [depɛ′ʃe] #3 *v. tr.* **1.** to dispatch. **2.** to hurry, to expedite (work). || **se dépêcher** *v. pron.* to hurry (o.s.) up; to make haste: *Dépêchez-vous!*, Hurry up!

dépeigné, -e [depɛ′ɲe] *adj.* uncombed, dishevelled (hair). || **dépeigner** #3 *v. tr.* to dishevel, [Fam.] muss one's hair.

dépeindre [de′pɛ̃:dr], **dépeignant** [dep|ɛ′ɲɑ̃], **dépeint** [-ɛ̃] #36 *v. tr.* to depict; to describe.

dépendance [depɑ̃′d|ɑ̃:s] *n.f.* [pays] dependency; dependence, subordination: *être sous la* ∼ *de qqun*, to be under s.o.'s domination. || *n.fpl.* outbuildings, annexes, appendages (to). || **dépendant, -e** [-ɑ̃(:t)] *adj.* dependent (on). || **dépendre**[1] [de′pɑ̃:dr] #42 *v. intr.* **1.** to depend (on, *de*): *Cela dépend de vous*, It depends on you. **2.** to come under: *Les préfets dépendent du Ministère de l'Intérieur*, Prefects come under the Ministry of the Interior.

dépendre[2] #42 *v. tr.* [un objet pendu] to take down.

dépens [de′pɑ̃] *n.mpl.* costs, expense: *à ses* ∼, at one's own risk; *Il vit aux* ∼ *de son oncle*, → He is living off his uncle; *Ils ont appris à leurs* ∼ *que* . . ., They learned, to their cost, that . . . ; [Fig.] *rire aux* ∼ *de qqun*, to laugh at s.o., to make fun of s.o.

dépense [de′p|ɑ̃:s] *n.f.* **1.** expense, expenditure: *regarder à la* ∼, to pinch pennies. **2.** pantry, storage room. || **dépenser** [-ɑ̃′se] #3 *v. tr.* to spend; to consume, to use. || **se dépenser** *v. pron.* to exert o.s.; *sans compter* ∼, to spare no effort. || **dépensi|er, -ère** [-ɑ̃′sj|e, -ɛ:r] *adj.* extravagant, spendthrift: *Elle est vraiment dépensière*, She is/a real spendthrift, really extravagant/.

déperdition [depɛrdi′sjõ] *n.f.* loss; wastage; diminution.

dépérir [depe′ri:r] #17 *v. intr.* **1.** [Pers.] to waste, pine away; [plante] to wither; [force] to weaken, to grow weak. **2.** [Fig.] [entreprise] to decline.

dépeupler [depœ′ple] #3 *v. tr.* **1.** to depopulate. **2.** to clear, thin (a forest); to empty, clear (a lake, pond, region) of living things.

dépister [depis′te] #3 *v. tr.* **1.** to detect, to spot, to pick up the trail of. **2.** to put (s.o.) off the/track, trail/.

dépit [de′pi] *n.m.* spite, vexation, resentment: *masquer son* ∼, to conceal one's resentment; *par* ∼, out of spite; *en* ∼ *de*, in spite of, despite. || **dépiter** [-′te] #3 *v. tr.* to vex, upset. || **se dépiter** *v. pron.* to take offence, to be annoyed.

déplacé, -e [deplas|e] *adj.* out of place, misplaced. || **déplacement** [-′mɑ̃] *n.m.* **1.** displacement, removal, shifting; travelling: *frais de* ∼, travelling expenses. **2.** [Naut.] displacement: ∼ *de 1000 tonnes*, displacement of 1000 tons. || **déplacer** [-e] #4 *v. tr.* **1.** to displace, move, shift; [Naut.] to have a displacement of: *Ce bateau déplace dix mille tonnes (d'eau)*; This ship has a displacement of ten thousand tons. **2.** to transfer (an employee). || **se déplacer** *v. pron.* to change one's place; to travel.

déplaire [de′pl|ɛ:r] #49 *v. intr.* to displease, to be unpleasant: *Cela me déplaît*, I don't like that; *Ne vous en déplaise*, No offence meant, With all due respect to you. || **déplaisant** [-ɛ′zɑ̃] *adj.* disagreeable, unpleasant. || **déplaisir** [-ɛ'ziːr] *n.m.* displeasure.

dépliant [depli'j|ɑ̃] *n.m.* (printed) folder. || *adj.* folding. || **déplier** [-e] #3 *v. tr.* to unfold.

déploiement [deplwa'mɑ̃] *n.m.* unfolding; [voiles] unfurling; [Mil.] deployment; [Fig.] show, display (of riches, jewels, &c.).

déplorable [deplɔ'r|abl] *adj.* lamentable, deplorable. || **déplorer** [-e] #3 *v. tr.* to deplore.

déployer [deplwa'je] #12 *v. tr.* **1.** to unfold, unfurl (a flag, a sail). **2.** [Fig.] to spread out, to display; [Mil.] to deploy: ~ *un grand courage,* to display great courage; *rire à gorge déployée,* → to laugh uproariously.

déplu [de'ply] cf. DÉPLAIRE.

déplumer [deply'me] #3 *v. tr.* to pluck. || **se déplumer** *v. pron.* to moult; [Fam.] to grow bald.

dépoli [depɔ'li] *adj.* ground, frosted (glass).

déportation [depɔrt|a'sjɔ̃] *n.f.* deportation. || **déporté, -e** [-e] *adj.* deported (person). || *n.* convict; [Polit.] deported prisoner, deportee. || **déportement** [-ə'mɑ̃] *n.m.* [seldom used in the plural] misbehaviour. || **déporter** #3 *v. tr.* to deport.

déposant, -e [depo'z|ɑ̃(ːt)] *n.* **1.** depositor. **2.** [Jur.] deponent, witness. || **déposé, -e** [-e] *adj.* entered; registered: *marque déposée,* registered trade mark. || **déposer** [-e] #3 *v. tr.* **1.** to put down: ~ *un voyageur,* to drop off a passenger; ~ *une couronne,* to place a wreath; ~ *les armes,* to lay down one's arms; ~ *son bilan,* to go bankrupt. **2.** to depose (a king). **3.** to deposit (money), to check: ~ *son manteau au vestiaire,* to check one's coat at the checkroom. **4.** to introduce (a bill); to lodge (a complaint); to make (a motion); to register (a trade mark). || *v. intr.* to give evidence, to testify. || **dépositaire** [-i'tɛːr] *n.m.* [Jur.] trustee; [Com.] agent. || **déposition** [-i'sjɔ̃] *n.f.* **1.** deposing (of a king, pope, &c.). **2.** [Jur.] deposition, sworn statement, testimony (of a witness).

déposséder [depɔse'de] #10 *v. tr.* [de ses biens] to dispossess; [de sa place, charge, &c.] to oust.

dépôt [de'po] *n.m.* **1.** deposition, placing: ~ *légal* (*d'un livre*), copyright privilege (of a book); ~ *d'une marque de fabrique,* registering of a trade mark; ~ *d'une couronne de fleurs,* placing of a wreath; ~ *d'une somme,* depositing of a sum. **2.** deposit: *en* ~, on deposit, in safe keeping; *mettre qqch. en* ~, to deposit sth.; *faire un* ~ *en banque,* to make a deposit at the bank. **3.** terminal, storage barn (for buses); warehouse, store (house); (baggage) depot; [Jur.] jail; [Mil.] depot: ~ *de la préfecture de police,* central police station, jail (in Paris); *envoyer au* ~, to send to jail. **4.** deposit (of a river, glacier); settlings (of still liquids); scale (in a boiler, &c.). || **dépotoir** [depɔ'twaːr] *n.m.* dump(ing-ground).

dépouille [de'puj] *n.f.* skin (shed by certain animals); hide, skin (of an animal): ~ *mortelle,* mortal remains. || *n.fpl.* spoils (of war). || **dépouillement** [-'mɑ̃] *n.* **1.** [privation de ses biens] despoiling. **2.** scrutiny, examination. **3.** ~ *du scrutin,* counting of the ballots. || **dépouiller** [-e] #3 *v. tr.* **1.** to skin (an animal). **2.** to strip (a tree of its branches, leaves, bark), a person (of his clothes); to take the scales off (a fish); to shave (the hair off). **3.** to deprive (s.o. of sth.); to take (sth.) from; to pillage, sack: ~ *un voyageur de son argent,* to take a traveller's money; ~ *qqun de son emploi,* to take s.o.'s job away; ~ *qqun de ses droits,* to deprive s.o. of his rights. **4.** to go over (documents), to analyze; to count (the ballots); to go through (one's mail). || **se dépouiller** *v. pron.* to shed (one's clothes; of certain animals, the skin).

dépourvu [depur'vy] *adj.* bereft, devoid of, destitute: ~ *de bon sens,* devoid of (any) sense: *pris au* ~, taken unawares.

dépravation [deprav|a'sjɔ̃] *n.f.* depravity; corruption. || **dépraver** [-e] #3 *v. tr.* to pervert, corrupt.

dépréciation [depresj|a'sjɔ̃] *n.f.* depreciation. || **déprécier** [-e] #3 *v. tr.* to depreciate, lower the value of (sth.); underrate. || **se déprécier** *v. pron.* [chose] to fall in value; [personne] to depreciate o.s.

dépression [deprɛ'sjɔ̃] *n.f.* depression, hollow; [météorologie] fall in pressure; [Méd., Écon.] depression.

déprimant, -e [depri'm|ɑ̃(ːt)] *adj.* depressing (climate). || **déprimé, -e** [-e] *adj.* depressed. || **déprimer** [-e] #3 *v. tr.* to depress.

depuis [də'pɥi] *prép.* **1.** since: *Il habite ici* ~ *1950,* He has been living here since 1950. **2.** for: *Nous sommes ici* ~ *deux jours,* We have been here for two days. **3.** from: ~ *le matin jusqu'au soir,* from morning till night: ~ *l'Atlantique jusqu'au Pacifique,* from the Atlantic to the Pacific. **4.** ~ *quand?,* How long?, [ironique] Since when? || **depuis que** *conj.* since: ~ *qu'il est parti,* since he left. *adv.* since, afterwards:

Je ne l'ai pas revu ~, I have not seen him since.

députation [depyt|a'sjõ] *n.f.* **1.** delegation; deputation. **2.** [Parliament] membership: *Il est candidat à la* ~, He is running for Parliament. || **député** [-e] *n.m.* **1.** member of Parliament; [US] congressman; © ~ *de l'arrière-banc*, back bencher. **2.** [sens général] delegate. || **députer** [-e] #3 *v. tr.* to delegate, depute, send (as representative).

déraciner [derasi'ne] #3 *v. tr.* **1.** to uproot. **2.** [Fig.] to eradicate, remove, stamp out: ~ *une erreur*, to eliminate an error.

déraillement [derɑj|'mɑ̃] *n.m.* derailment; [par ext.] train wreck. || **dérailler** [-e] #3 *v. intr.* **1.** to go off the track, to be derailed: *faire* ~, to derail. **2.** [Fig. & Fam.] to go off one's rocker; to talk nonsense. || **dérailleur** [-œ:r] *n.m.* [bicyclette] gearshift.

déraison [derɛ'z|õ] *n.f.* unreasonableness, folly. || **déraisonnable** [-ɔ'nabl] *adj.* unreasonable, senseless. || **déraisonner** [-ɔ'ne] #3 *v. intr.* [délirer] to rave; [dérailler] to talk nonsense.

dérangement [derɑ̃ʒ|'mɑ̃] *n.m.* disorder, trouble; [atmosphérique] disturbance; [de l'estomac] upset; [de l'esprit] disturbance. || **déranger** [-e] #5 *v. tr.* **1.** to put out of order, to disturb. **2.** to trouble, disturb, bother: *J'espère que je ne vous dérange pas* I hope I am not disturbing you. || **se déranger** *v. pron.* to go to some trouble, to inconvenience o.s.; to get out of order, to become deranged.

dérapage [dera'p|a:ʒ] *n.m.* skidding. || **déraper** [-e] #3 *v. intr.* to skid.

†**derechef** [dər'ʃɛf] *adv.* [moins employé que DE NOUVEAU] again.

déréglé, -e [der|e'gle] *adj.* [machine, &c.] out of order; [morale] dissolute; [pouls] irregular; [estomac] upset, unsettled. || **dérèglement** [-ɛglə'mɑ̃] *n.m.* **1.** faulty operation (of machinery): *par suite du* ~ *des appareils*, because the equipment was not working properly. **2.** dissoluteness: *vivre dans le* ~, to live a dissolute life. || **dérégler** [-e'gle] #10 *v. tr.* [le temps, l'estomac] to upset, unsettle; [machine, &c.] to put out of order.

dérision [deri'z|jõ] *n.f.* mockery, derision: *tourner en* ~, to ridicule. || **dérisoire** [-wa:r] *adj.* ridiculous; [prix] ridiculously low.

dérivati|f, -ve [deriva|'tif, -ti:v] *adj.* derivative. || **dérivation** [-'sjõ] *n.f.* **1.** [Gram., Alg.] derivation; [cours d'eau] diversion. **2.** [déviation] deviation, drift. || **dérivé** [deri've] *n.m.* derivative. || **dérive** [de'ri:v] **1.** *n.f.* drift; leeway: *aller à la* ~, to drift, to be/drifting, adrift/. **2.** [Naut.] dropkeel; [avion] rudder. || **dériver** [deri've] #3 *v. tr.* **1.** to divert (a stream); to shunt, switch (a train). **2.** [Fig. & Gram.] to derive (a word from, *de*). || *v. intr.* **1.** [Gram.] to derive (from, *de*). **2.** [Fig.] to spring, stem (from, *de*); to originate (in, *de*): *Tous ces malheurs dérivent de la guerre*, All these calamities spring from the war. || *v. intr.* [bateau, avion, projectile] to drift (off course).

derni|er, -ère [dɛr'nj|e, -ɛ:r] *adj.* **1.** last, final: *mettre la dernière main à un ouvrage*, to give the finishing touches to a work; *en* ~ *lieu*, finally; *son* ~ *livre*, his last book. **2.** last, latest: *la dernière mode*, the latest fashion; *son* ~ *livre*, his latest book. **3.** top: *au* ~ *étage*, on the top floor. **4.** lowest: *C'est notre* ~ *prix*, It's our lowest price. **5.** utmost, highest: *au* ~ *degré*, to the nth degree: *Ils sont du* ~ *bien*, They are on the best of terms. || **dernièrement** [-ɛr'mɑ̃] *adv.* lately, recently: *tout* ~, only recently.

dérobé, -e [derɔ'be] *adj.* [escalier, porte] secret, hidden: *à la dérobée*, secretly, stealthily, by stealth. || **dérober** #3 *v. tr.* **1.** to steal (from, *à*); to make off with: ~ *de l'argent*, to steal money from s.o.; ~ *à qqun le mérite qui lui est dû*, to steal from s.o. the merit which is his due; ~ *quelques heures à son travail*, to steal a few hours from one's work **2.** [Fig.] to hide, shield: *La brume dérobe le paysage à la vue*, The fog hides the countryside from view; ~ *qqun au danger*, to shield s.o. from danger. || **se dérober** *v. pron.* **1.** to evade, shirk, shun: ~ *à son devoir*, to shirk one's duty; ~ *à la publicité*, to shun the spotlight: *Il se déroba aux compliments*, He got away as they tried to compliment him. **2.** to fail: *Ses jambes se dérobèrent sous lui*, His legs buckled at the knees.

dérouler [deru'le] #3 *v. tr.* **1.** to unroll, unreel. **2.** [Fig.] to unfold, to spread out: ~ *ses plans*, to unfold one's plans. || **se dérouler** *v. pron.* to take place, to unfold: *La cérémonie s'est déroulée dans la cour*, The ceremony took place in the yard.

déroutant, -e [deru't|ɑ̃(:t)] *adj.* baffling, bewildering; disconcerting. || **dérouté, -e** [-e] *adj.* baffled, bewildered. || **déroute** [de'rut] *n.f.* rout: *mettre en* ~, to (put to) rout; *en pleine* ~, in full flight. || **dérouter** [-e] #3 *v. tr.* to deroute (a train, ship, &c.); [Fig.] to baffle, bewilder, disconcert.

derrière [dɛ'rjɛːr] *n.m.* back, rear; [Fam.] [gens] backside; [animaux] rump. || *adv.* behind: *rester ~*, to stay behind; *par ~*, from behind; the back way; secretly. || *prép.* behind: *se cacher ~ la porte,* to hide behind the door; *avoir qqch. ~ la tête,* to have sth. in the back of one's mind.

des [dɛ] [contraction of *de les* cf. DE] *art. déf.* **1.** of: *les fenêtres ~ chambres,* the windows of the bedrooms. **2.** from: *Il vient ~ Etats-Unis,* He comes from the United States. || *art. part. J'ai mangé ~ fruits,* I ate some fruit; *Il vend ~ fruits,* He sells fruit.

dès [dɛ] *prép* **1.** [time] from, since; as/early, soon/as: *~ l'enfance,* from/since/childhood; *~ à présent,* → from now on, henceforth; *~ son retour,* immediately on his return; *~ son arrivée . . .*, as soon as he arrives . . . ; *~ 1953,* as early as 1953. **2.** [place] (right) from; after: *Il a été malade ~ Winnipeg,* He has been sick right from Winnipeg; *~ la porte, il commença à crier,* As soon as he entered the door, he began to shout. **3.** [Loc. adv.] *~ lors,* ever since, consequently. **4.** *conj. ~ que,* as soon as.

désabusé, -e [dezaby'ze] *adj.* undeceived, disillusioned. || **désabuser** #3 *v. tr.* [désenchanter] to disillusion; [ouvrir les yeux] to open s.o.'s eyes.

désaccord [deza'k|ɔːr] *n.m.* **1.** discord, disagreement, disharmony: *être en ~ avec qqun,* to be at variance with s.o., to disagree with s.o. **2.** contradiction: *ses actions sont en ~ avec ses paroles,* his actions contradict his words. || **désaccordé, -e** [-ɔr'de] *adj.* out of tune. || **désaccorder** [-ɔr'de] #3 *v. tr.* [seldom used except in speaking of a musical instrument] to put out of tune.

désagréable [dezagre'abl] *adj.* disagreeable, unpleasant.

désagréger [dezagre'ʒe] #7 *v. tr.* to break up, disintegrate, loosen. || **se désagréger** *v. pron.* to disintegrate.

désagrément [dezagre'mɑ̃] *n.m.* unpleasantness.

désaltérer [dezalte're] #10 *v. tr.* to quench (s.o.'s) thirst.

désappointement [dezapwɛ̃t|'mɑ̃] *n.m.* disappointment. || **désappointer** [-e] #3 *v. tr.* to disappoint.

désapprobat|eur, -rice [dezaprɔba|'tœːr, -'tris] *adj.* [air, murmure, ton] disapproving. || *n.* disapproving person. || **désapprobation** [-'sjɔ̃] *n.f.* disapproval. || **désapprouver** [dezapru've] #3 *v. tr.* to disapprove of, to object to (sth.).

désarçonner [dezarsɔ'ne] #3 *v. tr.* [cavalier] to unhorse, throw; [Fig.] to floor, dumbfound (s.o.), to take the wind out of s.o.'s sail.

désarmant, -e [-ɑ̃(ː t)] *adj.* [Fig.] disarming. || **désarmé, -e** [-e] *adj.* disarmed. || **désarmement** [dezarm|ə'mɑ̃] *n.m.* [action] disarming; [résultat] disarmament. || **désarmer** [-e] #3 *v. tr.* **1.** to disarm (s.o.); to uncock (a gun). **2.** to disarm, appease: *~ la colère de qqun,* to appease s.o.'s anger. || *v. intr.* **1.** to disarm; to disband (one's forces). **2.** [Fig.] (anger) to abate.

désarroi [deza'rwa] *n.m.* confusion, disorder.

désastre [de'zastr] *n.m.* disaster. || **désastreu|x, -se** [-ø(ː z)] *adj.* disastrous.

désavantage [dezavɑ̃'t|aːʒ] *n.m.* disadvantage, drawback. || **désavantager** [-a'ʒe] #5 *v. tr.* to put at a disadvantage.

désaveu [deza'v|ø] *n.m.* disavowal, repudiation; [Jur.] disowning. || **désavouer** [-we] #3 *v. tr.* to disown; to repudiate, disavow.

descellé, -e [desɛ'le] *adj.* unsealed. || **desceller** [desɛ'le] #3 *v. tr.* **1.** to unseal. **2.** to tear out (from masonry).

descendance [desɑ̃'d|ɑːs] *n.f.* descent, lineage; [coll.] descendants. || **descendant, -e** [-ɑ̃(ː t)] *n.* descendant, offspring.

descendre [dɛ'sɑ̃ːdr] #42 *v. intr.* **1.** to go down, to come down. **2.** [de train, de bicyclette] to get off; [d'auto] to get out. **3.** [à un hôtel] to stop (at, *à*). **4.** [origine] to descend (from, *de*). **5.** *faire ~*, to bring down, to send down. || *v. tr.* **1.** [pente, rivière] to go down, to come down, to drop down. **2.** to take down, to bring down, to lower: *Il m'a descendu en ville,* He gave me a lift downtown. || **descente** [dɛ'sɑ̃ːt] *n.f.* **1.** coming down, going down, getting out of or off the plane. **2.** raid: *une ~ de police,* a police raid; *faire une ~ à,* to raid. **3.** *~ de lit,* bedside rug.

descripti|f, -ve [deskrip|'tif, -'tiːv] *adj.* descriptive. || **description** [-'sjɔ̃] *n.f.* description, [action] describing; [de brevet] specification.

désemparé, -e [dezɑ̃pa're] *adj.* **1.** disabled, in distress. **2.** [Fig.] in distress. || **désemparer** #3 *v. tr.* **1.** [un bâtiment ennemi] to put out of action, to disable; [Fig., une personne] to disconcert. **2.** †to leave [seldom used in this sense except in the following expression] *sans ~*, without stopping.

désenchantement [dezɑ̃ʃɑ̃t|'mɑ̃] *n.m.* disenchantment, [état] disillusionment, [action] disillusioning. || **désenchanter** [-e] #3 *v. tr.* to disenchant, disillusion.

déséquilibre [dezeki'libr] *n.m.* lack of balance. || **déséquilibré, -e** [-e] *adj.* unbalanced. || **déséquilibrer** [-e] #3 *v. tr.* to unbalance, to throw s.o. off (his, her) balance.

désert, -e [de'z|ɛːr, -ɛrt] *adj.* deserted; [désolé] lonely, wild. || *n.m.* **1.** desert; [ext.] wilderness. || *n.m.* © clearing (in forest). || **déserté, -e** *adj.* deserted, forsaken. || **déserter** [-ɛr'te] #3 *v. tr.* to desert, to forsake (one's post, the fields, one's home, &c.). || *v. intr.* to desert (from the armed forces). || **déserteur** [-ɛr|'tœːr] *n.m.* deserter. || **désertion** [-'sjõ] *n.f.* desertion (of a party, &c.; from the army, &c.). || **désertique** [-'tik] *adj.* desert-like: *région* ~, desert-like region.

désespérant, -e [dezɛspe'r|ɑ̃(ːt)] *adj.* hopeless; [qui désole] distressing, [plus fort] heart-rending. || **désespéré, -e** [-e] *adj.* disheartened; [plus fort] hopeless, desperate. || **désespérément** [-e'mɑ̃] *adv.* desperately; [en perdant espoir] despairingly. || **désespérer** [-e] #10 *v. intr.* to despair (of, *de*), to give up hope for: *On désespère de le sauver*, His life is despaired of. || *v. tr.* to reduce to despair: *être complètement désespéré* to be reduced to complete despair. || **désespoir** [dezɛs'pwaːr] *n.m.* despair, desperation: *en ~ de cause*, as a last resort; *être au ~*, to be in despair; *mettre au ~*, to drive to despair; *avec l'énergie du ~*, in desperation.

déshabillé, -e [dezabi'je] *adj.* undressed. || *n.m.* **1.** wrapper, dressing gown. **2.** *en ~*, in dishabille, partly dressed. || **déshabiller** #3 *v. tr.* **1.** to undress: *~ (Saint) Pierre pour habiller (Saint) Paul*, to rob Peter to pay Paul. **2.** [Fig.] to expose: *Les poètes déshabillent l'homme*, Poets expose (the weaknesses of man). || **se déshabiller** *v. pron.* to undress (o.s.).

déshabituer [dezabi'tɥe] #3 *v. tr.* to break (s.o.) of (a habit). || **se déshabituer** *v. pron.* to break (o.s.) of (a habit).

déshériter [dezeri'te] #3 *v. tr.* to disinherit.

déshonneur [dezɔ'n|œːr] *n.m.* dishonour, disgrace. || **déshonoré, -e** [-ɔ're] *adj.* dishonoured, disgraced. || **déshonorer** #3 *v. tr.* to dishonour, to disgrace. || **se déshonorer** *v. pron.* to disgrace o.s.

déshydrater [dezidra'te] #3 to dehydrate.

désignation [deziɲ|a'sjõ] *n.f.* **1.** designation, pointing out (of s.o., sth., a place). **2.** description, designation (of goods, &c.). **3.** nomination (for an office). || **désigné, -e** [-e] *adj.* [Pers., heure] designated; represented, nominated: *Il est tout ~ pour cela*, He is just right for it. || **désigner** [-e] #3 *v. tr.* **1.** to designate; [du doigt] to point out; [*à*] to call to the attention of; [mérite, succès, qualité] to mark out for; [marchandise] to describe. **2.** to nominate (s.o. to a post, office); [Mil.] to detail (for a duty).

désillusion [dezily'zj|õ] *n.f.* disillusionment. || **désillusionner** [-ɔ'ne] #3 *v. tr.* to disillusion.

désinfectant [dezɛ̃fɛk|'tɑ̃] *adj. & n.m.* disinfectant. || **désinfecter** [-'te] #3 *v. tr.* to disinfect. || **désinfection** [-'sjõ] *n.f.* disinfecting.

désintéressé, -e [dezɛ̃terɛ's|e] *adj.* **1.** disinterested, impartial. **2.** having no interests at stake, no longer concerned. || **désintéressement** [-mɑ̃] *n.m.* **1.** paying (of creditors, &c.). **2.** [oubli de soi] unselfishness. || **désintéresser** [-e] #3 *v. tr.* to indemnify; [créanciers] to pay off; [associé] to buy out. || **se désintéresser** *v. pron.* **1.** to lose (one's) interest (in, *de*). **2.** to dissociate o.s. (from, *de*); to give up one's interests (in, *de*).

désinvolte [dezɛ̃'vɔlt] *adj.* casual, offhand, free and easy. || **désinvolture** [-yːr] *n.f.* offhandedness, unrestraint, casual manner.

désir [de'z|iːr] *n.m.* wish, desire: *satisfaire aux désirs de qqun*, to satisfy, to gratify s.o.'s desires, wishes. || **désirable** [-i'rabl] *adj.* desirable: *peu ~*, undesirable. || **désirer** [-i're] #3 *v. tr.* to wish, to desire, to want: *Que désirez-vous?*, What would you like?, [vendeuse] May I help you?; *Cela laisse beaucoup à ~*, It leaves much to be desired. || **désireu|x, -se** [-i'rø(ːz)] *adj.* wishing (to, *de*), anxious (to).

désister, se [sə dezis'te] #3 *v. pron.* [de] to withdraw (from).

désobéir [dezɔbe|'iːr] #17 *v. intr.* to disobey (s.o., *à qqun*); to break (a rule, *à un règlement*). || **désobéissance** [-i'sɑ̃ːs] *n.f.* disobedience. || **désobéissant, -e** [-i'sɑ̃(ːt)] *adj.* disobedient.

désobligeant, -e [dezɔbli'ʒ|ɑ̃(ːt)] *adj.* discourteous, uncivil: *Ce serait ~ de refuser*, It would be ungracious to refuse. || **désobliger** [-e] #5 *v. tr.* to offend.

désodorisant [dezɔdɔrizɑ̃'] *n.m.* deodorizer.

désœuvré, -e [dezœ'vre] *adj.* idle, at a loose end. || *n.* a man, lady/of leisure: *les riches désœuvrés*, the idle rich.

désolant, -e [dezɔ'l|ɑ̃(ːt)] *adj.* sad, distressing. || **désolation** [-a'sj*f.* **1.** [õ] *n.*action] desolation, ravaging (of a country, &c.); [état] desolateness. **2.** distress, grief. || **désolé, -e** *adj.* **1.** desolated, devastated (country). **2.** aggrieved; very sorry. || **désoler** [-e] #3 *v. tr.* **1.** to desolate, to devastate (a country); [décimer] to desolate (a city, an army, &c.). **2.** to distress.

désordonné, -e [dezɔrdɔ'ne] *adj.* **1.** disorderly, untidy: *une course désordonnée*, a mad rush. || **désordre** *n.m.* **1.** disorder; untidiness; confusion; *en* ~, [chambre, cheveux, tenue, &c.] untidy, disorderly; [papiers, notes, &c.] in disorder, confusion; *mettre en* ~, to disarrange. **2.** *des désordres*, violence, rioting.

désorganisation [dezɔrganiz|a'sjõ] *n.f.* disorganization. || **désorganiser** [-e] #3 *v. tr.* to disorganize.

désorienté, -e [dezɔrjɑ̃'te] *adj.* bewildered; puzzled; at a loss: *être tout* ~, to be all twisted. || **désorienter** #3 *v. tr.* **1.** to make (s.o.) lose his bearings. **2.** [Fig.] to bewilder (s.o.).

désormais [dezɔr'mɛ] *adv.* from now on, henceforth; hereafter, in the future.

despote [dɛs'pɔt] *n.m.* despot. || **despotique** [-ik] *adj.* despotic.

desquels, desquelles [dɛ'kɛl] *pron. rel. pl.* [used instead of de lesquels and de lesquelles]. cf. LEQUEL [Pers.] of, for/whom; [chose] of, for/which.

dessaler [desa'le] #3 *v. tr.* **1.** to make less salty; to soak the salt out of (meat, fish, &c.). **2.** [Fig.] to put (s.o.) up to snuff.

desséchant, -e [deʃɛ's|ɑ̃(:t)] *adj.* **1.** drying, withering (wind). **2.** [Fig.] narrowing (doctrine, study). || **desséché, -e** [-e] *adj.* [état] dry; [résultat d'une action] dried up. || **dessèchement** ['mɑ̃] *n.m.* **1.** [naturel] drying up, [artificiel] drying. **2.** [Fig.] withering. || **dessécher** [-e] #10 *v. tr.* **1.** to dry, to wither (a plant), to parch (the throat). **2.** to drain (a swamp). **3.** to wither, to emaciate. **4.** to narrow (the mind). || **se dessécher** *v. pron.* to dry up, to become desiccated.

dessein [de'sɛ̃] *n.m.* **1.** design, scheme. **2.** intention: *avoir* ~ *de faire qqch.*, to intend to do sth.; *à* ~, intentionally; © *sans* ~, rather stupid, foolish.

desserrer [desɛ're] #3 *v. tr.* **1.** to loosen (a belt, a knot, a screw, one's hold on sth., &c.). **2.** to spread out (the ranks). || **se desserrer** *v. pron.* [étau, vis] to loosen, to come loose.

dessert [de'sɛ:r] *n.m.* dessert.

desservant [desɛr'v|ɑ̃] *n.m.* [Rel.] officiating priest. || **desservir** [-i:r] #28 *v. tr.* **1.** to clear (the table); [absol.] to clear up. **2.** [Rel.] to officiate (in a parish, &c.); [moyen de transport, &c.] to stop at, to serve.

dessin [de's|ɛ̃] *n.m.* **1.** drawing, sketch: ~ *à main levée*, freehand drawing; ~ *animé*, cartoon; *dessins humoristiques*, comics, funnies. **2.** [contour] design, form, outline. || **dessinat|eur, -rice** [-in|a'tœ:r, -a'tris] **1.** *n.* [publicité] illustrator; drawer. **2.** [industrie] draughtsman; designer. || **dessiné, -e** [-e] *adj.* drawn, designed. || **dessiner** [-e] #3 *v. tr.* **1.** to draw (sth.); [rapidement] to sketch: [Tech.] to draught, to design. **2.** [Fig.] to show the outline of. || **se dessiner** *v. pron.* **1.** to draw o.s. **2.** [montagne, arbre, &c.] to stand out, to be outlined (against, *sur*); to take form (in the darkness, fog, &c.).

dessous[1] [də'su] *adv.* underneath, below: *Cela se met* ~, It goes under it; *au-* ~, *en* ~, underneath, below: *Il habite* ~, He lives below; *par* ~, underneath. || **au-dessous de** *loc. prép.* below: ~ *la moyenne*, below average; ~ *quarante ans*, below forty.

dessous[2] [də'su] *n.m.* **1.** underside: ~ *de plat*, dish stand; *connaître le* ~ *des cartes*, to have inside information. **2.** *avoir le* ~, to be defeated.

dessus [də'sy] *adv.* above; on, upon. || **en** ~, *loc. adv. & prép.* at, on/the top; above. || **de** ~, from off . . . || **en** ~ **de**, on the top of, above. || **par** ~ above, over: ~ *le marché*, into the bargain; ~ *tout*, above all. || *n.m.* top; cover; [Fig.] *prendre le* ~, to get over it; *avoir le* ~, to have the upper hand; [sur qqun] to get the upper hand.

destin [dɛs'tɛ̃] *n.m.* fate, destiny.

destinataire [dɛstin|a'tɛ:r] *n.m/f.* [lettre, message, télégramme] addressee; [cheque, &c.] payee. || **destination** [-a'sjõ] *n.f.* **1.** purpose: *Cette machine n'a pas d'autre* ~, This machine has no other purpose. **2.** destination: *se diriger vers telle* ~, to set out for a certain destination; *arriver à sa* ~, to arrive at o.'s destination; *à* ~ *de* [lettre, colis, &c.] addressed to, [train] → to; [bateau] bound for. || **destiné, -e** [-e] *adj.* **1.** intended (for, *à*), destined (to be, *à être*). || **destinée** [-e] *n.f.* destiny, fate: *accomplir sa* ~, to fulfil one's destiny. || **destiner** [-e] #3 *v. tr.* to intend (for, *à*). || **se destiner** *v. pron.* to plan to enter (a profession): *Il se destine à l'enseignement*, He plans to become a teacher.

destituer [dɛsti't|ɥe] #3 *v. tr.* to dismiss, discharge (from a position, an office).

|| **destitution** [-y'sjõ] *n.f.* dismissal, removal (from office).
destruct|eur, -rice [dɛstryk|'tœ:r, -'tris] *n.* destroyer. || *adj.* destructive. || **destruction** [-'sjõ] *n.f.* destruction.
désu|et, -ète [de'sɥɛ(t)] *adj.* outmoded, out-of-date.
désunion [dezy'n|jõ] *n.f.* discord. || **désunir** [-i:r] #17 *v. tr.* to break up; to separate.
détaché, -e [deta'ʃ|e] *adj.* untied, unfastened; separate; [Fig.] detached: *pièces détachées,* spare parts. || **détachement** [-'mɑ̃] *n.m.* **1.** detachment, unconcern, indifference. **2.** detachment, separation: ~ *volontaire de ses amis,* voluntary detachment, separation from his friends. **3.** [Mil.] detachment. || **détacher** [-e] #3 *v. tr.* **1.** to untie, to unfasten. **2.** to take out or off: ~ *suivant le pointillé,* Tear out along the dotted line. **3.** to detach, to separate (a province from a country, &c.). **4.** [Mil.] to detach. || **se détacher** *v. pron.* **1.** to get loose, untied, to separate, to detach o.s. (from, *de*). **2.** to stand out (against a background, *sur un fond*).
détail [de'taj] *n.m.* **1.** [Com.] retail: *vendre au* ~ , to sell retail; *marchand au* ~ , retail merchant; *prix de* ~ , retail price. **2.** detail, particular: *se perdre dans/le, (les)/détail(s),* not to be able to see the forest for (the) trees; *entrer dans les détails,* to go into details; *tous les détails,* full particulars; *C'est un* ~ , It's a mere detail. || **détaillant, -e** [-ɑ̃(:t)] *n.* retailer. || *adj.* retail (merchant). || **détaillé, -e** [-e] *adj.* detailed, in detail. || **détailler** [-e] #3 *v. tr.* **1.** [vendre] to retail; [couper] to cut up (meat). **2.** [Fig.] to tell in detail, to give the/details, particulars/(of); to enumerate.
détective [detɛk'ti:v] *n.m.* detective: *agence de détectives privés,* private detective agency.
déteindre [de't|ɛ̃:dr], **déteignant** [-ɛ'ɲɑ̃], **déteint** [-ɛ̃] #36 *v. tr.* [artificiel] to bleach; [naturel] to fade (a cloth, &c.). || *v. intr.* to fade: ~ *sur,* to come off on; [Fig.] to influence (s.o.).
détendre [de't|ɑ̃:dr] #42 *v. tr.* **1.** to loosen, to slacken (a string, rope, cord, &c.); to relax (one's muscles); to unbend (one's arm, leg, &c.): [Fig.] ~ *son esprit,* to relieve the strain on one's mind. **2.** to lower the pressure (of a gas). || **se détendre** *v. pron.* **1.** [ressort, arc, corde] to get loose, to slacken; [muscles, traits, membres] to relax. **2.** [Fig., esprit, Pers.] to relax; [rapports, situation] to become less strained. || **détendu, -e** [-ɑ̃'dy] *adj.* **1.** slack, loose (rope, cable, &c.). **2.** [Fig.] relaxed (person, &c.).
détenir [det'ni:r] #22 *v. tr.* to retain (objects in pawn, &c.) to have, possess (a secret, the power, &c.); to hold (a grade, a position, a record, &c.); to detain, hold (a prisoner, &c.).
détente [de'tɑ̃:t] *n.f.* **1.** trigger (of arm): *appuyer sur la* ~ , to press the trigger; [Fig.] *Il est dur à la* ~ , He is close-fisted. **2.** release (of spring), expansion (of gas). **3.** relaxation: *une* ~ , a relaxation of tensions.
détention [detɑ̃'sjõ] *n.f.* [le fait d'avoir] possession; holding; [criminel, &c.] detention, holding. || **détenu, -e** [det'ny] *adj.* detained, imprisoned. || *n.* prisoner.
détergent [detɛr'ʒɑ̃] *n.m.* detergent.
détérioration [deterjɔr|a'sjõ] *n.f.* [dommage] damage; [de qualité] deterioration. || **détériorer** [-e] #3 *v. tr.* [endommager] to damage (sth.); [le temps] to get worse; to impair (one's health, &c.). || **se détériorer** *v. pron.* to deteriorate.
déterminant, -e [determi'n|ɑ̃(:t)] *adj.* determining. || *n.m.* [Math.] determinant. || **détermination** [-a'sjõ] *n.f.* **1.** determination; [Math.] calculation. **2.** determination, decision: *faire preuve de* ~ , to show determination. || **déterminé, -e** [-e] *adj.* **1.** certain, particular (point, place, time, meaning, &c.). **2.** determined, resolute. || **déterminer** [-e] #3 *v. tr.* **1.** to determine. **2.** to cause: *événements qui peuvent* ~ *une guerre,* events which may cause a war. || **se déterminer** *v. pron.* [Pers.] to decide, to make up one's mind; [une distance, un temps] to be determined.
déterrer [dete're] #3 *v. tr.* to dig up, unearth.
détestable [detɛs't|abl] *adj.* detestable, thoroughly disagreeable. || **déteste, -e** [-e] *adj.* detested; hated. || **détester** [-e] #3 *v. tr.* to detest, hate.
détonateur [detɔn|a'tœ:r] *n.m.* [d'un explosif] detonator. || **détonation** [-a'sjõ] *n.f.* **1.** [bruit] detonation, explosion; [Fam.] bang; [d'arme à feu] report. **2.** [Fig.] loud noise. || **détoner** [-e] #3 *v. intr.* [bombe, dynamite, &c.] to explode: *faire* ~ *qqch.,* to detonate, explode; [Fam.] to set off sth.
détour [de't|u:r] *n.m.* **1.** turn, bend; *pl.* windings (of a river, road, &c.): *au* ~ *du chemin,* → where the road/turns, bends/; *les tours et les détours de qqch.,* the twistings and windings, ins and outs of sth. **2.** detour, roundabout way: *faire un long* ~ ,

to make a long detour, → to go (by) a roundabout way. **3.** [Fig.] roundabout way (of doing, saying sth.): *plein de ~*, devious; *pas tant de détours, aux faits!*, → Don't be so devious, get to the facts!; *sans détour(s)*, plain(ly), frank(ly). || **détourné, -e** [-ur'n|e] *adj.* **1.** [chemin, &c.] roundabout, indirect. **2.** [Fig.] [moyen] devious; [reproche, allusion] indirect. || **détournement** [-ə'mɑ̃] *n.m.* **1.** diversion (of a river). **2.** [Jur.] embezzlement, misappropriation (of funds); abduction (of a minor). || **détourner** [-e] #3 *v. tr.* **1.** to divert (a river, a convoy, &c.); to deflect (a blow); to lead (s.o.) out of one's way. **2.** [Fig.] to change (a conversation); to turn (a question) aside; to divert (s.o.'s attention, anger, suspicions, &c.); to twist (the meaning of sth.). **2.** to turn (s.o.) aside (from an occupation, a work, a goal, &c.). **3.** to arrest, turn away (the eyes, head, face). **4.** [Jur.] to embezzle, misappropriate (funds); to abduct (a minor). || **se détourner** *v. pron.* to turn away (from, *de*).

détract|eur, -rice [detrak't|œ:r, -ris] *n.* detractor, sharp critic. || *adj.* sharply critical.

détraqué, -e [detra'ke] *adj.* **1.** [machine] out of order. **2.** [Fig.] [temps] unsettled; [Fam.] upset (health, nerves), unbalanced (mind). || *n.* unbalanced person. || **détraquer** #3 *v. tr.* to put (a machine) out of order; to upset (the stomach, nerves); [Fig. & Fam.] to derange (one's mind). || **se détraquer** *v. pron.* [machine, &c.] to break down; [estomac, nerfs, &c.] to become upset; [montre] to get out of order.

détrempé, -e [detrɑ̃'pe] *adj.* sodden. || **détremper** #3 *v. tr.* **1.** to mix (colours, mortar, &c.) (with water); to soak (the ground, a road, &c.): *Les chemins sont détrempés*, The roads are sodden, have turned to mud. **2.** to soften (steel); [Fig.] to soften (one's character).

détresse [de'trɛs] *n.f.* distress.

détriment [detri'mɑ̃] *n.m.* detriment, disadvantage.

détritus [detri'tys] *n.m.* refuse, rubbish.

détroit [de'trwa] *n.m.* strait: *le Détroit de Belle-Isle*, the Strait of Belle Isle.

détromper [detrõ'pe] #3 *v. tr.* to set (s.o.) straight, right; to undeceive. || **se détromper** *v. pron.* to set o.s. straight; [Fam.] to get wise.

détrôner [detro'ne] #3 *v. tr.* to depose, to dethrone.

détruire [de'trɥ|i:r] #56 *v. tr.* to destroy, ruin. || **se détruire** *v. pron.* [chose] to go to ruin; [personne] to destroy o.s.; [réciproquement] to destroy each other, one another. || **détruit, -e** [-i(t)] *adj.* ruined, destroyed.

dette [dɛt] *n.f.* debt: *faire des dettes*, to run into debt.

deuil [dœ:j] *n.m.* **1.** bereavement, loss. **2.** [action] mourning: *être en ~ de qqun*, to be in mourning for s.o.; [Fam.] *faire son ~ de qqch.*, to resign o.s. to the loss of sth.

deux [dø] *adj.* **1.** [cardinal number, invariable] two; [précédé de "les"] both: *avoir ~ yeux*, to have two eyes, [mais] *les ~ yeux*, both eyes; [aussi] *tous (les) ~*, both; *à ~*, together; *Mettez-vous à ~ pour le faire*, → Do it together; *L'amour et l'amitié, cela fait ~*, Love and friendship are two very different things. **2.** [ordinal number] second: *tome ~*, volume two, → second volume; *Richard ~*, Richard the Second; *tous les ~ du mois*, every second of the month, [mais] *tous les ~ mois*, every second month. || *n.m.* **1.** two: *~ et ~ font quatre*, two and two/are, make/four; *Compter de ~ en ~/pur ~/*, to count by twos; *(Aujourd'hui) Nous sommes le ~*, It is the second (today); [Fam.] *en moins de ~*, in two /shakes, seconds/. **2.** [le chiffre] two: *le ~ arabe*, the Arabic two. || **deuxième** [-'zjɛm] *adj.* **1.** [ordinal number] second: *Habiter au ~ (étage)*, To live on the © second, [Fr.] third floor; *voyager en ~ (classe)*, to travel second class. || *n.* second. || **deuxièmement** [-zjɛm'mɑ̃] *adv.* secondly. || **deux points** [dø'pwɛ̃] *n.m. inv.* colon.

dévaler [deva'le] #3 *v. intr.* **1.** [inches, &c.] roll/ slide, tumble, &c./down. **2.** [terrain en pente] to fall away.

dévaliser [devali'ze] #3 *v. tr.* to rob (s.o.); to burglarize (a house).

dévalorisation [devalɔriza'sjõ] *n.f.* devaluation, depreciation, fall in value.

devancer [dəvɑ̃'se] #4 *v. tr.* **1.** to get ahead of (s.o.), to outstrip, to steal a march on. **2.** to do sth. before the appointed time: *~ l'appel*, to enlist before one is called; *~ une objection*, to forestall an objection; *~ un désir*, to anticipate a wish.

devant [də'vɑ̃] *prép.* in front of, before; in the eyes of (the law, God); in the face of (danger): *aller droit ~ soi*, (to go) straight ahead; *laisser qqun passer ~ soi*, to let s.o. go before one (in space and time); [Fig.] *avoir du temps ~ soi*, to have some free time. || *n.m.* front (part); [peinture] foreground: *prendre les devants*, to get there first. || au-devant [od'vɑ̃] *adv.* in front, ahead: *Prendre des places* ~ , To take seats in front. || **au-devant de** [od'vɑ̃ də] *loc. prép.* to meet: *aller* ~ *ses amis,* to go to meet one's friends; *aller* ~ *des désirs, des souhaits de qqun,* to anticipate s.o.'s desires, wishes. || **de devant** [dəd'vɑ̃] *loc. prép.* from in front of: *Ôtez-vous* ~ *la voiture,* Get out from in front of the car. || **par-devant** [pardə'vɑ̃] *loc. prép.* [action] in front of, in the presence of (a notary, judge, &c.). || *adv.* in front, ahead: *Prendre des places* ~ , To take seats in front.

devanture [d(ə)vɑ̃'ty:r] *n.f.* front (of store), store window.

dévasté, -e [devas'te] *adj.* devastated; [Fig.] ruined. || **dévaster** #3 *v. tr.* to devastate; [Fig.] to ruin.

déveine [de'vɛn] *n.f.* (run of) bad luck: *être/dans la, en/*~ , to be having (a run of) bad luck; *avoir la* ~ , to be unlucky.

développement [devlɔp|'mɑ̃] *n.m.* development; growth; unfolding. || **développer [-e]** #3 *v. tr.* **1.** to develop: ~ *une pellicule,* to develop a film. **2.** to expand, develop, make stronger: ~ *un sujet,* to develop, to work out a topic. **3.** to unwrap, unfold, spread out. || **se développer** *v. pron.* to develop, expand, grow, unfold.

devenir [dəv'ni:r], **devenu** [də'vny] #22 *v. intr.* **1.** to become, grow, get, turn: *Il devint plus irritable,* He grew more irritable; *C'est à* ~ *fou,* It's enough to drive you crazy. **2.** to become, happen: *Qu'est-il devenu?,* What's become of him?; *Que devenez-vous?,* What are you doing?; *Il ne sait que* ~ , He does not know what to do. || *n.m.* growth, development: *être en perpétuel* ~ , to be in a state of flux.

dévergondage [devɛrgõ'da:ʒ] *n.m.* dissoluteness, licentiousness, shamelessness.

déverser [devɛr'se] #3 *v. tr.* to pour; to dump. *v. intr.* to lean, slope. || **se déverser** *v. pron.* to pour out, to spill out.

dévêtir [devɛ'ti:r] #42 *v. tr.* to undress (a child, a sick person, a wounded person). || **se dévêtir** *v. pron.* to undress o.s.

déviation [devja'sjõ] *n.f.* **1.** deviation, deflection (from). **2.** [road] detour.

dévider [devi|'de] #3 *v. tr.* [du fil, &c.] to unwind (from the spindle, a skein, a ball, a roll, &c.); [Fig.] [flot de paroles, &c.] to reel off; [son chapelet] to tell. || **dévidoir** [-'dwa:r] *n.m.* [de jardinier, de pompier, &c.] reel; winder; [cabestan] cable drum.

dévier [de'vje] #3 *v. intr.* [de] to deviate (from), to swerve, to go off course: *faire* ~ , to make (sth., s.o.) deviate, swerve, go off course; [Fig.] *Il ne dévie jamais de ses principes,* He never deviates, swerves from his principles. || *v. tr.* to deflect; [la colonne vertébrale] to deform. || **se dévier** *v. pron.* to grow crooked; [bois] to warp.

devin, -eresse [dəv|ɛ̃, -in'rɛs] *n.* soothsayer, fortune-teller: [Fig. & Fam.] *Je ne suis pas* ~ *!,* I'm no fortune-teller! || **deviner** [-i'ne] #3 *v. tr.* **1.** to divine, to read the future. **2.** [arriver à connaître] to guess; [soupçonner] to suspect; to figure out (s.o.): *Vous devinez le reste,* You can guess the rest; *Je vous le laisse à* ~ , I'll leave you to figure it out. || **devinette** [-i'nɛt] *n.f.* riddle, puzzle: *poser, proposer/une* ~ , to ask a riddle; *jouer aux devinettes,* to play at guessing games.

devis [də'vi] *n.m.* estimate.

dévisager [deviza'ʒe] #5 *v. tr.* **1.** to disfigure (s.o.); to scratch, claw (s.o.'s) face. **2.** to stare (s.o.) in the face; to stare at.

devise [də'vi:z] *n.f.* device, motto; [publicité] slogan.

deviser [dəvi'ze] #3 *v. intr.* to chat.

dévisser [devi'se] #3 *v. tr.* to unscrew.

dévoilement [devwal|'mɑ̃] *n.m.* © unveiling (of a statue). || **dévoiler** [-e] #3 *v. tr.* **1.** to reveal, to disclose (a secret). **2.** © to unveil (a statue). || **se dévoiler** [sə devwa'l|e] *v. pron.* to reveal, disclose itself.

devoir [də'vwa:r] *n.m.* **1.** duty, obligation; *pl.* respects: *s'acquitter d'un* ~ , to discharge a duty; *se mettre en* ~ *de,* to get about; *Je crois de mon* ~ *de le prévenir,* I feel I should tell him. **2.** [Scol.] homework, written assignment. || **devoir** [də'vwa:r], **devant** [də'vɑ̃], **dû** [dy] #34 *v. tr.* **1.** to owe: ~ *de l'argent,* to owe money. **2.** [followed by inf.] (a) to be supposed to: *Je dois partir demain,* I am (supposed) to go tomorrow. (b) must: *Il devra le faire,* He will have to do it, He must do it; *Il a dû partir,* He had to go, He must have gone. (c) ought to, should: *Il devrait le faire,* He ought to do it, He should do it.

dévolu, -e [devɔ'ly] *adj.* [Jur.] devolving (upon). || *n.m.* claim: *jeter son* ~ *sur* (un bénéfice), to lay claim to (a benefice); [Fig.] (sur qqun) to have designs (on s.o.).

dévorant [devɔ'r|ɑ̃(:t)] *adj.* consuming (thirst, fire, fever, passion, &c.). || **dévorer** [-e] #3 *v. tr.* **1.** to eat up, to devour, to swallow. **2.** [Fig.] to devour: ~ *qqun des yeux,* to gaze intently at s.o.

dévot, -e [de'v|o, -ɔt] *adj. & n.* pious, bigoted; sanctimonious, cf. DEVOUT. || **dévotion** [-ɔ'sjõ] *n.f.* devotion, devoutness: *être à la*

~ *de qqun*, to be completely devoted to s.o.; *faire ses dévotions*, to pray.

dévoué, -e [devwe] *adj.* devoted, loyal, faithful: *Votre tout* ~, Yours very truly. || **dévouement** [-|u'mɑ̃] *n.m.* [à] devotion to (s.o., sth.); self-sacrifice of (s.o.). || **dévouer** [-we] #3 *v. tr.* to dedicate, consecrate. || **se dévouer** *v. pron.* to devote o.s. (to, *à*), to dedicate o.s.

dévoyer [devwa'je] #12 *v. tr.* [Fig.] to lead astray. || **se dévoyer** *v. pron.* to stray (from the strait and narrow way).

dextérité [dɛksteri'te] *n.f.* **1.** [mains, &c.] dexterity, agility. **2.** [Fig.] skill: *avec* ~, skilfully, deftly.

diabète [dja'b|ɛt] *n.m.* diabetes. || **diabétique** [-e'tik] *adj. & n.* diabetic.

diable [djɑ:bl] *n.m.* **1.** devil, demon. **2.** devilish person, scoundrel; *petit* ~, scamp, imp. **3.** *un grand* ~, a strapping fellow. **4.** [jouet] Jack-in-the-box; [chariot] porter's dolly. **5.** [Loc.] *envoyer qqun au* ~, to send s.o. to blazes; *Comment* ~ *a-t-il pu croire cela!*, How the devil could he think that!; *faire le* ~ *à quatre*, to carry on, to be boisterous; *faire un bruit de tous les diables*, to make the devil of a row; *tirer le* ~ *par la queue*, to be hard up. || **diablement** [djɑbl|ə'mɑ̃] *adv.* devilishly, [plus souvent] terribly, extremely. || **diablerie** [-ə'ri] *n.f.* deviltry; mischievousness, mischief. || **diablotin** [-ɔ'tɛ̃] *n.m.* (little) imp, scamp; [plus fort, moins poli] little devil. || **diabolique** [djabɔ'lik] *adj.* diabolical, fiendish; devilish.

diacre [djakr] *n.m.* deacon.

diagnostic [djagnɔs'tik] *n.m* diagnosis. || **diagnostiquer** [-c] #3 *v. tr.* to diagnose.

diagonal, -e [djagɔ'nal] *adj. & n(f).* diagonal.

diagramme [dja'gram] *n.m.* diagram.

dialecte [dja'lɛkt] *n.m.* dialect. || **dialectique** [djalɛk'tik] *adj.* dialectic. || *n.f.* dialectics.

dialogue [dja'lɔg] *n.m.* conversation (between two people); [Théâtre] dialogue. || **dialoguer** [-e] #3 *v. intr.* to converse, talk. || *v. tr.* [un roman, &c.] [pour la scène] to put in dialogue form.

diamant [dja'mɑ̃] *n.m.* diamond; diamond ring. || **diamantaire** [-'tɛ:r] *adj.* diamond-like. || *n.m.* diamond-cutter, cf. LAPIDAIRE, JOAILLIER.

diamétralement [djametra|'mɑ̃] *adv.* diametrically: ~ *opposé*, diametrically opposed.

diamètre [dja'mɛ:tr] *n.m.* diameter.

Diane [djan] *n.f.* = Diana, Diane.

diantre! [djɑ̃:tr] *interj.* the deuce!

diapason [djapa'zɔ̃] *n.m.* **1.** [registre] range. **2.** [instrument] tuning fork; diapason: [Fig.] *être au* ~, to be in tune.

diaphane [dja'fan] *adj.* transparent.

diaphragme [dja'fragm] *n.m.* diaphragm.

diapositive [djapozi'ti:v] *n.f.* slide.

diapré, -e [dja'pre] *adj.* mottled.

diarrhée [dja're] *n.f.* diarrhœa.

diatribe [dja'trib] *n.f.* sharp criticism, diatribe.

dichotomie [dikɔtɔ'mi] *n.f.* dichotomy.

dictateur [dikta't|:œr] *n.m.* dictator. || **dictature** [-y:r] *n.f.* dictatorship.

dictée [dik'te] *n.f.* **1.** [action] dictation: *écrire sous la* ~ *de qqun*, to write sth. from dictation (from s.o.); [Fig.] *la* ~ *de la raison*, the dictates of reason. **2.** [école] dictation. || **dicter** #3 *v. tr.* **1.** to dictate (a letter, &c.). **2.** to dictate, to prescribe.

diction [dik'sjɔ̃] *n.f.* diction, style.

dictionnaire [diksjɔ'nɛ:r] *n.m.* dictionary; [Géog.] gazetteer; *C'est un/vrai* ~, ~ *vivant/*, He's a walking dictionary; *faire (une traduction, &c.) à coup de* ~, to do (a translation, &c.) by constantly referring to the dictionary.

dicton [dik'tɔ̃] *n.m.* saying.

didactique [didak'tik] *adj.* didactic. || *n.f.* didactics.

dièse [djɛ:z] *n.m.* [Mus.] sharp.

diesel [dje'zɛl] *n.m.* diesel.

diète[1] [djɛt] *n.f.* [Méd.] diet, regimen; [complète] fast: *se mettre à la* ~, to go on a/low, restricted/diet; to eat nothing; to fast; ~ *lactée*, milk diet.

diète[2] [djɛt] *n.f.* diet, assembly.

diététicien, -ne [dieteti'si|ɛ̃, ɛn] *n.* dietician.

Dieu [djø] *n.m.* God [traditionally less casually used in English than in French]: *Mon* ~, well; *pour l'amour de* ~, for goodness' sake; *le bon* ~, the Good Lord; *A* ~ *ne plaise*, The Lord forbid; *Dieu sait ce que . . .*, Heaven only knows.

diffamation [difama'sjɔ̃] *n.f.* defamation, slander.

diffamer [difa'me] #3 *v. tr.* to defame; [oralement] to slander, [par écrit] to libel.

différemment [difera'mɑ̃] *adv.* differently.

différence [dife'r|ɑ̃:s] *n.f.* difference, [plus recherché] disparity; [écart] discrepancy. || **différencier** [-ɑ̃'sje] #3 *v. tr.* to differentiate, to distinguish [*de*, from sth., s.o.; between two things]: *On ne peut pas les* ~, It is impossible to/differentiate, distinguish/between them; to tell them apart. || **se différencier** *v. pron.* to be distinguishable (from), to differentiate/o.s., themselves/ (from).

différend [dife'rɑ̃] *n.m.* difference, disagreement, dispute: *régler un* ~, to adjust, settle/a/difference, disagreement, dispute/; *avoir un* ~ *avec*, to be at variance with.

différent, **-e** [dife'r|ɑ̃(:t)] *adj.* **1.** different, unlike. **2.** different, several, various: *de différentes sortes*, of various kinds. || **différentiel, -le** [-ɑ̃'sjɛl] *adj.* [Math.] differential (calculus, equation, &c.); [Méc]. differential (gear(s), &c.); [Com.] discriminatory, discriminating (tariff, duty). || *n.f.* [Math.] differential. || *n.m.* differential.

différer [dife're] #10 *v. tr.* to defer, [plus courant] to postpone, to put off. || *v. intr.* to differ.

difficile [difi|'sil] *adj.* **1.** difficult, hard; [délicat] difficult, awkward (situation, position, &c.). **2.** [Pers.] difficult, hard to please, exacting; fastidious; [cheval] stubborn, hard (to handle). **3.** [chemin, terrain] rugged. || *n.m.* difficulty,/difficult, hard/part: *Le* ~, *c'est que . . .*, The difficulty, The difficult, hard part/ is that . . . || **difficilement** [-sil'mɑ̃] *adv.* with difficulty. || **difficulté** [-kyl'te] *n.f.* **1.** difficulty: *se heurter à une* ~, to run up against a difficulty; *surmonter une* ~, to overcome a difficulty. **2.** objection: *faire des difficultés*, to raise objections. **3.** difficulty, trouble: *être en* ~ *avec qqun*, to be at odds with s.o.

difforme [di'fɔrm] *adj.* deformed, misshapen. || **difformité** [-i'te] *n.f.* deformity.

diffraction [difrak'sjõ] *n.f.* diffraction.

diffus, -e [di'f|y(:z)] *adj.* **1.** diffused (light, rays, &c.). **2.** [Fig.] diffuse, [Fam.] long-winded (style, speaker, writer).

diffuser [-y'ze] #3 *v. tr.* **1.** to diffuse, to spread. **2.** [TSF] to broadcast, cf. RADIODIFFUSER. **3.** [Fig.] to broadcast, to spread (news, ideas, &c.); [des livres, &c.] to distribute, to send out, to disseminate. || **diffusion** [-y'zjõ] *n.f.* **1.** diffusion (of light, rays, &c.), spreading of, propagation of (knowledge, ideas, a language). **2.** [TSF] broadcasting, transmission; [ext.] coverage.

digérer [diʒ|e're] #10 *v. tr.* **1.** to digest: *Il digère mal*, → He has a poor digestion. **2.** [Fig.] to digest, [Fam.] to mull over (a thought, a new idea, &c.); [Fam.] to swallow, to be able to stomach (an insult, an affront): *C'est dur à* ~, It's hard to swallow. || **digestible** [-ɛs'tibl] *adj.* digestible. || **digesti|f, -ve** [-ɛs|'tif, -ti:v] *n.m.* & *adj.* digestive. || **digestion** [-'tjõ] *n.f.* digestion.

digital, -e [diʒi'tal] *adj.* → finger: *empreintes digitales*, fingerprints.

digne [diɲ] *adj.* [de] deserving, [plus souvent] worthy; [avant le nom] worthy, honourable; [après le nom] dignified: *un* ~ *homme*, a worthy man, [mais] *un homme* ~, a dignified man; ~ *de foi*, trustworthy, credible; *être* ~ *de*, to deserve to be, to be worthy of; *Ce n'est pas* ~ *de lui*, It's not like him.

dignitaire [-i't|ɛ:r] *n.m.* dignitary, office-holder. || **dignité** [-e] *n.f.* **1.** title, rank, †dignity. **2.** dignity, pride: *ne pas croire de sa* ~ *de faire qqch.*, to believe it to be beneath one's dignity to do sth.

digression [digrɛ'sjõ] *n.f.* digression.

digue [dig] *n.f.* [le long d'une rivière, &c.] dike; [en mer] sea wall, [brise-lames] breakwater; [Fig.] barrier, obstacle.

dilapider [dilapi'de] #3 *v. tr.* to squander, waste.

dilatation [dilat|a'sjõ] *n.f.* expansion (of a tire, balloon, &c.); [Méd.] expansion, dilation (of the heart, veins, &c.); [Phys.] dilation. || **dilater** [-e] #3 *v. tr.* **1.** [Phys.] to expand (sth. by heat); [Méd.] to dilate, [le cœur] to enlarge. **2.** [Fig.] to swell. || **se dilater** *v. pron.* to dilate, to expand.

dilemme [di'lɛm] *n.m.* dilemma, quandary: *être devant un* ~, to be in a/dilemma, quandary/.

dilettante [dilɛ'tɑ̃:t] *n. m/f.* dilettante.

diligence [dili'ʒ|ɑ̃:s] *n.f.* **1.** application; haste, speed: *faire* ~, to hurry; *en toute* ~, in a hurry; *faire preuve de* ~, to be speedy. **2.** stage coach, diligence. || **diligent, -e** [-ɑ̃(:t)] *adj.* diligent, prompt, speedy, quick.

diluer [di'l|ɥe] #3 *v. tr.* to dilute [*dans*, with], to water down. || **dilution** [-y'sjõ] *n.f.* diluting, watering down.

diluvien, -ne [dily'vj|ɛ̃, -ɛn] *adj.* [Géol.] diluvial (deposits, rocks, &c.); torrential (rain(s), &c.).

dimanche [di'mɑ̃:ʃ] *n.m.* Sunday: *le* ~ *de Pâques*, Easter Sunday; ~ *des Rameaux*, Palm Sunday; *un chauffeur du* ~, Sunday driver.

dîme [dim] *n.f.* tithe, tithing.

dimension [dimɑ̃'sjõ] *n.f.* dimension: *De quelles dimensions?*, Of what size?; *une nouvelle* ~, a new dimension.

diminué, -e [dimi'n|ɥe] *adj.* [Arch.] tapered (column); [Mus.] diminished (note); reduced (in size, activity); [santé] weakened, incapacitated. || **diminuer** #3 *v. tr.* to cut down, decrease, diminish; [longueur] to shorten; [la colère, &c.]

to lessen; to lower (prices); to lessen (a disadvantage). || **diminuti|f, -ve** [-y|'tif, -'ti:v] *adj. & n.m.* diminutive. || **diminution** [-'sjõ] *n.f.* decrease, reduction, lowering, lessening.

dinde [dɛ̃:d] *n.f.* **1.** turkey (-hen). **2.** [Fig.] goose, foolish woman. || **dindon** [dɛ̃'dõ] *n.m.* male turkey: *être le* ~ *de la farce*, to be the dupe, [Fam.] sucker.

dîner [di'n|e] *n.m.* dinner; dinner party. || #3 *v. intr.* **1.** to dine, to have dinner, © to have supper: ~ *en ville*, to eat out. **2.** [in rural France & Canada] to have midday dinner, to have lunch. © *salle à* ~, dining-room; restaurant. || **dîneu|r, -se** [-œ:r, -ø:z] *n.* diner.

dingo [dɛ̃'go] *adj.* **1.** dingo [Australian wild dog]. **2.** [Fig.] *être* ~, to be wacky, crazy.

dinosaure [dinɔ'zo:r] *n.m.* dinosaur.

diocèse [djɔ'sɛ:z] *n.m.* diocese.

diphtérie [difte'ri] *n.f.* diphtheria.

diphtongue [dif'tõ:g] *n.f.* diphthong.

diplomate [diplɔ'ma|t] *n.m.* **1.** diplomat. **2.** [Fig.] diplomat, tactful person: *Il est très* ~, He is very diplomatic. || **diplomatie** [-'si] *n.f.* **1.** diplomacy; [Fig.] diplomacy, tact. **2.** diplomatic service: *entrer dans la* ~, to enter the diplomatic service. || **diplomatique** [-'tik] *adj.* diplomatic; [Fig.] diplomatic, tactful.

diplôme [di'pl|o:m] *n.m.* **1.** charter, official document. **2.** diploma, certificate: *conférer, décerner/un* ~, to confer, to award/a diploma, certificate/; ~ *de bachelier, de maître ès arts*, bachelor's, master's degree. || **diplômé, -e** [-o'me] *adj.* certified, with a diploma. || *n.* graduate.

dire [di:r] #45 *v. tr.* to say, to tell, to speak: *Il me l'a dit*, He told me; *Qu'a-t-il dit?*, What did he say?; *à l'heure dite*, at the appointed time; *aussitôt dit, aussitôt fait*, no sooner said than done; *autrement dit*, in other words; *à vrai* ~, to tell the truth, strictly speaking; *c'est-à-* ~, that is to say; *C'est beaucoup* ~, That's going rather far; *C'est pas peu* ~, That's saying a lot; *Cela va sans* ~, It goes without saying; *comme on dit*, as the saying goes; *A qui le dites-vous?*, You're telling me!; *Dire que . . .*, To think that . . . ; *Dites-lui bien des choses de ma part*, Give him my regards, Say "hello" for me; *Dites donc!*, Hey!, Say!, I say!; *Il ne se l'est pas fait* ~ *deux fois*, He did not have to be told twice; *Il n'y a pas à* ~, Make no mistake about it; *Qui ne dit mot consent*, Silence means consent; *Tenez-vous-le pour dit*, You've been warned; *Tout n'est pas dit*, The last word is not said. || **se dire** *v. pron.* to say to o.s.; to say, tell/each other; to call o.s., to claim to be/(a friend, a painter, &c.); [mot, expression, &c.] to be/said, used/.

direct, -e [di'rɛkt] *adj.* **1.** direct, straight. **2.** [train] through. || **directement** [-ə'mɑ̃] *adv.* directly.

directeur [dirɛk|'tœ:r] *n.m.* director, manager, head: ~ *d'un journal*, editor; ~ *de ministère*, deputy minister, head of a branch; ~ *du personnel*, personnel manager; ~ *d'une prison*, [U.S.] warden, [Br.] governor; ~ *d'un théâtre*, manager; ~ *spirituel*, confessor. || *adj.* guiding, steering, directing. || **direction** [-'sjõ] *n.f.* **1.** direction, management. **2.** direction, way: *changer de* ~, to change directions; *la mauvaise* ~, the wrong way; © DIRECTION, ONE WAY. **3.** [Auto.] steering; [avion] *gouvernail de* ~, rudder.

dirigé, -e [diri'ʒe] *adj.* directed, managed.

dirigeable [diri'ʒ|abl] *adj.* steerable. || *n.m.* dirigible, airship. || **dirigeant, -e** [-ɑ̃(:t)] *adj.* ruling, governing, [plus général] leading (class, &c.). || *n.* leader. || **diriger** [-e] #5 *v. tr.* **1.** to direct, [gérer] to manage; [artillerie] to direct (fire); to drive, lead (a horse); to steer (a car, ship); [orchestre] to conduct: ~ *sur*, [colis, qqun] to send to; [Fig., les yeux, l'attention] to turn (one's eyes, attention) on. || **se diriger** *v. pron.* to head/for, towards/, to go towards.

dis, disais, disant, dise, cf. DIRE.

discernement [disɛrn|ə'mɑ̃] *n.m.* **1.** [action] discerning, distinguishing. **2.** discernment, discrimination, judgment. || **discerner** [-e] #3 *v. tr.* to distinguish, to discern, to perceive, [plus courant] to make out: ~ *le vrai du faux*, to distinguish truth from fiction.

disciple [di'sipl] *n.m.* disciple, follower.

disciplinaire [disipli'nɛ:r] *adj.* disciplinary. || *n.m.* disciplinarian.

discipline [disi'plin] *n.f.* **1.** discipline, branch (of learning, &c.). **2.** discipline, order. **3.** whip. || **discipliné, -e** [-e] *adj.* disciplined. || **discipliner** [-e] #3 *v. tr.* to discipline (a class; [Fig.] one's mind, instincts, &c.); to master (the forces of nature, &c.).

discontinuer [diskõti'nɥe] #3 *v. tr.* to discontinue: *sans* ~, without a break.

discordant, -e [diskɔr'dɑ̃(:t)] *adj.* [voix, sons, &c.] discordant; [opinions, &c.] conflicting; [couleurs] clashing. || **discorde** [dis'kɔrd] *n.f.* discord: [Fig.] *une pomme de* ~, a bone of contention.

discourir [disku'ri:r] #24 *v. tr.* to hold forth. || **discours** [dis'ku:r] *n.m.* **1.** speech: *faire, prononcer un* ~, to deliver a speech; *le* ~ *du Trône*, the speech from the throne. **2.** discourse, treatise. **3.** [Ling.] speech: *les parties du* ~, the parts of speech; *le* ~ *direct*, direct speech.

discourtois, -e [diskur'twa(:z)] *adj.* discourteous; unmannerly.

discrédit [diskre'di] *n.m.* discredit. || **discréditer** [-'te] #3 *v. tr.* to discredit. || **se discréditer** *v. pron.* to discredit o.s.

discr|et, -ète [dis'kr|ɛ(t)] *adj.* **1.** discreet, unobtrusive. **2.** [Math.] discrete. || **discrètement** [-ɛt'mɑ̃] *adv.* discreetly; quietly. || **discrétion** [-e'sjɔ̃] *n.f.* **1.** discretion: *à la* ~ *de*, at the discretion of; *à* ~, unlimited; *se rendre à* ~, to surrender unconditionally. **2.** discretion, unobtrusiveness: *avec tact et* ~, tactfully and discreetly.

discriminer [diskrimi'ne] #3 *v. tr.* to discriminate.

disculper [diskyl'pe] #3 *v. tr.* to exonerate, clear. || **se disculper** *v. pron.* to clear o.s.

discussion [disky|'sjɔ̃] *n.f.* discussion, [plus formel] debate, [vive et orageuse] argument. || **discutable** [-'tabl] *adj.* questionable, doubtful. || **discuté, -e** [-'te] *adj.* discussed, debated, talked over: *Il est très* ~, He is often criticized. || **discuter** [-'te] #3 *v. tr. & intr.* to discuss, [plus formel] to debate; [vif et orageux] to argue; [Fam. et amical] talk over: ~ *un débiteur*, to inquire into the assets of a debtor.

disert, -e [di'z|ɛ:r, -ɛrt] *adj.* fluent, articulate.

disette [di'zɛt] *n.f.* scarcity, lack, want, †dearth.

diseu|r, -se [di'z|œ:r, -ø:z] *n.m.* teller: [seldom used except in certain expressions]: *diseuse de bonne aventure*, fortune-teller; *un grand* ~, a good talker. cf. DIRE.

disgrâce [diz'gr|ɑ:s] *n.f.* **1.** disgrace, disfavour: *s'attirer, être dans/la* ~ *de qqun*, to draw, to be in/s.o.'s disfavour. **2.** [Fig., revers] misfortune, difficulty, †adversity: *pour comble de* ~, to top off/his, her, their/misfortune, to make things worse. || **disgracié, -e** [-a'sj|e] *adj.* **1.** out of favour, disgraced. **2.** [Fig.] [de, par/la nature] deformed, ugly; [de la fortune] unfortunate. || **disgracier** [-e] #3 *v. tr.* to disgrace. || **disgracieu|x, -se** [-ø(:z)] *adj.* [geste] ungraceful, awkward; [ornement, &c.] ugly; [visage] ugly, disfigured; [corps] deformed, awkward.

disjoindre [diz'ʒw|ɛ̃:dr], **disjoignant** [-a'ɲɑ̃], **disjoint** [-ɛ̃] #36 *v. tr.* **1.** to separate. **2.** [Jur.] to dissociate, to separate (two claims). || **se disjoindre** *v. pron.* to separate, to come apart. || **disjoint, -e** [-ɛ̃(:t)] *adj.* separate, separated. || **disjoncteur** [dizʒɔ̃k'-t|œ:r] *n.m.* circuit-breaker; (automatic) switch. || **disjoncti|f, -ve** [-if, -i:v] *adj.* disjunctive.

disloqué, -e [dislɔ'ke] *adj.* [siège, &c.] rickety; [démarche] disjointed, awkward; [coude, épaule, &c.] out of joint. || **disloquer** #3 *v. tr.* [os] to dislocate; [machine, meuble, &c.] to break up, to put out of action. || **se disloquer** *v. pron.* **1.** to come apart, to get out of joint. **2.** [cortège] to break up, to disperse.

disparaître [dispa'r|ɛ:tr], **disparu** [-y] #40 *v. intr.* **1.** to disappear, vanish; ~ *à la vue, aux yeux*, to/disappear, vanish/from sight: *faire* ~, to remove. **2.** [surtout à l'imparfait] to be/veiled, hidden/.

disparate [dispa'rat] *adj.* ill-assorted, disparate; [sons] jarring. || *n.f.* disparity.

disparité [dispari'te] *n.f.* disparity.

disparition [dispari'sjɔ̃] *n.f.* disappearance. || **disparu, -e** [dispa'ry] *adj.* disappeared, dead, extinct; [Mil.] missing.

dispendieu|x, -se [dispɑ̃'djø(:z)] *adj.* [Esp. ©] expensive [→ use CHER].

dispensaire [dispɑ̃'sɛ:r] *n.m.* dispensary.

dispense [dis'p|ɑ̃:s] *n.f.* **1.** dispensation. **2.** exemption. || **dispensé, -e** [-ɑ̃'se] *adj.* **1.** distributed, given. **2.** exempted (from military service); excused. || **dispenser** [-ɑ̃'se] #3 *v. tr.* **1.** to dispense, distribute. **2.** to excuse, exempt (from, *de*), to spare [with change of subject]: *Je vous dispense des détails*, You can spare me the details; *Je vous dispense de vos observations*, You may keep your remarks to yourself. || **se dispenser de** *v. pron.* to dispense with, to do without.

dispersé, -e [dispɛr's|e] *adj.* scattered, dispersed. || **disperser** #3 *v. tr.* **1.** to disperse, to scatter; [étendre] to spread (out). **2.** [Fig.] to spread, to disperse (one's efforts). || **se disperser** *v. pron.* to scatter, to disperse; [Fig.] to spread (o.s. out, out one's activity, &c.). || **dispersion** [-jɔ̃] *n.f.* dispersion, scattering.

disponibilité [dispɔnibili'te] *n.f.* availability; [au pl.] available funds, liquid assets: *en* ~, [fonctionnaire, Mil.] temporarily unattached, retired on half pay. || **disponible** [dispɔ'nibl] *adj.* available; [fonctionnaire] unattached, retired on half pay.

dispos, -e [dis'p|o(:z)] *adj.* [esprit] alert; [en bonne forme] fit; [humeur] cheerful:

frais et ~, refreshed. || **disposé, -e** [-o'z|e] *adj.* **1.** arranged; [espace] laid out: ~ *alphabétiquement*, alphabetically arranged. **2.** prepared, inclined (to, *à*): *Il est bien* ~ *pour vous*, He is well disposed toward you. || **disposer** [-e] #3 *v. tr.* **1.** to arrange, to lay out, to fix. **2.** to prepare, to incline (to, *à*). || *v. intr.* **1.** to have at one's disposal, to control: *Il dispose de ressources considérables*, Considerable resources are available to him. **2.** to use: *Disposez de moi*, Please call on me; *Vous pouvez en* ~, You may use it. **3.** *Vous pouvez* ~, You may go now.

dispositif [-i'tif] *n.m.* device, mechanism.

disposition [-i'sjõ] *n.f.* **1.** arrangement: *prendre ses dispositions pour*, to arrange to, to be prepared to. **2.** disposal: *se mettre à la* ~ *de qqun*, to place o.s. at s.o.'s disposal. || **3.** aptitude: *Il a des dispositions pour le dessin*, He has an aptitude for drawing. **4.** clause: *les dispositions de la loi*, the provisions of the act.

disproportion [disprɔpɔr'sjõ] *n.f.* disproportion.

disputable [dispy'tabl] *adj.* disputable, debatable, arguable.

dispute [dis'pyt] *n.f.* **1.** quarrel. **2.** debate, competition. || **disputé, -e** [-e] *adj.* contested: *un match chaudement* ~, a hard-fought game. || **disputer** [-e] #3 *v. intr.* to quarrel; to vie: *le* ~ *à qqun en bravoure*, to vie with s.o. in bravery. || *v. tr.* **1.** to fight over: ~ *le terrain*, to fight for every inch of ground. **2.** [Fam.] to quarrel with: *Il me dispute tout le temps*, He's constantly picking a quarrel with me.

disqualification [diskalifika'sjõ] *n.f.* disqualification. || **disqualifier** [diskali'fje] #3 *v. tr.* to disqualify.

disque [disk] *n.m.* **1.** [Sport] discus: *lancer le* ~, to throw the discus. **2.** [communications] disc, signal: ~ *d'appel*, signal. **3.** [Mus.] record, disc: *tourne-*~, record-player.

dissection [dissɛk'sjõ] *n.f.* dissection.

dissemblable [disɑ̃'bl|abl] *adj.* dissimilar (*à*, *de*, to), unlike: *en cela* ~ *des autres mères*, in that/dissimilar to, unlike/ other mothers. || **dissemblance** [-ɑ̃:s] *n.f.* dissimilarity, unlikeness: *Il y a une grande* ~ *entre ces deux sœurs*, These two sisters are not at all alike.

disséminer [disemi'ne] #3 *v. tr.* to disseminate.

dissension [disɑ̃|'sjõ] *n.f.* dissension; *les dissensions*, internal strife. || **dissentiment** [-ti'mɑ̃] *n.m.* disagreement, dissent.

disséquer [dise'ke] #10 *v. tr.* to dissect.

dissertation [disɛrt|a'sjõ] *n.f.* dissertation, thesis; [moins important] essay, paper, composition. || **disserter** [-e] #3 *v. intr.* to dissert, to hold forth (on a subject).

dissidence [disi'dɑ̃:s] *n.f.* [Polit.] dissidence; [Fig.] dissent.

dissident, -e [disi'dɑ̃(:t)] *adj.* dissident. || *n.* dissenter, nonconformist.

dissimulat|eur, -rice [disimyla|'tœ:r, -'tris] *n.* dissembler. || **dissimulation** [-'sjõ] *n.f.* dissimulation, deceitfulness: *agir avec* ~, to act deceitfully. || **dissimulé, -e** [disimy'le] *adj.* **1.** hidden, concealed, dissembled: *avec un plaisir non* ~, with obvious enjoyment; *porte dissimulée*, hidden, secret door. **2.** deceptive; secretive: *C'est un homme très* ~, He's a very deceptive, secretive man. || **dissimuler** [disimy'le] #3 *v. tr.* to hide, to conceal, to dissemble: *ne rien* ~, to conceal nothing. || **se dissimuler** *v. pron.* to keep out of sight; to conceal o.s., to hide.

dissipat|eur, -rice [disip|a'tœ:r, -a'tris] *adj.* wasteful, extravagant. || **dissipation** [-a'sjõ] *n.f.* [gaspillage] dissipation, wasting; [Fig.] [de l'esprit, de l'attention] distraction; [des élèves] bad behaviour; [débauche] dissipation. || **dissipé, -e** [-e] *adj.* **1.** dispersed; cleared; **2.** [Scol.] inattentive: *Il est très* ~, He won't keep still. || **dissiper** [-e] #3 *v. tr.* **1.** to disperse, to clear, to dispel: *La police a dispersé les manifestants*, The police broke up the demonstration; *Il a dissipé mes craintes*, He dispelled my fears. **2.** to dissipate, to waste. **3.** to distract the attention of (fellow students). || **se dissiper** *v. pron.* **1.** to lift, to clear. **2.** to become restless and inattentive.

dissocié, -e [disɔ'sje] *adj.* [éléments] dissociated, scattered; [Fig., famille] broken up. || **dissocier** #3 *v. tr.* to separate, to dissociate, to divorce. || **se dissocier** *v. pron.* [corps] to come apart, to break up; [groupe politique] to split.

dissolu, -e [disɔ'ly] *adj.* dissolute, corrupt (life, person). || **dissolution** [-'sjõ] *n.f.* **1.** [Phys.] [action] dissolving; [résultat] dissolution. **2.** dissolution (of organization). **3.** [moral] dissoluteness.

dissolvant, -e [disɔl'vɑ̃(:t)] *adj.* solvent; [Fig.] [doctrine] corrupting; [climat] enervating. || *n.m.* [Fig. & Lit.] solvent.

dissonance [disɔ'n|ɑ̃:s] *n.f.* dissonance; [Mus.] discord. || **dissonant, -e** [-ɑ̃(:t)] *adj.* [son] discordant, harsh; dissonant.

dissoudre [di's|udr], **dissolvant** [-ɔl'vɑ̃], **dissous** [-u], **dissoute** [-ut] #55 *v. tr.* [Note that this verb has no simple past tense.]

1. to dissolve: *L'eau dissout le sucre,* Water dissolves sugar. **2.** [Fig.] to dissolve, [plus Fam.] to break up.
dissou|s, -te [di'su(t)] *adj.* dissolved; broken up.
dissuader [disɥa'de] #3 *v. tr.* to dissuade (from); [Fam.] to talk (s.o.) out of (sth., doing sth.).
distance [dis't|ɑ:s] *n.f.* **1.** distance, way: *à une courte* ~, a short distance away; *parcourir une* ~, to cover a distance; *A quelle* ~ ?, How far?; *table des distances,* mileage chart; *commande à* ~, remote control. **2.** interval. **3.** difference, distance: *tenir qqun à* ~, to keep s.o. at a distance. || **distancer** [-ɑ̃'se] #4 *v. tr.* to distance, [plus souvent] to outdistance, [plus Fam.] to outstrip, [dans une course, &c.] to outrun, → to leave behind: *se laisser* ~, to be/outdistanced, outstripped, outrun, left behind/, to drop behind. || **distant, -e** [-ɑ̃(:t)] *adj.* [de] **1.** distant (from); [plus général] away; apart: *Cette ville est distante d'environ cinq milles,* That city is about five miles away; *Ces deux villes sont distantes d'environ cinq milles l'une de l'autre,* Those two cities are about five miles apart. **2.** [Fig., Pers.] distant, aloof, standoffish.
distendre [dis'tɑ̃:dr] #42 *v. tr.* [gonfler] to distend, [la peau, un muscle, &c.] to swell (up); to overstretch, to pull.
distension [distɑ̃'sjɔ̃] *n.f.* distension.
distillation [distil|a'sjɔ̃] *n.f.* distillation. || **distiller** [-e] #3 *v. tr.* to distil. || **distillerie** [-'ri] *n.f.* distillery.
distinct, -e [dis't|ɛ̃(:kt)] *adj.* **1.** distinct, separate: *couleurs qui sont bien distinctes les unes des autres,* colours which are clearly/distinct, separate/ from each other. **2.** distinct, clear: *parler d'une voix distincte,* to speak in a/distinct, clear/ voice. || **distinctement** [-ɛ̃ktə'mɑ̃] *adv.* distinctly. || **distincti|f, -ve** [-ɛ̃k'tif, -ɛ̃k'ti:v] *adj.* distinctive: *les traits distinctifs,* distinguishing features. || **distinction** [-ɛ̃k'sjɔ̃] *n.f.* **1.** [action] distinction, differentiation, separation. **2.** distinction: *homme sans* ~, undistinguished man; *air de* ~, distinguished air, manner. || **distingué, -e** [-'ɛ̃ge] *adj.* distinguished, refined (manners); [personne bien connue] eminent. || **distinguer** [-ɛ̃ge] #3 *v. tr.* **1.** to distinguish, to differentiate, to tell apart. **2.** to distinguish, to make out, to perceive. **3.** to single out, to honour. || **se distinguer** *v. pron.* **1.** to distinguish (o.s.); to gain distinction: [Péj.] to be conspicuous; [une personne, une chose, d'un groupe] to stand out: *Son style se distingue par sa pureté,* His style stands out because of its purity; [Péj.] *Oh! Monsieur veut* ~ *!,* Oh! You want to be different! **2.** to be distinguishable, to stand out: *Les maisons se distinguent sur la pente de la colline,* The houses can be seen on the hillside.
distraction [distr|ak'sjɔ̃] *n.f.* **1.** distraction, inattention, absent-mindedness, [ext.]: *avoir une* ~, to make a slip; *Il est sujet à des distractions,* He's often very absent-minded. **2.** entertainment, amusement, relaxation: *Est-ce que les distractions ici sont chères?,* Are amusements expensive here? || **distraire** [-ɛ:r], **distrayant** [-ɛ'jɑ̃], **distrait** [-ɛ] #38 *v. tr.* [Note that this verb has no simple past tense.] **1.** [de] to separate; [détourner] to divert, to misappropriate (funds); [épargner] to set aside (funds, &c.). **2.** to distract, divert. **3.** ~ *qqun,* to amuse, to entertain s.o. || **se distraire** *v. pron.* to relax; to amuse, to entertain o.s.; to be amused, entertained: *Je me distrais en lisant ce livre,* I/relax, amuse myself, entertain myself/by reading this book. || **distrait, -e** [-ɛ(t)] *adj.* [Fig.] inattentive, absent-minded. || **distrayant, -e** [-ɛ'jɑ̃(:t)] *adj.* entertaining, amusing.
distribuer [distrib|ɥe] #3 *v. tr.* **1.** to distribute, to pass out, to hand out, to issue. **2.** ~ *le courrier,* to deliver the mail. || **distribut|eur, -rice** [-y'tœ:r, -y'tris] *n.* distributor: ~ *automatique,* vending machine. || **distribution** [-y'sjɔ̃] *n.f.* distribution, [plus Fam.] handing out, issuing (of food, clothes, equipment, &c. to soldiers); delivery (of mail); [Théât.] casting [et ext.] the cast; (des prix dans une école) graduation exercises.
district [dis'trikt] *n.m.* district.
dit; **dites**, cf. DIRE.
divaguer [diva'ge] #3 *v. intr.* [Fig.] [en parlant] to wander, to ramble; [moins Fam.] to digress.
divan [di'vɑ̃] *n.m.* couch: *lit-* ~, studio couch, continental bed; [avec bras] chesterfield.
divergence [divɛr'ʒ|ɑ̃:s] *n.f.* **1.** dispersion (of light rays); divergence (of two straight lines, &c.). **2.** [Fig.] divergence, difference (in ideas between two ways of thinking, points of view, &c.). || **divergent, -e** [-ɑ̃(:t)] *adj.* divergent. || **diverger** [-e] #5 *v. intr.* to diverge to hold different views; [routes, lignes de chemin de fer, &c.] to branch off.
divers, -e [di'v|ɛ:r, -ɛrs] *adj.* **1.** †varying, changing. **2.** [*pl.*] different, various: *pour diverses raisons,* for various reasons; *à*

différentes reprises, several times. **3.** miscellaneous: *frais* ~, miscellaneous expenses; *fait* ~, news item. || **diversifier** [-ɛrsi'fje] #3 *v. tr.* to diversify, to vary.

diversion [divɛr's|jõ] *n.f.* [Mil.] diversive action, diversion, change: *faire* ~, to make a change.

diversité [-i'te] *n.f.* diversity, variety: *une grande* ~ *de goûts,* a great/variety, diversity/of tastes.

divertir [divɛr't|i:r] #17 *v. tr.* **1.** to divert, to turn away. **2.** to amuse, to entertain. || **se divertir** *v. pron.* to amuse o.s.; to laugh (at, *de*). || **divertissant, -e** [-i'sɑ̃(:t)] *adj.* diverting; [plus courant] amusing, entertaining. || **divertissement** [-is'mɑ̃] *n.m.* entertainment, amusement; pastime.

dividende [divi'dɑ̃:d] *n.m.* **1.** [Math.] dividend. **2.** [Fin.] dividend: *toucher un* ~, to receive a dividend.

divin, -e [di'v|ɛ̃, -in] *adj.* **1.** divine, holy: *monarchie de droit* ~, rule by divine right; *La Divine Comédie,* The Divine Comedy; *l'office* ~, divine service. **2.** divine, superb, heavenly: *une musique divine,* a/divine, superb, heavenly/music.

divination [divina'sjõ] *n.f.* divining; [augure] soothsaying; [prévision] foresight.

divinité [divini'te] *n.f.* **1.** divinity. **2.** deity.

diviser [divi'z|e] #3 *v. tr.* **1.** to divide. **2.** to separate, to divide: *Ils sont très divisés,* They don't agree. || **se diviser** *v. pron.* to divide; [Math.] to be divisible by; [livre, &c.] to be divided (into, *en*). || **diviseur** [-œ:r] *n.m.* divisor. || **divisible** [-ibl] *adj.* divisible. || **division** [-jõ] *n.f.* **1.** division, dividing. **2.** division, part, [du savoir humain] branch, division; [de la société] class, division; [Adm.] department, branch; [Mil. & Mar.] division; [école] class. **3.** dissension, discord: *semer la* ~ *dans une famille,* to sow dissension, discord in a family; [Sport] league cf. © LIGUE.

divorce [di'vɔrs] *n.m.* [Jur.] divorce; [Fig.] contradiction, divorce. || **divorcé, -e** [-e] *adj.* divorced. || **divorcer** [-e] #4 *v. tr.* to divorce: *Ils ont divorcé,* They were divorced; *Elle a divorcé d'avec son second mari,* She divorced her second husband.

divulgation [divylg|a'sjõ] *n.f.* divulging, disclosure. || **divulguer** [-e] #3 *v. tr.* to divulge, disclose.

dix [di] [devant h aspiré ou consonne]; [diz] [devant voyelle ou h muet]; [dis] [à la fin d'un groupe de mots]; [dis] [employé seul, et dans les dates] *adj.* **1.** ten. **2.** [les rois, les papes, les dates] tenth: *Charles* ~, Charles the Tenth; *le* ~ *mars,* March (the) tenth, the tenth of March; *le* ~ *du mois,* the tenth (day) of the month. || *n.m.* ten: ~ *et* ~ *font vingt,* ten and ten/are, make/twenty. || **dix-huit** [di|'zɥit] *adj. & n.m.* eighteen; [la date, les rois, &c.] the eighteenth. || **dix-huitième** [-zɥi'tjɛm] *adj. & n.* eighteenth. || **dixième** [-'zjɛm] *adj. & n.* tenth: *les neuf dixièmes du total,* nine-tenths of the total. || **dix-neuf** [diz'nœf] *adj. & n.* nineteen. || **dix-neuvième** [diznœ'vjɛm] *adj. & n.* nineteenth. || **dix-sept** [dis'sɛt] *adj. & n.* seventeen. || **dix-septième** [dissɛ'tjɛm] *adj. & n.* seventeenth. || **dizaine** [-'zɛn] *n.f.* **1.** [Math.] tens: *colonne des dizaines,* tens column. **2.** about ten, ten or so: *Il y a une* ~ *d'années,* about ten years ago, ten or so years ago; *une bonne* ~ *d'œufs,* at least/about/ten eggs, ten or so eggs.

do [do] *n.m.* [Mus.] C.

docile [dɔ'sil] *adj.* docile, obedient; meek. || **docilité** [-i'te] *n.f.* docility, meekness, submissiveness.

dock [dɔk] *n.m.* [bassin, col] dock; [hangars, &c.] warehouse. || **docker** [-ɛ:r] *n.m.* docker, stevedore.

docte [dɔkt] *adj.* learned.

docteur [-œ:r] *n.m.* **1.** doctor, physician. **2.** doctor: *Il est* ~ *de l'université Harvard,* He received his Ph.D. from Harvard. **3.** scholar, doctor: *les docteurs de l'Église,* the Doctors of the Church. || **doctoral, -e** [-ɔ'ral] *adj.* **1.** doctoral. **2.** [Fig.] pedantic, pompous. || **doctorat** [-ɔ'ra] *n.m.* doctorate, doctor's degree: ~ *ès lettres, ès sciences,* doctorate in Letters, in Science; *passer un* ~ *en histoire,* to take a doctor's degree in History; *une thèse de* ~, a doctoral dissertation. || **doctoresse** [-ɔ'rɛs] *n.f.* [less used than *femme docteur* or *Madame le docteur*] woman doctor.

doctrinaire [dɔktri'nɛ:r] *adj.* doctrinaire, dogmatic. || *n.m.* dogmatist.

doctrine [dɔk'trin] *n.f.* doctrine.

document [dɔky'mɑ̃] *n.m.* document: *fournir des documents à l'appui d'une affirmation,* to document a statement. || **documentaire** [-'tɛ:r] *adj.* documentary: *film* ~, documentary, instructional/film. || **documentation** [-ta'sjõ] *n.f.* pertaining to documents; documentation. || **documenter** [-'te] #3 *v. tr.* to document, to supply with information (on, *sur*).

dodeliner [dɔdli'ne] #3 *v. tr.* to dandle (a child on one's knees), to nod (one's head). || *v. intr.* ~ *de la tête,* to nod.

dodo [do'do] *n.m.* [nursery word] **1.** *aller faire* ~, to go bye-bye. **2.** cot, bed.

dodu, -e [dɔ'dy] *adj.* plump, chubby: *un bébé* ~, a/plump, chubby/baby.

dogmatique [dɔgma'tik] *adj.* dogmatic. || **dogme** [dɔgm] *n.m.* dogma.

dogue [dɔg] *n.m.* (type of) mastiff.

doigt [dwa] *n.m.* **1.** finger: ~ *de pied*, toe; *avoir les doigts palmés*, to be web-fingered, web-toed; *le petit* ~, the little finger. **2.** [form] finger: *avoir la forme d'un* ~, to be finger-shaped. **3.** [mesure] finger: *deux doigts de vin*, just a little wine; *à deux doigts de sa perte*, within an ace of his ruin; *Il s'en est fallu d'un* ~, It was a close call, It was very close. **4.** [Loc.]: *indiquer du* ~, to point out; *menacer qqun du* ~, to wave one's finger at s.o.; *mettre le* ~ *sur la plaie*, to hit the nail on the head; *se mettre le* ~ *dans l'œil*, to be all wet; *mon petit* ~ *me l'a dit*, a little bird told me; *savoir sur le bout du* ~, to have at one's fingertips; *taper sur les doigts à qqun*, to rap s.o.

doigté [-'te] *n.m.* **1.** [Mus.] fingering. **2.** [Fig.] adroitness, tact: *manquer de* ~, to lack adroitness, tact.

doléance [dɔle'ɑ̃:s] *n.f.* complaint, grievance: *faire ses doléances à qqun*, to tell s.o. about one's grievances.

dolent, -e [dɔ'lɑ̃(:t)] *adj.* [physique] painful; [malheureux] doleful, mournful.

dollar [dɔ'la:r] *n.m.* dollar: *un billet de cinq dollars*, a five-dollar bill; *une pièce d'un* ~ *en argent*, a silver dollar.

domaine [dɔ'mɛn] *n.m.* **1.** estate, domain, property. **2.** [Fig.] domain, realm, sphere, field: *Ce n'est pas de son* ~, It's not in his line; *dans tous les domaines*, in all areas.

dôme [do:m] *n.m.* **1.** dome, cupola; canopy (of foliage). **2.** rounded summit, dome.

domesticité [dɔmɛstisi'te] *n.f.* [état] domesticity; [staff] household. || **domestique** [dɔmɛs'tik] *adj.* domestic. || *n.* servant. || **domestiqué, -e** [-e] *adj.* domesticated, tamed (animal). || **domestiquer** [-e] #3 *v. tr.* to domesticate, to tame.

domicile [dɔmi'sil] *n.m.* abode; [Jur.] domicile, address: *élire* ~, to come to live; to live (at, *à*); *livrer à* ~, to deliver; *livraison à* ~, free delivery; *donner des leçons à* ~, to give private lessons at the homes of one's pupils. || **domicilié, -e** [-je] *adj.* living, residing, domiciled (at, *à*).

domicilier (se) [(sə) dɔmisi'lje] #3 *v. tr. & pron.* to reside, to dwell, to take up residence.

dominant, -e [dɔmi'n|ɑ̃(:t)] *adj.* predominating. || **dominat|eur, -rice** [-a'tœ:r, -a'tris] *adj.* domineering. || **domination** [-a'sjõ] *n.f.* domination, rule. || **dominer** [dɔmi'ne] #3 *v. tr.* to overcome, to control, to rule. || *v. intr.* to predominate: ~ *ses passions*, to control one's passion; to stand out. || **se dominer** *v. pron.* to control o.s.

dominicain, -e [dɔmini'k|ɛ̃, -ɛn] *adj. & n.* Dominican.

Dominicaine (République) [repyblik dɔmini'kɛn] *n.f.* Dominican Republic.

Dominion [dɔmi'njɔn] *n.m.* Dominion: *le* ~ *du Canada*, the Dominion of Canada.

Dominique (La) [(la) dɔmi'nik] *n.f.* Dominica.

domino [dɔmi'no] *n.m.* [game] domino.

dommage [dɔ'm|a:ʒ] *n.m.* **1.** damage, harm, [blessure] injury; [tort] wrong: ~ *causé à un tiers*, injury to a third party; *demander des dommages-/et/ intérêts*, to sue for damages. **2.** *Quel* ~ *!*, What a shame!; *C'est vraiment* ~, It's really a shame. || **dommageable** [-a'ʒabl] *adj.* harmful, prejudicial.

dompe [dõ:p] © [Pop.] *n.f.* dump cf. DÉPOTOIR.

dompter [dõ't|e] #3 *v. tr.* **1.** to tame; [cheval] to break (in). **2.** to subdue, overcome (an enemy, a rowdy class, the forces of nature, anger, &c.). || **dompteu|r, -se** [-œ:r, -ø:z] *n.* tamer, trainer.

don [dõ] *n.m.* present; [à une église, à une œuvre charitable] donation; gift: *faire* ~ *de qqch. à qqun*, to/give, present/sth. to s.o.; talent; *avoir le* ~ *de l'à-propos*, to have the/gift, talent/of saying the right thing. || **donataire** [dɔna|'tɛ:r] *n.* beneficiary. || **donateu|r, -rice** [-'tœ:r, -'tris] *n.* donor; [plus Fam.] giver: ~ *de sang*, blood donor. || **donation** [-'sjõ] *n.f.* donation, contribution; [à titre gratuit] gift; [à titre onéreux] grant.

donc [do:k] *conj.* **1.** [conséquence] so, therefore, consequently, †hence. **2.** [pour revenir à un sujet] as: *Je disais* ~ *que . . .*, As I was saying . . . **3.** [pour exprimer la surprise, l'incrédulité, et pour être emphatique] [ne se traduit pas directement, mais par un équivalent qui n'est souvent que l'accent que l'on met sur la phrase] *Écrivez-lui* ~ *tout de suite!*, Write to him right away!; *Venez* ~ *!, On vous attend*, Come on (then)! We're waiting for you!; *Allons* ~ *!*, Go on!, You're kidding!, [emphatique] Let's go (then); [surprise] What next!; *Vous aviez* ~ *oublié!*, You forgot (didn't you)!; *Pensez-* ~ *!*, Just think; *Dis* ~ *Jacques! Passe-moi ton crayon*; Say, Jack! Lend me your pencil; *Qu'y a-t-il* ~ *!*, What's the matter/anyway, anyhow?/

dondaine [dɔ̃'dɛn] *n.f.* © **1.** flirt, fickle female: *une vraie petite ~*, a real flirt. **2.** fat and pink and pretty: *Elle est bien ~ !*, She's (nice and) fat and pink and pretty!

donjon [dɔ̃'ʒɔ̃] *n.m.* keep (of a castle).

donne [dɔn] *n.f.* [cartes] deal: *perdre sa ~*, to lose one's deal.

donné, -e [dɔ'ne] *adj.* given; [spectacle, &c.] presented: *à cheval ~ on ne regarde pas la bride*, don't look a gift horse in the mouth; *Mais, c'est ~*, But, that's giving it away; *en un temps ~*, at/in/a given time. || **étant donné** [etɑ̃dɔ'ne] *loc. prép.* given; knowing: *~ son intelligence . . .*, Knowing his intelligence . . . || **étant donné que,** *loc. conj.* [followed by the indicative] inasmuch as, considering that.

donnée [dɔ'ne] *n.f.* **1.** datum *pl.* data **2.** *les données d'une pièce*, the central idea of a play.

donner [dɔ'n|e] #3 *v. tr.* **1.** to give, to give away. **2.** [Loc.] *~ le branle à*, to start; *~ les cartes*, to deal; *~ lieu à*, to give rise to; *~ la mort*, to kill; *~ une pièce*, to put on a play; *~ raison à*, to side with; *~ de la voix*, to bark; *Je vous le donne en mille*, You'll never guess. || *v. intr.* [Loc.] *~ sur le jardin*, to look out on the garden; *Le soleil donne dans cette pièce*, The sun shines into this room; *~ dans une embuscade*, to fall into an ambush; *~ dans un travers*, to indulge a weakness; *~ de la tête dans*, to bump one's head against; *~ tête baissée dans*, to rush headlong into. || **se donner** *v. pron.* **1.** to devote o.s. (to, *à*). **2.** [spectacle] to be/played, presented. **3.** *~ du mal*, to take trouble; *~ la mort*, to take one's life. **4.** to pass o.s. off as, to pretend to be. **5.** to give each other, one another. || **donneu|r, -se** [-œːr, -øːz] *n.* **1.** giver (of advice, compliments, &c.); [cartes] dealer, [de sang] donor. **2.** [Com.] [d'aval] backer, guarantor; [à la grosse aventure] underwriter.

dont [dɔ̃] *pron. rel. sing. & plur.* whose, of whom, of which: *L'homme ~ je vous ai parlé*, The man I spoke of; *L'homme ~ vous connaissez le fils*, The man whose son you know; *La fenêtre ~ vous avez cassé le carreau*, The window you broke the pane in.

dorade [dɔ'rad] *n.f.* dorado, sea bream.

doré, -e [dɔ're] *adj.* golden, gilt, gilded: *cheveux dorés*, golden hair; *viande dorée*, browned meat. || © *n.m.* wall-eyed pike, yellow pike.

dorénavant [dɔrena'vɑ̃] *adv.* henceforth, from now on, in the future.

dorer [dɔ're] #3 *v. tr.* **1.** [avec de l'or] gild; [un gâteau] to glaze; [la pilule, au propre et au figuré] to sugar coat a (pill). **2.** [Fig.] to tint, touch (qqch.) with gold. || **se dorer** *v. pron.* to turn golden brown; to get sun-tanned.

dorloter [dɔrlɔ'te] #3 *v. tr.* to coddle, pamper (a child, one's wife, &c.). || **se dorloter** *v. pron.* to pamper o.s.

dormant, -e [dɔr'm|ɑ̃(:t)] *adj.* **1.** sleeping [seldom used except in La Belle au bois dormant, Sleeping Beauty, and in Heraldry: *animal ~*, dormant animal]. **2.** still, stagnant, standing (water); dormant (passions). || **dormeu|r, -se** [-œːr, -øːz] *n.* [personne] sleeper; [qui aime dormir] sleepyhead; [Péj.] sluggard. || **dormir** [-iːr] #21 *v. intr.* **1.** to sleep, to be asleep. **2.** to go to sleep: *Il est l'heure de ~*, It's time to go to sleep. **3.** [Fig.] to lie dormant, to stagnate: *l'eau qui dort*, still water. **4.** [Loc.] *~ debout*, to sleep standing up; *une histoire à ~ debout*, a cock-and-bull story. || **dormiti|f, -ve** [-i'tif, -i'tiːv] *adj. & n.m.* [Méd.] soporific.

dorsal, -e [dɔr'sal] *adj.*: *épine dorsale*, backbone.

dortoir [dɔr'twaːr] *n.m.* dormitory.

dorure [dɔ'ryːr] *n.f.* **1.** [action] gilding (of a ceiling, picture frame, &c.); [sur tranches] gilt edging; glazing (of a cake, pastry). **2.** [Fig.] gilding (of a style).

dos [do] *n.m.* **1.** back; reverse: *avoir mal au ~*, to have a backache; *de ~*, from the back; *~ à ~*, back to back; *voir au ~*, see the reverse side. **2.** [Loc.] *avoir bon ~*, to have a broad back; *en avoir plein le ~*, to be fed up; *dès qu'il a le ~ tourné*, as soon as his back is turned; *faire le gros ~*, to arch one's back; *mettre sur le ~ de qqun*, to blame s.o. for; *se mettre qqun à ~*, to make an enemy of s.o.; *passer la main dans le ~ à qqun*, to flatter s.o.; *tourner le ~ à qqun*, to turn one's back on.

dosage [do'zaːʒ] *n.m.* [Méd.] dosing; [Chim.] measuring (of the quantity). || **dose** [doːz] *n.f.* [Méd.] dose; [quantité] quantity, amount: [Fig.] *donner par petites doses*, to dole out. || **doser** [do'ze] #3 *v. tr.* [Méd.] *déterminer la dose*, to measure out (a medicine).

dossier [do'sje] *n.m.* **1.** back (of a chair). **2.** [Jur.] [d'une affaire] file, record (on an affair): *classer les pièces d'un ~*, to arrange the papers in a file.

dot [dɔt] *n.f.* dowry, marriage settlement: *constituer une ~*, to provide for a dowry; *coureur de ~*, fortune-hunter.

dotation [-a'sjõ] *n.f.* endowment foundation (of a hospital, university, &c.); equipment (of a factory, army, &c.). || **doter** [-e] #3 *v. tr.* **1.** to give a dowry to (one's daughter, &c.); to endow (a foundation, a hospital, a library, &c.) with; to equip (a factory with new machines, an army with new weapons).

douane [dwan] *n.f.* customs; custom house: *déclaration de la* ~, custom declaration; *visite de la* ~, custom examination; *passer la* ~, to go through customs; *faire passer en* ~, to clear through customs; *droit de* ~, custom duty. || **douani|er, -ère** [-je, -jɛ:r] *adj.* customs: *politique douanière,* customs policy. || *n.m.* custom officer.

doublage [du'bla:ʒ] *n.m.* doubling (of threads): [Cin.] dubbing in; lining (of an article of clothing); sheathing, sheeting (of the hull of a ship). || **double** [dubl] *adj.* **1.** double, twofold: *C'est un mot à* ~ *sens,* It is a word with a double meaning; *fermer à double tour,* to double-lock, → to bolt and lock. **2.** [Fig., Pers., âme, jeu] deceitful; double dealing; [vie] double. || *n.m.* **1.** double; two times, twice|as much: *J'en veux le* ~, I want twice as much; *augmenter du* ~, to double; *jouer quitte ou* ~, to play double or nothing; *payer (le)* ~, to pay double, twice as much; *voir* ~, to see double; *plus du* ~, more than double. **2.** double, [copie exacte] duplicate, copy. **3.** [tennis] doubles: ~ *messieurs, dames, mixte,* men's, ladies' mixed doubles. || **en double** [ɑ̃'dubl] *loc. adv.* in two, twofold, in duplicate. || **doublement** [dubl|ə'mɑ̃] *adv.* doubly. || *n.m.* doubling (of a consonant, &c.). || **doubler** [-e] #3 *v. tr. & intr.* **1.** to double, to fold in two: ~ *le pas,* to quicken one's step. **2.** to line (with, *de*). **3.** to round (a cape); to pass (a car). **4.** [Théâ.] to stand in for (an actor] to understudy. **5.** [Cin.] to dub || **doublure** [-y:r] *n.f.* **1.** lining. **2.** [Théâ.] understudy.

douce [dus] cf. DOUX.

douce-amère [dus|a'mɛ:r] *n.f.* bitter-sweet.

doucement ['mɑ̃] *adv.* **1.** softly, quietly. **2.** easy!, go easy, take it easy, not so fast.

doucereu|x, -se [-ə'rø(:z)] *adj.* sickly sweet (taste); sugary (words, tone); mealy-mouthed (person).

doucettement [dusɛt'mɑ̃] *adv.* [Fam.] very softly, quietly.

douceur [dusœ:r] *n.f.* **1.** [au goût] sweetness: *aimer les douceurs,* to like sweet things; [à l'oreille] softness, sweetness; [au toucher] softness; [l'air, l'atmosphère, la température, la saison, &c.] mildness. **2.** charm, pleasantness; gentleness: *conter des douceurs à une femme,* to whisper sweet nothings to a woman.

douche [duʃ] *n.f.* **1.** shower: *prendre une* ~, to take a shower. **2.** [Fig. & Fam.] [réprimande] raking over the coals; [déception] cold shower. || **doucher** [-e] #3 *v. tr.* to shower, douse; to give a shower bath.

doué, -e [dwe] *adj.* gifted, talented: *Il est* ~ *pour le chant,* He is gifted in singing. || **douer** #3 *v. tr.* to endow [when speaking of God, nature or fortune].

douille [duj] *n.f.* **1.** socket: *visser une ampoule dans une* ~ *de lampe,* to screw a (light) bulb into a lamp socket. **2.** (cartridge, shell) case.

douillet, -te [du'jɛ(t)] *adj.* **1.** soft (pillow, bed, &c.); [peau] tender, delicate. **2.** [Pers.] sensitive, effeminate. || [du'jɛt] *n.f.* quilted wrap. || *n.* mollycoddle.

douleur [du'l|œ:r] *n.f.* **1.** [Phys.] pain, ache; [plus généralisé] suffering: *provoquer la* ~, to cause pain, suffering; *adoucir une* ~, to relieve a pain, an ache, suffering. **2.** [morale] suffering, grief, sorrow. || **douloureusement** [-urøz'mɑ̃] *adv.* painfully, sorrowfully. || **douloureu|x, -se** [-u'rø(:z)] *adj.* **1.** [physiquement] painful, aching. **2.** [moralement] sorrowful, sad; grievous.

doute [dut] *n.m.* doubt, [présentement] misgiving: *être/en, dans le/*~, to be in doubt; *Cela est hors de* ~, There is no question about it; *d'un air de* ~, doubtfully, with misgiving; *mettre qqch. en* ~, to question sth.; *avoir un* ~ *sur,* to have doubts/about, as to/; *Il n'y a pas l'ombre d'un* ~, There is not the shadow of a doubt; *Il n'y a pas de* ~ *qu'il ne vienne,* There is no doubt/that he will come, about his coming/; *Sans* ~ *!,* Of course!, No doubt!; *Elle arrivera sans* ~ *ce soir,* She will come this evening no doubt. || **douter** [-e] #3 *v. intr.* **1.** [de] to doubt (the reality of sth., the authenticity of sth.); to have doubts/about, as to/: *J'en doute fort,* I doubt it very much; *Doutez-vous de ma parole?,* Do you doubt my word?, Are you doubting my word? || **se douter** *v. pron.* [de] [qqch., &c. de louche] to suspect; to imagine, to guess; to think so: *Je m'en doutais (bien) !,* I thought so!; I/guessed, thought/as much; *Je me doute de ce que c'est,* I can/guess, imagine/what it is; *Il ne se doutait de rien,* He didn't suspect a thing. || **douteu|x, -se** [-ø(:z)] *adj.* **1.** doubtful, dubious; [discutable] questionable; [jour, lumière] dim. **2.** [suspect] doubtful, suspicious.

douve [du:v] *n.f.* **1.** [d'un château] moat; [Agric.] drainage ditch; [de steeplechase] water jump. **2.** [des tonneaux] stave.

Douvres [du:vr] *n.m.* Dover.

dou|x, -ce [du(s)] *adj.* **1.** [au goût] sweet; [à l'oreille] soft, melodious; [à l'odorat] sweet-smelling; [au toucher] soft; [l'air] mild; [lumière] soft. **2.** pleasant, charming: *faire les yeux doux,* to make eyes at s.o. **3.** gentle. || *adv.* softly, quietly: *filer ~*, to obey quietly, to tiptoe around; *en douce,* on the quiet.

douzaine [du'zɛn] *n.f.* **1.** dozen: *Les œufs se vendent à la ~*, Eggs are sold by the dozen. **2.** about twelve: *d'ici une ~ d'années,* about twelve years from now. || **douze** [du:z] *adj. inv.* **1.** twelve. **2.** [les rois, &c.; les mois] twelfth: *Louis XII,* Louis the Twelfth; *le 12,* on the twelfth. || **douzième** [du'zjɛm] *adj. & n.* twelfth.

doyen, -ne [dwa'j|ɛ̃, -ɛn] *n.* dean (of a faculty); [d'âge] senior.

dragée [dra'ʒe] *n.f.* **1.** candied almond: [Fig.] *tenir la ~ haute à qqun,* to make s.o. pay through the nose (for sth.). **2.** [Pharm.] sugar-coated pill.

dragon [dra'gõ] *n.m.* **1.** dragon: [Mil.] dragoon. **2.** [Fig.] [personne intraitable] old battle-axe.

drague [drag] *n.f.* [machine] dredger; [filet] dragnet; [pour retrouver des objets perdus dans l'eau] drag. || **draguer** [-e] #3 *v. tr.* [pour enlever la vase] to dredge; [pour pêcher] to drag; [pour enlever les mines] to sweep. || **dragueur** [-œ:r] *n.m.* dredge; [de mines] minesweeper.

drain [drɛ̃] *n.m.* drain, drainpipe. || **drainer** [drɛ'ne] #3 *v. tr.* to drain; [Fin.] to drain off.

dramatique [drama't|ik] *adj.* dramatic. || **dramatiser** [-i'ze] #3 *v. tr.* to dramatize [also Fig.]. || **dramaturge** [-yrʒ] *n.* playwright, dramatist. || **drame** [dram] *n.m.* drama; [plus général] play.

drap [drɑ] *n.m.* cloth; [de lit] sheet: [Fig.] *être dans de beaux draps,* to be in a pretty pickle, to be in the soup.

drapeau [dra'po] *n.m.* flag; [Mil.] colours: *être sous les drapeaux,* to be in the service(s).

draper [dra'p|e] #3 *v. tr.* to drape (something/with, in/a cloth, &c.). || **se draper** *v. pron.* to drape o.s. (in): *~ dans sa dignité,* to make a show of one's dignity. || **draperie** [-'ri] *n.f.* **1.** drapery. **2.** cloth /business, trade/.

drapier [dra'pje] *n.m.* cloth merchant, draper.

drave [dra:v] © *n.f.* drive: *faire la ~*, to make a (log) drive; *aller à la ~*, to go on a (log) drive; © "flottage"; floating, log-running. || **draver** [dra'v|e] #3 © *v. tr.* to float, drive. || **draveur** [-œ:r] © *n.m.* "flotteur"; driver, wood-floater, raftman; logger (who makes log drives).

dressage [drɛ's|a:ʒ] *n.m.* **1.** erection, putting up of (a tent, scaffold, &c.); pitching (of a tent). **2.** trimming, dressing (of a piece of wood). **3.** training (of animals); breaking (in) (of a horse). || **dresser** [-e] #3 *v. tr.* **1.** to raise, erect, pitch (a tent): *~ l'oreille,* to prick up one's ears; *~ la tête,* to lift one's head. **2.** to lay, set, prepare: *~ la table,* to set the table. **3.** to draw up (a list), to make (a plan). **4.** to square (a block of stone), to straighten (a rod). **5.** to train, drill. || **se dresser** *v. pron.* **1.** to stand up, to sit up. **2.** to stand, rise: *Une montagne se dresse à l'horizon,* A mountain rises on the horizon. **3.** to rise against (an enemy). || **dresseur** [-œ:r] *n.m.* trainer. || **dressoir** [-wa:r] *n.m.* sideboard, china cabinet.

drogue [drɔg] *n.f.* drug. || **droguer** [-e] #3 *v. tr.* [Péj.] to drug. || **se droguer** *v. pron.* to drug o.s.; to take drugs. || **droguiste** [-ist] *n.m.* druggist.

droit, -e [drwa(t)] *adj.* **1.** straight, erect: *veston ~*, single-breasted coat; *Tenez-vous ~*, Stand up straight. **2.** upright: *Mettez-le ~*, Put it right. **3.** right: *la main droite,* the right hand; *à main droite,* on the right. **4.** straight, honest. || *adv.* straight: *~ devant soi,* straight ahead. || *n.m.* **1.** right: *avoir ~ à,* to have a right to; *avoir des droits sur,* to have rights over; *faire ~ à,* to accede to (a request). **2.** fee: *~ d'auteur,* royalty; *~ de reproduction,* copyright; *~ de douane,* custom duty; *droits de succession,* estate duties. **3.** law: *étudiant en ~*, law student; *faire son ~*, to study law; *de ~*, by right; *A qui de ~*, To whom it may concern. || **droite** [drwat] *n.f.* **1.** right: *à, sur/votre ~*, on your right; *à ~*, to, on/the right; *à ~ et à gauche, de ~ et de gauche,* right and left; *Garder la ~*, Keep to the right. **2.** [Pol.] The Right [the Conservatives]. **3.** [boxe] right. || **droiti|er, -ère** [drwa|'tje, -'tjɛ:r] *adj. & n.* right-handed.

droiture [drwa'ty:r] *n.f.* honesty, uprightness, integrity.

drôlatique [drola'tik] *adj.* funny, amusing, comic.

drôle [dro:l] *n.m.* rascal, scamp, scoundrel;

strange character. || *adj.* **1.** funny, comical: *Comme c'est ~ !,* Isn't that funny!; *C'est ~, ça,* That's funny. **2.** [bizarre] queer, odd, strange: *C'est ~ ça !,* That's /strange, queer, odd/!; *Comme c'est ~ !,* That's really/odd, queer, strange/!; *Cela me fait un ~ d'effet,* That gives me a strange feeling; *Quelle ~ d'idée,* What a/strange, odd, queer/idea!; [Fam.] *C'est un ~ de type,* He's a queer bird; *avoir un ~ d'aspect,* to have a/queer, strange, odd/look. || **drôlerie** [drol'ri] *n.f.* [Fam.] gag; humour (of a story, a situation), funniness.

dru, -e [dry] *adj.* [herbe, blé, neige, &c.] thick; [cheveux] straight, thick. || *adv.* [pousser] thick, thickly; fast.

du [dy] *art. déf.* [contraction of *de le*; cf. DE, LE]: *Il vient ~ Canada,* He is from Canada. || *art. partitif m. sing.* [cf. DES] some, part of the: *Je prendrai ~ thé,* I'll have some tea.

dû, due [dy] cf. DEVOIR || *adj.* due, owing. || *n.m.* what one owes; one's due: *payer son ~,* to pay one's debt, one's share; *donner à chacun son ~,* to give each his due.

dubitati|f, -ve [dybita|'tif, -'ti:v] *adj.* dubious, doubtful.

duc [dyk] *n.m.* **1.** duke. **2.** horned owl. || **duchesse** [dy'ʃɛs] *n.f.* duchess.

duel [dɥɛl] *n.m.* **1.** duel: *se battre en ~,* to fight a duel. **2.** [Gram.] dual. || **duelliste** [-ist] *n.m.* duellist.

dûment [dy'mɑ̃] *adv.* duly, in due form, properly.

dune [dyn] *n.f.* dune.

Dunkerque [dœ̃'kɛrk] *n.f.* Dunkirk.

duo [dy'o] *n.m.* duo, duet.

dupe [dyp] *n.f.* dupe, [Fam.] sucker. || **duper** [-e] #3 *v. tr.* to trick, fool; to take in; [plus Lit.] to dupe; [tricher] to cheat. || **duperie** [-'ri] *n.f.* trickery. || **dupeu|r, -se** [-œ:r, -ø:z] *n.* cheat, trickster, swindler; [Fam.] sharper.

duplicata [dyplika't|a] *n.m.* (second) copy; duplicate. || **duplicateur** [-œ:r] *n.m.* duplicating machine, duplicator.

duplicité [dyplisi'te] *n.f.* duplicity, hypocrisy.

duquel [dy'kɛl] *pron. rel. m. sing. & pron. interrog. m. sing.* cf. LEQUEL.

dur, -e [dy:r] *adj.* **1.** hard: *du pain ~,* stale bread; *de la viande dure,* tough meat; *des œufs durs,* hard-boiled eggs; *brosse dure,* stiff brush. **2.** hard, difficult: *~ à ouvrir,* hard to open; *~ à mener,* hard to control; *~ de l'oreille,* hard of hearing. **3.** harsh, unfeeling, [Fam.] hard-boiled. **4.** fierce, severe: *de durs combats,* fierce fighting. || *adv.* hard. || *n. un ~,* a tough one.

durable [dy'rɑ̃] *adj.* lasting, durable.

durant [dy'rɑ̃] *prép.* during: *parler une heure ~,* to talk for a whole hour.

durci, -e [dyr's|i] *adj.* hardened. || **durcir** [-i:r] #17 *v. tr.* to harden, toughen. *v. intr.* to harden; [raidir] to stiffen. || **se durcir** *v. pron.* to become hard, to harden, stiffen. || **durcissement** [-is'mɑ̃] *n.m.* **1.** hardening (of clay, cement, earth, tissues, arteries, &c.); toughening (of the skin), **2.** [Fig.] stiffening (of enemy resistance); hardening (of an attitude).

dure [dy:r] *n.f.* something hard: *coucher sur la ~,* to sleep on the/ground, floor/; *en voir de dures,* [Fam.] to have a tough time.

durée [dy're] *n.f.* duration, length, term, period: *pour la ~ de la guerre,* for the duration of the war; *élu pour une ~ de quatre ans,* elected for a four-year term; *tâche de longue ~,* a long-term project; *de courte ~,* short-lived.

durement [dyr'mɑ̃] *adv.* severely (tried); harshly, roughly (brought up); [regarder, parler, traiter] harshly.

durer [dy're] #3 *v. intr.* **1.** to last, to go on: *Le temps lui dure,* Time hangs heavy on him. **2.** to last, endure, to wear well.

dureté [dyr'te] *n.f.* **1.** hardness (of glass, rock, diamonds, &c.); toughness (of meat); stiffness (of a brush, the beard, &c.). **2.** [Fig.] hardness (of water); hardness, difficulty (of hearing). **3.** hardness, harshness (of a sound, a voice); hardness (of a face), ruggedness (of condition); severity, harshness (of a punishment). **4.** [manque de sensibilité] hardness, harshness, severity: *dire des duretés à qqun,* to speak harsh words to s.o.; [plus Fam.] to say mean things to s.o.

durillon [dyri'jõ] *n.m.* callus, callosity.

duvet [dy'v|ɛ] *n.m.* down. || **duveté, -e** [-'te] *adj.* fuzzy, downy. || **duveteu|x, -se** [-'tø(:z)] *adj.* downy, fluffy; fuzzy.

dynamique [dina'mi|k] *adj.* dynamic. || *n.f.* [étude] dynamics. || **dynamisme** [-sm] *n.m.* [Phil.] dynamism; [énergie] drive push, energy.

dynamite [dina'mit] *n.f.* dynamite. || **dynamiter** [-e] #3 *v. tr.* to dynamite, to blow up.

dynamo [dina'mo] *n.f.* [Electr.] dynamo.

dynastie [dinas'ti] *n.f.* dynasty.

dysenterie [disɑ̃'tri] *n.f.* dysentery.

dyspepsie [dispɛp|'si] *n.f.* dyspepsia. || **dyspeptique** [-'tik] *adj.* dyspeptic.

E, e [ø, © e] *n.m.* [letter] E, e: *un e muet,* a silent e; é, è [e accent aigu, e accent grave].

eau [o] *n.f.* **1.** water: ~ *minérale,* mineral water; *suer sang et* ~, to sweat blood and tears; *être en* ~, to perspire profusely; ~ *douce,* fresh water; ~ *dure,* hard water; ~ *de mer,* ~ *salée,* salt water; ~ *de source,* spring water; ~ *vive,* running water. **2.** ~ *de Javel,* Javel water; ~ *de Cologne,* cologne water; ~ *lourde,* heavy water. **3.** [Naut.] *faire eau,* to leak. || *pl.* **les eaux**: *aller aux eaux,* to go to a spa; *aller voir* ~, to go and see the waterworks; © *eaux vives,* swift current.

eau-de-vie [od'vi] *n.f.* brandy; spirits.

ébahi, -e [eba|'i] *adj.* dumbfounded, astounded, flabbergasted, amazed. || **ébahir** [-'i:r] #17 *v.tr.* to astound, to flabbergast, to dumbfound, to amaze. || **ébahissement** [-is'mɑ̃] *n.m.* amazement, astonishment.

ébats [e'ba] *n.mpl.* [seldom used except in the plural]: *prendre ses* ~, to run and play; [oiseaux, animaux] to frolic, gambol || **s'ébattre** [-tr] #43 *v. pron.* [enfants] to run and play, [oiseaux, animaux] to frolic, gambol.

ébauche [e'b|o:ʃ] *n.f.* **1.** sketch, outline; rough draft. **2.** [Fig.] beginnings, outline. || **ébaucher** [-o'ʃe] #3 *v. tr.* to rough-hew (a beam); to rough out (a sculpture, &c.); to sketch (out), to outline (a project, a work).

ébène [e'b|ɛn] *n.f.* ebony. || **ébéniste** [-e'nist] *n.m.* cabinet-maker. || **ébénisterie** [-enist'ri] *n.f.* cabinet-making.

ébloui, -e [eblu|i] *adj.* dazzled, blinded, fascinated. || **éblouir** [-'i:r] #17 *v. tr.* **1.** [lumière brillante] to dazzle, to blind. **2.** to dazzle, to fascinate. || **éblouissant, -e** [-i'sɑ̃(:t)] *adj.* [lumière] blinding, glaring, dazzling; [teint] radiant. || **éblouissement** [-is'mɑ̃] *n.m.* glare, dazzle, splendour; [Méd.] dizziness: *avoir des éblouissements,* to have dizzy spells.

éborgner [ebɔr'ɲe] #3 *v. tr.* to blind in one eye.

ébouillanter [ebujɑ̃'te] #3 *v. tr.* to scald; [légumes, noix, &c.] to blanch. || **s'ébouillanter** *v. pron.* to scald o.s.

éboulement [ebul|'mɑ̃] *n.m.* fall of rock, landslide: *Attention aux éboulements,* Falling Rock. || **ébouler** [-e] #3 *v. tr.* to tear down. || *v. intr.* to slide down. || **s'ébouler** *v. pron.* to slide down, to fall down. || **éboulis** [-i] *n.m.* fallen rock.

ébouriffant, -e [eburi'f|ɑ̃(:t)] *adj.* startling, amazing. || **ébouriffé, -e** [-e] *adj.* [cheveux] rumpled, dishevelled, ruffled. || **ébouriffer** [-e] #3 *v. tr.* to rumple, dishevel (the hair).

ébranlé, -e [ebrɑ̃'l|e] *adj.* shaken, weakened, loosened. || **ébranlement** [-'mɑ̃] *n.m.* **1.** shaking; [vitres] rattling; shock, violent disturbance. **2.** [Fig.] undermining, weakening (of a fortune), shaking (of an empire), weakening, breaking (of one's health); [nerveux] shock; [cœur] weakening. || **ébranler** [-e] #3 *v. tr.* **1.** to start, set in motion; to shake; [vitres] to rattle. **2.** to shake, weaken (a building, an enemy, &c.) to loosen, to knock loose (a tooth). || **s'ébranler** *v. pron.* to swing; [plus rapide] to shake, to get under way, to move off.

ébréché, -e [ebre'ʃe] *adj.* [instrument tranchant] nicked; [choses cassantes] chipped; [ext., montagne, crête] notched; [Fig., réputation] dented. || **ébrécher** [-e] #10 *v. tr.* **1.** to nick, notch; [choses cassantes] to chip; [instrument tranchant] to nick; [ext.] to dull, blunt. **2.** [Fig. & Fam.] to make a hole in (a fortune); to damage (a reputation). || **s'ébrécher** *v. pron.* to chip (a tooth), to nick (a sword, &c.).

ébriété [ebrije'te] *n.f.* intoxication, drunkenness: *en état d'* ~, drunk.

ébrouement [ebru|'mɑ̃] *n.m.* [cheval] snort (ing). || **s'ébrouer** [-'e] #3 *v. pron.* **1.** [cheval] to snort. **2.** [oiseaux] to flutter about (in water, dust); [Pers.] to snort and shake o.s.

ébruiter [ebrɥi'te] #3 *v. tr.* to spread around, to make (sth.) known. || **s'ébruiter** *v. pron.* to become known, to spread.

ébullition [ebyli'sjõ] *n.f.* **1.** boiling. **2.** [Fig.] turmoil, commotion.

écaille [e'kaj] *n.f.* scale; [huître] shell. || **écailler** [-e] #3 *v. tr.* [poisson, &c.] to scale; [huître] to open; to chip off. || **s'écailler** *v. pron.* to peel, scale, flake.

écale [e'kal] *n.f.* [noix, noisettes, œuf, &c.] shell; [petits pois, fèves, haricots, &c.] pod. || **écaler** [-e] #3 *v. tr.* [noix, noisettes, &c., pois, fèves, haricots] to shell.

écarlate [ekar'lat] *n.f. & adj.* scarlet.

écarquillé, -e [ekarki'je] *adj.* opened wide: *les yeux écarquillés,* wide-eyed, goggle-eyed. || **écarquiller** #3 *v. tr.* to open wide (one's eyes).

écart[1] [e'ka:r] *n.m.* **1.** distance, difference/between (two things), spreading, diverging; [épaule d'un cheval] sprain, strain;

[danse] splits; [Artil.] error (in range). **2.** [brusque] swerve, [cheval, &c.] shying: *faire un* ~, [Pers.] to jump, step/aside; [voiture, &c.] to swerve; [cheval, &c.] to shy, to jump aside. **3.** [Fig.] flights (of imagination); slip (of behaviour); [de la jeunesse] errors; [d'un orateur] digression: *à l'écart*, at a distance, away, isolated.

écart[2] [e'ka:r] *n.m.* [cartes] discard. || **écarté, -e** [ekar't|e] *adj.* **1.** separated, spread out; [doigts, bras, jambes, &c.] spread apart. **2.** [candidat] rejected, eliminated; [idée, hypothèse] brushed aside; eliminated (from power). **3.** [endroit] isolated, solitary, remote. || **écartement** [-ə'mɑ̃] *n.m.* **1.** spreading (of the arms, legs, &c.) **2.** [poteaux, essieux, &c.] distance, space/between; [rails] gauge. || **écarter**[1] [-e] #3 *v. tr.* **1.** to separate, to draw apart, to open; to spread (one's legs). **2.** to move away (from, *de*); [Fig.] to brush, turn/aside, to eliminate (a candidate).

écarter[2] #3 *v. tr.* [cartes] to discard. || **s'écarter** [sekar'te] *v. pron.* **1.** to spread out, to draw apart; to fall back. **2.** to move away from (sth., s.o.); to move back (to let s.o. pass), to fall back. **3.** [Fig.] to stray (from the right road, from one's subject, from tradition, from the beaten paths); to deviate (from one's principles, &c.); © to lose one's way.

ecclésiastique [ɛklezjas'tik] *adj.* ecclesiastical, clerical. || *n.m.* clergyman, ecclesiastic.

écervelé, -e [esɛrvə'le] *adj.* scatter-brained, thoughtless. || *n.* scatter-brain, harum-scarum.

échafaud [eʃa'fo] *n.m.* scaffold. || **échafaudage** [eʃafo'd|a:ʒ] *n.m.* **1.** scaffolding: *dresser un* ~, to put up, build/scaffolding. **2.** [ext.] a stack, pile (of cards, furniture, hair). **3.** [Fig.] structure: *Tout cet ~ s'est écroulé*, The whole structure came tumbling down. || **échafauder** [-e] #3 *v. tr.* to build a scaffold; [Fig., plans, &c.] to construct.

échalote [eʃa'lɔt] *n.f.* shallot.

échancré, -e [eʃɑ̃'kr|e] *adj.* [robe, chemise, corsage] low-cut; [Bot., feuilles] indented; [littoral, rivage] indented. || **échancrer** [-e] #3 *v. tr.* to notch (a board); to indent; [couture] to cut (a dress) low (at the neck). || **échancrure** [-y:r] *n.f.* notch, cut, hollowing out, groove; [rivage] indentation; [couture] opening.

échange [e'ʃ|ɑ̃:ʒ] *n.m.* exchange, interchange; [entre pays] trade, commerce, exchange; [de produits] barter: *faire un ~ de qqch. contre qqch.*, to exchange, barter, trade/sth. for sth. || **échangeable** [-ɑ̃'ʒ|abl] *adj.* exchangeable: [marchandise d'un magasin] returnable. || **échangeai, &c.** cf. ÉCHANGER. || **échanger** [-e] #5 *v. tr.* to exchange; [Com.] to trade; [Fam.] to swap.

échantillon [eʃɑ̃ti'j|õ] *n.m.* **1.** sample; [tissu, &c.] sample, swatch; [ext.] specimen (of water for analysis): *cahier d'échantillons*, sample book. **2.** [Fig.] sample, example. || **échantillonner** [-ɔ'ne] #3 *v. tr.* to make, prepare/samples (of sth.).

échappatoire [eʃap|a'twa:r] *n.f.* subterfuge; way out, loophole. || **échappé, -e** [-e] *n.* fugitive, runaway. || **échappée** [-e] *n.f.* **1.** vista. **2.** escape (of game, &c.); [Sport] spurt. || **échappement** [-'mɑ̃] *n.m.* [Méc.] escape, outlet, exhaust. || **échapper** [-e] #3 *v. intr.* **1.** to escape (from, *de*), to leak: ~ *à un accident*, almost to have an accident. **2.** to slip out: *L'assiette lui a échappé des mains*, The plate fell out of his hands; *La remarque lui/a échappé, est échappée*, The remark slipped out; *laisser ~ une occasion*, to miss an opportunity. **3.** to elude: *Son nom m'échappe*, I can't remember his name. **4.** to be overlooked: *Il ne m'a pas échappé que*, I have noticed that. || **s'échapper** *v. pron.* **1.** to escape. **2.** to come out of.

écharde [e'ʃard] *n.f.* splinter.

écharpe [e'ʃarp] *n.f.* **1.** sash. **2.** sling: *le bras en* ~, with his arm in a sling. **3.** scarf.

écharper [eʃar'pe] #3 *v. tr.* to slash, to cut; [Fam.] to manhandle, to lynch.

échasse [e'ʃas] *n.f.* stilt: *marcher sur des échasses*, to walk on stilts. || **échassier** [-je] *n.m.* [Orn.] wader.

échauder [eʃo'de] #3 *v. tr.* to scald: [Fig.] *se faire ~ dans une affaire*, to get fleeced in a deal. || **s'échauder** *v. pron.* to get scalded.

échauffement [eʃof'mɑ̃] *n.m.* [oven] heating; [Méd.] chafing. || **échauffer** [eʃo'fe] #3 *v. tr.* **1.** to heat; [moins fort] to warm (gradually). **2.** [Fig.] to excite; to stir (the imagination, the blood); [la tête, les oreilles de qqun] to anger (s.o.), to make (s.o.) angry. || **s'échauffer** *v. pron.* **1.** [en courant] to get/warm, hot/; [Sport] to warm up (before a game, &c.). **2.** [Fig., conversation, querelle] to warm up, [plus sérieux] to become heated.

échauffourée [eʃofu're] *n.f.* scuffle, skirmish.

échéance [eʃe|'ɑ̃:s] *n.f.* **1.** [d'un acte, d'une lettre de change, &c.] (date of) maturity; date on which (sth.) falls due: *payable à* ~, payable at maturity. **2.** [délai] term, from date: *à deux mois d'* ~, at two months from date; [bill, loan, note, &c.] *à/longue, courte* ~, long, short/term. || **échéant** [-ɑ̃] *adj.* [Com.] falling due, payable; [Loc.] *le cas échéant*, should the occasion arise, if needs be, if necessary.

échec [e'ʃɛk] *n.m.* **1.** setback, defeat: *subir un* ~, to suffer a setback; *tenir en* ~, to hold in check. **2.** [*pl.*, jeu] chess: *jouer aux échecs*, to play chess; ~ *et mat*, checkmate; *mettre* ~ *et mat*, to checkmate.

échelle [e'ʃɛl] *n.f.* **1.** ladder: ~ *pliante*, stepladder; ~ *de sauvetage*, fire escape; *faire la courte* ~ *à qqun*, to give s.o. a hand up. **2.** [Fig.] scale: ~ *mobile*, sliding scale; *sur une grande* ~, on a large scale. || **échelon** [e'ʃl|ɔ̃] *n.m.* **1.** rung (of a ladder); step, degree (of a scale): *par échelons*, by degrees; *d'* ~ *en* ~, step by step. **2.** [Mil.] échelon. || **échelonnement** [-ɔn'mɑ̃] *n.m.* [troupes, paiements] spreading out. || **échelonner** [-ɔ'ne] #3 *v. tr.* **1.** [Mil.] to space (troops). **2.** to spread (deliveries, payments, work) out (over a period of time); to graduate, grade/(colours in a picture); [congés] to stagger. || **s'échelonner** *v. pron.* [choses] to be spread (out) over (an area); to spread (out).

écheveau [eʃ(ə)'vo] *n.m.* [laine] hank; [mesure] skein.

échevelé, -e [eʃəv'le] *adj.* **1.** [Pers., tête, perruque] dishevelled, tousled, [cheveux] dishevelled, tousled, rumpled. **2.** [Fig.] [danse, passion] wild; [histoire] mixed-up; [style] disorderly.

†**échevin** [eʃ'vɛ̃] *n.m.* alderman.

échine [e'ʃin] *n.f.* spine, backbone.

échiquier [eʃi'kje] *n.m.* exchequer; [échecs] chess board.

écho [e'ko] *n.m.* **1.** echo: *faire* ~ *à*, to echo. **2.** [nouvelle] news, gossip. **3.** [Pers.] echo, parrot.

échoir [e'ʃ|wa:r], **échéant** [-e'ɑ̃], **échu** [-y] #32 *v. intr.* [seldom used except in 3rd person]. **1.** [le gros lot] to fall (to s.o., *à qqun*). **2.** [billets, &c.] to mature, to fall, become/due; [un terme, le loyer, &c.] to expire, run out: *intérêts échus*, accrued interest.

†**échoppe** [e'ʃɔp] *n.f.* stall, booth, small workshop.

échotier [ekɔ'tje] *n.m.* (gossip-) columnist.

échoué, -e [e'ʃwe] *adj.* grounded, stranded, beached. || **échouer** #3 *v. intr.* **1.** to run aground; [à marée basse] to be stranded; [contre, sur/un écueil] to hit a rock, to be wrecked (on the rocks): *faire* ~, [à la plage] to beach; [sur un écueil] to wreck (on the rocks). **2.** [Fig.] [plans, projets, entreprise, mariage, &c.] to fail, [Fam.] to go on the rocks; ~ *à un examen*, to fail an exam; *faire* ~ (*qqch.*), to wreck, ruin (sth.); [Fam.] to queer (s.o.'s plans). || *v. tr.* to beach. || **s'échouer** *v. pron.* **1.** to run aground, to be wrecked. **2.** [Fig.] to end up (at a place).

échu, -e p.p. d'ÉCHOIR; due, falling due.

éclaboussé, -e [eklabu's|e] *adj.* splashed, spattered. || **éclabousser** #3 *v. tr.* **1.** to splash, (be)spatter. **2.** [scandale] to besmirch. || **s'éclabousser** *v. pron.* to splatter, splash (o.s.). || **éclaboussure** [-y:r] *n.f.* splash, spot (of ink, mud, &c.).

éclair [e'kl|ɛ:r] *n.m.* **1.** flash of lightning; [ext.] flash (of reflected light); [*pl.*] lightning: *rapide comme l'* ~, quick as/lightning, a flash/. **2.** [Fig.] flash (of good sense, lucidity); stroke (of genius). **3.** [Cul.] éclair. || **éclairage** [-ɛ'ra:ʒ] *n.m.* lighting.

éclairci, -e [-ɛr'si] *adj.* clearer, clarified. || *n.f.* gap, break (in clouds); clearing (in woods). || **éclaircir** [-ɛr'si:r] #17 *v. tr.* **1.** [vent] to clear (sky); to clear (voice). **2.** to lighten (a colour); to brighten (silverware, &c.), to thin (a soup, wine, &c.); to thin (growing plants, hair, the number of branches on a tree, &c.). **3.** [Fig.] to clear up (a question, a misunderstanding); to clarify, explain, elucidate (a point, an idea), to solve (a mystery). || **s'éclaircir** *v. pron.* **1.** [ciel] to clear; [temps] to clear up; [brouillard] to thin, clear. **2.** [couleur] to lighten, to fade; [liquide, cheveux] to thin, to/get, become/thin. **3.** [Fig.] to clear up, to become clear, to be clarified. || **éclaircissement** [-ɛrsis'mɑ̃] *n.m.* **1.** thinning (of a forest). **2.** explanation, clarification: explanatory note: *donner des éclaircissements sur qqch.*, to explain, clarify sth.

éclairé, -e [-ɛ're] *adj.* **1.** lighted, lit. **2.** [Pers.] well-informed, up-to-date; [Rel., Pol.] enlightened. || **éclairement** [-ɛr'mɑ̃] *n.m.* lighting, illumination (of a surface). || **éclairer** [-ɛ're] #3 *v. tr.* **1.** [soleil, lune, lampe, lumière] to light; [Pers.] to light (up) (a room), to turn the lights on (in a room); [qqun] to give (s.o.) some light; [Fig.] [la joie, &c.] to light up (s.o.'s face, &c.). **2.** [Fig.] to enlighten, inform; [Fam.] to let (s.o.) in on (sth.). **3.** [Mil.]

to reconnoitre for (an army, &c.). || *v. intr.* [mal, bien] to give a (bad, good) light; [à peine] to give (hardly any) light. || **s'éclairer** *v. pron.* **1.** to become light, to light up [also Fig.]. **2.** [Fig.] [problème, difficulté] to become clear; [réciproque] to enlighten each other. || **éclaireur** [eklɛ'r|œ:r] *n.m.* [Mil.] scout; [scoutisme] Boy Scout. || **éclaireuse** [-ø:z] *n.f.* © Girl Guide, [US] Girl Scout.

éclat [e'kla] *n.m.* **1.** [morceau] splinter, chip, piece; [bombe] fragment; [long, mince] sliver: *voler en éclats,* [bois] to be splintered; to (be) shatter(ed). **2.** [bruit] clap, peal, burst (of thunder); [trompette] blast; [de voix] [*pl.*] shouting, burst (of voices); [de joie, de colère] (out)burst: *partir d'un ~ de rire,* to burst out laughing; *rire aux éclats,* to roar with laughter. **3.** [lumière] brightness, [plus intense] brilliancy, glare; [d'une pierre précieuse, d'un métal, &c.] [dur] glitter, [doux] lustre, shine, [des couleurs] vividness, brilliancy; [apparition brusque] flash (of light, of a gun), [des yeux, du regard] brightness: *faire perdre l' ~* , to tarnish, to dull; *sans ~*, dull; *donner de l' ~ à qqch.*, to brighten sth. **4.** [Fig.] [dans la presse, société, &c.] stir, publicity; scandal, [Fam.] noise: *faire un ~* , to make a stir, to create a scandal, to cause publicity; *sans ~* , quietly. **5.** [Fig.] [d'une femme] radiance; [du style, &c.] brilliancy, [d'un nom] prestige: *avoir de l' ~* , [beauté] to be radiant, [style] brilliant; [nom] to have prestige; *être dans tout l' ~ de sa beauté,* to be radiantly beautiful; *perdre son ~* , to fade; *une action d' ~* , a brilliant action, feat.

éclatant, -e [-'tɑ̃(:t)] *adj.* **1.** [lumière] bright, brilliant; glittering, sparkling; vivid, cf. ÉCLAT. **2.** [sourire, beauté] radiant. **3.** [son] blaring (of a trumpet); [voix, rire] noisy, loud, ringing. **4.** [Fig.] brilliant (success, victory). || **éclatement** [-t'mɑ̃] *n.m.* exploding, explosion, bursting (of a bomb, boiler, &c.); [conduite] bursting; [Méd.] rupture; [pneu] blowout.

éclater [-'te] #3 *v. intr.* **1.** [chaudière, bombe, &c.] to burst, to explode, to blow up; [pneu] to blow out; [wood] to split (open): *faire ~ qqch.*, to shatter, burst, explode, blow up, split, **2.** [son] [applaudissements] to burst/forth, out/; [trompette] to blare (out); [rire] to burst out; [en sanglots] to burst into: *~ de rire,* to burst out laughing. **3.** [Fig.] [incendie, maladie, guerre, dispute, rires, &c.] to break out; [scandale, nouvelle] to break; [émotion] to burst: *laisser ~* (*une émotion*), to give vent to (an emotion). **4.** [Fig.] [faiblesse, innocence, partialité, &c.] to be manifest, evident.

éclipse [e'klips] *n.f.* eclipse. || **éclipser** [-e] #3 *v. tr.* **1.** to eclipse. **2.** [Fig.] to eclipse, outshine, overshadow s.o. || **s'éclipser** *v. pron.* **1.** [soleil] to become eclipsed; [paysage] to hide itself (behind the fog). **2.** [Fig.] to vanish, disappear.

éclopé, -e [eklɔ'pe] *adj.* crippled, lame. || *n.* cripple.

éclore [e'kl|ɔ:r], **éclosant** [-o'zɑ̃], **éclos** [-o] #53 *v. intr.* [Note that this verb is not used in the 1st & 2nd person plur. pres. ind., in the simple past and in the imperf. ind.]. **1.** conj. ÊTRE [œufs] to hatch: *faire ~* , to hatch. **2.** [par analogie] [bourgeon] to open; [fleur] to bloom, blossom. **3.** [Fig.] to break forth, to dawn. || **éclos, éclot** cf. ÉCLORE. || **éclosion** [-o'zjõ] *n.f.* hatching, blooming, dawning.

écluse [e'kly:z] *n.f.* [bassin] lock, sluice; [ext., portes d'écluse] sluice gate, floodgate.

écœurant, -e [ekœ'r|ɑ̃(:t)] *adj.* **1.** nauseating (odour, food). **2.** [Fig.] [procédé, flatteries, spectacle, &c.] disgusting. || **écœuranterie** [-ɑ̃'tri] © [Fam.] *n.f.* cf. ÉCŒUREMENT. || **écœurement** [-'mɑ̃] *n.m.* nausea; [Fig.] disgust; [causé par des échecs] discouragement: *être/pris, saisi/d' ~* , to be nauseated, disgusted. || **écœurer** [-e] #3 *v. tr.* **1.** to nauseate, to sicken. **2.** [Fig.] to disgust; [décourager] to dishearten.

école [e'kɔl] *n.f.* **1.** school (college, institute, faculty, &c., ☞ but no exact equivalence is possible); [bâtiment] school house, school building: *~ d'application,* model school; *~ des beaux-arts,* school of fine arts; *~ dentaire,* dental school, school of dentistry; *~ d'art dramatique,* school of dramatic arts; *~ d'arts et métiers,* trade school; *~ confessionnelle* (Fr. *école libre*) denominational school; *~ d'équitation,* riding academy, riding school; [Fr.] *~ de guerre,* staff or military college; *~ maternelle,* nursery school, kindergarten; [Fr.] *~ militaire,* military college; *~ mixte,* co-educational school; *~ normale,* teachers' college, © normal school; *~ normale supérieure,* college of education; *~ paroissiale,* parochial school; © *école polytechnique,* school of engineering, Polytechnic Institute; *~ primaire,* primary school, elementary school; *~ privée,* private school; *~ publique,* public school; *~ secondaire,* high school; © ~ *séparée*, separate school; ~ *sur rails*, railway school cars; ~ *technique*, technical school. **2.** school [of thought] doctrine, system: *faire* ~ , [Pers.] to start a doctrine, to be an authority on; [idées] to spread. **3.** [Loc.] *aller à l'* ~ , to go to school; *entrer à l'* ~ (*Polytechnique*) to be admitted to the (Polytechnic) Institute; *sortir d'une* ~ , to graduate (from).

écoli|er, -ère [ekɔ'l|je, -ɛːr] *adj.* [manières, goûts] schoolboy; [la gent] school (children): *papier* ~ , foolscap. || *n.* **1.** schoolboy, schoolgirl, pupil [below grade six, generally]; cf. LYCÉEN, COLLÉGIEN, ÉTUDIANT; *le chemin des écoliers*, the longest way. **2.** [Fig.] novice, learner, beginner.

éconduire [ekõ'dɥ|iːr], **éconduisant** [-i'zã], **éconduit** [-i] #56 *v. tr.* [solliciteur, prétendant, visiteur] to show (s.o.)/(to) the door, out/; [moins poli] to put (s.o.) out; [sans ménagement] to throw, kick/(s.o.) out: *être éconduit*, to meet with a polite refusal.

économat [ekɔnɔ'ma] *n.m.* [charge] treasurership; [bureau] treasurer's office [université, collège] bursar's office. || **économe** [ekɔ'nɔm] *adj.* economical, sparing, frugal, thrifty. || *n.* treasurer; [collège, université] bursar. || **économie** [-i] *n.f.* **1.** economy; †management: ~ *politique*, political economy. **2.** economy, arrangement (of the body); [d'une entreprise] set-up. **3.** a saving, economy; [*pl.*] savings, economies, nest-egg: *faire des économies*, to save (up); *réaliser une* ~ *de 30 cents*, to save 30 cents. **4.** thrift: *avoir de l'* ~ , to be thrifty, *avec* ~ , thriftily, frugally. || **économique** [-ik] *adj.* **1.** [qui réduit les frais] economical; [bon marché] cheap, inexpensive. **2.** [science, Hist., Géog., guerre, &c.] économic. || *n.f.* economics. || **économiser** [-i'ze] #3 *v. tr.* **1.** to economize, to save; to put by. **2.** [Fig.] [temps, force] to save; [paroles] not to waste. || **économiste** [-ist] *n.* economist.

écope [e'kɔp] *n.f.* scoop, ladle. || **écoper** [-e] #3 *v. tr.* to bail out. || *v. intr.* **1.** to bail out. **2.** to catch it, to suffer.

écorce [e'kɔrs] *n.f.* **1.** [arbres] bark; [noix, châtaigne] shell cf. ÉCALE; [melon, pastèque, &c.] rind; [orange, citron, &c.] peel, peeling cf. PELURE; [terrestre] crust; cf. CROÛTE: © *canot m d'écorce*, bark canoe. **2.** [Fig.] shell, outside. || **écorcer** [-e] #4 *v. tr.* to skin (a tree, orange, melon, &c.), to shell (nuts).

écorcher [ekɔr'ʃ|e] #3 *v. tr.* **1.** to skin (an animal). **2.** [épines, &c.] to scratch (one's arms, legs, hands, &c.); [ext.] to scratch, scrape, graze (a wall, tree, &c.), to scratch (the soil); [boisson] to burn, bite (the throat); [Fig.] [sons] to grate on (the ears); [une langue, un mot] to murder; [clients] to fleece. || **écorchure** [-yːr] *n.f.* scratch, abrasion.

écorner [ekɔr'ne] #3 *v. tr.* **1.** to dehorn (animals): to chip the corner off of (a rock, dish, book, &c.); [route] to cut a corner off of (one's property). **2.** [Fig.] to cut down (a pension); to make a (large) dent in (one's/fortune, provisions/).

écossais, -e [ekɔ'sɛ(ːz)] *adj.* Scottish, Scotch; [tissu] plaid; [douche] alternately hot and cold. || *n.m.* Scot, Scotsman, Scotchman; [dialect] Scots; [tissu] plaid. || *n.f.* Scotswoman, Scotchwoman, Scot. || **Écosse (l')** [(l) e'kɔs] *n.f.* Scotland; *la Nouvelle-Écosse*, Nova Scotia.

écosser [ekɔ'se] #3 *v. tr.* to shell, husk, shuck (peas, beans, &c.).

écot [e'ko] *n.m.* share, quota; score, bill.

écoulement [ekul|'mã] *n.m.* [liquide] flow, draining; [d'une foule d'un lieu] dispersal, exit; [temps] passing; [d'un champ] drainage; [de marchandises] flow; sale, turnover. || **écouler** [-e] #3 *v. tr.* [des marchandises] to sell, to dispose of. **s'écouler** *v. pron.* **1.** [liquide] to flow out, to escape, [fuite] to leak; [temps] to pass, elapse, [vite] to fly; [une foule] to come out, to exit; [marchandises] to flow, [vendre] to sell. **2.** [Fig.] [richesse, bonheur] to slip away.

écourter [ekur'te] #3 *v. tr.* to shorten (a skirt, a dress); to cut short (a trip, a stay, a visit); [la queue, les oreilles] to crop; [acte, discours, chapitre] to shorten, to cut (down).

écoute [e'kut] *n.f.* **1.** listening: [à la radio] *se mettre à l'* ~ , to turn on the radio; *être, rester|à l'* ~ , to be, keep listening (to sth.): *Ne quittez pas l'* ~ , → One moment please, Don't turn your dial! **2.** [pl.] *être aux écoutes*, [à la dérobée] to eavesdrop; [à ce qui se passe autour de soi] to keep one's ears open. **3.** listening post; *organiser l'* ~ , to set up a group of listening posts. || **écouté, -e** [-e] *adj.* influential, carrying weight. || **écouter** [-e] #3 *v. tr.* **1.** to listen to: *Écoutez !*, [protestation] Listen!, Look here!; I'll tell you what! **2.** listen to, heed, pay attention to (advice, counsel, a warning, &c.). || **s'écouter** *v. pron.* to listen to o.s.

|| **écouteur** [-œːr] *n.m.* [Tél.] earphone; [le tout] receiver. cf. RÉCEPTEUR.

écran [e'krɑ̃] *n.m.* screen; [Photo.] filter.

écrasant, -e [ekrɑ'z|ɑ̃(ːt)] *adj.* **1.** [poids, masse, &c.] crushing. **2.** [Fig.] crushing, overwhelming. || **écrasé, -e** [-e] *adj.* crushed, squashed; [par une voiture, un train] run over; [nez, visage] flat. || **écrasement** [-'mɑ̃] *n.m.* **1.** [action] crushing, flattening out. **2.** [Fig.] (crushing) defeat, stamping out (of a revolt). **écraser** [-e] #3 *v. tr.* **1.** to crush [si la chose contient du liquide] to squash: *se faire* ~ *(par un train, une voiture, &c.)*, → to be, get/ run over (by a train, a car, &c.). **2.** [Fig.] [travail] to swamp; [responsabilité, &c.] to crush; to crush, overwhelm (an adversary, an enemy, &c.); to be overcome/by, with/shame, &c. || **s'écraser** *v. pron.* [avion] to crash [*sur le sol*, into the ground; *contre une montagne*, into, against/a mountain]; [fruits, en tombant] to squash; to be squashed, bruised.

écrémer [ekre'm|e] #10 *v. tr.* to take the cream off, to skim. || **écrémeuse** [-øːz] *n.f.* (cream) separator.

écrevisse [ekrə'vis] *n.f.* crayfish, crawfish.

écrier, s' [sekri'je] #3 *v. pron.* to cry out (in anger, surprise, fear, &c.).

écrin [e'krɛ̃] *n.m.* jewel case, case, casket.

écrire [e'kr|iːr], **écrivant** [-i'vɑ̃], **écrit** [-i] #48 *v. tr.* to write, [coucher sur papier] to write down: *l'art d'* ~, the art of writing; *machine à* ~, typewriter. || **s'écrire** *v. pron.* to be written: *Cela se dit, mais ne s'écrit pas,* That's written but not said; *Comment ce mot s'écrit-il?*, How do you/write, spell/that word? || **écrit** [-i] *n.m.* **1.** writing: *par* ~, in writing; *coucher par* ~, to put in writing. **2.** [ouvrage] pamphlet, [plus grand] work, treatise; [pl.] writings (of s.o.). **3.** written exam(ination). || **écriteau** [-i'to] *n.m.* sign, notice. || **écriture** [-i'tyːr] *n.f.* **1.** (hand)-writing: *reconnaître l'* ~ *de qqun*, to recognize s.o.'s writing. **2.** *Com.* [pl.] accounts, [sing.] entry: *tenir les écritures*, to keep the accounts; *commis aux écritures*, accounting clerk. **3.** [Rel.] (Holy) Scripture, the Scriptures, Holy Writ. || **écrivain** [-i'vɛ̃] *n.m.* writer, author: *une femme* ~, an authoress, a woman writer. || **écrivais,** &c. cf. ÉCRIRE.

écrou [e'kru] *n.m.* [d'un boulon] nut; *serrer un* ~, to tighten a nut. || **écrouer** [-'e] #3 *v. tr.* to jail, to book.

écroulé, -e [ekru'l|e] *adj.* **1.** [maison] which has/fallen in, collapsed/; [mur] which has/fallen, crumbled/down. **2.** [Fig.] collapsed, ruined (hopes); [Fam., Pers.] collapsed, slumped (in a chair, on a bed). || **écroulement** [-'mɑ̃] *n.m.* **1.** [soudain] collapse; [éboulement] crumbling; [caverne, maison, &c.] falling in. **2.** [Fig.] collapse (of an empire, project, fortune, system), ruin (of one's hopes); [santé, raison] breaking down, ruin. || **s'écrouler** [sekru'le] #3 *v. pron.* **1.** to collapse, to fall in, [sous une charge] to give way. **2.** [Fig.] to collapse, [espérances] to be ruined. **3.** [Fam.] ~ *dans un fauteuil*, to flop into, collapse into/a chair; ~ *sur un lit* to flop down on (to), collapse on (to)/ a bed.

écru, -e [e'kry] *adj.* (toile, &c.) unbleached; [soie] raw.

écueil [e'kœj] *n.m.* **1.** (under water) rock, reef, sandbank. **2.** [Fig.] stumbling block; snag.

écuelle [e'kɥɛl] *n.f.* porringer, trencher; bowl.

éculé, -e [eky'le] *adj.* worn down at the heels: *talon* ~, run-down heel. || éculer #3 *v. tr.* (un soulier) to wear down at the heel.

écume [e'kym] *n.f.* **1.** [sur un liquide agité, chauffé, ou qui fermente] foam, froth, bubbles; [sale] scum; [d'un métal en fusion] dross, scum. **2.** [salive, sueur mousseuse] froth, foam: *(Un cheval) qui a l'* ~ *à la bouche*, (A horse) frothing at the mouth. || **écumer** [-e] #3 *v. intr.* to foam, froth, bubble: *Il écumait*, He was frothing at the mouth. || *v. tr.* **1.** to skim off (the foam, froth). **2.** [Fig.] to scour (the seas); to skim off (the richest part of sth.). **écumeur** [-œːr] *n.m.* [Fig.] [de mer] sea-rover, pirate; [de marmite] pot-licker, hanger-on. **écumeu|x, -se** [-ø(ːz)] *adj.* [état] foamy, frothy, bubbly; [action] foaming, frothing, bubbling. || **écumoire** [-waːr] *n.f.* skimmer.

écureuil [eky'rœj] *n.m.* squirrel: ~ *de terre,* cf. CITELLE.

écurie [eky'ri] *n.f.* **1.** horse stable; [ext.] © stable, barn. **2.** stable (of race horses).

écusson [eky'sõ] *n.m.* escutcheon, coat of arms.

édenté, -e [edɑ̃'te] *adj.* toothless. || **édenter** #3 *v. tr.* [arracher] to pull (s.o.'s) teeth out, [briser] to knock, break (s.o.'s) teeth out; [un peigne] to break the teeth out of (a comb).

édicter [edik'te] #3 *v. tr.* **1.** to enact; [une loi, un statut] to decree. **2.** [Fig.] to decree, to pronounce.

édifiant, -e [edi'f|jɑ̃(ːt)] *adj.* edifying, uplifting. || **édification** [-ika'sjõ] *n.f.* **1.**

[palais, monument, ville] erection, construction, building. **2.** [Fig.] construction, building (of an empire, literary work). **3.** [moral] edification, improvement: *pour votre* ~ , for your edification. ‖ **édifice** [-is] *n.m.* building, structure.

édifier [-je] #3 *v. tr.* **1.** [not often used except for large buildings.] cf. CONSTRUIRE, BÂTIR; to erect, construct (a temple, palace, &c.). **2.** [Fig.] to build (up) (an empire); to elaborate, construct (a system, theory). **3.** [moral] to edify, to enlighten: ~ *qqun sur qqch.*, to enlighten s.o. about sth.

Édimbourg [edɛ̃'bu:r] *n.* Edinburgh.

édit [e'di] *n.m.* edict, decree. ‖ **éditer** [-'te] #3 *v. tr.* to publish. ‖ **édit|eur, -rice** [-'tœ:r, -'tris] *n.* publisher [× L'anglais *editor* se rend par *rédacteur, directeur (d'un journal)*]; [une société] publishers, publishing house. ‖ **édition** [-'sjõ] *n.f.* **1.** [action] publishing, publication; [chose éditée] edition, issue, publication; [au *pl.* + nom de la maison] publishing company, publisher(s). **2.** book trade. ‖ **éditorial** [-tɔ'rjal] *adj. & n.* editorial. ‖ **éditorialiste** [-ist] *n.m.* editorial writer.

Édouard [e'dwa:r] *n.m.* = Edward.

édredon [edrə'dõ] *n.m. & adj.* eiderdown (quilt).

éducat|eur, -rice [edyka|'tœ:r, -'tris] *n.* educator. ‖ *adj.* educational. ‖ **éducati|f, -ve** [-'tif, -'ti:v] *adj.* educational, educative. ‖ **éducation** [-sjõ] *n.f.* **1.** education; [réflexes, l'œil, l'oreille, sens, mémoire] training, education: *l'* ~ *nouvelle*, progressive education; *faire l'* ~ *de*, to educate. **2.** education, upbringing. ‖ **éduquer** [edy'ke] #3 *v. tr.* to educate, bring up, train (a child); [l'esprit, la volonté] to train, discipline.

effaçage [efa's|a:ʒ] *ou* **effacement** [-'mã] *n.m.* **1.** erasing, rubbing out. **2.** [Fig.] erasing; wiping away (of sins, of a memory, by time); [de soi-même] self-effacement. ‖ © **efface** [e'fas] [élastique] *n.f.* [= Fr. *gomme* (à effacer)] eraser. ‖ **effacé, -e** [efa'se] *adj.* erased, rubbed out. **1.** [par l'usure] worn away, [couleur] faded; [Fig.] [de la mémoire] erased, faded/(from). **2.** [menton] receding, [poitrine] hollow; [Fig.] retiring (person, ways, manner). ‖ **effacer** #4 *v. tr.* **1.** to efface; [avec une gomme] to erase, rub out; [le temps, l'usure] to efface, wear away; [le soleil] to fade (colours); [d'une liste] to delete. **2.** [Fig.] to erase, rub out; [de sa mémoire] to erase, blot out; [de la carte] to wipe off. ‖ **s'effacer** *v. pron.* **1.** to be erased, rubbed out; [inscription, effigie] to wear away, become obliterated; [lumière, jour, couleur] to fade. **2.** [pour laisser passer qqun] to stand aside; [Fig.] to take a back seat. **3.** [Fig.] to fade (from one's memory).

effarant, -e [ɛfa'r|ã(:t)] *adj.* startling, alarming, frightening. ‖ **effaré, -e** [-e] *adj.* frightened; [plus fort] terrorized; alarmed *être* ~ , to be alarmed, shocked. ‖ **effarement** [-'mã] *n.m.* fright. ‖ **effarer** [-e] #3 *v. tr.* to frighten, alarm; to shock. ‖ **s'effarer** *v. pron.* to get scared, to take fright; to become bewildered.

effaroucher [ɛfaru'ʃe] #3 *v. tr.* [less used than EFFRAYER]. **1.** to frighten, scare (an animal). **2.** to frighten away (candidates, clients, &c.). ‖ **s'effaroucher** *v. pron.* (cheval) to take fright, to become frightened; [Pers.] to become alarmed; to take offence; [pudeur] to be offended.

effecti|f, -ve [ɛfɛk't|if, -i:v] *adj.* effective, real, actual. ‖ *n.m.* strength (of a regiment). ‖ **effectivement** *adv.* really, actually: *et* ~ *il s'en est occupé*, and he *did* take care of it; *bénéfice* ~ *réalisé*, profit actually made.

effectuer [ɛfɛk'tɥe] #3 *v. tr.* to effect, carry out, make (a retreat, an experiment, reforms, &c.). ‖ **s'effectuer** *v. pron.* to be made, effected, carried out.

efféminé, -e [ɛfemi'ne] *adj.* effeminate.

effervescence [ɛfɛrvɛ'sã:s] *n.f.* effervescence, excitement. ‖ **effervescent, -e** [ɛfɛrvɛ'sã(:t)] *adj.* effervescent.

effet [ɛ'fɛ] *n.m.* **1.** effect, result: *mettre à* ~ , to put into effect; *prendre* ~ , to take, go into effect; *efforts sans* ~ , ineffective, ineffectual efforts; *faire l'* ~ *de*, to give the impression of, to strike (s.o.) as; *l'* ~ *voulu*, the desired effect, results; *faire de l'* ~ , to be effective, to be striking; *faire un drôle d'* ~ *à*, to give (s.o.) a strange feeling. **2.** [de commerce] bill (of exchange) [in its most general meaning]. **3.** *pl.* effects, property, estate; [Fam.] things: *mettre ses* ~ *dans une valise*, to put one's things in a suitcase. ‖ **à cet effet** *loc. adv.* to this end, for that purpose. ‖ **en effet** *loc. adv.* [No exact English equivalent. The general meaning is *indeed*; often omitted altogether in English. Do not confuse with *en fait*, in fact. *En effet* means that things are as expected: sure enough, → do, did]: *Il a dit que cela arriverait et en effet c'est arrivé*, He said it would happen, and it did.

effeuiller [ɛfœ'je] #3 *v. tr.* **1.** to pluck the

leaves from (a tree, plant, flower, &c.). **2.** [Fig.] to destroy slowly. || **s'effeuiller** *v. pron.* to shed/its, their/leaves.

efficace [ɛfi'kas] *adj.* effective, efficient, efficacious; [personne compétente] competent. || **efficacité** [-i'te] *n.f.* efficacy, effectiveness; [productivité d'une machine, organisation] efficiency; [d'une personne] effectiveness, competence.

effilé, -e [ɛfi'le] *adj.* **1.** unravelled, frayed (cloth, &c.). **2.** [crayon] sharpened; [doigts] tapering. || **effiler** #3 *v. tr.* [étoffe] to unravel, to fray. **2.** to sharpen (a pencil, stick, &c.). || **s'effiler** *v. pron.* to unravel, to fray.

effilocher [ɛfilɔ'e] #3 *v. tr.* to ravel out, to fray.

efflanqué, -e [ɛflɑ̃'ke] *adj.* [animal] scrawny; [Fam., Pers.] lanky, lean.

effleurer [ɛflœ're] #3 *v. tr.* **1.** to pluck, pick/flowers (from a plant). cf. DÉPOUILLER. **2.** [de choses assez lourdes] to graze; [de choses légères] to brush; to skim, touch lightly. **3.** [Fig.] to dent, damage (one's reputation); to cross (one's mind), to touch on (a subject): *Il n'a fait qu'* ~ *le sujet*, He did not really come to grips with his topic.

effondré, -e [ɛfɔ̃'dr|e] *adj.* **1.** [toit] caved in, collapsed. **2.** [Fig., Pers.] prostrated. || **effondrement** [-ə'mɑ] *n.m.* **1.** [d'une voûte, d'un plafond, &c.] caving in, collapse, collapsing; falling in. **2.** [Fig.] collapse, collapsing, crumbling (of an empire, a government, a public person, a resistance, &c.). || **effondrer** [-e] #3 *v. tr.* [la terre] to work, break up (the soil). || **s'effondrer** *v. pron.* **1.** [toit, poutre, plancher, &c.] to cave in, collapse; [voiture, Pers.] to collapse. **2.** [Fig.] [coureur, empire, espérances, &c.] to collapse; [prix] to drop, slump.

efforcer, s' [sɛfɔr'se] #4 *v. pron.* [de + inf.] to strive, endeavour, make every effort [to, *de*]. || **effort** [ɛ'fɔːr] *n.m.* effort, endeavour, [qui force] strain; [de l'eau, du vent, d'une tempête] force; [qui tend à allonger, à tordre, à couper, &c.] stress: *faire un* ~ , make an effort; [Fam.] to make a reduction (in price); *faire* ~ *sur soi-même*, to get a hold of o.s.; *sans* ~ , without effort, effortlessly.

effraction [ɛfrak'sjɔ̃] *n.f.* house-breaking.

effraie, &c. cf. EFFRAYER.

effranger [ɛfrɑ̃'ʒe] #5 *v. tr.* [tissu] to fray.

effrayant, -e [ɛfrɛ'j|ɑ̃(:t)] *adj.* dreadful, awful, terrible. || **effrayé, -e** [-e] *adj.* frightened, scared (by sth.). || **effrayer** #11 *v. tr.* to frighten, scare. || **s'effrayer** *v. pron.* [de] to become, get/frightened, scared (of); to take fright (at).

effréné, -e [ɛfre'ne] *adj.* [Fig.] unrestrained, [plus littéraire] unbridled; wild.

effriter [ɛfri'te] #3 *v. tr.* †**1.** to wear out (the soil). **2.** to break up (chunks of earth, &c.). **3.** [Fig., majorité, pouvoir, autorité] to erode. || **s'effriter** *v. pron.* to crumble away.

effroi [ɛ'frwa] *n.m.* fear, [plus grand] terror; fright.

effronté, -e [ɛfrɔ̃'t|e] *adj.* impudent, brazen, shameless; [Fam.] cheeky (Pers., air, attitude, &c.). || *n.* impudent,/brazen, shameless/person. || **effronterie** [-'ri] *n.f.* impudence, brazenness, shamelessness: *nier avec* ~ , to deny brazenly, impudently, shamelessly.

effroyable [ɛfrwa'jabl] *adj.* horrible, terrible, frightful; [ext.] [dépenses, distance, &c.] incredible.

effusion [ɛfy'zjɔ̃] *n.f.* **1.** effusion, pouring out; [moins littéraire] flood, flow, gushing; [de sang] bloodshed, [plus littéraire] shedding (of blood). **2.** [Fig.] [d'amour, de charité, de tendresse, &c.] effusion, outpouring, flood; *avec* ~ , [parler, manifester qqch.] effusively, [remercier, accueillir, &c.] warmly.

égaie, &c. cf. ÉGAYER.

égal, -e [e'g|al] *mpl.* **égaux** [-o] *adj.* **1.** [de même quantité, dimension, nature, &c.] equal: *être sans* ~ , [Pers.] cannot be/equalled, matched, matchless (beauty); *n'avoir point d'* ~ , to have no equal, to be matchless; *n'avoir d'* ~ *que qqch.*, to be /equalled, matched/only by sth.; *traiter d'* ~ *à* ~ *avec qqun*, to deal with s.o. as an equal, to deal on equal terms with s.o. **2.** [pas, mouvement, &c.] regular, even; [sans aspérités] smooth, even. **3.** [Fig.] [style] smooth, even; [caractère, humeur] even. **4.** [indifférence] the same: *Cela m'est* (*parfaitement*) ~ , It's all the same to me, → It makes (absolutely) no difference to me; *Cela vous est* ~ *que* . . . , Do you mind if . . . , Is it all the same to you if . . . || **également** [-al'mɑ̃] *adv.* [d'une manière égale] equally; [aussi] also, as well. || **égaler** [-a'le] #3 *v. tr.* **1.** to equal, [valoir autant que] to match. **2.** to put on a par.

égalisat|eur, -rice [-ali|za'tœːr, -za'tris] *adj.* [Sport.] tying. || **égaliser** [-'ze] #3 *v. tr.* to equalize, to even; [Sport.] to tie, to even (the score); [rendre plan] to smooth, level, to make even. || **égalité** [-'te] *n.f.* **1.** [signe de] equal; [algébrique] equation, equality; cf. EQUAL (plus un nom comme *length, size, weight,* &c.); [prix] uniformity; [entre les hommes] equality: ~ *de deux lignes,* two lines of equal length; ~ *de deux angles,* two angles of equal size; *à* ~, [tennis] deuce, [parier] at even odds, [être à] to be tied, even; [arriver] to tie, to be tied; [Fam.] neck and neck. **2.** [d'un mouvement] regularity; [d'une surface] evenness, smoothness; [Fig.] [humeur, caractère, &c.] evenness.

égard [e'ga:r] *n.m.* **1.** consideration, taking into account: *avoir* ~ *à,* to consider, take into/account, consideration/; *eu* ~ *à,* [loc. prép.] considering; *à l'* ~ *de* [loc. prép.] with/regard, respect/to; *à mon, ton, son, &c.* ~, to(ward) me, you, him, &c.; *à tous (les) égards* [loc. adv.] in every respect, in all respects; *à cet* ~, in that respect, on that score; *sans* ~ *pour* [loc. prép.] without considering, in spite of. **2.** respect, consideration: *par* ~ *pour,* out of/respect, consideration/for; *avoir/des, beaucoup d'/égards pour,* to be considerate (of), to have (a lot of) respect for (s.o.).

égaré, -e [ega'r|e] *adj.* lost, strayed; [chose] lost, mislaid; [air, yeux] wild, bewildered. || *n.* wild person, lunatic. || **égarement** [-'mɑ̃] *n.m.* **1.** straying. **2.** [Fig.] frenzy (of anger, sorrow), (drunken) frenzy; wandering (of the mind, senses): *dans un moment d'* ~, in a wild moment. || **égarer** [-e] #3 *v. tr.* **1.** to get (s.o.) lost; to lose/mislay (sth.): ~ *ses pas,* to lose one's way. **2.** [Fig.] to confuse, to lead astray, to make (one) lose one's head; to affect s.o. mentally. || **s'égarer** *v. pron.* to get, be/lost; [loin de] to stray (from); to wander, to get on the wrong track.

égayer [egɛ'je] #11 *v. tr.* to cheer up (a person); to enliven (a conversation); [avec de la couleur, des fleurs, &c.] to brighten up (a room, &c.); to brighten. || **s'égayer** *v. pron.* to cheer o.s. up: ~ *aux dépens de qqun,* to have a good laugh at s.o.'s expense.

Égée, la mer [la mɛr e'ʒe] *n.f.* (the) Aegean Sea.

égide [e'ʒid] *n.f.* shield, protection: *sous l'* ~ *de,* under the sponsorship of.

églantier [eglɑ̃'t|je] *n.m.* wild rosebush. || **églantine** [-in] *n.f.* wild rose.

église [e'gli:z] *n.f.* **1.** [avec une majuscule] the Church: *l'Église chrétienne,* the Christian Church. **2.** [avec une minuscule] church; meeting house.

égoïsme [egɔ'is|m] *n.m.* selfishness, egoism, egotism. || **égoïste** [-t] *adj.* selfish, egotistic, egotistical. || *n.* egotist, selfish person.

égorger [egɔr'ʒe] #5 *v. tr.* to cut (an animal's) throat; [Fam.] to stick (an animal); [ext.] to massacre, slaughter (s.o.); [Fam.] to slit s.o.'s throat.

égosiller, s' [segozi'je] #3 *v. pron.* [Pers.] to shout, sing o.s. hoarse; [oiseau] to be singing away (with all its might).

égout [e'gu] *n.m.* **1.** [action] draining, drainage; [liquide qui égoutte] drip. **2.** drain; spout; [souterrain] sewer. || **égouttement** [-t'mɑ̃] *n.m.* dripping, draining. || **égoutter** [-'te] #3 *v. tr.* to drain (off), [goutte à goutte] to drip. || **s'égoutter** *v. pron.* to drain, [goutte à goutte] to drip. || **égouttoir** [-'twa:r] *n.m.* drain/board, rack/.

égratigner [egrati'ɲ|e] #3 *v. tr.* to scratch (the skin, [par analogie] a piece of furniture); [Fig.] to scratch, sting. || **égratignure** [-y:r] *n.f.* scratch [aussi au Fig.]: *se faire des égratignures,* to scratch o.s.

égrener [egrə'ne] #9 *v. tr.* to shell (peas), to husk (wheat); to gin (cotton); to take the seeds out of (grapes); ~ *son chapelet,* to tell one's beads. || **s'égrener** *v. pron.* [blé] to shell (out).

Égypte [e'ʒip|t] *n.f.* Egypt. || **égyptien, -ne** [-'sjɛ̃, -'sjɛn] *adj.* Egyptian, from, of/ Egypt. || *n.* Egyptian.

eh [e] *interj.* [étonnement] Well!; [interpellation] Hey!; ~ *bien!,* Well!, Well now!; ~ *quoi!,* So!; ~ *là!* Hey there!

éhonté, -e [eɔ̃'te] *adj.* shameless: *un mensonge* ~, a barefaced lie.

eider [e'dɛ:r] *n.m.* eider duck [× *eiderdown* cf. ÉDREDON].

Eire [ɛ:r] *n.m.* Eire. cf. IRELAND.

éjaculer [eʒaky'le] #3 *v. tr.* to ejaculate [× is not used in the Fig. sense].

éjecter [eʒɛk|'te] #3 *v. tr.* to eject. || **éjecteur** [-'tœ:r] *n.m.* ejector. || **éjection** [-'sjɔ̃] *n.f.* ejection.

élaborer [elabɔ're] #3 *v. tr.* to prepare, to draft, to work out.

élaguer [ela'ge] #3 *v. tr.* [arbre] to prune, [branches] to lop off; [Fig.] to condense, to curtail.

élan[1] [e'lɑ̃] *n.m.* **1.** [pour s'élancer] spring; [une fois lancé] impetus, momentum; [vagues, torrent] dash: *prendre son* ~, to get up some speed, to start running for a jump, [pour sauter] to take a (short) run, to run (and jump); *perdre son* ~, to lose one's momentum, speed; [Fig.] *donner de l'* ~ *à une entreprise,* to give a business a (good) start, send-off. **2.** [Fig.] outburst; impulse; [de l'imagination] flight: *avoir de* ~, to have spirit, [des troupes] dash; *avec* ~, with spirit, dash, enthusiasm.

élan[2] *n.m.* elk; [d'Amérique] moose. cf. ORIGNAL.

élancé, -e [elɑ̃'s|e] *adj.* tall and slender. || **élancement** [-'mɑ̃] *n.m.* **1.** spring(ing), leap(ing). **2.** [Fig.] [vers Dieu, l'infini] transport, yearning; [douleur] twinge, shooting pain. || **élancer** [-e] #4 *v. intr.* to throb: *le pouce m'élance*, my thumb is throbbing. || **s'élancer** *v. pron.* **1.** to rush, spring (forward, out of a room, after s.o., &c.); [à travers, dans] to throw o.s. (through, into); [sur] to pounce (on), throw o.s./[animal] itself/(on, at); [vers] to make a/rush, dash towards. **2.** [liquide] to shoot, spurt/out (of sth.); [vagues, &c.] to throw themselves (against sth.). **3.** [Fig.] [à la conquête] to set out (to conquer); [âme] to spring, rise (toward God).

élargi, -e [elar'ʒ|i] *adj.* [route] widened, broadened. || **élargir** [-i:r] #17 *v. tr.* **1.** [rue, chemin, trottoir, &c.] to widen; [jupe, veste, ceinture, &c.] to let out; [épaules] to broaden; [souliers] to stretch. **2.** [Fig.] to broaden, extend; [l'esprit, l'intelligence] to broaden, develop. **3.** to release (a prisoner). || **s'élargir** *v. pron.* to get wider, broader; to widen, broaden; [chaussure] to stretch; [morale, discipline] to become more lax, less stringent; [les idées, les amis, &c.] to have more scope.

élasticité [elastisi'te] *n.f.* elasticity; spring, buoyancy. || **élastique** [elas'tik] *adj.* **1.** elastic; stretchy (socks); [balle] rubber. **2.** [Fig., règlements] which can be stretched. || *n.m.* elastic; rubber band.

élect|eur, -rice [elɛk|'tœ:r, -'tris] *n.* †**1.** elector (of the Holy Roman Empire). **2.** voter, [moins souvent] elector: *Mes chers électeurs et électrices*, Constituents; *droit m d'* ~, franchise, the right to vote. || *mpl.* electorate. || **élection** [-'sjɔ̃] *n.f.* election: ~ *complémentaire*, by-election; *d'* ~, choice. || **électoral, -e** [-tɔ'ral] *adj.* electoral: *le corps* ~, the electorate.

électricien [elɛktri'sjɛ̃] *n.m.* electrician.

électricité [elɛktri|si'te] *n.f.* electricity: [Fig.] *Il y avait de l'* ~ *dans l'air*, You could feel the electricity in the air. || **électrification** [-fika'sjɔ̃] *n.f.* electrification. || **électrifier** [-'fje] #3 *v. tr.* to provide with electricity, to electrify. [× Is not used in a fig. sense as is the English verb to ELECTRIFY cf. ÉLECTRISER. || **électrique** [-k] *adj.* **1.** electrical, electric. **2.** [Fig.] electrifying, thrilling (effect, impression, &c.). || **électrisant, -e** [-'zɑ̃(:t)] *adj.* electrifying. || **électriser** [-'ze] #3 *v. tr.* **1.** to electrify. **2.** [Fig.] to electrify, thrill, inspire (an audience, s.o.'s imagination, &c.). || **électrocuter** [elɛktr|ɔky'te] #3 *v. tr.* to electrocute (a criminal). || **électrocution** [-ɔky'sjɔ̃] *n.f.* electrocution. || **électrode** [-ɔd] *n.f.* electrode, (electrical) pole. || **électron** [elɛk'trɔ̃] *n.m.* electron.

électronique [-ɔ'nik] *adj.* electronic. || *n.f.* electronics.

élégamment [eleg|a'mɑ̃] *adv.* elegantly, stylishly, smartly. || **élégance** [-ɑ̃:s] *n.f.* [des formes] beauty, elegance; [dans l'habillement] style, elegance; [ext.] d'un public, d'une assistance] stylishness, elegance; [d'une strophe, phrase, tournure, &c.] aptness, [d'un auteur, du style, d'une époque] refinement. || **élégant, -e** [-ɑ̃(:t)] *adj.* stylish, elegant. || *n.* [homme] dandy, swell; [femme] belle.

élégiaque [ele'ʒjak] *adj.* elegiac. || **élégie** [ele'ʒi] *n.f.* elegy.

élément [ele'mɑ̃] *n.m.* element: *des éléments de réponse*, material for an answer. || **élémentaire** [-'tɛ:r] *adj.* **1.** elementary; [installation] rudimentary; [étude] elementary, → basic, beginning. **2.** elemental.

éléphant, -e [ele'fɑ̃(:t)] *n.* elephant.

élevage [el'va:ʒ] *n.m.* raising, breeding.

élévat|eur, -rice [eleva|'tœ:r, -'tris] *adj.* elevating, raising. || *n.m.* elevator. || **élévation** [-'sjɔ̃] *n.f.* **1.** lifting, raising. **2.** elevation, height. **3.** nobility, distinction: *l'* ~ *de son esprit*, his high-mindedness.

élève [e'lɛ:v] *n. m/f.* pupil; student.

élevé, -e [el'v|e] *adj.* [terrain, bâtiment, plafond, &c.] high; [esprit, caractère, pensée, style, &c.] lofty, noble; [enfant] brought up, raised, → educated: *mal* ~, badly/brought up, raised, → ill-bred; *être d'une taille élevée*, to be tall. || **élever** [-e] #9 *v. tr.* **1.** to raise, to lift, to make higher. **2.** to raise, to increase (a rate, &c.). **3.** to build, to erect. **4.** to raise, to bring up (children). || **s'élever** *v. pron.* **1.** to rise, to go up. **2.** [Fig.] to rise, to come up, to arise: ~ *contre qqch.*, to oppose sth.; ~ *au-dessus de son ressentiment*, to rise above one's resentment. **3.** to rise, to increase, to number, to amount to: *La population s'élève à cent mille habitants*, The population numbers a hundred thousand. **4.** to be put up, to be built, to stand. || **éleveu|r, -se** [-œ:r, -ø:z] *n.* [d'animaux domestiques] breeder, rancher.

†**elfe** [ɛlf] *n.m.* elf.

élider [eli|'de] #3 *v. tr.* [Gram.] to elide.

éligible [eli'ʒibl] *adj.* eligible.

élimination [elimin|a'sjɔ̃] *n.f.* elimination. || **éliminatoire** [-a'twa:r] *adj.* resulting in elimination; (mark; trial, test, &c.). || *n.f.* [Sport.] elimination. || **éliminer** [-e] #3 *v. tr.* to eliminate.

élire [e'l|i:r], **élisant** [-i'zɑ̃], **élu** [-y] #49 *v. tr.* **1.** to elect; [candidat] to return. **2.** to choose: ~ *un arbitre*, to elect, choose/ a referee. || **élis, élisais, &c. élit.** cf. ÉLIRE.

Élisabeth [eliza'bɛt] *n.f.* = Elizabeth, [Fam.] Beth, Betty.

élision [eli|'zjõ] *n.f* [Gram.]. elision.

élite [e'lit] *n.f.* elite, choice [used only to refer to persons.] cf. CHOIX: *d'* ~ , [régiment, troupe] crack, picked, [une seule personne] top-notch, (hand-) picked.

elle, -s [ɛl] *pron. pers. f.* **1.** [en parlant des personnes du genre fém., des animaux femelles, quelques objets personnifiés comme un bateau, les pays, &c.] [sujet] she, *pl.* they; [précédé d'une préposition] her, *pl.* them. **2.** [en parlant des objets et des animaux dont on ne sait pas s'ils sont mâles ou femelles] [sujet et régime] it, *pl.* [sujet] they, [précédé d'une préposition] them: *être à* ~ , to be hers (its), her (its) + le nom de l'objet; *Elle ne pense qu'à* ~ , She thinks only of herself. || **elle-même** [-'mɛ:m] *pl.* **elles-mêmes** *pron. pers. emphatique f.sing.* **1.** [sujet] she, it, *pl.* they + un accent de force; she + herself, *pl.* they + themselves: ~ *l'a dit*, She said it herself, She said it. **2.** [régime] herself, itself, *pl.* themselves.

élocution [elɔky'sjõ] *n.f.* elocution.

éloge [e'lɔʒ] *n.m.* **1.** [discours] eulogy, citation; [funèbre] oration. **2.** praise: *digne d'* ~ , praiseworthy; *faire l'* ~ *de*, to praise; to sing (s.o.'s, sth.'s) praises; *être à son* ~ , to be to one's credit. || **élogieu|x, -se** [-ʒjø(:z)] *adj.* laudatory: *commentaires mpl* ~ , laudatory comments.

éloigné, -e [elwa'ɲ|e] *adj.* **1.** remote, distant, away (from); [l'un de l'autre, de sa famille, &c.] separated: ~ *de 15 pieds*, 15 feet/away, distant/; *parent* ~ , distant relative. **2.** [Fig.] far (removed), remote (from the truth, my idea, &c.): *Rien n'est plus* ~ *de mes idées*, Nothing is further from my ideas. || **éloignement** [-'mɑ̃] *n.m.* **1.** [action d'éloigner] removal, removing. **2.** distance; [d'une personne] absence. **3.** [Fig.] dislike, aversion. || **éloigner** [-e] #3 *v. tr.* **1.** to remove; to put, push (farther) away; [une chose d'une autre, dans le temps, l'espace] to separate; [verres concaves] to make (sth.) seem a long way off; [une personne] to send (s.o.) away; [dans le temps] to retard, put off (sth.). **2.** [Fig.] to exclude, to keep, to turn (from, *de*). || **s'éloigner** *v. pron.* **1.** [sciemment] to leave, go away (*de*, from); [accidentellement] to lose (one's way), to stray from (the road, path, &c.): ~ *à pas lents*, to walk slowly away; ~ *furtivement*, to sneak away. **2.** [dans le temps] to fade (into the past).

éloquence [elɔ'k|ɑ̃:s] *n.f.* eloquence. || **éloquent, -e** [-ɑ̃(:t)] *adj.* eloquent.

élu, -e [e'ly] *adj.* [Théol.] chosen (people), blessed. || *n.* [du suffrage] elected candidate; [de Dieu] chosen.

élucider [elysi'de] #3 *v. tr.* to elucidate, explain, clarify (a question, a passage).

éluder [ely'de] #3 *v. tr.* to elude (a problem); to evade (a question).

Élysées [eli'ze] *adj. pl.*: *Champs-* ~ , [Paris] Champs Élysées; [Myth.] Elysian Fields.

émacié, -e [ema'sje] *adj.* emaciated.

émail [e'maj] *n.m.* enamel. || **émaillé, -e** [-e] *adj.* enamelled. || **émailler** #3 *v. tr.* **1.** to enamel. **2.** [Fig.] [fleurs] to dot (the fields, &c.); [texte, discours] to sprinkle (*de*, with) (quotations, metaphors, &c.).

émancipation [emɑ̃sip|a'sjõ] *n.f.* emancipation, liberation, freeing. || **émancipé, -e** [-e] *adj.* emancipated, liberated, freed. || **émanciper** [-e] #3 *v. tr.* to emancipate, to liberate, to free.

émaner [ema'ne] #3 *v. intr.* **1.** [de] [lumière, chaleur, gaz, &c.] to emanate, to come (from). **2.** [Fig.] [pouvoir législatif, l'autorité de la nation, la loi morale, &c.] to originate (with, in, *de*).

émarger [emar'ʒe] #5 *v. intr.* to sign (in the margin and against one's name): *Il emarge au budget*, He is on the payroll.

emballage [ɑ̃ba'l|a:ʒ] *n.m.* **1.** [action] packing: *frais de port et d'* ~ , packing and shipping charges. **2.** [matériel] packing (material); [ext.] container box, carton. **3.** [Sport.] final spurt (in a race). || **emballé, -e** [-e] *adj.* **1.** packed. **2.** [cheval] bolting; [Fam., d'une personne] carried away. || **emballement** [-'mɑ̃] *n.m.* [cheval] bolting, running away; [Fam., d'une personne] carrying away: *être prompt aux emballements*, to be easily carried away. || **emballer** [-e] #3 *v. tr.* **1.** to pack. **2.** [Fig.] to kick off, to bawl out. **3.** [Fig.] to carry away, to excite: *Il est très emballé*, It appeals to him tremendously. || **s'emballer** [sɑ̃ba'le] *v. pron.* [cheval] to bolt, run away; [Pers.] to be carried away, to get excited. || **emballeur** [ɑ̃ba'lœ:r] *n.m.* packer.

embarcadère [ɑ̃barka|'dɛ:r] *n.m.* [Naut.] landing; [plus permanent] wharf, quay.

|| **embarcation** [-'sjõ] *n.f.* (small) boat; [nom générique] small craft.
embardée [ɑ̃bar'de] *n.f.* lurch; [navire, avion] lurch, yaw; [Auto.] swerve: *faire une* ~, to lurch, swerve.
embarquement [ɑ̃bark|ə'mɑ̃] *n.m.* [de personnes] embarkation; [de choses] loading, shipping. || **embarquer** [-e] #3 *v. tr.* **1.** [Pers.] to embark, take on board; [choses] to load, take on board; [Fam.] to pick up, arrest (a criminal). **2.** [une lame, de l'eau, &c.] to ship (a wave, water). **3.** [Fig.] to involve (in an affair). || *v. intr.* to go on board. || **s'embarquer** *v. pron.* **1.** to board, go aboard (a ship); to board, get on (a plane, train), to get in (a car). **2.** [Fig.] to embark/upon, in/ (an affair, &c.): ~ *dans une aventure,* to embark upon an adventure.
embarras [ɑ̃ba'r|ɑ] *n.m.* **1.** [malles, colis, &c.] pile, stack; [circulation] pile-up, traffic jam: [Méd.] obstruction, [de l'estomac] upset, trouble. **2.** difficulty, [plus fam.] fuss: *faire des* ~, to be fussy, particular; *faire de l'* ~, to make a fuss. **3.** [dans les affaires, &c.] confusion. **4.** [manque d'argent] difficult position, difficulty. **5.** [gêne] embarrassment. || **embarrassant, -e** [-a'sɑ̃(:t)] *adj.* [colis, bagages, &c.] awkward, cumbersome; [Fig.] [situation, position, &c.] embarrassing, awkward; [question, &c.] difficult. || **embarrassé, -e** [-a'se] *adj.* **1.** [table, &c.] encumbered; [rue] obstructed, crowded; [les mains] full; [estomac] upset; [dans qqch.] tangled up, caught (in); [raisonnement, situation] confused, mixed up. **2.**: *être* ~ *de ses mains, de sa personne, &c.*, not to know what to do with one's hands, o.s., &c.; [financière--ment] to be financially embarrassed. **3.** [pour répondre] hard put to it, at a loss (to do . . .). **4.** worried, embarrassed. || **embarrasser** [-a'se] #3 *v. tr.* **1.** [la circulation, &c.] to hinder, to hamper [colis, paquet, &c.] to get in one's way; to upset (one's stomach). **2.** [Fig.] to encumber (one's style, the action of a play, &c.) to confuse, mix up (a question, an affair, &c.); to bother (s.o.); [interloquer] to perplex, confuse (s.o.). || **s'embarrasser** *v. pron.* **1.** [de] to be burdened (with); to burden o.s. (with s.o., debts, other people's worries, &c.). **2.** [de] to worry o.s., bother (about): *Que cela ne vous embarrasse pas!,* Don't let that/ worry, bother/you!; ~ *d'un rien,* → to make a mountain out of a molehill. **3.** [dans] [s'emmêler] to get tangled up (in); [se prendre] to get caught (in) [also in the Fig. sense].
embaucher [ɑ̃bo'ʃe] #3 *v. tr.* to hire.
embaumé, -e [ɑ̃bo'm|e] *adj.* **1.** embalmed. **2.** sweet-smelling. || **embaumement** [-'mɑ̃] *n.m.* [cadavre] embalming. || **embaumer** [-e] #3 *v. tr.* to embalm (a dead body); to make (a room, one's clothes, &c.) smell sweet. || **embaumeur** [-œ:r] *n.m.* embalmer.
embellir [ɑ̃bɛ'li:r] #17 *v. tr.* to embellish, beautify (an object, place), to embellish (the truth, a story); to make (a person) more beautiful, [Pers.] to grow more beautiful. || *v. intr.* [action, AVOIR; état ÊTRE] [Pers.] to become, grow/more beautiful. || **s'embellir** *v. pron.* to make o.s. more beautiful. || **embellissement** [ɑ̃bɛlis'mɑ̃] *n.m.* **1.** [d'une personne] adornment; beautifying, beautification. **2.** [Fig., d'un texte, &c.] embellishment.
embêtant, -e [ɑ̃bɛ't|ɑ̃(:t)] *adj.* tiresome, annoying. || **embêté, -e** [ɑ̃bɛ'te] *adj.* worried, bored, irritated; [Fam.] fed up. || **embêtement** [-'mɑ̃] *n.m.* bother, nuisance. || **embêter** [-e] #3 *v. tr.* [ennuyer] to bore; [causer du souci] to worry; [agacer] to annoy, bother; © [embarrasser] to stump, embarrass.
emblée (d') [dɑ̃'ble] *loc. adv.* then and there, on the spot; right from the first.
emblématique [ɑ̃blema'tik] *adj.* emblematic. || **emblème** [ɑ̃'blɛ:m] *n.m.* emblem; symbol.
emboîter [ɑ̃bwa'te] #3 *v. tr.* to fit (sth.) into (sth.); to fit (shingles, tiles, &c.) together; to mesh (cog wheels): ~ *le pas à qqun,* to fall into step with s.o. || **s'emboîter** *v. pron.* to fit together, to fit into.
embonpoint [ɑ̃bõ'pwɛ̃] *n.m.* stoutness: *prendre de l'* ~, to put on weight.
embouché, -e [ɑ̃bu'ʃ|e] *adj.* mouthed: *être mal* ~, to use foul language. || **emboucher** [-e] #3 *v. tr.* **1.** [instrument de musique] to put (a horn, clarinet, &c.) to one's mouth; [Fig.] ~ *la trompette,* to take a lofty tone. **2.** to put (a bit) in a (horse's mouth); [Naut.] to enter into (the mouth of a river, bay, &c.). || **embouchure** [-y:r] *n.f.* **1.** [Mus.] mouthpiece; embouchure (wind instrument). **2.** opening; mouth (of a river, bay, &c.).
embourber [ɑ̃bur'be] #3 *v. tr.* **1.** to bog (sth.) down. **2.** [Fig.] to mire (s.o. in vice, &c.). || **s'embourber** *v. pron.* to get bogged down, stuck in the mud.
embouteillage [ɑ̃butɛ'j|a:ʒ] *n.m.* **1.** bottling (up). **2.** [Fig.] [circulation] jam, tie-up, congestion. || **embouteiller** [-e] #3 *v. tr.* **1.**

to bottle, to put into bottles. **2.** [Fig.] to bottle up, to tie up.

emboutir [ãbu'ti:r] #17 *v. tr.* **1.** [au marteau] to beat out, hammer (a metal); [au repoussoir] to stamp. **2.** [revêtir de métal] to emboss. **3.** [heurter] slam into (sth.). || **s'emboutir** *v. pron.* to collide.

embranchement [ãbrãʃ|'mã] *n.m.* [division] branching off; [point de jonction] fork, branch; [ligne secondaire] [du chemin de fer] branch line, junction.

embrasé, -e [ã'brɑ'z|e] *adj.* ablaze, fiery. || **embrasement** [-'mã] *n.m.* **1.** conflagration, burning. **2.** [Fig.] flare-up. || **embraser** [-e] #3 *v. tr.* **1.** to set on fire, to set aflame, to light up. **2.** [Fig.] to inflame. || **s'embraser** *v. pron.* to be set ablaze.

embrassade [ãbra's|ad] *n.f.* embrace, kissing. || **embrasse** [ã'bras] *n.f.* **1.** embrace. **2.** loop, curtain-holder. || **embrassement** [-'mã] *n.m.* embrace. || **embrasser** [-e] #3 *v. tr.* **1.** to embrace, to hug (s.o., [Fig.] qqch.); to reach around (sth.); [donner des baisers] to kiss (s.o.). **2.** [Fig.] to adopt (a religion, *la vie religieuse*); to espouse (a cause, an interest), to enter into (a profession); [entreprendre] to take on. **3.** to embrace, to include, to cover. || **s'embrasser** *v. pron.* to embrace, to kiss.

embrayage [ãbrɛ'i|a:ʒ] *n.m.* **1.** [action] putting (a machine) into gear; [l'organe] clutch, [plus général] coupling: *laisser le pied sur l'* ~, to ride the clutch. **2.** [le fait d'attacher] connecting, coupling. || **embrayé, -e** [-e] *adj.* in gear. || **embrayer** #11 *v. tr.* to couple; to put into gear. || *v. intr.* **1.** to let in the clutch. **2.** to start work, to get going.

embrouillé, -e [ãbru'j|e] *adj.* entangled, tangled up, mixed up. || **embrouillement** [-'mã] *n.m.* tangling, mixing. || **embrouiller** [-e] #3 *v. tr.* **1.** to (en)tangle (things) up. **2.** [Fig.] to mix, tangle (an affair, a situation, one's sentences, &c.): ~ *les idées*, to confuse one's thoughts. || **s'embrouiller** *v. pron.* to get tangled, to get mixed up.

embrumé, -e [ãbry'me] *adj.* misty, foggy. || **embrumer** #3 *v. tr.* to cover with mist. || **s'embrumer** *v. pron.* to become foggy, misty.

embrun [ã'brœ̃] *n.m.* spray.

embryon [ãbri'jõ] *n.m.* embryo. || **embryonnaire** [ãbrijɔ'nɛ:r] *adj.* embryonic.

embûche [ã'byʃ] *n.f.* ambush; trap: *dresser des embûches à qqun*, to lay a trap for s.o.

embuer [ãbɥe] #3 *v. tr.* to cloud (eyes); to dim; to steam over.

embuscade [ãbys'k|ad] *n.f.* ambush; trap. || **embusqué, -e** *n.* shirker. || **embusquer** [-e] #3 *v. tr.* to put in ambush, to put under cover. || **s'embusquer** *v. pron.* **1.** to lie in ambush, to wait for. **2.** to get a safe job [in wartime], to shirk one's duty.

éméché, -e [emɛ'ʃe] *adj.* [Fam.] tipsy.

émender [emã'de] #3 *v. tr.* to emend.

émeraude [em'ro:d] *n.f.* emerald.

émerger [emɛr'ʒe] #5 *v. intr.* to emerge, to appear.

émeri [em'ri] *n.m.* emery: *papier, toile/* ~, emery/paper, cloth/.

émérite [eme'rit] *adj.* first-rate, experienced.

émerveillé, -e [emɛrvɛ'j|e] *adj.* filled with wonder. || **émerveillement** [-'mã] *n.m.* feeling of wonder, amazement. || **émerveiller** [-e] #3 *v. tr.* to amaze, to fill with /wonder, admiration/.

émett|eur, -rice [em|ɛ'tœ:r, -ɛ'tris] *n.* [Fin.] issuer (of banknotes); [radio] transmitter. || **émettre** [-ɛtr] **émettant** [-ɛ'tã] **émis** [-i] #44 *v. tr.* **1.** to utter (a sound). **2.** to express (an opinion). **3.** to issue (paper currency); to float (a loan). **4.** to transmit (a broadcast).

émeus, émeut cf. ÉMOUVOIR.

émeute [e'mø:t] *n.f.* riot. || **émeutier** [emø'tje] *n.m.* rioter.

émiettement [emjɛt'mã] *n.m.* crumbling. || **émietter** [emjɛ'te] #3 *v. tr.* to crumble, to fritter.

émigrant, -e [emi'grã(:t)] *adj.* emigrating. || *n.* emigrant. || **émigration** [emigra'sjõ] *n.f.* emigration (of people); migration (of birds). || **émigré, -e** [emi'gre] emigrant; †[Revolution] †émigré. || **émigrer** [emi'gre] #3 *v. intr.* [gens] to emigrate; [oiseaux] to migrate.

éminemment [emin|a'mã] *adv.* eminently; to a high degree. || **éminence** [emi'nã:s] *n.f.* eminence, height; [Fig.] prominence. || **éminent, -e** [-ã(:t)] *adj.* eminent, distinguished; high (position).

émis, -e [e'mi(:z)] cf. ÉMETTRE.

émissaire [emi'sɛ:r] *n.m.* emissary, envoy.

émission [emi'sjõ] *n.f.* **1.** issue (of currency); floating (of loan): *institut d'* ~, bank of issue. **2.** [radio] broadcast, transmission.

emmagasinage [ãmagazi|'na:ʒ] *n.m.* storing up [in a warehouse]; [Com.] warehousing. || **emmagasiner** [-'ne] #3 *v. tr.* to store up.

emmailloter [ãmajɔ'te] #3 *v. tr.* to swathe.

emmancher [ãmã'ʃe] #3 *v. tr.* to put a handle to (a hammer, &c.): [Fig.] *bien emmanché*, off to a good start.

emmêlé, -e [ãmɛ'le] *adj.* entangled, tangled up, in a tangle. || **emmêler** #3 *v. tr.* to entangle; to mix up, to muddle. || **s'emmêler** *v. pron.* to become entangled, to get tangled up.

emménagement [ãmena|ʒ'mã] *n.m.* removal [cf. DÉMÉNAGEMENT] moving in. || **emménager** [-'ʒe] #5 *v. tr.* to move into (a new house, &c.).

emmener [ãm'ne] #9 *v. tr.* [used only of persons.] **1.** to take away. **2.** to take along.

emmitoufler [ãmitu'fle] #3 *v. tr.* to muffle up, to swaddle.

emmurer [ãmy're] #3 *v. tr.* to wall in; to immure (a victim).

émoi [e'mwa] *n.m.* emotion, excitement, trepidation: *mettre en* ~, to excite, to put into a flutter. || **émoti|f, -ve** [emɔ'tif] *adj.* [Pers.] emotional; [trouble] emotive. || **émotion** [emɔ'sj|õ] *n.f.* emotion, excitement. || **émotionnant, -e** [-ɔ'nã(:t)] *adj.* stirring, moving.

émotionner [emɔsjɔ'ne] #3 *v. tr.* to move, to stir. || **s'émotionner** *v. pron.* to get/ excited, flustered/.

émousser [emu'se] #3 *v. tr.* to blunt (a knife); [Fig.] to dull. || **s'émousser** *v. pron.* to get blunt; to dull.

émouvais, &c. cf. ÉMOUVOIR. || **émouvant, -e** [emu'v|ã(:t)] *adj.* moving, stirring, touching. || **émouvoir** [-wa:r] **émouvant, ému** [e'my] #33 *v. tr.* to move, to stir, to arouse, to affect. || **s'émouvoir** *v. pron.* to be moved, to get excited.

empailler [ãpɑ'je] #3 *v. tr.* [animaux] to stuff.

empaquetage [ãpak't|a:ʒ] *n.m.* packaging, packing. || **empaqueter** [-e] #8 *v. tr.* to wrap up, to pack (up), to package. || **empaquette, &c.** cf. EMPAQUETER.

emparer, s' [sãpa're] #3 *v. pron.*: ~ *de qqch.*, to pick up, to grab, to seize, to lay one's hands on: *Il s'en est emparé*, He got hold of it.

empattement [ãpat'mã] *n.m.* [mur] footing; [Auto.] wheelbase (of a car).

empêchement [ãpɛʃ|'mã] *n.m.* hindrance, impediment: *mettre* ~ *à qqch.*, to prevent sth. || **empêcher** [-e] #3 *v. tr.* to prevent, to stop (from, de); to hinder. || **s'empêcher** *v. pron.* to stop o.s. (from doing, *de faire*): *Il ne peut pas s'en empêcher*, He can't help himself.

empereur [ãp'rœ:r] *n.m.* emperor.

empèse [ãp|ɛ:z] cf. EMPESER. || **empesé, -e** [-ə'ze] *adj.* stiff, stuffy, wooden. || **empeser** #9 *v. tr.* to starch.

empester [ãpɛs'te] #3 *v. intr.* [odeur désagréable] to stink (of); [odeur forte] to reek (with).

empêtrer [ãpɛ'tre] #3 *v. tr.* to hamper; [Fig.] to saddle s.o. (*de*, with). || **s'empêtrer** *v. pron.* to/get, become/entangled (in).

emphase [ã'fɑ:z] *n.f.* [×] bombast, pomposity. || **emphatique** [ãfa'tik] *adj.* [×] bombastic, pompous.

empiétement [ãpje|t'mã] *n.m.* encroachment (*sur*, on, upon). || **empiéter** [-'te] #10 *v. intr.* to encroach (*sur*, upon).

empiler [ãpi'le] #3 *v. tr.* to pile up; [argot] *se faire* ~, to be had.

empire [ã'pi:r] *n.m.* **1.** empire, dominion: *avoir de l'* ~ *sur soi-même*, to have self-control. **2.** rule, sway, power: *prendre de l'* ~ *sur qqun*, to exercise power over s.o.; *sous l'* ~ *de la colère*, impelled by anger.

empirer [ãpi're] #3 *v. tr.* conj. AVOIR (action), ÊTRE (état), to make worse. || *v. intr.* to worsen, to grow worse.

empirique [ãpi'rik] *adj.* empirical. || *n.m.* empiric, empiricist.

empiriquement [ãpirik'mã] *adv.* empirically; by rule of thumb.

emplacement [ãplas'mã] *n.m.* site, location (of building); [Mil.] emplacement.

emplette [ã'plɛt] *n.f.* purchase: *faire des emplettes*, to go shopping; *faire* ~ *de qqch.*, to buy sth.

emplir [ã'pl|i:r] #17 *v. tr.* to fill. cf. REMPLIR. || **emplissant** [-i'sã] cf. EMPLIR.

emploi [ã'plwa] *n.m.* **1.** use: *mode d'* ~, directions for use; ~ *du temps*, schedule, timetable. **2.** job, employment, post, occupation: *offres fpl d'* ~, want ads, "help wanted." || **emploie, &c.; emploierai, &c.** cf. EMPLOYER. || **employé, -e** [-'je] cf. EMPLOYER. || *n.* clerical worker, clerk; employee. || **employer** #12 *v. tr.* **1.** [objet] to use. **2.** [Pers.] to employ.

empocher [ãpɔ'ʃe] #3 *v. tr.* to pocket; [Fig.] to net (profits).

empoigner [ãpwa'ɲe] #3 *v. tr.* **1.** to grasp, to grab, to get hold of. **2.** [fig.] to move deeply.

empois [ã'pwa] *n.m.* starch.

empoisonnement [ãpwaz|ɔn'mã] *n.m.* poisoning. || **empoisonner** [-ɔne] #3 *v. tr.* **1.** to poison. **2.** [Fig.] to embitter, to poison. || **s'empoisonner** *v. pron.* to take poison, to poison o.s.

emporté, -e [ãpɔr't|e] *adj.* impetuous, hot-tempered: *d'un caractère* ~, easily angered. || **emportement** [-ə'mã] *n.m.* fit (of anger), transport (of anger, joy, love).

emporte-pièce [ãpɔrtə'pjɛs] *n.m. inv.* [Méc.] cutter, punch; [Fig.] *à l'* ~, trenchant, cutting.

emporter [-e] #3 *v. tr.* **1.** [of things only]

to take away, to take along: *emporté par le vent*, blown/off, away; *emporté par la mer*, washed away; *se laisser ~ (par un sentiment)* to be carried away. **2.** [Loc.] *l' ~ sur qqun*, to get the upper hand over s.o. || **s'emporter** *v. pron.* to lose one's temper (with, *contre*).

empourpré, -e [ãpur'pre] *adj.* set aglow. || **empourprer** #3 *v. tr.* to spread a glow over. || **s'empourprer** *v. pron.* **1.** [visage] to flush. **2.** [ciel] to turn/crimson, purple/.

empreignais, &c., empreignant, empreins, &c. cf. EMPREINDRE. || **empreindre** [ã'prɛ̃:dr] #36 *v. tr.* **1.** to stamp, to imprint. **2.** to give an expression of: *le visage empreint de tristesse*, his face expressing sadness.

empreinte [ã'prɛ̃:t] *n.f.* **1.** impression, print: *~ des roues*, wheel tracks; *empreintes digitales*, fingerprints. **2.** [Fig.] stamp (of intelligence, genius).

empressé, -e [ãprɛ's|e] *adj.* eager; zealous. || **empressement** [-'mã] *n.m.* eagerness, readiness, alacrity. || **s'empresser** *v. pron.* to be eager, to hasten (to, *de*): *~ auprès de qqun*, to be most attentive to s.o.'s needs, to make a fuss of s.o.

emprise [ã'pri:z] *n.f.* expropriation; right of way; [Fig.] ascendancy (*sur*, over). || **emprisonnement** [ãpriz|ɔn'mã] *n.m.* imprisonment, custody. || **emprisonner** [-ɔ'ne] #3 *v. tr.* to imprison, to jail.

emprunt [ã'prœ̃] *n.m.* borrowing; loan: *d' ~*, feigned, assumed: *émettre un ~*, to float a loan; *contracter un ~*, to raise a loan; *à titre d' ~*, as a loan, on loan. || **emprunté, -e** [-'te] *adj.* awkward, ill at ease. || **emprunter** [-'te] #3 *v. tr.* **1.** to borrow. **2.** to assume (a name). **3.** [traffic] to go along: *Le cortège empruntera la rue Sherbrooke*, The procession will go along S. Street. || **emprunteur** [-'tœ:r] *n.m.* borrower.

ému, -e [e'my] cf. ÉMOUVOIR. || *adj.* moved, touched, excited, agitated; upset: *~ jusqu'aux larmes*, moved to tears; *en termes émus*, movingly.

émulation [emyla'sjõ] *n.f.* rivalry.

émus, &c. cf. ÉMOUVOIR.

en [ã] *prép.* **1.** in: *être ~ transe*, to be in a trance; *~ été*, in summer; *~ son honneur*, in his honour. **2.** to: *aller ~ France*, to go to F.; *d'année ~ année*, from year to year. **3.** into: *traduire ~*, to translate into. **4.** at: *~ guerre*, at war; *~ mer*, at sea. **5.** on: *~ congé*, on leave. **6.** by: *~ chemin de fer*, by rail. **7.** of, made of: *C'est ~ or*, It's made of gold. || *adv. & pron. invar.* [avoids repetition of noun or is part of an idiom]: *Il ~ partira le 8*, He will sail from there on the 8th; *Je m' ~ trouve mieux*, I feel better for it; *Nous ~ parlons*, We are discussing it; *Prenez-~*, Take some; *Il ne l'a pas fait, mais il ~ est capable*, He did not do it, but he/is capable of it, could have done it/; *Il ~ est ainsi*, That's the way it is; *Si le cœur vous ~ dit*, If you feel like it; *Où ~ sommes-nous restés?*, Where did we stop?

encabaner, s' [sãkaba'ne] © *v. pron.* to hole up, dig in/for the winter.

encadrement [ãkadr|ə'mã] *n.m.* framing, framework, [Mil.] officering (of unit). || **encadrer** [-e] #3 *v. tr.* **1.** to frame (in) to set. **2.** to staff (an organization), to officer (an army unit).

encaisse [ã'kɛ:s] *n.f.* [Com.] cash in hand.

encaissé, -e [ãkɛ'se] *adj.* [rivière] deeply embanked; [route] sunken.

encaisser [ãkɛ'se] #3 *v. tr.* [Com.] to collect (funds); to receive (accounts); [Fig.] *~ des coups*, to take (heavy) punishment; to put up (with). || **encaisseur** [œ:r] *n.m.* collector, [chèque] payee.

encan [ã'kã] *n.m.* public auction: *vendre (qqch.) à l' ~*, © *faire un ~*, to sell (sth.) by auction; *mettre qqch. à l' ~*, to put sth. up for auction. || **encanter** [-'te] © *v. tr.* auctioneer.

encastrer [ãkas'tre] #3 *v. tr.* to let . . . in, to fit in, to build in.

encaustique [ãkos'tik] *n.f.* (floor-, furniture-) wax polish. || **encaustiquer** [-e] #3 *v. tr.* to polish (with wax).

enceindre [ã|'sɛ:dr] #36 *v. tr.* to enclose. || **enceinte** [-'sɛ:t] *n.f.* enclosure; (city) walls, ramparts. || *adj. f.* pregnant, expectant.

encens [ã'sã] *n.m.* **1.** incense. **2.** [Fig.] flattery: *donner de l' ~*, to flatter, to show flattery to. || **encensement** [-s'mã] *n.m.* incensing; flattery. || **encenser** [-'se] #3 *v. tr.* to incense (to burn incense to); to flatter. || **encensoir** [-'swa:r] *n.m.* censer: *donner des coups d' ~*, to flatter, to adulate.

encercler [ãsɛr'kle] #3 *v. tr.* to surround.

enchaînement [ãʃɛn|'mã] *n.m.* **1.** chaining (up). **2.** chain, series, sequence, concatenation. || **enchaîner** [-e] #3 *v. tr. & intr.* **1.** to chain up. **2.** to connect (ideas).

enchanté, -e [ãʃã|'te] *adj.* **1.** enchanted, charmed. **2.** delighted: *~ de vous voir!*, delighted to see you. || **enchantement** [-t(ə)'mã] *n.m.* enchantment, spell; [Fig.] delight. || **enchanter** #3 *v. tr.* **1.** to enchant, to bewitch. **2.** [Fig.] to charm, to delight. || **enchant|eur, -eresse** [-tœ:r,

-t(ə)'res] *adj.* enchanting, entrancing. || **enchanteur** [-'tœːr] *n.m.* enchanter, magician.

enchâsser [ɑ̃ʃɑ'se] #3 *v. tr.* to enshrine; to insert; to set: ~ *une perle*, to set a pearl (*dans*, in).

enchère [ɑ̃|ʃɛːr] *n.f.* bid, bidding. || *n.fpl.* auction: *vente aux enchères*, sale by auction, auction sale. cf. ENCAN. || **enchérir** [-ʃe'riːr] #17 *v. tr.* to bid for; [Fig.] ~ *sur*, to outbid; to outdo. || *v. intr.* [prix] to rise. || **enchérisseur** [-ʃeri'sœːr] *n.m.* bidder.

enchevêtrement [ɑ̃ʃəvɛtr|ə'mɑ̃] *n.m.* tangling, entangling; tangle, jumble, network; criss-cross. || **enchevêtrer** [-e] #3 *v. tr.* to tangle up. || **s'enchevêtrer** *v. pron.* to become, be/entangled.

enclin, -e [ɑ̃'kl|ɛ̃, -in] *adj.* inclined, disposed, prone (to, *à*).

enclore [ɑ̃|'klɔːr] #53 *v. tr.* to enclose. || **enclos** [-'klo] *n.m.* enclosure.

enclume [ɑ̃'klym] *n.f.* anvil: [Fig.] *être pris entre le marteau et l'* ~, to be between the devil and the deep (sea).

encoche [ɑ̃'kɔʃ] *n.f.* notch; [petit] nick; [ouverture] slot. || **encocher** [-e] #3 *v. tr.* to notch, nick.

encoignure [ɑ̃kwa'ɲyːr] *n.f.* corner, angle.

encolure [ɑ̃kɔ'lyːr] *n.f.* neckline (of dress); size (in collars); neck (of horse).

encombrant, -e [ɑ̃kɔ̃'brɑ̃(ːt)] *adj.* cumbersome, bulky. || **encombre** [ɑ̃'kɔ̃ːbr] *n.m.* *sans* ~, safely. || **encombré, -e** [ɑ̃'kɔ̃'br|e] *adj.* crowded, cluttered up (with, *de*). || **encombrement** [-ə'mɑ̃] *n.m.* obstruction, stoppage; [circulation] (traffic) jam; crowd(ing); [d'un objet] floor space; measurements. || **encombrer** [-e] #3 *v. tr.* to crowd; [circulation] to block (up), to jam; [Fig.] to load (one's memory; *de*, with); [Péj.] to be saddled with. || **s'encombrer** *v. pron.* to hamper, burden o.s. (*de*, with).

encontre [ɑ̃'kɔ̃ːtr] [Loc.] *à l'* ~ *de*, in opposition to, against: *aller à l'* ~ *des désirs de qqun*, to go against s.o.'s wishes.

encore [ɑ̃'kɔːr] *adv.* **1.** still: *Il est* ~ *ici*, He is still here; ~ *mieux*, still better. **2.** yet: *pas* ~, not yet. **3.** more, again: *En voulez-vous* ~ ?, Do you want some more?; ~ *une fois*, once again. **4.** only: *Si* ~ *vous m'en aviez parlé*, If only you had told me; ~ *que*, although.

encourageant, -e [ɑ̃kura'ʒ|ɑ̃(ːt)] *adj.* encouraging, heartening, favourable. || **encouragement** [-'mɑ̃] *n.m.* encouragement, incentive. || **encourager** [-e] #5 *v. tr.* **1.** to encourage, to hearten, to support, to favour. **2.** © to patronize, to give business to. || **s'encourager** *v. pron.* © to cheer up.

encourir [ɑ̃ku'r|iːr], **encourant** [-ɑ̃], **encouru** [-y] #24 *v. tr.* [dépenses] to incur; [châtiment] to draw upon o.s.

encrassement [ɑ̃kras'mɑ̃] *n.m.* fouling. || **s'encrasser** [sɑ̃kra'se] #3 *v. pron.* to (get) dirty; [machine] to stop up, clog; [arme] to foul; [cheminée] to soot up.

encre [ɑ̃ːkr] *n.f.* ink: ~ *de Chine*, India ink; ~ *d'impression*, printer's ink. || **encrier** [ɑ̃kri'e] *n.m.* inkwell, inkstand.

encroûter, (s') [(s)ɑ̃kru'te] #3 *v. pron.* to become prejudiced, hidebound, rusty, &c.

encyclique [ɑ̃si'klik] *adj.* encyclical (letter). || *n.f.* encyclical.

encyclopédie [ɑ̃siklope'di] *n.f.* encyclopaedia.

endenté, -e [ɑ̃dɑ̃'te] *adj.* toothed, cogged (wheel): *roue* ~, cog wheel. || **endenter** [ɑ̃dɑ̃'te] #3 *v. tr.* [Méc.] to supply with teeth; [assembler] to indent; [roue] to cog.

endetter [ɑ̃dɛ'te] #3 *v. tr.* to get (s.o.) into debt. || **s'endetter** *v. pron.* to run into debt.

endiablé, -e [ɑ̃djɑ'ble] *adj.* wild; frenzied, full of vim.

endiguement [ɑ̃dig|'mɑ̃] *n.m.* damming; containment. || **endiguer** [-e] #3 *v. tr.* **1.** to dam up, to dike. **2.** [Fig.] to stay, to stem, to check.

endimanché, -e [ɑ̃dimɑ̃'ʃe] *adj.* in one's Sunday best. || **s'endimancher** #3 *v. pron.* to put on one's Sunday best.

endive [ɑ̃'diːv] *n.f.* endive.

endolori, -e [ɑ̃dɔlɔ'ri] *adj.* painful, sore.

endommageai, &c., cf. ENDOMMAGER. || **endommagé, -e** [ɑ̃dɔma'ʒe] *adj.* damaged. || **endommager** #5 *v. tr.* to damage. || **s'endommager** *v. pron.* to suffer damage.

endormais, &c., endormant cf. ENDORMIR. || **endormi, -e** [ɑ̃dɔr'm|i] *adj.* **1.** asleep, sleeping. **2.** [passion] dormant. **3.** [membre] numb. || *n.* [Fam.] slowpoke. || **endormir** [-iːr] #21 *v. tr.* **1.** to put to sleep: ~ *qqun en chantant*, to sing (s.o.) to sleep. **2.** [Méd.] to anæsthetize. **3.** [Fig. & Fam.] to bore. **4.** [Fig.] to put off (with promises, excuses). || **s'endormir** *v. pron.* to fall asleep, to go to sleep.

endors, endort, cf. ENDORMIR.

endosser [ɑ̃do'se] #3 *v. tr.* **1.** to put on (clothes). **2.** [Fig.] to take on (responsibility); to endorse (a cheque).

endroit [ɑ̃'drwa] *n.m.* **1.** place, spot. **2.** right side (of material): *mettre à l'* ~, to put on right side out. **3.** *à l'* ~ *de*, toward, with regard to.

enduire [ɑ̃'dɥ|iːr] **enduisant** [-i'zɑ̃] **enduit** [-i] #56 *v. tr.* to coat, to plaster (*de*, with);

[Péj.] to smear, daub. || **enduit** [ɑ̃'dɥi] *n.m.* coat, coating.

endurance [ɑ̃dy'rɑ̃:s] *n.f.* endurance, stamina || **endurant, -e** [ɑ̃dy'rɑ̃(:t)] *adj.* enduring; patient, long-suffering.

endurci, -e [ɑ̃dyr's|i] *adj.* **1.** hardened: *~ à la fatigue*, inured to fatigue. **2.** hard, callous. **3.** hardened, inveterate. || **endurcir** [-i:r] #17 *v. tr.* to harden, to toughen. || **s'endurcir** *v. pron.* to become hard, tough, callous. || **endurcissant** [-i'sɑ̃] cf. ENDURCIR. || **endurcissement** [-is'mɑ̃] *n.m.* hardness; [Fig.] obduracy.

endurer [ɑ̃dy're] #3 *v. tr.* to endure; [tolérer] to bear, put up with; [nég.] †brook.

énergétique [enɛrʒ|e'tik] *adj.* relating to industrial power: *ressources énergétiques*, power. || **énergie** [-i] *n.f.* **1.** energy, vigour, firmness. **2.** power: *~ hydraulique*, water power. || **énergique** [-ik] *adj.* energetic; vigorous, strenuous; strong, drastic (measures). || **énergiquement** [-ik'mɑ̃] *adv.* energetically.

énervant, -e [enɛr'vɑ̃(:t)] *adj.* enervating; [Fig.] irksome, irritating; exhausting.

énervé, -e [enɛr'v|e] *adj.* irritated. || **énervement** [-ə'mɑ̃] *n.m.* nervousness, irritation. || **énerver** [-e] #3 *v. tr.* **1.** to enervate. **2.** to exasperate.

enfance [ɑ̃'fɑ̃:s] *n.f.* childhood; boyhood, girlhood: *retomber en ~*, to be in one's dotage. || **enfant** [ɑ̃'fɑ̃] *n.m/f.* **1.** child, *pl.* children; boy, youngster, little girl: *livres pour enfants*, children's books. **2.** descendant. **3.** *mes enfants!*, fellows!, lads! || **enfantement** [-t'mɑ̃] *n.m.* childbirth; parturition. || **enfanter** [-'te] #3 *v. tr. & intr.* to beget, to give birth to. || **enfantillage** [-ti'ja:ʒ] *n.m.* [Péj.] childishness. || **enfantin, -e** [-'tɛ̃, -'tin] *adj.* **1.** childlike. **2.** [Péj.] childish, infantile.

enfariné, -e [ɑ̃fari'ne] *adj.* covered with flour. || **enfariner** #3 *v. tr.* to cover with flour.

enfer [ɑ̃'fɛ:r] *n.m.* hell; [pl.] the underworld, Hades: *aller, mener/un train d' ~*, to go/full speed, hell-for-leather.

enfermer [ɑ̃fɛr'me] #3 *v. tr.* **1.** to enclose. **2.** to lock up; [Fig.] to bottle up. **3.** to confine, to shut in. || **s'enfermer** *v. pron.* to closet o.s.; [Fig.] to wrap o.s. up (in, *dans*).

enferrer [ɑ̃fɛ're] #3 *v. tr.* to run through, to skewer: *Il l'enferra avec son épée*, He ran his sword through him. || **s'enferrer** *v. pron.* **1.** to be caught (on sharp point, spike). **2.** [Fig.] to contradict o.s.; to flounder (*dans*, in).

enfiévré, -e [ɑ̃fje'vre] *adj.* feverish. || **enfiévrer** #10 *v. tr.* to make feverish.

enfilade [ɑ̃fi'l|ad] *n.f.* **1.** series, suite, row: *des pièces en ~*, rooms that open into each other. **2.** [Mil.] enfilade: *prendre en ~*, to enfilade. || **enfiler** [-e] #3 *v. tr.* to thread (a needle); to go through (a street); to put on (clothes).

enfin [ɑ̃'fɛ̃] *adv.* **1.** finally; at last; in short. **2.** anyway; well! well!; that's that.

enflammé, -e [ɑ̃fla'me] *adj.* fiery, eloquent. || **enflammer** #3 *v. tr.* **1.** to ignite. **2.** to inflame, to fire, to excite. || **s'enflammer** *v. pron.* to catch fire; to become inflamed.

enflé, -e [ɑ̃|'fle] *adj.* swollen. || **enfler** #3 *v. tr.* to swell, to inflate. || *v. intr.* to swell. || **s'enfler** *v. pron.* to swell. || **enflure** [-'fly:r] *n.f.* swelling; [Fig., style] bombast.

enfonçai, &c. cf. ENFONCER. || **enfoncé, -e** [ɑ̃fõ's|e] *adj.* **1.** sunken, deep. **2.** broken. || **enfoncement** [-'mɑ̃] *n.m.* driving in (of nail); breaking open, down (of door, window); deep insertion. || **enfoncer** [-e] #4 *v. tr.* **1.** to drive in, to push in. **2.** to break down, in, open: *~ une porte*, to break a door open. || *v. intr.* to sink, to subside. || **s'enfoncer** *v. pron.* to sink, to settle; to go deep (into the woods).

enfoui, -e [ɑ̃'fw|i] *adj.* buried. || **enfouir** [-i:r] #17 *v. tr.* to bury.

enfourcher [ɑ̃fur'ʃe] #3 *v. tr.* **1.** to mount, to get astride (a horse, a bicycle). **2.** to thrust a pitchfork into (s.o.).

enfreignais, &c. cf. ENFREINDRE. || **enfreindre** [ɑ̃'frɛ̃:dr] #36 *v. tr.* to infringe, to break. || **enfreins, enfreint** cf. ENFREINDRE.

enfui [ɑ̃'fɥi], **enfuyant** [-'jɑ̃] cf. S'ENFUIR. || **s'enfuir** [sɑ̃'fɥi:r] #27 *v. pron.* to run away, to escape.

enfumer [ɑ̃fy'me] #3 *v. tr.* to fill with smoke; to smoke (vermin) out; [Fig., cerveau] to cloud.

engagé, -e [ɑ̃ga'ʒe] *adj.* pawned; [Fam.] in hock. || *n.m.* [Mil.] enlisted man.

engageai, &c. cf. ENGAGER. || **engageant, -e** [-ɑ̃(:t)] *adj.* engaging, winning. || **engagement** [ɑ̃gaʒ|'mɑ̃] *n.m.* **1.** pledge, promise, commitment. **2.** hiring, appointment. **3.** [Mil.] voluntary enlistment. **4.** [Mil.] engagement, action. || **engager** [-e] #5 *v. tr.* **1.** to pledge, to commit. **2.** to engage, to hire. **3.** to start, to begin. **4.** to urge: *Je l'ai engagé à le faire*, I urged him to do it. || **s'engager** *v. pron.* **1.** to promise, to commit o.s. (to, *à*). **2.** to begin: *L'opération est mal engagée*, The operation was not started right. **3.** to turn into (a street).

engelure [ɑ̃ʒ'ly:r] *n.f.* chilblain.

engendrer [ɑ̃ʒɑ̃'dre] #3 *v. tr.* **1.** to beget, to give birth to. **2.** to engender, to bring about.

engin [ɑ̃'ʒɛ̃] *n.m.* machine; appliance; weapon: ~ *de pêche*, fishing tackle; ~ *téléguidé*, guided missile.

engivré, -e [ɑ̃ʒi'vre] *adj.* covered with frost, frosted all over.

englober [ɑ̃glɔ'be] #3 *v. tr.* to merge, put together (*dans*, in); [Fig.] to comprehend, include.

engloutir [ɑ̃glu|'ti:r] #17 *v. tr.* to gobble (one's food); to swallow up; [Fig.] to engulf, devour. || **s'engloutir** *v. pron.* [bateau] to sink, go down. || **engloutissement** [-tis'mɑ̃] *n.m.* swallowing up; [Naut.] sinking.

engoncé, -e [ɑ̃gɔ̃'se] *adj.* bundled up (*dans*, in); awkward. || **engoncer** [ɑ̃gɔ̃'se] #4 *v. tr.* to bundle up, to cramp.

engorgé, -e [ɑ̃gɔr'ʒ|e] *adj.* blocked, choked up, obstructed; [Méd.] congested. || **engorgement** [-ə'mɑ̃] *n.m.* blocking, choking, obstruction; [Méd.] congestion. || **engorger**]-e[#5 *v. tr.* to block, choke up, obstruct; [Méd.] to congest. || **s'engorger** *v. pron.* to get/blocked, obstructed, [pump] fouled, [Méd.] congested/.

engoué, -e [ɑ̃'gwe] *adj.* infatuated (*de*, with). || **engouement** [ɑ̃gu'mɑ̃] *n.m.* infatuation (*pour*, with). || **s'engouer** [sɑ̃'gwe] #3 *v. pron.* to become infatuated (*de*, with).

engouffrer [ɑ̃gu'fre] #3 *v. tr.* to engulf. || **s'engouffrer** [sɑ̃gu'fre] *v. pron.* to rush, to dash, to pour (into, *dans*).

engoulevent [ɑ̃gul'vɑ̃] *n.m.* nighthawk.

engourdi, -e [ɑ̃gur|'di] *adj.* [de froid] numb, benumbed; [de sommeil] drowsy. || **engourdir** [-'di:r] #17 *v. tr.* to/grow, become/numb (&c.). || **engourdissement** [-dis'mɑ̃] *n.m.* numbness; drowsiness; [Fig.] dullness.

engrais [ɑ̃'grɛ] *n.m.* [fumier] manure: ~ *chimique*, fertilizer. || **engraissage** [-'sa:ʒ] *n.m.* [bétail] fattening. || **engraisser** [ɑ̃grɛ'se] #3 *v. tr.* **1.** to fatten. **2.** to fertilize. || *v. intr.* to grow fat, to put on weight. || **s'engraisser** *v. pron.* to grow rich.

engranger [ɑ̃grɑ̃'ʒe] #5 *v. tr.* to get in (crops); to put (crops) in the barn.

engrenage [ɑ̃grə|'na:ʒ] *n.m.* gears. || **engrener** [-'ne] #9 *v. tr.* [Méc.] to engage, put in gear. || **s'engrener** *v. pron.* to mesh with one another, to work into one another.

engueuler [ɑ̃gœ'le] #3 *v. tr.* to tell off, [Fam.] to bawl out.

enguirlander [ɑ̃girlɑ̃'de] #3 *v. tr.* **1.** to adorn with garlands, wreaths, to wreathe, to festoon. **2.** [Fam.] to bawl out.

enhardi, -e [ɑ̃ar'd|i] *adj.* emboldened. || **enhardir** [-i:r] #17 *v. tr.* to embolden, to encourage. || **s'enhardir** [sɑ̃ar'di:r] *v. pron.* to make bold to to pluck up courage (to, *à*).

énigmatique [enigma'tik] *adj.* enigmatic, perplexing. || **énigme** [e'nigm] *n.f.* enigma, riddle.

enivrant, -e [ɑ̃ni'vr|ɑ̃(:t)] *adj.* intoxicating, rapturous. || **enivrement** [-ə'mɑ̃] *n.m.* intoxication. || **enivrer** [-e] #3 *v. tr.* **1.** to intoxicate, to inebriate. **2.** [Fig.] to intoxicate, to elate. || **s'enivrer** *v. pron.* **1.** to get drunk. **2.** [Fig.] to become enraptured.

enjambée [ɑ̃ʒɑ̃'be] *n.f.* stride. || **enjamber** #3 *v. tr.* to stride over (an obstacle); to be astride; to span (a river).

enjeu [ɑ̃'ʒø] *n.m.* stake (betting).

enjoindre [ɑ̃'ʒw|ɛ̃:dr] **enjoignant** [-ɛ'ɲɑ̃] **enjoint** [-ɛ̃] #36 *v. tr.* to order (*à qqun de*, s.o. to): *Il lui a été enjoint de . . .*, He was directed to . . . .

enjolivé, -e [ɑ̃ʒɔli|'ve] *adj.* embellished, adorned. || **enjoliver** #3 *v. tr.* **1.** to beautify, to embellish. **2.** to touch up, to embroider (a story). || **enjoliveur** [-'vœ:r] *n.m.* [Auto] hub cap.

enjoué, -e [ɑ̃'ʒwe] *adj.* playful, sprightly.

enlaçai, &c. cf. ENLACER. || **enlacement** [ɑ̃las'mɑ̃] *n.m.* clasp; lacing, interweaving. || **enlacer** [ɑ̃la'se] #4 *v. tr.* to clasp, to embrace.

enlaidir [ɑ̃lɛ'di:r] #17 *v. tr.* to disfigure, to make ugly. || *v. intr.* to grow ugly.

enlevant, -e [ɑ̃l'vɑ̃(:t)] *adj.* [Fam.] rousing, stirring. || **enlèvement** [ɑ̃lɛv'mɑ̃] *n.m.* removal, carrying off; [Mil.] storming; [of a person] kidnapping, abduction.

enlever [ɑ̃l've] #9 *v. tr.* **1.** to remove, to take off, to take down (a curtain), to take up (a rug): ~ *qqch.* à *qqun*, to take sth. away from s.o. [☞ On précise l'action au moyen d'un verbe + *off* ou *away*]: [objet] take away, carry off; [objets qui traînent] clear away; ~ *en frottant*, to rub off. **2.** to kidnap (a person), to capture (a city). || **s'enlever** *v. pron.* **1.** to rise (in the air). **2.** to come off. **3.** to sell well: *Cela s'enlève comme des petits pains*, It sells like hot cakes.

enluminé, -e [ɑ̃lymi'n|e] *adj.* **1.** illuminated. **2.** made colourful, vivid. **3.** [visage] ruddy, red. || **enluminer** #3 *v. tr.* **1.** to illuminate. **2.** to make colourful, vivid. || **enlumineur** [-œ:r] *n.m.* illuminator.

|| **enluminure** [-y:r] *n.f.* illumination; colouring; high complexion.

enneigé, -e [ãnɛ'ʒ|e] *adj.* snowy. || **enneigement** [-'mã] *n.m.* snowfall, snow conditions [for skiing]. || **enneiger** [-e] #5 *v. tr.* to cover with snow.

ennemi, -e [en'mi] *n.* enemy; foe: *être l' ~ de qqch.*, to be opposed to sth. || *adj.* hostile, opposed, inimical.

ennoblir [ãnɔ'bl|i:r] #17 *v. tr.* to ennoble (life, work); to lift up, elevate (thoughts, mind). || **ennoblissement** [-is'mã] *n.m.* ennoblement, [Fig.] exaltation; (also *anoblissement*).

ennui [ã'nɥi] *n.m.* **1.** worry, trouble: *s'attirer des ennuis*, to get into trouble; *des ennuis d'argent*, money trouble. **2.** boredom: *mourir d' ~*, to be bored to death. || **ennuyant, -e** [ãnɥi'j|ã(:t)] *adj.* [esp. ©] **1.** vexing, troubling, annoying. **2.** boring. || **ennuyé, -e** [-e] *adj.* vexed, troubled, annoyed. || **ennuyer** [-'e] #12 *v. tr.* **1.** to annoy, to trouble: *Est-ce que cela vous ennuirait si . . .*, Would you mind if . . . . **2.** to bore. || **s'ennuyer** [sãnɥi'je] *v. pron.* to be bored: *~ de qqun*, to miss s.o.; *~ à mourir*, to be bored to death. || **ennuyeux, -se** [ãnɥi'jø(:z)] *adj.* **1.** annoying, vexing. **2.** boring, tedious.

énoncé [enɔ̃'se] *n.m.* statement; wording; mention. || **énoncer** #4 *v. tr.* to state, set forth (facts, ideas, opinions); to articulate (word, syllable). || **s'énoncer** *v. pron.* to be stated: *Le principe s'énonce comme suit*, This principle is stated as follows.

enorgueillir (s') [sãnɔrgə'ji:r] #17 *v. pron.* to get, grow/proud (*de*, of); to pride o.s. (*de*, upon).

énorme [e'nɔrm] *adj.* huge, enormous, vast; [Fig.] overwhelming, tremendous. || **énormément** [-e'mã] *adv.* enormously, tremendously: *~ de*, a great many. || **énormité** [-i'te] *n.f.* vastness, enormity.

enquérais, &c. cf. ENQUÉRIR. || **enquérir (s')** [sãke'ri:r] #23 *v. pron.* conj. ÊTRE. to inquire, to ask (about, after, *de*). || **enquerrai, &c.** cf. ENQUÉRIR.

enquête [ã'k|ɛ:t] *n.f.* inquiry, investigation; *procéder à une ~*, to investigate; *l'inspecteur chargé de l' ~*, the inspector in charge of the case. || **enquêter** [ɛ't|e] #3 *v. intr.* to inquire, to investigate. || **enquêteu|r, -se** [-œ:r, -ø:z] *n.* inquirer (also enquirer).

enquière, &c., enquiers, &c., enquis cf. ENQUÉRIR.

enraciner [ãrasi'ne] #3 *v. tr.* to root; [Fig.] to root, instil: *préjugés enracinés*, deep-rooted prejudice. || **s'enraciner** *v. pron.* to take root; to become rooted.

enragé, -e [ãra'ʒe] *adj.* **1.** [chien] mad, affected with rabies. **2.** enraged, desperate, crazy: *joueur ~*, card, gambling/fiend. || **enrager** #5 *v. intr.* to be furious: *faire ~*, to infuriate, to get a rise out of s.o.

enrayer [ãrɛ'je] #11 *v. tr.* [mécanisme] to jam, lock; [Fig., épidémie, &c.] to check, stop. || **s'enrayer** *v. pron.* [arme] to jam.

enregistré, -e [ãr(ə)ʒis'tr|e] *adj.*: *bagages enregistrés*, checked baggage. || **enregistrement** [-ə'mã] *n.m.* registration; [voix] recording: *~ sur bande*, tape recording; [bagages] checking. || **enregistrer** [-e] #3 *v. tr.* to register; [voix] to record; [bagages] to check. || **enregistreu|r, -se** [-œ:r, -ø:z] *n.* [Pers.] recorder, registrar. || *adj.*: *thermomètre ~*, recording thermometer.

enrhumé, -e [ãry'me] *adj.* with a cold: *Il est fortement ~*, He has a bad cold. || **enrhumer** #3 *v. tr.* to give a cold to. || **s'enrhumer** [sãry'me] *v. pron.* to catch a cold.

enrichir [ãri|'ʃi:r] #17 *v. tr.* to make (s.o.) wealthy, to enrich. || **s'enrichir** *v. pron.* to become rich, to make a fortune. || **enrichissement** [-ʃis'mã] *n.m.* accumulation of wealth; [Fig.] enrichment.

enrôlement [ãrol'mã] *n.m.* enrolment; [Mil.] enlistment. || **(s') enrôler** [(s)ãro'le] #3 *v. tr. & pron.* to enrol; [Mil.] to enlist.

enroué, -e [ã'rwe] *adj.* hoarse, husky (voice). || **enrouement** [ãru'mã] *n.m.* hoarseness, huskiness. || **s'enrouer** [sã'rwe] #3 *v. pron.* to grow hoarse.

enrouler (s') [(s)ãru'le] #3 *v. tr. & pron.* to wrap, fold (*autour de*, around); [en cercle] to coil up; [en rouleau] to roll up.

ensabler [ãsa'ble] #3 *v. tr.* [boucher] to silt up. || **s'ensabler** *v. pron.* to silt up; [navire] to strand, to run aground.

ensanglanté, -e [ãsãglã'te] *adj.* bloodstained, gory. || **ensanglanter** #3 *v. tr.* to stain, cover/with blood; [Fig.] to drench in blood.

enseignant [ãsɛ'ɲã] cf. ENSEIGNER. || *n.mpl.* *les enseignants*, teachers, all members of the teaching profession.

enseigne [ã'sɛɲ] *n.f.* **1.** sign (of store). **2.** [Naut.] sub-lieutenant. **3.** [Mil.] ensign (colours). **4.** [Loc.] *à telles enseignes que*, so that.

enseignement [ã'sɛɲ|(ə)'mã] *n.m.* **1.** teaching, instruction, education, educational system: *la gratuité de l' ~*, free education. **2.** [Fig.] lesson: *tirer un ~ de qqch.*, to draw a lesson from sth. || **enseigner** [-e] #3 *v. tr.* to teach, to instruct.

ensemble [ã'sã:bl] *adv.* together: *Ils sont*

mal ~, They don't get along. || *n.m.* **1.** whole, entirety: *dans l'* ~, on the whole, by and large; *une vue d'* ~, an overall picture. **2.** cohesion, unity: *avec* ~, in harmony. **3.** [couture] ensemble.

ensemencer [ɑ̃smɑ̃'se] #4 *v. tr.* to sow (a field).

enserrer [ɑ̃sɛ're] #3 *v. tr.* to clasp; to enclose.

ensevelir [ɑ̃səv|'liːr] #17 *v. tr.* to bury, inter: to shroud; [Fig.] to bury (*sous*, under). || **ensevelissement** [-lis'mɑ̃] *n.m.* burying, shrouding.

ensoleillé, -e [ɑ̃sɔlɛ'je] *adj.* sunny, sunlit.

ensommeillé, -e [ɑ̃sɔmɛ'je] *adj.* sleepy, drowsy.

ensorcelant, -e [ɑ̃sɔrs|ə'lɑ̃(ːt)] *adj.* bewitching. || **ensorceler** [-ə'le] #8 *v. tr.* to bewitch, to cast a spell on. || **ensorcelle, &c.** cf. ENSORCELER. || **ensorcellement** [-ɛl'mɑ̃] *n.m.* spell; [Fig.] enchantment.

ensuite [ɑ̃'sɥit] *adv.* afterwards, then: ~ *?*, What then?, Anything else?

ensuivre (s') [sɑ̃'sɥiːvr] #51 *v. pron.* [☞ Used only in the infinitive and 3rd pers.; + indic. in the affirmative; + subjunc. in the neg. or interrog.] to ensue, follow: *il s'ensuit que*, it follows that . . . .

entacher [ɑ̃ta'ʃe] #3 *v. tr.* to taint (*de*, with); [Jur.]: *entaché de nullité*, null and void.

entaille [ɑ̃'t|ɑːj] *n.f.* notch; [plus petit] nick; [blessure] cut, gash. || **entailler** [-ɑ'je] #3 *v. tr.* to notch, nick; to cut, gash.

entame [ɑ̃'tam] *n.f.* the top slice of a roast. || **entamer** [-e] #3 *v. tr.* to start: ~ *des négociations*, to start negotiations; ~ *une bouteille*, to start a bottle; ~ *un gigot*, to cut the first slice of a leg of lamb.

entassé, -e [ɑ̃tɑ|'se] *adj.* stacked up, packed. || **entassement** [-s'mɑ̃] *n.m.* heap; [Fig.] accumulation. || **entasser** #3 *v. tr.* to heap, to pile, to stack up: ~ *les gens dans un lieu*, to pack people into a place.

entend, entends, entendais, entendis, &c. cf. ENTENDRE.

entendement [ɑ̃tɑ̃d'mɑ̃] *n.m.* understanding, comprehension.

entendre [ɑ̃'t|ɑ̃ːdr] **entendant** [-ɑ̃'dɑ̃] **entendu** [-ɑ̃'dy] #42 *v. tr.* **1.** to hear: *Je lui ai entendu dire que*, I have heard him say that . . . ; ~ *dire que*, to hear that. **2.** to listen: *Il n'a rien voulu* ~, He would not listen. **3.** to understand: *Il n'y entend rien*, He doesn't know the first thing about it; *laisser* ~, to give to understand, to hint, to imply. **4.** to mean: *Qu'entendez-vous par là?*, What do you mean by that?; *J'entends qu'il le fasse*, I insist that he do it. || **s'entendre** *v. pron.* **1.** to hear o.s. **2.** to get along (with, *avec*): *Ils s'entendent bien*, They get along. **3.** to know: *Il s'entend à ce genre de travail*, He is very good at this sort of thing. || **entendu, -e** [ɑ̃tɑ̃'dy] *adj.* **1.** understood, agreed: *C'est* ~ *!*, Agreed!, All right!; *bien* ~, of course. **2.** expert (in, *à*). *n.m. faire l'* ~, to pretend to understand.

enténébré, -e [ɑ̃tene'bre] *adj.* dark, in darkness, gloomy. || **enténébrer** #9 *v. tr.* to plunge in darkness.

entente [ɑ̃'tɑ̃ːt] *n.f.* **1.** understanding, agreement: *en venir à une* ~, to come to an agreement. **2.** [= meaning] *expression à double* ~, double meaning, †double entendre.

enterrement [ɑ̃tɛr|'mɑ̃] *n.m.* **1.** funeral. **2.** [Fig.] shelving (of a question). || **enterrer** [-e] #3 *v. tr.* **1.** to bury, to inter. **2.** to bury, to plant. **3.** [Fig.] to shelve, to sidetrack a question. **4.** [Fig.] to outlive: *Il vous enterrera tous*, He will outlive every one of you. || **s'enterrer** *v. pron.* **1.** to dig o.s. in. **2.** [Fig.] to bury o.s.

en-tête [ɑ̃'tɛːt] *pl.* **en-têtes** *n.m.* head(ing): *papier m à* ~, (official) letterhead.

entêté, -e [ɑ̃tɛ't|e] *adj.* stubborn; [Péj.] pig-headed, obstinate. || **entêtement** [-'mɑ̃] *n.m.* stubbornness, obstinacy; [Péj.] pig-headedness. || **entêter** [ɑ̃tɛ'te] #3 *v. tr.* [boisson] to go to s.o.'s head; [parfum] to give a headache to. || **s'entêter** [sɑ̃tɛ'te] #3 *v. pron.*: ~ *à*, to persist in (+ *ing*), to stick stubbornly to.

enthousiasmant, -e [ɑ̃tuzjas'mɑ̃(ːt)] *adj.* thrilling, fascinating. || **enthousiasme** [ɑ̃tu'zjasm|] *n.m.* enthusiasm, rapture: *sans* ~, half-heartedly. || **enthousiasmé, -e** [-e] *adj.* fired, enraptured (by, *par*). || **enthousiasmer** #3 *v. tr.* to enrapture, to thrill. || **s'enthousiasmer** [sɑ̃tuzjas'me] *v. pron.* to become enthusiastic (over, *de*). || **enthousiaste** [ɑ̃tu'zjast] *adj.* enthusiastic. || *n.m/f.* enthusiast (for, *de*).

entiché, -e [ɑ̃ti'ʃ|e] *adj.* infatuated (with, *de*), [Fam.] crazy (about, *de*). || **entichement** [-'mɑ̃] *n.m.* infatuation. || **s'enticher** #3 *v. pron.* to be infatuated (*de*, with).

enti|er, -ère [ɑ̃'tj|e, -ɛːr] *adj.* entire; whole; complete. || *n.m.* whole, entirety: *en* ~, entirely, wholly, completely. || **entièrement** [-ɛr'mɑ̃] *adv.* entirely; wholly; completely.

entomologie [ɑ̃tɔmɔlɔ'ʒi] *n.f.* entomology.

entonner[1] [ɑ̃tɔ|'ne] #3 *v. tr.* to strike up (a song).

entonner[2] #3 *v. tr.* [Fam.] to funnel (into, *dans*). || **entonnoir** [-'nwa:r] *n.m.* funnel.

entorse [ɑ̃'tɔrs] *n.f.* sprain, wrench, twist, strain: [Fig.] *donner une ~ à*, to twist, to distort.

entortiller [ɑ̃tɔrti'je] #3 *v. tr.* to twist, twine (round); [Fam.] to trick. || **s'entortiller** *v. pron.* to twist, coil (*autour de*, around).

entour [ɑ̃'tu:r] *n.m.*: *à l' ~ (de)*, round about, around.

entourage [ɑ̃tu'r|a:ʒ] *n.m.* **1.** associates, entourage. **2.** setting, environment. || **entouré, -e** [-e] *adj.* surrounded, enclosed (with, *de*); attended (by, *de*): *Il était très ~*, Many people came up to him; *S.H. le Maire, ~ des membres du Conseil*, His Worship the Mayor/supported, attended/by the members of the council. || **entourer** #3 *v. tr.* to enclose, to surround: *les bois qui nous entourent*, the woods around us. || **s'entourer (de)** *v. pron.* to gather round o.s.

entr'acte [ɑ̃'trakt] *n.m.* intermission; [Br.] interval.

entr'aide [ɑ̃'trɛ:d] *n.f. inv.* mutual assistance.

entr'aider (s') [sɑ̃trɛ'de] #3 *v. pron.* to help one another.

entrailles [ɑ̃'trɑ:j] *n.fpl.* intestines, bowels; [Fig.] heart, compassion, affection: *sans ~*, heartless, unfeeling.

entrain [ɑ̃'tr|ɛ̃] *n.m.* zest; high spirits; [Fam.] pep: *sans ~*, half-heartedly. || **entraînant, -e** [-ɛ'nɑ̃(:t)] *adj.* stirring, martial. || **entraînement** [-ɛn'mɑ̃] *n.m.* **1.** training. **2.** attraction, temptation. || **entraîner** [-ɛ'ne] #3 *v. tr.* **1.** to entail, to involve. **2.** to carry/away, along/: *se laisser ~*, to allow o.s. to be carried away. **3.** to train; [athlète] to coach; to set the pace. || **entraîneur** [-ɛ'nœ:r] *n.m.* pacemaker.

entrave [ɑ̃'tr|a:v] *n.f.* **1.** shackle, fetter. **2.** [Fig.] hindrance, obstacle, impediment. || **entraver** [-a've] #3 *v. tr.* to shackle, fetter; [Fig.] to hinder.

entre[1] cf. ENTRER.

entre[2] [ɑ̃:tr] *prép.* between; among: *~ les mains de qqun*, in(to) s.o.'s hands; *d' ~*, among; [with pers. pronouns] of: *l'un d' ~ eux*, one of them.

entre(-),[3] prefix showing interdependence as in the following:

entrebâillé, -e [ɑ̃trəbɑ'je] *adj.* ajar. || **entrebâiller** #3 *v. tr.* to set ajar, to half open. || **s'entrebâiller** *v. pron.* to half open, to open partially.

entrechoquer [ɑ̃trəʃɔ'ke] #3 *v. tr.* to bump together. || **s'entrechoquer** *v. pron.* to knock together; to clash.

entrecôte [ɑ̃trə'ko:t] *n.f.* rib of beef.

entrecoupé, -e [ɑ̃trəku'pe] *adj.* broken, fitful. || **entrecouper** #3 *v. tr.* to interrupt, to intersperse. || **s'entrecouper** *v. pron.* to intersect.

entrecroiser (s') [(s)ɑ̃trəkrwa'ze] #3 *v. tr. & pron.* to intersect, to interlace.

entrée [ɑ̃'tre] *n.f.* entrance, entry, admission: *droit d' ~*, admission fee; *~ interdite*, No Admittance; *avoir ses entrées chez qqun*, to be on intimate terms with s.o.

entrefaite [ɑ̃trə'fɛt] *n.f.*: *loc. adv. sur ces entrefaites*, meanwhile.

entrefilet [ɑ̃trəfi'lɛ] *n.m.* [journal] notice, short; item.

entregent [ɑ̃trə'ʒɑ̃] *n.m.* tact and address; tact and discretion; savoir faire.

entrelaçai, &c. cf. ENTRELACER. || **entrelacement** [ɑ̃trəlɑs|'mɑ̃] *n.m.* interlacing, interweaving. || **entrelacer** [-e] #4 *v. tr.* to interlace, to interweave, to intertwine.

entremêlé, -e [ɑ̃trəmɛ'le] *adj.* intermingled (with, *de*). || **entremêler** #3 *v. tr.* to intermingle, to intersperse.

entremets [ɑ̃trə'mɛ] *n.m.* savoury, sweet.

entremise [ɑ̃trə'mi:z] *n.f.* intervention: *par l' ~ de*, through (the courtesy, agency/of).

entrepont [ɑ̃trə'pɔ̃] *n.m.* [Naut.] steerage (space) between decks.

entreposage [ɑ̃trəpo'za:ʒ] *n.m.* warehousing; [en douane] bonding. || **entreposer** [ɑ̃trəpo'ze] #3 *v. tr.* to store; [en douane] to bond, place in bond. || **entrepôt** [ɑ̃trə'po] *n.m.* warehouse; [des douanes] bonded warehouse.

entreprenant, -e [ɑ̃trəpr|ə'nɑ̃(:t)] *adj.* enterprising, forward-looking. || **entreprendre** [-ɑ̃:dr], **entreprenant** [-ə'nɑ̃], **entrepris** [-i] #41 *v. tr.* **1.** to undertake; to start, to enter upon; to contract for. || **entrepreneur** [-ə'nœ:r] *n.m.* [×] contractor: *~ de pompes funèbres*, funeral director. || **entreprise** [-i:z] *n.f.* undertaking, venture; business, concern: *esprit d' ~*, enterprise.

entrer #3 *v. intr.* [conj. ÊTRE] to enter, to go in, to come in: *~ dans une pièce*, to enter a room, to go, to come/into a room; *faire ~*, to show in; *~ en passant*, to drop in; *~ dans sa vingtième année*, to begin one's twentieth year; *~ au Collège royal militaire*, to enter the Royal Military College; *~ au chemin de fer*, to get a job with the railroad.

entre-regarder (s') [sɑ̃trərəgar'de] *v. pron.*

to look at one another, to exchange glances.

entre-temps [ɑ̃trəˈtɑ̃] *adv. & n(m).* meanwhile.

entretenir [ɑ̃trətˈn|iːr], **entretenant** [-ɑ̃], **entretenu** [-y] #22 *v. tr.* to maintain, to keep (up): ~ *une conversation,* to carry on a conversation; ~ *de bons rapports avec qqun,* to be on good terms with s.o.; ~ *des soupçons,* to harbour suspicion; ~ *qqun de qqch.,* to discuss a topic with s.o. || **s'entretenir** *v. pron.* to converse, to talk.

entretien [ɑ̃trəˈtjɛ̃] *n.m.* maintenance, upkeep; support (of family); clothes; conversation: *subvenir à l'* ~ *de qqun,* to support s.o.

entre-tuer (s') [sɑ̃trəˈtɥe] #3 *v. pron.* to kill one another.

entreverrai [ɑ̃trəv|ɛˈre], **entrevis** [-i], **entrevoie** [-wa] cf. ENTREVOIR.

entrevoir [ɑ̃trəˈv|waːr], **entrevoyant** [-waˈjɑ̃], **entrevu** [-y] #32 *v. tr.* **1.** to catch sight of, to catch a glimpse of: *laisser* ~ *qqch. à qqun,* to drop a hint to s.o. about sth. **2.** to foresee. || **entrevue** [-y] *n.f.* interview.

entr'ouvert, -e [ɑ̃truˈv|ɛːr, -ɛrt] *adj.* half-open, ajar; parted (lips). || **entr'ouvrir** [-riːr], **entr'ouvrant, entr'ouvert** #25 *v. tr.* to open/a little, part way/. || **s'entr'ouvrir** *v. pron.* to open part way.

énumération [enymer|aˈsjõ] *n.f.* enumerating; enumeration. || **énumérer** [-e] #10 *v. tr.* to enumerate, to count, to tick off.

envahir [ɑ̃va|ˈiːr] #17 *v. tr.* to invade, to overrun, to overgrow, to encroach upon. || **envahissant, -e** [-iˈsɑ̃(ːt)] *adj.* invading; [Fig.] encroaching. || **envahissement** [-isˈmɑ̃] *n.m.* invasion; [Fig.] encroachment. || **envahisseu|r, -se** [-iˈsœːr, -iˈsøːz] *n.* invader. || *adj.* invading; [Fig.] encroaching.

enveloppe [ɑ̃vˈlɔp] *n.f.* envelope: *mettre sous* ~ , to slip into an envelope. || **enveloppement** [-ˈmɑ̃] *n.m.* envelopment; [Fig.] wrapping up, surrounding; [Méd.] ~ *humide,* wet compress. || **envelopper** [-e] #3 *v. tr.* **1.** to envelop, to wrap (up). **2.** to shroud (in mystery). **3.** [Mil.] to surround (the enemy).

envenimer [ɑ̃vniˈme] #3 *v. tr.* **1.** to poison, to inflame. **2.** to fan (quarrel), to embitter. || **s'envenimer** *v. pron.* to fester; [Fig.] to rankle.

envergure [ɑ̃vɛrˈgyːr] *n.f.* **1.** [Naut.] spread of sail. **2.** [Aéro.] wing span. **3.** [Fig.] calibre, scope, scale (of activity).

enverrai, &c. cf. ENVOYER.

envers [ɑ̃ˈvɛːr] *prép.* towards, to, with regard to: *Il a agi honnêtement* ~ *nous,* He has dealt honourably with us. || *n.m.* reverse (side); back (of material): *à l'* ~ , the wrong way round; inside out; upside down; back to front; topsy-turvy: *avoir la tête à l'* ~ , to be very/upset, confused/.

envi [ɑ̃ˈvi] *n.m.*: *à l'* ~ , in emulation.

enviable [ɑ̃ˈvjabl] *adj.* enviable: *peu* ~ , unfortunate, unpleasant.

envie [ɑ̃ˈv|i] *n.f.* **1.** desire, longing, inclination; want: *avoir* ~ *de faire qqch.,* to feel like doing sth.; *avoir bien* ~ *de,* to have a good mind to; *faire* ~ *à qqun,* to make s.o. envious, to excite s.o.'s desire. **2.** envy: *porter* ~ *à qqun,* to envy s.o. || **envier** [-je] #3 *v. tr.* to covet, to envy, to begrudge. || **envieu|x, -se** [-jø(ːz)] *adj.* envious, jealous.

environ [ɑ̃viˈr|õ] *adv.* about; nearly. || **environnant, -e** [-ɔˈnɑ̃(ːt)] *adj.* surrounding. || **environner** [-ɔˈne] #3 *v. tr.* to surround, to encompass. || **environs** [-õ] *n.mpl.* surroundings, neighbourhood.

envisager [ɑ̃vizaˈʒe] #5 *v. tr.* to consider, to contemplate, to anticipate: *Il envisage de partir demain,* He is thinking of leaving tomorrow.

envoi [ɑ̃ˈvwa] *n.m.* **1.** sending, shipping, dispatch: *lettre d'* ~ , covering letter. **2.** parcel, consignment: ~ *d'argent,* remittance.

envoie, &c. cf. ENVOYER.

envol [ɑ̃ˈvɔl] *n.m.* [oiseaux] taking flight; [Aéro.] take-off, start: *piste d'* ~ , runway; *pont d'* ~ , flight deck. || **envolée** [-e] *n.f.* taking off; © flight. || **envoler (s')** [sɑ̃vɔˈle] #3 *v. pron.* to fly away; to be blown away; [Aéro.] to take off.

envoyé, -e [ɑ̃vwaˈje] *n.m.* messenger, envoy; [Journ.] correspondent. || **envoyer** #13 *v. tr.* to send, to dispatch: ~ *chercher,* to send for; ~ *dire,* to send word; © *Envoyez fort!,* Go to it!

épais, -se [eˈp|ɛ(ːs)] *adj.* thick; [cheveux] bushy; [forêt] dense; [nuit] pitch-black; [esprit] dull, slow; *peu* ~ , thin. || *adv.* thick(ly). || **épaisseur** [-ɛˈsœːr] *n.f.* **1.** thickness; depth (of a layer): *Le mur a deux pieds d'* ~ , The wall is two feet thick; ~ *d'un cheveu,* hair's-breadth; *peu d'* ~ , thinness. **2.** [feuillage] density, thickness; [nuit] blackness. **3.** [esprit] slowness, dullness. || **épaissi, -e** [-ɛˈsi] *adj.* thicker, stouter. || **épaissir** [-ɛˈsiːr] #17 *v. tr.* to make thicker; [Cul.] to thicken; to darken || *v. intr.* to thicken, to become thick; to grow stout; [nuit] to deepen; [esprit] to grow dull. || **s'épaissir** *v. pron.* to thicken; [traits] to coarsen; [corps] to grow fat.

|| **épaississement** [-ɛsisˈmɑ̃] *n.m.* thickening.

épanchement [epɑ̃ʃ|ˈmɑ̃] *n.m.* **1.** discharge, overflow (of liquid): ~ *de bile*, bilious attack, [Fig.] fit of temper. **2.** unburdening (of mind, heart); effusion (of feelings): *en veine d'* ~, in an expansive mood; *épanchements de l'amitié*, demonstrative affection. || **épancher** [-e] #3 *v. tr.* **1.** to pour out. **2.** [Fig.] to unburden: ~ *sa bile*, to vent one's spleen, to rail (against s.o., *contre qqun*). || **s'épancher** *v. pron.* **1.** to pour out, to overflow. **2.** to unbosom o.s.

épandre [eˈpɑ̃:dr], **épandu** [epɑ̃ˈdy] #42 *v. tr.* to spread; to pour out; to scatter. || **s'épandre** *v. pron.* to spread; [liquide] to flow out.

épanoui, -e [epaˈnw|i] *adj.* **1.** in full bloom. **2.** [Fig.] beaming: *rire* ~, broad grin. || **épanouir** [-i:r] #17 *v. tr.* to make (flowers) bloom. || **s'épanouir** *v. pron.* **1.** to open out, to bloom, to blossom. **2.** [visage] to light up, to beam. **3.** [Fig.] to develop fully. || **épanouissement** [-isˈmɑ̃] *n.m.* **1.** blooming, blossoming. **2.** [visage] beaming: *l'* ~ *de son visage*, his beaming face. **3.** [Fig.] full bloom, fruition.

épargnant, -e [eparˈɲ|ɑ̃(:t)] *adj.* thrifty. || *n.* person who saves money. || **épargné, -e** [-e] *adj.* saved; spared. || **épargne** [eˈparɲ] *n.f.* **1.** saving, economy, thrift. **2.** savings: *caisse d'* ~, savings bank; *l'* ~ *privée*, private investors. || **épargner** [-e] #3 *v. tr. & intr.* **1.** to save, to save up, to economize: *Qui épargne, gagne*, Waste not, want not. **2.** to save, to spare: ~ *de la peine à qqun*, to spare s.o. trouble. **3.** to spare, to show mercy to: *Personne n'a été épargné*, Nobody was spared.

éparpillé, -e [eparpi|ˈje] *adj.* scattered. || **éparpillement** [-jˈmɑ̃] *n.m.* scattering, dispersion. || **éparpiller** #3 *v. tr.* **1.** to scatter, to spread out. **2.** to dissipate, to fritter away (time, money). || **s'éparpiller** *v. pron.* to scatter, to disperse.

épars, -e [eˈp|a:r, -ars] *adj.* **1.** scattered. **2.** dishevelled (hair).

épatant, -e [epaˈtɑ̃(:t)] *adj.* [Fam.] wonderful; terrific: *Ce n'est pas bien* ~, It's nothing special. || **épate** [eˈpat] *n.f.*: [Fam.] *faire de l'* ~, to try to impress people. || **épaté, -e** [-e] *adj.* **1.** flabbergasted. **2.** [nez] flat. || **épater** [-e] #3 *v. tr.* [Fam.] to amaze, stagger; *pour* ~ *le bourgeois*, to shock respectable people. || **s'épater** *v. pron.* [Fam.] to get rattled: *Il ne s'épate pas facilement*, He is not easily impressed.

épaule [eˈpo:l] *n.f.* shoulder: ~ *contre* ~, shoulder to shoulder; *large d'épaules*, broad-shouldered; *lever, hausser / les épaules*, to shrug one's shoulders; [Fig.] *donner un coup d'* ~ *à qqun*, to help s.o. || **épaulement** [epol|ˈmɑ̃] *n.m.* shoulder-piece, shoulder. || **épauler** [-e] #3 *v. tr.* **1.** [to bring a rifle to the shoulder] to take aim. **2.** [Fam.] to help, to back up. || **épaulette** [-ɛt] *n.f.* **1.** [underclothing] shoulder strap. **2.** [Mil.] epaulette: *gagner ses épaulettes*, to win one's spurs; to become an officer.

épave [eˈpa:v] *n.f.* wreck; *pl.* [flottantes] flotsam; [jeté dans l'eau] jetsam.

épée [eˈpe] *n.f.* sword: *coup d'* ~, sword thrust; *se battre à l'* ~, to fight with swords; *passer au fil de l'* ~, to put to the sword; *tirer l'* ~, to draw one's sword; *pousser qqun, l'* ~ *dans les reins*, to prod s.o.; *donner des coups d'* ~ *dans l'eau*, to beat the air.

épeler [eˈple] #8 *v. tr.* to spell; [message] to spell out. || **s'épeler** *v. pron.* to be spelled.

éperdu, -e [epɛrˈdy] *adj.* **1.** [Pers.] distracted, bewildered: ~ *de douleur*, wild with/pain, grief/; ~ *de joie*, wild with delight. **2.** [emotion]: *résistance éperdue*, desperate resistance; *amour* ~, passionate love. || **éperdument** [-ˈmɑ̃] *adv.* madly, desperately, distractedly: *aimer* ~, to love to distraction; ~ *amoureux*, head over heels in love; *Je m'en moque* ~, I could not care less.

éperlan [epɛrˈlɑ̃] *n.m.* smelt.

éperon [eˈpr|ɔ̃] *n.m.* **1.** spur: *donner de l'* ~ *à son cheval*, to clap spurs to one's horse. **2.** [Fig.] spur, stimulus. || **éperonner** [-ɔˈne] #3 *v. tr.* to put spurs to (one's horse), to spur on, to prod.

épervier [epɛrˈvje] *n.m.* hawk.

éphémère [efeˈmɛ:r] *adj.* ephemeral; short-lived, fleeting.

épi [eˈpi] *n.m.* **1.** ear, head (of grain); spike (of flower): *blé en* ~, wheat in the head. **2.** [de cheveux] cowlick.

épice [eˈpis] *n.f.* spice: *pain d'* ~, gingerbread. || **épicé, -e** [-e] *adj.* highly/spiced, hot/(food); naughty (story). || **épicer** #4 *v. tr.* to spice (food).

épicerie [-epiˈs|ri] *n.f.* **1.** groceries. **2.** grocery store. **3.** grocery trade.

épici|er, -ère [epiˈs|je, -jɛ:r] *n.* grocer.

épicurien, -ne [epikyˈrj|ɛ̃, -ɛn] *adj. & n.* epicurean.

épidémie [epideˈmi] *n.f.* epidemic. || **épidémique** [-k] *adj.* epidemic(al), widespread.

épiderme [epiˈdɛrm] *n.m.* [Med.] epidermis; [Fam.] skin, hide.

épier [e'pje] #3 *v. tr.* **1.** to spy upon, to watch. **2.** to be on the look-out for, to watch for, to listen for; ~ *l'arrivée du facteur*, to watch for the mailman.

épilatoire [epila'twa:r] *adj.* depilatory. || **épiler** [epi'le] #3 *v. tr.* to pluck (eyebrows); to remove (hair).

épinard [epi'na:r] *n.m.* spinach: *épinards/au naturel, en branches/*, boiled spinach.

épine [e'pin] *n.f.* **1.** thorn, thorn bush: ~ *blanche*, hawthorn; ~ *noire*, blackthorn. **2.** ~ *dorsale*, spine, backbone.

épinette [epi'nɛt] © *n.f.* spruce: ~ *blanche*, white spruce; ~ *noire*, black spruce; ~ *rouge*, tamarack, red spruce; *gomme d'* ~, spruce gum; *bière d'* ~, spruce beer.

épineu|x, -se [epi'nø(:z)] *adj.* thorny, prickly; [Fig.] thorny, ticklish.

épingle [e'pɛ̃:gl] *n.f.* pin: ~ *à chapeau*, hatpin; ~ *à cheveux*, hairpin; ~ *à linge*, clothes peg; *tiré à quatre épingles*, immaculate, spick and span. || **épingler** [epɛ̃'gle] #3 *v. tr.* to pin, to fasten with a pin.

Épiphanie (l') [lepifa'ni] *n.f.* Epiphany.

épique [e'pik] *adj.* epic.

épiscopal, -e [episkɔ'pal] *adj.* episcopal. || **épiscopat** [episkɔ'pa] *n.m.* **1.** episcopate, the Bishops. **2.** episcopacy.

épisode [epi'zɔd] *n.m.* episode. || **épisodique** [-ik] *adj.* episodic.

épistolaire [epistɔ'lɛ:r] *adj.* epistolary.

épithète [epi'tɛt] *n.f.* epithet.

épître [e'pitr] *n.f.* epistle: *l'Épître*, the Epistle.

épluchage [eply'ʃ|a:ʒ] *n.m.* **1.** peeling, paring (of fruit, potatoes). **2.** cleaning (of feathers, fur). || **éplucher** [-e] #3 *v. tr.* **1.** to peel, to pare. **2.** to clean, to go over (accounts) minutely. || **épluchette** [-ɛt] © *n.f.* ~ *de blé d'Inde*, corn-husking bee.

éponge [e'põ:ʒ] *n.f.* sponge: *passer l'* ~ *sur qqch.*, to let bygones be bygones. || **épongé, -e** [epõ'ʒe] *adj.* mopped up. || **éponger** [epõ'ʒe] #5 *v. tr.* to sponge off, to mop up.

épopée [epɔ'pe] *n.f.* epic poem.

époque [e'pɔk] *n.f.* **1.** epoch, era, age: *qui fait* ~, epoch-making; *des meubles d'* ~, period furniture. **2.** time, period, date: *À quelle* ~ *?*, When was that?

épouse [e'pu:z] *n.f.* wife, spouse, cf. ÉPOUX. || **épouser** [epu'ze] #3 *v. tr.* **1.** to marry: *demander à une jeune fille de l'* ~, to propose to a girl. **2.** [Fig.] to espouse, to follow.

épousseter [epus'te] #8 *v. tr.* to dust. || **époussette, &c.** cf. ÉPOUSSETER.

épouvantable [epuvɑ̃'tabl] *adj.* dreadful, horrible, frightful; shocking; appalling: © [Fam.] *C'est beau* ~, It's awfully nice, It's mighty fine.

épouvantail [epuvɑ̃'taj] *n.m.* **1.** scarecrow. **2.** [Fam.] bogyman, bugaboo.

épouvante [epu'v|ɑ̃:t] *n.f.* terror, fright: *jeter, porter/l'épouvante dans un pays*, to spread terror in a country. || **épouvanté, -e** [-ɑ̃'te] *adj.* terror-stricken. || **épouvanter** #3 *v. tr.* to terrify, to scare.

époux [e'pu] *n.m.* husband; spouse: *les deux époux*, the married couple [☞ Official term only; normally use MARI, FEMME].

éprendre, s' [se'prɑ̃:dr] #41 *v. pron.* to fall in love, to become infatuated (*de*, with).

épreuve [e'prœ:v] *n.f.* **1.** test: *mettre à l'* ~, to test. **2.** [Scol.] examination: *épreuves orales*, oral examinations. **3.** trial, ordeal: *des épreuves*, hardships. **4.** [Impr.] proof: *corriger les épreuves*, to proof read.

épris, -e [e'pri(:z)] *adj.* in love, infatuated.

éprouvé, -e [epru'v|e] *adj.* **1.** tested. **2.** tried, sorely tried: *Il a été très* ~ *par la mort de . . .*, He was very much aggrieved by the death of . . . || **éprouver** [-e] #3 *v. tr.* **1.** to test, to try, to put to the test. **2.** to feel, to experience.

éprouvette [epru'vɛt] *n.f.* test-tube.

épuisant, -e [epɥi'z|ɑ̃(:t)] *adj.* exhausting, gruelling. || **épuisé, -e** [-e] *adj.* **1.** exhausted. **2.** [mine] worked out. **3.** [livre] out of print. || **épuisement** [-'mɑ̃] *n.m.* exhaustion: ~ *nerveux*, nervous breakdown. || **épuiser** [-e] #3 *v. tr.* **1.** to exhaust: ~ *ses forces*, to exhaust one's strength, to wear o.s. out; ~ *la patience de qqun*, to wear out s.o.'s patience. **2.** to use up; to sell out (an article). || **s'épuiser** *v. pron.* to run out, to wear out.

épuisette [epɥi'zɛt] *n.f.* scoop, bailer.

épuration [epyra'sjõ] *n.f.* **1.** purification, cleansing. **2.** [Pol.] purge. **3.** weeding-out process.

épure [e'py:r] *n.f.* working drawing.

épurer [epy're] #3 *v. tr.* to purify, filter (gas, water); to refine (oil, metals); to purify (morals); to weed out, purge (persons); to expurgate.

équarri, -e [ekɑ'r|i] *adj.* squared. || **équarrir** [-i:r] #17 *v. tr.* **1.** to square (timber). **2.** [cheval mort] to cut up. || **équarrisseur** [-i'sœ:r] *n.m.* knacker.

équateur [ekwa'tœ:r] *n.m.* equator. || **l'Équateur** [Géog.] *n.m.* Ecuador.

équation [ekwa'sjõ] *n.f.* equation.

équatorial, -e [ekwatɔ'rjal] *adj.* equatorial.
équerre [e'kɛ:r] *n.f.*: ~ *à dessin,* setsquare; ~ *en T,* T-square.
équestre [e'kɛstr] *adj.* equestrian.
équilibre [eki'libr] *n.m.* equilibrium, balance; poise: *mettre qqch. en* ~, to balance sth.; *perdre l'* ~, to lose one's balance. || **équilibrer** [-e] #3 *v. tr.* to balance. || **s'équilibrer** *v. pron.* to balance. || **équilibriste** [-ist] *n.m/f* aerialist.
équinoxe [eki'nɔks] *n.m.* equinox: ~ /*de printemps, d'automne*/, vernal, autumnal/ equinox; *d'* ~, equinoctial.
équipage [eki'pa:ʒ] *n.m.* crew: *maître d'* ~, boatswain. || **équipe** [e'kip] *n.f.* **1.** gang, working party, crew, team: ~ *sociale,* team of social workers. **2.** [Sport] team. **3.** shift: ~ *de nuit,* night shift. || **équipée** *n.f.* escapade, prank. || **équipement** [-'mɑ̃] *n.m.* outfit, equipment; [Mil.] kit. || **équiper** [-e] #3 *v. tr.* to equip, to fit out; © to dirty, to splash; *mal équipé,* in a (sorry) mess.
équipi|er, -ère [-je, -jɛ:r] *n.* member of the team.
équitable [eki'tabl] *adj.* equitable, fair, just, reasonable. || **équitablement** [-ə'mɑ̃] *adv.* equitably.
équitation [ekita'sjõ] *n.f.* (horseback) riding, horsemanship: *école d'* ~, riding school.
équité [eki'te] *n.f.* equity.
équivalent, -e [ekiva'lɑ̃(:t)] *adj.* equivalent. || *n.m.* equivalent.
équivoque [eki'vɔk] *adj.* **1.** equivocal, ambiguous (words). **2.** questionable, doubtful, dubious (conduct). || *n.f.* ambiguity: *sans* ~, unequivocal(ly).
érable [e'rabl] *n.m.* maple tree: ~ *à sucre,* sugar maple. || **érablière** [-i'jɛ:r] *n.f.* © maple grove.
érafler [erɑ'fl|e] #3 *v. tr.* to scuff. || **éraflure** [-y:r] *n.f.* slight scratch, abrasion.
éraillé, -e [erɑ'je] *adj.* frayed; [voix] hoarse, husky; [disque] scratchy. || **érailler** #3 *v. tr.* to fray; to scratch. || **s'érailler** *v. pron.* to fray, become frayed; [voix] to become husky; [disque] to get scratchy.
ère [ɛ:r] *n.f.* era.
érection [erɛk'sjõ] *n.f.* erection.
éreinté, -e [erɛ̃'te] *adj.* dog-tired, all in. || **éreinter** #3 *v. tr.* **1.** to tire out. **2.** [Fig.] to tear apart, to knock.
Érié (le lac) [lə lake'rje] *n.m.* Lake Erie.
ériger [eri'ʒe] #5 *v. tr.* [monument] to erect; [instituer] to establish, set up: ~ *en principe,* to lay down as a principle. || **s'ériger** *v. pron.* to set up (*en,* as).
ermitage [ɛrmi'ta:ʒ] *n.m.* hermitage. || **ermite** [ɛr'mit] *n.m.* hermit.
érosion [ero'zjõ] *n.f.* erosion.
érotique [erɔ'tik] *adj.* erotic.
errant, -e [ɛ'r|ɑ̃(:t)] *adj.* wandering: *le Juif* ~, the wandering Jew. || **errements** [ɛ'mɑ̃] *n.mpl.* **1.** way, behaviour. **2.** vagaries, tricks. || **errer** [-e] #3 *v. intr.* **1.** to wander, to roam, to ramble. **2.** to be mistaken. || **erreur** [ɛ'rœ:r] *n.f.* **1.** mistake, slip, error. **2.** fallacy, delusion.
erroné, -e [ɛrɔ'ne] *adj.* erroneous.
érudit, -e [ery'd|i(t)] *adj.* erudite, learned. || *n.* scholar. || **érudition** [-i'sjõ] *n.f.* erudition, learning, scholarship.
éruption [eryp'sjõ] *n.f.* **1.** [volcan] eruption: *entrer en* ~, to erupt. **2.** [Méd.] rash.
es, est, êtes cf. ÊTRE.
ès [ɛs] *prép.* in, of: *docteur* ~ *lettres,* doctor of letters.
escabeau [ɛska'bo] *n.m.* **1.** step ladder. **2.** †wooden stool.
escadre [ɛs'kadr] *n.f.* squadron. || **escadrille** [-i:j] *n.f.* [Aéro.] flight. || **escadron** [-õ] *n.m.* [Mil.] troop: *chef d'* ~, [cavalry & artillery] major.
escalade [ɛska'lad] *n.f.* scaling, climbing, clambering. || **escalader** [-e] #3 *v. tr.* to scale; [mur] to climb over.
escale [ɛs'kal] *n.f.* **1.** port of call. **2.** call: *faire* ~ *à Halifax,* to put in at Halifax; *vol sans* ~, nonstop flight.
escalier [ɛska'lje] *n.m.* stairs; staircase: ~ *roulant,* escalator; ~ *de sauvetage,* fire escape.
escamotable [ɛskamɔ't|abl] *adj.* retractable: *train d'atterrissage* ~, retractable undercarriage. || **escamotage** [-a:ʒ] *n.m.* sleight of hand; smuggling away; [Péj.] shirking, dodging; juggling, conjuring. || **escamoter** [-e] #3 *v. tr.* to conjure away; to spirit away; to skip (a question).
escapade [ɛska'pad] *n.f.* escapade, prank.
escargot [ɛskar'go] *n.m.* snail.
escarmouche [ɛskar'muʃ] *n.f.* skirmish. || **escarmoucher** [-e] #3 *v. intr.* to skirmish.
†**escarole** [ɛska'rɔl] *n.f.* endive.
escarpé, -e [ɛskar'pe] *adj.* steep, sheer; rugged.
escarpin [ɛskar'pɛ̃] *n.m.* dancing shoe; pump; court shoe.
escient [ɛ'sjɑ̃] *n.m.*: *à bon* ~, knowingly, purposely.
esclaffer, s' [sɛskla'fe] #3 *v. pron.* to guffaw.
esclandre [ɛs'klɑ̃:dr] *n.m.* scandal; [tapage] row, disturbance.
esclavage [ɛskl|a'va:ʒ] *n.m.* slavery; bondage: *mettre en* ~, to enslave. || **esclave**

[-aːv] *n.m/f.* slave: *être l' ~ de qqch.*, to be a slave to sth. || **Esclaves (le lac des)** *n.m.* Slave Lake.
escogriffe [ɛskɔ'grif] *n.m.*: *grand ~*, big lout.
escompte [ɛs'k|õːt] *n.m.* **1.** [Com.] discount, rebate: *~ de caisse*, cash discount; *taux d' ~*, discount rate; *prendre à l' ~ une traite de commerce*, to discount a bill of exchange. || **escompter** [-õ'te] #3 *v. tr.* to discount; [Fig.] to anticipate.
escorte [ɛs'kɔrt] *n.f.* escort: *faire ~ à*, to escort, to attend. || **escorter** [-e] #3 *v. tr.* to escort, to attend.
†**escouade** [ɛs'kwad] *n.f.* [Mil.] section.
escrime [ɛs'krim] *n.f.* fencing: *faire de l' ~*, to fence. || **escrimer** [ɛskri'me] #3 *v. intr.* to fence. || **s'escrimer** [sɛskri'me] #3 *v. pron.* [Fig.] to exert o.s.
escroc [ɛs'kro] *n.m.* swindler, sharper. || **escroquer** [ɛskrɔ|'ke] #3 *v. tr.* to swindle (*à*, out of). || **escroquerie** [-'kri] *n.f.* swindle.
ésotérique [ezɔte'rik] *adj.* esoteric.
espace [ɛs'p|ɑːs] *n.m.* space; room; distance; interval (of space, time); void, infinity: *~ interplanétaire*, space. || **espacement** [-asmɑ̃] *n.m.* interval; [action] spacing (out). || **espacer** [-e] #4 *v. tr.* to separate, space.
espadrille [ɛspa'drij] *n.f.* rope-soled shoe; sandal.
Espagne [ɛs'paɲ] *n.f.* Spain. || **espagnol, -e** [-ɔl] *adj.* Spanish. || *n.* Spaniard.
espèce [ɛs'pɛs] *n.f.* species; kind; sort: *~ d'idiot!*, you crazy fool!
espérance [ɛspe'r|ɑ̃ːs] *n.f.* hope, expectation. || **espérer** [-e] #10 *v. tr.* to hope: *Il espère une augmentation*, He is hoping for a raise; © [& Fam.] to wait for, expect.
espiègle [ɛs'pjɛgl] *adj. & n.* mischievous, roguish (person). || **espièglerie** [-ə'ri] *n.f.* mischievousness; prank.
espion, -ne [ɛs'pj|õ, -ɔn] *n.* spy; secret agent. || **espionnage** [-ɔ'naːʒ] *n.m.* spying, espionage. || **espionner** [-ɔ'ne] #3 *v. tr.* to spy on (s.o.). || *v. intr.* to be a spy.
espoir [ɛs'pwaːr] *n.m.* hope; hopefulness: *sans ~*, → hopeless.
esprit [ɛs'pri] *n.m.* **1.** mind: *Il me vient à l' ~*, It occurs to me. **2.** wit: *Il a beaucoup d' ~*, He is very witty. **3.** spirit; ghost: *le Saint-Esprit*, the Holy Ghost.
esquimau, -de [ɛskim|o, -oːd] *pl.* **esquimaux** [-o] *adj. & n.* Eskimo.
esquisse [ɛs'kis] *n.f.* sketch, draft, outline. || **esquisser** [-e] #3 *v. tr.* **1.** to sketch. **2.** to outline.
esquiver [ɛski've] #3 *v. tr.* to avoid, to dodge, to duck (a blow); to evade (a question).
essai [ɛ'sɛ] *n.m.* **1.** trial, test: *à l' ~*, on a trial basis. **2.** attempt.
essaim [ɛ'sɛ̃] *n.m.* swarm (of bees). || **essaimer** [ɛsɛ'me] #3 *v. intr.* to swarm.
essart(s) [ɛ'saːr] © *n.m(pl.)* clearing (in forest) cf. DÉSERT.
essayage [ɛsɛ'jaːʒ] *n.m.* fitting, try-on (of clothes): *trois essayages*, three fittings. || **essayer** [-e] #11 *v. tr.* **1.** [moyen] to try; [vêtement] to try on; [rôle] to try out. **2.** to try, to attempt (to, *de*).
essence [ɛ'sɑ̃ːs] *n.f.* **1.** essence. **2.** gas(oline), [Br.] petrol. **3.** kind, species (of tree, &c.). || **essentiel, -le** [ɛsɑ̃'sjɛl] *adj.* essential. || *n.m.* the main point.
essieu [ɛ'sjø] *n.m.* axle (-tree).
essor [ɛ'sɔːr] *n.m.* flight (of a bird): *prendre son ~*, to take wing, to soar, [Fig.] to expand, to make great strides.
essorer [ɛsɔ'r|e] #3 *v. tr.* to wring (linen) dry, to dry. || **essoreuse** [-øːz] *n.f.* wringer.
essoufflé, -e [ɛsu'fl|e] *adj.* out of breath. || **essoufflement** [-ə'mɑ̃] *n.m.* breathlessness. || **essouffler** [-e] #3 *v. tr.* to get (s.o.) out of breath. || **s'essouffler** *v. pron.* to get out of breath.
essuie [ɛsɥi-] cf. ESSUYER. || **essuie-glace** [-'glas] *n.m. inv.* windshield-wiper. || **essuie-mains** [-'mɛ̃] *n.m. inv.* hand towel. || **essuyage** [-'jaːʒ] *n.m.* wiping, drying. || **essuyer** [-'je] #12 *v. tr.* to wipe; [objet humide] to dry; [poussière] to dust [Fig.] to suffer (a setback), to meet with (a refusal). || **s'essuyer** *v. pron.* to mop one's brow: *~ les yeux*, to wipe one's eyes.
est[1], cf. ÊTRE. || **est-ce que, est-ce qui** [☞ A set formula giving emphasis to questions (cf. QUE, QUI), used mostly in the spoken language to avoid inverting word order]: *Est-ce que vous irez?* (= Irez-vous?), Will you be going?; *Qui est-ce qui est là?* (= Qui est là?), Who's there?; *Qu'est-ce que vous dites?* (= Que dites-vous?), What are you saying?; *Lequel est-ce que vous voulez?* (= Lequel voulez-vous?), Which (one) do you want?
est[2] [ɛst] *n.m.* East.
estaminet [ɛstami'nɛ] *n.m.* [Fr.] public-house, wine shop.
esthéticien, -ne [ɛsteti'sj|ɛ̃, -ɛn] *n.* beauty specialist. || **esthétique** [ɛste'tik] *adj.* aesthetic. || *n.f.* aesthetics.
estimable [ɛsti'mabl] *adj.* worthy, respectable. || **estimat|eur, -rice** [ɛstima|'tœːr, -'tris] *n.* appraiser, valuer. || **estimation** [-'sjõ] *n.f.* estimation, assessment, appraisal. || **estime** [ɛs'tim] *n.f.* esteem:

tenir en ~, to think highly of, to esteem. || **estimer** [-e] #3 *v. tr.* **1.** to estimate, to value. **2.** to esteem, to think well of.

estival, -e [ɛsti'val] *adj.* summer (dress, plant). || **estivant** [ɛsti'vɑ̃] *n.m.* vacation|ist (-er); tourist.

estomac [ɛsto'ma] *n.m.* stomach: *avoir l'* ~ */creux, dans les talons/*, to be very hungry; *avoir mal à l'* ~, to have stomach ache; *avoir l'* ~ *dérangé*, to have a stomach upset. || **estomaqué, -e** [ɛstɔma'ke] *adj.* flabbergasted.

estomper [ɛstõ'pe] #3 *v. tr.* **1.** [dessin] to shade off, to rub away. **2.** [Fig.] to rub away, to blur. || **s'estomper** *v. pron.* to become blurred, to fade.

estrade [ɛs'trad] *n.f.* stand.

estran [ɛs'trɑ̃] *n.m.* strand, cf. © BATTURE.

estropié, -e [ɛstrɔ'pje] *adj.* crippled, disabled, maimed. || *n.* a cripple: *les estropiés*, the halt. || **estropier** #3 *v. tr.* **1.** to cripple, to disable. **2.** [Fig.] to murder (music, a language); to mispronounce.

estuaire [ɛs'tɥɛ:r] *n.m.* estuary.

estudiantin, -e [ɛstydjɑ̃'t|ɛ̃, -in] *adj.* collegiate: *esprit* ~, student spirit.

esturgeon [ɛstyr'ʒõ] *n.m.* sturgeon.

et [e] *conj.* **1.** and. *Vous* ~ *moi*, Both you and I. **2.** What about: *Et vous?*, What about you?

étable [e'tabl] *n.f.* cowshed, barn; © stable.

établi [eta'bli] *n.m.* work bench.

établir [eta'bl|i:r] #17 *v. tr.* **1.** to set up, to establish, to introduce. **2.** to strike (a balance). **3.** to prove, to substantiate. **4.** to make out (a document). || **s'établir** *v. pron.* to establish o.s., to set up house, to set up headquarters: *venir* ~ *à*, to move to. || **établissement** [-is'mɑ̃] *n.m.* **1.** setting up, establishment, introduction. **2.** making out (of a document). **3.** institution; firm; settlement: *un* ~ *scolaire*, an academic institution; *les Établissements Durand*, Durand and Co.

étage [e'ta:ʒ] *n.m.* **1.** storey, floor; flight of stairs: *le dernier* ~, the top floor; *encore un* ~, one more flight. **2.** tier, range. || **étagé, -e** [eta'ʒ|e] *adj.* terraced, rising in tiers. || **étagère** [-ɛ:r] *n.f.* whatnot, shelf.

étain [e'tɛ̃] *n.m.* tin; pewter.

étais, &c. cf. ÊTRE.

étalage [eta'l|a:ʒ] *n.m.* **1.** display (of goods) window-dressing: *mettre qqch. à l'* ~, to put sth. on display. **2.** [Fig., showing off] *faire* ~ *de*, to show off, to parade.

étalé, -e [-e] *adj.* spread out: *largement* ~, sprawling. || **étalement** [-'mɑ̃] *n.m.* spreading, staggering, spacing. || **étaler** [-e] #3 *v. tr.* **1.** to spread out, to display. **2.** to parade, to flaunt. || **s'étaler** *v. pron.* to spread out, to sprawl.

étalon [eta'l|õ] *n.m.* **1.** stallion; stud horse. **2.** standard (of weights, &c.); yardstick: [Fin.] *l'* ~ *or*, the gold standard; *le mètre* ~, the standard metre. || **étalonnage** [-ɔ'na:ʒ] *n.m.* standardization. || **étalonner** [-ɔ'ne] #3 *v. tr.* to standardize, to calibrate.

étamé, -e [eta'me] *adj.* tinned. || **étamer** #3 *v. tr.* to coat with tin, to tin.

étamine [eta'min] *n.f.* [cloth] bunting; [Bot.] stamen.

étampe [e'tɑ̃:p] *n.f.* stamp, die; [Tech.] punch; © rubber stamp. || **étamper** [-e] *v. tr.* to stamp, to punch.

étanche [e't|ɑ̃:ʃ] *adj.* impervious (to, *à*): ~ *à l'eau*, watertight; ~ *à l'air*, airtight; *cloison* ~, bulkhead. || **étanchéité** [-ɑ̃ʃei'te] *n.f.* watertightness, imperviousness. || **étancher** [-ɑ̃'ʃe] #3 *v. tr.* [sang] to stanch; [soif] to slake, to quench.

étang [e'tɑ̃] *n.m.* pond, pool.

étant [e'tɑ̃] cf. ÊTRE.

étape [e'tap] *n.f.* stage (of journey, development, &c.): *par petites étapes*, in easy stages; [Fig.] *brûler les étapes*, to go full speed ahead.

état [e'ta] *n.m.* **1.** state, condition: ~ *d'esprit*, frame of mind; *en* ~ *d'ivresse*, intoxicated; *en tout* ~ *de cause*, in any case; *être en* ~ *de*, to be in a position to; *être hors d'* ~ *de*, to be incapable of, unfit for; *être dans tous ses états*, to be terribly upset; ~ *d'urgence*, emergency. **2.** statement, list, return: *faire* ~ *de qqch.*, to include sth., to allow for sth. **3.** status: ~ *civil* [on form], married or single; *le registre de l'* ~ *civil*, vital statistics. **4.** occupation: *menuisier de son* ~, a carpenter by trade. **5.** state: *homme d'État*, statesman.

état-major [-ma'ʒɔ:r] *n.m.* staff, general staff: *officier d'* ~, staff officer.

États [e'ta] *n.mpl.* © the (United) States (of America). || **États-Unis** [-zy'ni] *n.mpl.* United States of America (US, U.S.A.).

étau [e'to] *n.m.* vice [also spelt *vise*], clamp.

étayer [etɛ'je] #11 *v. tr.* to stay, prop (up), shore (up).

etc. [ɛtsete'ra], © [ɛtʃete'rɑ] [abbr. of *et cetera*] &c.

été[1] [e'te] *n.m.* summer: *en* ~, in summer; © *l'* ~ *des sauvages*, Indian summer (= [Fr.] *l'* ~ *de la Saint-Martin*).

été[2] [e'te] cf. ÊTRE.

éteignais, &c., éteigne, &c., éteignant, cf.

ÉTEINDRE. || **éteignoir** [etɛ'ɲwa:r] *n.m.* (candle) extinguisher. || **éteindre** [e'tɛ̃:dr], **éteignant** [etɛ'ɲɑ̃], **éteint** [e'tɛ̃] #36 *v. tr.* [lumière, gaz, &c.] to put out, to extinguish; [Fig.] to deaden, to dim; to obliterate; [soif] to quench; [dette] to pay off. || **s'éteindre** *v. pron.* to go out, to burn out; [Pers.] to die. **éteins, &c.** cf. ÉTEINDRE.

éteint, -e [e'tɛ̃(:t)] *adj.* [feu, &c.] put out, extinct; [dette] paid off; [Fig.] dying, faded, dim.

étend, étendais, &c. cf. ÉTENDRE.

étendard [etɑ̃'da:r] *n.m.* **1.** standard. **2.** [cavalry] regimental colours.

étendre [e'tɑ̃:dr], **étendant, étendu** #42 *v. tr.* **1.** to spread; to spread out; to stretch out. **2.** to extend, to broaden. **3.** to dilute. || **s'étendre** *v. pron.* **1.** to lie, to stretch out, to extend. **2.** to lie down. **3.** to dwell, to elaborate (on, *sur*). || **étendu, -e** [etɑ̃'dy] *adj.* **1.** [surface] wide; [ailes] outspread; [connaissance] extensive. **2.** diluted. || **étendue** [etɑ̃'dy] *n.f.* **1.** stretch. **2.** extent, dimensions, range (of knowledge).

éternel, -le [etɛr'n|ɛl] *adj.* eternal; everlasting; endless: *le Père Éternel*, the Eternal Father. || **éternellement** [-ɛl'mɑ̃] *adv.* eternally, everlastingly.

éterniser [-i'ze] #3 *v. tr.* to eternize; [le nom de qqun] to immortalize. || **s'éterniser** *v. pron.* [Fam.] to drag on; [visiteur] to wear out o.'s welcome. || **éternité** [-i'te] *n.f.* eternity: *de toute ~, adv.* from time immemorial, from all eternity; *Il y a une ~ que je ne l'ai vu(e)*, It's ages since I saw/him, her/.

éternuement [etɛr|ny'mɑ̃] *n.m.* sneezing, sneeze. || **éternuer** [-'nɥe] #3 *v. intr.* to sneeze.

êtes [ɛt] cf. ÊTRE.

éther [e'tɛ:r] *n.m.* ether. || **éthéré, -e** [ete're] *adj.* ethereal.

ethnique [ɛt'n|ik] *adj.* ethnic(al). || **ethnographe** [-ɔ'graf] *n.m.* ethnographer. || **ethnographie** [-ɔgra'fi] *n.f.* ethnography. || **ethnologie** [-ɔlɔ'ʒi] *n.f.* ethnology.

étincelant, -e [etɛ̃s|'lɑ̃(:t)] *adj.* sparkling, glittering. || **étinceler** [-'le] #8 *v. intr.* to sparkle, to glitter. || **étincelle, &c.** cf. ÉTINCELER. || **étincelle** [-ɛl] *n.f.* spark.

étiqueter [etik|'te] #9 *v. tr.* to label, to tag. || **étiquette** [-ɛt] *n.f.* **1.** label, sticker, tag. **2.** étiquette, good manners.

étiré, -e [eti're] *adj.* stretched, [village] straggling. || **étirer** #3 *v. tr.* to stretch, draw/out. || **s'étirer** *v. pron.* to stretch.

étoffe [e'tɔf] *n.f.* **1.** material; stuff, fabric; [Fam.] the makings: *Il a l' ~ d'un bon chef*, He has the makings of a good leader. || **étoffer** [-e] #3 *v. tr.* to (put) stuff (into); [Fig.] to pad (out); to fill in.

étoile [e'twal] *n.f.* star: *~ filante*, shooting star; *ciel semé d'étoiles*, starlit sky; *coucher à la belle ~*, to sleep out of doors; *remercier sa bonne ~*, to thank one's lucky stars. || **étoilé, -e** [-e] *adj.* starry, starlit: *la Bannière étoilée*, the Star-spangled Banner. || **étoiler** [-e] #3 *v. tr.* to stud, to bespangle with stars.

étole [e'tɔl] *n.f.* stole.

étonnamment [etɔna'mɑ̃] *adv.* amazingly, wonderfully. || **étonnant, -e** [etɔ'n|ɑ̃(:t)] *adj.* surprising, astonishing, amazing: *Ce n'est pas ~ que*, No wonder that . . . || **étonné, -e** [-e] *adj.* surprised. || **étonnement** [-'mɑ̃] *n.m.* surprise, amazement, astonishment. || **étonner** [-e] #3 *v. tr.* to surprise, to amaze, to astonish. || **s'étonner** *v. pron.* to be surprised, to wonder.

étouffant, -e [etu'f|ɑ̃(:t)] *adj.* stifling, sultry. || **étouffement** [-'mɑ̃] *n.m.* suffocation, stifling. || **étouffer** [-e] #3 *v. tr.* to choke, to stifle: *~ un cri*, to smother a cry; *~ une affaire*, to hush up a case. || *v. intr.* **1.** to choke. **2.** to be unbearably hot: *On étouffe ici*, This place is like an oven.

étourderie [eturd|ə'ri] *n.f.* **1.** thoughtlessness, absentmindedness. **2.** careless act or blunder. || **étourdi, -e** [-i] *adj.* thoughtless, careless. || *n.* scatterbrain. || **étourdiment** [-i'mɑ̃] *adv.* thoughtlessly, without thinking. || **étourdir** [-i:r] #17 *v. tr.* to stun, to daze; to deafen. || **s'étourdir** *v. pron.* to forget one's troubles. || **étourdissant, -e** [-i'sɑ̃(:t)] *adj.* deafening, dizzying. || **étourdissement** [-is'mɑ̃] *n.m.* giddiness, spell of dizziness.

étourneau [etur'no] *n.m.* [Orn.] starling.

étrange [e'tr|ɑ̃:ʒ] *adj.* strange; odd: *chose ~*, oddly enough. || **étrangement** [-ɑ̃ʒ'mɑ̃] *adv.* strangely. || **étrang|er, -ère** [-ɑ̃'ʒe, -ɑ̃'ʒɛ:r] *adj.* **1.** foreign: *le ministère des Affaires étrangères* [= © *Affaires extérieures*], the Department of External Affairs, [Br.] the Foreign Office, [US] the State Department. **2.** strange, unfamiliar. **3.** irrelevant: *~ à la question*, beside the point. || *n.* **1.** foreigner, alien. **2.** stranger. || *n.m.* foreign countries: *à l' ~*, abroad. || **étrangeté** [-ə'te] *n.f.* strangeness; [chose] strange thing.

étranglement [etrɑ̃gl|ə'mɑ̃] *n.m.* strangling, strangulation: *goulot d' ~*, bottleneck. || **étrangler** [-e] #3 *v. tr.* to strangle; to choke. || **étrangleur** [etrɑ̃'glœ:r] *n.m.* [Auto.] choke.

être [ɛ:tr] *n.m.* being, existence, reality: *l'Être suprême*, the Supreme Being; ~

humain, human being; *Quel* ~ *!*, What a fellow! || **être, étant** [e'tɑ̃], **été** [e'te] *v. intr. & aux.* [conj. AVOIR] **1.** to be: *Où êtes-vous?*, Where are you?; *Il est de Toronto*, He is from T.; *Il est d'un caractère irritable*, He is irritable by nature; ~ *bien avec qqun*, to be on good terms with s.o.; *Il n'est plus*, He has passed away. **2.** to belong: *C'est à moi*, It belongs to me, It's mine; *C'est à vous de jouer*, [cartes] It's your lead, [échecs, dames] It's your move. **3.** [In compound tenses] to be, to go: *J'y ai été*, I went there, I've been there. **4.** [Impers.] *Il est* [= Il y a] There is, There are. **5.** [Loc.]: *Il est à plaindre*, He is to be pitied; *Il n'en est rien*, Such is not the case; *Où en sommes-nous?*, How far along are we?; *Je n'en suis pas*, Count me out; *J'en suis encore à me demander si*, I am still wondering if . . . ; *J'en suis pour ma peine*, I have nothing to show for it; *Je n'y suis plus*, I don't follow [☞ as opposed to: I am no longer there, cf. §1]; *y* ~ *pour qqch.*, [thing] to be a factor, [person] to be partly responsible; *Je n'y suis pour rien*, Don't blame me for it; *Ça y est!*, That's done!; Here we go again!; He's done it again!; *Cette fois, ça y est!*, That did the trick!; *Nous y sommes!*, This is it!; *Je n'y suis pour personne*, I am not to be disturbed.

étreindre [e'trɛ̃:dr], **étreignant** [etrɛ'ɲɑ̃], **étreint** [e'trɛ̃] #36 *v. tr.* **1.** to embrace, to hug. **2.** to grasp, to grip: *Qui trop embrasse mal étreint*, Grasp all, lose all. || **étreinte** [e'trɛ̃:t] *n.f.* **1.** embrace, hug. **2.** grasp, grip, clasp. **3.** pressure (of want).

étrenne [e'trɛ:n] *n.f.pl.* **1.** *étrennes*, New Year's gift. **2.** first use (of sth.). || **étrenner** #3 *v. tr.* to try/put on/for the first time.

étrier [etri'je] *n.m.* stirrup: *avoir le pied à l'* ~ , to be off to a good start.

étriqué, -e [etri'ke] *adj.* skimpy, scanty, narrow, cramped.

étroit, -e [e'trw|a(t)] *adj.* **1.** narrow: ~ *d'esprit*, narrow-minded. **2.** close, strict: *une étroite parenté*, a close relationship: *à l'* ~ , pinched, cramped for room. || **étroitement** [-at'mɑ̃] *adv.* narrowly. || **étroitesse** [-a'tɛs] *n.f.* narrowness, tightness: ~ *d'esprit*, narrow-mindedness.

étude [e'tyd] *n.f.* **1.** study: *programme d'études*, curriculum; *faire ses études à*, to be educated at; *à l'* ~ , under study. **2.** study hall. **3.** [Fr.] office of certain lawyers: ~ *de notaire*, notary's office. || **étudiant, -e** [-jɑ̃(:t)] *n.* student, undergraduate: ~ *en médecine*, medical student. || **étudié, -e** [-je] *adj.* **1.** carefully studied, elaborate: *Nos prix sont très étudiés*, Our prices are the keenest. **2.** designed (for, *en vue de*). || **étudier** [-je] #3 *v. tr. & intr.* to study, to examine, to look into.

étui [e'tɥi] *n.m.* case box, cover: ~ *à lunettes*, spectacle case; ~ *à cigares*, cigar case; ~ *de revolver*, holster.

étymologie [etimɔlɔ'ʒi] *n.f.* etymology.

eu, eue, eus, eues, eûmes, eurent, eut, eûtes. cf. AVOIR.

Eucharistie [økaris'ti] *n.f.* Eucharist; the Lord's Supper.

Europe [ø'rɔp] *n.f.* Europe. || **européen, -ne** [-e'ɛ̃, -e'ɛn] *adj. & n.* European.

eux, eux-mêmes [ø, ø'mɛ:m] *pron. pers.* **1.** them: *avec eux*, with them; *eux-mêmes*, themselves. **2.** [disjunctive] they: *Eux, ils y sont allés*, They went.

évacuation [eva'kɥ|a'sjɔ̃] *n.f.* evacuation. || **évacué, -e** [-e] *n.* evacuee. || **évacuer** [-e] #3 *v. tr.* **1.** to evacuate. **2.** to abandon ship.

évadé [eva'de] *n.m.* fugitive. || **s'évader** [seva'de] #3 *v. pron.* to escape, break loose (*de*, from).

évaluation [evalɥ|a'sjɔ̃] *n.f.* valuation, appraisal, assessment. || **évaluer** [-e] #3 *v. tr.* to value, estimate.

évangéliser [evɑ̃ʒeli'ze] #3 *v. tr.* to evangelize. || **évangéliste** [evɑ̃ʒe'list] *n.m.* Evangelist. || **évangile** [evɑ̃'ʒil] *n.m.* Gospel: *l'* ~ *selon saint Jean*, the Gospel according to St. John; *parole d'* ~ , Gospel truth.

évanoui, -e [eva'nwi] *adj.* **1.** vanished, gone. **2.** in a faint, in a swoon. || **s'évanouir** [seva'nwi:r] #17 *v. pron.* **1.** to vanish, to melt away. **2.** to faint, to swoon. || **évanouissement** [evanwis'mɑ̃] *n.m.* **1.** vanishing, melting away, disappearance. **2.** faint, swoon.

évaporation [evapɔra'sjɔ̃] *n.f.* evaporation. || **évaporé, -e** [evapɔ're] *n.* feather-brained person. || **évaporer** #3 *v. tr.* to evaporate. || **s'évaporer** *v. pron.* **1.** to evaporate. **2.** [Fig.] to vanish into thin air.

évasi|f, -ve [eva'z|if, -i:v] *adj.* evasive. || **évasion** [-jɔ̃] *n.f.* escape, flight; evasion, quibble.

Ève [ɛv] *n.f.* Eve: [Fig.] *Je ne le connais ni d'* ~ , *ni d'Adam*, I do not know him from Adam.

évêché [evɛ'ʃe] *n.m.* bishopric, diocese, see; bishop's palace; cathedral city.

éveil [e'vɛ:j] *n.m.* **1.** awakening. **2.** warning; hint; alarm: *mettre qqun en* ~ , to put s.o. on his guard. || **éveillé, -e** [evɛ'je] *adj.* **1.** awake. **2.** quick, alert. || **éveiller** #3 *v. tr.*

to awake, to rouse, to arouse. || **s'éveiller** *v. pron.* to wake up.

événement [evɛn'mɑ̃] *n.m.* event, occurrence, incident; development: *attendre la tournure que prendront les événements,* to await further developments.

éventail [evɑ̃'t|aj] *pl.* **éventails** [-aj] **1.** fan. **2.** spread (of prices). || **éventé, -e** [-e] *adj.* flat, stale. || **éventer** [-e] #3 *v. tr.* **1.** to air. **2.** to spoil (wine) by exposure. 3. to get wind of (a secret). || **s'éventer** *v. pron.* to spoil, to go flat.

éventrer [evɑ̃'tre] #3 *v. tr.* **1.** to disembowel, to eviscerate. **2.** to break, tear/open.

éventualité [evɑ̃tɥ|ali'te] *n.f.* possibility, contingency, eventuality. || **éventuel, -le** [-ɛl] *adj.* possible, contingent: × EVENTUAL. || **éventuellement** [-ɛl'mɑ̃] [×] *adv.* possibly; on occasion; if need be.

évêque [e'vɛ:k] *n.m.* bishop.

évertuer, s' [sevɛr'tɥe] #3 *v. pron.* to struggle, to do o.'s best (*à*, to).

évidemment [evid|a'mɑ̃] *adv.* obviously, clearly. || **évidence** [-ɑ̃:s] *n.f.* obviousness, clearness; the facts: *se rendre à l'* ~ , to bow to facts; *nier l'* ~ , to fly in the face of facts; *mettre en* ~ , to show up, reveal, display. || **évident, -e** [-ɑ̃(:t)] *adj.* obvious, plain.

évier [e'vje] *n.m.* sink.

évincer [evɛ̃'se] #4 *v. tr.* to supplant, displace; [Jur.] to evict, oust.

éviter [evi'te] #3 *v. tr.* **1.** to avoid; to dodge. **2.** [épargner] to save, to spare (s.o.): *Cela vous évitera la peine de le faire,* It will save you the trouble of doing it.

évocat|eur, -rice [evɔka't|œ:r, -ris] *adj.* evocative. || **évocation** [evɔka'sjõ] *n.f.* evocation.

évolué, -e [evɔ'l|ɥe] *adj.* far along in its development; sophisticated. || **évoluer** [-ɥe] #3 *v. intr.* **1.** to evolve, to develop. **2.** to perform evolutions, to move about. || **évolution** [-y'sjõ] *n.f.* **1.** evolution, development, trend. **2.** *pl.* evolutions, movements.

évoquer [evɔ'ke] #3 *v. tr.* to evoke, to recall, to call up.

exacerber [ɛgzasɛr'be] #3 *v. tr.* to exacerbate.

exact, -e [ɛg'za|(kt)] *adj.* **1.** accurate: *C'est* ~ , That's right. **2.** punctual. || **exactement** [-ktə'mɑ̃] *adv.* exactly, precisely. || **exactitude** [-kti'tyd] *n.f.* **1.** accuracy, correctness. **2.** punctuality.

exagération [ɛgzaʒer|a'sjõ] *n.f.* exaggeration; excess; overstatement. || **exagéré, -e** [-e] *adj.* exaggerated, overdone. || **exagérer** [-e] #10 *v. tr. & intr.* **1.** [en paroles] to exaggerate, to overstate: ~ *l'importance de,* to overrate. **2.** [en action] to overdo.

exaltant, -e [ɛgzal't|ɑ̃(:t) *adj.* exalting, thrilling. || **exalté, -e** [-e] *adj.* hotheaded. || **exalter** [-e] #3 *v. tr.* **1.** to exalt, to praise. **2.** to uplift, to excite, to intensify. || **s'exalter** *v. pron.* to grow enthusiastic.

examen [ɛgza'm|ɛ̃] *n.m.* **1.** examination, test: *passer, se présenter à/un* ~ , to take an examination; *être reçu à un* ~ , to pass an examination; *être refusé, échouer/à un* ~ , to fail an examination; *faire passer un* ~ , to give an examination; ~ *d'entrée,* entrance examination; ~ *de fin d'année,* final examination. **2.** examination, scrutiny: *un* ~ *approfondi,* a thorough examination. || **examinat|eur, -rice** [-in|a'tœ:r, -a'tris] *n.* examiner: *jury d'examinateurs,* board of examiners. || **examiner** [-e] #3 *v. tr.* to examine, to scrutinize, to look into.

exaspérer [ɛgzaspe're] #10 *v. tr.* to aggravate; to exasperate.

exaucer [ɛgzo'se] #4 *v. tr.* to grant, fulfil (a wish, &c.): *Ma prière a été exaucée,* My prayer has been heard.

excavation [ɛkskava'sjõ] *n.f.* excavation; digging; cavity.

excédent, [ɛkse'd|ɑ̃] *n.m.* excess: *en* ~ , in excess; ~ *de bagages,* excess baggage. || **excéder** [-e] #10 *v. tr.* **1.** to exceed, surpass; to overdraw (a bank account). **2.** to tire (s.o.) out; to importune (s.o.), tax (s.o.'s) patience.

excellemment [ɛksɛla'mɑ̃] *adv.* excellently, pre-eminently.

excellence [ɛksɛ'l|ɑ̃:s] *n.f.* **1.** excellence. **2.** excellency: *Votre Excellence,* Your Excellency, Your Grace. || **excellent, -e** [-ɑ̃(:t)] *adj.* excellent, worthy: *un* ~ *homme,* a kind man. || **exceller** [-e] #3 *v. tr.* to excel, to be very good (at, *en*).

excentricité [ɛksɑ̃trisi'te] *n.f.* eccentricity; [d'un quartier, &c.] remoteness. || **excentrique** [ɛksɑ̃'trik] *adj.* **1.** eccentric, bizarre, odd. **2.** [cercles, &c.] eccentric, off centre; [quartier] peripheral, outlying. || *n.* an eccentric person, a crank.

excepté, -e [ɛksɛp|'te] *adj.* excepted: *mon ami* ~ , my friend excepted. || *prép.* except, with the exception that. ~ *que,* except that. || **excepter** [-'te] #3 *v. tr.* to except, to exclude. || **exception** [-'sjõ] *n.f.* exception: *faire une* ~ *à,* to make an exception to; *faire* ~ *à une règle,* to be an exception to a rule; *à l'* ~ *de,* except, save. || **exceptionnel, -le** [-sjɔ'nɛl] *adj.* exceptional, unusual, extraordinary: *lois ex-*

ceptionnelles, emergency legislation. || **exceptionnellement** [-mɑ̃] *adv.* exceptionally.

excès [ɛk'sɛ] *n.m. inv.* **1.** excess: *à l'* ~, too (much); *commettre un* ~ *de pouvoir*, to exceed one's powers. **2.** *pl.* excesses; debauch, overindulgence. || **excessi|f, -ve** [-'sif, -'si:v] *adj.* excessive; undue (optimism); exorbitant; immoderate; inordinate (pride). || **excessivement** [ɛksɛsiv'mɑ̃] *adv.* excessively, extremely.

excitable [ɛksi't|abl] *adj.* excitable. || **excitant, -e** [-ɑ̃(:t)] *adj.* exciting, stimulating. || *n.m.* stimulant. || **excité, -e** [-e] *adj.* overexcited, all worked up. || **exciter** [-e] #3 *v. tr.* to arouse, to incite, to excite. || **s'exciter** *v. pron.* to get worked up.

exclamati|f, -ve [ɛksklama|'tif, -ti:v] *adj.* exclamatory. || **exclamation** [-'sjɔ̃] *n.f.* exclamation: *point d'* ~ , exclamation mark. || **s'exclamer** [sɛkskla'me] #3 *v. pron.* to exclaim.

exclure [ɛks'kly:r], **excluant** [ɛkskly'ɑ̃], **exclu** [ɛks'kly] #58 *v. tr.* to exclude, shut out, leave out (s.o., sth.); to be incompatible with (sth.). || **exclusi|f, -ve** [ɛkskly'zi|f, -i:v] *adj.* **1.** exclusive, sole. **2.** [×] intolerant. || **exclusion** [-jɔ̃] *n.f.* exclusion. || **exclusivement** [-iv'mɑ̃] *adv.* exclusively.

exclusivité [ɛksklyzivi'te] *n.f.* exclusiveness; [Com.] exclusive rights.

excommunication [ɛkskɔmyn|ika'sjɔ̃] *n.f.* excommunication. || **excommunier** [-je] #3 *v. tr.* to excommunicate.

excorier [ɛkskɔ'rje] #3 *v. tr.* to excoriate. **s'excorier** *v. pron.* to peel off.

excroissance [ɛkskrwa'sɑ̃:s] *n.f.* excrescence, outgrowth.

excursion [ɛkskyr|'sjɔ̃] *n.f.* outing, sightseeing tour. || **excursionniste** [-sjɔ'nist] *n.m/f & adj.* tourist.

excuse [ɛks'k|y:z] *n.f.* **1.** excuse. **2.** *pl.* excuses, apology: *présenter ses excuses*, to apologize. || **excusé, -e** [-y'ze] *adj.* excused: *Vous êtes tout* ~ , You don't have to apologize. || **excuser** [-y'ze] #3 *v. tr.* to excuse: *Veuillez l'* ~ *de n'avoir pas écrit*, Please excuse him for not writing; © *Excusez!*, Pardon (me)!, Excuse me! [= Fr. PARDON]. || **s'excuser** *v. pron.* to apologize (for, *de*).

exécrable [ɛgze'kra|bl] *adj.* execrable; abominable. || **exécrablement** [-blə'mɑ̃] *adv.* abominably. || **exécration** [-'sjɔ̃] *n.f.* execration, detestation. || **exécrer** [ɛgze'kre] #10 *v. tr.* to execrate.

exécutant [ɛgzeky'tɑ̃] *n.m.* [Mus.] performer, musician. || **exécuter** [ɛgzeky'te] #3 *v. tr.* **1.** to carry out, to execute (an order), to fulfil (a promise); to accomplish, to do (a piece of work). **2.** to execute (a criminal). || **s'exécuter** *v. pron.* to comply, to bow. || **exécuti|f, -ve** [ɛgzeky|'tif, -'ti:v] *adj.* executive. || *n.m.* © the executive (committee), cf. BUREAU, DIRECTION. || **exécution** [-'sjɔ̃] *n.f.* **1.** execution (of an order), fulfilment (of a promise), achievement. **2.** execution (of a criminal).

exemplaire [ɛgzɑ̃'plɛ:r] *adj.* model, exemplary. || *n.m.* copy: *un* ~ *dédicacé*, an autographed copy.

exemple [ɛg'zɑ̃:pl] *n.m.* **1.** example, instance: *sans* ~ , unprecedented; *par* ~ , for example, e.g.; *par* ~ *!*, The idea!, You don't say!; *Ça par* ~ *!*, That's a bit thick! **2.** model: *prendre* ~ *sur*, to model o.s. on.

exempt, -e [ɛg'zɑ̃|(:t)] *adj.* exempt, free, immune (*de*, from) || **exempter** [-'te] #3 *v. tr.* to exempt, excuse (*de*, from).

exerçai, &c. cf. EXERCER. || **exercé, -e** [ɛgzɛr's|e] *adj.* trained, seasoned. || **exercer** #4 *v. tr.* **1.** to exercise, to train, to drill. **2.** to practise (medicine), to perform (a function). **3.** to exert (an influence). || **s'exercer** *v. pron.* to drill, to practise.

exercice [-is] *n.m.* **1.** exercise, practice, drill. **2.** discharge, performance (of a duty, a function). **3.** financial year.

exhalaison [ɛgzal|ɛ'zɔ̃] *n.f.* exhalation, fume. || **exhaler** [-e] #3 *v. tr.* to exhale, to give out: ~ *sa mauvaise humeur*, to air one's discontent, [Fam.] to gripe; ~ *le dernier soupir*, to breathe one's last, to give up the ghost.

exhausser [ɛgzo'se] #3 *v. tr.* to raise [× do not confuse with EXAUCER].

exhausti|f, -ve [ɛgzos't|if, -i:v] *adj.* exhaustive.

exhiber [ɛgzi'be] #3 *v. tr.* to exhibit; to show (a ticket, a passport).

exhibition [ɛgzibi'sjɔ̃] *n.f.* exhibition.

exhorter [ɛgzɔr'te] #3 *v. tr.* to exhort, to urge (to do, *à faire*).

exhumer [ɛgzy'me] #3 *v. tr.* to exhume, dig up; [Fig.] to bring to light.

exigeant, -e [ɛgzi'ʒ|ɑ̃(:t)] *adj.* exacting, demanding. || **exigence** [-ɑ̃:s] *n.f.* demand, requirement, exigency. || **exiger** [-e] #5 *v. tr.* to demand, to exact, to require: *Il a exigé que je le fasse*, He insisted on my doing it. || **exigible** [-ibl] *adj.* demandable, → on demand.

exigu, -ë [ɛgzi'g|y] *adj.* tiny, cramped, inadequate; diminutive; slender (income). || **exiguïté** [-ɥi'te] *n.f.* insufficiency; diminutiveness, small size; slenderness (income).

exil [ɛg'zil] *n.m.* exile, banishment. || **exilé,**

-e [-e] *n.* exile. ‖ **exiler** [-e] ♯3 *v. tr.* to exile, to banish. ‖ **s'exiler** *v. pron.* to go into exile.

existence [ɛgzis't|ɑ̃:s] *n.f.* existence; life, way of life. ‖ **exister** [-e] ♯3 *v. intr.* to exist, to live, to be.

exode [ɛg'zɔd] *n.m.* flight, exodus; [Rel.] Exodus.

exonérer [ɛgzɔne're] ♯10 *v. tr.* to exonerate, to relieve, to exempt (from, *de*).

exorbitant, -e [ɛgzɔrbi'tɑ̃(:t)] *adj.* exorbitant, extravagant; [Péj.] outrageous.

exorciser [ɛgzɔrsi'ze] ♯3 *v. tr.* to exorcise.

exotique [ɛgzɔ'tik] *adj.* foreign, exotic.

expansi|f, -ve [ɛkspɑ̃'s|if, -i:v] *adj.* expansive. ‖ **expansion** [ɛkspɑ̃'sjõ] *n.f.* expansion; spread (of knowledge, &c.).

expatrier [ɛkspatri'je] ♯3 *v. tr.* to banish, exile. ‖ **s'expatrier** *v. pron.* to expatriate o.s.

expectative [ɛkspɛkta'ti:v] *n.f.* expectation, anticipation.

expédient, -e [ɛkspe'djɑ̃(:t)] *adj.* expedient, advisable. ‖ [ɛkspe'djɑ̃] *n.m.* makeshift: *vivre d'expédients,* to live from hand to mouth.

expédier [ɛkspe'd|je] ♯3 *v. tr.* **1.** to dispatch, to finish, to complete. **2.** to send, to ship, to forward. ‖ **expédit|eur, -rice** [-i|'tœ:r, -'tris] *n.* sender (of telegram, letter); shipper, consigner (of goods); forwarding agent: *Expéditeur: J. Dupont,* from J.D. ‖ **expéditi|f, -ve** [-'tif, -'ti:v] *adj.* expeditious, speedy. ‖ **expédition** [-'sjõ] *n.f.* **1.** dispatch (of business). **2.** dispatch, forwarding, sending: *bulletin d'* ~, waybill. **3.** copy (of legal document). ‖ **expéditionnaire** [-sjɔ'nɛ:r] *adj.* expeditionary: *corps m* ~, expeditionary force. ‖ *n.m.* shipper; shipping clerk.

expérience [ɛkspe|rjɑ̃:s] *n.f.* **1.** experience: *avoir l'* ~ *de,* to be experienced in; *faire l'* ~ *de qqch.,* to experience sth. **2.** [×] experiment, test, trial: *faire une* ~, to make an experiment. ‖ **expérimental,** [-rimɑ̃'tal] *adj.* experimental. ‖ **expérimenté, -e** [-rimɑ̃'te] *adj.* experienced, trained. ‖ **expérimenter** ♯3 *v. tr.* to experiment with, to try out, to test. ‖ *v. intr.* to make experiments.

expert, -e [ɛks'p|ɛ:r, -ɛrt] *adj.* expert, skilled (*en,* in). ‖ *n.* expert, connoisseur; [Com.] valuer: ~ *-comptable,* chartered accountant. ‖ **expertise** [-ɛr'ti:z] *n.f.* appraisal, valuation. ‖ **expertiser** -ɛrti'ze] ♯3 *v. tr.* to appraise, value.

expiable [ɛks'pjabl] *adj.* expiable. ‖ **expiation** [ɛkspi(j)a'sjõ] *n.f.* expiation, atonement (*de,* for). ‖ **expier** [ɛks'pje] ♯3 *v. tr.* to expiate, to atone for.

expiration [ɛkspira'sjõ] *n.f.* expiration, breathing out; [terminaison] end, expiration. ‖ **expirer** [ɛkspi're] ♯3 *v. tr.* to breathe out. ‖ *v. intr.* **1.** to expire, to die. **2.** to expire, to run out, to be up.

explicable [ɛkspli'ka|bl] *adj.* explicable. ‖ **explicati|f, -ve** [-'tif, -'ti:v] *adj.* explanatory: *Notice explicative,* Directions (for use); prefatory note.

explication [ɛksplik|a'sjõ] *n.f.* explanation: *avoir une* ~ *avec qqun,* to have it out with s.o. ‖ **expliquer** [-e] ♯3 *v. tr.* to explain, to interpret, to account for. ‖ **s'expliquer** *v. pron.* **1.** to explain one's actions. **2.** to understand: *Je ne m'explique pas pourquoi . . ,* I can't understand why . . .

exploit [ɛks'plwa] *n.m.* exploit, achievement, feat.

exploitant [ɛksplwa't|ɑ̃] *n.m.* farmer; operator. ‖ **exploitation** [-a'sjõ] *n.f.* **1.** working (of a mine), cultivation (of land), development (of resources). **2.** [Péj.] exploitation. ‖ **exploiter** [-e] ♯3 *v. tr.* **1.** to work (a mine), to till (the land). **2.** [Péj.] to exploit. ‖ **exploiteu|r, -se** [-œ:r, -ø:z] *n.* [Péj.] exploiter.

explorat|eur, -rice [ɛksplɔr|a'tœ:r, -a'tris] *n.* explorer. ‖ *adj.* exploring. ‖ **explorer** [-e] ♯3 *v. tr.* to explore.

exploser [ɛksplo'z|e] ♯3 *v. tr.* [also causative, *faire* ~] to explode, go off, blow up; [Fig.] to burst (with anger). ‖ **explosif** [-if] *n.m.* explosive. ‖ **explosi|f, -ve** [-if, -i:v] *adj.* explosive. ‖ **explosion** [-jõ] *n.f.* explosion, blowing up: *faire* ~, to blow up, go off; [Tech.] *moteur à* ~, internal combustion engine; [Fig.] (out)-burst.

exportat|eur, -rice [ɛkspɔr|ta'tœ:r, -ta'tris] *n.* exporter. ‖ *adj.* exporting. ‖ **exportation** [-ta'sjõ] *n.f.* export (trade). ‖ **exporter** [-'te] ♯3 *v. tr.* to export.

exposant, -e [ɛkspo'z|ɑ̃(:t)] *n.* [Jur.] petitioner; exhibitor; [Math.] exponent. ‖ **exposé, -e** [-e] *adj.* on show, displayed. ‖ *n.m.* statement, account. ‖ **exposer** [-e] ♯3 *v. tr.* **1.** to show, to display. **2.** to set forth, to expound. ‖ **s'exposer** *v. pron.* to expose o.s. (to, *à*); to lay o.s. open (to). ‖ **exposition** [-i'sjõ] *n.f.* **1.** show, exhibition: *l'* ~ *d'horticulture,* the Flower Show. **2.** aspect, orientation (of a house). **3.** [mort] lying in state.

exprès, expresse [ɛks'prɛ(s)] *adj.* express, distinct, explicit (instructions, &c.); © [lettre] special delivery. ‖ *adv.* on purpose, intentionally. || **express** [ɛks'prɛs] *adj. & n.m. inv.* express (train).

expressi|f, -ve [ɛksprɛ's|if, -i:v] *adj.* expressive. || **expression** [-jõ] *n.f.* **1.** expression. **2.** expressiveness. **3.** expression, phrase. || **expressivement** [-iv'mɑ̃] *adv.* expressively. || **exprimer** [ɛkspri'me] #3 *v. tr.* to express, to give utterance to. || **s'exprimer** *v. pron.* to express o.s.

expropriation [ɛksprɔpri|a'sjõ] *n.f.* expropriation. || **exproprier** [-'e] #3 *v. tr.* to expropriate.

expulser [ɛkspyl's|e] #3 *v. tr.* to expel, to eject; to evict (a tenant); to deport (an alien). || **expulsion** [-jõ] *n.f.* expulsion, deportation.

expurgation [ɛkspyr|ga'sjõ] *n.f.* expurgation. || **expurger** [-'ʒe] #5 *v. tr.* to expurgate.

exquis, -e [ɛks'ki(:z)] *adj.* exquisite; [mets] delicious.

extase [ɛks't|a:z] *n.f.* ecstasy, rapture, trance. || **extasié, -e** [-a'zje] *adj.* in ecstasy, enraptured. || **s'extasier** [sɛksta'zje] #3 *v. pron.* to be enraptured, [Fam.] to enthuse, to rave (over, *sur*).

extensible [ɛkstɑ̃|'sibl] *adj.* extensible. || **extensi|f, -ve** [-'sif, -'si:v] *adj.* [× depending on the use of large areas] extensive. || **extension** [-'sjõ] *n.f.* **1.** extension. **2.** development, growth: *prendre de l'* ~, to expand; *par* ~, in a wider sense.

exténuant, -e [ɛkste'nɥ|ɑ̃(:t)] *adj.* exhausting. || **exténué, -e** [-e] *adj.* exhausted. || **exténuer** [-e] #3 *v. tr.* to exhaust, to wear out. || **s'exténuer** *v. pron.* to work o.s. to death.

extérieur, -e [ɛkste'rjœ:r] *adj.* exterior, outer, external: *le monde* ~, the outside world; *politique extérieure*, foreign policy; © *le ministère des Affaires extérieures*, the Department of External Affairs. || *n.m.* exterior, outside: *à l'* ~ *(de)*, outside. || **extérioriser** [ɛksterjɔri'ze] #3 *v. tr.* to exteriorize.

exterminat|eur, -rice [ɛkstɛrmi|na'tœ:r] *adj.* exterminating. || *n.* exterminator. || **extermination** [-na'sjõ] *n.f.* extermination. || **exterminer** [-ne] #3 *v. tr.* to wipe, stamp/out; to exterminate.

externat [ɛkstɛr'na] *n.m.* dayschool: © ~ *classique*, classical college (for day pupils). || **externe** [ɛks'tɛrn] *adj.* external, outside. || *n.* day pupil; [Med.] nonresident (medical) student.

extinction [ɛkstɛ̃k'sjõ] *n.f.* **1.** putting out (of fire, light): *l'* ~ *des feux*, lights out. **2.** extinction.

extirper [ɛkstir'pe] #3 *v. tr.* to eradicate.

extorquer [ɛkstɔr'ke] #3 *v. tr.* [de l'argent, des aveux] to extort (*à*, from).

extra [ɛks'tra] *adj. invar.* extra-special; first-rate. || *n.m.* something extra: *les extras*, hired servants. || **extra-** *préfixe* beyond, extra-.

extraction [ɛkstrak'sjõ] *n.f.* **1.** extraction; mining (of coal); production (of oil). **2.** parentage, lineage, descent. || **extraie, extrais, extrait, &c.** cf. EXTRAIRE. || **extraire** [ɛks'tr|ɛ:r], **extrayant** [-ɛ'jɑ̃], **extrait** [-ɛ] #38 *v. tr.* [Note that this verb has no simple past.] to extract, to pull out, to draw; to mine. || **extrait** [ɛks'trɛ] *n.m.* extract, excerpt: ~ *de naissance*, birth certificate.

extraordinaire [ɛkstraɔrdi'n|ɛ:r] *adj.* extraordinary; unusual. || **extraordinairement** [-ɛr'mɑ̃] *adv.* inordinately, extraordinarily.

extravagance [ɛkstrava'g|ɑ̃:s] *n.f.* extravagance; wastefulness; absurdity; excessiveness: *faire des extravagances*, to do foolish things. || **extravagant, -e** [-ɑ̃(:t) *adj.* extravagant, absurd. || **extravaguer** [ɛkstrava'ge] #3 *v. intr.* to talk extravagantly, to rave, to talk nonsense.

extrayais, &c. cf. EXTRAIRE.

extrême [ɛks'tr|ɛ:m] *adj.* extreme; farthest; intense, excessive: *l'* ~ *-Orient*, the Far East; *à l'* ~, in the extreme. || **extrêmement** [-ɛm'mɑ̃] *adv.* extremely. || **extrémité** [-emi'te] *n.f.* extremity, very end, tip; extremity, last degree; extreme(s): *être à toute* ~, to be at death's door.

exubérance [ɛgzybe'r|ɑ̃:s] *n.f.* exuberance; superabundance. || **exubérant, -e** [-ɑ̃(:t)] *adj.* exuberant; [végétation] luxuriant.

exultant, -e [ɛgzyl't|ɑ̃(:t)] *adj.* exulting. || **exulter** [-e] #3 *v. intr.* to exult.

F, f [ɛf] *n.m.* [letter] F, f; [abrév.] franc: NF= nouveau franc; [on cars] = France.
fa [fa] *n.m.* [Mus.] fa.
fable [fɑ:bl] *n.f.* fable, tale.
fabricant [fabri'k|ɑ̃] *n.m.* manufacturer, maker. || **fabricateur** [-a'tœ:r] *n.m.* fabricator. || **fabrication** [-a'sjõ] *n.f.* **1.** making, manufacturing. **2.** make: ~ *canadienne*, made in Canada; ~ *en série*, mass production. **3.** [fausses nouvelles] fabrication. || **fabrique** [fa'brik] *n.f.* **1.** factory, mill, works: *marque de* ~, trade mark. **2.** fabric (of a church); *conseil m de* ~, fabric council, vestry. || **fabriqué, -e** [-e] *adj.* **1.** made, manufactured. **2.** made up. || **fabriquer** [-e] #3 *v. tr.* **1.** to make, to manufacture. **2.** to make up, fabricate (a story, an alibi, gossip, &c.); to forge.
fabuleu|x, -se [faby'lø(:z)] *adj.* **1.** fabled, imaginary. **2.** fabulous, incredible.
façade [fa'sad] *n.f.* front, façade.
face [fas] *n.f.* **1.** face, countenance: *sauver la* ~, to save face; *perdre la* ~, to lose face; *faire* ~ *à*, to face; *faire volte-* ~, to turn around; *en* ~ *de*, facing, across from, opposite; *considéré sur toutes ses faces*, considered in all its aspects. **2.** [pièce] obverse: *pile ou* ~, heads or tails. || **facette** [fa'sɛt] *n.f.* facet.
fâché, -e [fɑ'ʃ|e] *adj.* **1.** angry, cross: ~ *avec qqun*, at odds with s.o. **2.** vexed, annoyed. || **fâcher** [-e] #3 *v. tr.* **1.** to make angry. **2.** to irritate, to annoy. || **se fâcher** *v. pron.* to get/angry, mad/ (at, *contre*; over, *de*): ~ *avec qqun*, to fall out with s.o. || **fâcheu|x, -se** [-ø(:z)] *adj.* unfortunate, annoying; [situation] awkward. || *n.* nuisance, bore.
facial, -e [fa'sjal] *adj.* facial, of the face; *massage m* ~, facial (massage).
facile [fa'sil] *adj.* easy, simple: *Il est* ~ *à vivre*, He is easy to get along with. || **facilement** [-'mɑ̃] *adv.* easily, simply. || **facilité** [-i'te] *n.f.* facility, ease; [à faire qqch.] gift (for doing sth.), ease (in doing sth.); *facilités de paiement*, easy terms; [disposition] readiness. || **faciliter** [-i'te] #3 *v. tr.* to facilitate, make easier.
façon [fa's|õ] *n.f.* **1.** making: *payer tant pour la* ~, to pay so much for the making of a garment; *tailleur à* ~, jobbing tailor. **2.** workmanship. **3.** way, manner: *De quelle* ~ *?*, In what way?; *La* ~ *dont vous vous y prenez*, The way you go about it; *de toute* ~, anyway; *en aucune* ~, in no way; *de (telle)* ~ *que*, in such a way that. **4.** ceremony: *sans* ~, without ceremony, informal(ly); *faire des façons*, to stand on ceremony. || **façonner** [-ɔ'ne] #3 *v. tr.* to form, shape, mould; to fashion.
facteur [fak'tœ:r] *n.m.* **1.** factor. **2.** postman; © mailman, cf. POSTILLON.
factice [fak'tis] *adj.* artificial.
faction [fak'sjõ] *n.f.* **1.** faction, party, group. **2.** guard duty: *être de* ~, to be on guard (duty); *monter la* ~, to stand guard.
facture [fak'ty:r] *n.f.* **1.** workmanship. **2.** invoice, bill: *établir une* ~, to make out an invoice; *acquitter une* ~, to receipt a bill.
facultati|f, -ve [fakylta't|if, -i:v] *adj.* optional, elective: *arrêt* ~ *de l'autobus*, bus stops when signalled; *arrêt* ~ *d'un train*, flag stop.
faculté [fakyl'te] *n.f.* **1.** power, right; privilege: *avoir la* ~ *de faire qqch.*, to have the/right, power/to do sth. **2.** [du corps, de l'âme] faculty, power: *être en possession de toutes ses facultés*, to be in possession of all one's faculties. **3.** [Scol.] faculty: *la Faculté*, the medical profession.
fadaises [fa'dɛ:z] *n.fpl.* nonsense; [Fam.] drivel.
fade [fad] *adj.* tasteless, flat, insipid, stale.
fadeur [fa'dœ:r] *n.f.* pointlessness, insipidity, tameness.
fagot [fa'go] *n.m.* fagot, bundle of sticks.
faible [fɛbl] *adj.* **1.** [Pers.] weak, feeble. **2.** [son, lumière] faint, slight. **3.** [choses] inadequate, small, slight: *L'écart est très* ~, The difference is very small. || *n.m.* **1.** weak point, weakness. **2.** weakling: *les faibles d'esprit*, the feebleminded. || **faiblement** [-ə'mɑ̃] *adv.* weakly, slightly. || **faiblesse** [-ɛs] *n.f.* weakness; feebleness; deficiency. || **faiblir** [-i:r] #17 *v. intr.* **1.** to grow weak; [vent] to die down, to decrease. **2.** to weaken, to yield. || **faiblissant, -e** [-i'sɑ̃(:t)] *adj.* weakening.
faïence [fa'jɑ̃:s] *n.f.* earthenware, crockery.
faille[1] [fa:j] cf. FALLOIR.
faille[2] *n.f.* [Géog.] fault.
failli[1] [fa'j|i] cf. FAILLIR.
failli[2] *n. & adj.* bankrupt. || **faillir** [-i:r] #19 *v. intr.* [The infinitive, compound tenses, past are the only forms in regular use.] **1.** to fail (in, *à*), to be derelict. **2.** → almost, nearly: *Il a failli tomber*, He almost fell. || **faillite** [-it] *n.f.* **1.** bankruptcy: *faire* ~ to go bankrupt; *être déclaré en* ~, to be declared bankrupt. **2.** failure: *la* ~ *d'une expérience*, the failure of an experiment.
faim [fɛ̃] *n.f.* hunger: *avoir* ~, to be hungry; *avoir* ~ *de qqch.*, to be hungry for sth.; *manger à sa* ~, to eat one's fill;

mourir de ~, to be dying of hunger, → to be/starving, starved/.

fainéant, -e [fene'ɑ̃(:t)] *adj.* lazy, indolent. || *n.* loafer, [Fam.] lazy bum.

faire [fɛ:r], **faisant** [fə'zɑ̃], **fait** [fɛ] #37 *v. tr.* **1.** to make: ~ *du café,* to make coffee; ~ *le lit,* to make the bed; ~ *une faute,* to make a mistake; ~ *des progrès,* to make progress; ~ *fortune,* to make a fortune; *En quoi est-ce fait?,* What is it made of?; *Il fera un bon professeur,* He will make a good teacher; *Deux fois deux font quatre,* Two times two/are, make/ four; *Cela fait dix dollars en tout,* The whole thing comes to ten dollars. **2.** to do: ~ *une chambre,* to do a room; ~ *un travail,* to do a job; *Cela vous fera du bien,* It will do you good; *Vous n'avez rien à* ~ *ici,* You have no business here; *Qu'est-ce que vous en avez fait?,* What did you do with it? **3.** [activités diverses]: ~ *du théâtre,* to be on the stage; ~ *du tennis,* to play tennis; ~ *du commerce,* to be in business; ~ *de la température,* to run a temperature. **4.** [avec divers objets]: ~ *une promenade,* to take a walk; ~ *des vers,* to write poetry; ~ *une dissertation,* to write a paper; ~ *un somme,* to take a nap; ~ *une carte,* to draw a map; ~ *une conférence,* to give a lecture; ~ *deux milles à pied,* to walk two miles. **5.** [in verbal phrases rendered by specific English verbs]: ~ *bon accueil à,* to welcome; ~ *une génuflexion,* to genuflect; ~ *appel à,* to appeal to, to call in; ~ *écho à,* to echo; ~ *la cuisine,* to cook; ~ *de la peinture,* to paint; ~ *du ski,* to ski, ~ *oui de la tête,* to nod. **6.** [Impers.] to be: *Il fait froid,* It is cold; *Il fait chaud,* It is hot; *Il fait beau,* It is fine; *Il fait (du) soleil,* The sun is out; *Il fait du vent,* It is windy; *Il se fait tard,* It is getting late. **7.** [causatif] to make, to have: *Il le fait travailler,* He makes him work; *Il voudrait nous faire croire que . . . ,* He would have us believe that . . . ; *Faites-le entrer,* Show him in; ~ *réparer une montre,* to have a watch fixed; ~ ~ *un complet,* to have a suit made; *se* ~ *raser,* to get a shave; *se* ~ *tuer,* to get killed. || **8.** faire + que: *Cela fait que . . . ,* So . . . ; ~ *en sorte que,* to see to it that; *Il ne fait que parler,* He talks all the time. || **9.** *v. intr.* to do, to act: *faire à sa guise,* to do as one pleases; *faire pour le mieux,* to do what's best; *C'est bien fait pour lui!,* Serves him right!; *Laissez-moi faire,* Leave it to me; *Vous feriez bien de partir,* You'd be well advised to go; *J'aurais vite fait de l'en empêcher,* I would soon stop him; *Rien n'y fait,* It's all in vain; *Il aura fort à* ~, His work will be cut out for him. **10.** [Loc.] *Que* ~ *?, Qu'y* ~ *?,* What can we do?; *Je n'ai que* ~ *de vos conseils,* I don't need your advice; © *Ça va* ~ *!,* That'll do! || **se faire** *v. pron.* to be made, to be done: *Le cidre se fait avec des pommes,* Cider is made with apples; *Cela se fait en quatre tailles,* It comes in four sizes; *Cela ne se fait pas,* It is not done; *Comment se fait-il que . . . ?,* How is it that . . . ?; *Il s'est fait prêtre,* He became a priest; ~ *une idée de,* to conceive, [Fam.] to figure out; ~ *à une idée,* to get used to an idea; ~ *du souci,* to worry: *Ne vous en faites pas,* Don't worry, Relax.

fais, &c., fait, fasse, &c. cf. FAIRE.

faisable [fə'zabl] *adj.* practicable, feasible.

faisan [fɛ'zɑ̃] *n.m.* pheasant. || **faisandé, -e** [-'de] *adj.* tainted, corrupt, deliquescent. || **faisander** [-'de] #3 *v. tr.* to hang meat till it gets high.

faisant [fə'zɑ̃] cf. FAIRE. || *adj.*: *chemin* ~, en route, while on the way.

faisceau [fɛ'so] *n.m.* **1.** bundle. **2.** [fusils] stack. **3.** [lumière] beam. **4.** accumulation: *un* ~ *de preuves,* cumulative evidence.

faiseu|r, -se [fə'zœ:r] *n.* **1.** doer, maker: *un bon* ~, a good tailor. **2.** [Fig.] a quack, a show-off.

fait,[1] **-e** [fɛ(t)] cf. FAIRE.

fait[2] [fɛ] *n.m.* fact: *en* ~, in fact; *dire son* ~ *à qqun,* to tell s.o. off; *être au* ~ *de,* to be acquainted with; *en venir au* ~, to come to the point.

faîte [fɛ:t] *n.m.* top, summit, ridge.

†faix [fɛ] *n.m.* [Fig.] burden, load, weight.

falaise [fa'lɛ:z] *n.f.* cliff; bluff.

fale © [fal] [aussi **falle**] *n.f.* **1.** [d'un oiseau] crop cf. JABOT; [d'un animal] chest: *Le chat a une belle* ~ *blanche,* The cat has a handsome white chest; *avoir la* ~ *basse,* to have an empty crop, → to be hungry; [Fig.] to look crestfallen, to be all in. **2.** [partie du vêtement] ruffle, jabot, frill.

fallait, fallut cf. FALLOIR.

falloir [fa'l|wa:r] #29 *v. impers.* [used only in third person sing.] **1.** [need]: *Il lui faut dix dollars,* He needs ten dollars, He must have ten dollars; *Il faut deux heures,* It takes two hours; *faire ce qu'il faut quand il le faut,* to do what is needed when it's needed; *l'homme qu'il me faut,* the man I need; *s'il le faut,* if needed. **2.** [obligation, necessity]: *Il faut partir,* We must go; *Il ne fallait pas le lui dire,* You should not have told him; *Il ne faut pas qu'il le sache,* He must not know; *comme il faut,* [*adv.*]

correctly, [*adj.*] respectable; *parler plus qu'il ne faut*, to speak more than one should; *Il fallait voir*, You should have seen it. 3. [to be wanting]: *Il s'en faut de beaucoup qu'il soit prêt*, He is far from ready; *tant s'en faut*, far from it; *Il s'en est fallu de peu qu'il réussisse*, He was very nearly successful. || **fallu** [-y] cf. FALLOIR.

falsification [falsif|ika'sjõ] *n.f.* [de ce qui est mangé] adulteration; [d'un document, des monnaies, d'une pièce d'identité, &c.] forgery; [Fig., de l'histoire, de la vérité, &c.] falsification. || **falsifier** [-je] #3 *v. tr.* [nourriture] to adulterate; [la vérité] to falsify; [un document, un billet de banque, une pièce d'identité, &c.] to counterfeit, to falsify.

famé, -e [fa'me] *adj.* [seldom used without the adverb *mal*] *mal* ~, disreputable.

famélique [fame'lik] *adj.* [air, &c.] starving, half-starved (look, &c.) hungry.

fameu|x, -se [fa'mø(:z)] *adj.* **1.** famous, renowned. **2.** [Fam.] terrific, outstanding, egregious.

familial, -e [fami'lj|al] *adj.* family, domestic: *allocation familiale*, family allowance. || **familiariser** [-ari'ze] #3 *v. tr.* to familiarize (s.o. with sth.). || **se familiariser** *v. pron.* to familiarize o.s. (with, *avec*). || **familiarité** [-ari'te] *n.f.* familiarity: *être dans la* ~ *de qqun*, to be (very) familiar with s.o.: *La* ~ *engendre le mépris*, Familiarity breeds contempt. || *pl.* **familiarités,** liberties: *se permettre des familiarités avec qqun*, to take liberties with s.o. || **famili|er, -ère** [-e, ɛ:r] *adj.* familiar: *une voix familière*, a familiar voice; *Cela m'est* ~, I am familiar with it. || *n.m.* intimate, close, friend (of important person). || **familièrement** [-ɛr'mã] *adv.* familiarly.

famille [fa'mi:j] *n.f.* family: *nom de* ~, family, last/name; *air de* ~, family resemblance; *en* ~, in the family, [chez soi] at home; © *être/en* ~, *partie pour la/* ~, to be pregnant.

famine [fa'min] *n.f.* famine: *budget de* ~, starvation budget.

fanal [fa'nal] *n.m.* lantern; red light; beacon.

fanatique [fana'ti|k] *adj.* fanatical. || *n.* fanatic; ~ *de*, enthusiast for, devotee of. || **fanatisme** [-sm] *n.m.* fanaticism.

fané, -e [fan|e] *adj.* **1.** faded, wilted. **2.** [foin] turned over. || **faner** [-e] #3 *v. tr.* **1.** to fade, to wilt. **2.** to turn over (mown grass), to make hay. || **faneu|r, -se** [-œ:r, -ø:z] *n.m.* [Pers.] haymaker; *f.* [machine] tedder, haymaker.

fanfare [fã'fa:r] *n.f.* **1.** [air] fanfare, flourish. **2.** [orchestre] brass band.

fanfaron, -ne [fãfa'r|õ, -ɔn] *adj.* boastful, bragging. || *n.* boaster, braggart. || **fanfaronnade** [-ɔ'nad] *n.f.* bragging, boasting.

fange [fã:ʒ] *n.f.* filth, muck, mire; [boue] mud. || **fangeu|x, -se** [fã'ʒø(:z)] *adj.* muddy, filthy.

fantaisie [fãtɛ'zi] *n.f.* **1.** fancy, whim. **2.** fantasy, imagination. || **fantaisiste** [-st] *adj.* [chose] fanciful, [Pers.] whimsical: *explication* ~, fanciful explanation.

fantassin [fãta'sɛ̃] *n.m.* infantryman, foot soldier.

fantastique [fãtas'tik] *adj.* [imagination] fanciful, wild; [incroyable] fantastic; [Fam.] incredible.

fantoche [fã'tɔʃ] *n(m).* puppet, marionette.

fantôme [fã'to:m] *n.m.* phantom, ghost, shadow.

faon [fã] *n.m.* fawn.

faraud, -e [fa'r|o(:d)] *adj.* swanky. || *n.m.* **1.** fop, swell: *faire le* ~, to show off. **2.** © boy friend, steady beau. || **farauder** [-o'de] #3 *v. tr.* © to go with, to court (a girl).

farce[1] [fars] *n.f.* **1.** [Théâ.] farce, slapstick. **2.** practical joke: *faire une* ~ *à qqun*, to play a trick on s.o. **3.** © ~ *plate*, off-colour joke. || *adj.* comical, funny.

farce[2] [fars] *n.f.* dressing, stuffing.

farceur [far'sœ:r] *n.m.* practical joker, phoney, humbug.

farci, -e [-i] *adj.* **1.** [volaille, &c.] stuffed. **2.** [Fig.] stuffed, crammed (with, *de*). || **farcir** [-i:r] #17 *v. tr.* **1.** [Cul.] to stuff (with, *de*). **2.** [Fig.] to stuff, to cram.

fard [fa:r] *n.m.* make up, [Fig.] disguise: *sans* ~, plain, unvarnished; plainly. || **fardé, -e** [far'de] *adj.* made-up; [exagéré] rouged.

fardeau [far'do] *n.m.* load, burden: *le* ~ *des ans*, the weight of years.

farder [far'de] #3 *v. tr.* to make up (an actor, &c.); [Fig.] to disguise (the truth, one's intentions, &c.). || **se farder** *v. pron.* to make up one's face, to apply make-up.

farine [fa'rin] *n.f.* flour; meal: ~ *d'avoine*, oatmeal. || **farineu|x, -se** [-ø(:z)] *adj.* mealy; farinaceous.

farouche [fa'ruʃ] *adj.* **1.** wild, unsociable, shy. **2.** stubborn, grim, fierce.

fascicule [fasi'kyl] *n.m.* **1.** bundle. **2.** fascicle, instalment, number (of publication). **3.** [Fr.] ~ *de mobilisation*, marching orders (in soldier's paybook).

fascination [fasin|a'sjõ] *n.f.* fascination, charm. || **fasciner** [-e] #3 *v. tr.* to fascinate, charm.

fascisme [fa'sism] *n.m.* fascism.
fasse, &c. cf. FAIRE.
faste [fast] *n.m.* pomp, magnificence; display; ostentation.
fastidieu|x, -se [fasti'djø(:z)] *adj.* dull, tedious, tiresome. [×] cf. FASTIDIOUS.
fastueusement [fastɥ|øz'mɑ̃] *adv.* ostentatiously. ‖ **fastueu|x, -se** [-ø(:z)] *adj.* [Péj.] ostentatious, showy.
fat [fat] *adj.* conceited, foppish. ‖ *n.m.*: *C'est un* ~, He is full of himself.
fatal, -e [fatal] *adj.* **1.** inevitable, fatal: *C'était* ~, It was inevitable, It had to happen. **2.** fatal: *un coup* ~, a deadly blow. ‖ **fatalité** [-i'te] *n.f.* fatality, inevitability.
fatigant, -e [fati'gɑ̃(:t)] *adj.* tiring, fatiguing; tiresome, tedious. ‖ **fatigue** [fa'tig] *n.f.* fatigue, tiredness, strain: *tomber, être mort/de* ~, to be dead tired; *vêtements de* ~, work clothes. ‖ **fatigué, -e** [-e] *adj.* tired; [vêtements] worn; [livre] well-thumbed. ‖ **fatiguer** [-e] #3 *v. tr.* **1.** to tire, to strain: *Cela fatigue la vue*, It strains your eyes. **2.** [Fig.] to wear out: ~ *qqun de demandes répétées*, to wear out s.o. with continual requests. ‖ *v. intr.* to strain, to labour. ‖ **se fatiguer** *v. pron.* to get tired.
fatras [fa'tra] *n.m.* jumble, hodgepodge.
fatuité [fatɥi'te] *n.f.* conceit, fatuousness, cf. FAT.
faubourg [fo'bu:r] *n.m.* suburb. ‖ **faubourien, -ne** [fobu'rj|ɛ̃, -ɛn] *adj.* working-class; common; vulgar. ‖ *n.* suburbanite.
fauchage [fo'ʃ|a:ʒ] *n.m.* mowing. ‖ **fauché, -e** [-e] *adj.* **1.** mown. **2.** [Fam.] broke. ‖ **faucher** [-e] #3 *v. tr.* **1.** to mow, to cut. **2.** [Fig.] to mow down. **3.** [Fam.] to swipe. ‖ **faucheu|r, -se** [-œ:r, -ø:z] *n.* mower, reaper. ‖ *n.f.* [machine] mower, mowing machine. ‖ **faucheux** [-ø] *n.m.* [araignée] daddy-long-legs.
faucille [fo'si:j] *n.f.* sickle, reaping hook.
faucon [fo'kõ] *n.m.* falcon: ~ *émerillon*, pigeon hawk; ~ *pèlerin*, peregrine hawk.
faudrait cf. FALLOIR.
faufiler [fofi'le] #3 *v. tr.* to baste. ‖ **se faufiler** *v. pron.* to thread one's way (through, *dans*).
faussaire [fo's|ɛ:r] *n.* forger. ‖ **fausser** [-e] #3 *v. tr.* **1.** to falsify, to distort (the facts, a report, &c.). **2.** to warp: *Son éducation lui a faussé l'esprit*, His education warped his mind. **3.** to bend, to twist (a tool, a key). **4.** ~ *compagnie à qqun*, to give him the slip. ‖ **fausseté** [-te] *n.f.* falseness, deceitfulness, double dealing.
faut cf. FAILLIR & FALLOIR.
faute [fo:t] *n.f.* **1.** lack, want: ~ *de temps*, for lack of time. **2.** mistake, fault: ~ *de genre*, mistake in gender; ~ *d'impression*, misprint; *A qui la* ~ ?, Whose fault is it?; *rejeter la* ~ *sur*, to throw the blame on; *sans* ~, without fail. **3.** sin, offence. **4.** [Sport.] foul.
fauteuil [fo'tœ:j] *n.m.* armchair; easy chair; [Théât.] seat.
fauti|f, -ve [fo't|if, -i:v] *adj.* faulty, wrong; at fault.
fauve [fo:v] *adj.* [colour] fawn; tawny; [smell] musky. ‖ *n.m.* **1.** [colour] fawn. **2.** wild beast [lion, tiger]: *la chasse aux fauves*, big-game hunting.
fauvette [fo'vɛt] *n.f.* warbler.
faux [fo], **fausse** [fo:s] *adj.* **1.** false, erroneous: *idée fausse*, fallacy; *fausse nouvelle*, false report; *faire fausse route*, to go astray; *faire un* ~ *pas*, to stumble, to slip; *faire* ~ *bond à qqun*, to let s.o. down. **2.** false, deceitful, treacherous: *C'est un* ~ *bonhomme*, He is a slippery customer. ‖ *adv.* out of tune, off key. ‖ *n.m. le* ~, what is false; *un* ~, a forgery. ‖ **faux-col** [fo|'kɔl] *n.m., pl.* **faux-cols** [detachable] collar. ‖ **faux-fuyant** [-fɥi'jɑ̃] *n.m.* subterfuge, pretext. ‖ **faux-monnayeur** [-mɔnɛ'jœ:r] *n.m.* counterfeiter.
faveur [fa'v|œ:r] *n.f.* favour: *en* ~ *de*, in favour of, for; *à la* ~ *de*, under cover of, on the strength of; *être en* ~ *auprès de*, to find favour with; *billet de* ~, complimentary ticket. ‖ **favorable** [-ɔ'rabl] *adj.* favourable. ‖ **favori, -te** [-ɔ'ri(t)] *adj.* favourite. ‖ *n.* favourite. ‖ *n.mpl.* sideburns. ‖ **favorisé, -e** [-ɔri'ze] *adj.* favoured. ‖ **favoriser** [-ɔri'ze] #3 *v. tr.* **1.** to favour, to discriminate in favour of. **2.** to promote, to help, to facilitate. ‖ **favoritisme** [-ɔri'tism] *n.m.* favouritism; patronage.
fayot [fa'jo] *n.m.* [Fam.] kidney bean.
fécond, -e [fe'k|õ(:d)] *adj.* fruitful, fertile. ‖ **féconder** [-õ'de] #3 *v. tr.* to fertilize; to enrich. ‖ **fécondité** [-õdi'te] *n.f.* fertility, fecundity, fruitfulness.
fécule [fe'kyl] *n.f.* starch. ‖ **féculent, -e** [-ɑ̃(:t)] *adj.* starchy. ‖ *n.m.* starchy food.
fédéral, -e [fede'ral] *adj.* federal. ‖ © *n.m.* the Federal Government: *Le* ~ *lance un nouvel emprunt*, The Federal Government is floating a new loan. ‖ **fédération** [federa'sjõ] *n.f.* federation. ‖ **fédérer (se)** [(sə) fede're] #10 *v. tr. & pron.* to federate.
fée [fe] *n.f.* fairy: *conte de fées*, fairy tale; *le pays des fées*, fairyland. ‖ **féerie** [-'ri] *n.f.* enchantment; fairy show. ‖ **féerique** [-'rik] *adj.* fairy-like, enchanting.

feindre [fɛ̃:dr] #36 *v. tr.* to pretend, make believe, sham: ∼ *de faire qqch.*, to pretend to do sth. || **feins** cf. FEINDRE. || **feint, -e** [fɛ̃(:t)] *adj.* put on; sham: *maladie feinte*, sham illness. || **feinte** [fɛ̃:t] *n.f.* sham, pretence, feint.

fêler [fɛ'le] #3 *v. tr.* to crack.

félicitation [felisita'sjõ] *n.f.* congratulation: *Je vous en fais mes félicitations*, I congratulate you on it. || **félicité** [felisi'te] *n.f.* felicity, happiness, bliss. || **féliciter** #3 *v. tr.* to congratulate, compliment (on, for, *de*).

félin, -e [fe'l|ɛ̃, -in] *adj. & n.* feline.

fêlure [fɛ'ly:r] *n.f.* crack.

femelle [fə'mɛl] *n.f.* female [animal only], she [as noun].

féminin, -e [femi'n|ɛ̃, -in] *adj.* feminine; female: *le sexe* ∼, the female sex. || *n.m.* feminine gender: *au* ∼, in the feminine. || **féminisme** [-ism] *n.m.* feminism. || **féministe** [-ist] *adj. & n.* feminist. || **féminité** [-i'te] *n.f.* femininity, womanliness. || **femme** [fam] *n.f.* **1.** woman: ∼ *de chambre*, chambermaid, housemaid; ∼ *de ménage*, cleaning woman. **2.** wife: *prendre* ∼, to get married.

fenaison [fənɛ'zõ] *n.f.* haymaking, tedding.

fendais, &c. cf. FENDRE.

fendiller [fɑ̃di'je] #3 *v. tr.* to chap [of wood], to crack, [of glaze] to crackle. || **se fendiller** *v. pron.* to chap, to crack, to crackle.

fendre [fɑ̃:dr], **fendant** [fɑ̃'d|ɑ̃], **fendu** [-y] #42 *v. tr.* to split, to chop, to cleave: ∼ *l'eau*, to cut through the water; ∼ *la foule*, to push one's way through the crowd; *geler à pierre* ∼, to freeze hard; *à* ∼ *l'âme*, heart-rending. || **se fendre** *v. pron.* to crack, to split. || **fendu** cf. FENDRE.

fenêtre [fə'nɛ:tr] *n.f.* window, casement: ∼ *en saillie*, bay window; ∼ *à guillotine*, sash window.

fente [fɑ̃:t] *n.f.* crack, slit, fissure, chink.

féodal, -e [feɔ'dal] *adj.* feudal.

fer [fɛ:r] *n.m.* **1.** iron: *battre le* ∼ *pendant qu'il est chaud*, strike while the iron is hot; ∼ *forgé*, wrought iron; *fil de* ∼, wire; *chemin de* ∼, railway. **2.** ∼ *à cheval*, horseshoe; ∼ *à friser*, curling iron; ∼ *à repasser*, iron; *donner un coup de* ∼ *à*, to press; ∼ *à souder*, soldering iron; *croiser le* ∼ *avec qqun*, to cross swords with s.o.; *remuer le* ∼ *dans la plaie*, to rub it in; *les fers*, fetters, captivity: *être dans les fers*, to be in fetters. **3.** head (of tool), point (of weapon): ∼ *de lance*, spearhead.

ferai, &c. cf. FAIRE.

fer-blanc [fɛr'blɑ̃] *pl.* **fers-blancs** *n.m.* tin-coated iron, tinplate, tin. || **ferblanterie** [-'tri] *n.f.* articles made of tin, tinware. || **ferblantier** [-'tje] *n.m.* tinsmith.

férié [fe'rje] *adj. un jour* ∼, holiday.

fermage [fɛr'ma:ʒ] *n.m.* farm rent.

ferme[1] [fɛrm] *n.f.* farm; farmhouse: *le travail de la* ∼, farming.

ferme[2] *adj.* firm, steady, steadfast: *attendre de pied* ∼, to be ready. || *adv.* firmly; hard.

fermé, -e [fɛr'me] *adj.* [Fig.] unresponsive, imperious.

ferment [fɛr'mɑ̃] *n.m.* ferment; leaven, yeast. || **fermentation** [-ta'sjõ] *n.f.* fermentation. || **fermenté, -e** [-'te] *adj.* fermented. || **fermenter** [-'te] #3 *v. intr.* to ferment.

fermer [fɛr'me] #3 *v. tr.* to shut, to close, to turn off: ∼ *à clef*, to lock, ∼ *au verrou*, to bolt; ∼ *la maison*, to lock up; ∼ *les yeux*, to close one's eyes (to, *sur*). || *v. intr.* to close, to close down: *Nous fermons à 5 heures*, We close at five; *L'usine a dû* ∼, The plant had to close down.

fermeté [fɛrmə'te] *n.f.* firmness, steadfastness.

fermeture [fɛrmə'ty:r] *n.f.* **1.** shutting, closing; shutdown, lockout (of factories). **2.** fastening: ∼ *éclair*, zip fastener, zipper.

fermi|er, -ère [fɛr'mj|e, ɛ:r] *adj.* → farming. *n.* **1.** [×] tenant farmer, cf. FARMER; *la fermière*, the farmer's wife. **2.** © farmer.

fermoir [fɛr'mwa:r] *n.m.* clasp.

féroce [fe'rɔs] *adj.* ferocious; fierce; wild; [Fam.] huge (appetite). || **férocité** [-i'te] *n.f.* ferocity; fierceness; wildness; [Fam.] hugeness (of appetite).

ferraille [fɛ'rɑ:j] *n.f.* scrap iron: *mettre à la* ∼, to scrap.

ferré, -e [fɛ'r|e] *adj.* iron-/shod, tipped/: *voie* ∼, railway, railway line; *souliers ferrés*, hobnailed shoes; [Fig.] well up (on, *sur*): *être très* ∼ *sur un sujet*, to know a subject inside out. || **ferrer** [fɛ'r|e] #3 *v. tr.* to strengthen with iron: ∼ *un cheval*, to shoe a horse; ∼ *un lacet*, to tag a lace; [fish] to strike. || **ferreu|x, -se** [-ø(:z)] *adj.* ferrous, of iron. || **ferrure** [-y:r] *n.f.* **1.** ironwork, iron binding; (door) fitting. **2.** shoeing (of horse).

fertile [fɛr'til] *adj.* fertile, fruitful. || **fertiliser** [-i'ze] #3 *v. tr.* to fertilize. || **fertilité** [-i'te] *n.f.* fertility.

féru, -e [fe'ry] *adj.*: *être* ∼ *de*, to be in love with, to be very much struck with.

fervent, -e [fɛr'v|ɑ̃(:t)] *adj.* fervent; enthusiastic. || *n.* enthusiast. || **ferveur** [-œ:r] *n.f.* fervour; zeal.

fesse [fɛs] *n.f.* buttock; *pl.* buttocks, bottom, rump. || **fessée** [-e] *n.f.* spanking. || **fesser** [-e] #3 *v. tr.* to spank; © to hit; to happen on.

festin [fɛs'tɛ̃] *n.m.* feast, banquet.

festival [fɛsti'val] *n.m.* festival (of art, music).

feston [fɛs't|õ] *n.m.* festoon. || **festonner** [-ɔ'ne] #3 *v. tr.* to festoon (with, *de*).

festoyer [fɛstwa'je] #12 *v. intr.* to feast.

fête [fɛ:t] *n.f.* celebration; feast; saint's day: ~ *patronale*, patron saint's day; ~ *légale*, legal holiday; *faire* ~ *à qqun*, to welcome, entertain s.o.; *faire la* ~, to lead a gay life; *se faire une* ~ *de*, to take particular pleasure in; *faire des fêtes à qqun*, to make a fuss of s.o.; *la Fête-Dieu*, Corpus Christi Day; *la Fête de la Confédération*, Confederation Day; *la Fête du Travail*, Labour Day; *le jour de la Fête nationale*, © Confederation Day, [Fr.] Bastille Day, [US] Independence Day. || **fêter** [fɛ'te] #3 *v. tr.* **1.** to keep, to observe (as a holiday): ~ *la Saint-Nicolas*, to keep St. Nicholas Day. **2.** to welcome, to fete.

fétiche [fe'tiʃ] *n.m.* fetish.

fétide [fe'tid] *adj.* fetid, stinking, rank. || **fétidité** [-i'te] *n.f.* fetid smell.

fétu [fe'ty] *n.m.* (bit of) straw.

feu,[1] **-x** [fø] *n.m.* **1.** fire: *mettre le* ~ *à qqch.*, to set sth. on fire; ~ *d'artifice*, fireworks; ~ *de joie*, bonfire; ~ *follet*, will-o'-the-wisp; ~ *de paille*, flash in the pan; *aller au* ~, to be fireproof. **2.** fire, firing: *faire* ~, to fire (at, *sur*); *faire long* ~, to hang fire. **3.** light: *Donnez-moi du* ~, Give me a light; ~ *de circulation*, traffic light; *feu de Bengale*, Bengal light. **4.** [Fig.] *prendre* ~, to flare up.

feu,[2] **-e** [fø] *adj.* late, deceased: ~ *ma mère*, my late mother.

feuillage [fœ'ja:ʒ] *n.m.* foliage, leaves.

feuille [fœ:j] *n.f.* **1.** leaf: *arbre à feuilles persistantes*, evergreen; *arbre à feuilles caduques*, deciduous tree. **2.** sheet: ~ *volante*, loose sheet; *cahier à feuilles mobiles*, loose-leaf notebook; ~ *d'étain*, tinfoil. || **feuillet** [fœ'j|ɛ] *n.m.* sheet. || **feuilleté, -e** [-'te] *adj.*: *gâteau* ~, puff cake. || *n.m.* puff paste. || **feuilleter** [-'te] #8 *v. tr.* to glance through (a book).

feuilleton [-'tõ] *n.m.* serial; (newspaper) column. || **feuilletoniste** [fœjtɔ'nist] *n.m.* columnist, [journaux] feature writer.

feuillu, -e [-y] *adj.* leafy; [arbre] © deciduous.

feutre [fø:tr] *n.m.* **1.** felt. **2.** felt hat. || **feutré, -e** [-e] *adj.* felt; padded: [Fig.] *à pas feutrés*, stealthily.

fève [fɛ:v] *n.f.* bean, broad bean: © ~ *de Lima*, Lima bean; *fèves au lard*, pork and beans; © *fèves jaunes*, wax beans (also *petites fèves*); © *fèves vertes*, string beans, cf. [Fr.] HARICOT SEC.

février [fevri'je] *n.m.* February.

fi! [fi] *interj.* shame!: *faire* ~ *de*, to look down on, to set little store by, to spurn.

fiable [fjabl] © *adj.* reliable.

fiacre [fjakr] *n.m.* (horse-drawn) cab.

fiançai, &c. cf. FIANCER. || **fiançailles** [fjɑ̃'s|ɑ:j] *n.fpl.* engagement (to be married); †betrothal. || **fiancé, -e** [-e] *n. & adj.* betrothed. || **fiancer** [-e] #4 *v. tr.* to arrange the engagement of, to get engaged. || **se fiancer** *v. pron.* to get engaged.

fiasco [fjas'ko] *n.m.* failure, [Fam.] flop: *faire* ~, to fail, to come to naught.

fibre [fibr] *n.f.* fibre; thread; feeling, sensibility: *avoir la* ~ *sensible*, to be easily moved. || **fibreu|x, -se** [-ø(:z)] *adj.* fibrous, stringy.

ficeler [fis'le] #8 *v. tr.* to tie up; to tie with string; to cord. || **ficelle,**[1] **ficellerai, &c.** cf. FICELER. || **ficelle**[2] [fi'sɛl] *n.f.* string; twine; [Fig.] *tirer les ficelles*, to pull strings.

fiche [fiʃ] *n.f.* **1.** peg, pin. **2.** slip (of paper), index card. || **ficher** [-e] #3 *v. tr.* **1.** to drive (a stake) into (the ground). **2.** [Fam.] to throw, to give: *Il l'a fichu à la porte*, He threw him out; *Il lui a fichu un coup de pied*, He kicked him; *Fichez-moi la paix*, Lay off me. || **se ficher** *v. pron.* [Fam.] to snap one's fingers (at, *de*): *Je me fiche de ce qu'il pense*, I don't care a hoot about what he thinks. || **fichier** [-je] *n.m.* index card box, card index.

fichtre! [fiʃtr] *interj.* Good Lord!, Goodness; My word!; I should say! || **fichtrement** [fiʃtrə'mɑ̃] *adv.* [Fam.] awfully, terribly.

fichu,[1] **-e** [fi'ʃy] *adj.* **1.** [before noun] wretched. **2.** [with ÊTRE] sunk, done for.

fichu[2] [fi'ʃy] *n.m.* kerchief.

ficti|f, -ve [fik'tif, -'ti:v] *adj.* fictitious. || **fiction** [-'sjõ] *n.f.* fiction: *La réalité dépasse la* ~, Truth is stranger than fiction.

fidèle [fi'd|ɛl] *adj.* **1.** faithful, loyal. **2.** [récit, mémoire] accurate. || *n.*: *C'est un* ~, He is very loyal; *les fidèles*, the faithful, the congregation. || **fidèlement** [-ɛl'mɑ̃] *adv.* faithfully, loyally. || **fidélité** [-eli'te] *n.f.* **1.** faithfulness; loyalty: *une*

~ *à toute épreuve*, an unswerving loyalty. **2.** reliability; honesty; accuracy.

fiducie [fidy'si] *n.f.* [Jur., Fin.] trust: *société, compagnie/de* ~, trust company.

fieffé, -e [fjɛ'fe] *adj.* arrant, rank, downright, regular (coward, liar).

fiel [fjɛl] *n.m.* bile, gall; [Fig.] bitterness; [Fig.] malice: ~ *et absinthe*, gall and wormwood.

fier,[1] **se** [sə'fje] #3 *v. pron.* to trust, to rely, to depend: *Vous pouvez vous* ~ *à lui*, You can trust him; *On peut s'y* ~, You can depend on it.

fi|er,[2] **-ère** [fjɛ:r] *adj.* **1.** proud, haughty. **2.** [Fam.] regular: *C'est un* ~ *homme*, He is quite a man; *C'est un homme* ~, He is a proud man. || **fièrement** [fjɛr|'mɑ̃] *adv.* proudly, haughtily. || **fierté** [-'te] *n.f.* pride; spirit; dignity; [Péj.] haughtiness.

fièvre [fjɛ:vr] *n.f.* fever; [Fig.] excitement: *avoir de la* ~, to have a fever. || **fiévreusement** [fjɛvr|øz'mɑ̃] *adv.* feverishly. || **fiévreu|x, -se** [-ø(:z)] *adj.* feverish; agitated: *déployer une activité fiévreuse*, to bustle.

fifre [fifr] *n.m.* [Mus.] fife; fife-player; fifer; [Fig.] *sous-* ~, underling.

figé, -e [fi'ʒe] *adj.* fixed, rooted (to the spot): *expression figée*, idiom, set phrase; [Fig.] wooden expression, deadpan. || **figer** #5 *v. tr.* to congeal; to curdle, set; to fix. || **se figer** *v. pron.* to congeal, to set.

fignoler [fiɲɔ'le] #3 *v. intr.* to be fussy, finicky. || *v. tr.* to work carefully at.

figue [fig] *n.f.* fig. || **figuier** [-je] *n.m.* fig tree.

figurant, -e [figy'r|ɑ̃(:t)] *n.* [Théât., Cin.] supernumerary.

figurati|f,-ve [figyra't|if, -i:v] *adj.* figurative.

figuration [-a'sjɔ̃] *n.f.* **1.** representation. **2.** the supernumeraries (in a play).

figure [fi'g|y:r] *n.f.* **1.** face: *se laver la* ~, to wash one's face; *faire* ~ *de*, to appear as; *faire bonne* ~, to show to advantage. **2.** illustration, diagram, figure. || **figuré, -e** [-y're] *adj.* figurative (style, language): *au* ~, in a figurative sense. || **figurer** [-y're] #3 *v. tr.* to represent, to show. **2.** *v. intr.* to appear: *Son nom ne figure pas sur la liste*, His name does not appear on the list. || **se figurer** *v. pron.* to imagine.

fil [fil] *n.m.* **1.** fibre. **2.** thread, yarn: *cousu de* ~ *blanc*, obvious; *donner du* ~ *à retordre*, to give a lot of trouble; *ne tenir qu'à un* ~, to hang by a thread; *le* ~ *d'un discours*, the thread of a discourse; *fils de la Vierge*, gossamer. **3.** wire: ~ *électrique*, electric wire; ~ *de fer barbelé*, barbed wire; *donner un coup de* ~, to give a ring, to phone; *à l'autre bout du* ~, at the other end of the line. **4.**: *le* ~ *du bois*, the grain of wood; *aller au* ~ *de l'eau*, to drift downstream. **5.** edge: *passer au* ~ *de l'épée*, to put to the sword. || **filament** [-a'mɑ̃] *n.m.* filament, fibre.

filant, -e [fi'lɑ̃(:t)] *adj.*: *liquide* ~, ropy liquid; *étoile filante*, shooting star.

filasse [fi'la|s] *n.f.* tow: *cheveux couleur* ~, flaxen hair. || **filateur** [-'tœ:r] *n.m.* owner of a spinning mill; spinner. || **filature** [-'ty:r] *n.f.* [usine] cotton, spinning/mill; [opération] spinning; [Fig.] shadowing, [Fam.] tailing (of s.o.).

file [fil] *n.f.* line; [Mil.] file, rank: *à la* ~, in a row; *se mettre à la* ~, to line up; *une* ~ *de voitures*, a line of cars; *chef de* ~, leader; *en* ~ *indienne*, in single file. || **filer** [-e] #3 *v. tr.* **1.** to spin; [Naut.] to pay out (a cable); [Fig.] ~ *une scène*, to spin out a scene; ~ *doux*, to go easy. **2.** to shadow, to tail. || *v. intr.* **1.** to flow thickly; [lampe] to smoke. **2.** to fly, to speed along: ~ *à l'anglaise*, to take French leave; ~ *entre les mains*, to slip through one's fingers.

filet[1] [-ɛ] *n.m.* **1.** filament. **2.** [vis] thread. **3.** [Impr.] thin line. **4.** [écoulement] trickle. **5.**: *un* ~ *de voix*, a thin voice. **6.** [Culin.] fillet.

filet[2] *n.m.* **1.** net, hockey net: *coup de* ~, catch, haul (fish); ~ *à provisions*, shopping bag. **2.** (baggage) rack.

fileter [-'te] #8 *v. tr.* [d'une vis, &c.] to thread; [tirer un métal] to draw wire.

filiale [fi'ljal] *n.f.* [Com.] subsidiary company.

filière [fi'ljɛ:r] *n.f.* **1.** draw-, die-/plate; [Fig.] channels: *passer par la* ~, to go through (the usual) channels. **2.** © [abus.] filing cabinet, files.

fille [fi:j] *n.f.* **1.** daughter. **2.** girl: *petite* ~, little girl; *jeune* ~, young girl, young woman; *vieille* ~, old maid; *rester* ~, to remain single; ~ *-mère*, unmarried mother; ~ *de salle*, ~ *de ferme*, servant. [Except in a few expressions *fille* is derogatory when used alone.] || **fillette** [fi'jɛt] *n.f.* young girl (up to 14.)

filleul, -e [fi'jœl] *n.* godson *m*, goddaughter *f.*

film [film] *n.m.* film, moving picture, movie: *le grand* ~, the feature; ~ *en exclusivité*, first-run movie. || **filmage** [-a:ʒ] *n.m.* filming. || **filmer** [-e] #3 *v. tr.* to film.

filon [fi'lɔ̃] *n.m.* vein, lode; [Fig.] *trouver le* ~, to strike oil.

filou [fi'lu] *n.m.* cheater, swindler, crook. || **filouter** [-'te] #3 *v. tr.* to rob: ~ *qqch. à qqun*, to do s.o. out of sth.

fils [fis] *n.m.* son; *petit-* ~ , grandson: *C'est bien le ~ de son père,* He is a chip off the old block.

filtrage [fil'tr|a:ʒ] *n.m.* filtration, straining [also Fig.]. || **filtrant, -e** [-ɑ̃(:t)] *adj.* filtering; *virus* ~ , filterable virus. || **filtre** [filtr] *n.m.* [corps poreux] filter; [passoire] strainer; [Electr.] filter: [Fr.] (coffee) percolator; [Fr.] *café-* ~ , percolated coffee. || **filtrer** [-e] #3 *v. tr.* to filter (a liquid, light, sounds); [à travers un corps percé de trous] to strain; [Fig.] to screen (the news, &c.). || *v. intr.* to filter, to seep (through, *à travers*).

fin[1] [fɛ̃] *n.f.* **1.** end; close: *tirer à sa* ~ , to be coming to an end; *à la* ~ , in the end, finally; *mot de la* ~ , clincher. **2.** goal, objective, aim: *mener à bonne* ~ , to bring to a successful end; *arriver à ses fins,* to gain one's end; *Qui veut la ~ veut les moyens,* → The end justifies the means; *à toutes fins utiles,* for your information; *à seule ~ de,* for the sole purpose of.

fin,[2] **-e** [fɛ̃, fin] *adj.* **1.** last [only in the following]: *au ~ fond de,* at the very end of; *savoir le ~ mot d'une histoire,* to get to the bottom of a story; *être ~ prêt,* to be absolutely ready. **2.** pure, fine, choice; *or* ~ , fine gold. **3.** discriminating, delicate; slender, sharp, subtle: *jouer au plus ~ avec qqun,* to try to outsmart s.o.

final, -e [fi'nal] *pl.* **-s** *adj.* final, last. || *n.f.* [Gram.] final vowel, consonant; [Mus.] finale; [Sport.] final game, final: *quart de* ~ , quarter-finals; *demi-* ~ , semi-finals. || **finalement** [-'mɑ̃] *adv.* finally: *Il en est ~ résulté que . . . ,* The end result has been that . . . || **finaliste** [-ist] *n.f.* finalist. || **finalité** [-i'te] *n.f.* finality.

finance [fi'n|ɑ̃:s] *n.f.* finance: *Ministère des Finances,* © Department of Finance; [Br.] Treasury; [US] Treasury (Department). || **financer** [-ɑ̃'se] #4 *v. tr.* to finance. || **financi|er, -ère** [-ɑ̃'sj|e, -ɛ:r] *adj.* financial: *marché* ~ , money market. || *n.m.* financier.

finasser [fina'se] #3 *v. intr.* to finagle, manœuvre.

finaud, -e [fi'n|o(:d)] *adj.* foxy, cunning, sly. || *n.* foxy grandpa, finagler. || **finauderie** [-od'ri] *n.f.* foxiness, finagling.

fine [fin] *n.f.* brandy (of extra quality).

finement [fin|'mɑ̃] *adv.* finely, delicately, exquisitely. || **finesse** [-ɛs] *n.f.* **1.** delicacy, exquisiteness, fineness. **2.** *pl.* fine points, niceties: *les finesses de la langue,* the niceties of speech.

fini, -e [fi'n|i] *adj.* **1.** completed. **2.** finished, done for: *Il est* ~ , He has nothing more to give; He is played out. || *n.m.* the finish. || **finir** [-i:r] #17 *v. tr.* to complete, to finish, to end. || *v. intr.* **1.** to end: *Tout est bien qui finit bien,* All's well that ends well. **2.** finally: *Il a fini par comprendre,* He finally understood. **3.** to be through (doing): *Il a fini de parler,* He has finished speaking; *Finis!,* Stop it!; *Il n'a pas encore fini de manger?,* He is still eating? **4.** *en finir,* to make an end of it; *Il faut en* ~ , This can't go on; *Quand il s'y met, il n'en finit plus,* When he starts, he never stops. || **finissant, -e** [-i'sɑ̃(:t)] *adj.* declining. || *n.* [Scol.] © *les finissants,* the seniors, the graduating students. || **finisseu|r, -se** [-i's|œ:r, -ø:z] *n.* finisher.

finlandais, -e [fɛ̃lɑ̃'dɛ(:z)] *adj.* Finnish; of, from/Finland. || *n.* Finn. || **Finlande** [fɛ̃'lɑ̃:d] *n.f.* Finland.

fiole [fjɔl] *n.f.* small bottle, phial.

firmament [firma'mɑ̃] *n.m.* firmament.

firme [firm] *n.f.* [entreprise] firm.

fis, &c. cf. FAIRE.

fisc [fisk] *n.m.* © Department of Finance; [US] Internal Revenue; [Br.] Exchequer, Inland Revenue: *les agents du* ~ , revenue/officials, authorities/; tax collector. || **fiscal, -e** [-al] *adj.* fiscal; → taxation: *lois fiscales,* taxation laws. || **fiscalité** [-ali'te] *n.f.* taxation, tax system.

fission [fi'sjõ] *n.f.* fission.

fissure [fi'sy:r] *n.f.* fissure, crack; [Fig.] crack, break.

fixation [fiksa'sjõ] *n.f.* fixing; [d'une population] settling; fixation. || **fixe** [fiks] *adj.* fixed; [un œil, regard] glassy; [date, moment, prix, &c.] fixed, regular; [règles] definite: *sans domicile* ~ , of no fixed abode; *idée* ~ , obsession. || *n.* fixed /income, revenue, salary/. || **fixement** [-ə'mɑ̃] *adv.* steadily, firmly: *regarder ~ qqun,* to stare at s.o. || **fixer** [-e] #3 *v. tr.* **1.** to fasten. **2.** [population] to settle. **3.** to fix (one's eye, a picture, &c.): ~ *qqun,* to stare at s.o.; *pour ~ les idées,* for the sake of argument. || **se fixer** *v. pron.* **1.** to be fastened (to, *à*). **2.** to settle.

flacon [fla'kõ] *n.m.* small bottle: ~ *de parfum,* bottle of perfume.

flagellation [flaʒɛl|a'sjõ] *n.f.* scourging, whipping. || **flageller** [-e] #3 *v. tr.* to scourge, to whip.

flageoler [flaʒɔ'le] #3 *v. intr.* to shake, to tremble.

flagrant, -e [fla'grɑ̃(:t)] *adj.* flagrant: *être pris en ~ délit,* to be caught/in the act, red-handed/; *une injustice flagrante,* a glaring injustice; *d'une façon flagrante,* openly, pointedly, deliberately.

flair [flɛ:r] *n.m.* [odorat] (keen) smell; [Fig.] flair, talent: *avoir du ~ pour*, to have a/flair, talent, nose/for. || **flairer** [flɛ're] #3 *v. tr.* **1.** [used mostly for animals known to have a keen smell] to sniff, smell. **2.** [Fig., soupçonner] to smell, to suspect: *~ qqch.*, to smell a rat.

flamand, -e [fla'mɑ̃(:d)] *adj.* Flemish.

flambant, -e [flɑ̃'b|ɑ̃(:t)] *adj.* flaming, blazing: *~ neuf*, brand-new. || **flambé, -e** [-e] *adj.* [volaille, &c.] singed; [omelette, crêpes] flambee; [Fig. & Fam.] done for, finished, washed up. || *n.f.* blaze, blazing fire. || **flambeau** [-o] *n.m.* **1.** torch; large candle: *marche aux flambeaux*, torch-light parade. **2.** [Fig.] light (of faith, truth, reason, progress, &c.). **3.** [d'or, &c.] candlestick. || **flamber** [-e] #3 *v. intr.* to flame, to blaze; to burn. || *v. tr.* to singe (a chicken, duck, &c.); [stériliser] to sterilize.

flamboie, &c. cf. FLAMBOYER. || **flamboiement** [flɑ̃bwa|'mɑ̃] *n.m.* blaze; [moins éclatant] glow. || **flamboyant, -e** [-'jɑ̃(:t)] *adj.* **1.** blazing, flaming. **2.** [Arch.] flamboyant. || **flamboyer** [-'je] #12 *v. intr.* to blaze, to flame; to glitter.

flamme [flɑ:m] *n.f.* **1.** flame, flare. **2.** [Fig.] fire, flame. **3.** [bannière] pendant, pennon. || **flammèche** [fla'mɛʃ] *n.f.* firebrand.

flan [flɑ̃] *n.m.* [Culin.] custard (pie); [d'une monnaie, d'une médaille, d'argent, d'un disque] blank.

flanc [flɑ̃] *n.m.* side, flank: *se coucher sur le ~*, to sleep on one's side; *être sur le ~*, to be laid up; *prêter le ~ à la critique*, to be open to criticism.

flancher [flɑ̃'ʃe] #3 *v. intr.* to weaken, to fail: *C'est le cœur qui flanche*, His heart is going; *Les troupes ont flanché*, The troops gave way.

Flandre, (la) [(la)flɑ̃:dr], **les Flandres** *n.f.* Flanders.

flanelle [fla'nɛl] *n.f.* flannel.

flâner [flɑ'n|e] #3 *v. intr.* to stroll, to saunter. || **flânerie** [-'ri] *n.f.* lounging, idling. || **flâneu|r, -se** [-œ:r, -ø:z] *n.* idler; [en promenade] stroller.

flanquer[1] [flɑ̃'ke] #3 *v. tr.* to flank (by, *de*).

flanquer[2] #3 *v. tr.* **1.** to fling, throw; [Fam.] chuck: *~ un coup à qqun*, to take a swing at, to hit/s.o.; *~ une gifle, une volée/à qqun*, to slap, beat/s.o.; *~ qqun à la/porte, rue/*, to throw, chuck/s.o. out; *avoir envie de tout ~ en l'air*, to feel like chucking the whole thing. **2.** [donner] to hit one with: *C'est un climat qui vous flanque les fièvres*, It's the kind of climate where you get malaria. || **se flanquer** *v. pron.* [par terre, volontairement] to throw o.s. (on the/ground, floor) [accidentellement], to crash (to the ground, floor).

flaque [flak] *n.f.* puddle, pool.

flasque [flask] *adj.* [chair] flabby, flaccid; [Fig., style] flaccid, weak.

flatter [fla't|e] #3 *v. tr.* to flatter, to please, charm. || **se flatter** *v. pron.* **1.** [vanité] to flatter o.s. **2.** [confiance] to be confident, to take credit: *Je me flatte de réussir*, I am confident I can succeed; *Je me flatte de l'avoir aidé*, I take credit for having helped him. || **flatterie** [-'ri] *n.f.* flattery. || **flatteu|r, -se** [-œ:r, -ø:z] *adj.* flattering, pleasing (words, language, &c.); [Pers.] flattering. || *n.* flatterer.

fléau [fle'o] *n.m.* [Agric.] flail; [balance] beam; [Fig.] scourge, plague.

flèche [flɛʃ] *n.f.* **1.** arrow: *en ~*, like an arrow; *étui à flèches*, quiver; *tirer une ~*, to shoot an arrow; *Il fait ~ de tout bois*, He makes silk purses out of sows' ears. **2.** spire. **3.** [grue] boom, [Br.] jib. **4.**: *attelés en ~*, hitched one in front of the other. || **fléchette** [fle'ʃɛt] *n.f.* dart.

fléchir [fle'ʃ|i:r] #17 *v. tr.* **1.** [un arc, le corps, les membres, &c.] to bend; *~ le genou*, → to kneel. **2.** [Fig.] [adoucir] to move (one's judges, &c.); [la cruauté, la dureté, la rigueur de qqun] to soften; [la colère de qqun] to melt: *se laisser ~*, → to relent, yield, give in. || *v. intr.* **1.** [sous un poids] to bend, to give way; [lâcher pied] to give way; [voix] to fade, weaken; [prix] to decline, fall off. **2.** [Fig.] to wane, to give way. || **fléchissement** [-is'mɑ̃] *n.m.* bending, giving way; *~ d'une courbe, d'un graphique, &c.*, decline; [des cours en bourse, des prix] decline; [d'une résolution, &c.] weakening: *des signes de ~*, signs of weakening.

flegmatique [flɛgma'tik] *adj.* phlegmatic, stolid; calm, cool. || **flegme** [flɛgm] *n.m.* [mucosité] phlegm; [Fig., caractère, &c.] stolidity, composure.

flétan [fle'tɑ̃] *n.m.* halibut.

flétri, -e [fle'tr|i] *adj.* [fleurs, peau, visage, &c.] withered; [fruit] blighted; [Fig., charme, beauté, &c.] faded. || **flétrir**[1] [-i:r] #17 *v. tr.* [soleil, vent, &c.] to wither (a plant, &c.); [Fig., salir] to stain, to sully. || **se flétrir** *v. pron.* [plants] to wither, [beauty] to fade.

flétrir[2] #17 *v. tr.* [marquer au fer rouge] to brand; [ext.] to denounce.

flétrissant[1] [-i'sɑ̃] *adj.* withering, fading.

flétrissant[2] [-i'sɑ̃(:t)] *adj.* withering (condemnation); scathing (words).

flétrissure[1] [-i'sy:r] *n.f.* withering, fading.

flétrissure[2] *n.f.* [action] branding (of criminals), [la marque] brand; [Fig.] blot, stigma.

fleur [flœ:r] *n.f.* **1.** flower, bloom, [arbre fruitier] blossom: *en ~*, in bloom, in blossom; [Fig.] [de l'innocence] bloom; [de l'âge] prime (of life); [de la jeunesse, de l'armée, &c.] flower; [du langage, de l'éloquence, &c.] flourish; [de farine] (fine) white flour; [Hér.] *~ -de-lis*, fleur-de-lis. **2.** [*pl.*] [de vin, vinaigre, &c.] mould (on the surface): *à ~ de*, even, level/with, close to (the ground, the water, &c.): *avoir les yeux à ~ de tête*, to have protruding eyes, to be goggle-eyed; *à ~ de peau*, skin deep. **3.** © flour. †**fleuraison** [flœr|ɛ'zõ] cf. FLORAISON. || **fleur de mai** [-dɔ'mɛ] *n.f.* mayflower.

fleuret [-ɛ] *n.m.* [escrime] foil.

fleurette [-ɛt] *n.f.* small flower; [Poét.] sentimental verse: *conter ~ à qqun*, to whisper sweet nothings to s.o., to flirt with s.o.

fleuri, -e [flœ'r|i] *adj.* [en fleur] in/flower, bloom/; [couvert de fleurs] covered with flowers; [Fig.] [chemin, sentier, &c.] flower-strewn; [orné de fleurs] flowery, flowered; [Fig., style, termes, &c.] flowery; [joues, nez] florid. || **fleurir** [-i:r] #17 *v. intr.* **1.** to flower, blossom. **2.** [Fig.] to flourish. [☞ In this sense the present participle is often FLORISSANT and the imperfect *florissais*, &c. from the obsolete verb *florir*]: *Le romantisme /fleurissait, florissait/en France au . . . ,* Romanticism flourished in F. in the . . . . || *v. tr.* to decorate with flowers. || **fleuriste** [-ist] *n.m./f.* florist.

fleuve [flœ:v] *n.m.* river; [Fig.] stream.

flexibilité [flɛksibili'te] *n.f.* flexibility, pliancy. || **flexible** [flɛk's|ibl] *adj.* flexible, pliable, supple [aussi au Fig.] || **flexion** [-jõ] *n.f.* bending, sagging; [Gram.] inflexion, ending.

flic [flik] *n.m.* [Fam.] cop; [Fr.] *Vingt-deux, voilà les flics!*, Cheese it, the cops!

flirt [flœrt] *n.m.* **1.** flirting, flirtation: *être en ~ avec qqun*, to be flirting with s.o. **2.** *n.m/f.* boy friend, girl friend. || **flirter** [-e] #3 *v. intr.* to flirt.

flocon [flɔ'k|õ] *n.m.* tuft (of wool, cotton, &c.); flake (of snow, &c.): *flocons d'avoine*, flakes of oats; wisp (of fog, smoke, &c.). || **floconneu|x, -se** [-ɔ'nø(:z)] *adj.* fleecy.

floraison [flɔrɛ'zõ] *n.f.* [action] blooming, blossoming, flowering; [période] blossoming time: *Cette plante a deux floraisons par année*, → This plant blooms twice a year; *en pleine ~*, in full/bloom, blossom, flower/.

Floride (la) [(la)flɔ'rid] *n.f.* Florida.

florin [flɔ'rɛ̃] *n.m.* [Br.] florin; [Holland] florin, guilder.

florissais, &c. cf. FLEURIR. || **florissant, -e** [flɔri'sɑ̃(:t)] *adj.* flourishing, [qui prospère] prosperous; [santé] glowing.

flot [flo] *n.m.* **1.** wave: *être à ~*, to be afloat;[Fig.] to be on one's feet financially. **2.** flow, flood, flood tide; [Poét. & Fig.] billows: *un ~ de larmes*, a flood of tears; *à flots*, in torrents, in a stream; *Le soleil entre à flots*, The sun streams in; The room is flooded with sunlight; *des flots de fumée*, billows of smoke; *un ~ de paroles*, a flow of words. || **flottage** [flɔ't|a:ʒ] *n.m.* floating, drive; [Au Canada, le flottage prend le nom de DRAVE.] || **flottaison** [-ɛ'zõ] *n.f.* floating: *ligne de ~*, waterline. || **flottant, -e** [-ɑ̃(:t)] *adj.* **1.** floating. **2.** [vêtement] loose. **3.** [moral] irresolute, wavering. || **flotte** [flɔt] *n.f.* **1.** fleet: *~ marchande*, merchant marine. **2.** [Fam.] rain, water. || **flottement** [-mɑ̃] *n.m.* **1.** floating. **2.** [Fig.] wavering, hesitation, swaying. || **flotter** [-e] #3 *v. intr.* **1.** to float. **2.** [Fig.] to waver; [Fam.] to rain. || *v. tr.* to float (sth.). || **flotteur** [-œ:r] *n.m.* float. || **flottille** [-ij] *n.f.* flotilla.

flou, -e [flu] *adj.* **1.** blurred, hazy, soft. **2.** out of focus, blurred. || *n.m.* blur, haziness.

fluctuant, -e [flyk'tɥ|ɑ̃(:t)] *adj.* fluctuating. || **fluctuation** [-a'sjõ] *n.f.* fluctuation, ups and downs. || **fluctuer** [-e] #3 *v. intr.* to fluctuate.

fluet, -te [fly'ɛ(t)] *adj.* slender, slight.

fluide [fly'id] *adj.* [encre, huile, &c.] thin; [Fig.] fluid, flowing (style, prose); [fluctuant] fluid (situation). || *n.m.* fluid.

fluorescent, -e [flɥɔrɛ'sɑ̃(:t)] *adj.* fluorescent (lighting, &c.).

flûte [flyt] *n.f.* **1.** flute: *~ à bec*, recorder. **2.** champagne glass. **3.** [Fam.] leg: *se tirer des flûtes*, to hit the road. **4.** [Fam.] Shucks! || **flûté, -e** [-e] *adj.* high; fluted. || **flûtiste** [-ist] *n.m./f.* flutist, flautist.

fluvial, -e [fly'vjal] *adj.* → river, fluvial: *port ~*, river harbour.

flux [fly] *n.m.* flow, tide; [grande quantité] flood (of money, words, insults); [ext.] current; *~ et reflux*, ebb and flow. || **fluxion** [flyk'sjõ] *n.f.* [Méd.] inflammation; bad cold (in the chest, &c.).

foi [fwa] *n.f.* **1.** faith; promise: *faire ~ de*, to prove (the authenticity of) sth.; [of text in one language] to be binding; *exemplaire qui fait ~*, master copy, &c.;

[Jur.] *En ~ de quoi*, In witness whereof; *de bonne ~*, *adv.* in good faith, sincerely, *adj.* trustworthy, sincere; *de mauvaise ~*, *adj.* dishonest; *adv.* dishonestly; *digne de ~*, trustworthy; *ajouter ~ à*, to believe, to credit. **2.** credit, trust: *avoir ~ en*, to have faith in, to trust. **3.** [Rel.] faith, belief: *prêcher la ~*, to preach the faith.

foie [fwa] *n.m.* liver: *maladie de ~*, disease of the liver, liver trouble; *foies de volaille*, chicken livers.

foin [fwɛ̃] *n.m.* **1.** hay: *rhume des foins*, hay fever; *chercher une aiguille dans une botte de ~*, to look for a needle in a haystack; *faire les foins*, to make hay. **2.** © [Fam.] dough.

foire [fwaːr] *n.f.* **1.** fair. **2.** [Fam.] chaos, mess: *C'est la ~ ici!*, Things are pretty chaotic.

foireu|x, -se [fwa'rø(ːz)] [Fam.] *adj.* scared; jittery; diarrhetic.

fois [fwa] *n.f.* time. [☞ Avec *une, deux, première* et *deuxième*, employer *once* et *twice*]: *chaque ~*, every time; [Fam.] *des ~*, sometimes; *des fois que . . .*, in case . . .; *à la ~*, *loc. adv.* at once, at the same time; *maintes et maintes ~*, time and (time) again.

foison [fwa'z|õ] *n.f.* [only in] *à ~*, in abundance. || **foisonner** [-ɔ'ne] #3 *v. intr.* to abound, to teem.

fol, -le [fɔl] cf. FOU.

folâtre [fɔ'lɑːtr] *adj.* playful, full of fun: *Ce n'est pas ~*, It's not much fun. || **folâtrer** [-ɑ'tre] #3 *v. intr.* [Pers.] to amuse o.s., to dally; [animaux] to frolic, to frisk.

folie [fɔ'li] *n.f.* folly, madness: *aimer à la ~*, to love passionately; *coup de ~*, a crazy idea; *faire une ~*, to do sth. crazy; *C'eût été ~*, It would have been folly to . . .

folle [fɔl] *n.f.* [aliénée] mad woman, lunatic; [qui manque de jugement] foolish/woman, girl/. || *adj.* cf. FOU. || **follement** [-'mɑ̃] *adv.* foolishly, unreasonably, passionately, extremely.

fomenter [fɔmɑ̃'te] #3 *v. tr.* [☞ Seldom used except in Fig. sense] to foment, to stir up.

foncé, -e [fõ's|e] *adj.* dark; [couleur profonde] deep. || **foncer** [-e] #4 *v. tr.* [couleur] to darken, deepen, to make it darker. || *v. intr.* [se précipiter] to rush (at, *sur*; into, *dans*); [attaquer] to charge (at, *sur*; into, *dans*); [aller très vite] to be really/going, flying/: *~ tête baissée*, to rush headlong.

fonci|er, -ère [fõ'sj|e, -ɛːr] *adj.* **1.** [propriété] real (estate); [propriétaire] land(owner); [rente; impôt, © contribution] land. **2.** [qualités, aptitudes, &c.] innate; [différence] fundamental.

fonction [fõk'sj|õ] *n.f.* **1.** duty, function; [Fr.] *la ~ publique*, Civil Service. **2.** [charge] position, post: *se démettre de ses fonctions*, to resign. **3.** role, function: *faire ~ de*, to/serve, act/as . . . **4.** [Math.] function: *en ~ de*, in terms of. || **fonctionnaire** [-ɔ'nɛːr] *n.m.* civil servant. || **fonctionner** [-ɔ'ne] #3 *v. intr.* to work, to operate, to function: *faire ~*, to operate.

fond [fõ] *n.m.* **1.** bottom: *de ~ en comble*, from top to bottom; *râcler les fonds de tiroir*, to scrape the bottom of the barrel. **2.** back (of a room), far end (of a garden); background (of a picture), core (of a problem); *toile de ~*, backdrop; *au ~ de moi*, deep in me; *au ~*, actually, really; *à ~*, thoroughly, fully, deeply, tight; *à ~ de train*, at full speed. **3.** foundation: *faire ~ sur*, to rely on; *article de ~*, editorial; *vague de ~*, ground swell. || **fond** cf. FONDRE.

fondamental, -e [fõdamɑ̃'tal] *adj.* fundamental, basic: *le français ~*, basic French.

fondant, -e [fõ'dɑ̃(ːt)] *adj.* melting [par analogie *juteux*] juicy. || *n.m.* melting quality; [bonbon] fondant, © fudge.

fondat|eur, -rice [fõda|'tœːr, -'tris] *n.* founder. || **fondation** [-'sjõ] *n.f.* **1.** [d'une construction] foundation; [action] founding, foundation. **2.** [dotation] endowment (of a hospital, &c.); establishment, setting up (of an award, bursary, &c.). || **fondé, -e** [fõ'de] *adj.* authorized: *Je suis ~ à croire que*, I am justified in thinking that . . . || *n. ~ de pouvoir*, proxy. || **fondement** [fod|'mɑ̃] *n.m.* **1.** basis, foundation: *sans ~*, without foundation. unfounded. **2.** [Méd.] rectum. || **fonder** [-e] #3 *v. tr.* to lay the foundations (of sth.); [bâtir] to build; [créer] to found (a city, an empire); to form (a commission, an organization); [doter] to endow (a hospital, library, &c.); to establish (a family, a home). || se **fonder** *v. pron.* **1.** [baser] to base, to place. **2.** to make, to establish (a reputation); to base one's argument (on, *sur*).

fonderie [fõd|'ri] *n.f.* [action] casting, smelting; [usine, atelier] foundry, smelter. || **fondeur** [-œːr] *n.m.* [Pers.] founder, smelter. || **fondre** [fõːdr], **fondant, fondu** #42 *v. tr.* **1.** to melt (ice), to smelt (a metal); [Fig.] to melt. **2.** to cast. **3.** to melt, to dissolve (sugar); to fuse (two elements); to blend (colours). || *v. intr.* **1.** to melt: *faire* ~, to melt; ~ *en larmes,* to burst into tears. **2.** [Fig., brume, argent, richesses, &c.] to melt away. **3.** [oiseau] to swoop down (on, *sur*); to fall upon (an enemy); [projectiles] to hit; [l'orage] to rain (on, *sur*).

fondrière [fõdri'jɛːr] *n.f.* quagmire, bog: © ~ *de mousse,* ~ *moussue,* muskeg.

fonds [fõ] *n.m.* **1.** property, land: *bien-fonds,* real estate. **2.** business, store: *vendre son* ~, to sell one's business. **3.** capital, stock, funds. **4.** [Fig.] fund: ~ *de connaissances,* fund of knowledge.

fondu [fõ'dy] *n.m.* [art] the blending. || **fondu, -e** cf. FONDRE. || *adj.* melted, molten (metal); cast (in metal); [Fig.] blended, dissolved.

font cf. FAIRE.

fontaine [fõ'tɛn] *n.f.* fountain.

fonte [fõːt] *n.f.* **1.** [action] melting; casting, founding (of metals). **2.** [Métal] cast iron.

fonts [fõ] *n.mpl.*: *tenir un enfant sur les* ~ *baptismaux,* to hold a child over, to present a child at/ the baptismal font.

forage [fɔ'raːʒ] *n.m.* drilling.

forain, -e [fɔ'r|ɛ̃, -ɛn] *adj.* itinerant: *marchand* ~, itinerant vendor, peddler; *fête foraine,* carnival. || *n.m.* carnival operator.

forçai, &c. cf. FORCER.

forçat [fɔr'sa] *n.m.* convict.

force [fɔrs] *n.f.* **1.** strength, force: *à* ~ *de,* by dint of; *à* ~ *de travail,* by working so hard; *à toute* ~, absolutely; *être de première* ~, to be tops (in, *en*); *être de* ~ *à faire qqch.,* to be strong enough to do sth. **2.** *pl.* strength: *Ses forces la trahirent,* Her strength failed her. **3.** [*pl.* & Mil.] forces: *les forces françaises de l'Intérieur,* the French Forces of the Interior.

forcément [fɔrse'mɑ̃] *adv.* inevitably.

forcené [fɔrsə'ne] *n.m.* madman.

forcer [fɔr'se] #4 *v. tr. & intr.* **1.** to force, to compel (to, *à*). **2.** to force one's way through: ~ *une porte,* to break a door open; ~ *le détroit,* to break through the straits.

forer [fɔ're] #3 *v. tr.* to bore; to drill.

foresti|er, -ère [fɔrɛs'tj|e, -ɛːr] *adj.* → forestry (school, industries).

foret [fɔ'rɛ] *n.m.* drill.

forêt [fɔ'rɛ] *n.f.* forest; woods: *la Forêt Noire,* the Black Forest.

foreuse [fɔ'røːz] *n.f.* [Tech.] drill.

forfait[1] [fɔr'fɛ] *n.m.* crime, outrage.

forfait[2] [fɔr'fɛ] *n.m.* contract; package deal: *à* ~, for a lump sum.

forfanterie [fɔrfɑ̃t'ri] *n.f.* braggadocio; bragging.

forge [fɔrʒ] *n.f.* forge; blacksmith's shop. || **forgé, -e** [-e] *adj.* made; [Fig.] forged: *fer* ~, wrought iron. || **forgeai, &c.** [-e] cf. FORGER. || **forger** [-e] #5 *v. tr.* **1.** to forge (metal). **2.** to coin (a word). **3.** to forge, to fabricate (a document). || **forgeron** [fɔrʒə'rõ] *n.m.* blacksmith.

formaliser, se [(sə)fɔrmali|ze] #3 *v. pron.* to take offence, take sth. amiss: *J'espère que vous ne vous formaliserez pas si . . .,* I hope you won't mind if . . .

formalité [-'te] *n.f.* formality: *formalités (administratives),* formalities, red tape.

format [fɔr'ma] *n.m.* [×] size (of paper).

formation [fɔrma'sjõ] *n.f.* **1.** formation. **2.** education, training.

forme [fɔrm] *n.f.* shape; form: *en bonne* ~, in order, in due form; *être en pleine* ~, to be at the top of one's form.

formel, -le [-ɛl] *adj.* formal; explicit. || **formellement** [fɔrmɛl'mɑ̃] *adv.* absolutely; definitely; in set terms.

former [-e] #3 *v. tr.* **1.** to form. **2.** to train, educate; to bring up (children). **3.** to produce (a sound, a piece of work). || **se former** *v. pron.* to form.

formidable [fɔrmi'dabl] *adj.* formidable; dreadful; [Fam.] wonderful, terrific.

Formose [fɔr'moːz] *n.f.* Formosa.

formule [fɔr'myl] *n.f.* **1.** formula. **2.** form: [lettre] ~ *de politesse,* complimentary close. || **formuler** [-e] #3 *v. tr.* to express, to compose, to draw up; [Math.] to reduce to a formula.

fort, -e [fɔːr, fɔrt] *adj.* **1.** strong. **2.** skilful. **3.** violent, heavy, severe. **4.** stout: *C'est trop* ~, It is a bit thick; *Je me fais* ~ *de l'en empêcher,* I am confident I can stop him. || *adv.* very, greatly, exceedingly. || *n.m.* **1.** strong man: *les forts,* the strong. **2.** height: *au* ~ *de l'été,* in the height of summer. **3.** *Ce n'est pas son* ~, It's not his strong point. || **fortement** [fɔrtə'mɑ̃] *adv.* strongly; vigorously; exceedingly.

forteresse [fɔrtə'rɛs] *n.f.* fortress, stronghold.

fortifiant, -e [fɔrti|'fjɑ̃(ːt)] *adj.* fortifying, invigorating. || *n.m.* tonic. || **fortifier** [-'fje] #3 *v. tr.* to strengthen; to fortify; [Fig.] to confirm (opinions).

fortuit, -e [fɔr'tɥi(t)] *adj.* fortuitous, accidental.

fortune [fɔr'tyn] *n.f.* **1.** fortune, wealth: *faire* ~, to become rich, to make a fortune. **2.** luck: *faire contre mauvaise* ~

bon cœur, to put a good face on the matter. || **fortuné, -e** [-e] *adj.* **1.** fortunate, lucky. **2.** rich, wealthy.

fosse [fo:s] *n.f.* **1.** hole, pit: ~ *d'aisance*, cesspool. **2.** grave: ~ *commune*, common grave. || **fossé** [fɔ'se] *n.m.* ditch; drain; trench.

fossette [fɔ'sɛt] *n.f.* dimple.

fossile [fɔ'sil] *adj.* fossil. || *n.m.* fossil; [Fig.] old. || **fossiliser, se** [fɔsili'ze] #3 *v. pron.* to fossilize.

fossoyeur [fɔswa'jœ:r] *n.m.* grave-digger.

fou [fu], **fol** [fɔl], **folle** [fɔl] *adj.* [*fol* is used in the masculine before vowel or mute h] mad, crazy, insane: *être* ~ *de qqun*, to be madly in love with s.o.; *être* ~ *à lier*, to be raving mad. || **fou** [fu] *n.* madman; lunatic: *asile de fous*, lunatic asylum; *s'amuser comme un* ~, to have the time of one's life. || **fou de Bassan** [fudba'sɑ̃] *n.m.* gannet.

foudre [fudr] *n.f.* lightning, thunderbolt: *frappé par la* ~, struck by lightning. || **foudroie, &c.** cf. FOUDROYER. || **foudroyant, -e** [-wa'jɑ̃(:t)] *adj.* sudden and terrible; → lightning: *à une vitesse foudroyante*, at lightning speed. || **foudroyé, -e** [-wa'je] *adj.* struck by lightning. || **foudroyer** #12 *v. tr.* to strike with thunder; to strike dead; to shatter, crush, ruin, confound.

fouet [fwɛ] *n.m.* whip: *donner le* ~ *à*, to whip; *faire claquer son* ~, to crack one's whip; *coup de* ~, stimulus. || **fouetter** [-'te] #3 *v. tr.* to whip, lash, flog, beat.

fougère [fu'ʒɛ:r] *n.f.* fern.

fougue [fug] *n.f.* impetuosity, dash. || **fougueu|x, -se** [-ø(:z)] *adj.* impetuous.

fouille [fu:j] *n.f.* **1.** excavation, [Archéol.] digging. **2.** search. || **fouiller** [fu'je] #3 *v. tr.* **1.** to excavate, to dig. **2.** to search. || **se fouiller** *v. pron.* **1.** to feel in one's pocket. **2.** *Il peut* ~, He can kiss it goodbye. || **fouillis** [fu'ji] *n.m.* mess, jumble, muddle.

fouine, fouinette [fwin, fwi'nɛt] *n.f.* marten.

foulard [fu'la:r] *n.m.* silk scarf.

foule [ful] *n.f.* crowd, mob; populace: *en* ~, in great numbers, in crowds.

fouler [fu'le] #3 *v. tr.* **1.** to tread (on): ~ *aux pieds*, to trample on. **2.** to oppress. **3.** to sprain: *Il s'est foulé le poignet*, He sprained his wrist; [Fig.] *Il ne se foule pas*, He does not exert himself. || **foulure** [fu'ly:r] *n.f.* sprain; strain.

four [fu:r] *n.m.* **1.** oven; [à chaux] kiln. **2.** [Théât. & Fam.] failure: *La pièce a été un* ~, The play was a flop.

fourbe [furb] *adj.* knavish. || *n.m/f.* knave, cheat. || **fourberie** [-ə'ri] *n.f.* knavery, deceitfulness.

fourbi [fur'bi] *n.m.* [Fam.] goods and chattels, paraphernalia: *tout le* ~, the whole stuff, all that junk.

fourbir [fur'bi:r] #17 *v. tr.* to furbish.

fourbu, -e [fur'by] *adj.* exhausted, tired out, fagged out.

fourche [furʃ] *n.f.* fork; pitchfork. || **fourcher** [-e] #3 *v. intr.* **1.** to fork. **2.** [Loc.] *La langue lui a fourché*, He made a slip of the tongue.

fourchette [-ɛt] *n.f.* [utensil] fork: *déjeuner m à la* ~, substantial breakfast; *Il a un bon coup de* ~, He is a good trencherman.

fourchu, -e [-y] *adj.* **1.** forked. **2.** cloven: *pied* ~, cloven hoof.

fourgon [fur'gɔ̃] *n.m.* **1.** [Rail.] baggage car; [Br.] luggage van. **2.** [Mil.] wagon. **3.** ~ *bancaire*, armoured car.

fourmi [fur'mi] *n.f.* ant: ~ *blanche*, termite. || **fourmilière** [-'ljɛ:r] *n.f.* ant-hill, ant-heap. || **fourmillement** [-j'mɑ̃] *n.m.* tingling sensation. || **fourmiller** [-'je] #3 *v. intr.* **1.** to swarm (with), to abound (in); [Fam.] to be crawling (with): *Les rues fourmillent de gens*, The streets are swarming with people. **2.** to tingle.

fournaise [fur'n|ɛ:z] *n.f.* **1.** [Fig.] very hot place: *C'est une* ~, It's just like an oven. **2.** © [abus.] furnace.

fourneau [-o] *n.m.* (cooking) stove: *haut* ~, [*pl.* hauts fourneaux] blast furnace.

fourni, -e [furni] *adj.* furnished, provided with; [cheveux, &c.] thick; [sourcils] bushy. cf. FOURNIR.

fourniment [furni'mɑ̃] *n.m.* outfit, paraphernalia.

fournir [fur'n|i:r] #17 *v. tr.* to supply, to provide: ~ *qqch. à qqun*, to supply s.o. with sth. || *v. intr.* [at cards] to follow suit. || **fournisseur** [-i'sœ:r] *n.m.* purveyor, supplier; tradesman. || **fourniture** [-i'ty:r] *n.f.* supply: *fournitures scolaires*, school supplies.

fourrage [fu'ra:ʒ] *n.m.* fodder. || **fourrager** [-a'ʒe] #5 *v. intr.* **1.** to forage. **2.** [Fig.] to rummage (through, *dans*).

fourré, -e [fu're] *adj.* lined with fur: *manteau* ~, fur-lined coat. || *n.m.* thicket.

fourreau [fu'ro] *n.m.* scabbard; sheath; cover; case; [robe] sheath dress.

fourrer [fu're] #3 *v. tr.* to thrust, to cram, to stuff; [Fam.] ~ *son nez dans qqch.*, to stick one's nose into sth. || **se fourrer** *v. pron.* to push one's way (into, *dans*). || **fourreur** [fu'r|œ:r] *n.m.* furrier. || **fourrure** [-y:r] *n.f.* fur: *manteau de* ~, fur coat.

fourvoie, &c. cf. FOURVOYER. || **fourvoyer**

[furvwa'je] #12 *v. tr.* to mislead, lead astray. || **se fourvoyer** *v. pron.* to go astray, to blunder.

foutre [futr], **foutu** [fu'ty]; © **fouter** *v. tr. & pron.* [in slang expressions—more vulgar than FICHER]: *Je m'en fous,* I don't care; *Foutez-moi la paix!,* Leave me alone! *Il est foutu!* He's a goner.

foyer [fwa'je] *n.m.* **1.** hearth, fireplace. **2.** [Théât.] foyer, lobby: ~ *des artistes,* greenroom. **3.** home. **4.** [optique] focus: *verres à double* ~, bifocals. **5.** centre, seat, hotbed.

fracas [fra'k|ɑ] *n.m.* **1.** crash, shattering noise. **2.** [Fig.] fanfare. || **fracasser** [-a'se] #3 *v. tr.* to shatter; to break (sth.) into pieces.

fraction [frak'sj|ɔ̃] *n.f.* fraction, portion. || **fractionner** [-ɔ'ne] #3 *v. tr.* to divide into fractions, to segment.

fracture [frak't|y:r] *n.f.* fracture. || **fracturer** [-y're] #3 *v. tr.* to fracture, to break: *Il s'est fracturé la jambe,* He broke his leg.

fragile [fra'ʒil] *adj.* fragile; brittle; frail (character, health); slender. || **fragilité** [-i'te] *n.f.* fragility.

fragment [frag'mɑ̃] *n.m.* fragment; chip (of stone, &c.); snatch, scrap. || **fragmentaire** [-'tɛ:r] *adj.* fragmentary. || **fragmentation** [-ta'sjɔ̃] *n.f.* fragmentation, breaking up (into, *en*).

frai [frɛ] *n.m.* spawn; spawning.

fraîche [frɛ:ʃ] cf. FRAIS. || **fraîchement** [frɛʃ|'mɑ̃] *adv.* **1.** freshly. **2.** recently, newly. **3.** coldly: *Il a été* ~ *reçu,* He was received without enthusiasm. || **fraîcheur** [-œ:r] *n.f.* **1.** coolness. **2.** freshness, bloom (of youth). || **fraîchir** [-i:r] #17 *v. intr.* **1.** [vent] to freshen. **2.** [température] to turn colder.

frais[1], **fraîche** [frɛ, frɛ:ʃ] *adj.* **1.** cool. **2.** fresh. **3.** recent: *de fraîche date,* recently. || *n.m.* coolness, fresh air: *prendre le* ~, to go out in the cool of the evening; *mettre au* ~, to put in a cool place.

frais[2] [frɛ] *n.pl.* expense, cost; costs (of lawsuit): *à peu de* ~, inexpensively; *à grands* ~, expensively, at great cost; ~ *d'affranchissement,* postage; ~ *de déplacement,* travel expenses; ~ *d'envoi,* shipping charges; ~ *de séjour,* per diem, living expenses; *couvrir ses* ~, to break even; *en être pour ses* ~, to have nothing to show for it; *se mettre en* ~, to put o.s. out.

fraise [frɛ:z] *n.f.* strawberry. || **fraisier** [frɛ'zje] *n.m.* strawberry plant.

framboise [frɑ̃'bw|a:z] *n.f.* raspberry. || **framboisier** [-a'zje] *n.m.* raspberry bush.

franc,[1] **franche** [frɑ̃, frɑ̃:ʃ] *adj.* **1.** frank, sincere: ~ *et loyal,* above board. **2.** exempt, clear: ~ *de port,* postpaid; *huit jours francs,* one clear week. || *adv.* frankly: *parler* ~, to speak frankly.

franc[2] [frɑ̃] *n.m.* [money] franc: *nouveaux francs,* new francs.

franc-maçon [frɑ̃ma's|ɔ̃] *n.m.* Freemason. || **la Franc-maçonnerie** [-ɔn'ri] *n.f.* Freemasonry.

français, -e [frɑ̃'sɛ(:z)] *adj.* **1.** French; [Fig.] *petit déjeuner à la française,* → Continental breakfast [☞ For other uses, see FRENCH]. **2.** © (French-speaking) Canadian, French-Canadian: *le régime* ~ *(au Canada),* the French régime; *pied* ~, French foot; *pain* ~, French bread, French stick. cf. BAGUETTE. || **Français, -e** *n.* French|man, -woman: *C'est un* ~, He is a Frenchman, He is French; © He is a (French-) Canadian; *les Français,* the French, © the French-Canadians. || **français** *n.m. le* ~ [= la langue française], French: *Parlez-vous* ~ *?,* Do you speak French?; *J'apprends le* ~, I am learning French; *le professeur de* ~, the French/master, teacher/. || **France, (la)** [(la)frɑ̃:s] *n.f.* France.

franchement [frɑ̃ʃ'mɑ̃] *adv.* **1.** frankly, sincerely; unreservedly. **2.** very: *Il a été* ~ *désagréable,* He was really very unpleasant.

franchir [frɑ̃'ʃi:r] #17 *v. tr.* **1.** to cross, to jump over: ~ *à gué,* to ford. **2.** to cover (a distance).

franchise [frɑ̃'ʃi:z] *n.f.* **1.** exemption; freedom (of a city); ~ *postale,* franking privilege, frank. **2.** frankness, sincerity, candour: *en toute* ~, quite frankly.

franco[1] [frɑ̃'ko] *adv.* free of charge. || © **Franco,**[2] **Franco-Américain, -e** [frɑ̃koameri'k|ɛ̃, -ɛn] *adj.* Franco-American.

frange [frɑ̃:ʒ] *n.f.* fringe: *à* ~, fringed.

frappant, -e [fra'pɑ̃(:t)] *adj.* striking; impressive.

frappe [frap] *n.f.* minting (of coins); stamp (on coins and medals); [typing] touch: *faute de* ~, typing mistake. || **frappé, -e** [-e] *adj.* **1.** struck: *Il en a été très* ~, He was very much struck by that. **2.** iced: *champagne* ~, iced champagne. **3.** coined: *bien* ~, well done, effective. || **frapper** [-e] #3 *v. tr. & intr.* to hit; to knock; to strike [also Fig.]; to ice (wines, &c.). || **se frapper** *v. pron.* [Fam.] to worry: *Ne te frappe pas,* Relax, take it easy.

fraternel, -le [fratɛr'n|ɛl] *adj.* brotherly,

fraternal. || **fraternité** [-i'te] *n.f.* fraternity, brotherhood.

fraude [fro:d] *n.f.* fraud, deceit: *rentrer en* ~, to smuggle in; *la* ~ *fiscale*, tax evasion. || **frauder** [fro'd|e] #3 *v. tr.* to defraud. || **fraudeur** [-œ:r] *n.m.* cheat, smuggler. || **frauduleu|x, -se** [-y'lø(:z)] *adj.* fraudulent.

frayer [-e] #11 *v. tr.* to open (a path): *se* ~ *un chemin*, to push one's way (through, *à travers*). || *v. intr.* **1.** to associate (with, *avec*). **2.** [poisson] to spawn.

frayeur [frɛ'jœ:r] *n.f.* fear, dread, fright.

fredaine [frə'dɛn] *n.f.* frolic, prank.

fredonner [frədɔ'ne] #3 *v. tr.* to hum.

frégate [fre'gat] *n.f.* [Naut.] frigate: ~ *météorologique*, weather ship; [Orn.] frigatebird.

frein [frɛ̃] *n.m.* **1.** bit, bridle: *ronger son* ~, to champ the bit. **2.** brake: ~ *à main*, emergency (brake); ~ *à pied*, foot brake; *mettre le* ~, to put the brake on; *donner un coup de* ~, to slam the brakes on. **3.** [Fig.] check, curb: *mettre un* ~ *à qqch.*, to curb, to check sth. || **freiner** [frɛ'ne] #3 *v. tr. & intr.* **1.** to put the brakes on. **2.** to curb, to check.

frelater [frəla'te] #3 *v. tr.* to adulterate.

frêle [frɛ:l] *adj.* frail, slender.

frelon [frə'lõ] *n.m.* hornet.

frémir [fre'm|i:r] #17 *v. intr.* to shudder: *Je frémis rien que d'y penser*, I shudder at the mere thought of it; ~ *de colère*, to tremble, to shake with anger. || **frémissement** [-is'mɑ̃] *n.m.* shudder, trembling, shaking.

frêne [frɛ:n] *n.m.* ash: ~ *d'Amérique*, white ash.

frénésie [frene|'zi] *n.f.* frenzy. || **frénétique** [-'tik] *adj.* frantic; frenzied: *applaudissements frénétiques*, wild applause. || **frénétiquement** [-tik'mɑ̃] *adv.* frantically.

fréquemment [frek|a'mɑ̃] *adv.* frequently. || **fréquence** [-ɑ̃:s] *n.f.* frequency; quickness (of pulse). || **fréquent, -e** [-ɑ̃(:t)] *adj.* frequent; rapid (pulse). || **fréquentation** [frekɑ̃t|a'sjõ] *n.f.* **1.** frequentation, frequenting: ~ *scolaire*, school attendance. **2.** company: *ses mauvaises fréquentations*, the bad company he keeps. || **fréquenté, -e** [-e] *adj.* frequented: *un endroit peu* ~, a rather deserted spot. || **fréquenter** [-e] #3 *v. tr.* to associate with, to keep company with: ~ *une école*, to attend a school; ~ *une jeune fille*, to go steady with a girl. || *v. intr.* to go frequently (to s.o.'s house).

frère [frɛ:r] *n.m.* **1.** brother. **2.** [Rel.] brother, friar: ~ *convers*, lay brother.

fresque [frɛsk] *n.f.* fresco.

fret [frɛ] *n.m.* freight.

fréter [fre'te] #10 *v. tr.* to charter.

frétiller [freti'je] #3 *v. intr.* to wriggle.

fretin [frə'tɛ̃] *n.m.* [usual. in] *menu* ~, small fry.

friand, -e [fri'j|ɑ̃(:d)] *adj.* **1.** fond (of food, candy, &c.): *Il est* ~ *de bonbons*, He loves candy. **2.** delicate, dainty (food). || **friandise** [-ɑ̃'di:z] *n.f.* dainties, goodies, sweet food.

friche [friʃ] *n.f.* waste land: *mettre (un terrain) en* ~, to let (a piece of land) lie fallow. cf. DÉFRICHER.

friction [frik'sj|õ] *n.f.* **1.** shampoo. **2.** rubbing: *alcool m à* ~, rubbing alcohol; *faire une* ~, to rub. || **frictionner** [-ɔ'ne] #3 *v. tr.* to rub (a part of the body). || **se frictionner,** *v. pr.* to rub o.s.

frigidaire [friʒi'dɛ:r] [Fr.] *n.m.* refrigerator.

frigorifier [frigɔri'f|je] #3 *v. tr.* to freeze (meat). || **frigorifique** [-ik] *adj.* refrigerating.

frileu|x, -se [fri'lø(:z)] *adj.* [Pers.] susceptible to the cold.

frimas [fri'mɑ] *n.mpl.* icy mist.

fringant, -e [frɛ̃'gɑ̃(:t)] *adj.* prancing, dashing.

fripé, -e [fri'p|e] *adj.* rumpled; jaded. || **friper** [-e] #3 *v. tr.* to rumple, to crush (dress). || **fripier** [-je] *n.m.* second-hand clothes dealer: *chez le* ~, in a hand-me-down shop.

fripon, -ne [fri'p|õ] *n.* cheat, swindler, rascal: *Il est très* ~, He is a rascal. || **friponnerie** [-ɔn'ri] *n.f.* rascality, cheating.

fripouille [-uj] *n.f.* a scoundrel.

frire [fri:r] #56 *v. tr. & intr.* to fry.

frise [fri:z] *n.f.* frieze.

frisé, -e [fri'ze] *adj.* **1.** curled. **2.** [naturellement] curly. || **friser** #3 *v. tr.* **1.** to curl. **2.** to have a narrow escape from (death, &c.), to sail pretty close to (dishonesty). || *v. intr.* to curl.

frisson [fri's|õ] *n.m.* shivering: *Cela me donne le* ~, It gives me the shivers. || **frissonner** [-ɔ'ne] #3 *v. intr.* to shiver, to shudder.

frit, -e [fri(t)] cf. FRIRE. || *adj.* fried: © *patates frites*, French-fried potatoes. || **frites** [frit] *n.fpl.* French fries. || **friture** [-y:r] *n.f.* frying; frying fat; [Fr.] fried fish.

frivole [fri'vɔl] *adj.* [things] idle, empty, trivial, trifling; [Pers.] frivolous. || *n.m.* triviality, trifles. || **frivolité** [-i'te] *n.f.* frivolity, trifles.

froid, -e [frwa|(d)] *adj.* **1.** cold: *Il fait* ~, It is cold; *animal à sang ~*, cold-blooded animal. **2.** cold, indifferent: *Cela ne me fait ni chaud ni ~*, It does not affect me one way or the other. **3.** cold, unemotional, self-possessed: *sang-~*, composure. || *n.m.* **1.** cold: *avoir ~*, to be cold: *J'ai ~ aux mains*, → My hands are cold; *prendre ~*, to catch cold. **2.** coldness: *Nous sommes en ~*, We are on the outs, not on speaking terms. || **froidement** [-d'mɑ̃] *adv.* coldly, in cold blood. || **froideur** [-'dœːr] *n.f.* coldness; chilliness; lukewarmness, coolness; indifference.

froissement [frwas|'mɑ̃] *n.m.* **1.** rumpling. **2.** [Fig.] vexation, clash, incompatibility. || **froisser** [-e] #3 *v. tr.* **1.** to rumple, to crumple: *Il froissa la lettre*, He crumpled up the letter; *un bruit de papier froissé*, the crackling of paper. **2.** to offend, to hurt the feelings of, to slight. || **se froisser** *v. pron.* to take offence.

frôlement [frol|'mɑ̃] *n.m.* grazing, light touch. || **frôler** [-e] #3 *v. tr.* to graze, to brush slightly against.

fromage [frɔ'maːʒ] *n.m.* cheese.

froment [frɔ'mɑ̃] *n.m.* wheat.

fronçai, &c. cf. FRONCER. || **fronce** [frɔ̃ːs] *n.f.* pucker, crease. || **froncement** [frɔ̃s|'mɑ̃] *n.m.* puckering; *~ de sourcils*, frowning. || **froncer** [-e] #4 *v. tr.* **1.** to pucker, to crease. **2.** to knit one's brows; to frown.

fronde [frɔ̃ːd] *n.f.* [weapon] sling; [Méd.] chin bandage; [Fr. Hist.] *La Fronde*, the Fronde.

front [frɔ̃] *n.m.* **1.** forehead; expression, face: *courber le ~*, to bow one's head; *relever le ~*, to hold one's head high again. **2.** [Mil.] front: *faire ~ à*, to turn and face, *heurter de ~*, to affront: *attaquer de ~*, to make a frontal attack; *de ~*, abreast. **3.** boldness, impudence: *avoir le ~ de*, to have the nerve to.

frontière [frɔ̃'tjɛːr] *n.f.* boundary; frontier; border.

frottement [frɔt|'mɑ̃] *n.m.* rubbing, friction. || **frotter** [-e] #3 *v. tr.* to rub, to rub down; to strike (a match); to polish. || **se frotter** *v. pron.* **1.** to rub o.s. **2.**: *~ à qqun*, to take on s.o.: *Il vaut mieux qu'il ne vienne pas s'y frotter*, He had better keep away.

froufrou [fru'fru] *n.m.* rustling (of silk, &c.).

frousse [frus] *n.f.* fear: *avoir la ~*, to be in a blue funk.

fructifier [frykt|i'fje] #3 *v. intr.* to bear fruit, to be fruitful. || **fructueu|x, -se** [-ɥø(ːz)] *adj.* fruitful, profitable.

frugal, -e [fry'gal] *adj.* [Pers.] **1.** frugal, abstemious. **2.** [repas] simple.

fruit [frɥi] *n.m.* fruit: *des fruits*, fruit; [différentes sortes de fruits], fruits; *le ~ de son travail*, the result of his work. || **fruitier** [-'tje] *adj.* fruit-bearing: *arbre ~*, fruit tree. || *n.m.* greengrocer.

fruste [fryst] *adj.* **1.** [médaille] worn. **2.** [Pers.] rough, uncouth: *un homme excellent sous des dehors un peu frustes*, a rough diamond.

frustrer [frys'tre] #3 *v. tr.* to deprive, to defraud: *~ qqun de qqch.*, to do s.o. out of sth.

fugace [fy'gas] *adj.* fleeting, evanescent.

fugiti|f, -ve [fyʒi't|if, -iːv] *adj.* fleeting, fugitive. || *n.* fugitive.

fugue [fyg] *n.f.* escapade, prank.

fui, &c. cf. FUIR. || **fuir** [fɥiːr], **fuyant** [fɥi'jɑ̃], **fui** [fɥi] #27 *v. intr.* to flee, to run away, to fly. || *v. tr.* to run away from, to avoid. || **fuite** [fɥit] *n.f.* **1.** flight: *mettre en ~*, to put to flight; *prendre la ~*, to run away. **2.** leak.

fulgurant, -e [fylgy'rɑ̃(ːt)] *adj.* flashing; [douleur] stabbing.

fulminer [fylmi'ne] #3 *v. intr.* to fulminate (against, *contre*).

fumant, -e [fy'm|ɑ̃(ːt)] *adj.* smoking. || **fume-cigarette** [-siga'rɛt] *n.m.* cigarette-holder. || **fumée** [-e] *n.f.* smoke: *pas de ~ sans feu*, no smoke without fire. || **fumer**[1] [-e] #3 *v. intr.* to smoke. || *v. tr.* to smoke (meat).

fumer[2] [-e] #3 *v. tr.* to spread manure over (a field), to fertilize.

fûmes cf. ÊTRE.

fumet [-ɛ] *n.m.* flavour (of meat, wine).

fumeur, -se [-œːr, -øːz] *n. & adj.* smoker: *Il est grand ~*, He is a heavy smoker. || **fumeu|x, -se** [-ø(ːz)] *adj.* smoky, heady (wine); foggy (ideas).

fumier [fy'mje] *n.m.* **1.** manure: *tas de ~*, dung heap. **2.** muck, garbage.

fumiste [fy'mist] *n.m.* **1.** chimney builder. **2.** humbug. || **fumisterie** [-ə'ri] *n.f.* **1.** chimney-building. **2.** (piece of) humbug.

fumoir [fy'mwaːr] *n.m.* [Br., Fr.] smoking-room.

Fundy (la baie de) [(labɛd)fɔ̃'di] *n.f.* Bay of Fundy.

funèbre [fy'nɛbr] *adj.* funereal; mournful: *pompes funèbres*, funeral service; *entrepreneur de pompes funèbres*, funeral director; *marche ~*, death march.

funérailles [fyne'raːj] *n.fpl.* state funeral; © funeral.

funeste [fy'nɛst] *adj.* fatal, disastrous.

funiculaire [fyniky'lɛːr] *n.m.* cable railway.

fur [fyːr] *n.m.* [in phrase]: *au ~ et à mesure*, (in proportion) as.

furent cf. ÊTRE.

furet [fy'r|ɛ] *n.m.* ferret. || **fureter** [-'te] #3 *v. intr.* to rummage, to snoop, to ferret out.
fureur [fy'r|œ:r] *n.f.* fury, passion: *entrer en* ~, to get into a passion; *passer sa* ~ *sur qqun*, to vent one's anger on s.o.; *faire* ~, to be the rage. || **furie** [-i] *n.f.* **1.** fury, rage. **2.** termagant. || **furieusement** [-jøz'mã] *adv.* furiously; [Fam.] terrifically. || **furieu|x, -se** [-jø(:z)] *adj.* furious: mad; fierce; raging: *fou* ~, raving lunatic.
furoncle [fy'rõ:kl] *n.m.* boil.
furti|f, -ve [fyr't|if, -i:v] *adj.* furtive, stealthy, secret. || **furtivement** [-iv'mã] *adv.* furtively.
fus cf. ÊTRE.
fusain [fy'zɛ̃] *n.m.* **1.** spindle tree. **2.** charcoal. **3.** charcoal sketch.
fuseau [fy'zo] *n.m.* **1.** spindle: *en* ~, spindly, tapering. **2.** zone: ~ *horaire*, time zone.
fusée [fy'ze] *n.f.* **1.** rocket. **2.** burst (of laughter).
fuselage [fyz'l|a:ʒ] *n.m.* [Aéro.] fuselage. || **fuselé, -e** [-e] *adj.* tapered, tapering; slender (fingers, legs, &c.).
fuser [fy'ze] #3 *v. intr.* to fizz, to spurt: *Des rires fusèrent*, Laughter burst out.
fusible [fy'zibl] *adj.* fusible. || *n.m.* [Elect.] fuse.
fusil [fy'zi] *n.m.* **1.** †musket; [chasse] gun; [guerre] rifle: *changer son* ~ *d'épaule*, to change one's tactics, one's outlook. **2.** [pour aiguiser] steel. || **fusiller** [-'je] #3 *v. tr.* to shoot (collectively and repeatedly): *On se fusillait presque à bout portant*, The shooting was at close quarters; *Il a été fusillé*, He was executed by a firing squad.
fusion [fy'zj|õ] *n.f.* **1.** melting; smelting: *plomb en* ~, molten lead. **2.** fusion. **3.** [Com.] merger. || **fusionner** [-ɔ'ne] #3 *v. tr. & intr.* to combine, to merge.
fut cf. ÊTRE.
fût [fy] *n.m.* **1.** keg. **2.** shaft (of column).
futaie [fy'tɛ] *n.f.* stand of tall trees, stand of timber.
†**futaille** [fy'tɑ:j] *n.f.* barrel, cask.
futé, -e [fy'te] *adj.* sharp, quick.
fûtes cf. ÊTRE.
futile [fy'til] *adj.* futile; trifling. || **futilement** [-'mã] *adv.* in a futile way. || **futilité** [-i'te] *n.f.* futility; [*pl.*] nonsense, trivia.
futur, -e [fy'ty:r] *adj.* future: *la vie* ~, the life to come. || *n.m.* **1.** future (tense). **2.** fiancé, fiancée.
fuyais, fuyons cf. FUIR. || **fuyant, -e** [fɥi'j|ã(:t)] *adj.* **1.** flying, fleeing. **2.** [forehead, chin, &c.] receding; retreating. || **fuyard, -e** [-a:r, -ard] *n.* fugitive.

G

G, g [ʒe] *n.m.* [letter] G, g.
gabarit [gaba'ri] *n.m.* gauge, model; [Tech.] template, mould.
gâcher [ga'ʃ|e] #3 *v. tr.* [ciment] to mix; [Fig.] to spoil; [travail] to bungle; [vie] to ruin. || **gâchette** [-ɛt] *n.f.* [fusil] trigger. || **gâcheu|r, -se** [-œ:r, -ø:z] *n.* bungler.
gâchis [gɑ'ʃi] *n.m.* mess, muddle: *En voilà un beau* ~ *!*, Here's a fine kettle of fish.
gaffe [gaf] *n.f.* boat hook; [Fam.] blunder, faux pas, boner: *faire une* ~, to pull a boner. || **gaffer** [-e] #3 *v. tr.* [Naut.] to hook. || *v. intr.* to blunder; to put one's foot into it. || **gaffeur** [-œ:r] *n.m.* blunderer.
gaga [ga'ga] *adj.* [Fam.] senile, gaga.
gage [ga:ʒ] *n.m.* **1.** security given, pawn: *mettre en* ~, to pawn; [jeux] forfeit. **2.** *mpl* [domestic help] wages: *être aux gages de qqun*, to be in s.o.'s pay. || **gager** [ga'ʒ|e] *v. tr.* **1.** to hire; to pay wages to, to pay (s.o.). **2.** to bet, wager. || **gageure** [-y:r] *n.f.* bet, wager.
gagnant, -e [gɑ'ɲ|ã(:t)] *adj.* winning (player). *n.* winner (in a wager). || **gagne-pain** [-'pɛ̃] *n.m. inv.* livelihood: *C'est son* ~, That's his bread and butter.
gagner [-e] #3 *v. tr. & intr.* **1.** to gain: ~ *du terrain*, to gain ground; *Il y gagnera*, He stands to gain; *Il gagne à être connu*, He improves on acquaintance. **2.** to earn: ~ *sa vie*, to earn a living. **3.** to win: ~ *la partie*, to win the game.
gai [ge, gɛ] *adj.* merry; gay; cheerful; jolly; in good spirits: *une pièce gaie*, a bright room.

|| **gaiement** [-'mɑ̃] *adv.* merrily, gaily. || **gaieté** [-'te] *n.f.* merriment, gaiety; mirth, glee; cheerfulness.

gaillard, -e [ga'j|a:r, -ard] *adj.* **1.** merry, jolly, jaunty. **2.** strong, stalwart. **3.** risqué, ribald. || *n.* strapping fellow, jolly old blade; buxom wench. || *n.m.* ~ *d'avant,* forecastle; ~ *d'arrière,* quarter-deck. || **gaillardement** [-ardə'mɑ̃] *adv.* merrily, heartily, lustily.

gain [gɛ̃] *n.m.* **1.** gain, profit: *donner* ~ *de cause à qqun,* to decide in s.o.'s favour. **2.** earnings. **3.** winnings.

gaine [gɛ:n] *n.f.* **1.** [couteau] sheath; case; [épée] scabbard. **2.** [corset] girdle.

gala [ga'la] *n.m.* gala: *habit m de* ~, formal wear.

galamment [gal|a'mɑ̃] *adv.* in a courtly way, courteously. || **galant, -e** [-ɑ̃(:t)] *adj.* attentive (to women); agreeable (person); gallant, courteous, generous; noble: *C'est un* ~ *homme,* He is a man of honour; *C'est un homme* ~, He is very attentive to women. || *n.m.* lover, gallant; womanizer. || **galanterie** [-ɑ̃'tri] *n.f.* gallantry; attentions [to women].

gale [gal] *n.f.* mange: *méchant comme la* ~, very spiteful.

galère [ga'l|ɛ:r] *n.f.* [Naut.] galley (ship); [Fig.] drudgery: *Qu'allait-il faire dans cette galère?,* What business had he there?

galerie [gal'ri] *n.f.* **1.** gallery; corridor; © porch. **2.** [Théât.] gallery: *Il fait cela pour la* ~, He is showing off. **3.** [de tableaux] picture gallery.

galérien [-e'rjɛ̃] *n.m.* †galley slave; convict.

galet [ga'lɛ] *n.m.* **1.** pebble: *une plage de galets,* a shingle beach **2.** [Méc.] roller bearings.

galette [ga'lɛt] *n.f.* **1.** [cake] "galette," sea-biscuit. **2.** [Sl,] dough.

Galilée (la) [(la) gali'le] *n.f.* Galilee. || **galiléen, -ne** [galile|'ɛ̃, -ɛn] *n. & adj.* Galilean.

galimatias [galima'tjɑ] *n.m.* gibberish.

galipote [gali'pɔt] *n.f.* © spree: *courir la* ~, to go on a spree.

Galles [gal] *n.f. Le pays de* ~, Wales; *la Nouvelle* ~ *du Sud,* New South Wales.

gallicisme [gali|'sism] *n.m.* gallicism. || **gallique** [-k] *adj.* Gallic.

gallois, -e [ga'lwa(:z)] *adj.* Welsh. || *n. m/f* Welshman, Welshwoman.

gallon [ga'lõ] *n.m.* © gallon: ~ *impérial,* imperial gallon; ~ *américain,* US gallon.

galoches [ga'lɔʃ] *n.fpl* clogs.

galon [ga'l|õ] *n.m.* **1.** lace, trimming, tape, braid. **2.** [Mil.] stripe. || **galonné, -e** [-ɔ'ne] *adj.* **1.** braided, laced. **2.** [Fam.] the brass.

galop [ga'l|o] *n.m.* gallop [also Fig.]: *au* ~, at a gallop. || **galopade** [-ɔ'pad] *n.f.* gallop, galloping. || **galoper** [-ɔ'pe] #3 *v. tr. & intr.* to gallop: *phtisie galopante,* galloping consumption.

galopin [galɔ'pɛ̃] *n.m.* young rascal, scamp.

galvaniser [galvani'ze] #3 *v. tr.* to galvanize.

gambade [gɑ̃'bad] *n.f.* skip, gambol. || **gambader** [-e] #3 *v. intr.* to skip, gambol.

gamelle [ga'mɛl] *n.f.* mess tin.

gamin, -e [ga'm|ɛ̃, -in] *n. m/f* youngster, boy; hoyden, chit of a girl. || **gaminerie** [-in'ri] *n.f.* child's prank, joke.

gamme [gam] *n.f.* [Mus.] scale; [couleurs] range; [outils] set, range; [série de produits] variety.

gang [gaɲ] © *n.f.* [Fam.] gang.

gangrène [gɑ̃'grɛn] *n.f.* [Méd.] gangrene.

gangster [gɑ̃gs'tɛ:r] *n.m.* gangster.

gant [gɑ̃] *n.m.* glove: ~ *de boxe,* boxing glove; *Cela lui va comme un* ~, It suits him to a T; *Il prend des gants pour lui parler,* He handles him with kid gloves. || **ganté, -e** [-'te] *adj.* gloved. || **ganter** [-'te] #3 *v. tr.* to put gloves on (s.o.). || **se** ~ *v. pron.* to put on one's gloves; to put gloves on. || **ganterie** [-'tri] *n.f.* glove-trade; glove-making; glove factory.

garage [ga'r|a:ʒ] *n.m.* **1.** garage. **2.** shunting: *voie de* ~, siding. || **garagiste** [-a'ʒist] *n.m.* garage man.

garance [ga'rɑ̃:s] *n.f.* madder(-wort). || *adj. inv.* madder(-red).

garant, -e [ga'r|ɑ̃(:t)] *n.m. & adj.* guarantee: *se porter* ~ *de,* to vouch for. || **garantie** [-ɑ̃'ti] *n.f.* warranty; guarantee; security. || **garantir** [-ɑ̃'ti:r] *v. tr.* **1.** to guarantee; to warrant; to vouch for. **2.** to preserve from, protect against (heat, cold).

garçon [gar'sõ] *n.m.* boy; lad, © son; restaurant: ~ *(de café),* waiter; *beau* ~, good-looking, handsome/boy; [Fam.] *vieux* ~, bachelor; *brave* ~, good fellow. || **garçonnet** [-ɔ'nɛ] *n.m.* little boy, †lad. || **garçonnière** [-ɔ'njɛ:r] *n.f.* bachelor's apartment.

garde[1] [gard] *n.f.* **1.** guard: *monter la* ~, to stand guard; *faire bonne* ~, to keep good watch; *sous bonne* ~, well guarded; *chien de* ~, watchdog. **2.** custody: *avoir la* ~ *de,* to be in charge of; *laissé à la* ~ *de,* left in the care of. **3.** attention: *être en* ~ *contre,* to be on one's guard against; *mettre en* ~ *contre,* to caution against; *prendre* ~ *de,* to be careful not to. **4.** hilt (of sword); *page de* ~, flyleaf.

garde[2] *n.m.* guard, keeper; watchman. || **garde-boue** [-ə'bu] *n.m.* fender; [Br.] wing, cf. AILE. || **garde-champêtre** [-ʃɑ̃'pɛ:tr] *n.m.* [Fr.] rural police. || **garde-chasse** [gardə|'ʃas] *n.m.* game-keeper. || **garde-côte** [-'ko:t] *n.m.* [Pers.] coastguard; [bateau] coastguard vessel. || **garde-fou** [-'fu] *n.m.* parapet; [Rail.] hand rail. || **garde-frein** [-'frɛ̃] *n.m.* brakeman. || **garde-malade** [-ma'lad] *n.f./m.* [hospital, &c.] nurse. || **garde-manger** [-mɑ̃'ʒe] *n.m.* larder, pantry, ice box.

garder [-e] #3 *v. tr.* **1.** to keep, retain: ~ *qqch. en bon état*, to keep sth. in good repair. **2.** to protect, to watch over, to guard: ~ *à vue*, to keep under close watch. **3.** to tend, to look after: ~ *les vaches*, to watch cows. || **se** ~ (de) *v. pron.* to be careful not to: *Gardez-vous-en bien*, Be sure you don't do that. || **garderie** [-ə'ri] *n.f.* nursery cf. CRÈCHE. || **gardien, -ne** [-jɛ̃, -jɛn] *n.* guardian, keeper, caretaker; attendant; © [US] (prison) guard. || *adj.* guardian: *ange* ~, guardian angel.

gare[1] [ga:r] *n.f.* [railway] station.

gare[2] [ga:r] *Interj.* Look out!, Beware!

garé, -e [ga're] *adj.* (train) on a siding; [auto] parked. || **garer** #3 *v. tr.* to shunt (a train); to park (a car). || **se** ~ *v. pron.* to get out of the way; [train] to run on to a siding, to shunt; [auto] to park.

gargariser [gargari|'ze] #3 *v. tr.* to gargle. || **se gargariser** *v. pron.* to gargle (one's throat); [Fig. & Fam.] to wet one's whistle. || **gargarisme** [-sm] *n.m.* gargle, gargling.

gargote [gar'gɔt] *n.f.* cheap eating house; [Fam.] greasy spoon.

gargouillement, gargouillis [garguj|'mɑ̃, -i] *n.m.* gurglings; rumble. || **gargouiller** [-e] #3 *v. intr.* to gurgle.

garnement [garnə'mɑ̃] *n.m.* scamp, rascal, good-for-nothing.

garni [gar'n|i] *n.m.* (furnished) room: *habiter un* ~, to live in a rooming house. || **garnir** [-i:r] #17 *v. tr.* to provide, fit (with, *de*), to adorn; to trim (material), to garnish (a dish). || **se** ~ *v. pron.* to fill: *Les sièges de devant se garnissent plus vite*, The seats in front are filled first.

garnison [garni'zõ] *n.f.* garrison.

garniture [garni'ty:r] *n.f.* **1.** fittings. **2.** trimming(s). 3. [plat] garnishing.

Garonne (la) [(la) ga'rɔn] *n.f.* the Garonne.

garrocher [garɔ'ʃe] © #3 *v. tr.*: ~ *des pierres*, to throw/stones, rocks/.

garrotter [garɔ'te] #3 *v. tr.* to tie, bind (a person) securely, to pinion.

gars, gas [ga] *n.m. inv.* [Fam.] lad, fellow: *hé!, les* ~ *!*, hi, fellows!

Gascogne (La) [gas'k|ɔɲ] *n.f.* Gascony. || **Gascon** [-õ] *n.m.* Gascon.

gasparot [gaspa'ro] ou **gaspareau** © *n.m.* alewife.

Gaspésie [gaspe'z|i] *n.f.* Gaspé Peninsula: *Parc* (*national*) *de la* ~, Gaspesian Park. || **gaspésien, -ne** [-jɛ̃, -jɛn] *adj. & n.* (belonging to) Gaspé.

gaspiller [gaspi'je] #3 *v. tr.* to waste, squander; to fritter away (time, money).

gastrique [gas'trik] *adj.* gastric: *suc* ~ gastric juice. || **gastronome** [gastrɔ'nɔm] *n.m.* gastronome, lover of good food.

gâteau [ga'to] *pl.* -x *n.m.* cake: ~ *des Rois*, Twelfth Night cake.

gâter [ga't|e] #3 *v. tr.* to spoil, taint (meat): *un enfant gâté*, a spoiled child: *Il va tout* ~, He's going to spoil everything. || **se** ~ *v. pron.* to spoil, deteriorate; to go to waste: *Le temps se gâte*, It looks like rain. || **gâterie** [-'ri] *n.f.* spoiling; pampering. || *n.pl. des gâteries*, treats. || **gâteu|x, -se** [-ø(:z)] *adj.* doddering.

gauche [go:ʃ] *adj.* **1.** left. **2.** [Fig.] awkward. || *n.f.* left hand, left side: *à* ~, to the left, on the left; *à* ~ *de*, to the left of; [Polit.] *la Gauche*, the Left. || **gauchement** [goʃ|'mɑ̃] *adv.* awkwardly, clumsily. || **gauch|er, -ère** [-e, -ɛ:r] *adj.* left-handed. || *n.* left-handed person. || **gaucherie** [goʃ'ri] *n.f.* awkwardness, clumsiness; gaucherie. || **gauchir** [-i:r] #17 *v. tr. & intr.* to warp. || **gauchissement** [-is'mɑ̃] *n.m.* warping, getting out of line.

gaudriole [godri'jɔl] *n.f.* broad joke.

gaufre [go:fr] *n.f.* **1.** honeycomb. **2.** waffle. #3. © gopher. || **gaufrier** [gofri'je] *n.m.* waffle iron.

gaule [go:l] *n.f.* pole.

Gaule [go:l] *n.f.* Gaul.

gauler [go'le] #3 *v. tr.* to bring down (fruit) with a pole.

gaulois, -e [go'lwa(:z)] *adj. & n.* Gaulish, Gallic: *esprit m* ~ Gallic wit, humour.

gaver [ga've] #3 *v. tr.* to cram; to stuff. || **se gaver** *v. pron.* to cram (o.s.) with food.

gaz [gɑ:z] *n.m. inv.* **1.** gas: *usine à* ~, gasworks; ~ *en cylindre*, bottled gas; *masque à* ~, gasmask; ~ *naturel*, natural, gas. **2.** © [abus.] gas, gasoline.

gazette [ga'zɛt] *n.f.* newspaper, gazette.

gazeu|x, -e [gɑ'z|ø(:z)] *adj.* gaseous: *eau gazeuse*, soda water.

gazoline [-ɔ'lin] © *n.f.* gasoline, gas.

gazon [ga'z|õ] *n.m.* grass; turf; [plot]

lawn. || **gazonner** [-ɔ'ne] #3 *v. tr.* to cover with turf; to seed (lawn).

gazouillement [gazuj|'mɑ̃] *n.m.* twittering, warbling. || **gazouiller** [gazu'je] #3 *v. intr.* [oiseau] to twitter, chirp, warble; [enfant] to prattle. **gazouillis** [-i] *n.m.* chirping.

geai [ʒe] *n.m.* jay: ~ *du Canada,* Canada jay.

géant, -e [ʒe'ɑ̃(:t)] *n.* giant(ess). || *adj.* giant, gigantic.

geindre [ʒɛ̃:dr] #36 *v. intr.* to whine, moan.

gel [ʒɛl] *n.m.* frost. || **gelée** [ʒə'le] *n.f.* **1.** frost. **2.** [Cul.] jelly: ~ *de coing,* quince jelly. || **geler** #9 *v. tr. & intr.* to freeze, congeal: *Il gèle à pierre fendre,* It's freezing hard.

gélinotte [ʒeli'nɔt] *n.f.* hazel-grouse, cf. PERDRIX.

gémir [ʒe'm|i:r] #17 *v. intr.* to groan, moan: *Il gémit sur son sort,* He feels sorry for himself. || **gémissement** [-is'mɑ̃] *n.m.* groan, moan, wail; groaning, moaning.

gênant, -e [ʒɛ'nɑ̃(:t)] *adj.* troublesome, embarrassing.

gencive [ʒɑ̃'si:v] *n.f.* gum.

gendarme [ʒɑ̃'darm] *n.m.* [Fr.] gendarme; [Fam.] virago. || **gendarmer (se)** [səʒɑ̃dar'me] #3 *v. pron.* to watch out; to struggle (*contre,* against). || **gendarmerie** [-ə'ri] *n.f.* [Fr.] gendarmerie; © *Gendarmerie Royale,* Royal Canadian Mounted Police.

gendre [ʒɑ̃:dr] *n.m.* son-in-law.

gêne [ʒɛ:n] *n.f.* **1.** constraint, embarrassment: *sans* ~ , casual, rude. **2.** inconvenience, money difficulties: *être dans la* ~ , to be hard up, to be in straitened circumstances. || **gêner** [ʒɛ'ne] #3 *v. tr.* **1.** to impede, disturb, bother: *Il ne s'est pas gêné pour le dire,* He did not hesitate to tell it. **2.** to embarrass financially, *Il est très gêné en ce moment,* He is rather short just now. 3. to embarrass: *Il se sentit très gêné,* He felt very much embarrassed. || se ~ *v. pron.* to go out of one's way, to put o.s. to some trouble: *Il ne se gêne pas,* He is pretty casual.

général [ʒene'r|al] *pl.* **généraux** [-o] *adj.* general; universal: *en* ~ , generally, in general; *répétition générale,* dress rehearsal. || *n.m.* general: ~ *de brigade,* brigadier; [US] brigadier general.

générale [-al] *n.f.* **1.** the general's wife: *la* ~ *X,* the wife of General X. **2.** *battre la* ~ , to call the men to arms. || **généralement** [-al'mɑ̃] *adv.* generally, in general. || **généralisation** [-aliza'sjɔ̃] *n.f.* generalization || **généraliser** [-ali'ze] #3 *v. tr.* to generalize. || se ~ *v. pron.* to become more general, to spread. || **généralité** [-ali'te] *n.f.* generality.

générateur [ʒenera|'tœ:r] *n.m.* generator; [vapeur] boiler; dynamo. || **génération** [-'sjɔ̃] *n.f.* generation, descent.

généreusement [ʒener|øz'mɑ̃] *adv.* generously.

généreu|x, -se [-ø(:z)] *adj.* **1.** †noble; courageous. **2.** generous.

générique [ʒene'rik] *n.m.* [Théât.] cast; [Cin.] (production) credits and cast. || *adj.* generic.

générosité [-ozi'te] *n.f.* generosity, liberality, benevolence.

Gênes [ʒɛ:n] *n.f.* Genoa.

genèse [ʒə'nɛ:z] *n.f.* genesis; beginning.

genêt [ʒə'nɛ] *n.m.* [Bot.] broom.

Genève [ʒ(ə)'nɛ:v] *n.f.* Geneva. || **genevois, -e** [ʒən'vwa(:z)] *n. & adj.* Genevan.

genévrier [ʒənevri'je] *n.m.* juniper.

génial, -e [ʒe'n|jal] *pl.* **géniaux** [-jo] *adj.* brilliant: *poète* ~ , poet of genius; *une idée* ~ , a brainwave. || **génie** [-i] *n.m.* **1.** genius. **2.** engineering: *le* ~ *civil,* civil engineering; *Il a fait son service dans le* ~ , He served with the Engineers.

génisse [ʒe'nis] *n.f.* heifer.

génital, -e [ʒeni'tal] *adj.* genital: *Les parties génitales,* genitals.

genou [ʒə'nu] *pl.* **-x** *n.m.* knee: *plier le* ~ , to bend the knee; *se mettre à* ~ , to kneel (down).

genre [ʒɑ̃:r] *n.m.* **1.** kind; species; genius: *le* ~ *humain,* the human race. **2.** [Gram.] gender.

gens [ʒɑ̃] *n.m.pl.* **1.** people: *de braves* ~ , good people; ~ *du monde,* society people; ~ *de maison,* servants; ~ *de mer,* seamen; †~ *de robe,* magistrates; †~ *d'épée,* soldiers; †~ *d'église,* clergy /clerics/. **2.** †servants, retinue: *ses* ~ , his/servants, men/. **3.** nations: *le droit des* ~ , the law of nations.

gentil, -le [ʒɑ̃'t|i(:j)] *adj.* nice; kind; †of gentle birth: *Il a été très* ~ *avec moi,* He was very nice to me. || *n.m.* gentile; pagan. || **gentilhomme** [-i'jɔm] *pl.* **gentilshommes** *n.m.* nobleman. || **gentillesse** [i'jɛs] *n.f.* kindness; nice action. || **gentiment** [-i'mɑ̃] *adv.* nicely, gracefully.

gentleman [ʒɛntlə'man] *n.m.* gentleman.

génuflexion [ʒenyflɛk'sjɔ̃] *n.f.* genuflection: *faire une* ~ , to genuflect.

géographe [ʒeɔ'graf] *n.m.* geographer. || **géographie** [-i] *n.f.* geography. || **géographique** [-ik] *adj.* geographical.

geôle [ʒo:l] *n.f.* jail, prison. || **geôlier** [ʒo'lje] *n.m.* jailer.

géomètre [ʒeɔ'mɛ:tr] *n.m.* geometer: ~

arpenteur, land-surveyor. || **géométrie** [ʒeɔme'tri] *n.f.* geometry. || **géométrique** [-k] *adj.* geometrical: *progression* ~, geometrical progression.

Georges [ʒɔrʒ] *n.m.* = George. || **Géorgie (la)** [(la) ʒeɔr'ʒi] *n.f.* Georgia. || **Géorgienne (la baie)** [(la bɛ) ʒɔr'ʒjɛn] *n.f.* Georgian Bay.

gérance [ʒe'rɑ̃:s] *n.f.* management, administration. || **gérant, -e** [ʒe'rɑ̃(:t)] *n. m/f* manager, administrator.

gerbe [ʒɛrb] *n.f.* sheaf (of wheat &c.); shower (of sparks).

gercer [ʒɛr's|e] #4 *v. tr. & intr.* [earth, skin] to crack: *Il a les lèvres gercées*, His lips are chapped. || **gerçure** [-y:r] *n.f.* chap; [lèvres] crack.

gérer [ʒe're] #10 *v. tr.* [Com.] to conduct, manage: ~ *un hôtel*, to run a hotel.

germain, -e [ʒɛr'm|ɛ̃, -ɛn] *adj. cousin* ~, first cousin; *issu de* ~, second cousin.

germanique [-a'nik] *adj.* Germanic.

germe [ʒɛrm] *n.m.* germ. || **germer** [-e] #3 *v. intr.* to sprout. || **germicide** [-i'sid] *adj.* germicidal. || *n.m.* germicide. || **germination** [ʒɛrmina'sjɔ̃] *n.f.* germination.

gérondif [ʒerɔ̃'dif] *n.m.* [Gram.] gerund; gerundive.

†**gésir** [ʒe'zi:r] #63 *v. intr.* to lie: *ci-gît*, here lies (buried).

geste [ʒɛst] *n.f.* deed, exploit: *faits et gestes*, conduct: *être au courant des faits et gestes de quelqu'un*, to know what s.o. is doing. || *n.m.* gesture: *faire un* ~, to gesture; *D'un* ~ *il lui fit signe de s'asseoir*, He motioned him to a seat. || **gesticuler** [-iky'le] #3 *v. intr.* to gesticulate, to use gestures.

gestion [ʒɛs'tjɔ̃] *n.f.* administration, management.

geyser [ʒe'zɛ:r] *n.m.* geyser.

ghetto [gɛ'to] *n.m.* ghetto.

gibecière [ʒib'sjɛ:r] *n.f.* game bag.

†**giberne** [ʒi'bɛrn] *n.f.* cartridge (-box), pouch.

gibet [ʒi'bɛ] *n.m.* gallows.

gibier [ʒi'bje] *n.m.* game: *gros* ~, forest game; *menu* ~, small game.

giboulée [ʒibu'le] *n.f.* April shower; hailstorm.

giboyeu|x, -se [ʒibwa'jø(:z)] *adj.* full of game.

Gibraltar (Le Détroit de) [ʒibral'ta:r] *n.m.* (Strait of) Gibraltar.

gicler [ʒi'kle] #3 *v. intr.* to squirt, to spurt out. || **gicleur** [ʒi'klœ:r] *n.m.* atomiser; jet; [auto] spray nozzle.

gifle [ʒifl] *n.f.* slap in the face; box on the ear. || **gifler** [-e] #3 *v. tr.* to slap (s.o.) in the face; to box s.o.'s ear.

gigantesque [ʒigɑ̃'tɛsk] *adj.* gigantic, huge.

gigogne [ʒi'gɔɲ] *n.f. Mère* ~, mother of a big family; Mother Goose; *table* ~, nest of tables.

gigot [ʒi'go] *n.m.* leg of mutton.

gigoter [ʒigɔ'te] #3 *v. intr.* [Fam.] to fidget.

gigue [ʒig] *n.f.* [Fam.] leg; [dance] jig.

gilet [ʒi'lɛ] *n.m.* [US] vest; [Br.] waistcoat. || © [abus.] coat cf. VESTON; pullover.

Gilles [ʒil] *n.m.* = Giles.

gin [dʒin] *n.m.* gin.

gingembre [ʒɛ̃'ʒɑ̃:br] *n.m.* ginger.

girafe [ʒi'raf] *n.f.* giraffe.

girofle [ʒi'rɔfl] *n.m.* clove: *clou de* ~, clove.

giron [ʒi'rɔ̃] *n.m.* lap; [Fig.] bosom.

girouette [ʒi'rwɛt] *n.f.* weathercock, vane.

gisement [ʒiz'mɑ̃] *n.m.* **1.** [Min.] layer, bed. **2.** [Naut.] bearing.

gît [ʒi] cf. GÉSIR.

gitan, -e [ʒi't|ɑ̃, -an] *n. & adj.* gipsy.

gîte [ʒit] *n.m.* lodging; form (of a hare); [Min.] deposit, layer; [Naut.] *n.f.*: *donner de la* ~, to heel. || **gîter** [-e] #3 *v. intr.* [Pers.] to lodge, sleep; [oiseaux] to perch.

givre [ʒi:vr] *n.m.* hoar frost, rime [ailes d'avion] ice. || **givrer** [ʒi'vre] *v. intr.* to frost, ice.

glabre [glɑ:br] *adj.* smooth, beardless (face).

glaçage [gla'sa:ʒ] *n.m.* icing [on cakes]. || **glace** [glas] *n.f.* **1.** ice: *rompre la* ~, to break the ice; *pris dans les glaces*, frozen in. **2.** ice cream: *une* ~ *au chocolat*, chocolate ice cream. **3.** mirror, pane: *lève-*~, window-raiser. || **glacé, -e** [-e] *adj.* **1.** frozen, frosty, iced: *thé* ~, iced tea. **2.** chilled, terribly cold. || **glacer** [-e] #4 *v. tr.* **1.** to freeze, to turn to ice. **2.** [Fig.] to chill, to strike with horror. || **glacial, -e** [-jal] *pl.* **glacials** [-jal] *adj.* frozen, glacial, icy: *des façons glaciales*, an icy manner. || **glaciaire** [-jɛ:r] *adj.* glacial. || **glacier** [-je] *n.m.* **1.** glacier, ice field. **2.** ice cream vendor. || **glacière** [-jɛ:r] *n.f.* ice box [also Fig.].

glaçon [-ɔ̃] *n.m.* icicle; [in rivers, &c.] floe.

gladiateur [gladja'tœ:r] *n.m.* gladiator.

glaïeul [gla'jœl] *pl.* **-s** *n.m.* [iris] gladiolus, pl. gladioli.

glaise [glɛ:z] *n.f.* clay. || **glaiser** [glɛ'z|e] #3 *v. tr.* to cover with clay, loam. || **glaiseu|x, -se** [-ø(:z)] *adj.* clayey, loamy.

gland [glɑ̃] *n.m.* **1.** [chêne] acorn. **2.** [rideau] tassel.

glande [glɑ̃ːd] *n.f.* gland. ‖ **glandulaire** [glɑ̃dy'lɛːr] *adj.* glandular.

glaner [gla'ne] #3 *v. intr.* to glean.

glapir [gla'p|iːr] #17 *v. intr.* [chien] to yelp; [Fig.] to scream, screech. ‖ **glapissant, -e** [-i'sɑ̃(ːt)] *adj.* yelping; screaming; screeching; shrill. ‖ **glapissement** [-is'mɑ̃] *n.m.* [dogs] yelping; [persons] screeching, screaming, squeaking.

glas [glɑ] *n.m.* death knell: *sonner le ∼*, to toll the knell.

glauque [gloːk] *adj.* glaucous.

glèbe [glɛb] *n.f.* [motte] clod; [terre] soil, land. [×].

glissade [gli's|ad] *n.f.* slide; slip; [dancing] glissade; slide; [en montagne] glissade. ‖ **glissant, -e** [-ɑ̃(ːt)] *adj.* slippery: *il fait ∼*, it's slippery; *chaussée glissante en cas de pluie*, slippery when wet; [Fig.] ticklish: *un terrain ∼*, a ticklish matter. ‖ **glissement** [-'mɑ̃] *n.m.* slipping; sliding. ‖ **glisser** [-e] #3 *v. tr. & intr.* **1.** to slip: *∼ entre les doigts*, to slip through one's fingers. **2.** [rainure, glace] to slide. **3.** to glide. **4.** [Fig.] to pass over lightly: *∼ sur une chose désagréable*, not to dwell on sth. unpleasant. ‖ **se ∼** *v. pron.* to slip (in, out, through, *en*). ‖ **glissière** [-jɛːr] *n.f.* sliding arrangement: *à ∼*, sliding; *fermeture f à ∼*, zipper. ‖ **glissoire** [-waːr] *n.f.* *∼ à tabagane*, © toboggan slide.

global, -e [glɔ'b|al] *pl.* **globaux** [-o] *adj.* global. ‖ **globe** [glɔb] *n.m.* globe, sphere.

globule [glɔ'byl] *n.f.* [air] globule; [eau, sang] drop.

gloire [glwaːr] *n.f.* glory; fame; splendour; halo: *se faire ∼ de*, to take great pride in; *mettre sa ∼ à*, to glory in; *rendre ∼ à*, to glorify, praise highly. ‖ **glorieu|x, -se** [glɔ'rjø(ːz)] *adj.* glorious; conceited; glorified (saint). ‖ **glorifier** [glɔri'fje] #3 *v. tr.* to glorify; to praise. ‖ **gloriole** [glɔ'rjɔl] *n.f.* vanity.

glose [gloːz] *n.f.* gloss, comment; criticism. ‖ **gloser** [glo'ze] #3 *v. tr.* to gloss, to comment upon. ‖ *v. intr.* to criticize; to find fault (*sur*, with).

glossaire [glɔ'sɛːr] *n.m.* glossary.

glotte [glɔt] *n.f.* glottis.

glouglou [glu'glu] *n.m.* gurgling. ‖ **glouglouter** [-'te] *v. intr.* [eau] to gurgle; [dindon] to gobble.

gloussement [glus|'mɑ̃] *n.m.* [poule] cluck, clucking; [dindon] gobble, gobbling; [Fam., Pers.] chuckle, chuckling. ‖ **glousser** [-e] #3 *v. intr.* [poule] to cluck; [dindon] gobble; [Fam., Pers.] chuckle.

glouton[1] [glu'tɔ̃] *n.m.* wolverine.

glouton[2] [glu't|ɔ̃] *adj.* gluttonous, greedy. ‖ **gloutonnerie** [-ɔn'ri] *n.f.* gluttony.

glu [gly] *n.f.* bird lime. ‖ **gluant, -e** [-ɑ̃(ːt)] *adj.* sticky, gummy.

glycérine [glise'rin] *n.f.* glycerine.

go (tout de) [tud'go] *adv.* at once; there and then.

gobelet [gɔ'blɛ] *n.m.* tin cup.

gobe-mouches [gɔb'muʃ] *n.m.* **1.** flycatcher. **2.** [Fig.] simpleton, sucker. ‖ **gober** [gɔ'b|e] #3 *v. tr.* to gulp, to swallow [also Fig.]: *∼ un œuf*, to suck an egg. ‖ **gobeu|r, -se** [-œːr, -øːz] *n.* [Fig.] gullible person.

godille [gɔ'd|iːj] *n.f.* stern oar; scull. ‖ **godiller** [-i'je] #3 *v. intr.* to scull.

godillot [gɔdi'jo] *n.m.* [Fam.] soldier's shoe.

goéland [gɔe'lɑ̃] *n.m.* gull, sea gull.

goélette [gɔe'lɛt] *n.f.* schooner; sea-swallow.

goglu [gɔ'gly] © *n.m.* bobolink.

gogo (à) [ago'go] *loc. adv.* galore; *avoir tout à ∼*, to live in clover.

goguenard, -e [gɔg'n|aːr, -ard] *adj.* bantering, jeering.

goinfre [gwɛ̃ːfr] *n.m.* glutton. ‖ **goinfrerie** [gwɛ̃frə'ri] *n.f.* gluttony.

goitre [gwaːtr] *n.m.* [Méd.] goitre. ‖ **goitreu|x, -se** [gwa'trø(ːz)] *adj.* [Méd.] goitrous. ‖ *n.* goitrous person.

golf [gɔlf] *n.m.* [Sport] golf.

golfe [gɔlf] *n.m.* gulf.

golfer [gɔl'fe] #3 *v. intr.* to play golf. ‖ **golfeur** [-œːr] *n.m.* golfer.

gomme [gɔm] *n.f.* [pour effacer] eraser; [substance] gum: *∼ à mâcher*, chewing gum; *∼ élastique*, india-rubber; *∼ laque*, shellac; *∼ d'épinette*, spruce gum; *∼ de sapin*, balsam. ‖ **gommé, -e** [-e] *adj.* gummed: *œillets gommés*, gummed reinforcements. ‖ **gommer** [-e] #3 *v. tr.* **1.** to gum. **2.** to erase, to rub out. ‖ **gommeu|x, -se** [-ø(ːz)] *adj.* gummy. ‖ *n.m.* [Fam.] fop.

gommier [-je] *n.m.* gum tree.

gond [gɔ̃] *n.m.* hinge: [Fig.] *être hors de ses gonds*, to be unhinged, beside oneself.

gondolant, -e [gɔ̃dɔ'lɑ̃(ːt)] *adj.* [Fam.] screamingly funny. ‖ **gondole** [gɔ̃'dɔl] *n.f.* gondola. ‖ **gondolé, -e** [-e] *adj.* warped, buckled. ‖ **gondoler** [-e] *v. tr.* to swell, to warp. ‖ **se ∼** *v. pron.* to swell, to warp. ‖ **gondolier** [gɔ̃dɔ'lje] *n.m.* gondolier.

gonflage [gɔ̃'fl|aːʒ] *n.m.* swelling. ‖ **gonflé, -e** [-e] *adj.* swollen, bulging (with, *de*). ‖ **gonflement** [-ə'mɑ̃] *n.m.* swelling, bulge, inflation, distension. ‖ **gonfler** [-e] #3 *v. tr.* to swell, inflate, distend.

gong [gɔ̃ːg] *n.m.* gong.

goret [gɔ'rɛ] *n.m.* young pig.
gorge [gɔrʒ] *n.f.* throat: *avoir mal à la* ~, to have a sore throat; *à pleine* ~, at the top of one's voice; *avoir la* ~ *serrée*, to have a lump in one's throat; *rire à* ~ *déployée*, to roar with laughter; *rendre* ~, to disgorge. || **gorgée** [-e] *n.f.* mouthful (of liquid). || **gorger** [-e] #5 *v. tr.* to gorge, stuff.
gorille [gɔ'ri:j] *n.m.* gorilla.
gosier [go'zje] *n.m.* throat, gullet: *à plein* ~, at the top of one's voice.
gosse [gɔs] *n. m/f* [Fam.] kid.
gosser [gɔs'e] *v. tr.* © to whittle.
gothique [gɔ'tik] *adj.* Gothic (nation, art, writing). || *n.m.* Gothic art. || *n.f.* Gothic script.
gouache [gwaʃ] *n.f.* [Art] gouache.
gouailler [gwɑ'j|e] #3 *v. tr.* [Fam.] to rag. || **gouailleu|r, -se** [-œ:r, -ø:z] *adj.* mocking.
goudron [gu'dr|õ] *n.m.* tar. || **goudronné, -e** [-ɔ'ne] *adj.* tarred. || **goudronner** [-ɔ'ne] #3 *v. tr.* to tar.
gouffre [gufr] *n.m.* chasm, gulf: †*les gouffres amers*, †the briny deep.
goujat [gu'ʒɑ] *n.m.* cad.
goujon [gu'ʒõ] *n.m.* chub: *taquiner le* ~, to go fishing [for small freshwater fish].
goulet [gu'l|ɛ] *n.m.* narrow entrance (of bay), narrows.
goulot [-o] *n.m.* [d'une bouteille, &c.] neck: *boire au* ~ *d'une cruche*, to drink (directly) from a pitcher; ~ *d'étranglement*, bottleneck.
goulu, -e [gu'ly] *adj.* greedy; gluttonous. || **goulûment** [-mɑ̃] *adv.* greedily, voraciously.
goupille [gu'pi:j] *n.f.* [Tech.] pin; [fendue] cotter pin. || **goupiller** [gupi'je] #3 *v. tr.* [Fam.] to manage, arrange; [Tech.] to pin; [écrou] to cotter.
gourd, -e [gu:r, gurd] *adj.* stiff; benumbed.
gourde [gurd] *n.f.* **1.** flask; [Fig. & Fam.] clod, dolt. **2.** [Haïti] gourd.
gourdin [gur'dɛ̃] *n.m.* club, cudgel.
gourmand, -e [gur'mɑ̃(:d)] *adj.* **1.** greedy. **2.** enjoying one's food: *Il est très* ~, He's a real trencherman. || *n.* gourmet.
gourmander [gurmɑ̃'de] #3 *v. tr.* to chide, lecture.
gourmandise [gurmɑ̃'di:z] *n.f.* **1.** gluttony, greed. **2.** love of good food. || *n.f.pl.* delicacies.
gourme [gurm] *n.f.* [enfant] impetigo; [animaux] distemper.
gourmet [gur'mɛ] *n.m.* gourmet; connoisseur.
gourmette [gur'mɛt] [×] *n.f.* [bride] curb; [chaîne de montre] watch chain.
gousse [gus] *n.f.* pod, shell: ~ *d'ail*, clove of garlic; © *tites fèves en* ~, green beans.
gousset [gu'sɛ] *n.m.* watch pocket, fob; [Fig.] *avoir le* ~ *vide*, not to have a cent in one's pocket.
goût [gu] *n.m.* **1.** taste. **2.** flavour, taste: *Cela a bon* ~, It's very tasty. **3.** good taste: *fait avec* ~, done with taste, arranged tastefully. **4.** taste, preference, liking: *prendre* ~ *à qqch.*, to develop an interest in, a taste for, sth.; *chacun selon son* ~, everyone to his own taste. || **goûté, -e** [-'te] *adj.* [acteur, écrivain, &c.] appreciated, enjoyed. || **goûter** [-'te] *n.m.* (mid-afternoon) snack, lunch, afternoon tea. || *v. tr.* **1.** to taste: ~ *un mets*, to taste a dish. **2.** to savour, relish. **3.** [Fig.] to enjoy. || *v. intr.* **1.** to taste: *Goûtez-y pour voir*, Taste it to find out. **2.** to experience, taste: *Ayant goûté au pouvoir, il ne peut s'en passer*, Having tasted power, he cannot do without it. **3.** to have a mid-afternoon snack, to have afternoon tea.
goutte[1] [gut] *n.f.* **1.** drop: *se ressembler comme deux gouttes d'eau*, to look as alike as two peas in a pod; ~ *à* ~, drop by drop; by drops. **2.** [used for negative of certain verbs] *Je n'y vois* ~, I can't see a thing; *Il n'y entend* ~, He doesn't understand the first thing about it.
goutte[2] [gut] *n.f.* [maladie] gout.
gouttelette [-'lɛt] *n.f.* small drop; droplet.
gouttière [gu'tjɛ:r] *n.f.* **1.** eavestrough, gutter (of roof). **2.** [Méd.] splint.
gouvernail [guvɛr'n|aj] *n.m.* rudder, helm: ~ *de profondeur*, [Aér.] elevator. || **gouvernant, -e** [-ɑ̃(:t)] *adj.* ruling, governing (class, powers). || *n.f.* [éducation] governess; [ménage] housekeeper. || *n.m.pl.* those who govern; [coll.] government. || **gouverné, -e** [-e] *adj.* governed; controlled. || *n.m.pl.* the governed. || **gouvernement** [-ə'mɑ̃] *n.m.* **1.** government. **2.** [maison] management: *avoir le* ~ *de*, to manage, govern. || **gouverner** [-e] #3 *v. tr.* **1.** to steer. **2.** to govern, control, rule. || **se** ~ *v. pron.* to/govern, control/o.s. || **gouverneur** [-œ:r] *n.m.* governor: ~ *général*, governor general; © *lieutenant-*~, lieutenant governor.
grâce [grɑ:s] *n.f.* **1.** favour, kindness: *Faites-moi la* ~ *de*, Be kind enough to; *s'attirer les bonnes grâces de qqun*, to get into s.o.'s good graces; ~ *à*, thanks to. **2.** [Rel.] grace: *action de* ~, thanksgiving. **3.** mercy: *demander* ~, to ask for mercy; *faire* ~ *à qqun*, to pardon s.o.; *Je vous fais* ~ *du reste*, I'll spare you the

rest. **4.** grace, gracefulness. **5.** *de bonne* ~, willingly; *de mauvaise* ~, unwillingly. || **gracier** [gra'sje] *v. tr.* [Jur.] to pardon. || **gracieusement** [-jøz'mɑ̃] *adv.* [aimablement] courteously, graciously; [gratuitement] free of charge; [avec grâce] gracefully. || **gracieuseté** [-jøz'te] *n.f.* graciousness; amiability, kindness: ~ *de*, compliments of . . . , courtesy of . . . || **gracieu|x, -se** [-jø(:z)] *adj.* **1.** gracious, courteous. **2.** graceful, charming. **3.** free; benevolent: *à titre* ~, free of charge.

gracile [-il] *adj.* slender, slim.

gradation [grada'sjõ] *n.f.* gradation.

grade [grad] *n.m.* **1.** [Mil.] rank. **2.** [Scol.] degree: *conférer un* ~, to confer a degree; *la collation des grades*, conferring degrees, © convocation, [US] commencement. **3.** [Loc. & Fam.]: *en prendre pour son* ~, to get it in the neck. || **gradé** [-e] *n.m.* non-commissioned officer [souvent *non-com.*].

gradin [gra'dɛ̃] *n.m.* [marche] step; [banc] bench, seat (in a tier of benches); *disposé en gradins*, arranged in tiers.

graduation [gradɥa'sjõ] *n.f.* graduation; [échelle] scale. || **graduel, -le** [gra'dɥ|ɛl] *adj.* gradual. || **graduellement** [mɑ̃] *adv.* gradually, by degrees, little by little. || **graduer** [-e] #3 *v. tr.* to graduate (a thermometer, ruler, &c.); [augmenter graduellement] to grade, graduate.

grain [grɛ̃] *n.m.* **1.** grain, kernel: ~ *de raisin*, grape; ~ *de groseille*, currant; ~ *de café*, bean. **2.** [coll.] seed. **3.** [coll.] grain, wheat. **4.** particle (of sand), speck (of dust). **5.** texture, grain.

graine [grɛn] *n.f.* seed; [l'œuf du ver à soie] egg: *monter en* ~, to run to seed.

graissage [grɛ'sa:ʒ] *n.m.* lubrication, greasing. || **graisse** [grɛ:s] *n.f.* [sur un animal, personne vivante] fat; grease. || **graisser** [grɛ's|e] #3 *v. tr.* [lubrifier] to grease, lubricate; ~ *la patte à qqun*, to grease s.o.'s palm, to bribe s.o. || **graisseu|x, -se** [-ø(:z)] *adj.* greasy, oily; [tissu] fatty.

grammaire [gram'm|ɛ:r] *n.f.* grammar. || **grammairien, -ne** [gram(m)ɛ'rj|ɛ̃, -ɛn] *n.* grammarian. || **grammatical, -e** [-ati'kal] *adj.* grammatical.

gramme [gram] *n.m.* gram.

gramophone [gramɔ'fɔn] *n.m.* gramophone.

grand, -e [grɑ̃(:d)] *adj.* **1.** large, big: *une grande salle*, a large room; *au* ~ *air*, in the open; *au* ~ *jour*, in broad daylight; ~ *-livre*, ledger; ~ *route*, highway; *C'est* ~ *comme un mouchoir de poche*, You couldn't swing a cat in it. **2.** tall: *un* ~ *arbre*, a tall tree; *un homme* ~, a tall man. **3.** grown up: *Les grandes personnes*, grown ups; *Quand tu seras* ~, When you are a man. **4.** great: *un* ~ *homme*, a great man. **5.** ~ *escalier*, grand staircase; *Grand-Maître*, Grand Master. || **Grande-Bretagne** [grɑ̃dbrə'taɲ] *n.f.* (Great) Britain. || **grand-chose** [grɑ|-'ʃo:z] *n.* [used only with negation] much: *Il ne dit pas* ~, He does not say much. || **grand-duc** [-'dyk] *n.m.* **1.** grand-duke. **2.** great horned owl. || **grandement** [grɑ̃d'mɑ̃] *adv.* highly, greatly, largely; grandly, handsomely.

grandeur [grɑ̃'d|œ:r] *n.f.* **1.** size: *De quelle* ~ *est-ce?*, How big is it?; ~ *nature*, life size. **2.** largeness, bigness; magnitude, importance. **3.** greatness: *Regarder qqun du haut de sa* ~, to look down at s.o., to assume a lofty manner with s.o.

grandiloquence [grɑ̃dilɔ'k|ɑ̃:s] *n.f.* [Pers.] grandiloquence; [style] bombast. || **grandiloquent, -e** [-ɑ̃(:t)] *adj.* grandiloquent, bombastic.

grandiose [grɑ̃'djo:z] *adj.* grandiose.

grandir [-i:r] #17 *v. intr.* **1.** to get larger, bigger, more important, to increase, grow. **2.** to get taller, to grow up. || *v. tr.* **1.** to make (s.o.) appear taller. **2.** to give more stature, to heighten, ennoble. || **grandissant, -e** [-i'sɑ̃(:t)] *adj.* growing, increasing. || **grandissement** [grɑ̃dis'mɑ̃] *n.m.* growth.

grand-maman [grɑ̃|ma'mɑ̃] *n.f.* grandma. || **grand-mère** [-'mɛ:r] *n.f.* grandmother. || **grand-messe** [-'mɛs] *n.f.* High Mass. || **grand-oncle** [-'tõ:kl] *n.m.* great-uncle. || **grand-papa** [-pa'pa] *n.m.* grandpa. || **grands-parents** [-pa'rɑ̃] *n.m.pl.* grandparents. || **grand-père** [-'pɛ:r] *n.m.* grandfather. || **grand-route** [grɑ̃'rut] *n.f.* highway, main road. || **grand-rue** [-'ry] *n.f.* main street. || **grand-tante** [-'tɑ̃:t] *n.f.* great-aunt.

Grands Lacs (les) [(le) grɑ̃'lak] *n.m.pl.* Great Lakes.

grange [grɑ̃:ʒ] *n.f.* barn.

granit [gra'ni(t)] *n.m.* granite. || **granitique** [grani'tik] *adj.* granitic.

granulation [granyla'sjõ] *n.f.* granulation. || **granule** [gra'nyl] *n.f.* granule. || **granuler** [-e] #3 *v. tr.* to granulate. || **granuleu|x, -se** [-ø(:z)] *adj.* granular, granulous.

graphie [gra'fi] *n.f.* spelling; alphabet letter, graph. || **graphique** [gra'fik] *adj.* graphic: *dessin* ~, industrial drawing. || *n.m.* [appliqué aux sciences] graph; [dessin] diagram.

grappe [grap] *n.f.* cluster, bunch: ~ *de raisin*, bunch of grapes.

grappin [-ɛ̃] *n.m.* [petite ancre] grapnel; [crochet d'abordage] grappling hook; [par extension] hook; [de pêche] gaff; [Fam.] *mettre le ~ sur qqun*, to get one's hooks into s.o.

gras, -se [grɑ(:s)] *adj.* **1.** fat; fatty: *bouillon ~*, meat broth; *jour ~*, meat day; *Mardi-Gras*, Shrove Tuesday; *contes ~*, smutty stories. **2.** [enduit de graisse] greasy, oily; [visqueux] thick. **3.** [Fig.] [sol] rich; generous: *faire la grasse matinée*, to sleep late. || **grassouillet, -te** [grɑsu'jɛ(t)] *adj.* plump, chubby.

gratification [gratif|ika'sjõ] *n.f.* bonus, gratuity. || **gratifier** [-je] #3 *v. tr.* to bestow; to reward: *~ qqun de qqch.*, to bestow sth. on s.o., to reward s.o. with sth.

gratin [gra'tɛ̃] *n.m.* [Cul.]: *au ~*, browned (potatoes, &c.): [Fig.] *le gratin*, the upper/crust, set/.

gratis [gra'tis] *adj.* free (of charge): *entrée ~*, admission free.

gratitude [grati'tyd] *n.f.* gratitude.

grattage [gra'ta:ʒ] *n.m.* [d'une surface] scratching, scraping; [effacement] erasure, rubbing. || **gratte** [grat] *n.f.* scraper; © (snow-) plough. || **gratte-ciel** [grat|'sjɛl] *n.m. inv.* skyscraper. || **gratter** [-e] *v. tr.* **1.** to scratch, scrape. **2.** [effacer] to scratch out. || **se ~** *v. pron.* to scratch o.s. || **grattoir** [-wa:r] *n.m.* scraper; [de bureau] eraser (knife).

gratuit, -e [gra'tɥi|(t)] *adj.* **1.** free, gratuitous. **2.** [Fig.] unfounded, gratuitous. || **gratuité** [-'te] *n.f.* **1.** exemption from fee or charge. **2.** gratuitousness. || **gratuitement** [-t'mɑ̃] *adv.* **1.** gratis, free. **2.** groundlessly: *accuser qqun ~*, to accuse s.o. without/reason, proof/.

grave [gra:v] *adj.* **1.** solemn, grave: *le visage ~*, with a solemn face. **2.** serious, grave, important, far-reaching. **3.** [son] low, deep.

graveleu|x, -se [grav|'lø(:z)] *adj.* [terre] gravelly; [propos] spicy, licentious; [Méd.] containing gravel. || **gravelle** [-ɛl] *n.f.* **1.** [Méd.] gravel, kidney stones. **2.** © gravel, grit.

gravement [grav|'mɑ̃] *adv.* **1.** solemnly. **2.** seriously, gravely.

graver [-e] #3 *v. tr.* [au burin] to engrave; [à l'eau forte] to etch; [Fig.] to stamp (in one's memory). || **graveur** [-œ:r] *n.m.* engraver, etcher.

gravier [gra'vj|e] *n.m.* gravel; [très petit] grit. || **gravière** [-ɛ:r] *n.f.* gravel pit.

gravir [gra'vi:r] #17 *v. tr.* to climb (a hill, a mountain, a stair, &c.); [à pied] to walk up; [à cheval] to ride up; [en voiture] to drive up.

gravitation [gravita'sjõ] *n.f.* gravitation.

gravité [gravi'te] *n.f.* gravity.

gravure [gra'vy:r] *n.f.* **1.** engraving; [d'eau forte] etching; [au trait] line engraving; [sur bois] woodcut; [en taille-douce] copper-plate (engraving); [disque] cutting. **2.** [reproduction] print, engraving; [par extension] picture.

gré [gre] *n.m.* **1.** will, liking; [used only in]: *à son ~*, to one's liking; *au ~ du vent*, as the wind blows. **2.** *bon ~, mal ~*, willy-nilly; *de ~ ou de force*, willy-nilly. **3.** *de ~ à ~*, by mutual consent. **4.** *de son plein ~*, willingly. **5.** *contre le ~ de*, against the wishes of. **6.** *savoir ~ de*, to appreciate.

grec, -que [grɛk] *adj.* Greek; *renvoyer aux calendes grecques*, to put off indefinitely. || **Grèce** [grɛ:s] *n.f.* Greece. || **grecque** [grɛk] cf. GREC.

gredin, -e [grə'd|ɛ̃, -in] *n.m/f* scoundrel.

gréement [gre|'mɑ̃] *n.m.* rigging. || **gréer** [-'e] #3 *v. tr.* to rig (up). || **(se) gréer** [sə grɛ'je] © *v. pron.* [Fam.] to equip o.s.; to get dressed.

greffe[1] [grɛf] *n.m.* clerk's registry/office.

greffe[2] *n.f.* graft; [action] grafting. || **greffer** [-e] #3 *v. tr.* to graft.

greffier [-je] *n.m.* clerk, recorder, court reporter: *~ de la Chambre*, Clerk of the House.

Grégoire [gre'gwa:r] *n.m.* = Gregory. || **grégorien, -ne** [grego'rj|ɛ̃, -ɛn] *adj.*: *calendrier ~*, Gregorian calendar; *musique grégorienne*, Gregorian music.

grêle [grɛ:l] *adj.* **1.** slender, slim: *l'intestin ~*, the small intestine. **2.** [son] shrill. || *n.f.* **1.** hail. **2.** shower (of blows, bullets). || **grêlé, -e** [grɛ'l|e] struck by hail; pock-marked. || **grêler** [-e] #3 *v. imp.* to hail. || *v. tr.* to damage (a garden) by hail. || **grêlon** [-õ] *n.m.* hailstone.

grelot [grə'lo] *n.m.* (harness) bell: *attacher le ~*, to bell the cat; *avoir les grelots*, to/shake, shiver/with fear.

grelottant, -e [grəlɔ't|ɑ̃(:t)] *adj.* trembling. || **grelotter** [-e] #3 *v. intr.* [personne] to shake, shiver; [grelot] to tinkle, jingle.

grenade [grə'nad] *n.f.* **1.** [fruit] pomegranate. **2.** [petite bombe] grenade. || **grenadier** [-je] *n.m.* **1.** [arbre] pomegranate tree. **2.** [personne] grenadier.

grenaille [grə'nɑ:j] *n.f.* [de plomb, &c.] (lead) shot, buckshot.

grenier [grə'nje] *n.m.* **1.** loft: *~ à foin*, hay loft. **2.** attic. **3.** granary, bread basket.

grenouille [grə'nuj] *n.f.* frog.

grès [grɛ] *n.m.* sandstone; [poteries] stoneware.

grésil [gre'zi|(l)] *n.m.* sleet. || **grésillement** [-j'mɑ̃] *n.m.* **1.** [du feu] crackling; [d'une friture] sizzling. **2.** [du grillon] chirping. **3.** [TV, Tél.] buzzing. || **grésiller** [-'je] #3 *v. intr.* **1.** to sleet. **2.** [huile sur le feu] to sizzle.

grève [grɛ:v] *n.f.* **1.** (sea) shore, strand, beach. **2.** strike: *faire la* ~, to strike; *être en* ~, to be on strike; ~ *de la faim*, hunger strike; ~ *perlée*, slow-down, go-slow strike; ~ *sur le tas*, sitdown strike; *briseur de* ~, strike-breaker.

grever [grə've] #9 *v. tr.* to burden (with, *de*).

gréviste [gre'vist] *n.* striker, cf. GRÈVE 2.

gribouillage [gribu'j|a:ʒ] *n.m.* scribbling, scrawling. || **gribouille** [gri'buj] *n.m.* muddle-headed person. || **gribouillé, -e** [-e] *adj.* scribbled, scrawled. || **gribouiller** [-e] #3 *v. intr.* [écrire] to scribble, scrawl; [peindre] to daub. || *v. tr.* to scribble (off) (a letter, note, &c.).

grief [gri'jɛf] *n.m.* grievance, complaint; objection. || **grièvement** [grijɛv'mɑ̃] *adv.* [☞ used only in]: ~ *blessé*, severely wounded.

griffe [grif] *n.f.* **1.** [animaux, oiseaux de proie] claw; [oiseaux de proie] talon; [Tech.] grip, hook, catch; [Bot.] tendril: *donner un coup de* ~, to scratch, [plus grave] to claw. **2.** [signature] stamp; [empreinte personnelle] mark, stamp: *Cette œuvre porte sa* ~, This work carries his stamp. || **griffer** [-e] #3 *v. tr.* to scratch; [plus grave] to claw.

griffonnage [-ɔ'na:ʒ] *n.m.* scrawl, scribble. || **griffonner** [-ɔ'ne] #3 *v. tr.* [dessiner, écrire] to scrawl, scribble; [Fig.] to scribble off (a letter, &c.).

grignoter [griɲɔ'te] #3 *v. tr.* to nibble (on, at); [en rongeant] to gnaw; [Fig.] [son capital, &c.] to fritter away; [un adversaire] to wear down.

gril [gri] *n.m.* gridiron, grill: [Fig.] *être sur le* ~, to be on tenterhooks.

grillade [gri'jad] *n.f.* © [×] side pork, halfback; [Fr.] grill; [collective for] steak, chop.

grillage [-'ja:ʒ] *n.m.* **1.** roasting; [metal] burning; [cloth] singeing. **2.** grill, trellis, lattice-work. || **grillager** [grija'ʒe] #5 *v. tr.* to lattice, grate. || **grille** [gri:j] *n.f.* **1.** grating; bars; railing. **2.** [porte] gate. **3.** [fourneau] grate; [Elect.] grid. || **grille-pain** [grij|'pɛ̃] *n.m.* toaster. || **griller**[1] [-e] #3 *v. tr.* **1.** to grill, broil; [marrons, café, amandes, &c.] to roast; [Mét.] to burn; [étoffe] to singe; [Elect.] to burn out; [pain] to toast. **2.** [Fig.] to long: *Il grillait de lui être présenté*, He could hardly wait to be introduced to her.

griller[2] [-e] #3 *v. tr.* to put a grill on (an opening); to bar (a window, &c.), cf. GRILLAGER.

grillon [gri'jɔ̃] *n.m.* cricket: *Les grillons font cri-cri*, Crickets go chirp-chirp.

grimaçant, -e [grima'sɑ̃(:t)] *adj.* twisted, grimacing (face, mouth, &c.); gaping (shoes). || **grimace** [gri'mas] *n.f.* **1.** face; grimace: *faire la* ~ *à qqun*, to/pull, make/ a face at s.o. || **grimacer** [-e] #4 *v. intr.* to grimace, make a wry face.

grimer [gri'me] #3 *v. tr.* [Théât.] to make up (an actor). || **se grimer** *v. pron.* to make up s.o.

grimpant, -e [grɛ̃'p|ɑ̃(:t)] *adj.* climbing: *plantes grimpantes*, creepers. || **grimpé, -e** [-e] *adj.* [sur qqch.] perched. || **grimper** [-e] #3 *v. intr.* to climb, scale: ~ *à un arbre*, to climb a tree; ~ *sur le toit*, to climb on to the roof. || **grimpeu|r, -se** [-œ:r, -ø:z] *adj.* [animal] climbing. || *n.m.* climbing bird, climber.

grincement [grɛ̃s|'mɑ̃] *n.m.* [clef] grating; [craie] screeching; [plume] scratching; [bois] squeak; [dents] gnashing, grinding. || **grincer** [-e] #4 *v. intr.* [des dents] to grind, grit; [choses en fer] to grate; [choses en bois] to creak.

grincheu|x, -se [grɛ̃'ʃø(:z)] *adj.* grumpy, touchy. || *n.* grumbler, complainer.

grippe [grip] *n.f.* **1.** flu, influenza: *une attaque de* ~, a bout of flu. **2.** sudden dislike: *prendre qqun en* ~, to take a dislike to s.o. || **grippé, -e** [-e] *adj.* *être* ~, to have the flu. || **gripper** [-e] #3 *v. tr.* **1.** to seize: *grippe-sou*, penny-pincher. **2.** to snatch, grasp. || **se gripper** *v. pron.* to get stuck.

gris, -e [gri(:z)] *adj.* **1.** grey: *substance grise*, grey matter. **2.** dull, grey: *un temps* ~, a grey day. || *n.m.* grey.

grisant, -e [gri'z|ɑ̃(:t)] *adj.* dizzying; [alcool] intoxicating.

grisâtre [-ɑ:tr] *adj.* greyish, dull grey.

griser [-e] #3 *v. tr.* to intoxicate, to make dizzy: *Les succès l'ont grisé*, His success has gone to his head. || **se** ~ *v. pron.* to get tipsy, to become intoxicated. || **griserie** [-'ri] *n.f.* intoxication, exhilaration.

grisette [-ɛt] *n.f.* (frivolous) working girl, factory girl.

grisonnant, -e [-ɔ'nɑ̃(:t)] *adj.* [homme, barbe] greying. || **grisonner** [-ɔ'ne] #3 *v. intr.* to turn grey, to grizzle.

grive [gri:v] *n.f.* thrush; © [= merle américain] robin.

grivois, -e [gri'vwa(:z)] *adj.* suggestive, smutty; licentious.
Groënland [groɛn'lɑ̃:d] *n.m.* Greenland. || **Groënlandais, -se** [-ɛ(:z)] *adj.* Greenlandic. || *n. m/f* Greenlander.
grognement [grɔɲ|'mɑ̃] *n.m.* [cri du cochon] grunt; [personnes] grumbling, growl. || **grogner** [-e] #3 *v. intr.* [cochon, &c.] to grunt; [chien, &c.] to growl; [Fam.] [personne] to growl, grumble. || **grogneu|r, -se** [grɔ'ɲ|œ:r, -ø:z] *adj.* grumbling, [Fam.] griping. || *n.m.* grumbler. || **grognon, -ne** [-õ, -ɔn] *adj.* grumpy.
groin [gro'ɛ̃] [×] *n.m.* [cochon, &c.] snout.
grommeler [grɔm'le] #8 *v. intr.* to mutter, grumble; [chien] to growl. || *v. tr.* to mutter, growl (insults, &c.).
grondant, -e [grõ'd|ɑ̃(:t)] *adj.* [animal] growling; [canons, bataille, tonnerre, &c.] rumbling; [moteur, avion, rivière, &c.] roaring. || **grondement** [-'mɑ̃] *n.m.* [animal] growl; [bataille, tonnerre] rumble; [moteur, eau] roar. || **gronder** [-e] #3 *v. intr.* to growl; to rumble; to roar. || *v. tr.* to scold. || **gronderie** [-'ri] *n.f.* scolding. || **grondeu|r, -se** [grõ'd|œ:r, -ø:z] *adj.* scolding, grumbling. || *n.m.* scold, grumbler.
gros, -se [gro(:s)] *adj.* **1.** [Esp. ©] big, large; thick, heavy. **2.** fat, stout: *un* ~ *homme*, a fat man. **3.** swollen: *le cœur* ~, with a heavy heart. **4.** pregnant. **5.** [Loc.] *un* ~ *bonnet*, a big wig; *le* ~ *lot*, the jackpot; *un* ~ *mot*, a bad word; *un* ~ *bon sens*, horse sense. || *adv.* big: *écrire* ~, to write big; *jouer* ~, to play for high stakes; *Il y a* ~ *à parier que*, You can bet your bottom dollar that; *en gros*, *loc. adv.* **1.** wholesale. **2.** roughly. || *n.m.* [gro] **1.** bulk, main body (of an army). **2.** wholesale: *commerce en* ~, wholesale trade. **3.** stout person.
groseille [gro'z|ɛ:j] *n.f.* [rouge, noire] currant; [verte] gooseberry. || **groseillier** [-ɛ'je] *n.m.* currant,/gooseberry/bush.
grosse [gro:s] *adj.* cf. GROS. || *n.f.* [Jur.] (enlarged) copy; probate; [Com.] gross, twelve dozen. || **grossesse** [gro's|ɛs] *n.f.* pregnancy. || **grosseur** [-œ:r] *n.f.* [volume] size; [enflure] swelling: *être de la* ~ *de*, to be the size of.
grossi|er, -ère [gro'sj|e, -ɛ:r] *adj.* **1.** coarse, rough. **2.** rude, vulgar. || **grossièreté** [-ɛr'te] *n.f.* **1.** coarseness, roughness. **2.** rudeness, vulgarity, coarse language.
grossir [gros|i:r] #17 *v. intr.* **1.** to grow larger, bigger, to increase. **2.** to put on weight, to get fat. || *v. tr.* **1.** to swell, to increase. **2.** to make (s.o.) look bigger. || **grossissant, -e** [-i'sɑ̃(:t)] *adj.* swelling, growing (crowd, &c.). || **grossissement** [-is'mɑ̃] *n.m.* **1.** growth (of a person, tumour, &c.); growing larger. **2.** [optique] magnifying || **grossiste** [-ist] *n.m.* wholesaler.
grotesque [grɔ'tɛsk] *adj.* grotesque; [ridicule] ridiculous.
grotte [grɔt] *n.f.* grotto; cavern, cave.
grouiller [gru'je] #3 *v. intr.* to swarm about (on, in, *sur*, *dans*); [de] to teem, be alive (with, *de*); [Fam.] *Grouille-toi!*, Get a move on!
groupe [grup] *n.m.* group: ~ *sanguin*, blood group. || **groupement** [-'mɑ̃] *n.m.* **1.** [action] grouping. **2.** association, organization. || **grouper** [-e] #3 *v. tr.* to group, to arrange into a group.
grue [gry] *n.f.* **1.** [Zool.] crane. **2.** [machine] crane: *faire le pied de* ~, to stand and wait. **3.** [Fam.] prostitute.
gruger [gry'ʒe] #5 *v. tr.* [Fig.] to fleece (s.o.).
grumeau [gry'mo] *n.m.* lump.
gué [ge] *n.m.* ford: *traverser une rivière à* ~, to ford a river. || **guéable** [-'abl] *adj.* fordable.
guenille [gə'ni:j] *n.f.* rag; [pl.] tatters.
guêpe [gɛ:p] *n.f.* wasp: *avoir une taille de* ~, to have an hour-glass figure. || **guêpier** [ge'pje] *n.m.* wasp's nest: *tomber dans un* ~, to get into trouble.
guère [gɛ:r] *adv.* used with *ne*: not much. **1.** *Il n'en a* ~, He does not have much of it. **2.** *Je ne le vois plus* ~, I hardly see him any more. **3.** *Il ne lui reste* ~ *que deux jours*, He has only about two days left.
guéret [ge'rɛ] *n.m.* cultivated field; farmland.
guéri, -e [ge'ri] *adj.* healed, cured.
guéridon [geri'dõ] *n.m.* pedestal table; one-legged table.
guérilla [geri'ja] *n.f.* guerilla warfare; guerilla band.
guérir [ge'ri:r] #17 *v. tr.* [a wound, s.o.] to heal; [a sickness, s.o.] to cure; [Fig.] to cure, remedy (a hurt, all things, &c.). || *v. intr.* [plaie, blessure] to heal; [personne, animal, &c.] to get well; to recover (from, *de*). || **se** ~ *v. pron.* to get well, recover: *Il s'en est guéri*, He got over it. || **guérison** [-i'zõ] *n.f.* healing, cure, recovery. || **guérisseu|r, -se** [-i'sœ:r, -i'sø:z] *n. m/f* healer.
guérite [ge'rit] *n.f.* [Mil.] sentry box; [ch. de fer] signal box.
guerre [gɛ:r] *n.f.* war, warfare: *en* ~, at war; *entrer en* ~, to go to war; *faire*

la ~ , to make war (on, *à*); *l'époque d'avant-* ~ , pre-war days; *le ministère de la* ~ , © the Department of National Defence, [US] the Department of Defense, [Br.] the War Office. || **guerri|er, -ère** [gɛ'r|je, -ɛ:r] *adj.* warlike; martial. || **guerrier** [-je] *n.m.* warrior. || **guerrière** [-jɛ:r] *n.f.* amazon. || **guerroyer** [-wa'je] #12 *v. intr.* to wage war (on, *contre*).

guet [gɛ] *n.m.* watch, look-out; night watch: *faire le* ~ , *être au* ~ , to be on the look-out. || **guet-apens** [-ta'pɑ̃] *n.m.* ambush, trap.

guêtre [gɛ:tr] *n.f.* gaiter, legging.

guetter [ge'te] #3 *v. tr.* to watch, to watch for, to listen for: *Le chat guette la souris,* The cat watches the mouse; ~ *l'arrivée du facteur,* to watch for the mailman.

guetteur [-'tœ:r] *n.m.* look-out, sentinel.

gueulard, -e [gœ'l|a:r, -ard] *adj.* loud-mouthed, noisy. || *n.m.* [Fam.] loudmouth, blowhard.

gueule [gœl] *n.f.* **1.** [animaux] mouth; jaws: *Se jeter dans la* ~ *du loup,* To put one's head in the lion's mouth. **2.** [Fam.] [personne] mug: *avoir la* ~ *de bois,* to have a hangover; *casser la* ~ *à qqun,* to beat s.o. up; *aller se faire casser la* ~ , to go and risk one's life [in war]. **3.** opening, mouth; [cannon] muzzle, mouth. || **gueuler** [-e] #3 *v. intr.* to bellow.

gueu|x, -se [gø(:z)] *n.f.* beggar, vagabond. || *adj.* poverty-stricken.

gui [gi] *n.m.* mistletoe.

guichet [gi'ʃɛ] *n.m.* **1.** †small door. **2.** © wicket, [US] window, [Br.] position: *s'adresser au* ~ *d'à côté,* next wicket, please; *jouer à guichets fermés,* to play to a full house.

guide [gid] *n.m.* guide; [livre] guidebook; [scoutisme] girl guide. || *n.f.* [rêne] rein. || **guider** [-e] #3 *v. tr.* to guide, lead, direct. || **guidon** [-õ] *n.m.* [fusil] front sight; [bicyclette, &c.] handlebar; [Mil.] pennant.

guigne [giɲ] *n.f.* [Fam.] bad luck.

guigner]gi'ɲe] #3 *v. tr.* to peep, to peer at, to ogle; [Fig.] to covet.

guignol [gi'ɲɔl] *n.m.* [marionnette] hand puppet; [personne ridicule] clown, character; [Théât.] Punch and Judy show.

guignolée [giɲɔ'le] © *n.f.* house-to-house collection for the poor; charity drive.

Guillaume [gi'jo:m] *n.m.* = William.

guillemet [gij'mɛ] *n.m.* quotation mark: *ouvrir les guillemets,* to quote; *fermer les guillemets,* to end a quotation.

guilleret, -te [gij'rɛ(t)] *adj.* brisk, gay, sprightly, merry.

guillotine [gijɔ'tin] *n.f.* guillotine: *à* ~ , sliding (up and down); *fenêtre à* ~ , sash window. || **guillotiner** [-e] #3 *v. tr.* to guillotine.

guimauve [gi'mo:v] *n.f.* [pâte de] marsh-mallow.

guimbarde [gɛ̃'bard] *n.f.* **1.** [Fam.] jalopy, rattletrap. **2.** [Mus.] Jew's harp.

guindé, -e [gɛ̃'de] *adj.* affected; stiff.

guinder [gɛ̃'de] #3 *v. tr.* to hoist; [Fig., affecter] to strain, to force. || **se guinder** *v. pron.* to behave in an affected manner.

Guinée [gi'ne] *n.f.* Guinea: *la Nouvelle-Guinée,* New Guinea.

guirlande [gir'lɑ̃:d] *n.f.* garland; [circulaire] wreath.

guise [gi:z] *n.f.* **1.** manner, way [☞ seldom used except in the following]: *à sa* ~ , as one likes, pleases; *en* ~ *de,* by way of, as.

guitare [gi'ta:r] *n.f.* guitar: *pincer la* ~ , to strum.

gustati|f, -ve [gysta't|if, -i:v] *adj.* gustatory: *papilles gustatives,* taste buds.

guttural, -e [gyty'ral] *adj.* guttural. || *n.f.* guttural (sound).

Guyane (la) [la gɥi'jan] *n.f.* Guiana.

gymnase [ʒim'n|ɑ:z] *n.m.* gymnasium, gym. || **gymnaste** [-ast] *n.m.* gymnast. || **gymnastique** [-as'tik] *adj.* gymnastic. || *n.f.* gymnastics.

gyroscope [ʒirɔs'kɔp] *n.m.* gyroscope. || **gyroscopique** [-ik] *adj.* gyroscopic.

H

H, h [aʃ] *n.m.* [alphabet] La lettre H; le H. [☞ There is no "h" sound in Standard French; the letter H must be treated (1) as a purely graphic sign, without any effect on the pronunciation, or, (2) as preventing *liaison*; in the latter case, an asterisk has been placed in front of the phonetic transcription.]

habile [a'bil] *adj.* clever, skilful; able, capable. || **habilement** [-'mɑ̃] *adv.* cleverly, skilfully. || **habileté** [-'te] *n.f.* cleverness, skill.

habiliter [abili'te] #3 *v. tr.* to qualify, to entitle; to empower.

habillé, -e [abi|'je] *adj.* **1.** dressed (up). **2.** dressy: *Il est* ~, he is dressed (up); *Cela fait plus* ~, It is more dressy. || **habillement** [-j'mɑ̃] *n.m.* clothing, clothes. || **habiller** #3 *v. tr.* **1.** to dress. **2.** to be becoming, to suit: *Cette robe l'habille bien*, That dress is becoming to her. **3.** [Fig.] ~ *sa pensée*, to clothe one's thoughts. || **s'habiller** *v. pron.* to dress (o.s.); to buy one's clothes: *Cet enfant ne peut pas encore* ~ *tout seul*, This child cannot dress himself yet; *Elle s'habille chez X*, She buys her clothes at X's.

habit [a'bi] *n.m.* [usual. pl.] clothes [*vêtement* is the usual word]: *un habit*, a dress suit, [Fam.] tails; *se mettre en* ~, to put on evening clothes; *marchand d'habits*, old clothes man.

habitant [abi't|ɑ̃] *n.m.* **1.** inhabitant; resident; -dweller. [☞ ou utilisez un adjectif de localité: ~ *de l'Alaska*, Alaskan]. **2.** © habitant; French settler [in Canada], farmer, cf. PAYSAN. || **habitation** [-a'sjõ] *n.f.* house, dwelling: *maison d'* ~, dwelling-house, residence; © *L'* ~ *Jacques Cartier*, The Jacques Cartier house. || **habité, -e** [-e] *adj.* inhabited, lived in. || **habiter** #3 *v. tr. & intr.* to live (in), inhabit; to live, reside (at): *Où habitez-vous?*, Where do you live? Where are you living?; *Il habite* (à) *Montréal*, He lives in Montreal.

habitude [abi't|yd] *n.f.* habit, custom, practice: *avoir l'* ~ *de*, to have, be in/ the habit of; *prendre l'* ~ *de*, to get into the habit of; *J'en ai perdu l'* ~, I got out of it; *d'* ~, usually. || **habitué, -e** [-ɥe] *adj.* accustomed (*à*, to). || *n.*: *un habitué*, a regular patron (of café, theatre, movie): *les habitués des théâtres*, theatre-goers. || **habituel, -le** [-ɥɛl] *adj.* usual, customary. || **habituellement** [-mɑ̃] *adv.* usually. || **habituer** [-ɥe] #3 *v. tr.* to use, to accustom. || **s'habituer** *v. pron.* to get used, to become accustomed (*à*, to).

hâbleur, -euse [ɑ'bl|œ:r, -ø:z] *n.m.* braggart, boaster: *Il est* ~, → He likes to brag.

hache [*aʃ] *n.f.* axe. || **haché, -e** [-e] chopped up: *viande hachée*, chopped, minced/ meat; *bifteck haché*, hamburger. || **hacher,** #3 *v. tr.* to chop up: *hacher menu*, to mince. || **hachette** [-ɛt] *n.f.* hatchet. || **hachis** [-i] *n.m.* hash; minced meat. || **hachoir** [-wa:r] *n.m.* cleaver: ~ *mécanique*, chopping-knife. || **hachures** [-'y:r] *n.f.pl.* shading, hatching. || **hachurer** [-y're] #3 *v. tr.* to hatch, to shade (with a series of parallel lines).

hagard, -e [*a'g|a:r, -ard] *adj.* wild (-looking), [×] cf. HAGGARD.

haï, haïe [*a'i] cf. HAÏR.

haie [*ɛ] *n.f.* hedge: ~ *vive*, quickset hedge.

haillon [*ɑ'jõ] *n.m.* rag; old clothes, tatters: *en haillons*, in rags/tatters/.

haine [*ɛ:n] *n.f.* †hate; hatred: *avoir qqun en* ~, to hate s.o.; *nourrir de la* ~ *contre qqun*, to nurse a hatred against s.o. || **†haineu|x, -se** [ɛ'nø(:z)] spiteful, hateful, → full of hatred.

haïr [*a'i:r] **haïssant, haï** #18 *v. tr. & intr.* to hate; to detest. cf. DÉTESTER. || **haïssable** [*ai'sabl] *adj.* hateful, detestable; © mischievous: *un enfant* ~, a little brat.

hais; hait [*ɛ] cf. HAÏR.

Haïti [ai|'ti] [Géo.] Haiti. || **haïtien, -ne** [-'sjɛ̃, -'sjɛn] *adj.* Haitian.

hâle [*ɑ:l] *n.m.* tan. || **hâlé, -e** [ɑ'le] (sun-) tanned.

haleine [a'lɛ:n] *n.f.* breath; wind; *courir à perdre* ~, to run as fast as one can; *être hors d'* ~, to be out of breath; *reprendre* ~, *to catch one's breath*; [Fig.] *un ouvrage de longue* ~, a long-term project.

haler[1] [*ɑ'le] #3 *v. tr.* to tow, to take in tow.

hâler[2] [*ɑ'le] #3 *v. tr.* to tan (the skin).

haletant, -e [al't|ɑ̃(:t)] *adj.* panting; out of breath. || **haleter** [-e] #8 *v. intr.* to pant; to be out of breath.

halette &c.; haletterai &c. cf. HALETER.

Haligonien, -ne [aligɔnj|ɛ̃, -ɛn] © *n.* (natif d'Halifax) Haligonian.

halle [*al] *n.f.* market; market-place [usual. covered]: *Les Halles* (in Paris), Les Halles, The Central Market; *la Halle aux grains*, the Grain Exchange; *la Halle aux vins*, the Wine Market. || ***hallettes** [*a'lɛt] *n.f.pl.* provisions (store), grocer's (store), © market.

hallucination [alysina'sjõ] *n.f.* hallucination.

halte [*alt] *n.f.* 1. stopping place, stopover: *faire* ~, to stop, (come to a) halt. [Rail.] whistle-stop. 2. *interj. Halte!* Stop!
hamac [*a'mak] *n.m.* hammock.
†**hameau** [*a'mo] *n.m.* hamlet.
hameçon [am'sõ] *n.m.* (fish-) hook: *prendre à l'* ~, to hook (a fish); [Fig.] bait.
hampe [*ɑ̃:p] *n.f.* [drapeau] staff; pole.
hanche [*ɑ̃:ʃ] *n.f.* hip; [animal] haunch: *les deux poings sur les hanches,* with arms akimbo.
handicap [*ɑ̃di|'kap] *n.m.* handicap. ‖ **handicaper** [-ka'pe] #3 *v. tr.* to handicap.
hangar [*ɑ̃'ga:r] *n.m.* shed, [aviation] hangar.
hanneton [*an'tõ] *n.m.* June bug, cockchafer.
Hansard, le [*ɑ̃'sa:r] © *n.m.* [journal officiel des débats parlementaires], the Hansard.
hanté, -e [ɑ̃'t|e] *adj.* haunted. ‖ **hanter** #3 *v. tr.* to haunt; [Fig.] to frequent; [†] to associate with: *Dis-moi qui tu hantes, je te dirai qui tu es,* → A man is known by the company he keeps. ‖ **hantise** [-i:z] *n.f.* obsession *f*: *avoir la* ~ *de,* → to be obsessed by.
happer [*a'pe] #3 *v. tr.* to snatch (up), catch.
harangue [*a'rɑ̃:g] *n.f.* harangue, speech.
haranguer [*arɑ̃'ge] #3 *v. tr.* to harangue; [Fam.] to orate.
harassement [*aras'mɑ̃] *n.m.* harassment.
harcèlement [*arsɛl'mɑ̃] *n.m.* harassing, teasing. ‖ **harceler** [*arsə'le] #8 *v. tr.* to harass, worry; to harry (an enemy); [débiteur] to dun; [Fig.] to pester: *harcelé de créanciers,* → riddled with debts.
hardi, -e [*ar'd|i] *adj.* daring, bold; brazen, [×] HARDY. ‖ interj. *hardi!* go to it! ‖ **hardiesse** [-jɛs] *n.f.* boldness, daring: *la* ~ *de ces paroles,* such bold words. ‖ **hardiment** [-i'mɑ̃] *adv.* boldly; daringly.
hareng [*a'rɑ̃] *n.m.* herring: © *faux* ~, alewife; ~ *saur,* red herring; ~ *fumé,* kipper.
hargneu|x, -se [*ar'ɲø(:z)] *adj.* [chien] snarling; [person] peevish; cantankerous.
haricot [*ari'ko] *n.m.* bean [× often called FÈVE in Canada]: *haricots verts,* French, string/beans; © *haricots en biais,* French beans; *haricots au four,* baked beans.
harmonica [armoni'ka] *n.m.* harmonica, mouth-organ.
harmonie [armɔ'n|i] *n.f.* harmony, concord; [Mus.] band. ‖ **harmonieusement** [-jøz'mɑ̃] *adv.* harmoniously. ‖ **harmonieu|x, -se,** [-jø(:z)] *adj.* harmonious, musical: [Fig.] *de formes harmonieuses,* well-matched, well-proportioned. ‖ **harmonique** [-ik] *n.m.* harmonics, overtones.
harnachement [*arnaʃ'mɑ̃] *n.m.* harness; [Fam.] equipment.
harnacher [*arnaʃ|e] #3 *v. tr.* to harness (a horse), [Fig.] to rig out (a person). ‖ **harnais** [*ar'nɛ] *n.m.* harness.
harpe [*ar|p] *n.f.* harp. ‖ **harpiste** *n.m.f.* ['pist] harpist; †harper.
harpon [*ar'põ] *n.m.* harpoon.
hasard [*a'z|a:r] *n.m.* chance: *au* ~, at random, by guess; *par* ~, by chance, by accident; *un heureux* ~, a happy coincidence, a lucky chance; *les hasards de la guerre,* fortune of war. ‖ **hasarder** [-ar'de] #3 *v. tr.* to risk, to venture. ‖ **se hasarder** *v. pron.* to venture, to take the risk (of, *à*). ‖ **hasardeu|x, -se** [-ar'dø(:z)] *adj.* risky, uncertain.
hâte [*a:t] *n.f.* haste; hurry: *faire qqch. à la* ~, to do sth./hastily, in a hurry, hurriedly/; *en toute* ~, with all possible speed; *avoir hâte de,* → to be eager to. ‖ **hâter** [*ɑ'te] #3 *v. tr.* to hasten, to hurry; to expedite. ‖ **se hâter** *v. pron.* to make haste, to hurry: *Il se hâta d'en sortir,* → He hurried out; *Hâtez-vous* (= *Dépêchez-vous!*) Hurry up! ‖ **hâti|f, -ve** [*ɑ't|if, -i:v] *adj.* hurried; early. ‖ **hâtivement** [-iv'mɑ̃] *adv.* hastily, hurriedly.
hausse [*o:s] *n.f.* rise (in prices) [© and US. of wage or salary, *raise*]; upward trend; [Mil.] back-sight (of a gun), range: *la* ~ *des prix,* → higher prices; *en* ~, rising. ‖ **haussement** [*os'mɑ̃] *n.m.* [d'épaules] shrug. ‖ **hausser** [*o'se] #3 *v. tr.* to raise, to shrug (one's shoulders). ‖ **se hausser,** *v. pron.* to raise oneself: ~ *sur la pointe des pieds,* to stand on tiptoe.
haut, -e [*o(:t)] *adj.* high, tall, upper: *une haute fenêtre,* a tall window; *la haute mer,* the high seas; *La marée est haute,* The tide is in; *le* ~ *bout de la table,* the head of the table; *la Chambre haute,* the Upper House; *le Haut-Canada,* Upper Canada; *la haute bourgeoisie,* the upper middle class (mais *grand bourgeois*); *la haute,* the upper crust; *la haute couture,* fashion, dressmaking (mais *grand couturier*); *la main haute,* with uplifted hand; *la tête haute,* holding up one's head; ~ *en couleur,* high-coloured, with a florid complexion; *parler* ~, to speak out; *gagner* ~ *la main,* to win hands down; *le prendre de* ~, to assume a lofty tone; *plus* ~ [in book], above; *en* ~, at the top, upstairs. ‖ **haut** *n.m.* the top; *tomber de son* ~, to be

dumbfounded. || **hautain, -e** [*o'tǀɛ̃, -ɛn] *adj.* haughty.

hautbois [*o'bwɑ] *n.m.* [Mus.] oboe; oboe-player (also *un hautboïste*). || **haut(s)-fourneau(x)** [*ofur'no] *n.m.(pl.)* blast-furnace. || **haut-parleur(s)** [*opar'lœːr] *n.m.(pl.)* loud-speaker.

hauteur [*o'tœːr] *n.f.* **1.** height, altitude (of ground, land); hill, higher ground, point of vantage: *Quelle est la ~ de ce mur?* How high is this wall?; *les hauteurs entourant la ville,* the hills around the city; *l'avion prend de la ~,* the plane climbs; *à la ~ de,* at the height of, level with: *Comme ils arrivaient à sa ~,* As they drew level with him; *à la ~ de Terre-Neuve,* off Newfoundland; [Fig.] *se montrer à la ~ /des circonstances, de la situation/,* to be/equal to the task, up to par/; *ne pas être à la ~ du sujet,* to be out of one's depth. **2.** haughtiness, arrogance: *regarder qqun de toute sa ~,* to look down on s.o.; *parler avec ~,* to speak loftily, in a lordly manner. **3.** *hauteur musicale,* pitch.

haute-ville [*ot'vil] *n.f.* © Upper town: [*à Québec*] Upper Quebec.

hauturiǀer, -ère [*oty'rjǀe, -ɛːr] *adj.*: *navigation hauturière,* deep-sea shipping.

Havane (La), [(la) *a'van] *n.f.* Havana. || *n.m. un havane,* a Havana cigar.

hâve [*ɑːv] *adj.* haggard, gaunt.

†**havre** [*ɑːvr] *n.m.* harbour; [Fig.] haven. [Often used in place names, cf. HAVRE SAINT-PIERRE, HAVRE DE GRÂCE, &c.]; *le Havre,* Havre (France).

Hawaii, Hawaï [awɑǀ'i] *n.fpl.* Hawaii: *les îles ~,* the Hawaiian Islands. || **hawaïen, -ne** [-jɛ̃, -jɛn] *adj.* Hawaiian.

Haye (La) [la'ɛ] *n.f.* The Hague.

hé! hep! [he, hɛp] *interj.* hey, hey you! just a minute!

hebdomadaire [ɛbdɔma'dɛːr] *adj.* weekly. || *n.m.* [Fam.: *hebdo*] weekly (paper, magazine).

hébergement [eberʒəǀ'mɑ̃] *n.m.* quartering, lodging; *centre d' ~,* shelter, centre for displaced persons. || **héberger** [-ǀe] #5 *v. tr.* to lodge, put up; to house.

hébété [ebe'te] *adj.* dazed, stupefied. || **hébéter** [ebe'te] #10 *v. tr.* to stupefy, to daze. || **hébétude** [ebe'tyd] *n.f.* stupefaction, stupidity, idiocy.

hébraïque [ebrǀa'ik] *adj.* Hebrew: *la langue ~,* (the) Hebrew (language). || **hébreu,** *pl.* **-x** [-'ø] *n.m.* **1.** a Hebrew; [usual. pl.] *les Hébreux,* the Hebrews, the Jews. [→ *In the fem. use* JUIVE.] **2.** [langue] Hebrew: *La langue de l'état d'Israël est l'hébreu,* Hebrew is the (official) language of Israel. **3.** *adj.* Hebrew, Jewish. *Le peuple ~,* the Jews, the Jewish people.

Hébrides (les) [(lez) e'brid] *n.fpl.* the Hebrides; *les Nouvelles- ~* : the New Hebrides.

hectare [ɛk'taːr] *n.m.* [abbr. **ha.**] hectare. || **hecto-** [ɛktɔ-] [a Greek prefix meaning a hundred]: || **hectogramme** [abbr. **hecto**] *n.m.* hectogram. || **hectolitre** *n.m.* [abbr. **hl.**] hectolitre. || **hectomètre** *n.m.* [abbr. **hm.**] hectometre.

hein [*ɛ̃] *int. exclam.* What! [L'intonation varie suivant qu'on demande ou qu'on exprime l'incrédulité.]; No! || *interrog.* What? Isn't it?: *On y va, ~ ?* We are going, aren't we?

hélas! [e'lɑːs] *int.* [rather literary in France, more common in French Canada] †alas; sad to say.

Hélène [e'lɛːn] *n.f.* = Helen.

héler [*e'le] #10 *v. tr.* to hail (a taxi, s.o.).

hélice [e'lis] *n.f.* [navire] screw, propeller, [avion] propeller: *navire à deux ~,* twin-screw vessel.

hélicoptère [eliǀkɔp'tɛːr] *n.m.* helicopter. || **héligare** [-'gaːr] *n.f.* helicopter terminal. || **héliport** [-'pɔːr] *n.m.* helicopter landing station, heliport.

hellène [e'lɛːn] *adj.* Hellenic. || *n.m/f* Hellene: *les Hellènes,* the Greeks. || **hellénique** [ɛle'nik] *adj.* Greek, Hellenic; Hellenistic. || **helléniste** *n.m/f* Hellenist.

helvète [ɛl'vǀɛt] *adj. & n.* Swiss; Helvetian [☞ the usual term is SUISSE]. || **helvétique** [-e'tik] *adj.* Swiss: *la Confédération ~,* the Swiss Confederation.

hémi + [emi-] [Greek prefix meaning half]: **hémisphère** [emi'sfɛːr] *n.m.* hemisphere.

hémorragie [emɔra'ʒi] *n.f.* h(a)emorrhage.

hennir [*a'niːr, ©*ɛ'nǀiːr] #17 *v. intr.* to neigh, to whinny. || **hennissement** [-is'mɑ̃] *n.m.* neighing, whinnying (of horses, &c.).

Henri, Henry [*ɑ̃'ri] *n.m.* = Henry. || **Henriette** [*ɑ̃'rjɛt] *n.f.* = Henrietta.

héraut [*e'ro] *n.m.* herald [× Do not confuse with HÉROS].

herbage [ɛr'bǀaːʒ] *n.m.* pasture, grazing-, land. || **herbe** [ɛrb] *n.f.* grass [cf. GAZON] weed, herb: © *~ à la puce,* poison ivy; *mauvaises herbes,* weeds; *fines herbes,* seasoning herbs. || **herbeux** ou **herbu, -e** [ɛr'bǀø, -y] *adj.* grassy. || **herboriste** [-ɔ'rist] *n.m.* herbalist.

héréditaire [erediǀ'tɛːr] *adj.* hereditary. || **hérédité** [-'te] *n.f.* heredity.

hérésie [ere'zi] *n.f.* heresy. || **hérétique** ere'tik] *adj.* heretical. *n. m/f.* heretic.

(se) hérisser [eri'sǀe] ♯3 *v. tr.* to bristle up; [cheveux] to stand on end; [Fig.] to bristle with, to be covered with. ǁ **hérisson** [-õ] *n.m.* hedgehog. ǁ *adj.* © [Fig.] touchy.

héritage [eri'tǀa:ʒ] *n.m.* **1.** inheritance: *faire un* ~ , to inherit, come into some property. **2.** [Fig.] heritage. ǁ **hériter** (de) [-e] ♯3 *v. tr.* to inherit: *hériter/(d')une propriété, (d')une somme d'argent/*, to inherit/ a piece of property, a sum of money/. ǁ **héritiǀer, -ère** [-je, -jɛ:r] *n.* heir, heiress.

hermine [ɛr'min] *n.* ermine; stoat. cf. BELETTE.

hernie [*ɛr'ni] *n.f.* hernia, rupture.

héroïne [erɔ'in] cf. HÉROS; heroine. ǁ **héroïque** [erɔ'ik] *adj. m/f.* heroic(al), brave. ǁ **héroïquement** [-'mɑ̃] *adv.* like a hero, heroically. ǁ **héroïsme** [-'ism] *n.m.* heroism.

héron [*e'rõ] *n.m.* heron.

héros [*e'ro] *n.m/f.* [HÉROÏNE] hero; heroine [× Do not confuse with HÉRAUT] *agir en* ~ , to behave heroically.

herse [*ɛrs] *n.f.* harrow. ǁ **herser** [-e] ♯3 *v. tr.* to harrow.

hésitant, -e [ezi'tǀɑ̃(:t)] *adj.* hesitating, undecided: *d'une voix hésitante*, in a faltering voice. ǁ **hésitation** [-a'sjõ] *n.f.* hesitation; uncertainty: *sans* ~ , unhesitatingly. ǁ **hésiter** [-e] ♯3 *v. intr.* to hesitate; to waver, to falter: *ne pas hésiter à . . .* , → to feel free to . . . .

hétéroclite [eterɔ'klit] *adj.* odd, unusual: *assemblage* ~ , conglomeration.

hêtre [*ɛ:tr] *n.m.* beech (-tree).

heure [œ:r] *n.f.* hour, o'clock; time, moment. **1.** time: *à l'* ~ , 1. on time, 2. per hour (of speed); *à l'* ~ *actuelle*, at this time, at the present time; *à quelle* ~ , at what time; *de bonne* ~ , early; *à la bonne* ~ *!*, fine! good (for you, &c.)! (Fr.) ~ *d'été* © ~ *avancée*, daylight saving time; ~ *normale*, standard time; ~ *avancée de l'Est*, Eastern Daylight Saving Time; ~ *de l'Atlantique*, Atlantic Time; ~ *des Prairies*, Central Time; ~ *des Montagnes*, Mountain Time; ~ *du Pacifique*, Pacific Time. **2.** time, hour, o'clock: *Quelle* ~ *est-il?*, What time is it?; *Il est une* ~ , It is one o'clock; *Il est une* ~ *dix*, It is ten past (after) one; *Il est une* ~ */et quart, un quart/*, It is/a quarter past one, one fifteen/; *Il est une* ~ *et demie*, It is half past one; *Il est une* ~ *trente*, It is one thirty; *Il est deux heures moins vingt*, It is twenty to two; *Il est deux heures moins le quart*, It is a quarter to two; *Il est six heures au plus*, It is six (o'clock) at the latest; *Il est six heures précises*, it is exactly six; *Il est six heures passées*, it is past six; *Avez-vous l'* ~ *exacte?*, Do you have the correct time? *Cinq heures vont sonner*, It is about to strike five; *Cinq heures viennent de sonner*, It's just/gone, struck/five; *à l'* ~ */fixée, convenue*, at the appointed time; *fixer une* ~ , to set a time; *à une* ~ */avancée, tardive/*, at a late hour; *à une* ~ *indue*, at an unusually late hour; *à une* ~ *convenable*, at a reasonable hour; *toutes les heures*, every hour, hourly; *jusqu'à une* ~ *avancée de la nuit*, until the small hours of the morning. **3.** [Loc.] *de bonne* ~ , early; *tout à l'* ~ , (1) presently, (2) a while back; *À tout à l'* ~ , See you later.

heureusement [œrøz'mɑ̃] *adv.* luckily, fortunately, happily: ~ *que vous étiez là*, → It's a good thing you were there! ~ *!* → I should hope so! I should hope not! [d'après le contexte].

heureuǀx, -se [œ'rǀø, -ø:z] *adj.* happy, pleased; lucky, fortunate: *Je suis (très) heureux de . . .* , it gives me (great) pleasure to . . . , I am glad to . . . ; *Il est* ~ *que* [+ subj.], it is fortunate that. . . .

heurt [*œ:r] *n.m.* [sudden noise made by sth. knocking against sth. else] blow, [sur du bois] knock, [sur du métal] clang, [sourd] thump, [mat] thud; [loc.] *sans heurts*, smoothly. ǁ **heurter** [œr'te] ♯3 *v. tr.* **1.** to bump against, to run against, to knock against. **2.** [Fig.] antagonize. ǁ **se heurter** *v. pron.* to bump into, to collide with/each other, one another; ~ *à un obstacle*, to come up against/a difficulty, an obstacle/, to hit a snag.

hiberner [ibɛr'ne] ♯3 *v. intr.* to hibernate.

hibou, *pl.* **-x** [*i'bu] *n.m.* owl.

hic! [*ik] *n.m.*: *Voilà le* ~ *!*, There's the rub!

hideuǀx, -se [*i'dǀø, -ø:z] *adj.* hideous.

hier [i'jɛ:r] *adv.* yesterday; †of yore: *avant-* ~ , (the) day before yesterday; ~ *matin*, yesterday morning; ~ *soir*, last evening, last night.

hiérarchie [jerar'ʃi] *n.f.* hierarchy.

hilarant, -e [ila'rɑ̃] *adj.* mirth-provoking. ǁ **hilare** [i'la:r] *adj.* hilarious. ǁ **hilarité** [-i'te] *n.f.* hilarity, laughter.

hindou [ɛ̃'du] *adj. & n.* Hindoo.

hippique [i(p)'pǀik] *adj.*: *concours m* ~ , horse-show. ǁ **hippodrome** [-ɔ'dro:m] *n.m.* race-track (for horses); circus. ǁ **hippomobile** [-ɔmɔ'bil] *adj. m/f*: *véhicule* ~ horsedrawn vehicle.

hippopotame [-ɔpɔ'tam] *n.m.* hippopotamus; [Fam.] hippo.

hirondelle [irõ'dɛl] *n.f.* swallow.

hirsute [ir'syt] *adj.* hirsute, shaggy; unkempt.

hisser [*i'se] #3 *v. tr.* to hoist, raise, lift, pull up: ~ *un drapeau,* to hoist a flag. || **se hisser** *v. pron.* to pull o.s. up, in, into, &c.

histoire [is't|wa:r] *n.f.* **1.** story, tale: *l'* ~ *du Petit Chaperon rouge,* the story of Little Red Riding Hood. **2.** history: *l'* ~ *du Canada,* Canadian history. **3.** fabrication: *raconter des histoires,* to tell a song and dance; *une* ~ *à dormir debout,* a shaggy dog story; *faire des histoires,* to make no end of a fuss. || **historien** [-ɔ'rjɛ̃] *n.m.* historian; history teacher. || **historique** [-ɔ'rik] *adj.* **1.** historical: *un roman* ~, a historical novel. **2.** historic: *un événement* ~ , an historic event. || *n.m. faire l'* ~ *d'une affaire,* to retrace the development of a case.

hiver [i'v|ɛ:r] *n.m.* winter: *en* ~ , in winter; *les mois d'* ~ , the winter months. || **hiverner** [-ɛr'ne] #3 *v. intr.* **1.** to winter, to take up winter quarters. **2.** [animaux] to hibernate.

hochement [ɔʃ|'mɑ̃] *n.m.* shaking. || **hocher** [-e] #3 *v. tr.*, to shake: ~ *la tête,* to shake one's head [doubtfully rather than negatively]. || **hochet** [*ɔ'ʃɛ] *n.m.* rattle, toy.

hockey [*ɔ'ke] *n.m.* [Sport] hockey; © *partie f de* ~ , hockey game; ~ *sur glace,* ice hockey; © *joueur m de* ~ , hockey player.

holà [*ɔ'la] *interj.* [when calling s.o.'s attention] Hey! Say! Ahoy! [when hailing a ship] [× Do not confuse with OH!]; [Fig.] *mettre le holà,* to put a stop (to, *à*).

hollandais, -e [*ɔllɑ̃d|ɛ, -ɛ:z] *adj.* Dutch. || *n.* Dutchman, Dutchwoman. || **Hollande (la)** [(la) *ɔl'lɑ̃:d] [Official name is PAYS-BAS in Fr.] Holland; the Netherlands.

homard [*ɔ'ma:r] *n.m.* lobster.

homicide [ɔmi'sid] *adj.* murderous, homicidal. || *n.m.* ~ *volontaire* [wilful] murder; ~/*involontaire, par imprudence,* manslaughter.

hommage [ɔ'ma:ʒ] *n.m.* homage, tribute, compliment(s), respects: *faire* ~ *de qqch. à qqun,* to present s.o. with sth. (as a token of respect); *rendre* ~ *à qqun,* to pay tribute to; ~ *de l'auteur,* compliments of the author; *présenter ses* ~ *à qqun,* to pay o.'s respects to s.o.

homme [ɔm] *n.m.* **1.** man [as opposed to woman, FEMME], *pl.* men: ~ *de bien,* good man; ~ *de cœur,* kind man; ~ *d'affaires,* businessman; ~ *politique,* statesman, politician; ~ *de lettres,* writer, author; ~ *d'église,* cleric, churchman; ~ *de peine,* labourer, odd-job man; ~ *de paille,* figurehead; ~ *du monde,* gentleman, ~ *comme il faut,* respectable man. cf. MONSIEUR, MESSIEURS. **2.** man [as a genus]: *L'* ~ *est mortel,* Man is mortal; *le musée de l'* ~ , the Museum of Natural History; *les sciences de l'* ~ , social sciences; *les droits de l'* ~ , human rights. (*La déclaration des*) *droits de l'* ~ , (the bill of) human rights.

homogène [ɔmɔ'ʒɛ:n] *adj.* homogeneous. || **homogénéité** [ɔmɔʒenei'te] *n.f.* homogeneity.

homonyme [ɔmɔ'nim] *adj.* homonymous. || *n.m.* **1.** homonym. **2.** namesake.

homosexuel, -le [ɔmosɛk'sɥɛl] *adj. & n.* homosexual.

Honduras (le) [(lə) *õdy'ras] *n.m.* [Géog.] Honduras: *le* ~ *britannique,* British Honduras.

Hongrie, la [*õ'gr|i] *n.f.* Hungary. || **hongrois, -e** [-wa, -wa:z] **1.** *adj.* Hungarian; **2.** *n.* (the) Hungarian (language).

honnête [ɔ'n|ɛ:t] *adj.* honest; straightforward; ☞ *C'est un* ~ *homme,* He is a gentleman; *C'est un homme* ~ , He is an/honest, upright/man; *C'est une* ~ *femme,* She is a respectable woman. || **honnêtement** [-ɛt'mɑ̃] *adv.* honestly; decently. || **honnêteté** [-ɛt'te] *n.f.* honesty.

honneur [ɔ'n|œ:r] *n.m.* **1.** honour: *en l'* ~ *de,* in honour of; *J'ai l'* ~ *de,* I beg to; *Faites-moi l'* ~ *de,* Allow me to; *demoiselle d'* ~ , bridesmaid; *faire* ~ *à,* to do honour to; *faire les honneurs,* to do the honours; *rendre les* ~ , to present arms; *rendre les derniers honneurs à,* to pay the last honours to; *mort au champ d'* ~ , killed in action. **2.** credit: *Il vous fait* ~ . He does you credit; *faire* ~ *à ses échéances,* to meet one's bills. || **honorabilité** [-ɔrabili'te] *n.f.* respectability, good name. || **honorable** [-ɔ'rabl] *adj.* honourable, respectable. || **honorablement** [-ɔrablə'mɑ̃] *adv.* honourably: ~ *connu,* enjoying a good reputation, in good standing; *Il s'en est tiré* ~ , He did creditably. || **honoraire** [-ɔ'rɛ:r] *adj.* honorary: *professeur* ~ , professor emeritus. || *n.m.pl.* honorarium, fee(s); [avocat] retainer. || **honorer** [-ɔ're] #3 *v. tr.* to honour s.o.; to do honour. cf. HONNEUR. || **s'honorer (de),** *v. pron.* to pride oneself (on having done sth.). || **honorifique** [-ɔri'fik] *adj.* honorific: *distinction* ~ , award; distinction.

honte [*õ:t] *n.f.* **1.** shame; disgrace,

infamy; *sans* ~, unashamedly: *avoir* ~ *de*, to be ashamed (of); *faire* ~ *à qqun*, to put s.o. to shame, to make s.o. ashamed, to disgrace; *C'est une honte!*, It's a shame, a disgrace; It's scandalous. **2.** *fausse honte*, bashfulness, self-consciousness. || **honteu|x, -se** [*ɔ̃t|ø, -ø:z] *adj.* **1.** [personne] ashamed (of, *de*). **2.** [action] shameful, disgraceful.

hôpita|l, -ux [ɔpi'tal] *n.m.* hospital: *aller à l'* ~, to go to the hospital; to be hospitalized.

hoquet [*ɔ'kɛ] *n.m.* hiccup: *avoir le* ~, to have the hiccups.

horaire [ɔ'rɛ:r] *adj.* hourly: *tarif* ~, hourly rate. || *n.m.* time-table, schedule.

horizon [ɔri'zõ] *n.m.* horizon: *à l'* ~, on the horizon. || **horizontal** [-tal] *adj.* horizontal. || **horizontalement** [-tal'mɑ̃] *adv.* horizontally.

horloge [ɔr'lɔ:ʒ] *n.f.* clock (esp. town or church clock): *L'* ~ *marque deux heures, Il est deux heures à l'* ~, It's two o'clock by the clock; *L'* ~ *sonne deux heures,* The clock strikes two. || **horloger** [-e] *n.m.* watchmaker; clockmaker. || **horlogerie** [-'ri] *n.f.* watchmaker's store or trade: *un mouvement d'* ~, clockwork, movement (of a clock).

hormis [ɔr'mi] *prep.* except, save (for), but for, with the exception of.

horreur [ɔ'r|œ:r] *n.f.* **1.** horror, dread, disgust: *avoir* ~ *de*, to dislike intensely. **2.** dreadful thing, spectacle, ugly person. || **horrible** [-ibl] *adj.* horrible; hideous, atrocious. || **horriblement** [-iblə'mɑ̃] *adv.* horribly, frightfully.

horrifiant, -e [ɔri'fjɑ̃(:t)] *adj.* horrifying. || **horrifier** [ɔri'fje] #3 *v. tr.* to horrify.

hors [ɔ:r] *prep.* **1.** out (of), outside (of): ~ *d'ici!* Get out!; ~ *ligne*, exceptional; ~ *tout*, overall (measurements). **2.** [mostly used in set phrases] past, beyond, save: ~ *d'atteinte*, out of reach; ~ *de combat*, disabled; ~ *de danger*, out of danger; ~ *de doute*, unquestionable; ~ *d'haleine*, out of breath; ~ *de prix*, extravagant; ~ *de saison*, untimely; ~ *de soi*, frantic, beside o.s. || **hors-bord** [-'bɔ:r] *n.m.* outboard (motor-boat). || **hors-concours** [-kõ'ku:r] *n.m.* in a class by himself. || **hors-d'œuvre** [-'dœvr] *n.m. inv.* [*usual. pl.*] hors d'œuvre. || **hors-la-loi** [-la'lwa] *n.m.* outlaw.

horticulture [ɔrtikyl'ty:r] *n.f.* horticulture: *exposition d'* ~, flower show.

hospice [ɔs'pis] *n.m.* hospital, home: ~ *de vieillards*, old people's home.

hospitali|er, -ère [ɔspita'l|je, -'jɛ:r] *adj.* **1.** related to hospitals: *le personnel* ~, hospital personnel. **2.** hospitable. || **hospitaliser** [-i'ze] #3 *v. tr.* to hospitalize; to admit to a home. || **hospitalité** [-i'te] *n.f.* hospitality; welcome.

hostie [ɔs'ti] *n.f.* [Rel.] host, (consecrated) wafer; *la Sainte Hostie*, the Holy Sacrament [cf. ESPÈCES].

hostile [ɔs'til] *adj.* hostile, inimical, unfriendly. [× In the case of *hostile forces*, use ENNEMI.] || **hostilité** [-i'te] *n.f.* hostility, ill-will: *manifester de l'* ~ *contre*, to show hostility towards, (*pl.*) *les hostilités*, act of warfare: *ouvrir, cesser les* ~, to begin, to cease hostilities.

hôt|e[1], -esse [o:t, o'tɛs] *m.* host; M.C. [= Master of Ceremonies]; innkeeper, †landlord.

hôte[2] [o:t] *n.m.* guest, visitor; lodger, inmate: *recevoir ses hôtes sans cérémonie*, to receive one's guests informally. || **hôtel** [o't|ɛl] *n.m.* **1.** hotel: *descendre à l'* ~, to stay at a hotel; *maître d'* ~, head waiter; ~ *meublé*, residential hotel. **2.** ~ *particulier*, town house, mansion: *maître d'* ~, butler; head waiter. **3.** *Hôtel de ville*, town hall, city hall. **4.** *Hôtel des Postes*, General Post Office. || **hôteli|er, -ère** [-ə'lje, -ə'ljɛ:r] **1.** *n.m.f.* hotel manager. **2.** *adj.* → hotel: *l'industrie hôtelière*, the hotel industry. || **hôtesse** [o'tɛs] *n.f.* hostess, landlady: ~ *de l'air*, air hostess, stewardess. cf. HÔTE[1].

houblon [*u'blõ] *n.m.* [Bot.] hop(s).

houe [*u] *n.f.* hoe. || **houer** [*u'e] #3 *v. tr.* to hoe.

houille [*u:j] *n.f.* **1.** coal (as source of energy), cf. CHARBON: *mine de* ~, cf. HOUILLÈRE. **2.** source of energy, e.g. *la* ~ *blanche*, water-power, hydro-electric power; *la* ~ *bleue*, wind-power, tide power. || **houillère** [*u'jɛ:r] *n.f.* coal-mine, colliery, coal pit.

houle [*ul] *n.f.* [Naut.] swell. || **houleu|x, -se** [-ø, -ø:z] *adj.* **1.** rather rough. **2.** [Fig.] turbulent, openly hostile [of meeting].

houppe [*up] *n.f.* tuft (of hair); tassel; powder-puff.

housse [*us] *n.f.* slip-cover; dust-sheet; jacket [of a gun].

houx [*u] *n.m.* holly.

huard [*y'a:r] © *n.m.* loon.

hublot [*y'blo] *n.m.* port-hole.

Hudson [yd'sõ] *n.*: *la baie d'* ~, Hudson Bay; *la Compagnie de la baie d'* ~, Hudson's Bay Company, HBC; *le détroit d'* ~, Hudson Strait; [fleuve des É.-U.] *l'Hudson*, the Hudson.

hue! [hy] *interj.* (to horse) giddy up! gee up!

huée(s) [*y'e] *n.f. usual. pl.* boos, booing. || **huer** [*y'e] #3 *v. intr.* to boo, to hiss. || *v. tr.* to boo s.o.

huile [ɥil] *n.f.* **1.** oil: *sardines à l' ~*, sardines in oil; *~ d'olives,* olive oil; *~ de ricin,* castor oil; *~ à salade,* salad oil; *à l' ~ et au vinaigre,* with French dressing. **2.** © *~ de charbon,* coal-oil; *~ de chauffage,* fuel/heating, oil; © *fournaise f à l' ~*, oil furnace. [Tech.] *~ lourde,* diesel fuel; *~ à moteur,* motor oil; *~ de freins,* brake fluid; *~ de graissage,/* lubricating, machine/oil. [Loc.] *une ~*, a big shot; *les huiles,* the VIP's. || **huiler** [-e] #3 *v. tr.* to oil; to grease. || **huileu|x, -se** [-ø, -ø:z] *adj.* oily. || **huilier** [-je] *n.m.* cruet. [The two bottles or vials which contain French dressing, usually held together in one piece. cf. VINAIGRIER.]

†**huis** [*ɥi] *n.m.* [Loc.] : *à ~ clos,* behind closed doors; in camera. || **huissier** [-'sje] *n.m.* **1.** writ server, bailiff. **2.** court attendant, court crier, court bailiff.

huit [*ɥit] + vowel and silent *h*; [ɥi] before a consonant; [ɥit] finally. *adj.* eight; eighth: *dans ~ jours,* in a week, within a week; *il y a ~ jours,* a week ago; *il y aura ~ jours demain,* it will be a week tomorrow; *tous les ~ jours,* every week, weekly. || *n.m. le ~*, the eighth (of the month); the eight (of clubs, &c.); the 8 (bus, street-car, &c.): *de demain en ~*, a week from tomorrow. || **huitaine** [-'tɛn] *n.f.* about eight: *remis à ~*, postponed for a week. || **huitième** [-'tjɛm] *n.m.* eighth; the eighth. || **huitièmement** [-tjɛm'mɑ̃] *adv.* eight.

huître [ɥitr] *n.f.* oyster: *coquille f d' ~*, oyster shell. © *partie f d'huitres,* oyster party; clam-bake.

hum [hœm] *interj.* hmm, uhmm. **1.** I say! **2.** Well!

humain [y'm|ɛ̃, -ɛn] *adj.* **1.** human, pertaining to man: *le genre ~*, mankind. **2.** humane, kind, considerate. **3.** *n.m.pl. les humains,* men, mankind, the human race, cf. HUMANITÉ below. || **humainement** [-ɛn'mɑ̃] *adv.* humanly; humanely: *tout ce qu'il est ~ possible de faire,* all that it is humanly possible to do. || **s'humaniser** [-ani'ze] #3 *v. pron.* to become/civilized, more human/; [Fig.] to unbend. || **humaniste** [-a'nist] **1.** *adj.* humanistic. **2.** *n.m.* a humanist, a classical scholar. || **humanitaire** [-ani'tɛ:r] *adj.* humanitarian. || **humanité** [-ani'te] *n.f.* **1.** humanity, humaneness: *avec ~*, humanly, in a humane manner. **2.** mankind. **3.** *n.f.pl.* the humanities: *faire ses ~*, to receive a classical education.

humble [œ̃:bl] *adj.* humble; meek, modest: *les humbles,* the lowly. || **humblement** [-ə'mɑ̃] *adv.* humbly; meekly. cf. HUMILITÉ.

humecter [ymɛk'te] #3 *v. tr.* to sprinkle, to moisten, to dampen: *~ le linge,* to sprinkle linen (before ironing).

humeur [y'mœ:r] *n.f.* [× HUMOUR] **1.** humour, mood: *être/de bonne, de mauvaise/ ~*, to be in a/good, bad/mood. **2.** temper, disposition: *avoir l' ~ triste,* to have an unhappy disposition. **3.** humour: *les quatre ~*, the cardinal humours.

humide [-y'mid] *adj.* damp [humide et froid], humid [humide et chaud], dank [humide et malsain], moist [humide et tiède]. || **humidité** [-i'te] *n.f.* dampness, humidity, moisture.

humiliant, -e [ɥmi'l|jɑ̃, -jɑ̃:t] *adj.* humiliating. || **humiliation** [-ja'sjɔ̃] *n.f.* humiliation. || **humilier** [-je] #3 *v. tr.* to humiliate s.o., to abuse s.o. || **s'humilier** *v. pron.* to humble o.s.: *~ devant qqun,* to grovel, to eat/crow, humble pie/. **humilité** [-i'te] *n.f.* humility, meekness, humbleness, cf. HUMBLE.

humoriste [ym|ɔ'rist] *n.m.* humorist, humorous writer. || **humoristique** [-ɔris'tik] *adj.* humoristic; witty. || **humour** [-u:r] *n.m.* humour; wit. [Do not confuse with HUMEUR]: *avoir le sens de l' ~*, to have a sense of humour.

hurlement [*ɥrl|ə'mɑ̃] *n.m.* howling, howl; yell, shriek; scream: *pousser un ~*, to howl, yell, shriek, scream. || **hurler** [-e] #3 *v. intr.* to howl (wolves, &c.), to yell, to shriek: *~ de frayeur,* to scream with terror.

Huron, -ne [*y'r|ɔ̃, -ɔn] *adj. & n.* Huron; a Huron [Indian tribe]: *le lac ~*, Huron Lake. || **Huronie** [-ɔ'ni] © *n.f.* Huron country.

hussard [*ɥ'sa:r] *n.m.* hussar.

hutte [*ɥt] *n.f.* hut, cabin.

hybride [i'brid] *adj. & n.m.* hybrid.

hydraulique [idrɔ'lik] *adj.* hydraulic.

hydravion [idra'vjɔ̃] *n.m.* sea plane; *~ à coque,* flying boat.

hydrogène [idrɔ'ʒɛ:n] *n.m.* hydrogen.

hygiène [i'ʒj|ɛ:n] *n.f.* hygiène: *~ mentale,* mental/health, hygiene/. || **hygiénique** [-e'nik] *adj.* hygienic, healthy: *papier ~*, toilet paper.

hymne [imn] **1.** *n.m.* anthem: *l' ~ national,* the national anthem. **2.** *n.f.* hymn.

hypnose [ip'no:z] *n.f.* hypnosis. || **hyp-**

notique [ipnɔtik] *adj.* hypnotic. || **hypnotiser** [ipnɔti'ze] #3 *v. tr.* to hypnotize.
hypocrisie [ipɔkr|i'zi] *n.f.* hypocrisy. || **hypocrite** [-it] *adj.* hypocritical; *n.m.* hypocrite. || **hypocritement** [-it'mã] *adv.* hypocritically.
hypodermique [ipɔdɛrmik] *adj.* hypodermic, hypodermal: *injection* ~, hypodermic injection shot.
hypothécaire [ipɔte'kɛ:r] *adj.* on mortgage. || **hypothèque** [ipɔ't|ɛk] *n.f.* mortgage. || **hypothéquer** [-e'ke] #10 *v. tr.* to mortgage (a house, &c.).
hypothèse [ipɔt|ɛ:z] *n.f.* hypothesis; supposition: *émettre une* ~, to put forward a theory. || **hypothétique** [-e'tik] *adj.* hypothetical; improbable.
hystérie [iste'ri] *n.f.* hysteria.

I

I, i [i] *n.m.* the letter I, i: *Mettre les points sur les i,* To cross one's t's, and dot one's i's.
ibid. cf. IBIDEM.
ibidem [ibi'dɛm] *adv.* ibidem.
ibis [i'bis] *n.m.* ibis.
Iceberg [iz'bɛrg] *n.m.* iceberg.
ici [i'si] *adv.* **1.** here (ou selon le contexte: up here, down here, over here, back here, in here, out here); [au téléphone] *Ici Jean,* This is John; [radio] *Ici Montréal,* This is Montreal (calling); *par ici,* through here, this way; *par ici la sortie,* this way out; *ici-bas,* in this world. **2.** now [in phrases such as: *jusqu'ici,* up to now; *d'ici demain,* before tomorrow: *d'ici peu,* before long; *d'ici là,* in the meantime].
iconoclaste [ikɔnɔ'klast] *n.m/f.* iconoclast. || *adj.* iconoclastic.
Idaho (l') [aida'o] *n.m.* Idaho.
idéal, -e [ide'al] *pl.* **idéals, idéaux** [ide'al, ide'o] *adj.* **1.** [imaginaire] imaginary. **2.** [parfait] ideal. || *n.m.* [*pl.* idéals, idéaux] ideal. || **idéaliser** [-i'ze] #3 *v. tr.* to idealize. || **idéaliste** [-ist] *adj.* idealistic *n.* idealist.
idée [i'de] *n.f.* idea, notion, thought: *se faire des idées,* to imagine things; ~ *fixe,* obsession.
idem [i'dɛm] *adv.* idem, ditto.
identification [idãti|fika'sjõ] *n.f.* identification; identifying. || **identifier** [-'fje] #3 *v. tr.* to identify. || **s'identifier** *v. pr.* to/be, become/identified.
identique [idã'ti|k] *adj.* identical. || **identité** [-'te] *n.f.* identity; *carte f d'* ~, identity card; *papiers d'* ~, identification.
idéologie [ideɔlɔ'ʒi] *n.f.* ideology.
idiomatique [idjoma'tik] *adj.* idiomatic.
idiosyncrasie [idjosɛ̃kra'zi] *n.f.* idiosyncrasy.
idiot, -e [i'dj|o, -ɔt] *adj.* idiotic, stupid. || *n.* idiot, numskull.
idiotisme [idjɔ'tism] *n.m.* idiom, idiomatic expression.
idolâtre [idɔ'lɑ:tr] *n.m.* idolater, *f.* idolatress. || *adj.* idolatrous.
idole [i'dɔl] *n.f.* idol.
idylle [i'dil] *n.f.* idyll.
if [if] *n.m.* [Bot.] yew(-tree): ~ *du Canada,* ground hemlock, dwarf yew.
igloo, iglou [i'glu] *n.m.* © igloo.
ignifuge [iɲi'f|y:ʒ] *adj.* non-inflammable. || *n.m.* fireproofing (substance). || **ignifuger** [-y'ʒe] #5 *v. tr.* to fireproof.
ignoble [i'ɲɔbl] *adj.* base, mean, vile; disgraceful.
ignominie [iɲɔmi'ni] *n.f.* ignominy. || **ignominieu|x, -se** [iɲɔmi'njø(:z) *adj.* ignominious.
ignorance [iɲɔ'r|ã:s] *n.f.* ignorance. || **ignorant, -e** [-ã(:t)] *adj.* ignorant. || *n.m.* ignoramus. || **ignorer** [-e] #3 *v. tr.* **1.** [ne pas savoir] not to know: *Je l'ignorais,* I did not know. **2.** [ne pas tenir compte de] to ignore: *Il m'ignore,* He ignores me; [×] cf. TO IGNORE.
il [i(l)] *pl.* **ils** [il] *pron. pers. m.* [used only as subject of verb] **1.** [êtres mâles] he. **2.** [choses] it. **3.** [pl. dans tous les cas] they.
île [il] *n.f.* island, isle: *les îles Britanniques,*

the British Isles; *les ~ Anglo-Normandes,* the Channel Islands; *l'Île du Prince-de-Galles,* Prince of Wales Island; *l'Île du Prince-Édouard,* Prince Edward Island.

illégal, -e [ille'g|al] *adj.* illegal, unlawful. || **illégalement** [-al'mɑ̃] *adv.* illegally. || **illégalité** [-ali'te] *n.f.* illegality, unlawfulness.

illégitime [illeʒi'tim] *adj.* illegitimate, unlawful, unjustified: *enfant ~*, illegitimate child; *conclusion ~*, unjustified, invalid conclusion. || **illégitimité** [-i'te] *n.f.* illegitimacy.

illettré [illɛ'tre] *adj.* illiterate; uneducated.

illicite [illi'sit] *adj.* illicit; foul (blow).

illimité, -e [illimi'te] *adj.* unlimited; [sans borne] boundless; [congé] indefinite.

illisible [illi'zibl] *adj.* [caractères] illegible; [livre] unreadable.

illogique [illɔ'ʒik] *adj.* illogical.

illumination [illymin|a'sjõ] *n.f.* **1.** [éclairage] floodlighting: *aller voir les illuminations,* to go and see the floodlit buildings. **2.** [Fig.] illumination; brain wave. || **illuminé, -e** [-e] *adj.* (all) lit up, brightly lit; [Fig.] illuminated, visionary. || *n.* visionary. || **illuminer** [-e] *v. tr.* to light up, to floodlight. || *v. intr.* to illuminate.

illusion [illy'z|jõ] *n.f.* illusion *f*; [fausse] delusion: *une ~ d'optique,* an optical illusion; *se faire des illusions,* to delude o.s.; *faire ~*, to be deceptive, to have a deceptive appearance. || **illusionner** [-jɔ'ne] #3 *v. tr.* to delude. || **s'illusionner** *v. pron.* to/delude, deceive/o.s. || **illusoire** [-wa:r] *adj.* illusory.

illustrateur [illystra'tœ:r] *n.m.* illustrator (of books, comic strips, &c.). || **illustration** [-'sjõ] *n.f.* [gravure] illustration, picture; [action] illustrating.

illustre [il'lystr] *adj.* famous, renowned, illustrious. || **illustré, -e** [-e] *adj.* illustrated. || *n.m.* [Journ.] magazine. || **illustrer** #3 *v. tr.* **1.** to make illustrious. **2.** to illustrate (with notes, explanations, pictures, &c.).

îlot [i'lo] *n.m.* **1.** islet, small island. **2.** [maisons] block: *chef d' ~*, air-raid warden.

ils [il] cf. IL.

image [i'm|a:ʒ] *n.f.* picture; [miroir] image, reflection; [ressemblance] likeness, resemblance; [Lit.] image, figure (of speech). || **imagé, -e** [-a'ʒe] *adj.* [style] full of images. || **imager** #5 *v. tr.* [style] to adorn with figures of speech.

imaginable [imaʒi'n|abl] *adj.* imaginable. || **imaginaire** [-ɛ:r] *adj.* imaginary, fancied (illness, &c.). || **imaginati|f, -ve** [-a'tif, -a'ti:v] *adj.* imaginative. || **imagination** [-a'sjõ] *n.f.* imagination, fancy. || **imaginer** [-e] #3 *v. tr.* to imagine, to conceive. || **s'imaginer** [simaʒi'ne] *v. pr.* to picture to o.s.; to picture o.s.; to think, to imagine.

imbécile [ɛ̃be'sil] *adj.* foolish. || *n.m.* imbecile, fool, dolt. || **imbécilité** [-i'te] *n.f.* foolishness, stupidity, idiocy.

imberbe [ɛ̃'bɛrb] *adj.* beardless.

imbiber [ɛ̃bi'be] *v. tr.* to soak, to steep.

imbriquer [ɛ̃bri'ke] #3 *v. tr.* [tiles] to overlap.

imbroglio [ɛ̃brɔ'ljo] *n.m.* confusion, mix-up.

imbu, -e [ɛ̃'by] *adj.* imbued (with, *de*), steeped (in, *de*).

imbuvable [ɛ̃by'vabl] *adj.* undrinkable; [Fig. & Fam.] impossible.

imitable [imi'ta|bl] *adj.* imitable. || **imitat|eur, -rice** [-'tœ:r, -'tris] *adj.* imitative. || *n.m.* imitator; [mime] mimic. || **imitation** [-'sjõ] *n.f.* imitation, [action] imitating; copy(ing); *à l' ~ de,* on the same lines as, imitating. || **imité, -e** [imi'te] *adj.* imitated, copied; [marbre, &c.] → imitation. || **imiter** #3 *v. tr.* to imitate; [copier] to copy; [mimer] to mimic, ape.

immaculé, -e [immaky'le] *adj.* immaculate, spotless.

immangeable [ɛ̃mɑ̃'ʒabl] *adj.* uneatable.

immanquable [ɛ̃mɑ̃'kabl] *adj.* infallible. || **immanquablement** [-ə'mɑ̃] *adv.* inevitably.

immatriculation [imatrikyl|a'sjõ] *n.f.* registration; [Schol.] matriculation. || **immatriculer** [-e] #3 *v. tr.* to register; [Schol.] to matriculate.

immédiat, -e [ime'dj|a(t)] *adj.* immediate. || **immédiatement** [-at'mɑ̃] *adj.* immediately.

immense [im'm|ɑ:s] *adj.* immense; huge; vast. || **immensité** [-ɑ̃si'te] *n.f.* immensity, hugeness; vastness.

immergé, -e [imɛr|'ʒe] *adj.* submerged, under water. || **immerger** [-'ʒe] #5 *v. tr.* to immerse, to submerge. || **immersion** [-'sjõ] *n.f.* immersion, plunging.

immeuble [im'mœbl] *n.m.* **1.** [large] house, building: *un ~ de douze étages,* a twelve-story building; *~ de rapport,* apartment house. **2.** [biens-fonds] real estate.

immigrant, -e [imi'gr|ɑ̃(:t)] *adj. & n.* immigrant. || **immigration** [-a'sjõ] *n.f.* immigration. || **immigré, -e** [-e] *adj. & n.* immigrant. || **immigrer** #3 *v. intr.* to immigrate (to, *en*).

imminence [immi'n|ɑ̃:s] *n.f.* imminence. || **imminent, -e** [-ɑ̃(:t)] *adj.* imminent, impending.

immiscer (s') [simi'se] #4 *v. pr.* to interfere with, to meddle with.

immobile [immɔ'bil] *adj.* motionless, still: *se tenir* ~, to stand still. || **immobili|er, -ère** [-je, -jɛːr] *adj.* immovable, → real estate: *biens immobiliers,* real estate; *agence immobilière,* real estate agency. || **immobilisation** [-iza'sjõ] *n.f.* immobilization, tying up. || **immobiliser** [-i'ze] #3 *v. tr.* to immobilize, to tie up. || **immobilité** [-i'te] *n.f.* immobility; stillness.

immodéré, -e [immɔde're] *adj.* unreasonable, exaggerated, immoderate.

immolation [imɔ'l|a'sjõ] *n.f.* immolation. || **immoler** [e] #3 *v. tr.* to immolate.

immonde [im'mõːd] *adj.* foul, filthy; [Rel.] unclean. || **immondices** [imõ'dis] *n.fpl.* filth, refuse, garbage.

immoral, -e [immɔ'ral] *adj.* immoral. || **immoralité** [-i'te] *n.f.* immorality.

immortaliser [immɔrt|ali'ze] #3 *v. tr.* to immortalize. || **s'immortaliser** *v. pron.* to win immortality (for o.s.). || **immortalité** [immɔrt|ali'te] *n.f.* immortality. || **immortel, -le** [-ɛl] *adj.* immortal; [Fig.] everlasting. || *n.* immortal.

immuable [im'mɥabl] *adj.* immutable; unchangeable.

immunisé, -e [immyni|'ze] *adj.* [contre une maladie] immunized; [Fig.] immune (to, *contre*). || **immuniser** #3 *v. tr.* [Méd.] to immunize; [Fig.] to make immune. || **immunité** [-'te] *n.f.* immunity (from, *à l'égard de*).

impair, -e [ɛ̃'pɛːr] *adj.* odd: *Trois est un nombre* ~, Three is an odd number. || *n.m.* [Fam.] blunder.

impardonnable [ɛ̃pardɔ'nabl] *adj.* unpardonable, unforgivable.

imparfait, -e [ɛ̃par'fɛ(t)] *adj.* imperfect, defective. || *n.m.* [Gram.] imperfect (tense).

impartial, -e [ɛ̃par'sj|al] *adj.* impartial.

impassable [ɛ̃pɑ'sabl] *adj.* impassable.

impasse [ɛ̃'pɑːs] *n.f.* dead-end street, blind alley; [jeu de cartes] finesse; [Fig.] impasse, deadlock.

impassible [ɛpa'sibl] *adj.* impassive.

impatience [ɛ̃pa'sj|ɑ̃ːs] *n.f.* impatience; eagerness. || **impatient, -e** [-ɑ̃(ːt)] *adj.* impatient, eager: ~ *d'arriver,* eager to get there; ~ *de toute contrainte,* rejecting any kind of restraint. || **impatienter** [ɑ̃'te] #3 *v. tr.* to irritate, to make impatient. || **s'impatienter** *v. pr.* to get impatient.

impayable [ɛ̃pɛ'jabl] *adj.* **1.** invaluable. **2.** priceless, inimitable; very funny: *Il est* ~ (*dans ce rôle*), He is priceless (in that role).

impeccable [ɛ̃pɛ'kabl] *adj.* faultless, impeccable. || **impeccablement** [-ə'mɑ̃] *adv.* faultlessly, impeccably.

impénétrable [ɛ̃pene'trabl] *adj.* impenetrable; [au liquide] impervious; [mystère, figure, &c.] inscrutable, unfathomable.

impérati|f, -ve [ɛ̃perat|if, -iːv] *adj.* imperative. || *n.m.* [Gram.] imperative (mood).

impératrice [-ris] *n.f.* empress.

imperceptible [ɛ̃pɛrsɛp'tibl] *adj.* imperceptible.

imperfection [ɛ̃pɛrfɛk'sjõ] *n.f.* imperfection.

impérial, -e [ɛ̃pe'rjal] *adj.* imperial. || **impériale** *n.f.* **1.** deck (of bus): *autobus à* ~, double-decker. **2.** game of cards. **3.** Van Dyke beard.

impérialisme [ɛ̃perja'lism] *n.m.* imperialism.

impérieu|x, -se [ɛ̃pe'rjø(ːz)] *adj.* imperious; [caractère, &c.] domineering; urgent, pressing (need).

impérissable [ɛ̃peri'sabl] *adj.* imperishable, undying.

imperméabiliser [ɛ̃pɛrmeab|ili'ze] #3 *v. tr.* to waterproof. || **imperméable** [-l] *adj.* impermeable; [Fig.] impervious (*à*, to); waterproof. || *n.m.* raincoat.

impersonnel, -le [ɛ̃pɛrsɔ'nɛl] *adj.* impersonal.

impertinence [ɛ̃pɛrti'n|ɑ̃ːs] *n.f.* impertinence; [Fam.] nerve, cheek. || **impertinent, -e** [-ɑ̃(ːt)] *adj.* impertinent; [Fam.] cheeky, nervy.

imperturbable [ɛ̃pɛrtyr'babl] *adj.* imperturbable; unruffled.

impétrant, -e [ɛ̃pe'trɑ̃(ːt)] *adj. & n.* holder (of diploma); [Schol.] graduand.

impétueu|x, -se [ɛ̃pe'tɥ|ø(ːz)] *adj.* impetuous, rash. || **impétuosité** [-ozi'te] *n.f.* impetuosity, rashness.

impie [ɛ̃'p|i] *adj.* impious, ungodly. || **impiété** [-je'te] *n.f.* ungodliness, impiety.

impitoyable [ɛ̃pitwa'jabl] *adj.* pitiless, merciless, relentless.

implacable [ɛ̃pla'kabl] *adj.* implacable; relentless.

implanter [ɛ̃plɑ̃'te] #3 *v. tr.* to implant, to plant; [Méd., Fig.] to implant. || **s'implanter** *v. pron.* to take root; [Fig.] ~ *chez qqun,* to thrust o.s. on s.o.

implicite [ɛ̃pli'sit] *adj.* implicit.

impliquer [ɛ̃pli'ke] #3 *v. tr.* **1.** to implicate. **2.** to imply.

implorer [ɛ̃plɔ're] #3 *v. tr.* to implore, beseech.

impoli [ɛ̃pɔ'li] *adj.* impolite, rude (to, *envers, avec*). || **impolitesse** [-'tɛs] *n.f.* impoliteness, rudeness, discourtesy.

impondérable [ɛ̃põde′rabl] *adj.* imponderable. *n.pl.* imponderables.
importance [ɛpɔr′t|ɑ:s] *n.f.* importance; [numérique] size: *avoir de l'* ~, to matter; *être d'une* ~ *capitale*, to be vital (*pour*, to); *sans grande* ~, not particularly important. || **important, -e** [-ɑ̃(:t)] *adj.* important, of consequence: *faire l'* ~, to be self-important; [Fam.] to act big. || *n.m.*: *l'important*, the main thing.
importat|eur, -rice [ɛ̃pɔrt|a′tœ:r, -a′tris] *adj.* importing. || *n.m.* importer. || **importation** [-a′sjõ] *n.f.* [action] importation; [product] import. || **importer**[1] [-e] #3 *v. tr.* to import.
importer[2] *v. intr.* to be of importance, to matter (to, *à*): *Il importe de le faire*, It is important to do it; *Il importe qu'il le fasse*, It is important that he should do it; *N'importe!* It does not matter, Never mind; *n'importe qui*, anyone; *n'importe quoi*, anything; *n'importe quand*, any time; *n'importe où*, anywhere; *n'importe comment*, anyhow; *Peu importe*, It matters little; *Qu'importe!*, It makes no difference, It does not matter.
importun, -e [ɛ̃pɔrt|œ̃, -yn] *adj.* importunate, bothersome: *Il craint de vous être* ~, He is afraid of bothering you. || **importun** [-œ̃] *n.m.* bore, pest. || **importuner** [-y′ne] #3 *v. tr.* to importune, bother; [plus fort] to pester, harass.
imposable [ɛ̃po′zabl] *adj.* taxable.
imposant, -e [ɛ̃po′zɑ̃(:t)] *adj.* imposing, impressive.
imposé, -e [ɛ̃po′z|e] *adj.* fixed; taxed; prescribed: *prix* ~, fixed price; ~ *sur le revenu*, taxed on income; *tâche f imposée*, prescribed task. || **imposer** #3 *v. tr.* **1.** to impose, to thrust on, to inflict (on, *à*). **2.** to tax. **3.** [Rel.] ~ *les mains*, to lay on hands. || *v. intr. en* ~ *à*, to impress. || **s'imposer** *v. pr.* **1.** to assume, to force on o.s. (an obligation). **2.** to tax o.s. **3.** to be necessary: *Son remplacement s'imposait*, It had become necessary to replace him. **4.** to assert o.s., to command respect, to take over. || **imposition** [-i′sjõ] *n.f.* imposing, levying; taxation.
impossibilité [ɛposib|ili′te] *n.f.* impossibility: *dans l'* ~ *de*, to find it impossible to; *mettre qqun dans l'* ~ *de*, to make it impossible for s.o. to. || **impossible** [-l] *adj.* impossible (to, *de*). || *n.m.* what seems impossible: *Je ferai l'* ~ *pour vous aider*, I'll do all I can, I'll do my utmost to help you.
imposteur [ɛ̃pɔs′t|œ:r] *n.m.* impostor. || **imposture** [-y:r] *n.f.* imposture, deception.

impôt [ɛ̃′po] *n.m.* tax: ~ *sur le revenu*, income tax; ~ *foncier*, property tax.
impotent, -e [ɛ̃pɔ′tɑ̃(:t)] *adj.* crippled, bedridden. || *n.* cripple.
impraticable [ɛ̃prati′kabl] *adj.* **1.** impractical, unworkable. **2.** [route] impassable.
imprécis, -e [ɛ̃pre′si(:z)] *adj.* vague. || **imprécision** [ɛ̃presi′zjõ] *n.f.* [expression] vagueness; [idée] haziness.
imprégner [ɛpre′ɲe] *v. tr.* to impregnate, to permeate.
impression [ɛ̃prɛ′sj|õ] *n.f.* **1.** impression: *produire une mauvaise* ~, to create a bad impression; *avoir l'* ~ *que*, to be under the impression that. **2.** print, printing: *faute d'* ~, misprint. || **impressionnant, -e** [-ɔ′nɑ̃(:t)] *adj.* impressive. || **impressionner** [-ɔ′ne] #3 *v. tr.* to impress, to affect. || **impressionniste** [ɛ̃prɛsjɔ′nist] *adj.* impressionistic.
imprévisible [ɛ̃prev|i′zibl] *adj.* unforeseeable. || **imprévoyant, -e** [-wa′jɑ̃(:t)] *adj.* lacking foresight, improvident. || **imprévu, -e** [-y] *adj.* unforeseen. || *n.m.* (the) unexpected.
imprimé, -e [ɛ̃pri′m|e] *adj.* printed. || *n.m.* print, printed material; [poste] printed matter, second-class mail. || **imprimer** [-e] #3 *v. tr.* **1.** [avec l'encre] to print; [pression] to imprint. **2.** to impart (a movement). || **imprimerie** [-′ri] *n.f.* printing; printing office, print shop. || **imprimeur** [-œ:r] *n.m.* printer: © *l'* ~ *de la Reine*, the Queen's Printer.
improbable [ɛ̃prɔ′babl] *adj.* improbable, unlikely.
impromptu [ɛ̃prõp′ty] *adj. inv. & adv.* impromptu. || *n.m.* [Mus.] impromptu.
impropre [ɛ̃′prɔpr] *adj.* improper, unfit (for, *à*). || **impropriété** [-ie′te] *n.f.* impropriety, unfitness.
improvisation [ɛ̃prɔviz|a′sjõ] *n.f.* improvisation; (en parlant) extemporization, adlibbing. || **improviser** [-e] #3 *v. tr.* to improvise, to extemporize, to ad-lib. || **improviste** (à l') [alɛ̃prɔ′vist] *loc. adv.* unexpectedly; without warning.
imprudence [ɛ̃pry′dɑ̃:s] *n.f.* rashness, imprudence; *commettre une* ~, to do sth. foolish; *Ne faites pas d'imprudences*, Don't do anything foolish. || **imprudent, -e** [-ɑ̃(:t)] *adj.* rash, foolish.
impudence [ɛ̃py′d|ɑ̃:s] *n.f.* impudence, audacity; [Fam.] cheek. || **impudent, -e** [-ɑ̃(:t)] *adj.* impudent; cheeky.
impudeur [-œ:r] *n.f.* immodesty, indecency. || **impudique** [ɛ̃py′dik] *adj.* immodest, unchaste.

impuissance [ɛ̃pɥisɑ̃:s] *n.f.* powerlessness; inability; [sexuelle] impotence: *être dans l'* ~ *de faire qqch.*, to be powerless to do sth. || **impuissant, -e** [-ɑ̃(:t) *adj.* powerless, incapable; impotent; [sans effet] unavailing.

impulsi|f, -ve [ɛ̃pyl's|if, -i:v] *adj.* impulsive. || **impulsion** [-jɔ̃] *n.f.* impulse, impetus, impulsion.

impunément [ɛ̃pyne'mɑ̃] *adv.* with impunity.

impuni, -e [ɛ̃py'ni] *adj.* unpunished. || **impunité** [-'te] *n.f.* impunity.

impur, -e [ɛ̃'p|y:r] *adj.* impure, tainted; lewd, immodest. || **impureté** [-yr'te] *n.f.* impurity; uncleanness.

imputer [ɛ̃py'te] #3 *v. tr.* **1.** to impute (to, *à*): *La chose m'a été imputée*, The matter was laid at my door. **2.** to charge (to an account).

inabordable [inabɔr'dabl] *adj.* [personne] unapproachable; [lieu] inaccessible; [prix] prohibitive.

inaccessible [inaksɛ'sibl] *adj.* inaccessible, out of reach; [Fig.] unattainable; [personne] unapproachable.

inaccoutumé, -e [inakuty'me] *adj.* unaccustomed; [inhabituel] unusual.

inachevé, -e [inaʃ've] *adj.* unfinished, incomplete.

inacti|f, -ve [inak'tif, -'ti:v] *adj.* inactive; [bourse] dull. || **inaction** [-'ɔjɔ̃] *n.f.* inaction.

inadmissible [inadmi'sibl] *adj.* (prétention) inadmissible: *C'est* ~, It is out of the question.

inadvertance [inadvɛr'tɑ̃:s] *n.f.* oversight: *par* ~, inadvertently.

inanimé, -e [inani'me] *adj.* [corps] inanimate, lifeless; [regard] dull; [Pers.] unconscious.

inanité [inani'te] *n.f.* inanity, futility.

inanition [inani'sjɔ̃] *n.* inanition: *tomber d'* ~, to starve to death.

inapaisé, -e [inapɛ'ze] *adj.* unappeased, unassuaged.

inaperçu, -e [inapɛr'sy] *adj.* unseen, unperceived: *passer* ~, to go unnoticed.

inappréciable [inapre'sjabl] *adj.* **1.** invaluable. **2.** negligible.

inassouvi, -e [inasu'vi] *adj.* unsatisfied, unsated.

inattendu, -e [inatɑ̃'dy] *adj.* unexpected.

inattenti|f, -ve [inatɑ̃'t|if, -i:v] *adj.* inattentive.

inauguration [inogyra'sjɔ̃] *n.f.* [monument] inauguration; [statue] unveiling; [Fig., campagne politique, &c.] beginning, opening. || **inaugurer** [inogy're] #3 *v. tr.* [mettre en pratique pour la première fois] to inaugurate; to unveil (a monument); to usher in.

incalculable [ɛ̃kalky'labl] *adj.* incalculable.

incapable [ɛ̃ka'pa|bl] *adj.* **1.** incapable (of, *de*). **2.** [absol.] incompetent. || **incapacité** [-si'te] *n.f.* incapacity, inability; [physique] disability.

incarcération [ɛ̃karser|a'sjɔ̃] *n.f.* incarceration. || **incarcérer** [-e] #10 *v. tr.* [Jur.] to incarcerate.

incarnation [ɛ̃karn|a'sjɔ̃] *n.f.* [Rel.] incarnation; [Fig.] embodiment. || **incarné, -e** [-e] *adj.* incarnate: *ongle* ~, ingrowing nail. || **incarner** [-e] #3 *v. tr.* to incarnate, to embody. || **s'incarner** *v. pron.* to become incarnate; [Méd.] to grow in.

incartade [ɛ̃kar'tad] *n.f.* prank, faux pas; *faire une* ~, to shy; [Fig.] to blunder.

incassable [ɛ̃kɑ'sabl] *adj.* unbreakable.

incendiaire [ɛ̃sɑ̃'djɛ:r] *n. m/f.* incendiary, [Fam.] fire bug. || *adj.* incendiary.

incendie [ɛ̃sɑ̃'d|i] *n.m.* fire: ~ *de forêt*, forest fire; ~ *volontaire*, arson. || **incendier** [-je] #3 *v. tr.* to set on fire.

incertain, -e [ɛ̃sɛr't|ɛ̃, -ɛn] *adj.* uncertain, doubtful, vague; [temps] unsettled. || **incertitude** [-i'tyd] *n.f.* uncertainty, doubt, hesitation: *être dans l'* ~, to be uncertain.

incessamment [ɛ̃sɛ's|a'mɑ̃] *adv.* **1.** incessantly. **2.** any time now. || **incessant, -e** [-ɑ̃(:t)] *adj.* incessant, ceaseless.

inceste [ɛ̃'sɛst] *n.m.* incest.

incident [ɛ̃si'dɑ̃] *n.m.* incident; event; *incidents de la journée*, events of the day. || *adj.* incidental; [Gram.] subordinate, relative.

incinérateur [ɛ̃siner|a'tœ:r] *n.m.* incinerator. || **incinération** [-a'sjɔ̃] *n.f.* **1.** incineration. **2.** cremation. || **incinérer** [-e] #10 *v. tr.* **1.** to incinerate. **2.** to cremate.

incisi|f, -ve [ɛ̃si'z|if, -i:v] *adj.* incisive.

incision [ɛ̃si'zjɔ̃] *n.f.* incision, lancing; [arbre] tapping: *faire une* ~, to lance, tap.

inciter [ɛ̃si'te] #3 *v. tr.* to incite; [Fam.] to stir up.

inclinaison [ɛ̃klin|ɛ'zɔ̃] *n.f.* inclination, [pente] slope; [Tech.] gradient. || **inclination** [-a'sjɔ̃] *n.f.* **1.** inclination, disposition: *avoir de l'* ~, to have a taste (*pour*, for). **2.** †bent, attachment. || **incliner** [ɛ̃kli'ne] #3 *v. tr.* to lower, to bend, to lean, to tilt: ~ *la tête*, to lean one's head forward, to bow. || *v. intr.* **1.** to slant, to be at a slant, to tilt. **2.** to incline, to be inclined (to, *à*). || **s'incliner** *v. pr.* **1.** to bow, to nod. **2.** to bow, to yield: *Il s'est incliné devant mes raisons*, He deferred to my reasons.

inclure [ɛ̃'kl|y:r] #58 *v. tr.* to include, enclose. || **inclus, -e** [-y(:z)] *adj.* included, enclosed: *ci-* ~, enclosed herewith.
inclusi|f, -ve [ɛ̃kly'z|if, -i:v] *adj.* inclusive. || **inclusivement** [-iv'mɑ̃] *adv.* inclusively.
incognito [ɛ̃kɔɲi'to] *adj. & n.m.* incognito: *garder l'* ~, to keep o.'s identity secret.
incohérence [ɛ̃kɔe'r|ɑ̃:s] *n.f.* incoherence. || **incohérent, -e** [-ɑ̃(:t)] *adj.*: *des idées incohérentes,* incoherent thoughts.
incolore [ɛ̃kɔ'lɔ:r] *adj.* colourless.
incomber [ɛ̃kɔ̃'be] *v. intr.* to be incumbent (on, *à*), to devolve (upon).
incombustible [ɛ̃kɔ̃bys'tibl] *adj.* incombustible.
incommode [ɛ̃kɔ'mɔd] *adj.* inconvenient, awkward. || **incommoder** [-e] #3 *v. tr.* to bother, to cause physical discomfort to: *incommodé par la chaleur,* made uncomfortable by the heat.
incomparable [ɛ̃kɔ̃pa'rabl] *adj.* incomparable, unrivalled.
incompatible [ɛ̃kɔ̃pa'tibl] *adj.* incompatible.
incompétence [ɛ̃kɔ̃pe't|ɑ̃:s] *n.f.* incompetence. || **incompétent, -e** [-ɑ̃(:t)] *adj.* incompetent; not qualified.
incompl|et, -ète [ɛ̃kɔ̃'plɛ(t)] *adj.* incomplete; unfinished.
incompréhensible [ɛ̃kɔ̃preɑ̃'s|ibl] *adj.* incomprehensible; inexplicable. || **incompréhension** [-jɔ̃] *n.f.* incomprehension. || **incompris, -e** [ɛ̃kɔ̃'pri(:z)] *adj.* misunderstood. || *n.* [Pers.] → misunderstood.
inconcevable [ɛ̃kosə'vabl] *adj.* inconceivable.
inconduite [ɛ̃kɔ̃'dɥit] *n.f.* misconduct, misbehaviour.
incongru, -e [ɛ̃kɔ̃'gry] *adj.* incongruous. || **incongruité** [ɛ̃kɔ̃gryi'te] *n.f.* incongruity.
inconnu, -e [ɛ̃kɔ'ny] *adj.* unknown (*de,* to); strange. || *n.m.* stranger. || *n.f.* [Math.] unknown.
inconsciemment [ɛ̃kɔ̃|sja'mɑ̃] *adv.* unconsciously. || **inconscience** [-'sjɑ̃:s] *n.f.* unconsciousness; [folie] senselessness. || **inconscient, -e** [-sjɑ̃(:t)] *adj.* unconscious; unaware (of, *de*).
inconséquence [ɛ̃kɔ̃se'kɑ̃:s] *n.f.* inconsequence; [acte, paroles] indiscretion. || **inconséquent, -e** [ɛ̃kɔ̃se'kɑ̃(:t)] *adj.* [choses] illogical, inconsistent; [personne] inconsistent.
inconsidéré, -e [ɛ̃kɔ̃side're] *adj.* inconsiderate, thoughtless.
inconsistance [ɛ̃kɔ̃sis't|ɑ̃:s] *n.f.* lack of consistence; [substance] yielding; [Fig.] [Pers.] inconsistency, [character] flabbiness. || **inconsistant, -e** [-ɑ̃(:t)] *adj.* [×] lacking in consistence; [Fig.] [Pers.] inconsistent; [character] flabby.
inconsolable [ɛ̃kɔ̃sɔ'labl] *adj.* inconsolable.
inconstant, -e [ɛ̃kɔ̃s'tɑ̃(:t)] *adj.* inconstant, unstable; [fidélité] fickle.
incontestable [ɛ̃kɔ̃tɛs'tabl] *adj.* unquestionable, indisputable. || **incontestablement** [-ə'mɑ̃] *adv.* unquestionably.
inconvenance [ɛ̃kɔ̃v'n|ɑ̃:s] *n.f.* impropriety. || **inconvenant, -e** [-ɑ̃(:t)] *adj.* improper, indecent.
inconvénient [ɛ̃kɔ̃ve'njɑ̃] *n.m.* inconvenience; objection; disadvantage: *Je n'y vois pas d'* ~, I have no objection to that.
incorporer [ɛ̃kɔrpɔ're] #3 *v. tr.* to incorporate; [mélange] to mix; to embody.
incorrect [ɛ̃kɔ'rɛkt] *adj.* incorrect, wrong; [inexact] inaccurate.
incorrigible [ɛ̃kɔri'ʒibl] *adj.* incorrigible.
incrédule [ɛ̃kre'dyl] *adj.* incredulous, unbelieving; sceptical. || *n.* sceptic; [non-croyant] unbeliever.
incriminer [ɛ̃krimi'ne] #3 *v. tr.* to incriminate.
incroyable [ɛ̃krwa'jabl] *adj.* unbelievable, incredible.
incrusté, -e [ɛ̃krys'te] *adj.* inlaid. || **incruster** #3 *v. tr.* to incrust; [Tech.] to fur. || **s'incruster** *v. pron.* [Fig., idée, préjugé] to take root, to become ingrained.
inculpation [ɛ̃kylp|a'sjɔ̃] *n.f.* charge, indictment: *sous l'* ~ *de,* on a charge of. || **inculpé, -e** [-e] *adj.* charged (with, *de*); accused (of, *de*). || *n.* accused, defendant. || **inculper** [-e] #3 *v. tr.* to charge (*de,* with), to accuse (*de,* of); [Jur.] to indict.
inculquer [ɛ̃kyl'ke] #3 *v. tr.* to inculcate.
inculte [ɛ̃'kylt] *adj.* uncultivated; [Fig.] uncouth.
incursion [ɛ̃kyr'sjɔ̃] *n.f.* [Mil.] foray, raid; [Fig.] incursion.
Inde, l' [ɛ̃:d] *n.f.* India; *les Indes,* India; *les Indes Occidentales,* the West Indies; [Hist.] *les Indes Orientales Néerlandaises,* the Dutch East Indies; © *blé d'* ~, corn, maize.
indécis, -e [ɛ̃de'si|(:z)] *adj.* undecided, uncertain; [flou] indistinct, blurred. || **indécision** [-'zjɔ̃] *n.f.* indecision.
indéfini, -e [ɛ̃defi'ni] *adj.* indefinite, undefined. || **indéfinissable** [-'sabl] *adj.* undefinable.
indéfrisable [ɛ̃defri'zabl] *adj. n.f.* permanent (wave).
indélicat, -e [ɛ̃deli'ka(t)] *adj.* unscrupulous, dishonest.
indemne [ɛ̃'dɛmn] *adj.* unhurt; undamaged: *Il s'en est tiré* ~, He came out of it with-

out a scratch. || **indemniser** [i'ze] #3 *v. tr.* to indemnify. || **indemnité** [-i'te] *n.f.* **1.** indemnity, compensation. **2.** salary: ~ *parlementaire*, M.P.'s salary. **3.** allowance: ~ *de séjour*, per diem.

indéniable [ɛ̃de'njabl] *adj.* undeniable.

indépendance [ɛ̃depɑ̃'d|ɑ̃:s] *n.f.* independence. || **indépendant, -e** [-ɑ̃(:t)] *adj.* independent.

indescriptible [ɛ̃dɛskrip'tibl] *adj.* indescribable, → that baffles description.

indésirable [ɛ̃dezi'rabl] *adj. & n.* undesirable.

indéterminé, -e [ɛ̃detɛrmi'ne] *adj.* undetermined; vague.

index [ɛ̃'dɛks] *n.m.* **1.** forefinger. **2.** index. **3.** [Rel.] the Index: *mettre à l'Index*, to place on the Index. **4.** [de cadran] pointer.

indicat|eur, -rice [ɛ̃dika|'tœ:r, -'tris] *adj.* indicating: *poteau* ~ , signpost. || *n.m.* [Rail.] timetable; [police] informer; [instrument] gauge, indicator. || **indicati|f, -ve** [-'tif, -'ti:v] *adj.* indicative (of, *de*): *à titre* ~ , as an indication, as a rough approximation. || *n.m.* [Gram.] indicative (mood); [Radio] signal. || **indication** [-'sjɔ̃] *n.f.* **1.** indication, direction: *les indications que vous m'avez données*, the information you gave me.

indice [ɛ̃'dis] *n.m.* **1.** indication, sign; [police] informer. **2.** index: *l'* ~ *du coût de la vie*, the cost-of-living index.

indicible [ɛ̃di'sibl] *adj.* unutterable, inexpressible, beyond expression.

indien, -ne [ɛ̃'dj|ɛ̃, -ɛn] *adj.* Indian: *l'Océan Indien*, the Indian Ocean. || *n.*: *un Indien*, [Inde] an Indian; [Amérique] an Indian, an Amerindian: *la loi des Indiens*, the Indian Act.

indifféremment [ɛ̃difer|a'mɑ̃] *adv.* **1.** [avec indifférence] indifferently. **2.** [sans préférence] indiscriminately: *Il parle les deux langues* ~ , He speaks both languages equally well. || **indifférence** [-ɑ̃:s] *n.f.* indifference; unconcern. || **indifférent, -e** [-ɑ̃(:t)] *adj.* indifferent; uninterested: *Cela m'est* ~ , It makes no difference to me; *parler de choses indifférentes*, to talk about this and that.

indigence [ɛ̃di'ʒɑ̃:s] *n.f.* [poverty] indigence; [Fig.] lack, want.

indigène [ɛ̃di'ʒɛ:n] *adj.* [plante] indigenous; [population] native. || *n.* native.

indigent, -e [ɛ̃di'ʒɑ̃(:t)] *adj.* destitute: *végétation indigente*, scrub. || *n.* pauper: *les indigents*, the needy.

indigeste [ɛ̃di'ʒɛst] *adj.* indigestible, [Fig.] stodgy. || **indigestion** [-jɔ̃] *n.f.* indigestion: *avoir une* ~ , to have indigestion.

indignation [ɛ̃diɲa'sjɔ̃] *n.f.* indignation. || **indigne** [ɛ̃'diɲ] unworthy. || **indigné, -e** [-e] indignant, disgusted, outraged (over, *de*). || **indigner** [-e] #3 *v. tr.* to arouse the indignation of, to revolt. || **s'indigner** *v. pron.* to become indignant, to be revolted (by, *contre*). || **indignité** [-i'te] *n.f.* **1.** unworthiness, vileness. **2.** [affront] indignity.

indigo [ɛ̃di'go] *adj. invar.* [couleur] indigo blue.

indiquer [ɛ̃di'ke] #3 *v. tr.* to indicate, to show, [du doigt] to point out: ~ *qqun*, to give the name of, to recommend s.o.

indirect, -e [ɛ̃di'rɛkt] *adj.* indirect; [Fig.] devious. || **indirectement** [-ə'mɑ̃] *adv.* indirectly, deviously.

indiscipliné, -e [ɛ̃disipli'ne] *adj.* undisciplined, unruly.

indiscr|et, -ète [ɛ̃dis'kr|ɛ(t)] *adj.* indiscreet; [curieux] inquisitive, [Péj.] prying, [Fam.] nosy; [bavard] talkative. || **indiscrétion** [-e'sjɔ̃] *n.f.* indiscretion: *sans* ~ , if I may ask, I don't want to pry, but . . .

indiscutable [ɛ̃disky'tabl] *adj.* unquestionable.

indispensable [ɛ̃dispɑ̃'sabl] *adj.* indispensable, (absolutely) necessary. || *n.m.* bare necessities: *ne faire que le strict* ~ , to do only what is strictly necessary.

indisponible [ɛ̃dispɔ'nibl] *adj.* unavailable; [héritage] entailed; [biens] inalienable.

indisposé, -e [ɛ̃dispo'z|e] *adj.* indisposed, upset. || **indisposer** [-e] #3 *v. tr.* to indispose, upset: *Le cidre m'indispose*, Cider doesn't agree with me. || **indisposition** [-i'sjɔ̃] *n.f.* indisposition, slight illness.

indissolubilité [ɛ̃disɔlyb|ili'te] *n.f.* indissolubility; [Chem.] insolubility. || **indissoluble** [-l] *adj.* indissoluble; [Chem.] insoluble.

indistinct, -e [ɛ̃dis'tɛ̃(:kt)] *adj.* indistinct; [lumière] dim, [ligne] blurred.

individu [ɛ̃divi'd|y] *n.m.* individual; [personne quelconque] character, customer, chap: *C'est un drôle d'* ~ , He's a queer character. || **individualiser** [-ɥali'ze] #3 *v. tr.* to individualize. || **individuel, -le** [-ɥɛl] *adj.* individual. || **individuellement** [-ɥɛl'mɑ̃] *adv.* individually.

Indochine, l' [ɛ̃dɔ'ʃin] *n.f.* Indo-China. || **indochinois, -e** [-wa(:z)] *adj. & n.* Indo-Chinese.

indolence [ɛ̃dɔ'l|ɑ̃:s] *n.f.* indolence. || **indolent, -e** [-ɑ̃(:t)] *adj.* indolent.

indomptable [ɛ̃dɔ̃'tabl] *adj.* indomitable, untamable; unconquerable.

Indonésie, l' [ɛ̃dɔne'z|i] *n.f.* Indonesia. || **indo-**

nésien, -ne [-jɛ̃, -jɛn] *adj.* Indonesian. || **Indonésien, -ne** *n.* Indonesian.

indu, -e [ɛ̃'dy] *adj.* [heure] unreasonable; [remarques] unwarranted, unfounded; †not due.

indubitable [ɛ̃dybi'tabl] *adj.* beyond doubt, unquestionable. || **indubitablement** [-ə'mɑ̃] *adv.* unquestionably, undoubtedly.

induction [ɛ̃dyk'sjɔ̃] *n.f.* induction.

induire [ɛ̃'dɥi:r] #56 *v. tr.* **1.** to lead: *~ en erreur*, to lead astray; *~ en tentation*, to lead into temptation. **2.** to infer. **3.** [Phys.] to induce.

indulgence [ɛ̃dyl|'ʒ|ɑ̃:s] *n.f.* indulgence, leniency: *user d'~ envers*, to be lenient towards. || **indulgent, -e** [-ɑ̃(:t)] *adj.* indulgent, lenient.

indûment [ɛ̃dy'mɑ̃] *adv.* unduly, without permission.

industrie [ɛ̃dys'tri] *n.f.* **1.** skill, resourcefulness: *chevalier d'~*, confidence man. **2.** industry. || **industriel, -le** [-ɛl] *adj.* industrial: *office de la propriété industrielle*, Patent Office. || *n.m.* manufacturer, industrialist. || **industrieu|x, -se** [-ø(:z)] *adj.* [habile] skilful, resourceful. × INDUSTRIOUS.

inébranlable [inebrɑ̃'labl] *adj.* unshakable, immovable, as steady as a rock.

inédit, -e [ine'di(t)] *adj.* unpublished, published for the first time. || *n.m.* unpublished material.

ineffaçable [inefa'sabl] *adj.* indelible.

inefficace [inefi'kas] *adj.* ineffective, ineffectual. || **inefficacité** [-i'te] *n.f.* inefficacy, inefficiency.

inégal, -e [ine'gal] *adj.* **1.** [surface] rough, uneven. **2.** [travail] unequal, uneven. **3.** irregular. || **inégalé, -e** [-e] *adj.* unequalled, unparalleled, unrivalled. || **inégalité** [-i'te] *n.f.* inequality; unevenness; irregularity; roughness.

inepte [i'nɛp|t] *adj.* inept, inane. || **ineptie** [-'si] *n.f.* ineptitude, absurdity.

inépuisable [inepɥi'zabl] *adj.* inexhaustible.

inerte [i'nɛr|t] *adj.* inert; limp, lifeless: *matière ~*, inert matter; *main ~*, limp hand. || **inertie** [-'si] *n.f.* [Phys.]: *force d'~*, force of inertia; [Fig., Pers.] inertia, apathy: *force d'~*, passive resistance.

inespéré, -e [inɛspe're] *adj.* unhoped for.

inestimable [inɛsti'mabl] *adj.* inestimable, priceless.

inévitable [inevi'tabl] *adj.* inevitable, unavoidable. || **inévitablement** [-ə'mɑ̃] *adv.* inevitably.

inexact, -e [ineg'za|(kt)] *adj.* inaccurate, inexact; [Pers.] unpunctual, never on time. || **inexactitude** [-kti'tyd] *n.f.* inaccuracy, inexactitude; [Pers.] lack of punctuality.

inexcusable [inɛksky'zabl] *adj.* inexcusable.

inexistant, -e [inɛgzis'tɑ̃(:t)] *adj.* nonexistent.

inexorable [inɛgzɔ'rabl] *adj.* [Pers.] inexorable, unrelenting; [Fig., law, fate] harsh, inexorable.

inexpérience [inɛkspe'r|jɑ̃:s] *n.f.* inexperience, lack of experience. || **inexpérimenté, -e** [-imɑ̃'te] *adj.* inexperienced.

inexplicable [inɛkspli'kabl] *adj.* inexplicable, unexplainable.

inexprimable [inɛkspri'mabl] *adj.* inexpressible, unutterable.

in extenso [inɛkstɛ̃'so] *loc. adv.* [report, &c.] verbatim; in toto.

infaillible [ɛ̃fa'jibl] *adj.* infallible. || **infailliblement** [-ə'mɑ̃] *adv.* inevitably, infallibly.

infâme [ɛ̃'fɑ:m] *adj.* infamous, shameful. || **infamie** [ɛ̃fa'mi] *n.f.* infamy, infamous act.

infanterie [ɛ̃fɑ̃t'ri] *n.f.* infantry.

infatigable [ɛ̃fati'gabl] *adj.* indefatigable, untiring, tireless.

infatuation [ɛ̃fatɥa'sjɔ̃] *n.f.* infatuation.

infatuer [ɛ̃fa'tɥe] #3 *v. tr.* to infatuate. || **s'infatuer** *v. pron.* to become infatuated (*de*, with): *infatué de soi*, conceited.

infect, -e [ɛ̃'fɛkt] *adj.* foul, rotten, putrid. || **infecter** [-e] #3 *v. tr.* to infect, contaminate. || **infectieu|x, -se** [ɛ̃fɛk'sjø(:z)] *adj.* infectious. || **infection** [ɛ̃fɛk'sjɔ̃] *n.f.* infection.

inférer [ɛ̃fe're] #10 *v. tr.* to infer.

inférieur, -e [ɛ̃fe'rj|œ:r] *adj.* inferior; lower. || **infériorité** [-ɔri'te] *n.f.* inferiority.

infernal, -e [ɛ̃fɛr'nal] *adj.* infernal.

infester [ɛ̃fɛs'te] #3 *v. tr.* to infest, overrun (*de*, with).

infidèle [ɛ̃fi'd|ɛl] *adj.* unfaithful. || *n.* [often plur.] infidel. || **infidélité** [-eli'te] *n.f.* infidelity, unfaithfulness; [action] unfaithfulness, faithlessness; [Rel.] unbelief.

infiltrer, s' [sɛ̃fil'tre] #3 *v. pron.* **1.** to seep (into, *dans*). **2.** [Fig.] to infiltrate.

infime [ɛ̃'fim] *adj.* very small, negligible, trifling.

infini, -e [ɛ̃fi'ni] *adj.* infinite; endless; immeasurable, boundless. || *n.m.* the infinite: *à l'~*, infinitely, ad infinitum. || **infiniment** [-'mɑ̃] *adv.* infinitely; [aimable, agréable, &c.] extremely, infinitely: *regretter ~*, to be terribly sorry (for).

infinitif [-'tif] *n.m.* infinitive (mood).

infirme [ɛ̃'firm] *adj.* crippled, disabled. || *n. m/f.* cripple, invalid. || **infirmerie** [-ə'ri] *n.f.* infirmary, sick bay. || **infirmier** [-'je] *n.m.* attendant, male nurse; [Mil.] orderly. || **infirmière** [-'jɛ:r] *n.f.* nurse: ~ *major*, matron. || **infirmité** [-i'te] *n.f.* infirmity; (physical) disability.

inflammabilité [ɛ̃flamabili'te] *n.f.* inflammability.

inflammation [ɛ̃flama'sjõ] *n.f.* inflammation.

inflation [ɛ̃fla'sjõ] *n.f.* inflation.

inflexible [ɛ̃flɛk'sibl] *adj.* inflexible, unyielding.

inflexion [ɛ̃flɛk'sjõ] *n.f.* inflexion (or inflection); [attitude] change.

infliger [ɛ̃fli'ʒe] #5 *v. tr.* to inflict (on, *à*): ~ *un châtiment à qqun*, to inflict a punishment on s.o.

influence [ɛ̃fly|'ɑ̃:s] *n.f.* influence: *exercer une* ~, to exert an influence. || **influencer** [-ɑ̃'se] #4 *v. tr.* to influence. || **influent, -e** [-ɑ̃(:t)] *adj.* influential.

influenza [ɛ̃flyɑ̃'za] *n.f.* influenza, [Fam.] flu.

influer [ɛ̃fly'e] #3 *v. intr.* to have an effect (on, *sur*), to influence.

informat|eur, -rice [ɛ̃fɔrma|'tœ:r, -'tris] *n.* informant. || **information** [-'sjõ] *n.f.* **1.** information, news: *informations de presse*, press reports; *aller aux informations*, to inquire. **2.** [Jur.] investigation.

informe [ɛ̃'fɔrm] *adj.* formless, shapeless; [laid] unshapely; [Fig., document] all over the place, disorganized.

informer [ɛ̃fɔr'me] #3 *v. tr.* to inform, to notify. || *v. intr.* to start proceedings (against, *contre*). || **s'informer (de)** *v. pron.* to inquire, to find out.

infortune [ɛ̃fɔr'tyn] *n.f.* misfortune; calamity. || **infortuné, -e** [-e] *adj.* unfortunate.

infraction [ɛ̃frak'sjõ] *n.f.* infraction, violation: ~ *aux règlements*, breach of regulations.

infranchissable [ɛ̃frɑʃi'sabl] *adj.* [obstacle matériel] impassable.

infroissable [ɛ̃frwa'sabl] *adj.* [tissu] wrinkle-proof.

infructueu|x, -se [ɛ̃fryk'tɥø(:z)] *adj.* fruitless, unproductive; [efforts] unavailing.

infuser [ɛ̃fy'z|e] #3 *v. tr. & intr.* to infuse, to brew; to inject; to stand: *Laissez-le* ~ *deux minutes*, Let it stand two minutes. || **infusion** [-jõ] *n.f.* infusion.

ingénier (s') à [sɛ̃ʒe'nje] #3 *v. pron.* to rack one's brains: ~ *à se faire comprendre*, to strive hard to make o.s. understood.

ingénieur [ɛ̃ʒe'njœ:r] *n.m.* engineer: ~ *chimiste*, chemical engineer; ~ *-conseil*, consulting engineer; ~ *des mines*, mining engineer; ~ *-électricien*, electrical engineer; ~ *-mécanicien*, mechanical engineer.

ingénieusement [ɛ̃ʒe|njøz'mɑ̃] *adv.* ingeniously. || **ingénieu|x, -se** [-njø(:z)] *adj.* ingenious, inventive, resourceful. || **ingéniosité** [-njozi'te] *n.f.* ingenuity.

ingénu, -e [ɛ̃ʒe'ny] *adj.* ingenuous; artless; simple. || *n.* naive person. || **ingénument** [-'mɑ̃] *adv.* ingenuously, naively.

ingérer [ɛ̃ʒe're] #10 *v. tr.* to ingest. || **s'ingérer (dans)** *v. pron.* to meddle (in), to interfere (with).

ingrat, -e [ɛ̃'gra|(t)] *adj.* [Pers.] ungrateful; [travail] thankless; tedious; [âge] difficult; [paysage] unappealing. || *n.*: *C'est un* ~, → He has no gratitude. || **ingratitude** [-ti'tyd] *n.f.* ingratitude, ungratefulness.

ingrédient [ɛ̃gre'djɑ̃] *n.m.* ingredient.

inhabile [ina'bil] *adj.* unskilful, awkward, unfit (for, *à*); [Jur.] unqualified.

inhabitable [inabi't|abl] *adj.* uninhabitable. || **inhabité, -e** [-e] *adj.* uninhabited.

inhérent, -e [ine'rɑ̃(:t)] *adj.* inherent (in, *à*).

inhibition [inibi'sjõ] *n.f.* inhibition.

inhospitali|er, -ère [inɔspita'lj|e, -ɛ:r] *adj.* inhospitable.

inhumain, -e [iny'm|ɛ̃, -ɛn] *adj.* inhuman, beastly.

inhumer [iny'me] *v. tr.* to bury, to inter.

inimitable [inimi'tabl] *adj.* inimitable.

inimitié [inimi'tje] *n.f.* enmity: *leur* ~, the bad feeling between them.

inintelligible [inɛ̃teli'ʒibl] *adj.* unintelligible.

ininterrompu, -e [ɛ̃tɛrõ'py] *adj.* uninterrupted, continuous.

inique [i'nik] *adj.* iniquitous, unrighteous. || **iniquité** [-i'te] *n.f.* iniquity, unrighteousness.

initial, -e [ini'sjal] *adj.* initial; [original] original, first. || *n.f.* initial: *signer de ses initiales*, to initial.

initiative [inisja'ti:v] *n.f.* initiative: *avoir l'esprit d'* ~, to be resourceful.

initié, -e [ini'sje] *adj.* & *n.* initiated. || **initier** #3 *v. tr.* to initiate; to introduce: ~ *à une société*, to initiate into a society; ~ *à un jeu*, to introduce to a game.

injecté, -e [ɛ̃ʒɛk|'te] *adj.* [yeux] bloodshot; [visage] flushed, congested. || **injecter** [-'te] #3 *v. tr.* to inject. || **s'injecter** *v. pron.* to become congested, [yeux] to become bloodshot. || **injection** [-'sjõ] *n.f.* injection.

injonction [ɛ̃ʒõk'sjõ] *n.f.* injunction: © ~ *de la Cour*, court order.

injure [ɛ̃'ʒ|y:r] *n.f.* injury, wrong; [parole] insult. || **injurier** [-y'rj|e] #3 *v. tr.* to abuse; [avec paroles] to insult, to call (s.o.) names. || **injurieu|x, -se** [-ø(:z)] *adj.* insulting, abusive.

injuste [ɛ̃'ʒyst] *adj.* unjust, unfair. || **injustice** [-is] *n.f.* injustice, wrong: *commettre une* ~, to commit an injustice, to do wrong.

inlassable [ɛ̃la'sabl] *adj.* [Pers.] tireless, indefatigable; [efforts] untiring. || **inlassablement** [-ə'mɑ̃] *adv.* tirelessly, indefatigably, untiringly.

inné, -e [in'ne] *adj.* innate.

innocence [inɔ's|ɑ̃:s] *n.f.* innocence; [d'un propos] harmlessness. || **innocent, -e** [-ɑ̃(:t)] *adj.* innocent; harmless. || *n.* [Péj.] innocent soul. || **innocenter** [-ɑ̃'te] #3 *v. tr.* to exonerate, to clear.

innombrable [inɔ̃'brabl] *adj.* innumerable, numberless.

innommable [inɔ'mabl] *adj.* unmentionable.

innovation [inɔv|a'sjɔ̃] *n.f.* innovation. || **innover** [-e] #3 *v. tr.* to innovate.

inoccupé, -e [inɔky'pe] *adj.* [lieu] unoccupied, vacant; [Pers.] idle.

inoculer [inɔky'le] #3 *v. tr.* [Méd.] to inoculate (against, *contre*); [Fig.] to inoculate; to instil (into, *à*).

inodore [inɔ'dɔ:r] *adj.* odourless.

inoffensi|f, -ve [inɔfɑ̃'s|if, -i:v] *adj.* inoffensive.

inondation [inɔ̃d|a'sjɔ̃] *n.f.* inundation, flood. || **inondé, -e** [-e] *adj.* flooded; [Fig.] inundated, swamped (with, *de*). || **inonder** [-e] #3 *v. tr.* to flood; [Fig.] to inundate.

inopportun, -e [inɔpɔr't|œ̃, -yn] *adj.* inopportune, untimely.

inoubliable [inubli'abl] *adj.* unforgettable.

inouï, -e [i'nwi] *adj.* unheard of, extraordinary.

inoxydable [inɔksi'dabl] *adj.* rust-proof, stainless.

inqualifiable [ɛ̃kali'fjabl] *adj.* unqualifiable, scandalous: *conduite* ~, unspeakable behaviour.

inqui|et, -ète [ɛ̃'kj|ɛ(t)] *adj.* uneasy, worried, disturbed (about, *au sujet de*). || **inquiétant, -e** [-e'tɑ̃(:t)] *adj.* disturbing, disquieting. || **inquiéter** [-e'te] #10 *v. tr.* to make uneasy, to worry, to disturb. || **s'inquiéter** *v. pron.* to feel uneasy, to worry (about, *de*). || **inquiétude** [-e'tyd] *n.f.* uneasiness, worry.

inquisition [ɛ̃kizi'sjɔ̃] *n.f.* inquisition.

insaisissable [ɛ̃sɛzi'sabl] *adj.* **1.** [Jur.] not seizable, unattachable. **2.** [Fig.] evanescent, imperceptible, intangible.

insalubre [ɛ̃sa'lybr] *adj.* [of climate, land] unhealthy.

insanité [ɛ̃sani'te] *n.f.* insanity.

insatiable [ɛ̃sa'sjabl] *adj.* insatiable.

inscription [ɛ̃skr|ip'sjɔ̃] *n.f.* **1.** inscription. **2.** [formalité] registration, enrolment: *frais d'* ~, registration fee. || **inscrire** [-i:r] #48 *v. tr.* **1.** to inscribe, to write down; to enter. **2.** to register: *se faire* ~, to register. || **s'inscrire** *v. pron.* to register. || **inscrit, -e** [-i(t)] *adj.* inscribed, registered. || *n.m.* registered student: ~ *maritime*, registered seaman.

inscrutable [ɛ̃skry'tabl] *adj.* inscrutable.

insecte [ɛ̃'sɛkt] *n.m.* insect; [Fam.] bug. || **insecticide** [-i'sid] *adj.* & *n.m.* insecticide; [Fam.] bug-killer.

insensé, -e [ɛ̃sɑ̃'se] *adj.* crazy, senseless. || *n.m.* madman. || *n.f.* madwoman.

insensible [ɛ̃sɑ̃'sibl] *adj.* **1.** insensitive, unfeeling: *Il est* ~ *au froid*, He does not feel the cold. **2.** imperceptible, insensible.

inséparable [ɛ̃sepa'rabl] *adj.* inseparable.

insérer [ɛ̃se're] #10 *v. tr.* to insert, to put in.

insidieu|x, -se [ɛ̃si'djø(:z)] *adj.* insidious.

insigne [ɛ̃'siɲ] *adj.* signal, conspicuous, noteworthy. || *n.m.* badge, mark. || *n.m.pl.* insignia.

insignifiant, -e [ɛ̃siɲi'fjɑ̃(:t)] *adj.* insignificant, trivial; trifling, nominal.

insinuant, -e [ɛ̃si'nɥ|ɑ̃(:t)] *adj.* insinuating, ingratiating. || **insinuer** [-e] #3 *v. tr.* to insinuate, to imply. || **s'insinuer** *v. pron.* to insinuate o.s., to worm one's way (into, *dans*).

insipide [ɛ̃si'pid] *adj.* insipid, flat, tasteless.

insistance [ɛ̃sis't|ɑ̃:s] *n.f.* insistence: *sur l'* ~ *de*, → pressed by. || **insister** [-e] #3 *v. intr.* to insist: ~ *sur qqch.*, to insist on sth., to stress, to emphasize; *Je n'ai pas voulu* ~, I did not want to stress the point; *Il a insisté pour que vous y soyez*, He insisted on your being included.

insolation [ɛ̃sɔla'sjɔ̃] *n.f.* exposure to the sun; sunstroke.

insolence [ɛ̃sɔ'l|ɑ̃:s] *n.f.* insolence. || **insolent, -e** [-ɑ̃(:t)] *adj.* insolent.

insolite [ɛ̃sɔ'lit] *adj.* unaccustomed, unusual.

insoluble [ɛ̃sɔ'lybl] *adj.* insoluble.

insolvable [ɛ̃sɔl'vabl] *adj.* insolvent.

insomnie [ɛ̃sɔm'ni] *n.f.* insomnia, sleeplessness.

insonore [ɛ̃sɔ'n|ɔ:r] *adj.* **1.** noiseless. **2.** sound-proofed. || **insonorisation** [-ɔriza'sjɔ̃] *n.f.* sound-proofing. || **insonoriser** [-ɔri'ze] #3 *v. tr.* to sound-proof.

insouciance [ɛ̃su'sj|ɑ̃:s] *n.f.* carelessness; unconcern (for, *de*): *vivre dans l'* ~, to lead a carefree life. || **insouciant, -e** [-ɑ̃(:t)] *adj.* careless; unconcerned;

thoughtless. || **insoucieu|x, -se** [ɛ̃su'sjø(:z)] *adj.* careless, heedless.

insoumis, -e [ɛ̃su'mi(:z)] *adj.* [enfant] unruly; [peuple] rejecting the rule of colonial power, unconquered; [soldat] evading conscription. || **insoumission** [ɛ̃sumi'sjɔ̃] *n.f.* unsubmissiveness, insubordination; [Mil.] defaulting.

insoupçonné, -e [ɛ̃supsɔ'ne] *adj.* unsuspected.

inspecter [ɛ̃spɛk'te] #3 *v. tr.* to inspect. || **inspect|eur, -rice** [-'tœ:r, -'tris] *n.* inspector; [police] police inspector, police sergeant; [grand magasin] floorwalker. || **inspection** [-'sjɔ̃] *n.f.* inspection.

inspiration [ɛ̃spir|a'sjɔ̃] *n.f.* inspiration. || **inspirer** [-e] #3 *v. tr.* to inspire.

instable [ɛ̃'stabl] *adj.* unstable, unreliable, erratic.

installation [ɛ̃stala'sjɔ̃] *n.f.* induction (of a magistrate, &c.); [Tech., action] installation, fitting up; [équipement] plant, equipment, fittings (of a shop, a factory); [Electr.] putting in. || **installer** [ɛ̃sta'le] #3 *v. tr.* to install, to set up; [famille] to settle; [commodité] to put in: ~ *l'électricité,* to put in electric light. || **s'installer** *v. pron.* to settle down, to set up headquarters or shop.

instamment [ɛ̃sta'mɑ̃] *adv.* earnestly, urgently.

instance [ɛ̃s'tɑ̃:s] *n.f.* instancy, solicitation.

instant [ɛ̃s'tɑ̃] *adj.* pressing, urgent. || *n.* moment, instant.

instaurer [ɛ̃stɔ're] #3 *v. tr.* to found, to establish.

instigation [ɛ̃stiga'sjɔ̃] *n.f.* instigation.

instinct [ɛ̃s'tɛ̃] *n.m.* instinct. || **instincti|f, -ve** [-kt|if, -i:v] *adj.* instinctive. || **instinctivement** [-iv'mɑ̃] *adv.* instinctively.

instituer [ɛ̃sti'tɥe] #3 *v. tr.* to found, to establish, to set up (an order, &c.); [Jur.] to appoint (an heir), to institute (*une poursuite,* proceedings). || **institut|-eur, -rice** [ɛ̃stity't|œ:r, -ris] *n.* [elementary, primary schools] school-/master, teacher; schoolmistress.

institution [ɛ̃stity'sjɔ̃] *n.f.* [établissement] institution, establishment, founding; [école] academy, establishment, private school. || *pl.* institutions (of a country).

instruct|eur, -rice [ɛ̃stryk'tœ:r, -'tris] *adj. & n.* instructor: [Mil.] *sergent* ~, drill instructor; [Jur.] *juge* ~, examining magistrate. || **instructi|f, -ve** [-'tif, -'ti:v] *adj.* instructive. || **instruction** [-'sjɔ̃] *n.f.* [information] instruction, guidance; [learning] education: *avoir de l'* ~, to be educated; *sans* ~, uneducated; [Jur.] preliminary examination: *juge m d'* ~, examining magistrate. || *pl.* directions, instructions: *instructions permanentes,* standing orders. || **instruire** [ɛ̃s'trɥi:r] #56 *v. tr.* [renseigner] to inform (of, *de*), to tell; [enseigner] to instruct, teach; [Jur.] to prepare; [soldiers] to train, drill. || **instruit, -e** [ɛ̃s'trɥi(t)] *adj.* educated.

instrument [ɛ̃stry'mɑ̃] *n.m.* [Tech.] instrument, tool; [Jur.] instrument, deed: ~ *de musique,* musical instrument; [Fig., Pers.] *servir d'* ~ *à qqun,* to be used as a tool by s.o. || **instrumental, -e** [-'tal] *adj.* instrumental.

insu [ɛ̃'sy] *n.m.* [used only in the loc.]: *à l'* ~ *de* (qqun), unknown to (s.o.).

insubordonné, -e [ɛ̃sybɔrdɔ'ne] *adj.* insubordinate.

insuffisance [ɛ̃syfi'z|ɑ̃:s] *n.f.* [incapacity] insufficiency, inadequacy; [lack] shortage. || **insuffisant, -e** [-ɑ̃(:t)] *adj.* insufficient, inadequate.

insulaire [ɛ̃sy'lɛ:r] *adj.* insular. || *n.m/f.* islander.

insulte [ɛ̃'sylt] *n.f.* insult: *faire* ~ *à,* to offend. || **insulter** [-e] #3 *v. tr.* to insult, offend (s.o.).

insupportable [ɛ̃sypɔr'tabl] *adj.* unbearable, provoking.

insurgé, -e [ɛ̃syr'ʒe] *adj. & n.* (*m*). || insurgent, rebel. || **s'insurger** #5 *v. pron.* to revolt, to rebel (*contre,* against).

intarissable [ɛ̃tari'sabl] *adj.* [source] inexhaustible; [imagination] unfailing.

intégral, -e [ɛ̃te'gral] *adj.* integral, complete. || *n.f.* [Math.] integral.

intègre [ɛ̃'tɛ:gr] *adj.* honest, upright.

intégrer [ɛ̃te'gre] #10 *v. tr.* to integrate (*dans,* into). || **s'intégrer** *v. pron.* to combine (*dans,* with); to form an integral part (*dans,* of).

intellect [ɛ̃tɛ'lɛkt] *n.m.* intellect.

intellectuel, -le [ɛ̃tɛlɛk'tɥɛl] *adj. & n.* intellectual.

intelligence [ɛ̃tɛli'ʒ|ɑ̃:s] *n.f.* [faculty] intelligence, understanding; terms: *être d'* ~ *avec qqun,* to have an agreement with s.o. || **intelligent, -e** [-ɑ̃(:t)] *adj.* intelligent, clever.

intelligible [ɛ̃tɛli'ʒibl] *adj.* [texte, discours] intelligible, clear: [voix] distinct.

intendance [ɛ̃tɑ̃'dɑ̃:s] *n.f.* administration, management.

intendant [ɛ̃tɑ̃'dɑ̃] *n.m.* (super)intendent; steward.

intense [ɛ̃'t|ɑ̃:s] *adj.* intense; [bombardment, &c.] severe; [couleur] deep, rich; [fièvre] high; [froid] severe. || **intensité** [-ɑ̃si'te] *n.f.* intensity; [vent] force; [courant électrique] strength.

intenter [ɛ̃tɑ̃'te] #3 *v. tr.* to bring an action, to institute proceedings (against, *à*).

intention [ɛ̃tɑ̃'sj|õ] *n.f.* **1.** intention, [Jur.] intent: *avoir l' ~ de,* to intend to; *à l' ~ de,* for, intended for; *sans ~*, unintentionally. || **intentionné, -e** [ɛ̃tɑ̃sjɔ'ne] *adj.* disposed, motivated: *bien ~*, well-disposed; *mal ~* , ill-disposed. || **intentionnel, -le** [-ɔ'nɛl] *adj.* intentional, deliberate. || **intentionnellement** [-'mɑ̃] *adv.* intentionally, deliberately.

inter [ɛ̃'tɛ:r] *n.m.* long-distance (telephone).

intercaler [ɛ̃tɛrka'le] #3 *v. tr.* to interpolate.

intercéder [ɛ̃tɛrse'de] #10 *v. intr.* to intercede (with, *auprès de*).

intercepter [ɛ̃tɛrsɛp'te] #3 *v. tr.* to intercept; to cut off.

intercession [ɛ̃tɛrsɛ'sjõ] *n.f.* intercession.

interdiction [ɛ̃tɛrd|ik'sjõ] *n.f.* forbidding, prohibition, interdiction. || **interdire** [-i:r] #46 *v. tr.* to forbid, to prohibit: *Il est formellement interdit de . . .*, It is strictly prohibited to . . . || **interdit, -e** [-i(t)] *adj.* **1.** forbidden, prohibited; [Mil.] off limits: *entrée interdite,* no admittance; *passage ~* , no thoroughfare. **2.** dumbfounded, taken aback.

intéressant, -e [ɛ̃terɛ|sɑ̃(:t)] *adj.* interesting. || **intéressé, -e** [-'se] *adj.* **1.** interested: *être ~ dans une affaire,* to have an interest in a business. **2.** interested, self-seeking. || *n.m.*: *l'intéressé,* the person concerned, the applicant. || **intéresser** [-e] #3 *v. tr.* **1.** to interest, to arouse the interest of. **2.** to concern. **3.** [Fin.] to interest, to give a financial interest (in, *à*). || **s'intéresser** *v. pron.* to take an interest (*à*, in).

intérêt [-ɛ] *n.m.* **1.** interest, concern: *l' ~ qu'il vous porte,* the interest he takes in you; *prendre de l' ~ à qqch.*, to be interested in sth. **2.** advantage: *Vous avez ~ à le faire,* It's in your interest to do so; *Il y aurait ~ à,* It would be advisable to. **3.** [Fin.] interest: *Il a de gros intérêts dans cette affaire,* He has important interests in that business; *payer des intérêts,* to pay interest.

interférence [ɛ̃tɛrfe'rɑ̃:s] *n.f.* interference.

intérieur, -e [ɛ̃te'rj|œ:r] *adj.* inside, inner, interior. || *n.m.* interior, inside; home: *C'est une femme d' ~* , She is very much interested in her home; *à l' ~* , indoors, inside; le ministre de l'Intérieur, [Br.] the Home Secretary, [U.S.] the Secretary of the Interior. || **intérieurement** [-œr'mɑ̃] *adv.* inwardly.

intérim [ɛ̃te'rim] *n.m.* interim: *par ~* , provisional; *chef de l'opposition par ~* , acting leader of the Opposition; *dans l' ~* , meanwhile, in the meantime.

interjection [ɛ̃tɛrʒɛk'sjõ] *n.f.* interjection; exclamation.

interlocut|eur, -rice [ɛ̃tɛrlɔky't|œ:r, -ris] *n.* the other person in a conversation: *mon ~* , the man I was speaking with.

interlude [ɛ̃tɛr'lyd] *n.m.* interlude.

intermédiaire [ɛ̃tɛrme'djɛ:r] *adj.* intermediate. || *n.m.* intermediary, [Com.] middleman: *par l' ~ de,* through.

interminable [ɛ̃tɛrmi'nabl] *adj.* interminable, endless.

intermittent, -e [ɛ̃tɛrmi'tɑ̃(:t)] *adj.* intermittent.

internat [ɛ̃tɛr'na] *n.m.* [Scol.] boarding school; boarding school life: *L' ~ ne lui vaut rien,* → It's not good for him to be a boarder; [Méd.] internship.

international, -e [ɛ̃tɛrnasjɔ'nal] *adj.* international.

interne [ɛ̃'tɛrn] *adj.* internal; interior. || *n.* [Scol.] boarder, resident student; [Méd.] intern. || **interné, -e** [-e] *adj.* confined, interned. || *n.* internee. || **internement** [ɛ̃tɛrnə'mɑ̃] *n.m.* internment, commitment (in a mental hospital). || **interner** [-e] #3 *v. tr.* to intern.

interpeller [ɛ̃tɛrpɛ'le] #3 *v. tr.* **1.** to hail, to call out to, to challenge. **2.** [Polit.] to interpellate.

interprétation [ɛ̃tɛrpr|eta'sjõ] *n.f.* **1.** interpretation. **2.** [artistique] rendition, rendering, interpretation. || **interprète** [-ɛt] *n.m/f.* **1.** interpreter. **2.** artist, actor, actress. **3.** [Fig.] *Soyez mon ~ auprès de lui,* → Convey to him what I feel. || **interpréter** [-e'te] #10 *v. tr.* **1.** to interpret, to translate orally. **2.** to interpret, to explain. **3.** to interpret, to render; to act: *Le rôle a été très bien interprété,* The part was well done.

interprovincial, -e [ɛ̃tɛrprɔvɛ̃'sjal] *adj.* interprovincial.

interrogat|eur, -rice [ɛ̃tɛrɔ|ga'tœ:r, -ris] *adj.* questioning. || *n.* examiner, interrogator. || **interrogati|f, -ve** [-ga'tif, -i:v] *adj.* interrogative. || **interrogation** [-ga'sjõ] *n.f.* **1.** oral examination: *~ écrite,* test, quiz. **2.** examining: *point d' ~* , question mark. || **interrogatoire** [-ga'twa:r] *n.m.* examination, examining: *contre- ~* , cross-examination. || **interroger** [-'ʒe] #5 *v. tr.* to examine, question.

interrompre [ɛ̃tɛ'r|õ:pr] #52A *v. tr.* to interrupt, to stop, to discontinue, to break: *Excusez-moi de vous ~* , Excuse me for interrupting. || **s'interrompre**

v. pron. to stop, to pause. || **interrompu, -e** [-ɔ̃'py] cf. INTERROMPRE. || *adj.* interrupted, broken off, discontinued.
interrupt|eur, -rice [-yp'tœ:r, -yp'tris] *adj.* interrupting. || *n.m.* **1.** [mécanisme] switch, circuit-breaker, cut-out. **2.** [Pers.] interrupter. || **interruption** [-yp'sjɔ̃] *n.f.* interruption; [Electr.] break (in, *de*): *sans* ~, without a break.
intersection [ɛ̃tɛrsɛk'sjɔ̃] *n.f.* intersection.
interurbain, -e [ɛ̃tɛryr'b|ɛ̃, -ɛn] *adj.* intercity. || *n.m.* [Tél.] long distance.
intervalle [ɛ̃tɛr'val] *n.m.* [espace] distance; [temps] interval; [Mus.] interval: *par intervalles*, in places, at times; *dans l'* ~, in the meantime.
intervenir [ɛ̃tɛrv|ə'ni:r] #22 *v. intr.* **1.** to intervene, to step in. **2.** to occur. || **intervention** [-ɑ̃'sjɔ̃] *n.f.* intervention; [Péj.] interference: ~ *chirurgicale*, operation, surgery.
intervertir [ɛ̃tɛrvɛr'ti:r] #3 *v. tr.* to invert; [l'ordre] to reverse.
interview [ɛ̃tɛr'vju] *n.f.* interview: *solliciter une* ~, to ask for an interview. || **interviewer** [-(v)e] #3 *v. tr.* to interview (s.o.). || *n.m.* interviewer.
intestin, -e [ɛ̃tɛst|ɛ̃, in] *adj.* internal: *luttes intestines*, internal strife. || *n.m.* intestine. || **intestinal, -e** [-i'nal] *adj.* intestinal.
intime [ɛ̃'tim] *adj.* inner, inward, intimate: *conviction* ~, inner conviction; *ami* ~, intimate friend; *Ils sont très intimes*, They are very close. || *n.m.* intimate, close/friend.
intimer [ɛ̃ti'me] #3 *v. tr.* **1.** to give (an order): *Il lui intima l'ordre d'arrêter*, He ordered him to stop. **2.** [Jur.] to summons to appear.
intimider [ɛ̃timi'de] #3 *v. tr.* to intimidate; [Fam.] to browbeat.
intimité [ɛ̃timi'te] *n.f.* intimacy; privacy.
intitulé, -e [ɛ̃tity'le] *adj.* entitled, called. || *n.m.* title. || **intituler** #3 *v. tr.* to entitle.
intolérable [ɛ̃tɔle'r|abl] *adj.* intolerable. || **intolérance** [-ɑ̃:s] *n.f.* intolerance.
intonation [ɛ̃tɔna'sjɔ̃] *n.f.* intonation.
intoxication [ɛ̃tɔksik|a'sjɔ̃] *n.f.* poisoning. || **intoxiqué, -e** [-e] *adj.* poisoned. || **intoxiquer** [-e] #3 *v. tr.* to poison.
intraitable [ɛ̃trɛ'tabl] *adj.* **1.** adamant, uncompromising. **2.** [Méd.] that cannot be treated.
intransigeance [ɛ̃trɑ̃zi'ʒɑ̃:s] *n.f.* refusal to compromise, stubbornness. || **intransigeant, -e** [-ɑ̃(:t)] *adj.* intransigent, uncompromising.
intransiti|f, -ve [ɛ̃trɑ̃zi't|if, -i:v] *adj.* intransitive.
intrépide [ɛ̃tre'pid] *adj.* dauntless, fearless. || **intrépidité** [-i'te] *n.f.* intrepidity, dauntlessness.
intrigant, -e [ɛ̃tri'gɑ̃(:t)] *adj.* intriguing, scheming. || *n.* intriguer, schemer; [Fam.] wire-puller. || **intrigue** [ɛ̃'trig] *n.f.* **1.** intrigue: *intrigues de couloir*, lobbying. **2.** [récit] plot. || **intriguer** [-e] #3 *v. tr.* to intrigue, puzzle. || *v. intr.* to intrigue, scheme.
introduction [ɛ̃trɔdyk'sjɔ̃] *n.f.* introduction: *lettre d'* ~, letter of introduction; letting in, bringing in, admission. || **introduire** [ɛ̃trɔ'dɥi:r] #56 *v. tr.* to introduce, to bring in: ~ *qqun dans sa famille*, to bring s.o. into one's family; *Il fut immédiatement introduit*, He was immediately shown in; ~ *une nouvelle mode*, to start a new fashion.
introuvable [ɛ̃tru'vabl] *adj.* impossible to find, not to be found.
intrus, -e [ɛ̃'try(:z)] *adj.* intruding. || *n.* intruder.
intuition [ɛ̃tɥi'sjɔ̃] *n.f.* intuition, insight.
inusable [iny'zabl] *adj.* indestructible, that wears for ever.
inusité, -e [inyzi'te] *adj.* unusual; unused, obsolete.
inutile [iny'til] *adj.* useless, unnecessary. || **inutilement** [-'mɑ̃] *adv.* in vain.
inutilisable [-i'zabl] *adj.* unusable, worthless. || **inutilisé, -e** [-i'ze] *adj.* unused.
inutilité [-i'te] *n.f.* uselessness.
invalide [ɛ̃va'lid] *adj.* **1.** disabled, crippled. **2.** [Jur.] not valid. || *n.m.* disabled soldier. || **invalider** [-e] #3 *v. tr.* to invalidate, to nullify; [député] to unseat. || **invalidité** [-i'te] *n.f.* **1.** disability. **2.** invalidity.
invariable [ɛ̃va'rjabl] *adj.* invariable, constant.
invasion [ɛ̃va'zjɔ̃] *n.f.* invasion.
invective [ɛ̃vɛk'ti:v] *n.f.* invective; *pl.* abuse.
invendable [ɛ̃vɑ̃'d|abl] *adj.* unsalable: *être* ~, to be a drug on the market. || **invendu, -e** [-y] *adj.* unsold. || *n. les invendus*, unsold/copies, articles.
inventaire [ɛ̃vɑ̃'tɛ:r] *n.m.* inventory, stocktaking: *faire l'* ~ *de*, to take stock of.
inventer [ɛ̃vɑ̃'|tɛ:r] #3 *v. tr.* **1.** to invent: *Il n'a pas inventé le fil à couper le beurre*, He won't set the Thames on fire. || **invent|eur, -rice** [-tœ:r, -'tris] *adj.* inventive. *n.m.* inventor. || **inventi|f, -ve** [-'tif, -'ti:v] *adj.* inventive, creative. || **invention** [-sjɔ̃] *n.f.* **1.** invention, device, contrivance. **2.** [faculté] inventiveness, imagination. **3.** [mensonge] invention.
inverse [ɛ̃'vɛrs] *adj.* reverse, opposite:

faire l' ~ *de*, to do the opposite of; *en sens* ~, in the opposite direction. || **inversion** [ɛ̃vɛr'sjõ] *n.f.* inversion. || **invertir** [ɛ̃vɛr'ti:r] #17 *v. tr.* to invert.
investigat|eur, -rice [ɛ̃vɛstiga't|œ:r, -ris] *adj.* searching. || *n.* investigator.
investir [ɛ̃vɛs'ti:r] #17 *v. tr.* to invest: ~ *qqun de sa confiance*, to place one's confidence in s.o.
invétéré -e [ɛ̃vete're] *adj.* inveterate, confirmed.
invincible [ɛ̃vɛ̃'sibl] *adj.* invincible, unconquerable; [argument] unanswerable.
invisible [ɛ̃vɛ̃'sibl] *adj.* invisible; unseen.
invitation [ɛ̃vit|a'sjõ] *n.f.* invitation. || **invité, -e** [-e] *adj.* invited. || *n.* guest: *Nous avions des invités*, → We had company. || **inviter** [-e] #3 *v. tr.* to invite; to call upon (to, *à*).
invocation [ɛ̃vɔka'sjõ] *n.f.* invocation.
involontaire [ɛ̃vɔlõ'tɛ:r] *adj.* involuntary.
invoquer [ɛ̃vɔ'ke] #3 *v. tr.* to invoke, to appeal to.
invraisemblable [ɛ̃vrɛsɑ̃'bl|abl] *adj.* unlikely; improbable, hard to believe. || **invraisemblance** [-ɑ̃:s] *n.f.* improbability, unlikelihood.
invulnérable [ɛ̃vylne'rabl] *adj.* invulnerable.
iode [jɔd] *n.m.* iodine.
ion [jõ] *n.m.* ion.
Iowa, l' [lajɔ'wa] *n.m.* Iowa.
irai, &c. Cf. ALLER.
Irak, l' [li'rak] *n.m.* Iraq.
Iran, l' [li'rɑ̃] *n.m.* Iran.
irascible [ira'sibl] *adj.* irascible.
iridescence [iridɛ'sɑ̃:s] *n.f.* iridescence.
iris [i'ris] *n.m.* iris, flag.
irlandais, -e [irlɑ̃'dɛ(:z)] *adj.* Irish. || *n.* Irishman, Irishwoman. || **Irlande, l'** [lir'lɑ̃:d] *n.f.* Ireland: †*État libre d'* ~, Irish Free State; *mer d'* ~, Irish Sea.
ironie [irɔ'ni] *n.f.* irony. || **ironique** [-k] *adj.* ironical. || **ironiquement** [-k'mɑ̃] *adv.* ironically.
irons, iront [i'rõ] cf. ALLER.
irradier [irra'dje] #3 *v. tr.* to irradiate. || *v. intr.* to radiate, irradiate.
irraisonné, -e [irrɛzɔ'ne] *adj.* unreasoned, unreasoning.
irrationnel, -le [irrasjɔ'nɛl] *adj.* irrational.
irréalisable [irreali'zabl] *adj.* impossible, not feasible.
irrécupérable [irrekype'rabl] *adj.* unrecoverable.
irréel, -le [irre'ɛl] *adj.* unreal.
irréfléchi, -e [irrefle'ʃi] *adj.* thoughtless, spontaneous.
irrégulier, -ère [irregy'lj|e, -ɛ:r] *adj.* irregular.
irrémédiable [irreme'djabl] *adj.* irremediable.
irréparable [irrepa'rabl] *adj.* irreparable.
irréprochable [irreprɔ'ʃabl] *adj.* irreproachable, impeccable.
irrésistible [irrezis'tibl] *adj.* irresistible.
irrésolu, -e [irrezɔ'ly] *adj.* **1.** [problème] unsolved. **2.** [Pers.] irresolute.
irrespectueu|x, -se [irrɛspɛk'tɥø(:z)] *adj.* disrespectful, uncivil.
irrespirable [irrɛspi'rabl] *adj.* unbreathable; [Fig.] stifling.
irresponsable [irrɛspõ'sabl] *adj.* irresponsible.
irrévérencieu|x, -se [irreverɑ̃'sjø(:z)] *adj.* irreverent.
irrigation [iriga'sjõ] *n.f.* irrigation, dry farming.
irritable [iri't|abl] *adj.* irritable, peevish; (very) sensitive (to irritants). || **irritant, -e** [-ɑ̃(:t)] *adj.* irritating. || **irritation** [-a'sjõ] *n.f.* irritation, anger; [Méd.] irritation. || **irrité, -e** [-e] *adj.* irritated. || **irriter** #3 *v. tr.* to irritate.
irruption [iryp'sjõ] *n.f.* irruption: *faire* ~, to burst (into, *dans*).
Islande, l' [lislɑ̃:d] *n.f.* Iceland.
isolant, -e [izɔ'l|ɑ̃(:t)] *adj.* insulating. || *n.m.* insulator. || **isolat|eur, -rice** [-a'tœ:r, -a'tris] *adj.* insulating. || *n.m.* insulator. || **isolé, -e** [-e] *adj.* **1.** isolated. **2.** [Electr.] insulated. || **isolément** [-e'mɑ̃] *adv.* separately, independently. || **isolement** [-'mɑ̃] *n.m.* **1.** isolation, seclusion; [moral] loneliness. **2.** insulation. || **isoler** [-e] #3 *v. tr.* **1.** to isolate. **2.** [Electr.] to insulate. || **isoloir** [-wa:r] *n.m.* **1.** insulator, insulating table. **2.** polling booth.
Israël [izra'ɛl] *n.m.* Israel. || **israélien, -ne** [-jɛ̃, -jɛn] *adj.* Israeli. || **Israélien, -ne** *n.* Israeli. || **israélite** [-it] *adj.* Jewish. || *n.m/f.* Jew.
issu, -e (de) [i'sy] *adj.* born (of); descended (from). || **issue** *n.f.* **1.** exit, outlet. **2.** issue, outcome, result: *à l'* ~ *de*, at the end of.
isthme [ism] *n.m.* isthmus.
Italie, l' [lita'li] *n.f.* Italy. || **italien, -ne** [-jɛ̃, -jɛn] *adj.* Italian. || **Italien, -ne** *n.* Italian.
italique [ita'lik] *adj.* Italic; [Impr.] italics: *mettre en* ~, to italicize.
itinéraire [itine'rɛ:r] *n.m.* itinerary, route.
ivoire [i'vwa:r] *n.m.* ivory.
ivre [i:vr] *adj.* drunk: ~*-mort* [ivrə'mɔ:r], dead drunk. || **ivresse** [i'vr|ɛs] *n.f.* drunkenness; intoxication; [Fig.] rapture, intoxication. || **ivrogne, -sse** [-ɔɲ, -ɔ'ɲɛs] *adj.* given to drinking, often drunk. || *n.* drunkard. || **ivrognerie** [-ɔɲ'ri] *n.f.* drunkenness, heavy drinking.

J

J, j [ʒi] *n.m.* the letter J, j.
j' cf. JE.
jabot [ʒa'bo] *n.m.* [oiseau] crop; [chemise] frill.
jachère [ʒa'ʃɛ:r] *n.f.* fallow: *être en* ~, to lie fallow.
jacinthe [ʒa'sɛ̃:t] *n.f.* [Bot.] hyacinth.
Jacques [ʒɑ:k] *n.m.* = James: *la rue Saint-* ~, St. James St.
†**jadis** [ʒa'dis] *adv.* formerly: *au temps* ~, in the old days.
jaillir [ʒa'j|i:r] #17 *v. intr.* to gush, spout, spurt out, spring. || **jaillissement** [-is'mɑ̃] *n.m.* gushing, spouting, spurting.
jais [ʒɛ] *n.m.* jet: *noir de* ~, jet black.
jalon [ʒa'l|ɔ̃] *n.m.* surveying staff; [mostly Fig.] landmark. || **jalonner** [-ɔ'ne] #3 *v. tr.* to stake out (an area, a road, &c.); to mark at intervals (with, *de*).
jalousement [ʒaluz'mɑ̃] *adv.* jealously. || **jalouser** [-u'ze] #3 *v. tr.* to be envious of (a rival, a neighbour, s.o.'s good fortune, &c.). || **jalousie** [u'zi] *n.f.* **1.** jealousy. **2.** venetian blind. cf. STORE. || **jalou|x, -se** [ʒa'l|u(:z)] *adj.* jealous; envious; [Fig.] †anxious (to succeed, &c.). || *n.m.* jealous person.
Jamaïque, la [ʒama'ik] *n.f.* Jamaica.
jamais [ʒa'mɛ] *adv.* **1.** never, not . . . ever: *Ne dites* ~ *cela,* Never say that, Don't ever say that; *Jamais de la vie!,* Nothing doing!, It's out of the question. **2.** ever; for ever: *à jamais,* for ever; *à tout* ~, for ever and ever; *presque* ~, hardly ever; *si* ~ (+ *indic.*), if ever.
jambe [ʒɑ̃:b] *n.f.* leg; [*N.B.* legs of table, chair, &c., cf. PIED]: *courir à toutes jambes,* to run as fast as one can; *prendre ses jambes à son cou,* to take to one's heels.
jambon [ʒɑ̃'bɔ̃] *n.m.* ham.
James, la Baie [la bɛ 'ʤe:mz] *n.f.* James Bay.
jante [ʒɑ̃:t] *n.f.* felloe, rim.
janvier [ʒɑ̃'vje] *n.m.* January. cf. AVRIL.
Japon, le [ʒa'p|ɔ̃] *n.m.* Japan: *la mer du* ~, the Sea of Japan. || **japonais, -e** [-ɔ'nɛ(:z)] *adj.* Japanese. || **Japonais, -e** *n.* Japanese.
jappement [ʒap|'mɑ̃] *n.m.* [chien, chacal] yelping, yapping. || **japper** [-e] #3 *v. intr.* to yelp, yap.
jaquette [ʒa'kɛt] *n.f.* morning coat, cutaway coat; © (woman's) nightgown.
jardin [ʒar'd|ɛ̃] *n.m.* garden, gardens, park: *Jardin botanique,* Botanical Gardens; ~ *potager,* vegetable garden; ~ *[d'enfants,* © *d'enfance,* kindergarten. || **jardiner** [-i'ne] #3 *v. tr.* to garden. || **jardinet** [-i'nɛ] *n.m.* small garden. || **jardini|er, -ère** [-i'nje, -i'njɛ:r] *n.* gardener. || **jardinière** [-i'njɛ:r] *n.f.* **1.** flower stand. **2.** mixed salad.
jargon [ʒar'gɔ̃] *n.m.* jargon, lingo.
jarre [ʒa:r] *n.f.* (earthenware) jar.
jarret [ʒa'rɛ] *n.m.* ham, hock, muscle of the leg: *avoir de bons jarrets,* to have strong legs. || **jarretelle** [ʒar'tɛl] *n.f.* garter. || **jarretière** [ʒar'tjɛ:r] *n.f.* garter: *L'Ordre de la Jarretière,* the Order of the Garter.
jars [ʒa:r] *n.m.* gander.
jaser [ʒɑ'z|e] #3 *v. intr.* to gossip: *Cela a fait beaucoup* ~, It caused a good deal of gossip; © to chat, talk. || **jaseu|r, -se** [-œ:r, -ø:z] *adj.* gossip: *Il est très* ~, He is quite a gossip; ~ *du cèdre,* cedar waxwing.
jasmin [ʒas'mɛ̃] *n.m.* jasmine, jessamine.
jauge [ʒo:ʒ] *n.f.* gauge; [Naut.] tonnage. || **jauger** [ʒo'ʒe] #5 *v. tr.* to gauge, to measure; [Naut.] to have a capacity of: *Ce navire jauge 10,000 tonnes,* This ship is ten thousand tons.
jaunâtre [ʒo'nɑ:tr] *adj.* yellowish; [peau, &c.] sallow. || **jaune** [ʒo:n] *adj.* yellow, (light) brown: *rire* ~, to laugh on the wrong side of the mouth. || *n.m.* **1.** yellow. **2.** yolk. **3.** strike-breaker, [Br.] blackleg. || **jauni, -e** [ʒo'n|i] *adj.* turned yellow; yellowed. || **jaunir** [-i:r] #17 *v. intr.* to turn yellow; *v. tr.* to dye yellow, to stain: *jauni par le tabac,* tobacco-stained; [© au repassage] to scorch. || **jaunisse** [-is] *n.f.* jaundice.
Javel, eau de [ʒa'v|ɛl] *n.f.* Javel water.
javeler [ʒav'le] #8 *v. tr.* to lay in loose sheaves. || **javelle** [ʒa'v.ɛl] *nf.* swath.
javelliser [ʒav|eli'ze] #3 *v. tr.* to chlorinate (water).
jazz [ʤa:z] *n.m.* jazz.
je [ʒə] (j' before vowel or mute *h*) *pron.* [☞ used only as subject of a verb] I: *Je sais,* I know; *Que sais-je?,* What do I know? Cf. MOI.
Jean [ʒɑ̃] *n.m.* = John, [Fam.] Johnny. || **Jeanne** [ʒan] *n.f.* = Joan, Jean, Jane: ~ *d'Arc,* Joan of Arc. || **Jeannette** [-ɛt] *n.f.* = Janet, Jeanette. || **Jeannot** [-o] = Jackie.
jeep [ʒi:p] [© dʒi:p] *n.f.* jeep.
Jésuite [ʒe'zɥit] *n.m.* **1.** Jesuit. **2.** [Fig., Péj.]: *Il est très* ~, He is very jesuitical.
Jésus [ʒe'zy] *n.m.* Jesus; Jesus Christ; *après J.C.,* → A.D.; *avant J.-C.* → B.C.
jet [ʒɛ] *n.m.* throw(ing), cast(ing); [liquide]

jet, spurt: ~ *d'eau*, fountain; [lumière] flash; [Loc.] *d'un seul* ~, in one sweep: *C'est du premier* ~, It's a first draught.

jetée [ʒə'te] *n.f.* [Naut.] jetty, pier.

jeter [ʒə'te] #3 *v. tr.* **1.** to throw; [avec violence] to hurl, to fling; [négligemment] to toss: ~ *qqch. à la figure de qqun*, to throw sth. into s.o.'s face; ~ *ses armes*, to throw down one's arms; ~ *ce qui ne sert plus*, to throw away what can no longer be used; ~ *bas*, to tear down. **2.** [Loc.] ~ *l'ancre*, to drop the anchor; ~ *un coup d'œil*, to cast a glance; ~ *les fondements*, to lay the foundations; ~ *sur le papier*, to jot down. || **se jeter** *v. pron.* to/throw, fling/o.s. (on, *sur*), to pounce upon; ~ */tête baissée, à corps perdu/sur*, to rush headlong into.

jeton [ʒə'tõ] *n.m.* token, counter; [Tél.] slug: ~ *de présence*, attendance fee.

jeu [ʒø] *n.m.* **1.** game, play: *avoir beau* ~, to have a good hand, [Fig.] to be in a good position (to, *de*); *avoir du* ~, to have a good hand; *être dans le* ~, to be in on the game; *Ce n'est pas de* ~, It is not fair; *jouer franc* ~, to play fair; *montrer son* ~, to show one's hand; *être vieux* ~, to be outmoded. **2.** gamble: *être en* ~, to be at stake; *mettre en* ~, to stake; *jouer gros* ~, to play for high stakes. **3.** acting, play. **4.** deck (of cards), set (of tools). **5.** working, play: *entrer en* ~, to operate; *donner du* ~, to give some leeway, to loosen.

jeudi [ʒø'di] *n.m.* Thursday, cf. LUNDI.

jeun, à [a'ʒœ̃] *loc. adv.* [nourriture] on an empty stomach; [boisson] sober.

jeune [ʒœn] *adj.* young, [in comparison] younger: *un* ~ *homme*, a young man; *une* ~ *fille*, a girl; *mon* ~ *frère*, my younger brother; *Pline le* ~, Pliny the Younger. || *n.mpl. les jeunes*, the younger/set, generation/.

jeûne [ʒø:n] *n.m.* fast, fasting: *rompre le* ~, to break the fast; *le* ~ *eucharistique*, the fast for communion. || **jeûner** [ʒø'ne] #3 *v. intr.* to fast.

jeunesse [ʒœ'nɛs] *n.f.* **1.** youth; boyhood, girlhood, young days: *dans la fleur de la* ~, in the prime of youth. **2.** [coll.] young people, youth.

joailli|er, -ère [ʒwɑ'j|e, -ɛ:r] *n.* jeweller.

joie [ʒwa] *n.f.* joy; mirth, gaiety: †*être comblé de* ~, to be overwhelmed with joy; *pleurer de* ~, to weep for joy.

joindre [ʒwɛ̃:dr], **joignant** [ʒwa'ɲɑ̃], **joint** [ʒwɛ̃] #36 *v. tr.* **1.** to join, connect; [mains] to clasp. **2.** to combine, add; to enclose: ~ *l'utile à l'agréable*, to combine business with pleasure; *Je joins à ma lettre*, I enclose. **3.** to catch, reach (a person). || *v. intr.* to fit: *La porte ne joint pas bien*, The door does not fit. || **joint, -e** [ʒwɛ̃(:t)] *adj.* joined, added, enclosed: *ci-joint*, enclosed herewith; *pièces jointes*, enclosures. || **joint** [ʒwɛ̃] *n.m.* joint; junction; [Fig.] *trouver le* ~, to find a way, to hit upon a plan. || **jointure** [-'ty:r] *n.f.* joint; [doigt] knuckle.

joli, -e [ʒɔ'li] *adj.* pretty; nice, neat; attractive, pleasing: *C'est très* ~, It is very pretty. || *n.m.* [Iron.] *C'est du joli!*, That's a fine mess. || **joliment** [-'mɑ̃] *adv.* prettily; [Fam.] extremely; much: *C'est* ~ *dommage*, That is really too bad.

jonc [ʒõ] *n.m.* **1.** rush, cane. **2.** © wedding ring.

joncher [ʒõ'ʃe] #3 *v. tr.* to strew: ~ *le sol de fleurs*, to strew, litter/the ground with flowers.

jonction [ʒõk'sjõ] *n.f.* junction: *Les deux armées opérèrent leur* ~, The two armies came together.

jongler [ʒõ'gl|e] #3 *v. intr.* to juggle (*avec*, with); [Fig.] to be an expert (at, *avec*). || **jongleur** [-œ:r] *n.m.* minstrel; juggler; trickster.

jonquille [ʒõ'ki:j] *n.f.* daffodil.

joue [ʒu] *n.f.* cheek: *mettre en* ~, to take aim at, to cover s.o. (with a gun); *En* ~ *!*, Aim!

jouer [ʒw|e] #3 *v. intr.* **1.** to play, to amuse o.s.: ~ *aux cartes*, to play cards; ~ *du piano*, to play the piano; *A vous de* ~ *!*, It's your/turn, move/; [Fig.] ~ *avec une idée*, to toy with an idea. **2.** to gamble: ~ *à la Bourse*, to play the stock market; ~ *gros jeu*, to play for high stakes. || *v. tr.* to act, to perform: ~ *le rôle de*, to play the part of; ~ *la comédie*, to put on a play, [Fig.] to put on an act; ~ *un tour à qqun*, to play a trick on s.o. || **se jouer (de)** *v. pron.* to make fun (of), to mock, to make a fool of: ~ *des difficultés*, to handle things with the greatest of ease. || **jouet** [-ɛ] *n.m.* toy; [Fig.] laughing-stock; *être le* ~ *des circonstances*, to be a toy in the hands of fate. || **joueu|r, -se** [-œ:r, -ø:z] *n.* **1.** player [mostly with sports, games, &c.; for musical instruments, use compounds in *-iste*, e.g. a violin player, → un violoniste; for theatre plays, use *acteur*, *actrice*.] **2.** gambler; speculator.

joug [ʒug] *n.m.* yoke.

†**jouir (de)** [ʒwi:r] #17 *v. intr.* to enjoy: *Il jouit d'une bonne santé*, He enjoys good health. || **jouissance** [ʒwi'sɑ̃:s] *n.f.* enjoy-

ment, use: *avoir la ~ du jardin*, to have the use of the garden.

joujou [ʒu'ʒu] *pl.* **-x** *n.m.* [Fam.] toy, plaything: *faire ~*, to play. cf. JOUET.

jour [ʒu:r] *n.m.* **1.** day: *le ~ de l'an*, New Year's Day; *~ férié*, holiday; *~ ouvrable*, workday; *~ de semaine*, weekday; *au ~ le ~*, from day to day; *vivre au ~ le ~*, to live from hand to mouth; *A un de ces jours!*, Be seeing you!; *de ~ en ~*, from day to day; *de nos jours*, nowadays; *du ~ au lendemain*, overnight; *mettre à ~*, to bring up to date. **2.** daylight: *Il fait (grand) jour*, It is (broad) daylight; *au petit ~*, at daybreak; *au grand ~*, in broad daylight; *faire le ~ sur une affaire*, to throw light on a matter; *mettre au ~*, to bring to light; *présenter sous un certain ~*, to present in a certain light; *donner le ~ à*, to give birth to; *voir le ~*, to be born. **3.** opening.

Jourdain, le [ʒur'dɛ̃] *n.m.* the Jordan.

journal [ʒur'n|al] *n.m.* **1.** newspaper; [savant] journal: *kiosque à journaux*, newstand. **2.** diary: *tenir un ~*, to keep a diary. || **journali|er, -ère** [-a'lje, -a'ljɛ:r] *adj.* daily. || *n.m.* journeyman, labourer. || **journalisme** [-a'lism] *n.m.* journalism. || **journaliste** [-a'list] *n. m/f* journalist.

journée [-e] *n.f.* day [from morning till night], daytime, day's work: *la ~ du 13 mai*, the day of May 13th; *dans la ~*, in the daytime; *toute la ~*, all day long; *passer toute la ~ à . . .*, to spend the whole day on . . . ; *travailler à la ~*, to work by the day; *homme de ~*, day labourer; *femme de ~*, cleaning woman. || **journellement** [-ɛl'mɑ̃] *adv.* daily.

joute [ʒut] *n.f.* †joust, tilting-match; © game, contest, match; *~ de hockey*, hockey game.

jovial [ʒɔ'vj|al] *pl.* **jovials** ou **joviaux** [-al, -o] *adj.* jovial, debonair.

joyau [ʒwa'jo] *n.m.* jewel.

joyeusement [ʒwaøz'mɑ̃] *adv.* joyfully, cheerfully. || **joyeu|x, -se** [ʒwa'jø(:z)] *adj.* excited; glad; merry. cf. JOIE.

jubilation [ʒybila'sjɔ̃] *n.f.* jubilation.

jubilé [ʒybi'le] *n.m.* jubilee; golden wedding.

jubiler [ʒybi'l|e] #3 *v. intr.* to be jubilant.

jucher, se [ʒy'ʃe] #3 *v. pron.* to roost, to perch.

judaïque [ʒyda'ik] *adj.* Judaic. || **judaïsme** [ʒyda'ism] *n.m.* Judaism.

Judée, la [ʒy'de] *n.f.* Judæa.

judiciaire [ʒydi|'sjɛ:r] *adj.* judicial; [Med.] forensic. || **judicieu|x, -se** [-'sjø(:z)] *adj.* judicious, sensible: *peu ~*, → injudicious.

juge [ʒy:ʒ] *n.m.* judge; justice: *~ de la Cour Suprême*, Justice of the (U.S.) Supreme Court; *~ de paix*, justice of the peace.

jugement [ʒyʒ|'mɑ̃] *n.m.* **1.** judgment; opinion; good sense: *Il a beaucoup de ~*, He is very sound; *porter un ~ sur*, to pass judgment on. **2.** [Jur.] trial, sentence: *passer en ~*, to be brought up for trial; *prononcer un ~*, to pass sentence. || **juger** [-e] #5 *v. tr.* **1.** to judge, to estimate: *~ bon de*, *~ à propos de*, to see fit to. **2.** to try (before a judge): *~ un procès*, to try a case. || *v. intr.* *~ de*, to have an opinion on, to judge: *Je suis mal placé pour en ~*, I am not in a position to judge; *A vous d'en ~*, You be the judge.

jui|f, -ve [ʒy|if, -i:v] *adj.* Jewish. || **Jui|f, -ve** *n.* Jew, Jewess; Hebrew cf. ISRAÉLIEN; ISRAÉLITE.

juillet [ʒɥi'jɛ] *n.m.* July, cf. AVRIL.

juin [ʒɥɛ̃, ʒɥœ̃, © ʒy'œ̃] *n.m.* June, cf. AVRIL.

Julie [ʒy'l|i] *n.f.* = Julia. || **Juliette** [-jɛt] *n.f.* = Juliet.

jume|au, -lle[1] [ʒy'm|o, -ɛl] *adj.* & *n.* twin (brother, sister): *son ~*, his twin brother; *lits jumeaux*, twin beds. || **jumelé, -e** [-'le] *adj.* arranged in pairs, coupled, twin: *villes jumelées*, twin cities. || **jumeler** #8 *v. tr.* to couple, to join. || **jumelles**[2] [-ɛl] *n.f. usual. plur.* binoculars, field glasses: *~ de théâtre*, opera glasses.

jument [ʒy'mɑ̃] *n.f.* mare.

jungle [ʒɔ̃:gl] *n.f.* jungle.

junte [ʒɔ̃:t] *n.f.* : *~ militaire*, military junta.

jupe [ʒyp] *n.f.* skirt (dress). || **jupon** [-ɔ̃] *n.m.* petticoat.

juré [ʒy'r|e] *n.m.* juror, juryman: [Fr.] *Messieurs les jurés*, gentlemen, members of the jury.

jurement [ʒyr'mɑ̃] *n.m.* oath.

jurer [-e] #3 *v. tr.* & *intr.* **1.** to swear; to promise, to swear by, to take an oath: *Je jure de* (+ *inf.*), I swear to . . . ; *Je jure que* (+ *futur*), I swear that; *Je jure par*, I swear by; *se ~ amitié*, to take an oath of friendship. **2.** to swear, blaspheme, cf. JURON. **3.** to clash (of sounds, colours, &c.).

juridiction [ʒyridik'sjɔ̃] *n.f.* jurisdiction. || **juridique** [ʒyri'dik] *adj.* juridical, legal. || **jurisprudence** [ʒyrispry'dɑ̃:s] *n.f.* jurisprudence.

juron [ʒy'rɔ̃] *n.m.* oath, blasphemy.

jury [ʒy'ri] *n.m.* **1.** [Jur.] jury. **2.** [Scol.] board of examiners, the examiners. **3.** [épreuve] the judges.

jus [ʒy] *n.m.* **1.** juice: *un ~ de fruit, de raisin*: fruit juice, grape juice. **2.** [Culin.] gravy: *le ~ de rôti*, stock, pan gravy (of a roast).

jusque, jusqu'à, jusqu'au [ʒysk(ə), -a, -o] *prép.* **1.** [temps] until, till, up to, down to: *jusqu'à présent*, until now, to this day; *jusque-là*, until then; *jusqu'ici*, till now, so far. **2.** [espace] as far as, up to, down to: *Jusqu'où êtes-vous allé?*, How far did you go?; *jusqu'ici*, up, down/to here; *jusque-là*, up, down/to there. **3.** [progression] to: *jusqu'au bout*, to the end, all the way; *jusqu'au dernier*, to the last one; *jusque-là*, up to that point. **4.** even: *Jusqu'aux enfants qui sont venus*, Even the children came. || *conj. jusqu'à ce que* (+ subj.) until: *Jusqu'à ce qu'il vienne*, Until he comes.

juste [ʒyst] *adj.* **1.** just, fair, lawful. **2.** correct, right, tone: *Le compte est ~*, The account is correct. || *n.m.* upright, righteous person. || *adv. chanter ~*, to sing in tune; *comme de ~*, needless to say; *J'y suis arrivé tout ~*, I just managed it. || **justement** [-ə'mɑ̃] *adv.* **1.** justly, properly. **2.** precisely: *~, je viens de le voir*, It so happens I've just seen him. || **justesse** [-ɛs] *n.f.* **1.** exactness, precision: *avec ~*, rightfully, properly. **2.** [Mus.] exact pitch. **3.** [Loc.] *arriver de ~*, to cut it fine.

justice [-is] *n.f.* **1.** justice: *le ministère de la Justice*, the Department of Justice: *haute cour de ~*, high court of justice; *poursuivre, traduire en ~*, to hale into court, to bring an action against. **2.** justice, fairness: *traiter qqun avec ~*, to treat s.o. fairly; *rendre ~ à qqun*, to give s.o. credit. || **justicier** [-i'sje] *n.m.* **1.** lover of justice. **2.** judge, justiciary. || **justification** [-ifika'sjɔ̃] *n.f.* justification, †vindication. || **justifier** [-i'fje] #3 *v. tr.* to justify, to vindicate. || **se justifier** *v. pron.* to justify, clear o.s. (of, *de*).

jute [ʒyt] *n.m.* jute.

juteu|x, -se [ʒy'tø(:z)] *adj.* juicy, cf. JUS.

juvénile [ʒyve'nil] *adj.* [×] youthful.

K

K, k [kɑ] the letter K, k.

kaki [ka'ki] *n.m. & adj. invar.* khaki.

kangourou [kɑ̃gu'ru] *n.m.* kangaroo.

Kansas, le [kɑ̃'zɑ:s] *n.m.* Kansas.

kayac, kayak [ka'jak] *n.m.* kayak.

Kentucky, le [kɛntɔ'ke] *n.m.* Kentucky.

képi [ke'pi] *n.m.* [French army] kepi.

kidnapper [kidna'pe] #3 *v. tr.* to kidnap.

kif-kif [kif'kif] [Fr.] *adj. invar.* all the same: [Fam.] *C'est ~ (bourricot)*, It is as broad as it is long, It's much of a muchness.

kilo [ki'l|o] [abbr. of KILOGRAMME] *n.m.* kilo. || **kilogramme** [-ɔ'gram] [= 2.2046 lbs] *n.m.* kilogram. || **kilométrage** [-ɔme'tra:ʒ] *n.m.* [© cf. MILLAGE] number of kilometres, → mileage. || **kilomètre** [-ɔ'mɛ:tr] [= km: 3280.8 feet] *n.m.* kilometre: *16 kilomètres*, 10 miles. || **kilométrique** [-ɔme'trik] *adj.* pertaining to kilometres: *borne ~*, milestone.

kiosque [kjɔsk] *n.m.* [Mus.] bandstand; [journaux] news-stand.

klaxon [klak's|ɔ̃] *n.m.* [Fr.] (motor) horn. cf. AVERTISSEUR. || **klaxonner** [-ɔ'ne] #3 *v. intr.* to honk (one's horn).

Klondike, le [klɔn'dajk] *n.m.* Klondike.

knock-out [nɔka'ut] *n.m.* knockout: *mettre ~*, to knock (s.o.) out. || **K.-O.** [kɑ'o] *n.m.* [cf. KNOCK-OUT] K.O.; k.o.: *être K.-O.*, to be K.O.ed.

kyste [kist] *n.m.* cyst.

L, l [ɛl] *n.m.* [letter] L: *l mouillé(e)*, palatal L.

l' [☞ Elided form of *art.* and *pron.* **le, la** occurring before nouns or verbs beginning with vowel or mute *h*: *l'ami*, the friend, *l'orange*, the orange; *je l'entends*, I hear/him/her. cf. LE].

la[1] [la] *art. déf.* cf. LE.

la[2] [la] *n.m.* [Music] A: *donner le* ~, to sound the A; [Fig.] to set the tone.

là [la] *adv.* **1.** there; here: *Mettez ça* ~, Put it there; *Je suis* ~, I am here; *Est-ce qu'il est* ~ ? Is he in?, Is he about?; *Il n'était pas* ~, He was/out, out of town; *Nous en sommes* ~, We have come to that. **2.** [as part of adverbials] **là-bas** [la'bɑ], over there; **là-dedans** [lad(ə)'dɑ̃] in there, in that (receptacle); **là-dessous** [lad(ə)'su], under there, under this, under that; **là-dessus** [la'd(ə)sy], on this, on that; [Fig.] thereupon; **là-haut** [la'o], up there. **3.** [with CE, CET, CETTE]: *cet homme-là*, that man. **4.** [to soothe] *Là! ne pleure plus!* Come now, don't cry any more.

†**labeur** [la'bœːr] *n.m.* [×] labour, work.

laboratoire [labɔra'twaːr] *n.m.* laboratory.

laborieusement [labɔrjøz'mɑ̃] *adv.* painstakingly, laboriously. ‖ **laboriou|x, -se** [labɔ'rjø, -øːz] *adj.* **1.** hard-working, laborious. **2.** *les classes laborieuses*, the working classes.

labour [la'b|uːr] *n.m.* [×] **1.** ploughing; **2.** [*pl.*] ploughed fields. ‖ **labourage** [-u'raːʒ] *n.m.* ploughing, tillage. ‖ **labourer** [-u're] #3 *v. tr.* to plough; [Fig.] to scratch, cut: *Elle lui a labouré la figure de ses ongles*, She scratched his face all over. ‖ *v. intr.* to plough. ‖ **laboureur** [-u'rœːr] *n.m.* [×] ploughman.

Labrador, (le) [labra'dɔːr] Labrador.

labyrinthe [labi'rɛ̃ːt] *n.m.* labyrinth; maze.

lac [lak] *n.m.* lake: *le* ~ *Erié*, Lake Erie; *les Grands Lacs*, the Great Lakes.

lacer [lɑ'ɔ|e], #4 *v. tr.* to lace (up).

lacérer [lase're] #10 *v. tr.* to tear, to lacerate.

lacet [la'sɛ] *n.m.* **1.** lace: ~ *de soulier*, shoelace. **2.** snare, noose. **3.** hairpin bend [of zigzagging road]: *route en* ~, switchback: *La route monte en lacets*, The road zigzags up the mountain.

lâche [lɑːʃ] *adj.* [rope] slack; [knot] loose; [Fig.] cowardly. ‖ *n.m.* coward. ‖ **lâcher** [lɑ'ʃ|e] #3 *v. tr.* **1.** to let go, to release, to let loose, to turn loose: *Il dut* ~ *prise*, He had to let go; ~ *un coup de feu*, to fire a shot; ~ *la bride à un cheval*, to give a horse his head; ~ *un chien*, to turn a dog loose; ~ *pied*, to flinch. **2.** [Fig.] to drop, to blurt out: ~ *ses amis*, to drop one's friends; ~ *un mot*, to blurt out a word. ‖ **lâcheté** [-ʃ'te] *n.f.* cowardice, faint-heartedness.

lacté [lak'te] *adj.* milky: *la Voie lactée*, the Milky Way; → milk: *régime* ~, milk diet.

lacune [la'kyn] *n.f.* gap, deficiency.

là-dedans [lad(ə)'dɑ̃] *adv.* cf. LÀ. ‖ **là-dessous** [lad(ə)'su] *adv.* cf. LÀ. ‖ **là-dessus** [lad(ə)'sy] *adv.* cf. LÀ.

ladre [lɑːdr] *adj.* stingy, niggardly. ‖ *n.m.* miser.

là-haut [la'o] cf. LÀ.

laï|c, -que [la'ik] *adj.* lay, secular: *l'apostolat* ~, the lay Apostolate; undenominational: *école* ~, undenominational school. ‖ *n.m.* layman, lay person; *les laïques*, the laity.

laid, -e [lɛ, lɛd] plain, [US] homely, ugly; improper, shabby: *Ce qu'il a fait là est bien* ~, That was a shabby trick. ‖ **laideur** [-'dœːr] *n.f.* plainness, [US] homeliness, ugliness; shabbiness (of action).

lainage [lɛ'naːʒ] *n.m.* woollen goods, woollens. ‖ **laine** [lɛn] *n.f.* wool: *chaussettes de* ~, woollen socks; ~ *d'acier*, steel wool; [Fig.] *le bas de* ~ (of French peasant), savings, nest-egg; *manger la* ~ *sur le dos à qqun*, to fleece s.o. ‖ **laineu|x, -se** [-ø, -øːz] *adj.* woolly.

laïque cf. LAIC.

laisse[1] [lɛs] *n.f.* leash.

laisse[2] cf. LAISSER.

laisser [lɛ'se] #3 *v. tr.* **1.** to leave (endroit, personne, travail), to quit (travail): *Il n'a rien laissé*, He made a clean sweep. **2.** to leave, to let: *Laissez-le tranquille*, Let him alone. 3. to let, to allow: *Il m'a laissé sortir*, He let me out; *Il s'est laissé guider*, He allowed himself to be guided; *Ne vous laissez pas faire*, Fight, hit back. **4.** to let have: *Je vous le laisse pour cinq dollars*, I'll let you have it for five dollars. **5.** [Loc.] *Laissons cela*, Let's forget (about) it; *Cela ne laisse pas de m'inquiéter*, I can't help being worried. ‖ **laisser-aller** [-ra'le] *n.m. inv.* carelessness, negligence, slovenliness (in dress, speech, manners]. ‖ **laissez-passer** [-pɑ'se] *n.m. inv.* pass, permit.

lait [lɛ] *n.m.* milk: ~ /*concentré, condensé*/, condensed milk; ~ *écrémé*, skim milk; *petit* ~, whey; ~ *de poule* eggnog; *dents de* ~, first teeth; *frère de* ~, foster-brother. ‖ **laitage** [-'taːʒ] *n.m.*

dairy products. || **laitance** [-'tɑ̃:s] *n.f.* milt, roe. || **laiterie** [-t'ri] *n.f.* dairy, dairy-farming. || **laiteu|x, -se** [-'tø, -'tø:z] *adj.* milky. || **laiti|er, -ère** [-'tje, -'tjɛ:r] *adj.* dairy: *une vache laitière*, a milch cow; *l'industrie laitière*, the dairy industry. || *n.* milkman, milkmaid.

laiton [lɛ'tõ] *n.m.* brass.

laitue [lɛ'ty] *n.f.* lettuce.

lambeau [lɑ̃'bo] *n.m.* tatter, shred.

lambin, -e [lɑ̃'b|ɛ̃, -in] *adj.* [Fam.] slow. || *n.* dawdler. || **lambiner** [-i'ne] #3 *v. intr.* to dawdle.

lambris [lɑ̃'bri] *n.m.* panelling, wainscoting; (plaster) ceiling: *vivre sous des* ~ *dorés*, to live in a luxurious setting. || **lambrisser** [-'se] #3 *v. tr.* to panel, wainscot, plaster.

lame [lam] *n.f.* **1.** blade; [jalousie] slat; [patin] runner; [métal] thin blade. **2.** wave: *brise-lames*, breakwater; *le creux des lames*, the trough of the sea; *une* ~ *de fond*, a ground swell. || **lamelle** [-ɛl] *n.f.* lamelle, thin strip; *lamelles de plomb* (aux fenêtres), latticework.

lamentable [lamɑ̃'t|abl] *adj.* lamentable, regrettable, piteous: *un accident* ~, a lamentable accident; *un incident* ~, a regrettable incident; *un échec* ~, a piteous failure; [Fam.] *Il a été* ~, He was hopeless. || **lamentation** [-a'sjõ] *n.f.* lamentation, wailing. || **lamenter (se)** [-e] #3 *v. pron.* to moan, to wail. ||

laminer [lami'n|e] #3 *v. tr.* to laminate, to roll out. || **laminoir** [-wa:r] *n.m.* rolling mill.

lampadaire [lɑ̃pa'dɛ:r] *n.m.* tall lamppost, lamp standard. || **lampant** [lɑ̃'pɑ̃] *adj.* refined: *pétrole* ~, kerosene. || **lampe** [lɑ̃:p] *n.f.* lamp; [radio] tube: ~ *à arc*, arc lamp; ~ *à pétrole*, kerosene lamp; ~ (*électrique*) *de poche*, flashlight, [Br.] torch; ~ *-tempête*, hurricane lamp; *pâlir sous la* ~, to burn the midnight oil; *mettre sa* ~ *sous le boisseau*, to hide one's light under a bushel. || **lampion** [lɑ̃'p|jõ] *n.m.* Chinese lantern; © [Rel.] candle. || **lampiste** [-ist] *n.m.* lamp-maker; lamplighter [in charge of lamp in railway station]; [Sl.] scapegoat, fall guy.

lance [lɑ̃:s] *n.f.* [weapon] lance, spear; (d'arrosage) hose. || **lancé** [lɑ̃'s|e] *adj.*: *Il est très* ~, He's in the swim. || **lance-flammes** [lɑ̃s|'flɑ:m] *n.m. inv.* flame-thrower. || **lance-pierres** [-'pjɛ:r] *n.m. inv.* sling. || **lance-torpille** [-tɔr'pi:j] *n.m. inv.* torpedo tube. || **lancement** [-'mɑ̃] *n.m.* [action] throwing; [bateau] launching; [Fig.] bringing out, launching (of a book, play, &c.). || **lancer** [-e], **(-çant)** #4 *v. tr.* **1.** to throw, to fling, to pitch; ~ *des pierres*, to throw stones; ~ *des bombes*, to drop bombs. **2.** to issue; to launch; to introduce: ~ *un navire*, to launch a ship; ~ *un nouveau produit*, to introduce a new product; ~ *un appel*, to issue, to send out/a call; ~ *un coup d'œil*, to give a glance. || **se lancer** *v. pron.* **1.** [passive sense] to be thrown; to be started: *la balle se lance avec une raquette*, The ball is hit with a racket. **2.** [active sense] to launch out: ~ *dans la traduction*, to take up translation. || *n.m.* [action] throwing, launching, casting. || **lanceur** [-œ:r] © *n.m.* [Sport] pitcher.

lancinant, -e [-i'nɑ̃, -i'nɑ̃:t] *adj.* shooting: *une douleur lancinante*, a gnawing pain, a twinge.

landau, -s [lɑ̃'do] *n.m.* **1.** landau. **2.** baby carriage, cf. CARROSSE.

lande [lɑ̃:d] *n.f.* moor, heath.

langage [lɑ̃'ga:ʒ] *n.m.* language, speech.

lange [lɑ̃:ʒ] *n.m.* diaper.

langoureu|x, -se [lɑ̃gu'r|ø, -ø:z] *adj.* languid; languishing; languorous.

langouste [lɑ̃'gust] *n.f.* spiny lobster, rock lobster, (sea) crawfish.

langue [lɑ̃:g] *n.f.* **1.** tongue: *mauvaise* ~, backbiter, scandalmonger; *donner sa* ~ *au chat*, to give up; *délier la* ~ *à qqun*, to loosen s.o.'s tongue; *tirer la* ~ *à qqun*, to stick one's tongue out at s.o.; (*avoir*) *la* ~ *bien pendue*, (to have) the gift of the gab. **2.** language: *langues vivantes*, modern languages. **3.** [Fig.] strip (of land). || **languette** [lɑ̃'gɛt] *n.f.* flap, strip (of paper, &c.).

langueur [lɑ̃'gœ:r] *n.f.* languor. || **languir** [lɑ̃'g|i:r], **languissant** [-i'sɑ̃], **langui** [-i] #17 *v. intr.* to languish, to pine away. || **languissant, -e** [-i'sɑ̃(:t)] *adj.* languishing; inactive.

lanière [la'njɛ:r] *n.f.* thong; lash.

lanterne [lɑ̃'tɛrn] *n.f.* lantern: ~ *-tempête*, hurricane lamp; ~ *vénitienne*, Japanese lantern, [Br.] Chinese lantern; ~ *magique*, magic lantern; *prendre des vessies pour des lanternes*, to labour under a false impression, to be taken in; ~ *sourde*, dark lantern. || **lanterner** [-e] #3 *v. intr.* to dawdle; to string along.

laper [la'pe] #3 *v. tr.* [of animal] to lap up (milk, water, &c.).

lapereau [lap'ro] *n.m.* young rabbit.

lapidaire [lapi|'dɛ:r] *n.m.* lapidary. || *adj.* lapidary; [style] concise, terse. || **lapider** [-'de] #3 *v. tr.* to lapidate; stone to death.

lapin [la'pɛ̃] *n.m.* rabbit: ~ *de garenne*, wild rabbit.

lapsus [lap'sys] *n.m.* slip; lapse; ~ *calami,* slip of the pen, clerical error.

laquaiche [la'kɛʃ] © *n.f.* mooneye.

laquais [la'kɛ] *n.m.* footman, lackey.

laque [lak] *n.f.* lacquer.

laquelle [la'kɛl] *pron. interrog. & rel. f. pl.* **lesquelles,** cf. LEQUEL.

laquer [lake] #3 *v. tr.* to lacquer; to japan.

larcin [lar'sɛ̃] *n.m.* petty larceny, theft.

lard [la:r] *n.m.* [×] bacon; © lard. || **larder** [lar'de] #3 *v. tr.* to lard.

lardon [lar'dõ] *n.m.* lardoon, piece of bacon (for larding); [Fig.] jest, taunt.

large [larʒ] *adj.* wide; broad: *être ~ de carrure,* to be broad-shouldered; [Fig.] generous, liberal: *Il a l'esprit ~ ,* He is broadminded. [Loc.] *ne pas en mener ~ ,* not to feel very courageous; *pour une ~ part, dans une ~ mesure,* to a large extent, largely. || *n.m.* **1.** width, breath: *ayant trois pieds de ~ ,* three feet/wide, in width/. **2.** [sea] open sea: *prendre le ~ ,* to head out to sea; [Fig. & Fam.] to take off; *au ~ ,* in the offing; *au ~ de Terre-Neuve,* off Newfoundland. || **largesse** [-ɛs] *n.f.* bounty; liberality, generosity; *pl.* gifts: *faire des largesses (à),* to be/ generous, open-handed/(with). || **largeur** [-œ:r] *n.f.* **1.** width, breadth: *qui a trente pieds de ~ ,* thirty feet/wide, in breadth/. **2.** [Fig.] broadness (of outlook): *~ d'esprit,* broadmindedness.

larguer [lar'ge] #3 *v. tr.* [Naut.] to let go: *~ l'amarre,* to cast off; [ballon] to release.

larme [larm] *n.f.* tear: *avoir les larmes aux yeux,* to have tears in one's eyes; *verser des larmes,* to shed tears. || **larmoyant, -e** [-wa'jɑ̃(:t)] *adj.* lachrymose, tearful; [*yeux*] watering. || **larmoyer** [-wa'je] ++12 *v. intr.* to water; [Péj.] to snivel.

†**larron** [la'rõ] *n.m.* thief, robber: *Ils s'entendent comme larrons en foire,* They are as thick as thieves.

larve [larv] *n.f.* larva. || **larvé, -e** [larve] *adj.* embryonic.

laryngite [larɛ̃'ʒit] *n.f.* laryngitis.

larynx [la'rɛ̃:ks] *n.m.* larynx.

las, -se [lɑ, lɑ:s] *adj.* [rather literary. cf. FATIGUÉ] weary. || **lasser** [lɑ'se] #3 *v. tr.* to tire, to weary. || **se lasser** *v. pron.* to grow weary: *sans se ~ ,* unceasingly; *se ~ de (qqun, qqch.),* to get tired of (s.o., sth.). || **lassitude** [lasi'tyd] *n.f.* weariness.

latent, -e [la'tɑ̃(:t)] *adj.* latent.

latéra|l, -ux [late'r|al, -o] *adj.* lateral, → side: *porte latérale,* side door.

latin, -e [la't|ɛ̃, -in] *n.m.* Latin. || *n.m.* [language] Latin: [Loc.] *J'y perds mon ~ ,* → It's all Greek to me.

latitude [lati'tyd] *n.f.* latitude; [Fig.] scope, freedom.

latte [lat] *n.f.* lath. || **lattis** [-i] *n.m.* lath-work, lattice(-work).

lauréat, -e [lɔre'a(t)] *n. & adj.* (prize-) winner, †laureate.

Laurent [lɔ'rɑ̃] *n.m.* = Lawrence, [Fam.] Larry. || **Laurentides, les** [-'tid] *n.f.pl.* [Géog.] the Laurentians: *le Parc des ~ ,* the Laurentides Park. || **Laurentien -ne** [-'sjɛ̃, -'sjɛn] © *adj. & n.* Laurentian, of Quebec.

laurier [lɔ'rje] *n.m.* laurel, [Fig. usual. pl.] laurels, glory: *s'endormir sur ses lauriers,* to rest on o.'s/laurels, oars.

lavable [la'v|abl] *adj.* washable. || **lavabo** *n.m.* **1.** washbowl. **2.** [w.c.] washroom. **3.** [R.C.] the washing of fingers. || **lavage** [-a:ʒ] *n.m.* washing.

lavande [la'vɑ̃:d] *n.f.* lavender.

lave [la:v] *n.f.* lava.

lave[2] [la:v] cf. LAVER.

lavement [lav|'mɑ̃] *n.m.* (rectal) injection. [☞ Do not confuse with LAVAGE.] ||**laver** [-e] #3 *v. tr.* to wash: *~ la vaisselle,* to wash up. || **se laver** *v. pr.* to wash (oneself): *~ les mains,* to wash o.'s hands. || **lavette** [-ɛt] *n.f.* dish cloth. || **laveu|r, -se** [-œ:r, -ø:z] *n.m/f* washer: *~ de vaisselle,* dish-washer; *laveuse f mécanique,* also *machine f à laver,* washing machine. || **lavoir** [-wa:r] *n.m.* wash-house.

laxati|f, -ve [laksa't|if, -i:v] *adj.* laxative.

layette [lɛ'jɛt] *n.f.* baby trousseau.

le, la, les[1] [lə, la, lɛ] *art. déf.* [*le, la* become *l'* before vowel or mute *h*]. **1.** [présentant un objet déterminé, un être type, une nation] the: *la maison,* the house; *les livres que vous avez,* the books you have; *le lion (en général)* the lion; *les Russes,* the Russians. **2.** [présentant une catégorie, une entité, ne se traduit pas devant un nom, se traduit devant un adjectif substantivé] *les livres,* books; *l'eau,* water; *le lundi,* on Mondays; *Il apprend le russe,* He is learning Russian; *les Anglais* (en général), English people; *le Canada,* Canada; *le maréchal Foch,* Marshal Foch; *le beau,* the beautiful; *les aveugles,* the blind. **3.** → *adj. poss.: Fermez les yeux,* Shut your eyes. **4.** *art. indéf.:* → *dix sous la douzaine,* a dime a dozen.

le, la, les[2] [lə, la, lɛ] *pron. pers.* [same elision rules as for article]. **1.** him, her, it, them: *Je l'ai vue,* I saw her; *Donnez-les-lui,* Give them to him. **2.** [ne se traduit pas en remplacement d'un adjectif ou d'un nom employé comme tel] *Je le suis*, I am. **3.** [représentant un membre de phrase] so: *Je le pense*, I think so.

lécher [le'ʃe] #10 *v. tr.* to lick: *un style léché*, an ornate style.

leçon [lə'sõ] *n.f.* **1.** lesson: *réciter sa ~*, to say one's lesson. **2.** version. **3.** [Fig.] lesson, warning: *Que cela vous serve de ~*, Let that be a lesson to you; *Je lui ai fait la ~*, I lectured him; *donner une bonne ~ à qqun*, to teach s.o. a lesson.

lect|eur, -trice [lɛk't|œ:r, -ris] *n.* assistant, tutor. || **lecture** [-y:r] *n.f.* reading.

ledit [lə'di] *f.* **ladite** [la'dit] *adj.* [Jur.] the aforesaid, the above-mentioned.

légal, -aux [le'g|al, -o] *adj.* legal, lawful, statutory; [Méd.] forensic. || **légaliser** [-ali'ze] #3 *v. tr.* to make legal, legalize; [signature] to certify, to authenticate.

légataire [lega'tɛ:r] *n.* legatee; *~ universel*, residuary legatee.

légation [lega'sjõ] *n.f.* legation.

légendaire [leʒɑ̃'dɛ:r] *n.m. & adj.* legendary. || **légende** [le'ʒɑ̃:d] *n.f.* **1.** legend, myth. **2.** legend, caption.

lég|er, -ère [le'ʒ|e, -ɛ:r] *adj.* **1.** light, slight: *un ~ accent*, a slight accent; *avoir le cœur ~*, to be carefree, lighthearted. **2.** frivolous: *parler à la légère*, to speak inconsiderately. || **légèrement** [-ɛr'mɑ̃] *adv.* lightly, slightly. || **légèreté** [-ɛr'te] *n.f.* lightness; nimbleness, agility; levity, frivolity, thoughtlessness: *agir avec ~*, to act thoughtlessly.

légiférer [leʒife're] #10 *v. intr.* to legislate.

légion [le'ʒjõ] *n.f.* legion: *la Légion d'Honneur*, the Legion of Honour; *la Légion Étrangère*, the Foreign Legion; *Ils sont ~*, Their name is legion.

législat|eur, -rice [leʒisla|'tœ:r, -'tris] *n.* legislator, lawmaker. || **législati|f, -ve** [-'tif, -'ti:v] *adj.* legislative. || **législation** [-'sjõ] *n.f.* legislation, law. || **législature** [-'ty:r] *n.f.* legislature: © [Polit.] *la Législature provinciale*, the Provincial Legislature. || **légiste** [le'ʒist] *n.m.* legist: *médecin-~*, court pathologist, medico-legal expert.

légitimation [leʒitima'sjõ] *n.f.* legitimization, recognition. || **légitime** [leʒi'tim] legitimate, lawful: *C'est un cas de ~ défense*, He did it in self-defence. || **légitimement** [-'mɑ̃] *adv.* legitimately, lawful; justifiably. || **légitimer** [-e] #3 *v. tr.* to legitimate, to authorize, to justify: *~ un enfant*, to legitimate a child. || **légitimité** [-i'te] *n.f.* legitimacy, lawfulness.

legs [lɛ] *n.m.* legacy, bequest. || **lègue**, &c. cf. LÉGUER. || **léguer** [le'ge] #10 *v. tr.* to bequeath, to will.

légume [le'gym] *n.m.* vegetable: *légumes verts*, greens, [Fam.] *grosse ~*, big shot.

Léman, le lac [le'mɑ̃] *n.m.* Lake (of) Geneva, Lake Leman.

lendemain [lɑ̃d'mɛ̃] *n.m.* **1.** next day: *le ~ matin*, the next morning. **2.** [Fig.] morrow: *au ~ de la guerre*, on the morrow of the war; *sans ~*, short-lived. **3.** [Loc.] *du jour au ~*, overnight.

lent, -e [lɑ̃, lɑ̃:t] *adj.* slow, dilatory, tardy. || **lentement** [-t'mɑ̃] *adv.* slowly. || **lenteur** [-'tœ:r] *n.f.* slowness, sluggishness, dilatoriness.

lentille [lɑ̃'ti:j] *n.f.* [Bot.] lentil; [Opt.] lens.

léopard [leɔ'pa:r] *n.m.* leopard.

lèpre [lɛpr] *n.f.* leprosy. || **lépreu|x, -se** [le'pr|ø, -ø:z] *adj.* leprous. || *n.* leper. || **léproserie** [-oz'ri] *n.f.* leper-house.

lequel, laquelle, *pl.* **lesquels, lesquelles** [lə'kɛl, la'kɛl, le'kɛl] [contracted forms are used in conjunction with *à* and *de*: *auquel, auxquels, auxquelles*; *duquel, desquels, desquelles.*] **1.** *adj.* which: *auquel cas*, in which case. **2.** *pron. rel.* who, whom, whose, which, that: *Il était avec son frère et son neveu, lequel venait d'arriver*, He was with his brother and his nephew, who had just arrived; *L'ami avec lequel j'y suis allé*, The friend with whom I went; *Le livre auquel vous faites allusion*, The book to which you refer; *L'étudiant au père duquel vous avez écrit*, The student whose father you wrote to. **3.** *pron. interrog.* which: *Lequel est le vôtre?*, Which (one) is yours?

les [le] *art. & pron.* cf. LE.

lèse, &c. cf. LÉSER. || **lèse** [lɛ:z] *adj. f.* [Used only before nouns in compound expressions.]: *~ -majesté*, lese-majesty. || **léser** [le'ze] #10 *v. tr.* to wrong, to injure: *Ses intérêts s'en trouvèrent lésés*, It turned out to be detrimental to his interest.

lésiner [lezi'ne] #3 *v. intr.* to be stingy, niggardly, to stint.

lésion [le'zjõ] *n.f.* lesion, injury.

lesquel|s, -les [le'kɛl] *cf.* LEQUEL.

lessivage [lɛsi'va:ʒ] *n.m.* washing, scrubbing. || **lessive** [lɛ's|i:v] *n.f.* **1.** [action de laver] washing: *faire la ~*, to do the washing. **2.** [linge à laver] wash. **3.** [détergent liquide] lye. || **lessiver** [-i've] #3 *v. tr.* to wash. || **lessiveuse** [-i'vø:z] *n.f.* [qui va sur le feu] wash-boiler; [mécanique] washing machine.

lest [lɛst] *n.m.* ballast.

leste [lɛst] *adj.* quick, agile, nimble; [parole, blague, &c.] off-colour. || **lestement** [-ə'mɑ̃] *adv.* nimbly, deftly. || **lester** [-e] #3 *v. tr.* to ballast, to weigh. || **se lester** *v. pron.* to refresh the inner man.

léthargie [letar'ʒi] *n.f.* lethargy, apathy. || **léthargique** [-k] *adj.* lethargic, apathetic.

Lettonie [lɛtɔ'ni] *n.f.* Latvia.

lettré [lɛ'tre] *adj.* learned; educated. || *n.m.* scholar. || **lettre** [lɛtr] *n.f.* **1.** letter: (~) *majuscule*, capital (letter); *à la* ~, to the letter; *en toutes lettres*, in full; [Fig.] *Il me l'a dit en toutes lettres*, He told me in so many words. **2.** letter: *mettre une* ~ *à la poste*, to mail a letter; ~ *de faire-part*, announcement; ~ *de change*, bill of exchange; ~ *de voiture*, bill of lading; *Ce règlement est* ~ *morte*, This regulation is a dead letter. **3.** *pl.* letters, literature: *homme de lettres*, man of letters; *la Faculté des lettres et des sciences*, the Faculty of arts and science.

leur [lœːr] *adj. poss.* their: ~ *père*, their father; *leurs enfants*, their children. || *pron. poss.* [always preceded by *le, la, les*] *Ils ont les leurs*, They have theirs. || *n.pl.* friends, family: *Serez-vous des leurs demain?*, Will you be at their party tomorrow? || *pron. pers. inv.* them, to them: *Je* ~ *ai dit*, I told them.

leurre [lœːr] *n.m.* delusion. || **leurrer** [lœ're] #3 *v. tr.* to deceive, to delude. || **se leurrer** *v. pron.* to delude o.s.

levage [l(ə)'vaːʒ] *n.m.* lifting (up), hoisting: *appareil de* ~, hoist.

levain [lə'vɛ̃] *n.m.* leaven, yeast: *pain sans* ~, unleavened bread.

levant [lə'v|ɑ̃] *n.m.* east, sunrise, orient; → eastern: *exposition au* ~, eastern exposure; *le Levant*, the Near East, the Levant. || *adj.* rising: *le soleil* ~, the rising sun. || **levé, -e** [-e] *adj.* up: *Il est* ~, He is up; *au pied* ~, unexpectedly, off hand; *dessin à main levée*, freehand drawing; *voter à mains levées*, to vote by a show of hands. || *n.m.* mapping, charting [also LEVER]. || *n.f.* removal: *la* ~ *du corps*, the removal of the body; *la* ~ *des punitions*, cancelling detentions; *la* ~ *des lettres*, mail collection; *la* ~ *des impôts*, levying taxes; *la* ~ *des troupes*, levying troops; ~ *de terre*, embankment, levee. || **lève, lèverai,** &c. cf. LEVER. || **lever** [-e] #9 *v. tr.* to raise, to lift: ~ *l'ancre*, to weigh anchor; ~ *un enfant*, to get up a child; ~ *le courrier*, to collect the mail; ~ *un plan*, to draw a plan; ~ *une punition*, to remit a punishment; ~ *des troupes, des impôts*, to levy troops, taxes; ~ *la séance*, to adjourn the meeting; ~ *le pied*, to abscond. || **se lever** *v. pron.* to rise, to spring up, to get up [d'un lit], to stand up [d'un siége]. || **lever** *n.m.* rising: *dès son* ~, as soon as he/gets, got/up; *le* ~ *du soleil*, sunrise; *le* ~ *du roi*, the King's levee; *un* ~ *de rideau*, a curtain raiser.

levier [lə'vje] *n.m.* lever; *ouvrir au moyen d'un* ~, to pry open, [Br.] to prize.

levraut [le'vro] *n.m.* leveret; young hare.

lèvre [lɛːvr] *n.f.* lip: *serrer les lèvres*, to purse one's lips; *du bout des lèvres*, half-heartedly.

lévrier [levri'je] *n.m.* greyhound.

levure [l[ə]'vyːr] *n.f.* yeast; ~ *anglaise*, baking powder, cf. POUDRE.

lexical, -aux [lɛksi|'kal|-'ko] *adj.* lexical. || **lexicographe** [-kɔ'graf] *n.m.* lexicographer. || **lexicographie** [-kɔgra'fi] *n.f.* lexicography. || **lexicologie** [-[k]ɔlɔ'ʒi] *n.f.* lexicology. || **lexique** [lɛk'sik] *n.m.* vocabulary, lexicon; shorter dictionary.

lézard [le'zaːr] *n.m.* lizard: [Fig. & Fam.] *faire le* ~, to lounge about, to loaf. || **lézarde** [le'zard] *n.f.* crack, cranny, split. || **lézardé, -e** [-e] *adj.* cracked, crannied. || **lézarder** [-e] #3 *v. tr. & intr.* to bask in the sun, to laze about. || **se lézarder** *v. pron.* to crack, split.

liaison [ljɛ'zɔ̃] *n.f.* **1.** link, tie, connection, co-ordination. **2.** love affair. **3.** [Ling.] liaison. **4.** [Mil.] liaison: *officier de* ~, liaison officer. **5.** [Mus.] slur.

liane [ljan] *n.f.* liana, bindweed.

liant, -e [lj|ɑ̃, -ɑ̃ːt] *adj.* friendly, sociable. || *n.m.*: *mettre du* ~, to make people feel at ease; *liants*, various kinds of cement.

liard [ljaːr] *n.m.* farthing: *pas un* ~, not a red cent.

liasse [ljas] *n.f.* wad, bundle (of papers): *une* ~ *de billets*, a wad, [US] roll/of paper money.

Liban [li'bɑ̃] *n.m.* Lebanon. || **libanais, -e** [liba'nɛ(ːz)] *adj. & n.* Lebanese.

libation [liba'sjɔ̃] *n.f.* libation, potation: *après de copieuses libations*, after copious potations.

libellé [libɛ'l|e] *n.m.* wording, phrasing. || **libeller** [-e] #3 *v. tr.* to draw up; to word (documents); to make out (a cheque).

libellule [libɛ'lyl] *n.f.* dragonfly, [Fam.] darning-needle.

libéral, -e [libe'ral] *adj. le parti* ~, the Liberal party; *une politique libérale*, a liberal policy; *une interprétation libérale*, a broad interpretation. || **libéralisme** [-ism] *n.m.* liberalism: [Polit. Econ].

~ *économique*, laissez faire. || **libéralité** [-i'te] *n.f.* liberality, generousness; *pl.* largesse.

libérat|eur, -rice [libera|'tœ:r, -'tris] *adj.* liberating, delivering: *pouvoir* ~, releasing power. || *n.* liberator, deliverer; rescuer. || **libération** [-'sjõ] *n.f.* liberation, freeing; release; discharge (of a prisoner); [Fr.] *La Libération*, Liberation. || **libère,** &c. cf. LIBÉRER. || **libéré, -e** [libe're] *adj.* freed, released, discharged. || *n.* discharged prisoner. || **libérer** #10 *v. tr.* to free, to liberate, to release, to discharge. || **se libérer (de)** *v. pron.* to free o.s. (from), to become emancipated (from); to disengage o.s. [d'une obligation].

Libéria, le [libe'rja] *n.m.* Liberia.

liberté [libɛr't|e] *n.f.* freedom; liberty; free will: *mettre en* ~ *(sous caution)*, to release (on bail); *avoir des moments de* ~, to have some free time.

libertin, -e [-ɛ̃, -in] *adj.* libertine, profligate, licentious. || *n.m.* libertine; †freethinker.

libraire [li'br|ɛ:r] *n.m.* bookseller [× LIBRARIAN]. || **librairie** [-ɛ'ri] *n.f.* **1.** book store, book shop. **2.** book trade.

libre [libr] *adj.* **1.** free (to), at liberty (to): ~ *à vous de refuser*, You may refuse if you wish. **2.** disengaged: *Il n'est pas* ~, He is engaged. **3.** clear, unobstructed: *La voie est* ~, The road is clear; *port* ~ *de glaces*, warm-water port. **4.** free, unrestrained: *des propos un peu libres*, risky talk. **5.** Poet. *des vers libres*, irregular verse. || **libre-échange** [-e'ʃɑ̃:ʒ] *n.m.* free trade. || **librement** [-ə'mɑ̃] *adv.* freely.

Libye [li'bi] *n.f.* Libya.

†**lice** [lis] *n.f.* lists: *entrer en* ~, to enter the lists.

licence [li's|ɑ̃:s] *n.f.* **1.** permission; permit, © licence. **2.** [Schol.] [academic degree giving the right to teach]. **3.** [moral] licence, licentiousness. **4.** [Poet.] licence. || **licencié, -e** [-a'sje] © [abus.] licensed; [Fr.] licentiate: ~ *ès lettres*, [approx.] Master of Arts.

licenciement [-ɑ̃si'mɑ̃] *n.m.* [soldats] disbandment; [ouvriers] lay-off. || **licencier** [-ɑ̃sje] #3 *v. tr.* [soldats] to disband; [ouvriers] to lay off. || **licencieu|x, -se** [-ɑ̃'sjø, -ɑ̃'sjø:z] *adj.* licentious.

lichen [li'kɛn] *n.m.* [Bot.] lichen.

licite [li'sit] *adj.* lawful, licit.

lie [li] *n.f.* dregs, lees; [Fig.] scum: *(couleur) lie de vin*, maroon.

lié, -e [lje] *adj.* **1.** bound, tied: *Il a les mains liées*, His hands are tied. **2.** connected: *Les deux choses ne sont pas nécessairement liées*, The two things are not necessarily connected; [amis] close, intimate.

liège [ljɛ:ʒ] *n.m.* cork: *chêne-liège*, cork-oak; [pêche] float.

lien [ljɛ̃] *n.m.* tie, bond; link, connection. || **lier** [lje] #3 *v. tr.* **1.** to tie, to bind; to link, to connect: ~ *conversation avec*, to fall into conversation with; *se* ~ *d'amitié*, to become fast friends. **2.** [Mus.] to slur. **3.** [Culin.] to thicken.

lierre [ljɛ:r] *n.m.* ivy.

†**liesse** [ljɛs] *n.f.* joy, glee: *être en* ~, to rejoice, to celebrate, to be merrymaking.

lieu, -x [ljø] *n.m.* place, spot: ~ *commun*, commonplace, truism; ~ *géométrique*, locus; *sur les lieux*, on the spot, on the scene; *en tous lieux*, everywhere; *en aucun* ~, nowhere; *en quelque* ~ *que* ..., wherever; [Fig.] *en haut* ~, high up, in government circles; *l'état des lieux*, the condition of the premises; *Il y a* ~ *de croire*, I have every reason to think; *avoir* ~, to take place; *tenir* ~ *de*, to take the place of; *en second* ~, secondly.

lieue [ljø] *n.f.* league (about three miles); [Fig.] *être à cent lieues de*, to be far from.

lieu|r, -se [ljœ:r, ljø:z] *n.* binder; [machine] self-binder.

lieutenant [ljøt'nɑ̃] *n.m.* lieutenant. || **Lieutenant-gouverneur** [-guvɛr'nœ:r] © *n.m.* Lieutenant-Governor.

lièvre [ljɛ:vr] *n.m.* hare; ~ *d'Amérique*, snowshoe rabbit; ~ *des prairies*, jack rabbit; [Fig.] *courir deux lièvres à la fois*, to have too many irons in the fire; [Fig.] *lever le* ~, to raise an awkward question.

ligature [liga|'ty:r] *n.f.* binding; ligature: *mettre une* ~, to apply a tourniquet. || **ligaturer** [-ty're] #3 *v. tr.* to bind, to tie; [Surgery & Bot.] to apply a tourniquet.

lignage [li'ɲa:ʒ] *n.m.* lineage: *un homme de haut* ~, a man of high birth. || **ligne** [liɲ] *n.f.* line: *en* ~ *droite*, in a straight line; *descendant en* ~ *directe*, direct descendant; *les grandes lignes d'un projet*, the outline of a plan; [Rail] *grandes lignes et lignes de banlieue*, main and suburban lines; *la* ~ *de partage des eaux*, the watershed, the divide; *être en première* ~, to be in the/firing line, line of fire/. || **lignée** [-e] *n.f.* lineage, progeny.

ligneu|x, -se [li'ɲ|ø, -ø:z] *adj.* woody, ligneous.

ligoter [ligɔ'te] #3 *v. tr.* to tie up.

ligue [lig] *n.f.* league: [Hist.] *la Sainte Ligue*, the Holy League; conspiracy: *la*

~ *de ses ennemis*, the conspiracy of his enemies; © abus. *La ~ Nationale de Hockey*, National Hockey League. cf. DIVISION. || **liguer** [-e] #3 *v. tr.* to band, to league. || **se liguer** *v. pron.* to unite, to combine, to join forces. || **ligueu|r, -se** [-œ:r, -ø:z] *adj. & n.* leaguer.

lilas [li'lɑ] *adj. & n.m.* lilac.

Lima [li'ma] *n.* Lima: © *fèves de ~*, Lima beans.

limace [li'mas] *n.f.* slug. || **limaçon** [-õ] *n.m.* snail.

limaille [li'mɑ:j] *n.f.* filings: ~ *de fer*, iron filings.

limande [li'mɑ̃:d] *n.f.* [Br.] dab, © flounder.

limbes [lɛ̃:b] *n.mpl.* [Rel.] Limbo.

lime[1] [lim] *n.f.* file: ~ *à ongles*, nail file. || **lime**[2] *n.f.* lime. || **limer** [-e] #3 *v. tr.* to file; [Fig.] to polish.

limier [li'mje] *n.m.* bloodhound; [Fig.] sleuth.

liminaire [limi'nɛ:r] *adj.* prefatory.

limitati|f, -ve [limita|'tif, -'ti:v] *adj.* limitative. || **limitation** [-'sjõ] *n.f.* limit, restriction: *sans ~ de temps*, without a time limit. || **limite** [li'mit] *n.f.* limit, boundary; [plur.] bounds: *sans limites*, unlimited, unbounded; maximum: *vitesse ~*, maximum speed; *au 31 décembre, dernière ~*, not later than December 31st. || **limité, -e** [-e] *adj.* limited. || **limiter** [-e] #3 *v. tr.* to limit, to restrict; [Géog.] to bound. || **limitrophe** [-'rɔf] *adj.* adjacent (de, *to*); bordering (on).

limogeai, &c. cf. LIMOGER. || **limoger** [limɔ'ʒe] #5 *v. tr.* [Fam.] to relieve from command, to shelve.

limon [li'mõ] *n.m.* **1.** silt; [Fig.] clay. **2.** lime, lemon. **3.** [cart] shaft. || **limonade** [limɔ'nad] *n.f.* [approx.] ginger ale, soft drink, cf. LIQUEUR.

limousine [limu'zin] *n.f.* [Auto.] limousine, © sedan.

limpide [lɛ̃'pid] *adj.* clear, crystal clear, limpid. || **limpidité** [-i'te] *n.f.* limpidity.

lin [lɛ̃] *n.m.* Bot. **1.** flax: *fil de ~*, flaxen thread. **2.** linseed: *huile de ~*, linseed oil. **3.** linen: *toile de ~*, linen.

linéament [linea'mɑ̃] *n.m.* [trait] feature; [ébauche] sketch.

linceul [lɛ̃'sœ:l] *n.m.* shroud.

linge [lɛ̃:ʒ] *n.m.* linen: ~ *de table*, table linen; underwear: *du ~ de rechange*, a change of underwear; clothes: *pince à ~*, clothespin; *corde à ~*, clothesline; *étendre le ~*, to hang out the clothes; *pâle comme un ~*, as white as a sheet. || **lingerie** [lɛ̃ʒ'ri] *n.f.* **1.** linen goods. **2.** underwear, [US, de femme] lingerie. **3.** linen room.

lingot [lɛ'go] *n.m.* [Metal.] ingot: *de l'or en lingots*, bullion; [Impr.] slug.

linguiste [lɛ̃'gɥist] *n.m.* (scientific) linguist. || **linguistique** [lɛ̃gɥis'tik] *n.f.* linguistics.

linoléum [linɔle'ɔm] *n.m.* linoleum.

linteau [lɛ̃'to] *n.m.* lintel.

lion, -ne [ljõ, ljɔn] *n.* lion: ~ *de mer*, sea lion; ~ *de montagne* [also *puma, couguar*], mountain lion; [Fig.] *la part du ~*, the lion's share. [Astr.] Leo. || **lionceau** [ljõ'so] *n.m.* lion/whelp, cub/.

lippe [lip] *n.f.* thick lower lip: *faire la ~*, to pout.

liquéfaction [likefak'sjõ] *n.f.* liquefaction. || **liquéfier** [like'fje] #3 *v. tr.* to liquefy. || **se liquéfier** *v. pron.* to liquefy.

liqueur [li'kœ:r] *n.f.* **1.** liqueur, cordial: *la chartreuse est une ~*, chartreuse is a liqueur. **2.** †liquid: *l'équilibre des liqueurs*, the equilibrium of liquids. **3.** © liquor, drink: *la Commission des liqueurs du Québec*, the Quebec Liquor Commission; © *liqueurs douces*, soft drinks.

liquidation [likida'sjõ] *n.f.* liquidation, winding-up; [Stock Exchange] account-day; [vente] clearance.

liquide [li'kid] *n.m.* liquid; fluid. || *adj.* liquid, fluid: *argent ~*, ready money, cash. || **liquider** [-e] #3 *v. tr.* to liquidate, wind up; to sell off, clear; [Fam.] to get rid of (s.o.).

liquoreu|x, -se [likɔ'r|ø, -ø:z] *adj.* [du vin] sweet and strong.

lire [li:r], **lisant** [li'zɑ̃], **lu** [ly] #49 *v. tr.* to read, to peruse: *on lit dans le Star*, it says in the Star; ~ *à haute voix*, to read out, to read aloud. || **se lire** *v. pron.* to be read. *Ce livre se lit beaucoup*, This book is much read; *Cela se lit facilement*, It's very readable; *la surprise se lisait sur son visage*, → surprise was on/his, her/face; /his, her/face showed surprise.

lis[1] [lis] *n.m.* lily [also LYS] [Her.] *fleur-de-~* [flœrde'li], fleur-de-lis.

lis[2], **lise**[1], &c. cf. LIRE. || **Lise**[2] [li:z], *n.pr.* = Lizzie.

Lisbonne [lis'bɔn] *n.f.* Lisbon.

liseré [liz're] *n.m.* border, edge.

liseron [liz'rõ] *n.m.* [Bot.] bindweed.

liseu|r, -se [li'z|œ:r, ø:z] *n.* person who reads much. || *n.f.* book mark; book cover; bed jacket; reading lamp. || **lisibilité** [lizibili'te] *n.f.* legibility. || **lisible** [li'zibl] *adj.* legible. || **lisiblement** [-ə'mɑ̃] *adv.* legibly.

lisière [li'zjɛ:r] *n.f.* [d'un bois, d'un village] edge; [d'une étoffe] list, selvage.

lisse [lis] *adj.* smooth; sleek. || **lisser** [-e] #3 *v. tr.* to smooth, to smooth over.

liste [list] *n.f.* list, roll; register (of voters); panel (of juries); roster: *dresser une* ~, to draw up a list.

lit[1] [li] *n.m.* **1.** bed, bedstead; cot: *se mettre au* ~, to go to bed; *au saut du* ~, immediately upon getting up; *dessus de* ~, bedspread; ~ *de sangle*, ~ *étroit*, cot; ~ *cage*, folding cot; *le* ~ *d'un fleuve*, the bed of a river. **2.** marriage: *les enfants du premier* ~, the children by the first marriage.

lit[2] cf. LIRE.

litanie [lita'ni] *n.f.* [Rel.] litany; [Fig.] tedious enumeration.

literie [li|'tri] *n.f.* bedding. || **litière** [-'tjɛ:r] *n.f.* litter; *faire* ~ *de*, to trample.

litige [li't|i:ʒ] *n.m.* litigation, dispute; *le point en* ~, the point at issue. || **litigieu|x, -se** [-i'ʒjø(:z)] *adj.* litigious: *un point* ~, a bone of contention.

litre [litr] *n.m.* litre, [US] liter [= about 1 quart].

littéraire [lite'r|ɛ:r] *adj.* literary. || **littéral, -e** [-al] *adj.* literal. || **littéralement** [al'mɑ̃] *adv.* literally. || **littérateur** [-a'tœ:r] *n.m.* literary man, man of letters. || **littérature** [-a'ty:r] *n.f.* literature: *se lancer dans la* ~, to/take up, begin/writing.

littoral, -e [litɔ'ral] *adj.* littoral, coastal, || **littoral** *n.m.* littoral, seaboard, coastline.

Lituanie [litɥa'ni] *n.f.* Lithuania.

liturgie [lityr'ʒi] *n.f.* liturgy. || **liturgique** [-k] *adj.* liturgic, liturgical.

livide [li'vid] *adj.* livid, white, wan. || **lividité** [-i'te] *n.f.* lividity, lividness.

Livourne [li'vurn] *n.* Leghorn.

livrable [li'vr|a:bl] *adj.* deliverable. || **livraison** [-ɛ'zɔ̃] *n.f.* **1.** delivery: *défaut de* ~, non-delivery; *comptant sans* ~, cash and carry; *P.S.L.*, C.O.D.; ~ *à domicile*, → We deliver. **2.** [book] part, instalment; [magazine] issue, copy, number; *par* ~, in parts.

livre[1] [li:vr] *n.m.* book: *faire un* ~, to write a book; ~ *de classe*, school book; *feuilleter un* ~, to glance through a book; [Comp.] *porter au grand* ~, to post; *teneur de livres*, bookkeeper; *le grand* ~, the ledger; ~ *de bord*, ship's/journal, register/, log; [aviation] log.

livre[2] [= lb] *n.f.* **1.** pound: *Le sucre se vend à la* ~, Sugar is sold by the pound. **2.** [= £] ~ *sterling*, pound (sterling).

livre[3] cf. LIVRER. || **livré, -e** [li'vre] cf. LIVRER: abandoned; addicted (to): ~ *à lui-même*, left to his own devices, abandoned; ~ *à la boisson*, addicted to drinking; ~ *à l'oubli*, consigned to oblivion.

†**livrée** [li'vre] *n.f.* livery; *gens de* ~, house servants.

livrer [li'vre] #3 *v. tr.* **1.** to deliver (goods). **2.** to surrender; to betray: ~ *une ville*, to surrender a city; *Il fut livré par ses amis*, He was betrayed by his friends. **3.** to wage (a fight): ~ *une bataille*, to fight a battle. **se livrer** (à) *v. pron.* to surrender (to); [Fig.] to indulge in: *Il se livrait à son passe-temps favori*, He was indulging in his favourite pastime; ~ *à des voies de fait*, to use violence.

livresque [li'vrɛsk] *adj.* bookish. || **livret** [li'vrɛ] *n.m.* booklet; libretto (of an opera); ~ *de l'étudiant*, student's record book; ~ *militaire*, service record book.

livreur [li'vrœ:r] *n.m.* delivery/man, boy/.

lobe [lɔb] *n.m.* lobe: ~ *de l'oreille*, earlobe.

local, -e [lɔ'kal] *adj.* local. || *n.m.* place, premises: *locaux mpl commerciaux*, office space. || **localisation** [-iza'sjɔ̃] *n.f.* localization. || **localiser** [-i'ze] #3 *v. tr.* to localize. || **se localiser** *v. pron.* to be localized. || **localité** [-i'te] *n.f.* locality, place, village.

locataire [lɔka|'tɛ:r] *n.* tenant (of land, building); lodger (in s.o.'s house); [Jur.] lessee. || **locati|f, -ve** [-'tif, -'ti:v] *adj.* pertaining to rent, tenant: *la valeur locative d'une maison*, the rental value of a house; *réparations locatives*, tenant repairs. || *n.m.* [Gram.] locative. || **location** [-'sjɔ̃] *n.f.* renting, hiring: *en* ~, for hire; ~ *de machines à écrire*, → We rent typewriters; [Théât., Rail.] ~ *des places*; [seat] reservation(s), cf. GARDE.

locomotion [lɔkɔmɔ'sjɔ̃] *n.f.* locomotion: *Quels sont vos moyens de* ~ ?, What kind of transportation do you have? || **locomotive** [lɔkɔmɔ'ti:v] *n.f.* locomotive, engine; ~ *de train de marchandises*, freight engine.

locution [lɔky'sjɔ̃] *n.f.* phrase, locution, expression.

loge [lɔ:ʒ] *n.f.* lodge; [Théât.] (spectator's) box, (actor's) dressing room; [wild animal show] cage. || **logé, -e** [-e] *adj.* lodged; [of wine] bottled, in a cask. || **logeai(s), logeons,** cf. LOGER. || **logement** [-'mɑ̃] *n.m.* lodging(s), quarters, accommodation(s); [Mil.] billeting; small apartment: *la crise du* ~, the housing shortage; *billet de* ~, billet. || **loger** [-e] #5 *v. intr.* to live, to stay: *Où logez-vous ?*, Where are you staying? *v. tr.* to house, to accommodate: *Nous pouvons* ~ *cinq* *personnes,* We can accommodate five persons; [Mil.] to billet: *logé(s) chez l'habitant,* billeted in private homes. || **se loger** *v. pron.* to find a place to stay; ~ *une balle dans la tête,* to put a bullet through one's head. || **logeu|r, -se** [-œ:r, -ø:z] *n.* rooming-house keeper.; © roomer.

logique [lɔ'ʒik] *adj.* **1.** logical. **2.** *n.f.* logic.

logis [lɔ'ʒi] *n.m.* house, home, dwelling: *au* ~, at home; †*la folle du* ~, imagination.

loi [lwa] *n.f.* law, rule: **1.** *faire la* ~, to lay down the law; *faire la* ~ *chez soi,* to rule the roost; *cette tradition fait* ~, this tradition is law; **2.** law, legislation, act of Parliament: *les lois pénales,* penal laws, ~ *exceptionnelle,* emergency legislation; *abroger une* ~, to repeal a law; *faire des lois,* to legislate; *avoir force de* ~, to be law; *projet de* ~, bill; *homme de* ~, lawyer; *aux yeux de la* ~, in the eye of the law; *hors-la-loi,* outlaw.

loin [lwɛ̃] *adv.* far, far away, far off: *au* ~, in the distance; afar; *de* ~, from afar, at a distance; *de* ~ *en* ~, at intervals; ~ *de moi la pensée de,* far be it from me to; *il y a* ~ *de . . . à . . .*, it is a far cry from . . . to . . . ; ~ *des yeux,* ~ *du cœur,* out of sight, out of mind; *Il y a* ~ *de la coupe aux lèvres,* There is many a slip between cup and lip. || **lointain, -e** [-'tɛ̃, -'tɛn] *adj.* far; distant, faraway, remote; early: *mes plus lointains souvenirs,* my earliest memories. || *n.m.* distance: *dans le* ~, in the distance.

loir [lwa:r] *n.m.* dormouse: *dormir comme un* ~, to sleep like a log.

Loire (la) [la'lwa:r] *n.f.* (the) Loire.

loisible [lwa'zibl] *adj.* permissible: *Il vous est* ~ *de . . .*, /You may, You are free to/. . . .

loisir [lwa'zi:r] *n.m.* leisure, spare time: *à* ~, at leisure; *occuper ses loisirs à qqch.,* to spend one's spare time doing sth.

London ['lɔndən] [Ontario] *n.* London. || **Londres** [lɔ̃:dr] *n.f.* London [UK].

long, longue [lɔ̃, lɔ̃:g] *adj.* long; slow: *un* ~ *voyage,* a long journey; *Il a été* ~ *à s'en rendre compte,* He was slow in realizing it; *à la longue,* in the long run; *avoir le bras* ~, to be influential; *avoir les dents longues,* to be greedy. || *n.m.* length: *une règle de douze pouces de* ~, a ruler twelve inches long; *en* ~, lengthwise; *étendu de tout son* ~, lying full length; *de* ~ *en large,* up and down, back and forth; *Il en sait* ~, He has inside information; *Cela en dit* ~, It speaks volumes. || *loc. prép. le* ~ *de,* along. || **longanimité** [-ganimi'te] *n.f.* forbearance, long-suffering. || **long-courrier** [lɔ̃ku'rje] *n.m.* ocean-going ship; overseas liner. || **long cours** [lɔ̃'ku:r] *n.m.* offshore navigation: *capitaine au* ~, merchant marine captain, master mariner.

longe[1] [lɔ̃:ʒ] *n.f.* tether. || **longe**[2] *n.f.* loin (of veal).

longer [lɔ̃'ʒe] #5 *v. tr.* **1.** to/go, walk, run/ along: *Nous longions la rivière,* We were walking along the river. **2.** to/lie, extend along, skirt/: *le petit bois qui longe la route,* the little wood (which extends) along the road.

longévité [lɔ̃ʒevi'te] *n.f.* longevity, life expectancy.

longitude [lɔ̃ʒi'tyd] *n.f.* longitude. || **longitudinal, -e** [-i'nal] *adj.* longitudinal: *coupe f longitudinale,* lengthwise section.

longtemps [lɔ̃|'tɑ̃] *adv.* long, a long time: *aussi* ~ *que vous voudrez,* as long as you wish; *pendant* ~, for a long time; *Il n'en a plus pour* ~, He will soon be through, He isn't long for this world.

longuement [lɔ̃|g'mɑ̃] *adv.* long, a long time; at length. || **longueur** [-'gœ:r] *n.f.* **1.** length: *dans le sens de la* ~, lengthwise; *mesure de* ~, linear measure. **2.** lengthiness: *la* ~ *de ses discours,* the lengthiness of his speeches; *à* ~ *de journée,* all the livelong day; *traîner en* ~, to drag. **3.** (at the races) a length, a head: *il a gagné d'une* ~, he won by a/length, head/. || **longue-vue** [lɔ̃g'vy] *pl.* **longues-vues** *n.f.* telescope, spy glass, [Br.] glass.

†**lopin** [lɔ'pɛ̃] *n.m.* small piece, portion: ~ *de terre,* parcel of land. cf. LOT.

loquace [lɔ'kwas] *adj.* talkative, garrulous, loquacious. || **loquacité** [-i'te] *n.f.* talkativeness, garrulity, loquacity.

loque [lɔk] *n.f.* rag: *une* ~ *humaine,* a human wreck.

loquet [lɔ'kɛ] *n.m.* latch: *La porte était fermée au* ~, The door was on the latch.

loqueteu|x, -se [lɔk't|ø, -ø:z] *adj.* ragged, tattered.

lorgner [lɔr'ɲ|e] #3 *v. tr.* **1.** to look sidelong at, to ogle, to leer. **2.** to covet, to have one's eye on. || **lorgnette** [-ɛt] *n.f.* binoculars, opera glass(es): *regarder par le petit bout de la* ~, to pay too much attention to petty details. || **lorgnon** [-ɔ̃] *n.m.* pince-nez.

lors [lɔ:r] *adv.* then, at that time; ~ *de,* at the time of; *depuis* ~, since then; *dès* ~, consequently; *pour* ~, therefore; ~ *même que,* even though.

lorsque [lɔrsk(ə)] *conj.* when; at the time that.
losange [lɔ'zɑ̃:ʒ] *n.m.* diamond (shape).
lot [lo] *n.m.* share, portion, lot; prize: *le gros* ~, the highest prize, [US] the jackpot; batch: *un* ~ *de marchandises,* a batch of goods; premium: *obligation(s) à lots,* premium bond(s); © [abus.] parcel of land; cf. LOPIN.
loterie [lɔ'tri] *n.f.* lottery, raffle.
loti, -e [lɔ'ti] *adj.*: *bien* ~, well/off, fixed/; *Il est bien mal* ~, Things did not go too well for him.
lotion [lɔ'sjõ] *n.f.* wash; lotion: ~ *capillaire,* hair lotion.
lotir [lɔ't|i:r] #17 *v. tr.* to parcel out (land). || **lotissement** [-is'mɑ̃] *n.m.* parcelling out; [town planning] development.
lotus [lo'tys] *n.m.* [Bot.] lotus.
louable [lwabl, © lu'abl] *adj.* laudable, commendable, praiseworthy.
louage [lwa:ʒ, © lu'[a:]ʒ] *n.m.* hire: *une bicyclette de* ~, a hired bicycle; *une voiture de* ~, a hack.
louange [lwɑ̃:ʒ, © lu'ɑ̃:ʒ] *n.f.* praise: *à la* ~ *de,* in praise of. || **louanger** [luɑ̃'ʒ|e] #5 *v. tr.* to praise exceedingly. || **louangeu|r, -se** [-œ:r, -ø:z] *adj.* laudatory. || *n.* one who lavishes praise.
louche[1] [luʃ] **1.** cross-eyed, squinting. **2.** ambiguous, suspicious, equivocal; [Slang] phony. || *n.m.* something suspicious: *Il y a du* ~ *là-dedans,* I smell a rat.
louche[2] *n.f.* ladle.
loucher [-e] #3 *v. intr.* to squint, to be cross-eyed.
loué, -e [lwe, © lu'e] cf. LOUER. || *adj.* [on a seat at the theatre] engaged, reserved. || **louer**[1] #3 *v. tr.* to let, let out, rent; to lease; to hire, hire out; [Théât.] to book, reserve (a seat). || **se louer** *v. pron.* to be rented, to rent: *Cette maison se loue $200 par mois,* This house rents for $200 a month.
louer[2] #3 *v. tr.* to praise, laud, commend. || **se louer** *v. pron.* to praise o.s.: ~ *de,* to be very happy about; *Je n'ai eu qu'à me louer de ses services,* → He has proved most satisfactory. || **loueu|r, -se** [lwœ:r, lwø:z] *n.* person hiring out vehicles, horses, boats, &c.
loufoque [lu'fɔk] *adj.* dotty. || *n.m.* crackpot.
Louis [lwi] *n.m.* = Louis, Lewis. || **Louisbourg** [lwi'bu:r] *n.m.* [Géog.] © Louisburg. || **Louise** [lwi:z] *n.f.* Louise. || **Louisiane** [lwi'zjan] *n.f.* [Géog.] Louisiana.
loup [lu] *n.m.* **1.** wolf: *une bande de loups,* a pack of wolves; *à pas de* ~, stealthily; *crier au* ~, to cry wolf; *avoir une faim de* ~, to be ravenous; *Il fait un froid de* ~, It is bitterly cold; *Il faut hurler avec les loups,* In Rome do as the Romans do; *se jeter dans la gueule du* ~, to put one's head in the lion's mouth; [time] *entre chien et* ~, at dusk; ~ *de mer,* [fish] wolf eel, [sailor] salt, sea dog; *saut de* ~, ditch; *tête de* ~, pope's head. **2.** mask: *porter un* ~ *de velours,* to wear a velvet mask. **3.** error, cf. LOUVE.
loup-cervier [-sɛr'vje] *n.m.* lynx.
loupe [lup] *n.f.* **1.** magnifying glass. **2.** wen.
louper [lu'pe] #3 *v. tr. & intr.* [Sl.] to/ bungle, muff, goof/.
loup-garou [luga'ru] *n.m.* werewolf.
lourd, -e [lu:r, -d] *adj.* heavy, [US Fam.] hefty; [climat] sultry; clumsy; dull, ponderous: *l'industrie lourde,* heavy industry; *un* ~ *colis,* a heavy package; *un* ~ *après-midi de juillet,* a sultry July afternoon; *un style* ~, a clumsy style; *un esprit* ~, a dull mind. || **lourdaud, -e** [lur'd|o, -to:d] *adj.* clumsy, dull. || *n.* clumsy/fellow *m,* woman *f*/, lout. || **lourdement** [-ə'mɑ̃] *adv.* heavily; clumsily: *rouler* ~, to lumber along. || **lourderie** [lurdə'ri] *n.f.* clumsiness; bad blunder. || **lourdeur** [-œ:r] *n.f.* heaviness; sultriness; clumsiness; dullness.
loutre [lutr] *n.f.* otter.
louve [lu:v] *n.f.* she-wolf. || **louveteau** [luv'to] *n.m.* **1.** wolf cub. **2.** cub (in the Boy Scouts).
louvoyer [luvwa'je] #12 *v. intr.* **1.** [Naut.] to tack. **2.** [Fig.] to manœuvre, to act evasively.
loyal, -e, -aux [lwa'j|al, -o] *adj.* honest, straightforward, upright. || **loyalement** [-al'mɑ̃] *adv.* honestly, fairly, [Fam.] squarely. || **loyalisme** [-a'lism] *n.m.* loyalty. || **loyaliste** [-a'list] *n.m.* [Can. Hist.] Loyalists, Tories. || **loyauté** [-o'te] *n.f.* honesty, fairness, uprightness.
loyer [lwa'je] *n.m.* rent, rental: *Il est en retard pour son* ~, He is behind with his rent.
lu, cf. LIRE.
lubie [ly'bi] *n.f.* whim, fad.
lubricité [lybri|si'te] *n.f.* lewdness.
lubrifiant, -e [-'fjɑ̃(:t)] *adj.* lubricating. || *n.m.* lubricant.
lubrique [-k] *adj.* lewd.
lucarne [ly'karn] *n.f.* dormer window, skylight.
lucide [ly'sid] *adj.* lucid, clear; clear-headed. || **lucidité** [-i'te] *n.f.* lucidity, lucidness; clear-headedness.

luciole [ly'sjɔl] *n.f.* firefly.
lucrati|f, -ve [lykrat|if, -i:v] *adj.* lucrative, profitable.
luette [lɥɛt] *n.f.* uvula.
lueur [lɥœ:r, © ly'œ:r] *n.f.* [less strong than LUMIÈRE] light: *à la ~ des flammes*, in the firelight; gleam, [tremblotante] glimmer: *une faible ~ d'espoir*, a faint glimmer of hope; [d'objet incandescent] glow: *la ~ des braises*, the glow of embers; [rapide] flash: *la ~ d'un éclair*, a flash of lightning.
luge [ly:ʒ] *n.f.* [Fr.] sled. cf. TRAÎNE.
lugubre [ly'gybr] *adj.* dismal, dreary, lugubrious, mournful.
lui[1] [lɥi] *pr. pers.* 3e pers. sing., can be all three genders. **1.** [emphatic for *il*] he: *Elle restera, ~ partira*, She will stay, he will go. **2.** [as indirect object] him, her, it: *Donnez- ~ à manger*, Give/him, her, it/sth. to eat. **3.** [with prep.] him, it: *avec ~* [person] with him; *avec ~* [animal] with it. **4.** [to express possession] *C'est à ~*, It's/his, his own, its own/. **5.** [for emphasis] *une façon bien à ~ de*, a way of/his, its/own; /his, its/own way.
lui[2] [lɥi] cf. LUIRE. || **luire** [-:r], **luisant** [-'zɑ̃], **lui** [lɥi] #57 *v. intr.* [Note that this verb is no longer used in the simple past.] [répandre ou réfléchir de la lumière] to shine: *Le soleil luit*, The sun shines; *L'acier luit au soleil*, Steel shines in the sunlight; [d'une lumière pâle] to gleam; [rougeoyante] to glow; [tremblotante] to glimmer; [avec le luisant d'une surface mouillée] to glisten; [d'une surface sombre] to glint; [Fig.] to dawn: *L'espoir luit de nouveau*, Hope dawns once more.
luis, cf. LUIRE. || **luisant, -e** [-'zɑ̃ :t] *adj.* shining, gleaming: *une lame luisante*, a shining blade; [glossy]: *du satin ~*, glossy satin; *ver ~*, glow-worm. || *n.m.* gloss, glossiness, sheen.
lumbago [lɔ̃ba'go] *n.m.* lumbago.
lumière [lym|jɛ:r] *n.f.* light: *la ~ artificielle*, artificial light; *faire la ~ sur . . .*, to shed some light on . . . ; *mettre en ~*, bring out in the light; *à la ~*, in the light; *avoir des lumières de qqch.*, to have knowledge of sth.; *Ce fut un trait de ~*, It came to him in a flash; [person] *C'est une ~*, He is a luminary; [Tech.] sight; steamport; touch hole.
lumignon [-i'ɲɔ̃] *n.m.* candle end, guttering candle. || **lumineu|x, -se** [-i'nø(:z)] *adj.* bright, brilliant. || **luminosité** [-inozi'te] *n.f.* luminosity.
lunaire [ly'n|ɛ:r] *adj.* lunar. || **lunatique** [-a'tik] *adj.* erratic, capricious.
lunch [lɔnʃ] © *n.m.* lunch, [Fr.] buffet lunch. || **luncher** [-e] #3 *v. intr.* to have a buffet lunch; © to lunch.
lundi [lœ̃'di] *n.m.* Monday: *le ~*, on Mondays; *~ prochain*, next Monday; *de ~ en huit*, a week from Monday; [on a letter] *Lundi 18 janvier 1960*, Monday, Jan. 18, 1960.
lune [lyn] *n.f.* moon: *rayon de ~*, moonbeam; *clair de ~*, moonlight; *~ de miel*, honeymoon; *être dans la ~*, to be daydreaming. || **luné, -e** [-e] *adj.* moon-shaped; [Fig.]: *bien, mal/ ~*, in a/good, bad/ mood.
lunette [-ɛt] *n.f.* telescope, spyglass; *pl.* spectacles, eyeglasses; [fortifications] lunette; [volaille] wishbone.
†**lurette** [ly'rɛt] *n.f.*: *Il y a belle ~*, That was a long time ago. || †**luron** [ly'r|ɔ̃] *n.m.* jolly fellow: *joyeux ~*, gay dog. || **luronne** [-ɔn] *n.f.* buxom wench.
lus, &c. cf. LIRE.
lustre [lystr] *n.m.* **1.** lustre, gloss. **2.** chandelier. 3. †lustrum, interval of five years. || **lustrer** [-e] #3 *v. tr.* to lustre, to smooth, to make smooth, to make smooth and shiny.
luth [lyt] *n.m.* lute.
luthérien, -ne [lyterj|ɛ̃, -ɛn] *adj.* & *n.* [Rel.] Lutheran.
luthier [ly'tje] *n.m.* violin-maker.
lutin [ly'tɛ̃] *n.m.* imp, (mischievous) sprite, elf, goblin.
lutrin [ly'trɛ̃] *n.m.* lectern; © reading stand, music stand.
lutte [lyt] *n.f.* struggle, contest, fight: *de haute ~*, after much wrestling; [Sport.] wrestling: *~ gréco-romaine*, French wrestling. || **lutter** [-e] #3 *v. intr.* to fight, struggle, contend, [Sport.] wrestle. || **lutteu|r, -se** [-œ:r, -ø:z] *n* wrestler.
luxe [lyks] *n.m.* luxury: *~ de mauvais goût*, showiness, tawdriness; profusion: *avec un ~ de détails*, with a wealth of details.
luxueu|x, -se [-ɥø, -ɥø:z] *adj.* luxurious. [× LUXURIOUS.]
luxure [lyk'sy:r] *n.f.* [×] lust, lewdness. || **luxuriance** [lyksy'rj|ɑ̃:s] *n.f.* [×] luxuriance. || **luxuriant, -e** [-ɑ̃, -ɑ̃:t] *adj.* [×] luxuriant. || **luxurieu|x, -se** [lyksy'rj|ø, ø:z] *adj.* [×] lewd, lustful.
luzerne [ly'zɛrn] *n.f.* [Bot.] lucerne, [US] alfalfa.
lycée [li'se] *n.m.* [Fr.] public high school, college [includes first two years of University]; © [abus.] independent private school. || **lycéen, -ne** [-'ɛ̃, -'ɛn] [Fr.] high-school/boy, girl/, student.

lymphatique [lɛ̃fɑ'tik] *adj. & n.* lymphatic; [Fig.] sluggish. || **lymphe** [lɛ̃:f] *n.f.* lymph.
lynchage [lɛ̃'ʃ|a:ʒ] *n.m.* lynching. || **lyncher** [-e] #3 *v. tr.* to lynch (a person).
lynx [lɛ̃:ks] *n.m.* lynx, bobcat: *avoir des yeux de* ~, to be lynx-eyed.
Lyon [ljõ] *n.* Lyons. || **Lyonnais, -e** *adj. & n.* (Native of) Lyons.
lyre [li:r] *n.f.* lyre. || **lyrique** [li'r|ik] *adj.* lyric, lyrical. || *n.m.* lyric. || **lyrisme** [-ism] *n.m.* lyricism.
lys [lis] *n.m.* cf. LIS[1].

M

M,[1] **m** [ɛm] *n.m.* [letter] M, m.
M.[2] *pl.* **MM.** [= monsieur, messieurs. ☞ The abbr. is always followed by the family name.] Mr., *pl.* Messrs.: *M. Ladouceur*, Mr. Ladouceur; *MM. Ladouceur et Lavoie*, Messrs. Ladouceur and Lavoie.
m' contraction of **me**: *il m'a dit*, he told me.
ma [ma] *adj. poss. f.* my. cf. MON.
maboul, -e [ma'bul] *adj.* [Fam.] balmy, off his rocker.
macabre [ma'kɑ:br] *adj.* macabre, gruesome.
macadam [maka'dam] *n.m.* hard surface, pavement. || **macadamiser** [-i'ze] #3 *v. tr.* to pave.
macareux [maka'rø] *n.m.* puffin.
macaron [maka'rõ] *n.m.* macaroon.
macaroni [makarɔ'ni] *n.m. inv.* macaroni.
macération [masera'sjõ] *n.f.* maceration, soaking; [Fig.] mortifying of the flesh. || **macérer** [mase're] #10 *v. tr.* to macerate: *faire* ~, to soak, to steep; [Fig., la chair] to mortify.
mâché, -e [mɑ'ʃə] *adj.* chewed: *papier* ~, papier-mâché.
mâchefer [mɑʃ'fɛ:r] *n.m.* clinker.
mâcher [mɑ'ʃe] #3 *v. tr.* to chew: [Fig.] ~ *le travail à qqun*, to prepare the work for s.o., to do all the work for s.o.; *ne pas* ~ *ses mots*, not to mince matters.
machiavélique [makjave'lik] *adj.* Machiavellian.
machin, -e [ma|'ʃɛ̃, ʃin], *n.* [Fam., = chose] gadget, jigger; [Pers.] what's-his-name.
machinal, -e [maʃi'na|l] *adj.* mechanical. || **machinalement** [-l'mɑ̃] *adv.* mechanically.
machination [-'sjõ] *n.f.* machination, scheme, plot.
machine [ma'ʃin] *n.f.* engine, machine: ~ *à vapeur*, steam engine; *la chambre aux machines*, the engine-room; ~ *à coudre*, sewing-machine; ~ *à écrire*, typewriter; ~ *-outil*, machine tool; *faire* ~ *arrière*, to back up, to go in reverse; *les machines*, machinery.
machiner [-e] #3 *v. tr.* to scheme, plot.
machinerie [-'ri] *n.f.* [coll.] machinery; [endroit] engine-room. || **machiniste** [-ist] *n.m.* engineer, bus driver; [Théât.] stage hand, scene shifter.
mâchoire [mɑ'ʃwa:r] *n.f.* jaw(-bone).
mâchonner [mɑʃɔ'ne] #3 *v. tr.* to chew, munch; [Fig.] to mutter, mumble.
mâchurer [maʃy're] #3 *v. tr.* to bruise, [métal] to crush.
maçon [ma's|õ] *n.m.* mason, bricklayer: *Franc-maçon*, Free-Mason. || **maçonner** [-ɔ'ne] #3 *v. tr.* to build with stone and mortar, to put together. || **maçonnerie** [-ɔn'ri] *n.f.* masonry, stonework; [short for] Freemasonry.
maculer [maky'le] #3 *v. tr. & intr.* to stain, blot.
Madagascar [madagas'ka:r] *n.m.* Madagascar.
madame [ma'dam] *n.f.* [*pl.* **mesdames** [mɛ'dam]] **1.** [with family name] Mrs.: *Mme Martin*, Mrs. Martin. **2.** [without family name] Madam, *pl.* Ladies. **3.** *Madame la présidente*, Madam Chairman; *Madame est servie*, Dinner is served.
madeleine [mad'l|ɛn] *n.f.* [form of] sponge cake. || **Madeleine** (les Îles de la) *n.f.pl.* Magdalen Islands. || **Madeleine** *n.pr.f.* = Magdalen(e).
madelinot, -e [-i'n|o, -ɔt] © *n. & adj.* relating to the Magdalen Islands.

mademoiselle [madmwa'zɛl] [*pl.* mesdemoiselles] Miss [presque toujours suivi du nom de famille] *Mademoiselle Martin,* Miss Martin; *Mesdemoiselles Martin,* the Misses Martin.
madone [ma'dɔn] *n.f.* madonna.
madré, -e [mɑ'dre] *adj.* sly, crafty.
madrier [madri'e] *n.m.* beam.
madrig|al, -aux [madri'g|al, -o] *n.m.* madrigal.
maestro [maɛs'tro] *n.m.* maestro.
mafflu, -e [ma'fly] *adj.* heavy-jowled.
maganer [maga'ne] © #3 *v. tr.* to ill-treat, tire out (s.o.); to damage (sth.).
magasin [maga'z|ɛ̃] *n.m.* **1.** store, shop: *avoir en* ~, to have in stock; *les grands* ~, department stores. **2.** warehouse. **3.** [fusil] magazine. || **magasinage** [-i'na:ʒ] *n.m.* **1.** warehousing, storing. **2.** © shopping: *faire du* ~, to go shopping. **magasiner** [-i'ne] #3 *v. tr.* © to go shopping. || **magasinier** [-i'nje] *n.m.* warehouseman, storekeeper.
magazine [maga'zin] *n.m.* [périodique] magazine.
mage [ma:ʒ] *n.m.* magus: *les trois Rois Mages,* the Three Magi, the Three Wise Men.
Magellan (le détroit de) [maʒɛl'lɑ̃] *n.m.* (Strait of) Magellan.
magicien, -ne [maʒi'sj|ɛ̃, -ɛn] *n.* magician, wizard. || **magie** [ma'ʒi] *n.f.* magic. || **magique** [-k] *adj.* magic, magical: *d'un coup de sa baguette* ~, with a touch of his wand; *tapis* ~, flying carpet.
magistère [maʒis't|ɛ:r] *n.m.* [intellectual authority exercised by master over disciples]: *exercer un* ~, to have disciples.
magistral, -e [-ral] *adj.* **1.** [ton] magistral. **2.** masterly. **3.** → lecture: *un cours* ~ a lecture course.
magistrat [-ra] *n.m.* magistrate, judge. || **magistrature** [-'ty:r] *n.f.* magistracy, judgeship; [Coll.] the Bench: *entrer dans la* ~, to become a judge.
magnanime [maɲa'nim] *adj.* magnanimous.
magnat [ma'ɲa] *n.m.* magnate, tycoon.
magnétique [maɲe't|ik] *adj.* magnetic.
magnéto [-o] *n.f.* magneto.
magnificence [maɲifi|'sɑ̃:s] *n.f.* magnificence, lavishness, stateliness.
magnifique [-k] *adj.* magnificent; wonderful: *Il a fait un temps* ~, It's been a glorious day. || **magnifiquement** [-k'mɑ̃] *adv.* magnificently.
mai [mɛ] © [me] *n.m.* May, cf. AVRIL.
maigre [mɛ:gr] *adj.* **1.** thin, lean, gaunt: ~ *comme un clou,* as thin as a nail. **2.** meagre, slender: *ses maigres ressources,* his slender resources; *un* ~ *repas,* a scanty meal. **3.** meatless: *un repas* ~, a meatless meal; *faire* ~, to abstain from meat. || **maigreur** [mɛ'g|rœ:r] *n.f.* thinness, gauntness, emaciation. || **maigri, -e** [-i] *adj.* → thinner. || **maigrichon, -ne** [-i'ʃ|ɔ̃, -ɔn] *adj.* small and skinny. || **maigriot|** **-e** [-i|'o, -'ɔt] *adj.* small and skinny. || **maigrir** [-i:r] #17 *v. intr.* to lose weight, to get thinner.
mail [ma:j] *pl.* **mails** *n.m.* mall.
maille[1] [mɑ:j] *n.f.* [tricot] stitch; [filet] mesh, loop; [chaînon] link: *cotte de mailles,* coat of mail.
maille[2] *n.f.* [old copper coin]: *n'avoir ni sou ni* ~, not to have a red cent; *avoir* ~ *à partir avec qqun,* to have a bone to pick with s.o.
maillon [mɑ'jɔ̃] *n.m.* link (of a chain).
maillot [ma'jo] *n.m.* [bain] swimming suit; [de corps] undershirt; [sport] jersey; [danseuse, acrobate] tights.
main [mɛ̃] *n.f.* **1.** hand. **2.** [papier] quire. **3.** [Loc.] *coup de* ~, raid; ~*-d'œuvre,* labour, manpower; ~ *à laver,* face cloth; *écrit de sa* ~, written in his (own) hand; *à portée de la* ~, *sous la* ~, within reach; *aller la* ~ *dans la* ~, to go hand in hand; *avoir la haute* ~ *sur,* to control; (*donner*) *de la* ~ *à la* ~, (to give) privately; (*préparer*) *de longue* ~, (to prepare) carefully; *de* ~ *de maître,* in a masterly fashion; *demander la* ~ *d'une femme,* to ask for a woman's hand; *donner les mains à qqch,* to be in favour of sth.; *en un tour de* ~, in a jiffy; *en venir aux mains,* to come to blows; *faire* ~ *basse sur,* to grab; *se faire la* ~, to get one's hand in; *se frotter les mains,* to rub one's hands; *haut la* ~, without any difficulty, easily; *haut les mains!,* hands up!; *se laver les mains de qqch.,* to wash one's hands of sth.; *lever la* ~ *sur qqch.,* to lay one's hand on sth.; *mettre la dernière* ~ *à qqch.,* to put the finishing touch on sth.; *ne pas y aller de* ~ *morte,* not to pull one's punches; *passer la* ~, to let s.o. else take over; *porter la* ~ *sur qqun,* to hit s.o.; *prendre en* ~, to take in hand; *prêter la* ~ *à qqch.,* to be a party to sth.; *prêter* ~ *forte,* to give strong support, to assist; *serrer la main à qqun,* to shake hands with s.o.; *tendre la* ~ *à qqun,* to hold one's hand to s.o.; *y tenir la* ~, to see to it.
Maine (le) [(lə)'mɛn] *n.m.* Maine.
maint, -e [mɛ̃(:t)] *adj.* many: *maintes fois,*

many a time; *à maintes reprises,* time and again.

maintenant [mɛ̃t'nɑ̃] *adv.* now.

maintenir [mɛ̃t|'ni:r] #22 *v. tr.* to maintain, keep, preserve. || **se ~** *v. pr.* to keep, stay, continue. || **maintien** [-jɛ̃] *n.m.* maintenance; [du corps] bearing.

maire [mɛ:r] *n.m.* mayor. || **mairesse** [mɛ'r|ɛs] *n.f.* mayoress, mayor's wife. || **mairie** [-i] *n.f.* town hall.

mais [mɛ] *adv.* but: *~ oui, bien sûr,* why yes, certainly; *~ non,* of course not, certainly not.

maïs [ma'is] *n.m.* corn; [Br.] Indian corn; [colour] maize; *un épi de ~* , an ear of corn, a corn cob; *potage de ~* , hominy.

maison [mɛ'z|õ] *n.f.* **1.** house, home: *à la ~* , at home, home; *~ de bois,* frame house; *~ de rapport,* apartment house; *~ de santé,* nursing home. **2.** firm, house, establishment: *Ils travaillent tous deux pour la même ~* , They both work for the same firm. || **maisonnée** [-ɔ'ne] *n.f.* household. || **maisonnette** [-ɔ'nɛt] *n.f.* small house, cottage.

maître [mɛ:tr] *n.m.* **1.** master, owner: *~ de maison,* master of the house; householder. **2.** master, expert: *~ charpentier,* master carpenter; *coup de ~* , masterstroke; *être passé ~ en,* to be a past master in; *se rendre ~ de,* to master, conquer. **3.** master, teacher: *~ d'école,* school master; *livre du ~* , teacher's manual, key. **4.** [Loc.] *maître-autel,* high altar; *~ chanteur,* blackmailer; *~ d'hôtel,* headwaiter, butler. || **maîtresse** [mɛ'trɛs] *n.f.* **1.** mistress: *~ de maison,* lady of the house; housewife; [Com.] householder. **2.** teacher.

maîtrise [-'tr|i:z] *n.f.* **1.** mastery, command: *~ de soi,* self-control. **2.** master's (degree). || **maîtriser** [-i'ze] #3 *v. tr.* to master, to subdue, to control.

majesté [maʒɛs't|e] *n.f.* majesty. || **majestueusement** [-ɥøz'mɑ̃] *adv.* majestically. || **majestueu|x, -se** [-ɥø(:z)] *adj.* stately, majestic.

majeur [ma'ʒœ:r] *adj.* **1.** major, important: *avoir une raison majeure de . . . ,* to have a special reason to . . . ; *un cas de force majeure,* a case of absolute necessity; act of God. **2.** of age. **3.** [Mus.] major.

major [ma'ʒ|ɔ:r] *n.m.* **1.** [Milit.] © major, †army doctor. **2.** [Loc.] *être le ~ de sa promotion,* to be the head of one's class; *état- ~* , staff; headquarters' staff; *sergent- ~* , sergeant major; *tambour- ~* , drum major.

majorité [-ɔri'te] *n.f.* **1.** majority: *une ~ écrasante,* an overwhelming majority. **2.** coming of age: *à sa ~* , when he comes of age.

Majorque [ma'ʒɔrk] *n.f.* Majorca.

majuscule [maʒɥs'kyl] *adj.* capital (letter). || *n.f.* capital letter.

mal [mal] *adj.* bad, evil, wicked: *bon an, ~ an,* year in, year out. || *adv.* badly, bad: *être ~ avec qqun,* to be on bad terms with s.o.; *être ~ disposé envers qqun,* to be unfavourably disposed toward s.o.; *Il est ~ venu de s'en plaindre,* He should not be the one to complain; *pas ~* , (a) not bad: *Cela n'a pas ~ marché,* It went pretty well; (b) many: *Il y avait pas ~ de gens,* There were quite a few people. || *n.m.* **1.** pain: *avoir ~ aux dents,* to have a toothache; *avoir ~ au doigt,* to have a sore finger; *avoir ~ au cœur,* to be sick to one's stomach; *avoir le ~ de mer,* to be seasick; *avoir le ~ du pays,* to be homesick; *faire ~ à qqun,* to hurt s.o. **2.** pains, trouble: *Il se donne beaucoup de ~* , He is very painstaking; *J'ai du ~ à le croire,* I find it difficult to believe that. **3.** wrong, injury: *faire du ~ à qqun,* to harm s.o.; *dire du ~ de qqun,* to speak ill of s.o. **4.** wrong, evil, wickedness: *le bien et le ~* , right and wrong.

M.A.L.: *Membre de l'Assemblée législative*: M.L.A., Member of the Legislative Assembly.

malade [ma'lad] *adj.* ill, sick. || *n.mf.* sick person, patient. || **maladie** [-i] *n.f.* illness, sickness, disease: *relever de ~* , to convalesce; [Fig.] *Il va en faire une ~* , He'll be terribly upset over it. || **maladi|f, -ve** [-if, -i:v] *adj.* sickly.

maladresse [mala'dr|ɛs] *n.f.* blunder: *commettre une ~* , to make a blunder, to blunder. || **maladroit, -e** [-wa(t)] *adj.* clumsy, awkward. || *n.* clumsy person, butter-fingers. || **maladroitement** [-wat'mɑ̃] *adv.* clumsily, awkwardly.

Malais, -e (États) [ma'lɛ] *n.m.* Malay States.

malaise [ma'l|ɛ:z] *n.m.* discomfort; uneasiness: *avoir, ressentir un ~* , not to feel well.

malaisé [-ɛ'ze] *adj.* difficult.

Malaisie [malɛ'zi] *n.f.* Malaya.

malard [ma'la:r] *n.m.* mallard.

malaxage [malak's|a:ʒ] *n.m.* kneading (of dough); working (of butter); massaging (of muscles). || **malaxer** [-e] #3 *v. tr.* to knead (bread); to work (butter); to massage (muscles). || **malaxeu|r, -se** [-œ:r, -ø:z] *n.* mixer, mixing machine.

Malbaie (La) [la mal'be] *n.f.* © Murray Bay.

malchance [mal'ʃ|ɑ̃:s] *n.f.* ill, bad luck: *une* ~, a bit of bad luck; *par* ~, unluckily. || **malchanceu|x, -se** [-ɑ̃'sø(:z)] *adj.* unlucky.

mâle [mɑ:l] *adj.* male, masculine. || *n.m.* male.

malédiction [maledik'sjõ] *n.f.* curse.

maléfique [male'fik] *adj.* harmful, maleficent.

malencontreux, -se [malɑ̃kõ'trø(:z)] *adj.* untimely, unfortunate.

malentendu [malɑ̃tɑ̃'dy] *n.m.* misunderstanding.

malfaisance [malfə'zɑ̃:s] *n.f.* mischievousness; evil-doing. || **malfaisant, -e** [malfə'zɑ̃(:t)] *adj.* malevolent, harmful.

malfait|eur, -rice [malfɛ't|œ:r, -ris] *n.* evildoer; thief.

malfamé, -e [malfa'me] *adj.* of ill repute.

malgré [mal'gre] *prép.* in spite of; despite.

malheur [ma'l|œ:r] *n.m.* misfortune, unhappiness: *jouer de* ~, to be unlucky; *porter* ~ *à qqun*, to bring bad luck to s.o.; *pour comble de* ~, to make things worse; *Un* ~ *ne vient jamais seul*, It never rains but it pours. || **malheureusement** [-œrøz'mɑ̃] *adv.* unfortunately. || **malheureu|x, -se** [-œ'rø(:z)] *adj.* [personne] unhappy; [événement] unfortunate.

malhonnête [malɔ'n|ɛ:t] *adj.* dishonest; rude, uncivil. || **malhonnêtement** [-ɛt'mɑ̃] *adv.* dishonestly. || **malhonnêteté** [-ɛt'te] *n.f.* dishonesty.

malice [ma'lis] *n.f.* malice; mischievousness; *Il n'y voit pas de* ~, He does not see any harm in it; *avoir un air plein de* ~, to have a sly look; *faire une* ~ *à qqun*, to play a trick on s.o. || **malicieu|x, -se** [-jø(:z)] *adj.* mischievous, [×] malicious.

mali|n, -gne [ma'l|ɛ̃, -iɲ] *adj.* cunning, shrewd, sharp; malignant; © bad, wicked: ~ *comme un renard*, as sly as a fox; *fièvre maligne*, malignant fever; *Ce n'est pas* ~, There's nothing to it. || *n.* sly fox.

malingre [ma'lɛ̃:gr] *adj.* weakly, puny.

malle [mal] *n.f.* **1.** trunk: *faire ses malles*, to pack (up). **2.** mail boat; © mail. || **maller** [-e] *v. tr.* © to mail.

mallette [-ɛt] *n.f.* suitcase; small trunk.

malmener [mal|mə'ne] #9 *v. tr.* to bully, rough up.

malpropre [-'prɔpr] *adj.* dirty, not clean; [Fig.] indecent.

malsain, -e [-'s|ɛ̃, -ɛn] *adj.* unhealthy.

Malte [malt] *n.f.* Malta.

maltraiter [mal|trɛ'te] #3 *v. tr.* to ill-treat, ill-use.

malveillance [-vɛ'jɑ̃:s] *n.f.* malevolence, ill-will, desire to harm. || **malveillant, -e** [malvɛ'jɑ̃ (:t)] *adj.* malevolent, spiteful.

malversation [-vɛrsa'sjõ] *n.f.* malversation, corruption.

maman [mɑ̃'mɑ̃] *n.f.* ma(ma); mummy: *grand-* ~, grandma.

mamelle [ma'm|ɛl] *n.f.* [personne] breast; [animal] udder. || **mamelon** [-'lõ] *n.m.* nipple, teat; [butte] hillock.

Man (l'île de) [man] *n.f.* The Isle of Man.

†**manant** [ma'nɑ̃] *n.m.* villain; boor, clodhopper.

manche[1] [mɑ̃:ʃ] *n.f.* **1.** sleeve: *être dans la* ~ *de qqun*, to be in his good books; *C'est une autre paire de manches*, That's (quite) another pair of shoes. **2.** [à air] shaft. **3.** [jeux] round, [cartes] hand, [tennis] set, [baseball] inning. **4.** [Géog.] *la Manche*, the English Channel.

manche[2] [mɑ̃:ʃ] *n.m.* handle: ~ *à balai*, (a) broomstick, (b) [Aviat.] joystick: [Fig.] *être du côté du* ~, to have the whiphand.

manchette [mɑ̃'ʃ|ɛt] *n.f.* cuff: *boutons de* ~, cuff-links.

manchon [-õ] *n.m.* **1.** muff. **2.** [Tech.] casing, sleeve. **3.** [à gaz] mantle.

manchot, -te [mɑ̃'ʃ|o, -ɔt] *adj.* one-handed; one-armed. || *n.m.* one-armed person.

mandarine [mɑ̃da'rin] *n.f.* tangerine.

mandat [mɑ̃'da] *n.m.* **1.** mandate. **2.** [député] term. **3.** warrant. **4.** [postal] money order: *un* ~ *de vingt dollars*, a money order for twenty dollars. || **mandat-poste** [-'pɔst] *n.m.* postal money order.

mandataire [-'tɛ:r] *n.m.* representative; proxy.

mander [mɑ̃'de] #3 *v. tr.* to summon, call; †to report; to announce.

manège [ma'nɛ:ʒ] *n.m.* training; [lieu] riding-school; [chevaux de bois] merry-go-round; [Fig.] trick, little game.

manette [ma'nɛt] *n.f.* handle, hand-lever.

manganèse [mɑ̃ga'nɛ:z] *n.m.* manganese.

mangeaille [mɑ̃'ʒ|ɑ:j] *n.f.* [Péj.] food; [Fam.] grub. || **mangeoire** [-wa:r] *n.f.* manger. || **manger** [-e] #5 *v. tr.* to eat: ~ *du bout des lèvres*, to nibble at; ~ *à sa faim*, to eat one's fill; ~ *comme quatre*, to eat like a horse; [Fig.] to squander: *donner à* ~ *à*, to feed. || **mangeu|r, -se** [-œ:r, -ø:z] *n.* eater: *un gros* ~, a big eater.

maniable [ma'njabl] *adj.* manageable, easy to handle.

maniaque [ma'njak] *adj.* fussy, finicky. || *n.* crank, fuss-budget.

manie [ma'n|i] *n.f.* mania; passion; craze, fad: *avoir la* ~ *de faire qqch.*, to have a mania for doing sth.

manier [-je] #3 *v. tr.* to handle; to use.

manière [ma'nj|ɛ:r] *n.f.* manner; way: *d'une ~ ou d'une autre*, one way or another; *en aucune ~*, by no means; *de ~ que*, so that; *de ~ à*, so as to; *~ de voir*, point of view. || **maniéré, -e** [-e're] *adj.* affected.

manifeste [mani'fɛst] *adj.* manifest, evident, obvious. || *n.m.* manifesto. || **manifester** [-e] #3 *v. tr.* **1.** to manifest, show: *~ l'intention de*, to express a desire to. **2.** to demonstrate.

Manille [ma'ni:j] *n.f.* Manila.

manipule [mani'pyl] *n.m.* maniple.

manipuler [-e] #3 *v. tr.* to manipulate, handle.

Manitoba (le) [(lə) manitɔ'b|a] *n.m.* Manitoba. || **manitobain|-e** [-ɛ̃, -ɛn] © *adj. & n.* Manitoban.

Manitou [mani'tu] *n.m.* manito, manitou: [Fam.] *le grand ~*, the big boss, the great white father.

manivelle [mani'vɛl] *n.f.* crank, winch.

mannequin [man'kɛ̃] *n.m.* **1.** dress form, dummy. **2.** mannequin, model.

manœuvre [ma'n|œ:vr] *n.f.* **1.** manœuvre; [trains] shunting; handling. **2.** [Mil.] manœuvres, army manœuvres. **3.** [Fig.] scheme, manœuvring. || *n.m.* unskilled labourer. || **manœuvrer** [-œ'vre] #3 *v. tr.* to manœuvre, operate, handle. || *v. intr.* to manœuvre; [Fig.] to scheme: *Il sait ~*, He is a skilful operator.

manoir [ma'nwa:r] *n.m.* †manor; country residence.

manomètre [manɔ'mɛ:tr] *n.m.* manometer; pressure gauge.

manque [mɑ̃:k] *n.m.* lack, shortage; [Loc.]: *~ de*, for want of.

manqué, -e [mɑ̃'ke] *adj.* unsuccessful, abortive: *C'est un avocat ~*, He should have been a lawyer; *un coup ~*, a flop, miss; *une vie manquée*, a wasted life.

manquer #3 *v. intr.* **1.** to fail; [fusil] to misfire: *~ à sa parole*, to break one's word; *~ à qqun*, to show disrespect to s.o.; *sans ~*, without fail; *Je n'y manquerai pas*, I won't fail to do it; *Il a manqué de tomber*, He almost fell. **2.** to be lacking, to be without: *Les vivres vinrent à ~*, They ran out of food; *Nous en manquons*, We are out of it; *~ à l'appel*, to be missing. **3.** to be missed: *Vous nous manquez beaucoup*, → We miss you very much. || *v. tr.* to miss: *Il a manqué son coup*, He missed; *Il a manqué son examen*, He flunked his exam. || *v. impers.* to be missing: *Il en manque deux*, There are two missing; *Il ne manquerait plus que cela*, I should say not.

mansarde [mɑ̃'sard] *n.f.* [toit] mansard; [chambre] attic room, garret; [fenêtre] dormer (window).

mansuétude [mɑ̃sɥe'tyd] *n.f.* meekness, forbearance, mansuetude.

manteau [mɑ̃'to] *n.m.* [sans manches] mantle, cloak; [avec manches] coat; [cheminée] mantelpiece: [Fig.] *sous le ~*, sub rosa.

manucure [many'ky:r] *n.m.* manicure.

manuel, -le [ma'nɥɛl] *adj.* manual; [Scol.] *travaux manuels*, manual training. || *n.m.* manual, handbook.

manufacture [manyfak'ty:r] *n.f.* [usine] factory, plant; [action] manufacture.

manuscrit, -e [manys'kri(t)] *adj.* handwritten. || *n.m.* manuscript.

manutention [manytɑ̃'sjɔ̃] *n.f.* **1.** handling: *frais de ~*, handling charges. **2.** [Mil.] bakery.

maquereau [mak'ro] *n.m.* mackerel; [Fig. & Fam.] pimp.

maquette [ma'kɛt] *n.f.* [réduite] model; [grandeur nature] mock-up.

maquillage [maki'j|a:ʒ] *n.m.* make up. || **maquillé** [-e] *adj.* [visage] made up; [tableau] faked. || **maquiller** [-e] #3 *v. tr.* to make up; to fake; [Fig.] to gloss over. || **se ~** *v. pr.* to make up.

maquis [ma'ki] *n.m.* **1.** bush. **2.** underground resistance, maquis.

maraîch|er, -ère [marɛ'ʃ|e, -ɛ:r] *adj.* truck-gardening. || *n.m.* truck-gardener.

marais [ma'rɛ] *n.m.* salt marsh.

marâtre [ma'rɑ:tr] *adj.* cruel mother; †stepmother.

maraude [ma'r|o:d] *n.f.* **1.** stealing from gardens, pilfering. **2.** [taxi] *en ~*, cruising. || **marauder** [-o'de] #3 *v. intr.* **1.** to steal fruit from gardens; to go pilfering. || **maraudeu|r, -se** [-o'd|œ:r, -ø:z] *n.* marauder: *C'est un ~*, He goes about robbing gardens.

marbre [marbr] *n.m.* marble; [baseball] © home plate. || **marbré, -e** [-e] *adj.* marbled, mottled. || **marbrer** #3 *v. tr.* to marble, mottle.

marc [ma:r] *n.m.* **1.** [weight or money] mark. **2.** [de raisin] marc, pulp; [de café] grounds; [de thé] leaves.

Marc [mark] *n.m.* = Mark.

marchand, -e [mar'ʃɑ̃(:d)] *adj.* marketable: *valeur marchande*, sale value; *marine marchande*, mercantile marine; *ville marchande*, trading city. || *n.* shopkeeper, storekeeper, dealer: *~ ambulant*, vendor; †merchant. || **marchandage** [-ɑ̃'d|a:ʒ] *n.m.* bargaining; [Péj.] haggling. || **marchander** [-e] #3 *v. tr.* **1.** to bargain; [Péj.] to haggle.

2. to price. 3. to grudge. || **marchandise** [-i:z] *n.f.* goods, wares, merchandise; freight: *train de marchandises,* freight (train).

marche [marʃ] *n.f.* 1. walk, walking: *à cinq minutes de ~*, five minutes walk from here; *Il aime la ~*, He likes walking. 2. movement, running, operation: *en état de ~*, in running order; *quand le train est en ~*, when the train is in motion; *faire ~ arrière,* to back up, to reverse. 3. [Mil.] march. 4. step: *Attention à la ~ !,* Watch your step!

marché [mar'ʃe] *n.m.* 1. market: *la place du ~*, the market square; © grocery. 2. marketing, shopping: *faire son ~*, to do the marketing, to get the groceries. 3. deal, bargain: *conclure un ~*, to strike a bargain; *par-dessus le ~*, into the bargain; *bon ~*, cheap; *faire bon ~ de,* to set little store by.

marchepied [marʃə'pje] *n.m.* 1. folding step, running board. 2. [Fig.] stepping-stone.

marcher [mar'ʃe] #3 *v. intr.* 1. to walk, tread: *~ au pas,* to walk in step; *~ à grands pas,* to stride; *~ sur qqch.,* to tread on sth.; *~ sur les pieds à qqun,* to push s.o. around. 2. [Mil.] to march. 3. to work, run, operate: *Cette usine marche nuit et jour,* This plant operates day and night.

mardi [mar'di] *n.m.* Tuesday: *Mardi gras,* Shrove Tuesday, cf. LUNDI.

mare [ma:r] *n.f.* pool, pond.

marécage [mare'k|a:ʒ] *n.m.* marsh, bog, swamp. || **marécageu|x, -se** [-a'ʒø(:z)] *adj.* swampy, marshy.

maréchal [mare'ʃal] *n.m.* [ferrant] blacksmith, farrier; [Milit.] Marshal.

maréchal des logis [mare'ʃal de lɔ'ʒi] *n.m.* (cavalry, artillery) sergeant.

marée [ma're] *n.f.* tide: *~ descendante,* ebb tide; *~ montante,* flood tide.

marelle [ma'rɛl] *n.f.* hop-scotch.

marge [marʒ] *n.f.* [autour d'une page écrite] border; [à gauche d'une page écrite] margin; [bord] edge; [Fig.] margin, leeway.

marguerite [margə'rit] *n.f.* daisy.

Marguerite [margə'rit] *n.f.* = Margaret.

marguillier [margi'je] *n.m.* churchwarden.

mari [ma'ri] *n.m.* husband.

mariage [ma'rj|a:ʒ] *n.m.* marriage; wedding; married life. || **marié, -e** [-e] *adj.* married, wedded. || *n.m.* bridegroom. || *n.f.* bride.

Marie [ma'ri] *n.f.* = Mary.

marier [ma'rje] #3 *v. tr.* 1. to marry, join in wedlock. 2. to marry off; *On la maria à un ingénieur,* She was married off to an engineer. 3. [Fig.] to blend, harmonize. || **se ~** *v. pr.* to get married.

marin [ma'r|ɛ̃] *adj.* marine; sea-going. || *n.m.* sailor, seaman.

marinades [mari'nad] © *n.fpl.* pickles.

marine [-in] *n.f.* 1. navy: *la ~ de guerre,* the navy; *la ~ marchande,* the mercantile marine. 2. seascape.

mariné, -e [mari'ne] *adj.* [Culin.] marinated. || **mariner** #3 *v. tr.* to marinate.

maringouin [marɛ̃'gwɛ̃] *n.m.* © mosquito; [Fr.] crane-fly, daddy-long-legs.

marini|er, -ère [mari'nj|e, -ɛ:r] *adj.* marine, naval. || *n.m.* waterman.

marionnette [marjɔ'nɛt] *n.f.* [à gant] puppet; [à fil] marionette: *théâtre de marionnettes,* puppet show.

maritime [mari'tim] *adj.* maritime: © *Les Provinces maritimes,* The Maritime Provinces, the Maritimes; *un habitant des Provinces maritimes,* a Maritimer.

maritorne [mari'tɔrn] *n.f.* slut, sloven.

mark [mark] *n.m.* [monnaie allemande] mark.

marmelade [marmə'lad] *n.f.* marmalade: *~ de pommes,* apple sauce.

marmite [mar'mit] *n.f.* pot: [Fig.] *faire bouillir la ~*, to keep the pot boiling.

marmonner [marmɔ'ne] #3 *v. tr.* to mumble, mutter.

marmot [mar'mo] *n.m.* toddler, brat; [Fig.] *croquer le ~*, to cool one's heels.

marmotte [mar'mɔt] *n.f.* marmot; © gopher, groundhog: *~ du Canada* (ou: *siffleux*), whistler, woodchuck.

marmotter [marmɔ'te] #3 *v. tr.* to mutter, mumble.

Maroc, le [(lə) ma'rɔk] *n.m.* Morocco. || **marocain, -e** [-ɛ̃, -ɛn] *adj.* Moroccan.

maroquin [marɔ'k|ɛ̃] *n.m.* Morocco leather. || **maroquinerie** [-in'ri] *n.f.* leather goods.

marquant, -e [mar'kɑ̃(:t)] *adj.* prominent; striking.

marque [mark] *n.f.* 1. mark, sign. 2. [Com.] make, brand: *De quelle ~ est votre voiture?,* What make is your car?; *une ~ de cigarettes,* a brand of cigarettes. 3. distinction: *un visiteur de ~*, a distinguished visitor. || **marqué, -e** [-e] *adj.* marked, pronounced. || **marquer** #3 *v. tr.* 1. to mark; [au fer rouge] to brand. 2. [Sport.] to score. 3. [Fig.] to indicate, to express, to show: *Il ne marque pas son âge,* He does not look his age. || *v. intr.* to leave a mark.

marqueterie [markə'tri] *n.f.* marquetry, inlay.

marquis [mar'k|i] *n.m.* marquis. || **marquise**

[-i:z] *n.f.* **1.** marchioness. **2.** awning, marquee.
marraine [ma'rɛn] *n.f.* godmother, [ext.] sponsor.
marre [ma:r] *n.f.* [only in]: *en avoir* ~, to be fed up.
marron [ma'r|õ] *adj.* **1.** brown, tan: *souliers marron*, tan shoes. **2.** [nègre] runaway, [courtier, avocat] unlicensed. || *n.m.* chestnut: *tirer les marrons du feu*, to do the dirty work (for s.o. else). || **marronnier** [-ɔ'nje] *n.m.* chestnut-tree: ~ *d'Inde*, horse chestnut.
mars[1] [mars] *n.m.* March. || **Mars**[2] *n.m.* [planète] Mars.
marseillais, -e [marsɛ'jɛ(:z)] *adj.* & *n.* Marseillais: *la Marseillaise*, the Marseillaise.
Marseille [mar'sɛ:j] *n.f.* Marseilles.
marsouin [mar'swɛ̃] *n.m.* porpoise; ~ *commun* (ou *pourcil*) herring hog, harbour porpoise.
marteau [mar't|o] *n.m.* **1.** hammer: ~ *de porte*, knocker; ~ *-pilon*, sledge-hammer, power hammer. **2.** [poisson] hammerhead. **3.** [Loc.] *être pris entre le* ~ *et l'enclume*, to get it from both sides.
marteler [-ə'le] #8 *v. tr.* to hammer at; to pound.
Marthe [mart] *n.f.* = Martha.
martial, -e [mar'sjal] *adj.* martial.
martinet[1] [marti'nɛ] *n.m.* martinet: ~ *ramoneur*, chimney swift.
martinet[2] *n.m.* cat-o'-nine-tails; carpet beater.
Martiniquais, -e [martini'kɛ(:z)] *n.* & *adj.* native, inhabitant of Martinique. || **Martinique, (la)** [(la) marti'nik] *n.f.* Martinique.
martin-pêcheur [martɛ̃pɛ'ʃœ:r] *n.m.* kingfisher.
martre [martr] *n.f.* marten: ~ *d'Amérique*, pine marten, American sable; ~ *de Pennant*, black cat.
martyr, -e [mar't|i:r] *n.* martyr. || **martyre** [-i:r] *n.m.* martyrdom: *souffrir le* ~, to suffer martyrdom. || **martyriser** [-iri'ze] #3 *v. tr.* to martyr; [Fig.] to torture, torment.
Maryland, (le) [(lə) mari'lɑ̃:d] *n.m.* Maryland.
mascotte [mas'kɔt] *n.f.* mascot.
Mascoutain, -e [masku't|ɛ̃, -ɛn] *n.* inhabitant, native/of St. Hyacinthe. Que.
masculin, -e [masky'l|ɛ̃, -in] *adj.* masculine, male; mannish: *genre* ~, masculine gender; *sexe* ~, male sex; *Elle a l'air* ~, She has a mannish look.
maskinongé [maskinõ'ʒe] © *n.m.* muskellunge; lunge; musky.
masque [mask] *n.m.* mask; [Fig.] *arracher le* ~ *à qqun*, to unmask s.o. || **masqué, -e** [-e] *adj.* [visage] masked; [ext.] disguised: *bal* ~, fancy dress ball. || **masquer** #3 *v. tr.* to mask, put a mask on (s.o.); [Fig.] to conceal, hide.
Massachusetts, (le) [(lə) masaʃy'sɛts] *n.m.* Massachusetts.
massacre [ma'sakr] *n.m.* massacre, slaughter. || **massacrer** [-e] #3 *v. tr.* to massacre, slaughter.
massage [ma'sa:ʒ] *n.m.* massage.
masse[1] [mas] *n.f.* mass, bulk: *en* ~, in the mass; *les masses*, the masses.
masse[2] *n.* mace; sledge-hammer.
masser [-e] #3 *v. tr.* **1.** to mass, to assemble. **2.** to massage.
masseu|r, -se [ma'sœ:r] *n.* masseur *m*, masseuse *f.*
massi|f, -ve [ma's|if, -i:v] *adj.* solid, massive. || *n.m.* **1.** [Géog.] massif. **2.** [jardin] *les massifs*, shrubbery.
massue [ma'sy] *n.f.* [war] club; [Fig.] *un coup de* ~, a staggering blow.
mastic [mas'tik] *n.m.* mastic; putty. || **mastiquer** [-e] #3 *v. tr.* **1.** to chew. **2.** to putty, to fill with mastic.
masure [ma'zy:r] *n.f.* (tumble-down) shack, shanty.
mat, -e [mat] *adj.* **1.** dull, flat, lustreless, mat: *un son* ~, a thud. **2.** checkmated: *faire échec et* ~, to checkmate.
mât [mɑ] *n.m.* mast; pole.
match [matʃ] *n.m.* [Sport.] match, game.
matelas [mat'lɑ] *n.m.* mattress.
matelasser [-se] #3 *v. tr.* to pad, to cushion.
matelot [mat'lo] *n.m.* sailor, seaman.
mater [ma'te] #3 *v. tr.* to break in, to subdue, to curb, to tame.
mâter [mɑ'te] #3 *v. tr.* to mast, to provide with masts.
matérialiser [materj|ali'ze] #3 *v. tr.* to materialize. || **matériau, -x** [mate'rjo] *n.m.* (building) material; [Fig. pl.] materials. || **matériel, -le** [-ɛl] *adj.* material, real. || *n.m.* material, equipment; aid: ~ *audio-visuel*, audio-visual aids; ~ *d'enseignement*, instructional material [× MATERIAL].
maternel, -le [matɛr'n|ɛl] *adj.* maternal; motherly: *école maternelle*, sub primary; *langue maternelle*, mother tongue; *grand-père* ~, maternal grandfather; *un sentiment* ~, a motherly feeling. || **maternité** [-i'te] *n.f.* maternity, motherhood; maternity hospital.

mathématicien, -ne [matemati|'sjɛ̃, -'sjɛn] *n.* mathematician. || **mathématique** [-k] *adj.* mathematical. || *n.fpl.* mathematics; [abbr. Fam.] math.

matière [ma'tjɛ:r] *n.f.* matter; subject matter; material.

matin[1] [ma'tɛ̃] *n.m.* morning: *de grand* ~, early in the morning; *du* ~ *au soir,* morning, noon and night.

mâtin[2] [mɑ'tɛ̃] *n.m.* [chien] mastif.

matinal, -e [mati'n|al] *adj.* morning: *une promenade matinale,* a morning walk; *être* ~, to be an early riser; *Vous êtes* ~ *aujourd'hui,* You are early today. || **matinée** [-e] *n.f.* **1.** morning: *passer la* ~, to spend the morning; *dans la* ~, sometime in the morning; *faire la grasse* ~, to sleep late. **2.** [Théât.] afternoon performance, matinée.

matois, -e [ma'twa(:z)] *adj.* sly, shrewd. || *n.m.* a sly dog.

matou [ma'tu] *n.m.* tom-cat.

matraque [ma'trak] *n.f.* club, night stick.

matricule [matri'kyl] *n.f.* roll, register. || *n.m.* regimental number (of a soldier); *numéro* ~, registration number, serial number.

maturité [matyri'te] *n.f.* maturity: *avec* ~, maturely.

maudire [mo'd|i:r] #47 *v. tr.* to curse, to damn. || **maudit, -e** [-i(t)] *adj.* cursed, accursed; damned.

maugréer [mogre'e] #3 *v. intr.* to mutter, to fume (at, *contre*).

maure [mo:r] *adj.* Moorish. || *n. les Maures,* the Moors.

maussade [mo'sad] *adj.* **1.** [caractère] sullen, surly. **2.** [temps] dull, gloomy.

mauvais, -e [mɔ'vɛ(:z)] *adj.* **1.** bad, evil, wicked; poor: *La mer est mauvaise,* The sea is rough; *Il fait* ~ *temps,* The weather is bad; *une mauvaise tête,* a sorehead; *avoir mauvaise mine,* to look bad, ill; *avoir mauvais caractère,* to be cantankerous; *prendre en mauvaise part,* to take exception to. || *adv.* bad: *sentir* ~, to smell bad, to stink.

mauve [mo:v] *adj.* mauve, purple. || *n.f.* cf. GOÉLAND.

maxime [mak'sim] *n.f.* maxim.

maximum [maksi'mɔm] *adj. & n.m.* maximum.

mayonnaise [majɔ'nɛ:z] *n.f.* mayonnaise.

mazout [ma'zu] *n.m.* fuel oil.

me [mə] *pron. pers.* [dir.] me, [ind.] to me: *Il m'a frappé,* He hit me; *Il me parle,* He is speaking to me. || *pron. réfl.* myself: *Je me suis demandé,* I asked myself, I wondered.

méandre [me'ɑ̃:dr] *n.m.* meander.

mécanicien, -ne [mekani|'sjɛ̃, -'sjɛn] *n.* mechanic; [Rail.] engineer, [Br.] engine-driver. || **mécanique** [-k] *adj.* mechanical. || *n.f.* mechanics. || **mécaniser** [mekani'ze] #3 *v. tr.* to mechanize. || **mécanisme** [meka'nism] *n.m.* mechanism.

méchamment [meʃ|a'mɑ̃] *adv.* spitefully, nastily, meanly. || **méchanceté** [-ɑ̃s'te] *n.f.* [adult] wickedness, meanness; [enfant] naughtiness, mischievousness. || **méchant, -e** [-ɑ̃(:t)] *adj.* **1.** bad, nasty, mean: *de méchante humeur,* in a bad mood; [enfant] naughty; *Chien* ~, Beware the dog. **2.** poor: *une méchante valise,* a wretched suitcase. || *n.* mean person: *les méchants,* the wicked; *Méchant !,* You naughty child!

mèche [mɛʃ] *n.f.* **1.** [lampe] wick. **2.** [fouet] lash. **3.** [explosif] fuse. **4.** [vrille] bit. **5.** [Loc.] *éventer la* ~, to catch on to the trick; *vendre la* ~, to let the cat out of the bag; [Fam.] *Il n'y a pas* ~, It is impossible, [Fam.] No soap; *être de* ~ *avec qqun,* to be in cahoots with s.o.

mécompte [me'kõ:t] *n.m.* disappointment.

méconnaissable [mekɔn|ɛ'sabl] *adj.* unrecognizable, changed out of recognition. || **méconnaître** [-ɛ:tr] **méconnaissant** [-ɛ'sɑ̃] **méconnu** [-y] #40 *v. tr.* to fail to recognize; to ignore, to disregard.

mécontent, -e [mekõ't|ɑ̃(:t)] *adj.* dissatisfied, disgruntled. || **mécontentement** [-ɑ̃t'mɑ̃] *n.m.* discontent, dissatisfaction.

Mecque, (la) [(la)'mɛk] *n.f.* Mecca.

mécréant, -e [mekre'ɑ̃(:t)] *adj.* unbelieving. || *n.* unbeliever.

médaille [me'da:j] *n.f.* medal: *C'est le revers de la* ~, You have to take the rough with the smooth.

médecin [met's|ɛ̃] *n.m.* physician: ~ *ordinaire,* family doctor, general practitioner; *femme* ~, woman doctor. || **médecine** [-in] *n.f.* medicine: *étudiants en* ~, medical students.

médiation [medja'sjõ] *n.f.* mediation.

médical, -e [medi'ka|l] *adj.* medical. || **médicament** [-'mɑ̃] *n.m.* medicine, drug.

médiéval, -e [medje'val] *adj.* mediæval.

médiocre [medjɔkr] *adj.* mediocre, average. || **médiocrité** [-i'te] *n.f.* mediocrity.

médire [me'd|i:r] #46 *v. intr.* to speak ill (of, *de*), to disparage, to run down. || **médisance** [-i'zɑ̃:s] *n.f.* malicious gossip.

méditation [medit|a'sjõ] *n.f.* meditation. || **méditer** [-e] #3 *v. intr.* to meditate, to be deep in thought, to muse (on, *sur*). || *v. tr.* to ponder, to meditate.

Méditerranée (la) [(la) mediterа'ne] *n.f.* Mediterranean.
médius [me'djys] *n.m.* middle finger.
méduse [me'dy:z] *n.f.* jelly fish.
méfait [me'fɛ] *n.m.* misdeed.
méfiance [me'fj|ɑ̃:s] *n.f.* distrust. || **méfiant, -e** [-ɑ̃(:t)] *adj.* distrustful. || **méfier (se)** [-e] #3 *v. pron.* to distrust, to be suspicious of: *Il ne se méfiait de rien,* He did not suspect a thing.
mégarde [me'gard] *n.f.* [only in:] *par* ~, inadvertently, unawares.
mégère [me'ʒɛ:r] *n.f.* [femme] shrew: [Lit.] *La Mégère apprivoisée,* The Taming of the Shrew.
mégot [me'go] *n.m.* cigar (or cigarette) butt.
meilleur, -e [mɛ'jœ:r] *adj.* better: *le* ~, the better, the best; ~ *marché,* cheaper.
mélancolie [melɑ̃kɔ'li] *n.f.* melancholy, sadness. || **mélancolique** [-k] *adj.* melancholy; sad, gloomy.
mélange [me'l|ɑ̃:ʒ] *n.m.* [action] mixing, [résultat] mixture, blend. || **mélanger** [-ɑ̃'ʒe] #5 *v. tr.* to mix; [soigneusement] to blend.
mélasse [mɛ'las] *n.f.* molasses, [Br.] treacle.
mêlée [mɛ'le] *n.f.* free-for-all, melee, scuffle. || **mêler** #3 *v. tr.* to mix, to mix up: *être mêlé à une affaire,* to be involved in a case. || **se mêler** *v. pron.* **1.** to interfere (with, *de*): *Mêlez-vous de ce qui vous regarde!,* You keep out of this. **2.** to dabble (in, *de*).
mélèze [me'lɛ:z] *n.m.* larch, cf. TAMARAC.
mélodie [melɔd|i] *n.f.* melody. || **mélodieu|x, -se** [-jø(:z)] *adj.* melodious, tuneful.
mélodrame [melɔ'dram] *n.m.* melodrama.
melon [mə'lõ] *n.m.* **1.** melon: ~ *d'eau,* watermelon. **2.** derby (hat), [Br.] bowler.
membrane [mɑ̃'bran] *n.f.* membrane.
membre [mɑ̃:br] *n.m.* [corps] limb: *trembler de tous ses membres,* to shake all over; [société] member: *le nombre des membres,* the membership.
même [mɛ:m] *adj.* **1.** same: *le* ~ *jour,* the same day. **2.** very: *le jour* ~, on that very day. **3.** self: *lui-* ~, himself. || *adv.* even: ~ *lui,* even he; *de* ~, in the same way, likewise.
mémoire[1] [me'mwa:r] *n.f.* memory: *avoir une bonne* ~, to have a retentive memory; *faire qqch. de* ~, to do sth. from memory; *se rafraîchir la* ~, to refresh one's memory; *pour* ~, for the record. || **mémoire**[2] *n.m.* **1.** memorandum, paper; [Scol.] thesis, honours paper. **2.** *pl.* memoirs.
mémorable [memɔ'rabl] *adj.* memorable.
menaçant, -e [məna'sɑ̃(:t)] *adj.* threatening; menacing. || **menace** [mə'nas] *n.f.* threat, menace: *proférer des menaces,* to threaten, to utter threats. || **menacer** [-e] #4 *v. tr.* to threaten, to menace: ~ *ruine,* to be about to fall apart.
ménage [me'n|a:ʒ] *n.m.* **1.** housekeeping, household: *articles de* ~, household utensils; *faire le* ~, to do the housework; © *le grand* ~, spring cleaning; *pain de* ~, home-made bread; *femme de* ~, cleaning woman; *faire des ménages,* to work as a cleaning woman. **2.** married couple: *faire bon* ~, to get along well. || **ménagement** [-aʒ'mɑ̃] *n.m.* care, caution: *Allez-y avec* ~, Go easy; *parler sans* ~, to speak bluntly.
ménager [-a'ʒe] #5 *v. tr.* **1.** to husband, to use sparingly: ~ *sa santé,* to take good care of one's health; *Qui veut voyager loin ménage sa monture,* Slow and steady wins the race. **2.** to deal gently with (s.o.): *Il faut le* ~, You must not antagonize him. **3.** to plan, to arrange, to effect: ~ *une entrevue,* to arrange an interview, ~ *une surprise,* to have a surprise in store; ~ *une ouverture,* to make a hole. || **ménage|r, -ère** [-a'ʒ|e, -ɛ:r] *adj.* **1.** → household: *l'enseignement* ~, home economics; *travaux ménagers,* housework. **2.** using sparingly: ~ *de ses deniers,* thrifty. || **ménagère** [-ɛ:r] *n.f.* housewife; [esp. ©] housekeeper: *C'est une bonne* ~, She is a good housekeeper.
ménagerie [menaʒ'ri] *n.f.* menagerie.
mendiant, -e [mɑ̃'d|jɑ̃(:t)] *n.* beggar. || **mendicité** [-isi'te] *n.f.* begging. || **mendier** [-je] #3 *v. tr. & intr.* to beg (for).
mené [me'ne] © *n.m.* minnow.
menée [mə'ne] *n.f.* [usual. pl.] **1.** intrigues. **2.** tracks of deer.
mener [mə'ne] #9 *v. tr.* **1.** to take: *Menez-le chez le docteur,* Take him to the doctor. **2.** to lead, to guide, to conduct: ~ *une enquête,* to conduct an investigation; ~ *à bien,* to achieve, to bring to a successful conclusion; *Elle le mène par le bout du nez,* He is a henpecked husband.
†**ménestrel** [menɛs'trɛl] *n.m.* minstrel.
meneur [mə'nœ:r] *n.m.* leader, ringleader.
menotte [mə'nɔt] *n.f.* little hand. || *n.fpl.* handcuffs; [Fam.] bracelets: *passer, mettre/les* ~ *à qqun,* to handcuff s.o., to put the handcuffs on s.o.
mensonge [mɑ̃'sõ:ʒ] *n.m.* lie, falsehood. || **mensong|er, -ère** [mɑ̃sõ'ʒ|e, -ɛ:r] *adj.* lying, deceitful; deceptive.
mensualité [mɑ̃sɥ|ali'te] *n.f.* monthly/

payment, instalment/. || **mensuel, -le** [-ɛl] *adj.* monthly.

mensurable [mɑ̃sy'rabl] *adj.* measurable.

mental, -e [mɑ̃'tal] *adj.* mental.

mentalité [mɑ̃tali'te] *n.f.* mentality; tenour of mind.

menteu|r, -se [mɑ̃t|œ:r, -ø:z] *adj.* lying; [moins grave] fibbing; [apparence] deceptive. || *n.* liar, [moins grave] fibber.

menthe [mɑ̃:t] *n.f.* mint: ~ *poivrée*, peppermint.

mention [mɑ̃'sj|ɔ̃] *n.f.* mention: *faire ~ de*, to mention. || **mentionner** [-ɔ'ne] #3 *v. tr.* to mention; to name (s.o.).

mentir [mɑ̃'ti:r] #26 *v. intr.* to lie, to tell a lie, [moins grave] to fib.

menton [mɑ̃'tɔ̃] *n.m.* chin.

menu, -e [mə'ny] *adj.* small, tiny: *menue monnaie*, small change. || *adv.* small: *hacher ~*, to chop fine. || *n.m.* menu, bill of fare.

menuet [mə'nɥɛ] *n.m.* minuet.

menuiserie [mənɥiz|'ri] *n.f.* carpentry; woodwork. || **menuisier** [-je] *n.m.* carpenter, [Br.] joiner.

méprendre (se) [(sə) me'pr|ɑ̃:dr] **méprenant** [-ə'nɑ̃] **mépris** [-i] #41 *v. pron.* to make a mistake (on, *sur*), to misunderstand: *Il s'est mépris sur mes intentions*, He misunderstood my intentions.

mépris [-i] *n.m.* contempt, scorn. || **méprisable** [-i'zabl] *adj.* contemptible, despicable. || **méprisant, -e** [-i'zɑ̃(:t)] *adj.* contemptuous, scornful. || **méprise** [-i:z] *n.f.* mistake. || **mépriser** [-i'ze] #3 *v. tr.* to despise, scorn, to spurn.

mer [mɛ:r] *n.f.* sea: *en pleine ~*, on the high seas; *jeter à la ~ (d'un navire)*, to throw overboard: *d'une ~ à l'autre*, from coast to coast; *toutes les mers du monde*, the seven seas; *(la) mer de Béring*, (the) Bering Sea.

mercanti [mɛrkɑ̃'ti] *n.m.* profiteer. || **mercantile** [-l] *adj.* mercantile; [Péj.] profiteering.

mercenaire [mɛrsə'nɛ:r] *n. m/f.* mercenary.

mercerie [mɛrsə'ri] *n.f.* small wares, [US] notions; notions store: © ~ *pour hommes*, haberdashery.

merci [mɛr'si] *n.f.* mercy: *être à la ~ de qqun*, to be at s.o.'s mercy; *demander ~ à qqun*, to ask s.o. for mercy; *sans ~*, merciless, without mercy. || *n.m.* thank you, thanks: *Merci (oui)*, Yes, please; thanks; *Merci (non)*, No, thanks.

merci|er, -ère [mɛr'sj|e, -ɛ:r] *n.* haberdasher.

mercredi [mɛrkrə'di] *n.m.* Wednesday: ~ *des Cendres*, Ash Wednesday, cf. LUNDI.

mercure [mɛr'ky:r] *n.m.* mercury, quicksilver.

mère [mɛ:r] *n.f.* mother; [cheval] dam: *grand'- ~*, grandmother; *belle- ~*, **1.** stepmother, **2.** mother-in-law: *la maison ~*, the head office.

méridien [mɛri'dj|ɛ̃] *n.m.* meridian. || **méridional, -e** [-ɔ'nal] *adj.* Southern. || **Méridional, -e** *n.* Southerner, person from the South.

méritant, -e [meri'tɑ̃(:t)] *adj.* deserving; worthy. || **mérite** [me'rit] *n.m.* merit; worth: *revendiquer le ~ de*, to claim credit for. || **mériter** [-e] #3 *v. tr.* to merit; to deserve. || *v. intr.* [used in the expression] *bien ~ de* (sa patrie), to deserve well of. || **méritoire** [-wa:r] *adj.* meritorious, deserving.

merlan [mɛr'lɑ̃] *n.m.* pollock, whiting.

merle [mɛrl] *n.m.* blackbird: ~ *bleu*, bluebird; ~ *américain* [cf. GRIVE] robin. **2.** [Fig.] *C'est un fin ~*, He is a shrewd one.

merveille [mɛr'v|ɛ:j] *n.f.* marvel, wonder: *les Sept Merveilles du monde*, the Seven Wonders of the World; *à ~*, wonderfully (well); *se porter à ~*, to be in the best of health. || **merveilleu|x, -se** [-ɛ'jø(:z)] *adj.* marvellous, wonderful. || *n.m. le ~*, the supernatural.

mes [mɛ, mez] *adj. poss. m/f. plur.* my. cf. MON.

mésalliance [meza'ljɑ̃:s] *n.f.* misalliance: *Elle a fait une ~*, She married beneath herself.

mésange [me'zɑ̃:ʒ] *n.f.* chickadee.

mésaventure [mezavɑ̃'ty:r] *n.f.* mishap; misadventure; misfortune.

mesdames [mɛ'dam] *n.fpl.* ladies, cf. MADAME.

mesdemoiselles [mɛdmwa'zɛl] *n.fpl.* ladies, cf. MADEMOISELLE.

mésentente [mezɑ̃'tɑ̃:t] *n.f.* misunderstanding, disagreement.

mésestimer [mezɛsti'me] #3 *v. tr.* to underestimate, underrate.

mésintelligence [mezɛ̃tɛli'ʒɑ̃:s] *n.f.* misunderstanding, disagreement.

mesquin, -e [mɛs'k|ɛ̃, -in] *adj.* mean; petty. || **mesquinerie** [-in'ri] *n.f.* pettiness.

mess [mɛs] *n.m.* (officers') mess.

message [mɛ'sa:ʒ] *n.m.* message. || **messager, -ère** [-a'ʒ|e, -ɛ:r] *n.m.* messenger, carrier.

messagerie [mɛsaʒ'ri] *n.f.* express (transport), shipping service; *train de ~*, fast freight.

messe [mɛs] *n.f.* [Rel.] mass: *la grand- ~*, high mass; *servant m de ~*, altar-boy.

messieurs [mɛ'sjø] *n.mpl.*: [oralement]

gentlemen; [par écrit] Dear Sirs; [Abr.] Messrs, cf. MONSIEUR.

Messine [mɛ'sin] *n.f.* Messina: *le détroit de ~*, the Strait of Messina.

mesurable [məzy'r|abl] *adj.* measurable. || **mesurage** [-a:ʒ] *n.m.* measuring. || **mesure** [mə'z|y:r] *n.f.* **1.** measurement, measure: *On va prendre vos mesures*, We'll take your measurements; *fait sur mesures*, made to/measure, order/; *faire bonne ~*, to give full measure; *outre ~*, excessively; *dans la ~ du possible*, in so far as possible. **2.** measure, step, action: *Il faut prendre des mesures*, We must act. **3.** measure, moderation. **4.** rhythm, time: *battre la ~*, to keep time. || **mesuré, -e** [-y're] *adj.* [pas] measured, regular; [Fig., voix] even, well controlled. || **mesurer** #3 *v. tr.* to measure; to appreciate. || **se mesurer** *v. pron.* to pit o.s. (against, *avec*).

mésuser [mezy'ze] #3 *v. intr.* to misuse (s.o., *de qqun*).

met [mɛ] cf. METTRE.

métabolisme [metabɔ'lism] *n.m.* metabolism.

métal [me'tal] *n.m.* metal. || **métallique** [-ik] *adj.* metallic. || **métalloïde** [-ɔ'id] *n.m.* metalloid, non-metal. || **métallurgie** [-yr'ʒi] *n.f.* metallurgy. || **métallurgiste** [-yr'ʒist] *n.m.* steelworker.

métamorphose [metamɔr'fo:z] *n.f.* metamorphosis.

métaphore [meta'fɔ:r] *n.f.* metaphor.

métaphysique [metafi'zik] *n.f.* metaphysics.

métayer [mete'je] *n.m.* share cropper, tenant farmer.

météo [mete'o] *n.f.* [Fam.] weather/forecast, report/; weather bureau. || **météorologie** [meteɔrɔlɔ'ʒi] *n.f.* meteorology.

méthode [me'tɔd] *n.f.* method (of doing sth., *pour faire qqch.*), system; *avoir de la ~*, to be methodical. || **méthodique** [-ik] *adj.* methodical, systematic.

méticuleu|x, -se [metiky'lø(:z)] *adj.* meticulous.

métier [me'tje] *n.m.* **1.** trade, occupation, business: *soldat de ~*, professional soldier. **2.** loom: *mettre sur le ~*, to undertake, to start.

métis, -se [me'ti(s)] [me'tis] *adj.* half-breed, cross-breed; [chien] mongrel; [plante] hybrid. || *n.* [Pers.] half-breed; [chien] mongrel.

métrage [me'tra:ʒ] *n.m.* length (in metres); footage (in feet); [action] measuring: *film de long ~*, a feature-length film; *un film de court ~*, a short (film). || **mètre** [mɛ:tr] *n.m.* metre, metre stick [about $1\frac{1}{10}$ yards], [équivalent pour la traduction] yard. || **métrique** [me'trik] *adj.* metric, metrical.

métro (le) [me'tro] *n.m.* [abbr. of MÉTROPOLITAIN] subway; [Br.] tube.

métropole [metrɔ'pɔl] *n.f.* **1.** metropolis. **2.** mother country.

métropolitain, -e [-i't|ɛ̃, -ɛn] *adj.* metropolitan; continental: *territoire m ~ des États-Unis d'Amérique*, continental United States of America; *les forces métropolitaines*, the home forces; © *l'agglomération f métropolitaine*, Greater Montreal. || *n.m.* [Rel.] metropolitan; [Rail.] Paris subway.

mets[1] [mɛ] *n.m.* dish, food.

mets[2] [mɛ] cf. METTRE.

mettable [mɛ't|abl] *adj.* wearable.

metteur [-œ:r] *n.m.* [gens] *~ en œuvre*, setter; [Théât.] *~ en scène*, director.

mettre [mɛt|r] **mettant** [-ɑ̃] **mis** [mi] #44 *v. tr.* **1.** to put: *~ debout*, to stand; *~ à plat*, to lay down. **2.** [Loc.] *~ en colère*, to make angry; *~ de côté*, to set aside, to save; *~ à l'épreuve*, to test; *~ en état*, to repair, to fix; *~ le feu à*, to set fire to; *~ en mesure*, to enable (to, *de*); *~ en pièces*, to break up; *~ au point*, to overhaul, to develop; *~ la table*, to set the table; *~ du temps à faire qqch.*, to take time to do sth.; *~ un vêtement*, to put on a garment. || **se mettre** *v. pron.*: *~ à*, to begin; *~ en colère*, to get angry; *~ debout*, to stand up; *~ à un endroit*, to sit or to stand at some place; *~ en frais*, to exert o.s.; *~ au lit*, to go to bed; *~ mal avec qqun*, to quarrel with s.o.; *~ en route*, to set out, to start; *~ en tête de*, to get one's mind set on; *~ à table*, to sit down to eat.

meuble [mœbl] *adj.* movable: [sol] loose: *biens meubles*, chattels; movables. || *n.m.* a piece of furniture; [au pl.] furniture. || **meublé, -e** [-e] *adj.* & *n.m.* furnished: *habiter en meublé*, to live in lodgings. || **meubler** #3 *v. tr.* to furnish; [Fig.] *se ~ l'esprit*, to enrich one's mind (with, *de*).

meuglement [møglə'mɑ̃] *n.m.* lowing; mooing (of cattle, &c.).

meuh [mø] [Onomat.] moo [of a cow, &c.].

meule [mœl] *n.f.* **1.** [de moulin] millstone, [pour aiguiser] grindstone; [de fromage] round cheese. **2.** [tas de foin, &c.] stack.

meuni|er, -ère [mø'nj|e, -ɛ:r] *n.* miller, miller's wife.

meurs [mœ:r] cf. MOURIR.

meurtre [mœrtr] *n.m.* murder. || **meurtri|er, -ère** [-i'j|e, -ɛ:r] *adj.* murderous, deadly.

|| *n.* murderer. || *n.f.* murderess; [de tir] loophole.
meurtrir [mœr'tr|i:r] #17 *v. tr.* to bruise. || **meurtrissure** [-i'sy:r] *n.f.* bruise.
meute [mø:t] *n.f.* pack.
meuvent [mœv] cf. MOUVOIR.
mévente [me'vɑ̃:t] *n.f.* slump, drop in sales.
mexicain, -e [mɛksi'k|ɛ̃, -ɛn] *adj.* & *n.* Mexican.
Mexico [mɛksi'ko] *n.m.* Mexico City. || **Mexique, (le)** [(lə) mɛk'sik] *n.m.* Mexico: *le golfe du* ~, the Gulf of Mexico.
mi [mi] *n.m.* [Mus.] mi. || *adv.* mid, half, semi-: *à* ~ *-chemin*, half-way; *à* ~ *-côte*, half-way/up, down/; *à la* ~ *-septembre*, in mid-September.
miaulement [mjol|'mɑ̃] *n.m.* miaow. || **miauler** [-e] #3 *v. intr.* to miaow; †to mew.
mica [mi'ka] *n.m.* mica.
miche [miʃ] *n.f.* (round) loaf (of bread).
Michel [mi'ʃɛl] *n.m.* = Michael, [Fam.] Mike, Mickey.
Michigan, (le) [(lə) miʃi'gɑ̃] *n.m.* Michigan: *le lac* ~, Lake Michigan.
micmac [mik'mak] *n.m.* [Fam.] trick; fiddle, fiddling. || **Micmac** [Amérindien] Micmac, the Micmac (nation).
mi-corps (à) [ami'kɔ:r] *loc. adv.* up to the waist; *saisir à* ~, to take hold around the waist.
micro [mi'kro] *n.m.* mike. || **microbe** [mi'krɔb] *n.m.* microbe, germ. || **microphone** [mikrɔ'fɔn] *n.m.* microphone. || **microscope** [mikrɔs'kɔp] *n.m.* microscope: *observer au* ~, to observe through a microscope. || **microsillon** [mikrosi'jõ] *adj.* long playing: *(disque)* ~, long-playing record, [Fam.] LP.
midi [mi'di] *n.m.* **1.** noon, twelve o'clock, midday. **2.** the South (of France, Italy).
mie [mi] *n.f.* crumb, soft part (of bread).
miel [mjɛl] *n.m.* honey: *lune de* ~, honeymoon. || **mielleu|x, -se** [-ø(:z)] *adj.* [goût] honey, of honey; [Fig.] honeyed (words, &c.).
mien, -ne [mjɛ̃, mjɛn] *poss. adj.* of mine: †*un mien cousin*, a cousin of mine. || *poss. pr.* [used with le, la, les] mine: *Voici/le mien, la mienne*, Here is mine; *Voici/les miens, les miennes*, Here are mine; *Les miens*, My family.
miette [mjɛt] *n.f.* crumb.
mieux [mjø] *adv.* better, best: *aimer* ~, to prefer; *à qui* ~ ~, one trying to outdo the other; *tant* ~, so much the better; *Je ne demande pas* ~, I don't mind if I do; *faire de son* ~, to do one's best; *Le* ~ *est l'ennemi du bien*, Leave well enough alone; *J'agirai au* ~ *de vos intérêts*, I'll do what's best for you.
mièvre [mjɛ:vr] *adj.* delicate, dainty.
mignard, -e [mi'ɲ|a:r, -ard] *adj.* mincing. || **mignardise** [-ar'di:z] *n.f.* [Péj.] mincing manner.
mignon, -ne [mi'ɲ|õ, -ɔn] *adj.* cute; dainty; darling; [child] sweet, cute; dainty.
migraine [mi'grɛn] *n.f.* headache.
migration [migra'sjõ] *n.f.* migration. || **migratoire** [migra'twa:r] *adj.* migratory.
mijoter [miʒɔ'te] #3 *v. intr.* to simmer. || *v. tr.* & *Fig.* to concoct, to cook up: *Ils mijotent quelque chose*, Something is brewing.
mil[1] [mil] *adj.* thousand (in dates): ~ *neuf cent trente*, nineteen hundred and thirty.
mil[2] [mi:j] *n.m.* cf. MILLET.
milan [mi'lɑ̃] *n.m.* [oiseau] kite.
Milan [mi'lɑ] *n.m.* Milan.
milice [mi'lis] *n.f.* militia.
milieu, -x [mi'ljø] *n.m.* **1.** middle, centre: *au beau* ~ *de*, in the very midst of; *le juste* ~, the happy medium, the golden mean. **2.** environment, milieu, set.
militaire [mili'tɛ:r] *adj.* military, → army: *installation militaire*, army installation. || *n.m.* soldier.
militarisme [milita'rism] *n.m.* militarism.
***millage** [mi'la:ʒ] *n.m.* mileage, cf. [Fr.] KILOMÉTRAGE.
mille[1] [mil] *adj. card.* thousand: ~ *un*, one thousand and one; *deux* ~, two thousand.
mille[2] *n.m.* mile: ~ *carré*, square mile; ~ *marin*, nautical mile.
Mille-Îles (la rivière des) [mi'lil] © *n.f.* Thousand-Island River.
millet [mi'jɛ] *n.m.* [Bot.] millet; millet-grass; canary-seed.
milliaire [mi'ljɛ:r] *adj. borne* ~, milestone.
milliard [mi'lj|a:r] *n.m.* billion, [Br.] milliard: *cinq milliards*, five billion. || **milliardaire** [-ar'dɛ:r] *n.m.* → millionaire [based on the difference between francs and dollars].
millième [mi'ljɛm] *n.m.* thousandth.
millier [mi'lje] *n.m.* thousand: *plusieurs milliers de personnes*, several thousand people.
million [mi'ljõ] *n.m.* million: *deux millions*, two million. || **millionième** [-ɔ'njɛm] *adj.* & *n.m.* millionth. || **millionnaire** [-ɔ'nɛ:r] *n.m.* millionaire.
mi-mât [mi'mɑ] *adv. loc. à* ~, at half-mast.
mime [mim] *n. m/f.* mime, mimic. || **mimer** [-e] #3 *v. intr.* & *tr.* to mimic; to mime.
mimosa [mimo'za] *n.m.* mimosa.

minable [mi'nabl] *adj.* **1.** pitiful, shabby, wretched. **2.** that can be mined.
minauder [mino'de] #3 *v. intr.* to simper.
mince [mɛ̃:s] *adj.* **1.** thin, slim, slender: *un livre* ~, a thin book; *une taille* ~, a slim figure. **2.** [Fig.] scanty, slender. || **minceur** [mɛ̃'sœ:r] *n.f.* thinness, slimness.
mine [min] *n.f.* **1.** look, appearance; *avoir bonne* ~, to look well; *juger sur la* ~, to judge (people) by appearances; *faire* ~ *de*, to pretend; *Il a fait* ~ *de refuser*, He seemed to be about to refuse; *faire grise* ~ *à qqun*, to give s.o. the cold shoulder. || *n.f.* **1.** mine, pit. **2.** [crayon] lead. || **miner** [-e] #3 *v. tr.* to mine, [Fig.] to undermine, sap: *Le surmenage a miné sa santé*, Overwork has impaired his health.
minerai [-'rɛ] *n.m.* ore.
minér|al, -aux [-e'r|al, -o] *adj.* mineral: *eau minérale*, mineral water; *chimie minérale*, inorganic chemistry. || *n.m.* mineral. || **minéralogie** [mineralɔ'ʒi] *n.f.* mineralogy. || **minéralogiste** [mineralɔ'ʒist] *n.m.* mineralogist.
minet [mi'nɛ] *n.m.* pussy.
mineur[1] [mi'nœ:r] *adj.* under age. || *n.m.* minor.
mineur[2] *n.m.* miner.
miniature [minja'ty:r] *n.f.* miniature, small scale: *en* ~, (in) miniature; tiny; on a small scale.
minime [mi'nim] *adj.* small: *pour une somme* ~, for a nominal fee.
minimum [mini'mɔm] *n.m.* minimum.
ministère [minis't|ɛ:r] *n.m.* Department, [Br.] Ministry, Office: ~ *de la Justice*, Department of Justice. || **ministériel, -le** [-e'rjɛl] *adj.* ministerial. || **ministre** [mi'nistr] *n.m.* **1.** minister, [US] Secretary: © *premier* ~, [Federal] Prime Minister, [Provincial] Premier: *Ministre des Finances*, Minister of Finance; [Br.] Chancellor of the Exchequer, [US] Secretary of the Treasury. **2.** minister, pastor (clergy).
Minnesota, (le) [(lə) minəso'ta] *n.m.* Minnesota.
minois [mi'nwa] *n.m.* face, countenance.
minorité [minɔri'te] *n.f.* minority.
Minorque [mi'nɔrk] *n.f.* Minorca.
minot [mi'no] © *n.m.* peck.
minoterie [-ɔt'ri] *n.f.* **1.** (flour) mill. **2.** flour industry. || **minotier** [-ɔ'tje] *adj.* miller, flour-mill owner.
minuit [mi'nɥi] *n.m.* midnight, twelve o'clock (at night).
minuscule [minys'kyl] *adj.* tiny. || *n.f.* small letter, lower case letter.
minute[1] [mi'nyt] *n.f.* minute.
minute[2] *n.f.* original draft.
minuterie [-'ri] *n.f.* motion work (of a clock); automatic time switch.
minutie [miny's|i] *n.f.* minute detail; [qui n'est pas important] trifle- ~ *-s*, minutiae. || **minutieu|x, -se** [-jø(:z)] *adj.* meticulous, thorough, detailed.
mioche [mjɔʃ] *n.m.* brat.
mi-pente [mi'pɑ̃:t] *adv.*: *à* ~, half-way up, half-way down.
miracle [mi'ra:kl] *n.m.* miracle, wonder: *faire des miracles*, to work wonders. || **miraculeusement** [-akyløz'mɑ̃] *adv.* miraculously. || **miraculeu|x, -se** [-aky'lø(:z)] *adj.* miraculous.
mirage [mi'ra:ʒ] *n.m.* mirage.
mire [mi:r] *n.f.* **1.** sight: *ligne de* ~, line of sight; *point de* ~, aim; [Fig.] centre of attraction. **2.** surveyor's rod.
mirer [mi'r|e] #3 *v. tr.* to fix one's eye on: ~ *des œufs*, to candle eggs; ~ *qqch.*, to have one's eye on sth. || **se** ~ *v. pr.* to look at o.s., to be reflected. || **miroir** [-wa:r] *n.m.* mirror; looking-glass: © *œuf au* ~, egg sunny side up.
miroitant, -e [mirwa't|ɑ̃(:t)] *adj.* glistening, shining: [eau] shimmering. || **miroiter** [-e] #3 *v. intr.* to glitter, glisten; [eau] shimmer: *faire* ~ *qqch. aux yeux de qqun*, to dangle sth. before s.o.
mis [mi] cf. METTRE.
misaine [mizɛn] *n.f. mât de* ~, foremast.
misanthrope [mizɑ̃'trɔp] *n.m.* misanthrope. || *adj.* misanthropic.
mise [mi:z] *n.f.* **1.** putting, placing: ~ *en action*, realization, implementation; ~ *à exécution*, carrying out; ~ *en marche*, starting; ~ *en œuvre*, putting into action; ~ *au point*, overhauling; [moteur] tuning up; [modèle] development; [question] clarification; ~ *en scène*, staging; ~ *en vente*, (putting on) sale; ~ *en vigueur*, enforcement. **2.** [au jeu] stake; [enchère] bid; [habillement] dress, attire; *Cela n'est pas de* ~, It is not proper, suitable.
miser [mi'ze] #3 *v. intr.* [parier] to bet, to wager; [enchères] to bid. || *v. tr.* to stake, to bid.
misérable [mize'rabl] *adj.* **1.** wretched, miserable. **2.** destitute. **3.** worthless. || *n.m.* wretch, scoundrel. || **misérablement** [-ə'mɑ̃] *adv.* miserably, wretchedly. || **misère** [mi'zɛ:r] *n.f.* **1.** [matérielle] want, utter poverty. **2.** [morale] misery: *faire des misères à qqun*, to tease s.o. unmercifully. || **miséricorde** [mizeri'kɔrd] *n.f.* mercy: *faire* ~ *à qqun*, to give mercy

to s.o. || **miséricordieu|x, -se** [-jø(:z)] *adj.* merciful.
missel [mi'sɛl] *n.m.* missal, prayer-book.
missile [mi'sil] *adj. & n.m.* missile.
mission [mi'sj|õ] *n.f.* mission; assignment; [Rel.] mission. || **missionnaire** [-ɔ'nɛ:r] *n.m.* missionary.
Mississipi, (le) [(lə) misisi'pi] *n.m.*The Mississipi.
Missouri, (le) [(lə) misu'ri] *n.m.* The Missouri.
mit [mi] cf. METTRE..
mitaine [mi'tɛn] *n.f.* **1.** mitten. **2.** © church.
mite [mit] *n.f.* [étoffe] moth; [fromage] mite. || **mité, -e** [-e] *adj.* [fourrures, &c.] moth-eaten; [fromages, &c.] full of mites.
mi-temps [mi'tɑ̃] *n.m.* half-time.
miteu|x, -se [mi'tø(:z)] *adj.* moth-eaten, shabby (looking).
mitiger [miti'ʒe] #5 *v. tr.* to mitigate: *avec un plaisir mitigé*, with mixed feelings.
mitoyen, -ne [mitwa'j|ɛ̃, -ɛn] *adj.* dividing two properties: *mur* ~, party wall.
mitraille [mi'tr|ɑ:j] *n.f.* grape-shot. || **mitrailler** [-ɑje] #9 *v. tr.* to machine-gun.
mitraillette [-ɑ'jɛt] *n.f.* submachine gun, tommy gun.
mitrailleuse [-a'jø:z] *n.f.* machine-gun.
mitre [mitr] *n.f.* mitre: ~ *de cheminée*, rain cowl (on a chimney).
mi-voix (à) [ami'vwa] *adv.* [parler] in a low voice, under one's breath.
mixte [mikst] *adj.* mixed; [commission] joint; co-educational. || **mixture** [-y:r] *n.f.* mixture.
Mlle [madmwa'zɛl], **Mlles** [mɛdmwa'zɛl] abbr. of Mademoiselle and Mesdemoiselles: must be followed by family name as Miss is in English: *Mlle Gagné*, Miss Gagné.
Mme [ma'dam], **Mmes** [mɛ'dam] abbr. of Madame and Mesdames; must be followed by family name as Mrs. is in English: *Mme Dupont*, Mrs. Dupont.
MM. [mɛ'sjø] cf. M.
mobile [mɔ'bil] *adj.* mobile, movable; changeable *n.m.* **1.** moving body. **2.** motive.
mobili|er, -ère [mɔbi'lj|e, -ɛ:r] *adj.* movable, personal: *biens mobiliers*, chattels. || *n.m.* furniture: ~ *de chambre à coucher*, bedroom suite.
mobilisation [mɔbiliz|a'sjõ] *n.f.* mobilization. || **mobiliser** [-e] #3 *v. tr.* [des troupes, des ressources, &c.] to mobilize.
mobilité [mɔbili'te] *n.f.* mobility; [Fig.] changeableness.
mocassin [mɔka'sɛ̃] *n.m.* moccasin.
moche [mɔʃ] *adj.* [Slang] lousy; ugly.
mode[1] [mɔd] *n.f.* fashion: *ne plus être à la* ~, to be out of style: *à la* ~, fashionable, in style. || *n.fpl.* millinery; *magasin de modes*, boutique.
mode[2] [mɔd] *n.m.* **1.** mode, method: ~ *d'emploi*, directions for use. **2.** [Gram.] mood. **3.** [Mus.] mode.
modèle [mɔ'd|ɛl] *adj.* model. *n.m.* model; pattern: *prendre* ~ *sur qqun*, to take s.o. as a model. || **modelé** [-le] *n.m.* modelling.
modeler #9 *v. tr.* to model, make a model of (sth.); [Fig.] to/model, shape/. || **se** ~, *v. pr.* to model o.s. (after, *sur*).
modérat|eur, -rice [mɔder|a'tœ:r, -a'tris] *adj.* moderating, restraining. || *n.m.* moderator. || **modération** [-a'sjõ] *n.f.* moderation. || **modéré, -e** [-e] *adj.* moderate, restrained. || **modérer** #10 *v. tr. & intr.* to moderate, reduce; [Fig.] to moderate, restrain. || **se** ~ *v. pron.* to restrain o.s.
moderne [mɔ'dɛrn] *adj.* modern: *d'un style très* ~, modernistic. || **moderniser** [-i'ze] #7 *v. tr.* to modernize.
modeste [mɔ'dɛst] *adj.* modest; unassuming. || **modestie** [-i] *n.f.* modesty, unassuming manner.
modification [mɔdif|ika'sjõ] *n.f.* modification, alteration. || **modifier** [-je] #3 *v. tr.* to modify, alter.
modique [mɔ'dik] *adj.* small: *pour un prix* ~, at a low price.
modiste [mɔ'dist] *n.f.* milliner.
moduler [mɔdy'le] #3 *v. tr. & intr.* to modulate.
moelle [mwal] *n.f.* [os] marrow; [plante] pith: *jusqu'à la moelle*, right to the marrow. || **moelleu|x, -se** [mwa'lø(:z)] *adj.* **1.** full of marrow. **2.** soft.
moellon [mwa'lõ] *n.m.* rubble; building stone.
moeurs [mœrs] *n.fpl.* customs, ways, morals; habits (of animals).
moi [mwa] *pron. pers. m. & f.s.* **1.** [as indirect object]: *Donnez-* ~ *le livre*, Give me the book; *Il est venu vers* ~, He came toward me; *C'est à* ~, It's mine; *Un ami à* ~, A friend of mine. **2.** [for emphasis, with *me* and *je*]: *Il m'a écrit à* ~, He wrote to me; *Moi, je n'irai pas*, As for me, I won't go. || **moi-même** [-'mɛ:m] *pron. pers. m. & f.s.* [used for emphasis] myself.
moignon [mwa'ɲõ] *n.m.* [jambe, arbre] stump.
moindre [mwɛ̃:dr] *adj.* **1.** lesser: *le* ~ *mal*,

the lesser of two evils. **2.** least, slightest: *sans la ~ difficulté*, without the least trouble.

moine [mwan] *n.m.* monk; [utensil] bed warmer; [toy] top.

moineau [mwa'no] *n.m.* sparrow.

moins [mwɛ̃] *adv.* less, fewer; [Math.] minus, take away: *le ~*, the least; *au ~*, at least; *du ~*, at least, at any rate; *pas le ~ du monde*, not in the least; *en ~ de rien*, in no time at all; *rien ~ que*, anything but.

mois [mwɑ] *n.m.* month: *une fois par ~*, once a month.

moisi, -e [mwa'z|i] *adj.* mouldy, musty, mildewy. || *n.m.* mould, mildew, mustiness: *sentir le ~*, to have a musty smell. || **moisir** [-i:r] #17 *v. intr.* to become mouldy, rot.

moisson [mwa's|õ] *n.f.* [ce qu'on récolte] harvest; [action] harvesting; [saison] harvest/time, season/: *faire la ~*, to harvest; *rentrer la ~*, to/bring, get/in the harvest. || **moissonner** [-ɔ'ne] #3 *v. tr.* to harvest, reap. || **moissonneu|r, -se** [-ɔ'nœ:r, -ɔ'nø:z] *n.* [Pers.] reaper. || *n.f.* [Tech.] reaper: *moissonneuse-lieuse*, binder; *moissonneuse-batteuse*, combine.

moite [mwat] *adj.* moist, damp. || **moiteur** [-œ:r] *n.f.* moistness, dampness; [froide] clamminess.

moitié [mwa'tje] *n.f.* half: *à ~*, half; *à ~ cuit*, half cooked; *couper par ~*, to cut in/half, two/.

mol [mɔl] cf. MOU. **1.** soft, limp, flabby. **2.** slack, spineless.

molaire [mɔ'lɛ:r] *n.f.* [dent] molar.

môle [mo:l] *n.m.* [jetée] breakwater.

molécule [mɔle'kyl] *n.f.* molecule.

molester [mɔlɛs'te] #3 *v. tr.* to molest.

mollement [mɔl'mɑ̃] *adv.* softly, gently; feebly, indolently.

mollesse [mɔ'lɛs] *n.f.* **1.** softness, [muscle] flabbiness. **2.** slackness, lack of backbone.

mollet, -te [mɔ'lɛ(t)] *adj.* soft; [œuf] soft-boiled. || *n.m.* [de la jambe] calf.

molletière [mɔl'tjɛ:r] *n.f.* [bande] puttee.

molleton [mɔl'tõ] *n.m.* swansdown; flannel.

mollir [mɔ'li:r] #17 *v. intr.* to soften; [vent] to abate; [résistance] to weaken.

moment [mɔ'mɑ̃] *n.m.* moment, time: *à ce ~ -là*, then; *en ce ~*, now, at this time; *d'un ~ à l'autre*, any time; *par ~*, now and then; *sur le ~*, on the spur of the moment; *au ~ où*, (at a time) when; *du ~ que*, since; *C'est le bon ~*, Now is the time. || **momentané, -e** [-ta'ne] *adj.* momentary.

momie [mɔ'mi] *n.f.* mummy; [Fam.] moss-back, fogey.

mon [mõ] *m*, **ma** [ma] *f*, **mes** [mɛ] *pl.*; *adj. poss.* my.

monacal, -e [mɔnɑ'kɑl] *adj.* monastic; monkish.

Monaco [mɔna'ko] *n.m.* Monaco.

monarchie [mɔnar|'ʃi] *n.f.* [Pol.] monarchy. || **monarque** [-k] *n.m.* monarch, sovereign.

monastère [mɔnas'tɛ:r] *n.m.* monastery. || **monastique** [mɔnas'tik] *adj.* monastic.

monceau, -x [mõ'so] *n.m.* heap, pile.

mondain, -e [mõ'd|ɛ̃, -ɛn] *adj.* **1.** worldly, mundane. **2.** social: *Il est très ~*, He is a socialite. || **mondanité** [-ani'te] *n.f.* **1.** worldliness, mundaneness. **2.** *pl.* social events, society news.

monde [mõ:d] *n.m.* **1.** world: *dans le ~ entier*, all over the world; *mettre au ~*, to give birth to; *venir au ~*, to be born. **2.** people: *tout le ~*, everybody; *Il n'y avait pas grand ~*, There were not many people; *avoir du ~*, to have company. **3.** society: *Je le vois dans le ~*, I meet him socially. || **mondial, -e** [mõ'djal] *adj.* **1.** → world: *la seconde Guerre mondiale*, the Second World War. **2.** world-wide: *réputation mondiale*, world-wide fame.

monétaire [mɔne'tɛ:r] *adj.* monetary.

Mongolie, la [(la) mõgɔ'li] *n.f.* Mongolia.

Monique [mɔ'nik] *n.f.* = Monica.

monit|eur, -rice [mɔni't|œ:r, -ris] *n.* monitor, instructor; [Sport.] coach; pupil helper.

monnaie [mɔ'nɛ] *n.f.* **1.** (small) change: *Avez-vous la ~ de dix dollars*, Do you have change for ten dollars; *une pièce de ~*, a coin. **2.** currency: *battre ~*, to issue currency; [Fig.] to raise money. || **monnayer** [-'je] #11 *v. tr.* **1.** to mint. **2.** to exchange for money, to market.

monogamie [mɔnɔga'mi] *n.f.* monogamy.

monologue [mɔnɔ'lɔg] *n.m.* monologue. || **monologuer** [-e] #3 *v. intr.* to talk in a monologue.

monoplan [mɔnɔ'plɑ̃] *adj.* & *n.m.* monoplane.

monopole [mɔnɔ'pɔl] *n.m.* monopoly. || **monopoliser** [-i'ze] #3 *v. tr.* to monopolize.

monosyllabe [mɔnɔsil'lab] *adj.* [Gram.] monosyllabic. || *n.m.* monosyllable.

monotone [mɔnɔ'tɔn] *adj.* monotonous; dull; [pays] featureless. || **monotonie** [-i] *n.f.* monotony; sameness.

monseigneur [mõsɛ'ɲœ:r] *n.m.* [duc] His, Your/Grace; [prince] His, Your/Royal Highness; [archevêque] His, Your/Grace: *pince-~*, short crowbar, jimmy.

monsieur [mœ'sjø] *pl.* **messieurs** [mɛ'sjø] *n.m.* **1.** [avec le nom de famille] Mr. *pl.* Messrs. **2.** [à un supérieur] Sir. **3.** [épistolaire] Dear Sir; *Cher* ~, Dear Mr. X. **4.** somebody, †gentleman: *Un* ~ *vous demande*, Somebody wants to see you.

monstre [mõːstr] *adj.* huge, mammoth. || *n.m.* monster. || **monstrueusement** [-øz'mɑ̃] *adv.* monstrously. || **monstrueu|x, -se** [mõstry|'ø(ːz)] *adj.* [enfant, &c.] deformed; [Fig.] gigantic, huge (size); [crime] monstrous. || **monstruosité** [-ozi'te] *n.f.* monstrosity.

mont [mõ] *n.m.* mountain, [noms de lieu] mount: *par monts et par vaux*, over hill and dale; ~ *Eisenhower*, Mount Eisenhower; ~ *Old Chief*, Old Chief Mountain.

montage [mõ'taːʒ] *n.m.* **1.** raising, taking up. **2.** [joyau] setting. **3.** [machine] assembling. **4.** [Ciné.] montage.

montagnard, -e [mõta'ɲ|aːr, -ard] *n.* mountaineer. || **montagne** [mõ'taɲ] *n.f.* mountain. || **montagneu|x, -se** [-ø(ːz)] *adj.* mountainous; hilly.

Montana, le [(lə) mõta'na] *n.m.* Montana.

montant, -e [mõ'tɑ(ːt)] *adj.* [qui monte] rising, ascending; [chemin] uphill; [robe] high-necked. || *n.m.* [échelle] upright; [d'un compte] total, sum, amount.

Mont Blanc, le [ləmõ'blɑ̃] *n.m.* Mont Blanc.

mont-de-piété [mõdpje'te] *n.m.* pawnshop.

monté, -e [mõ'te] *adj.* [à cheval] mounted; [en qqch.] equipped (with sth.); *coup* ~, put-up job; [Pers.] *être* ~, to be all worked up. || **montée** *n.f.* slope; [Tech.] gradient; [l'action] climbing.

monter #3 *v. intr.* **1.** to go up, to come up, to rise, to get higher: ~ *dans un train*, to get on a train; ~ *dans une voiture*, to get into a car; ~ *à cheval*, to get on a horse, to go horseback riding; ~ *à une échelle*, to climb a ladder; ~ *sur les planches*, to go on the stage; ~ *sur le trône*, to ascend the throne; *Le vin vous monte à la tête*, Wine goes to your head; *faire* ~ *qqun dans sa voiture*, to give s.o. a lift. || **se monter** *v. pron.* **1.** to rise, to amount (to, *à*). **2.** to provide o.s. (with, *en*). **3.** ~ *la tête*: to get all excited. || *v. tr.* **1.** to take up, to bring up. **2.** to set (a stone), to assemble, erect (a structure). **3.** to stock (a store). **4.** to stage (a play). **5.** ~ *la tête à qqun*, to get s.o. all worked up.

montre[1] [mõːtr] *n.f.* watch: une ~ *-bracelet*, a wrist watch; *Ma* ~ *avance*, My watch/gains, is fast/; *Ma* ~ *retarde*, My watch/loses, is slow/; *Ma* ~ *va bien*, My watch keeps good time.

montre[2] *n.f.* show, display: *en* ~, in the window; *faire* ~ *de*, to display, to parade.

Montréal [mõre'al] *n.m.* Montreal: *la Commission de transport de* ~, the Montreal Transport Commission. || **Montréalais, -e** [-ɛ(ːz)] *n.* Montrealer. || *adj.* → Montreal, from M.

montrer [mõ'tre] #3 *v. tr.* to show, to exhibit, to display: ~ *du doigt*, to point out. || **se montrer** *v. pron.* **1.** to appear. **2.** to be: *Il s'est montré très patient*, He was very patient.

montueu|x, -se [mõtɥø(ːz)] *adj.* rolling, hilly.

monture [mõ'tyːr] *n.f.* [cheval, &c.] mount; [d'une machine, &c.] mounting, frame; [joyau] mounting, setting; [le travail de] assembling, putting together.

monument [mɔny'mɑ] *n.m.* monument. || **monumental, -e** [-tal] *adj.* monumental.

moquer [mɔ'k|e] #3 *v. pron.* to make fun (of, *de*), to laugh (at), to mock: *Je m'en moque*, I don't care. || **moquerie** [-'ri] *n.f.* jeer, mockery: *être en butte aux moqueries*, to be a butt to ridicule. || **moqueu|r, -se** [-œːr, -øːz] *adj.* mocking, scoffing, jeering; derisive (laugh): *Il est très* ~, He likes to make fun of people. || **moqueur-chat** [-œr'ʃa] *n.* catbird. || **moqueur polyglotte** *n.* mockingbird.

moral, -e [mɔ'ral] *adj.* moral: *certitude morale*, moral certainty. || *n.m.* morale: *faire monter le* ~, to boost the morale; *remonter le* ~ *à qqun*, to raise s.o.'s spirits. || **morale** *n.f.* **1.** morality, ethics, morals: *faire la* ~ *à qqun*, to lecture s.o. **2.** moral (of story). || **moraliser** [i'ze] #3 *v. intr.* to moralize. || *v. tr.* [réprimander] to lecture. || **moralité** [-i'te] *n.f.* morality

morbide [mɔr'bid] *adj.* morbid

morbleu [mɔr'blø] *interj.* [Fam.] Golly!

morceau, -x [mɔr's|o] *n.m.* piece, bit; morsel, cut: *mettre en morceaux*, to break into pieces; *les bas morceaux*, the cheap cuts. || **morceler** [-ə'le] #8 *v. tr.* to cut into pieces, to break up.

mord [mɔːr] cf. MORDRE. || **mordant, -e** [mɔr'd|ɑ̃(ːt)] caustic, biting, cutting. || *n.m.* causticity.

mordicus [mɔrdi'kys] *adv.* tenaciously: *Il y tient* ~, He's dead set on it.

mordiller [mɔrdi'je] #3 *v. tr.* to nibble at.

mordoré, -e [mɔrdɔ're] *adj.* reddish brown, bronze.

mordre [mɔrdr] #42 *v. tr.* to bite; [acide] to eat; [Fig.] *s'en* ~ *les doigts*, to regret bitterly; to kick o.s. for. || *v. intr.* to bite (into, *à*); [Fig.] to get one's teeth into (French, Latin, &c.).

morfondre [mɔr'fõ:dr] #42 *v. tr.* to chill (s.o.). || **morfondre (se)** *v. pron.* to be/ frozen, chilled/to the bone; [s'ennuyer] to be bored, to mope; [attendre] to cool one's heels.

morgue [mɔrg] *n.f.* **1.** haughtiness, stuck-up ways. **2.** morgue.

moribond, -e [mɔri'bõ(:d)] *adj.* dying, moribund.

morigéner [mɔriʒe'ne] #10 *v. tr.* to take to task; to scold.

morillon [mɔri'jõ] *n.m.* [oiseau] duck; ~ *à dos blanc,* canvas-back duck.

morne [mɔrn] *adj.* dismal, gloomy; [Pers.] glum; [silence] dejected; [couleur] dismal, dull; [paysage] bleak, dismal.

mornifle [mɔr'nifl] *n.f.* slap.

morose [mɔ'ro:z] *adj.* morose; surly.

mors [mɔ:r] *n.m.* [bride] bit: *prendre le ~ aux dents,* to take the bit between one's teeth.

morse [mɔrs] *n.m.* walrus.

morsure [mɔr'sy:r] *n.f.* bite; [action] biting.

mort [mɔ:r] cf. MOURIR. || *adj.* dead: *au point ~*, at a standstill, [Auto.] in(to) neutral; *être ~ de fatigue,* to be dead-tired; *la morte-saison,* slack time; *eau morte,* still water. || *n.* dead person: *faire le ~*, **1.** to play dead. **2.** [bridge] to/be, play/the dummy. || *n.f.* death: *être à l'article de la ~*, to be at death's door; *mettre à ~*, to put to death; *se donner la ~*, to take one's life; *trouver la ~ dans un accident,* to lose one's life in an accident. || **mortalité** [mɔrt|ali'te] *n.f.* mortality; death rate. || **mortel, -le** [-ɛl] *adj.* mortal; deadly; [blessure] fatal.

mortier [mɔr'tje] *n.m.* **1.** [récipient] mortar. **2.** [liant] mortar. **3.** [arme] mortar.

mortifiant, -e [mɔrti'fj|ɑ̃(:t)] *adj.* mortifying. || **mortifier** [-e] #3 *v. tr.* **1.** [viande] to tenderize. **2.** [Fig.] to mortify.

mort-né, -e [mɔ:r'ne] *adj.* **1.** still-born. **2.** [Fig.] abortive.

mortuaire [mɔr'tɥɛ:r] *adj.* mortuary; © *salon m ~*, funeral/home, parlour/; *drap m ~*, pall; *service m ~*, burial service.

morue [mɔ'ry] *n.f.* cod (-fish); *petite ~* [© poulamon *m*] tomcod.

morve [mɔrv] *n.f.* **1.** [chevaux] glanders. **2.** [gens] mucus, [Fam.] snot.

mosaïque [mɔza'ik] *n.f.* mosaic.

Moscou [mɔs'ku] *n.m.* Moscow.

mosquée [mɔs'ke] *n.f.* mosque.

mot [mo] *n.m.* word, saying: *mots croisés,* crossword puzzle; *selon, suivant/le ~ de X,* as X/says, puts it/; *~ à ~*, word by word; *~ pour ~*, word for word, verbatim; *au bas ~*, at the least; *bon ~*, joke; *comprendre à demi- ~*, to take a hint; *gros mots,* bad words; *grands mots,* big words; *envoyer un ~*, to drop a line; *~ de passe,* password; *~ d'ordre,* slogan, motto; *prendre qqun au ~*, to take s.o. at his word; *parler de qqch. à mots couverts,* to hint at sth.; *avoir toujours le ~ pour rire,* to be always cracking jokes; *savoir le fin ~ de l'affaire,* to get to the bottom of it; *le ~ de l'énigme,* the answer to the riddle.

mot|eur, -rice [mɔ't|œ:r, -ris] *adj.* moving, driving: *force motrice,* power; *roues motrices,* driving wheels. || *n.m.* engine, motor, driving force: *~ à explosion,* internal-combustion engine; *~ à réaction,* jet engine.

motif [mɔ'tif] *n.m.* **1.** reason, motive. **2.** theme, motif.

motion [mɔ'sj|õ] *n.f.* motion: *déposer une ~*, to make a motion; *appuyer une ~*, to second a motion. || **motionnaire** [-ɔ'nɛ:r] © *n.m.* mover.

motiver [mɔti've] #3 *v. tr.* to justify.

moto [mɔ't|o] *n.f.* [= MOTOCYCLETTE] motor bike. || **motocyclette** [-ɔsi'klɛt] *n.f.* motor cycle.

motorisé, -e [-ɔri'ze] *adj.* motorized.

motte [mɔt] *n.f.* [de terre] clod; [butte] mound; [beurre, &c.] lump; pat.

mou [mu] **molle** [mɔl] *adj.* [*mou* becomes *mol* before vowel or mute e; *pl.* **mous**] soft; limp; flabby; slack; spineless; © *balle-molle,* soft ball.

mouchard, -e [mu'ʃ|a:r, -ard] *adj.* stool pigeon, squealer. || **moucharder** [-ar'de] #3 *v. intr.* to spy; to squeal (*sur qqun,* on s.o.).

mouche [muʃ] *n.f.* **1.** fly: *~ à miel,* honey bee; © *~ à cheval,* horsefly, cf. TAON; *Quelle ~ vous pique?,* What's eating you?; *prendre la ~*, to take offence, to get riled. **2.** beauty spot. **3.** [cible] bull's eye: *faire ~*, to hit the bull's eye.

moucher [mu'ʃe] #3 *v. tr.* to blow one's nose; to snuff (a candle); to trim (the frayed ends of a rope); [Fig.] to tell (s.o.) off. || **se moucher** *v. pron.* to blow one's nose.

moucherolle [muʃ'rɔl] *n.m.* fly-catcher.

moucheron [muʃ'rõ] *n.m.* gnat; [de chandelle] snuff; [petit garçon] small boy.

moucheté, -e [muʃ'te] *adj.* **1.** [tacheté] spotted, speckled. **2.** [fleuret] buttoned. || **moucheter** #8 *v. tr.* to spot, to speckle; [fleuret] to button.

mouchoir [mu'ʃwa:r] *n.m.* handkerchief:

C'est grand comme un ~ de poche, You couldn't swing a cat.

moud, mouds [mu] cf. MOUDRE. ‖ **moudre** [mudr], **moulant** [mu|'lɑ̃], **moulu** [-y] #76 *v. tr.* to grind.

moue [mu] *n.f.* pout: *faire la ~*, to pout.

mouette [mwɛt] *n.f.* (sea-)gull.

mouffette [mu'fɛt] [also called *bête f puante*] *n.f.* skunk, Alaska sable.

moufle [mufl] *n.f.* mitten, mitt. ‖ *n.m.* pulley block.

mouflon [mu'flõ] *n.m.* bighorn, rocky mountain sheep.

mouillage [mu'j|a:ʒ] *n.m.* **1.** wetting. **2.** watering (of wine). **3.** anchorage. ‖ **mouillé, -e** [-e] *adj.* **1.** wet. **2.** at anchor. **3.** [Ling.] palatalized. ‖ **mouiller** #3 *v. tr.* to wet; cf. HUMECTER; *~ l'ancre*, to drop anchor; [Ling.] to palatalize; [bateau, &c.] to moor; © [Fam.] to rain. ‖ **se mouiller** *v. pron.* to get wet.

moulage[1] [mu'la:ʒ] *n.m.* [métaux] casting; [empreinte] mould; [reproduction] cast.

moulage[2] *n.m.* grinding, milling.

moulais, &c. [mu'lɛ] cf. MOUDRE.

moule[1] [mul] *n.m.* mould, form.

moule[2] [mul] *n.f.* [mollusque] mussel; [Fig. & Fam.] muscle head.

moulé, -e *adj.* **1.** moulded, cast. **2.** *en lettres moulées*, in block letters. **3.** [Pers.] *bien ~*, shapely. ‖ *n.m. le moulé*, print. ‖ **mouler** #3 *v. tr.* to mould, [métal] to cast; to fit closely. ‖ **se mouler** *v. pron.* to model o.s. (after, *sur*).

moulin [mu'l|ɛ̃] *n.m.* mill: *porter de l'eau à son ~*, to take grist to one's mill; *~ à vent*, windmill; *~ à café*, coffee grinder; © [abus.] ~ à *papier*, paper mill.

moulinet [-i'nɛ] *n.m.* winch; [canne à pêche] reel; [porte de barrière] turnstile: *faire le ~ avec un bâton*, to twirl a stick.

moulu, -e [mu'ly] *adj.* ground, powdered; [Fig., Fam.] aching all over; done up.

moulure [mu'ly:r] *n.f.* moulding.

mourais, &c. cf. MOURIR.

mourant, -e [mu'r|ɑ̃(:t)] *adj.* dying; [voix] faltering. ‖ *n. m/f* dying person. ‖ **mourir** [-i:r] #62 *v. intr.* to die: *~ de faim*, to die of starvation; [Fig.] to starve; *~ de froid*, to freeze to death; *les bruits qui meurent au loin*, the sounds that die away.

mousse[1] [mus] *n.f.* **1.** moss. **2.** [eau] foam. **3.** [bière] froth, foam, head. **4.** [savon] lather, suds; [Cul.] mousse.

mousse[2] *n.m.* ship boy. ‖ *adj.* dull (point, knife, ‖ &c.).

mousseline [mus'lin] *n.f.* muslin: *~ de soie*, chiffon.

mousser [mu'se] #3 *v. intr.* to foam, to froth; [savon] to lather, to make suds: *faire ~ du savon*, to work up a good lather; [Fig.] *faire ~ qqun*, to boost s.o.'s stock, to give s.o. a plug.

mousseu|x, -se [mu'sø(:z)] *adj.* **1.** mossy. **2** [bière] frothy, foamy. **3.** vin] sparkling. **4.** [savon] lathery, sudsy.

mousson [mu'sõ] *n.f.* monsoon.

moussu, -e [mu'sy] *adj.* mossy; moss-grown.

moustache [mus'taʃ] *n.f.* moustache.

moustiquaire [musti'kɛ:r] *n.f.* mosquito-net. ‖ **moustique** [mus'tik] *n.m.* mosquito.

moût [mu] *n.m.* [de vin] must; [de bière] wort.

moutard [mu'ta:r] *n.m.* kid.

moutarde [mu'tard] *n.f.* mustard: *La ~ lui est montée au nez*, He got mad.

moute [mut] © *n.m.* = mouton.

mouton [mu't|õ] *n.m.* [animal] sheep; [viande, fourrure] mutton; [sur la mer] white horses, whitecaps; [Loc.] *doux comme un ~*, as gentle as a lamb; *Revenons à nos moutons*, Let's get back to our subject; *Ce sont des moutons de Panurge*, They act like sheep. ‖ **moutonnant, -e** [-ɔ'nɑ̃(:t)] *adj.* [mer] covered with white caps. ‖ (**mère**) **moutonne** [-on] © *n.f.* ewe, cf. BREBIS. ‖ **moutonner** [-ɔ'ne] #3 *v. tr.* to curl. ‖ *v. intr.* to break into whitecaps. ‖ **moutonneu|x, -se** [-ɔ'nø(:z)] *adj.* [nuage] fleecy; [mer] covered with whitecaps.

mouture [mu'ty:r] *n.f.* **1.** grinding. **2.** mixture of wheat, rye and barley. **3.** milling feed.

mouvais, &c. cf. MOUVOIR.

mouvant, -e [mu'v|ɑ̃(:t)] cf. MOUVOIR. ‖ *adj.* moving, in motion; *sables mouvants*, quicksands. ‖ **mouvement** [-'mɑ̃] *n.m.* **1.** movement, motion: *mettre en ~*, to set in motion. **2.** [sol] undulation. **3.** [cœur] feeling: *un ~ de colère*, a fit of anger. **4.** [Méc.] movement, works. ‖ **mouvementé, -e** [-mɑ̃'te] *adj.* [discussion] lively; [vie] eventful; [sol] hilly, broken.

mouvoir [-wa:r] #33 *v. tr.* to move. cf. MÛ.

moyen[1], **-ne** [mwa'j|ɛ̃, -ɛn] *adj.* average, intermediate, medium, ordinary: *le Français ~*, the average Frenchman, the man in the street; *le Moyen Age*, the Middle Ages; *le cours ~*, the intermediate course; *Il est très ~*, He is very ordinary.

moyen[2] [-ɛ̃] *n.m.* means, way, manner: *Par quel ~ ?*, How?; *au ~ de*, by means of; *moyens de transport*, transportation;

employer les grands moyens, to resort to drastic actions.
moyennant [-ɛ'nɑ̃] *prép.* in exchange for.
moyenne [-ɛn] *n.f.* average; [Tech.] mean; [Scol.] pass mark: *en* ~, on/an, the/ average.
moyeu [mwa'jø] *n.m.* hub.
mû, mue [my] *p.p.* de MOUVOIR: **1.** driven, propelled: ~ *à la vapeur*, steam-driven. **2.** [Fig.] impelled, motivated.
mucosité [mykɔzi'te] *n.f.* mucosity, mucus.
mue [my] *n.f.* [plumage] moulting; [poils] shedding; [peau] sloughing; [voix] changing. || **muer** #3 *v. intr.* to moult, shed; to slough off; [voix] to break, change.
muet, -te [mɥɛ(t)] *adj.* dumb, mute, silent; [lettre, film] silent; [d'étonnement] speechless; *être sourd-* ~, to be deaf and dumb. || *n.* mute.
mufle [myfl] *n.m.* **1.** muzzle. **2.** cad.
mugir [my'ʒ|i:r] #17 *v. intr.* to bellow, †to low; [vent] to howl; [vagues] to roar. || **mugissement** [-is'mɑ̃] *n.m.* bellowing; lowing; [vents] howling; [vagues] roaring.
muguet [my'gɛ] *n.m.* lily-of-the-valley.
mulâtre, -sse [my'l|ɑ:tr, -ɑ'trɛs] *n.* mulatto *m*, mulatress *f*.
mule[1] [myl] *n.f.* [animal] she-mule.
mule[2] *n.f.* mule.
mulet [-ɛ] *n.m.* [animal] mule; [poisson] chub, fall fish. || **muletier** [-'tje] *n.m.* mule driver: *chemin* ~, bridle path.
mulot [my'lo] *n.m.* field mouse.
multicolore [myltikɔ'lɔ:r] *adj.* multi-coloured, many-coloured.
multiple [myl'tipl] *adj. & n.m.* multiple.
multiplicande [-i'kɑ̃:d] *n.m.* multiplicand. || **multiplicateur** [-ika'tœ:r] *n.m.* multiplier. || **multiplication** [-ika'sjɔ̃] *n.f.* multiplication. || **multiplier** [-i'e] #3 *v. tr. & intr.* to multiply.
multitude [mylti'tyd] *n.f.* crowd, multitude.
muni, -e [my'ni] *adj.* provided with, fitted with, → with.
municipal, -e [mynisi'pal] *adj.* municipal, → town: *conseil* ~, town, city/council. || **municipalité** [-i'te] *n.f.* municipality, town(ship).
munificence [mynifi'sɑ̃:s] *n.f.* munificence.
munir [my'ni:r] #17 *v. tr.* to provide, to equip, to fit (with, *de*). || **se munir** *v. pron.* to provide o.s. (with, *de*). || **munitions** [myni'sjɔ̃] *n.fpl.* **1.** ammunition. **2.** †stores, supplies: *pain de munition*, army bread.
muqueu|x, -se [my'k|ø(:z)] *adj.* mucous. || **muqueuse** [-ø:z] *n.f.* mucous membrane.
mur [my:r] *n.m.* wall: ~ *de soutènement*, retaining wall; ~ *intérieur*, partition; ~ *du son*, sound barrier; *mettre qqun au pied du mur*, to corner s.o.
mûr, -e *adj.* ripe, mature: *d'âge* ~, middle-aged.
muraille [my'rɑ:j] *n.f.* (high) wall; rampart.
mural, -e [my'ral] *adj.* mural: *peinture murale*, mural (painting).
mûre [my:r] *n.f.* mulberry, blackberry.
murer [my're] #3 *v. tr.* [espace] to wall in, [ouverture] to wall up.
mûrier [my'rje] *n.m.* blackberry bush.
mûrir [my'r|i:r] #17 *v. tr.* [été, blé, fruits] to ripen; [Pers.] to mature. || *v. intr.* [fruits] to ripen, to get ripe; [Pers.] to mature; [une affaire] to develop. || **mûrissant, -e** [-i'sɑ̃(:t)] *adj.* ripening, maturing.
murmurant, -e [myrmy'rɑ̃(:t)] *adj.* murmuring, babbling. || **murmure** [myr'my:r] *n.m.* murmur, muttering. || **murmurer** [myrmy're] #3 *v. tr. & intr.* to murmur, to mutter.
musaraigne [myza'rɛɲ] *n.f.* shrew.
musarder [myzar'de] #3 *v. intr.* to dawdle, fiddle.
muscade [mys'kad] *n.f.* [épice] nutmeg; magician's ball; *Passez* ~, Now you see it, now you don't.
muscle [mysk|l] *n.m.* muscle, [coll.] brawn. || **musclé, -e** [-le] *adj.* muscular. || **musculaire** [-y'lɛ:r] *adj.* muscular. || **musculeu|x, -se** [-y'lø(:z)] *adj.* muscular.
muse [my:z] *n.f.* muse.
museau [my'zo] *n.m.* muzzle; [Fig.] mug.
musée [my'ze] *n.m.* museum.
museler [myz|'le] #8 *v. tr.* to muzzle; [Fig.] to silence. || **muselière** [-ə'ljɛ:r] *n.f.* muzzle.
muser [my'ze] #3 *v. intr.* to dawdle, idle.
musette [my'zɛt] *n.f.* [Mus.] bagpipes; [de cheval] nose-bag; [pour outils, &c.] kit bag; [Mil.] haversack.
muséum [myze'ɔm] *n.m.* [natural history] museum.
musical, -e [myzi|'kal] *adj.* musical. || **music-hall** [-'kɔl] *n.m.* music hall. || **musicien, -ne** [-'sjɛ̃, -'sjɛn] *adj. & n.* musician. || **musique** [-k] *n.f.* music.
musqué, -e [mys'ke] *adj.* musk; *poire musquée*, musk-pear; *rat-* ~, muskrat. || **musquer** #3 *v. tr.* to perfume with musk.
musulman, -e [myzyl'm|ɑ̃, -an] *adj.* Moslem. || **Musulman, -e** *n.* Moslem.
mutation [myta'sjɔ̃] *n.f.* mutation.
mutilation [mytil|a'sjɔ̃] *n.f.* **1.** maiming, mutilation. **2.** defacement. || **mutilé, -e** [-e] *adj.* mutilated, maimed, disabled; [statue, édifice, &c.] defaced, mutilated. || *n.* disabled person: ~ *de guerre*, disabled

war-veteran. || **mutiler** #3 *v. tr.* to mutilate, maim; to deface.
mutin, -e [my't|ɛ̃, -in] *adj.* mischievous, roguish. || *n.m.* mutineer, rioter. || **mutiner** [-i'ne] #3 to incite to rebellion; || **se mutiner** *v. pron.* to mutiny. || **mutinerie** [-in'ri] *n.f.* mutiny.
mutisme [my'tism] *n.m.* **1.** silence. **2.** dumbness.
mutuel, -le [my'tɥɛl] *adj.* mutual, reciprocal. || *n.f.* mutual society. || **mutuellement** [-'mɑ̃] *adv.* mutually, reciprocally.
myope [mjɔp] *adj.* near-sighted, myopic. || **myopie** [-i] *n.f.* near, short/-sightedness; myopia.
myosotis [mjɔzɔ'tis] *n.m.* forget-me-not.
myriade [mi'rjad] *n.f.* myriad.
myrte [mirt] *n.m.* myrtle.
mystère [mis'tɛːr] *n.m.* mystery; [Théât.] mystery play: *faire ~ de qqch.*, to be very mysterious about sth.; *Il n'en fait pas ~*, He makes no bones about it. || **mystérieusement** [-erjøz'mɑ̃] *adv.* mysteriously. || **mystérieu|x, -se** [-e'rjø(ːz)] *adj.* mysterious.
mysticisme [misti'sism] *n.m.* mysticism.
mystification [mistif|ika'sjõ] *n.f.* hoax. || **mystifier** [-je] #3 *v. tr.* to hoax; to mystify.
mystique [mis'tik] *adj.* mystical. || *n.* [Pers.] mystic. || *n.f.* mystical theology, mystique.
mythe [mit] *n.m.* myth. || **mythique** [-ik] *adj.* mythical. || **mythologie** [ɔlɔ'ʒi] *n.f.* mythology.

N

N, n [ɛn] *n.m.* [letter] N. || **n'** cf. NE.
nacelle [na'sɛl] *n.f.* skiff; gondola (of an airship).
nacre [nakr] *n.f.* mother of pearl. || **nacré, -e** [-e] *adj.* pearly.
nage [naːʒ] *n.f.* **1.** swimming: *traverser la rivière à la ~*, → to swim across the river. **2.** [Naut.] rowing, sculling. **3.** [Fig.] sweat, perspiration: *être en ~*, to be in a sweat. || **nageoire** [na'ʒwaːr] *n.f.* fin (of a fish). || **nager** [na'ʒ|e] #5 *v. intr.* **1.** to swim; to float [esp. SURNAGER]; [Fig.] *Le bouchon nage sur l'eau*, The cork floats on the water; *Il nage dans la joie*, → He's perfectly happy, He is the image of bliss; [Fam.] *Il sait ~*, He knows how to handle himself. **2.** [Naut.] to row, to scull. || **nageur** [-œːr] *n.m.*, **nageuse** [-øːz] *n.f.* swimmer: */Il, Elle/nage bien*, /He's, She's/a good swimmer: *maître m nageur* lifeguard (at swimming pool, etc.).
†**naguère(s)** [na'gɛːr] *adv.* not long ago, lately; [abus.] formerly.
naïf, naïve [na|'if, -'iːv] *adj.* naive, ingenuous; artless. || *n.* simpleton, fool.
nain, -e [nɛ̃, nɛn] *adj.* dwarfish, diminutive. || *n.* dwarf, midget.
nais cf. NAÎTRE.
naissance [nɛ's|ɑ̃ːs] *n.f.* **1.** birth: *acte m de ~*, birth certificate; *date f de ~*, date of birth; *anniversaire m de ~*, *jour m de ~*, birthday; *lieu m de ~*, birth place; *être de haute ~*, to be of noble birth. cf. NAÎTRE, NÉ. *donner ~ à un fils*, to give birth to a son. **2.** [Fig.] beginning, rise; dawn: *donner ~ à*, to give rise to; *prendre ~*, to rise, to originate; *La rivière Saint-Maurice prend ~ dans les Laurentides*, The Saint Maurice River rises in the Laurentians. || **naissant, -e** [-ɑ̃, -ɑ̃ːt] *adj.* new-born, in its infancy; growing, dawning.
naître [nɛːtr], **naissant, né** #39 *v. intr.*, conj. ÊTRE. **1.** to be born [☞ Use present tense in French; ☞ Remarquez l'emploi du passé en anglais]: *Je suis né(e) en 1938*, I was born in 1938; *Quand êtes-vous né(e)?*, When were you born?; *Je l'ai vu naître*, → I have known him since birth; *né de parents français*, of French parentage; *née d'une mère française*, born of a French mother. **2.** [Fig.] to begin, arise (from), originate (in), spring up: *Le Rhône naît en Suisse*, The Rhone rises, originates/in Switzerland; *faire ~ (des soupçons)*, to arouse suspicion.

naïvement [naiv|'mɑ̃] *adv.* naively, ingenuously. || **naïveté** [-'te] *n.f.* ingenuousness, candour; [Péj.] silliness.

Napoléon [napɔle|'ɔ̃] *n. pr.* Napoleon || *n.m.* napoleon [former gold coin worth 20 francs]. || **napoléonien, -ne** [-ɔ'njɛ̃, -ɔnjɛn] *adj.* Napoleonic.

nappe [nap] *n.f.* **1.** tablecloth, cloth; [Relig.] *nappe f d'autel,* altar cloth. **2.** ~ *d'eau,* sheet of water. || **napperon** [-rɔ̃] *n.m.* place mat; doily.

naquis &c. cf. NAÎTRE.

narcisse [nar'sis] *n.m.* narcissus: ~ *des prés,* daffodil.

narcotique [narkɔ'tik] *adj. & n.m.* narcotic; [Fam.] drug.

narguer [nar'ge] #3 *v. tr.* to flout; to snap one's fingers at s.o.

narine [na'rin] *n.f.* nostril (of man), cf. NASEAU.

narquois, -e [narkwa(:z)] *adj.* bantering.

narrat|eur, -rice [nar|a'tœ:r, -a'tris] *n.m.* narrator, story-teller. || **narration** [-a'sjɔ̃] *n.f.* narrative, account (of incident); [Educ.] essay. || †**narrer** [-e] #3 *v. tr.* to narrate, relate (a story, events).

nasal, -e, pl. -aux [na'z|al, -o] *adj.* nasal. || **nasale** *n.f.* [Phon.] nasal. || **naseau,** *pl.* **-x** [-o] *n.m.* nostril (of animals), cf. NARINE. || **nasillard, -e** [nazi|'ja:r, -'jard] *adj.*: *voix nasillarde,* nasal twang.

natal, -e(s) *pl.* **nataux** (rare) [na't|al, -o] *adj.* native: *le pays natal,* one's native country. || *n.m.* **Natal** [Geog.] Natal (in South Africa). || **natalité** [-ali'te] *n.f.* birthrate.

natation [nata'sjɔ̃] *n.f.* swimming (as sport) [cf. NAGE]: *pratiquer la* ~, to go in for swimming.

nati|f, -ve [na't|if, -i:v] *adj.* native [not often used in French] → NÉ, RESSORTISSANT.

nation [na'sj|ɔ̃] *n.f.* nation. || **national, -e** [-ɔ'nal] *adj.* national: *L'hymne m* ~, the national anthem; [Fr.] *l'Assemblée f nationale,* the National Assembly. || **nationaux** [-ɔ'no] *n.mpl.* nationals, native citizens, cf. RESSORTISSANT. || **nationaliser** #3 *v. tr.* to nationalize (an industry, &c.). || **nationaliste** [-ɔna'list] *adj.* nationalistic: *La Chine* ~, Nationalist China. || *n.m.* nationalist. || **nationalité** [-ɔnali'te] *n.f.* citizenship, nationality: *changer de* ~, to change one's citizenship; *prendre la* ~ *canadienne,* → to become a Canadian citizen.

nativité [nativi'te] *n.f.* [Relig.] Nativity, cf. NOËL; birth, cf. NAISSANCE.

natte [nat|] *n.f.* **1.** mat, matting. **2.** [hair]: *une* ~ *dans le dos,* a pigtail. || **natter** [-e] #3 *v. tr.* to mat; to braid (hair).

naturalisation [natyraliz|a'sjɔ̃] *n.f.* naturalization. || **naturaliser** [-e] #3 *v. tr.* to naturalize: *se faire* ~, to get naturalized, to become a citizen [of Canada, &c.].

naturalisme [natyra'lism] *n.m.* naturalism.

nature [na't|y:r] *n.f.* **1.** nature; countryside [as opposed to cities]: *Les beautés de la* ~ [often printed with capital N], The beauties of nature. **2.** kind, sort; essence: *un crime contre* ~, an unnatural/repulsive/crime; *payer en* ~, to pay in kind; *Quelle est la* ~ *de ce sol?,* What kind of soil is it?. **3.** character, disposition: *la* ~ *humaine,* human nature; *Il est de* ~ *tranquille,* He has a quiet disposition. **4.** life: *dessiner d'après* ~, to draw/from life, from the actual object/; ~ *morte,* still life [a type of painting]. **5.** plain: *pommes de terre* ~, (plain) boiled potatoes; *café* ~, black coffee. **6.** [Loc.] *de* ~ *à,* of a nature to, likely to: *des arguments de* ~ *à lui faire changer d'idée,* arguments likely to change his mind. || **naturel, -le** [-y'rɛl] *adj.* **1.** natural: *le gaz* ~, natural gas; *de grandeur naturelle,* life-size. **2.** natural, unaffected, unsophisticated: *un jeu* ~, a natural style (of acting). || **naturel** *n.m.* **1.** †native: *les naturels,* the natives. **2.** character, disposition: *d'un* ~ *aimable,* with an amiable disposition. **3.** [attitude] ease, unaffectedness. || **naturellement** [-yrɛl'mɑ̃] *adv.* naturally, unaffectedly; of course! [☞ répétez l'auxiliaire: *of course, I did,* &c.].

naufrage [no'fr|a:ʒ] *n.m.* shipwreck; *faire* ~, to be shipwrecked. || **naufragé, -e** [-a'ʒe] *adj. & n.* shipwrecked (person); survivor, †castaway.

nauséabond, -e [nozea'b|ɔ̃, -ɔ̃:d] *adj.* nauseating, foul-smelling. || **nausée** [no'ze] *n.f.* [often *pl.*] nausea; [Fig.] loathing: *avoir des nausées,* to have nausea; *cela me donne la* ~, it makes me sick.

nautique [no'tik] *adj.* nautical; [sports] aquatic.

naval, -e, *mpl.* **navals** [na'val] *adj.* naval, of the navy; nautical: *chantier* ~, *chantier de construction navale,* shipyard, shipbuilding yard; *guerre navale,* war at sea; *École Navale,* Naval Academy.

navet [na'vɛ] *n.m.* turnip: [Fig.] *avoir du sang de* ~, to be spineless.

navette[1] [na'vɛt] *n.f.* (weaver's) shuttle; [mostly Fig.] shuttle (line): *faire la* ~ (entre 2 points), to ply between . . . , to go back and forth.

navette[2] [na'vɛt] © *n.f.* wild turnip.

navigabilité [navi|gabili'te] *n.f.* [rivière]

navigability; [navire] seaworthiness; [avion] airworthiness. || **navigable** [-gabl] *adj.* navigable, seaworthy, airworthy. || **navigant** [-gɑ̃] *adj. le personnel* ~, sea-going personnel, flying personnel. || **navigateur** [-ga'tœ:r] *n.m.* [gen. & tech.] navigator, †seafarer.

navigation [-ga'sjõ] *n.f.* navigation; sailing; shipping: *La* ~ *sur le Saint-Laurent est ouverte six mois par an,* The St. Lawrence is open to shipping six months a year; *compagnie de* ~, steamship line; ~ *au long cours,* sailing across the seas, in ocean-going ships [as opposed to coastwise sailing, LE CABOTAGE]; *La* ~ *à vapeur a remplacé la* ~ *à voile,* Steamships have taken the place of sailing ships; ~ *de plaisance,* boating, yachting. || **naviguer** [-ge] #3 *v. intr.* **1.** to sail, to navigate; to steer (a course); to sail (on board a ship, as a sailor). **2.** [Fig.] to know how to steer one's course in life: [Péj.] *Il sait* ~, He gets around.

navire [na'vi:r] *n.m.* [refers to large craft, cf. BATEAU] ship, †vessel: ~ *de commerce,* merchantman, commercial ship; ~ *de guerre,* warship; *le mouvement des navires,* shipping news.

navrant, -e [nɑ'vr|ɑ̃, ɑ̃:t] *adj.* distressing: [Fam.] *C'est* ~ *!,* It's a great pity!, What a shame!, It's pathetic!. || **navré, -e** [-e] *adj.* (deeply) sorry for, distressed: *Je suis* ~ *de vous avoir fait attendre,* I am very sorry to have kept you waiting; †*avoir le cœur* ~, to be broken-hearted. || **navrer** #3 *v. tr.* to distress s.o., to pain.

nazaréen, -ne [nazare|'ɛ̃, -'ɛn] *adj.* of Nazareth; Nazarene: *Jésus le Nazaréen,* Jesus of Nazareth.

ne[1] [nə, n] *adv.* [*n'* before a vowel or a mute h] no, not [rarely used alone, cf. AUCUN, GUÈRE, JAMAIS, NI . . . NI, PERSONNE, PLUS, QUE, RIEN, etc.].

ne[2] [expl. rather literary] *Je crains qu'il* ~ *refuse,* I am afraid he may turn us down; *Si je* ~ *m'abuse,* If I am not mistaken.

né, -e [ne] [past part., *m & f* of *naître*] born: *Je suis* ~ *à Toronto en 1945,* I was born in Toronto in 1945; *Madame X née Y,* Mrs. X, whose maiden name was Y, Mrs. X, nee Y; *être bien* ~, to be of noble birth; *nouveau-*~, new-born baby; *premier-*~, pl. *premier-nés,* f. *premier-née* or *première-née,* first-born (child).

néanmoins [neɑ̃'mwɛ̃] *adv.* nevertheless.

néant [ne'ɑ̃] *n.m.* [Lit.] nothingness; nothing, void, nullity: *tirer . . . du* ~, to create . . . out of nothing; [on a return] ~, nil.

nébuleuse [neby'lø:z] *n.f.* [Astron.] nebula. || **nébuleu|x, -se** [-ø, -ø:z] *adj.* cloudy; nebulous, hazy: *un esprit* ~, an obscure mind. || **nébulosité** [-ozi'te] *n.f.* cloudiness.

nécessaire [nese|'sɛ:r] *adj.* necessary; unavoidable [cf. → IL FAUT, AVOIR BESOIN]. || *n.m.* **1.** kit, dressing case: ~ *à couture,* sewing kit. **2.** [Fig.] that which is necessary: *faire le* ~, → to take care of it; *Il manque de tout, même du* ~, He is absolutely destitute, even of the barest necessities (of life). || **nécessairement** [-sɛr'mɑ̃] *adv.* necessarily, inevitably. || **nécessité** [-si'te] *n.f.* **1.** necessity; [Théât.] [de l'intrigue] requirements: *de toute* ~, of necessity, necessarily; *mettre (qqun) dans la* ~ *de (faire qqch),* to compel (s.o. to do sth.); *être dans la* ~ *de (faire qqch.),* to be compelled (to do sth.); *les nécessités de l'intrigue,* the requirements of the plot. **2.** need, want: †*Il est dans la* ~, He is in great need. || **nécessiter** #3 *v. tr.* to require, to demand: *Ceci nécessite une explication,* This/requires, calls for/an explanation. || **nécessiteu|x, -se** [-si'tø, -si'tø:z] *n. & adj.* a pauper: *les* ~, the needy.

néerlandais, -e [neɛrlɑ̃'dɛ(:z)] *adj. & n.* Dutch.

nef [nɛf] *n.f.* **1.** vessel, ship. **2.** [Arch.] nave.

néfaste [ne'fast] *adj.* ill-fated, unlucky; harmful (*à, de*).

négati|f, -ve [nega|'tif, -'ti:v] *adj.* negative. || *n.m.* [Photo.] negative. || **négation** [-'sjõ] *n.f.* negation, denial; [Gram.] negative. || **négative** [-'ti:v] *n.f.*: *se maintenir sur la* ~, to adopt a negative attitude.

négligé, -e [negli|'ʒe] *adj.* **1.** careless (in appearance); slovenly. **2.** neglected, unheeded. **3.** neglected, overlooked. || *n.m.* [costume] negligee; dishabille. || **négligeable** [-'ʒabl] *adj.* negligible, trifling. || **négligemment** [-ʒa'mɑ̃] *adv.* negligently; carelessly; [Pej.] casually. || **négligence** [-'ʒɑ̃:s] *n.f.* neglect, carelessness; negligence, oversight. || **négligent, -e** [-ʒɑ̃(:t)] *adj.* negligent, careless. || **négliger** [-'ʒe] #5 *v. tr.* to neglect (*de,* to), to ignore, to disregard (a piece of advice); ~ *sa mise,* to be careless about one's clothes. || **se négliger** *v. pron.* to become/careless, slovenly/(about one's health, &c.).

†**négoce** [ne'gɔs] *n.m.* [Com.] trade, business. || **négociant** [-jɑ̃] *n.m.* merchant, dealer: ~ *en vins,* wine dealer.

négociation [negɔ|sja'sjõ] *n.f.* [traité] negotiation; [Com.] transaction. || **négocier** [-'sje] #3 *v. tr.* to negotiate (a treaty).

nègre [nɛ:gr] *n.m.* **1.** Negro, coloured man. [☞ use *noir, Africain* or *homme de couleur*]. **2.** [Arg.] stooge; ghost. ‖ *adj.* Negro, black. ‖ **négresse** [ne'grɛs] *n.f.* Negro woman, coloured woman.

neige [nɛ:ʒ] *n.f.* snow: *~ fondue*, wet snow, [Br.] sleet; *tempête f, de ~*, snowstorm; *train m de ~*, ski train. ‖ **neiger** [nɛ|'ʒe] #5 *v. impers.* to snow: *Il neige*, It is snowing; *Il neige beaucoup à Québec*, Q. (city) has heavy snowfalls. ‖ **neigeu|x, -se** [-'ʒø, -'ʒø:z] *adj.* snowy; [sommet] snow-covered; [Fig.] snow-white.

nénuphar [neny'fa:r] *n.m.* water-lily.

Néo- [neo-] *préf.*: Neo-, New-: *Néo-Canadien, m*, New Canadian; *Néo-Zélandais m*, New-Zealand(er).

népotisme [nepɔ'tism] *n.m.* nepotism.

nerf [nɛ:r] *n.m.* [Méd.] nerve; [abus.] sinew; [Fig.] energy, pep: *avoir du ~*, to be energetic, vigorous: *taper sur les nerfs de qqun*, to get into s.o.'s hair. ‖ **nerveu|x, -se** [-vø(:z)] *adj.* nervous, high-strung; [énergique] sinewy, wiry; [style] forceful. ‖ **nervosité** [-vozi'te] *n.f.* excitability; irritability.

nervure [nɛr'vy:r] *n.f.* [Bot.] nervure, nerve.

n'est-ce pas [nɛs'pɑ] *loc. verb.* **1.** [☞ Fin de phrase qui se rend sur le modèle de *is it not?* (si la phrase est affirmative) ou *is it?* (si la phrase est négative), en reprenant le verbe auxiliaire de la phrase ou en employant le verbe *do* si le verbe principal n'a pas d'auxiliaire ou n'est pas lui-même un auxiliaire]: *Il est là, n'est-ce pas?*, He is in, isn't he?; *On peut le faire renouveler, n'est-ce pas?*, It can be renewed, can't it?; *Vous l'avez vu, n'est-ce pas?*, You saw him, didn't you?; *Vous y avez été, n'est-ce pas?*, You've been there, haven't you?; *Il ne comprend pas, n'est-ce pas?*, He doesn't understand, does he?; *Il faut que ça parte ce soir, n'est-ce pas?*, It must go tonight, mustn't it? **2.** [renforcement] *Oui, n'est-ce pas!*, Yes, of course!; *Non, n'est-ce pas?*, I shouldn't think so; [tic de langage], you know, . . . [ne pas confondre avec la construction régulière *N'est-ce pas lui qui . . . ?*, Wasn't he the one who . . . ?].

net, -te [nɛt] *adj.* **1.** clean, spotless, tidy [Fr. ☞ PROPRE]. **2.** clear, distinct. **3.** [Fin.] *bénéfice ~*, net return. ‖ *adv.* cleanly; clearly, plainly: *s'arrêter ~*, to stop, pull up/short. ‖ **nettement** [nɛt'mɑ̃] *adv.* cleanly; distinctly; plainly. ‖ **netteté** [-'te] *n.f.* cleanness, neatness; clearness.

nettoiement [nɛtwa|'mɑ̃] *n.m.*: *service de ~*, garbage, refuse/disposal. ‖ **nettoyage** [-'ja:ʒ] *n.m.* cleaning: *~ à sec*, French, dry/cleaning; *grand ~*, spring cleaning. ‖ **nettoyer** [-'je] #12 *v. tr.* to cleanse, clean; [vaisselle] to wash up; [casserole] to scour: *~ à sec*, to dryclean; [Fam.] to clear out. ‖ **se nettoyer** *v. pron.* [Pers.] to clean o.s., to wash. ‖ **nettoyeur** [-'jœ:r] *n.m.* cleaner; [vêtements] dry-cleaner.

neu|f, -ve [nœf, nœ:v] *adj.* [☞ *neuf* = new, just out of the shop, factory; *nouveau* = new, recent, i.e. *le nouvel an*, the New Year.] new: *comme ~*, as good as new; [Fig.] fresh, [Péj.] raw, green: *regarder d'un œil ~*, → to take a fresh view of things. ‖ *n.m.* new: *habillé de ~*, dressed in new clothes; [Fam.] *Quoi de ~ ?*, What news?; *remettre à ~*, [© [Pop.] *en ~*], to renovate; [Fam.] to do up like new.

neuf [nœf] [nœv in *neuf ans, neuf heures.*] *adj. num.* nine.

neurologie [nørɔlɔ'ʒi] *n.f.* neurology.

neutraliser [nøtrali|'ze] #3 *v. tr.* to neutralize. ‖ **neutralité** [-'te] *n.f.* neutrality. ‖ **neutre** [nø:tr] *adj. & n.m.* [Gram.] neuter; [Pol.] neutral: *rester ~*, not to take sides; © [abus.] neutral, cf. POINT MORT.

neuvième [nœ'vjɛm] *adj. & n.m.* ninth.

neveu [nə'vø] *n.m.* nephew.

névralgie [nevral'ʒi] *n.f.* neuralgia.

nez [ne] *n.m*, nose; [odorat] scent: *avoir du ~*, to have a/good nose, flair/for; *faire qqch. au ~ de qqun*, to do sth. under s.o.'s nose; © *mettre*/[Fr.] *fourrer*/*son ~ dans*, to stick one's nose into, to pry into; [Fam.] *à vue de ~*, at a guess.

ni [ni] *conj.*: *ni . . . ni*, neither . . . nor.

niais, -e [nj|ɛ, -ɛ:z] *adj.* silly, foolish. ‖ *n.m.* fool.

niche [niʃ] *n.f.* [à chien] kennel; [de statue] niche.

nichée [ni'ʃe] *n.f.* nestful (of birds), brood (of chicks, &c.); [Fig.] swarm (of children). ‖ **nicher** #3 *v. intr.* [oiseau] to nest, perch. ‖ **se nicher** *v. pron.* to nest; [Fig.] to nestle.

nickel [ni'kɛl] *n.m.* nickel. ‖ **nickeler** [ni'kle] #8 *v. tr.* to nickel-plate.

nid [ni] *n.m.* nest; [Fig.] lovenest, cosy home.

nièce [njɛs] *n.f.* niece.

nier [nje] #3 *v. tr.*: *~ que* [†subj.], to deny that . . . ; *~ être . . .*, to deny being . . .

nigaud, -e [ni'go(:d)] *n.* fool; [Fam.] sap, fathead. ‖ *adj.* silly, foolish.

niveau [ni|'vo] *n.m.* level: *~ d'eau*, water

level; *au ~ de*, on a level with; [Fig.] on a par with; *au ~ de la mer*, at sea-level; *être de ~*, to be (on a) level; [oil, gas] gauge; [ch. de fer] *passage à ~*, railway crossing, /level, grade/crossing. || **niveler** [-v'le] ‡8 *v. tr.* to level (a plot of land); [mesurer] to survey. cf. ARPENTEUR. || **nivellement** [-vɛl'mɑ̃] *n.m.* levelling; surveying.

noble [nɔbl] *adj.* noble; [Fig.] noble, generous; [style] lofty. || *n.* nobleman, noblewoman. || **noblesse** [nɔ'blɛs] *n.f.* nobility: *la petite ~*, the gentry.

noce [nɔs] *n.f.* wedding: *repas de ~*, wedding banquet; [Fam.] *faire la ~*, to go/on a spree, on a bender/. || *n.fpl.* marriage: *voyage de ~*, honeymoon (trip); *épouser qqun en secondes ~*, to become s.o.'s second/husband, wife/.

noceur [nɔ'sœ:r] *n.m.* reveller, rake.

noci|f, -ve [nɔ|'sif, -'si:v] *adj.* harmful; [Tech.] noxious. || **nocivité** [-sivi'te] *n.f.* harmfulness, noxiousness.

nocturne [nɔk'tyrn] *adj.* of the night, nocturnal.

Noël [nɔ'ɛl] *n.m.* [☞ but *la Noël* — la fête de N.] Christmas: *la veille de ~*, Christmas Eve; [Pop.] *le père ~*, Santa Claus.

nœud [nø] *n.m.* knot: *faire, défaire/un ~*, to tie, untie/a knot; [cravate] bow(tie); [Phys.] node; [Naut.]: *filer 10 nœuds*, to make ten knots; [Fig.] bond, tie.

noir, -e [nwa:r] *adj.* **1.** [couleur] black: *la race noire*, the Negro race; *tableau m ~*, blackboard. **2.** [absence de lumière] dark: *Il fait ~*, It is (getting) dark. **3.** [Fig.]: *des idées noires*, (to have) the blues; *une misère noire*, utter poverty. || *n.m.* **1.** [couleur] black. **2.** black (man), Negro; *les Noirs*, Negroes, coloured people. cf. NÈGRE. || **noirâtre** [nwa'r|ɑtr] *adj.* [Péj.] blackish. || **noirceur** [-sœ:r] *n.f.* blackness; darkness; [Fam.] *la ~*, dusk, gloaming. || **noircir** [-'si:r] ‡17 *v. tr.* to blacken, darken; [une réputation] to slander. || *v. intr.* to grow, turn /black.

noisetier [nwaz|'tje] *n.m.* hazel (tree). || **noisette** [-ɛt] *n.f.* hazel nut. || *adj.* (nut-) brown, hazel.

noix [nwɑ] *n.f. inv.* nut; walnut.

nom [nɔ̃] *n.m.* **1.** name: *~ de famille*, surname; *~ de jeune fille*, maiden name; †*avoir ~ X*, to be named X; *du ~ de X*, named X, X by name (cf. S'APPELER); *connu sous le ~ de*, going under the name of. **2.** [réputation] name, fame: *se faire un ~*, to achieve, win/fame. **3.** [Exclam.] *~ d'une pipe!*, *~ d'un chien!*, Dash (it)!

nomade [nɔ'mad] *n.m.* nomad. || *adj.* nomadic; migratory.

nombre [nɔ̃:br] *n.m.* [Math.] **1.** number; quantity; *un grand ~ (de gens)*, a large number (of people); *~ entier*, integer; *~ pair*, even number; *~ impair*, odd number; *~ premier*, prime number. **2.** multitude; majority; *en ~ écrasant*, (by) an overwhelming majority; *surpasser ses adversaires en ~*, to outnumber o.'s enemies; *compter au ~ de*, to be ranked with, among; *sans ~*, countless, → a multitude of. || **nombreu|x, -se** [-ø, -ø:z] *adj.* numerous, many; *Il a de ~ enfants*, → He has a large family; *famille nombreuse*, large family.

nombril [nɔ̃'bri] *n.m.* [Anat.] navel: [Fig.] *Il se prend pour le ~ du monde*, He thinks he is God's gift to the world.

nominal, -e [nɔmi'na|l] *adj.* nominal; [Gram.] *phrase nominale*, noun clause: *appel ~*, rollcall. || **nominalement** [-l'mɑ̃] *adv.* by name, nominally. || **nominati|f, -ve** [-'tif, -'ti:v] *adj.* nominative, of names: [action] registered.

nomination [-'sjɔ̃] *n.f.* appointment [× NOMINATION].

nommé, -e [nɔ'm|e] *adj.* called; *le ~*, the said; *arriver à point ~*, to arrive in the nick of time. || **nommément** [-e'mɑ̃] *adv.* by name; in so many words. || **nommer** ‡3 *v. tr.* **1.** to name; to give a name; to mention by name: *Il n'a pas été nommé*, His name was not mentioned. **2.** to name, appoint: *Il a été nommé gouverneur*, He has been appointed Governor. || **se nommer** *v. pron.* to be named, called; to give one's name: †*Comment vous nommez-vous?*, → What is your name? [use S'APPELER].

non[1] [nɔ̃] *adv.* **1.** no: *non, non*, no, not at all: *Il a dit ~*, He refused; *Il a dit que ~*, He said he had not, was not, would not, &c. [répéter le verbe de la principale]; *~ pas*, indeed no; [Loc.] *ni moi ~ plus*, nor I either [cf. NI]. **2.** not: *~ seulement*, not only. || *n.m. répondre par un ~*, to answer negatively.

non[2] [Negative prefix in compounds non-, un-, in-: *~-être*, nonbeing; with adjectives, often without hyphen: *~ solvable*, insolvent.] || **non-combattant** *adj.* noncombatant. || **non-existant** [nɔnɛgzis'tɑ̃] *adj.* nonexistent. || **non-intervention** *n.f.* non-intervention. || **non-sens** [nɔ̃'sɑ̃:s] *n.m.* meaningless (act, thing).

nonce [nɔ̃:s] *n.m.*: *le ~ du Pape, le ~ apostolique*, Papal Nuncio.

nonchalamment [nõʃal|a'mɑ̃] *adv.* unconcernedly, nonchalantly. || **nonchalance** [-ɑ̃:s] *n.f.* unconcern, indifference. || **nonchalant, -e** [-ɑ̃, -ɑ̃:t] *adj.* nonchalant, unconcerned; *avoir une attitude nonchalante,* → to lounge.

nonobstant [nɔnɔp'stɑ̃] *prép.* notwithstanding. || *adv.* nevertheless. || **nonobstant que** *loc. conj.* although.

nord [nɔ:r] *n.m.* north: *se diriger vers le* ~, to go northward; *Il habite le* ~ *de la France,* He lives in the north of France; *La Belgique est au* ~ *de la France,* Belgium is north of France; *le Nord canadien,* the Canadian Northland; *le grand Nord,* the frozen North; *le pôle* ~, the North Pole; *la mer du Nord,* the North Sea; *le* ~ *de la France,* northern France; *l'Irlande du* ~, Northern Ireland; *un vent du* ~, a northerly wind; *perdre le* ~, to be out of o.'s mind. || **nord-africain, -e** [nɔr(d) afri'k|ɛ̃, -ɛn] *adj.* North African. || **nord-américain, -e** [nɔr(d)ameri'k|ɛ̃, -ɛn] *adj.* North American.

nord-est [nɔr(d)ɛst] *n.m.* north-east; north-east wind.

nordique [nɔr'dik] *adj. & n.* Nordic.

nord-ouest [nɔr(d)wɛst] *n.m.* north-west: *les Territoires du* ~, the North-West Territories [abr.: NWT]; north-west wind, cf. NOROIT.

normal, -e [nɔr'mal] *adj.* normal, usual; standard. cf. NORME. *École normale,* Teachers' College. © Normal School; || **normaliser** [-i'ze] #3 *v. tr.* to normalize, standardize.

normand, -e [nɔrm|ɑ̃, -ɑ̃:d] *adj. & n.* Norman [from Normandy]; [Hist.] Norseman, Northman: *répondre en* ~, to answer evasively; *les îles Anglo-Normandes,* the Channel Islands. || **Normandie** [-ɑ̃'di] *n.f.* Normandy.

norme [nɔrm] *n.f.* norm, standard.

noroit [nɔ'rwa] *n.m.* north-west (wind): *le vent souffle du* ~, the wind blows from the N.W.

Norvège [nɔr'vɛ:ʒ] *n.f.* Norway. || **norvégien, -ne** [nɔrve'ʒj|ɛ̃, -ɛn] *n. & adj.* Norwegian.

nos [no] *adj. poss. pl.* cf. NOTRE.

nostalgie [nɔstal'ʒi] *n.f.* nostalgia; homesickness. || **nostalgique** [-k] *adj.* nostalgic, wistful.

notable [nɔ'tabl] *adj.* notable, noteworthy. || *n.m.* a prominent person; *les notables,* the leading citizens.

notaire [nɔ'tɛ:r] *n.m.* notary, lawyer: © ~ *public,* notary public.

notamment [nɔta'mɑ̃] *adv.* particularly, especially.

note [nɔt] *n.f.* note, memo; [école] mark, grade; [Com.] bill, account; [Mus.] note: *prendre des notes,* to take notes; *prendre (bonne) note de qqch.,* to take (careful) note of sth.; *régler une* ~, to pay a bill. [Fig.] *payer la* ~, to foot the bill, [Fam.] to pick up the tab.

noter [-e] #3 *v. tr.* to note, take note, to make a mental note; to jot down: *bien noté, mal noté,* in good standing, not in good standing. || **notice** [-is] *n.f.* note, introduction.

notifier [-i'fje] #3 *v. tr.* to signify, to make known.

notion [nɔ'sjõ] *n.f.* notion, idea: *avoir des notions de,* to have an elementary knowledge of.

notoire [nɔ't|wa:r] *adj.* well-known, notorious [× ce mot est souvent péjoratif]: *un fait* ~, a well-known fact. || **notoriété** [-ɔrje'te] *n.f.* notoriety, repute; notoriousness: *Il est de* ~ *publique que,* It is common knowledge that . . .

notre [nɔtr] *adj. poss. m. & f.*; **nos** *pl.* our: [Rel.] *Notre-Dame,* Our Lady; [Géog.] *la baie de Notre-Dame,* Notre Dame Bay (Nfld.).

nôtre (le) [(lə)no:tr] *pron. poss.* [☞ used in conj. with def. article]: *le nôtre m, la nôtre f, les nôtres mfpl.* ours: *Cette maison est la* ~, This house is ours, → This is our house. || **les nôtres** *n.pl.* our/ people, friends, side, party, &c./. || †*adj. poss.*: *Ce pays qui est nôtre,* This country of ours.

nouer [nwe] #3 *v. tr.* to tie, knot; [Fig.] to devise, to establish: *une intrigue bien nouée,* a well-contrived plot; ~ *des relations avec qqun,* to become acquainted with s.o. || **se nouer** *v. pron.* to twist (into knots), to knit; [fruit] to set. || **noueu|x, -se** [nw|ø, -ø:z] *adj.* knotty, [Fig.] gnarled. cf. NŒUD.

nouilles [nu:j] *n.fpl.* noodles, spaghetti: *soupe aux* ~, noodle soup.

nourri, -e [nu'r|i] *adj.* fed: *bien* ~, *mal* ~, well-fed, ill-fed; [Fig.] steeped in, versed in (classics, &c.). || **nourrice** [-is] *n.f.* nurse [☞ in Fr. applies only to women], wet nurse; [Auto] service tank, jerrican. || **nourrici|er, -ère** [-i'sje, -i'sjɛ:r] *adj.* nutritive: *père* ~, foster-father. || **nourrir** [-i:r] #17 *v. tr.* **1.** to feed, nourish; to nurse (infant). **2.** to raise (animals); to bring up (children). **3.** [Fig.] to harbour, entertain (feelings), to cherish (hope): ~ *des ressentiments contre qqun,* to bear s.o. ill will, to harbour ill feelings against s.o. || **se nourrir** *v. pron.* to feed o.s., to live (upon, *de*): *L'homme ne se nourrit pas que de pain,* Man does not live by bread alone; *Les écureuils se nourrissent de noix,* Squirrels feed on nuts. || **nourrissant, -e** [-i'sɑ̃, -i'sɑ̃:t] *adj.* nourishing; [Tech.] nutritious, rich. || **nourrisson** [-i'sɔ̃] *n.m.* [no *f.* form] infant. || **nourriture** [-i'ty:r] *n.f.* (less frequently used than *food*) [cf. CUISINE, RÉGIME, ALIMENT, ALIMENTATION] **1.** food, nourishment, [budget familial] groceries, food. **2.** board, keep: *Il gagne sa* ~, He earns his keep.

nous [nu] *pron. pers.* **1.** We [sujet du verbe]. **2.** us [objet du verbe ou de la préposition]: *Il s'est adressé à* ~, He came to us; *entre lui et* ~, between him and us. **3.** [object of reflexive verbs] ourselves; each other, one another: [s'aimer], *nous nous aimons,* we love one another; *entre* ~, between/ ourselves, us/: [Loc.] *chez* ~, at home. cf. CHEZ SOI, at our place. **4.** †we [☞ meaning: "I", in scientific or literary style: in this case, the verb does not agree in number]: ~ *sommes persuadé que . . . ,* we are convinced that . . . || **nous-même(s)** [-'mɛ:m] *pron. pers. pl.* **1.** ourselves: *Nous l'avons fait nous-mêmes,* We made it ourselves. cf. SOI-MÊME. **2.** [☞ very formal style]: *ce que nous pensons de nous-même,* what we think of ourself. cf. NOUS §4.

nouv|eau, nouv|elle [nuv|o, -ɛl] *adj.* [☞ use **nouvel** [-ɛl] before m. nouns beginning with a vowel or mute *h*: *le nouvel an,* New Year]. **1.** [precedes nouns] new, additional, another, further: *une nouvelle voiture,* a new car [i.e. added to another one previously acquired]; *une nouvelle aventure de . . . ,* another adventure of . . . ; *un nouveau venu,* a new-comer; *jusqu'à nouvel ordre,* until further notice; [Loc.] *le Nouveau Monde,* the New World; *le Nouveau Testament,* the New Testament. [cf. various place names with NOUVEAU-]. **2.** [follows noun] new, fresh, recent, new-style, novel: *une voiture nouvelle,* a new car [new design, new model]; *du vin nouveau,* new wine [new vintage]; *un monde nouveau,* a new, better world. **3.** [☞ in that position, contrasts with NEUF, which means *new,* recently bought]: *un chapeau nouveau,* a new(-style) hat; *un chapeau neuf,* a new hat; *une voiture neuve,* a new car [not used or second-hand]. **4.** (Loc. adv.) *à* ~, again, all over again [introducing new features]; *de* ~, again [for the second time]: *tout* ~, *tout beau,* A new broom sweeps clean. || *n.m.*: *il y a du* ~, there's something new; [École] *un nouveau,* a new pupil; a freshman. || **Nouveau-Brunswick (le)** [nuvo-brɔn'zwik] *n.m.* [Géog.] New Brunswick. || **Nouveau-Mexique (le),** [-mɛk'sik] New Mexico. || **nouveau-né** *pl.* **nouveaunés** [-ne] new-born child. || **Nouveau-Québec (le),** [-ke'bɛk] New Quebec. || **nouveauté** [-o'te] *n.f.* **1.** novelty, innovation; [Com.] fancy articles, new line, latest model. **2.** *n.fpl.* [Com.] dry goods: *un magasin de nouveautés,* a dry-goods store.

nouvelle, -s [-ɛl] *n.f. often pl.* **1.** news; account (of incident): *une* ~, a piece of news; *Quelles sont les nouvelles?,* What is the news?; *Donnez-moi de vos nouvelles,* Let me hear from you; *écouter les nouvelles (à la radio),* to listen to the news (bulletin); *Pas de nouvelles, bonnes nouvelles,* No news is good news; *recevoir des nouvelles de qqun,* to hear from s.o. [Fig.] *Vous m'en direz des nouvelles,* You'll be delighted with it; I'm sure you'll like it. [Journ.] ~ *sensationnelle,* scoop. **2.** *n.f.* (short-) story. || **Nouvelle-Angleterre (la)** [la nuvɛl|ɑ̃glə'tɛ:r] *n.f.* New England. || **Nouvelle-Calédonie (la)** [-kaledɔ'ni] *n.f.* New Caledonia. || **Nouvelle-Écosse (la)** [-e'kɔs] *n.f.* Nova Scotia. || **Nouvelle-Guinée (la)** [-gi'ne] *n.f.* New Guinea. || **Nouvelles-Hébrides (les)** [-ze'brid] *n.fpl.* The New Hebrides. || **nouvellement** [nuvɛl'mɑ̃] *adv.* newly, lately. || **Nouvelle-Orléans (la)** [-ɔrle'ɑ̃] *n.f.* New Orleans (US). || **Nouvelle-Zélande (la)** [-ze'lɑ̃:d] *n.f.* New Zealand.

novembre [nɔ'vɑ̃:br] *n.m.* November.

novice [nɔ'vis] *n.* novice, probationer (religious orders), tyro, beginner cf. APPRENTI. || *adj.* new, inexperienced. || **noviciat** [-ja] *n.m.* novitiate.

noyade [nwa'jad] *n.f.* drowning, cf. NOYER[1].

noyau *n.m.* pl. **noyaux** [nwa'jo] **1.** stone (of fruit); *fruits à* ~, stone fruit; *ôter les noyaux de,* to stone (fruit). cf. PÉPIN. **2.** core; inner part (of). **3.** [Phys.] nucleus. || **noyauter** [-'te] #3 *v. tr.* to set up locals (in a labour union) or cells (in organization).

noyé, -e [nwa'je] *n.m. un* ~, a drowned person. *adj.* drowned: [Fig.] *les yeux noyés de larmes,* /his, her/eyes filled with tears.

noyer[1] [nwa'je] #12 *v. tr.* **1.** to drown. **2.** [Fig.] to sink, to submerge: ~ *son chagrin dans l'alcool,* to drown one's sorrow in drink. **3.** [Tech.] to countersink, to set in (screws, nails): ~ *dans du béton,* to countersink . . . in concrete. || **se noyer**

v. pron. **1.** to drown (o.s.) [volontairement]; to be drowned [accidentellement]: *Il s'est noyé dans le Saint-Laurent,* He was drowned in the St. Lawrence. **2.** [Fig.] to be plunged into (*dans*), to get lost: *Il se noie dans un verre d'eau,* He makes a mountain out of a molehill; *noyé dans la foule,* lost in the crowd.

noyer[2] [nwa'je] *n.m.* walnut(tree) cf. NOIX: *meubles en* ~, walnut furniture.

nu, -e [ny] *adj.* **1.** naked, bare; [☞ usually preceded by *tout*]: *être tout* ~, to be stark naked; *aller nu-pieds,* to go barefoot, barefooted; *être nu-tête,* to be bareheaded → avoir la tête nue. **2.** [Fig.] plain [i.e. easily perceptible]; unadorned, naked, bare; *des murs nus,* bare walls; *la vérité toute nue,* the naked truth; *cela se voit à l'œil* ~, anyone can see that; it hits you in the eye [cf. *cela saute aux yeux*]. || *n.m.* the nude; nudity. [Art] *un* ~, a nude: *mettre à* ~, to lay bare, to strip; [Fig.] to expose (an evil).

nuage [nɥ|a:ʒ, © ny'a:ʒ] *n.m.* **1.** cloud; mist: *Le ciel se couvre de nuages,* The sky is clouding over; *Les nuages se dissipent,* It is clearing up, The clouds are breaking up; [Fig.] *dans les nuages,* up in the clouds, day-dreaming. **2.** [Fig.] gloom; shadow; unpleasantness: [Lit.] *un nuage passa sur son front,* a shadow clouded his brow; *un nuage de* (*lait, &c.*), a drop of (milk, &c.). || **nuageu|x, -se** [-a'ʒø, -a'ʒø:z] *adj.* cloudy.

nuance [nɥɑ̃:s] *n.f.* shade, hue; shade of meaning, nuance: *avoir le sens des nuances,* to have a feeling for subtlety, nuance. || **nuancé, -e** [nɥɑ̃s|e] *adj.* nicely shaded; subtly expressed; subtle. || **nuancer** [-e] #4 *v. tr.* to shade (colours); to qualify (a statement); to express subtly.

nucléaire [nykle'ɛ:r] *adj.* nuclear: *physique* ~, nuclear physics. || **nucléon** [nykle'õ] *n.m.* nucleon.

nudisme [ny'dism] *n.m.* nudism.

nudité [nydi'te] *n.f.* nudity; nakedness.

nue[1] [ny] *n.f.* usual pl. **nues** [Lit.] cloud, clouds, skies: *porter/élever jusqu'aux nues,* to praise to the skies; *se perdre dans les nues,* to lose o.s. in the clouds; *tomber des nues,* to be flabbergasted.

†**nue**[2], **nues**[2] [ny] cf. NU.

†**nuée** [nɥe] *n.f.* often pl. **nuées** cloud; host, multitude, swarm: *une* ~ *de sauterelles,* a swarm of locusts.

nuire [nɥi|:r], **nuisant** [-'zɑ̃], **nui** [nɥi] #57 *v. intr.* to harm, to hurt, to be injurious (to, *à*): *Cela vous nuira,* It will hurt your chances; *Son attitude lui a beaucoup nui,* His attitude did him a great deal of harm. || **se nuire** *v. pron.*: ~ (*à soi-même*), to hurt o.s. || **nuisible** [-zibl] *adj.* harmful, injurious, detrimental: *les animaux nuisibles,* pests, vermin; *une plante* ~, weed; ~ *à nos intérêts,* detrimental to our interests; ~ *à la santé,* injurious to one's health.

nuit[1] [nɥi] cf. NUIRE.

nuit[2] [nɥi] *n.f.* night, night-time; darkness, dark: *à la* ~ *tombante/à la tombée de la* ~, at nightfall; *Il fait* ~, It is dark; *Il fait* ~ *noire,* It is pitch dark; *passer une bonne* ~, to have a good night's sleep; *une* ~ *blanche,* a sleepless night; *Il travaille la* ~, He works at night; *de* ~, by night; *cette* ~ (passée], last night; *cette* ~ (à venir), tonight; *la* ~ *des Rois,* Twelfth Night; © *lettre de* ~, night letter. || †**nuitamment** [-ta'mɑ̃] *adv.* by night.

nul, -le [nyl] **1.** *adj. indéf.* [☞ precedes nouns + *ne*] no, not any: ~ *espoir n'est permis,* there is no hope (whatsoever); *nulle part,* nowhere. **2.** *adj. qualif.* [☞ follows the noun]: *Son influence est nulle,* He has no influence; *nul et non avenu,* null and void; *Ils ont fait partie nulle,* It was a draw. **3.** †*pron. ind.* no one, nobody: ~ *ne le sait,* nobody knows. || **nullement** [-'mɑ̃] *adv.* not at all, by no means. || **nullité** [-li'te] *n.f.* **1.** nullity (d'un acte légal). **2.** incapacity: *Il est d'une* ~ *rare,* He is completely devoid of intelligence. **3.** [Fig.] cipher: *C'est une* ~, He is a lightweight.

numéraire [nyme'r|ɛ:r] *n.m.* gold or gold coins. || **numéral, -e** [-al] *adj.* numeral. || **numérique** [-ik] *adj.* numerical. || **numériquement** [-ik'mɑ̃] *adv.* numerically.

numéro [-o] *n.m.* **1.** number (of ticket, house, room, &c.): *Avez-vous son* ~ *de téléphone?,* Do you have his/her phone number? **2.** issue (of a periodical): *dans le prochain* ~, in the next issue. || **numérotage** [-ɔ'ta:ʒ] *n.m.,* **numérotation** [-ɔta'sjõ] *n.f.* numbering. || **numéroter** [-ɔte] #3 *v. tr.* to number.

nuptial, -e, pl. **nuptiaux** [nypsj|al, -o] *adj.* nuptial, bridal: *marche nuptiale,* wedding march; *bénédiction nuptiale,* nuptial blessing.

nuque [nyk] *n.f.* nape (of the neck).

nutriti|f, -ve [nytri|'tif, -'ti:v] *adj.* nutritive, nutritious. || **nutrition** [-'sjõ] *n.f.* nutrition, food.

nylon [ni'lõ] *n.m.* nylon.

O, o *n.m.* [letter] O, o.
oasis [ɔa'zis] *n.f.* oasis.
obéir [ɔ'be|'i:r] #17 *v. intr.* to obey: ~ *à un ordre,* to obey an order; ~ *à qqun,* to obey s.o.; *se faire* ~, to enforce one's orders; [Fam.] to make it stick. || **obéissance** [-i'sɑ̃:s] *n.f.* obedience: *Il lui doit* ~, He must obey him. || **obéissant, -e** [-i'sɑ̃, -ɑ̃:t] *adj.* obedient.
obèse [o'bɛ:z] *adj.* obese, fat. || **obésité** [obezi'te] *n.f.* corpulence.
objecter [ɔbʒɛk'te] #3 *v. tr.* [✕] to raise an objection. || **objecti|f, -ve** [ɔbʒɛk't|if, -i:v] *adj.* & *n(m).* objective. || **objection** [ɔbʒɛk'sjõ] *n.f.* objection: *soulever une* ~, to raise an objection.
objet [ɔb'ʒɛ] *n.m.* **1.** object, thing, article. **2.** subject, matter: *Cela fera l'* ~ *d'une seconde conférence,* It will be taken up in a second lecture. **3.** object, purpose: *Quel est l'* ~ *de sa visite?,* What is his visit about?
obligation [ɔblig|a'sjõ] *n.f.* obligation, duty: *remplir une* ~, to fulfil an obligation; *être dans l'* ~ *de,* to be obliged to, to feel compelled to. || **obligatoire** [-a'twa:r] *adj.* obligatory, compulsory: *instruction* ~, compulsory education; *Arrêt* ~ *de l'autobus,* → All buses stop here. || **obligatoirement** [-atwar'mɑ̃] *adv.* → (one) must . . . , it is compulsory . . . , *pas* ~, not necessarily.
obligé, -e [ɔbli|'ʒe] *adj.* obliged, bound: *Je vous suis très* ~, I am much obliged to you. || **obligeance** [-'ʒɑ̃:s] *n.f.* kindness: *avoir l'* ~ *de faire qqch.,* to be kind enough to do sth. || **obligeant, -e** [-'ʒɑ̃(:t)] *adj.* obliging, kind: *C'est très* ~ *de votre part (de),* It is very kind of you (to). || **obliger** [ɔbli'ʒe] #5 *v. tr.* **1.** to compel, to oblige: *Il m'a obligé à le faire,* He compelled me to do it; *Noblesse oblige,* Privilege entails responsibility. **2.** to please, to accommodate, to oblige: *Vous m'obligeriez beaucoup en le faisant,* You would greatly oblige me by doing it.
oblique [ɔ'blik] *adj.* oblique, slanting; [Fig.] devious. || **obliquer** [-e] #3 *v. intr.* to swerve (to the left, to the right, *à gauche, à droite*).
oblitérer [ɔblite're] #10 *v. tr.* to postmark, to cancel; [Fig.] to obliterate, to erase.
obscène [ɔp'sɛ:n] *adj.* obscene, smutty. || **obscénité** [ɔpseni'te] *n.f.* obscenity.
obscur, -e [ɔps'k|y:r] *adj.* **1.** dark. **2.** [Fig.] obscure. || **obscurcir** [-yr'si:r] #17 *v. tr.* to darken, to dim. || **s'obscurcir** *v. pron.* to grow, to become dark, to darken; to cloud over. || **obscurcissement** [-yrsis'mɑ̃] *n.m.* darkening; [Mil.] blackout. || **obscurément** [-'yre'mɑ̃] *adv.* obscurely. || **obscurité** [-yri'te] *n.f.* [nuit] darkness; [Fig.] obscurity.
obsédant, -e [ɔpse'dɑ̃(:t)] *adj.* haunting. || **obséder** [ɔpse'de] #10 *v. tr.* to obsess, haunt; [Pej.] to importune.
obsèques [ɔp'sɛk] *n.f. pl.* funeral.
obséquieu|x, -se [ɔpse'kjø(:z)] *adj.* obsequious, fawning.
observance [ɔpsɛr'vɑ̃:s] *n.f.* observance.
observat|eur, -rice [ɔpsɛrva|'tœ:r, -'tris] *n.* observer. || *adj.* observant. || **observation** [-'sjõ] *n.f.* **1.** [loi, fête, &c.] observance. **2.** [action de regarder] observation: *être en* ~, to be under observation. **3.** critical remark, observation: *faire des observations à qqun,* to pick on s.o., to find fault with s.o. || **observatoire** [-'twa:r] *n.* observatory. || **observer** [ɔpsɛr've] #3 *v. tr.* **1.** [règlement] to observe, to keep. **2.** to watch, to observe. **3.** *faire* ~ *qqch. à qqun,* to point out sth. to s.o.
obsession [ɔpsɛ'sjõ] *n.f.* obsession.
obstacle [ɔps'takl] *n.m.* obstacle: *faire, mettre* ~ *à qqch.,* to stand in the way of sth., to oppose sth.; *course d'obstacles,* obstacle race.
obstination [ɔpstin|a'sjõ] *n.f.* obstinacy, stubbornness. || **obstiné, -e** [-e] *adj.* stubborn, obstinate; [résistance] dogged. || **obstinément** [-e'mɑ̃] *adv.* stubbornly, doggedly. || **s'obstiner** [-e] #3 *v. pron.* to show obstinacy: ~ *à faire qqch.* (*dans une attitude*), to persist in (doing sth.); [Fam.] © to argue, gainsay
obstruction [ɔpstr|yk'sjõ] *n.f.* obstruction, clogging; [US Pol.] filibustering. || **obstruer** [-y'e] #3 *v. tr.* to obstruct, block; [conduit] to clog.
obtempérer [ɔptɑ̃pe're] #10 *v. tr.*: ~ *à un ordre,* to comply with an order, to obey.
obtenir [ɔptə'ni:r] #22 *v. tr.* to get, to procure, to obtain: ~ *un permis,* to obtain a permit; *Il obtint de rester,* He got permission to stay; *J'ai obtenu qu'on le garde,* I got them to keep him on.
obturer [ɔpty're] #3 *v. tr.* to stop; [dent] to fill.
obtus, -e [ɔp'ty(:z)] *adj.* obtuse; [Fig.] dull.
obus [o'by] *n.m.* shell.
obvier [ɔb'vje] #3 *v. tr.*: ~ *à un inconvénient,* to obviate a drawback.
occasion [ɔka'zj|õ] *n.f.* **1.** occasion, opportunity: *en toute* ~, on every occasion; *à l'* ~, on occasion; *à l'* ~ *de son anniversaire,* for his birthday; *profiter de*

l' ~ pour, to take the opportunity to. **2.** cause: *Ce n'est pas une ~ de se réjouir*, There is no cause to celebrate. **3.** bargain, value: *d' ~*, second-hand. || **occasionnel, -le** [-ɔ'nɛl] *adj.* occasional. || **occasionnellement** [-ɔnɛl'mɑ̃] *adv.* occasionally, only on occasion. || **occasionner** [-ɔ'ne] #3 *v. tr.* to cause, to bring about, to produce: *Les passages à niveau occasionnent de nombreux accidents*, Grade-crossings cause many accidents.

occident [ɔksi'dɑ̃] *n.m.* the West; West. || **occidental, -e** [-'tal] *adj.* western, westerly. || **(les) occidentaux** [-'to] *n.mpl.* the West.

occupant, -e [ɔky'p|ɑ̃, -ɑ̃:t] *n.* occupant: *le droit du premier ~*, the right of occupancy. || **occupation** [-a'sjõ] *n.f.* **1.** occupation, job, business, employment, work: *vaquer à ses occupations*, to go about o.'s business. **2.** occupation; occupancy, capture: *l' ~ d'un territoire*, the occupation of a territory. || **occupé, -e** [-e] *adj.* **1.** busy, occupied, engaged (in): *Il est trop ~ pour vous recevoir*, He is too busy to see you. **2.** seized, occupied: *en territoire ~*, (in) occupied territory; [sur une porte] *occupé*, engaged (≠ *libre*, vacant). || **occuper** [-e] #3 *v. tr.* **1.** to employ, to occupy. **2.** to hold, to occupy: *Cette place est-elle occupée?*, Is this seat vacant? || **s'occuper (de, à)** *v. pron.* to concern o.s. with, to take care of, to handle: *C'est lui qui s'occupe de ces questions-là*, He handles that side of the business; *Il s'occupe d'importation*, He is in the import business; *Occupez-vous de ce qui vous regarde*, Mind your own business.

occurrence [ɔky'rɑ̃:s] *n.f.* occurrence; juncture.

océan [ɔse|'ɑ̃] *n.m.* ocean: *l' ~ Pacifique*, the Pacific Ocean; *d'un ~ à l'autre*, © → from coast to coast. || **Océanie** [-a'ni] *n.f.* Oceania (Oceanica), (the) South Sea Islands. || **océanique** [-a'nik] *adj.* ocean-going. || *n.m.* © liner, ocean-going ship; [Fr.] TRANSATLANTIQUE. || **océanographie** [-anogra'fi] *n.f.* oceanography.

ocre [ɔkr] *n.f.* ochre.

octave [ɔk'ta:v] *n.f.* [Mus.] octave.

octobre [ɔk'tɔbr] *n.m.* October: *le 10 octobre 1958*, October 10, 1958; cf. AVRIL.

octroi [ɔk'trwa] *n.m.* **1.** grant. **2.** †tollhouse (at entrance of city to collect municipal taxes); toll dues: *marchandises soumises à l' ~*, goods liable to duty. || **octroyer** [-'je] #12 *v. tr.* to grant, to concede. || **s'octroyer** *v. pron.* to take (often unduly): *Il s'est octroyé un jour de plus*, He decided he was entitled to an extra day.

oculaire [ɔky'l|ɛ:r] *adj.* ocular (cf. OEIL): *témoin ~*, eye-witness. || **oculiste** [-ist] *n.m.* oculist. cf. OPTOMÉTRISTE.

ode [ɔd] *n.f.* ode.

odeur [ɔ'dœ:r] *n.f.* smell, odour; scent, perfume: [Fig., R.C.] *mourir en ~ de sainteté*, to die in the odour of sanctity.

odieu|x, -se [ɔ'djø(:z)] *adj.* hateful, odious, repulsive: *Il s'est rendu ~*, He made himself unbearable. || †*n.m.* odium.

odorant, -e [ɔdɔ'r|ɑ̃, -ɑ̃:t] *adj.* fragrant, sweet-smelling: *un parfum ~*, a fragrant perfume; ≠INODORE. || **odorat** [-a] *n.m.* (the sense of) smell.

œil, yeux [œ:j] [jø] *n.m.* **1.** eye, eyes: *clin d' ~*, wink: *en un clin d' ~*, in the twinkling of an eye; *coup d' ~*, glance; *d'un coup d' ~*, at a glance; *à vue d' ~*, visibly; *visible à l' ~ nu*, visible to the naked eye; *se battre l' ~ de qqch.*, not to give a curse about sth.; *ne dormir que d'un ~*, to sleep with one eye open; *faire de l' ~ à qqun*, to make eyes at s.o.; *ouvrir l' ~*, to keep one's eyes open; *voir d'un mauvais ~*, to look askance at; *voir les choses du même ~ que qqun*, to see eye to eye with s.o.; *d'un ~ critique*, critically; *n'avoir d'yeux que pour qqun*, to be interested only in s.o.; *n'avoir pas froid aux yeux*, not to be easily scared; *Cela coûte les yeux de la tête*, It costs a fortune; *Cela crève les yeux*, It stares you in the face; *dévorer qqun des yeux*, to feast one's eyes on s.o.; *entre quatre (z')yeux*, privately; *faire les yeux doux à qqun*, to make eyes at s.o.; *faire les gros yeux à qqun*, to glare at s.o.; *fermer les yeux sur qqch.*, to look the other way; *fixer les yeux sur*, to stare at; *lever les yeux*, to look up; *Loin des yeux, loin du cœur*, Out of sight, out of mind; *Cela m'a ouvert les yeux*, It was an eye-opener; *Cela saute aux yeux*, It's pretty obvious. **2.** *~ -de-bœuf*, round window; *~ -de-perdrix*, (soft) corn. || **œillère** [œ'jɛ:r] *n.f.* [usual. plur.] blinker(s). || **œillet**[1] [œ'jɛ] *n.m.* eyelet: *œillets gommés*, gummed reinforcements.

œillet[2] [œ'jɛ] *n.m.* carnation; clove-pink.

œuf [œf] *n.m.* [pl. **œufs**] [ø] egg; *œufs de poisson*, spawn, roe; *blanc d' ~*, egg white; *jaune d' ~*, yolk; *~ /frit, sur le plat/*, fried egg; *œufs brouillés*, scrambled eggs; *~ à la coque*, boiled egg; *~ dur*, hard-boiled egg; *plein comme un ~*, chock-full.

œuvre [œ:vr] *n.f.* [not to be confused with OUVRAGE] **1.** work: *chef-d' ~*, masterpiece; *~ d'art*, work of art; *Les œuvres complètes de Balzac*, Balzac's collected works. **2.** [Loc.] *se mettre à l' ~*, to get to work; *mettre en ~*, to implement, to use; *mettre tout en ~*, to leave no stone unturned; *à pied d' ~*, ready to start work; *la main-d' ~*, labour, manpower; *les bonnes œuvres*, charities; *être le fils de ses œuvres*, to be a self-made man. || *n.m. l' ~ de Chopin*, the whole of Chopin's work; *le gros ~*, the main part of a building; *le grand ~*, the philosopher's stone.

offense [ɔ'f|ɑ̃:s] *n.f.* offence, wrong: *commettre une ~*, to do wrong; *faire ~ à qqun*, to offend s.o.; *réparer une ~*, to make amends. || **offensé, -e** [-ɑ̃'se] *adj.* offended. || *n. l'offensé*, the offended party. || **offenser** #3 *v. tr.* to offend: *soit dit sans vous ~*, with all due respect to you. || **s'offenser** *v. pron.* to be offended (by, *de*), to take offence (at, *de*). || **offensi|f, -ve** [ɔfɑ̃'s|if, -i:v] *adj.* offensive. **offensive** *n.f.* [Mil.] offensive.

offert [ɔ'fɛ:r] cf. OFFRIR. || **offertoire** [ɔfɛr'twa:r] *n.m.* [R.C.] Offertory.

office [ɔ'fis] *n.m.* **1.** office, duty: *d' ~*, ex officio; *faire ~ de*, to act as; *exercer un ~*, to perform a function. **2.** divine worship, service: *aller aux offices*, to go to church. **3.** Board, Council: *l'Office national du film*, the National Film Board. **4.** pantry; servants' quarters.

officiant [ɔfi'sjɑ̃] *adj. & n.m.* officiant.

officiel, -le [-sjɛl] *adj.* official, formal: *un avis ~*, an official notice; *protestation officielle*, formal protest. || *les officiels n.m. pl.* the official party. || **officiellement** [-sjɛl'mɑ̃] *adv.* officially, formally.

officier[1] [ɔfi'sje] *n.m.* officer [× But not "officer" of a Company. cf. OFFICER]: *~ /de marine, de terre, de l'air*, naval, army, air officer; *~ d'état-major*, staff officer; *~ supérieur*, field officer; *sous-~*, non-commissioned officer; [Fig.] *Officier d'Académie*, holder of academic honours (for service); [Fr.] *Officier ministériel*, [Fr.] notary, notary public, solicitor.

officier[2] [ɔfi'sje] #3 *v. intr.* to officiate.

officieu|x, -se [ɔfi'sjø(:z)] *adj.* zealous, unofficial.

offrande [ɑ̃:d] *n.f.* offering. || **offrant** [ɔfr|ɑ̃] *adj. & n.m.* bidder: *le plus ~*, the highest bidder. || **offre**[1] [ɔfr] *n.f.* offer; [enchères] bid; [Com.] tender. || **offre**[2] cf. OFFRIR.

offrir [ɔ'fri:r] **offrant, offert** [ɔ'fɛ:r] #25 *v. tr.* **1.** to offer: *Il a offert sa voiture*, He offered his car. **2.** to give: *Il lui a offert un cadeau*, He gave him a present; *~ ses condoléanees*, to express sympathy. **3.** to present; to offer: *Cette solution offre plusieurs avantages*, This solution presents several advantages. || **s'offrir** *v. pron.* to present o.s.; *~ comme volontaire*, to volunteer.

offusquer [ɔfys'ke] #3 *v. tr.* to dazzle; [Fig.] to offend. || **s' ~ de** *v. pr.* to take offence at.

oh! [o] *interj.* O!, oh!

Ohio, l' [ɔ'jo] *n.m.* Ohio.

oie [wa, wɑ] *n.f.* goose (pl. geese): *~ sauvage*, cf. OUTARDE, wild goose.

oignon, ognon [ɔ'ɲõ] *n.m.* **1.** onion: *soupe à l' ~*, onion soup; *en rang d'oignons*, in one row. **2.** [tulipe] bulb. **3.** bunion.

oiseau, -x [wa'zo] *n.m.* bird; *à vol d' ~*, as the crow flies; *~ de basse-cour*, barnyard fowl; *~ de proie*, bird of prey. || **oiseau-mouche** *n.m.* [pl. **oiseaux-mouches**] humming bird.

oiseu|x, -se [wa'zø(:z)] *adj.* idle, useless.

oisi|f, -ve [wa'zi|f, -i:v] *adj.* idle, lazy; unemployed. || **oisiveté** [-v'te] *n.f.* idleness.

oison [wa'zõ] *n.m.* gosling, cf. OIE.

ojibwa [ɔʒi'bwa] © *n.m.* Ojibwa(y).

Oklahoma, (l') [oklaɔ'ma] *n.m.* Oklahoma.

olive [ɔ'li:v] *n.f.* olive: *huile d' ~*, olive oil. || **Olive**[1] *n.f.* = Olive, Olivia.

olivier [ɔli'vje] *n.m.* olive tree. || **Olivier** *n.m.* Oliver.

omble [õ:bl] *n.*: *~ de fontaine* (ou: truite de ruisseau, rouge, saumonée, mouchetée), brook, speckled, red/trout; *~ grise* (truite/grise, de lac/), lake trout.

ombrage [õ'br|a:ʒ] *n.m.* **1.** shade. **2.** [Fig.] umbrage: *prendre ~ de*, to take umbrage at. || **ombrager** [-a'ʒ|e] #5 *v. tr.* to give shade, to spread over. || **ombrageu|x, -se** [-ø(:z)] *adj.* suspicious, distrustful, ready to take offence; [cheval] shy, skittish. || **ombre** [õ:br] *n.f.* **1.** shade: *à l' ~ d'un arbre*, in the shade of a tree. **2.** shadow: *projeter une ~*, to cast a shadow. **3.** shadow, ghost: *sans l' ~ d'un doute*, without the shadow of a doubt; *Il n'est plus que l' ~ de lui-même*, He is but the shadow of his former self. || **ombrelle** [õ'brɛl] *n.f.* sunshade. || **ombrer** [õ'bre] *v. tr.* to shade (a drawing).

omelette [ɔm'lɛt] *n.f.* omelet.

omettre [ɔ'm|ɛtr] **omettant** [-ɛ'tɑ̃] **omis** [-i] #44 *v. tr.* to omit, to leave out. || **omission** [-i'sjõ] *n.f.* omission, oversight. || **omis** cf. OMETTRE.

omoplate [ɔmɔ'plat] *n.f.* shoulderblade.

on [õ, õn+] *indef. pron.* [☞ Only sing.;

takes 3rd pers. sing. verb forms]. The liaison form, as in *on est* [ɔ̃nɛ] is easily confused with a negative form *on n'est* [ɔ̃nɛ]. **1.** one, they, you, people [☞ *On* is gen. used to avoid passive forms in French]: *on sait que*, it is generally known (that); *on dit* (*que*), it is said, they say; *Qu'en dira-t-on?*, What will people say? **2.** we [often replaces the 2nd pers. plur. *nous*] *On y va?*, Shall we go? [N.B. Insert *t* in questions when verb ends in a vowel: *Y va-t-on?*]

once [ɔ̃:s] [= oz.] *n.f.*: ~ *troy*, ounce troy; ~ *de liquide*, fluid ounce.

oncle [ɔ̃:kl] *n.m.* uncle.

onction [ɔ̃k'sjɔ̃] *n.f.* **1.** [R.C.] anointing. **2.** unction, unctuousness. || **onctueu|x, -se** [ɔ̃k'tɥø(:z)] *adj.* unctuous; [Fig.] bland, suave.

ondatra [ɔ̃da'tra] *n.* (ou *rat musqué*), muskrat.

onde [ɔ̃:d] *n.f.* **1.** water; the sea: *les ondes amères*, the briny deep. **2.** [Phys.] wave: *poste à ondes courtes*, short-wave (radio) set; *grandes ondes*, long waves.

ondée [ɔ̃'de] *n.f.* shower.

ondoyant, -e [ɔ̃dwa|'jɑ̃(:t)] *adj.* undulating, swaying; [Fig.] illusive. || **ondoyer** [-'je] #12 *v. tr.* to undulate; [eau] to ripple.

ondulant, -e [ɔ̃dy'lɑ̃(:t)] *adj.* undulating, waving. || **ondulation** [-a'sjɔ̃] *n.f.* wave (of hair): *se faire faire une* ~ *permanente*, to have a permanent wave; *ondulations de terrain*, rolling land. || **onduler** [ɔ̃dy'l|e] #3 *v. tr. & intr.* to wave, to undulate. || **onduleu|x, -se** [-ø(:z)] *adj.* undulous, wavy.

onéreu|x, -se [ɔne'rø(:z)] *adj.* expensive; [dépense] heavy.

ongle [ɔ̃:gl] *n.m.* (finger-)nail: *se faire les ongles*, to do one's nails; *payer rubis sur l'* ~ , to pay on the nail; *être* (*qqch.*) *jusqu'au bout des ongles*, to be (sth.) to the finger-tips.

onguent [ɔ̃'gɑ̃] *n.m.* ointment, salve.

ont [ɔ̃] cf. AVOIR.

Ontario [ɔ̃ta'rj|o] *n.m.* Ontario; (*le lac*) *Ontario*, Lake O. || **Ontarien, -ne** [-ɛ̃, -ɛn] *n.* Ontarian, (from) Ontario.

onze [ɔ̃:z] *adj. card. & n.m.* [N.B. *le onze*] eleven, eleventh: *le* ~ *du mois de mai*, on the eleventh of May; [Sport.] *le onze français*, the French /team, eleven/. || **onzième** [ɔ̃'ziɛm] *adj. & n.m.* eleventh.

opaque [ɔ'pak] *adj. m/f* opaque.

opéra [ɔpe'ra] *n.m.*: ~ *bouffe*, opera bouffe; ~ *comique*, comic opera; *le grand* ~, grand opera.

opérat|eur, -rice [opera'tœ:r, -a'tris] *n.* operator. [×: This term is restricted in French to certain occupations]: *opérateur de cinéma*, cameraman. cf. EXPLOITANT.

opération [ɔper|a'sjɔ̃] *n.f.* operation, performance; [Méd.] operation; [Com.] *une* ~ *financière*, a financial transaction; [Mil.] *le théâtre des opérations*, the theatre of war; [Méd.] *subir une* ~ , to undergo an operation; *effectuer une* ~, to perform an operation. cf. INTERVENTION; [Math.] *les quatre opérations*, the four/operations, sums/. || **opérer** [-e] #10 *v. tr.* to operate, to bring about (a change, &c.); [Méd.] to operate upon; *se faire* ~ , to have an operation; *Il vient d'être opéré de l'appendicite*, He has just been operated on for appendicitis.

opérette [-ɛt] *n.f.* musical comedy, operetta.

opiner [ɔpi'ne] #3 *v. intr.* to be of opinion (for/against, *pour/contre*).

opiniâtre [ɔpi|njɑ:tr] *adj.* stubborn, obstinate, headstrong. || **opiniâtreté** [-njatrə'te] *n.f.* stubbornness, obstinacy.

opinion [ɔpi'njɔ̃] *n.f.* opinion: *sondage d'* ~ , public opinion poll, Gallup poll; *se former une* ~ , to form an opinion; *partager une* ~ , to share an opinion.

opium [ɔ'pjɔm] *n.m.* opium.

opossum [opɔ'sɔm] *n.m.* opossum.

opportun, -e [ɔpɔr|'tœ̃, -'tyn] *adj.* opportune, timely. || **opportunité** [-tyni'te] *n.f.* [×] opportuneness, seasonableness.

opposant [ɔpo'z|ɑ̃] *n.m.* opposed: *deux opposants*, two opponents. || **opposé, -e** [-e] *adj.* opposite; over against; [Fig.] opposed to, contrary: *diamétralement opposés*, po'es apart. || **opposé** *n.m.* the contrary, the reverse, the opposite: *à l'* ~ *de*, contrary to . . . . || **opposer** #3 *v. tr.* **1.** to oppose, to object. **2.** to place face-to-face, to contrast. || **s'opposer** *v. pron.* to oppose: *Il s'y est opposé*, He opposed it, He came out against it, He set his face against it. || **opposition** [-i'sjɔ̃] *n.f.* **1.** opposition, obstacle: *se heurter à une forte* ~ , to meet with considerable opposition; *faire* ~ *à un chèque*, to stop a cheque; *faire* ~ *à un jugement*, to appeal a judgment. **2.** contrast.

oppresser [ɔprɛ|'se] #3 *v. tr.* to oppress. || **oppression** [-sjɔ̃] *n.f.* oppression.

opprimer [ɔpri'me] #3 *v. tr.* to oppress, crush down.

opprobre [ɔ'prɔbr] *n.m.* opprobrium, disgrace.

opter [ɔp'te] #3 *v. tr.*: ~ *pour qqch.*, to decide in favour of sth.

opticien [ɔpti'sjɛ̃] *n.m.* optician.

optimisme [ɔpti|'mism] *n.m.* optimism. || **optimiste** [-mist] *n.m.* optimist. || *adj. m/f* optimistic.

option [ɔp'sjõ] *n.f.* option, choice (*sur*, on).

optique [ɔp'tik] *n.f.* optics. || *adj. m/f* optical.

optométriste [ɔptɔme'trist] *n.m.* optometrist; cf. [Fr.] OCULISTE *m.*

opulence [ɔpu'lã:s] *n.f.* opulence, riches, plenty, affluence: *nager dans l'* ~ , to live on Easy Street.

or[1] [ɔ:r] *n.m.* gold: *valoir son pesant d'* ~ , to be worth one's weight in gold; *rouler sur l'* ~ , to be rolling (in money).

or[2] *conj.* [☞ Always at the beginning of a clause; followed by a comma; strongly stressed in speaking, and followed by a silence.] [☞ Often missing altogether in English.] Now, . . . ; But, . . . ; Well, . . .

oracle [ɔ'ra:kl] *n.m.* oracle.

orage [ɔ'ra:ʒ] *n.m.* thunderstorm: *Le temps est à l'* ~ , A storm is brewing; storm, turmoil: *tenir tête à l'* ~ , to face the music. || **orageu|x, -se** [-ø(:z)] *adj.* stormy, tempestuous: *entrevue orageuse*, stormy interview.

oraison [ɔrɛ'zõ] *n.f.* prayer; †oration.

oral, -e [ɔ'ral] *adj.* oral. || *n.m.* oral examination.

orange [ɔ'r|ɑ:ʒ] *n.f.* orange. || *adj.* orange. || **orangé -e** [-ɑ̃'ʒe] *adj.* orange-coloured. || **orangeade** [-ɑ̃'ʒad] *n.f.* orangeade, orange juice. || **oranger** [-ɑ̃'ʒe] *n.m.* orange tree. || **orangiste** [-ɑ̃'ʒist] *n. & adj.* © Orangeman.

orateur [ɔra'tœ:r] *n.m.* orator, speaker; © [Pol.] *l'Orateur*, the Speaker of the House of Commons. || **oratoire**[1] [ɔra'twa:r] *adj.* oratorical: *l'art* ~ , the art of public speaking. || **oratoire**[2] *n.m.* oratory, chapel, shrine.

orbe [ɔrb] *n.m.* orb, globe.

orbite [ɔr'bit] *n.f.* orbit; [œil] socket.

orchestre [ɔr'kɛstr] *n.m.* orchestra; [smaller] band; *chef d'* ~ , conductor; *diriger un* ~ , to conduct an orchestra; *un* ~ *de six musiciens*, a six-piece band.

orchidée [ɔrki'de] *n.f.* orchid.

ordinaire [ɔrdi'nɛ:r] *adj.* ordinary, common, usual, customary; [Fig.] mediocre: *d'* ~ , usually, ordinarily; *comme à l'* ~ , as usual. || *n.m.* **1.** [Mil.] mess: *manger à l'* ~ , to eat at the mess; [Rel.] *l'Ordinaire*, the Bishop. **2.** daily fare; © *faire l'* ~, to cook.

ordinal, -e [ɔrdi'nal] *adj.* ordinal (number).

ordinand [ɔrdi'n|ɑ̃] *n.m.* [Rel.] candidate (for ordination). || **ordination** [-a'sjõ] *n.f.* [Rel.] ordination.

ordonnance [ɔrdɔ|'nɑ̃:s] *n.f.* **1.** order, prescription. **2.** statute, regulation. **3.** grouping, disposition. || **ordonnat|eur, -rice** [-na'tœ:r, -na'tris] *n.* master of ceremonies. || **ordonné, -e** [-'ne] *adj.* orderly, tidy; [Rel.] ordained. || **ordonner** #3 *v. tr.* **1.** to order; to command, cf. DÉCRÉTER: *On a ordonné la réouverture des magasins*, The re-opening of the stores has been ordered. **2.** to set in order, to clean: *une maison bien ordonnée*, a well-kept house. **3.** [Rel.] to ordain: *Il a été ordonné prêtre*, He has been ordained to the priesthood. **4.** [Med.] to prescribe.

ordre [ɔrdr] *n.m.* **1.** order: *donner un* ~ , to give an order; *intimer à qqun l'* ~ *de*, to order s.o. to; *exécuter un* ~ , to carry out an order; *servir sous les ordres de qqun*, to serve under s.o.; *rappeler à l'* ~ , to call to order; *l'* ~ *du jour*, the agenda; *payer à l'* ~ *de* . . . , to pay to the order of . . . **2.** order, tidiness: *avoir de l'* ~ , to be tidy, orderly, systematic; *mettre en* ~ , to tidy up; *maintenir l'* ~ , to keep order; *rétablir l'* ~ , to restore order; *ne pas troubler l'* ~, to keep the peace. **3.** decoration: *l'Ordre du Bain*, the Order of the Bath. **4.** *les ordres*, holy orders: *entrer dans les ordres*, to be ordained.

ordure [ɔr'dy:r] *n.f.* garbage, rubbish, filth.

Orégon, (l') [ɔre'gõ] *n.m.* Oregon.

oreille [ɔ'r|ɛ:j] *n.f.* ear: *avoir mal à l'* ~ , to have earache; *avoir l'* ~ *juste*, to have a good ear; *avoir l'* ~ *fine*, to have a quick ear; *être dur d'* ~ , to be hard of hearing; *écouter d'une* ~ *distraite*, to listen without paying much attention; *avoir la puce à l'* ~ , to be alerted; *échauffer les oreilles à qqun*, to get s.o.'s dander up; *faire la sourde* ~ *à*, to turn a deaf ear to; *se faire tirer l'* ~, to consent grudgingly; *frotter les oreilles à qqun*, to box s.o.'s ears; to give s.o. a good talking to; *prêter l'* ~ *à*, to listen to; *rabattre les oreilles à qqun*, to keep repeating the same thing to s.o.; *tendre l'* ~, to prick up one's ears.

oreiller [-e'je] *n.m.* pillow. || **oreillette** [-ɛ'jɛt] *n.f.* **1.** [Anat.] auricle (of the heart). **2.** ear flap: *fauteuil à oreillettes*, wing chair. || **oreillons** [-ɛ'jõ] *n.mpl.* the mumps.

Orénoque, l' [lɔre'nɔk] *n.m.* the Orinoco (River).

orfèvre [ɔr'fɛ:vr] *n.m.* goldsmith.

organe [ɔr'gan] *n.m.* cf. ORGUE. **1.** organ

(of the body): *L'œil est l' ~ de la vue,* The eye is the organ of sight. **2.** medium; voice; spokesman, mouthpiece, organ: *La TV est un excellent ~ de diffusion de la pensée,* TV is an excellent medium for the diffusion of ideas; *Ce journal est l' ~ du parti,* This paper is the organ of the party. || **organique** [-ik] *adj.* organic.

organisat|eur, -rice [ɔrganiza'tœ:r, -a'tris] *n.* organizer. || **organisation** [-a'sjõ] *n.f.* organization, arrangement; agency [= U.N.]: *Organisation des Nations Unies* [= ONU], United Nations Organization [= UN] || **organiser** [ɔrgani'z|e] #3 *v. tr.* to organize, to arrange. || **organisme** [ɔrga'nism] *n.m.* organization, agency: [Med.] system.

organiste [ɔrga'nist] *n.m.* organist.

orge [ɔrʒ] *n.f.* barley.

orgue [ɔrg] *n.m.* (fem. in pl.) [Mus.] organ: *tribune d'orgues,* organ loft.

orgueil [ɔr'gœ:j] *n.m.* pride, arrogance: *tirer ~ de,* to point with pride to, to take pride in. || **orgueilleu|x, -se** [ɔrgœ'jø(:z)] *adj.* proud, arrogant. || *n.m. pl.* the proud.

Orient [ɔ'rjɑ̃] *n.m.* **1.** Orient; East: *l'Extrême ~* , (the) Far East; *le Moyen ~* , the Middle East. **2.** [perle] orient, water. || **oriental,** *f.* **-e** [-'tal] *adj. & n.m.* Eastern; oriental. cf. OCCIDENTAL: *les Orientaux,* Orientals. [NB. *oriental* applies mostly to the Eastern hemisphere, China, Japan, &c. For *Eastern Canada,* use: le Canada de l'Est.]

orientation [ɔrjɑ̃t|a'sjõ] *n.f.* orientation; trend; guidance: *~ professionnelle,* vocational guidance. || **orienter** [-e] #3 *v. tr.* to orient; to direct; to guide; to set (map) by the compass: *une maison bien orientée,* a house with a good exposure. || **s'orienter** *v. pron.* to take one's bearings; to know one's way about: *On s'oriente à l'aide d'une carte,* You use a map to find your way around. || **orienteur** [-œ:r] *n.m.* counsellor, adviser, director: *~ professionnel,* guidance counsellor.

orifice [ɔri'fis] *n.m.* opening, hole.

originaire [ɔriʒi'nɛ:r] *adj.* native (of, *de*); → from: *Il est ~ de Québec,* He was born in Quebec City, He is from Quebec City.

origin|al, -e [ɔriʒi|'nal] *adj.* original; queer, peculiar, odd. || *n.* character, an eccentric; original (of a text): *l'original et deux copies,* the original and two copies. || **originalité** [-nali'te] *n.f.* originality.

origine [ɔri'ʒin] *n.f.* origin, source; descent, birth, extraction: *tirer son ~ de,* to originate from, with; *dès l' ~* , from the beginning; *à l' ~* , in the beginning; *d' ~ française,* of French extraction; *être à l' ~ de,* to be responsible for, to initiate. || **originel, -le** [-ɛl] *adj.* original; *le péché ~* , original sin; [×] cf. ORIGINAL.

origna|l, *pl.* **-ux** [ɔri'ɲ|al, -o] © *n.m.* moose: *panache (d' ~),* antlers, rack (of a moose).

oriole [ɔ'rjɔl] *n.f.* oriole.

orme [ɔrm] *n.m.* elm.

ornement [ɔrnə'mɑ̃] *n.m.* ornament, adornment, decoration: [R.C.] *les ornements sacerdotaux,* vestments. || **ornemental, -e** [-'tal] *adj.* ornamental. || **ornementation** [-ta'sjõ] *n.f.* decoration, embellishment, ornamentation. || **orner** [ɔr'ne] #3 *v. tr.* to adorn, to decorate; to embellish, to ornament.

ornière [ɔr'njɛ:r] *n.f.* rut, groove: *chemin à ~* , rutted road; [Fig.] *sortir de l' ~* , to get out of the rut.

ornithologie [ɔrnitɔlɔ'ʒi] *n.f.* ornithology.

orphelin, -e [ɔrfə'l|ɛ̃, -in] *adj. & n. m/f:* orphan. || **orphelinat** [-i'na] *n.m.* orphanage.

orteil [ɔr'tɛ:j] *n.m.* toe.

orthodoxe [ɔrtɔ'dɔks] *adj.* orthodox.

orthographe [ɔrtɔ'graf] *n.f.* spelling: *faute d' ~* , misspelling. || **orthographier** [-je] #3 *v. tr.* to spell.

ortie [ɔr'ti] *n.f.* nettle.

os [ɔs] *n.m.* ☞ *pl. unchanged,* [o]: bone: *ronger un ~* , to pick a bone; *être trempé jusqu'aux ~,* to be wet to the skin; to be wet through and through.

osciller [ɔsi'le] #3 *v. intr.* to oscillate.

osé, -e [o'ze] *adj.* daring, bold. [×: applies to actions, not to men], cf. INTRÉPIDE. || **oser** #3 *v. tr. & intr.* to dare, to venture.

oseille [o'zɛ:j] *n.f.* sorrel.

osier [o'zje] *n.m.* willow; *panier d' ~* , wicker basket.

ossapan [ɔsa'pɑ̃] *n.m.* [© écureuil volant] flying squirrel.

ossature [ɔs|a'ty:r] *n.f.* bone structure, framework, skeleton. || **†ossements** [-'mɑ̃] *n.mpl.* remains (of the dead); bones. || **osseu|x, -se** [-ø, -ø:z] *adj.* bony.

ostensible [ɔstɑ̃'sibl] *adj.* ostensible, patent.

ostensoir [ɔstɑ̃'swa:r] *n.m.* monstrance.

ostentation [ɔstɑ̃ta'sjõ] *n.f.* [Pej.] show, display.

otage [ɔ'ta:ʒ] *n.m.* hostage.

otarie [ɔta'ri] *n.f.* sea lion.

ôter [o'te] #3 *v. tr.* to remove; to take off, away; to deprive s.o. of sth.: *Ôtez votre chapeau,* Take off your hat; *ôter une tache* *d'un vêtement,* to remove a stain from an article of clothing. || **s'ôter** *v. pron.* to get away, to remove o.s.: *Ôtez-vous de là,* Get out of there; *Ôtez-vous du chemin,* Stand aside, Get out of the road, Get out of the way.

Ottawa [ɔta'wa] *n.f.* [Géog.] Ottawa. cf. OUTAOUAIS.

ou[1] [u] *conj.* [× Do not confuse with next entry]: or; either; else; *ou . . . ou . . .* , either . . . or; /*ou bien, ou alors*/ [stronger forms], or else.

où[2] [u] *adv.* affirm. (where) and interrog. (where?) where: *Où est-il?,* Where is he?; *Où suis-ie?,* Where am I? || *rel. pron.*/at, in, to, through/which; when: *D'où venez-vous,* Where are you from?; *Où allez-vous?,* Where are you going?; *Où en êtes-vous?,* How far have you got (with your work)?; *Par où est-il passé?,* Where, Which way/did he go?; *le temps où, le moment où,* the time when; *l'occasion où,* the occasion on which . . .

ouananiche © [wana'niʃ] *n.f.* land-locked salmon, wananish.

ouaouaron [wawa'rõ] © *n.m.* bullfrog.

ouapiti [wapi'ti] *n.m.* cf. CERF.

ouate [wat] *n.f.* [☞ *la ouate*] wadding, cotton wool. || **ouater** [wa'te] #3 *v. tr.* to wad, to pad.

oubli [u'bli] *n.m.* oblivion; oversight, omission: †*tomber dans l'* ∼, to sink into oblivion. || **oublier** [-'je] #3 *v. tr.* to forget, to neglect: *J'ai oublié de vous avertir,* I forgot to warn you. || **s'oublier** *v. pron.* to forget o.s. (i.e., not to be selfish); to be forgotten: *C'est une chose qui ne s'oublie pas facilement,* It is sth. that is not easily forgotten.|| **oublieu|x, -se** [-'jø, -'jø:z] *adj.* [Lit.] forgetful: *être* ∼ *de ses devoirs,* to be unmindful of one's duties, to be remiss.

ouest [west] *n.m.* west; westerly, western: *à l'* ∼ *de Montréal,* west of Montreal; *dans l'* ∼ *de la France,* in western France; *les Provinces de l'* ∼ , the Western Provinces; *Il habite l'* ∼ , He lives in the West.

oui [wi] *adv.* yes; *mais oui!,* yes indeed; certainly: *dire ni oui ni non,* to say neither yes nor no. || *n.m.*: *pour un* ∼ , *pour un non,* for no reason at all, at the slightest excuse; [Pol.] *les oui et les non,* the ayes and the nays.

ouï-dire [wi'di:r] *n.m. inv.* hearsay. || **ouïe** [wi] *n.f.* **1.** [sens] hearing: *avoir l'* ∼ *fine,* to be sharp of hearing. **2.** [poisson] *pl.* gill(s). || **ouïr** [wi:r] #60 *v. tr.* [rare] to hear.

ouragan [ura'gɑ̃] *n.m.* hurricane.

ourdir [ur'd|i:r] #17 *v. tr.* **1.** to warp. **2.** [Fig.] ∼ *un complot,* to hatch a plot. || **ourdisseu|r, -se** [-i'sœ:r, -i'sø:z] *n.* warper.

ourler [ur'le] #3 *v. tr.* to hem. || **ourlet** [ur'lɛ] *n.m.* hem.

ours [urs] *n.m.* pl. unchanged [in the pl., both [urs], [u:r] are heard] bear: ∼ *blanc,* polar bear; ∼ *brun,* brown bear, ∼ *gris,* grizzlly: *vendre la peau de l'* ∼ *avant de l'avoir tué,* to count one's chickens before they are hatched; *le Grand lac de l'Ours,* Great Bear Lake. || **ourse** [urs] *n.f.* she-bear; [Astr.] *la Grande Ourse,* the Big Dipper; *la Petite Ourse,* the Little Dipper. || **ourson** [-õ] *n.m.* bear's cub.

ouste [ust] *Interj.* Out, Off you go!

outaouais, -e [uta|'wɛ, -'wɛ:z] *adj.* © up, from, of Ottawa: *la rivière Outaouais, l'Outaouais,* the Ottawa river; [Fam.] *un Outaouais,* a resident of Ottawa.

outarde [u'tard] © *n.f.* Canada goose (également appelée *bernache*).

outil [u'ti] *n.m.* tool, implement. || **outillage** [-ja:ʒ] *n.m.* set of tools, equipment: *l'* ∼ *d'un port,* docking facilities. || **outiller** [-'je] #3 *v. tr.* to equip, to supply (with tools). || **s'outiller** *v. pron.* to tool up.

outrage [u'tra:ʒ] *n.m.* **1.** outrage, flagrant insult: *faire* ∼ *à qqun,* to outrage s.o., to commit an outrage against s.o. **2.** [Jur.] contempt: ∼ *à la justice,* contempt of court.|| **outrager** [-e] #5 *v. tr.* to outrage, to insult. || **outrageusement** [-øz'mɑ̃] *adv.* exceedingly. || **outrageu|x, -se** [-ø(:z)] *adj.* outrageous, insulting.

outrance [u'trɑ̃:s] *n.f.* excess: *à* ∼ , to the limit, to the death.

outre[1] [u:tr] *prép.* **1.** in addition to, apart from. †**2.** beyond: ∼ *-Atlantique,* across the Atlantic. || *adv.* further: *en* ∼ , moreover; *passer* ∼ (*à un ordre*), to ignore (an order); [Jur.] to overrule.

outre[2] [u:tr] *n.f.* (goatskin) water bottle.

outré [u'tre] *adj.* **1.** exaggerated, overdone. **2.** revolted, incensed: *J'en suis* ∼ , I am revolted by it.

outrecuidance [utrəkɥi'dɑ̃:s] *n.f.* presumption; audacity; insolence. || **outrecuidant, -e** [utrəkɥi'dɑ̃(:t)] *adj.* presumptuous, insolent; © [US] fresh.

outremer [utrə'mɛ:r] *n.m.* ultramarine. || **outre-mer** *adv.* overseas. || **outrepasser** [utrəpɑ'se] #3 *v. tr.* to go beyond, to exceed (orders, &c.).

outrer [u'tre] #3 *v. tr.* [Fig.] to provoke.

ouvert, -e [u'v|ɛ:r, -ɛrt] *adj.* opened; open;

on; [Fig.] exposed, unprotected; frank: *Laissez la porte ouverte,* Leave the door open; *Le compteur est* ~ , The meter is (turned) on; *lire Shakespeare à livre* ~ , to read S. at sight; *parler à cœur* ~ , to speak frankly. ‖ **ouvertement** [-ɛrtə'mɑ̃] *adv.* admittedly, openly. ‖ **ouverture** [-ɛr'ty:r] *n.f.* opening, hole, gap; [Mus.] overture: *l'* ~ *de la/chasse, pêche/,* the opening of the/hunting, fishing/season; *l'* ~ *de Guillaume Tell,* the William Tell Overture; *l'* ~ *du parlement fédéral,* the opening of the Federal Parliament; [Com.] *heures d'* ~ , business hours. ‖ **ouvrable** [u'vrabl] *adj.*: *jour* ~ , working day.

ouvrage [u'vra:ʒ] *n.m.* [stresses workmanship or manual labour more than ŒUVRE.] **1.** work, handiwork: *panier à* ~ , work basket; ~ *d'art,* [coll. for] bridge, viaduct, tunnel: *sans* ~ , unemployed; *avoir du cœur à l'* ~ , to enjoy one's work. **2.** book, treatise, text: ~ *technique,* technical book.

ouvreu|r, -se [u'vr|œ:r, -ø:z] *n.* (esp. f.): attendant, usher.

ouvri|er, -ère [uvri'j|e, -ɛ:r] **1.** *n.* worker, workman, mechanic; labourer: *les ouvriers du bâtiment,* workers in the building trades; *les ouvrières du vêtement,* garment workers. ‖ *adj.* working, worker: *la classe ouvrière,* the working class; *le mouvement* ~ , the labour movement; *cheville ouvrière,* kingpin.

ouvrir [u'vri:r] **ouvrant, ouvert** [u'vɛ:r] #25 *v. tr.* to open, to throw open, to turn up: ~ *la porte,* to open the door; *aller* ~ , to answer the door; ~ *le gaz,* to turn on the gas; *se faire* ~ , to be let in, [Fig.] ~ *son cœur à qqun,* to open one's heart to s.o.; ~ *un compte en banque,* to open an account in a bank.

oval, -e [ɔ'val] *adj. & n.m.* oval; egg-shaped.

ovation [ɔva'sjõ] *n.f.* ovation.

oxyder (s') [(s)ɔksi'de] #3 *v. tr. & pron.* to oxidize.

oxygène [ɔksi'ʒɛn] *n.m.* oxygen

P

P, p [pe] *n.m.* (the letter) P, p.

pacage [pa'ka:ʒ] *n.m.* pasture.

pacificat|eur, -rice [pasifika't|œ:r, -ris] *n. m/f* pacifier. ‖ *adj.* pacifying, peace-making. ‖ **pacification** [pasifikasjõ] *n.f.* pacification. ‖ **pacifier** [pasi'fje] #3 *v. tr.* [pays] to pacify; [personne] to appease. ‖ **se pacifier** *v. pr.* to calm down. ‖ **pacifique** [pasi'fik] *adj.* peace-loving, pacific: *le Pacifique,* the Pacific Ocean. ‖ **pacifiquement** [-'mɑ̃] *adv.* peaceably, quietly. ‖ **pacifisme** [pasi'fism] *n.m.* pacifism.

pacotille [pakɔ'tij] *n.f.*: *marchandises de* ~ , shoddy goods; trash.

pacte [pakt] *n.m.* pact, agreement; covenant. ‖ **pactiser** [-i'ze] #3 *v. intr.*: ~ *avec l'ennemi,* to treat with the enemy; ~ *avec sa conscience,* to compromise with o.'s conscience.

padre [pa'dre] © *n.m.* [R.C.] padre cf. AUMÔNIER.

paf [paf] **1.** *interj.* [onomat.] bang! **2.** *adj. inv.* [Fam.] tipsy, tight.

pagaie[1] [pa'gɛ] *n.f.* (canoe) paddle.

pagaïe,[2] **pagaille** [pa'ga:j] *n.f.* [pej.] mess, disorder: *en* ~ , at random; [slang] snafu.

paganisme [paga'nism] *n.m.* paganism; [Col.] heathendom.

pagayer [pagɛ'je] #11 *v. intr. & tr.* to paddle, cf. PAGAIE [1].

page[1] [pa:ʒ] *n.f.* page (of a book): *de la première à la dernière* ~ , from cover to cover; [Fig.] *être à la* ~ , to be up to date.

page[2] [pa:ʒ] *n.m.* page boy.

paie,[1] &c. cf. PAYER. ‖ **paie**[2] [pɛ] *n.f.* [ouvrier] wages: *jour m de* ~ , payday. cf. PAYE. ‖ **paiement** [pɛ'mɑ̃] *n.m.* payment: *effectuer un* ~ , to make a payment.

païen, -ne [pa'j|ɛ̃, -ɛn] *adj. & n.* pagan; [Péj.] heathen.

paillasse [pa'jas] *n.f.* **1.** straw mattress, pallet. *n.m.* buffoon. || **paillasson** [-õ] *n.m.* (door-) mat. || **paille** [pɑ:j] *n.* **1.** straw; chaff: *chapeau de* ~ , straw hat; *jaune* ~ , straw-coloured; †*être sur la* ~ , to be penniless. **2.** mote: *la* ~ *et la poutre*, the mote and the beam. **3.** flaw. || **pailleter** [paj'te] #8 *v. tr.* to spangle. || **paillette** [pa'jɛt] *n.f.* spangle; flake (of mica, &c.), grain (of gold).

pain [pɛ̃] *n.m.* **1.** bread, loaf: *du* ~ , bread; *un* ~ , a loaf; *un petit* ~ , a roll; ~ *de ménage*, © ~ *canadien*, home-made bread; ~ *grillé*, toast; ~ *bis*, brown bread, whole-wheat bread; © ~ *français*, French bread; ~ *d'épice*, gingerbread; *Il a du* ~ *sur la planche*, He has money put by. His work is cut out for him; *Il l'a eu pour une bouchée de* ~ , He bought it for a song. **2.** cake: *un* ~ *de savon*, a cake of soap; *un* ~ *de sucre*, a sugar loaf; *un* ~ *à cacheter*, a sealing wafer.

pair [pɛ:r] *adj. & n.m.* equal, even (number) cf. IMPAIR: *Les numéros pairs (d'une rue)*, the even numbers (of a street); *au* ~ , at par; with room and board, but no salary; *aller de* ~ *avec*, to be on a par with; *hors (de) pair*, unrivalled. || **Pair** [pɛ:r] *n.m.* peer, equal: *la Chambre des Pairs* [Br.] the House of Lords. || **paire** [pɛ:r] *n.f.* pair; couple, brace (of dogs, &c.): *une* ~ *de ciseaux*, a pair of scissors.

paisible [pɛ'zibl] *adj.* peaceful, quiet, calm, cf. PAIX. || **paisiblement** [-ə'mɑ̃] *adv.* peacefully.

paître [pɛ:tr] #72 *v. tr.* [cattle] to graze. || *v. intr.* to feed, graze; [Fam.] *envoyer (qqun)* ~ , to send s.o. packing.

paix [pɛ] *n.f.* peace; quiet, stillness, peacefulness; [Polit.] *signer la* ~ , to sign a peace treaty; *laisser la* ~ *à qqun*, to leave s.o. alone.

Pakistan, le [pakis'tɑ̃] *n.m.* Pakistan.

palais [pa'lɛ] *n.m.* **1.** palace; courthouse, law courts: *(le)* ~ *du Commerce*, (the) Show Mart; ~ *de Justice*, courthouse. **2.** palate (roof of the mouth).

palan [pa'lɑ̃] *n.m.* pulley block; tackle.

pale [pal] *n.f.* blade (of oar, propeller).

pâle [pɑ:l] *adj.* pale, pallid, colourless: ~ *comme un linge*, as white as a sheet; ~ *de rage*, livid with rage; *teint* ~ , light complexion; †*visage* ~ , paleface; *bleu* ~ , pale blue.

palefrenier [palfrə'nje] *n.m.* groom.

Palestine [palɛs'tin] *n.f.* Palestine; [Rel. geog.] Holy Land.

paletot [pal'to] *n.m.* topcoat, overcoat.

palette [pa'lɛt] *n.f.* [rame] blade, paddle; palette.

pâleur [pɑ'lœ:r] *n.f.* pallor.

palier [pa'lje] *n.m.* **1.** landing (of staircase); cf. ÉTAGE: [Fr.] *Ils demeurent sur le même* ~ (i.e. au même étage), They live on the same floor. **2.** stage, level: *en* ~ , on the level; *La courbe marque un* ~ , The graph/shows a plateau, levels off.

pâlir [pɑl|i:r] #17 *v. intr.* to grow, to turn pale, to blench: *faire* ~ , to throw into the shade, to outshine.

palissade [pali'sad] *n.f.* paling, picket fence; palisade, [d'un fort] stockade.

pâlissant, -e [-i'sɑ̃, -i'sɑ̃:t] *adj.* turning pale.

palliatif [pallja'tif] *n.m.* palliative.

†**pallier** [pal'lj|e] #3 *v. tr.* to palliate, to mitigate: *pour* ~ *ce défaut*, in order to offset this weakness.

palme [palm] *n.f.* **1.** palm: *remporter la* ~ , to bear the palm. **2.** fin (for skin-diving). || **palmé, -e** [-e] *adj.* webbed: *aux pieds palmés*, web-footed. || **palmier** [-je] *n.m.* palm-tree. || **palmipède** [-i'pɛd] *n.m. & adj.* palmiped, web-footed.

pâlot, -te [palo, -ɔt] *adj.* pale.

palpable [pal'pabl] *adj.* palpable; [Fig.] tangible. || **palper** [pal'pe] #3 *v. tr.* to feel, to touch.

palpitant, -e [palpi't|ɑ̃, -ɑ̃:t] *adj.* palpitating, throbbing; [Fig.] thrilling. || **palpitation** [-a'sjõ] *n.f.* throb, quiver; thrill; palpitation. || **palpiter** [-e] #3 *v. intr.* to throb, to quiver, to flutter.

pamphlet [pɑ̃'flɛ] *n.m.* [×] lampoon, satirical pamphlet, cf. BROCHURE.

pamplemousse [pɑ̃plə'mus] *n.m.* grapefruit.

pan[1] [pɑ̃] *n.m.* [d'habit] skirt, tail; [de polyèdre] side; [de mur] part: *à pans coupés*, canted.

pan[2]! [pɑ̃] *interj.* [*onomat.*] Bang! cf. PAO, PAF.

panacée [pana'se] *n.f.* panacea.

panache [pa'naʃ] *n.m.* plume; [Fig.] flourish, florid style; [Loc.] *faire* ~ , [car] to turn over. || **panacher** [-e] #3 *v. tr. & intr.* to mix, to variegate.

panais [pa'nɛ] *n.m.* parsnip.

Panama [pana'ma] *n.m.* Panama: *zone du canal de* ~ , Panama Canal Zone; *un panama*, a Panama hat.

pancarte [pɑ̃'kart] *n.f.* notice, sign; placard, showcard.

pancréas [pɑ̃kre'a:s] *n.m.* pancreas.

paneterie [pant'ri] © *n.f.* cupboards (in kitchen); bread-store. || **panetière** [pan'tjɛ:r] *n.f.* bread bag, bread bin.

panier [pa'nje] *n.m.* **1.** basket, hamper; waste basket: *jeter au* ~ , to throw away; *C'est à mettre au même* ~ , They go together; ~ *à ouvrage*, work basket; ~ *à salade*, salad washer [Fig.] patrol wagon; *le dessus du* ~, the cream of the crop; *être un* ~ *percé*, to be a spendthrift. || **2.** [couture] hoop.

panique [pa'nik] *n.f.* panic: *être pris de* ~, to panic.

panne [pan] *n.f.* **1.** breakdown (of car, &c.), failure: *avoir une* ~, to have engine trouble; *avoir une* ~ *d'essence*, to run out of gas; *Il y a eu une* ~ *d'électricité*, The power was off. **2.** [Naut.] *être en* ~, to lie to; *mettre en* ~, to heave to; [voilier] *rester en* ~, to be becalmed.

panneau [pa'no] *n.m.* panel; *panneaux*, panels, panelling.

panorama [panɔra'ma] *n.m.* panorama.

panse [pɑ̃:s] *n.f.* belly, paunch.

pansement [pɑ̃s|'mɑ̃] *n.m.* dressing (of wounds): *faire un* ~ *d'urgence*, to put on a first-aid dressing. || **panser** [-e] #3 *v. tr.* to dress, bandage (wounds). [☞ Do not confuse with PENSER, to think.]

pantalon [pɑ̃ta'lɔ̃] *n.m.* (pair of) trousers; pants.

pantelant, -e [pɑ̃t'lɑ̃(:t)] *adj.* panting.

panthère [pɑ̃'tɛ:r] *n.f.* panther; © mountain lion.

pantin [pɑ̃'tɛ̃] *n.m.* puppet: ~ *articulé*, string puppet.

pantomime [pɑ̃tɔ'mim] *n.f.* pantomime.

pantouflard [pɑ̃tu'fla:r] *n.m.* [Fam. & Péj.] a stay-at-home.

pantoufle [pɑ̃'tufl] *n.f.* [usual. pl.] slipper(s): *être en pantoufles*, to be wearing slippers.

pao [pau] © *onomat.* Bang!

paon, -ne [pɑ̃, pan] *n.* peacock, pea-hen.

papa [pa'pa] *n.m.* [Fam.] dad, daddy.

papal, -e [pa'p|al] *adj.* papal. || **papauté** [-o'te] *n.f.* Papacy. || **pape** [pap] *n.m.* the Pope.

paperasse [pap'ras] *n.f.* [péj.] papers, paper work, red tape. || **paperasserie** [-'ri] *n.f.* red tape. || **paperassi|er, -ère** [-'sje, -'sjɛ:r] *adj.* given to red tape.

papeterie [pap(ə)t'ri] *n.f.* **1.** paper mill; paper trade. **2.** stationery; stationer's: *librairie-papeterie*, book store. || **papetier** [pap(ə)'tje] *n.m.* stationer; paper mill worker.

papier [pa'pje] *n.m.* paper: ~ *collant*, gummed tape; ~ *d'emballage*, brown paper; ~ *à en-tête*, letterhead; ~ *hygiénique*, toilet paper; ~ *à lettres*, letter paper, note paper; ~ *-monnaie*, paper money; ~ *paraffiné*, waxed paper, ~ *peint*, wall paper, ~ *de soie*, tissue paper; ~ *de verre*, sandpaper: [Fig., Journ.] *faire un* ~ *sur*, to cover (a story); *être dans les petits papiers de qqun*, to be in s.o.'s good books; *Ça marche bien sur le* ~, It works well on paper.

papille [pa'pi:j] *n.f.* papilla: ~ *gustative*, taste bud.

papillon [papi|'jɔ̃] *n.m.* butterfly; ~ *de nuit*, moth. || **papilloter** [-jɔ'te] #3 *v. intr.* [œil] to blink; [lumière] to flicker.

papiste [pa'pist] *n. & adj.* papist, popish.

Pâque(s) [pɑ:k] *n.m. usual. pl.* Easter: *la pâque, f.* passover; *la semaine de* ~, Easter week; *la fête de* ~, Easter (Sunday); *à* ~ *ou à la Trinité*, when the cows come home. [☞ *n.f.* in the following instances]: *faire ses Pâques*, to take communion at Easter; *Pâques fleuries*, Palm Sunday.

paquebot [pak'bo] *n.m.* [Naut.] steamer; [large vessel] liner: *paquebot-poste m.*, mail steamer, cf. MALLE.

pâquerette [pɑk'rɛt] *n.f.* daisy.

paquet [pa'kɛ] *n.m.* **1.** parcel, package; bundle: *faire un* ~, to make up a parcel; [Fig.] *faire ses paquets*, to pack up, to leave; ~ *recommandé*, registered parcel; [Fam.] *un* ~ *(de . . .)*, a lot (of . . .), a batch (of). cf. COLIS. **2.** *risquer le* ~, to chance it.

par [pa:r] *prép.* **1.** by: ~ *erreur*, by mistake. **2.** through, out of: ~ *le trou de la serrure*, through the keyhole; ~ *la fenêtre*, out of the window. **3.** on, in: ~ *une belle journée*, on a fine day; ~ *gros temps*, in rough weather. **4.** per; a, an: *dix dollars* ~ *jour*, ten dollars a day. **5.** from: ~ *un sentiment de culpabilité*, from a sense of guilt. **6.** [Loc. adv.] || **par avion** [-a'vjɔ̃] by air mail, by air. || **par-ci, par-là** [parsi, par'la] here and there. || **par delà** [par|də'la] beyond. || **par derrière** [dɛ'rjɛ:r] at the back, the back way. || **par devant** [də'vɑ̃] in front, before. || **par ici** [pari'si] this way. || **par là,** that way, thereby: *en passer* ~, to knuckle under. || **par le bas, par en bas** [-lə'bɑ, -ɑ̃'bɑ] from, through/the bottom, along the lower road. || **par le haut, par en haut** [-lə'o, -ɑ̃'o] from, through/the top, along the upper road.

para [pa'ra] *n.m.* [Fam.] paratrooper.

parachute [para'ʃyt] *n.m.* parachute: *sauter en* ~, to parachute, to bail out.

parade [pa'rad] *n.f.* show [× for *Xmas, Easter/parade*, use *défilé m*]; [Fig.] *faire* ~ *de*, to display / show off . . . ; *à la* ~, on parade; *être exposé sur un lit de* ~, to lie in state. || **parader** [para'de] #3 *v. intr.* to show off.

paradis [para'di] *n.m.* **1.** paradise. **2.** [Théât.] top gallery, [Br.] the gods.

paradoxe [para'dɔks] *n.m.* paradox.
parages [pa'ra:ʒ] *n.m.pl.* region, area: *dans ces* ~ , around here, in these parts.
paragraphe [para'graf] *n.m.* paragraph.
parais, paraît, &c. cf. PARAÎTRE.
paraître [pa'r|ɛ:tr], **paraissant** [-ɛ'sɑ̃], **paru** [-y] #40 *v. intr.* **1.** to appear. **2.** to show off: *Il aime* ~ , He likes to impress people. **3.** to come out: *vient de* ~ , just out; *faire* ~ , to publish. **4.** to seem, to look: *Il paraît se plaire ici,* He seems to like it here. **5.** [Loc. impers.] *Il paraît que la bourse monte,* It seems that the stock market is going up; *à ce qu'il paraît,* so it would seem.
parallèle [paral'lɛl] *adj. & n. m/f.* parallel: *établir un* ~ , to draw a parallel; *le 60ᵉ* ~ , the 60th parallel; *tracer une* ~ , to draw a parallel.
paralyser [parali'z|e] #3 *v. tr.* to paralyze; [Fig.] to hamper, to hamstring. || **paralysie** [-i] *n.f.* paralysis; palsy.
parapet [para'pɛ] *n.m.* parapet; breastwork.
paraphe [pa'raf] *n.m.* **1.** paraph, flourish (after signature). **2.** (one's) initials: *apposer son* ~ (au bas d'un document officiel), to initial.
paraphrase [para'fra:z] *n.f.* paraphrase.
parapluie [para'plɥi] *n.m.* umbrella.
parasite [para'zit] *n.m.* parasite, sponger. || **parasitisme** [-ism] *n.m.* [Biol., Méd.] parasitism; sponging.
parasol [para'sɔl] *n.m.* parasol, sunshade.
paratonnerre [paratɔ'nɛ:r] *n.m.* lightning rod.
paravent [para'vɑ̃] *n.m.* folding screen.
parbleu [par'blø] *interj.* Rather!, Sure!, You bet!
parc [park] *n.m.* **1.** park. **2.** [propriété privée] grounds: *le* ~ *de l'hôtel,* the hotel grounds. || **parcage** [-a:ʒ] *n.m.* parking lot; penning in (of sheep).
parcelle [par'sɛl] *n.f.* particle; lot, plot.
parce que ['pars(ə)kə] *conj.* because [☞ not to be confused with *par ce que* . . . , by what . . .].
parchemin [parʃə'mɛ̃] *n.m.* parchment.
parcimonieu|x, -se [parsimɔ'njø(:z)] *adj.* parsimonious.
parcourir [parku'r|i:r], **parcourant** [-ɑ̃] **parcouru** [-y] #24 *v. tr.* to cover, to go all over, to glance through: *Il a parcouru la distance en une heure,* He covered the distance in one hour; *Il a parcouru toute la ville,* He went all over the town; *Je ne l'ai que parcouru,* I only glanced through it.
parcours,[1] cf. PARCOURIR.
parcours[2] [par'ku:r] *n.m.* distance covered, route; run, trip: *sur tout le* ~ , along the route; *Il lit pendant le* ~ , He reads during the trip.
parcourt, cf. PARCOURIR.
par-dessous [pardə'su] *adv.* underneath. || **par-dessus** [pardə'sy] *prép., adv.* over, on top: ~ *la clôture,* over the fence; *Mettez-le* ~ , Put it on top.
pardessus [pardə'sy] *n.m.* [pl. unchanged] **1.** overcoat. **2.** *pl.* © overshoes.
pardon [par'd|ɔ̃] *n.m.* **1.** forgiveness, pardon: *pardon!,* I beg your pardon, excuse me, sorry!; *Je vous en demande* ~ , Please forgive me; *demander* ~ *à qqun de qqch.,* to ask s.o.'s pardon for sth. **2.** pilgrimage (in Brittany). || **pardonnable** [-ɔ'nabl] *adj.* excusable, pardonable. || **pardonner** [-ɔ'ne] #3 *v. tr.* to forgive, to pardon; to excuse: *pardonnez-moi si* . . . , excuse me if . . . ; ~ *à qqun d'avoir fait qqch.,* to forgive s.o. for having done sth.
pare-brise [par'bri:z] *n.m.* windshield. || **pare-chocs** [par'ʃɔk] *n.m.* [Auto.] bumper.
pareil, -le [pa'rɛj] *adj.* **1.** same, identical, alike: *J'en voudrais un* ~ , I'd like one exactly like it. **2.** similar: *demain à pareille heure,* same time tomorrow; *Je n'ai jamais rien vu de* ~ , I have never seen anything like it. **3.** such, such a: *Comment a-t-il pu dire une chose pareille,* How could he say such a thing! || *n.* equal, match: *Il n'a pas son* ~ , He does not have his equal; *C'est du* ~ *au même,* It's six of one and half a dozen of the other; *sans* ~ , unequalled; *rendre la pareille à qqun,* to pay s.o. back in his own coin. || **pareillement** [-'mɑ̃] *adv.* likewise.
parement [par'mɑ̃] *n.m.* ornament; [de manche] cuff, [de col] facing; [de pierre] facing.
parent, -e [pa'rɑ̃|(:t)] *n.* **1.** *m.pl.*: *les parents,* the father and mother, the parents; *l'Association des Parents d'élèves,* © *l'École des Parents,* the Parent-Teacher Association (P.T.A.), the Home & School Ass'n; *ses grands-parents,* his/her/grandparents. **2.** relative, relation: *un proche* ~ , a close relative; *le plus proche* ~ , the next of kin. || **parenté** [-'te] *n.f.* relationship, kinship; © relatives.
parenthèse [parɑ̃'tɛ:z] *n.f.* parenthesis: *entre parenthèses,* **1.** between parentheses. **2.** [Fig.] incidentally, by the way.
parer [pa'r|e] #3 *v. tr.* **1.** to adorn. **2.**

to parry, to ward off (a blow, *un coup*). 3. to provide: ~ *aux besoins immédiats*, to provide for immediate needs. || **se parer** *v. pron.* to adorn o.s., to put on one's best finery.

paresse [pa'rɛs] *n.f.* laziness, idleness: ~ *d'esprit*, mental laziness. || **paresser** [-e] #3 *v. intr.* to laze about. || **paresseusement** [-øz mã] *adv.* lazily. || **paresseu|x, -se** [-ø(:z)] *adj.* lazy. || *n.* lazy fellow.

parfait, -e [par'fɛ|(t)] *adj.* perfect; complete, full. || *Interj.* Capital!: *C'est ~ !*, That's fine. || **parfaitement** [-t'mã] *adv.* perfectly; undoubtedly, exactly. [☞ A strong form of assent, often *mais ~ !* = DEFINITELY,] of course! certainly!

parfois [par'fwa] *adv.* sometimes, occasionally, at times, once in a while.

parfum [par'f|œ̃] *n.m.* perfume, fragrance, scent; [of wines] bouquet. || **parfumer** [-y'me] #3 *v. tr.* to perfume. || **se parfumer** *v. pron.* to use perfume (on o.s.). || **parfumerie** [-ym'ri] *n.f.* perfumery. || **parfumeu|r, -se** [-y'mœ:r, -y'mø:z] *n.* perfumer.

pari [pa'r|i] *n.m.* bet, wager. || **parier** [-je] #3 *v. tr.* to bet, to wager.

Paris [pa'ri] *n.m.* Paris. || **parisien, -ne** [-'zjɛ̃, -'zjɛn] *n. & adj.* Parisian.

parjure [par'ʒ|y:r] *n.m.* perjury: *commettre un ~*, to commit perjury. || *n. m/f* perjurer. || *adj.* perjured: *un témoin ~*, a perjured witness. || **se parjurer** [-y're] #3 *v. pron.* to perjure o.s.

parlant, -e [par'l|ã(:t)] *adj.* talking: *un film ~*, a talking picture; *le sujet ~*, the native speaker (of a language).

parlement [-ə'mã] *n.* parliament: *au ~*, in Parliament. || **parlementaire** [-'tɛ:r] *adj.* parliamentary; → Parliament: © *la Colline ~*, Parliament Hill. || *n.m.* white flag bearer (to arrange truce). || **parlementer** [-te] #3 *v. tr.* to parley.

parler[1] [parl|e] #3 *v. tr. & intr.* to speak, to talk: *Il parle bien*, He is a good speaker; *N'en parlons plus*, Let's say no more about it; *Il n'en a pas parlé*, He did not mention it; ~ *plusieurs langues*, to speak several languages; *Ils ne se parlent plus*, They are no longer on speaking terms; *Tu parles*, [Slang] And how! || **parler**[2] *n.m.* speech, way of speaking, dialect, language: *La Société du bon ~ français*, The Association for the Encouragement of Pure French; *un ~ régional*, a regional dialect; *avoir son franc ~*, to speak one's mind, not to mince words. || **parleur** [-œ:r] talker [only in]: *un beau ~*, a windbag, a glib talker; *haut- ~*, loudspeaker. || **parloir** [-wa:r] *n.m.* parlour.

parmi [par'mi] *prép.* among.

parodie [parɔ'd|i] *n.f.* parody. || **parodier** [-je] #3 *v. tr.* to parody; to travesty; to burlesque.

paroi [pa'rwa] *n.f.* partition, wall; inner side.

paroisse [pa'rw|a:s] *n.f.* parish. || **paroissial, -e** [parwa'sj|al] *adj.* parochial, → parish. || **paroissien, -ne** [-ɛ̃, -ɛn] *n.* 1. parishioner. 2. prayer-book.

parole [pa'rɔl] *n.f.* 1. word, saying: *ses propres paroles*, his, her/own words; *Il a pris la ~ à la réunion*, He spoke at the meeting; *Il ne m'adresse jamais la ~*, He never speaks to me; *donner la ~ à*, to recognize; *Il a la ~*, He has the floor; *Il a la ~ facile*, He speaks easily. 2. promise, word (of honour): *Je vous donne ma ~*, I give you my word; *libéré sur ~*, released on parole.

paroxysme [parɔk'sism] *n.m.* paroxysm, culminating point.

parquer [par'ke] #3 *v. tr.* 1. to pen (sheep). 2. to park (vehicle).

parquet [par'kɛ] *n.m.* 1. hardwood floor. 2. [Jur. Fr.] public prosecutor's office. 3. [Bourse] ring.

parrain [pa'r|ɛ̃] *n.m.* 1. godfather: *être ~ de*, to stand godfather to. 2. sponsor. || **parrainage** [-ɛ'na:ʒ] *n.m.* sponsorship.

pars, cf. PARTIR.

parsemer [parsə'me] # 9 *v. tr.* to strew, dot, sprinkle.

part [pa:r] *n.f.* part, share, lot, side, interest: *à ~*, aside; *autre ~*, elsewhere; *quelque ~*, somewhere; *J'ai vu ça quelque ~*, That rings a bell; *nulle ~*, nowhere; *d'une ~*, on the one hand; *d'autre ~*, on the other hand; *de la ~ de*, from; *pour ma ~*, as for me, I for one; *prendre ~ à*, to take part in; *faire la ~ de*, to make allowance for; *faire ~ de*, to announce; *faire- ~*, announcement.

partage [par'ta|:ʒ] *n.m.* sharing, division, partition: *faire le ~ de*, to share, to divide; *le ~ de la Pologne*, the partition of Poland; *échoir en ~ à qqun*, to fall to s.o.'s lot; [Fig.] *sans partage*, undivided. || **partager** [-'ʒe] #5 *v. tr.* to share, to divide [Argot] to divvy: *Je partage votre avis*, I share your views; *Les avis sont partagés*, Opinions are divided.

partance [par'tã:s] *n.f.* departure: *en ~ pour . . .*, bound for . . . .

partenaire [partə'nɛ:r] *n.m.* partner.

parterre [par'tɛ:r] *n.m.* flower-bed; [Théât.] pit.

parti [par'ti] *n.m.* **1.** party; side, part, cause: *un ~ politique,* a political party; *prendre le ~ de qqun,* to take s.o.'s side; *prendre ~ pour . . . contre . . . ,* to side with . . . , against; *être de ~ pris,* to be prejudiced. **2.** decision, course of action: *prendre le ~ de faire qqch.,* to decide to do sth.; *en prendre son ~ ,* to be resigned to it. **3.** advantage: *tirer ~ de,* to take advantage of, to turn to account; *tirer le meilleur ~ de,* to make the most of. **4.** *faire un mauvais ~ à,* to rough up, to set upon.

parti, -e [par'ti] cf. PARTIR.

partial, -e [par'sjal] *adj.* partial, biased, one-sided. || **partialité** [-i'te] *n.f.* partiality, bias.

participation [partisipa'sjõ] *n.f.* contribution (à œuvre de charité), participation (à organisation). || **participe** [parti'sip] *n.m.* [Gram.] participle. || **participer** [-e] #3 *v. intr.* to share (in, *à*); to take part (in, *à*); to partake (of, *de*).

particulariser [partikylari|'ze] #3 *v. tr.* to particularize; to specify. || **particularité** [-'te] *n.f.* peculiarity, characteristic; detail.

particule [parti'kyl] *n.f.* particle.

particuli|er, -ère [partiku'lj|e, -ɛːr] *adj.* particular, peculiar, special; odd, extraordinary. [Fig.] personal: *les intérêts particuliers,* private interests; *un talent ~ (de),* a special talent (for); *un cas ~ ,* a special, an unusual/case; *une chambre particulière,* a private room; *Cela lui est ~ ,* It is peculiar to him. || †*n.m.* private citizen, person; individual: *en ~ ,* privately, as a private citizen. || **particulièrement** [-ɛr'mã] *adv.* in particular, particularly, especially.

partie [par|'ti] *n.f.* **1.** part, share, lot: *chanter la ~ de ténor,* to sing the tenor part; *les parties du corps,* the parts of the body; *faire ~ de,* to be part of, to be a member of. **2.** line of business, occupation: *Ce n'est pas sa ~ ,* It is not his line. **3.** game, contest: *faire une ~ de tennis,* to play a game of tennis; *Nous avons fait ~ nulle,* It was a tie; *faire la ~ belle à qqun,* to make it easy for s.o. **4.** party: *avoir affaire à forte ~ ,* to have s.o. to reckon with; *se porter ~ civile,* to put in a claim for damages; *avoir ~ liée avec qqun,* to be in league with s.o. **5.** [gathering] party: © *~ d'huîtres,* oyster party. **6.** [Loc.] *en grande ~ ,* largely; *prendre à ~ ,* to take to task. || **partiel, -le** [-'sjɛl] *adj.* partial, in part. || **partiellement** [-sjɛl'mã] *adv.* partially, partly.

partir [par'tiːr], **partant, parti** #26 *v. intr.* **1.** to leave, to go away: *~ en vacances,* to go on one's vacation; *~ du pied gauche,* to get off on the wrong foot. **2.** to go off: *Le fusil partit tout seul,* The rifle went off by itself. **3.** *faire ~ ,* to send off; to wipe off (a stain, *une tache*). **4.** *~ à rire,* to burst out laughing: *Cela part d'un bon cœur,* It is meant kindly. **5.** to part: *avoir maille à ~ avec qqun,* to have a bone to pick with s.o. **6.** [Loc.] *à ~ de,* from; after: *à ~ de maintenant,* from now on.

partisan, -ne [parti'zã] *n. m/f* supporter; believer (in, *de*); [Mil.] guer(r)illa: *guerre f de partisans,* guerilla warfare.

partition [parti'sjõ] *n.f.* [Mus.] score [× PARTITION].

partout [par'tu] *adv.* everywhere: *~ où,* wherever; *~ ailleurs,* anywhere else.

paru [pa'ry] cf. PARAÎTRE.

parure [pa'ryːr] *n.f.* ornament; finery; set of jewellery.

parution [pary'sjõ] *n.f.* appearance; [livres] publication.

parvenir [parvə'n|iːr], **parvenant** [-ã], **parvenu** [-y] #22 *v. intr.* conj. ÊTRE. **1.** to reach: *Votre lettre m'est parvenue hier,* Your letter reached me yesterday. **2.** to succeed (in, *à*). || **parvenu, -e** [-y] cf. PARVENIR. || *n.m.* parvenu, upstart, vulgarian.

parviendrai; parvienne; parviens; parvient; parvins, &c. cf. PARVENIR.

pas[1] [pɑ] *n.m.* **1.** step, pace; footprint, footfall; walk, gait: *faire quelques ~ ,* to take a few steps; *être au ~ ,* to be in step; *ne pas être au ~ ,* to be out of step; *marcher à grands ~ ,* to stride; *~ à ~ ,* step by step; *à ~ comptés,* with measured tread; *à ~ de loup, à ~ feutrés,* stealthily; *avancer à ~ de géant,* to make rapid strides; *allonger, hâter le ~ ,* to quicken one's pace; *retourner sur ses ~ ,* to retrace one's steps; *faire un faux ~ ,* to slip; *J'y vais de ce ~ ,* I am going there right away; *emboîter le ~ ,* to follow in the footsteps of. **2.** [Fig.] *un ~ de clerc,* a blunder; *un mauvais ~ ,* a fix, a hole; *avoir le ~ sur,* to have precedence over; *céder le ~ à,* to stand aside for. **3.** threshold; strait: *sur le ~ de sa porte,* on his doorstep; *le Pas de Calais,* the Straits of Dover.

pas[2] [pɑ] *adv.* [second half of neg. form *ne . . . pas*; the *ne* is often slurred in quick speech; the stress is on *pas*]: *Je ne sais ~ ,* I don't know; *Je n'en ai ~ ,* I don't have any; *Ne ~ signer,* Do not sign; *~ du tout,* not at all; *presque ~ ,* hardly any.

pascal, -e [pas'kal] *adj.* Paschal: *le temps* ~, Eastertide, cf. PÂQUES.

passable [pɑ'sabl] *adj.* [route] passable; [Fig.] tolerable, fair. || **passablement** [-ə'mã] *adv.* tolerably, fairly.

passage [pa's|a:ʒ] *n.m.* passage, crossing: ~ *couvert*, breezeway; ~ *à niveau*, railway crossing, grade crossing; *barrer le* ~, to block the way; *livrer* ~, to let through; *s'ouvrir, se frayer un* ~, to push one's way through. || **passage|r, -ère** [-a'ʒe, -a'ʒɛ:r] *n.* [×] passenger (on ship, plane). || *adj.* passing, fleeting.

passant, -e [-ã(:t)] *n.* passer-by. *adj.* frequented: *une rue passante*, a busy street. || **passe** [pɑ:s] *n.f.* pass [at football, in hypnotism]; channel, fairway; [Fig.] *être en* ~ *de réussir*, to be about to succeed; *être dans une mauvaise* ~, to be in a tight spot; *mot de* ~, password. || **passé, -e** [pɑ'se] *adj.* past, gone by; faded: *Il a quarante ans passés*, He is over forty; *la semaine passée*, last week; *une couleur passée*, a faded colour. || *n.m.* past; [Gram.] the past tense: *dans le* ~, in the past; *mettre le verbe au* ~, to put the verb in the past. || *prép.* after, past, beyond: ~ *dix heures*, after ten o'clock; ~ *le coin*, beyond the corner. || **passe-partout** [-par'tu] *n.m.* master key: [cadre] passe-partout. || **passe-passe** [pɑs'pɑ:s]: *un tour de* ~, a sleight of hand. || **passeport** [pɑs'pɔ:r] *n.m.* passport.

passer [pɑ'se] #3 *v. intr.* [☞ conj. AVOIR & ÊTRE] **1.** to go by, to walk by, to ride by [according to transportation used]: *regarder* ~ *les gens*, to watch people go by; *en passant*, in passing. **2.** to go, to come (by way of, *par*): *Par où êtes-vous passé?* Which way did you go? **3.** to drop in, to stop by: *Je passerai vous prendre à neuf heures*, I'll stop by for you at nine. **4.** *en* ~ *par là*, to yield, to knuckle under. **5.** to pass, to slip by: *le temps passe vite*, time goes quickly; *faire* ~ *le temps*, to while time away. **6.** to pass away: *Mes paroles ne passeront pas*, My words shall not pass away. **7.** *Passons!*, Let's skip it!, Never mind! **8.** ~ *outre à* (une objection), to override. **9.** ~ *pour*, to be regarded as: *Il peut se faire* ~ *pour russe*, He can pass himself off as a Russian. **10.** [Loc.] *faire* ~, to send through, to get through (a message); *faire* ~ *une douleur*, to relieve a pain. || *v. pron.* **1.** to happen: *Qu'est-ce qui se passe?*, What's happening?, What's going on? **2.** to do without: *Il faudra s'en* ~, We'll have to do without it. || *v. tr.* **1.** to get through, across, to ferry: ~ *qqch. en contrebande*, to smuggle sth. through; ~ *les gens en bac*, to ferry people across. **2.** to pass: *Passez-moi le sel*, Pass me the salt. **3.** to get over, across: ~ *une rivière*, to get across a river. **4.** [time] to spend: ~ *la soirée à lire*, to spend the evening reading. **5.** to take (an exam, *un examen*): *Il m'a fait* ~ *un test*, He gave me a test. **6.** to put or slip on: ~ *un veston*, to put on a coat. **7.** to excuse: *passez-moi l'expression*, if I may use the phrase. **8.** to go on (one's way, *son chemin*).

passerelle [pɑs'rɛl] *n.f.* foot bridge; [Naut.] bridge; gangway.

passe-temps [pɑs'tã] *n.m. inv.* pastime.

†passeur [pɑ'sœ:r] *n.m.* ferry man, cf. TRAVERSE.

passible [pa'sibl] *adj.* liable (to/for, *de*).

passi|f, -ve [pa's|if, -i:v] *adj.* passive, submissive. || *n.m.* passive form.

passion [pa'sj|õ] *n.f.* **1.** passion: *à la* ~, passionately. **2.** agony, great suffering: *la* ~ *de Notre-Seigneur*, the Passion of our Lord. || **passionnant, -e** [-ɔ'nã(:t)] *adj.* thrilling, fascinating. || **passionné, -e** [-ɔ'ne] *adj.* passionate, impassioned, passionately fond of. || **passionnel, -le** [-ɔ'nɛl] *adj.* motivated by passion: *crime* ~, crime due to jealousy. || **passionnément** [-ɔne'mã] *adv.* passionately. || **passionner** [-ɔ'ne] #3 *v. tr.* to arouse, to excite the interest of. || **se passionner** *v. pron.* to be passionately fond of: *Il se passionne pour la philatélie*, → Stamp-collecting is a passion with him.

passoire [pa'swa:r] *n.f.* strainer: ~ *à légumes*, colander.

pastel [pas'tɛl] *n.m.* pastel.

pastèque [pas'tɛk] *n.f.* watermelon, cf. MELON.

pasteur [pas'tœ:r] *n.m.* [Prot.] minister, clergyman; [Fig.] shepherd.

pasteuriser [pastœri'ze] #3 *v. tr.* to pasteurize.

pastiche [pas'tiʃ] *n.m.* pastiche.

pastille [pas'ti:j] *n.f.* **1.** lozenge, pastille. **2.** patch.

pastoral, -e [pastɔ|'ral] *adj.* pastoral. || **pastorale** *n.f.* pastoral (play, poem). || **pastorat** [-ra] *n.m.* pastorate, pastorage.

patate [pa'tat] *n.f.* [usual in Canada, Fam. in Fr.] potato: *patates frites*, © French fries, cf. POMME DE TERRE.

patauger [pato'ʒ|e] #5 *v. intr.* to paddle; flounder.

pâte [pɑ:t] *n.f.* paste, dough, batter: *pâtes (d'Italie)*, spaghetti and macaroni; ~ *à papier*, wood pulp; *mettre la main à* *la ~*, to lend a hand, to put one's hand to the plough. **pâté** [pɑ'te] *n.m.* **1.** pie, patty. **2.** blot (of ink). **3.** *~ de maisons,* block. || **pâtée** *n.f.* dog food [when dished out]; *donner sa ~ au chien,* to feed the dog.

patelin [pat'lɛ̃] *n.m.* **1.** native village. **2.** [Péj.] small place.

patent, -e [pa|'tɑ̃] *adj.* patent, obvious. || **patente** [-'tɑ̃:t] *n.f.* **1.** licence: *payer ~*, to be licensed. **2.** © thingummy, gadget: *toute la ~*, the whole works. || **patenter** [-tɑ̃'te] #3 *v. tr.* to license: *agent m patenté,* licensed dealer.

pater [pɑ'tɛ:r] *n.m.* the Lord's Prayer; pater noster.

patère [pa'tɛ:r] *n.f.* hat peg; coat peg; clothes tree, costumer.

paternel, -le [patɛr|'nɛl] *adj.* paternal; [Fig.] fatherly, kindly. || **paternité** [-ni'te] *n.f.* paternity, fatherhood; [Fig.] authorship.

pâteu|x, -se [pɑ'tø(:z)] *adj.* pasty; [Fig.] thick (voice); coated (tongue).

pathétique [pate'tik] *adj.* pathetic, moving.

pathologie [patɔlɔ'ʒi] *n.f.* pathology.

pâti [pɑ'ti] *p.p. of* PÂTIR.

patiemment [pasja'mɑ̃] *adv.* patiently.

patience [pa'sj|ɑ̃:s] *n.f.* patience: *jeu de ~*, jigsaw puzzle; *prendre ~*, to be patient; *s'armer de ~*, to be prepared to wait; *prendre son mal en ~*, to learn to live with it; *être à bout de ~*, to be out of patience; *mettre la ~ de qqun à une rude épreuve,* to try s.o.'s patience sorely, *faire une ~*, to play solitaire. || **patient, -e** [-ɑ(:t)] *adj. & n.* patient. || **patienter** [-ɑ̃'te] #3 *v. intr.* to be patient, to exercise patience.

patin [pa'tɛ̃] *n.m.* © runner, skate. *~ à roulettes,* roller skate; [frein] shoe. || **patiner** [pati'ne] #3 *v. intr.* **1.** to skate; **2.** (of vehicle) to have no traction, to skid. || **patinette** [pati|'nɛt] *n.f.* scooter. || **patineu|r, -se** [-'nœ:r, -'nø:z] *n. m/f* skater. || **patinoire** [-'nwa:r] *n.f.* skating arena, rink.

pâtir [pɑ't|i:r], **pâtissant** [-i'sɑ̃], **pâti** [-i] #17 *v. intr.* to suffer: *Sa santé en a beaucoup pâti,* → His health is the worse for it.

pâtisserie [pɑtis|'ri] *n.f.* **1.** pastry. **2.** pastry shop, bakery. || **pâtissier, ère** [-je, -jɛ:r] *n.m./f.* pastry cook, baker.

patois [pa'twɑ] *n.m.* **1.** patois; [Péj.] jargon. **2.** © verbal tic, cliché.

†**pâtre** [pɑ:tr] *n.m.* herdsman, shepherd.

patriarche [patri'arʃ] *n.m.* patriarch.

Patrice [pa'tris] *n.m.* = Patrick.

patrie [pa'tri] *n.f.* native land, fatherland: *mère- ~*, mother country, cf. PAYS[3]. || **patrimoine** [-'mwan] *n.m.* heritage.

patriote [patri'jɔt] *n. m/f.* patriot. || *adj.* patriotic. || **patriotique** [patrijɔ'tik] *adj.* patriotic. || **patriotisme** [patrijɔ'tism] *n.m.* patriotism.

patron, -ne [pa'tr|ɔ̃, -ɔn] *n.* **1.** [×] employer, owner (of concern); [Coll.] boss; [Naut.] master, captain, skipper. cf. CLIENTÈLE. **2.** patron (saint): *Les saints Patrons du Canada,* The patron saints of Canada. **3.** pattern, model: *Ils sont taillés sur le même ~*, They are very much alike.

patronage [patrɔ|'na:ʒ] *n.m.* **1.** patronage, support. **2.** [Rel.] social club (for children). || **patronal, -e** [-'nal] *adj.* **1.** of the patron saint. **2.** *syndicat m ~*, employer's association. || **patronat** [-'na] *n.m.* management.

patronyme [patrɔ'nim] *n.m.* family name.

patrouille [pa'truj] *n.f.* patrol: *aller en ~*, to patrol. || **patrouiller** [-e] #3 *v. tr. & intr.* to patrol.

patte [pat] *n.f.* **1.** [animal] paw, [oiseau] foot, [insecte] leg, [Fam.] leg, foot, hand: *marcher à quatre pattes,* to crawl on one's hands and knees; *faire ~ de velours,* to draw in one's claws; *donner un coup de ~ à qqun,* to give s.o. a dig; *tomber sous la ~ de qqun,* to fall into s.o.'s clutches; *graisser la ~ à qqun,* to grease s.o.'s palm. **2.** [narrow part of article such as flap, tab]: *~ d'épaule,* shoulder strap.

pâturage [pɑtyra:ʒ] *n.m.* pasture(land). || **pâture** [pɑ|'ty:r] *n.f.* [animaux] feed, fodder; [Fig.] food. || **pâturer** [-ty're] #3 *v. tr. & intr.* to graze, feed (on).

paume [po:m] *n.f.* palm (of the hand).

paupière [po'pjɛ:r] *n.f.* eyelid.

pause [po:z] *n.f.* pause, interval: *faire une ~*, to pause, stop.

pauvre [po:vr] *adj. m. & f.* **1.** poor, indigent. **2.** pitiful, wretched, unlucky; ☞ N.B.: *un ~ homme,* a poor man (to be pitied); *un homme ~*, a poor man (without money); *un pays ~*, a poor country (no resources); *une terre ~*, unproductive soil. || **pauvre,** *f* **pauvresse** [po:vr, po'vrɛs] *n.* pauper; beggar; N.B. *les pauvres,* the poor. || **pauvreté** [povrə'te] *n.f.* poverty.

pavé [pa've] *n.m.* pavement, street, paving stone: *jeter qqun sur le ~*, to turn s.o. out of house and home, of a job. || **paver** [pa've] #3 *v. tr.* to pave.

pavillon [pavi'jɔ̃] *n.m.* **1.** tent, pavilion. **2.** detached house or building: *le ~ de chimie,* the chemistry building. **3.** bell (of trumpet). **4.** [Naut.] flag, colours: *un navire battant ~ anglais,* a ship flying the

British flag; *clouer son* ~ , to nail one's colours to the mast; *amener son* ~ , to strike one's colours; [Fig.] *baisser* ~ , to knuckle under.

pavoiser [pavwa'ze] #3 *v. tr.* to deck with flags.

pavot [pa'vo] *n.m.* poppy.

payable [pɛ'jabl] *adj.* payable. || **payant, -e** [pɛ'jɑ̃] *adj.* paying, charged for. || **paye** [pɛj] *also* **paie** [pɛ] *n.f.* [solde, traitement] wages, pay: *jour de paye,* payday. || **payement** [pɛjmɑ̃] also **paiement** [pɛ'mɑ̃] *n.m.* payment.

payer [pɛ'j|e], #11 *v. tr.* **1.** to pay (a sum, s.o.), to pay for (sth.): *Combien le lui avez-vous payé?,* How much did you pay him for it?; ~ *à boire,* to stand a drink. **2.** to reward, to atone for (crime): ~ *de retour,* to pay back, to reciprocate; *Il me le paiera,* I'll get my own back; [Fig.] ~ *d'audace,* to bluff one's way in (or out); ~ *de sa personne,* not to spare o.s. || *v. pron.*: *se payer qqch.,* to treat o.s. to sth.; [Fig.] *se* ~ *la tête de qqun,* to make fun of s.o. || **payeur** [-œ:r] *n.m.* payer; [Mil.] paymaster; [banque] teller.

pays [pe'ji] *n.m.* **1.** country, land; countryside. **2.** native land, country: *De quel* ~ *êtes-vous?,* [Fam.] Where are you from?; ~ *natal,* native land, homeland; *avoir le mal du* ~ , to be homesick. **3.** ©: *au* ~ , in Quebec, in Canada; *sucre m du* ~ , maple sugar; *étoffe f du* ~ , homespun; *les vieux* ~ , *les* ~ *d'Europe,* the old countries; [P.Q.] *les* ~ *d'en haut,* the North. || **Pays-Bas, (les)** [(lɛ)peji'bɑ] *n.mpl.* The Netherlands.

paysage [-'za:ʒ] *n.m.* landscape, scenery, landscape painting.

paysan, -ne [-'zɑ̃, -'zan] *n.m./f.* peasant; farmer; cf. HABITANT. || *adj.* rustic, peasant; countrified.

péage [pe'a|:ʒ] *n.m.* [droit de] toll; [*bureau de* ~] toll house: *payer un droit de* ~ , to pay toll; *pont à* ~ , toll bridge. || **péager** [-'ʒe] *n.m.* toll-keeper.

peau [po] *n.f. pl.* **peaux** [po] **1.** [porc, chèvre, mouton] skin: *une serviette en* ~ *de porc,* a pigskin briefcase. **2.** [éléphant, vache] hide: *en* ~ *de vache,* in cowhide. **3.** [fruit] peel, skin: ~ *d'orange,* orange peel, ~ *de banane,* banana skin. **4.** [Fig.] *Je ne voudrais pas être dans sa* ~ , I would not want to be in his shoes. || **Peau(x)-Rouge(s)** [po'ru:ʒ] *n.m.* (*pl*) Red Indians, Redskin, cf. SAUVAGE.

pécan [pe'kɑ̃] *n.m.* pecan.

pécan(t) [pe'kɑ̃] © *n.m.* marten.

pécane [pe'kan] *n.f.* pecan.

pêche[1] [pɛ:ʃ] *n.f.* peach.

pêche[2] [pɛ:ʃ] *n.f.* fishing: *aller à la* ~ *au saumon,* to go salmon fishing; *La* (*saison de la*) ~ *est ouverte,* The fishing season is open; *la* ~ *à la ligne,* angling; *la* ~ *au filet,* net fishing; *une canne à* ~ , a fishing rod; *une barque de* ~ , a fishing boat.

péché [pe'ʃe] *n.m.* sin, trespass: ~ *mortel,* deadly sin; ~ *véniel,* venal sin; *pardonnez-nous nos péchés,* forgive us our trespasses; ~ *mignon,* besetting sin. || **pécher** #10 *v. intr.* to sin (against, *contre*): ~ *par excès,* to exceed, to overshoot the mark; ~ *par défaut,* to fall short of.

pêcher[1] [pɛ'ʃe, pe'ʃe] *n.m.* peach tree.

pêcher[2] [pɛ'ʃe] #3 *v. tr.* to fish (for): ~ *le saumon,* to fish for salmon; [Fig.] *Où avez-vous pêché cela?,* Where did you get that? || *v. intr.* to catch fish: ~ *à la ligne,* to fish with hook and line, to angle; ~ *en eau trouble,* to fish in troubled waters; ~ *par excès,* to overshoot the mark; ~ *par défaut,* to fall short of the mark.

pécheresse [peʃ'rɛs] *n.f.* cf. PÉCHEUR.

pêcherie [pɛʃ'ri, peʃ'ri] *n.f.* fishery: *Ministère des pêcheries,* Department of Fisheries.

péche|ur, -resse [pe'ʃœ:r, peʃ'rɛs] *n. m/f* sinner; offender.

pêcheu|r, -se [pɛ|'ʃœ:r, -'ʃø:z] *n. m/* fisherman, -woman; *village de pêcheurs,* → fishing village.

pectoral [pɛktɔ'ral] *adj.* [croix] pectoral.

pécule [pe'kyl] *n.m.* savings, nest-egg.

pécuniaire [peky'njɛ:r] *adj.* pecuniary.

pédagogie [pedagɔ'ʒi] *n.f.* pedagogy. || **pédagogique** [pedagɔ'ʒik] *adj.* pedagogic. || **pédagogue** [peda'gɔg] *n.m.* pedagogue.

pédale [pe'dal] *n.f.* pedal: ~ *d'embrayage,* clutch (pedal); *frein à* ~ , foot brake. || **pédaler** [-e] #3 *v. intr.* to pedal, cycle.

pédant, -e [pe'dɑ̃(:t)] *adj.* pedantic. || *n. m/f* pedant. || **pédanterie** [-'tri] *n.f.* pedantry.

pédestre [pe'dɛstr] *adj.* [×] pedestrian.

pègre [pɛ:gr] *n.f.* thieves, [Sl.] whizz mob.

peignant[1] [pɛ'ɲɑ̃] *p. pr.* de PEIGNER.

peignant[2] [pɛ'ɲ|ɑ̃] *p. pr.* de PEINDRE.

peignais, peigne, cf. PEINDRE.

peigne [pɛɲ] *n.m.* comb: (*se*) *donner un coup de* ~ , to run a comb through one's hair. || **peigner** [-e] #3 *v. tr.* to comb (one's hair, s.o.'s hair) [confusion is possible between forms of peigner and peindre]. || **se peigner** *v. pron.* to comb one's hair.

peignez, peignis, &c., cf. PEINDRE.

peignoir [pɛ'ɲwa:r] *n.m.* negligé, house-coat, dressing gown.

peindre [pɛ̃:dr], **peignant**[2] [pɛɲɑ̃], **peint** [pɛ̃] #36 *v. tr.* to paint; [Fig.] to represent, to depict, to describe. [Fr. Can. distinguishes between PEINDRE (to paint a portrait, &c.) and PEINTURER (to paint a house): ~ *en blanc, en bleu, &c.*, to paint white, blue, &c. || **se peindre** *v. pron.* to show: *La surprise se peignait sur son visage,* → Surprise was written on his face.

peine [pɛn] *n.f.* **1.** punishment, penalty: *la ~ capitale,* capital punishment; *sous ~ de,* under penalty of; *purger une ~*, to serve a sentence. **2.** pain, grief: *faire de la ~ à qqun,* to hurt s.o.'s feelings; *Elle fait ~ à voir,* It is pathetic. **3.** trouble, difficulty: *avoir de la ~ à faire qqch.*, to have trouble in doing sth.; *Cela m'a donné beaucoup de ~*, It gave me a lot of trouble; *se donner la ~ de,* to take the trouble to, to go out of one's way to; *valoir la ~*, to be worth while; *conter ses peines,* to tell one's troubles; *être en ~*, to be troubled. **4.** [Loc.] *à ~*, hardly, scarcely. || **peiné, -e** [-e] *adj.* grieved, pained. || **peiner** [-e] #3 *v. tr. & intr.* **1.** to pain, to grieve. **2.** to work hard, to labour.

peins, peint, cf. PEINDRE. || **peint, -e** [pɛ(:t)] *adj.* painted: *papier ~*, wall paper. || **peintre** [pɛ̃:tr] *n.m.* painter: ~ *en bâtiment,* house-painter. || **peinture** [pɛ̃'t|y:r] *n.f.* paint; painting, picture: ~ *à l'huile,* oil painting; *faire de la ~*, to paint (pictures); *Attention à la ~*, Wet paint. || **peinturer** [-y're] #3 *v. tr.* © to paint (a house, &c.); to daub.

péjorati|f, -ve [peʒɔra't|if, -i:v] *adj.* pejorative, disparaging, derogatory.

Pékin [pe'kɛ̃] *n.m.* Peking, Peiping.

pelage [pə'la:ʒ] [animaux] hair, coat; fur.

pêle-mêle ['pɛlmɛl] *adv.* pell-mell, helter-skelter. *n.m. inv.* jumble, medley.

peler [pəle] #9 *v. tr.* [fruit] to peel; [écorce] to peel off. || *v. intr.* to peel off.

pèlerin, -e (rare) [pɛl'rɛ̃] *n.m.* pilgrim. || **pèlerinage** [pɛlri'na:ʒ] *n.m.* pilgrimage. || **pèlerine** [pɛl'rin] *n.f.* cape; hooded cape.

pélican [peli'kɑ̃] *n.m.* pelican.

pelisse [pə'lis] *n.f.* fur-lined coat, cf. CAPOT.

pelle [pɛl] *n.f.* [terre] shovel; [ménage] dustpan; [four] peel, paddle: ~ *mécanique,* steam shovel; *ramasser une ~*, to come a cropper. || **pelletée** [pɛl'te] *n.f.* shovelful. || **pelleter** [pɛl'te] #8 *v. tr.* to shovel.

pelleterie [pɛlt'ri] *n.f.* [peaux] furs; the fur trade.

pellicule [pɛli'kyl] *n.f.* **1.** pellicle; [huile, &c.] film. **2.** [photo] film. **3.** *pellicules,* dandruff.

pelote [plɔt] *n.f.* **1.** ball (of string): ~ *à épingles,* pincushion; [Fig.] *faire sa ~*, to make o.'s pile. **2.** [Sport.]: ~ *basque,* pelota. || **peloter** [-ə] #3 *v. tr.* to wind into a ball; [Fig. & Fam.] to pet, paw.

peloton [plɔ't|õ] *n.m.* **1.** small ball (of wool, cotton, &c.). **2.** troop (of cavalry): ~ *d'exécution,* firing squad. || **pelotonner** [-ɔ'ne] #3 *v. tr.* to wind into a ball. || **se pelotonner** #3 *v. pron.* to curl up, to snuggle.

pelouse [pə'lu:z] *n.f.* lawn; plot of grass.

pelure [pə'ly:r] *n.f.* [pomme] peel; [oignon] skin; [légumes] paring; [fromage] rind; [Fig.] *papier ~*, onion-skin paper; *une ~*, a carbon copy.

pénal, -e, -aux [pe'n|al, -o] *adj.* penal. || **pénalisation** [-aliza'sjõ] *n.f.* penalization. || **pénalité** [-ali'te] *n.f.* penalty.

penaud, -e [pə'no(:d)] *adj.* crestfallen.

penchant [pɑ̃'ʃ|ɑ̃] *n.m.* inclination, tendency, leaning: *avoir un ~ pour,* to have a tendency toward, to be partial to; *suivre son ~*, to follow one's bent.

pencher [-e] #3 *v. intr.* to lean, to incline: *Cela penche d'un côté,* It leans to one side; *Il penche vers cette solution,* He inclines toward this solution; *faire ~ la balance,* to tip the scale. || *v. tr.* to incline, to tilt: *la tête penchée,* with head bowed. || **se pencher** *v. pron.* to lean, to bend: ~ *sur son travail,* to bend over one's work.

pend, pende, pends, &c. cf. PENDRE.

pendable [pɑ̃'dabl] *adj.* that deserves hanging; [Fig.] outrageous. || **pendaison** [pɑ̃dɛ'zõ] *n.f.* (death by) hanging.

pendant[1] [pɑ̃'d|ɑ̃] *p. pr.* de PENDRE.

pendant, -e[2] [ɑ̃-(:t)] *adj.* hanging; undecided, pending. || *n.m.* counterpart.

pendant[3] [pɑ̃'dɑ̃] *prép.* [période] during; [temps mesuré] for; [distance] for: ~ *la guerre,* during the war; ~ *six mois,* for six months; ~ *des kilomètres,* for miles. || **pendant que** *conj.* while: ~ *vous y êtes,* while you are at it.

penderie [pɑ̃'dri] *n.f.* closet, wardrobe.

pendre [pɑ̃:dr], **pendant** [pɑ̃'dɑ̃], **pendu** [pɑ̃'dy] # 42 *v. tr.* to hang up (sth.), to hang (s.o.). || *v. intr.* to hang (down), to be suspended (from). || **se pendre** *v. pron.* to hang o.s. || **pendu, -e** [pɑ̃'dy] *adj.* hanging, hung up, [condamné] hanged:

~ *à un clou*, hanging from a nail. || *n.* s.o. who has been hanged.

pendule [pɑ̃'dyl] *n.m.* pendulum. || *n.f.* clock: ~ *de voyage*, travelling clock.

pénétrable [pene|'trabl] *adj.* penetrable. || **pénétrant, -e** [-'trɑ̃(:t)] *adj.* penetrating; [vent] piercing; [odeur] pungent; [esprit] shrewd. || **pénétration** [-tra'sjõ] *n.f.* penetration; [Fig.] insight, shrewdness. || **pénétrer** [pene'tre] #10 *v. tr.* to penetrate, to invade, to go through; || [usual. as *v. intr.*] to penetrate, to enter: *Il pénétra dans la pièce*, He entered the room.

pénible [pe'nibl] *adj.* hard, difficult, gruelling; painful, distressing. || **péniblement** [-ə'mɑ̃] *adv.* painfully.

péniche [pe'niʃ] *n.f.* canal boat, barge.

pénicilline [penisi'lin] *n.f.* penicillin.

péninsule [penɛ̃'syl] *n.f.* peninsula.

pénitence [peni't|ɑ̃:s] *n.f.* repentance, penitence, penance: *être en* ~, to be in disgrace; *mettre un enfant en* ~, to punish a child; *faire* ~, to do penance. || **pénitencier** [-ɑ̃'sje] *n.m.* penal settlement; penitentiary. || **pénitent, -e** [-ɑ̃(:t)] *adj.* repentant, contrite. || **pénitentiaire** [-ɑ̃'sjɛ:r] *adj.* penitentiary.

Pennsylvanie, Pensylvanie [pɛnsilva'ni] *n.f.* Pennsylvania.

pénombre [pe'nõ:br] *n.f.* semi-darkness, penumbra.

pensée¹ [pɑ̃'se] *n.f.* pansy.

pensée² [pɑ̃'s|e] *n.f.* thought, thoughts: *le confident de sa* ~, the confidant of his thoughts. || **penser** [-e] #3 *v. tr. & intr.* to think: *Qu'en pensez-vous?*, What do you think of it?; *Avez-vous pensé à le faire?*, Did you think of doing it?; *Faites-moi* ~ *à lui en parler*, Remind me to mention it to him; *N'y pensez plus*, Forget it. || **penseur** [-œ:r] *n.m.* thinker. || **pensi|f, -ve** [-if, -i:v] *adj.* thoughtful, pensive.

pension [pɑ̃'sj|õ] *n.f.* **1.** board and lodging; boarding-house; boarding school (the latter usual. called PENSIONNAT): *prendre* ~ *chez qqun*, to board and room with s.o.; *être en* ~ *à*, to be boarding at. **2.** pension; annuity: ~ *de vieillesse*, old-age pension. || **pensionnaire** [-ɔ'nɛ:r] *n.m. & f.* **1.** boarder. **2.** paying guest. || **pensionnat** [pɑ̃sjɔ'na] *n.m.* boarding school.

pente [pɑ̃:t] *n.f.* slope, gradient; [Fig.] propensity (for); bent: *la rue est en* ~, the street is sloping; ~ *de ski*, ski run.

Pentecôte [pɑ̃t'ko:t] *n.f.* [Rel.] Whitsun(tide); [Jewish] Pentecost: *Dimanche de la* ~, Whit Sunday.

pénurie [peny'ri] *n.f.* scarcity, penury, lack.

pépin [pe'p|ɛ̃] *n.m.* [orange] pip; [raisin] stone. || **pépinière** [-i'njɛ:r] *n.f.* [tree] nursery; training school. || **pépiniériste** [-inje'rist] *n.m.* nurseryman.

pépite [pe'pit] *n.f.* nugget.

perçant, -e [pɛr'sɑ(:t)] *adj.* piercing, penetrating, shrill. || **perce** [pɛrs] *n.f.* bore; [tonneau] *mettre en* ~, to broach.

percée [pɛr'se] *n.f.* break, opening; [Fig.] break-through.

percement [-ə'mɑ̃] *n.m.* opening, boring, perforation, breaking through.

percepteur [pɛrsɛp|'tœ:r] *n.m.* tax-collector. || **perceptible** [-'tibl] *adj.* **1.** perceptible, noticeable, audible. **2.** [tax] collectable. || **perception** [-'sjõ] *n.f.* [connaissance] perception; [impôts] collection; [office] collector's office.

percer [pɛr'se] #4 *v. tr.* to pierce; [trou] to bore, drill; [Fig.] to penetrate, break through. || *v. intr.* to pierce, break through.

perceuse [pɛr'sø:z] *n.f.* drill; punch.

percevoir [pɛrsə'vwa:r] #34 *v. tr.* **1.** to perceive, to sense. **2.** to collect.

perche¹ [pɛrʃ] pole; [Fig.] *tendre la* ~ *à qqun*, to/give, lend/s.o. a hand.

perche² [pɛrʃ], © **perchaude** [-o:d] *n.f.* [poisson] (yellow, American) perch.

percher [-e] #3 *v. intr.* to perch, to roost. || **perchoir** [-wa:r] *n.m.* perch.

perclus, -e [pɛr'kly(:z)] *adj.* stiff, unable to move: ~ *de douleurs*, crippled with rheumatism.

percussion [pɛrky'sjõ] *n.f.* percussion. || **percuter** [-'te] *v. tr.* #3 to strike; [Méd.] to percuss. || **percuteur** [-'tœ:r] *n.m.* firing pin.

perdant, -e [pɛr|'dɑ̃(:t)] *adj.* losing. || *n.* loser. || **perdition** [-di'sjõ] *n.f.*: *en* ~, in distress.

perdre [pɛrdr], **perdu** [pɛr'dy] #42 *v. tr.* **1.** to/lose, get rid of: [Fig.] ~ *la tête*, to lose one's/head, wits. **2.** to waste, corrupt, deprave: ~ *du temps*, to waste time. || *v. intr.* to/lose, be a loser/(at cards, &c.); [of vessels] to leak. || **se perdre** *v. pron.* to lose one's way, be lost; [custom] to disappear; [food] to spoil.

perdreau [pɛr'dro] *n.m.* young partridge. || **perdrix** [pɛr'dri] *n.f.* partridge; © grouse, cf. TÉTRAS; © ~ *grise*, ruffed grouse.

perdu, -e [pɛr'dy] *adj.* lost; wasted, ruined; spoilt, bewildered; remote, out of the way: *Le bureau des objets perdus*, The Lost and Found Office; *à temps* ~, in one's spare time; *endroit* ~, out-of-the-way place; *à corps* ~, recklessly.

père [pɛːr] *n.m.* father; (pl. Litt.) forefathers, ancestors: *le ~ de famille,* the head of the family; *le Saint-Père,* the Pope, the Holy Father; © *Les Pères de la Confédération,* the Fathers of Confederation; *le Père Noël,* Santa (Claus). cf. PAPA.
péremptoire [perɑ̃p'twaːr] *adj.* peremptory.
perfection [pɛrfɛk'sj|õ] *n.f.* perfection, completion, realization. || **perfectionnement** [-ɔn'mɑ̃] *n.m.* perfecting; improvement: *cours de ~,* refresher course. || **perfectionner** [-ɔ'ne] #3 *v. tr.* to improve, to perfect. || **se perfectionner** *v. pron.* to improve, to perfect/o.s.
perfide [pɛr'fid] *adj.* perfidious, treacherous, false. || **perfidie** [-i] *n.f.* treachery, perfidy.
perforatrice [pɛrfɔr|a'tris] *n.f.* drill. || **perforer** [-e] #3 *v. tr.* to drill, to bore (through), to perforate.
péril [pe'ri|l] *n.m.* peril, danger, risk: *au péril de sa vie,* at the risk of one's life; *mettre en ~,* to put in danger, to jeopardize. || **périlleu|x, -se** [-'jø, -'jøːz] *adj.* perilous, hazardous: *saut m ~,* somersault; *faire le saut périlleux,* to turn a somersault.
périmé [peri'me] *adj.* no longer valid, expired, lapsed; outdated.
périmètre [peri'mɛːtr] *n.m.* perimeter, circumference.
période [pe'rjɔd] *n.f.* period: [Hist.] age, era. || **périodique** [-ik] *adj.* periodic; [revue] periodical. *n.* periodical, journal. || **périodiquement** [-ik'mɑ̃] *adv.* at regular intervals.
péripétie [peripe'si] *n.f.* [usual. pl.] the twists and turns.
périphérie [perife'ri] *n.f.* periphery.
périphrase [peri'fraːz] *n.f.* periphrase.
périr [pe'r|iːr] #17 *v. intr.* to perish, to die. || **périssable** [-i'sabl] *adj.* perishable.
perle [pɛrl] *n.f.* pearl; [verroterie] bead; [Fig.] gem, → priceless person. || **perlé, -e** [-e] *adj.* pearly; [Fig.] finicky: *grève f perlée,* go-slow, slow-down/strike. || **perler** [-e] #3 *v. tr.* [sueur] to bead.
permanence [pɛrma'n|ɑ̃ːs] *n.f.* permanen|ce, -cy; [bureau] headquarters, secretariat: *ouvert en ~,* open/at all hours, without interruption/. || **permanent, -e** [-ɑ̃, -ɑ̃ːt] *adj.* permanent, lasting; non-stop (show). || **permanente** *n.f.* permanent wave.
permettre [pɛr'm|ɛtr], **permis** [-i] #44 *v. tr.* to permit; to allow, let; to suffer: *~ à qqun de faire qqch.,* to let s.o. do sth. || **se permettre** *v. pron.* to venture (to, *de*): *~ une remarque,* to allow o.s. (to make) a remark. || **permis** [-i] *n.m.* licence, permit: *~ de conduire,* driver's licence. || **permis, -e** [-i(ːz)] *adj.* permitted, lawful: *Ce n'est pas ~,* → This is forbidden. || **permission** [-i'sjõ] *n.f.* permission; [Mil.] furlough, leave. || **permissionnaire** [-isjɔ'nɛːr] *n.m.* soldier on leave, furlough.
permuter [pɛrmy'te] #3 *v. tr. & intr.* to exchange, to change over.
pernicieux, -se [pɛrni'sjø(ːz)] *adj.* pernicious, harmful, injurious.
péroraison [perɔrɛ'zõ] *n.f.* peroration.
perpendiculaire [pɛrpɑ̃diky'lɛːr] *adj. & n(f).* perpendicular.
perpétrer [pɛrpe'tre] #10 *v. tr.* to perpetrate, to commit.
perpétuel, -le [pɛrpe|'tɥɛl] *adj.* perpetual, everlasting, endless. || **perpétuer** [-'tɥe] #3 *v. tr.* to perpetuate. || **perpétuité** [pɛrpetɥi'te] *n.f.* perpetuity: *à ~,* for ever.
perplexe [pɛr'plɛks] *adj.* perplexed, puzzled. || **perplexité** [-i'te] *n.f.* perplexity.
perquisition [pɛrkizi'sj|õ] *n.f.* search: *mandat de ~,* search warrant. || **perquisitionner** [-ɔ'ne] #3 *v. tr.* to search.
perron [pɛ'rõ] *n.m.* (front) steps.
perroquet [pɛrɔ'kɛ] *n.m.* parrot. || **perruche** [pɛ'ryʃ] *n.f.* hen parrot; parakeet.
perruque [pɛ'ryk] *n.f.* wig; [Hist.] peruke.
Persan, -ne [pɛr's|ɑ̃, -an] *adj. & n.* Persian, cf. IRAN. || **Perse** [pɛrs] *n.f.* Persia. cf. IRAN. *adj. & n.* [antique] Persian.
persécuter [pɛrseky|'te] #3 *v. tr.* to persecute, to pester, to worry. || **persécution** [-'sjõ] *n.f.* persecution.
persévérance [pɛrseve'r|ɑ̃ːs] *n.f.* perseverance, persistance. || **persévérer** [-e] #10 *v. intr.* to persevere, to persist.
persienne [pɛr'sjɛn] *n.f.* shutter, [US] blind.
persiflage [pɛrsi'flaːʒ] *n.m.* persiflage, flippant tone.
persil [pɛr'si] *n.m.* parsley.
Persique (golfe) [pɛr'sik] *n.m.* Persian Gulf.
persistance [pɛrsis't|ɑ̃ːs] *n.f.* persistence, persistency, continuance. || **persistant, -e** [ɑ̃-, -ɑ̃ːt] *adj.* persistent, continuous. || **persister** [-e] #3 *v. intr.* to persist (in, *à*), to insist; to continue, to remain unchanged, unabated.
personnage [pɛrsɔ'n|aːʒ] *n.m.* [célèbre] figure, personage; person; [Théâtre] character; rôle. || **personnalité** [-ali'te] *n.f.* personality: [= personnage] person of position; [invités] guests of honour. || **personne** [pɛr'sɔn] *n.f.* **1.** person: *grande ~,* adult, grown-up; †*jeune ~,* girl. **2.** one's own/person, self/; appearance: *en ~,* in person; *payer de sa ~,* not to spare one's efforts; *bien de sa ~,* good

looking, handsome. || *pron. m.* anyone, anybody; no one, nobody: [Fam.] *~ n'est venu?*, Did anybody come? No one came?; *Il n'y a ~*, There is nobody in here. || **personnel, -le** [-ɛl] *adj.* personal; intimate; private, selfish. || *n.m.* staff; personnel: *~ administratif*, officers (of a company); *~ enseignant*, the Faculty; *~ navigant*, flight crew. || **personnellement** [-ɛl'mɑ̃] *adv.* personally: in person, oneself. || **personnifier** [-i'fje] #3 *v. tr.* to personify; [Fig.] to embody.

perspective [pɛrspɛk'tiːv] *n.f.* perspective, prospect, vista: *en ~*, in prospect.

perspicace [pɛrspi'kas] *adj.* shrewd, perspicacious, discerning. || **perspicacité** [-i'te] *n.f.* perspicacity, shrewdness, penetration.

persuader [pɛrsɥa|'de] #3 *v. intr.* to persuade, to convince: *~ à qqun de faire qqch.*, to persuade s.o. to do sth. || **persuasi|f, -ive** [-'zif, -'ziːv] *adj.* persuasive, convincing. || **persuasion** [-'zjõ] *n.f.* persuasion, (firm) belief, conviction: *force de ~*, persuasiveness.

perte [pɛrt] *n.f.* loss; waste(fulness): *à ~*, at a loss; *à ~ de vue*, as far as the eye can see; *~ de temps*, waste of time; *courir à sa ~*, to go to the dogs; to ride for a fall.

pertinent, -e [pɛrti'n|ɑ̃, -ɑ̃ːt] *adj.* pertinent, relevant.

perturbat|eur, -rice [pɛrtyrba't|œːr, -ris] *n. m/f.* trouble-maker, heckler. || *adj.* disturbing. || **perturbation** [pɛrtyrba'sjõ] *n.f.* perturbation.

péruvien, -ne [pery'vj|ɛ̃, -ɛn] *adj. & n.* Peruvian; of Peru.

pervers, -e [pɛrv|ɛːr, -ɛrs] *adj.* perverted, depraved, wicked. || *n.* pervert, evil person. || **perversité** [-ɛrsi'te] *n.f.* perversion, perversity. || **pervertir** [-ɛr'tiːr] #17 *v. tr.* to pervert, to corrupt.

pesage [pə'z|aːʒ] *n.m.* weighing, weighing in; weighing-in enclosure, paddock.

pesant [-ɑ̃] *n.m.* *valoir son ~ d'or*, to be worth one's weight in gold. || **pesant, -e** [-ɑ̃(:t)] *adj.* heavy; [allure] sluggish; [Fig.] irksome: *dormir d'un sommeil ~*, → to sleep heavily, to be sound asleep. || **pesanteur** [-ɑ̃'tœːr] *n.f.* heaviness, sluggishness; [Phys.] gravity [→ for *weight* use POIDS]. || **pesée** [-e] *n.f.* weighing. || **peser** [-e] #9 *v. tr.* to weigh (out); [Fig.] to bear (on, *sur*); to consider, think over: *~ le pour et le contre*, to weigh the pros and cons. || *v. intr.* to weigh; [Fig.] to be/ of weight, of importance/: *combien cela pèse-t-il?* How much does it weigh?; [Fig.] *L'ennui me pèse*, I am bored to death.

pessimisme [pɛsi'mis|m] *n.m.* pessimism. || **pessimiste** [-t] *adj.* pessimistic. || *n.m.* pessimist.

peste [pɛst] *n.f.* plague; [Pers.] pest, nuisance. || **pestiféré** [-ife're] *adj.* plagued, plague-stricken. || **pestilence** [-i'lɑ̃ːs] *n.f.* plague, pestilence, contagious disease.

pet [pɛ(t)] *n.m.* [Vulg.] fart.

pétale [pe'tal] *n.m.* petal.

pétarade [pet|a'rad] *n.f.* cracking (of fireworks); [indoor] back firing. || **pétard** [-aːr] *n.m.* firecracker; [Mil.] petard; [Fam.] *faire du ~*, to kick up a row; [Fam.] backside. || **pète** &c. cf. PÉTER. || **péter** [-e] #10 *v. intr. & tr.* [Vulg.] to fart; [Fam.] to crack (off), [ballon] to burst.

pétillant, -e [peti'j|ɑ̃(:t)] *adj.* [fire] crackling, [vin, esprit] sparkling. || **pétillement** [-'mɑ̃] *n.m.* crackling, sparkling, fizz(ing). || **pétiller** [-e] #3 *v. intr.* to crackle, to sparkle, to fizz.

petiot, -e [pə'tj|o, -ɔt] *n.* little/boy, girl/, tiny child.

petit, -e [pəti(t)] *adj.* **1.** small, little, short: *une petite chambre*, a small room; *le ~ doigt*, the little finger; *Il est plus ~ que son frère*, He is shorter than his brother. **2.** young: *quand j'étais ~*, when I was a boy; *un animal et ses petits*, an animal and its young; *une lionne et ses petits*, a lioness and her cubs. **3.** petty, small. **4.** [in compounds] *le ~ déjeuner*, breakfast; *ses petits-enfants*, his grandchildren; *sa petite-fille*, his granddaughter; *son ~ -fils*, his grandson; *un ~ garçon*, a little boy; *au ~ jour*, at daybreak; *le ~ -lait*, whey; *~ nom*, first name; *~ pain*, roll; *petits pois*, peas; *petites tables*, separate tables; *petite tenue*, undress; *petite vitesse*, slow freight; *petite vérole*, smallpox. || **petit-duc** [pəti'dyk] *n.m.* [Ornith.] screech owl.

petitesse [p(ə)ti'tɛs] *n.f.* **1.** smallness; **2.** insignificance, pettiness.

pétition [peti'sjõ] *n.f.* petition: *faire une ~ de principe*, to beg the question.

petit-lait [p(ə)ti'lɛ] *n.m.* whey: [Fig.] *boire du ~*, to lap it up.

pétoncle [pe'tõːkl] *n.m.* scallop.

pétrifier [petri'fje] #3 *v. tr.* to petrify. || *v. intr.* to turn into stone.

pétrin [pe'tr|ɛ̃] *n.m.* kneading trough; [Fig.] *être dans le ~*, to be in a/fix, mess/. || **pétrir** [-iːr] #17 *v. tr.* to knead (the dough); [Fig.] to steep (in), mould.

pétrole [pe'trɔl] *n.m.* petroleum, rock oil;

kerosene: *puits m de ~*, oil well; *trouver du ~*, to strike oil. || **pétrolier** [-je] *n.m.* [Naut.] oil tanker. || **pétroli|er, -ière,** [-je, -jɛːr] *adj.*: *industrie pétrolière*, oil industry; (*valeurs*) *pétrolières*, oil shares. || **pétrolifère** [-i'fɛːr] *adj.* oil-bearing.

peu [pø] *adv.* little, not much; few, not many: *~ de temps*, little, not much/time; *~ de fautes*, few, not many/mistakes; *~ à ~*, little by little; *à ~ près*, nearly; *quelque ~*, somewhat. || *n.m.* little, few: *le ~ que j'ai*, what/little, few/I have.

peuplade [pœ'plad] *n.f.* tribe, primitive people. || **peuple** [pœpl] *n.m.* people, nation: *le ~*, the people, the masses, the working classes; *Le ~ canadien*, The Canadian nation, people; Canadians. || **peupler** [-e] #3 *v. tr.* to people (with inhabitants); to stock (with animals). || *v. intr.* to multiply, to breed.

peuplier [pœpli'je] *n.m.* poplar; © aspen: *~ baumier*, balm poplar, cottonwood.

peur [pœːr] *n.f.* **1.** fear; [soudaine] fright: [Fam.] *une ~ bleue*, a blue funk; *avoir ~ (de)*, to be afraid (of); *faire ~ (à)*, to scare, to frighten (s.o.); *sans ~*, fearless(ly). **2.** [Loc.] *de ~ de*, for fear of; *de ~ que*, lest, in case [+ subj.] || **peureu|x, -se** [pœ'rø(ːz)] *adj.* timid, fearful, timorous, nervous.

peut [pø] cf. POUVOIR. || **peut-être** [pø'tɛːtr] *adv.* perhaps, maybe; [abs.] possibly: *~ que oui*, perhaps so; *~ que non*, perhaps not. [☞ Invert pronoun & verb after ~ : *peut-être avez-vous entendu parler de . . .*, perhaps you have heard of . . .].

peuve [pœv] cf. POUVOIR. || **peux** [pø] cf. POUVOIR.

phare [faːr] *n.m.* [port] lighthouse; [aviation] beacon; [auto] (head)light.

pharmaceutique [farmasø'tik] *adj.* pharmaceutical. || **pharmacie** [farma's|i] *n.f.* pharmacy, drug store; dispensary. || **pharmacien, -ne** [-sjɛ̃, -sjɛ̃n] *n.* pharmacist, druggist; (dispensing) chemist.

phase [fɑːz] *n.f.* phase; [lune] phasis; [Fig.] stage.

phénoménal, -e [fenɔme'nal] *adj.* phenomenal, remarkable, surprising. || **phénomène** [fenɔ'mɛn] *n.m.* phenomenon; [Fig.] freak; [Fam.] (queer) character.

philanthropie [filɑ̃trɔ'pi] *n.f.* philanthropy.

Philippe [fi'lip] *n.m.* = Philip. || **Philippines (les)** [(le)fili'pin] *n.f. pl.* The Philippine Islands; The Philippines.

philologie [filɔlɔ'ʒi] *n.f.* philology.

philosophe [filɔ'zɔf] *n.m.* philosopher. || *adj.* philosophical. || **philosophie** [-i] *n.f.* philosophy. || **philosophique** [-ik] *adj.* philosophical.

phobie [fɔ'bi] *n.f.* phobia.

phone [fɔn] *n.m.* speech-sound. || **phonétique** [-e'tik] *adj.* phonetic. || *n.f.* phonetics. || **phoniatrie** [-jɑ'tri] *n.f.* speech therapy. || **phonique** [-ik] *adj.*: *isolation ~*, sound proofing. || **phono(graphe)** [-o('graf)] *n.m.* [abr. *phono*] phonograph; record-player. || **phonologie** [-ɔlɔ'ʒi] *n.f.* phonemics.

phoque [fɔk] *n.m.* seal.

phosphate [fɔs'fat] *n.m.* phosphate. || **phosphore** [fɔs'fɔːr] *n.m.* phosphorus.

photo [fo'to] *n.f.* [Fam.] photo. || **photocopie** [-kɔ'pi] *n.f.* photostat. || **photogénique** [-ʒe'nik] *adj.* photogenic, photographing well: *Il est ~*, He takes a good picture. || **photographe** [-'graf] *n.m.* photographer. || **photographie** [-gra'fi] *n.f.* [abr. *photo*] photography; photograph, picture: *prendre des photographies*, to take pictures. || **photographier** [-gra'fje] #3 *v. tr. & intr.* to photograph, take a picture of.|| **photographique** [-gra'fik] *adj.* photographic. || **photostat** [-stat] *n.m.* photostat, photostatic copy.

phrase [fraːz] *n.f.* [Gram. ×] sentence; [abus.] phrase; [music] phrase.

physicien [fizi'sjɛ̃] *n.m.* physicist. || **physiologie** [fizjɔlɔ'ʒi] *n.f.* physiology. || **physionomie** [fizjɔnɔ'mi] *n.f.* features, face; [choses] aspect.

physique [fi'zik] *adj.* physical, material. || *n.f.* physics. || *n.m.* physique, appearance (of a person).

piaffer [pja'fe] #3 *v. intr.* to prance, paw the ground; [Fig.] to fume, strain at the leash.

piailler [pjɑ'je] #3 *v. intr.* to squall, chirp.

pianiste [pja'nist] *n. m/f.* pianist. || **piano** [pja'no] *n.m.* piano: *~ droit*, upright piano, *~ à queue*, grand piano

piastre [pjastr] © *n.f.* [Fam.] dollar: *un cinq piastres*, a five-dollar bill. [☞ came into use with the English regime and is still widely used; DOLLAR is comparatively recent].

pic [pik] *n.m.* [outil] pick, pickaxe; [montagne] peak: *à ~*, sheer; [Fig.] *tomber à ~*, to happen, to arrive in the nick of time.

pic(-vert) [pi'vɛːr] *n.m.* woodpecker.

picaillon, picasson [pi|kɑ'jõ, -ka'sõ] © *n.m.* hack, worn-out old horse.

pichet [pi'ʃɛ] *n.m.* pitcher, jug.

pichou [pi'ʃu] © *n.m.* lynx. cf. LOUP-CERVIER.

pick-up [pi'kɔp] *n.m.* record-player.

picote [pi'kɔt] © *n.f.*: *grosse* ~, smallpox, variola; ~ *volante, petite* ~, varicella, chickenpox.

picoter [pikɔ'te] #3 *v. tr.* to prick; to peck (at): ~ *les yeux,* to sting one's eyes, to make your eyes smart.

pie [pi] *n.f.* magpie; ~ *-grièche f* shrike; [Fig.] shrew.

pièce [pjɛs] *n.f.* **1.** patch: *mettre une* ~ *à un vêtement,* to patch a garment. **2.** room: *un appartement de cinq pièces,* a five-room apartment. **3.** play: *une* ~ *de Molière,* a play by Molière. **4.** coin, piece: *une* ~ *de cinquante sous,* a fifty-cent piece. **5.** [Milit.] gun: ~ *de marine,* naval gun. **6.** part: ~ *de rechange,* spare part. **7.** document: ~ *d'identité,* identification. **8.** bolt: ~ *d'étoffe,* bolt of cloth. **9.** ~ *d'eau,* ornamental pond. **10.** [Loc.] *dix dollars* ~, ten dollars a piece; *faire* ~ *à qqun,* to play a trick on s.o.

pied [pje] *n.m.* **1.** foot: *aller à* ~, to walk; *coup de* ~, kick; *donner un coup de* ~ *à qqun,* to kick s.o.; *doigt de* ~, toe; *sur la pointe des pieds,* on tiptoe; *marcher sur la pointe des pieds,* to tiptoe; *de* ~ *en cap,* from top to toe; *nu-pieds, pieds nus,* barefoot(ed). **2.** [measure, abbr. as *pi.*] foot: *mesurer, avoir six pieds de haut,* to be six/foot tall, feet high. **3.** [mur] base, foot; [arbre] foot; [meuble] leg; [salade] head; © ~ *de roi,* folding ruler. **4.** [Loc.] *au* ~ *levé,* offhand; *avoir le* ~ *marin,* to have one's sea-legs; *fouler aux pieds,* to trample under foot; *lâcher* ~, to give way; *ne pas lâcher* ~, to stand one's ground; *se lever du* ~ *gauche,* to get up on the wrong side of the bed; *marcher sur les pieds à qqun,* to tread on s.o.'s corns; *mettre à* ~, to dismiss, fire; *mettre les pieds dans le plat,* to put one's foot in it; *mettre* ~ *à terre,* to dismount; *mettre sur* ~, to set up; *ne pas se moucher du* ~, to think no small beer of o.s.; *perdre* ~, to be out of one's depth; *prendre* ~, to gain a foothold; *taper du* ~, to stamp one's foot.

pied-à-terre [pjeta'tɛ:r] *n.m.inv.* (small) occasional lodgings.

piédestal [pjedɛs'tal] *n.m.* pedestal.

piège [pjɛ:ʒ] *n.m.* trap: *tendre un* ~ *à qqun,* to lay a trap for s.o.; *prendre au* ~, to catch in a trap, to trap.

pierre [pjɛ:r] *n.f.* **1.** stone: *un mur de* ~, a stone wall; *une maison en* ~, a stone house; ~ *de taille,* freestone; ~ *de touche,* touchstone, acid test; ~ *angulaire,* cornerstone. **2.** [caillou] stone, rock. [Can. English often uses *rock* in this sense.] cf. ROCHE. || **Pierre** [pjɛ:r] *n.m.* = Peter; [Fam.] Pete. || **pierreries** [pjɛr'ri] *n.fpl.* gems, precious stones. || **pierreu|x, -se** [pjɛ'rø(:z)] *adj.* stony.

piété [pje'te] *n.f.* devotion, devoutness. || †**mont-de-piété** [mõdpje'te] *n.m.* pawn shop, cf. CRÉDIT.

piétiner [pjeti'ne] #3 *v. tr.* to stamp down, to trample. || *v. intr.* #3 to stamp, to mark time.

piéton [pje'tõ] *n.m.* pedestrian.

piètre [pjɛtr] *adj.* poor, shabby, wretched.

pieu [pjø] *n.m.* post, pile, stake.

pieu|x, -se [pjø(:z)] *adj.* devout, dutiful.

pigeon [pi'ʒ|õ] *n.m.* pigeon: ~ *voyageur,* homing pigeon. || **pigeonnier** [-ɔ'nje] *n.m.* pigeonhouse, dovecot.

pignon [pi'ɲõ] *n.m.* gable: *Il a* ~ *sur rue,* He's a man of property.

pile[1] [pil] *n.f.* [amas] heap, stack; [pont] pier; [Electr.] battery: ~ *sèche,* dry cell; ~ *atomique,* atomic pile [cf. RÉACTEUR].

pile[2] *n.f.* tail: ~ *ou face,* heads or tails; *jouer à* ~ *ou face,* to toss for it; [Fam.] *s'arrêter* ~, to come to an abrupt halt, to stop dead.

piler [pi'le] #3 *v. tr.* to grind, to crush.

pilier [pi'lje] *n.m.* pillar, column, support.

pillage [pi'j|a:ʒ] *n.m.* looting, pillaging; *mettre au* ~, to loot. || **pillard** [-a:r] *adj.* looting, plundering. || *n.* plunderer. || **piller** [-e] #3 *v. tr.* **1.** to loot, to plunder. **2.** [Fig.] to plagiarize.

pilon [pi'l|õ] *n.m.* **1.** pestle. **2.** rammer: *mettre au* ~, to destroy. **3.** [poulet] drumstick. **4.** wooden leg. || **pilonner** [-ɔ'ne] #3 *v. tr.* to pound.

pilotage [pilɔ'ta:ʒ] *n.m.* **1.** piloting. **2.** pile-driving. || **pilote** [pi'lɔt] *n.m.* pilot: ~ *d'essai,* test pilot; © ~ *de la brousse,* bush pilot. || **piloter** [-e] #3 *v. tr.* to pilot (a ship); to fly (a plane); to steer (a car); [Fig.] to guide, to act as s.o.'s guide; to show s.o. over (a city, &c.). || **pilotis** [pilɔ'ti] *n.m.* piles, piling.

pilule [pi'lyl] *n.f.* pill; [Fig.] *dorer la* ~ *à qqun,* to sugar-coat the pill for s.o.

pimbina [pɛ̃bi'na] cf. VIORNE.

piment [pi'mɑ̃] *n.m.* **1.** spice. **2.** [Bot.] pimento. || **pimenter** [-'te] #3 *v. tr.* to spice, to give spice to.

pimpant, -e [pɛ̃'pɑ̃(:t)] *adj.* smart, stylishly dressed, spruce.

pin [pɛ̃] *n.m.* [Bot.] pine(tree): *pomme f de* ~, (fir)cone: © ~ *blanc,* white pine; ~ *rouge,* red pine; ~ *gris,* jack pine.

pince [pɛ̃:s] *n.f.* often *plur.* pliers; [à épiler] tweezers; [à sucre] sugar tongs;

[homard] claws; [levier] crowbar. || **pincé, -e** [pɛ's|e] *adj.* prim, cold, tight-lipped.

pinceau [pɛ̃'so] *n.m.* (paint-)brush.

pincée [pɛ̃'s|e] *n.f.* pinch: *une ~ de sel,* a pinch of salt. || **pincer** [-e] #4 *v. tr.* to pinch; [guitare] to pluck; [lèvres] to purse. || **pincette** [-ɛt] *n.f.* tongs, tweezers.

pinçon [-õ] *n.m.* bruise, mark left by a pinch.

pingouin [pɛ̃'gwɛ̃] *n.m.* penguin; auk.

pinson [pɛ̃'sõ] *n.m.* finch; chaffinch; [Fam.] sparrow [Fam. *moineau*], chippie.

pintade [pɛ̃'tad] *n.f.* guinea-hen.

pinte [pɛ̃:t] © *n.f.* quart [✕ = 2 pints]; [Fig.] *se faire une ~ de bon sang,* to have a good laugh.

pioche [pjɔʃ] *n.f.* pick(axe); mattock [cf. PELLE]; [Fig.] *tête de ~*, stubborn, obstinate. || **piocher** [-e] #3 *v. tr. & intr.* to dig (with a pick); to whack; [Fam.] to work hard at, to grind away at: *piocher son français,* to work hard at one's French.

pion [pjõ] *n.m.* [échecs] pawn; [dames] man: *damer le ~ à,* to beat s.o. hollow; [Fr. schools] proctor.

pionnier [pjɔ'nje] *n.m.* pioneer: *faire œuvre de ~*, to break new ground.

pipe [pip] *n.f.* pipe: [☞] *fumer la ~*, to smoke a pipe; [Fam.] *casser sa ~*, to kick the bucket. || **pipeau** [pi'po] *n.m.* shepherd's pipe; bird-call; lime twig. || **pipée** [pi'pe] *n.f.* bird-snare. || **piper** #3 *v. intr.* to peep, to chirp: *Il n'a pas pipé,* He said not a word. || *v. tr.* to snare, to dupe: *des cartes pipées,* marked cards.

piquant, -e [pi'k|ɑ̃(:t)] *adj.* prickly, stinging, [sauce] hot; [remarque] biting, sharp; [scène] exciting. || *n.* [fleur, &c.] prickle; [insecte, &c.] sting; [porc-épic] quill; [Fig.] piquant, [réponse, &c.] sharpness, pungency.

piqué, -e [pi'ke] *adj.* [par les insectes] bitten, stung; [vin] sour. || **piqué** *n.m.* [étoffe] quilt, piqué; [avion] *descendre en ~*, to nosedive.

pique [pik] *n.f.* [arme] pike; [cartes] spades *n.pl.*: *la dame de ~*, the queen of spades. || **pique-assiette** [pika'sjɛt] *n.m.* sponger. || **pique-bois** [pik'bwɑ] © *n.m. inv.* woodpecker. cf. PIC. || **pique-nique** [pik'nik] *n.m.* picnic. || **piquer** [pi'k|e] #3 *v. tr.* to prick; [insectes] to bite, sting; [à travers] to stick; [Fig.] to pique; to rouse, stimulate; [avion] to dive: *Un moustique m'a piqué,* → I've been bitten by a mosquito; *~ la curiosité de,* to arouse s.o.'s curiosity. || **se piquer** *v. pron.* to prick o.s. (e.g. with a needle); *~ (de),* to take offence (from); [être fier de] to take pride in.

piquet [pi'k|e] *n.m.* **1.** post, stake, peg. **2.** [jeu] piquet. || **piqueter** ['te] #8 *v. tr.* **1.** to stake out. **2.** to spot, to dot.

piqueur [pi'kø] *n.m.* **1.** huntsman. **2.** outrider. || **piqueuse** [pi'kø:z] *n.f.* stitcher. || **piqûre** [-y:r] *n.f.* sting, bite (of insect); [Méd.] shot, injection [couture] stitching.

pirate [pi'rat] *n.m.* pirate.

pire [pi:r] [Irr. compar. of MAL] *adj.* worse: *la ~ tempête de l'année,* the worst storm of the year. || *n.m. le ~*, the worst. ☞ [This is a noun; cf. PIS].

pirogue [pi'rɔg] *n.f.* dugout canoe, pirogue.

pirouette [pi'rwɛt] *n.f.* pirouette. || **pirouetter** [-e] #3 *v. intr.* to pirouette.

pis[1] [pi] *adv.* worse. cf. MAL: *au ~ aller,* as a last resource; *aller de mal en ~*, to go from bad to worse. || *adj.* worse: *Tant ~ pour vous!,* You've had it! || *n.m. le pis,* the worst: *mettre les choses au ~*, to assume the worst.

pis[2] [pi] *n.m.* udder.

piscine [pi'sin] *n.f.* swimming pool.

pissenlit [pisɑ̃'li] *n.m.* dandelion.

pisser [pi'se] # 3 *v. tr. & intr.* [Vulg.] to piss.

piste [pist] *n.f.* [sport] track; [ski] trail; [aérodrome] airstrip, runway; [Fig.] clue, track: *être sur une fausse ~*, to be barking up the wrong tree. || **pister** [pist'e] #3 *v. tr.* to track (game); [police, &c.] to shadow.

†**pistole** [pis'tɔl] *n.f.* pistole [former gold coin; in place names, cf. TROIS PISTOLES].

pistolet [pistɔ'lɛ] *n.m.* pistol; *~ à peinture,* spray gun; *~ à dessiner*, French curve.

piston [pis't|õ] *n.m.* piston; [Fam.] *avoir du ~ (auprès de),* to have some pull (with). || **pistonner** [-ɔ'ne] #3 *v. tr.* [Fig.] to back (a candidate): *Il est très pistonné,* He has influential friends.

piteu|x, -se [pi'tø(:z)] *adj.* pitiful, sorry: *en ~ état,* in a sorry state.

pitié [pi'tje] *n.f.* pity, mercy, compassion: *avoir ~ de,* to/take, have/pity on, to feel sorry for; → to pity: *faire ~ à, exciter la ~ de (qqun),* to excite s.o.'s pity; *par ~*, out of compassion.

piton [pi'tõ] *n.m.* **1.** screw ring. **2.** [montagne] peak.

pitou [pi'tu] © *n.m.* [☞ the usual pet name for a dog] dog; tyke.

pitoyable [pitwa'jabl] *adj.* pitiful.

pittoresque [pitɔ'rɛsk] *adj.* picturesque.

pivert [pi'vɛ:r] *n.m.* cf. PIC.

pivot [pi|'vo] *n.m.* pivot, swivel. || **pivoter**

[-vɔ'te] #3 *v. intr.* to pivot, to swing around.

placage [pla'ka:ʒ] *n.m.* [bois] veneer(ing); [metal] plating.

plaçai [pla'se] cf. PLACER.

placard [pla'k|a:r] *n.m.* **1.** cupboard, closet. **2.** poster. **3.** galley (proof). || **placarder** [-ar'de] #3 *v. tr.* to post, stick up.

place [plas] *n.f.* **1.** room: *Il n'y a plus de ~*, There is no more room. **2.** seat: *Cette ~ est-elle libre?*, Is this seat taken? **3.** square: *la plus grande ~ de la ville*, the largest square in the city. **4.** position, job: *Il a perdu sa ~*, He's lost his job. **5.** Loc. *sur ~*, on the spot; *à la ~ de*, instead of; *Mettez-vous à ma ~*, Put yourself in my place; *remettre qqun à sa ~*, to take s.o. down a peg or two; *prendre ~*, to/ sit, stand; *faire ~ à*, to make room for. || **placement** [-'mɑ̃] *n.m.* **1.** [Fin.] investment. **2.** employment: *bureau de ~*, employment agency. || **placer** [-e] #4 *v. tr.* **1.** to place, [chose] to set, [personne] to give a seat to: *être bien placé*, to have a good seat. **2.** [argent] to invest. || **se placer** *v. pron.* **1.** to place o.s., to stand, to sit. **2.** to get a job (as, *comme*).

placide [pla'sid] *adj.* placid, unruffled, calm.

plafond [pla'fõ] *n.m.* ceiling. || **plafonnier** [plafɔ'nje] *n.m.* ceiling light.

plage [pla:ʒ] *n.f.* beach; [seaside] resort.

plagiaire [pla'ʒj|ɛ:r] *adj.* plagiarizing. || *n.m.* plagiarist. || **plagiat** [-a] *n.m.* plagiarism. || **plagier** [-e] #3 *v. tr.* to plagiarize.

plaider [plɛ'd|e] #3 *v. intr.* **1.** to plead (for, *pour*). **2.** [avocat] to present a case in court. **3.** [plaignant] to go to law. || *v. tr.* to plead: *~ sa cause*, to plead o.'s cause. || **plaideur** [-œ:r] *n.m.* suitor, petitioner, litigant. || **plaidoirie** [-wa'ri] *n.f.* pleading, lawyer's speech. || **plaidoyer** [-wa'je] *n.m.* plea, argument.

plaie [plɛ] *n.f.* wound, cut, sore; [Fig.] plague, bane.

plaignant, -e [plɛ'ɲɑ̃] *n. m/f* plaintiff.

plaigne(s) cf. PLAINDRE.

plain [plɛ̃] *adj.*: *de ~ -pied*, on the/same, one/floor; level with.

plaindre [plɛ̃:dr], **plaignant** [plɛ'ɲɑ̃], **plaint** [plɛ̃] #36 *v. tr.* to pity s.o., have pity on s.o., be sorry for s.o.: *Je vous plains*, I feel sorry for you. || **se plaindre** *v. pron.* to complain (*à*, to; *de*, about); to grumble, to moan.

plaine[1] [plɛn] *n.f.* plain; field: *les plaines de l'Ouest*, the Plains. || **plaine**[2] *n.f.* © plane (tree).

plains [plɛ̃] cf. PLAINDRE.

plainte [plɛ̃:t] *n.f.* complaint, reproach; [son] moan, whine; [law] *déposer une ~ contre qqun*, to lodge a complaint against s.o. || **plainti|f, -ve** [plɛ̃t|if, -i:v] *adj.* complaining: [voix] plaintive; [attitude] doleful. || **plaintivement** [-iv'mɑ̃] *adv.* plaintively.

plaire [plɛ:r] **plaisant, plu** #49 *v. intr.* **1.** to please: *~ à qqun*, to please s.o.; *Cela m'a plu*, → I enjoyed it; *Cela ne me plaît pas*, I don't care for it. **2.** [abs.] to please, be pleasing: *s'il vous plaît*, (if you) please (abr. SVP); *Fermez la porte, s'il vous plaît*, Please close the door; *comme il vous plaira*, as you like (it). || **se plaire** *v. pron.* to take delight (*à*, in); to like, to love: *Je me plais à la campagne*, I like it in the country.

plaisais, &c. [plɛ'zɛ] cf. PLAIRE.

plaisance [plɛ'z|ɑ̃:s] *n.f.* [Naut.] [boating, yachting]: *navire m de ~*, yacht, pleasure boat. || **plaisancier** [-ɑ̃'sje] *n.m.* yacht, yachtsman. || **plaisant** [-ɑ̃] *n.m.* joker: *mauvais ~*, practical joker. || **plaisant, -e** [-ɑ̃(:t)] *adj.* funny, humorous; pleasant. || **plaisanter** [-ɑ̃'te] #3 *v. tr.* to joke, make fun of: *en plaisantant*, for fun. || **plaisanterie** [-ɑ̃t'ri] *n.f.* joke; [parole] witticism, humour.

plaisir [plɛ'zi:r] *n.m.* **1.** pleasure, delight: *avec ~*, willingly, with pleasure; *avoir/ trouver, prendre du/ ~ à qqch.*, to take/ pleasure, delight/in . . . ; *faire ~ à*, to give pleasure to . . . . **2.** consent, approbation; [Formules polies] *J'ai le (grand) ~ de . . .*, It gives me (great) pleasure to . . . ; *Faites-moi le ~ de . . .*, Be so kind as to . . . ; [as a polite but very firm request]: Please see to it that . . . . || **plaît** [plɛ] cf. PLAIRE. + *plaît-il?*, (I) beg your pardon?; [Fam.] *ça me plaît*, I like it.

plan[1] [plɑ̃] *n.m.* **1.** plan (of a house); map (of a city); [Géom.] plane: *au premier ~*, in the foreground; *à l'arrière-~*, in the background; [Photo] *gros ~*, close-up. **2.** [projet] plan, project; [Péj.] scheme: *laisser qqun en ~*, to leave s.o. in the lurch. **plan,**[2] **-e** [plɑ̃, plan] *adj.* flat, even (ground). || **planche** [plɑ̃:ʃ] *adj.* ©: *un terrain ~*, a flat, level/tract of land. || **planche** [plɑ̃:ʃ] *n.f.* board, plank; [jardin] bed; [Fig.] *~ de salut*, sheet-anchor. || **plancher** [plɑ̃ʃ|e] *n.m.* floor (× but *first floor, &c.* → ÉTAGE). || **planchette** [-ɛt] *n.f.* small board.

planer [pla'n|e] #3 *v. intr.* to glide (on wings), to soar (into the air); [Fig.] to hang (over, *sur*). || *v. tr.* to plane (down).

planète [pla'nɛt] *n.f.* planet.

planeur [pla'nœ:r] *n.m.* glider.

planification [planifika'sjõ] *n.f.* planning.

planquer [plɑ̃'ke] #3 *v. tr.* [Fam.] to hide. || **se planquer** *v. pron.* to hide out.

plant [plɑ̃] *n.m.* seedling, [jeune arbre] sapling. || **plantation** [-ta'sjõ] *n.f.* planting; [grande ferme] plantation.

plante [plɑ̃:t] *n.f.* **1.** plant: *Jardin des Plantes,* Botanical Gardens. **2.** sole (of the foot). || **planté** [plɑ̃'t|e] *adj.* [Fig.] *bien* ~, well set-up. || **planter** [-e] #3 *v. tr.* to plant; [Fig.] to set (up); [Fam.] ~ *là* (*qqun*), to give (s.o.) the slip. || **se** ~, *v. pron.* to stand in front of, remain standing. || **planteur** [-œ:r] *n.m.* planter, grower; plantation-owner. || **plantoir** [-wa:r] *n.m.* dibble.

plantureu|x, -se [plɑty'rø(:z)] *adj.* abundant, fertile, plentiful, rich.

plaque [plak] *n.f.* [métal, photo] plate; [décoration, &c.] plaque; badge (of policeman). || **plaqué** [-e] *adj.* plated; [bois] veneered. || *n.m.* plated (metal). || **plaquer** [-e] #3 *v. tr.* [métal] to plate (with, *de*); [bois] to veneer; [Fig.] ~ *un accord* (*sur le piano*), to strike a chord; [Fam.] to jilt, abandon. || **plaquette** [-ɛt] *n.f.* **1.** small/plate, slab/. **2.** thin book, pamphlet.

plastique [plas'tik] *adj.* plastic. || *n.f.* plastic art. || *n.m.* plastics.

plastron [plas|'trõ] *n.m.* **1.** shirtfront. **2.** breastplate, plastron. || **plastronner** [-trɔ'ne] #3 *v. tr.* to swagger, strut.

plat, -e [plɑ, plat] *adj.* flat, even, level; [Fig. ©] dull: *farce plate,* corny joke; *à* ~, lying flat; *être à* ~ *-ventre,* → to lie flat on one's/face, stomach/. || **plat** [plɑ] *n.m.* dish; course (of a meal): *œufs sur le* ~, fried eggs; [partie plate] flat.

Plata (Rio de la) [(rio də la) pla'ta] *n.f.* the Plate River, [Br.] the River Plate.

platane [pla'tan] *n.m.* plane tree; ~ *d'occident* [© *sycomore*], sycamore.

plateau [pla'to] *n.m.* **1.** tray. **2.** plateau, tableland. **3.** [théâtre] stage.

plate-bande [plat'bɑ̃:d] *n.f.* flowerbed.

platée [pla'te] *n.f.* dishful, plateful.

plate-forme [plat'fɔrm] *pl.* **plates-formes** *n.f.* platform: *wagon* ~, flatcar.

platine [pla'tin] *n.m.* platinum.

platitude [plati'tyd] *n.f.* **1.** flatness, dullness. **2.** platitude.

plâtre [plɑ:tr] *n.m.* plaster. || **plâtrer** [plɑ'tre] #3 *v. tr.* to plaster.

plausible [plo'zibl] *adj.* plausible.

plébiscite [plebi'sit] *n.m.* plebiscite.

plein, -e [plɛ̃, plɛn] *adj.* **1.** full, filled (with, *de*): *un verre* ~, a full glass; ~ *comme un œuf,* chock-full; *Il est* ~ *de lui-même,* He is full of himself. **2.** full, complete: *la pleine lune,* the full moon; *en* ~ *jour,* in broad daylight; *en* ~ *air,* in the open, outdoors; *en pleine mer,* on the high seas; *en* ~ *centre de la ville,* right in the centre of the town. || *n.m.* [Loc.] *faire le* ~ (*d'essence*), to/fill, tank/up; *battre son* ~, to be in full swing.

plénipotentiaire [plenipɔtɑ̃'sjɛ:r] *adj.* & *n.m.* plenipotentiary.

plénitude [pleni'tyd] *n.f.* (over-)abundance, ful(l)ness; plenitude.

†**pleur** [plœ:r]: *verser un* ~, to shed a tear; *en pleurs,* in tears. || **pleurer** [plœ'r|e] #3 *v. intr.* to weep, [Fam.] to cry; ~ *de joie,* to weep for joy; [de froid] *Mes yeux pleuraient de froid,* My eyes were running. || *v. tr.* to mourn s.o. || **pleurnichard, -e** [-ni'ʃa:r, -ni'ʃard] *adj.* whimpering, snivelling. || **pleurnicher** [-ni'ʃe] #3 *v. intr.* to whimper, snivel; [chien] to whine.

pleut [plø], **pleuve** [plœv] cf. PLEUVOIR. || **pleuvoir** [plœ'vwa:r] #77 *v. imp.* to rain: *Il pleut,* It is raining; *Il va pleuvoir,* It is going to rain; *Il pleut/à verse, à seaux, à boire debout/,* It is raining buckets; It is raining cats and dogs. [N.B. © *Fam.* il mouille = il pleut, cf. PLUIE.]

pli [pli] *n.m.* **1.** fold; *faux* ~, crease, wrinkle; [terrain] undulation; [habitude] habit. **2.** [postes] message, letter; envelope: *sous* ~ *cacheté,* in a sealed envelope; *sous ce* ~, enclosed, herewith; *sous* ~ *séparé,* under separate cover. || **pliable** [pli'j|abl] *adj.* pliable. || **pliage** *n.m.* folding. || **pliant, -e** [-ɑ̃(:t)] *adj.* folding (chair); pliable, flexible. || **plier** [-e] #3 *v. tr. & intr.* to fold (up); to bow; to bend; [Fig.] to give way, yield: ~ *bagages,* to fold up; ~ *du linge,* to fold up linen; *Le pont plia sous son poids.* The bridge/gave, bent/under his weight. || **plisser** [pli'se] #3 *v. tr.* to pleat, crease; [lèvres] to pucker.

plomb [plõ] *n.m.* lead; [de chasse] shot; *sous* ~ *de douane,* in bond, bonded; [Fam.] *un plomb,* a fuse. || **plombage** [-'ba:ʒ] *n.m.* filling, stopping (of teeth). || **plombé, -e** [-be] *adj.* [teint] leaden; [douanes] in bond, sealed; [dent] filled, stopped. || **plomber** [-'be] #3 *v. tr.* **1.** to seal with lead. **2.** to [illegible] (teeth). **3.** to plumb. || **plomberie** [-b'ri] *n.f.* plumber('s); plumbing. || **plombier** [-'bje] *n.m.* plumber.

plongée [plõ'ʒ|e] *n.f.* dive, plunge; [terrain] dip. || **plongeon** [-õ] *n.m.* dive: *faire* *un* ~, → to dive; to duck; [oiseau] loon cf. HUARD. || **plonger** [-e] *v. tr.* #5 to plunge, to immerse, dip. || *v. intr.* to dive, to submerge; to duck; [navire] to pitch. || **se plonger (dans)** #5 *v. pron.* to plunge, [Fig.] to get immersed in, to pore over. || **plongeur, -euse** [-œ:r, -ø:z] *n.* **1.** diver. **2.** dishwasher.

ployer [plwa'je] #12 *v. tr. & intr.* to bend. cf. PLIER.

plu[1] [ply] cf. PLAIRE.

plu[2] [ply] cf. PLEUVOIR.

pluie [plɥi] *n.f.* rain: *le régime des pluies,* the rainfall; *la* ~, rain; *une* ~, a shower; *une* ~ */battante, diluvienne/,* a downpour; *Le temps est à la* ~, It looks like rain; *un jour de* ~, a rainy day, cf. PLEUVOIR.

plumage [ply'ma:ʒ] *n.m.* plumage, feathers. || **plume** [plym] *n.f.* **1.** feather, plume. **2.** pen; © fountain-pen [= Fr. *stylo*]. || **plumeau** [-o] *n.m.* (feather-) duster. || **plumer** [-e] #3 *v. tr.* to pluck (fowls); [Fig.] to fleece; © [Fam.] to peel (potatoes, &c.). || **plumier** [-je] *n.m.* [école] pen box.

plupart (la) [ply'pa:r] *n.f.*: *La* ~ *des gens ne le font pas,* Most people don't do it.

pluriel [ply'rjɛl] *n.m.* plural: *au* ~, in the plural.

plus[1] [Two pronunciations: [plys] meaning *more* and [ply] meaning *no more,* when the word comes at the end of a clause. ☞ Never used before: antérieur, extérieur, inférieur, intérieur, majeur, meilleur, mineur, moindre, pire, postérieur, supérieur, ultérieur.] *adv.* **1.** more, -er (than, *que*): ~ *tard,* later; ~ *difficile,* more difficult. **2.** *ne* . . . ~, no more, not any more; no longer, not any longer: *Nous ne les voyons* ~, We don't see them any more; *Il n'y est* ~, He is no longer there. **3.** the most, -est; best: *au* ~, at most; *d'autant* ~, all the more so; *celui que j'aime le* ~, the one (whom, that) I love the most. **4.** [Loc.] *de* ~, moreover, besides; *ni* ~ *ni moins,* neither more nor less; *qui* ~ *est,* what is more . . . , moreover; *tout au* ~, at/the most, the outside, best/; *sans* ~ *tarder,* without further delay.

plus[2], **plut** [ply] cf. PLAIRE.

plusieurs [ply'zjœ:r] *adj. pl. & pron. indéf.* several, some.

plutôt [ply'to] *adv.* rather (*que,* than) [× Do not confuse with *plus tôt* (*que*), earlier (than).]

pluvieu|x, -se [ply'vjø(:z)] *adj.* rainy, wet.

pneu [pnø] *n.m.* [abr. de *pneumatique*] tire [Br. tyre]: ~ *de/secours, rechange/,* spare (tire). || **pneumatique** [-ma'tik] *adj.* pneumatic. *n.m.* **1.** tire. **2.** [Paris] special delivery letter, [abbr. **pneu**].

pneumonie [pnømɔ'ni] *n.f.* pneumonia.

poche [pɔʃ] *n.f.* **1.** pocket. **2.** pouch, bag; © *une* ~ *de farine,* a peck of flour. || **poché** [-e] *adj.*: *œuf m* ~, poached egg; *œil m* ~, black eye; "shiner". || **pochette** [-ɛt] *n.f.* **1.** small pocket, folder: ~ *à disque,* record jacket; [Tech.] kit. **2.** fancy handkerchief; [allumettes] book.

poêle[1] [pwa:l] *n.m.* **1.** stove; © [abus.] kitchen stove [Fr. CUISINIÈRE]. || *n.m.* pall; canopy.

poêle[2] *n.f.*: ~ *(à frire),* frying pan.

poème [pɔ|'ɛm] *n.m.* poem. || **poésie** [-e'zi] *n.f.* poetry; [poème] poem, piece of poetry. || **poète** [-ɛt] *n.m.* poet. || **poétesse** [-e'tɛs] *n.f.* poetess. || **poétique** [-e'tik] *adj.* poetic(al).

poids [pwɑ] *n.m.* pl. unchanged. **1.** weight: *les* ~ *et mesures,* weights and measures; *un* ~ *d'une livre,* a weight of one pound; *vendre qqch. au* ~, to sell sth. by weight, by the pound; ~ */brut, net/,* /gross, net/ weight. **2.** weight, burden, load; [Fig.] importance; *le* ~ *des ans,* the weight of years; *avoir du* ~, to be of weight, of consequence.

poignant, -e [pwa'ɲɑ̃(:t)] *adj.* poignant, keen.

poignard [pwa'ɲ|a:r] *n.m.* dagger. || **poignarder** [-ar'de] #3 *v. tr.* to stab, knife.

poigne [pwaɲ] *n.f.* grip, grasp: *un homme à* ~, a strong-willed man. || **poignée** [-e] *n.f.* **1.** handful: ~ *de main,* handshake. **2.** [porte] handle, [revolver] grip; [outil] haft. || **poigner** [-e] © #3 *v. tr.* to grasp; [Fig.] *Il s'est fait* ~, He got caught. || **poignet** [-ɛ] *n.m.* wrist; [de chemise] cuff.

poil [pwal] *n.m.* hair (of animals; of persons, other than that of the head → LES CHEVEUX); bristle; *à longs poils,* shaggy, long-haired (= *poilu*). || **poilu, -e** [-y] hairy, shaggy; [Hist.] French soldier.

poinçon [pwɛ̃'s|ɔ̃] *n.m.* **1.** punch. **2.** [monnaie] stamp. **3.** [garantie] hallmark. || **poinçonner** [-ɔ'ne] #3 *v. tr.* to punch; to stamp.

poindre [pwɛ̃:dr] #36 *v. intr.* to begin to appear, to dawn; to sprout.

poing [pwɛ̃] *n.m.* fist; clenched hand: *dormir à poings fermés,* to sleep like a/log, top/; *donner un coup de* ~ *à qqun,* to hit, to give (s.o.) a blow.

point [pwɛ̃] *n.m.* **1.** speck, dot, mark: ~ *et virgule,* semicolon; *deux points,* colon; ~ *d'exclamation,* exclamation mark; ~ *d'interrogation,* question mark.

2. [Fig.] point: *Il a insisté sur ce ~*, He stressed that point. 3. point, degree: *~ d'ébullition*, boiling point. 4. [Scol.] point, mark: *perdre des points*, to lose points; *marquer des points*, to score; *bon ~*, good mark. 5. stitch: *~ de côté*, stitch in the side; *~ de suture*, stitch. 6. [Loc.] *venir à ~*, to come at the right moment; *cuit à ~*, done to a turn; *être sur le ~ de partir*, to be about to leave; *être au ~*, to be/ready, in good shape, in focus/; *mettre au ~*, to develop, to focus; [Auto.] *être au ~ mort*, to be in neutral. || **pointage** *n.m.* 1. [gun] laying. 2. checking. || **pointe** [pwɛ̃:t] *n.f.* 1. point; sharp end, tip (of knife): *en ~*, tapering; *marcher sur la ~ des pieds*, to tiptoe. 2. nail, tack. 3. [Géog.] cape, point: *Pointe St-Charles*, Point St. Charles. || **pointeur** [-œ:r] *n.m.* [Mil.] pointer, marker: [vérificateur] checker. || **pointillé** [-i'je] *n.m.* dotted line. || **pointilleu|x, -se** [-i'jø(:z)] *adj.* particular, fastidious. || **pointu, -e** [-y] *adj.* sharp, pointed. || **pointure** [-y:r] *n.f.* size, number (of shirts, shoes, gloves, &c.).

poire [pwa:r] *n.f.* pear; [caoutchouc] bulb; [Loc.] *une ~ pour la soif*, a nest-egg; *couper la ~ en deux*, to split the difference; [Fig., Fam.] dupe, sucker.

poireau [pwa'ro] *n.m.* leek.

poireauter [pwarɔ'te] #3 *v. intr.* to kick o.'s heels.

poirier [pwa'rje] *n.m.* pear tree.

pois [pwɑ] *n.m. inv.* pea(s): *~ verts, petits ~*, green peas; *soupe aux ~*, pea soup; [motif] polka dot. [× Do not confuse with POIDS.]

poison [pwa'zõ] *n.m.* poison; [Fig.] venom.

poisson [pwa's|õ] *n.m.*: *du ~*, fish; *beaucoup de poissons*, a lot of fish; *~ d'eau douce*, fresh-water fish; *~ de mer*, salt-water fish; *~ rouge*, gold fish; © *~ / des chenaux, des Trois-Rivières/*, tomcod, frostfish. || **poissonnerie** [-ɔn'ri] *n.f.* fish market. || **poissonneu|x, -se** [-ɔ'nø(:z)] *adj.* / full of, abounding in/fish. || **poissonni|er, -ère** [-ɔ'nj|e, -ɛ:r] *n.* fish dealer, [Br.] fishmonger.

poitrail [pwa'tra:j] *n.m.* breast (of a horse).

poitrinaire [pwatri'nɛ:r] *adj.* consumptive. || **poitrine** [pwa'trin] *n.f.* chest; [dame] bust; breast; † lungs.

poivre [pwa:vr] *n.m.* pepper. || **poivrer** [pwa'vr|e] #3 *v. tr.* to pepper. || **poivrier** [-i'je] *n.m.* 1. pepper-plant. 2. pepper-shaker. || **poivrière** [-i'jɛ:r] *n.f.* 1. pepper box. 2. corner turret.

poix [pwɑ] *n.f.* pitch.

polaire [pɔ'lɛ:r] *adj.* polar, of the pole: *l'étoile ~*, the north star. || **pôle** [po:l] *n.m.* pole: *le ~ /nord, sud/*, the / North, South/Pole.

polémique [pɔle'mik] *n.f.* polemic; polemics.

poli, -e [pɔ'li] *adj.* 1. polished, glossy. 2. polite; civil, courteous. || *n.m.* polish, gloss.

police [pɔ'lis] *n.f.* 1. police; constabulary; *agent (de ~)*, policeman, [Fam.] cop; *la ~ de Montréal*, the Montreal Police (Force); © *n.f.* policeman; [Fig.] *faire la ~*, to keep order. 2. *~ d'assurance*, insurance policy. || **policer** [-e] #4 *v. tr.* 1. to civilize. 2. to police, to control. || **policier** [-je] *n.m.* plain-clothes man, detective; © constable.

poliment [pɔli'mɑ̃] *adv.* politely.

polio(myélite), [pɔ'ljo(mje'lit)] *n.f.* polio (myelitis); infantile paralysis.

polir [pɔ'li:r] #17 *v. tr.* to polish; [Fig.] to lick . . . into shape. || **polisseu|r, -se** [pɔli's|œ:r, -ø:z] *n.* polisher, French-polisher. || **polissoir** [-wa:r] *n.m.* polisher, polishing machine or tool, buffer.

polisson, -ne [pɔli's|õ, -ɔn] *n.* scamp, rascal. || *adj.* smutty; *regard ~*, leer. **polissonnerie** [pɔlisɔn'ri] *n.f.* depravity, [enfant] mischievousness, [acte] lewdness, [plaisanterie] dirtiness.

politesse [pɔli'tɛs] politeness, good breeding.

politicien [pɔliti'sj|ɛ̃, -ɛn] *n.m.* [Péj.] politician. || **politique** [pɔli'tik] *adj.* political; *homme ~*, statesman; [Fig.] prudent, wise. || *n.f. la ~*, politics; public affairs; [Fig.] policy (of a company, &c.).

polluer [pɔl'lqe] #3 *v. tr.* to pollute, defile. || **pollution** [pɔly'sjõ] *n.f.* pollution.

Pologne [pɔ'lɔ|ɲ] *n.f.* Poland. || **polonais, -e** [-'nɛ(:z)] *adj.* Polish. || *n.* Pole; [langue] Polish.

poltron, -ne [pɔl'tr|õ, -ɔn] *n.* coward. || *adj.* cowardly. || **poltronnerie** [-ɔn'ri] *n.f.* cowardice.

polycopier [pɔlikɔ'pje] #3 *v. tr.* to mimeograph. || **polyglotte** [pɔli'glɔt] *n.m.* linguist. || **polygone** [pɔli'gɔn] *n.m.* polygon.

Polynésie [pɔline'zi] *n.f.* Polynesia.

pommade [pɔ'mad] *n.f.* pomade, [lèvres] salve. || **pommader** [-e] #3 || *v. tr.* to pomade (one's hair).

pomme [pɔm] *n.f.* 1. apple; *~ de terre*, potato [often abbr. to *pomme*]; [Fr.] *~ frites*, French fries. 2. [round objects] ball; [canne] knob; head (of lettuce), cf. PIED; *~ de pin*, cone; [Fig.] *~ de discorde*, bone of contention. || **pommelé, -e**

[le] *adj.* mottled, dappled (sky). || **pommette** [-ɛt] *n.f.* **1.** cheek-bone. **2.** © crab apple. || **pommetier** [-(ə)'tje] © *n.m.* hawthorn tree. || **pommier** [-je] *n.m.* apple tree.
pompe[1] [pɔ̃:p] *n.f.* pomp, ceremony; [Fr.] *pompes funèbres,* undertaker, funeral parlour.
pompe[2] *n.f.* pump. || **pomper** [pɔ̃'p|e] #3 *v. tr.* to pump; to suck up.
pompeu|x, -se [-ø(:z)] *adj.* pompous; [style] highfalutin.
pompier [pɔ̃'pje] *n.m.* fireman. || *adj.* conventional, uninspired.
pompon [pɔ̃'pɔ̃] *n.m.* tassel; [Mil.] pompon.
ponce [pɔ̃:s] *adj.*: *pierre f* ~, pumice (stone). || **poncer** [pɔ̃'se] #4 *v. tr.* to pumice, pounce.
ponci|f, -ve [pɔ̃'s|if, -i:v] *adj.* trite, commonplace. || *n.m.* conventional piece of work.
ponctualité [pɔ̃ktɥali'te] *n.f.* punctuality.
ponctuation [pɔ̃ktɥa'sjɔ̃] *n.f.* punctuation.
ponctuel, -le [pɔ̃k'tɥɛl] *adj.* punctual, prompt.
pondération [pɔ̃der|a'sjɔ̃] *n.f.* balance. || **pondéré, -e** [-e] *adj.* [Fig.] sensible, moderate.
pondre [pɔ̃:dr], #42 *v. tr.* to lay eggs. || **pondu** [pɔ̃'dy] cf. PONDRE.
pont [pɔ̃] *n.m.* **1.** bridge; [Naut.] deck; [Auto.] ~ *arrière,* rear axle: *le Pont Jacques Cartier,* the Jacques Cartier Bridge; [Fr.] *Ponts & Chaussées,* Roads Department; ~ *suspendu,* suspension bridge; ~ *tournant,* swing bridge; ~ *aérien,* airlift; ~ *-levis,* drawbridge. **2.** [Fr.] *faire le* ~, to have a long weekend.
pontife [pɔ̃'tif]: *le Souverain* ~, the Pope. || **pontificat** [-i'ka] *n.m.* [R.C.] the Holy See; [temps] pontificate.
ponton [pɔ̃'tɔ̃] *n.m.* pontoon.
populace [pɔpy'l|as] *n.f.* [Péj. ×] rabble, mob. || **populaire** [-ɛ:r] *adj.* popular; [Péj.] vulgar, common. || **popularité** [-ari'te] *n.f.* popularity. || **population** [-a'sjɔ̃] *n.f.* population. || **populeu|x, -se** [-ø(:z)] *adj.* populous, thickly-settled. || **populo** [pɔpy'lo] *n.m.* [Fam. & Péj.] the common crowd, the rabble, the mob.
porc [pɔ:r] *n.m.* [vivant] pig, hog; cf. COCHON; [viande] pork; [injure] dirty swine.
porcelaine [pɔrsə'lɛn] *n.f.* china, chinaware.
porc-épic [pɔrke'pik] *n.m.* [pl. -s, -s] hedgehog; porcupine.
porche [pɔrʃ] *n.m.* porch; portico.
porcher [pɔr'ʃ|e] *n.m.* swineherd. || **porcherie** [-ə'ri] *n.f.* pigsty.
pore [pɔ:r] *n.m.* pore. || **poreu|x-, -se** [pɔ'rø(:z)] *adj.* porous.
port[1] [pɔ:r] *n.m.* port, harbour; wharf; seaport (town): ~ *de mer,* seaport; [Fig.] haven, refuge: *arriver à bon* ~, to arrive safely.
port[2] *n.m.* **1.** bearing. **2.** carrying: *le* ~ *d'une arme prohibée,* carrying a weapon without a permit. **3.** postage, shipping charges.
portage [pɔr't|a:ʒ] *n.m.* © portage. || **portager** [-a'ʒe] #5 *v. intr.* © to portage.
portail [pɔr'ta:j] *n.m.* gate.
portant [pɔr'tɑ̃] [Loc.]: *à bout* ~, point-blank.
portati|f, -ve [pɔrta't|if, -i:v] *adj.* portable.
porte [pɔrt] *n.f.* door, doorway; gate, gateway; entrance: ~ *à deux battants,* double door; ~ *-fenêtre,* French window; ~ *cochère,* carriage entrance; ~ *à soufflets,* folding door; *pousser la* ~, to push the door open, to push the door to; *forcer la* ~, to break the door open, [Fig.] to force admittance; *un bruit de* ~ *qu'on ferme,* the slam of a door. || **porte-avions** [pɔrt|a'vjɔ̃] *n.m. inv.* aircraft carrier. || **porte-bagages** [-ba'ga:ʒ] *n.m. inv.* carrier. || **porte-bannière** [-ba'njɛ:r] *n.m. inv.* standard-bearer. || **porte-bonheur** [-bɔ'nœ:r] *n.m. inv.* good-luck charm. || **porte-cartes** [-ə'kart] *n.m. inv.* card case. || **porte-cigarettes** [-siga'rɛt] *n.m. inv.* cigarette case. || **porte-couteau** [-ku'to] *n.m. inv.* knife rest. || **porte-drapeau** [-dra'po] *n.m. inv.* colour-bearer. || **porte-malheur** [-ma'lœ:r] *n.m. inv.* → that brings ill luck. || **porte-mine** [-ə'min] *n.m. inv.* mechanical pencil. || **porte-monnaie** [-mɔ'nɛ] *n.m. inv.* change purse. || **porte-parapluies** [-para'plɥi] *n.m. inv.* umbrella stand. || **porte-parole** [-pa'rɔl] *n.m. inv.* spokesman. || **porte-savon** [-sa'vɔ̃] *n.m. inv.* soap dish. || **porte-serviettes** [-sɛr'vjɛt] *n.m. inv.* towel rack.
porté, -e [pɔr'te] *adj.* carried; [Fig.] prone, given (to, *à*). || **portée** [pɔr'te] *n.f.* **1.** litter. **2.** [texte] import, significance. 3. [Mus.] stave. **4.** reach, range: *à* ~ *de la main,* within reach; *hors de la* ~ *de,* beyond the reach of; *hors de* ~, out of range.
portefeuille [pɔrtə'fœ:j] *n.m.* **1.** billfold, wallet. **2.** portfolio, office. || **portemanteau** [pɔrtmɑ̃'to] *n.m.* coat/rack, hanger/. || **porte-plume** [-ə'plym] *n.m.* penholder.
porter [pɔr't|e] #3 *v. tr. & intr.* **1.** to carry, take, bear: *Portez ce livre au bureau,* Take this book to the office; ~ *dans sa poche,* to carry in one's pocket; ~ *les armes,* to bear arms. **2.** to wear: ~

le deuil, to be in mourning; ~ *une montre-bracelet*, to wear a wristwatch. **3.** to yield, to bear: ~ *fruit*, to bear fruit; ~ *intérêt*, to bear interest. **4.** to/prove effective, tell, go, come home: *Le coup a porté*, The blow went home. **5.** [Loc.] ~ *un jugement sur*, to pass judgment on; ~ *témoignage*, to bear witness; ~ *un toast*, to propose a toast; *être porté(e) à*, to be inclined to. || **se porter** *v. pron.* **1.** to be (in good or bad health): *Il se porte bien*, He is well. **2.** to be/carried, worn: *Le brassard se porte au bras gauche*, The armlet is worn on the left arm. **3.** to move: ~ *au devant de qqun*, to go to meet s.o. || **porteu|r, -se** [-œːr, -øːz] *n.* [Rail., &c.] porter; [Fin.] holder: *donner ses bagages au* ~, give one's baggage to the porter; *faire un chèque au* ~, make a cheque out to the bearer.

portier [pɔr'tǀje] *n.m.* porter, janitor. || **portière** [-jɛːr] *n.f.* **1.** (carriage, car) door. **2.** portiere. || **portillon** [-i'jõ] *n.m.* gate.

portion [pɔr'sjõ] *n.f.* portion; share.

porto [pɔr'to] *n.m.* port (wine).

Porto Rico [pɔrtori'ko] *n.m.* Puerto Rico.

portrait [pɔr'trɛ] *n.m.* portrait; [Fig.] likeness, image.

pose [poːz] *n.f.* **1.** laying down; setting down: ~ *de la première pierre (d'un édifice)*, laying of the cornerstone. **2.** [Fig.] pose, attitude. **3.** [Photo.] exposure. || **posé, -e** [po'ze] *adj.* laid, set; [Fig.] sedate. || **poser** [po'ze] #3 *v. tr.* **1.** to/put, plan, set: [*à* plat] to lay; [debout] to stand. **2.** to put down: *Posez ça là-bas*, Put that down over there. **3.** [Math.] to put down: *Je pose neuf et je retiens un*, I put down nine and carry one. || *v. intr.* **1.** to sit (for one's picture). **2.** to pose, to assume a pose. || **se poser** *v. pron.* **1.** to perch, to alight, [avion] to come down. **2.** [Fig.] to pose: ~ *en*, to pose as; ~ *en défenseur de*, to act as the champion of.

poseu|r, -se [po'zœːr] *n.* poseur, snob, attitudinizer; [Fam.] phony.

positi|f, -ve [pozi|'tif, -tiːv] *adj.* **1.** actual, real. **2.** [Photo.] positive, print. || **positivement** [-tiv'mɑ̃] *adv.* absolutely, completely.

position [pozi'sjõ] *n.f.* position, place.

possédé, -e [pɔse'de] *adj.* possessed; [fou] maniac. || *n.* madman. || **posséder** [pɔse'de] #10 *v. tr.* to possess, to own, to have; [Fig.] to know perfectly, to have a command of: ~ *une propriété*, to own a piece of land; *Il possède le français à fond*, He has perfect command of French. || **se posséder** *v. pron.* to contain o.s., to control o.s. || †**possesseur** [pɔsɛ|'sœːr] owner, proprietor, → *propriétaire*. || **possession** [-'sjõ] *n.f.* ownership; property; †possession, colony.

possibilité [pɔsibili'te] *n.f.* possibility. || **possible** [pɔ'sibl] *adj.* possible; *Il est* ~ *qu'* [= *il se peut qu'*] *il le fasse*, → He might do it yet; *Il est* ~ *de* [= *on peut*] *le faire*, → It can be done; *C'est bien* ~, It's very likely; *Pas* ~ *!*, You don't say! || **possible** *n.m. faire (tout) son* ~ *pour*, to do one's/utmost, very best/to. . . .

postal, -e [pɔs'tal] *adj.* postal; *carte postale*, post-card; *colis* ~, parcel post.

poste[1] [pɔst] *n.m.* **1.** station; [Mil.] post: ~ *de douane*, port of entry; post, job: *être à son* ~, to be on duty.

poste[2] [pɔst] *n.m.* **1.** station; [Fr.] ~ *d'essence*, gas, service/station; ~ *d'incendie*, fire station; ~ *de secours*, first-aid station; [TSF] ~ *émetteur*, broadcasting station. **2.** set; ~ *de radio*, [Fr.] ~ *(de TSF)*, radio set.

poste[3] [pɔst] et pl. **Postes 1.** *n.f.* (pl) post, postal services: *Postes royales*, Royal mail; [Fr.] PTT [= Postes, Télégraphes et Téléphones], © *Ministère des Postes*, Post Office Department; © *Ministre des Postes*, Postmaster General; © *maître de* ~, postmaster; *bureau de* ~, (post-office) station. **2.** *n.f.* mail, [Br.] post; *mettre une lettre à la* ~, to mail a letter.

poster[1] [pɔs'te] #3 *v. tr.* to station, to post. || **se poster** *v. pron.* to take up one's/stand, post/, to lie in waiting.

***poster**[2] [pɔs'te] *v. tr.* to mail, post (a letter).

postérieur, -e [pɔste'rjœːr] *adj.* posterior, back; later, subsequent. (≠ ANTÉRIEUR). || *n.m.* [Fam.] behind, backside. || **postérité** [pɔsteri'te] *n.f.* posterity.

post-gradué, -e [pɔst|grady'e] © *adj. & n.* postgraduate.

posthume [pɔs'tym] *adj.* posthumous.

postiche [pɔs'tiʃ] *adj.* superadded; false.

posti|er, -ère [pɔs't|je, -jɛːr] *n.* [Fr.] postal employee; © mail-carrier.

***postillon** [pɔsti'jõ] *n.m.* postilion, courier; © postman [cf. Fr. FACTEUR].

post-scolaire [-skɔ'lɛːr] *adj.*: *enseignement* ~, adult education.

post-scriptum [pɔstskrip'tɔm] *n.m.* postscript.

postulant, -e [pɔsty'l|ɑ̃(ːt)] *n.* applicant, candidate. || **postulat** [-a] *n.m.* postulate. || **postuler** [-e] #3 *v. tr.* **1.** to postulate. **2.** to apply for (a job).

posture [pɔs'tyːr] *n.f.* posture; stance.

pot [po] *n.m.* pot; jug, jar: ~ *au lait*, milk jug; ~ *de peinture*, can; ~ */à, de/ fleurs*, flower pot; ~ *de chambre*, chamber (-pot); [Auto.] ~ *d'échappement*, muffler; [Culin.] *pot-au-feu*, hot-pot; [Loc.] *pot-de-vin*, bribe, graft; *manger à la fortune du* ~, to take pot luck; *tourner autour du* ~, to beat about the bush.

potable [pɔ'tabl] *adj.*: *eau* ~, drinking water.

potage [pɔ't|a:ʒ] *n.m.* [Culin.] soup [a more refined word than *soupe*]. || **potag|er, -ère** [-a'ʒe, -a'ʒɛ:r] *adj.* & *n.*: *le (jardin) potager*, vegetable garden; *plantes potagères*, herbs.

potasse [pɔ'tas] *n.f.* potash.

poteau [po'to] *n.m.* post, pole: [Fr.] ~ *indicateur*, signpost; ~ *télégraphique, téléphonique*, telegraph, telephone pole.

potelé, -e [pɔt'le] *adj.* plump, [bébé] chubby.

potence [pɔ'tɑ̃:s] *n.f.* gallows; [Tech.] bracket.

potentiel, -le [pɔtɑ̃'sjɛl] *adj.* potential.

poterie [pɔt|'ri] *n.f.* pottery, earthenware. || **potier** [-je] *n.m.* potter.

potin [pɔ'tɛ̃] *n.m.* **1.** [esp. pl.] gossip. **2.** [Fam.] row, racket: *faire du* ~, to kick up a row. || **potiner** [pɔti'ne] #3 *v. intr.* to gossip.

†**potion** [pɔ'sjõ] *n.f.* potion, draught.

potiron [pɔti'rõ] *n.m.* pumpkin.

pou, *pl.* **-x** [pu] *n.m.* louse (*pl.* lice).

poubelle [pu'bɛl] *n.f.* garbage can; dustbin.

pouce [pus] *n.m.* **1.** [main] thumb; [pied] big toe: [Fig.] *manger sur le* ~, to have a snack; *se tourner les pouces*, to loaf. **2.** inch [© abbr. *po.*] **3.** © hitch-hiking: *faire du* ~, to hitch-hike.

poudre [pudr] *n.f.* powder; [à canon] gun powder; [Fig.] dust: *réduire en* ~, to grind to powder; *café en* ~, instant coffee; *sucre en* ~, granulated sugar © icing sugar; © ~ *à pâte*, baking powder. cf. LEVURE; *(se) mettre de la* ~, to powder one's nose. || **poudrer** [-e] #3 *v. tr.* to (sprinkle with) powder. || **se poudrer** *v. pron.* to powder one's face. || **poudrerie** [-ə'ri] © *n.f.* **1.** blizzard; drifting snow. **2.** powder factory. || **poudrette** [-ɛt] © *n.f.* powderpuff. || **poudreu|x, -se** [-ø(:z)] dusty: © *neige poudreuse*, powdered snow. || **poudrier** [-i'je] *n.m.* powder compact. || **poudrière** [-i'jɛ:r] *n.f.* powder magazine.

pouilleu|x, -se [pu'jø(:z)] *adj.* lousy, covered with lice, cf. POU.

poulailler [pulɑ'je] *n.m.* henhouse.

poulain [pu'lɛ̃] *n.m.* foal, colt (fem. *pouliche*, filly).

poulamon [pula'mõ] © *n.m.* tomcod.

poule [pul] *n.f.* hen; fowl: ~ *d'eau*, water. hen; © ~ *des prairies*, prairie chicken; ~ *d'Inde*, hen-turkey; *chair f de* ~, gooseflesh; [Fig.] [Fam.] ~ *mouillée*, → molly coddle; namby-pamby; †[Sl.] doll. || **poulet** [-ɛ] *n.m.* [N.B. The feminine **poulette** [-ɛt], pullet, is rare.] chicken: ~ *rôti*, roast, barbecued/chicken; *soupe au* ~, chicken soup.

pouliche [pu'liʃ] *n.f.* filly [cf. POULAIN].

poulie [pu'li] *n.f.* pulley; block.

poulpe [pulp] *n.m.* octopus.

pouls [pu] *n.m.* pulse.

poumon [pu'mõ] *n.m.* lung.

poupe [pup] *n.f.* [Naut.] stern.

poupée [pu'p|e] *n.f.* doll: *jouer à la* ~, to play (with) dolls. || **poupon** [-õ] *n.m.* [Fam.] baby. || **pouponnière** [-ɔ'njɛ:r] *n.f.* nursery.

pour [pu:r] **1.** *prep.* [used with nouns] for, for the sake of; to: ~ *dix dollars*, for ten dollars; *Faites-le* ~ *moi*, Do it for my sake; ~ *moi, cela n'a pas d'importance*, To me, it is not important; *Il a été très bon* ~ *moi*, He was very good to me. **2.** *prép.* [used with verbs]: [aim] in order to; [cause] for, because: *Je l'ai fait* ~ *vous aider*, I did it to help you; *Il a échoué* ~ *s'y être pris trop tard*, He failed because he made too late a start. **3.** *conj.* so that; for . . . to: *Écartez-vous* ~ *que je puisse voir*, Stand aside so that I can see; ~ *qu'il ait agi ainsi, il doit y avoir une raison*, For him to act thus, there must be a reason. **4.** [Loc.] ~ *ainsi dire*, so to speak; ~ *cent*, per cent; ~ *ce qui est du reste*, as for the remainder; ~ *rire*, for a joke; *le* ~ *et le contre*, the pros and cons.

pourboire [pur'bwa:r] *n.m.* tip: ~ *compris*, tip included.

pourceau [pur'so] *n.m.* [Pej.] hog, swine, cf. PORC.

pour cent [pur'sɑ̃] [Loc.] per cent. || **pourcentage** [-'ta:ʒ] *n.m.* percentage.

pourchasser [purʃa'se] #3 *v. tr.* to chase (s.o.) around, to pursue.

pourcil [pur'si] *n.m.* © cf. MARSOUIN.

pourfendre [pur'fɑ̃:dr] #42 *v. tr.* to cleave asunder.

pourlécher (se) [purle'ʃe] #10 *v. tr.* to lick one's chops, lips.

pourparlers [purpar'le] *n.m.pl.* parley, talks; negotiations.

pourpre [purpr] *adj.* purple, crimson. || *n.f.* [Fig.] purple.

pour que cf. POUR §3.

pourquoi [pur'kwa] *adv.* why; wherefore; what . . . for?: ~ *pas?*, Why not?

|| *conj.* Why, what for: *c'est ~ ; voici, voilà ~ . . .* , that's why; therefore. *n.m.*: *le ~ (de)*, the reason why; the whys and the wherefores.

pourrai &c. cf. POUVOIR.

pourri, -e [pu'r|i] *adj.* rotten; [Fam.] spoiled. **pourrir** [-i:r], **pourrissant** [-i'sɑ̃], **pourri** [-i] #17 *v. tr. & intr.* to rot, to become rotten; [Fig.] to corrupt, to become corrupted; [Fam.] to spoil. || **pourriture** [-i'ty:r] *n.f.* decay, rot; [Fig.] corruption.

poursuis, poursuit, cf. POURSUIVRE.

poursuite [pur'sɥ|it] *n.f.* pursuit; chase; *n.pl.* [Law] suit, action: *entamer des poursuites contre*, to bring an action against. || **poursuivant** [-i'vɑ̃] *n.m.* [Law] plaintiff, prosecutor. || **poursuivre** [-i:vr] #51 *v. tr.* **1.** to pursue, chase, run after; [Fig.] to follow up, proceed with; persecute, annoy. **2.** [Law]: *poursuivre qqun en justice*, to sue, to bring an action against s.o. || *v. intr.* **poursuivre**: to go on, carry on, continue.

pourtant [pur'tɑ̃] *adv.* yet, however; nevertheless.

pourtour [pur'tu:r] *n.m.* circumference.

pourvoi [pur'vw|a] *n.m.* [Law] appeal. || **pourvoir** [-a:r] *équivalent de* #71 *v. intr.* to provide (*à*, for); to attend (*à*, to); to furnish (*de*, with). || **se pourvoir** *v. pron.* to provide o.s. (*de*, with); [Law] to appeal. || **pourvu** [pur'vy] *adj.* (well) provided (*de*, with): *bien ~ des choses de ce monde*, → with an abundance of worldly goods. || **pourvu que** *conj.* provided [+ subj.]; [Exclam.] Let's hope that . . .

pousse [pus] *n.f.* [Bot.] shoot. || **poussée** [-e] *n.f.* thrust, push; pressure: *sous la ~ de l'opinion publique*, under pressure from public opinion. cf. POUSSER. || **pousser** [-e] #3 *v. tr.* **1.** to push, to shove: *Ne poussez pas*, Don't push; *~ une porte*, to push a door/open, to/. **2.** to urge, to egg on: **3.** [Loc.] *~ un cri*, to utter a cry; *~ un soupir*, to heave a sigh. || *v. intr.* **1.** to grow: *faire ~* , to grow, [US] to raise. **2.** to push on: *Il a poussé jusqu'à Lyon*, He pushed on to Lyons. || **se pousser** *v. pron.* to push forward: *Il s'est poussé au premier rang*, He pushed his way through to the first row; to move aside: *Pousse-toi!*, Move over!

poussière [pu'sj|ɛ:r] *n.f.* dust; powder, cf. POUDRE. || **poussiéreu|x, -se** [-e'rø(:z)] *adj.* dusty.

poussi|f, -ve [pu's|if, -i:v] *adj.* pursy, wheezy.

poussin [pu'sɛ̃] *n.m.* chick.

poutre [putr] *n.f.* beam; [steel] girder. || **poutrelle** [-ɛl] *n.f.* small girder.

pouvais &c. cf. POUVOIR.

pouvoir [pu'v|wa:r], **pouvant** [-ɑ̃], **pu** [py] #70 *v. intr. & occasionally tr.* **1.** to be able to, can: *Je ne peux pas y arriver*, I can't manage it; *Je n'en peux plus*, I am worn out; *Je n'y peux rien*, I can't help it. **2.** to be allowed to, may: *Vous pouvez partir*, You may go. **3.** to be likely to, may: *Il peut pleuvoir*, It may rain; *Puis-je vous aider?*, May I help you?; *Puisse-t-il venir!*, May he come!; *Il a pu oublier*, He may have forgotten; *Ça peut valoir deux dollars*, It may cost two dollars. **4.** *impers. Il se peut qu'il accepte*, He may agree; *Il se pourrait qu'il arrive plus tôt*, He might conceivably arrive sooner.

prairie [prɛ'ri] *n.f.* meadow; prairie: © *les Provinces des Prairies*, the Prairie Provinces; © *la rivière des Prairies*, the Back River.

praticable [prati|'kabl] *adj.* **1.** practicable, feasible. **2.** [roads] passable, cf. CARROSSABLE. || **praticien** [-'sjɛ̃] *n.m.* practitioner. || **pratiquant, -e** [-'kɑ̃(:t)] *adj.* churchgoing. || **pratique** [pra'tik] *adj.* practical, convenient: *esprit ~* , matter-of-fact. || *n.f.* **1.** practice; observance: *mettre en ~* , to put into practice; *la ~ des affaires*, business experience. **2.** habit, custom: *c'est la pratique ici de*, → it is customary here to . . . **3.** practice (of sports): *avoir de la ~* , to be in good shape; to have experience (mostly manual or physical). **4.** †custom, customers. || **pratiquement** [-'mɑ̃] *adv.* practically. || **pratiquer** [-e] #3 *v. tr.* [profession] to practise, exercise. *~ la médecine*, to practise as a doctor; [Fig.] *~ un chemin, une route (à travers la forêt)*, to open up a road. [× For musical practice, language practice, &c. cf. TRAVAILLER.]

pré [pre] *n.m.* meadow, cf. PRAIRIE.

préalable [prea'labl] *adj.* previous, prior: *au ~* , previously; prior to.

préambule [preɑ̃'byl] *n.m.* preamble.

préau [pre'o] *n.m.* [école] covered playground; shed.

préavis [prea'vi] *n.m.* advance notice.

précaire [pre'kɛ:r] *adj.* precarious.

précaution [preko'sj|õ] *n.f.* precaution; care, caution: *avec ~* , carefully, with care. || **précautionner** [-ɔ'ne] #3 *v. tr.* to forewarn (s.o. against doing . . .). || *se ~ v. pron.* to provide (*contre*, against).

précédemment [preseda'mɑ̃] *adv.* previously; before, earlier. || **précédent** [prese'd|ɑ̃] *n.m.* precedent: *sans*

~, unprecedented. || *adj.* preceding, former. || **précéder** [-e] #10 *v. tr.* to go/ before, in front of/; to precede.

précepte [pre'sɛpt] *n.m.* precept. || **pré-cept|eur, -rice** [-œ:r, -ris] *n.* (private) tutor.

prêche [prɛ:ʃ] *n.m.* sermon. || **prêcher** [prɛ'ʃ|e] #3 *v. tr.* to preach (upon, *sur*), to deliver a sermon, cf. PREDICATION; [Fam.] to repeat, to harp upon. || **prê-cheur** [-'œ:r] *n.m. & adj.* preacher.

précieusement [presjøz'mɑ̃] *adv.* preciously; carefully. || **précieu|x, -se** [pre'sj|ø(:z)] *adj.* **1.** precious, rare, costly, valuable: *pierre f précieuse,* gem. **2.** affected. || **préciosité** [-ozi'te] *n.f.* affectation, cf. PRÉCIEUX.

précipice [presi'pis] *n.m.* precipice; chasm, void.

précipitation [presipit|a'sjɔ̃] *n.f.* hurry, haste. || **précipité, -e** [-e] *adj.* hurried; hasty, sudden. || **précipiter** #3 *v. tr.* to precipitate (events), hasten. || **se** ~ *v. pron.* to throw o.s., rush (into, *dans, sur*).

précis [pre's|i] *n.m.* abstract: ~ *d'histoire,* historical abstract. || **précis, -e** [-i(:z)] *adj.* precise; exact; formal. || **précisément** [-ize'mɑ̃] *adv.* precisely; just so; as you say. || **préciser** [-i'ze] #3 *v. tr.* to specify; to clarify, to define exactly. || **précision** [-i'zjɔ̃] *n.f.* precision; preciseness, accuracy.

précité [presi'te] *adj.* above(-mentioned).

précoce [pre'kɔs] *adj.* [maturation] early; [enfant] precocious.

préconçu [prekɔ̃'sy] *adj.* preconceived.

préconiser [prekɔni'ze] #3 *v. tr.* to advocate, recommend.

précurseur [prekyr'sœ:r] *n.m.* forerunner, precursor. *adj. m.*: *un signe* ~, a/warning, premonitory/sign.

prédécesseur [predesɛ'sœ:r] *n.m.* predecessor.

prédestiné [predɛsti'ne] *adj.* predestined, foreordained. || **prédestiner** #3 *v. tr.* to predestinate.

prédicateur [predika|'tœ:r] *n.m.* preacher. || **prédication** [-sjɔ̃] *n.f.* preaching.

prédiction [pred|ik'sjɔ̃] *n.f.* prediction, prophecy; [Mét.] forecast. || **prédire** [-i:r], **prédisant** [i'zɑ̃], **prédit** [-i] #46 *v. tr.* to predict, foretell; [temps] to forecast.

prédisposer [predispo'ze] #3 *v. tr.* to predispose. || **prédisposition** [predispozi'sjɔ̃] *n.f.* predisposition; prejudice, prepossession.

prédominance [predɔmi'n|ɑ:s] *n.f.* predominance. || **prédominer** [-e] #3 *v. intr.* to predominate, prevail.

préfabriqué [prefabri'ke] *adj.*: *maison préfabriquée,* prefab(ricated house).

préface [pre'fas] *n.f.* preface, foreword.

préfecture [prefɛk'ty:r] *n.f.* [Fr.] prefecture, district; head town (of district): [Fr.] ~ *de police,* police headquarters.

préférable [prefe'r|abl] *adj.* preferable. || **préféré, -e** [-e] *adj.* favourite; preferred: *mon auteur* ~, my favourite author. || **pré-férence** [-ɑ̃:s] *n.f.* preference, partiality (for). || **préférer** [-e] #10 *v. tr.* to prefer; to be partial to: *Je préfère le café noir,* I'd rather have black coffee.

préfet [pre'fɛ] *n.m.* [Fr.] prefect: ~ *de police,* commissioner of police; ~ *des études,* tutor.

préfixe [pre'fiks] *n.m.* prefix.

préhistorique [preistɔ'rik] *adj.* prehistoric.

préjudice [preʒy'dis] *n.m.* injury, detriment; [×] prejudice, but cf. PRÉJUGÉ: *sans* ~ *de,* without prejudice to; *porter* ~ *à,* to be prejudicial to (the interests of). || **préjudiciable** [-jabl] *adj.* prejudicial, detrimental (to, *à*).

préjugé [preʒu'ʒe] *n.m.* prejudice, bias: *avoir des préjugés contre qqun* →, to be prejudiced against s.o.

prélasser (se) [prela'se] #3 *v. pron.* to lounge (in an armchair), to take it easy.

prélat [pre'la] *n.m.* [R.C.] prelate: ~ *domestique,* domestic prelate, Monsignor.

prélèvement [pre|lɛv'mɑ̃] *n.m.* levy; [Tech.] sample. || **prélever** [-lə've] #9 *v. tr.* to set aside; to levy (a sum).

préliminaire [prelimi'nɛ:r] *adj.* preliminary; prerequisite.

prélude [pre'lyd] *n.m.* prelude (to, *à*). || **préluder** [-e] #3 *v. intr.* to prelude (to, *à*).

prématuré, -e [prematy're] *adj.* premature.

préméditation [premedit|a'sjɔ̃] *n.f.* premeditation: *avec* ~, wilful. || **pré-méditer** [-e] #3 *v. tr.* to premeditate.

premi|er, -ère [prə'mj|e, -ɛ:r] *adj.* first: *en* ~ *lieu,* in the first place; *matières premières,* raw materials; ~ *ministre,* prime minister. || *n.m.* **1.** the first one: *Il habite au* ~, He lives on the/[Fr.] second, © ground/floor; *le* ~ *du mois,* the first of the month; *le* ~ *juin,* the first of June; *Il est le* ~ *de sa classe,* He stands first in his class. **2.** the former [of two; cf. *ce dernier,* the latter]. || *n.f.* **1.** the first one. **2.** [Loc.] *voyage en première,* to travel first (class); *être en première,* [Fr.] to be in/the twelfth grade, low (gear); *soir de première,* first night. || **première-ment** [-ɛr'mɑ̃] *adv.* first(ly). || **premier-né** [-e'ne] *n.m.* first born.

prémunir [premy'ni:r] #17 *v. tr.* to guard,

warn (against, *contre*). || **se** ~ *v. pron.* to guard, provide (against, *contre*).

prenant, -e [prə'nɑ̃(:t)] *adj.* captivating, fascinating, cf. PRENDRE.

prendre [prɑ̃:dr], **prenant** [prə'nɑ̃], **pris** [pri] #41 **1.** *v. tr.* to take, catch, capture: *Cela prend du temps,* It takes time; *Vous allez* ~ *froid,* You'll catch cold; *Je vous y prends!,* I have caught you (at it)!; *C'est à* ~ *ou à laisser,* Take it or leave it; *passer* ~ *qqun,* to call for s.o. **2.** *v. intr.* to/form, set, start: *La glace prend à 0° C.,* Ice forms at 0 degrees C.; *Cela n'a pas pris,* It did not set; *Le feu a pris dans le sous-sol,* The fire started in the basement; [Loc.] ~ *au plus court,* to take a short cut. || **se prendre** *v. pron.* **1.** to/freeze, congeal, get caught: ~ *à un clou,* to catch on a nail. **2.** [Loc.] ~ *d'amitié pour qqun,* to take a liking to s.o.; *Il ne sait comment s'y prendre,* He does not know how to go about it; *Ne vous en prenez pas à moi,* Don't blame me for it.

prenne [prɛn] cf. PRENDRE.

prénom [pre'nõ] *n.m.* Christian name; given name; first name: *Donnez vos nom et prénoms,* Give your last name and your first names.

préoccupation [preɔkyp|a'sjõ] *n.f.* care, worry; anxiety. || **préoccupé, -e** [-e] *adj.* preoccupied, worried. || **(se) préoccuper** [-e] #3 *v. tr. & pron.* to preoccupy (with, *de*); to be preoccupied, worried; to provide (for, *de*); *se* ~ *de,* to give one's attention to, to see to.

préparatifs [prepara|'tif] *n.mpl.* preparations (for, *de*). || **préparation** [-'sjõ] *n.f.* preparation (for, *pour/à*). || **préparatoire** [-'twa:r] *adj.* preparatory. || **préparer** [prepa're] #3 *v. tr.* to prepare, get ready. || **se préparer (à)** *v. pron.* to prepare o.s. (for), to get ready (for): *Préparez-vous!,* Get ready!

prépondérant, -e [prepõde'rɑ̃(:t)] *adj.* preponderant: *voix f prépondérante,* casting vote.

préposé, -e [prepo'z|e] *n.* (man, woman; officer, official) in charge (of, *à*). || **préposer** [-e] #3 *v. tr.* to put . . . in charge (of, *à*); to appoint. || **préposition** [-i'sjõ] *n.f.* preposition.

près[1] [prɛ] *adv.* **1.** near, close by: *Il habite tout* ~ , He lives/close by, next door/; *être* ~ *de,* to be near; [Fig.] *étudier qqch. de* ~ , to scrutinize, to study closely. **2.** nearly, almost: *à peu* ~ , almost; *à peu de chose* ~ , pretty near(ly); *à beaucoup* ~ , by a long way, nowhere near. [× Do not confuse with PRÊT, q.v.]

†**près**[2] *prép.* near, close; with, attached to: *conseiller culturel près l'ambassade de France,* Cultural attaché to the French Embassy.

présage [pre'z|a:ʒ] *n.m.* omen. || **présager** [-a'ʒe] #5 *v. tr.* to forebode; [prévoir] to predict.

presbyte [prɛs'bit] *adj.* far-sighted, long-sighted.

presbytère [prɛsbi'tɛ:r] *n.m.* [R.C.] rectory; vicarage.

presbytérien, -ne [prɛsbite'rj|ɛ̃, -ɛn] *adj. & n.* Presbyterian: *L'Église Presbytérienne,* The Presbyterian Church.

prescription [prɛskrip'sjõ] *n.f.* prescription; medical prescription cf. ORDONNANCE. || **prescrire** [prɛs'kr|i:r] **prescrivant** [-i'vɑ̃], **prescrit** [-i] #48 *v. tr.* to prescribe, enjoin.

prescrit[1], **-e** [prɛs'kri(t)] cf. PRESCRIRE. || **prescrit**[2], **-e** *adj.* set, appointed: *délai* ~ , deadline.

présence [pre'z|ɑ̃:s] *n.f.* presence; attendance (at school, ceremony, &c.): ~ *d'esprit,* presence of mind; *feuille de* ~ , time sheet. || **présent, -e** [-ɑ̃(:t)] *adj.* present: *être* ~ *à* (*une cérémonie*), to be (present) at/to attend/(a ceremony); [celui-ci] *le présent article,* this article. || *n.m.* **1.** the present, present time; [Gram.] present tense: *à* ~ , at the present time, now; *jusqu'à* ~ , up to now, until now; *pour le* ~ , for the time being; *vivre dans le* ~ , to live in the present. **2.** present company: *les présents et les absents,* those present and those absent. **3.** gift cf. CADEAU: *donner, recevoir des présents,* to give, to receive presents, gifts. || **présentable** [-ɑ̃'tabl] *adj.* presentable; suitable. || **présentation** [-ɑ̃ta'sjõ] *n.f.* presentation; introduction. || **présenter** [-ɑ̃'te] #3 *v. tr.* **1.** to present; to give away (prize); to offer, pay (compliments). **2.** to introduce: *permettez-moi de vous* ~ *M. Tremblay,* /allow me to, may I/introduce Mr. T.; [Fig.] to present, to offer: *Ce problème présente plusieurs difficultés,* This problem presents several difficulties. || **se présenter** *v. pron.* to report, introduce o.s. (*à,* to); to present itself: *le cas ne s'est pas présenté* →, this (case) did not arise before, this has never come up before.

préservati|f, -ve [prezɛrv|a'tif, -ati:v] *adj.* preservative (against, *contre*). || **préservation** [-a'sjõ] *n.f.* preservation, protection. || **préserver** [-e] #3 *v. tr.* to preserve (from, *de*); to keep safe. || **se préserver** *v. pron.* to guard, defend o.s. (against, *de*).

présidence [prezi'd|ã:s] *n.f.* presidency; [Parl.] the Chair. || **président, -e** [-ã(:t)] *n.* **1.** president (e.g. of the United States): ~ *du Conseil,* [Fr.] Prime Minister. **2.** Chairman (of board, &c.): *Monsieur le Président,* Mr. Chairman; *Madame la Présidente,* Madam Chairman. || **présidentiel, -le** [-ã'sjɛl] *adj.* presidential; the President's . . . . ||**présider** [-e] #3 *v. tr.* to preside (at, over a meeting). || *v. intr.* to preside, act as chairman.

présompti|f, -ve [prezõp|'tif, -ti:v] *adj.* presumptive, presumed. || **présomption** [-'sjõ] *n.f.* presumption; conceit. || **présomptueu|x, -se** [-'tɥø(:z)] *adj.* presumptuous, bold.

presque [prɛsk, © -ə] *adv.* **1.** almost, nearly: ~ *parfait,* almost perfect. **2.** hardly, scarcely: ~ *pas,* hardly at all; ~ *jamais,* hardly ever; *il n'en reste* ~ *plus,* there is/scarcely, hardly/any left. || **presqu'île** [prɛs'kil] *n.f.* peninsula.

pressant, -e [prɛ'sã(:t)] *adj.* pressing (need), urgent (appeal). || **presse** [prɛ:s] *n.f.* **1.** haste, hurry; pressure. [Fam.] *Il n'y a pas de* ~, There is no hurry; cf. PRESSER §2. **2.** crowd (→ foule). **3.** press, letterpress: *Ce livre va sous* ~ *en juin,* This book goes to press in June; *Presses Universitaires,* University Press. **4.** newspapers; the press: *La nouvelle fut annoncée dans la* ~, The news was announced in the papers; *La* ~ *du soir* (= Les journaux du soir), The evening papers.

pressé, -e [prɛ's|e] *adj.* **1.** pressed (for time), hurried, in haste. **2.** pressed (for space), crowded, close. **3.** [Fig.] urgent: *un pli* ~, an urgent message; *Ça n'est pas* ~, → It can wait.

pressentiment [presã|ti'mã] *n.m.* presentiment; [Fam.] hunch: *avoir un* ~, to feel in one's bones. || **pressentir** [-'ti:r] #26 *v. tr.* to feel; [Fam.] to have a hunch; [chercher à savoir] to sound (s.o.) out, to approach s.o.

presse-papiers [prɛs-pa'pje] *n.m. inv.* paperweight. || **presse-purée** [-py're] *n.m. invar.* potato-masher.

presser [prɛ's|e] #3 *v. tr.* **1.** to press, to squeeze: ~ *un bouton,* to push a button. **2.** to hurry, hasten. || *v. intr.* to be urgent: *rien ne presse,* there is no hurry. || *v. pron.* to hurry, make haste: *pressons-nous,* let's hurry; [les uns sur les autres] to crowd, mill. || **pression** [-jõ] *n.f.* pressure: *faire* ~ *sur qqun,* to put pressure on s.o.; *bouton-* ~ *m,* dome fastener; ~ *artérielle,* blood pressure. || **pressoir** [prɛ|'swa:r] *n.m.* (wine)press. || **pressurer** [-sy're] #3 *v. tr.* to squeeze (out); [Fig.] to grind.

prestation [prɛsta'sjõ] *n.f.* payment; tax money; taking of an oath.

preste [prɛst] *adj.* nimble; quick. || **prestement** [-ə'mã] *adv.* deftly, quickly. || **prestesse** [-ɛs] *n.f.* nimbleness. || **prestidigitateur** [-idizita'tœ:r] *n.m.* conjuror. || **prestidigitation** [-idiʒita'sjõ] *n.f.* sleight of hand: *tour de* ~, conjuring trick.

prestige [prɛs't|i:ʒ] *n.m.* reputation. || **prestigieu|x, -se** [-i'ʒjø(:z)] *adj.* glamorous, of distinction; amazing.

présumer [prezy'me] #3 *v. tr. & intr.* to presume (upon, *de*).

prêt,[1] **-e** [prɛ(t)] *adj.* ready (to, *à*); prepared (for, *à*): *se tenir* ~, to keep o.s. in readiness; *Êtes-vous* ~ ?, Are you ready?

prêt[2] [prɛ] *n.m.* loan: *consentir un* ~ *à,* to grant a loan to; ~ *à terme,* time loan; ~ *hypothécaire,* mortgage.

prétendant [pretã'dã] *n.m.* candidate, claimant; [couronne] pretender; suitor.

prétendre [pre't|ã:dr] **prétendu** [-ã'dy] #42 *v. tr.* to claim, to pretend to; to maintain: *Il prétend avoir raison,* He claims to be right. || **prétendu, -e** [-ã'dy] *adj.* supposed, would-be. || **prétentieu|x, -se** [-ã'sjø(:z)] *adj.* pretentious, affected, ostentatious. || **prétention** [-ã'sjõ] *n.f.* claim, pretension; wish, wishful thinking: *avoir des prétentions (à),* to lay claim to, to claim.

prêter [prɛ't|e] #3 *v. tr.* **1.** to lend, to loan; [Fig.] ~ *secours à,* to give help to; ~ *de l'argent,* to lend money; [Fig.] ~ *l'oreille à,* to listen to. **2.** to attribute, to impart (to, *à*). || **se prêter (à)** *v. pron.* to yield to, to countenance.

prétérit [prete'rit] *n.m.* preterite.

prêteur [-œ:r] *n.* lender.

prétexte [pre'tekst] *n.m.* pretext: *sous* ~ *de,* under the pretence of . . . [+ ing]. || **prétexter** [-e] #3 *v. tr.* [= prendre prétexte de], to make pretext of, to pretend to.

prêtre [prɛ:tr] *n.m.* priest, minister. || **prêtresse** [prɛ'tr|ɛs] *n.f.* priestess. || **prêtrise** [-i:z] *n.f.* priesthood.

preuve [prœ:v] *n.f.* proof, evidence; [Fig.] token: *faire* ~ *de courage,* to show courage; *faire ses preuves,* to prove o.s.; [Math.] *faire la* ~ *d'une opération,* to prove an operation; *fournir des preuves,* to give evidence; *une* ~ *de plus,* one more piece of evidence.

preux [prø] †*n.m.* valiant knight. || †*adj. m.* valiant, gallant.

prévaloir [preva'lwa:r] #29 *v. intr.* to prevail. || **se** ~ *v. pron.* to take advantage, avail o.s. (of, *de*).

prévenance [prev'nɑ̃:s] *n.f.* kindness, kind attention. || **prévenant, -e** [prev'nɑ̃(:t)] *adj.* kind; anxious to please, obliging.

prévenir [-i:r], **prévenant, prévenu** [-y] #22 *v. tr.* **1.** to anticipate, to forestall. **2.** to prevent: *Mieux vaut* ~ *que guérir*, Prevention is better than cure. **3.** to notify, to inform: *Prévenez-moi quand il arrivera*, Let me know when he comes. || **préventi|f, -ve** [prevɑ̃|'tif, -'ti:v] *adj.* preventive. || **prévention** [-'sjɔ̃] *n.f.* prejudice, bias: *avoir des préventions contre*, to be prejudiced against. || **préventivement** [-tiv'mɑ̃] *adv.* preventively, previously. || **prévenu, -e** *adj.* prejudiced (against, *contre*) || *n.* [Fr. law] *le* ~, the defendant.

préviens cf. PRÉVENIR.

prévis &c., prévoie &c. cf. PRÉVOIR. || **prévision** [prev|i'zjɔ̃] *n.f.* conjecture; [temps] forecast: *en* ~ *de*, in anticipation of . . . || **prévoir** [-wa:r] #32 *v. tr.* to foresee, anticipate: *Il a tout prévu*, He thought of everything; [temps] to forecast. || **prévoyance** [-wa'jɑ̃:s] *n.f.* foresight; prudence, wisdom. || **prévoyant, -e** [-wa'jɑ̃(:t)] *adj.* prudent, careful, provident. || **prévu, -e** [-y] foreseen, anticipated.

prier [pri'j|e] #3 *v. tr.* to pray; to beseech, request: *prier Dieu*, to pray to God; *sans se faire* ~, willingly; *Je vous en prie*, Please do!; *Je vous prie de bien vouloir*, You are requested to kindly; Please . . . || **prière** [-ɛ:r] *n.f.* prayer; request: *adresser une* ~ *à*, to say a prayer to; *exaucer une* ~, to answer a prayer; ~ *de . . .* →, please (a stronger form than S.V.P. q.v.): ~ *de ne pas plier*, → Please do not fold.

primaire [pri'm|ɛ:r] *adj.* primary; elementary: *école* ~, primary, elementary school (as opposed to *École secondaire*); [Fr.; Péj.] uneducated mind, bigoted. || **primauté** [-o'te] *n.f.* supremacy. || **prime** [prim] *n.f.* premium (on insurance policy); bonus: *de* ~ *abord*, to begin with, at first sight. || **primer** [-e] #3 *v. tr.* to excel, take priority over . . . : *être primé*, to be awarded (a medal, &c.).

primesauti|er, -ère [primso'tj|e, -ɛ:r] *adj.* quick, quick-witted; impulsive.

primeur [-œ:r] *n.f.* **1.** early vegetable. **2.** prime; first fruit, first bloom. **3.** [Journ.] scoop.

primevère [prim'vɛ:r] *n.f.* primrose.

primiti|f, -ve [primi't|if, -i:v] *adj.* primitive, early; first. || **primitivement** [-iv'mɑ̃] *adv.* in the first place, originally. || **primo** [pri'mo] *adv.* firstly, in the first place. || **primordial, -e** [primɔr'djal] *adj.* primary.

prince, princesse [prɛ̃:s, prɛ̃'sɛs] *n.* prince, princess: *Le Prince de Galles*, The Prince of Wales; *l'Île du Prince-Édouard*, Prince Edward Island. || **princi|er, -ère** [prɛ̃'s|je, -jɛ:r] *adj.* princely.

principal, -e [-i'pal] *adj.* principal, main, chief: *l'objectif* ~ (as against *l'objectif secondaire*), the main, chief object. || *n.m.* chief, principal (person, thing); principal (of a school). *Le* ~ *est que* (+ *subj.*), The main thing is that . . . || **principalement** [-ipal'mɑ̃] *adv.* chiefly, principally. || **principe** [prɛ̃'sip] *n.m.* basis, principle; [*pl.*] principles.

printani|er, -ère [prɛ̃ta'nj|e, -ɛ:r] *adj.* spring(-like). || **printemps** [prɛ̃'tɑ̃] *n.m.* spring(time); [Fig.] prime: *au* ~, in spring.

priorité [priɔri'te] *n.f.* priority, precedence (over, *sur*); [Route] right of way: ~ *à droite, à gauche*, yield to oncoming traffic.

pris,[1] -e [pri(:z)] cf. PRENDRE.

pris,[2] -e *adj.* taken, caught; set, frozen. || **prise** [pri:z] *n.f.* taking, capture; hold; pinch (of snuff): *la* ~ *de la Bastille*, the fall of the Bastille; *lâcher* ~, to let go; *être aux prises avec qqun*, to be at odds with s.o.; *donner* ~ *à la critique*, to be open to criticism; *avoir* ~ *sur qqun*, to have a hold on s.o.

priser[1] [pri'z|e] #3 *v. tr.* [estimer] to value.

priser[2] #3 [*v. tr.*] [tobacco] to take snuff.

priseur [-œ:r] *n.m.* [Fr.]: *commissaire-* ~, auctioneer, appraiser.

prisme [prism] *n.m.* prism.

prison [pri'z|ɔ̃] *n.f.* prison, jail: *condamner qqun à la* ~, to imprison. || **prisonni|er, -ère** [-ɔ'nje, -ɔ'njɛ:r] *n.* prisoner.

privation [priva'sjɔ̃] *n.f.* privation, want (of). || **privé, -e** [pri've] *adj.* private, intimate: *la vie* ~, private life; *Conseil* ~, Privy Council. [×] Private [on a door] → *Défense d'entrer* or *Interdit au public*. || ~ *de*, deprived of, without. || **priver (de)** [-e] #3 *v. tr.* to deprive (s.o. of). || **se priver (de)** *v. pron.* to deprive o.s. (of); to do without; to abstain (from).

privilège [privi'l|ɛ:ʒ] *n.m.* privilege; licence. || **privilégier** [-e'ʒje] #3 *v. tr.* to privilege.

prix [pri] *n.m.* **1.** price, cost, rate; worth, value: *à tout* ~, at all costs; *hors de* ~, extravagant; *le* ~ *de la vie*, the cost of living; *Cela n'a pas de* ~, It's priceless; *attacher du* ~ *à qqch.*, to value sth. highly; ~ *courant*, price list; ~ *de revient*, cost price. **2.** prize, regard: *remporter un*

~ , to win a prize; *décerner un* ~ , to award a prize.

probabilité [prɔbabili'te] *n.f.* probability, likelihood: *selon toute* ~ , in all probability. || **probable** [prɔ'babl] *adj.* probable, likely. || **probablement** [-ə'mɑ̃] *adv.* probably, likely, in all probability.

probant, -e [prɔ'bɑ̃(:t)] *adj.* convincing; [Jur.] conclusive.

probe [prɔb] *adj.* honest, upright. || **probité** [-i'te] *n.f.* honesty, uprightness.

problématique [prɔbl|ema'tik] *adj.* doubtful, questionable. || **problème** [-ɛm] *n.m.* problem [×] cf. DIFFICULTÉ.

procédé [prɔse'd|e] *n.m.* [Tech.] process; attitude; [*pl.*] dealings. || **procéder** [-e] #10 *v. intr.* **1.** to proceed (to, *à*); to go on with: ~ *à des réparations*, to undertake repairs. **2.** (+ *de*) to proceed, to arise (from). || **procédure** [-y:r] *n.f.* [code] procedure; proceedings. || **procès** [prɔ'sɛ] *n.m.* case, lawsuit; trial: *intenter un* ~ *à*, to file suit against, to prosecute s.o.; *subir un* ~ , to be tried. || **procès-verb|al,** [-vɛr'b|al] *pl.* **-aux** [-o] *n.m.* minutes (of a meeting), report; [police] ticket.

prochain, -e [prɔ'ʃ|ɛ̃, ɛn] *adj.* **1.** near: *à une prochaine occasion*, in the near future; *sentant sa fin prochaine*, feeling his end near. **2.** next: *la prochaine fois*, next time. *n.m.* fellow-being, neighbour. || **prochainement** [-ɛn'mɑ̃] *adv.* shortly: ~ *sur cet écran*, coming soon.

proche [prɔʃ] *adj.* near: *la ville la plus* ~ , the nearest town; *le plus* ~ *parent*, the next of kin; *Son départ était* ~ , → He was about to leave. || *n.m. pl.*: *ses proches*, his close relatives.

proclamer [prɔkla'me] #3 *v. tr.* to proclaim.

procuration [prɔkyr|a'sjõ] *n.f.* [Jur.] power of attorney; proxy.

procurer [-e] #3 *v. tr.* to procure, get (for, *à*). || **se procurer** *v. pron.* to get, secure; [acheter] to buy, obtain: ~ *de l'argent*, to raise money. || **procureur** [-œ:r] *n.m.* **1.** [Jur.] proxy; attorney; ~ *de la*/© *Couronne*, [Fr.] *République*/, public prosecutor. **2.** [Rel.] bursar, purveyor.

prodigalité [prɔdigali'te] *n.f.* prodigality, lavishness.

prodige [prɔ'd|i:ʒ] *n.m.* prodigy, wonder: *un enfant* ~ , a wonder child. || **prodigieu|x, -se** [-i'ʒø(:z)] *adj.* prodigious, wonderful.

prodigue [prɔ'dig] *adj.* prodigal; lavish, wasteful. || *n.m.* prodigal, squanderer. || **prodiguer** [-e] #3 *v. tr.* [son bien] to waste, squander; [Fig.] to be lavish of: ~ *des soins à*, to tend, minister to s.o. || **se prodiguer** *v. pron.* not to spare o.s.

product|eur, -rice [prɔdyk|'tœ:r, -'tris] || *adj.* productive. *n.* producer, processer. || **producti|f, -ve** [-'tiʃ, -'ti:v] *adj.* productive. || **production** [-'sjõ] *n.f.* **1.** production. **2.** produce.

produire [prɔ'dɥ|i:r], **produisant** [-i'zɑ̃], **produit** [-i] #56 *v. tr.* **1.** to produce, to bring about. **2.** to/yield, bear (fruit), grow. || **se produire** *v. pron.* **1.** to be produced. **2.** to happen. **3.** to show o.s.: *Il aime* ~ , → He likes to be in the public eye.

produit [-i] *n.m.* product: *produits manufacturés*, manufactured products; *produits agricoles*, farm produce.

proéminent, -e [prɔemi'nɑ̃(:t)] *adj.* prominent, salient.

profanat|eur, -rice [prɔfana|'tœ:r, -'tris] *n.* profaner, desecrator. || **profanation** [-'sjõ] *n.f.* desecration, sacrilege.

profane [prɔ'fan] *adj.* profane; [Fig.] lay. || *n.* [Fig.] layman. || **profaner** [-e] #3 *v. tr.* to profane, desecrate.

proférer [prɔfe're] #10 *v. tr.* [injures, &c.] to utter.

professer [prɔfɛ's|e] #3 *v. tr.* [déclarer] to profess; [Scol.] to teach. || **professeur** [-œ:r] *n.m.* teacher; [université] professor. || **profession** [-jõ] *n.f.* profession, calling, business: [Fr.] *les professions libérales*, the professions. || **professionnel, -le** [-jɔ'nɛl] *adj.* **1.** [not amateur] professional: *enseignement* ~ , vocational education. **2.** © professional [= law, medicine, &c.] cf. LIBÉRAL. || *n.* © *les professionnels* [= [Fr.] les professions libérales]. || **professoral, -e** [-ɔ'ral] *adj.* professorial: *le corps* ~ , the faculty (of a university). || **professorat** [-ɔ'ra] *n.m.* teaching; [chair] professorship.

profil [prɔ'fil] *n.m.* profile; [Fig.] outline. || **profiler (se)** [-e] #3 *v. pron.* to be outlined (against, *sur*).

profit [prɔ'fi] *n.m.* profit, gain, benefit: *mettre à* ~ , to/use, turn to account; *tirer* ~ *de*, to profit by; to benefit by, from; *profits et pertes*, profit and loss. || **profitable** [-'tabl] *adj.* profitable, advantageous. || **profiter** [-'te] #3 *v. intr.* to profit (by, *de*), to gain by: ~ *d'une occasion*, to take advantage of an opportunity; *Il a bien profité des cours*, He derived much benefit from the courses. || **profiteur** [-'tœ:r] *n.m.* profiteer.

profond, -e [prɔ'fõ|(:d)] *adj.* deep; profound; [sommeil] sound; [nuit] dark; ☞ *peu* ~ , shallow. || **profondément**

[-de'mɑ̃] *adv.* deeply, profoundly, soundly: *dormir* ~, to be sound asleep, sleep soundly. ‖ **profondeur** [-'dœ:r] *n.f.* depth.

profusion [prɔfy'zjɔ̃] *n.f.* profusion, abundance: *à* ~, galore [→ q.v.].

progéniture [prɔʒeni'ty:r] *n.f.* offspring.

prognose [prɔg'no:z] *n.f.* prognosis.

programme [prɔ'gram] *n.m.* program; [politique] platform; [plan] scheme, plan; ~ *d'études*, curriculum, syllabus; [réunion] agenda.

progrès [prɔ'grɛ] *n.m. invar.* progress, improvement; development: *Cet élève fait de grands* ~, That student is making /good, excellent/progress. ‖ **progresser** [-'se] #3 *v. intr.* to show improvement, advance (toward, *vers*), progress, make headway. ‖ **progressi|f, -ve** [-'sif, -'si:v] *adj.* progressive. ‖ **progression** [-'sjɔ̃] *n.f.* progression; [mouvement] progress. ‖ **progressivement** [-siv'mɑ̃] *adv.* progressively, by stages.

prohiber [prɔi'b|e] #3 *v. tr.* to forbid, prohibit. ‖ **prohibiti|f, -ve** [-i'tif, -i'ti:v] *adj.* prohibitive. ‖ **prohibition** [-i'sjɔ̃] *n.f.* forbidding, prohibition.

proie [prwa] *n.f.* prey; [chasse] quarry: [Fig.] *en* ~ *à*, a prey to.

projecteur [prɔʒɛk|'tœ:r] *n.m.* searchlight; [Théât.] spotlight. ‖ **projectile** [-'til] *n.m.* missile, projectile: ~ *téléguidé*, (guided) missile. ‖ **projection** [-'sjɔ̃] *n.f.* throwing; [×] projection, cf. SAILLIE.

projet [prɔ'ʒ|ɛ] *n.m.* project, design, plan, idea; [de lettre] draught; *faire des projets*, to make plans; ~ *de loi*, bill. ‖ **projeter** [-'te] #8 *v. tr.* to plan, to design; to project; to throw: ~ *un voyage*, to plan a trip; ~ *dans l'avenir*, to project into the future; *Il a été projeté par-dessus le guidon*, He flew over the handlebar.

prolétaire [prɔle't|ɛ:r] *n.m.* proletarian. ‖ **prolétariat** [-a'rja] *n.m.* proletariat, proletarianism.

prolixe [prɔ'liks] *adj.* lengthy, wordy, verbose, long-winded. ‖ **prolixité** [-i'te] *n.f.* prolixity, verbosity, wordiness.

prologue [prɔ'lɔg] *n.m.* prologue.

prolongation [prɔlɔ̃ga'sjɔ̃] *n.f.* prolongation, extension, lengthening. ‖ **prolonge** [prɔ'l|ɔ̃:ʒ] *n.f.* gun-carriage. ‖ **prolongement** [-ɔ̃ʒ'mɑ̃] *n.m.* extension, prolongation, protraction, lengthening. ‖ **prolonger** [-ɔ̃'ʒe] #5 *v. tr.* to prolong; to extend; to draw out, to lengthen. ‖ **se prolonger** *v. pron.* to continue, to be extended, prolonged: *La réunion se prolongea jusqu'à l'aube*, The meeting continued until daybreak.

promenade [prɔm|'nad] *n.f.* [can be translated only by specifying mode of transportation]: *faire une* ~, to take [à pied] a walk, [en voiture] a drive, a ride, [à bicyclette, à cheval] a ride; [en bateau] a boat ride. ‖ **promener** [-'ne] #9 *v. tr.* **1.** to take out for a walk, a drive, &c. **2.** to parade, to show, to pass. ‖ **se promener** *v. pron.* to go for a walk, a drive, a ride, a sail, &c., to stroll, to ramble. ‖ **promeneur** [-'nœ:r] *n.m.* stroller, walker: *les promeneurs*, people out for a walk. ‖ **promenoir** [-(ə)'nwa:r] *n.m.* covered walk.

promesse [prɔ'm|ɛs] *n.f.* promise: *faire une* ~, to make a promise; *tenir sa* ~, to keep/a, one's/promise, *manquer à sa* ~, to break one's promise. ‖ **prometteu|r, -se** [-ɛ'tœ:r, -ɛ'tø:z] *adj.* promising, one who makes rash promises. ‖ **promettre** [-ɛtr] **promettant** [-ɛ'tɑ̃], **promis** [-i] #44 *v. tr.* to promise: *promettre qqch. à qqun*, to promise sth. to s.o. ‖ *v. intr.* to be promising, to have a big future in store, to look promising, to bid fair (to, *de*). ‖ **se promettre (de)** *v. pron.* to promise o.s. to, to resolve to. ‖ **promis, -e** [-i(:z)] *adj.* promised, intended: *la Terre promise*, the Promised Land. ‖ **promis, -e** [-i(:z)] *n.* [in countrified use] fiancé, fiancée, future husband or wife.

promiscuité [prɔmiskɥi'te] *n.f.* promiscuity, promiscuousness.

promontoire [prɔmɔ̃'twa:r] *n.m.* promontory, headland.

promot|eur, -rice [prɔmɔ|'tœ:r, -tris] *n.* promoter, prime mover. ‖ **promotion** [-'sjɔ̃] *n.f.* promotion, [Sch.] class: *Ils sont de la même* ~, They were in the same class.

†**prompt, -e** [prɔ̃|(:t)] *adj.* prompt, quick; sudden; [Fig.] hasty: *avoir l'esprit* ~, to have a quick mind. ‖ **promptement** [-t'mɑ̃] *adv.* promptly, quickly. cf. RAPIDEMENT, VITE. ‖ **promptitude** [-pti'tyd] *n.f.* promptitude, promptness.

promu, -e [prɔ'my] *adj.* promoted, advanced.

promulguer [prɔmyl'ge] *v. tr.* to promulgate, to declare.

prône [pro:n] *n.m.* sermon. ‖ **prôner** [pro'ne] #3 *v. tr.* to advocate, to extol.

pronom [prɔ'nɔ̃] *n.m.* pronoun.

prononcer [prɔnɔ̃'s|e] #4 *v. tr.* to pronounce; to deliver (a speech); to pass (judgment), to pronounce (sentence). ‖ **se prononcer** *v. pron.* **1.** to be pronounced: *Le t ne se prononce pas*, The t is silent. **2.** to declare o.s., to express an opinion (on, *sur*). || **prononciation** [-ja'sjõ] *n.f.* pronunciation.

pronostic [prɔnɔs'tik] *n.m.* prognosis, prognostic: *ses pronostics*, his prognostication.

propagande [prɔpa|'gɑ̃:d] *n.f.* propaganda, advertising: ~ *à domicile*, canvassing. || **propagandiste** [-gɑ̃'dist] *n.m.* propagandist. || **propagation** [-ga'sjõ] *n.f.* propagation. || **propager** [-'ʒe] #5 *v. tr.* to propagate, to spread. || **se propager** *v. pron.* to spread: *La lumière se propage plus vite que le son*, Light travels faster than sound.

propension [prɔpɑ̃'sjõ] *n.f.* propensity, inclination, tendency.

prophète [prɔ'f|ɛt] *n.m.* prophet. || **prophétie** [-e'si] *n.f.* prophecy. || **prophétique** [-e'tik] *adj.* prophetic. || **prophétiser** [-eti'ze] #3 *v. tr.* to prophesy, to predict, to foretell.

propice [prɔ'pis] *adj.* well chosen, auspicious, †propitious, opportune. || **propitiation** [prɔpisja'sjõ] *n.f.* propitiation, atonement.

proportion [prɔpɔr'sj|õ] *n.f.* proportion, part, portion: *assumer des proportions*, to assume dimensions. || **proportionné, -e** [-ɔ'ne] *adj.* proportioned, proportionate (to, *à*): *un homme bien* ~ , a well-built man. || **proportionnel, -le** [-ɔ'nɛl] *adj.* proportional: *directement* ~ *à*, in direct ratio to. || **proportionnelle** [-ɔ'nɛl] *n.f.* proportional representation. || **proportionnellement** [-ɔnɛl'mɑ̃] *adv.* proportionally. || **proportionner** [-ɔ'ne] #3 *v. tr.* to proportion, adjust.

propos [prɔ'po] *n.m.* **1.** remark(s); gossip: *ses* ~ , what he said; *tenir des* ~ *flatteurs sur le compte de*, to make flattering remarks on. **2.** purpose, design: *mon* ~ *est de montrer . . .* , my purpose is to show . . . **3.** [Loc.] *à* ~ (*adj.*) appropriate: *juger à* ~ *de . . .*, to see fit to . . . ; *à* ~ (*adv.*) by the way, incidentally; appropriately: *venir à* ~ , to come at the right moment; *à* ~ *de* (*prép.*) in connection with.

proposer [-'ze] #3 *v. tr.* **1.** to propose, to suggest, to offer: *Je le lui ai proposé*, I suggested it to him; *Je lui ai proposé d'y aller*, I suggested to him that we should go. **2.** to move, to recommend, to nominate: *être proposé pour une promotion*, to be recommended for a promotion. || **se proposer** *v. pron.* to volunteer (for, *pour*), to offer o.s.: ~ *de faire qqch.*, to intend to do sth. || **proposition** [-zi'sjõ] *n.f.* proposal, suggestion, proposition: ~ *de loi*, bill.

propre[1] [prɔpr] *adj.* own, intrinsic, proper: *avoir qqch. en* ~ , to possess sth. in one's own right; *remis en mains propres*, delivered personally; *son* ~ *père*, his own father; [Gram.] *nom* ~ , proper noun; *sens* ~ , literal meaning; *au* ~ *et au figuré*, literally and figuratively. ☞ Distinguish between: *son* ~ *mouchoir*, his own handkerchief, and *son mouchoir* ~ , his clean handkerchief.

propre[2] *adj.* clean; tidy, neat: *avoir les mains propres*, to have clean hands.

proprement[1] [-ə'mɑ̃] *adv.* properly, suitably, appropriately: ~ *dit*, *à* ~ *parler*, strictly speaking.

proprement[2] [-ə'mɑ̃] *adv.* cleanly; tidily, neatly.

propreté [-ə'te] *n.f.* cleanliness; tidiness, neatness: *d'une* ~ *immaculée*, spotlessly clean.

propriétaire [-ije'tɛ:r] *n.m.* owner; landlord, householder; landowner. || **propriété** [-ije'te] *n.f.* **1.** property, ownership. **2.** estate, real estate. **3.** property, quality: *Quelles sont les propriétés de ce corps?*, What are the properties of this/body, material/? **4.** appropriateness: *la* ~ *des termes*, the exact use of words.

propulseur [prɔpyl'sœ:r] *adj.* propelling, propulsive. || *n.m.* propeller.

prorata [prɔra'ta] *n.m. inv.* proportional share: *fixer au* ~ , to prorate; *loc. adv. au* ~ , on a pro rata basis; *loc. prép. au* ~ *de*, proportionately to.

prorogation [prɔrɔga'sjõ] *n.f.* prorogation, extension, protraction.

prosaïque [prɔza'ik] *adj.* prosaic, flat, dull.

proscription [prɔskr|ip'sjõ] *n.f.* proscription, rejection, denunciation. || **proscrire** [-i:r] #48 *v. tr.* to proscribe, to prohibit, to exile, to banish, to ban, to reject. || **proscrit, -e** [-i(t)] *adj.* banned, rejected, banished. || *n.m.* exile.

prose [pro:z] *n.f.* prose.

prospecteur [prɔspɛk't|œ:r] *n.* prospector.

prospectus [-ys] *n.m.* handbill, leaflet.

prospère [prɔs'pɛ:r] *adj.* prosperous, flourishing. || **prospérer** [prɔspe'r|e] #10 *v. intr.* to prosper, to become prosperous, to thrive. || **prospérité** [-i'te] *n.f.* prosperity, success, welfare.

prosternation [prɔstɛrn|a'sjõ] *n.f.* prostration. || **prosterner** [-e] #3 *v. tr.* to prostrate. || **se prosterner** *v. pron.* to prostrate o.s.; [Péj.] to grovel.

prostituée [prɔsti'tɥe] *n.f.* prostitute.

prostituer [prɔsti'tɥe] #3 *v. tr.* to prostitute, to misuse. || **se prostituer** *v. pron.* to prostitute o.s.

prostration [prɔstra'sjõ] *n.f.* prostration.
protagoniste [prɔtagɔ'nist] *n. m/f.* protagonist.
protect|eur, -rice [prɔt|ɛk'tœ:r, -ɛk'tris] *adj.* **1.** protective. **2.** patronizing, condescending. || *n.* protector, defender, patron. || **protection** [-ɛk'sjõ] *n.f.* protection; patronage; [Assur.] coverage. || **protectorat** [-ɛktɔ'ra] *n.m.* protectorate. || **protégé** [prɔte'ʒe] *n.m.* protégé; favourite. || **protégée** *n.f.* protégée. || **protéger** [-e'ʒe] #7 *v. tr.* to protect, to shield: *se ~ du froid,* to protect o.s. from the cold.
protéine [prɔte'in] *n.f.* protein.
protestant, -e [prɔtɛs't|ã(:t)] *adj.* Protestant. || *n.* Protestant: ☞ *Il est protestant,* He is a Protestant. || **protestantisme** [-ã'tism] *n.m.* Protestantism.
protestation [-a'sjõ] *n.f.* protest, protestation: *élever une ~* , to lodge a protest. || **protester** [-e] #3 *v. intr.* to protest: *~ contre qqch.*, to protest against sth.; *~ de son innocence,* to protest one's innocence; *~ un billet,* to protest a bill.
protocole [prɔtɔ'kɔl] *n.m.* protocol; etiquette.
proue [pru] *n.f.* [Naut.] bow, prow, stem.
prouesse [pru'ɛs] *n.f.* valour, prowess: *ses prouesses,* his prowess.
prouver [pru've] #3 *v. tr.* to prove, to show.
provenance [prɔv'n|ã:s] *n.f.* source, origin, beginnings.
provençal, -e [prɔv|ã'sal] *adj.* from Provence. || **Provence, la** [-ã:s] *n.f.* Provence.
provenir(de) [prɔv'ni:r] #22 *v. intr.* to arise, proceed (from); to come (from).
proverbe [prɔ'vɛrb] *n.m.* proverb. || **proverbial, -e** [-jal] *adj.* proverbial. || **proverbialement** [-jal'mã] *adv.* proverbially.
providence [prɔvi'd|ã:s] *n.f.* providence. || **providentiel, -le** [-ã'sjɛl] *adj.* providential, opportune. || **providentiellement** [-ãsjɛl-'mã] *adv.* providentially.
proviens, provient, &c. cf. PROVENIR.
province [prɔ'v|ɛ̃:s] *n.f.* **1.** province: *la ~ de Québec,* the Province of Quebec; © *les Provinces maritimes,* the Maritime Provinces, the Maritimes; *un habitant des Provinces maritimes,* a Maritimer. **2.** *la province* [Fr.] the country (outside Paris), the provinces: *Il a débuté en province,* He started in another town than Paris. || **provincial, -e** [-ɛ̃'sjal] *adj.* **1.** provincial: *le gouvernement ~* , the Provincial Government. **2.** provincial, parochial, countrified. [× Do not confuse with PROVENÇAL.] || *n.* **1.** provincial, not a Parisian, country cousin. **2.** [R.C.] Provincial.
provins, &c. cf. PROVENIR.
proviseur [prɔvi'zœ:r] *n.m.* [Fr. Lycée] = headmaster.
provision [prɔvi'zjõ] *n.f.* **1.** *sing.* stock; stock in hand: *faire ~ de (farine, huile, &c.),* to stock up on (flour, oil, &c.). ☞ **2.** *pl.* stock, supply; shopping: *aller aux provisions,* to go shopping, to do the marketing; *faire des ~* , to stock up on, lay in a store of.
provisoire [prɔvizw|a:r] *adj.* provisional, temporary: *expédient m ~* , emergency measure. || **provisoirement** [-ar'mã] *adv.* temporarily, provisionally.
provocant, -e [prɔvɔ'k|ã(:t)] *adj.* provoking, provocative; alluring, suggestive. || **provocat|eur, -rice** [-a'tœ:r, -a'tris] *adj.* provoking, provocative: *agent ~*, agitator. || *n.* provoker, aggressor. || **provocation** [-a'sjõ] *n.f.* provocation, instigation. || **provoquer** [-e] #3 *v. tr.* **1.** to cause, to bring about, to produce. **2.** to provoke: *~ en duel,* to challenge to a duel.
proximité [prɔksimi'te] *n.f.* proximity, vicinity, nearness.
pruche [pryʃ] © *n.f.* hemlock.
prude [pryd] *adj.* prudish. || *n.f.* prude.
prudemment [pryd|a'mã] *adv.* cautiously, discreetly. || **prudence** [-ã:s] *n.f.* prudence, caution: *agir avec ~* , to act/with caution, discretion/wiscly. || **prudent, -e** [-ã(:t) *adj.* prudent, cautious, wary.
pruderie [pryd'ri] *n.f.* prudishness.
prune [pryn] *n.f.* [×] plum: *(prune) reine claude,* greengage; [Fam.] *y aller pour des prunes,* to go on a fool's errand. || **pruneau** [-o] *n.m.* prune. || **prunelle** [-ɛl] *n.f.* **1.** sloc; sloc gin. **2.** eyeball; [Fig.] apple of the eye: *Il y tient comme à la ~ de ses yeux,* It is the apple of his eye. **3.** [tissu] prunella. || **prunier** [-je] *n.m.* plum tree.
Prusse, la [prys] *n.f.* Prussia: *bleu de ~* , Prussian blue.
psalmodier [psalmɔ'dje] #3 *v. tr.* to recite psalms; [Fig.] to mumble. || **psaume** [pso:m] *n.m.* psalm.
P.S.D. [peɛs'de] [= Parti social démocratique] © *n.* C.C.F. [= Commonwealth Cooperative Federation].
pseudo- [psød|o] *prefix in compounds,* pseudo-, would-be. || **pseudonyme** [-ɔ'nim] *n.m.* pen-name, assumed name; nom de plume.
psychanalyse [psikana'li:z] *n.f.* psycho-

analysis. || **psychique** [psi|'ʃik] *adj.* psychic, psychical. || **psychologie** [-kɔlɔ'ʒi] *n.f.* psychology. || **psychologique** [-kɔlɔ'ʒik] *adj.* psychological. || **psychologue** [-kɔ'lɔg] *n.m.* psychologist.

pu, pus, put [py] cf. POUVOIR.

puant, -e [pɥɑ̃|(:t) py'ɑ̃(:t)] *adj.* stinking, foul-smelling. || **puanteur** [-'tœ:r] *n.f.* stench, stink.

pubère [py'b|ɛ:r] *adj.* pubescent. || **puberté** [-ɛr'te] *n.f.* puberty.

public[1] [py'blik] *n.m.* public, audience: *Avis au* ~ , Public/notice, warning/; *parler en* ~ , to speak in public; *le grand* ~ , the general public; *le* ~ *des théâtres*, the theatre-going public; *Le* ~ *était nombreux*, The audience was large.

publi|c[2], **-que** [py'bli|k] *adj.* public; [ext.] notorious [often Pej.]: *rendre (une nouvelle) publique*, to announce, to reveal; *services mpl publics*, public/utilities, services/; *la fonction publique*, civil service. || **publication** [-ka'sjɔ̃] *n.f.* publication; publishing. cf. PUBLIER.

publiciste [-'sist] *n.m.* **1.** †journalist. **2.** publicity agent, ad man. || **publicité** [-si'te] *n.f.* publicity; advertising; advertising space (in newspaper): *faire de la* ~ *autour d'une affaire*, to advertise, publicize an event. || **publier** [-'je] #3 *v. tr.* to publish, to issue (a book, a statement); to edit: *publié avec une notice et des notes par*, edited by; to proclaim, to make known. [× but the publisher, in French, is L'ÉDITEUR]. || **publiquement** [-k'mɑ̃] *adv.* in public, publicly; in the open.

puce [pys] *n.f.* flea: *secouer les puces à qqun*, to haul s.o. over the coals, to jump on s.o.

pudeur [py'd|œ:r] *n.f.* modesty, decency. || **pudibond, -e** [-i'bɔ̃(:d)] *adj.* prudish. || **pudibonderie** [-ibɔ̃d'ri] *n.f.* prudishness. || **pudique** [-ik] *adj.* modest, chaste, decent.

pue [py] cf. PUER.

puer [pɥe © py'e] #3 *v. tr. & intr.* to smell bad, to stink, to reek.

puéril, -e [pɥe'ril] *adj.* childish, puerile, infantile. || **puérilement** [-'mɑ̃] *adv.* childishly. || **puérilité** [-i'te] *n.f.* childishness, puerility.

puis [pɥi] *adv.* then, next, afterwards: *et* ~ , besides, moreover.

puisatier [pɥiz|a'tje] *n.m.* well-digger, cf. PUITS.

puiser [-e] #3 *v. tr.* to draw. || *v. intr.* to draw (upon, *à, dans*): ~ *dans une bourse*, to dip into a purse.

puisque [pɥisk] *conj.* since, as, seeing that.

puissamment [pɥisa'mɑ̃] *adv.* powerfully, potently. **puissance** [pui's|ɑ̃:s] *n.f.* power, force: *les petites puissances*, the lesser powers; *la* ~ *d'un moteur*, the (horse) power of an engine; *élever un nombre à la 3e* ~ , to raise a number to the third power; *en* ~ , potentially; *en* ~ *de mari*, under marital control. || **puissant, -e** [-ɑ̃(:t)] *adj.* powerful, potent, mighty, influential: *le Tout-Puissant*, God Almighty.

puisse, &c. [pɥis] cf. POUVOIR.

puits [pɥi] *n.m. invar.* [eau] well; [charbon] pit; [mine] shaft: *creuser un* ~ , to dig, drill, a well; *tirer de l'eau au* ~ , to draw water from the well; *un* ~ *de pétrole*, an oil well.

pulluler [pylly'le] #3 *v. intr.* to swarm, to teem, to multiply.

pulmonaire [pylmɔ'nɛ:r] *adj.* pulmonary, of the lungs.

pulpe [pylp] *n.f.* pulp; © (wood) pulp.

pulsation [pylsa'sjɔ̃] *n.f.* pulsation, beat(ing), throb(bing).

pulvérisateur [pylveriz|atœ:r] *n.m.* atomizer, spray, vaporizer, spraying equipment. || **pulvérisation** [-a'sjɔ̃] *n.f.* pulverization. || **pulvériser** [-e] #3 *v. tr.* **1.** to pulverize. **2.** [Fig.] to demolish, to smash, to pulverize.

puma [py'ma] *n.m.* puma, cougar, mountain lion.

punaise [py'nɛ:z] *n.f.* **1.** [insecte] bedbug. **2.** [clou] thumbtack, [Br.] drawing pin.

punch [pɔ̃:ʃ] [pɔnʃ] *n.m*. punch [a drink].

punir [pyn|i:r] #17 *v. tr.* to punish. || **punissant** [-i'sɑ̃] cf. PUNIR. || **punition** [-i'sjɔ̃] *n.f.* punishment: *infliger une* ~ *à qqun*, to punish s.o.

pupille[1] [py|'pil © -'pi:j] *n. m/f.* ward.

pupille[2] *n.f.* pupil (of the eye).

pupitre [py'pitr] *n.m.* [bureau, classe] desk; lectern; music stand.

pur, -e [py:r] *adj.* **1.** pure, clear, unadulterated: *de l'eau pure*, plain water; *Il prend son vin* ~ , He drinks his wine straight; *un* ~ *sang*, a thoroughbred; *par pure bonté*, out of pure kindness. **2.** pure, innocent.

purée [py're] *n.f.* purée, mash: ~ *de pommes de terre*, mashed potatoes; [Sl.] *être dans la* ~ , to be broke.

pureté [pyr'te] *n.f.* purity; innocence.

purgati|f, -ve [pyrga|'tif, -ti:v] *adj.* purgative, purging. || **purgatif** [-'tif] *n.m.* purgative, cathartic. || **purgation** [-'sjɔ̃] *n.f.* purging, purgation.

purgatoire [-twa:r] *n.m.* purgatory.

purge [pyrʒ] *n.f.* purge, purgative, cathartic; paying off (of mortgage). || **purger** [-e] #5 *v. tr.* **1.** to purge. **2.** to pay off: ~ *une peine*, to serve a sentence.

purification [pyrif|ika'sjõ] *n.f.* purification, cleansing. || **purifier** [-je] #3 *v. tr.* to purify, cleanse.

puriste [py'rist] *n. m/f.* purist. || *adj.* puristic.

puritain, -e [pyri't|ɛ̃, -ɛn] *n. & adj. m/f* Puritan. || **puritanisme** [-a'nism] *n.m.* puritanism.

pus¹ [py] cf. POUVOIR.

pus² [py] *n.m.* pus, matter.

pustule [pys'tyl] *n.f.* pimple, pustule.

putois [py'twa] *n.m.* skunk, polecat.

putréfaction [pytr|efak'sjõ] *n.f.* putrefaction, rotting, decomposition, decaying. || **putréfier** [-e'fje] #3 *v. tr.* to rot, to putrefy, to decompose, to decay. || **putride** [-id] *adj.* putrid, rotten, decomposed.

pygmée [pig'me] *n.m.* pygmy.

pyjama [piʒa'ma] *n.m.* pajamas: *un* ~, a pair of pajamas.

Pyrénées, les [pire'ne] *n.f.pl.* The Pyrenees.

Q

Q, q [ky, © kə] *n.m.* Q, q; cf. A.

qu' cf. QUE.

quadragénaire [kwadraʒe'nɛ:r] *adj. & n.m./f.* quadragenarian. || **quadrangulaire** [kwadrɑ̃gy'lɛ:r] *adj.* four-angled.

quadrillage [kadri|'ja:ʒ] *n.m.* **1.** cross-ruling. **2.** [pattern] chequer-work; grid. || **quadrillé-e** [-'je] *adj.* cross-ruled; chequered.

quadruple [ka'drypl] *adj.* quadruple, four-fold.

quai [ke, kɛ] *n.m.* **1.** [harbour] quay, pier, wharf: *Nous serons à ~ à 7 heures,* We'll dock at 7. **2.** [station] platform, track: *Quai 3,* Track 3, [Br.] Platform 3.

qualificatif, -ve [kalifika|'tif, 'ti:v] *adj.* [Gram.] qualifying (adjective). || **qualification** [-'sjõ] *n.f.* [×] title, qualification. || **qualifier** [kali'fje] #3 *v. tr.* to qualify (sth.); to give s.o. the name of, to call s.o. a name.

qualité [kali'te] *n.f.* quality, grade, qualification, capacity: *bœuf de première ~*, choice beef; *en ~ de,* in the capacity of; *avoir ~ pour,* to be qualified to, to be authorized to; *avoir les qualités requises pour une tâche,* to be fitted for an assignment; *une personne de ~*, a person of noble birth.

quand [kɑ̃] *adv.* **1.** when, whenever [× cf. où]: *~ reviendrez-vous?,* When are you coming back?; *Depuis ~ habitez-vous Toronto?* How long have you been living in Toronto?; *Pour ~ voulez-vous ce costume?,* When do you want this outfit?; *Venez ~ vous voudrez,* Come whenever you like. **2.** While, at the time when: *J'étais là ~ le facteur est arrivé,* I was there when the postman came. **3.** quand (même), quand bien même, (even) though, even if . . . : *Quand même il viendrait, je ne lui parlerai pas,* Even if he does come, I will not speak to him; *Je le ferai quand même!,* I'll do it just the same.

quant à [kɑ̃'ta] *loc. prép.* as for: *~ à moi,* as for me; *rester sur son quant-à-soi,* to remain aloof.

quantième [kɑ̃'tiɛm] *n.m. le ~ du mois,* day of the month, date. || **quantitati|f, -ve** [kɑ̃ti|ta'tif, -'ti:v] *adj.* quantitative (analysis). || **quantité** [-'te] *n.f.* **1.** quantity; abundance, plenty; amount, supply: *avoir . . . en ~*, to have plenty of . . . ; *avoir (du pétrole) en ~*, to have a large supply (of oil). **2.** a great/many, deal of/: *~ de gens disent,* many people say.

quantum [kwɑ̃'tɔm] *n.m.* [société] quorum; [Math.] quantum.

quarantaine [karɑ̃'tɛn] *n.f.* about forty; *une ~ de personnes,* about forty; *approcher de la ~*, to be close to forty. || **quarante** [ka'r|ɑ̃:t] *adj. & n.m.* forty. || **quarantième** [-ɑ̃'tjɛm] *adj. & n.m.* fortieth.

quart [ka:r] *n.m.* fourth (part); quarter (of an hour): *une heure et ~*, a quarter past one; *un ~ d'heure,* a quarter of an hour; [Naut.] watch: *prendre le ~*, to go on watch; *être de ~*, to be on watch.

quartier [kar'tje] *n.m.* **1.** fourth part,

†quarter; quarter (of the moon). **2.** neighbourhood, section, district: *les beaux quartiers*, upper class residential district; *le ~ des affaires*, the business section, downtown. **3.** large cut (of meat), section (of orange). **4.** barracks, armoury.

†**quasi** [ka'zi] *adv.* as if, almost (as if). ‖ **quasiment** [-'mɑ̃] *adv.* [Colloq.] as you might say, in a manner of speaking, as it were.

quatorze [ka'tɔrz] *adj. & n.m.* fourteen; [date] *le ~*, the fourteenth; *Louis Quatorze*, Louis the Fourteenth. ‖ **quatorzième** [-jɛm] *adj. & n.m.* fourteenth.

quatrain [ka'trɛ̃] *n.m.* quatrain.

quatre [katr] *adj. & n.m.* four: *monter un escalier ~ à ~*, to run up the stairs, to take the stairs four at a time; *marcher à ~ pattes*, to crawl on hands and knees, to go on all fours; [Fam.] *se mettre en ~ pour lui faire plaisir*, to/do anything, tie oneself in(to) knots/to please s.o. ‖ [R.C.] **les quatre-temps** [always pl.] Ember days. ‖ **quatre-vingts** [-ə'vɛ̃] *adj. & n.m.* [☞ takes no *s* when followed by another number] eighty. ‖ **quatre-vingt-dix** [-əvɛ̃'dis] ninety. ‖ **quatrième** [-i'jɛm] *adj. & n.* fourth.

quatuor [kwa'tɥɔːr] *n.m.* [Mus.] quartet.

que, qu'[1] [kə, k] *pron. rel.* whom [souvent omis], that, which: *l'homme ~ j'ai vu*, the man (whom) I saw; *la lettre ~ j'ai écrite*, the letter (that) I wrote; *Sa lettre, ~ je n'ai reçue qu'après . . .*, His letter, which I received only afterwards . . . ; *le jour qu'il est venu*, the day on which he came, the day when he came. ‖ *pron. interrog.* what: *Que désirez-vous?*, What would you like? cf. also QU'EST-CE QUE.

que, qu'[2] *conj.* **1.** that [souvent omis]: *Il a dit qu'il viendrait*, He said (that) he would come. **2.** [after comp.] than, as: *plus grand ~ moi*, taller than I; *aussi grand ~ moi*, as tall as I. **3.** till, until: *Attendez qu'il vienne*, Wait till he comes. **4.** [to express wish] let: *Qu'il le dise!*, Let him say so; *~ Dieu vous bénisse!*, God bless you! **5.** [with OU] whether: *Qu'il parte ou non . . .*, Whether he goes or not . . . **6.** [to avoid repeating conjunction]: *S'il vient et ~ je n'y sois pas*, If he comes and I am not there . . . . **7.** rendered by *if* in other clause: *Il viendrait ~ cela ne m'étonnerait pas*, I would not be surprised if he came. **8.** since: *Il y a huit jours qu'il est arrivé*, It is a week since he came. **9.** but, except: *personne ~ vous*, no one but you. *adv.* [exclamatory] how, what: *~ de livres!*, What a lot of books!; *~ c'est grand!*, How big it is! ‖ **ne . . . que** *adv.* only: *Je n'en veux qu'un*, I want only one; *Il n'a fait que passer*, He only stopped by.

Québec [ke'b|ɛk] [☞ Do not confuse the *city* with the *Province* of the same name; cf. below **1** and **2.**] **1.** *n.f.* Quebec (City), the City of Quebec: *habiter ~*, to live in Q. City; *à ~*, at Q. **2.** *n.m.* = La Province de ~, [*abbr.* P.Q. or Qué.], (the Province of) Quebec, [*abbr.* Que.]: *habiter le ~*, to live in Q.; *au ~*, in Q.; *le Nouveau-Québec*, New Q.; **3.** © [Loc.] *faire/passer/un ~*, to take s.o. in. ‖ **québecois, -e** [-e'kwa(ːz)] *adj. & n.* of, from Quebec; Quebec(k)er.

quel, quelle; quels, quelles [kɛl] **1.** *adj.* what; what sort of: *Quelle heure est-il?*, What time is it?; *Quelle pointure chaussez-vous?*, What size (of) shoes do you wear?; *Quelle route prenons-nous?*, Which, What/road do we take?, Which, What/way do we go? **2.** what: *Quel homme!* What a man! *Quelle chance!* What luck! **3.** *Quel que . . .* whoever, whatever: *quelle que soit la difficulté*, whatever the difficulty; [Loc.] *tel quel*, as is. [→ tel]. [× Do not confuse *quelle qu'elle, quel qu'il* with QUELQUE[2].]

quelconque [kɛl'kɔ̃ːk] *adj.* **1.** any, whatever: *pour une raison ~*, for some (any) reason. **2.** commonplace, indifferent. [Colloq.] *Il est très ~*, He is very ordinary.

quelque,[1] *pl.* **quelques** [kɛlk(ə)] *adj.* some, any; some [+ in compounds]: *il y a quelques années*, some, several/years ago; *il y a ~ temps*, some time ago; *~ part*, somewhere; *~ chose*, something, [indéf.] anything.

quelque[2] *adv.* (*inv.*) some, about; †however: *Il y avait ~ mille personnes*, There were about one thousand persons (in the room, &c.); *~ peu*, somewhat. [× Do not confuse with QUEL]; †*~ difficile que ce soit . . .*, no matter how difficult . . . , however difficult it may be. . . . ‖ **quelquefois** [-ə'fwa] sometimes, at times, occasionally. ‖ **quelqu'un, -e** [kɛl'k|œ̃, -yn] *pron. ind.* someone; somebody; anybody, anyone. ‖ **quelques-uns, quelques-unes** [kɛlkə|'zœ̃, -'zyn] *pron. ind. pl.* some, any, a few: *Y en avait-il ~ ?*, Were there any?

quémander [kemɑ̃'de] #3 *v. intr.* to beg (from door to door). ‖ *v. tr.* to beg for, solicit.

querelle [kə'rɛl] *n.f.* quarrel, row; fight: *chercher ~ à*, to pick a quarrel with;

La Querelle des Anciens et des Modernes, The quarrel of the Ancients and the Moderns. || **se quereller** [səkərɛ'le] #3 *v. pron.* to quarrel (with, *avec*), to have words (about, *à propos de*). || **querelleu|r, -se** [-œ:r, -ø:z] *adj. & n.* quarrelsome.

qu'est-ce que [kɛsk|ə] *pron. int.* [set formula emphasizing QUE, used, as an object, of things only]: ~ *vous voulez?*, What do you want?; ~ *ça fait?*, What does it matter?

qu'est-ce qui [kɛs'ki] *pron. int.* [set formula emphasizing QUI, as a subject, of things only] what: ~ *se passe?*, What's going on?

question [kɛs'tj|õ] *n.f.* **1.** question, interrogation; query: *adresser, poser/une* ~ *à . . .*, to ask . . . a question; *répondre à une* ~, to reply to a question. **2.** point, issue; problem: [Pol.] ~ *de confiance*, vote of confidence; *La deuxième* ~ *de l'ordre du jour*, The second item on the agenda; *il n'est pas* ~ *de . . .*, is out of the question; *la* ~ *est de savoir si*, the question is whether . . . ; *De quoi est-il* ~ *?* [also *De quoi s'agit-il?*], What is it about?, What is involved here?; *résoudre une* ~, to solve a problem. || **questionnaire** [-ɔ'nɛ:r] *n.m.* questionnaire; (Gallup) poll. || **questionner** [-ɔ'ne] #3 *v. tr.* to ask s.o., to question s.o. (about, *sur*): *Il a été questionné par la police*, He was questioned by the police.

quête [kɛ:t] *n.f.* **1.** collection (at church); drive (charity): *Faire une* ~ *pour les pauvres*, to take up a collection for the poor. **2.** [Fig.] quest, search: *se mettre en* ~ *de*, to set out in search of. . . . ||**quêter** [kɛ't|e] #3 *v. tr.* to collect (money), to ask for donations, to beg for (votes, praise, compliments). || **quêteur** [-œ:r] & © **quêteux** [-ø] *n.m.* collector; beggar; canvasser.

queue [kø] *n.f.* **1.** tail: [Fig.] *Cela n'a ni* ~ *ni tête*, I can't make head or tail of it. **2.** Stem (of flowers); handle (of saucepans); end; (billiard) cue; train (of robes). **3.** [Fig.] rear; queue, line: *être à la* ~, *en* ~, to be in the rear; *faire la* ~, *faire* ~ *(à un guichet, &c.)*, to line up, to queue up, to stand in line.

qui [ki] *pron. rel.* who, whom; which, that: *Les gens* ~ *réfléchissent*, People who think; *L'employé à* ~ *il s'est adressé*, The clerk to whom he spoke; *Sa maison,* ~ *est hypothéquée . . .*, His house, which is mortgaged . . . ; *Le livre* ~ *est sur la table . . .*, The book (that is) on the table . . . ; ~ *que vous soyez*, Whoever you may be; *N'en parlez à* ~ *que ce soit*, Mention it to no one; [in set phrases]: *N'importe* ~ *vous le dira*, Anyone will tell you; *Je ne sais* ~ *lui en a parlé*, I don't know who told him. || *pron. int.* [only of people] who, whom, whose, which: ~ *est venu?*, Who came?; *A* ~ *est ce livre?*, Whose book is this?; ~ *de vous?*, Which of you?

quiconque [ki'kõ:k] *pr. rel. ind.* whoever, whomever, whichever: ~ *parlera sera puni*, Anyone who speaks shall be punished.

qui est-ce que [kiɛskə] *pron. int.* [set formula giving emphasis to QUE, used as an object, of people] who: *A qui est-ce qu'il faut s'adresser?*, To whom should one apply? Who(m) should one apply to?

qui est-ce qui [kiɛski] *pron. int.* [set formula giving emphasis to QUI, used as a subject, of people], who: ~ *vous l'a dit?*, Who told you?

quignon [ki'ɲõ] *n.m.*: ~ *de pain*, chunk, hunk (of bread).

quille[1] [ki:j] *n.f.* keel (of a boat).

quille[2] [ki:j] *n.f.* [bowling] pin: *jeu de quilles*, bowling alley; *jouer aux quilles*, to bowl; *Comme un chien dans un jeu de quilles*, Like a bull in a china shop. || © **quilleu|r, -se** [ki'j|œ:r, -ø:z] *n.* bowler.

quincaillerie [kɛ̃kaj|'ri] *n.f.* hardware. || **quincaillier** [-e] *n.m.* hardware dealer.

quinine [ki'nin] *n.f.* quinine.

quinquenn|al, -ale, *pl.* **-aux, -ales** [kɛ̃kɛn|al, -o] quinquennial: *Plan* ~, Five-year plan.

quintal [kɛ̃'tal] *n.m.* quintal, a hundredweight [Abr. cwt = 112 lbs]; ~ *métrique*, *quintal* [= 100 kilos, 220.46 lbs].

quinte [kɛ̃:t] *n.f.* [Mus.] fifth; a fit (of coughing). || **quinteu|x, -se** [kɛ̃'t|ø, -ø:z] *adj.* cantankerous, contentious. || **quintuple** [kɛ̃'typl] *adj. & n.m.* fivefold. || **quintupl|és, -ées** [-e] *n. & adj.* quintuplets. || **quintupler** #3 *v. tr. & intr.* to increase fivefold.

quinzaine [kɛ̃'zɛn] *n.f.* about fifteen; two weeks. || **quinze** [kɛ̃:z] *adj. & n.m.* fifteen; fifteenth: *dans* ~ *jours*, in two weeks' time. || **quinzième** [kɛ̃'zjɛm] *adj. & n.m.* fifteenth.

qui que [kikə] ☞ *pr. complexe* [+ subj.] whoever; anyone, no one: ~ *vous soyez . . .*, whoever you are; ~ *ce soit qui vous l'ait dit*, . . . No matter who told you, . . . cf. QUI, QUOI.

quittance [ki'tɑ̃:s] *n.f.* receipt, bill (gas,

electricity): *donner ~ à*, to give a receipt.

quitte [kit] *adj.* clear (of debts), free (from obligation): *tenir quelqu'un ~*, to release s.o.; *Je vous en tiens ~*, I won't hold you to it; *Nous sommes quittes*, Now we are quits; *~ à recommencer*, even if we have to start all over again; *Il en a été ~ pour une réprimande*, He was let off with a warning.

quitter [ki'te] #3 *v. tr.* to leave, to take off, to give up: *~ qqun*, to leave s.o.; *~ un endroit*, to leave a place, *~ un vêtement*, to take off a garment; *~ sa place*, to give up one's job.

qui-vive [ki'vi:v] *n.m.* challenge word, password: *Qui vive?*, Who goes there?; *se tenir sur le ~*, to be on the lookout, on the alert.

quoi[1] [kwa] *pron. rel.* what, which: *Ce à ~ il travaille . . .*, What he is working at . . . ; *faute de ~*, failing which; *sans ~*, otherwise; *moyennant ~*, in exchange for which; *Comme ~ il est difficile de contenter tout le monde*, Which goes to show it's hard to please everybody; *Il n'y a pas de ~ s'alarmer*, There is no cause for alarm; ***Il a juste de ~ payer son loyer***, He has just enough to pay the rent; *un je ne sais ~*, a little something; *n'importe ~*, anything.

quoi[2] *pron. int.* what: *~ de nouveau?*, What's new?; *A ~ cela sert-il?*, What is it for?; *A ~ bon?*, What's the use?; *En ~ puis-je vous être utile?*, What can I do for you?; *Quoi?*, What?, What did you say? *interj. Quoi!*, What!, You don't say!

quoique, quoiqu' [kwak(ə)] *conj.* although, though (+subj.) [Do not confuse with QUOI QUE]: *Quoiqu'il ne m'ait rien dit, je . . .*, Although he said nothing to me, I . . . .

quoi que, quoi qu' ['kwak(ə)] *pron. ind. neutre, + subj.* whatever, however: *Quoi qu'il dise*, Whatever he may say, No matter what he says; *Il a refusé de faire ~ ce soit*, He refused to do anything whatever; *Quoi qu'il en soit*, However that may be, Be that as it may.

quote-part [kɔt'pa:r] *n.f.* share, quota.

quotidien, -ne [kɔtidj|ɛ̃, -ɛn] *adj.* daily; *notre pain ~*, our daily bread. || **quotidiennement** [-ɛn'mɑ̃] *abv.* daily, every-day.

quotient [kɔ'sjɑ̃] *n.m.* quotient: *~ intellectuel*, **I.Q.**

R

R, r [ɛ:r] *n.m.* the letter R, r. || *R* [on letters] [= RECOMMANDÉ], *R* [= *Registered*]. || *R.F.* [= République française], the French Republic; *R.S.V.P.* [= répondre, s'il vous plaît], *RSVP*.

rabâcher [rabɑ'ʃe] #3 *v. tr.* to keep on repeating (sth.). || *v. intr.* to harp on (one string).

rabais [ra'bɛ] *n.m.* reduction, discount, rebate: *acheter au ~*, to buy/ at a reduced price, in a bargain basement; *vingt pour cent de ~*, twenty per cent off; *faire un ~ sur . . .*, to allow a reduction on . . . || **rabaisser** [rabɛ'se] #3 *v. tr.* to lower: [Fig.] to reduce, detract from.

rabat, rabats [ra'ba] cf. RABATTRE. || **rabat-joie** [-'ʒwa] *n.m. invar.* kill-joy, [Fam.] wet blanket. || **rabatteur** [-'tœʀ] *n.m.* [chasse] beater.

rabattre [ra'bat|r] #43 *v. tr.* **1.** to lower, put down, fold up. **2.** to lower, reduce: *Je n'en rabattrai pas un centime*, I won't come down a penny more; *Il faut ~ la moitié de ce qu'il dit*, You have to discount half of what he says; *Il a fallu en ~*, They had to come down a peg or two. **3.** to flush: *~ le gibier*, /to flush, to beat up/game. || **se rabattre** *v. pron.* **1.** to fold: *table qui se rabat*, folding table. **2.** to fall back: *L'armée se rabattit sur la ville*, The army fell back upon the town. || **rabattu, -e** [-y] cf. RABATTRE. || *adj.* [couture] turned down (seam).

rabbin [ra'bɛ̃] *n.m.* rabbi.

râblé, -e [ra'ble] *adj.* strong; husky.
rabot [ra'b|o] *n.m.* [menuiserie, &c.] plane. || **raboter** [-ɔ'te] #3 *v. tr.* to plane (down) (a door, &c.). || **raboteu|x, -se** [-ɔ'tø(:z)] *adj.* rough, uneven: *un terrain ~*, rugged terrain; *un bois ~*, knotty wood; *un style ~*, an unpolished style.
rabougri [rabu'gri] *adj.* stunted, dwarfed.
racaille [ra'kɑ:j] *n.f.* rabble, riffraff.
raccommodage [rakɔmɔ'd|a:ʒ] *n.m.* mending; [socks] darning; [clothes] patching. || **raccommodement** [-'mɑ̃] *n.m.* reconciliation. || **raccommoder** [rakɔmɔ'de] #3 *v. tr.* **1.** to mend, repair [clothing; also crockery, furniture, &c.]; [repriser] to darn (socks, stockings); [rapiécer] to patch. **2.** to reconcile, patch up a quarrel between (two persons).
raccord [ra'k|ɔ:r] *n.m.* fittings; connection. || **raccorder** [-ɔrde] #3 *v. tr.* to join, connect.
raccourci [rakur's|i] cf. RACCOURCIR. || *adj.* shortened, abridged. || *n.m.* short cut; [Loc.] *en ~*, in abbreviated form. || **raccourcir** [-i:r] #17 *v. tr.* to shorten. *v. intr.* [preferably SE RACCOURCIR]. || **se raccourcir** *v. pron.* to grow shorter; cf. RÉTRÉCIR.
raccrocher [rakrɔ'ʃe] #3 *v. tr.* to hang up (again). || *v. intr.* to hang up (the phone receiver). || **se raccrocher** (à) *v. pron.* to cling to, to hang on to.
race [ras] *n.f.* **1.** [humaine] race. **2.** [d'animaux] breed: *un cheval de ~*, a thoroughbred (horse).
rachat [ra'ʃ|a] *n.m.* **1.** buying back, repurchase (of goods); cashing in (of bonds) ransom (of prisoners) **2.** [Fig.] atonement (for o.'s sins); redemption (of mankind). || **rachète, rachèterai** cf. RACHETER. || **racheter** [-'te] #9 *v. tr.* **1.** to buy back, to repurchase (goods, &c.); to cash in (bonds, &c.); to ransom (prisoners). **2.** to buy again: *~ du même tissu*, to buy some more of the same fabric. **3.** [Fig.] to atone for, to redeem: *~ son passé*, to atone for o.'s past; *Jésus-Christ est mort pour ~ les hommes*, Christ died to redeem mankind.
racine [ra'sin] *n.f.* root (of plant, tree, hair, word, &c.): *prendre ~*, to take root; [Fig.] *couper le mal dans sa ~*, to strike at the root of (the) evil; *~ carrée*, square root.
raclée [rɑ'kle] *n.f.* beating, [Fam.] licking; *administrer/flanquer/une ~ à qqun*, [Fam.] to lick s.o.
racler [rɑ'kl|e] #3 *v. tr.* to scrape. || **racloir** [-wa:r] *n.m.* scraper. || **raclure** [-y:r] *n.f.* scrapings *npl.*
raconter [rakõ'te] #3 *v. tr.* to tell, relate (a story, a tale): *Je vous raconterai cela plus tard*, I'll tell you all about it later.
raconteur [rakõ'tœ:r] *n.m.* raconteur; story-teller.
racorni, -e [rakɔr'ni] *adj.* hardened, shrivelled; [Fig.] hardened (feelings), narrow (mind). || **racornir** [rakɔr'ni:r] #17 *v. tr.* to harden, to shrivel.
radar [ra'da:r] *n.m.* radar.
rade [rad] *n.f.* [Naut.] roads, roadstead.
radeau [ra'do] *n.m.* raft: *~ de sauvetage*, liferaft.
radiat|eur, -rice [radja|'tœ:r, -'tris] *adj.* radiating, radiant. || *n.m.* [chauffage d'un logement, refroidissement d'un moteur] radiator; (space, electric) heater. || **radiation**[1] [-'sjõ] *n.f.* [Phys.] radiation. || **radiation**[2] *n.f.* crossing out, deletion.
radical, e [radi'kal] *adj.* [Polit., Math., Méd., &c.] radical. || *n.m.* radical.
radier [ra'dje] #3 *v. tr.* to strike/off, out/; to cross out. || *v. intr.* [chaleur, &c.] to radiate; [lumière] to gleam; [joie] to beam.
radieu|x, -se [ra'djø(:z)] *adj.* radiant, beaming; [sourire] dazzling; [journée] glorious.
radio [ra'djo] *n.f.* [radiophonie] radio; [esp. Naut.] wireless: *à la ~*, on the radio, on the air. || *n.m.* **1.** wireless, radio/operator. **2.** © [poste, appareil de T.S.F.] radio, radio set; [esp. Naut.] wireless, wireless set. || **radiodiffuser** [radjodify'ze] #3 *v. tr.* to broadcast. || **radiodiffusion** [radjodify'zjõ] *n.f.* broad casting. || **radiogramme** [-'gram] *n.m.* **1.** X-ray (photograph). **2.** radio message. || **radioguidé, -e** [-gi'de] *adj.*: *projectile ~*, guided missile.
radis [ra'di] *n.m.* radish.
radium [ra'djɔm] *n.m.* radium.
radius [ra'djys] *n.m.* radius.
radotage [radɔ't|a:ʒ] *n.m.* drivel; rambling, idle talk. || **radoter** [-e] #3 *v. intr.* to/talk, speak/drivel, to/talk, speak/(utter) nonsense; to rant on.
radoucir [radu'si:r] #17 *v. tr.* to calm (s.o.) (down), to mollify, pacify (s.o.): [Fig.] *La pluie a radouci le temps*, The rain has brought milder weather. || **se radoucir** *v. pron.* to calm down; [temps] to grow milder.
rafale [ra'fal] *n.f.* **1.** squall, gust (of wind): *vent à rafales*, gusty wind; *temps à rafales*, squally weather. **2.** [mitrailleuse, &c.] burst of fire.

raffermir [rafɛr'mi:r] #17 *v. tr.* to harden (again); to strengthen; [Fig.] [courage] to consolidate; to brace (up); [voix] to become steady.

raffinage [rafi'n|a:ʒ] *n.m.* refining (of oil, sugar, &c.). || **raffiné, -e** [-e] *adj.* refined. || **raffinement** [-'mɑ̃] *n.m.* **1.** [raffinage] refining. **2.** refinement, subtlety (of expression, style, &c.). || **raffiner** #3 *v. tr.* to refine, to bring to a fine point. || **raffinerie** [-'ri] *n.f.* refinery.

raffoler [rafɔ'le] #3 *v. intr.* to dote (*de*, on): *~ de qqch.*, [Fam.] to be /wild, crazy/ about sth.

rafle [rɑ:fl] *n.f.* **1.** [bunch of grapes] stalk; [corn] corncob. **2.** [police] raid. **3.** © [abus.] rummage sale. || **rafler** [rɑ'fle] #3 *v. tr.* to sweep/away, off/; to carry/away, off/; [Fam.] to swipe.

rafraîchir [rafrɛ'ʃ|i:r] #17 *v. tr.* **1.** to cool (wine, &c.); to refresh, cool off (a person); to air (an apartment). **2.** [Fig.] to freshen up, to brighten up, to revive, to refresh: *~ un tableau*, to brighten up a picture; *Je vais vous ~ la mémoire*, I'm going to refresh your memory. || *v. intr.* [vin, &c.] to cool; [Pers.] to refresh o.s.: *On a mis le vin à ~*, The wine was put (away) to cool. || **se rafraîchir** *v. pron.* **1.** [temps] to turn cooler. **2.** to refresh o.s. || **rafraîchissant** [-i'sɑ̃], *adj.* refreshing, cooling: *C'est très ~*, → It quenches your thirst. || **rafraîchissement** [-is'mɑ̃] *n.m.* cooling; || *pl.* [Fig.] cool drinks.

ragaillardir [ragajar'di:r] #17 *v. tr.* to cheer (s.o.) up: *Cela vous ragaillardit*, [Fam.] It's a good pick-me-up.

rage [ra:ʒ] *n.f.* rage, fury; [chiens] rabies: *écumer de ~*, to froth at the mouth; *La bataille, La tempête, L'incendie faisait ~*, The/battle, storm, fire/was raging; *avoir une ~ de dents*, to have a raging toothache; *Cela fait ~*, It's all the rage. || **rager** [ra'ʒ|e] #5 *v. intr.* to rage; to be enraged; to boil, fume (with rage). || **rageu|r, -se** [-œ:r, -ø:z] *adj.* passionate, bad- (hot-, ill-) -tempered.

ragoût [ra'gu] *n.m.* stew, ragout.

ragoûtant, -e [ragu'tɑ̃(:t)] *adj.* tempting, inviting [usual. neg.]: *Ce n'est pas très ~*, It's not very inviting.

raid [rɛd] *n.m.* [Mil.] raid; [avion] long-distance flight.

raide [rɛd] *adj.* **1.** stiff (limbs, bristles, corpse); taut, tight (rope, drum); straight and swift (bullet or arrow shot, flight of bird, &c.); steep (hill, stairway): *marcher sur la corde ~*, to walk/the, a/tightrope [also Fig.] **2.** [Fig.] stiff, stubborn, unbending, unyielding, rigid (attitude, disposition); strong, forceful, vigorous: *se tenir ~*, to hold o.s. stiffly; *une riposte ~*, a stinging retort; *Ça, c'est un peu ~ !*, That's a bit steep! || *adv.* swift, straight, suddenly: *aller ~ comme une balle*, to go like a shot; *tomber ~ mort*, to drop dead. || **raideur** [-œ:r] *n.f.* stiffness (of limbs, bristles, attitude); swift accuracy, vigour: *saluer avec ~*, to greet stiffly. || **raidir** [-i:r] #17 *v. tr.* to stiffen (sth.); to tighten, pull taut (rope, &c.). || *v. intr.* [preferably SE RAIDIR]. || **se raidir** *v. pron.* **1.** to stiffen (up); [corde, &c.] to tighten, grow taut. **2.** [Fig.] [contre le malheur, la douleur] to brace o.s. (against).

raie,[1] **raierai** cf. RAYER.

raie[2] [rɛ] *n.f.* **1.** [au crayon, &c.] line, stroke; [tissu; zèbre, tigre] stripe: *faire une ~*, to draw, make a line; *tissu à raies noires*, black-striped material. **2.** [cheveux] part, [esp. Br.] parting: *faire sa ~*, → to part o.'s hair.

raie[3] *n.f.* [poisson] ray, skate.

raifort [re'fɔ:r] *n.m.* horseradish.

rail [ra:j] *n.m.* [Rail.] rail; *pl.* [voie ferrée] rails, track.

railler [ra'j|e] #3 *v. tr.* to make fun of (s.o.), [Fam.] to kid, josh (s.o.): *Il ne peut supporter qu'on le raille*, He can't stand being/made fun of, kidded/. || *v. intr.* to joke, [Fam.] kid: *Allons, vous raillez!*, Oh come now, you're/joking!, kidding!; *Je ne raille point*, I'm not joking a bit. || **se railler de** *v. pron.* to make fun of, to laugh at [more usual, SE MOQUER DE]. || **raillerie** [-'ri] *n.f.* joking, [Fam.] kidding: *Il n'entend pas la ~*, → He can't/take a joke, stand being made fun of. || **railleu|r, -se** [-œ:r, -ø:z] *adj.* joking, bantering; scoffing, mocking. || *n.* joker, banterer; scoffer.

rainure [rɛ'ny:r] *n.f.* groove.

raisin [re'zɛ̃] *n.m.* grapes: */le, du/ ~*, grapes; *un ~*, a (variety of) grape; *une grappe de ~*, a bunch of grapes; *un grain de ~*, a (single) grape; *raisins secs*, raisins; *raisins de Corinthe*, (dried) currants, cf. CURRANT.

raison [rɛ'zɔ̃] *n.f.* **1.** reason, cause, good sense: *en ~ de*, because of; *Cela n'a plus de ~ d'être*, It does not make sense any more; *avoir des raisons suffisantes de . . .*, to have adequate grounds for . . .; *~ de plus, à plus forte ~*, the more the reason; *comme de ~*, justifiably; *avoir ~*, to be right; *avoir des raisons de penser . . .*, to have reason to think; *se faire une ~*, to resign o.s.; *entendre ~*, to listen to reason; *faire entendre* ~ *à qqun*, to bring s.o. to reason; *donner* ~ *à*, to decide in s.o.'s favour; *On lui a demandé la* ~ *de sa conduite*, He was asked to account for his behaviour; *Il devra en rendre* ~, He will have to account for it; *J'ai fini par avoir* ~ *de son opposition*, I finally overcame his opposition; *plus que de* ~, to excess; *sans rime ni* ~, without rhyme or reason. **2.** ~ *sociale*, name (of business firm). **3.** ratio, rate: *en* ~ *directe* (*inverse*), in direct (inverse) ratio; *à* ~ *de*, at the rate of. || **raisonné, -e** [rezɔ'n|e] cf. RAISONNER. || *adj.* reasoned, rational. || **raisonnement** [-'mɑ̃] *n.m.* reasoning. || **raisonner** [-e] #3 *v. intr.* to reason. || *v. tr.* to reason out (a problem), to think through. || **se raisonner** *v. pron.* to reason with o.s. || **raisonneu|r, -se** [-œ:r, -ø:z] *adj.* reasoning, rational; [péj.] argumentative. || *n.* arguer.

rajeuni, -e [raʒœ'n|i] *adj.* younger, rejuvenated. || **rajeunir** [-i:r] #17 *v. tr.* to rejuvenate; to make (s.o.) look younger; to renovate: *Cette coiffure la rajeunit de dix ans*, That hair-do makes her look ten years younger. || *v. intr.* to grow young again, to look younger.

rajouter [raʒu'te] #3 *v. tr.* to add (again, more).

rajuster [raʒys'te] #3 *v. tr.* to readjust, to set right. || **se rajuster** *v. pron.* to readjust (o.s., one's dress).

râle[1] [rɑ:l] *n.m.* **1.** râle (de la mort), death rattle. **2.** [Méd.] râle.

râle[2] *n.m.* [oiseau] rail.

ralenti [ralɑ̃'t|i] *n.m.* slow motion: *film tourné au ralenti*, slow-motion film, picture; [moteur] *tourner au ralenti*, to idle; [usine, &c.] *marcher au ralenti*, to curtail, slow/down/production. || **ralentir** [-i:r] #17 *v. tr.* to slow down, slow up, slacken (pace); to moderate (o.'s zeal, ardour, efforts). || *v. intr.* to slow/down up: *Ralentir!*, (Go) slow(ly)! || **se ralentir** *v. pron.* [marche, vitesse, activité, &c.] to slow down, to drop off: *Pendant l'été les affaires se ralentissent ici*, During the summer business drops off here.

râler [rɑ'le] #3 *v. intr.* to rattle in o's throat; to be at o.'s last gasp; [Fam.] to grumble, [Fam.] grouch.

ralliement [ral|i'mɑ̃] *n.m.* rallying; [Mil.] rallying word; countersign. || **rallier** [-je] #3 *v. tr.* to rally, join. || **se rallier (à)** *v. pron.* to rally.

rallonge [ra'l|ɔ̃:ʒ] *n.f.* extra piece; [table] (extra) leaf. || **rallonger** [-ɔ̃'ʒe] #5 *v. tr.* to lengthen, make . . . longer; to extend (a shelf, a table); to lengthen, let down (a skirt).

rallumer [raly'me] #3 *v. tr.* [lampe, feu] to relight; [espoir] to rekindle, revive.

ramage [ra'ma:ʒ] *n.m.* **1.** [oiseaux] warbling, chirping. **2.** [sur une étoffe] flower, flowering.

ramassage [rama's|a:ʒ] *n.m.* gathering, collecting; picking up.

ramassé, -e [ramɑ'se] *adj.* stocky, thick-set; [Fig.] compact.

ramasser [ramɑ'se] #3 *v. tr.* **1.** [single item] to pick up (a glove &c.). **2.** [scattered items] to gather together, to collect, assemble; to/gather, pick/up: ~ *du bois*, to gather, collect (fire)wood; [Fig.] ~ *ses forces*, to muster o.'s strength; ~ *de l'argent*, to pick up some money. || **se ramasser** *v. pron.* to pick o.s. up; [pour sauter, &c.] to brace o.s. || **ramassis** [-i] *n.m.* [choses] heap, jumble; [Pers., Péj.] pack, crowd.

rame[1] [ram] *n.f.* oar. cf. AVIRON.

rame[2] *n.f.* ream (of paper).

rameau [ra'mo] *n.m.* branch, sprig; [fleuri] sprig: [RC] *le dimanche des Rameaux*, Palm Sunday.

ramène, &c., ramènerai cf. RAMENER. || **ramener** [ram'ne] #9 *v. tr.* **1.** bring back, take back; lead back: ~ *qqun chez lui en voiture*, to drive s.o. home; ~ *qqch. de la ville*, to bring sth. back from town; ~ *les vaches*, to bring in the cows (from pasture); [Fig.] ~ *qqun à la vraie foi*, → to bring s.o. back to the fold. **2.** to reduce: ~ *qqch. à sa plus simple expression*, to reduce sth. to its simplest expression; *Il ramène tout à lui*, He is self-centred. **3.** [la paix, l'ordre, l'abondance] to restore.

ramer [ra'me] #3 *v. intr.* to row cf. NAGER[2].

ramification [ramif|ika'sjɔ̃] *n.f.* [arbre] ramification, ramifying; [Rail., science] branch; [filon] spur. || **se ramifier** [-je] #3 *v. pron.* [arbre] to branch out; [Fig.] to extend.

ramollir [ramɔ'li:r] #17 *v. tr.* [corps dur] to soften; [courage] to weaken, enervate. || se **ramollir** *v. pron.* [corps dur] to grow soft, to soften; [cerveau] to give way.

ramoner [ramɔ'n|e] #3 *v. tr.* to sweep (chimneys). || **ramoneur** [-œ:r] *n.m.* chimney-sweep(er).

rampe [rɑ̃:p] *n.f.* **1.** [vers une plate-forme; chemin qui monte jusqu'à une autoroute, &c.] ramp; [more usual. PENTE] grade, gradient (of road, railroad track). **2.** [escalier] banister. **3.** [aéroport] runway lights; [Théât.] footlights: *La pièce n'a* *pas passé la* ~, The play didn't get across; *être sous les feux de la* ~, → to be in the limelight. **ramper** [rɑ̃'pe] #3 *v. intr.* [reptile, pers.] to crawl, creep; [lierre, vigne] to creep: /*entrer, sortir, monter*/*en rampant*, to crawl/in, out, up; [Fig.] ~ *devant ses supérieurs*, to grovel before o.'s superiors.

rancart [rɑ̃'ka:r] *n.m.* refuse, trash: *mettre qqch. au* ~, to cast aside; [Fig.] to shelve (a topic, a decision).

rance [rɑ̃:s] *adj.* [beurre, huile, &c.] rancid: *sentir le* ~, to smell rancid.

ranch [rɑ̃:ʃ] *n.m.* ranch.

rancir [rɑ̃'si:r] #17 *v. intr.* [beurre, huile, &c.] to go, turn rancid.

rancoeur [rɑ̃'kœ:r] *n.f.* rancour, animosity.

rançon [rɑ̃'sõ] *n.f.* ransom: *mettre qqun à* (*la*) ~, to hold s.o. for ransom.

rançonner [rɑ̃sɔ'ne] #3 *v. tr.* to ransom.

rancune [rɑ̃'kyn] *n.f.* grudge, hard feelings: *avoir de la* ~ *contre qqun*, to have a grudge against s.o.; *Je ne lui garde pas* ~ *de cela*, I don't hold any grudge against him for that; *Sans* ~ *!*, → No hard feelings! ‖ **rancuni|er, -ère** [-je, -jɛ:r] *adj.* [caractère, &c.] vindictive.

randonnée [rɑ̃dɔ'ne *n.f.* long walk, ride or drive; ramble; tour].

rang [rɑ̃] *n.m.* **1.** row, rank, line: *Il s'était assis au premier* ~, He sat in the first row; *se mettre en* ~ *d'oignons*, to stand in a line; [Milit.] *par rangs de quatre*, four abreast; *sur deux rangs*, two deep; *former les rangs*, to fall in; *rompre les rangs*, to fall out; *serrer les rangs*, to close ranks; *Il est sorti du* ~, He rose from the ranks; *se mettre sur les rangs*, to become a candidate. **2.** rank, status, (social) station: *un homme de son* ~, a man/of his rank, of his station; *Il vient au second* ~, → He ranks second. **3.** © [group of adjacent farms served by a single road, or (more usual) the road itself] concession.

rangé [-'ʒe] cf. RANGER. ‖ *adj.* **1.** tidy, neat, well-ordered, orderly; steady, regular: *un bureau bien* ~, a tidy desk; *un homme* ~, an orderly man; *mener une vie rangée*, to lead an orderly life. **2.** *en bataille rangée*, in pitched battle. ‖ **rangée** [-'ʒe] *n.f.* row. ‖ **ranger** #5 *v. tr.* **1.** to arrange, to range: ~ *par ordre alphabétique*, to arrange in alphabetical order; *Les troupes étaient rangées le long du fleuve*, The troops were drawn up along the river. **2.** to put away, to put out of the way: *Rangez vos affaires*, Put your things away. **3.** to tidy (up): *Range ta chambre*, Tidy up your room. **4.** to rate, to rank: *On le range parmi les meilleurs*, He is rated among the best. ‖ **se ranger** *v. pron.* **1.** to range o.s.: *Ils se rangèrent de chaque côté*, They ranged themselves on each side. **2.** [Fig.] to side (with), to align o.s. with: *Il se rangea à mon avis*, He agreed with me. **3.** to stand aside, to make way: *Rangez-vous sur le côté*, Move over to the side. **4.** to settle down: *Il s'est rangé*, He settled down (to a quiet, orderly life).

ranimer [rani'me] #3 *v. tr.* [un mort] to bring to life; [personne évanouie, noyée] to bring . . . to, to revive; [Fig.] [feu] to stir up, to get . . . going again; [espoir] to revive, to rekindle; [conversation] to give a fillip to. ‖ **se ranimer** *v. pron.* [d'une personne évanouie, noyée] to come to, to regain consciousness.

rapace [ra'pas] *adj.* [vautour, &c.]; [Fig.] [usurier, &c.] rapacious, predatory. ‖ *n.m.* bird of prey.

rapatriement [rapatri|'mɑ̃] *n.m.* repatriation. ‖ **rapatrier** [-'je] #3 *v. tr.* to repatriate.

râpe [rɑ:p] *n.f.* **1.** [lime à grosses aspérités] rasp. ‖ **2.** grater: ~ *à fromage, à muscade*, cheese-, nutmeg-grater. ‖ **râpé** [rɑ'pe] cf. RÂPER *adj.* **1.** grated: *fromage* ~, grated cheese. **2.** [Fig.] [vêtements] threadbare, shabby. ‖ **râper** #3 *v. tr.* to grate (with grater or rasp).

rapetisser [rapti'se] #3 *v. tr.* to make smaller. ‖ *v. intr.* [lainage] to shrink; [jours] to shorten, to draw in. ‖ **se rapetisser** *v. pron.* to get smaller, to shrink, to shorten.

rapide [ra'pid] *adj.* **1.** rapid, swift, speedy; [vite] fast, quick. **2.** [pente] steep, sharp. ‖ *n.m.* **1.** [usual. *pl.*: *les rapides*] rapid [habituellement au pl.: the rapids]: *sauter les* ~, to shoot the rapids. **2.** [Rail.] express (train). ‖ **rapidement** [-'mɑ̃] *adv.* rapidly, swiftly, speedily; [vite] fast, quickly. ‖ **rapidité** [-i'te] *n.f.* **1.** rapidity, swiftness, speed. **2.** [pente] steepness.

rapiécer [rapje'se] #6 *v. tr.* [pantalons, &c.] to patch.

rapière [ra'pjɛ:r] *n.f.* rapier.

rappel [ra'p|ɛl] *n.m.* **1.** recall, calling back (of s.o., sth.); [d'un prêt de banque, &c.] calling in (of); [d'un décret] repeal; [Théât.] curtain call, encore; [Milit.] [réservistes] call-up: [Parl.]: ~ *à l'ordre*, call to order; *battre le* ~, to call in all men. **2.** [compte échu, &c.] reminder: *lettre de* ~, letter of reminder. ‖ **rappeler** [-'le] #8 *v. tr.* **1.** [au téléphone] to call (s.o.) again, back: *Je vous rappellerai demain*, I'll/call you back, phone you back/

tomorrow. **2.** to recall (s.o.), to call (s.o.) back; [chien] to call . . . off: ~ *un ambassadeur,* to recall an ambassador; ~ *au pouvoir,* to recall to power; *Ses affaires l'ont rappelé à Montréal,* → He has been called back to Montreal on business; ~ *à la vie,* to recall to life [also Fig.]; ~ *qqun à l'ordre,* to call s.o. to order. **3.** to call (sth.) back: ~ *un prêt de banque,* to call in a bank loan. **4.** to remind (s.o. of): *Vous me rappelez qqun que je connaissais autrefois,* You remind me of s.o. I used to know. || **se rappeler** *v. pron.* to recall (to mind), to remember, to recollect.

rapport [ra'p|ɔːr] *n.m.* **1.** [sol] yield, [capital] return: *immeuble de* ~ , apartment house. **2.** report: /*faire, rédiger, déposer*/*un* ~ , to/make, draft, submit/a report. **3.** relation, relationship, connection, link, bearing: *Cela n'a aucun* ~ *avec le sujet,* That has no bearing upon the subject; *Mettez-le en* ~ *avec mon frère,* Put him in touch with my brother; *Les rapports entre les deux pays se sont tendus,* Relations between the two countries have become strained; *en* ~ *avec sa dignité,* in keeping with his dignity; *par* ~ *à,* in comparison with, compared with, with respect to, as regards; *sous tous les rapports,* in all respects. **4.** [Math., &c.] ratio. || **rapporter** [-ɔr'te] #3 *v. tr.* **1.** to bring back (sth.); [livre emprunté, &c.] to take back, to return; [chien, gibier] to retrieve; [chien, objet lancé] to fetch: [Fig.] *Il n'en a rapporté que des coups,* → All he got for his trouble was a good thrashing. **2.** to bring in, to bear, to yield; to pay: *Les arbres fruitiers rapportent beaucoup cette année,* The fruit trees are/bearing, producing/well this year; *un placement qui rapporte six pour cent,* an investment that/yields, brings in, pays/six per cent [cf. also *v. intr.* **1**]. **3.** to report (a fact, &c.). **4.** to relate (to): ~ *l'effet à sa cause,* to relate the effect to its cause. **5.** [Compt.] to post: ~ *un article,* to post an entry. **6.** to repeal, revoke, rescind (a decree, &c.) || *v. intr.* **1.** to bear, produce; to be profitable: *Les pommiers rapportent bien,* The apple trees are bearing well; *une affaire qui rapporte,* → a paying business. **2.** [Péj.] to tell tales (about s.o.); [absol.] to bear, carry, tell tales. || **se rapporter** *v. pron.*. **1.** to relate (*à,* to): *L'adjectif se rapporte au nom,* The adjective is governed by the noun. **2.** *s'en rapporter à qqun, au témoignage de qqun,* to be guided, go by s.o.'s judgment: *Je m'en rapporte à vous,* → You be the judge. cf. S'EN REMETTRE À. || **rapporteu|r, -se** [-ɔr't|œːr, -øːz] *n.* telltale, tattler; [école] sneaker. || *n.m.* [Math., &c.] protractor.

rapprochement [raprɔʃ|mɑ̃] *n.m.* [d'objets concrets] bringing together; [Fig.] [de deux personnes, deux familles] reconciliation; [de faits, d'idées] comparison; [Polit.] rapprochement, restoration. || **rapprocher** [-e] #3 *v. tr.* **1.** to bring, move (sth.) near again; to bring, draw (sth.) closer: *Il a rapproché sa chaise de la table,* He drew his chair closer to the table; *Les jumelles rapprochent les objets,* Binoculars bring objects closer; [Fig.] *Le besoin rapproche les hommes,* Common necessity draws people together; ~ *des partis opposés,* to reconcile opposing parties. **2.** [textes, idées, &c.] to compare. || **se rapprocher** *v. pron.* **1.** to come, draw (still, ever) closer; [Fig.] to resemble, to approximate: *L'ennemi se rapprochait,* The enemy was drawing ever closer; *Je me suis rapproché de mon travail,* I've moved closer to my job; *Leur plan se rapproche du nôtre sur plusieurs points,* Their plan resembles ours in a number of respects. **2.** [personnes, nations] to draw closer; to become reconciled.

rapt [rapt] *n.m.* [Jur.] abduction; [d'enfant] kidnapping.

raquette *n.f.* **1.** [Sport] (tennis) racket. **2.** © snowshoe. || © **raquetteur** [-œːr] *n.m.* snowshoer.

rare [raːr] *adj.* **1.** [timbre, livre, perle]; [Fig.] [génie] rare; [provisions, &c.] scarce: *Vous vous faites* ~ *ces derniers temps,* → We haven't been seeing much of you lately. **2.** [herbe, cheveux] sparse, scanty. || **rarement** [rar|'mɑ̃] *adv.* rarely, seldom. || **rareté** [-'te] *n.f.* **1.** shortage, scarcity (of goods, manpower, &c.). cf. PÉNURIE. **2.** curio: *une collection de raretés,* a collection of curios. **3.** rarity (of the atmosphere).

ras, -e [ra(ːz)] *adj.* **1.** [barbe] close-shaven; [cheveux] close-cropped; [mesure] level; [velours] smooth, short-napped: *chien à poil* ~ , → short-haired dog; *en rase campagne,* in flat, open country; *Ajoutez deux cuillerées à thé rases de sucre,* Add two level teaspoonfuls of sugar. **2.** *faire table rase de qqch.,* to make a clean sweep of sth. || *n.m.* [surtout dans la locution *au, à, ras (de)*]: *vaisseau chargé au* ~ *de l'eau,* vessel loaded to the water line; [oiseaux, avions] *voler au* ~ *du sol,* → to skim (along) the ground; *verser à* ~ *bord,* to fill (glass, &c.) to the brim, brim full.

rasant, -e [rɑ'zɑ̃(:t)] *adj.* dull, boring.
raser [ra'z|e] #3 *v. tr.* **1.** to shave (off) (s.o.'s beard, moustache); to shave (s.o.'s head): *On avait rasé la tête des prisonniers,* The prisoners' heads had been shaved; *se faire* ~, to/have, get/a shave; *rasé de près,* close-shaven; *complètement rasé,* clean-shaven. **2.** [immeuble, forteresse, ville] to raze, to level. **3.** to graze, to brush (by, past), to skim (along, close to): *La balle lui rasa l'oreille,* The bullet grazed his ear; [oiseau, avion] ~ *le sol, l'eau,* to skim/along, close to/the ground, the water. **4.** © *J'ai rasé de manquer le train,* I all but missed, I came within an inch of missing/the train. cf. FAILLIR. **2.** ‖ **se raser** *v. pron.* to shave.
raseur [rɑ'zœ:r] *n.m.* [Fam.] bore.
rasoir [-wa:r] *n.m.* razor: ~ *de sûreté,* safety razor; ~ *à manche,* © ~ *droit,* straight razor; *cuir à* ~, (razor) strap; ~ *électrique,* electric/shaver, razor.
rassasier [rasa'zje] #3 *v. tr.* to satisfy, appease, satiate (person; hunger, desire): ~ *ses yeux de qqch.,* to feast o.'s eyes on sth. ‖ **se rassasier** *v. pron.* to eat, have o.'s fill (of sth.): ~ /*de pâtisseries, des plaisirs de la vie*/, to have o.'s fill of/ pastries, life's pleasures.
rassembler [rasɑ̃'ble] #3 *v. tr.* **1.** to gather together (again), gather in (dispersed flocks, &c.). **2.** to muster, levy (troops, forces); to assemble, gather together (documents, evidence, materials): ~ *ses idées,* to collect o.'s thoughts; ~ *ses forces,* to muster, summon (all) o.'s strength. ‖ **se rassembler** *v. pron.* to assemble, to gather together. cf. SE RÉUNIR.
rasseoir [ra's|wa:r] #30 & 31 *v. tr.* © [Péj.] to put (s.o.) in his place. cf. RABAISSER. ‖ **se rasseoir** *v. pron.* to sit down, take o.'s seat, again.
rasséréner [rasere'ne] #10 *v. tr.* [temps] to clear up; [Pers.] to calm; to restore s.o.'s composure. ‖ **se rasséréner** *v. pron.* [ciel] to clear up; [Pers.] to become calm again, to regain o.'s composure.
rasseyais cf. RASSEOIR.
rassis[1], **-e** [ra'si(:z)] *adj.* **1.** calm, sober, solid (person; disposition, temperament): *personne de sens* ~, person of/poised, well-balanced/judgment; *esprit* ~, calm disposition. **2.** stale: *pain* ~, stale bread.
rassis[2] cf. RASSEOIR.
rassoie, rassois, cf. RASSEOIR.
rassurant, -e [rasy'rɑ̃(:t)] *adj.* reassuring, heartening. ‖ **rassurer** [rasy're] #3 *v. tr.* to reassure (s.o.), to put, set (s.o.'s) mind at rest, at ease (about sth.). ‖ **se rassurer** *v. pron.* to reassure o.s., to be reassured, to put, set, o.'s mind at rest, at ease (about sth.).
rat [ra] *n.m.* **1.** rat: ~ *des champs,* field mouse, cf. CAMPAGNOL; ~ *musqué,* muskrat; ~ *à bourse,* gopher, cf. GAUFRE. **3.**; ~ *d'eau,* water rat, [Br.] *aussi,* water vole; *mort aux rats,* rat poison. **2.** [Fig., pers.]: *C'est un vrai* ~, He's a regular miser, [Fam.] tightwad; ~ *de bibliothèque* bookworm; [navire] ~ *de cale,* stowaway; ~ *d'hôtel,* hotel thief.
ratatiné, -e [ratati'n|e] cf. RATATINER. ‖ *adj.* [pomme, &c.] shrivelled, [Pers., figure, &c.] shrivelled up, wizened. ‖ **ratatiner** [-e] #3 *v. tr.* [seldom used, cf. SE RATATINER]. ‖ **se ratatiner** *v. pron.* [pomme, figure, personne] to shrivel (up), shrink, become shrunken or wizened; to crinkle (up).
rate[1] [rat] *n.f.* female rat.
rate[2] [rat] *n.f.* spleen: *dilater la* ~ (*à qqun*), to make (s.o.) laugh.
raté, -e [ra'te] *adj.* miscarried, ineffectual: *coup* ~, bad shot, miss; misfire; [avion] *atterrissage* ~, bad landing; *L'affaire est ratée,* [Fam.] It's a flop; *Ce fut une vie ratée,* His life was a failure. ‖ *n.* [Pers.] failure.
râteau [rɑ'to] *n.m.* rake. ‖ **râteler** #8 *v. tr.* to rake (up).
râtelier[1] [ratə'lje] *n.m.* rack [écurie, et dans un sens plus général]: [Fig.] *manger à deux râteliers,* to have a foot in both camps; to derive o.'s income from two sources; ~ *d'armes.* gun rack; ~ *à pipes,* pipe rack.
râtelier[2] *n.m.* set of false teeth, denture.
rater [ra'te] #3 *v. intr.* **1.** [fusil, machine] to misfire. **2.** [affaire] to fail, miscarry, come to nothing. ‖ *v. tr.* [coup de fusil] to miss: ~ *son coup,* to miss o.'s shot, to miss the mark; *coup qui rate le but,* bad shot; [Fam.] ~ *son train,* to miss o.'s train.
ratifier [rati'fje] #3 *v. tr.* to ratify (a treaty, an agreement); to approve, confirm (a decision, an opinion): ~ *une nomination,* to confirm a nomination.
ration [rɑ'sjõ] *n.f.* ration, pittance; [Mil.] rations. ‖ **rationnement** [rasjɔn|'mɑ̃] *n.m.* rationing: *ticket m de* ~, rationing coupon, food coupon. ‖ **rationner** [-e] #3 *v. tr.* [qqun, un produit]: ~ *le beurre,* to ration butter.
ratisser [rati'se] #3 *v. tr.* to rake (leaves, a lawn, a path). cf. RÂTEAU.

raton laveur [ratõla'vœ:r] (= © *chat sauvage*) *n.m.* raccoon.

rattacher [rata'ʃe] #3 *v. tr.* **1.** to fasten, tie again. **2.** to bind: *les liens qui le rattachent à son pays,* the ties that bind him to his country. ‖ **se rattacher** (à) *v. pron.* to be related, linked to: *Cela se rattache à une autre question,* This relates to another question.

rattraper [ratra'pe] #3 *v. tr.* **1.** to recapture; to catch again: [Fam.] *On ne m'y rattrapera pas!, Bien fin qui m'y rattrapera!,* → Once bitten, twice shy!; *Je vous rattraperai!,* I'll get even with you! **2.** to overtake; to catch (s.o.) up, catch up with (s.o.). **3.** to recover (o.'s money, o.'s health): ~ *le temps perdu,* to make up for lost time. ‖ **se rattraper** *v. pron.* **1.** to catch hold (of): ~ *à une branche,* to catch hold of a branch. **2.**: ~ *de ses pertes,* to make good, to recoup o.'s losses. **3.** [blunder, mistake]: *Il se rattrapa par une phrase habile,* He saved himself by a clever remark.

rature [ra't|y:r] *n.f.* erasure, crossing out: *faire des ratures,* to cross (words, &c.) out. ‖ **raturer** [-y're] #3 *v. tr.* to cross out.

rauque [ro:k] *adj.* [voix, &c.] hoarse, raucous, harsh.

ravage [ra'v|a:ʒ] *n.m.* damage, destruction, devastation: *faire des ravages,* to play havoc; ravage (of war, disease, passion). ‖ **ravager** [-a'ʒe] #5 *v. tr.* to ravage, devastate; to lay (a country) waste, play havoc with (sth.): *visage ravagé,* pock-marked face; *visage ravagé par la douleur,* face ravaged by grief.

ravalement [raval'mã] *n.m.* [arbre] trimming down; [bois] thinning; [dans un mur] recess; [propriété] resurfacing, repainting; [Fig.] disparagement, defamation. ‖ **ravaler** [rava'le] #3 *v. tr.* **1.** to swallow (sth.) again, down: ~ *un sanglot,* to choke down a sob; [Fam.] ~ *ses paroles,* to eat o.'s words. **2.** to reduce, drag (s.o.) down (to the level of slavery, of the beasts). **3.** to disparage, decry, run (s.o. or sth.) down: ~ *la gloire d'un homme,* to decry a man's fame.

ravauder [ravo'de] #3 *v. tr.* to mend, to patch; to darn.

ravi, -e [ra'vi] *adj.* **1.** delighted, overjoyed. **2.** †entranced, enraptured.

ravigoter [ravigɔ'te] #3 *v. tr.* [Fam.] [physiquement] to revive; [moralement] to cheer up.

ravilir [ravi'li:r] #17 *v. tr.* to debase, degrade.

ravin [ra'vɛ̃] *n.m.* ravine, gully.

ravir [ra'vi:r] #17 *v. tr.* **1.** to carry off, to snatch away, to rob: [Fig.] *On lui a ravi son honneur,* He has been robbed of his honour. **2.** to delight, enrapture: *être habillée à* ~, to be bewitchingly dressed; *jouer, chanter à* ~, to play, sing divinely.

raviser (se) [ravi'ze] #3 *v. pron.* to change o.'s mind; to think better of it.

ravissant, -e [ravi's|ã(:t)] *adj.* delightful, charming, enchanting. ‖ **ravissement** [-'mã] *n.m.* rapture(s), delight, ecstasy.

ravitaillement [ravitaj|'mã] *n.m.* supplying; supplies; food: *aller au* ~, to go get food; [Br. & Fr.] *Ministère du* ~, Ministry of Food; *carte de* ~, ration card; *organisateur de* ~, food-controller. ‖ **ravitailler** [-e] #3 *v. tr.* to supply. ‖ **se ravitailler** *v. pron.* to lay, bring, in (fresh) supplies (of, *en*).

raviver [ravi've] #3 *v. tr.* **1.** to revive (the fire; s.o.'s strength, &c.). **2.** to brighten up, touch up (colours); to reopen (an old wound).

rayer [rɛ'je] #11 *v. tr.* **1.** to scratch (glass); to rule, line (paper); to stripe, streak (fabric, material); to rifle (a gun). **2.** to strike, cut out (a word, line): *On vous a rayé de la liste,* You have been struck off the list; [Fam. & Fig.] *Je l'ai rayé de mes papiers,* I crossed him off my list.

rayon[1] [rɛ'j|ɔ̃] *n.m.* **1.** ray, beam (of light); [Fig.] ray, gleam (of hope): ~ *de lune,* moonbeam; *un faible* ~ *de lumière,* a faint gleam of light; [Phys.] [rayons X] X-rays. **2.** ~ *visuel,* [Phys.] line of sight; range of vision. **3.** radius (of a circle): *dans un* ~ *de deux milles,* within a two-mile radius; ~ *d'action,* radius. **4.** spoke, arm; point (of a star): *étoile à cinq rayons,* five-pointed star.

rayon[2] *n.m.* **1.** shelf (of a cupboard, a bookcase): [plur.] set of shelves, bookcase, shelf space. **2.** [Com.] department: *chef de* ~, buyer, floorwalker, [Br.] shopwalker; [Fam.] *Ce n'est pas mon* ~, That's not in my line. ‖ **rayonnage** [-ɔ'na:ʒ] *n.m.* shelving, shelves.

rayonnant, -e [-ɔ'nã(:t)] *adj.* **1.** radiant, beaming (light, face); radiant (beauty). **2.** [Phys.] radiant (heat); *pouvoir* ~ *d'une antenne,* transmitting power of an aerial; *matière rayonnante,* radio-active matter.

rayonne [rɛ'jɔn] *n.f.* rayon.

rayonnement [rɛj|ɔn'mã] *n.m.* **1.** radiation (of light, heat, &c.); radiance, shining: [Fig.] *le* ~ *d'une idée,* the wide appeal of an idea. **2.** radiance (of the face); [Télév., &c.] coverage. ‖ **rayonner** [-ɔ'ne] #3 *v. intr.* **1.** to radiate, give out (radiations);

to cast rays. **2.** [Fig.] to beam, to be radiant. **3.** [Fig.] to radiate: *Les routes rayonnent autour de la capitale*, The highways radiate from the capital.

rayure [-yːr] *n.f.* stripe; scratch, groove; rifling (of a gun): *à rayures*, striped.

raz de marée [radmaˈre] *n.m.* bore, tidal wave.

razzia [raˈzja] *n.f.* incursion, raid, foray.

réacteur [reakˈtœːr] *n.m.* [Elect.] reactor; choke; [Aviat.] jet engine: ~ *nucléaire*, nuclear reactor, cf. PILE. ‖ **réactif** [-ˈtif] *n.m.* [Chimie] reagent. ‖ **réaction** [-ˈsjõ] *n.f.* **1.** reaction; kick (of a rifle): *moteur à* ~, jet engine; *avions à* ~, jet aircraft; ~ *en chaîne*, chain reaction. **2.** [Fig.] reaction, conservatism, [hence] → *la réaction*, the ultra-conservatives. ‖ **réactionnaire** [-sjɔˈnɛːr] *adj. & n.* [Polit.] reactionary; [Hist.] Tory, ultra-conservative.

réadaptation [readapt|aˈsjõ] *n.f.* **1.** readaptation: ~ *professionnelle*, occupational retraining. **2.** [social work] rehabilitation: ~ *des handicapés*, rehabilitation of the handicapped. ‖ **réadapter** [-e] #3 *v. tr.* to rehabilitate.

réagir [reaˈʒiːr] #17 *v. intr.* **1.** [corps, forces] to react (against, on): ~ *réciproquement*, to interact. **2.** [Fig.] ~ *violemment*, to react violently.

réalisable [realiˈz|abl] *adj.* feasible; practical. ‖ **réalisat|eur, -rice** [-aˈtœːr, -aˈtris] *n.* **1.** one who realizes, accomplishes, achieves (a design, purpose). **2.** [Télé.] producer. ‖ **réalisation** [-aˈsjõ] *n.f.* realization (of dreams, hopes); achievement, accomplishment (of a design, purpose); fulfilment. ‖ **réaliser** [-e] #3 *v. tr.* **1.** to realize (hopes, dreams, plans); to carry out, bring to fruition (a plan, an undertaking); to achieve, accomplish. [× abus. to realize, understand.] **2.** [Ciné.] to produce.

réalisme [reaˈli|sm] *n.m.* [Phil.; Art; Lit.] realism. ‖ **réaliste** [-st] *n.m.* realist. ‖ *adj.* realistic. ‖ **réalité** [-te] *n.f.* reality; [Fam.] the facts: *en* ~, actually; *en venir à la* ~, to get, come down/to brass tacks; *s'en tenir aux réalités*, to stick to the facts.

rébarbati|f, -ve [rebarbaˈt|if, -iːv] *adj.* forbidding, unprepossessing.

rebattre [rəˈbatr] #43 *v. tr.* to beat, hammer again: [Fig.] ~ *les cartes*, to reshuffle the cards.

rebelle [rəˈbɛl] *adj.* rebellious (person, spirit); refractory (person, horse); unworkable (material); stubborn, obstinate (fever). ‖ *n.* rebel. ‖ **rebeller, se** [rəbɛˈle] #3 *v. pron.* to rebel, rise, revolt (against). ‖ **rébellion** [rebɛˈljõ] *n.f.* rebellion, rising, revolt.

rebiffer, se [rəbiˈfe] #3 *v. pron.* to jib, [Fam.] to get o.'s dander up, to bridle at, to kick over the traces.

rebond [rəˈbõ] *n.m.* rebound. ‖ **rebondi, -e** [-di] *adj.* rounded; chubby (cheeks); plump (body). ‖ **rebondir** [-diːr] #17 *v. intr.* **1.** to rebound, bounce. **2.**: [Fig.] *L'affaire rebondit*, The case is taking a new turn. ‖ **rebondissement** [-disˈmɑ̃] *n.m.* rebound; [Fig.] repercussion, new development.

rebord [rəˈbɔːr] *n.m.* edge, border, rim; [hat] brim; [garment] hem; lip (of cup): ~ *d'une fenêtre*, window sill, window ledge.

rebours [rəˈbuːr] *n.m.*: *à, au* ~, against the grain; [Fig.] the wrong way; backwards: *prendre tout à* ~, to take everything the wrong way; *compliment à* ~, backhanded compliment.

rebrousse-poil (à) [arbrusˈpwal] *loc. adv.* against the grain: *caresser qqun* ~, to ruffle a person's feathers; *prendre/qqun, qqch./*~, to take/s.o., sth./the wrong way.

rebrousser [rəbruˈse] #3 *v. tr.* to turn up, brush up (hair, nap): [Fam.] ~ *qqun*, to rub s.o. the wrong way; ~ *chemin*, to retrace o.s' steps; *faire* ~ *chemin à qqun*, to make s.o. turn back. ‖ **se rebrousser** *v. pron.* [edge of tool] to turn (up); [nail, point] to bend back, curl up.

rebuffade [rəbyˈfad] *n.f.* rebuff, repulse.

rébus [reˈbys] *n.m.* riddle: *parler par* ~, to speak in riddles.

rebut [rəˈby] *n.m.* waste, discard: *papier de* ~, wastepaper; *vêtements de* ~, castoff clothing; [Indus.] *pièces de* ~, rejects; [Admin.] *bureau de* ~, dead-letter office; *mettre qqch. au* ~, to throw away, to scrap, to discard; [Fam.] ~ *de la société*, the scum of society. ‖ **rebutant, -e** [-ˈtɑ̃(ːt)] *adj.* wearisome, dull, tedious. ‖ **rebuter** [-ˈte] #3 *v. tr.* to repel, to discourage: *se laisser* ~, to allow o.s. to be discouraged.

récalcitrant, -e [rekalsiˈtrɑ̃(ːt)] *adj.* recalcitrant, refractory.

recaler [rəkaˈle] #3 *v. tr.* [Fam.] to fail, flunk (s.o.) in an examination: *être recalé*, [Fam.] to fail, flunk (out).

récapitulati|f, -ve [rekapityl|aˈtif, -aˈtiːv] *adj.* recapitulatory. ‖ **récapitulation** [-aˈsjõ] *n.f.* recapitulation, summing up; summary. ‖ **récapituler** [-e] #3 *v. tr.* to recapitulate, sum up; to summarize.

recel [rə's|ɛl] *n.m.* receiving stolen goods. || **receler** [-e'le] #10 *v. tr.* to receive stolen goods. || **receleur** [-e'lœ:r] *n.m.* receiver of stolen goods; fence.
récemment [resa'mɑ̃] *adv.* recently, lately, of late.
recensement [rəsɑ̃s|'mɑ̃] *n.m.* enumeration; census; counting (of votes). || **recenser** [-e] #3 *v. tr.* to take the census (of a country, a town); to count (votes); to enumerate. || **recenseu|r, -se** [-œ:r, -ø:z] *n.* census-taker, enumerator; teller (of votes).
récent, -e [re'sɑ̃(:t)] *adj.* recent.
récépissé [resepi'se] *n.m.* acknowledgment (of receipt, of a complaint); [Com.] receipt.
réceptacle [resɛp'takl] *n.m.* receptacle.
récept|eur, -rice [resɛp|'tœ:r, -'tris] *adj.* receiving (apparatus, set). || *n.m.* [Tél., Radio] receiver. || **réception** [-'sjɔ̃] *n.f.* **1.** receipt (of a letter, an order); taking delivery (of goods): *accuser ~ de qqch.*, to acknowledge receipt of sth. **2.** approval (of a machine for operation, of a play for performance). **3.** admission (of a new member to a society). **4.** [social life] reception; at-home; party. **5.** reception (by telephone, telegraph, radio). **6.** [hotel] registration desk. || **réceptionnaire** [-sjɔ'nɛ:r] *adj.* receiving (clerk, agent). || *n.* consignee. || **réceptionniste** [-sjɔ'nist] *n.* © receptionist, desk clerk.
recette [rə'sɛt] *n.f.* **1.** receipts, takings. **2.** collection of debts, bills, taxes; receivership, revenue office. **3.** [Culin.] recipe.
recevable [rəsə'v|abl] *adj.* [excuse, offre, appel] admissible; receivable. || **receveu|r, -se** [-œ:r, -ø:z] *n.* **1.** receiver (of sth.); addressee (of telegram). **2.** tax collector; © *Receveur général du Canada*, Receiver-General of Canada. **3.** © catcher (in baseball, softball). **4.** [Fr., Br.] conductor (bus, streetcar, &c.); [Théât., &c.] ticket-taker. || **recevoir** [-wa:r], **reçu** [rə'sy] #34 *v. tr.* **1.** to receive; to catch (a ball, water in a container). **2.** to receive, welcome (s.o.); to entertain (friends); to hold a reception. **3.** to accommodate, have room for (ships, vehicles; tourists). **4.** to admit (to a school); *être reçu à un examen*, to pass an examination; *être reçu premier*, to come out first. 5. [Fig.] to accept, admit of (opinions, excuses); to approve of (customs, manners): *Ce passage peut ~ diverses interprétations*, This passage can admit of several interpretations.
rechange [rə'ʃɑ̃:ʒ] *n.m.* replacement: *pièces de ~*, spare parts.
réchapper [reʃa'pe] #3 *v. intr.* to escape: *~ d'un péril*, to escape from a peril; *~ d'une maladie*, to get over an illness; *Il n'en réchappera pas*, → It's all up with him.
recharger [rəʃar'ʒe] #3 *v. tr.* to reload (vehicle, weapon); to recharge (battery); to attack again.
réchaud [re'ʃo] *n.m.* **1.** portable stove. **2.** hot plate, chafing dish: *mettre un plat au ~*, → to keep a dish hot. || **réchauffer** [-'fe] #3 *v. tr.* **1.** to warm (up); to chafe (limbs). **2.** [Fig.] rekindle, revive (feelings, friendship): [Fam.] *Cela me réchauffe le cœur de l'entendre*, It does my heart good to hear him.
recherche [rə'ʃɛrʃ] *n.f.* **1.** quest, search, pursuit (for, after): *être à la ~ de qqun, de qqch.*, → to be looking for s.o., sth.; [Fam.] to be on the lookout for sth.; *aller, partir, se mettre/à la ~ de qqun, de qqch.*, to set off in search of s.o., sth.; to go and look for s.o., sth.; [mines] *~ de filons*, prospecting. **2.** research, investigation: *recherches scientifiques*, scientific research; *faire des recherches (sur)*, to do research (in). **3.** refinement, elegance, affectation (of style); refinement (of cruelty): *style sans ~*, → plain, unadorned style. || **recherché, -e** [-e] *adj.* **1.**: *article ~*, article in demand; *personne très recherchée*, person much sought after. **2.** choice, select, elaborate, exquisite (jewels, clothes): *toilette recherchée*, dress of studied elegance. **3.** [style] studied, mannered, laboured, affected, far-fetched. || *n.m.*: *éviter le ~*, to avoid affectation. || **rechercher** [-e] #3 *v. tr.* **1.** to search for, search into, inquire into (causes, &c.); to track down (defects, crimes): *La police le recherche*, He is wanted by the police. **2.** to seek after, to canvass (favours, friendship, support, praise); to cultivate.
rechigné, -e [rəʃi'ɲ|e] *adj.* bad-tempered, surly (person), sullen. || **rechignement** [-'mɑ̃] *n.m.* sullenness. || **rechigner** [-e] #3 *v. intr.* [Fam.] to balk (at sth.): *Il ne rechigne pas à l'ouvrage*, He doesn't balk at /is not afraid of/hard work.
rechute [rə'ʃyt] *n.f.* [Méd.] relapse, setback.
récidive [resi'd|i:v] *n.f.* [Méd.] recurrence, reappearance; [Jur.] second offence. || **récidiver** [-i've] #3 *v. intr.* to/relapse into, return to/crime. || **récidiviste** [-i'vist] *n.* habitual criminal, recidivist, /old, second/offender.
récif [re'sif] *n.m.* reef: *heurter un ~*, to run on to a reef.

récipient [resi'pjɑ̃] *n.m.* container, vessel, receptacle.

réciprocité [resiprɔ|si'te] *n.f.* reciprocity; interchange. || **réciproque** [-k] *adj.* reciprocal, converse; mutual. || *n.f.* [Math., Logic] converse, opposite: *La ~ n'est pas vraie,* The converse is not true. || **réciproquement** [-k'mɑ̃] *adv.* reciprocally, conversely.

récit [re'si] *n.m.* narrative, narration; account, recital, story, relation (of events): *faire un ~ exact de qqch.*, to give an exact account of sth. || **réciter** [-'te] #3 *v. tr.* to recite (a poem, a lesson).

réclamant, -e [reklɑ'm|ɑ̃(:t)] *n.* claimant. || **réclamation** [-a'sjõ] *n.f.* **1.** complaint; objection, protest. **2.** [Jur., Admin.] claim, demand; notice of claim: *faire la ~ d'une créance,* to demand payment of a debt. || **réclame** [re'kl|ɑ:m] *n.f.* **1.** advertising: *faire de la ~*, to advertise, [Fam.] boost; [Com.] *articles de ~*, special offer (to promote sales): *en ~*, reduced. **2.** advertisement: *~ lumineuse,* illuminated sign; *~ à éclipse,* → flashing sign. || **réclamer** [-ɑ'me] #3 *v. intr.* **1.** to complain, lodge a complaint: *~ contre qqch.*, to/protest against, object to/sth.; *~ auprès de qqun,* to lodge a complaint with s.o.; [Jur.] *~ contre une décision,* to appeal against a decision. **2.**: *~ en faveur de qqun,* to/intercede, plead/in s.o.'s behalf. || *v. tr.* **1.** to claim, lay claim to (sth.): *~ son droit,* to claim o.'s right; to /claim, demand/(sth.) back. **2.** to crave, beg, call for (sth.): [Théât.] *L'auditoire a réclamé l'auteur,* The audience called for the author. **3.** *~ qqch. de qqun,* to require sth. of s.o.: *Ceci réclame beaucoup de soin,* This requires a good deal of attention. || **se réclamer** *v. pron.*: *~ de qqun, de qqch.*, to appeal to s.o., sth.; to quote s.o. as o.'s authority (for a statement); to claim kinship with s.o: *Vous pouvez vous réclamer de moi,* → You may use my name as a reference.

réclamiste [reklɑ'mist] *n.m.* [Fam.] advertiser, ad man.

réclusion [rekly'zjõ] *n.f.* seclusion; [prison] solitary confinement.

recoin [rə'kwɛ̃] *n.m.* nook, cranny, recess: *coins et recoins,* nooks and crannies.

reçois, reçoit; reçoive, &c. cf. RECEVOIR.

recoller [rəkɔ'le] #3 *v. tr.* **1.** to paste, glue, stick/together again. **2.** [Slang] to flunk again: *Il s'est fait ~*, He flunked again.

récolte [re'kɔlt] *n.f.* **1.** harvesting, reaping (of cereals). **2.** [Fig.] collecting (of documents, information). **3.** harvest, crop(s); vintage (of grapes): *~ sur pied,* → standing crops; *rentrer la ~*, to get the harvest in; *~ exceptionnelle,* [Fam.] bumper crop. || **récolter** [-e] #3 *v. tr.* to reap, to harvest, gather in (crops); to collect.

recommandable [rəkɔmɑ̃'d|abl] *adj.* **1.** reputable, estimable, decent, respectable: *personne peu ~*, undesirable person. **2.** advisable. || **recommandation** [-a'sjõ] *n.f.* **1.** recommendation (of a person): *lettre de ~*, letter of introduction. **2.** recommendation, injunction, advice. **3.** registration (of a letter). || **recommander** [-e] *v. tr.* **1.** to recommend (a person, a hotel); [Rel.] to commend (o.'s soul to God); *~ à l'attention de qqun,* to call s.o.'s attention to. **2.** to enjoin: *Je vous recommande de ne pas faire cela,* I advise you not to do that. **3.** to register (a letter, a parcel). || **se recommander** *v. pron.* **1.** *~ à qqun,* to seek s.o.'s protection; *Je me recommande à son bon souvenir,* I wish to be remembered to him. **2.**: *~ de qqun,* to give s.o. as a reference; *Il se recommande de lui-même,* He is his own recommendation.

recommencer [rəkɔmɑ̃'se] #3 *v. tr. & intr.* to begin, start again: [Fam.] *C'est toujours à ~*, → There's no end to it; *Le voilà qui recommence!,* → He's at it again!

récompense [rekõ'p|ɑ̃:s] *n.f.* reward: *en ~ de,* in return for, as a reward for. || **récompenser** [-ɑ̃'se] #3 *v. tr.* to reward (s.o.): *~ qqun de qqch.*, to reward s.o. for sth.

réconciliation [rekɑ̃silj|a'sjõ] *n.f.* reconciliation. || **réconcilier** [-e] #3 *v. tr.* to reconcile (persons): *Les voilà réconciliés,* Now they are friends again. || **se réconcilier** *v. pron.*: **1.** *~/à, avec/qqun,* to make it up with s.o.; *~ avec Dieu,* to make o.'s peace with God. **2.** [réfléchi] *Ils se sont réconciliés,* → They are friends again.

reconduire [rəkõ'dɥ|i:r] #56 *v. tr.* to take, see, show (s.o.) back, out, home, &c.: *Il l'a reconduite chez elle,* He/drove, walked/her home; *Reconduisez Monsieur,* Show Mr. X. out; *~ un étranger à la frontière,* to expel an alien. || **reconduis, reconduit,** cf. RECONDUIRE. || **reconduite** [-it] *n.f.* [action] escorting, accompanying, seeing (s.o.) home, to the door, &c.: *Il m'a fait un bout de ~*, He accompanied me part of the way home.

réconfort [rekõ'f|ɔ:r] *n.m.* comfort, consolation. || **réconfortant, -e** [-ɔr't|ɑ̃(:t)] *adj.* consoling. || *n.m.* tonic, stimulant. || **réconforter** [-e] #3 *v. tr.* **1.** to fortify, revive, refresh (s.o.); to act as a tonic to (s.o.). **2.** to comfort, console; to cheer (s.o.) up. || **se réconforter** *v. pron.* **1.** to take refreshment, to recuperate. **2.** to cheer up.

reconnaissable [rəkɔnɛ's|abl] *adj.* ~ *à*, recognizable by, from: *Il n'est plus* ~, → You wouldn't know him. || **reconnaissance** [-ɑ̃:s] *n.f.* **1.** recognition (of a person, an object): *sourire de* ~, smile of recognition. **2.** gratitude, thankfulness: *témoigner de la* ~ *à qqun de qqch.*, to show gratitude to s.o. for sth.; *un sourire de* ~, a grateful smile; *avec* ~, gratefully, thankfully. **3.** recognition, acknowledgment: *en* ~ *de*, in recognition of; ~ *de dette*, I.O.U. **4.** [Mil.] reconnoitring, reconnaissance: *faire une* ~, *aller en* ~, to reconnoitre. **5.** [Naut.] charting. || **reconnaissant, -e** [-ɑ̃(:t)] *adj.* grateful (*envers qqun de qqch.*, to s.o. for sth.).

reconnaître [rəkɔ'n|ɛ:tr] #40 *v. tr.* **1.** to recognize, to know again, to identify: *Je l'ai reconnu tout de suite*, I knew him at once. **2.** to admit, to concede, to acknowledge. **3.** [Mil.] to reconnoitre. || **se reconnaître** *v. pron.* to find o.'s bearings: *Je n'arrive pas à m'y* ~, I can't make head or tail of it. || **reconnu** [-y] cf. RECONNAÎTRE.

reconstituant [rəkɔ̃sti|'tyɑ̃] *n.m.* [Med.] tonic. || **reconstituer** [-'tye] #3 *v. tr.* to reconstitute, restore; [crime] to reconstruct; [réserves] to build up.

reconstruction [rəkɔ̃str|yk'sjɔ̃] *n.f.* reconstruction, rebuilding. || **reconstruire** [-ɥi:r] #56 *v. tr.* to rebuild; [Fig.] to reconstruct (*à partir de*, from).

recopier [rəkɔ'pje] #3 *v. tr.* to recopy, to copy (over), to make another copy of.

record [rə'kɔ:r] *n.m.* record: *battre un* ~, to break a record; *détenir un* ~, to hold a record.

recoucher [rəku'ʃe] #3 *v. tr.* to put back to bed, to put to bed again. || *v. intr.* to sleep again (at same place). || **se recoucher** *v. pron.* **1.** to go back to bed. **2.** to lie down again.

recoupement [rəkup|'mɑ̃] *n.m.* check: *permettre un* ~, to provide a way of checking. || **recouper** [-e] #3 *v. tr.* [Fig.] to cut . . . again; to cross-check.

recourais, &c., cf. RECOURIR.

recourbé, -e [rəkur'be] *adj.* curved, bent. || **recourber** #3 *v. tr.* to curve. || **se recourber**, *v. pron.* to curve, to bend.

recoure, recourez, &c., cf. RECOURIR.

recourir [rəku'ri:r] #24 *v. int.* **1.** to run again. **2.** to resort (to, *à*). || **recouru** cf. RECOURIR.

recours [rə'ku:r] *n.m.* recourse, resort, resource, appeal: *avoir* ~ *à*, to resort to, to ask for the help of (s.o.); ~ *en grâce*, petition for pardon.

recouvert, -e [rəku'v|ɛ:r, -ɛrt], cf. RECOUVRIR.

recouvrable [rəku|'vrabl] *adj.* recoverable. || **recouvrement** [-vrə'mɑ̃] *n.m.* recovery (of debts, &c.); collection (of funds); [une chose par-dessus une autre] overlap. || **recouvrer** [-'vre] #3 *v. tr.* to recover; [dette] to collect: *$10 à* ~, $10 outstanding.

recouvrir [rəku'v|ri:r] **recouvrant** [-rɑ̃], **recouvert** [-ɛ:r] #25 *v. tr.* **1.** to re-cover, to cover again. **2.** to cover (*de*, with); [Fig.] to mask. || **se recouvrir** *v. pron.*: ~ *en partie*, to overlap.

récréati|f, -ve [rekrea|tif, -'ti:v] *adj.* amusing: [Scol.] *séance récréative*, show. || **récréation** [rekreasjɔ̃] *n.f.* recreation, amusement, relaxation; [Scol.] recess: *en* ~, at recess, at play; *cour de* ~, playground; *salle de* ~, recreation hall. || **récréer** [rekre|'e] #3 *v. tr.* to amuse, to entertain. || **se récréer** *v. pron.* to relax, to amuse o.s.

récrier, se [sə rekri'je] #3 *v. pron.* to protest; to express loudly: *se* ~ *d'admiration*, to be loud in o.'s praise.

récriminer [rekrimi'ne] #3 *v. intr.* to recriminate (*contre*, against).

récrire [re'kr|i:r], **récrivant** [-i'vɑ̃], **récrit** [-i] #48 *v. tr.* to rewrite; to write again.

recrue [rə'kry] *n.f.* [person] recruit; [action] recruiting. || **recrutement** [-t'mɑ̃] *n.m.* recruiting. || **recruter** [-'te] #3 *v. tr.* to recruit.

rectangle [rɛk'tɑ̃:gl] *n.m.* rectangle. || *adj.* right-angled.

rectification [rɛktif|ika'sjɔ̃] *n.f.* rectification. || **rectifier** [-je] #3 *v. tr.* to rectify, set . . . right.

rectiligne [rɛkti'liɲ] *adj.* rectilinear; in a straight line.

rectitude [rɛkti'tyd] *n.f.* rectitude, integrity.

reçu [rə'sy] *n.m.* receipt, cf. RECEVOIR. || **reçu, -e** *adj.* received; [examen] passed, admitted; †customary, usual.

recueil [rə'kœ:j] *n.m.* collection (of songs); → collected (papers, &c.); [ouvrage] miscellany.

recueillement [rəkœj|'mɑ̃] *n.m.* solemn /calm, quiet/; quietude, composure. || **recueillir** [-i:r] #20 *v. tr.* to gather, collect (items of information): to take . . . in, to adopt (an orphan). || **se recueillir**

v. pron. to collect o.s., one's thoughts; to reflect, ponder.
recul [rə'kyl] *n.m.* backward movement, step; loss (of ground); [fusil] recoil. || **reculer** [-e] #3 *v. tr.* to back, to move back; [remettre à plus tard] to put off (until . . .). || *v. intr.* to back (up); to/fall, step/back; [fusil] to recoil; [renoncer à une entreprise] to back out: ~ *devant qqch.*, to shrink from doing sth.: *ne* ~ *devant aucun sacrifice*, to spare no effort. || **se reculer** *v. pron.* to/fall, step, move/ back. || **à reculons** [ar(ə)ky'lõ] *loc. adv.* backwards: *entrer* ~ *dans*, to back into.
récupérer [rekype're] #10 *v. tr.* to recover; to recuperate.
récurer [reky're] #3 *v. tr.* to scour (silver, &c.).
reçus [rə'sy] cf. RECEVOIR. || **reçus** cf. REÇU.
récuser [reky'ze] #3 *v. tr.* to take exception to. || **se récuser** *v. pron.* to/decline, refuse/to give one's opinion.
rédact|eur, -rice [redak|'tœ:r, -'tris] *n.* writer: ~ *en chef*, editor (of a magazine, paper, &c.); ~ *gérant*, managing editor. || **rédaction** [-'sjõ] *n.f.* [d'un texte] drawing-up, drafting; [le texte lui-même] language; [Journ.] editorial staff; editors: *secrétaire de* ~, associate editor; *comité de* ~, editorial board.
redescendre [rədɛ'sɑ̃:dr] #42 *v. intr.* [conj. with ÊTRE] to come down again. || *v. tr.* [*conj.* with AVOIR] to take down (again).
redevable [rədə'v|abl] *adj.* indebted (*de*, for; *à*, to). || **redevance** [-ɑ̃:s] *n.f.* dues, rent.
redevenir [rədəv'ni:r] #22 *v. intr.* to become . . . again.
rédiger [redi'ʒe] #5 *v. tr.* [un texte] to draw up; [un journal] to edit; [une ordonnance] to write out.
redingote [rədɛ̃'gɔt] *n.f.* frockcoat.
redire [rə'di:r] #45 *v. tr.* to/tell, say/ . . . again; to repeat: [Fig.] *trouver à* ~ *à*, to blame, to find fault with. || **redite** [rə'dit] *n.f.* [Péj.] repetition.
redonner [rədɔ'ne] #3 *v. tr.* to give . . . again, a second time; [foi] to restore.
redoubler [rədu'ble] #3 *v. tr.* to redouble (*de*, with); to increase: ~ *ses efforts*, to strive hard (at, *pour*); [école] to repeat; to take the . . . grade over.
redoutable [rədu't|abl] *adj.* formidable; dreaded. || **redoute** [rə'dut] *n.f.* [Mil.] redoubt; [Fig.] stronghold. || **redouter** [-e] #3 *v. tr.* to dread: *Je redoute de passer cet examen*, I can't bear to think about this exam.
redressement [rədrɛ's|mɑ̃] *n.m.* straightening up; [Fig.] recovery, upward movement. || **redresser** [-e] #3 *v. tr.* to straighten; [la tête] to hold up . . . (again); [des torts] to set . . . to rights. || **se redresser** *v. pron.* to straighten up, to get straight again; [assis] to sit upright; [debout] to stand upright; [navire]: *Le navire se redressa*, The ship righted herself.
réduction [red|yk'sjõ] *n.f.* reduction; price cut. || **réduire** [-ɥi:r] #56 *v. tr.* to reduce (*en esclavage*, to slavery): ~ *à la famine*, to drive . . . to starvation; to starve out; [frais] to cut down (expenses). || **se réduire** *v. pron.* to be reduced (*à*, to); to be converted (into, *en*). || **réduit, -e** [re'dɥi(t)] cf. RÉDUIRE. || *adj.*: *prix réduits*, cut rates, reduced prices.
réel [re'ɛl] *n.m.* reality. || **réel, -le** *adj.* real; [qui a lieu réellement] actual. || **réellement** [-mɑ̃] *adv.* really; actually.
refaire [rə'fɛ:r] #37 *v. tr.* to/make, do/ . . . again; [reconstruire] to rebuild: *Refaites-le!*, Do it again!; *faire* ~, to have . . . done again. || **se refaire** *v. pron.* to recover (one's health); [Fam.] to make one's losses good. || **réfection** [refɛk'sjõ] *n.f.* restoration: *route en* ~, road under repair, [Br.] road up.
réfectoire [refɛk'twa:r] *n.m.* refectory, dining hall.
référence [refe'rɑ̃:s] *n.f.* reference. || **se référer** [sərefe're] #10 *v. pron.* to refer (*à*, to).
refermer [rəfɛr'me] #3 *v. tr.* to/shut, close/again. || **se refermer** *v. pron.* to close again.
refiler [rəfi'le] #3 *v. tr.*: ~ (*une fausse pièce*) *à qqun*, to palm off (a bad coin) on s.o.
réfléchi, -e [refle'ʃ|i] *adj.* [lumière] reflected; [esprit] reflective, thoughtful; [décision] deliberate. || **réfléchir** [-i:r] #17 *v. tr.* **1.** to reflect (light, &c.). **2.** [pensée] to reflect, think, ponder (*à*, upon; *sur*, over): *Cela donne à* ~, It makes one /think, wonder/; *Réfléchissez-y!*, Think it over! || **se réfléchir** *v. pron.*: *La lumière se réfléchit dans le miroir*, Light is reflected in the mirror. || **réflecteur** [reflɛk'tœ:r] *n.m.* reflector; [Theatre] spotlight.
reflet [rə'fl|ɛ] *n.m.* reflection; [rapide] flash; [sombre] glint; [coloré] gleam, glow. cf. RÉFLÉCHIR[1]. || **refléter** [-e'te] #10 *v. tr.* to reflect.
réflexe [re'flɛks] *n.m.* reflex.
réflexion [reflɛk'sjõ] *n.f.* reflection: *faire* ~ *sur* . . . , to think . . . over; *faire un*

effort de ~, to try to recall. cf. RÉFLÉCHIR[2].
refluer [rəfly'e] #3 *v. intr.* [Naut.] to ebb; [Fig.] to surge (back). || **reflux** [rə'fly] *n.m.* [Naut.] ebb (tide).
refonte [rə'fõ:t] *n.f.* [mostly Fig.] recasting, remodelling.
réformateur [refɔrma'tœ:r] *n.m.* reformer. || *adj.* reformist. || **réformation** [refɔrma'sjõ] *n.f.* reformation; reform.
réforme [re'fɔrm] *n.f.* reform; [Hist.] *La Réforme*, (the) Reformation; [Mil.] discharge (for physical incapacity). || **réformé, e** [-e] *adj.* [soldat] disabled; discharged for physical incapacity; [Église] Protestant. || **réformer** [refɔr'me] #3 *v. tr.* to reform; [Mil.] to discharge (for physical incapacity). || **se réformer** *v. pron.* to reform.
reformer [refɔr'me] #3 *v. tr.* to re-form: [Mil.] ~ *les rangs*, to fall in again. || **se reformer** *v. pron.* to re-form, to take shape again; [Mil.] to form up again.
refoulement [rəful|'mɑ̃] *n.m.* repulsing, driving back; [Polit.] roll-back. || **refouler** [-e] #3 *v. tr.* [Tech.] to compress, stem; [Mil.] to repulse, drive back; [à la frontière] to turn back; [Ch. de fer] to back; [sanglot] to choke back. || *v. intr.* to flow back; [Fig.] *refoulé*, inhibited.
réfractaire [refrak'tɛ:r] *adj.* [sens moral] rebellious, insubordinate; [à un agent externe] = proof; fireproof. || *n.m.* insubordinate (soldier).
réfraction [refrak'sjõ] *n.f.* refraction.
refrain [rəfrɛ̃] *n.m.* [Mus.] chorus.
refréner [rəfre'ne] *v. tr.* [ses passions, &c.] to curb, control.
réfrigérant, -e [refriʒe'r|ɑ̃(:t)] *adj.* refrigerating; [mélange] freezing. || **réfrigérateur** [-a'tœ:r] *n.m.* **1.** refrigerator, [Fam.] frig. || **réfrigération** [-a'sjõ] *n.f.* refrigeration. || **réfrigérer** [-e] #10 *v. tr.* to refrigerate.
refroidi, -e [rəfrwa'd|i] *adj.* cooled, chilled, cf. REFROIDIR. || **refroidir** [-i:r] #17 *v. tr.* to cool, chill; [Fig.] to damp, cool. || *v. intr.* to grow colder, to cool down. || **se refroidir** *v. pron.* [température] to grow colder; [Méd.] to catch a chill; [Péj.] to cool down. || **refroidissement** [-is'mɑ̃] *n.m.* cooling (down); fall (in temperature); [moteur] *à* ~ *par/eau, air/*, water-, air-/cooled (engine); [Méd.] chill.
refuge [rə'fy:ʒ] *n.m.* refuge; [Fig.] refuge, asylum; [de piétons] island, boulevard. || **réfugié, -e** [refy'ʒje] *n.* refugee. || **se réfugier** #3 *v. pron.* to take refuge (*chez*, with); [Péj.] to take refuge (*dans*, in), to fall back (*dans*, on).
refus [rə'fy] *n.m.* refusal; [en réponse à une offre de repas, &c.] *Ce n'est pas de* ~, → I'd be glad to. || **refuser** [-'ze] #3 *v. tr.* to refuse [+ inf.]; to decline, turn down [an invitation]; [candidat] to fail; [Fam.] to flunk; [Fig.] to deny: *Il se vit* ~ *le visa américain*, He was denied an American visa. || *v. intr.* to refuse. || **se refuser** *v. pron.* to deny o.s.: *Il ne se refuse rien*; [Fam.] He puts jam on it; ~ *à*, to refuse, decline/to do . . . .
réfuter [refy'te] #3 *v. tr.* to refute, disprove.
regagner [rəgɑ'ɲe] #3 *v. tr.* **1.** to get back, win back (one's money); [temps] to make up (for lost time). **2.** [mouvement]: ~ *son domicile*, to return, go back/home.
regain [rə'gɛ̃] *n.m.* [foin] second growth, aftercrop; [Fig.] aftermath: ~ *de vie*, new lease of life.
régal [re'gal] *pl.* **régals** *n.m.* [Culin.] exquisite food, dainty dish; [Fig.] treat. || **régaler** [-e] #3 *v. tr.* to treat, †regale one's friends (*de*, with); [Fam.] †*C'est moi qui régale* (→ *c'est ma tournée*), The drinks are, this one is/, on me. || **se régaler** *v. pron.* to feast (*de*, on).
regard [rə'ga:r] *n.m.* look; [fixe] stare; [hostile] glare; [rapide] glance: ~ *interrogateur*, quizzical look; *Tous les regards sont fixés sur X*, → X is the cynosure of all eyes. || **regarder** [rəgar'de] #3 *v. tr.* **1.** to look at; [fixement] to gaze at; [rapidement] to glance at; to behold; [succinctement] to have a look at; [une partie de football] to watch. **2.** [Fig.] to concern: *Ça le regarde*, That's up to him; *Cela ne vous regarde pas*, This is/no business of yours, none of your business/; [juger] to regard, consider; [maison] to face [west, south]. || *v. intr.* to look: ~ *par la fenêtre*, [vers l'extérieur] to look out of the window; [vers l'intérieur] to look in through the window; [longuement] to gaze; [droit devant soi] to look (straight) ahead; [fixement] to stare; [derrière soi] to look back; [par le trou de la serrure] to peep through the keyhole; [Fig.] ~ *à la dépense*, to watch the expense; to be economical; *y* ~ *à deux fois avant de . . .*, to think twice before [+ ing]. || **se regarder** *v. pron.* to look at o.s. (in a mirror); [v. réciproque] to look at one another.
régate [re'gat] *n.f.* regatta.
régence [re'ʒɑ̃:s] *n.f.* regency.
régénération [reʒener|a'sjõ] *n.f.* regeneration; [monde] regeneration, reform. || **régénérer** [-e] #10 *v. tr.* to regenerate.
régent [re'ʒɑ̃] *n.m.* regent.

régie [re'ʒi] *n.f.* [Admin.] commission, Board, office: ~ *des alcools*, liquor commission, &c.; [Fr.] [impôts] Excise office: *droit de* ~, excise tax, cf. ACCISE.

regimber [rəʒɛ̃'be] #3 *v. tr.* to back (*contre*, at): [Fig.] to revolt; [Fam.] to kick against.

régime [re'ʒim] *n.m.* **1.** [mode de vie] regime; diet: *suivre un* ~, to (be on a special) diet; ~ *amaigrissant*, reducing diet; [bananes] bunch; [moteur] speed. **2.** [Polit.] regime, rule, political system; © *le* ~ *français*, the French regime; [Gram.] predicate.

régiment [reʒi'mɑ̃] *n.m.* regiment. || **régimentaire** [-'tɛːr] *adj.* regimental.

région [re'ʒj|ɔ̃] *n.f.* region; area, district. || **régional, -e** [-ɔ'nal] *adj.* regional. || **régionale** [-ɔ'nal] *n.f.* [société] branch. || **régionalisme** [-ɔna'lism] *n.m.* regionalism.

régir [re'ʒ|iːr] #17 *v. tr.* to rule; [Admin.] to manage, administer; [Gram.] to govern. || **régisseur** [-i'sœːr] *n.m.* [propriété] agent, manager; [TV] floor-manager, stage-manager.

registraire [rəʒis'trɛːr] © *n.m.* registrar: *Registraire général du Canada*, Registrar General of Canada. || **registre** [rə'ʒistr] *n.m.* register, record: *tenir* ~ *de*, to keep a record of; [des délibérations] minutes; [Fr.] ~ *du Commerce*, Trade Registrar; [voix] range, compass.

réglage [re'glaːʒ] *n.m.* setting, adjustment; [radio, TV, Auto.] tuning. || **règle** [rɛgl] *n.f.* rule(r): ~ *à calcul*, sliderule; [règlement] rule; *en* ~, correct, in order; *membre en* ~ *avec le trésor*, member in good standing; *se mettre en* ~ *avec*, to comply with (the law, &c.); ~ /*absolue, immuable*/, hard and fast rule; *en* ~ *générale*, as a rule. || **réglé, -e** [re'gle] *adj.* [papier] ruled; [travail] steady, regular; [vie] well-regulated. || **règlement** [rɛglə'mɑ̃] *n.m.* regulation, rule; [d'une admin.] statute; [de police] bylaw: ~ *intérieur*, rules of procedure; *rappel au* ~, point of order. || **réglementaire** [-tɛːr] *adj.* regular; regulation: *tenue* ~, regulation uniform. || **réglementairement** [-tɛr'mɑ̃] *adv.* [Fam.] according to the book. || **réglementation** [-ta'sjɔ̃] *n.f.* regulation, control. || **réglementer** [-'te] #3 *v. tr.* to regulate, control.

régler [re'gle] #10 *v. tr.* **1.** [comptes] to settle, pay. **2.** [ses affaires] to put in order; [montre] to regulate; [radio, TV, moteur] to tune; [différend] to settle; [Fam.] ~ *son compte à qqun*, to square up with s.o.

règne[1] [rɛːɲ] *n.m.* **1.** reign: *sous le* ~ *d'Elizabeth II*, in the reign of Elizabeth II. **2.** [Bot., Zool.] kingdom: *le* ~ *végétal*, the vegetable kingdom.

règne[2], &c. cf. RÉGNER.

régner [re'ɲe] #10 *v. intr.* to reign, rule (*sur*, over); [Fig.] to reign, prevail.

regorger [rəgɔr'ʒe] #5 *v. intr.* to overflow; [Fig.] to abound (*de*, in); to be crowded (*de*, with).

régression [regrɛ'sjɔ̃] *n.f.* regression; throw-back; [Fig.] decline.

regret [rə'grɛ] *n.m.* regret, sorrow (*de*, for): *être au* ~ /*de . . . , de ne . . .* /to be sorry /to have to . . . , not to be able to . . ./; *à* ~, with regret, reluctantly. || **regrettable** [-'tabl] *adj.* regrettable, to be deplored: *Il est* ~ *que*, It is a pity that. || **regretter** [-'te] #3 *v. tr.* **1.** to regret (s.o., sth.); ~ *d'avoir fait qqch.*, to be sorry (for having done sth.). **2.** [un absent] to miss s.o., to regret s.o.'s absence.

régulariser [regylari|'ze] #3 *v. tr.* to regularize, standardize; [Fig.] to clear up [an irregular state of affairs]. || **régularité** [-'te] *n.f.* [mouvement] steadiness, regularity; [du caractère] evenness. || **réguli|er, -ère** [regy'lj|e, -ɛːr] *adj.* [mouvement] regular, steady; [habitude] regular, methodical; [passeport] valid, [vie] orderly. || **régulièrement** [-ɛr'mɑ̃] *adv.* regularly, steadily; according to regulations.

réhabiliter [reabili'te] #3 *v. tr.* to rehabilitate: ~ *la mémoire de qqun*, to clear s.o.'s name. || **se réhabiliter** *v. pron.* to rehabilitate o.s.; to clear one's good name.

rehausser [rəo'se] #3 *v. tr.* to raise; [couleur] to touch up (*de*, with); [Fig.] to enhance.

réimprimer [reɛ̃pri'me] #3 *v. tr.* to reprint.

rein [rɛ̃] *n.m.* [Anat.] kidney; *les reins*, the back: [Fig.] *se ceindre les reins*, to gird (up) one's loins; [Fig.] *avoir les reins solides*, to be very strong.

reine [rɛːn] *n.f.* queen: *la Reine*, the Queen; *la Reine-mère*, the Queen-mother; *service de la* ~, on Her Majesty's Service; [Géog.] *détroit de la Reine-Charlotte*, Queen Charlotte Sound. || **reinette** [rɛ'nɛt] *n.f.*: (*pomme de*) ~, rennet, pippin.

réintégration [reɛ̃tegr|a'sjɔ̃] *n.f.* [fonctionnaire] reinstatement; return: ~ *à la vie civile*, rehabilitation. || **réintégrer** [-e] #10 *v. tr.* to reinstate (s.o. in one's employ): ~ *son domicile*, to return home [after having left it].

rejaillir [rəʒa'j|iːr] #17 *v. intr.* to rebound, bounce back; [boue] to splash; [lumière] to be/reflected, thrown back/; [Fig.] to reflect (*sur*, on). || **rejaillissement** [-is'mɑ̃] *n.m.* bouncing back, rebounding; splashing; spurting; reflection.

rejet [rə'zɛ] *n.m.* casting up; [Fam.] reject, throw-away; [Jur.] dismissal. || **rejeter** [rəʒ(ə)'te] #8 *v. tr.* **1.** to throw back: ~ *un poisson dans l'eau*, to throw a fish back in the water. **2.** to cast up, to wash up: *des débris rejetés sur le rivage*, wreckage cast up on the shore; *La mer a rejeté son corps deux jours plus tard*, His body was washed up two days later. **3.** ~ *le blâme sur autrui*, to/place, throw/the blame on others. **4.** [Jur.] ~ *un appel*, to/dismiss, reject, turn down/an appeal.

rejeton [rəʒ'tõ] *n.m.* shoot (of plant, tree): *pousser des rejetons*, to send forth shoots; [Fig.] scion, offspring, descendant.

rejette, &c. cf. REJETER.

rejoigne, &c., rejoignis, &c., cf. REJOINDRE. || **rejoindre** [rə'ʒw|ɛ̃:dr] **rejoignant** [-a'ɲɑ̃] **rejoint** [-ɛ̃] #36 *v. tr.* **1.** to meet (by arrangement): *Rejoignez-moi à quatre heures*, Meet me at four o'clock. **2.** to join (one's ancestors). **3.** to join again, to reach: *Il rejoindra sa famille plus tard*, He will join his family later; *Je n'ai pas pu le rejoindre (au téléphone)*, I could not reach him. **4.** to report to: *Il doit* ~ *son unité immédiatement*, He must report to his unit at once. || **rejoins, rejoint** cf. REJOINDRE.

réjoui, -e [re'ʒwi] *adj.* cheerful, jolly. || **réjouir** [re'ʒw|i:r] **réjouissant** [-i'sɑ̃] **réjoui** [-i] #17 *v. tr.* to gladden, cheer: *Cela nous réjouit le cœur*, That/cheers us tremendously, gladdens our hearts; *une nouvelle réjouissante*, cheering news; *le visage réjoui*, with a beaming countenance. || **se réjouir** *v. pron.* to take delight, pleasure (in); to be delighted (to): *Je me réjouis de vous voir*, I am delighted to see you. || **réjouissance** [-i'sɑ̃:s] *n.f.* rejoicing, celebration: *les réjouissances*, the festivities. || **réjouissant, -e** [-i'sɑ̃(:t)] *adj.* pleasant: *Ce n'est pas très* ~, It's not a very cheering prospect.

relâche [rə'l|ɑ:ʃ] *n.m.* **1.** respite, let up: *travailler sans* ~, to work unremittingly. **2.** [Théât.] ~ *dimanche soir*, no performance Sunday evening. **3.** [Naut.] *n.f. faire* ~ *à*, to call at.

relâcher [-ɑ'ʃe] #3 *v. tr.* **1.** to slacken, to loosen (ropes, bonds, &c.); to relax (pressure, discipline). **2.** to release (a prisoner). || **se relâcher** *v. pron.* to slacken, loosen, (be)come loose (rope, shoelaces, &c.); to relax (in one's efforts); [Fig.] *Son ardeur se relâche*, His, her/ardour is cooling; *Les mœurs se sont relâchées*, Morals have grown lax.

relaie, &c., cf. RELAYER.

relais [rə'lɛ] *n.m.* [stage coach] stage; [workmen] shift; [Radio, TV] hook-up.

relancer [rəlɑ̃'se] #4 *v. tr.* **1.** to throw again; to start again. **2.** [tennis] ~ *la balle*, to return a stroke (esp. service). **3.** to harass (s.o.); to hound (s.o.). || *v. intr.* [poker, bridge, &c.] to raise the bid.

relater [rəla'te] #3 *v. tr.* [fait] to state; [histoire] to tell, relate. || **relati|f, -ve** [rəla|'tif, -'ti:v] *adj.* relative. || **relation** [-'sjõ] *n.f.* relation, relationship, connection; *pl.* relations: *relations d'affaires*, business relations; *être en relations avec qqun*, to be in/communication, touch/with s.o.; *le cercle des relations*, (one's) (business) connections; *avoir des relations*, to have influential friends; [Rail.] *relations directes*, through connections.

relativement [rəlativ'mɑ̃] *adv.* relatively; comparatively. || **relativité** [rəlativi'te] *n.f.* relativity.

relayer [rəlɛ'je] #11 *v. tr.* **1.** to relieve (guard, worker on previous shift, &c.). **2.** to relay (a message). || *v. intr.* to change horses (at relay station). || **se relayer** *v. pron.* to work in shifts, relays.

relègue, &c., cf. RELÉGUER. || **reléguer** [rəle'ge] #10 *v. tr.* to relegate, to consign.

relève [rə'l|ɛ:v] *n.f.* [Mil.] relief (force); [Fig.] the new generation. || **relevé** [rəl've] cf. RELEVER. || *adj.* **1.** raised (in relief) cf. RELIEF. **2.** [style, langage, sentiments] lofty, elevated; [pensées, sentiments] noble. **3.** [sauce, &c.] spicy, tangy, highly seasoned. **4.** *virage* ~, graded curve || *n.m.* **1.** list, check list, statement: ~ *de compte*, (bank) statement. **2.** survey, check: *faire le* ~ *de qqch.*, to survey (land, &c.); to note, check, list (from text, &c.). || **relèvement** [-ɛv'mɑ̃] *n.m.* [économique] recovery; [prix] raising (*de*, of), rise (*de*, in); [impôts] increase; [Naut.] bearing; [moral] recovery, improvement. || **relever** [rəl've] #9 *v. tr.* **1.** to set up again (chair, stand, &c.). **2.** to raise, lift up, pull up (o.'s head, garment, &c.). **3.** to revive (spirits), to restore (country). **4.** to change, to relieve: *La sentinelle est relevée toutes les deux heures*, The sentry is changed every two hours; *Il a été relevé de son commandement*, He has been relieved of his command. **5.** to release: *Elle a été relevée de ses vœux*, She was released from her vows. **6.** to note, to pick up: ~ *des exemples*, to list examples. **7.** to enhance, to set off (beauty, character). **8.** to season (sauce, dish). || *v. intr.* **1.** to come under (authority, category, &c.). **2.** ~ *de maladie,* to recover from illness. || **se relever** *v. pron.* to pick o.s. up; to recover.

relief [rə'ljɛf] *n.m.* **1.** relief: *carte en* ~, relief map; *donner du* ~ *à, mettre en* ~, to set off; cf. RELEVER. **2.** *pl.* leftovers, scraps (from a meal).

relier [rə'lj|e] #3 *v. tr.* **1.** to bind (books, &c.). **2.** to link, connect: *Une autoroute relie les deux villes,* An express highway links the two cities. || **relieur** [-œ:r] *n.m.* bookbinder.

religieusement [rəliʒj|øz'mɑ̃] *adv.* religiously.

religieu|x, -se [-ø(:z)] *adj.* religious. || *n.m.* monk, brother. *f.* nun, sister. || **religion** [-õ] *n.f.* religion: *entrer en* ~, to take one's vows.

relique [rə'lik] *n.f.* relic.

relire [rə'l|i:r], **relisant** [-i'zɑ̃], **relu** [-y] #49 *v. tr.* to re-read, to read again. || **relis, relit** cf. RELIRE.

reliure [rə'ljy:r] *n.f.* binding (of book); bookbinding.

reluire [rə'lɥ|i:r], **reluisant** [-i'zɑ̃], **relui** [-i] #57 *v. intr.* [briller] to shine; [étinceler] to glitter, sparkle: *faire* ~ *qqch.,* to/polish up, shine up/sth. || **reluis, reluit** cf. RELUIRE. || **reluisant, -e** *adj.* gleaming, shiny, glossy.

relus, &c., cf. RELIRE.

remanier [rəma'nje] #21 *v. tr.* to adapt, revamp, revise (novel, play, &c.); reshuffle (Cabinet).

remarquable [rəmar'kabl] *adj.* remarkable; worthy of note, noteworthy. || **remarque** [rə'mark] *n.f.* observation, remark. || **remarquer** [-e] #3 *v. tr.* to notice, observe: *faire* ~ *qqch. à qqun,* to point out sth. to s.o.; *se faire* ~, to make o.s. conspicuous.

rembarquer [rɑ̃bar'ke] #3 *v. tr.* to re-embark, reload (sth.). || *v. intr.* [personne] to re-embark, go back on board. || **se rembarquer** *v. pron.* to re-embark, go back on board.

remblai [rɑ̃'blɛ] *n.m.* **1.** fill, filling material (esp. earth). **2.** [construction de routes ou de voies ferrées] embankment. || **remblaie, &c. remblaierai, &c.** cf. REMBLAYER. || **remblayer** [-'je] #11 *v. tr.* **1.** to fill (hollow). **2.** [terrassement] to embank, bank up.

rembourrer [rɑ̃bu|'re] #3 *v. tr.* to upholster (a piece of furniture); to stuff, to pad (a mattress, &c.). || **rembourreur** [-'rœ:r] © *n.m.* upholsterer, cf. TAPISSIER.

remboursement [rɑ̃burs|ə'mɑ̃] *n.m.* reimbursement, repayment, refund(ing); [bons, &c.] redemption, redeeming: *livraison contre* ~, C.O.D. (cash on delivery). || **rembourser** [-e] #3 *v. tr.* [somme] to refund; [personne ou argent] to reimburse, to repay, to pay back.

rembrunir [rɑ̃bry'ni:r] #17 *v. tr.* to sadden. || **se rembrunir** *v. pron.* to darken, to get cloudy: *Le temps se rembrunit,* The weather is clouding up; *Son visage se rembrunit,* His brow clouded over.

remède [rə|'mɛ:d] *n.m.* remedy, cure; [Fig.] *porter* ~ *à,* → to remedy (a situation). || **remédier** [-me'dje] #3 *v. intr.* to cure, remedy (*à*); [Fig., perte] to make good.

remerciement [rəmɛrs|i'mɑ̃] *n.m.* thanks [no sing.]: *faire ses remerciements à qqun de qqch.,* to express o.'s thanks to s.o. for sth.; *un vote de* ~, a vote of thanks. || **remercier** [-je] #3 *v. tr.* **1.** to thank: *Je vous remercie de vos bonnes lignes,* I thank you for your kind letter. **2.** to dismiss, discharge (servant, employee).

remet, remets, cf. REMETTRE. || **remettre** [rə'mɛt|r] **remettant** [-ɑ̃] **remis** [rə'mi] #44 *v. tr.* **1.** [chapeau, &c.] to put (sth.) back (in its place); to put back on, put on again; to restore (sth., s.o.) to its, his former state: *Remettez-le dans le fichier,* Put it back in the index file; ~ *un os,* to set a bone; ~ *qqch. en état,* to/fix, repair/ sth.; *Les vacances m'ont remis(e),* My vacation/has put me back in trim, has made me myself again. **2.** to hand (over), to deliver (letter, telegram); to remit (sum of money due); to turn over, entrust (sth. to s.o.). **3.** to postpone, put off: *Ne remettez pas à demain ce que vous pouvez faire aujourd'hui,* Never put off till tomorrow what you can do today; *C'est partie remise,* [Fam.] I'll take a rain check on that. || **se remettre** *v. pron.* **1.** to start off, start in, again: ~ *en route,* to resume o.'s journey, to set off on o'.s way again; ~ *au travail,* to get back to work. **2.** to recover (from an illness); to regain (o.'s composure); [temps] to clear up: *Remettez-vous!,* Pull yourself together!; *Le temps s'est remis,* The weather has/cleared up, turned pleasant again. **3.** *s'en remettre à qqun,* to refer to someone: *Je m'en remets à votre bienveillance,* I trust to your kindness.

réminiscence [remini'sɑ̃:s] *n.f.* reminiscence, recollection.

remis, remise[1], cf. REMETTRE. || **remise**[2] rə'm|i:z] *n.f.* **1.** [colis] delivery; [retard] postponement. **2.** [Tech.] shed; [Com.] remittance; commission, discount: ~ *de* 5%, 5 per cent discount. || **remiser** [-i'ze]

#3 *v. tr.* [ranger] to put/up, away/; [voiture] to park, to garage.

remontant [rəmõ'tɑ̃] *n.m.* tonic, [Fam.] pick-me-up. || **remonter** [rəmõ'te] #3 *v. intr.* **1.** to go (come) up again; to ride up: *Cette jupe remonte constamment,* This skirt keeps riding up. **2.** to go back, to date back: *Cela remonte à 1800,* It goes back to 1800. || *v. tr.* **1.** to go (come) up again; to go up: *~ l'escalier,* to go back up the stairs; *~ un fleuve,* to go up a river. **2.** [horloge] to wind up. **3.** [vêtement] to pull up. **4.** to take, bring back up. **5.** to stimulate, revive: *Cela remonte,* It's a [Fam.] pick-me-up. || **se remonter** *v. pron.* to recuperate, to get rested up.

remontrance [rəmõ'tr|ɑ̃:s] *n.f.* remonstrance, expostulation. || **remontrer** [-e] #3 *v. intr.*: *en ~ à qqun,* to know better (than); to outdo, best/s.o. || *v. tr.* to show again; [Fig.] to stress, point out.

remords [rə'mɔ:r] *n.m.* remorse: [surtout au pl.] *avoir, éprouver/des remords (de qqch.),* to feel remorse (over sth.).

remorque [rə'mɔrk] *n.f.* **1.** [Auto.] trailer. **2.** *(câble de) ~,* tow-rope, [Naut.] towline, hawser; *à la ~,* in tow. || **remorquer** [-e] #3 *v. tr.* to tow; to haul: *Les trains sont maintenant remorqués par des locomotives à moteur Diesel,* Trains are now hauled by Diesel engines. || **remorqueur** [-œ:r] *n.m.* [Naut.] tugboat, tug.

remous [rə'mu] *n.m. invar.* [often pl.] swirl, eddy; [d'un bateau] wash; [Fig.] stir, commotion.

rempart [rɑ̃'pa:r] *n.m.* rampart.

remplaçant, -e [rɑ̃plɑ̃'s|ɑ̃(:t)] *n.* substitute. || **remplacement** [-'mɑ̃] *n.m.* replacement; substitution: *en ~ de,* in place of. || **remplacer** [rɑ̃pla'se] #4 *v. tr.* to replace, substitute for.

remplir [rɑ̃'pl|i:r], **remplissant** [-i'sɑ̃], **rempli** [-i] #17 *v. tr.* **1.** to fill, fill up. **2.** to refill, replenish. **3.** to fill out (a form), to fill in (a blank). **4.** to fulfil (o.'s obligations).

remporter [rɑ̃pɔr'te] #3 *v. tr.* **1.** to take back. **2.** to win, to carry off (a prize).

remue-ménage [rəmyme'na:ʒ] *n.m. inv.* hullabaloo, [Fam.] rumpus. || **remuer** [rə'mɥe] #3 *v. tr.* [jambe, bras] to move; [meubles, &c.] to move, move about; [sol] to turn over; [café] to stir; [Fig.] to move, stir: *Il en fut très remué,* He was very much moved; *~ ciel et terre,* to move heaven and earth. || *v. intr.* to move. || **se remuer** *v. pron.* to move, to bestir o.s.

rémunérat|eur, -rice [remynera|'tœ:r, -'tris] *adj.* profitable, remunerative. || **rémunération** [-'sjõ] *n.f.* remuneration; compensation, payment. || **rémunérer** [remyne're] #10 *v. tr.* to remunerate, reward (*de,* for).

renais, renaît, renaissant, cf. RENAÎTRE. || **renaissance** [rən|ɛ'sɑ̃:s] *n.f.* **1.** revival, rebirth, renascence. **2.** [Hist.] Renaissance. || **renaître** [-ɛ:tr] #39 *v. intr.* [This verb, having no past participle, has no compound tenses.] to be reborn, to be revived. || **renaquis, &c.** cf. RENAÎTRE.

renard [rə'na:r] *n.m.* fox.

renchérir [rɑ̃ʃe'ri:r] #17 *v. intr.* **1.** to go up in price. **2.** to go one better (than, *sur*).

rencontre [rɑ̃'k|õ:tr] *n.f.* meeting, encounter cf. ESCARMOUCHE: *faire la ~ de qqun,* to meet s.o. (by chance); *aller à la ~ de qqun,* to go to meet s.o. || **rencontrer** [-õ'tre] #3 *v. tr.* to meet (by chance); encounter, run into (s.o.); to run across, chance upon (passage in book, &c.). || **se rencontrer** *v. pron.* **1.** to meet (by chance or by arrangement): *Ils se rencontrent souvent,* They/meet, see each other/often. **2.** to be encountered, met with: *Cette qualité se rencontre rarement,* This quality is not often met with.

rendement[rɑ̃d'mɑ̃] *n.m.* efficiency; [récolte] yield; [machine] output; [placement] return, profit.

rendez-vous [rɑ̃de'vu] *n.m. inv.* appointment, engagement, date: *prendre ~,* to make an appointment.

rendre [rɑ̃:dr], **rendant** [rɑ̃'dɑ̃], **rendu** [rɑ̃'dy] #42 *v. tr.* **1.** to give back, return (sth. to s.o.); [argent] to repay, pay back; [santé, liberté] to restore; [hommage, service, compte, &c.] to render; [terre] to yield, produce; [placement] to pay, bring in, yield: *~ le bien pour le mal,* to return good for evil; *~ à qqun la monnaie d'un dollar,* to give s.o. change for a dollar; *~ la pareille à qqun,* to give s.o. tit for tat, to repay s.o. in kind; *Je n'ai pas de comptes à vous rendre,* → I'm not accountable to you. **2.** to surrender, hand over, turn over, turn in (arms, &c.): *~ son âme (à Dieu),* to die, pass away, pass on. **3.** to throw up. **4.** [devant un adjectif] to make: *Son livre l'a rendu célèbre,* His book made him famous. || **se rendre** *v. pron.* **1.** to go, proceed, betake o.s.: *~ à Paris,*/to go, to proceed/to Paris. **2.** to make, render, o.s.: *~ utile,* to make o.s. useful. **3.** [Mil.] to surrender. || **rendu, -e** cf. RENDRE. || *adj.*: *être ~,* to be worn out. || *n.m.* returned article: [Loc.] *un prêté pour un ~,* tit for tat.

rêne [rɛ:n] *n.f.* [surtout au pluriel] rein.

renfermé [rɑ̃fɛr'me] *adj.* **1.** close-mouthed, self-contained. **2.** [odeur d'une chambre] musty, stale: *sentir le* ~, to have a musty smell. **renfermer** #3 *v. tr.* to contain. || **se renfermer** *v. pron.* to restrict, confine s.o.: *Il se renferme étroitement dans son sujet*, He stays within his topic; ~ *en soi-même*, to retire into o.s.

renfler [rɑ̃'fle] #3 *v. tr.* to bulge, to swell.

renflouer [rɑ̃flu'e] #3 *v. tr.* [Naut.] to refloat; [Fig.] to salvage.

renfoncement [rɑ̃fõs|'mɑ̃] *n.m.* [mur] recess; [objet] dent. || **renfoncer** [-e] #4 *v. tr.* to dent; [chapeau] to pull down (over one's ears); [mur] to set back, recess. || **se renfoncer** *v. pron.* to recede, to go in.

renforcement [rɑ̃fɔrs|ə'mɑ̃] *n.m.* strengthening, reinforcing; [d'un mur] bracing; [son] intensifying; [Fig.] hardening. || **renforcer** [-e] #4 *v. tr.* to strengthen, reinforce; to intensify; [Fig.] to harden. || **renfort** [rɑ̃'fɔːr] *n.m.* [usual. pl.] reinforcement.

renfrogné, -e [rɑ̃frɔ'ɲe] *adj.* sullen, glum. || **se renfrogner** #3 *v. intr. & pron.* to scowl.

rengorger, se [rɑ̃gɔr'ʒe] #5 *v. pron.* [pigeon] to puff up; [Fig.] to swell visibly.

renier [rə'nje] #3 *v. tr.* to disown (o.'s son); to repudiate, deny (a doctrine), to abjure (o.'s faith).

renifler [rəni'fle] #3 *v. tr. & intr.* to sniff, snort, snuffle.

renne [rɛn] *n.m.* reindeer.

renom [rə'nõ] *n.m.* renown, repute. || **renommé, -e** [rənɔ'me] *adj.* renowned, noted. || **renommée** *n.f.* fame, renown; rumour, hearsay; reputation.

renommer [rənɔ'me] #3 *v. tr.* to reappoint, re-elect.

renoncement [rənõs'mɑ̃] *n.m.* renouncement, giving up (of, *à*); [abnégation] renunciation: ~ *de soi-même*, self-/denial, sacrifice/. || **renoncer** [rənõ's|e] #4 *v. intr.* to renounce, waive, swear off: ~ *à une prétention*, to renounce a claim; ~ *à un droit*, to waive a right; ~ *au tabac*, to swear off tobacco; ~ *à la lutte*, to give up the struggle. || **renonciation** [-ja'sjõ] *n.f.* [Jur.] renunciation, disclaimer; waiver.

renoncule [rənõ'kyl] *n.f.* ranunculus: ~ (*âcre*), [Fam.] [bouton d'or], buttercup.

renouer [rə'nwe] #3 *v. tr.* [cheveux] to tie up; [ruban] to retie, tie again, reknot: [Fig.] [relations] to renew, [conversation] to resume.

renouveau [rənu'vo] *n.m.* [season] spring(tide, time), coming of spring; [Fig.] revival. || **renouvelable** *adj.* renewable. || **renouveler** [rənuv'le] #8 *v. tr.* to renew, to revive, to renovate; [Com.] to repeat (an order); [Fig.] to change, restore. || **se renouveler** *v. pron.* to renew, renovate/ o.s.; [Fig.] to bring new life in; to rejuvenate. || **renouvellement** [-ɛl'mɑ̃] *n.m.* renewal, revival, renovation.

rénover [renɔ've] #3 *v. tr.* to renovate, renew; [Jur.] to renew.

renseignement [rɑ̃sɛɲ|'mɑ̃] *n.m.* **1.** (*un*) *renseignement*, a piece of information; (*des*) *renseignements*, information: *prendre des renseignements* (*sur*), to get information (on). **2.** [Mil.] *pl.* intelligence: *officier de renseignements*, intelligence officer. || **renseigner** [-e] #3 *v. tr.* to inform: *Il n'a pas pu me* ~, He could not give me the information. || **se renseigner** *v. pron.* to inquire, to find out.

rente [rɑ̃ːt] *n.f.* [surtout au pluriel] income, revenue: *vivre de ses rentes*, to live on o.'s income; ~ *viagère*, annuity, life endowment. || **renti|er, -ère** [rɑ̃'tj|e, -ɛːr] *n.* person living on a private income or an annuity; annuitant.

rentrée [rɑ̃'tre] *n.f.* **1.** return; reconvening (of legislative body, &c.), reopening (of school): *à sa* ~ *au Canada*, on his return to Canada; *à la* ~ *du Parlement*, when Parliament reconvenes; *la* ~ *des classes*, reopening of school. **2.** bringing in, gathering: *la* ~ *de la récolte*, the bringing in of the harvest. || **rentrer** [rɑ̃'tre] #3 *v. intr.* **1.** to enter again. **2.** to go, come home, to return: *A quelle heure rentre-t-il?*, What time does he come home? **3.** [Fig.]: ~ *dans le bon chemin*, to turn over a new leaf. || *v. tr.* to bring in: *faire* ~ *les impôts*, to collect taxes.

renverrai, &c. cf. RENVOYER.

renversant, e [rɑ̃vɛr'sɑ̃(ːt)] *adj.* fantastic.

renverse [rɑ̃'vɛrs] *n.f.*: *tomber à la* ~, to fall on o.'s back, [Fig.] to be bowled over.

renversement [rɑ̃vɛrsə'mɑ̃] *n.m.* [meuble] upsetting, overturning; [liquide] spilling; [mur] throwing down; [Phys., image, polarity] reversal; [Naut.] [vent] shifting, [marée] turn; [Mus., Fin.] inversion; [Polit.] overthrow (of the government).

renverser [-e] #3 *v. tr. & intr.* **1.** to turn upside down, turn over, overturn, invert; [Fig.] to overthrow, subvert (a government). **2.** to knock down, knock over (vase, pedestrian, &c.); to spill (wine, &c.). **3.** to reverse (an engine; [Fig.] a proposition): ~ *les rôles*, to reverse roles, turn the tables.

renvoi [rɑ̃'vwa] *n.m.* **1.** return. **2.** dismissal, discharge (of employee). **3.** reference (to source material; to higher authority). **4.** belch; [Fam.] burp; [Med.] eructation: *Le bébé a fait un renvoi*, The baby has burped. || **renvoie, renvoies,** cf. RENVOYER. || **renvoyer** [-'je] #13 *v. tr. &* © *intr.* **1.** to send (sth.) back, return (sth.). **2.** to dismiss, discharge, [Fam.] fire (an employee) cf. CONGÉDIER. **3.** to refer (person, case, &c., to another place).

réouverture [reuvɛr'ty:r] *n.f.* reopening.

repaire [rə'pɛ:r] *n.m.* [animaux sauvages, bandits] den: [Fam.] hangout.

repaître [rə'pɛ:tr] #40 *v. tr.* [animals] to feed; to graze; [Fig.] to fill (with, *de*): *~ ses yeux de*, to feast one's eyes on. || **se repaître** *v. pron.* to eat one's fill: [Fig.] *~ de sang*, to wallow in blood.

répand, répands cf. RÉPANDRE. || **répandre** [re'p|ɑ̃:dr] **répandant** [-ɑ̃'dɑ̃] **répandu** [-ɑ̃'dy] #42 *v. tr.* **1.** [sable; [Fig.] rumeur, nouvelle] to spread; [lumière] shed; [odeur] to give off. **2.** [vin, &c.] to spill cf. RENVERSER; [larmes, sang] to shed cf. VERSER. || **se répandre** *v. pron.* **1.** [odeur, infection; [Fig.] rumeur, opinion, &c.] to spread; [liquide renversé] to spill, run (all over sth.); **2.** [Fig.] *~ en éloges*, to be loud in one's praise. || **répandu** [-ɑ̃'dy] *adj.* common, prevalent, widespread, [opinion] widely held, [revue] with a wide circulation.

réparable [repa'rabl] *adj.* [broken, torn object] repairable, mendable, → that can be fixed; [erreur] → corrigible, which can be put right; [perte] retrievable.

reparaître [rəpa'r|ɛ:tr], **reparaissant** [-ɛ'sɑ̃], **reparu** [-y] #40 *v. intr.* to reappear; [Fam.] to show up again, turn up again.

réparat|eur, -rice [repara|'tœ:r, -'tris] *adj.* restoring, refreshing. || *n.* repairer, mender. || **réparation** [repar|a'sjõ] *n.f.* [machine, chaussures] repairing, repair; [vêtements] mending: *atelier de ~*, repair shop; [Fig.] reparation, amends: *réparations de guerre*, war reparations; *faire ~*, to make amends. || **réparer** [-e] #3 *v. tr.* to repair, fix, mend; [Fig.] to make up for, make amends for [une faute, un tort].

reparler [rəpar'le] #3 *v. intr.* to speak again: *~ de qqch.*, to discuss sth. again, to mention it again.

repars, repart, cf. REPARTIR.

repartie [rəpar'ti] *n.f.* repartee, (quick) rejoinder; [Péj.] retort.

repartir [rəpar't|i:r], **repartant** [-ɑ̃], **reparti** [-i] #26 *v. intr.* **1.** [Conj. ÊTRE] to set out again. **2.** [Conj. AVOIR] to retort, to reply.

répartir [repar't|i:r] #17 *v. tr.* to distribute, to divide, to share: *répartis en six groupes*, divided into six groups; *versements répartis sur six mois*, payments spread out over six months; *Les livres furent répartis entre eux*, The books were distributed among them. || **se répartir** *v. pron.* to break up; [Adm.] to break down. || **répartition** [-i'sjõ] *n.f.* distribution, sharing out; [impôt] assessment; breakdown.

reparu, reparus, &c. cf. REPARAÎTRE.

repas [rə'pa] *n.m.* meal: *faire/prendre/un ~*, to take a meal; © *~ complet*, full-course meal [as opposed to *~ léger*, snack].

repassage [rəpɑ'sa:ʒ] *n.m.* [river] recrossing; [linge] ironing; [lame] whetting, stropping; [Fig., Scol.] going over (a lesson), review. || **repasse** [rə'pɑ:s] *n.f.* © cf. REPASSAGE. || **repasser** [rəpɑ's|e] #3 *v. tr. & intr.* **1.** to pass again, to drop in again, to cross over again. **2.** to go over, check over, review (sth.) **3.** to iron (clothes). **4.** to strop (a razor); to whet (a tool on a whetstone). || **repasseur** [-œ:r] *n.m.* grinder. || **repasseuse** [-ø:z] *n.f.* ironer.

repêcher [rəpɛ'ʃe] #3 *v. tr.* to fish out, recover (object from water); [Fam.] to give s.o. a second chance.

repenti, -e [rəpɑ̃'ti] *adj.* repentant. || **se repentir** [sərpɑ̃'ti:r] #26 *v. pron.* to repent: *se ~ de qqch.*, to repent sth.; *Il s'en repentira*, He will be sorry (for it).

répercussion [repɛrky|'sjõ] *n.f.* repercussion; *pl.* [Fig.] consequences. || **répercuter** [-'te] #3 *v. tr.* [chaleur] reflect; [son] reverberate. || **se répercuter** *v. pron.* [lumière] to be reflected; [son] to reverberate; [Fig.] to have/repercussions, consequences/.

repère [rə|'pɛ:r] *n.m.* point of reference, [Fig.] landmark. || **repérer** [-pe're] #10 *v. tr.* to put a reference mark on (an instrument); [Ciné.] to synchronize; [Mil.] to locate, to spot (a submarine, &c.); [Fam.] to spot.

répertoire [repɛr'twa:r] *n.m.* [catalogue] repertory; [Théâ.] repertoire.

répète, &c. [re'p|ɛt] cf. RÉPÉTER. || **répéter** [-e'te] #10 *v. tr.* **1.** to repeat. **2.** [Théât.] to rehearse. || **répétit|eur, -rice** [-eti|'tœ:r, -'tris] *n.* **1.** private tutor, coach. **2.** [Fr. lycée] assistant master; teaching fellow, section-leader. || **répétition** [-'sjõ] *n.f.* **1.** repetition (of action, words, &c.): *fusil à ~*, repeating rifle. **2.** [Théât.] rehearsal: *~ générale*, dress rehearsal.

répit [re'pi] *n.m.* respite: *sans ~*, → unceasingly; *prendre un moment de ~*, to pause, let up.

replacer [rəpla'se] #4 *v. tr.* to put back, to

replace. [Fin.] to reinvest, plough back (profits).

repl|et, -ète [rəˈplɛ(t)] *adj.* fat, plump, stout.

repli [rəˈpli] *n.m.* **1.** fold, recess: *les plis et replis,* the innermost recesses. **2.** [terrain] dip, depression. **3.** [Mil.] falling back. || **replier** [-ˈje] #3 *v. tr.* to fold up again, refold. || **se replier** *v. pron.* [Mil.] to withdraw, fall back.

réplique [reˈplik] *n.f.* rejoinder, retort. || **répliquer** [-e] #3 *v. tr. & intr.* to retort, rejoin; [enfants] to answer back: *Ne réplique pas!,* Don't answer back!

replonger [rəplõˈʒe] #5 *v. tr. & intr.* to dive again. || **se replonger** *v. pron.*: [Fig.] to get back into.

répond, réponds, cf. RÉPONDRE. || **répondre** [reˈp|õ:dr] **répondant** [-õˈdɑ̃], **répondu** [-õˈdy] #42 *v. intr.* **1.** to answer, to reply: *Il y a répondu,* He answered it, replied to it. **2.** to meet: ~ *à un besoin pressant,* to meet a pressing need. **3.** to vouch (for, *de*), to be accountable (for, *de*): *Je vous en réponds!,* You can take my word for it!, Mark my words! || **réponse** [-õ:s] *n.f.* answer, reply; response.

reportage [rəpɔrˈta:ʒ] *n.m.* [Journ., TV, &c.] feature story: *Il a fait un* ~ *sur le Japon,* He wrote "on the spot" articles about Japan.

reporter [rəpɔrˈte] #3 *v. tr.* **1.** to take back. **2.** to postpone (till, *à*): *reporté à une date ultérieure,* postponed to a later date. **3.** [Comp.] to carry, bring forward. || **se reporter** *v. pron.* to refer (to, *à*).

repos [rəˈpo] *n.m.* rest; [Fig.] peace: *en* ~, at rest; *de tout* ~, reliable, dependable; [Mil.] *Repos!,* At ease!; [Tech., Mach.] *au* ~, not running. || **reposant, -e** [-ˈzɑ̃(:t)] *adj.* restful. || **reposé, -e** [-ˈze] *adj.* refreshed, relaxed: calm: *à tête reposée,* at leisure. || **reposer** [-ˈze] #3 *v. tr. & intr.* **1.** to put down again. **2.** to rest (one's head on a pillow, &c.). **3.** to lie: *Ici repose . . . ,* Here lies . . . || **se reposer** *v. pron.* **1.** to rest, to take a rest. **2.** to rely: *Je m'en repose sur vous,* I rely on you.

repoussant, -e [rəpuˈs|ɑ̃(:t)] *adj.* repulsive: *d'une laideur repoussante,* repulsively ugly. || **repousser** [-e] #3 *v. tr. & intr.* **1.** to push back, shove back; to push away, shove away; [attaque] to repulse, to drive back, repulse, repel; [les avances de qqun] to repel, resist; [offre, demande] to reject. **2.** to grow again. || **repoussoir** [-wa:r] *n.m.*: [Fig.] *servir de* ~ *à,* to act as a foil to.

répréhensible [repreɑ̃|ˈsibl] *adj.* reprehensible. || **répréhensi|f, -ve** [-ˈsif, -si:v] *adj.* reprehensible.

reprenais, &c., reprend, reprends, reprenne, cf. REPRENDRE. || **reprendre** [rəˈpr|ɑ̃:dr], **reprenant** [-əˈnɑ̃], **repris** [-i] #41 *v. tr. & intr.* **1.** to take back or again; to regain, to resume: ~ *connaissance,* to regain consciousness. **2.** to correct, to find fault with: *Je ne vois rien à y* ~, I find no fault with it. **3.** to start again, to resume; to improve, to pick up: *Les affaires reprennent,* Business is picking up.

représailles [rəpreˈza:j] *n.fpl.* reprisal(s), retaliation.

représentant, -e [rəprezɑ̃ˈt|ɑ̃(:t)] *adj.* representative. || *n.m.* representative; [Com.] agent, representative. || **représentation** [-aˈsjõ] *n.f.* **1.** representation. **2.** [Théât.] performance. **3.** [Com.] agency: *avoir la* ~ *exclusive* (*de*), → to be sole agent(s) (for); *frais de* ~, entertainment allowance, expense account. || **représenter** [-e] #3 *v. tr.* **1.** to represent (a firm, government, &c.); to act as agent(s) (for firm, &c.). **2.** [tableau, &c.] to represent, depict, portray; [symbole] to stand for, take the place of. **3.** [pièce] to perform, give, put on, show. || *v. intr.*: *Il représente bien,* He makes a good showing, cuts a good figure.

réprimander [reprimɑ̃ˈde] #3 *v. tr.* to reprimand, rebuke (s.o.); to take (s.o.) to task.

réprimer [repriˈme] #3 *v. tr.* to suppress; to put down: ~ *un sourire,* to suppress a smile; ~ *une insurrection,* to suppress, to put down an insurrection.

repris, &c. cf. REPRENDRE.

reprisage [rəpr|iˈza:ʒ] *n.m.* darning, mending; © ~ *invisible,* invisible mending. || **reprise** [-i:z] *n.f.* **1.** resumption, revival: *à plusieurs reprises,* several times. **2.** retaking, recapture. **3.** darning: *faire une* ~ *à,* → to darn. || **repriser** [-e] #3 *v. tr.* [bas] to darn; [robe] to mend.

réprobat|eur, -rice [reprɔba|ˈtœ:r, -ˈtris] *adj.* reproachful, reproving. || **réprobation** [-ˈsjõ] *n.f.* reprobation.

reproche [rəˈprɔʃ] *n.m.* reproach: *faire des reproches à qqun,* to reproach, upbraid (s.o.), take (s.o.) to task; *d'un air de* ~, reproachfully. || **reprocher** [-e] #3 *v. tr.*: ~ *qqch. à qqun,* to reproach s.o. with sth., to blame s.o. for sth.; to begrudge (s.o., sth.). || **se reprocher** *v. pron.* to blame o.s. for.

reproduction [rəprɔdykˈsjõ] *n.f.* reproduction; [imprimerie] duplicating; [art] reproduction, copy: *droits de* ~ *réservés,* copyright reserved. || **reproduire** [rəprɔ'dɥ|i:r] **reproduisant** [-i'zɑ̃] **reproduit** [-i] #56 *v. tr.* to reproduce. || **se reproduire** *v. pron.* to be reproduced; to happen again; [Physiol.] to breed.

réprouvé, -e [repru've] *adj.* rejected; disapproved of. || *n.*: *les réprouvés*, the damned; [Fam.] outcast. || **réprouver** #3 *v. tr.* to disapprove of; [Rel.] to damn, reprobate.

reptile [rɛp'til] *n.m.* reptile.

repu, -e [rə'py] *adj.* [Péj.] full, satiated.

républicain, -e [repybli'k|ɛ̃, -ɛn] *adj. & n.* republican. || **république** [repy'blik] *n.f.* republic.

répudier [repy'dje] #3 *v. tr.* to repudiate; [Fig.] to reject.

répugnance [repy'ɲ|ɑ̃:s] *n.f.* aversion, loathing, extreme dislike (for, *pour*). || **répugnant, -e** [-ɑ̃(:t)] *adj.* repugnant, loathsome. || **répugner** [-e] #3 *v. intr.* to be repugnant, loathsome, revolting (to, *à*): *Il me répugnerait de faire une telle chose*, → The very thought of doing such a thing revolts me.

répulsi|f, -ve [repyl's|if, -i:v] *adj.* repellent; [Fig.] repulsive. || **répulsion** [-jɔ̃] *n.f.* repulsion; [Fig.] distaste, aversion (*pour*, for).

réputation [repyt|a'sjɔ̃] *n.f.* reputation, repute: *Il jouit d'une bonne ~*, He/has, enjoys/a good reputation, He is a man of good repute. || **réputé, -e** [-e] *adj.* renowned, of high repute. || **réputer** #3 *v. tr.* [☞ mostly used in passive]: to be /considered, reputed/to; *être réputé coupable*, to be deemed guilty.

requérir [rək|e'ri:r] #23 *v. tr.* to go for; [exiger] to demand, to call upon s.o. (to do sth.); [Fig.] to call for.

requête [rə'kɛ:t] *n.f.* request; petition.

requin [rə'kɛ̃] *n.m.* shark.

requis, -e [rə'ki(:z)] *adj.* required, requisite: *conditions requises* (*pour se présenter à un examen*), prerequisites. || **réquisition** [rekizi'sj|ɔ̃] *n.f.* requisition: *droit de ~*, eminent domain. || **réquisitionner** [-ɔ'ne] #3 *v. tr.* to requisition, to commandeer.

rescousse [rɛs'kus] *n.f.*: *venir à la ~ de*, to come to the rescue.

réseau [re'zo] *n.m.* network, system: *~ ferroviaire, routier*, railway, road system.

réserve [re'zɛrv] *n.f.* **1.** reservation, reserve: *~ de places*, reservation of seats; *en ~*, in reserve; *mettre en ~*, to reserve, /put, set/aside; cf. RECHANGE; *vivres de ~*, emergency rations; *officier de ~*, Reserve officer; *fonds de ~*, reserve fund; *sans ~*, unreservedly; *sous ~ de*, contingent upon, subject to. **2.** reserve, aloofness (of character). || **réservé, -e** [-e] *adj.* reserved; [Fig.] reserved, aloof, uncommunicative. || **réserver** [-e] #3 *v. tr.* to reserve, set aside, put aside; to store up, save up, lay by (provisions, &c.). || **réservoir** [rezɛr'vwa:r] *n.m.* tank; reservoir: *~ à gaz*, gasometer.

résidence [rezi|'dɑ̃:s] *n.f.* residence, home: *changer de ~*, to move. || **résident, -e** ['dɑ̃(:t)] *n.* [Jur.] resident. || **résidentiel, -le** [-dɑ̃'sjɛl] *adj.* residential. || **résider** [-'de] #3 *v. intr.* to reside, live; [Fig.] to consist (*en*, in).

résidu [rezi'dy] *n.m.* residue; [Fig.] residuum.

résignation [reziɲ|a'sjɔ̃] *n.f.* [×] resignation, submissiveness: *avec ~*, resignedly. || **résigner** [-e] #3 *v. tr.* to relinquish: *~ ses fonctions*, to resign. || **se résigner** (**à**) *v. pron.* to resign, reconcile o.s. (to).

résiliation [rezilj|a'sjɔ̃] *n.f.* [d'un contrat] cancellation. || **résilier** [-e] #3 *v. tr.* [Jur., Com.] to cancel, annul.

résille [re'zi:j] *n.f.* hair net.

résine [re'zin] *n.f.* resin. || **résineu|x, -se** [-ø(:z)] *adj.* [bois] resinous; [forêt] evergreen, coniferous.

résistance [rezis't|ɑ:s] *n.f.* resistance (to, *à*): *opposer une ~ acharnée*, to fight stubbornly; endurance, stamina; [Polit.] Resistance; [Fig.] *pièce de ~*, principal dish or feature. || **résistant, -e** [-ɑ̃(:t)] *adj.* rugged, resistant, tough: *couleur résistante*, fast colour. || **résister** [-e] #3 *v. intr.* to resist, to hold out against, to withstand: *~ à la tentation*, to resist temptation; *Le fort résistait encore*, The fort was still holding out; *~ à l'assaut*, to withstand the assault.

résolu [rezɔ'ly] cf. RÉSOUDRE. || **résolument** [-mɑ̃'] *adv.* resolutely, determinedly. || **résolution** [-'sjɔ̃] *n.f.* resolution, determination: *prendre la ~ de*, to resolve to; solution (of a problem); [Jur.] cancellation.

résolvais, résolve, cf. RÉSOUDRE.

résonance [rezɔ'n|ɑ̃:s] *n.f.* resonance; [Fig.] repercussion, overtone. || **résonnant, -e** [-ɑ̃(:t)] *adj.* resounding; [voix] booming. || **résonner** [rezɔ'ne] #3 *v. intr.* to resound, [sound] reverberate; [endroit] to echo, to ring.

résoudre [re'z|udr], **résolvant** [-ɔl'vɑ̃], **résolu** [-ɔ'ly], ou **résous** [-u] #55 *v. tr.* [problem] to solve; [question] to settle; to resolve, decide: *j'ai résolu de* [+ inf.] . . . , I have/

decided, resolved/to . . . || **se résoudre** (à) *v. pron.* to resolve, to decide upon [as last resort]. || **résous, résout,** cf. RÉSOUDRE.

respect [rɛs'pɛ] *n.m.* respect, regard: *manquer de ~ à qqun,* to be disrespectful to; *sauf votre ~ ,* if you'll pardon my saying so; *présenter ses respects à,* to pay o.'s respects to. || **respectabilité** [-ktabili'te] *n.f.* respectability. || **respectable** [-k'tabl] *adj.* **1.** respectable, worthy of respect. **2.** fairly large: *un nombre ~ ,* a fairly large number. || **respecter** [-k'te] #3 *v. tr.* to respect, reverence; to have regard for: *~ le sommeil de qqun,* to be careful not to disturb s.o.'s sleep. || **se respecter** *v. pron.* to have self-respect.

respecti|f, -ve [rɛspɛk't|if, -i:v] *adj.* respective. || **respectivement** [-iv'mɑ̃] *adv.* respectively.

respectueu|x, -se [rɛspɛk'tɥø(:z)] *adj.* respectful (to, *envers*): *~ des lois,* law-abiding; [obéissant], dutiful.

respiration [rɛspir|a'sjõ] *n.f.* breathing, respiration: *avoir la ~ difficile,* to breathe with difficulty; [Fam.] *Cela m'a coupé la ~ ,* That took my breath away. || **respirer** [-ɛ] #3 *v. intr.* to breathe: *n'avoir pas le temps de ~ ,* not to have time to catch o.'s breath. || *v. tr.* to express, to manifest: *Il respire la santé,* He is the picture of health.

resplendir [rɛsplɑ̃'d|i:r] #17 *v. intr.* to be resplendent (with, *de*); to shine, to glow. || **resplendissant, -e** [-i'sɑ̃(:t)] cf. RESPLENDIR. || *adj.* resplendent, shining, glowing: *être ~ de santé,* to be glowing with health.

responsabilité [rɛspõsa|bili'te] *n.f.* responsibility, accountability, liability: *avoir la ~ de qqch.,* to be responsible for sth.; *sous sa propre ~ ,* on o.'s own responsibility; *~ civile,* civil liability. || **responsable** [-bl] *adj.* responsible, accountable, liable, answerable: *Le gouvernement est ~ devant le Parlement,* The government is responsible to Parliament; *~ des dommages,* liable for the damage.

ressaisir [rəsɛ'zi:r] #17 *v. tr.* to seize again, to recover possession of sth. or s.o., to recapture. || **se ressaisir** *v. pron.* to regain o.'s self-control, to recover: *~ de qqch.,* to seize possession of sth. again.

ressemblance [rəsɑ̃'bl|ɑ̃:s] *n.f.* resemblance, likeness. || **ressemblant, -e** [-ɑ̃(:t)] cf. RESSEMBLER. || *adj.*: *C'est ~ ,* It's a good likeness. || **ressembler** [-e] #3 *v. intr.* to resemble, to look like, to be like: *Il ressemble à son père,* He looks like his father; *Cela ne lui ressemble pas,* That's not a bit like him. || **se ressembler** *v. pron.* to look alike.

ressemelage [rəsəm|'la:ʒ] *n.m.* resoling. || **ressemeler** [-'le] #8 *v. tr.* to sole, to resole.

ressens, ressent, cf. RESSENTIR.

ressentiment [rəsɑ̃ti'mɑ̃] *n.m.* resentment (at, against, *de, contre*).

ressentir [rəsɑ̃'t|i:r] #26 *v. tr.* **1.** to feel, experience (emotion, sensation, shock, &c.). **2.** to resent (insult, &c.). || **se ressentir** *v. pron.* to feel the effects (of, *de*).

resserrer [rəsɛ're] #3 *v. tr.* **1.** to draw tighter: [Fig.] *~ les liens,* to strengthen the bonds. **2.** to narrow, confine, constrict, restrict. **3.** to put away, put back. || **se resserrer** *v. pron.* to narrow, to contract.

ressors, ressort,[1] cf. RESSORTIR. [1 & 2]

ressort[2] [rə'sɔ:r] *n.m.* **1.** spring. **2.** springiness, resilience. **3.** incentive, motive. **4.** jurisdiction, competence: *Ce n'est pas de mon ~ ,* It is not within my competence; *en dernier ~ ,* as a last resort.

ressortir[1] [rəsɔr't|i:r], **ressortant** [-ɑ̃], **ressorti** [-i] [Conj. AVOIR & ÊTRE.] #26 *v. intr.* **1.** to come out again, go out again. **2.** to be evident: *faire ~ ,* to bring out, to emphasize. || *v. tr.* to take or bring out again.

ressortir[2] [-i:r], **ressortissant** [-i'sɑ̃], **ressorti** [-i] #17 *v. intr.* to be within the competence (of, *à*): *~ à une juridiction,* to come under a jurisdiction. || **ressortissant, -e** [-i'sɑ̃(:t)] || *adj.* subject (to, *à*). || *n.m.* national (of a country).

ressource [rə'surs] *n.f.* resource; resourcefulness; [plur.] resources, means: *être sans ressources,* to be penniless; *être à bout de ressources,* to be at the end of o.'s tether, to be down and out.

ressusciter [rəsysi'te] #3 *v. tr.* to restore to life, to resuscitate, to raise from the dead; [Fig.] to revive. || *v. intr.* to rise from the dead.

restant, -e [rɛs'tɑ̃(:t)] *adj.* remaining, left: *poste restante,* general delivery. || *n.m.* rest, remainder.

restaurant [rɛstɔ'r|ɑ̃] *n.m.* restaurant, café; © lunchroom.

restauration [-a'sjõ] *n.f.* restoration, restoring. || **restaurer** [-e] #3 *v. tr.* to restore; to re-establish; to refresh (s.o.). || **se restaurer** *v. pron.* to eat.

restauroute [rɛstɔ'rut] *n.m.* curb-service.

reste [rɛst] *n.m.* rest, remainder, balance; [plur.] leavings, remains: *les restes de Napoléon,* Napoleon's remains; *savoir accommoder les restes,* to know how to deal with left-overs; [Loc.] *avoir de* *l'argent de ~*, to have money to spare; *au ~, du ~*, moreover; *partir sans demander son ~*, to slink away. || **rester** [-e] #3 *v. intr.* to remain, to be left (over); to stay: *Il ne me reste qu'à partir*, The only thing left for me to do is to leave; *La situation reste critique*, → The situation is still critical.

restituer [resti|'tɥe] #3 *v. tr.* to return, to restore. || *v. intr.* © to vomit. || **restitution** [-ty'sjõ] *n.f.* restitution, return.

restreindre [rɛs'tr|ɛ̃:dr] #36 *v. tr.* to restrict, limit; to curtail, cut down (expenses, production, rights, authority). || **se restreindre** *v. pron.* to cut down expenses, to retrench; *~ à*, to limit o.s. to. || **restreint, -e** [-ɛ̃(:t)] cf. RESTREINDRE. || *adj.* restricted, limited, confined: *édition à tirage ~*, limited edition. || **restriction** [-ik'sjõ] *n.f.* restriction, limitation: *sans ~*, unreservedly; *~ mentale*, mental reservation.

résultant, -e [rezul't|ɑ̃(:t)] *adj.* resultant. || **résultat** [-a] *n.m.* result; consequence, outcome, issue: *sans ~*, vain, of no avail; *avoir pour ~ de*, to result in. || **résulter** [-e] #3 *v. intr.* [used in the 3rd person only] to result (from, *de*), follow, ensue: *Il en résulte que ...*, The result is that ..., It follows that ...

résumé [rezy'me] *n.m.* summary, summing up, abstract: *en ~*, to sum up. || **résumer** #3 *v. tr.* to summarize, to sum up.

résurrection [rezurɛk'sjõ] *n.f.* resurrection; [Fig.] revival.

rétablir [reta'bl|i:r] #17 *v. tr.* to restore. || **se rétablir** *v. pron.* to recover one's health; [Com., les affaires] to be looking up. || **rétablissement** [-is'mɑ̃] *n.m.* restoration, reinstatement; [santé] recovery.

retard [rə't|a:r] *n.m.* delay: *être en ~*, to be late, to be behind; *en ~ sur son époque*, behind the times; *avoir une heure de ~*, to be an hour late; *mettre en ~*, to make (s.o.) late. || **retardataire** [-arda'tɛ:r] *adj. & n.* tardy, late, latecomer. || **retardé, -e** [-ar'de] cf. RETARDER. || **retarder** #3 *v. tr.* to delay, make late: *Cela m'a retardé*, It delayed me; to put off; to set back: *~ la pendule d'une heure*, to set the clock back one hour. || *v. intr.* to be slow: *Ma montre retarde de cinq minutes*, My watch is five minutes slow.

retenir [rət'n|i:r] **retenu** [-y] #22 *v. tr.* **1.** to keep, to hold, to hold back. **2.** to detain: *Il est en retard parce qu'on l'a retenu*, He is late because he was detained. **3.** to note, to remember: *Retenez bien ceci*, Remember this. **4.** to retain; to reserve: *~ les services d'un avocat*, to retain a lawyer; *~ sa place*, to make o.'s reservations. || **se retenir** *v. pron.* to cling (to, *à*); to refrain (from, *de*).

retentir [rətɑ̃'t|i:r] #17 *v. intr.* to resound, ring, reverberate, re-echo (with, *de*): *La maison a retenti des cris des enfants*, The house rang with the children's shouting. || **retentissant** [-i'sa(:t)] cf. RETENTIR. || *adj.* resounding, sonorous.

retenu, -e [rət'ny] cf. RETENIR. || **retenue** *n.f.* [Compt.] deduction; [Scol.] detention; [Math.] carry-over; [morale] restraint, moderation.

réticence [reti'sɑ̃:s] *n.f.* reticence, reserve.

retiendrai, retienne, retiens, retient, cf. RETENIR.

réti|f, -ve [re't|if, -i:v] *adj.* [cheval] restive; [Fig.] stubborn.

retins cf. RETENIR.

retiré, -e [rəti're] cf. RETIRER. || *adj.* [endroit] sequestered, secluded. || **retirer** #3 *v. tr.* **1.** to withdraw, take back, pull out. **2.** to take off, to remove. **3.** [Fig.] to derive: *Les avantages qu'il en a retirés ...*, The benefits he derived from it ... || **se retirer** *v. pron.* to withdraw, to retire: *L'ennemi s'est retiré*, The enemy withdrew; *~ des affaires*, to retire from business; *~ dans sa chambre*, to retire to o.'s room.

retombée [rətõ'be] *n.f.* [draperies] fall; [Phys.]: *retombées radio-actives*, fall-out. || **retomber** [rətõ'be] #3 *v. intr.* conj. ÊTRE. **1.** to fall (down) again. **2.** to hang (down), come down (over, *sur*). **3.** [Fig.] to relapse, to sink back: *~ dans les mêmes errements*, to relapse into the same old ways; *~ dans l'oubli*, to sink back into oblivion; *~ sur ses pieds*, to land on o.'s feet.

retors, -e [rət|ɔ:r, -ɔrs] *adj.* twisted; [Fig.] wily, crafty.

retoucher [rətu'ʃe] #3 *v. tr.* to touch up.

retour [rə't|u:r] *n.m.* **1.** return: *par ~ du courrier*, by return mail; *être de ~*, to be back; *payer de ~*, to return a favour. **2.** turn, bend, angle: *en ~ d'équerre*, at right angles. **3.** reversal, vicissitude: *un ~ d'opinion*, a reversal of opinion. || **retourner** [-ur'ne] #3 *v. intr.* [conj. AVOIR & ÊTRE.] to go again, go back, return. || *v. tr.* **1.** to send back, return. **2.** to turn over, turn out: *~ ses poches*, to turn out o.'s pockets. || **se retourner** *v. pron.* to turn around, look back; [Fig.] *Je n'ai pas le temps de me retourner*, I don't know whether I am coming or going; ~ *contre qqun*, to turn against s.o.

retracer [rətra'se] #4 *v. tr.* **1.** to draw again. **2.** to relate; to locate.

rétracter [retrak'te] #3 *v. tr.* to take back, to withdraw. || se **rétracter** *v. pron.* to retract, to eat o.'s words.

retrait [rə'trɛ] *n.m.* [matériaux] shrinking; [marée] running out; [banque] withdrawal, drawing out (of funds): *en* ~ , [*Loc. adv.*] set back from.

retraite [rə'trɛt] *n.f.* **1.** retreat, withdrawal; [défilé] tattoo: *battre en* ~ , to retreat; *couper la* ~ *à qqun*, to cut off s o.'s retreat. **2.** retirement, pension: *prendre sa* ~ , to retire; *toucher sa* ~ , to draw o.'s pension; *en* ~ , retired. **3.** [Cath.] retreat. || **retraité, -e** [-e] *adj.* pensioned off. || *n.* pensioner.

retranchement [rətrɑ̃ʃ|'mɑ̃] *n.m.* **1.** [Mil.] retrenchment, entrenchment. **2.** retrenchment, curtailment. || **retrancher** [-e] #3 *v. tr.* to reduce, to retrench. || **se retrancher** *v. pron.* to entrench o.s., to dig o.s. in.

rétréci, -e [retre's|i:r] cf. RÉTRÉCIR. || *adj.* shrunk. || **rétrécir** [-i] #17 *v. tr. & intr.* to make narrower, to narrow: *faire* ~ , to shrink. || **se rétrécir** *v. pron.* [tissu] to shrink; [espace] to narrow, to get narrower. || **rétrécissement** [-is'mɑ̃] *n.m.* [tissu] shrinking; [space] narrowing, narrowness.

rétribuer [retri'b|ɥe] #3 *v. tr.* to pay, remunerate, reward: *bien rétribué*, well paid. || **rétribution** [-y'sjõ] *n.f.* payment, compensation, remuneration.

rétroacti|f, -ve [retroak't|if, -i:v] *adj.* retroactive.

rétrograde [retrɔ|'grad] *adj.* retrograde, backward. || **rétrospecti|f, -ve** [-spɛk't|if, -i:v] *adj.* retrospective.

retrousser [rətru'se] #3 *v. tr.* to roll or turn up: ~ *ses manches*, to roll up o.'s sleeves; ~ *la lèvre*, to curl o.'s lip; ~ *sa jupe*, to /tuck, pull/up o.'s skirt; *nez retroussé*, snub, turned-up nose.

retrouver [rətru've] #3 *v. tr.* **1.** to find again. **2.** to meet again: *Je vous retrouverai devant la poste*, I'll meet you outside the post office. || **se retrouver** *v. pron.* **1.** to find o.s. again; to find o.'s way. **2.** to meet again.

rétroviseur [retrɔvi'zœ:r] *n.m.* rear-view mirror.

réuni, -e [rey'n|i] cf. RÉUNIR. || **réunion** [-jõ] *n.f.* **1.** meeting, gathering. **2.** bringing or joining together. **3.** reunion. || **réunir** [-i:r] #17 *v. tr.* to join, unite, bring together, convene, collect: ~ *le comité*, to call the committee together; ~ *le Parlement*, to convene Parliament; ~ *des fonds*, to raise funds. || **se réunir** *v. pron.* to meet, to come together.

réussi, -e [rey's|i] cf. RÉUSSIR. || *adj.* successful. || **réussir** [-i:r] #17 *v. intr.* to succeed (in, *à*); to be successful, to thrive: ~ *à un examen*, to pass an examination; *ne pas* ~ *à un examen*, to fail an examination; *Cela lui réussit*, He thrives on it; *Puissiez-vous* ~ *!*, More power to you! || *v. tr.* to perform successfully: *Il réussit très bien les mots croisés*, He is very good at crossword puzzles. || **réussite** [-it] *n.f.* **1.** success: *calculer les chances de* ~ , to figure out the odds. **2.** [jeu] solitaire, patience: *faire une* ~ , to play a game of solitaire.

revanche [rə'vɑ̃:ʃ] *n.f.* revenge: *prendre sa* ~ , to get even (with, *sur*); *en* ~ , on the other hand.

rêve [rɛ:v] *n.m.* dream: *faire de beaux rêves*, to have pleasant dreams; *C'est le* ~ *!*, It's perfect!

revêche [rə'vɛ:ʃ] *adj.* sullen, crabbed.

revécus, &c. cf. REVIVRE.

réveil [re'v|ɛ:j] *n.m.* **1.** awakening, waking up: *dès son* ~ , as soon as he wakes up; *Le* ~ *a été rude*, It was a rude awakening. **2.** alarm clock. || **réveille-matin** [-ɛjma'tɛ̃] *n.m. inv.* alarm clock. || **réveiller** [-ɛ'je] #3 *v. tr.* to awake; to awaken; to wake up, to rouse, to arouse; to revive. || **se réveiller** *v. pron.* to awake; to wake up. || **réveillon** [-ɛ'j|õ] *n.m.* midnight supper on Christmas Eve or New Year's Eve. || **réveillonner** [-ɔ'ne] #3 *v. intr.* to have late supper on Christmas or New Year's Eve.

révélat|eur, -rice [revel|a'tœ:r, -a'tris] *adj.* revealing, telltale. || **révélation** [-a'sjõ] *n.f.* revelation, disclosure: *Quelle* ~ *!*, What an eye-opener! || **révéler** [-e] #10 *v. tr.* to reveal, disclose; [Fig.] to show, display. || **se révéler** *v. pron.* [pers.] to show, reveal o.s. (as); [fait] to come out.

revenant [rəv'nɑ̃(:t)] *n.* ghost.

revendication [rəvɑ̃dik|a'sjõ] *n.f.* claim, demand: *les revendications de la Chine*, the Chinese claims. || **revendiquer** [-e] #3 *v. tr.* to claim, lay claim to, to insist on.

revenir [rəv'n|i:r], **revenu** [-y] #22 *v. intr.* conj. ÊTRE. **1.** to come back, come again, to return, to recur: *On ne peut pas* ~ *en arrière*, There is no turning the clock back. **2.** to amount (to, *à*): *Cela revient à dix dollars*, It costs ten dollars. **3.** to suit, to please: *Il a un genre qui ne me revient pas* I don't care for his manner. **4.** to recover (from, *de*): *Il n'en est pas encore revenu*, He has not got over it yet.

revenu [rəv'ny] *n.m.* income, [État] revenue: *impôt sur le* ~, income tax; *Il dépense plus que son* ~, He lives beyond his means.

rêver [rɛ've] #3 *v. tr. & intr.* **1.** [en dormant] to dream (of, *à*). **2.** [éveillé] to dream; to muse, to daydream: *Vous rêvez!*, You must be out of your mind.

réverbération [revɛrbera'sjõ] *n.f.* reverberation.

†**réverbère** [revɛrb|ɛ:r] *n.m.* street lamp. || **réverbérer** [-e're] #10 *v. tr.* to reflect, to reverberate.

révérence [reve'r|ɑ̃:s] *n.f.* **1.** reverence. **2.** bow, curtsy: *faire la* ~, to curtsy; *tirer sa* ~, to make o.'s bow. || **révérencieu|x, -se** [-ɑ̃'sjø(:z)] *adj.* reverent, respectful. || **révérend, -e** [-ɑ̃(:d)] *adj.* reverend.

révérer [reve're] #10 *v. tr.* to revere, to reverence; to respect.

rêverie [rɛv'ri] *n.f.* daydreaming, musing, reverie.

revers [rə'vɛ:r] *n.m.* reverse (side); [veston] lapel; [main] back; [médaille] obverse; [Sport] backhand; [Fig.] reverse, setback.

reverser [rəvɛr'se] #3 *v. tr.* to pour back; to pay back.

revêtement [rəvɛt|'mɑ̃] *n.m.* surfacing, facing, revetment: *mur de* ~, retaining wall.

revêtir [-i:r] #42 *v. tr.* to put on, to deck o.s. with: *revêtu de ses habits du dimanche*, all decked out; [Fig.] *revêtu de sa signature*, bearing his signature.

rêveu|r, -se [rɛ'v|œ:r, -ø:z] *adj.* dreamy, musing: *d'un air* ~, with a dreamy look. || *n.m.* **dreamer, daydreamer.**

revient[1] [rə vjɛ̃] cf. REVENIR.

revient[2] *n.m.*: *prix m de* ~, cost price, manufacturing cost.

revis,[1] **revit,**[1] **&c.** cf. REVIVRE.

revis,[2] **revit.**[2] **&c.** cf. REVOIR.

reviser, réviser [rəvi'z|e], [revi'z|e] #3 *v. tr.* to revise; [moteur] to overhaul. || **revision, révision** [-jõ] *n.f.* revision; [Scol. & Jur.] review; [Méc.] overhauling: [Mil.] *Conseil de* ~, medical board for inducted men.

revivais, revive, cf. REVIVRE. || **revivre** [rəv|i:vr] **revivant** [-i'vɑ̃] **revécu** [-e'ky] #52 *v. intr.* to live again; [Fig.] to revive: *se sentir* ~, to feel a new man.

revoie, &c.; revois; revoit cf. REVOIR. || **revoir** [rə'vwa:r] *n.m.*: *au* ~, goodbye for now, [Fam.] see you later. || **revoir** [rə'v|wa:r] **revoyant** [-wa'jɑ̃] **revu** [-y] #32 *v. tr.* **1.** to see again, to meet again, to revisit. **2.** to look over again, to review, to revise: ~ *ses notes*, to review o.'s notes; *entièrement revu et corrigé*, completely revised. || **se revoir** *v. pron.* to see, meet . . ./again.

révoltant, -e [revɔl'tɑ̃(:t)] *adj.* revolting; shocking. || **révolte** [re'vɔlt] *n.f.* revolt, rebellion. || **révolté, -e** [-e] *n.* rebel. || **révolter** #3 *v. tr.* to rouse, excite; to make s.o. rebel; [Fig.] to shock. || **se révolter** *v. pron.* to rebel, rise (against); [Fig.] to be shocked (at, *devant*).

révolu, -e [revɔ'ly] *adj.* accomplished, completed: *avoir 21 ans révolus*, to be over 21.

révolution [-'sjõ] *n.f.* revolution; [mouvement] rotation. || **révolutionnaire** [-sjɔ'nɛ:r] *adj.* revolutionary; [Fig.] amazing, new. || *n.m.* revolutionist. || **révolutionner** [-'sjɔ'ne] #3 *v. tr.* to revolutionize, change completely.

revolver [revɔl'vɛ:r] *n.m.* revolver, gun: *poche f* ~, hip pocket.

révoquer [revɔ'ke] #3 *v. tr.* [ordre] to revoke, countermand; [fonctionnaire] to dismiss.

revoyais, revoyez, &c. cf. REVOIR.

revu, -e cf. REVOIR. || **revue** [rə'vy] *n.f.* **1.** review: *faire la* ~ *de*, to inspect, look over (papers, &c.); *passer des troupes en* ~, → to review. **2.** [périodique] review; [périodique scientifique] journal; [critique] review; [Théât.] musical comedy.

rez-de-chaussée [redʃo'se] *n.m. inv.* ground, main floor: *au* ~, on the/main floor, [©, US] first floor.

rhabiller [rabi'je] #3 *v. tr.* to dress . . . again; [Tech.] to repair. || **se rhabiller** *v. pron.* to get dressed again; to change, dress (for dinner).

rhapsodie [rapsɔ'di] *n.f.* rhapsody.

rhénan, -e [re'n|ɑ̃, -an] *adj.* Rhenish, (of the) Rhine. || **Rhénanie, la** [-a'ni] *n.f.* Rhineland. *cf.* RHIN.

rhétorique [retɔ'rik] *n.f.* rhetoric; © [collège] sophomore year.

Rhin, le [(lə)rɛ̃] *n.m.* the Rhine (river).

rhinocéros [rinɔse'rɔs] *n.m. inv.* rhinoceros.

Rhode-Island, le [(lə)rɔdaj'land] *n.m.* [Géog., U.S.] Rhode Island.

Rhodésie, la [(la)rɔde'zi] *n.f.* Rhodesia: *la* ~ */du Nord, du Sud/*, Northern, Southern/Rhodesia.

Rhône, le [(lə)ro:n] *n.m.* The Rhone (river).

rhubarbe [ry'barb] *n.f.* rhubarb.

rhum [rɔm] *n.m.* rum.

rhumatisme [ryma'tism] *n.m.* rheumatism.

rhume [rym] *n.m.* cold (in the head): ~ *des foins*, hay fever.

ri [ri] cf. RIRE. || **riant, -e** [-'ɑ̃(:t)] *adj.*

laughing, smiling: *Il l'a dit en* ~, He said it for fun [= pour rire]; [spectacle] pleasant, cheerful.

ribambelle [ribɑ̃'bɛl] *n.f.* [Fam.] long string (of insults, &c.); swarm (of children).

ricanement [rikan|'mɑ̃] *n.m.* sneer. || **ricaner** [-e] #3 *v. intr.* to sneer, snigger.

richard [ri'ʃa:r] *n.m.* [Fam., Péj.] money-bags. || **riche** [riʃ] *adj.* rich (in, *en*), wealthy; [Fig.] abundant, plentiful; [sol] fertile. || *n.m.* rich man; *les riches*, the rich.

Richelieu, le [(lə)riʃə'ljø] *n.m.* [P.Q.] the Richelieu (river).

richement [riʃ|'mɑ̃] *adv.* richly. || **richesse** [-ɛs] *n.f.* riches, wealth; [Fig.] richness, copiousness; *les richesses* (*d'un pays*), natural resources. || **richissime** [-i'sim] *adj.* rolling in money.

ricin [ri'sɛ̃] *n.m.* castor-oil plant, bean: *huile f de* ~, castor oil.

ricocher [rikɔ'ʃ|e] #3 *v. intr.* to ricochet; [Fig.] to rebound. || **ricochet** [-ɛ] *n.m.* ricochet, ducks and drakes; *faire des ricochets*, to skip (stones); [Fig.] *par* ~, indirectly.

ride [rid] *n.f.* wrinkle (on face); ripple (on water, sand). || **ridé, -e** [-e] *adj.* wrinkled; rippling.

rideau [ri'do] *n.m.* curtain; [écran] screen: ~ *de fumée*, smoke screen; ~ *d'arbres*, line of trees; [Théât., Polit.] ~ *de fer*, iron curtain; *baisser le* ~, to drop the curtain.

rider [ri'de] #3 *v. tr.* to wrinkle; [eau] to ripple. || **se rider** *v. pron.* to get wrinkled; to shrivel up.

ridicule [ridi'kyl] *adj.* ridiculous; absurd, ludicrous. || *n.m.* ridicule; ridiculousness: *tourner . . . en* ~, to ridicule; *les ridicules* (*d'une société*), foibles. || **ridiculiser** [-i'ze] #3 *v. tr.* to ridicule.

rie [ri] cf. RIRE.

rien [rjɛ̃] *adv.* anything, nothing: *Il n'a* ~ *dit*, He said nothing, He did not say anything; *Je n'y suis pour* ~, I have nothing to do with this; ~ *du tout*, nothing at all; ~ *de neuf*, nothing new; *ne faire semblant de* ~, to look unconcerned, not to seem to mind; *comme si de* ~ *n'était*, as if everything was all right; *se trouver sans* ~ *à faire*, to be at a loose end. || *n.m.* trifle, mere nothing: *pour un* ~, for a trifle; *Il se fâche pour un* ~, The least thing makes him angry; *en un* ~ *de temps*, in no time at all.

rieu|r, -se [rjœ:r, rjø:z] *adj.* laughing, joking. || *n.m.* laugher, mocker.

rigide [ri'ʒid] *adj.* **1.** rigid; [droit] erect; [durci] stiff, taut. **2.** [Fig., sens moral] strict, severe, unbending. || **rigidité** [-i'te] *n.f.* rigidity, rigidness; stiffness; strictness.

rigolade [rigɔ'l|ad] *n.f.* [Fam.] good time, good laugh; fun; buffoonery.

rigole [ri'gɔl] *n.f.* (small) ditch, drain.

rigoler [rigɔ'le] #3 *v. intr.* [Fam., esp. Fr.] to laugh (heartily); to have a good time, to have great fun. || **rigolo** [-o] *adj.* [Fam.] jolly, funny.

rigoureusement [rig|urøz'mɑ̃] *adv.* rigorously; strictly, exactly. || **rigoureu|x, -se** [-u'rø(:z)] *adj.* rigorous, strict; [Fig.] hard, severe: *un hiver* ~, a severe winter. || **rigueur** [-œ:r] *n.f.* **1.** [précision] rigour, exactness: *à la* ~, strictly speaking; if necessary, at a pinch. **2.** [Fig.] severity, sternness; sharpness, inclemency: *de* ~, strictly enforced, de rigueur; *tenir* ~ *à qqun*, to refuse to forgive s.o.

rime [rim] *n.f.* rhyme; [Fig.] verse. || **rimer** [-e] #3 *v. tr. & intr.* to rhyme; to write poetry.

rinçage [rɛ̃'s|a:ʒ] *n.m.* rinsing. || **rinçai(s)** cf. RINCER. || **rincer** [-e] #4 *v. tr.* to rinse (out), to wash; [verres] to swill.

Rio de la Plata [riodəlapla'ta] *n.m.* the River Plate.

riposte [ri'pɔst] *n.f.* repartee, retort. || **riposter** [-e] #3 *v. intr.* to answer, retort.

rire [ri:r] **riant** [ri'ɑ̃] **ri** [ri] #50 *v. intr.* **1.** to laugh: *se mettre à* ~, to laugh; *éclater de* ~, to burst out laughing; ~ *aux éclats*, to roar with laughter; ~ *aux larmes*, to laugh till one cries; ~ */jaune, du bout des lèvres*, to force a laugh; ~ *tout bas*, to titter. || **2.** [Fig.] to laugh, smile: *pour* ~, for fun; *Il n'y a pas de quoi* ~, This is no laughing matter; *se* ~ *de qqun*, to laugh at s.o. || *n.m.* laugh(ter); laughing.

ris[1] [ri] *n.m.* sweetbread: ~ *de veau*, calf's sweetbread.

ris[2] [ri] cf. RIRE. || †*n.mpl.* laughter. || **risée** [-'ze] *n.f.* **1.** laugh(ter); [Fig.] derision, mockery: *être la* ~ *de*, to be the laughingstock of. **2.** [Naut.] gust, squall (of wind). || **risette** [-'zɛt] *n.f.* pretty smile: *faire* ~ *à*, to smile sweetly at. || **risible** [-'zibl] *adj.* laughable; [pers.] ridiculous.

risque [risk] *n.m.* risk, danger: *courir le* ~ *de*, to run the risk of [+ *-ing*]; *à ses risques et périls*, at one's own risk; *à tout* ~, at all hazards; [Assur., &c.] risk. || **risque-tout** [-ə'tu] *n.m. inv.* dare-devil. || **risquer** [-e] #3 *v. tr.* to risk, venture (one's life, &c.): ~ *le tout pour le tout*, It's neck or nothing. || *v. intr.* ~ *de*, to run the risk of.

rissoler [risɔ'le] #3 *v. tr.* [Culin.] to brown.

ristourne [ris'turn] *n.f.* rebate, return; refund.

rite [rit] *n.m.* rite; ritual, ceremony. || **rituel, -le** [-ɥɛl] *adj.* ritual; traditional.

rivage [ri'va:ʒ] *n.m.* [lac, mer] shore, strand.

rival, -e [ri'val] *adj. & n.* rival. || *n.* rival, competitor. || **rivaliser** [-i'ze] #3 *v. intr.* to rival (in, *de*); to compete with. || **rivalité** [-i'te] *n.f.* rivalry; competition.

rive [ri:v] *n.f.* [lac, mer] shore; [rivière] bank.

river [ri've] #3 *v. tr.* to rivet; [Tech. & Fig.] to clench.

riverain, -e [riv|'rɛ̃, -'rɛn] *adj.* riverside. || *n.* riverside, lakeshore/resident. || **rivière** [-jɛ:r] *n.f.* river, stream; [diamants] necklace; © (large) river = [Fr. FLEUVE]; *la Rivière (à) la Paix*, Peace River; *la Rivière des Prairies*, the Back River (Que.).

riz [ri] *n.m.* rice. || **rizière** [-'zjɛ:r] *n.f.* rice /field, paddy/.

robe [rɔb] *n.f.* dress; [habillée] gown; [de professeur] gown; †robe; [animal] coat: ~ *d'intérieur*, housecoat; ~ *de chambre*, dressing gown.

robine [rɔ'bin] © *n.f.* [Fam.] moonshine.

robinet [rɔbi'nɛ] *n.m.* faucet; tap: *fermer, ouvrir/un* ~, to turn/off, on/a faucet.

robineux [rɔbi'nø] © [Fam.] *n.m.* moonshiner.

robuste [rɔ'byst] *adj.* strong, robust; sturdy. || **robustesse** [-ɛs] *n.f.* strength, robustness; sturdiness.

roc [rɔk] *n.m.* [large mass of stone] rock. || **rocaille** [-a:j] © *n.f.* rock garden. || **rocailleu|x, -se** [-a'jø(:z)] *adj.* rocky, stony; [Fig.] harsh.

roche [rɔʃ] *n.f.* [×] **1.** [mass of rock] rock. **2.** [large stone] boulder; © [piece of stone] rock, stone: © *tirer des roches*, to throw rocks, cf. GARROCHER. || **rocher** [-e] *n.m.* [large mass of stone, in landscape] rock, crag. || **rocheu|x, -se** [-ø(:z)] *adj.* rocky, stony: *les (Montagnes) Rocheuses fpl.*, the Rocky Mountains, the Rockies.

rodage [rɔ'd|a:ʒ] *n.m.* [Auto.] breaking-in (of motor); *en* ~, "new car." || **roder** [-e] #3 *v. tr.* [Auto.] to break in (motor).

rôder [ro'd|e] #3 *v. intr.* to prowl, lurk. || **rôdeur** [-œ:r] *n.m.* prowler, vagrant.

Rogations (les) [(le) rɔga'sjõ] *n.fpl.* [Cath.] Rogations.

Roger-bontemps [rɔʒebõ'tã] *adj. & n.m. inv.* © happy-go-lucky (fellow).

rogner [rɔ'ɲe] #3 *v. tr.* to pare (nails), to trim (paper); [Fig.] to curtail.

rognon [rɔ'ɲõ] *n.m.* [Culin.] kidney. cf. REIN.

roi [rwa] *n.m.* king; [Rel.] *le Jour des Rois*, Twelfth Night.

†roide ☞ Stylistic variant of RAIDE.

roitelet [rwat'lɛ] *n.m.* [petit roi] kinglet; [oiseau] wren.

rôle [ro:l] *n.m.* **1.** [Théât., &c.] part: *jouer le* ~ *de*, to act the part of . . .; [Fig.] role, character: *jouer un* ~, to play a role. **2.** roster; [d'équipage] muster roll; *à tour de* ~, in turn, by turns.

romain, -e [rɔm|ɛ̃, -ɛn] *adj. & n.* [of, from Rome] Roman: *chiffre* ~, Roman numeral.

roman,[1] **-e** [-ã, -an] *adj.* **1.** [Ling.] Romance: *Le français est une langue romane*, French is a Romance language. **2.** [Arch.] romanesque [×]: *une église romane*, a romanesque church.

roman,[2] novel: ~ *policier*, detective story; [coll.] *romans*, fiction.

romance [-ã:s] *n.f.* [×] song.

romanci|er, -ère [-ã'sj|e, -ɛ:r] *n.* novelist.

romand, -e [-ã(:d)] *adj.*: *Suisse romande*, French (-speaking) Switzerland.

romanesque [-a'nɛsk] *adj.* romantic, imaginative. || **romantique** [-ã'tik] *adj. & n.* Romantic [Art, littérature]. || **romantisme** [-ã'tism] *n.m.* Romanticism (Art, littérature).

rompe, romps, rompt, cf. ROMPRE.

rompre [rõ:pr], **rompant** [rõ'p|ã], **rompu** [-y] #52A *v. tr.* to break, to burst: *Les eaux rompirent les digues*, The waters broke through the dams; ~ *les relations diplomatiques*, to break off diplomatic relations; ~ *l'enchantement*, to break the spell; ~ *un traité*, to break a treaty; *On l'a applaudi à tout* ~, He brought down the house. || *v. intr.* to break off (with, *avec.*) || **se rompre** *v. pron.* to break, to snap, to collapse. || **rompu, -e** [-y] cf. ROMPRE. || *adj.* **1.** broken: *à bâtons rompus*, desultory; desultorily. **2.** tired out. **3.** experienced, trained (in, *à*): ~ *aux affaires*, experienced in business.

ronce [rõ:s] *n.f.* bramble; *ronce(s) artificielle(s)*, barbed wire [also (*fil de fer*) *barbelé*].

rond, -e [rõ(:d)] *adj.* **1.** round. **2.** [Fig.] direct, straightforward: *Il est* ~ *en affaires*, He goes straight to the point. || *n.m.* ring, circle: ~ *de serviette*, napkin ring; ~ *de cuir*, [Fig.] clerk, pen-pusher; *tourner en* ~, to go round in circles; *Cela ne tourne pas* ~, It is not working smoothly. || **ronde** [rõ:d] *n.f.* round: *l'agent qui fait sa* ~, the policeman on his beat; round dance; radius: *à dix lieues à la* ~ for twenty-five miles around. || **rondelet, -te** [rõd'lɛ(t)] *adj.* plump; [Fig.]: *Il s'est fait une somme rondelette,* He made a tidy little sum. || **rondelle** [rõ'dɛl] *n.f.* small round slice or disc: ~ *de robinet,* washer; © [Sport] puck. || **rondement** [rõd|'mɑ̃] *adv.* roundly, briskly: *Il a mené la chose* ~, He made short work of it; *parler* ~, to be blunt. || **rondeur** [-œ:r] *n.f.* **1.** roundness, rotundity, fulness. **2.** [Fig.] frankness, directness. || **rondin** [rõ'dɛ̃] *n.m.* round log or bar: *cabane en* ~, log cabin. || **rond-point** [rõ'pwɛ̃] *pl.* **ronds-points** *n.m.* circular intersection, (traffic) circle; [Br.] circus.

ronflement [rõfl|ə'mɑ̃] *n.m.* **1.** snore, snoring. **2.** [Fig.] whirring, buzz, hum.

ronfler [-e] #3 *v. intr.* **1.** to snore. **2.** [Fig.] to hum, to whir: [Fam.] *Ça ronfle!*, Things are humming.

ronger [rõ|'ʒe] #5 *v. tr.* to gnaw (at); to corrode: *se* ~ *les ongles,* to chew o.'s nails; ~ *son frein,* to champ at the bit; *La jalousie le ronge,* He is consumed with jealousy. || **se ronger** *v. pron.* to fret. || **rongeur** [-'ʒœ:r] *n.m.* rodent.

ronronnement [rõrɔn|'mɑ̃] *n.m.* **1.** [chat] purr, purring. **2.** [Fig.] purr(ing); hum, drone. || **ronronner** [-e] #3 *v. intr.* **1.** [chat] to purr. **2.** [Fig.] to purr, to hum, to drone.

roquette [rɔ'kɛt] *n.f.* [Mil.] rocket.

rosace [ro'zas] *n.f.* rose window.

rosaire [ro'zɛ:r] *n.m.* rosary.

rosbif [rɔs'bif] [Fr.] *n.m.* roast beef.

rose [ro:z] *n.f.* rose: ~ *trémière,* hollyhock.

rose *adj.* pink: *voir la vie en* ~, to see life through rose-coloured glasses; *Tout n'est pas* ~ *dans la vie,* Life is not all beer and skittles, Life is not all a bed of roses. || **rosé, -e** [ro'ze] *adj.* rosy, rose-coloured: *vin* ~, rosy wine.

roseau [ro'zo] *n.m.* reed.

rosée [ro'ze] *n.f.* dew: *goutte de* ~, dewdrop.

rosette [ro'zɛt] *n.f.* small rose; rosette, bow: *la* ~ *de la Légion d'honneur,* the rosette of the Legion of Honour.

rosier [ro'zje] *n.m.* rosebush. || **rosier églantier** *n.m.* sweetbrier.

rosse [rɔs] *adj.* [Fam.] nasty, beastly, very strict: *une comédie* ~, a cynical play. || *n.f.* nasty person, [Argot] stinker, slavedriver: *C'est une petite* ~, She's a little beast. || **rosser** #3 *v. tr.* to beat up.

rossignol [rɔsi'ɲɔl] *n.m.* **1.** nightingale. **2.** skeleton key. **3.** piece of junk.

rôti, -e [ro't|i] cf. RÔTIR. || *n.m.* roast. || **rôtie** *n.f.* piece of toast: ~ *à l'anglaise,* Welsh rarebit (or rabbit). || **rôtir** [-i:r] #17 *v. tr. & intr.* **1.** [viande] to toast. **2.** [pain] to toast. || **se rôtir** *v. pron.* [Fig.] *se* ~ *devant le feu,* to toast o.s. by the fire. || **rôtisserie** [-is'ri] *n.f.* grillroom, barbecue.

rouage [rwa:ʒ] *n.m.* wheels, wheelwork; [Fig.] cog: *n'être qu'un* ~, to be just a cog.

roublard, -e [ru'bl|a:r, -ard] *adj.* cunning, crafty, astute. || *n.m. & f.* wily person.

roucoulement [rukul'mɑ̃] *n.m.* cooing. || **roucouler** [-e] #3 *v. intr.* to coo.

roue [ru] *n.f.* wheel: *cinquième* ~ *à un carrosse,* useless person; *faire la* ~, to strut, to show off; ~ *libre,* freewheel; *Il m'a mis des bâtons dans les roues,* He put a spoke in my wheel.

rouge [ru:ʒ] *adj.* red: *voir* ~, [Fam.] to see red; *se fâcher tout* ~, to lose one's temper; *les habits rouges,* the redcoats; *la Rivière* ~, Red River. || *n.m.* red: *chauffé au* ~, red hot. || **rougeâtre** [ru'ʒ|ɑ:tr] *adj.* reddish. || **rougeaud, -e** [-o] *adj.* red-faced. || *n.m.* red-faced, ruddy-faced/person. || **rouge-gorge** [ruʒ'gɔrʒ] *n.m.* robin (redbreast).

rougeole [ru'ʒɔl] *n.f.* measles.

rougeur [ru'ʒ|œ:r] *n.f.* redness; [du visage] blush, flush; [*pl.*] red blotches. || **rougi, -e,** cf. ROUGIR || *adj.*: *eau rougie,* wine diluted with water; *les mains rougies par le froid,* his hands red with cold. || **rougir** [-i:r] #17 *v. tr.* to turn sth. red, to redden. || *v. intr.* to redden; [visage] to blush, to flush. || **rougissant, -e** [-i'sɑ̃(:t)] *adj.* [Fig.] blushing, flushing; reddening, turning red.

rouille [ruj] *n.f.* rust, rustiness: *tache de* ~, rust stain. || **rouiller** [-e] #3 *v. tr.* **1.** [métal) to rust, to make rusty. **2.** [plante] to mildew, to blight. || *v. intr.* to rust, to get rusty. || **se rouiller** *v. pron.* to rust, to get rusty; [Fig.] to get rusty, to get out of practice.

roulade [ru'lad] *n.f.* [Mus.] roulade, run; [oiseau] trill.

roulant, -e [ru'lɑ̃] *adj.* rolling: *escalier m* ~, escalator; [chemin] good; [Rail.] *matériel* ~, rolling stock; [Fam.] killing, funny.

rouleau [ru'lo] *n.m.* roller; [de papier] roll; [de film] spool; [Culin.] rolling pin. || **roulement** [rul|'mɑ̃] *n.m.* **1.** roll, rolling, running: ~ *à billes,* ball bearing. **2.** rotation: *par* ~, in rotation. **3.** rattle, clatter. || **rouler** [-e] #3 *v. tr.* to roll, to wheel; [Fam.] to cheat; [Loc.] ~ *carrosse,* to live in great style. || *v. intr.* to roll (up,

down, along): *Cette voiture a beaucoup roulé,* This car has a lot of mileage. || **se rouler** *v. pron.* to roll.
roulier [ru'lje] *n.m.* teamster.
roulis [ru'li] *n.m.* [Naut.] roll(ing).
roulotte [ru'lɔt] *n.f.* trailer, house on wheels, [Br.] caravan.
Roumanie [ruma'ni] *n.f.* Rumania.
rousse [rus] cf. ROUX. || *n.f.* red-haired woman, redhead; [Fr., Slang] the police. || **rousseur** [-œ:r] *n.f.*: *tache de* ~, freckle.
roussin [ru'sɛ̃] *n.m.* **1.** cob. **2.** police spy.
roussir [-i:r] #17 *v. tr.* to brown; [cheveux] to singe; [linge] to scorch.
route [rut] *n.f.* road, way, route: *en* ~, on the way; *se mettre en* ~, to set out, to start out; *grand-route,* highway; *faire fausse* ~, to go astray, to be on the wrong track; *faire* ~ *avec qqun,* to travel with s.o.; *barrer la* ~, to block the way; *la Route transcanadienne,* Trans-Canada Highway. || **routi|er, -ère** [-'tj|e, -ɛ:r] *adj.* → road: *circulation routière,* road traffic; *carte routière,* road map; *transports routiers,* road transport, trucking. || **routier** *n.m.* [scout] rover; truckman: *un vieux* ~, an old campaigner.
routine [ru'tin] *n.f.* refusal to change: *être l'esclave de la* ~, to be set in one's ways, to do things by rote. || **routini|er, -ère** [-j|e, -ɛ:r] *adj.* [Fam.] stick-in-the-mud.
rouvert [ru'v|ɛ:r] cf. ROUVRIR. || **rouvrir** [-ri:r] #25 *v. tr.* to open again, to reopen. || **se rouvrir** *v. pron.* to open again, to reopen.
rou|x, -sse [ru(s)] *adj.* reddish brown, russet; [cheveux] red, auburn; [beurre] brown. || *n.m.* red-haired person; brown sauce. cf. ROUSSE.
royal, -e [rwa'jal] *adj.* royal, regal, kingly. || **royaliste** [-ist] *adj.* & *n.m.* & *f.* royalist. || **royaume** [rwa'j|o:m] *n.m.* kingdom; realm: *le Royaume-Uni,* the United Kingdom; *le* ~ *des cieux,* the kingdom of heaven. || **royauté** [-o'te] *n.f.* monarchy: *sous la* ~, under the kings; royalty.
RSVP [= Répondez, s'il vous plaît], RSVP.
ruade [rɥad] *n.f.* kick (of a horse): *lancer une* ~ *à,* to kick at, [Fig.] to hit out at.
ruban [ry'bɑ̃] *n.m.* **1.** ribbon, band, tape: *gagner le* ~ *bleu,* to win the blue ribbon; ~ *de chapeau,* hatband; ~ *magnétique,* magnetic tape. **2.** measuring tape, tape measure.
rubis [ry'bi] *n.m.* ruby: *payer* ~ *sur l'ongle,* [Fam.] to pay on the nail; *montre montée sur* ~, jewelled watch.
ruche [ryʃ] *n.f.* beehive; [Fig.] hive.
rude [ryd] *adj.* rough, rugged, uncouth; severe, hard, dreary: *L'année a été* ~, The year was hard; *mettre à une* ~ *épreuve,* to test severely; *de rudes combats,* severe fighting; *une voix* ~, a gruff voice. || **rudement** [-'mɑ̃] *adv.* roughly, harshly, hard; [Fam.] extremely: *C'est* ~ *bon,* [Fam.] It's awfully good. || **rudesse** [-ɛs] *n.f.* roughness, uncouthness; severity; harshness, gruffness: *traiter avec* ~, to bully.
rudiment [rydi'mɑ̃] *n.m.* rudiment, element. || **rudimentaire** [-'tɛ:r] *adj.* elementary.
rudoiement [rydwa|'mɑ̃] *n.m.* bullying. || **rudoyer** [-'je] #12 *v. tr.* to browbeat.
rue [ry] *n.f.* street; road: ~ *barrée,* no thoroughfare, closed for repairs; *demeurer, habiter/rue Principale,* to live on Main Street; *l'homme de la* ~, the man in the street.
ruée [rɥe] *n.f.* rush, onrush, surge: [Hist.] *la* ~ *vers l'or,* the Gold Rush.
ruelle [rɥɛl] *n.f.* lane, alley; © back street.
ruer [rɥe] #3 *v. intr.* to kick: ~ *dans les brancards,* to kick over the traces. || **se ruer** *v. pron.* to rush (at, *sur*).
rugby [ryg'bi] *n.m.* rugby.
rugi [ry'ʒ|i] cf. RUGIR. || **rugir** [-i:r] #17 *v. intr.* to roar, bellow. || **rugissement** [-is'mɑ̃] *n.m.* roar(ing), bellowing.
rugueu|x, -se [ry'gø(:z)] *adj.* rough, rugged.
ruine [rɥin] *n.f.* ruin; [Fig.] decline, decay, downfall: *être en ruines,* to lie in ruins; *tomber en ruines,* to fall in ruins; *maison en ruines,* tumble-down house; *Ce fut sa* ~, That was his downfall. || **ruine-babines** [-ba'bin] *n.m. inv.* © [Mus., Fam.] mouth organ, harmonica. || **ruiner** [-e] #3 *v. tr.* to ruin. || **se ruiner** *v. pron.* to ruin o.s. || **ruineu|x, -se** [-ø(:z)] *adj.* ruinous.
ruisseau, x [rɥi'so] *n.m.* **1.** stream, brook. **2.** gutter.
ruisselant, -e [ryis|'lɑ̃(:t)] cf. RUISSELER. || *adj.* streaming (with, *de*). || **ruisseler** [-'le] #8 *v. intr.* to stream, run, flow (down): *Il ruisselait,* He was dripping with perspiration. || **ruissellement** [-ɛl'mɑ̃] *n.m.* streaming, running, flowing: *le* ~ *des lumières,* the glittering lights.
rumeur [ry'mœ:r] *n.f.* **1.** distant hum, roar: *la* ~ *de l'océan,* the roar of the sea. **2.** rumour: *la* ~ *publique,* public opinion.
ruminer [rymi'ne] #3 *v. tr.* to ruminate; to ponder, turn over in one's mind. || *v. intr.* to chew the cud; [Fig.] to think things over, to ruminate.
Rupert, la Terre de [latɛrdəry'pɛ:r] © Rupert's Land.

rupture [ryp'ty:r] *n.f.* breaking; [Pers.] parting, separation; [contrat] annulment, breach; [os] fracture.
rural, -e [ry'r|al] *adj.* rural, → country: *la vie rurale*, country life. || *n.mpl. les ruraux* [-o] the country people.
ruse [ry:z] *n.f.* trick, ruse, dodge; cunning: *~ de guerre*, stratagem. || **rusé, -e** [ry'ze] *adj.* cunning, crafty, tricky.
russe [rys] *adj.* Russian. || *n.m. & f.* Russian. || **Russie** [-i] *n.f.*: *la ~ /d'Europe, d'Asie*, Russia/in Europe, in Asia; *la Russie blanche*, White Russia.
rusticité [rysti|si'te] *n.f.* **1.** rusticity, primitiveness, simplicity, coarseness. **2.** [plantes] hardiness. || **rustique** [-k] *adj.* rustic, rural, countrified. || *n.m.* peasant, rustic. || **rustre** [rystr] *adj.* boorish, churlish. || *n.m.* boor, churl.
rutabaga [rytaba'ga] *n.m.* Swedish turnip; swede.
rutilant, -e [ryti'l|ɑ̃(:t)] cf. RUTILER. || *adj.* glittering. || **rutiler** [-e] #3 *v. intr.* to shine, to glitter.
rythme [ritm] *n.m.* rhythm; pace, rate. || **rythmique** [-ik] *adj.* rhythmic(al).

S

S, s [ɛs] *n.f.* [letter] S, s: *faire des s*, to zigzag; *sentier en s*, winding path.
s' cf. SE.
sa [sa] *pron. poss.* his, her. cf. SON.
sabbat [sa'ba] *n.m.* **1.** sabbath. **2.** witches' meeting. **3.** racket.
sable[1] [sɑ:bl] *adj.* [Hér.] sable.
sable[2] [sɑ:bl] *n.m.* **1.** sand: *le marchand de ~*, the sandman; *sables mouvants*, shifting sands, quicksands. || **sabler** [sɑ'bl|e] #3 *v. tr.* **1.** to sand, to gravel: *une allée sablée*, a gravelled walk. **2.** to toss off: *~ le champagne*. to toss off a glass of champagne. || **sableuse** [-ø:z] *n.f.* sander, sand blaster. || **sableu|x, -se** [-ø(:z)] *adj.* sandy. || **sablier** [-i'je] *n.m.* sandglass, hourglass. || **sablière** [-i'jɛ:r] *n.f.* sand pit, gravel pit; [locomotive] sandbox. || **sablonneu|x, -se** [-ɔ'nø(:z)] *adj.* sandy.
sabot [sa'bo] *n.m.* **1.** wooden shoe, clog: [Loc.] *Je vous vois venir avec vos gros sabots*, I am on to your game; *travailler comme un ~*, to do a wretched job. **2.** [cheval] hoof. **3.** [véhicule] skid, shoe.
sabotage [sabɔ't|a:ʒ] *n.m.* sabotage. **saboter** [-e] #3 *v. tr.* to sabotage.
sabre [sɑ:br] *n.m.* sabre, broadsword. || **sabrer** [sɑ:bre] #3 *v. tr. & intr.* to strike with a sabre, to cut down: [Fig.] *~ un texte*, to make drastic cuts in a text; *~ un travail*, to botch a piece of work.
sac [sak] *n.m.* sack, bag, pouch: *~ à provisions*, shopping bag; *~ / à main, de dame/*, handbag, purse; *course en sacs*, sack race; *~ de couchage*, sleeping bag; *~ de montagne*, rucksack; *~ de soldat*, pack, knapsack; [Loc.] *mettre à ~*, to sack; *prendre la main dans le ~*, to catch red-handed; *vider son ~*, to get things off one's chest.
saccade [sa'kad] *n.f.* jerk, twitch, pull, jolt: *Elle travaille par saccades*, She works by fits and starts. || **saccadé, -e** [-e] *adj.* jerky, staccato: *respiration saccadée*, irregular breathing.
saccager [saka'ʒe] #5 *v. tr.* to sack, pillage, plunder (a town); to ransack (a building or a room); to put in great disorder, to mess up.
sacerdoce [sasɛr'dɔ|s] *n.m.* [church] priesthood, ministry: [Fig.] *Pour lui, c'est un ~*, He is dedicated. || **sacerdotal, -e** [-'tal] *adj.* [Rel.] sacerdotal, priestly, priestlike (manner).
sachant [sa'ʃɑ̃] *cf.* SAVOIR.
sache, &c. cf. SAVOIR.
sacoche [sa'kɔʃ] *n.f.* bag, satchel, money bag, tool bag; © (lady's) handbag.
sacre [sakr] *n.m.* [évêque, &c.] consecration; [souverain] coronation. || **sacré, -e** [-e] *adj.* holy, sacred; [Fam.] cursed, damned: *Il n'a pas le feu ~*, His heart isn't in it; *Il a le feu ~*, He is dedicated.
sacrement [-ə'mɑ̃] *n.m.* sacrament: *adminis-*

trer les derniers sacrements, to administer the last rites. || **sacrer** [-e] #3 *v. tr.* to anoint, to crown, to consecrate (bishop, &c.). || *v. intr.* to swear, to curse. || **sacreur** [-œ:r] © *n.m.* blasphemer.

sacrifice [-i'fis] *n.m.* sacrifice, renunciation: *faire le ~ de*, to sacrifice. || **sacrifier** [-i'fje] #3 *v. tr.* to sacrifice; to immolate; to renounce, give up; to devote.

sacrilège [-i'lɛ:ʒ] *n.m.* sacrilege. || *adj.* sacrilegious.

sacristain [-is'tɛ̃] *n.m.* sacristan, verger, sexton. || **sacristie** [-is'ti] *n.f.* vestry, sacristy.

sadisme [sa'dism] *n.m.* sadism.

safran [sa'frɑ̃] *adj.* saffron yellow. || *n.m.* saffron.

sagace [sa'gas] *adj.* shrewd, discerning, sagacious. || **sagacité** [-i'te] *n.f.* shrewdness, sagacity. || **sage** [sa:ʒ] *adj.* wise, well-advised; [enfant] good, well-behaved. || *n.m.* wise man, sage. || **sage-femme** [saʒ|'fam] *n.f.* midwife. || **sagement** [-'mɑ̃] *adv.* wisely, sensibly. || **sagesse** [-ɛs] *n.f.* wisdom; good behaviour; chastity.

sagittaire [saʒi'tɛ:r] *n.m.* [Bot.] arrowhead.

Saguenay, le [sag'ne] *n.m.* [rivière] Saguenay River.

saignant, -e [sɛ'ɲ|ɑ̃(:t)] *adj.* bleeding: [Bot.] © *cœurs saignants*, bleeding hearts; [Culin.] rare, underdone.

saignée [-e] *n.f.* **1.** bleeding, blood-letting. **2.** bend of the arm. || **saignement** [-'mɑ̃] *n.m.* bleeding: *~ de nez*, nosebleed. || **saigner** [-e] #3 *v. intr.* to bleed: *~ du nez*, to have a nosebleed. || *v. tr.* to bleed; to draw, let blood from: *~ un porc*, to bleed, stick/a pig; *~ à blanc*, to bleed white. || **se saigner** *v. pron.*: *~ aux quatre veines pour qqun*, to pinch and scrape for s.o.

saillant, -e [sa'j|ɑ̃(:t)] *adj.* salient, striking: *pommettes saillantes*, prominent cheekbones; *dents saillantes*,/buck, projecting/ teeth. || **saillie** [-i] *n.f.* projection, protrusion, relief; ledge; sally, witticism: *faire ~, être en ~*, to jut out, to protrude. || **saillir** [-i:r] #19 *v. intr.* to jut out, stand out, project.

sain, -e [sɛ̃, sɛn] *adj.* healthy, wholesome, sound: *~ et sauf*, safe (and sound); *arriver ~ et sauf*, to arrive safely.

saindoux [sɛ̃'du] *n.m.* [×] lard.

saint, -e [sɛ̃|(:t)] *adj.* holy, saintly: *Vendredi ~*, Good Friday; *Terre Sainte*, Holy Land; *Saint-Esprit*, Holy/Ghost, Spirit/; *Saint-Graal*, Holy Grail; *Saint-Siège*, Holy See; *sainte nitouche*, sanctimonious person: *Elle a un petit air sainte nitouche*, She looks as if butter would not melt in her mouth. || *n.* saint: *le ~ des saints*, the inner sanctum, the holy of holies. || **Saint, -e** [☞ First part of numerous place-names. Note that the abbreviated form is not normally used in France; in ©, use *St-*, not *St.* The following are some important *saint-* compounds which are usually translated.] **Saint-Domingue** [-dɔ'mɛ̃:g] San Domingo; **St-Jacques** [-'ʒɑ:k] St. James: *la rue ~*, St. James Street; **St-Jean** [-'ʒɑ̃] St. John: *la Saint-Jean*, Midsummer Day; *la procession de la Saint-Jean-Baptiste*, the St. Jean Baptiste Parade; **St-Jean (P.Q.)**, St. Johns, St. Jean, P.Q.; **St-Jean (N.B.)**, St. John, N.B.; **St-Jean (Terre-Neuve)**, St. John's, Nfld; **le lac St-Jean**, Lake St. John; **Saint-Laurent** (le) [-lɔ'rɑ̃] *n.m.* [Géog.] St. Lawrence River: *la voie maritime du ~*, the St. Lawrence Seaway; **Saint-Martin** [-mar'tɛ̃] *n.f.* Martinmas; **Saint-Maurice** (le) [-mɔ'ris] *n.m.* [Géog.] St. Maurice River; **Saint-Michel** [-mi'ʃɛl] *n.f.* Michaelmas. || **saintement** [-t'mɑ̃] *adv.* in a saintly manner: *vivre ~*, to lead a/ godly, righteous/life. || **sainteté** [-t'te] *n.f.* holiness, sanctity, saintliness: *Sa Sainteté*, His Holiness.

sais, sait cf. SAVOIR.

saisie [se'z|i] *n.f.* [Jur.] seizure, distraint. || **saisir** #17 *v. tr.* **1.** to seize, to get hold of, to pick up; [Jur.] to distrain, to foreclose. **2.** [Fig.] to grasp, to catch: *Je n'ai pas très bien saisi le sens de ses paroles*, I did not quite catch what he said; *~ l'occasion*, to take the opportunity. || **se ~ de** *v. pr.* to lay hold of; to arrest. || **saisissant, -e** [-i'sɑ̃(:t)] *adj.* striking, thrilling. || **saisissement** [-is'mɑ̃] *n.m.* surprise, shock.

saison [sɛ'z|ɔ̃] *n.f.* season; time: *de ~*, in season, seasonable, timely; *hors de ~*, out of season, untimely; *en cette ~ de l'année*, at this time of the year; *faire une ~ à Vichy*, to take a cure at Vichy. || **saisonni|er, -ère** [-ɔ'nje] *adj.* seasonal: *travailleur ~*, seasonal worker.

salade [sa'lad] *n.f.* salad, © lettuce; [Fam.] jumble, hodgepodge: *Quelle ~ !*, What a mess!, What a jumble! || **saladier** [-je] *n.m.* salad bowl.

salaire [sa'lɛ:r] *n.m.* wages, pay, salary; retribution.

salaison [salɛ'zɔ̃] *n.f.* [poisson] salting; [lard] curing; *salaisons*, salt provisions.

salarié, -e [sala'rje] *adj.* paid, salaried.

|| *n.m.* wage-earner. || **salarier** #3 *v. tr.* to pay a wage to.
salaud, -e [sa'lo(:d)] *n.* [vulgar & seldom *f.*] stinker, bastard. || © *adj.* dirty, muddy, cf. SALE.
sale [sal] *adj.* soiled, dirty, filthy; [Fam., before noun]: ~ *bête*, dirty dog; ~ *type*, a bad egg; *jouer un* ~ *tour à qqun*, to play a dirty trick on s.o.
salé, -e [sa'le] *adj.* **1.** salted, salt; corned: *eau salée*, salt water; *bœuf* ~, corned beef; © *lard* ~, salt pork. **2.** spicy, risqué: *une histoire salée*, a dirty story. || *n.m. petit salé*, salt pork. || **Salé, le Grand Lac** *n.m.* Great Salt Lake.
salement [sal'mɑ̃] *adv.* dirtily, nastily, disgustingly.
saler [sa'le] #3 *v. tr.* to salt, to cure, to pickle; [Fig.] to overcharge, to pad (a bill).
saleté [salte] *n.f.* dirt, filth: *d'une* ~ *repoussante*, → filthy; dirtiness; [Fig.] obscenity; dirty trick.
sali, :-e cf. SALIR.
salière [sa'l|jɛ:r] *n.f.* salt/cellar, shaker/; [cuisine] salt box.
salin, -e [-ɛ̃, -in] *adj.* salt, saline, briny, salty. || *n.m.* salt marsh. || *n.f.* salt works, rock-salt mine, fish-curing establishment.
salir [sa'li:r] #17 *v. tr.* **1.** to make dirty; to soil; to foul. **2.** to defile, to hurt o.'s reputation. || **se** ~, *v. pr.* to get dirty, soil: *Cette robe se salit très vite*, This dress soils easily. || **salissant, -e** [sali'sɑ(:t)] cf. SALIR. *adj.*: *C'est très* ~, It shows the dirt.
salive [sa'li:v] *n.f.* saliva, spittle. || **saliver** #3 *v. intr.* to salivate, to secrete saliva.
salle [sal] *n.f.* room: ~ *à manger*, dining room; ~ *de bain*, bathroom; ~ (*commune*), livingroom; ~ *de jeu*, playroom; ~ *d'attente*, waiting room; ~ *d'hôpital*, ward; ~ *de cinéma*, movie theatre; ~ *de/concert, conférence/*, auditorium; ~ (*de théatre*), house; ~ *de cours*, lecture, class room; ~ *d'étude*, [privée] schoolroom, [école] study hall; ~ *des professeurs*, staff room; ~ *de quilles*, bowling alley.
saloir [sa'lwa:r] *n.m.* salting tub; [Cul.] salt-sprinkler.
salon [sa'lõ] *n.m.* **1.** drawing room, sitting-room, parlour: *jeux de* ~, parlour games; *fréquenter les salons*, to move in fashionable circles. **2.** [public rooms]: ~ *de coiffure*, barber shop; ~ *de thé*, tea room. **3.** exhibition: ~ *de peinture*, art exhibition; ~ *de l'automobile*, motor show.
salopette [salɔ'pɛt] *n.f.* (workman's, child's) overalls, dungarees.
salpêtre [sal'pɛ:tr] *n.m.* saltpetre, potassium nitrate.
salsepareille [salspa'rɛ:j] *n.f.* sarsaparilla.
saltimbanque [saltɛ̃'bɑ̃:k] *n.m.* mountebank, member of a travelling circus; [Fig.] charlatan.
salubre [sa'lybr] *adj.* salubrious, healthy, wholesome: *un climat* ~, a healthy climate. || **salubrité** [-i'te] *n.f.* salubrity, salubriousness, wholesomeness.
saluer [sa'lɥe] #3 *v. tr.* to greet; to bow to; to salute; †to hail: *ne pas* ~ *qqun*, to cut s.o. dead; ~ *bien bas*, to bow and scrape.
salut [sa'ly] *n.m.* **1.** salvation: *l'Armée du* ~, the Salvation Army; *faire son* ~, to work out o.'s salvation; safety: *le* ~ *public*, public safety. **2.** salute, greeting. || **salutaire** [-'tɛ:r] *adj.* salutary, beneficial. || **salutation** [-ta'sjõ] *n.f.* salutation, greeting: [in letter] *Veuillez agréer mes sincères salutations*, Yours truly; [R.C.] *la* ~ *angélique*, the Hail Mary.
Salvador, le [salva'dɔ:r] *n.m.* El Salvador.
salve [salv] *n.f.* salvo, salute: *tirer une* ~, to fire a salvo, a salute; ~ *d'applaudissements*, burst of applause; *feu de* ~, volley fire.
samedi [sam'di] *n.m.* Saturday: ~ *saint*, Holy Saturday, Easter Eve cf. LUNDI.
sanctifier [sɑ̃kti'fje] #3 *v. tr.* to sanctify, hallow: *que Votre nom soit sanctifié*, hallowed be Thy name.
sanction [sɑ̃k'sj|õ] *n.f.* **1.** sanction, assent: ~ *royale*, royal assent. **2.** penalty: *prendre des sanctions contre qqun*, to penalize, to take action against s.o. || **sanctionner** [-ɔ'ne] #3 *v. tr.* **1.** to sanction, approve. **2.** to punish, penalize.
sanctuaire [sɑ̃k'tɥɛ:r] *n.m.* **1.** sanctuary, shrine. **2.** sanctuary, asylum.
sandale [sɑ̃'dal] *n.f.* sandal, gym shoe: [Fig.] *Il a secoué la poussière de ses sandales*, He shook the dust off his feet.
sandwich [sɑ̃'dwiʃ] *n.m.* sandwich: *homme-*~, sandwich-man.
sang [sɑ̃] *n.m.* **1.** blood: *effusion de* ~, bloodshed; *les yeux injectés de* ~, with; bloodshot eyes; *banque de* ~, blood bank; *suer* ~ *et eau*, to sweat blood; (*cheval*) *pur* ~, thoroughbred; ~*-froid*, composure; *se faire du mauvais* ~, to worry, to fret. **2.** extraction, stock. || **sanglant, -e** [sɑ̃'glɑ̃(:t)] *adj.* **1.** bloody, blood-stained, sanguinary. **2.** cruel, harsh: *des reproches sanglants*, cutting reproach; *un affront* ~, an outrageous affront.

sangle [sɑ̃:gl] *n.f.* strap, belt. || **sangler** #3 *v. tr.* [cheval] to girth; [colis] to strap.
sanglier [sɑ̃gli'je] *n.m.* wild boar: ~ *d'Amérique*, peccary.
sanglot [sɑ̃'gl|o] *n.m.* sob. || **sangloter** [-ɔ'te] #3 *v. intr.* to sob.
sangsue [sɑ̃'sy] *n.f.* leech; [Fig.] extortioner, blood-sucker.
sanguin, -e [sɑ̃g|ɛ̃, -in] *adj.* **1.** [Anat.] sanguineous; of blood: *le système* ~, the blood vessels. **2.** [couleur] red-tinged: *(orange f) sanguine*, blood-orange. **3.** [Pers.] full-blooded, sanguine. || **sanguinaire** [-i'nɛ:r] *adj.* sanguinary; [Fig.] bloodthirsty; [combat] bloody. || *n.f.* [Bot.] ~ *du Canada*, bloodroot. || **sanguinolent** [-inɔ'lɑ̃(:t)] *adj.* bleeding, blood-stained.
sanitaire [sani'tɛ:r] *adj.* sanitary: *matériel* ~, medical stores.
sans [sɑ̃] *prép.* without; free (of, from); but for; were it not for: ~ *cesse*, unceasingly; ~ *doute*, doubtlessly, no doubt; ~ *fin*, unending; ~ *quoi*, else, otherwise; *être* ~ *le sou*, to be penniless. || **sans-abri** [z-u'bri] *n.pl.* homeless: *initiatives en faveur des* ~, measures to help the homeless. || **sans-cœur** [-'kœ:r] *n.m.* & *f.* heartless person. || **sans-fil** [-'fil] *inv.* [télégraphie] wireless. || **sans-gêne** [-'ʒɛ:n] *n.m.* over-familiarity; off-handedness. || **sans-souci** [-su'si] *n. m/f* [person] easy-going; carefree.
sansonnet [sɑ̃sɔ'nɛ] *n.m.* cf. ÉTOURNEAU.
santé [sɑ̃'te] *n.f.* **1.** health; well-being: *avoir une excellente* ~, to be in perfect health; *une* ~ *de fer*, an iron constitution; *respirer la* ~, to look the picture of health. **2.** [Fr.] *Ministère de la* ~ *publique*, Ministry of Health (& Welfare); [Fr.] *La Santé* [a prison in Paris]; *maison f de* ~, nursing home; mental hospital.
saoul, saouler cf. SOÛL, SOÛLER.
saper [sa'p|e] #3 *v. tr.* to sap, undermine. || **sapeur** [-œ:r] *n.m.* [Mil.] sapper, pioneer: [Fr. Paris] ~ *-pompier m* fireman.
saphir [sa'fi:r] *n.m.* sapphire.
sapin [sa'p|ɛ̃] *n.m.* [Bot.] © fir (-tree); [Fr.] spruce (-fir): ~ *baumier*, balsam fir; ~ *de Douglas*, Douglas fir. || **sapinière** [-i'njɛ:r] *n.f.* spruce grove.
sapristi [sapris'ti] *interj.* by Jove! hang it!
sarbacane [sarba'kan] *n.f.* pea-shooter.
sarcasme [sar'kasm] *n.m.* sarcasm; taunt.
sarcelle [sar'sɛl] *n.f.* teal.
sarcler [sar'kle] #3 *v. tr.* [champ] to clean; [jardin] to weed; [légumes] to hoe.
Sardaigne, la [sar'dɛɲ] *n.f.* Sardinia.
sardine [sar'din] *n.f.* sardine.
sardonique [sardɔ'nik] *adj.* sardonic.
sarrasin [sara'zɛ̃] *n.m.* buckwheat; [Hist.] Saracen.
sarriette [sa'rjɛt] *n.f.* savoury.
sas [sɑ] *n.m.* sieve; [Tech.] lock-chamber.
Saskatchewan [saskatʃɔ'wan] *n.* [☞ No agreement on gender.] Saskatchewan. || **Saskatchewan, la** *n.f.* the Saskatchewan (river).
sasser [sɑ'se] #3 *v. tr.* to sift.
Satan [sa'tɑ̃] *n.m.* Satan.
satellite [satɛ'lit] *n.m.* satellite: ~ *artificiel*, man-made satellite; [Fam.] sputnik.
satiété [sasje'te] *n.f.* satiety, surfeit: *manger à* ~, to eat one's fill.
satin [sa't|ɛ̃] *n.m.* satin. || **satiné** [-i'ne] *adj.* smooth (as satin, velvet); [paper] (high-) glazed.
satire [sa't|i:r] *n.f.* satire, lampoon. || **satirique** [-i'rik] *adj.* satirical.
satisfaction [satisf|ak'sjõ] *n.f.* **1.** satisfaction, gratification, contentment: *tirer* ~ *de*, to gain comfort from . . . **2.** reparation, amends.
satisfaire [-ɛ:r] **satisfaisant** [-ə'zɑ̃] **satisfait** [-ɛ] #37 *v. intr.* to satisfy: ~ *à des conditions*, to meet requirements. || *v. tr.* to please, to give satisfaction to (s.o.): ~ *l'attente de qqun*, to come up to s.o.'s expectations. || **satisfaisant, -e** [-ə'zɑ̃(:t)] *adj.* satisfying, satisfactory: *peu* ~, unsatisfactory. || **satisfait, -e** [-ɛ(t)] *adj.* satisfied, contented. || **satisfis, &c.** cf. SATISFAIRE.
saturer [saty're] #3 *v. tr.* to saturate.
Saturne [sa'tyrn] *n.m.* Saturn.
sauce [so:s] *n.f.* **1.** [jus de cuisson] gravy. **2.** [condiment] sauce; ~ *aux tomates*, catsup.
saucisse [so'sis] *n.f.* sausage. || **saucisson** [-õ] *n.m.* salami.
sau|f,[1] **-ve** [so:f, so:v] *adj.* safe: *sain et* ~, unscathed, unhurt.
sauf[2] *prep.* save, except: ~ *correction*, subject to correction; ~ *accidents*, barring accidents; ~ *-conduit m*, safe-conduct.
sauge [so:ʒ] *n.f.* [Bot.] sage.
saugrenu, -e [sogrə'ny] *adj.* absurd, preposterous, ridiculous.
saule [so:l] *n.m.* willow: ~ *pleureur*, weeping willow.
sault [so] *n.m.* [Géo.] fall(s), cf. LONG SAULT [Modern spelling SAUT]: *Sault-Sainte-Marie*, "The Soo."
saumon [so'mõ] *n.m.* salmon: © ~ *sockeye*, © sockeye salmon.

saumure [so'my:r] *n.f.* brine, pickling.
saupoudrer [sopu'dre] #3 *v. tr.* to sprinkle, powder, dust (with, *de*).
saur [sɔ:r] *adj.* smoked: *hareng* ~, red herring.
saurai(s), &c. cf. SAVOIR.
saut [so] *n.m.* leap, jump, vault: ~ *périlleux*, somersault; *faire un* ~, to take a leap; *faire un* ~ *vers la porte*, to make a bee-line for the door; [route] ~ *-de-mouton m*, cloverleaf intersection. || **saute** [so:t] *n.f.*: ~ *de vent*, sudden /change, turn/, jump [wind, prices, &c.]. || **sauté, -e** [so't|e] *adj.* [Culin.] sauté: *rognons sautés*, sautéed kidneys. || **saute-mouton** [-mu'tõ] *n.m.* [jeu] leap-frog. || **sauter** [-e] #3 *v. tr.* **1.** to leap, to jump; [mine] to explode, blow up; [chaudière] to burst: ~ *à pieds joints*, to do a standing jump; ~ *à cloche-pied*, to hop (on one foot); ~ *de joie*, to leap for joy. **2.** [Fig.] to be obvious: *Cela saute aux yeux*, It is/obvious, plain as a pike-staff/; to omit, to skip (a passage from a text); [Culin.] to fry quickly. cf. SAUTÉ.
sauterelle [sot|'rɛl] *n.f.* grasshopper; [African] locust.
sauterie [-'ri] *n.f.* dance, "hop." || **sauteu|r, -se** [-œ:r, -ø:z] *n.* leaper; [Fig.] mountebank. || *adj.* jumping. || **sautillant, -e** [-i'jɑ̃(:t)] *adj.* jumping, hopping, dancing (person, child); jumpy, jerky (step, style). || **sautillement** [-ij'mɑ̃] *n.m.* jumping, skipping; [oiseaux] hopping. || **sautiller** [-i'je] #3 *v. intr.* to skip, jump (about); [oiseau] to hop (about).
sautoir [so'twa:r] *n.m.* St. Andrew's cross; [woman's] long neck chain; *en* ~, crosswise, around o.'s neck.
sauvage [so'v|a:ʒ] © [sɔ'va:ʒ] *adj.* **1.** [animal, pays] wild; [animal] wild, untamed. **2.** savage, uncivilized: © Indian: *traîne f* ~, toboggan; © *langues fpl sauvages*, Amerindian languages. **3.** [Fig.] shy, unsociable. || *n.m.* [☞ the fem. **sauvagesse** [-a'ʒɛs] is rare] savage; © Indian, Amerindian [fem. squaw]: *agent m des sauvages*, Indian agent; *été m des sauvages*, Indian summer; [Fig.] *attendre les sauvages*, to be expecting; *les sauvages sont passés*, a baby/is, was/ born; cf. FEU. || **sauvagerie** [-aʒ'ri] *n.f.* (state of) savagery, savageness; [Fig.] shyness, coyness.
sauve [so:v] cf. SAUF: ~ *qui peut!*, Every man for himself!; *un sauve-qui-peut*, a stampede. || **sauvegarde** [sov'gard] *n.f.* **1.** safeguard, safe-keeping. **2.** safe-conduct. || **sauvegarder** [-e] #3 *v. tr.* to safeguard, protect.
sauver [so'v|e] #3 *v. tr.* to save (from, *de* . . .); [accident] to rescue; [libérer] to deliver, free. || **se sauver** *v. pron.* to save o.s.; [de prison, &c.] to escape, get away; [Fig.] to run away; [Fam.] *Sauvez-vous!*, Beat it!, Scram! || **sauvetage** [-'ta:ʒ] *n.m.* **1.** life-saving, rescue: *ceinture f de* ~, lifebelt; lifepreserver; *canot m de* ~, lifeboat; *échelle f de* ~, fire-escape. **2.** salvage (of ship, goods). || **sauveteur** [-'tœ:r] *n. & adj.* [No fem.] rescuer; lifesaver, lifeguard. || **sauveur** [-œ:r] *n. & adj.* deliverer; [Rel.] Saviour.
savais, &c. cf. SAVOIR.
savamment [sava'mɑ̃] *adv.* learnedly.
savane [sa'van] © *n.f.* [treeless plain] savanna(h).
savant, -e [sa'v|ɑ̃(:t)] *adj.* learned; scholarly; [Fig.] clever: *chien* ~, performing dog. || **savant** [-ɑ̃] *n.m.* scholar; [science] scientist [×].
savate [sa'vat] *n.f.* slipper; [Fig.] old shoe: *traîner la* ~, to be down at the heels.
saveur [sa'vœ:r] *n.f.* flavour, taste: *sans* ~, tasteless, insipid; [Fig.] pungency (of style): *observations pleines de* ~, pungent remarks.
Savoie, la [sa'vwa] *n.f.* Savoy. || **Savoyard, -e** [-'ja:r, -'jard] *adj. & n.* (from) Savoy.
savoir [sa'vwa:r], **sachant** [sa'ʃɑ̃], **su** [sy] #69 *v. tr.* **1.** to know: ~ *par cœur*, to know by heart; *Il sait l'anglais*, He knows English. **2.** can: *Il sait nager*, He can swim. **3.** to know, to be aware of, to be informed of, to hear: *faire* ~ *qqch. à qqun*, to let s.o. know sth.; ~ *pertinemment*, to know for a fact; *Je savais qu'il viendrait*, I knew he was coming; *J'ai su qu'il viendrait*, I heard he was coming; *Je crois* ~ *qu'il est candidat*, I understand he has applied; *Je crois* ~ *pourquoi*, I think I know why; *Je le savais malade*, I knew he was ill; *Je sais quelqu'un qui* . . . , I know of s.o. who . . . ; *pas que je sache*, not that I know of; *Cela a fini par se* ~, It finally came out. || **savoir-faire** [savwar|'fɛ:r] *n.m.* know-how. || **savoir-vivre** [-'vi:vr] *n.m.* **1.** manners: *Il manque de* ~, He has no manners. **2.** etiquette: *manuel de* ~, etiquette book.
savon [sa'v|õ] *n.m.* soap; ~ *en paillettes*, soap flakes; ~ *de Marseille*, yellow soap; ~ *blanc*, Castile soap; *eau f de* ~, soap suds; [Fig.] scolding, rebuke: *Je lui ai passé un* ~, I gave him a dressing-down, I let him have it, [Fam.] I bawled

him out. || **savonnage** [-ɔ'na:ʒ] *n.m.* **1.** [also EAU DE SAVON] soaping. **2.** (= action de savonner) soap washing. || **savonner** [-ɔ'ne] #3 *v. tr.* to soap, wash with soap; to lather. || **se savonner** *v. pron.* to bear washing, to wash (of fabrics); to soap oneself. || **savonnette** [-ɔ'nɛt] *n.f.* (cake of) toilet-soap; © shaving-brush. || **savonneu|x, -se** [-ɔ'nø(:z)] *adj.* soapy (water); *terre f savonneuse* (= terre *f* à Foulon), Fuller's earth.

savons[1] [sa'võ] cf. SAVOIR.

savons[2] cf. SAVON.

savourer [savu'r|e] #3 *v. tr.* [goûter] to taste slowly; [Fig.] to relish, enjoy: ~ *une plaisanterie,* to gloat over a joke. || **savoureu|x, -se** [-ø(:z)] *adj.* savoury, tasty; [Fig.] enjoyable.

saxophone [saksɔ'fɔn] *n.m.* saxophone; [personne] saxophonist.

saynète [sɛ'nɛt] *n.f.* playlet, sketch.

scabreu|x, -se [ska'brø(:z)] *adj.* difficult, risky (work), indelicate (allusion); improper, scabrous (tale, conduct).

scalpel [skal'pɛl] *n.m.* scalpel.

scandale [skɑ̃'dal] *n.m.* evil example; scandal; shame: *crier au* ~, to cry shame. || **scandaleu|x, -se** [-ø(:z)] *adj.* scandalous; shameful. || **scandaliser** [-i'ze] #3 *v. tr.* to scandalize; to shock, to cause offense to (s.o.), to lead (s.o.) astray. || **se scandaliser** *v. pron.* to be shocked.

scander [skɑ̃'de] #3 *v. tr.* to scan (verse); to stress (a phrase).

scandinave [skɑ̃di'n|a:v] *adj. & n.* Scandinavian. || **Scandinavie** [-a'vi] *n.f.* Scandinavia.

scaphandre [ska'f|ɑ̃:dr] *n.m.* diving suit; diver. || **scaphandrier** [-ɑ̃dri'je] *n.m.* (deep sea) diver.

scarabée [skara'be] *n.m.* beetle; scarab.

scarlatine [skarla'tin] *adj. & n.f.* (*fièvre*) ~, scarlet fever, scarlatina.

sceau [so] *n.m.* seal; [Fig.] mark, stamp: ~ *de l'état,* state seal.

scélérat, -e [sele'ra|(t)] *adj.* wicked, villainous; crafty, cunning. || *n.m.* scoundrel, villain. || **scélératesse** [-'tɛs] *n.f.* villainy, baseness.

sceller [sɛ'l|e] #3 *v. tr.* [lettre] to seal (up); [fixer] to fasten, fix in (a post, etc.). || **scellés** [-e] *n.mpl.* [Jur.] seal: *mettre les* ~ (*à* . . .), to put . . . under seal.

scénario [sena'r|jo] *n.m.* scenario, script [of movie, etc.]. || **scénariste** [-ist] *n.m.* scenarist. || **scène** [sɛ:n] *n.f.* **1.** [Théâtre] stage; *mise f en* ~, staging, (stage-) setting; *metteur m en* ~, producer. **2.** scene (of action): *La* ~ *se passe à Québec,* The action takes place in Q. **3.** angry discussion, flare-up: *faire une* ~, to make a scene; ~ *de famille,* family wrangle.

scepticisme [sɛpti|'sism] *n.m.* scepticism. || **sceptique** [-k] *adj.* sceptical. || *n.m.* sceptic.

sceptre [sɛptr] *n.m.* sceptre.

schéma [ʃe'ma] *n.m.* diagram; (sketch-) plan.

schizophrène [skizɔ'frɛ:n] *adj.* schizophrenic.

sciatique [sja'tik] *adj.* sciatic. || *n.m.* sciatic nerve. || *n.f.* sciatica.

scie [si] *n.f.* saw: © ~ *à deux mains,* cross-cut saw; ~ *à ruban,* band saw; [Fig.] bore; nuisance.

sciemment [sja'mɑ̃] *adv.* purposely, knowingly. || **science** [sjɑ̃:s] *n.f.* **1.** science, learning: *les sciences de l'homme,* social sciences; *homme de* ~, scientist. **2.** [Fig.] knowledge, skill, know-how: *savoir de* ~ *certaine,* to know for a fact. || **scientifique** [sjɑ̃ti'fik] *adj.* scientific. || *n.m.* scientist [×].

scier [sje] #3 *v. tr.* to saw (off), to cut down: [Fig.] ~ *le dos à qqun,* to bore s.o. stiff. || **scierie** [si'ri] *n.f.* saw mill, lumber mill.

scinder [sɛ̃'de] #3 *v. tr.* to divide, split up (into, *en*).

scintillant, -e [sɛ̃ti'j|ɑ̃(:t)] *adj.* scintillating; [étoile] †winking; [style] sparkling. || **scintillement** [-'mɑ̃] *n.m.* glitter, sparkle; sparkling. || **scintiller** [-e] #3 *v. intr.* to glitter; [étoile] twinkle; [tisons] sparkle, flicker.

scission [si'sjõ] *n.f.* scission, split, cleavage; [Polit.] secession.

sciure [sjy:r] *n.f.*: ~ *de bois,* sawdust.

scolaire [skɔ'lɛ:r] *adj.* academic: *année* ~, academic (scholastic, school) year; *succès* ~, academic achievement; *fréquentation* ~, school attendance; © *commission* ~, school board; *radio* ~, educational broadcast; *bulletin* ~, report card; *autobus* ~, school bus; *matériel* ~, school equipment; *fournitures* ~ *s,* school supplies; *manuel* ~, textbook. || **scolarité** [-ari'te] *n.f.* (term of) residence [at colleges, &c.]; *frais de* ~, tuition (fees).

scolasticat [skɔlasti'ka] *n.m.* scholasticate. || **scolastique** [skɔlas'tik] *n.m. & adj.* [Philos.] scholastic. || *n.f.* scholastic philosophy.

scout [skut] *n.m.* boy scout [cf. ÉCLAIREUR, GUIDE]. || **scoutisme** [-ism] *n.m.* Boy Scout movement; scouting: *faire du* ~, to be a/boy, girl/scout. || **scoutmestre** [-'mɛstr] © *n.m.* scoutmaster.

scrupule [skry'pyl] *n.m.* scruple; doubt, qualm (of conscience): *se faire un ~ de*, to have scruples about sth., → to scruple [+ inf.]. || **scrupuleusement** [-øz'mɑ̃] *adv.* scrupulously; precisely. || **scrupuleu|x, -se** [-ø(:z)] *adj.* scrupulous; precise, punctilious.

scruter [skry'te] #3 *v. tr.* to scrutinize, investigate.

scrutin [skry'tɛ̃] *n.m.* ballot, vote: *~ secret*, secret ballot; [élection] poll.

sculpter [skyl't|e] #3 *v. tr.* to sculpture, [bois] to carve. || **sculpteur** [-œ:r] *n.m.* sculptor: *~ sur bois*, wood-carver. || **sculpture** [-y:r] *n.f.* sculpture; carving, carved work.

se [sə, s] s' [☞ before vowel or mute *h*] *pron. pers. 3e pers.* **1.** himself, herself, itself, oneself, themselves: *Il s'est lavé*, He washed himself; *Ils se sont lavés*, They washed themselves; *Elle s'est baignée*, She went swimming; *Il s'en moque*, He does not care. **2.** [réciproque] each other; [plusieurs] one another: *Ils se sont parlé*, They spoke to each other. **3.** [☞ rendered by passive verb] *Les oranges se vendent à la douzaine*, Oranges are sold by the dozen; *Cela ne se fait pas*, This is not done.

séance [se'ɑ̃:s] *n.f.* **1.** sitting, session, [assemblée] meeting: *tenir ~*, to meet; *~ publique*, open meeting: [Loc.] *~ tenante*, there and then, at once. **2.** [cinéma] show, performance; [spiritisme] seance.

séant [se'ɑ̃] *n.m.*: *se mettre sur son ~*, to sit up. || *adj.* becoming, fitting, cf. BIENSÉANT.

seau [so] *n.m.* [☞ Do not confuse with SCEAU], pail; bucket [☞ © wooden buckets are called SEAU [so, sjo], metal containers CHAUDIÈRE]; *~ à incendie*, fire-bucket; [Loc.] *il pleut à seaux*, it is raining cats and dogs.

sébile [se'bil] *n.f.* (wooden) bowl.

sec, sèche [sɛk, sɛʃ] *adj.* **1.** dry; [pays] arid; [langue] parched; [vin] dry: *mettre un étang à ~*, to drain a pond; *nettoyage à ~*, dry cleaning; *Tenir au ~*, Keep in a dry place; *traverser* (*une rivière*) *à pied ~*, to cross (a river) dry-shod; *figues sèches*, dried figs; *raisins secs*, raisins; *pois secs*, split peas. **2.** [Fig.] dry, sharp, unfeeling; [visage] plain; [voix] harsh, curt; [accueil] cool; [ton] incisive; [bruit] sharp: *claquement ~*, snap [cf. BRUIT]; *une perte sèche*, a total loss; *un fruit ~*, a failure, a dud. **3.** [Loc. Fam.] *être à ~*, to be /broke, on the rocks/; *en cinq ~*, in no time at all, in a jiffy.

sécession [sesɛ'sjõ] *n.f.* secession: *faire ~*, → to secede.

sèche[1], **seiche** [sɛʃ] *n.f.* cuttle (fish).

sèche[2] [sɛʃ] cf. SEC. || **sèchement** [-'mɑ̃] *adv.* [Fig.] curtly, dryly, sharply, bluntly. || **sécher** [se'ʃ|e] #10 *v. tr.* to dry, dry up; to cure, season (meat): *faire ~ au soleil*, to dry in the sun; *se sécher*, to dry o.s.; dry up! || *v. intr.* to dry up; [Fig.] to pine away, wither (away), fret: *Il sèche d'ennui*, He's/pining, wasting/ away; *~ sur pied*, to languish, to pine away, to fret; [School] (Fam.) *~ à un examen*, to flunk; *~ un cours*, to cut class. || **sécheresse** [-'rɛs] *n.f.* dryness (of the air, throat); [manque de pluie] drought; [traits] leanness, spareness; [manières] curtness, coldness; [style] barrenness. || **séchoir** [-wa:r] *n.m.* [Tech.] drying-room; dryer, drying apparatus; [linge] clothes-horse.

second, -e[1] [sə'gõ(:d)], [zgõ(:d)] *adj.* [= deuxième] second: *en ~ lieu*, in the second place; [Fig.] *sans ~*, matchless, peerless, unparalleled; *~ associé*, junior partner. *n.m.* **1.** assistant, second (in command): *commander en ~*, to be second in command; [Marine] first mate, first (chief) officer. **2.** [étage] second floor, © third floor: *habiter au ~*, to live on the third floor. || **secondaire** [səgõ'dɛ:r], [zgõ'dɛ:r] *adj.* secondary; minor: *question d'intérêt ~*, question of minor interest, side-issue; [Enseignement] *études fpl* secondaires,secondary/classical/ education.

seconde[2] [sə'gõ:d], [zgõ:d] *n.f.* second (of time, angle); [Typo.] second proof, revision; [Train, &c.] second class: *voyager en ~*, to travel second class.

secondé [səgõ'de], [zgõ'de] *adj.* assisted by: *~ admirablement par*, → with the able assistance of . . . .

secondement [səgõd'mɑ̃], [zgõd'mɑ̃] *adv.* secondly, in the second place.

seconder [səgõ'de], [zgõ'de] #3 *v. tr.* to second, assist (s.o.) to back up, promote (interests, plans).

secouer [sə'kwe] #3 *v. tr.* to shake, throw off; [violemment] to toss; [cahot] to jolt, jerk; [Fig.] to rouse. || **se secouer** *v. pron.* to shake o.s.; [Fig.] to pull o.s. together.

secourable [səku'rabl] *adj.* helping, helpful.

secoure, secours [sə'ku:r] cf. SECOURIR.

secourir [səku'ri:r] #24 *v. tr.* to help, aid; *porter secours à*, to rescue. || **secours**

[sə'ku:r] *n.m.* help, assistance, aid; [bienfaisance] relief: *venir au ~ de qqun*, to come to the rescue of, to rescue s.o.; *porter ~ à*, to bring assistance, relief to; *au ~ !*, help!; *porte f de ~*, emergency door; *roue f de ~*, spare wheel; *des secours mpl*, supplies, relief.

secousse [sə'kus] *n.f.* shake, jerk, [véhicule & Fig.] jolt; © *attendre une/petite, bonne/ ~*, to wait (for quite a while).

secr|et, -ète [sə'kr|ɛ(t)] *adj.* [chose] secret, private, [personne] reserved, secretive; [lieu, &c.] hidden. || **secret** [-ɛ] *n.m.* secret, privacy, secrecy: *en ~*, secretly; *dans le plus grand ~*, on the/Q.T., q.t. /.

secrétaire [səkre't|ɛ:r] *n.m./f.* **1.** [personne] secretary, clerk: *~ d'État*, Secretary of State; *sous-~ d'État*, Under-Secretary of State. **2.** [meuble] (writing-)desk. || **secrétariat** [-a'rja] *n.m.* [charge] secretaryship, [bureau] secretary's office, secretariat.

secrète [sə'krɛt] *n.f.* (R.C.) secrets (at Mass).

secrètement [səkrɛt'mɑ̃] *adv.* secretly, in secret.

sécrétion [sekre'sjõ] *n.f.* secretion.

secte [sɛkt] *n.f.* [Rel.] sect, denomination.

secteur [sɛk|'tœ:r] *n.m.* [Geom., &c.] sector; [ville] section, district, [pays, région] area, district. || **section** [-'sjõ] *n.f.* section, division, [Mil.] platoon. || **sectionner** [-sjɔ'ne] #3 *v. tr.* to divide; to sever, cut off.

séculaire [seky'l|ɛ:r] *adj.* secular, centenarian; [Fig.] ancient, [coutume, &c.] time-honoured.

séculi|er, -ère [-je, -jɛ:r] *adj.* worldly; [ordre, clergé] secular.

sécurité [sekyri'te] *n.f.* [sauvegarde] security, safety, guarantee, collateral; [sentiment] confidence.

sédatif [seda't|if, -i:v] *adj.* sedative, quieting. || *n.m.* sedative.

sédentaire [sedɑ̃'tɛ:r] *adj.* sedentary; fixed, settled.

sédition [sedi'sjõ] *n.f.* sedition.

séduct|eur, -rice [sedyk|'tœ:r, -'tris] *n.* seducer. || *adj.* seductive, bewitching. || **séduction** [-'sjõ] *n.f.* seduction, enticement. || **séduire** [se'dɥ|i:r] **séduisant** [-i'zɑ̃] **séduit** [-i] #56 *v. tr.* to seduce, charm, bewitch (s.o.); [tromper] to bribe. || **séduis, séduisais,** etc. cf. SÉDUIRE. || **séduisant, -e** [-i'zɑ̃(:t)] *adj.* seductive, beguiling, fascinating; engaging, promising.

segment [sɛg'mɑ̃] *n.m.* [partie] segment, [Auto.] (motor) ring: *segments de frein*, brake shoes. || **segmentaire** [-'tɛ:r] *adj.* segmental.

ségrégation [segrega'sjõ] *n.f.* segregation.

seigle [sɛgl] *n.m.* rye.

seigneur [sɛ'ɲ|œ:r] *n.m.* lord, nobleman; master: *Notre-Seigneur*, Our Lord. || **seigneurial, -e** [-œ'rjal] *adj.* **1.** seigniorial, manorial. **2.** [Fig.] lordly. || **seigneurie** [-œ'ri] *n.f.* **1.** [domaine] seigniory; manor. **2.** [dignité] lordship.

sein [sɛ̃] *n.m.* [femme] breast, bosom, [ext.] womb: *donner le ~ à un enfant*, to nurse a child; [Fig.] *au ~ de*, in the/midst, middle, heart/of . . . .

seine[1] [sɛ:n] *n.f.* [filet] seine.

Seine,[2] **la** [la'sɛ:n] *n.f.* [fleuve] the Seine.

seing [sɛ̃] *n.m.* signature, signing.

seize [sɛ:z] *n.m.* sixteen. || **seizième** [sɛ'zjɛm] *adj.* (the) sixteenth.

séjour [se'ʒ|u:r] *n.m.* stay, visit: *pièce de ~*, living-room; *visa de ~*, visitor's visa. || **séjourner** [-ur'ne] #3 *v. intr.* to stay, to reside.

sel [sɛl] *n.m.* salt; [Fig.] wit, humour; [conversation] spice.

selle [sɛl] *n.f.* **1.** [monture] saddle. **2.** stool: *aller à la ~*, to have a bowel movement. || **seller** [-e] #3 *v. tr.* to saddle: *~ les chevaux*, to saddle up. || **sellette** [-ɛt] *n.f.* **1.** small saddle. **2.** [Fig.] *être sur la ~*, to be on the carpet.

selon [s(ə)'lõ] *prép.* according to: *~ que* [+ *ind.*], according as; *~ lui*, in his opinion.

semailles [sə'mɑ:j] *n.fpl.* sowing, seed(ing): *le temps des ~*, sowing season, seed-time.

semaine [sə'mɛn] *n.f.* week; [salaire] week's wages, [travail] week's work: [Fr.] *~ anglaise*, five-day week; *faire la ~ anglaise*, to work five days a week; *en ~*, during the week; [Rel.] (*la*) *Semaine Sainte*, (the) Holy Week; *Je le ferai la ~ des*/[Fr.] *quatre*, © *trois*/*jeudis*, I will do it in a week of two Sundays.

sémaphore [sema'fɔ:r] *n.m.* semaphore.

semblable [sɑ̃'blabl] *adj.* similar (to, *à*), such (as), like. || *n.m.* [Pers.] equal, fellow-/being, creature/. || **semblablement** [-ə'mɑ̃] *adv.* likewise, similarly, in the same way.

semblant [sɑ̃'bl|ɑ̃] *n.m.* appearance: *faire ~*, to pretend (to, *de*); *ne faire ~ de rien*, to seem unconcerned, to seem to take no notice; *faux ~*, trick. || **sembler** [-e] #3 *v. intr.* to seem, to appear: *Il semble qu'il ne viendra pas*, It looks as if he will not come; *Il me semble encore l'entendre*, I can still hear him.

sème, sèmerai, &c. cf. SEMER.

semelle [sə'mɛl] *n.f.* sole; [intérieure] sock; [chaussette, bas] foot: *ne pas reculer d'une ~*, to stand one's ground; *battre la ~*, to stamp one's feet.
semence [sə'mɑ̃:s] *n.f.* seed; [homme] semen. || **semer** [sə'me] #9 *v. tr.* to sow; [Fig.] to scatter, to spread; [Fam.] to leave behind, to shake off.
semestre [sə'mɛstr] *n.m.* [école] semester; half-year. || **semestriel, -le** [səmɛstri'ɛl] *adj.* semi-annual.
semeur [sə'mœ:r] *n.m.* sower; disseminator.
semi- [səmi-] *adj.* semi-, semi: *~ circulaire* semi-circular; *~ automatique*, semi-automatic.
séminaire [semi'nɛ:r] *n.m.* **1.** [Rel.] seminary. **2.** [Scol.] seminar.
sémitique [semi'tik] *adj.* Semitic.
semonce [sə'mõ:s] *n.f.* reprimand, [Fam.] dressing-down: *s'attirer une verte ~*, to be sharply rebuked.
sénat [se'na] *n.m.* senate: © *Président du Sénat*, Speaker of the Senate. || **sénateur** [-'tœ:r] *n.m.* senator.
sénescence [senɛ'sɑ̃:s] *n.f.* senescence.
sénile [se'nil] *adj.* senile, elderly.
sens[1] [sɑ̃:s] *n.m.* **1.** meaning. **2.** sense: *le ~ commun*, common sense: *C'est contraire au bon ~*, It does not make sense; *en dépit du bon ~*, in a senseless manner. **3.** sense: *le ~ de l'ouïe*, the sense of hearing; *les cinq ~*, the five senses.
sens,[2] **sent** [sɑ̃] cf. SENTIR.
sensation [sɑ̃sa'sj|õ] *n.f.* sensation, feeling; excitement. || **sensationnel, -le** [-ɔ'nɛl] *adj.* sensational, exciting.
sensé, -e [sɑ̃'se] *adj.* [Pers.] sensible; [décision] sound, reasonable. [× CENSÉ.]
sensibilité [sɑ̃sibili'te] *n.f.* sensitivity, sensitiveness, feelings. || **sensible** [sɑ̃sibl] *adj.* **1.** sensitive (to, *à*). **2.** perceptible, noticeable: *progrès sensibles*, marked, good/progress. **3.** sore. || **sensiblement** [-ə'mɑ̃] *adv.* noticeably, perceptibly. || **sensiblerie** [-ə'ri] *n.f.* sentimentality.
sensualité [sɑ̃sɥ|ali'te] *n.f.* sensuality; voluptuousness. || **sensuel, -le** [-ɛl] *adj.* sensual; voluptuous.
sentais, sente, sentis, &c. cf. SENTIR.
sentier [sɑ̃'tje] *n.m.* (foot)path: *hors des sentiers battus*; [Fig.] off the beaten track.
sentiment [sɑ̃ti'mɑ̃] *n.m.* feeling; [impression] sentiment, opinion: *avoir le ~ intime de* (*qqch.*), to feel (sth.) in one's bones. || **sentimental, -e** [-'tal] *adj.* sentimental, [mièvre] mawkish; [Fam.] namby-pamby. || **sentimentalement** [-tal'mɑ̃] *adv.* sentimentally. || **sentimentalité** [-tali'te] *n.f.* sentimentality.
sentinelle [sɑ̃ti'nɛl] *n.f.* sentinel, sentry.
sentir [sɑ̃t|i:r] **sentant** [-ɑ̃], **senti** [-i] #26 *v. tr.* to smell: *Je le sens*, I can smell it; *Cela sent le renfermé*, It has a musty smell; [Fig.] *Je ne peux pas le ~*, I can't stand him. **2.** to feel: *Il m'a fait ~ que j'étais de trop*, He made me feel unwelcome. || **se sentir** *v. pron.* to feel: *Il se sent fatigué*, He feels tired.
seoir [swa:r] **séant, seyant** [se'ɑ̃, sɛ'jɑ̃] #66 *v. intr.* to suit, become, be becoming: *Il ne lui sied pas d'agir ainsi*, It does not become him to behave that way.
séparable [sepa'r|abl] *adj.* separable, distinguishable. || **séparation** [-a'sjõ] *n.f.* separation, severing; [mur] partition. ||**séparé, -e** [sepa'r|e] *adj.* separate, distinct. || **séparément** [-e'mɑ̃] *adv.* separately, asunder, apart. || **séparer** [-e] #3 *v. tr.* to separate, divide, part; to draw apart. || **se séparer** *v. pron.* to separate, to part (from, *de*), to part company, [réunion] to break up: *~ en*, to divide into.
sept [sɛt] *n.m. & adj.* seven: *le ~ avril*, the seventh of April.
septembre [sɛp'tɑ̃:br] *n.m.* (the month of) September.
septième [sɛ'tjɛm] *adj. num. & n.m.* (the, one) seventh.
Sept-Iles [sɛ'til] *n.f.* © Sept-Iles [sometimes translated by Seven Islands].
septuagénaire [sɛptɥaʒe'nɛ:r] *n. & adj.* septuagenarian.
sépulcre [se'pylkr] *n.m.* sepulchre. ||**sépulture** [sepyl'ty:r] *n.f.* **1.** burial ground, burial place. **2.** interment, burial.
serai, &c. cf. ÊTRE.
séraphin [sera'f|ɛ̃] *n.m.* © *C'est un vrai ~*, He's a real stingy fellow. || **séraphique** [-ik] *adj.* seraphic(al).
serein[1], **-e** [sə'r|ɛ̃, -ɛn] *adj.* [Pers.] serene, calm, placid; [ciel] cloudless, clear.
serein[2] *n.m.* night dew.
sérénade [sere'nad] *n.f.* serenade: *donner /une, la/ ~ à* (*qqun*), to serenade (s.o.).
†**serf** [sɛrf] *n.m.* [Hist.] serf; [ext.] slave. || *adj.* **ser|f, -ve** [sɛrf, sɛrv] *adj.* in bondage: *condition serve*, serfdom.
sergent [sɛr'ʒɑ̃] *n.m.* **1.** [armée] sergeant: *~ d'armes*, sergeant-at-arms; *~ de ville*, constable, policeman. **2.** [menuiserie] clamp.
série [se'ri] *n.f.* series, succession: *production en ~*, mass production.
sérieusement [serjøz'mɑ̃] *adv.* seriously, in earnest: *Je parle ~*, I mean it. || **sérieu|x, -se** [se'rjø(:z)] *adj.* serious, earnest;

thorough. || *n.* seriousness: *prendre au* ~, to take seriously; *garder son* ~, to keep a straight face.

serin [s(ə)'rɛ̃] *n.m.* **1.** canary(-bird). **2.** [Pers.] simpleton, ninny.

seringue [s(ə)'rɛ̃:g] *n.f.* syringe.

serment [sɛr'mɑ̃] *n.m.* oath, swearing; [Fig.] promise: *prêter* ~, to take an oath, to be sworn in.

sermon [sɛr'm|õ] *n.m.* sermon; [réprimande] lecture, admonition. || **sermonner** [-ɔ'ne] #3 *v. tr.* [réprimander] to lecture, to sermonize (s.o.).

serpe [sɛrp] *n.f.* billhook.

serpent [sɛr'pɑ̃] *n.m.* snake, serpent: ~ *à sonnettes*, rattlesnake. || **serpenter** [-'te] #3 *v. intr.* [route, &c.] to wind, [rivière] to meander. || **serpentin** [-'tɛ̃] *n.m.* [tuyau] coil; [alambic] worm; [papier] streamer.

serpillière [sɛrpi'ljɛ:r] *n.f.* burlap; sacking, packing-cloth.

serpolet [sɛrpɔ'lɛ] *n.m.* [Bot.] thyme.

serre[1] [sɛ:r] *n.f.* [plantes] greenhouse.

serre[2] *n.f.* [oiseau de proie] claw, talon.

serré, -e [sɛ're] *adj.* [vêtement, &c.] tight, [rang, espace] narrow, close; [bref] compact, condensed: *avoir le cœur* ~, to be heavy-hearted.

serre-frein [sɛr'frɛ̃] *n.m.* *inv.* [Rail.] brakeman.

serrement [sɛr|'mɑ̃] *n.m.* squeezing, pressing: ~ *de cœur*, pang, heaviness of heart; ~ *de mains*, hand-shake. || **serrer** [-e] #3 *v. tr.* to squeeze, press, tighten; to be tight, to hold tight, to clasp: *Cela me serre*, It's too tight; ~ *une vis*, to tighten a screw; ~ *les rangs*, to close ranks; ~ *qqun contre son cœur*, to hug close; ~ *la main à qqun*, to shake hands with s.o.; ~ *le cœur*, to make sad, to grieve; ~ *une question*, to examine a question more closely. || **se serrer** *v. pron.* to stand, to sit closer; to huddle.

serre-tête [sɛr'tɛ:t] *n.m.* *inv.* headband, kerchief.

serrure [sɛ'r|y:r] *n.f.* lock: *(le) trou de la* ~, keyhole. || **serrurier** [-y'rje] *n.m.* locksmith.

sers, sert cf. SERVIR.

servant [sɛr'v|ɑ̃] *n.m.* gunner: ~ *de messe*, altar boy. || **servante** [-ɑ̃:t] *n.f.* maid. || **serveur** [-œ:r] *n.m.* waiter, bartender. || **serveuse** [-ø:z] *n.f.* waitress, barmaid.

serviable [-jabl] *adj.* obliging.

service [sɛr'vis] *n.m.* **1.** help, favour: *rendre un* ~ *à qqun*, to help s.o.; *Qu'y a-t-il pour votre* ~ *?*, What can I do for you? **2.** service, duty, employ: *être au* ~ *de qqun*, to be employed by s.o.; *restaurant libre-* ~, self-service restaurant; *Le* ~ *est compris*, The tip is included; *être de* ~, to be on duty; *avoir vingt ans de services*, to have worked twenty years; ~ *militaire*, conscription, draft, © [abus.] *Service civil*, Civil service; *hors de* ~, out of/use, order/. **3.** set: ~ *à café*, coffee set. **4.** [tennis] service. **5.** [repas] course: *un dîner à trois services*, a three-course dinner; [hotel] *premier service*, first call for dinner, first seating. **6.** [Rel.] service.

serviette [sɛr'vjɛt] *n.f.* [table] napkin, serviette; [toilette] towel; [porte-documents] briefcase, portfolio, bag.

servile [sɛr'vil] *adj.* servile, menial; slavish.

servir [sɛr'v|i:r] #28 *v. tr.* to serve, to wait on, to be of help. || **se servir** *v. pron.* to help o.s.; to use, make use of: ~ *d'un outil*, to use a tool.

serviteur [-i'tœ:r] *n.m.* servant.

servitude [sɛrvi'tyd] *n.f.* servitude, slavery.

ses [sɛ] *adj. poss. 3e pers. m/f.pl.* his (own); her (own); its (own); one's (own).

session [sɛ'sjõ] *n.f.* session, sitting.

seuil [sœ:j] *n.m.* threshold, doorstep.

seul, -e [sœl] *adj.* alone, by o.s.; single, sole; lonely: *être* ~, to be alone; *un* ~ *exemple*, a single instance; *le* ~ *survivant*, the sole survivor; *Il se sent* ~, He feels lonely. || **seulement** [-'mɑ̃] *adv.* only, solely, merely; [restriction] but. || †**seulet, -te** [-ɛ(t)] *adj.* [poét.] lonely, all alone.

sève [sɛ:v] *n.f.* [plante] sap; [Fig.] vim and vigour, vitality.

sévère [se'v|ɛ:r] *adj.* strict, severe, stern. || **sévérité** [-eri'te] *n.f.* strictness, severity, sternness.

sevrer [sə'vre] #9 *v. tr.* to wean (a baby); [Fig.] to deprive (of, *de*).

sexe [sɛks] *n.m.* sex: *le beau* ~, the fair sex.

sextant [sɛks'tɑ̃] *n.m.* sextant.

sextuor [sɛks't|ɥɔ:r] *n.m.* [Mus.] sextet.

sextuple [-ypl] *adj.* sixfold, sextuple. || *n.* sextuple.

seyait, &c. cf. SEOIR.

seyant[1] [sɛ'jɑ̃] cf. SEOIR.

seyant[2] *adj.* [robe] becoming.

shilling [ʃi'liŋ] *n.m.* shilling.

si[1] [si] *conj.* **1.** if: *Si vous avez le temps*, If you have time; *Si je le dis, c'est que c'est vrai*, If I say so, it's because it's true. **2.** whether, if: *Je ne sais s'il viendra*, I don't know whether he'll come. **3.** suppose: *Et s'il oubliait?*, And what if he forgets?, Suppose he forgets. **4.** [to suggest] *Si on allait au cinéma?*, How about going to a movie? || *adv.* **1.** so: *Il* *est* ~ *fort*, He is so strong; *Ce n'est pas* ~ *facile que ça*, It's not as easy as all that, It's not that easy; *si bien que . . .*, so that . . . [expressing consequence]. **2.** however, no matter how: *si prudent qu'il soit*, no matter how careful he is. **3.** [to contradict negative statement] yes: *Vous ne le saviez pas? Si!* You did not know? Yes, I did.

si[2] *n.m.* [Mus.] si, B.

Sibérie, la [sibe'ri] *n.f.* Siberia.

Sicile, la [si'sil] *n.f.* Sicily. || **sicilien, -ne** [-jɛ̃, -jɛn] *adj. & n.* Sicilian.

sidéré, -e [side're] *adj.* [Pers.] flabbergasted, dumbfounded.

siècle [sjɛkl] *n.m.* **1.** century; [ext.] period, age. **2.** [Rel.] the world, things mundane.

sied, cf. SEOIR.

siège [sj|ɛ:ʒ] *n.m.* **1.** seat; [Anat.] seat, bottom. **2.** head office. **3.** [Mil.] siege. **4.** *le Saint-Siège*, the Holy See. || **siéger** [-e'ʒe] #7 *v. intr.* to sit; to be in session.

sien, -ne (le, la) [sjɛ̃, -ɛn] *pron. poss. 3e pers.* one's, his, hers, its. || *n.*: *y mettre du* ~, to be cooperative; *les siens*, one's (own)/people, relatives/; *faire des siennes*, to be up to one's usual tricks.

sieste [sjɛst] *n.f.* siesta, (afternoon) nap: *faire une courte* ~, to have forty winks.

sifflement [sifl|ə'mɑ̃] *n.m.* [modulé] whistle, whistling; [serpent, vapeur] hiss(ing); [baguette] swish; [balle de fusil] whiz(zing). || **siffler** [-e] #3 *v. tr. & intr.* [en modulant] to whistle; [serpent, vapeur] to hiss, [baguette] to swish; [balle] to whiz: ~ *un acteur*, to hiss, to boo an actor. || **sifflet** [-ɛ] *n.m.* whistle: [Fam.] *Cela lui a coupé le* ~, That held him, That did the trick; [Théât.] *les sifflets*, the boos; *essuyer les sifflets*, to be booed, hissed.

siffleux [-ø] *n.m.* © cf. MARMOTTE.

signal [si'ɲal] *n.m.* signal: ~ *d'alarme*, emergency signal, [Br.] communication cord; ~ *de manœuvre*, dial tone; ~ *pas libre*, the 'busy' signal; *signaux lumineux*, traffic lights. || **signalé, -e** [-e] *adj.* remarkable: *Il m'a rendu un* ~ *service*, He did me a/distinct, great/favour. || **signalement** [-'mã] *n.m.* description. || **signaler** [-e] #3 *v. tr.* to point out, to indicate: *Il m'a signalé plusieurs erreurs dans ce texte*, He pointed out to me several errors in the text.

signature [siɲa'ty:r] *n.f.* signature: *apposer sa* ~, to sign, to affix one's signature; *revêtu de sa* ~, furnished with one's signature.

signe [siɲ] *n.m.* sign, mark, symbol; [témoignage] token: ~ *de tête*, nod; *faire le* ~ *de la croix*, to make the sign of the cross; *faire* ~ *(à qqun)*, to beckon to s.o., to sign to s.o. (to, *de*). || **signer** [-e] #3 *v. tr.* to sign. || **se signer** *v. pron.* to cross o.s., to make the sign of the cross.

signet [-ɛ] *n.m.* bookmark.

signification [siɲif|ika'sjõ] *n.f.* meaning; significance. || **signifier** [-je] #3 *v. tr.* to mean, signify; to notify (sth. to s.o., *qqch. à qqun*).

silence [si'l|ɑ̃:s] *n.m.* silence, quiet, stillness; [Mus.] rest: *Gardez le* ~, *s.v.p.!*, Keep silence, please! Be quiet, please!; *passer (qqch.) sous* ~, to omit (sth.); *réduire qqun au* ~, *imposer* ~ *à qqun*, to silence s.o. || **silencieusement** [ɑ̃sjøz'mɑ̃] *adv.* silently. || **silencieu|x, -se** [-ɑ̃'sjø(:z)] *adj.* silent, quiet, still. || *n.m.* [Auto.] muffler, silencer.

Silésie, la [sile'z|i] *n.f.* Silesia. || **Silésien, -ne** [-jɛ̃, -jɛn] *adj. & n.* Silesian.

silhouette [si'lwɛt] *n.f.* silhouette, profile.

sillage [si'ja:ʒ] *n.m.* wake.

sillon [si'j|õ] *n.m.* [charrue] furrow, [ride] wrinkle, [disque, &c.] groove. || **sillonner** [-ɔ'ne] #3 *v. tr.* [champ] to furrow, to plough; [front, &c.] to wrinkle; [éclairs] to streak (across the sky).

similarité [similari'te] *n.f.* similarity, likeness.

simili- [simili] [prefix used in the sense of "imitation" of sth.] simili- [employé comme adj. préposé] imitation: ~ *-cuir*, leatherette.

simple [sɛ̃:pl] *adj.* **1.** simple; ordinary, common: ~ *soldat*, private (soldier). **2.** single. **3.** easy, plain: ~ *comme bonjour*, as easy as ABC. || **simplicité** [sɛ̃pli|si'te] *n.f.* simplicity; plainness. || **simplifier** [-'fje] #3 *v. tr.* to simplify.

simulacre [simy'l|akr] *n.m.* semblance, sham: *un* ~ *de procès*, a/mockery, travesty/of a trial.

simuler [-e] #3 *v. tr.* to simulate, feign, sham, pretend.

sincère [sɛ̃'s|ɛ:r] *adj.* sincere, openhearted, genuine, frank, true, honest. || **sincèrement** [-ɛr'mɑ̃] *adv.* sincerely, frankly, truly. || **sincérité** [-eri'te] *n.f.* sincerity, open-heartedness, truthfulness, honesty.

Singapour [sɛ̃ga'pu:r] *n.f.* Singapore.

singe [sɛ̃:ʒ] *n.m.* monkey, ape. || **singer** [sɛ̃'ʒ|e] #5 *v. tr.* to ape, to mimic, to imitate (s.o., sth.). || **singerie** [-'ri] *n.f.* monkey trick, antic, grimace, mimicry.

singulariser [sɛ̃gyl|ari'ze] #3 *v. tr.* to make conspicuous, queer, strange. || **se singula-**

riser *v. pron.* to make o.s. conspicuous: *Il aime se ~* , He likes to be different. || **singularité** [-ari'te] *n.f.* singularity, strangeness, queerness, peculiarity.

singuli|er, -ère [-je, -jɛ:r] *adj.* **1.** strange, peculiar, singular. **2.** [Gram.] singular. || **singulièrement** [-jɛr'mɑ̃] *adv.* singularly, strangely, particularly.

sinistre [si'nistr] *adj.* sinister, evil, ominous. || *n.m.* disaster, tragedy.

sinon [si'nõ] *conj.* if not, otherwise; except, unless.

sinueu|x, -se [si'nɥ|ø(:z)] *adj.* sinuous, [route] winding, [ligne] wavy, [cours d'eau] meandering. || **sinuosité** [-ozi'te] *n.f.* winding, meandering, sinuosity.

Sion [si'õ] *n.m.* Mount Zion.

sionisme [sjɔ'nism] *n.m.* Zionism.

siphon [si'fõ] *n.m.* siphon.

sire [si:r] *n.m.* Sir, †sire [when addressing a sovereign]: *un/pauvre, triste/ ~* , a poor wretch.

sirène [si'rɛ:n] *n.f.* siren, [Naut.] fog-horn; [Mythol.] mermaid.

sirop [si'ro] *n.m.* syrup.

siroter [sirɔ'te] #3 *v. tr.* to sip; to tipple.

sis, -e [si(:z)] *adj.* situated, located.

site [sit] *n.m.* site, location.

sitôt [si'to] *adv.* *~ que*, as soon as; *~ dit*, *~ fait*, no sooner said than done.

sittelle [si'tɛl] *n.f.* nuthatch; [Fam.] crin-crin *m*, pic bleu *m*.

situation [sitɥ|a'sjõ] *n.f.* **1.** [lieu] situation, location, place; [Naut.] bearings. **2.** [occupation] position, job. **3.** [Fig.] position: *être dans une ~ embarrassante*, to be in an awkward position.

situer [-e] #3 *v. tr.* to locate, to situate.

six [sis, siz, si] *n.m. & adj. num.* six: *le ~ février 1960*, February 6, 1960. || **sixième (le, la)** [si'zjɛm] *adj. num. & n.m.* (the) sixth.

ski [ski] *n.m.* [Sport.] ski: *Faites-vous du ~ ?*, Do you ski? || **skieu|r, -se** [skj|œ:r, -ø:z] *n.* skier.

slave [sla:v] *adj.* [ethnique] Slavic, [langue] Slavonic. || *n.* Slav.

smoking [smɔ'kiɲ] *n.m.* tuxedo, dinner jacket.

snack-bar [snak'ba:r] *n.m.* snack (-bar) *m*; © casse-croûte *m*.

sobre [sɔbr] *adj.* [Pers.] abstemious, temperate, moderate [× SOBER]; [lignes, &c.] sober, quiet. || **sobriété** [-ije'te] *n.f.* [Pers.] temperance, moderation; [lignes, style] sobriety.

sobriquet [sɔbri'kɛ] *n.m.* nickname.

soc [sɔk] *n.m.* ploughshare.

sociable [sɔ'sja|bl] *adj.* sociable, affable. || **social, -e** [-l] *adj.* social. || **socialiste** [-'list] *adj.* socialist.

sociétaire [sɔsje't|ɛ:r] *n. m/f.* (full) member. || **société** [-e] *n.f.* society, association; [Com.] company, firm: *faire ~ avec qqun*, to form a partnership with s.o.; *La Société Radio-Canada*, The Canadian Broadcasting Corporation.

socque [sɔk] *n.f.* clog; [théâtre antique] sock. || **socquette** [-ɛt] *n.f.* [Fr., ankle] sock.

Socrate [sɔ'krat] *n.m.* Socrates. || **socratique** [-ik] *adj.* Socratic.

sœur [sœ:r] *n.f.* **1.** sister: *belle- ~* , sister-in-law. **2.** [Rel.] nun, sister.

sofa [sɔ'fa] *n.m.* sofa, couch, © chesterfield.

soi [swa] *pron. pers. réfl. 3e pers. sing.* [souvent suivi de *-même*] himself, herself, itself, oneself: *être chez ~* , to be at home; *Cela va de ~* , That goes without saying.

soi-disant [-di'zɑ̃] *adj. inv.* so-called, would-be, pretended.

soie [swa] *n.f.* **1.** silk: *papier de ~* , tissue paper. **2.** [cochon] bristle. || **soierie** [-'ri] *n.f.* **1.** silk(s). **2.** silk trade.

soif [swaf] *n.f.* thirst: *avoir ~* , to be thirsty; to thirst (for): *garder une poire pour la ~* , to put by for a rainy day; *mourir de ~* , to die of thirst.

soigné, -e [swa ɲ|e] *adj.* careful, neat: *travail ~* , fine workmanship; [tenue] well-groomed. || **soigner** [-e] #3 *v. tr.* to take care of, to look after; [malade] to nurse; to do carefully: *~ son style*, to polish one's style. || **se soigner** *v. pron.* to take care of o.s.

soigneusement [-øz'mɑ̃] *adv.* carefully. || **soigneu|x, -se** [-ø(:z)] *adj.* careful, painstaking.

soi-même [swa'mɛ:m] cf. SOI.

soin [swɛ̃] *n.m.* care: *aux bons soins de M.X.*, (to the) care of Mr. X.; *être aux petits soins /avec, auprès de/(qqun)*, to wait on (s.o.) hand and foot, to fuss over (s.o.); *mettre un ~ infini à faire qqch.*, to take great pains to do sth. || *n.mpl.* care: *les soins médicaux*, medical care.

soir [swa:r] *n.m.* evening, night: *ce ~* , this evening, tonight; *hier (au) ~* , last /evening, night/; *cours du ~* , evening class. || **soirée** [swa're] *n.f.* **1.** evening: *passer la ~* , to spend the evening. **2.** party: *aller à une ~* , to go to a party (in the evening).

sois, &c. cf. ÊTRE.

soit[1] [swa] cf. ÊTRE.

soit[2] [swa] *conj.* (usual, repeated) either . . .

or, whether . . . or: ~ *lui*, ~ *moi*, either he or I; ~ *qu'il vienne ou qu'il ne vienne pas*, whether he comes or not. || *adv.* all right!

soixantaine [swasɑ̃'tɛn] *n.f.* (about) sixty: *Il est dans la* ~, He is about sixty years of age, [Fam.] He is in his sixties. || **soixante** [swa's|ɑ̃:t] *n.m. & adj. num.* sixty. || **soixantième** [-ɑ̃'tjɛm] *adj.* sixtieth.

sol[1] [sɔl] *n.m.* **1.** ground: *sur le* ~, on the ground. **2.** soil: ~ *fertile*, fertile soil.

sol[2] *n.m.* [Mus.] sol, G.

solaire [sɔ'lɛ:r] *adj.* solar.

soldat [sɔl'da] *n.m.* soldier: *simple* ~, private.

solde[1] [sɔld] *n.m.* **1.** [Fin.] balance. **2.** [Com.] clearance sale.

solde[2] *n.f.* [Mil.] pay: [Fig.] *être à la* ~ (*de qqun*), to be in s.o.'s pay; *être en demi-* ~, to be on half pay.

solder [-e] #3 *v. tr.* **1.** [compte] to settle, to pay (off). **2.** [Com.] to clear (goods). || **se solder** *v. pron.* to result in: *L'opération se solde par un bénéfice*, The transaction leaves a profit.

soleil [sɔ'lɛ:j] *n.m.* sun; [lumière et chaleur] sunshine; [fleur] sunflower; © [R.C.] monstrance: *coucher de* ~, sunset; *lever du* ~, sunrise.

solennel, -le [sɔla'n|ɛl] *adj.* solemn; [air] pompous. || **solennellement** [-ɛl'mɑ̃] *adv.* solemnly, pompously. || **solennité** [-i'te] *n.f.* solemnity, ceremony.

solfège [sɔl'fɛ:ʒ] *n.m.* [Mus.] solfeggio; solmization: *faire du* ~, to run over one's scales, to solmizate.

solide [sɔ'lid] *adj.* strong, durable. || *n.m.* solid. || **solidement** [-'mɑ̃] *adv.* strongly, firmly, steadfastly. || **solidifier** [-i'fje] #3 *v. tr.* to solidify. || **se solidifier** *v. pron.* to solidify, become solid. || **solidité** [-i'te] *n.f.* solidity; [Fig.] strength, firmness.

soliste [sɔ'list] *n. m/f.* soloist.

solitaire [sɔli't|ɛ:r] *adj.* solitary, lonely, single. || *n.m.* recluse. || **solitairement** [-ɛr'mɑ̃] *adv.* solitarily, all by o.s. || **solitude** [-yd] *n.f.* solitude; solitariness, loneliness.

solive [sɔ'l|i:v] *n.f.* joist. || **soliveau** [-i'vo] *n.m.* small joist.

solliciter [sɔlisi't|e] #3 *v. tr.* to solicit, to beg, to request. || **solliciteu|r, -se** [-œ:r, -ø:z] *n.* solicitor, petitioner. || **sollicitude** [-yd] *n.f.* solicitude, concern, care.

soluble [sɔ'ly|bl] *adj.* [substance] soluble; [question, problem] solvable.

solution [-'sjõ] *n.f.* [substance] solution; [problème, &c.] solving.

solvable [sɔl'vabl] *adj.* [Com.] solvent.

sombre [sõ:br] *adj.* **1.** dark. **2.** [Fig.] gloomy, sombre. **3.** [ciel] overcast, cloudy. || **sombrer** [sõ'bre] #3 *v. intr.* to sink, founder; [Fig.] to collapse.

sommaire [sɔ'm|ɛ:r] *adj.* summary, abridged, brief. || *n.m.* summary, abridgment. || **sommairement** [-ɛr'mɑ̃] *adv.* summarily, briefly.

sommation [sɔmma'sjõ] *n.f.* [Jur.] summons.

somme[1] [sɔm] *n.f.* **1.** [argent] amount. **2.** [addition] sum: *une* ~ *de connaissances*, a body of knowledge. **3.** burden: *bête de* ~, beast of burden.

somme[2] *n.m.* nap: *faire un* ~, to take a nap; *faire un petit* ~, to have forty winks. || **sommeil** [-ɛ:j] *n.m.* sleep, [état] sleepiness: *avoir* ~, to/be, feel/sleepy; *tomber de* ~, not to be able to keep one's eyes open. || **sommeiller** [-ɛ'je] #3 *v. intr.* to doze.

sommer [sɔ'me] #3 *v. tr.* to call upon: ~ *qqun de faire qqch.*, to call upon s.o. to do sth., to demand that he do sth.

sommes, cf. ÊTRE.

sommet [sɔ'mɛ] *n.m.* summit, top: [Pol.] *conférence f au* ~, conference at the summit.

sommier [sɔ'mje] *n.m.* box springs.

somnambule [sɔmn|ɑ̃'byl] *n.m.* sleep-walker.

somnifère [-i'fɛ:r] *adj.* somniferous. || *n.m.* sleeping tablet, opiate.

somnolence [-ɔ'lɑ̃:s] *n.f.* sleepiness, drowsiness. || **somnolent, -e** [-ɔ'lɑ̃(:t)] *adj.* sleepy, drowsy; somnolent. || **somnoler** [-ɔ'le] #3 *v. intr.* to doze (off).

somptueu|x, -se [sõp'tɥø(:z)] *adj.* sumptuous, luxurious.

son[1] [sõ] *adj. poss. m.sg. 3e pers.* [before a vowel or silent h, the feminine form is the same as the masc. *son*] his (own); her (own); its (own); one's (own).

son[2] *n.m.* sound, tone: *le mur du* ~, sound barrier.

son[3] *n.m.* bran.

sonate [sɔ'nat] *n.f.* sonata.

sondage [sõ'd|a:ʒ] *n.m.* sounding; [mine] boring; [Méd. &c.] probe: *le* ~ *de l'opinion publique*, the polling of public opinion; *pl.* sampling techniques. || **sonder** [-e] *v. tr.* [Naut.] to sound; [Méd.] to probe; [Fig.] to test.

songe [sõ:ʒ] *n.m.* dream, dreaming. || **songe-creux** [sõʒ'krø] *n.m.* [☞ no change in the plural] dreamer, visionary. || **songer** [sõ'ʒ|e] #5 *v. intr.* **1.** to dream (about sth.), to muse. **2.** to think (of doing, *à faire*). || **songerie** [-'ri] *n.f.* dreaming, musing; reverie. || **songeu|r, -se** [-œːr, -øːz] *n. m/f* dreamer. *adj.* dreamy, thoughtful.

sonnaille [sɔ'naːj] *n.f.* cattle bell.

sonnant, -e [sɔ'n|ɑ̃(ːt)] *adj.* ringing, sounding: *payer en espèces sonnantes,* to pay in hard cash.

sonner [-e] #3 *v. tr.* to ring (the bell), to sound (the bugle, &c.), to blow (a horn, trumpet): *sonnez le concierge,* ring for the janitor. || *v. intr.* [cloche] ring; [cor] to blow; to sound; [horloge] to strike.

sonnerie [-'ri] *n.f.* ringing, chimes.

sonnet [sɔ'nɛ] *n.m.* sonnet.

sonnette [-ɛt] *n.f.* bell, door bell: *Tirez la ~, s.v.p.,* Ring the bell, please.

sonore [sɔ'n|ɔːr] *adj.* sonorous, sounding; [voyelle, consonne] voiced. || **sonorité** [-ɔri'te] *n.f.* sonority, sonorousness.

sont [sõ] *v.* ÊTRE.

soprano [sɔpra'no] *n.m.* soprano.

sorbet [sɔr'bɛ] *n.m.* sherbet.

sorbier [sɔr'bje] *n.m.* sorb tree: *~ d'Amérique,* American mountain ash.

sorcellerie [sɔrs|ɛl'ri] *n.f.* witchcraft, sorcery, black magic. || **sorcier** [-je] *n.m.* sorcerer, wizard. || **sorcière** [-jɛːr] *n.f.* sorceress, witch.

sordide [sɔr'did] *adj.* [sale] squalid, filthy; [avarice, &c.] sordid, mean; [Fig.] vile.

Sorlingues (les îles) [sɔr'lɛ̃ːg] *n.f.pl.* Scilly Islands.

sort [sɔːr] *n.m.* **1.** destiny, fate; hazard, chance: *Le ~ en est jeté!,* The die is cast! **2.** charm, spell: *jeter un ~ / à, sur/qqun,* to/throw, cast/a spell/on, over/s.o.

sortable [sɔr't|abl] *adj.* [personne] acceptable, suitable.

sortant [-ɑ̃] *adj.* outgoing: *le numéro ~,* the winning number; *le président ~,* the immediate past-president.

sorte [sɔrt] *n.f.* sort, kind, type: *de la ~,* thus; *de (telle) ~ que . . .,* so that . . .; *faire en ~ que . . .,* to see to it that. . . .

sorti, -e [sɔr'ti] *p.p.* of SORTIR.

sortie [sɔr'ti] *n.f.* **1.** going out, coming out; way out, exit: *Par ici la ~,* This way out; *~ de secours,* emergency exit, fire escape. **2.** outburst: *Il m'a fait une ~,* He bawled me out. **3.** [siège] sortie.

sortilège [sɔrti'lɛːʒ] *n.m.* spell, charm, sortilège, magic.

sortir[1] [sɔr'tiːr] #26 *v. intr.* **1.** to/go, get, come, walk/out. **2.** [origine] to come of, from; to originate with. || *n. au ~ de,* on/coming, getting/out of.

sortir[2] #26 *v. tr.* [note that this verb is conjugated with the auxiliary AVOIR] to /bring, take/(sth.) out.

sosie [sɔ'zi] *n.m.* double.

sot, -te [so, sɔt] *adj.* foolish, stupid, silly. || *n.* fool, blockhead, ass: *C'est un ~ en trois lettres,* He is/a downright fool, an absolute dunce/. || **sottise** [sɔ'tiːz] *n.f.* foolishness, stupidity, silliness: *Ce sont des sottises!,* (It's) nonsense!; *Dire des sottises à (qqun),* To/abuse, insult/ (s.o.), call (s.o.) names.

sou [su] *n.m.* copper, penny, © [Fam.] cent: *un trente sous,* [25 cent coin] a quarter; *être sans le ~,* to be penniless; */brillant, propre/comme un ~ neuf,* spick and span (new); *Il n'a pas laissé un ~ à ses héritiers,* He cut his heirs off without a /dime, penny/.

soubassement [subɑs'mɑ̃] *n.m.* [église, maison] basement; [Arch.] base, subfoundation.

soubresaut [subrə'so] *n.m.* [véhicule] jolt, start; [personne] jump, start.

soubrette [su'brɛt] *n.f.* soubrette, waiting- / maid, woman/.

souche [suʃ] *n.f.* [arbre] stump, stock; [famille, généalogie] origin, source, founder (of a family); [chèque] counterfoil, stub.

souci[1] [su's|i] *n.m.* concern, care, anxiety, worry: *C'est le/cadet, moindre/de mes soucis,* It does not worry me in the least, It's the least of my worries; *se faire du ~ au sujet de qqch.,* to worry about sth.

souci[2] *n.m.* [Bot.] marigold.

soucier (se) [-je] #3 *v.* (*pron.*) to bother, to care, to worry (about, *de*), to be concerned (with, *de*): *Je m'en soucie comme de l'an quarante,* I don't care a/straw, button/for it. || **soucieu|x, se** [-jø(ːz)] *adj.* [personne, air] concerned, worried, anxious.

soucoupe [su'kup] *n.f.* saucer: *~ volante,* flying saucer.

soudage [su'daːʒ] *n.m.* © cf. SOUDURE.

soudain [su'd|ɛ̃] *adv.* cf. SOUDAINEMENT. *adj.* sudden, unexpected, abrupt. || **soudainement** [-ɛn'mɑ̃] *adv.* suddenly, all of a sudden, out of the blue.

Soudan [su'dɑ̃] *n.m.* The Sudan.

soudard [su'daːr] *n.m.* [Mil.] [Péj.] ruffian.

soude [sud] *n.f.* soda: *bicarbonate m de ~,* sodium bicarbonate.

souder [su'de] #3 *v. tr.* to solder, to weld (metals); [Fig.] to join (two things, &c.).

soudoyer [sudwa'je] #12 *v. tr.* [Péj.] to hire, to bribe.

soudure [su'dyːr] *n.f.* solder(ing), welding; [Fig.] joining; [Fig.] *faire la ~,* to tide over.

soue [su] *n.f.* (pig) sty.

soufflage [su'fla:ʒ] *n.m.* [verre] glass-blowing. || **souffle** [sufl] *n.m.* [respiration] breath, breathing; puff (of air): *être à bout de* ~, to be (completely) out of breath; [Fig.] *ne tenir qu'à un* ~, to hang by a thread. || **soufflé** [-e] *adj.* puffed, puffy: *blé/riz* ~, puffed/wheat, rice. || *n.* [Culin.] soufflé. || **souffler** [-e] #3 *v. tr.* to blow (sth.); [bougie] to blow out; [rôle] to prompt: *ne pas* ~ *mot* (*de qqch.*), not to/breathe, utter/a word (of sth.). || *v. intr.* [vent] to blow; [respirer] to catch o.'s breath.

soufflet [-ɛ] *n.m.* **1.** slap (in the face), box (on the ear); [Fig.] insult: *donner/flanquer/un* ~ *à qqun*, to slap s.o.'s face. **2.** [forge] bellows. || **souffleter** [-ə'te] #8 *v. tr.* to slap (s.o.) in the face; [Fig.] to insult (s.o.).

souffleur [su'flœ:r] *n.m.* [things] blower; [Théât.] prompter.

souffrance [su'fr|ɑ̃:s] *n.f.* suffering, pain, ailment: *endurer des souffrances atroces*, to suffer agonizing pain; *compte en* ~, overdue account: *marchandises en* ~, unclaimed, undelivered/goods. || **souffrant, -e** [-ɑ̃(:t)] *adj.* suffering, ailing, sickly. || **souffre-douleur** [sufr|ədu'lœ:r] *n.m. inv.* *être le* ~ *de*, to be persecuted by, to be the butt for the jokes of. || **souffreteu|x, -se** [-ə'tø(:z)] ailing, sickly; stunted. || **souffrir** [-i:r] #25 *v. intr.* to suffer, to be in pain: ~ *du froid*, to suffer from cold. || *v. tr.* to suffer, to endure; to allow, tolerate (sth.): *Je ne le souffrirai pas*, I won't stand for it.

soufre [sufr] *n.m.* sulphur, †brimstone.

souhait [swɛ] *n.m.* wish: *exprimer un* ~, to express a desire; *A vos souhaits!*, God bless you!; *avoir tout à* ~, to have everything to one's/wish, liking/. || **souhaitable** [-'tabl] *adj.* desirable. || **souhaiter** [-'te] #3 *v. tr.* to wish (for sth.), to desire.

souiller [su'j|e] #3 *v. tr.* to soil, stain, dirty; [reputation, &c.] to blemish. || **souillon** [-õ] *n. m/f.* [usual. a woman] slut. || **souillure** [-y:r] *n.f.* soil, stain, spot, blot; [Fig.] blemish, defilement.

soûl, -e [su, sul] *adj.* cf. SAOUL. || [su] *n.m.* (one's) fill; [Fig.] heart's content: *manger tout son* ~, to eat one's fill.

soulagement [sulaʒ|'mɑ̃] *n.m.* relief (from sth.), comfort, alleviation. || **soulager** [-e] #5 *v. tr.* to relieve, comfort, alleviate.

soûlaud [su'l|o] *n.m.* [Vulg.] drunk, drunkard. || **soûler** [-e] #3 *v. tr.* to intoxicate, to make (s.o.) drunk; [saturer] to fill, satiate. || **se soûler** *v. pron.* to get drunk; to have one's fill (of, *de*).

soulèvement [sulɛv'mɑ̃] *n.m.* heaving: [estomac] rising; [Fig.] upheaval, insurrection. || **soulever** [sul've] #9 *v. tr.* **1.** to lift (up), to raise. **2.** [Fig.] to raise (a question); to rouse (a mob); ~ *le cœur*, to nauseate. || **se soulever** *v. pron.* **1.** to raise o.s. **2.** to rise (up), to revolt.

soulier [su'lje] *n.m.* shoe.

souligné, -e [suli'ɲe] *adj.* underlined; [Fig.] emphasized. || **souligner** #3 *v. tr.* to underline; [Fig.] to stress, to emphasize.

soumettre [su'm|ɛtr] #44 *v. tr.* to submit (s.o., sth.), to conquer (s.o.); [question, &c.] to refer (sth.) to (s.o.). || **se soumettre** *v. pr.* to yield (to, *à*); [règlements, &c.] to comply (with), to knuckle/under, down/. || **soumis, -e** [-i(:z)] *adj.* **1.** obedient, docile; [pupil, son, &c.] submissive. **2.** subject to, liable to (a duty). || **soumission** [-i'sjõ] *n.f.* **1.** submission, obedience; surrender: *faire sa* ~ *à qqun*, to/yield, surrender/to s.o. **2.** tender (for a contract).

soupape [su'pap] *n.f.* valve.

soupçon [sup's|õ] *n.m.* suspicion, distrust; surmise. || **soupçonner** [-ɔ'ne] #3 *v. tr.* to suspect (s.o., sth.), to surmise. || **soupçonneusement** [-ɔnøz'mɑ̃] *adv.* suspiciously, distrustfully. || **soupçonneu|x, -se** [-ɔ'nø(:z)] *adj.* suspicious, distrustful.

soupe [sup] *n.f.* soup: [Fig.] *trempé comme une* ~, drenched to the skin: *Il est très* ~ *au lait*, He has a low boiling-point.

soupente [su'pɑ̃:t] *n.f.* garret, loft.

souper [su'pe] #3 *v. intr.* to have (o.'s) supper: [Fam.] *J'en ai soupé!*, I am fed up with it! || *n.m.* supper; [© in Canada, = dinner].

soupeser [supə'ze] #9 *v. tr.* to weigh in o.'s hand, to try the weight of.

soupière [su'pjɛ:r] *n.f.* soup tureen.

soupir [su'pi:r] *n.m.* **1.** sigh, gasp: *pousser un* ~, to heave a sigh; *rendre le dernier* ~, to pass away, to breathe o.'s last. **2.** [Mus.] crotchet (-rest).

soupirail *pl.* **aux** [supi'r|a:j, -o] *n.m.* basement window.

soupirant [supi'r|ɑ̃] *n.m.* lover, wooer, suitor. || **soupirer** [-e] #3 *v. tr. & intr.* to sigh, to gasp; [Fig.] to long (for, *après*).

souple [supl] *adj.* flexible, pliant; [Fig.] compliant, versatile. || **souplesse** [-ɛs] *n.f.* flexibility, pliancy; [Fig.] compliance.

source [surs] *n.f.* source, spring: *prendre sa* ~ *dans*, to have its source in; [Fig.] to originate in; *de* ~, from the heart; *de bonne* ~, reliably, from a reliable source.

sourcil [sur'si] *n.m.* (eye)brow: *froncer les sourcils*, to frown; [réflexion] to knit o.'s brows. || **sourciller** [-je] #3 *v. intr.* [usually negative] to frown, to wince: *sans ~*, without turning a hair.

sourd, -e [su:r, surd] *adj.* [audition] deaf; [bruit] rumbling: *~ comme un pot*, stone deaf.

sourdine [sur'din] *n.f.* sordino: *en ~*, muted, [Fig.] on the sly; *mettre en ~*, to soft-pedal.

sourd-muet [sur'mɥɛ] *f.* **sourde-muette** [surd'mɥɛt] *pl.* **sourd(e)s- muet(te)s** [sur'mɥɛ, surd'mɥɛt] *adj. & n.* deaf-and-dumb (person).

sourdre [surdr] #42 *v. intr.* to rise, to spring (up); to gush (forth), to well up.

souriant, -e [su'rjɑ̃(:t)] *adj.* smiling: *tout en ~*, beaming.

souriceau [suri's|o] *n.m.* small mouse.

souricière [-jɛ:r] *n.f.* **1.** mousetrap. **2.** snare.

sourire [su'ri:r] #50 *v. intr.* to smile (upon, at, *à*): [Fig.] *Cela me sourit*, It appeals to me. || *n.m.* smile, [large] grin; [hautain] smirk.

souris[1] [su'ri] *n.f.* mouse.

souris[2] *n.m.* cf. SOURIRE.

sournois, -e [sur'nw|a(:z)] *adj.* sly, cunning; [manières] devious, underhand(ed). || *n.m.* sneak. || **sournoisement** [-az'mɑ̃] *adv.* cunningly, slyly. || **sournoiserie** [-az'ri] *n.f.* cunning, slyness, underhandedness.

sous [su] *prép.* under, below, beneath: *~ la main*, at hand; *~ peu*, before long; *~ la pluie*, in the rain; *~ le soleil*, under the sun; *~ un tunnel*, in a tunnel. || **sous-bois** [su'bwɑ] *n.m.* undergrowth. || **sous-chef** [su'ʃɛf] *pl.* **sous-chefs** *n.m.* [bureau] deputy head clerk. || **souscripteur** [suskr|ip-'tœ:r] *n.m.* subscriber. || **souscription** [-ip'sjɔ̃] *n.f.* subscription, subscribing; signature, complimentary close. || **souscrire** [-i:r] #48 *v. tr.* to subscribe (money, to sign (a document). || *v. intr.* [Fig.] to agree to (sth.), to endorse. || **souscrit, -e** [-i(t)] p.p. of SOUSCRIRE. || **sous-diaconat** [sudjak|ɔ'na] *n.m.* [Rel.] subdeaconship. || **sous-diacre** [-r] *n.m.* subdeacon. || **sous-directeur** [sudirɛk'tœ:r] *n.m.* assistant-manager, vice-president. || **sous-entendre** [suzɑ̃t|ɑ̃:dr] #42 *v. tr.* to imply. || **sous-entendu** [-ɑ̃'dy] *adj.* implied, understood. || *n.m.* implication. || **sous-entente** [-ɑ̃:t] *n.f.* mental reservation. || **sous-fifre** [su'fifr] *n.m.* [Fig.] second fiddle. || **sous-jacent, -e** [suʒa'sɑ̃(:t)] *adj.* underlying, subjacent. || **sous-lieutenant** [suljøt'nɑ̃] *n.m.* [Mil.] second lieutenant. || **sous-locataire** [sulɔka|-'tɛ:r] *n. m/f* subtenant. || **sous-location** [-'sjɔ̃] *n.f.* subletting. || **sous-louer** [su'lwe] #3 *v. tr.* to sublet. || **sous-main** [su'mɛ̃] *n.m. pl.* sous-mains, blotter. || **sous-marin** [suma'rɛ̃] *n.m.* submarine. *adj.* submarine, underwater. || **sous-ministre** [sumi'nistr] *pl.* **sous-ministres** © *n.m.* deputy-minister. || **sous-officier** [suzɔfi'sje] *n.m.* [Mil.] *pl.* **sous-officiers** non-commissioned officer. || **sous-ordre** [su'zɔrdr] *n.m. pl. inv.* subordinate: *en ~*, as an underling. || **sous-préfecture** [suprefɛk'ty:r] *n.f. pl.* **sous-préfectures** sub-prefecture. || **sous-préfet** [supre'fɛ] *n.m.* sub-prefect. || **sous-principal** [suprɛ̃si'pal] *n.m.* vice-principal. || **sous-secrétaire** [susəkre'tɛ:r] *n. m/f* under-secretary: © *~ d'État adjoint*, Assistant Under-Secretary of State. || **soussigné, -e** [susi'ɲe] *adj.* undersigned: *Je, ~, certifie que . . .*, I, the undersigned, certify that . . . . || **sous-sol** [su'sɔl] *pl.* **sous-sols** *n.m.* **1.** basement. **2.** subsoil. || **sous-titre** [su'titr] *n.m.* subtitle.

soustraire [sus'trɛ:r] #38 *v. tr.* [Math.] to subtract; to take (sth.) away; to steal. || **se ~** *v. pr.* to escape (from, *à*).

sous-traitant [sutrɛ'tɑ̃] *n.m.* sub-contractor.

soutane [su'tan] *n.f.* cassock, soutane.

soute [sut] *n.f.* [bateau] store-room, bunker.

soutenance [sut'nɑ̃:s] *n.f.* *~ de thèse*, defence of a thesis.

soutènement [sutɛn'mɑ̃] *n.m.* *mur de ~*, retaining wall.

soutenir [sut'ni:r] #22 *v. tr.* **1.** to support, to prop (up). **2.** to support, to side with, to defend. **3.** to stand, to sustain, to resist (an attack). **4.** to support, to provide for. || *v. intr.* **1.** [food] to be sustaining. **2.** [Fig.] to maintain. || **soutenu, -e** [sut'ny] *adj.* [intérêt, &c.] sustained, constant, steady; [style, &c.] lofty, elevated.

souterrain, -e [sute'r|ɛ̃, -ɛn] *adj.* underground (passage, &c.); [Fig.] underhand, subterranean. || *n.m.* underground (passage).

soutien [su'tjɛ̃] *n.m.* support, stay; [personne] supporter (of a family, &c.): *Il est ~ de famille*, He helps support a family. || **soutien-gorge** [-'gɔrʒ] *n.m.* brassière × BRASSIÈRE *n.f.*

soutirer [suti're] #3 *v. tr.* [vin, &c.] to draw (sth.) off; [Fig.] to worm (sth.) out (from s.o.).

†**souvenance** [suv'nɑ̃:s] *n.f.* recollection.

souvenir (se) [səsuv'ni:r] *v. pr.* see #22 to remember (sth.), to bear (sth.) in mind, to recollect (sth.). || [suv'ni:r] *n.m.* **1.**

recollection, †remembrance, memory. **2.** keepsake; souvenir.

souvent [su'vɑ̃] *adv.* often, frequently.

souverain, -e [suv'r|ɛ̃, -ɛn] *n. m/f.* sovereign, monarch. ‖ *adj. remède* ~, excellent remedy. ‖ **souverainement** [-ɛn'mɑ̃] *adv.* extremely, supremely, utterly. ‖ **souveraineté** [-ɛn'te] *n.f.* sovereignty.

soviet [sɔ'vj|ɛt] *n.m.* [Polit.] Soviet. ‖ **soviétique** [-e'tik] *adj.* Soviet: *l'Union des Républiques socialistes soviétiques*, the Union of (the) Socialist Soviet Republics.

soya, soja [sɔ'ja, sɔ'ʒa] *n.m.* soybean.

soyeu|x, -se [swa'jø(:z)] *adj.* silky, silken.

spacieu|x, -se [spa'sjø(:z)] *adj.* spacious, roomy.

spaghetti [spagɛ'ti] *n.m.pl.* [singular in © = du spaghetti] spaghetti.

spahi [spa'i] *pl.* **spahis** *n.m.* [Mil.] spahi, spahee.

sparadrap [spara'dra] *n.m.* [Fr.] (sticking-, adhesive) plaster.

spasme [spasm] *n.m.* spasm. ‖ **spasmodique** [spasmɔ'dik] *adj.* spasmodic.

spatial, -e [spa'sjal] *adj.* → space: *recherches spatiales*, space research.

speaker [spi'kɛ:r] *n.m.* [Fr.] cf. ANNONCEUR; (radio) announcer.

spéci|al, -aux [spe'sj|al, -o] *adj.* (e)special, particular, peculiar. ‖ **spécialement** [-al'mɑ̃] *adv.* (e)specially, particularly, peculiarly. ‖ **spécialiser** [-ali'ze] #3 *v. tr.* to specialize. ‖ se ~ *v. pr.* to specialize (in, *en*); [Schol.] to honour (in, *en*). ‖ **spécialiste** [-a'list] *n.m.* specialist (in, *de*), expert (in, *en*). ‖ **spécialité** [-ali'te] *n.f.* speciality.

spécieu|x, -se [spe'sjø(:z)] *adj.* specious, misleading.

spécifier [spesi'fje] #3 *v. tr.* to specify.

spécifique [spesi'fik] *adj.* specific.

spécimen [spesi'mɛn] *n.m.* specimen, sample.

spectacle [spɛk'ta|kl] *n.m.* **1.** sight, scene. **2.** show, play: *Spectacles* [listed in newspaper]. *Amusements*: *monter un* ~, to put on a show. **3.** [Fig. & Loc.] *se donner en* ~, to make a spectacle of o.s. ‖ **spectat|eur, -rice** [-'tœ:r, -'tris] *n.* spectator, bystander, onlooker; [théâtre] a member of the audience: *les spectateurs*, the audience.

spectre [spɛktr] *n.m.* ghost, spectre; [couleurs] spectrum.

spéculat|eur, -rice [spekyla|'tœ:r, -tris] *n. m/f.* [thoughts] speculator, theorizer; [Fin.] speculator. ‖ **spéculati|f, -ve** [-'tif, -'ti:v] *adj.* speculative. ‖ **spéculation** [-'sjɔ̃] *n.f.* speculation; [thoughts] theory, conjecture; [Fin.] operations. ‖ **spéculer** [speky'le] #3 *v. tr.* [thoughts] to speculate, cogitate (upon, *sur*); [Fin.] to speculate (in, *sur*).

sperme [spɛrm] *n.m.* sperm.

sphère [sfɛ:r] *n.f.* sphere. ‖ **sphérique** [sfe'rik] *adj.* spherical.

sphinx [sfɛ̃:ks] *n.m.* [Mythol.] **1.** sphinx. **2.** [insecte] hawk moth.

spinal, -e [spi'nal] *adj.* spinal.

spir|al, -aux [spi'r|al, -o] *adj.* spiral. ‖ [spi'ral] *n.m.* [montre] hair spring.

spiritisme [spiri'tism] *n.m.* spiritualism.

spirituel, -le [spiri'tɥɛl] *adj.* **1.** spiritual. **2.** witty. ‖ *n.m.* spirituality, things spiritual. ‖ **spirituellement** [-'mɑ̃] *adv.* **1.** spiritually. **2.** wittily.

splendeur [splɑ̃'d|œ:r] *n.f.* splendour, glory.

splendide [-id] *adj.* splendid; [jour, &c.] glorious.

spoliation [spɔlj|a'sjɔ̃] *n.f.* spoliation, despoiling, plunder. ‖ **spolier** [-e] #3 *v. tr.* to despoil, to rob, to plunder.

spontané, -e [spɔ̃ta'ne] *adj.* spontaneous: *allumage spontané*, self-ignition. ‖ **spontanéité** [-i'te] *n.f.* spontaneity, spontaneousness. ‖ **spontanément** [-'mɑ̃] *adv.* spontaneously, of his own accord.

sport [spɔ:r] *n.m.* sport: *Il s'intéresse aux sports*, He is very much interested in sports. ‖ **sporti|f, -ve** [spɔr't|if, -i:v] *adj.* sporting (activities, spirit, publication).

spoutnik [sput'nik] *n.m.* sputnik; cf. BÉBÉ-LUNE.

square [skwa:r] *n.m.* square cf. CARRÉ.

squelette [skə'lɛt] *n.m.* skeleton.

stabiliser [stabili|'ze] #3 *v. tr.* to stabilize; to steady. ‖ **stabilité** [-'te] *n.f.* stability; steadiness; firmness. ‖ **stable** [stabl] *adj.* stable, firm, steady.

stade[1] [stad] *n.m.* stage: *à ce* ~, at this stage.

stade[2] *n.m.* stadium, arena.

stage [sta:ʒ] *n.m.* **1.** [term of] probation, period of instruction, qualifying period. **2.** [refresher] course, workshop, clinic. ‖ **stagiaire** [sta'ʒjɛ:r] *n.m/f.* trainee, probationer; [Educ.] exchange teacher.

stagner [sta'ɲe] #3 *v. intr.* to stagnate.

stalle [stal] *n.f.* [chœur] stall; [écurie] stall.

stance [stɑ̃:s] *n.f.* [Poet.] stanza.

standardiser [stɑ̃dardi|'ze] #3 *v. tr.* to standardize. ‖ **standardiste** [-st] *n.f.* [Tel.] (switchboard) operator.

station [sta'sj|ɔ̃] *n.f.* station; [arrêt] pause: *petite* ~, whistle stop; ~ *intermédiaire*, wayside station; ~ *balnéaire*, seaside resort; ~ *climatique*, health resort; ~ *de sports d'hiver*, winter sport resort; [Fr.] ~ *-service*, service station; ~

thermale, watering place; ~ *touristique*, tourist centre. || **stationnaire** [-ɔ'nɛ:r] *adj.* stationary. || *n.m.* coastguard vessel. || **stationnement** [-ɔn'mɑ̃] *n.m.* [Auto] parking; standing: ~ *interdit*, No parking. || **stationner** [-ɔ'ne] #3 *v. intr.* [Auto] to park (a car).
statique [sta'tik] *adj.* static. || *n.f.* statics.
statistique [statis'tik] *adj.* statistical. || *n.f.* statistics.
statue [sta'ty] *n.f.* statue.
statuer [sta'tɥe] #3 *v. tr. & intr.* to rule (upon sth.).
stature [sta'ty:r] *n.f.* stature, height, size.
statut [sta'ty] *n.m.* statute.
stéatite [stea'tit] *n.f.* steatite, French chalk.
stellaire [stɛl'lɛ:r] *adj.* stellar.
sténographe [stenɔ'graf] *n.m/f.* stenographer, shorthandwriter. || **sténographie** [-i] *n.f.* stenography, shorthand. || **sténographier** [-je] #3 *v. tr.* to take down in shorthand.
stentor [stɑ̃'tɔ:r] *n.m.* stentor: *voix f de* ~, stentorian voice.
stérile [ste'ril] *adj.* sterile, unfruitful; barren; childless; unproductive. || **stériliser** [-i'ze] #3 *v. tr.* to sterilize.
sterne [stɛrn] *n.m.* tern.
stigmate [stig'mat] *n.m.* stigma, scar, brand; pock mark.
stimulant, -e [stimy'l|ɑ̃(:t)] *adj.* stimulating. || *n.m.* stimulant. || **stimuler** [-e] #3 *v. tr.* to stimulate, to rouse (s.o.).
stipuler [stipy'le] #3 *v. tr.* to stipulate.
stoïcisme [stɔi'sism] *n.m.* stoicism.
stoppage [stɔ'p|a:ʒ] *n.m.* [Fr.] invisible mending. || **stopper** [-e] #3 *v. intr.* to stop. || *v. tr.* to mend invisibly.
store [stɔ:r] *n.m.* (Venetian) blind.
strabisme [stra'bism] *n.m.* squint(ing).
strapontin [strapɔ̃'tɛ̃] *n.m.* attached folding seat, jump seat.
stratagème [strata'ʒɛ:m] *n.m.* stratagem.
stratégie [strate'ʒi] *n.f.* strategy.
strict, -e [strik(t)] *adj.* strict, severe, rigid. || **strictement** [-ə'mɑ̃] *adv.* strictly, severely, rigidly.
strident, -e [stri'dɑ̃(:t)] *adj.* shrill, harsh, grating.
strie [stri] *n.f.* streak (of lightning, &c.), [rayure] stripe.
strontium [strɔ̃'sjɔm] *n.m.* strontium.
strophe [strɔf] *n.f.* [Poét.] verse, stanza.
structural, -e [strykty'ral] *adj.* structural. || **structure** [stryk'ty:r] *n.f.* structure, construction.
strychnine [strik'nin] *n.f.* strychnine.
stuc [styk] *n.m.* stucco.
studieu|x, -se [sty'djø(:z)] *adj.* studious.
stupéfaction [stypef|ak'sjɔ̃] *n.f.* amazement. || **stupéfait, -e** [-ɛ(t)] *adj.* amazed, astonished (at, *de*). || **stupéfiant, -e** [-jɑ̃(:t)] *adj.* astounding. || *n.m.* narcotic. || **stupéfié, -e** [-je] cf. STUPÉFAIT. || **stupéfier** [-je] #3 *v. tr.* to amaze, astound. || **stupeur** [stypœ:r] *n.f.* amazement.
stupide [sty'pid] *adj.* stupid. || **stupidité** *n.f.* stupidity.
style [stil] *n.m.* style.
stylet [sti'lɛ] *n.m.* stiletto.
stylo [sti'l|o] *n.m.* fountain pen. cf. STYLOGRAPHE: ~ *à bille*, ball-point pen. || **stylographe** [-ɔ'graf] *n.m.* [usual. abbreviated in stylo] fountain pen. || **stylomine** [-ɔ'min] *n.m.* mechanical pencil.
su, -e [sy] cf. SAVOIR. || *n.m.* knowledge: *au vu et au* ~ *de tous*, to everybody's knowledge.
suaire [sɥɛ:r] *n.m.* shroud.
suave [sɥa:v] *adj.* bland, suave. || **suavité** [sɥavi'te] *n.f.* blandness, suavity.
subalterne [sybal'tɛrn] *adj. & n.* subordinate, inferior.
subconscient, -e [sybkɔ̃'sjɑ̃(:t)] *adj. & n(m).* subconscious.
subir [sy'b|i:r] #17 *v. tr.* to undergo (sth.), to suffer (sth., s.o.).
subit, -e [-i(t)] *adj.* unexpected. || **subitement** [-it'mɑ̃] *adv.* suddenly, unexpectedly.
subjecti|f, -ve [sybʒɛk't|if, -i:v] *adj.* subjective.
subjoncti|f, -ve [subʒɔ̃k't|if, -i:v] *adj. & n.m.* [Gram.] subjunctive (mood).
subjuguer [sybʒy'ge] #3 *v. tr.* to subdue, to subjugate (s.o.).
sublime [sy'blim] *adj.* sublime.
submerger [sybmɛr'ʒe] #5 *v. tr.* to submerge, to drown.
submersible [sybmɛr'sibl] *adj.* submersible. || *n.m.* submarine.
subordination [sybɔrdina'sjɔ̃] *n.f.* subordination. || **subordonné, -e** [sybɔrdɔ'ne] *adj. & n.* subordinate.
subreptice [sybrɛp'tis] *adj.* surreptitious.
subséquent, -e [sybse'kɑ̃(:t)] *adj.* subsequent.
subsidiaire [sybsi'djɛ:r] *adj.* subsidiary.
substance [syps't|ɑ̃:s] *n.f.* substance, matter. || **substantiel, -le** [-ɑ̃'sjɛl] *adj.* substantial.
substanti|f, -ve [sypstɑ̃'t|if, -i:v] *adj.* [Gram.] substantive. || *n.m.* substantive, noun.
substituer [sypsti'tɥe] #3 *v. tr.* to substitute (for, *à*): ~ *A à B*, to substitute A for B, to replace B by A. || **substitut** [sypsti'ty] *n.m.* substitute; [administration] deputy (to s.o.).
subterfuge [syptɛr'fy:ʒ] *n.m.* subterfuge.

subtil, -e [syp'til] *adj.* subtle; [esprit] keen, sharp; fine: *une distinction* ~, a nice distinction. || **subtiliser** [-i'ze] #3 *v. tr.* to subtilize, filch. || **subtilité** [-i'te] *n.f.* subtlety, shrewdness.
subvenir [sybvə'ni:r] #22 *v. tr.* to supply, provide. || **subvention** [sybvɑ̃'sj|õ] *n.f.* grant, subsidy. || **subventionner** [-ɔ'ne] #3 *v. tr.* to subsidize.
subversi|f, -ve [sybvɛr's|if, -i:v] *adj.* subversive.
suc [syk] *n.m.* juice; [Fig.] (quint)essence.
succédané [sykseda'ne] *n.m.* substitute (for sth.).
succéder [sykse'de] #10 *v. intr.* to succeed: *Il a succédé à son père,* He succeeded his father; [chronologie] to come after, to follow.
succès [syk'sɛ] *n.m.* success: *remporter un* ~, to score a success; [Théât.] *remporter un* ~ *fou,* to bring down the house.
successeur [syksɛ's|œ:r] *n.m.* successor. || **successi|f, -ve** [-if, -i:v] *adj.* successive. || **successivement** [-iv'mɑ̃] *adv.* successively, in succession.
succinct, -e [syk's|ɛ̃(:t)] *adj.* succinct, brief, concise. || **succinctement** [-ɛ̃t'mɑ̃] *adv.* succinctly, briefly, concisely.
succion [syk'sjõ] *n.f.* suction, sucking.
succomber [sykõ'be] #3 *v. intr.* to succumb, to yield (to sth.); to die.
succulent, -e [syky'lɑ̃(:t)] *adj.* succulent, juicy.
succursale [sykyr'sal] *n.f.* branch.
suce [sys] *n.f.* © cf. TÉTINE. || **sucer** [-e] #4 *v. tr.* to suck, to suck (sth.) in. || **sucette** [-ɛ] *n.* sucker. || **suçon** [-õ] *n.m.* cf. SUCETTE.
sucre [sykr] *n.m.* sugar: ~ *en morceaux,* lump sugar; ~ *en poudre,* granulated sugar; [Br.] castor sugar; ~ *d'érable,* maple sugar; © *partie de sucre,* sugaring party; [Fig.] *casser du* ~ *sur le dos de qqun,* to run s.o. down. || **sucré, -e** [-e] *adj.* sugared, sugary, sweet(ened); [Fig.] demure. || **sucrer** [-e [#3 *v. tr.* to sweeten. || **sucrerie** [-ə'ri] *n.f.* **1.** sugar refinery; © maple bush, sugar bush. **2.** *pl.* sweets: *aimer les sucreries,* to have a sweet tooth. || **sucrier, -ère** [-i'je, -i'jɛ:r] *adj.* (pertaining to) sugar. || *n.m.* **1.** sugar bowl. **2.** sugar-maker.
sud [syd] *n.m.* south: *du* ~, [pays] southern, [direction] southerly. || **sud-est** [-'ɛst] *n.m.* southeast. || **sud-ouest** [-'wɛst] *n.m.* southwest.
Suède, la [sɥɛd] *n.f.* Sweden. || **suédois, -e** [sɥe'dwa(:z)] *adj.* Swedish. || *n.* Swede.
suer [sɥe] #3 *v. intr.* to sweat, to perspire. || **sueur** [sɥœ:r] *n.f.* sweat, perspiration.
Suez [sɥɛ:z] *n.m.* Suez: *le canal de* ~, the Suez Canal.
suffire [sy'f|i:r] #46 *v. intr.* to be sufficient, enough, to suffice: *Ça suffit!,* Skip it!; *Ça suffit pour aujourd'hui!,* Call it a day!; *se* ~ *(à soi-même),* to be self-sufficient. || **suffisamment** [-iza'mɑ̃] *adv.* sufficiently, enough. || **suffisance** [-i'zɑ̃:s] *n.f.* **1.** sufficiency. **2.** cockiness, conceit. || **suffisant, -e** [-i'zɑ̃(:t)] *adj.* **1.** sufficient, enough. **2.** cocky, conceited.
suffixe [sy'fiks] *n.m.* [Gram.] suffix.
suffoquer [syfɔ'ke] #3 *v. tr.* to suffocate, to choke: [Fig.] *être, rester/suffoqué,* to be flabbergasted. || *v. intr.* to choke.
suffrage [sy'fra:ʒ] *n.m.* vote, suffrage: *donner ses suffrages à qqun,* to vote for s.o.; *le* ~ *universel,* universal suffrage.
suggérer [sygʒ|e're] #10 *v. tr.* to suggest. || **suggesti|f, -ve** [-ɛs't|if, -i:v] *adj.* suggestive, evocative. || **suggestion** [-jõ] *n.f.* suggestion. || **suggestionner** [-jɔ'ne] #3 *v. tr.* to suggest; to prompt.
suicide [sɥi'sid] *n.m.* suicide. || **suicider (se)** [-e] #3 *v. pron.* to commit suicide, to take one's own life.
suie [sɥi] *n.f.* soot.
suif [sɥif] *n.m.* tallow: [Fam.] *donner un* ~ *à qqun,* to give s.o. a dressing down.
suint [sɥɛ̃] *n.m.* grease (in wool).
suintement [sɥɛ̃t|'mɑ̃] *n.m.* oozing, leak. || **suinter** [-e] #3 *v. intr.* to ooze, seep; [goutte à goutte] to trickle; [blessure] to run.
suisse [sɥis] © *n.m.*: ~ *barré,* chipmunk cf. TAMIAS.
Suisse *n.f.* Switzerland. || *adj.* Swiss. || *n.m.* **1.** [*f.* **Suissesse**] Swiss. **2.** [église] beadle.
suite [sɥit] *n.f.* **1.** continuation, sequel: *donner* ~ *à,* to take up, to follow up; *pour* ~ *à donner,* for action; *Ce livre a une* ~, This book has a sequel; *La* ~ *au prochain numéro,* To be continued; *par la* ~, eventually; *tout de* ~, immediately. **2.** result, consequence: *à la* ~ *de,* as a result of, following; *Il mourut des suites de l'accident,* He died as a result of the accident. **3.** succession, sequence: *la* ~ *des événements,* the sequence of events. **4.** retinue, suite, party: *le président et sa* ~, the President and his party; [Fig.] *venir à la* ~ *de,* to come in the train of. **5.** coherence, consistency: *avoir de la* ~ *dans les idées,* to think coherently.
suivant[1], -e [sɥi'vɑ̃(:t)] *adj.* following, next. || *n.m.* follower, disciple.
suivant[2] [sɥi'vɑ̃] *prép.* according to.

suivre [sɥi:vr] #51 *v. tr. & intr.* to follow; to/go, come/after: *Prière de faire* ~, Please forward; ~ *un cours,* to take a course.

sujet, -te [sy'ʒ|ɛ(t)] *adj.* subject (to, *à*). || **sujet** [-ɛ] *n.m.* **1.** [Gram.] subject. **2.** subject, matter, topic. **3.** [Pers.] subject: *C'est un mauvais* ~, He's a bad lot. **4.** [Loc.] *avoir* ~ *de,* to have reason to.

sujétion [-e'sjõ] *n.f.* subjection, bondage, slavery; liability (to, *à*).

sulfate [syl'f|at] *n.m.* sulphate.

sulfite [-it] *n.m.* sulphite.

sulfure [-y:r] *n.m.* sulphide. || **sulfureu|x, -se** [-y'rø(:z)] *adj.* sulphurous. || **sulfurique** [-y'rik] *adj.* sulphuric.

sultan [syl't|ɑ̃] *n.m.* sultan. || **sultane** [-an] *n.f.* sultana.

sumac [sy'mak] *n.m.* [vénéneux, toxique] poison ivy, cow itch. cf. HERBE.

superbe [sy'pɛrb] *adj.* superb, magnificent, stately; [Péj.] haughty, vainglorious. || *n.m.* vainglorious man: *Les Superbes,* The Proud. || *n.f.* [Péj.] haughtiness, vainglory.

superficie [sypɛrfi's|i] *n.f.* area (of a country, &c.). || **superficiel, -le** [-jɛl] *adj.* superficial; [esprit] shallow.

superflu [sypɛr'fly] *adj.* superfluous; redundant; useless. || *n.m.* superfluity.

supérieur, -e [sype'rj|œ:r] *adj.* superior; [classe, étage, &c.] upper; © *le Lac Supérieur,* Lake Superior. || *n.* [R.C.] Father, Mother/Superior. || **supérieurement** [-œr'mɑ̃] *adv.* superlatively. || **supériorité** [-ɔri'te] *n.f.* superiority: *reconnaître la* ~ *de qqun,* to take off one's hat to s.o.

superlatif, -ve [sypɛrla't|if, -i:v] *adj. & n.m.* superlative.

superposer [sypɛrpo'ze] #3 *v. tr.* to superpose, to stack; to superimpose.

superstitieu|x, -se [sypɛrsti'sj|ø(:z)] *adj.* superstitious. || **superstition** [-õ] *n.f.* superstition.

supplanter [syplɑ̃'te] #3 *v. tr.* to supplant.

suppléant, -e [syple|'ɑ̃(:t)] *adj.* substitute, assistant: *professeur* ~, substitute teacher. || *n.m.* substitute. || **suppléer** [-e] #3 *v. tr.* **1.** to complete, to supplement: *Je suppléerai le reste,* I'll make up the balance. **2.** to help, assist; to be the stand-in of.

supplément [syple'mɑ̃] *n.m.* supplement, additional/sum, amount/: *en* ~, additional. || **supplémentaire** [-'tɛ:r] *adj.* supplementary, additional: *faire des heures supplémentaires,* to work overtime.

suppliant, -e [sypli'ɑ̃(:t)] *adj.* [voix, &c.] supplicating, suppliant, entreating. || **supplication** [syplika'sjõ] *n.f.* supplication, beseeching.

supplice [sy'plis] *n.m.* torment, ordeal: [Fig.] *être au* ~, to be tormented, to be racked with pain.

supplier [sypli'e] #3 *v. tr.* to implore, to entreat, to beseech (s.o.). || **supplique** [sy'plik] *n.f.* supplication, entreaty: *présenter une* ~, to petition.

support [sy'p|ɔ:r] *n.m.* support, stand, prop; © coat-hanger. || **supportable** [-ɔr'tabl] *adj.* bearable (pain, &c.), sufferable. || **supporter** [-ɔr'te] #3 *v. tr.* to bear, to suffer (s.o., sth.), to put up with (sth., s.o.), to tolerate.

supposé, -e [sypo'z|e] *adj.* supposed, implied; [Péj.] pretended. || **supposer** [-e] #3 *v. tr.* **1.** to suppose. **2.** to imply, to assume, to presuppose. || **supposition** [-i'sjõ] *n.f.* supposition, implication, assumption, hypothesis; [Péj.] forgery (of a legal deed).

suppôt [sy'po] *n.m.* tool, agent, myrmidon.

suppression [syprɛ'sjõ] *n.f.* suppression, removing; abatement. || **supprimer** [sypri'me] #3 *v. tr.* to do away with, to abolish, to discontinue: ~ *qqun,* to do away with s.o.

suppurer [sypy're] #3 *v. intr.* to suppurate.

supputer [sypy'te] #3 *v. tr.* to weigh, to calculate (chances, &c.).

suprématie [syprema'si] *n.f.* supremacy. || **suprême** [sy'prɛm] *adj.* supreme, paramount: *Cour* ~, Supreme Court.

sur[1] [sy:r] *prép.* **1.** on, in [avec mouvement sur une surface] across, down: ~ *le toit,* on the roof; ~ *un cahier,* in a notebook, ~ *une photo,* in a picture; *La pluie coule* ~ *les vitres,* The rain runs down the panes. **2.** [Fig.] on, about, as to: *écrire* ~ *un sujet,* to write on a topic; *pressenti* ~ *ses intentions,* sounded as to his intentions. **3.** over, on: *avoir de l'influence* ~, to have influence on. **4.** out of: *dix* ~ *vingt,* ten out of twenty. **5.** [divers] *juger* ~ *les apparences,* to judge by appearances; *chanter* ~ *un air,* to sing to a tune; ~ *ce,* thereupon.

sur,[2] **-e** *adj.* sour, tart.

sûr,[3] **-e** *adj.* **1.** sure, certain: *J'en suis* ~, I am positive. **2.** secure, safe: *mettre (qqch.) en lieu* ~, to put (sth.) in a place of safety. **3.** reliable, trustworthy; infallible: *à coup* ~, for/sure, certain/; *de source sûre,* reliably.

surabondance [syrabõ'd|ɑ̃:s] *n.f.* superabundance, profusion. || **surabondant, -e** [-ɑ̃(:t)] *adj.* superabundant, profuse.

|| **surabonder** [-e] #3 *v. tr.* to superabound, overflow with.
suralimentation [syralimɑ̃t|a'sjõ] *n.f.* overfeeding. || **suralimenter** [-e] #3 *v. tr.* to overfeed.
suranné, -e [syra'ne] *adj.* old-fashioned, out-of-date.
surcharger [syrʃar'ʒe] #5 *v. tr.* to overload (s.o., sth.).
surchauffer [syrʃo'fe] #3 *v. tr.* to overheat.
surcroît [syr'krwa] *n.m.* excess, increase, surplus: *par* ~, in addition.
surdité [syrdi'te] *n.f.* deafness.
sureau [sy'ro] *n.m.* elder: ~ *bleu*, mountain elder; ~ */blanc, du Canada,* Canadian elder.
surélévation [syrel|eva'sjõ] *n.f.* raising; part raised. || **surélever** [-'ve] #9 *v. tr.* to raise higher.
sûrement [syr'mɑ̃] *adv.* surely, for sure, certainly.
surestimer [syrɛsti'me] #3 *v. tr.* to overestimate, to overrate.
sûreté [syr'te] *n.f.* **1.** security, safety: *serrure de* ~, safety lock; *en* ~, safe. **2.** sureness, unerringness, control (of gestures).
surette [sy'rɛt] *n.f.* © cf. OSEILLE.
surévaluer [syreva'lɥe] #3 *v. tr.* to overestimate.
surexcité, -e [syrɛksi'te] *adj.* overexcited, stirred up. || **surexciter** #3 *v. tr.* to overexcite (s.o.).
surface [syr'fas] *n.f.* surface, area: [sous-marin] *remonter à la* ~, to surface.
surgir [syr'ʒi:r] #17 *v. intr.* to emerge, to arise, to loom.
surhumain, -e [syry'm|ɛ̃, -ɛn] *adj.* superhuman.
surimposer [syrɛ̃po'ze] #3 *v. tr.* **1.** to superimpose. **2.** to overtax (s.o.).
surintendant, -e [syrɛ̃tɑ̃'dɑ̃(:t)] *n.* superintendent, overseer.
surir [sy'ri:r] #17 *v. intr.* to turn sour.
surlendemain [syrlɑ̃d'mɛ̃] *n.m.* (the) second day after.
surmenage [syrmə'n|a:ʒ] *n.m.* overwork (-ing), physical/intellectual/strain: *Pas de* ~ *!,* Take it easy! || **surmené, -e** [-e] *adj.* overworked, exhausted, overtired. || **surmener** #9 *v. tr.* to overwork (s.o.), to overtire (s.o.).
surmonter [syrmõ'te] #3 *v. tr.* to surmount, to overcome (a difficulty).
surmultiplication [syrmyltiplika'sjõ] *n.f.* [Auto] overdrive.
surnager [syrna'ʒe] #5 *v. intr.* to/float, swim/on the surface.
surnaturel, -le [syrnaty'rɛl] *adj.* supernatural. || *n.m.*: (*le*) ~, (the) supernatural.
surnom [syr'n|õ] *n.m.* nickname. [×] SURNAME.
surnombre [syr'nõ:br] *n.m.* cf. SURPLUS.
surnommer [syrnɔ'me] #3 *v. tr.* to nickname, to call (s.o.).
surnuméraire [syrnyme'rɛ:r] *adj.* supernumerary, in excess. || *n.m.* supernumerary.
suroît [sy'rwɑ] *n.m.* [Naut.] South-west; sou'-wester (wind); [chapeau] sou'wester.
surpasser [syrpɑ'se] #3 *v. tr.* to surpass, to outdo (s.o.). || **se** ~ *v. pr.* to outdo o.s.
surpeuplé, -e [syrpœ'pl|e] *adj.* overpopulated (country); overcrowded. || **surpeuplement** [-ə'mɑ̃] *n.m.* over-population, overcrowding. || **surpeupler** #3 *v. tr* to over-populate, to overcrowd.
surplis [syr'pli] *n.m.* [R.C.] surplice.
surplomber [syrplõ'be] #3 *v. tr. & intr.* to overhang.
surplus [syr'plys] *n.m.* surplus, excess: ~ *de marchandises,* surplus goods.
surpoids [syr'pwɑ] *n.m.* overweight.
surprenant, -e [syrpr|ə'nɑ̃(:t)] *adj.* surprising, amazing. || **surprendre** [-ɑ̃:dr] #41 *v. tr.* **1.** to surprise, to amaze. **2.** to take by surprise. **3.** to overhear. || **surpris, -e** [-i(:z)] *adj.* surprised, amazed (by, *par,* at, *de*). || **surprise** [-i:z] *n.f.* surprise, astonishment, amazement: *boîte f à* ~, Jack-in-the-box.
surproduction [syrprɔdyk'sjõ] *n.f.* overproduction.
surréalisme [syrea'lis|m] *n.m.* [Art] surrealism. || **surréaliste** [-t] *adj.* surrealistic. || *n.m/f.* surrealist.
sursaut [syr'so] *n.m.* start: *en* ~, with a start. || **sursauter** [-'te] #3 *v. intr.* to give a start; *faire un* ~, to give a/start, jump.
sursis [syr'si] *n.m.* surcease, respite, reprieve; [Milit.] deferment.
surtaxe [syr'taks] *n.f.* overcharge; surtax.
surtout[1] [syr'tu] *adv.* above all, (e)specially, chiefly.
surtout[2] *n.m.* overcoat, surtout.
surveillance [syrvɛ'j|ɑ̃:s] *n.f.* watch, supervision: *exercer une* ~ *de tous les instants,* to watch ceaselessly. || **surveillant, -e** [-ɑ̃(:t)] *n.m/f.* supervisor, watchman. || **surveille** [syrv|ɛ:j] *n.f.* © two days before. || **surveiller** [-ɛ'je] #3 *v. tr.* to supervise, to watch (over), to observe closely. || **se** ~, *v. pr.* [Fig.] to be on one's best behaviour.
survenant, -e [syrvə'n|ɑ̃(:t)] *n.* ©chance-comer, unexpected guest. || **survenir** [-i:r]

#22 *v. intr.* to/happen, arrive/unexpectedly, to take place.

survivance [syrv|i'vɑ̃:s] *n.f.* survival. || **survivant, -e** [-i'vɑ̃(:t)] *adj.* surviving. || *n.m.* survivor. || **survivre** [-i:vr] #52 *v. intr.* to survive: *Il n'a pas survécu à son père,* He did not survive his father.

survoler [syrvɔ'le] #3 *v. tr.* to fly over (a country, &c.).

sus[1] [sys] [*prép.*] *courir* ~ *à l'ennemi,* to rush at the enemy.

sus[2] [sys] *en* ~ *de* (*qqch.*), in addition to (sth.).

sus- [sys, syz] [*préf.*] sus-.

susceptibilité [sysɛptibili'te] *n.f.* touchiness. || **susceptible** [sysɛp'tibl] *adj.* susceptible, capable (of), liable (to); [personne] sensitive, touchy.

susciter [sysi'te] #3 *v. tr.* to create, to bring about.

suscription [syskrip'sjõ] *n.f.* superscription.

susdit, -e [syz'di(t)] *adj.* & *n.* above-mentioned, aforesaid.

susmentionné, -e [sysmɑ̃sjɔ'ne] cf. SUSDIT.

suspect, -e [syspɛ|(kt)] *adj.* suspicious, suspect(ed). || *n.m.* [personne] suspect. || **suspecter** [-k'te] #3 *v. tr.* to suspect.

suspendre [sys'p|ɑ̃:dr] #42 *v. tr.* **1.** to hang (up). **2.** to suspend (an official); to interrupt: *La séance est suspendue,* There will be a short break. || **suspendu, -e** [-ɑ̃'dy] *adj.* suspended, hanging; interrupted, delayed; [Jur.] deferred. || *adj.* hanging; suspended; interrupted: *pont* ~, suspension bridge. || **suspension** [-ɑ̃'sjõ] *n.f.* hanging (up); [ressorts] suspension; [personne] suspension; [séance] break, interruption: *points de* ~, dots, suspension points.

suspicion [syspi'sjõ] *n.f.* distrust.

susurrer [sysy're] #3 *v. tr.* to whisper, murmur.

susvisé [syzvi'ze] *adj.* above-mentioned.

suture [sy't|y:r] *n.f.* [Med.] suture: *point de* ~, stitch; [Ling.] juncture. || **suturer** [-y're] #3 *v. tr.* to sew (sth.) up; to join.

Suzanne [sy'zan] *n.f.* Susan.

svelte [zvɛlt] *adj.* [taille] slim, slender. || **sveltesse** [-ɛs] *n.f.* slimness, slenderness.

S.V.P. [ɛzve'pe] [on letters and signs, abbreviation of *s'il vous plaît*] please.

sycomore [sikɔ'mɔ:r] *n.m.* sycamore. cf. PLATANE.

syllabe [si(l)'lab] *n.f.* syllable. || **syllabique** [-ik] *adj.* syllabic.

symbole [sɛ̃'bɔl] *n.m.* symbol: *le Symbole des Apôtres,* The Apostles' Creed. || **symbolique** [-ik] *adj.* symbolic(al): *un versement, une contribution/* ~, a token contribution. || **symboliser** [-i'ze] #3 *v. tr.* to symbolize, to represent (sth.).

symétrie [sime'tri] *n.f.* symmetry. || **symétrique** [-k] *adj.* symmetrical.

sympathie [sɛ̃pa'ti] *n.f.* **1.** liking: *éprouver de la* ~ *pour qqun,* to like s.o., to have a liking for s.o. **2.** © condolence: *offrir ses sympathies à qqun,* to offer one's sympathy to s.o. || **sympathique** [-k] *adj.* [personne] likeable; [atmosphere] congenial. || **sympathisant** [-'zɑ̃] *n.m.* follower, fellow-traveller. || **sympathiser** [-'ze] #3 *v. intr.* to feel congenial ([×] sympathize).

symphonie [sɛ̃fɔ'ni] *n.f.* symphony. || **symphonique** [-k] *adj.* symphonic (orchestra, &c.).

symptôme [sɛ̃p'to:m] *n.m.* [Méd.] symptom; sign.

synagogue [sina'gɔg] *n.f.* synagogue.

synchroniser [sɛ̃krɔni'ze] #3 *v. tr.* to synchronize.

syncope [sɛ̃'kɔp] *n.f.* syncope; faint.

syndicat [sɛ̃di'ka] *n.m.* (trade) union: *les syndicats,* organized labour.

synonyme [sinɔ'nim] *adj.* & *n.m.* synonym.

synthèse [sɛ̃'tɛ:z] *n.f.* synthesis. || **synthétique** [sɛ̃te'tik] *adj.* synthetic.

syntoniser [sɛ̃tɔni'ze] #3 *v. tr.* © [radio, TV] to tune in, to listen in (to), to dial (a program, station).

syphilis [sifi'lis] *n.f.* syphilis.

Syrie [si'ri] *n.f.* Syria.

systématique [sistema'tik] *adj.* systematic.

système [sis'tɛm] *n.m.* system.

T

T, t [te] *n.m.* [letter] T, t.

t' [☞ Link with following vowel] [elided form of TE, pers. pron. 2nd pers. sing.]: *T'a-t-il prévenu?*, Did he tell you?

ta [ta] *adj. poss. 2ᵉ pers. fém. sing.* your; your own; thy; thy own. cf. TON.

tabac [ta'ba] *n.m.* tobacco; ~ *à chiquer*, chewing tobacco; ~ *à priser*, snuff; *blague à* ~, tobacco pouch; *débit de* ~, tobacco shop; [Fam.] *passer à* ~, to beat up; *coup de* ~, [Mil.] sudden and violent attack; [Naut.] violent storm. ‖ **tabagie** [-'ʒi] *n.f.* room reeking of tobacco smoke; © [abus.] smoking-room. ‖ **tabatière** [-'tjɛːr] *n.f.* **1.** snuff box. **2.** skylight.

tabernacle [tabɛr'nakl] *n.m.* [Rel.] tabernacle.

table [tabl] *n.f.* **1.** table: *mettre la* ~, to set the table; *A* ~ *!*, Dinner, Lunch/is served!, [Fam.] Come and get it!; *se mettre à* ~, to sit down to a meal; *la* ~ *et le logement*, board and lodging; *tenir* ~ *ouverte*, to keep open house; *faire* ~ *rase*, to make a clean sweep; *la Sainte* ~, the communion table, the altar rail. **2.** table: ~ *des matières*, table of contents.

tableau [-o] *n.m.* board; ~ *noir*, blackboard; [Auto] ~ *de bord*, dashboard; ~ *d'honneur*, honour roll; painting, picture; ~ *d'avancement*, seniority list; *mettre sous forme de* ~, to tabulate.

tabler [-e] #3 *v. intr.* to count, reckon (*sur qqch.*, on sth.).

tablette [-ɛt] *n.f.* shelf (of a closet); mantelpiece; writing pad; (chocolate) bar.

tablier [tabli'je] *n.m.* apron; pinafore; hood (of a chimney); flooring (of a bridge).

tabou [ta'bu] *n.m.* taboo. ‖ *adj.*: *sujets tabous*, forbidden subjects.

tabouret [tabu'rɛ] *n.m.* stool; footstool; ~ *de piano*, piano stool.

tac [tak] *n.m.*: *le tic-tac* (*d'une montre*), the tick-tock (of a watch); [Fig.] *répondre du* ~ *au* ~, to make a lightning retort.

tache [taʃ] *n.f.* [de couleur] stain; [d'encre] blot; [de liquide] blob; [de graisse] smear; [ronde] spot; [petite] speck; [qui rend trouble] blur: *Il y a une* ~ *sur la vitre*, There is a blur on the windowpane; [sur la peau] blemish; [Fig.] flaw, taint: *faire* ~ *sur*, to mar the appearance of; *faire* ~ *d'huile*, to spread; ~ *originelle*, original sin; ~ *du soleil*, sun spot; ~ *de rousseur*, freckle; *sans* ~, spotless, unblemished.

tâche [tɑːʃ] *n.f.* work, assignment, task, job: *prendre à* ~ *de faire qqch.*, to set one's heart on doing sth.; *se mettre*, [Fam.] *s'atteler à la* ~, to undertake to do sth.; *travail à la* ~, piecework; *ouvrier à la* ~, jobbing workman. ‖ **tâcher** [tɑ'ʃe] #3 *v. intr.* to try, endeavour (to, *de*).

tacher [-e] #3 *v. tr.* to stain, spot; to mar, blemish. ‖ **se tacher** *v. pron.* to soil, stain; to get soiled.

tacheter [taʃ'te] #8 *v. tr.* to spot.

tacite [ta'sit] *adj.* tacit, implied.

taciturne [tasi'tyrn] *adj.* silent, taciturn.

tacot [ta'ko] [Fr.] *n.m.* [Fam.] jalopy; heap, cf. BAZOU.

tact [takt] *n.m.* tact: *plein de* ~, tactful; *dépourvu de* ~, tactless; *avec* ~, tactfully; *manquer de* ~, to act tactlessly.

tactile [tak'til] *adj.* tactile.

tactique [tak'tik] *n.f.* **1.** [Mil.] tactics. **2.** tactics, manœuvring, approach. ‖ *adj.* tactical.

taffetas [taf'tɑ] *n.m.* taffeta; ~ *gommé*, adhesive tape.

taie [tɛ] *n.f.* [d'oreiller] pillow case; [sur l'œil] film.

taille [tɑːj] *n.f.* **1.** cutting, clipping, †tally: *la* ~ *du diamant*, diamond cutting; *pierre de* ~, freestone; *la* ~ *des haies*, hedge clipping; *la* ~ *du boulanger*, baker's tally. **2.** height: *de grande* ~, very tall; *de* ~ *moyenne*, of middle height; **3.** waist: *de forte* ~, stout; *prendre par la taille*, to take by the waist [This is the usual meaning in ©]. **4.** size: *Ce veston n'est pas à votre* ~, This coat is not your size. **5.** [Loc.] *être de* ~ *à*, to be quite capable of. ‖ **taillé, -e** [tɑ'j|e] cf. TAILLER. ‖ *adj.* cut: *verre, cristal* ~, cut glass. ‖ **taille-crayon** [-krɛ'jõ] *n.m. inv.* pencil-sharpener. ‖ **tailler** [-e] #3 *v. tr.* [pierre, verre] to cut; [bois] [avec une hache] to carve, to hew; [avec un couteau] to whittle: ~ *un crayon*, to sharpen a pencil; ~ *une haie*, to clip a hedge; ~ *en biseau*, to bevel; ~ *en pièces*, to wipe out. ‖ **tailleur** [-œːr] *n.m.* cutter: ~ *de pierre*, stone-cutter; tailor: *craie de* ~, French chalk; (*costume*) ~, (tailored) suit.

taillis [ta'ji] *n.m. invar.* thicket, copse.

taire [tɛːr] **taisant** [tɛ'zɑ̃] **tu** [ty] #49 *v. tr.* [☞ Note that this verb is not used in the passive.] to keep back, withhold, leave /unsaid, untold/: *faire* ~, to silence. ‖**se taire** *v. pron.* **1.** to/remain, fall/silent. **2.** [impoli] *Tais-toi!*, *Taisez-vous!*, Shut up! **3.** *Il a promis de* ~, He promised not to tell.

tais, tait cf. TAIRE.
talc [talk] *n.m.* talcum powder.
talent [ta'lɑ̃] *n.m.* talent, ability: *un homme de* ~, a gifted man; *avoir du* ~, to be talented. || **talentueu|x, -se** [-'tɥø(:z)] *adj.* talented.
talion [ta'ljõ] *n.m.* talion; *loi du* ~, law of retaliation: *appliquer la loi du* ~, → to retaliate.
talisman [talis'mɑ̃] *n.m.* talisman.
talon [ta'l|õ] *n.m.* heel: ~ *Louis XV*, French heel; *tourner les* ~, to turn on one's heel; *avoir l'estomac dans les talons*, to feel ravenous; ~ *(de souche)*, stub. || **talonner** [-ɔ'ne] #3 *v. tr.* to harass.
talus [ta'ly] *n.m.* slope, bank.
tamarac [tama'rak] *n.m.* © [= mélèze d'Amérique] tamarack. cf. ÉPINETTE ROUGE.
tambour [tɑ̃'b|u:r] *n.m.* **1.** drum: *battre le* ~, to beat a drum; *sans* ~ *ni trompette*, quietly; ~ *battant*, with drums beating, [Fig.] quickly, vigorously. **2.** drummer: ~ *major*, drum major; ~ *de ville*, town crier. **3.** [Auto.] ~ *de freins*, brake drum; *porte à* ~, revolving door. || **tambouriner** [-uri'ne] #3 *v. tr. & intr.* to patter, to beat a tattoo.
tamias [ta'mja:s] *n.m.*: ~*rayé*, chipmunk, cf. SUISSE.
tamis [ta'mi] *n.m.* sieve.
Tamise, la [ta'mi:z] *n.f.* The Thames (River).
tamiser [tami'ze] #3 *v. tr.* to sift; [lumière] to veil, soften.
tampon [tɑ̃'p|õ] *n.m.* **1.** stopper, plug: ~ *d'ouate*, pad, dab. **2.** [cachet] rubber stamp. **3.** [Rail.] buffer. || **tamponnement** [-ɔn'mɑ̃] *n.m.* collision (of trains), plugging. || **tamponner** [-ɔ'ne] #3 *v. tr.* **1.** to plug, rub with a pad, dab. **2.** [Rail.] to collide; to bump into.
tan [tɑ̃] *n.m.* tan. *adj. inv.* tan (-coloured).
tancer [tɑ̃'se] #4 *v. tr.* to scold, rate: ~ *vertement qqun*, to scold s.o. severely, [Fam.] read s.o. the Riot Act.
tanche [tɑ̃:ʃ] *n.f.* tench.
tandis que [tɑ̃'di k(ə)] *conj.* **1.** while, as: *Il joue* ~ *je travaille*, He plays while I work. **2.** whereas: *Il est pauvre tandis qu'elle est riche*, He is poor whereas she is rich.
tangage [tɑ̃'ga:ʒ] *n.m.* pitching (and tossing).
tangara [tɑ̃ga'ra] *n.m.* tanager, redbird.
tangent, -e [tɑ̃'ʒ|ɑ̃(:t)] *adj.* tangent. || **tangente** [-ɑ̃:t] *n.f.* tangent; [Fig. & Fam.] *prendre la* ~, to slip away.
Tanger [tɑ̃'ʒe] *n.m.* Tangier.
tangible [tɑ̃'ʒibl] *adj.* tangible.
tanguer [tɑ̃'ge] #3 *v. intr.* to pitch.
tanière [ta'njɛ:r] *n.f.* cave, den, lair. [Fig. & Fam.] *demeurer dans sa* ~, to be unsociable.
tank [tɑ̃:k] *n.m.* [Mil.] tank. cf. CHAR DE COMBAT.
tannage [ta'na:ʒ] *n.m.* tanning, dressing (of skins).
tannant, -e [ta'n|ɑ̃(:t)] *adj.* © boring, bothering: *Que c'est donc* ~ *!*, What a bore it is!
tanner [-e] #3 *v. tr.* to tan, dress, cure (skins); © [Fam.] to bore: *être tanné de . . .*, to be fed up with. . . . || **tannerie** [-'ri] *n.f.* tannery. || **tanneur** [-œ:r] *n.m.* tanner.
tant [tɑ̃] *adv.* & [with *que*] *loc. conj.* **1.** [degree] so, so much, so long, so well: *Il a* ~ *hésité*, He hesitated so long; *Il a* ~ *insisté que j'ai accepté*, He insisted so much that I agreed; *Rien ne lui plaît* ~ *que la musique*, There's nothing he likes as well as music. **2.** [quantity] so much, so many: *Il y a passé* ~ *de temps,* ~ *d'heures que . . .*, He spent so much time, so many hours on it that . . . ; [indefinite] *Vous aurez* ~ *pour ce travail*, You will get so much for this job. **3.** [duration] as long as: ~ *que vous serez là, nous resterons*, As long as you are here, we'll stay. **4.** [equally] as well . . . as, both . . . : *Il réussit* ~ *par son travail que par son talent*, He succeeds/both by his work and his ability, as well by his work as his ability/. **5.** [Loc.] ~ *mieux*, so much the better; ~ *pis*, It can't be helped, Never mind; ~ *bien que mal*, not too well; ~ *soit peu*, ever so little; ~ *s'en faut*, far from it; *si* ~ *est que . . .* [+ subj.], if it is true that . . . : *Si* ~ *est qu'il s'y intéresse*, Assuming that he is interested; *en* ~ *que*, as: *en* ~ *magistrat*, in his capacity as a judge. || *n.m. le* ~ *pour cent*, the percentage.
tante [tɑ̃:t] *n.f.* aunt; *grand-* ~, great aunt: ~ *par alliance*, aunt by marriage; [Fam. for pawn shop] *chez ma* ~, at my uncle's.
tantôt [tɑ̃'to] *adv.* [with a v. in the future] by and by, in a short while: *Il viendra* ~, He will come by and by; © [with a v. in the past tense] a short while ago, just now: *Comme je l'ai dit* ~, As I said earlier; [with a v. in the pres. tense] soon: *Il est* ~ *midi*, It will soon be noon; *À* ~ *!*, [Fr.] See you this afternoon, see you soon; ~ . . . ~, sometimes . . . sometimes, now . . . then, now . . . now: ~

montant ~ *descendant*, sometimes rising, sometimes descending.
taon [tɑ̃] *n.m.* horsefly.
tapage [ta'p|aːʒ] *n.m.* noise, uproar, din; [Fam.] racket, row: *faire du* ~, to be very noisy, to kick up a row. || **tapageu|r, -se** [-a'ʒœːr, -a'ʒøːz] *adj.* noisy, uproarious rowdy; [vêtement] loud, flashy; [manières] blustering: *Elle porte une toilette tapageuse*, She is wearing a flashy outfit.
tape [tap] *n.f.* slap, rap. || **tapé, -e** [-e] *adj.* [Fam.] to the point: *C'est* ~, That wraps it up. || **taper** [-e] #3 *v. tr. & intr.* **1.** ~ *sur qqun*, to beat s.o.; ~ *du pied*, to stamp one's foot. **2.** to touch (for a loan). **3.** to type: *Il apprend à* ~ *à la machine*, He is learning to type. **4.** [Loc.] ~ *dans l'œil*, to be attractive (to, *à*): *Elle lui a tapé dans l'œil*, He is quite taken with her.
tapi, tapis cf. TAPIR.
tapinois [tapi'nwa] *adv.* : *en* ~, stealthily.
tapir¹ (se) [səta'piːr] #17 *v. pron.* to crouch.
tapir² [ta'piːr] *n.m.* tapir.
tapis¹ [ta'pi] *n.m.* [floor] carpet, rug; [table] table cover: ~ *vert*, gambling table; ~ *roulant*, conveyor belt; [Fig.] *venir sur le* ~, to crop up (in the course of conversation).
tapis² cf. TAPIR¹.
tapisser [tapi's|e] #3 *v. tr.* to hang (with, *de*); [mur] to paper; [Fig.] to line, to cover. || **tapisserie** [-'ri] *n.f.* tapestry; wall paper; cf. PAPIER PEINT; [Fig.] *faire* ~, to be a wallflower. || **tapissi|er, -ère** [-je, -jɛːr] *n.* **1.** upholsterer. **2.** paper hanger.
tapoter [tapɔ'te] #3 *v. tr.* to thrum, tap, rap; ~ *un air* (*au piano*), to play a tune (on the piano).
taquet [ta'kɛ] *n.m.* cleat.
taquin, -e [tak|ɛ̃, -in] *adj.* teasing. *n.* tease. || **taquiner** [-i'ne] #3 *v. tr.* to tease; [Fam.] to kid; ~ *le goujon*, to go fishing. || **taquinerie** [-in'ri] *n.f.* teasing; [Fam.] kidding.
tard [taːr] *adv.* late: *se lever* ~, to get up late; *Il se fait* ~, It is getting late; *pas plus* ~ *que*, no later than; *plus* ~, later, after; *tôt ou* ~, sooner or later; *sur le* ~, late/in the evening, in life/. || **tarder** [tar'd|e] #3 *v. intr.* to delay; *sans* ~, without delay; ~ *à*, to be long in: *Il tarde à répondre*, His answer is long in coming; *ne pas* ~ *à*, to do sth. soon: *Il ne tarda pas à se rendre compte*, He soon realized. || *v. impers.*: *Il me tarde de le voir*, I long to see him; [Lit.] *Il lui tarde que vous veniez*, He is anxious for you to be here. || **tardi|f, -ve** [-if, -iːv] *adj.* late, belated: *à une heure tardive*, at a late hour. || **tardivement** *adv.* belatedly.
tare [taːr] *n.f.* [poids] tare; [défaut] defect, blemish; [héréditaire] taint.
targette [tar'ʒɛt] *n.f.* slide-bolt.
targuer (se) [sətar'ge] #3 *v. pron.* to pride o.s. on, boast of, (*de*).
tari, -e [ta'ri] cf. TARIR.
tarif [ta'rif] *n.m.* price list; schedule of charges; rates; tariff; ~ *douanier*, customs tariff; ~ *des abonnements*, subscription rates; ~ *ordinaire*, ordinary rates; ~ /*du courrier, de la poste*/ *recommandé*(*e*), registered mail rates; ~ *de la poste aérienne*, air mail rates.
tarir [ta'riːr] #17 *v. tr.* to dry up; to exhaust; to drain. || *v. intr.*: *Il ne tarit pas sur ce sujet*, He can talk about it for hours.
tarte [tart] *n.f.* pie, [Br.] tart. || **tartelette** *n.f.* [ə'lɛt] tart, [Br.] tartlet.
tartine [-in] *n.f.* slice of bread and/butter, jam, &c./: ~ *de beurre*, slice of buttered bread; *des tartines de beurre*, bread and butter; [Fig.] long, prosy article.
tas [tɑ] *n.m. invar.* **1.** heap, pile: *mettre en* ~, to heap up; *un* ~ *de foin*, a haycock; [Fig.] *la grève sur le* ~, a sit-down strike. **2.** lot: *un* ~ *de lettres à écrire*, a lot of letters to write.
tasse¹ [tɑːs] *n.f.* cup: ~ *à café*, coffee cup; ~ *de café*, cup of coffee.
tasse² cf. TASSER.
tassé, -e [tɑ's|e] cf. TASSER.
tasseau [ta'so] *n.m.* bracket, clamp.
tasser [-e] #3 *v. tr.* to heap, to pile up; to compress; to squeeze; to pack. || **se tasser** *v. pron.* to settle, subside, sink; [Fam.] to huddle.
tâter [tɑ'te] #3 *v. tr. & intr.* to feel, touch; to try: ~ *le terrain*, to see how the land lies, to throw out feelers; to sound: ~ *de*, to taste. || **se tâter** *v. pron.* to examine o.s.: ~ *pour savoir si*, to wonder if.
tâtonner [tat|ɔ'ne] #3 *v. intr.* to feel o.'s way in the dark; to grope; to fumble; [Fig.] to hesitate. || **tâtons** [-õ] *adv.*: *à* ~, gropingly; *chercher à* ~, to grope for.
tatouage [ta'tw|aːʒ] *n.m.* tattoo. || **tatouer** [-e] #3 *v. tr.* to tattoo.
taudis [to'di] *n.m.* hovel: *un quartier de* ~, a slum area.
taupe [toːp] *n.f.* mole: *myope comme une* ~, very nearsighted, as blind as a bat; [peau] moleskin. || **taupinière** [topi'njɛːr] *n.f.* molehill.
taureau [to'ro] *n.m.* bull; *course de*

taureaux, bull fight; *prendre le ~ par les cornes*, to take the bull by the horns.

taux [to] *n.m.* rate: *le ~ des naissances*, the birth rate; *le ~ d'escompte*, the bank rate.

taverne [ta'vɛrn] *n.f.* tavern, beer parlour, [Br.] pub; © *pilier de ~*, bar lounger.

taxe [taks] *n.f.* tax, rate, duty: *~ de séjour*, non-resident tax; pegged price. || **taxer** [-e] #3 *v. tr.* to tax; to assess; to fix the price of: *~ la viande*, to fix the price of meat; [Fig.] to charge: *~ qqun de*, to charge s.o. with. || **se taxer** (de) *v. pron.* to accuse o.s. (of).

taxi [tak'si] *n.m.* taxi(cab).

tchécoslovaque [tʃekɔslɔ'vak] *adj. & n.* Czechoslovak(ian). || **Tchécoslovaquie** [-i] *n.f.* Czechoslovakia, Czecho-Slovakia.

tchèque [tʃɛk] *adj. & n.* Czech.

te [tə] *pron. pers. 2e pers. sing.* you, yourself, †thee, thyself: *Je ~ parle*, I am talking to you; *Tu ~ regardes*, You are looking at yourself.

technicien, -ne [tɛkni'sj|ɛ̃, -ɛn] *n.* technician. || **technique** [tɛk'nik] *adj.* technical: *détails techniques*, technicalities. || *n.f.* technique.

technologie [tɛknɔlɔ'ʒi] *n.f.* technology.

teignais, &c. cf. TEINDRE.

teigne[1] *n.f.* tinea; ringworm; [Bot.] scurf.

teigne[2] cf. TEINDRE.

teindre [tɛ̃:dr] **teignant** [tɛ'ɲɑ̃], **teint** [tɛ̃] #36 *v. tr.* **1.** to dye: *~ qqch. en vert*, to dye sth. green. **2.** to tinge, stain.

teins [tɛ̃] cf. TEINDRE.

teint[1] cf. TEINDRE.

teint[2] [tɛ̃] *n.m.* **1.** dye, colour: *garanti bon ~*, fast colour. **2.** complexion: *~ clair*, light complexion. || **teinte** [tɛ̃:t] *n.f.* tint, shade, hue, colour: *demi-~*, mezzotint. || **teinter** [tɛ̃'t|e] #3 *v. tr.* to tint. || **teinture** [y:r] *n.f.* dye; dyeing; [Chim.] tincture. || **teinturier** [-y'rje] *n.m.* dyer, cleaner.

tel -le [tɛl] *adj. indef.* such, like, as: *avec une telle violence que . . .*, with such force that . . . ; *Il est ~ que vous l'avez vu*, He is the same as when you saw him; *des exemples tels que ceux qu'il nous a donnés*, examples like those he gave us; *Telles furent ses paroles*, Those were his words; *~ père, ~ fils*, Like father, like son; *~ ou ~ détail*, this or that detail; *~ quel*, as is; *~ est pris qui croyait prendre*, He is often caught who thought he would do the catching; *de telle sorte que*, so that; *Un ~*, So and so.

télégramme [tele'|gram] *n.m.* telegram, wire: *commander par ~*, to wire for.

télégraphe [-'graf] *n.m.* telegraph; © a person who votes in place of s.o. else. || **télégraphie** [-'grafi] *n.f.* telegraphy; T.S.F. [= ~ sans fil]; radio, wireless. || **télégraphier** [-gra'fje] #3 *v. tr.* to telegraph, wire. || **télégraphique** [-gra'fik] *adj.* telegraphic; *style ~*, telegraphic style, telegraphese. || **télégraphiste** [-gra'fist] *n.* telegraph/operator, messenger/.

téléguidé [-gi'de] *adj.* guided: *projectile m, engin m ~*, guided missile.

télé'journal [-ʒur'nal] *n.m.* [Télév.] newscast.

télémètre [-'mɛ:tr] *n.m.* range finder.

télépathie [telepa'ti] *n.f.* telepathy.

téléphone [-'fɔn] *n.m.* (tele)phone; *~ automatique*, dial phone; *~ interurbain*, long distance phone; *~ public*, pay telephone, pay station; *commander par ~*, to telephone for; *appeler au ~*, to ring up; *annuaire du ~*, phone book; *coup de ~*, ring: *Je vous donnerai un coup de ~*, I'll give you a ring. || **téléphoner** [-e] #3 *v. tr.* to (tele)phone, to call, ring up. || **téléphoniste** [-ist] *n.* telephone operator; [réparateur] lineman.

téléprojectile [-prɔʒɛk'til] *n.m.* [Mil.] guided missile.

télérécepteur [teleresɛp'tœ:r] *n.m.* television set.

télescope [telɛs'kɔp] *n.m.* telescope || **télescoper** [-e] #3 *v. tr.* [trains] to telescope.

téléspectat|eur, -rice [telespɛkta't|œ:r, -ris] *n.* televiewer.

télévisé, -e [televi'z|e] *adj.*: *journal télévisé*, newscast. || **téléviser** [-e] #3 *v. tr.* to televise. || **téléviseur** [-œ:r] *n.m.* [Fr.] T.V. set. || **télévision** [-jõ] *n.f.* television: *appareil de ~*, [Fam.] © T.V.: T.V. set; *transmettre par ~*, to televise, *regarder la ~*, to watch T.V.; *à la ~*, on T.V. [the Fr. fam. abbreviation is: *la télé*].

telle [tɛl] cf. TEL.

tellement [-'mɑ̃] *adv.* **1.** [degree] so, so much. **2.** [quantity, with *de*] so much, so many: *Il a eu ~ d'ennuis*, He had so many troubles; *~ que . . .*, (+ Ind.) to such an extent that. . . .

tel quel [-'kɛl] cf. TEL.

†tels, telles [tɛl] cf. TEL.

téméraire [teme'r|ɛ:r] *adj.* rash, reckless: *Charles le Téméraire*, Charles the Bold. || **témérité** [-i'te] *n.f.* rashness, recklessness.

témoignage [temwa'ɲ|a:ʒ] *n.m.* testimony, evidence: *en ~ de quoi*, in witness whereof; *en ~ d'amitié*, in token of o.'s friendship; *faux ~*, perjury. || **témoigner** [-e] #3 *v. intr.* to testify, to give evidence.

|| *v. tr.* to show: *On lui a témoigné beaucoup d'égards,* He was shown every consideration. || **témoin** [te'mwɛ̃] *n.m.* witness: ~ *à charge,* witness for the prosecution; ~ *à décharge,* witness for the defense; *faux* ~ , perjurer; ~ *oculaire,* eye witness; *prendre à* ~ , to call to witness: *Je vous prends à* ~ *que* (+ ind.) . . . , You can bear witness that . . . ; © *témoins de Jéhovah,* Jehovah's Witnesses.

tempe [tɑ̃:p] *n.f.* [human body] temple.

tempérament [tɑ̃pera'mɑ̃] *n.m.* **1.** temperament, temper, disposition. **2.** adjustment: *acheter à* ~ , to buy on the instalment plan.

tempérance [tɑ̃pe'rɑ̃:s] *n.f.* temperance, moderation.

température [tɑ̃pera'ty:r] *n.f.* **1.** temperature, © weather. **2.** fever: *faire de la* ~ , to run a temperature.

tempéré, -e [tɑ̃pe'r|e] *adj.* moderate, temperate: *zone tempérée,* temperate zone; [style] restrained, sober. || **tempérer** [-e] #10 *v. tr.* to temper; to mitigate.

tempête [tɑ̃'pɛ:t] *n.f.* storm, tempest; ~ *de neige,* snowstorm; ~ *de sable,* sandstorm; ~ *de poussière,* dust storm; *Il fait une* ~ , A storm is blowing; [Fig.] *affronter la* ~ , to face the music; *une* ~ *dans un verre d'eau,* a storm in a teacup; *Qui sème le vent récolte la* ~ , He who sows the wind shall reap the whirlwind.

temple [tɑ̃:pl] *n.m.* temple; [Protestant] church, [in Britain] chapel.

temporaire [tɑ̃pɔ'r|ɛ:r] *adj.* temporary. || **temporel, -le** [-ɛl] *adj.* temporal; secular. || **temporiser** [-i'ze] #3 *v. intr.* to temporize, to procrastinate; to stall.

temps [tɑ̃] *n.m.* **1.** time: *emploi du* ~ , time table; *passer son* ~ , to spend o.'s time; *faire passer le* ~ , to while the time away; *gagner du* ~ , to save time; *chercher à gagner du* ~ , to stall; *perdre son* ~ , to waste o.'s time; *perdre du* ~ , to lose time; *rattraper le* ~ *perdu,* to make up for lost time; *avoir fait son* ~ , to have seen better days; *à* ~ , in time; *au* ~ *jadis,* in olden days; *dans le* ~ , formerly; *de mon* ~ , in my day; *de* ~ *en* ~ , occasionally; *de tout* ~ , always; *en* ~ *et lieu,* in due course; *en un rien de* ~ , in no time at all. **2.** [Gram.] tense: *les* ~ *de l'indicatif,* the indicative tenses. **3.** weather: *par gros* ~ , in rough weather; *Quel* ~ *fait-il?,* What is the weather like?; *Le* ~ *se met au beau,* It's clearing up; [Fig.] *Il fait la pluie et le beau* ~ , What he says goes.

tenace [tə'nas] *adj.* tenacious; stubborn: *mémoire* ~ , retentive memory. || **ténacité** [tenasi'te] *n.f.* tenacity, tenaciousness.

tenaille(s) [tə'n|ɑ:j] *n.f.* pincers. || **tenaillé, -e** [-ɑ'je] *adj.* [Fig.] racked, tortured (by remorse); ~ *par la soif, la faim,* gnawed by thirst, hunger. || **tenailler** [-ɑ'je] #3 *v. tr.* [Fig.] to torture; to rack.

tenais, &c. cf. TENIR.

tenanci|er, -ère [tənɑ̃'sj|e, -ɛ:r] *n.* holder; keeper, manager; [Hist.] *franc-*~ , freeholder: *le* ~ *d'un tripot,* a gambling-house operator.

tenant [tə'nɑ̃] *n.m.* **1.** champion, supporter (of an idea). **2.** [Loc.] *d'un seul* ~ , in one piece; *les tenants et aboutissants,* the ins and outs. || *adj.*: *séance tenante,* there and then.

tend [tɑ̃] cf. TENDRE.

tendance [tɑ̃'d|ɑ̃:s] *n.f.* **1.** tendency: *Il a* ~ *à temporiser,* He is apt to stall. **2.** trend: *Une nouvelle* ~ *se fait jour,* A new trend is developing. || **tendanci|eux, -euse** [-ɑ̃'sjø(:z)] *adj.* tendentious, one-sided.

tendeur [tɑ̃'dœ:r] *n.m.* stretcher; shoe tree.

tendon [tɑ̃'dõ] *n.m.* tendon, sinew.

tendre[1] [tɑ̃:dr] *adj.* **1.** tender, soft; fond, loving, affectionate. **2.** early, young, new: *dès la plus* ~ *enfance,* from early childhood.

tendre[2] [tɑ̃:dr] **tendu** [tɑ̃'dy] #42 *v. tr. & intr.* **1.** to stretch, strain, tighten: ~ *un arc,* to bend a bow; ~ *un piège,* to lay a trap; ~ *l'oreille,* to strain one's ear. **2.** to spread, hang: ~ *un mur de papier gris,* to hang a wall with grey paper. **3.** to /hold, reach/out, proffer: *Je lui tendis la main,* I held out my hand to him. **4.** to aim (at, *à*). || **se tendre** *v. pron.* to become stretched, taut.

tendrement [-ə'mɑ̃] *adv.* tenderly, fondly.

tendresse [tɑ̃'drɛs] *n.f.* tenderness, fondness; [pl.] endearments, caresses.

tendu,[1] **-e** [tɑ̃'dy] cf. TENDRE.

tendu,[2] **-e** [tɑ̃'dy] *adj.* **1.** tense, taut. **2.** hung (with, *de*).

ténèbres [te'n|ɛbr] *n.f.pl.* darkness, gloom. || **ténébr|eux, -euse** [-e'brø(:z)] *adj.* dark, gloomy.

teneur[1] [tə'nœ:r] *n.m.* ~ *de livres,* book-keeper.

teneur[2] *n.f.* [document] text, substance, gist, tenor; [minerai] grade.

tenir [tə'n|i:r] **tenu** [-y] #22 *v. tr.* **1.** to hold, keep, have: ~ *bon,* to hold fast; ~ *conseil,* to hold a meeting; ~ *rigueur à qqun de qqch.,* to hold sth. against s.o.; ~ *les comptes,* to keep accounts; ~ *la maison,* to keep house; ~ *un magasin,* to keep, run a store; ~ *un article,* to carry an article; ~ *parole*, to keep one's word; ~ *de bonne source*, to have on good authority; *Nous le tenons!*, We've got him!; ~ *à distance*, to keep at arm's length; ~ *les enfants*, to manage children; ~ *des propos*, to make remarks; *Cela ne tient pas debout*, It does not make sense. **2.** to hold, consider: *Il ne se tient pas pour battu*, He won't admit defeat; ~ *en haute estime*, to regard highly. **3.** to take up: *Cela tient beaucoup de place*, It takes up a lot of space. || *v. intr.* ~ *à qqch.*, to care for sth.; *Cela tient à la fatigue*, It's caused by fatigue; ~ *à faire qqch.*, to insist on doing sth.; ~ *de qqun*, to take after s.o.; *Il ne tient qu'à vous de*, It's up to you to. || **se tenir** *v. pron.* to stand, sit; to behave (well, badly): *s'en tenir à*, to limit o.s. to.

tennis [tɛ'nis] *n.m.* tennis; tennis court: ~ *de table*, ping-pong; *faire du* ~, to play tennis.

tension [tɑ̃'sjɔ̃] *n.f.* tension, tenseness, tautness: ~ *artérielle*, blood pressure; *faire de la* ~, to have high blood pressure; [Electr.] *ligne à haute* ~, power line.

tentacule [tɑ̃ta'kyl] *n.f.* tentacle, feeler.

tentation [tɑ̃ta'sjɔ̃] *n.f.* temptation: *induire en* ~, to lead into temptation.

tentative [tɑ̃ta'ti:v] *n.f.* attempt.

tente [tɑ̃:t] *n.f.* tent; *dresser la* ~, to pitch the tent; *dormir sous la* ~, to sleep under canvas.

tenter [tɑ̃'te] #3 *v. tr.* to tempt, to entice. || *v. intr.* to attempt (to, *de*), to try (to, *de*).

tenture [tɑ̃'ty:r] *n.f.* hangings, tapestry; wallpaper; © curtain, drape: *des tentures bleues*, blue drapes.

tenu, -e [tə'ny] cf. TENIR.

tenue [tə'ny] *n.f.* **1.** holding, keeping: *pour la bonne* ~ *de la maison*, for good housekeeping; ~ *des livres*, bookkeeping. **2.** behaviour, sense of form, decorum: *bonne* ~, good behaviour; *avoir de la* ~, to behave well, to keep one's form, to be dignified. **3.** dress: *grande* ~, full dress; *petite* ~, undress; ~ *de corvée*, fatigue dress; ~ *de soirée*, evening dress, formal; ~ *de ville*, [Mil.] walking-out uniform, [invitation] semi-formal. **4.** firmness: *bonne* ~ *des pétrolières*, firmness of oil shares.

térébenthine [terebɑ̃'tin] *n.f.* turpentine.

tergiverser [tɛrʒivɛr'se] #3 *v. intr.* to dillydally, to vacillate, to back and fill.

terme [tɛrm] *n.m.* **1.** limit, end: *au* ~ *de sa vie*, at the end of his life; *mettre un* ~ *à*, to put an end to; *avant* ~, prematurely. **2.** term, quarter: *le jour du* ~, quarter day, rent day; *payer son* ~, to pay one's rent. **3.** term, word: *en ces termes*, in these /terms, words/; *être en bons termes*, to be on friendly terms; *en termes de métier*, in technical language; *termes de marine*, nautical terms.

terminaison [tɛrmin|ɛ'zɔ̃] *n.f.* ending; termination.

terminer [-e] #3 *v. tr. & intr.* **1.** to limit, to bound: *Un cours d'eau termine la propriété*, The estate is bounded by a stream. **2.** to end, to conclude: *Il termina en remerciant*, He concluded with an expression of thanks. || **se terminer** *v. pron.* to end, to close, to terminate: *Le contrat se termine le 15*, The contract terminates on the 15th; *Le mot se termine par un s*, The word ends in an s.

terminologie [tɛrminɔlɔ'ʒi] *n.f.*terminology.

terminus [tɛrmi'nys] *n.m.* terminal, [Br.] terminus.

termite ['tɛrmit] *n.m.* termite.

terne [tɛrn] *adj.* dull, tame, lustreless, colourless. || **ternir** [-i:r] #17 *v. tr.* to dull, tarnish; [Fig.] to sully, besmirch (a reputation), tarnish.

terrain [tɛ'r|ɛ̃] *n.m.* **1.** ground: ~ *de jeux*, playground; ~ *de manœuvres*, parade ground; ~ *d'aviation*, airfield; ~ *vague*, vacant lot, ~ *à bâtir*, building plot. **2.** [Mil.] terrain: ~ *difficile pour ce genre d'opérations*, terrain unsuited for this type of warfare; *accidents de* ~, uneven, broken ground. **3.** [Loc.]/*gagner, perdre/ du* ~,/to gain, lose/ground; *préparer le* ~, to pave the way; *reconnaître le* ~, to reconnoitre; *s'engager sur un* ~ *dangereux*, to skate on thin ice; *être sur son* ~, to be on familiar ground; *ne pas être sur son* ~, to be out of one's depth; *une rencontre sur le* ~, a duel.

terrasse [-as] *n.f.* terrace; sidewalk section of café. || **terrasser** [-a'se] #3 *v. tr.* **1.** to bank, to embank, to bank up. **2.** to strike down, to throw down, to overpower. **3.** to stun, to dismay, to hit hard: *terrassé par cette nouvelle*, stunned by the news; *terrassé par la maladie*, stricken by illness. || **terrassier** [-a'sje] *n.m.* ditch-digger, [Br.] navvy.

terre [tɛ:r] *n.f.* **1.** [planète] earth: *tremblement de* ~, earthquake; *entre ciel et* ~, between heaven and earth; *remuer ciel et* ~, to move heaven and earth. **2.** [opposé à *mer*] land: *descendre à* ~, to go on shore; *par voie de* ~, overland; *la* ~ *ferme*, the mainland. **3.** [opposé à *ciel*] land, ground: *l'armée de* ~, the land forces. **4.** [substance] earth, soil, dirt: ~ *cuite,* terracotta; ~ *de Sienne,* sienna; *vase de* ~ , earthen vase. **5.** [étendue] piece of land, property, farm, estate: *vivre sur ses* ~ , to live on one's farm: ~ *arable,* arable land; ~ *sainte,* consecrated land; *porter en* ~ , to bury, to inter. 6. [Loc.] *par* ~ , on the floor, on the ground; *tomber par* ~ , to fall down; *tout flanquer par* ~ , to upset the apple cart; *mettre pied à* ~ , to dismount; *ventre à* ~ , at full speed.

Terre de Baffin [tɛr|dəba'fɛ̃] *n.f.* Baffin Island. || **Terre de Feu** [-də'fø] *n.f.* Tierra del Fuego. || **Terre-neuvas** [-a] *n.m. inv.* Newfoundland fishermen or boats (from Brittany). || **Terre-Neuve** [-'nœv] *n.f.* Newfoundland. || **terre-neuve** *n.m.* Newfoundland dog. || **Terre-neuvien, -ne** [-nœ'v|jɛ̃, -jɛn] *n.m.f.* **1.** Newfoundlander. **2.** [Fr.] Newfoundland fisherman or boat (from Brittany). || **terre-plein** [tɛr'plɛ̃] *n.m.* platform; strip; filled-in ground.

terreau [tɛ'r|o] *n.m.* compost.

terrer [-e] #3 *v. tr.* [plante] to earth (up); [semences] to bury. || **se terrer** *v. pron.* to burrow, to dig o.s. in, to entrench o.s.

terrestre [-ɛstr] *adj.* terrestrial, earthly, worldly; → ground: *les forces terrestres,* the ground forces.

terreur [tɛ'rœ:r] *n.f.* terror, dread, fright; *la Terreur,* the Reign of Terror.

terreu|x, -se [tɛ'rø(:z)] *adj.* earthy; muddy; [teint] sallow.

terrible [tɛ'ribl] *adj.* terrible, dreadful: *enfant* ~ , enfant terrible.

terrier [tɛ'rje] *n.m.* **1.** [d'un animal] hole, earth. **2.** [chien] terrier.

terrifiant, -e [tɛri'fj|ɑ̃(:t)] *adj.* frightening, appalling. || **terrifier** [-e] #3 *v. tr.* to terrify, to frighten, to appal.

terrine [tɛ'rin] *n.f.* earthen pan; terrine.

territoire [tɛri'twa:r] *n.m.* territory; district.

terroir [tɛ'rwa:r] *n.m.* soil; [Fig.] homeland: *les chansons du* ~ , folk songs.

terroriser [tɛrɔri'ze] #3 *v. tr.* to terrorize, to browbeat.

tertre [tɛrtr] *n.m.* hillock, mound, knoll.

tes [tɛ] *adj. poss. pl. 2^e^ pers. sing.* cf. TON.

tesson [tɛ'sõ] *n.m.* shard; ~ *de pot,* potsherd; ~ *de bouteille,* fragment of broken bottle.

test [tɛst] *n.m.* test.

testament [tɛsta'mɑ̃] *n.m.*: *faire son* ~ , to make one's will; *laisser par* ~ , to will, to bequeath.

têtard [tɛ'ta:r] *n.m.* **1.** [grenouille] tadpole, [US] polliwog. **2.** [arbre] pollard.

tête [tɛ:t] *n.f.* **1.** head: *baisser la* ~ , to duck, to hang one's head; *hocher la* ~ , to nod doubtfully; *piquer une* ~ , to dive; *saluer qqun de la* ~ , to nod to s.o.; *de* ~ , mentally; *la* ~ *en bas,* upside down; *la* ~ *la première,* headlong, headforemost; *coup de* ~ , butt; *donner de la* ~ *contre,* to bump one's head against. **2.** hair: *se laver la* ~ , to wash one's hair. **3.** [referring to character] © *une* ~ *chaude,* a hothead, *une mauvaise* ~ , a troublemaker; *une* ~ *de linotte,* a scatterbrain. **4.** front: *en* ~ , in front; /*marcher, venir*/*en* ~ , to lead; *être à la* ~ *de,* to head, to be in charge of. **5.** [Loc. & Fig.] *à* ~ *reposée,* at one's leisure; *avoir la* ~ *près du bonnet,* to have a low boiling point; *avoir du travail par-dessus la* ~ , to be swamped with work; *en avoir par-dessus la* ~ , to be sick and tired of; *en* ~ *à* ~ *avec,* alone with; *faire un coup de* ~ , to act rashly; *faire la* ~ , to sulk; *faire une* ~ , to wear a long face: *J'aimerais voir la* ~ *que vous feriez si . . .* , I'd like to see your face if . . . ; *laver la* ~ *à qqun,* to give s.o. a good talking-to; *monter la* ~ *à qqun,* to get s.o. all/ excited, stirred up/; *n'avoir ni queue ni* ~ , not to make sense; *n'en faire qu'à sa* ~ , to be a law unto o.s.; *ne pas savoir où donner de la* ~ , to go round in circles; *se cogner la* ~ *contre les murs,* to run one's head against a stone wall; *se creuser la* ~ , to rack one's brains; *se mettre en* ~ *de,* to get it into one's head to; *se payer la* ~ *de qqun,* to pull s.o.'s leg; *tenir* ~ *à,* to stand up to; *tourner la* ~ *à qqun,* to turn s.o.'s head; *tout ce qui lui passe par la* ~ , anything that comes through his head. || **tête-à-tête** [tɛta'tɛ:t] *n.m. inv.* private conversation.

tétée [te'te] *n.f.* sucking.

téter [te't|e] #10 *v. tr.* to suck: *donner à* ~ , to suckle. || **tétine** [-in] *n.f.* nipple.

tétras [te'trɑ] *n.m.*: [Orn.] ~ *des savanes,* cf. PERDRIX.

têtu, -e [tɛ'ty] *adj.* stubborn, pigheaded: ~ *comme une mule,* mulish.

teutonique [tøtɔ'nik] *adj.* Teutonic.

texte [tɛkst] *n.m.* text, passage, excerpt; statement, wording.

textile [tɛks'til] *adj. & n.m.* textile.

textuel, -le [tɛks'tɥɛl] *adj.* textual, verbatim. || **textuellement** [-'mɑ̃] *adv.* verbatim, in so many words.

texture [tɛks'ty:r] *n.f.* texture.

Thaïlande [tai'lɑ̃:d] *n.f.* Thailand.

thé [te] *n.m.* tea, tea plant; tea party: © ~ *des bois*, wintergreen.

théâtral, -e [tea'tr|al] *pl.* **théâtraux** [-o] *adj.* theatrical; dramatic, stagy. || **théâtre** [te'ɑ:tr] *n.m.* **1.** theatre, stage: *une pièce de* ~, a play; *faire du* ~, to go on the stage. **2.** [Fig.] theatre, scene: *être le* ~ *d'un drame*, to be the scene of a tragedy; *le* ~ *des opérations en Corée*, the Korean theatre of war; *coup de* ~, sudden development.

théière [te'jɛ:r] *n.f.* teapot.

thème [tɛm] *n.m.* **1.** theme. **2.** [school translation from mother into foreign tongue]: composition, prose, cf. VERSION.

théologie [teɔlɔ'ʒi] *n.f.* theology.

théorème [teɔ'rɛm] *n.m.* theorem.

théorie [teɔ'ri] *n.f.* **1.** theory, doctrine. **2.** procession. || **théorique** [-k] *adj.* theoretical. || **théoriquement** [-k'mɑ̃] *adv.* in theory.

thérapeutique [terap|ø'tik] *adj.* therapeutic. || *n.f.* therapeutics. || **thérapie** [-i] *n.f.* [Méd.] therapy: ~ *par le travail*, occupational therapy.

Thérèse [te'rɛ:z] *n.f.* Theresa.

thermal, -e [tɛr'm|al] *pl.* **thermaux** [-o] *adj.* thermal: *eaux thermales*, hot springs; *station thermale*, watering-place.

thermomètre [-ɔ'mɛ:tr] *n.m.* thermometer: ~ *à minima et à maxima*, registering thermometer; *le* ~ *marque* 72°, the thermometer stands at 72°.

thermostat [tɛrmɔs'ta] *n.m.* thermostat.

thésauriser [tezɔri'ze] #3 *v. intr.* to hoard.

thèse [tɛ:z] *n.f.* thesis: *soutenir une* ~, to defend a thesis.

T(h)ibet [ti'bɛ] *n.m.* Tibet.

thon [tõ] *n.m.* [Br.] tunny (fish), ©, [US] tuna (-fish).

thuya [ty'ja] *n.m.* [Bot.] arbor vitae: ~ *de l'Est*, Eastern white cedar; ~ *géant*, Western red cedar. cf. CÈDRE.

thym [tɛ̃] *n.m.* thyme.

thyroïde [tirɔ'id] *adj.* & *n(f)* thyroid.

tiare [tja:r] *n.f.* tiara; [Fig.] papacy.

tibia [ti'bja] *n.m.* shin.

tic [tik] *n.m.* [Med.] tie, twitching; mannerism.

ticket [ti'kɛ] *n.m.* ticket; check.

tic-tac [tik'tak] *n.m.* ticking, tick-tack.

tiède [tjɛd] *adj.* warm, lukewarm, [Péj.] tepid; [Fig.] lukewarm, cool. || **tiédeur** [tje'd|œ:r] *n.f.* lack of warmth, indifference. || **tiédir** [-i:r] #17 *v. tr.* to make lukewarm. || *v. intr.* to get lukewarm.

tien, -ne [tjɛ̃, tjɛn] *adj. poss. 2ᵉ pers. sing.* cf. MIEN; your: *le tien, la tienne*, yours; *les tiens*, yours, your people.

tiendrai, tienne, tient cf. TENIR.

tiens,[1] **tenez** [tjɛ̃, tə'ne] *interj.* Here! Here you are! Look here! cf. TENIR.

tiens[2] cf. TIEN.

tierce[1] [tjɛrs] cf. TIERS.

tierce[2] *n.f.* [escrime, carte] tierce.

tier|s,[1] **-ce** [tjɛ:r, tjɛrs] *adj.* third.

tier|s,[2] **-ce** *n.m.* **1.** third. **2.** third person, third party.

tige [ti:ʒ] *n.f.* stalk, stem, vine; [piston] rod; [clé] shank; [botte] leg; [genealogy] stock.

tigre, -sse [tigr, ti'grɛs] *n.* tiger, tigress.

tilleul [ti'jœl] *n.m.* linden: ~ *d'Amérique*, basswood.

timbale [tɛ̃'bal] *n.f.* goblet, cup; [Culin.] pie dish; [Mus.] kettledrum.

timbrage [tɛ̃'br|a:ʒ] *n.m.* stamping: *dispensé du* ~, post free. || **timbre** *n.m.* **1.** bell, buzzer. **2.** [Mus.] timbre, tone. **3.** stamp: *timbre-poste*, [*pl.* timbres-poste], postage stamp; ~ *de la poste*, postmark. || **timbré** [-e] *adj.* stamped (paper, document): *papier* ~, stamped paper; *voix bien timbrée*, ringing voice; [Fam.] cracked, a little touched. || **timbrer** [-e] #3 *v. tr.* to stamp.

timide [ti'mid] *adj.* shy, self-conscious, bashful. || **timidité** [-i'te] *n.f.* shyness, self-consciousness, bashfulness.

timon [ti'm|õ] *n.m.* [véhicule] pole; †[navire] holm. || **timonier** [-ɔ'nje] *n.m.* **1.** [Naut.] man at the wheel. **2.** wheel horse.

timoré, -e [timɔ're] *adj.* timid, timorous.

tinette [ti'nɛt] © *n.f.* [×] (butter) tub: *Ça ne prendra pas goût de* ~, It won't take a year and a day, It won't hang fire.

tins, &c. cf. TENIR.

tintamarre [tɛ̃ta'ma:r] *n.m.* racket, uproar, hullabaloo.

tintement [tɛ̃t|'mɑ̃] *n.m.* [cloche] toll, tolling; [clochette] tinkle, tinkling: *avoir des tintements d'oreille*, to have a singing in one's ears. || **tinter** [-e] #3 *v. tr.* & *intr.* [cloche] to ring, to toll; [clochette] to tinkle; [grelot] to jingle; [monnaie entrechoquée] to chink; [verres entrechoqués] to clink; [oreilles] to sing.

tintouin [tɛ̃'twɛ̃] *n.m.* trouble: *donner du* ~, to be no end of trouble, to be a headache.

tique [tik] *n.f.* tick, cattle tick.

tir [ti:r] *n.m.* **1.** shooting; firing; rifle practice; gunnery. **2.** rifle range; shooting gallery; ~ *à l'arc*, archery; ~ *à la cible*, target firing; *exercice de* ~, target practice, firing drill.

tirage [ti'r|a:ʒ] *n.m.* **1.** drawing, pulling, towing; difficulties. **2.** draught (of a chimney). **3.** printing (of photographs); circulation (of a newspaper). **4.** [Loc.] ~ *au sort*, drawing lots, draught lottery; ~ *à part*, offprint. **5.** [Fig.] tussle, tension.

tiraillement [-ɑj'mɑ̃] *n.m.* [often plur.] **1.** pain, cramp. **2.** tension: *Il y a des tiraillements entre eux*, They are at loggerheads. || **tirailler** [-ɑ'je] #3 *v. tr.* to pull about, to tug (at). || *v. intr.* to snipe (at), to skirmish. || **se tirailler** *v. pron.* © to tussle, scuffle. || **tirailleur** [-ɑ'jœːr] *n.m.* sharpshooter, skirmisher: *déployer en* ~, to deploy in extended order.

tire[1] [tiːr] *n.f.* pull, tug, tugging: *voleur à la* ~, pickpocket. cf. TIRER. || **tire-au-flanc** [tir|o'flɑ̃] *n.m. invar.* shirker, malingerer. || **tire-bouchon** [-bu'ʃõ] *n.m.* [*pl.* des tire-bouchons] corkscrew. || **tire-d'aile** [-'dɛl] *n.m.* swift flight: *à* ~, at full speed; *s'envoler à* ~, to fly swiftly away.

tire[2] [tiːr] *n.f.* © molasses candy, taffy; taffy pull: © ~ *sur la neige*, (maple) taffy on the snow.

tirelire [tir'liːr] *n.f.* money box, [Fam.] piggy-bank.

tirer [ti're] #3 *v. tr. & intr.* **1.** to pull, haul, drag, tug, draw: ~ *un train*, to haul a train; ~ *sur un aviron*, to tug at an oar; ~ *qqun par la manche*, to tug at s.o.'s sleeve; ~ *une ligne, les rideaux, une épée*, to draw a line, the curtains, a sword. **2.** to shoot, to fire: ~ *un coup de feu*, to fire a shot. **3.** to print, to run off: ~ *quatre épreuves d'un cliché*, to make four prints of a negative. **4.** [Fig.] to draw, to deduce, to derive: ~ *une conclusion*, to draw a conclusion; ~ *son nom de*, to derive one's name from. **5.** [Loc.] ~ *à sa fin*, to draw to an end; ~ *au clair*, to clarify; ~ *au sort*, to draw lots; ~ *en longueur*, to drag out; ~ *la couverture à soi*, to hog; ~ *la langue*, to stick out one's tongue; ~ *le diable par la queue*, to be hard up; ~ *les cartes*, to tell fortunes; ~ *les vers du nez à qqun*, to worm a secret out of s.o. **6.** *tiré par les cheveux*, far-fetched; ~ *parti de*, to make use of, to turn to account; ~ *son épingle du jeu*, to retrieve one's stake, to come out even; ~ *une épine du pied à qqun*, to get s.o. out of a fix. **7.** © ~ *les vaches*, to milk the cows. cf. TRAIRE. || **se tirer de** *v. pron.* to extricate o.s.: ~ *d'affaire*, to pull through; *On peut s'en tirer avec dix dollars*, You can manage on ten dollars.

tiret [ti'rɛ] *n.m.* dash.

tireur [ti'rœːr] *n.m.* **1.** [the user of a firearm]: *être bon* ~, to be a good marksman, a good shot. **2.** [chèque] drawer. || **tireuse de cartes** *n.f.* fortune-teller.

tiroir [ti'rwaːr] *n.m.* drawer; [Méc.] slide, slide valve; [Fig.] *roman à tiroirs*, episodic novel.

tiroir-caisse [ti'war'kɛːs] *n.m.* till.

tisane [ti'zan] *n.f.* herbs (tea).

tison [ti'z|õ] *n.m.* ember, live coal; firebrand: *allumette-* ~, fusee. || **tisonner** [-ɔ'ne] #3 *v. intr.* to poke. || **tisonnier** [-ɔ'nje] *n.m.* poker.

tissage [ti's|aːʒ] *n.m.* weaving; weaving mill. || **tisser** [-e] #3 *v. tr.* to weave. || **tisserand** [-'rɑ̃] *n.m.* weaver.

tissu [-y] *n.m.* fabric; material; [Fig.] *un* ~ *de mensonges*, a pack of lies.

titre [titr] *n.m.* **1.** [livre] title; [chapitre] heading; [Journ.] headline. **2.** right, claim: *son principal* ~ *de gloire*, his chief claim to fame. **3.** [pl.] qualifications. **4.** [Jur.] deed, title deed. **5.** [argent, or] standard. **6.** [pl., Fin.] securities. **7.** [Loc.] *à* ~ *de*, as in the capacity of; *à juste* ~, rightfully; *à* ~ *gratuit*, free of charge; *à* ~ *onéreux*, for a price.

titrer [-e] #3 *v. tr.* [Journ.] to title, give a title to; [Tech.] to titrate, assay.

tituber [tity'be] #3 *v. intr.* to stagger, to reel, to weave.

titulaire [tity'l|ɛːr] *adj.* titular, regular: *professeur m* ~ full professor. || *n.m.* incumbent, occupant, holder: ~ *d'un passeport*, holder of a passport. || **titulariser** [-ari'ze] #3 *v. tr.* to appoint as titular, give tenure to.

toast[1] [toːst] *n.m.* toast, health: *porter un* ~, to propose a toast; *porter un* ~ *à*, to drink to s.o.'s health.

toast[2] *n.m.* [© *n.f.*] toast: *un* ~, a piece of toast; [pl.] *des toasts*, toast.

tocsin [tɔk'sɛ̃] *n.m.* alarm bell; [signal] tocsin.

toge [tɔʒ] *n.f.* [romain] toga; [Scol.] gown.

tohu-bohu [tɔybɔ'y] *n.m. inv.* hubbub, hurly-burly, confusion.

toi [twa] *pron. pers. 2e pers. sing.* cf. TU.

toile [twal] *n.f.* **1.** [tissu] cloth, [fine] linen, [rude] canvas: ~ *cirée*, oilcloth; ~ *de fond*, backdrop. **2.** painting. **3.** [araignée] (spider's) web.

toilette [twa'lɛt] *n.f.* **1.** dressing table; toilet set: *nécessaire de* ~, toilet kit. **2.** washing; dressing: *faire sa* ~, to wash; *faire un brin de* ~, to wash up. 3. dress: *aimer la* ~, to be fond of clothes. **4.** lavatory, bathroom.

toiser [twa'ze] #3 *v. tr.* to measure, size up.
toison [twa'zõ] *n.f.* fleece; shock (of hair).
toit [twa] *n.m.* **1.** roof; housetop: *crier sur les toits*, to proclaim. **2.** home, house: *habiter sous le même* ~, to share the same house. || **toiture** [-'ty:r] *n.f.* roof (-ing).
tôle [to:l] *n.f.* sheet iron: ~ *ondulée*, corrugated iron; ~ *de blindage*, armour plate.
tolérable [tɔle'r|abl] *adj.* tolerable, acceptable. || **tolérance** [-ɑ̃:s] *n.f.* tolerance; [mesure] allowance: *avec* ~, tolerantly; *par* ~, on sufferance. || **tolérant, -e** [-ɑ̃(:t)] *adj.* tolerant. || **tolérer** [-e] #10 *v. tr.* to tolerate, put up with; to allow; to bear, endure.
tomate [tɔ'mat] *n.f.* tomato; © [slang] buck [— $1].
tombal, -e [tõ'bal] *adj.*: *pierre* ~, tombstone.
tombant, -e [tõ'bɑ̃(:t)] *adj.* falling, drooping: *à la nuit tombante*, towards nightfall.
tombe [tõ:b] *n.f.* tomb, grave. || **tombeau** [tõ'bo] *n.m.* tombstone, grave: *descendre au* ~, to go to one's grave; *à* ~ *ouvert*, at breakneck speed.
tombée [tõ'be] *n.f.*: *la* ~ *de la nuit*, nightfall; *avant la* ~ *de la nuit*, before dark.
tomber [-e] #3 *v. intr. & tr.* **1.** to fall, drop: *Le thermomètre est tombé à zéro*, The mercury dropped down to zero; *Sa colère est tombée*, His anger subsided; *Le vent est tombé*, The wind has gone down; *Les plis tombent bien*, The folds hang well; ~ *dans l'oubli*, to sink into oblivion; ~ *en poussière*, to crumble into dust; ~ *du ciel*, to arrive unexpectedly; ~ *sur qqun*, to run into s.o.; *La conversation tomba sur X*, Conversation turned to X; *faire* ~ *en tirant*, to pull down; *faire* ~ *en poussant*, to push down; *laisser* ~, to drop. **2.** *v. tr.* to throw (a wrestler), down (a play). **3.** *v. impers. Il tombe de l'eau*, It's raining.
ton[1] [tõ] *adj. poss. 2e pers. m. sing.* [Also *f* before a *f* word beginning with a written vowel or mute h] your: *ton ami, ton amie*, your friend [cf. also TA, TES].
ton[2] [tõ] *n.m.* tone; [Mus.] pitch; [couleur] shade, tint; [Fig.] *bon* ~, good/manners, form/; *donner le* ~, to set the pace. || **tonalité** [tɔnali'te] *n.f.* [Mus.] tonality.
tondeur [tõ'd|œ:r] *n.m.* sheepshearer. || **tondeuse** [-ø:z] *n.f.* **1.** clipper, **2.** lawnmower.
tondre [tõ:dr], **tondu** [tõ'dy] #42 *v. tr.* [cheveux] to clip, cut close; [mouton] to shear; [pelouse] to mow; [Fig.] ~ *un œuf*, to skin a flint.
tondu[1] cf. TONDRE.
tondu,[2] **-e** [tõ'dy] *adj.* shorn, fleeced.
tonique [tɔ'nik] *adj.* tonic, stressed; [climat] bracing. || *n.f.* keynote. || *n.m.* tonic drug.
tonitruant, -e [tonitry|'ɑ̃(:t)] *adj.* vociferous.
tonnage [tɔ'na:ʒ] *n.m.* tonnage.
tonne [tɔn] *n.f.* ton: ~ *métrique*, metric ton.
tonneau, *pl.* **-x** [tɔ'n|o] *n.m.* cask, barrel: *petit* ~, keg.
tonnelier [-ə'lje] *n.m.* cooper, bottler.
tonnelle [tɔ'nɛl] *n.f.* arbor; bower.
tonner [tɔ'n|e] #3 *v. intr. impers.* to thunder. || **tonnerre** [-ɛ:r] *n.m.* thunder: *un coup de* ~, a thunderclap; [Fig.] thundering noise.
tonsure [tõ'sy:r] *n.f.* [R.C.] tonsure: *recevoir la* ~, to enter the priesthood.
topaze [tɔ'pa:z] *n.f.* topaz.
topinambour [tɔpinɑ̃'bu:r] *n.m.* Jerusalem artichoke.
topographie [tɔpɔgra'fi] *n.f.* topography.
toqué, -e [tɔ'ke] *adj.* cracked, crazy; [Fam.] nuts.
torche [tɔrʃ] *n.f.* torch; [paille] twist.
torchère [tɔr'ʃɛ:r] *n.f.* candelabrum, floor lamp.
torchis [tɔr'ʃi] *n.m.* [mixture of clay and straw] adobe.
torchon [tɔr'ʃõ] *n.m.* (dish) towel.
tordant[1] [tɔr'dɑ̃] cf. TORDRE.
tordant,[2] **-e** [tɔr'd|ɑ̃(:t)] *adj.* [Fam.] screamingly funny, side-splitting.
tordre [-r], **tordu** [-y] #42 *v. tr.* to wring, twist; to wring out. || **se tordre** *v. pron.* to twist, writhe: ~ *de rire*, to split with laughter.
Toronto [tɔrõ't|o] *n.m.* Toronto. || **torontois, -e** [-wa(:z)] *n. & adj.* Torontonian.
torpeur [tɔr'pœ:r] *n.f.* torpor, stupor: *tirer qqun de sa* ~, to arouse s.o.
torpille [tɔr'p|i:j] *n.f.* **1.** torpedo: *tube lance-* ~, torpedo tube. **2.** [Icht.] cramp fish. || **torpiller** [-i'je] #3 *v. tr.* to torpedo. || **torpilleur** [-i'jœ:r] *n.m.* torpedo boat; *contre-* ~, destroyer.
torréfier [tɔre'fje] #3 *v. tr.* to roast (coffee).
torrent [tɔ'rɑ̃] *n.m.* torrent; flood, flow, stream. || **torrentiel, -le** [tɔrɑ̃'sjɛl] *adj.* torrential: *pluie torrentielle*, pouring rain, downpour.
torride [tɔ'rid] *adj.* scorching, broiling.
tors, -e [tɔ:r, tɔrs] *adj.* [fil] twisted; [jambe] crooked.

torsade [tɔr'sad] *n.f.* twisted/cord, fringe/, coil, torsade.
torse [tɔrs] *n.m.* trunk; torso.
torsion [tɔr'sjõ] *n.f.* twisting.
tort [tɔːr] *n.m.* wrong, damage, injury, harm, hurt; [Jur.] tort, misfeasance: *avoir* ~, to be wrong; *donner* ~ *à qqun*, to decide against s.o.; *faire* ~ *à*, to wrong; *à* ~, wrongly; *à* ~ *et à travers*, at random, haphazardly; *parler à* ~ *et à travers*, to speak out of turn; *à* ~ *ou à raison*, rightly or wrongly.
torticolis [tɔrtikɔ'li] *n.m.* stiff neck.
tortiller [tɔrti'je] #3 *v. tr.* to twist, twirl. || **se tortiller** *v. pron.* to wriggle, squirm.
tortue [tɔr'ty] *n.f.* turtle, tortoise.
tortueu|x, -se [tɔr'ty|ø(ːz)] *adj.* winding, twisting; tortuous, underhanded.
torture [tɔr't|yːr] *n.f.* torture. || **torturer** [-y're] #3 *v. tr.* to torture, rack; to tantalize; to distort.
tôt [to] *adv.* soon; early: *le plus* ~ *possible*, as soon as possible, at your earliest convenience; ~ *ou tard*, sooner or later.
total, -e [tɔ't|al] *pl.* **totaux** [-o] *adj.* total, whole, entire, complete; utter, universal; aggregate, gross. || *n.m.* whole, sum total: *grand* ~, grand total; *faire le* ~ *de*, to add, sum up; *atteindre le* ~ *de*, to total. || **totaliser** [-ali'ze] #3 *v. tr.* to totalize; to add up; to tot up.
totalitaire [tɔtali'tɛːr] *adj.* totalitarian. || **totalitarisme** [tɔtalita'rism] *n.m.* totalitarianism.
totalité [-ali'te] *n.f.* totality, entirety, whole: *en* ~, wholly, totally, altogether.
totem [tɔ'tɛm] *n.m.* totem.
touage [tuaːʒ] *n.m.* towing.
toucan [tu'kɑ̃] *n.m.* toucan.
touchant, -e [tuʃɑ(ːt)] *adj.* touching, moving. || *prep.* concerning, regarding.
touche [tuʃ] *n.f.* [piano] key; [violon] fingerboard; [orgue] stop; [escrime] hit; [peinture] style; [bétail] goad, drove; [Fam.] look; *pierre de* ~, touchstone; || **touche-à-tout** [-a'tu] *n.m.* meddler, busybody; jack-of-all-trades.
toucher [-e] #3 *v. tr.* **1.** to touch: *N'y touchez pas*, Don't touch it; *Prière de ne pas* ~, Please do not touch. **2.** to move: *C'était touchant*, It was moving. **3.** to concern: *Cela ne me touche pas*, It is no concern of mine. **4.** [special phrases] ~ *de l'argent*, to draw money; ~ *un attelage*, to goad a yoke of oxen; ~ *un chèque*, to cash a cheque; ~ *du piano*, to be able to play the piano; ~ *un port*, to call at a port; ~ *au but*, to be about to achieve one's aim; *en* ~ *un mot*, to mention it briefly. || *v. intr.* to touch, be close to, adjoin. || *n.m.* (sense of) touch, feeling. || **se toucher** *v. pron.* to touch, be contiguous.
touffe [tuf] *n.f.* [cheveux, laine] tuft; [herbe] wisp.
touffu, -e [tu'fy] *adj.* bushy; [arbre] leafy; [végétation] thick, dense; [style] bombastic.
toujours [tu'ʒuːr] *adv.* **1.** always, ever: *Il répond* ~, He always answers; ~ *changeant*, ever-changing; *pour* ~, for ever. **2.** still: *Il est* ~ *là?*, Is he still there?; *Il n'est* ~ *pas arrivé*, He still has not come. **3.** [Loc.] ~ *est-il que* . . . , The fact remains that . . .
toundra [tun'dra] *n.f.* tundra.
toupet [tu'pɛ] *n.m.* [cheveux] tuft, forelock; bang(s); [Fig. & Fam.] cheek, nerve: *Quel* ~ *!*, What a nerve!; *avoir du* ~, to be cheeky.
toupie [tu'pi] *n.f.* spinning top: *ronfler comme une* ~, to snore like a hippo.
tour[1] [tuːr] *n.f.* tower; [échecs] rook, castle; [Mil.] turret: ~ *de guet*, look-out tower; [Fig.] ~ *d'ivoire*, ivory tower.
tour[2] *n.m.* **1.** turn: *A qui le* ~ *?*, Whose turn is it? **2.** stroll, walk: *sortir faire un* ~, to go out for a stroll. **3.** tour: *faire le* ~ *du pâté de maisons*, to walk, drive around the block; *faire le* ~ *d'un pays*, to tour a country; *faire le* ~ *d'une île par mer*, to circumnavigate an island; *faire tout le* ~, to go all the way round. **4.** trick: *jouer un* ~ *à qqun*, to play a trick on s.o. **5.** [Loc.] *à* ~ *de bras*, with all o.'s might; *avec un* ~ *de main*, with a sleight of hand; *en un* ~ *de main*, in a jiffy.
tour[3] *n.m.* [de potier] throwing wheel; [de tourneur] turning lathe; [à fileter] screw-cutting lathe; [Fig.] *fait au* ~, beautifully made.
tourbe[1] [turb] *n.f.* herd, mob.
tourbe[2] *n.f.* peat; © sod.
tourbillon [turbi'j|õ] *n.m.* whirl, vortex; [d'eau] whirlpool; [de vent] whirlwind; [Fig.] hurly-burly. || **tourbillonner** [-ɔ'ne] #3 *v. intr.* to whirl round; to eddy; to swirl.
tourelle [tu'rɛl] *n.f.* turret.
tourillon [turi'jõ] *n.m.* axle; trunnion, journal; spindle.
tourisme [tu'ris|m] *n.m.* touring; tourist trade: *auto de* ~, touring car. || **touriste** [-t] *n.* tourist, sight-seer.
tourment [tur'mɑ̃] *n.m.* torment, torture, sorrow. || **tourmente** [tur'mɑ̃t] *n.f.* storm, gale, blizzard; turmoil. || **tourmenter**

[turmɑ̃'te] #3 *v. tr.* to torment; to plague, trouble, worry; to bother. || **se tourmenter** *v. pron.* to worry, fret.

tournant, -e [tur'nɑ̃(:t)] *adj.* turning, revolving, rotating. || *n.m.* turn, bend, corner; turning point.

tournebroche [turnə'brɔʃ] *n.m.* turnspit.

tournedos [turnə'do] *n.m.* filet mignon.

tournée [tur'ne] *n.f,* round, tour; [Fam.] drinks: *Je paie la ~*, © *Je paie la traite,* The drinks are on me.

tournemain [turnə'mɛ̃] *n.m. en un ~*, in a split second, in a jiffy.

tourner [tur'ne] #3 *v. tr. & intr.* **1.** to turn: *~ le dos à qqun,* to turn one's back on s.o.; *~ les talons,* to turn on one's heel; *Les succès lui ont tourné la tête,* His success has gone to his head; *~ bride,* to turn back; *~ un film,* to shoot a picture; *~ une lettre,* to write a good letter; *~ un obstacle,* to get around an obstacle; *~ l'ennemi,* to outflank the enemy; *se ~ les pouces,* to twiddle one's thumbs; *~ autour du pot,* to beat around the bush; *~ en ridicule,* to ridicule; *~ et retourner une idée dans la tête,* to turn an idea over in one's mind. **2.** to turn, spin, rotate: *~ en rond,* to go around in circles; *La tête me tourne,* My head is swimming; *~ au tragique,* to take a tragic turn; *Le lait a tourné,* The milk has gone sour. || **se tourner** *v. pron.* to turn (towards, *vers*).

tourne-pierre [turnə'pjɛ:r] *pl.* **tourne-pierres** *n.m.* turnstone.

tournesol [turnə'sɔl] *n.m.* sunflower.

tournevis [turnə'vis] *n.m.* screw-driver.

tourniquet [turni'kɛ] *n.m.* turnstile; revolving stand; [Méd.] tourniquet.

tourniquette [turni'kɛt] *n.f.* © [— petite tornade] twister; © [Méd.] tourniquet.

tournoi [tur'nwa] *n.m.* tournament.

tournoyer [turnwa'je] #12 *v. intr.* to turn round and round, wheel, whirl; [eau] to eddy.

tournure [tur'ny:r] *n.f.* [événements] turn, course (of events): *Cela dépendra de la ~ des événements,* It will depend on developments; [personne] shape; [langue] construction; [vêtement] bustle.

tourte[1] [turt] *n.f.* pie: *~ aux pommes,* apple pie.

tourte[2] *n.f.* cf. PIGEON VOYAGEUR.

tourtereau, *pl.* **-x** [turtə'r|o] *n.m.* young turtle dove; [pl. & Fig.] pair of lovers.

tourterelle [-ɛl] *n.f.* turtle-dove.

tourtière [tur'tjɛ:r] *n.f.* pie dish, pie pan; © pie, cf. TOURTE[1].

tous [tu, tus] cf. TOUT.

Toussaint (la) [tu'sɛ̃] *n.f.* [R.C.] All Saints' Day: *la veille de la ~*, Hallowe'en.

tousser [tu'se] #3 *v. intr.* to cough; [ironiquement] to hem.

tout,[1] **toute, tous, toutes** [tu, tut, tus, tut] *adj.* **1.** whole, entire, all: *toute la journée,* the whole day, all day. **2.** all: *tous les hommes*: all men. **3.** any, each: *Tout étudiant qui . . .*, Any student who . . . ; *à toute heure,* at any time. **4.** [Loc.] *à tout bout de champ,* on the slightest excuse; *à tout coup,* every time; *à toutes jambes,* as fast as possible; *à toute vapeur,* full steam ahead; *à toute volée,* loud and clear; *à tout hasard,* just in case; *à tout prix,* at all costs; *à tout propos,* at every turn; *À tout seigneur, tout honneur,* Honour to whom honour is due; *toute affaire cessante,* dropping everything else; *toute proportion gardée,* other things being equal; *le Tout Paris des premières,* the upper crust.

tout[2] [tu] *adv.* all, quite, completely: *~ en larmes,* all in tears. **2.** [Loc.] *parler ~ bas,* to talk in a whisper; *~ à côté de,* right next to; *~ au plus,* at most; *~ à coup,* suddenly; *~ à fait,* quite; *~ à l'heure,* presently; *~ de même,* however; *~ neuf,* brand new; *~ nu,* stark naked; *rien du ~*, nothing at all. **3.** [used with gerund] *~ en marchant,* while walking; *~ en prenant le café,* over the coffee. **4.** [used with *que*] *~ jeune qu'il était,* young as he was, despite his youth.

tout[3] *n.m.* whole: *Le ~ est plus grand que la partie,* The whole is greater than the part; *Le ~ est de savoir si . . .*, The main thing is to know if . . . ; *risquer le ~ pour le ~*, to go the whole way.

tout[4], **tous, toutes** [tu, tus, tut] *pron.* **1.** all, everything, anything: *Tout est sens dessus dessous,* Everything is topsy turvy; *~ ce que j'ai dit,* all I said; *~ ce qui peut être réparé,* anything that can be repaired; *Ils sont tous venus,* They all came; *Ils sont venus tous les deux,* They both came. **2.** [Loc.] *~ compté,* all things considered; *à ~ prendre,* on the whole.

toute, toutes cf. TOUT.

toutefois [tut'fwa] *adv.* yet, however, nevertheless.

toute-puissance [tutpɥi'sɑ̃:s] *n.f.* almightiness. || **tout-puissant** [tupɥi'sɑ̃] *f.* **toute-puissante** [tutpɥi'sɑ̃:t] *m.pl.* **tout-puissants** [tupɥi'sɑ̃] *f.pl.* **toutes-puissantes** *adj.* all powerful, almighty. *n.m. le Tout-Puissant,* the Almighty.

tout-petit [tupə'ti] *n.m.* toddler.

toux [tu] *n.f.* cough, coughing: *une quinte de* ~, a fit of coughing.

toxine [tɔk'sin] *n.f.* toxin.

toxique [tɔk'sik] *adj.* toxic. || *n.m.* poison.

tracas [tra'k|ɑ] *n.m.* trouble, worry, annoyance. || **tracasser** [-a'se] #3 *v. tr.* to worry. || **se tracasser** *v. pron.* to worry, fuss.

trace [tras] *n.f.* **1.** footprint, trail; [gibier] spoor, scent: *être sur la* ~ *de qqun*, to be on s.o.'s trail; *marcher sur les traces de qqun*, to follow in s.o.'s footsteps. **2.** trace, vestige, clue: *ne pas trouver* ~ *de*, to find no/trace, mention, record/of; *des traces de poison*, traces of poison. ||**tracé** [-e] *n.m.* line, proposed line, drawing lay-out. || **tracer** #4 *v. tr.* to draw: ~ *les grandes lignes de*, to outline.

trachée [tra'ʃe] *n.f.* trachea; ~ *artère*, windpipe.

tracteur [trak'tœ:r] *n.m.* tractor; traction engine: ~ *agricole*, farm tractor.

traction [trak'sjõ] *n.f.* traction, pulling; pull; tractive power: *(auto) à* ~ *avant*, with front-wheel drive.

tradition [tradi'sj|õ] *n.f.* tradition, custom. || **traditionalisme** [tradisjɔna'lism] *n.m.* traditionalism. || **traditionaliste** [tradisjɔna'list] *n.m.* traditionalist. || **traditionnel, -le** [-ɔ'nɛl] *adj.* traditional.

traduct|eur, -rice [tradyk|'tœ:r, -'tris] *n.* translator. || **traduction** [-'sjõ] *n.f.* translation, rendering: ~ *inexacte*, mistranslation. || **traduire** [tra'dɥ|i:r], **traduisant** [-i'zɑ̃], **traduit** [-i] #56 *v. tr.* **1.** to translate. **2.** ~ *en justice*, to prosecute, hale into court.

trafic [tra'fik] *n.m.* [×] traffic, trading, dealing: *faire* ~ *de qqch.*, to traffic, deal in sth.

trafiquant [trafi'k|ɑ̃] *n.m.* trafficker, trader. || **trafiquer** [-e] #3 *v. intr.* to traffic, deal, trade.

tragédie [traʒe'd|i] *n.f.* tragedy. || **tragédien, -ne** [-jɛ̃, -jɛn] *n.* tragedian, tragic actor. || **tragi-comédie** [traʒikɔm|e'di] *n.f.* tragi-comedy. || **tragi-comique** [-ik] *adj.* tragi-comical. || **tragique** [tra'ʒik] *adj.* tragic. || *n.m.*: *prendre les choses au* ~, to dramatize.

trahir [tra|'i:r] #17 *v. tr.* **1.** to betray, be false to: *Ses forces le trahirent*, His strength failed him. **2.** to betray, reveal. || **se trahir** *v. pron.* to give o.s. away. || **trahison** [-i'zõ] *n.f.* betrayal, betraying, treachery; [Jur.] treason.

train [trɛ̃] *n.m.* **1.** pace, rate, speed: *aller bon* ~, to move at a brisk pace; *à fond de* ~, at full speed. **2.** style, way, manner: ~ *de vie*, standing; *mener un* ~ *de vie paisible*, to live quietly; *mener grand* ~, to live/in the grand manner, on a grand scale. **3.** [Fam.] noise, row, racket: *faire du* ~, to be noisy. **4.** [animal] quarters; [véhicule]: ~ *avant*, front/end, carriage/; ~ *arrière*, rear/end, carriage/; [avion] ~ *d'atterrissage*, landing gear. **5.** [Rail.] train: *prendre un* ~, to/take, catch/a train; ~ *de voyageurs*, passenger train; ~ *de marchandises*, freight train, [Br.] goods train; ~ *de banlieue*, suburban train; ~ *direct*, through train; ~ *express*, fast train; ~ *à destination de . . .*, → train to . . . ; ~ *de neige*, snow train; *chef de* ~, [US], © conductor, [Br.] guard. **6.** way, course: *mettre qqch. en* ~, to start sth.; *être en* ~ *de*, to be (+ pres. part.): *je suis en* ~ *d'écrire*, I am writing. **7.** © [ferme] *faire le* ~, to do (the) chores (on a farm).

traînard [trɛ'na:r] *n.m.* [Milit.] straggler; laggard, slow poke.

traîne [trɛ:n] *n.f.* [robe] train; [corde] drag; dragnet; *à la* ~, in tow; © ~ *sauvage*, toboggan.

traîneau, *pl.* **-x** [trɛ'n|o] *n.m.* sled; [explorateur] sledge; [à chevaux] sleigh.

traînée [-e] *n.f.* [de lumière] trail, train, streak; [de poudre, fumée] train: *se répandre comme une* ~ *de poudre*, to spread like wildfire; [Fam.] streetwalker.

traîner [-e] #3 *v. tr.* to drag, draw, haul, lug: ~ *les pieds*, to shuffle. || *v. intr.* to drag: ~ *en longueur*, to drag; to lie about: *Des jouets traînaient par terre*, Toys were lying about. || **se traîner** *v. pron.* to crawl, limp.

traintrain [trɛ̃'trɛ̃] *n.m.* daily round of occupations, routine.

traire [trɛ:r], **trayant** [trɛ'jɑ̃], **trait** [trɛ] #38 [Note that this verb is not used in the simple past.] to milk.

trait [trɛ] *n.m.* **1.** arrow, bolt, shaft, dart: *Il partit comme un* ~, He was off like a shot. **2.** [harnais] trace. **3.** [dessin] dash, stroke, line; [visage] feature. **4.** [action] deed: ~ *d'héroïsme*, heroic deed. **5.** [Loc.] *avoir* ~ *à*, to be about, refer to; *boire d'un* ~, to gulp down, quaff; *cheval de* ~, draught horse; *tracer à grands traits*, to outline; ~ *pour* ~, exactly; ~ *d'union*, hyphen, [Fig.] connecting link.

traitable [trɛ'tabl] *adj.* tractable, negotiable.

traite [trɛt] *n.f.* **1.** stretch: *tout d'une* ~, at a stretch. **2.** trading, traffic: ~ *des blanches*, white slave traffic. **3.** draught:

émettre une ~ sur, to issue a draught on. **4.** milking. **5.** © treat: *payer une ~*, to stand a round; *payer la ~ à qqun*, to treat s.o.

traité [trɛ'te] *n.m.* **1.** treatise. **2.** treaty, compact: *conclure un ~*, to sign a treaty.

traitement [trɛt|'mɑ̃] *n.m.* **1.** treatment: *mauvais traitements*, ill usage, cruelty. **2.** salary.

traiter [-e] #3 *v. tr. & intr.* **1.** to treat. **2.** to call: *Il le traita d'avare*, He called him a miser. **3.** to receive: *J'ai été très bien traité*, I was very well received. **4.** to transact, negotiate. || **traiteur** [trɛ'tœ:r] *n.m.* caterer.

traître, traîtresse [trɛ:tr], [trɛ'trɛs] *adj.* treacherous; false; [animal] vicious; *pas un ~ mot*, not a single word. || *n.* traitor; [melodrama] villain: *donner un coup en ~*, to hit below the belt. || **traîtrise** [trɛ'tri:z] *n.f.* treachery.

trajet [tra'ʒe] *n.m.* distance, run, trip, [mer] passage, [avion] flight.

tralala [trala'la] *n.m.* fuss.

trame [tram] *n.f.* woof, web: *la ~ de nos jours*, the web of our life. || **tramer** [-e] #3 *v. tr.* to contrive: *~ un complot*, to hatch a plot. || **se tramer** *v. pron. Il se trame qqch. contre lui*, There is sth. afoot against him.

tramontane [tramõ'tan] *n.f.* north star; (dans la Méditerranée) tramontana, north wind: *perdre la ~*, to lose one's bearings.

tramway [tram'we] *n.m.* streetcar, trolley car, [Br.] tram.

tranchant, -e [trɑ̃'ʃɑ̃(:t)] *adj.* sharp, cutting, [ton] peremptory, trenchant; [couleur] glaring. || *n.m.*: *C'est/une arme, un argument/à deux tranchants*, It cuts both ways.

tranche [trɑ̃:ʃ] *n.f.* slice, [lard] rasher; [livre] edges; [programme] section, portion; [vie] cross section; *doré sur ~*, gilt-edged.

tranchée [trɑ̃'ʃe] *n.f.* trench, ditch; *pl.* colic, gripes.

trancher [trɑ̃'ʃe] #3 *v. tr.* to cut off, sever; to slice; [Fig.] to decide, settle. || *v. intr.* to decide peremptorily, be positive; [couleurs] to contrast, stand out.

tranquille [trɑ̃'kil] *adj.* quiet, unconcerned; undisturbed: *Laissez-moi ~*, leave me alone; *Soyez ~, il n'y a pas de danger*, Have no fear, there is no danger. || **tranquillement** [-'mɑ̃] *adv.* quietly, calmly. || **tranquillisant,**[1] **-e** [-i'zɑ̃(:t)] cf. TRANQUILLISER. || **tranquillisant**[2] *n.m.* [Méd.] tranquillizer. || **tranquilliser** [-i'ze] #3 *v. tr.* to reassure, set s.o.'s mind at rest. || **tranquillité** [-i'te] *n.f.* peace, quiet; tranquillity.

transaction [trɑ̃zak'sjõ] *n.f.* **1.** transaction, *pl.* dealings. **2.** compromise.

transaméricain, -e [trɑ̃zameri'k|ɛ̃, -ɛn] © *adj.* transamerican.

transatlantique [trɑ̃zatlɑ̃'tik] *adj.* transatlantic. || *n.m.* **1.** liner: *la Compagnie générale transatlantique*, the French Line. **2.** deck chair.

transborder [trɑ̃zbɔr'd|e] #3 *v. tr.* to tranship; to transfer; to ferry across. || **transbordeur** [-œ:r] *n.m.* **1.** tender. **2.** train ferry. **3.** *pont ~*, aerial ferry.

transcanadien, -ne [trɑ̃skana'dj|ɛ̃, -ɛn] © *adj.* Trans-Canada: *la route ~*, Trans-Canada Highway.

transcontinental, -e [trɑ̃skõtinɑ̃'t|al] *pl.* **transcontinentaux** [-o] transcontinental.

transcription [trɑ̃skrip'sjõ] *n.f.* transcription; transcript; copy. || **transcrire** [trɑ̃s'kr|i:r], **transcrivant** [-i'vɑ̃], **transcrit** [-i] #48 *v. tr.* to transcribe.

transept [trɑ̃'sɛpt] *n.m.* transept.

transférer [trɑ̃sfe're] #10 *v. tr.* to transfer; to convey; to move, remove.

transfigurer [trɑ̃sfigy're] #3 *v. tr.* to transfigure. || **se transfigurer** *v. pron.* to be transfigured.

transformateur [trɑ̃sfɔrm|a'tœ:r] *n.m.* [Electr.] transformer. || **transformation** [-a'sjõ] *n.f.* **1.** transformation; conversion. **2.** wig, toupee. || **transformer** [-e] #3 *v. tr.* to transform; to alter; to convert. || **se transformer** *v. pron.* to be transformed.

transfuge [trɑ̃s'fy:ʒ] *n.m.* turncoat.

transfusion [trɑ̃sfy'zjõ] *n.f.* transfusion: *~ de sang*, blood transfusion.

transgresser [trɑ̃zgrɛ's|e] #3 *v. tr.* to transgress; to trespass against; to infringe; to contravene. || **transgresseur** [-œ:r] *n.m.* transgresser, trespasser.

transi,[1] **-e** [trɑ̃'si] cf. TRANSIR.

transi,[2] **-e** [trɑ̃'zi] *adj.* chilled (to the marrow); benumbed.

transiger [trɑ̃zi'ʒe] #5 *v. intr.* to compromise.

transir [trɑ̃'si:r] #17 *v. tr. & intr.* [Used only in the inf., pres. ind., past. part. and in the compound tenses.] to chill.

transistron [trɑ̃zis'trõ] *n.m.* [Electr.] transistor.

transiti|f, -ve [trɑ̃zi't|if, -i:v] *adj.* transitive.

transition [trɑ̃zi|'sjõ] *n.f.* transition: *sans ~*, abruptly; *pour faire ~*, to introduce a new topic. || **transitoire** [-'twa:r] *adj.* transitory, transient; transit: *pays ~*, transit country. || *n.m.* forwarding, shipping/agent.

Transjordanie [trɑ̃zʒɔrda'ni] *n.f.* Transjordan(ia).

transmettre [trɑ̃s'm|ɛtr], **transmis** #44 *v. tr.* to transmit, forward, convey, hand, relay. || **transmis, -e** [-i(:z)] cf. TRANSMETTRE. || **transmission** [-i'sjõ] *n.f.* transmission, transmittal, transfer; [machine] drive: *chaîne de* ~ , gear chain; [Auto.] transmission: ~ *automatique,* automatic transmission; [pl. Milit.] communications, signals.

transmuer [trɑ̃smy'e] #3 *v. tr.* to transmute (*en,* into).

transparence [trɑ̃spa'r|ɑ̃:s] *n.f.* transparency. || **transparent, -e** [-ɑ̃:t] *adj.* transparent, pellucid.

transpercer [trɑ̃spɛr'se] #4 *v. tr.* to transpierce; to transfix; to get through: ~ *d'un coup de poignard,* to stab.

transpiration [trɑ̃spir|a'sjõ] *n.f.* sweat, perspiration, perspiring. || **transpirer** [-e] #3 *v. intr.* **1.** to sweat, perspire. **2.** [Fig.] to transpire.

transplanter [trɑ̃splɑ̃'te] #3 *v. tr.* to transplant.

transport [trɑ̃s'p|ɔ:r] *n.m.* transport, transportation, conveyance, haulage, freight; [†sentiment] ecstasy, rapture, transport; © [Fam.] *Modère tes transports,* Take it easy. || **transporter** [-ɔr'te] #3 *v. tr.* to carry, transport, remove; [Comm.] to carry over; [sentiment] to enrapture, ravish, transport. || **se transporter** *v. pron.* to transport o.s.; †to repair.

transposer [trɑ̃spo'ze] #3 *v. tr.* to transpose; to transmute.

transversal, -e [trazvɛr's|al] *adj.* transverse, transversal: *rue transversale,* cross street.

trapèze [tra'pɛ:z] *n.m.* [acrobat] trapeze; [Géom.] trapezium.

trappe [trap] *n.f.* trap, trapdoor; pitfall; [abbaye] *la Trappe,* Trappist monastery. || **trapper** [-e] #3 *v. intr.* © to hunt by trapping. || **trappeur** [-œ:r] *n.m.* trapper: *le métier de* ~ , trapping; *faire le métier de* ~ , to trap. || **trappiste** [-ist] *n.m.* [R.C.] Trappist. || *adj.*: *les Pères trappistes,* the Trappist Fathers.

trapu, -e [tra'py] *adj.* thickset, squat.

traquenard [trak'na:r] *n.m.* trap, pitfall.

traquer [tra'ke] #3 *v. tr.* to hunt out, bring to bay, track down.

traumatisme [troma'tism] *n.m.* trauma.

travail[1] [tra'v|a:j] *n.m.* **1.** work: ~ *manuel,* manual work. **2.** labour: *le Ministère du Travail,* the Ministry of Labour. **3.** employment, job: *sans* ~ , jobless. **4.** workmanship: ~ *soigné,* fine workmanship. **5.** [Scol.] ~ *écrit,* (term) paper. **6.** travail: *femme en* ~ , woman in labour. **7.** [pl.] *travaux,* works: *le Ministère des Travaux publics,* © the Department of Public Works; *travaux forcés,* hard labour; ~ *ménagers,* housework. **8.** [Loc.] ~ *à forfait,* job work; ~ *à la pièce,* piece work; ~ *à la six, quatre, deux,* slapdash work.

travail[2] *pl.* **-s** *n.m.* sling, stocks, brake.

travaillant, -e [-a'jɑ̃(:t)] *adj.* hard-working, industrious. || *n.m.* © *les travaillants,* the working people; *un bon* ~ , **a** hard-working man.

travaillé,[1] **-e** [-a'je] cf. TRAVAILLER. || **travaillé,**[2] **-e** *adj.* elaborate; laboured: *un style très* ~ , a carefully wrought style; *du pain* ~ , light bread. || **travailler** [-a'je] #3 *v. intr.* **1.** to work, to be at work: *faire* ~ , to put to work. **2.** to warp: *Le bois vert travaille,* Unseasoned wood warps. || *v. tr.* **1.** to work: ~ *le beurre,* to work butter; ~ *la terre,* to till the land; ~ *son style,* to work at one's style. **2.** to worry, to upset, to stir up: *Qu'est-ce qui le travaille?,* What's worrying him? || **travailleur** [-a'jœ:r] *n.m.* worker, employee: ~ *scientifique,* scientist. || *adj.* [*f.* **travailleuse**] hardworking, industrious. || **travaux** [-o] *n.mpl.* [sing. TRAVAIL *q.v.*]

travée [tra've] *n.f.* [pont] span; [bâtiment] bay; row of seats.

travers [tra'vɛrs] *n.m.* **1.** breadth: *deux* ~ *de doigt,* two finger's breadth; *à* ~ , across, through: *à* ~ *champs,* across the fields; *à* ~ *bois,* through the woods; *à* ~ *le mur,* through the wall; *en* ~ *de,* across: *en* ~ *de la page,* across the page; *de* ~ , awry: *Il m'a regardé de* ~ , He gave me a black look. **2.** fault, foible, failing: *parler à tort et à* ~ , to talk out of turn.

traverse [tra'vɛrs] *n.f.* **1.** cross beam. **2.** crossroad, short cut. **3.** [Rail.] sleeper, tie. **4.** © ~ *de chemin de fer,* grade crossing, [Br.] level crossing. **5.** © ferry boat. cf. BAC. **6.** [Fig.] *se mettre à la* ~ , to stand in the way; *essuyer des traverses,* to suffer setbacks. || **traversée** [-e] *n.f.* crossing, voyage: *faire une bonne* ~ , to have a good crossing. || **traverser** [-e] #3 *v. tr. & intr.* to cross,/get, cut/across: ~ *en courant,* to run across; *L'idée lui a traversé l'esprit,* The idea flashed through /his, her/mind. || **traversier** [-je] *n.m.* © ferryboat; [personne] ferryman. cf. BAC.

traversin [travɛr'sɛ̃] *n.m.* bolster [of bed].

travesti, -e [travɛs|'ti] *adj.* disguised (*en*, as); [Péj.] travestied. ‖ **travestir** [-'ti:r] ♯17 *v. tr.* to disguise.

trayais, &c., trayant. cf. TRAIRE.

trébucher [treby'ʃe] ♯3 *v. intr.* to stumble: *marcher en trébuchant*, to stagger along; *faire* ~ *qqun*, to trip s.o.

trèfle [trɛfl] *n.m.* **1.** clover. **2.** [aux cartes] clubs: *atout* ~ , clubs are trumps.

treillis [trɛ'ji] *n.m.* trellis, lattice: ~ *métallique*, wire mesh.

treize [trɛ:z] *adj. & n.m. inv.* thirteen. ‖ **treizième** [trɛ'zjɛm] *adj. ord. & n.* thirteenth.

tréma [tre'mɑ] *n.m.* diaeresis (as in *maïs*).

tremblant, -e [trɑ̃'blɑ̃(:t)] *adj.* trembling, shaking, shaky, flickering: *les mains tremblantes*, with shaky hands; *d'une voix tremblante*, in a quavering voice.

tremble[1] [trɑ̃:bl] *n.m.* [Bot.] aspen.

tremble[2] cf. TREMBLER.

tremblement [trɑ̃bl|ə'mɑ̃] *n.m.* trembling, shaking, quivering: ~ *de terre*, earthquake; [Fig.] *tout le* ~ , the whole caboodle. ‖ **trembler** [-e] ♯3 *v. intr.* to tremble, to shake, to quiver, to shudder: *Il tremblait de tous ses membres*, He was shaking all over; *Il tremble à la pensée de . . .*, It makes him shudder to think of . . . ‖ **trembloter** [-ɔ'te] ♯3 *v. intr.* to tremble, to quiver: *lumière tremblotante*, glimmering light.

trémière [tre'mjɛ:r] *adj.f.*: *rose* ~ , hollyhock.

trémousser (se) [tremu'se] ♯3 *v. pron.* **1.** to dance, [Fam.] to shake a leg. **2.** [Fig.] to exert o.s.

trempe[1] [trɑ̃:p] *n.f.* **1.** tempering (of steel, *de l'acier*). **2.** [Fig.] stamp, character: *d'une autre* ~ , of another calibre.

trempe[2] *adj.* © wet; perspiring profusely. cf. TREMPÉ.

trempe[3] cf. TREMPER.

trempé, -e [trɑ̃'pe] cf. TREMPER. *adj.* **1.** soaked (through), sopping wet: ~ *jusqu'aux os*, wet to the skin. **2.** tempered. **3.** strong: *à l'esprit bien* ~ , strong-minded. ‖ **tremper** [trɑ̃'pe] ♯3 *v. tr.* **1.** to dip, to dunk: ~ *sa plume dans l'encre*, to dip one's pen in ink; ~ *du pain dans du café*, to dunk bread in coffee. **2.** to soak: *faire* ~ , to soak; ~ *la soupe*, to put bread in soup. **3.** [acier] to temper. **4.** to be involved: *Il a trempé dans cette affaire*, He is involved in it.

tremplin [trɑ̃'plɛ̃] *n.m.* springboard: *se faire un* ~ *de*, to use as a springboard, a stepping-stone. cf. PLONGEON.

trentaine [trɑ̃'tɛn] *n.f.* about thirty: *Il est dans la* ~ , He is about thirty. ‖ **trente** [trɑ̃:t] *adj. & n.m.* thirty; thirtieth: *le* ~ *mars*, March 30; © *un trente-sous*, a quarter, two bits; *être sur son trente-et-un*, to be in one's best finery, to be all dressed up; [Fam.] *en voir trente-six chandelles*, to see stars. ‖ **trentième** [trɑ̃'tjɛm] *adj. & n.* thirtieth.

†**trépas** [tre'pɑ] *n.m.* death; †*passer de vie à* ~ , to pass away. ‖ **trépassé, -e** *adj. & n.* dead (person) deceased: *les trépassés*, the dead. ‖ **trépasser** [-'se] ♯3 *v. intr.* [× Do not confuse with TRESPASS] to die, pass away.

trépidant, -e [trepi'dɑ̃(:t)] *adj.* agitated: *une vie trépidante*, a hectic life.

trépidation [trepida'sjõ] *n.f.* trepidation, tremor; [forte] jar; [vitres, véhicules, &c.] vibration; [Fig.] agitation, flurry.

trépigner [trepi'ɲ|e] ♯3 *v. intr.* to stamp one's feet, to dance: ~ *de joie*, to exult, to dance with joy; ~ *de colère*, to be hopping mad. ‖ **trépignement** [-'mɑ̃] *n.m.* stamping (with the feet).

très [trɛ] *adv.* very; very much, greatly; †most: *Le très Haut*, God Almighty; *J'ai eu* ~ *froid*, I was very cold; *Vous êtes* ~ *aimable*, You are/most, very/ kind; *être* ~ *reconnaissant à*, to be greatly indebted to. [☞ for emphasis] *très, très*: *C'est* ~ , ~ *bien!*, That is very, very good!; *le très honorable*, the Right Honourable.

trésor [tre'z|ɔ:r] *n.m.* **1.** treasure; †hoard; treasure house. **2.** Treasury; [Fin.] *Bon du Trésor*, Treasury bill. **3.** [Fig.] dear, darling: *C'est un* ~ , He is/sweet a, dear/. ‖ **trésorerie** [-ɔr'ri] *n.f.* treasury. ‖ **trésorier, -ère** [-ɔ'rj|e, -ɛ:r] *n.* treasurer.

tressaillement [trɛsaj|'mɑ̃] *n.m.* start, quiver. ‖ **tressaillir** [-i:r], **tressaillant** [-ɑ̃], **tressailli** [-i] ♯19 *v. intr.* to (give a) start: ~ *de joie*, to thrill with joy; *faire* ~ , to startle.

tresse [trɛs] *n.f.* braid (of hair), †plait. ‖ **tresser** [-e] ♯3 *v. tr.* to weave; to braid, †to plait.

tréteau [tre'to] *n.m.* trestle; [pl.] *les tréteaux*, the stage.

treuil [trœj] *n.m.* windlass, [Naut.] winch.

trêve [trɛ:v] *n.f.* **1.** truce: *faire* ~ , to call a halt; ~ *de plaisanteries!*, enough joking! **2.** respite: *sans* ~ , unremittingly.

tri [tri] *n.m.* sorting (of mail); selection. ‖ **triage** [-'ja:ʒ] *n.m.* [Rail.] *gare de* ~ , classification yard, freight yard, [Br.] marshalling yard.

triangle [tri'|ɑ̃:gl] *n.m.* triangle: ~ /*équilatéral, isocèle*/, equilateral, isosceles/

triangle. || **triangulaire** [-ɑ̃gu'lɛːr] *adj.* triangular.
tribord [tri'bɔːr] *n.m.* [Naut.] starboard.
tribu [tri'by] *n.f.* tribe.
tribulation [tribyla'sjõ] *n.f.* *usual. pl.* tribulation, adversity.
tribun|al, *pl.* **-aux** [triby'n|al, -o] *n.m.* court (of justice), tribunal: *comparaître devant un* ~, to stand trial.
tribune [tri'byn] *n.f.* **1.** [orateur] rostrum: *monter à la* ~, to take the floor, to go before the House. **2.** [spectateurs] gallery, grandstand. **3.** ~ *-libre*, forum.
†**tribut** [tri'by] *n.m.* tribute [esp. Fig.]: *payer le* ~ *à la gloire*, to pay the price for glory. || **tributaire** [-'tɛːr] *adj.* tributary; dependent (on, *de*).
tricher [tri'ʃ|e] #3 *v. tr. & intr.* to cheat: ~ *aux cartes*, to cheat at cards. || **tricherie** [-'ri] *n.f.* cheating, trickery. || **tricheu|r, -se** [-œːr, -øːz] *n.* cheat, card-sharper, trickster.
tricolore [trikɔ'lɔːr] *adj.* tricolour(ed): *le drapeau* ~, the French flag, the Tricolour.
tricorne [tri'kɔrn] *n.m.* cocked hat.
tricot [tri'k|o] *n.m.* knitting; knitted garment, sweater. || **tricoter** [-ɔ'te] #3 *v. tr. & intr.* to knit.
tricycle [tri'sikl] *n.m.* tricycle.
trier [tri'je] #3 *v. tr.* to sort out (mail), select; [Fig.] *trié sur le volet*, select; hand-picked.
trifluvien, -ne [trifly'vj|ɛ̃, -ɛn] © *adj. & n.* (resident) of Three Rivers.
trigonométrie [trigɔnɔme'tri] *n.f.* trigonometry.
trille [triːj] *n.f.* trill.
trimbaler [trɛ̃ba'le] #3 *v. tr.* to cart/about, along/. || **se trimbaler** *v. pron.* [Fam.] to trail: *Il faut* ~ *à l'autre bout de la ville*, You have to trail over to the other end of town.
trimer [tri'me] #3 *v. intr.* to slave.
trimestre [tri'mɛstr] *n.m.* term; quarter (i.e. three months). || **trimestriel, -le** [-i'ɛl] *adj.* quarterly.
tringle [trɛ̃ːgl] *n.f.* rod: ~ *de rideau*, curtain rod.
trinité [trini'te] *n.f.* trinity: [Rel.] *la Sainte Trinité*, the Holy Trinity; [Géog.] *baie de la Trinité* (T.-N.), Trinity Bay (Nfld.).
trinquer [trɛ̃'ke] #3 *v. intr.* to touch, clink glasses, to drink to one another's health.
trio [tri'o] *n.m.* trio.
triomphal, -e [triõ'f|al] *pl.* **triomphaux** [-o] *adj.* triumphant, triumphal: *une marche triomphale*, a triumphal march. || **triomphalement** [-al'mɑ̃] *adv.* triumphantly.
|| **triomphant, -e** [-ɑ̃(ːt)] *adj.* triumphant: *être tout* ~, to be cock-a-hoop. || **triomphat|eur, -rice** [-a'tœːr, -a'tris] *adj.* victorious, triumphant. || *n.* victor, conqueror. || **triomphe** [tri|'õːf] *n.m.* triumph: *arc de* ~, triumphal arch. || **triompher** [-õ'fe] #3 *v. intr.* to triumph (over, *de*), overcome; to exult, be triumphant.
tripatouiller [tripatu'je] #3 *v. tr.* [Fam.] to fiddle, tamper with; to garble (news); to paw over.
tripe [trip] *n.f.* tripe; [Fam.] guts, entrails.
triple [tripl] *adj. & n.m.* triple, threefold; treble; three times: *Je vous en donne le* ~, I'm giving you three times as much. || **tripler** [-e] #3 *v. tr. & intr.* to treble, to triple. || **triplicata** [-ika'ta] *n.m.* triplicate; *faire un acte en* ~, to draw up a deed in triplicate.
Tripolitaine [tripɔli'tɛn] *n.f.* Tripolitania.
tripot [tri'po] *n.m.* gambling den.
tripoter [tripɔ'te] #3 *v. tr.* [Péj.] to mess, meddle/with; [argent] to speculate; [Fig.] to intrigue. || *v. intr.* to mess about.
trique [trik] *n.f.* cudgel, club: *donner des coups de* ~ *à qqun*, to beat s.o. up.
trisaïeul, -e [triza'jœl] *n.* great-great-/grandfather, grandmother/; [pl.] **trisaïeuls,** great-great-grandparents.
triste [trist] *adj.* sad, sorrowful, gloomy, wretched; dreary: *Il a le vin* ~, Drinking makes him gloomy. || **tristement** [-ə'mɑ̃] *adv.* sadly, sorrowfully, gloomily, wretchedly. || **tristesse** [-ɛs] *n.f.* sadness, gloom, melancholy [endroit, temps] dreariness: *être plongé dans la* ~, → to brood.
trivial, -e [tri'vjal] *adj.* **1.** [×] common, trite. **2.** vulgar.
troc [trɔk] *n.m.* barter: *faire un* ~, to swap.
troglodyte [trɔglɔ'dit] *n.m.* **1.** cave-dweller, troglodyte. **2.** [Ornith.] wren.
trognon [trɔ'ɲõ] *n.m.* core, stump: ~ *de chou*, cabbage stump, [Fig. & Fam.] pint-sized.
trois [trwɑ] *adj. & n.m.* three, third: ~ *frères*, three brothers; *le* ~ *mai*, the third of May; *le* ~ *de cœur*, the three of hearts. || **troisième** [-'zjɛm] *adj. & n.* third; *au* ~, on the third floor: *voyager en* ~, to travel third (class). || **trois-quarts** [-'kaːr] *n.m.pl. inv.* three-quarter(s): *un portrait pris de* ~, a three-quarter portrait.
Trois-Rivières [-ri'vjɛːr] *n.f.pl.* Three Rivers.
trombone [trõ'bɔn] *n.m.* **1.** trombone. **2.** paper clip.

trompe [trõːp] *n.f.* **1.** [Mus.] horn. **2.** [éléphant] trunk.

tromper [trõ'p|e] #3 *v. tr.* to deceive, to fool, to cheat, [conjoint] to be unfaithful to: *se laisser* ~, to be taken in; ~ *l'ennui*, †to beguile tedium; ~ *la vigilance*, to elude vigilance. || **se tromper** *v. pron.* to make a mistake, to be mistaken. || **tromperie** [-'ri] *n.f.* deceit; cheating; delusion.

trompette [trõ'pɛt] *n.f.* trumpet. || *n.m.* trumpeter: *nez en* ~, turned-up nose.

trompeu|r, -se [trõ'p|œːr, -øːz] *adj.* **1.** deceitful: *une femme trompeuse*, a deceitful woman. **2.** deceptive, misleading: *Les apparences sont trompeuses*, Appearances are deceptive.

tronc [trõ] *n.m.* **1.** trunk: *un* ~ *d'arbre*, a tree trunk. **2.** box: *le* ~ *pour les pauvres*, the poor box, the alms box.

tronçon [-'sõ] *n.m.* stump; [voie ferrée] section, portion.

trône [troːn] *n.m.* throne. || **trôner** [tro'ne] #3 *v. intr.* **1.** to lord it over. **2.** to sit on the throne.

tronquer [trõ'ke] #3 *v. tr.* **1.** to truncate. **2.** [Fig.] to mutilate.

trop [tro] *adv.* too, too much, over: ~ *peu*, too little; ~ *lourd*, overweight: *par* ~, overly, *de* ~, to excess. || *n.m.* excess.

trophée [trɔ'fe] *n.m.* trophy.

tropical, -e [trɔpi'kal] *adj.* tropical. || **tropique** [trɔ'pik] *n.m.* tropic.

troquer [trɔ'ke] #3 *v. tr.* to exchange, to barter, [Fam.] to swap.

trot [tro] *n.m.* trot: *aller au* ~, to trot; *aller au petit* ~, to jog along; [Fig.] *mener une affaire au grand* ~, to make short work of it. || **trotter** [trɔ't|e] #3 *v. intr.* to trot: *J'ai trotté toute la matinée*, I've been/running around, on the go/ all morning; *C'est un air qui me trotte par la tête*, That tune keeps running through my head. || **trotteur** [-œːr] *n.m.* trotter: *course de trotteurs*, harness racing.

trottiner [-i'ne] #3 *v. intr.* [cheval] to trot short; [Fig.] to/trot, toddle/about.

trottinette [-i'nɛt] *n.f.* scooter.

trottoir [trɔ'twaːr] *n.m.* sidewalk: *le bord du* ~, the curb; *faire le* ~, to be a street-walker.

trou [tru] *n.m.* hole: ~ *de la serrure*, keyhole; ~ *d'une aiguille*, the eye of a needle; *boire comme un* ~, to drink like a fish.

trouble[1] [trubl] *adj.* blurred, muddy, unsettled, troubled: *la vue* ~, blurred vision; *un temps* ~, unsettled weather; [Fig.] *une situation* ~, a confused situation; *pêcher en eau* ~, to fish in troubled waters.

trouble[2] *n.m.* commotion, disturbance, confusion, trouble: *troubles émotionnels*, emotional maladjustments.

trouble-fête [-ə'fɛːt] *n. inv.*: *être un* ~, to be a/wet blanket, killjoy/.

troubler [-e] #3 *v. tr.* **1.** to blur, to make muddy. **2.** disturb, trouble, worry, confuse, upset. || **se troubler** *v. pron.* to become muddy, cloudy; [Fig.] to lose one's composure, to get confused.

troué, -e [tru'e] *adj.* in holes, with a hole in it: ~ *aux coudes*, out-at-elbows. || **trouée** *n.f.* gap, hole, breach, opening; [Mil.] breakthrough: *la Trouée de Belfort*, the Belfort Gap. || **trouer** #3 *v. tr.* to make a hole (or holes) in, break through: *Tu as encore troué ton pantalon*, You've worn holes in your trousers again; *Il a troué le mur*, He cut holes in the wall; *L'ennemi a troué nos lignes*, The enemy broke through our lines.

trouille [truj] *n.f.* [Fam.] cold feet: *avoir la* ~, to have cold feet, to funk it.

troupe [trup] *n.f.* **1.** band, body, party; [Théât.] troupe. **2.** [Mil.] troop: *les troupes*, the troops; *homme de* ~, private, buck private.

troupeau, *pl.* **-x** [-o] *n.m.* [petit bétail] flock; [gros bétail] herd: *Attention aux troupeaux*, Cattle crossing; [Fig.] crowd, mob.

troupier [-je] *n.m.* private, soldier: *un vieux* ~, an old campaigner.

trousse [trus] *n.f.* **1.** case, kit: ~ *de couture*, sewing kit; ~ *de voyage*, travelling case; ~ *d'outils*, tool kit; ~ *de secours*, emergency/first-aid/kit. **2.** *avoir qqun à ses trousses*, to have s.o. at one's heels.

trousseau, *pl.* **-x** [-o] *n.m.* [clefs] bunch of keys; [vêtements] outfit, kit; [mariée] trousseau.

trouvaille [tru'v|ɑːj] *n.f.* a find: *Quelle* ~ *!*, What a/find, discovery, godsend/!

trouvé,[1] **-e** [-e] cf. TROUVER.

trouvé,[2] **-e** *adj.* found: *enfant* ~, foundling. || **trouver** [-e] #3 *v. tr.* to find, get, invent, discover; think of: *Comment trouvez-vous ma coiffure?*, What do you think of my hair-do?; *Il commença à* ~ *le temps long*, Time hung heavy on his hands. || **se trouver** *v. pron.* to be found, to be: *Cela se trouve difficilement*, It is hard to come by; *Je ne sais pas où cela se trouve*, I don't know where it is.

truc [tryk] *n.m.* [Fam.] trick, knack, gadget, dodge, gimmick.

trucage [-aːʒ] *n.m.* faking.

truchement or **trucheman** [tryʃ'mɑ̃] *n.m.*: *par le ~ de*, through, thanks to.
truie [trɥi] *n.f.* sow.
truite [trɥit] *n.f.* trout cf. OMBLE; *~ mouchetée*, speckled trout.
tsuga du Canada [tsy'ga] *n.m.* © Canadian /white/Eastern/hemlock, spruce. cf. SAPIN DU CANADA, PRUCHE, PIN NOIR.
T.S.V.P. = [Tournez, s'il vous plaît], P.T.O., over.
tu,[1] te, toi [ty], [tə], [twa] *pron. pers. 2e pers. sing.* **1.** [archaic] *tu, toi*, thou; *te, toi*, thee; *te* [reflexive] thyself. **2.** [used with small children, or within the family, or with class mates and army 'buddies'] you.
tu,[2] tue, tues, tus [ty] cf. TAIRE.
tu,[3] -e [ty] cf. TAIRE.
tube [tyb] *n.m.* **1.** tube, pipe: *~ acoustique*, speaking tube. **2.** [Anat.] duct; *le ~ digestif*, the digestive tract. **3.** [Fam.] silk hat.
tuberculeu|x, se [tybɛrky'l|ø(:z)] *adj.* tubercular, tuberculous. || *n.* tubercular. || **tuberculose** [-o:z] *n.f.* tuberculosis.
tue, tues, &c. cf. TUER.
tuer [tɥe] #3 *v. tr.* to kill, to destroy: *~ le temps*, to kill time; *se faire ~*, to get killed. || **se tuer** *v. pron.* to be killed; to kill o.s.: *Il s'est tué dans un accident de montagne*, He was killed in a mountaineering accident.
tue-tête (à) [aty'tɛ:t] *loc. adv.* at the top of one's voice; *crier à ~*, to yell.
tuile [tɥil] *n.f.* tile; [Fam.] bore, bad blow: *Quelle ~ !*, What a/bore, nasty blow/!
tulipe [ty'lip] *n.f.* tulip.
tumeur [ty'mœ:r] *n.f.* tumour.
tumulte [ty'mylt] *n.m.* tumult, uproar, hubbub, turmoil, commotion. || **tumultueusement** [-ɥøz'mɑ̃] *adv.* noisily, boisterously, tumultuously. || **tumultueu|x-, se** [-ɥø(:z)] *adj.* tumultuous, riotous, stormy, disorderly, noisy: *une vie tumultueuse*, a stormy life.
tunique [ty'nik] *n.f.* tunic.
Tunisie [tyni'zi] *n.f.* Tunisia; †Tunis.
tunnel [ty'nɛl] *n.m.* tunnel: *passer sous un ~*, to go through a tunnel.
tuque [tyk] *n.f.* © [= bonnet d'hiver] tuque, stocking cap. cf. CASQUE.
turbine [tyr'bin] *n.f.* turbine.
turboréacteur [tyr'boreak'tœ:r] *n.m.* turbo-jet.
turbulent, -e [tyrby'lɑ̃(:t)] *adj.* turbulent; romping; boisterous.
turc [tyrk] *adj. m.* Turkish. || *n.m.* Turk: *fort comme un ~*, strong as an ox; *tête de ~*, [Sl.] butt, goat. || **turque** [tyrk] *adj.f.* Turkish; *à la ~*, in the Turkish way: *assis à la ~*, sitting cross-legged; *installation à la ~*, seatless toilet. || *n.f.* Turk, Turkish woman. || **Turquie** [-i] *n.f.* Turkey.
turquoise [tyr'kwa:z] *n.f.* turquoise.
tus, &c. cf. TAIRE.
tutelle [ty'tɛl] *n.f.* tutelage, protection; guardianship; [droit international] trusteeship. cf. MANDAT. || **tut|eur,[1] -rice** [ty't|œ:r, -ris] *n* guardian, [Québec] tutor.
tuteur[2] *n.m.* [Hort.] prop, support, stake.
tutoie [ty'twa], &c. cf. TUTOYER. || **tutoyer** [-'je] #12 *v. tr.* to use the familiar form of address, to be on familiar terms with s.o.: *Ils se tutoyent*, → They are on a first-name basis.
tuyau, *pl.* **-x** [tɥi'jo] *n.m.* pipe, tube, piping: *~ d'échappement*, exhaust; *~ d'arrosage*, garden hose; *~ d'incendie*, fire hose; [Fig.] tip: *avoir des tuyaux sur qqch.*, to have inside information on sth.
tympan [tɛ̃'pɑ̃] *n.m.* eardrum.
type [tip] *n.m.* **1.** type, standard model. **2.** fellow, chap: *Quel ~ !*, What a character!; *C'est un drôle de ~*, He's a queer fellow; *C'est un chic ~*, He's a wonderful guy. || **typique** [-ik] *adj.* typical, representative, true to type.
typographe [tipɔ'graf] *n.m.* typesetter, compositor.
tyran[1] *n.m.* [Ornith.] kingbird.
tyran[2] [ti'r|ɑ̃] *n.m.* tyrant. || **tyrannie** [-a'ni] *n.f.* tyranny. || **tyrannique** [-a'nik] *adj.* tyrannical, domineering. || **tyranniser** [-ani'ze] #3 *v. tr.* to tyrannize, boss.

U, u [y] *n.m. invar.* U, u: [Chem.] *un tube en U*, a U-shaped tube.

Ukraine [y'krɛn] *n.f. l'* ~, the Ukraine. || **ukrainien, -ne** [-jɛ̃, -jɛn] *adj.* Ukrainian.

ulcère [yl'sɛːr] *n.m.* ulcer.

ultérieur, -e [ylte'rjœːr] *adj.* later, subsequent: *une séance ultérieure*, a later meeting. || **ultérieurement** [ylterjœr'mɑ̃] *adv.* later on, subsequently.

ultimatum [yltima'tɔm] *n.m.* ultimatum.

ultime [yl'tim] *adj.* last, final, ultimate; last minute: *une ~ recommandation*, a final recommendation.

ultraviolet, -te [yltravjɔ'lɛ(t)] *adj.* ultraviolet.

un[1] pl. **uns** [œ̃] *n.m.* one; number one; [the sing. *un* is not used with *l'* when referring to the number]: *Le un gagne*, Number one wins. cf. UNIÈME. || *pron.* one (person, thing): *les uns*, some [as opposed to *les autres*, the others]; *l'* ~ *et l'autre*, both; *ni l'* ~ *ni l'autre*, neither (one of them); *l'* ~ *l'autre*, each other, one another. || *loc. adv.* ~ *à* ~, one by one.

un[2], **une** pl. **des** [œ̃, yn, de] *indef. art.* a, an, one: *C'est ~ Canadien, ~ Américain*, He is a Canadian, an American; ~ *appartement d'une pièce*, a one-room apartment; ~ *homme et une femme*, a man and a woman; ~ *jour que . . .*, one day when . . . , on a day when . . . . || **un, une** *indef. pron.* [used in connection with *en*; has no plural form]: *J'en veux ~, une*, I want one, cf. EN.

unanime [yna'nim] *adj.* unanimous, of one mind: *Nous sommes unanimes à déclarer que . . .*, We are unanimous in declaring that . . . . || **unanimité** [ynanimi'te] *n.f.* unanimity: *être élu à l'* ~, to be elected unanimously.

Ungava [œ̃ga'va] *n.m. l'* ~, Ungava; *la baie d'* ~, Ungava Bay.

uni, -e [y'ni] *adj.* **1.** united: *les États-Unis*, the United States; *Ils sont très unis*, They are devoted to each other; *une famille très unie*, a very closely-knit family. **2.** smooth, plain, [of colour] solid.

uni . . . [y'ni +] [prefix meaning one, single: *unilatéral*, one-sided, unilateral].

unième [y'njɛm] *adj. ord.* [used only in compounds] first: *vingt et ~*, twenty-first.

unification [ynifika'sjɔ̃] *n.f.* unification, streamlining. || **unifier** [yni'fje] #3, *v. tr.* to unify, to streamline. || **s'unifier** *v. pron.* to merge, to consolidate, to become unified.

uniforme [yni'fɔrm] *adj.* uniform; unrelieved. || *n.m.* uniform: *être en ~*, to be in uniform; *être en grand ~*, to be in full-dress uniform. || **uniformément** [ynifɔrme'mɑ̃] *adv.* evenly, without variation, uniformly. || **uniformité** [ynifɔrmi'te] *n.f.* uniformity.

unilatéral, -e [ynilate'ral] *adj.* unilateral.

union [y'njɔ̃] *n.f.* **1.** union, society, association: © [abus.] ~ *ouvrière*, trade union: *l'Union Sud-Africaine*, the Union of South Africa. **2.** unity, concord, agreement. **3.** marriage. **4.** [Méc.] union-joint, coupling.

unique [y'nik] *adj.* only, single, the only one; unique: *Il est fils ~*, He is an only son; *rue à sens ~*, one-way street; *chemin de fer à voie ~*, single-track railway; *une occasion ~*, a unique opportunity; ~ *au monde*, the only one in the world. || **uniquement** [ynik'mɑ̃] *adv.* solely.

unir [y'niːr] **unissant, uni,** #17, *v. tr.* to unite, to join, to connect. || **s'unir** (**à**) *v. pron.* to unite, to join forces (with). || **unisson** [yni'sɔ̃] *n.m.* unison: *à l'* ~, in unison.

unité [yni'te] *n.f.* **1.** unity, concord. **2.** unit: ~ *de longueur, de poids*, unit of length, of weight. **3.** [Naut.] [type of ship, class of warship] ship, craft, vessel: *les petites unités*, small craft; *les grandes unités*, large ships; [Mil.] unit.

univers [yni'vɛːr] *n.m. invar.* universe. || **universalité** [yniversali'te] *n.f.* **1.** totality. **2.** universality. || **universel, -le** [yniver'sɛl] *adj.* universal: *légataire ~*, sole legatee.

universitaire [yniversi'tɛːr] *adj.* university, academic: *un grade ~*, a university degree; *année ~*, college year, academic session; *Cercle ~*, Faculty Club; **domaine ~*, campus. || *n.* teacher, professor. || **université** [yniversi'te] *n.f.* university; college: *l'Université de Montréal*, the University of Montreal; *aller à l'* ~, to go to (the) university, [US] to go to college.

uranium [yra'njɔm] *n.m.* uranium.

urbain, -e [yr'b|ɛ̃, -ɛn] *adj.* city, urban: *la vie urbaine*, city life. || **urbanisme** [yrba'nism] *n.m.* town-planning. || **urbanité** [yrbani'te] *n.f.* urbanity, polish.

urgence [yr'ʒɑ̃ːs] *n.f.* **1.** urgency, pressing need: *faire qqch. d'* ~, to do sth. at once, to give priority to sth. **2.** emergency: *état d'* ~, state of emergency; *En cas d'* ~, *appeler . . .*, In case of emergency, call . . .; [Chir.] *opérer qqun d'* ~, to perform an emergency operation; *transporter qqun d'* ~ *à*, to rush s.o. to; *convoquer d'* ~ *un comité*, to call an emergency meeting of a committee; *Il a* *été appelé d'* ~, He received an urgent call. || **urgent, -e** [yr'ʒ|ɑ̃, -ɑ̃:t] *adj.* urgent, pressing; [on a letter] Rush; [Med.] *cas* ~, emergency.

urine [y'rin] *n.f.* urine. || **uriner** [-e] #3 *v. intr.* to urinate.

urne [yrn] *n.f.* **1.** urn. **2.** ballot box: *aller aux urnes*, to go to the polls.

U.R.S.S. [yɛrɛs'ɛs] *n.m.* [= Union des républiques socialistes soviétiques], USSR [= Union of Soviet Socialist Republics].

Uruguay [yry'ge] *n.m. l'* ~, Uruguay.

usage [y'za:ʒ] *n.m.* **1.** custom, practice, usage: *Ce n'est pas l'* ~ *de . . .*, It is not the custom to . . . ; [Ling.] *l'* ~ *(de la langue)*, usage. **2.** use, enjoyment: *pour l'* ~ *externe*, for external use only; *faire (bon)* ~ *de*, to make (good) use of. **3.** wear: *hors d'* ~, out of order, [clothes] worn out; *faire bon* ~, to wear well. || **usagé, -e** [yza'ʒe] *adj.* worn out, not new; [especially in Canada] second-hand, cf. OCCASION. || **usager** [yza'ʒe] *n.m.* user: *les usagers/du gaz, du métro*, those who use/gas, the subway; gas users, subway riders.

usé, -e [y'ze] *adj.* worn out, worn away; [expression] hackneyed: *Les marches sont usées*, The steps are worn away; ~ *jusqu'à la corde*, threadbare. || **user** [y'ze] #3, *v. intr.*: ~ *de*, to make use of; ~ *de prudence*, to exercise care; ~ *de douceur*, to deal gently; [☞ for most meanings of *to use*, cf. SE SERVIR DE, UTILISER, EMPLOYER.] || *v. tr.* to wear out: ~ *ses vêtements*, to wear out one's clothes. || **s'user** *v. pron.* [choses] to wear out, [personnes] to wear o.s. out: *Le tissu s'use vite*, This material wears out quickly; *Il s'est usé à la tâche*, He wore himself out on the job.

usine [y'zin] *n.f.* plant, factory, mill, works: ~ *à gaz*, gas works; ~ *électrique*, power station; ~ *d'aviation*, aircraft factory; *un ouvrier d'* ~, a factory worker. || **usiner** [yzi'ne] #3, *v. tr.* [Metal] to tool, to machine.

usité, -e [yzi'te] *adj.* in common use.

ustensile [ystɑ̃'sil] *n.m.* utensil.

usuel, -le [y'zɥɛl] *adj.* in common use: *l'anglais* ~, everyday English.

usure[1] [y'zy:r] *n.f.* wear and tear: *une guerre d'* ~, a war of attrition.

usure[2] [y'zy:r] *n.f.* usury [charging excessive interest on loans]: [Fig.] *rendre qqch. avec* ~, to repay with/usury, excessive interest. || **usurier** [yzy'rje] *n.m.* usurer.

usurpat|eur, -rice [yzyrpa|'tœ:r, -'tris] *adj.* usurping. || *n.* usurper. || †**usurper** [yzyr'pe] #3, *v. tr.* to usurp.

Utah [y'ta] *n.m. l'* ~, Utah.

utile [y'til] *adj.* useful, of use: *se rendre* ~, to make o.s. useful; *En quoi puis-je vous être* ~ *?*, What can I do for you?, Is there anything I can do?; *en temps* ~, in due course. || *n.m.* usefulness: *joindre l'* ~ *à l'agréable*, to combine work with pleasure. || **utilement** [ytil'mɑ̃] *adv.* usefully. || **utilisable** [ytili'zabl] *adj.* usable. || **utilisation** [ytiliza'sjɔ̃] *n.f.* use, utilization. || **utiliser** [ytili'ze] #3, *v. tr.* to use, to make use of. || **utilité** [ytili'te] *n.f.* usefulness, utility, value: *d'aucune* ~, of no use whatever; *sans* ~, useless; *d'* ~ *publique*, of service to the public.

utopie [ytɔ'pi] *n.f.* utopia.

V

V, v [ve] *n.m. invar.* V, v.

va[1] [va, © vɑ] *interj.* **1.** It's O.K.!, It's all right!: *Va, je ne te hais pas*, I don't really hate you; *Va, ne t'en fais pas*, It's O.K.! Don't worry about it; *Je t'aime bien,* ~ !, I like you a lot! **2.** agreed, O.K.: *Va pour /une partie d'échecs, cinq dollars/*, Agreed for a game of chess, five dollars it will be.

va[2], **vas; vais; vont** [va; vɛ; vɔ̃] cf. ALLER.

vacance [va'kɑ̃:s] *n.f.* **1.** [sing.] vacancy; opening. **2.** [pl.] vacation, holidays: *grandes vacances*, summer holidays, summer vacation; *passer ses vacances dans les Laurentides*, to spend one's holidays, vacation, in the Laurentians. || **vacanci|er, -ère** [vakɑ̃'sj|e, -ɛːr] *n.* vacationer.

vacant, -e [va'k|ɑ̃, -ɑ̃ːt] *adj.* vacant, empty; unoccupied, tenantless: *appartement ~*, apartment for rent; *place vacante*, vacancy (in a firm, &c.).

vacarme [va'karm] *n.m.* noise, din, racket.

vaccin [vak'sɛ̃] *n.m.* vaccine. || **vaccination** [vaksina'sjõ] *n.f.* vaccination, inoculation. || **vacciner** [vaksi'ne] #3, *v. tr.* **1.** to vaccinate (s.o. against smallpox and polio); *se faire ~*, to be vaccinated (*contre*, for, against). **2.** to inoculate; *se faire ~*, to be inoculated (for/against/ typhoid fever and typhus).

vache [vaʃ] *n.f.* cow; *~ à lait*, milk cow, †milch cow; *parler français comme une ~ espagnole*, to murder the French language. || **vacher**[1] [va'ʃe] *n.m.* cowherd, buckaroo, cow-boy.

vacher[2] [va'ʃe] *n.m.* cowbird; cf. ÉTOURNEAU.

vacillant, -e [vasi'j|ɑ̃, -ɑ̃ːt] *adj.* **1.** flickering, wavering. **2.** [Fig.] wavering, vacillating. || **vaciller** [vasi'je] #3, *v. intr.* **1.** [lumière] to flicker, to waver. **2.** to be unsteady, to wobble (on one's legs). **3.** [Fig.] to vacillate (in a decision, &c.).

vacuum [vaky'ɔm] *n.m.* vacuum.

va-et-vient [vae'vjɛ̃] *n.m. invar.* moving to and fro, coming and going; see-saw motion, oscillation: *Il y avait beaucoup de ~ dans la pièce*, There was a lot of coming and going in the room.

vagabond, -e [vaga'b|õ, -õːd] *n. & adj.* vagrant, vagabond. || **vagabonder** [vagabõ'de] #3 *v. intr.* to wander, to rove.

vagon cf. WAGON.

vague[1] [vag] *n.f.* wave, billow. *Les vagues déferlent sur le rivage*, the waves break on the shore; *une ~ de chaleur*, a heat wave.

vague[2] [vag] *adj.* **1.** vague; hazy, indefinite: *un regard ~*, a vacant/stare, look. **2.** waste, empty; uncultivated: *terrain ~*, vacant lot. || *n.m.* vagueness, uncertainty. || **vaguement** [vag'mɑ̃] *adv.* dimly, vaguely, vacantly.

vaillamment [vaja'mɑ̃] *adv.* valiantly. || **vaillance** [va'jɑ̃ːs] *n.f.* bravery, valour. || **vaillant, -e** [va'j|ɑ̃, -ɑ̃ːt] *adj.* brave, gallant, valiant: *Il n'a pas un sou ~*, He hasn't a red cent (to his name).

vaille, &c. [vɑj] cf. VALOIR.

vain, -e [vɛ̃, vɛn] *adj.* **1.** vain, idle, empty: *de vaines promesses*, empty promises. **2.** vain, unavailing: *en ~*, in vain; *vains efforts*, futile efforts. **3.** vain, conceited.

vainc, vaincs [vɛ̃] cf. VAINCRE.

vainement [vɛn'mɑ̃] *adv.* vainly, in vain.

vaincre [vɛ̃ːkr] **vainquant, vaincu,** #35, *v. tr.* to defeat, conquer; [Fig.] to overcome (fear). || *v. intr.* to conquer. || **vaincu, -e** [vɛ̃'ky] *adj.* vanquished, conquered: *s'avouer ~*, to admit defeat. || *n. les vaincus*, the conquered, the losers. || **vainquais; vainque** [vɛ̃'kɛ, vɛ̃ːk]. || **vainqueur** [vɛ̃'kœːr] *n.m.* victor; winner (of a competition). || *adj.* [no fem.] victorious, conquering.

vainquez; vainquis; vainquons [vɛ̃'ke, vɛ̃'ki, vɛ̃'kõ] cf. VAINCRE.

vais cf. ALLER.

†**vaisseau**, pl. **-x** [vɛ'so] *n.m.* **1.** vessel, [large sailing] ship. [For modern ships, use NAVIRE, BATEAU, UNITÉ]; [Fig.] *brûler ses vaisseaux*, to burn one's boats, to burn one's bridges. **2.** †©vessel, pan; [Arch.] nave (of a church); *~ sanguin*, blood vessel.

vaisselle [vɛ'sɛl] *n.f.* plates, dishes, china; table ware: *faire la ~*, to do the dishes; [Br.] to wash up; *machine à laver la ~*, dish-washer.

val cf. VALLÉE.

valable [va'labl] *adj.* valid: *une excuse ~*, a valid excuse; *Ce billet est ~ un mois*, This ticket is good for one month.

valet [va'lɛ] *n.m.* **1.** valet. **2.** jack: *le ~ de pique*, the jack of spades.

valeur [va'lœːr] *n.f.* **1.** value, worth: *mettre en ~*, to show to advantage, to develop (a country); *envoyer en ~ déclarée*, to insure (a parcel); *un homme de ~*, a very able man. **2.** [Com.] security, stock. **3.** valour, courage. **4.** © [Bus.] value(s), bargain. **5.** © *de ~*, too bad, unfortunate: *C'est de ~ qu'il ne soit pas venu*, It's too bad he didn't come. **valeureu|x, -se** [valœ'r|ø, -øːz] *adj.* gallant.

valide [va'lid] *adj.* valid; sound, able-bodied; [Fig.] good. || **valider** [-e] #3 *v. tr.* to validate (a passport). || **validité** [validi'te] *n.f.* validity.

valise [va'liːz] *n.f.* suitcase: *faire ses valises*, to pack (one's bags) [© often refers to a large trunk].

vallée [va'le] *n.f.* valley: *la ~ du Saint-Laurent*, the St. Lawrence Valley.

valoir [va'lwaːr] **valant, valu,** #29, *v. intr.* to be worth: *Cela ne vaut rien*, It is worth nothing; *Cela vaut mieux que rien*, It is better than nothing; *faire ~*, to set off to advantage, to use to advantage; *Une couleur fait ~ l'autre*, One colour sets off the other; *faire ~ ses terres*, to develop one's land; *faire ~ des fonds*, to invest funds profitably; *faire ~ ses raisons*, to put forward one's reasons; *faire ~ que . . .*, to argue that . . .; *se faire* ~, to assert oneself, to show off. || *v. tr.* **1.** to equal: *Les deux se valent,* One is as good as the other. **2.** to bring, to earn: *Cela lui a valu une gratification,* It got him a bonus. || *v. impers. Il vaut mieux attendre,* We had better wait, It would be better to wait; *Autant vaut y renoncer,* We might as well give up; *Mieux vaut tard que jamais,* Better late than never.

valse [vals] *n.f.* [Mus.] waltz. || **valser** [val'se] #3, *v. intr.* to waltz; *faire ~ qqun,* to waltz with s.o.

valve [valv] *n.f.* valve.

Vancouver [vɑ̃ku'vɛːr] [Topon.] *l'île de ~,* Vancouver Island.

vandale [vɑ̃'dal] *n.m.* vandal. || **vandalisme** [vɑ̃da'lism] *n.m.* vandalism.

vanille [va'niːj] *n.f.* vanilla.

vanité [vani'te] *n.f.* vanity, conceit; uselessness, folly: *tirer ~ de sa fortune,* to be conceited about one's fortune. || **vaniteu|x, -se** [vani|'tø, -'tøːz] *adj.* vain, conceited.

vanne [van] *n.f.* flood-gate (in a dam); © [abus]. truck.

vantard [vɑ̃'taːr] *n.m.* braggart, swaggerer. || *adj.* bragging, boastful. || **vantardise** [vɑ̃tar'diːz] *n.f.* bragging, boasting. || **vanter** [vɑ̃'te] #3, *v. tr.* to praise, to extol (s.o.'s qualities); to boost, push (a product on the market). || **se vanter** *v. pron.* to boast, to brag: ~ *de son succès,* to brag about one's success.

vapeur[1] [va'pœːr] *n.f.* **1.** steam. **2.** mist, vapour: [Fig.] *filer à toute ~,* to go at full speed; *machine à ~,* steam engine; *bain de ~,* steam bath.

vapeur[2] [va'pœːr] *n.m.* [Naut.] steamship, steamer.

vaquer [va'ke] #3, *v. intr.* **1.** to take a recess: *Les classes vaqueront demain,* There will be no school tomorrow. **2.** to devote one's attention to: ~ *à ses affaires,* to go about one's business.

vareuse [va'røːz] *n.f.* pea-jacket; [Mar.] jumper; [Army] blouse.

variable [va'rjabl] *adj.* changeable, variable: *temps ~,* changeable temperature, weather. || **variation** [varja'sjɔ̃] *n.f.* variation. || **varié, -e** [va'rje] *adj.* varying, changing, fluctuating; varied, †variegated (colours). || **varier** [va'rje] #3, *v. tr.* to vary, to diversify: ~ *son alimentation,* to vary one's diet. || *v. intr.* to vary, to fluctuate, to depend.

variété [varje'te] *n.f.* variety, range.

Varsovie [varsɔ'vi] *n.f.* [Topon.] Warsaw.

vas cf. ALLER.

vase[1] [vɑːz] *n.m.* vase; vessel; [Rel.] ~*sacré,* sacred vessel.

vase[2] [vɑːz] *n.f.* slime; mud.

vaseline [vaz'lin] *n.f.* vaseline.

vaste [vast] *adj.* **1.** large, spacious, vast [Eng. *vast* is larger than Fr. *vaste*]: *les vastes plaines de l'Ouest canadien,* the vast plains of the Canadian West. **2.** [Fig.] great, ambitious: *de vastes projets,* ambitious projects.

Vatican [vati'kɑ̃] *n.m. le ~* , the Vatican: *la Cité du ~* , the Vatican City.

vaudeville [vod'vil] *n.m.* light comedy, vaudeville.

vaudra, &c. cf. VALOIR.

vau-l'eau [vo'lo] *adv. phr.*: *s'en aller à ~,* to drift; [Fig.] to go to pot.

vaurien, -ne [vo'rj|ɛ̃, -ɛn] *n.* worthless person, rotter, good-for-nothing.

vaut [vo] cf. VALOIR.

vautour [vo'tuːr] *n.m.* vulture.

vaux cf. VALOIR.

veau [vo] *n.m.* [animal] calf; [viande] veal; [cuir] calfskin: *un rôti de ~,* a veal roast; *pleurer comme un ~,* to blubber; [Zool.] ~ *marin,* seal cf. PHOQUE.

vécu, -e [ve'ky] *adj.* experienced, true to life: *un film, un roman ~,* a true-life movie, novel; cf. VIVRE.

vedette [və'dɛt] *n.f.* **1.** [Ciné., TV] star, leading man, leading lady; *mettre en ~,* to highlight; *tenir la ~,* to play the lead, the title role. **2.** [Naut.] launch, patrol boat.

végétal, -e [veʒe'tal] *adj.* vegetable: *le règne ~* , the vegetable kingdom. || *n.m.* [sing.] plant; [pl.] vegetation. || **végétation** [veʒeta'sjɔ̃] *n.f.* vegetation. || **végéter** [veʒe'te] #10, *v. intr.* to vegetate.

véhémence [vee'mɑ̃ːs] *n.f.* vehemence. || **véhément, -e** [vee'mɑ̃(ːt)] *adj.* vehement.

véhicule [vei'kyl] *n.m.* [générique] vehicle: ~ *à moteur,* motor vehicle.

veille [vɛːj] *n.f.* **1.** vigil, watching; sitting (at night), wakefulness: *entre la ~ et le sommeil,* between waking and sleeping. **2.** day or evening before, eve: *la ~ des examens,* the day before exams; *Je l'ai vu la ~ au soir,* I saw him the night before; *la ~ de Noël,* Christmas Eve. || **veillée** [vɛ'je] *n.f.* **1.** [the time between supper and bedtime] evening: ~ *funèbre,* wake. **2.** social evening; © evening party; © [Fam.] *un casseux de ~,* a wet blanket. || **veiller** [vɛ'je] #3, *v. intr.* **1.** to keep a vigil; to stay up, sit up (with a sick person); ~ *jusqu'au jour,* to sit up all night; ~ *fort avant dans la nuit,* to burn the midnight oil. **2.** to watch over, ~ *aux* *intérêts de qqun*, to look after s.o.'s interests; ~ *à*, to see to. || *v. tr.* to sit up with (a sick person). || **veilleu|r, -se** [vɛ'j|œ:r, -ø:z] *n.* vigil keeper; [*m.*] watchman: ~ *de nuit*, night watchman; [*f.*] night light: *mettre* (*une lumière*) *en veilleuse*, to turn (a light) down (low).

veinard, -e [vɛ'n|a:r, -ard] [Fam.] *adj.* lucky. || *n.* lucky dog, lucky girl. || **veine** [vɛ:n] *n.f.* **1.** vein. **2.** mood: *être en* ~ *de faire qqch.*, to be in the mood to do sth. **3.** [Fam.] luck: *avoir de la* ~, to be lucky.

vélo [ve'lo] *n.m.* [Fam.] bike, [Br.] (push) bike: *aller à* ~, to ride a bike; *Nous y sommes allés en* ~, We went, rode/there on our bikes.

vélocité [velɔsi'te] *n.f.* velocity, speed.

velours [v(ə)'lu:r] *n.m.* velvet; [Fig.] *être sur le* ~, to be in clover; *faire patte de* ~, to pull in one's claws, to go easy.

velouté, -e [vəlu'te] *adj.* velvety; [vin] mellow.

venaison [vənɛ'zõ] *n.f.* venison.

venant [v(ə)'nã] *n.m.*: *à tout* ~, to anybody.

vendange [vã'dã:ʒ] *n.f.* [usual. pl.] grape harvest: *faire les vendanges*, to gather, pick the grapes.

vendeu|r, -se [vãd|œ:r, -ø:z] *n.* clerk, salesman, saleswoman: *une vendeuse de magasin*, a store clerk. || **vendre** [vã:dr], **vendant, vendu,** #42, *v. tr.* to sell: *maison à* ~, house for sale; ~ *aux enchères*, to sell by auction; ~/*au détail, en gros*, to retail, to wholesale; ~ *sa conscience*, to sell one's soul; ~ *la peau de l'ours avant de l'avoir tué*, to count one's chicken before they are hatched. || **vendu, -e** [vã'dy] *n.* traitor; person who has sold out to s.o.

vendredi [vãdrə'di] *n.m.* Friday: *Vendredi Saint*, Good Friday cf. LUNDI.

vénéneu|x, -se [vene'nø(:z)] *adj.* [mushroom, &c.] poisonous.

vénérable [vene'ra:bl] *adj.* venerable. || **vénération** *n.f.* veneration. || **vénérer** [vene're] #10, *v. tr.* to respect, to venerate, to honour: ~ *un bienfaiteur*, to respect/honour/a benefactor.

Vénézuéla [vene|zɥɛ'la] *n.m.* Venezuela. || **Vénézuélien** [-zɥe'ljɛ̃] *n.* (*& adj.*) Venezuelan.

vengeance [vã'ʒã:s] *n.f.* revenge, vengeance: *tirer* ~ *de*, to get revenge on (s.o.) for (sth.). || **venger** [vã'ʒe] #5, *v. tr.* to avenge (s.o., an insult). || **se venger** *v. pron.* to revenge o.s., to have one's revenge. || **vengeur, vengeresse** [vã'ʒœ:r, vãʒ(ə)'rɛs] *n.m./f.* avenger, revenger. || *adj.* avenging.

véniel, -le [ve'njɛl] *adj.* venial.

venimeu|x, -se [vəni'mø(:z)] *adj.* venomous (snake, &c.); [Fig.] spiteful, venomous.

venir [v(ə)'ni:r], **venant, venu,** #22, *v. intr.* **1.** to come: *Venez avec nous*, Come with us; *Faites-le* ~, Have him come, Get him to come; *Il l'a fait* ~, He sent for him, her, it. **2.** [Loc.] *en* ~ *à l'essentiel*, to get down to the point; *Où voulez-vous en* ~*?*, What are you getting at?; *Il me vient à l'esprit que . . .*, It occurs to me that . . .; *voir* ~, to wait and see; *dans les temps à* ~, in days to come. **3.** [aux. de passé immédiat]: *Il vient* (*tout juste*) *de partir*, He has just left.

Venise [v(ə)'ni:z] *n.f.* Venice. || **vénitien, -ne** [veni'sj|ɛ̃, -ɛn] *adj.* Venetian; © *store m.* ~, Venetian blind.

vent [vã] *n.m.* **1.** wind: *Il fait du* ~, It is windy; *par grand* ~, in a high wind; *un coup de* ~, a gust of wind; *Le* ~ *souffle en tempête*, The wind, It/is blowing a gale; [Naut.] ~ *debout, arrière*, head, tail wind. **2.** [Mus.] *les vents*, the woodwinds. **3.** [Fig.] *avoir* ~ *d'une affaire*, to get wind of an incident.

Vent [vã] [Topon.] *les Îles du* ~, the Windward Islands; *les Îles sous le* ~, the Leeward Islands.

vente [vã:t] *n.f.* sale cf. VENDRE: *mettre qqch. en* ~, to put sth. on sale; *en* ~ *à*, on sale at; ~ *à crédit*, credit sale; ~ *à terme*, time-payment sale; ~ *à tempérament*, instalment selling.

venter [vã'te] #3, *v. impers.*: *Il vente*, It is windy.

ventilateur [vãtila'tœ:r] *n.m.* electric fan [ventilator].

ventre [vã:tr] *n.m.* stomach, belly, abdomen, [Fam.] paunch: *être à plat* ~, to be lying flat on one's stomach; [Fam.] *avoir mal au* ~, to have a stomach ache; *courir* ~ *à terre*, to run at full speed; *prendre du* ~, to get fat, to become paunchy.

venu, venue cf. VENIR.

venu, -e [v(ə)'ny] *n.* comer [never used alone]; one who comes: *le premier* ~, *la première venue*, the first person who happens along; *le dernier* ~, the last one to arrive. || **venue** [v(ə)'ny] *n.f.* coming, arrival: *Avisez-moi de votre* ~, Let me know (in advance) that you are coming, Notify me of your arrival; *Après plusieurs allées et venues . . .*, After going back and forth several times . . .

vêpres [vɛ:pr] *n.f. pl.* vespers; evensong.

ver [vɛ:r] *n.m.* worm [do not confuse pl. (*les*) *vers* with VERS,[1] VERS[2]]: *un* ~ *à soie, de terre*, a silkworm, an earthworm; *nu comme un* ~, stark naked; [Fig.] *tirer les* *vers du nez à qqun*, to worm information out of s.o., to pump s.o.

verbal, -e [vɛr'bal] *adj.* verbal.

verbe [vɛrb] *n.m.* [Gram.] verb; [Fig.] *avoir le ~ haut*, to talk loud.

verdâtre [vɛr'dɑ:tr] *adj.* greenish.

verdeur [vɛr'dœ:r] *n.f.* greenness (of lumber, fruit); immaturity; [Fig.] *la ~ de l'âge*, the vigour of youth; *la ~ de ses paroles*, his blunt words.

verdict [vɛr'dikt] *n.m.* verdict: *Le jury rend son ~*, The jury returns its verdict.

verdir [vɛr'di:r] #17 *v. intr.* to grow/turn/ green. ‖ **verdure** [vɛr'dy:r] *n.f.* **1.** greenery, foliage. **2.** greens [for decoration or as green vegetables].

véreu|x, -se [ve|rø, -'rø:z] *adj.* worm-eaten, rotten; [Fig.] dishonest, shaky.

verge [vɛrʒ] *n.f.* **1.** rod. **2.** [Med.] penis. **3.** © yard, yardstick [YARD].

verger [vɛr'ʒe] *n.m.* orchard.

verglas [vɛr'glɑ] *n.m.* ice; glare, glaze/of ice: *routes couvertes de ~*, roads slick with ice.

véridique [veri'dik] *adj.* veracious, truthful.

vérificateur [verifika'tœ:r] *n.m.* auditor. ‖ **vérifier** [veri'fje] #3, *v. tr.* to verify, to check; to audit: *~ un compte*, to check a calculation, an account; *~ si tout est prêt*, to make sure that everything is ready.

véritable [veri'tabl] *adj.* real, genuine: *or ~*, real gold; *un ami ~*, a real friend. ‖ **vérité** [veri'te] *n.f.* truth; *jurer de dire la ~*, to swear to tell the truth; *Ce que je vous dis là, c'est la pure ~*, What I'm telling you is the absolute truth; *La ~ finit toujours par se savoir*, Truth will out; *Je lui ai dit ses quatre vérités*, I gave him a piece of my mind, I told him a few home truths.

vermeil, -le [vɛr'mɛ:j] *adj.* rosy; ruby; bright red: *des lèvres vermeilles*, ruby lips. ‖ **vermeil** *n.m.* silver-gilt: *une médaille de ~*, a silver-gilt medal.

vermine [vɛr'min] *n.f.* vermin.

Vermont [vɛr'mõ] *n.m.* Vermont.

vermoulu, -e [vɛrmu'ly] *adj.* worm-eaten; [Fig.] decrepit, shaky.

vernaculaire [vɛrnaky'lɛ:r] *adj.* & *n.m.* vernacular.

verni- -e [vɛr'ni] *adj.* **1.** *souliers vernis*, patent-leather shoes. **2.** [Fam., Fig.] lucky: *Il est ~*, His luck always holds. ‖ **vernir** [vɛrni:r], **vernissant, verni,** #17, *v. tr.* to varnish. ‖ **vernis** [vɛr'ni] *n.m.* varnish: [Fig.] *un ~ d'élégance*, a veneer of elegance. ‖ **vernissage** [vɛrni'sa:ʒ] *n.m.* **1.** varnishing. **2.** private viewing (of pictures).

vérole [ve'rɔl] *n.f.* pox: *petite ~*, smallpox.

verrai, &c. [vɛ're] cf. VOIR.

verre [vɛ:r] *n.m.* **1.** [dans lequel on boit] glass, tumbler: *boire dans un ~*, to drink from a glass; [Fig.] *une tempête dans un ~ d'eau*, a storm in a tea cup. **2.** glass: *articles de ~*, glassware; *du ~ taillé*, cut glass; *~ dépoli*, frosted glass; *~ à vitre* cf. CARREAU, sheet, window glass; *papier de ~*, sandpaper; *~ de montre*, watch crystal; *~ de lampe*, chimney, (lantern) globe. **3.** [Optic.] [always pl. *verres*] glasses; lenses: *porter des verres* cf. LUNETTES, to wear glasses; *verres de contact*, contact lenses.

verrou [vɛ'ru] *n.m.* bolt, bar: *pousser le ~*, to bolt the door; *tirer les verrous*, to unbolt the door; *être sous les verrous*, to be locked up. ‖ **verrouiller** [vɛru'je] #3 *v. tr.* to bolt (a door).

vers[1] [vɛ:r] *prep.* **1.** toward(s). **2.** about: *aller ~ la fenêtre*, to go toward the window; *Il est venu ~ deux heures*, He came about two o'clock.

vers[2] [vɛ:r] *n.m. invar.* line (of poetry): *faire, écrire des ~*, to write poetry; *en ~*, in verse.

vers[3] cf. VER.

versant [vɛr'sɑ̃] *n.m.* slope, side (of a valley): *venir de l'autre ~ de la montagne*, to come from the other side of the mountain.

versatile [vɛrsa'til] *adj.* changeable, fickle. [×] cf. VERSATILE.

verse [vɛrs] *à verse, adv. phr.* in torrents: *Il pleut à verse*, It's raining cats and dogs.

versé, -e [vɛr'se] *adj.* experienced, versed in, well versed: *Il est ~ dans les affaires*, He is an experienced businessman. ‖ **versement** [vɛrsə'mɑ̃] *n.m.* payment, instalment; deposit.

verser [vɛr'se]# 3, *v. tr.* **1.** to pour: *~ du vin dans un verre*, to pour wine into a glass. **2.** to deposit, to pay: *~ de l'argent à la banque*, to deposit money in the bank; *L'argent a été versé à mon compte*, The money was paid into my account. ‖ *v. intr.* to overturn: *La voiture a versé dans le fossé*, The car overturned in the ditch.

version [vɛr'sjõ] *n.f.* **1.** [School] translation [from the foreign into the native language]. **2.** version: *Sa ~ de l'accident*, His version of the accident.

vert, -e [vɛ:r, vɛrt] *adj.* **1.** green. **2.** [Fig.] [fruit, &c.] green, unripe; [personne, animal] vigorous: *encore ~ malgré son âge*, still hale and hearty. **3.** [Fig.] *se mettre au ~*, to go and relax in the country.

vertébral, -e [vɛrte'bral] *adj.* vertebral; *colonne f vertébrale*, spinal column, the spine. || **vertèbre** [vɛr'tɛ:br] *n.f.* vertebra.

vertement [vɛrtə'mɑ̃] *adv.* sharply: *Je l'ai tancé* ~, I spoke sharply to him.

vertical, -e [vɛrti'kal] *adj.* vertical, upright.

vertige [vɛr'ti:ʒ] *n.m.* dizziness: *avoir le* ~, to be, to feel dizzy; *avoir facilement le* ~, to have a bad head for heights; *être sujet à des vertiges*, to have dizzy spells. || **vertigineu|x, -se** [vɛrtiʒin|ø, -ø:z] *adj.* dizzy, giddy: *vitesse vertigineuse*, breath-taking speed.

vertu [vɛr'ty] *n.f.* virtue. || **en vertu de** *prep. phr.* by virtue of. || **vertueu|x, -se** [vɛr'tɥ|ø, -ø:z] *adj.* virtuous, righteous, chaste.

vésicule [vezi'kyl] *n.f.* vesicle; ~ *biliaire*, gall bladder.

vessie [ve'si] *n.f.* bladder.

veste [vɛst] *n.f.* × jacket; © [Abus.] vest, waistcoat.

vestiaire [vɛs'tjɛ:r] *n.m.* checkroom, [Br.] cloakroom; locker room [adjacent à la salle de gymnastique].

vestibule [vɛsti'byl] *n.m.* [maison particulière] hall, hallway; [théâtre, hôtel, immeuble] lobby, foyer.

vestige [vɛs'ti:ʒ] *n.m.* vestiges, remains: *les vestiges d'une civilisation*, the vestiges of a civilization.

veston [vɛs'tõ] *n.m.* [suit] coat, jacket: *endosser/passer, mettre/son* ~, to put on one's/(sports) coat, jacket; [Fr.] *complet veston*, lounge suit.

Vésuve [ve'zy:v] *n.m.* [Topon.] Vesuvius.

vêt; vêts [vɛ] cf. VÊTIR.

vêtement [vɛt'mɑ̃] *n.m.* garment, clothes, clothing: *un* ~, a garment, *le* ~, cf. NOURRITURE, LOGEMENT, clothes; *ses vêtements*, his, her/clothes; *passer ses vêtements*, to put on one's clothes.

vétéran [veterɑ̃] *n.m.* veteran, old soldier.

vétérinaire [veterinɛ:r] *n.m.* veterinary surgeon, veterinarian, [Fam.] vet. || *adj.* veterinary: *école* ~, veterinary school.

vêtir [vɛ'ti:r] **vêtant, vêtu**, #42, *v. tr.* to clothe, to dress. || **se vêtir** *v. pron.* to dress.

veto [ve'to] *n.m.* veto: *mettre son* ~ *à qqch.*, to veto sth.

veuf, veuve [vœf, vœ:v] *adj.* widowed: *devenu* ~, left a widower. || *n.* widower, widow.

veuille, veuillez [vœ:j, vœ'je] cf. VOULOIR.

veut; veux [vø] cf. VOULOIR.

veuve cf. VEUF.

vexer [vɛk'se] #3, *v. tr.* to pique [seulement au passif], to offend, to annoy: *Cela l'a vexé*, He was piqued, It annoyed him. [×] cf. VEX.

viable [vjabl] *adj.* viable, likely to live.

viaduc [vja'dyk] *n.m.* viaduct.

viag|er, -ère [vjaʒ|e, -ɛ:r] *adj.* limited to one's lifetime: *rente viagère*, life annuity. || **viager** *n.m. placer de l'argent en* ~, to purchase a life annuity.

viande [vjɑ̃:d] *n.f.* meat.

viatique [vja'tik] *n.m.* [R.C.] Holy Viaticum: *donner la communion en* ~, to give the Holy Viaticum; [Fig.] viaticum.

vibrant, -e [vi'br|ɑ̃, -ɑ̃:t] *adj.* **1.** vibrating. **2.** [Fig.] ringing (voice); stirring (speech). || **vibration** [vibra'sjõ] *n.f.* vibration; resonance (of voice). || **vibrer** [vi'bre] #3, *v. intr.* **1.** to vibrate. **2.** [Fig.] to be touched, moved; *faire* ~ *qqun*, to move s.o.

vicaire [vi'kɛ:ɛr] *n.m.* **1.** curate, assistant priest. **2.** vicar: ~ *apostolique*, Vicar Apostolic; *Vicaire de Jésus-Christ*, Vicar of Christ. || **vicariat** [vika'rja] *n.m.* [R.C.] vicariate.

vice-[1] . . . [vis . . .] [prefix meaning "in the place of"]: ~ *président*, vice-president.

vice[2] [vis] *n.m.* vice, bad habit. || **vicieu|x, -se** [vi'sjø(:z)] *adj.* vicious; [emploi], wrong use; [cheval], unsound.

victime [vik'tim] *n.f.* victim, casualty: *Il est sur la liste des victimes*, He is on the casualty list; *Il a été* ~ *d'un accident*, He was killed (or injured) in an accident; *Il a été* ~ *de sa sévérité*, He fell a victim to his own rashness.

victoire [vik'twa:r] *n.f.* victory. || **victorieu|x, -se** [viktɔ'rj|ø, -ø:z] *adj.* victorious.

Victoria [viktɔ'rja] *n.f.* [Topon.]: *l'île de* ~, Victoria Island.

vide [vid] *adj. m/f.* empty, vacant: *revenir les mains vides*, to come back empty-handed; *des mots vides de sens*, meaningless words; *une place* ~, a vacant seat. || *n.m.* **1.** emptiness: *le* ~ *de la maison*, the emptiness of the house. **2.** vacuum [absence d'air ou de puissance]: *La nature a horreur du* ~, Nature abhors a vacuum; *faire le* ~, to create a vacuum. **3.** void [absence de ce qui nous est cher]: *Sa mort laisse un* ~, His death leaves a void. **4.** [Loc.]: *faire le* ~ *autour de qqun*, to isolate s.o., to drive s.o.'s friends away. || **vidé, -e** [vi'de] *adj.* **1.** *poulet* ~, drawn chicken. **2.** [Fig., Fam.]: *Je suis complètement* ~, I am (completely) exhausted, worn-out. || **vider** [vi'de] #3, *v. tr.* **1.** to empty: ~ *un tiroir*, to empty a drawer; ~ *son verre d'un trait*, to drain one's glass; ~ *les lieux*, to clear out. **2.** to clean, draw:

~ *un poisson*, to clean a fish; ~ *une volaille*, to draw a fowl. **3.** [Fig.] ~ *une question*, to settle a question.

vie [vi] *n.f.* **1.** life, existence: *pour la* ~, for life; *Jamais de la* ~, Not on your life; *sans* ~, lifeless; *sauver la* ~ *à qqun*, to save s.o.'s life; *rendre la* ~ *dure à qqun*, to give s.o. a hard time; *Je ne l'ai jamais vu de ma* ~, I have never seen him in my life. **2.** living: *gagner sa* ~, to earn one's living; *le coût de la* ~, the cost of living.

vieil, -le [vjɛj] *adj.* cf. VIEUX.

vieillard [vjɛ'ja:r] *n.m.* old man; *des vieillards*, old people. || **vieille** [vjɛj] *n.f.* (or *vieille femme*) old woman cf. VIEUX. || **vieillesse** [vjɛ'jɛs] *n.f.* old age. || **vieillir** [vjɛ'ji:r] **vieillissant; vieilli,** #17, *v. intr.* **1.** to grow old, to age. **2.** [Fig.] to go out of style. || *v. tr.* to make s.o. look older: *Cette robe vous vieillit*, That dress makes you look older.

viendra; vienne cf. VENIR.

Vienne [vjɛn] *n.f.* [Topon.] [in Austria] Vienna; [in France] Vienne.

viens, vient cf. VENIR.

vierge [vjɛrʒ] *n.f.* virgin; *la Sainte Vierge*, the Holy Virgin. || *adj.* virgin: *une forêt* ~, a virgin forest; [Topon.] *les Îles Vierges*, the Virgin Islands.

Viet-Nam [vjɛt'nam] *n.m.* [Topon.] Viet Nam [formerly *Indo-China*, l'Indo-Chine]; *le* ~/*Sud, Nord*, Southern, Northern/Viet Nam. || **vietnami|en, -enne** [vjɛtna'mj|ɛ̃, -ɛn] *adj.* Vietnamese.

vieux, vieille [vjø, vjɛj] [The form *vieil* is used before m. sing. n. which begin with a vowel or a mute *h*; *vieux* is *invar.*] *adj.* **1.** old in years: *se faire* ~, to grow old, to age; *une vieille fille*, an old maid; *un vieil ami*, an old friend, a friend of old standing; ~ *comme la terre*, as old as the hills; © *le* ~ *pays*, the Old Country. **2.** old-fashioned: *être* ~ *jeu*, to be old-fashioned. || **vieux, vieille** *n.m. & f.* **1.** old person: *le* ~, the old man; *les* ~, the old people; *jeunes et* ~, young and old. **2.** [sing. & Fam.] *mon* ~, old boy, old man; *ma vieille*, old girl.

vif, vive [vif, vi:v] *adj.* **1.** alive, living: *eau vive*, spring water; *foi vive*, unshakable faith; *haie vive*, quickset hedge; *Il faut le capturer mort ou* ~, He must be captured dead or alive. **2.** [Fig.] lively, energetic: *un enfant* ~, a lively, energetic child; *de vifs reproches*, sharp criticism; *un* ~ *plaisir*, a keen pleasure. **3.** quick, animated, impetuous: *imagination vive*, quick lively imagination; *des yeux vifs*, bright eyes; *une attaque vive*, a sudden, impetuous attack. **4.** bright, intense, sharp: *des couleurs vives*, bright, intense colours. **5.** heartfelt, hearty: *Nos plus vives félicitations*, Our heartiest congratulations. || **vif** *n.m.*: *trancher dans le* ~, to act drastically; *Il a été piqué au* ~, He was stung to the quick; *entrer dans le* ~ *du sujet*, to get to the heart of the matter.

vigilance [viʒi'lɑ̃:s] *n.f.* vigilance, watchfulness; caution. || **vigilant, -e** [viʒi'lɑ̃, -ɑ̃:t] *adj.* vigilant, watchful; cautious.

vigne [viɲ] *n.f.* vine; vineyard.

vignette [vi'ɲɛt] *n.f.* vignette, cut.

vigoureusement [vigurøz'mɑ̃] *adv.* vigorously. || **vigoureu|x, -se** [vigu'r|ø, -ø:z] *adj.* vigorous, strong. || **vigueur** [vi'gœ:r] *n.f.* vigour, strength: *mettre une loi en* ~, to enforce a law; *entrer en* ~, to come into force; *Le traité est encore en* ~, The treaty is still in force.

vil, -e [vil] *adj.* **1.** cheap, of little value: *acheter à* ~ *prix*, to buy at a very cheap price, to buy dirt cheap. **2.** [Fig.] vile, despicable.

vilain, -e [vi'l|ɛ̃, -ɛn] *adj.* **1.** nasty, villainous: *vilaine action*, villainous act; *de vilaines gens*, nasty people; *jouer un* ~ *tour à*, to play a dirty trick on. **2.** disagreeable, unpleasant: ~ *temps*, bad weather; ~ *incident*, an unpleasant incident. **3.** ugly: ~ *comme tout*, ugly as anything; *une vilaine blessure*, an ugly wound. **4.** [of child] naughty, bad. || **vilenie** [vilə'ni] *n.f.* **1.** nastiness, meanness, foul action: *lui faire des vilenies*, to play dirty tricks on him. **2.** abusive language: *dire des vilenies*, to use abusive language.

villa [vil'la] *n.f.* villa, elegant country home.

village [vi'la:ʒ] *n.m.* village. || **villageois, -e** [vila'ʒ|wa, -wa:z] *n.* rustic, villager. || *adj.* country- (dance, &c.), rustic.

ville [vil] *n.f.* town, city: *en* ~, in town; *dans la* ~, inside the town, within the city limits; *aller en* ~, to go to town, to go downtown; *habiter hors de la* ~, to live out of town; *dîner en* ~, to eat downtown, to dine out; *Hôtel de* ~, City Hall; ~ *sainte* [e.g. Rome, Jérusalem, la Mecque], Holy City.

villégiature [villeʒja'ty:r] *n.f.* [used in the sing. only] stay in the country: *être en* ~, to be staying at a summer resort.

Ville-Marie [vilma'ri] *n.f.* [Topon.] [former name of the City of Montreal] Ville-Marie.

Ville-Reine [vil'rɛ:n] *n.f.* [Topon.] [titre attribué à la ville de Toronto] Queen City.

vin [vɛ̃] *n.m.* wine: *être entre deux vins*, to be

half-drunk; *Il a mis de l'eau dans son* ~, He has toned down his demands, He is now easier to deal with.
vinaigre [vi'nɛ:gr] *n.m.* vinegar.
vinaigrette [vinɛ'grɛt] *n.f.* vinaigrette sauce; French dressing.
vindicati|f, -ve [vɛ̃dika't|if, -i:v] *adj.* vindictive, vengeful.
vingt [vɛ̃] *n.m. & adj.* twenty; †score. || **vingtaine** [vɛ̃'tɛn] *n.f.* about twenty: *une* ~ *de feuilles,* about twenty sheets. || **vingt-deux** [vɛ̃d'dø] *n.m.* twenty-two. || **vingt-et-un** [vɛ̃te'œ̃] *n.m.* twenty-one. || **vingtième** [vɛ̃'tjɛm] *n.m. & adj. ord.* twentieth.
vins[1], **&c.** cf. VENIR.
vins[2] cf. VIN.
violation [vjɔla'sjõ] *n.f.* violation, infringement; desecration.
viole [vjɔl] *n.f.* viola.
violemment [vjɔla'mɑ̃] *adv.* violently. || **violence** [vjɔ'lɑ̃:s] *n.f.* violence, force: *faire* ~ *à,* to do violence to, to violate; *user de* ~ *envers qqun,* to use violence, force on s.o. || **violent, -e** [vjɔ'l|ɑ̃, -ɑ̃:t] *adj.* violent: *mourir de mort violente,* to die a violent death; *tempête violente,* violent storm.
violer [vjɔ'le] #3, *v. tr.* [Fig.] to violate, to break (an agreement, a promise).
violet, -te [vjɔ'l|ɛ, -ɛt] *adj.* purple, violet. || **violette** *n.f.* [Bot.] violet.
violon [vjɔ'lõ] *n.m.* **1.** [Mus.] violin; [Fig.] ~ *d'Ingres,* hobby. **2.** [Fam.] prison cells: *mettre qqun au* ~, to lock s.o. up. || **violoneux** [vjɔlɔ'nø] *n.m.* [Fam.] fiddler. || **violoniste** [vjɔlɔ'nist] *n.m.* violinist.
violoncelle [vjɔlõ'sɛl] *n.m.* [Mus.] cello. || **violoncelliste** [vjɔlõsɛ'list] *n.m.* violoncellist, cellist.
viorne [vjɔrn] *n.f.* [Bot.] ~ *d'Amérique* [Vulg. *pimbina*], cranberry tree.
vipère [vi'pɛ:r] *n.f.* viper.
virage [vi'ra:ʒ] *n.m.* turning; [Auto.] sharp curve: *prendre un* ~, to take a curve; ~ *en épingle à cheveux,* hair-pin turn; ~ *sur place,* U-turn; [on signs] *Virages sur trois milles,* Winding road (for three miles); [on signs] *Pas de* ~ *à gauche,* No left turn. || **virement** [vir'mɑ̃] *n.m.* [Fin.] transfer (*à,* to). || **virer** [vi'rɛ] #3, *v. tr. & intr.* **1.** to turn: [Naut.] ~ *de bord,* to back about, to turn about. **2.** to change to another colour: *Le tournesol vire au rouge au contact des acides,* Litmus is turned red by acid. **3.** to transfer: *La somme a été virée à mon compte,* The sum was transferred to my account.
virgin|al, -ale [virʒi'nal] *adj.* virgin.
Virginie [virʒi'ni] *n.f.* [Topon.] Virginia: *tabac de* ~, Virginia (tobacco).
virgule [vir'gyl] *n.f.* comma: *point et* ~, semicolon; [Fr.] *trois* ~ *cinq* (3.5), three point five.
viril, -e [vi'ril] *adj.* virile.
virtuose [virty'o:z] *n.m.* virtuoso.
virulent, -e [viry'lɑ̃(:t)] *adj.* virulent.
vis[1], **&c.** [vi] cf. VOIR.
vis[2]; **vit** [vi] cf. VIVRE.
vis[3] [vis] *n.f.* [Tech.] screw: *escalier en* ~, winding stairs, circular stairway; [Fig.] *serrer la* ~ *à qqun,* to tighten the screws on s.o., to put the screws on s.o.
visage [vi'za:ʒ] *n.m.* face; [Fig.] *voir qqun sous son vrai* ~, to see s.o. in his true colours; ~ *pâle,* paleface; [Fig.] *faire bon, mauvais* ~ *à qqun,* to greet s.o. cordially, to scowl at s.o.
vis-à-vis [viza'vi] *adv. phr.* opposite: *Ils se faisaient* ~, They faced each other. || **vis-à-vis de** *prep. phr.* toward(s).
viser [vi'ze] #3, *v. tr. & intr.* to aim (at); [Fig.] ~ *plus haut,* to set one's sights higher.
visible [vi'zibl] *adj.* **1.** visible, perceptible: *être* ~ *à l'œil nu,* to be visible to the naked eye. **2.** able to be visited: *Madame n'est pas* ~, Mrs. A. is not at home; *être* ~ *pour qqun,* to be in to s.o. || **visiblement** [viziblə'mɑ̃] *adv.* visibly; obviously, clearly.
visière [vi'zjɛ:r] *n.f.* visor (of a helmet), peak (of a cap).
vision [vi'zjõ] *n.f.* **1.** [faculty of the eye] sight, eyesight, vision: *Sa* ~ *n'est pas claire,* His, Her/eyesight is poor. **2.** [Fig.] vision: *avoir une* ~ *nette de la situation,* to see the situation clearly. **3.** vision: *avoir des visions,* to see visions.
visite [vi'zit] **1.** visit, call: *aller en* ~, to pay a visit, to go visiting; *faire des visites,* to go visiting; *rendre* ~ *à qqun,* to visit s.o.; *rendre à qqun sa* ~, to return s.o.'s visit; *carte de* ~, calling card; [hospital] *heures de* ~, visiting hours. **2.** inspection, examination: [customs] *la* ~ *des bagages,* baggage inspection; *passer une* ~ *médicale,* to have a medical examination. || **visiter** [vizi'te] #3, *v. tr.* **1.** to visit (sth.) [The Fr. verb is used in the sense of *to pay a visit to s.o.* only when this is done in a professional capacity]. **2.** to examine: ~ *un malade,* to visit a patient; ~ *un monument,* to visit a monument; ~ *les bagages,* to inspect baggage. || **visit|eur, -euse** [vizi't|œ:r, -ø:z] *n.* visitor, caller.
vison [vi'zõ] *n.m.* [Zool.] [also Pop. *fouine f, fouinette f*] mink.

visser [vi'se] #3 *v. tr.* [écrou] to screw on (a nut); [vis] to screw in, to drive (a screw): ~ *une serrure à la porte,* to screw a lock to the door.
Vistule [vis'tyl] *n.f.* [Topon.] Vistula.
visuel, -le [vi'zɥɛl] *adj.* visual.
vital, -e [vi'tal] *adj.* vital; [Fig.] essential.
vitamine [vita'min] *n.f.* vitamin.
vite [vit] *adv.* quickly, fast; speedily; rapidly: *Venez ~ !,* Come quickly!; *Faites ~ !,* Hurry up!; *Faites cela aussi ~ que possible, le plus ~ possible, au plus ~,* Do this as quickly as possible, as fast as you can. ‖ **vitesse** [vi'tɛs] *n.f.* speed, velocity, rapidity, quickness: ~ *moyenne,* average speed; ~ *initiale (de projectile),* muzzle velocity; *la ~ acquise,* (the) momentum; *à toute ~,* at full speed; *limite de ~,* speed (limit); [Auto.] *boîte de ~,* transmission (box); [Auto.] *changer de ~,* to change/shift, gears; *diminuer de ~,* to slow down; *changement de ~,* gearshift; *en/première, deuxième, troisième, ~,* in low, second, high/gear.
vitrage [vi'tra:ʒ] *n.m.* fitting (of windows) with panes, glazing; [Coll.] window-panes, window-space; glass partition; panes (of a building). ‖ **vitr|ail, -aux** [vitr|a:j, -o] *n.m.* stained-glass window: *les vitraux (d'une église),* the stained glass (of a church). ‖ **vitre** [vitr] *n.f.* (window-) pane: [Fam., Fig.] *casser les vitres,* to make a scandal. ‖ **vitr|eux, -euse** [vi'tr|ø, -ø:z] *adj.* glassy; [used in tech. context] vitreous: *yeux ~,* glassy eyes; *éclat ~ (de certaines pierres),* vitreous lustre (of some stones). ‖ **vitrine** [vi'trin] *n.f.* shop, store window; show case.
vitriol [vitri'jɔl] *n.m.* vitriol.
vivace [vi'vas] *adj.* [Bot.] hardy; [Fig.] enduring, vivid. ‖ **vivacité** [-i'te] *n.f.* liveliness, vivacity, vivaciousness.
vivant, -e [vi'v|ɑ̃, -ɑ̃:t] *adj.* **1.** living, alive. **2.** [Fig.] lively, lifelike, animated, stimulating: *un cours ~,* a stimulating course. ‖ **vivant** *n.m.* living being: *les vivants et les morts,* the living and the dead; *un bon ~,* a happy-go-lucky person. ‖ **du vivant de** *prep.* during the life of, in the lifetime of.
vive[1]**; vivez; vivons; &c.** cf. VIVRE.
vive[2] cf. VIF.
vive[3] [vi:v] *interj.* Long live . . . !: *Vive la Reine!,* Long live the Queen!; *Vive(nt) les Alliés!,* Long live the Allies!, Hurrah for the Allies!
vivement [viv'mɑ̃] *adv.* quickly, briskly, vigorously, sharply.
vivoir [vi'vwa:r] © *n.m.* living-room; sitting-room; [Br.] lounge.
vivre [vi:vr] **vivant, vécu,** #52, *v. intr,* **1.** to live, to exist: ~ *au jour le jour.* to live from day to day; *savoir ~,* to know how to get along; *apprendre à ~ à qqun,* to teach s.o. some manners; *ne pas rencontrer âme qui vive,* not to meet a living soul; *Qui vivra verra,* Time will tell; *Qui vive?* Who goes there? **2.** to live, †to dwell: ~ *à la campagne,* to live in the country; ~ *seul,* to live alone; *Il fait bon ~ ici,* Life is pleasant here. **3.** to last: *Sa gloire vivra éternellement,* His glory will last, live/forever. **4.** to live on, to subsist on: ~ *de légumes,* to live on vegetables, to be a vegetarian; ~ *de la charité publique,* to live on public charity. ‖ **vivre** *n.m.* [us. pl. *vivres*] food; provisions, supplies (of food), [Mil.] rations: *couper les vivres à qqun,* to cut off s.o.'s supplies; *Les vivres vinrent à manquer,* The provisions ran out, They ran out of food.
vocabulaire [vɔkaby'lɛ:r] *n.m.* vocabulary: *test m de ~,* word test.
vocal, -e [vɔ'kal] *adj.* vocal.
vocation [vɔka'sjõ] *n.f.* vocation, calling: ~ *sacerdotale,* sacerdotal/priestly/vocation.
vociférant, -e [vɔsife'rɑ̃(:t)] *adj.* vociferous, clamorous.
vociférer [vɔsife're] #10, *v. tr.* to shout, to yell: ~ *(des injures) contre qqun,* to shout (insults) at s.o. ‖ *v. intr.*: *Il a vociféré,* He was vociferous.
vœu, pl. **-x** [vø] *n.m.* **1.** vow: *faire un ~,* to make a vow; *faire ~ de,* to vow to; [Rel.] *prononcer ses vœux,* to take one's vows. **2.** wish: *présenter ses vœux (à),* to offer one's best wishes (to); *Nos vœux vous accompagnent,* → We wish you well; *Avec mes meilleurs vœux,* With my best wishes; *exaucer un ~,* to fulfil a wish.
vogue [vɔg] *n.f.* fashion: *être en ~,* to be in vogue, in fashion, in style; to be popular.
voguer [vɔ'ge] #3, *v. intr.* [rather literary] to sail, to float.
voici [vwa'si] *prep.* [Note that *voici* is being replaced in most expressions by VOILÀ.] here is, here are: *Le ~,* Here he is; *Le ~ qui arrive,* Here he comes; *Voici, Madame,* Here you are, Mrs. A.; *Voici mon livre,* This is my book; *En ~ un autre,* Here is another one; *Nous y ~,* Here we are; *Mon père que ~ va vous parler,* My father here is going to speak to you; *Voici trois semaines qu'il est parti,* He's been gone three weeks.
voie[1] [vwa] *n.f.* **1.** road, way: *une ~ romaine,* a Roman road; *une route à quatre voies,*

a four-lane highway; *la ~ lactée*, the Milky Way; *les voies navigables*, waterways; *la ~ maritime du Saint-Laurent*, the St. Lawrence Seaway. **2.** track, gauge: *~ ferrée*, railway track; *traverser la ~ ferrée*, to cross the railway tracks; *chemin de fer à ~ unique, à ~ étroite*, single-track, narrow-gauge/railway. **3.** tract: *voies respiratoires*, respiratory tract. **4.** [Naut.] *~ d'eau*, leak (in a ship). **5.** [way of travel]: *par ~ de terre*, by land; *par la ~ des airs*, by air. **6.** [Fig., Loc.] *les voies de Dieu*, the ways of God; *être dans la bonne ~ , être sur la ~* , to be on the right track; *être en bonne ~* , to be doing well, to be improving; *s'engager dans une ~ dangereuse*, to take a dangerous course; *en ~ de guérison*, on the road to recovery; *en ~ d'achèvement*, nearing completion.

voie[2], **voies, &c.** [vwa] cf. VOIR.

voilà [vwa'la] *prep.* **1.** [Usually denotes things or persons some distance away] there is, there are: *Me ~ !* Here I am!; *Voilà Philippe*, There is Philip; *Le ~ qui arrive*, There he comes; *la table que ~* , that table (there); *En ~ un qui fera son chemin*, There is s.o. who will get ahead; *Ne ~ -t-il pas qu'il pleut!* Well! Now it's raining! **2.** [Used in the sense of *ago* (cf. IL Y A)]: *Voilà deux ans qu'il est mort*, He died two years ago, It's now two years since he died. **3.** [Used to refer to things already mentioned in the conversation]: *Les oranges, les pommes, les bananes, ~ ce qu'il y a de bon pour la santé*, Oranges, apples, bananas, these are things which are good for the health; *Voilà pourquoi . . .*, That's why . . . ; *Voilà où . . .*, That's where . . . ; *Voilà tout*, That's all, That's that; *Voilà une bonne idée*, That's/There's a good idea; *La ~ bien!* That's just like her! **4.** [Absolute]: *Voilà, Monsieur*, There you are, Sir; *Voilà, c'est fait*, There, it's done, finished; *Et ~ !* And that's that. **5.** suddenly: *. . . et ~ qu'un orage nous force à chercher un abri*, . . . when suddenly a storm forced us to seek shelter.

voile[1] [vwal] *n.f.* [Naut.] **1.** sail; [Coll.] canvas: *faire ~* , to make sail, to sail; *mettre à la ~* , to set sail; *toutes voiles déployées, dehors*, under canvas. **2.** sailboat.

voile[2] [vwal] *n.m.* veil: [Rel.] *prendre le ~* , to take the veil, to become a nun.|| **voilé, -e** [vwa'le] *adj.* **1.** veiled. **2.** [Mec.] buckled, bent (wheel). **3.** [Photo.] blurred, out of focus. **4.** [Fig.]: *avoir la voix voilée*, to have a hoarse, husky voice. || **voiler** [vwa'le] #3, *v. tr.* **1.** to veil, to hide from view. **2.** [Mec.] to twist, to buckle, to bend (a wheel). **3.** [Photo.] to blur. **4.** [Fig.] to dissimulate, to dissemble, to conceal (one's intentions, thoughts).

voilier [vwa'lje] *n.m.* [Naut.] **1.** sailing ship, sailboat. **2.** sailmaker.

voir [vwa:r] **voyant, vu,** #32, *v. tr.* **1.** to see, to witness: *~ un accident*, to see, to witness an accident; *Je vois mal*, I can't see well [because my eyesight is poor]; *J'y vois mal*, I can't see well [because the light is poor]; [Fam.] *~ trente-six chandelles*, to see stars; [Fig.] *~ rouge*, to see red; *Je ne peux pas le ~* , I can't stand (the sight of) him; [Fig.] *~ le jour*, to see the light of day, to be born. **2.** to examine: *Voyez ce tableau*, Look at this picture; *C'est à ~* , That's (a question) to be taken up, studied up later. **3.** to visit: *aller ~ (un musée)*, to visit (a museum); *~ souvent son médecin*, to visit one's doctor often. **4.** to meet, to encounter: *Je l'ai vu ce matin*, I saw, met him this morning; *On voit dans ce livre de nombreuses citations*, Numerous quotations are found in this book. **5.** [Fig.] to understand, to know: *~ loin*, to be far-sighted; *Il ne voit pas plus loin que le bout de son nez*, He can't see any farther than the end of his nose; *Je commence à ~ clair*, I'm beginning to see the light; *Il m'a fait ~ que je n'étais pas indispensable*, He showed me that I was not indispensable; *à ce que je vois . . .*, as far as I can see . . . **6.** [way of regarding sth.]: *se faire bien ~ de qqun*, to gain s.o.'s favour, goodwill; *mal ~ les choses*, not to have the proper perspective; *Tout bon professeur a sa manière de ~* , Every good teacher has his own way of looking at things. **7.** [connection]: *Cela n'a rien à ~ avec mon travail*, That has nothing to do with my work. || *v. intr.* [form of encouragement]: *Voyons, il n'y a pas lieu de désespérer*, Come, come, there is no reason to give up hope; *Voyons, qu'est-ce que nous allons faire?* Let me see, what do we do next? || **se voir** *v. pron.* to see o.s.; to see one another; [Fig.] to be obvious: *Ils se voient tous les jours*, They meet every day, They see each other every day; [Fig.] *Cela se voit*, That's obvious; *Cela se voit tous les jours*, It happens every day.

voirie [vwa'ri] *n.f.* department of roads and highways; garbage dump.

vois cf. VOIR.

voisin, -e [vwa'z|ɛ̃, -in] *n.* neighbour. || *adj.* neighbouring, near, adjoining; similar: *deux pièces voisines*, adjoining rooms.

|| **voisinage** [vwazi'na:ʒ] *n.m.* proximity, vicinity; neighbourhood: *Tout le ~ en parle*, The whole neighbourhood is talking (about it); *Le ~ de la mer lui plaisait*, The proximity of the sea appealed to him.

voit cf. VOIR.

voiture [vwa'ty:r] *n.f.* vehicle; (railroad, motor-) car; (horse-drawn) carriage: *ranger sa ~*, to park one's car; *aller en ~*, to go by car, to drive; *~ d'occasion*, used car; *En ~!* All aboard!; *~ de pompier*, fire engine; *~ d'enfant*, baby carriage; *petite ~ (de malade)*, wheel-chair; *petite ~ (automobile)*, small car.

voix [vwa] *n.f.* **1.** voice: *baisser, élever/la ~*, to lower, raise/one's voice; *parler à ~ /haute, basse*, to speak in a/loud, low voice; *lire à haute ~*, to read aloud. **2.** [Fig.] vote: *une majorité de dix ~*, a majority of ten votes; *avoir ~ prépondérante*, to have the deciding vote.

vol[1] [vɔl] *n.m.* flight, flying: *prendre son ~*, to take flight, to fly away, [Aero.] to take off; *au ~*, on the wing, in flight; *en plein ~*, in flight; *~ de nuit*, night flight; *mille heures de ~*, a thousand hours of flying time; *~ nº 103*, flight No. 103; *un ~ de canards*, a flight of ducks.

vol[2] [vɔl] *n.m.* theft, stealing, robbery: *commettre un ~*, to commit a robbery; *~ à la tire*, purse snatching, pocket-picking; *~ à main armée*, armed robbery.

volaille [vɔ'lɑ:j] *n.f.* poultry, fowl, chicken: *élever de la ~*, to raise poultry; *J'ai acheté une ~, deux volailles, au marché*, I bought one fowl, two fowls, at the market; *foies de volaille*, chicken livers.

volant [vɔ'lɑ̃] *n.m.* [Auto.] steering wheel; [Mec.] fly wheel; blade (of a windmill); [Tailor.] flounce (of a dress); [Sport] bird [in badminton]; [Fig.] reserve: [Comm.] *~ de sécurité*, security reserve. || **volant, -e** [vɔ'l|ɑ̃, -ɑ̃:t] *adj.* flying: *poisson ~*, flying fish; *feuille volante*, loose leaf.

volatile [vɔla'til] *n.m. & f.* winged creature; domestic fowl.

volcan [vɔl'kɑ̃] *n.m.* volcano: *Le ~ se réveille*, The volcano is coming to life, shows signs of life; *Le ~ fait éruption*, The volcano is erupting; *Le ~ lance, vomit/des torrents de lave*, The volcano throws out, spews out/torrents of lava. || **volcanique** [vɔlka'nik] *adj.* volcanic.

volée [vɔ'le] *n.f.* **1.** flight, flying: *~ de moineaux*, flight of sparrows. **2.** volley (of missiles, of blows); © *donner une ~ à (un enfant)*, to give (a child) a spanking; © [Pop.] *Tu vas manger une bonne ~*, You are going to get a good beating, thrashing. **3.** peal (of bells). **4.** [Loc.] *(attraper) à la ~*, (to catch) in the air, on the fly; [Fig.] *saisir l'occasion à la ~*, to take prompt advantage of an opportunity, to take time by the forelock.

voler[1] [vɔle] #3, *v. intr.* to fly; [Fig.] *~ au secours de qqun*, to fly to s.o.'s rescue; [Fig.] *Le cheval vole autour de la piste*, The horse flies around the track.

voler[2] [vɔle] #3, *v. tr.* to steal, to rob: *~ qqch. à qqun*, to steal sth. from s.o., to rob s.o. of sth.; *Je me suis fait ~*, I was robbed.

volet [vɔ'lɛ] *n.m.* shutter, blind.

voleter [vɔl'te], **voletant, voleté,** #8, *v. intr.* to flutter; to flit [short distances].

voleu|r, -se [vɔ'l|œ:r, -ø:z] *n.* thief, robber: *~ à l'étalage*, shop-lifter; *~ à la tire*, pickpocket; *~ de grand chemin*, highwayman; [Fam.] *pincer un ~*, to catch, to nab/a thief; *Au ~!*, Stop thief!

volition [vɔli'sjɔ̃] *n.f.* volition.

volontaire [vɔlɔ̃'tɛ:r] *adj.* **1.** voluntary. **2.** wilful, obstinate: *enfant ~*, wilful, spoiled child. || *n.m.* volunteer: *s'offrir comme ~*, to volunteer. || **volontairement** [vɔlɔ̃tɛr'mɑ̃] *adv.* **1.** voluntarily. **2.** wilfully. || **volonté** [vɔlɔ̃'te] *n.f.* **1.** will, moral strength: *faire preuve de bonne ~*, to be cooperative; *avoir la ~ de réussir*, to have the will to succeed; *faire qqch. de sa propre ~*, to do sth. of one's free will; *à ~*, at will. **2.** wishes, desires: *agir contre, à l'encontre de la ~ de qqun*, to do sth. against s.o.'s wishes; *exécuter les volontés de qqun*, to carry out the wishes of s.o.; [Fam.] *faire ses quatre volontés*, to do just as one pleases; *dernières volontés*, last wishes, [Jur.] (last) will (and testament). || **volontiers** [vɔlɔ̃'tje] *adv.* willingly, gladly.

volt [vɔlt] *n.m.* volt.

volte-face [vɔltə'fas] *n.f. invar.* about-turn, about-face; *faire ~*, to make an about-turn, [Fig.] [decision, order, &c.] to reverse o.s.

voltiger [vɔlti'ʒe], **voltigeant,** #5, *v. intr.* [used only for light things: leaves, bees, &c.] **1.** to flit, to flutter about: *~ de fleur en fleur*, to flit from flower to flower. **2.** to flutter: *Une feuille de papier voltige au vent*, A piece of paper flutters in the wind.

volubilité [vɔlybili'te] *n.f.* volubility: *parler avec ~*, to be a glib, voluble talker, speaker.

volume [vɔ'lym] *n.m.* **1.** volume, tome: *ouvrage en trois volumes*, three-volume work. **2.** bulk, volume, mass. || **volumineu|x, -se**

[vɔlymi'n|ø, -ø:z] *adj.* voluminous, bulky.
volupté [vɔlyp'te] *n.f.* voluptuousness: *faire qqch. avec* ~ , to revel in doing sth.; [Loc.] *avec* ~ , voluptuously.
vomir [vɔ'mi:r], **vomissant, vomi,** #17, *v. tr.* **1.** to vomit, to throw up. **2.** [Fig.]: *Le volcan vomit des torrents de lave,* The volcano spews out torrents of lava. || **vomissement** [vomis'mɑ̃] *n.m.* vomiting.
vont cf. ALLER.
vos [vo] *poss. pron. m. & f. pl.* cf. VOTRE.
votant [vɔ'tɑ̃] *n.m.* voter.
vote [vɔt] *n.m.* vote; voting, ballot: *droit de* ~ , right to vote; franchise; *bulletin de* ~ , ballot; *loi en cours de* ~ , bill before the House; *passer un projet de loi au* ~ , to vote on a proposed bill; ~ *affirmatif,* yea(s); ~ *négatif,* nay(s), [Br.] no(es). || **voter** [vɔ'te] #3, *v. intr.* to vote. || *v. tr.* to pass: ~ *une loi,* to pass a law.
votre, pl. **vos** [vɔtr, vo] *poss. adj.* [agrees with the thing modified and not with the possessor] your: *Est-ce* ~ *livre?* Is this your book?; ~ *fils et vos filles,* your son and your daughters; *vos frère et sœur,* your brother and sister.
vôtre [vo:tr] *poss. pron. m. & f.* [determinative; is always preceded by *le, la* or *les* according to the gender and number of the thing referred to] yours: *Ce n'est pas mon chapeau; c'est le* ~ , That is not my hat; it's yours; [In a few fixed expressions, the article is omitted]: *Je suis tout* ~ , I am entirely at your service; *Considérez ma maison comme (la)* ~ , → Make yourself (entirely) at home.
voudrai, &c. [vu'dre] cf. VOULOIR.
vouer [vwe] #3, *v. tr.* **1.** to vow, to promise: *Il m'a voué son amitié,* He promised to be my friend. **2.** to consecrate, to dedicate: ~ *un temple à Dieu,* to dedicate a temple (to God). **3.** to be destined for, to be headed for: *Cette pièce est vouée à un grand succès,* This play is sure to be a great success; *voué à un échec,* doomed to failure. || **se vouer à** *v. pron.* to devote o.s. to.
vouloir [vu'lwa:r], **voulant, voulu,** #65, *v. tr.* **1.** to want, to wish, to try: *J'en veux un,* I want one; *Je veux partir,* I want to go; *Je veux qu'il vienne,* I want him to come; *Il a voulu s'échapper,* He tried to escape; *J'aurais voulu qu'il le sache,* I wish he had been told. **2.** to insist on: *Il veut absolument qu'on écrive à l'encre,* He insists on our writing in ink; *Il a voulu venir,* He insisted on coming. **3.** to like: *Comme vous voudrez,* As you like it; *Je voudrais que vous veniez,* I'd like you to come. **4.** *vouloir bien,* to be willing. **5.** *Veuillez . . . ,* Please . . . : *Veuillez vous asseoir,* Please be seated; *Veuillez me faire savoir,* Kindly let me know. **6.** to mean: *Il l'a fait sans le* ~ , He did not mean to do it; *Qu'est-ce que cela veut dire?* What does it mean? **7.** [Loc.] *en* ~ *à,* to bear a grudge against . . . || **voulu, -e** [vu'ly] *adj.* deliberate, intentional: *avec une impolitesse voulue,* with intentional rudeness.
vous [vu] *pers. pron. 2nd pers. pl.* [In polite speech, can refer to one person only, though remaining grammatically plur.] you, yourself: *Vous désirez?* What would you like?, May I help you?; *De vous à moi . . . ,* Between you and me . . . || **vous-mêmes,** [in polite speech, when addressing a single person] **vous-même,** yourself.
voûte [vut] *n.f.* vault, arch; [Poet.] *la* ~ *des cieux,* the sky. || **voûté, -e** [vu'te] *adj.* rounded, arched, stooped: *des épaules voûtées,* rounded shoulders. || **voûter** [vu'te] #3, *v. tr.* to cover with an arch. || **se voûter** *v. pron.* to stoop, to become bent, round-shouldered.
voyage [vwa'ja:ʒ] *n.m.* trip, journey; voyage: *préparer un* ~ , to prepare for a trip; *partir en* ~ , to go on a trip; *être en* ~ , to be away, to be on a trip; *faire un* ~ *(d'agrément),* to take a (pleasure) trip; *Bon* ~ *!* Have a good trip!; *agence de* ~ , travel agency; ~ *de noces,* honeymoon (trip). || **voyager** [vwa'ja:ʒ] **voyageant,** #5, *v. intr.* to travel, to go on a trip: ~ *en voiture, par avion,* to travel by car, by plane; ~ *par le train,* to travel by train. || **voyageu|r, -se** [vwaja'ʒ|œ:r, -ø:z] *n.* traveller; [dans un train, un autobus, &c.] passenger; [© Hist.] *les Voyageurs,* the Voyageurs. || *adj.* travelling: *commis* ~ , travelling salesman; *pigeon* ~ , carrier homing/pigeon, [Fig.] wanderer.
voyais, &c. cf. VOIR.
voyant, -e [vwa'j|ɑ̃, -ɑ̃:t] *adj.* loud, showy, gaudy: *couleur voyante,* gaudy colour. || *n.* seer, fortune-teller cf. VOIR.
voyelle [vwa'jɛl] *n.f.* [Phon.] vowel.
voyou [vwa'ju] *n.m.* [Fam.] guttersnipe, hoodlum, hooligan: *se conduire en* ~ , to be rowdy.
vrai, -e [vrɛ] *adj.* true, real, genuine: *une histoire vraie,* a true story; *un* ~ *Français,* a real Frenchman; *un* ~ *diamant,* a genuine diamond; [Fam.] *Vous allez venir, pas* ~ *?* You are going to come, aren't you? || **vrai** *n.m.* truth: *aimer le* ~ , to love truth; *le* ~ *de l'affaire,* the truth of the matter; *à* ~ *dire,* to tell the truth; [Fam.] *Il est parti pour de* ~ *?* Has he gone

for sure? || **vraiment** [vrɛ'mɑ̃] *adv.* really, truly; *Vraiment?* Really? Is that right?

vraisemblable [vrɛsɑ̃'blabl] *adj.* likely, probable: *Ce n'est pas du tout* ~, It is not at all likely. || **vraisemblablement** [vrɛsɑ̃blablə'mɑ̃] *adv.* probably, very likely. || **vraisemblance** [vrɛsɑ̃'blɑ̃:s] *n.f.* probability, likelihood: *selon toute* ~, in all probability.

vrille [vri:j] *n.f.* **1.** drill. **2.** [Bot.] tendril (of a plant). **3.** [Aero.] spin: *chute en* ~, tail spin. || **vriller** [vrije] #3, *v. tr.* to bore a hole (with a drill); ~ *une planche,* to bore a hole in a board.

vu, -e [vy] *adj.* seen, regarded: *être mal* ~ *de,* to be out of favour with, to be held in poor esteem by; [Loc.] *au* ~ *et au su de* (*tous*), openly, with everyone's knowledge. || **vu** *prep.* considering, seeing: *Vu la difficulté du travail . . .,* Considering the difficulty of the work . . . || **vu que** *conj.* *Vu que M. X ne s'est pas présenté . . .,* Whereas, considering that Mr. X did not appear . . . || **vue** *n.f.* **1.** (eye) sight, vision: *connaître qqun de* ~, to know s.o. by sight; *perdre qqun de* ~, to lose sight of s.o., [Fig.] to lose touch with s.o.; *à* ~ *d'œil,* visibly; *à perte de* ~, as far as the eye can reach; *payable à* ~, payable on demand. **2.** view: ~ *à vol d'oiseau,* bird's eye view; *On a une belle* ~ *d'ici,* The view is fine from here; *point de* ~, vantage point, [Fig.] point of view. **3.** view, picture: *une* ~ *de Montréal,* a view of Montreal. **4.** [plur.] © *vues* (*animées*), moving pictures. **5.** [plur., Fig.] view, opinion: *les vues du gouvernement à ce sujet,* the government's views about this. **6.** [plur., Fig.] *avoir des vues sur,* to have designs on. **7.** [Loc.] *en* ~ *de,* in order to [× IN VIEW OF] cf. VOIR.

vulcaniser [vylkani'ze] #3 *v. tr.* to vulcanize.

vulgaire [vyl'gɛ:r] *adj.* vulgar, common: *le français* ~, substandard French. || **vulgariser** [vylgari|'ze] #3, *v. tr.* to popularize. || **vulgarité** [-'te] *n.f.* vulgarity.

vulnérable [vylne'rabl] *adj.* vulnerable.

W

W, w [dublə've] *n.m. invar.* [Rarely used in French, except in foreign words, mostly English] W, w.

wagon [also **vagon**] [va'gõ] *n.m.* [Rail.] car, [Br.] carriage: ~ *-restaurant,* dining-car, diner; ~ *-lit* [pl. wagons-lits], sleeping-car, sleeper; ~ *-salon,* parlour-car, club-car; ~ *de première* (*classe*), first-class car, pullman; ~ *de seconde* (*classe*), second-class car, coach; ~ *de voyageurs,* passenger car; ~ *de marchandises,* freight car; ~ *couvert,* box car; ~ *ouvert,* gondola; ~ *plate-forme,* flat car.

Washington [waʃiŋ'tœn] *n.m.* (l'état de) Washington; *Washington, D.C.,* (la ville de) W.

waters cf. W.C.

watt [wat] *n.m.* [Electr.] watt; *kilowatt m,* kilowatt; *kilowatt-heure m,* kilowatt-hour.

W.C. [dublə've'se, ve'se, wa'tɛ:r] *n.m. us. pl.* [→ In France, *W.C.* has displaced the older *cabinets* (*d'aisance*), *vespasienne,* still used in Canada] toilet, rest-room: *Où sont les* ~ *?* Where is the toilet? cf. TOILETTE.

whisk(e)y [wis'ki] *n.m.* whisky [terme général désignant diverses marques].

whist [wist] *n.m.* whist [sorte de jeu de cartes]: *jouer au* ~, to play whist.

wigwam [wig'wam] *n.m.* wigwam.

Wisconsin [wiskõ'sɛ̃] *n.m. le* ~, Wisconsin [U.S.A.].

Wyoming [wajo'miŋ] *n.m. le* ~, Wyoming [U.S.A.].

X

X, x [iks] *n.m. invar.* [rarely found initially; doubles with *s* to form plur. nouns and adjectives, e.g. *chou*, pl. *choux*. Used in algebra: *un x* [œ̃'niks] to denote an unknown quantity. The sign X is also used in France as a check sign (√), hence the phrase *faire un X*, *faire une croix*] X, x: *Monsieur X* [denoting an unknown person], Mr. X; (*les*) *rayons X* [rɛjõ'iks], X-rays.

Xérès [ke'rɛ:s] *n.m.* sherry (wine) [of late also called (*le*) *sherry* [ʃɛ're]].

xylophone [gzilo'fɔn] *n.m.* [Mus.] xylophone.

Y

Y, y [i'grɛk] *n.m. invar.* [Called *i grec*. Rarely used initially, it is found usually in place of **i** as the final letter of family and place names, e.g. *Passy*, *Vichy*, where it sounds like [i]. Elsewhere, it has the three phonetic values of [j], [ij] or [i]]: Y, y.

y [i + consonant and finally; j + vowel; ij + vowel in careful speech] *adv.* there; within; at home: *Allez-* ~ , Get going, Go to it, Go (right) ahead; *Allons-* ~ , Let's go (there); *J'* ~ *vais*, I am going there; *il* ~ *a*, there is, there are; *Combien* ~ *a-t-il de cents dans un dollar?* How many cents are there in a dollar?; *Y est-il?*, Is he there?; *Y es-tu?*, *Y êtes-vous?*, Are you there?; *Il* ~ *a deux jours que . . .*, It is two days since . . . ; *Il* ~ *a cinq milles . . .*, It is five miles . . . . || *pron.* to, at, in, by + a noun or a pronoun such as him, her, it, them, used as predicate: *Je l'ai fait sans* ~ *penser*, I did it without thinking (of it); *Je n'* ~ *crois pas*, → I don't believe it; *Ça* ~ *est!*, It's done!, That's it!, I knew it!; *J'* ~ *suis*, I've got it; *Je n'* ~ *suis pour rien*, Don't blame me for it.

yacht [jɔt] *n.m.* [Naut.] yacht [also *bateau m de plaisance*]. || **yachting** [jak'tiŋ] *n.m.* yachting, sailing.

Yankee [jaŋ'ki] *n.m.* Yankee.

yeux [jø] *n.m.* [plur. of ŒIL] eyes: *Elle a les* ~ *noirs*, *bleus*, → She has/black, blue/ eyes; *Il a des* ~/*de lynx*, *de chat*, He has the eyes/of a lynx, of a cat; [Fig.] *jeter de la poudre aux* ~ *de qqun*, to pull the wool over s.o.'s eyes; *Cela saute aux* ~ , It is obvious; *Cela coûte les* ~ *de la tête*, It costs a fortune; *faire les gros* ~ *à qqun*, to glare at s.o., *faire les doux* ~ *à qqun*, to make eyes at s.o.; *loin des* ~ , *loin du cœur*, out of sight, out of mind.

Yougoslavie [jugosla'vi] *n.f. la* ~ , Yugoslavia [also spelled *Jugo-Slavia*].

Yukon [ju'kõ] *n.m. le* ~ , Yukon.

Z, z [zɛd] *n.m. invar.* [Rare initially but frequent in final position, where it is often mute as in *nez, allez* [ne, a'le]] Z, z.

zèbre [zɛbr] *n.m.* [Zool.] zebra; [Fam., Fig.] *un drôle de* ~, a queer customer. || **zébrure** [ze'bry:r] *n.f. us. pl.* stripe(s).

zèle [zɛ:l] *n.m.* zeal, ardour: *avec* ~, eagerly, zealously; *Il fait du* ~, He is an eager-beaver; [Fam.] *Pas de* ~ !, Take it easy!, Don't overdo it! **zélé, -e** [ze'le] *adj.* zealous, eager.

zénith [ze'nit] *n.m.* zenith.

zéro [ze'ro] *n.m.* **1.** zero; naught; 0 → [In calling out numbers, use *zéro*, e.g. 0032 [zeroze'rotrwa'dø]]: [Phys.] *le* ~, the freezing-point [in centigrade]; *Le thermomètre est à* ~, The thermometer is down to zero, It is zero; [Sch.] *Zéro de conduite*, Zero in conduct; [Fig.] *recommencer à* ~, to start again from scratch, to start all over again. **2.** [Fig.] *un* ~, a mere cipher, a nobody.

zézayer [zezɛ'je] #11, *v. intr.* to lisp.

zibeline [zib'lin] *n.f.* [Zool.] sable; *martre* ~, sable marten.

zigzag [zig'zag] *n.m.* zigzag: *faire des zigzags*, to weave, to stagger, to move in zigzags. || **zigzaguer** [zigza'ge] #3, *v. intr.* to zigzag, to weave.

zinc [☞ zɛ̃:g] *n.m.* zinc.

zodiaque [zɔ'djak] *n.m.* zodiac.

zone [zo:n] *n.f.* zone, area, belt: *la* ~ *verte*, the green belt (around a city) cf. CEINTURE, Fr. *la zone*; *de seconde* ~, second-rate.

zoo [zo, esp. © zu] *n.m.* zoo: *le* ~ *de Granby*, Granby Zoo.

zoologie [zoɔlɔ'ʒi] *n.f.* zoology. || **zoologique** [zoɔlɔʒik] *adj.* zoological: *jardin* ~, zoo. || **zoologiste** [zoɔlɔʒist] *n.m.* zoologist.

zut [zyt] *interj.* [Fam.] darn it!: [Fam.] *avoir un œil qui dit* ~ *à l'autre*, to squint, to be cock-eyed.

ENGLISH-FRENCH/ANGLAIS-FRANÇAIS

A, a [ej] *pl.* **A's, a's. 1.** [letter] le A *m*, les A. **2.** [Mus.] la *m*. ‖ **A-1** ['ej'wʌn] also **A number 1,** excellent, de première/qualité *f*, catégorie *f*, classe *f*/.

a, an [ə ou accentué ej] *art. indéf.* [devant une voyelle ou *h* non prononcé, devient *an* [ən]. **1.** un, une: *~ boy and (~) girl*, un garçon et une fille; [transposed] *such ~ small house*, une si petite maison; *too hard ~ question*, une question trop difficile; *half an hour*, une demi-heure. **2.** [omitted in Fr.] *She is an actress*, Elle est actrice; [but with qualifying adj.] *She is ~ famous actress*, C'est une actrice célèbre; [×] *Mr. Jones, ~ teacher at our school . . .*, M. Jones, professeur à notre école . . . ; *What ~ disappointment!*, Quelle déception!; *He left in ~ car*, Il est parti en auto; *He was disguised as ~ policeman*, Il était déguisé en policier; *As ~ pianist, he excels*, Comme pianiste, il excelle; × [French compounds] *An officer's uniform was missing*, Il manquait un uniforme d'officier [= a uniform for officers], Il manquait l'uniforme d'un officier [= one particular officer's uniform]. **3.** [replaced by the def. art. in Fr.] le, la: *Give me ~ half*, Donnez-m'en la moitié; *He has ~ small nose*, Il a le nez petit. **4.** [replaced by the partitive in Fr. after a general negative] *I haven't got ~ stamp*, Je n'ai pas de timbre; [but emphatically] *I haven't ~ friend in the world*, Je n'ai pas un seul ami au monde; [specific negative] × *It isn't ~ mouse, it's ~ rat*, Ce n'est pas une souris, c'est un rat. **5.** [distributively] le, la; par, à, de: *a dollar ~ pound*, un dollar la livre; *twice ~ month*, deux fois par mois; *He earns two dollars an hour*, Il gagne deux dollars (de) l'heure; *The car was going 60 miles an hour*, La voiture faisait 60 milles à l'heure.

A.B. ['ej'bij]. cf. B.A.

aback [ə'bæk] *adv.*: *to be taken ~*, être/pris au dépourvu, déconcerté/.

abandon [ə'bændən] *v. tr.* [give up] abandonner, quitter; [leave] laisser, délaisser; [Fig.] *to ~ o.s. to (despair, &c.)*, se laisser aller (au désespoir, &c.). ‖ *n.* [freedom from restraint] abandon *m*; [Pej.] laisser-aller *m*. ‖ **abandoned** [-d] *adj.* [deserted] déserté, délaissé, abandonné; [Fig.] immoral, déréglé. ‖ **abandonment** [-mənt] *n.* abandon *m*.

abase [ə'bejs] *v. tr.* abaisser: *to ~ o.s.*: s'abaisser, s'humilier. ‖ **abasement** [-mənt] *n.* abaissement *m*, humiliation *f*.

abash [ə'bæʃ] *v. tr.* décontenancer.

abashed [ə'bæʃd] *adj.* confus (*at*, de).

abate [ə'bejt] *v. tr.* diminuer, réduire. ‖ *v. intr.* faiblir, se calmer: *The wind has abated*, Le vent s'est calmé.

abbey ['æbɪ] *n.* abbaye *f*. ‖ **abbot** ['æbət] *n.* [Rel.] (père) abbé *m*.

abbreviate [ə'bɹijvɪˌejt] *v. tr.* abréger (en, *to*). ‖ **abbreviation** [əˌbɹijvɪ'ejʃən] *n.* abréviation *f* [☞ En anglais, les abréviations sont suivies d'un point: Dr. = Doctor; ☞ In French, periods are used only if the last letter of the abbreviation is not the last letter of the word, e.g. *M.* = Monsieur, but *Mme* = Madame].

ABC *pl.* **ABC's** [ˌejˌbij'sij(z)] *n.* l'alphabet *m*; [Fig.] *He doesn't even know his ABC's*, Il ne sait ni A ni B.

abdicate ['æbdɪˌkejt] *v. intr.* abdiquer

abdomen ['æbdəmən] *n.* abdomen *m*.

abdominal [əb'dɑmɪnḷ] *adj.* abdominal.

abduct [əb'dʌk|t] *v. tr.* enlever. ‖ **abduction** [-ʃən] *n.* enlèvement *m*.

abed [ə'bɛd] *adv.* au lit.

aberration [ˌæbə'ejʃən] *n.* aberration *f*.

abet [ə'bɛt] *v. tr.* [-tt-] être complice de: *aiding and abetting*, complicité *f*.

abeyance [ə'bejəns] *n.* [seulement dans l'expression] *in ~*, en suspens.

abhor [əb'hɔə] *v. tr.* [-rr-] détester. ‖**abhorrence** [-əns] *n.* aversion *f* (pour qqun, qqch.); [hatred] horreur *f* (de qqch.).

†**abide** [ə'bajd], **abided** [-əd] or **abode** [ə'bowd] *v. intr.* rester, demeurer (*at/in*, dans); *to ~ by a promise*, rester fidèle à une promesse. ‖ *v. tr.* subir (une épreuve); attendre (une occasion).

abiding [ə'bajdɪŋ] *adj.* durable.

ability [ə'bɪlɪtɪ] *n.* **1.** capacité *f* (de faire qqch.): *to the best of my ~*, de mon mieux. **2.** capacité *f*, talent *m*; [×] [cleverness] habileté *f*: *a man of (great) ~*, un homme (très) capable.

abject ['æbdʒɛkt] *adj.* abject.

abjure [əb'dʒuwə] *v. tr.* abjurer (ses erreurs); renier; renoncer à (ses droits).

able ['ejbḷ] *adj.* **1.** doué (physiquement,

intellectuellement). **2.** [Pers.] habile, capable; [thing] bien fait: *an ~ physician,* un médecin compétent; *an ~ piece o, work,* une œuvre de talent. **3.** [☞ Sert d'infinitif à CAN] *to be ~*, pouvoir, savoir: *Is he ~ to do this work?,* Pourra-t-il, Saura-t-il/faire ce travail?; *Are you able* [= *in a position*] *to make a down payment?,* Êtes-vous/en mesure de, à même de/faire un premier paiement? [☞ © *être capable de* is often used in Canada where *pouvoir* would be better: *capable* should be restricted to "physically able" to do, or "mentally equipped" for, sth.]. cf. CAN. || **able-bodied** [-ˌbɑdɪd] *adj.* bien constitué; [Fr. Mil.] bon pour le service; [seaman] breveté, de 1ère classe. || **ably** [-ɪ] *adv.* habilement; avec science.

abnormal [ˌæb'nɔɚml̩] *adj.* anormal. || **abnormality** [ˌæbnɔɚ'mælətɪ] *n.* anomalie *f.*

aboard [ə'bɔɚd] *adv.* à bord: *to go ~*, monter à bord; [Rail.] *All ~!,* En voiture! || *prép.* à bord de: *~ the Queen Mary,* à bord du Queen Mary.

abolish [ə'bɑlɪʃ] *v. tr.* abolir, supprimer. || **abolition** [æbə'lɪʃən] *n.* abolition *f,* suppression *f.*

A-bomb ['ejˌbɑm] *n.* bombe *f* atomique.

abominable [ə'bɑmɪn|əbl̩] *adj.* abominable; horrible (à voir). || **abominate** [-ejt] *v. tr.* détester, avoir . . . en horreur.

aboriginal [ˌæbɚ'ɪdʒɪn|l̩] *adj. & n.* aborigène (*m*). || **aborigene** [-ij] *n.* aborigène *m.f.*

abortive [ə'bɔɚtɪv] *adj.* manqué, avorté.

abound [ə'bawnd] *v. intr.* **1.** [plentiful] abonder: *Game abounds in this district,* Le gibier abonde dans cette région. **2.** [well supplied with] être riche en, avoir en abondance: *Alberta abounds in oil,* L'Alberta/possède du pétrole en abondance, est riche en pétrole/.

about [ə'bawt] *prép.* [cf. also AROUND] **1.** [concerning] sur, au sujet de, à propos de, de: *a book ~ Italians,* un livre sur les Italiens; *She worries ~ me,* Elle s'inquiète à mon sujet; *He came* (*to see me*) *~ the gas bill,* Il est venu me voir à propos de la note du gaz; *to speak ~*, parler de; *What are you thinking ~?,* A quoi pensez-vous?; *About what?,* A quel sujet?; *What is it ~?,* De quoi s'agit-il?; *What ~ you?,* Et vous?; *What ~ going to a show?,* Si on allait au cinéma?; *About next year . . . ,* A propos de l'année prochaine . . . . **2.** [approximately] à peu près, environ, vers: [with numeral, *-aine*]: *~ the same* (*thing*), à peu près la même chose; *He is ~ 20* (*years old*), Il a 20 ans environ; *There were ~ ten* (*of them*), Il y en avait/à peu près dix, environ dix, une dizaine; *Come ~ 3* (*o'clock*), Venez vers trois heures; (*It's*) *~ time!,* Ce n'est pas trop tôt! **3.** [in various directions] *to walk ~ the room, the park,* se promener (de long en large) dans la pièce, (un peu partout) dans le parc; *to look ~ the room,* parcourir la pièce des yeux; [see also under other verbs]. **4.** [in connection with] *There is sth. strange ~ her,* Elle a qqch. d'étrange. **5.** *to be ~ to,* aller, être sur le point de: *As I was ~ to say . . . ,* Comme j'allais le dire . . . ; *He was ~ to lose his temper,* Il était sur le point de s'emporter. **6.** [Loc.] *the way to go ~ it, sth.,* la façon de s'y prendre; *Be quick ~ it!,* Faites vite!; *While you're ~ it . . . ,* Pendant que vous y êtes. . . . || *adv.* [cf. AROUND] **1.** [almost] presque: *I'm* (*just*) *~ dead,* Je suis presque mort. **2.** [in various directions] par ci, par là; partout; de tous côtés: *to walk ~*, marcher de long en large; *to stand ~*, rester/autour, dans le voisinage, là, &c./; [see also under other verbs].

above [ə'bʌv] *prép.* au-dessus de (l'horizon, de tout soupçon, &c.): *~ all,* surtout, avant tout; *the rank ~ mine,* le rang supérieur au mien; *above our expectations,* au-delà de nos espoirs. || *adv.* au-dessus: *from ~*, d'en haut; [Com.] *as ~*, comme ci-dessus; *See ~*, Voir plus haut; *Heavens ~!* Cieux! || **above-mentioned** [-ˌmɛnʃənd] *adj.* [Com.] susvisé, précité, susmentionné, ci-dessus.

abrasive [ə'bɹejsɪv] *adj. & n.* abrasif (*m*).

abreast [ə'bɹɛst] *adv.* de front.

abridge [ə'bɹɪdʒ] *v. tr.* abréger (un ouvrage); †priver (qqun de ses droits).

abroad [ə'bɹɔd] *adv.* à l'étranger: *to go ~*, aller à l'étranger; [out] dehors, [Fig.] qui court: *A rumour is ~*, Le bruit court (que . . .).

abrogate ['æbɹəˌgejt] *v. tr.* abroger (une loi).

abrupt [ə'bɹʌpt] *adj.* [departure, &c.] brusque, précipité; [slope] abrupt; [style] heurté; [manners] brusque. || **abruptly** [-lɪ] *adv.* brusquement, soudain(ement).

abscess ['æbsɛs] *n.* abcès *m.*

abscond [əb'skɑnd] *v. intr.* lever le pied.

absence ['æbsn̩|s] *n.* **1.** absence *f,* éloignement *m*: *in the ~ of Mr. X,* en l'absence de M. X; *excused ~*, absence motivée; *~ record,* → registre *m* des présences; *on leave of ~*, en congé *m,* [Mil.] en permission *f.* **2.** manque *m* (de): *in the ~*

of, à défaut de. || **absent** [-t] *adj.* absent (de, *from*). || *v. tr. to* ~ *o.s. from*, s'absenter de. || **absentee** [ˌæbsn̩'tij] *n.* absent *m.* || **absent-minded** [ˌæbsn̩t'majndəd] *adj.* distrait. || **absent-mindedness** [-nəs] *n.* distraction *f.* || **in absentia** [ɪnˌæb'sɛnʃɪə] *adv.* [law] par contumace; [Univ.] in absentia.

absolute ['æbsəˌluwt] *adj.* absolu, total: [without limits] ~ *freedom*, liberté absolue; ~ *alcohol*, alcool absolu; [perfect] véritable, certain: ~ *proof*: preuve certaine. || **absolutely** [-lɪ] *adv.* absolument; totalement: ~ *forbidden*, formellement interdit.

absolution [ˌæbsə'luwʃən] *n.* [R.C.] absolution *f*; [funeral] absoute *f.* || **absolve** [əb'zɔlv] *v. tr.* **1.** absoudre (qqun de ses fautes, de tout blâme); [R.C.] donner l'absolution (à qqun). **2.** dégager (qqun de ses obligations).

absorb [əb'zɔɚb] *v. tr.* absorber. || **absorbent** [-ənt] *adj. & n.* absorbant *m*: ~ *cotton*, coton *m* hydrophile. || **absorbing** [-ɪŋ] *adj.* absorbant; [Fig.] absorbant, → qui ne laisse aucun répit.

abstain [əb'stejn] *v. intr.* s'abstenir (de, *from*). || **abstainer** [-ɚ] *n.* → qui s'abstient de . . . : *total abstainer* [from alcohol], personne *f*/qui ne boit pas d'alcool, [Fam.] au régime sec/. || **abstemious** [əb'stijmjəs] *adj.* sobre; abstinent. || **abstinence** ['æbstɪnəns] *n.* abstinence *f.*

abstract [əb'stɹæk|t] *adj.* abstrait. || ['æbstɹækt] *n.* abrégé *m*, résumé *m* (d'une communication scientifique), précis *m.* || *v. tr.* **1.** abstraire, séparer (de, *from*); [Fig.] faire abstraction de. **2.** abréger, résumer (un texte). || **abstraction** [əb'stɹæk|ʃən] *n.* abstraction *f*, distraction *f*; vol *m.* || **abstractly** [-tlɪ] *adv.* d'une manière abstraite, en théorie. || **abstractness** [-tnəs] *n.* nature *f* abstraite, caractère *m* abstrait.

abstruse [ˌæb'stɹuws] *adj.* abstrus.

absurd [əb'zɚd] *adj.* absurde: *Don't be* ~*!*, Ne soyez pas ridicule! || **absurdity** [-ɪtɪ] *n.* absurdité *f.*

abundance [ə'bʌndən|s] *n.* abondance *f*, prospérité *f*: *to have an* ~ *of*, avoir (qqch.) en abondance. || **abundant** [-t] *adj.* abondant (en, *in*).

abuse [ə'bjuws] *n.* **1.** abus *m* (de pouvoir, &c.). **2.** insultes *fpl.*; injures *fpl.* || *v. tr.* [ə'bjuwz] **1.** abuser de, maltraiter (qqun). **2.** insulter (qqun); médire de (qqun). || **abusive** [-ɪv] *adj.* abusif; injurieux, grossier.

abysmal [ə'bɪsməl] *adj.* insondable.

abyss [ə'bɪs] *n.* abîme *m.*

A.C. ['ejˌsij] [= alternating current], courant *m* alternatif, cf. D.C.

academic(al) [ˌækə'dɛmɪk(l̩)] *adj.* [learned society] académique, [Univ.] universitaire, académique; [Sch.] scolaire: ~ *achievement*, succès *m* scolaire; ~ *attainment*, niveau *m* d'instruction; ~ *subject*, matière *f* fondamentale; ~ *year*, année *f* scolaire. || **Academy** [ə'kædəmɪ] *n.* [learned society] académie *f*; [private school] école *f.* © académie *f*; [Fr.] pensionnat *m*, collège *m.*

Acadia [ə'kejdɪə] *n.* © l'Acadie *f.* || **Acadian** [-n] *adj. & n.* acadien; [dialect] l'acadien *m.*

accede [ˌæk'sijd] *v. intr.* [request] accéder (à, *to*): [throne] monter sur le trône.

accelerate [ək'sɛlɚˌejt] *v. tr.* accélérer. || **acceleration** [əkˌsɛlɚ'ejʃən] *n.* accélération *f.* || **accelerator** [ək'sɛlɚˌejtɚ] *n.* accélérateur *m.*

accent ['æksɛnt] *n.* [speech] accent *m*: *a foreign* ~, (parler avec) un accent étranger; [on letters] accent (aigu, grave, circonflexe). || **accentuate** [ək'sɛntuwejt] *v. tr.* accentuer (un mot); [Fig.] insister, appuyer sur (une idée).

accept [ək'sɛpt] *v. tr.* accepter (un cadeau, une offre); [believe] admettre: *a widely accepted theory*, une théorie généralement admise. || **acceptable** [-əbl̩] *adj.* [worth accepting] acceptable; [satisfactory] agréable. || **acceptance** [-əns] *n.* acceptation *f*; [approval] approbation *f*; [favourable] réception *f.*

access ['æksɛs] *n.* **1.** accès *m* (à une bibliothèque, &c.); [Univ.] admission *f.* **2.** [Med.] accès (de fièvre), crise *f* (de paludisme, &c.). || **accessible** [ək'sɛs|ɪbl̩] *adj.* accessible, facile d'accès.

accession [ˌæk'sɛʃən] *n.* accession *f*, avènement *m.*

accessory [-ɚː] *n.* [part] accessoire *m*; [law] complice.

accident ['æksɪdənt] *n.* [Tech.] accident *m*: *a traffic* ~, un accident de la circulation; [unfortunate happening] contretemps *m*; malheur *m*: [Fig.] *by* ~, par hasard. || **accidental** [ˌæksɪ'dɛntl̩] *adj.* [caused by accident] accidentel; [chance] fortuit; [non-essential] accessoire. || **accidentally** [-ɪ] *adv.* accidentellement, par hasard.

acclaim [ə'klejm] *v. tr.* acclamer, applaudir. || **acclamation** [ˌæklə'mejʃən] *n.* acclamation *f*: [oral vote] © *to be elected by* ~, être élu sans concurrent.

acclimatize [ə'klajməˌtajz] *v. tr.* acclimater.

accommodate [ə'kɑməˌdej|t] *v. tr.* [room] loger, avoir de la place pour (qqun, qqch.); [Fig.] rendre service à (qqun), obliger (qqun); [oblige] accommoder; [views] concilier. || **accommodating** [ə'kɑməˌdejtɪŋ] *adj.* accommodant, obligeant. || **accommodation** [əˌkɑmə'dejʃən] *n.* [lodging] logement *m*, place *f*; *to have ~ for 50 persons*, → pouvoir/loger, recevoir/50 personnes, avoir de la place pour . . . ; [Fig.] accommodement *m*; adaptation *f*: *~ train*, train *m* omnibus.

accompaniment [ə'kʌmp|n̩ɪmənt] *n.* [Esp. Mus.] accompagnement *m*. || **accompanist** [-ənɪst] *n.* accompagnateur. || **accompany** [-ənɪ] *v. tr.* [go along with] accompagner: *to be accompanied by*, être/accompagné, escorté/de . . . , [happen with] s'accompagner de . . . ; [Mus.] accompagner.

accomplice [ə'kɑmplɪs] *n.* complice.

accomplish [ə'kɑmplɪʃ] *v. tr.* accomplir (son devoir); atteindre, réaliser (un but): *He accomplished nothing*, Il n'est arrivé à rien. || **accomplished** [-t] *adj.* [done] accompli, réalisé; [Fig.] accompli, parfait. || **accomplishment** [-mənt] *n.* réalisation *f*, accomplissement *m*; [skill] talent *m*.

accord [ə'koɚd] *n.* accord *m*; consentement *m* : *of one's own ~*, spontanément, de (son) propre gré; *with one ~*, d'un commun accord, à l'unanimité. || *v. intr.* s'accorder, s'entendre (avec). || *v. tr.* accorder, concéder (une faveur). || **accordance** [-n̩s] *n.* accord *m*; conformité *f*: *in ~ with*, conformément à . . . , au mieux (des intérêts de . . .). || **according** [-ɪŋ] *adv.* *~ as*, selon que [+ indic.]; *~ to*, selon, suivant; d'après (saint Thomas, &c.); *~ to whether*, selon que [+ indic.] || **accordingly** [-ɪŋlɪ] *adv.* en conséquence; [therefore] par conséquent.

accost [ə'kɑst] *v. tr.* [Fig.] accoster, aborder.

account [ə'kawnt] *n.* **1.** [bank, &c.] compte *m* (en banque, bancaire): *savings ~*, © compte d'épargne; *current ~*, compte courant: *to open an ~*, ouvrir un compte. **2.** compte, facture *f*: *I settled my ~*, J'ai réglé/mon compte, ma facture/; *on ~*, en acompte, à compte. **3.** [report] rapport *m*, compte rendu, récit *m* (d'un événement), description *f* (d'une situation): *to give an ~ of*, rendre compte de. **4.** [consideration, esteem, regard] cas *m*, estime *f*: *to take (s.o., sth.) into ~*, tenir compte de (qqun, qqch.); prendre (qqch.) en considération; *on no ~*, à aucun prix, sous aucun prétexte, en aucun cas. **5.** [worth] importance *f*, valeur *f*: *of no ~*, sans importance; profit *m*, avantage *m*: *to turn (sth.) to o.'s ~*, tirer/parti, avantage/de (qqch.). **6.** [reason, cause] raison *f*, explication *f*: *on ~ of*, étant donné, vu, à cause de. || **account** *v. tr.* [deem] considérer (comme), estimer: *X was accounted innocent*, On estima que X était innocent. || *v. intr.* [be responsible for] répondre (de qqch., *for sth.*); [action, conduct, &c.] rendre compte (de), justifier (de qqch., *for sth.*). || **accountable** [-əbl̩] *adj.* [pers.] responsable (de qqch. envers qqun, *for sth. to s.o.*); [thing] justifiable, explicable. || **accountancy** [-ənsɪ] *n.* [profession] comptabilité *f*; tenue *f* des livres. || **accountant** [-ənt] *n.* comptable *m*: *Chartered Accountant*, Expert *m* comptable, © comptable agréé. || **accounting** [-ɪŋ] *n.* comptabilité *f*.

accrue [ə'kɹuw] *v. intr.* résulter (*from*, de).

accumulate [ə'kjuwmjəˌlejt] *v. tr. & intr.* (s')accumuler, (s')entasser. || **accumulator** [-ɚ] [Br.] *n.* accumulateur *m*, cf. BATTERY.

accuracy ['ækjɚə|sɪ] *n.* précision *f*, exactitude *f*; [remark] justesse *f*. || **accurate** [-t] *adj.* précis, exact; [remark] juste.

accusation [ækˌjuw'zejʃən] *n.* accusation *f*. || **accuse** [ə'kjuwz] *v. tr.* accuser (qqun de qqch., *s.o. of sth.*).

accustom [ə'kʌstəm] *v. tr.* accoutumer, habituer (à, *to*). || **accustomed** [-d] *adj.* habituel, accoutumé: *to get ~ to*, → s'habituer à, s'accoutumer à.

ace [ejs] *n.* as *m*; [Fig.] héros *m*, [Fam.] as *m*: [Loc.] *within an ~ of*, à deux doigts de.

ache [ejk] *n.* douleur *f*, mal *m*: *headache*, mal *m* de tête; *to have a headache*, avoir mal à la tête; *toothache*, mal de dents [cf. below]. || *v. intr.* faire mal à, avoir mal à: *My head aches*, Ma tête me fait mal, J'ai mal à la tête; [Fig.] *to ~ to*, brûler de (faire qqch.); *to ~ for*, soupirer (après qqch.).

achievable [a'tʃijvəbl̩] *adj.* [task] faisable; [goal] possible.

achieve [ə'ʧijv] *v. tr.* **1.** mener (qqch.) à bien, réaliser (une œuvre), accomplir (une tâche); remporter (une victoire). **2.** [get by effort] acquérir, obtenir. || **achievement** [-mənt] *n.* [thing] réalisation *f*; [feat] exploit *m*, prouesse *f*; [act] réussite *f*.

acid ['æsɪd] *adj. & n.* acide (*m*): [Fig.] *the ~ test*, la pierre *f* de touche. || **acidity** [æ'sɪdɪtɪ] *n.* acidité *f*.

acknowledge [ək'nɑləʤ] *v. tr.* [admit to be true] reconnaître (le bien-fondé de), admettre; [a fault] avouer, confesser; [a letter] répondre (à une lettre), accuser réception (d'une lettre). || **acknowledgment** [-mənt] *n.* **1.** reconnaissance *f* (d'un tort); aveu *m*: *acknowledgments,* remerciements *mpl* (d'un auteur à ses collaborateurs, &c.). **2.** [letter] accusé *m* de réception.

acme ['ækmɪ] *n.* [Fig.] sommet *m.*

acorn ['ejkɔə˞n] *n.* gland *m* (d'un chêne).

acoustics [ə'kuwstɪks] *n. sing.* acoustique *f.*

acquaint [ə'kwejnt] *v. tr.* **1.** faire savoir (qqch. à qqun), faire part (à qqun de qqch., *with*), informer (qqun de qqch., *with*). **2.** [to meet, to know]: *They became acquainted in 1940,* Ils se sont connus en 1940; *to get acquainted* (*with*), faire (la) connaissance (de qqun); *to be acquainted with,* connaître, savoir (un fait). || **acquaintance** [-əns] *n.* [person] connaissance *f*; [knowledge] *to make the* ∼ *of,* faire la connaissance de.

acquiesce [ˌækwɪ'ɛs] *v. intr.* acquiescer (à, *in*). || **acquiescence** [-əns] *n.* acquiescement *m.* || **acquiescent** [-ənt] *adj.* accommodant; → qui ne dit pas non.

acquire [ə'kwajə˞] *v. tr.* acquérir, acheter (une propriété); prendre (une habitude); [knowledge] apprendre. || **acquirement** [-mənt] *n.* acquisition *f*; (*pl.*) connaissances *fpl,* érudition *f.* || **acquisition** [ˌækwɪ'zɪʃən] *n.* acquisition *f.* || **acquisitive** [ə'kwɪzɪtɪv] *adj.* âpre au gain, avide.

acquit [ə'kwɪt] *v. tr.* [-tt-] acquitter (un prévenu); exonérer (de, *of*). || *v. intr.* s'acquitter (d'une tâche); *to* ∼ *o.s. well,* se distinguer; [debt, &c.] s'acquitter, se libérer (d'une dette). || **acquittal** [-l̩] *n.* [Jur.] acquittement *m*; [debt, &c.] décharge *f.*

acre ['ejkə˞] *n.* acre *f.* © acres, domaine *m,* terres *fpl.* || **acreage** [-əʤ] *n.* superficie *f* (en acres).

acrid ['ækɹɪd] *adj.* âcre; acerbe.

acrimonious [ˌækɹɪ'mownɪəs] *adj.* acrimonieux. || **acrimony** ['ækɹɪˌmownɪ] *n.* acrimonie *f.*

acrobat ['ækɹəˌbæt] *n.* acrobate *m/f.* || **acrobatics** [ˌækɹə'bætɪks] *n.* acrobaties *fpl.*

across [ə'kɹɔs] *prép.* **1.** à travers: ∼ *country,* à travers champs; *He pulled it* ∼ *the room,* Il l'a tiré à travers la pièce; [→ often better transposed, using *traverser*] *He went/ran/* ∼ *the street,* Il a traversé la rue (en courant); *to jump* ∼ *sth.,* sauter par-dessus qqch.; [see other verbs of motion]. **2.** [crosswise] en travers de: *He laid it* ∼ *the table,* Il l'a posé en travers de la table. **3.** [on the other side] de l'autre côté: *He lives* ∼ *the street,* Il habite de l'autre côté de la rue. || *adv.* en travers, à travers: *Lay it* ∼, Mettez-le en travers; *Pull it* ∼, Tirez-le à travers; *a lake* 500 *feet* ∼, un lac large de cinq cents pieds; *to go* ∼, traverser; [see also under other verbs].

act [ækt] *n.* **1.** [deed] acte *m*; [process] action *f*: *in the* ∼ *of,* en train de; *to catch s.o. in the* ∼ *of,* prendre qqun en flagrant délit de; [Bible] *Acts of the Apostles,* Actes des Apôtres. **2.** [Jur.] loi *f*; [text] acte *m*: *the British North America* ∼, l'Acte de l'Amérique du Nord britannique; ∼ *of God,* force *f* majeure, cas *m* fortuit; ∼ *of Parliament,* loi *f.* **3.** [Thea.] acte; [artist] numéro *m.* || *v. tr.* jouer (une pièce de théâtre): ∼ *the fool,* faire l'imbécile. || *v. intr.* agir (sur, *on*): ∼ *as,* faire fonction de, agir en qualité de; [Fam.] ∼ *up,* faire des siennes. || **acting** [-ɪŋ] *adj.* **1.** qui agit, actif. **2.** suppléant: ∼ *chairman,* président *m* par intérim. || *n.* jeu *m* (des acteurs). || **action** ['ækʃən] *n.* **1.** [process] action *f*; [thing done] geste *m*; [motor] fonctionnement *m*: *out of* ∼, ne fonctionne pas, cf. ORDER; [Mil.] combat *m*: *killed in* ∼, mort au champ d'honneur; (*pl.*) conduite *f.* **2.** [Br. law] cf. SUIT. || **active** ['æktɪv] *adj.* actif: *to take an* ∼ *part in,* prendre une part active à; [volcano] en activité; [lively] alerte; [Gram.] ∼ *voice,* la voix active; [Mil.] *on* ∼ *service,* en service actif; en campagne. || **actively** [-lɪ] *adv.* activement. || **activity** [æk'tɪvɪtɪ] *n.* activité *f*; (*pl.*) fonctions *fpl*; occupations *fpl* (d'une personne), (le) rayon d'action (d'un groupe, d'une société): *anti-American* ∼, menées *fpl* anti-américaines.

actor ['ækt|ə˞] *n.* acteur *m.* || **actress** [-ɹəs] *n.* actrice *f.*

actual ['ækʧuwl̩] *adj.* [×] véritable, réel: *in* ∼ *life,* dans la vie réelle. || **actuality** [ˌækʧuw'ælətɪ] *n.* [×] réalité *f,* existence *f* effective. || **actually** [-lɪ] *adv.* [×] en réalité, réellement: *what he* ∼ *thought,* ce qu'il pensait/en fait, effectivement/.

actuary ['æktjuwˌɛəɪ] *n.* actuaire *m.*

acumen ['ækjəmən] *n.* [Fig.] pénétration *f.*

acute [ə'kjuwt] *adj.* aigu; [keen] pénétrant; [pain] vif; [shortage] → crise *f* de, manque presque total de . . . [angle, accent] aigu. || **acutely** [-lɪ] *adv.* d'une manière/aiguë, pénétrante/. || **acuteness** [-nəs] *n.* acuité *f* (des sens), finesse *f.*

A.D. ['ej'dij] [= Anno Domini]: *the third century A.D.*; *250 A.D.*, le troisième siècle après J.C.; 250 ap. J.C.; [Lit.†] en l'an de grâce 250.

ad [æd] *n.* [= ADVERTISEMENT]: *to place an ad* (*in the paper*), mettre, insérer/ une annonce (dans un journal); *classified ads*, petites annonces *fpl*; © annonces classées.

adage ['ædədʒ] *n.* adage *m.*

adamant ['ædəmənt] *adj.* intraitable.

adapt [ə'dæpt] *v. tr.* adapter (à, *to*); *to ~ o.s. to*, s'adapter à (son milieu, &c.). || **adaptable** [-əbḷ] *adj.* adaptable, souple. || **adaptation** [ˌædæp'tejʃən] *n.* adaptation *f.*

add [æd] *v. tr.* ajouter (à, *to*); *to ~ up*, additionner. || *v. intr.* additionner: *adding-machine*, machine *f* à calculer.

addendum [ə'dɛndəm] *n.* supplément *m.*

adder [-ɚ] *n.* vipère *f.*

addict ['ædɪkt] *n.* [person] . . . qui s'adonne à: *drug ~*, toxicomane *m/f.* || *v. tr.* [ə'dɪkt] s'adonner (à, *to*).

addition [ə'dɪʃən] *n.* **1.** [process] addition *f*; [result] somme *f.* || **2.** [thing added] supplément *m*, surcroît *m*: *~ (to a house)*, nouvelle aile *f*, nouvelle partie (d'une maison); annexe *f* (d'un bâtiment); *in ~*, de plus, en outre; *in ~ to . . .*, en plus de . . . || **additional** [-ḷ] *adj.* [added] supplémentaire, additionnel, [general] nouveau.

address [ə'dɹɛs] *n.* **1.** adresse *f* (postale). **2.** [speech] allocution *f*, discours *m*; © adresse *f*: *~ in reply to the speech from the Throne*, adresse en réponse au discours du Trône. || *v. tr.* **1.** mettre une adresse (sur une lettre), *adresser une lettre. **2.** adresser la parole à (un auditoire); s'adresser à (qqun), aborder qqun. **3.** [to apply o.s. to] étudier, considérer: *if we address ourselves first to . . .*, si nous considérons en premier lieu . . . || **addressee** [ˌædɹɛs'ij] *n.* destinataire *m* (d'une lettre).

adduce [ə'djuws] *v. tr.* alléguer; fournir (une preuve).

adept [ə'dɛpt] *adj.* expert, initié; habile à. || ['ædɛpt] *n.* expert *m.*

adequate ['ædəkwət] *adj.* suffisant (à, *to*); [well suited to] à la hauteur (des circonstances, &c.), adéquat.

adhere [əd'hijɚ] *v. intr.* adhérer; [Fig.] s'en tenir (à, *to*), maintenir (une décision, &c.). || **adherence** [-əns] *n.* [×] adhésion *f* (à un parti, &c.). || **adherent** [-ənt] *n.* [party, &c.] adhérent, -e; partisan *m.* || **adhesion** [əd'hijʒən] *n.* **1.** adhésion *f*, approbation *f.* **2.** [sticking] adhérence *f.* || **adhesive** [əd'hijsɪv] *adj.* adhésif, collant: [gummed] gommé: *~ tape*, sparadrap *m.*

adjacent [ə'dʒejsənt] *adj.* avoisinant, voisin; [Tech.] adjacent; *~ to*, qui touche à, contigu à.

adjective ['ædʒəktɪv] *n.* adjectif *m.*

adjoin [ə'dʒojn] *v. tr.* être contigu, toucher (à). || **adjoining** [-ɪŋ] *adj.* contigu, voisin.

adjourn [ə'dʒɚn] *v. tr.* ajourner (un travail à plus tard); [meeting] lever la séance. || *v. intr.* passer (*to another part of the house*, dans une autre pièce). || **adjournment** [-mənt] *n.* ajournement *m* (à une date ultérieure).

adjudicate [ə'dʒuwdɪˌkejt] *v. tr. & intr.* juger, se prononcer sur. || **adjudication** [əˌdʒuwdɪ'kejʃən] *n.* [×] jugement *m*, arrêt *m.* || **adjudicator** [ə'dʒuwdɪ'kejtɚ] *n.* juge *m*, arbitre *m.*

adjudge [ə'dʒʌdʒ] *v. tr.* [award] adjuger; [Jur.] juger, déclarer (coupable); condamner à (un an de prison, &c.).

adjunct [ˌædʒ'ʌnkt] *n.* adjoint *m*; [Fig.] auxiliaire *m*, accessoire *m.*

adjure [ə'dʒuwɚ] *v. tr.* adjurer.

adjust [ə'dʒʌst] *v. tr.* ajuster, régler (un appareil); [settle] régler (une affaire). || *v. intr. to ~ o.s. to*, s'adapter (aux circonstances, &c.). || **adjustment** [-mənt] *n.* [Tech.] ajustement *m*, réglage *m*; [TV] mise *f* au point; [settlement] arrangement *m.*

adjutant ['ædʒətənt] *n.* adjudant-major *m* [× adjudant].

ad lib. [= ad libitum] [ˌæd'lɪb] *adv.* [Fam.] à discrétion; à volonté. || *v. tr.* improviser.

administer [əd'mɪnɪstɚ] *v. tr.* [Com.] administrer (une société), gérer (une entreprise commerciale); [Fig.] *to ~ justice*, rendre la justice; [oath] faire prêter serment; [Rel.] *to ~ the last rites to*, administrer les derniers sacrements à (un mourant).

administration [ədˌmɪnɪ'stɹejʃən] *n.* **1.** [Com.] administration *f* (d'une société), gestion *f* (d'une entreprise commerciale). **2.** [Pol.] gouvernement *m*: *under the Truman ~*, sous le gouvernement Truman. **3.** administration *f* (d'un médicament). || **administrative** [əd'mɪnɪˌstɹejt|əv] *adj.* administratif. || **administrator** [-ɚ] *n.* administrateur *m.*

admirable ['ædmɚəbḷ] *adj.* admirable. || **admirably** [-ɪ] *adv.* admirablement.

admiral ['ædmɚəl] *n.* amiral *m.* || **admiralty** [-tɪ] *n.* amirauté *f*, [Fr.] Ministère *m* de la marine.

admiration [ˌædmɪ'ɹejʃən] *n.* admiration *f*; estime *f.* || **admire** [əd'majɚ] *v. tr.* admirer (qqun, qqch.); [less strong] aimer, estimer (qqun, qqch.). || **admirer**

[-ɚ] *n.* admirat|eur *m*, -rice *f.* || **admiringly** [-ɪŋlɪ] *adv.* avec admiration.

admissible [əd'mɪ|sɪbl̩] *adj.* admissible; [Jur.] recevable. || **admission** [-ʃən]. **1.** accès (à, *to*); admission *f* (à un concours, &c.): *No* ~ , Défense d'entrer; Défense de pénétrer (sur ce chantier, &c.); *No* ~ *except on business*, Défense d'entrer sans motif de service; → Le public n'est pas admis ici. **2.** (prix *m* d')entrée *f*: ~ *fees*, droits *mpl* d'inscription. **3.** admission *f*, concession *f*; aveu *m*, cf. ADMETTRE.

admit [əd'mɪt] *v. tr.* **1.** admettre (un fait); reconnaître (une erreur); [allow] permettre: *It must be admitted that*, Il faut reconnaître que . . . . **2.** permettre l'entrée (à qqun): *He was admitted*, On le fit entrer, Il eut accès à; *to be admitted to the bar*, être reçu au barreau. || **admittance** [-n̩s] entrée *f*, accès *m*: *to force* ~ , forcer la porte de; *No* ~ , Entrée interdite. cf. ADMISSION. || **admittedly** [-ədlɪ] *adv.* d'une façon évidente, ouvertement: ~ , *you may be right, but* . . . , Je veux bien reconnaître que vous avez sans doute raison, mais . . . .

admonish [əd'mɑnɪʃ] *v. tr.* admonester (un enfant); prévenir (qqun): *He was admonished not to* . . . , On l'a prévenu de ne pas [+ inf.]; [urge] exhorter (à, *to*). || **admonition** [ˌædmə'nɪʃən] *n.* conseil *m*; [stronger] admonestation *f*, réprimande *f*.

ado [ə'duw] *n.* **1.** bruit *m*, vacarme *m*: [Loc.] *much* ~ *about nothing*, beaucoup de bruit pour rien. **2.** façons *fpl*: *without any further* ~ , sans plus.

adobe [ə'dowbɪ] *n.* adobe *m.*

adolescence [ˌædə'lɛsən|s] *n.* adolescence *f.* || **adolescent** [-t] *adj.* & *n.* adolescent *m*, cf.

adopt [ə'dɑpt] *v. tr.* **adopter** (une attitude, un enfant). || **adopted** [-d] *adj.* d'adoption: ~ *child*, enfant adoptif. || **adoption** [ə'dɑpʃən] *n.* adoption *f.* || **adoptive** [ə'dɑptɪv] *adj.*: ~ *father*, père *m* adoptif.

adorable [ə'dɔɚəbl̩] *adj.* adorable; [Fam.] adorable, charmant. || **adoration** [ˌædɚ'ejʃən] *n.* adoration *f.* || **adore** [ə'dɔɚ] *v. tr.* adorer; [Fam.] idolâtrer, adorer, aimer passionnément. || **adorer** [-ɚ] adorat|eur *m*, -rice *f.* || **adoring** [-ɪŋ] *adj.* qui adore, qui idolâtre.

adorn [ə'dɔɚn] *v. tr.* orner, parer (de, *with*). || **adornment** [-mənt] *n.* parure *f*, ornement *m.*

adrift [ə'dɹɪft] *adv.* [Naut.] à la dérive; [Fig.] à l'aventure.

adroit [ə'dɹojt] *adj.* adroit, habile.

adulation [ˌædʒə'lejʃən] *n.* adulation *f.*

adult [ə'dʌlt] *adj.* & *n.* ['ædʌlt] adulte *m/f.*

adulterate [ə'dʌlt|əˌejt] *v. tr.* adultérer (un texte), falsifier (un texte, un médicament). || **adulteration** [əˌdʌltɚ'ejʃən] *n.* falsification *f* (d'un texte, &c.); [thing] produit *m*, (texte, &c.) falsifié. || **adulterer** [-ɚɚ] **adulteress** [-ɹəs] *adj.* & *n.* adultère *m/f.* || **adultery** [-ɚɪ] *n.* adultère *m.*

advance [əd'væns] *n.* **1.** [space] avance *f* (de troupes, &c.): *in* ~ *of*, en avant de. **2.** [progress] avancement *m*, progrès *m*; [rise] augmentation *f*; hausse *f* (des prix). || *pl.* avances *fpl.* **3.** [time] avance *f*: *in* ~, à l'avance, d'avance; [Com.] paiement *m* anticipé. || **advance** *v. tr.* avancer (l'heure, de l'argent, une opinion); [make progress] faire avancer; [prices] élever, hausser (les prix); [rank] promouvoir (à, *to*). || *v. intr.* [move forward] avancer; [come forward] s'avancer; [make progress] progresser. || **advanced** [-t] *adj.* avancé; [in years] âgé; [Fig.] en avance (sur les autres); [ideas] d'avant-garde, progressif. || **advancement** [-mənt] *n.* avancement *m*, progrès *m*; [rank] promotion *f*, avancement.

advantage [əd'væntədʒ] *n.* **1.** avantage *m*, intérêt *m*: *to take* ~ *of*, tirer parti de, profiter de, [unfair advantage] abuser de; *to be to s.o.'s* ~ *to* . . . , y aller de l'intérêt de qqun de . . . . **2.** supériorité *f* (du nombre): *to show (off) to* ~ , mettre (qqch.) en valeur, faire valoir; *of* ~ , d'utilité publique; *to the best* ~ , avantageusement. || **advantageous** [ˌædvən'tejdʒəs] *adj.* avantageux.

advent ['ædvɛnt] *n.* venue *f*, arrivée *f*; [Rel.] l'Avent *m.* || **Adventist Church** [æd'vɛntɪstˌtʃɚtʃ] Église *f* adventiste.

adventure [əd'vɛntʃɚ] *n.* aventure *f*: *spirit of* ~ , esprit *m* aventureux; [Com.] entreprise *f*, spéculation *f*/hasardeuse. || *v. tr.* aventurer, hasarder (de, *to*). || **adventurer** [-ɚ] *n.* aventurier *m*, [Pej.] chevalier *m* d'industrie. || **adventurous** [-əs] *adj.* aventureux, hardi; [Com.] entreprenant.

adverb ['ædvɚb] *n.* [Gram.] adverbe *m.*

adverbial [ˌæd'vɚbɪl̩] *adj.* adverbial.

adversary ['ædvɚˌsɛɚɪ] *n.* adversaire *m.*

adverse [əd'vɚs] *adj.* [unfavourable] adverse; [unfriendly] hostile; [wind] contraire. || **adversity** [-ɪtɪ] *n.* adversité *f.*

advertise ['ædvɚˌtajz] *v. tr.* annoncer (une vente); faire de la/publicité, réclame/ pour (un produit). || *v. intr.* faire de la /publicité, réclame/, © annoncer, insérer une annonce (dans un journal): *to* ~ *for a job*, mettre une annonce. || **advertisement** [əd'vɚtɪsmənt] *n.* annonce *f*, réclame *f.* || **advertiser** [ˈædvərtajzər] *n.* annoncier *m.* || **advertising** [ˈædvərˌtajz|ɪŋ] *n.* la publicité, [advertisements] réclame *f*: ~ *agency*, agence *f* de publicité, conseil *m* en publicité; ~ *campaign*, campagne (de publicité).

advice [ədˈvajs] *n.* [coll.] opinion *f*, avis *m*; conseil *m* [☞ usual. pl.]: *a piece of* ~, *some* ~, un conseil; *to get legal* ~, consulter un avocat. || **advisable** [ədˈvajzəbḷ] *adj.* [to be recommended] indiqué, judicieux, opportun. || **advise** [ədˈvajz] *v. tr.* **1.** conseiller: *to* ~ *s.o. to*, conseiller à qqun de . . . ; [stronger] engager qqun à [+ inf.]; *to* ~ *s.o./not to do, against doing/sth.*, déconseiller à qqun de faire qqch. **2.** informer, avertir (qqun de qqch.). || **advis|er, -or** [-ər] *n.* [legal, &c.] conseiller *m*; *spiritual* ~, directeur *m* de conscience. || **advisory** [-ərɪ] *adj.* consultatif.

advocacy [ˈædvə|kəsɪ] *n.* plaidoyer *m* (en faveur de), défense *f.* || **advocate** [-ˌkejt] *n.* avocat; [Fig.] défenseur *m* (d'une cause), partisan *m* (d'une réforme, &c.). || *v. tr.* préconiser, plaider en faveur de.

aerate [ˈɛərˌejt] *v. tr.* aérer (une pièce). cf. AIR: *aerated water*, eau gazeuse. || **aeration** [ɛərˈejʃən] *n.* aération *f.* || **aerial** [ˈɛərɪəl] *adj.* aérien. || *n.* [radio, &c.] antenne *f.*

aerodrome [ˈɛər|əˌdɹowm], **aeroplane** [-əˌplejn] cf. AIRPORT, AIRPLANE. || **aeronautics** [ɛərəˈnɔtɪks] *n.* l'aéronautique *f.*

aesthetic(s) [ɛsˈθɛtɪk] *adj.* esthétique. || *n.* esthétique *f.*

aether, ether [ˈijθər] *n.* éther *m.*

†**afar** [əˈfɑər] *adv.* de loin: ~ *off*, au loin.

affability [æfəˈbɪlɪtɪ] *n.* affabilité *f.* || **affable** [ˈæfəbḷ] *adj.* affable.

affair [əˈfɛər] *n.* **1.** affaire *f*; *affairs*, affaires *fpl.* **2.** [vague term] chose *f*, événement *m*: *love* ~, épisode *m* amoureux, liaison *f.*

affect[1] [əˈfɛkt] *v. tr.* affecter; avoir un effet sur, influer sur: *to be (deeply) affected by*, être (profondément)/touché, ému/par; *That does not* ~ *me one way or the other*, Cela ne me fait ni chaud ni froid, Ça m'est égal.

affect[2] *v. tr.* [pretend] affecter (l'ignorance, &c.); [be fond of] rechercher, faire étalage de; [assume] feindre, afficher. || **affectation** [ˌæfɛkˈtejʃən] *n.* affectation *f*; [Pej.] ostentation *f.* || **affected** [əˈfɛktəd] *adj.* **1.** affecté, ému. **2.** affecté, feint.

affection [əˈfɛkʃən] *n.* affection *f*, tendresse *f*; [Med.] affection *f*, maladie *f.* || **affectionate** [-ət] *adj.* affectueux.

affidavit [æfɪˈdejvɪt] *n.* [law] © affidavit *m*; [Fr.] déclaration *f* sous serment.

affiliate [əˈfɪlɪ|ˌejt] *v. tr. & intr.* (s')affilier (à, *with*). || *n.* [-ət] société *f* affiliée.

affirm [əˈfərm] *v. tr.* affirmer (que, *that*), déclarer solennellement que; [confirm] confirmer, ratifier. || **affirmation** [ˌæfərˈmejʃən] *n.* affirmation *f*; déclaration *f* (solennelle). || **affirmative** [əˈfərmətɪv] *adj.* affirmatif. || *n.* [answer] affirmative *f.*

affix [əˈfɪks] *v. tr.* attacher, coller, joindre.

afflict [əˈflɪk|t] *v. tr.* affliger (de, *with*); [distress] tourmenter. || **affliction** [-ʃən] *n.* affliction *f*, chagrin *m.*

affluence [ˈæfluwən|s] *n.* [×] opulence *f*, richesses *fpl*; [pers.] affluence *f.* || **affluent** [-t] *adj.* opulent, riche. || *n.* [river] affluent *m.*

afford [əˈfɔərd] *v. tr.* **1.** se permettre de, pouvoir; avoir les moyens de (+ inf.): *I can* ~ *to wait*, Je peux attendre; *I can't* ~ *a car*, Mes moyens ne me permettent pas, Je n'ai pas les moyens d'avoir/une auto. **2.** [yield] donner, fournir.

affront [əˈfɹʌnt] *v. tr.* offenser, insulter. || *n.* affront *m*, insulte *f.*

afield [əˈfijld] *adv.*: *far, further/* ~, loin, très loin. || **afire** [əˈfajər] *adj. & adv.* en feu. || **afloat** [əˈflowt] *adj. & adv.* à flot; [Fig.] [rumours, &c.] en circulation. cf. AFOOT. || **afoot** [əˈfʊt] *adv.* [on foot] sur pied, [walking] à pied; [Fig.] en circulation, en cours.

A.F. (of) L. = American Federation of Labor = © Congrès *m* américain du travail.

aforesaid [əˈfɔərˌsɛd] *adj.* susdit, précité.

aforethought [əˈfɔərˌθɔt] *adj.* prémédité: *with malice* ~, avec préméditation.

afraid [əˈfɹejd] *adj.* **1.** effrayé (de, *to*): *to make s.o.* ~, → faire peur à qqun; *to be* ~ *of (s.o., sth.)*, avoir peur de, craindre (qqun, qqch.); *to be* ~ *that*, craindre que (+ ne + subj.). **2.** [esp. Br.] *to be* ~ *that* . . . , regretter que . . . ; *I'm* ~ *I don't know*, Je ne le sais malheureusement pas; *I'm* ~ *so!*, J'ai bien peur que oui!

afresh [əˈfɹɛʃ] *adv.* de nouveau.

Africa [ˈæfɹɪkə] *n.* l'Afrique *f*: *to, in* ~, en Afrique; *North* ~, l'Afrique du Nord; *South* ~, l'Union *f* sud-africaine. || **African** [-n] *adj. & n.* africain, -e.

after [ˈæftər] *adv.* après, ensuite, plus tard: *to come* ~, venir après; *I'll see you* ~, Je vous verrai/après, plus tard/; *What happened* ~ *?*, Qu'est-ce qui est arrivé /après, ensuite?; *I never saw him* ~, Je ne l'ai plus jamais revu; *a week* ~, une semaine/après, plus tard/; *the week*

~, la semaine d'après; [cf. DAY]. || *prép.* **1.** après: ~ *class*, après la classe; ~ *you*, après vous; *to run* ~ *s.o.*, courir après qqun; *to be* ~ *sth.*, chercher qqch.; *What are you* ~ ?, Où en voulez-vous venir?; ~ *all*, malgré tout; ~ *a few days*, au bout de quelques jours; *day* ~ *day*, jour après jour; *page* ~ *page*, page sur page; ☞ ~ *finishing*, après avoir fini. **2.** [according to] d'après, selon, suivant. || *conj.* après que [+ indic.]: *We always had to put everything away* ~ *he had finished*, Nous devions toujours tout ranger après qu'il avait fini; ☞ *We put away everything*, ~ *he had finished*, Nous avons tout rangé, après qu'il a fini, [in formal style] Nous rangeâmes tout, après qu'il eut fini; ☞ [if the subject of both clauses is the same, Fr. prefers a participial or noun phrase] *After I had finished, I put everything away*, Après avoir fini, j'ai tout rangé/[or formally] je rangeai tout/; *After I am ready/have finished/, you will be glad*, Après que je serai prêt/j'aurai fini/, vous serez content; *After you leave, don't forget to write*, Après votre départ, n'oubliez pas d'écrire; [a noun phrase may often be used when the subjects are different] *After the plane landed, the crowd began to leave*, Après l'atterrissage de l'avion, la foule commença à se disperser.

aftermath [-ˌmæθ] *n.* [result] suites *fpl.*

afternoon [-'nuwn] *n.* après-midi *m/f*: *at 3 (o'clock) in the* ~, à 3 heures de l'après-midi; *on the* ~ *of the 3rd*, l'après-midi du 3; ~ *tea*, le thé; l'heure *f* du thé; *Good* ~ *!*, Bonjour! cf. GOOD.

aftertaste [-ˌtejst] *n.* arrière-goût *m.*

afterthought [ˌ-θɔt] *n.* réflexion *f* après coup; [Loc.] esprit *m* d'escalier.

afterward(s) [-wɚd(z)] *adv.* après, ensuite, plus tard, [cf. AFTER adv.].

again [ə'gɛn, ə'gejn] *adv.* **1.** re- [+ verb]; de nouveau, encore: *I saw him* ~, Je l'ai revu; *He woke up* ~, Il se réveilla de nouveau; *What! You* ~ *!*, Comment! Vous encore!; [Fam.] *Here we are/go/* ~, Nous y revoilà; *Don't do it* ~ *!*, Ne le fais plus! Ne recommence pas!; *Never* ~ *!*, Jamais plus!; ~ *and* ~, maintes et maintes fois; *He did it* ~ *and* ~, Il l'a fait et refait; *He woke up* ~ *and* ~, Il s'est réveillé à plusieurs reprises; *now and* ~, de temps en temps. **2.** aussi: *(twice) as/much, big/* ~, (deux fois) autant/aussi grand/. **3.** d'ailleurs: . . . *and (then)* ~, *I need the money*, . . . et d'ailleurs, j'ai besoin de l'argent.

against [ə'gɛnst, moins souvent ə'gejnst] *prép.* **1.** contre: *to fight* ~, se battre contre; ~ *the wall*, contre le mur; *Are you for or* ~ ?, Êtes-vous pour ou contre?; *I have nothing* ~ */it, your doing it/*, Je n'y vois pas d'inconvénient, Je ne vois pas d'inconvénient à ce que vous le fassiez; *to be* ~ *sth.*, être/contre, opposé à/qqch.; *the charge* ~ *him*, → l'accusation portée contre lui; ~ *a green background*, sur un fond vert. **2.** en prévision de: *to lay away supplies* ~ *a hard winter*, mettre des provisions de côté en prévision d'un hiver rigoureux.

age [ejdʒ] *n.* **1.** âge *m*: *old* ~, vieillesse *f*; *to come of* ~, atteindre sa majorité; *under* ~, mineur: *What's your* ~ ?, Quel âge/as-tu, avez-vous/? **2.** âge, *m.* période *f*: *the Stone Age*, l'Âge de la pierre: [Fig.] *I haven't seen you for ages*, Il y a des siècles qu'on ne s'est pas vu; *the Middle Ages*, le Moyen Âge. || **age** *v. tr. & intr.* vieillir. || **aged** [-d] *adj.* âgé (de): *the* ~, les vieillards, [Fam.] les vieux; *middle-* ~, entre deux âges, d'âge mûr; [wine, whisky] vieilli. || **ageless** [-ləs] *adj.* sans âge; éternellement jeune. || **agelong** [-ˌlɔŋ] *adj.* éternel, qui n'en finit pas.

agency ['ejdʒənsɪ] *n.* [Com.] agence *f*; [UN.] institution *f* spécialisée; [Fig.] action *f*, entremise *f* (*through*, par).

agenda [ə'dʒɛndə] *n.* programme *m*; *on the* ~, à l'ordre du jour.

agent ['ejdʒənt] *n.* agent *m*; [Com.] représentant *m*: ~ *for X*, concessionnaire *m* de (la maison) X; [Chem.] agent.

agglomeration [əˌglɑmə'ejʃən] *n.* conglomérat *m*; agglomération *f.*

aggrandizement [ə'gɹænˌdɪzmənt] *n.* développement *m*, accroissement *m* (de puissance, richesse).

aggravate ['ægɹəˌvejt] *v. tr.* aggraver; [Fam. = irritate] agacer, exaspérer. || **aggravation** [ˌægɹə'vejʃən] *n.* aggravation *f*; [Fam.] irritation *f.*

aggregate ['ægɹəˌgejt] *n.* total *m*, masse *f*: *in the* ~, en bloc. || *adj.* total; pris en bloc, collectif. || **aggregation** [ˌægɹə'gejʃən] *n.* assemblage *m*, foule *f.*

aggression [ə'gɹɛ|ʃən] *n.* agression *f.* || **aggressive** [-sɪv] *adj.* agressif; [Fig.] [×] énergique, entreprenant. || **aggressor** [-ɚ] *n.* agresseur *m.*

aggrieve [ə'gɹijv] *v. tr.* chagriner, [unjustly] froisser.

aghast [ə'gæst] *adj.* stupéfait, atterré.

agile ['ædʒajl] *adj.* [fingers, &c.] agile || **agility** [ə'dʒɪlɪtɪ] *n.* agilité *f.*

agitate [ˈædʒɪˌtejt] *v. tr.* agiter, troubler; [argue] débattre (une question). || *v. intr.*: *to ~ for*, faire campagne pour. || **agitation** [ˌædʒɪˈtejʃən] *n.* agitation *f*; discussion *f*, campagne *f* (en faveur de, contre/*for*, *against*). || **agitator** [ˈædʒɪˌtejtər] *n.* agitateur *m*; [Pol.] meneur *m*.

aglow [əˈglow] *adj.* rougeoyant. cf. GLOW.

agnostic [ˌægˈnastɪk] *adj. & n.* agnostique.

ago [əˈgow] *adj.* il y a [☞ always precedes in Fr.]: *Three days ~*, Il y a trois jours; *A little while ~*, Tout à l'heure. || *adv.* il y a: *long ~*, il y a longtemps; *not long ~*, récemment, dernièrement; *How long ~ is it since . . .*, Combien de temps y a-t-il que . . . ?

agog [əˈgag] *adj.* en émoi.

agonize [ˈægən|ajz] *v. intr.* souffrir cruellement; [Fig.] être au supplice. || *v. tr.* torturer, faire souffrir. || **agonizing** [-ajzɪŋ] *adj.* atroce; [Fig.] cruel, terrible. || **agony** [-ɪ] *n.* douleur *f* intense; [death throes] agonie *f*; [Fig.] angoisse *f*; [Br. press] *~ column*, messages *mpl* personnels.

agrarian [əˈgɹɛərɪən] *adj.* agraire. || *n.* agrarien *m*.

agree [əˈgɹij] *v. intr.* **1.** consentir à; être d'accord (pour, *in*): *He agreed with us*, Il a été de notre avis; *He agreed to do it*, Il a accepté de le faire. **2.** convenir à: [food] *This does not ~ with me*, Cela ne me convient pas, → Je ne peux pas le supporter; [Gram.] s'accorder (avec, *with*; en, *in*); *agreed!*, convenu! || **agreeable** [-əbl̩] *adj.* agréable; [ready to agree] consentant, prêt à accepter; [suitable] approprié. || **agreement** [-mənt] *n.* entente *f*, accord *m*: *to be in ~*, être d'accord; [Jur., Com.] convention *f*, pacte *m*: *to come to an ~*, tomber, se mettre/d'accord.

agricultural [ˌægɹɪˈkʌltjər|l̩] *adj.* agricole. || **agriculture** *n.* agriculture *f*, culture *f* (de la terre). || **agriculturist** [-ɪst] *n.* agriculteur *m*.

aground [əˈgɹawnd] *adv.* à la côte: *to run ~*, s'échouer.

ahead [əˈhɛd] *adv.* **1.** [place] en avant; de l'avant: *to be* (*up*) *~*, être en avant; *to go* (*up*) *~*, [also Fig.] aller de l'avant/avancer; [Fig.] *Go ~!*, Allez-y!; *to get ~ of*, dépasser; *to stay ~ of*, garder son avance sur; *Full speed ~!*, En avant toute!; *~ of*, devant; *It is straight ~* (*of you*), C'est tout droit (devant vous). **2.** [time] en avance, d'avance: *to/be, arrive/ ~ of time*, être/arriver/en avance (sur l'horaire); *to/be, arrive/an hour ~ of schedule*, avoir une heure d'avance sur l'horaire; [clock] *to be ~*, avancer; *to look, see/ ~*, prévoir.

aid [ejd] *n.* **1.** aide *f*, assistance *f*: *mutual ~*, assistance mutuelle; *by the ~ of*, à l'aide de; *in ~ of*, au bénéfice de. **2.** secours *mpl*, soins *mpl*: *first ~*, les premiers secours; appareil *m* (de prothèse): [Pedag.] *audio-visual ~*, matériel *m*/audio-visuel, didactique/; **3.** [Pers.] aide *m* assistant *m*: *aide-de-camp*, aide de camp. || *v. tr.* secourir, aider (qqun à faire qqch.).

ail [ejl] *v. intr.* souffrir: *He is ailing*, Il dépérit; [Fig.] *What ails you?*, Qu'est-ce qui ne va pas? || **ailing** [-ɪŋ] *adj.* maladif, souffreteux. || **ailment** [-mənt] *n.* mal *m*, [slight] malaise *m*.

aim [ejm] *n.* visée *f*; [target] cible *f*, but *m*: *to take ~ at*, → viser; [Fig.] dessein *m*, but. || *v. tr.* [gun] pointer; [blow] lancer, donner. || *v. intr.* viser (at, . . .) mettre . . . en joue; [Fig.] viser, aspirer (à, *at*): *to ~ at happiness*, aspirer au bonheur. || **aimless** [-ləs] *adj.* sans but. || **aimlessly** [-ləslɪ] *adv.* sans but, au hasard.

ain't [ejnt] © [Vulg. = am, is, are/not; has, have/not] cf. BE, HAVE.

air [ɛər] *n.* **1.** air *m*: *to get a breath of fresh ~*, aller prendre l'air; *~ brakes*, freins *mpl* à air comprimé; *~ -conditioned*, climatisé; [light wind] brise *f*. **2.** [space overhead] air: *in the ~*, dans l'air; *by ~*, par avion; *~ -borne*, aéroporté; [Fig.] *in the ~*, (propos) en l'air; [radio] *on the ~*, sur les ondes. **3.** [bearing] air, allure *f*: *to give o.s. airs*, faire des manières. || *adj.* aérien: *~ mail*, poste aérienne, → par avion; *~ base*, base aérienne; *~ force*, armée *f* de l'air, aviation *f* militaire; *the Air Force*, l'aviation. cf. RCAF. || **air** *v. tr.* aérer (une pièce); [Fig.] exposer (son opinion). || **aircraft** [-ˌkɹæft] *n. inv.* avion *m*, appareil *m*, [ICAO] aéronef *m*. || **airdrome** [-ˌdɹowm] *n.* aérodrome *m*. || **airfield** [-ˌfijld] *n.* champ *m* d'aviation. || **airgraph** [-ˌgɹæf] *n.* aérogramme *m*. || **air hostess** [-ˌhowstəs] *n.* hôtesse *f* de l'air. || **airline** [-ˌlajn] *n.* compagnie *f* /d'aviation, aérienne/. || **airliner** [-ər] *n.* avion *m* de ligne, © aérobus *m*. || **airman** [-mən] *n.* aviateur *m*. || **airplane** [-ˌplejn] *n.* avion *m*. || **air pocket** [-ˌpakət] *n.* poche *f*, trou *m*/d'air. || **airport** [-ˌpɔərt] *n.*: *land ~*, aéroport *m* terrestre; *water ~*, hydroaéroport *m*. || **air route** [-ˌɹuwt] *n.* ligne *f* aérienne. || **air sickness** [-ˌsɪknəs] *n.* mal *m* de l'air. || **airstop** [-ˌstap] *n.* escale *f* aérienne. || **airstrip** [-ˌstɹɪp] *n.* piste *f* d'atterrissage. || **airtight** [-ˌtajt] *adj.*

hermétique(ment clos); étanche. || **air-woman** [-ˌwʊmən] *n.* aviatrice *f.*
airy [ˈɛəɪ] *adj.* aéré, ventilé; [Fig.] gracieux, léger; [promesse] en l'air.
aisle [ajl] *n.* [church] bas-côté *m*, nef *f* latérale: *centre* ~, allée *f* centrale; *to walk down the* ~, conduire (qqun) à l'autel.
ajar [əˈdʒɑə] *adj.* [door] entr'ouvert.
akin [əˈkɪn] *adj.* apparenté (*to*, à), tenant (*to*, de).
alacrity [əˈlækɹɪtɪ] *n.* empressement *m.*
alarm [əˈlɑəm] *n.* [state] alarme *f*, inquiétude *f*; [warning] alerte *f*; [device] avertisseur *m* (d'incendie, &c.): ~ *clock*, réveil *m*, réveille-matin *m*; ~ *bell*, tocsin *m.* || *v. tr.* alarmer, effrayer: *to become alarmed*, s'alarmer, s'effrayer (de, *at*).
alarming [əˈlɑəmɪŋ] *adj.* alarmant.
alas [əˈlæs] *interj.* hélas!
Alaska [əˈlæskə] *n.* Alaska *f*; *to, in* ~, en Alaska: *the* ~ *Highway*, la route de l'A. || **Alaskan** [-n] *adj. & n.* de l'A., d'A.
albatross [ˈælbəˌtɹɔs] *n.* [bird] albatros *m.*
†**albeit** [ɔlˈbijɪt] *conj.* quoique, bien que [+ subj.] [cf. ALTHOUGH].
album [ˈælbəm] *n.* album *m.*
alcohol [ˈælkəˌhɔl] *n.* alcool *m.* || **alcoholic** [-ɪk] *adj.* alcoolique; [containing some alcohol] alcoolisé. || **alcoholism** [-ɪsm] *n.* alcoolisme *m.*
alder|man [ˈɔldəmən] *pl.* **-men** *n.* conseiller *m* municipal; † © échevin *m.*
ale [ejl] *n.* bière *f* (anglaise), ale *f.*
alert [əˈlət] *adj.* [mind] éveillé, vif; [body] alerte. || *n.* alerte *f*: *on the* ~, en état *m* d'alerte, [Fig.] être/sur ses gardes, sur le qui-vive. || *v. tr.* [Mil.] donner/l'alerte, l'alarme *f*/. || **alertness** [-nəs] *n.* vigueur *f* (d'esprit); verdeur *f* (physique).
Alexander [æləksˈændə] *n.* = Alexandre *m.*
alfalfa [ælfˈælfə] *n.* luzerne *f.*
algebra [ˈældʒəbɹə] *n.* algèbre *f.*
Algon|quian, -quin [ælˈgɒnkwɪn] *n.* © Algonquin *m.*
alias [ˈejlɪəs] *adv.* autrement dit. || *n.* nom *m* d'emprunt.
alibi [ˈælɪˌbaj] alibi *m*; excuse *f.*
alien [ˈejlɪən] *adj. & n.* étranger *m*, étrangère *f* (à, *to*). || **alienate** [-ejt] *v. tr.* aliéner, éloigner (de, *from*).
alight[1] [əˈlajt] *v. intr.* débarquer (de bateau, de train, d'avion) [otherwise use *descendre*]: descendre (de cheval, de bicyclette), mettre pied à terre; [bird] se poser; [Aero.] se poser; [on land] atterrir [at sea] amerrir; [on the moon] alunir.
alight[2] *adj. & adv.* éclairé, illuminé; [Fig.] ~ *with joy*, illuminé de joie, radieux.
align [əˈlajn] *v. tr.* aligner. || **alignment** [-mənt] *n.* alignement *m.*
alike [əˈlajk] *adj.* pareil, -le *f*, semblable (à, *to*): *to be* ~ *to . . .*, → ressembler à: *They are both* ~, Ils, Elles/se ressemblent/ beaucoup, tout à fait/. || *adv.* également, de la même façon.
alimony [ˈælɪˌmownɪ] *n.* pension *f* alimentaire.
alive [əˈlajv] *adj.* vivant, en vie: *He is still* ~, Il est toujours en vie, → Il vit encore; *the most famous artist* ~, le plus fameux artiste de notre temps; *The place is* ~ *with worms*, Cet endroit est grouillant de vers; [Fig.] actif, sensible: *to be* ~ *to . . .*, être sensible à . . . ; *Look* ~ *!*, Dépêche-toi.
alkali [ˈælkəˌlaj] *n.* alcali *m.*
all [ɔl] *adj.* tout, toute; *pl.* tous, toutes: ~ */that, this/*, tout/cela, ceci/; ~ *men*, ~ *the men*, tous les hommes; ~ *Canada*, tout le Canada; *All chalk is not white*, Toute la craie n'est pas blanche; [every] *All crime is found out eventually*, Tout crime finit par être découvert; ~ *the way*, tout le long du chemin; *to go* ~ *the way*, aller jusqu'au bout; *For /with/* ~ *his charm*, Malgré (tout) son charme; [cf. HOUR, SPEED]. || *pron.* tout, toute; *pl.* tous [tus], toutes: *That's* ~ *(that) (I see)*, C'est tout (ce que je vois); ~ *(of) /that, this/*, tout cela/ceci/; ~ *who(m)*, tous ceux, toutes celles/qui (que, dont, &c.); ~ *of the pie*, toute la tarte, la tarte toute entière; *All of you were there*, Vous étiez là/tous, toutes/; *He knows* ~ *(four) of us*, Il nous connaît/tous, toutes/ (les quatre); *All you have to do is to . . .*, Vous n'avez qu'à . . . ; *once and for* ~, une fois pour toutes; *($10) in* ~, (dix dollars) en tout; ~ *in* ~ */when* ~ *is said and done*, somme toute/en dernière analyse; *(not, nothing, &c.) at* ~, (pas, rien, &c.) du tout; *Do you skate at* ~ *?*, Savez-vous patiner un peu?, Allez-vous jamais patiner?; *If he complains at* ~, Pour peu qu'il se plaigne, Si jamais il se plaint; ~ *but*, presque; *She* ~ *but failed*, Elle a failli échouer. || *adv.* tout(e)(s) [for agreement cf. TOUT]; entièrement: *They are* ~ *alone*, Ils, Elles/ sont/tout seuls, toutes seules/; *She is* ~ *ears*, Elle est tout oreilles; *It isn't* ~ *true*, Ce n'est pas entièrement vrai; ~ *the better*, tant mieux; ~ *the more because . . .*, d'autant plus que . . . ; *It is* ~ *too true*, Ce n'est que trop vrai; ~ *at once*,

[suddenly] tout à coup, [all at the same time] tout d'un coup. || *n.* tout *m*, totalité *f*: *He lost his* ~, Il a perdu la totalité /de ses biens, de son argent/; *This is my* ~, C'est mon tout; *I'll do my* ~, Je ferai/de mon mieux, tout ce que je pourrai/.

allay [ə'lej] *v. tr.* calmer, apaiser.

allegation [ælə'gejʃən] *n.* allégation *f.* || **allege** [ə'lɛʤ] *v. tr.* alléguer, prétendre (que + indic.). || **alleged** [-d] *adj.* [raison, fait] allégué; [criminel] présumé.

allegiance [ə'lijʤəns] *n.* fidélité *f*, obéissance *f* (à, *to*).

allegory ['ælə,gɔəɪ] *n.* allégorie *f.*

Allen ['ælən] *n.* = Alain *m.*

allergic [ə'lərʤɪk] *adj.* allergique: *to be* ~ *to* . . ., ne pas supporter . . .

allergy ['ælərʤɪ] *n.* allergie *f.*

alleviate [ə'lijvɪ,ejt] *v. tr.* alléger (la souffrance), consoler (un chagrin), soulager (une peine).

alley ['ælɪ] *n.* [back ~] ruelle *f*: *blind* ~, impasse *f* [also Fig.]; [garden] allée *f*; *bowling* ~, © salle *f* de quilles.

alliance [ə'lajəns] *n.* alliance *f*; [agreement] entente *f.* || **allied** ['ælajd] *adj.* allié; [Com.] associé; [subject] connexe. || **Allies, the** [-s] les Alliés. cf. ALLY.

allocate [,ælə'kej|t] *v. tr.* allouer, attribuer. || **allocation** [-ʃən] *n.* allocation *f*, attribution *f.*

allot [ə'lɑt] *v. tr.* [-tt-] assigner (à, *to*). || **allotment** [ə'lɑtmənt] *n.* attribution *f*, part *f* allouée.

allow [ə'ləw] *v. tr.* **1.** [permit] permettre (à qqun de faire qqch.): *We are not allowed to use a dictionary*, On ne nous permet pas de nous servir d'un dictionnaire; *Smoking is not allowed*, Il est défendu de fumer; *May I be allowed to* . . ., Pourrais-je . . . [+ inf.], Aurais-je la permission de . . . . **2.** [acknowledge] admettre (une opinion): *to* ~ *for*, tenir compte de; [give] allouer (une somme d'argent). || **allowable** [-əbḷ] *adj.* admissible, permis(sible). || **allowance** [-əns] *n.* **1.** [money] pension *f*, allocation *f*; *weekly* ~ (for children), argent *m* de poche; *monthly* ~, mensualité *f*; *family* ~, allocations *fpl* familiales. **2.** [on used car] remise *f*; [food] ration *f*; [Com.] rabais *m.* **3.** [permission] permission *f*, prévision *f*: *to make* ~ *for* . . ., prévoir . . ., faire la part de. . . .

alloy ['æloj] *n.* alliage *m.* || *v. tr.* allier.

all right [ɔl'ɹajt], [Fam.] **alright** *adv.* parfait, [health] en bonne santé; [morals] bien, irréprochable: *He is* ~ *now* [après un accident], Il va bien maintenant; *Is it* ~ *for me to* . . . ?, Ai-je le droit de . . ., Puis-je . . . ? || *interj. All right!*, Très bien!, Parfait!

allude [ə'luwd] *v. intr.* faire allusion (à, *to*).

allure [ə'luwər] *v. tr.* attirer, séduire. || **allurement** [-mənt] *n.* charme *m*, séduction *f.* || **alluring** [-ɪŋ] *adj.* séduisant.

allusion [ə'luw|ʒən] *n.* allusion *f.* || **allusive** [-sɪv] *adj.* allusif, par allusion.

ally ['æləj] *pl.* **allies** *n.* allié *m.* || [ə'laj] *v. intr.* (s')allier à; [by marriage] entrer (dans une famille). cf. ALLIED.

almanac ['ælmə,næk] *n.* almanach *m.*

almighty [ɔl'məjtɪ] *adj.* tout-puissant *m*, toute-puissante *f.* || *n. the Almighty*, le Tout-Puissant, Dieu *m.*

almond ['ɑmənd] *n.* amande *f.*

almost ['ɔl,mowst] *adv.* presque; à peu près: ~ *blind*, presque aveugle; [= approximately] ~ *the same thing*, à peu près la même chose; *I* ~ *fell*, → J'ai failli tomber.

alms [ɑmz] *n.* (*pl.*) aumône *f*: *to give* ~, faire/l'aumône, la charité/.

aloft [ə'lɑft] *adv.* en haut; dans la mâture.

alone [ə'lown] *adj.* **1.** seul; tout seul; seul à seul: *He is* (*all*) ~ *tonight*, Il est (tout) seul ce soir; *He* ~ *knew*, Lui seul savait, Il n'y avait que lui qui savait, Il était le seul à savoir; *She did it* (*all*) ~, Elle l'a fait/toute seule, elle-même/; *I want to speak to you* ~, Je veux vous parler seul à seul; *In* (*the province of*) *Ontario* ~ . . ., Dans la seule province d'Ontario . . . **2.** *to leave, let*/ ~ /: *Leave me* ~*!*, Laissez-moi (tranquille), Laissez-moi faire!; *Leave that* ~ *!*, Laissez cela!, Ne touchez pas à cela!; *Let well enough* ~, Le mieux est l'ennemi du bien; [to say nothing of] *let* ~ . . ., sans parler de. . . .

along [ə'lɔŋ] *prép.* le long de: *The houses* (*which are*) ~ *the road*, Les maisons/qui sont le long de la route, qui bordent la route/; *to go* ~ (*beside*) *a wall, &c.*, aller le long d'un mur, longer un mur; *all* ~ *the way*, tout le long du chemin; *all* ~ *the line*, sur toute la ligne; [see also under other verbs]. || *adv.* [dénote une idée de progression après certains verbes] *He'll be* ~ *shortly*, Il arrivera d'ici peu; *He is well* ~ *in his work*, → Son travail avance bien; ~ *with*, avec, en même temps que; [Fig.] *to go* ~ *with s.o.* (on some matter), être d'accord avec qqun (sur tel point particulier). || **alongside** [-,sajd] *prép. & adv.* le long de; à côté de: [Naut.] *to come* ~, accoster; venir à quai.

aloof [ə'luwf] *adv. & adj.* à l'écart, séparé (de, *from*): *to stand* ~, se tenir à l'écart. || **aloofness** [-nəs] *n.* froideur *f*, réserve *f* (vis-à-vis de).

aloud [ə'lawd] *adv.* à haute voix, (tout) haut: *to read* ~, lire à haute voix.

alp [ælp] *n.* [montagne élevée] alpe *f. The Alps*, les Alpes *fpl.*

alphabet ['ælfəbət] *n.* alphabet *m.* || **alphabetical** [ˌælfə'bɛtɪkl̩] *adj.* alphabétique. || **alphabetically** [-ɪ] *adv.* en ordre alphabétique.

already [ol'ɹɛdɪ] *adv.* [☞ Ne pas confondre avec *all ready.*] déjà: *I've* ~ *told you*, Je vous l'ai déjà dit.

alright [ɔlɹəjt] [Fam.] cf. ALL RIGHT.

Alsace ['ælsæs] *n.* Alsace *f.* || **Alsatian** [æl'sejʃən] *adj. & n.* alsacien (*m*), -e (*f*).

also ['ɔlsow] *adv.* **1.** aussi: *I* ~, moi aussi; [emphatic] *I* ~ *saw* . . . , moi aussi, je vis . . . cf. TOO. **2.** [connective] également, de plus [☞ Never begin a Fr. sentence with *aussi* in this connection, use *de plus*]: [on theatres] *also*: au même programme.

altar ['ɔltɚ] *n.* [Rel.] autel *m*: ~ *boy*, enfant *m* de chœur; ~ *cloth*, nappe *f* d'autel.

alter ['ɔltɚ] *v. tr.* modifier; retoucher (un vêtement); [make very different] changer, remanier. || *v. intr.* changer, se modifier. || **alteration** [ɔltɚ'ejʃən] *n.* modification *f*, changement *m*; rectification *f* (d'un vêtement); [Com.] *alterations*, transformations *fpl* (d'un magasin).

altercation [ˌɑltɚ'kejʃən] *n.* altercation *f.*

alternate ['ɔltɚˌnejt] *v. tr. & intr.* alterner; [do by turns] faire chacun son tour; [Elect.] *alternating current* (*A.C.*), courant *m* alternatif, l'alternatif *m*, cf. DIRECT. || *adj.* [ɔl'tɚnət] [passive] alterné; [active] alternatif; [by turns] réciproque; [assemblies] ~ (*delegate*), suppléant *m.* || **alternately** [-lɪ] *adv.* alternativement, tour à tour. || **alternation** [ˌɔltɚ'nejʃən] *n.* alternance *f.* || **alternative** [ɔl'tɚnətɪv] *adj.* alternatif; [choice between 2 solutions] de remplacement. || *n.* [☞ choix entre 2 possibilités] alternative *f*; solution *f* /de rechange, de remplacement/.

although [ɔl'ðow] *conj.* bien que, quoique [+ *subjunc.*]: *Although I arrived late, he welcomed me*, Bien que je sois arrivé en retard, il m'a fait bon accueil; *Although* (*I am*) *young, I have been around the world*, Quoique (je sois) jeune, Tout jeune que je suis/, j'ai fait le tour du monde; *Although he respected me, he* . . . , Bien qu'il me respectât, il . . . , [or avoiding the Imperfect Subjunc.] En dépit de son respect pour moi, il. . . .

altitude ['ɔltɪˌtuwd] *n.* altitude *f.*

altogether [ˌɔltə'gɛðɚ] *adv.* **1.** [wholly] tout à fait, complètement, absolument: *He is* ~ *wrong*, → Il se trompe tout à fait, Il a complètement tort. **2.** [all included] en tout: *How many were there* ~ *?*, Combien y en avait-il en tout?

altruism [ˌɑl'tɹuwɪzm] *n.* altruisme *m.*

aluminum [ə'luwmɪnəm] *n.* aluminium *m.*

alumn|us [ə'lʌmn|əs] *pl.* **-i** [-aj] *n.* [university] diplômé *m*; ancien élève *m*, ancien *m.* || **alumn|a** [ə'lʌmn|ə] *pl.* **-ae** [-ij] *n.* diplômée *f*; ancienne élève *f*, ancienne *f.*

always ['ɔlwejz, 'ɔlwəz] *adv.* **1.** [at all times] toujours; en permanence: *The store is* ~ *open*, Le magasin est ouvert en permanence. **2.** [all the time] tout le temps, à chaque instant: *He is* ~ *fidgeting*, Il remue tout le temps.

am ['æm] cf. BE.

a.m. ['ejˌem] [= ante meridiem] © a.m.; [Fr.] du matin [☞ in France, hours are counted from 0 to 24]: *at 2* ~, à deux heures du matin [☞ on écrit aussi A.M.].

A.M. cf. M.A.

amalgamate [ə'mælgə'mejt] *v. tr. & intr.* amalgamer.

amass [ə'mæs] *v. tr.* amasser.

amateur ['æmətʃɚ] *n.* amateur *m.* || **amateurish** [-ɪʃ] *adj.* d'amateur; [Pej.] inexpérimenté.

amaze [ə'mejz] *v. tr.* étonner, surprendre, [wonder] émerveiller: *to be amazed at*, s'étonner, s'émerveiller de; [beyond words] *to be amazed*, être stupéfait. || **amazement** [-mənt] *n.* étonnement *m*; [stunning] stupeur *f.* || **amazing** [-ɪŋ] *adj.* étonnant; [very surprising] inouï.

ambassador [əm'bæsədɚ] *n.* ambassadeur *m*, ambassadrice *f.*

amber ['æmbɚ] *n.* ambre *f.* || *adj.* ambré.

ambidextrous [ˌæmbɪ'dɛkstɹəs] *adj.* ambidextre.

ambiguity [ˌæmbɪ'gjuwɪtɪ] *n.* ambiguïté *f.* || **ambiguous** [æm'bɪgjuwəs] *adj.* ambigu *m*, ambiguë *f.*

ambition [æm'bɪʃ|ən] *n.* ambition *f.* || **ambitious** [-əs] *adj.* [person, project] ambitieux: *to be* ~ *of*, ambitionner (qqch.).

amble ['æmbl̩] *v. intr.* aller l'amble.

ambulance ['æmbjələns] *n.* ambulance *f*: *Ambulance Corps*, corps *m*, service *m*/ d'ambulanciers.

ambush ['æmbuʃ] *n.* embuscade *f*, guet-apens *m*; [Fig.] embûche *f* [us. pl.]. || **ambush** *v. tr.* attirer (qqun) dans un guet-apens; surprendre (l'ennemi) dans une embuscade; [Fig.] tendre des embûches à (qqun). || *v. intr.* s'embusquer.

ameliorate [ə'mijlɪɚ,ejt] *v. tr.* améliorer. *v. intr.* s'améliorer. || **amelioration** [ə,mijlɪɚ'ejʃən] *n.* amélioration *f.*

amen ['ej'mɛn] *Int. inv.* amen.

amenable [ə'mijnəbl̩] *adj.* soumis, docile: ~ *to persuasion*, docile, ouvert/aux suggestions; [Law] responsable.

amend [ə'mɛnd] *v. tr.* [change] corriger, modifier (un texte, &c.); [improve] se corriger, (s')améliorer: *to ~ one's conduct*, s'amender. || **amendment** [-mənt] *n.* [Law] amendement *m*, rectification *f*; modification *f*; [change for the better] amélioration *f.* || **amends** [-z] *n.pl.* réparation *f*, dédommagement *m* (pour un dommage subi ou causé): [Fig.] *to make ~ for*, (se) racheter; dédommager de; réparer (une faute).

amenity [ə'mɛnɪtɪ] *n.* aménité *f*: *the amenities of a place*, ce qui fait l'agrément d'un lieu.

America [ə'mɛɚɪkə] *n.* [Geog.] l'Amérique *f*; *in/to/ ~*, en Amérique; *the Americas*, les (trois) Amériques, le Nouveau Monde; [Coll.] les États-Unis *mpl* (d'Amérique). || **American** [-n] *adj. & n.* américain, -e: [hotel] ~ *plan*, chambre *f* et pension *f.* || **Americanism** [-nɪzm] *n.* [expression, custom, &c.] américanisme *m.* || **Amerindian** [,æmɚ'ɪndɪən] *adj. & n.* amérindien: ~ *languages*, langues amérindiennes [pour les distinguer des langues indiennes]

amiable ['ejmɪəbl̩] *adj.* aimable; [good-natured] affable, ouvert. || **amiably** [-ɪ] *adv.* avec amabilité, amicalement. || **amicable** ['æmɪkəbl̩] *adj.* [doublet de AMIABLE] amical; [settlement] à l'amiable.

†**amid** [ə'mɪd], **amidst** [ə'mɪdst] *prép.* au milieu de, parmi [cf. AMONG 1.].

amiss [ə'mɪs] *adv.* mal: *to take (sth.) ~*, prendre (qqch.)/en mauvaise part, mal/. || *adj.* mal, fautif: *Is it ~ to . . . ?*, Est-ce mal de . . . ?

amity ['æmɪtɪ] *n.* amitié *f*, concorde *f*, bonne intelligence *f*: ~ *pledge*, pacte *m* d'amitié.

ammonia [ə'mown|jə] *n.* [Chem.] ammoniaque *f.* || **ammoniac** [-ɪ,æk] *adj.* ammoniac *m*, -aque *f.*

ammunition [,æmjə'nɪʃən] *collective n.* [arms] munitions *fpl*: *a round of ~*, cartouche *f*, [gun] coup *m.*

amnesia [æm'nijʒə] *n.* amnésie *f.*

amnesty ['æmnəstɪ] *n.* amnistie *f.* || *v. tr.* amnistier (un détenu).

among [ə'mʌŋ], †**amongst** [ə'mʌŋst] *prép.* **1.** [amid] parmi, au milieu de [the crowd, the trees, the spectators, &c.]: *from ~*, (du milieu) de. **2.** [with] chez, avec, parmi: *Among Frenchmen, such an opinion is rare*, Chez, Parmi/les Français, une telle opinion est rare; *He spends his time ~ his books*, Il passe son temps/avec, parmi/ses livres. **3.** [in the number of] au nombre de, parmi, entre: *Among the spectators were . . .*, Au nombre des, Parmi les/spectateurs se trouvaient . . . ; *They are ~ those who . . .*, Ils sont (du nombre) de, parmi/ceux qui . . . ; *That book is the best ~ modern novels*, Ce livre est le meilleur des romans contemporains; ~ *them*, ~ *the (whole) lot*, [persons] parmi/eux, elles/, [things] dans le nombre; *some ~ them*, [persons] certains/parmi, d'entre/ eux, [things] certains; ~ *others*, entre autres; *Blessed art thou ~ women*, Vous êtes bénie entre toutes les femmes. **4.** [between] entre: *Divide it ~ you*, Divisez-le entre vous; *They fought ~ themselves*, Ils se sont battus entre eux.

amoral ['æmɚəl] *adj.* amoral.

amorous ['æmɚəs] *adj.* amoureux; d'amour. || **amorously** [-lɪ] *adv.* amoureusement.

amortization [,æmɚtajz'ejʃən] *n.* amortissement *m.* || **amortize** ['æmɚtajz] *v. tr.* [Fin.] amortir (une dette, une hypothèque).

amount [ə'mawnt] *n.* [sum] montant *m*, somme *f*; [total] total *m*; [Fig.] quantité *f*: *a large ~ of (patience, &c.)*, une forte dose de (patience), → (avoir) beaucoup de . . . ; *to the ~ of*, jusqu'à concurrence de. || **amount** *v. intr.* se monter, s'élever (*to*, à): *The total amounted to* $100, Le total s'élevait à cent dollars; [Fig.] revenir: *It amounts to the same thing*, Cela revient au même; *It does not ~ to much*, Ce n'est pas grand'chose.

amphibian [,æm'fɪbɪən] *adj. & n.* amphibie (*m*).

amphitheatre ['æmfɪ,θijətɚ] *n.* amphithéâtre *m.*

ample ['æmpl̩] *adj.* ample, [roomy] spacieux; [sufficient] suffisant, abondant: *an ~ room*, une pièce spacieuse. || **amplifier** ['æmplɪfaj|ɚ] *n.* [Tech.] amplificateur *m.* || **amplify** *v. tr.* amplifier; [theory] développer. || **amply** ['æmplɪ] *adv.* amplement, suffisamment.

amputate ['æmpjə,tejt] *v. tr.* amputer. || **amputation** [,æmpjə'tejʃən] *n.* amputation *f.* || **amputee** ['æmpjə,tij] *n.* amputé, -e.

amuck [ə′mʌk] *adv.* [seulement dans l'expression] *to run* ~ , se mettre à courir comme un fou furieux.

amuse [ə′mjuwz] *v. tr.* amuser, divertir (qqun). || *v. intr.* (s')amuser (*oneself with*, à [+ verb], de [+ n.]). || **amusement** [-mənt] *n.* amusement *m.* || **amusing** [-ɪŋ] *adj.* amusant, [causing laughter] drôle, comique.

an [æn] [ən] cf. A.

Anabaptist [′ænə͵bæptɪst] *n.* & *adj.* anabaptiste *m.*

anachronism [ə′nækɹə͵nɪzm] *n.* anachronisme *m.*

anæmia [ə′nijm|jə] *n.* anémie *f.* || **anæmic** [-:k] *adj.* anémique.

anæsthesia [͵ænəs|′θijʒə] *n.* anesthésie *f.* || **anæsthetic** [-′θɛtɪk] *adj.* & *n.* anesthésique (*m*).

analogous [ə′nælə|gəs] *adj.* analogue (*to*, à). || **analogy** [-ʤɪ] *n.* analogie *f* (*to, with*, avec): *to draw an* ~ *from*, citer un cas semblable pris dans . . .

analysis [ə′næləsɪs] *n.* analyse *f.* || **analyze** [′ænəlajz] *v. tr.* analyser, faire l'analyse de.

anarchism [′ænɚkɪs|m] *n.* anarchisme *m.* || **anarchist** [-t] *adj.* & *n.* anarchiste (*m/f*).

anarchy [′ænɚkɪ] *n.* anarchie *f.*

anatomic [͵ænə′tɑmɪk] *adj.* anatomique.

anatomy [ə′nætəmɪ] *n.* anatomie *f.*

ancestor [′ænsɛst|ɚ] *n.* ancêtre *m*, [more personal] aïeul *m*, aïeux *mpl.* || **ancestral** [-ɹəl] *adj.* ancestral. || **ancestry** [-ɹɪ] *n.* ancêtres *mpl*, [lineage] lignage *m.*

anchor [′æŋkɚ] *n.* [Naut.] ancre *f*: *at* ~ , à l'ancre, mouillé; *to cast* ~ , jeter l'ancre, mouiller. || *v. tr. to* ~ *a ship*, mouiller, jeter l'ancre; [Fig.] (s')ancrer, (se) fixer fermement. || **anchorage** [-əʤ] *n.* mouillage *m.*

ancient [′ejnʃənt] *adj.* **1.** [pertaining to Antiquity] antique; ancien [follows *n.*]: ~ *Greece*, la Grèce ancienne. **2.** [of great age] ancien, -ne [follows *n.*]: *an* ~ *custom*, une coutume ancienne; [precedes *n.*] *the* ~ *capital of Ireland*, l'ancienne capitale de l'Irlande [e.g. no longer existing]. || *n.* Ancien *m*: *the Ancients*, les Anciens, l'Antiquité classique.

and [ænd] [ən(d)] *conj.* et; [cf. BOTH]: [special uses] *two/hundred, thousand/* ~ *three*, deux/cent, mille/trois; *more* ~ *more* (*difficult*), de plus en plus difficile; *I tried* ~ *tried*, J'ai essayé tant et plus; *I turned over* ~ *over*, Je me suis tourné et retourné; *Go* ~ *see*, Allez voir; *Try* ~ *help*, Essayez d'aider; *without eating* ~ *drinking*, sans boire ni manger; *You can't do that* ~ *not be caught*, Vous ne pourrez pas faire cela sans vous faire attraper; *coffee* ~ *milk*, du café au lait; *ham* ~ *eggs*, → des œufs au jambon.

Andes (the) [′ændɪz] *n.* les Andes *fpl.*

Andrew [′ændɹuw] *n.* = André *m.*

anecdote [′ænək͵dowt] *n.* anecdote *f.*

†**anew** [ə′njuw] *adv.* de, à/nouveau.

angel [′ejnʤ|] *n.* ange *m.* || **angelic** [æn′ʤɛlɪk] *adj.* angélique, d'ange.

anger [′æŋgɚ] *n.* colère *f*, irritation *f.* || *v. tr.* mettre (qqun) en colère, irriter (qqun). || *v. intr.* se fâcher, se mettre en colère.

angina [͵æn′ʤajnə] *n.* angine *f.*

angle¹ [′æŋg|] *n.* angle *m*; [Fig.] tournant *m* (d'une route); aspect *m* (d'une question), point *m* de vue.

angle² *v. intr.* pêcher (à la ligne): [Fig.] *to* ~ *for* (*sth.*), essayer d'attraper qqch. || **angler** [-ɚ] *n.* pêcheur *m* (à la ligne).

Anglican [′æŋglɪkən] *adj.* & *n.* [Relig.] anglican; *the* ~ *Church*, l'Église anglicane; [US] anglais.

anglicism [′æŋglɪ|sɪzm] *n.* [Ling.] anglicisme *m.* || **anglicize** [-͵sajz] *v. tr.* [to make English] (s')angliciser [☞ l'anglais peut *angliciser* des mots français en les adoptant; le français peut *s'angliciser* en adoptant un grand nombre de mots ou de tournures anglaises].

angling [′æŋglɪŋ] *n.* pêche *f* à la ligne.

Anglo- [æŋglow-] *prefix*: ~ *-Catholic Church*, l'Église *f* anglo-catholique; ~ *-Norman*, Anglo-normand *m*; ~ *-Saxon* Anglo-saxon.

angrily [′æŋgɹɪlɪ] *adv.* avec colère, cf. ANGER. || **angry** [′æŋgɹɪ] *adj.* fâché, irrité: *to be* ~ *with s.o.*, être fâché, en colère/ contre qqun; *to be* ~ *at sth.*, s'irriter de qqch.; [Fig.] *an* ~ *sky*, un ciel menaçant; ~ *words*, des paroles/de colère, enflammées/; ~ *wound*, blessure *f* irritée.

anguish [′æŋgwɪʃ] *n.* angoisse *f*; tourment *m* [usual. pl.]. || **anguished** [-t] *adj.* angoissé, tourmenté.

angular [′æŋgjəlɚ] *adj.* [Geom.] angulaire; [Fig.] anguleux.

animal [′ænɪməl] *n.* & *adj.* animal (*m*); [dumb] bête *f*: ~ *kingdom*, règne *m* animal.

animate [′ænɪ͵mejt] *v. tr.* [give life to] animer; [encourage] encourager, stimuler. || **animate(d)** *adj.* animé; [Fig.] animé, vivant: (*animated*) *cartoon*, dessins *mpl* animés. || **animation** [͵ænɪ′mejʃən] *n.* animation *f*, [Fig.] verve *f*, vie *f.*

animosity [ˌænɪ'mɑsɪtɪ], also **animus** ['ænɪməs] *n.* animosité *f* (*for*, contre).
ankle ['æŋkl] *n.* cheville *f.*
annals ['ænəlz] *n.pl.* annales *fpl.*
annex [æ'nɛks] *v. tr.* (s')annexer (un territoire); joindre (un document à une lettre). || *n.* ['ænɛks] annexe *f.* || **annexation** [ˌænɛks'ejʃən] *n.* annexion *f* (d'un territoire). || **annexed** *adj.* [Com.] (document) ci-joint, (lettre) ci-jointe.
annihilate [ə'najɪˌlejt] *v. tr.* anéantir (un ennemi), annihiler (les efforts de qqun). || **annihilation** [əˌnajɪ'lejʃən] *n.* anéantissement *m.*
anniversary [ˌænɪ'vɚsərɪ] *n. & adj.* anniversaire (*m*) (de naissance, &c.).
annotate ['ænəˌtejt] *v. tr.* [comment] annoter (un texte), mettre des notes.
announce [ə'nawns] *v. tr.* annoncer (*to*, à): *to ~ a guest*, annoncer un invité. || **announcement** [-mənt] *n.* avis *m*; annonce *f* (à la radio, &c.). || **announcer** [-ɚ] *n.* [Radio] speaker *m*, © annonceur *m*: *woman ~*, speakerine *f.*
annoy [ə'noj] *v. tr.* contrarier, importuner; [hurt] harasser (un ennemi), vexer (qqun). || **annoyance** [-əns] *n.* désagrément *m*; [bother] ennui *m*; [stronger] contrariété *f.* || **annoying** [-ɪŋ] *adj.* ennuyeux; [disturbing] contrariant, fâcheux: *This is very ~*, C'est un contretemps fâcheux.
annual ['ænjuwəl] *adj.* annuel. || *n.* [publication] annuaire *m.* || **annually** [-ɪ] *adv.* annuellement.
annuity [ə'njuwɪtɪ] *n.* annuité *f*: *life ~*, pension *f* viagère.
annul [ə'nʌl] *v. tr.* [-ll-] annuler (un contrat); abroger (une loi); casser (un jugement).
annunciation [əˌnʌnsɪ'ejʃən] *n.* annonciation *f.*
anoint [ə'nojnt] *v. tr.* oindre.
anomalous [ə'nɑməl|əs] *adj.* anormal. || **anomalously** [-əslɪ] *adv.* d'une manière anormale.
anonymous [ə'nɑnɪməs] *adj.* anonyme. || **anonymously** [-lɪ] *adv.* anonymement, → d'une façon anonyme.
another [ə'nʌðɚ] *adj. & pron.* cf. OTHER: [different] un(e) autre; [similar] un(e) /autre, second(e); [additional] encore un(e): *One said this, ~ said that*, Tel disait ceci, tel autre disait cela; *They hate one ~*, Ils se détestent (les uns les autres, l'un l'autre); *with one ~*, les uns avec les autres.
answer ['ænsɚ] *n.* réponse *f*: *to give an ~*, → répondre; *in ~ to*, en réponse à (votre lettre du . . . , &c.); [oral] réponse *f*, réplique *f*; [Fig.] *to know all the answers*, avoir réponse à tout; [to a problem] solution *f* (d'un problème). || **answer** *v. intr.* **1.** répondre (à qqun, à une lettre): *to ~ s.o.'s question*, répondre à une question (posée par qqun). **2.** [Fig.] *to ~ the door*, aller ouvrir; *to ~ the call*, répondre à l'appel (*to*, de); répondre à (l'attente de, &c.): *to ~ the purpose*, faire l'affaire; *to ~ for* (*sth., s.o.*), répondre de (qqch., qqun).
ant [ænt] *n.* fourmi *f*; *~ -hill*, fourmilière *f.*
antagonism [æn'tægə|nɪzm] *n.* antagonisme *m*, hostilité *f.* || **antagonize** [-ˌnajz] *v. tr.* blesser, offusquer (qqun), rendre (qqun) hostile: *Don't ~ him*, Ne vous en faites pas un ennemi.
Antarctic [ænt'ɑɚtɪk] *adj. & n.* antarctique (*m*).
ante- [æntɪ-] *préf.* anté-, pré-, anti-, as in: *antecedent adj. & n.*, antécédent (*m*). || *antechamber n.* antichambre *f.* || *antedate* (a cheque) *v. tr.* antidater. || *antenatal adj.* prénatal. || *anteroom n.* antichambre *f*, salle *f* d'attente.
antelope ['æntəlowp] *n.* antilope *f.*
antenna [æn'tɛnə] *pl.* **-s** *n.* antenne *f*: *TV ~*, antenne de TV.
anthem ['ænθəm] *n.* hymne *m* (national); [Rel.] antienne *f.*
anthology [ˌæn'θɑlədʒɪ] *n.* anthologie *f.*
Anthony ['ænθənɪ] *n.* Antoine *m.*
anthropology [ˌænθɹə'pɑlədʒɪ] *n.* anthropologie *f.*
anti- [æntɪ-] *préf.* [= contre, anti-] as in: *antibiotic*, antibiotique *m*; *antifreeze*, antigel *m*; *antipathy*, antipathie *f*; *antiseptic*, antiseptique *m.*
anticipate [æn'tɪsɪˌpejt] *v. tr.* **1.** [foresee] prévoir (à l'avance); [ahead of time] anticiper. **2.** [expect] s'attendre à, compter que; [eagerly] se promettre (du plaisir, de bonnes vacances, &c.). **3.** [be ahead] devancer, prévenir. || **anticipation** [ænˌtɪsɪ'pejʃən] *n.* anticipation *f*, prévision *f.*
anticlerical [ˌæntɪ'klɛɚɪkl̩] *adj.* anticlérical. || **anticlericalism** [-ɪzm] *n.* anticléricalisme *m.*
anticlimax [ˌæntɪ'klajmæks] *n.* [Gram.] anticlimax *m*; [Fam.] dégringolade *f.*
antics ['æntɪks] *n.pl.* bouffonneries *fpl*, cabrioles *fpl.*
antidote ['æntɪˌdowt] *n.* antidote *m.*
Antilles, the [æn'tilijz] *n.* [Geog.] les Antilles *fpl*: *the/Greater, Lesser/ ~*, les /Grandes, Petites/Antilles [cf. WEST].

antipathy [æn'tɪpəθɪ] *n.* antipathie *f* (*to*, pour).

antiquary ['æntɪ|ˌkwɛəɪ] *n.* [×] amateur *m* de choses anciennes. ‖ **antiquated** [-ˌkwejtəd] *adj.* vieilli, démodé. ‖ **antique** [æn'tijk] *adj.* **1.** [old fashioned] ancien [cf. × ANCIENT]. **2.** [ancient Greece & Rome] antique. ‖ *n.pl.* antiquités *fpl*: ~ *dealer*, antiquaire *m.* ‖ **antiquity** [æn'tɪkwətɪ] *n.* l'antiquité *f*, le monde *m* antique.

antiseptic [ˌæntɪ'septɪk] *adj.* & *n.* antiseptique (*m*).

antithesis [ˌæn'tɪθəsɪs] *n.* antithèse *f.* ‖ **antithetical** [ˌæntɪ'θɛtɪkḷ] *adj.* antithétique.

antler ['æntlər] *n.* andouiller *m.*

anvil ['ænvḷ] *n.* enclume *f.*

anxiety [æŋ'zajətɪ] *n.* **1.** [anxious feeling] inquiétude *f*, anxiété *f.* **2.** [desire] vif désir *m*, ambition *f* (de faire qqch.). ‖ **anxious** ['æŋkʃəs] *adj.* [× avoid Fr. *anxieux*] **1.** inquiet (*for*, de), angoissé. **2.** [Fig.] désireux, → désirer vivement: *I am* (*most*) ~ *to . . .*, Je désire vivement . . ., Je tiens beaucoup à ce que . . . [+ subjunc.]; *He is* ~ *to see you*, → Il vous attend avec impatience. ‖ **anxiously** [-lɪ] *adv.* avec inquiétude; avec impatience, vivement.

any ['ɛnɪ] *adj.* **1.** [interrog., = *some*] du, de la, de l', des: *Have you* (*got*) ~ *bread*/ ~ *oranges*/?, Avez-vous/du pain, des oranges/? **2.** [neg., = *no*] ne . . . pas de; ne . . . aucun(e): *I don't have* ~ *bread*/ ~ *oranges*/, Je n'ai pas/de pain, d'oranges/; *You won't have* ~ *difficulty*, Vous n'aurez /pas de, aucune/difficulté; *without* ~ *reason* (*at all*), sans aucune raison. **3.** [indef., = *no matter which*] n'importe quel(le); [after neg.] ne . . . aucun(e); quelconque: *You may choose* ~ *book*, Vous pouvez choisir n'importe quel livre; *You won't find it in* ~ *book* (*at all*), Vous ne le trouverez dans aucun livre; × *You shouldn't read just* ~ *book*, Vous ne devriez pas lire n'importe quel livre; *Take* ~ *card*, Tirez une carte quelconque. **4.** [indef. = *every*] tout: *Any doctor*/*who knows his profession, worthy of the name*/ *will tell you so*, Tout docteur qui connaît son métier, digne du nom/vous le dira; [cf. MOMENT, PRICE, RATE]. **5.** [condit. = *the slightest*] le moindre: *If you have* ~ *difficulty* (*at all*) *. . .*, Si vous avez la moindre difficulté . . . . ‖ *pron.* **1.** [interrog.] en: *Do you see* ~ (*of it*/*them*/)*?*, En voyez-vous?. **2.** [neg.] en: *I don't see* ~ (*of it*/*them*/), Je n'en vois pas. **3.** [indef.] n'importe lequel; tout: *Any* (*of them*) *will do*, N'importe lequel fera l'affaire; *Keep* ~ (*of it*/*them*/) *you find*, Gardez/tout ce, tous ceux, toutes celles/que vous trouverez. ‖ *adv.* [before a comparative, not translated]: *I don't want* ~ *more*, Je n'en veux plus.

anybody ['ɛnɪˌbʌdɪ], **anyone** ['ɛnɪˌwʌn] *pron.* **1.** [interrog.] quelqu'un: *Do you see* ~ *?*, Voyez-vous quelqu'un? **2.** [neg.] ne . . . personne: *I don't see* ~, Je ne vois personne; *without* ~, sans personne. **3.** [indef.] n'importe qui; qui que ce/soit, fût/; quiconque, tout le monde, tous (ceux qui): *Anybody can do it*, N'importe qui peut le faire; *That doesn't suit* ~, Cela ne convient à personne; *She won't go out with just* ~, Elle ne veut pas sortir avec n'importe qui; *Anybody likes him*, Tout le monde l'aime; *Anyone who wants to come must hurry*, Tous ceux qui veulent venir, doivent se dépêcher.

anyhow ['ɛnɪˌhaw] *adv.* **1.** [no matter how] n'importe comment: *He does his work* ~, Il fait son travail n'importe comment; *Anyhow he does it, his work is worthless*, N'importe comment il le fait, son travail ne vaut rien. **2.** [nevertheless] quand même; *I know it's raining, but I'm going* ~, Je sais bien qu'il pleut, mais j'y vais quand même. **3.** [at any rate] en tout cas, de toute façon; quoi qu'il en soit; enfin: *Anyhow, it isn't snowing*, En tout cas, il ne neige pas; *Anyhow, I knew it already*, De toute façon, je le savais déjà; *Anyhow, we've got to do sth*, Quoi qu'il en soit, il faut faire qqch.; *Anyhow, to cut a long story short . . .*, Enfin, pour abréger . . . . **4** [after questions] enfin: *What is he doing* ~ *?*, Qu'est-ce qu'il fait enfin?

anyone ['ɛnɪˌwʌn] cf. ANYBODY.

anything ['ɛnɪˌθɪŋ] *pron.* **1.** [interrog.] quelque chose: *Do you see* ~ *?*, Vous voyez qqch.? **2.** [neg.] ne . . . rien: *I don't see* ~, Je ne vois rien; *without* ~, sans rien. **3.** [indef.] n'importe quoi, quoi que ce/soit, fût/; tout (ce que): *He eats* ~, Il mange n'importe quoi; *Don't meddle with* ~, Ne touchez/à rien, pas à quoi que ce soit/; × *He won't be happy with just* ~, Il ne se contentera pas de n'importe quoi; *He likes* ~, → Tout lui plaît; *Pay attention to* ~ *he says*, Faites attention à tout ce qu'il dit; *It's as simple as* ~, C'est simple comme tout; *He's working like* ~, Il travaille tant qu'il peut. **4.** ne . . . rien: *Have you ever seen* ~ *so beautiful?*, Avez-vous jamais rien vu d'aussi beau?

anyway ['ɛnɪ,wɛj] cf. ANYHOW.

anywhere ['ɛnɪ,wɛɚ] *adv.* **1.** [interrog.] quelque part: *Have you seen it ~ ?*, L'avez-vous vu quelque part?. **2.** [neg.] ne . . . nulle part: *I haven't seen it ~*, Je ne l'ai vu nulle part. **3.** [indef.] n'importe où; ne . . . nulle part; partout (où), où que [+ *subjunc.*]: *Leave it ~*, Laissez-le n'importe où; *I can't find it ~ (at all)*, Je ne le trouve nulle part; *I can't leave it just ~*, Je ne peux pas le laisser n'importe où; *You can see that ~*, → Cela se voit partout; *Anywhere I go, I see him*, Partout où je vais, Où que j'aille, /je le vois.

apart [ə'pɑɚt] *adv.* **1.** à l'écart, à part; séparé: *to stand ~*, se tenir à l'écart: *to move ~*, s'écarter. **2.** (mettre) en pièces; distinguer: *to take . . . ~*, démonter, mettre en pièces; *to come ~*, se défaire, tomber en morceaux; *to tell (two things) ~*, distinguer (deux choses) l'une de l'autre.

apartment [ə'pɑɚtmənt] *n.* [abbr. *apt.*, in Fr. *App.*] **1.** pièce *f*, chambre *f* (dans un logement); © [abus.] appartement *m*. **2.** [set of rooms] appartement *m*: *~ house*, maison *f* de rapport, © conciergerie *f*.

apathy ['æpəθɪ] *n.* apathie *f*.

ape [ejp] *n.* grand singe *m*; [ext.] singe *m*, guenon *f*. ‖ *v. tr.* singer, imiter (qqun).

aperture ['æpɚtʃɚ] *n.* orifice *m*; [camera, &c.] ouverture *f*; [Ling.] aperture *f*.

apex ['æpɛks] *n.* sommet *m*.

aphorism ['ɛjfɚɪzm] *n.* aphorisme *m*.

apiece [ə'pijs] *adv.* (la) pièce *inv.*, chacun: *a dollar ~*, un dollar pièce.

apologetic [ə'pɑlə|,dʒɛtɪk] *adj.* prêt à s'excuser, humble. ‖ **apologize** [-,dʒəjz] *v. intr.* s'excuser (*for*, de; *to*, auprès de), présenter, faire/ses excuses. ‖ **apology** [-dʒɪ] *n.* **1.** excuse *f* (*for*, de) [☞ usually pl. as in *I demand an ~*, J'exige des excuses]. **2.** [defense] apologie *f*.

apostle [ə'pɑsl̩] *n.* apôtre *m*. ‖ **apostleship** *n.* apostolat *m*. ‖ **apostolic(al)** [æpə'stɑlɪk(l̩)] *adj.* apostolique.

apostrophe [ə'pɑstɹə,fɪ] *n.* apostrophe *f*.

appal(l) [ə'pɔl] *v. tr.* terrifier, épouvanter. consterner, atterrer.

Appalachians [,æpə'lejʃəns] *n.* = *the Appalachian Mountains*, les Appalaches *fpl*.

appalling [ɚ'pɔlɪŋ] *adj.* terrifiant, épouvantable.

apparatus [æpɚ'ætəs] *n.pl. inv.* & **-es** appareil *m*; [piece of machinery] dispositif *m*.

apparel [ə'pæɚl̩] *n.* [coll.] vêtements *mpl*.

apparent [ə'pæɚənt] *adj.* apparent; [obvious] évident; *heir ~*, héritier *m* présomptif. ‖ **apparently** [-lɪ] *adv.* en apparence, visiblement; [Fig.] apparemment.

apparition [,æpɚ'ɪʃən] *n.* apparition *f*, fantôme *m*.

appeal [ə'pijl] *v. intr.* **1.** [Jur.] faire, interjeter/appel (à, *to*); en appeler (de, *from*); réclamer (contre, *from*). **2.** avoir recours (à, *de*). **3.** se sentir attiré (par, vers): *It appeals to me*, Cela/me plait, m'attire/. ‖ **appealing** [-ɪŋ] *adj.* touchant, attirant.

appear [ə'pijɚ] *v. intr.* [come in sight] apparaître, se manifester; [seem] paraître, sembler, avoir l'air; [book] paraître, sortir; [on the stage] se produire; [Court] comparaître (devant, *before*): *He appears intelligent*, Il/semble, paraît, a l'air/ intelligent; *He appeared to have understood*, Il/paraissait, avait l'air, [less certain] semblait/avoir compris; *It appears that . . .* [true], Il paraît que + indic., [not true] Il semble que + subjunc.; *It appears to me that . . .*, [certain] Il me paraît que + indic., [less certain] Il me semble que + indic.; *(so) it appears*, à ce qu'il paraît. ‖ **appearance** [-əns] *n.* [act] apparition *f*; [sight] apparence *f*; aspect *m*: *to put in an ~*, faire acte de présence; [book] publication *f*; [Théâ.] représentation *f*: *first ~*, début(s) *m(pl)*; [Jur.] comparution *f* (devant un tribunal); *by all appearances*, selon toute apparence; *to keep up appearances*, sauver les apparences.

appease [ə'pijz] *v. tr.* apaiser, tranquilliser, calmer. ‖ **appeasement** [-mənt] *n.* apaisement *m*, conciliation *f*.

appendage [ə'pɛndɪdʒ] *n.* accessoire *m*.

appendicitis [ə,pɛndɪ'sajtɪs] *n.* appendicite *f*.

appendix [ə'pɛndɪks] *n.* appendice *m*.

appertain [,æpɚ'tejn] *v. intr.* se rapporter (*to*, à).

appetite ['æpətaj|t] *n.* appétit *m*; [Fig.] soif *f*, désir *m* (de, *for*). ‖ **appetizer** [-zɚ] *n.* [drink] apéritif *m*; [Food] hors-d'œuvres *mpl*. ‖ **appetizing** [-zɪŋ] *adj.* appétissant; [Fig.] alléchant.

applaud [ə'plɑ|d] *v. tr.* applaudir (qqun). ‖ *v. intr.* applaudir à (une idée); approuver. ‖ **applause** [-s] *n.* [Coll.] applaudissements *mpl*.

apple ['æpl̩] *n.* pomme *f*: *~ tree*, pommier *m*; *~ jack*, alcool *m* de cidre; [Fr.] calvados *m*; [Fig.] *the ~ of o.'s eyes*, la prunelle *f* de ses yeux. ‖ **apple pie** *n.* © tarte *f* aux pommes: [Fig.] *in ~ order*, en ordre parfait. ‖ **apple sauce** *n.* compote *f*, marmelade *f*/de pommes;

[Sl.] blague *f*, baratin *m*. || **apple turnover** *n*. chausson *m* aux pommes.

appliance [ə'plajəns] *n*. appareil *m*, dispositif *m*: *electrical* ~, accessoire *m*, appareil *m*/électrique; *household appliances*, appareillage *m* électrique; appareil électroménager.

applicable ['æplɪk|əbl̩] *adj*. applicable, approprié (à, *to*). || **applicant** [-ənt] *n*. postulant *m*, candidat *m*, [Jur.] demandeur *m*, demanderesse *f*. || **application** [æplɪ'kejʃən] *n*. **1.** application *f* (d'un enduit vernis). **2.** demande *f* d'emploi, candidature *f*, démarche *f*: *to make an* ~ (*for the post of*), poser sa candidature (au poste de . . .); *letter of* ~, demande *f* d'emploi. || **apply** [ə'plaj] *v. tr*. appliquer (un vernis, une règle, &c.). || *v. intr*. **1.**: *to* ~ *for* (*a job*), faire une demande (d'emploi), solliciter/poser sa candidature à/un poste; *to* ~ *to*, s'adresser à. **2.** [rule] s'appliquer (à, *to*).

appoint [ə'pojnt] *v. tr*. [office] désigner, nommer (à, *to*); [time] assigner (un temps); [prescribe] établir, instituer; [set time] décider, convenir (d'une heure, d'un rendez-vous); [equip] équiper, meubler: *well-appointed*, bien/équipé, monté, installé/. || **appointment** [-mənt] *n*. nomination *f* (à un poste); [position] situation *f*; [time] rendez-vous *m* (chez le coiffeur, le dentiste, &c.); *appointments*, installation *f*, équipement *m*.

apportion [ə'pɔɚʃən] *v. tr*. répartir.

appraisal [ə'pɹejz|əl] *n*. estimation *f*, évaluation *f*. || **appraise** *v. tr*. évaluer, estimer. || **appraiser** [-ɚ] *n*. expert *m*, évaluateur *m*: *official* ~, [Fr.] commissaire-priseur *m*.

appreciable [ə'pɹijʃ|əbl] *adj*. appréciable. || **appreciate** [-ɪˌejt] *v. tr*. **1.** apprécier (une qualité, une valeur, un art). **2.** [be thankful for] être reconnaissant à qqun de: *I would* ~ *it if you would . . .*, J'aimerais que vous [+ *subj*.]. || *v. intr*. [rise in value] augmenter (de valeur), prendre de la valeur. || **appreciation** [əˌpɹijʃɪ'ejʃən] *n*. appréciation *f*; [Comm.] hausse *f* (des prix), augmentation *f* (de valeur). || **appreciative** [ə'pɹijʃɪətɪv] *adj*. qui sait apprécier; reconnaissant.

apprehend [ˌæpɹɪ'hɛn|d] *v. tr*. arrêter, appréhender (un criminel); saisir, comprendre (un texte); appréhender, craindre (une mauvaise nouvelle). || **apprehension** [-ʃən] *n*. [arrest] arrestation *f*; [dread] crainte *f*; [understanding] compréhension *f*. || **apprehensive** [-sɪv] *adj*. inquiet: *to be* ~ *of*, craindre.

apprentice [ə'pɹɛntɪs] *n*. apprenti (plombier, menuisier, &c.); [Fig.] élève *m* & *f*, débutant *m*. || **apprenticeship** [-ˌʃɪp] *n*. apprentissage *m*.

approach [ə'pɹowtʃ] *n*. [action] approche *f*; [access] entrée *f*, accès *m* (à, *to*); [Fig.] façon *f* de procéder, manière *f* de voir, point de vue *m*: *The Latin* ~ *to T.V.* → La façon dont les peuples latins envisagent la télévision. || *npl*. abords *mpl* (d'une propriété); [Fig.] avances *fpl*. || *v. tr*. approcher, aborder (qqun, une question); s'approcher de (qqun, qqch.).

approbation [ˌæpɹə'bejʃən] *n*. approbation *f*.

appropriate [ə'pɹowpɹɪət] *adj*. approprié, indiqué. || *v. tr*. [ə'pɹowpɹɪˌejt] affecter, attribuer (à, *to*). [take for o.s.] s'approprier. || **appropriation** [əˌpɹowpɹɪ'ejʃən] *n*. **1.** appropriation *f*, prise *f* de possession; **2.** [Admin.] sommes *fpl*; crédits *mpl* budgétaires.

approval [ə'pɹuwv|l] *n*. approbation *f*, ratification *f* (d'une décision): *on* ~, à condition, à l'essai. || **approve** *v. tr*. [commend] approuver; ratifier (un projet); [sanction] consentir à.

approximate [ə'pɹɑksɪmət] *adj*. approximatif; [very near] proche, approché. || *v. tr*. [ə'pɹɑksɪˌmejt] approcher (de); [come near] se rapprocher de (qqch.). || **approximately** [ə'pɹɑksɪmətlɪ] *adv*. à peu près, approximativement.

apricot ['æpɹɪkɑt] *n*. abricot *m*.

April ['ejpɹɪl] *n*. avril *m*: ~ *fool joke*, poisson *m* d'avril; *April 15, 1961*, le 15 avril 1961; *Monday, April the 15th*, (le) lundi 15 avril; *in* ~, en avril, au mois d'avril.

apron ['ejpɹən] *n*. tablier *m*.

apt. [= APARTMENT].

apt [æpt] *adj*. enclin, porté (à, *to*); [quick to learn] apte (à, *to*); doué (pour, *to*); [fitting] qui vient à propos, pertinent. || **aptitude** [-ɪˌtjuwd] *n*. aptitude *f*, talent *m*, habileté *f*: *scholastic* ~, aptitude à l'étude.

aquarium [ə'kwɛɚɪəm] *n*. aquarium *m*. || **aquatic** [ə'kwɑtɪk] *adj*. & *n*. [plante, sport] aquatique. || **aqueduct** ['ækwəˌdʌkt] *n*. aqueduc *m*.

Arab ['æɚəb] *n*. Arabe *m/f*. || *adj*.: *the* ~ *League*, la Ligue arabe. || **Arabia** [ə'ɹejbɪə] *n*. Arabie *f*. || **Arabian** [-n] *adj*. arabe, d'Arabie: *the* ~ *sea*, la mer d'Oman; *the* ~ *nights*, les mille et une nuits. || **Arabic** ['æɚəbɪk] *adj*. [language] (l')arabe *m*; [figures] chiffre *m* arabe.

arable ['æɚəbl̩] *adj*. arable.

arbiter ['ɑɚbajtɚ] *n*. arbitre *m*. || **arbitrament**

[ɑɚ'bɪtɹəmənt] *n.* arbitrage *m*, sentence *f.* || **arbitrary** ['ɑɚbɪ|ˌtɹɛɚɪ] *adj.* arbitraire; sommaire. || **arbitrate** [-ˌtɹejt] *v. tr.* arbitrer, juger. || **arbitration** [ˌɑɚbɪ'tɹejʃən] *n.* arbitrage *m.* || **arbitrator** ['ɑɚbɪˌtɹejtɚ] *n.* [Jur.] arbitre *m*, juge *m*.

arbour ['ɑɚbɚ] *n.* tonnelle *f.*

arc [ɑɚk] *n.* [Elect.] arc *m*: ~ *welding*, soudure *f* à l'arc. || **arcade** [ɑɚ'kejd] *n.* arcades *fpl*, passage *m*.

arch[1] [ɑɚʧ] *n.* [bridge] arche *f*; [monument] arc *m* (de triomphe, &c.); [Arch.] voûte *f*, cintre *m*; [foot] cambrure *f.* || *v. tr.* arquer; voûter. || **arch**[2] *adj.* **1.** archi-, principal, grand; [Pej.] fieffé. **2.** espiègle, moqueur.

archaic [ˌɑɚ'kejɪk] *adj.* archaïque.

archangel ['ɑɚkˌejnʤl] *n.* archange *m.* || **archbishop** [aɚtʃ'bɪʃəp] *n.* archevêque *m.*

archipelago [ˌɑɚkɪ'pɛləgow] *n.* archipel *m.*

architect ['ɑɚkɪtɛk|t] *n.* architecte *m*: *landscape* ~, architecte *m* paysagiste. || **architecture** [-ʧɚ] *n.* architecture *f.*

archives ['ɑɚkajvz] *n.pl.* [Adm.] archives *fpl.*

archway ['ɑɚʧˌwej] *n.* voûte *f*, portail *m*.

Arctic ['ɑɚtɪk] *n.* & *adj.* l'Arctique (*m*): *the* ~ *Ocean*, l'Océan *m* (glacial) Arctique; *arctics*, bottes *f* polaires.

ardent ['ɑɚdənt] *adj.* ardent, passionné. || **ardour** ['ɑɚdɚ] *n.* ardeur *f*, zèle *m*.

arduous ['ɑɚdjuwəs] *adj.* ardu, pénible.

are cf. BE.

area ['ɛɚɪə] *n.* [Geom.] aire *f*, surface *f*; [region] région *f*; espace *m*; [Fig.] domaine *m*: *burnt-over* ~, © brûlis *m*, brûlés *mpl*, bois *mpl* brûlés.

arena [ə'ɹijnə] *n.* stade *m*; [Sport] © aréna *f*, patinoire *f*; [Fr.] arène *f.*

aren't [ɑɚnt] are not, cf. TO BE; also [Sub-standard] *ain't*.

argue ['ɑɚgjuw] *v. intr.* argumenter (pour, contre qqch.), discuter (avec qqun), disputer (sur qqch.). || *v. tr.* soutenir, discuter (une question); débattre (un point); soutenir (une chose). || **argument** ['ɑɚgjəmənt] *n.* [reasoning] argument *m*; [Collect.] argumentation *f*; [disagreement] dispute *f*, discussion *f*; [debate] débat *m.* || **argumentative** [ˌɑɚgjə'mɛntətɪv] *adj.* raisonneur, qui aime à discutailler.

arid ['æɚɪd] *adj.* aride, sec. || **aridity** [æɚ'ɪdɪtɪ] *n.* aridité *f*, sécheresse *f.*

aright [ə'ɹajt] *adv.* bien, juste.

arise [ə'ɹajz], **arose** [ə'ɹowz], **arisen** [ə'ɹɪzn̩] *v. intr.* survenir, s'élever; [result] provenir, résulter (*from*, de).

aristocracy [ˌæɚɪs'tɑkɹəsɪ] *n.* aristocratie *f*, élite *f.* || **aristocrat** [æ'ɹɪstəkɹæt] *n.* aristocrate *m* & *f.* || **aristocratic** [ˌæɹɪstə'kɹætɪk] *adj.* aristocratique.

arithmetic [ə'ɹɪθmətɪk] *n.* arithmétique *f.*

ark [ɑɚk] *n.* [Bible] *Noah's* ~, l'arche *f* de Noé.

arm[1] [ɑɚm] *n.* bras *m*: *at* ~ *'s length*, → à bout de bras; ~ *in* ~, bras dessus, bras dessous; ~ *band*, brassard *m.* || **arm**[2] *n.* [weapon] arme *f.* || *v. tr.* armer (qqun). || *v. intr.* s'armer (pour, *for*). || **armament** [-əmənt] *n.* armement *m*: *conventional* ~, armement *m* de type classique. || **armature** [-əʧɚ] *n.* armature *f*; [Elect.] induit *m.*

arm-band ['ɑɚmˌbænd] *n.* brassard *m.*

armchair [-ˌtʃɛɚ] *n.* fauteuil *m.* || **armful** [-ˌfʊl] brassée *f.*

armistice [-ɪstɪs] *n.* armistice *f.*

armour [-ɚ] *n.* armure *f*, cuirasse *f*, blindage *m* (d'un véhicule): *a suit of* ~, (une) armure. || *v. tr.* blinder, cuirasser (un véhicule, &c.). || **armoured** [-ɚd] *adj.* blindé, cuirassé. || **armoury** [-ɚɪ] *n.* armurerie *f*; arsenal *m*, caserne *f.*

armpit [-ˌpɪt] *n.* [Anat.] aisselle *f.*

army ['ɑɚmɪ] *n.* armée *f*; [crowd] multitude *f.* || *adj.* militaire; de l'armée.

aroma [ə'ɹowmə] *n.* arome *m.* || **aromatic** [ˌæɚə'mætɪk] *adj.* aromatique. || **aromatize** [ə'ɹowməˌtajz] *v. tr.* parfumer, aromatiser.

arose cf. ARISE.

around [ə'ɹawnd] [cf. also ABOUT] *adv.* autour; alentour: *a house with a fence (all)* ~ *(it)*, une maison avec une barrière (tout) autour; *to roam* ~, rôder alentour; [Fam.] *I saw him* ~, Je l'ai vu ça et là; [see also under other verbs]. || *prép.* autour de: ~ *the house*, autour de la maison; *the men* ~ *him*, → les hommes qui l'entourent; ~ *6 o'clock*, vers six heures.

arouse [ə'ɹawz] *v. tr.* éveiller, réveiller (l'enthousiasme); susciter (l'intérêt); réveiller, secouer (qqun).

arpent ['ɑɚpənt] © *n.* arpent *m*.

arraign [ə'rejn] *v. tr.* traduire (*before a court*, devant un tribunal).

arrange [ə'ɹejnʤ] *v. tr.* arranger, disposer; [settle] régler (une affaire); [come to an agreement] convenir de. || **arrangement** [-mənt] *n.* arrangement *m*, préparatif *m*; combinaison *f* (d'objets, &c.): *make arrangements*, prendre des dispositions.

array [ə'ɹej] *v. tr.* ranger, disposer; [adorn] orner. || *n.* [battle] ordre *m*, formation *f*; [force] troupe *f.* || **arrear** [ə'ɹijɚ] *n.* retard *m*: *in* ~, arriéré; *arrears npl.* arriéré *m*; [Com.] arrérages *mpl.*

arrest [ə'ɹɛst] *n.* arrestation *f*: *to put under*

~ , arrêter qqun; [Mil.] mettre aux arrêts *mpl.* || *v. tr.* **1.** arrêter (qqun, qqch.); [stop] prévenir (un danger); [Jur.] surseoir (à un jugement). **2.** retenir (l'attention de qqun): *an arresting personality*, une personnalité attachante.

arrival [ə'ɹajv|l̩] *n.* [Pers., trains, &c.] arrivée *f*, [goods] arrivage *m.* || **arrive** *v. intr.* arriver, parvenir (à, *at*; dans, *in*): *to ~ at a decision*, prendre une décision; [reach] aboutir à une décision.

arrogance ['æɚəgən|s] *n.* arrogance *f.* || **arrogant** [-t] *adj.* arrogant.

arrow ['æɚow] *n.* flèche *f*: *~ head*, pointe *f* de flèche.

arsenal ['ɑɚsənəl] *n.* arsenal *m.*

arson ['ɑɚsən] *n.* incendie *m* volontaire.

art[1] [ɑɚt] *n.* **1.** art *m*; *Fine Arts*, les Beaux-Arts. **2.** artifice *m*; [Pej.] ruse *f.*

†art[2] cf. TO BE [☞ *thou art*, forme vieillie de la 2e pers. sing. indic. prés. en usage dans les prières.]

artery [-ɚɪ] *n.* [Anat.] artère *f*; [Fig.] artère, grande route *f.*

artful [-fl̩] *adj.* rusé; [clever] adroit, ingénieux.

arthritic [ˌɑɚθ|'ɹɪtɪk] *adj.* arthritique. || **arthritis** [-'ɹajtɪs] *n.* arthritisme *m.*

artichoke ['ɑɚtɪˌʧowk] *n.* artichaut *m*; *Jerusalem ~*, topinambour *m.*

article ['ɑɚtɪkl̩] *n.* [Gram., newspaper, &c.] article *m*; [Jur.] clause *f*; [item] objet *m.*

articulate [ɑɚ'tɪkjələt] *adj.* articulé, manifeste, intelligible. || *v. tr.* [ɑɚ'tɪkjəˌlejt] articuler, énoncer. || **articulation** [ˌɑɚtɪkjə'lejʃən] *n.* articulation *f.*

artifice ['ɑɚtɪfɪs] *n.* artifice *m*, ruse *f.* || **artificial** [ɑɚtɪ'fɪʃəl] *adj.* artificiel; [Pej.] feint.

artillery [ɑɚ'tɪlɚɪ] *n.* artillerie *f.* || **artilleryman** [-ˌmæn] *n.* artilleur *m.*

artisan ['ɑɚtɪˌzæn] *n.* artisan *m.*

artist [ɑɚtɪst] *n.* artiste *m/f.* || **artistic** [ɑɚ'tɪstɪk] *adj.* artistique. || **artistry** ['ɑɚtɪstɹɪ] *n.* art *m.*

artless ['ɑɚtləs] *adj.* naïf, ingénu.

as [æz, *unaccented* əz] **1.** [in the way (that)] comme: *~ always*, comme toujours; *Do ~ I do*, Faites comme moi; *Do it ~ you were told*, Faites-le comme on vous a dit de le faire. **2.** [to the degree (that)] aussi . . . (que), si . . . (que); comme: *He is (just) ~ tall / ~ I, ~ I am/*, Il est (tout) aussi grand (que moi); *Have you seen anything ~ beautiful (~ that)?*, Avez-vous jamais rien vu/d'aussi, de si/beau (que cela)?; *He isn't/ ~, so/clever (~ you think)*, Il n'est pas/aussi, si/intelligent (que vous croyez); *It's ~ easy ~ anything*, C'est facile comme tout; [cf. FAR, MUCH, WELL]. **3.** [in the role of] en; de; comme; à titre de; en tant que; en (la) qualité de: *He acted ~ a (good) father*, Il a agi en (bon) père; *He was/disguised, dressed/ ~ a pirate*, Il était/déguisé, habillé/en pirate; *Treat him ~ a friend*, Traitez-le en ami; *His job ~ teacher*, Son poste de professeur; *That serves ~ a table*, Ceci sert de table; *I use it ~ a table*, Cela me sert de table, Je m'en sers comme table; *He was admitted ~* [with the rights of] *an observer*, Il fut admis /comme, à titre d'/observateur; *As a doctor* [permanent role], *I advise you against it*, Comme médecin, je vous le déconseille; *As a neighbour* [a less usual role], *I wish I could help*, En tant que voisin, je voudrais bien pouvoir aider; *As* [in his capacity of] *chairman, he presided over the meeting*, En sa qualité de président, il présidait la réunion; *Stylistics (considered) ~ a science*, La stylistique en tant que science. **4.** [during the time that] comme, au moment où; (tout) en . . . -ant; pendant que: *As I passed the house . . .*, Comme je passais devant la maison . . . ; *(Just) ~ he reached the gate . . .*, Au moment (même) où il arriva devant la grille . . . ; [both clauses have same subject] *As I worked I listened to the radio*, [Tout] en travaillant, j'ai écouté la radio; *He lay still ~ the doctor cleaned his wound*, Il resta tranquille pendant que le médecin lui nettoyait sa blessure; *one day ~ . . .*, un jour que . . . ; *He was quite clever ~ a boy*, (Étant) enfant, Dans son enfance/, Il était très intelligent. **5.** [in proportion as] (au fur et) à mesure que: *As the hour passed, he felt increasingly nervous*, (Au fur et) à mesure que l'heure passait, il s'énervait de plus en plus; *I'll send them to you ~ they arrive*, Je vous les enverrai (au fur et) à mesure qu'ils arriveront. **6.** [because] comme, puisque; parce que: *As it's getting late, I'll have to leave you*, Comme, Puisqu'/il se fait tard, il faudra que je vous quitte; *He sat down, ~ he was tired*, Il s'assit parce qu'il était fatigué. **7.** [which] qui, que, dont; ce qui; comme: *He said the same (thing) ~ you (did)*, Il a dit la même chose que vous; *He took only such things/ ~ he found, ~ he needed/*, Il n'a pris que les choses/qu'il a trouvées, dont il avait besoin/; *He is gone, ~ is obvious*, Il est parti,/ce qui est évident, comme ça se voit/; *As you can see, I have just started*, Comme vous voyez, je viens de commencer. **8.** [avec *such*] comme, tel(le) que: *Some animals, such ~ dogs and cats, like meat*, Certains animaux/comme, tels que/les chiens et les chats, aiment la viande. **9.** [though] tout . . . que [+ *indic.*], si . . que [+ *subjonc.*]: *Brave ~ they are, they are afraid to go in*, Tout courageux qu'ils sont, Si courageux qu'ils soient/, ils ont peur d'entrer. **10.** [and so also] et . . . aussi, de même que: *He was disgusted, ~ was I*, Il était dégoûté/de même que moi, et moi aussi/. [Special uses, cf. FAR, FOLLOW, MUCH, SOON, WELL, YET. ‖ **as for** (me, &c.) quant à (moi), en ce qui (me) concerne. ‖ **as from** [cf. AS OF]. ‖ **as if** comme; comme si: *He ran ~ (he were) frightened*, Il courait comme s'il avait peur; *As if incapable of speaking...*, Comme incapable de parler . . . ; *~ to say sth.*, comme pour dire qqch.; [×] *He looks ~ he were sick*, Il a l'air malade; [×] *He/looks, seems/ ~ he were going to be sick*, → On dirait qu'il va être malade. ‖ **as is** tel quel: *I'll take it ~*, Je le prendrai tel quel. ‖ **as it is** déjà, comme ça: *Things are bad enough ~*, Les choses/vont déjà assez mal, vont assez mal comme ça/; *As it is, I'll have to work this evening too*, Les choses étant ainsi, je devrai travailler ce soir aussi. ‖ **as it were**, pour ainsi dire. ‖ **as of** (tomorrow) à partir de, à compter de (demain). ‖ **as regards** [cf. AS FOR]. ‖ **as though** [cf. AS IF]. ‖ **as to** sur, au sujet de; quant à: *He was mistaken ~ the colour of her dress*, Il s'est trompé sur la couleur de sa robe; *~ you . . .*, quant à vous . . . ‖ **so as to** (come, &c.) de façon à (venir, &c.).

asbestos [æz'bɛstəs] *n.* amiante *f.*

ascend [ə'sɛn|d] *v. tr.* gravir, monter; [mountain] faire l'ascension de; [river] remonter. ‖ *v. intr.* s'élever. ‖ **ascension** [-ʃən] *n.* ascension *f*: *~ Day*, l'Ascension *f.* ‖ **ascent** [-t] *n.* ascension *f*, montée *f.*

ascertain [ˌæsər'tejn] *v. tr.* vérifier (si), s'assurer de; [determine] s'informer (auprès de, *from*).

ascetic [ə'sijtɪk] *adj.* ascétique.

ascribe [ə'skɹajb] *v. tr.* attribuer (*to*, à). ‖ **ascription** [ə'skɹɪpʃən] *n.* attribution *f.*

ash[1] [æʃ] *n.* cendre *f*: *~ -coloured*, cendré; *~ tray*, cendrier *m*; [Rel.] *Ash Wednesday*, Mercredi *m* des Cendres. ‖ **ashes,** *npl.* cendres *fpl* (du foyer); [Fig.] dépouille mortelle.

ash[2] *n.* [Bot.] frêne *m*: (*American*) *mountain ~*, sorbier *m* (d'Amérique); *white ~*, frêne *m* d'Amérique.

ashamed [ə'ʃejmd] *adj.* qui a honte (*of*, de), honteux: *to be ~*, → avoir honte *f* [cf. SHAME].

ashen ['æʃn̩] *adj.* couleur *f* de cendre.

ashore [ə'ʃɔər] *adv.* [Naut.] à terre, sur terre: *to run ~*, (s')échouer; *to go ~*, débarquer.

Asia ['ejʒə] *n.* [Geog.] l'Asie *f*: *~ Minor*, l'Asie Mineure. ‖ **Asiatic** [ˌejʒɪ'ætɪk], **Asian** ['ejʒən] *adj. & n.* asiatique *m, f.*

aside [ə'sajd] *adv.* à part, à l'écart, de côté: *to put one's troubles ~*, mettre ses ennuis de côté; *~ from*, outre, en plus de; [Fam.] à l'exception de: *joking ~*, plaisanterie à part. ‖ *n.* [Théât.] aparté *m.*

ask [æsk] *v. intr.* [for sth.] demander (qqch. à qqun): *to ~ for help*, demander du secours; *to ~ s.o. to dinner*, inviter qqun à dîner; *He was asked to speak*, On le pria de prononcer un discours; *to ~ after*, demander des nouvelles de; [Fig.] *to be asking for sth.*, aller au devant des ennuis, © se mettre au blanc. ‖ *v. tr.* [a question] poser (une question), demander: *Why don't you ~ ?*, Pourquoi ne demandez-vous pas?; *Ask him*, Demandez (-le)-lui, Interrogez-le.

askance [ə'skæns] *adv.* de travers: *to look ~ at*, regarder de travers.

askew [ə'skjuw] *adv.* obliquement, de travers.

asleep [ə'slijp] *adj. & adv.* endormi; [Fig.] engourdi: *to fall ~*, s'endormir; *to be ~*, dormir; *to be fast ~*, dormir à poings fermés.

asparagus [ə'spærəgəs] *n. coll.* asperges *fpl*: *a stick of ~*, une asperge.

aspect ['æspɛkt] *n.* aspect *m*, air *m* (d'une personne, &c.); orientation *f*, exposition *f* (d'une fenêtre au soleil), face *f* (d'un mur à l'ouest, à l'est).

aspen ['æspən] *n.* [Bot.] peuplier *m*, tremble *m.*

aspersion [ə'spərʒən] *n.* aspersion *f*; [Fig.] propos *m* défavorable: *to cast ~ on*, dénigrer.

asphalt(um) ['æsˌfɔlt] *n.* asphalte *m.*

asphyxiate [ˌæs'fɪksɪˌejt] *v. tr.* asphyxier.

aspiration [ˌæspər'ejʃən] *n.* aspiration *f*; [breathing] souffle *m*, inspiration *f.* ‖ **aspire** [ə'spajər] *v. intr.* aspirer, prétendre (*to*, à): *an aspiring young man*, un jeune plein d'ambition.

aspirin ['æspərɪn] *n.* aspirine *f.*

ass [æs] *n.* [☞ tendance à éviter *ass* et à le remplacer par DONKEY] âne *m*; [Fig.] âne *m*, imbécile *m*: *she- ~*, ânesse *f.*

assail [ə'sejl] *v. tr.* assaillir, attaquer.

|| **assailant** [-ənt] *n.* assaillant *m*, agresseur *m.*

assassin [ə'sæsɪn] *n.* assassin *m.* || **assassinate** [-ˌejt] *v. tr.* assassiner. || **assassination** [əˌsæsɪn'ejʃən] *n.* assassinat *m.*

assault [ə'sɔlt] *n.* attaque *f*; [Mil.] assaut *m*; [Law] agression *f*: *~ and battery*, voies *fpl* de fait. || *v. tr.* attaquer, donner l'assaut à . . . .

assemble [ə'sɛmbḷ] *v. tr.* [people] assembler, réunir; [parts] monter. || *v. intr.* se réunir, s'assembler. || **assembly** [-ɪ] *n.* assemblée *f*, réunion *f*: *~ room*, salle *f* de réunion; *~ line*, chaîne *f* de montage; [Pol.] *Legislative Assembly*, © Assemblée législative.

assent [ə'sɛnt] *n.* assentiment (*to*, à): © *royal ~* , sanction *f* royale. || *v. intr.* donner son assentiment, acquiescer (*to*, à).

assert [ə'sɚ|t] *v. tr.* affirmer, soutenir, déclarer (ses idées, ses opinions); revendiquer (un privilège, un droit), faire valoir (un point de vue, un plan). || **assertion** [-ʃən] *n.* assertion *f* (d'une idée); revendication *f* (d'un droit); défense *f* (d'un principe). || **assertive** [ə'sɚtɪv] *adj.* qui aime s'affirmer.

assess [ə'sɛs] *v. tr.* imposer, taxer (une propriété, &c.); [estimate] évaluer, estimer (une fortune, des dommages, &c.). || **assessment** [-mənt] *n.* imposition *f*, taxation *f*; évaluation *f.*

asset ['æsɛt] *n.* qualité *f*, avantage *m*: *Being able to speak both languages is a real ~* , La possession des deux langues est un avantage certain; *He is a real ~ /to our organization*, C'est/un des piliers, une des lumières/de notre organisation. || **assets** *n.pl.* [Com.] avoirs *mpl*; actif *m.*

assiduity [æsɪ'djuwɪtɪ] *n.* assiduité *f.* || **assiduous** [æ'sɪdjuwəs] *adj.* [diligent] assidu; [polite] empressé.

assign [ə'sajn] *v. tr.* assigner (une tâche à qqun); désigner (qqun à un poste); fixer, déterminer (une date); [Jur.] céder, tranférer (un droit, une propriété). || **assignment** [-mənt] *n.* attribution *f* (de qqch. à qqun); [duty] mission *f*, affectation *f* (de qqun à un poste, une mission); [School] devoir *m*, travail *m*; [Jur.] cession *f*, transfert *m* (de titres, &c.).

assimilate [æ'sɪmɪlejt] *v. tr.* assimiler (une nourriture, un enseignement); [Fig.] [liken] assimiler, comparer (*to*, à). || **assimilation** [ˌæsɪmɪ'lejʃən] *n.* assimilation *f.*

assist [ə'sɪst] *v. tr.* [help] aider, assister (qqun) (*in*, à); [be associated with] collaborer avec. || **assistance** [-əns] *n.* aide *f*, concours *m*: *to come to s.o.'s ~* , venir /en aide à, au secours de/qqun; *with the able ~ of*, → admirablement secondé par . . . . || **assistant** [-ənt] *n.* adjoint *m*; [lab.] garçon *m* (de laboratoire), préparateur *m*, [helper] aide *m*: *~ professor*, chargé *m* de cours, © professeur *m* assistant.

assizes [ə'sajzəs] *n.pl.* [Law] assises *fpl.*

associate [ə'sowʃɪˌejt] *v. tr.* associer, unir (*with*, à, avec), joindre (qqch. à). || *v. intr.* s'associer, s'unir (à, avec); fréquenter (*with s.o., a group*, qqun, un groupe). || **associate** [ə'sowʃət] [-ʃɪət] *n.* associé *m*; membre *m* (d'une association), collègue *m* (d'une institution); [Fam.] compagnon *m*, compagne *f*, camarade *m, f*; [Law] *associates*, consorts *mpl.* || *adj.* associé, allié (à); [Pej.] complice (*with*, de): *~ professor*, maître *m* de conférences, © professeur *m* agrégé. || **association** [ə'sowsɪˌejʃən] *n.* **1.** association *f*; [professional] groupement *m* (professionnel, &c.), société *f* (savante), groupe *m* (sportif, &c.). **2.** [Psych.] rapport *m* (avec qqun, qqch.); association *f* (des idées); [*pl.*] souvenirs *mpl.* **3.** [Sport] *~ football*, soccer *m*, (football) association.

assort [ə'sɔɚt] *v. tr.* **1.** trier, classer (des objets); assortir: *assorted candy*, bonbons assortis. **2.** [with] fréquenter (qqun). || **assortment** [-mənt] *n.* tri *m*, classement *m*; assortiment *m.*

assuage [ə'swejʤ] *v. tr.* calmer, apaiser.

assume [ə'sjuwm] *v. tr.* **1.** [take on] assumer (une responsabilité); s'attribuer /prendre, s'arroger/(des droits, des privilèges). **2.** [take for granted] supposer (qqch.). || *v. intr.* supposer (que + *Ind.*); affecter (de + *Inf.*): *assuming that . . .* , on supposant que . . . . || **assumed** [-d] *adj.* [name] d'emprunt: *under an ~ name*, sous un faux nom. || **assuming** [-ɪŋ] *adj.* prétentieux. || **assumption** [ə'sʌmpʃən] *n.* supposition *f*, présomption *f*; [boldness] arrogance *f*; [R.C.] l'Assomption *f.*

assurance [ə'sjɚ|əns] *n.* [certainty] assurance *f*, certitude *f*; [declaration] promesse *f*, affirmation *f*; [insurance] assurance *f*, garantie *f.* || **assure** *v. tr.* assurer, affirmer avec certitude (que + *Ind.*); [insurance] assurer (une maison, &c.). || **assured** [-d] *adj.* [confident] assuré, sûr (de soi); [insurance] assuré; [sure] sûr, certain: *You may/rest, be/~ that . . .*, Vous pouvez être sûr de . . . / que . . . /. || **assuredly** [-ədlɪ] *adv.* assurément, sans aucun doute.

asterisk ['æstərɪsk] *n.* astérisque *m.*

astern [ə'stɚn] *adv.* [Naut.] à l'arrière (de); [behind] en arrière de.

asthma ['æzmə] *n.* asthme *m.*

astir [ə'stɚ] *adv.* en émoi; debout, levé.

astonish [ə'stɑnɪʃ] *v. tr.* étonner, surprendre (qqun): *to be astonished,* s'étonner (*at,* de). ‖ **astonishing** [-ɪŋ] *adj.* étonnant, surprenant. ‖ **astonishment** [-mənt] *n.* étonnement *m,* surprise *f.*

astound [ə'stawnd] *v. tr.* stupéfier, ébahir: *an astounding success,* un succès foudroyant.

astray [ə'stɹej] *adv.* hors du bon chemin: *to go* ~, s'égarer; *to lead s.o.* ~, égarer, perdre/qqun.

astride [ə'stɹajd] *adv. & adj.* [a chair, &c.] à cheval sur; [bicycle] à califourchon sur.

astronomer [ə'stɹɑnəm|ɚ] *n.* astronome *m.* ‖ **astronomical** [ˌæstɹə'nɑmɪkl̩] *adj.* astronomique. ‖ **astronomy** [ə'stɹɑnəmɪ] *n.* astronomie *f.*

astute [ə'stuwt] *adj.* habile, sagace.

asunder [ə'sʌndɚ] *adv.* en deux: *to tear* ~, déchirer en deux.

asylum [ə'sajləm] *n.* †asile *m,* hospice *m* d'aliénés; hôpital *m*; [Fig.] asile *m,* refuge *m.*

at [æt] *prep.* **1.** [location] à; chez: ~ *Dorval,* ~ *(the) school, &c.,* à Dorval, à l'école, &c.; ~ */George's, the doctor's, the dentist/,* chez/Georges, le médecin, le dentiste/. **2.** [time] à: ~ *(half past) five (o'clock)* à cinq heures (et demie). **3.** [price] à: ~ *four dollars apiece,* à quatre dollars la pièce. **4.** [activity] en: *He is /good, weak/* ~ *algebra,* Il est/fort, faible/ en algèbre. **5.** [special uses: see also under other nouns and verbs]: ~ *the/most, earliest/,* au plus, au plus tôt; *to come in, go out/* ~ *the door,* entrer, sortir/par la porte; *What's he* ~ *?,* Qu'est-ce qu'il fait?; *He's hard* ~ *it,* Il y travaille ferme; *I saw him* ~ *it,* Je l'ai vu faire; *While you're* ~ *it . . . ,* Pendant que vous y êtes . . . ; *Where are we* ~ *?,* Où en sommes-nous?; *He's* ~ *it again,* Le voilà qui recommence; *Don't let me catch you* ~ *it again!* Que je t'y reprenne!

ate cf. EAT.

atheism ['ejθij|ˌɪzm] *n.* athéisme *m.* ‖ **atheist** [-ˌɪst] *n.* athée *m/f.*

athlete ['æθlijt] *n.* athlète *m, f.* ‖ **athletic** [æθ'lɛtɪk] *adj.* athlétique. ‖ **athletics** [-ɪks] *n.* **1.** [sing.] athlétisme *m.* **2.** [pl.] gymnastique *f.*

at home [æt'howm] *adv.* chez/soi, nous, lui, moi, &c./, cf. HOME.

Atlantic [ət'læntɪk] *n. & adj.* (l'océan *m*) Atlantique *m,* l'Atlantique: © *the* ~ *Provinces,* les Provinces atlantiques: *the* ~ *Charter,* la Charte (de l')Atlantique.

atlas ['ætləs] *n.* atlas *m.*

atmosphere ['ætməs|ˌfijɚ] *n.* atmosphère *f.* ‖ **atmospheric** [-ˌfɛɚɪk] *adj.* atmosphérique.

atom [ætəm] *n.* [Phys., Chem.] atome *m*; ~ *bomb, A-bomb,* bombe *f* atomique. ‖ **atomic**(al) [ə'tɑmɪk(l̩)] *adj.* atomique: ~ *energy,* énergie *f* nucléaire; ~ *weight,* poids *m* atomique. ‖ **atomics** [-s] *n.* [a science] atomistique *f.*

†atone (for) [ə'town] *v. intr.* expier, racheter (une faute, &c.). ‖ **atonement** [-mənt] *n.* expiation *f,* rachat *m* (d'une faute); [Rel.] Rédemption *f.*

atop [ə'tɑp] *adv.*: ~ *Mount-Royal,* sur le, en haut du/Mont Royal.

atrocious [ə'tɹowʃəs] *adj.* atroce. ‖ **atrocity** [ə'tɹɑsɪtɪ] *n.* atrocité *f.*

attach [ə'tætʃ] *v. tr. & intr.* **1.** (s')attacher (*to,* à); [one's signature] apposer (sa signature au bas d'un document). **2.** [responsibility, blame] faire retomber (*to,* sur): *The blame attaches to you,* Le blâme retombe sur vous, La faute en est à vous. **3.** [Law] saisir (un salaire, des biens). ‖ **attachment** [-mənt] *n.* attachement *m* (*to,* à, pour); [thing attached] pièce *f* annexe; [Tech.] mécanisme *m,* dispositif *m*; [Law] saisie *f,* saisie-arrêt *f.*

attack [ə'tæk] *n.* attaque *f*; [Mil.] offensive *f*; [assault] agression *f*; [Fig.] atteinte *f* (à la réputation); [Med.] attaque *f* (cardiaque), crise *f* (de nerfs), accès *m* (de fièvre). ‖ **attack** *v. tr.* attaquer, assaillir (une victime); s'attaquer, se mettre/à (une tâche). ‖ *v. intr.* attaquer, passer à l'attaque. ‖ **attacker** [-ɚ] *n.* assaillant *m* attaquant *m.*

attain [ə'tejn] *v. tr.* atteindre; [Fig.] parvenir (*to,* à), acquérir (une compétence, &c.). ‖ **attainment** [-mənt] *n.* [us. pl. *-s*] réalisation *f*; [person] connaissances *fpl,* savoir *m.*

attempt [ə'tɛmpt] *n.* essai *m*; [unsuccessful] effort *m,* tentative *f* (infructueuse): *to make an* ~ *at,* → tenter de, essayer de; [criminal] attentat *m* (*on,* contre). ‖ **attempt** *v. intr.* tenter de, essayer de, tâcher de (+ *Inf.*).

attend [ə'tɛnd] *v. tr.* **1.** assister à (une cérémonie): *to* ~ *lectures,* suivre des cours; *to* ~ *courses at the University,* aller à, fréquenter/l'Université. **2.** faire attention (*to,* à); [care for] soigner: *to* ~ *upon s.o.,* servir qqun (au restaurant); *to* ~ *to sth.,* s'occuper de qqch., †vaquer à une affaire. **3.** découler de, accompagner.

|| **attendance** [-əns] *n.* **1.** assistance *f*, présence *f*: *school* ~, fréquentation *f* scolaire. **2.** service *m* (d'hôtel, &c.); soins *mpl* (médicaux): *doctor in* ~, médecin/traitant, de service/. || **attendant** [-ənt] *n.* domestique *m*, assistant *m*: *attendants*, suite *f*, cortège *m*; *medical* ~, médecin. || *adj.* résultant de, découlant de; qui suit (un cortège), qui dépend (d'un fait).

attention [ə'tɛn|ʃən] *n.* **1.** attention *f*: *to pay* ~ *to*, faire attention à; *to call s.o.'s* ~ *to* (*a fact*), porter (un fait) à l'attention de . . . , → faire remarquer . . . à; *to draw away s.o.'s* ~ *from*, détourner l'attention de qqun de . . . **2.** [to please] prévenance *f*; égards *mpl*, soins *mpl*: *to devote one's* ~ *to*, se donner à, [person] avoir des égards envers . . . **3.** [Mil.] *Attention!*, Garde à vous!: *to come to* ~, se mettre au garde à vous; [Com.] *Attention Mr. X*, à l'attention de M. X. || **attentive** [-tɪv] *adj.* attent/if, -ve; [to please] prévenant.

attenuate [ə'tɛnjuwˌejt] *v. tr.* atténuer; diluer. || **attenuation** [əˌtɛnjuw'ejʃən] *n.* atténuation *f* (d'une peine, &c.).

attest [ə'tɛst] *v. tr.* attester, certifier (qqch., que qqun est . . .). || **attestation** [ˌætɛs-'tejʃən] *n.* [Law] déposition *f*, témoignage *f*.

attic ['ætɪk] *n.* grenier *m*; mansarde *f*.

attire [ə'tajɚ] *v. tr.* habiller (*in*, de). || *n.* mise *f*.

attitude ['ætɪˌtjuwd] *n.* attitude *f*.

attorney (at law) [ə'tɚnɪ] *n.* [Law] avoué *m*; © avocat *m*; chef *m* du contentieux: *Attorney-general*, © Procureur général; *Crown* ~, © Procureur *m* de la Couronne

attract [ə'tɹæk|t] *v. tr.* attirer (*to*, à); [Fig.] attirer, fasciner. || **attraction** [-ʃən] *n.* [Phys.] attraction *f*; [Fig.] attrait *m*, séduction *f*. || **attractive** [-tɪv] *adj.* [thing] attrayant; [person] attirant, séduisant; [magnet] attractif.

attribute [ə'tɹɪbjuwt] *v. tr.* attribuer (*to*, à); [wrongly] prêter (une qualité, &c., à qqun). || *n.* ['ætɹɪbjuwt] attribut *m*, caractéristique *f*. || **attribution** [ˌætɹɪ-'bjuwʃən] *n.* attribution *f*, prérogative *f*.

attrition [ə'tɹɪʃən] *n.* usure *f*: *war of* ~, guerre *f* d'usure.

auburn ['ɔbɚn] *adj.* [hair] châtain roux, roux.

auction ['ɔkʃən] *n.* vente *f* aux enchères, © encan *m*: *sold by* ~, mis aux enchères; ~ *room*, salle *f* des ventes. || **auction** *v. tr.* vendre (qqch.) aux enchères. || **auctioneer** [ˌɔkʃən'ijɚ] *n.* [Fr.] commissaire-priseur *m*, © encanteur *m*.

audacious [ɔ'dejʃəs] *adj.* audacieux. || **audacity** [ɔ'dæsɪtɪ] *n.* audace *f*.

audible ['ɔdɪbl̩] *adj.* audible; perceptible (à l'oreille). || **audience** ['ɔdɪəns] *n.* **1.** [a gathering] auditoire *m*, public *m*; auditeurs *mpl*, spectateurs *mpl*; [Fig.] audience *f*: *This book had a large* ~, Ce livre a atteint le grand public. **2.** [hearing] audience *f* (du tribunal); [R.C.] audience *f* (pontificale). || **audit** ['ɔdɪt] *v. tr.* [accounts] apurer, vérifier (des comptes); [college] suivre un cours en auditeur. || *n.* apurement *m*, vérification *f* (de comptes); bilan *m*. || **audition** [ɔ'dɪʃən] *n.* audition *f*; [Physiol.] ouïe *f*. || **auditor** ['ɔdɪtɚ] *n.* auditeur *m*; [accounts] vérificateur *m*: © [Parlem.] *Auditor General*, Auditeur général. || **auditorium** [ˌɔdɪ'tɔɚɪəm] *n.* salle *f* (de réunion, de concerts, &c.); [university] amphithéâtre *m*.

†**aught** [ɔt] *n.* & *pron.* quelque chose: *For* ~ *I know*, (Pour) autant que je le sache; A ma connaissance.

augment [ɔg'mɛnt] *v. tr.* augmenter. || **augmentation** [ˌɔgmɛn'tejʃən] *n.* augmentation *f*.

August[1] ['ɔgəst] *n.* (le mois d') août *m*: *in* ~, en août.

august[2] [ɔ'gʌst] *adj.* auguste, solennel.

aunt [ænt] *n.* tante *f*.

aurora borealis cf. NORTHERN LIGHTS.

†**auspices** ['ɔspɪˌsijz] *n.* [patronage]: *under the auspices of*, sous les auspices de . . . || **auspicious** [ɔs'pɪʃəs] *adj.* propice, favorable.

austere [ɔ'stijɚ] *adj.* austère. || **austerity** [ɔ'stɛɚɪtɪ] *n.* austérité *f*; [Econ.] restrictions *fpl*.

Australia [ɔ'stɹejljə] *n.* [Geog.] l'Australie *f*; le Commonwealth d'Australie. || **Australian** [-n] *adj.* & *n.* australien, -ne.

Austria ['ɔstɹɪə] *n.* [Geog.] l'Autriche *f*. || **Austrian** [-n] *adj.* & *n.* autrichien, -ne.

authentic(al) [ɔ'θɛntɪk(l̩)] *adj.* authentique; qui fait foi. || **authenticity** [ɔˌθɛn'tɪsɪtɪ] *n.* authenticité *f*.

author ['ɔθɚ] *n.* auteur *m*, écrivain *m*: *authoress*, (femme) auteur *m*.

authoritative [ə'θɔɚɪˌtejtɪv] *adj.* **1.** autorisé; [argument] d'autorité. **2.** [commanding] autoritaire. || **authoritatively** [-lɪ] *adv.* **1.** de source autorisée. **2.** avec autorité, péremptoirement. || **authority** [ə'θɔɚɪtɪ] *n.* **1.** autorité *f* (*over*, sur): *the authorities*, les autorités *fpl*, l'administration *f*; *Port of London Authority*, Port autonome de Londres. **2.** mandat *m* (d'un policier, &c.); source *f* (d'information); [Fig.]

expert *m*: *to be an ~ on . . .*, faire autorité en matière de . . . . || **authorization** [ˌɔθɚaj'zejʃən] *n.* autorisation *f.* || **authorize** ['ɔθɚˌajz] *v. tr.* autoriser (qqch., qqun à faire qqch.); donner pouvoir/mandat/ (à qqun + *Inf.*). || **authorized** [-d] *adj.* autorisé: [Prot.] **Authorized Version** = Traduction *f* autorisée.

auto[1] ['ɔtow] pl. **-s** cf. AUTOMOBILE: ~ *court*, motel *m*, [Fr.] auto-relais *m.* || **auto body** [-ˌbɑdɪ] *n.* carrosserie *f* automobile.

auto-[2] [ɔtə] *préf.* auto- [= self]: *autobiography*, autobiographie *f*; *automat*, (restautant) automatique; &c. [☞ this prefix is often rendered in French by *servo-*]. || **automatic** [ɔtə'mætɪk] *adj.* automatique: ~ *transmission*, transmission *f* automatique. || **automatically** [-lɪ] *adv.* automatiquement; [reflex] machinalement; [Fig.] d'office. || **automation** [ɔtə'mejʃən] *n.* [Indust.] automa(tisa)tion *f.*

automobile ['ɔtəməˌbijl] *n.* [☞ In French Canada, this word is often treated as *m*; so are the trade names of cars: *le Ford*, *&c.*, which in Fr. are *f*] automobile *f*, [Fam.] auto *f*, voiture *f* [☞ the Fam. *auto* corresponds to CAR]. || **automotive** [ɔtə'mowtɪv] *adj.* (de l')automobile: *the ~ industry*, l'industrie de l'automobile.

autonomous [ɔ'tɔnəm|əs] *adj.* autonome. || **autonomy** [-ɪ] *n.* autonomie *f.*

autumn ['ɔtəm] *n.* automne *m*, cf. FALL.

auxiliary [ɔg'zɪljɚɪ] *adj. & n.* auxiliaire (*m*).

†**avail** [ə'vejl] *n.* utilité *f*, avantage *m*, service *m*: *This is of no ~ to (me)*, Cela /ne (me) servira à rien, ne (me) sera d'aucune utilité/. || **avail** *v. intr.* profiter, se servir (de qqch.). || **available** [-əbl̩] *adj.* **1.** [that can be used] disponible, à la disposition de (qqun). **2.** [that can be had] que l'on peut se procurer; en vente (chez).

avarice ['ævɚɪs] *n.* cupidité *f.*

avaricious [ˌævɚ'ɪʃəs] *adj.* [person] avare.

avenge [ə'vɛnʤ] *v. tr.* venger (qqun) (*for*, de): *to ~ an offence on s.o.*, se venger d'une offense sur qqun. || **avenger** [-ɚ] *n.* vengeur *m*, vengeresse *f.*

avenue ['ævn̩juw] *abr.* **Ave.** *n.* avenue *f*; [also Fr.] boulevard *m*: *He lives on X ~*, Il habite (l')avenue X.

average ['ævɹəʤ] *n.* moyenne *f*; chiffre *m*, prix *m*/moyen, valeur *f* moyenne: *above the ~*, au-dessus de la moyenne; *on an ~*, en moyenne. || *adj.* moyen, normal: ~ *price*, prix moyen; ~ *mind*, esprit dans la moyenne. || *v. tr.* prendre la moyenne de. || *v. intr.* se monter à, compter: *to ~ 12 hours' work a day*, compter/faire une moyenne de/12 heures par jour.

†**averse** [ə'vɚs] *adj.* hostile (à), opposé (à): *to be ~ from*, répugner à (+ *Inf.*). || **aversion** [ə'vɚʒən] *n.* aversion *f*, répugnance *f.* || †**avert** [ə'vɚt] *v. tr.* détourner (qqch. de qqun); écarter (*from*, de).

aviation [ˌævɪ'ejʃən] *n.* aviation *f*: *International Civil Aviation Organization (ICAO)*, Organisation de l'aviation civile internationale (OACI). || **aviator** ['ævɪˌejtɚ] *n.* aviat|eur *m*, -trice *f.*

avid ['ævɪd] *adj.* avide. || **avidity** [æ'vɪdɪtɪ] *n.* avidité *f.*

avocation [ˌævə'kejʃən] *n.* distraction *f*, passe-temps favori.

avoid [ə'vojd] *v. tr.* éviter (qqun, qqch.), se soustraire à (une tâche); [Jur.] annuler (une clause). || **avoidable** [-əbl̩] *adj.* évitable, → qu'on peut éviter. || **avoidance** [-əns] *n.* abstention *f* (*of*, de); [Jur.] annulation *f* (d'une clause, &c.).

†**avow** [ə'vaw] *v. tr.* avouer, admettre (une erreur). || **avowal** [-əl] *n.* aveu *m*, déclaration *f.* || **avowed** [-d] *adj.* avéré: *an avowed preference for*, une préférence marquée pour. || **avowedly** [-ədlɪ] *adv.* ouvertement, → de son propre aveu.

†**await** [ə'wejt] *v. tr.* attendre; [Fig.] guetter [☞ pour les sens habituels, cf. WAIT].

awake [ə'wejk], **awoke** [ə'wowk] or **awaked** *v. tr.* éveiller (qqun), réveiller (qqun); [Fig.] exciter (de l'intérêt). || *v. intr.* s'éveiller, se réveiller; [Fig.] prendre conscience (*to sth.*, de qqch.). || **awake** *adj.* (r)éveillé: *wide ~*, bien éveillé; [Fig.] intelligent, fin. || **awaken** cf. AWAKE. || **awakening** [-ənɪŋ] *n.* (r)éveil *m*; [Pej.] désappointement *m.*

award [ə'wɔɚd] *n.* prix *m*, récompense *f*; bourse *f*; [Law] jugement *m* arbitral, décision *f.* || *v. tr.* décerner (un prix), accorder (une récompense): *He was awarded first prize*, On lui décerna le premier prix.

aware [ə'wɛɚ] *adj.*: *to be ~ of sth.*, être/au courant de, instruit de/qqch., ne pas ignorer. || **awareness** [-nəs] *n.* conscience *f* (d'un fait, &c.): ~ *of one's/audience, public, &c.*/, (la) connaissance *f*/de son public, du marché/.

away [ə'wej] *adv.* **1.** loin; absent; à: *I left it ~ back on the road*, Je l'ai laissé loin derrière nous sur la route; *It's far ~*, C'est bien loin (d'ici); *He is ~*, Il est absent/en voyage/, → il n'est pas là; †*Away (with you)!*, Allez-vous-en!;

†*Away with it!*, Enlevez (ça)!; *It is* 10 *miles* ~ *(from here)*, C'est à 10 milles (d'ici); [see also under other verbs of motion: GO, COME, TAKE, &c.]. **2.** [après un verbe, exprime l'idée d'un processus continu ou graduel; after a verb, expresses an idea of continual or gradual process]: *He worked* ~ *at his assignment*, → Il a travaillé avec énergie à son devoir; *He kept pounding* ~ *until* . . . , Il continua à cogner jusqu'à ce que . . . ; *The steps are worn* ~, → Les marches sont usées (à force d'avoir servi).

†**awe** [ɔ] *n.* crainte *f*, terreur *f* (religieuse); respect *m*: *to stand in* ~ *of*, craindre, redouter. || **awful** [ˈɔfḷ] *adj.* terrible; solennel, imposant; [Fam.] impossible, insupportable. || **awfully** [-ɪ] *adv.* [Fam.] beaucoup, énormément, terriblement: *He is* ~ *nice*, → C'est/un amour, un chou/.

awhile [əˈwajl] *adv.* pendant quelque temps, quelques instants; un instant.

awkward [ˈɔkwərd] *adj.* [person] maladroit, gauche, © gêné; [tool] incommode, peu maniable; [circumstance] embarrassant, délicat: *This was an* ~ *situation*, La situation était délicate. || **awkwardly** [-lɪ] *adv.* gauchement, maladroitement. || **awkwardness** [-nəs] *n.* gaucherie *f*, maladresse *f*; embarras *m* (d'une situation).

awning [ˈɔnɪŋ] *n.* tente *f*; auvent *m*, marquise *f* (de théâtre, d'hôtel).

awoke cf. AWAKE.

ax(e) [æks] *pl.* **axes** [-əs] *n.* hache *f*.

axis [ˈæksɪz] pl. **axes** [-sijz] *n.* axe *m*; [Hist., Pol.] *the Axis*, [ˈæksɪs], l'Axe (Rome-Berlin-Tokyo).

axle [ˈæksḷ] *n.* essieu *m*; [Tech.] arbre *m*.

†**aye** [aj] *n.* oui *m*; [Pol.] vote *m* affirmatif: *The "ayes" have it*, Le vote est pour.

Azores (the) [əˈzɔərz] *n.* [Geog.] les Açores *fpl.*

azure [ˈæʒər] *n.* azur *m*, bleu *m* azur. || *adj.* d'azur, bleu azur *inv.*

B

B, b [bij] *n.* **1.** [lettre] le B. **2.** [Mus.] [dans la notation alphabétique, désigne la note ré] si *m*: *B flat*, si bémol.

B.A. [ˈbijˈej] *abr.* cf. BACHELOR OF ARTS.

babble [ˈbæbl] *n.* babil *m* (des enfants, &c.); [Pej.] caquetage *m*, bavardage *m* (de commères). || *v. intr.* [baby, &c.] babiller; [people] caqueter, bavarder; [brook, stream] murmurer. || **babbling** [-ɪŋ] *n.* cf. BABBLE. || *adj.* bavard, babillard; [brook, stream] murmurant.

baby [ˈbejbɪ] *n.* bébé *m*, petit(e) enfant. || *adj.* petit, jeune; d'enfant, enfantin: ~ *carriage*, voiture *f*, © carrosse *m*/ d'enfant; ~*-sitter*, gardienne *f* d'enfant(s). || *v. tr.* dorloter.

baccalaureate [ˌbækəˈlɔərət] *n.* baccalauréat *m* (ès arts, &c.).

bach (it) [ˈbætʃɪt] [Fam.] *v. intr.* vivre en /célibataire, vieux garçon/. || **bachelor** [ˈbætʃlər] *n.* **1.** célibataire *m*, [Fam.] (vieux) garçon *m*. **2.** [Sch.] bacheli|er *m*, -ère *f*: *Bachelor of Arts, of Science, of Divinity* (*degree*), (diplôme *m* de) bachelier ès arts [Fr. ès lettres], ès sciences, en théologie.

bacillus [bæˈsɪləs] *n.* [Biol.] bacille m.

back[1] [bæk] *n.* **1.** dos *m* (de qqun, d'un animal); [lower part] les reins *mpl*: *I have a backache*, J'ai mal aux reins; *behind s.o.'s* ~, derrière qqun, [Fig.] à l'insu de qqun; *to turn one's* ~ *on*, montrer, tourner/le dos à; *to/put, get/s.o.'s* ~ *up*, mettre qqun en colère, faire sortir qqun de ses gonds; *to fall on one's* ~, tomber à la renverse; *with one's* ~ *to the wall*, acculé au mur. **2.** le derrière *m* (de la tête, d'un bâtiment); l'arrière *m* (d'un bâtiment, d'un véhicule); le revers *m* (de la main); le verso *m* (d'une page, d'un chèque, d'un document); le dossier *m* (d'une chaise, d'un fauteuil): *at the* ~, derrière, [inside] au fond (de la salle); ~ *to front*, sens *m* devant derrière. || *adj.* de derrière: [Phon.] ~ *vowel*, voyelle postérieure; [Auto.] ~ *light*, feu *m* arrière. || *adv.* **1.** en arrière: *to jump* ~, sauter en arrière; *to go, drive, &c.*/~, retourner, rentrer, revenir/à pied, en voiture, &c.; *to send, bring*/~, renvoyer, rapporter; *to hit, pay*/~, rendre/un coup, de l'argent/; ~ *from the road*, à quelque distance de la route. **2.** *I'll be* ~ /*in an hour, in a moment*/, Je serai de retour dans une heure/dans un instant/; ~ *to school*, rentrée *f* (des classes); *a few years* ~, il y a quelques années, ~ *in 1940*, (déjà) en 1940.

back[2] [bæk] *v. tr.* **1.** renforcer (un mur, une carte); financer (une entreprise); parier sur; soutenir (une entreprise); [Fam.] protéger, [Fr.] pistonner (qqun); appuyer (des arguments). **2.** reculer (qqun, qqch.); faire reculer (qqun, un cheval): *to* ~ *the car into the garage*, [Fr.] rentrer la voiture dans le garage en marche arrière, © reculer l'auto dans le garage. || *v. intr.* reculer: *to* ~ /*into, out of*/*the garage*, entrer dans le, sortir du/garage en marche arrière/; © reculer dans le garage, sortir du garage/en reculant; *to* ~ /*up, down, across, the street*, [Fr.] monter, descendre, traverser la rue en marche arrière. || **back away** *v. intr.* [person, animal] s'éloigner à reculons; [Fig.] se dérober à: *to* ~ *from a difficult job*, se soustraire/se dérober/à une tâche difficile. || **back down** *v. tr.* (faire) descendre à reculons: *to* ~ *the hill*, descendre la côte à reculons. || *v. intr.* renoncer (à un projet); abandonner (une poursuite, une réclamation, une prétention); filer doux. || **back in** *v. tr. & intr.* (faire) (r)entrer à reculons; [car] en marche arrière. || **back out** *v. tr. & intr.* (faire) sortir à reculons, [car] en marche arrière. || *v. intr.* abandonner, retirer, sa promesse: *to* ~ *of a bargain*, revenir sur sa parole, sa décision. || **back up** *v. tr. & intr.* (faire) reculer. || **back bencher** [-ˌbɛntʃɚ] *n.* © député *m* de l'arrière-ban. || **backbone** [-ˌbown] colonne *f* vertébrale; [Fig.] partie *f* essentielle, cheville *f* ouvrière; armature *f*; caractère *m*, énergie *f*. || **background** [-ˌgrawnd] *n.* fond *m*, arrière-plan *m*; [Fig.] culture *f* (générale), expérience *f*.

backhand [ˈbæk|ˌhænd] *adj.* du revers de la main: ~ *stroke*, revers *m*.

backing [-ɪŋ] *n.* soutien *m*, appui *m*.

backlog [-ˌlɔg] *n.* [Fig.] arriéré *m*, accumulation *f* (de travaux en souffrance).

backslide [-ˌslajd], **backslid** [-ˌslɪd], **backslid(den)** [-ˌslɪdn̩] *v. intr.* récidiver; retomber (dans ses mauvaises habitudes).

backward [-wɚd] *adj.* **1.** (mouvement) rétrograde, en arrière; (enfant, pays) arriéré; (élève) lent. **2.** *Don't be* ~ *!*, Ne soyez pas timide!. || *adv.* [cf. BACKWARDS. || **backward(s)** *adv.* (se déplacer) en arrière, (marcher) à reculons, (tomber) à la renverse: *to count* ~, compter à rebours.

backwater [-ˌwɔtɚ] *n.* bras *m* mort (de rivière); [Fig.] mare *f* stagnante.

backwoods [-ˌwʊdz] *n.* bois *mpl* non exploités: *in the* ~, au fond des bois.

bacon [ˈbejkən] *n.* **1.** lard *m.* **2.** bacon *m.*

bacteria [bækˈtijɚɪə] *n.pl.* [Biol.] bactéries *fpl.*

bad[1] cf. BID.

bad[2] [bæd] *adj.* [☞ comp. WORSE, superl. WORST] **1.** mauvais; de mauvaise qualité; incorrect; [ill] malade; [food] gâté, pourri; [coin] faux; [teeth] carié: *a* ~ *egg*, un œuf pourri; *a* ~ *cold*, un gros rhume; *a* ~ *headache*, un violent mal de tête; ~ *luck*, malchance *f*, [Fam.] poisse *f*; ~ *language*, des mots grossiers. **2.** [Loc.] *to go* ~, se gâter; *to be* ~ *at*, être maladroit à; *from* ~ *to worse*, de mal en pis; *to be in a* ~ *way*, être en mauvais état; *That's not* ~ *!*, Ce n'est pas (si) mal!; (*It's*) *too* ~ (*that*), (C'est) dommage (que + *subjunc.*); *It's very* ~ *of you to . . .*, C'est très mal à vous de . . . ; *He is on* ~ *terms with his neighbour*, Il est/mal, en mauvais termes/avec son voisin; *That looks* ~, Les choses/affaires/vont mal; *You look* ~, Vous avez mauvaise mine; *I feel* ~, Je ne me sens pas (très) bien.

bade cf. BID.

badge [bæʤ] *n.* [distinction] insigne *m*; [workman's, &c.] plaque *f*.

badger [ˈbæʤɚ] *n.* [animal] blaireau *m*: ~ *-legged*, [person] boiteux. || *v. tr.* harceler (qqun).

badly [ˈbædlɪ] *adv.* **1.** mal. **2.** grièvement (blessé): *He is not doing* ~, Il se débrouille pas mal; *He did* ~, → Il a raté (son examen, &c.); *He is* ~ *off*, Il est dans une situation précaire; *I'm* ~ *off for shirts*, J'ai grand besoin de chemises; *He wants that* ~, Il en a grande envie.

badminton [ˈbædmɪntən] *n.* badminton *m.*

badness [ˈbædŋəs] *n.* méchanceté *f* (d'une personne); mauvaise qualité *f*; mauvais état *m* (d'un chemin, &c.).

bad-tempered [bædˈtɛmpɚd] *adj.* [person] qui a (un) mauvais caractère, susceptible, méchant; [horse] vicieux, rétif.

Baffin Island (Land) [bæfɪn|ˈɑjlənd] *n.* ©

l'île, †la terre/de Baffin. || **Baffin's Bay** [-zˌbej] *n.* la/baie, mer/de Baffin.

baffle [ˈbæfl̩] *v. tr.* [Fig.] dérouter (qqun), déjouer (les plans de qqun): *It baffles analysis,* → Cela échappe à l'analyse. || **baffling** [-ɪŋ] *adj.* déconcertant.

bag [bæg] *n.* **1.** sac *m*; [handbag] sac (à main), © bourse *f*, sacoche *f*; cornet *m* (de bonbons); [leather] sacoche *f* (de bicyclette, &c.): *paper* ~, sac en papier; *to let the cat out of the* ~, vendre la mèche. **2.** chasse *f*: *to make a good* ~, faire bonne chasse. || *v. tr.* [-gg-] **1.** mettre (qqch.) en sac. **2.** abattre, tuer (du gibier). || *v. intr.* se gonfler; [garment] faire poche.

baggage [-əʤ] *n.* bagages *mpl*; [Mil.] équipement *m*: ~ *car,* fourgon *m* (à bagages); ~ *check,* bulletin *m* de bagages; ~ *tag,* étiquette; ~ *truck,* chariot *m* à bagages.

bagpipe [-ˌpajp] *n.* [Mus.] cornemuse *f*.

bail[1] [bejl] *n.* [Jur.] (liberté sous) caution *f*: *to hold (s.o.) on* ~, garder (qqun) sous caution. || *v. tr.* [bail out] donner caution pour (qqun); [Fam.] aider.

bail[2] *n.* [Naut.] écope *f*. || *v. tr. to* ~ *(a boat) out,* vider l'eau (d'une chaloupe).

bait [bejt] *n.* [on a trap] amorce *f*; appât *m* (d'un hameçon). || *v. tr.* **1.** [fishing] amorcer (un hameçon). **2.** [Fig.] harceler (qqun).

bake [bejk] *v. tr.* [of bread] faire (le pain); (faire) cuire (qqch.) au four. || *v. intr.* [bread] cuire (au four); [Fig.] cuire (au soleil); [earth] se durcir, se dessécher (au soleil). || **baked** *adj.* [Fig., Pers.] à bout, épuisé. || **baker** [-ɚ] *n.* boulanger *m*. || **bakery** [-əɪ] *n.* boulangerie *f*. || **baking pan** [-ɪŋˌpæn *n.* tourtière *f*. || **baking powder** [-ˌpawdɚ] *n.* © poudre *f* à pâte; levure *f* chimique, [Fr.] levure *f* alsacienne.

balance [ˈbæləns] *n.* **1.** équilibre *m*: *to keep one's* ~, se (main)tenir en équilibre; *out of, off*/~, déséquilibré. **2.** balance *f*: *to hang in the* ~, être, rester/en balance. **3.** [Fin.] solde *m*; [Fig.] reste *m*. **4.** stabilité (de caractère). || *v. tr.* **1.** peser (les conséquences). **2.** mettre, maintenir en équilibre; équilibrer (le budget). **3.** solder (un compte), régler (les livres). **4.** compenser, faire contre-poids à (qqch.). || **balanced** [-t] *adj.* [person, thing] équilibré: *(well-)* ~ *diet,* régime *m* synthétique. || **balance sheet** [-ˌʃijt] *n.* bilan *m*. || **balance wheel** [-ˌwijl] *n.* balancier *m*.

balcony [ˈbalkənɪ] *n.* balcon *m*.

bald [bɔld] *adj.* **1.** chauve. **2.** [Fig.] [hill] dénudé; [style] sec; [truth] simple. || **baldness** [-nəs] *n.* calvitie *f*.

bale [bejl] *n.* [cotton, &c.] ballot *m* (de marchandises); botte *f* (de foin). || *v. tr.* emballer (de la marchandise). || **baler** [-ɚ] *n.* emballeur *m*, emballeuse *f*.

balk [bɔk] *n.* **1.** poutre *f*. **2.** contretemps *m*, déception *f*; obstacle *m*. || *v. tr.* contrarier, faire obstacle à (qqun), [s.o.'s projects, plans] déjouer, frustrer. || *v. intr.* [horse] se dérober; [pers.] reculer (*at*, devant).

Balkan [ˈbɔlkən] *adj.* *(the)* ~ *Mountains,* (les) Balkans *mpl*; *(the)* ~ *States,* (les) États *mpl* balkaniques; *(the)* ~ *Peninsula,* (la) péninsule des Balkans.

ball [bɔl] *n.* **1.** balle *f* (de tennis, de baseball, &c.); [large, hollow] ballon *m* (de football, basketball, &c.); bille *f* (de billard); boule *f* (de neige); boulet *m* (de canon, de viande); pelote *f* (de laine); [any round object] boule *f*: *to roll up in a* ~, (se) rouler en boule. **2.** © [Sport: = *ball game*] baseball *m*; rugby *m*: *to play* ~, jouer au baseball, au rugby; [Fig.] [Fam.] coopérer. **3.** [dance] bal *m*. || *v. tr.* & *intr. to* ~ *up,* (se) mettre en boule; (s')embrouiller; *to be completely balled up,* être complètement embrouillé.

ballast [ˈbæləst] *n.* lest *m*.

ball bearings [bɔl bɛɚɪŋz] *n.pl.* roulements *mpl* à billes.

ballet [ˈbælej] *n.* ballet *m*.

balloon [bəˈluwn] *n.* ballon *m*. || *v. intr.* [sleeve] ballonner.

ballot [ˈbælət] *n.* scrutin *m*, vote *m*: ~ *box,* urne *f* (électorale).

balm [bɔm] *n.* baume *m*. || *v. tr.* embaumer, parfumer (qqch.). || **balmy** [-ɪ] *adj.* embaumé, parfumé.

baloney [bəˈlownɪ] [Fam.] *n.* boniments *mpl*, bêtises *fpl*.

balsam [ˈbɔlsəm] *n.* © gomme *f* de sapin; [Fr.] baume *m* du Canada: ~ *fir,* sapin *m* (d'Amérique).

Baltic [ˈbɔltɪk] *adj.* **1.** [sea] Baltique *f*, [trade, cities] de la Baltique. **2.** [ports, states] balte.

bamboo [bæmˈbuw] *n.* bambou *m*.

ban [bæn] *n.* **1.** interdiction *f*; [Com.] embargo *m*: *to put a* ~ *on sth.,* interdire qqch. **2.** *pl.* bans *mpl*: *marriage banns,* bans, promesse *f* de mariage. || *v. tr.* [-nn-] interdire (qqun, qqch.), mettre (un livre) à l'index, mettre (qqun) hors la loi.

banal [ˈbejnl̩] *adj.* banal, médiocre.

banana [bəˈnænə] *n.* banane *f*: ~ *tree,* bananier *m*.

band[1] [bænd] *n.* **1.** [strip, belt] bande *f* (de métal, de papier, de tissu); [ribbon, tape] ruban *m*: *elastic* ~, bande élastique, © élastique *m*. **2.** [stripe on things] raie *f*, [on clothes] rayure *f*. **3.** bande *f* (de voleurs, de loups, etc.), troupe *f* (d'étudiants, etc.). || *v. tr.*: *to* ~ *together*, (se) réunir en bande, (se) liguer; [mob] s'ameuter.

band[2] *n.* orchestre *m*; (la) musique *f* (du régiment): *brass* ~, fanfare *f*; *bandsman*, musicien *m*.

bandage [-ədʒ] *n.* bandage *m*; [dressing] pansement *m*; [blindfold] bandeau *m*. || *v. tr.* [tie up] bander (un bras cassé, une plaie); [dress] mettre un pansement (sur une plaie, à un doigt, etc.).

bandit [-ɪt] *n.* bandit *m*.

bandy [-ɪ] *adj.* [limb] croche, tordu, [legs] arqué. || *v. tr.* [people] (se) renvoyer (la balle), échanger (des coups, des insultes). || **bandylegged** [-ɪˌlɛgəd] *adj.* [person] bancal, aux jambes arquées.

bang [bæŋ] *n.* **1.** [blow] coup *m* (violent); [noise] (grand) bruit *m*, fracas *m*; détonation *f* (d'arme à feu); claquement *m* (de porte). **2.** frange *f* (de cheveux). || *interj.* pan!; boum! || *v. tr. & intr.* frapper (qqch.) avec bruit; claquer (une porte); [pound] cogner: *to* ~ *on the table* (*with one's fist*), frapper sur la table (du poing).

banish [ˈbænɪʃ] *v. tr.* bannir (qqch., qqun), exiler (qqun), [ideas, fear] chasser. || **banishment** [-mənt] *n.* exil *m*, bannissement *m*.

banister [ˈbænɪstə˞] *n.* balustrade *f*, rampe *f* (d'escalier).

bank[1] [bæŋk] *n.* **1.** [slope] talus *m*, remblai *m*; banc *m* (de sable): *snow* ~, © banc *m* de neige; [Mar.] haut-fond *m*, banc: *the Grand Banks*, le Grand Banc (de Terre-Neuve). **2.** rive *f* (d'une rivière); bord *m* (d'un lac); [steep] berge *f*. **3.** [avion] virage *m* (sur l'aile). || *v. tr. & intr.*: *to* ~ *up*, amonceler, s'amonceler [neige, etc.]. || *v. intr.* [avion] virer (sur l'aile).

bank[2] *n.* [Fin.] banque *f*: ~ *account*, compte *m* en banque; *savings* ~, caisse *f* d'épargne: (*the*) ~ *of Canada*, (la) Banque du Canada. || *v. intr.* avoir (de l'argent) en banque; [Fam.] *to* ~ *on* (*sth.*), compter sur (qqch.). || *v. tr.* déposer (de l'argent) en banque.

bank[3] *n.* banc *m* (de rameur), rangée *f* (de touches), clavier *m*.

banker [-ə˞] *n.* **1.** banquier *m*. **2.** [operating on Banks off Newfoundland] terre-neuvien, terre-neuvas [*n.m, & adj.*]. || **banking** *n.* profession *f* de banquier, de banque; opérations *fpl* bancaires., || **bank note** [-ˌnowt] *n.* billet *m* (de banque). || **bankrupt** [-ɹʌpt] *adj.* en faillite, ruiné: *to go* ~, faire faillite. || **bankruptcy** [-ɹʌpsɪ] *n.* banqueroute *f*, faillite *f*.

banner [ˈbænə˞] *n.* bannière *f*, étendard *m*. || *adj.* [US] principal.

banquet [ˈbæŋkwət] *n.* banquet *m*. || *v. intr.* banqueter, festoyer.

banter [ˈbæntə˞] *n.* plaisanterie *f*; taquinerie *f*; raillerie *f*. || *v. intr.* plaisanter, taquiner, railler (qqun).

baptism [ˈbæp|tɪzm] *n.* [Rel.] baptême *m*: *to administer* ~ *to s.o.*, administrer le baptême à qqun, baptiser qqun. || **Baptist** [-tɪst] *n.* [Rel.] baptiste *m, f*: *John the* ~, [Bibl.] Saint Jean-Baptiste. || **baptize** [-ˌtajz] *v. tr.* baptiser: *to* ~ *s.o.*, administrer le baptême à qqun, baptiser qqun.

bar[1] [bɑə˞] *n.* **1.** barre *f* (de fer, de chocolat); barreaux *mpl* (d'une cage), grilles *fpl* (d'une prison); [Fig.] obstacle *m*, empêchement *m*. **2.** barre *f*, ligne *f*; [Mus.] mesure *f*; [Jur.] barre *f* (des accusés): © ~ *of the House*, barre de la Chambre. **3.** [drinking establishment] bar *m*: *candy* ~, confiserie *f*; *soda* ~, limonaderie *f*; *snack* ~, *casse-croûte *m*; *bartender*, garçon *m*. || *v. tr.* [-rr-] **1.** barrer (une porte) [× in ©, this usually means *to lock*]: *to* ~ *o.s. in*, se barricader (chez soi, &c.); [Fig.] *to* ~ *the way to*, barrer la route à. **2.** empêcher; exclure.

bar[2] (also: barring) *prép.* sauf, à l'exception de: ~ *none*, sans exception; *Barring delay, I'll arrive on Tuesday*, A moins d'être retenu, j'arriverai mardi.

barb [bɑə˞b] *n.* barbe *f*, barbelure *f* (d'une flèche); barbillon *m* (d'un hameçon); arête *f* (d'un épi).

barbarian [bɑə˞|ˈbɛə˞ən] *adj. & n.* [people, manners, &c.] barbare. || **barbaric** [-bæə˞ɪk] *adj.* [action, treatment] barbare. || **barbarous** [ˈbɑə˞bə˞əs] *adj.* cf. BARBARIC.

barbecue [ˈbɑə˞bɪˌkjuw] *n.* **1.** [US, ©] [animal, especially chicken] rôti *m*; gril *m*. **2.** © rôtisserie *f* .|| *v. tr.* rôtir (un animal) à la broche.

barbed wire [ˈbɑə˞bdˈwəjə˞] *n.* [fil *m* de fer) barbelé, (du) barbelé *m*, (des) barbelés *mpl*.

barber [ˈbɑə˞bə˞] *n.* coiffeur *m*; © barbier *m*: ~ *shop*, salon *m* de coiffure/de coiffeur/.

bare [bɛə˞] *adj.* **1.** nu; (paysage, arbre) dénudé; (chambre) vide; (cou) découvert: *to lay* ~, mettre à nu, exposer; dévoiler (un secret). **2.** [plain] simple: *the bare facts of the matter*, la vérité toute simple, la vérité en quelques traits. **3.** [scanty] (tout) juste; faible: *to earn a ~ living*, gagner tout juste de quoi vivre; *a ~ majority*, une faible majorité; *the ~ idea is enough to . . .*, la seule idée suffit à . . . **4.** [Mesures] faible: *2¼" ~*, 2 po. ¼ faible. || *v. tr.* mettre (qqch.) à nu, découvrir (une plaie, &c.); découvrir (la tête). || **barefoot(ed)** *adj.* aux pieds nus. *adv.* pieds nus, nu-pieds. || **bare-headed** *adj.* nu-tête || **barely** *adv.* tout juste, à peine, tout au plus: *He has ~ enough*, Il en a à peine, tout juste, assez; *He is ~ fifteen*, Il a quinze ans tout au plus; *He ~ escaped*, C'est tout juste s'il a échappé.

bargain ['bɑɚgən] *n.* **1.** marché *m*: *to make, drive/a ~ with s.o.*, faire, conclure/ un marché avec qqun; convenir avec qqun (de . . .); *to drive a hard ~*, (chercher à) imposer des conditions très dures; *to get the best of a ~*, avoir le dessus (dans un marché); *It's a ~!*, C'est entendu!; *into the ~*, par-dessus le marché, en plus/. **2.** occasion *f*, affaire *f*; © aubaine *f*: *to find a good ~*, trouver /une (belle) occasion, une bonne affaire/. || *v. intr.* conclure un marché (avec qqun), marchander (avec qqun pour avoir qqch.): *I didn't ~ on that!, That's more than I bargained for!*/, Je ne m'attendais pas à cela! || **bargaining** [-ɪŋ] *n.* marchandage *m*; [labour] négociations *fpl*, entente *f*.

barge [bɑɚʤ] *n.* chaland *m*.

bark[1] [bɑɚk] *n.* écorce *f* (d'arbre). || *v. tr.* écorcer (un arbre).

bark[2] *n.* aboiement *m* (d'un chien). || *v. intr.* aboyer.

barley ['bɑɚlɪ] *n.* orge *f*.

barmy ['bɑɚmɪ] *adj.* [Fam.] crazy.

barn [bɑɚn] *n.* [grain] grange *f*; [horses] écurie *f*; [cows, &c.] étable *f*: *~ dance*, danse *f* champêtre. || **barnyard** [-ˌjɑɚd] *n.* basse-cour *f*.

barometer [bə'ɹɑmətɚ] *n.* baromètre *m*: *the ~ is/falling, rising/*, le baromètre descend/monte.

baron ['bæɚən] *n.* **1.** baron *m*. **2.** [money] [US, ©] magnat *m* (de la finance, &c.).

barracks ['bæɚəks] *n.pl.* [army] caserne *f*, baraquements *mpl*.

barrage [bə'ɹɑʒ] *n.* [dam, Mil.] barrage *m*.

barrel[1] ['bæɚəl] *n.* [US] [mesure de pétrole valant 42 gallons = (Fr.) 159 litres] baril *m* (de pétrole).

barrel[2] *n.* **1.** tonneau *m*, fût *m*, [small] baril *m* (de vin, &c.); caque *f* (de harengs); seau *m* (à biscuits). **2.** canon *m* (de fusil): *double-barrelled, adj.* à deux coups. || *v. tr.* mettre (qqch.) en baril, embariller, (en)caquer (du hareng); mettre (du vin) en fût, entonner (du vin).

barren ['bæɚən] *adj.* **1.** stérile (en), improductif, aride. **2.** désertique, nu: *(the) Barren Lands*, (les) Terres Stériles/ subarctiques, toundra *f*. **3.** (sujet) ingrat, terne. || *n.* (*usual. pl.*) désert *m*, toundra *f*. || **barrenness** [-nəs] *n.* stérilité *f*. || **barrens** [-z] *n.* © cf. BARREN.

barricade ['bæɚɪˌkejd] *n.* barricade *f*. || *v. tr.* barricader.

barrier ['bæɚɪɚ] *n.* barrière *f*; [Fig.] obstacle *m*: *sound ~*, mur *m* du son.

barrister ['bæɚɪstɚ] *n.* avocat *m*.

barrow[1] ['bæɚow] *n.* [wheel-] brouette *f*. || *v. tr.* brouetter (de la terre).

barrow[2] *n.* [mound] tumulus *m*.

bartender ['bɑɚˌtendɚ] *n.* barman *m*.

barter ['bɑɚtɚ] *n.* troc *m*. || *v. tr.* troquer (des objets).

base[1] [bejs] *adj.* [character] bas, ignoble; [Metal] vil.

base[2] *n.* **1.** base *f*; fondement *m*, fondations *fpl*. **2.** [Mil., Av., Chem.] base *f*. **3.** [Sport] but *m*. || *v. tr.* baser, fonder établir (*on*, sur).

baseball [-ˌbɔl] *n.* [Sport] **1.** baseball *m*, © balle *f* au camp. **2.** balle *f* (de baseball).

baseless ['bejsləs] *adj.* sans fondement.

basement [-mənt] *n.* cave *f* (d'une maison); sous-sol *m* (d'un magasin, &c.).

baseness [-nəs] *n.* bassesse *f*.

bashful ['bæʃfl̩] *adj.* timide. || **bashfulness** [-nəs] *n.* timidité *f*.

basic ['bejsɪk] *adj.* fondamental, de base; essentiel: *~ vocabulary*, vocabulaire de base; *~ needs*, besoins essentiels; *~ features*, les grandes lignes (d'un projet); *Basic French*, le français élémentaire.

basilica [bə'sɪlɪkə] *n.* basilique *f*.

basin ['bejsn̩] *n.* bassin *m*: *the Mississippi ~*, le bassin du Mississippi; *washbasin*, [stand] lavabo *m*; [separate bowl] cuvette *f*: *Holy Water ~*, bénitier *m*.

basis ['bejsɪs] pl. **bases** ['bejsɪjz] *n.* base *f*; fondement *m*: *There is no ~ to his opinion*, Son opinion est sans fondement.

bask [bæsk] *v. intr.* se chauffer (au soleil/ devant le feu, &c.).

basket ['bæskət] *n.* **1.** panier *m* (avec poignées), corbeille *f* (sans poignées): *waste(paper) ~*, corbeille à papier; *laundry ~*, corbeille à linge; *bread- ~*, corbeille à pain. || **basketball** [-ˌbɔl] *n.* basket-ball *m*, © ballon-panier *m*.

|| **basketmaker** [-ˌmejkɚ] *n.* vannier *m.* || **basketwork** [-ˌwɚk] *n.* vannerie *f.*

bass[1] [bejs] *n. & adj.* [Mus.] basse *f*: *~ voice,* voix *f* de basse; *double ~,* contrebasse *f.*

bass[2] [bæs] *n.* achigan *m*: *calico/straw-berry/~,* crapet *m,* calicot *m*; *rock ~ (red eye),* achigan de roche, crapet gris, vert ou noir; *striped ~ (rock fish),* bar *m* d'Amérique; *large-mouth ~,* achigan à grande bouche; *small-mouth ~,* achigan à petite bouche.

bassoon [bəˈsuwn] *n.* [instrument] basson *m.* || **bassoonist** [-ɪst] *n.* [person] basson *m.*

bastard [ˈbæstɚd] *adj. & n.* [illegitimate] bâtard *m.*

baste[1] [bejst] *v. tr.* [meat] arroser.

baste[2] *v. tr.* [sewing] bâtir; faufiler.

Bastille [bæsˈtijl] *n.* [Hist.] (la) Bastille: *~ day,* [Fr.] le 14 juillet.

bat[1] [bæt] *n.* [baseball] bâton *m*;[Sport] crosse *f.* || *v. tr.* [-tt-] [baseball] © frapper (la balle).

bat[2] *n.* chauve-souris *f.*

batch [bætʃ] *n.* **1.** [bread] fournée *f.* **2.** [people] bande *f*; [things] tas *m,* (grande) quantité *f.*

bath [bæθ] *n.* **1.** bain *m*: *to have, to take a ~,* prendre un bain (dans une baignoire). **2.** baignoire *f*; salle *f* de bain: *He is in the ~,* Il est dans la baignoire; *room with ~,* chambre *f* avec salle de bain. **3.** *the Order of the Bath* [Br.], l'Ordre *m* du Bain. **4.** *v. tr.* baigner (le bébé).

bathe [bejð] *v. tr. & intr.* (se) baigner. || **bathe, bathing** *n.* bain *m*: [Br.] *go for a bath, go bathing,* aller se baigner; †*bathing resort,* †station *f* balnéaire; plage *f*: *the bathing is fine here,* l'eau est bonne ici. || **bather** [-ɚ] *n.* baigneur *m,* baigneuse *f.* || **bathrobe** [ˈbæθˌɹowb] *n.* peignoir *m* (de bain). || **bathroom** [-ˌɹuwm] *n.* salle *f* de bain. || **bathtub** [-ˌtʌb] *n.* baignoire *f.*

baton [bæˈtɑn] *n.* bâton *m*; [orchestra] baguette *f.*

battalion [bəˈtæljən] *n.* [army] bataillon *m.*

batter[1] [ˈbætɚ] *v. tr.* [fortress, &c.] battre (en brèche), frapper; ébranler (qqch.); bossuer (un chapeau, &c.). || *n.* [Baseball] © frappeur *m.*

batter[2] *n.* [cake, pie] pâte *f* lisse.

battery [-ɪ] *n.* **1.** [dry cell] pile *f* (électrique); [Auto.] accumulateur *m.* **2.** [Mil.] batterie *f.* **3.** *assault and ~,* voies *fpl* de fait, attaque *f* sournoise (contre qqun).

battle [ˈbætl] *n.* **1.** bataille *f,* [engagement] combat *m*: *to fight a ~,* livrer (une) bataille/un combat/; *a naval ~,* un combat naval; *That's half the ~,* C'est bataille à moitié gagnée. **2.** lutte *f*: *the ~ against cancer,* la lutte contre le cancer. || *v. tr. & intr.* combattre, se battre; lutter (contre, against). || **battledress** [-ˌdɹɛs] *n.* tenue *f* de campagne. || **battlefield** [-ˌfijld] *n.* champ *m* de bataille. || **battleship** [-ˌʃɪp] *n.* [Naut.] cuirassé *m.*

bawdy [ˈbɔdɪ] *adj.* obscène, impudique.

bawl [bɔl] *n.* cri *m.* || *v. intr.* crier (à tue-tête). || *v. tr.* [Fam.] *to ~ out (s.o.),* réprimander, [Fam.] engueuler (qqun).

bay[1] [bej] *n.* **1.** baie *f*; [cove] anse *f*: *the Bay of Biscay,* le golfe de Gascogne; *Hudson's Bay,* la Baie d'Hudson. **2.** *~ window,* fenêtre *f*/en saillie, en baie/.

bay[2] *n.* aboiement *m*: *to be at ~,* être aux abois; *to keep the enemy at ~,* tenir l'ennemi en échec. || *v. intr.* aboyer.

bay[3] *n.* [Bot.] laurier *m* [also bay tree].

bayonet [ˈbejənət] *n.* baïonnette *f.* || *v. tr.* tuer/percer (qqun)/d'un coup de baïonnette.

bayou [ˈbəjuw] *n.* [US] bayou *m.*

bazaar [bəˈzɑɚ] *n.* **1.** [Oriental] bazar *m.* **2.** vente *f* (de charité).

BBC [ˌbijˌbijˈsij] *n.* [= British Broadcasting Corporation] la B.B.C. [labebeˈse].

B.D. [ˈbijˈdij] *abbr.* [= BACHELOR OF DIVINITY.]

be [bij], **was** [wʌz], **been** [bijn] [bɪn] *v. intr.* ☞ A. [pers. constructions] **1.** [+ n. or pron.] être: *He is a doctor,* Il est médecin; *He is the doctor,* C'est le médecin; *They, Those/are the ones who . . .,* Ce sont ceux-là qui . . .; *Seeing is believing,* Voir c'est croire; *the main thing is to . . .,* l'essentiel, (c')est de . . .; *What's that?,* Qu'est-ce que c'est?; *What's that to me?,* Qu'est-ce que cela me fait?; *if I were you,* si j'étais/de vous, à votre place/. **2.** [+ adj. or number] être; avoir; aller: *It, That/is easy to do that,* Il est facile de faire cela; *He is young,* Il est jeune; *How old is he?,* Quel âge a-t-il?; *He is 15 (years old),* Il a 15 ans; *The garden is 40 feet long,* Le jardin/a 40 pieds de long, est long de 40 pieds/; *I'm/thirsty, hungry, hot, cold, sleepy, right, wrong, afraid, ashamed/,* J'ai/soif, faim, chaud, froid, sommeil, raison, tort, peur, honte/; *His feet are cold,* Il a froid aux pieds; *His eyes are blue,* Il a les yeux bleus; *How are you? I'm fine,* Comment allez-vous? Je vais bien. **3.** [+ adv.] être; [position, also] se trouver: *The book is there, on the table,* Le livre/est, se trouve/ là, sur la table; *How long/have, had/you been here?,* Depuis/quand, combien de temps/êtes-vous, étiez-vous/ici?; *Here,*

There/is the book, Voici, Voilà/le livre; *Here he is,* Le voici; *Where, How far/are you (in the book)?,* Où en êtes-vous (dans le livre)?; *My birthday is tomorrow,* Mon anniversaire tombe demain; *Today is Tuesday,* C'est/Nous sommes/aujourd'hui mardi. **4.** [alone] être; exister: *To ~ or not to ~* , Être ou ne pas être; *The biggest liar that ever was,* Le plus grand menteur qui ait jamais existé; †*It is no more,* Cela/n'est, n'existe/plus; †*time was when* . . . , il fut un temps où . . .; *That may (well) ~* , Cela se peut (bien); *however that may ~* , quoi qu'il en soit; *Let him ~* , Laissez-le tranquille; *as/is, was/,* tel(le) quel(le). **5.** [= go, come] être, aller, venir: *He has been to Europe,* Il/a été, est allé/en Europe; *Has he been here today?,* Est-il/venu, passé/aujourd'hui?; *I've been to see it,* J'ai été, Je suis allé/le voir, Je l'ai déjà vu; *(Now) I've been and forgotten again!,* Voilà que j'ai encore oublié! ☞ **B.** [impers. constructions] **1.** [+ *n., pron.*] être: *Who is it?,* Qui est-ce, Qui est là?; *It's me [It's I,* C'est moi; *It is they who are wrong,* C'est, Ce sont/eux qui ont tort; *It's a long way from here,* C'est loin d'ici; *It's time to get up,* C'est, Il est/l'heure de se lever; *What/time, day, date/is it?,* Quelle heure est-il?, Quel jour/est-ce, sommes-nous/(aujourd'hui)?, Quelle est la date (aujourd'hui)?; *It is 3.30 (o'clock),* Il est 3 heures et demie; *It's/Tuesday, the 30th/,* Nous sommes/mardi, le trente/; *It is/daylight, a nice day/,* Il fait/jour, beau/; *What a nice day it is!,* Quelle belle journée!; *it/is, has been/months since,* il y a, voilà/des mois que . . . (ne); *What is it?,* Qu'est-ce que c'est!, Que voulez-vous?, Qu'est-ce qu'il y a? **2.** [+ adv.] être; y avoir: *It is so,* C'est ainsi; *Isn't it so?,* N'est-ce pas?; *There/is, was/a book on the table,* Il y/a, avait/un livre sur la table; *There/are, were/no letters in the box,* Il n'y/a, avait/pas de lettres dans la boite; *There must ~ one,* Il doit y en avoir un(e); *Once upon a time there was . . .,* Il était une fois . . . ; *how is it that . . . ?,* comment se fait-il que [+ subjunc.], D'où vient que [+ indic.]?; *if it had not been for me . . . ,* sans moi . . . . ☞ **C.** [as part of verbal constructions] **1.** [+ pr.p.] [×: no literal translation; use *en train de* + inf.] *He/is, was, will be/reading,* Il/lit, lisait, lira/; *He/has, had/been doing it for a long time,* Il le/fait, faisait/depuis longtemps; *I/have, had/just been talking to him.* Je/viens, venais/de lui parler; *They/have, had/been studying all morning,* Ils/ont, avaient/passé (toute) la matinée à étudier, Ils/ont, avaient/étudié toute la matinée; *They are doing it right now,* Ils sont en train de le faire en ce moment. **2.** [+ p.p.] être [+ p.p.]; [☞ When no agent is indicated use *on* + active or reflexive forms] *It was done by my father,* Cela a été fait par mon père, → Mon père l'a fait; *It was done yesterday,* → On l'a fait hier; *That is not done,* Cela ne se fait pas; × *I was given the money by my father,* → Mon père m'a donné l'argent. **3.** [+ inf.] [idée d'intention, de nécessité, de possibilité]: *I/am, was/to meet him here,* Je/dois, devais/le retrouver ici; *What am I to do now?,* Que dois-je faire maintenant?; *What is to be done?,* Que faire?; *if he were to find out . . . ,* s'il apprenait . . . ; *even if he were to come back . . . ,* quand (bien) même il reviendrait . . . , même s'il revenait . . . , †dût-il revenir . . . ; *How was I to know?,* Comment pouvais-je (le) savoir?; *It was to be found everywhere,* On pouvait en trouver partout; [×] *the problem (which is) to be solved,* → le problème à résoudre; *He was to ~ /pitied, congratulated/,* Il était à plaindre, Il méritait des félicitations. ☞ **D.** [elliptical uses] *(Are you willing to help me?) I am,* — Oui, (Monsieur, &c.); *You are glad, aren't you? I am not,* Vous êtes content, n'est-ce pas? — Non (je ne le suis pas); *(I'm sorry), You are?* → Vraiment?; *He is taller than I am,* Il est plus grand que moi.

beach [bijtʃ] *n.* plage *f.* ‖ *v. tr.* échouer; tirer (une) embarcation à sec. ‖ **beached** [-t] échoué. ‖ **beachhead** [-ˌhɛd] *n.* tête *f* de pont, de plage.

beacon [ˈbijkən] *n.* **1.** [light] phare *m*; [Naut.] balise *f.* **2.** [fire] signal *m.* ‖ *v. tr.* baliser (une route). ‖ *v. intr.* signaliser.

bead [bijd] *n.* **1.** [glass, &c.] perle *f* (de verroterie, &c.); goutte *f*, perle *f* (de sueur, de rosée): *Beads of perspiration stood out on his forehead,* La sueur perlait sur son front, Il suait à grosses gouttes. **2.** [R.C.] grain *m* (de chapelet): *to recite/tell/one's beads,* réciter, dire/son chapelet. ‖ *v. tr.* orner (qqun, qqch.) de perles.

beadle [bijdl] *n.* [Rel.] bedeau *m.*

beak [bijk] *n.* **1.** bec *m* (d'oiseau). **2.** pointe *f* (en forme de bec); [Fig.] nez *m* crochu.

beaker [ˈbijkər] *n.* gobelet *m*, coupe *f*; [Chem.] bécher *m.*

beam [bijm] *n.* poutre *f*; fléau *m* (d'une balance); [light] rayon *m*, faisceau *m* (d'un phare); [radio] ondes *fpl* dirigées; [Fig.] sourire *m* [radieux]. || *v. tr.* lancer, darder (des rayons); diriger (des ondes); [Fig.] rayonner (de plaisir, de joie). || **beaming** [-ɪŋ] *adj.* [Pers., face] rayonnant, radieux.

bean [bijn] *n.* haricot *m,* © fève *f* [Acadie, Fr.] fayot *m*: *French beans, string beans,* haricots verts, © haricots en biais; *baked beans,* haricots au four, cassoulet *m*; *pork and beans,* © fèves au lard; *Lima beans,* soissons *mpl,* © fèves de Lima; [Fig.] *to spill the beans,* éventer la mèche; [Fam.] *I haven't got a* ~, Je n'ai pas le sou.

bear[1] [bɛɚ], **bore** [bɔɚ], **born(e)** [-n] [☞ Dans la plupart des cas, le participe passé est **borne**; toutefois, on écrit **born** dans les tournures passives se rapportant à la naissance: *He was born in . . . ,* Il est né en . . .] *v. tr.* **1.** [carry] porter, supporter; *to* ~ *a burden,* supporter un fardeau; [Fig.] *to* ~ *in mind,* garder présent/à l'esprit, à la mémoire/. **2.** [endure] supporter, tolérer, endurer: *I can't* ~ *the noise,* Je ne peux (pas)/supporter, endurer/ce bruit; *Grin and* ~ *it!,* Prenez-le avec le sourire! **3.** yield, porter, produire (des fruits): *to* ~ *interest,* porter intérêt. **4.** [give birth to] enfanter, donner naissance à: *When were you born?* Quand êtes-vous né? [☞ Notice present tense in auxiliary]. **5.** [relate, show] offrir (des rapports), présenter (une analogie): *to* ~ *comparison with,* soutenir la comparaison avec; *to* ~ *marks of wear,* porter des traces d'usure. **6.** [Jur.]: *This document bears the seal of . . . ,* Ce document est revêtu du sceau de . . . ; *to* ~ *witness to,* porter témoignage sur. || *v. intr.* **1.** souffrir, endurer: *to* ~ *with s.o.,* se montrer patient envers qqun. **2.** se diriger vers: ~ *to the right,* Prenez à droite [Naut.] *The ship bore due north,* Le navire fit route droit au nord. **3.** agir (*on,* sur); se rapporter (*on,* à): *to bring to* ~ , mettre en action. || **bear down** [ˈbɛɚ|ˈdawn] *v. tr.* vaincre, défaire (un ennemi). || *v. intr.* s'approcher (*on,* de), se précipiter (*on,* vers). || **bear out** [-ˈawt] *v. tr.* prouver, confirmer (un argument). || **bear up** [-ˈʌp] *v. tr.* soutenir (qqun). || *v. intr.* tenir bon, se montrer courageux.

bear[2] *n.* ours *m,* [she-bear] ourse *f*: *The Great Bear* [Astr.], la Grande Ourse.

bearable [-əbl̩] *adj.* [pain, etc.] supportable.

beard [bijɚd] *n.* barbe *f*; barbiche *f* (d'une chèvre): *to have/wear/a* ~ , avoir de la barbe, porter la barbe. || *v. tr.* défier, narguer (qqun): *to* ~ *the lion* (*or a person*) affronter qqun. || **bearded** [-əd] *adj.* [person] barbu, à barbe. || **beardless** [-ləs] *adj.* imberbe.

bearer [ˈbɛəɚ] *n.* **1.** [person] porteur *m.* **2.** [thing] support *m*: *ensign* -~ , porte-drapeau *m*; *stretcher* ~ , brancardier *m.*

bearing [bɛɚɪŋ] *n.* **1.** [Tech.] coussinet *m*: *ball* ~ , roulement *m* à bille; ~ *surface,* plan *m* d'appui. **2.** [Fig.] conduite *f*; [physic.] port *m* (de tête, &c.). **3.** relation *f,* rapport *m*: *This has no* ~ *on the problem,* → Ceci n'a rien à voir avec la question. **4.** *pl.* orientation *f*: *to take one's bearings,* s'orienter; [Fig.] *to lose one's bearings,* perdre le nord.

bearskin [ˈbɛɚˌskɪn] *n.* peau *f* d'ours.

beast [bijst] *n.* **1.** bête *f* (domestique ou sauvage), quadrupède *m,* animal *m* (domestique ou sauvage); tête *f* de bétail. **2.** [Fig.] brute *f,* sale type *m,* dégoûtant personnage *m.* || **beastly** [-lɪ] *adj.* brutal, bestial; [Fig.] sale, dégoûtant, infect.

beat[1] [bijt] *n.* **1.** coup *m,* battement *m* (du cœur), pulsation *f*; batterie *f* (de tambour). **2.** [Mus.] mesure *f,* temps *m.* **3.** ronde *f* (d'un agent de police); secteur *m,* parcours *m* (d'une sentinelle); itinéraire *m,* tournée *f* (d'un facteur). **4.** cf. BEATNIK.

beat[2] [bijt], **beat, beaten** [-n̩] *v. tr.* **1.** battre, frapper: [Mus.] *to* ~ *time,* battre la mesure; [Fig.] *to* ~ *the air,* donner des coups d'épée dans l'eau; [Sl.] *Beat it!,* File! **2.** surpasser, vaincre, battre (qqun): *to* ~ *the record,* battre le record; *to* ~ *s.o. hollow,* battre qqun à plate couture; *to* ~ *s.o. to it,* devancer qqun; [Fam.] *That beats me!,* Ça me dépasse!, Je n'en sais rien!; *That beats everything!,* Ça, c'est le comble! **3.** aplatir (le fer); fouler (un sentier). **4.** battre, fouetter (les œufs, la crème). **5.** faire une battue (dans les bois): [Fam.] *to* ~ *about the bush,* tourner autour du pot; *Let's not* ~ *about the bush!,* Allons (droit) au fait!; *to* ~ *a retreat,* battre en retraite, [Fam.] reculer (devant un obstacle). || **beat down** *v. tr.* (r)abattre; marchander avec qqun (sur le prix de qqch.). || **beat in(to)** *v. tr.* enfoncer. || **beat on** *v. intr.* [sun] frapper (sur nos têtes); [rain] cingler qqun. || **beaten** *adj.* battu, vaincu: *off the* ~ *track,* hors des sentiers battus, inusité. || **beater** *n.* [machine] batteur *m* (à œufs), fouet *m*; battoir *m.*

beatitude [bijˈætɪˌtuwd] *n.* béatitude *f.*

beatnik [ˈbijtnɪk] *n.* beatnik *m.* || *adj.* fatigué, malade de vivre.

beau [bow] *pl.* **beaus, beaux** *n.* galant *m*, amoureux *m.*

beautiful [ˈbjuwtɪf|l̩] *adj.* beau; ravissant, charmant; magnifique, admirable. || **beautifully** [-ɪ] *adv.* admirablement, magnifiquement. || **beautify** [ˈbjuwtɪˌfaj] *v. tr.* embellir, enjoliver. || **beauty** [ˈbjuwtɪ] *n.* **1.** beauté *f*, charme *m*: ~ *care*, soins *mpl* de beauté; ~ *parlour*, salon *m* de beauté. **2.** [a woman] une belle *f*, une beauté *f*: [Fig.] *That's the ~ of it!*, C'est le plus beau de l'affaire!

beaver [ˈbijvɚ] *n.* castor *m*: ~ *hat*, chapeau *m* de castor: *to work like a ~*, travailler comme un nègre; [Fam.] *He is an eager ~*, Il veut faire du zèle. || © Hist. [a monetary unit] un castor.

B.C. [ˈbijˈsij] *abr.* **1.** (Before Christ) *the Third Century ~ /240 ~*, le troisième siècle avant J.-C./240 av. J.-C. || **2.** = © *British Columbia*, la Colombie-Britannique.

became cf. BECOME.

because [bij|ˈkʌz] [-ˈkɔz] *conj.* parce que: *It is ~ . . .*, C'est (parce) que . . . ; *all the more ~*, d'autant plus que; ~ *of*, à cause de.

beckon [ˈbɛkn̩] *v. intr.* faire signe (à qqun, *to s.o.*).

become [bijˈkʌm], **became** [bijˈkejm], **become** *v. intr.* **1.** devenir: *He is becoming more experienced*, Il devient/commence à être/plus expérimenté; *She became a doctor*, Elle est devenue/s'est faite/ médecin. [☞ *become* + adj. may often be translated by a single word]: *to ~ worried, accustomed, red, old, &c.*, → s'inquiéter, s'accoutumer, rougir, vieillir, &c.; *As timber becomes more valuable*, → Avec la revalorisation du bois. **2.** *to ~ of*, devenir: *What has ~ of them?*, Que sont-ils devenus? || *v. tr.* aller (bien): *That hair style doesn't ~ her*, Cette coiffure ne lui va pas (bien). || **becoming** [-ɪŋ] *adj.* qui va bien (à qqun), seyant; convenable, qui convient: *a ~ dress*, une robe qui lui/va, allait/bien; *Your attitude is hardly ~*, Votre attitude n'est guère convenable, Voilà une attitude qui ne vous convient guère.

bed [bɛd] *n.* **1.** lit *m*: *single, double ~*, lit à une place, à deux places; *twin beds*, lits jumeaux; *to be in ~*, être au lit, être couché; *to go to ~*, (aller) se coucher; *to get into ~*, se mettre au lit; *to stay in ~*, [in the morning] faire la grasse matinée, [illness] garder le lit; *to get out of ~*, se lever/descendre, sauter/du lit; *to get out of ~ on the wrong side*, se lever du pied gauche; *to make the ~*, faire le lit. **2.** lit *m* (d'une rivière); plate-bande *f* (de fleurs); [Geol.] gisement *m*, couche *f*. || **bedclothes** [-ˌklowðz] *n.* les couvertures *fpl* (et les draps *mpl*). || **bedding** [-ɪŋ] *n.* la literie *f*. || **bedroom** [-ˌɹuwm] *n.* chambre *f* (à coucher). || **bedside** [-ˌsajd] *n.* [head of bed] chevet *m*; [edge] bord *m* du lit; [space] ruelle *f* (près du mur): *to be at s.o.'s ~*, être au chevet de qqun. || **bedspread** [-ˌspɹɛd] *n.* dessus *m* de lit; [quilt] couvre-pieds *m invar.* || **bedspring** [-ˌspɹɪŋ] *n.* les ressorts *mpl*; [part supporting mattress] sommier *m.* || **bedtime** [-ˌtajm] *n.* l'heure du coucher: *It's ~ !*, Il est l'heure d'aller se coucher!; *It's (long) past your ~ !*, Tu devrais être déjà couché (depuis longtemps)!

bee [bij] *n.* **1.** abeille *f*: *a swarm of bees*, un essaim d'abeilles; [Fig.] *to have a ~ in one's bonnet*, avoir une idée fixe; *to make a ~ line for*, se diriger en droite ligne sur. **2.** réunion *f* (de travail), © corvée *f*: *spelling ~*, concours *m* d'orthographe.

beech [bijʧ] *n.* hêtre *m.* || **beechnut** [-ˌnʌt] *n.* faîne *f*.

beef [bijf] *n.* [invar. au pl.] [Cul.] bœuf *m* (à cuire ou à bouillir): *corned ~*, salaison *f* de bœuf, bœuf salé; ~ *tenderloin*, filet *m* de bœuf, *roast ~*, rôti de bœuf, [Fr.] rosbif *m.* || *v. intr.* [Fam.] rouspéter. || **beefsteak** [-ˌstejk] *n.* bifteck *m*, © steak *m.*

beehive [ˈbijˌhajv] *n.* ruche *f*.

been cf. BE.

beer [bijr] *n.* [☞ l'anglais distingue entre *beer* et *ale*, le français distingue entre *bière brune* et *bière blonde*] bière *f*: *draught ~*, bière sous pression; © ~ *parlour*, © taverne *f*.

beet [bijt] *n.* betterave *f*.

beetle[1] [ˈbijtl̩] *n.* escarbot *m*, scarabée *m.*

beetle[2] *v. intr.* [rocks, etc.] surplomber (qqch. *over sth.*), faire saillie. || **~-browed**, [-ˌbrawd] *adj.* **1.** [person] aux sourcils /épais, proéminents/. **2.** [person] [Fig.] menaçant, sévère.

befall [bɪˈfɔl], **befell** [-ɛl], **befallen** [-ɔln̩] *v. tr. & intr.* arriver/survenir/à (qqun).

befit [bəˈfɪt] *v. tr.* [-tt-] convenir à, incomber à: *It does not ~ you to . . .*, Il ne vous sied pas de . . . || **befitting** [bɪˈfɪtɪŋ] *adj.* convenable, seyant.

before [bɪˈfɔɚ] *adv.* **1.** [in space] en avant: *to go (on) before*, aller en avant; ~ *and behind*, devant et derrière; *This adjective generally comes ~*, D'habitude cet adjectif précède le nom, Cet adjectif se place normalement devant (le substantif). **2.** [in time] avant, auparavant: *two hours* ~ , deux heures/avant, auparavant/; *the year* ~ , l'année/d'avant, précédente/; *the day* ~ , le jour d'avant, la veille; *Where have I seen him* ~ *?*, Où est-ce que je l'ai déjà vu? *I never heard such a thing* ~ *!*, Je n'ai encore jamais entendu dire une chose pareille!; *Why didn't you say so* ~ *?*, Il fallait le dire tout de suite!, Vous auriez dû le dire plus tôt! || *prép.* **1.** [in space] devant: ~ *my eyes*, sous mes yeux; *to appear* ~ *a judge*, comparaître par devant un juge. **2.** [in time] avant. || *conj.* avant que (+ subjunc.); plutôt que de.

beforehand [-ˌhænd] *adv.* à l'avance; d'avance.

befriend [bɪ'fɹɛnd] *v. tr.* **1.** traiter (qqun) en ami, devenir l'ami de qqun. **2.** secourir, aider (qqun).

beg [beg] [-gg-] *v. intr.* [for] mendier, tendre la main [*mendier* is both *intr.* and *tr.*]. || *v. tr.* prier [stronger] supplier (qqun de + inf.), demander (qqch.) [comme une faveur]: *to* ~ *the question*, faire une pétition de principe; *(I)* ~ *your pardon!*, Excusez-moi!, (Je vous demande) pardon!; *(I)* ~ *your pardon?*, Vous dites?, Plaît-il?, Pardon?

began cf. BEGIN.

†**beget** [bɪ'gɛt], **begot** [bɪ'gɑt], ††**begat** [bɪ'gæt]; **begot(ten)** [bɪ'gɑtn̩] *v. tr.* engendrer; [Fig.] engendrer, causer (des répercussions, &c.).

beggar ['bɛg|ɚ] *n.* mendiant *m*, mendiante *f*; pauvre *m*, pauvresse *f*. || *v. tr.* réduire (qqun) à la mendicité, mettre (qqun) sur la paille. || **begging** [-ɪŋ] *n.* mendicité *f*.

begin [bɪ'g|ɪn], **began** [-æn], **begun** [-ʌn] *v. tr. & intr.* commencer (*with*, *by*, par): *to* ~ *with*, pour commencer; *to* ~ [+ *ing*], commencer/à, de/, se mettre à [+ inf.]; *He began studying French in 1959*, Il s'est mis à étudier le français/en 1959. || **beginner** [-ɪnɚ] *n.* commençant, -e *m/f* débutant, -e *m/f*: *He is only a* ~, → Il ne fait que/commencer, débuter/. || **beginning** [-ɪnɪŋ] *n.* commencement *m*, début *m*; origine *f*; naissance *f*.

begotten cf. BEGET: *God's only* ~ *Son*, le Fils unique de Dieu.

begrudge [bɪ'gɹʌʤ] *v. tr.* envier, être jaloux de; reprocher (un avantage) à.

beguile [bɪ'gajl] *v. tr.* tromper, faire passer (l'attente, le temps).

begun cf. BEGIN.

behalf [bɪ'hæf] *n.*: *in* ~ *of*, en faveur de; *on* ~ *of*, au nom de; *on my* ~ , de ma part, en mon nom.

behave [bɪ'hejv] *v. intr.* **1.** se conduire, agir. **2.** être sage, agir prudemment. || **behaviour** [-jɚ] *n.* **1.** conduite *f*, tenue *f*. **2.** [façon d'agir] (bonnes, mauvaises) manières; [ethnology] comportement *m* (social).

behead [bɪ'hɛd] *v. tr.* décapiter (qqun).

beheld cf. BEHOLD.

behest [bɪ'hɛst] *n.* ordre *m*: *at his* ~ , sur son ordre.

behind [bɪ'hajnd] *adv.* [general area, directions] par derrière; [precise position, or order] derrière; [distance behind] en arrière; [late] en retard: *and there is a garden* ~ , et il y a un jardin par derrière; *He was stabbed from* ~ , Il a été poignardé par derrière; (*to come out*) *from* ~ , (sortir) de derrière; *There is a porch* ~ , Il y a un porche derrière; *The band was* ~ , La musique était/derrière, [some distance back] en arrière/; *He was ten miles* ~ , Il était en arrière de dix milles; *I am* ~ */with, in/my work*, Je suis en retard dans mon travail [see also verbs]. || *prép.* derrière; [progress] en arrière de; [time] en retard sur: *It's* ~ *him*, C'est derrière lui; *Look* ~ *it*, Regardez derrière; *He is* ~ *his brother in his school work*, Il est en arrière de son frère dans ses études; *The train is* ~ *schedule*, Le train est en retard (sur l'horaire); *I'm* ~ *you!*, Je vous suis, [Fig.] Je suis pour vous, Vous pouvez compter sur moi. || *n.* derrière *m*.

†**behold** [bɪ'howld], **beheld, beheld** [bɪ'hɛld] *v. tr.* regarder, contempler. || **behold** *interj.* ~ *!*, (et) voilà (que . . .).

beholden [bɪ'howldn̩] *adj. To be* ~ *to s.o.*, Être redevable à qqun (de, *for*).

behove [bɪ'howv] *v. tr.* [Fig.] appartenir à, incomber à.

being[1] cf. BE.

being[2] *n.* **1.** être *m*: (*a*) *human* ~ , (un) être humain; *human beings*, le genre humain. **2.** existence *f*, nature *f*; *to be in* ~ , exister. **3.** [Loc.] *for the time* ~ , pour le moment [cf. BE].

belated [bɪ'lejtəd] *adj.* [person] attardé, en retard; [arrival] tardif.

belch [bɛltʃ] *v. intr.* [Vulg.] roter; éructer. || *v. tr.* vomir (de la fumée, des flammes). || *n.* [Vulg.] rot *m*, éructation *f*; vomissement *m* (de fumée, de flammes).

Belgian ['bɛldʒ|ən] *adj. & n.* belge *m & f*. || **Belgium** [-əm] *n.* (la) Belgique *f*: *in, to/* ~ , en B.

belie [bɪ'laj] *pr. p.* **belying** *v. tr.* démentir; donner un démenti à.

belief [bɪ'lij|f] *n.* croyance (*en*, in) *f*; conviction *f*, foi *f* (religieuse); confiance (en qqun): *to the best of my* ~ , pour autant que je (le) sache. || **believable** [-vəbl] *adj.* croyable. || **believe** [-v] *v. tr.* croire (une affirmation), ajouter foi (à une parole); penser, estimer: *I* ~ *you*, Je vous crois; *I* ~ *so*, Je crois que oui; *I* ~ *he is right*, Je pense qu'il a raison. || *v. intr.* croire (*in*, à); avoir foi (en qqun, qqch.): *to* ~ *in God*, croire en Dieu; *to make* ~ , faire semblant, supposer. || **believer** [-vər] *n.* croyant, -e. || **believing** [-viŋ] *adj.* **1.** [person] croyant. **2.** [Pej.] crédule.

belittle [bɪ'lɪtl̩] *v. tr.* déprécier, discréditer (qqun); rabaisser, amoindrir (qqch.).

bell [bɛl] *n.* **1.** cloche *f* (d'église); appel *m*, sonnerie *f* (du téléphone), timbre *m* (de bicyclette), sonnette *f* (de porte); [small] clochette *f*, grelot *m*: *church bells*, cloches *fpl*; *to ring a* ~ , sonner (une cloche); *the passing* ~ , le glas *m*; *handbell*, *altar-* ~ , clochette *f*; *bellboy*, chasseur *m* (d'hôtel). **2.** [Naut.] coup *m* de cloche; la demie *f*.

belle [bɛl] *n.* [terme affectif, très souvent péjoratif] (la) belle *f*, (une) beauté *f*.

belligerent [bə'lɪʤərənt] *adj.* [= fond of fighting] belliqueux; [= at war] belligérant. || *n.* nation *f* belligérante.

bellow ['bɛlow] *n.* beuglement *m*, mugissement *m*. || *v. intr.* beugler, mugir.

bellows [-z] *n. pl.* soufflet *m*.

belly [bɛlɪ] *n.* ventre *m*: ~ *ache*, mal *m*/de ventre, d'estomac/.

belong [bɪ'lɔŋ] [bə'lɔŋ] *v. intr.* appartenir (à qqun, qqch.), être (à qqun); être membre, faire partie de (tel groupe, pays): *He belongs to this Association*, Il/fait partie, est membre/de cette association; *This belongs to me*, → Ceci m'appartient, C'est à moi; [*absol.*] *He belongs here*, Il est chez lui, Il se sent chez lui/ici. || **belongings** [-ɪŋz] *n.pl* effets *mpl* personnels, affaires *fpl*.

beloved [bɪ'lʌvəd] *adj.* bien-aimé [never used before the noun], cher; chéri.

below [bɪ'low] *prép.* sous, au-dessous de. || *adv.* dessous, au-dessous: *down* ~ , en bas; *see* ~ , cf. ci-dessous, voir plus loin.

belt [bɛlt] *n.* ceinture *f*; [Mil.] ceinturon *m*; [Medic.] bande *f*; [Geog.] zone *f*; fuseau *m* (horaire): [Fig.] *to hit below the* ~ , porter (à qqun) un coup en traître; ~ *work*, travail à la chaîne. || *v. tr.* ceindre, ceinturer; entourer (d'une ceinture, d'une bande).

bemoan [bɪ'mown] *v. tr.* [Fig.] pleurer sur.

bench [bɛnʧ] *n.* **1.** banc *m*; banquette *f* (de restaurant); gradin *m* (d'amphithéâtre); établi *m* (de menuisier). **2.** *the Bench*, la Cour, la magistrature; siège *m* du juge: *the Queen's Bench*, © tribunal *m* du Banc de la Reine.

bend [bɛnd], **bent, bent** [bɛnt] *v. tr.* **1.** courber, plier (une barre de fer); faire plier, fléchir (le genou); incliner (la tête); tendre (un arc). **2.** *To* ~ *one's steps towards*, diriger, porter/ses pas (vers un endroit), se diriger vers. || *v. intr.* **1.** plier, se (re)courber: *The branch began to* ~ , La branche commença à plier. **2.** se baisser, se pencher: *He bent to the ground and picked up a stone*, Il se baissa pour ramasser une pierre; *to* ~ *over*, se pencher (en avant); [Fig.] *to* ~ *to*, fléchir devant, se plier à; *I bent to his will*, Je me pliai à sa volonté, cf. BENT. || *n.* **1.** courbure *f*; [rope] nœud *m*; [limb] pli *m*. **2.** [road] tournant *m*; courbe *f*, virage *m*: *There is a sharp* ~ *in the road here*, → La route fait ici un coude brusque; *hairpin* ~ , virage en épingle à cheveux. **3.** *the bends*, *npl.* mal *m* des caissons.

beneath [bɪ'nijθ] *adv.* dessous; [lower] au-dessous. || *prép.* [under] sous; [lower] au-dessous de: [Fig.] *It's* ~ *him to do that*, Il est indigne de lui de faire cela.

Benedictine [ˌbɛnə'dɪktɪn] *n.* & *adj.* **1.** [R.C.] Bénédictin *m*. **2.** [liqueur] bénédictine *f*.

benediction [ˌbɛnə'dɪkʃən] *n.* bénédiction *f*.

benefac|tor, -tress ['bɛnəˌfæk|tər, -tɹəs] *n.* bienfai|teur, -trice.

benefice ['bɛnəfəs] *n.* [Rel.] bénéfice *m* (du clergé); [× Au sens commercial, cf. BENEFIT]. || **beneficent** [ˌbɛnə'fɪʃ|ənt] *adj.* [kind] bienfaisant. || **beneficial** [-əl] *adj.* [helpful] avantageux, salutaire (*pour*, *à*, to). || **benefit** ['bɛnɪfət] *n.* profit *m*, bénéfice *m*; secours *m*: *unemployment* ~ , indemnité *f*/prestation *f*/de chômage: ~ *society*, société *f* de secours mutuel; *for his* ~ , à son profit; *for your* ~ , *let me . . .* , à votre intention, permettez-moi de . . . || *v. tr.* faire du bien à, profiter à (qqun). || *v. intr.*: *to* ~ *from, by*, profiter de, se trouver bien de (qqch.); gagner (à).

benevolence [bə'nɛvələn|s] *n.* **1.** bienveillance *f*. **2.** bienfaisance *f*. || **benevolent** [-t] *adj.* **1.** [person] bienveillant (*to*, envers). **2.** [charity] bienfaisant.

benign [bə'najn] *adj.* **1.** [person] affable, bienfaisant, doux. **2.** [drug, etc.] bénin,

bénigne. || **benignant** [bə'nɪgnənt] *adj.* [person] bienveillant, bon.
bent[1] cf. BEND.
bent[2] *n.* penchant *m*, inclination *f*, tendance *f.* || *adj.* courbé, penché; plié: *to be ~ on* (*doing . . .*), être décidé/résolu/à (+ *inf.*).
benzene, benzine [bɛn'zijn] *n.* benzine *f.*
bequeath [bɪ'kw|ijθ] *v. tr.* léguer (à, *to*). || **bequest** [-ɛst] *n.* legs *m.*
berate [bɪ'ɹejt] *v. tr.* gronder: *to ~ s.o. for sth.*, reprocher qqch. à qqun.
bereave [bɪ'ɹ|ijv], **bereft** [-ɛft] or **bereaved** [-ijvd] *v. tr.* priver, déposséder (de, *of*): *The bereaved*, **La** famille du défunt. || **bereavement** [-ijvmənt] *n.* deuil *m*, perte *f* (d'un parent).
bereft cf. BEREAVE.
beret [bə'ɹej] ['bɛəɹ] *n.* béret *m.*
Bermuda(s) [bə'mjuwdə] *n*(*pl*) [Géog.] les Bermudes *fpl*: *in, to ~*, aux B.; *~ shorts*, © bermudas *mpl.*
berry ['bɛəɹ] *n.* [Bot.] baie *f*; grain *m* (de café).
berth [bəθ] *n.* couchette *f*, lit *m* (de cabine); [Naut.] mouillage *m*, poste *m* d'amarrage (d'un bateau); †poste *m*, emploi *m*: *to give* (*s.o., sth.*) *a wide ~*, éviter soigneusement (qqun, qqch.); se garder d'approcher (qqun).
Bertha [bəθə] *n.* = Berthe.
†beseech [bɪ'sijtʃ], **besought, besought** [bɪ'sɑt] *v. tr.* implorer/supplier/(Dieu).
beset [bɪ'sɛt], **beset, beset** *v. tr.* serrer (de près), entourer (de, *with*); [wounds] assaillir, couvrir (de, *with*): *besetting sin*, péché mignon.
beside [bɪ'sajd] *prép.* **1.** à côté de, auprès de: *Sit ~ me*, Asseyez-vous à côté de moi. **2.** excepté, à part, †hormis: *Who was there ~ yourself?*, Qu'y avait-il à part vous?; [Loc.] *He was ~ himself*, Il était /hors de lui, dans tous ses états/; *This is ~ the point*, Ceci est hors de propos. || **besides** [bɪ'sajdz] *prép.* outre, à part. cf. BESIDE 2. || *adv.* **1.** en outre, de plus. **2.** du reste, d'ailleurs.
besiege [bɪ'sijdʒ] *v. tr.* assiéger (une place forte).
besought [bɪ'sɑt] cf. BESEECH.
best [bɛst] *adj.* [superlatif de GOOD] **1.** le meilleur, la meilleure, les meilleurs: *The ~ hotel in town*, Le meilleur hôtel de la ville. **2.** [in conjunction with THING] le mieux: *The ~ thing to do*, Le mieux (serait de . . .), Ce qu'il y a de mieux à faire. **3.** [PART] *The ~ part of* (*the day, &c.*), La plus grande partie (de la journée, &c.). || *adv.* le mieux; le plus: *at ~*, (en mettant les choses) au mieux; *Who reads ~ ?*, Quel est celui qui lit le mieux?; *I like this book ~*, C'est le livre que j'aime/le mieux, le plus/que je préfère/; *You know ~*, →C'est vous qui êtes le mieux placé pour en juger; *I had ~* (*go home early*), → Il vaut mieux (que je rentre de bonne heure). || *n.* ce qu'il y a de mieux, le summum (de . . .), [Fam.] la crème, le dessus du panier: *We want/the ~, nothing but the ~/*, Nous voulons (avoir) ce qu'il y a de mieux; *I did my ~ to finish the work on time*, J'ai fait de mon mieux/mon possible/pour terminer le travail à temps; *to be at one's ~*, se surpasser, [Fam.] être en pleine forme; *He was at his ~* (*in Hamlet*), → Il s'est surpassé (dans le rôle de Hamlet); *He can run with the ~*, Il se classe parmi les meilleurs coureurs; *All for the ~*, Ç'aurait pu être pire, Après tout, ça n'est pas si mal; *to get the ~ of*, l'emporter sur, avoir l'avantage (sur), avoir le dessus (de); *to make the ~ of*, tirer le meilleur parti de; *to the ~ of my ability*, → du mieux que j'ai pu; *to the ~ of my knowledge*, du meilleur de ma connaissance.
bestial ['bɛstʃəl] *adj.* bestial. || **bestiality** [ˌbɛstʃɪ'ælɪtɪ] *n.* bestialité *f.*
bestow [bɪ'stow] *v. tr.* accorder (une faveur), donner (qqch.) (*on s.o.*, à qqun).
best seller [ˌbɛst'sɛlə] *n.* **1.** livre *m*/à succès, à fort tirage/. **2.** auteur *m* à gros tirage.
bet [bɛt] *n.* pari *m*, gageure *f.* || **bet, bet** *or* **betted** *v. tr.* parier, © gager. || *v. intr.* faire un pari: *You ~ !*, Je vous crois!, [Fam.] Tu paries!
betray [bɪ'tɹej] *v. tr.* trahir, tromper (qqun), révéler (un fait). || **betrayal** [-l] *n.* trahison *f.* || **betrayer** [-ə] *n.* traître, -esse.
†betroth [bɪ'tɹowð] *v. tr.* fiancer (des jeunes gens). || **betrothal** [-əl] *n.* fiançailles *fpl.* || **betrothed** [-d] *adj.* & *n.* fiancé, -e.
better[1] cf. BETTOR.
better[2] [cf. GOOD] [bɛtə] *adj. compar.* meilleur; mieux; [cleverer] plus fort; [more virtuous] plus sage, &c. cf. GOOD: *He is a ~ student than you think*, C'est un meilleur élève que vous ne croyez; *That's ~*, C'est mieux, Voilà qui est mieux; *to get ~*, [things] s'améliorer; [Pers.] se remettre (d'une maladie); [improve] faire mieux; *I/am, feel/ ~ today*, Je vais, Je me sens/mieux aujourd'hui; *Which* (*one*) *is ~ ?*, Lequel vaut mieux?; *It is ~ to say nothing*, Il vaut mieux se taire; *to go one ~*, renchérir; *the ~ part* (*of Sunday*), la plus

grande partie (du dimanche). || *adv. compar.* mieux: *so much the* ~ , tant mieux; *I like it* ~ *than the other one,* Je l'aime mieux que l'autre; *You had* ~ *not do that,* Vous fer(i)ez mieux de ne pas faire cela; *He thought* ~ *of it,* Il/s'est ravisé, a changé d'avis/; *He thought* ~ *of me for it,* Il m'en estimait davantage; *His brother is* ~ *known than he,* Son frère est plus connu que lui; *Now I know* ~ , → Maintenant, j'ai plus d'expérience; Maintenant, je sais; Maintenant, je suis fixé (sur le compte de qqun). || *n.* mieux *m*: [Pers., usual. *pl.*] supérieurs *mpl*: *to change for the* ~ , changer pour le mieux; *to get the* ~ *of s.o.,* l'emporter sur qqun; [Fam.] avoir qqun; *to get the* ~ *of sth.,* vaincre, surmonter/qqch. || *v. tr.* rendre meilleur, améliorer; surpasser (qqch.): *to* ~ *o.s.,* améliorer sa position. || **better half** *n.* (ma) (chère) épouse *f,* (mon) épouse. || **betterment** [-mənt] *n.* amélioration *f* (d'une situation, etc.).

betting [bɛtɪŋ] *n.* pari *m.*

bettor [bɛtər] *n.* parieur *m,* © gageur *m,* cf. BET.

between [bɪ'twijn] *prep.* entre, à: ~ *us,* entre nous; *There is a fence* ~ *the two lots,* /Il y a une barrière entre, Une barrière sépare/les deux terrains; ~ *now and Christmas,* d'ici (à) Noël, *We ate the pie* ~ *us,* Nous avons mangé la tarte à nous/deux, trois, &c.

beverage ['bɛvɹədʒ] *n.* boisson *f* (en général); © breuvage *m.* || **beverages** *pl.* [-z] **1.** boissons gazeuses, limonades *fpl.* **2.** [alcoholic] bière *f,* vin *m.*

bevy ['bɛvɪ] *n.* bande *f,* essaim *m.*

bewail [bɪ'wejl] *v. tr.* déplorer.

†**beware** [bɪ'wɛər] *v. intr.* [ce verbe n'est usité qu'à l'infinitif et à l'impératif] prendre garde (*of,* à): ~ *of the dog!,* Prenez garde au chien/Attention! Chien méchant!; se méfier de, se défier de.

bewilder [bɪ'wɪldər] *v. tr.* désorienter; [Fam.] ahurir. || **bewildered** [-d] *adj.* désorienté; [Fam.] ahuri, abasourdi. || **bewildering** [-ɪŋ] *adj.* déroutant; [Fam.] ahurissant. || **bewilderment** [-mənt] *n.* trouble *m*; [Fam.] ahurissement *m.*

bewitch [bɪ'wɪtʃ] *v. tr.* ensorceler (qqun); [Fam.] enchanter (qqun).

beyond [bɪ'jɑnd] *adv.* au-delà, plus loin. || *prép.* au-delà de; plus loin que; [exceeding] au-dessus de; [later than] après; [besides] en dehors de; [in set expressions] outre: ~/*the sea, the mountains,* au-delà/de la mer, des montagnes; *Our school is* ~ *the city hall,* Notre école est plus loin que l'hôtel de ville; *to go* ~ *the limit,* dépasser les bornes; *It's* ~ *my strength,* C'est au-dessus de mes forces; *That is* ~ *my wildest hopes,* Cela dépasse mes espoirs les plus extravagants; *It's* ~ *me,* Cela me dépasse; ~ *the first of April, no further applications will be accepted,* Après le premier avril, on n'acceptera plus de demandes; *I have nothing* ~ *personal effects to declare,* Je n'ai rien à déclarer en dehors des effets personnels; ~ *reach,* hors de portée; ~ *doubt,* hors de doute; ~ *measure,* outre mesure; ~ *the sea(s),* outre-mer, &c.

bias ['bajəs] *n.* [slant] biais *m*: *on the* ~ , en biais; [Fig.] parti pris *m,* préjugé *m,* penchant *m* (*for,* pour; *against,* contre). || *v. tr.* faire pencher; [Fig.] influencer (qqun). || *adv.* de biais, de travers. || **biassed** [-t] *adj.* partial: *to be* ~ *against,* avoir des préventions contre.

Bible ['bajbl̩] *n.* Bible *f,* livre(s) saint(s) *m(pl).*: [Fig.] *This book is my Bible,* Ce livre est mon bréviaire. || **biblical** ['bɪblɪkl̩] *adj.* biblique.

bibliography [bɪblɪ'ɑgɹəfɪ] *n.* bibliographie *f.*

bicker ['bɪkər] *v. intr.* se chamailler.

bicycle ['bajsəkl̩] *n.* bicyclette *f,* © bicycle *m*: *on a, by*/~ , à, [Fam.] en/bicyclette. || *v. intr.* [travel] aller (quelque part) à bicyclette; [activity] faire/de la bicyclette, du cyclisme/. || **bicyclist** [-ɪst] *n.* cycliste *m/f.*

bid[1] [bɪd] *n.* offre *f*; [auction] enchère *f,* tentative *f*; [bridge] annonce *f*: *to make a* ~ *for sth.,* essayer/d'avoir, de faire/ qqch.

bid[2] [bɪd] *v. tr.* **1. bad(e)** [bæd], **bidden** [bɪdn̩], **bidding** [bɪdɪŋ] dire, ordonner, donner l'ordre (à qqun de faire qqch.): *I bade him wait,* Je lui ai dit d'attendre; *to* ~ *s.o. goodday,* souhaiter le bonjour à qqun; *to* ~ *s.o. farewell,* dire adieu à qqun. || **2. bid, bid, bidding** offrir; [auction] faire une offre, mettre une enchère, (*for, on, sth.,* sur qqch.); [bridge] annoncer (une couleur). || **bid up** [bɪd|'ʌp] *v. tr. & intr.* surenchérir: *to bid s.o. up,* faire surenchérir qqun; *to bid sth. up,* surenchérir. || **bidder** [-ər] *n.*: *to the highest* ~ , au plus offrant. || **bidding** [-ɪŋ] *n.* ordres *mpl*; invitation *f.*

†**bide** [bajd] *v. tr.*: *to* ~ *o's time,* attendre le bon moment/le moment favorable. || *v. intr.* rester, demeurer (chez soi).

bier [bijər] *n.* **1.** civière *f.* **2.** corbillard *m.*

bifocals [ˌbaj'fowkls] *n.pl.* [Opt.] verres *mpl* à double foyer.

big [bɪg] *adj.* [-gg-] grand; gros; fort; important: [☞ The distinction between *grand* and *gros* depends largely on usage; *grand* has the idea of *tall* or *large* and *gros* of bulk; in France, *grand* is used more often than *gros*, while in Canada, the reverse is true]: *a ~ man*, [tall] un homme (de) grande taille, [fat] un gros homme; *a ~ woman*, une forte femme; *a big/boy, girl/*, [= growing up] un grand garçon, une grande (jeune) fille/; [Fig.] *a ~ voice*, une voix forte; *the Big Three*, les trois Grands; *a ~ decision*, une décision importante; *a ~ firm*, une société importante; *a ~ deal*, une grosse affaire; *to get/grow, big(ger)/*, [taller, larger] grandir; [bulkier] grossir; *~ enough to* . . . , de taille à . . . ‖ *adv. to/see, think/~* , voir grand; *to/act, talk/~* , faire l'important, se vanter. ‖ **big horn** [-ˌhɔɚn] *n.* mouflon *m.* ‖ **bigness** [-nəs] *n.* grosseur *f*, grande taille. ‖ **big wig** [-ˌwɪg] *n.* [Fam.] gros bonnet *m.*

bigot [ˈbɪgət] *n.* bigot, -e, fanatique *mf.* ‖ **bigoted** [-əd] *adj.* [attitude, reaction] bigot, sectaire, [person] à l'esprit étroit. ‖ **bigotry** [-ɹɪ] *n.* [religion] bigoterie *f*, [politics] fanatisme *m*, sectarisme *m.*

bike [bajk] *n.* [Fam.] vélo *m.*

bile [bajl] *n.* [gall] bile *f*; [Fig.] colère *f.*

bilingual [ˌbajlɪŋgwəl] *adj.* & *n.* bilingue, (rédigé) en deux langues. ‖ **bilingualism** [-ɪzm] *n.* bilinguisme *m.*

bilious [ˈbɪljəs] *adj.* [health] bilieux; [Fig., Pers.] colérique.

bilk [bɪlk] *v. tr.* [Fam.] tromper, attraper: *to be bilked of sth.*, se faire voler qqch.; *to be bilked in a deal*, se faire attraper dans une affaire.

bill[1] [bɪl] *n.* **1.** [Com.] facture *f*, compte *m*; note *f* (d'hôtel); addition *f* (de restaurant). **2.** affiche *f*: *billboard*, panneau-réclame *m*; *Post no Bills*, → Défense d'afficher. **3.** [bank] lettre *f* de change, traite *f*; billet *m* (de banque). **4.** [Pol.] projet *m* de loi, © bill *m*: *private ~* , bill *m* (d'intérêt) privé; *Bill of Rights*, Déclaration *f* des Droits de l'Homme; *~ of lading*, connaissement *m.* ‖ *v. tr.* facturer (des marchandises); afficher, placarder.

bill[2] [bɪl] *n.* **1.** bec *m* (d'oiseau). **2.** [Geog.] promontoire *m*, bec *m.* ‖ *v. intr.* se becqueter.

billet [ˈbɪlət] *n.* **1.** [stick] billette *f* (de bois, d'acier). **2.** [army] billet *m* (de logement). ‖ *v. tr.* [army] donner un billet de logement à (un soldat), loger (un soldat) chez l'habitant.

billfold [ˈbɪlˌfowld] *n.* portefeuille *m.*

billiards [ˈbɪljɚd(z)] *n.* billard *m*: *to have a game of ~* , faire une partie de billard; *to play ~* , jouer au billard; *billiard cue*, queue *f* de billard; *billiard-table*, billard *m.*

billion [ˈbɪljən] *n.* [number] [Br.] trillion *m*, (US, ©) milliard *m*, billion *m.*

billow [ˈbɪlow] *n.* [sea] houle *f*, lame *f*, vague(s) *f(pl).* ‖ *v. intr.* [sea] s'élever/se soulever/en vagues. ‖ **billowy** [-ɪ] *adj.* [sea] houleux, ondoyant.

bin [bɪn] *n.* coffre *m*; huche *f* (à pain), bac *m* (à ordures): [Br.] *dustbin*, boîte à ordure. cf. GARBAGE.

bind [bajnd], **bound, bound** [bawnd] *v. tr.* **1.** attacher (avec une corde); lier, ligoter (les mains); serrer, fixer (un objet à un autre); panser, bander (une blessure); border (un chapeau); relier (un livre). **2.** [Fig.] confirmer (une entente); obliger, forcer (qqun à faire qqch.). ‖ **binder** [ˈbajnd|ɚ] *n.* **1.** [person] lieur *m*; [book] relieur *m.* **2.** [band] attache *f.* **3.** [Agric.] moissonneuse-lieuse *f.* ‖ **binding**[1] [-ɪŋ] *n.* reliure *f* (d'un livre). ‖ **binding**[2] *adj.* [law] obligatoire: *This text shall be ~* , Ce texte fera foi.

binge [bɪnʤ] [Fam.] *n.* virée *f*: *to go on a ~* , faire une virée.

bingo [ˈbɪŋgow] *n.* © [game] bingo *m.*

bio- [ˌbajow] *préf.* bio-. ‖ **biographer** [bajˈɑgɹəf|ɚ] *n.* biographe *m.* ‖ **biography** [-ɪ] *n.* biographie *f.* ‖ **biologist** [bajˈɑləʤɪ|st] *n.* biologiste *m.* ‖ **biology** *n.* biologie *f.*

birch [bɚtʃ] *n.* bouleau *m.*

bird [bɚd] *n.* oiseau *m*; [Culin.] volaille *f*; gibier *m* (à plumes): *~ of prey*, rapace *m*, oiseau *m* de proie; [Fig.] type *m*, individu *m*: *Birds of a feather flock together*, Qui sent la caque sent le hareng, Ce sont des gens du même acabit; *To kill two birds with one stone*, Faire d'une pierre deux coups; *a bird's eye view*, vue *f* à vol d'oiseau.

biretta [bɪˈɹɛtə] *n.* [R.C.] barrette *f.*

birth [bɚθ] *n.* naissance *f*; [Fig.] origine *f*, début *m*: *to give ~ (to a son, daughter)*, donner naissance (à un fils, une fille)/ mettre (un enfant) au monde; *~ certificate*, acte *m* de naissance; *~ -place*, lieu *m* de naissance, pays *m* (natal); *~ rate*, natalité *f*; [right] droit *m* d'aînesse. ‖ **birthday** [-ˌdej] *n.* anniversaire *m* (de naissance); [saint's day] fête *f*: *~ party*, fête *f*; *~ present*, cadeau *m* de fête; *the Queen's Birthday*, Fête de la Reine.

biscuit [ˈbɪskət] *n.* **1.** biscuit *m.* **2.** gâteau *m* sec.

bisect [ˌbajˈsɛkt] *v. tr.* couper en deux parties égales.

bishop [ˈbɪʃəp] *n.* **1.** évêque *m*: *~'s palace,* palais *m* épiscopal, évêché *m*. **2.** [Chess] fou *m*. || **bishopric** [-ɹɪk] *n.* évêché *m*, diocèse *m*.

bison [ˈbajsən, bajzən] *n.* [*pl.* unchanged] bison *m*.

bit[1] [bɪt] *n.* **1.** morceau *m*, fragment *m*; [Fam.] un peu, un bout de: *a ~ of bread,* un peu de pain; *to do one's ~*, faire sa part; *He is a ~ silly,* Il est un peu toqué; *not a ~*, pas du tout; *a ~ of/news, advice,* une nouvelle, un conseil. **2.** [tool] mèche *f*; [bridle] mors *m*.

bit[2] cf. BITE.

bitch [bɪʧ] *n.* chienne *f*.

bite [bajt], **bit** [bɪt], **bitten** [ˈbɪtn̩] *v. tr.* mordre; [insects] piquer; [wind] couper: *a biting wind,* vent qui vous coupe la figure; brûler: *His fingers are bitten by frost,* Le froid lui brûle les doigts; *to ~ one's nails,* se ronger les ongles. || *n.* **1.** coup *m* de dent; morsure *f*; [insecte] piqûre *f*. **2.** bouchée *f*; morceau *m*: *Let's have a ~*, Allons casser la croûte! || **biting** [ˈbajtɪŋ] *adj.* mordant, piquant. || **bitten** cf. BITE.

bitter [ˈbɪtɚ] *adj.* [food] amer; [wine] aigre; [wind] aigre, piquant; [cold] rigoureux, cinglant; [remorse] cuisant; [hatred] acharné: *to the ~ end,* jusqu'au bout. || **bitterly** [-lɪ] *adv.* amèrement, avec amertume; [Fig.] aigrement: *It was ~ cold,* Il faisait/un froid extrême, extrêmement froid/. || **bitterness** [-nəs] *n.* amertume *f*, rigueur *f* (de l'hiver, du temps); aigreur *f* (d'un propos); acrimonie *f* (d'un sentiment); rancune *f*. || **bitter-sweet** [-ˌswijt] *n.* [plant] douce-amère *f*. || *adj.* aigre-doux.

black [blæk] *adj.* noir; sombre: *~ eye,* œil poché, [Fam.] au beurre noir; *~ blizzard,* © blizzard *m* noir. || *n.* [colour] noir *m*; [dress] *in ~*, en deuil; [negro] noir *m*, nègre *m*; *~-out,* obscurcissement *m*. || *v. tr.* noircir (qqch.). || **blackberry** [-ˌbɛɚɪ] *n.* mûre *f* (de ronce). || **blackbird** [-ˌbɚd] *n.* merle *m*. || **blackboard** [-ˌboɚd] *n.* [School] tableau *m* (noir). || **blacken** [-n̩] *v. tr. & intr.* noircir. || **Blackfoot** [-ˌfut] *n.* [Indian] Pied-Noir *m*. || **blackmail** [-ˌmejl] *n.* chantage *m*. || *v. tr.* faire chanter (qqun). || **blackness** [-nəs] *n.* noirceur *f*. || **black pudding** [-ˈpudɪŋ] *n.* boudin *m*.

bladder [ˈblædɚ] *n.* vessie *f*.

blade [blejd] *n.* lame *f* (de couteau, de rasoir, d'épée, de feuille, de scie); épée *f*, sabre *m*; brin *m* (d'herbe); pale *f* (d'aviron, d'hélice); plat *m* (de la langue); [Fam.] (solide) gaillard *m*.

blame [blejm] *n.* blâme *m*, reproches *mpl.*, condamnation *f*; faute *f*, responsabilité *f*. || *v. tr.* blâmer, condamner (qqun de qqch., *for sth.*); reprocher (qqch.) à (qqun): *to ~ s.o. for sth.*, s'en prendre à qqun de qqch. || **blameless** [-ləs] *adj.* innocent, irréprochable.

bland [blænd] *adj.* doux, aimable.

blank [blæŋk] *n.* blanc *m*, vide *m* (sur un document); trou *m*, lacune *f* (de mémoire). || *adj.* [paper] blanc; [cheque] en blanc; [page] vierge; [look, face] vague, perdu; déconcerté: *point ~*, de but en blanc, [shooting] à bout portant; formule *f*.

blanket [ˈblæŋkət] *n.* couverture *f* (de lit, de cheval); [Fig.] *wet ~*, (un) rabat-joie. || *v. tr.* mettre une couverture à (qqch.); [Fig.] (re)couvrir; étouffer (un scandale).

blare [blɛɚ] *n.* bruit *m* (retentissant, prolongé), bruit de trompettes. || *v. tr.* sonner (de la trompette). || *v. intr.* résonner.

blaspheme [ˌblæsˈfijm] *v. intr.* blasphémer. || **blasphemer** [-ɚ] *n.* blasphémateur *m*, © sacreur *m*. || **blasphemous** [ˈblæsfəm|əs] *adj.* [person] blasphémat|eur, -rice; [words] blasphématoire. || **blasphemy** [-ɪ] *n.* blasphème *m*.

blast [blæst] *n.* **1.** [wind] rafale *f*, coup *m* de vent; souffle *m* (d'une explosion); air *m* (chaud, froid). **2.** [noises] coup *m* (de sifflet), sonnerie *f* (de) trompette, explosion *f*. **3.** [Fig.] *in full ~*, en pleine activité: *~ furnace n.* haut fourneau *m*. || *v. tr.* faire sauter (à la dynamite); [Fig.] détruire; anéantir; ruiner.

blatant [ˈblejtn̩t] *adj.* criant.

blaze [blejz] *n.* flambée *f*, flamme *f*; [sun] flamboiement *m*; [colours, jewels] éclat *m*; [Fig.] accès *m* (de colère). || *v. intr.* [fire] flamber; [© colours, sun] flamboyer; [precious stones, metal] étinceler; [costume] resplendir; [Fig.] être embrasé, enflammé (de colère). || *v. tr.* claironner, proclamer (une nouvelle); marquer, griffer (un arbre).

blazer [ˈblejzɚ] *n.* blazer *m*.

bleach [blijʧ] *v. tr.* blanchir; (hair) oxygéner. || *v. intr.* pâlir, blanchir.

bleak [blijk] *adj.* froid, exposé au vent; désolé, désert.

bleat [blijt] *n.* bêlement *m*. || *v. intr.* bêler.

bled cf. BLEED.

bleed [blijd], **bled**, **bled** [blɛd] *v. tr.* (faire) saigner (qqun); [Fig.] saigner (*white,* à blanc), gruger (qqun), extorquer de l'argent à (qqun). || *v. intr.* saigner, perdre du sang, perdre sa sève; [water, gas] fuir; [Fig.] éprouver de la compassion (pour qqun). || **bleeding** [-ɪŋ] *n.* saignement *m,* hémorragie *f.*

blemish [blɛmɪʃ] *n.* **1.** défaut *m,* imperfection *f.* **2.** tache *f,* tare *f.* || *v. tr.* **1.** tacher, entacher, souiller. **2.** abîmer, gâter (un travail).

blench[1] [blɛntʃ] *v. intr.* sourciller; broncher.

blench[2] *v. intr.* pâlir, blêmir. || *v. tr.* blanchir, faire pâlir (une couleur).

blend [blɛnd], **blended** [-əd] or **blent** [blɛnt] *v. tr.* mélanger (à, *with*); fondre (des couleurs); réunir. || *v. intr.* [colours, sounds] se marier, se fondre. || *n.* mélange *m.*

bless [blɛs] *v. tr.* [☞ × blesser] bénir, donner une bénédiction (à qqun); consacrer (une cloche); bénir (qqun) de (qqch.): *to be blessed with,* avoir le bonheur de . . . || **blessed** [-əd] *adj.* béni, -e, [by priest] bénit, -e; saint, bienheureux. || **blessing** [-ɪŋ] *n.* bénédiction *f*; grâce *f* (de Dieu): *to ask a* ~, dire le bénédicité; [Fig.] avantage *m,* bienfait *m* (de l'instruction, &c.).

blew cf. BLOW.

blight [blajt] *n.* **1.** rouille *f*; [food] brouissure *f.* **2.** peste *f*; fléau *m.*

blighter [-ɚ] *n.* [Fam. & Pej.] type *m.*

blind [blajnd] *adj.* aveugle; [track] invisible; [window] aveugle: ~ *in one eye,* borgne; ~ *alley,* impasse *f*; [Fig.] *to be* ~ *to sth.,* fermer les yeux sur qqch. || *adv.* à l'aveuglette: *to fly* ~, voler sans visibilité. || *v. tr.* aveugler (qqun), rendre (qqun) aveugle; bander les yeux à. || *n.* **1.** *the* ~ (*pl.*), les aveugles. **2.** store *m*; abat-jour *m*; [Fig.] feinte *f,* façade *f*; *Venetian* ~, jalousie *f,* © store *m* vénitien. || **blindfold** [-ˌfowld] *v. tr.* bander les yeux à. || *adv.* les yeux bandés. || *n.* bandeau *m.* || **blinding** [-ɪŋ] *adj.* (of light, snow) aveuglant. || **blindly** [-lɪ] *adv.* aveuglément, à l'aveuglette. || **blindness** [-nəs] *n.* cécité *f*; [Fig.] aveuglement *m.*

blink [blɪŋk] *v. intr.* cligner des yeux, battre des paupières; [light] clignoter; [Fig.] fermer les yeux (*at,* sur). || *n.* clignotement *m* (des yeux, de la lumière), lueur *f* intermittente. || **blinker** [-ɚ] *n.* œillère *f*; [traffic light] feu *m* clignotant, clignotant *m.*

bliss [blɪs] *n.* béatitude *f,* félicité *f.* || **blissful** [-fl̩] *adj.* bienheureux. || **blissfulness** [-fl̩nəs] *n.* béatitude *f.*

blister [ˈblɪstɚ] *n.* ampoule *f* (sur la peau); (paint) boursouflure *f,* cloque *f.* || *v. tr. & intr.* boursoufler.

blizzard [ˈblɪzɚd] *n.* /rafale *f,* tempête *f*/de neige, © poudrerie *f*: *black* ~, poudrerie *f* noire.

bloat [blowt] *v. tr.* enfler, gonfler. || **bloated** [-əd] *adj.* bouffi, boursouflé.

bloc [blɑk] *n.* [Pol.] bloc *m*: *en bloc,* d'un seul bloc, en bloc.

block [blɑk] *n.* **1.** bloc *m* (de marbre, de fer), quartier *m* (de roche); morceau *m* (de bois); [street] pâté *m* de maisons: *two blocks away,* → à deux rues de là; deux coins de rue plus loin. **2.** [traffic] encombrement *m*; embouteillage *m.* **3.** [printing] cliché *m*; ~ *letter,* lettre *f* moulée: *in* ~ *letters,* en caractères d'imprimerie. || *v. tr.* obstruer, boucher; barrer (le passage); [Fig.] entraver; gêner.

blockade [ˌblɑˈkejd] *n.* blocus *m.* || *v. tr.* faire le blocus de.

blockhead [ˈblɑkˌhɛd] *n.* imbécile *m*; idiot *m*; crétin *m.*

blond(e) [blɑnd] *adj. & n.* blond, -e. || *n.* [man] blond; [girl] blonde.

blood [blʌd] *n.* sang *m*: ~ *bank,* banque *f* de sang; [Fig.] tempérament *m,* état *m* d'esprit; *in cold* ~, de sang froid; *in bad* ~, méchamment; [Fig.] liens *mpl* de famille, parenté *f*; ~ *is thicker than water,* l'appel de la race; *warm-blooded,* (animal) à sang chaud. || **bloodless** [-ləs] *adj.* exsangue. || **bloodshed** [-ˌʃɛd] *n.* effusion *f* de sang. || **bloodsucker** [-ˌsʌkɚ] *n.* sangsue *f.* || **bloodthirsty** [-θɚstɪ] *adj.* cruel, sanguinaire. || **bloody** [-ɪ] *adj.* sanglant, ensanglanté.

bloom [bluwm] *n.* floraison *f,* fleur *f*; épanouissement *m* (de la beauté, &c.); velouté *m* (du raisin), duvet *m* (d'une pêche). || *v. intr.* être en fleur, fleurir, être en (pleine) floraison; s'épanouir.

blossom [ˈblɑsəm] *n.* fleur *f* (d'un arbre, &c.); fleuraison *f*: *in* ~, en fleur. || *v. intr.* [tree] fleurir; [Fig.] se développer, s'épanouir.

blot [blɑt] *n.* tache *f,* pâté *m* (d'encre); [Fig.] souillure *f.* || **[-tt-]** *v. tr.* salir, tacher, barbouiller, faire un pâté (d'encre); [= dry] sécher l'encre (d'une lettre), passer le buvard sur (l'encre): *blotting paper,* (papier) buvard *m*: *to* ~ *out,* effacer, masquer (qqch.); [Fig.] exterminer. || **blotter** [-ɚ] *n.* buvard *m.*

blouse [blawz] *n.* [Cost.] blouse *f*; [Mil.] vareuse *f* (de soldat).

blow[1] [blow] *n.* coup *m* (de poing, de bâton): *to come to blows,* en venir aux coups; coup *m* de vent, souffle *m*; [Fig.] coup *m,* choc *m.*

blow[2] [blow], **blew** [bluw], **blown** [blown] *v. intr.* [wind] souffler, venter; [electric bulb] griller; [fuse] sauter, fondre; [tire] éclater; [curtains] ballotter, voler (dans le vent), s'enfler. || *v. tr.* chasser, pousser (en soufflant); essouffler (qqun), faire voler, éclater (qqch.); gonfler (un ballon): *to ~ one's nose*, se moucher; *to ~ one's brains out*, se brûler la cervelle. || **blow in** [ˈblow|ɪn] arriver à l'improviste; *to ~ out* (*a candle*), souffler (une bougie); *to ~ up*, exploser; agrandir (une photo).

blower [-ɚ] *n.* souffleur *m*, soufflerie *f*.

blown cf. BLOW.

blowout [-awt] *n.* éclatement *m* (d'un. pneu). || **blow up** [-ˌʌp] *v. tr.* [photo] agrandir. || *n.* explosion *f* (de colère). krach *m* (d'une maison de commerce).

blue [bluw] *adj.* bleu, bleuté; *sky ~*, azur; [Fig.] triste, cafardeux: *to feel ~*, avoir le cafard; *once in a ~ moon*, tous les trente-six du mois; [hockey] *~ line*, la ligne bleue. || *n.* bleu *m*, azur *m*: *the ~*, la mer *f*; le ciel: *out of the ~*, soudainement; [Fig.] *the blues*, cafard *m*, idées *fpl* noires. || **bluebell** [-ˌbɛl] *n.* campanule *f*. || **blueberry** [-ˌbɛəɪ] *n.* airelle *f* du Canada; [Pop.] bleuet/bluet *m*. || **bluebird** [-ˌbɚd] *n.* © merle *m* bleu. || **blue jay** [-ˌʤej] *n.* geai *m* bleu. || **bluenose** [-ˌnowz] *n.* habitant *m* de la Nouvelle-Écosse. || **blueprint** [-ˌpɹɪnt] *n.* plan *m*; devis *mpl*.

bluff[1] [blʌf] *n.* **1.** © falaise *f*, escarpement *m*. **2.** [of trees] boqueteau *m*. || *adj.* escarpé; [Pers.] bourru.

bluff[2] *n.* bluff *m*. || *v. tr. & intr.* bluffer.

blunder [ˈblʌndɚ] *n.* gaffe *f*, bourde *f*, impair *m*. || *v. intr.* faire/une gaffe, des gaffes/, gaffer. || **blunderer** [-ɚ] *n.* gaffeur *m*, maladroit *m*.

blunt [blʌnt] *adj.* [edge] émoussé; [point] épointé; [Fig.] brusque, rude: *a ~ answer*, une réponse brutale. || *v. tr.* émousser, épointer.

blur [blɚ] *v. tr.* [-rr-] brouiller, estomper; [Fig.] ternir, troubler. || *n.* brouillard *m*; [Fig.] ternissure *f*, faille *f*.

blurt [-t] *v, tr.*: *to ~ out* (a secret, &c.), lâcher.

blush [blʌʃ] *n.* rougeur *f* (de honte, de modestie); incarnat *m* (d'une rose): *at the first ~*, de prime abord/à première vue/au premier abord. || *v. intr.* rougir (de timidité, de honte), devenir rouge (de honte).

bluster [ˈblʌstɚ] *n.* rodomontade *f*. || *v. intr.* souffler en tempête; faire le malin.

boar [bɔɚ] *n.* sanglier *m*.

board [boɚd] *n.* **1.** planche *f*; [small] planchette *f*; [school] tableau *m* (noir); [notices] écriteau *m*; [ironing] planche à repasser. **2.** table *f*; pension *f*; *room and ~*, pension *f* complète; *boarding house*, pension *f*; *boarding school*, pensionnat *m*, internat *m*. **3.** [group of administrators] comité *m*; conseil *m* (des gouverneurs), d'administration, &c.): *~ of Trade*, Chambre de commerce; © *National Harbours ~*, Conseil *m* des ports nationaux; *~ of examiners*, bureau des/examens, examinateurs/; *school ~*, © *Board of School Commission(ers)*, © *~ of Education*, © commission *f* scolaire. **4.** bord *m* (d'un navire): *on ~ the ship*, à bord; *on ~ the train*, dans le train. **5.** [Loc.] *the boards*, les planches *fpl* (le théâtre); *above ~*, franc, loyal. || *v. tr.* **1.** planchéier (une salle). **2.** aborder (un rivage), monter à bord (d'un bateau, train). || *v. intr.* aller à bord, aborder, prendre un navire à l'abordage; monter (dans un train); [Fam.] © s'embarquer (dans un train); être en pension. || **boarder** [-ɚ] *n.* pensionnaire *m/f*; (in a school) interne *m/f*.

boast [bowst] *v. intr.* se vanter (de qqch.). || *n.* vanterie *f*, vantardise *f*; gloriole *f*. || **boastful** [-fl] *adj.* vantard, prétentieux. || **boasting** [-ɪŋ] *n.* cf. BOAST.

boat [bowt] *n.* bateau *m*; embarcation *f*; [row ~] © chaloupe *f*, [Fr.] canot *m*; [ship] navire *m*: *in, by/ ~*, en bateau; [Fig.] *in the same ~*, dans le même cas. || *v. intr.* se promener, aller en bateau, en chaloupe. || *v. tr.* mettre, transporter (qqch.)/en bateau, dans une chaloupe. || **boathouse** [-ˌhaws] *n.* hangar *m* à bateaux. || **boating** [-ɪŋ] *n.* [sport] canotage *m*. || †**boatman** [mən] *n.* navigateur *m*, marin *m*.

bob[1] [bɑb] *v. intr.* [-bb-] se balancer (sur l'eau), sautiller: *to ~ up*, surgir d'on ne sait où.

bob[2] *n.* [car] pendant *m*; [curl] coiffure *f* à la Jeanne d'Arc; [curtsy] révérence; [angling] bouchon *m* (de la ligne); [Br. Fam.] = shilling.

bobby pin [ˈbɑbɪˌpɪn] *n.* [hair] épingle *f* à cheveux, © pince *f* à cheveux, pincette *f*. cf. HAIRPIN.

bobby-socks [ˈbɑbɪˌsɑks] *n.pl.* socquettes *fpl*. || **bobby-soxer** [-ɚ] *n.* [Fam.] jeune admiratrice *f*.

bobolink [ˈbɑbəˌlɪŋk] *n.* [Orn.] © goglu *m*.

†**bode** [bowd] *v. tr.* prédire. || *v. intr.* [Pej.] présager.

bodice [ˈbɑdɪs] *n.* corsage *m*.

bodiless [ˈbɑdɪ|ləs] *adj.* sans corps, immatériel. || **bodily** [-lɪ] *adj.* corporel, physique;

matériel || *adv.* corporellement; [Fig.] [action] en groupe, solidairement.

body [ˈbɑdɪ] *n.* **1.** corps *m* [dead] cadavre *m*, [literary usage] dépouille *f* (mortelle); [collective] société *f*, recueil *m*; [water, people] masse *f*; [Jur.] corporation *f*; collège *m* (électoral); (une) personne *f*; (un) type *m*. **2.** [Aut.] carrosserie *f*. || **body-guard** [-ˌgɑɚd] *n.* **1.** [coll.] garde *f* du corps. **2.** [man] garde *f* du corps. || **body shell** [-ʃɛl] *n.* [snail, &c.] coque *f*.

bog [bɑg] *n.* marais *m.* || [-gg-] *v. intr. to ~ down*, s'enliser. || **boggy** [-ɪ] *adj.* marécageux.

bogus [ˈbowgəs] *adj.* faux.

Bohemia [bowˈhijmɪə] *n.* la Bohème. || **Bohemian** *adj.* bohème.

boil[1] [bojl] *n.* furoncle *m*, [Fam.] clou *m*.

boil[2] [bojl] *v. intr.* (of liquids) bouillir, bouillonner; [Fig.] être transporté (de fureur). || *v. tr.* faire bouillir (un liquide); [Culin.] (faire) cuire (des légumes) à l'eau; lessiver (le linge): *The milk is boiling over*, Le lait/se sauve, © renverse. || *n.*: *to bring to the ~*, porter à l'ébullition; *to come to the ~*, commencer à bouillir. || **boiler** [-ɚ] *n.* chaudière *f*, bouilloire *f*; bain-marie *m.f.* || **boiling** [-ɪŋ] *n.* ébullition *f*: *the ~ -point*, point *m* d'ébullition.

boisterous [ˈbojstɚəs] *adj.* bruyant; [agitated] turbulent.

bold [bowld] *adj.* hardi, intrépide; audacieux, téméraire; [Pej.] effronté, impudent; [of a cliff] escarpé, à pic *inv.*; [of a line] prononcé. || **boldly** [-lɪ] *adv.* hardiment, audacieusement; [Pej.] effrontément. || **boldness** [-nəs] *n.* audace *f*; [Pej.] insolence *f*.

bolster [ˈbowlstɚ] *n.* [bed] traversin *m*; [Tech.] coussin(et) *m.* || *v. tr.* appuyer: *to ~ up (with)*, soutenir (de).

bolt [bowlt] *n.* boulon *m*; cheville *f*, goupille *f*; †carreau *m* (d'arbalète); éclair *m*, coup *m* de foudre; verrou *m* (de porte), pêne *m* (de serrure); [Fig.] départ *m* précipité; pièce *f* de toile, de papier tenture. || *v. tr.* verrouiller (une porte), mettre le(s) verrou(s); engloutir (sa nourriture), expédier (un repas); © virer son capot de bord, abandonner (son parti politique). || *v. intr.* prendre la poudre d'escampette, déguerpir; sortir précipitamment; [Fig.] prendre le mors aux dents.

bomb [bɑm] *n.* [atom, explosive] bombe *f*. || *v. tr.* [war] bombarder (une ville, &c.).

bombard [ˌbɑmˈbɑɚd] *v. tr.* bombarder; [Fig.] assaillir (de questions, &c.).

bombastic [-ˈbæstɪk] *adj.* [style] ampoulé, grandiloquent.

bomber [-ɚ] *n.* [Aero.] bombardier *m.* || **bombing** [-ɪŋ] *n.* bombardement *m*.

bona fide [ˈbownəˌfajdi] *adj.* réel, authentique, de profession.

bond [bɑnd] *n.* **1.** lien *m*; chaîne *f*; attache *f*. **2.** [Jur.] engagement *m*; obligation *f*; contrat *m*. **3.** bon *m* (de la défense nationale, de la victoire, &c.); © obligation *f* (de la victoire). || **bondage** [-əʤ] *n.* servitude *f*; [Fig.] esclavage *m*.

bone [bown] *n.* os *m*; *fish ~*, arête *f*; *pl.* [of dead person] ossements *mpl*; [Arg.] dominos *mpl*, dés à jouer; [Mus.] cliquettes *fpl*; baleines *fpl* (de corset). || *v. tr.* désosser (une viande); enlever les arêtes (d'un poisson): *to feel in one's bones*, avoir un pressentiment, avoir le sentiment intime de qqch.; *to have a ~ to pick with s.o.*, avoir maille à partir avec qqun; *to make no bones about doing sth.*, ne pas hésiter à faire qqch.; [Fam.] *to ~ up (on sth.)*, bûcher (qqch.).

boner [ˈbownɚ] [Fam.] *n.* gaffe *f*.

bonfire [ˈbɑnˌfajɚ] *n.* feu *m* de joie, de bivouac; [camp, beach] bûcher *m*.

bonnet [ˈbɑnət] *n.* [headgear] bonnet *m* (de femme); [Br.] capot *m* (d'automobile). cf. HOOD. || *v. tr.* mettre un bonnet à (qqun).

bonspiel [ˈbɑnˌspijl] *n.* bonspiel *m*, joute *f* de curling.

bonus [ˈbownəs] *n.pl.* **bonuses,** boni *m*, prime *f*, part *f* de bénéfice: *cost-of-living ~*, indemnité *f* de cherté de vie; [Fin.] *~ on shares*, bonification *f* sur les actions.

bony [-ɪ] *adj.* osseux; [Fig.] anguleux.

boo [buw] *interj.* hou! || *v. tr.* huer, chahuter.

book [buk] *n.* **1.** livre *m*; [opera] livret *m*; [record, stud, account] registre *m*; [copy] cahier *m*: *to be in s.o.'s/good, bad/ books*, être, ne pas être/dans les papiers de qqun; *to keep books*, tenir les livres/la comptabilité/; *to quote ~, chapter and verse*, → mettre les points sur les i. **2.** [composés avec *book* en deuxième élément]: © *examination book*, copie *f* d'examen; *colouring ~*, album *m* à colorier; *copy ~, exercise ~*, cahier *m*; *note~*, carnet *m* (de notes); *school-~*, livre de classe ; *story ~*, livre d'histoires [≠ *history ~*, livre d'histoire]. **3.** [composés avec *book* suivi d'une épithète]: *bookbinder*, relieur *m*; *bookbinding*, reliure *f*; *bookcase*, [shelves] bibliothèque *f*; *~ cover*, couverture *f* (de livre); *~ jacket*, liseuse *f*, jaquette *f*; *~keeper*, teneur *m* de livres, comptable *m*, cf. ACCOUNTANT;

~*keeping*, tenue *f* des livres, comptabilité *f*; *booklet*, livret *m*, brochure *f*; ~ *mark(er)*, signet *m*; ~ *of matches*, ~ *matches*, allumettes *fpl* en carnet; *bookseller*, libraire *m*; *second-hand bookseller*, bouquiniste *m*; ~ *shelf*, rayon *m* (de bibliothèque); ~ *shop*, ~ *store*, librairie *f*; ~ *trade*, (le) commerce *m* du livre; *bookworm*, rat *m* de bibliothèque. || **book** *v. tr.* inscrire, porter (qqch.) au compte de; [surtout Br.] retenir (une place, un billet): *The theatres are all booked up*, → Les théâtres jouent à/[Fr.] bureaux/© guichets/fermés; *The hotels were booked solid*, → Les hôtels/étaient pleins, refusaient du monde. || **booking** [-ɪŋ] *n.* [Br.] enregistrement *m* (des colis): ~ *office*, [Br.] **1.** guichet *m* des billets, cf. TICKET. **2.** bureau *m* des messageries, cf. EXPRESS.

boom [buwm] *n.* **1.** [wind, &c.] grondement *m*; bourdonnement *m*; ronflement *m* (de l'orgue); mugissement *m* (des vagues). **2.** [commerce] expansion *f* rapide, croissance *f* phénoménale: ~ *town*, ville *f* champignon. || *v. intr.* gronder, mugir; prospérer.

boomerang [ˈbuwmɚˌɪæŋ] *n.* choc *m* en retour, boumerang *m.* || *v. intr.* agir comme un boumerang.

boon [buwn] *n.* faveur *f*; [blessing] atout *m*, avantage *m.*

boor [buwɚ] *n.* rustre *m*, lourdaud *m.* || **boorish** *adj.* balourd, fruste.

boost [buwst] *v. tr.* [Fam.] pousser, hisser/(fortement); [Com.] augmenter, hausser/(les prix): *to* ~ *a product*, faire mousser un article.

booster [ˈbuwstɚ] *n.* **1.** qqun qui aime faire de la reclame. **2.** [Electr.] survolteur *m*

boot [buwt] *n.* **1.** chaussure *f*; botte *f*; bottine *f.* **2.** caisson *m*, [Br. Auto] coffre *m* (à bagages). || *v. tr.* botter (le derrière de qqun), donner un coup de pied à (qqun).

booty [-tɪ] *n.* butin *m.*

bordage [ˈbɔɚdədʒ] © *n.* bordages *mpl.*

border [ˈboɚdɚ] *n.* **1.** bord *m* (d'un lac), lisière *f* (d'un bois), bordure *f* (d'une route); frontière *f*, confins *mpl* (d'un pays). **2.** bordure *f* (d'un tapis), cordon *m* (de gazon); encadrement *m*; baguette *f* (sur le papier) à lettres. || *v. tr.* border (une route), lisérer (un mouchoir), encadrer (un panneau). || *v. intr. to* ~ *on*, confiner à (un territoire) être près de (qqch.), friser (la grossièreté). || **borderline** [-ˌlajn] *n.* ligne *f* de démarcation: *a* ~ *case*, un cas limite.

bore[1] [boɚ] *v. tr.* creuser, forer, percer (un trou). || *n.* calibre *m* (d'un tuyau, d'un canon).

bore[2] cf. BEAR.

bore[3] *v. tr.* ennuyer; [Fam.] assommer: *to be bored to death*, s'ennuyer à mourir. || *n.* [Fam.] raseur *m*, casse-pieds *m*; [thing] ennui *m*, corvée *f.* || **boredom** [-dəm] *n.* ennui *m.*

born [boɚn] *p.p. to be* ~, naître, venir au monde; *He was* ~ *in Montreal*, Il est né, Il naquit/à Montréal. || *adj.* (-) né, -e: *She is a* ~ *dancer*, C'est une danseuse-née, Elle est née danseuse; de naissance: *He is Canadian* ~, C'est un Canadien de naissance; *a Canadian* ~ *and bred*, un Canadien authentique, © un Canadien pure laine.

borne cf. BEAR.

borough [ˈbɚow] *n.* [US] ville *f*; [Pej.] bourg *m*; [Br.] circonscription *f* électorale; [New York] arrondissement *m.*

borrow [ˈboɚow] *v. tr.* emprunter (*sth. from s.o.*, qqch. à qqun). || *v. intr.* faire un emprunt. || **borrowed** [-d] *adj.* [look, manners] d'emprunt, faux. || **borrower** [-ɚ] *n.* emprunteur *m*, emprunteuse *f.* || **borrowing** [-ɪŋ] *n.* emprunt *m.*

bosom [ˈbuzəm] *n.* poitrine *f*, sein *m*; [Fig.] sein *m*, cœur *m*: ~ *friend*, ami(e) intime.

boss [bɔs] *n.* patron *m*, chef *m* (de chantier), contremaître *m* (d'atelier); [Fam.] patron *m*, patronne *f*, © bourgeois *m*; [US] chef *m* de file, leader *m* (de syndicat). || *v. tr.* [généralement Péj.] régenter; diriger (une affaire, une organisation).

both [bowθ] *adj.* deux: ~ *books*, les deux livres; *with* ~ *hands*, à deux mains. || *pron.* les deux; tou(te)s les deux, l'un(e) et l'autre: ~ *of these books*, ces deux livres; *Both are here*, Les deux, L'un et l'autre/sont ici; *He wants* ~, Il veut/les deux, l'un et l'autre/; ~ *of them are here*, Ils sont ici tous (les) deux; *He saw/them* ~, ~ *of them*, Il les a vus tous (les) deux. || *conj.* aussi bien (. . .) que; à la fois . . . et; [et . . . et . . . is outmoded]: *Both my brother and I are here*, Mon frère et moi sommes ici tous (les) deux; *a girl* ~ *beautiful and clever*, une jeune fille/à la fois belle et intelligente, aussi belle qu'intelligente/; ~ *in Canada and in France*, aussi bien, tant/au Canada qu'en France.

bother [ˈbɑðɚ] *n.* **1.** ennui *m*; tracas *m*; souci *m.* **2.** difficulté *f*; problème *m*; [Pers.] importun *m*; fâcheux *m*, [Fam.] casse-pieds *m.* || *v. tr.* **1.** importuner, ©

achaler: *Don't ~ me!*, Ne viens pas/m'importuner, [Fam.] m'embêter, © m'achaler/; *He is always bothering his brother*, Il passe son temps à importuner son frère. **2.** déranger: *Don't ~ to get up*, Ne vous dérangez pas. **3.** ennuyer: *His being late bothers me*, Son retard m'ennuie. **4.** gêner; incommoder: *These shoes ~ me*, Ces souliers me gênent; *His sore throat bothers his speech*, Son mal de gorge l'incommode quand il parle. **5.** embarrasser: *Your question really bothers me*, Votre question m'embarrasse vraiment. || *v. intr.* se tracasser: *Don't ~ (about it)!*, Ne vous dérangez pas (pour ça)!, [worry] Ne vous tracassez pas! || **bothersome** [-səm] *adj.* ennuyeux.

bottle [ˌbɑtḷ] *n.* bouteille *f*; [small] flacon *m*, fiole *f* (de médicaments); [big] bocal *m*: *hot water ~*, bouillotte *f*; *feeding ~*, biberon *m*; *vacuum ~*, bouteille isolante. || *v. tr.* embouteiller (du vin, du lait), mettre (un liquide) en bouteilles. || **bottleneck** [-ˌnɛk] **1.** *n.* embouteillage *m* (de la circulation). **2.** goulot *m* (de production).

bottom [ˈbɑtṃ] **1.** *n.* bas (d'une page), fond *m* (de la mer); dessous *m* (d'un verre, d'une assiette); siège *m* (d'une chaise). **2.** vallée *f*, terre *f* d'alluvion. **3.** postérieur *m*, derrière *m* (d'une personne); fondement *m*, base *f* (d'une histoire); fond *m*, carène *f* (d'un navire); navire *m*. || *adj.* inférieur, du bas; dernier. || *v. tr.* (re)-mettre un fond (à une boîte), un siège (à une chaise); [Fig.] baser, fonder (un argument) sur (qqch.).

bough [baw] *n.* rameau *m*, branche *f*.

bought cf. BUY.

boulder [ˈbowldɚ] *n.* rocher *m*; (grosse) roche *f*.

boulevard [ˈbuləˌvɑɚd] *n.* boulevard *m*, (grande) avenue *f*; [strip of green on middle of highways] terre-plein *m*, © mail *m*.

bounce [bawns] *n.* **1.** [ball] bond *m*, rebondissement *m*; [person] saut *m*. **2.** vantardise *f*. **3.** [Fam.] [US, ©] expulsion *f*, renvoi *m*: [Fam.] *to get the ~*, être/mis à la porte, flanqué dehors. || *v. intr.* **1.** ball, [person] (re)bondir, sauter. **2.** se vanter. || *v. tr.* [US, ©] expulser (qqun), mettre (qqun) à la porte.

bound cf. BIND.

bound [bawnd] *adj.* **1.** relié. **2.** forcé; dans l'obligation de; *He is ~ to come*, Il viendra forcément, nécessairement; Il est assuré qu'il viendra; Il va certainement venir. **3.** (for) à destination de; *The train ~ for Quebec leaves at 4 o'clock*, Le train à destination de Québec part à 4 heures. || *n.* limite *f*; borne *f*: *Out of Bounds*, Interdit; *within ~*, dans la juste mesure; *within the ~ of possibility*, dans les limites du possible; *to know no bounds*, dépasser les limites. || *v. tr.* **1.** borner; mettre des bornes à; fixer des limites à. **2.** délimiter; situer les frontières de. || *v. intr.* **1.** [ball] rebondir. **2.** bondir; sauter.

boundary [ˈbawnd|ɚɪ] *n.* limite *f*, bornes *fpl*; [Pol.] frontière *f*. || **boundless** [-ləs] *adj.* sans borne, sans limite.

bountiful [ˈbawntɪ|fḷ] *adj.* **1.** [person] bon, généreux, libéral. **2.** [thing] abondant. || **bounty** *n.* bonté *f*, générosité *f*, largesse *f* (d'une personne); [bonus] prime *f*.

bouquet [bowˈkej] *n.* bouquet *m* (de fleurs); bouquet *m* (d'un vin).

bout [bawt] *n.* accès *m*: *~ of malaria*, accès de paludisme; *drinking-~*, beuverie *f*.

bow[1] [bow] *n.* arc *m*; [Mus.] archet *m* (de violon), coup *m* d'archet; nœud *m* (de ruban); courbure *f*. || *v. tr.* arquer, courber (qqch.).

bow[2] [baw] *v. intr.* s'incliner, baisser la tête; faire une génuflexion, une courbette. || *v. tr.* incliner (la tête), fléchir (le genou); courber; voûter (le dos). || *n.* salut *m*, révérence *f*.

bowel [ˈbawəl] *n.* intestin *m*; [Fam.] boyau *m*: [Fig.] *the bowels of the earth*, les entrailles *fpl* de la terre.

bowl [bowl] *n.* bol *m* (en porcelaine); gamelle *f* (en fer); boule *f* (de cristal); fourneau *m* (d'une pipe); cuvette *f* (de compas); [Sp.] boule *f*; [indoor] quille *f*: *toilet ~*, (la) cuvette *f* du cabinet.

bow-legged [ˈbowˌlegɪd] *adj.* bancal, *pl.* bancals.

bowler (hat) [ˈbowlɚˌ(hæt)] *n.* (chapeau *m*) melon *m*. || **bowling** [ˈbowlɪŋ] *n.* (jeu *m* de) boules, [indoor] quilles *fpl*: *~ alley*, boulodrome *m*.

box[1] [bɑks] *n.* boîte *f*; coffre *m*; [small] coffret *m*, [large wooden] caisse *f*; siège *m* (du cocher, du chauffeur); [Theat.] loge *f* (au théâtre); guérite *f* (d'une sentinelle); gifle *f*, claque *f*: || *v. tr.* mettre (qqch.) en boîte, encaisser, encartonner (qqch.): *to ~ s.o.'s ears*, gifler qqun. || *v. intr.* boxer, faire de la boxe.

box[2] (wood) *n.* buis *m*.

boxer [-ɚ] *n.* boxeur *m*, pugiliste *m*. || **boxing** [ɪŋ] *n.* la boxe: *~-glove*, gant *m* de boxe.

Boxing Day [ˈbɑksɪŋˌdej] *n.* Jour *m* des étrennes.

boy [boj] *n.* **1.** garçon *m*; [young] enfant *m*; [☞ when "son" is meant, use *fils m*]: *when I was a* ~ , dans ma jeunesse, dans mon jeune/temps, age/: [Sch.] *old* ~ , ancien (élève): *How are you, old* ~ *?*, Comment ça va, mon vieux?; *Oh* ~ *!*, Chouette alors!; ~ *scout*, scout *m*, éclaireur *m.* **2.** boy *m* domestique *m* indigène.

boycott [-ˌkɑt] *n.* boycottage *m.* || *v. tr.* [-tt-] boycotter.

boyhood [-ˌhud] *n.* enfance *f*, adolescence *f.* || **boyish** [-ɪʃ] *adj.* enfantin; [Pej.] puéril.

bra [bɹɑ] cf. BRASSIERE.

brace [bɹejs] *n.* [Tech.] attache *f*; support *m*; croisillon *m* (d'une fenêtre); [Mus.] accolade *f.* || **brace (up)** [-ˈʌp] *v. tr.* étayer, soutenir; [Fig.] fortifier, remonter (le moral de qqun). || *inv.* couple *f* (de canards, de perdrix), paire *f* (de pistolets).

bracelet [-lət] *n.* bracelet *m.*

braces [-əz] *n.pl.* [Br.] bretelles *fpl.*

bracken [ˈbɹækən] *n.* fougère *f.*

bracket [ˈbɹækət] *n.* support *m*; [construction] tasseau *m*; applique *f*; [Typog.] accolade *f*, [square] crochet *m*, [round] parenthèse *f*; [Admin.] échelon *m*, niveau *m.* || *v. tr.* mettre entre crochets; [Fig.] réunir (sous une même rubrique).

brag [bɹæg] *v. intr.* [-gg-] se vanter (de, *of, about*). || **braggart** [-ɚt] *n.* fanfaron *m*, hâbleur *m.*

braid [bɹejd] *n.* tresse *f*, natte *f*; liséré *m.* || *v. tr.* tresser, natter; garnir d'un liséré.

brain [bɹejn] *n.* cerveau *m*; [sheep, &c.] cervelle *f*; *pl.* intelligence *f*: [Fig.] *a bird-*~ , une tête de linotte; *to cudgel o.'s.* ~ , se creuser la cervelle. || *v. tr.* assommer, défoncer le crâne (à qqun). || **brainstorm** [-ˌstɔɚm] *n.* accès *m* de folie. || **brainwashing** [-ˌwɑʃɪŋ] *n.* [Polit., &c.] vidage *m* de crâne. cf. BOURRAGE. || **brain wave** [-wejv] *n.* trouvaille *f*, idée de génie. || **brainy** [-ɪ] *adj.* intelligent, doué.

brake [bɹejk] *n.* frein *m.* || *v. tr. & intr.* freiner, arrêter; [Auto.] appliquer le frein (sur les roues). || **brakeman** [-mən] *n.* [Rail.] serre-frein *m.*

bramble [ˈbɹæmbl̩] *n.* ronce *f* sauvage. || **brambleberry** [-ˌbɛɚɪ] *n.* mûre *f.*

bran [bɹæn] *n.* son *m.*

branch [bɹæntʃ] *n.* branche *f*, rameau *m* (d'un arbre, d'une famille); bras *m* (d'un fleuve); embranchement *m* (d'une route, d'un chemin de fer); succursale *f*, filiale *f* (d'une compagnie, d'une banque); [Post Office] bureau *m*: ~ *office*, agence *f.* || *v. intr.* [tree] ~ *forth*, pousser des branches; [society] ~ *out*, se ramifier, s'étendre; [road] bifurquer.

brand [bɹænd] *n.* **1.** marque *f* (de fabrique); sorte *f*; [Fig.] flétrissure *f*, stigmate *f.* **2.** [fire] brandon *m*, tison *m*: *a* ~ *-new car*, → une auto flambant neuve. || *v. tr.* marquer (des bestiaux) au fer rouge; [Fig.] flétrir, stigmatiser (qqun).

brandish [-ɪʃ] *v. tr.* [sword, stick] brandir.

brandy [-ɪ] *n.* eau-de-vie *f.*

brass [bɹæs] *n.* [☞ the distinction between *brass* and *copper* is rarely observed in current French] cuivre *m* (jaune); laiton *m*; [Mus.]: *the* ~ *(section)*, *the brasses*, les cuivres *mpl*; [Fam.] *the brass*, les officiers supérieurs. || **brass band** [-ˈbænd] *n.* fanfare *f.*

brassiere [bɹəˈzijɚ] *n.* soutien-gorge *m inv.* cf. BRA.

brasswork [ˈbɹæsˌwɚk] *n.* [coll.] les cuivres *mpl* (d'une cuisine, d'un bateau, &c.).

brat [bɹæt] *n.* [Pej.] enfant *m/f* espiègle, © haïssable.

brave [bɹejv] *adj.* brave, courageux; †de belle apparence, élégant; fameux. || *n.* brave *m*, guerrier indien (d'Amérique). || *v. tr.* braver, défier (un adversaire), affronter (un danger). || **bravery** [-ɚɪ] *n.* bravoure *f.*

bravo [ˈbɹævow] *n. & interj.* bravo (*m*).

brawl [bɹɔl] *n.* [noisy fight] bagarre *f*, rixe *f.* || *v. intr.* [fight] se quereller (bruyamment), se bagarrer.

brawn [bɹɔn] *n.* muscle *m.* || **brawny** [-ɪ] *adj.* fort, musclé.

bray [bɹej] *v. intr.* braire.

brazen [ˈbɹejzn̩] *adj.* **1.** d'airain. **2.** [Fig. & Pej.] effronté, impudent.

brazier [ˈbɹejʒiɚ] *n.* brasero *m.*

Brazil [bɹəˈzɪl] *n.* le Brésil: *in, to* ~ , au B.; ~ *nut*, noix *f* du Brésil. || **Brazilian** [-jən] *adj. & n.* brésilien, -ne.

breach [bɹijtʃ] *n.* brèche *f*; [Fig.] infraction *f* (à la loi), violation *f*: ~ *of the peace*, attentat *m* à l'ordre public.

bread [bɹɛd] *n.* **1.** (du) pain *m*: *a slice of* ~ , une tranche de pain; *a loaf of* ~ , un pain; *brown* ~ , pain bis, © brun/; *French* ~ , baguette *f*, © pain français; *stale* ~ , pain rassis; ~ *and butter*, tartines *fpl* de beurre. **2.** [Fig.] nourriture *f*, subsistance *f*: *to earn one's* ~ , gagner /sa vie, son pain/; ~ *-winner*, gagne-pain *m*, [person] soutien *m* de famille.

breadth [bɹɛdθ] *n.* largeur *f*; dimension *f* cf. BROAD; envergure *f* (des ailes d'un oiseau, d'un avion); [Fig.] largeur *f* (d'esprit).

break [bɹejk], **broke** [bɹowk], **broken** [bɹowkn̩] *v. tr.* **1.** casser; briser; rompre [☞ The distinction between these verbs is largely a matter of usage, esp. in the [Fig.]; however, as a guide = CASSER: to break in several pieces, often accidentally, but not necessarily beyond repair: *casser un bras, un verre*; [Fig.] *un jugement*; = BRISER: to smash beyond repair: *briser une glace, un verre*, [Fig.] *le cœur*; = ROMPRE: to break in two: *rompre du pain, un bâton*, [Fig.] *le silence, une promesse*]. **2.** interrompre (une activité, le courant); amortir (un choc, un coup); enfreindre (un règlement); troubler (l'ordre public): *to ~ the news to s.o.*, apprendre une nouvelle à qqun; [Fig.] *~ (new) ground*, faire œuvre de pionnier. || *v. intr.* se casser; se briser; se rompre [☞ See note on BREAK *tr.* **1.**]; [weather] changer [health] s'altérer; [spirits] être abattu; [war, storm] éclater; [news] être annoncé, se savoir; [day] se lever, poindre: *to ~ with/s.o., sth.*, rompre avec qqun, qqch.; *to ~ loose*, s'échapper (de), [Fig.] se déchaîner; *to ~ open*, forcer, enfoncer. || *n.* rupture *f*; interruption *f*; ouverture *f*; arrêt *m*; changement *m* (de temps); [day] point *m* du jour; pause *f*, repos *m*, récréation *f*: *to make a bad ~*, faire une gaffe; *to make a ~ for it*, s'échapper. || **breakaway** [-ə'wej] *v. tr. & intr.* (se) détacher; s'échapper. || **break down** [-'dawn] *v. tr.* abattre, démolir; enfoncer (une porte); analyser, décomposer; vaincre, briser. || *v. intr.* s'effondrer; [health] s'altérer; [fail] échouer; [machine] se détraquer, avoir une panne; [person] tomber malade, fondre en larmes. || **break forth** [-'fɔɚθ] *v. intr.* jaillir; éclater. || **break in** [-'ɪn] *v. tr.* enfoncer (une porte); dresser (un domestique); roder (un moteur). || *v. intr.* intervenir; entrer par effraction (dans une maison); interrompre: *to ~ upon*, interrompre; envahir. || **break-in** [-ɪn] *n.* effraction *f*. || **break into** [-'ɪntuw] *v. intr.* entrer, ouvrir de force; éclater (en sanglots, de rire); fondre (en larmes); tomber (en morceaux). || **break off** [-'ɑf] *v. tr.* rompre; interrompre. || *v. intr.* se détacher; interrompre, arrêter; prendre un repos; [Mil.] *Break off!* Rompez! || **break out** [-'awt] *v. intr.* s'évader; [war, disease] éclater; se couvrir (de boutons); s'exclamer. || **break through** [-'θɹuw] *v. tr. & intr.* enfoncer; [sun, troops] percer. || **break up** [-'ʌp] *v. tr.* mettre en morceaux, démolir; défoncer (un terrain); disperser (une foule); interrompre, arrêter (une discussion); diviser; décomposer. || *v. intr.* se désagréger; [meeting] se séparer; [road] se défoncer; [ice] débâcler.

breakable ['bɹejk|əbl̩] *adj.* fragile. || **breakage** [-əʤ] *n.* [action] rupture *f*; [result] || casse *f*. || **breakdown** [-ˌdawn] *n.* débâcle *f* (de pourparlers); rupture *f* (de négociations); dépression *f* (nerveuse); analyse *f*; [mechanical] panne *f*: *to have a ~*, être en panne.

breakfast ['bɹɛkfəst] *n.* petit déjeuner, © déjeuner *m*. || *v. intr.* prendre le (petit) déjeuner.

breaking ['bɹejkɪŋ] *adj.*: *~ point*, point *m* de rupture. || **breakthrough** [-ˌθɹuw] *n.* percée *f*. || **breakup** [-ˌʌp] *n.* fin *f*; dissolution *f*; [ice] (grande) débâcle *f*. || **breakwater** ['bɹejkˌwɔtɚ] *n.* brise-lames *m*.

breast [bɹɛst] *n.* **1.** poitrine *f*; [horse] poitrail *m*; [Fig.] cœur *m*. **2.** devant *m* (d'un habit); proue *f* (d'un navire); [Anat.] sein *m*, mamelle *f*. || *v. intr.* lutter contre.

breath [bɹɛθ] *n.* respiration *f*, haleine *f*, souffle *m*: *to be out of ~*, être hors d'haleine; *to catch one's ~*, reprendre haleine; *to be short of ~*, être essoufflé.

breathe ['bɹijθ] *v. intr.* respirer, souffler, prendre haleine. || *v. tr.* aspirer, exhaler (l'air): *to ~ one's last*, rendre le dernier soupir.

breathless [-ləs] *adj.* essoufflé; [panting] haletant, hors d'haleine; [Fig.] confondu, interdit.

bred cf. BREED: *well-bred*, bien élevé.

breeches ['bɹijʧəz] *n.pl.* culotte *f*.

breed [bɹijd], **bred, bred** ['bɹɛd] *v. tr.* engendrer, produire (qqun, qqch.), donner naissance à (qqun, qqch.); élever (un animal), éduquer (un enfant). || *v. intr.* [animals, human beings] se reproduire; [Fig.] [ideas] se propager. || **breeder** [-ɚ] *n.* **1.** éleveur *m* (d'animaux); [Fig.] éducat|eur, -rice. **2.** [horse] étalon *m*. || **breeding** [-ɪŋ] *n.* procréation *f*; [Fig.] éducation *f*; [animals] élevage *m*.

breeze [bɹijz] *n.* brise *f*, vent *m* assez fort. || **breezeway** [-ˌwej] *n.* corridor *m* (entre deux maisons), passage *m* couvert. || **breezy** [-ɪ] *adj.* [of weather] frais, fraîche; [Fig.] animé, jovial, désinvolte.

†**brethren** ['bɹɛðɹən] *n. pl.* cf. BROTHER (mes) frères [pluriel archaïque, utilisé dans la langue liturgique].

breviary ['bɹijvɪˌɛɚɪ] *n.* [Eccl.] bréviaire *m*.

brevity [bɹɛvɪtɪ] *n.* [shortness] brièveté *f*; [terseness] concision *f*.

brew [bɹuw] *v. tr.* [ale] brasser; [tea] faire infuser; [Fig., mischief] comploter. || **brewer** [-ɚ] *n.* brasseur *m.* || **brewery** [-ɚɪ] *n.* brasserie *f.*

bribe [bɹajb] *n.* pot-de-vin *m,* présent *m* malhonnête, appât *m.* || *v. tr.* acheter, corrompre (un fonctionnaire), soudoyer (qqun), [Fam.] graisser (la patte à) qqun; suborner (un témoin). || **bribery** [-ɚɪ] *n.* corruption *f* (de fonctionnaire); pot-de-vin *m.*

brick [bɹɪk] *n.* brique *f*; pain *m* (de savon); bloc *m* (de thé): *a* ~ *house,* une maison /en, de/briques; [Loc.] *to drop a* ~, (se) mettre les pieds dans les plats, faire une gaffe; *To make bricks without straw,* faire un miracle. || *v. tr.* garnir (un bâtiment, &c.) en briques, briqueter (un mur, &c.). || **bricklayer** [-ˌlejɚ] *n.* maçon *m.* || **brickwork** [-ˌwɚk] *n.* mur *m* (en brique), maçonnerie *f.*

bridal [bɹajd|l] *adj.* conjugal, nuptial. || **bride** *n.* **1.** fiancée *f,* future *f.* **2.** nouvelle mariée, épousée *f.*

bridegroom [-ˌgɹuwm] *n.* **1.** futur *m.* **2.** nouveau marié *m*: *the bride and* ~, **1.** les futurs conjoints *mpl.* **2.** les nouveaux mariés *mpl.* || **bridesmaid** [-zˌmejd] *n.* demoiselle *f* d'honneur.

bridge [ˈbɹɪʤ] *n.* **1.** pont *m*: *the Victoria* ~, le pont Victoria; ~ *street,* la rue du pont; [Nau.] passerelle *f* (de commandement); [nose] arête *f*; [Dent.] pont *m*; chevalet *m* (d'un violon). **2.** [card game] bridge *m*: *to play* ~, jouer au bridge. || *v. tr.* jeter un pont (sur, *over*); relier; [Fig.] *to* ~ *a gap,* combler une lacune.

bridle [ˈbɹajdl] *n.* [horse] bride *f*; [Fig.] frein *m.* || *v. tr.* brider (un cheval); [Fig.] maîtriser (une impulsion). || **bridlepath** [-ˌpæθ] *n.* piste *f,* allée *f*/cavalière.

brief [bɹijf] *adj.* bref *m,* brève *f*; court, de (très) courte durée, passager; [terse] concis: *in* ~, en un mot, en bref. || *n.* **1.** [R.C.] bref *m* (du Pape). **2.** court exposé *m,* résumé *m*; [Jur.] requête *f,* © bref *m*; dossier *m* (d'une procédure). || **briefcase** [-ˌkejs] *n.* serviette *f.* || **briefing** [-ɪŋ] *n.* instructions *fpl* verbales. || **briefs** *npl.* culottes *fpl* de dame. || **briefly** [-lɪ] *adv.* brièvement, en bref.

brigade [bɹɪˈgejd] *n.* brigade *f.* || **brigadier** [bɹɪgəˈdijɚ] *n.* général *m* de brigade, © brigadier *m.*

bright [ˈbɹajt] *adj.* **1.** [eyes] brillant, lumineux; [sun] éclatant; [fire] vif; [steel] poli; [day] clair. **2.** [mind] intelligent, vif: *a* ~ *pupil,* un élève brillant. || **bright(ly)** [-lɪ] *adv.* clair: *the sun was shining* ~, le soleil brillait clair. || **brighten** [-n̩] *v. tr.* [colours, &c.] faire briller (qqch.); polir (les cuivres); [Fig.] égayer (l'existence). || *v. intr.* s'éclairer. || **brightness** [-nəs] *n.* [colour] éclat *m,* clarté *f*; splendeur *f*; [Fig.] gaieté *f.*

brilliance [bɹɪljəns] *n.* lustre *m,* éclat *m.* || **brilliant** [ˈbɹɪljənt] *adj.* brillant, éclatant, lumineux; [Fig.] (of a person), brillant, intelligent.

brim [bɹɪm] *n.* bord *m* (d'un verre, d'une coupe, d'un chapeau): *to fill* (*a glass, cup, bucket, &c.*) *to the* ~, remplir (un verre, une tasse, un seau, &c.) jusqu'au bord, à ras bord; [glass, cup, &c.] *to be full to the* ~, être plein jusqu'au bord, déborder. || *v. tr.* [-mm-] remplir (un verre, &c.) jusqu'au bord. || *v. intr. to* ~ *over,* déborder; [Fig.] [person] être débordant (de, *with*). || **brimful** [-fʊl] *adj.* plein à déborder (*of,* de).

brine [bɹajn] *n.* eau *f* salée, saumure *f.*

bring [bɹɪŋ], **brought** [bɹɑt], **brought** *v. tr.* [carry] apporter; [otherwise] amener; transporter; [Fig.] amener (qqun à faire qqch.); apporter/une nouvelle du secours/; (s') attirer (des ennuis); porter (bonheur à qqun); porter (à la connaissance de qqun); faire venir (des larmes aux yeux de qqun); intenter (un procès): *to* ~ *into*/*action, play*/, mettre en œuvre; *He can't* ~ *himself to do it,* Il ne peut pas se résoudre à le faire. || **bring about** [-əˈbawt] *v. tr.* amener, causer; provoquer, entraîner (un résultat désagréable); opérer, effectuer (un changement). || **bring around** [-əˈɹawnd] apporter (qqch.), amener (qqun) (chez . . .); convertir (qqun); ranimer (qqun). || **bring back** [-ˈbæk] *v. tr.* ramener; [carry] rapporter; [return sth.] rapporter, rendre; rappeler (un souvenir): *to* ~ *word that,* revenir avec le message que . . . || **bring down** [-ˈdawn] *v. tr.* descendre (qqch.), faire descendre (qqun); abattre (un homme, un avion, un arbre, &c.); réduire (le prix); donner un coup de . . . sur qqch.; [Fig.] s'attirer (un ennui): [Theatre] *to* ~ *the house,* faire crouler la salle (par les applaudissements). || **bring forth** [-ˈfɔɚθ] *v. tr.* produire; provoquer; mettre (des enfants) au monde; [animals] mettre bas (des petits). || **bring forward** [-ˈfɔɚwɚd] *v. tr.* avancer (une chaise, un argument); présenter (une suggestion); reporter (une somme). || **bring in** [-ˈɪn] *v. tr.* apporter (qqch. dans . . .), [inside] rentrer qqch.;

faire entrer (qqun); introduire (une idée); présenter (un projet de loi); rendre (un verdict); rapporter (une somme d'argent, de l'intérêt). || **bring off** [-'ɑf] *v. tr.* réussir qqch. || **bring on** [-'ɑn] *v. tr.* causer; amener; provoquer, entraîner (un ennui). || **bring out** [-'awt] *v. tr.* apporter (qqch.) dehors, sortir (qqch.); faire sortir (qqun); publier (un livre); lancer (une nouvelle mode); faire ressortir (une qualité). || **bring to** [-'tuw] *v. tr.* ranimer (qqun). || **bring together** [-tə'gɛðɚ] *v. tr.* réunir; réconcilier; mettre en présence. || **bring up** [-'ʌp] *v. tr.* monter (qqch.); faire monter (qqun); élever (un enfant); rendre, vomir; soulever (une question). || *v. intr.* rendre, vomir.

brink [bɹɪŋk] *n.* bord *m*: *on the ~ of,* à deux doigts de . . . , sur le bord de (l'abîme, &c.).

brisk [bɹɪsk] *adj.* vif *m*, vive *f*, animé: *to move at a ~ pace,* aller à vive allure, marcher bon train. || **briskly** [-lɪ] *adv.* avec célérité, vivement, à vive allure.

bristle [bɹɪsl̩] *v. intr.* se hérisser (de); [Fig.] *bristling with difficulties,* hérissé de difficultés. || **bristly** [-ɪ] *adj.* hérissé, raide.

Britain ['bɹɪtn̩] *n.* [Hist.] Bretagne *f* (insulaire). || **Great ~** , la Grande-Bretagne: *in, to*/ ~ , en Grande-Bretagne.

Britanny [-ɪ] *n.* [a French province] la Bretagne.

British ['bɹɪtɪʃ] *adj.* britannique; d'Angleterre, anglais. || *n.* [coll.]: *the ~* , les Britanniques *mpl.* || **British America** *n.* l'Amérique britannique, le Canada. || **British Columbia** [-kə'lʌmbjə] *n.* © la Colombie Britannique (sometimes called *Colombie canadienne*). || **British Commonwealth of Nations** cf. COMMONWEALTH. || **Britisher** [-ɚ] *n.* Anglais *m*, -e *f*; sujet *m* britannique. || **British Isles (the)** *n.* les Îles Britanniques. || **Briton** ['bɹɪtn̩] *n.* sujet *m* britannique.

brittle ['bɹɪtl̩] *adj.* [ice, glass, &c.] fragile, [cast iron] cassant.

broach [bɹowtʃ] *n.* **1.** foret *m*, mèche *f* à percer. **2.** broche *f.* || *v. tr.* mettre (un tonneau) en perce, percer; [Fig.] entamer (un sujet de conversation).

broad [bɹɑd] *adj.* **1.** [wide] large, vaste: *a ~ expanse of water,* une vaste étendue d'eau. **2.** [Fig.] large, vaste: *a ~ outlook,* un large horizon; *~ ideas,* des idées larges; *~ outlines,* les grandes lignes (d'un projet). **3.** [accent] fort, prononcé; complet: *It was ~ daylight,* Il faisait/complètement, tout à fait/jour.

broadcast [-ˌkæst] *n.* radiodiffusion *f*, émission *f* (radiophonique): *educational ~*, radio *f* scolaire. || *v. tr. & intr.* radiodiffuser, émettre (un programme) sur les ondes; répandre (des nouvelles), semer (des idées) à tout vent.

broaden [-n̩] *v. tr. & intr.* élargir. || **broadly** [-lɪ] *adv.* largement: *~ speaking,* grosso modo. || **broad-minded** [-'majndəd] *adj.* à l'esprit large, large d'esprit.

broil [bɹojl] *n.* bagarre *f*, rixe *f.* || *v. tr.* griller, faire cuire sur le gril. || **broiler** [-ɚ] *n.* gril *m.* || **broiling** [-ɪŋ] *adj.* ardent, brûlant.

broke[1] cf. BREAK.

broke[2] [bɹowk] *adj.* [Fam.] fauché, © cassé.

broken cf. BREAK.

broker ['bɹowkɚ] *n.* courtier *m*: *custom house ~* , courtier en douane; *stock ~*, courtier en valeurs. || **brokerage** [-ədʒ] *n.* courtage *m.*

bronchia ['bɹɑnkɪə] *n.pl.* bronches *fpl.* || **bronchial** [-l] *adj.* bronchial, des bronches. || **bronchitis** [bɹɑn'kajtɪs] *n.* bronchite *f.*

bronze [bɹɑnz] *n.* bronze *m.* || *v. tr. & intr.* bronzer.

brooch [bɹowtʃ] *n.* [clasp] broche *f*, épingle *f.*

brood [bɹuwd] *n.* couvée *f.* || *v. tr.* couver (des œufs); [danger] peser sur. || *v. intr.* couver, menacer: [Fig.] *to ~ over,* méditer sur.

brook[1] [bɹuk] *n.* ruisseau *m.*

brook[2] *v. tr.* [usual, neg.] (ne pas) tolérer, endurer, souffrir, digérer (qqch.).

broom [bɹuwm] *n.* **1.** balai *m.* **2.** [bush] genêt *m.*

broth [bɹɑθ] *n.* bouillon *m*; potage *m.*

brother ['bɹʌðɚ] *pl.* **-s** [abbr. Com. *Bros.*] **1.** frère *m*: *elder ~* , frère aîné; *younger ~* , frère cadet; [Rel.] frère: *mes (chers) frères,* my dear brethren. **2.** confrère *m*; frère d'armes; [Fam.] mon vieux; [Rel.] frère: *Brother Raphael,* Frère R. [☞ Le pluriel ici est *brothers.*] || **brotherhood** [-ˌhud] *n.* fraternité *f*; [group of people] confrérie *f.* || **brother-in-law** [-ɪnˌlɔ] *n.* beau-frère *m* (*pl.* beaux-frères). || **brotherliness** [-lɪnəs] *n.* fraternité *f*, amour *m* fraternel. || **brotherly** [-lɪ] *adj.* fraternel.

brought cf. BRING.

brow [bɹaw] *n.* **1.** sourcil *m*; [Fig.] front *m.* **2.** sommet *m* (d'une colline). || **browbeat** [-ˌbijt] *v. tr.* intimider (qqun), malmener (qqun); agir par intimidation, traiter (qqun) avec hauteur.

brown [bɹawn] *adj.* brun, (de couleur) sombre, [tan-coloured] marron; (pain) bis, (beurre) roux, noir; [Fig.] rembruni; [Cul., meat] rissolé. || *v. tr.* brunir; [Cul.] rissoler, gratiner; [Fam.] *to be browned off*, en avoir/jusque par-dessus la tête, plein le dos/.

browse [bɹawz] *v. tr.* brouter, paître.

bruise [bɹuwz] *n.* contusion *f*, meurtrissure *f*, bleu *m*; [Fig.] froissement *m*; écrasement *m*. || *v. tr.* meurtrir, contusionner, [Fig.] froisser; broyer, écraser. || *v. intr.* se meurtrir, se froisser.

brunette [bɹuw'nɛt] *n.* [×] brune *f*.

brunt [bɹʌnt] *n.* choc *m*, assaut *m*; violence *f*: [Fig.] *to bear the ~ of*, faire tous les frais de (qqch.), pay er de sa personne.

brush [bɹʌʃ] *n.* brosse *f* (à habit), balai *m*, [paint] pinceau *m*; escarmouche *f*; algarade *f*; queue *f* (d'un renard), coup *m* de brosse (à un vêtement); effleurement *m*: *They are tarred with the same ~*, [Fig.] On peut les mettre dans le même panier. || *v. tr.* brosser, balayer: *to ~ away*, ôter avec une brosse; essuyer (une larme); effleurer, raser, frôler; passer rapidement: *to ~ up one's French*, se remettre à l'étude du français; *to ~ up one's clothes*, donner un coup de brosse à ses vêtements. || **brushwood** [-ˌwud] *n.* broussailles *fpl*.

brusque [bɹʌsk] *adj.* brusque, rude, bourru. || **brusqueness** [-nəs] *n.* rudesse *f*, brusquerie *f*.

Brussels [bɹʌsəlz] *n.* Bruxelles: *~ sprout*, chou *m* de Bruxelles.

brutal ['bɹuwtḷ] *adj.* brutal; [instinct] déchaîné, sans frein. || **brutality** [bɹuw'tælɪtɪ] *n.* brutalité *f*. || **brute** [bɹuwt] *n.* brute *f*; [animal] animal *m*, bête *f*. || *adj.* brutal, grossier. || **brutish** [-ɪʃ] *adj.* brutal, de brute.

B.Sc. [ˌbijˌess'sij] [= Bachelor of Science] bachelier *m* ès sciences.

bubble ['bʌbəl] *n.* **1.** bulle *f* (d'air, de savon); bouillon *m* (dans un liquide); soufflure *f* (dans le verre). **2.** [Fig.] illusion *f*, chimère *f*, tromperie *f*. || *v. intr.* [water] bouillonner, dégager des bulles; [wine] pétiller; [liquid poured] glouglouter; [Fig.] *~ over*, déborder (de joie, d'enthousiasme).

buck [bʌk] *n.* **1.** mâle *m* (chèvre, lièvre, lapin, antilope, mouton) [☞ or use special word: BOUC, BÉLIER, &c.]. **2.** [Sl.] dollar *m*, © tomate *f*: [Loc.] *to pass the ~ to*, mettre (ça) sur le dos de (qqun). || *v. tr.* lutter contre: *to ~ up s.o.*, remonter le moral à qqun. || *v. intr.*: *to ~ up*, reprendre courage.

bucket [bʌkət] *n.* seau *m* (d'eau), [wooden] baquet *m*: [Fam.] *to kick the ~*, casser sa pipe.

buckle ['bʌkḷ] *n.* boucle *f*, agrafe *f*; [Tech.] gauchissement *m* (d'une surface), flambage *m* (d'une tige de métal). || *v. tr.* boucler (une valise, un soulier), agrafer, attacher (une redingote, une ceinture); [Tech.] gauchir, déjeter, voiler (une roue), faire flamber (une tige de métal). || *v. intr.* [of belt, &c.] se boucler: *to ~ (down) to (work)*, s'appliquer à (un travail).

buckskin ['bʌkˌskɪn] *n.* (peau *f* de) daim *m*.

buckwheat ['bʌkˌwijt] *n.* [Pop.] blé *m* noir, sarrasin *m*.

bud [bʌd] *n.* [Bot.] bouton *m*, bourgeon *m*; [Fig.] germe *m*: *to nip in the ~*, étouffer dans l'œuf. || *v. intr.* **[-dd-]** [tree] bourgeonner, [flower] commencer à éclore, pousser des boutons; [Fig.] [talents] se montrer, apparaître.

buddy [-ɪ] *n.* [Fam.] camarade *m*, copain *m*.

budge [bʌʤ] *v. tr.* bouger, remuer, déplacer (qqun, qqch.). || *v. intr.* [to move] bouger, remuer, se déplacer: *Don't ~ from that spot!*, Ne bouge pas de là!

budget ['bʌʤət] *n.* **1.** [Fin.] budget *m*: *~ speech*, exposé *m* budgétaire, © discours *m* du budget. **2.** recueil *m* (d'histoires), collection *f* (de documents), paquet *m* (de lettres), tas *m* (de papiers). || *v. tr.* inscrire, porter/(une dépense) au budget.

buff [bʌf] *n.* couleur *f* chamois.

buffalo ['bʌfəlow] *pl.* **-es** [or Coll.] **buffalo** *n.* **1.** bison *m* (d'Amérique). **2.** [Africa, &c.] buffle *m*.

buffer ['bʌfr] *n.* [Rail.] tampon; [Auto.] pare chocs *m*.

buffet[1] [bʌ'fej] *n.* [sideboard; counter] buffet *m*.

buffet[2] ['bʌfət] *n.* [wind] coup *m* (violent et répété). || *v. tr.* [wind, sea] frapper (violemment).

bug [bʌg] *n.* [Zool.] insecte *m* [en général]; [Br.] punaise *f*; [Fam.] bestiole *f*, © bibite *f*; [Fig.] [Fam.] *He is a big ~*, C'est/un grand manitou, une grosse légume, une huile/.

buggy ['bʌgɪ] *n.* © buggy, boghei, boghey *m*; landau *m*, voiture *f* d'enfant.

bugle [bjuwgḷ] *n.* clairon *m*. || *v. intr.* claironner.

build [bɪld], **built** [bɪlt], **built** *v. tr.* (faire) bâtir, (faire) construire (une maison): *I am having a house built*, Je me fais bâtir (une maison); [Fig.] édifier (une réputation, &c.); compter sur: *We can ~ upon* *his honesty*, Nous pouvons/compter, faire fond/sur son honnêteté. || *n.* structure *f*; [person] taille *f*, stature *f*. || **builder** [-ɚ] *n.* constructeur, *m*, entrepreneur *m*. || **building** [-ɪŋ] *n.* construction *f*, bâtiment *m*: *school* ~ , école *f*. || *attrib.*: ~ *materials*, matériaux *mpl* de construction; ~ *trades*, corps *mpl* de métiers, industries *fpl* du bâtiment. || **buildup** [-ˌʌp] *n.* mise *f* en valeur, développement *m*; publicité *f* (tapageuse). || **built** cf. BUILD; bâti, façonné: [person] *well-* ~ , bien proportionné, fort; ~ *-up area*, agglomération *f* (urbaine).

bulb [bʌlb] *n.* [Bot.] bulbe *f*, oignon *m*; ampoule *f* (électrique).

Bulgaria [bʌlˈgɛɚiə] *n.* Bulgarie *f*. || **Bulgarian** [-n] *n. & adj.* Bulgare.

bulge [bʌldʒ] *n.* renflement *m*, bosse *f*: [Hist.] *the Battle of the Bulge*, l'offensive *f* des Ardennes. || *v. intr.* (se) gonfler: *bulging pockets*, des poches gonflées (d'objets); *bulging eyes*, des yeux exorbités.

bulk [bʌlk] *n.* volume *m*, masse *f*: *the* ~ *of*, la/plus grande partie de, totalité de . . ./; *in* ~ , en vrac, en gros. || *v. intr.* occuper une place importante; [Fig.] avoir de l'importance. || **bulky** [-ɪ] *adj.* volumineux, encombrant.

bull[1] [bul] *n.* **1.** taureau *m*; mâle *m* (d'un animal): ~ *elephant*, éléphant *m* mâle. **2.** joueur *m* à la hausse: ~ *market*, marché à la hausse [≠ bear]: [Fig.] *to take the* ~ *by the horns*, prendre le taureau par les cornes; *like a* ~ *in a china shop*, comme un chien dans un jeu de quilles.

bull[2] *n.* bulle *f* (papale, du Pape).

bulldog [-dɑg] *n.* bouledogue *m*.

bulldozer [-ˌdowzɚ] *n.* niveleuse *f*, bélier *m* mécanique, bulldozer *m*.

bullet [ˈbulət] *n.* balle *f* (de fusil, de revolver).

bulletin [ˈbulətn̩] *n.* bulletin *m* (de nouvelles, &c.); communiqué *m*: ~ *board*, tableau *m* d'affichage, © babillard *m*.

bullfight [-ˌfajt] *n.* course *f*, combat *m* de taureaux.

bullfrog [-ˌfɹɑg] *n.* © ouaouaron *m*.

bullion [ˈbuljən] *n.* lingot *m*; or *m* en barre.

bull's-eye [-zˌaj]: *to hit the* ~ , faire mouche, [Fam.] taper dans le mille.

bully [ˈbulɪ] *n.* fanfaron *m*, matamore *m*. || **bully**! [Fam.] chic!, épatant! || **bully beef** [-ˌbijf] *n.* bœuf *m* en conserve, [Fam.] singe *m*.

bum [bum] [Fam.] *n.* clochard, voyou. || *adj.* [Fam.] de camelote: *a* ~ *steer*, un faux renseignement. || *v. intr.* vivre aux crochets des autres.

bumblebee [ˈbʌmbl̩ˌbij] *n.* bourdon *m*.

bump [bʌmp] *n.* coup *m*, choc *m* (sourd); bosse *f*; [Road] cahot *m*, [Fr.] cassis *m*. || *v. tr.* cogner, frapper (une auto). || *v. intr.* se heurter, entrer en collision (avec): *to* ~ *against sth.*, heurter qqch.; *to* ~ *along*, avancer en cahotant; *to* ~ *into s.o.*, heurter qqun, [Fig.] rencontrer (qqun) (par hasard).

bumper [-ɚ] *n.* [Auto.] pare-chocs *m*.

bumpkin [ˈbʌmˌkɪn] *n.* rustre *m*.

bumptious [ˈbʌmpʃəs] *adj.* suffisant, prétentieux.

bumpy [ˈbʌmpɪ] *adj.* [road] raboteux, inégal.

bun [bʌn] *n.* **1.** petit pain *m*, © brioche *f*. **2.** [hair] chignon *m*.

bunch [bʌntʃ] *n.* groupe *m* (de personnes, d'objets); bouquet *m* (de fleurs), botte *f* (d'oignons); grappe *f* (de raisins), régime *m* (de bananes); trousseau *m* (de clés); [Fam.] bande *f* (d'amis, de voyous), tas *m* (de choses). || *v. tr.* grouper (des amis, des gens), botteler (des oignons); mettre, lier (des fleurs) en bouquet. || *v. intr.* [of people] se presser, se serrer (ensemble), se pelotonner (les uns contre les autres).

bundle [ˈbʌndl̩] *n.* paquet *m* (de linge, d'effets) liasse *f* (de papier, de lettres), fagot *m* (de bois). || *v. tr.* empaqueter (du linge), mettre (des lettres) en liasse, lier (des asperges) en bottes: *to* ~ *up*, emmitoufler, [object] empaqueter.

bungalow [ˈbʌŋgəˌlow] *n.* bungalow *m*, villa *f* (sans étage).

bungle [ˈbʌŋgl̩] *n.* gâchis *m*. || *v. tr.* gâcher (un travail).

bunk [bʌnk] *n.* **1.** couchette *f*; [Fam.] pieu *m*, plumard *m*. **2.** [nonsense] de la blague, des bêtises. || *v. intr.* dormir (à la dure); se coucher.

bunker [-ɚ] *n.* soute *f* (à charbon, &c.); [Mil.] casemate *f*.

bunny [ˈbʌnɪ] *n.* [Fam.] jeannot-lapin *m*; [US] écureuil *m*.

bunt [bʌnt] *n.* [Sport] coup *m* retenu.

buoy [boj] *n.* bouée *f*. || *v. tr.*: *to* ~ *up*, soutenir (sur l'eau). || **buoyancy** [-ənsɪ] *n.* flottabilité *f*; poussée *f* (d'un liquide). || **buoyant** [-ənt] *adj.* léger, qui flotte (bien).

burden [ˈbɚdn̩] *n.* fardeau *m*, charge *f*: *beast of* ~ , bête *f* de somme; [Fig.] *to be a* ~ *to s.o.*, être à la charge de qqun. || **burdensome** [-səm] *adj.* lourd, pesant: [Fig.] fâcheux, ennuyeux.

bureau [ˈbjuwɚow] *n.* **1.** [piece of furniture] commode *f*; [Br.] bureau *m*, secrétaire *m*.

2. [building] office *m* (de renseignements): *Travel* ~, Agence *f* de voyage; [Gov.] bureau *m*, service *m* gouvernemental: *the Weather* ~, Services météorologiques.

burglar ['bɚglɚ] *n.* cambrioleur *m.* ‖ **burglary** [-ɪ] *n.* cambriolage *m.*

Burgundian [bɚ'gʌndɪən] *n.* Bourguignon, -ne. ‖ **Burgundy** ['bɚgəndɪ] *n.* **1.** la Bourgogne. **2.** [wine] un bourgogne.

burial ['bɛɚɪəl] *n.* enterrement *m*, inhumation *f*, sépulture *f*: ~ *ground*, ~ *place*, cimetière *m*; [individual tomb] sépulture *f*.

burlap ['bɚlæp] *n.* toile *f* (à sac), toile de jute.

burly ['bɚlɪ] *adj.* **1.** volumineux; [Pers.] corpulent. **2.** bruyant.

burn [bɚn] **burnt** or **burned** [-t] [-d] *v. tr.* brûler, réduire (qqch.) en cendres; détruire par le feu: *The lamp was burning bright*, La lampe brûlait intensément, brillait d'un vif éclat. ‖ *v. intr.* être en flammes, en feu; [Fig.] brûler (de): *The house burnt down*, La maison a complètement brûlé. ‖ **burner** [-ɚ] *n.* [gas] brûleur *m* (à gaz, &c.), bec *m* (de gaz). ‖ **burning** [-ɪŋ] *n.* brûlure *f*; [fire] incendie *m.* ‖ *adj.* brûlant; en feu, enflammé.

burnish ['bɚnɪʃ] *v. tr.* brunir, polir (un métal).

burnt cf. BURN.

burrow ['bɚow] *n.* terrier *m* (de lapin).

bursar ['bɚsɚ] *n.* économe *m* (d'un collège). ‖ **bursary** [-ɪ] *n.* [award] bourse *f*.

burst [bɚst], **burst, burst** *v. intr.* fendre; éclater (de rire); exploser, se rompre, jaillir; fondre (sur qqun, en larmes). ‖ *v. tr.* crever (violemment), fendre, rompre. ‖ *n.* explosion *f*, fracas *m* (du tonnerre), éclat *m* (de rire); débordement *m*, transport *m*, élan *m* (de joie, de colère).

bury [bɛɚɪ] *v. tr.* enterrer, ensevelir (un mort); inhumer (une dépouille mortelle); [Fig.] enfoncer, plonger, cacher: *He buried his head in his hands*, Il se cacha le visage entre les mains.

bus [bʌs] *pl.* **buses, busses** [-əz] *n.* **1.** [in town] autobus *m inv.* **2.** [intercity] [Fr.] autocar *m*, car *m* (routier); © autobus *m.*

bush [buʃ] *n.* **1.** buisson *m*; taillis *m.* **2.** *the* ~ *country*, la brousse *f*: ~ *pilot*, pilote *m* de brousse; *to live in the* ~, vivre dans les bois.

bushel [bʌʃəl] *n.* [grain] boisseau *m.*

bushy [-ɪ] *adj.* touffu, épais; [hair] en broussailles; [beard] épais.

business ['bɪznəs] *n.* [inv. au pl., sauf 5: businesses] **1.** [concern] occupation *f*, affaire *f*, rôle *m*: *It is his* ~ *to*, C'est à lui de; *It is none of your* ~, *Mind your own* ~, Occupez-vous, Mêlez-vous/de vos affaires, de ce qui vous regarde/; *to make it o.'s* ~ *to*, se charger de; *You had no* ~ *doing that*, Vous n'aviez pas le droit de faire cela. **2.** [matter] affaire *f*: *a sorry* ~, une triste affaire; *the* ~ *of the /meeting, day/*, l'ordre *m* du jour; *State your* ~, → Quel est l'objet de votre visite?; *to have* ~ *with s.o.*, avoir affaire à qqun; *Let's get down to* ~, (Allons) au fait. **3.** [profession] métier *m*, profession *f*: *What* ~ *is he in, What is his (line of)* ~ *?*, Quel est son métier, Quelle est sa profession?; *He is in the fur* ~, Il travaille dans la fourrure; *He knows his* ~, Il connaît son affaire. **4.** [Com.] les affaires *fpl*, commerce *m*: ~ *is good*, Les affaires vont bien; *to lose* ~, perdre de la clientèle; *to go into, be in/* ~, entrer, être/dans les affaires; *to set up in* ~, s'établir; *to be out of* ~, être retiré des affaires; *to do* ~ *with s.o.*, faire des affaires avec qqun; *to do a land-office* ~, faire des affaires d'or; *on* ~, pour affaires; ~ *is* ~, Les affaires sont les affaires; *to talk* ~, parler affaires; [Fam.] *to mean* ~, parler sérieusement, ne pas plaisanter. **5.** [enterprise] fonds *m* de commerce; affaire *f*; maison *f*; entreprise *f*; établissement *m*: *He manages an important* ~, Il dirige une grosse affaire; *big* ~, les grosses entreprises. ‖ *attrib.* des affaires: ~ *man*, homme *m* d'affaires; ~ *college*, institut *m* d'études commerciales; ~ *hours*, heures *fpl* d'ouverture; ~ *section*, quartier *m* commerçant; ~ *suit*, costume *m* de ville. ‖ **businesslike** [-ˌlajk] *adj.* [Pers., mind] propre aux affaires, pratique, positif, sérieux.

bust[1] *n.* buste *m.*

bust[2] [bʌst] [Fam.] *v. tr.* ruiner, démolir: [Fam.] *to go* ~, faire faillite.

bustle ['bʌsḷ] *v. intr.* s'affairer. ‖ *n.* affairement *m*, remue-ménage *m. inv.*

busy [bɪzɪ] *adj.* affairé, occupé (*at*, à): *a* ~ *street*, une rue achalandée: *I am* ~, Je suis occupé; [Pers.] actif, empressé. ‖ *v. tr.*: *to* ~ *o.s. with*, s'occuper de; [Pej.] se mêler de. ‖ **busybody** [-ˌbɑdɪ] *n.* important *m*, la mouche du coche, © Ti-Jos connaissant.

but [bʌt] *conj.* **1.** mais: *He is tired* ~ *(he is) happy*, Il est fatigué, mais (il est) heureux; *Nobody*, ~ *nobody can come in here*, Personne, mais là personne, ne peut entrer ici. **2.** [= that . . . not] *Who knows*

~ (*that*, [*Fam.*] *what*) *he may be right?*, Qui sait s'il n'a pas raison?; ~ *that I know him to be home* . . . , Si je ne le savais pas chez lui . . . ; *He is not so sick* ~ *he can stand up*, Il n'est pas si malade qu'il ne puisse (pas) se tenir debout; *He never speaks* ~ *she interrupts him*, Il ne parle jamais sans qu'elle l'interrompe; *not* ~ *that* . . . , non que [+ subjunc.]. **3.** [= that] *I don't doubt* ~ (*that*, [*Fam.*] *what*) *you may be right*, Je ne doute pas que vous n'ayez raison. **4.** [= not] *I cannot* ~ *think that* . . . , Je ne peux pas m'empêcher de, Il m'est impossible de ne pas/croire que . . . || *prép.* **1.** sauf, à part; plutôt que; sinon: *everyone* ~ *him, all* ~ *he*, tous sauf lui; *No one* ~ */him, he/can do it*, Personne/sauf, à part/lui ne pourra, Il n'y a que lui qui puisse/le faire; *Anything* ~ *that*, Tout/plutôt que, à part/cela; *He is anything* ~ *shy*, Il n'est rien moins que timide; *There is nothing for it* ~ *to* . . . , Il n'y a, On n'a/qu'à . . . ; *What could I say* ~ . . . , Que pouvais-je dire sinon . . . ; *the last* ~ *one*, l'avant-derni|er, -ère. **2.** ~ *for*, sans; à part; si ce n'était . . . ; ~ *for him, I'd be ruined*, Sans lui, je serais perdu; ~ *for that, we are finished*, A part cela, nous avons fini; ~ *for the fact that he is sick* . . . , (Si ce) n'était qu'il est malade . . . **3.** *all* ~ , presque; *He all* ~ *failed*, Il a failli échouer, C'était tout juste s'il n'a pas échoué. || *adv.* ne . . . que; seulement: *He is* ~ *15*, Il n'a que 15 ans; *I had* ~ *begun*, Je n'avais fait que commencer; *If I could* ~ . . . , Si je pouvais seulement . . . ; *Had I* ~ *known!*, Si j'avais su!; ~ *last week*, pas plus tard que la semaine dernière.

butcher [ˈbutʃɚ] *n.* boucher *m*; ~*'s* (*shop*), boucherie *f*. || *v. tr.* massacrer; [Fam.] charcuter. || **butchery** [-ɪ] *n.* [Fig.] boucherie *f*.

butler [ˈbʌtlɚ] *n.* maître d'hôtel *m*.

butt¹ [bʌt] *n.* [end] gros bout *m*; [stump] bout; [cigarette] mégot *m*.

butt² *n.* [Mil.] cible *f*: *the butts*, le stand de tir; [Fig.] cible: *to be the* ~ *of*, être la/cible, victime/de . . . || *v. intr.* frapper à coups de tête; buter (*against*, contre): [Fig.] *to* ~ *into a conversation, &c.*, se mêler à, s'immiscer dans/une conversation, &c.

butter [-ɚ] *n.* beurre *m*: *brown* ~ , beurre noir; *peanut* ~ , beurre d'arachide; ~ *dish*, beurrier *m*. || *v. tr.* beurrer.

buttercup [-ɚˌkʌp] *n.* bouton *m* d'or.

butterfly [-ˌflaj] *n.* papillon *m*.

buttermilk [ˈbʌtɚˌmɪlk] *n.* petit-lait *m*.

butterscotch [-ˌskɑtʃ] *n.* caramel *m*.

buttock [ˈbʌtək] *n.* **1.** fesse *f*. || *pl.* [Pers.] le derrière, le postérieur, les fesses. **2.** [animal] croupe *f*.

button [-n̩] *n.* bouton *m*. || *v. tr.* boutonner (son pardessus, &c.). || *v. intr.* se boutonner.

buttonhole [-ˌhowl] *n.* boutonnière *f*. || *v. tr.* [Fig.] retenir qqun par la veste, s'accrocher à qqun.

buttress [ˈbʌtɹəs] *n.* arc-boutant *m*. || *v. tr.* arc-bouter; soutenir.

buxom [ˈbʌksəm] *adj.* [usual. fem.] accorte.

buy [baj], **bought** [bɔt], **bought** *v. tr.* acheter; acquérir, faire l'acquisition de; [Fig.] payer (cher sa liberté, &c.); [Fam.] *I'll buy*, Je marche, D'accord. || *n.*: *a good* ~ , une/affaire, occasion/(à ne pas manquer). || **buy back** *v. tr.* racheter. || **buyer** [-ɚ] *n.* **1.** acheteur *m*, client *m*. **2.** acheteur *m* [pour le compte d'un magasin]. || **buy off** [ˈbaj|ˈɔf] *v. tr.* se débarrasser (de qqun) à prix d'argent, désintéresser qqun. || **buy out** [-ˈawt] *v. tr.* désintéresser (qqun); s'assurer/l'exclusivité de, la totalité des parts de/ . . . || **buy up** [-ˈʌp] *v. tr.* acheter en bloc.

buzz [bʌz] *n.* [insects] bourdonnement *m*: ~ *saw*, scie *f* circulaire; [conversation] murmure *m* (des voix). || *v. intr.* [insects] bourdonner; [voice] murmurer, marmotter; [motor] vrombir. || *v. tr.* lancer, répandre (une rumeur); [Aviat.] faire du rase-mottes (au-dessus de); [Fam.] *to* ~ *about*, s'affairer; ~ *off*, Filez! [Tel.] Raccrochez!

buzzard [-ɚd] *n.* buse *f*; busard *m*.

buzzer [-ɚ] *n.* vibreur *m*, vibrateur *m*.

by [baj] *prép.* **1.** [position] [= near] près de; [= beside] à côté de: *by o.s.*, tout seul; *to go* ~ *a store*, passer devant un magasin. **2.** [via] par: ~ *plane*, par avion; ~ */land, sea, air/*, par/terre, mer/, par la voie des airs. **3.** [not later than] avant, pour, d'ici, pas plus tard que; à . . . (déjà): [future] *I'll be back* ~ *6 o'clock*, Je serai de retour/avant, pour, pas plus tard que/6 heures; ~ *this time*, ~ *now*, déjà. **4.** [agent after passive verb] par; de: *This book is* ~ *our teacher*, Ce livre est/par, de/notre professeur; [☞ *de* usual. replaces *par* after: être/suivi, précédé, accompagné, aimé, préféré, détesté, admiré, respecté, &c./.] **5.** [means] par; en [+ pres. part.]; à; de: ~ *heart*, par cœur; *to come* ~ *boat*, venir/en, par le/bateau; *One learns ~ studying*, On apprend en étudiant; *to/begin, finish/ ~ doing sth.*, commencer, finir/par faire qqch. **6.** [according to] d'après, selon; à: *By what I can see*, D'après ce que je vois; *Judging ~ . . .*, A en juger par . . . ; *~ my watch*, à ma montre; *~ /the pound, the month, the dozen/*, à la livre, au mois, à la douzaine. **7.** [to the extent of] de: *~ far*, de /beaucoup, loin/; *wider ~ 10 feet*, plus large de 10 pieds; *20 feet ~ 30*, vingt pieds sur trente. **8.** *to do well ~ s.o.*, agir bien envers qqun; *one ~ one*, un/par, à/un. || *adv.* près: *close ~* , tout près; *to put sth. ~* , mettre qqch. de côté; (*taking it*) *~ and large*, à tout prendre, d'une manière générale; *~ and ~* , peu après; plus tard. || **by-election** *n.* élection *f*/partielle, complémentaire/.

bye-bye! ['bajbaj] [Fam.] *interj.* © bonjour! [Fr.] salut!, au revoir!; [snobbish] bye-bye!

bygone ['bajgɑn] *adj.* passé, ancien. || *n.pl.*: *Let bygones be bygones*, N'en parlons plus, Passons l'éponge, [Fam.] C'est de l'histoire ancienne.

bystander ['baj,stændɚ] *n.* assistant *m*, spectateur *m.*

byword ['baj,wɚd] *n.* dicton *m*: *to be a ~* , être proverbial.

C

C, c [sij] pl. **C's, c's** [sijz] *n.* **1.** [lettre] C, c. **2.** [Mus.] do *m*, †ut *m.* || **cc, c.c.** *abr.* [= cubic centimetre(s)] *n.* centimètre(s) *m* cube(s).

cab [kæb] *n.* voiture *f* de place; taxi *m*; [truck] cabine *f*: *to call a ~* , héler un taxi. || **cab-driver** [-,dɹajvɚ] *n.* chauffeur *m* de taxi; †cocher *m.* || **cab stand** [-,stænd] *n.* station *f* de taxis.

cabbage ['kæbədʒ] *n.* chou *m.*

cabin ['kæbɪn] *n.* **1.** [shed] cabane *f*; [hut] case *f*: *Uncle Tom's ~* , La case de l'Oncle Tom. **2.** poste *m* de conduite, [avion] carlingue *f*; [ship] cabine *f.* || **cabinet** [-ət] *n.* **1.** meuble *m* à tiroirs: *filing ~* , classeur *m*, fichier *m*; *~ -maker*, ébéniste *m.* **2.** [small room] cabinet *m.* **3.** cabinet *m*; conseil *m* (des ministres): *~ minister*, ministre *m* d'état; *to form a ~* , former un ministère.

cable ['kejbḷ] *n.* **1.** [electric, &c.] câble *m.* **2.** câble [cf. CABLEGRAM]. || *v. tr. & intr.* câbler (à qqun). || **cablegram** [-,gɹæm] *n.* câblogramme *m.*

caboose [kə'buws] *n.* **1.** [Rail.] fourgon *m* de queue. **2.** [Naut.] cuisine *f.*

cackle ['kækḷ] *n.* caquet *m.* || *v. tr.* caqueter, bavarder; [laugh] ricaner.

cactus ['kækt|əs] *pl.* **cacti** [-aj] *n.* cactus *m.*

cad [kæd] *n.* mufle *m.*

cadence ['kejdəns] *n.* [music, rhythm] cadence *f.*

cadet [kə'dɛt] *n.* [school, army] © cadet *m*; [Fr.] élève-officier *m.*

cadge [kædʒ] [Fam.] *v. tr. & intr.* se faire donner, mendier.

café [kə'fej] *n.* café *m*, restaurant *m.* || **cafeteria** [kæfə'tijɚɪə] *n.* cafétéria *f*, © *m.*

cage [kejdʒ] *n.* **1.** cage *f.* **2.** cabine *f* (d'ascenseur). || *v. tr.* mettre en cage.

cagey ['kejdʒɪ] [Fam.] *adj.* prudent, circonspect.

Cairo ['kajɚow] *n.* [Geog.] Le Caire *m.*

cajole [kə'dʒowl] *v. tr.* cajoler.

cake [kejk] *n.* gâteau *m*; [fruit- ~] cake *m*; tablette *f* (de chocolat); pain *m* (de savon); [toilet ~] savonnette *f*; tourteau *m* (pour les bestiaux); masse *f* coagulée, croûte *f* (de boue, de ciment). || *v. intr.* [mud] former une croûte; [blood] s'agglutiner: *caked with*, couvert d'une croûte de.

calaboose ['kælə,buws] *n.* [US] [Colloq.] prison *f*, violon *m.*

calamity [kə'læmɪtɪ] *n.* [plague, &c.] calamité *f*; [misfortune] malheur *m.*

calcium ['kælsɪəm] *n.* calcium *m.*

calculate ['kælkjə,lejt] *v. tr. & intr.* calculer: [Fig.] *to ~ on sth.*, compter sur qqch.; *calculated to*, de nature à. || **calculating machine** [-ɪŋmə,ʃijn] *n.* machine *f* à calculer. || **calculation** [,kælkjə'lejʃən] *n.* [mathematics] calcul *m*, compte *m*; *pl. calculations*, [Fig.] conjectures *fpl*, prévisions *fpl*. || **calculus** ['kælkjələs] *n.* **1.** [mathematics] calcul *m* (infinitésimal). **2.** [Med.] calcul *m* (biliaire, &c.).

caldron ['kɔldɹən] *n.* chaudron *m*.

calendar ['kæləndɚ] *n.* calendrier *m*; [Univ.] annuaire *m*: *~ year*, année *f* civile.

calf [kæf] *pl.* **calves** [kævz] *n.* **1.** veau *m*. **2.** petit *m* (de certains animaux). **3.** [person] mollet *m* (de la jambe). || **calfskin** ['kæf,skɪn] *n.* [leather, bookbinding] veau *m*.

calibrate ['kælɪ,bɹejt] *v. tr.* [scale, thermometer, gauge] calibrer. || **calibre** ['kælɪbɚ] *n.* [gauge, diameter] calibre *m*: *of another ~*, [Fig.] [person, &c.] d'une autre trempe.

calico ['kælɪkow] *n.* [fabric] calicot *m*: *printed ~*, (de l') indienne *f*.

call[1] [kɔl] *n.* **1.** [shout] appel *m*, cri *m* (d'appel); [bugle] sonnerie *f* (de clairon): *telephone ~*, coup *m* de téléphone, appel *m* téléphonique; *to be on ~*, être disponible, prêt à répondre (à un appel). **2.** [duty] obligation *f*, vocation *f*: *to answer the ~*, répondre à sa vocation; *to have (no) call to . . .*, (n') être (pas) dans l'obligation de . . ., (n') avoir (aucune) raison de . . . **3.** visite *f*: *to pay s.o. a ~*, passer chez qqun, rendre visite à qqun.

call[2] [kɔl] *v. tr.* **1.** appeler (qqun); crier (qqch.; à qqun de faire qqch.): *to ~ the roll*, faire l'appel. **2.** [summon] appeler, faire venir (qqun); convoquer (une réunion); décréter, ordonner/(une grève); [wake] réveiller: *to ~ to mind*, rappeler; *to ~ attention to sth.*, *to ~ sth. to s.o.'s attention*, porter qqch. à l'attention (de qqun); *to ~ to order*, rappeler à l'ordre. **3.** [name] appeler; traiter, qualifier/(de): *He is called Peter*, Il s'appelle Pierre; *He calls himself an expert*, Il se croit expert; *He called him a liar*, Il l'a traité de menteur; *to ~ s.o. names*, dire des injures à qqun; *He is called after his uncle*, Il porte le nom de son oncle. || *v. intr.* faire une visite: passer/se rendre/se présenter/chez qqun. || **call** + *preposition* [☞ on notera que certains de ces verbes se recouvrent partiellement] || **call aside,** *v. tr.* prendre (qqun) à part. || **call at** ['s], passer chez qqun; rendre visite à qqun [☞ Il s'agit d'une courte visite; voir CALL ON]. || **call away,** *v. tr.* appeler; s'absenter: *to be called away on business*, s'absenter pour affaires. || **call back,** *v. tr.* rappeler (qqun); rappeler (qqun au téléphone); *~ me back at 7*, rappelez-moi à sept heures. || **call down,** *v. tr.* faire descendre; invoquer; [Fam.] gronder (qqun). || **call for,** *v. intr.* **1.** demander, exiger: *This calls for a celebration*, → Ça s'arrose; *to ~ for an apology*, exiger des excuses. **2.** aller chercher (qqch., qqun): *He called for his hat*, Il est passé/venu/chercher son chapeau. || **call in,** *v. tr.* faire entrer (qqun), faire rentrer [qqun qui connaît déjà la maison]; avoir recours à (un spécialiste, &c.): *to ~ in the police*, appeler/faire venir/la police. || **call off,** *v. tr.* décommander (un rendez-vous), annuler (un marché), rompre (des négociations). || **call on,** *v. intr.* **1.** rendre visite à qqun [visite assez longue; voir CALL AT]. **2.** s'adresser à qqun, inviter qqun à faire qqch. || **call out,** *v. tr.* [shout] crier; réclamer (qqch.) à grands cris. || **call up,** *v. tr.* **1.** évoquer (un souvenir), remettre en mémoire. **2.** appeler (qqun au téléphone); faire monter, [army] mobiliser. || **call upon,** *v. intr.* **1.** passer (chez qqun); faire appel (à qqun): *I call upon Mr. X to address the meeting*, → Je donne la parole à M. X, J'invite M. X à prendre la parole. || **caller** [-ɚ] *n.* visiteur *m*, visiteuse *f*. || **calling** [-ɪŋ] *n.* **1.** appel *m*; [meeting] convocation *f*. **2.** état *m*, profession *f*, vocation *f*.

callous ['kæləs] *adj.* [hands, &c.] calleux; [Fig.] [person] sans cœur, [heart] endurci, sans pitié. || **callus** ['kæləs] *n.* [on hands] callosité *f*.

calm [kɑm] *v. tr.* **1.** calmer, tranquilliser: *~ yourself!*, Remettez-vous!. **2.** calmer, adoucir (la douleur, &c.). || *v. intr.* [storm, pain] *to ~ down*, se calmer, s'apaiser. || *adj.* calme, tranquille. || *n.* calme *m*; tranquillité *f*: [Naut.] *dead ~*, calme plat. || **calmly** [-lɪ] *adv.* avec calme; calmement; tranquillement, sans s'émouvoir. || **calmness** [-nəs] *n.* calme *m*, tranquillité *f*.

calorie ['kælɚɪ] *n.* [physics, dietetics] calorie *f*.

calumet ['kæljuw,mɛt] *n.* calumet *m* (de paix).

calumniate [kə'lʌmnɪ,ejt] *v. tr.* calomnier (qqun). || **calumny** ['kæləmnɪ] *n.* calomnie *f*.

Calvary ['kælvɚɪ] *n.* [Bibl.] (*Mount*) *~*, le Calvaire *m*.

calves cf. CALF.

calyx ['kejlɪ|ks] *pl.* **calyces** [-,sijz] *n.* [flower] calice *m*.

came cf. COME.

camel [kæml̩] *n.* chameau *m.*

camera [ˈkæmərə] *pl.* **-s** *n.* **1.** appareil *m* (photographique); [cinema] caméra *f.* **2.** [Loc.] *in* ~, à huis clos.

camouflage [ˈkæməˌflæʒ] *n.* camouflage *m.* || *v. tr.* camoufler.

camp [kæmp] *n.* camp *m*; [site] campement *m*: *summer* ~, colonie *f* de vacances; © camp d'été, chalet *m* d'été; *to pitch* (*a*) ~, établir un camp; *to/strike, break* (*up*)/ ~, lever le camp; ~ *-bed,* lit *m* de camp; ~ *stool,* pliant *m.* || *v. intr. to* ~ (*out*), camper. || **campaign** [kæmˈpejn] *n.* campagne *f* (militaire, électorale): *to/lead, conduct/a* ~ *against s.o.*, mener (une) campagne contre qqun. || *v. intr.* faire (une) campagne. || **camping** [ˈkæmpɪŋ] *n.* campement *m*; [sport] camping *m*: *to go* ~, faire du camping; ~ *ground,* terrain *m* de camping. || **campus** [ˈkæmpəs] *n.* *domaine *m* universitaire, © campus *m*: ~ *activities,* vie *f* universitaire.

can[1] [kæn], **could** [kʊd] [On supplée l'inf. & les part. par BE ABLE, q.v.]. *v.* [☞ *can* possède un sens prés. & fut.; *could* a une valeur de passé & de cond.] **1.** [ability] pouvoir; savoir [cf. also **2.**]: *I can't come now,* Je ne peux pas venir maintenant; *I* ~ *come tomorrow,* Je pourrai venir demain; *I couldn't know,* Je ne pouvais pas le savoir; *I couldn't find you yesterday,* Je n'ai pas pu vous trouver hier; *He could do it if he wanted to,* Il pourrait le faire s'il le voulait; *He* ~ *have done it,* Il aurait pu le faire; *I/can't, couldn't/say,* Je ne saurais dire; *He is as nice as could be,* Il est on ne peut plus gentil, Il ne saurait être plus aimable; *How could you do that?,* Comment avez-vous pu faire une chose pareille!(?). **2.** [know how] savoir: *Can you swim?,* Savez-vous nager? [in the same tenses as 1.]. **3.** [Fam. permission] pouvoir: *He says I can't go,* Il dit que je ne/peux, pourrai/pas y aller [in the same tenses as 1.]. **4.** [possibility] se pouvoir: *That can happen occasionally,* Il se peut que ça se produise parfois; *Can it be* (*that . . .*)?, Se peut-il (que . . .)?. **5.** [no translation]: actual occurrence; *I* ~ *see him from here,* Je le vois d'ici; *I can't find my tie,* Je ne trouve pas ma cravate; *I can't understand* (*why*), Je ne comprends pas (pourquoi); *He* ~ *be quite difficult,* Il est /parfois, souvent/très difficile.

can[2] [kæn] *n.* [liquids] bidon *m*; burette *f* (à l'huile); [food] boîte *f* (de conserve): ~ *-opener,* ouvre-boîte *m.* || *v. tr.* **[-nn-]** mettre (des aliments)/en conserve, en boîte.

Canada [ˈkænədə] *n.* le Canada *m*: *in* ~, au Canada, †en C.; *to* ~, au Canada, †en C.; *throughout* ~, d'un bout à l'autre du C. || **Canadian** [kəˈnejdɪən] *adj.* canadien, canadienne; (*the*) ~ *Pacific* (*Railway*), (le) Pacifique-Canadien; *the* ~ *government,* le gouvernement/du Canada, canadien/; *the National Conference of Canadian Universities,* l'Office national des universités (canadiennes). || **Canadian** *n.* Canadien *m*, -ne *f.*

canal [kəˈnæl] *n* [Panama, &c.] canal *m.*

canasta [kəˈnæstə] *n.* © canasta *m* [Fr. *f*].

cancel [ˈkænsəl] *v. tr.* **[-ll-]** **1.** annuler, résilier (un contrat). **2.** contremander, décommander (un rendez-vous, &c.); biffer (un mot); oblitérer (un timbre). || **cancellation** [ˌkænsəˈlejʃən] *n.* annulation *f.*

cancer [ˈkænsər] *n.* cancer *m*: *the* ~ *Institute,* l'Institut du Cancer; *to suffer from* ~, être atteint du cancer. || **cancerous** [-əs] *adj.* [person, organ] cancéreux.

candid [ˈkændɪd] *adj.* [×] franc, loyal: *a* ~ *opinion,* une opinion franche.

candidacy [ˈkændɪdəsɪ] *n.* candidature *f*: *to support s.o.'s* ~ *for . . .*, soutenir la candidature de qqun (au poste de . . .). || **candidate** [ˈkændɪˌdejt] *n.* candidat *m*: *to become a* ~, → faire acte de candidature.

candidly [ˈkændɪdlɪ] *adv.* franchement, de bonne foi.

candied [ˈkændɪd] *adj.* [fruit] confit.

candle [ˈkændl̩] *n.* [wax] bougie *f*; [tallow] chandelle *f*; [church] cierge *m.* || **candle-light** [-ˌlajt] *n.*: *by* ~, à la chandelle; [Phys.] ~ *power,* bougie *f.* || **candlestick** [-ˌstɪk] *n.* [×] chandelier *m*, [flat] bougeoir *m.*

candour [ˈkændər] *n.* [×] franchise *f*, bonne foi *f* [cf. CANDID].

candy [ˈkændɪ] *n.* bonbon *m*: ~ */shop, store/,* confiserie *f.*

cane [kejn] *n.* [walking stick] canne *f*; [sugar] canne *f* (à sucre): ~ *sugar,* sucre *m* de canne.

canine [ˈkejnajn] *adj.* canin *m*, -e *f*: ~ *tooth,* canine *f.*

canker [ˈkæŋkər] *n.* chancre *m.*

canned [kæn|d] *adj.* en conserve [cf. CAN 2.]: ~ *goods,* conserves *fpl* alimentaires. || **cannery** [-ərɪ] *n.* fabrique *f* de conserves.

cannily [ˈkænɪlɪ] *adv.* prudemment, avec prudence.

cannon [ˈkænən] *n.* canon *m*, pièce *f* (d'artillerie) [cf. GUN]: ~ *ball,* boulet *m* de canon; *within* ~ *shot,* à portée de canon; [Coll.] artillerie *f.* || **cannonade** [-ˌejd] *n.* canonnade *f.* || *v. tr.* canonner. || **cannoneer** [-ˌijɚ] *n.* canonnier *m.*

cannot [ˈkænɑt] = *can not* [qui s'écrit habituellement en un seul mot] [cf. CAN[1]].

canny [kænɪ] *adj.* prudent, sagace.

canoe [kəˈnuw] *n. Canadian* ~, canoë *m*: *in a, by*/~, en canoë; © canot *m*; [large] pirogue *f.*

canon [ˈkænən] *n.* [Eccl.] chanoine *m.* || **canonic(al)** [kəˈnɑnɪkḷ] *adj.* [law] canonique. || **canonize** [ˈkænəˌnajz] *v. tr.* [Rel.] canoniser.

canopy [ˈkænəpɪ] *n.* dais *m* (d'un trône); †baldaquin *m* (d'un lit).

can't [kænt] = cannot, cf. CAN[1].

cantaloup(e) [ˈkæntəˌlowp] *n.* [melon] cantaloup *m.*

cantankerous [kənˈtæŋkɚəs] *adj.* [person, mood] bourru, revêche, acariâtre.

canteen [kænˈtijn] *n.* **1.** [restaurant] cantine *f.* **2.** bidon *m* (pour l'eau).

canter [ˈkæntɚ] *n.* [horse] petit galop *m.* || *v. intr.* aller au petit galop.

canvas[1] [ˈkænvəs] *n.* toile *f*; [art] toile; [camping] toile de tente: *under* ~, sous la tente; [Naut.] voiles *fpl*: *under* ~, toutes voiles dehors.

canvas(s)[2] inspection *f*; campagne *f* électorale (à domicile), © cabale *f*; démarchage *m.* || *v. tr.* examiner (soigneusement); [élection] solliciter des voix, © faire la cabale. || **canvasser** [-ɚ] *n.* démarcheur *m*, solliciteur *m*, © cabaleur *m.* || **canvassing** [-ɪŋ] *n.* campagne *f* électorale, sondage *m* d'opinion (à domicile), © cabale *f*; démarchage *m.*

canyon [ˈkænjən] *n.* cañon *m*, [valley] gorge *f*, défilé *m.*

cap [kæp] *n.* casquette *f*; © casque *m*: *fur cap*, casque de poil; képi *m* (d'un soldat); toque *f*, mortier *m* [insigne universitaire]: ~ *and gown*, la toge et le mortier; [Tech.] capsule *f* (d'une bouteille, d'une cartouche); [Rail.] *red-* ~, porteur *m.* || *v. tr.* [-pp-] capsuler; [Fig.] coiffer, couronner; surpasser: *to* ~ *it all*, pour comble de [fill in with noun]. || **cap.** [abbr.] majuscule *f*: *small caps*, petites capitales *fpl.*

capability [ˌkejpəˈbɪlɪtɪ] *n.* capacité *f*, aptitude *f.* || **capable** [ˈkejpəbḷ] *adj.* capable (*de*, of); susceptible (de faire qqch.); [doctor, &c.] compétent. [☞ Often best rendered by POUVOIR].

capacious [kəˈpejʃəs] *adj.* ample, vaste, spacieux. || **capacity** [kəˈpæsɪtɪ] *n.* **1.** capacité *f*, contenance *f*: *house filled to* ~, salle *f* comble. **2.** capacité *f*; aptitude *f*: *to show one's* ~, donner sa mesure; *mental* ~, aptitude mentale, intelligence *f.* **3.** compétence *f* (légale): *In my* ~ *as (chairman)*, En tant que (président).

cape[1] [kejp] *n.* pèlerine *f*; cape *f.*

cape[2] *n.* cap *m*; promontoire *m*: *Cape Breton Island*, l'île *f* du Cap Breton.

caper [-ɚ] *n.* cabriole *f.* || *v. intr.* cabrioler.

capital [ˈkæpɪtḷ] *n.* [money] capital *m*, capitaux *mpl*; [letter] (lettre) majuscule *f*; [column] chapiteau *m*; [city] capitale *f* (d'un pays, &c.). || *adj.* capital, essentiel; [good] excellent, parfait: ~ *city*, capitale *f*; ~ *punishment*, peine capitale/de mort/; *It is of* ~ *importance*, C'est de la plus haute importance; *Capital!*, Fameux! || **capitalism** [-ɪzm] *n.* [economics, politics] capitalisme *m.* || **capitalist** [-ɪst] *n.* & *adj.* capitaliste (*m*). || **capitalize** [-ˌajz] *v. tr.* **1.** capitaliser; [Fig.] miser sur: *to* ~ *on s.o.'s errors*, tirer parti des erreurs/fautes/ de qqun. **2.** écrire (un mot) avec une majuscule.

Capitol [ˈkæpɪtḷ] *n.* [Washington, D.C.] le Capitole *m.*

capitulate [kəˈpɪtjəˌlejt] *v. intr.* capituler. || **capitulation** [kəˌpɪtjəˈlejʃən] *n.* capitulation *f.*

caprice [kəˈpɹijs] *n.* [whim, mood, fancy] caprice *m.* || **capricious** [kəˈpɹɪʃəs] *adj.* capricieux.

capsize [kæpˈsajz] *v. intr.* [boat] chavirer. || *v. tr.* faire chavirer (une chaloupe, &c.).

capstan [ˈkæpstən] *n.* [Naut.] cabestan *m.*

capsule [ˈkæpsjəl] *n.* capsule *f.*

captain [ˈkæptən] *n.* chef *m*, capitaine *m*; chef *m* d'équipe; [ship's] commandant *m*: [RCAF] *Group Captain*, colonel *m* (d'aviation), © capitaine *m* de groupe.

caption [ˈkæpʃən] *n.* légende *f* (d'un texte), sous-titre *m.* || **captious** [ˈkæpʃəs] *adj.* [person] chicaneux, pointilleux, [Pej.] critique; [argument] captieux.

captivate [ˈkæptɪ|ˌvejt] *v. tr.* [charm] captiver (qqun). || **captive** [-v] *adj.* & *n.* capt|if, -ive, prisonni|er, -ère. || **captivity** [kæpˈtɪvɪtɪ] *n.* captivité *f.* || **capture** [ˈkæptʃɚ] *n.* capture *f*, [loot] prise *f* (de butin, &c.). || *v. tr.* capturer (un vaisseau); prendre (une ville); capter (des ondes).

car [kɑɚ] *n.* **1.** [Auto] automobile *f*, auto *f*, [© *m*] voiture *f*: *used* ~, voiture d'occasion [N.B. *car* in French means a bus]. **2.** [Rail.] wagon *m*, [passengers] voiture *f*: *dining* ~, wagon-restaurant *m*; *freight* ~, wagon *m* de marchandises; *sleeping* ~, wagon-lit *m.* **3.** nacelle *f* (d'un ballon); cabine *f* (d'ascenseur), ascenseur *m*.

caravan [ˈkæəəˌvæn] *n*. **1.** [desert, gypsies] caravane *f*, convoi *m* (de voyageurs). **2.** [truck] roulotte *f* [d'ordinaire, on emploie le mot VAN]; [Br.] remorque *f* (automobile).

caraway [ˈkæəəˌwej] *n*. anis *m*.

carbolic [kɑəˈbɑlɪk] *adj*. [acid] phénique. || **carbon** [ˈkɑəbən] *n*. carbone *m*.: *~ dioxide*, acide *m* carbonique; *~ monoxide*, oxyde *m* de carbone; *~ tet(rachloride)*, tétrachlorure *m* de carbone; *~ paper*, (papier) carbone; *~ copy*, [typed] double *m*, pelure *f*. || **carbonate** [-ejt] *n*. carbonate *m*. || **carbonic** [kɑəˈbɑnɪk] *adj*. carbonique.

carburettor [ˈkɑəbəˌɛtə] *n*. [car] carburateur *m*.

carcase [ˈkɑəkəs] *n*. carcasse *f*; cadavre *m*.

card [kɑəd] *n*. **1.** carte *f* (à jouer): *to have a game of cards*, faire une partie de cartes; *playing cards*, cartes (à jouer); *to play cards*, jouer aux cartes; *a deck of cards*, un jeu de cartes; *~ -player*, joueur *m* de cartes. **2.** carte *f* (de visite, d'affaire); [index] fiche *f*; [report] bulletin *m* scolaire. **3.** [Loc.] *It's in the cards*, C'est tout/fort/probable; *to put one's cards on the table*, mettre cartes sur table. || **cardboard** [-ˌboəd] *n*. carton *m*: *~ box*, boîte *f* en carton.

cardiac [ˈkɑədɪˌæk] *adj*. cardiaque.

cardinal [ˈkɑədn̩əl] *adj*. [number, point] cardinal. || *n*. **1.** [R.C.] cardinal *m*. **2.** [bird] cardinal *m*.

cardiograph [ˌkɑədɪəˈɡɹæf] *n*. cardiographe *m*.

care [kɛə] *n*. **1.** [anxiety] souci *m*; inquiétude *f*. **2.** [caution] soin *m*, attention *f*: *Handle with ~*, → Fragile; *Take ~ !*, Faites attention!; *to take ~ of*, → s'occuper de; *to take ~ to*, avoir soin de; *beauty ~*, soins de beauté. **3.** charge *f*; tenue *f*; [upkeep] entretien *m*: *~ of X*, (*c/o*), aux bons soins de, (a/s); *want of ~*, incurie *f*, négligence *f*. || **care** *v. intr.* **1.** (*about*) se soucier de, porter attention à: [Fam.] *I couldn't ~ less*, Ce que ça pouvait bien m'être égal; Ça me laissait complètement froid. *I don't ~ (a hoot, &c.)*, Ça m'est égal, [Fam.] Je m'en fiche; *What do you ~ ?* Qu'est-ce que ça peut vous faire? **2.** désirer, vouloir, aimer: *Would anyone ~ for coffee?*, Qqun désire-t-il du café? *if you ~ to join us*, si vous voulez vous joindre à nous; *if you ~ to*, si le cœur vous en dit; *I don't ~ for it*, Je n'y tiens pas; *I don't ~ to (do that)*, Ça ne me dit rien (de faire ça); *She cares a great deal for him*, Elle tient beaucoup à lui. **3.** s'occuper de (qqun); soigner un malade.

careen [kəˈɹijn] *v. tr.* faire coucher (un navire) sur le côté. || *v. intr.* donner de la bande.

career [kəˈɹijə] *n*. **1.** carrière *f*: *to take up a ~*, embrasser une carrière. **2.** course *f*.

careful [ˈkɛə|fl̩] *adj*. **1.** soigneux (de, *of*): *to be ~ of*, avoir (bien) soin de; *he was ~ not to . . .*, il eut bien soin de ne pas . . . **2.** prudent, circonspect: *Do be ~ !*, Prenez garde, → Surtout faites attention! **3.** bien pesé: *after ~ /thought, consideration/*, tout bien pesé. || **carefully** [-fl̩ɪ] *adv*. **1.** soigneusement, avec soin, attentivement. **2.** prudemment, avec circonspection. || **careless** [-ləs] *adj*. **1.** (of, about) insouciant (de); nonchalant: *a ~ remark*, une observation à la légère, irréfléchie; *~ mistake*, faute *f* d'inattention. **2.**; négligent, sans soin. || **carelessly** [-ləslɪ] *adv*. avec insouciance, négligemment, sans soin. || **carelessness** [-ləsnəs] *n*. négligence *f*; insouciance *f*.

caress [kəˈɹɛs] *n*. caresse *f*. || *v. tr.* caresser.

caretaker [ˈkɛə|ˌtejkə] *n*. concierge *m* (d'un immeuble), gardien *m* (d'un local, bureau). || **careworn** [-ˌwoən] *adj*. dévoré/rongé/par le(s) souci(s).

cargo [ˈkɑəgow] *n*. cargaison *f* (d'un bateau, &c.); fret *m*; *~ boat*, cargo *m*.

caribou [ˈkæəɪˌbuw] *pl.* **-s** *n*. © caribou *m*.

caricature [ˈkæəɪkətʃə] *n*. caricature *f*. || *v. tr.* caricaturer (qqun).

carillon [kəˈɹɪljən] *n*. carillon *m*.

car(r)iole [ˈkæəɪˌol] © *n*. carriole *f* [cf. CARRYALL].

carious [ˈkæəɪəs] *adj*. [teeth] carié.

carnal [ˈkɑənl̩] *adj*. charnel.

carnation [kɑəˈnejʃən] *n*. **1.** teint *m*. **2.** [Bot.] œillet *m*.

carnival [ˈkɑənɪvəl] *n*. carnaval *m*.

carnivorous [kɑəˈnɪvərəs] *adj*. [animal] carnivore.

carol [ˈkæəəl] *n*. chant *m*, [Christmas] cantique *m* (de Noël).

Carolina [kæəəˈlajnə] *n*.: *North ~*, *South ~*, la Caroline du Nord, du Sud.

carouse [kəˈɹawz] *n*. beuverie *f*. || *v. intr.* prendre part à une beuverie.

carp [kɑəp] *n*. carpe *f*; [vulg.] © castor *m* [cf. SUCKER].

carpenter [ˈkɑəpən|tə] *n*. charpentier *m*, [joiner] menuisier *m*: *carpenter's shop*, atelier *m* de menuiserie. || **carpentry** [-tɹɪ] *n*. charpenterie *f*, menuiserie *f*.

carpet [ˈkɑəpət] *n*. tapis *m*; [wall to wall] moquette *f*: [Fig.] *on the ~*, sur le tapis;

carpeting, les tapis; *bedside* ~ , descente *f* de lit. || *v. tr.* recouvrir d'un tapis.
carriage [ˈkæəɪʤ] *n.* **1.** transport *m*; port *m*: ~ *free*, ~ *paid*, franco de port, port payé. **2.** voiture *f*; [royal] carrosse *m*; [Rail.] voiture *f*, wagon *m*; attelage *m*. **3.** [bearing] maintien *m*, port *m*, allure *f*. || **carrier** [ˈkæəɪɚ] *n.* transporteur *m*; [errands] commissionnaire *m*; [rack] porte-bagages *m*: (aircraft) ~ , [Mil.] porte-avion *m*; *mail-* ~ , facteur *m*.
carrion [ˈkæəɪən] *n.* charogne *f*.
carrot [ˈkæəət] *n.* carotte *f*.
carry [ˈkæəɪ] *v. tr.* **1.** porter, supporter [☞ le verbe anglais est souvent précisé par une postposition, voir plus loin]: *to* ~ *a watch*, porter une montre sur soi; *the walls* ~ *the roof*, les murs (sup)portent le toit. **2.** [goods, &c.] transporter (par voie ferrée, par camion, &c.); transmettre (un signal); [take away] emporter. **3.** [body] se tenir, porter; supporter: *He carries himself/erect, straight/*, Il se tient très droit; *He carries his head high*, Il porte la tête haute. **4.** [in distance] porter: *His voice carries well*, sa voix porte/bien, loin/; avoir/une importance, une portée/: *His words* ~ *a lot of weight*, Ses paroles/ont une grande portée, sont d'un grand poids/; [Journ.] publier: The Globe *carries an article on . . .*, *Le Globe* publie/donne/un article sur . . . **5.** [vote] adopter, faire adopter/une proposition: *carried!*, adopté!; *to* ~ *o's point*, imposer sa manière de voir; *to* ~ *sth. into effect*, mettre qqch. à exécution. **6.** [Arith.] retenir, effectuer une retenue. || **carry across** [-əˈkɹɑs] *v. tr.* transporter (qqch.) de l'autre côté. || **carry along** [-əˈlɔŋ] *v. tr.* entraîner, emporter. || **carry away** [-əˈwej]: *v. tr.* *He is carried away by his feelings*, Il est emporté par ses émotions. || **carry back** [-ˈbæk] *v. tr.* rapporter (qqch.); ramener (qqun), remmener (qqun). || **carry down** [-ˌdawn] *v. tr.* descendre (qqch.). || **carry forward** [-ˈfɔəwəd] *v. tr.* [an item] reporter (un article). || **carry off** [-ˈɑf] *v. tr.* [the prize], remporter (le prix). || **carry on** [-ˈɑn] *v. tr.* poursuivre; continuer (une tradition); exercer (un commerce); entretenir (une correspondance); soutenir (une conversation). || *v. intr. to* ~ *during s.o.'s absence*, continuer le travail, diriger les affaires en l'absence de qqun; persévérer; persister; se comporter: *I shall* ~ *to the end*, j'irai jusqu'au bout; *I don't like the way he carries on*, Je n'aime pas ses façons; *Don't* ~ *like that*, Ne vous emballez pas comme ça! || **carry out** [-awt] *v. tr.* porter dehors; mettre à exécution, effectuer; remplir (des instructions); exécuter (un programme); exercer (un mandat); s'acquitter (d'une fonction): *to* ~ *the law*, appliquer la loi. || **carry over** [-ˈowvɚ] *v. tr.* transporter de l'autre côté; reporter. || **carry through** [-θɹuw] *v. tr.* transporter (qqch.); mener (une entreprise) à bonne fin. || **carry up** [-ˈʌp] *v. tr.* monter (qqch.).
carryall © [ˈkæəɪˌɔl] *n.* carriole *f*, charrette *f*.
cart [kɑət] *n.* charrette *f*; [Mil.] fourgon *m*: ~ *horse*, cheval *m* de trait; ~ *load*, chargement *m*, charretée *f*. || *v. tr.* charrier, charroyer: *to* ~ *away*, enlever, ramasser. || **cartage** [-əʤ] *n.* transport *m*.
cartel [ˌkɑəˈtɛl] *n.* [Com.] cartel *m*.
carton [ˈkɑətn̩] *n.* boîte *f* (en carton); [cigarettes] cartouche *f*.
cartoon [kɑəˈtuwn] *n.* caricature *f*; [cinéma] dessin(s) animé(s) *m(pl)*. || **cartoonist** [-ɪst] *n.* caricaturiste *m*.
cartridge [ˈkɑətɹɪʤ] *n.* **1.** cartouche *f*. **2.** [Phot.] (pellicule *f* en) bobine *f*.
carve [kɑəv] *v. tr.* **1.** sculpter; [flat] graver. **2.** [meat] découper (un poulet): *to* ~ *one's way*, se tailler un chemin; *to* ~ *up a country*, démembrer un pays. || **carver** [-ɚ] *n.* **1.** [wood-] sculpteur *m*. **2.** graveur *m*, ciseleur *m*. **3.** découpeur *m*. || **carving** [-ɪŋ] *n.* **1.** [wood] sculpture *f*. **2.** [metal] gravure *f*, ciselure *f*. **3.** [meat] découpage *m*. || **carving knife** [-ɪŋˌnajf] *n.* couteau *m* à découper (la viande).
cascade [kæsˈkejd] *n.* cascade *f*.
case[1] [kejs] *n.* **1.** cas *m*: [Loc.] *the* ~ *in point*, le cas dont il s'agit; *a* ~ *in point*, un cas d'espèce; *should the* ~ *occur*, → le cas échéant; *That is not the* ~ , Ce n'est pas le cas; Il n'en est rien; *if that is the* ~ , s'il en est ainsi; *That is often the* ~ , Cela arrive souvent; *in any* ~ , en tout cas; dans tous les cas; de toute/manière, façon; *as the* ~ *may be*, selon le cas; *in no* ~ , en aucun cas; *in that* ~ , dans ce cas (-là); *In* ~ *I can't come . . .*, Au cas où je ne pourrais pas venir . . . ; *Take your umbrella in* ~ *it rains*, Prenez votre parapluie pour le cas où il pleuvrait; *in* ~ *not*, au cas contraire; *just in* ~ , à tout hasard; *in most cases*, en général. **2.** cause *f*, affaire *f*, [Jur.] procès *m*: *to state the* ~ , faire l'exposé des faits; *the* ~ *for the Crown*, l'accusation *f*. **3.** caisse *f*, colis *m*. **4.** étui *m*; écrin *m*; boîte *f* (de violon); boîtier *m* (de montre); caisse (de piano): *filing* ~ , carton *m*. **5.** couverture

f: *pillow* ~ , taie *f* d'oreiller. **6.** [Gram.] cas (de la flexion nominale): *the* ~ *-endings*, les flexions casuelles.

case[2] [kejs] *v. tr.* **1.** encaisser: *to* ~ *foods* (*up*), encaisser des marchandises. **2.** envelopper; cartonner (un livre).

casement [-mənt] *n.* croisée *f*, fenêtre *f*.

cash [kæʃ] *n.* [money] espèces *fpl*; argent *m* liquide: ~ *down*, argent comptant; ~ *on delivery* (*parcel*), (colis) payable contre remboursement; ~ *register*, caisse *f* enregistreuse; *to be out of* ~, ne pas avoir d'argent comptant; être à sec, n'être pas en fonds. || *v. tr.* toucher (un chèque), encaisser (un chèque, un coupon): [Fam.] *to* ~ *in on*, faire un profit sur, tirer parti de (qqch.). || **cashier** [kæ'ʃɪjər] *n.* caissi/er *m*, -ère *f* (d'une banque, d'un magasin, &c.).

cask [kæsk] *n.* [wine, beer, &c.] tonneau *m*, fût *m*.

casket [-ət] *n.* **1.** coffret *m* (à lettres, à bijoux, &c.). **2.** cercueil *m* [cf. COFFIN].

casserole ['kæsər,owl] *n.* [baking dish] casserole *f*.

cassock ['kæsək] *n.* [R.C.] soutane *f*.

cast[1] [kæst] *n.* **1.** [throw] jet *m* (de pierre); coup *m* (de dés); lancer *m* (du filet). **2.** [iron] fonte *f*; [statue] moulage *m*, plâtre *m*: *cast iron*, fonte *f*; *plaster cast*, moulage au plâtre, [broken limb] plâtre *m*. **3.** [Fig.] ~ *of features*, expression *f* (du visage): ~ *of mind*, tournure *f* d'esprit. **4.** [Théâtre] distribution *f* (des rôles).

cast[2], **cast, cast** *v. tr.* **1.** jeter (l'ancre, &c.); lancer (une pierre); projeter (une ombre): *to* ~ *in one's lot with s.o.*, épouser le parti de qqun, partager le sort de qqun; *The die is* ~, Le sort en est jeté; [Naut.] *to* ~ *the line*, lancer la ligne. **2.** fondre (du métal); mouler (un cylindre); couler (une statue): ~ *in one piece*, moulé en bloc. **3.** [Théâtre] distribuer (les rôles d'une pièce); assigner (un rôle à qqun). **4.** [a vote, ballot] voter: *number of votes* ~ , nombre de voix recueillies, nombre de personnes qui ont voté. || **cast about** [-ə'bawt] *v. intr.* (one's eyes) promener (ses regards) de tous côtés; (for an excuse) chercher (un prétexte). || †**cast aside** [-əsajd] *v. intr.* se défaire de, mettre (qqch.) de côté/au rancart/. || †**cast away** [-ə'wej] *v. intr.* **1.** jeter au loin. **2.** [Fig.] rejeter. || **castaway** ['kæstə,wej] *n.* naufragé *m*. || †**cast back** [-'bæk] *v. intr.* **1.** renvoyer (une pierre, &c.); [Fig.] ramener, reporter (ses pensées, &c.) en arrière. || **cast down** [-'dawn] *v. intr.* jeter bas; [Fig.] baisser (les yeux, le regard, &c.): [Fig.] *to be* ~ , être abattu/déprimé/. || **cast off** [-'ɔf] *v. tr.* **1.** larguer une amarre; [Fig.] (*to be*) (être) renié par sa famille; †**2.** se dévêtir (de ses vêtements). || **cast-off** [-,ɑf] *adj.* [clothing, &c.] de rebut: ~ *clothing*, vêtements de rebut, défroques. || **cast-off** [-,ɔf] *n.* [from society] au ban de. || **cast out** [-'awt] *v. intr.* [pers.] mettre dehors; [demons] exorciser. || **cast up** [-'ʌp] *v. intr.* (one's eyes), lever (les yeux au ciel); [sea, ocean, &c.] rejeter (qqch. sur la rive).

castanets [,kæstən'ɛts] *n.pl.* castagnettes *fpl*.

caste [kæst] *n.* caste *f*.

caster[1] ['kæstər] *n.* [cf. CASTOR **1**].

caster[2] *n.* **1.** [metal] fondeur *m*. **2.** jeteur *m* (de sorts, &c.).

†**castigate** ['kæstɪ,gejt] *v. tr.* châtier, punir (qqun).

†**casting** ['kæstɪŋ] *adj. The chairman has the* ~ *vote*, la voix du président est prépondérante; *to give the* ~ *vote*, départager les voix. || *n.* †**1.** jet *m* (d'une pierre). **2.** moulage *m*; fonte *f*. **3.** distribution *f* des rôles.

castle ['kæsl̩] *n.* **1.** château *m*. **2.** [chess] tour *m*. || *v. intr.* [chess] roquer.

castor ['kæstər] [also *caster*] *n.* **1.** roulette *f* (de fauteuil, &c.). **2.** [Br.] salière *f*; poivrière *f*. **3.** ~ *oil*, huile *f* de ricin; © huile de castor.

casual ['kæʒuwəl] *adj.* **1.** fortuit; accidentel. **2.** insouciant: *to give a* ~ *answer*, répondre d'un air désinvolte; *to engage in* ~ *conversation*, parler de choses et d'autres; ~ *labour*, main-d'œuvre d'emploi intermittent; ~ *labourer*, homme *m* à l'heure; ~ *profit*, produit *m* casuel. || **casually** [-lɪ] *adv.* **1.** fortuitement; par hasard; en passant. **2.** négligemment; avec désinvolture. || **casualty** [-tɪ] *n.* accident *m*; blessé *m*, mort *m*; [Mil.] *casualties*, les pertes *fpl*.

cat [kæt] *n.* chat *m*, chatte *f*: *tomcat*, matou *m*; [Fig.] *to let the* ~ *out of the bag*, vendre la mèche.

cataclysm ['kætə,klɪzm] *n.* cataclysme *m*.

catacomb ['kætə,kowm] *n.* catacombe *f*.

catafalque ['kætə,fɔlk] *n.* [funeral] catafalque *m*.

catalogue ['kætəlɔg] [also **-og**] *n.* catalogue *m*, [small] liste *f*; [price list] prix-courant *m*; [university] programme *m*, annuaire *m*. || *v. tr.* cataloguer.

catapult ['kætə,pult] *n.* catapulte *f*.

cataract ['kætər,ækt] *n.* cataracte *f*.

catarrh [kə'tɑər] *n.* catarrhe *m*.

catastrophe [kə'tæstɹəfɪ] *n.* catastrophe *f*.

catch[1] [kætʃ] **caught, caught** [kɔt] *v. tr.* **1.**

attraper (une balle), prendre (un poisson, le train), saisir: *to ~ hold of*, saisir, s'accrocher à (une branche, un espoir). **2.** [Fig.] attraper (un voleur), (sur)prendre: *He was caught redhanded*, Il fut pris la main dans le sac; comprendre: *I didn't ~ what you said*, Je n'ai pas compris (saisi) ce que vous disiez; *You can't ~ me!* Ça ne prend pas (avec moi). **3.** [become caught] (s')accrocher (à) (une branche); attraper (une maladie); se laisser surprendre (par un orage, &c.): *A nail caught my coat*, Un clou a accroché mon veston; *I caught a cold*, J'ai attrapé un rhume; *A sound caught my ear*, Un son me frappa l'oreille. **4.** [become lighted] s'allumer, prendre (feu): *The house caught fire*, La maison prit feu. || **catch on** [-'ɑn] *v. intr.* comprendre/à demi-mot/à mots couverts/; devenir/célèbre/populaire. || **catch out** [-'awt] *v. tr.* prendre (qqun) sur le fait. || **catch up** [-'ʌp] *v. intr.* (with), rattraper (un retard, une personne). || *v. tr.* s'emparer (vivement) de; interrompre constamment (un orateur).

catch[2] [kætʃ] *n.* [fish, game] prise *f*; [Pej.] attrape *f*; [advantageous] aubaine *f*, [fastener] cliquet *m*: *~ word, phrase*, réclame *f*, slogan *m*. [Fam.] *There's a ~ to it*, C'est une attrape. || **catching** [-ɪŋ] *adj.* **1.** contagieux; infectieux. **2.** [du rire] communicatif. **3.** [d'un air, d'une mélodie] entraînant; facile à retenir.

catchup *n.* cf. CATSUP.

catchword ['kætʃˌwɚd] *n.* mot *m*, expression *f*/à la mode.

catchy ['kætʃɪ] *adj.* [tune, &c.] facile à retenir, entraînant; [objection, question] insidieux.

catechism ['kætəkɪzm] *n.* [Rel.] catéchisme *m*.

categorical [ˌkætə'gɔɚɪkl] *adj.* [answer, &c.] catégorique. || **category** ['kætəˌgɔɚɪ] *n.* catégorie *f*.

cater ['kejtɚ] *v. intr.* [at a party] approvisionner (qqun, *for s.o.*). || **caterer** [-ɚ] *n.* pourvoyeur *m*, fournisseur *m* (en victuailles, &c.).

caterpillar ['kætɚˌpɪlɚ] *n.* **1.** chenille *f*. **2.** auto-chenille *f*; tracteur *m*: *~ wheel*, roue *f* à chenille.

catfish ['kætˌfɪʃ] *n.* poisson-chat *m*, © barbotte *f*: *spotted ~*, barbue *f*.

cathedral [kə'θijdɹəl] *n.* cathédrale *f*. || *adj.*: *~ town*, ville *f* épiscopale.

cathode ['kæθowd] *n.* cathode *f*.

Catholic ['kæθ(ə)lɪk] *adj.* **1.** catholique: [Rel.] *the Roman Catholic Church*, l'Église catholique (romaine). **2.** [mind] large, universel. || *n.* [Rel.] catholique. || **Catholicism** [kə'θɔləsɪzəm] *n.* [Rel.] catholicisme *m*.

catnap ['kætˌnæp] *n.* (un) somme *m*.

catsup ['kɛtʃəp] [also *catchup, ketchup*] *n.* sauce *f* tomate (épicée).

cattle ['kætl̩] *n. invar.* [rig] bétail *m*; [pl.] bestiaux *mpl*: *horned ~*, bêtes *fpl* à cornes; *~ -drover*, bouvier *m*; *~ -lifter*, voleur *m* de bétail; *~ shed*, étable *f*; *~ truck*, fourgon *m* à bestiaux. || **cattleman** [-ˌmæn] *n.* **1.** conducteur *m* de bétail; bouvier *m*. **2.** éleveur *m*, propriétaire *m*/ de bétail.

catty ['kætɪ] *adj.* [Fam.] rosse.

Caucasian [kɔ'kejʒən] *n. & adj.* Caucasien, -ne.

caucus ['kɔkəs] *n.* [Polit.] © caucus *m*, réunion *f* secrète.

caught cf. CATCH.

cauliflower ['kɔlɪˌflawɚ] *n.* [vegetable] chou-fleur *m*.

causal ['kɔzl̩] *adj.* causal. || **causation** [ˌkɔz'ejʃən] *n.* cause *f*; rapport *m* de cause à effet.

cause [kɔz] *n.* **1.** cause *f*. **2.** raison *f*, motif *m*: *~ for celebration*, raison, motif/de réjouissance; *to have (good) ~ for believing*, avoir (tout) lieu de croire . . . **3.** [Jur.] cause *f*, procès *m*. || *v. tr.* causer, occasionner: *to ~ a fire*, déterminer un incendie; *to ~ s.o. to do sth.*, faire faire qqch. à qqun.

causeway [-ˌwej] *n.* chaussée *f*.

caustic ['kɔstɪk] *adj.* caustique.

caution ['kɔʃən] *n.* **1.** précaution *f*; prudence *f*: *to do sth. with great ~*, faire qqch. avec de grands ménagements. **2.** avis *m*; avertissement *m*: *Caution!*, Attention!; *to inflict a punishment as a ~ to others*, infliger une punition pour l'exemple. || *v. tr.* avertir (qqun); mettre (qqun) sur ses gardes: *to ~ s.o. against sth.*, mettre qqun en garde contre qqch. || **cautious** ['kɔʃəs] *adj.* circonspect; prudent: *to be ~ in doing sth.*, faire qqch. avec circonspection; *to play a ~ game*, jouer serré. || **cautiously** [-lɪ] *adv.* avec circonspection; prudemment; avec ménagement(s). || **cautiousness** [-nəs] *n.* circonspection *f*, prudence *f*.

cavalcade ['kævl̩ˌkejd] *n.* cavalcade *f*. || **cavalry** ['kævl̩ɹɪ] *n.* cavalerie *f*.

cave [kejv] *n.* [×] caverne *f*; repaire *m*, antre *m*: *~ man, ~ dweller*, homme des cavernes, [Fig.] brute *f*, butor *m*. || *v. intr.* *to ~ in*, s'effondrer, s'ébouler; [Fig.] céder, se rendre. || **cavern** ['kævɚn] *n.* caverne *f*.

caviar(e) ['kævɪˌɑɚ] *n.* [food] caviar *m*: *It is ~ to the general*, [Fig.] C'est trop fin pour la foule.
cavity ['kævɪtɪ] *n.* cavité *f*; [tooth] carie *f*.
cavort [kə'vɔɚt] *v. intr.* [Fam.] caracoler, gambader.
caw [kɔ] *n.* croassement *m* (d'un corbeau). || *v. intr.* [crow] croasser.
cayenne [kaj'ɛn] *n.* poivre *m* rouge.
cayman ['kejmən] *n.* [alligator] caïman *m*.
C.B.C. [ˌsij,bij'sij] *abr.* Radio-Canada.
c.c. [= cubic centimetres] cc. [=centimètre *m* cube].
C.C.F. [ˌsijˌsij'ɛf] [=Commonwealth Co-operative Federation]; © *n.* P.S.D. [=Parti social démocratique].
cease [sijs] *v. intr.* cesser (*de*, to), s'arrêter: *to ~ doing sth.*, cesser de faire qqch.; *to ~ work*, arrêter le travail/les travaux/. || *n.* cesse *f*: *without ~*, sans cesse/répit/. || **ceaseless** [-ləs] *adj.* incessant. || **ceaselessly** [-ləslɪ] *adv.* sans cesse.
cedar ['sijdɚ] *n.* thuya *m*, © cèdre *m*: *yellow ~*, cyprès *m* jaune.
cede [sijd] *v. tr.* céder.
ceiling ['sijlɪŋ] *n.* plafond *m*: *~/light, lamp*, plafonnier *m*; [Com.] plafond *m*, maximum *m*: *~ price*, prix *m* maximum.
celebrant ['sɛlə|bɹənt] *n.* [Eccl.] célébrant *m*, officiant *m*. || **celebrate** [-ˌbɹejt] *v. tr.* célébrer (la mémoire de qqun), fêter (qqch.): *Let's ~ !*, Ça s'arrose! || **celebrated** [-ˌbɹejtəd] *adj.* [person] célèbre. || **celebration** [ˌsɛlə'bɹejʃən] *n.* célébration *f* (d'une fête); fête *f*. || **celebrity** [sə'lɛbɹɪtɪ] *n.* célébrité *f*; renommée *f*.
celery ['sɛlərɪ] *n.* céleri *m*: *head of ~*, pied *m* de céleri.
celestial [sə'lɛstʃəl] *adj.* [body, &c.] céleste.
celibacy ['sɛlɪ|bəsɪ] *n.* célibat *m*. || **celibate** [-ˌbejt] *n.* & *adj.* célibataire.
cell [sɛl] *n.* **1.** cellule *f*; cachot *m*. **2.** alvéole *f*; compartiment *m*; cellule *f*; élément *m* (de pile): *dry ~*, pile *f* sèche. || **cellar** ['sɛlɚ] *n.* cave *f*; [food store] cellier *m*.
cello ['tʃɛlow] *n.* violoncelle *m*.
cement [sə'mɛnt] *n.* ciment *m*. || *v. tr.* cimenter (des pierres); [Fig.] cimenter, consolider (une amitié).
cemetery ['sɛməˌtɛɚɪ] *n.* cimetière *m*.
censer ['sɛnsɚ] *n.* [R.C.] encensoir *m*: *~-bearer*, [in church] thuriféraire *m*.
censor ['sɛnsɚ] *n.* censeur *m*: *The Board of Censors*, la censure. || *v. tr.* censurer. || **censored** [-d] *adj.* interdit (par la censure); expurgé. || **censorship** [-ˌʃɪp] *n.* censure *f*. || **censure** ['sɛnʃɚ] *n.* censure *f*. || *v. tr.* censurer; blâmer.
census ['sɛnsəs] *n.* recensement *m*.
cent [sɛnt] *n.* [coin] cent *m*, © †centin *m*, [Fam.] sou *m*: *a 25 ~ piece, a quarter*, © un trente-sous *m*; *I haven't got a red ~*, Je n'ai pas/le sou, un rouge liard/; *per ~* [= %], pour cent [= %]; pourcentage *m*.
centenarian [sɛntə'nɛɚɪən] *n.* [person] centenaire. || **centenary** [sɛn'tɛn|ɚɪ] *adj.* centenaire, séculaire. || *n.* **1.** (une) centaine (d'années). **2.** [hundredth anniversary] centenaire *m*. || **centennial** [-jəl] *adj.* centenaire. || *n.* centenaire *m*, centième anniversaire *m*.
center cf. CENTRE.
centesimal [sɛn'tɛsɪml̩] *adj.* le centième (de ...), la 100ᵉ partie (de ...); [thermomètre] centigrade *m*. || **centigrade** ['sɛntɪˌgɹejd] *adj.* centigrade: *~ thermometer*, thermomètre *m* centigrade. || **centimetre** [also **centimeter**] ['sɛntɪˌmijtɚ] *n.* centimètre *m*. || **centipede** [-ˌpijd] *n.* [insect] mille-pattes *m. invar.*, scolopendre *m*.
central ['sɛntɹəl] *adj.* central; [Fig.] bien situé, stratégique: *a ~ location* (*in town*), → emplacement/bien situé, idéal. || *n.* central *m* (téléphonique).
centralize ['sɛntɹəˌlajz] *v. tr.* centraliser.
centre [also **center**] ['sɛntɚ] *n.* **1.** centre *m* (d'un cercle); milieu *m* (d'une table); foyer *m* (d'érudition, d'infection): *in the ~*, au centre; *~ of attraction*, clou *m* (d'une fête, &c.): *shopping ~*, centre commercial, place *f* marchande, © [abus.] centre d'achat. **2.** [employé comme adj.] central, du centre: *the ~ arch*, l'arche/centrale, du centre. || *v. tr.* placer (qqch.) au centre, centrer; [Fig.] (se) concentrer: *to ~ /in, on, round/sth.*, se concentrer/dans, sur/qqch.
centrifugal [sɛn'tɹɪ|fəgl̩] *adj.* [force, &c.] centrifuge. || **centripetal** [-pətl̩] *adj.* [force, &c.] centripète.
century ['sɛntʃɚɪ] *n.* siècle *m*: *in the nineteenth ~*, au dix-neuvième siècle.
ceramic [sɚ'æmɪk] *adj.* céramique. || **ceramics** [-s] *n.* céramique *f*.
cereal ['sijɚɪəl] *n.* **1.** céréale *f*. **2.** [breakfast food] © céréale *f*.
cerebral ['sɛɚəbɹəl] *adj.* cérébral.
ceremonial [sɛɚə'mownɪ|əl] *n.* cérémonial *m*. || *adj.* de cérémonie. || **ceremonially** [-əlɪ] *adv.* en grande cérémonie. || **ceremonious** [-əs] *adj.* cérémonieux, solennel. || **ceremoniously** [-əslɪ] *adv.* cérémonieusement, solennellement. || **ceremony** ['sɛɚəˌmownɪ] *n.* cérémonie *f*: *to*

attend a ~, assister à une cérémonie; *with* ~, solennellement; *without* ~, sans/cérémonie, façon/; *to stand (up)on* ~, faire des façons.

certain ['sɚtn̩] *adj.* [sure, settled, not named] certain; [sure, reliable] sûr: *It's (a)* ~ *(thing)*, C'est une chose certaine; [indef.] *a* ~ */thing, Mr. X/*, une certaine chose, un certain Monsieur X; [indef.] ~ *people*, certaines gens [no partitive], certains *mpl*; ~ *of*, certain, sûr/de; *She is* ~ *to find out*, Elle le saura sûrement, Il est certain qu'elle le saura; *I am not* ~ *(that) he knows*, Je ne suis pas certain(e) qu'il (le) sache; *for* ~, sans (aucun) doute, certainement, sûrement; *I'll do it for* ~, Je le ferai sans faute; *to make* ~ *of (sth.)*, s'assurer de (qqch.). || **certainly** [-lı] *adv.* certainement, sûrement, assurément: *Certainly!*, Bien sûr!; *Certainly not!*, Bien sûr que non; [emphatic] *I* ~ *wish I knew*, Je voudrais bien savoir; *He* ~ *needs it*, Il en a bien besoin. || **certainty** [-tı] *n.* certitude *f*; assurance *f*.

certificate [sɚ'tıfıkət] *n.* certificat *m* (d'aptitude): *to make out a* ~, établir un certificat; [school] diplôme *m*, brevet *m*; [État civil] acte *m*: *birth* ~, acte de naissance; *death* ~, acte de décès. || **certify** ['sɚtıˌfaj] *v. tr.* certifier, déclarer (qqch. conforme à . . . , que qqch. est conforme à . . . , &c.); [Com.] garantir (la qualité d'un produit). || **certitude** ['sɚtıˌtjuwd] *n.* certitude *f*, assurance *f*.

cessation [sə'sejʃən] *n.* cessation *f*, arrêt *m*.

Ceylon [sı'lɑn] *n.* [Geog.] Ceylan: *in, to/* ~, à Ceylan.

cf. *abr.* [= compare] voir . . .

chafe [tʃejf] *v. tr.* frictionner; écorcher par le frottement. *v. intr.* [Lit. & Fig.] s'irriter.

chaff [tʃæf] *n.* **1.** balle *f* (du grain). **2.** raillerie *f*. || *v. tr.* plaisanter.

chagrin [ʃə'gɹın] *n.* vive contrariété *f*.

chain [tʃejn] *n.* [mountain] chaîne *f*; [mesure] chaînée *f*; [pl.] †fers *mpl*, entraves *fpl*: [Fig.] *in chains*, dans les fers, en prison; [Phys.] ~ *reaction*, réaction *f*/en chaîne, caténaire; ~ *store*, succursale *f* de grand magasin; ~ *stitch*, [knitting] point *m* de chaînette; ~ *work*, travail *m* à la chaîne. || *v. tr.* enchaîner, attacher /avec, par/une chaîne; tenir (qqun) en prison; réduire (qqun) en esclavage.

chair [tʃɛɚ] *n.* **1.** chaise *f*; siège *m*; chaire *f* (d'un professeur): *arm* ~, fauteuil *m*; [ship] *deck* ~, chaise longue, transat(lantique) *m*; *high* ~, chaise d'enfant; *rocking* ~, (chaise) berceuse *f*, © chaise berçante; *Please take a* ~, Veuillez/vous asseoir, prendre un siège. **2.** fauteuil, siège/présidentiel; [Fig.] le président, la présidence: *to take the* ~, présider (une réunion); *to leave the* ~, lever la séance. || *v. tr.* **1.** présider (une réunion), prendre la présidence (d'une assemblée). **2.** porter (qqun) en triomphe. || **chairman** [-mən] *n.* président *m*, présidente *f*: *Mr. Chairman*, Monsieur le président; *Madam Chairman*, Madame la présidente. || **chairmanship** [mənˌʃıp] *n.* présidence *f*: *under the* ~ *of*, présidé par.

chalet ['ʃælej] *n.* [mountain, ski] chalet *m*.

chalice ['tʃælıs] *n.* **1.** †coupe *f*. **2.** [Rel.] calice *m*.

chalk [tʃɔk] *n.* **1.** [blackboard] craie *f*: [Loc.] *by a long* ~, à beaucoup près, cf. SHOT. **2.** [limestone] calcaire *m*: ~ *pit*, carrière *f* de craie, crayère *f*, plâtrière *f*. || *v. tr.* écrire/marquer/(qqch.) à la craie; blanchir (sa figure, ses habits) à la craie; *to* ~ *out*, tracer (un plan, &c.) à la craie; *to* ~ *up (sth.)*, inscrire (qqch.)/sur un tableau, dans sa mémoire/; hausser, augmenter/(les prix). || **chalky** [-ı] *adj.* [substance] de craie, crayeux; [deposit] calcaire.

challenge ['tʃæləndʒ] *n.* **1.** défi *m*; provocation *f*. **2.** sommation *f* (par une sentinelle); qui-vive!. || *v. tr.* **1.** défier (qqun au combat); provoquer (qqun en duel); porter un défi à (un champion). **2.** interpeller. **3.** disputer; relever (une affirmation); mettre en/question, doute/(la parole de qqun). **4.** récuser (un juré).

chamber ['tʃejmbɚ] *n.* salle *f*, pièce *f*; [×] chambre *f* [cf. ROOM]; ~ *music*, musique de chambre; [Br.] *chambers*, bureaux *mpl*, locaux *mpl*: *Chamber of Commerce*, Chambre de commerce; [Parl.] *Lower Chamber*, Chambre des Communes; *Upper Chamber*, © le Sénat, [Br.] Chambre des Lords. || **chambermaid** [-ˌmejd], *n.* femme *f* de chambre.

chamois ['ʃæmı] *n.* chamois *m*: ~ *leather*, (peau *f* de) chamois.

champagne [ʃæm'pejn] *n.* vin *m* de Champagne; champagne *m*.

champion ['tʃæmpıən] *n.* champion *m*. || *v. tr.* soutenir, défendre/(une cause); prendre fait et cause pour (qqun). || **championship** [-ˌʃıp] *n.* championnat *m*.

chance [tʃæns] *n.* **1.** hasard *m*: *by (any)* ~, par hasard. **2.** occasion *f*: *The chances are that . . .*, Il y a des chances que + subjunc.; *to have a good* ~ *to*, avoir une belle occasion de; *to stand a* ~ *of*, avoir des chances de; *He hasn't*/*a, the least*/ ~ (*of...*), Il n'a pas la moindre chance (de . . .); *his last* ~ , sa dernière chance; *Now's your* ~ *!*, C'est le moment (d'y aller); *Give me a* ~ *!*, Un peu de patience, voyons! **3.** risque *m*: *to take chances*, courir des risques. || *attrib*. fortuit, accidentel: *a* ~ *meeting*, une rencontre /d'occasion, fortuite/. || *v. tr.* risquer: *I'll* ~ *it!*, → Arrive que pourra! || *v. intr. to* ~ *to do sth.*, → faire qqch. par hasard: *It chanced that* . . . , Il se trouva que . . .

chancellor [ˈtʃænsələ˞] *n.* **1.** [politics] chancelier *m.* **2.** [university] chancelier *m.*

chandelier [ˌʃændəˈlijə˞] *n.* [×] lustre *m.*

change [tʃejndʒ] *n.* **1.** changement *m*: ~ *for the*/*better, worse*, changement en/ mieux, mal; *to make a* ~ , apporter un changement; *for a* ~ , pour changer. **2.** linge *m* de rechange; [small change] (petite) monnaie *f*: *Do you have* ~ *for a dollar?*, Avez-vous la monnaie d'un dollar?; *to*/*get, make*/ ~ , faire de la monnaie. || *v. tr.* changer (de l'argent); [from one to another] changer de (vêtements, &c.); changer, transformer (en, *in*: *to* ~ *for sth. better*, changer contre qqch. de mieux; *to* ~ *for the better*, s'améliorer. || **changeable** [-əbl̩] *adj.* [weather] variable. || **changeless** [-ləs] *adj.* immuable, invariable. || **changing** [-ɪŋ] *n.* changement *m*; [Mil.] relève *f.* (de la garde). || *adj.* changeant.

channel [ˈtʃænl̩] *n.* **1.** canal *m*; [TV] canal; [Geog.] bras *m* de mer: *the English* ~ , la Manche; *the Channel Islands*, les îles Anglo-Normandes; [river] chenal *m*, lit *m*; [harbour] passe *f.* **2.** [Fig.] canal *m*. voie *f*: *through the channels of diplomacy*, par voie diplomatique. || *v. tr.* [-ll-] **1.** creuser des rigoles dans (un terrain). **2.** canneler; rainurer: *to* ~ *out a groove*, tailler une rainure; évider (une lame de sable).

chant [tʃænt] *n.* [church, funeral] chant *m* (religieux, funèbre). || *v. tr.* & *intr.* chanter (un chant liturgique, funèbre); psalmodier.

chaos [ˈkejɑs] *n.* chaos *m.*

chaotic [ˌkejˈɑtɪk] *adj.* chaotique; anarchique.

chap[1] [tʃæp] *n.* [hand] gerçure *f*, [skin] crevasse *f.* || *v. tr.* & *intr.* [-pp-] [hand] (se) gercer, [skin] (se) crevasser.

chap[2] *n.* individu *m*; [Fam.] type *m*; [affectionate] garçon *m*: [Br.] *old* ~ , mon vieux; *He is an odd* ~ , C'est un drôle de bonhomme.

chapel [ˈtʃæpl̩] *n.* chapelle *f*: *funeral* ~ , © salon *m* mortuaire.

chaperon [ˈʃæpə˞own] *n.* [lady] chaperon *m.* || *v. tr.* chaperonner (une jeune fille).

chaplain [ˈtʃæplən] *n.* [Rel.] aumônier *m*: *army* ~ , aumônier militaire.

chaplet [ˈtʃæplət] *n.* [Rel.] chapelet *m.* cf. BEADS.

chapter [ˈtʃæptə˞] *n.* **1.** chapitre *m*: *to give* ~ *and verse*, citer ses autorités; fournir des documents. **2.** [Rel.] chapitre (de chanoines); [association] régionale *f.*

char[1] [tʃɑə˞] [-rr-] *v. tr.* & *intr.* (se) carboniser.

char[2] *n.* [esp. Br.] petit travail *m*; ménages *mpl*: ~ *woman*, femme *f* de ménage. cf. CHORE.

character [ˈkæə˞əktə˞] *n.* **1.** caractère *m*, nature *f*; réputation *f*: *to have a*/*good, bad*/ ~ , avoir une/bonne, mauvaise/ réputation. **2** caractéristique *f*, marque *f* distinctive: *in his* ~ *of* (*president*, *&c.*), en (sa) qualité de (président, &c.). **3.** personnage *m* (d'une pièce); ~ *actor*, acteur *m* de genre. **4.** [Typ.] caractère *m*, lettre *f.* **5.** [Fam.] *a suspicious* ~ , un individu louche. || **characteristic** [ˌkæə˞əktə˞ˈɪstɪk] *adj.* caractéristique. || *n.* caractéristique *f*; trait *m*, caractère *m* distinctif. || **characterize** [ˈkæə˞əktə˞ˌajz] *v. tr.* caractériser.

charcoal [ˈtʃɑə˞ˌkowl] *n.* charbon *m* de bois, [Art] fusain *m.* || *adj.* [colour] anthracite.

charge [tʃɑə˞dʒ] *n.* **1.** charge *f*, soin(s) *m*(*pl*); [duty] fonction *f*: *in* (*the*) ~ *of*, aux soins de, à la charge de; [official] *the man in* ~ , le préposé (à . . .); *to take* ~ *of*, avoir soin de; *to be in* ~ *of*, être chargé de; avoir/le commandement, la responsabilité/de. **2.** prix *m*: *free of* ~ , *no* ~ , [gift] gratuit; [postage] franco, [invar.], franc de port; *cover* ~ , [restaurant] couvert *m.* **3.** consigne *f*, dépôt *m*: *No* ~ , [for a bottle] [Fr.] Pas de consigne, © Pas de dépôt. **4.** accusation *f* [law] chef *m* d'accusation: *on a* ~ *of*, sous l'inculpation de. **5.** [enemy] charge *f*, attaque *f.* || *v. tr.* **1.** [load] charger (*s.o. with sth.*, qqun de qqch.); [battery] charger. **2.** [crime] accuser (*s.o. with sth.*, qqun de qqch.); [fault] imputer (*s.o. with sth.*, qqch. à qqun). **3.** demander (un prix, une somme): *How much did he* ~ *you?*, Combien vous l'a-t-il fait payer?; *Charge this to my account*, Portez cela sur mon compte; *To whom should this be charged?*, A qui/faut-il, devrons-nous/envoyer la facture?; *charged* (*to . . .*), à débiter; à mettre sur le compte (de). **4.** [enemy, &c.] charger; foncer sur (qqun).

charitable [ˈʧæəɪt|əbl̩] *adj.* charitable; [association, &c.] de charité. || **charity** [-ɪ] *n.* **1.** charité *f*: *out of* ~ , *for* ~ *'s sake*, par charité. **2.** acte *m* de charité; action *f* charitable; aumônes *fpl*; bienfaisance *f*: *to live on* ~ , vivre d'aumônes. **3.** [charities] œuvre *f* de/bienfaisance, charité/.

charlatan [ˈʃɑələtən] *n.* charlatan *m.*

charm [ʧɑəm] *n.* **1.** charme *m*; sort *m.* **2.** porte-bonheur *m.* **3.** charme; agrément *m*: *not to be devoid of* ~ , ne pas manquer de charme. || *v. tr.* charmer; enchanter. || **charming** [-ɪŋ] *adj.* charmant, ravissant. || **charmingly** [-ɪŋlɪ]] *adv.* d'une manière /charmante, ravissante/.

chart [ʧɑət] *n.* **1.** carte *f* (marine): ~ */house, room/*, chambre des cartes; *wind* ~ , carte des vents. **2.** [statistics] graphique *m*; diagramme *m*; tableau *m* (de graissage). || *v. tr.* **1.** porter (un rocher, &c.) sur une carte, dresser la carte (d'une côte, &c.); faire l'hydrographie (d'une mer, &c.). **2.** établir le graphique (d'une série de relèvements).

charter [ˈʧɑətə] *n.* charte *f.* || *v. tr.* accorder une charte: [hire] louer; noliser.

chary [ˈtʃæəɪ] *adj.* **1.** prudent. **2.** peu prodigue (*of*, de).

chase [ʧejs] *n.* **1.** chasse *f*; poursuite *f*: *to give* ~ *to s.o.*, donner la chasse à qqun; *to/go, be/on a wild goose* ~ , courir après la lune. **2.** [Sport] chasse *f* à courre. || *v. tr.* chasser; pourchasser (le cerf); poursuivre: *to* ~ */away, out/(a dog)*, chasser (un chien). || *v. intr. to* ~ *after sth.*, partir à la poursuite de qqch.; [Fam.] *to* ~ *around looking for sth.*, cavaler partout pour trouver qqch.

chasm [ˈkæzm] *n.* crevasse *f* (dans la terre); abîme *m.*

chassis [ˈʧæsɪ] *n. invar.* châssis *m.*

chaste [ʧejst] *adj.* pur, innocent; [style] simple. || **chastise** [ʧæsˈtajz] *v. tr.* châtier (qqun pour qqch.). || **chastisement** [-mənt] *n.* châtiment *m*, punition *f.* || **chastity** [ˈʧæstɪtɪ] *n.* chasteté *f*; [style] simplicité *f.*

chat [ʧæt] *n.* causerie *f*; [Fam.] *to have a* ~, faire un brin de causette. || *v. intr.* [-tt-] causer, bavarder. || **chatter** [-ə] *n.* bavardage *m.* || *v. intr.* bavarder, jaser; [teeth] claquer des dents. || **chattering** [-əɪŋ] *n.* bavardage *m*; [birds, children] jasement *m*, babil *m*; claquement *m* (des dents).

chatty [-ɪ] *adj.* causeur, bavard.

chauffeur [ˈʃowfə] *n.* chauffeur *m*, conducteur *m* (d'auto). || *v. tr.* conduire (une auto).

cheap [ʧijp] *adj.* **1.** (à) bon marché; pas cher: *to buy sth.* ~ , acheter qqch. à bon marché; *cheaper*, meilleur marché, moins cher: *dirt* ~ , à vil prix, pour rien. **2.** de peu de valeur: ~ *goods*, camelote *f*; [Fig.] *to feel* ~ , se sentir honteux; ~ *music*, musiquette *f.* || **cheapen** [-n̩] *v. tr.* diminuer la valeur de (qqch.); [Fig.] déprécier, amoindrir. || **cheaply** [-lɪ] *adv.* (à) bon marché; à bas prix; [Fig.] à peu de frais: *He got off* ~ , Il en est quitte à bon compte. || **cheapness** [-nəs] *n.* **1.** modicité *f*, bas prix *m* (d'une marchandise). **2.** qualité *f* inférieure (d'une chose); bassesse *f* (d'une personne).

cheat [ʧijt] *n.* fourberie *f*, escroquerie *f*; tricherie *f*; [person] fourbe *m*, escroc *m*; tricheu|r *m*, -se *f.* || *v. tr.* escroquer, tromper (qqun); [at cards] tricher (aux cartes).

check[1] [ʧɛk] *n.* **1.** [chess] échec *m*: *to (give)* ~ *(to) the king*, faire échec au roi. **2.** échec *m*, revers *m*: *to/keep, hold/(s.o.) in* ~ , tenir (qqun) en échec; [door, &c.] arrêt *m*; frein *m.* **3.** contrôle *m*, vérification *f*: *to keep a* ~ *on (sth.)* contrôler (qqch.). **4.** billet *m*, ticket *m*, jeton *m*: ~ *-room*, vestiaire; *baggage* ~ , bulletin *m* de bagages. **5.** [US] [bank] chèque *m.* || *v. tr.* **1.** [chess, person] faire échec à (qqun, qqch.), mettre (qqun, qqch.) en échec; [tears] refouler; [passion] refréner; [enemy] contenir; [attack] arrêter. **2.** [child] réprimander. **3.** [finance] vérifier, épurer/(un compte); [proofs] reviser: *to* ~ *(off)*, pointer (des/mots, noms/sur une liste); *to* ~ *(up on) information*, contrôler des renseignements; *to* ~ *one's bags through*, enregistrer ses bagages.

check[2] cf. CHEQUE.

checkbook cf. CHEQUEBOOK.

checker cf. CHEQUER.

checkered cf. CHEQUERED.

checkmate [ˈtʃɛkˌmejt] *n.* échec et mat *m.* || *v. tr.* faire échec et mat.

check-off [-ˌɔf] *n.* [US] déduction *f* à la source (des cotisations syndicales). || **checkroom** [-ˌɹuwm] *n.* **1.** bureau *m* d'enregistrement des bagages. **2.** [clothes] vestiaire *m*; [baggage] consigne *f.* || **check-up** [-ˌʌp] *n.* examen *m* médical.

cheek [ʧijk] *n.* **1.** joue *f*; ~ *bone*, pommette *f*: *(He said it) with his tongue in his cheek*, → Il n'en pensait rien; → Il n'en pensait pas un mot. **2.** [Fig.] toupet *m*; effronterie *f*; impudence *f*. ‖ **cheeky** [-ɪ] *adj*. effronté.

cheer [ʧijɚ] *n*. **1.** bonne humeur *f*, gaieté *f*: *words of* ~, parole *f* d'encouragement. **2.** (bonne) chère *f*. **3.** *cheers pl*. acclamations *fpl*; bravos *mpl*; vivats *mpl*: *Three cheers for X!*, Vive X!; *loud cheers*, vifs applaudissements *mpl*; [college] ~ *-leader*, chef de claque. ‖ ~ (*up*), *v. tr*. **1.** encourager, relever le moral de/qqun: *Cheer up!*, Courage! **2.** acclamer, applaudir (qqun): *to* ~ *s.o. on* (*to*), encourager qqun (à). ‖ *v. intr*. pousser/des hourras, des vivats; applaudir. ‖ **cheerful** [-fḷ] *adj*. [person] gai; de bonne humeur; allègre; [place] d'aspect agréable; riant; [news] encourageant. ‖ **cheerfully** [-fḷɪ] *adv*. **1.** gaiement; allègrement. **2.** de bon cœur; volontiers. ‖ **cheerfulness** [-fḷnəs] *n*. gaieté *f*, allégresse *f*. ‖ **cheerless** [-ləs] *adj*. [person] abattu, morne; [room, &c.] triste, déprimant.

cheese [ʧijz] *n*. fromage *m*: *cottage* ~, fromage blanc, © fromage en grains.

chef [ʃɛf] *n*. [cuisinier] chef *m*, maître-queux *m*.

chemical [ˈkɛmɪkḷ] *adj*. chimique: ~ *warfare*, guerre *f* des gaz; ~ *balance*, balance *f* de laboratoire. ‖ *n*. produit *m* chimique; drogue *f*. ‖ **chemically** [-ɪ] *adv*. chimiquement. ‖ **chemist** [ˈkɛmɪst] *n*. **1.** chimiste *m*: *analytical* ~, chimiste (analyste). **2.** [Br.] pharmacien *m*: ~ *'s shop*, pharmacie *f*. ‖ **chemistry** [-ɹɪ] *n*. chimie *f*.

cheque [ʧɛk] *n*. chèque *m*: *to write a* ~, faire un chèque; *traveller's* ~, chèque de voyage. ‖ **chequebook** [-ˌbʊk] *n*. carnet *m* de chèques. ‖ **chequer** [-ɚ] *n*. [pattern] quadrillage *m*: ~ *board*, damier *m*; **chequers** *pl* [US] © jeu *m* de dames: *Do you play* ~ *?*, Jouez-vous aux dames? ‖ *v. tr*. [fabric] quadriller (qqch.). ‖ **chequered** [-ɚd] *adj* [fabric, shirt, &c.] quadrillé, à carreaux, © carreauté; [coloured] bigarré; [Fig.] varié.

cherish [ˈʧɛɚɪʃ] *v. tr*. chérir; soigner (un enfant): [Fig.] *to* ~ *a hope*, nourrir un espoir.

cherry [ˈʧɛɚɪ] *n*. cerise *f*: ~ *stone*, noyau *m* de cerise; ~ *-tree*, *-wood*, cerisier *m*.

cherub [ˈʧɛɚəb] *n*. chérubin *m*.

chess [ʧɛs] *n*. échecs *mpl*: *to play* ~, jouer aux échecs; ~ *board*, échiquier *m*. ‖ **chessman** [-ˌmæn] *n*. pièce *f*.

chest [ʧɛst] *n*. **1.** poitrine *f*: *to get it off one's* ~, dire ce qu'on a sur le cœur. **2.** coffre *m*; caisse *f*: ~ (*of drawers*), commode *f*.

chesterfield [ˈʧɛstɚˌfijld] *n*.© sofa *m*, canapé *m*.

chestnut [ˈʧɛstˌnʌt] *n*. [edible] marron *m*, châtaigne *f*.; [tree] châtaignier *m* d'Amérique: *horse* ~, marron *m* (d'Inde). ‖ *adj*. [hair] châtain; [horse] alezan.

chew [ʧuw] *n*. [tobacco] chique *f*. ‖ *v. tr*. [food] mâcher: *to* ~ (*sth.*) *up*, [food] mastiquer, bien mâcher (un aliment); [coat, &c.] mettre en pièces, déchiqueter; [tobacco] chiquer; *to* ~ *over* (*an idea*), [Fig.] ruminer (une idée). ‖ **chewing** [-ɪŋ] *n*. mastication *f*: ~ *gum*, gomme *f* à mâcher, © gomme *f*.

chick [ʧɪk] *n*. poussin *m*: ~ *-pea*, pois *m* chiche. ‖ **chickadee** [-ədɪ] *n*. © cf. TITMOUSE. ‖ **chicken** [ˈʧɪkən] *n*. poulet *m*; [Med.] ~ *pox*, varicelle *f*; [Fig.] ~ *-hearted*, poltron *m*, -ne *f*, poule *f* mouillée.

chicory [ˈʧɪkɚɪ] *n*. [Bot.] chicorée *f*, [broad-leaved] endive *f*.

chid cf. CHIDE.

chide [ʧajd], **chid** [ʧɪd], **chidden** [-ṇ], **chided** [ˈʧajd|əd] *v. tr*. gronder, réprimander, blâmer (qqun); reprocher (à qqun d'avoir fait qqch., *s.o. for sth.*). ‖ **chiding** [-ɪŋ] *n*. réprimande *f*, [scold] gronderie *f*.

chief [ʧijf] *pl*. **-s** *n*. chef *m* (d'un bureau, &c.): *the* ~, le patron, © le bourgeois; © *fire-* ~, chef des pompiers; (*commander*)*-in-* ~, (commandant) en chef. ‖ *adj*. [part, role, &c.] principal, essentiel, premier. ‖ **chiefly** [-lɪ] *adv*. principalement, essentiellement, avant tout, surtout. ‖ **chieftain** [-tən] *n*. chef *m* (de tribu, de scouts).

chiffon [ʃɪˈfɑn] *n*. [thin fabric, lace, &c.] chiffon *m*; gaze *f*; [Culin.] (gâteau *m*) mousseline.

chilblain [ˈʧɪlˌblejn] *n*. engelure *f*.

child [ʧajld] *n*. **children** *pl*. [ˈʧɪldɹən] enfant *m/f*.; [coll.] (le) petit, (la) petite: †*from a* ~, dès l'enfance; (*woman*) *with* ~, [pregnant] (femme) enceinte; *school-age* ~, enfant d'âge scolaire; †*our children's children*, †nos arrière-neveux. ‖ **childbearing** [ˈʧajld|ˌbɛɚɪŋ] *n*. grossesse *f*, gestation *f*. ‖ **childbirth** [-ˌbɚθ] *n*. accouchement *m*. ‖ **childhood** [-ˌhʊd] *n*. enfance *f*: *to be in one's second* ~, être (re)tombé en enfance. ‖ **childish** [-ɪʃ] *adj*. enfantin, d'enfant; [Fig.] puéril. ‖ **childishly** [-ɪʃlɪ] *adv*./en, comme un/enfant. ‖ **childless** [-ləs] *adj*. [couple] sans enfant. ‖ **childlike** [-ˌlajk] *adj*. [Fig.] enfantin, naïf. ‖ **child murder** [-ˌmɚdɚ] *n*. infanticide *m*.

children cf. CHILD.

Chile [ˈʧɪlɪ] *n.* le Chili. || **Chilian** *adj.* & *n.* chilien, -ne.

chil(l)i [ˈʧɪlɪ] *n.* [red pepper] piment *m.*

chill [ʧɪl] *n.* [weather, feeling] froid *m*: *to take, catch/a ~*, prendre froid; *to take the ~ off sth.*, faire tiédir qqch.; [drink] rafraîchissement *m*; [fear, &c.] frisson *m.* || *adj.* froid, refroidi. || *v. tr.* refroidir, glacer (une boisson); [champagne] frapper; faire frissonner (qqun). **chilled** [-d] *adj.* [person] transi; [meat] frigorifié. || **chilling** [-ɪŋ] *n.* refroidissement *m.* || **chilly** [-ɪ] *adj.* [room] froid; [person] frileux; [Fig.] [person] distant; [reception] glacial.

chime [ʧajm] *n.* [bells] carillon *m*; [sounds] harmonie *f.* || *v. intr.* [bells] carillonner; [sounds, &c.] être en harmonie (avec, *with*); [Fig.] *~ in (with s.o.)*, s'accorder (avec qqun); ajouter son mot. || *v. tr.* mettre (les cloches) en mouvement; sonner (les cloches).

chimney [ˈʧɪmnɪ] *n.* cheminée *f*: *lamp ~*, verre *m* de lampe. || **chimney hook** [-ˌhʊk] *n.* crémaillère *f.* || **chimney-sweep** [-ˌswijp] *n.* ramoneur *m.*

chimpanzee [ˌtʃɪmpn̩ˈzij] *n.* chimpanzé *m.*

chin [ʧɪn] *n.* menton *m*: *~ cough*, coqueluche *f*; *~ rest*, [violin] mentonnière *f*; *~ strap*, jugulaire *f.*

china[1] [ˈʧajnə] *n.* porcelaine *f*; vaisselle *f* de porcelaine; faïence *f* fine: *~ closet*, vaisselier *m*; *Dresden ~*, porcelaine de Saxe.

China[2] *n.* (la) Chine: *in, to/ ~*, en Chine; *from ~ to Peru*, d'un bout du monde à l'autre. || **Chinese** [ˌʧajˈnijz] *adj.* & *n.* [people] chinois; [language] le chinois, la langue chinoise; *~ laundry*, © le chinois.

chink [ʧɪŋk] *n.* [crack] fente *f*; [log-house] crevasse *f.*

Chinook [ʃɪˈnʊk] *n.* [Ind.] chinook *m.* || © *n.* [warm wind] le chinook.

chip [ʧɪp] *n.* [wood] copeau *m*; éclat *m*, fragment *m* (de verre, &c.): *(potato) chips*, (pommes *fpl* de terre, © patates *fpl*) frites *fpl.* || **[-pp-]** *v. tr.* [china, glass, stone, &c.] ébrécher: *to ~ a hole in the ice*, tailler un trou dans la glace.

chipmunk [-ˌmʌŋk] *n.* tamias *m* rayé; [Fam.] suisse *m.*

chippie [-ɪ] [= chipping sparrow] *n.* pinson *m* familier, © moineau *m.*

chiropodist [kəˈɑpədɪst] *n.* pédicure *m.*

chiropractic [ˌkajəowˈpɹæk|tɪk] *n.* chiropra(c)tique *f.* || **chiropractor** [ˈkajəowˌpɹæktə] *n.* chiro(praticien) *m.*

chirp [ʧəp] *n.* gazouillement *m*, gazouillis *m* (d'un oiseau). || *v. intr.* [birds] gazouiller. || **chirping** [-ɪŋ] *n.* gazouillement *m*, ramage *m* (d'un oiseau).

chisel [ˈʧɪzl̩] *n.* ciseau *m* (à froid). || *v. tr.* ciseler (le bois, la pierre, le métal): [Sl.] *to ~ s.o. out of ten dollars*, escroquer dix dollars à qqun. || **chiseller** [-ə] *n.* [Sl.] escroc *m.*

chivalrous [ˈʃɪvl̩ɹ|əs] *adj.* [gentlemanly] chevaleresque; [person, manners] courtois. || **chivalry** [-ɪ] *n.* chevalerie *f*, esprit *m* chevaleresque, courtoisie *f.*

chive(s) [ʧajvz] *n.(pl.)* ciboulette *f.*

chlorate [ˈklɔə|ejt] *n.* chlorate *m.* || **chloric** [-ɪk] *adj.* chlorique. || **chloride** [-ajd] *n.* chlorure *m.* || **chlorine** [-ɪn] *n.* chlore *m.* || **chloroform** [-əˌfɔəm] *n.* chloroforme *m.* || **chlorophyl(l)** [-əˌfɪl] *n.* chlorophylle *f.*

chock [ʧɑk] *n.* [Naut.] poulie *f.* || **chockfull** [-ˈful] *adj.* plein (comme un œuf), comble.

chocolate [ˈʧɑkələt] *n.* chocolat *m*: *~ bar*, tablette *f* de chocolat; *~ -maker*, chocolatier *m*; *~ pot*, chocolatière *f.* || *adj.* [colour] chocolat *invar.*

choice [ʧojs] *n.* choix *m*; [person's] préférence *f*; variété *f*, assortiment *m* (d'articles, &c.): *by ~*, par goût, volontairement; *for ~*, de préférence. || *adj.* [piece, item] de choix, recherché; [food] délicat; [wine, &c.] fin.

choir [kwajə] *n.* [church, singers] chœur *m*: *~ boy*, [church] enfant *m* de chœur; *~ master*, maître *m* de chapelle.

choke [ʧowk] *n.* [Auto.] starter *m.* || *v. tr.* étouffer, étrangler, suffoquer (qqun, qqch.); obstruer, boucher (qqch.). || *v. intr.* (s')étouffer, (s')étrangler, suffoquer (de, *with*); [clog] s'obstruer, se boucher.

chokecherry [ˈʧowkˌʧɛəɪ] © *n.* cerise *f* à grappes.

cholera [ˈkɑlərə] *n.* [Med.] choléra *m.*

choose [ʧuwz] **chose** [ʧowz] **chosen** [-n̩] *v. tr.* choisir (qqun, qqch.); adopter (qqch.); préférer (qqun, qqch.); décider (de, *to*): *He was chosen president*, On l'a choisi comme président; *I cannot ~ but study*, Je ne peux faire autrement qu'étudier; *I'll go when I ~*, J'irai quand il me plaira. || **choosing** [-ɪŋ] *n.* choix *m*: *the difficulty of ~*, l'embarras *m* du choix.

choosy [ˈʧuwzɪ] [Fam.] *adj.* difficile.

chop [ʧɑp] *n.* **1.** [cleaver, axe, large knife] coup *m* (violent). **2.** [pork, mutton] côtelette *f.* **3.** [waves] clapotis *m*: *to lick one's chops*, se (pour) lécher les babines. || *v. tr.* **[-pp-]** [weed, &c.] couper, fendre [to pieces] hacher. || *v. intr.* [sea] clapoter. || **chop down** [-ˈdawn] *v. tr.* [tree] abattre.

|| **chop off** [-'ɔf] *v. tr.* trancher, couper (qqch.). || **chop up** [-'ʌp] *v. tr.* tailler, hacher (en morceaux). || **chopper** [-ɚ] *n.* [food-, vegetable-] hachoir *m*; fendoir *m*; [meat] couperet *m*. || **choppy** [-ɪ] *adj.* [sea] clapoteux, agité. || **chopsticks** [-ˌstɪks] *n.pl.* [eating] baguettes *fpl.*

choral ['kɔɚəl] *adj.* [singing] choral *m*. || **choral**(e) [kə'ɹæl] *n.* [Mus.] choral *m*. || **choralist** ['kɔɚəlɪst] *n.* [choir] chanteur *m*, choriste *m*.

chord [kɔɚd] *n.* [string] †corde *f*; [Mus.] accord *m*.

chore [ʧɔɚ] *n.* corvée *f*, (dure) besogne *f*.

chorus [kɔɚəs] *pl.* **-es**, *n.* chœur *m* (de chant). || *v. intr.* chanter en chœur. || *v. tr.* répéter, chanter (un refrain) en chœur.

chose cf. CHOOSE. || **chosen** [ʧowzn̩] *adj.* choisi: *the* ~, les élus *mpl.*

chow [ʧaw] *n.* [Sl.] la soupe, la boustifaille. || **chowder** [-dɚ] *n.* [Culin.] soupe *f* au poisson, © le chowder.

chrism ['kɹɪzm] *n.* [Rel.] (le saint) chrême *m*. || **Christ** [kɹajst] *n.* le Christ, Jésus-Christ *m*. || **christen** ['kɹɪsn̩] *v. tr.* baptiser (qqun, un navire): *to* ~ *a child after s.o.*, donner à un enfant le nom de qqun. || **Christendom** [-dəm] *n.* (la) chrétienté *f*. || **christening** [-ɪŋ] *n.* baptême *m*. || **Christian** ['kɹɪsʧən] *adj.* chrétien: *the* ~ *era*, l'ère *f* chrétienne: ~ *name*, prénom *m*. || *n.* chrétien *m*, chrétienne *f*: *to behave like a decent* ~, [Fig.] se conduire en homme civilisé. || **Christianity** [ˌkɹɪstʃɪ'ænɪtɪ] *n.* christianisme *m*. || **Christmas (Xmas)** ['kɹɪsməs] *n.* Noël *m*; la (fête de) Noël *f*: ~ *carol*, chant *m* de Noël, cantique *m* de Noël; ~ *eve*, la veille de Noël, la nuit de Noël, la veillée de Noël; ~ *day*, le jour de Noël, Noël; *Merry* ~ *!*, Joyeux Noël!

chrome [kɹowm] *adj.* chromé. || **chromium** [-ɪəm] *n.* chrome *m*.

chronic ['kɹɑnɪk] *adj.* [disease, &c.] chronique.

chronicle [-l̩] *n.* [record] chronique *f*. || *v. tr.* raconter, relater (des faits); écrire la chronique de (qqch.). || **chronicler** [-l̩ɚ] *n.* chroniqueur *m*.

chronological [kɹɑnə'lɑʤɪkl̩] *adj.* chronologique. || **chronology** [kɹə'nɑləʤɪ] *n.* chronologie *f*. || **chronometer** [kɹə'nɑmətɚ] *n.* [watch] chronomètre *m*.

chrysal|id, -is ['kɹɪsəlɪd, -ɪs] *n.* [butterfly, &c.] chrysalide *f*.

chrysanthemum [kɹɪz'ænθəməm] *n.* chrysanthème *m*.

chubby ['ʧʌbɪ] *adj.* [Pers.] joufflu, [hand] potelé, [body] dodu.

chuck [ʧʌk] *v. tr.* [Fam.] jeter, [Fam.] balancer, © envoyer.

chuckle ['ʧʌkl̩] *n.* ricanement *m*, rire /étouffé, bas/. || *v. intr.* rire/sous cape, dans sa barbe/.

chuck wagon ['ʧʌkˌwægən] *n.* roulante *f*. cf. STAMPEDE.

chum [ʧʌm] *n.* [Fam.] copain *m*, camarade *m*, intime *m*. || **chummy** [-ɪ] *adj.* [Pers.] intime, amical; [Fam.] copain.

chump [ʧʌmp] *n.* [Fig.] imbécile *m*, lourdaud *m*, idiot *m*.

chunk [ʧʌŋk] *n.* gros morceau, tronçon *m* (de bois); quignon *m* (de pain). || **chunky** [-ɪ] *adj.* Pers.] trapu.

church [ʧɚʧ] *n.* [R.C.] église *f*; [Protestant] temple *m*; [organization] l'Église *f*: *the Church of England*, l'Église anglicane; *to go to* ~, aller/à l'église, au temple. || **church-goer** [-ˌgowɚ] *n.* pratiquant, -e. || **churchman** [-mən] *n.* ecclésiastique *m*. || **church service** [-ˌsɚvɪs] *n.* office *m*/ service *m*/ divin. || **churchyard** [-ˌjɑɚd] *n.* cimetière *m*.

churn [ʧɚn] *v. tr.* battre (le beurre); [Fig.] faire bouillonner (l'eau, &c.).

chute [ʃuwt] *n.* chute *f* à linge; chute *f*, rapides *mpl*; [Fam.] parachute *m*.

ciborium [sɪ'bɔɚɪəm] *pl.* **ciboria** *n.* [Rel.] ciboire *m*.

cicada [sɪ'kɑdə] *n.* cigalle *f*.

cider ['sajdɚ] *n.* cidre *m*.

cigar [sɪ'gɑɚ] *n.* cigare *m*: ~ *case*, étui *m* à cigares; *to be a* ~ *-smoker*, → fumer le cigare; ~ *-holder*, fume-, porte-/ cigare *m*; *Have a* ~ *!*, Prenez donc un cigare!, Un cigare?; © ~ *store*, [Fr.] bureau *m* de tabac; © tabagie *f*.

cigarette [sɪgɚ'ɛt] *n.* cigarette *f*: ~ *case*, étui *m* à cigarettes; ~ *-holder*, fume-, porte-/cigarette *m*; *cork-tipped* ~, cigarette (à) bout liège; *packet of* ~ *paper*, cahier *m* de papier à cigarettes.

cinch [sɪnʃ] *n.* **1.** [girth] sangle *f*. **2.** [Fam.] *It's a* ~ *!*, [easy] C'est enfantin! || *v. tr.* [fasten] sangler (un colis, &c.).

cinder ['sɪndɚ] *n.* braise *f*; [*pl.*] escarbilles *fpl.* || **Cinderella** [ˌsɪndɚ'ɛlə] *n.* Cendrillon *f*.

cinema ['sɪnəmə] *n.* cinéma *m*.

cinnamon ['sɪnəmən] *n.* cannelle *f*.

cipher ['sajfɚ] *n.* zéro *m*; chiffre *m*; code *m* secret, chiffre *m*: *in* ~, en chiffre, chiffré. || *v. tr.* chiffrer (un message).

circle ['sɚkl̩] *n.* cercle *m*; [Fig.; usual. pl.] milieu *m*, monde *m* (littéraire, &c.); [Pej.] coterie *f*: *vicious* ~, cercle vicieux; *to remain in one's family* ~, rester, demeurer/au sein de sa famille. || *v. tr.*

entourer, encercler, faire le tour de (qqch.). || *v. intr. to* ~ */around, about/* (*sth.*), tournoyer autour de (qqch.); *to* ~ *round,* [thing] circuler.

circuit ['sɚkət] *n.* circuit *m* (électrique, &c.); circuit *m,* parcours *m*: *short* ~, court-circuit.

circuitous ['sɚkətəs] *adj.* détourné, indirect.

circular ['sɚkjələr] *adj.* circulaire. || *n.* [advertisement] circulaire *f.* || **circularize** [-ajz] *v. tr.* [customers, &c.] envoyer des circulaires à. || **circularly** [-lɪ] *adv.* en/cercle, rond/. || **circulate** ['sɚkjəˌlejt] *v. tr.* mettre (qqch.) en circulation; [book] faire circuler; [news] faire courir, répandre: *circulating library,* bibliothèque circulante. || **circulation** [ˌsɚkjə'lejʃən] *n.* **1.** [blood, &c.] circulation *f.* **2.** tirage *m* (d'un journal).

circumference [sɚ'kʌmfɚəns] *n.* circonférence *f.* || **circumflex** ['sɚkəmˌflɛks] *n. & adj.* [accent] circonflexe (*m*). || **circumlocution** [ˌsɚkəmlə'kjuwʃən] *n.* circonlocution *f.* || **circumscribe** ['sɚkəm|-ˌskɹajb] *v. tr.* circonscrire. || **circumspect** [-ˌspɛkt] *adj.* circonspect, méfiant. || **circumspection** [ˌsɚkəm'spɛkʃən] *n.* circonspection *f,* méfiance *f,* prudence *f.*

circumstance ['sɚkəmˌstæns] *n.* circonstance *f,* occasion *f*; [story, &c.] fait *m,* détail *m*; événement *m*: *circumstances, pl.* moyens *mpl* (de/fortune, subsistance/); *in no circumstances,* sous aucun prétexte, en aucun cas; *in/under/the circumstances,* dans ces conditions, si tel est le cas.

circumstantial [ˌsɚkm̩'stænʃəl] *adj.* indirect: ~ *evidence,* preuves par déduction.

circumvent ['sɚkmˌvɛnt] *v. tr.* circonvenir.

circus ['sɚkəs] *n.* cirque *m* (de rochers, &c.); [Br.] [traffic] rond-point *m.*

cistern ['sɪstɚn] *n.* réservoir *m.*

citadel ['sɪtədəl] *n.* citadelle *f.*

citation [saj'tejʃən] *n.* [Mil. Law] citation *f*; [award] présentation *f* (d'un candidat), mention *f.* || **cite** [sajt] *v. tr.* citer, mentionner [cf. QUOTE].

citizen ['sɪtɪzən] *n.* **1.** citoyen, -ne, habitant *m* (d'un pays, d'une ville). **2.** [townsman] citadin, -e. || **citizenry** [-ɹɪ] *n.* [coll.] les citoyens *mpl.* || **citizenship** [-ˌʃɪp] *n.* citoyenneté *f,* qualité *f* de citoyen, droit *m* de cité: © *Department of Citizenship and Immigration,* Ministère de la citoyenneté et de l'immigration.

citrus ['sɪtɹəs] *n.* agrumes *mpl.*

city [sɪtɪ] *n.* ville *f*; cité *f*: *Quebec City,* la ville de Québec; *the City of Montreal,* la /ville, © [abus.] cité/de Montréal; *City Hall,* Hôtel *m* de Ville, mairie *f*; [Br.] The City, la Cité de Londres. || *attrib.* municipal: ~ *council,* conseil *m* municipal.

civic ['sɪvɪk] *adj.* civique: *civics,* instruction *f* civique. || **civil** ['sɪvl̩] *adj.* **1.** [marriage, &c.] civil; [rights, &c.] civique: ~ *engineering,* génie *m* civil; ~ *government,* administration *f* centrale; [government] *Civil Service,* (la) fonction *f* publique, © (le) service *m* civil; [U.S. Hist.] *the Civil war,* la guerre de Sécession. **2.** [Pers.] courtois, poli. || **civilian** [sɪ'vɪljən] *adj.* [life, clothes, &c.] civil. || *n.* civil *m,* [Fam.] pékin *m.* || **civility** [sɪ'vɪlɪtɪ] *n.* civilité *f,* courtoisie *f,* politesse *f.* || **civilization** [sɪvɪlaj'zejʃən] *n.* civilisation *f.* || **civilize** ['sɪvɪlajz] *v. tr.* civiliser (un pays): *to become civilized,* se civiliser.

clad cf. CLOTHE.

claim [klejm] *n.* **1.** réclamation *f,* revendication *f*; titre *m,* droit *m* (à qqch., *to sth.*): *to/make, put in/a* ~ (*for sth.*), faire une réclamation (pour qqch.). **2.** [mining] concession *f.* || *v. tr.* réclamer, revendiquer (qqch.), [one's rights, &c.] faire valoir (ses droits); s'attribuer, prétendre à/(qqch.). || **claimant** [-ənt] *n.* réclamant, -e; [Law] *rightful* ~, ayant droit *m.*

clam [klæm] *n.* clam *m,* [Fr.] palourde *f.*

clamber ['klæmbɚ] *v. intr.*: *to* ~ *up,* grimper, escalader; *to* ~ *down,* dégringoler.

clammy ['klæmɪ] *adj.* [cold] humide, [hands, &c.] moite, [sticky] visqueux.

clamorous ['klæmɚ|əs] *adj.* bruyant. || **clamour** *n.* clameur *f,* grand cri *m.* || *v. intr.* vociférer: *to* ~ *for,* réclamer à grands cris.

clamp [klæmp] *n.* crampon *m*; agrafe *f.* || *v. tr.* fixer (par des crampons, agrafes), assujétir.

clan [klæn] *n.* clan *m*; [Fig.] coterie *f,* chapelle *f.*

clandestine ['klændəˌstajn] *adj.* clandestin.

clang [klæŋ] also **clank** [klæŋk] *n.* [☞ dénote un bruit fort, métallique] bruit *m* (métallique), choc *m*; cliquetis *m.* || *v. intr.* [loud] résonner, retentir.

clannish ['klænɪʃ] *adj.* fermé.

clap [klæp] *n.* battement *m,* claquement *m* (de mains, d'ailes, &c.), [hand] claque *f*; coup *m* (de tonnerre); applaudissements *mpl.* || *v. tr.* **[-pp-]** battre, claquer (des mains, des ailes); applaudir (qqun); [lid, cover, &c.] (re)fermer bruyamment (qqch.). || *v. intr.* [lid, cover, &c.] battre, claquer, se (re)fermer bruyamment; [people] applaudir.

claret ['klæɚət] *n.* [wine] bordeaux *m*: ~ *-colour, n.* grenat *m.*

clarify [ˈklæɚɪˌfaj] *v. tr.* clarifier (un liquide, une situation), éclaircir (un liquide, &c.); [Fig.] élucider (une question).

clarinet [ˌklæɚɪˈnɛt] *n.* clarinette *f.* || **clarion** [ˈklæɚɪən] *n.* clairon *m.*

clarity [ˈklæɚɪtɪ] *n.* clarté *f.* pureté *f.*

clash [klæʃ] *n.* **1.** choc *m*, bruit *m* (métallique fort). **2.** conflit *m*, opposition *f.* || *v. intr.* se heurter, s'entrechoquer; [Fig.] venir en conflit (avec, *with*), s'opposer à, se heurter à. || *v. tr.* heurter (violemment), choquer (deux objets métalliques l'un contre l'autre).

clasp [klæsp] *n.* fermoir *m*, agrafe *f*; poignée *f* de mains, étreinte *f.* || *v. tr.* agrafer; serrer la main; étreindre, prendre qqun dans ses bras.

class [klæs] *n.* **1.** [social] classe *f*: *the working* ~, la classe ouvrière; [train] *in first* ~, en première classe. **2.** [Sch.] classe *f*; cours *m*: *in* ~, en classe; *after* ~, après la classe; *to/go to, attend/a* ~, aller à, suivre/un cours; *evening classes*, cours *mpl* du soir; *the* ~ *of (19)61*, [Sch.] la promotion de 1961, [Mil.] la classe de 1961. **3.** [sort] catégorie *f*, genre *m*: *in a* ~ *by itself*, unique; [Sch.] *a degree with First Class Honours*, diplôme *m* avec mention très bien. **4.** [style, Fam.] *He has no* ~, Il n'a pas de classe. || *v. tr.* classer.

classic [-ɪk] *adj. & n.* classique: *the classics*, les classiques. || **classical** [-ɪkl] *adj.* classique. || **classicism** [-ɪˌsɪzm] *n.* classicisme *m.* || **classicist** [-ɪˌsɪst] *n.* classique *m.* || **classification** [ˌklæsɪfɪˈkejʃən] *n.* classification *f*, groupement *m.* || **classify** [ˈklæsɪˌfaj] *v. tr.* **1.** classer, [group according to system] classifier. **2.** *classified*, secret, confidentiel; [Com.] *classified ads*, petites annonces.

classmate [ˈklæsˌmejt] *n.* [Sch.] camarade *m/f*, condisciple *m.* || **classroom** [-ˌɹuwm] *n.* la classe, salle *f* de classe.

clatter [ˈklætɚ] *n.* bruit *m* (de vaisselle, ferraille, &c.), vacarme *m*, fracas *m* (des rails, &c.). || *v. intr.* [dishes, &c.] faire/un fracas, du bruit/; [voices, &c.] mener/le, un/vacarme.

clause [klɔz] *n.* article *m* (d'un texte); clause *f* (d'un contrat); [Gram.] proposition *f*, membre *f* de phrase.

clavichord [ˈklævɪˌkɔɚd] *n.* [Mus.] clavecin *m.*

clavicle [ˈklævɪ|kl] *n.* [collar-bone] clavicule *f.* ||

claw [klɔ] *n.* [animal] griffe *f*; [crab] pince *f.* || *v. tr.* griffer, déchirer.

clay [klej] *n.* (terre-) glaise *f*, argile *f*: ~ *pit*, glaisière *f*, argilière *f.* || **clayish** [-ɪʃ] *adj.* [soil] argileux.

clean [klijn] *adj.* propre [☞ follows noun], net; [Fig.] pur: *spotlessly* ~, → d'une propreté immaculée. || *adv.* totalement, tout à fait, absolument, complètement; net: ~ *-shaven*, [face, Pers.] glabre. || *v. tr.* nettoyer, [boots, shoes] cirer, [fish] vider; purifier (l'atmosphère, &c.). || **clean-cut** [-ˌkʌt] *adj.* [young man] [Fig.] net, élégant, bien mis. || **cleaner** [-ɚ] *n.* [Pers.] laveur *m* (de carreaux, &c.), nettoyeu|r, -se; [product] détacheur *m*; *pl.* [shop] le teinturier, la teinturerie: *vacuum* ~, [dust] aspirateur *m.* || **clean-handed** [-ˌhændəd] *adj.* [Pers.] aux mains propres; [Fig.] honnête, probe. || **cleaning** [-ɪŋ] *n.* [room, house] nettoyage *m*; [suit] dégraissage *m.* || **cleaning woman** [-ˌwʊmən] *n.* femme *f* de/journée, ménage/. || **cleanliness** [ˈklɛnlɪnəs] *n.* propreté *f* (d'un endroit, &c.); [Fig.] pureté *f* (de cœur, &c.). || **cleanly** [ˈklijn|lɪ] *adv.* proprement, nettement, bien. || *adj.* propre. || **cleanness** [-nəs] *n.* physical, [moral] propreté *f*; [outline, &c.] netteté *f*; [Fig.] honnêteté *f.* || **clean out** [-ˈawt] *v. tr.* décrasser, nettoyer (qqch.) à fond. || **clean up** [-ˈʌp] *v. tr.* nettoyer, [house, room] © faire le ménage de (qqch.); débarbouiller (qqun). || *n.* nettoyage *m.*

cleanse [klɛnz] *v. tr.* nettoyer, curer (une fosse d'aisance, &c.); [Fig.] purifier. || **cleanser** [-ɚ] *n.* produit *m* de nettoyage, [soap] détersif *m*, © nettoyeur *m.*

clear [klijɚ] *adj.* clair, net, pur; [thing] évident, manifeste; [Pers.] convaincu, sûr (de qqch., *about sth.*); [way, space] dégagé, libre: *The coast is* ~, Le champ est libre; *to make it* ~ *to s.o.*, faire comprendre qqch. à qqun; *to make it* ~ *that*, préciser que; *All* ~*!*, Fin d'alerte; *to stand* ~ *(of sth.)*, s'écarter, rester éloigné de qqch.; *to keep* ~ *of sth.*, éviter qqch. || **clear** *v. tr.* [voice, &c.] éclaircir, clarifier (qqch.); [piece of ground] déblayer, défricher; [line, way] dégager; [room] faire évacuer (la salle); [Com.] solder, liquider; [law] libérer, exonérer (qqun d'une accusation, *s.o. of a charge*); [clean] nettoyer (qqch.): ~ *the table, please*, Enlevez le couvert, Desservez la table,/s'il vous plaît; [letter-box] lever (les lettres). || **clearance** [-əns] *n.* [tunnel, &c.] hauteur *f*, espace *m* libre; [customs] dédouanage *m*, dédouanement *m*; [way] dégagement *m*; déblaiement *m* (d'un terrain, &c.): [Com.] ~ *sale*, liquidation *f*, vente *f* de soldes. || **clear away** [ə'wej] *v. tr.* enlever (qqch.). || *v. intr.* [Pers.] faire place. || **clear-cut** [-'kʌt] *adj.* [sharp] net, tranché; [Fig.] absolu. || **clearing** [-ɪŋ] *n.* éclaircissement *m*; dédouanage *m*, dédouanement *m*; [way, space, &c.]; dégagement *m*, déblaiement *m*; [land] défrichement *m*; [open place] clairière *f*, © essarts *mpl*, désert *m*; [Fin.] [account] liquidation *f*, [debt] acquittement *m*, [cheque] compensation *f*; [law] désinculpation *f*. || **clearly** [-lɪ] *adv.* clairement, avec clarté, nettement; [speak] d'une façon distincte. || **clearness** [-nəs] *n.* [sky, explanation, &c.] clarté *f*; [contour, picture, &c.] netteté *f*; [air, water, &c.] transparence *f*; [Fig.] lucidité *f* (d'un esprit, &c.) transparence *f*. || **clear off** [-'ɔf] *v. tr.* [obligations, debts] se dégager de (qqch.), s'acquitter de (qqch.); [Fam.] se débarrasser de (qqch.). || **clear out** [-'awt] *v. tr.* enlever (qqch.), nettoyer (qqch.) à fond. || *v. intr.* [Fam.] [skedaddle] déguerpir. || **clear up** [-ʌp] *v. tr.* [problem, matter] élucider, résoudre (une énigme, &c.). || *v. intr.* [weather] s'éclaircir, se mettre au beau; [Fig.] se rasséréner.

cleavage ['klijvədʒ] *n.* [Tech.] clivage *m*; [Fig.] scission *f*, division *f*.

cleave[1] [klijv], **clove/cleft** [klowv/klɛft], **cloven/cleft** ['klovən] *v. tr.* fendre. || *v. intr.* se fendre (en deux) [plus souvent, on emploie SPLIT]. || **cleaver** ['klijvɚ] *n.* [meat] hachoir *m*.

cleave[2], **cleaved, cleaved** [klijvd] *v. intr.* (se) coller (à, *to*); [Bibl.] [Fig.] s'attacher (à une personne).

clef [klɛf] *n.* [Mus.] clef *f* (de sol, de fa, &c.).

cleft [klɛft] cf. CLEAVE. || *n.* fente *f*, crevasse *f* (dans un rocher, &c.). || *adj.* ~ *palate*, fissure *f* palatine.

clemency ['klɛmən|sɪ] *n.* clémence *f*, †merci *f*. || **clement** [-t] *adj.* clément, [weather] doux, tempéré.

clench [klɛntʃ] *v. tr.* serrer (les poings), tenir fermement.

clergy ['klɚdʒɪ] *n.* clergé *m*. || **clergyman** [-mən] *n.* ecclésiastique *m*; ministre *m*, pasteur *m*/protestant.

cleric ['klɛɚɪk] *n.* ecclésiastique *m*.

clerical ['klɛɚɪkḷ] *adj.* [pertaining to clergy] clérical, ecclésiastique: ~ *error*, faute *f* de copiste; ~ *work*, travail *m* d'écritures, de bureau: *owing to a* ~ *error*, par suite d'une erreur matérielle. || **clerk** [klɚk] *n.* **1.** employé *m*, commis *m* (de bureau); clerc *m* (de notaire); [store] vendeur *m*: ~ *of the House*, © [Parl.] greffier *m* de la Chambre. **2.** [church] clerc *m*, ecclésiastique *m*.

clever ['klɛvɚ] *adj.* [Pers.] adroit, [answer, &c.] intelligent, fin, habile: *He is* ~ *at mathematics*, Il est/doué pour, fort en/mathématiques. || **cleverly** [-lɪ] *adv.* adroitement, habilement, intelligemment. || **cleverness** ['klɛvɚnəs] *n.* habileté *f*, adresse *f*; ingéniosité *f*, intelligence *f*.

clew [kluw] [US] cf. CLUE.

cliché [klɪ'ʃej] *n.* [trite] cliché *m*.

click [klɪk] *n.* **1.** [heels] bruit *m* sec; claquement *m* (de langue); clic *m*. **2.** déclic *m*. **3.** [Mach.] cliquet *m*. || *v. intr.* faire un déclic; [Fam.] réussir.

client ['klajənt] *n.* client *m*, -e *f*. || **clientele** [ˌklajṇ'tɛl] *n.* clientèle *f*: [store, &c.] *to have a large* ~, être bien achalandé.

cliff [klɪf] *n.* falaise *f*, rocher *m* escarpé.

climate ['klajmət] *n.* climat *m*.

climax ['klajmæks] *n.* point *m* culminant; comble *m*; sommet *m*: *to reach a* ~, atteindre son apogée.

climb [klajm] *n.* [mountain, stairs] ascension *f*, escalade *f*. || *v. tr.* **(up)** [mountain] faire l'ascension de, escalader; [hill, slope] gravir; [stairs] monter. || *v. intr.* [wall] grimper (sur, *over*), [tree] monter (dans, *up*), grimper (à, *up*). || **climb down** [-'dawn] *v. intr.* dégringoler; [Fig.] déchanter, en rabattre; [Fam.] se dégonfler. || *n.* descente *f*, reculade *f*; [Fig.] défaite *f*, déconfiture *f*. || **climber** [-ɚ] *n.* **1.** [person, animal] grimpeur *m*; [mountain-] alpiniste *m*, *f*; [vine] plante *f* grimpante. **2.** [US] © [social] arriviste *m*, *f*. || **climbing** [-ɪŋ] *n.* ascension *f* (d'une montagne), escalade *f* (d'un mur, &c.); alpinisme *m*.

clinch [klintʃ] *v. tr.* river (deux pièces de fer, &c.): [Fig.] *to* ~ *a bargain*, boucler une affaire, un marché.

cling [klɪŋ], **clung, clung** [klʌŋ] *v. intr.* s'accrocher, se cramponner (à, *to*); se serrer, se coller (contre qqun); [Fig.] adhérer (à une croyance, &c., *to a belief*).

clinic ['klɪnɪk] *n.* clinique *f*, [out-patient] dispensaire *m*. || **clinical** [-ḷ] *adj.* clinique.

clink [klɪŋk] *n.* [☞ petit bruit cristallin] tintement *m*. || *v. intr.* tinter; faire tinter.

clip [klɪp] *n.* **1.** [sheep] tonte *f*. **2.** taloche *f*, [fist, stick] coup sec. **3.** pince *f*, chargeur *m* (de fusil); [Loc.] *at a fast* ~, à/bonne, toute/vitesse; *paper* ~, trombone *m*, attache *f*. || **clip** *v. tr.* **[-pp-]** couper (ras, avec des ciseaux); tailler (les cheveux); tondre (un chien); rogner; [Fig.] avaler (ses mots). || **clipper** [-ɚ] *n.* tondeuse *f*; [Naut.] voilier *m* de course, [Naut., Aero.] clipper *m*. || **clipping** [-ɪŋ] *n.* [hair, sheep] tonte *f*; taille *f* (des cheveux), [horse] tondage *m*; [press, newspaper] coupure *f* (de journal); [ticket] poinçonnage *m*; *clippings pl.* rognures *fpl*, chutes *fpl*.

clique [klijk] *n.* clique *f*, chapelle *f*.

cloak [klowk] *n.* manteau *m*; [Fig.] manteau *m*, voile *m*. || *v. tr.* recouvrir (d'un manteau); voiler, masquer, cacher (sous un manteau, un voile). || **cloak-room** [-ˌɹuwm] *n.* vestiaire *m*; [Br.] consigne *f*; (de gare) [cf. CHECK].

clock [klɑk] *n.* [big, wall] horloge *f*; pendule *f*, [portable] montre *f*: *It is 4 o'clock*, Il est 4 heures; *One cannot put the ~ back*, On ne peut revenir en arrière; *alarm ~*, réveil *m*, réveille-matin, *inv.*; *The ~ is fast*, L'horloge avance. || **clock** *v. tr.* [time] minuter, chronométrer (une course, &c.): [sports] ~ (*s.o.*)/*in*, *out*/, pointer (qqun)/à l'arrivée, au départ/. || **clockwise** [-ˌwajz] *adv.* [movement] dans le sens des aiguilles d'une montre. || **clockwork** [-ˌwɚk] *n.* mouvement *m* (d'horlogerie); rouages *mpl* (d'une montre): [Fig.] *Everything went like ~*, Tout/s'est bien passé, a marché comme sur des roulettes/.

clod [klɑd] *n.* **1.** motte *f* (de terre). **2.** [Fig.] benêt *m*, lourdaud *m*.

clog [klɑg] [-gg-] *v. tr.* boucher, engorger (un tuyau); entraver (la circulation), arrêter.

cloister [ˈklojstɚ] *n.* cloître *m*.

close[1] [klowz] *v. tr.* fermer, © barrer (une porte, &c.); terminer, conclure, arrêter (un débat, une discussion, une séance); (res)serrer les rangs, &c.): [night-club, factory] ~ *down*, fermer (qqch.) définitivement; ~ *up*, fermer (une boutique), mettre une barrière à (qqch.), interdire l'accès à (une rue, &c.). || *v. intr.* [store, &c.] fermer, [meeting, &c.] se clore: se terminer, tirer à sa fin: ~ *in* [weather] s'assombrir, se couvrir, [fog, night] tomber; ~ *up*, [Pers.] se taire. || **close**[2] *n.* (en)clos *m* enceinte *f*, clôture *f*; [meeting, &c.] clôture *f*, fermeture *f*; [session, speech, &c.] conclusion *f*, fin *f*: *draw to a ~*, se terminer, prendre fin.

close[2] [klows] *adj.* **1.** fermé, clos; [air, atmosphere] lourd, renfermé. **2.** proche (de, *to*), [space] étroit, [game, order] serré: *to have a ~ shave*, l'échapper belle. **3.** [Pers.] avare, mesquin: *~-mouthed*, [Pers.] laconique, peu loquace. **4.** secret, hermétique; [friendship, &c.] intime. **5.** [examination, &c.] rigoureux, attentif. || *adv.* **1.** étroitement, hermétiquement: *~-fitting*, [clothes, &c.] ajusté, collant. **2.** (de) près, à proximité (de, *to*): *~-shaven*, [Pers.] rasé de près. || **closely** [-lɪ] *adv.* étroitement, de près, [shaven, shorn] ras *inv.*; rigoureusement, attentivement; [Fig.] [disputed] chaudement. || **closeness** [-nəs] *n.* manque *m* d'air; étroitesse *f*, exiguïté *f* (d'un endroit); proximité *f*; [friendship] intimité *f*; rigueur *f* (d'une traduction, &c.); [Pers.] avarice *f*, mesquinerie *f*. || **closet** [klɑzət] *n.* [study] cabinet *m*; [for clothes] garde-robe *f*, armoire *f*, placard *m*: *water-~*, cabinet *m* d'aisance, [Fam.] les cabinets. || *v. tr.* enfermer (qqun) dans un cabinet.

close-up [-ˌʌp] *n.* [Photo., Cin., &c.] premier plan *m*, close-up *m*. || **closure** [ˈklowʒɚ] *n.* clôture *f*.

clot [klɑt] *n.* **1.** [blood] caillot *m*. **2.** [Fig.] niais *m*, benêt *m*. || *v. intr.* [-tt-] [blood] se coaguler, [milk] se cailler. || *v. tr.* [blood] coaguler, [milk] cailler.

cloth [klɑθ] *n.* [linen, &c.] drap *m*, toile *f*, linge *m*; [woollen, &c.] tissu *m*, étoffe *f*; [rag] guenille *f*, torchon *m*; nappe *f*; [Fig.] le clergé: *to lay the ~*, mettre la nappe, mettre, dresser/le couvert; *face ~*, gant *m* de toilette, © débarbouillette *f*; *table ~*, nappe *f*; *wash ~*, cf. FACE ~.

clothe [klowð], **clothed** [-d] or **clad** [klæd] *v. tr.* habiller, (re)vêtir (*in*, *with*, de). || **clothes** [klowðz] *n.pl.* vêtements *mpl*, habits *mpl*, linge *m*: *in plain ~*, en civil; *Put on your ~*, Habille-toi, Habillez-vous; *Take off your ~*, Déshabille-toi, Déshabillez-vous. || **clothes closet** [-ˌklɑzət] *n.* garde-robe *f*, [Fr.] penderie *f*, placard *m*. || **clothesline** [-ˌlajn] *n.* corde *f* à linge. || **clothes peg** [-ˌpɛg] *n.* pince *f* à linge. || **clothier** [ˈklowðɪɚ] *n.* drapier *m*; marchand *m* de/confections, drap/. || **clothing** [ˈklowðɪŋ] *n.* **1.** habillement *m*, vêtement(s) *m(pl)*, [wear] linge *m*. **2.** [nun's] prise *f* de voile.

cloud [klawd] *n.* nuage *m*, †nue *f*, nuée *f*: *to drop from the clouds*, [Fig.] tomber des nues; *Every ~ has a silver lining*, [Prov.] Après la pluie le beau temps; [on glass] buée *f*. || **cloud** *v. tr.* couvrir (le ciel) de nuages; voiler, obscurcir, assombrir (qqch.). || *v. intr.* [sky] *to ~ /over, up/*, se couvrir (de nuages); se voiler, s'obscurcir, s'assombrir. || **cloudberry** [-ˌbɛɚɪ] *n.* ronce *f* petit-mûrier. || **cloudburst** [-ˌbɚst] *n.* averse *f*, trombe *f*, rafale *f* de pluie. || **cloudiness** [-ɪnəs] *n.* nébulosité *f*; [Fig.] morosité *f*. || **cloudless** [-ləs] *adj.* [sky, life] sans nuage, serein, clair. || **cloudy**

[-ɪ] *adj.* [sky, weather] nuageux, couvert; [Fig., notions, &c.] nébuleux.

clove[1] [klowv] *n.* clou *m* de girofle: ~ *of garlic*, gousse *f* d'ail.

clove[2], **cloven** cf. CLEAVE.

clover ['klowvɚ] *n.* trèfle *m*: *sweet* ~, mélitot *m*, [Fam.] trèfle d'odeur: *to be like a pig in* ~, [Fig.] être comme un coq en pâte.

clown [klawn] *n.* clown *m*, bouffon *m*. || *v. intr.* faire le/clown, bouffon/.

club [klʌb] *n.* [stick] massue *f*, gourdin *m*; [bat] crosse *f*, club *m* (de golf); [cards] trèfle *m*; [Sport., charities, &c.] association *f*, société *f*: *social* ~, cercle *m*, société *f*/d'entr'aide; [Pol., Lit.] cercle *m*, club *m*. || *v. tr.* [-bb-] frapper, assommer (qqun) à coups de/massue, gourdin. || *v. intr.* [people] former/un club, un groupe, une association. || **clubfoot** [-ˌfʊt] *n.* pied bot. || **clubhouse** [-ˌhaws] *n.* cercle *m*, club *m*.

cluck [klʌk] *v. intr.* [hen] glousser. || *n.* gloussement *m*.

clue [kluw] *n.* [detective story, &c.] [Fig.] fil *m* (conducteur), piste *f*, indice *m*.: *I haven't got a* ~, Je n'ai pas la moindre idée (de cela), Je n'en sais rien.

clump [klʌmp] *n.* [trees] bouquet *m* d'arbres, massif *m*; [earth] motte *f* (de terre).

clumsy ['klʌmzɪ] *adj.* [Pers., movement] lourd, gauche, maladroit; [body] disgracieux, informe.

clung cf. CLING.

cluster ['klʌstɚ] *n.* groupe *m*, ensemble *m*; [fruit, flowers] grappe *f*, [bananas] régime *m*. || *v. tr.* grouper (ensemble), rassembler. || *v. intr. to* ~ *(a)round*, se grouper, se rassembler (autour de).

clutch [klʌtʃ] *n.* **1.** [bird of prey] serre *f*, griffe *f*; [Fig.] griffe, prise *f*. **2.** [car] embrayage *m*. || *v. tr.* empoigner, [grasp] (en)serrer, saisir (qqun, qqch.).

clutter ['klʌtɚ] *v. tr.* [+ **up**] encombrer (de, *with*).

cm. [= centimetre] *n.* centimètre *m*.

CNR [ˌsijˌɛn'ɑɚ], **CN** [ˌsij'ɛn] [= Canadian National Railways] Chemins *mpl* de fer nationaux du Canada, le Canadien National.

Co. 1. [= COMPANY, Cie [= COMPAGNIE]: *Co. Ltd.*, © Cie Ltée, [Fr.] S.A. [Société Anonyme]. **2.** [= COUNTY]. || **C.O.** ['sij'ow] [= Commanding Officer]. || **C/o** [= care of], A/s [= aux bons soins de].

coach [kowtʃ] *n.* **1.** †carrosse *m*; [car] voiture *f*; [train] voiture *f* (de voyageurs); autocar *m*, autobus *m*: *stage* ~, diligence *f*. **2.** [Pers.] répétiteur *m* (d'anglais, &c.); [Sport] entraîneur *m* (d'une équipe). || **coach** *v. tr.* donner des leçons particulières à (qqun); entraîner (une équipe). || **coaching** [-ɪŋ] *n.* leçons *fpl.* particulières, répétitions *fpl*; [Sport] entraînement *m*. || **coachman** [-mən] *n.* cocher *m*, [stage-coach] conducteur *m*.

coadjutor [kow'ædʒətɚ] *n.* collaborateur *m*, aide *m*: [R.C.] *Coadjutor Bishop*: évêque *m* coadjuteur.

coagulate [kow'ægjəˌlejt] *v. tr.* [clot] coaguler (le sang, &c.), faire cailler. || *v. intr.* se coaguler, se cailler.

coal [kowl] *n.* **1.** charbon *m*, [unmined] houille *f*. **2.** morceau *m* de charbon: *hard* ~, anthracite *m*; *live coals*, charbons ardents, braise *f*; ~ *dust*, poussier *m* (de charbon); *coalfield*, bassin *m* houiller; ~ *mine*, mine *f* de houille, houillère *f*; ~ *-miner*, houilleur *m*, mineur *m*; ~ *oil*, pétrole *m*, © huile *f* de charbon; ~ *tar*, goudron *m* de houille. || **coal** *v. tr.* [ship, &c.] approvisionner (qqch.) en charbon. || *v. intr.* [ship, house, &c.] s'approvisionner en charbon. || **coaler** [-ɚ] *n.* [navire] charbonnier *m*.

coalesce [ˌkowl̩'ɛs] *v. intr.* s'unir.

coalition [ˌkowl̩'ɪʃən] *n.* coalition *f*.

coarse [kɔɚs] *adj.* grossier, rude; [salt] gros; [sugar] brut. || **coarseness** [-nəs] *n.* [fabric, person, manners, character] grossièreté *f*, rudesse *f*; [Fig.] brutalité *f*.

coast [kowst] *n.* [seashore] côte *f*, littoral *m*, rivage *m*: *from* ~ *to* ~, © d'un océan à l'autre, d'une mer à l'autre. || *v. tr.*: ~ *down (sth.)*, descendre (une pente, &c.) en roue libre. || *v. intr.* [vessel] caboter. || **coastal** [-l̩] *adj.* [Naut.] côtier; littoral. || **coaster** [-ɚ] *n.* **1.** [Naut.] caboteur *m*. **2.** dessous *m* de/bouteille, carafe, verre/. || **coastguard** [-ˌgɑɚd] *n.* garde-côte *m*, *pl.* gardes-côte. || **coastline** [-ˌlajn] *n.* littoral *m*.

coat [kowt] *n.* **1.** [man's] habit *m*, veston *m*; [winter, man's] pardessus *m*, [woman's] manteau *m*; [horse, &c.] robe *f*, [snake] peau *f*. **2.** [paint, &c.] couche *f*, enduit *m*: [Her.] ~ *of arms*, armes *fpl*, armoiries *fpl*; *morning* ~, jaquette *f*; *tail* ~, [man's] frac *m*: *Cut your* ~ *according to your cloth*, [Prov.] Selon ta bourse gouverne ta bouche. || **coat** *v. tr.* (re)couvrir, enduire (de, *with*). **coat-hanger** [-ˌhæŋɚ] *n.* porte-manteau *m*, cintre *m*. || **coating** [-ɪŋ] *n.* couche *f*, enduit *m*.

coax [kowks] *v. tr.*: *to* ~ *s.o. into sth.*, persuader qqun (à force de cajoleries); amadouer.

cob [kɑb] *n.* épi *m* de maïs/© de blé d'Inde/: *corn on the* ~, maïs en épi.
cobalt ['kowbɔlt] *n.* cobalt *m*: ~ *bomb,* bombe *f* au cobalt.
cobble ['kɑbl̩] *v. tr.* [shoes] raccommoder, ressemeler. || **cobbler** [-ɚ] *n.* †savetier *m*, cordonnier *m*. [-ɚ]. || **cobblestone** [-ˌstown] *n.* [Coll.] pavé *m*, pavés *mpl.*
cobweb ['kɑbˌwɛb] *n.* toile *f* (d'araignée).
cocaine [ˌkow'kejn] *n.* cocaïne *f.*
cock[1] [kɑk] *n.* **1.** [rooster] coq *m*; [-bird] (oiseau *m*) mâle (*m*): *It's a* ~ *-and-bull story,* [Fig.] C'est une histoire à dormir debout; [Fig.] *He is the* ~ *of the walk,* C'est le coq/du village, de la paroisse/; ~ *-a-doodle-do,* coquerico *m*, cocorico *m*; *at* ~ *crow,* au premier chant du coq. **2.** [gas, fuel, water] robinet *m*. **3.** [pile] meulon *m* (de foin). **4.** [gun] chien *m* (de fusil): *safety* ~, cran *m* d'arrêt. || **cock** *v. tr.* **1.** armer (un fusil). **2.** mettre (le foin) en meulons.
cock[2] *n.* [turn up] retroussis *m*, retroussement *m* (d'un chapeau, &c.): ~ *of the eye,* clignement *m* d'œil, œillade *f*. || *v. tr.* [one's hat] relever, retrousser, mettre (qqch.) de côté. || **cockeyed** [-ˌajd] *adj.* **1.** [Pers.] qui louche, © coq-l'œil. **2.** [thing] de/biais, travers, côté/; ~ *notion,* idée *f* biscornue.
cockle ['kɑkl̩] *n.* [mollusk] bucarde *f*, clovisse *f*: *to play at hot cockles,* jouer à la main chaude; *It warms the cockles of my heart,* Cela me réchauffe le cœur.
cockney ['kɑknɪ] *adj.*: [Br.] ~ *accent,* accent *m*/faubourien de Londres, cockney/. || *n.* cockney *m.*
cockpit ['kɑk|ˌpɪt] *n.* **1.** arène *f* de combats de coqs. **2.** carlingue *f* (d'un avion).
cockroach [-ˌɹowʧ] *n.* blatte *f*, cafard *m*; © coquerelle *f.*
cocksure [-ʃɚ] *adj.* **1.** sûr et certain. **2.** [Pers.] cf. COCKY.
cocktail [-ˌtejl] *n.* cocktail *m*, © coquetel *m.*
cocky ['kɑkɪ] *adj.* [Pers.] suffisant, outrecuidant, impertinent, qui a du toupet.
cocoa ['kow|kow] *n.* cacao *m*: ~ *bean,* graine *f*, fève *f*/de cacao; ~ *tree,* cacaotier *m*, cacaoyer *m.*
cocoanut [also **coconut**] [-kənʌt] *n.* noix *f* de coco.
cocoon [kɑ'kuwn] *n.* cocon *m.*
cod [kɑd] *n.* morue *f*: ~ *bank,* banc *m* de morues; ~ *-fisher,* morutier *m*, moruyer *m*; ~ *-liver oil,* huile *f* de foie de morue; © *tomcod,* poisson *m* des chenaux; poulamon *m.*
C.O.D. [ˌsijˌow'dij] *loc.* [= cash on delivery] contre remboursement *m.*
coddle ['kɑdl̩] *v. tr.* dorloter.
code [kowd] *n.* code *m*; [secret] chiffre *m*: ~ *message,* message *m* chiffré; [Fig.] éthique *f*: [Med.] ~ *of ethics,* déontologie *f.*
codicil ['kɑdɪˌsɪl] *n.* codicille *m.*
codify [-ɪfaj] *v. tr.* codifier.
co-ed ['kowˌɛd] *n.* élève *f* d'école mixte; étudiante *f*. || **co-education** [ˌkowɛʤə'kejʃən] *n.* coéducation *f.*
coerce [kow'ɚ|s] *v. tr.* contraindre, forcer. || **coercion** [-ʃən] *n.* coercition *f.*
coexistence [ˌkowəks'ɪstəns] *n.* coexistence *f.*
coffee ['kɑfɪ] *n.* café *m*: ~ *bean,* grain *m* de café; ~ *pot,* cafetière *f*; *black* ~, café/nature *inv.*, noir/; *white* ~, café /au lait, crème/*inv.*
coffer ['kɑfɚ] *n.* coffre *m* (à argent), boîte *f* (à outils); [valuables] cassette *f.*
coffin ['kɑfɪn] *n.* cercueil *m*, bière *f.*
cog [kɑg] *n.* dent *f* (d'engrenage): *cogwheel,* roue *f* dentée.
cogency ['kowʤən|sɪ] *n.* force *f* (de persuasion), puissance *f*. || **cogent** [-t] *adj.* fort, puissant; [arguments] convaincant.
cogitate ['kɑʤɪˌtejt] *v. intr.* méditer.
cognizance ['kɑgnɪzn̩s] *n.* connaissance *f*: *to take* ~ *of,* tenir compte de.
coherent [kow'hijɚənt] *adj.* cohérent; [reasoning] logique, qui se tient. || **cohesion** [kow'hijʒən] *n.* cohésion *f*; [reasoning] logique *f* (interne), structure *f.*
coiffeur [kwɑ|'fjɚ] *n.* coiffeur *m* de dames. || **coiffure** [-fjuwɚ] *n.* coiffure *f.*
coil [kojl] *n.* [wire, &c.] enroulement *m*; [hair, &c.] rouleau *m*; [twist] torsade *f* (de cheveux); [Electr.] bobine *f*; serpentin *m* (de radiateur); [wind] repli *m* (d'un serpent, &c.); [Fig.] [smoke] tourbillon *m*. || **coil** *v. tr.* [wire, cable, &c.] enrouler, bobiner. || **coil around** (sth.) [-ə'ɹawnd] *v. intr.* [vine, &c.] s'enrouler autour de (qqch.). || **coil up** [-'ʌp] *v. intr.* [snake, &c.] s'enrouler (sur soi-même), [animal] se mettre en rond.
coin [kojn] *n.* pièce *f* de monnaie; monnaie *f*: ~ *of the realm,* espèces *fpl*, cf. CURRENCY; *to pay s.o.* (*back*) *in his own* ~, [Fig.] rendre à qqun la monnaie de sa pièce. || *v. tr.* [government] battre (monnaie); frapper (la monnaie, des médailles); [Fig.] inventer (une expression, &c.): [Fig.] *They are coining money,* Ils font des affaires d'or, Ils s'enrichissent à vue d'œil. || **coinage** [-əʤ] *n.* monnaie *f*; frappe *f* (de la monnaie); [Fig.] invention *f* (d'un mot, &c.).

coincide [kowɪn'sajd] *v. intr.* coïncider (avec, *with*), correspondre (à). || **coincidence** [kow'ɪnsɪdəns] *n.* coïncidence *f* [dans le temps, dans l'espace].
coke [kowk] *n.* [fuel] coke *m.*
Col. [also **Colo.**] [= Colorado].
colander ['kʌləndɚ] *n.* passoire *f.*
cold [kowld] *adj.* froid: *to get* ~, se refroidir; *Are you* ~?, As-tu, Avez-vous/froid?; *It is* ~, [weather] Il fait froid, [thing] Il, Elle/est froid(e); *My hands are* ~, J'ai les mains glacées, J'ai froid aux mains; [Fig.] *That leaves me* ~, Cela ne me fait ni chaud ni froid. || *n.* **1.** froid *m*: ~ *wave*, [weather] vague *f* de froid. **2.** rhume *m*: *to catch* (*a*) ~, attraper un rhume, s'enrhumer; prendre froid: *cold sore*, © feu *m*/sauvage, volage; herpès *m*; ~ *storage*, entrepôt *m* frigorifique. || **cold-blooded** [-ˌblʌdəd] *adj.* à sang froid; [Fig.] insensible, [action] délibéré. || **coldly** [-li] *adv.* froidement, avec froideur. || **coldness** [-nəs] *n.* **1.** [atmosphere] froideur *f*, [climate, weather] froidure *f.* **2.** [Fig.] [unfriendliness] froid *m*, froideur *f.*
cole-slaw ['kowlˌslɔ] *n.* salade *f* de chou, cole-slaw *m.*
collaborate [kə'læbɚˌejt] *v. intr.* collaborer (à, *to*; avec, *with*). || **collaboration** [kəˌlæbɚ'ejʃən] *n.* collaboration *f*, aide *f.*
collapse [kə'læps] *v. intr.* s'effondrer, s'écrouler, s'affaisser: *The roof collapsed under the weight*, Le toit s'est effondré sous le poids; [Fig.] s'effondrer, perdre tout courage. || *n.* effondrement *m*, écroulement *m*, affaissement *m.* || **collapsible** [-ɪbl̩] *adj.* pliant, démontable.
collar ['kɑlɚ] *n.* [shirt, dress] col *m*; [horse, &c.] collier *m*: ~ *bone*, clavicule *f.* || *v. tr.* mettre la main sur (qqun, qqch.), [grab] pincer, attraper (qqun, qqch.).
colleague ['kɑlijg] *n.* collègue *m/f.*
collect [kə'lɛk|t] *v. tr.* [things, information] recueillir, [papers, documents] (r)amasser, [people] rassembler; [stamps] collectionner; [taxes] percevoir; [money, debt, &c.] recouvrer, encaisser: [Pers.] *to* ~ *o.s.*, se ressaisir, se reprendre; [parcel] *Collect on delivery*, en port dû. || *n.* [Rel.] collecte *f.* || **collection** [-ʃən] *n.* [gathering] collection *f* (d'objets); [money, bills] recouvrement *m*, [taxes] perception *f*, encaissement *m* (d'un dû); levée *f* (des lettres); [picking up] ramassage *m*; [charities, church] quête *f*, collecte *f.* || **collective** [-tɪv] *adj.* [noun, &c.] collectif. **collector** [-tɚ] *n.* collectionneur *m* (de timbres, d'objets d'art, &c.); percepteur *m* (d'impôts, &c.); receveur *m* (des douanes); [charities, church] quêteur *m*: *ticket-* ~, contrôleur *m.*
college ['kɑlədʒ] *n.* **1.** [university] © collège *m* universitaire, université *f*: [US] *to go to* ~, aller à l'université; ~ *professor*, professeur *m* de faculté. **2.** collège *m*: © *classical* ~, collège *m* classique; ~ *course*, études *fpl* secondaires, © cours *m* classique: *to go to* ~, faire ses humanités. **3.** école *f* (militaire, navale, de musique, &c.): ~ *of education*, école normale supérieure; *Teachers'* ~, école normale. || **collegiate** [kə'lijdʒət *adj.* © collégial; [studies] secondaire.
collide [kə'lajd] *v. intr.* [vehicles, &c.] entrer en collision, se heurter.
collier ['kɑljɚ] *n.* [coal] houilleur *m*, mineur *m.* || **colliery** [-ɪ] *n.* houillère *f*, mine *f* de charbon.
collision [kə'lɪʒən] *n.* collision *f.*
colloquial [kə'lowkwɪəl] [☞ not formal, but correct] *adj.* [speech] familier, de la conversation: ~ *English*, l'anglais (parlé) familier/courant, de la conversation/.
Colombia [kə'lʌmbɪə] *n.* [Géog.] la Colombie *f.*
colon ['kowlən] *n.* **1.** [punctuation] deux-points *m.* **2.** ['kɑlən] [intestine] colon *m.*
colonel [kɚnl̩] *n.* colonel *m.*
colonial [kə'lownɪəl] *adj.* colonial. || **colonist** ['kɑlənɪst] *n.* colon *m.* || **colonization** [ˌkɑlən'aj'zejʃən] *n.* colonisation *f.* || **colonize** ['kɑlən|ˌajz] *v. tr.* coloniser (une région). || **colony** [-ɪ] *n.* [settlement, group, territory] colonie *f.*
color cf. COLOUR.
Colorado [kɑlə'ɹædow] *n.* le Colorado.
colossal [kə'lɑsl̩] *adj.* colossal.
colour ['kʌlɚ] *n.* couleur *f*; coloris *m* (d'un tableau, &c.); [complexion] couleurs *fpl*, teint *m*; *pl.* [Fig.] [flag] couleurs *fpl*, pavillon *m*: *to strike one's* ~, baisser pavillon, se rendre à l'ennemi; *to be off* ~, n'être pas dans son assiette; ~ *-blind*, daltonien, daltoniste. || *v. tr.* colorer (qqch.), mettre de la couleur à (qqch.); colorier (un dessin); [Fig.] imager (une description); déguiser, dénaturer (les faits, la vérité). || **coloured** [-d] *adj.* coloré, colorié: [race] ~ *people*, gens *mpl*, personnes *fpl*/de couleur; [Fig.] [style] imagé, pittoresque. || **colourful** [-fl̩] *adj.* coloré; [Fig.] pittoresque, imagé. || **colouring** [-ɪŋ] *n.* coloration *f*; coloriage *m*, coloris *m* (d'un dessin, &c.). || **colourless** [-ləs] *adj.* incolore, sans couleur, terne.
colt [kowlt] *n.* poulain *m.*

Columbia [kə'lʌmbɪə] *n.* [River] la Colombie; *British ~*, la Colombie-Britannique: *in, to B.C.*, en Colombie-Britannique. || **Columbus (Christopher)** [kə'lʌmbəs] *n.* Christophe Colomb.

column [kɑləm] *n.* colonne *f*; [article] chronique *f.* || **columnist** [-nɪst] *n.* [Journ.] chroniqueur *m* (sportif, &c.), collaborateur *m* attitré (d'un journal).

coma ['kowmə] *n.* coma *m.*

comb [kowm] *n.* peigne *m*; rayon *m* de miel; crête *f* de coq: *small ~*, peigne fin. || *v. tr.* peigner: *to ~ one's hair*, se peigner; *to ~ one's hair rapidly*, -> se donner un coup de peigne; [Fam.] faire une rafle (dans un lieu); [police] chercher partout. || *v. intr.* [waves] déferler (sur, *over*).

combat ['kɑmbæt] *n.* [fight] combat *m.* || *v. tr.* combattre (qqch.), se battre contre (qqch., qqun). || *v. intr.* [kəm'bæt] lutter (avec, contre qqun, qqch., *with, against s.o., sth.*). || **combatant** [-ənt] *adj. & n.* [soldier, forces] combattant (*m*).

comber [kowmə˞] *n.* **1.** [Pers.] peigneu|r, -se; [wool] cardeu|r, -se. **2.** [wave] brisant *m*

combination [kɑmbɪ'nejʃən] *n.* **1.** combinaison *f* (d'éléments, &c.), ligue *f*, coalition *f* (d'intérêts, &c.). **2.** *pl.* [men, women] sous-vêtements *mpl.* || **combine** ['kɑmbajn] **1.** *n.* [Ind.] cartel *m.* **2.** [Agric.] moissonneuse-batteuse *f.* || *v. tr.* [kəm'bajn] [elements] combiner (avec qqch., *with sth.*), [efforts, forces] (ré)-unir, allier (avec, à, *with*). || *v. intr.* [elements, &c.] se combiner (avec qqch., *with sth.*), [join] s'unir (à, *with*), s'allier (à, avec, *with*); [leagues, &c.] fusionner. || **combined** [-d] *adj.* combiné, [efforts, &c.] réuni; [Indus., Com.] fusionné.

combustible [kəm'bʌs|tɪbḷ] *adj.* combustible. || *n.* combustible *m.* || **combustion** [-tʃən] *n.* combustion *f.*

come [kʌm], **came** [kejm], **come** [kʌm] *v. intr.* **1.** venir, arriver: *to ~ again*, revenir; *to ~ home (again)*, rentrer (chez soi); *Come/and, to/see me*, Venez me voir; *He came late*, Il arriva tard; *(I'm) coming!*, Voilà!, J'arrive/; *Come! Come!*, Voyons!; *Come (now)!*, Allons (donc)!; *Easy ~, easy go*, Cela s'en va aussi facilement que c'est venu; *coming Sunday*, dimanche prochain; *in the weeks to ~*, dans les semaines à venir; *for a long time to ~*, pendant longtemps. **2.** [origin] venir; provenir; résulter: *This wine comes from France*, Ce vin vient de France; *This word comes from French*, Ce mot (pro)vient du français; *Where do you ~ from?*, D'où êtes-vous?; *What university does he ~ from?*, De quelle université sort-il?; *What came of it?*, Qu'est-ce qui en a résulté?; *That's what comes of ~ + -ing*, Voilà ce qui arrive quand on. . . . **3.** [get to] en venir, en arriver, en être: *He has ~ to realize that . . .*, Il/en est venu à, a fini par/ comprendre que . . . ; *If it comes to that*, Si on en arrive là; *I haven't ~ to that yet*, Je n'en suis pas encore là; *When it comes to + -ing*, Pour ce qui est de + infin. **4.** [happen] arriver: *Come what may*, Advienne que pourra, Quoi qu'il arrive; *Now that I ~ to think of it*, Maintenant que j'y pense; *How (does it) ~ (that) . . .*, Comment se fait-il que + subjunc., D'où vient que + indic. **5.** [amount] s'élever: *The bill comes to $10*, La note s'élève à $10. **6.** [with part., adj.]: *to ~ /undone, untied, &c./*, se/défaire, dénouer,/&c./; *to ~ true*, se réaliser; *That comes/easy, natural/to you (to)*, Cela vous est/facile, naturel/de. || **come about** [-ə'bawt] *v. intr* arriver, se produire; [Naut.] changer de direction. || **come across** [-ə'kɹɑs] *v. intr.* traverser; trouver, rencontrer (par hasard). || **come after** [-'æftə˞] *v. intr.* suivre, venir après. **come along** [-ə'lɔŋ] *v. intr.* accompagner; [happen] arriver; [progress] marcher: *~!*, Mais venez donc!; *How are things coming along?*, Où en êtes-vous?, (Alors) ça marche (bien)? || **come apart** [-ə'pɑə˞t] *v. intr.* se séparer. || **come around** [-ə'ɹawnd] *v. intr.* faire le tour (de); venir voir (qqun); [time] revenir; reprendre connaissance; se rallier (à une opinion). || **come at** [-ˌæt] *v. intr.* attaquer; s'approcher de. || **come away** [-ə'wej] *v. intr.* s'en aller; s'éloigner: *Come away (from there)!*, Va-t-en de là! || **come back** [-'bæk] *v. intr.* revenir; en revenir (à ce qu'on disait); revenir en vogue. || **come before** [-bɪ'fɔə˞] *v. intr.* précéder; [be more important] venir en premier; être considéré par; comparaître devant (un tribunal). || **come between** [-bɪ'twijn] *v. intr.* intervenir, s'interposer (entre). || **come by** [-'baj] *v. intr.* passer par, devant; obtenir. || **come down** [-'dawn] *v. intr.* descendre; [price] baisser; [rain] tomber; [story] être transmis; [building] être démoli; s'écrouler: *He has ~ to cheating*, Il en est venu à tricher; *It all comes down to/this, whether . . . /*, Tout se réduit à/ceci, savoir si . . . /. || **come forth** [-'fɔə˞θ] *v. intr.* sortir; paraître || **come forward** [-'fɔə˞wə˞d] *v. intr.* s'avancer;

se présenter. || **come in** [-'ɪn] *v. intr.* entrer; [again] rentrer; [tide] monter; [race] arriver; [fashion] s'introduire; [money] rentrer: *to ~ for sth.*, recevoir (une part de) qqch.; *to ~ handy*, être utile. || **come into** [-'ɪntuw] *v. intr.* entrer dans; hériter de (qqch.); participer à. || **come off** [-'ɔf] *v. intr.* descendre de; se détacher, se décoller, partir; [happen] avoir lieu, réussir; [escape] s'en tirer. || **come on** [-'ɑn] *v. intr.* s'avancer; [progress] faire des progrès; arriver; commencer: *Come on!*, Venez!, [disbelief or hurrying] Allons! Allons!; *to feel a headache coming on*, se sentir gagner par un mal de tête. || **come out** [-'awt] *v. intr.* sortir; [stain] partir; [sun] se montrer; [truth] se découvrir; [book] paraître; [buds] s'ouvrir; réussir, finir bien; [escape] s'en tirer; [girl] faire ses débuts dans le monde; [sum] se monter (à): *to ~ for s.o.*, se déclarer pour qqun. || **come over** [-'owvər] *v. intr.* traverser; [feeling] gagner, prendre/(qqun); venir voir (qqun); se convertir (à une opinion). || **come through** [-θɹuw] *v. intr.* traverser, passer par; s'en tirer, se tirer (d'une affaire). || **come to** [-'tuw] *v. intr.* reprendre connaissance. || **come together** [-tə'gɛðər] *v. intr.* se réunir, se rassembler. || **come under** [-'ʌndər] *v. intr.* subir (une influence); tomber (dans une catégorie); ressortir (d'une autorité). || **come up** [-'ʌp] *v. intr.* monter; [plants] pousser; [reach] atteindre, arriver à; [question] être soulevé: *to ~ to an opponent*, égaler, valoir/un adversaire; *to ~ against sth.*, se heurter à qqch.; *to ~ with s.o.*, rattraper qqun; *to ~ with sth.*, trouver (qqch.). || **come upon** [-ə'pɑn] *v. intr.* [emotion] saisir (qqun); rencontrer, trouver (par hasard), tomber sur.

comeback ['kʌm,bæk] *n.* retour *m* (en vogue, au pouvoir); [retort] réplique *f*: *You won't have any ~*, Vous ne pourrez pas vous plaindre.

comedian [kə'mijdɪən] *n.* **1.** comédien, -ne; [Pers.] comique *m.* **2.** auteur *m* comique.

comedown ['kʌm,dawn] *n.* dégradation *f*, chute *f*, déchéance *f.*

comedy ['kɑmədɪ] *n.* **1.** [Thea.] comédie *f.* **2.** [art] le comique *m*: *musical ~*, opéra *m* bouffe; *slapstick ~*, farce *f.*

comeliness ['kʌmlɪnəs] *n.* beauté *f*, grâce *f.* || **comely** ['kʌmlɪ] *adj.* avenant, gracieux; †convenable.

comet ['kɑmət] *n.* [star] comète *f.*

comfort ['kʌmfərt] *v. tr.* consoler, soulager, donner du réconfort à (qqun), réconforter (qqun). || *n.* **1.** consolation *f*, soulagement *m*, réconfort *m*: *That is cold ~*, C'est une piètre consolation. **2.** confort *m*, vie *f* facile, aises *fpl.* || **comfortable** [-əbl̩] *adj.* confortable; [warmth, &c.] agréable; [space] commode, [way, &c.] facile; [Pers.] à l'aise: *It's ~ here*, On est bien ici. || **comfortably** [-əblɪ] *adv.* confortablement, [installed, &c.] à l'aise. || **comforter** [-ər] *n.* **1.** [Pers.] consolat|eur, -rice. **2.** [quilt, counterpane] courtepointe *f*, couvre-pied *m*, © confortable *m*; [scarf] cache-nez *m.* || **comforting** [-ɪŋ] *adj.* réconfortant, consolant. || **comfortless** [-ləs] *adj.* [Pers.] désolé, triste; [position, &c.] incommode.

comic ['kɑmɪk] *adj.* comique: *~ opera*, opéra *m* bouffe. || *n.* comédien *m*, -ne *f.* || **comical** [-l] *adj.* [situation, pers.] comique, drôle. || **comics** [-s] *n.pl.* dessins *mpl* humoristiques, bandes *fpl* dessinées, histoires *fpl* en images: *crime ~*, roman policier en images.

comma ['kɑmə] *n.* [Gram.] virgule *f.*

command [kə'mænd] *n.* [army, &c.] commandement *m*; ordre *m*; autorité *f*: *under the ~ of*, sous/le commandement, les ordres/de; *to be in ~*, → commander; *to have full ~ (of)*, être entièrement maître (de), avoir la pleine disposition (de); *to have a ~ of French*, posséder (parfaitement) le français. || *v. tr.* **1.** [army, &c.] commander, gouverner; [Pers.] être/maître, -sse/de; [order] commander, ordonner (à qqun de faire qqch., *s.o. to do sth.*); [thing] posséder (qqch.), avoir (qqch.) à sa disposition. || **commander** [-ər] *n.* [Army] commandant *m*; [Navy] capitaine *m* (de vaisseau), [Fr.] de frégate: *~-in-chief*, commandant *m* en chef. || **commanding** [-ɪŋ] *adj.* **1.**: *~ officer*, commandant *m*, [Mil.] chef *m* de corps. **2.** [authoritative] imposant, d'autorité. **3.** [position] dominant. || **commandment** [-mənt] *n.* commandement *m* (de Dieu).

commemorate [kə'mɛmər,ejt] *v. tr.* commémorer, célébrer (un anniversaire). || **commemoration** [kə,mɛmər'ejʃən] *n.* commémoration *f*: *in ~ of*, en/souvenir *m*, mémoire *f* de.

commence [kə'mɛns] *v. tr. & intr.* commencer. || **commencement** [-mənt] *n.* **1.** commencement *m*, début *m.* **2.** [Univ.] collation *f* des/grades, diplômes/: *~ exercise*, (cérémonie *f* de) collation *f* des/grades, diplômes/.

commend [kə'mɛnd] *v. tr.* recommander (qqun, qqch.); [praise] louer; [entrust]

confier (qqch. à qqun, *sth. to s.o.*). || **commendable** [-əbl] *adj.* [Pers., action] louable, recommandable, digne d'éloges. || **commendation** [kamən'dejʃən] *n.* louange *f*, éloge(s) *m(pl) words of* ~, félicitations *fpl.*

comment ['kamɛnt] *n.* commentaire *m*, [remark] observation *f*: *No* ~!, Sans commentaire, Je n'ai rien à dire. || *v. tr.* commenter (un texte), faire des/commentaires, observations/(sur qqch., *on sth.*). || **commentary** ['kamn̩ˌtɛəɪ] *n.* commentaire *m* (*on*, de). || **commentator** [kamən'tejtər] *n.* commentat|eur *m*, -rice *f* (à la radio, &c.).

commerce ['kamər̩s] *n.* (le) commerce *m*: [Quebec], (*Junior*) *Chamber of Commerce*, (la) Chambre de commerce (des jeunes). || **commercial** [kə'mərʃəl] *adj.* [trade, business] commercial, [agreement, article, &c.] de commerce: [bills, cheques, &c.] ~ *papers*, papiers *mpl* d'affaires.

commiserate [kə'mɪzərˌejt] *v. tr.* avoir de la commisération pour.

commissar ['kamɪsaər] *n.* [USSR] commissaire *m* (du peuple). || **commissary** ['kamɪˌsɛəɪ] *n.* commissaire *m*, [Mil.] intendant *m*; [store] cantine *f.*

commission [kə'mɪʃən] *n.* commission *f*, délégation *f* (de pouvoirs), [authority] mandat *m*; [rank] brevet *m* (d'officier); [profit] pourcentage *m*; [crime] perpétration *f*: *Royal Commission* (*of Enquiry*), *Commission f royale d'enquête.* || *v. tr.* [give powers] charger (qqun de faire qqch., *s.o. to do sth.*), commissionner (un agent), confier un mandat à (qqun). || **commissioned** [-d] *adj.* [agent, delegate] autorisé, commissionné, muni de pouvoirs: [army] ~ *officer*, officier *m*; *non-* ~ *officer*, sous-officier *m*. || **commissioner** [-ər] *n.* [Sch., &c.] commissaire *m*; membre *m* d'une commission: *The Trade Commissioner of Canada*, (le) Délégué commercial du Canada.

commit [kə'mɪt] *v. tr.* [action, crime, &c.] commettre; [entrust] confier (qqch. à qqun, *sth. to s.o.'s care*); [Law] envoyer (qqun en prison): *to* ~ *o.s.*, se compromettre, s'engager; *to* ~ *suicide*, se suicider; *to* ~ (*sth.*) *to memory*, apprendre (qqch.) par cœur. || **commitment** [-mənt] *n.* **1.** engagement *m* (financier). **2.** emprisonnement *m*; mandat *m* de dépôt.

committee [kə'mɪtɪ] *n.* comité *m*, commission *f* (parlementaire, &c.): *Reception* ~, comité *m* d'accueil.

commodity [kə'madɪtɪ] *n.* [Com., fabricated] marchandise *f*, denrée *f*, produit *m*: ~ *prices*, (les) prix *mpl* des/denrées, produits de base/.

commodore ['kamədɔər] *n.* [navy] [Br.] chef *m* de division (par intérim), © [US] commodore *m*: *Air Commodore*, © commodore *m* de l'air; [Fr.] général de brigade aérienne.

common ['kamən] *adj.* commun, général; [people, things] ordinaire; [usual] courant; [low] vulgaire: ~ *law*, droit *m* coutumier. || *n.* **1.** [land] commune *f*. **2.** *pl.* [Br.] © *The House of Commons*, la Chambre des Communes, les Communes *fpl.* || **commonly** [-lɪ] *adv.* communément, ordinairement, généralement. || **commonness** [-nəs] *n* [action, &c.] fréquence *f*; [cheapness] banalité *f*; [people] vulgarité *f.*

commonplace [-ˌplejs] *n.* lieu commun, banalité *f*. || *adj.* banal, ordinaire. || **common sense** [-'sɛns] *n.* le sens commun, © le bon sens *m*. || **commonweal** [-ˌwijl] *n.* le bien public. || **commonwealth** [-ˌwɛlθ] *n.* [Pol., citizenry] (l')État *m*, (la) chose publique: *The* (*British*) *Commonwealth* (*of Nations*), le Commonwealth.

communal ['kamjənəl] *adj.* communal → de la commune.

commune[1] [kə'mjuwn] *v. intr.* converser: *to* ~ *with o.s.*, se recueillir, se renfermer en soi-même.

commune[2] ['kamjuwn] *n.* [local administration] commune *f.*

communicable [kə'mjuwnɪ|kəbl̩] *adj.* communicable; [disease] contagieux.

communicant [-kənt] *n.* [Rel.] communiant *m*, -e *f*: *to be a regular* ~, fréquenter les sacrements. || **communicate** [-ˌkejt] *v. tr.* [news, message, &c.] communiquer, transmettre (qqch.). || *v. intr.* **1.** [access, contact] communiquer (avec qqun, qqch., *with s.o., sth.*). **2.** [Rel.] communier. || **communication** [kəˌmjuwnɪ'kejʃən] *n.* [contact, connection] communication *f*; [information] message *m*, communiqué *m*. || **communicative** [kə'mjuwn|ɪkətɪv] *adj.* [connective; sociable] communicatif. || **communion** [-jən] *n.* [relationship, sharing] communion: [Rel.] *to receive Holy Communion*, recevoir la (Sainte) Communion, communier. || **communism** ['kamjə|nɪzm] *n.* [Pol.] communisme *m*. || **Communist** [-nɪst] *n.* communiste *m/f*. || *adj. Communist China*, la Chine communiste. || **community** [kə'mjuwnɪtɪ] *n.* [people] communauté *f*, société *f*, collectivité *f*, groupe *m*, [place] localité *f*: ~ *centre*, salle *f* paroissiale, centre *m* communautaire; [relief fund] ~ *chest,* caisse *f* de secours.

commutation [ˌkɑmjəˈtejʃən] *n.* [Phil.] commutation *f* (de peine, d'unités); [US] ~ *ticket*, carte *f* d'abonnement (au chemin de fer). || **commute** [kəˈmjuwt] *v. tr.* commuer (en, *to*). || *v. intr.* habiter en banlieue. || **commuter** [-ɚ] *n.* abonné *m* (-e *f*) (des lignes de banlieue); [Pej.] banlieusard *m.*

compact [ˈkɑmpækt] *n.* **1.** [alliance] pacte *m*, [agreement] convention *f.* **2.** [toilet] poudrier *m*, boîte *f* à poudre. || [kəmˈpækt] *adj.* compact, serré, dense, concis. || *v. tr.* [pack] serrer, tasser, condenser (qqch.).

companion [kəmˈpænjən] *n.* compagn|on *m*, -e *f*, [Sch., &c.] camarade *m*/*f*. || **companionship** [-ʃɪp] *n.* compagnie *f*, société *f*, camaraderie *f*. || **company** [ˈkʌmpənɪ] *n.* [group] compagnie *f*; [gathering] assistance *f*; [Ind.] société *f* (par actions), © compagnie *f*; [association] troupe *f* (de comédiens, &c.): *in the* ~ *of*, en compagnie de; *to keep s.o.* ~, tenir compagnie à qqun; *to keep /good, bad/* ~, fréquenter la/bonne, mauvaise/compagnie; *We are having* ~ *for dinner*, Nous avons du monde à dîner.

comparable [ˈkɑmpɚəbḷ] *adj.* comparable. || **comparative** [kəmˈpæɚətɪv] *adj.* comparatif, [linguistics, &c.] comparé. || **compare** [kəmˈpɛɚ] *v. tr.* comparer (à, avec, *to*, *with*). || *v. intr.* être comparable (à, *with*), se comparer (à, *with*). || *n.*: *beyond* ~, sans comparaison, inégalable, hors pair, sans pareil. || **comparison** [kəmˈpæɚɪsən] *n.* comparaison *f*: *in* ~ *with*, en comparaison de, comparé à.

compartment [kəmˈpɑɚtmənt] *n.* compartiment *m*; local *m* (séparé), cabinet *m.*

compass [ˈkʌmpəs] *n.* boussole *f*: (*a*) *pair of compasses*, (un) compas; limites *fpl* (d'une enceinte); [voice, &c.] portée *f*, étendue *f*. || *v. tr.* faire le tour de, parcourir (qqch.), entourer (qqun); [Fig.] embrasser (qqch.).

compassion [kəmˈpæʃən] *n.* compassion *f*, pitié *f*. || **compassionate** [-ət] *adj.* compatissant, charitable (*to*/*towards*, envers).

compatible [kəmˈpætɪbḷ] *adj.* compatible; qui va de pair avec.

compatriot [kəmˈpejtɹɪət] *n.* compatriote *m.*

compel [kəmˈpɛl] *v. tr.* [-ll-] forcer, contraindre (qqun de), obliger (qqun/à, de/). || **compelling** [kəmˈpɛlɪŋ] *adj.* [motive] impérieux.

compensate [ˈkɑmpṇˌsejt] *v. tr.* compenser: *to* ~ *s.o. for* . . . , dédommager qqun de . . . .|| **compensation** [ˌkɑmpṇˈsejʃən] *n.* compensation *f*; dédommagement *m*; [fee] honoraires *mpl*, traitement *m.*

compete [kəmˈpijt] *v. intr.* concourir (pour qqch., *for sth.*); faire concurrence (à qqun, *with*, *against*/*s.o.*).

competence [ˈkɑmpətən|s] *n.* **1.** compétence *f* (en qqch., *in sth.*), aptitude(s) *f*(*pl*) (pour, *in*), [official's] attributions *fpl.* **2.** moyens *mpl* de subsistance. || **competency** [-sɪ] *n.* cf. COMPETENCE. || **competent** [-t] *adj.* [Pers.] compétent (en, pour, *in*), apte (à, *in*); [means, knowledge] suffisant. || **competing** [kəmˈpijtɪŋ] *adj.* en concurrence avec (qqun). || **competition** [ˌkɑmpəˈtiʃən] *n.* concurrence *f*, rivalité; concours *m*; compétition *f* (sportive). || **competitive** [kəmˈpɛtɪtɪv] *adj.* : ~ *examination*, concours *m.* || **competitor** [kəmˈpɛtitɚ] *n.* concurrent, -e, rival, -e; [Sport] compétiteur *m.*

compile [kəmˈpajl] *v. tr.* compiler.

complacent [kəmˈplejsənt] *adj.* complaisant, affable; content de soi.

complain [kəmˈplejn] *v. intr.* se plaindre (de qqch., *about sth.*), réclamer; [Fig.] pleurer, se lamenter. || **complaint** [-t] *n.* **1.** plainte *f*, grief *m*, réclamation *f*. **2.** mal *m*, maladie *f*.

complaisant [kəmˈplejzṇt] *adj.* bien disposé.

complement [ˈkɑmpləmənt] *n.* [Gram.] complément *m*; [full quantity] complément *m*, reste *m*: *to have o.'s full* ~ *of* . . ., avoir tout (son esprit, toutes les grâces, &c.); *to have a full* ~, être au grand complet.

complete [kəmˈplijt] *adj.* [finished] complet, terminé, achevé, [whole] entier; [thorough] accompli, parfait. || *v. tr.* [finish] compléter, terminer, achever; [achieve] accomplir, parfaire; [make whole] remplir (un questionnaire). || **completely** [-lɪ] *adv.* complètement, absolument. || **completeness** [-nəs] *n.* état *m* complet, plénitude *f*; perfection *f*: *for the sake of* ~, → pour être complet. || **completion** [kəmˈplijʃən] *n.* [act of completing] achèvement *m*; perfection *f*.

complex [kəmˈplɛks] *adj.* complexe, composé; compliqué. || *n.* [ˈkɑmplɛks] **1.** [inferiority, superiority] complexe *m.* **2.** groupe *m* industriel, usine *f* polyvalente. || **complexion** [kəmˈplɛk|ʃən] *n.* teint *m*; [Fig.] caractère *m*: *This puts a different* ~ *on the matter*, Cela change tout. || **complexity** [-sɪtɪ] *n.* complexité *f*; [Fig.] complication *f*.

compliance [kəm'plajən|s] *n.* acquiescement *m,* obéissance *f*: *in ~ with,* aux termes de (la loi, &c.), conformément à . . . . || **compliant** [-t] *adj.* obligeant, obéissant.
complicate ['kamplɪˌkejt] *v. tr.* compliquer. || **complicated** [-əd] *adj.* compliqué, complexe. || **complication** [ˌkamplɪ'kejʃən] *n.* complication *f.*
compliment ['kamplɪmənt] *n.* compliment *m,* félicitation *f,* hommage *m*: *to pay s.o. a ~ ,* faire un compliment à qqun; *With the compliments of the author,* Hommage de l'auteur. || *v. tr.* complimenter (qqun), féliciter (qqun) de (qqch.). || **complimentary** [ˌkamplɪ'mentərɪ] *adj.* flatteur, élogieux; en hommage: *~ ticket,* billet *m* de faveur.
comply [kəm'plaj] + *with v. intr.* accéder (à, *with*); remplir (certaines conditions), se soumettre (à certaines conditions). || **complying** [-ɪŋ] *adj.* accommodant, conciliant.
component [kəm'pownənt] *n.* composant *m*; élément *m* constitutif, partie *f* essentielle; [Math.] composante *f.* || *adj.* composant.
compose [kəm'pows] *v. tr.* [song, poem] composer, [letter, &c.] écrire, rédiger; [mind, o.s.] calmer, tranquilliser: *to ~ o.s.* (*to*), se disposer (à); *to be composed of,* se composer, être composé/de. || **composed** [-d] *adj.* [Pers., mind] calme, assuré. || **composedly** [-ədlɪ] *adv.* calmement, avec/assurance, sang-froid/. || **composer** [-ər] *n.* [Mus.] composit|eur *m,* -rice *f*; auteur *m* (d'une chanson). || **composite** ['kampəzɪt] *adj.* composé, [Archit. & Fig.] composite. || **composition** [kampə'zɪʃən] *n.* [Mus., make-up, mixture] composition *f,* [Sch.] [own language] composition *f,* [foreign language] thème *m*; [settlement] arrangement *m,* entente *f.* || **composure** [kəm'powʒər] *n.* sang-froid *m,* calme *m,* maîtrise *f* de soi.
compound ['kamˌpawnd] *n.* [chemical, &c.] composé *m,* composition *f.* || *adj.* [word, interest, &c.] composé. || *v. tr.* [kəm'pawnd] **1.** composer, [mix] combiner, mêler (des éléments, &c.). **2.** arranger, [debt] régler. || *v. intr.* [come to terms] composer, s'arranger (avec qqun, qqch., *with s.o., sth.*).
comprehend [kampɹɪ'hɛn|d] *v. tr.* [understand, include] comprendre. || **comprehensible** [-sɪbl̩] *adj.* compréhensible, intelligible. || **comprehension** [-ʃən] *n.* compréhension *f.* || **comprehensive** [-sɪv] *adj.* compréhensif; [inclusive] étendu, complet, total: *a ~ report,* une vue d'ensemble. || **comprehensively** [-sɪvlɪ] *adv.* en bloc, en général. || **comprehensiveness** [-sɪvnəs] *n.* étendue *f,* portée (d'un jugement, &c.).
compress [kəm'pɹɛs] *v. tr.* comprimer; [Fig.] condenser, resserrer. || *n.* ['kampɹɛs] compresse *f.* || **compression** [kəm'pɹɛʃən] *n.* compression *f.*
comprise [kəm'pɹajz] *v. tr.* [include] comprendre, [consist of] contenir.
compromise ['kampɹəˌmajz] *n.* compromis *m,* transaction *f.* || *v. tr.* compromettre (sa réputation, &c.). || *v. intr.* transiger.
comptroller [kən'tɹowlər] *n.* **1.** contrôleur *m*; [Fin.] vérificateur *m* (de comptes): © *Comptroller of the Treasury,* © *Contrôleur* m *du Trésor.* **2.** [device] cf. CONTROLLER.
compulsion [kəm'pʌl|ʃən] *n.* contrainte *f.* || **compulsive** [kəm'pʌlsɪv] *adj.* (désir, envie) insurmontable. || **compulsory** [-sərɪ] *adj.* [education, &c.] obligatoire.
computation [kampjə'tejʃən] *n.* calcul *m,* supputation *f.* || **compute** [kəm'pjuwt]. *v. tr.* calculer, supputer.
comrade ['kamɹæd] *n.* [work, Sch., play] camarade *m/f,* [mate] compagn|on *m,* -e *f*; [Fam.] copain *m,* copine *f.*
concave [kan'kejv] *adj.* concave.
conceal [kən'sijl] *v. tr,* cacher, dissimuler (*sth. from s.o.,* qqch. à qqun).
concede [kən'sijd] *v. tr.* concéder, admettre, [grant] accorder; [Pol.] reconnaître, admettre (sa défaite).
conceit [kən'sijt] *n.* vanité *f.*
conceited [kən'sijtəd] *adj.* [Pers.] vaniteux, suffisant, prétentieux.
conceivable [kən'sijv|əbl̩] *adj* [imaginable] concevable. || **conceive** *v. tr.* concevoir. || *v. intr.* (s')imaginer.
concentrate ['kansənˌtɹejt] *v. tr.* [liquid, &c.] concentrer (qqch.). || *n.* concentré *m.* || *v. intr.* [attention] se concentrer (sur qqch., *on sth.*). || **concentration** [ˌkansən'tɹejʃən] *n.* [liquid, troops, &c.] concentration *f.*
concept ['kanˌsɛpt] *n.* concept *m*; idée *f.* || **conception** [kən'sɛpʃən] *n.* conception *f,* idée *f,* notion *f*: [R.C.] *the Immaculate Conception,* l'Immaculée Conception; *pl.* philosophie *f* (de la vie).
concern [kən'sərn] *n.* **1.** [généralement dans des circonstances graves] souci *m* (que l'on a de); part *f* (que l'on prend à): *a deep ~ for . . . ,* être profondément soucieux de . . . , être préoccupé par . . . . **2.** [en bonne part] intérêt *m* (que l'on porte à): *This is not my ~ ,* → Cela ne

me regarde pas, cf. CONCERN *v.*; *to show no ~ for*, n'avoir aucun égard envers (qqun), être indifférent devant (qqch.). **3.** [Com.] affaire *f*, maison *f* (de commerce), firme *f*, entreprise *f*. ‖ *v. tr.* **1.** concerner (qqun): *As far as I am concerned*, En ce qui me concerne, → Pour ma part; *This does not ~ you*, Cela ne vous regarde pas; *to be concerned in*, prendre part à (un mouvement, &c.). **2.** intéresser: *to be concerned in*, être intéressé dans (une affaire); *the persons concerned*, les intéressés; *to whom it may ~*, à qui de droit. **3.** préoccuper; se préoccuper de, se faire du souci à propos de: *to be concerned about*, se préoccuper de (la santé de qqun), être inquiet (au sujet) de . . . . ‖ **concerning** [-ɪŋ] prep. concernant; à l'égard de, au sujet de.

concert [ˈkɑnsɚt] *n.* **1.** concert *m*: *to attend a ~*, assister à un concert. **2.** accord *m*, harmonie *f*: *in ~*, (faire qqch.) de concert. ‖ *v. tr.* [kənˈsɚt] [plan together] concerter. ‖ *v. intr.* [people] se concerter.

concession [kənˈsɛʃən] *n.* **1.** concession *f*: *as a ~ towards*, par concession envers. **2.** [mines, &c.] concession *f*; © *~ road*, rang *m*.

conciliate [kənˈsɪlɪˌejt] *v. tr.* concilier (des opinions divergentes, &c.).

concise [kənˈsajs] *adj.* [brief] concis; [book] abrégé: *the Concise Oxford*, le petit Oxford. ‖ **concisely** [-lɪ] *adv.* avec concision. ‖ **conciseness** [-nəs] *n.* concision *f*.

conclude [kənˈkluw|d] *v. tr.* **1.** [agreement, &c.] conclure; terminer (qqch.), décider (une question). **2.** juger, estimer (que). ‖ *v. intr.* [finish] conclure, se terminer. ‖ **conclusion** [-ʒən] *n.* conclusion *f*, fin *f*: *in ~*, en conclusion, → pour conclure; *to come to a ~*, [end] se terminer, [decide] en venir à une conclusion; *to draw a ~*, tirer une conclusion; *to jump to conclusions*, se faire des idées; *It's a foregone ~*, C'était prévu. ‖ **conclusive** [-zɪv] *adj.* [argument, &c.] concluant, décisif.

concoct [kənˈkɑk|t] *v. tr.* préparer (un plat); imaginer, élaborer (une excuse); machiner (une intrigue). ‖ **concoction** [-ʃən] *n.* mélange *m*; [Fig.] élaboration *f* (d'un plan).

concord [ˈkɑnkɔɚd] *n.* [agreement] concorde *f*, entente *f*, harmonie *f*; pacte *m*, accord *m*.

concourse [ˈkɑnkɔɚs] *n.* **1.** [people, circumstances] concours *m*; rassemblement *m* (de gens). **2.** [station] salle *f* des pas perdus.

concrete [kɑnˈkɹijt] *adj.* [real, specific] concret. ‖ *n.* [ˈkɑnˌkɹijt] ciment *m*, béton *m*. ‖ *v. tr.* [building] cimenter, bétonner (des fondations, &c.).

concur [kənˈkɚ] *v. intr.* **1.** s'accorder, être d'accord (avec, *with*). **2.** s'unir (à, *with*). ‖ **concurrence** [-əns] *n.* **1.** approbation *f*; identité *f* (de vues). **2.** [×] concours *m* (de circonstances), coïncidence *f* (d'action). ‖ **concurrent** [kənˈkɚənt] *adj.* tendant au même but; du même avis. ‖ **concurrently** [-lɪ] *adv.* concurremment.

concussion [kənˈkʌʃən] *n.* ébranlement *m*, commotion *f*.

condemn [kənˈdɛm] *v. tr.* condamner (*to*, à); blâmer (qqun). ‖ **condemnation** [ˌkandɛmˈnejʃən] *n.* condamnation *f*, blâme *m*.

condensation [ˌkandɛnˈsejʃən] *n.* [gases, &c.] condensation *f*; [Fig.] résumé *m*, abrégé *m* (d'un cours). ‖ **condense** [kənˈdɛns] *v. tr.* [gas, sentence, &c.] condenser; [liquid, &c.] concentrer; [Fig.] abréger (une expression, &c.). ‖ *v. intr.* [gas, &c.] se condenser; [Fig.] [style, &c.] se resserrer. ‖ **condenser** [-ɚ] *n.* [electricity, &c.] condensateur *m*.

condescend [kandɪˈsɛn|d] *v. intr.* condescendre (à, *to*), accepter de. ‖ **condescension** [-ʃən] *n.* condescendance *f*.

condiment [ˈkandɪmənt] *n.* [spices, &c.] condiment *m*.

condition [kənˈdɪʃən] *n.* [stipulation] condition *f*; [financial, &c.] situation *f*; [health, &c.] état *m*: [social] rang *m*. ‖ *v. tr.* imposer des conditions à (qqch.); [Tech.] conditionner (qqch.). ‖ **conditional** [-l̩] *adj.* conditionnel: *~ on (sth.)*, dépendant de (qqch.). ‖ *n.* [Gram.] le conditionnel (*m*).

conditioned [kənˈdɪʃənd] *adj.* conditionné: *air-~*, climatisé.

condole [kənˈdowl] *v. intr.* s'affliger (avec qqun, *with s.o.*); présenter ses, faire des/ condoléances (à qqun, *with s.o.*). ‖ **condolence** [-əns] *n.* condoléance *f*.

condone [kənˈdown] *v. tr.* **1.** pardonner à, être indulgent envers. **2.** fermer les yeux sur (qqch. de répréhensible).

conduce (to) [kənˈdjuws] *v. tr.* contribuer (à), conduire (à). ‖ **conducive (to)** [-ɪv] *adj.* qui contribue (à) . . . , favorable (à).

conduct [ˈkandʌkt] *n.* [behaviour, management] conduite *f*; [management] gestion *f*, direction *f*. ‖ [kənˈdʌkt] *v. tr.* [guide] conduire (qqun, qqch.); [business, firm] gérer; diriger (un orchestre, &c.); [experiment] effectuer. ‖ **conductor** [-ɚ] *n.* **1.**

[business] directeur *m*; chef *m* d'orchestre; chef *m* de train; [bus] receveur *m*; contrôleur *m* (des billets). **2.** [physical] conducteur *m* (du son, &c.): *lightning* ~, paratonnerre *m*.
conduit ['kandwɪt] *n.* conduit *m*, tuyau *m*.
cone [kown] *n.* [solid] cône *m*; [ice-cream] cornet *m*; [pine] pomme *f* de pin.
con(e)y ['kownɪ] *n.* [†animal; fur] lapin *m*: ~ *wool*, poil *m* de lapin.
confection [kən'fɛkʃən] *n.* bonbon, cf. CONFECTIONERY. || **confectioner** [-ɚ] *n.* confiseur *m.* || **confectionery**]-ˌɛəɪ] *n.* confiserie *f*; bonbons *mpl.*
confederacy [kən'fɛdɚ|əsɪ] *n.* [Pol., &c.] confédération *f.* || **confederate** [-ˌɛjt] *v. tr.* confédérer (des États). || *v. intr.* se confédérer (avec, *with*). || *n.* [-ət] [state, †[US] soldiers, &c.] confédéré *m.* || **confederation** [kənˌfɛdɚ'ejʃən] *n.* confédération *f* (de pays, &c.); © *The Fathers of Confederation*, Les Pères de la Confédération.
confer [kən'fɚ] *v. tr.* [-rr-] [bestow] conférer (un grade, &c. à qqun, *a title, &c. on s.o.*). || *v. intr.* [talk things over] conférer, tenir une conférence, être en consultation (avec qqun, *with s.o.*). || **conference** ['kanfɚəns] *n.* [association] conférence *f*, consultation *f* (médicale); [meeting] congrès *m* (professionnel); [talk] entretien *m.* || **conferment** [kən'fɚmənt] *n.* [Acad.] collation *f* (d'un grade, titre, &c.).
confess [kən'fɛ|s] *v. tr.* [one's sins, error] confesser, avouer, [R.C.] entendre (qqun) en confession; [Fig.] *I must* ~ *that* . . . , Je dois avouer que . . . || *v. intr.* faire des aveux; *to* ~ *to sth.*, avouer qqch. || **confession** [-ʃən] *n.* [Rel.] confession *f*; aveu *m* (de qqch.). *to go to* ~, aller à confesse. || **confessional** [-ʃənl̩] *adj.* [Sch., &c.] confessionnel. || *n.* [R.C.] confessionnal *m.* || **confessor** [-sɚ] *n.* [Rel.] confesseur *m.*
confidant [ˌkanfɪ'dant] *n.* confident *m.* || **confidante** *n.* confidente *f.* || **confide** [kən'fajd] *v. tr.* [entrust] confier (un secret, une charge, &c.); avouer (qqch.). || *v. intr.* se confier (à qqun), se fier (*in*, à). || **confidence** ['kanfɪdən|s] *n.* **1.** [secret] confidence *f.* **2.** [trust] confiance *f*, (*in*, en); [boldness] assurance *f.* || **confident** [-t] *adj.* [Pers.] confiant, certain, assuré, sûr. || **confidential** [ˌkanfɪ'dɛnʃəl] *adj.* [top secret] confidentiel: intime; [reliable] de confiance, sûr. || **confidentially** [-ɪ] *adv.* confidentiellement, en confidence.
confine [kən'fajn] *v. tr.* **1.** confiner (à, *to*), borner/: *to* ~ *oneself to*, se borner à, se limiter à. **2.** enfermer dans; [unlawfully] séquestrer: *to be confined to one's room*, garder la chambre; *to be confined*, accoucher. || **confinement** [-mənt] *n.* détention *f*, emprisonnement *m*; [childbirth] accouchement *m*, couches *fpl*; *in* ~, en prison.
confirm [kən'fɚm] *v. tr.* [statement, appointment] confirmer; [rumour, &c.] corroborer; [nomination] ratifier; [situation, authority, &c.] (r)affermir, assurer; [Rel.] confirmer (un enfant). || **confirmation** [ˌkanfɚ'mejʃən] *n.* [statement; church] confirmation *f*, [nomination] ratification *f*; [authority, &c.] raffermissement *m*, [opinion, &c.] corroboration *f*.
confiscate ['kanfɪsˌkejt] *v. tr.* saisir, confisquer [le verbe anglais s'applique surtout à des saisies d'État].
conflagration [ˌkanflə'gɹejʃən] *n.* conflagration *f*, incendie *m*.
conflict ['kanˌflɪkt] *n.* conflit *m*, lutte *f.* || *v. intr.* [kən'flɪkt]: *to* ~ *with*, entrer en conflit avec, s'opposer à, lutter contre.
conform [kən'fɔɚm] *v. tr.* (se) conformer (à, *to*), s'aligner sur (un modèle). || **conformable** [-əbl̩] *adj.* conforme (à, *to*); docile, souple. || **conformist** [kən'fɔɚmɪst] *n.* conformiste *m.* || **conformity** [-ɪtɪ] *n.* conformité *f* (à, *with, to*); soumission *f*, conformisme *m*.
confound [kən'fawnd] *v. tr.* [mix up] confondre (qqch. avec qqch. d'autre); [puzzle] confondre (qqun); [Fam.] *Confound him!*, Que le diable l'emporte. || **confounded** [-əd] *adj.* [Fam.] Satané, © maudit.
confront [kən'fɹʌnt] *v. tr.* confronter (deux points de vue); faire face à (un ennemi); *to be confronted with* (*a problem*): se trouver devant/être mis en face d'/une difficulté.
confuse [kən'fjuwz] *v. tr.* confondre; mêler, embrouiller (une question, des arguments); déconcerter, embrouiller (qqun); © mêler qqun: *This is* (*all*) *very confusing*, C'est très troublant → On n'y comprend plus rien. || **confused** [-d] *adj.* confus, trouble. || **confusedly** [-ədlɪ] *adv.* confusément, indistinctement. || **confusing** [-ɪŋ] *adj.* [ease, circumstance, &c.] déroutant, peu clair, embrouillant. || **confusion** [kən'fjuwʒən] *n.* [mistaking, bewilderment] confusion *f*, désordre *m*; [Pers.] désarroi *m*, honte *f* (extrême).
confutation [ˌkanfjuw'tejʃən] *n.* réfutation *f.* || **confute** [kən'fjuwt] *v. tr.* [to

prove false] réfuter (un argument); convaincre (qqun) d'erreur.

congeal [kən'ʤijl] *v. tr.* (se) congeler; [thicken] (se) prendre, (se) solidifier; [blood] (se) coaguler; [Fig.] se figer.

congenial [kən'ʤijnjəl] *adj.* agréable, qui convient bien à; [Pers.] sympathique (*with*, à). || **congeniality** [kən,ʤijnɪ'ælɪtɪ] *n.* affinité *f* (*with*, *for*, avec).

congest [kən'ʤɛst] *v. tr.* [Med.] congestionner; [Fig.] encombrer.

congestion [kən'ʤɛstʃən] *n.* [Med.] congestion *f.*

conglomerate [kən'glɑmər|ət] *n.* [cemented mass] conglomérat *m*, agglomération *f.* || *adj.* [clustered] congloméré, aggloméré. || *v. tr.* [-,ejt] conglomérer, agglomérer (des cailloux, &c.).

congratulate [kən'gɹætʃə,lejt] *v. tr.* féliciter (qqun de qqch., *s.o. on sth.*). || **congratulations** [kən,gɹætʃə'lejʃəns] *n.pl.* félicitations *fpl.*

congregate ['kɑŋgɹə,gejt] *v. tr.* [people, things] rassembler, réunir. || *v. intr.* [people] s'assembler, se réunir. || **congregation** [,kɑŋgɹə'gejʃən] *n.* assemblée *f*; [Rel.] les fidèles (réunis pour le culte).

congress ['kɑŋgɹəs] *n.* congrès *m*: *the Congress* [U.S. Senate and House of Representatives] le Congrès. || **congress|man' -woman** [-mən] [-,wʊmən] *n.* [US] député *m*, -e *f.*

congruence ['kɑŋgɹuwəns] *n.* cf. CONGRUITY. || **congruity** [kən'gɹuwɪtɪ] *n.* conformité *f* (avec, *with*).

conifer ['kɑnɪfər] *n.* [tree] conifère *m.*

conjecture [kən'ʤɛktʃər] *n.* conjecture *f*, supposition *f.* || *v. tr.* conjecturer.

conjugate ['kɑnʤə,gejt] *v. tr.* conjuguer (un verbe, des efforts). || **conjugation** [,kɑnʤə'gejʃən] *n.* [Gram.] conjugaison *f.*

conjunction [kən'ʤʌŋkʃən] *n.* [Gram.] conjonction *f*: *in ~ with*, conjointement, en collaboration/avec.

conjure[1] [kən'ʤuwər] *v. tr.* conjurer (le sort), conjurer (contre l'État, &c.).

conjure[2] ['kɑnʤər] *v. tr. & intr.* escamoter, faire des tours de passe-passe: *to ~ up* (*a spirit*), évoquer (un esprit), conjurer (le diable).

connect [kə'nɛk|t] *v. tr.* (ré)unir, relier, attacher, joindre (à, *to*, *with*); [Elect.] brancher (un appareil); [bus, train, &c.] faire la correspondance (avec, *with*). || **connection** [-ʃən] *n.* union *f*, [air, &c.] liaison *f*, jonction *f*, communication *f*, [bus, train] correspondance *f*; [family, business, friendship] relation *f*: *in this ~*, à ce propos, dans cet ordre d'idées; *I don't see the ~*, Je ne saisis pas le rapport.

connive [kə'najv] *v. intr.* fermer les yeux (sur, *at*), être de connivence (avec, *with*).

connoisseur [kɑnɪ'sər] *n.* [expert] connaisseur *m.*

connotation [,kɑnə'tejʃən] *n.* évocation *f*, suggestion *f.* || **connote** [kə'nowt] *v. tr.* évoquer, suggérer.

conquer ['kɑŋkər] *v. tr.* vaincre (un ennemi), conquérir (un territoire, une ville, &c.); dompter (ses passions). || **conquering** [-ɪŋ] *adj.* conquérant, victorieux, triomphant. || **conqueror** [-ər] conquérant *m*, vainqueur *m*, triomphateur *m.* || **conquest** ['kɑŋkwɛst] *n.* conquête *f.*

conscience ['kɑnʃəns] *n.* conscience *f*: [Pers.] *~ -stricken*, pris, rongé/de remords; *to search one's ~*, examiner sa conscience; *in all ~*, en vérité, certes. || **conscientious** [,kɑnʃɪ'ɛnʃəs] *adj.* consciencieux: *~ objector*, objecteur *m* de conscience. || **conscientiousness** [-nəs] *n.* conscience *f*, droiture *f.* || **conscious** ['kɑnʃəs] *adj.* **1.** conscient: *to be ~ of sth.*, avoir conscience de qqch.; *to become ~ of sth.*, s'apercevoir de qqch.; *to be(come) ~ that ...*, avoir le sentiment que. **2.** avoir sa connaissance: *to become ~*, reprendre connaissance. || **consciousness** [-nəs] *n.* [awareness] conscience *f*; [state] connaissance *f*; sentiment *m*, perception *f* (de qqch.).

conscript [kən'skɹɪpt] *v. tr.* [Mil.] appeler (qqun) sous les drapeaux; réquisitionner (qqch.); [Fig.] enrôler (qqun). || *n.* ['kɑnskɹɪpt] [Mil.] conscrit *m*, recrue *f.* || **conscription** [kən'skɹɪpʃən] *n.* service *m* militaire (obligatoire), © conscription *f.*

consecrate ['kɑnsə,kɹejt] *v. tr.* [a church to worship] consacrer; sacrer (un évêque); canoniser (un saint); *consecrated ground*, terre sainte. || **consecration** [,kɑnsə'kɹejʃən] *n.* consécration *f.*

consecutive [kən'sɛkjətɪv] *adj.* consécuti|f, -ve.

consent [kən'sɛnt] *v. intr.* consentir, donner son assentiment (à qqch., *to sth.*). || *n.* consentement *m*, assentiment *m*; accord *m* (donné à qqch., *to sth.*).

consequence ['kɑnsəkwən|s] *n.* conséquence *f*, effet *m*, résultat *m*, suites *fpl*; importance *f*: *It's of no ~*, Cela n'a pas d'importance. || **consequent** [-t] *adj.* [resulting] en conséquence (de qqch., *upon sth.*); [consistent] conséquent. || **consequential** [,kɑnsə'kwɛnʃəl] *adj* . **1.** [resulting] conséquent. **2.** [Pers.] important; [self-important] suffisant.

|| **consequently** ['kɑnsəkwəntlɪ] *adv.* par conséquent; conséquemment.
conservation [kɑnsə'vejʃən] *n.* conservation *f* (des forêts, &c.), préservation *f.* || **conservative** [kən'sɚvətɪv] *adj.* & *n.* [political party, &c.] conservat|eur, -rice. || **conservatory** [kən'sɚvəˌtoɚɪ] *n.* [Mus.] conservatoire *m*; [greenhouse] serre *f.*
conserve [kən'sɚv] *v. tr.* conserver.
consider [kən'sɪdɚ] *v. tr.* considérer; prendre (une demande, &c.) en considération, examiner (qqch.); avoir égard à (qqun, qqch.); réfléchir à (qqch.): *to ~ s.o. (as) a friend,* considérer qqun comme un ami; *to ~ /s.o., sth./ridiculous,* tenir/qqun, qqch./pour ridicule, trouver /qqun, qqch./ridicule; *I ~ that . . . ,* J'estime que . . . , → A mon avis.
considerable [-əbl̩] *adj.* considérable; important; [personality] éminent.
considerate [-ət] *adj.* prévenant, attentif; réfléchi. || **consideration** [kənˌsɪdɚ'ejʃən] *n.* [thought, esteem] considération *f*; [deliberation] réflexion *f,* examen *m*; [money] dédommagement *m*: *to give careful ~ (to sth.),* réfléchir mûrement (à qqch.): *to take sth. into ~,* tenir compte de qqch.; *for a ~,* à titre onéreux; *out of ~ for s.o.,* par égard pour qqun; *money is no ~,* sans regarder à la dépense. || **considering** [kən'sɪdɚɪŋ] *prep.* eu égard à. || *conj.* étant donné/(qqch.): *~ that,* vu, attendu/que.
consign [kən'sajn] *v. tr.* confier (à, *to*); [Com.] expédier (à, sur) par messageries, &c.; envoyer (des marchandises) en consignation. || **consignment** [-mənt] *n.* [Com.] envoi *m*; consignation *f*; [shipment received] arrivage *m* (de poisson, &c.).
consist [kən'sɪst] *v. intr.* consister (*of sth.,* en qqch.; *in sth.,* dans qqch.), se composer (*of sth.,* de qqch.); *to ~ in doing (sth.),* consister à faire (qqch.). || **consistency** [-ənsɪ] *n.* **1.** consistance *f* (d'une pâte); [Fig.] fermeté *f* (de qqun). **2.** compatibilité *f,* esprit *m* de suite. || **consistent** [-ənt] *adj.* compatible (avec, *with*), [reasoning] logique, conséquent.
consolation [kɑnsə'lejʃən] *n.* consolation *f.* || **console**[1] [kən'sowl] *v. tr.* consoler (qqun de qqch.).
console[2] ['kɑnsowl] *n.* buffet *m* (d'orgue), orgue *m*; [table] console *f.*
consolidate [kən'sɑlɪˌdejt] *v. tr.* **1.** consolider (un meuble, une position). **2.** réunir, amalgamer. || *v. intr.* se consolider.
consommé ['kɑnsəˌmej] *n.* consommé *m.*
consonant ['kɑnsənənt] *adj.* consonant, en harmonie, compatible (avec, *with*). || *n.* [Phon.] consonne *f.*
consort [kən'soɚt] *v. intr.* s'associer (à, *with*), s'entendre avec.
conspicuous [kən'spɪkjuwəs] *adj.* (très) visible, évident; [Fig.] [noteworthy] remarquable, de premier plan: *to make o.s. ~* se faire remarquer, s'afficher.
conspiracy [kən'spɪjɚə|sɪ] *n.* conspiration *f.* || **conspirator** [-tɚ] *n.* conspirateur *m.* || **conspire** [kən'spajɚ] *v. tr.* [in secret] conspirer (*against,* contre); contribuer.
constable ['kɑnstəbl̩] *n.* policier *m,* agent *m* (de police); © constable *m*: *chief ~,* commissaire *m* de police, © directeur *m* de la Police. || **constabulary** [kən'stæbjəˌlɛəɪ] *n.* force *f* policière, police *f* (de la ville), © force constabulaire.
constancy ['kɑnstən|sɪ] *n.* constance *f,* persévérance *f.* || **constant** [-t] *adj.* [unchanging, loyal] constant, [weather, &c.] stable, invariable. || *n.* [Math.] constante *f.*
constellation [ˌkɑnstə'lejʃən] *n.* constellation *f.*
consternation [ˌkɑnstɚ'nejʃən] *n.* consternation *f.*
constituency [kən'stɪtjuwən|sɪ] *n.* [Pol.] électeurs *mpl,* circonscription électorale. || **constituent** [-t] *adj.* **1.** [element, part] constituant, constitutif, essentiel. **2.** [Pol.] électoral. || *n.* **1.** élément *m*/de base, essentiel/. **2.** [Pol.] électeur *m.*
constitute ['kɑnstɪˌtjuwt] *v. tr.* **1.** constituer, organiser (qqch.). **2.** [Pol.] élire (qqun). || **constitution** [ˌkɑnstɪ'tjuwʃən] *n.* [makeup] constitution *f,* composition *f,* organisation *f*; santé *f,* constitution *f.* || **constitutional** [-l] *adj.* [law, &c.] constitutionnel.
constrain [kən'stɹejn] *v. tr.* contraindre (qqun), [feelings, &c.] réprimer (qqch.); gêner (qqun); retenir (qqun) de force. || **constraint** [-t] *n.* [compulsion] contrainte *f*; [manners] gêne *f,* retenue *f.*
constrict [kən'stɹɪkt] *v. tr.* resserrer. || **constricted** [-əd] *adj.* → à l'étroit.
construct [kən'stɹʌk|t] *v. tr.* construire, édifier, bâtir (qqch.). || **construction** [-ʃən] *n.* [building] construction *f,* édifice *m,* [foundation] édification *f*; [Gram.] construction (d'une phrase). **2.** [statement] interprétation *f,* explication *f.* || **constructive** [-tɪv] *adj.* [suggestion, criticism, &c.] pratique, constructif. || **construe** [kən'stɹuw] *v. tr.* **1.** traduire (un texte). **2.** [judgment, statement, text] interpréter, donner une explication de (qqch.).
consul ['kɑnsəl] *n.* consul *m*: *the French ~,*

le consul de France. || **consulate** [-ət] *n.* consulat *m.*
consult [kən'sʌlt] *v. tr.* consulter (qqun, qqch.). || *v. intr.* conférer, délibérer. || **consultant** [kən'sʌltənt] *n.* médecin *m* consultant; expert-conseil *m.* || **consultation** [ˌkɑnsəl'tejʃən] *n.* consultation *f* (médicale, &c.). || **consulting** [kən'sʌltɪŋ]: ~ *lawyer,* avocat-conseil *m,* conseil *m* juridique.
consumable [kən'sjuwm|əbl̩] *adj.* [food, wares] consommable, [food] comestible; [destroyable] consumable. || **consume** *v. tr.* [food, &c.] consommer; [eat up] consumer, dévorer; [waste away] gaspiller (son temps, sa fortune). || **consumer** [-ɚ] *n.* [Com., &c.] consommat|eur, -rice. || **consuming** [-ɪŋ] *adj.* [fire, love, &c.] consumant; [Fig.] dévorant.
consummate ['kɑnsəmejt] *v. tr.* [fulfil] consommer (qqch.); parfaire (qqch.). || [kən'sʌmət] *adj.* [complete] consommé, achevé, parfait.
consummation [ˌkɑnsə'mejʃən] *n.* consommation *f,* achèvement *m.*
consumption [kən'sʌmp|ʃən] *n.* **1.** consommation *f* (d'aliments, &c.). **2.** tuberculose *f,* phtisie *f,* || **consumptive** [-tɪv] *adj.* [Pers.] tuberculeux.
contact ['kɑntækt] *n.* contact *m,* [touching] attouchement *m;* [connection] rapport *m* (avec qqun, *with s.o.*): *He has business contacts in Toronto,* Il a des/relations commerciales, correspondants/à T.; ~ *lenses,* verres *mpl* de contact. || *v. tr.* [kən'tækt] prendre, entrer en/contact, communication, rapport/avec (qqun, *s.o.*).
contactor [-ɚ] *n.* [Elect.] interrupteur *m* automatique.
contagion [kən'tej|dʒən] *n.* contagion *f.* || **contagious** [-dʒəs] *adj.* [disease] contagieux.
contain [kən'tejn] *v. tr.* **1.** contenir, renfermer. **2.** [Fig.] maîtriser, retenir (ses instincts, ses sentiments). || **container** [-ɚ] *n.* récipient *m,* boîte *f.*
contaminate [kən'tæmɪˌnejt] *v. tr.* contaminer (qqun), polluer (l'eau), infecter (l'atmosphère). || **contamination** [kənˌtæmɪ'nejʃən] *n.* contamination *f,* pollution *f,* infection *f.*
contemplate ['kɑntəmˌplejt] *v. tr.* [look at] contempler; [intend] projeter (qqch.), avoir (qqch.) en vue; [expect] espérer. || **contemplation** [ˌkɑntəm'plejʃən] *n.* contemplation *f,* méditation *f;* projet *m.*
contemporary [kən'tɛmpɚˌɛɚɪ] *adj.* contemporain (de, *with*). || *n.* contemporain *m.*
contempt [kən'tɛmpt] *n.* mépris *m,* dédain *m:* [Jur.] ~ *of court,* refus *m* de comparaître, contumace *f,* outrage *m* à la Cour. || **contemptible** [-ɪbl̩] *adj.* méprisable, à dédaigner. || **contemptuous** [-uwəs] *adj.* [Pers., look] méprisant, dédaigneux.
contend [kən'tɛnd] *v. intr.* lutter, combattre (pour, *for;* contre, *against, with*); concourir (pour qqch., *for sth.*); prétendre, affirmer, soutenir (que).
content[1] [kən'tɛnt] *adj.* content, satisfait (de, *with*). || *n.* contentement *m,* satisfaction *f.* || *v. tr.* contenter, satisfaire (qqun).
content[2] ['kɑntɛnt] *n.* contenance *f,* capacité *f* (d'un récipient); teneur *f* (d'un discours, &c.). || **contents** [-z] *n.pl.* contenu *m* (d'une boîte): [book] *table of* ~, table *f* des matières.
contented [kən'tɛntəd] *adj.* content, satisfait (de, *with*). || **contentedly** [-lɪ] *adv.* avec satisfaction/; sans se plaindre.
contention [kən'tɛnʃ|ən] *n.* lutte *f,* controverse *f,* dispute *f,* contention *f,* débat *m;* assertion *f,* affirmation *f:* [Fig.] *a bone of* ~, une pomme de discorde. || **contentious** [-əs] *adj.* [point] contentieux, litigieux; [Pers.] querelleur.
contentment [kən'tɛntmənt] *n.* contentement *m,* satisfaction *f.*
contents, cf. CONTENT[2].
contest ['kɑntɛst] *n.* concours *m,* débat *m* (oratoire, &c.), lutte *f,* combat *m,* dispute *f.* || *v. tr.* [kən'tɛst] contester, débattre (qqch.). || *v. intr.* lutter, se disputer, rivaliser (avec qqun, *with s.o.*).
context ['kɑntɛkst] *n.* contexte *m.*
contiguity [kɑntɪ'gjuwɪtɪ] *n.* contiguïté *f.* || **contiguous** [kən'tɪgjuwəs] *adj.* contigu, -uë (à, avec, *with*), attenant (à, *with*), voisin (de, *with*).
continence ['kɑntɪnən|s] *n.* continence *f,* chasteté *f.* || **continent**[1] [-t] *adj.* continent, chaste.
continent[2] *n.* [Geog.] continent *m.* || **continental** [ˌkɑntɪn'ɛntl̩] *adj.* continental: ~ *bed,* divan *m;* ~ *divide,* ligne *f* de partage des eaux.
contingence [kɑn'tɪndʒən|s] *n.* cf. CONTINGENCY. || **contingency** [-sɪ] *n.* contingence *f;* hasard *m,* éventualité *f.* || **contingent** [-t] *adj.* contingent, aléatoire, éventuel: *to be* ~ *upon sth.,* dépendre de qqch. || *n.* [troops] contingent *m.*
continual [kən'tɪnjuw|əl] *adj.* continuel, ininterrompu. || **continually** [-əlɪ] *adv.* continuellement, sans/interruption, arrêt/. || **continuance** [-əns] *n.* continuation *f,* continuité *f;* durée *f.* || **continuation** [kənˌtɪnjuw'ejʃən] *n.* continuation *f,*

prolongation *f*; durée *f*; suite *f*. || **continue** [kən'tınjuw] *v. tr.* continuer, poursuivre (un travail); perpétuer, prolonger, maintenir. || *v. intr.* continuer (à, de), persister (à), demeurer, durer: *To be continued,* À suivre. || **continuity** [ˌkɑntı'nuwıtı] *n.* continuité *f*; scénario *m*. || **continuous** [kən'tınjuwəs] *adj.* continu. || **continuously** [-lı] *adv.* continûment, sans /cesse, arrêt/.

contortion [kən'tɔɚʃən] *n.* [odd twist] contorsion *f*.

contour ['kɑntuwɚ] *n.* contour *m*.

contraband ['kɑntɹəˌbænd] *n.* [smuggling] contrebande *f*.

contract ['kɑntɹækt] *n.* **1.** contrat *m*, convention *f*, pacte *m*. **2.** [work] entreprise *f* à forfait, soumission *f*. || *v. tr.* [kən'tɹækt] [shrink] resserrer, rétrécir, raccourcir; contracter (un mariage, une maladie), froncer (les sourcils). || *v. intr.* **1.** se contracter, se resserrer, se rétrécir. **2.** traiter, s'engager (à qqch., *for sth.*), soumissionner. || **contractor** [-ɚ] *n.* [work] entrepreneur *m*; adjudicataire *m*.

contradict [ˌkɑntɹə'dık|t] *v. tr.* contredire (qqun), démentir (une rumeur, &c.). || **contradiction** [-ʃən] *n.* contradiction *f*, démenti *m*. || **contradictory** [-tɚı] *adj.* [statement, &c.] contradictoire. || **contrariness** [kən'tɹɛɚı|nəs] *n.* esprit *m* de contradiction. || **contrariwise** [-ˌwajz] *adv.* en sens opposé. || **contrary** ['kɑntɹɚı] *adj.* **1.** contraire, opposé (à, *to*): *on the* ~ , au contraire. **2.** [kən'tɹɛɚı] [perverse] hostile, contrariant. || *n.* contraire *m*, opposé *m*.

contrast ['kɑntɹæst] *n.* contraste *m*. || *v. tr.* [kən'tɹæst] (faire) contraster (qqch. avec qqch., *sth. with sth.*). || *v. intr.* [colour, pattern, &c.] contraster, faire contraste.

contribute [kən'tɹıbjuwt] *v. tr.* [amount] contribuer pour (qqch.), [assistance, &c.] fournir. || *v. intr.* [participate] contribuer (à qqch., *to sth.*), [achievement, success] concourir (à); [newspaper, institution] collaborer (à). || **contribution** [kɑntɹı'bjuwʃən] *n.* contribution *f*, participation *f*, [charities] souscription *f* (à qqch., *to sth.*); [share, bringing] part *f*, apport *m* (dans, *to*); [newspaper, periodical] article *m*, [general] collaboration *f*. || **contributor** [kən'tɹıbjətɚ] *n.* [Lit.] collaborat|eur, -rice (d'une revue, &c., *to a quarterly, journal,* &c.); [charities, &c.] souscripteur *m*.

contrite [kən'tɹajt] *adj.* contrit.

contrition [kən'tɹıʃən] *n.* [regret] contrition *f*; [Rel.] *act of* ~ , acte *m* de contrition.

contrivance [kən'tɹajv|əns] *n.* invention *f*, plan *m*; expédient *m* [gadget] dispositif *m*. || **contrive** *v. tr.* inventer, imaginer, arranger (un plan, &c.). || **contriver** [-ɚ] *n.* [schemer] inventeur *m*, auteur *m*.

control [kən'tɹowl] *n.* autorité *f*, influence *f*, [keeping down] contrainte *f* (sur, *over*); [power] maîtrise *f* (d'une situation, &c.); [check] surveillance *f*, [government, &c.] contrôle *m* (de, *on, over*). || *v. tr.* avoir de l'autorité sur (qqun, qqch.); réprimer (ses impulsions, &c.); maîtriser (qqch.); [check] surveiller, contrôler (qqch.); [regulate] régler (qqch.). || **controller** [-ɚ] *n.* **1.** cf. COMPTROLLER. **2.** appareil *m* de contrôle.

controversial [ˌkɑntɹə'vɚʃıəl] *adj.* → prêtant à controverse.

controversy ['kɑntɹəˌvɚsı] *n.* [debate] controverse *f*.

contumacious [kɑntjuw'mejʃəs] *adj.* [Pers.] rebelle, récalcitrant; [Jur.] contumace. || **contumaciously** [-lı] *adv.* obstinément. || **contumacy** ['kɑntjuwməsı] *n.* [Jur.] contumace *f*.

conundrum [kə'nʌndɹəm] *n.* devinette *f*; énigme *f*.

convalesce [kɑnvə'lɛs] *v. intr.* [Pers.] être en convalescence. || **convalescence** [-əns] *n.* convalescence *f*.

convene [kən'vijn] *v. tr.* [meeting, &c.] convoquer, réunir. || *v. intr.* [people] se réunir, s'assembler.

convenience [-jəns] *n.* commodité *f*, aise *f*; *pl.* confort *m* (moderne): *Please answer at your earliest* ~ , Veuillez répondre /aussitôt, dès/que possible. || **convenient** [-jənt] *adj.* commode, pratique.

convent ['kɑnvənt] *n.* **1.** [nuns] couvent *m*. **2.** pensionnat *m* (pour jeunes filles), couvent *m*.

convention [kən'vɛnʃən] *n.* **1.** [custom] convention *f*: *conventions pl.* l'étiquette *f*, les bienséances *fpl*; [agreement] contrat *m*, accord *m*. **2.** [professional, Pol., &c.] réunion *f*, assemblée *f*, congrès *m*, © convention *f*. || **conventional** [-l̩] *adj.* [customary] conventionnel, de convention; [model, type, brand] classique, traditionnel, ordinaire: ~ *armaments,* des armes classiques.

converge [kən'vɚʤ] *v. intr.* converger.

conversant [kən'vɚsənt] *adj.* [Fam.] versé (dans, *with sth.*), familier (avec un sujet, &c.). || **conversation** [kɑnvɚ'sejʃən] *n.* conversation *f*, entretien *m*: *to carry on a* ~ , faire la conversation. || **conversational** [-l̩] *adj.* de (la) conversation. || **converse** [kən'vɚs] *v. intr.* converser, causer, s'entretenir (avec qqun, *with s.o.*). || *adj.*

['kɑnvɚs] inverse, réciproque. || *n.* **1.** [talk] entretien *m*, conversation *f*. **2.** contrepartie *f*.

conversion [kən'vɚ|ʒən] *n.* conversion *f*. || **convert** [-t] *v. tr.* convertir (*to*, à), changer, transformer. || *n.* ['kɑnvɚt] [Rel.] converti, -e. || **convertible** [kən'-vɚtıbl̩] *adj.* [Pers.] convertissable; [thing] convertible, transformable. || *n.* [car] décapotable *f*.

convex [kɑn'vɛks] *adj.* convexe.

convey [kən'vej] *v. tr.* transporter; transmettre (qqch.); [Fig.] exprimer, présenter (des remerciements, &c.); [Jur.] céder (un titre). || **conveyance** [-əns] *n.* transport *m*, transmission *f*; [Jur.] transfert *m*, cession *f* (d'un titre).

convict ['kɑnvıkt] *n.* condamné, -e, forçat *m*. || *v. tr.* [kən'vık|t] [crime] convaincre (qqun de qqch.); condamner, déclarer (qqun) coupable. || **conviction** [-ʃən] *n.* **1.** [belief] conviction *f*; persuasion *f*. **2.** [law] condamnation *f* (d'un prévenu): *to act from* ~, agir par conviction.

convince [kən'vıns] *v. tr.* convaincre, persuader (qqun de qqch., *s.o. of sth.*). || **convincing** [-ıŋ] *adj.* convaincant.

convivial [kən'vıvıəl] *adj.* → plein d'entrain; où règne la bonne humeur.

convocation [kɑnvə'kejʃən] *n.* convocation *f* (d'une assemblée); [Rel.] assemblée *f*. || **convoke** [kən'vowk] || *v. tr.* [summon] convoquer (une assemblée).

convoy ['kɑnvoj] *n.* convoi *m*, [ship] escorte *f*. || *v. tr.* [protect, accompany] convoyer, escorter (une flotte, &c.).

convulsion [kən'vʌlʃən] *n.* [spasm] convulsion *f*; [Fig., Fam.] *to be in convulsions*, se tordre de rire.

coo [kuw] *n.* roucoulement *m* (de pigeon, colombe). || *v. intr.* [pigeon, dove] roucouler. || **cooing** [-ıŋ] *n.* roucoulement *m*.

cook [kʊk] *n.* [male] cuisinier *m*, [female] cuisinière *f*. || *v. tr.* (faire) cuire (qqch.); faire (le dîner). || *v. intr.* faire la cuisine. || **cookery** [-ɚı] *n.* art *m* culinaire, (la) cuisine *f*: *cook(ery) book*, livre *m* de recettes. || **cookie** [-ı] *n.* biscuit *m*, gâteau sec *m* (Br. *biscuit*): ~ *sheet*, tôle *f* à biscuits. || **cooking** [-ıŋ] *n.* **1.** cuisson *f* (d'une viande). **2.** cf. COOKERY.

cool [kuwl] *adj.* [weather, &c.] frais, [drink] rafraîchissant; [mood] calme, flegmatique; [reception] froid, distant. *It is* ~, Il fait frais; *It is getting cooler*, Le temps se rafraîchit; [Fig.] *to keep* ~, garder son sang-froid. || *n.* (le) frais, (la) fraîcheur. || *v. intr.* [weather, water, &c.] se rafraîchir, (se) refroidir: [Pers.] *to* ~ *down*, se calmer, reprendre son sang-froid; [feeling] *to* ~ *off*, tiédir, se refroidir. || **cooler** [-ɚ] *n.* [device] refroidisseur *m*, [system] réfrigérant *m*; réfrigérateur *m*; garde-manger *m*, © dépense *f*; [US, Sl.] prison *f*. || **cooling** [-ıŋ] *adj.* rafraîchissant, refroidissant. || *n.* rafraîchissement *m*, refroidissement *m*. || **coolness** [-nəs] *n.* [weather] fraîcheur *f*; [disposition] flegme *m*, calme *m*, sang-froid *m*, [reception] froideur *f*.

coon [kuwn] *n.* abr. de **raccoon**; [US, Pej., Sl.] nègre.

coop [kuwp] *n.* poulailler *m*; mue *f*. || *v. tr.*: *to* ~ *up*, claquemurer.

cooper [-ɚ] *n.* tonnelier *m*.

co-operate [kow'ɑpɚˌejt] *v. intr.* [Pers.] collaborer, coopérer (avec qqun à qqch., *with s.o. in sth.*), [thing] contribuer (à, *in*). || **co-operative** [kow'ɑpɚətıv] *adj.* [Com.] coopératif: *to be* ~, faire preuve de bonne volonté. || *n.* [Com.] coopérative *f* (de consommation, &c.).

co-ordinate [kow'ɔɚdın|ˌejt] *v. tr.* coordonner. || *adj.* [-ət] coordonné. || *n.* [Math.] coordonnée *f*.

cop [kɑp] *n.* [Fam.] [Fr.] flic *m*, © (une) police.

cope[1] [kowp] *v. intr.* tenir tête (à qqun, *with s.o.*), être aux prises (avec qqch., *with sth.*); être à la hauteur (d'une tâche).

cope[2] *n.* **1.** [R.C.] chape. **2.** voûte *f*/céleste, des cieux/.

copious ['kowpıəs] *adj.* copieux, abondant.

copper ['kɑpɚ] *n.* **1.** cuivre *m*. **2.** *coppers pl.* petite monnaie, [Fam.] sous *mpl.* || *adj.* de, en/cuivre. || **coppersmith** [-ˌsmıθ] *n.* chaudronnier *m*.

coppice ['kɑpıs] *n.*, **copse** [kɑps] *n.* taillis *m*.

copula ['kɑpjə|lə] *pl.* **copulas**, *n.* [Gram.] copule *f*.

copy ['kɑpı] *n.* [duplicate, imitation] copie *f*, [text, notes] transcription *f*, [letter, document] double *m*; [newspaper] numéro *m*, [book] exemplaire *m*: [assignment, &c.] sujet *m* d'article, copie: *fair* ~, copie *f* au/propre, net/; *rough* ~, brouillon *m*. || *v. tr.* copier, imiter (qqun, qqch.), [painting] reproduire (qqch.); [style, poem] pasticher: *to* ~ *out*, copier, transcrire/qqch. || **copyright** [-ˌɹajt] *n.* droit *m* d'auteur, propriété *f* littéraire.

coquetry [kow'kɛt|ɹı] *n.* [flirt] coquetterie *f*. || **coquette** *n.* coquette *f*. || *v. intr.* flirter (avec qqun, *with s.o.*).

coral ['kɔɚəl] *n.* corail *m*: ~ *reef*, banc *m* de corail. || *adj.* [colour] de corail.

cord [kɔɚd] *n.* [wood, rope, &c.] corde *f*, cordon *m*, ficelle *f*; [Elect.] fil *m*: *spinal* ~, moelle *f* épinière. || *v. tr.* attacher, lier (avec une corde), corder (un paquet, &c.).

cordial [kɔɚdɪəl] *adj.* [hearty] cordial. || *n.* [liqueur, &c.] cordial *m*.

cordon [kɔɚdn̩] *n.* [policemen; ribbon] cordon *m*.

corduroy [ˈkɔɚdɚoj] *n.* velours *m*/à côtes, côtelé/: ~ *road*, © portage ponté, [Fr.] chemin *m* de rondins.

core [kɔɚ] *n.* [wood, argument, question] cœur *m*; [heart] fond *m*; [apple] trognon *m*; [magnet] noyau *m*: *He is Canadian to the* ~, Il est/profondément, foncièrement/canadien. || **core** *v. tr.* [apple, &c.] vider: ~ *out*, enlever le/cœur, noyau/de (qqch.), [corn, &c.] extirper.

cork [kɔɚk] *n.* **1.** liège *m*: ~ *tree*, chêne-liège *m*. **2.** bouchon *m* (de bouteille). || *v. tr.* [bottle] *to* ~ *up*, boucher (une bouteille). || **corkage** [-əʤ] *n.* couvert *m*. cf. COVER. || **corking** [-ɪŋ] *n.* bouchage *m*. || **corkscrew** [-ˌskɹuw] *n.* tire-bouchon *m*. || *adj.* en tire-bouchon.

cormorant [ˈkɔɚmɚənt] *n.* cormoran *m*.

corn [kɔɚn] *n.* **1.** © blé *m* d'Inde, [Fr.] maïs *m*: © ~ *husk*, © épluchette *f* de blé d'Inde. **2.** [Br.] [cereals] grain *m* blé *m*. **3.** [foot] cor *m*, durillon *m*. || *v. tr.* saler (de la viande de bœuf).

corner [ˈkɔɚnɚ] *n.* coin *m*, angle *m*, [nook.] encoignure *f*; [road] virage *m*, tournant *m*: ~ *stone*, pierre *f*/angulaire, d'angle/. || *v. tr.* monopoliser, accaparer (une marchandise, &c.); [Fig.] mettre (qqun) au pied du mur, cerner (qqun).

cornet [kɔɚˈnɛt] *n.* **1.** [nun's] cornette *f*. **2.** [Mus.] cornet *m* (à pistons). **3.** [paper] cornet *m*.

cornfield [ˈkɔɚnˌfijld] *n.* champ *m* de maïs, blé *m* d'Inde; [Br.] champ *m* de blé.

cornice [ˈkɔɚnɪs] *n.* corniche *f*.

cornstarch [ˈkɔɚn|ˌstɑɚʧ] *n.* fécule *f* de maïs.

corny [-ɪ] *adj.* [Fam.] pompier *invar.*

coronation [kɔɚəˈnejʃən] *n.* [ceremony] couronnement *m*.

coroner [ˈkɔɚənɚ] *n.* [law] coroner *m*.

coronet [ˈkɔɚəˌnɛt] *n.* petite couronne, [lady's] diadème *m*.

corporal [ˈkɔɚpɚəl] *adj.* corporel. || *n.* [army] caporal *m* (d'infanterie); [R.C.] corporal *m*.

corporate [ˈkɔɚpɚət] *adj.* organisé, constitué.

corporation [kɔɚpɚˈejʃən] *n.* [trade, &c.] corporation *f*; [law] société *f*, © compagnie *f*; personne/morale, civile/: *The Canadian Broadcasting Corporation*, Radio-Canada.

corps [kɔɚ] *pl.* **corps** [kɔɚz] *n.* [army, diplomatic] corps *m*; groupe *m*, association *f*.

corpse [kɔɚps] *n.* [dead] corps *m*, cadavre *m*, dépouille *f* (mortelle).

corpulence [ˈkɔɚpjələns] *n.* corpulence *f*, embonpoint *m*.

corpus [ˈkɔɚpəs] *n.* [body, collection] corpus *m* (de lois, &c.): [R.C.] *Corpus Christi*, la Fête-Dieu.

corpuscle [ˈkɔɚpəsl] *n.* corpuscule *m*; [blood] globule *m* (rouge, blanc).

corral [kəˈɹæl] *n.* enclos *m*, corral *m*.

correct [kəˈɹɛk|t] *v. tr.* [homework, habit] corriger, [opinion, blunder] rectifier; [s.o.] reprendre, semoncer. || *adj.* [information, data] correct, exact, [answer] juste; [manners, action] bienséant, convenable, de bon goût. || **correction** [-ʃən] *n.* [proofs, homework, error, punishment] correction *f*; [blunder, data] rectification *f*; [punishment] punition *f*. || **correctly** [-tlɪ] *adv.* correctement, exactement, justement; convenablement, comme il faut. || **correctness** [-tnəs] *n.* [manners, &c.] correction *f*, bienséance *f*, convenance *f*; [accuracy] exactitude *f*, justesse *f*. || **corrector** [-tɚ] *n.* [proof, &c.] correct|eur, -rice.

correlate [ˈkɔɚəˈˌlejt] *v. tr.* mettre qqch. en rapport avec, établir un rapport/une relation/(entre, *with*). || **correlated** [-əd] *adj. The two things are not* ~, Il n'y a aucun rapport entre. . . . || **correlation** [kɔɚəˈleiʃən] *n.* relation *f*, corrélation *f*, rapport *m*.

correspond [kɔɚəˈspɑnd] *v. intr.* [agree, write] correspondre (à, avec, *to, with*), s'harmoniser (avec qqch., qqun, *with, to sth., s.o.*). || **correspondence** [-əns] *n.* [agreement, writing] correspondance *f* (à, avec, *to, with*); harmonie *f*, accord *m*. || **correspondent** [-ənt] *n.* correspondant *m*: [journalist] envoyé spécial. || **corresponding** [-ɪŋ] *adj.* correspondant, se rapportant, conforme (à, *to*).

corridor [ˈkɔɚɪdɚ] *n.* corridor *m*, couloir *m*.

corroborate [kəˈɹɑbɚˌejt] *v. tr.* confirmer, corroborer.

corrode [kəˈɹow|d] *v. tr.* [metal] corroder, ronger. || **corrosive** [-sɪv] *adj. & n.* [liquid, &c.] corrosi|f, -ve (*m*).

corrupt [kəˈɹʌp|t] *v. tr.* corrompre. || *v. intr.* se corrompre. || *adj.* corrompu. || **corruption** [-ʃən] *n.* corruption *f*.

corsage [kɔɚ'sɑʤ] *n.* bouquet *m* de corsage.
corset ['kɔɚsət] *n.* corset *m*: ~ *bone*, baleine *f* de corset.
cortege ['kɔɚˌtɛʒ] *n.* cortège *m.*
corvette [kɔɚ'vɛt] *n.* [warship] corvette *f.*
cosmetics [kɑs'mɛtɪks] *n.pl.* cosmétique(s) *f(pl).*
cosmic ['kɑzmɪk] *adj.* cosmique.
cosmopolitan [kɑsmə'pɑlɪtn̩] *adj.* cosmopolite.
cost [kɑst] *n.* coût *m* (d'une marchandise, &c.), prix *m* (d'un article); [expense(s)] frais *mpl*: *the ~ of living*, le coût de la vie; *at ~ price*, au prix coûtant; *at the ~ of*, au prix de; *at any ~*, *at all costs*, à tout prix; [Fig.] *to my ~*, à mes dépens. || *v. intr.* coûter. || *v. tr.* [Com.] évaluer le prix (d'un ouvrage, &c.); établir le prix de revient de (qqch.). || **costly** [-lɪ] *adj.* coûteux; précieux, de grand prix.
costume ['kɑstjuwm] *n.* costume *m*: ~ *ball*, bal *m* costumé. || *v. tr.* [stage] costumer (qqun). || **costumer** [-ɚ] *n.* [US] costumier *m.*
cosy ['kowzɪ] *adj.* [choses] douillet, intime.
cot[1] [kɑt] *n.* [baby] couchette *f*; [folding] lit *m*/de camp, pliant/.
cot[2] *n.* abri *m*; chaumière *f.*
cottage ['kɑtəʤ] *n.* **1.** villa *f* (à la campagne, &c.); © chalet *m*, camp *m.* **2.** [Br.] chaumière *f.*
cotton ['kɑtn̩] *n.* [fiber, cloth] coton *m*: ~ *plant*, ~ *tree*, cotonnier *m*; *absorbent* ~, coton hydrophile; *printed* ~, indienne *f.* || *v. intr.* [Fam.] éprouver de la sympathie (pour qqun, *to s.o.*); se lier d'amitié (avec qqun, *to s.o.*).
couch [kawʧ] *n.* sofa *m*, canapé *m*, divan *m*; lit *m* (pour une personne). || *v. tr.* [express] rédiger, exprimer.
cough [kɔf] *n.* toux *f.* || *v. intr.* tousser.
could cf. CAN[1]. || **couldn't** ['kʊdn̩t] = could not. cf. CAN[1].
council ['kawnsəl] *n.* **1.** conseil *m*: © [government] *Privy Council*, Conseil privé; *Legislative Council*, © Conseil législatif. || **2.** [church] concile *m.* || **councillor** [-ɚ]: *City ~*, conseiller municipal, † © échevin *m.*
counsel ['kawnsəl] *n.* **1.** conseil *m*; délibération *f.* **2.** secret *m*, dessein (secret): *to keep one's own ~*, garder le secret. **3.** [law] (avocat-) conseil *m*: *Queen's*, *King's*/ ~, conseil *m*/de la reine, du roi/. cf. COUNCIL. || *v. tr.* conseiller (qqun sur qqch.). || **counsellor** [-ɚ] *n.* conseiller; [law] avocat. cf. COUNCILLOR.

count[1] [kawnt] *n.* compte *m*, total *m*, addition *f*; dépouillement *m* (des votes); dénombrement *m* (de la population). [Jur.] chef *m* d'accusation: *to keep ~ (of sth.)*, compter, tenir le compte (de)/qqch.; *to lose ~*, perdre/le compte, [Fig.] la notion/(de qqch.). || *v. tr.* compter, dénombrer; calculer; dépouiller (un scrutin): *to ~ one's chickens before they are hatched*, [Prov.] vendre la peau de l'ours avant de l'avoir tué. || *v. intr.* compter (parmi) être au nombre de; [Fig.] avoir de l'importance: *to ~ on s.o.*, compter sur qqun (pour faire qqch.); *to ~ on doing sth.*, compter faire qqch. || **count in** [-'ɪn] *v. tr.* comprendre, compter. || **count out** [-'awt] *v. tr.* compter (un à un): *You can ~ me out*, Ne comptez pas sur moi.
count[2] *n.* [title] comte *m* [☞ fem. **countess**].
countenance ['kawntənəns] *n.* **1.** [face] air *m*, mine *f*; physionomie *f*: *His ~ fell*, → La consternation se peignit sur son visage. **2.** [support] appui *m*, encouragement *m.* **3.** sérieux *m*, calme *m*: *to keep one's ~*, garder son sérieux; *to put s.o. out of ~*, → déconcerter qqun, embarrasser qqun. || *v. tr.* appuyer, favoriser (un projet, &c.).
counter[1] ['kawntɚ] *n.* **1.** [piece of metal] jeton *m*; [shop] comptoir *m*, [large store] rayon *m*; [exhibition] stand; [open air ground] kiosque *m.* **2.** [Pers.] compteur *m.*
counter[2] *adj.* contraire, opposé (à, *to*). || *adv.* contrairement (à, *to*); en sens inverse (de). || *v. tr.* opposer à, rétorquer: [Loc.] *to run ~ to*, aller à l'encontre de.
counter- *Préf.* indiquant l'opposition, la correspondance, et correspondant au français *contre-*: || **counteract** [-'ækt] *v. tr.* contrebalancer, neutraliser (une influence). || **counterattack** [-ə'tæk] *n.* contre-attaque *f.* || *v. intr.* contre-attaquer. || **counterclockwise** [ˌkawntɚ'klɑkˌwajz] *adj. & adv.* à l'inverse des aiguilles d'une montre. || **counterfeit** [-fət] *n.* contrefaçon *f*; [coin] fausse monnaie *f*, faux billet *m.* || *adj.* faux, imité. || *v. tr.* imiter, fabriquer (de la fausse monnaie). || **countermand** [-'mænd] *n.* contre-ordre *m.* || *v. tr.* contremander. || **counterpart** [-ˌpɑɚt] *n.* contrepartie *f*, pendant *m.* || **counterpoise** [-ˌpojz] *n.* contrepoids *m.* || *v. tr.* faire contrepoids à, contrebalancer, compenser.
countess ['kawntəs] *n.* comtesse *f.*
counting-house ['kawnt|ɪŋˌhaws] *n.* [business] comptoir *m*, caisse *f*, bureau(x)

m(pl). || **countless** [-ləs] *adj.* innombrable.

country ['kʌntɹɪ] *n.* **1.** pays *m*, région *f*, contrée *f*: *The Old Country*, la Mère Patrie, © les Vieux Pays. **2.** [rural districts] (la) campagne; [Fr.] (la) province (par opposition à Paris, la capitale), *in the* ~, à la campagne; *across* ~, à travers champs. || *adj.* de la campagne, champêtre, paysan, rural: ~ *club*, club *m* champêtre. || **country|man, -woman** [-mən] [-ˌwʊmən] *n.* **1.** (con)-citoyen *m*, -ne *f*, compatriote *m/f*. **2.** campagnard, -e.

county ['kawntɪ] *n.* comté *m*: *Argenteuil County*, comté d'Argenteuil: ~ *line*, limite *f*/de, du/comté.

coupé [kuw'pej] *n.* [Auto., carriage] coupé *m*.

couple ['kʌpl̩] *n.* [number, animals, persons] couple *m*; ménage *m* (d'époux): *We spent a* ~ *of days in Montreal*, Nous avons passé/deux, © une couple de/jours à Montréal. || *v. tr.* (ac)coupler (des animaux, des objets), mettre (deux personnes, choses) ensemble; associer (deux idées, &c.); joindre, unir (deux personnes, choses). || **coupling** [-ɪŋ] *n.* accouplement *m*.

coupon ['kuwpɑn] *n.* [Fin.] coupon *m*; [Com.] bon *m* (-prime): *ration* ~, ticket *m* de rationnement.

courage ['kɚədʒ] *n.* courage *m*. || **courageous** [kɚ'ejdʒəs] *adj.* courageux.

courier ['kɚɪɚ] *n.* courrier *m*; [travel] guide *m*, cicerone *m*.

course [kɔɚs] *n.* [river, events, education] cours *m*, courant *m*, marche *f* (des affaires); route *f*, direction *f*: *In the* ~ *of*, au cours de, *In due* ~, en temps utile, après quelque temps; *to take its* ~, suivre son cours; [Sch.] *to take a* ~, suivre un cours; [Naut.] *to set a* ~ *for*, mettre le cap sur; *of* ~, naturellement, bien sûr; *a matter of* ~, une chose qui va sans dire. **2.** plat *m*, service *m* (d'un repas). **3.** terrain *m* (de course, de golf). || *v. tr.* [race] faire courir (un animal). || *v. intr.* [blood, water] †courir, circuler, couler.

court [kɔɚt] *n.* Cour *f* (royale); [law] cour *f*, tribunal *m*.; [Sport] court *m* (de tennis): *to have a friend at* ~, avoir un ami/en haut lieu, influent/; ~ *day*, jour *m* d'audience; ~*house*, palais *m* de justice; ~ *-martial*, conseil *m* de guerre. || *v. tr.* courtiser (une femme), fréquenter (une jeune fille), faire la cour (à qqun); aller au devant de (la mort, &c.). || **courteous** ['kɚtɪəs] *adj.* poli, courtois (envers qqun, *to*). || **courtesy** ['kɚtəsɪ] *n.* courtoisie *f*, politesse *f*: ~ *of Eaton's*, gracieuseté *f* de (la maison) Eaton; *This soap is a* ~ *of XYZ*, Ce savon vous est offert par XYZ. || **courtship** ['kɔɚt|ˌʃɪp] *n.* [woo] → faire la cour à . . . .

courtyard [-ˌjɑɚd] *n.* cour *f* (d'une maison).

cousin ['kʌzn̩] *n.* cousin *m*, cousine *f*: *first* ~, cousin(e) germain(e) *m/f*; *second* ~, cousin(e) issu(e) de germain.

cove [kowv] *n.* [bay] anse *f*, crique *f*.

covenant ['kʌvənənt] *n.* convention *f*, pacte *m*; [Bible] alliance *f*; [Hist.] le pacte (de la SDN).

cover ['kʌvɚ] *n.* couverture *f*: *He read the book from* ~ *to* ~, Il a lu le livre de la première page à la dernière; *covers pl.* cf. BEDCOVERS; couvercle *m* (de marmite); [letter, &c.] enveloppe *f*: *slip* ~, housse *f*; [postage] emballage *m*, pli *m*: *You will find under separate . . .* , Je vous envoie, sous pli séparé, . . . ; [Fig.] abri *m*, voile *m*, masque *m*: *to take* ~, se mettre à l'abri; *under* ~ *of darkness*, sous le couvert de la nuit; [restaurant] ~ *charge*, couvert *m*. || *v. tr.* couvrir (qqun, qqch.); [distance] parcourir, franchir; [facts, problem] comprendre, embrasser; [journalist] faire le reportage (d'un événement); défrayer (des dépenses); [scandal, &c.] *to* ~ *up* (*sth.*), dissimuler, cacher (qqch.); *covering letter*, lettre *f* d'accompagnement. || **coverage** ['kʌvɹədʒ] *n.* **1.** [radio, television, publicity, &c.] rayonnement *m*, champ *m* d'application, extension *f*, rayon *m* d'action; [action, newspaper, review, idea] portée *f*, diffusion *f*; [especially radio & television] (ampleur *f* du) public *m* atteint. **2.** [assurance] garantie *f*, protection *f*. **3.** [space] compte-rendu *m* (d'un événement *m*); variété *f*, diversité *f*/des informations.

covert ['kʌvɚt] *adj.* caché; [Fig.] secret: ~ *glance*, regard *m* dérobé.

covet ['kʌvət] *v. tr.* convoiter, désirer. || **covetous** [-əs] *adj.* avide, cupide.

cow[1] [kaw] *n.* vache *f*; femelle *f* (d'un phoque, d'un éléphant, &c.): *When the cows come home*, À Pâques ou à la Trinité, dans la semaine des/(Fr.) quatre, © trois/jeudis.

cow[2] [kɑw] *v. tr.* intimider, subjuguer.

coward [kawɚd] *n. & adj.* lâche (*m/f*), poltron, -ne: peureu|x, -se. || **cowardice** [-ɪs] *n.* couardise *f*, lâcheté *f*. || **cowardly** [-lɪ] *adv.* lâchement, en lâche, peureusement. || *adj.* [person, action] lâche.

cowbird [ˈkaw|ˌbɚd] *n.* vacher *m*, © étourneau *m*.
cowboy [-ˌboj] *n.* vacher *m*, cowboy *m*.
cower [ˈkawɚ] *v. intr.* se cacher, se tapir; reculer en tremblant.
cowl [kawl] *n.* capuchon *m*.
cowlick [ˈkaw|ˌlɪk] *n.* épi *m* de cheveux.
cowslip [-ˌslɪp] *n.* [flower] souci *m* des marais; [Br.] coucou *m*, primevère *f*.
coy [koj] *adj.* timide, réservé.
coyote [ˌkajowt] *n.* coyote *m*.
cozen [ˈkʌzn̩] *v. tr.* duper, tromper (qqun).
CPR [ˌsijˌpijˈɑɚ] [= Canadian Pacific Railway] le Pacifique-Canadien.
crab[1] [kɹæb] *n.* [shellfish] crabe *m*; cancre *m*.
crab[2] *n.* ~ *apple*, pomme *f* sauvage, © pommette *f*: ~ *tree*, pommier *m* sauvage, © pommetier *m*. || **crabbed [-d]** *adj.* **1.** [person] revêche, acariâtre, maussade. **2.** [handwriting, &c.] indéchiffrable, illisible.
crack [kɹæk] *n.* craquement *m* (des branches); coup *m* de feu, détonation (de fusil); fissure *f*, fente *f* (dans les rochers); crevasse *f*, gerçure *f* (de la peau). || *adj.* [Fam.] [regiment, &c.] d'élite, valeureux. || *v. tr.* [one's fingers] faire craquer; [whip] faire claquer; [china] fêler, fendiller; [wall] lézarder, crevasser; lancer (une plaisanterie). || *v. intr.* [branches, &c.] craquer; [whip] claquer; [rifle] éclater, péter; [china] se fêler, se fendiller; [skin] se gercer; [wall] se crevasser; [voice] muer (à la puberté). || **cracked** [-t] *adj.* fendu, crevassé; [pots, china] fêlé, fendillé; [wall] lézardé; [Fam.] [person] timbré, toqué. || **cracker** [-ɚ] *n.* [firework] pétard *m*; [boaster] vantard *m*; © biscuit *m* soda *inv.*; [Fr.] craquelin *m*. || **crackle** [-l̩] *v. intr.* [feu] pétiller; [paper, &c.] craqueter. || **crackling** [-lɪŋ] *n.* **1.** crépitement *m* (de la flamme, des buissons); pétillement *m* (de la flamme); craquètement *m* (du papier, &c.); craquèlement *m* (de la porcelaine, faïence). **2.** [pork] croquant *m*.
cradle [ˈkɹejdl̩] *n.* [baby's] berceau *m*. || *v. tr.* coucher (un enfant) dans un berceau; bercer (un enfant).
craft [kɹæft] *n.* **1.** métier *m*. **2.** habileté *f*; [Fam.] ruse *f*, fourberie *f*. **3.** [ship] bâtiment *m*, unité *f* (navale); [airplane] appareil *m*, cf. AIRCRAFT. || **craftsman** [-smən] *n.* artisan *m*, ouvrier *m*, homme *m* de métier. || **crafty** [-ɪ] *adj.* [person] rusé, roublard, astucieux.
crag [kɹæg] *n.* roc *m* abrupt, rocher *m*/escarpé, à pic/; pointe *f* de rocher.
cram [kɹæm] *v. tr.* **[-mm-]** remplir (qqch. de, *sth. with*), [room, &c.] encombrer; [Fig.] bourrer (le crâne), gorger (qqun de nourriture, *s.o. with food*). || **cramming** [-ɪŋ] *n.* [Fig.] bourrage *m* de crâne (à la veille des examens).
cramp [kɹæmp] *n.* crampe *f*, colique *f*. || *v. intr.* cramponner, restreindre, gêner. || **cramped** [-t] *adj.* [movement] gêné; [style] étriqué; [person] mal à l'aise.
cranberry [ˌkɹænˌbɛəɪ] *n.* canneberge *f*; © atoca *m*: ~ *shrub*, viorne d'Amérique; [Pop.] pimbina *m*.
crane [kɹejn] *n.* [bird, machine] grue *f*: *whooping* ~, grue blanche d'Amérique. || *v. intr.* tendre, allonger (le cou).
crank [kɹæŋk] *n.* manivelle *f* (d'auto); [idea] marotte *f*; [person] maniaque *m/f*, original *m*; [ship, person] instable. || *v. tr.* [car] *to* ~, faire partir/démarrer à la manivelle.
crankiness [-ɪnəs] *n.* humeur *f* capricieuse, irritabilité *f*; [ship] instabilité *f*.
crankshaft [-ˌʃæft] *n.* [car] vilebrequin *m*.
cranky [-ɪ] *adj.* capricieux, irritable.
cranny [ˈkɹænɪ] *n.* fente *f*, fissure *f*; [wall] lézarde *f*: *In every nook and* ~, Dans tous les coins et recoins.
crape [kɹejp] *n.* crêpe *m* (noir); ~ *band*, brassard *m* (de deuil).
crash [kɹæʃ] *n.* **1.** [noise] fracas *m*; écrasement *m*, chute *f* (d'un avion): ~ *landing*, atterrissage *m* forcé (sur un espace réduit); collision (de véhicules, &c.), accident *m*; catastrophe *f*; krach *m* (de Bourse): ~ *programme*, programme *m* d'urgence. **2.** (grosse) toile *f* (à serviettes, &c.). || *v. intr.* [noise] retentir, éclater; [cars] entrer en collision; [airplane] s'abattre, s'écraser (sur le sol, *down*). || *v. tr.* fracasser (qqch.).
crate [kɹejt] *n.* [box] cageot *m*; harasse *f*; mannequin *m*. || *v. tr.* [fruit, &c.] emballer (qqch. dans un cageot, &c.).
crater [ˈkɹejtɚ] *n.* [volcano] cratère *m*; *shell* ~, entonnoir *m*, cratère *m*.
cravat [kɹəˈvæt] *n.* **1.** cravate *f*. **2.** foulard *m*.
crave [kɹejv] *v. intr.* être avide, affamé (de qqch., *for sth.*); [Fig.] soupirer (après qqun, *for s.o.*). || *v. tr.* [s.o.'s pardon] implorer (qqch.); [the attention of the audience] solliciter (qqch.). || **craving [-ɪŋ]** *n.* (vif) désir (de, *for*): *to have a* ~ *for praise*, être assoiffé de louanges; ~ *for alcohol*, passion (*f*) de l'alcool.
crawfish [ˈkɹɔˌfɪʃ] *n.* cf. CRAYFISH.
crawl [kɹɔl] *v. intr.* [snake, &c.] ramper, glisser; [people, baby] se traîner; [rats

mice, &c.] grouiller (de, *with*); *He crawled to the other side of the road*, → Il gagna en rampant l'autre côté de la route. || *n.* [reptile] rampement *m*; [person] mouvement *m* traînant; [swimming] crawl *m*.

crayfish [ˈkɹejˌfɪʃ] *n.* **1.** [fresh-water] écrevisse *f*. **2.** [sea] langouste *f*.

crayon [ˈkɹejən] *n.* **1.** crayon *m* (de couleur, pastel); fusain *m*. **2.** crayon de couleur, fusain *m*. || *v. tr.* dessiner (qqch.) au pastel, crayon de couleur, fusain.

craze [kɹejz] *n.* [Fig.] manie *f*, engouement *m*, toquade *f* (de qqch., *for sth.*). || *v. tr.* (employé surtout au participe passé) *The poor fellow was half-crazed by fear*, Le pauvre homme était/à demi-fou de peur, → affolé par la peur/.

crazy [-ɪ] *adj.* [person, mind] fou, dérangé; [building, furniture, &c.] en mauvais état, croulant, branlant; *to go* ~ (*with*), devenir fou (de); *to drive s.o.* ~, rendre qqun fou; *to be* ~ *about*, raffoler de (qqch.), être fou de (qqun).

creak [kɹijk] *v. intr.* [door, wheel, &c.] grincer, crier; [shoes] craquer. || *n.* grincement *m* (d'une porte, &c.); craquement *m* (de souliers, &c.).

cream [kɹijm] *n.* crème *f*:|*whipped* ~, crème *f* fouettée; ~ *cheese*, fromage *m* à la crème; *hair* ~, cosmétique *m*; *shaving* ~, crème à/raser, barbe. || *adj.* café *m* au lait; crème *inv.* || *v. tr.* écrémer (le lait). || *v. intr.* [milk, &c.] crémer &c.; [beer] mousser. || **creamery** [-əɹɪ] *n.* crémerie *f*. || **creamy** [-ɪ] *adj.* crémeux.

crease [kɹijs] *n.* [clothes] pli *m*, faux pli. || *v. tr.* [clothes] plisser, faire/un pli, des plis/à (un pantalon, &c.); [dress, &c.] froisser, friper. || *v. intr.* [clothes] se plisser; [trousers, &c.] prendre un faux pli; [dress] se froisser, se friper.

create [ˌkɹijˈej|t] *v. tr.* créer (qqch.); [trouble] causer, engendrer, faire naître; [impression] produire; [fashion] lancer. || **creation** [-ʃən] *n.* [act, world, creatures, fashion] création *f*; [product] création *f*, œuvre *f*; produit *m*. || **creative** [-tɪv] *adj.* [esprit] créateur: ~ *writing*, création *f* littéraire. || **creator** [-tɚ] *n.* créateur *m*: *The Creator*, le Créateur, Dieu. || **creature** [ˈkɹijtʃɚ] *n.* créature *f*, être *m* (vivant); animal *m*.

creche [kɹɛʃ] *n.* crèche *f*; hospice *m* des enfants trouvés.

credence [ˈkɹijdəns] *n.* **1.** créance *f*, foi *f*, croyance *f*. **2.** [church] ~ (*table*), crédence *f*.

credentials [kɹəˈdɛnʃəls] *n.pl.* [testimonial] lettres *fpl* de créance; [license, &c.] papiers *mpl*, pièces *fpl* d'identité.

credible [ˈkɹɛdɪbl̩] *adj.* [person] digne de/créance, foi/; [story, &c.] croyable. || **credibly** [-ɪ] *adv.* de manière digne de/créance, foi/: *We are* ~ *informed* (*that*) . . . , → Nous savons de bonne source (que . . .).

credit [ˈkɹɛdɪt] *n.* foi *f*, créance *f*, croyance *f* (à qqch., *to sth.*); réputation *f*, influence *f*, crédit *m* (auprès de qqun, *with s.o.*); honneur *m*, mérite *m*; [Com.] crédit *m*, avoir *m*: ~ *card*, carte *f* de crédit: *to take* (*the*) ~ *for sth.*, s'attribuer le mérite de qqch.; *It does him* ~, Cela lui fait honneur; *to be a* ~ *to*, faire honneur à; *to give s.o.* ~ *for sth.*, rendre hommage à qqun de qqch.; *I gave him* ~ *for more sense*, → Je lui croyais plus de bon sens; [Com.] *on* ~, à crédit; *on the* ~ *side*, à l'actif. || *v. tr.* ajouter foi à (qqch.), accorder créance à (une nouvelle); attribuer, prêter (un pouvoir à qqun, *s.o. with a power*), reconnaître (une qualité à qqun, *s.o. with a quality*); [Com.] créditer (qqun d'une somme, *s.o. with a sum*). || **creditable** [-əbl̩] *adj.* [person] estimable; [praiseworthy] honorable. || **creditor** [-ɚ] *n.* créanci|er, -ère. || *adj.* [book-keeping] compte créditeur.

credulous [ˈkɹɛdjələs] *adj.* [person] crédule, naïf.

Cree [kɹij] *n. & adj.* [Amerindian language, tribe] cris.

creed [kɹijd] *n.* **1.** [religious] (profession *f* de) foi *f*, croyance *f*: *the* (*Apostles'*) *Creed*, le/Symbole des Apôtres, Credo/; *the Nicene Creed*, Le Symbole de Nicée.

creek [kɹijk] *n.* ruisseau *m*; [Br.] [little bay] crique *f*, anse *f*.

creel [kɹijl] *n.* panier *m* de pêche.

creep [kɹijp] **crept** [kɹɛpt] **crept** *v. intr.* [crawl] ramper, [baby] se glisser, se traîner; [plant] grimper: [Fig.] *to* ~ *in*, s'insinuer, s'installer doucement; *to* ~ *on*, cheminer, [Fig.] venir, avancer/à pas lents. || *n.* rampement *m*, grimpement *m*, cheminement *m*: *pl.* (*the*) *creeps*, [Fig.] (la) chair de poule. || **creeping** [-ɪŋ] *n.* cf. CREEP *n.* || **crept** cf. CREEP.

crescent [ˈkɹɛsənt] *n.* [moon, &c.] croissant *m*. || *adj.* en forme de/croissant, demi-lune/.

cress [kɹɛs] *n.* [plant] cresson *m*.

crest [kɹɛst] *n.* **1.** [rooster; wave; hill] crête *f*, [bird] huppe *f*, houppe *f*, [peacock] aigrette *f*, [wave, hill, &c.] sommet *m*. **2.** [coat of arms] armoiries *fpl*, écusson *m*. **3.** [helmet] cimier *m*. || *v. tr.* [Fig.] surmonter (qqch.). || **crestfallen** [-ˌfɔln̩] *adj.* [Pers.] abattu, [disconcerted] démonté; [look] penaud.

crevice [ˈkɹɛvɪs] *n.* [earth] crevasse *f*; [wall] lézarde *f*, [rock] fissure *f*, fente *f*.

crew [kɹuw] *n.* [ship, aircraft] (les membres *mpl* de l')équipage *m*, [aircraft] personnel *m* navigant; [ext.] équipe *f*. || **crewcut** [-ˌkʌt] *n.* cheveux *mpl* en brosse.

crib [kɹɪb] *n.* **1.** (petite) couchette *f* (de bébé); [cows, horses, &c.] mangeoire *f*, râtelier *m*, crèche *f*. **2.** plagiat *m* (d'un auteur, d'une œuvre); [Pej., Sch.] copie *f* (de notes, d'un corrigé). || *v. tr.* **[-bb-]** plagier (un auteur, une œuvre, *from*); [Pej., Sch.] copier (des notes, un corrigé). **2.** [Fig.] emmurer (qqun).

cricket[1] [ˈkɹɪkət] *n.* [insect] grillon *m*, © criquet *m*.

cricket[2] *n.* [Sport] cricket *m*.

crime [kɹajm] *n.* crime *m*, délit *m*, contravention *f*, infraction *f* pénale. || **criminal** [ˈkɹɪmɪnl̩] *n.* & *adj.* criminel *m*, coupable *m*: *criminal lawyer*, avocat *m* d'assises.

crimp [kɹɪmp] *n.* [stuff, &c.] gaufrage *m*, pli *m*; [hair] frisure *f*, crêpage *m*. || *v. tr.* gaufrer, friser, crêper; [shoe] emboutir (une empeigne). || **crimping** [-ɪŋ] *n.* [stuff] gaufrage *m*, plissement *m*, [hair] frisage *m*, crêpage *m*; [shoe] emboutissage *m*.

crimson [ˈkɹɪmzən] *n.* & *adj.* cramoisi, (*m*): [Fig.] *She turned* ~, Elle rougit, Elle devint/pourpre, toute cramoisie/.

cringe [kɹindʒ] *v. intr.* **1.** se dérober (à un coup). **2.** ramper. || **cringing** [-ɪŋ] *adj.* **1.** [gesture] craintif. **2.** [Pers.] servile, obséquieux.

crinkle [ˈkɹɪŋkl̩] *v. intr.* onduler, se rider. || *v. tr.* plisser, froisser.

cripple [ˈkɹɪpl̩] *n.* infirme *m*/*f*, estropié, -e; boiteu|x, -se. || *v. tr.* estropier (qqun), rendre (qqun) infirme; [Fig.] paralyser (des efforts, &c.).

crisis [ˈkɹajs|ɪs] *pl.* **crises** [-ijz] *n.* crise *f*.

crisp [kɹɪsp] *adj.* [food] croustillant; [brittle] cassant; [air] vif, piquant; [hair] crépu; [answer] tranchant. || *n.* *potato crisps*, [Fr.] pommes *fpl*/chips, pailles/.

criterion *pl.* **criteria** [kɹajˈtijɚə|n] *n.* critérium *m*, critère *m*; [Fam.] pierre *f* de touche.

critic [ˈkɹɪtɪk] *n.* [Lit., Mus.] critique *m*; [Pej.] critiqueur *m*. || **critical** [-l̩] *adj.* [Lit., &c.] critique; [point, situation, &c.] dangereux. || **critically** [-l̩ɪ] *adv.*/avec, en/ critique; [ill] dangereusement. || **criticism** [ˈkɹɪtɪ|sɪzm] *n.* critique *f*, jugement *m* (défavorable ou favorable) sur (qqun, qqch.). || **criticize** [-ˌsajz] *v. tr.* critiquer (qqun, qqch.), porter un jugement (favorable ou défavorable) sur; blâmer.

croak [kɹowk] *n.* [frog] coassement *m*; [raven] croassement *m*. || *v. intr.* [frog] coasser; [raven] croasser.

crochet [ˈkɹowʃej] *n.* **1.** crochet *m*. **2.** ouvrage *m*, dentelle *f*/au crochet. || *v. intr.* faire du crochet. || *v. tr.* faire (qqch.) au crochet.

crock [kɹɑk] *n.* **1.** cruche *f*; marmite *f*; pot *m* (de terre). || **crockery** [-ɚɪ] *n.* faïence *f*, poterie *f*.

crocodile [ˈkɹɑkəˌdajl] *n.* crocodile *m*: [Fig.] ~ *tears*, larmes *fpl* de/crocodile, commande/.

crony [ˈkɹownɪ] *n.* ami intime, vieil ami; [Fam.] un vieux copain, une vieille copine, [Fr.] un pote, © un chum.

crook [kɹʊk] *n.* **1.** croc *m*, crochet *m*; houlette *f* (de berger): *by hook or by* ~, coûte que coûte; ~ *of the arm*, pli *m* du bras. **2.** angle *m*, courbure *f*; détour *m*, coude *m* (d'une rivière, d'un sentier). 3. escroc *m*; chevalier *m* d'industrie. || **crook** *v. tr.* courber, recourber. || **crooked** [-əd] *adj.* **1.** courbé (en crosse); [nose] crochu, [handle, horns] recourbé; [wood, limbs] tors; [body] difforme; [hat, tie] de travers; [Fig., reasoning] tortu. **2.** [Pers., behaviour] tortueu|x, -se; malhonnête: ~ *counsels*, conseils *mpl* pervers; ~ *means*, moyens *mpl* obliques, détours *mpl*. || **crookedness** [-ədnəs] *n.* **1.** sinuosité *f* (d'un sentier). **2.** perversité *f* (de conduite). **3.** difformité *f* (d'un corps); [Fig.] © croche.

croon [kɹuwn] *v. intr.* chantonner. || **crooner** [-ɚ] *n.* chanteur *m* de charme.

crop [kɹɑp] *n.* [wheat, &c.] récolte *f*, moisson *f*, manche *m* (d'un fouet); jabot *m* (d'un oiseau); coupe *f*, tonte *f* (de cheveux): ~ *year*, campagne *f* agricole; *bumper* ~, récolte *f* exceptionnelle. || *v. tr.* **[-pp-]** [hair] couper, tondre; [hedge] tailler ras; [sheep, &c.] brouter (l'herbe). || *v. intr.* [field] donner une récolte; *to* ~ *up*, venir sur le tapis, surgir. || **cropper** [-ɚ] *n.* [Br.] *to come a* ~, faire faillite, se flanquer par terre, © faire patate. || **cropping** [-ɪŋ] *n.* coupe *f* (de cheveux, &c.); taille *f* (d'une haie, &c.); tonte *f* (de la laine); fauchage *m* (des foins, &c.); [animals] action *f* de brouter.

crosier [ˈkɹowʒɚ] *n.* [Rel.] crosse *f* (d'un évêque).

cross [kɹɑs] *n.* croix *f*: *the/Stations, Way of the Cross/*, le Chemin de la Croix; [genetics] croisement *m*, mélange *m* (de races); croisée *f* (des chemins); [Fig.] contrariété *f*: [person] ~ *-armed*, les bras croisés; *crossbeam*, traverse *f*; ~ *-bred* [animal, person], métis, -se, de sang mêlé; ~ *breed*, race croisée; ~ *-breeding*, métissage *m*, croisement *m* (de races); ~ *cut*, raccourci *m*, (chemin *m* de) traverse *f*; ~ *-examination*, contre-interrogatoire *m*; [person] ~ *-eyed*, qui louche; ~ *fire*, feu croisé; ~ *-grained*, (bois *m*) aux fibres irrégulières; ~ *-hatching*, contre-hachure *f*; ~ *-legged*, les jambes croisées; ~ *purpose*, but *m* contraire, contradiction *f*; ~ *-reference*, renvoi *m*; ~ *section*, coupe *f* transversale; ~ *-shaped*, en forme de croix. || *adj.* [person] maussade, fâché, de /mauvaise, méchante/humeur; [road, &c.] transversal; [answer, &c.] contrariant, contraire, opposé; *to be as* ~ *as two sticks*, être/de mauvais poil, d'une humeur massacrante/. || *v. tr.* croiser (deux bâtons, &c.); marquer (un mot, nom, &c.) d'une croix; mettre les barres à (ses t); franchir (le désert, l'océan), traverser (la rue, l'océan); *to* ~ *o.s.*, se signer; [Fig.] contrarier (qqun), contrecarrer (l'opinion de qqun). || **crossbar** [-ˌbɑɚ] *n.* traverse *f*; [football] barre *f* de but. || **crosse** *n.* cf. LACROSSE. || **cross-examine** [-ɪg'zæmɪn] *v. tr.* [law] contre-examiner (qqun), soumettre (qqun) à un contre interrogatoire. || *v. intr.* traverser, passer; [letters] se croiser. || **crossing** [-ɪŋ] *n.* croisement *m* (de lignes), rencontre *f*, intersection *f* (de voies); traversée *f* (de la rue, de l'océan): *level* ~, passage *m* à niveau; *Cattle* ~, Passage *m* de troupeaux, Attention aux troupeaux! || **cross-out** [-ˌawt] *v. tr.* biffer. || **crosspiece** [-ˌpijs] *n.* traverse *f*, entretoise *f*. || **crossroad** [-ˌɹowd] *n.* chemin *m* de traverse. || **crossroads** [-ˌɹowdz] *n.* intersection *f*. || **crosswise** [-ˌwajz] *adv.* en (forme de) croix, en travers; [band, ribbon] en sautoir. || **crossword** [-ˌwɚd] *n.* ~ *puzzle*, mots croisés. *pl.* [also crosswords].

crouch [kɹawtʃ] *v. intr.* s'accroupir, [dog] se tapir.

croup [kɹuwp] *n.* **1.** croupe *f* (d'un cheval). **2.** [disease] croup *m*.

crow[1] [kɹow] *n.* corneille *f*: *duck* ~, cormoran *m*: *as the* ~ *flies*, à vol d'oiseau; *crowbar*, pince *f* (à levier): [Fig.] *to eat* ~, venir à Canossa.

crow[2] *v. intr.* [rooster] chanter, pousser un cocorico; [baby] crier de joie; [Fig.] chanter victoire (sur, *over*).

crowd [kɹawd] *n.* foule *f* (de gens, de choses), [people] rassemblement *m*, affluence *f*. || *v. intr.* [people] *to* ~ (*in*), s'entasser, se presser en foule. || *v. tr.* [people] entasser, [things] serrer, [room, hall] remplir. || **crowded** [-əd] *adj.* [bus, &c.] bondé, encombré, [room, hall, &c.] plein à craquer.

crown [kɹawn] *n.* [king's, queen's, tooth, coin] couronne *f*, [Pol.] (la) Couronne *f*: © *Crown attorney*, procureur *m* de la Couronne; [head] sommet *m*; [hat] calotte *f*, fond *m*. || *v. tr.* [king, queen] couronner, sacrer; [Fig.] récompenser, honorer (qqun); achever (une œuvre); [building, &c.] être au sommet de (la colline, &c.). || **crowning** [-ɪŋ] *n.* couronnement *m*. cf. CORONATION. || *adj.* [Fig.] suprême, derni|er, -ère, final.

crozier *n.* cf. CROSIER.

crucial ['kɹuwʃəl] *adj.* [point] crucial, critique; [test, examination] définitif, décisif.

crucible ['kɹuwsɪbl̩] *n.* [foundry] creuset *m*.

crucifix ['kɹuwsɪfɪks] *n.* [Rel.] crucifix *m*. || **crucifixion** [ˌkɹuwsɪ'fɪkʃən] *n.* crucifixion *f*, crucifiement *m*. || **crucify** ['kɹuwsɪˌfaj] *v. tr.* crucifier (qqun).

crude [kɹuwd] *adj.* à l'état brut; [fruit] vert; [colour] cru; [Fig.] grossier, brutal. || **crudely** [-lɪ] *adv.* [Fig.] crûment, grossièrement. || **crudeness** [-nəs] *n.* crudité *f*.

cruel ['kɹuwl̩] *adj.* cruel, sans pitié. || **cruelly** [-ɪ] *adv.* cruellement. || **cruelty** [-tɪ] *n.* cruauté *f*.

cruet ['kɹuwət] *n.* [oil, vinegar] burette *f*.

cruise [kɹuwz] *n.* [ocean] croisière *f*. || *v. intr.* [ship] croiser; [taxi] faire la maraude. || **cruiser** [-ɚ] *n.* [ship] croiseur *m*.

crumb [kɹʌm] *n.* [bread] miette *f*; [Fig.] (un) tout petit peu, (un) brin (d'affection, &c.). || *v. tr.* [bread] émietter, réduire (qqch.) en miettes; [Cul.] paner (des côtelettes, &c.); enlever les miettes (de sur la table).

crumble ['kɹʌmbl̩] *v. tr.* pulvériser (qqch.), réduire (qqch.) en/miettes, poussière/. || *v. intr.* tomber en poussière: *to* ~ *down*, s'écrouler, tomber en ruines.

crumple ['kɹʌmpl̩] *v. tr.* [clothes] froisser, friper. || *v. intr.* se friper, se froisser.

crunch [kɹʌntʃ] *v. tr.* [chocolate, &c.] croquer (un aliment); broyer, écraser. || *v. intr.* [snow] crisser (sous les pas), craquer. || *n.* croquement *m*; craquement *m*, crissement *m* (de la neige).

crusade [kɹuw'sejd] *n.* [Hist.] croisade *f*. || *v. intr.* faire/une, la/croisade; [Fig.] être en campagne (contre, *against*). || **crusader** [-ɚ] *n.* croisé *m.*

crush [kɹʌʃ] *n.* écrasement *m*, bousculade *f*, [crowd] cohue *f*; [US, infatuation] béguin *m* (pour qqun, *on s.o.*): ~ *hat*, chapeau *m*, claque *m*, [US] chapeau mou. || *v. tr.* écraser (qqun, qqch.), broyer, aplatir (qqch.); [clothes] froisser. || **crushing** [-ɪŋ] *n.* écrasement *m*, broyage *m.* || *adj.* [pain, &c.] écrasant, accablant.

crust [kɹʌst] *n.* [bread, &c.] croûte *f*, dépôt *m*, couche *f* (de saleté, &c.). || *v. tr.* encroûter (qqch.), (re)couvrir (qqch.) d'une/croûte, couche/(de qqch.). || *v. intr.* se couvrir d'une/croûte, couche/(de qqch.). || **crusty** [-ɪ] *adj.* [bread] croûté; [Fig., Pers.] bourru, revêche.

crutch [kɹʌtʃ] *n.* béquille *f.*

crux [kɹʌks] *n.* **1.** point crucial; nœud *m* (d'un problème). **2.** difficulté *f.*

cry [kɹaj] *n.* cri *m* (de joie, douleur, &c.); proclamation *f*; clameur *f*; pleurs *mpl*; aboiement *m* (d'une meute de chiens): *to be within* ~, être à portée de voix; *to utter a* ~, pousser un cri; *crybaby*, pleurard, pleurnicheur. || *v. tr. & intr.* [shout] crier, pousser/un cri, des cris/; [exclaim] s'écrier; [weep] pleurer: *to* ~ *o.s. out*, pleurer toutes les larmes de son corps; *to* ~ *down* (*s.o., sth*). || *v. tr.* décrier, déprécier (qqun, qqch.); *to* ~ *out* (*sth.*) proclamer, crier (qqch.); *v. intr.* pousser les hauts cris, se récrier (contre, *against*). || **crying** [-ɪŋ] *adj.* [abus, &c.] criant; [Fig.] qui crève les yeux; [Pers.] pleurant. || *n.* cri(s) *m(pl)*; pleurs *mpl*, [outburst] larmes *fpl.*

crystal ['kɹɪstəl] *n.* cristal *m*, verre *m* (de montre). || *adj.* [water, &c.] de cristal, cristal'in, limpide. || **crystalline** [-ˌajn] *adj.* cristallin. || **crystallize** [ˌajz] *v. tr.* cristalliser. || *v. intr.* [sugar, salt] se cristalliser.

cu. [= CUBIC].

cub [kʌb] *n.* **1.** petit *m* (d'un animal sauvage), [fox] renardeau *m*, [lion] lionceau *m*, [wolf] louveteau *m*, [bear] ourson *m*; [young Boy Scout] louveteau *m.* **2.** [Fig.] jeune homme inexpérimenté, débutant *m.*

cube [kjuwb] *n.* [root, shape] cube *m*: [Math.] ~ *root*, racine *f* cubique. || *v. tr.* donner (à qqch.) la forme d'un cube; cuber (un nombre). || **cubic** [-ɪk] *adj.* [root, shape] cubique: ~ *centimetre*, centimètre *m* cube.

cubicle['kjuwbɪkḷ] *n.* chambre *f* minuscule; alcôve *f*, réduit *m.*

cuckoo ['kukuw] *n.* [bird] coucou *m*: ~ *clock*, coucou *m*; [Fig.] timbré.

cucumber ['kjuwˌkʌmbɚ] *n.* concombre *m.*

cud [kʌd] *n.* **1.** [ruminant] bol *m* alimentaire: *to chew the* ~, ruminer. **2.** chique *f* (de tabac).

cuddle ['kʌdḷ] *v. tr.* embrasser, étreindre, serrer (qqun) dans ses bras. || *v. intr.* se serrer (l'un contre l'autre), se blottir (dans les bras de qqun).

cudgel ['kʌdʒəl] *n.* [big stick] (gros) bâton *m*, gourdin *m*, brique *f.* || *v. tr.* [-ll-] bâtonner, rouer (qqun) de coups (de bâton), rosser (qqun); [Fig.] *to* ~ *o.'s brains*, se creuser la cervelle.

cue [kjuw] *n.* **1.** queue *f* (de billard); **2.** [Theat.] réplique *f.*

cuff [kʌf] *n.* **1.** manchette *f*; poignet *m* (de chemise); parement *m* (d'une manche); revers *m* (de pantalon): [Fam.] *on the* ~, à crédit; *off the* ~, impromptu, improvisé. **2.** [blow] taloche *f.*

culinary ['kʌlɪnɛɚɪ] *adj.* culinaire.

cull [kʌl] *v. tr.* (re)cueillir, choisir.

culminate ['kʌlmɪˌnejt] *v. intr.* se terminer (en qqch., *in sth*); [star] culminer, passer au méridien.

culprit ['kʌlpɹɪt] *n.* coupable *m/f*; [Jur.] inculpé, -e, prévenu, -e.

cult [kʌlt] *n.* culte *m.*

cultivate ['kʌltɪvejt] *v. tr.* cultiver (la terre); [Fig.] éduquer, élever, cultiver (l'esprit), pratiquer (un art). || **cultivated** [-əd] *adj.* cultivé; [Fig.] éduqué, cultivé. || **cultivation** [kʌltɪ'vejʃən] *n.* culture *f* (de la terre, de l'esprit). || **cultivator** ['kʌltɪˌvejtɚ] *n.* cultivateur *m*;[machine] motoculteur *m.* || **culture** ['kʌltʃɚ] *n.* culture *f*; civilisation *f.* || **cultured** ['kʌltʃɚd] *adj.* [mind, Pers.] cultivé, raffiné, lettré.

cumbersome ['kʌmbɚsəm] *adj.* encombrant, gênant, embarrassant.

cumulative ['kjuwmələtiv] *adj.* → qui s'accumule(nt), qui s'ajoute(nt).

cunning ['kʌnɪŋ] *n.* ruse *f*, adresse *f*, astuce *f*, [Pej.] fourberie *f.* || *adj.* rusé, astucieux; [US, Fam.] mignon.

cup [kʌp] *n.* [tea] tasse *f*, [wine, sport] coupe *f*; calice *m* (d'une fleur, de la messe): [Fig.] *to be in one's cups*, être/rond, un peu gris/; *This is not my* ~ *of tea*, Je ne mange pas de ce/pain-, plat-/là; [Br.] ~ *tie*, partie *f* de championnat, match *m* éliminatoire. || **[-pp-]** *v. tr.* mettre (ses mains) en forme de coupe: *He sheltered his cigarette in his cupped hand*, → Il abritait sa cigarette dans le creux de sa main. || **cupboard** ['kʌbɚd] *n.* [cabinet] armoire *f*; [closet] placard *m* (dans un mur).

cur [kɚ] *n.* [dog] roquet *m*; [Fig., Pers.] malotru *m.*
curable ['kjuwɚəbl̩] *adj.* [disease] curable, guérissable.
curate ['kjɚət] *n.* [Anglican] vicaire *m.* [× Ne pas confondre avec VICAR.]
curb [kɚb] *n.* bord *m*, bordure *f*, © chaîne *f* (du trottoir): [tourism] ~ *service*, restauroute *m*, auto-buffet *m*; [horse] gourmette *f*, [Fig.] frein *m.* ‖ *v. tr.* brider (un cheval); [Fig.] contenir, réprimer, refréner (ses sentiments), mettre un frein à (qqch.).
curd [kɚd] *n.* grumeaux *mpl*, caillebotte *f*: ~ *cheese*, © fromage *m* en grain. ‖ **curdle** [-l̩] *v. tr.* cailler (le lait). ‖ *v. intr.* [milk] se cailler; [blood, Fig.] se figer.
cure [kjuwɚ] *n.* guérison *f*, remède *m*, [treatment] cure *f*, [spiritual] charge *f.* ‖ *v. tr.* guérir (qqun, une maladie); saler, fumer (une viande).
curfew ['kɚfjuw] *n.* couvre-feu *m.*
curio ['kjuwɚɪow] *n.* [object] bibelot *m*, curiosité *f*, objet *m* rare. ‖ **curiosity** [kjuwɚɪ'ɑsɪtɪ] *n.* **1.** curiosité *f*: *to show* ~, manifester de la curiosité. **2.** cf. CURIO. ‖ **curious** ['kjuwɚɪəs] *adj.* [Pers.] curieux; [Pers., thing] étrange, bizarre. ‖ **curiously** [-lɪ] *adv.* curieusement, avec curiosité; de façon étrange.
curl [kɚl] *n.* [hair] boucle *f*, frisure *f*, [wire, smoke, &c.] spirale *f*, volute *f*. ‖ *v. tr.* boucler, friser (ses cheveux); (en)-rouler (qqch.): *to* ~ (*up*) *one's lip*, faire la moue. ‖ **curled** [-d] *adj.* [hair] bouclé, frisé; [paper, &c.] (en)roulé. ‖ **curlers** [-ɚz] *n.pl.* bigoudis *mpl*, frisettes *fpl.*
curlew ['kɚljuw] *n.* [bird] courlis *m*, courlieu *m.*
curling ['kɚlɪŋ] *n.* jeu *m* de palets sur la glace.
curly [kɚlɪ] *adj.* [hair] bouclé, frisé; [wire, &c.] spiralé.
currant [kɚənt] *n.* [berry] groseille *f*: *black* ~, cassis *m.* © gadelle noire; [bush] groseillier *m*; *dried* ~, raisin *m* de Corinthe.
currency ['kɚənsɪ] *n.* **1.** circulation *f*, cours *m* (d'une monnaie, d'une nouvelle, &c.). **2.** monnaie *f* (en circulation), espèces *fpl.* ‖ **current** ['kɚənt] *n.* courant *m* (électrique); cours *m* d'eau, fil *m* de l'eau: *direct* ~, courant continu; *alternating* ~, courant *m* alternatif. ‖ *adj.* [use] courant; [month, &c.] en cours. ‖ **currently** [-lɪ] *adv.* couramment; actuellement, à l'heure actuelle.
curriculum [kɚ'ɪkjələm] *n.* [Schol.] programme *m* (d'études).
curry ['kɚɪ] *n.* [sauce] cari *m.* ‖ *v. tr.* assaisonner, apprêter (un aliment) au cari; [horse] étriller: *to* ~ *favour with s.o.*, faire sa cour à qqun, rechercher les faveurs de qqun.
curse [kɚs] *n.* malédiction *f*; [oath] juron *m*; fléau *m*, calamité *f*, affliction *f.* ‖ *v. tr.* maudire (qqun). ‖ *v. intr.* blasphémer, jurer, sacrer.
cursory ['kɚsɚɪ] *adj.* rapide et superficiel.
curt [kɚt] *adj.* [answer] cassant, brusque, bref, sec.
curtail [kɚ'tejl] *v. tr.* [time] raccourcir, abréger; [expenses] réduire; [freedom] restreindre; [activities] diminuer; [amount] retrancher.
curtain ['kɚtn̩] *n.* [window, stage] rideau *m*: [Polit.] *the Iron Curtain*, le Rideau de Fer; ~ *-raiser*, lever *m* de rideau; ~ *rod*, tringle *f.* ‖ *v. tr.* garnir (qqch.) d'un rideau; cacher (qqch.) avec un rideau.
curts(e)y [kɚtsɪ] *n.* [bow of respect] révérence *f.* ‖ *v. intr.* [lady] tirer sa révérence, faire la révérence.
curve [kɚv] *n.* courbe *f*; virage *m*, coude *m*, tournant *m* (d'une route). ‖ *v. tr.* courber, recourber (qqch.). ‖ *v. intr.* se courber, décrire une courbe. ‖ **curved** [-d] *adj.* courbe, courbé, recourbé, en coude.
cushion ['kuʃən] *n.* coussin *m*; [Mech.] matelas *m* (de vapeur); [billiards] bande *f.* ‖ *v. tr.* [seat, &c.] garnir (qqch.) d'un coussin, de coussins; amortir (un choc). ‖ **cushioned** [-d] *adj.* garni de coussins; [jolt] amorti.
custard ['kʌstɚd] *n.* [dessert] crème *f* (renversée), flan *m*, © cossetarde *f.*
custodian [kʌs'towdɪən] *n.* gardien, ne; [museum] conservateur *m.* ‖ **custody** ['kʌstədɪ] *n.* garde *f*; surveillance *f* (d'un enfant, &c.); détention *f*: *to take* (*s.o.*) *into* ~, mettre, emmener (qqun) en prison; écrouer.
custom ['kʌstəm] *n.* coutume *f*; clientèle *f* (d'une entreprise, d'un magasin); *customs*, *n.pl.* douane *f*: *custom*(*s*) *duties*, droits *mpl* de douane; ~ *-built*, (fait, fabriqué) hors série; [clothes] ~ *-made*, fait sur mesure. ‖ **customary** [-cɚɪ] *adj.* coutumier, habituel, usuel, d'usage. ‖ **customer** [-ɚ] *n.* client *m*; [Fig., Péj.] type *m*, individu *m*, bonhomme *m*: *He is a queer* ~, C'est un/curieux, drôle/de bonhomme. ‖ **customhouse** [-ˌhaws] *n.* la douane *f*, les douanes *fpl.*
cut [kʌt] *n.* coup *m* (de couteau, sabre, &c.); coupe *f* (de cheveux); [wound] coupure *f*, entaille *f*; [Cul.] tranche *f* (de bœuf, &c.);

[Fig.] *the cheap cuts*, les bas morceaux; gravure *f* (sur métal); taille *f* (d'une pierre précieuse); réduction *f*; [Slang] part *f*, pourcentage *m*: *short* ~, raccourci *m*, chemin *m* de traverse. || **cut, cut, cut** *v. tr.* couper (de, *from*; dans, *out of*), (en)tailler, [slice] trancher, [chop] hacher, [first cut] entamer; tailler (une pierre); [engrave] graver; faire (ses dents); [cards] couper; [Fig.] piquer (qqun) au vif; éliminer, faire disparaître (qqch.); réduire (un prix): *to* ~ *a figure*, faire brillante figure; *to* ~ *and run*, filer (en vitesse), décamper, prendre ses jambes à son cou; *to* ~ *it fine*, faire (qqch.) de justesse, réussir tout juste: *That cuts both ways*, C'est un argument à deux tranchants; *to* ~ *a corner*, prendre un virage à la corde; [Fig.] *to* ~ *corners*, économiser du temps, de l'argent, &c.; *to* ~ *sth. short*, abréger qqch.; *to* ~ *it* ~ . . . , pour ne pas trop en dire . . . ; [Fam.] *to* ~/*a class, school*/, sécher un cours, faire l'école buissonnière. cf. COAT. || **cut across** [-ə'kras] *v. tr.* couper en travers. || *v. intr. to* ~ *country*, couper à travers champs. || **cut away** [-ə'wej] *v. tr.* couper. || **cut back** [-'bæk] *v. tr.* réduire, ralentir (la production). || **cutback** ['kʌtˌbæk] *n.* réduction *f*, ralentissement *m.* || **cut down** [-ˌdawn] *v. tr.* couper, abattre; réduire. || **cut in** [-'ɪn] *v. intr.* interrompre; [car] couper (la route à) (qqun); [conversation] s'interposer. || **cut off** [-'ɔf] *v. tr.* couper; supprimer (qqch.); déshériter (qqun). || **cut out** [-'awt] *v. tr.* couper; découper (une gravure); supprimer qqch.; éclipser, supplanter/(qqun): [Fam.] *Cut it out!*, Ça va!, (En voilà) assez!; *to be* ~ *for sth.*, avoir des dispositions pour qqch. || **cut up** [-'ʌp] *v. tr.* couper (en morceaux); [carve] découper; [chop] hacher (des légumes): [Fig.] *to be* ~ *about sth.*, être bouleversé par qqch.

cute [kjuwt] *adj.* [girl, child, &c.] mignon, -ne, gentil, -le © cute ; [Br.] rusé.

cutlery ['kʌtləɪ] *n.* [fabrication] coutellerie *f*; argenterie *f*; ustensiles *mpl* de table.

cutlet ['kʌtlət] *n.* [pork, &c.] côtelette *f*; [veal, fish] escalope *f.*

cut-rate ['kʌtˌɹejt] *adj.* bon marché, à prix réduit.

cutter ['kʌtɚ] *n.* **1.** [person] coupeur *m*; [instrument] coupoir *m.* **2.** [Naut.] cotre *m*, cutter *m.*

cutting ['kʌtɪŋ] *n.* **1.** tranchée *f.* **2.** bouture *f.*

cycle [sajkl̩] *n.* [movement] cycle *m*, période *f*; [bicycle] bicyclette *f.* || *v. intr.* faire de la bicyclette, aller à bicyclette. || **cycling** [-ɪŋ] *n.* cyclisme *m.*

cyclone ['sajklown] *n.* [storm] cyclone *m.*

cylinder ['sɪlɪndɚ] *n.* [shape, volume, car, locomotive] cylindre *m*; [revolver] barillet *m.*

cynic ['sɪnɪk] *n.* cynique. || **cynical** [-l̩] *adj.* cynique.

cypress ['sajpɹəs] *n.* [tree] cyprès *m.*

czar [zɑɚ] *n.* **1.** tsar *m*; empereur *m* (de Russie). **2.** [Fam.] grand patron, chef (incontesté), dictateur *m.*

Czech [ʧɛk] *n.* & *adj.* Tchèque (*m*/*f*). || **Czechoslovak** [-ow'slowvæk] *n.* & *adj.* Tchécoslovaque (*m*/*f*). || **Czechoslovakia** [ʧɛkowˌslow'vækɪə] *n.* Tchécoslovaquie *f.*

D

D, d [dij] *pl.* **D's, d's. 1.** [lettre] D, d; [Mus.] ré *m.*

D.A. ['dij'ej] [U.S.] cf. DISTRICT ATTORNEY. *n.* procureur *m*,

dab [dæb] *n.* tapotement *m*; petit coup *m*: *to give a* ~ *to*, toucher (légèrement). || *v. tr.* [-bb-] tapoter; [~ **up**] tamponner.

dabble [-l̩] *v. intr.* **1.** [in the water] barboter. **2.** [~ **in**] se mêler (de politique, &c.); faire un peu de (peinture, &c.).

dad, daddy [dæd(ɪ)] *n.* [Fam.] papa *m.*

daffodil ['dæfədɪl] *n.* [Bot.] narcisse *m.*

daft [dæft] *adj.* sot, faible d'esprit.

dagger ['dægɚ] *n.* poignard *m*; [Fig.]

at daggers drawn, à couteaux tirés; *to look daggers at . . . ,* lancer des regards furibonds à. . . .

dahlia ['dejljə] *n.* dahlia *m.*

daily ['dejlı] *adj.* quotidien; [work, &c.] journalier. || *n.* [newspaper] quotidien *m.* || *adv.* journellement, tous les jours, cf. DAY.

daintiness ['dejntı|nəs] *n.* délicatesse *f,* raffinement *m,* grâce *f.* || **dainty** *adj.* délicat; [food] raffiné; [person] gracieux; (femme) soignée. || *n. us. pl.* friandises *fpl.*

dairy ['dɛəˑı] *n.* laiterie *f*; [store] crémerie *f.* || **dairyman** [-ˌmən] *n.* crémier *m*; *~ farming,* industrie *f* laitière; *~ maid,* laitière *f.*

daisy ['dejzı] *n.* marguerite *f.*

†**dale** [dejl] *n.* petite vallée *f,* vallon *m*: *up hill and down ~ ,* par monts et par vaux.

dally ['dælı] *v. intr.* **1.** badiner (avec qqch., qqun); folâtrer. **2.** s'attarder, flâner.

dam [dæm] *n.* barrage *m,* digue *f.* || *v. tr.* [-mm-] [also *~ up*] endiguer; barrer (une rivière).

damage ['dæmədʒ] *n.* dégâts *mpl,* dommage *m*; [Fig.] tort *m,* préjudice *m*; *pl.* [cost] dommages-intérêts *mpl*: *to do ~ ,*/faire des dégâts; [Fig.] faire (du) tort/à. || *v. tr.* endommager, abîmer (qqch.); [Fig.] faire tort à, nuire à (qqun, qqch.); [Com.] *damaged foodstuffs,* nourriture *f* avariée.

Damascus [də'mæskəs] *n.* Damas.

damn [dæm] *v. tr.* [Rel.] damner; [criticize] condamner; [curse] maudire. || **damnation** [-'nejʃən] *n.* [Rel.] damnation *f*; condamnation *f.* || **damned** ['dæmd] *adj.* damné; condamné; [juron] sacré.

damp [dæmp] *adj.* humide; [skin] moite: *The weather is ~ ,* Il fait humide. || *v. tr.* humidifier; étouffer (un feu). || **dampen** [-ən] *v. tr.* **1.** [clothes] humecter; [cement] humidifier. **2.** [Fig.] refroidir (l'enthousiasme). || **dampness** [-nəs] *n.* humidité *f,* moiteur *f* (de la peau).

dance [dæns] *v. intr.* **1.** danser. **2.** sauter, gambader. || *v. tr.* danser (la valse, &c.). || *n.* **1.** danse *f*; [party] sauterie *f*; bal *m*; soirée *f,* matinée *f*/dansante: *~ hall,* salle *f* de danse; *~ floor,* piste *f* de danse. || **dancer** [-ɚ] *n.* danseu|r *m,* -se *f.* || **dancing** [-ıŋ] *n.* [art] la danse *f.*

dandelion ['dændıˌlajən] *n.* pissenlit *m.*

Dane [dejn] *pr. n.* Danois *m,* -e *f.*

danger ['dejndʒɚ] *n.* danger *m* (pour, *to*); péril *m*: *in ~ (of),* en danger (de). || **dangerous** [-əs] *adj.* dangereux; périlleux. || **dangerously** [-əslı] *adv.* dangereusement.

dangle ['dæŋgl] *v. intr.* pendiller, pendre: *with his legs dangling,* les jambes ballantes.

Danish ['dejnıʃ] *adj.* danois. || *n.* [Ling.] le danois.

dank [dæŋk] *adj.* humide, cf. FROID.

dapper ['dæpɚ] *adj.* [gentleman] bien mis, tiré à quatre épingles.

dare [dɛɚ], **dared** or †**durst,** *v. intr.* [à l'interrog, et au nég., la 3e pers. du sing. du prés. de l'ind. peut être *dare* suivi directement de l'infinitif] oser: *He /doesn't ~ to come, He dares not come/ here,* Il n'ose pas venir ici; *Don't you ~ !,* Que je t'y prenne!; *I ~ say (he'll come),* Sans doute, Je crois bien/(qu'il viendra). || *v. tr.* braver, défier (qqun, qqch.); affronter (le danger): *I ~ you (to) (do it),* Je vous mets au défi (de le faire) [Fam.] Chiche!/. || *n.* défi *m.* || **dare-devil** [-ˌdɛvl̩] *n.* [person] casse-cou *m. inv.* || **daring** [-ıŋ] *adj.* [person] intrépide, audacieux, hardi; [answer] effronté; [dress] osé. || *n.* hardiesse *f,* audace *f*; [Pej.] effronterie *f.* || **daringly** [-ıŋlı] *adv.* hardiment, audacieusement; effrontément.

dark [dɑɚk] *adj.* **1.** obscur, sombre: *It's getting ~ ,* La nuit tombe; *It is ~ ,* Il fait/sombre, nuit/. **2.** [colour, &c.] foncé, noir: *a ~ blue dress,* une robe bleu foncé. **3.** [scheme, &c.] secret; mauvais. **4.** [Fig.] [expression] triste, renfermé, sombre. || *n.* **1.** obscurité *f,* ténèbres *fpl*: *after ~ ,* la nuit tombée. **2.** [Fig.] *to/ leave, keep/s.o. in the ~ ,* → laisser qqun dans l'ignorance (d'un fait, &c.). || **darken** [-n̩] *v. tr.* **1.** obscurcir, assombrir (qqch.); [colour, &c.] brunir (la peau, &c.), foncer (une couleur, &c.). **2.** [Fig.] attrister (qqch.). || *v. intr.* [sky, &c.] s'obscurcir, s'assombrir; [skin, &c.] se foncer; [face] se rembrunir. || **darkness** [-nəs] *n.* obscurité *f*: [Fig.] *I am in complete ~ ,* Je suis dans le noir. || **darkroom** [-ˌɹuwm] *n.* chambre *f* noire. || **darky** [-ı] *n.* [Fam., Pej.] nègre *m.*

darling ['dɑɚlıŋ] *adj.* chéri, bien-aimé; [cute] mignon; favori. || *n.* chéri *m,* -e *f.*

darn [dɑɚn] *v. tr.* [socks, &c.] repriser, raccommoder: *darning needle,* aiguille *f* à repriser, © [insect] libellule *f,* demoiselle *f.* || *n.* reprise *f.* || *interj. Darn it!,* Zut!

dart [dɑɚt] *n.* **1.** dard *m*; [Fig.] [arrow] trait *m.* **2.** élan *m,* mouvement *m* (brusque et rapide). || *v. tr.* lancer (un regard); [shaft, &c.] décocher (une flèche, &c.). || *v. intr.* s'élancer: *to ~ /across, out, &c./,* traverser, sortir/comme une flèche/.

dash [dæʃ] *n.* **1.** choc *m* (violent), heurt *m*; élan *m* (impétueux). **2.** [character] fougue *f*, impétuosité *f*, brio *m*. **3.** trait *m*; [Gram.] tiret *m*. **4.** [small quantity] goutte *f*, larme *f* (de liquide, &c.); filet *m* (de crème): soupçon *m* (de sel, &c.); [colour] touche *f*, légère teinte; [Fig.] [humour] pointe *f*. **5.** course *f* (de 100m., &c.). || *v. tr.* heurter (qqun, qqch.); lancer (qqch. violemment); mettre (qqch.) en pièces; [proper & Fig.] fracasser. || *v. intr.* se précipiter, se ruer (sur qqun, qqch., *at s.o., sth*); se heurter (à, contre qqun, qqch., *against s.o., sth*); *to ~ /in, out, &c./*, /entrer, sortir, &c./en trombe.

dashboard [-ˌbɔɚd] *n.* [car] tableau *m* de bord. || **dashing** [-ɪŋ] *n.* brillant, plein d'allant.

dastardly [ˈdæstɚdlɪ] *adj.* lâche.

data [ˈdejtə] *n.pl.* données *fpl.*

date[1] [dejt] *n.* **1.** date *f*; [month] quantième *m*: *What ~ is it?* Quelle date sommes-nous?; [event, &c.] époque *f*: *out of ~*, démodé; *up to ~*, à la page; *to ~*, à ce jour; [Fin.] (*due*) *~*, échéance *f*, terme *m*. **2.** [persons of the opposite sex] rendez-vous *m*, sortie *f*. || *v. tr.* **1.** dater (un événement, &c.). **2.** [boy-friend, girl-friend] fréquenter; [Fam.] sortir avec (qqun). || *v. intr.* *It dates back to the seventeenth century*, Cela remonte au XVIIe siècle.

date[2] *n.* [fruit] datte *f*: *~ palm*, dattier *m*.

daub [dɔb] *v. tr.* enduire (de peinture); [Pej.] barbouiller. || *n.* enduit *m*; [Pej.] barbouillage *m*.

daughter [ˈdɔtɚ] *n.* fille *f*. || **daughter-in-law** [-ɪnˌlɔ] *n.* bru *f*; [son's wife] belle-fille *f*.

daunt [dɔnt] *v. tr.* effrayer, intimider, décourager (qqun). || **dauntless** [-ləs] *adj.* intrépide.

davenport [ˈdævn̩pɔɚt] *n.* sofa *m*; lit-divan *m*.

dawdle [dɔdl̩] *v. intr.* musarder, flâner.

dawn [dɔn] *n.* aube *f*, aurore *f*; [Fig.] commencement *m*. || *v. intr.* [daylight] poindre; [Fig.] commencer, (ap)paraître.

day [dej] *n.* **1.** [when counting, or as opposed to night] jour *m*; [considered as a period during which given events occur, or modified by a descriptive adj.] journée *f*: 10 *days ago*, il y a 10 jours; *every* (*other*) *~*, chaque jour, tous les (deux) jours; *~ and night*, jour et nuit; *once a ~*, une fois par jour; *from ~ to ~*, au jour le jour; *~ after ~*, jour après jour; *from one ~ to the next*, du jour au lendemain; *one, some/* (*fine*) *~*, un (beau) jour; *the other ~*, l'autre jour; *What ~* (*of the/week, month*) *is it?*, Quel jour, Quelle date/ sommes-nous?; *by ~*, le, de/jour; *by ~* (*light*), au jour; *by the ~*, à la journée; *I spent the ~* [+ *-ing*], J'ai passé la journée à [+ infin.]; *What a beautiful ~!*, Quelle belle journée!; *All ~* (*long*), toute la journée, tout le jour; *It's a nice ~*, → Il fait beau aujourd'hui; [Fam.] (*Let's*) *call it a ~*, → Ça suffit pour aujourd'hui; *a working ~*, un jour ouvrable. **2.** *the ~ before*, la veille, *the ~ before yesterday*, avant-hier; *the ~ after*, le lendemain; *the ~ after tomorrow*, après-demain. **3.** *usual. pl.* [time, period] temps *m*; époque *f*: *in those days*, en ce temps-là, à cette époque-là; (*in*) *these days*, de nos jours; *in my day*(*s*), de mon temps; *in the days when . . .*, du temps que . . . ; *in the good old days*, dans le bon vieux temps: *in/†olden, the old/days*, jadis, autrefois; *His days are numbered*, Ses jours sont comptés; *He has had his ~*, Il a fait son temps. **4.** fête *f*: [R.C.] *Corpus Christi Day*, (la) Fête-Dieu; *Commencement Day*, [Sch.] © (la) collation *f* des grades; [Fr.] la distribution des prix; *Labour Day*, la Fête du Travail; *Remembrance Day*, © Jour *m* du Souvenir, [Fr.] Jour *m* de l'Armistice. || **dayboy** [-ˌboj] *n.* (élève) externe *m*. || **daybreak** [-ˌbɹejk] *n.* aube *f*, aurore *f*: *at ~*, au point du jour. || **day dream** [-ˌdɹijm] *n.* rêverie *f*. || *v. intr.* rêver creux, rêvasser. || **day dreaming** [-ˌdɹijmɪŋ] *n.* songerie *f*, rêverie *f*. || **day labourer** [-ˌlejbɚɚ] *n.* journalier *m*. || **daylight** [-ˌlajt] *n.* lumière *f* du jour, le jour: *in broad ~*, en plein jour; [Fig.] *to see ~*, comprendre; *~ saving time*, heure *f* d'été; *Eastern Daylight Saving Time*, © heure avancée de l'est. || **daylily** [-ˌlɪlɪ] *n.* belle *f* de jour. || **dayliner** [-ˌlajnɚ] © *n.* autorail *m*. || **day nursery** [-ˌnɚsəɪ] *n.* garderie *f* (d'enfants), pouponnière *f*. || **day school** [-ˌskuwl] *n.* externat *m*. || **daytime** [-ˌtajm] *n.* journée *f*: *in the ~*, de jour, pendant la journée.

daze [dejz] *v. tr.* **1.** [drug, shock] stupéfier, hébéter; étourdir (qqun) d'un coup. **2.** [light] éblouir. || *n.* étourdissement *m*: *to be in a ~*, être stupéfié, hébété; ne plus savoir où on en est.

dazzle [ˈdæzl̩] *v. tr.* [intensity of light] éblouir. || *n.* éblouissement *m*. || **dazzling** [-ɪŋ] *adj.* [light] éblouissant, aveuglant.

D.C., [ˈdijˌsij] **1.** [= US, District of Columbia] district *m* de Columbia. **2. d.c.** [= *direct current*] courant continu, (le) continu *m*. cf. A.C.

deacon ['dijkn̩] *n.* [Rel.] diacre *m.*

dead [dɛd] *adv.* en plein; *~ centre*, en plein milieu; absolument; *You are ~ right*, Vous avez absolument raison; *~ tired*, éreinté, à bout; || *~ shot*, fin tireur. *n.* **1.** cœur *m*: *in/~ of/night, winter/*, au cœur de/la nuit, l'hiver/. **2.** *pl. the ~*, les morts *mpl.* || *adj.* **1.** mort, sans vie: *~ body*, cadavre *m*; *as ~ as a door-nail*, mort et bien mort; *the Dead Sea*, la mer Morte; *the ~ march*, la marche funèbre; [Fam.] *Drop ~!*, Tu peux crever! **2.** [Fig.] *~ to the world*, inerte, inanimé; [season] morte-saison *f*; [fire] éteint; [calm] plat; [letter] tombée au rebut; [loss, stop] total; [weight] mort; [wire] sans courant: *~ end*, impasse *f*, sans issue; *~ loss*, perte,/totale, sèche/; *to come to a ~ stop*, s'arrêter/sur place, brusquement. || **deaden** [-n̩] *v. tr.* amortir (un choc, un coup); assourdir, étouffer (un bruit, un son). || **deadline** [-lajn] *n.* date *f* limite, dernier délai *m.* || **deadlock** [-ˌlɑk] *n.* [Fig.] impasse *f.* || **deadly** [-lɪ] *adj.* [enemy, sin, &c.] mortel: *the seven ~ sins*, les sept péchés capitaux; [blow] fatal. || *adv.* mortellement.

deaf [dɛf] *adj.* sourd: [Fig.] *stone ~*, sourd comme un pot; *~ and dumb*, cf. DEAF-MUTE. || **deafen** [-n̩] *v. tr.* assourdir (qqun, qqch.); rendre (qqun) sourd. || **deafening** [-n̩ɪŋ] *adj.* [noise] assourdissant. || **deaf-mute** [ˌmjuwt] *adj.* sourd-muet. || **deafness** [-nəs] *n.* surdité *f.*

deal¹ [dijl], **dealt** [dɛlt], **dealt** [dɛlt] *v. intr.* **1.** traiter (avec qqun, de qqch.); s'occuper (de qqch.) **2.** [Com.] faire le commerce (de qqch., *in sth.*); commercer, négocier (avec qqun, *with s.o.*); acheter qqch. (chez, à/qqun); faire un marché (avec qqun) **3.** [behave] traiter (qqun), se conduire (envers qqun); s'y prendre (avec qqun). **4.** distribuer (les cartes).

deal² *v. tr.* [*also to ~ out*] donner, distribuer. || *n.* **1.** opération *f* (commerciale, financière); [Fin.] transaction *f*; [business] marché *m*, affaire *f*: *It's a ~*, C'est entendu, Marché conclu. **2.** [settlement] arrangement *m*, partage *m*: *to give* (*s.o.*) *a/fair, square/ ~*, donner (à qqun) son dû. **3.** *a/great, good/ ~ (of)*, beaucoup (de), bien (des). **4.** [cards] donne *f*: *It's your* (*turn to*) *~*, A vous de faire la donne. || **dealer** [-ər] *n.* négociant *m*; marchand *m*, vendeur *m*; [car, &c.] distributeur *m*; [cards] donneur *m.* || **dealing** [-ɪŋ] *n.* **1.** [behaviour] procédé *m*, conduite *f.* **2.** *pl.* relations *fpl*; rapports *mpl* (amicaux); [Pej.] manigances *fpl.*

dealt [dɛlt] cf. DEAL.

dean [dijn] *n.* [University & Ecc.] doyen *m.*

dear [dijər] *adj.* **1.** [affection] cher: *Dear Sir*, Monsieur, *Dear Mr. Jones*, Monsieur, [acquaintance] Cher Monsieur; *Dear John*, Mon cher Jean; *my ~ fellow*, mon cher (ami). **2.** [price] cher, précieux, coûteux: *to get dear*(*er*), (r)enchérir. || *n.* cher *m*, chère *f*: *My ~*, Cher ami, Chère amie. || *interj. Oh ~!*, *Dear me!*, Oh là là!, Mon Dieu! || **dearly** [-lɪ] *adv.* cher, chèrement; tendrement.

†**dearth** [dərθ] *n.* disette *f*, pénurie *f.*

death [dɛθ] *n.* mort *f*: *~ duties*, droits *mpl* de succession; *Death Valley*, la Vallée de la Mort; trépas *m*; [official] décès *m*; fin *f*, extinction *f*; [Fig.] ruine *f*: *to put to ~*, mettre à mort; *to freeze to ~*, mourir de froid; *to be frightened to ~*, mourir de peur; *to fight to the ~*, lutter à mort; *He will be the ~ of me*, Il me fera mourir (de rire); [Fam.] *She is ~ on noise*, Elle ne peut pas supporter le bruit. || **deathbed** [-ˌbɛd] *n.* lit *m* de mort: *He is on his ~*, Il est à l'article de la mort. || **death bell** [-ˌbɛl] *n.* glas *m.* || **deathrate** [-ˌɹejt] *n.* [demography] (taux de) mortalité. || **death rattle** [-ˌɹætl] *n.* râle *m* (de l'agonie). || **death warrant** [-ˌwɔərənt] *n.* arrêt *m* de mort.

debacle [dɪ'bækl̩] *n.* débâcle *f*; désastre *m.*

debar [dɪ'bɑər] *v. tr.* [**-rr-**] exclure, priver (qqun de qqch.).

debark [dɪ'bɑərk] *v. tr.* débarquer.

debase [dɪ'bejs] *v. tr.* abaisser, avilir, dégrader, altérer (la monnaie).

debate [dɪ'bejt] *n.* débat *m*, discussion *f*: [Hansard] *Debates of the House of Commons*, Débats *mpl* de la Chambre des Communes. || *v. tr.* débattre, discuter (une question). || *v. intr.* discuter (avec qqun sur qqch.).

debauch [dɪ'bɔtʃ] *n.* débauche *f.* || *v. tr.* débaucher. || **debauchery** [-ərɪ] *n.* débauche *f*, perversion *f.*

debilitate [dɪ'bɪlət|ejt] *v. tr.* affaiblir; [Med.] débiliter. || **debility** [-ɪ] *n.* faiblesse *f*; [Med.] débilité *f.*

debit ['dɛbɪt] *n.* débit *m*; *~ balance*, solde *m* débiteur. || *v. tr.* débiter, porter au débit de (un compte).

debris [də'bɹij] *n.* débris *mpl.*

debt [dɛt] *n.* [Fin.] dette *f*, créance *f*; [Fig.] obligation *f*: *to be $10 in ~*, être endetté de dix dollars; *to be out of ~*, ne plus avoir de dettes. || **debtor** [-ər] *n.* débit|eur *m*, rice *f.*

debunk [dɪ'bʌŋk] *v. tr.* [Fam.] déboulonner, rabaisser.

debut [ˈdejˌbjuw] *n.* début *m*: *to make one's* ~, faire ses débuts. || **debutante** [ˈdɛbjəˌtɑnt] *n.* débutante *f.*
decade [ˈdɛkejd] *n.* [period of ten years] décade *f*, décennie *f.*
decadence [ˈdɛkədən|s] *n.* décadence *f.* || **decadent** [-t] *adj.* décadent.
decamp [dɪˈkæmp] *v. intr.* décamper; [Fam.] plier bagage.
decant [dɪˈkænt] *v. tr.* décanter, transvaser (un liquide). || **decanter** [-ɚ] *n.* carafe *f.*
decapitate [dɪˈkæpɪˌtejt] *v. tr.* décapiter.
decay [dɪˈkej] *n.* **1.** décadence *f*; [building] délabrement *m*; [Fig.] déchéance *f*, ruine *f*, déclin *m*. **2.** pourriture *f*; carie *f* (dentaire). || *v. intr.* [carcase, &c.] se décomposer, pourrir; [tooth] se gâter, se carier; [building] se délabrer, tomber en ruine; [régime] tomber en décadence.
decease [dɪˈsijs] *v. intr.* décéder [Conj. ÊTRE]. || *n.* décès *m*. || **deceased** [-d] *n. & adj.* défunt *m*, -e *f.*
deceit [dɪˈsijt] *n.* tromperie *f*, supercherie *f*; fourberie *f.* || **deceitful** [-fḷ] *adj.* [person] trompeur, fourbe; [action] frauduleux; mensonger. || **deceitfully** [-fḷɪ] *adv.* faussement, frauduleusement. || **deceive** [dɪˈsijv] *v. tr.* tromper, leurrer (qqun), induire (qqun) en erreur: *to* ~ *o.s.*, s'abuser, se tromper. || **deceiver** [-ɚ] *n.* fourbe *m.*
decelerate [dɪˈsɛlɚˌejt] *v. tr. & intr.* ralentir.
December [dɪˈsɛmbɚ] *n.* décembre *m.*, cf. APRIL.
decency [ˈdijsṇsɪ] *n.* décence *f*; [proper behaviour] bienséance *f.* || **decent** [ˈdɪsənt] *adj.* [proper] convenable, bienséant; [modest] décent; [persons] respectable, convenable, comme il faut; [weather] beau; [food] bon, satisfaisant; [number, quantity] suffisant, convenable: *a* ~ *fellow*, un/bon, gentil/garçon; *It's very* ~ *of him*, C'est vraiment gentil à lui.
decentralize [dɪˈsɛntɹəˌlaiz] *v. tr.* décentraliser.
deception [dɪˈsɛpʃən] *n.* tromperie *f*; illusion *f.* || **deceptive** [dɪˈsɛptɪv] *adj.* trompeur.
decide [dɪˈsajd] *v. tr.* [question, &c.] trancher, décider (de qqch.): *That decided me to do it*, Cela m'a décidé à le faire; *It was decided to do it*, Il fut décidé de le faire. || *v. intr. to* ~ *to do sth.*, décider de, se décider à/, prendre la décision de/faire qqch. || **decided** [-əd] *adj.* décidé, résolu, ferme, indiscutable, complet. || **decidedly** [-ədlɪ] *adv.* décidément; résolument; incontestablement.
deciduous [dɪˈsɪdjuwəs] *adj.* à feuilles caduques; © feuillu.
decimal [ˈdɛsɪməl] *adj.* décimal: ~ *point*, point *m* décimal, virgule *f* décimale. [☞ au Canada, utilisez un point, en France une virgule; in France, a comma replaces a decimal point].
decimate [ˈdɛsəˌmejt] *v. tr.* décimer.
decipher [dɪˈsajfɚ] *v. tr.* déchiffrer.
decision [dəˈsɪʒən] *n.* décision *f*, résolution *f*; [Jur.] arrêt *m* (de Cour), jugement *m*: [Sport.] *to win a* ~, gagner un match. || **decisive** [dɪˈsajsɪv] *adj.* **1.** [action] décisi|f, -ve, concluant. **2.** [tone] tranchant, catégorique.
deck [dɛk] *n.* **1.** [Naut.] pont *m*: *foredeck*, gaillard *m* d'avant; *quarter* ~, gaillard *m* d'arrière; ~ *chair*, transat *m*, chaise *f* longue; [Fig.] *to be on* ~, être prêt pour l'action. **2.** jeu *m* (de cartes). || *v. tr.* [also ~ *out*] orner, décorer, parer (de qqch., *with sth.*): *She is all decked out*, Elle est sur son/trente-et-un, © trente-six.
declaim [dɪˈklejm] *v. intr.* déclamer.
declaration [ˌdɛkləˈejʃən] *n.* [statement] déclaration *f*; [official] communication *f*; [solemn] proclamation *f.* || **declare** [dɪˈklɛɚ] *v. tr.* déclarer; affirmer; [solemnly] proclamer.
declension [dɪˈklɛnʃən] *n.* [Gram.] déclinaison *f.*
decline [dɪˈklajn] *n.* pente *f*; [Fin., Com.] baisse *f*, diminution *f* (des prix, &c.); [Fig.] déclin *m*, décadence *f*; [Med.] consomption *f.* || *v. intr.* [prices, stocks, &c.] baisser, diminuer; [Fig.] décliner, tomber en décadence; [invitation, &c.] refuser (poliment) (de faire qqch.). || *v. tr.* [noun, adj.; invitation] décliner; refuser. || **declivity** [dɪˈklɪvɪtɪ] *n.* pente *f*, déclivité *f.*
decode [dɪˈkowd] *v. tr.* déchiffrer (un message).
decompose [dɪkəmˈpowz] *v. tr. & intr.* (se) décomposer.
decor [deˈkɔɚ] *n.* décor *m.*
decorate [ˈdɛkɚˌejt] *v. tr.* décorer, orner. || **decoration** [ˌdɛkɚˈejʃən] *n.* décoration *f*, ornement *m*, médaille *f.* || **decorative** [ˈdɛkɚətɪv] *adj.* décorati|f, *m* -ve *f.* || **decorum** [dɪˈkɔɚəm] *n.* décorum *m*, bienséance *f.*
decoy [dɪˈkoj] *n.* leurre *m*, appât *m.* || *v. tr.* attirer dans un piège, leurrer.
decrease [dɪˈkɹijs] *v. tr.* diminuer, réduire. || *v. intr.* diminuer, décroître. || *n.* diminution *f*, réduction *f.*
decree [dɪˈkɹɪj] *n.* [official] décret *m*; [Jur.] jugement *m*, arrêt *m.* || *v. tr.* décréter, ordonner.

decrepit [dɪ'kɹɛpɪt] *adj.* [person] décrépit, affaibli; [thing] qui tombe en ruine.

decry [dɪ'kɹaj] *v. tr.* décrier, dénigrer.

decuple ['dɛkjəpḷ] *n.* décuple *m.* || *v. tr. & intr.* (se) décupler.

dedicate ['dɛdɪˌkejt] *v. tr.* consacrer (une église); inaugurer (un bâtiment); dédier (une œuvre): *to ~ o.self to,* se vouer à. || **dedication** [ˌdɛdɪ'kejʃən] *n.* consécration *f*; inauguration *f*; dédicace *f* (d'une œuvre).

deduce [dɪ'd|uws] *v. tr.* déduire, inférer, conclure. || **deduct** [-ʌkt] *v. tr.* déduire, retrancher (*from*, de). || **deduction** [-ʌkʃən] *n.* déduction *f.*

deed [dijd] *n.* **1.** action *f*: *a ~ of valour,* un exploit; *a good ~*, une bonne action; *to do s.o. a good ~*, rendre service *m* à qqun. **2.** [legal] acte *m.*

†**deem** [dijm] *v. tr.* juger; estimer: *I ~ it useful to . . .*, Je crois utile, J'estime qu'il est utile/de . . . ; *He was deemed a rich man,* Il passait pour (être), Il était considéré comme/riche.

deep [dijp] *adj.* profond; [colour] foncé: [note] grave; [Fig.] profond, intense; [Pers.] rusé: *This well is* 100 *feet ~*, Ce puits/a 100 pieds de profondeur, est profond de 100 pieds/; *three ~*, sur trois rangs; *~ blue (flowers),* (des fleurs) bleu foncé; *That fellow is a ~ one,* C'est un malin, Il a plus d'un tour dans son sac; [Fam.] *to go (in) off the ~ end,* s'emporter, prendre les choses au tragique; *to be knee-deep in water,* être dans l'eau jusqu'aux genoux. || *adv.* profondément; plongé, absorbé (*dans*); très avant (dans): *to breathe ~*, respirer profondément; *~ in/thought, a book, debt/,* absorbé par ses pensées, absorbé, plongé/dans (la lecture d') un livre, cousu de dettes/; *~ in his heart,* au fond de son cœur; *~ in the night,* très avant dans la nuit; *Still waters run ~*, Il n'y a pire eau que l'eau qui dort. || **deep** *n.* **1.** *in the ~ of . . .*, en plein(e) . . . . †**2.** les profondeurs *fpl* (de l'océan). || **deepen** [-ṇ] *v. tr.* approfondir, rendre plus profond; [colour, &c.] foncer; [Fig.] intensifier. || *v. intr.* s'approfondir; [colour, &c.] se foncer; [shadow, &c.] s'épaissir; [Fig.] s'intensifier. || **deep-freeze** [-ˌfɹijz] *n.* [Fr.] frigo(rifique *m* de ménage), © glacière *f.* || **deeply** [-lɪ] *adv.* profondément; fort, extrêmement. || **deepness** [-nəs] *n.* profondeur *f*; [Fig.] ruse *f.*

deer [dijɚ] *n. inv.* cerf *m*; © chevreuil *m.*

deface [dɪ'fejs] *v. tr.* défigurer (qqun); [monument, work of art, &c.] mutiler: *The wall is defaced,* Le mur est dégradé.

defamation [ˌdɛfə'mejʃən] *n.* diffamation *f.* || **defame** [dɪ'fejm] *v. tr.* diffamer.

default [dɪ'fɔlt] *n.* défaut *m*: *by ~*, par défaut, par forfait; *in ~ of,* à défaut de. || *v. intr.* faire défaut (à), manquer (à un engagement).

defeat [dɪ'fijt] *n.* défaite *f*; [Fig.] échec *m,* insuccès *m.* || *v. tr.* vaincre, défaire, battre (qqun, qqch.); [Fig.] faire échouer, © frustrer ,[fr.] déjouer (un complot, &c.)

defeatism [dɪ'fijtɪzm] *n.* défaitisme *m.*

defect [dɪ'fɛkt] *n.* défaut *m*, imperfection *f*, || *v. intr.* faire défection. || **defective** [-ɪv] *adj.* défectueux, imparfait; [Gram.] défectif.

defence [dɪ'fɛns] *n.* [justification, protection, Jur.] défense *f*; [Univ.] soutenance *f* (de thèse): © *Department of National Defence,* ministère *m* de la Défense nationale; *in self ~*, en légitime défense. || **defenceless** [-ləs] *adj.* sans défense, désarmé. || **defenceman** [-mæn] © *n.* [hockey] joueur *m* de défense. || **defend** [dɪ'fɛnd] *v. tr.* [guard] défendre; protéger (contre qqch., *from sth.*); justifier (une opinion). || **defendable** [-əbḷ] *adj.* [person, case] défendable; [point of view, action] justifiable. || **defendant** [-ənt] *n.* [Jur.] défend|eur, *m*, -eresse *f.* || **defender** [-ɚ] *n.* défenseur *m.* || **defensive** [dɪ'fɛnsɪv] *adj.* défensif. || *n.* défensive *f.*

defer [dɪ'fɚ] *v. tr.* [-rr.] **1.** [put off] différer, ajourner. [× DÉFÉRER]. **2.** [refer] déférer (une cause à un tribunal). || *v. intr.* [yield courteously] déférer (à l'opinion de qqun).

deference ['dɛfɚəns] *n.* déférence *f*: *out of ~ to, in ~ to,* par déférence pour. || **deferential** [ˌdɛfɚ'ɛnʃəl] *adj.* déférent, respectueu|x *m*, -se *f.*

defiance [dɪ'fajən|s] *n.* défi *m*: *in ~ of,* au mépris de, en dépit de; *to set s.o. at ~*, défier qqun. || **defiant** [-t] *adj.* agressi|f *m*, -ve *f*, provocant.

deficiency [dɪ'fɪʃən|sɪ] *n.* manque *m*, insuffisance *f*, défaut *m* (de, *of*); [Fin.] déficit *m*; imperfection *f.* || **deficient** [-t] *adj.* défectueu|x *m*, -se *f*, insuffisant: *to be ~ in . . .*, manquer de. . . . || **deficit** ['dɛfɪsɪt] *n.* déficit *m.*

defile[1] ['dijˌfajl] *n.* défilé *m.* || *v. intr.* défiler.

defile[2] [dɪ'fajl] *v. tr.* souiller, polluer; [Fig.] ternir (une réputation, &c.). || **defilement** [dɪ'fajlmənt] *n.* souillure *f.*

define [dɪ'fajn] *v. tr.* définir (des termes), préciser, déterminer. || **definite** ['dɛfɪnɪt] *adj.* défini, précis, déterminé: *Be ~ !* Soyez précis!; *A ~ statement,* Une déclaration catégorique; [Gram.] défini.

|| **definitely** [-lɪ] *adv.* sans aucun doute, sans conteste, sans hésitation; absolument, décidément. || **definition** [ˌdɛfɪ'nɪʃən] *n.* définition *f.* || **definitive** [də'fɪnɪtɪv] *adj.* décisi|f *m,* -ve *f,* définiti|f *m,* -ve *f;* [Gram.] déterminatif.

deflate [dɪ'flej|t] *v. tr.* dégonfler. || **deflation** [-ʃən] *n.* dégonflement *m*; [Fin.] déflation *f.*

deflect [dɪ'flɛkt] *v. tr.* détourner, (faire) dévier. || *v. intr.* se détourner, dévier.

deform [dɪ'foɚm] *v. tr.* déformer, enlaidir. || **deformed** [-d] *adj.* difforme. || **deformity** [-ɪtɪ] *n.* difformité *f.*

defraud [dɪ'fɹɔd] *v. tr.* frauder, tromper; [Fig.] priver (de).

defray [dɪ'fɹej] *v. tr.* défrayer, payer: *to ~ expenses,* couvrir les dépenses.

defrost [dɪ'fɹɔst] *v. tr.* [windshield, &c.] dégivrer; [food] décongeler. || **defroster** [-ɚ] *n.* [device] dégivreur *m.* || **defrosting** [-ɪŋ] *n.* dégivrage *m.*

deft [dɛft] *adj.* adroit; [nimble] agile, habile.

defunct [dɪ'fʌŋkt] *adj.* défunt.

defy [dɪ'faj] *v. tr.* braver, défier, mettre au défi: *This problem defies solution,* Ce problème/résiste, se dérobe/à toute solution.

degenerate [dɪ'ʤɛnɚˌət] *adj.* dégénéré, abâtardi. || *n.* dégénéré *m.* || *v. intr.* [-ejt] dégénérer (dans, en).

degradation [ˌdɛgɹə'dejʃən] *n.* dégradation *f*; [Fig.] avilissement *m.* || **degrade** [dɪ'gɹejd] *v. tr.* dégrader; [Mil.] casser (un grade); [Fig.] avilir.

degree [dɪ'gɹij] *n.* **1.** [quantity] degré *m,* mesure *f*: *by degrees,* graduellement, peu à peu; *to a ~*, jusqu'à un certain point. **2.** [science] degré *m.* **3.** [Sch.] diplôme *m,* grade *m* (universitaire): *bachelor's ~*, baccalauréat *m*; *Where did you get your ~?*, Où avez-vous reçu votre diplôme?; *What degrees does he/have, hold/?*, Quels sont ses grades universitaires? cf. LICENCE, DOCTOR.

de-icer [dɪ'ajsɚ] *n.* dégivreur *m.*

deign [dejn] *v. intr.* daigner (faire qqch.). || *v. tr.* daigner, accorder (une réponse, &c.).

deity ['dijətɪ] *n.* divinité *f*; [Myth.] déité *f.*

dejected [dɪ'ʤɛk|təd] *adj.* abattu, triste, découragé, déprimé. || **dejection** [-ʃən] *n.* abattement *m,* découragement *m*; [Med.] évacuation *f,* déjection *f.*

delay [dɪ'lej] *n.* retard *m*: *to obtain a ~*, obtenir un sursis; *without ~*, sans/délai, retard/. || *v. tr.* retarder (qqun), différer (qqch.). || *v. intr.* tarder (à faire qqch., *in doing sth.*); [be late] s'attarder.

delectable [dɪ'lɛktəbl̩] *adj.* délectable, délicieu|x *m,* -se *f.*

delegate ['dɛləgət] *n.* délégué *m,* représentant *m.* || *v. tr.* ['dɛləˌgej|t] déléguer, députer. || **delegation** [-ʃən] *n.* délégation *f,* députation *f.*

delete [dɪ'lijt] *v. tr.* effacer, rayer: *to ~ a paragraph,* supprimer un paragraphe.

deliberate [dɪ'lɪbɹət] *adj.* **1.** délibéré, prémédité. **2.** circonspect, lent, réfléchi. || *v. intr.* [dɪ'lɪbɚejt] délibérer (sur, *upon*); réfléchir à. || **deliberately** [-lɪ] *adv.* de propos délibéré; posément. || **deliberation** [dɪlɪbɚ'ejʃən] *n.* délibération *f,* réflexion *f*; [debate] débats *mpl,* discussion *f.*

delicacy ['dɛlɪkəsɪ] *n.* **1.** délicatesse *f.* **2.** [Culin.] friandise *f,* mets *m* délicat.

delicate ['dɛlɪkət] *adj.* délicat; [wit] fin; [health] fragile, délicat. || **delicately** [-lɪ] *adv.* délicatement, avec délicatesse, finement. || **delicatessen** [ˌdɛlɪkə'tɛsən] *n.* [store & food] charcuterie *f.*

delicious [dɪ'lɪʃəs] *adj.* délicieu|x *m,* -se *f.*

delight [dɪ'lajt] *n.* délice *m*; [délice is *f* in the *pl.*] plaisir *m,* joie *f* (*to* de, + infin., pour + *n.*). || *v. tr.* charmer, enchanter (qqun), ravir, réjouir (qqun): *to be delighted to,* être/charmé, ravi, enchanté/de. || *v. intr.* se délecter (de qqch.); prendre plaisir (à faire qqch.). || **delightful** [-fl̩] *adj.* délicieu|x *m,* -se *f,* charmant, ravissant.

delineate [dɪ'lɪnɪˌejt] *v. tr.* tracer, esquisser, dessiner; [Fig.] décrire.

delinquency [də'lɪŋkwən|sɪ] *n.* délinquance *f*; [fault] délit *m*: *juvenile ~*, enfance *f* délinquante. || **delinquent** [-t] *n. & adj.* délinquant *m.*

delirious [dɪ'lijɚɪ|əs] *adj.* en délire, délirant: *To be ~*, → avoir le délire, délirer. || **delirium** [-əm] *n.* [Med.] délire *m.*

deliver [dɪ'lɪvɚ] *v. tr.* **1.** livrer (des marchandises, &c.), distribuer (le courrier, &c.); remettre (qqch. à qqun): *We ~*, → Livraison *f* à domicile. **2.** prononcer (une allocution, un discours); asséner (un coup, &c.); [free] délivrer, libérer (qqun, qqch.): *She has just been delivered of her baby,* Elle vient d'accoucher (d'un garçon, d'une fille). || **deliverance** [-əns] *n.* délivrance *f*; [of a woman] accouchement *m.* || **delivery** [-ɪ] *n.* **1.** livraison *f* (de marchandises, &c.); distribution *f* (de lettres, &c.); [handing over] remise *f* (de qqch.). **2.** [baseball, cricket] service *m,* lancer *m,* lancement *m.* **3.** [speech, &c.] débit *m* (oratoire), diction *f,* élocution *f.* **4.** [Med.] accouchement *m.* **5.** [setting free] délivrance *f* (de qqch.). || **delivery-man** [-ˌmæn] *n.* [Com.] livreur *m.* || **delivery truck** [-ˌtɹʌk] *n.* voiture *f*/camion *m*/de livraison. cf. VAN.

†**dell** [dɛl] *n.* vallon *m.*

delude [dɪ'luwd] *v. tr.* tromper, duper.

deluge ['dɛljuwʤ] *n.* déluge *m.* || *v. tr.* inonder (de, *with*).

delusion [dɪ'luw|ʒən] *n.* illusion *f*; erreur *f.* || **delusive** [-sɪv] *adj.* trompeur, décevant, illusoire.

de luxe, deluxe [dɪ'lʌks] *adj.* de (grand) luxe, de qualité.

delve [dɛlv] *v. tr.* [Fig.] fouiller.

demagogue [ˌdɛmə'gɑg] *n.* démagogue *m.*

demand [dɪ'mænd] *n.* **1.** [×] exigence *f*; [claim] revendication *f.* **2.** [Com.] demande *f*: *in great* ~, très demandé. || *v. tr.* [☞ mot très fort en anglais; comparer ASK] exiger, réclamer (qqch. à qqun); [call for] demander, réclamer. || **demanding** [-ɪŋ] *adj.* exigeant.

demean [dɪ'mijn] *v. intr.* **1.** se conduire, se comporter. **2.** [humble] abaisser, avilir. || **demeanour** [-ɚ] *n.* air *m*, maintien *m*; [behaviour] comportement *m.*

demented [dɪ'mɛntəd] *adj.* fou *m*, folle *f*; dément.

demerit [dɪ'mɛɚɪt] *n.* faute *f*; [driving, & Mil.] point *m* de mauvaise conduite; *the merits and demerits*, le pour et le contre.

demi- ['dɛmɪ-] préfixe correspondant à Fr. *demi*; cf. HALF.

demilitarize [dɪ'mɪlɪtɚˌajz] *v. tr.* démilitariser.

demobilization [dɪˌmowbɪlaj'zejʃən] *n.* démobilisation *f.* || **demobilize** [dɪ'mowbɪˌlajz] *v. tr.* démobiliser.

democracy [də'mɑkɹəsɪ] *n.* démocratie *f.* || **democrat** ['dɛməˌkɹæt] *n.* démocrate *m.* || **democratic** [ˌdɛmə'kɹætɪk] *adj.* démocratique; [USA] ~ *Party*, le parti démocrate.

demolish [dɪ'mɑlɪʃ] *v. tr.* démolir, détruire; [Fig.] dévorer.

demon ['dijmən] *n.* démon *m*; *a* ~ *for work*, un bourreau *m* de travail. || **demoniac** [dɪ'mownɪək] *adj.* démoniaque.

demonstrate ['dɛmənˌstɹej|t] *v. tr.* démontrer. || *v. intr.* [mob] manifester. || **demonstration** [-ʃən] *n.* démonstration *f*; [parade] manifestation *f*, défilé *m.* || **demonstrative** [də'mɑnstɹəˌtɪv] *adj.* démonstrati|f *m*, -ve *f.*

demoralize [dɪ'mɔɚəˌlajz] *v. tr.* corrompre, démoraliser (les troupes, le peuple).

demur [də'mɚ] *v. intr.* [-rr-] hésiter (*at*, à), faire des objections (contre, *at*).

demure [də'mjuwɚ] *adj.* réservé, d'une modestie *f* affectée: *She has a* ~ *look*, C'est une vraie Sainte-Nitouche.

den [dɛn] *n.* [animal] antre *m*; [thief] repaire *m*; [Fig.] cabinet *m* de travail.

denial [dɪ'najḷ] *n.* **1.** dénégation *f*, déni *m* (de justice); démenti *m*, un démenti catégorique. **2.** refus *m*: *self-* ~, abnégation *f.*

denim ['dɛnṃ] *n.* coutil *m.*

†**denizen** ['dɛnɪzən] *n.* habitant *m.*

Denmark ['dɛnˌmɑɚk] *n.* (le) Danemark *m.*

denomination [dɪˌnɑmɪn'ej|ʃən] *n.* dénomination *f*; [Rel.] culte *m*, secte *f*; [Fin.] valeur *f* d'une coupure. || **denominator** [dɪ'nɑmɪnˌejtɚ] *n.* [Math.] dénominateur *m.*

denote [dɪ'nowt] *v. tr.* dénoter, indiquer.

denounce [dɪ'nawns] *v. tr.* dénoncer; [treaty] dénoncer, rompre; s'élever contre (des abus).

dense [dɛns] *adj.* dense, épais, [crowd] compact; [Fig.] stupide. || **density** [-ɪtɪ] *n.* densité *f*, épaisseur *f*; [Fig.] stupidité *f.*

dent [dɛnt] *v. tr.* bosseler, cabosser; [blade, armour] ébrécher. || *n.* bosse *f*; [blade, armour] brèche *f.*

dental ['dɛnt|l] *adj.* **1.** [art, care, &c.] dentaire: ~ *office*, cabinet *m* dentaire. **2.** [Ling.] dental. || **dentifrice** [-ɪfɹɪs] *n.* pâte *f* dentifrice, dentifrice *m.* || **dentist** [-ɪst] *n.* dentiste *m.* || **denture** [-ʧɚ] *n.* fausses dents *fpl*; [Tech.] prothèse *f* dentaire; dentier *m.*

denude [dɪ'njuwd] *v. tr.* dénuder; dépouiller (de, *of*).

denunciation [dɪˌnʌnsɪ'ejʃən] *n.* dénonciation *f*; [treaty] rupture *f.*

deny [dɪ'naj] *v. tr.* **1.** nier; démentir (une rumeur, déclaration): *I* ~ *having done it*, Je nie l'avoir fait; *I* ~ *that he did it*, Je nie qu'il l'ait fait; *I don't* ~ *that he did it*, Je ne nie pas qu'il (ne)/l'ait, l'a/fait; *it can't be denied, there is no denying that . . .*, on ne saurait nier que . . . (ne) [+ subjunc., more rarely + indic.]. **2.** refuser, dénier (qqch. à qqun): *to* ~ *o.s. sth.*, se priver de qqch.

deodorant [dɪ'owdɚ|ənt] *n.* désodorisant *m.* || **deodorize** [-ˌajz] *v. tr. & intr.* désodoriser.

depart [dɪ'pɑɚt] *v. intr.* partir (*for*, pour), s'en aller, [habit] se départir de; s'écarter, s'éloigner (de qqch., *from sth.*); [Fig.] [die] †trépasser. || **departed** [-əd] *adj.* mort, défunt; *the* ~, les morts, les défunts *mpl.*

department [dɪ'pɑɚtmənt] *n.* **1.** [Adm.] service *m*, département *m*; [Univ.] institut *m*, section *f*: (*the*) *Department of Linguistics*, (la) section de Linguistique.

2. © ministère *m*: (*the*) *Department of External Affairs*, le ministère des Affaires extérieures. 3. ~ *store*, grand magasin *m*. 4. [Mil.] division *f*: [French administrative division] département *m*. || **departmental** [dɪˌpɑɚt'mɛntl̩] *adj*. départemental.

departure [dɪ'pɑɚtʃɚ] *n*. départ *m*; [Fig.] déviation *f*: ~ *from evil*, renonciation *f* au mal; ~ *from orders*, infraction *f* aux ordres.

depend [dɪ'pɛnd] *v. intr*. [rely, &c.] dépendre (de, *on*); compter (sur qqun, qqch.); *to* ~ *on s.o., sth.*, se fier (à): *You can* ~ *on him*, Vous pouvez/vous fier à lui, vous y fier/; *You can* ~ *on it*, Vous pouvez/compter là-dessus, y compter/. || **dependable** [-əbl̩] *adj*. [Pers.] digne de confiance, © fiable. || **dependant** [-ənt] cf. DEPENDENT. || **dependence** [-əns] *n*. 1. dépendance *f* (de, *on*), subordination *f* (à, *on*). 2. confiance *f*, (en, *on*). || **dependency** [-ənsɪ] *n*. dépendance *f*. || **dependent** [-ənt] *adj*. dépendant (de, *on*), relevant (de, *on*); à la charge (de, *on*); [Gram.] ~ *clause*, proposition subordonnée. || *n*. (personne) à charge; ayant droit *m*: *dependents*, charges *f* de famille.

depict [dɪ'pɪkt] *v. tr*. peindre; [describe] dépeindre, décrire (une situation, &c.).

deplane [dɪ'plejn] *v. intr*. descendre (d'avion).

deplete [dɪ'plijt] *v. tr*. [supplies] épuiser, vider.

deplorable [dɪ'plowɚ|əbl̩] *adj*. déplorable; [Pej.] lamentable. || **deplore** *v. tr*. déplorer, se lamenter sur.

deploy [dɪ'ploj] *v. tr. & intr*. [Mil.] déployer; se déployer.

deport [dɪ'pɔɚt] *v. tr*. 1. déporter; expulser. 2. [behave] se conduire, se comporter. || **deportation** [ˌdɪpɔɹ'tejʃən] *n*. déportation *f*, expulsion *f*. || **deportment** [dɪ'pɔɹtmənt] *n*. comportement *m*, tenue *f*, manières *fpl*.

depose [dɪ'powz] *v. tr*. [Pol.] déposer (un souverain). || *v. intr*. [Jur.] déposer, faire une déposition, témoigner. || **deposit** [dɪ'pɑzɪt] *n*. [money] dépôt *m*; [Geol.] dépôt, sédiment *m*; [Jur.] cautionnement *m*: [bank] *safety* ~ *box*, coffre *m*, © coffret *m* de sûreté. || *v. tr*. déposer (qqch.), mettre (qqch.) en/dépôt, consigne/. || **deposition** [ˌdɛpə'zɪʃən] *n*. déposition *f*, destitution *f* (d'un monarque); témoignage *m*. || **depositor** [dɪ'pɑzɪtɚ] *n*. déposant *m*. || **depot** ['dijpow] *n*. 1. [storage] magasin *m*, entrepôt *m*; [Mil.] dépôt *m*. 2. © gare *f*.

deprave [dɪ'pɹejv] *v. tr*. dépraver.

deprecate ['dɛpɹəˌkejt] *v. tr*. désapprouver.

depreciate [di'pɹijʃɪˌejt] *v. tr*. déprécier, faire baisser le prix de . . . . || *v. intr*. se déprécier, diminuer de valeur.

depreciation [dɪˌpɹɪʃɪ'ejʃən] *n*. dépréciation *f*.

depress [dɪ'pɹɛ|s] *v. tr*. baisser, abaisser; appuyer sur (un bouton, &c.); [prices] déprécier; [Pers.] attrister, décourager. || **depressed** [-st] *adj*. [Pers.] déprimé, abattu; [prices] bas. || **depression** [-ʃən] *n*. [low place] dépression *f*; [weather] dépression *f*; [Fin.] crise *f*, dépression *f* (économique); [gloominess] découragement *m*, abattement *m*.

deprive [dɪ'pɹajv] *v. tr*. priver, déposséder qqun (de, *of*).

dept. [= DEPARTMENT].

depth [dɛpθ] *n*. 1. profondeur *f*; [sea, &c.] fond *m*; [Fig.] intensité *f* (d'une douleur, &c.): *to be 50 feet in* ~, avoir 50 pieds de profondeur; *at a* ~ *of 50 feet*, par 50 pieds de fond; *in the* ~ *of winter*, en plein hiver; *to/be, get/out of one's* ~, [swimming] perdre pied, [Fig.] n'être pas à la hauteur. 2. *pl*.: *the depths* les profondeurs *fpl* (de l'océan), l'abîme *m*: *in the depths of despair*, dans le désespoir le plus profond.

deputation [ˌdɛpjə'tejʃən] *n*. députation *f*, délégation *f*. || **depute** [dɪ'pjuwt] *v. tr*. députer, déléguer (qqun). || **deputize** ['dɛpjəˌtajz] *v. tr*. nommer qqun. remplaçant, déléguer qqun. || *v. intr*. servir de remplaçant (à, *for*), remplacer qqun. || **deputy** ['dɛpjətɪ] *n*. [Pol.] député *m*; [Adm.] remplaçant *m*, adjoint *m*: ~ *chairman*, vice-président *m*; ~ *minister*, ministre *m* adjoint, © sous-ministre *m*.

derail [dɪ'ɹejl] *v. tr*. [train] (faire) dérailler.

derange [dɪ'ɹejndʒ] *v. tr*. 1. déranger (qqun, qqch.). 2. troubler, déranger (qqun).

derelict ['dɛɚəˌlɪkt] *adj*. [ship] abandonné; [in o.'s duty] coupable de négligence. || *n*. épave *f*.

deride [dɪ'ɹajd] *v. tr*. rire de, se moquer de; railler, ridiculiser. || **derision** [dɪ'ɹɪʒən] *n*. moquerie *f*, sujet *m*, objet *m*/de dérision.

derive [dɪ'ɹajv] *v. tr*. provenir, tirer (de, *from*), recevoir: [Fig.] *That child derives his good disposition from his mother*, Cet enfant tient son bon caractère de sa mère. || *v. intr*. dériver (de, *from*).

derogative, derogatory [dɪ'ɹɑgətɪv, dɪ'ɹɑgəˌtɔɚɪ] *adj*. péjoratif; [Jur.] dérogatoire.

derrick ['dɛɚɪk] *n*. grue *f*, [oil well] derrick *m*.

descend [dɪ'sɛnd] *v. intr*. [go down, come from] descendre (de, *from*); [Fig., Lit.]

tomber, fondre (sur, *upon*). ‖ *v. tr.* descendre. ‖ **descendant** [-ənt] *n.* [offspring] descendant *m*, -e *f*; rejeton *m.* ‖ **descent** [dɪ'sɛnt] *n.* **1.** [going, bringing down] descente *f.* **2.** [origin] descendance *f*: *of French* ~, d'origine française.

describe [dɪ'skɹajb] *v. tr.* décrire (qqun, qqch.), donner une description de (qqun, qqch.), signaler (un suspect). ‖ **description** [dɪ'skɹɪpʃən] *n.* description *f* (de qqch.), signalement *m* (de qqun); [Fig.] espèce *f*, genre *m*, sorte *f*.

desecrate ['dɛsəˌkɹejt] *v. tr.* profaner.

desert[1] ['dɛzɚt] *n.* désert *m.* ‖ *adj.* [not inhabited] désert; [barren] désertique.

desert[2] [dɪ'zɚt] *n. us. pl.* mérite *m*; [punishment] punition *f*: *to get one's just deserts*, recevoir/ce qu'on mérite, sa juste punition/. cf. DESERVE.

desert[3] [dɪ'zɚt] *v. tr.* déserter, abandonner, [Pers.] délaisser. ‖ **deserter** [-ɚ] *n.* [army] déserteur *m.* ‖ **desertion** [dɪ'zɚʃən] *n.* désertion *f*, abandon *m.*

deserve [dɪ'zɚv] *v. tr.* mériter, être digne de (qqch.): *to* ~ *well of* (*one's country, &c.*), bien mériter de (sa patrie, &c.). ‖ **deserved** [-d] *adj.* (bien) mérité. ‖ **deservedly** [-ədlɪ] *adv.* à juste titre; à bon droit; justement. ‖ **deserving** [-ɪŋ] *adj.* [Pers.] méritant, [Pers., action] de mérite; [action] méritoire.

desiccate ['dɛsəˌkejt] *v. tr.* dessécher.

design [dɪ'zajn] *n.* [graph] plan *m*; [outline] dessin *m*, schéma *m*; [fashion] modèle *m*; [object] type *m*; [Fig.] dessein *m*, but *m.* ‖ *v. tr.* dessiner (un plan), faire le plan de (qqch.); projeter (qqch.); destiner (qqch. à, *sth. for*).

designate ['dɛzɪgˌnejt] *v. tr.* désigner; nommer. ‖ *adj.* choisi, nommé. ‖ **designation** [ˌdɛzɪg'nejʃən] *n.* désignation *f.*

designedly [dɪ'zajn|ədlɪ] *adv.* à dessein, de propos délibéré. ‖ **designer** [-ɚ] *n.* auteur *m*, inventeur *m* (d'un projet, d'un plan); dessinateur *m* (de mode, d'auto, d'avion), décorateur *m* de théâtre; [building] architecte *m*; [Fig.] intrigant *m.* ‖ **designing** [-ɪŋ] *adj.* rusé, intrigant.

desirability [dɪˌzajɚ|ə'bɪlɪtɪ] *n.* utilité *f*, caractère *m* désirable. ‖ **desirable** [-əbḷ] *adj.* désirable, souhaitable, à désirer. ‖ **desire** [dɪ'zajɚ] *n.* désir *m*, souhait *m.* ‖ *v. tr.* [wish for] désirer (qqch.), avoir envie de (+ inf., *to*). ‖ **desirous** [-əs] *adj.* désireux (de, *of, to*), empressé (à, *to*): *he seemed* ~ *to* , → il paraissait/désirer, avoir envie de/. . . .

desist [dɪ'zɪst] *v. intr.* renoncer (à, *from*), abandonner (un projet).

desk [dɛsk] *n.* [Sch.] pupitre *m*, [office] bureau *m.*

desolate ['dɛsələt] *adj.* désert, inhabité, ravagé; désolé. ‖ *v. tr.* ['dɛsəˌlejt] dépeupler, ravager; [Pers.] désoler. ‖ **desolation** [ˌdɛsə'lejʃən] *n.* désolation *f*, ravage *m*, profonde misère.

despair [dɪs'pɛɚ] *n.* désespoir *m.* ‖ *v. intr.* désespérer (de, *of*), perdre espoir. ‖ **despairing** [-ɪŋ] *adj.* désespéré. ‖ **despairingly** [-ɪŋlɪ] *adv.* désespérément.

despatch [dɪ'spætʃ] *n.* **1.** envoi *m*, [news] dépêche *f*, [Com.] expédition *f.* **2.** [action] rapidité *f*, promptitude *f.* ‖ *v. tr.* **1.** [news] dépêcher, [goods, &c.] expédier, [mail, &c.] envoyer; tuer (qqun). **2.** [hasten] hâter, précipiter (qqch.).

desperate ['dɛspɚət] *adj.* désespéré; [fighting] furieux, acharné; [reckless] capable de tout; [serious condition] (état *m*) très grave. ‖ **desperately** [-lɪ] *adv.* avec l'énergie *f* du désespoir; [in love] éperdument (amoureux). ‖ **desperation** [ˌdɛspɚ'ejʃən] *n.* désespoir *m*; fureur *f.*

despicable ['dɛspɪkəbḷ] *adj.* méprisable. ‖ **despise** [dɪ'spajz] *v. tr.* mépriser (qqun).

despite [dɪ'spajt] *prép.* malgré, en dépit de. cf. SPITE.

despoil [dɪ'spojl] *v. tr.* dépouiller, spolier (de, *of*).

despond [dɪ'spɔnd] *v. intr.* se décourager (de, *of*). ‖ **despondency** [-ənsɪ] *n.* découragement *m*, abattement *m*, désespoir *m.* ‖ **despondent** [-ənt] *adj.* découragé, abattu, déprimé.

despot ['dɛspɑt] *n.* despote *m*, tyran *m.* ‖ **despotic** [ˌdɛs'pɑtɪk] *adj.* despotique, tyrannique. ‖ **despotism** ['dɛspəˌtɪzəm] *n.* despotisme *m*, tyrannie *f.*

dessert [də'zɚt] *n* dessert *m*, entremets *m.*

destination [ˌdɛstɪ'nejʃən] *n.* destination *f.* ‖ **destine** ['dɛstɪn] *v. tr.* destiner (à, *to, for*). ‖ **destiny** [-ɪ] *n.* destin *m*, destinée *f.*

destitute ['dɛstɪ'tjuwt] *adj.* dénué, dépourvu (de, *of*). ‖ **destitution** [ˌdɛstɪ'tjuwʃən] *n.* dénuement *m*, indigence *f.*

destroy [dɪ'stɹoj] *v. tr.* détruire, [kill, &c.] tuer, exterminer; [Fig.] ruiner. ‖ **destroyer** [-ɚ] *n.* **1.** [Pers.] destruct|eur, -rice. **2.** [Naut.] destroyer *m.* ‖ **destruction** [dɪ'stɹʌk|ʃən] *n.* destruction *f*, ruine *f.* ‖ **destructive** [-tɪv] *adj.* [influence, &c.] destructif, [element, agent] destructeur.

desultory ['dɛsḷtɚɪ] *adj.* → à bâtons rompus.

detach [dɪ'tætʃ] *v. tr.* détacher, séparer (de, *from*): *a semi-detached house*, une maison/jumelle, mitoyenne/. ‖ **detachment** [-mənt] *n.* détachement *m*, indifférence *f*; [Mil.] détachement *m.*

detail [ˈdijtejl] *n.* détail *m*, particularité *f*; [Mil.] détachement: *to go into details*, entrer dans les détails. ‖ *v. tr.* [dɪˈtejl] [Adm.] affecter (un fonctionnaire à un poste), [Mil.] détacher (un officier à une mission); [Fin., Com.] détailler (un compte, &c.). ‖ **detailed** [-d] *adj.* [description, &c.] détaillé, circonstancié.

detain [dɪˈtejn] *v. tr.* détenir (qqun en prison), arrêter (qqun), empêcher (qqun de partir): *I was detained*, J'ai été retenu.

detect [dɪˈtɛk|t] *v. tr.* découvrir, déceler; détecter; [Fig.] percevoir, apercevoir. ‖ **detection** [-ʃən] *n.* découverte *f.* ‖ **detective** [-tɪv] *n.* détective *m.*

detention [dɪˈtɛnʃən] *n.* action *f* de retenir; détention *f*; retard *m* forcé.

deter [dɪˈtɚ] [-rr-] *v. tr.* détourner, dissuader/(qqun de qqch., *s.o. from sth.*); empêcher, décourager/(qqun de faire qqch.).

detergent [dɪˈtɚʤənt] *n.* détersif *m.* ‖ *adj.* détersi|f *m*, -ve *f.*

deteriorate [dɪˈtijərɪɚ|ˌejt] *v. tr.* détériorer. ‖ *v. intr.* [become worse] empirer. ‖ **deterioration** [-ˌejʃən] *n.* détérioration *f.*

determinate [dɪˈtɚmɪnət] *adj.* déterminé, fixé; [resolute] résolu, décidé à. ‖ **determination** [dɪˌtɚmɪ|ˈnejʃən] *n.* **1.** détermination *f*, décision *f.* **2.** [calculation] fixation *f*; évaluation *f* (de prix, &c.). ‖ **determine** [-n] *v. tr.* déterminer, fixer, préciser (une date, &c.); [limit] délimiter (une responsabilité, &c.); [reaction] causer, produire/qqch. ‖ *v. intr.* décider (de + inf., *to*), se déterminer (à + inf., *to*). ‖ **determined** [-nd] *adj.* [thing, Pers.] déterminé, [Pers.] résolu (à faire qqch., *to do sth.*).

deterrent [dɪˈtɚənt] *adj.* & *n.* préventif *m*: *nuclear* ∼, force *f* de dissuasion.

detest [dɪˈtɛst] *v. tr.* détester.

detonate [ˈdɛtn̩ˌejt] *v. intr.* détoner. ‖ *v. tr.* faire détoner.

detour [ˈdɪjˌtuwɚ] *n.* [road traffic] déviation *f*, © détour *m*; [postal traffic] voie *f* détournée.

detract [dɪˈtɹækt] *v. tr.* & *intr.* diminuer, amoindrir, enlever (*from*, à).

detriment [ˈdɛtɹɪmənt] *n.* détriment *m*, préjudice *m*, dommage *m*: *It is no* ∼ *to . . .*, Cela ne nuit en rien à . . . ‖ **detrimental** [ˌdɛtɹɪˈmɛntl] *adj.* nuisible, préjudiciable (*to*, à).

deuce [duws] *n.* [cartes] deux; [tennis] égalité *f.* ‖ [fam.] diable *m*; [interj.] diantre!

devaluate [dɪˈvæljuwˌejt] *v. tr.* dévaluer.

devastate [ˈdɛvəˌstejt] *v. tr.* dévaster, ravager.

develop [dɪˈvɛləp] *v. tr.* **1.** développer; amplifier; perfectionner; [region] aménager, mettre en valeur. **2.** [Photog.] révéler (une plaque). ‖ *v. intr.* se développer; évoluer, progresser. ‖ **developer** [-ɚ] *n.* [Photog.] révélateur *m.* ‖ **development** [dɪˈvɛləpmənt] *n.* [growing; Photog.] développement *m*, amplification *f*; [phenomenon] évolution *f*; [city] progrès *m*: *to await further developments*, attendre la suite des événements.

deviate [ˈdijvɪˌejt] *v. intr.* dévier, s'écarter (de); [Fig.] s'égarer, donner dans l'erreur. ‖ **deviation** [ˌdijvɪˈejʃən] *n.* déviation *f*, écart *m*; [Naut.] changement *m* de route.

device [dɪˈvajs] *n.* mécanisme *m*, dispositif *m*, [Fam.] truc *m*; [Pej.] stratagème *m*: *to leave s.o. to /his, her/own devices*, laisser qqun se débrouiller/tout seul, toute seule/.

devil [ˈdɛv|l] *n.* diable *m*: *the Devil*, le Diable; [Fig.] démon *m*, un diable d'homme; *to be between the* ∼ *and the deep blue sea*, être pris entre deux feux; [Fam.] *There will be the* ∼ *to pay*, Les conséquences seront sérieuses, Cela pourra coûter cher; *How the* ∼ *!*, Comment diable! ‖ **devilish** [-ɪʃ] *adj.* diabolique, infernal.

devious [ˈdijvɪəs] *adj.* détourné, tortueux; ∼ *paths*, chemins sinueux; *by* ∼ *means*, par des moyens détournés.

devise [dɪˈvajz] *v. tr.* imaginer, inventer; [Pej.] tramer, ourdir (une machination); [Law] léguer (un bien immeuble).

devoid [dɪˈvojd] *adj.* dénué, dépourvu (*of*, de): ∼ *of care*, sans souci.

devolve [dɪˈvolv] *v. tr.* transmettre (à), déléguer (des pouvoirs à qqun). ‖ *v. intr.* échoir (à): *It devolves upon me*, C'est à moi qu'il incombe de, Il me revient de . . . .

devote [dɪˈvowt] *v. tr.* consacrer, vouer (sa vie, son temps), (*to*, à). ‖ **devoted** [-əd] *adj.* **1.** dévoué: *to be* ∼ *to one's friends*, se vouer à ses amis. **2.** consacré: *This period was* ∼ *to History*, Cette classe était consacrée à l'histoire. ‖ **devotion** [dɪˈvowʃən] *n.* [devoutness] dévotion *f*; [deep affection] dévouement *m*; *devotions*, prières *fpl*, †dévotions *fpl.*

devour [dɪˈvawɚ] *v. tr.* [food] dévorer.

devout [dɪˈvawt] *adj.* pieu|x *m*, -se *f*, sincère; dévot.

dew [djuw] *n.* rosée *f.* ‖ **dewy** [-ɪ] *adj.* /couvert, humide/de rosée; [Poet.] humide.

dexterity [ˌdɛks'tɛɚɪtɪ] *n.* dextérité *f,* adresse *f,* habileté *f.* || **dexterous** ['dekstɪəs] *adj.* adroit, habile.

diabetes [ˌdajə'bijtɪz] *n.* [Med.] diabète *m.*

diabolic [ˌdajə'bɑlɪk] *adj.* diabolique.

diagnose ['dajəgˌnows] *v. tr.* diagnostiquer. || **diagno|sis** [ˌdajəg'now|səs] *pl.* **-ses** [-sijz] *n.* diagnostic *m.*

diagonal [ˌdaj'ægənl] *adj.* diagonal. || *n.* diagonale *f.* || **diagonally** [-ɪ] *adv.* en diagonale.

diagram ['dajəˌgɪæm] *n.* diagramme *m,* schéma *m,* graphique *m.*

dial [dajl] *n.* [clock] cadran *m*; [Tel.] disque *m* d'appel: ~ *tone,* bourdonnement *m* d'appel. || *v. tr.* former, composer (un numéro).

dialect ['dajəˌlɛkt] *n.* dialecte *m.*

dialectic [ˌdajə'lɛktɪk] *adj.* & *n.f.* dialectique. || **dialectics** [-s] *n.* dialectique *f.*

dialogue ['dajəˌlɔg] *n.* dialogue *m,* entretien *m.* || *v. intr.* dialoguer, s'entretenir (avec, *with*).

diameter [daj'æmətɚ] *n.* [Geom.] diamètre *m.*

diametrically [ˌdajə'mɛtɪɪklɪ] *adv.* diamétralement.

diamond ['dajmənd] *n.* [jewel; glazier's] diamant *m*; [cards] carreau *m*; [baseball] © losange *m*: *baseball* ~ , terrain *m* de baseball; [Fig.] [Prov.] ~ *cut* ~ , A bon chat bon rat.

Diana [ˌdaj'ænə] *n.* = Diane *f.*

diaper ['dajpɚ] *n.* [baby] couche *f.*

diary ['dajɚɪ] *n.* agenda *m*; [daily account] journal *m.*

dibble ['dɪbl] *n.* [Agric.] plantoir *m.* || *v. tr.* planter (avec un plantoir).

dice [dajs] *n.pl.* cf. DIE[2] dés *mpl*: *to play* ~ , jouer aux dés; ~ *box,* cornet *m* (à dés); [Fam.] *No dice!,* Rien à faire! || *v. tr.* couper en cubes (des légumes).

dicker ['dɪkɚ] *v. intr.* marchander; manœuvrer pour avoir.

dictate [dɪk'tejt] *v. tr.* [letter, text, &c.] dicter. || *v. intr.* faire la loi (à qqun, *to s.o.*), donner des ordres (à qqun, *to s.o.*). || **dictation** [dɪk'tejʃən] *n.* dictée *f*: *to take (down) a* ~ , prendre en dictée. || **dictator** ['dɪkˌtejtɚ] *n.* dictateur *m.* || **dictatorial** [ˌdɪktə'tɔɚɪəl] *adj.* de dictateur, en dictateur. || **dictatorship** [dɪk'tejtɚˌʃɪp] *n.* dictature *f.*

diction ['dɪkʃən] *n.* diction *f*; débit *m* (de la parole). || **dictionary** ['dɪkʃənˌɛɚɪ] *n.* dictionnaire *m.*

did cf. DO. || **didn't** [= did not] cf. DO.

die[1] [daj] **dying** *v. intr.* mourir, périr (de, *of*); [animals] crever; [also Fig.] s'éteindre: *to* ~ *in one's sleep,* mourir, s'éteindre/ dans son sommeil; *to be dying,* se mourir; *He is dying for a drink,* Il meurt de soif; *I am dying to see it,* Je meurs d'envie de le voir. || **die away, out** [-əˌwej] [-ˌawt] *v. intr.* s'éteindre; s'affaiblir; disparaître. || **die down** [-ˌdawn] *v. intr.* se calmer, s'éteindre.

die[2] [daj] *pl.* **dice** *n.* dé *m* (à jouer): [Fig.] *The* ~ *is cast,* Le sort en est jeté.

die[3] [daj] *pl.* **dies** [-z] *n.* [Tech.] matrice *f,* coin *m.*

dieresis [daj'ɛɚəsɪs] *n.* [Gram.] tréma *m.*

diet ['dajət] *n.* **1.** alimentation *f,* nourriture *f.* **2.** diète *f,* régime *m* (alimentaire): *to put s.o. on a low* ~ , mettre qqun à la diète; *to put s.o. on a* ~ , mettre qqun au régime; *milk* ~ , régime lacté, diète lactée. || **dietary** ['dajəˌtɛɚɪ] *n.* régime *m* (alimentaire). || **dietetic** [ˌdajə|'tɛtɪk] *adj.* diététique. || **dietetics** [-'tɛtɪks] *n.* [science] diététique *f.* || **dietician, dietitian** [-'tɪʃən] *n.* diététicien *m,* -ne *f.*

differ ['dɪfɚ] *v. intr.* **1.** [be unlike] différer (de, *from*), être différent (de, *from*). **2.** [disagree] différer d'avis (avec qqun, *with s.o.*), ne pas être d'accord (avec qqun): *I beg to* ~ , Je ne suis pas d'accord. || **difference** ['dɪfɪ|əns] *n.* **1.** différence *f.* **2.** [disagreement] différend *m,* divergence *f* (d'opinion). || **different** [-ənt] *adj.* différent (de, *from*); autre (que); [various] différent, divers; [unusual] → qui sort de l'ordinaire: **1.** [= various]: *We have* ~ *ways of doing it,* Nous avons/différentes, diverses/façons de le faire; **2.** [dissimilar] Nous avons des façons différentes de le faire; *That's quite a* ~ *matter,* Ça, c'est/ autre chose, une autre affaire/; *sth. quite* ~ , qqch. qui sort vraiment de l'ordinaire. || **differential** [ˌdɪfɚ'ɛn|ʃəl] *adj.* & *n.* différentiel (*m*). || **differentiate** [-ʃɪˌejt] *v. tr.* différencier, distinguer (de, *from*); faire établir une/différence, distinction/entre. . . . || **differently** ['dɪfɪəntlɪ] *adv.* différemment.

difficult ['dɪfɪkəlt] *adj.* difficile, [task] ardu, [work, &c.] malaisé, pénible; [child, &c.] difficile, peu commode; *person* ~ *to get along with,* personne difficile à vivre. || **difficulty** [-ɪ] *n.* difficulté *f*: *with great* ~ , à grand peine; [bother] ennui *m,* embarras *m*: *in a* ~ , dans l'embarras; *to get out of a* ~ , se tirer/d'embarras, d'affaire/; obstacle (à), objection (à): *He made no* ~ *at my going out,* Il n'a pas fait d'objection à ce que je sorte.

diffidence ['dɪfɪdən|s] *n.* manque *m* de confiance (en soi-même), réserve *f.* || **diffi-**

dent [-t] *adj.* qui manque d'assurance (en soi-même), réservé.

diffuse [dɪ'fjuw|z] *v. tr.* [light, news] répandre, diffuser. || *adj.* [-s] [light] diffus; [writing, style] diffus, verbeux. || **diffusion** [dɪ'fjuwʒən] *n.* diffusion *f.*

dig [dɪg] **dug** [dʌg], **dug** *v. tr.* **[-gg-]** creuser (un trou, &c.); bêcher (la terre); [tunnel] percer: ~ *out*, extraire: extraire (qqch.): *to* ~ (*sth.*) *up*, déraciner (qqch.), [Fig.] mettre (un fait, &c.) à jour. || *v. intr.* ~ *into*, [work hard] piocher; ~ *in*, creuser une tranchée; [Fig.] *to* ~ *one's toes in*, se tenir de pied ferme; [US, Sl.] comprendre, [Fam.] piger. || *n.* creusage *m*; [Fig.] sarcasme *m*; *to have a* ~ *at sth.*, essayer qqch.; **digs** *n.pl.* [= DIGGINGS].

digest [daj'dʒɛst] *v. tr.* [food] digérer; [laws, documents, &c.] classer, compiler, résumer. || *n.* ['daj,dʒɛst] sommaire *m*, abrégé *m*; [laws, &c.] recueil *m*, †digeste *m*. || **digestible** [daj'dʒɛst|əbl̩] *adj.* digestible. || **digestion** [-tʃən] *n.* digestion *f.* || **digestive** [-ɪv] *adj.* digestif.

digger ['dɪgɚ] *n.* terrassier *m*: *gold-* ~, chercheur *m* d'or. || **digging** [-ɪŋ] *n.* **1.** [soil] creusage *m*, bêchage *m*, [ground] terrassement *m*, [excavation] fouille *f.* **2.** *diggings* mine *f*, gisement *m* (d'or, &c.); || **diggings, digs** [Br.] meublé *m*, garni *m*, [Argot.] turne *f.*

digit ['dɪdʒɪt] *n.* doigt *m*; [Math.] chiffre *m.*

dignified ['dɪgnɪ,faj|d] *adj.* digne, grave, emprunt de dignité; solennel. || **dignify** [faj] *v. tr.* donner de la dignité à, élever à une dignité; ennoblir. || **dignitary** ['dɪgnɪ|-,tɛɚɪ] *n.* dignitaire *m*; [church] prélat *m.* || **dignity** [-tɪ] *n.* dignité *f*; [rank] (haut) rang *m*; importance *f* (d'un personnage).

digress [daj'gɹɛ|s] *v. intr.* faire une digression; s'écarter (du sujet). || **digression** [-ʃən] *n.* [speech] digression *f.*

dike [dajk] *n.* [ditch] fossé *m*; [dam] digue *f.*

dilapidated [dɪ'læpɪ,dejtəd] *adj.* délabré: *to get* ~, se délabrer, tomber en ruines.

dilate [,daj'lejt] *v. tr.* dilater, distendre. || *v. intr.* se dilater, s'élargir, s'étendre. || **dilatory** ['dɪlə,tɔɚɪ] *adj.* lent, tardif: *a* ~ *answer*, une réponse dilatoire.

dilemma [dɪ'lɛmə] *n.* dilemme *m*; [Fig.] situation *f*, position *f*/embarrassante.

dilettante ['dɪlə,tɑnt] *n.* dilettante *m/f.*

diligence ['dɪlɪ,dʒən|s] *n.* diligence *f*, application *f*, assiduité *f* (au travail). || **diligent** [-t] *adj.* [Pers.] travailleur, appliqué, assidu.

dilute [dɪ'luwt] *v. tr.* diluer; [milk, wine] couper, étendre, mouiller; [Fig.] adoucir, atténuer (une opinion, une doctrine).

dim [dɪm] *adj.* **[-mm-]** faible, indistinct; [glow] sombre, obscur; [colour] terne; [Fig.] vague, imprécis: *to grow* ~, [light] baisser, s'éteindre, [sound, sight] s'affaiblir, [eyes] s'obscurcir, [colour] se ternir; [outline] s'effacer. || *v. tr.* **[-mm-]** obscurcir; affaiblir (la mémoire); baisser (une lumière, [Auto.] les phares); ternir (l'éclat). || *v. intr.* cf. *to grow* DIM.

dime [dajm] *n.* [coin] pièce *f* de dix cents, © (un) dix sous *m*: ~ *novel*, roman *m* populaire, roman de quatre sous (© de cinq sous).

dimension [dɪ'mɛnʃən] *n.* **1.** dimension *f*, mesure *f.* **2.** étendue *f.*

diminish [dɪ'mɪnɪʃ] *v. tr.* diminuer, réduire, amoindrir. || **diminution** [,dɪmɪ'nuwʃən] *n.* diminution *f*; réduction *f.* || **diminutive** [dɪ'mɪnjətɪv] *adj.* [very small] très petit, chétif. || *n.* [of a name] diminutif *m.*

dimity ['dɪmɪtɪ] *n.* [cotton cloth] basin *m.*

dimness ['dɪmnəs] *n.* obscurité *f*; [sight] faiblesse *f.*

dimple ['dɪmpl̩] *n.* [cheek, chin] fossette *f*; [on water] ride *f.*

din [dɪn] *v. tr.* **[-nn-]** assourdir, étourdir (qqun): *She dinned it into my ears*, Elle m'en a rebattu les oreilles. || *n.* (grand) bruit *m*, vacarme *m*; [Fam.] tapage *m*, tintamarre *m*; [arms] cliquetis *m.*

dine [dajn] *v. intr.* [Fr.] dîner, © souper; prendre le/[Fr.] dîner, © souper/. || *v. tr.* *to* ~ (*and wine*) *s.o.*, bien traiter qqun (au restaurant). || **diner** [-ɚ] *n.* [Pers.] dîneur *m*; [Rail.] voiture-restaurant *f.* [also dining car].

dingy ['dɪndʒɪ] *adj.* sale, terne; [soiled] défraîchi; [Fam.] miteux.

dinner ['dɪnɚ] *n.* [Fr.] dîner *m*, © souper *m*; [public] banquet *m*: *after* ~, [once] après dîner, [usual] après le dîner; *to have* ~, dîner; *to go out for* ~, dîner/en ville, chez des amis/; *at* ~ *-time*, à l'heure du dîner; ~ *jacket*, smoking *m.*

dint [dɪnt] *n.* [seulement dans l'expression] *by* ~ *of*, à force de.

diocese ['dajə,sijz] *n.* diocèse *m.*

dip [dɪp] *v. tr.* **[-pp-]** plonger, tremper, immerger; baisser (les phares): *to* ~ *water out* (*of a pot*), puiser de l'eau (dans un pot). || *v. intr.* plonger; descendre (subitement); [Fig.] baisser: *to* ~ *into a book*, feuilleter un livre. || *n.* plongeon *m*, immersion *f*, [Tech.] bain *m*, inclinaison *f*; dépression *f*; [swim] trempette *f*: *to have a* ~, faire trempette.

diphtheria [dɪf'θijɚɪə] *n.* [Med.] diphtérie *f.*

diphthong ['dɪfθɔŋ] *n.* [Phon.] diphtongue *f.*

diploma [dɪ'plowmə] *pl.* **-s,** *n.* diplôme *m.*
diplomacy [-sɪ] *n.* diplomatie *f.* || **diplomat** ['dɪplə,mæt] *n.* diplomate *m.* || **diplomatic** [,dɪplə'mætɪk] *adj.* diplomatique.
dipper ['dɪpɚ] *n.* [Pers.] plongeur *m*; [thing] cuiller *f* à pot; [stars] *the/Big, Little/Dipper,* la/Grande, Petite/Ourse.
dipt [dɪpt] -dipped. cf. DIP.
dire [dajɚ] *adj.* terrible, affreux: *in a ~ necessity,* → en dernière extrémité *f*; *to be in ~ straits,* être dans une misère noire.
direct [dɪ'ɹɛk|t] *adj.* [blow, route, &c.] direct; [line] droit; [answer, statement] catégorique; [Pers.] franc; [danger, &c.] immédiat, imminent; [Elect.] *~ current,* courant *m* continu. || *v. tr.* diriger (des hommes, une entreprise, son attention sur); indiquer le chemin à (qqun); donner l'ordre à (qqun de faire qqch.); [aim] orienter, braquer (*on,* sur): attirer (l'attention de qqun sur); adresser (une lettre à qqun); mettre (un film) en scène: *to ~ o.s to s.o.,* s'adresser à qqun; *Will you ~ me to . . . ?,* Voulez-vous m'indiquer le chemin pour aller à . . . ? || *v. intr.* commander; être metteur en scène. || **direction** [-ʃən] *n.* **1.** [guidance] direction *f*, administration *f* (d'une entreprise; mise *f* en scène (d'un film); [course] sens *m*, côté *m*, direction *f*: *under the ~ of,* sous la direction de; *in that ~ ,* de ce côté là, dans cette direction-là, dans ce sens-là; (*In*) *which ~ did he go?,* De quel côté est-il parti ?; *in all directions,* de tous côtés; *Are you going in my ~ ?,* Allez-vous de mon côté ? **2.** *pl. directions* instructions *fpl*: *Directions for use,* Mode *m* d'emploi. || **directive** [-tɪv] *n.* directive *f.* || **directly** [-tlɪ] *adv.* directement, tout droit; [esp. Br.] sur-le-champ, immédiatement. || **directness** [-tnəs] *n.* [Fig.] franchise *f*, spontanéité *f*; [character] droiture *f.* || **director** [dɪ'ɹɛktɚ] *n.* [institution, company, &c.] directeur *m*; membre *m* du Conseil d'administration; [enterprise] administrateur *m*; *Board of Directors,* Conseil *m* d'administration; [orchestra, &c.] chef *m.*
directory [dɪ'ɹɛktəɪ] *n.* **1.** [telephone] annuaire *m*; *business ~ ,* [Fr.] le Bottin; © l'Annuaire *m* du Commerce. **2.** conseil *m* d'administration.
dirge [dɚʤ] *n.* chant *m* funèbre.
dirt [dɚt] *n.* saleté *f*; ordure *f*; [body, suit] crasse *f*; [esp. moral] malpropreté *f*; [ground] *~ road,* chemin *m* de terre, route non goudronnée; boue *f*: *~ -cheap,* pour rien, sans valeur; [Fig.] *He treated her like ~ ,* Il la traitait d'une manière grossière, insultante; [Fig.] *to eat ~ ,* être obligé de s'abaisser, de faire des excuses; *cheap as ~ ,* sans valeur, commun; *to strike pay ~ ,* avoir du succès (dans une mine, une entreprise). || **dirty** [-ɪ] *adj.* sale, [Pers., &c.] malpropre, [shoe] crotté, [suit, &c.] crasseux; [Fig., language, style] ordurier, obscène; [weather] orageux, couvert. || *v. tr.* salir, souiller, encrasser.
dis- [dɪs-] correspond souvent à des mots français en **dé(s)-** [préfixe marquant le contraire ou l'éloignement indiqué par un trait vertical].
disability [,dɪzə'bɪlɪtɪ] *n.* incapacité *f.*
dis|able [dɪs'ejbḷ] *v. tr.* [physically] estropier, rendre incapable (de); [Law, Sport] disqualifier: *to be disabled,* être/ [Pers.] impotent, infirme, [ship] désemparé/.
dis|advantage [,dɪsəd'væntəʤ] *v. tr.* désavantager (qqun). || *n.* désavantage *m*; condition *f* défavorable: *to be at a ~ ,* être en état d'infériorité; [Com.] *to sell at a ~ ,* vendre à perte.
dis|agree [,dɪsə'gɹij] *v. intr.* [Pers.] être en désaccord (avec, *with*), différer/d'opinion, d'avis/; se/brouiller, fâcher/(avec qqun, *with s.o.*); [thing] ne pas convenir, être contraire (à, *with*). || **dis|agreeable** [-əbḷ] *adj.* désagréable, ennuyeux. || **dis|agreement** [-mənt] *n.* désaccord *m*, différence *f* (d'opinion, de vues); différend *m*; [Fam.] fâcherie *f*, brouille *f.*
disallow [,dɪsə'law] *v. tr.* rejeter, refuser.
dis|appear [,dɪsə'pijɚ] *v. intr.* disparaître [action = conj. AVOIR, state = conj. ÊTRE]; [Fig., thing] s'évanouir, [Pers.] mourir. || **dis|appearance** [-əns] *n.* disparition *f.*
disappoint [dɪsə'pojnt] *v. tr.* désappointer, décevoir (qqun), [not to keep one's word] faire faux bond à (qqun). || **disappointed** [-əd] *adj.* déçu, désenchanté; contrarié. || **disappointment** [-mənt] *n.* déception *f*, désappointement *m*; contretemps *m*; [Pers.] *He is a ~ ,* → Il n'a pas rendu ce qu'on attendait de lui.
disapprobation [dɪs,æpɹə'bejʃən] *n.* désapprobation *f.*
dis|approval [dɪsə'pɹuwv|ḷ] *n.* désapprobation *f.* || **dis|approve** *v. tr. & intr.* (of) désapprouver, trouver à redire à (qqun, qqch.).
dis|arm [dɪs'ɑɚm] *v. tr.* désarmer; [Fig.] apaiser (la colère de qqun). || **dis|armament** [-əmənt] *n.* désarmement *m.*
dis|arrange [dɪsə'ɹejnʤ] *v. tr.* déranger; mettre . . . en désordre. || **dis|array**

[dɪsə'ɹej] *v. tr.* [troops] mettre en déroute, en désarroi; mettre en désordre. ‖ *n.* désarroi *m,* désordre *m*: *in* ~, mi-vêtu, en partie déshabillé.

disaster [dɪz'æst|ɚ] *n.* désastre *m,* calamité *f,* grand malheur *m.* ‖ **disastrous** [-ɹəs] *adj.* désastreux.

dis|avow [dɪsə'vaw] *v. tr.* désavouer (qqun qqch.), renier (qqun).

dis|band [dɪs'bænd] *v. tr.* disperser; [dismiss] licencier. ‖ *v. intr.* se disperser.

dis|belief [ˌdɪsbə'lij|f] *n.* incrédulité *f.* ‖ **dis|believe** [-v] *v. tr.* refuser de croire (*in,* à): *to ~ every word of ...*, ne pas croire un traître mot de. . . .

disburse [dɪs'bɚs] *v. tr.* débourser (une somme d'argent). ‖ **disbursement** [-mənt] *n.* paiement *m,* débours *m*; [Com.] *pl.* déboursés *mpl.*

disc [dɪsk] *n.* [phonograph, &c.] disque *m*; © [Sport] rondelle *f* (de hockey).

discard ['dɪsˌkɑɚd] *n.* [cards] écart *m,* défausse *f*; objet *m* de rebut, déchet *m.* ‖ *v. tr.* [dɪs'kɑɚd] mettre de côté, écarter, jeter (qqch.); congédier (qqun); [cards] se défausser (de).

discern [dɪ'sɚn] *v. tr.* discerner, distinguer (*from,* de, d'avec). ‖ **discerning** [-ɪŋ] *adj.* judicieux, avisé. ‖ **discernment** [-mənt] *n.* discernement *m.*

dis|charge [dɪs'ʧɑɚʤ] *v. tr.* **1.** décharger (une arme à feu, un navire, des marchandises). **2.** renvoyer (de l'hôpital), congédier (un domestique); libérer (un prisonnier; démobiliser (un soldat); [Fig.] s'acquitter de, accomplir (un devoir); payer (une dette). ‖ *n.* ['dɪsˌʧɑɚʤ] décharge *f*; [dismissal] renvoi *m,* [more polite] congé; [prisoner] mise *f* en liberté, élargissement *m*; [soldier] démobilisation *f*; [duty] accomplissement *m*; [Com.] quittance *f*; [Med.] écoulement *m,* suppuration *f.*

disciple [dɪ'sajpḷ] *n.* disciple *m.* ‖ **disciplinary** ['dɪsɪplɪˌnɛɚɪ] *adj.* [mesure, loi] disciplinaire. ‖ **discipline** ['dɪsɪplɪn] *n.* [Mil., Sch., &c.] discipline *f*; [lawmaking] autorité *f,* pouvoir *m*; [punishment] châtiment *m.* ‖ *v. tr.* [soldiers, pupils, &c.] discipliner, soumettre (qqun) à la discipline; [punish] corriger, punir (qqun).

dis|claim [dɪs'klejm] *v. tr.* nier, désavouer, renier: [Law] *to ~ o.'s rights to,* renoncer à ses droits sur.

dis|close [dɪs'klow|z] *v. tr.* dévoiler, divulguer, découvrir, révéler (un secret, une intention, un but caché). ‖ **dis|closure** [-ʒɚ] *n.* divulgation *f,* révélation *f.*

dis|colour [dɪs'kʌlɚ] *v. tr.* décolorer.

discomfit [dɪs'kʌmfət] *v. tr.* [-tt-] mettre en déroute; [Fig.] déconcerter.

dis|comfort [dɪs'kʌmfɚt] *n.* incommodité *f,* gêne *f,* malaise *m*; manque *m* de confort. ‖ *v. tr.* incommoder, gêner.

disconcert [dɪskən'sɚt] *v. tr.* déconcerter, troubler, embarrasser.

dis|connect [dɪskən'ɛkt] *v. tr.* désunir, séparer; [Electr.] couper (le courant), débrancher; [Mec.] débrayer. ‖ **dis|connected** [-əd] *adj.* désuni, séparé, [Mec.] débrayé; [Electr.] débranché; [speech] décousu, incohérent.

disconsolate [dɪs'kɑnsələt] *adj.* désolé, inconsolable.

dis|content [ˌdɪskən'tɛnt] *n.* mécontentement *m.* ‖ *adj.* mécontent (*with,* de). ‖ *v. tr.* mécontenter (qqun).

dis|continuance [ˌdɪskən'tɪnjuw|əns] *n.* interruption *f,* suspension *f,* cessation *f*; [Jur.] abandon *m* (d'un procès). ‖ **dis|continue** [-] *v. tr.* interrompre, suspendre, cesser (de). ‖ **dis|continuity** [dɪsˌkɑntə'njuwətɪ] *n.* discontinuité *f.* ‖ **dis|continuous** [ˌdɪskən'tɪnjuwəs] *adj.* discontinu.

discord ['dɪskɔɚd] *n.* discorde *f,* désaccord *m,* désunion *f*; [Mus.] dissonance *f.* ‖ **discordant** [dɪs'kɔɚdənt] *adj.* (en) désaccord (avec, *from*); [Mus.] dissonant.

discount ['dɪskawnt] *n.* [Com., Fin.] escompte *m,* [price] rabais *m,* réduction *f,* remise *f.* ‖ *v. tr.* [dɪs'kawnt] escompter (une facture, &c.); [Fig.=disregard] ne pas tenir compte de.

dis|courage [dɪs'kɚəʤ] *v. tr.* décourager; dissuader (qqun de, *s.o. from*), se prononcer (contre un projet, &c.); *This practice should be discouraged,* Cette habitude, Cette pratique/devrait être abandonnée. ‖ **dis|couragement** [-mənt] *n.* découragement *m.*

discourse ['dɪskɔɚs] *n.* discours *m,* entretien *m,* conversation *f.* ‖ *v. intr.* discourir (de, sur, *on*); entretenir (qqun de qqch., *to s.o. about sth.*), converser (avec); s'entretenir (avec qqun de qqch.).

dis|courteous [dɪs'kɚt|ɪəs] *adj.* impoli, discourtois. ‖ **discourtesy** [-əsɪ] *n.* impolitesse *f,* manque *m* de courtoisie.

dis|cover [dɪ'skʌvɚ] *v. tr.* **1.** découvrir, faire la découverte de. **2.** †révéler. ‖ **discoverer** [-ɚ] *n.* découvreur *m,* inventeur *m.* ‖ **discovery** [-ɪ] *n.* découverte *f* (d'un pays, d'un microbe), révélation *f* (d'un complot, d'un secret).

discredit [dɪs'kɹɛdət] *n.* discrédit *m,* déshonneur *m.* ‖ *v. tr.* discréditer; jeter le doute (sur qqun): *He is discredited*, On n'a plus confiance en lui. || **discreditable** [dɪs'kɹɛdɪtəbl̩] *adj.* → peu honorable.

discreet [dɪs'kɹijt] *adj.* discret; [careful] prudent, circonspect. || **discreetly** [-lɪ] *adv.* discrètement.

discrepancy [dɪs'kɹɛpənsɪ] *n.* [entre deux faits] désaccord *m*, divergence *f*, contradiction *f*; [entre deux récits, chiffres] différence *f*.

discrete [dɪs'kɹijt] *adj.* [elements, parts, &c.] distinct, séparé. || **discretion** [dɪs'kɹɛʃən] *n.* discrétion *f*; [caution] prudence *f*, circonspection *f*; [wisdom] jugement *m*: *years of ~*, l'âge *m* de raison.

discriminate [dɪs'kɹɪmənˌejt] *v. tr.* distinguer (de, d'avec, *from*); établir une distinction (entre, *between*): *to ~ against*, faire une distinction contre. || **discriminating** [-ɪŋ] *adj.* plein de jugement, avisé. || **discrimination** [dɪs'kɹɪmə'nejʃən] *n.* discernement *m*, jugement *m*; distinction *f*.

discursive [dɪ'skɚsɪv] *adj.* décousu, sans suite, à bâtons rompus.

discus ['dɪskəs] *n.* disque *m*.

discuss [dɪ'skʌs] *v. tr.* [idea, question] discuter, débattre; parler de. || **discussion** [dɪs'kʌʃən] *n.* discussion *f*, débat *m*.

disdain [dɪs'dejn] *n.* dédain *m*, mépris *m*. || *v. tr.* dédaigner. || **disdainful** [-fl̩] *adj.* [Pers.] dédaigneux, méprisant.

disease [dɪ'zijz] *n.* maladie *f*; [ailment] mal *m*. || **diseased** [-d] *adj.* malade; [mind, &c.] troublé, dérangé.

dis|embark [ˌdɪsəm'bɑɚk] *v. tr.* & *intr.* [from a ship] débarquer (de). || **dis|embarkation** [dɪsˌɛmbɑɚ'kejʃən] *n.* débarquement *m*.

dis|engage [ˌdɪsn̩'gejʤ] *v. tr.* dégager, libérer (qqun, qqch de qqch.); [Mech.] débrayer. || **dis|engaged** [-d] *adj.* libre, inoccupé.

dis|entangle [ˌdɪsn̩'tæŋgəl] *v. tr.* démêler, débrouiller, dégager (de): *to ~ (o.s.) from a difficulty*, (se) tirer d'embarras.

disfavour [dɪs'fejvɚ] *n.* désapprobation *f*; défaveur *f*.

dis|figure [dɪs'fɪgɚ] *v. tr.* [face] défigurer; [picture, &c.] abîmer; enlaidir.

disfranchise [dɪs'fɹænˌʧajs] *v. tr.* enlever le droit de vote à.

dis|gorge [dis'gɔɚʤ] *v. tr.* vomir, dégorger; [Fam., objets volés] rendre gorge.

disgrace [dɪs'gɹejs] *n.* honte *f*: *It's a ~ !*, C'est une honte; déshonneur *m*; [out of favour] disgrâce *f*. || *v. tr.* déshonorer, faire honte/(à qqun). || **disgraceful** [-fl̩] *adj.* honteux (pour, *to*), déshonorant, dégradant.

disgruntled [dɪs'gɹʌntl̩d] *adj.* maussade, contrarié, mécontent (de, *at*).

disguise [dis'gajz] *n.* déguisement *m*; [Fig.] camouflage *m*, feinte *f*: *in ~* , déguisé. || *v. tr.* déguiser (*as*, en); [Fig.] travestir (les faits), farder (la vérité).

disgust [dɪs'gʌst] *n.* dégoût *m*, écœurement *m*. || *v. tr.* dégoûter, écœurer (qqun). || **disgusted** [-əd] *adj.* [Fig.] dégoûté, écœuré. || **disgusting** [-ɪŋ] *adj.* dégoûtant, écœurant; [sight] répugnant.

dish [dɪʃ] *n.* [container, food] plat *m*; [food] mets *m*, repas *m*: *to do the dishes*, laver, faire/la vaisselle. || *v. tr.* (up, out) servir (un aliment). || **dish cloth** [-ˌklɔθ] *n.* torchon *m*. || **dish rag** [-ˌɹæg] *n.* lavette *f*. || **dish-washer** [-ˌwɔʃɚ] *n.* machine *f* à laver la vaisselle || **dish water** [-ˌwɔtɚ] *n.* eau *f* de vaisselle.

dis|hearten [dɪs'hɑɚtn̩] *v. tr.* décourager (de, *from*; par, *by*), démoraliser: *disheartened by difficulties*, abattu par des difficultés.

dishevel [dɪ'ʃɛvl̩] *v. intr.* [-ll-] écheveler, ébouriffer: *dishevelled hair*, cheveux *mpl* en désordre.

dis|honest [dɪs'ɑnəst] *adj.* malhonnête; déloyal. || **dis|honesty** [-ɪ] *n.* malhonnêteté *f*. || **dis|honour** [dɪs'ɑnɚ] *n.* déshonneur *m*. || *v. tr.* déshonorer (qqun): *to ~ o.s.*, se couvrir de honte, ne pas faire honneur à un engagement; [Com.] *a dishonoured cheque*, un chèque impayé. || **dis|honourable** [-əbl̩] *adj.* déshonorant, honteux.

dis|illusion [dɪsɪ'luwʒən] *n.* désillusion *f*. || *v. tr.* désillusionner.

disinclination [dɪsˌɪnklə'nejʃən] *n.* aversion *f* (*for*, *to*, pour).

dis|infect [dɪsn̩'fɛkt] *v. tr.* [room, &c.] désinfecter. || **dis|infectant** [-ənt] *n.* désinfectant *m*.

dis|inherit [dɪsn̩'hɛɚɪt] *v. tr.* déshériter.

dis|integrate [dɪs|ɪntəˌgɹejt] *v. tr.* désagréger, désintégrer. || *v. intr.* se désagréger; [atom] se désintégrer.

dis|interested [dɪs'ɪntɹəstəd] *adj.* désintéressé; [Fam.] non intéressé; qui se désintéresse de, indifférent.

dis|join [dɪs'ʤojn] *v. tr.* disjoindre, désunir, détacher.

disjoint [dɪs'ʤojnt] *v. tr.* désarticuler.

disk cf. DISC.

dis|like [dɪs'lajk] *n.* antipathie *f* (envers qqun, *for s.o.*), aversion *f* (pour qqun, qqch.); dégoût *m* (pour un aliment, &c.). || *v. tr.* détester (qqun, qqch.), ne pas aimer (qqun, qqch.).

dis|locate ['dɪsləˌkejt] *v. tr.* [machine,

bone] disloquer; [business] désorganiser; [limbs] déboîter, luxer. || **dis|lodge** [dɪs'lɑʤ] *v. tr.* déloger, faire partir (*from*, de): *to ~ the enemy*, déloger l'ennemi.

dis|loyal [dɪs'lojl̩] *adj.* déloyal, infidèle, perfide. || **dis|loyalty** [-tɪ] *n.* déloyauté *f*, perfidie *f*.

dismal ['dɪsml̩] *adj.* sinistre, affreux: *a ~ day*, une journée morne; [Fam.] *~ results*, résultats lamentables.

dismantle [dɪs'mæntl̩] *v. tr.* désarmer (un navire), démanteler (une ville, une forteresse), démonter (une machine).

dismay [dɪs'mej] *n.* consternation *f*, effroi *m*, épouvante *f*. || *v. tr.* consterner, effrayer, épouvanter.

dismember [dɪs'mɛmbɚ] *v. tr.* démembrer.

dismiss [dɪs'mɪs] *v. tr.* congédier (qqun), donner son congé à (qqun), renvoyer (un domestique, &c.); [minister] destituer (qqun), licencier (un employé), [polite] remercier (qqun de ses services); [Pej.] mettre à la porte; [ideas, feelings, &c.] écarter: [Jur.] *to ~ a charge*, rendre une ordonnance de non-lieu; [Mil.] *~ !*, Rompez les rangs! || **dismissal** [-l̩] *n.* renvoi *m* (d'un employé), congédiement *m*, mise *f* à pied; [minister, &c.] destitution *f*, révocation *f*; [Jur.] rejet *m* d'un appel; acquittement *m* (d'un accusé).

dis|mount [dɪs'mawnt] *v. tr.* [horse] désarçonner, faire descendre (de); démonter (une arme, une pièce d'horlogerie). || *v. intr.* descendre (de cheval), mettre pied à terre.

dis|obedience [dɪsə'bijdɪən|s] *n.* désobéissance *f*. || **dis|obedient** [-t] *adj.* désobéissant. || **dis|obey** [ˌdɪsə'bej] *v. tr. & intr.* désobéir (à qqun, qqch.).

dis|oblige [ˌdɪsə'blajʤ] *v. tr.* désobliger (qqun).

dis|order [dɪs'ɔɚdɚ] *n.* désordre *m*; maladie *f*, dérangement *m*; [population] trouble *m*, émeute *f*. || *v. tr.* mettre en désordre, [maladie] troubler, déranger le cerveau. || **dis|orderly** [-lɪ] *adj.* en désordre; turbulent, déréglé.

dis|organization [dɪsˌɔɚgn̩aj'zejʃən] *n.* désorganisation *f*. || **dis|organize** [dɪs'ɔɚgn̩'ajz] *v. tr.* désorganiser.

dis|own [dɪs'own] *v. tr.* renier (sa famille, son pays); désavouer (une œuvre).

disparage [dɪs'pæɚəʤ] *v. tr.* déprécier (qqun, qqch.), discréditer (qqun), dénigrer; *a disparaging remark*, une remarque peu flatteuse. || **disparagement** [-mənt] *n*, dénigrement *m*, mépris *m*.

disparate ['dɪspɚət] *adj.* disparate: *disparates*, choses sans rapport, sans suite.

disparity [dɪs'pæɚɪtɪ] *n.* disparité *f*.

dis|passionate [dɪs'pæʃənət] *adj.* exempt de passion, calme, impartial.

dispatch [dɪs'pætʃ] cf. DESPATCH.

dispel [dɪs'pɛl] *v. tr.* **[-ll-]** dissiper, chasser, (des craintes, &c.).

dispensable [dɪs'pɛnsəbl̩] *adj.* secondaire, dont on peut se passer.

dispensary [dɪs'pɛnsɚɪ] *n.* [hospital] dispensaire *m*.

dispensation [dɪspən'sejʃən] *n.* [of Providence] grâce *f*, don *m*; dispense *f*, exemption *f* (d'un travail, d'une corvée). || **dispense** [dɪ'spɛns] *v. tr.* [alms] dispenser, distribuer. || *v. intr.* [×] exempter (d'une obligation): *to ~ with a rule*, ne pas observer une loi; *to ~ with s.o.*, se passer de qqun: [drugstore] exécuter une ordonnance, [hence Br.] *dispensing chemist*, pharmacien *m*. || **dispenser** [-ɚ] *n.* **1.** [person who gives] dispensat|eur, -rice. **2.** pharmacien *m*. **3.** [device] distributeur *m* automatique (de café, &c.).

dispersal [dɪs'pɚsl̩], **dispersion** [dɪs'pɚʒən] *n.* dispersion *f*, éparpillement *m*. || **disperse** [dɪs'pɚs] *v. tr.* disperser, [Fam.] éparpiller; distribuer, répandre, propager (une nouvelle).

dispirited [dɪs'pijɚɪtəd] *adj.* découragé, abattu.

dis|place [dɪs'plejs] *v. tr.* déplacer: *displaced person* (*D.P.*), réfugié *m*; [remove from position] muter, destituer (qqun de ses fonctions).

display [dɪ'splej] *n.* [store, &c.] étalage *m*; [show] manifestation *f*, déploiement *m* (de force, &c.), parade *f*, exposition *f*: *a ~ of bad manners*, un étalage de mauvaise éducation; *~ window*, vitrine *f*; *on ~*, exposé, en vitrine. || *v. tr.* étaler (qqch.), [show] faire montre de (qqun), manifester (qqch.), déployer (ses talents, &c.).

dis|please [dɪs'pl|ijz] *v. tr.* déplaire (à), mécontenter; contrarier. || **dis|pleasure** [-ɛʒɚ] *n.* mécontentement *m*, déplaisir *m*.

disport [dɪs'pɔɚt] *v. tr.*: *to ~ o.s.*, se divertir, s'amuser. || *v. intr.* folâtrer, s'ébattre.

disposal [dɪs'powzl̩] *n.* disposition *f*, répartition *f* (de qqch.); vente *f*: *to be at s.o.'s ~*, être à la disposition de qqun; *garbage ~*, enlèvement *m* des ordures. || **dispose** [dɪ'spowz] *v. tr.* disposer, arranger (qqch.), mettre de l'ordre dans (qqch.), disposer (qqun à faire qqch., *s.o. to do sth.*): *to be disposed to do sth.*, être disposé à faire qqch.; *well-, ill-/disposed*, bien, mal/intentionné. || **dispose (of)** [-ʌf] *v. intr.* se débarrasser (de qqch.); [unload] se défaire de (ses valeurs). ‖ **disposition** [ˌdɪspəˈzɪʃən] *n.* **1.** disposition *f*, arrangement *m.* **2.** [Pers.] tempérament *m*, caractère *m*: *a cheerful* ~ , un heureux caractère.

dis|possess [dɪspəˈzɛs] *v. tr.* déposséder (de, *of*); [Jur.] exproprier.

dis|prove [dɪsˈpɹuwv] *v. tr.* réfuter.

dispute [dɪˈspjuwt] *n.* [quarrelling] dispute *f* (au sujet de, *over*); [discussion] débat *m*: *beyond* ~ , incontestable. ‖ *v. tr.* [debate] discuter (une décision), [oppose] contester, [contend] disputer (qqch. à qqun). ‖ †*v. intr.* [fight, quarrel] se disputer (avec qqun, *with s.o.*).

dis|qualify [dɪsˈkwɔlɪˌfaj] *v. tr.* rendre (qqun) incapable de (faire qqch.); [Sport] disqualifier.

dis|regard [ˌdɪsɹəˈgɑɚd] *n.* insouciance *f*, indifférence *f*, (envers, *for*); [neglect] négligence *f.* ‖ *v. tr.* dédaigner (qqun, qqch.), négliger (qqch.), [advice, &c.] ne pas tenir compte de (qqch.), faire fi de (qqun, qqch.): *Disregard what I said*, Mettez que je n'ai rien dit.

disrepair [ˌdɪsɹəˈpɛɚ] *n.* mauvais état *m.*

dis|reputable [dɪsˈɹɛpjətəbḷ] *adj.* déshonorant; [clothes] minable: ~ *place*, endroit *m* mal famé; ~ *person*, de mauvaise réputation. ‖ **dis|repute** [dɪsɹəˈpjuwt] *n.*: *to be in, fall into*/ ~ , être, tomber/en discrédit; *to bring into* ~ , discréditer.

dis|respect [dɪsɹəˈspɛkt] *n.* manque *m* de respect (pour), irrévérence *f*, impertinence *f* (envers). ‖ **dis|respectful** [-fḷ] *adj.* irrespectueux: *to be* ~ *towards*, manquer de respect à.

disrupt [dɪsˈɹʌp|t] *v. tr.* rompre; interrompre (un service); [Fig.] bouleverser (des plans, &c.). ‖ **disruption** [-ʃən] *n.* rupture *f*; interruption *f.*

dis|satisfaction [dɪsˌsætɪsˈfækʃən] *n.* mécontentement *m* (de, *with*). ‖ **dis|satisfy** [dɪsˈsætɪsˌfaj] *v. tr.* mécontenter qqun (de qqch.), déplaire à qqun.

dissect [ˌdajˈsɛkt] *v. tr.* disséquer (un cadavre, un texte).

dissemble [dɪˈsɛmbḷ] *v. tr. & intr.* dissimuler.

disseminate [dɪˈsɛmɪnˌejt] *v. tr.* disséminer; [news] répandre.

dissension [dɪˈsɛn|ʃən] *n.* discussion *f*; désaccord *m.* ‖ **dissent** [-t] *v. intr.* différer d'avis, d'opinion (avec, *with*); [Rel.] être dissident. ‖ **dissenter** [dɪˈsɛntɚ] *n.* dissident *m*, opposant *m.*

dissertation [ˌdɪsɚˈtejʃən] *n.* dissertation *f* (littéraire); thèse *f.*

disservice [dɪsˈsɚvɪs] *n.* mauvais service *m*: *to do s.o. a* ~ , rendre un mauvais service à qqun.

dissidence [ˈdɪsədən|s] *n.* dissidence *f.* ‖ **dissident** [-t] *adj. & n.* dissident (*m*).

dis|similar [dɪˈsɪmɪlɚ] *adj.* différent (de, *to*), dissemblable.

dissimulation [dɪˌsɪmjəˈlejʃən] *n.* dissimulation *f*; hypocrisie *f*, duplicité *f.*

dissipate [dɪsɪˈpejt] *v. tr.* dissiper. ‖ **dissipation** [ˌdɪsɪˈpejʃən] *n.* dissipation *f.*

dissociate [dɪˈsowʃɪˌejt] *v. tr.* dissocier, séparer, désunir; [Fig.] désorganiser.

dissolute [dɪsəˈluwt] *adj.* [Pers.] dissolu, débauché. ‖ **dissolution** [ˌdɪsəˈluwʃən] *n.* dissolution *f*, débauche *f*; [Fig.] dissolution *f* (d'une société). ‖ **dissolve** [dɪˈzɑlv] *v. tr.* [proper and Fig.] dissoudre (qqch.); faire dissoudre (un comprimé, &c.); [Fig.] briser, détruire (des liens, l'unité, &c.), décomposer, désagréger (un tout, &c.). ‖ *v. intr.* [pill, &c.] se dissoudre: [Fig.] *She was found dissolved in tears*, → On la trouva/pleurant à chaudes larmes, tout en larmes/.

dissonance [ˈdɪsənən|s] *n.* dissonance *f.* ‖ **dissonant** [-t] *adj.* dissonant.

dissuade [dɪˈswejd] *v. tr.* dissuader (qqun de faire qqch.): *I dissuaded him from his purpose*, Je l'ai détourné de son projet.

distaff [ˈdɪstæf] *n.* quenouille *f*: *on the* ~ *side*, du côté maternel.

distance [ˈdɪstəns] *n.* **1.** [éloignement] distance *f*: *from a* ~ , → de loin; *The house is at a* ~ *from any railroad*, → La maison est éloignée de tout chemin de fer; [Tel.] *long* ~ , (le téléphone) interurbain *m*, © [abus.] (la) longue distance *f*: *to call s.o. long* ~ , appeler qqun à l'inter(urbain). **2.** *in the* ~ , dans le lointain, au loin. **3.** [time, Mus.] intervalle *m.* **4.** [Fig.] froideur *f*, réserve *f*: *to keep (s.o.) at a* ~ , tenir (qqun) à distance; *Keep your* ~ *!*, Gardez vos distances! ‖ **distant** [ˈdɪstənt] *adj.* éloigné, lointain; [Fig., Pers., manners] froid, hautain: *3 miles* ~ , à 3 milles (de distance).

dis|taste [dɪsˈtejst] *n.* dégoût *m* (de), aversion *f* (pour): *I have a real* ~ *for castor oil*, → L'huile de ricin m'inspire une vraie répugnance. ‖ **dis|tasteful** [-fḷ] *adj.* dégoûtant, répugnant; désagréable, antipathique.

distend [dɪˈstɛnd] *v. tr.* distendre (la peau, un ressort); [expand] dilater, gonfler (un ballon). ‖ *v. intr.* se distendre; se dilater; se gonfler.

distil [dɪˈstɪl] *v. tr.* [-ll-] distiller, secréter; faire tomber goutte à goutte; distiller (de la bière, des fleurs). ‖ **distillation** [ˌdɪstɪ-

ˈlejʃən] *n.* distillation *f.* || **distillery** [dɪˈstɪlərɪ] *n.* distillerie *f.*

distinct [dɪsˈtɪŋk|t] *adj.* distinct, différent (de, *from*); [voice, sound, &c.] net, clair; [quality] marqué: *to keep* ~ , distinguer entre. || **distinction** [-ʃən] *n.* distinction *f*: *to make a* ~ *between*, distinguer, faire une distinction/entre. || **distinctive** [-tɪv] *adj.* distinctif, [fashion, &c.] distingué: *a* ~ *flag*, un drapeau national. || **distinctly** [-tlɪ] *adv.* distinctement; clairement; décidément; [tell] expressément.

distinguish [dɪˈstɪŋgwɪʃ] *v. tr.* distinguer (entre, *between*); [sorts, &c.] déterminer; cf. DISTINGUER, DISCERNER: *to* ~ *truth from fiction*, discerner le vrai du faux; *to* ~ *o.s.*, se distinguer, se faire remarquer. || *v. intr.* distinguer, faire une distinction (entre, *between*). || **distinguished** [-t] *adj.* distingué, de distinction. || **distinguishing** [-ɪŋ] *adj.* distinctif, caractéristique.

distort [dɪˈstɔərt] *v. tr.* **1.** tordre, convulser. **2.** [Fig.] déformer, dénaturer (la vérité).

distract [dɪˈstɹæk|t] *v. tr.* détourner (l'attention); troubler, déranger (qqun); [upset] affoler; [entertain] distraire. || **distraction** [-ʃən] *n.* distraction *f*; [disturbance] confusion *f*, désordre *m*; affolement *m*: *to drive s.o. to* ~ , affoler qqun.

distress [dɪˈstɹɛs] *n.* détresse *f*; [deep sorrow] désarroi *m*, affliction *f*: *ship in* ~, navire *m* en détresse. || *v. tr.* affliger.

distribute [dɪˈstɹɪbjut] *v. tr.* distribuer, [tasks, &c., usual. equally] répartir; [arrange in order] disposer, agencer. || **distribution** [ˌdɪstɹɪˈbjuʃən] *n.* [act] distribution *f*, répartition *f*; [result] disposition *f*, agencement *m*; [Com.] vente *f*, écoulement *m* (de produits). || **distribut|or, -er** [dɪˈstɹɪbjətər] *n.* **1.** distribut|eur *m*, -rice *f* (de films, &c.). **2.** [Auto] distributeur *m* d'allumage, allumeur *m*.

district [ˈdɪstɹɪkt] *n.* [region] région *f*; [Adm.] territoire *m*, district *m*, secteur *m*, [electoral] circonscription *f*: [US] *District of Columbia*, district fédéral de C.; [US] *District Attorney*, procureur *m* de district; [Fr.] procureur *m*, cf. © CROWN ATTORNEY.

dis|trust [dɪsˈtɹʌst] *n.* méfiance *f*, défiance *f*. || *v. intr.* se méfier de. || **dis|trustful** [-fl̩] *adj.* méfiant, soupçonneux.

disturb [dɪˈstərb] *v. tr.* [bother] déranger (qqun, qqch.); [peace, &c.] troubler; [Fig.] inquiéter (qqun): *He is not to be disturbed on any account*, Il ne faut (pas) le déranger sous aucun prétexte. || **disturbance** [-əns] *n.* dérangement *m*, perturbation *f*; [riot] troubles *mpl*, désordres *mpl*; [upset] bouleversement *m*, [noise] vacarme *m*; [Fig.] inquiétude *f*.

dis|union [dɪsˈjuwn|jən] *n.* désunion *f*. || **dis|unite** [-ajt] *v. tr. & intr.* désunir.

dis|use [dɪsˈjuws] *n.* désuétude *f*; non-usage *m*: *fallen into* ~ , tombé en désuétude.

ditch [dɪtʃ] *n.* fossé *m.* || *v. tr.* [Arg.] se débarrasser de (qqch.); [Aero.] faire un amerrissage forcé.

dither [ˈdɪðər] *n.* tremblement: *to be in a* ~ , être très agité.

ditto [ˈdɪtow] *adv.* idem; [Com.] dito; et moi/aussi, de même, &c./.

ditty [ˈdɪtɪ] *n.* chansonnette *f*, petit poème.

divan [dɪˈvæn] *n.* divan *m.*

dive [dajv], **dived** [dajvd], **dived** [Fam.] **dove** [dowv] *v. intr.* plonger (dans, *into*); [airplane] exécuter un piqué, piquer. || *n.* **1.** plongeon *m*; [airplane] piqué *m*, [submarine] plongée *f*. **2.** [Arg.] gargotte *f*. || **diver** [ˈdajvər] *n.* plongeur *m*, scaphandrier *m*: *pearl* ~ , pêcheur *m* de perles.

diverge [dɪˈvərʤ] *v. intr.* diverger (de, *from*). || **divergence** [-əns] *n.* divergence *f* (d'opinions, &c.).

divers[1] [ˈdajvərz] *adj.* divers, plusieurs *inv.*: ~ *persons*, diverses personnes. || **divers**[2] cf. DIVER. || **diverse** [dɪˈvərs] *adj.* différent, varié: *a person of* ~ *opinions*, une personne d'opinions variées. || **diversion** [dɪˈvərʒən] *n.* diversion *f*; [amusement] divertissement *m*; détournement *m* (de circulation): *to create a* ~ , faire diversion. || **diversity** [dɪˈvərsətɪ] *n.* diversité *f*; variété *f*. || **divert** [dajˈvərt] *v. tr.* **1.** détourner, dévier (de, *from*). **2.** divertir, amuser.

divest [dɪˈvɛst] *v. tr.* dépouiller (de, *of*): *to* ~ *o.s. of*, se/dépouiller, priver/de.

divide [dɪˈvajd] *v. tr.* séparer (en, *into*), diviser (en, *into*); [equally] partager, répartir (en, *into*; entre, *among*); séparer, désunir; [Parl.] © aller aux voix. || *n.* [Geog.] ligne *f* de partage des eaux. || **dividend** [ˈdɪvɪˌdɛnd] *n.* dividende *m.* || **dividers** [dɪˈvajdərz] *n.pl.* compas *m* (de précision).

divine[1] [dɪˈvajn] *adj.* **1.** [of God] divin. **2.** superlatif, suprême; [taste, &c.] exquis. || *n.* théologien *m.*

divine[2] [dɪˈv|ajn] *v. tr.* deviner (qqch.), conjecturer. || **diviner** [-ajnər] cf. DIVINE[2] *n.* devin *m.* || **divinity** [-ɪnɪtɪ] *n.* **1.** divinité *f*. **2.** [Rel.] théologie *f*.

divisible [dɪˈvɪzɪbl] *adj.* divisible. || **division** [dɪˈvɪʒən] *n.* [dividing; part, group];

séparation; [Mil.] division *f*; [ideas, feelings] désaccord *m*, mésentente *f*; [Parl.] vote *m*. ‖ **divisor** [dɪ'vajzɚ] *n*. diviseur *m*.

divorce [dɪ'vɔɚs] *n*. divorce *m*; [Fig.] séparation *f*, [ideas, &c.] scission *f*. ‖ *v. tr.* divorcer (d'avec qqun, *s.o.*); [Jur.] divorcer (deux conjoints); [Fig.] séparer, désunir (deux choses).

divulge [dɪ'vʌlʤ] *v. tr.* divulguer.

Dixie (Land) ['dɪksɪˌ(lænd)] *n*. [US] les États du sud des É.-U.

dizziness ['dɪzɪ|nəs] *n*. étourdissement *m*, vertige *m*. ‖ **dizzy** *adj.* **1.** étourdi, chancelant. **2.** confus. **3.** vertigineux; [thoughtless] étourdi, évaporé; [silly] bête: *a ~ height*, une hauteur/extraordinaire, vertigineuse/; *I feel ~*, J'ai la tête qui tourne; *to have a ~ spell*, avoir le vertige.

do [duw], **did** [dɪd], **done** [dʌn] *3e pers. du sing. du prés.* **does** [dʌz] *v. tr.* **1.** faire [☞ Fr. prefers a more explicit verb to excessive repetition of *faire*: cf. also under accompanying words]: *to ~ again*, refaire; *I won't ~ it again*, Je ne recommencerai pas; *to ~ one's duty*, faire son devoir; *to ~ a painting*, faire, peindre/un tableau; *to ~ the dishes*, faire, laver/la vaisselle; *Did you ~ question 2?*, Avez-vous/fait, répondu à/la deuxième question?; *to ~ 60 miles an hour*, faire du soixante, aller à 60 milles à l'heure; *That isn't done*, Cela ne se fait pas, *It can't be done*, C'est impossible; *What is, How is it/to be done?*, Que, Comment/faire?; *What can I ~ for you?*, Que puis-je faire pour vous? [in store] Vous désirez, Madame?; *When in Rome, ~ as the Romans ~*, Il faut hurler avec les loups; [Fam.] *Nothing doing!*, Rien à faire!; *Well done!*, Bravo! **2.** [other uses] *to ~ s.o. out of sth.*, mettre qqun dedans pour qqch., filouter qqch. à qqun; [Fam.] *I've been done!*, On m'a roulé!; *I'll ~ no such thing!*, Je n'en ferai rien!; *to ~ a steak*, faire cuire un bifteck; *I like my meat well done*, J'aime la viande bien cuite. ‖ *v. intr.* **1.** [fare] aller; marcher: *How do you ~ ?*, Comment allez-vous?; *How are you doing?*, Ça/va, marche/?; *You're doing fine*, Vous vous défendez/bien, comme un roi/; *He will ~ well*, Il ira loin. **2.** [suffice] aller; suffire; faire l'affaire: *That will ~ !*, Assez!, Ça suffit!, Cela/fera l'affaire, ira/; *It wouldn't ~ for you to . . .*, Il ne faudrait pas que vous [+ subjunc.]; *to make ~ (with sth.)*, se débrouiller (avec qqch.). **3.** [finish] finir: *Another 5 minutes and I'm done*, Encore 5 minutes et j'aurai fini; *Is it done yet?*, Avez-vous fini?; *Have you done (contradicting?)*, Vous avez fini (de me contredire)?; *I/am, have/done with smoking* →, C'est fini, je ne fume plus. ‖ *v. aux.* **1.** [le prés., le prét. et l'impérat. de ~ s'emploient pour créer les formes négatives et inverties du verbe, sauf dans le cas des auxiliaires.] [× No direct translation in Fr.]: *I do not*, [*Fam.*] *don't/see it*, Je ne le vois pas; *You did not*, [*Fam.*] *didn't/say that, did you?*, Vous n'avez pas dit cela, n'est-ce pas?; *Don't interrupt (me)!*, Ne m'interrompez pas!; *Do, Did/you know him?*, Le connaissez-vous?, L'avez-vous connu?; *What/don't, didn't/you understand?*, Qu'est-ce que vous/ne comprenez pas, n'avez pas compris?/; *He sings well, doesn't he?*, Il chante bien, n'est-ce pas?; *Seldom does he admit his mistakes*, C'est rare qu'il reconnaisse ses fautes. **2.** [Le prés., le prét. et l'impérat. de ~ s'emploient pour créer une forme affirmative qui souligne le sens du verbe] [× No direct translation in Fr.]: [emphasis] (*Yes,*) *I* (*really*)/ *~ , did/understand!*, Mais si,/je comprends (bien), j'ai (bien) compris; *I ~ /think, hope) that . . .*, je crois, j'espère/bien que . . . ; *He does look silly*, (En effet), il a vraiment l'air bête; *I did try, but . . .*, J'ai essayé, c'est vrai, mais . . . ; *Do be quiet!*, Mais taisez-vous donc!; *Do try to be reasonable!*, Essayez donc d'être raisonnable, voyons!; *Do sit down*, Asseyez-vous donc, je vous en prie; *He didn't succeed, but he did try*, Il n'a pas réussi, mais il faut avouer qu'il a essayé. **3.** [Les différentes formes de ~ , et surtout le prés. et le prét. s'emploient pour éviter la répétition du verbe principal.] [× Rarely a direct translation in Fr.]: *I/come, came/here more often than you/do, did/*, Je viens, Je venais/plus souvent que vous; *Do you think so?—I did (so) then and I ~ now*, Vous (le) croyez?—Oui, je le croyais alors et je le crois maintenant; *I agree. Do(n't) you?*, Je suis d'accord. Et vous?; *I saw him.—You did?*, Je l'ai vu.—Vraiment?, C'est vrai?; *You won, didn't you?*, Vous avez gagné, n'est-ce pas?; *You don't smoke, do you?*, Vous ne fumez pas, n'est-ce pas? *Can, May/I come in?—Please ~ !*, (Est-ce que) je peux entrer?—Je vous en prie!; *Don't*, Ne faites pas cela!, Assez!; *So ~ I*, Moi aussi.

do. [= DITTO].

do away (*with*) [ˌduw|ə'wejˌwɪð] *v. intr.*

abolir qqch.; supprimer (qqch., qqun). || **do by** *v. intr.* traiter: *He did/well, badly/ by me*, Il m'a/bien, mal/traité. || **do for** ['duw,fɔɚ] *v. intr.*: *to ~ o.s.*, se débrouiller tout seul, tenir la maison soi-même; *He is done for*, Il est perdu. || [Arg.] **do in** [,duw'ɪn] *v. tr.* tuer (qqun). || **do over** ['duw'owvɚ] *v. tr.* refaire, recommencer (qqch.); refaire, repeindre (un appartement). || **do up** [,duw'ʌp] *v. tr.* [fasten] empaqueter, emballer, envelopper; faire, ficeler (un paquet); boutonner, agrafer, fermer; [house] remettre à neuf; [hair] se coiffer. || **do with** [du,wɪð] *v.* **1.** faire de: *What did you ~ /him, my tie/?*, Qu'avez-vous fait de/lui, ma cravate/?; *I didn't know what to ~ myself*, Je ne savais pas comment/passer le temps, cacher ma joie, ma gêne/. **2.** *What has that to ~ it?*, Je ne/saisis, vois/pas le rapport; *That has nothing to ~ it*, Cela n'a/rien à voir, aucun rapport/(avec l'affaire); *He had sth. to ~ it*, Il y était pour qqch.; *I had a lot to ~ him*, J'avais souvent affaire à lui. || *v. intr.*: *I could ~ a drink* (*of sth.*), Je boirais bien qqch.; *You can ~ a little advice*, Quelques conseils ne vous feraient pas de mal; *He does with very little sleep*, Il a besoin de très peu de sommeil. || **do without** ['duwɪð'awt] *v. intr.* se passer de.

doc [dɑk] *n.* [Fam.] toubib *m*, cf. DOCTOR.

docile ['dɑsajl] *adj.* **1.** docile, obéissant. **2.** attentif. || **docility** [da'sɪlɪtɪ] *n.* docilité *f.*

dock [dɑk] *n.* quai *m*, jetée *f*; [harbour] bassin *m*: *dry ~*, cale *f* sèche; [Jur.] banc *m* (des accusés). || *v. tr.* faire accoster (un navire); couper la queue à; retrancher (. . . sur une somme). || *v. intr.* accoster. || **docker** [-ɚ] *n.* docker *m*, débardeur *m.* cf. LONGSHOREMAN.

doctor ['dɑktɚ] *n.* médecin *m*; docteur *m* [applies only to medical doctors; normally, University professors, Ph.D's and other bearers of University titles should be called *Monsieur* and be referred to as M. X, Mme X]: *Hello, Doctor*, Bonjour, docteur; *There is Dr. X.*, Voilà le docteur X, © [abus.] Dr. X.; *Call the ~*, Faites venir le/médecin, docteur/; *Doctor and Mrs. Smith*, M. & Mme Smith; *Doctor S. Smith, M.D.*, M. S. Smith, docteur en médecine; *Doctor of Laws*, docteur en droit. || **doctorate** [-ət] *n.* also **Doctor's degree**, doctorat *m.*

doctrine ['dɑktɹɪn] *n.* doctrine *f.*

document ['dɑkjəmənt] *n.* document *m*; [Jur.] acte *m.* || *v. tr.* documenter.

documentary [,dɑkjə'mɛntəɪ] *adj.* & *n.* documentaire (*m*).

dodge [dɑʤ] *n.* écart *m* (de côté); [Fig.] détour *m*, stratagème *m.* || *v. tr.* [blow] éviter, esquiver; [Fig.] éluder (une question); contourner (la loi).

doe[1] [dow] *n.* [female deer] daine *f*, biche *f*; [female rabbit] lapine *f*; [female hare] hase *f.*

Doe[2] **John** ['ʤɑn'dow] *n.m.* conventionnel de l'Américain ou du Canadien moyen: correspond à © Jean-Baptiste, [Fr.] Durand.

doesn't [dʌznt] = does not, cf. DO.

†**doff** [dɑf] *v. tr.* ôter, enlever (un vêtement).

dog [dɔg] *n.* chien *m*; [Pers., Pej.] canaille *f*; [fire] chenet *m*: *a gay ~*, un bon vivant; *Lucky ~*, Veinard!; *~ show*, exposition *f* canine; *Prairie ~*, © *chien m des prairies*; *~ days*, (la) canicule; [Fig.] *to go to the dogs*, courir à sa perte. || **dog-eared** [-,ijɚd] *adj.* corné. || **dogfight** [-,fajt] *n.* [Mil., aviation] (combat *m*) corps à corps. || **dogged** [-əd] *adj.* tenace, opiniâtre, obstiné. || **doggedly** [-ədlɪ] *adv.* obstinément, avec acharnement. || **doggedness** [-ədnəs] *n.* ténacité *f*, opiniâtreté *f*, obstination *f.* || **dog house** [-,haws] *n.* niche *f* (à chien): [Fam.] *to be in the ~*, être en disgrâce.

dogma ['dɔgmə] *n.* dogme *m*; doctrine *f.* || **dogmatic** [,dɔg'mætɪk] *adj.* dogmatique.

dogsled ['dɑg,slɛd] *n.* © traîne *f*, traîneau *m*/à chiens. || **dogteam** [-,tijm] *n.* attelage *m* de chiens. || **dog-tired** [-'tajɚd] *adj.* rendu, à bout, éreinté. || **dogwood** [-,wʊd] *n.* [Bot.] cornouiller *m.*

doily ['dojlɪ] *n.* napperon *m.*

doings ['duwɪŋz] *n.pl.* [US] choses *fpl* faites, actions *fpl*; faits et gestes *mpl*; conduite *f.* || **do-it-yourself** ['duwɪt-,jɚ'sɛlf] *n.* travaux *mpl* d'amateur; bricolage *m.* || **do-it-yourselfer** [-ɚ] © *n.* bricoleur *m.* || **do-it-yourselfing** [-ɪŋ] © *n.* bricolage *m.*

dole [dowl] *n.* **1.** aumône *f.* **2.** petite part (de qqch.). **3.** [Br.] indemnité *f* de chômage. || **dole out** [-'awt] *v. tr.* distribuer parcimonieusement.

doleful ['dowlfl̩] *adj.* affligé; triste, dolent.

doll [dɑl] *n.* poupée *f*; [Sl.] pépée *f.*

dollar ['dɑlɚ] *n.* dollar *m*, © piastre *f*: *a dollar coin, a silver dollar*, une pièce d'un dollar, un dollar en argent; *a (one-) dollar bill*, un billet d'un dollar; [Fam.] un dollar; *a two-dollar bill*, un billet de deux dollars; [Fam.] © un deux dollars; *a five-dollar bill*, un billet de cinq dollars;

[Fam.] © un cinq dollars; *a half- ~*, © un cinquante sous.

dolly [dɑlɪ] *n.* **1.** [Fam.] poupée *f.* **2.** [transports] diable *m.*

dolphin [ˈdɑlfɪn] *n.* [whale] dauphin *m*; [buoy] bouée *f.*

dolt [dowlt] *n.* imbécile *m.*

domain [ˌdowˈmejn] *n.* domaine *m*, terres *fpl*; [Fig.] champ *m* (d'action); domaine (scientifique, médical, littéraire, &c.).

dome [dowm] *n.* dôme *m*; [inside] coupole *f.*

domestic [dəˈmɛstɪk] *adj.* [animal, care, task] domestique; [production] national; [produce] fabriqué au pays; [network] national, intérieur: *~ science*, enseignement ménager.

domesticate [dəˈmɛstɪˌkejt] *v. tr.* domestiquer.

domicile [ˈdɑmɪˌsajl] *n.* domicile *m*, résidence *f.*

dominant [ˈdɑmɪ|nənt] *adj.* dominant. || **dominate** [-ˌnejt] *v. tr.* dominer. || **domination** [ˌdɑmɪˈnejʃən] *n.* domination *f.* || **domineer** [-ˈnijɚ] *v. tr.* se montrer dominateur, tyranniser (*over*).

Dominican [dəˈmɪnɪkən] *adj. & n.* [Rel.] Dominicain; [Pol.] Dominicain, de Saint-Domingue: *the ~ Republic*, la République Dominicaine.

dominion [dəˈmɪnjən] *n.* **1.** [Pol.] souveraineté *f.* **2.** © *the Dominion of Canada*, †la Puissance, le Dominion/du Canada; le Canada: *Dominion Day*, fête *f* de la Confédération [1er juillet].

domino [ˈdɑmɪˌnow] *n.* **1.** [cloak] domino *m.* **2.** [game] dominos *mpl.*

†don [dɑn] *v. tr.* [-nn-] mettre, enfiler (un vêtement).

donate [ˈdowˌnej|t] *v. tr.* donner (à une œuvre, &c.); [bequeath] léguer. || **donation** [-ʃən] *n.* donation *f*; don *m.*

done [dʌn] cf. DO.

donkey [ˈdɑŋkɪ] *n.* âne *m*, baudet *m*; [Fig., Pers.] imbécile *m*, andouille *f*: *to ride a ~*, aller à (dos d') âne.

donor [ˈdownɚ] *n.* [money] donateur *m*; [blood] donneur *m* (de sang).

don't [downt] = do not; **doesn't** [dʌznt] = does not; **didn't** [dɪdnt] = did not. cf. DO. [☞ Formes généralement employées dans la langue parlée, pour éviter la mise en relief qui résulterait de l'accentuation de *not*; à éviter dans la prose soutenue.]

doom [duwm] *n.* **1.** sort *m.* **2.** mort *f*, jugement *m.* || *v. tr.* destiner, condamner qqun (à mourir, à sa perte). || **doomsday** [-zˌdej] *n.* jugement dernier.

door [dɔɚ] *n.* porte *f*; [car] portière *f*; [Fig.] accès *m*: *behind closed doors*, à huis clos. || **doorbell** [-ˌbɛl] *n.* sonnette *f*, timbre *m.* || **door handle** [-ˌhændl̩] *n.* bouton *m*, poignée *f*/de porte; bec-de-cane *m.* || **doorkeeper** [-ˌkijpɚ] *n.* portier *m.* || **doorstep** [-ˌstɛp] *n.* pas *m* de la porte, [threshold] seuil *m.* || **doorway** [-ˌwej] *n.* encadrement *m* de la porte; entrée *f*; [church] portail *m.*

dope [dowp] *n.* **1.** [Sl., drug] narcotique *m.* **2.** [oil, grease] lubrifiant *m.* **3.** [Arg.] information *f*, [Sl.] tuyau *m.*

dormant [ˈdɔɚmənt] *adj.* latent.

dormitory [ˈdɔɚmɪˌtɔɚɪ] *n.* [Sch.] dortoir *m.*

dormouse [ˈdɔɚˌmaws] *n. pl. -mice* [-ˌmajs] [animal] loir *m.*

dory [ˈdɔɚɪ] *n.* [Naut.] doris *m.*

dosage [ˈdows|əʤ] *n.* [Med.] dose *f*; [use] posologie *f.* || **dose** *n.* [remedy] dose *f*; quantité *f.* || *v. tr.* administrer (un médicament); médicamenter (qqun).

dot [dɑt] *n.* [Gram.] point *m*; pois *m* (sur une étoffe, cravate): *on the ~*, à l'heure dite. || *v. tr.* [-tt-] marquer (qqch.) avec des points, mettre un point sur: *dotted with*, parsemé de.

dotage [ˈdowt|əʤ] *n.* radotage *m*: *to be in one's ~*, être tombé en enfance. || **dotard** [-ɚd] *n.* radoteur *m.* || **dote** [dowt] *v. intr.* radoter: *to ~ (up)on s.o.*, être fou de . . . , raffoler de . . . .

dotty [ˈdɑtɪ] *adj.* **1.** marqué de points. **2.** [Fam.] toqué, timbré.

double [ˈdʌbl̩] *adj.* double: *~ the amount*, deux fois autant; [spelling] *~ r*, deux r; *~ bed*, lit *m* à deux places; *~ room*, chambre *f* à deux personnes. || *n.* double *m*; duplicata *m*; [Pers.] sosie *m*; [bridge] contre *m*: [Mil.] *at the ~*, au pas gymnastique. || *v. tr.* doubler; redoubler (ses efforts); serrer (les poings): *to ~ sth. up*, plier en deux. || *v. intr.* se doubler; [bridge] contrer: *to ~ back*, revenir sur ses pas; *to ~ up*, se plier en deux, partager une chambre avec qqun. || **double bass** [-ˈbejs] *n.* contre-basse *f.* || **double-breasted** [-ˈbɹɛstəd] *adj.* [coat] croisé. || **double-cross** [-ˌkɹɔs] *v. tr.* tromper qqun. || **double-deal(ing)** [-ˈdijlɪŋ] *n.* fourberie *f*, tromperie *f.* || **double talk** [-ˌtɔk] *n.* charabia *m.* || **double window** [-ˈwɪnˌdow] *n.* **1.** [à Montréal] châssis-doubles *mpl*; [Fr.] doubles fenêtres *fpl.* **2.** [à Toronto] fenêtre *f* à double volet [le contraire de la guillotine]; [châssis-double = *storm-window*].

doubt [dawt] *n.* doute *m*; hésitation *f*: *beyond (a) ~*, sans le moindre doute; *without (a) ~*, sans aucun doute; *No ~*

they will succeed, Ils réussiront certainement; *to be in* ~ , être/[Pers.] dans le doute, [thing] en doute/. || *v. tr.* douter de (qqun, qqch.), mettre (qqch.) en doute: *I* ~ *it,* J'en doute; *I* ~ *whether he will be able to do it,* Je crains qu'il ne, Je doute qu'il/puisse faire cela; *I don't* ~ *(but) he can do it,* Je ne doute pas qu'il (ne) puisse le faire. || *v. intr.* hésiter (à faire qqch.). || **doubtful** [-fḷ] *adj.* douteux; [Pers.] incertain, indécis; [subject, question] discutable, ambigu: *I'm* ~ *of that,* J'en doute. || **doubtless** [-ləs] *adv.* sans doute, très probablement.

dough [dow] *n.* [bread] pâte *f*; [Sl.] fric *m*, poignon *m*, © foin *m.* || †**doughboy** [-ˌboj] *n.* [US, Fam.] troufion *m*, fantassin *m.* ||**doughnut** [-ˌnʌt] *n.* beignet *m*, © beigne *m.*

†**doughty** [ˈdawtɪ] *adj.* [humorous] brave, vaillant: *a* ~ *knight,* un preux chevalier.

dour [ˈduwɚ] *adj.* dur, sévère.

douse [daws] *v. tr.* **1.** plonger (dans l'eau). **2.** asperger. **3.** éteindre (un feu, [Fam.] une lumière).

dove[1] [dʌv] *n.* colombe *f*: ~ *-cot,* pigeonnier *m.*

dove[2] cf. DIVE.

dowager [ˈdawədʒɚ] *n.* douairière *f.*

dowdy [ˈdawdɪ] *adj.* mal habillé, fagoté.

dower [ˈdawɚ] *n.* douaire *m*; dot *f.*

down[1] [dawn] *adv.* **1.** [with verbs of motion] en bas; par terre; → descendre: *to go* ~ , descendre, aller en bas; *to fall* ~ , tomber par terre; *to lay, &c.* ~ , poser qqch.: [elevator] *(Going) down!,* Pour descendre!; [on elevator button] ~ , Descente *f*; *nothing* ~ , pas de premier paiement, pas de dépôt préalable; [to dog] ~ *!,* A bas (les pattes)!, Couché! **2.** [with expression of position]: ~ *here,* ici; ~ *there,* là-bas; *He went* ~ *to New York,* Il est allé à New-York; *She is* ~ *at the university,* Elle est à l'université; *They are* ~ *from the country,* Ils sont arrivés/de province, de la campagne/; ~ *under,* [en Australie] aux antipodes; *His name, He/is* ~ *on the list,* Son nom, Il/est sur la liste; *head, upside/* ~ , la tête/en bas, sens dessus dessous/. **3.** [with v. *to be*]: (le soleil) est couché; (le lac, la marée) est bas, -se; (le vent, sa fièvre) est tombé, -e; (les prix)/ont baissé, sont en baisse/; *There's a tree* ~, Il y a un arbre par terre, Un arbre est tombé; [boxing] *He's* ~ *!,* Il est sur le tapis!; *I'll be right* ~ *!,* Je descends tout de suite!; *to be* ~ *and out,* avoir tout perdu, être sur la paille. **4.** [special uses] *to be* ~ *in the mouth,* être abattu; *to be* ~ *on s.o.,* en vouloir à qqun; *to be* ~ *with a fever,* avoir la fièvre, être malade de la fièvre; *Down with . . . !,* A bas . . . !; *One* ~ *, two to go,* Et d'un, deux à venir; *from . . . down to . . . ,* de . . . jusqu'à . . . . || *prép.* au bas de, en bas de; le long de: *He lives* ~ *the/hill, street/,* Il habite/au bas de la côte, en bas de la rue, plus loin dans la rue/; *to walk* ~ *the street,* descendre la rue, marcher le long de la rue; *He spilled it* ~ *his shirt front,* Il l'a renversé sur le devant de sa chemise. || *v. tr.* abattre; avaler (une boisson): *to* ~ *tools,* cesser le travail. || *adj.* descendant. || *n.* cf. UPS; [football] © essai *m.*

down[2] [dawn] *n.* dune *f*; [feathers] duvet *m.*

downfall [-ˌfɔl] *n.* destruction *f*, ruine *f*; forte/pluie, neige/: *That was his* ~ , C'est ce qui l'a perdu. || **downpour** [-ˌpɔɚ] *n.* forte averse *f.* || **downright** [-ˌɹajt] *adj.* véritable, intégral; franc; catégorique. || *adv.* vraiment; catégoriquement. **downstairs** [-ˌˈstɛɚz] *adj.* d'en bas, plus bas. || *adv.* en bas: *to fall* ~ , tomber en bas de l'escalier. || **downtown** [-ˈtawn] *n.* quartier *m* des affaires, centre(-ville) *m*: *situated in* ~ *Montreal,* situé au cœur (même) de Montréal. || *adv.* en ville, © dans le bas de la ville. || **downward** [-wɚd] *adj.* descendant. || *adv.* also **downwards** [-wɚdz] en bas, vers le bas.

dowry [ˈdawɚɪ] *n.* dot *f.*

doz. [= DOZEN].

doze [dowz] *n.* assoupissement *m*, somme *m.* || *v. intr.* sommeiller.

dozen [ˈdʌzn̩] [☞ *pl.* **dozens** [-z], mais **dozen** après un chiffre] douzaine *f*: *two* ~ *oysters,* deux douzaines d'huîtres; *half a* ~ , une demi-douzaine.

D.P. [ˈdijˈpij] [= *displaced person*] réfugié *m*, personne *f* déplacée.

Dr., Dr [= DOCTOR], D[r].

drab [dɹæb] *adj.* **1.** ennuyeux, terne, monotone. **2.** [colour] gris brun, © drab.

draft, draught [dɹæft] *n.* **1.** dessin *m*; brouillon *m*, premier jet (d'un texte); *rough* ~ , brouillon, esquisse *f.* **2.** [pulling] trait *m*, traction *f*, [Com.] tirage *m* (d'un effet); courant *m* d'air; [breathing] inhalation *f*; [Naut.] tirant *m* d'eau (d'un navire); gorgée *f* (d'eau, &c.); *bank* ~ , traite *f* de banque, lettre *f* de change; *to drink (sth.) at/one, a/* ~ , boire (qqch.) d'un/trait, seul coup/; ~ *beer,* bière *f*/à la pompe, au tonneau/. **3.** [US, Mil.] © conscription *f*, [Fr.] service *m* militaire (obligatoire). || *v. tr.* **1.** esquisser (un plan), dessiner (une ébauche), rédiger (un texte, un brouillon). **2.** [US, Mil.]

appeler (qqun sous les drapeaux) conscrire, mobiliser (des hommes). || **draftee** [dɹæf'tij] *n.* [US, Mil.] conscrit *m*, recrue *f.* || **draftsman** ['dɹæftsmən] *n.* dessinateur *m*, artiste *m.*

drag [dɹæg] *v. tr.* [-gg-] [heavily] traîner, tirer; [pond] draguer. || *v. intr.* traîner [Fig., lag behind] traîner, [time, &c.] s'éterniser: *to ~ along*, traîner; [Fig.] entraîner; *to ~ on*, traîner en longueur; *to ~ out*, tirer; prolonger; arracher (un aveu). || *n.* tirage *m*; drague *f*, [fishing] seine *f*; [Fig.] entrave *f*: *to be a ~ on s.o.*, être un boulet au pied de qqun. || **dragger** [-ɚ] © *n.* chalutier *m.* || **dragnet** [-ˌnɛt] *n.* **1.** [net] chalut *m.* **2.** [police] coup *m* de filet.

dragon [dɹægn̩] *n.* dragon *m.* || **dragonfly** [-ˌflaj] [Br.] *n.* libellule *f.*

drain [dɹejn] *n.* [street] égout *m*, [field] drain *m*, rigole *f.* || *v. intr.* [liquid] s'égoutter, s'écouler. || *v. tr.* [also **drain off**] faire égoutter (un liquide); drainer (un champ, &c.), mettre (qqch.) à sec. || **drainage** [-əʤ] *n.* drainage *m*, écoulement lent.

drake [dɹejk] *n.* canard *m* (mâle), malard *m.*; *to play ducks and drakes*, faire des ricochets.

drama ['dɹæmə] *n.* drame *m.* || **dramatic** [dɹə'mætɪk] *adj.* dramatique. || **dramatics** [-s] *n.pl.* art *m* dramatique. || **dramatist** ['dɹæmə|ˌtɪst] *n.* dramaturge *m*, auteur *m* dramatique. || **dramatize** [-ˌtajz] *v. tr.* **1.** porter à la scène. **2.** exprimer d'une façon théâtrale, dramatiser.

drank cf. DRINK.

drape [dɹejp] *n.* draperie *f*; *drapes*, rideau(x) *m(pl).* || *v. tr.* draper, tendre (des tentures). || **draper** [-ɚ] *n.* [Br.] drapier *m.* || **drapery** [-ɚɪ] *n.* draperie *f.*

drastic ['dɹæstɪk] *adj.* violent, énergique; draconien, rigoureux.

draught [dɹæft] cf. DRAFT. || **draughtsman** [-smən] cf. DRAFTSMAN. || **draughts** [-s] *n.pl.* jeu *m* de dames, les dames *fpl.* cf. CHEQUERS: *to play ~*, jouer aux dames. || **draught-board** [-ˌbɔɚd] *n.* damier *m.* cf. CHEQUERBOARD.

draw [dɹɔ] *n.* tirage *m* (au sort); loterie *f*; match *m* nul, partie *f* nulle: *to finish in a ~*, faire match nul, finir/à égalité, ex-aequo/. || *v. tr.* **1.** tirer; traîner (une voiture), haler (un chaland); baisser (les stores); arracher (une dent); vider (une volaille); étirer (du caramel), puiser (de l'eau dans qqch.), tirer (de l'eau de qqch.); toucher (de l'argent); *to ~ breath*, respirer; [Fig.] *to ~ a blank*, ne rien trouver; échouer. **2.** [Fig.] attirer (l'attention, &c.); entraîner, engager (qqun dans qqch., qqun à faire qqch.). **3.** tracer (une ligne); dessiner (qqch.); faire le portrait de (qqun). || *v. intr.* [chimney] tirer; [tea] infuser; [to move] →verb of motion: *to ~ near*, s'approcher; *to ~ aside*, s'écarter; [Fig.] *to ~ to an end*, tirer, toucher/à sa fin. || **draw away** [-əˌwej] *v. tr.* détourner. || *v. intr.* s'éloigner. || **draw back** [-'bæk] *v. tr.* retirer, ramener en arrière. || *v. intr.* reculer; s'en dédire. || **drawback** [-ˌbæk] *n.* inconvénient *m.* || **drawbridge** [-ˌbɹɪʤ] *n.* [Arch.] pont-levis *m.* || **draw down** [-'dawn] *v. tr.* tirer en bas; baisser; [Fig.] attirer. || **drawer** [-ɚ] *n.* tiroir *m*; [Fin.] tireur *m*; [Tech.] dessinat-|eur *m*, -rice *f*: *chest of drawers*, commode *f.* || [Br.] **drawers** [-ɚz] caleçon *m.* || **draw forth** [-'fɔɚθ] *v. tr.* tirer, sortir; [Fig.] provoquer. || **drawing** [dɹɔɪŋ] *n.* dessin *m*: *~ -room*, salon *m.* || **draw off** [-'ɔf] *v. tr.* retirer (ses gants); soutirer (du vin); [Fig.] détourner.

drawl [dɹɔl] *n.* [Ling.] accent *m* traînant.

drawn [dɹɔn] cf. DRAW. || **draw on** ['dɹɔ|'ɑn] *v. tr.* mettre (ses gants). || *v. intr.* s'avancer, s'approcher. || **draw out** *v. tr.* sortir, tirer; retirer (de l'argent); [outline] tracer; prolonger: [Fig.] *to draw s.o. out*, faire parler qqun. || **draw together** [-təˌgɛðɚ] *v. tr.* & *intr.* (se) rapprocher, (se) rassembler. || **draw up** [-'ʌp] *v. tr.* tirer /ramener/ en haut; lever; ranger (des troupes); dresser (une liste); établir (un document); approcher (qqch.). || *v. intr.* s'approcher (de); s'arrêter, s'aligner.

dread [dɹɛd] *n.* crainte *f*, terreur *f* (de qqun, qqch.): *to be in ~ of*, redouter. || *adj.* redoutable; redouté. || *v. tr.* redouter, craindre (qqun, qqch., que + ne + subjunc.). || **dreadful** [-fl̩] *adj.* redoutable; affreux.

dream [dɹijm] *n.* rêve *m*, †songe *m*; [daydream] rêverie *f*: *to have a ~*, rêver, faire un rêve. || **dream** [dɹijm] **dreamt** [dɹɛmt] **dreamt** also **dreamed, dreamed** [dɹijm|d] *v. intr.* rêver (de qqun, qqch., *of s.o., sth.*), [daydream] (à qqch., de + inf.): *I wouldn't ~ of it!*, J'en serais absolument incapable! || **dream up (sth.)** *v. tr.* imaginer, supposer, concevoir (qqch.). || **dreamer** [-ɚ] *n.* rêveur *m*, visionnaire *m*; fainéant *m.* || **dreamy** [-ɪ] *adj.* rêveur; (souvenir, &c.) vague.

dreary ['dɹijɚɪ] *adj.* triste, morne.

dredge [dɹɛʤ] *v. tr.* draguer. || **dredger** [-ɚ] *n.* dragueur *m.*

dregs [dɹɛgz] *n.pl.* lie *f*; [Fig.] lie (du peuple): *to the ~*, jusqu'à la lie.

drench [dɹɛntʃ] *v. tr.* mouiller, tremper (jusqu'aux os): *drenching rain*, pluie battante.

dress [dɹɛs] **dressed** [dɹɛst] *v. tr.* habiller, vêtir; décorer, orner; [Culin., skins, &c.] apprêter [esp. fowl] éviscérer; [wound] panser; [hair] (se) coiffer: [Fig.] *to be dressed to the /ears, hilt/*, être tiré à quatre épingles; *to* ~ *(s.o.) down*, [Fam.] passer un savon à (qqun). || *v. intr.* s'habiller, se vêtir: *to* ~ *up*, s'habiller, [evening] se mettre en habit (de soirée); [woman] se mettre en grande toilette. || **dress** *n.* [woman's] robe *f*; habillement *m*, [suit] tenue *f*, toilette *f*: [Theat.] ~ *rehearsal*, répétition générale, la générale; ~ *suit*, habit *m*. || **dresser** [-ɚ] *n.* coiffeuse *f*, commode *f*, [kitchen] buffet *m*, dressoir *m*. || **dressing** [-ɪŋ] *n.* [cooking] farce *f*, sauce *f*: *French* ~ , vinaigrette *f*; [action] toilette *f*: ~ *-gown*, robe *f* de chambre; [of wounds] pansement *m*; [Tech.] apprêt *m*; [Fam.] ~ *-down*, raclée *f*, [Sl.] engueulade *f*. || **dressmaker** [-ˌmejkɚ] *n.* couturi|er *m*, ère *f*. || **dressy** [-ɪ] *adj.* chic, élégant. || **drest** = dressed.

drew cf. DRAW.

dribble [ˈdɹɪbl̩] *n.* **1.** égouttement *m*; [mouth] bave *f*. **2.** [ball] dribble *m*. || *v. intr.* **1.** égoutter, baver. **2.** [ball] dribbler.

dried [dɹaj|d] *adj.* séché, sec; [milk] en poudre; cf. DRY[2]. || **drier** [-ɚ] *n.* **1.** [person] sécheur *m*; [hair] séchoir *m*; [clothes] sécheuse *f*. **2.** dessiccatif *m*.

drift [dɹɪft] *n.* poussée *m*; courant *m* (d'air, d'eau); [snow] © banc *m* de neige; [Fig.] direction *f*, tendance *f*; [meaning] portée *f* (des paroles). || *v. intr.* être chassé (par le vent, le courant); dériver: *driftwood*, bois *m* de grève; [Fig.] se laisser aller, aller à la dérive. || *v. tr.* chasser, pousser (devant soi).

drill[1] [dɹɪl] *v. tr.* percer, forer (un trou). || *n.* [Tech.] perceuse *f*, foret *m*; [bit] mèche *f*.

drill[2] *n.* exercice *m*; [troops] entraînement *m*, instruction *f*: ~ *book*, cahier *m* d'exercices. || *v. tr.* [Mil.] faire faire l'exercice à . . . , instruire (des troupes): ~ *ground*, terrain *m* d'exercice; [Fig.] former, entraîner (des élèves, &c.).

drilling [-ɪŋ] *n.* forage *m*.

drily cf. DRYLY.

drink [dɹɪŋk], **drank** [dɹæŋk], **drunk** [dɹʌŋk] *v. tr.* boire; [animal] boire, s'abreuver; [Fig.] absorber; [general] prendre (du lait, du café, &c. avec ses repas): *to* ~ */hard, like a fish/*, boire/sec, comme un trou/; *to* ~ *out of/a glass, a bottle/*, boire/dans un verre, à même la bouteille/; *to* ~ *in*, boire (les paroles de); boire avec avidité; *to* ~ *to*, boire à la santé de; porter un toast en l'honneur de; *to* ~ *up*, boire tout. || *v. intr.* boire, s'adonner à la boisson [implique qu'il s'agit de boisson alcoolique]. || *n.* **1.** [Fr.] boisson *f*, © breuvage *m*. **2.** boisson *f* (alcoolique); consommation *f*; [Fam.] "coup" *m*; "quelque chose": *to have/a* ~ , *something to* ~ , prendre qqch., [Fam.] boire un coup; *a long* ~, une (fine, &c.) à l'eau; *drinks*, rafraîchissements *mpl*. || **drinkable** [-əbl̩] *adj.* potable [eau, &c.], buvable. || **drinker** [-ɚ] *n.* buveur *m*, ivrogne *m*. || **drinking** [-ɪŋ] *adj.*: ~ *water*, eau *f* potable. || *n.* [habituel] l'alcoolisme *m*: *He is taking to* ~ , Il s'est mis à boire.

drip [dɹɪp] *n.* goutte *f*, liquide *m* qui tombe goutte à goutte. || *v. intr.* **[-pp-]** tomber goutte à goutte; être trempé. || *v. tr.* égoutter (qqch.). || **dripping** [-ɪŋ] *n.* gouttes *fpl.*: ~ *of trees*, bruit *m* des arbres qui s'égouttent; [cooking] *drippings*, graisse *f* (de rôti, &c.).

drive [dɹajv] *n.* **1.** promenade *f* (en voiture) [distance] étape *f* (en voiture): *to/go for, take/a* ~ , (aller) faire une promenade (en voiture); *It's a long* ~ *(from here)*, C'est loin d'ici (en voiture). **2.** avenue *f*, boulevard *m*. **3.** [Mech.] entraînement *m*, actionnement *m*, transmission *f*; [Fig. and proper] poussée *f* énergique: *front-wheel* ~ , traction *f* avant. **4.** [tennis] drive *m*. **5.** [community] campagne *f*. || **drive, drove** [dɹowv] **driven** [dɹɪvn̩] *v. tr.* pousser, chasser (devant soi); [incite] pousser (qqun à faire qqch.); conduire (une auto, un cheval, une affaire, &c.); actionner (une machine), enfoncer (un clou); [tunnel] forer, percer; conclure (un marché): *He drives me/mad, crazy/*, Il me rend fou; [Fig.] *to* ~ *(s.o.) from pillar to post*, renvoyer (qqun) de Caïphe à Pilate. || *v. intr.* [car] conduire, rouler (sur la route); aller (de A à B) en voiture: [Fig.] *What are you driving at?*, Où voulez-vous en venir? || **drive along** [ˈdɹajv|əˈlɔŋ] *v. tr.* chasser, pousser (devant soi); [car] rouler. || **drive away** [-əˈwej] *v. tr.* chasser, repousser (un envahisseur). || *v. intr.* partir, s'éloigner (en voiture). || **drive back** [-ˈbæk] *v. tr.* repousser; reconduire, ramener (qqun en voiture). || *v. intr.* retourner, revenir, rentrer (en voiture). || **drive in** [-ˈɪn] *v. tr.* enfoncer (qqch.); faire entrer (en voiture).

|| *v. intr.* entrer (en voiture). || **drive-in** [-ɪn] *adj.*: © ~ *movie,* cinéma *m* de plein air. || **drive off** [-ˈɔf] *v. tr.* repousser. || *v. intr.* partir (en voiture). || **drive on** [-ˈɑn] *v. tr.* pousser. || *v. intr.*: *drive on,* continuer sa route. || **drive out** [-ˈawt] *v. tr.* chasser. || *v. intr.* sortir (en voiture): *We'll ~ and see you,* Nous irons vous voir (en voiture).

drivel [ˈdɹɪvḷ] *n.* bave *f*; [nonsense] sottises *fpl.* || *v. intr.* [-ll-] baver; [habitually] dire, raconter/des sottises.

driven cf. DRIVE.

driver [-ɚ] *n.* [car] chauffeur *m,* [bus] conducteur; [horse-drawn vehicle] cocher *m*: *driver's license,* permis *m* de conduire. || **driving** [-ɪŋ] *n.* [car] conduite *f*; ~ *school,* [Fr.] auto-école *f.*

drizzle [ˈdɹɪzḷ] *n.* bruine *f.* || *v. intr.* brouillasser.

droll [dɹowl] *adj.* amusant, comique.

drone [dɹown] *n.* **1.** [bees] (faux) bourdon *m*; [Fig.] fainéant *m.* **2.** [noise] bourdonnement *m* (d'abeille, d'avion). || *v. intr.* bourdonner; ronronner.

droop [dɹuwp] *n.* position *f* penchée. || *v. intr.* (se) pencher, pendre; [Fig.] se décourager, s'affaiblir.

drop [dɹɑp] *n.* **1.** goutte *f* (d'un liquide), [small quantity] doigt *m* (de vin, &c.). **2.** [prices, &c.] chute *f,* baisse *f* (soudaine): [Fig.] *at the ~ (of a hat),* au signal; [Loc.] *to have the ~ on (s.o.),* avoir l'avantage sur (qqun). || *v. intr.* [-pp-] **1.** [liquid] tomber goutte à goutte. **2.** [barometer, &c.] tomber, [prices, &c.] baisser, s'abaisser, descendre; [Fig.] décliner. || *v. tr.* **1.** [liquid] verser; [thing] laisser tomber; laisser échapper (une parole); [letter, word] omettre, supprimer (qqch.); jeter, rejeter (qqch.); [employee] renvoyer; [Pers., Fam.] laisser tomber (qqun). || **drop in** [-ˈɪn] *v. intr.* passer, s'arrêter (chez qqun). || **drop out** [-ˈawt] *v. intr.* [Mil.] sortir des rangs; [Fig.] renoncer.

drought [dɹawt] *n.* sécheresse *f.*

drove[1] [dɹowv] *n.* troupeau *m* en marche.

drove[2] cf. DRIVE.

drown [dɹawn] *v. intr.* se noyer. || *v. tr.* noyer (qqun, qqch.). || **drowning** [-ɪŋ] *n.* [self; by others] noyade *f,* inondation *f* (d'une région, &c.).

drowse [dɹawz] *v. intr.* s'assoupir, sommeiller. || **drowsiness** [-ɪnəs] *n.* somnolence *f*; indolence *f.* || **drowsy** [-ɪ] *adj.* **1.** somnolent, assoupi. **2.** endormant.

drudge [dɹʌʤ] *n.* souffre-douleur *m,* homme *m,* femme *f*/de peine. || *v. intr.* travailler durement. || **drudgery** [-ɚɪ] *n.* corvée *f,* travail *m* pénible.

drug [dɹʌg] *n.* **1.** drogue *f,* produit *m* pharmaceutique. **2.** stupéfiant *m.* || *v. tr.* [-gg-] [poison] droguer (qqun). || **druggist** [-ɪst] *n.* pharmacien *m,* droguiste *m.* || **drugstore** [-ˌstɔɚ] *n.* pharmacie *f.*

drum [dɹʌm] *n.* tambour *m*: *ear-~,* tympan *m.* || *v. intr.* [-mm-] tambouriner, /jouer, battre/du tambour. || **drumbeater** [-ˌbijtɚ] *n.* [Pers.] tambour *m.* || **drummer** [-ɚ] *n.* [Pers.] tambour *m*; [US, Fam.] représentant *m* de commerce.

drunk cf. DRINK. || *adj.* ivre, [Fam.] soûl: *to get ~,* s'enivrer. || **drunkard** [ˈdɹʌnk|ɚd] *n.* ivrogne *m,* ivrognesse *f.* || **drunken** [-ən] *adj.* ivre; [Fam.] soûl; [Fig.] trempé. || **drunkenness** [-ənəs] *n.* ivresse *f*; [habitual] ivrognerie *f.*

dry [dɹaj] *adj.* sec, sèche; [country] aride; [well] tari; [Fig.] [course, &c.] abstrus: *~ goods,* [Com.] mercerie *f,* articles *mpl* de nouveautés; *~ goods store,* magasin *m* de nouveautés. || **dry** *v. tr.* (faire) sécher (qqch.), dessécher, tarir (une source, &c.). || *v. intr. to dry up* (se) sécher, se dessécher, s'assécher, [well] (se) tarir; [Fig.] [stop talking] rester court: *~ up !,* [Vulg.] La ferme! || **dry-cleaning** [-ˈklijnɪŋ] *n.* [garments] dégraissage *m,* nettoyage *m* à sec. || **drying** [-ɪŋ] cf. DRY. || *n.* séchage *m,* [ground] asséchement *m,* [clothes] essorage *m.* || **dryly** [-lɪ] *adv.* sèchement; [answer] d'un ton sec. || **dryness** [-nəs] *n.* sécheresse *f* (de l'atmosphère, d'un climat); aridité *f* (d'une région); [wit, statement] causticité *f.*

dual [djuwəl] *adj.* de deux, double. || **dualism** [-ɪsm] *n.* dualisme *m.*

dub [dʌb] *v. tr.* [-bb-] **1.** nommer (chevalier, &c.). **2.** doubler, post-synchroniser (un film).

dubious [ˈdjuwbɪəs] *adj.* [Pers.] indécis; [mind] vacillant; [question] douteux; [answer] équivoque.

duchess [ˈdʌtʃəs] *n.* [title] duchesse *f.*

duck[1] [dʌk] *v. intr.* baisser la tête, esquiver (un coup). || *v. tr.* [Fig.] esquiver, se dérober à (des coups). || *n.* plongeon *m* (de la tête); [boxing] esquive *f.*

duck[2] *n.* canard *m*; cane *f*; [term of affection] (mon) chou: *mallard ~,* canard/malard, ordinaire/; [Fig.] *It's like water off a duck's back,* C'est comme de l'eau sur le dos d'un canard; cf. DRAKE. || **duckling** [-lɪŋ] *n.* caneton *m.*

duct [dʌkt] *n.* conduit *m* (des larmes, &c.). || **ductile** [-ˌajl] *adj.* [metal] souple;

ductile; [wax] malléable; [Fig.] docile, complaisant.

dud [dʌd] *n.* obus *m* non explosé; raté *m.*

due [djuw, duw] *adj.* [account] échu, [amount] dû, exigible; [punishment, &c.] juste; [train, plane, person] attendu: [×] ~ *to* . . . , attendu que . . . , à cause de . . . ; *He will be here in* ~ *time,* Il viendra en temps voulu; [account] *to fall, become/* ~ , venir à échéance, échoir; *Your account is past* ~ , Votre compte est/échu, en souffrance. ‖ *n.* dû *m*: *to give the devil his* ~ , [Fig.] donner à chacun son dû, rendre à César ce qui est à César.

duel [djuwəl] *n.* duel *m.* ‖ *v. intr.* [-**ll**-] se battre en duel.

duet [djuw'ɛt] *n.* [Mus.] duo *m.*

duffle [dʌfl̩] *n.* molleton *m.* ‖ **duffle-coat** [-ˌkowt] *n.* duffle-coat *m.*

dug cf. DIG. ‖ **dugout** ['dʌgˌawt] *n.* abri *m* (creusé); [baseball] abri *m*; canot *m,* pirogue *f.*

duke [djuwk, duwk] *n.* [title] duc *m.*

dull [dʌl] *adj.* [colour; mind] terne, [point of a tool, blade] émoussé; [Fig.] (esprit, &c.) épais, obtus; [speech, &c.] ennuyeux; [weather, day] calme (et couvert); [Stock Exchange; mind, &c.] inactif; [sound] étouffé, sourd. ‖ **dull** *v. tr.* [tool] épointer, [blade] émousser; [sound] étouffer, assourdir. ‖ *v. intr.* [knife, tool] s'épointer, s'émousser; [colour, &c.] se ternir, perdre son éclat. ‖ **dullness** [-nəs] *n.* [colour, &c.] manque *m* d'éclat; [blade, tool] émoussement *m*; [Fig.] monotonie *f* (d'un discours, &c.), lourdeur *f,* épaisseur *f* (de l'esprit, du raisonnement, &c.); inactivité *f* (du marché, &c.).

duly [djuwlɪ] *adv.* dans la forme voulue, convenablement; en temps et lieu: *We* ~ *received your letter,* Nous avons bien reçu votre lettre.

dumb [dʌm] *adj.* muet, silencieux; [Fam.] stupide. ‖ **dumbfound** [-'fawnd] *v. tr.* réduire au silence; [Fam.] clouer le bec (à qqun). ‖ **dumbness** [-nəs] *n.* mutisme *m,* silence *m*; [Fam.] stupidité *f.*

dumb-waiter [ˌdʌm'wejtɚ] *n.* [Br.] desserte *f*; [US] monte-charge *m.*

dummy ['dʌmɪ] *n.* **1.** [shop] mannequin *m,* objet *m* factice. **2.** maquette *f*; contrefaçon *f*; [cards] mort *m.* **3.** [Fam.] crétin *m*; [business, Pol.] homme *m* de paille.

dump [dʌmp] *n.* © [refuse] dépotoir *m*; [Sl.] [joint] boîte *f,* baraque *f.* ‖ *v. tr. & intr.* décharger (des déchets, &c.): *No Dumping,* → Défense de déposer des ordures.

dumps [dʌmps] *n. to be in the* ~ , avoir le cafard.

dumpy [-ɪ] *adj.* [Pers.] trapu.

dun [dʌn] *n.* **1.** demande *f* pressante (de paiement, &c.). **2.** créancier *m* importun. ‖ *v. tr.* [-**nn**-] [for debts] relancer (qqun).

dunce [dʌns] *n.* sot *m,* âne *m*: ~ (*'s*) *cap,* bonnet *m* d'âne.

dune [djuwn] *n.* dune *f.*

dung [dʌŋ] *n.* fumier *m*: *cow* ~ , bouse *f* de vache; *horse* ~ , crottin *m.*

dungeon ['dʌnʤən] *n.* [×] cachot *m,* oubliettes *fpl.*

dunk [dʌŋk] [Fam.] *v. tr.* tremper (un croissant dans du café).

dupe [duwp] *n.* dupe *f.* ‖ *v. tr.* duper (qqun).

duplex [ˌduw'plɛks] *n.* maison *f* à deux appartements, © duplex.

duplicate ['duwplɪˌkejt] *adj.* double. ‖ *n.* duplicata *m,* double *m*; réplique *f*: *in* ~ , en double exemplaire *m.* ‖ *v. tr.* [texts] reproduire (qqch.) en double (exemplaire); polycopier (des textes, documents). ‖ **duplicating** [-ɪŋ] *n.* [texts] reproduction *f,* polycopie *f*: ~ *machine,* duplicateur *m,* machine *f* à polycopier. ‖ **duplicator** [-ɚ] *n.* cf. DUPLICATING.

duplicity [duw'plɪsɪtɪ] *n.* duplicité *f,* mauvaise foi *f,* dissimulation *f.*

durable ['djɚəbl̩] *adj.* durable, résistant (à la corrosion, &c.). ‖ **duration** [djɚ'ejʃən] *n.* durée *f,* laps *m* de temps: [war] *for the* ~ , pour la durée de la guerre.

during ['djɚɪŋ] *prep.* durant, pendant [☞ *durant* is less frequently used in Fr. than in ©]; ~ *the day,* pendant, au cours de/ la journée.

†**durst** cf. DARE.

dusk [dʌsk] *n.* crépuscule *m,* brune *f,* *at* ~ , au crépuscule, © à la brunante *f*; ombre *f.* ‖ **dusky** [-ɪ] *adj.* noirâtre; sombre: *a* ~ *belle,* une mulâtresse *f.*

dust [dʌst] *n.* [dirt] poussière *f,* sciure *f* (de bois); cf. BRAN: ~ *pan,* pelle *f,* [Fr.] ramasse-poussière *m,* © porte-poussière *m*; [Fig.] *to bite the* ~ , mordre la poussière; *to throw* ~ *in a person's eyes,* jeter de la poudre aux yeux (de qqun), en mettre plein la vue (à qqun). ‖ **dust** *v. tr.* épousseter (un meuble, &c.). ‖ **duster** [-ɚ] *n.* chiffon *m,* torchon *m*; [coat] blouse *f*; cache-poussière *m.* ‖ **dusty** [-ɪ] *adj.* poussiéreux, couvert de poussière, [road, &c.] poudreux; [look, surface] gris(âtre): [Fam.] *It's not so* ~ , Ce n'est pas mal du tout.

Dutch [dʌtʃ] *adj.* [nationality] hollandais, néerlandais, [thing, produce] de Hollande: ~ *treat,* © à la Bisaillon, [Fr.] chacun pour soi. || *n.* [language] le/hollandais, néerlandais/; *pl. the Dutch* [nationality] les Hollandais; *Pennsylvania* ~, l'allemand de Pennsylvanie. || **Dutchman, -woman** [-mən] [-ˌwUmən] *n.* Hollandais, -e.

dutiable [ˈdjuwtɪ|əbl̩] *adj.* taxable; [customs] soumis aux droits (de douane). || **dutiful** [-fl̩] *adj.* obéissant, respectueux. || **duty** [ˈdjuwtɪ] *n.* devoir *m,* obligation *f* (morale); fonction *f,* tâche *f* (professionnelle); droit *m* (de douane): *to be on* ~, [constable, &c.] être de service; *to be off* ~, être libre; *to do* ~ *(for s.o.),* [Mil.] remplacer (qqun).

dwarf [dwɔɚf] *adj.* nain. || *n.* **1.** [persons, animals, plants], nain *m,* -e *f.* **2.** [fairy tales] lutin *m.* || *v. tr.* empêcher de croître, rapetisser.

dwell [dwel] **dwelt** [-t] or **dwelled** [-d] *v. intr.* demeurer, résider (dans une ville, *in a town*), habiter (une ville, dans une ville): [Fig.] *to* ~ *on (a subject, &c.),* s'appesantir sur, mettre l'accent sur (qqch.). || **dweller** [-ɚ] *n.* [d'habitude employé comme deuxième élément d'un composé] habitant *m*: *city-* ~, citadin *m*; *country-* ~, [Fr.] paysan, © habitant *m.* [Ce terme est souvent péjoratif.] || **dwelling** [-ɪŋ] *n.* habitation *f,* demeure *f.* || **dwelt** cf. DWELL.

dwindle [dwɪndl̩] *v. intr.* diminuer, s'amoindrir: *to* ~ *away,* dépérir.

dye [daj] *pr. p.* **dyeing** [-ɪŋ] *v. tr.* teindre (une étoffe, &c.). || *n.* [colour] teinte *f*; [substance] teinture *f.* || **dyer** [-ɚ] *n.* teinturier *m.*

dying [-ɪŋ] *adj.* mourant; agonisant; moribond cf. DIE.

dynamic [dajˈnæmɪk] *adj.* **1.** dynamique. **2.** actif. **3.** vigoureux. || **dynamics** [-s] *npl.* [Mus.] nuances *fpl.* || **dynamite** [ˈdajnəˌmajt] *n.* dynamite *f.* || *v. tr.* dynamiter. || **dynamiter** [-ɚ] *n.* dynamiteur *m.* || **dynamo** [ˈdajnəˌmow] *n.* dynamo *f.*

dynasty [ˈdajnəstɪ] *n.* dynastie *f.*

dysentery [ˈdɪsn̩tɹɪ] *n.* dysenterie *f.*

dyspepsia [dɪsˈpɛpsɪə] *n.* dyspepsie *f,* mauvaise digestion *f.*

dz. cf. DOZEN.

E

E, e [ij] pl. **E's, e's** [-z]. **1.** [letter] le E *m,* les E. **2.** [Mus.] mi *m.*

ea. [= each].

each [ijtʃ] *adj.* chaque, tou(te)s les: ~ *one of,* chacun(e) de: ~ *and every,* chacun(e) de. || *pron.* **1.** chacun(e): *Each of them did it,* Chacun d'eux l'a fait, Ils l'ont fait chacun (de son côté); *one dollar* ~, un dollar chacun(e), [Fam.] chaque. **2.** se . . . (l'un(e) l'autre): *They hated* ~ *other,* Ils se détestaient (l'un l'autre, mutuellement); *They spoke to* ~ *other,* Ils se parlaient (l'un à l'autre); *to strike, flatter/* ~ *other,* s'entrefrapper, s'entre-louer.

eager [ˈijgɚ][*adj.* impatient (de); ardent, brûlant de: ~ *to start,* brûlant de commencer; *an* ~ *contest,* une épreuve âprement disputée; © *to be an* ~ *beaver,* faire /la mouche du coche, du zèle/. || **eagerly** [-lɪ] *adv.* impatiemment, avec impatience; avidement, avec ardeur. || **eagerness** [-nəs] *n.* impatience *f,* enthousiasme *m,* ardeur *f*; [Pej.] avidité *f.*

eagle [ˈijgl̩] *n.* [bird] aigle *m.*

ear[1] *n.* épi (de blé).

ear[2] [ijɚ] *n.* oreille *f*: *to play by* ~, jouer d'instinct; anse *f,* oreillette *f* (d'un vase); *to have sharp ears,* avoir l'oreille fine; *to have a good* ~, avoir l'oreille fine; *by* ~, d'oreille; *I am all ears,* → Je vous écoute; *to prick up one's ears,* dresser l'oreille; *to have sharp ears,* avoir /l'oreille, l'ouïe/ fine; *up to the ears in work,* être enterré/sous le, de/travail, être débordé. || **eardrop** [-ˌdrɑp] *n.* pendant *m* d'oreille. || **eardrum** [-ˌdɹʌm] *n.* tympan *m.* || **earflaps** [-ˌflæps] protège-oreilles *m.* || **ear trumpet** [-ˌtɹʌmpət] *n.* cornet *m* acoustique. cf. AID.

earl [ɚl] *n.* [Hist.] comte *m.*

earliness [ˈɚlɪ|nəs] *n.* **1.** heure *f* peu avancée (du jour). **2.** [death] heure prématurée. **3.** précocité *f.* || **early** *adv.* **1.** de bonne heure; tôt: *earlier,* plus tôt; *too* ~, trop tôt; *as* ~ *as possible,* le plus tôt possible; ~ (*in the morning*), (le matin) de bonne heure, (de grand) matin; ~ *in* . . ., au début de . . . ; *as* ~ *as* . . ., dès . . . ; *earlier than* . . ., avant . . . ; *You are* ~ *today,* → Vous êtes matinal aujourd'hui. **2.** prématurément. || *adj.* **1.** du début, premier; [art] primitif: *the* ~ *Canadians,* les premiers Canadiens; *at an* ~ *age,* dès l'enfance; *at an* ~ *date,* à une date/prochaine, rapprochée/; *in* (*the*) ~ *days,* dans l'ancien temps; ~ *in the nineteenth century,* au début du XIX siècle; *at the earliest,* au plus tôt; *He is an* ~ *riser.* → Il est matinal. **2.** précoce, hâtif.

earmark [ˈijɚ|ˌmɑɚk] *n.* marque *f* à l'oreille; [Fig.] marque distinctive, marque/de propriété, d'affectation, d'identité/; affectation *f.* || *v. tr.* **1.** marquer (des moutons à l'oreille). **2.** affecter à, assigner à, réserver pour; spécialiser (des fonds): *to* ~ *a sum for a payment,* assigner une somme à un paiement. || **earmarked** [-ˌmɑɚkt] *adj.* réservé, marqué, affecté à: ~ *gold,* or *m* en consigne (réservé, barré).

earn [ɚn] *v. tr.* gagner (un salaire, sa vie); [Fin.] rapporter (un intérêt); [Fig.] mériter, avoir droit à/(des félicitations, &c.).

earnest [ˈɚnəst] *adj.* **1.** [serious] sérieux, consciencieux; [firm in purpose] sincère, convaincu; [efforts, &c.] pressant, fervent. **2.** [important] important, sérieux: *in* ~, sérieusement, pour de bon; *to be in* ~, → être sérieux, ne pas plaisanter. || **earnestly** [-lɪ] *adv.* avec/ardeur, empressement/; avec conviction. || **earnestness** [-nəs] *n.* zèle *m,* ardeur *f*; conviction *f.*

earnings [ˈɚnɪŋz] *n.pl.* gain *m,* salaire *m*; [Fin.] profits *mpl,* bénéfices *mpl.*

earring [ˈijɚ-ˌɹɪŋ] *n.* boucle *f* d'oreille.

earth [ɚθ] *n.* **1.** [the planet] la terre; le monde; le globe terrestre. **2.** [Fig.] le monde; †ce bas monde; [inhabitants] les hommes *mpl*; l'humanité *f*; [worldly matters] affaires *fpl* d'ici-bas. **3.** [land] terre *f*; [soil] sol *m*; [Chem.] terre; [hole of a fox, &c.] terrier *m*; tanière *f.* **4.** [Loc.] *down to* ~, pratique, réaliste: *to come back to* ~, sortir de sa rêverie; *to run to* ~, découvrir, [Fam.] (finir par) mettre la main sur, dénicher; *How on* ~ . . . ?, Comment diantre (peut-on)?; *Why on* ~ . . . ?, Pourquoi diantre . . . ? || **earthen** [-n̩] *adj.* de, en/terre. || **earthenware** [-n̩ˌwɛɚ] *n.* faïence *f.* || **earthly** [-lɪ] *adj.* terrestre: [Fig.] concevable, possible: *There is no* ~ *reason for,* Il n'y a pas la moindre raison pour . . . || **earthquake** [-ˌkwejk] *n.* tremblement *m* de terre. || **earthwork** [-ˌwɚk] *n.* terrassement *m,* ouvrage *m* en terre. || **earthworm** [-ˌwɚm] *n.* lombric *m*; ver *m* de terre. || **earthy** [-ɪ] *adj.* terreux; de terre; [Fig.] de ce monde, matériel; [Pej.] grossier, terre à terre.

ease [ijz] *n.* **1.** aise *f*; [comfort] bien-être *m*; tranquillité *f*: *to take one's* ~, prendre ses aises; *at* ~, à l'aise [→ cf. § 2]; [natural] facilité *f,* aisance *f*: *with* ~, → aisément, facilement. **2.** *At* ~ *!,* Repos! || *v. tr.* [give relief] calmer, soulager; atténuer; [release from tension] détendre, soulager; [loosen] desserrer, relâcher; [move] déplacer (lentement et avec soin); modérer (sa vitesse). || *v. intr.* [Fig.] se détendre: *to* ~ */off, up/,* soulager; se relâcher, ralentir.

easel [ˈijzl̩] *n.* chevalet *m* (de peintre).

easily [ˈijzɪlɪ] *adv.* **1.** aisément, facilement; → sans difficulté, sans effort. **2.** avec calme, doucement. **3.** [Fig.] facilement, de loin: *He came in* ~ *first,* Il s'est classé bon premier.

east [ijst] *n.* est *m*; †orient *m*; *the East,* l'Orient, †le Levant; *the Near East,* le Proche-Orient; *the Middle East,* le Moyen-Orient; *the Far East,* l'Extrême-Orient; [US] *the East,* l'Est des États-Unis: *down East,* en Nouvelle-Angleterre. || *adj.* à, de/l'est: *an* ~ *wind,* un vent d'est. || *adv.* face à l'est, vers l'est, à l'est (*of,* de). || **East Germany** [-ˈʤɚmənɪ] [Geog.] l'Allemagne *f* de l'Est. || **East Indies** [-ˈɪndɪz] [Hist.] les Indes *fpl* Orientales; l'Asie *f* du sud-est.

Easter [ˈijstɚ] *n.* Pâques *m*: ~ *Day,* (le jour de) Pâques; ~ *Monday,* le lundi de Pâques: *Happy* ~ !, Joyeuses Pâques.

easterly [-lɪ] *adj. & adv.* d'est, de l'est. || **eastern** [-n] *adj.* **1.** vers l'est, face à l'est. **2.** d'orient, oriental; [Geog.] © *the* ~ *Townships,* les Cantons *m* de l'Est, *l'Estrie *f.* **3.** [US] de l'est des États-Unis; [Asia] asiatique; oriental. || **eastward** [ˈijstwɚd] *adj. & adv.* à l'est; vers, en direction de/l'est.

easy [ˈijzɪ] *adj.* **1.** facile, aisé: *It's* ~ *to*

see . . ., → On voit bien (que . . .); [life] tranquille; sans inquiétude; paisible; [Fig.] *~ circumstances*, [Fam.] *on ~ street*, à l'aise. **2.** facile, confortable: *~ terms*, conditions *fpl* faciles; *by ~ steps*, à petites étapes *fpl*; *an ~ chair*, un fauteuil confortable; [shoe] *an ~ fit*, → qui va bien, qui chausse bien; [Pej.] indolent, nonchalant: [ready to agree] facile, accommodant; [Com.] peu demandé. ‖ *adv.* aisément, facilement; [Fam.] *Take it ~ !*, Allez-y doucement; Pas de surmenage!; *He had to take things ~ for a bit*, Il a dû ralentir un peu le rythme; *Go ~ on . . .*, → N'abusez pas de . . . ‖ **easy chair** [-ˌtʃɛɚ] *n.* cf. ARMCHAIR. ‖ **easy-going** [-ˌgowɪŋ] *adj.* nonchalant; facile à vivre, [Fam.] qui ne se fait pas de bile.

eat [ijt], **ate** [ejt], **eaten** [ˈijtn] *v. tr. & intr.* manger; prendre un repas; [Fig.] *to ~ out*, ronger: *to ~ one's heart out*, se consumer de chagrin; *to ~ into*, [acid] corroder, attaquer; *to ~ one's words*, se rétracter; ravaler ses paroles; *to ~ up*, manger jusqu'à la dernière miette; dévorer. ‖ **eatable** [ˈijt|əbl] *adj.* comestible .‖ *n.pl.* victuailles *fpl.* ‖ **eaten** cf. EAT. [☞ Comme pour la plupart des phrases passives, transposer par le réfléchi]: *Ham is usually ~ cold*, → Le jambon se mange généralement froid. ‖ **eating** [-ɪŋ] *n.* nourriture *f*; [Fam.] le manger. ‖ **eats** [-s] *n.pl.* [Fam.] boustifaille *f.*

eaves [ijvz] *n. pl.* gouttière *f*; larmier *m.* ‖ **eavesdropper** [-ˌdɹɑpɚ] *n.* indiscret *m*; écouteur aux portes. ‖ **eavestrough** [-ˌtɹɔf] Ⓒ *n.* gouttière *f.*

ebb [ɛb] *n.* [Geo.] reflux *m*; [Fig.] déclin *m.* ‖ *v. tr.* refluer; [Fig.] décliner.

ebony [ˈɛbənɪ] *n.* ébène *f.*

ebullient [ɪˈbʊljənt] *adj.* bouillonnant; [Fig.] débordant, exubérant.

ebullition [ˌɛbəˈlɪʃən] *n.* ébullition *f*; [of feeling] transport *m*, explosion *f.*

eccentric [ˌɛkˈsɛntrɪk] *n. & adj.* excentrique, original. ‖ **eccentricity** [ˌɛksənˈtɹɪsɪtɪ] *n.* excentricité *f.*

ecclesiastic [əˌklijzɪˈæstɪk] *n. & adj.* ecclésiastique (*m*). ‖ **ecclesiastical** [-l̩] *adj.* ecclésiastique.

echo [ˈɛkow] pl. **echoes** [-z] *n.* écho *m.* ‖ *v. intr.* faire écho, résonner. ‖ *v. tr.* répéter; se faire l'écho de.

eclipse [ɪˈklɪps] *n.* éclipse *f.* ‖ *v. tr.* éclipser; [Fig.] surpasser.

economic [ɪkəˈnɑmɪk] *adj.* [principle, science] économique.

economical [-l̩] *adj.* [thrifty] économe; [cheap] économique. ‖ **economically** [-l̩ɪ] *adv.* économiquement. ‖ **economics** [-s] *n.* [science] économique *f*; économie *f* politique; [Fin.] situation *f* économique. ‖ **economist** [ɪˈkɑnə|mɪst] *n.* économiste. ‖ **economize** [-ˌmajz] *v. tr.* économiser, épargner; faire des économies (sur, *on*). ‖ **economy** [-mɪ] *n.* économie *f*; structure *f*, système *m*/économique; [thrift] économie, épargne *f*: *~ size*, format *m* économique; [efficient system] économie, agencement *m.*

ecstasy [ˈɛkstəsɪ] *n.* extase *f*, [Fig.] transport *m* (de joie); ravissement *m.* ‖ **ecstatically** [ɪkˈstætɪkl̩ɪ] *adv.* avec extase.

eddy [ˈɛdɪ] *n.* remous *m*; [wind] tourbillon *m.* ‖ *v. intr.* [water] faire des remous; [wind] tourbillonner.

edge [ɛʤ] *n.* **1.** tranchant *m*; [razor] fil *m*; *to take the ~ off*, émousser. **2.** bord *m*; limite *f*; [wood] lisière *f*; [page] bord, marge *f*; [beam, &c.] arête *f*, [rock] saillie *f.* **3.** [Fig.] acuité *f*, finesse *f*; [Fam.] avantage *m*: *on ~* , agacé, énervé; [Fam.] crispé: *to set on ~* , agacer; [Fam.] énerver, crisper. ‖ **edge** *v. tr.* **1.** border; [hem] ourler. **2.** affiler; aiguiser; affûter. ‖ *v. intr.* se faufiler; se glisser (*in*, parmi, dans); s'approcher tout doucement.

edible [ˈɛdɪbl̩] *adj.* comestible. ‖ **edibles** [-z] *n.pl.* comestibles *mpl.*

edict [ˈijdɪkt] *n.* édit *m.*

edifice [ˈɛdɪf|ɪs] *n.* édifice *m.* ‖ **edify** [-ˌfaj] *v. tr.* [Arch] édifier, construire; [Fig.] instruire, édifier.

edit [ˈɛdɪt] *v. tr.* [newspaper] rédiger; [book] préparer la publication de. ‖ **edition** [əˈdɪʃən] *n.* édition *f. limited ~* , édition à tirage limité. ‖ **editor** [ˈɛdɪtɚ] *n.* **1.** [×] annotateur *m*, éditeur *m* (d'un texte); auteur *m* (d'une édition critique). **2.** directeur *m* (d'une publication, d'un journal, d'une revue); *~ in chief*, rédacteur *m* en chef, rédacteur; *dramatic ~* , critique *m* dramatique; *sports ~* , rédacteur sportif; *managing ~* , rédacteur gérant; *associate ~* , secrétaire *m* de rédaction. ‖ **editorial** [ˌɛdɪˈtɔɚɪəl] *adj.* éditorial: *~ board*, comité *m* de rédaction. ‖ *n.* [newspaper] éditorial *m*; article *m* de fond. ‖ **editorship** [ˈɛdɪtɚˌʃɪp] *n.* [function] rédaction *f*; [post] poste *m* de/rédacteur en chef, directeur/; [publishing trade] éditeur *m*; directeur *m* (d'une maison d'édition).

educate [ˈɛʤəˌkejt] *v. tr.* donner de l'instruction à; instruire, faire l'éducation de; [animal] dresser: *to be well educated*, avoir reçu une bonne instruction; *Where were you educated?*, Où avez-vous fait vos études? || **education** [ˌɛʤəˈkejʃən] *n.* **1.** éducation *f*, formation *f*; [Sch.] enseignement *m*: *progressive* ~, l'éducation nouvelle: *adult* ~, enseignement post-scolaire; *Department of Education*, ministère *m* de l'Instruction publique. **2.** instruction *f*, connaissances *fpl*; bagage *m*: *general* ~, instruction de culture générale. **3.** pédagogie *f*: *Faculty of* ~, École *f* normale; institut *m* de pédagogie. || **educational** [-l̩] *adj.* **1.** d'éducation; d'enseignement; pédagogique. **2.** [informative] instructif; éducatif. || **educative** [ˈɛʤəˌkejt|ɪv] *adj.* éducat|eur, -rice; éducati|f, -ve. || **educator** [-ɚ] *n.* éducateur *m*, éducatrice *f*.

Edward [ˈɛdwɚd] *n.* = Édouard *m.*

eel [ijl] *n.*: *American* ~, anguille *f*; *conger* ~, anguille de roche; *sand* ~, équille *f*, anguille de sable.

†**e'en** [ijn] *adv.* [Poet. = *even*] même.

†**e'er** [ɛɚ] *adv.* [Poet. = *ever*] toujours, à jamais.

efface [ɪˈfejs] *v. tr.* effacer, faire disparaître; [Fig.] éclipser, effacer: *to* ~ *o.s.*, se tenir à l'écart.

effect [ɪˈfɛkt] *n.* effet *m* (*on*, sur); résultat *m*, conséquence *f*, action *f*: *to carry into* ~, mettre en œuvre, réaliser; *in* ~, en fait, en pratique; *to take* ~, prendre effet, [Law] entrer en vigueur; *of no* ~, sans effet, inutile; *to no* ~, en vain, sans résultat; *to that* ~, dans ce sens, à cet effet. || [pl.] effets *mpl*; biens *mpl* (personnels). || *v. tr.* effectuer, accomplir. || **effective** [-ɪv] *adj.* efficace, → qui produit/un, son/effet; [impression] saisissant, frappant; [law] en vigueur. || **effectively** [-ɪvlɪ] *adv.* **1.** avec effet; utilement. **2.** en réalité; effectivement. **3.** d'une façon frappante; d'une manière saisissante. || **effectual** [-ʃuwl̩] *adj.* **1.** efficace. **2.** valable. || **effectually** [-ʃuwl̩ɪ] *adv.* efficacement.

effeminate [ɪˈfɛmɪnət] *adj.* & *n.* efféminé.

effervescent [ˌɛfɚˈvɛsənt] *adj.* effervescent: ~ *beverages*, boissons gazeuses; [of person] bouillonnant.

effete [ɛˈfijt] *adj.* épuisé, usé; [of systems] cadu|c, -que.

efficacy [ˈɛfɪkəsɪ] *n.* efficacité *f*, énergie *f*; [of a machine] rendement *m*.

efficiency [ɪˈfɪʃən|sɪ] *n.* efficacité *f*, rendement *m*; compétence *f*, faculté *f* de travail; [soldier] discipline *f*; [machine] rendement *m*, travail *m* utile; [organization] méthode *f* (rationnelle): *certificate of* ~, brevet *m* d'aptitude; ~ *expert*, organisateur *m* spécialiste. || **efficient** [-t] *adj.* [Pers.] habile, compétent, apte; [☞ Philos.] efficient; [machine] efficace, de bon rendement: ~ *industry*, industrie *f* productive. || **efficiently** [-tlɪ] *adv.* efficacement; avec compétence.

effigy [ˈɛfɪʤɪ] *n.* effigie *f*.

effort [ˈɛfɚt] *n.* effort *m*, peine *f*; [Fig., usual. Pej.] œuvre *f*; travail *m*. || **effortless** [-ləs] *adj.* aisé, facile; style coulant. || **effortlessly** [-ləslɪ] *adv.* sans effort; [style] → qui coule de source.

effrontery [ɪˈfɹʌntɚɪ] *n.* effronterie *f*.

effulgence [ɛˈfulʤəns] *n.* éclat *m*, splendeur *f*; rayonnement *m*.

effusive [ɛˈfjuwsɪv] *adj.* démonstrati|f, -ve, expansi|f, -ve, exubérant: [Geol.] ~ *rock*, roche *f* d'épanchement.

e.g. [= for example] par exemple. [cf. aussi EX.]

egg [ɛg] *n.* œuf *m*. || **egg-beater** [-ˌbijtɚ] *n.* fouet *m* (à œufs), batteur *m* (à œufs). || **eggcup** [-ˌkʌp] *n.* coquetier *m*. || **egghead** [-ˌhɛd] [Fam.] *n.* & *adj.* intellectuel (*m*). || **eggplant** [-ˌplænt] *n.* aubergine *f*. || **egg-shaped** [-ˌʃejpt] *adj.* en forme d'œuf; ovoïde. || *v. tr.*: *to* ~ *on*, pousser qqun (à faire qqch.).

ego [ˈijgow] *n.* [Philos.] le moi. || **egoist** [ˈijgowɪst] *n.* égoïste *m*. || **egotism** [ˈɪjgətɪzm] *n.* égoïsme *m*.

egret [ˈɪjgɹət] *n.* aigrette *f*.

Egypt [ˈijʤəpt] *n.* l'Égypte *f*. || **Egyptian** [ɪˈʤɪpʃən] *adj.* & *n.* égyptien.

eh? [ej] © †*interj.* [habituellement interrog.] Hein?; Quoi?

eider [ˈajdɚ] *n.* [duck] eider *m*. || **eiderdown** [-ˌdawn] *n.* édredon *m*.

eight [ejt] *n.* **1.** huit *m*. **2.** [Sport] équipe *f* de huit rameurs; canot *m* à huit rameurs. || *adj.* huit: *to be* ~, avoir huit ans; [Fam.] *behind the* ~ *ball*, être dans le pétrin. || **eighteen** [ejˈtijn] *n.* dix-huit *m*. || **eighteenth** [-θ] *adj.* & *n.* dix-huitième (*m*). || **eighth** [ejtθ] *adj.* huitième. || *n.* huitième *m*; [date] huit *m*. || **eighty** [ˈejtɪ] *adj.* & *n.* quatre-vingts (*m*); ~ *-one*, ~ *-two*, quatre-vingt-un, quatre-vingt-deux.

either [ijðɚ] [ajðɚ] *adj.* & *pron.* [one or the other of two] l'un ou l'autre, l'une ou l'autre; [both] l'un et l'autre; l'une et l'autre; les deux: *on* ~ *side*, des deux côtés. || *conj.* ~ . . . *or* . . . , ou (bien) . . . ou (bien) . . . ; soit . . . soit . . . : ~ *come in or go out*, entrez ou sortez; *not* . . . ~ . . . , ne . . . non plus . . . : *I won't come* ~, Je ne viendrai pas non plus, Ni moi non plus.

eject [ɪ'ʤɛk|t] *v. tr.* jeter dehors; chasser; déposséder; [Med.] évacuer. ‖ **ejection** [-ʃən] *n.* expulsion *f*, dépossession *f*; [Med.] évacuation *f*, éjection *f*.

elaborate [ɪˌlæbɚ|ət] *adj.* élaboré, soigné, travaillé. ‖ [-ejt] *v. tr.* élaborer. ‖ *v. intr.* entrer dans les détails, préciser.

elapse [ɪ'læps] *v. intr.* s'écouler, passer.

elastic [ɪ'læstɪk] *adj.* élastique, flexible, souple. ‖ *n.* élastique *m*, bande *f* élastique. ‖ **elasticity** [ɪˌlæs'tɪsɪtɪ] *n.* élasticité *f*, flexibilité *f*, souplesse *f*.

elate [ɪ'lejt] *v. tr.* exalter, exciter, transporter: *to be elated*, exulter, être transporté de joie.

elbow ['ɛlbow] *n.* coude *m*; [Fig.] coude, tournant *m* (d'une route, &c.): [Loc.] *at one's* ~, (tout) près; à portée de la main; *out at* ~, loqueteux, déguenillé; [Fam.] ~ *grease*, huile *f* de/bras, coude/. ‖ *v. tr.* coudoyer: *to* ~ *o.'s way*, se frayer un chemin à coups de coude.

elder[1] ['ɛldɚ] *n.* [Bot.] sureau *m*.

elder[2] *adj.* **1.** [= older] aîné; plus âgé (de deux personnes). cf. OLD. **2.** [= senior] plus ancien, ayant préséance; supérieur. ‖ *n.* aîné *m*, aînée *f*; doyen *m*, doyenne *f*; [tribe] ancien *m*, chef *m*. ‖ **elderly** [-lɪ] *adj.* âgé, d'un certain âge: ~ *people*, vieilles gens. ‖ **eldest** ['ɛldəst] *adj.* aîné; le plus âgé.

elect [ɪ'lɛk|t] *v. tr.* élire; [Fig.] choisir; se décider/pour, en faveur de/; préférer. ‖ *adj.* élu (sans être encore entré en fonction): [US] *the President* ~, le nouveau Président; [Fig.] préféré; [Rel.] élu; sauvé. ‖ *n.* [Rel.] *the* ~, les élus *mpl*; le peuple des élus; [Fig.] les privilégiés *mpl*. ‖ **election** [-ʃən] *n.* élection *f*: *by-*~, élection/partielle, complémentaire/; *general* ~, élections *fpl* générales; [Fig.] choix *m*; élection, option *f*; [Rel.] salut *m*. ‖ **elector** [-tɚ] *n.* élect|eur *m*, -rice *f*. ‖ **electoral** [-tɚl] *adj.* électoral: ~ *district*, circonscription *f* (électorale). ‖ **electorate** [-tɚət] *n.* **1.** les électeurs *mpl*, le corps *m* électoral. **2.** droit *m* d'électeur.

electric [ɪ'lɛktɹɪk] *adj.* [also **electrical**] électrique: ~ *chair*, chaise *f* électrique; ~ *eel*, gymnote *f*; ~ *heater*, radiateur *m* électrique; [Fig.] passionnant; sensationnel. ‖ **electrically** [-lɪ] *adv.* électriquement, → à l'électricité. ‖ **electrician** [ɪˌlɛk'tɹɪ|ʃən] *n.* électricien *m*. ‖ **electricity** [-sɪtɪ] *n.* électricité *f*; courant *m* électrique. ‖ **electrify** [ɪ'lɛktɹ|ɪˌfaj] *v. tr.* électriser; [Fig.] frapper, faire frémir. ‖ **electrocute** [-əˌkjuwt] *v. tr.* électrocuter. ‖ **electrode** [-owd] *n.* électrode. ‖ **electromagnet** [ɪˌlɛktɹow|'mægnət] *n.* électro-aimant *m*. ‖ **electromagnetic** [-mə'gnɛtɪk] *adj.* électro-magnétique.

electron [ɪ'lɛktɹɑn] *n.* [Phys.] électron *m*. ‖ **electronic** [ɪˌlɛk'tɹɑnɪk] *adj.* électronique: ~ *brain*, cerveau *m* électronique. ‖ **electronics** [-s] *n.sing.* [science] l'électronique *f*. ‖ **electrostatics** [ɪˌlɛktɹə'stætɪks] *n.sing.* [science] l'électrostatique *f*.

elegance ['ɛləgən|s] *n.* élégance *f*. ‖ **elegant** [-t] *adj.* élégant, de bon goût.

element ['ɛləmənt] *n.* élément *m*; [Fig.] milieu *m*; [Mil.] formation *f*, unité *f*; *the elements, n.pl.* éléments *mpl*, rudiments *mpl*; [météorologie] les éléments *mpl*; [Rel.] le pain et le vin, les (saintes) espèces *fpl*. ‖ **elemental** [ˌɛlə'mɛnt|l] *adj.* des éléments; [Fig.] élémentaire; essentiel. ‖ **elementary** [-ɚɪ] *adj.* élémentaire; [Sch.] primaire.

elephant ['ɛləfənt] *n.* éléphant *m*.

elevate ['ɛləˌvejt] *v. tr.* élever; exalter, exciter; animer, égayer. ‖ **elevated** ['ɛləˌvejtəd] *adj.* élevé; (métro) aérien. ‖ **elevation** [ˌɛlə'vejʃən] *n.* **1.** altitude *f*, cote *f* d'altitude; [Top.] site *m*, éminence *f*; [Math.] élévation *f*; [Mil.] angle *m* de hausse; montage *m* (du grain, &c.). **2.** [Fig.] élévation (de pensée), grandeur *f*, dignité *f*. ‖ **elevator** ['ɛləˌvejtɚ] *n.* **1.** ascenseur *m*: *freight* ~, monte-charge *m*. **2.** élévateur *m* (à céréales), entrepôt *m*: *terminal* ~, élévateur-terminus *m*. **3.** [Aviat.] gouvernail *m*/de profondeur, d'altitude/.

eleven [ɪ'lɛvn̩] *n.* & *adj.* [date, &c.] onze *m*; [Sport] équipe *f* de onze joueurs. ‖ **eleventh** [-θ] *adj.* onzième: *at the eleventh hour*, à la onzième heure, au dernier moment.

elicit [ɪ'lɪsɪt] *v. tr.* **1.** faire jaillir, faire sortir; tirer. **2.** mettre au jour, découvrir; faire avouer.

elide [ɪ'lajd] *v. tr.* élider.

eligible ['ɛlɪʤəbl̩] *adj.* éligible, convenable; avantageux (à, pour).

eliminate [ɪ'lɪmɪ|nejt] *v. tr.* éliminer; écarter; omettre; exclure. ‖ **elimination** [-nˌejʃən] *n.* élimination *f*; [Sport] *pl.* (épreuves) éliminatoires *fpl*.

elision [ɪ'lɪʒən] *n.* élision *f*.

elixir [ɪ'lɪksɚ] *n.* élixir *m*.

Elizabeth [ɪ'lɪzəbəθ] *n.* = Élisabeth *f*.

elk [ɛlk] *n.* élan *m*.

ell [ɛl] *n.* annexe *f*.

ellipse [ɪ'lɪps] *n.* ellipse *f*.

elm [ɛlm] *n.* [Bot.] orme *m*.

elope [ɪ'lowp] *v. intr.* s'enfuir; se faire enlever.

eloquence [ˈɛləkwən|s] *n.* éloquence *f.* || **eloquent** [-t] *adj.* éloquent.

else [ɛls] *adv.* autrement, ou bien: *Hurry or ~ you'll be late,* Dépêchez-vous, /autrement, ou bien/vous serez en retard; *Do it, or ~ !,* Faites-le,/sans cela . . . , sinon/(gare à vous)! || *adj.* **1.** *Who ~ ?,* Qui d'autre?, Qui encore?; *somebody, someone,* [interrog.] *anybody, anyone/ ~ ,* quelqu'un d'autre, un autre; *nobody, no one, not . . . anybody, not anyone/ ~ ,* personne (d')autre, aucun autre/(. . . ne); [indef.] *anybody, anyone/ ~ ,* n'importe quelle autre personne, tout autre; *everybody, everyone/ ~ ,* tous les autres. **2.** *What else?,* Quoi encore, [store] Et avec cela?; *What ~ did you do?,* Qu'avez-vous fait d'autre?; *something,* [interrog.] *anything/ ~ ,* autre chose, quelque chose d'autre; *nothing ~ , not . . . anything ~ ,* rien (d')autre, [store] plus rien; [indef.] *anything ~ ,* n'importe quoi d'autre; *everything ~ ,* tout le reste. **3.** *little, not much/ ~ ,* pas grand-chose d'autre, ne . . . guère autre chose; *much ~ ,* encore beaucoup, bien d'autres choses. **4.** *where ~ ,* où ailleurs, en quel autre endroit; *somewhere,* [interrog.] *anywhere/ ~ ,* ailleurs, autre part; *nowhere, not . . . anywhere/ ~ ,* nulle part ailleurs, en aucun autre endroit; [indef.] *anywhere ~ ,* n'importe où ailleurs; *everywhere ~ ,* partout ailleurs. **5.** *How ~ ?,* De quelle autre/façon, manière/?; *When ~ ?,* A quel autre moment, A quelle autre date?; *Why ~ ?,* Pour quelle autre raison? || **elsewhere** [-ˌwɛɚ] *adv.* ailleurs; autre part.

elucidate [ɪˈluwsɪˌdejt] *v. tr.* éclaircir, élucider, expliquer. || **elucidation** [ɪˌluwsɪˈdejʃən] *n.* éclaircissement *m,* élucidation *f.*

elude [ɪˈluwd] *v. tr.* éluder, éviter, esquiver, échapper à.

emaciated [ɪˈmejʃɪˌejtəd] *adj.* décharné, squelettique.

emanate [ˈɛməˌnejt] *v. intr.* émaner. || **emanation** [ˌɛməˈnejʃən] *n.* émanation *f.*

emancipate [ɪˈmænsɪˌpejt] *v. tr.* émanciper, affranchir (de). || **emancipation** [ɪˌmænsɪˈpejʃən] *n.* émancipation *f.*

embalm [ɪmˈbɔm] *v. tr.* embaumer, conserver.

embankment [ɪmˈbæŋkmənt] *n.* terrassement *m,* remblai *m,* talus *m*; [of a river] digue *f,* quai *m*; construction *f* (de quais); encaissement *m.*

embargo [ɪmˈbɑɚgow] *n.* embargo *m.*

embark [ɪmˈbɑɚk] *v. tr.* embarquer; prendre à bord. || *v. intr.* s'embarquer.

embarrass [ɪmˈbæɚəs] *v. tr.* [perturb] embarrasser, gêner, déconcerter; [mix up] compliquer, embrouiller; [hinder] entraver, gêner: *to be embarrassed,* être [overwhelmed] confus, [undecided] embarrassé, [shy, moneyless] gêné.

embassy [ˈɛmbəsɪ] *n.* ambassade *f*: *the Canadian Embassy,* l'Ambassade du Canada.

embed [ɪmˈbɛd] *v. tr.* **[-dd-]** encastrer.

embellish [ɪmˈbɛlɪʃ] *v. tr.* embellir, orner; agrémenter (*with,* de).

ember [ˈɛmbɚ] *n.* **1.** braise *f,* cendre *f.* **2.** *Ember Days,* Quatre-Temps *mpl.*

embezzle [ɪmˈbɛzl̩] *v. tr.* détourner, s'approprier (des fonds). || **embezzlement** [-mənt] *n.* détournement *m* (de fonds).

embitter [ɪmˈbɪtɚ] *v. tr.* rendre amer, remplir d'amertume; empoisonner, envenimer; irriter, aigrir.

emblem [ˈɛmbləm] *n.* emblème *m,* symbole *m.*

embodiment [ɪmˈbɑdɪmənt] *n.* incarnation *f,* personnification *f.* || **embody** [ɪmˈbɑdɪ] *v. tr.* incorporer; personnifier, incarner, résumer, contenir; [Mil.] incorporer.

embolden [ɪmˈbowldn̩] *v. tr.* enhardir.

emboss [ɪmˈbɑs] *v. tr.* [metal] bosseler; [Sculp.] travailler en bosse; [engr.] graver en relief; [cutlery] damasquiner; [paper, leather] gaufrer; [linen] brocher.

embrace [ɪmˈbɹejs] *v. tr.* [clasp] embrasser, étreindre; [hug] serrer/dans ses bras, sur son cœur/; [Fig.] embrasser (une carrière, la foi chrétienne); adopter (une opinion); saisir (l'occasion); [include] inclure; comprendre; [surround] embrasser, entourer; enclore; comprendre. || *v. intr.* [to hug one another] s'embrasser, s'étreindre. || *n.* [esp. Fig.] accueil *m* chaleureux; *a tender ~ ,* → (Il, Elle/me prit) tendrement dans ses bras.

embranchment [ɪmˈbɹæntʃmənt] *n.* embranchement *m.*

embroider [ɪmˈbɹojdɚ] *v. tr.* broder, orner. || **embroidery** [-ɪ] *n.* **1.** broderie *f.* **2.** [trade] la broderie: *~ set,* nécessaire *m* à broder.

embryo [ˈɛmbɹɪˌow] *n.* embryon *m.*

emend [ɪˈmɛnd] *v. tr.* corriger, améliorer.

emerald [ˈɛmɹəld] *n.* émeraude *f.*

emerge [ɪˈmɚdʒ] *v. intr.* émerger, surgir; s'élever, se dégager, paraître.

emergency [-ənsɪ] *n.* événements *mpl* graves, situation *f* critique (inattendue), état *m* d'urgence, crise *f*: *war ~ ,* état de guerre; *at a time of ~ ,* en cas d'alarme. || *attrib.* de secours: *~ brakes,* freins *mpl* de secours; *~ legislation* loi *f* exceptionnelle; ~ *measure*, expédient *m* provisoire, mesure *f* de circonstance; ~ *rations*, vivres *mpl* de réserve; ~ *signal*, signal *m* d'appel.

emeritus [ɪ'mɛɚɪtəs] *adj.* honoraire [× émérite].

emery ['ɛməɪ] *n.* émeri *m.*

emigrant ['ɛmɪgɹ|ənt] *adj. & n.* émigrant *m*; [Pol.] émigré *m.* || **emigrate** [-ˌejt] *v. intr.* émigrer. || **emigration** [ˌɛmɪ'gɹejʃən] *n.* émigration *f.*

eminence ['ɛmɪnən|s] *n.* **1.** éminence *f*; réputation *f*; distinction *f.* **2.** élévation *f* (de terrain). **3.** [title] Éminence. || **eminent** [-t] *adj.* **1.** éminent, remarquable, illustre: *Most* ~, éminentissime. **2.** haut, élevé.

emissary ['ɛmɪˌsɛəɪ] *n.* émissaire *m*, messager *m.* || *adj.* émissaire.

emission [ɪ'mɪʃən] *n.* émission *f*; [gas] dégagement *m.*

emit [ɪ'mɪt] *v. tr.* émettre; [Chem.] exhaler.

emotion [ɪ'mowʃən] *n.* émotion *f.* || **emotional** [-l̩] *adj.* émoti|f, -ve, émotionnable, impressionnable.

emperor ['ɛmpɚɚ] *n.* empereur *m.*

emphasis ['ɛmfə|sɪs] *n.* [Gram.] accent *m* d'insistance; [style] mise *f* en relief; [Fig.] force *f*, insistance *f*: *with* ~ *on*, → en insistant particulièrement sur. [☞ Do not confuse with Fr. *emphase*, bombast]. || **emphasize** [-ˌsajz] *v. tr.* [Gram.] accentuer, mettre en relief; [Fig.] appuyer sur, souligner, faire ressortir: *to* ~ *the need for*, souligner le besoin urgent de . . . || **emphatic** [ɪm'fætɪk] *adj.* énergique, expressi|f, -ve, accentué, emphatique. || **emphatically** [-əlɪ] *adv.* énergiquement, expressivement; → avec/force, emphase/

empire ['ɛmpajɚ] *n.* **1.** empire *m.* **2.** autorités *fpl*, pouvoir *m* suprême.

empiric [ˌɛm'pijəɪ|k] *adj.* empirique. || **empiricism** [-ˌsɪzm] *n.* empirisme *m.*

employ [ɪm'ploj] *v. tr.* **1.** [use services of] employer, prendre à son emploi, donner du travail à; [keep busy] occuper, tenir occupé. **2.** [use] utiliser, employer, faire usage de, se servir de. || *n.* emploi *m*, occupation *f*: *to be in the* ~ *of*, être au service de, → employer qqun. || **employability** [ɪmˌplojə'bɪlɪtɪ] *n.* aptitude *f* (au travail). || **employable** [ɪm'ploj|əbl̩] *adj.* apte (au travail). || **employee** [-ij] *n.* employé *m*, -e *f.* || **employer** [-ɚ] *n.* patron *m.* || **employment** [-mənt] *n.* **1.** emploi *m* (de la main-d'œuvre); marché *m* du travail, embauchage *m.* **2.** [job] travail *m*; emploi *m*; occupation *f*; situation *f*; place *f*: *out of* ~, sans travail.

†**emporium** [ɛm'pɔɚɪəm] *n.* magasin *m*; entrepôt *m*; marché *m.*

empress ['ɛmpɹəs] *n.* impératrice *f.*

emptiness ['ɛmptɪ|nəs] *n.* vacuité *f*, vide *m*, néant *m*; [Fig.] vanité *f*, inanité *f*; [Pers.] nullité *f.* || **empty** *adj.* vide; [room] inoccupé; [country] inhabité, désert; [Fig.] vain, sans importance; dérisoire: *an* ~ *threat*, une vaine menace; ~*-handed*, les mains vides; ~ *-headed*, sans cervelle, écervelé; [Fam.] affamé, qui a faim. || *n.* emballage *m* vide, bouteille *f* vide. || *v. tr.* vider (*into*, dans). || *v. intr.* se vider; [river] se jeter.

emulate ['ɛmjəˌlejt] *v. tr.* tâcher d'égaler, égaler, imiter, suivre, rivaliser avec. || **emulation** [ˌɛmjə'lejʃən] *n.* émulation *f*: *to inspire* ~, exciter l'émulation.

enable [ɪn'ejbl̩] *v. tr.* **1.** rendre capable (*to*, de); mettre (qqun) à même de (faire). **2.** [Jur.] donner pouvoir à, habiliter.

enact [ɪ'nækt] *v. tr.* **1.** [Jur.] décréter, ordonner, statuer. **2.** [Theat.] représenter. **3.** accomplir.

enamel [ɪ'næməl] *n.* émail *m*; vernis *m*, laque *f*: ~ *work*, émaillure *f.* || *v. tr.* peindre en émail; émailler; vernir.

enamour [ɪ'næmɚ] *v. tr.* rendre amoureux, s'éprendre (de), se passionner (pour): *to become enamoured*, devenir amoureux (de).

encamp [ɪn'kæmp] *v. tr.* camper. || **encampment** [-mənt] *n.* campement *m.*

enchain [ɪn'ʧejn] *v. tr.* enchaîner.

enchant [ɪn'ʧænt] *v. tr.* enchanter, charmer. || **enchantment** [-mənt] *n.* enchantement *m.*

encircle [ɪn'sɚkl̩] *v. tr.* entourer, environner, encercler, ceindre.

enclose [ɪn'klow|z] *v. tr.* **1.** [shut in] enclore, clôturer; entourer. **2.** [include] inclure, renfermer; [in envelope] inclure, joindre, insérer: *enclosed* . . ., ci-joint . . ., sous ce pli . . . || **enclosure** [-ʒɚ] *n.* [fence] clôture *f*; [land] enceinte *f*; enclos *m*; †clos *m*; [Com.] pièce *f*/annexée, jointe/; annexe *f.*

encomium [ɛn'kowmɪəm] *n.* éloge *m*, panégyrique *m*, louange *f.*

encompass [ɪn'kʌmpəs] *v. tr.* **1.** entourer, environner, renfermer. **2.** venir à bout de, achever.

encore ['ɑnkɔɚ] *n.* [Theat.] rappel *m*; bis *m.* || *v. tr.* bisser.

encounter [ɪn'kawntɚ] *n.* **1.** rencontre *f.* **2.** combat *m*, choc *m*, bataille *f*, lutte *f*, assaut *m.* || *v. tr.* **1.** rencontrer. **2.** attaquer, combattre, affronter, essuyer, engager (le combat).

encourage [ɪn'kɚəʤ] *v. tr.* **1.** [increase

hope] encourager, enhardir; [give courage to] donner du cœur à; exhorter à; [incite] encourager à, pousser à. **2.** aider, favoriser; [Com.] stimuler; © encourager. || **encouragement** [-mənt] *n.* encouragement *m* (*from,* de la part de; *to,* à).

encroach [ɪn'kɹowtʃ] *v. intr.* empiéter (sur), abuser (de); [rights] anticiper sur.

encumber [ɪn'kʌmbɚ] *v. tr.* embarrasser; [debt] grever (de); [load] charger (de); accabler (de); [estate] hypothéquer.

encumbrance [ɪn'kʌmbɹəns] *n.* embarras *m,* charge *f.*

encyclopædia [ɪnˌsajklə'pijdɪə] *n.* encyclopédie *f.*

end [ɛnd] *n.* **1.** [conclusion] fin *f,* conclusion *f*: *at an* ~, fini, [supplies, &c.] épuisé; *at the* ~ (*of*), à la fin (de); *at the* ~ *of July,* [regular event] à la fin de, en fin/juillet, [single event] à la fin juillet: *to put an* ~ *to,* mettre/un terme, fin/à, en finir avec; *in the* ~, à la fin, à la longue; *to come to an* ~, s'achever, se terminer. **2.** [place where a thing stops] fin *f,* limite *f*; [time] terme *m*; [ruler, stick, &c.] bout *m,* extrémité *f*: *on* ~, debout, sur son extrémité; ~ *to* ~, bout à bout. **3.** [remote section of town] quartier *m*; [*Mile End* corresponds to Fr. *Bout du Monde, Point du Jour,* &c.]; [Tel. conversation] *at this* ~, *at your* ~, de mon côté, ici; de votre côté, chez vous. **4.** [purpose] but *m*; fin *f*; intention *f*; propos *m,* dessein *m.* **5.** [result] résultat *m*; conclusion *f*; issue *f*; dénouement *m.* **6.** [death] fin *f,* mort *f.* **7.** [fragment] reste *m*; fragment *m*; morceau *m*; débris *m*: *odds and ends,* bribes *fpl.* bouts *mpl.* **8.** [Loc.] ~ *of steel,* © [Rail.] bout *m* de la ligne, terminus *m*; *to be at a loose* ~, se trouver/sans rien à faire, sans occupation, désœuvré/; *to go off the deep* ~, perdre patience, se mettre en colère; *to make an* ~ *of,* s'arrêter (de faire); interrompre; cesser; mettre/fin, un terme/ à; *to make* (*both*) *ends meet,* joindre les deux bouts; *to the bitter* ~, jusqu'au bout. || **end** *v. tr.* [job, &c.] finir, achever, terminer; [kill] achever, supprimer. || *v. intr.* finir, se terminer; [lease, subscription, &c.] expirer; [year, season] s'achever, prendre fin: *to* ~ *up by* . . . , finir par faire . . . ; *to* ~ *up in* . . . , aboutir à . . . .

endanger [ɪn'dejnʤɚ] *v. tr.* mettre en danger; exposer; risquer.

endear [ɪn'dijɚ] *v. tr.* rendre cher (à). || **endearment** [-mənt] *n.* caresse *f*; attrait *m,* charme *m,* tendresse *f,* affection *f.*

endeavour [ɪn'dɛvɚ] *n.* effort *m*; tentative *f*; essai *m*; soin *m.* || *v. intr.* s'efforcer (de); chercher (à); viser (à).

ending ['ɛnd|ɪŋ] *n.* fin *f*; [story] conclusion *f,* dénouement *m*; [life] fin *f,* terme *f*; [Gram.] terminaison *f*; désinence *f.* || **endless** [-ləs] *adj.* interminable; [space] infini, sans bornes; [time] éternel; [noise, &c.] continuel, incessant; [speaker] intarissable; [chain, belt] sans fin.

endorse [ɪn'dɔɚs] *v. tr.* [Fin.] endosser (un chèque); viser (un passeport); [Fig.] approuver (une décision), sanctionner (un projet). || **endorsement** [-mənt] *n.* [Fin.] endos *m* (d'un chèque); [Fig.] appui *m,* approbation *f.* || **endorser** [-ɚ] *n.* [Fin.] endosseur *m.*

endow [ɪn'daw] *v. tr.* doter (de); doter; [Fig.] douer (de). || **endowment** [-mənt] *n.* dotation *f*; [Fig.] don *m,* qualité *f,* avantage *m.*

endue [ɪn'djuw] *v. tr.* revêtir (de); [qualities] douer (de).

endurance [ɪn'djuwɚ|əns] *n.* endurance *f,* patience *f*; souffrance *f*: *beyond* ~, insupportable. || **endure** *v. intr.* [last] durer; persister; [Fam.] tenir (bon). || *v. tr.* [undergo] supporter; [bear] endurer; souffrir; [tolerate] tolérer, subir. || **enduring** [-ɪŋ] *adj.* endurant, dur au mal; [lasting] durable.

enema ['ɛnəmə] *n.* lavement *m.*

enemy ['ɛnəmɪ] *n.* & *adj.* ennemi *m,* -e *f.*

energetic [ˌɛnɚ'ʤɛtɪk] *adj.* énergique. || **energy** ['ɛnɚʤɪ] *n.* énergie *f,* vigueur *f.*

enervate ['ɛnɚˌvejt] *v. tr.* énerver; affaiblir.

enfeeble [ɪn'fijbl̩] *v. tr.* affaiblir.

enfold, also **infold** [ɪn'fowld] *v. tr.* enrouler, envelopper; [embrace] embrasser, prendre dans ses bras.

enforce [ɪn'fɔɚs] *v. tr.* [force obedience] forcer, contraindre; imposer . . . (*on s.o.,* à qqun)/par la force, de force/: *to* ~ *the law,* faire respecter la loi. || **enforcement** [-mənt] *n.* contrainte *f*; [Jur.] application *f.*

enfranchise [ɪn'fɹænʧajz] *v. tr.* **1.** [slave] affranchir. **2.** [vote, Pers.] donner le droit de vote (à).

engage [ɪn'gejʤ] *v. tr.* engager (*to,* à): *to* ~ *o.s. to,* s'engager à; [hire] engager, embaucher (un domestique); [reserve] louer, retenir (des places); [attract] retenir (l'attention de qqun); [lock together] engrener; [gears] embrayer; [Mil.] engager (le combat): *to be engaged in* ,(a) être occupé à; [taxi] [Br.] *Are you engaged?,* → Êtes-vous libre?; [Tel.] *The line is engaged,* La ligne est occupée; (b) *to be engaged,* être fiancé(e) (*to,* à):

They/got, became/engaged last week, Ils se sont fiancés la semaine dernière. || *v. intr.* se livrer (à qqch.): *to ~ in discussion,* entrer en discussion. || **engagement** [-mənt] *n.* [pledge, Mil., &c.] engagement *m*; [promise to marry] fiançailles *fpl*; [appointment] rendez-vous *m*: *to make an ~*, fixer un rendez-vous, prendre date. || **engaging** [-ɪŋ] *adj.* attrayant, charmant.

engender [ɪn'ʤɛndər] *v. tr.* engendrer, faire naître.

engine ['ɛnʤɪn] *n.* [Auto.] moteur *m*; [Naut.] machine *f* [often pl.]: *~ room,* la chambre des machines; [Rail.] locomotive *f*; [†Hist.] engin *m*, machine *f*: *fire ~*, pompe *f* à incendie; *~-driver,* mécanicien *m*, cf. ENGINEER; *~ trouble,* panne *f* (de moteur). || **engineer** [ɛnʤɪ'nijər] *n.* mécanicien *m* (de locomotive, &c.); [expert] ingénieur *m*; [Mil.] soldat *m*, officier *m*/du génie; [radio, &c.] *sound ~*, ingénieur du son. || *v. tr.* construire; diriger les travaux [à titre d'ingénieur]; faire, tracer/les plans de; [Fig., Fam.] machiner, manigancer. || **engineering** [-ɪŋ] *n.* [science de l'ingénieur] génie *m*, génie civil; travaux *mpl*, ouvrages *mpl* d'art; travaux techniques; technique *f*; construction *f* mécanique: *agricultural ~*, génie agricole; *civil ~*, génie civil; *electrical ~*, technique /électrique, de l'électricité/, électrotechnique *f* (appliquée), électricité *f* industrielle; *marine ~*, construction *f* navale; *nuclear ~*, génie atomique; *mechanical ~*, équipement *m* en matériel [par opposition à *civil ~*, qui ne concerne que l'infrastructure d'une installation]; construction *f*/mécanique, de machines/; *~ departments,* services *mpl* techniques; *~ science,* technique *f* (industrielle); *~ trades,* métiers *mpl* de la mécanique; *~ work,* ouvrage *m* d'art, [Mil.] fortification *f* de campagne; *farm ~*, génie rural; *military ~*, génie militaire; *mining ~*, génie minier, art *m* des mines, technique *f* minière; *social ~*, technologie *f* sociale; *sales ~*, technique de vente; *structural ~*, technique de la construction; *electrical ~ industry,* électrotechnique *f*; *~ geology,* géologie *f* appliquée; *~ industry,* industrie *f* mécanique; *~ and craft industries,* mécanique *f* et artisanat *m*; *~ shop,* atelier *m*. **2.** étude *f*, projet *m*: *~ and design,* étude *f* et projet *m*; *methods ~*, étude *f* des méthodes. **3.** [Fig., Pej.] machinations *fpl*, manœuvres *fpl*, manigances *fpl*.

England ['ɪŋglənd] *n.* l'Angleterre *f*: *in, to/~*, en Angleterre.

English ['ɪŋglɪʃ] *adj.* anglais, d'Angleterre; © anglais, canadien-anglais: *the ~ Channel,* la Manche; [Mus.] *~ horn,* cor *m* anglais, oboe da caccia. || *n.* [coll.] *the ~*, les Anglais *mpl*; [langage] l'anglais: *to speak ~*, parler anglais; *in ~*, en anglais; *to study ~*, étudier l'anglais. || **English|man** [-mən] *pl.* **-men** [-mən] *n.* Anglais. || **English-speaking** [-ˌspijkɪŋ] *adj.* de langue, d'expression/anglaise; anglophone. || **English|woman** [-ˌwʊmən] *pl.* **-women** [-ˌwɪmən] *n.* Anglaise *f*.

engrave [ɪn'gɹejv] *v. tr.* graver. || **engraver** [-ər] *n.* [person] graveur *m*. || **engraving** [-ɪŋ] *n.* gravure *f*.

engross [ɪn'gɹows] *v. tr.* **1.** accaparer. **2.** absorber. **3.** [Jur.] grossoyer, copier.

engulf [ɪn'gʌlf] *v. tr.* engouffrer, engloutir.

enhance [ɪn'hæns] *v. tr.* rehausser, relever, augmenter; [price] aggraver.

enigma [ɪ'nɪgmə] *n.* énigme *f*.

enjoin [ɪn'ʤojn] *v. tr.* enjoindre, prescrire, recommander.

enjoy [ɪn'ʤoj] *v. tr.* **1.** aimer (*dancing,* &c., danser, &c.); prendre plaisir (à danser, &c.): *to ~ o.s.,* s'amuser, se divertir; *to ~ o.s. immensely,* s'en donner à cœur joie, s'amuser royalement. **2.** jouir (d'une bonne santé); disposer (d'une grande fortune). || **enjoyable** [-əbl] *adj.* agréable; plaisant; [spectacle] divertissant. || **enjoyment** [-mənt] *n.* plaisir *m*, satisfaction *f*; [Jur.] jouissance *f*.

enkindle [ɛn'kɪndl̩] *v. tr.* allumer; [Fig.] enflammer.

enlarge [ɪn'lɑərʤ] *v. tr.* **1.** agrandir, augmenter, étendre, développer; [Med.] hypertrophier. **2.** [Fig.] dilater. **3.** [Jur.] élargir. || **enlargement** [-mənt] *n.* agrandissement *m*; [Fig.] accroissement *m*.

enlighten [ɪn'lajtn̩] *v. tr.* **1.** éclairer; illuminer. **2.** [Fig.] éclaircir. || **enlightenment** [-mənt] *n.* éclaircissements *mpl* (*on,* sur): *the Age of Enlightenment,* le siècle des lumières.

enlist [ɪn'lɪst] *v. tr.* inscrire; [Mil.] enrôler, engager. || *v. intr.* s'enrôler, s'inscrire. || **enlistment** [-mənt] *n.* enrôlement *m*, engagement *m*.

enliven [ɪn'lajvən] *v. tr.* animer, vivifier, ranimer; activer, égayer, réjouir.

enmity ['ɛnmɪtɪ] *n.* inimitié *f*, hostilité *f*, haine *f*.

ennoble [ɪ'nowbl̩] *v. tr.* anoblir; [Fig.] ennoblir, illustrer.

enormous [ɪ'noərməs] *adj.* **1.** [huge] énorme, colossal. **2.** [outrageous] monstrueux, excessif; effrayant. || **enormously** [-lɪ] *adv.* énormément.

enough [ɪ'nʌf] *adj. & n.* assez, suffisamment/(de): (*That's*) ~, (En voilà) assez, Ça suffit; *I've had* ~ (*of this*), J'en ai assez; *Do you have* ~ *money* (*to*)?, Avez-vous assez, suffisamment/d'argent (pour)?; *more than* ~, plus qu'il n'en faut; *It is not* ~ *to be polite*, Il ne suffit pas d'être poli; *It was* ~ *to drive you crazy*, C'était à vous rendre fou; *He has* ~ *to live on*, Il a de quoi vivre; *One glance was* ~ (*to*), Il a suffi d'un seul coup d'œil (pour); *to leave well* ~ *alone*, Le mieux est l'ennemi du bien. || *adv.* assez, suffisamment; [Pej.] passablement: *He is tall* ~ (*to*), Il est /assez, suffisamment/grand (pour); *You know well* ~ *that . . .*, Vous savez très bien que . . . ; *Curiously* ~, Chose curieuse; *He plays well* ~, (*but*), Il ne joue pas mal, (mais); *I'm*/*happy, willing*/ ~ *to help*, (*but*), Je suis parfaitement d'accord pour aider, (mais).

enrage [ɪn'ɹejʤ] *v. tr.* exaspérer, irriter. faire enrager.

enrapture [ɪn'ɹæptʃɚ] *v. tr.* transporter (de joie), ravir.

enrich [ɪn'ɹɪtʃ] *v. tr.* enrichir; [soil] fertiliser.

enrol [ɪn'ɹowl] *v. tr.* [-ll-] enrôler; enregistrer, inscrire. || **enrolment** [-mənt] *n.* [action] enrôlement *m*, enregistrement *m*, inscription *f*.

enshroud [ɪn'ʃɹawd] *v. tr.* ensevelir; cacher, recouvrir.

ensign ['ɛnsajn] *n.* [flag] enseigne *f*, drapeau *m*; [mark] signe *m*, insigne *m*; signal *m*; [Mar., flag] enseigne *f*, pavillon *m*; [Mil., flag] drapeau *m*; [soldier] enseigne *m*: ~ *-bearer*, porte-enseigne *m*.

enslave [ɪn'slejv] *v. tr.* asservir, réduire à l'esclavage; assujettir.

ensnare [ɪn'snɛɚ] *v. tr.* prendre au piège; [Fig.] attraper, réduire, enjôler.

ensue [ɪn'suw] *v. tr.* s'ensuivre (*from*, de); suivre. || *v. intr.* résulter.

ensure [ɪn'ʃuwɚ] *v. tr.* assurer; garantir.

entail [ɪn'tejl] *v. tr.* [Jur.] substituer (à); [Fig.] léguer (à), imposer (à); entraîner, occasionner. || *n.* substitution *f*; [Fig.] transmission *f*; [property] bien *m* substitué, majorat *m*.

entangle [ɪn'tæŋgl̩] *v. tr.* emmêler, enchevêtrer, engager, embarrasser, embrouiller.

enter ['ɛntɚ] *v. tr.* **1.** entrer, pénétrer/(dans): *He entered the highway*, Il déboucha sur la grand-route. **2.** inscrire, porter (un nom sur une liste); s'inscrire à (une école, &c.); enregistrer; consigner par écrit; participer à, prendre part à. **3.** [Jur.] intenter (un procès); élever (une protestation contre); [customs] faire une déclaration. || *v. intr.* entrer, pénétrer (dans): *to* ~ *into an agreement*, conclure un marché; *to* ~ *into negotiations*, entamer des négociations; *to* ~ *into* (*the make-up of*), faire partie (intégrante) de; *to* ~ (*up*)*on*, entreprendre (un travail), débuter dans (une carrière), commencer.

enterprise ['ɛntɚˌpɹajz] *n.* entreprise *f*; esprit *m* d'entreprise, hardiesse *f*. || **enterprising** [-ɪŋ] *adj.* entreprenant, hardi.

entertain [ˌɛntɚ'tejn] *v. tr.* amuser, distraire; [receive guest] recevoir, offrir un dîner à (un invité, un hôte); [Fig.] prendre (qqch.) en considération; entretenir (un espoir); concevoir (un projet). || *v. intr.* recevoir, donner une réception. || **entertaining** [-ɪŋ] *adj.* amusant, divertissant; plaisant. || **entertainment** [-mənt] *n.* divertissement *m*; amusement *m*; [show] spectacle *m*; [Fig.] accueil *m*, hospitalité *f*, réception *f*.

enthral [ɪn'θɹɔl] *v. tr.* captiver, charmer; asservir, rendre esclave.

enthuse [ɪn'θuwz] [Fam.] *v. intr.* s'enthousiasmer (*over*, de).

enthusiasm [ɪn'θjuwzɪˌæs|m] *n.* enthousiasme *m*. || **enthusiast** [-t] *n.* enthousiaste *m*/*f*. || **enthusiastic** [ɛnˌθjuwzɪ'æstɪk] *adj.* enthousiaste.

entice [ɪn'tajs] *v. tr.* inciter (à), exciter, pousser (à); [allure] attirer, tenter, séduire, entraîner.

entire [ɪn'tajɚ] *adj.* [whole] entier, tout entier, complet; [text] intégral; [not broken] parfait, intact. || **entirely** [-lɪ] *adv.* entièrement, complètement, intégralement, totalement, pleinement. || **entirety** [-ətɪ] *n.* totalité *f*: *in its* ~, dans son entier.

entitle [ɪn'tajtl̩] *v. tr.* intituler, nommer; [Jur.] donner droit (à); mettre en droit.

entity ['ɛntɪtɪ] *n.* entité *f*, individualité *f*.

entomb [ɪn'tjuwm] *v. tr.* ensevelir.

entrails ['ɛntɹejlz] *n.pl.* entrailles *fpl.*

entrain [ɪn'tɹejn] *v. intr.* [Rail.] prendre le train, embarquer. || *v. tr.* mettre dans le train.

entrance ['ɛntɹəns] *n.* [action] entrée *f*; [door, &c.] entrée *f*, accès *m*; ~ *to . . .*, entrée de . . . , accès à . . . : *Tradesmen's* ~, Entrée de service; [right] droit *m* d'entrée; [to a university, &c.] admission *f*: ~ *examination*, examen *m* d'entrée.

entreat [ɪn'tɹijt] *v. tr.* supplier, conjurer, prier/(de); implorer. || **entreaty** [-ɪ] *n.* instances *fpl.*, supplication *f*, prière *f*, sollicitation *f*.

entree [ˈɑntɹej] *n.* [Culin.] entrée *f.* || **entree dish** [-ˌdɪʃ] *n.* plat *m* d'entrée.

entrench, also **intrench** [ɪnˈtɹɛntʃ] *v. tr.*: *to* ~ *o.s.*, [Mil. & Fig.] se retrancher.

entrepreneur [ˌɑntɹəpɹəˈnɚ] *n.* entrepreneur *m.*

entrust [ɪnˈtɹʌst] *v. tr.*: *to* ~ *s.o. with sth.*, charger qqun de faire qqch.; confier qqch. à qqun.

entry [ˈɛntɹɪ] *n.* **1.** [action] entrée *f.* **2.** [way] entrée, vestibule *m*, passage *m*; [in a book] entrée; [in a dictionary] article *m*, rubrique *f*; [bookkeeping] écriture *f*; [customs] *port of* ~, poste *m* douanier, poste de douane; [sports, exhibition] participant *m*, concurrent *m*; exposant *m*; [the thing shown] objet *m* exposé; [book, &c.] envoi *m*; [law] mise *f* en vigueur; [Mus.] entrée.

entwine [ɪnˈtwajn] *v. tr.* enlacer, entrelacer, entortiller. || *v. intr.* s'enlacer, s'entrelacer, s'entortiller.

enumerate [ɪˈnjuwmɚˌejt] *v. tr.* énumérer.

enunciate [ɪˈnʌnsɪˌejt] *v. tr.* énoncer, déclarer; prononcer, articuler.

envelop [ɪnˈvɛləp] *v. tr.* envelopper; [Mil.] cerner (l'ennemi). || **envelope** [ˈɛnvəˌlowp] *n.* enveloppe *f*; [Bot.] tunique *f*; [Math.] enveloppante *f.*

enviable [ˈɛnvɪə|bḷ] *adj.* enviable, digne d'envie. || **envious** [-s] *adj.* envieux, jaloux (de, *of*).

environ [ɪnˈvajɹən] *v. tr.* environner, entourer; [Mil.] cerner. || **environment** [-mənt] *n.* milieu *m*, entourage *m*; environnement *m.*

envisage [ɪnˈvɪzədʒ] *v. tr.* envisager; regarder . . . en face.

envoy [ˈɛnvɔj] *n.* **1.** [Pers.] envoyé *m* (diplomatique); [messenger] messager *m.* **2.** [Lit.] envoi *m.*

envy [ˈɛnvɪ] *n.* **1.** envie *f*, convoitise *f* (*at, of*, de, à l'égard de). **2.** objet *m* d'envie (de): *to be the* ~ *of*, → faire envie. || *v. tr.* envier (qqun); porter envie à; convoiter, envier (qqch./à qqun).

epaulet [ˌɛpəˈlɛt] *n.* épaulette *f.*

ephemeral [ɪˈfɛmərəl] *adj.* éphémère.

epic [ˈɛpɪk] *n.* poème *m* épique, épopée *f.* || *adj.* épique.

epicure [ˈɛpɪˌkjuwɚ] *n.* gourmet *m.*

epidemic [ɛpɪˈdɛmɪk] *n.* épidémie *f.* || *adj.* épidémique.

epigram [ˈɛpɪˌgɹæm] *n.* épigramme *m.*

epilepsy [ˈɛpɪˌlɛpsɪ] *n.* épilepsie *f.*

Epiphany [ɪˈpɪfənɪ] *n.* Épiphanie *f.*

episode [ˈɛpɪˌsowd] *n.* épisode *m.*

epistle [ɪˈpɪsḷ] *n.* épître *f.*

epitaph [ˈɛpɪˌtæf] *n.* épitaphe *f.*

epoch [ˈijpɑk] *n.* époque *f.*

equable [ˈɛkwəbḷ] *adj.* [caractère) égal.

equal [ˈijkwəl] *adj.* **1.** égal, équivalent (*to*, à); de même/valeur, force/: *on* ~ *terms*, sur un pied d'égalité. **2.** [even] égal; uniforme; [Fig.] *to be, feel/* ~ *to* [+ inf], être/de taille à, de force à, à même de/ faire . . . || *n.* [person or thing equal] pair *m*; égal *m*; pareil *m.* || *v. tr.* [-ll-] égaler; être, devenir/l'égal de. || **equality** [ɪˈkwɑlətɪ] *n.* égalité *f.* || **equalization** [ˌɪkwəlɪˈzejʃən] *n.* égalisation *f*; [Fin., Com.] péréquation *f*, compensation *f.* || **equalize** [ˈijkwəˌlajz] *v. tr.* égaliser, niveler. || *v. intr.* s'égaliser, se compenser, s'équilibrer.

equate [ɪˈkwej|t] *v. tr.* mettre en équation; assimiler. || **equation** [-ʒən] *n.* équation *f.*

equilibrium [ˌijkwəˈlɪbɹɪəm] *n.* équilibre *m.*

equip [ɪˈkwɪp] *v. tr.* [-pp-] équiper (*with*, de); [fit out] meubler; installer; [shop] outiller; [boat] armer; [organization] pourvoir; [instrument] monter, munir de.

equipment [-mənt] *n.* équipement *m.*

equitable [ˈɛkwɪt|əbḷ] *adj.* équitable, juste. || **equity** [-ɪ] *n.* équité *f*; [in property] part *f* résiduaire.

equivalence [ɪˈkwɪvələns] *n.* équivalence *f.* || **equivalent** [-t] *adj. & n.* équivalent *m.*

equivocal [ɪˈkwɪvɪkḷ] *adj.* équivoque.

equivocate [ɪˈkwɪvəˌkejt] *v. intr.* jouer sur les mots.

era [ˈijɹə] *n.* ère *f*, époque *f.*

eradicate [ɪˈɹædɪˌkejt] *v. tr.* **1.** arracher, extirper. **2.** déraciner.

erase [ɪˈɹejs] *v. tr.* effacer, raturer, oblitérer. || **eraser** [-ɚ] *n.* **1.** gomme *f* (à effacer), © efface *f.* **2.** brosse *f* (pour effacer le tableau noir).

erect [ɪˈɹɛkt] *v. tr.* dresser; [building] ériger; construire; élever; [Geom.] dresser (une perpendiculaire, &c.); [Tech.] monter; installer; établir, fonder.

erode [ɪˈɹow|d] *v. tr.* [rock] éroder; [metal] corroder. || *v. intr.* s'éroder, subir l'action de l'érosion. || **erosion** [-ʒən] *n.* érosion *f.*

erotic [ɪˈɹɑtɪk] *adj.* érotique.

err [ɚ] *v. intr.* se tromper, être erroné; s'écarter du droit chemin.

errand [ˈɛɚənd] *n.* **1.** [action] course *f*, commission *f*: *to run an* ~, faire une course; ~ *boy*, garçon *m* de courses. **2.** [purpose, object] message *m*, l'objet *m* de (ma) visite.

errant [ˈɛɚənt] *adj.* **1.** errant: *knight* ~, chevalier *m* errant. **2.** tombé dans l'erreur.

erratic [ɪˈɹætɪk] *adj.* [Geol.] erratique; [Fig.] errant; [queer] excentrique.

erroneous [ɪˌɹownɪəs] *adj.* erroné, faux, incorrect.

error [ˈɛɚɚ] *n.* **1.** [mistake] erreur *f*; faute *f*; [clerical] erreur matérielle; [Printer's] coquille *f*; [social] bévue *f*: *in* ~, par erreur; *to be in* ~, être dans l'erreur, se tromper; impair *m*. **2.** [opinion] erreur *f*, confusion *f*; [sin] errement *m*, péché *m*; faute *f*. **3.** [baseball] erreur *f*.

erudite [ˈɛɚuwˌdajt] *adj.* érudit, savant. || **erudition** [ˌɛɚuwˈdɪʃən] *n.* érudition *f*.

erupt [ɪˈɹʌp|t] *v. intr.* [volcano] entrer en, faire/éruption; [geysers] jaillir; [Fig.] se déchaîner, exploser; [tooth] pousser; percer. || **eruption** [-ʃən] *n.* **1.** éruption *f*; [Fig.] éclat *m*. **2.** [Med.] éruption (des dents); poussée *f* (de boutons). **3.** [Mil.] insurrection *f*.

escalator [ˈɛskəˌlejtɚ] *n.* escalier *m*/roulant, mécanique.

escapade [ˈɛskəˌpejd] *n.* escapade *f*, frasque *f*, fredaine *f*.

escape [ɪˈskejp] *v. intr.* **1.** s'évader (*from*, de); s'échapper, prendre la fuite; [Fig.] [get free from] fuir à, se dérober à (son devoir, &c.). **2.** [avoid] éviter; échapper (*from*, à); [steam, &c.] fuir; [fail to be noticed] échapper à, passer inaperçu. || *n.* évasion *f*; fuite *f*: *to have a narrow* ~, l'échapper belle; [way of escaping] *fire* ~, escalier *m* de sauvetage; échappatoire *f*; subterfuge *m*: ~ *clause*, clause/de résiliation, de sauvegarde/; [Fig.] évasion *f*; [gas, &c.] échappement *m*; fuite *f*; dégagement *m*. || **escapement** [ɪˈskejp|-mənt] *n.* issue *f*, passage *m*, libre cours *m*; sortie *f*, débouché *m*: ~ *of fish*, banc *m* de poisson; [Mec.] échappement *m*.

escapist [-ɪst] *adj.* d'évasion. || *n.* qui vit d'illusions.

†**eschew** [ɛsˈʃuw] *v. tr.* éviter (qqun, qqch.); fuir.

escort [ˈɛskɔɚt] *n.* escorte *f*: ~ *to a lady*, cavalier *m*.

Eskimo [ˈɛskɪˌmow] *pl.* **Eskimos** *n.* Esquimau *m*, -de *f*. || *adj.* esquimau, -de *f*.

esp. [= especially] spécialement. || **especial** [əˈspɛʃəl] *adj.* spécial; exceptionnel, particulier. cf. SPÉCIAL. || **especially** [-ɪ] *adv.* surtout; spécialement, en particulier.

espionage [ˈɛspɪəˌnɑʒ] *n.* espionnage *m*.

esquire [ˈɛskwajɚ] abbr. Esq., *n.* **1.** [mainly Br.] Monsieur: *John Smith, Esq.*, Monsieur John Smith. **2.** [Hist.] écuyer *m*.

essay [ˈɛsej] *n.* **1.** [Lit.] composition *f*, dissertation *f*, essai *m*. **2.** essai *m*, effort *m*, tentative *f*. || *v. tr.* [əˈsaj] essayer, tenter; mettre à l'épreuve.

essence [ˈɛsəns] *n.* essence *f*; [concentrated extract] essence, extrait *m*. || **essential** [ɪˈsɛnʃəl] *adj.* **1.** [constituting the essence of] essentiel, intégrant: ~ *oils*, huiles *fpl* essentielles. **2.** [Fig.] essentiel; capital; fondamental. || *n.* élément *m* /constitutif, fondamental/; l'essentiel *m*: *job essentials*, les ficelles, les trucs/du métier; *essentials of life*, objets *mpl* de première nécessité. || **essentially** [-ɪ] *adv.* essentiellement; au premier chef; principalement.

EST [= Eastern Standard Time] heure *f* normale de l'Est.

establish [ɪˈstæblɪʃ] *v. tr.* [set up] établir, édifier; fonder, créer; instituer; [Fig.] établir; asseoir; [by proof] démontrer; prouver. || **establishment** [-mənt] *n.* **1.** [business] établissement *m*, maison *f*: *business* ~, maison de commerce. **2.** [act] établissement (d'un gouvernement, &c.), création *f* (d'un système), fondation *f* (d'une maison d'affaires). **3.** [fact] établissement, constatation *f*.

estate [ɪˈstejt] *n.* **1.** [large piece of land] domaine *m*; propriété *f*; terres *fpl*; [property] *real* ~, biens *mpl* immobiliers; ~ *agent*, agent *m* immobilier; †bien *m*; biens *mpl*; possessions *fpl*. **2.** [condition] état *m*; rang *m*, condition *f*; [Hist.] *Estates General*, les États généraux; *the Third Estate*, le Tiers-État; la bourgeoisie.

esteem [ɪˈstijm] *v. tr.* **1.** [value] estimer, priser; [absol.] considérer, avoir une haute opinion (de qqun). **2.** [think] considérer, estimer, juger. || *n.* estime *f*.

estimable [ˈɛstɪməbl̩] *adj.* **1.** estimable. **2.** → que l'on peut évaluer. || **estimate** [ˈɛstɪ|mət] *n.* [statement] calcul *m*, évaluation *f*; [judgment] opinion *f*, appréciation *f*; [detailed] devis *m*, estimé *m*: [pl.] *estimates*, crédits *mpl*, budget *m* des dépenses; *budget estimates*, prévisions *fpl* budgétaires. || *v. tr.* [-ˌmejt] estimer, évaluer; [price] déterminer, fixer; [Fig.] juger, apprécier. || **estimation** [ˌɛstɪˈmejʃən] *n.* **1.** jugement *m*, estimation *f*, opinion *f*. **2.** considération *f*, estime *f*.

estrange [ɛˈstɹejndʒ] *v. tr.* aliéner, éloigner.

estuary [ˈɛstjuwˌɛɚɪ] *n.* estuaire *m*.

etc. [ɛtˈsɛtəɚə] [= et cetera, and so forth] etc., et cætera; ainsi de suite.

etch [ɛtʃ] *v. tr.* graver à l'eau forte; [Fig.] tracer, dessiner. || **etching** [-ɪŋ] *n.* gravure *f* à l'eau forte.

eternal [ɪˈtɚn|əl] *adj.* éternel, sans fin; continuel, incessant. || **eternity** [-ɪtɪ] *n.* éternité *f*.

ether [ˈijθɚ] *n.* éther *m.* || **ethereal** [ɪˈθijɚɪəl] *adj.* éthéré.
ethic [ˈɛθɪk] *n.* morale *f*; [Phil.] éthique *f.* || **ethical** [-l̩] *adj.* éthique, moral. || **ethics** [-s] *n.* morale *f*, éthique *f.*
ethnic [ˈɛθnɪk] *adj.* ethnique.
etiquette [ˈɛtɪkət] *n.* étiquette *f.*
etymology [ˌɛtɪˈmɑləʤɪ] *n.* étymologie *f.*
eucalyptus [ˌjuwkəˈlɪptəs] *n.* eucalyptus *m.*
Eucharist [ˈjuwkɚɪst] *n.* [Rel.] Eucharistie *f.*
eulogize [ˈjuwləˌʤaɪz] *v. tr.* faire l'éloge de. || **eulogy** [ˈjuwləʤɪ] *n.* panégyrique *m.*
euphemism [ˈjuwfəmˌɪzm] *n.* euphémisme *m.*
Eurasia [juwɚˈejʒə] *n.* [Geog.] Eurasie *f.* || **Eurasian** [-n] *adj.* eurasien *m*, -ne *f.*
Europe [ˈjuwɚəp] *n.* l'Europe *f*: *in, to* ~, en E. || **European** [ˌjuwɚəˈpijən] *adj. & n.* européen.
evacuate [ɪˈvækjuw|ˌejt] *v. tr.* évacuer, vider. || **evacuation** [-ˌejʃən] *n.* évacuation *f.*
evade [ɪˈvejd] *v. tr.* [pursuit] échapper; [difficulty] éviter; [blow] esquiver; [obligation] se soustraire à; [question] éluder.
evaluate [ɪˈvæljuwˌejt] *v. tr.* évaluer, estimer.
evangelical [ɪˌvænˈʤɛlɪkl] *adj.* évangélique.
evaporate [ɪˈvæpɚˌejt] *v. tr.* faire évaporer. || *v. intr.* s'évaporer; se vaporiser; [Fig.] se volatiliser. || **evaporation** [ɪˌvæpɚˈejʃən] *n.* évaporation *f.*
evasion [ɪˈvej|ʒən] *n.* dérobade *f* (*of*, à); [Pej.] échappatoire *f*, faux-fuyant *m.* || **evasive** [-sɪv] *adj.* évasif. || **evasively** [-sɪvlɪ] *adv.* évasivement.
eve [ijv] *n.* veille *f*: *on the* ~, à la veille (de); [Rel.] vigile *f*: *New Year's Eve*, la Saint-Sylvestre.
even[1] [ˈijvn̩] *adj.* [-er, -est] [surface] égal, uni; [intervals] égal, régulier; [rate] égal, régulier, uniforme; [number] pair; [sum] exact; [temper] (humeur) égale: *to make sth.* ~, aplanir (une surface), rendre . . . uniforme; *to get* ~ *with s.o.*, rattraper qqun, rendre la pareille à qqun; *to be* ~ *with*, être, arriver/au même niveau que, être quitte avec/qqun; *There's an* ~ *chance that*, Il y a des chances égales pour que [+ subj.] || *adv.* même; [with compar.] encore: *Even the birds were singing*, Les oiseaux mêmes chantaient; *I could* ~ *see the birds*, Je voyais même les oiseaux; *He wasn't* ~ *listening*, Il n'écoutait même pas; *Even/if, though/he came, he could do nothing*, Même s'il venait, Quand (bien) même il viendrait, Il viendrait qu'/il n'y pourrait rien; *I'll do it* ~ *though I am sick*, Je le ferai quoique je sois malade; ~ *so*, tout de même, précisément; †*Even as . . . so . . .*, De même que . . . de même . . . ; ~ *better, smaller, oftener, &c.*, encore/mieux, plus petit, plus souvent, &c.; *to break, come out/* ~, n'avoir ni profit ni perte. || **even**[2] *v. tr.* [level] niveler, mettre de niveau; aplanir; [make equal] égaliser; [be equal] égaler.
evening [ˈijvnɪŋ] *n.* soir *m*; soirée *f* [☞ for constructions, cf. MORNING]; [party] soirée *f*: *Good* ~ *!*, Bonsoir! || *attrib.*: *in* ~ *dress*, en tenue de soirée, [woman] en toilette de soirée, [man] en habit; ~ *paper*, journal *m* du soir.
evenly [ˈijvn̩lɪ] *adv.* uniment; régulièrement; uniformément; également; tranquillement.
event [ɪˈvɛnt] *n.* **1.** événement *m* (marquant): *passing events*, l'actualité *f*; [Sport] épreuve *f*, réunion *f* sportive: *at all events*, en tout état de cause, de toute manière. **2.** résultat *m*; conséquence *f*: *in the* ~ *of his turning down the offer . . .*, au cas où, dans le cas où/il n'accepterait pas l'offre . . . || **eventful** [-fl̩] *adj.* riche en événements; mémorable; marquant, mouvementé.
eventual [ɪˈvɛntʃuwəl] *adj.* **1.** [possible] éventuel, aléatoire. **2.** final, définitif. || **eventuality** [ɪˌvɛntʃuwˈælɪtɪ] *n.* éventualité *f.* || **eventually** [ɪˈvɛntʃuwəlɪ] *adv.* finalement, en fin de compte.
ever [ˈɛvɚ] *adv.* **1.** [at any time] jamais: *was there* ~ *. . .*, vit-on jamais . . . ; *A poet, if there* ~ *was one*, Poète, s'il en fut; *if* ~ *he should come back*, si jamais il devait revenir. **2.** [= at all times] toujours: *for* ~ *and* ~, *for* ~ *and a day*, pour toujours; à jamais; ~ *since*, depuis. **3.** [at intervals]† ~ *and anon*, de temps en temps [☞ NEVER avec verbe positif]: *Nobody* ~ *told me*, Personne ne m'a jamais dit (que . . .). [= at all] *Who* ~ *could have thought that . . .*, Qui diantre aurait (bien) pu penser que . . . ; *the /largest, biggest, worst/* ~, le plus grand, le pire . . . , la plus grande, la pire . . ./ de tous les temps, des temps modernes; † ~ *longer*, de plus en plus long; *It is* ~ *so easy*, C'est tout ce qu'il y a de facile; ~ *so much easier*, infiniment plus facile; ~ *so happy*, on ne peut plus heureux. || **evergreen** [-ˌgrijn] *adj.* toujours vert. || *n.* (plante *f*, arbre *m*) à feuillage persistant; conifère *m.* || **everlasting** [-ˌlæstɪŋ] *adj.* éternel; perpétuel; sans fin; [durable] inusable; interminable; persistant; [Pej.] lassant; fastidieux; interminable.
every [ˈɛvrɪ] *adj.* **1.** chaque; tou(te)s les; tout(e); chacun(e) de(s): ~ *day*, chaque

jour, tous les jours; ~ *other day,* tous les deux jours, un jour sur deux; *his ~ desire,* tous, chacun de/ses désirs; [gen. statement] ~ *Canadian knows that . . . ,* tout Canadien sait que . . . ; [Fam.] ~ *which way,* de tous les côtés, en désordre; ~ *one of them,* chacun, tous, tout le monde; ~ *one of you,* vous tous, chacun, -(e), de vous; ~ *man for himself,* chacun pour soi. **2.** [progression] de . . . en . . . : ~ *day he feels better,* Il va mieux de jour en jour; ~ *now and then,* de temps en temps; [position] de loin en loin. **3.** [emphatic] tout(e); toute sorte de: *to have ~ reason to . . . ,* avoir/tout lieu, toute raison/de . . . ; ~ *bit,* tout à fait; ~ *bit as . . . as,* tout aussi . . . que; *I wish you ~ success,* Je vous souhaite le succès le plus complet. || **everybody** [-ˌbɑdɪ] *pron. indef.* chacun *m,* chacune *f;* tous *mpl,* toutes *fpl;* tout le monde; le premier venu *m;* n'importe qui. || **everyday** [-ˌdej] *adj.* quotidien, → de chaque jour, de tous les jours; [clothes] ordinaire; [Pej.] banal; commun; [language] courant; usuel. || **everyman** [-ˌmæn] *n.* Monsieur Tout-le-monde, le Canadien moyen; © Baptiste; le Français moyen. || **everyone** [-ˌwʌn] *pron. indéf.* chacun; tout le monde, tous. || **everything** [-ˌθɪŋ] *pron. indef.* tout. || *n.* (chose) de première importance: *The news meant everything to us,* Cette nouvelle était pour nous /capitale, de première importance/. || **everywhere** [-ˈwɛɚ] *adv.* partout; en tous lieux; de tous côtés.

evict [ɪˈvɪkt] *v. tr.* expulser (de); [Fig.] évincer (de).

evidence [ˈɛvɪdən|s] *n.* évidence *f,* caractère *m* manifeste; [logic] conclusion *f;* preuve *f* (certaine); [Law] déposition *f: to give ~ ,* déposer, témoigner (en justice); *a piece of ~ ,* une preuve; [witness] témoin *m.* || *v. tr.* [show clearly] mettre en évidence, rendre évident; [prove] démontrer, illustrer. || **evident** [-t] *adj.* évident. || **evidently** [-tlɪ] *adv.* évidemment; de toute évidence, manifestement.

evil [ijvḷ] *adj.* [☞ comp. WORSE, superl. WORST, or *more evil, most evil*] [bad] mauvais; [wicked] méchant, malfaisant, néfaste; [spirit] malin. || *n.* **1.** mal *m.* **2.** malheur *m.* **3.** méchanceté *f,* perversité *f: to think ~ of s.o.,* penser du mal de qqun. || **evil-doer** [-ˌduwɚ] *n.* → mauvais, malfaisant. || **evil-minded** [-ˈmajndəd] *adj.* méchant, malintentionné.

evince [ɪˈvɪns] *v. tr.* manifester; faire preuve de; [intention] montrer.

evocation [ˌɛvəˈkejʃən] *n.* évocation *f.* || **evocative** [ɪˈvɑkətɪv] *adj.* évocat|eur, -rice. || **evoke** [ɪˈvowk] *v. tr.* évoquer, rappeler (un fait).

evolution [ˌɛvəˈluwʃən] *n.* **1.** développement *m;* [events] déroulement *m* (des faits, *mpl*); évolution *f.* **2.** [Phil., Biol.] évolution *f.* **3.** [Mil.] évolution *f,* mouvement *m* (de troupes *fpl,* de navires *mpl*). **4.** [heat, gas] dégagement *m* (de gaz, de chaleur). || **evolve** [ɪˈvɑlv] *v. tr.* **1.** développer, élaborer. **2.** [theory, argument] développer, déduire; [a conclusion] tirer, dégager. **3.** [heat, gas] dégager. || *v. intr.* évoluer (vers, *into*).

ewe [juw] *n.* brebis *f:* ~ *-lamb,* agnelle *f.*

ex. [⇒ EXAMPLE; EXCEPT].

ex- [ɛks-] *pref.* ancien, ex-: ~ *-president,* ancien président *m.*

exact [ɪgˈzækt] *adj.* **1.** [without any mistake] exact; juste; [accurate] précis. **2.** [severe] strict; sévère; rigoureux. || *v. tr.*: *to ~ (money) from s.o.,* extorquer (de l'argent) à qqun. || **exacting** [-ɪŋ] *adj.* difficile, exigeant; [work] ardu, épuisant. || **exactitude** [-tɪˌtjuwd] *n.* exactitude *f;* précision *f;* ponctualité *f.* || **exactly** [-lɪ] *adv.* **1.** exactement; avec précision. **2.** [just so] tout juste!; précisément!; parfaitement!, exactement!

exaggerate [ɪgˈzæʤɚˌejt] *v. tr.* exagérer. || **exaggeration** [ɪgˌzæʤɚˈejʃən] *n.* exagération *f.*

exalt [ɪgˈzɔlt] *v. tr.* exalter, transporter; [colours] intensifier, soutenir; [extol] exalter, porter aux nues. || **exaltation** [ɛgˌzɔlˈtejʃən] *n.* exaltation *f,* transport *m;* augmentation *f:* [Rel.] ~ *of the Cross,* glorification *f.*

exam [ɪgˈzæm] [Fam.] *n.* examen *m* (scolaire): *to take an ~ ,* se présenter à, passer/un examen. || **examination** [ɪgˌzæmɪˈnejʃən] *n.* **1.** examen *m;* vérification *f;* inspection *f;* [customs] visite *f.* **2.** [test] examen *m,* épreuve *f: entrance ~ ,* examen d'entrée; [Jur.] instruction *f.* || **examine** [ɪgˌzæmɪn] *v. tr.* **1.** examiner; inspecter; visiter; contrôler; [Jur.] instruire (une affaire); faire enquête sur; étudier (un dossier). **2.** [Sch.] interroger; faire subir un examen. || **examinee** [ɪgˌzæmɪˈnij] *n.* candidat *m* à un examen. || **examiner** [ɪgˈzæmɪnɚ] *n.* **1.** inspecteur *m;* vérificateur *m.* **2.** [Sch.] examinateur *m,* examinatrice *f.*

example [ɪgˈzæmpḷ] *n.* **1.** exemple *m;* [sample] échantillon *m,* spécimen *m;* [pattern] modèle *m;* [Fig.] idéal *m: for ~ ,* par exemple; *to set an ~ ,* donner l'exemple; prêcher d'exemple; *without ~*, sans exemple, sans précédent. **2.** [arithmetic] problème *m*.

exasperate [ɪg'zæspɚˌejt] *v. tr.* exaspérer (qqun), exacerber (une douleur).

excavate ['ɛkskəˌvejt] *v. tr.* [dig] creuser; [unearth] déterrer en creusant; [Archeol.] faire des fouilles.

exceed [ɪk'sijd] *v. tr.* dépasser, outrepasser; [quantity] excéder; [limits] dépasser; [Fig.] dépasser, surpasser; [Pej.] outrepasser (ses droits). || **exceedingly** [-ɪŋlɪ] *adv.* extrêmement, à l'extrême.

excel [ɪk'sɛl] *v. tr.* [-ll-] surpasser, dépasser; faire mieux que. || *v. intr.* exceller (*in*, à); briller, être éminent (*in*, en). || **excellence** ['ɛksələn|s] *n.* excellence *f*, supériorité *f*; mérite *m*, qualité *f*. || **Excellency** [-sɪ] *n.* [titre]: *Your ~*, Excellence *f*. || **excellent** [-t] *adj.* excellent; remarquable; [food, &c.] exquis, délicieux; [artist] accompli. || **excellently** [-tlɪ] *adv.* excellemment; de façon *f* remarquable; parfaitement; admirablement.

except [ɪk'sɛp|t] *prep.* excepté, à l'exception de; en dehors de, sauf; sinon; hormis. || *v. tr.* excepter, exclure; faire abstraction (*from*, de). || *v. intr.* soulever des objections (*against*, contre). || **excepting** [-tɪŋ] *prep.* excepté; à l'exception de; à l'exclusion de; sauf; hormis. || **exception** [-ʃən] *n.* **1.** exception *f* (*to*, à): *to be an ~ to*, faire exception à; *to make an ~ to*, faire une exception à. **2.** objection *f*, réserve *f*: *to take ~ to*, élever des objections contre, trouver à redire (à qqch.); [to resent] se froisser de, prendre . . . en mauvaise part. || **exceptionable** [-ʃənabl̩] *adj.* qui prête à /la critique, objection/. || **exceptional** [-ʃənl̩] *adj.* exceptionnel. || **exceptionally** [-ʃənl̩ɪ] *adv.* exceptionnellement, par exception.

excerpt ['ɛksɚpt] *n.* extrait *m* (d'un texte), passage *m*, citation *f*. || *v. tr.* extraire (un passage d'un texte), faire une citation (d'un ouvrage), citer des passages (d'un ouvrage). || **excerption** [ɪk'sɚpʃən] *n.* (Le fait de prélever des extraits d'un texte).

excess [ɪk'sɛs] *n.* excès *m*, excédent *m*, surplus *m*: *in ~ of*, en plus de; [Fig., usual. pl.] excès *m* (dans le boire ou le manger); intempérance *f*. || *adj.* excédentaire: *~ baggage*, excédent *m* de bagages. || **excessive** [-ɪv] *adj.* excessif; exagéré; immodéré, extrême. || **excessively** [-ɪvlɪ] *adv.* excessivement; à l'excès.

exchange [ɪks'ʧejnʤ] *v. tr. & intr.* échanger, [Pej.] troquer (*for*, contre); échanger, faire un échange de (*with*, avec). || *n.* **1.** échange *m*; [Pej.] troc *m*; [thing] objet *m* d'échange. **2.** [Com.] Bourse *f*: *Stock Exchange*, la Bourse (des valeurs). **3.** (opérations *fpl* de) change *m*; *foreign ~*, devises *fpl* étrangères; *the rate of ~*, le taux (du change). **4.** [Tel.] central *m* (téléphonique). || *adj.* au pair: *~ teacher*, stagiaire *m*. || **exchangeable** [-əbl] *adj.* échangeable (*for*, contre).

excise[1] ['ɛksajz] *n.* [duty] impôt *m* indirect; [esp. ©] accise *f*.

excise[2] [ɪk'sajz] *v. tr.* [remove] exciser, pratiquer l'excision *f* de.

excitable [ɪk'sajt|əbl̩] *adj.* excitable. || **excite** [ɪk'sajt] *v. tr.* **1.** exciter; stimuler (*to*, à). **2.** [move] émouvoir, agiter. **3.** [action] inciter à; pousser à; [Pej.] surexciter. **4.** [Electr.] exciter. || **excited** [-əd] *adj.* excité, énervé; [Pej.] agité, fiévreux; [Med., Electr.] excité; [Fig.] ému, bouleversé. || **excitement** [-mənt] *n.* excitation *f*; instigation *f*; invitation *f*; [Fig.] agitation *f*; émoi *m*; surexcitation *f*. || **exciting** [-ɪŋ] *adj.* [Med. or Pej.] excitant; [moving] émouvant, passionnant; palpitant d'intérêt; [book] captivant; [drama] empoignant.

exclaim [ɪks'klejm] *v. intr.* s'écrier, s'exclamer; protester (contre, *against*). || **exclamation** [ˌɛkskləˈmejʃən] *n.* exclamation *f*; [Gram.] *~ mark*, point *m* d'exclamation.

exclude [ɪks'kluw|d] *v. tr.* exclure de; [keep out] refuser d'admettre; [drive out] éliminer, rejeter, éliminer (de, *from*); [Fig.] écarter. || **excluding** [-dɪŋ] *prép.* ne comprenant pas, → non compris. || **exclusion** [-ʒən] *n.* exclusion *f* (de, *from*); expulsion *f*, renvoi *m*: *to the ~ of*, à l'exclusion de, hormis. || **exclusive** [-sɪv] *adj.* exclusif, unique; [limited] choisi, réservé, sélect; [fashionable] élégant, à la mode, chic; [Pej.] dédaigneux, distant; [opinion] entier, intolérant; [Loc.] *~ of*, non compris, non inclus; *~ rights*, droits/réservés, en exclusivité. || **exclusively** [-sɪvlɪ] *adv.* exclusivement. || **exclusiveness** [-sɪvnəs] *n.* exclusivité *f*.

excommunicate [ˌɛkskə|'mjuwnɪˌkejt] *v. tr.* excommunier. || **excommunication** [ˌmjuwnɪ'kejʃən] *n.* excommunication *f*.

excrement ['ɛkskɹəmənt] *n.* excrément *m*.

excruciating [ɪks'kɹuwʃɪˌejtɪŋ] *adj.* atroce.

exculpate ['ɛkskəlˌpejt] *v. tr.* disculper: *to ~ o.s. from*, se disculper de.

excursion [ɪk'skɚʒən] *n.* [voyage] excursion *f*: [Rail.] *~ train*, †train *m* de plaisir; [Mil.] raid *m*, sortie *f*.

excusable [ɪk'skjuw|zəbl̩] *adj.* excusable (de,

for). ‖ **excuse** [-s] *n.* excuse *f*; [plea] explication *f*, raison *f*; [pretext] prétexte *m*, défaite *f*: *to make excuses*, s'excuser; présenter des excuses (*to*, à; *for*, pour). ‖ *v. tr.* [-z] excuser; pardonner; fermer les yeux (sur); fournir une excuse à, donner des raisons de; [release from duty] *to be excused from*, être/libéré, dispensé/de; *Excuse me*, Excusez-moi; *Excuse/me for, my/being late*, Excusez-moi, Mes excuses/ d'être en retard.

execrable ['ɛksəkɹəbḷ] *adj.* exécrable, abominable.

execute ['ɛksəˌkjuwt] *v. tr.* exécuter, accomplir (un ordre, une mission); remplir (un devoir); [Jur.] appliquer (une loi); signer (un contrat, un document); exécuter (un jugement, un criminel). ‖ **execution** [ˌɛksə'kjuwʃən] *n.* [order] exécution *f*, accomplissement *m*; [duty] exercice *m*; [Jur.] [law] application *f*; [writ] saisie-exécution *f*. ‖ **executioner** [-ɚ] *n.* bourreau *m*, exécuteur *m* des hautes œuvres. ‖ **executive** [ɪg'zɛkjətɪv] *adj.* [pouvoir] exécutif; ~ *officers*, personnel *m*/de direction, administratif/, cadres *mpl*; ~ *office*, bureau *m* administratif. ‖ *n.* administrateur *m*, directeur *m*; [Fam.] *the* ~, l'exécutif *m* (d'un pays); le bureau (d'une association). ‖ **executor** [ɪg'zɛkjətɚ] *n.* exécuteur *m*.

exemplary [ɪks'ɛmpl|ɚɪ] *adj.* [held as example] exemplaire; [typical] typique. ‖ **exemplify** [-ɪˌfaj] *v. tr.* servir d'exemple; illustrer, donner un exemple de: *to* ~ *one's precepts*, prêcher d'exemple.

exempt [ɪg'zɛmpt] *adj.* [taxes, &c.] exempt (*from*, de); [service] exempté. ‖ *n.* exempté *m*. ‖ *v. tr.* exempter (*from*, de): *to* ~ *o.s. from*, s'exempter de; *to get exempted from*, se faire exempter de. ‖ **exemption** [-ʃən] *n.* exemption *f* (*from*, de); dispense *f*; [taxes] déductions *fpl*: ~ *from postage*, franchise *f* postale.

exercise ['ɛkzɚˌsajz] *n.* [Sch.] exercice *m*, devoir *m*; [Sport] exercice, gymnastique *f*; [Rel.] pratique *f*, observance *f*; [of virtue] exercice, mise *f* en pratique; *pl.* cérémonie *f*. ‖ *v. tr.* **1.** exercer; [Mil.] entraîner, exercer. **2.** pratiquer; [profession] exercer; mettre en pratique; [rights] user de, mettre en œuvre. **3.** contrarier, embarrasser. ‖ *v. intr.* s'exercer à, s'entraîner.

exert [ɪg'zɚ|t] *v. tr.* [influence] déployer: *to* ~ *o.s.*, se dépenser, mettre tout en œuvre (pour, *for*). ‖ **exertion** [-ʃən] *n.* effort *m*, exertion *f*; [power] exercice *m*.

exhalation [ˌɛkshə'lejʃən] *n.* [actions] exhalaison *f*, évaporation *f*; [result] exhalaison *f*, émanation *f*. ‖ **exhale** [ˌɛks'hejl] *v. tr.* [respiration] expirer, exhaler; [Fig.] exhaler, donner (libre) cours à (sa colère, &c.). ‖ *v. intr.* s'exhaler.

exhaust [ɪg'zɔs|t] *v. tr.* tarir; mettre à sec; [Fig.] épuiser; exténuer; [a subject] vider (un sujet); traiter à fond; faire le tour (d'une question). ‖ *n.* échappement *m*: ~ *-pipe*, tuyau *m* d'échappement. ‖ **exhaustion** [-tʃən] *n.* épuisement *m*. ‖ **exhaustive** [-tɪv] *adj.* **1.** complet, approfondi, étendu, à fond, très poussé. **2.** épuisant, accablant, exhaustif; [Agric.] exhaustif, épuisant. **3.** limitatif.

exhibit [ɪg'zɪbɪt] *v. tr.* [document, &c.] produire, présenter; [arts] exposer; [Fig.] faire/montre, preuve/de. ‖ *v. intr.* exposer. ‖ *n.* [Jur.] document *m*; [exhibition] objet *m*; exposé *m*; envoi *m*; exposition *f*. ‖ **exhibition** [ˌɛksɪ'bɪʃən] *n.* **1.** exposition *f* (de peinture, &c.); [law] exhibition *f* (de documents); [Fig., Pej.] étalage *m*: *to make an* ~ *of o.s.*, se donner en spectacle. **2.** [Sch. esp. Br.] bourse *f*.

exhilarate [ɪg'zɪlɚˌejt] *v. tr.* égayer, animer.

exhort [ɪg'zɔɚt] *v. tr.* exhorter, pousser, inciter (qqun à, *s.o. to*); recommander (qqch.).

exhume [ɪg'zjuwm] *v. tr.* exhumer, déterrer.

exigency ['ɛksɪdʒənsɪ] *n.* exigence *f*; urgence *f*. ‖ **exigent** ['ɛksədʒənt] *adj.* [pressing] urgent, pressant; [exacting] exigeant.

exiguous [ɪg'zɪgjuwəs] *adj.* exigu *m*, -uë *f*.

exile ['ɛkzajl] *n.* exil *m*; [Pers.] exilé. ‖ *v. tr.* exiler (de, *from*).

exist [ɪg'zɪst] *v. intr.* **1.** exister, être. **2.** [occur] se trouver, se rencontrer (*in*, dans). **3.** [live] vivre; subsister; durer. ‖ **existence** [-əns] *n.* **1.** [Philos.] être *m*. **2.** vie *f*, existence *f*. ‖ **existent** [-ənt] *adj.* existant. ‖ **existentialism** [ˌɛgzɪs'tɛnʃəlɪzm] *n.* [Philos.] existentialisme *m*. ‖ **existing** [ɪg'zɪstɪŋ] *adj.* existant; actuel, vivant.

exit ['ɛksɪt] *n.* [way out, also Theat.] sortie *f*.

exodus ['ɛksədəs] *n.* exode *m*; [Eccl.] Exode.

exonerate [ɪg'zɑnɚˌejt] *v. tr.* [charge, obligation] exempter, décharger, dispenser/de; [Fig., from/blame, an accusation/] disculper (de).

exorbitant [ɪg'zɔɚbɪtənt] *adj.* (demande, exigence) exorbitant; (prix) prohibitif.

exorcist ['ɛksɔɚˌsɪst] *n.* [Rel.] exorciste *m*.

exotic [ɪg'zɑtɪk] *adj.* exotique.

expand [ɪk'spæn|d] *v. tr.* [open out, unfold] étendre, déployer; [enlarge] élargir, [Med., Chem.] dilater; développer [Math., une équation], [Fig., une idée, un sujet].

|| *v. intr.* se dilater; s'étendre, se déployer; se développer, grandir. || **expanse** [-s] *n.* étendue *f*; [Tech.] expansion. || **expansion** [-ʃən] *n.* étendue *f*, élargissement *m*; [Tech.] dilatation *f*, développement *m* [Math., d'une équation], [Fig., d'une idée, d'un raisonnement]' || **expansive** [-sɪv] *adj.* étendu, large; [Chim.] dilatable, [Phys.] expansif; [Fig., Pers.] expansif, communicatif, démonstratif.

expatriate [ɛks'pejtɹɪˌejt] *v. tr.* exiler (qqun): *to ~ o.s.*, s'expatrier.

expect [ɪk'spɛkt] *v. tr.* **1.** [await] attendre, © [Fam.] espérer: *I ~ him at 4*, Je l'attends pour quatre heures. **2.** [rely] compter (sur), s'attendre à: *I ~ to see you at 4*, Je compte vous voir à quatre heures; *I did not ~ that*, Je ne m'y attendais pas. **3.** [desire] attendre (qqch. de qqun): *How do you ~ me to do that?*, Comment voulez-vous que je fasse cela?; *I ~ you to . . .*, Je tiens à ce que vous [+ subjonc.]; *You are expected to*, Vous êtes tenu de... **4.** [Fam.] penser, supposer, estimer: *I ~ so*, Je crois que oui; *to be expecting*, attendre/un bébé, un heureux événement/; © attendre les sauvages. || **expectancy** [-ənsɪ] *n.* attente *f*, expectative *f*. || **expectation** [ˌɛkspɛk'tejʃən] *n.* **1.** attente *f*, expectative *f*: *in ~*, en perspective. **2.** prévision *f*; probabilité *f*; *pl.* espérances *fpl.* || **expecting** [ɪks'pɛktɪŋ] *adj. to be ~*, © [Fam.] attendre les sauvages.

expectorate [ɪk'spɛktəˌejt] *v. tr. & intr.* expectorer.

expediency [ɪk'spijdɪən|sɪ] *n.* avantage *m*, utilité *f*, commodité *f*, convenance *f*: [Pej.] *political ~*, opportunisme *m* politique. || **expedient** [-t] *adj.* **1.** utile, avantageux. **2.** à propos, opportun. || *n.* expédient *m*.

expedite ['ɛkspəˌdajt] *v. tr.* [business] expédier. || **expedition** [ˌɛkspə'dɪʃən] *n.* **1.** [exploration] expédition *f*, voyage *m*; [Mil.] expédition *f*, campagne *f*; détachement *m*; troupes *fpl*, force *f*. **2.** célérité *f*; promptitude *f*; diligence *f*. || **expeditionary** [-ˌɛərɪ] *adj.* expéditionnaire.

expel [ɪk'spɛl] [-ll-] *v. tr.* expulser, exclure (*from*, de); [Sch.] renvoyer.

expend [ɪk'spɛn|d] *v. tr.* dépenser (son argent, ses efforts), épuiser (ses ressources). || **expenditure** [-dɪtʃər] *n.* [Fin.] dépense *f*.

expense [ɪk'spɛns] *n.* **1.** dépense *f*: *to go to the ~ of*, faire la dépense de; [pl.] dépenses *fpl*, frais *mpl*: *~ account*, frais professionnels. **2.** [Pej.] *at the ~ of*, aux dépens *mpl* de. || **expensive** [-ɪv] *adj.* coûteux, cher, → qui coûte cher, © dispendieux. || **expensively** [-ɪvlɪ] *adv.* → d'une façon/coûteuse, onéreuse/ [☞ or translate by adj.].

experience [ɪk'spijərɪəns] *n.* **1.** expérience *f*, acquis *m*: *to know from ~*, connaître par expérience; *~ meeting*, confession *f* publique; réunion *f* d'experts. **2.** expérience *f* vécue, aventure *f*, incident *m*; moment *m*, sensation *f*; épreuve *f*. || *v. tr.* éprouver, rencontrer, faire l'expérience de, passer par. || **experienced** [-t] *adj.* expérimenté (*in*, en); qui a/de l'expérience, du métier/; exercé, averti.

experiment [ɪk'spɛərɪmənt] *n.* expérience *f* (scientifique); essai *m*. || *v. tr.* expérimenter; faire/une expérience, un essai/ (*on*/*with*, sur/avec). || **experimental** [ɪkˌspɛər'mɛntl̩] *adj.* expérimental, → à titre d'expérience.

expert ['ɛkspərt] *n.* expert *m*; spécialiste *m*; technicien *m*: *efficiency ~*, spécialiste du rendement. || *adj.* expert; expérimenté; versé (*in*, dans/en): *~ advice*, avis *m* autorisé. || **expertness** [-nəs] *n.* maîtrise *f*.

expiate ['ɛkspɪˌejt] *v. tr.* expier.

expiration [ˌɛkspə'ɹejʃən] *n.* expiration *f*. || **expire** [ɪk'spajər] *v. intr.* [die, & Fig.] expirer.

explain [ɪks'plejn] *v. tr.* **1.** expliquer, mettre en lumière; interpréter. **2.** justifier; motiver: *to ~ away*, donner une explication satisfaisante de; *to ~ o.s.*, s'expliquer, se justifier, justifier sa conduite. || **explainable** [-əbl̩] *adj.* explicable. || **explanation** [ɛksplə'nejʃən] *n.* explication *f*; interprétation *f*. || **explanatory** [ɪks'plænətɔərɪ] *adj.* explicatif.

explicit [ɪks'plɪsɪt] *adj.* explicite.

explode [ɪks'plowd] *v. tr.* faire/exploser, éclater/; [Fig.] démontrer la fausseté de, réduire (un argument) à néant. || *v. intr.* exploser; [mine] sauter.

exploit ['ɛksplojt] *n.* exploit *m*, haut fait *m*. || *v. tr.* [ˌɪks'plojt] exploiter. || **exploitation** [ɛksˌploj'tejʃən] *n.* exploitation *f*. || **exploiter** [ɪks'plojtər] *n.* exploiteur *m*.

exploration [ˌɛksplɔə'ejʃən] *n.* [Geog.] exploration *f*; [Med.] examen *m*, sondage *m*; [Fig.] examen *m* attentif. || **explore** [ɪks'plɔər] *v. tr.* explorer; [Med.] explorer, sonder (une plaie); [Fig.] scruter, examiner attentivement. || **explorer** [-ər] *n.* explorat|eur *m*, -rice *f*.

explosion [ɪks'plow|ʒən] *n.* explosion *f*; éclat *m* (de rire); éclats *mpl* (de colère). || **explosive** [-zɪv] *adj.* explosif; (mélange) explosible, détonant; (caractère) irascible; [Phon.] occlusive *f*.

exponent [ɪk'spownənt] *n.* interprète *m* (d'une théorie); chef *m* de file (d'une école); [Math.] exposant *m.*
export [ɪk'spɔɚt] *v. tr.* exporter. || *n.* ['ɛkspɔɚt] exportation *f*; article *m* d'exportation. || **exporter** [ɪk'spɔɚtɚ] *n.* exportateur *m.*
expose [ɪk'spowz] *v. tr.* **1.** exposer (au soleil, à un danger); laisser sans protection. **2.** dénoncer, percer à jour, démasquer: *exposed industries*, industries *fpl* vulnérables; *exposed prices*, prix *mpl* concurrentiels. || **exposé** [ɛkˌspow'zej] *n.* exposé *m*; [Pej.] révélation *f*, mise *f* à jour (d'un scandale).
exposition [ˌɛkspə'zɪʃən] *n.* exposition *f* (*to*, à; *of*, de); [Lit.] exposé *m*; [Com.] exposition, foire *f* (commerciale).
expostulate [ɪk'spɑstʃəˌlejt] *v. intr.*: *to* ~ *with*, raisonner, en remontrer à/(qqun).
exposure [ɪk'spowʒɚ] *n.* exposition *f* (*to the cold*, au froid); [Photo.] pose *f*, exposition *f*; [Fig., Pej.] révélation *f* (d'un scandale, &c.); [Photo.] ~ *meter*, posomètre *m.*
expound [ɪk'spawnd] *v. tr.* expliquer, analyser (une théorie, &c.).
express [ɪks'pɹɛ|s] *v. tr.* **1.** [thoughts] exprimer: *to* ~ *o.s.*, s'exprimer, donner son avis; [wish] formuler; [attitude] témoigner; indiquer; [art] symboliser. **2.** extraire, exprimer (le jus d'une orange). || *adj.* [wish, &c.] formel, exprès; catégorique; [image] exact; fidèle: *He is the* ~ *image of his father*, C'est tout le portrait de son père; [train] express *m*: *an* ~ *company*, une compagnie de messageries. || *n.* [Rail.] express *m* (train); [post] exprès; message *m* par exprès; [Com.] compagnie *f*, agence *f*/de messageries.
expression [-ʃən] *n.* expression *f.* || **expressive** [-sɪv] *adj.* expressif: ~ *of*, → qui exprime, dénote . . . || **expressly** [-slɪ] *adv.* [on purpose] exprès; [stated] expressément. || **expressway** [-sˌwej] *n.* voie *f* rapide.
expropriate [ɛks'pɹowpɹɪˌejt] *v. tr.* exproprier; [Fig.] déposséder (qqun).
expulsion [ɪk'spʌlʃən] *n.* expulsion *f*; [from school] renvoi *m.*
expunge [ɪk'spʌndʒ] *v. tr.* supprimer.
expurgate ['ɛkspɚˌgejt] *v. tr.* expurger.
exquisite [ˌɛks'kwɪzɪt] *adj.* **1.** exquis, délicieux. **2.** recherché, choisi, raffiné. || **exquisiteness** [-nəs] *n.* perfection *f*; raffinement *m.*
extant [ɪk'stænt] *adj.* existant; [race, &c.] non éteint, encore vivant.
extemporaneous [ɪksˌtɛmpɚ'ejnɪəs] *adj.* improvisé.
extend [ɪks'tɛn|d] *v. tr.* étendre; allonger (son bras); tendre (la main); prolonger (une rue, un délai); [Fig., sympathy] faire preuve de, manifester; [help] accorder; souhaiter (la bien venue à qqun). || *v. intr.* s'étendre. || **extended** [-dəd] *adj.* étendu, prolongé. || **extension** [-ʃən] *n.* **1.** extension *f*, [space] étendue *f*, portée *f.* **2.** [time] délai *m*, prolongation *f.* **3.** diffusion *f*, vulgarisation *f*; *University* ~, ~ *courses*, cours *mpl*/publics, extra-muros, hors-cadres/. **4.** [Tel.] poste *m.* **5.** [bookkeeping] chiffrage *m*; tirage *m*; calcul *m.* || **extensive** [-sɪv] *adj.* [space] vaste, étendu; [Agric.] extensif; [Fig.] considérable, d'une grande portée. || **extensively** [-sɪvlɪ] *adv.* d'une manière étendue; [Fig.] considérablement; amplement; largement. || **extent** [-t] *n.* étendue *f*: *to a certain* ~, dans une certaine mesure.
extenuate [ɪk'stɛnjuwˌejt] *v. tr.* diminuer, affaiblir; [excuse in part] minimiser; *extenuating circumstances* circonstance *f* atténuante.
exterior [ɪk'stijɚɪɚ] *n.* [Cin.] extérieur *m*: *a pleasant* ~, des dehors plaisants. || *adj.* extérieur, du dehors; extrinsèque.
exterminate [ɪk'stɚmɪˌnejt] *v. tr.* exterminer. || **extermination** [ɪkˌstɚmɪ'nejʃən] *n.* extermination *f.*
external [ɪk'stɚnl] *adj.* extérieur; [superficial] externe, superficiel; étranger: © *Minister for External Affairs*, ministre des Affaires Extérieures: *for* ~ *use*, usage *m* externe.
extinct [ɪk'stɪŋ|kt] *adj.* [fire, volcano] éteint; [race] disparu. || **extinction** [-ʃən] *n.* extinction *f.* || **extinguish** [ɪk'stɪŋˌgwɪʃ] *v. tr.* [put out] éteindre; [destroy] tuer; anéantir (des espoirs, &c.).
extirpate ['ɛkstɚˌpejt] *v. tr.* extirper, déraciner.
extol [ɪk'stowl] *v. tr.* **[-ll-]** exalter, porter (qqun) aux nues.
extort [ɪk'stɔɚ|t] *v. tr.* extorquer, soutirer (*from*, à). || **extortion** [-ʃən] *n.* extorsion *f.*
extra ['ɛkstɹə] *adj.* supplémentaire; [Com.] de qualité supérieure, superfin, [Fam.] extra. || *adv.* en plus; en sus. || *n.* supplément *m*, extra *m*; [newspaper] édition *f* spéciale; [Cin.] figurant *m*; [servant] extra *m.*
extract ['ɛkstɹækt] *n.* extrait *m*; [Cul.] concentré *m.* || *v. tr.* [ɪk'stɹæk|t] extraire (*from*, de); [Fig.] extorquer, soutirer. || **extraction** [-ʃən] *n.* extraction *f.*
extradite ['ɛkstɹɛˌdajt] *v. tr.* extrader.
extraneous [ɪks'tɹejnɪəs] *adj.* étranger (*to*, à).
extraordinarily ['ɪks'tɹɔɚdɪnˌɛɚ|lɪ] *adv.*

extraordinairement, exceptionnellement. || **extraordinary** [-ɪ] *adj.* extraordinaire; exceptionnel, remarquable.

extravagance [ɪks'tɹævəgən|s] *n.* extravagance *f,* prodigalité *f*; [waste] gaspillage *m.* || **extravagant** [-t] *adj.* dépensier, prodigue; [price] exorbitant, prohibitif; [conduct] extravagant, outrancier.

extreme [ɪks'tɹijm] *adj.* **1.** [at the very end] extrême; le plus éloigné, la plus éloignée; dernier, dernière. **2.** [very great] extrême, intense; [too great] excessif, insupportable; [severe] extrême, rigoureux; [Pol.] extrémiste; [Rel.] ~ *unction,* l'extrême-onction *f.* || *n.* extrême *m*; *in the* ~, à l'extrême, au plus haut degré; *to go to extremes,* se porter aux extrêmes. || **extremely** [-lɪ] *adv.* extrêmement. || **extremity** [ɪks'tɹɛmɪtɪ] *n.* extrémité *f*; bout *m*; [Fig.] extrême degré *m,* summum *m*; [need] urgence *f*: [Anat.] *extremities,* les extrémités *fpl.*

extricate ['ɛkstɹɪˌkejt] *v. tr.* [set free] libérer; [Fig.] dégager, faire sortir (*from,* de).

exuberance [ɪg'zuwbɚən|s] *n.* exubérance *f.* || **exuberant** [-t] *adj.* exubérant; [vegetation] luxuriant.

exude [ɪks'juwd] *v. tr.* exsuder.

exult [ɪg'zʌlt] *v. intr.* exulter, jubiler. || **exultation** [ˌɛgzəl'tejʃən] *n.* exultation *f,* jubilation *f*; triomphe *m.*

eye [aj] *n.* **1.** œil *m, pl.* yeux; [Fig.] acuité *f* visuelle, vue *f,* regard *m.* **2.** [Tech.] œillet *m,* œilleton *m*; *hook and* ~, agrafe *f* et porte *f*; [needle] chas *m*; [potato] œil. **3.** [Loc.] *to have a good* ~ *for,* avoir le coup d'œil pour; *to catch s.o.'s* ~, tirer l'œil à qqun; *to sleep with one* ~ *open,* ne dormir que d'un œil; *to see with half an* ~, voir du premier coup d'œil; *to do sth. with one's eyes open,* faire qqch. en connaissance de cause; *to see* ~ *to* ~ *with s.o.,* voir les choses du même œil que qqun; *Keep your* ~ *open!,* Ouvrez l'œil!; [Fam.] *to keep one's eyes/peeled, skinned/,* ne pas avoir les yeux en poche; [Fam.] *My eye!,* Mince (alors)!, Mon œil!; *That's all my* ~ *!,* Tout ça, c'est de la blague!; *to be up to the eyes in work,* avoir du travail jusqu'au cou; *to keep an* ~ *on s.o.,* surveiller qqun; *with an* ~ *to,* en vue de; *in the public* ~, en vue; *to give s.o. the glad* ~, faire de l'œil à qqun; *in my eyes,* [Fig.] à mes yeux. || *v. tr.* [often Pej.] toiser; reluquer; examiner. || **eyeball** [-ˌbɔl] *n.* œil *m,* globe *m* (de l'œil). || **eyebrow** [-ˌbɹaw] *n.* sourcil *m.* || **eyelash** [-ˌlæʃ] *n.* cil *m.* || **eyelid** [-ˌlɪd] *n.* paupière *f.* || **eyesight** [-ˌsajt] *n.* vue *f.* || **eyesore** [-ˌsɔɚ] *n.* objet *m,* tableau *m*/ déplaisant. || **eyewitness** [-ˌwɪtnəs] *n.* témoin *m* oculaire.

F

F, f [ɛf] pl. **F's, f's** *n.* F, f *m,* la lettre f; [Mus.] fa *m.* || **F.** [= FAHRENHEIT, FEBRUARY, FRIDAY].

fable ['fejbl] *n.* fable *f*; légende *f.* || **fabled** [-d] *adj.* légendaire.

fabric ['fæbɹɪk] *n.* tissu *m*; textile *m*; [framework] structure *f.* || **fabricate** [-ejt] *v. tr.* construire, fabriquer; [assemble] monter; [Fig.] inventer (des excuses). || **fabrication** [ˌfæbɹɪ'kejʃən] *n.* fabrication *f.*; invention *f.* (d'histoires, &c.).

fabulous ['fæbjələs] *adj.* fabuleux, incroyable; [imaginary] imaginaire.

façade [fə'sɑd] *n.* façade *f.*

face [fejs] *n.* figure *f,* visage *m*; [expression] air *m,* mine *f,* grimace *f,* aspect *m*; [Fam.] front *m,* audace *f.*; surface *f,* devant *m*; façade *f*; face *f*; [clock] cadran *m*: ~ *to* ~, nez à nez, face à face; *on the* ~ *of it,* à première vue; ~ *massage,* massage *m* facial; *in the* ~ *of* (*difficulties, &c.*) malgré, envers et contre (tout); *to have the* ~ *to do sth.,* avoir l'aplomb de faire qqch.; *to keep a straight* ~, garder son sérieux; *to put a good* ~ *on it,* faire contre mauvaise fortune bon cœur; *at its* ~ *value,* selon sa valeur apparente, au pied de la lettre. || *v. tr.* affronter; faire face à; [house]

donner sur: *to ~ up to sth.*, faire face à qqch.

facet ['fæsət] *n.* facette *f*, aspect *m.*

facetious [fə'sijʃəs] *adj.* facétieux: *to be ~*, faire le plaisantin.

facile [ˌfæ'sijl] *adj.* facile.

facilitate [fə'sılı|tejt] *v. tr.* faciliter; [assist] aider. || **facility** [-tı] *n.* facilité *f*, aisance *f*; [Tech.] *facilities*, installations *fpl* (de radar, &c.) [→ specify: BÂTIMENTS, PISTES, LOCAUX, &c.]: *harbour facilities*, installations portuaires; [Adm.] dispositions *fpl.*

facing ['fejsıŋ] *n.* [covering] revêtement *m*; revers *m* (d'habit).

fact [fækt] *n.* **1.** fait *m.* **2.** dire(s): *We doubted his facts*: Nous avons mis en doute ses déclarations; *as a matter of ~*, en réalité; *to know for a ~*, savoir pertinemment; *in ~*, de fait [= in reality]; *In ~ . . .*, En fait; *The ~ is that . . .*, Le fait est, C'est/que . . . ; *Is it a ~ that?*, Est-ce vrai que . . . ?

factor [-ɚ] *n.* **1.** facteur *m*; élément *m.* **2.** [Math.] facteur *m.* **3.** agent *m*; intendant *m.* || **factorage** [-ɚəʤ] *n.* commission *f* (payée à un agent); courtage *m.*

factory [-ɚı] *n.* **1.** usine *f*; fabrique *f*; atelier *m.* **2.** [Com.] factorerie *f*; comptoir *m.*

factual ['fæktʃuwḷ] *adj.* factuel.

faculty ['fækəltı] *n.* faculté *f*: *Faculty club*, club *m* universitaire; *the faculty*, le corps *m* enseignant.

fad [fæd] *n.* [hobby] marotte *f*; [craze] mode *f.* vogue *f.* || **faddist** ['fædıst] *n.* maniaque *m*: *He is a ~*, Il a des marottes.

fade [fejd] *v. intr.* **1.** se faner, se flétrir. **2.** s'affaiblir, disparaître: [Radio, TV] *to ~ in*, apparaître graduellement, s'amplifier; *to ~ out*, se fondre. || *v. tr.* **1.** flétrir, faner (une fleur). **2.** décolorer (une étoffe). || **faded** [-əd] *adj.* fané; flétri; décoloré. || **fading** [-ıŋ] *adj.* s'évanouissant; disparaissant; se fanant.

fag [fæg] *v. intr.* [-gg-] peiner; s'éreinter. || *n.* **1.** corvée *f*, fatigue *f.* **2.** [Br.] [Fam.] cigarette *f.*

fail [fejl] *v. intr.* manquer; manquer, omettre, négliger/(de faire qqch.); ne pas réussir, échouer, [Fam.] rater; [weaken] baisser, s'affaiblir; [Com.] faire faillite; [Sch.] échouer, ne pas être reçu (à un examen): *Don't ~ to*, Ne manquez pas de; *You can't ~ to see it*, Vous ne pourrez pas manquer de le voir; *He failed to see it*, → Il ne l'a pas vu; *He failed to tell me*, Il a/omis, négligé/ de me le dire; *His efforts failed*, Sa tentative a échoué, Il a manqué son coup. || *v. tr.* manquer à; trahir, abandonner (qqun): [Sch.] échouer à (un examen), refuser (un candidat): *Words ~ me*, Les mots me manquent; *Don't ~ me*, Ne manquez pas à votre promesse; *His strength failed him*, Ses forces l'ont abandonné. || *n.*: *without ~*, sans faute; cf. FAILURE. || **failure** [-jɚ] *n.* échec *m*, insuccès *m*; [Pers.] raté *m*; [lack] manque *m*, défaut *m*; baisse *f*, affaiblissement *m*/(des facultés); [Sch.] échec *m*; [Tech.] panne *f* (d'électricité, &c.); [Com.] faillite *f*: *The play was a ~*, La pièce a fait four; *His ~ to /come, realize, &c./*, → Son/absence, incompréhension, &c./.

faint [fejnt] *adj.* pâle; faible; médiocre; timide; défaillant. || *v. intr.* s'évanouir; défaillir. || *n.* évanouissement *m*; défaillance *f.* || **faintly** [-lı] *adv.* faiblement; vaguement; légèrement. || **faintness** [-nəs] *n.* **1.** faiblesse *f*; légèreté *f.* **2.** timidité *f*; découragement *m.* **3.** malaise *m.*

fair [fɛɚ] *n.* exposition *f*, foire *f*, vente *f* de charité. || *adj.* juste; honnête, équitable; loyal; moyen, passable; (teint) clair; (chevelure) blond; [weather] ensoleillé; beau: *to play ~*, jouer franc jeu. || **fairly** [-lı] *adv.* honnêtement, équitablement; moyennement; raisonnablement. || **fairness** [-nəs] *n.* honnêteté *f*, équité *f*; loyauté *f*; beauté *f.*

fairway [-ˌwej] *n.* [Nau.] chenal *m.*

fairy [-ı] *n.* fée *f.* || *adj.* **1.** de(s) fée(s): *~ tale*, conte *m* de fées. **2.** féerique.

faith [fejθ] *n.* foi *f*; confiance *f*; croyance *f*; religion *f*; loyauté *f*: *in good ~*, de bonne foi; *to keep ~*, tenir ses engagements; *to break ~*, manquer à sa parole; *to have ~ in*, avoir confiance en. || **faithful** [-fḷ] *adj.* loyal; fidèle (*to*, à); exact. || *n.*: *the ~*, les fidèles *mpl.* || **faithfully** [-fḷı] *adv.* fidèlement; loyalement. || **faithless** [-ləs] *adj.* infidèle; déloyal; [to God] sans foi (en Dieu). || **faithlessness** [-ləsnəs] *n.* infidélité *f*; déloyauté *f.*

fake [fejk] *v. tr.* truquer; *n.* trucage.

falcon ['fɔlkṇ] *n.* faucon *m.*

fall [fɔl] *n.* **1.** [instantaneous] chute *f*; [gradual] descente *f*; [Fig.] chute (d'un empire); renversement *m* (d'un gouvernement); baisse *f* (des prix); éboulement *m* (des rochers); pente *f* (de la terre): *There has been a heavy ~ of snow*, → Il est tombé beaucoup de neige. **2.** automne *m*: *in the ~*, en automne; *the ~ term*, le semestre d'automne. 3. [usual. pl.] chute *f*; cascade *f*, [large] cataracte *f.* || **fall, fell** [fɛl], **fallen** [fɔlən], *v. intr.* **1.** tomber; [go, come/down] descendre:

[building] s'effondrer, s'écrouler; [star] filer; [face] s'allonger; [city] capituler; [tide, prices] baisser; [curtain] se baisser; [sea] se calmer; succomber (à une tentation de), périr; [begin] se mettre à; *to ~ flat*, s'aplatir; *Her eyes fell*, → Elle baissa les yeux; *The hills ~ towards the sea*, Les collines descendent vers la mer; *Rivers ~ into the ocean*, Les fleuves se jettent dans l'océan. **2.** [become] *to ~ sick*, tomber malade; *to ~ due*, échoir; *to ~ asleep*, s'endormir. **3.** *impers.*: *It falls on me to do it*, C'est à moi (qu'il incombe) de le faire. || **fall apart** [-ə'pɑɚt] *v. intr.* tomber en morceaux; s'écrouler; s'effondrer. || **fall away** [-ə'wej] *v. intr.* *to ~ from (s.o., sth.)*, abandonner. || **fall back** [-'bæk] *v. intr.* tomber en arrière; [Mil.] reculer; *to ~ on*: avoir recours à: *sth. to ~ back on*, qqch. en réserve. || **fall behind** [-bɪ'hajnd] *v. intr.* rester en arrière; perdre du terrain; [be surpassed] se laisser devancer (par qqun). || **fall down** [-'dawn] *v. intr.* tomber/[Pers.] à terre, [thing] par terre; [building] s'effondrer, s'écrouler; [Fig.] *to ~ on the job*, ne pas être à la hauteur. || **fallen** cf. FALL. || *adj.* [Fig.] déchu. || *n. the ~*, les morts. **fall for** [-'foɚ] *v. intr.* [Fam.] *to ~ for s.o.*, tomber amoureux, s'éprendre/de qqun; *to ~ for s.o.'s charms*, succomber aux charmes de qqun; adopter (un projet, &c.) avec enthousiasme; [trick] se laisser prendre à. || **fall in** [-'ɪn] *v. intr.* [building] s'écrouler, s'effondrer; [Mil.] former les rangs: *~ !*, A vos rangs!; *to ~ love with s.o.*, tomber amoureux, s'éprendre de qqun; *to ~ with a/request, proposal/*, accéder à une demande, accepter une proposition. || **fall in** [-ɪn] *n.* [Mil.] rassemblement *m.* || **fall into** [-'ɪntuw] *v. intr.* succomber, se laisser prendre (à un piège, &c.); prendre (l'habitude de faire qqch.). || **fall off** [-'ɔf] *v. intr.* tomber; [Fig.] diminuer. || **fall on, upon** [-'ɑn|ə'pɑn] *v. intr.* trouver (qqch.) par hasard, tomber sur (qqch.). || **fall out** [-'awt] *v. intr.* tomber (dehors); [Mil.] rompre les rangs: *~ !*, Rompez!; *to ~ with s.o.*, se brouiller avec qqun. || **fall out** [-ˌawt] *n.* [atomic] retombées *fpl* radioactives. || **fall over** [-'owvɚ] *v. intr.* [Pers.] tomber (à terre, à la renverse); [thing] se renverser: *to ~ an obstacle*, trébucher sur un obstacle. **fall through** [-θɹuw] *v. intr.* [plan] n'aboutir à rien, échouer. || **fall to** [-'tuw] *v. intr.* se mettre au travail, s'y mettre; attaquer (un repas). || **fall under** [-'ʌndɚ] *v. intr.* tomber sous; [be classified under] rentrer dans, relever de: *to ~ suspicion*, devenir suspect.

fallacy ['fæləsɪ] *n.* erreur *f*, idée *f* erronée.

fallible ['fælɪbl̩] *adj.* faillible.

fallow ['fælow] *n.* jachère *f*; sol *m* en friche. || *adj.* en friche: *to let lie ~* , laisser en friche.

false [fɔls] *adj.* faux, mensonger; artificiel; (fond) double: *to play a person ~* , trahir, tromper, tricher, rouler/qqun. || **falsehood** [-ˌhʊd] *n.* fausseté *f*; mensonge *m.* || **falsely** [-lɪ] *adv.* faussement, perfidement. || **falseness** [-nəs] *n.* fausseté *f.* || **falsification** [ˌfɔlsɪfɪ'kejʃən] *n.* [nourriture] adultération *f*, contrefaçon *f*; [d'un document, des monnaies, d'une pièce d'identité, &c.]; [Fig., de l'histoire, de la vérité, &c.] falsification. || **falsify** ['fɔlsɪ|faj] *v. tr.* falsifier; mentir (au sujet de qqch.). || **falsity** [-ɪtɪ] *n.* fausseté *f.*

falter ['fɔltɚ] *v. intr.* hésiter, perdre courage; [speech] balbutier; [stumble] chanceler. || *n.* tremblement *m*; balbutiement *m.*

fame [fejm] *n.* **1.** renommée *f*; renom *m.* **2.** réputation *f.* || **famed** [-d] *adj.* célèbre, renommé: *ill-~* , (quartier *m*) mal famé.

familiar [fə'mɪljɚ] *adj.* commun; familier; proche, intime; amical; familiarisé: *to be ~ with*, connaître; *to become ~ with*, se familiariser avec. || **familiarity** [fəˌmɪlɪ'æɚɪtɪ] *n.* familiarité *f*; intimité *f.* || **familiarize** [fə'mɪljəˌajz] *v. tr.* familiariser: *to ~ o.s. with*, se familiariser (avec qqun, qqch.).

family ['fæmɪlɪ] *n.* famille *f*: *~ name*, nom *m* de famille; *~ tree*, arbre *m* généalogique.

famine ['fæmɪn] *n.* famine *f*; misère *f*: *to cry ~* , crier misère.

famish ['fæmɪʃ] *v. tr.* affamer. || *v. intr.* mourir de faim: [Fig.] *I am famished!*, J'ai une faim de loup!

famous ['fejməs] *adj.* célèbre, renommé, fameux. || **famously** [-lɪ] *adv.* fameusement.

fan[1] [fæn] *n.* **1.** ventilateur *m*; [hand] éventail *m*: *electric ~* , ventilateur, *m* électrique, © éventail électrique. **2.** [Agric.] van *m.* || *v. tr.* [-nn-] éventer; attiser (le feu); vanner (le grain): [Mil.] *to ~ out*, se déployer.

fan[2] *n.* [Fam.] fervent *m*; passionné, enragé *m* (de sport); admirat|eur, -rice.

fanatic [fə'nætɪ|k] *n. & adj.* fanatique. || **fanaticism** [-sɪzm] *n.* fanatisme *m*; enthousiasme *m* excessif.

fanciful ['fænsɪ|fl̩] *adj.* **1.** étrange; capricieux. **2.** fantaisiste. **3.** imaginaire. || **fancy** *adj.* **1.** de fantaisie; ornemental. **2.** de luxe: *~ dress ball*, bal *m* costumé.

|| *n.* imagination *f*, fantaisie *f*; caprice *m*; illusion *f*; goût *m*. || *v. tr.* **1.** imaginer; s'imaginer. **2.** croire, penser; se sentir attiré vers.

fang [fæŋ] *n.* croc *m*; serre *f*; griffe *f*.

fantastic [fæn'tæstɪk] *adj.* fantastique, extravagant; (esprit) fantasque. || **fantasy** ['fæntəsɪ] *n.* [whim] caprice *m*, lubie *f*; fantaisie *f*, imagination *f*. cf. FANCY.

far [fɑɚ] *adj.* **farther** [-ðɚ], **farthest** [-ðəst] [cf. aussi FARTHER, FURTHER] lointain, éloigné: *the ~ side* (*of the house*), l'autre côté (de la maison). || *adv.* **1.** loin, au loin: *as ~ as* (*Toronto*), jusqu'à T.; *He will go ~*, Il ira loin; *How ~ is it to . . .*, A quelle distance se trouve . . . ?, → Combien y a-t-il d'ici à . . . ?, A combien est-on de . . . ?; *So ~ and no farther*, Jusque-là et pas plus loin; *So ~ so good*, C'est fort bien jusque-là, Jusqu'ici ça va bien; *to go too ~*, passer/la mesure, les bornes/. **2.** beaucoup, bien, de loin: *He was by ~ the best pupil*, C'était de loin le meilleur élève; *far from . . .*, loin de . . . ; *~ from it*, loin de là, → tant s'en faut; *It would be ~ better to . . .*, Il serait bien préférable de . . . ; *in so ~ as*, dans la mesure où; *so ~ as*, jusqu'à; *as ~ as . . .*, dans la mesure où . . . , pour autant que . . . ; *As ~ as I know*, → Si je ne me trompe, Pour autant que je sache . . . || **faraway** [-əˌwej] *adj.* lointain; éloigné; (regard) perdu dans le vague; (voix) éteinte. || **far-fetched** [-'fɛtʃt] *adj.* tiré par les cheveux, forcé; outré. || **far-flung** [-'flʌŋ] *adj.* **1.** lancé au loin. **2.** d'une vaste portée, considérable, étendu, d'une grande envergure, vaste. || **far-reaching** [-'ɹijtʃɪŋ] *adj.* de grande envergure; d'une grande portée. || **Far North** [-ˌnɔɚθ] *n.* le Grand Nord.

farce [fɑɚs] *n.* [play] farce *f*; [Fig.] spectacle *m* absurde, folie *f*.

fare [fɛɚ] *n.* **1.** prix *m* (du voyage, de la place, de la course); billet *m*; tarif *m*: *single ~*, (prix du) billet simple; *return ~*, *round trip ~*, prix d'un aller-et-retour. **2.** client *m*, voyageur *m*. **3.** nourriture: *bill of ~*, menu *m*, carte *f*. || *v. intr.* **1.** voyager. **2.** manger, se nourrir. **3.** se porter, avoir tel ou tel sort: *How did you ~ ?*, Comment ça s'est-il passé?

farewell [-'wɛl] *n.* **1.** adieu *m*: *to bid s.o. ~*, dire adieu à qqun. **2.** congé *m*: *to take one's ~ of*, prendre congé de. || *adj.* d'adieu: *a ~ call*, une visite d'adieu.

farm [fɑɚm] *n.* **1.** ferme *f* (*on a*, dans une); métairie *f*. || *v. tr.* cultiver; exploiter; affermer: *to ~ out*, donner à ferme. || **farmer** [-ɚ] *n.* fermier *m*; cultivateur *m*; © habitant *m*: *stock ~*, éleveur *m* (de bétail). || **farming** [-ɪŋ] *n.* culture *f*; agriculture *f*; exploitation *f* agricole. || *adj.* agricole.

farrier ['fæɚɪɚ] [Br.] *n.* maréchal-ferrant *m*.

farsighted [ˌfɑɚ'sajtəd] *adj.* presbyte; [Fig.] clairvoyant, prévoyant; perspicace. || **farsightedness** [-nəs] *n.* [Fig.] clairvoyance *f*; [Med.] presbytie *f*.

farther ['fɑɚð|ɚ] [comp. de FAR; voir aussi FURTHER.] *adj.* plus éloigné; autre, additionnel. || *adv.* plus loin, au-delà (de); davantage. || **farthest** [-əst] [sup. de FAR; voir aussi FURTHEST]. || *adj.* le plus éloigné. || *adv.* & *n.* le plus loin.

farthing [-ɪŋ] [Br.] *n.* liard *m*, sou *m*.

fascinate ['fæsɪˌnejt] *v. tr.* fasciner; [attract] séduire, attirer. || **fascination** [ˌfæsɪ'nejʃən] *n.* fascination *f*; [Fig.] attrait *m* (irrésistible).

fashion ['fæʃən] *n.* **1.** façon *f*; manière *f*; forme *f*; style *m*: *after the ~ of*, à la /lumière, façon/de; *in*, *after/a ~*, tant bien que mal. **2.** mode *f*; vogue *f*; ton *m*: *~ show*, défilé *m*, © parade *f*/de mode; présentation *f* de collection: *in ~*, à la mode, en vogue; *to go out of ~*, passer de mode, se démoder. || **fashion** *v. tr.* façonner; former; confectionner (une robe). || **fashionable** [-əbl] *adj.* **1.** à la mode, en vogue. **2.** élégant, fashionable.

fast[1] [fæst] *adj.* solide, fixe; [Fig.] fidèle: *to make* (*doors, &c.*) *fast*, → fixer, fermer (les portes, &c.); [couleur] bon, grand/teint *m*. || *adv.* ferme: *to hold ~*, tenir bon; *to stand ~* (*against*), tenir tête à, s'opposer courageusement à.

fast[2] *adj.* rapide, vite: *he's a ~ worker*, → il travaille vite; *~ train*, (train *m*) rapide *m*. || *adv.* vite, rapidement.

fast[3] *n.* jeûne *m*: *~ day*: jour *m* maigre. || *v. intr.* jeûner.

fasten ['fæsən] *v. tr.* **1.** fixer; attacher; fermer; amarrer (un bateau); agrafer. **2.** fixer (les yeux) sur: *to ~* (*up*)*on*, s'attacher, se fixer, se cramponner; imputer à. || **fastener** [-ɚ] *n.* attache *f*; agrafe *f*; *belt ~*, agrafe de courroie; [zipper] fermeture *f* éclair.

fastidious [fæ'stɪdɪəs] *adj.* × [hard to please] difficile, exigeant; [food] délicat.

fastness ['fæstnəs] *n.* **1.** fermeté *f*, constance *f*; rapidité *f*. **2.** place *f* forte.

fat [fæt] *adj.* [large] gros, [plump, greasy] gras: *to grow ~*, engraisser; [Fig.] riche, productif: *a ~ salary*, de gros émoluments; *a ~ soil*, un sol riche. || *n.* graisse *f*, [in meat] gras *m*.

fatal ['fejtḷ] *adj.* [causing death] mortel, fatal; [fateful] fatal, inévitable. || **fatality** [fə'tælɪtɪ] *n.* accident *m* (mortel), mortalité *f*; [destiny] fatalité *f*. || **fate** [fejt] *n.* le destin, le sort; [Fig.] la fortune; nécessité *f*. || **fated** [-əd] *adj.* décrété par le sort, inéluctable; condamné à . . . : *the ill-~ boy*, le malheureux enfant.

fateful ['fejtfḷ] *adj.* lourd de conséquences, décisif.

father ['fɑðɚ] *n.* père *m*; aieul *m*; ancêtre *m*: *the Our Father*, le Notre-Père: [R.C.] *Father Smith*, le père, l'abbé/Smith; *Good morning, Father*, Bonjour, mon père. || **fatherhood** [-ˌhʊd] *n.* paternité *f* [état]. || **father-in-law** [-ɪnˌlɔ] *n.* beau-père *m*. || **fatherland** [-ˌlænd] *n.* (mère-) patrie *f*. || **fatherless** [-ləs] *adj.* [child] sans père, orphelin. || **fatherly** [-lɪ] *adj.* paternel.

fathom ['fæðəm] *n.* [Meas.] brasse *f*. || *v. tr.* [Mar.] sonder; [Fig.] pénétrer, aller au fond de. . . . || **fathomless** [-ləs] *adj.* [Fig.] insondable, impénétrable.

fatigue [fə'tijg] *n.* **1.** fatigue *f*: *He bears up well against ~*, Il supporte bien la fatigue; *spent with ~*, sur les dents, rendu. **2.** [Mil.] corvée *f*: *on ~*, de corvée. || *v. tr.* fatiguer, lasser, importuner.

fatness ['fæt|nəs] *n.* **1.** embonpoint *m*; corpulence *f*; adiposité *f*. **2.** fertilité *f*. || **fatten** [-ṇ] *v. tr. & intr.* engraisser; prendre de l'embonpoint. || **fatty** [-ɪ] *adj.* gras; graisseux, adipeux.

fatuous ['fætʃuwəs] *adj.* sot, stupide.

faucet ['fɔsət] *n.* **1.** robinet *m* cf. TAP. **2.** fausset *m*, fosset *m* (d'un tonneau).

fault [fɔlt] *n.* défaut *m*; faute *f*; vice *m* (de construction); © manque *f* (dans un vêtement, un tissu, &c.); [Géol.] faille *f*: *at ~*, en défaut, fautif, coupable, dans l'erreur; *to find ~ with*, trouver à redire contre qqun; *It's not my ~*, Ce n'est pas (de) ma faute. || **fault-finder** [-ˌfajndɚ] *n.* mécontent *m*; critiqueur *m*. || **faultless** [-ləs] *adj.* sans faute, sans défaut; impeccable; irréprochable. || **faulty** [-ɪ] *adj.* défectueux; imparfait; incorrect; erroné; inexact.

favour ['fejvɚ] *n.* faveur *f*, grâce *f*; bonté *f*; service *m*: *to be in ~ with*, être dans les (petits) papiers de, être dans les bonnes grâces de; *to be in ~ of*, être partisan de; *to decide in s.o.'s ~*, donner gain de cause à qqun. || *v. tr.* favoriser, préférer; gratifier. || **favourable** [-əbḷ] *adj.* favorable bon. || **favourably** [-əbḷɪ] *adv.* favorablement; avantageusement. || **favourite** [-ɪt] *adj. & n.* favori *m*, favorite *f*. || **favouritism** [-ɪtɪzm] *n.* favoritisme *m*.

fawn[1] [fɔn] *n.* faon *m*. || *adj.* [colour] fauve.

fawn[2] *v. intr.* (upon) flatter, caresser; [Fig.] flatter bassement, courtiser. || **fawning** [-ɪŋ] *n.* [Fig.] servilité *f*, flatterie *f*.

fear [fijɚ] *n.* peur *f*, crainte *f*: *for ~ of*, de peur de; *without ~ or favour*, impartialement. || *v. tr.* craindre, redouter; [be afraid] avoir peur de, craindre (qqch.): *I ~ he will come*, J'ai peur, Je crains/qu'il ne vienne; *I ~ I don't know*, Je regrette, mais je ne le sais pas. || **fearful** [fḷ] *adj.* **1.** redoutable, effrayant. **2.** peureux, craintif. || **fearless** [-ləs] *adj.* intrépide; sans peur, courageux. || **fearlessness** [-ləsnəs] *n.* intrépidité *f*, bravoure *f*.

feasibility [ˌfijzɪ'bɪlɪtɪ] *n.* possibilité *f*, praticabilité *f*. || **feasible**]'fijzɪbḷ] *adj.* faisable, réalisable, praticable, exécutable.

feast [fijst] *n.* festin *m*; fête *f*. || *v. tr. & intr.* régaler; fêter: *to ~ o.'s eyes on*, se repaître de. || *v. intr.* festoyer; se régaler (*on*, de). || **feasting** [-ɪŋ] *n.* festoiement *n*; bonne chère *f*.

feat [fijt] *n.* prouesse *f*, exploit *m*; [Fig.] tour *m* de force; *feats of war*, faits d'armes.

feather ['fɛðɚ] *n.* plume *f*; plumage *m*: *Red ~ campaign*, collecte *f*, campagne *f* des œuvres de charité; *It's a ~ in his cap*, C'est une bonne note en sa faveur, C'est un fleuron à sa couronne. || *v. tr.* emplumer; empenner (une flèche): *to ~ one's nest*, faire son beurre, s'enrichir. || **featherweight** [-ˌwejt] *n.* [Sport.] poids-plume *m*. || **feathery** [-ɪ] *adj.* couvert de plumes.

feature ['fijtʃɚ] *n.* trait *m*, caractéristique *f*, particularité *f*; [Cin.] grand film *m*; [Journ.] reportage *m*; *pl.* traits *mpl*, visage *m*. || *v. tr.* **1.** caractériser, donner la vedette à. **2.** [Cin.] mettre au programme.

February ['fɛbɹuwˌɛəɪ] *n.* février *m*. cf. APRIL.

fed cf. FEED.

federal ['fɛdɹəl] *adj.* fédéral: © *Federal Government*, gouvernement *m* fédéral; [US, guerre civile] nordiste, fédéral; *The Federal Government floats a loan*, le Fédéral lance un nouvel emprunt. || **federate** ['fɛdɚɪt] *adj. & n.* fédéré. || **federation** [ˌfɛdɚ'ejʃən] *n.* fédération *f*; confédération *f*.

fee [fij] *n.* honoraires *mpl* (d'un médecin, d'un avocat, &c.); cachet *m* (d'un précepteur); salaire *m*; [Jur.] propriété *f* héréditaire: *tuition fees*, droits *mpl* de scolarité; *for a ~*, → en se faisant payer; contre honoraires; *for a ~*, contre honoraires; *for a nominal ~*, → pour presque rien; pour une/somme minime, symbolique.

feeble [fijbl̩] *adj.* faible, maladif: *to grow* ~, s'affaiblir; [Fig.] faible: *a* ~ *sound*, un son faible; ~ *attempts*, de faibles efforts *mpl.*

feed [fijd], **fed** [fɛd], **fed** *v. tr.* **1.** nourrir; donner à manger à; [cattle] faire paître. **2.** alimenter (une machine, le feu). || *v. intr.* manger, se nourrir. || *n.* **1.** fourrage *m*; alimentation *f.* **2.** [Fam.] repas *m.* || **feeder** [ˈfijdɚ] *n.* pourvoyeur *m*; [Mec.] alimenteur *m*; [Elect.] canal *m* d'amenée. || **feeding bottle** [-ɪŋˌbɑtl̩] *n.* biberon *m*; © bouteille *f.*

feel [fijl] *n.* [sense] toucher *m*; [feeling] sensation *f*: *to, by/the* ~, au toucher; *I have (got) the* ~ *of it now*, Je m'y suis habitué maintenant. || **feel, felt, felt** [fɛlt] *v. tr.* **1.** [physical] toucher (avec la main); tâter (le pouls, une étoffe); palper (un membre cassé, &c.): *to* ~ *one's way*, avancer, aller, marcher/à tâtons. **2.** [be aware of] sentir; [experience] éprouver (une sensation, un sentiment, une émotion); ressentir (une émotion, les effets de qqch.); [be sensitive to] être sensible à (la douleur); [Fig.] avoir l'impression (que): *I (can)* ~ *his heart beating*, Je sens battre son cœur, Je sens son cœur qui bat; *He felt it necessary to . . .*, Il jugea nécessaire de . . . ; *I feel (that) I am right*, Je sens que j'ai raison, J'ai l'impression d'avoir raison. || *v. intr.* se sentir: *How do you* ~ *?*, Comment vous sentez-vous?; *I* ~*/tired, sick/*, Je me sens/fatigué, malade/; *I* ~ *hungry, cold*, → J'ai/faim, froid/; *It feels cold in here*, Il fait froid ici; *He felt the better for it*, Il s'en trouva mieux; *What does it* ~ *like (to . . .)?*, Quelle impression est-ce que cela vous fait (de . . .)?; *I* ~ *like a cup of coffee*, J'aimerais bien, J'ai envie d'/une tasse de café; *I* ~ *like going now*, J'ai envie d'y aller maintenant; *He doesn't* ~ *(like) himself*, Il ne se sent pas bien; *I* ~ *as if I were . . .*, J'ai l'impression de . . . , Il me semble que. . . . || **feel about** [-əˈbawt] *v. intr.* tâtonner (pour qqch.) dans l'obscurité: *How do you* ~ *going to New York?*, Que dites-vous d'aller à New-York? || **feel for** [-ˈfɔɚ] chercher (qqch.) à tâtons; tâter pour trouver (qqch.): *to feel in one's pockets for sth.*, fouiller dans ses poches pour trouver qqch.; [sympathy] *I* ~ *you*, → Vous avez ma sympathie; *to* ~ *s.o. in his sorrow*, → prendre part à, partager/la douleur de qqun. || **feel up to** [-ˈʌpˌtuw]: *I don't* ~ *it*, → Je ne me sens pas assez bien pour, Je ne me sens pas de taille à/faire cela. || **feel with** [-ˈwɪð]: *to* ~ *s.o. in his sorrow*, → prendre part à, partager/la douleur de qqun. || **feeler** [-ɚ] *n.* [insect] antenne *f*, [cat] moustache *f*: [Fig.] *to throw out a* ~, lancer un ballon *m* d'essai.

feeling [-ɪŋ] *n.* [sense] toucher *m*; [physical] sensation *f.* (de froid, douleur); [mental] sentiment *m*; émotion *f*, sensibilité *f*: *I have/the, a/* ~ *that . . .*, J'ai le sentiment que . . . ; *a* ~ *for languages*, le sentiment des langues; *to have a* ~ *for music*, être sensible à la musique; *The general* ~ *is that . . .*, L'opinion, L'impression/générale est que . . . ; *You know my feelings on the matter*, Vous connaissez mes sentiments là-dessus; *good, ill/* ~, sympathie *f*, rancune *f*; *No hard feelings!*, Sans rancune!; *to hurt s.o.'s feelings*, blesser, froisser/qqun; *to suppress one's feelings*, se contenir; *to spare s.o.'s feelings*, épargner qqun; *to have no feelings*, ne pas avoir de cœur; *a man of (great)* ~, un homme (très) sensible; *to speak with* ~, parler avec/émotion, enthousiasme/. || *adj.* [un peu vieilli] [Pers.] sensible: [words, air] ému; [manner] tendre. || **feelingly** [-ɪŋlɪ] *adv.* avec émotion; avec âme.

feet [fijt] cf. FOOT.

feign [fejn] *v. tr. & intr.* feindre (colère, &c.); faire semblant, contrefaire: *to* ~ *a laugh*, faire semblant de rire; *in a feigned hand*, d'une écriture déguisée. || **feint** [-t] *n.* feinte *f*, artifice *m*: [Fig.] *to make a* ~ *of*, → feindre.

felicitate [fəˈlɪsɪˌtejt] *v. tr.* féliciter.

fell[1] cf. FALL. || **fell**[2] *v. tr.* **1.** [tree, adversary] abattre. **2.** rabattre (une couture).

fellow [ˈfɛlow] *n.* compagnon *m*; camarade *m*; collègue *m*; individu *m*; [Pej.] type *m*; membre *m* (d'une association). || **fellow citizen** [-ˈsɪtɪzən] *n.* concitoyen *m.* || **fellowship** [-ʃɪp] *n.* camaraderie *f*; association *f*; bourse *f* universitaire. || **fellow student** [-ˈstuwdənt] *n.* condisciple *m*; confrère *m* (de classe). || **fellow sufferer** [-ˈsʌfɚɚ] *n.* compagnon *m* de misère. || **fellow worker** [-ˈwɚkɚ] *n.* compagnon *m* (de travail).

felon [ˈfɛlən] *n.* [Jur.] criminel *m*; [Med.] panaris *m.* || *adj.* criminel; perfide. || **felony** [-ɪ] *n.* [Jur.] crime *m.*

felt[1] cf. FEEL.

felt[2] *n.* feutre *m.* || *adj.* en, de/feutre.

female [ˈfijˌmejl] *adj.* [Pers.] féminin; [animals, plants] femelle: ~ *friend*, amie; © ~ *bird* [= hen], la femelle. || *n.*

femme *f*, fille *f*; [animals, plants] femelle *f*.

feminine ['fɛmɪnɪn] *adj.* féminin, de femme; [Pej.] efféminé.

fen [fɛn] *n.* marais *m*; marécage *m*.

fence [fɛns] *n.* **1.** clôture *f*; barrière *f*, palissade *f*: *to sit on the* ~, être indécis; hésiter; se réserver. **2.** receleur *m*. || *v. tr.* **1.** clôturer; palissader. **2.** faire de l'escrime: *to* ~ *with*, éluder (une question).

fencing [-ɪŋ] *n.* [Sport.] escrime *f*.

fend [fɛnd] *v. intr.*: *to* ~ *off (a blow)*, parer, écarter (un coup); [Fam.] *to* ~ *for o.s.*, se débrouiller.

fender [-ɚ] *n.* [Br.] pare-chocs *m. inv.*; garde-boue *m. inv.*; [in front of a fireplace] garde-feu *m. inv.*; [Auto.] aile *f* [= Br. wing].

ferment ['fɚmɛnt] *n.* [substance] ferment *m*; [process] fermentation *f*; [Fig.] agitation *f*, effervescence *f*. || *v. intr.* fermenter; (wine) travailler. || **fermentation** [ˌfɚmən'tejʃən] *n.* fermentation *f*; [Fig.] effervescence *f* (des esprits).

fern [fɚn] *n.* fougère *f*.

ferocious [fɚ'owʃəs] *adj.* féroce, cruel. || **ferocity** [fɚ'ɑsɪtɪ] *n.* férocité *f*, cruauté *f*.

ferret ['fɛɚət] *n.* furet *m*. || *v. tr.* fureter; *to* ~ *out*, dénicher.

ferrous ['fɛɚəs] *adj.* ferreux.

ferrule ['fɛɚuwl] *n.* virole *f*; bague *f*; embout *m*.

ferry ['fɛɚɪ] *n.* bac *m*, © traversier *m*, traverse *f*. || *v. intr.*: *to* ~ *over a river*, passer (une rivière) en bac. || *v. tr.* transporter (des marchandises, &c.)/par mer, par avion/. || **ferry boat** [-ˌbowt] *n.* bac; © traversier *m*, traverse *f*. || **ferryman** [-mən] *n.* traversier *m*.

fertile ['fɚtajl] ['fɚtl̩] *adj.* fertile; riche. || **fertility** [fɚ'tɪlɪtɪ] *n.* fertilité *f*. || **fertilize** ['fɚtɪlajz] *v. tr.* fertiliser, [Biol.] féconder. || **fertilizer** [-ɚ] *n.* engrais *m*.

fervent ['fɚv|ənt] *adj.* [earnest] fervent; [hot] brûlant; [Fig.] vif, ardent: ~ *blood*, un sang *m* ardent. || **fervour** [-ɚ] *n.* zèle *m*, ferveur *f*; [heat] intense chaleur *f*.

fester ['fɛstɚ] *n.* [Med.] suppuration *f*; ulcère *m*. || *v. intr.* suppurer; ulcérer.

festival ['fɛstɪvəl] *n.* fête *f*; festival *m*; célébration *f*. || **festivity** [fɛs'tɪvɪtɪ] *n.* *n.* fête *f*, réjouissance *f*.

festoon [fɛs'tuwn] *n.* guirlande *f*; feston *m*.

fetch [fɛtʃ] *v. tr.* **1.** aller chercher; rapporter; amener. **2.** pousser (un gémissement, un soupir, &c.). **3.** [prix] atteindre. || *v. intr.*: *to* ~ *and carry*, faire de menus travaux; *to* ~ *up at a port*, arriver, parvenir à un port.

fetching ['fɛtʃɪŋ] *adj.* séduisant.

fete [fejt] *n.* fête *f*. || *v.*: *to be feted*, être fêté.

fetid ['fɛtɪd, 'fijtɪd] *adj.* fétide.

fetter ['fɛtɚ] *n.* fers *mpl* (pour les pieds); entraves *fpl* (pour les animaux); [Fig.] obstacles *mpl*. || *v. tr.* enchaîner, mettre aux fers; [Fig.] gêner dans les mouvements.

feud [fjuwd] *n.* **1.** querelle *f*; vendetta *f*. **2.** fief *m*. || **feudal** [-l̩] *adj.* féodal. || **feudalism** [-l̩ɪzm] *n.* féodalité *f*. || **feudality** [ˌfjuw'dælɪtɪ] *n.* féodalité *f*.

fever ['fijvɚ] *n.* fièvre *f*: *to run a* ~, avoir (de) la fièvre; *scarlet* ~, scarlatine *f*; *swamp* ~, malaria *f*, paludisme *m*. || **feverish** [-ɪʃ] *adj.* fiévreux, fébrile. || **feverishly** [-ɪʃlɪ] *adv.* fiévreusement; fébrilement. || **feverishness** [-ɪʃnəs] *n.* fébrilité *f*, (léger) accès *m* de fièvre.

few [fjuw] *adj.* **1.** peu de: *a* ~, quelques. **2.** peu nombreux: *such opportunities are* ~, de telles occasions sont rares. || *pron. indéf.* **1.** peu. **2.** quelques-uns *mpl*, quelques-unes *fpl*: *only a* ~ *know that . . .*, bien peu de gens savent que. . . .

fiancé(e) [ˌfij'ɑnsej] *n.* fiancé(e).

fib [fɪb] *n.* (petit) mensonge *m*. || *v. intr.* [-bb-] raconter des blagues. || **fibber** [-ɚ] *n.* menteur *m*, blagueur *m*.

fibre ['fajbɚ] *n.* fibre *f*. || **fibrous** ['fajbɹəs] *adj.* fibreux.

fickle ['fɪkl̩] *adj.* inconstant; [Psych.] instable. || **fickleness** [-nəs] *n.* inconstance *f*, instabilité *f*.

fiction ['fɪkʃən] *n.* **1.** romans *mpl*; ouvrages *mpl* d'imagination. **2.** fiction *f*. || **fictitious** [fɪk'tɪʃəs] *adj.* fictif, imaginaire; faux, mensonger.

fiddle ['fɪdl̩] *n.* violon *m*: ~ *stick*, archet *m*; *second* ~, sous fifre *m*; *to play second* ~, jouer un rôle secondaire. || *v. tr.* **1.** jouer du violon. **2.** [Fam.] se trémousser: *to* ~ *with sth.*, tripoter, toucher à/qqch.

fidelity [fɪ'dɛlɪtɪ] *n.* fidélité *f*; [accuracy] vérité *f*, exactitude *f*.

fidget ['fɪdʒət] *v. intr.* s'agiter; [child] se trémousser.

field [fijld] *n.* champ *m*, espace *m*; terrain *m*, champ (de baseball, &c.): [Fig.] domaine *m*: ~ *of study*, spécialité *f*; *coal* ~, bassin *m* houiller; ~ *of vision*, champ de vision: *landing* ~, terrain d'atterrissage; ~ *-day*, grand jour. || *v. tr.* [baseball] *to* ~ *the ball*, arrêter (et relancer) la balle. || *v. intr.* [baseball] tenir le champ (pour relancer la balle).

fiend [fijnd] *n.* diable *m*; [Fig.] démon *m* [woman] furie *f*. || **fiendish** [-ɪʃ] *adj.* diabolique, méchant.

fierce [fijɚs] *adj.* **1.** féroce, sauvage. **2.** furieux, violent. ‖ **fiercely** [-lɪ] *adv.* **1.** férocement. **2.** violemment. ‖ **fierceness** [-nəs] *n.* [lion, &c.] férocité *f*; [violence] brutalité *f*, violence *f*: *the ~ of the wind*, la violence du vent; [Fig.] fureur *f*, acharnement *m*.

fiery ['fajɚɪ] *adj.* [like fire] de feu, ardent; [Fig.] ardent, fougueux: *a ~ temper*, un tempérament *m*/irascible, ardent/.

fifteen [fɪf'tijn] *adj. num.* quinze. ‖ **fifteenth** [-θ] *adj. num.* **1.** quinzième. **2.** [Arith.] (un) quinzième, la quinzième partie d'un tout. ‖ **fifth** [fɪfθ] *adj. num.* **1.** cinquième. **2.** [Arith.] (un) cinquième; la cinquième partie d'un tout. ‖ **fiftieth** ['fɪftɪəθ] *adj.* cinquantième. ‖ **fifty** ['fɪftɪ] *adj. num.* cinquante: *to go ~-~*, partager moitié moitié.

fig [fɪg] *n.* figue *f*: *~ tree*, figuier *m*.

fight [fajt], **fought** [fɔt], **fought** *v. intr.* combattre, lutter; se quereller. ‖ *v. tr.* se battre/avec, contre/qqun: *to ~ a battle*, livrer bataille; *to ~ for one's own hand*, défendre ses propres intérêts; *to ~ with the gloves off*, ne pas ménager qqun. ‖ *n.* **1.** combat *m*, bataille *f*. **2.** lutte *f*: *hand-to-hand ~*, combat *m* corps-à-corps; *~ to the death*, combat *m* à outrance; *free ~*, mêlée *f* générale; *to show ~*, montrer les dents. ‖ **fighter** [-ɚ] *n.* **1.** combattant *m*; lutteur *m*. **2.** appareil *m* de combat; avion *m* de chasse. ‖ **fighting** [-ɪŋ] *n.* combats *mpl*, lutte *f*.

figment ['fɪgmənt] *n.* fiction *f*.

figurative ['fɪgjɚətɪv] *adj.* figuratif; [speech] figuré; *in a ~ sense*, au figuré.

figure ['fɪgɚ] *n.* forme *f*, apparence *f*; silhouette *f*; [woman] ligne *f*; taille *f*; [drawing] dessin *m*; [Math., Sport] figure *f*; [number] chiffre *m*; *pl.* calcul *m*, statistiques *fpl*: *the central ~ (of a drama)*, le pivot de l'action; *to cut a sorry ~* faire, piètre figure; [Art] *lay ~*, mannequin *m*; *What's the ~ ?*, Ça coûte combien?; *~ of speech*, figure *f* de rhétorique; métaphore *f*, façon *f* de parler. ‖ *v. tr.* **1.** figurer; représenter. **2.** estimer; calculer, penser: *to ~ out*, *v. intr.* se monter, se chiffrer; *v. tr.* supputer, calculer.

file¹ [fajl] *n.* **1.** classeur *m*: *spike ~*, pique-notes *m. inv.*; *card-index ~*, fichier *m*. **2.** dossier *m*. ‖ *v. tr.* classer, ranger.

file² *n.* file *f*: *in/single, Indian/ ~*, en file indienne, à la queue leu leu; *~-leader*, chef *m* de file.

file³ *n.* lime *f*: *three-cornered ~*, tiers-point *m*. ‖ *v. tr.* limer (le bois, le métal, &c.).

filial ['fijlɪəl] *adj.* filial: *~ duty*, devoir *m*/de fils, de fille/.

filing ['fajlɪŋ] *n.* **1.** classement *m*. **2.** limage *m*: *filings*, limaille *f* (de fer).

fill [fɪl] *v. tr.* (r)emplir; combler; plomber (une dent); occuper (un poste); exécuter (une commande); remplir (un questionnaire): *to ~ a part*, tenir un rôle; *to ~ in the date*, insérer la date; [Auto.] *~ her up!*, Faites le plein! ‖ *v. intr.* s'emplir, se remplir. ‖ **fill** *n.* **1.** charge *f*; plein *m*. **2.** suffisance *f*. **3.** [road] remblai *m*: *to eat o.'s ~*, manger à sa faim; *to drink o.'s ~*, boire à sa soif; *to have o.'s ~ of sth.*, être rassasié de qqch.

fillet ['fɪlət] *n.* **1.** ruban *m*, bandelette *f*, bandeau *m*. **2.** [viande] filet *m*.

filling ['fɪlɪŋ] *n.* **1.** (r)emplissage *m*. **2.** obturation (d'une dent): *~ of a vacancy*, nomination *f* (de qqun) à un poste; *~ station*, poste *m* d'essence.

filly [fɪlɪ] *n.* pouliche *f*.

film [fɪlm] *n.* **1.** couche *f* (d'huile, &c.); taie *f* (sur l'œil). **2.** [Photo.] pellicule *f*; [Cin.] film *m*, bande *f*. ‖ *v. tr.* filmer; tourner (une scène). ‖ *v. intr.*: *to ~ over*, se couvrir d'une pellicule.

filter ['fɪltɚ] *n.* [Photo.] filtre *m*. ‖ *v. tr.* filtrer. ‖ *v. intr.* s'infiltrer. ‖ **filter tip** [-ˌtɪp] *n.* bout-filtre *m*. ‖ *adj.*: *~ cigarettes*, cigarettes/à filtre, à bout-filtre/.

filth [fɪlθ] *n.* ordure *f*, [dirt] saleté(s) *f(pl)*; [Fig.] corruption *f*, souillure *f*. ‖ **filthy** [-ɪ] *adj.* sale; [foul] immonde.

fin [fɪn] *n.* nageoire *f* (de poisson); aileron *m* (d'avion, etc.).

final ['fajnl̩] *adj.* **1.** final; dernier. **2.** définitif. ‖ **finalist** [-ɪst] *n.* [Sport.] © finaliste *m*. ‖ **finally** [-ɪ] *adv.* finalement, enfin; définitivement: *He ~ did it*, → Il a fini par le faire. ‖ **finals** [-z] *npl.* [Sport] les (épreuves *fpl*) finales *fpl*.

finance [fɪ'næns] *n.* finance *f*; finances *fpl*: *high ~*, la haute finance; [Fam.] *His finances are low*, Ses fonds sont/bas, en baisse/. ‖ *v. tr.* ['fajnæns] financer; commanditer (une entreprise). ‖ **financial** [fɪ'nænʃəl] *adj.* financier; pécuniaire: *~ statement*, état *m* des finances; *~ year*, exercice *m* financier. ‖ **financier** [ˌfɪnən'sijɚ] *n.* financier *m*; bailleur *m* de fonds. ‖ **financing** [faj'nænsɪŋ] *n.* financement *m* (d'une entreprise).

finch [fɪntʃ] *n.* pinson *m*, roselin *m*.

find¹ [fajnd], **found, found** [fawnd] *v. tr.* trouver; [again] retrouver: *Where is it (to be) found?*, Où peut-on trouver cela?; *That is not to be found*, Cela est introuvable; *I ~ it easy to do that*, Je trouve, Il m'est/facile de faire cela; *You'll ~ that...* Vous verrez que ... ; *It has been found that ...*, On a constaté que; *It happened yesterday, I ~*, Cela est a arrivé hier, à ce que j'apprends; *to ~ s.o. guilty*, déclarer qqun coupable. || **find**[2] *n.* **1.** découverte *f.* **2.** trouvaille *f.* || **finder** ['fajnd|ɚ] *n.* personne *f* qui (trouve/trouvera/a trouvé) ... ; || **finding** [-ɪŋ] *n.* découverte *f*, invention *f*, [Jur.] verdict *m.* || **findings** [-ɪŋz] *n. pl.* conclusions (d'un comité d'enquête). || **find out** [-'awt] *v. tr.* trouver, découvrir; apprendre: *He found out where I was*, Il a/su, appris/où j'étais; *I'll ~ !*, Je le saurai!, *Find out!*, À vous de trouver!; *to ~ about sth.*, se renseigner sur qqch.; *to find s.o. out*, trouver qqun en défaut.

fine[1] [fajn] *n.* amende *f.* || *v. tr.* condamner (qqun) à une amende,

fine[2] [fajn] *adj.* [weather, &c.] beau, magnifique; [Pers.] excellent, distingué, superbe; [delicate] fin, délicat, raffiné, [also Fig.]; [Fam.] joli: *That's ~*, Voilà qui est parfait; *That's all very ~, but*, Tout cela est fort beau, mais; [Iron.] *A ~ thing!*, C'est du propre! || *adv.* bien; finement: *to cut sth. ~*, y arriver/tout juste, de justesse/. || **finely** [-lɪ] *adv.* finement, délicatement; magnifiquement; admirablement. || **fineness** [-nəs] *n.* finesse *f*, délicatesse *f*; excellence *f*; élégance *f*; [gold] titre *m* (de l'or).

finery [-ɚɪ] *n.* atours *mpl*, parure *f.*

finesse [fɪ'nɛs] *n.* finesse *f*; [cards] impasse *f.* || *v. intr.* finasser; faire une impasse.

finger ['fɪŋgɚ] *n.* doigt *m* (de la main, d'un gant, de pied, &c.): *first ~*, index *m*; *second, middle/ ~*, médius *m*, majeur *m*, doigt *m* du milieu; *third, ring/ ~*, annulaire *m*; *little ~*, auriculaire *m*, petit doigt *m.* || *v. tr.* **1.** manier, palper, tâter. **2.** chiper, dérober. **3.** [Pop.] *to ~ s.o.*, moucharder, vendre, doubler/ qqun. || **fingerboard** [-ˌbɔɚd] *n.* [Mus.] clavier *m* (du piano). || **fingernail** [-ˌnejl] *n.* ongle *m* (d'un doigt de la main). || **fingerprints** [-ˌpɹɪntz] *n.pl.* empreintes *fpl* digitales. || **fingertip** [-ˌtɪp] *n.* bout *m* du doigt.

finicky ['fɪnɪkɪ] *adj.* (trop) difficile, (trop) délicat.

finish ['fɪnɪʃ] *v. tr.* **1.** finir, terminer, achever; [Tech.] usiner (une pièce); [polish] parachever. **2.** [Fam.]: *My answer finished him*, Ma réponse l'a assommé. || *v. intr.* finir, prendre fin, cesser, se terminer: *to ~ first*, finir, arriver premier (dans une course, &c.); *to ~ doing sth.*, finir de faire qqch.; *to ~ by doing sth.*, finir par faire qqch.; *Are, Have/you finished?*, Avez-vous fini?; *I am finished with it*, → Je n'en ai plus besoin; [Fig.] *He is finished*, C'en est fait de lui, C'est un homme fini. || *n.* **1.** fin *f*; arrivée *f* (d'une course); conclusion *f.* **2.** fini *m*: *two-tone ~*, fini bicolore; *a fight to the ~*, une lutte à mort. || **finished** [-t] *adj.* **1.** fini, achevé, terminé. **2.** soigné, parfait: *a ~ speaker*, un orateur accompli.

Finland ['fɪn|lænd] *n.* la Finlande. || **Finn** *n.* Finnois *m*, -e *f.*

finnan haddie [ˌfɪnən'hædɪ] *n.* aiglefin *m* fumé.

Finnish ['fɪn|ɪʃ] *adj.* finlandais. || *n.* [language] finnois *m.*

fir [fɚ] *n.* sapin *m*: *balsam ~*, sapin baumier; *Douglas ~*, sapin de Douglas.

fire[1] [fajɚ] *v. tr.* **1.** mettre le feu à; allumer. **2.** congédier, renvoyer. || *v. intr.* faire feu, tirer (*at*, sur).

fire[2] *n.* feu *m*; [destructive] incendie *m*; [Fig.] flamme *f*, ardeur *f*; [Mil.] tir *m*: *to catch ~*, prendre feu; *to set ~ to*, mettre le feu à; *on ~*, en feu; *to/open, cease/ ~*, ouvrir, cesser/le feu; *to be under ~*, essuyer le feu. || **fire alarm** [-əˌlɑɚm] *n.* avertisseur *m* d'incendie. || **firearm** [-ˌɑɚm] *n.* arme *f* à feu. || **firebrand** [-ˌbɹænd] *n.* tison *m*, brandon *m.* || **firebreak** [-ˌbɹejk] *n.* © coupe-feu *m*; tranchée *f*, pare-feu *m*, garde feu *m.* || **firecracker** [-kɹækɚ] *n.* pétard *m.* || **fire department** [-dəˌpɑɚtmənt] [US] ©, [Br.] **fire brigade** [-bɹɪˌgejd], *n.* service *m* des incendies; pompiers *mpl.* || **fire drill** [-ˌdɹɪl] *n.* exercices *mpl* de sauvetage. || **fire engine** [-ˌɛndʒɪn] *n.* pompe *f* à incendie. || **fire escape** [-əˌskejp] *n.* échelle *f* de sauvetage. || **fire-extinguisher** [-əkˌstɪŋgwɪʃɚ] *n.* extincteur *m* (© d'incendie, chimique). || **firefly** [-ˌflaj] *n.* luciole *f*; © mouche *f* à feu. || **fire hall** [-ˌhɔl] *n.* © caserne *f* de pompiers. || **fire hose** [-ˌhowz] *n.* manche *f* d'incendie. || **fire house** [-ˌhaws] also **fire hall** [-ˌhɔl] *n.* poste *m*, caserne *f*/de(s) pompiers. || **fire-insurance** [-ɪnˌʃɚəns] *n.* assurance *f* contre l'incendie. || **fireman** [-mən] *n.* pompier *m.* || **fireplace** [-ˌplejs] *n.* foyer. || **fire plug** [-ˌplʌg] *n.* © borne-fontaine *f*; bouche *f* d'incendie. || **fireproof** [-ˌpɹuwf] *adj.* ignifuge; incombustible. || **firereel(s)** [-ˌɹijlz] [Ontario] *n.* cf. FIRE-ENGINE. || **fire sale** [-ˌsejl] *n.* vente *f* après incendie. || **fireside** [-ˌsajd] *n.* coin *m* du feu; [Fig.] le chez-soi, → intime (*adj.*). || **fire station** [ˌ-stejʃən] cf. FIREHOUSE. || **fire warden** [-ˌwɔɚdn̩] *n.* © garde-feu *m.* || **firewater** [-ˌwɔtɚ] *n.* [Hist.] eau-de-vie

f. || **fireworks** [-wɚks] *n.pl.* feu *m* d'artifice.
firm[1] [fɚm] *n.* [Com.] maison *f*/de commerce, d'affaires; société *f* commerciale; firme *f*: *legal ~*, bureau *m* d'avocats.
firm[2] *adj.* **1.** ferme, solide. **2.** fixe, stable. **3.** [Fig.] résolu, décidé: *as ~ as a rock*, inébranlable; *to stand ~*, tenir bon.
firmament [-əmənt] *n.* firmament *m.*
firmly [-lɪ] *adv.* fermement, solidement. || **firmness** [-nəs] *n.* fermeté *f*, solidité *f*; détermination *f.*
first [fɚst] *adj.* **1.** premier: *to live on the ~ floor*, demeurer au/premier (étage); © rez-de-chaussée/. **2.** unième: *seventy-first*, → soixante-et-onzième. || *adv.* premièrement, primo, en premier lieu; d'abord, pour commencer; pour la première fois; plutôt: *But ~ . . .*, Mais d'abord . . . ; *When I ~ came here*, Quand je suis venu ici pour la première fois: *I'll die ~ !*, Plutôt mourir. || *n.* **1.** le premier, la première: *to come in an easy ~*, arriver bon premier. **2.** commencement *m*; début *m*: *at ~*, au commencement, d'abord. || **first aid** [-'ejd] *n.* premiers secours *mpl*, premiers soins *mpl*: *~ kit*, trousse *f* de pansement. || **first class** [-'klæs] *adj.* (wagon) de première classe; (produit) de première qualité; (hôtel) de premier ordre. || **first quarter** [-ˌkwɔɚtɚ] *n.* [Astr.] le premier quartier (de la lune). || **first-rate** [-'ɹejt] *adj.* excellent; de première classe; fameux.
fisc [fɪsk] *n.* fisc *m.* || **fiscal** [fɪskl̩] *adj.* fiscal: *~ year*, exercice *m.*
fish [fɪʃ] [sens coll. *fish*] *pl.* **fishes** *n.* **1.** poisson *m.* **2.** [Fam.] personne *f*; individu *m*; type *m*: *He's a queer ~*, C'est un drôle de type; *fresh-water ~*, poisson *m* d'eau douce; *salt-water ~*, poisson de mer. || *v. tr.* **1.** pêcher (le saumon, la truite, &c.). **2.** [Fig.] fouiller; chercher (qqch. dans qqch.). || *v. intr.* pêcher: *to ~ for trout*, pêcher la truite. || **fish bone** [-ˌbown] *n.* arête *f* (de poisson). || **fishdealer** [-ˌdijlɚ] *n.* poissonnier *m*; marchand *m* de poisson. || **fisher** [-ɚ], **fisherman** [-mən] *pl.* **fishermen** [-mən] pêcheur *m.* || **fishery** [-ɚɪ] *n.* [business] pêche *f*; [place] pêcherie *f*: *Department of Fisheries*, ministère *m* des Pêcheries. || **fish-hook** [-hʊk] *n.* hameçon *m*; © ain *m*, aim *m.* || **fishing** ['fɪʃɪŋ] *n.* (la) pêche: *deep-sea ~*, la grande pêche. || **fishing rod** [-ˌrɑd] *n.* canne *f* à pêche. || **fish market** [-ˌmɑɚkət] *n.* marché *m* au poisson. || **fishstick** [-ˌstɪk] *n.* croquette *f* de poisson. || **fishy** [fɪʃɪ] *adj.* **1.** de poisson: *~ eyes*, yeux *mpl* vitreux. **2.** [Fig.] louche: *It looks ~*, ça n'a pas l'air honnête.

fissile [ˌfɪsajl] *adj.* [= **fissionable**] fissile, fissionnable, scissile: *~ material*, substance *f*, matière *f*/fissile. || **fission** ['fɪʃən] *n.* [Nucl.] fission *f.* || **fissure** ['fɪʃɚ] *n.* fissure *f*, [large crack] fente *f.* || *v. tr. & intr.* (se) fissurer, (se) fendre.
fist [fɪst] *n.* poing *m*: *to clench one's fists*, serrer les poings.
fistula [-jələ] *n.* [Med.] fistule *f.*
fit[1] [fɪt] *adj.* **[-tt-] 1.** [health] en bonne santé; [Sport.] en forme. **2.** *~ for*: bon, propre, convenable/à (qqch.); digne de (qqch., qqun); convenir à qqun; en état, capable/de faire (qqch.): *~ for nothing*, propre à rien; *~ for military service*, bon pour le service. **3.** *~ to* (+ inf.): bon, propre/à, digne de; en état, capable/de (faire qqch.): *~ to be used*, bon, /propre, en état/de servir; *~ to live*, digne de vivre; *~ to/wear, eat, drink/*, mettable, mangeable,/buvable, [safe] potable; [Fam.] *to be ~ to be tied*, être fou furieux; *to laugh ~ to die*, rire à en mourir. **4.** *to/think, see/ ~ to*, juger bon de; *as you think ~*, comme bon vous semblera.
fit[2] *n.* **1.** accès *m* (de folie, fièvre, &c.); crise *f* (de rage, larmes, nerfs, jalousie); quinte *f* (de toux): *to have a ~*, avoir une attaque [also Fig.]; *to go into fits of laughter*, avoir le fou rire; *by fits and starts*, par accès. **2.** ajustement *m*, coupe *f.*
fit[3] *v. tr.* [-tt-] [clothes] aller à (qqun), être à la taille de (qqun); habiller, chausser /(qqun); ajuster, adapter/(qqch. à qqch.); s'ajuster, s'adapter/à (qqch.); convenir à (l'occasion); emboîter (qqch. dans qqch.); équiper, munir/(qqch. de qqch.); préparer (qqun à qqch); [be suitable]: *It fits (you) perfectly*, Cela (vous) va à merveille. || *v. intr.* **[-tt-]** [clothes] bien aller (à qqun); s'ajuster, s'adapter/(à qqch.); s'emboîter, entrer, [be contained] tenir/(dans qqch.). || **fit in** [-'ɪn] *v. intr.* entrer, s'emboîter, [be contained] tenir/(dans qqch.); *to ~ with*, s'accorder avec; *not to ~*, détonner. || **fitness** [-nəs] *n.* aptitude *f* (*for, to*, à); à-propos *m* (d'une remarque); [physical] santé *f* physique; [Sport] bonne forme *f.* || **fit on** [-'an] *v. tr.* essayer [un habit). || **fit out** [-'awt] *v. tr.* équiper (*with*, de). || **fit together** [-təˌgɛðɚ] *v. intr.* aller ensemble; s'ajuster, s'adapter. || *v. tr.* monter (qqch.). || **fitted** [-əd] *adj.* [Tech.] ajusté, monté; [suitable] adapté (*to*, à); [pers.] fait (*to*, pour). || **fitter** [-ɚ] *n.* [Tech.] ajusteur *m*, monteur *m*; [Electr.] installateur *m*, [clothes] essayeur *m.*

|| **fitting** [-ɪŋ] *adj.* approprié (*to*, à), [proper] convenable; (remarque) à propos; [clothes] → qui va (bien, mal): *It is ~ that*..., Il est/convenable, juste/que [+ subj.] || *n.* **1.** essayage *m* (de vêtements). **2.** [*usual pl.*] installations *fpl* (d'un atelier); agencements *mpl*; fournitures *fpl*; accessoires *mpl*.

five [fajv] *adj. num.* cinq. || **fiver** [-ər] [Fam. or Sl.] billet *m* de cinq dollars, © un "cinq dollars."

fix [fɪks] *v. tr.* attacher; établir, fixer; réparer. || *n.* embarras *m*; mauvais pas *m*; difficulté *f*. || **fixed** [-t] *adj.* fixe, ferme: *~ smile*, sourire *m* figé. || **fixture** ['fɪkstʃər] *n.* appareil *m*; accessoire *m*: *lighting ~*, appareil *m* d'éclairage.

fizz [fɪz] *n.* pétillement *m*. || *v. intr.* pétiller. || **fizzle** ['fɪzl] *v. intr.* fuser, pétiller.

flabby ['flæbɪ] *adj.* flasque; mou *m*, molle *f*.

flaccid ['flæksɪd] *adj.* flasque; mou *m*, molle *f*, [Plus littéraire que le précédent].

flag [flæg] *n.* **1.** drapeau *m*, [Naut.] pavillon *m*; *~ at half-mast*, drapeau en berne. **2.** [stone] dalle *f*. **3.** [flower] glaïeul *m*. || *v. tr.* [-gg-] **1.** pavoiser. **2.** faire des signaux. || *v. intr.* languir, faiblir.

flagrant ['flejgɹənt] *adj.*: [×] scandaleux.

flagship ['flæg|ˌʃɪp] *n.* navire *m*, vaisseau *m*/amiral. || **flagstaff** [-ˌstæf] *n.* hampe *f* (d'un drapeau).

flail [flejl] *n.* [Agric.] fléau *m*. || *v. tr.* battre (le blé) au fléau.

flair [flɛər] *n.* flair *m* (politique), esprit *m* de finesse.

flake [flejk] *n.* flocon *m* (de neige); [scale, chip] écaille *f*: *corn flakes*, flocons *mpl* de maïs. || *v. intr.* tomber en flocons; s'écailler.

flamboyant [ˌflæm'bojənt] *adj.* flamboyant.

flame [flejm] *n.* flamme *f*; feu *m*; [Fig.] passion *f*; zèle *m*. || *v. intr.* flamber; s'enflammer; flamboyer: *Her cheeks flamed*, Le rouge lui monta aux joues. || **flaming** [-ɪŋ] *n.* flamboiement *m*. || *adj.* flamboyant; [Fig.] passionné; enflammé.

flamingo [flə'mɪŋgow] *n.* flamant *m*.

Flanders ['flændərz] *n.* la Flandre; [Hist.] les Flandres *fpl*: *in, to/ ~*, en Flandre.

flange [flændʒ] *n.* bride *f*; rebord *m*; jante *f* (d'une roue); patin *m* (d'un rail).

flank [flæŋk] *n.* flanc *m* (du corps humain) [Fig.] flanc *m* (d'une armée); côté *m* (d'un édifice). || *v. tr.* flanquer, (*with*, de); [Mil.] prendre . . . de flanc.

flannel ['flænḷ] *n.* flanelle *f*. || flannellette/ finette.

flap [flæp] *n.* **1.** coup *m* (d'aile); [noise] battement *m*. **2.** [hanging piece] pan *m* (d'étoffe), battant *m* (de table); [of an airplane] volet *m*. || *v. intr.* [-pp-] battre (des ailes, des bras); agiter (les bras).

flap'jack [-ˌdʒæk] *n.* **1.** crêpe *f*. **2.** poudrier *m*; © minaudière *f*.

flare [flɛər] *n.* lumière *f* intermittente, éclat *m*; fusée *f* éclairante. || *v. intr.*: étinceler [flame]: *to ~ up*, flamber (soudain); [Fig.] s'emporter.

flash [flæʃ] *n.* **1.** éclair *m*; éclat *m*; instant *m*; trait *m* (d'esprit): *in a ~*, en un clin d'œil; *news ~*, dernières nouvelles *fpl*; *a ~ of hope*, une lueur d'espoir; *~ of lightning*, éclair *m* (d'orage). || *v. intr.* **1.** flamboyer; lancer des étincelles; jeter des éclairs; [eyes] étinceler. **2.** jaillir; darder; [Fig.] *to ~ past*, passer comme un éclair. || *v. tr.* **1.** faire flamboyer (un sabre); faire étinceler (un bijou). **2.** projeter (un rayon de lumière); décocher (un sourire). **3.** répandre, transmettre (une nouvelle). || *n.* éclair *m*; [sabre] éclat: *It's a ~ in the pan*, C'est un feu de paille. || **flashlight** [-ˌlajt] *n.* lampe *f* de poche; [Photo.] lampe-éclair *f*. || **flashy** [-ɪ] *adj.* (vêtement) criard, voyant.

flask [flæsk] *n.* flacon *m*, gourde *f*; *the flasks*, les burettes *fpl*.

flat [flæt] *adj.* plat; uni: *a ~ tract of land*, © un terrain planche; [tire] à plat, dégonflé. cf. CREVAISON; monotone; fade: *~ beer*, bière éventée; terne: *~ colour*, couleur *f* mate; *~ sound*, son *m* sourd; [Mus.] bémol: *B ~ major*, si bémol majeur; [Sl.] fauché, à sec, © cassé. cf. BROKE; *~ nose*, nez *m* camus. || *n.* le plat *m* (d'un sabre, &c.); chambre *f* (meublée), appartement *m*, © plain-pied *m*; [tire] crevaison *f*; [shoal] bas fond *m*; terrain *m* plan; [Mus.] bémol *m*. || *adv* nettement: *to sing ~*, chanter faux, fausser; *to fall ~*, tomber à plat. || **flatly** [-lɪ] *adv.* carrément; nettement: *to deny sth. ~*, nier qqch. absolument. || **flatten** [-n] *v. tr.* aplatir; aplanir, [Metall.] laminer.

flatter [-ər] *v. tr.* flatter; [win over] amadouer: *to ~ o.s.*..., se flatter (de). || **flatterer** [-ərər] *n.* flatteur *m*. || **flattering** [-ərɪŋ] *adj.* flatteur, agréable: *a ~ compliment*, un compliment flatteur. || **flattery** [-ərɪ] *n.* flatterie *f*, louange *f* (vraie ou fausse).

flattop [-ˌtɑp] *n.* [airplane carrier] porte-avions *m*.

flaunt [flɔnt] *n.* étalage *m*, ostentation *f*. || *v. intr.* se pavaner, s'afficher. || *v. tr.* faire étalage de (son luxe).

flavour ['flejvər] *n.* **1.** goût *m*, saveur *f*; arôme *m*; bouquet *m* (du vin); parfum *m* (d'une glace). **2.** assaisonnement *m*. || *v. tr.*

1. assaisonner. 2. [Fig.] agrémenter. || **flavouring** [-'flejvərɪŋ] *n.* assaisonnement *m*, parfum *m*. || **flavourless** [-ləs] *adj.* insipide, sans saveur *f*.

flaw [flɔ] *n.* défaut *m*; [crack] paille *f*; [Fig.] erreur *f* (de raisonnement), [Jur.] vice *m* (de forme). || **flawless** [-ləs] *adj.* impeccable, sans défaut.

flax [flæks] *n.* lin *m*: *flax seed*, graine *f* de lin. || **flaxen** [-n̩] *adj.* de lin; blond.

flay [flej] *v. tr.* écorcher: *to ~ alive*, écorcher vif, [Fig.] critiquer sévèrement qqun.

flea [flij] *n.* puce *f*. || **fleabane** [-ˌbejn] *n.* [Bot.] © herbe *f* à (la) puce.

fleck [flɛk] *n.* (petite) tache *f*, moucheture *f*.

fled cf. FLEE.

flee [flij], **fled** [flɛd], **fled** *v. intr.* fuir; s'enfuir; se sauver. || *v. tr.* fuir, s'enfuir/de; [Fig.] fuir (un danger).

fleece [flijs] *n.* toison *f* (de mouton &c.) || *v. tr.* tondre (un mouton): [Fig.] dépouiller (qqun de son argent).

fleet[1] [flijt] *n.* [Naut. Aviat.] flotte *f*: *air fleet*, flotte aérienne; [railway cars, motor cars] train *m*; *~ of trucks*, parc *m* de camions.

fleet[2] *adj.* rapide; † *~ -footed*, au pied léger. || **fleeting** [-ɪŋ] *adj.* fugitif, éphémère.

Flemish ['flɛmɪʃ] *adj. & n.* flamand.

flesh [flɛʃ] *n.* chair *f*: *to eat ~* , faire gras; [exclusively used to indicate meat that is eaten] viande *f*; pulpe *f* (d'un fruit); le corps *m* (as opposed to the soul or spirit): [Fig.] *The spirit is willing but the ~ is weak*, L'esprit est prompt mais la chair est faible. || **flesh colour** [-ˌkʌlər] *n.* couleur *f* (de) chair. || **flesh-eater** [-ˌijtər] *n.* [animal] carnassier; [être humain] cannibale *m*. || **flesh wound** [-ˌwuwnd] *n.* blessure *f* dans les chairs. || **fleshy** [-ɪ] *adj.* charnu.

fleur-de-lis [ˌflərdə'lɪ] *n.* fleur *f* de lis. || *attrib.* fleurdelisé [e.g. the flag of the Province of Quebec].

flew cf. FLY.

flex [flɛks] *v. tr.* fléchir, plier, courber. || **flexibility** [flɛksɪ'bɪlɪtɪ] *n.* 1. flexibilité *f*. 2. [Fig.] souplesse *f* (d'esprit), complaisance *f* (à se laisser persuader). || **flexible** [flɛksɪbl] *adj.* flexible; souple. || **flexure** [flɛkʃər] *n.* courbure *f*; flexion *f*; fléchissement *m*.

flick [flɪk] *n.* petit coup *m*, [stroke] chiquenaude *f*: *at the ~ of a switch*, → en poussant un bouton.

flicker ['flɪkər] *n.* 1. [movement] vacillement *m*; tremblotement *m*; [eyelid] battement *m*. 2. [light] lueur *f* (tremblotante); 3. [bird] © pic *m* doré. || *v. intr.* clignoter; trembloter.

flier ['flajər] cf. FLYER.

flight [flajt] *n.* 1. vol *m*, distance *f* parcourue; escadrille *f*.: *maiden ~* , premier vol; *trial ~* , vol d'essai; [aircraft carrier] *~ deck*, pont *m* d'envol; *~ number 7 leaving in 5 minutes*, Le vol, © l'envolée numéro 7 part dans 5 minutes. 2. *~ of stairs*, escaliers *mpl*.

flighty ['flajtɪ] *adj.* léger, inconstant, frivole.

flimsy [flɪmzɪ] *adj.* [dress] léger; [froid] faible; [fabric] fragile, sans consistance; [Fig.] frivole. || *n.* (papier) pelure *f*.

flinch [flɪntʃ] *v. intr.* fléchir, reculer (from, devant): *without flinching*, sans hésiter, [Fam.] sans broncher.

fling [flɪŋ], **flung** [flʌŋ], **flung** *v. tr.* lancer (une balle); jeter (une pierre): *to ~ the door open*, → ouvrir brusquement la porte; [Fig.] décocher, lancer (des injures, &c.); *to ~ aside*, rejeter de côté; [Fig.] se départir de; *to ~ one's arms around s.o.'s neck*, se jeter, sauter/au cou de qqun; *to ~ back*, repousser violemment; *to ~ off*, se débarrasser (de ses vêtements); *to ~ out*, jeter . . . dehors, flanquer (qqun) à la porte; *to ~ up the window*, relever brusquement la fenêtre. || *v. intr.* s'élancer; se précipiter. || *n.* jet *m* (d'une pierre); [Fig.] essai *m*, tentative *f*: *to have one's ~* , jeter sa gourme.

flint [flɪnt] *n.* silex *m*; [lighter] pierre *f* (à briquet): [Fig.] *a heart of ~* , un cœur de pierre.

flip [flɪp] *n.* chiquenaude *f* cf. FLICK. || *v. tr.* [-pp-]: donner une chiquenaude à, chasser . . . d'une chiquenaude; tourner rapidement (une page): *to ~ over*, retourner (un disque). || *v. intr.*: *to ~ back*, revenir brusquement en arrière; *to ~ over*, se renverser (brusquement).

flippancy ['flɪpən|sɪ] *n.* désinvolture *f*. || **flippant** [-t] *adj.* désinvolte; irrévérencieux; [tongue] délié.

flirt [flərt] *n.* [girl] coquette *f*; flirteu|r, -se. || *v. intr.* flirter; [Fig.] *to ~ with an idea*, jouer avec, caresser/une idée. || **flirtation** [flər'tejʃən] *n.* flirt *m*.

flit [flɪt] *v. intr.* [-tt-] voleter, voltiger; [Fig.] *to ~ away*, passer rapidement, disparaître.

float [flowt] *v. intr.* flotter; nager (sur une surface liquide); [swimming] faire la planche; [Fig.] circuler: *A rumour is floating about that . . .* , Le bruit court que . . . || *v. tr.* 1. flotter (du bois); [Naut.] renflouer (un navire). 2. [Com.] lancer, fonder/une compagnie: *to ~ a loan*, émettre un emprunt. || *n.* flotteur *m*; [fishing] bouchon *m*, flotteur; [parade] char *m*. || **floater** [-ɚ] *n.* flotteur *m*; [assurance] police *f* flottante; [Fin.] titre *m* au porteur; [Pol.] faux électeur *m*, © télégraphe *m*. || **floating** [-ɪŋ] *adj.* **1.** flottant; à flot. **2.** libre, mobile: [Anat.] ~ *ribs*, fausses côtes *fpl*; ~ *population*, population *f* instable; ~ *capital*, fonds *m* de roulement. || *n.* flottement *m*; flottage *m* (du bois); [Com.] lancement *m* (d'une société commerciale); émission *f* (d'un emprunt).

flock [flɑk] *n.* troupeau *m*; [Fig.] bande *f*; foule *f*; *They arrived in flocks*, Ils arrivaient en foule; [Rel.]: *a pastor and his* ~, un pasteur et ses ouailles. || *v. intr.* affluer, aller en foule. || **flock in** [-'ɪn] *v. intr.* entrer en foule. || **flock together** [-tə'gɛðɚ] s'attrouper.

floe [flow] *n.* banquise *f*; [floating piece of ice] glaçon *m* (flottant), glace *f* flottante.

flog [flɑg] *v. tr.* [-gg-] fouetter, donner le fouet à. || **flogging** [-ɪŋ] *n.* le fouet; †flagellation *f*.

flood [flʌd] *v. intr.* **1.** [river], déborder, être en crue. **2.** [Auto.]: *The carburettor is flooded*, Le carburateur est noyé. || *v.tr.* inonder, noyer (un terrain, un pays); faire déborder (une rivière). || *n.* inondation *f*; [river] crue *f*; [mer] flux *m*, marée *f* montante; [Fig.] déluge *m*, flot *m*: *a* ~ *of light*, des flots de lumière; *a* ~ *of tears*, un torrent de larmes; *the Flood*, le Déluge. || **flooded** [-əd] *adj.* inondé, noyé. || **floodgate** [-ˌgejt] *n.* porte d'écluse. || **floodlight** [-ˌlajt] *n.* lumière *f* indirecte: ~ (*projector*), projecteur *m* de lumière; **phare** *m* **d'éclairage.** || **floodlighting** [-ˌlajtɪŋ] *n* éclairage *m* indirect. || **flood tide** [-ˌtajd] *n.* marée *f* montante.

floor [flɔɚ] *n.* **1.** [room] plancher *m*, parquet *m*: ~ *show*, spectacle *m* (de cabaret). **2.** [storey] étage *m*: *to live on the fourth* ~, habiter, demeurer/au quatrième (étage). [☞ In Europe, this would correspond to *le troisième étage*]. **3.** [Tech.] fond *m* (de l'océan); tablier *m* (d'un pont); prétoire *m* (d'un tribunal); parquet *m*, enceinte *f* (d'une assemblée législative). **4.** parole *f*: *Mr. X has the* ~, M. X a la parole; *to take the* ~, prendre la parole || **floor** *v. tr.* parqueter; carreler; [Fig.] terrasser (un adversaire); [Fam.] coller (un candidat à un examen). || **floor board** [-ˌbɔɚd] *n.* lame *f* (de parquet). || **floor polish** [-ˌpɑlɪʃ] *n.* cire *f* à parquet. || **floorwalker** [-ˌwɔkɚ] *n.* inspecteur *m* (d'un grand magasin).

flop [flɑp] *v. intr.* [-pp-] **1.** [Fam.] échouer (à), rater; [play] être un four. **2.** tomber lourdement, s'affaler (dans un fauteuil). || *n.* **1.** bruit *m* sourd. **2.** [Fig.] chute *f*, four *m*, échec *m*. **3.** dégringolade *f*, effondrement *m* (d'une monnaie, &c.). || [Sl.] **flophouse** [-ˌhaws] *n.* asile *m* de nuit.

florid ['flɔɚɪd] *adj.* [complexion] haut(e) en couleurs; [ornate] fleuri.

florist ['flɔɚɪst] *n.* fleuriste *m/f*.

floss ['flɑs] *n.* bourre *f* de soie.

flotilla [ˌflow'tɪlə] *n.* flottille *f*.

flotsam ['flɑtsəm] *n.* épave(s) *f* (*pl.*).

flounce ['flawns] *n.* volant *m* (de robe). || *v. intr.* [Fig.] s'élancer; sursauter.

flounder ['flawndɚ] *v. intr.* patauger: *to* ~ *along*, avancer en trébuchant; [Fig.] *to* ~ *in a speech*, patauger dans un discours.

flour ['flawɚ] *n.* farine *f*, © fleur *f*.

flourish ['flɚɪʃ] *n.* **1.** grand(s) geste(s) *m*(*pl.*); [épée] moulinet *m*. **2.** [handwriting] fioriture *f*; [signature] parafe *m*. **3.** langage *m* fleuri. **4.** [Mus.] prélude *m*, fanfare *f*: *to strike up a* ~, sonner une fanfare. || *v. intr.* **1.** fleurir. **2.** [Fig.] être florissant, prospérer: *Trade then flourished*, Alors le commerce florissait. **3.** parler en termes fleuris, pompeux. **4.** brandir, faire tournoyer (une épée, un bâton). **5.** [Mus.] sonner une fanfare. || *v. tr.* **1.** [broderie] fleurir. **2.** brandir. **3.** embellir de fleurs de rhétorique. **4.** parafer.

floury ['flawɚɪ] *adj.* enfariné.

flout [flawt] *n.* moquerie *f*, insulte *f*. || *v. tr.* se moquer (de qqun), narguer (qqun).

flow [flow] *n.* écoulement *m* (d'un liquide); courant *m* (électrique); afflux *m* (d'air, de sang à la tête); flux *m* (de la marée); [rate] débit *m*; [Fig.] flot *m* (de paroles). || *v. intr.* couler; [to drain] s'écouler; [spurt forth] jaillir; [Electr., blood] circuler; [tide] monter, remonter; [Fig., time] s'écouler; †[result] découler (de); †[abound] abonder (en). *ebb and* ~, flux *m* et reflux *m*; *Blood will* ~, Le sang va couler; *The rivers flow into the sea*, Les fleuves se jettent dans la mer. || **flow away** [-ə'wej] *v. intr.* s'écouler. || **flow back** [-'bæk] *v. intr.* refluer. || **flow in** [-'ɪn] [liquid] entrer; [people, money] affluer. || **flow out** [-'awt] *v. intr.* sortir; s'écouler. || **flow over** [-'owvɚ] *v. intr.* déborder.

flower ['flawɚ] *n.* **1.** fleur *f*: ~ *show*, exposition *f* d'horticulture; *in full* ~, en plein épanouissement; *to burst into* ~, fleurir. **2.** [Fig.] [army] élite *f*; [society] fine fleur: *to be in the* ~ *of one's age*, être dans la fleur de l'âge. || *v. intr.* fleurir. || **flower bed** [-ˌbɛd] *n.* plate-bande *f*.

flower girl [-ˌgɚl] *n.* bouquetière *f.* || **flower shop** [-ˌʃɑp] *n.* boutique *f* de fleuriste. || **flowered** [-d] *adj.* fleuri, épanoui (en fleur); [decorated with flowers] à fleurs. || **flowery** [-ɪ] *adj.* en fleurs; [style] fleuri.

flowing [flowɪŋ] *adj.* coulant; [style] facile: *a* ~ *tongue,* une langue bien pendue; *a* ~ *beard,* une barbe flottante.

flown cf. FLY.

flu [fluw] [abr. = influenza] *n.* [Fam.] la grippe.

fluctuate [ˈflʌktjuwˌejt] *v. intr.* osciller, [prices] varier; [Fig.] hésiter, flotter: *to* ~ *between hope and fear,* flotter entre l'espérance et la crainte. || **fluctuation** [ˌflʌktjuwˈejʃən] *n.* fluctuation *f*; variation *f* (des prix, des cours); [Fig.] incertitude *f*, hésitation *f*.

flue [fluw] *n.* tuyau *m* (de cheminée, d'échappement).

fluency [-ənsɪ] *n.* [speech] facilité *f*. || **fluent** [-ənt] *adj.* [style] coulant: *to speak* ~ *French* → parler couramment le français. || **fluently** [-əntlɪ] *adv.* couramment, d'abondance.

fluff [flʌf] *n.* duvet *m.* || **fluffy** [-ɪ] *adj.* duveteux.

fluid [ˈfluwɪd] *n.* fluide *m*, liquide *m*: *brake* ~, huile *f* de freins. || *adj.* fluide, liquide: ~ *ounce*: once *f* liquide.

fluke [fluwk] *n.* **1.** [Naut.] patte *f* d'ancre. **2.** coup *m* de chance.

flung cf. FLING.

flunk [flʌnk] *v. tr.* [Fam.] rater (un examen), coller (un candidat): *He flunked his exam,* Il a été recalé, © Il a coulé ses examens.

fluoridize [ˈfluwɚɪˌdajz] *v. tr.* verduniser (de l'eau).

flurry [ˈflɚɪ] *n.* [gust] coup *m* de vent: *snow* ~, légère chute *f* de neige; [Fig.] agitation *f*, hâte *f*. || *v. tr.* [Fig.] agiter, mettre en émoi.

flush [flʌʃ] *adj.* plein (à déborder); bien pourvu (d'argent); abondant; [level] à ras; [health] éclatant, frais, plein de vigueur; vigoureux: *to be* ~ *with,* être au/ras, niveau/de; *to be* ~ *with money,* [Br.] avoir de l'argent à revendre; [US] être généreux, donner largement. || *adv.* à ras, de niveau; [directly] droit. || *n.* rougeur *f*, afflux *m* de sang; [light] éclat *m*; [toilet] chasse *f* d'eau; [poker] flush *f*; [Fig.] éclat *m* (de beauté), accès *m* (de colère), transport *m* (de joie). || *v. tr.* [toilet] tirer la chasse d'eau; rincer; [hunt] faire lever. || *v. intr.* rougir; [birds] se lever. || **flushed** [-t] *adj.* empourpré, rouge.

fluster [ˈflʌstɚ] *n.* agitation *f*: *in a* ~, en émoi. || *v. tr.* déconcerter, ahurir, agiter (qqun): *to become flustered,* se troubler, perdre son sang-froid. cf. FLURRY.

flute [fluwt] *n.* **1.** flûte *f*. **2.** [Arch.] cannelure *f*. || *v. intr.* jouer de la flûte. || *v. tr.* canneler.

flutter [ˈflʌtɚ] *n.* **1.** émoi *m*, agitation: *I'm all of a* ~, je suis tout agité. **2.** battement *m* d'ailes. **3.** [Med.] palpitation *f*. || *v. tr.* agiter, mettre en désordre. || *v. int.* **1.** s'agiter. **2.** battre des ailes. **3.** [cœur] palpiter.

flux [flʌks] *n.* [tide] flux *m*; [Fig.] flottement *m*, incertitude *f*.

fly[1] [flaj] *n.* mouche *f*: *house* ~, mouche commune; *black* ~, © mouche noire; *horse, deer*/ ~, taon *m*; [pants] braguette *f*; [tent] auvent *m*.

fly,[2] **flew** [fluw], **flown** [flown] *v. intr.* **1.** [bird, plane] voler; [Pers.] prendre l'avion, aller (venir, &c.) en avion; piloter (un avion); [flag] flotter: *to* ~ *to New York,* prendre l'avion pour N.Y., aller à N.Y. en avion; *to* ~ *across the Atlantic,* → traverser l'Atlantique en avion; *to* ~ *over sth.,* survoler qqch; *to* ~ *away,* s'envoler. **2.** [rush] courir, se précipiter; [time] filer, s'enfuir; [sparks] jaillir: *to* ~ *to s.o.'s rescue,* courir, voler/au secours de qqun; *to* ~ *at s.o.,* s'élancer, sauter/sur qqun; *to* ~ *into a rage,* se mettre en fureur; *The door flew open,* La porte s'ouvrit brusquement; *to* ~ *into pieces,* voler en éclats; *to send s.o. flying,* envoyer (qqun) par terre; [Fam.] *to* ~ *off the handle,* s'emporter; *to let* ~, lâcher un coup (de fusil, de poing, &c.). **3.** fuir; s'enfuir, se sauver (de). cf. FLEE. || *v. tr.* piloter (un avion); survoler (une mer); amener (qqun), transporter (qqch.) en avion; faire voler (un modèle d'avion); battre (pavillon); fuir, éviter. || **flycatcher** [-ˌkætʃɚ] *n.* © moucherolle *f*. || **flyer, flier** [-ɚ] *n.* aviat|eur *m*, -rice *f*, pilote *m*; [Rail.] rapide *m*, express *m*; prospectus *m.* || **fly fishing** [-ˌfɪʃɪŋ] *n.* pêche *f* à la mouche. || **flying** [-ɪŋ] *adj.* **1.** volant; flottant, léger. **2.** rapide, court: *to pay a* ~ *visit to Montreal,* faire un voyage éclair à Montréal. || *n.* vol *m*; aviation *f*: ~ *boat,* hydravion *m*; ~ *club,* aéro-club *m*; ~ *field,* terrain *m* d'aviation; *night* ~, vol *m* de nuit; *instrument* ~, pilotage *m* sans visibilité; ~ *fish,* poisson *m* volant; ~ *saucer,* soucoupe *f* volante; [Fig.] *to come through with* ~ *colours,* remporter la victoire. || **fly-past** [-ˌpæst] *n.* défilé *m* aérien. || **flywheel** [-ˌwijl] *n.* volant *m.*

foal [fowl] *n.* poulain *m,* pouliche *f,* ânon *m.*

foam [fowm] *n.* [sea, &c.] écume *f*: ~ *rubber,* caoutchouc *m* mousse. || *v. intr.* écumer; [beer] mousser. || **foamy** (or: **foaming**) [-ɪ|ɪŋ] *adj.* écumeux, [beer] mousseux.

F.O.B. [= free on board] franco à bord, F.A.B.

focal ['fowk|l] *adj.* focal. || **focus** [-əs] *pl.* **foci** ['fowsaj] ou **focuses** ['fowkəsəs] *n.* foyer *m*; [Fig.] centre *m* (d'intérêt): *in* ~, au point. || *v. tr.* [-ss-] faire converger (*on,* sur); [Phot.] mettre au point. || *v. intr.* converger, se concentrer (*on,* sur).

fodder ['fadər] *n.* fourrage *m.*

foe [fow] *n.* ennemi *m*: *a* (*bitter*) ~ *to,* l'ennemi (acharné/implacable) de . . .

fog [fag] *n.* **1.** brouillard *m*; brume *f*: ~*-horn,* trompe *f,* corne *f*/de brume. **2.** [Phot.] voile *m.* || *v. tr.* [-gg-] s'embrumer; [Fig.] brouiller; [Phot.] voiler. || *v. intr.* se voiler; [window] s'embuer. || **foggy** [-ɪ] *adj.* brumeux; [Fig.] confus, flou.

foil [fɔjl] *n.* **1.** [Metall.] feuille *f.* **2.** [Sport] fleuret *m.* **3.** [Opt.] tain *m*; [Fig.] repoussoir *m.* || *v. tr.* déjouer, faire échouer.

fold [fowld] *n.* **1.** pli *m.* **2.** [sheep] bergerie *f.* || *v. tr.* **1.** plier. **2.** [sheep] parquer: *to* ~ *one's arms,* se croiser les bras; *to* ~ *sth. up,* replier qqch.; [Fam.] *to* ~ *up,* plier bagages, [collapse] s'effondrer. || **folder** [-ər] *n.* **1.** plieur *m* (de journaux, &c.). **2.** chemise *f,* dossier *m.* **3.** [Com.] dépliant *m*; prospectus *m* (plié). || **folding** [-ɪŋ] *adj.* pliant; repliable: ~ *camera,* appareil *m* pliant, folding *m*; ~ *chair,* chaise *f* pliante.

foliage ['fowlɪəʤ] *n.* feuillage *m,* †feuillée *f.*

folio ['fowlɪow] *n.* **1.** folio *m.* **2.** in folio *m.* || *v. tr.* paginer.

folk [fowk] *pl.* **folk, folks** [-s] *n.* **1.** peuple *m*: *country* ~, campagnards *mpl.* **2.** race *f*; nation *f.* **3.** *folks,* gens *mpl*; personnes *fpl*; *my* ~, les miens *mpl,* ma famille: *decent* ~, braves gens; *stage* ~, gens de théâtre; ~ *dance,* danse/campagnarde, rustique/. || **folklore** [-ˌlɔər] *n.* folklore *m*; traditions *fpl* populaires. || **folksy** [-sɪ] *adj.* [Fam.] sociable, liant; populaire.

follow ['falow] *v. tr.* **1.** suivre; marcher derrière, se suivre: *Follow me!,* Suivez-moi!; *Days* ~ *one another,* Les jours se suivent. **2.** découler de: *Misery follows war,* La guerre/sème, apporte/la misère. **3.** suivre, se conformer à: *to* ~ *s.o.'s advice,* suivre le conseil de qqun; *to* ~ *suit,* emboîter le pas (à qqun). **4.** suivre (un exposé), prêter attention à (un discours); comprendre (une explication); embrasser (la profession de . . .). || *v. intr.* **1.** aller, venir/à la suite de: *as follows,* comme suit; *to* ~ *close behind s.o.,* emboîter le pas à qqun; [Fig.] *to* ~ *in s.o.'s footsteps,* marcher dans les traces de qqun. **2.** s'ensuivre de, *It follows that,* Il s'ensuit que. || **follow up** [-'ʌp] *v. tr.* suivre (qqun, qqch.) de près; poursuivre (avec énergie); exploiter (un succès): *to* ~ *with,* faire suivre de: *to* ~ *a clue,* s'attacher à une indication. || **follower** [-ər] *n.* suivant *m*; disciple *m,* partisan *m.* || **following** [-ɪŋ] *adj.* suivant: *Please note the* ~, Prière de noter/la chose suivante, les faits suivants → ce qui suit/. || *n.* suite *f* (d'un prince); [Fam.] disciples *mpl,* partisans *mpl.*

folly ['falɪ] *n.* folie *f*; sottise *f,* bêtise *f.*

foment [ˌfow'mɛnt] *v. tr.* fomenter.

fond [fand] *adj.* **1.** affectueu|x, -se, aimant: *a* ~ *look,* un regard tendre. **2.** passionné (pour), fou (de). **3.** indulgent, bon (pour). **4.** (espoir) caressé, bercé, entretenu: *to be* ~ *of s.o.,* aimer, affectionner, avoir de l'attachement pour qqun; *they are* ~ *of each other,* ils s'aiment; *to be* ~ *of music,* être amateur de musique; *to be* ~ *of doing sth.,* aimer à faire qqch.

fondle [-l] *v. tr.* caresser, choyer.

fondly [-lɪ] *adv.* [passionately] follement, passionnément; [foolishly] naïvement. || **fondness** [-nəs] *n.* tendresse *f,* affection *f* (pour); passion *f* (pour), goût *m* (de).

font [fant] *n.* **1.** fonts *mpl* baptismaux. **2.** bénitier *m.*

food [fuwd] *n.* **1.** nourriture *f,* aliments *mpl*: *to take* ~, → s'alimenter: *Ministry of Food,* ministère *m* du Ravitaillement. **2.** [foodstuff] produits *m,* denrées *f*/alimentaires; alimentation *f.* [NB. In this sense avoid *nourriture*]: *Frozen foods,* produits congelés; *sea-food,* fruits *mpl* de mer, dégustation *f* de rocaille; *good* ~, → bonne cuisine *f*: ~ *and clothing,* le vivre et le vêtement; ~ *and drink,* le boire et le manger; *tinned* ~, des conserves *fpl*; [Fig.] *to give s.o.* ~ *for thought,* donner/à penser, à réfléchir/à qqun; donner matière à réflexion.

fool [fuwl] *n.* **1.** sot *m*; imbécile *m*; idiot *m.* **2.** fou *m* (du roi); bouffon *m*: *to play the* ~, faire/le pitre, l'idiot/. **3.** dupe: *to make a* ~ *of s.o.,* berner, mystifier/qqun; *silly* ~ *!,* espèce d'idiot! || *v. tr.* **1.** faire la bête: *stop fooling,* assez de bêtises. **2.** se payer la tête de (qqun), berner (qqun); *to* ~ *around,* gâcher son temps; flâner; *to* ~ *away,* dissiper, dilapider. || **foolhardy** [ˌfuwl'haərdɪ] *adj.* téméraire. || **foolish**

[-ɪʃ] *adj.* **1.** sot, étourdi; insensé, fou. **2.** absurde; ridicule. || **foolishly** [-ɪʃlɪ] *adv.* **1.** follement; étourdiment. **2.** sottement, bêtement. || **foolishness** [-ɪʃnəs] *n.* **1.** folie *f*; étourderie *f*. **2.** sottise *f*; bêtise *f*.

foolscap [ˈfʊlskæp] *n.* [Fr.] format *m* ministre.

foot [fʊt] *pl.* **feet** [fijt] *n.* **1.** pied *m* (d'homme, d'animal à sabot); patte *f* (d'un chat, d'un chien, d'oiseau): *to be on one's feet*, se tenir debout; *to stamp one's* ~, taper du pied. **2.** semelle *f*, pied *m* (d'un bas); bas bout *m* (d'une table); pied *m* (d'un lit); base *f* (d'une colonne); patte *f* (d'un verre à boire). **3.** [coll., Mil.] l'infanterie *f*. **4.** [Meas.] pied *m* (anglais): *A yard has three feet*, © Trois pieds font une verge. **5.** [poetry] pied *m*: [Loc.] *at the* ~ *of the page*, au bas de la page; *to find one's feet*, voler de ses propres ailes; *to have one* ~ *in the grave*, avoir un pied dans la tombe; *to put one's best* ~ *forward*, faire de son mieux; *to put one's* ~ *down*, faire acte d'autorité; *to put one's* ~ *in it*, se mettre les pieds dans les plats, faire une gaffe; *to set on* ~, (re)mettre sur pied, (r)établir; *to step off on the wrong* ~, partir du mauvais pied; prendre un mauvais départ; *on* ~, (1) à pied, (2) debout, (3) en train, sur pied; *under* ~, (être) dans le chemin de qqun); *to trample under* ~, fouler aux pieds. || *v. tr.* **1.** rempiéter (un bas); faire un pied à (un bas). **2.** *to* ~ *it*, marcher, faire le trajet à pied. || *v. intr.* **1.** danser. **2.** *to* ~ *(up) an account*, additionner un compte: *to* ~ *the bill*, payer la note, les dépenses; payer la casse. || **football** [-ˌbɔl] *n.* **1.** ballon *m*. **2.** le football. || **foot brake** [-ˌbɹejk] frein *m* à pied. || **foothold** [-ˌhowld] *n.* **1.** prise *f* pour le pied: *to get a* ~, prendre pied. **2.** [Fig.] point *m* d'appui. || **footing** [-ɪŋ] *n.* équilibre *m*: *to gain a* ~, prendre pied, s'implanter; *to be on an equal* ~ *with*, être sur un pied d'égalité avec; *to be on a friendly* ~, être en bons termes; ~ *(up)*, addition *f* (d'une colonne de chiffres). || **footlights** [-ˌlajts] *n.* [Theat.] rampe *f* (de la scène. || **footpath** [-ˌpæθ] *n.* sentier *m* (pour piétons). || **footprint** [-ˌpɹɪnt] *n.* empreinte *f* de pas. || **footstep** [-ˌstɛp] *n.* pas *m*; empreinte *f* de pas; marche *f* (d'escalier): *to follow in s.o.'s footsteps*, marcher sur les traces de qqun. || **footwear** [-ˌwɛɚ] *n.* chaussures *fpl*: *rubber* ~ chaussures *fpl* en caoutchouc.

fop [fɑp] *n.* fat *m*, dameret *m*, bellâtre *m*.

for [foɚ] *prep.* [☞ In some cases, the Fr. equivalent is not needed.] **1.** pour, au profit de: *Do this* ~ *me*, Faites ça pour moi; *ten* ~ *a dollar*, dix pour un dollar; *vote* ~ *X*, votez pour X; *books* ~ *children*, → livres *mpl* d'enfants. **2.** pour, par, à cause de: *The Niagara peninsula is famous* ~ *its fruit*, La péninsule de N. est renommée pour ses fruits; *He was named* ~ *his father*, → Il a reçu le nom de son père; *He was punished* ~ *stealing*, Il fut puni pour avoir volé. **3.** pour, dans la mesure où: *John is tall* ~ *his age*, Il est grand pour son âge. **4.** pour, en échange de: *He sold it* ~ *$100*, Il l'a vendu(e) cent dollars; *ten* ~ *a dollar*, dix pour un dollar; *a cheque* ~ *5 dollars*, un chèque de 5 dollars; ~ *nothing*, [Fam.] ~ *free*, pour rien, gratuit. **5.** pour, à destination de: *He left* ~ *Ottawa*, Il partit pour O.; *the train* ~ *O.*, le train (à destination) d'O. **6.** pour, à la place de, pour le compte de; *Do it* ~ *me*, Faites-le à ma place; *to sign* ~ *s.o.*, signer/à la place de, pour/qqun. **7.** pendant: *We walked* ~ */an hour, 3 miles/*, Nous marchâmes (pendant) une heure, trois milles; *He is going away* ~ *a month*, Il part pour un mois; *He will be gone* ~ *a month*, Il sera absent pendant un mois. **8.** il y a, depuis: *She has been in Quebec* ~ *three weeks*, Il y a trois semaines qu'elle est à Q., Elle est à Q. depuis trois semaines. [☞ Note tenses in Eng. & Fr.] **9.** [☞ No equivalent needed in Fr.]: *Write* ~ *our pamphlet*, Demandez notre brochure; *Call* ~ *a taxi*, Appelez un taxi; *A doctor was sent* ~, On alla chercher le docteur. **10.** en dépit de: ~ *all his faults*, en dépit de, malgré/tous ses défauts. **11.** en faveur de: *He is* ~ *co-education*, Il est/partisan de, pour/ l'enseignement mixte; *He is* ~ *doing it now*, Il est en faveur de le faire tout de suite. **12.** [infin. clause constructions] que, pour que, + subjunc.; de + infin.: *It is useless* ~ *me to do that*, Il est inutile que je fasse cela, Il m'est inutile de faire cela; *We did that* ~ *him to be happy*, Nous avons fait cela/pour qu'il soit heureux, pour le rendre heureux/; *It is* ~ *you to decide*, C'est à vous de décider; *He said* ~ *me to do that*, Il m'a dit de faire cela; *He said* ~ *that to be done*, Il a dit de faire cela. **13.** [Loc.] ~ *instance*, par exemple; ~ *a fact*, de source sûre; ~ *short*, en abrégé; ~ *Heaven's sake*, pour l'amour de Dieu, © pour l'amour; *What* ~ *?*, Pourquoi *?*; *What is that* ~ *?*, A quoi sert cela ? ; *He's* ~ *it!*, Il va se faire attraper; *He was no farther ahead* ~ *it*, Il n'en était pas plus avancé (pour cela); *For/myself, my part/*,

Pour/ma part, moi/, Quant à moi; ∼ *all I know*, pour autant que je sache; *word* ∼ *word*, mot pour mot. cf. BUT, AS. || *conj.* car, parce que: *Don't leave now,* ∼ *I have to speak to you,* Ne partez pas, car j'ai à vous parler.

F.O.R. [= free on rail] franco gare, franco sur wagon.

forage [ˈfɔɚəʤ] *n.* fourrage *m.*

foray [ˈfɔɚej] *n.* incursion *f*, raid *m*, razzia *f.* || *v. tr.* saccager, piller; faire une incursion dans (un pays).

forbade cf. FORBID.

†**forbear** [fɔɚ|ˈbɛɚ], **forbore** [-ˈbɔɚ], **forborne** [-ˈboɚn] *v. tr.* cesser, s'abstenir de (qqch.): *to* ∼ *reading*, cesser de lire. || *v. intr.* **1.** s'abstenir, s'empêcher/(de): *to* ∼ *from thinking of sth.*, se garder de penser à qqch. **2.** patienter. || [ˈfɔɚˌbɛɚ] *n.* ancêtre *m.*

forbid [fɚ|ˈbɪd], **forbade** [-ˈbæd], **forbid, forbidden** *v. tr.* **1.** défendre, prohiber. **2.** empêcher: *God forbid* (*that . . .*)*!*, A Dieu ne plaise (que + subj.)!; *I* ∼ *you the house,* Je vous interdis l'entrée de la maison. || **forbidden** [-ˈbɪdn̩] *adj.* interdit. || **forbidding** [-ˈbɪdɪŋ] *adj.* rebutant, rébarbatif: *a* ∼ *face*, un visage sinistre.

forbore cf. FORBEAR.

forborne cf. FORBEAR.

force [fɔɚs] *n.* **1.** [physical] force *f*, énergie *f*, puissance *f.* **2.** violence *f*; contrainte *f*: *by sheer* ∼ , à force de; [Fig.] *in* ∼ , en vigueur. **3.** influence *f*, autorité *f*; [number] corps *m* (de police, &c.): *the police* ∼ , la police; *office* ∼ , personnel *m* de bureau; [armed] *forces*, l'armée *f*; les forces *fpl* armées. || *v. tr.* contraindre, obliger, forcer (qqun à faire qqch.): *to* ∼ *sth. into*, faire entrer qqch. de force dans; *to* ∼ *out of*, arracher, faire sortir/de force (de). || *v. tr.*: *to* ∼ *a safe*, forcer un coffre-fort; *to* ∼ *a door*, enfoncer une porte. || **forced** [fɔɚst] *adj.* forcé.

forceful [ˈfoɚs|fl] *adj.* fort, puissant; [style] vigoureux. || **forcible** [-ɪbl̩] *adj.* violent, énergique. || **forcibly** [-ɪblɪ] *adv.* fortement, énergiquement; [using force] par, de/force.

ford [fɔɚd] *n.* gué *m.* || *v. tr.* passer, traverser/(une rivière) à gué.

fore[1] [fɔɚ] *adj.* antérieur, de devant: *the* ∼ *part*, la partie *f* antérieure, le devant *m.* || *n.*: *to come to the* ∼ , se mettre/en avant, au premier plan/. || **fore-**[2] [Préfixe indiquant une position ou un mouvement vers l'avant]. || **forearm** [-ˌɑɚm] *n.* avant-bras *m.* || *v. tr.* prémunir. || **forebode** [-ˈbowd] *v. tr.* pressentir; [predict] présager.

forecast [-ˈkæst], **forecast, forecast,** *v. tr.* prédire, pronostiquer (les événements, le temps). || *n.* [ˈfɔɚkæst] prédiction *f*, prévision *f*: *weather* ∼ , [Fr.] prévisions *fpl* météorologiques, © pronostics *mpl* de la température.

foreclosure [ˌfɔɚˈklowʒɚ] *n.* [Jur.] forclusion *f.*

forefather [-ˌfɑðɚ] *n.* ancêtre *m*, aïeul *m*, *pl.* aïeux.

forefinger [-ˌfɪŋgɚ] *n.* index *m.*

forefoot [-ˌfʊt] *n.* patte *f* de devant.

foregoing [ˈfɔɚ|ˌgowɪŋ] *adj.* précédent. || **foregone** [-gan] *adj.* décidé d'avance, prévu: *It was a* ∼ *conclusion*, L'issue (en) était fatale.

foreground [ˈfɔɚˌgɹawnd] *n.* premier plan *m*: *in the* ∼ , au premier plan.

forehead [ˈfoɚˌhɛd] *n.* front *m*: *receding* ∼ , front fuyant.

foreign [ˈfoɚɪn] *adj.* étranger (*to*, à): *a* ∼ *land*, un pays étranger; ∼ *service*, service *m* diplomatique; ∼ *trade*, commerce *m* extérieur. || **foreigner** [-ɚ] *n.* étrang|er, -ère.

forelock [ˈfɔɚ|ˌlɑk] *n.* mèche *f* (de cheveux) sur le front.

fore|man *pl.* **-men** [-mən] *n.* contremaître *m*, chef *m* d'équipe.

foremast [ˈfɔɚˌmæst] *n.* [Mar.] mât *m* de misaine.

foremost [-ˌmowst] *adj.* le premier [Fig.] le plus en vue: *to be first and* ∼ , être le premier dans tout. || *adv.* en premier, au premier rang: *I went* ∼ , Je marchais le premier.

forenoon [-ˌnuwn] *n.* matinée *f*, © avant-midi *m.* cf. MORNING.

forerunner [ˌɹʌnɚ] *n.* précurseur *m*, avant-coureur *m.*

foresaw cf. FORESEE. || **foresee** [fɔɚ|ˈsij] **foresaw** [-ˈsɔ] **foreseen** [-ˈsijn] *v. tr.* prévoir; entrevoir.

foresight [ˈfɔɚˌsajt] *n.* prévision *f*; prévoyance *f*; [rifle] mire *f*: *want of* ∼ , imprévoyance *f.*

forest [ˈfoɚəst] *n.* forêt *f.* || *attrib.* de la forêt: ∼ *-guard*, garde-forestier *m*; ∼ *tree*, arbre *m* forestier.

forestall [ˌfoɚˈstɔl] *v. tr.* anticiper, prévenir.

forester [ˈfɔɚəst|ɚ] *n.* garde-forestier *m.* || **forestry** [-ɪɪ] *n.* sylviculture *f*: *School of* ∼ , © École forestière, [Fr.] Eaux & forêts *fpl.*

foretell [fɔɚ|ˈtɛl], **foretold** [-ˈtowld], **foretold** *v. tr.* prédire, présager.

forethought [ˈfɔɚˌθɑt] *n.* prévoyance *f.*

forever [fɚˈɛvɚ] *adv.* **1.** pour jamais. **2.** toujours.

forewarn [ˌfɔɚˈwɔɚn] *v. tr.* avertir, prévenir.

foreword [ˈfɔɚˌwɚd] *n.* avant-propos *m.*

forfeit [ˈfɔɚfə|t] *n.* amende *f,* pénalité *f,* déchéance *f.* || *v. tr.* être déchu de, perdre; confisquer: *to ~ a right,* perdre un droit. || **forfeiture** [-tʃɚ] *n.* perte *f,* confiscation *f*; déchéance *f,* forfaiture *f.*

forgave cf. FORGIVE.

forge [fɔɚdʒ] *n.* forge *f.* || *v. tr.* forger (un métal); [Fig.] **1.** forger (une histoire, de toutes pièces), inventer. **2.** falsifier (un acte); contrefaire (une signature). || **forgery** [-ɚɪ] *n.* falsification *f,* contrefaçon *f*; [document, crime] faux *m.*

forget [fɚ|ˈgɛt] **forgot** [-ˈgɑt] **forgotten** [-ˈgɑtn̩] *v. tr.* **1.** oublier. **2.** perdre le souvenir de; omettre involontairement: *to ~ how time goes,* perdre la notion du temps: *to ~ o.s.,* s'oublier, se laisser aller, manquer aux bienséances; *I forgot myself,* Ça m'a échappé. || *v. intr.* oublier (*to,* de). || **forgetful** [-ˈgɛtfl̩] *adj.* **1.** oublieux: *He is very ~,* Il a (une) très mauvaise mémoire. **2.** distrait, négligent. || **forgetfulness** [-ˈgɛtfl̩nəs] *n.* **1.** manque *m* (habituel) de mémoire. **2.** négligence *f*; inattention *f*: *a moment of ~,* un moment d'oubli.

forget-me-not [fɚˈgɛtmɪˌnɑt] *n.* [Bot.] myosotis *m.*

forgive [fɚ|ˈgɪv], **forgave** [-ˈgejv], **forgiven** [-ˈgɪvn̩] *v. tr.* pardonner (qqch. à qqun), faire grâce (de qqch. à qqun). || **forgiveness** [-ˈgɪvnəs] *n.* **1.** pardon *m.* **2.** clémence *f*; indulgence *f*; [Rel.] [sins] absolution *f.* || **forgiving** *adj.* indulgent, clément; sans rancune.

forgo [-ˈgow], **forwent** [-ˈwɛnt], **forgone** [-ˈgɑn] *v. tr.* renoncer à, s'abstenir de/(qqch.).

forgot, forgotten cf. FORGET.

fork [fɔɚk] *n.* **1.** [food] fourchette *f*; [hay, &c.] fourche *f.* cf. PITCHFORK. **2.** [Fig.] bifurcation *f*; [river] © fourche *f*; [branch] branche *f* fourchue; [Mus.] *tuning fork,* diapason *m.* || *v. tr.* remuer à la fourche. || *v. intr.* [road] fourcher, bifurquer. || **forked** [-t] *adj.* fourchu.

forlorn [ˌfɔɚˈlɔɚn] *adj.* abandonné [Fig.] désespéré, perdu.

form [fɔɚm] *n.* **1.** [shape] forme *f*; silhouette *f*: *in the ~ of,* sous forme de; [text]: *~ and substance,* la forme et le fond. **2.** [metal] moule *m,* forme *f*; [Adm.] formule *f*: *printed ~,* imprimé *m*; *to fill/in, up/a ~,* remplir une formule, un formulaire. **3.** condition *f,* forme *f*: *in, out of/ ~,* être, ne pas être/en forme. **4.** sorte *f,* forme *f*: *Heat is a ~ of energy,* La chaleur est une forme de l'énergie. **5.** étiquette *f,* convenances *fpl*; formalité *f*: *good ~,* le bon ton, savoir-vivre *m*; *It's not good ~,* → Cela ne se fait pas; *a matter of ~,* une formalité; *for form's sake,* pour la forme. **6.** [Sch., Br. & Ont.] classe *f*; banc *m.* || **form** *v. tr.* former, façonner, donner la forme de (*after,* d'après, sur; *out of,* de); [Fig.] former (un gouvernement); organiser, constituer (une compagnie); *to ~ good habits,* contracter de bonnes habitudes; *to ~ an idea,* se faire une idée. || *v. intr.* se former, prendre forme de; devenir, se changer en: [Mil.] *to ~ into line,* se mettre en ligne; *to ~ into a square,* se former en carré, former le carré.

formal [ˈfɔɚməl] *adj.* **1.** [Techn.] formel. **2.** minutieux; affecté; formaliste. **3.** officiel, cérémonieu|x, -se: *~ dinner,* dîner *m*/prié, officiel/.

formality [fɚˈmælɪtɪ] *n.* formalité *f*: *a mere ~,* une simple formalité; [stiffness] → avec cérémonie, cf. FORMAL. || **formally** [ˈfɔɚməlɪ] *adv.* **1.** formellement, expressément; conformément à un rite établi. **2.** cérémonieusement, d'un ton guindé. || **formation** [fɚˈmejʃən] *n.* formation *f.* || **formative** [ˈfɔɚmətɪv] *adj.* de formation; formatif.

former [ˈfɔɚmɚ] *adj.* antérieur; précédent; ancien: *in ~ times,* à une époque reculée; *~ times,* le passé; *my ~ students,* mes anciens élèves; *her ~ letters,* ses lettres précédentes. || *pron.* celui-là *m,* celle-là *f,* ceux-là *mpl,* celles-là *fpl*: *of the two theories, I prefer the ~,* des deux théories, je préfère/celle-là, la première. || *adv.* autrefois, jadis; auparavant. || **formerly** [ˈfɔɚmɚlɪ] *adv.* anciennement, autrefois.

formidable [ˈfɔɚmɪdəbl̩] *adj.* redoutable, formidable.

formul|a [ˈfɔɚmjəl|ə] *pl.* **as** [-əz] **-ae** [-ɪ] *n.* formule *f,* modèle *m*; [Med.] recette *f* [Theol.] profession *f* de foi. || **formulate** [-ˌejt] *v. tr.* formuler; [Fig.] articuler, développer.

forsake [ˌfɔɚ|ˈsejk], **forsook** [-ˈsʊk], **forsaken** [-ˈsejkən] *v. tr.* abandonner, délaisser; renoncer à. || **forsaken** *adj.* délaissé; abandonné.

forswear [ˌfɔɚ|swɛɚ], **forswore** [-ˈswɔɚ], **forsworn** [-ˈswɔɚn] *v. tr.* **1.** abjurer, renier/qqch. **2.** *~ o.s.,* se parjurer.

fort [fɔɚt] *n.* fort *m*; forteresse *f*: [Fig.] *to hold the ~,* gérer la maison; assurer la permanence (en l'absence des chefs); *to hold a ~,* défendre une forteresse, tenir une position.

forth [fɔɚθ] *adv.* **1.** en avant, dehors: *to*

put ~, avancer; *to set* ~, avancer, exposer (une théorie); *back and* ~, de long en large; *and so* ~, (et) ainsi de suite; et cetera. **2.** dehors: *to sally* ~, sortir; se mettre en route.

forthcoming ['fɔɚθˌkʌmɪŋ] *adj.* [season, book] prêt à paraître, prochain. || **forthright** ['fɔɚθˌɹajt] *adj.* franc, qui va droit au but. || **forthwith** ['fɔɚθ'wɪð] *adv.* immédiatement, sans retard *m.*

fortieth ['fɔɚtɪəθ] *adj.* quarantième cf. FORTY.

fortification [ˌfɔɚtɪfɪ'kejʃən] *n.* fortification *f*, place *f* forte || **fortify** ['fɔɚtɪˌfaj] *v. tr.* fortifier (une ville, un poste); [Fig.] (r)affermir (le courage). || **fortitude** ['fɔɚtɪˌtjuwd] *n.* force *f* d'âme, courage *m* (dans la peine, dans l'adversité); patience *f.*

fortnight ['fɔɚtˌnajt] *n.* [surtout Br.] quinzaine *f* (de jours): *a* ~ *hence*, dans une quinzaine, d'aujourd'hui en quinze: *every* ~, tous les quinze jours; *tomorrow* ~, de demain en quinze.

fortress ['fɔɚtɹəs] *n.* forteresse *f.*

fortuitous [ˌfɔɚ'tjuwɪtəs] *adj.* fortuit, imprévu.

fortunate ['fɔɚtʃənət] *adj.* **1.** fortuné, heureux, © à l'aise: *to be* ~, avoir de la chance. || **fortunately** [-lɪ] *adv.* heureusement, par chance, par bonheur. || **fortune** ['fɔɚtʃən] *n.* **1.** fortune *f*; richesse *f*; biens *mpl.* **2.** destin(ée) *m(f)*, sort *m*; [luck] bonne, mauvaise/fortune: † ~ *favours him*, → La chance lui sourit; *to tell s.o.'s* ~, dire la bonne aventure à qqun, [by cards] tirer les cartes à qqun. || **fortune-teller** [ˌtelɚ] *n.* diseur *m*, diseuse *f*/de bonne aventure.

forty ['fɔɚtɪ] *adj.* quarante: *about* ~ *students*, une quarantaine d'étudiants; *she'll never see* ~ *again*, elle a passé la quarantaine.

forward ['fɔɚwɚd] *adv.* **1.** en avant: *Move* ~ *!*, Avancez!; *straight* ~, tout droit; *Forward!*, En avant!; *to put* ~, avancer (une opinion); *to push o.s.* ~, se mettre/ en avant, en vue/. **2.** à l'avant: *The crew's quarters are* ~, Le logement de l'équipage est à l'avant. || *adj.* avant; de, sur/l'avant; [Fig.] [child] précoce, en avance; [bold] audacieux, entreprenant; [Pej.]effronté.|| *n.* [Sport.] avant *m.* || *v. tr.* expédier, envoyer; *Please* ~, Prière de faire suivre; [Fig.] favoriser (un projet, &c.).

fossil ['fɑsɪl] *n. & adj.* fossile *m.*

foster ['fɑstɚ] *v. tr.* nourrir, élever (un enfant); [Fig.] stimuler, encourager. || *adj.* adopti|f, -ve, nourrici|er, -ère: ~ *-brother*, frère de lait; ~ *-father*, père adoptif; ~ *-mother*, mère adoptive.

fought cf. FIGHT.

foul [fawl] *adj.* immonde; infect; nauséabond; [water] bourbeux, trouble; [air] malsain, vicié; [weather] mauvais; [unpleasant] odieux, infâme; [behaviour] malhonnête; [language] grossier, ordurier. || *n.* [baseball] faute *f*; [boxing] coup/ irrégulier, bas/. || *v. tr.* **1.** souiller (un nid, &c.), salir. **2.** [Sport] violer la règle du jeu.

found[1] cf. FIND.

found[2] [fawnd] *v. tr.* **1.** fonder, créer, instituer. **2.** [Metall]. fondre (les métaux).

foundation [ˌfawn'dejʃən] *n.* fondation *f*, fondement *m*, base *f*: *the foundations of a building*, les fondements d'un édifice; *to dig the foundations*, creuser les fondations; ~ *stone*, pierre/d'angle, angulaire/; *to lay the* ~ *stone*, poser la première pierre; [Fig.] *the foundations of music*, les bases de la musique. **2.** établissement *m.* **3.** institution *f* dotée.

founder[1] ['fawnd|ɚ] *n.* fondat|eur, -rice.

founder[2] *n.* [Metall.] fondeur *m.*

foundling [-lɪŋ] *n.* enfant trouvé(e).

foundry [-ɹɪ] *n.* fonderie *f.*

fountain ['fawntən] *n.* fontaine *f*, jet *m* d'eau: ~ *pen*, stylo *m*; *soda* ~, *limonaderie *f.* [Fig.] source *f*, cause *f* première.

four [fɔɚ] *adj.* quatre: *on all fours*, à quatre pattes; ~ *-engined*, quadrimoteur *m*; ~ *-footed*, quadrupède; *the dog is a* ~ *-footed animal*, le chien est un quadrupède. || **fourscore** [-'skɔɚ] *adj.* quatre-vingts: *a man of* ~, un octogénaire. || **fourteen** [fɔɚ'tijn] *adj.* quatorze. || **fourteenth** [-θ] *adj.* quatorzième; [kings, days] quatorze: *Louis the* ~, Louis XIV; *on the* ~, le quatorze. || **fourth** [fɔɚθ] *adj.* quatrième. || *n.* quart *m*; [Mus.] quarte *f.* || **fourthly** [-lɪ] *adv.* quatrièmement.

fowl [fawl] *pl.* **fowls** **1.** oiseau *m*; [coll.] les oiseaux. **2.** [poultry] volaille *f*: *to keep fowls*, élever de la volaille.

fox [fɑks] *pl.* **foxes** [the female is VIXEN]. **1.** renard *m*: ~ *cub*, renardeau *m*; *a sly* ~, un madré, un fin matois. || **foxy** [-ɪ] *adj.* rusé, madré, astucieu|x, -se.

Fr. [= FRENCH] || **fr., frs.** [= FRANC, FRANCS].

fraction ['fɹæk|ʃən] *n.* fraction *f*; fragment *m.* || **fracture** [-tʃɚ] *n.* [bone] fracture *f*; rupture *f*; [Geol.] cassure *f.* || *v. tr.* briser, rompre; [Med.] fracturer. || *v. intr.* se briser, se rompre; [of limb] se fracturer.

fragile ['fɹædʒajl] *adj.* fragile; [delicate] frêle.

fragment ['fɹægmənt] *n.* fragment *m.*

fragrance ['fɹejgɹən|s] *n.* parfum *m*; bonne odeur *f.* || **fragrant** [-t] *adj.* parfumé, embaumé.

frail [fɹejl] *adj.* [Moral] fragile, faible; [body] frêle. || **frailty** [-tɪ] *n.* fragilité *f.*

frame]fɹejm] *n.* structure *f,* charpente *f,* forme *f*: ~ *of mind,* disposition *f* d'esprit; [picture, bicycle] cadre *m*; [embroidery] métier *m*; [window, car] châssis *m*; [bed] bois *m* de lit; [glasses] monture *f*; [Pers.] stature *f*: *a* ~ *house,* une maison en bois. || *v. tr.* former, charpenter, construire; encadrer (un tableau); inventer, ourdir (un complot); [Sl.] ~ *up,* coup monté. || **framework** [-ˌwɚk] *n.* charpente *f*; squelette *m.*

franc [fɹæŋk] *n.* franc *m*: *new French* ~, nouveau franc, NF; *a five* ~ *coin,* une pièce de cinq francs.

France [fɹæns] *n.* la France: *in, to/* ~, en France.

Frances [fɹænsəs] *n.f.* = Françoise.

franchise ['fɹæntʃajz] *n.f.* **1.** [Hist., Jur.] franchise *f,* privilège *m,* immunité *f*; [Com.] concession *f,* privilège *m.* **2.** [Pol.] droit *m* de vote.

Francis [fɹænsɪs] *n.m.* = François.

Francophile ['fɹæŋkow|ˌfajl] *adj.* & *n.* francophile (*m*). || **Francophobe** [-ˌfowb] *adj.* & *n.* francophobe (*m*).

frank [fɹæŋk] *adj.* franc, sincère; [action] franc, direct, ouvert. || *n.* franchise *f* postale. || *v. tr.* envoyer en franchise postale.

frankfurter [-ˌfɚtɚ] *n.* (saucisse *f* de) Francfort; [Fam.] **frank(s)** [-s] *n.*

frankly [-lɪ] *adv.* franchement, sincèrement.

frantic ['fɹæntɪk] *adj.* désespéré, ne sachant plus à quel saint se vouer.

fraternal [fɹə'tɚn|əl] *adj.* fraternel, de frère. || **fraternity** [-ɪtɪ] *n.* **1.** fraternité *f.* **2.** confrérie *f*; [Univ.] club *m* d'étudiants. || **fraternize** ['fɹætɚˌnajz] *v. intr.* fraterniser.

fraud [fɹɔd] *n.* fraude *f,* supercherie *f*; [Pers.] imposteur *m.* || **fraudulent** [-jələnt] *adj.* frauduleux.

fray [fɹej] *n.* échauffourée *f,* bagarre *f,* mêlée *f.* || *v. tr.* érailler, effiler. || *v. intr.* s'érailler, s'effiler. || *n.* éraillure *f.*

freak [fɹijk] *n.* caprice *m*; [of nature] phénomène *m.*; [Fam.] curiosité *f.*

freckle [fɹɛkl̩] *n.* tache *f* de rousseur || **freckled** [-d] *adj.* **1.** qui a des taches de rousseur. **2.** moucheté.

free [fɹij] *adj.* libre (*to, from,* de); [manner] désinvolte, sans façons; exempt de; [no cost] gratuit; généreux, libéral, [supply] copieux; *to set* ~, libérer, [slave] affranchir; *to give s.o. a* ~ *hand,* donner carte blanche à qqun; ~ *and easy,* désinvolte, cavalier, sans façons; ~ *lance,* (écrivain *m,* journaliste *m*) à son compte, indépendant; ~ *postage,* franc(o) de port; ~ *trade,* libre-échange *m*; ~ *thinker,* libre-penseur *m*; ~ *will,* libre arbitre *m*; ~ *wheel,* roue *f* libre. || *adv.* gratuit, gratis; franco: *delivered* ~, franco à domicile. || *v. tr.* **1.** délivrer, libérer; affranchir (un esclave). **2.** débarrasser (de); dégager. || **freedom** [-dəm] *n.* **1.** liberté *f,* indépendance *f.* **2.** franchise *f,* exemption *f.* **3.** sans-gêne *m.* || **freely** *adv.* **1.** librement; volontairement; sans contrainte. **2.** franchement. || **freemason** [-ˌmejsn̩] *n.* franc-maçon *m.* || **freemasonry** [-ˌmejsn̩ɹɪ] *n.* franc-maçonnerie *f.* || **free press** [-'pɹɛs] → liberté *f* de la presse.

freeze [fɹijz], **froze** [fɹowz], **frozen** [-n̩] *v. tr.* geler, congeler; [Fig.] glacer: *frozen meat,* viande *f* congelée. || *v. intr.* geler, se congeler: *Water freezes at* 32° *F,* L'eau gèle à 32 F; [Fig.] être glacé, transi. || **freezer** ['fɹijz|ɚ] *n.* (*home*) *freezer,* congélateur *m* (familial). || **freezing** [-ɪŋ] *n.* congélation *f*; gel *m*: ~ *point,* point *m* de congélation; *deep* ~, congélation (à basse température).

freight [fɹejt] *n.* **1.** fret *m*; chargement *m*; cargaison *f.* **2.** transport *m* (de marchandises): ~ *train,* train *m* de marchandises. || **freighter** [-ɚ] *n.* cargo *m.*

French [fɹɛntʃ] *n.* **1.** le français, la langue française; © le Canadien-français: *He speaks* ~ *quite well,* Il parle très bien (le) français; *Do you speak* ~ ?, Parlez-vous français ?; *I am learning* ~, J'apprends le français; ~ *-speaking,* francophone, → d'expression française; ~ *-speaking Canada,* le Canada français; ~ *-speaking Switzerland,* la Suisse romande. **2.** [Coll.] *the* ~, les Français; © les Canadiens français: *He is* ~, C'est un Français [☞ Use capital for noun only]; Il est français.

French *adj.* **1.** français (de France, d'Europe): *the* ~ *Regime,* le régime français au Canada; *the* ~ *Consul in Halifax,* le consul de France à Halifax; *the* ~ *representative,* le délégué de la France; [language] *to take* ~ *lessons,* prendre des leçons de français; *He is a good* ~ *speaker,* Il s'exprime bien en français, Il parle français couramment. **2.** canadien (français) cf. FRENCH CANADIAN [in Canada, the word French refers primarily to French Canadians]. **3.** [Loc.] ~ *artichoke,* artichaut *m* (comestible); ~ *bed,* lit *m* en portefeuille; ~ *blue,* outremer *m* artificiel; ~ *beans*, haricots *mpl* (verts, en biais); ~ *brandy*, cognac *m*; ~ *bread*, pain *m* (de fantaisie) © pain *m* français; ~ *briar*, bruyère *f*; pipe *f* de bruyère; ~ *bristles*, soies *fpl* (de sanglier); ~ *calf*; [shoes] calf, boxcalf *m*; ~ *cambric*, batiste *f*; mousseline *f* de coton; ~ *Canadian*, Canadien (français), Canadienne (française) cf. FRENCH 2; ~ *Canada*, (a) le Canada français; (b) la Nouvelle-France; le Québec; ~ *canvas*, toile *f* de tailleur; ~ *chalk*, craie *f* de tailleur; stéatite *f*; ~ *chestnut*, châtaigne *f*; marron *m* comestible; ~ *-cleaning*, nettoyage *m*, dégraissage *m*, [Fr.] nettoyage *m* américain; ~ *Coast*, © le Petit Nord; ~ *cuffs* [on pants], revers *mpl* (de pantalons); [sleeves] ~ *cuff*, manchette *f*; [art] ~ *curve*, pistolet *m*; ~ *drain*, puits *m* absorbant; [Culin.] ~ *dressing*, vinaigrette *f*; ~ *eaves*, gouttière *f*; ~ *endive*, chicorée *f*; ~ *foot*, © pied *m* francais [= 30, 4 cm.]; ~ *fried*, [also *French fries*], (pommes de terre) frites *fpl*, © patates *fpl* frites; ~ *frying*, friture *f*; ~ *heels*, talons *mpl* Louis XV; ~ *horn*, cor *m* (d'harmonie); ~ *ice cream*, crème *f* glacée; [Fr.] glace *f* (à la vanille, &c.); © crème à la glace (à la vanille, &c.); ~ *knitting*, queue *f* de rat; ~ *knot*, point *m* noué; ~ *lavender*, lavande *f*; *to take* ~ *leave*, filer à l'anglaise; ~ *Line*, La Compagnie *f* Générale Transatlantique; ~ *magpie*, pic-bois *m* moucheté; ~ *morocco*, maroquin *m*; [sea-food] ~ *mussel*, moule *f*; ~ *mustard*, moutarde *f* (de Dijon); ~ *nut*, marron *m* (comestible); [Fig.] ~ *pancake*, béret *m*; ~ *pastries*, pâtisseries *fpl*, © pâtisseries françaises; ~ *plum*, pruneau *m* d'Agen; ~ *polish*, vernis au tampon; ~ *polishing*, vernissage *m*, polissage *m*/au tampon; [Culin.] ~ (*pork*), porc *m* haché; ~ *rice*, épautre *m*; ~ *roll*, petit pain *m*; [Archit.] ~ *roof*, toit *m* à la Mansard; ~ *seam*, couture/rabattue, anglaise/; ~ *Shore*, © **1.** [West coast of Newfoundland, also *French Coast*; Treaty Shore] le petit Nord. **2.** [SW coast of Nova Scotia] Côte *f* aux Français; ~ *sole*, plie *f* limande *f*; [sewing] ~ *tack*, passant *m*; ~ *telephone*, combiné *m*; ~ *toast*, pain *m* perdu; canapé *m*; ~ *walnut*, noix *f* (comestible); ~ *wheat*, sarrasin *m* [also buckwheat]; ~ *wines*, © vins *mpl* français; [Fr.] vins *mpl* de France; ~ *wrestling*, lutte *f* gréco-romaine.

Frenchman *pl.* **men** [-mən] *n.m.* **1.** © Canadien-français *m*, Canadien *m*. **2.** Français *m*: *He is a* ~, C'est un Français, Il est français. **3.** vaisseau *m* (de guerre) français. || **Frenchwoman** [-ˌwumən] *pl.* **women** [-ˌwɪmən] *n.* **1.** © Canadienne-française, Canadienne *f.* **2.** Française *f.*

frenzied ['fɹɛnzɪ|d] *adj.* affolé, frénétique: ~ (*mob*), une foule furieuse.

frenzy *n.* frénésie *f*, [great excitement] délire *m*, folie *f.*

frequency ['fɹijkwənsɪ] *n.* fréquence *f.* || **frequent** [fɹɪ'kwənt] *v. tr.* fréquenter. || *adj.* ['fɹɪkwənt] fréquent; qui/arrive, se produit/souvent. || **frequently** [-lɪ] *adv.* fréquemment souvent.

fresh [fɹɛʃ] *adj.* **1.** fra|is, -iche: ~ *water*, eau douce. **2.** nouve|au, -lle: ~ *theory*, nouvelle théorie. **3.** désinvolte; impertinent. || **freshen** [-n̩] *v. tr.* rafraîchir. || *v. intr.* fraîchir; se rafraîchir. || **freshly** [-lɪ] *adv.* **1.** fraîchement. **2.** nouvellement.

fresh/man -men [-mən] *n.* étudiant *m* de première année; [Arg.] © navot *m*, gnochon *m*, [Fr.] bizuth *m*; novice *m* (dans/un art/une science).

freshness [-nəs] *n.* fraîcheur *f*; nouveauté *f.*

fret [fɹɛt] *n.* **1.** irritation *f*, agitation *f.* **2.** éraillure *f*, érosion *f*, usure *f.* **3.** [Arch.] grecque *f*; frette *f*: ~ *-saw*, scie *f* à découper. || *v. tr.* **[-tt-] 1.** inquiéter, tracasser (qqun). **2.** user, ronger, frotter. **3.** orner. || *v. intr.* s'irriter, se chagriner, se tourmenter.

friar ['fɹajɚ] *n.* moine *m*: [R.C.] *Grey* ~, Franciscain *m*; *Black* ~, Dominicain *m*; *White* ~, Carme *m.*

friction ['fɹɪkʃən] *n.* friction *f*; [rubbing] frottement *m*; [Fig.] désaccord *m*; [Elect.] ~ *tape*, ruban *m* isolant, [Fr.] chatterton *m.*

Friday ['fɹajdej] *n.* vendredi *m*: *Good* ~, Vendredi saint.

fridge [fɹɪʤ] *n.* [Fam.] [abr. de (re)frig(erator)] réfrigérateur *m*, [Fr.] frigidaire *m.*

fried cf. FRY.

friend ['fɹɛnd] *n.* ami, -e: *to make friends*, se faire des amis; *to make friends with s.o.*, se lier (d'amitié) avec qqun; *We are friends*, Nous sommes amis.

friendliness [-lɪnəs] *n.* disposition *f* amicale, bienveillance *f.* || **friendly** [-lɪ] *adj.* amical, sympathique: ~ *winds*, vents *mpl* propices: *a* ~ *country*, un pays ami. || *adv.* amicalement. || **friendship** [-ˌʃɪp] *n.* amitié *f*; sentiments *mpl*/d'amitié, amicaux/.

frig. cf. FRIDGE.

frigate ['fɹɪgət] *n.* frégate *f.*

fright [fɹajt] *n.* **1.** peur *f*; [stronger] frayeur *f*; [stronger still] épouvante *f*: *to take* ~, s'effrayer. **2.** [Fam.] épouvantail *m*;

personne *f* grotesque. || **frighten** [-n̩] *v. intr.* prendre peur, s'effrayer. || *v. tr.* effrayer, faire peur à; terrifier, épouvanter. || **frightful** [fl̩] *adj.* terrible, effroyable; [Fam.] désagréable, épouvantable. || **frightfully** [-fʊlɪ] *adv.* terriblement, effroyablement, affreusement.

frigid ['fɹɪʤɪd] *adj.* (très) froid; glacial; [Med.] frigide.

frill [fɹɪl] *n.* ruche *f,* jabot *m*; [*pl.*, Fig.] falbalas *mpl.*

fringe [fɹɪnʤ] *n.* [trimming] frange *f,* bordure *f*; [border] bord *m,* extrémité *f,* lisière *f* (d'un bois): *a* ~ *case,* un cas limite. || *v. tr.* [clothes] franger; [Fig.] border (une route); friser (la folie).

frippery ['fɹɪpɚɪ] *n.* camelote *f*; [gaudy] clinquant *m.*

frisk [fɹɪsk] *v. intr.* **1.** s'ébattre; gambader, folâtrer. **2.** [Sl.] palper, fouiller (qqun). *n.* gambade *f.* || **frisky** [-ɪ] *adj.* gai, vif, folâtre; [horse] fringant.

fritter ['fɹɪtɚ] *n.* beignet *m.* || *v. tr.* effriter; [Fig.] ~ *away,* gaspiller (son temps, &c.).

frivolity [fɹɪ'vɑlɪtɪ] *n.* frivolité *f.* || **frivolous** ['fɹɪvələs] *adj.* frivole; [trivial] futile, vain.

frizzle ['fɹɪzl̩] *v. tr.* faire/frire, griller/(du lard, &c.). || *v. intr.* grésiller; crépiter.

fro cf. TO AND FRO.

frock [fɹɑk] *n.* robe *f*; blouse *f*; [Rel.] froc *m*: ~ *-coat,* redingote *f.*

frog [fɹɑg] *n.* grenouille *f*; [Fig.] chat *m* dans la gorge. || **froggy** [-ɪ] *adj.* surnom donné aux Français. || **frogman** [-ˌmæn] *n.* homme-grenouille *m.*

frolic ['fɹɑlɪk] *n.* **1.** gaieté *f*; divertissements *mpl*; ébats *mpl.* **2.** bouffonnerie *f,* jeux *mpl.* **3.** espièglerie *f.* || *v. intr.* **1.** jouer, folâtrer, se divertir. **2.** jouer des tours, faire des fredaines.

from [fɹʌm] *prep.* **1.** [after verb of motion] de: *to come, take out, &c./* ~, venir sortir/de. **2.** [indicating motion after a verb of activity: ☞ use the prep. of position]: *to take sth.* ~ *the table,* prendre qqch. sur la table; *He learned it* ~ *a book,* Il l'a appris dans un livre; *to drink* ~ */a glass, the bottle/,* boire/dans un verre, à même la bouteille/. **3.** [origin] de; depuis: *Where are you* ~ *?,* D'où êtes-vous?; *passengers* ~ *Montreal,* les voyageurs/en provenance, venant/de M.; [on letter] From, Expéditeur; *Tell him* ~ *me that . . .,* Dites-lui de ma part que . . .; ~ *Toronto to Montreal,* de T. à M., depuis T. jusqu'à M.; ~ *Monday to Friday,* de lundi à vendredi, depuis lundi jusqu'à vendredi; (*as*) ~ *Tuesday,* à partir de mardi; ~ *the beginning,* depuis le début, [right ~] dès le début; ~ *time to time,* de temps en temps; ~ *door to door,* de porte en porte. **4.** [separation] de; à: *to separate, tell/* ~, séparer, distinguer/de; *to take sth.* ~ *s.o.,* prendre qqch. à qqun (cf. ENLEVER, ÔTER, ARRACHER, VOLER, EMPRUNTER, ÉCHAPPER, &c.); *far* ~, loin de. **5.** [other uses] *made* ~ *flour,* fait avec de la farine; [according to] ~ *what I hear,* d'après ce que j'apprends; [against] *shelter* ~ *the rain,* abri *m* contre la pluie; [because of] *to die* ~ *hunger,* mourir de faim; ~ *pity,* par pitié; *He fell sick* ~ *overeating,* Il tomba malade/d', pour/avoir trop mangé.

front [fɹʌnt] *n.* **1.** devant *m,* avant *m* (partie *f* antérieure); façade *f* (d'un édifice): *shirt* ~, le/devant, plastron/ d'une chemise; [Météor.] front *m*: *in* ~, devant, en avant, en tête; *at, in/the* ~, au premièr rang. **2.** [Mil.] le front (d'une armée); coalition *f*: [Pol.] *united* ~, front *m* commun. **3.** †[Anat.] front *m*; [Fig.] visage *m,* face *f*; attitude *f*; [Péj.] toupet *m*; front *m*; effronterie *f*; *in* ~ *of,* devant, en face de: *Look in* ~ *of you!,* Regardez devant vous! || *adj.* antérieur; de devant; (d')avant; de face: ~ *row,* premier rang; [vowel] antérieure, palatale; ~ *drive,* traction *f* avant; ~ *mounted engine,* moteur *m* avant; [Auto.] ~ *end,* train *m* avant. || *v. intr.* faire face à (qqch.); être tourné vers (qqch.): *windows that* ~ *the sea,* fenêtres qui donnent sur la mer. || *v. tr.* affronter; braver: *to* ~ *with,* confronter avec.

frontage ['fɹʌntəʤ] *n.* façade *f* (d'un édifice); [of a lot] largeur *f* (en bordure de la rue, &c.]; [exposure] exposition *f.* || **frontier** [fɹʌn'tijɚ] *n.* frontière *f,* confins *mpl.* (d'un pays, d'une zone): ~ *town,* ville frontière.

frost [fɹɑst] *n.* gelée *f*; [rime] givre *m*: *ground* ~, gelée blanche. || *v. tr.* **1.** geler; givrer (des vitres). **2.** [icing] glacer (un gâteau). || **frostbite** [-ˌbajt] *n.* [Méd.] engelure *f.* || **frostbitten** [-bɪtn̩] *adj.* gelé; brûlé par le froid. || **frosted** [-əd] *adj.* givré: ~ *glass,* verre *m* dépoli. || **frosty** [-ɪ] *adj.* [freezing] glacial, gelé: [covered with frost] givré, couvert de givre *m*; [Fig.] glacial.

froth [fɹɑθ] *n.* écume *f,* cf. FOAM; [on beer] © broue *f,* [Fr.] mousse *f.*

frown [fɹawn] *n.* froncement *m* de sourcils; regard *m* sévère. || *v. intr.* froncer le sourcil, se renfrogner: [Fig.] *to* ~ *upon sth.,* s'opposer à, être contraire à.

froze cf. FREEZE. || **frozen** cf. FREEZE. || *adj.* **1.** gelé; glacé; couvert (d'une couche) de glace. **2.** très froid; glacial. **3.** mort de froid; souffrant d'engelure. **4.** froid; insensible; sans coeur: ~ *to the spot in horror,* glacé, pétrifié/d'horreur; [Fin.] ~ *assets,* fonds *mpl* non liquides; © *Frozen North,* le Grand Nord (canadien).

fructify ['fɹʊktɪˌfaj] *v. tr.* féconder, fertiliser (une terre). || *v. intr.* produire son fruit.

frugal ['fɹuwgəl] *adj.* [meal] frugal, sobre; [saving] économe.

fruit [fɹuwt] *pl.* **fruits** [coll. fruit] *n.* **1.** fruit *m*; *dried* ~ , fruits *mpl* secs; *to bear* ~ , porter fruit; *the fruits of the earth,* les fruits de la terre. **2.** [Fig.] fruit *m*; résultat *m*; produit *m*.

frustrate ['fɹʌstɹejt] *v. tr.* **1.** frustrer (qqun de son dû]; tromper. **2.** faire échouer: *He frustrates our plans,* Il renverse nos projets. || **frustration** [fɹʌs'tɹejʃən] *n.* sentiment *m* d'impuissance, déception *f.*

fry [fɹaj] *v. tr.* faire frire: *fried eggs,* œufs sur le plat. || *v. intr.* frire. || *n.* **1.** friture *f*; plat *m* de viande frite. **2.** [Fr.] les gosses *m*; © les enfants, **3.** fretin *m*; alevin *m*: *small* ~ , menu fretin; le menu peuple; les petites gens. || **frying-pan** ['fɹajzŋˌpæn] *n.* poêle *f* (à frire): *to jump from the* ~ *into the fire,* tomber de Charybe en Scylla; tomber d'un mal dans un pire.

fudge [fʌʤ] *n.* fondant *m* (américain).

fuel [fjuwl] *n.* combustible *m*; [oil] carburant *m*; ~ *oil,* mazout *m*, © [abus.] huile *f.*

fugitive ['fjuwʤɪtɪv] *n.* fugitif *m*; [Army] déserteur *m*. || *adj.* fugiti/f, -ve, [fleeting] fugace.

fulcrum ['fʊlkɹəm] *n.* point *m* d'appui.

fulfil(l) [fʊl'fɪl] *v. tr.* [-ll-] **1.** accomplir (des prophéties). **2.** remplir (un engagement). **3.** combler: *to* ~ *a wish,* satisfaire un désir. || **fulfilment** [-mənt] *n.* accomplissement *m*.

full [fʊl] *adj.* **1.** plein, rempli: ~ *of (sth.),* plein de (qqch.); *look* ~ *of gratitude,* regard *m* chargé de reconnaissance; ~ *of hope,* rempli d'espoir. **2.** complet; entier: ~ *to the brim,* comble; ~ *meal,* repas *m* complet; ~ *weight,* poids *m* juste; ~ *measure,* mesure *f* comble; ~ *session,* assemblée *f* plénière; ~ *text,* texte *m* intégral; ~ *house,* salle *f* comble; ~ *professor,* professeur *m* titulaire; *at* ~ *speed,* à toute vitesse; *It lasted three* ~ *hours,* Cela a duré trois bonnes heures, Cela a bien duré trois heures; *The* ~ *purchase price will be refunded,* Le prix d'achat sera remboursé intégralement; [bus, &c.] ~ *up!,* complet! **3.** abondant, copieux: ~ *particulars,* tous les détails. **4.** [face, figure] plein; rond; (lèvres) fortes; (manche) bouffante; (vêtement) ample; [measures] fort: $2\frac{1}{4}''$ *full* = $2\frac{1}{4}$ po. fort. || *adv.* **1.** totalement; entièrement: *to know* ~ *well,* savoir parfaitement; juste; en plein: ~ *in the face,* en pleine figure; ~ *in the middle,* au beau milieu. || **full** *n.* **1.** plein: *The moon is at the* ~ , La lune est dans son plein. **2.** *in* ~ , tout au long; intégralement, in extenso: *name in* ~ , nom *m* en toutes lettres; [Fin.] *capital paid in* ~ , capital *m* entièrement versé. **3.** *to the* ~ , entièrement, complètement, intégralement. || **full-grown** [-ˌgɹown] *adj.* ayant atteint son plein développement, adulte.

fumble ['fʌmbl̩] *v. intr.* tâtonner, aller à tâtons: *to* ~ *about in the dark,* tâtonner dans l'obscurité; [Fam.] farfouiller.

fumes [fjuwmz] *n.pl* émanations *fpl* (nocives).

fumigate ['fjuwmɪˌgejt] *v. tr.* désinfecter par fumigation. || **fumigation** [ˌfjuwmɪ'gejʃən] *n.* fumigation *f.*

fun [fʌn] *n.* amusement *m*, gaieté *f*; plaisanterie *f*; *in, for/* ~ , pour rire; *to make* ~ *of s.o., to poke* ~ *at s.o.,* se moquer de qqun; *for the* ~ *of the thing,* histoire *f* de s'amuser; *to have* ~ , s'amuser, se divertir; *to have a lot of* ~ , s'amuser follement, © avoir un fun/vert, noir/; *He is a lot of* ~ , Il a toujours le mot pour rire; *It's* ~ , C'est amusant; © C'est le fun.

function ['fʌŋkʃən] *n.* [duty] fonction *f*; [gathering] cérémonie *f.* || *v. intr.* fonctionner (*as,* en qualité de), faire fonction de. || **functionary** [-ˌɛɹɪ] *n.* fonctionnaire *m* cf. CIVIL.

fund [fʌnd] *n.* **1.** fonds *m*; caisse *f.* **2.** [Fig.] *He has a* ~ *of knowledge,* Il possède un fonds d'érudition; *endowment* ~ , caisse de dotation; *to launch a* ~ *-raising campaign,* lancer une souscription. || **funds** [-z] *n.pl* **1.** fonds *m*, masse *f*, ressources *fpl* pécuniaires: *to make a call for* ~ , faire un appel de capital; *public* ~, les deniers/publics, de l'État. **2.** argent *m*; capital *m*.

fundamental [ˌfʌndə'mɛntl̩] *adj.* fondamental, essentiel.

funds, *cf.* FUND.

funeral ['fjuwnɹel] *n.* **1.** funérailles *fpl*; enterrement *m*; obsèques *fpl*: *to attend s.o.'s* ~ , assister à l'enterrement de qqun; aller aux funérailles de qqun. **2.** convoi *m*, cortège *m*/funèbre: *That is his (their)* ~ , Ça, c'est son (leur) affaire; © ~ *home,* © salon *m* mortuaire;

entrepreneur *m* de pompes funèbres. || *adj.* funèbre; funéraire; d'enterrement: ~ *insurance*, assurance *f* funéraire.

funk [fʌŋk] *n.* [Fam.] frousse *f*; trac *m*: *to be in a* (*blue*) ~, avoir une peur bleue; avoir la frousse.

funnel [ˈfʌnəl] *n.* entonnoir *m*; [ship] cheminée.

funny [ˈfʌnɪ] *adj.* **1.** drôle; comique; amusant: *None of your ~ tricks*, Pas de farces; Pas de blagues; *He is trying to be* ~, Il veut faire de l'esprit. **2.** curieux; bizarre: *Where did you get that ~ idea?*, Où avez-vous pris cette drôle d'idée?; *to taste* ~, avoir un drôle de goût.

fur [fɚ] *n.* **1.** [animal] pelage *m*; poil *m*; fourrure *f*. **2.** [pelt] fourrure *f*; [Com.] pelleteries *fpl*: ~ *coat*, manteau de fourrure: *She was wearing her furs at the ball*, Elle portait ses fourrures au bal. **3.** [Med.] [sur la langue] enduit *m* (blanchâtre). **4.** [Loc.] *to make the ~ fly*, se battre avec acharnement; *to stroke a person's ~ the wrong way*, prendre qqun à contre-poil, à rebrousse-poil; ~ *trade*, la pelleterie; la traite des fourrures; ~ *trader*, pelletier *m*; traiteur *m* de pelleteries.

furious [ˈfjuwɚɪəs] *adj.* furieux: *a ~ gale*, une violente tempête; *to grow* ~, se mettre dans une violente colère.

furl [fɚl] *v. tr.* [up] replier; [umbrella] rouler.

furlough [ˈfɚlow] *n.* [Mil.] permission *f* (*on*, en).

furnace [ˈfɝnəs] *n.* **1.** calorifère *m*, © fournaise *f*: *hot water* ~, calorifère *m* à eau chaude; *hot air* ~, calorifère *m* à air chaud; *blast* ~, haut fourneau. **2.** [Fig.] [hot place] fournaise. *She has been tried in the* ~, Elle s'est retrempée dans l'adversité.

furnish [ˈfɝnɪʃ] *v. tr.* **1.** fournir (*with*, de); donner: *The sun furnishes heat*, Le soleil donne de la chaleur. **2.** meubler, garnir (une maison): *furnished apartment*, appartement *m* meublé.

furnishings [ˈfɚnɪʃɪŋz] *n.*: *men's* ~, bonneterie *f* pour hommes; lingerie *f* pour hommes; chemiserie *f*.

furniture [ˈfɝnɪtʃɚ] *pl. inv. n.* meubles *mpl*; ameublement *m*; mobilier *m*: *piece of* ~, meuble *m*; *suite, set/of* ~, mobilier *m*; ~ *-van*, voiture *f* de déménagement.

furrow [ˈfɚˌow] *n.* sillon *m*; [wrinkle] ride *f*. || *v. intr.* sillonner; [wrinkle] rider.

further [ˈfɝð|ɚ] *adj.* plus éloigné, ultérieur; autre, nouveau. || *adv.* plus loin; de plus, encore. || *v. tr.* faciliter, favoriser, servir une cause, &c.). || **furthermore** [ˈfɚðɚˈmɔɚ] *adv.* de plus. || **furthest** [-əst] cf. FAR.

furtive [ˈfɚtɪv] *adj.* furtif: ~ *glance*, regard *m* à la dérobée.

fury [fjuwɚɪ] *n.* furie *f*, emportement *m*; [Fig.] femme *f* très méchante: *to get into a* ~, se mettre en fureur; *a fit of* ~, un accès de fureur.

fuse [fjuwz] *v. tr.* fondre. || *v. intr.* se fondre, se liquéfier. || *n.* [Elect.] plomb *m*, fusible *m* cf. FUZE.

fuselage [ˈfjuwzəˌlɑʒ] *n.* fuselage *m* (d'un avion).

fusion [ˈfjuwʒən] *n.* [metal] fonte *f*; [ice] fusion *f*.

fuss [fʌs] *n.* [noise] bruit *m*, fracas *m*; [bother] embarras *m*: *what a ~ !*, que d'histoires pour rien! || *v. intr.* faire beaucoup d'embarras pour peu de choses; faire l'important: *to ~ about*, s'agiter dans tous les sens sans raison. || **fussy** [ˈfʌsɪ] *adj.* **1.** tatillon. **2.** tarabiscoté.

futile [ˈfjuwtajl] *adj.* futile, peu important, sans valeur, sans effet.

future [ˈfjuwtʃɚ] *n.* **1.** avenir *m*; *in the* ~, à l'avenir; *in the near* ~, dans un avenir rapproché; à brève échéance; *to ruin one's* ~, briser son avenir. **2.** [Gram.] le (temps) futur: *a verb in the* ~, un verbe au futur. || *adj.* **1.** futur; à venir; d'avenir; *my ~ wife*, ma future, ma promise. **2.** [Gram.] *the ~ tense*, le (temps) futur.

fuze [fjuwz] *n.* fusée *f*; [wick] mèche *f*; [Elect.] fusible *m*.

fuzz [fʌz] *n.* duvet *m*. || **fuzzy** [-ɪ] *adj.* couvert de particules de/duvet, poussière/; [Fig.] (esprit) brumeux; [image] indistinct, flou.

G

G, g [ʤij] *pl.* G's, g's [-z]. **1.** [alphabet] le G *m.* **2.** [Mus.] sol *m.*

Ga. [= GEORGIA].

gab [gæb] *n.* faconde *f*: *to have the gift of the ~*, avoir la langue bien pendue.

gabble [ˈgæbḷ] *v. intr.* babiller, bavarder; [oies] caqueter. || *n.* bavardage *m*, caquet *m.*

gable [ˈgejbḷ] *n.* [Arch.] pignon *m.*

gad [gæd] *v. intr.* [**-dd-**]: *to ~ about*, vagabonder; courir la prétentaine.

gadfly [-ˌflaj] *n.* taon *m.*

gadget [ˈgæʤət] [Fam.] *n.* dispositif *m*, petite pièce *f*; [Fam.] truc *m*, machin *m.*

gag [gæg] *n.* bâillon *m*; [Fam.] gag *m*, plaisanterie *f.* || *v. tr.* [**-gg-**] bâillonner; réduire au silence. || *v. intr.* s'étouffer.

gage [gejʤ] cf. GAUGE.

gaggle [ˈgægḷ] *n.* troupeau *m* (d'oies).

gaiety, also **gayety** [ˈgejəti] *n.* gaieté *f*, allégresse *f*; éclat *m* (d'un costume).

gaily [ˈgejlɪ] *adv.* gaiement; [habillé] splendidement, avec éclat.

gain [gejn] *n.* gain *m*, profit *m*, avantage *m.* || *v. tr.* gagner (de l'argent, du temps, des amis); acquérir (une réputation); obtenir (une faveur, des renseignements); prendre (du poids); atteindre, gagner (une destination); *to ~ the upper hand*, prendre le dessus, *to ~ ground*, gagner du terrain. || *v. intr.* gagner; [clock] avancer: *to ~ by doing sth.*, gagner à faire qqch.; *to ~ (on s.o.)*, prendre de l'avance (sur qqun); [to catch up] rattraper qqun.

gait [gejt] *n.* [speed] allure *f*; [way of walking] démarche *f.*

gal., *pl.* **gals.** [= GALLON].

galaxy [ˈgæləksɪ] *n.* galaxie *f*, constellation *f*; [Fig.] brillante assemblée *f.*

gale [gejl] *n.* **1.** (coup de) vent *m*, tempête *f*: *It is blowing a ~*, Le vent souffle en tempête. **2.** [Fig.]: *gales of laughter*, éclats *mpl* de rire.

gall [gɔl] *n.* **1.** bile *f*, fiel *m*: *~ bladder*, vésicule *f* biliaire. **2.** [Fig.] amertume *f*; [Fam.] effronterie *f*, [Fam.] toupet *m.* **3.** écorchure *f*, irritation *f* (de la peau). || *v. tr.* [Fam.] exaspérer, vexer (qqun).

gallant[1] [ˈgælənt] *adj.* vaillant, courageux: *our ~ allies*, nos courageux alliés.

gallant[2] *adj.* galant (auprès des femmes). || **gallantry** [-ɹɪ] *n.* **1.** vaillance *f*, courage *m*; [Mil.] acte *m* de courage. **2.** galanterie *f.*

gallery [ˈgæləɹɪ] *n.* [Theat.] balcon *m*; [Art] musée *m*: *press ~*, tribune *f* de la presse.

Gallic [ˈgælɪk] *adj.* [Hist.] gaulois; [Fig.] français cf. GAUL. || **gallicism** [-əˌsɪzm] *n.* gallicisme *m.*

gallon [ˈgælən] *n.* © gallon *m*; [Fr.] gallon *m* [as loan-word, or convert to] litre *m*: *Imperial ~*, © gallon impérial; *US ~*, © gallon américain.

gallop [ˈgæləp] *n.* galop *m.* || *v. intr.* aller au galop, galoper. || *v. tr.* [**-pp-**] faire galoper (un cheval).

gallows [ˈgælowz] *n.pl.* potence *f.*

galoshes [gəˈlɔʃəs] *n.pl.* caoutchoucs *mpl*, © claques *fpl.*

gals. [= GALLONS].

gamble [gæmbḷ] *v. tr.* jouer (de l'argent); risquer: *to ~ sth. away*, perdre qqch. (au jeu); || *n.* risque *m*, affaire *f* de chance, spéculation *f* risquée: *It's a ~*, → C'est (assez) risqué.

game[1] [gejm] *n.* **1.** [the pastime] jeu *m*; [a contest] partie *f*; [match] match *m*, © partie *f* (de football), © joute *f* (de hockey): *Baseball is an interesting ~*, Le baseball est un jeu intéressant; *What about (having) a ~ of/tennis, bridge/?* Si on faisait une partie de/tennis, bridge/?; *What ~ were they playing?* A quel jeu jouaient-ils?; *They were playing a ~ of cards*, Ils jouaient aux cartes, Ils faisaient une partie de cartes; [Fig.] *to play the ~*, jouer franc jeu; *That's not playing the ~*, Ce n'est pas loyal; *~ of chance*, jeu de hasard. **2.** [Fam., = trick] manège: *m*: *What's your ~?*, Où voulez-vous en venir?; *The ~ is up!*, On a découvert le pot aux roses.

game[2] *n.inv.* gibier *m.inv.*: *~ -keeper*, © *~ warden*, garde-chasse *m; small ~*, menu gibier; *big ~*, les fauves.

game[3] *adj.* **1.** courageux, résolu: *to put up a ~ fight*, se battre avec l'énergie du désespoir; *I'm ~!* J'en suis!,/Comptez sur moi! **2.** [Fam.] estropié: *to have a ~ leg*, avoir une patte folle (= BOÎTER).

gamut [ˈgæmət] *n.* [Mus.] gamme *f.*

gander [ˈgændɚ] *n.* jars *m.*

gang [gæŋ] *n.* [Pej.] bande *f*, clique *f*; équipe *f* (d'ouvriers), cf. SHIFT. || **gang-plank** [-ˌplæŋk] *n.* passerelle *f.* || **gangster** [-stɚ] *n.* bandit *m*, gangster *m.* || **gangway** [-ˌwej] *n.* passage *m*; couloir *m*; [Naut.] coursive *f*; [Br.] passerelle *f.* || *interj. Gangway!*, Rangez-vous!

gannet [ˈgænət] *n.* [bird] fou *m* de Bassan.

gaol cf. JAIL.

gap [gæp] *n.* brèche *f* (dans un mur), ouverture *f* (dans une porte), trou *m* (dans une clôture); interstice *m* (des rochers); gorge *f* (de montagne); [Fig.] lacune *f*, vide *m.*

gape [gejp] *v. intr.* bâiller: *to ~ at*, regarder

bouche bée. || **gaping** [-ɪŋ] *adj.* [mouth, door] béant(e), grand(e) ouvert(e).
garage [gəˈɹæʤ] *n.* garage *m.*
garbage [ˈgɑɚbəʤ] *n.* ordures *fpl*, déchets *mpl*: ~ *can*, poubelle *f*; ~ *collector*, boueux *m*, © vidangeur *m*; ~ *dump*, dépotoir *m* (d'ordures). cf. NUISANCE.
garble [ˈgɑɚbl̩] *v. tr.* dénaturer (un texte).
garden [ˈgɑɚdn̩] *n.* jardin *m*: *kitchen, vegetable*/ ~, jardin potager; *rock* ~, (jardin de) rocaille *f.* || *v. intr.* jardiner, faire du jardinage. || **gardener** [-ɚ] *n.* jardini/er *m*, -ère *f.* || **gardening** [-ɪŋ] *n.* jardinage *m.*
gargle [ˈgɑɚgl] *v. tr.* gargariser. || *v. intr.* se gargariser. || *n.* gargarisme *m.*
garish [ˈgæɹɪʃ] *adj.* aux couleurs, aux lumières/crues; rutilant.
garlic [ˈgɑɚlɪk] *n.* ail *m.* (*pl* aulx); *clove of* ~, gousse *f* d'ail.
garment [gɑɚmənt] *n.* vêtement *m*: ~ *industry*, industrie *f* de la confection; ~ *worker*, travailleur *m* dans la confection.
garner [ˈgɑɚnɚ] *v. tr.* engranger; [Fig.] amasser, stocker (des provisions).
garnish [ˈgɑɚnɪʃ] *v. tr.* garnir (*with*, de).
garrison [ˈgæɚɪsn̩] *n.* garnison *f.* || *v. tr.* mettre une garnison dans, mettre des troupes en garnison dans.
garter [ˈgɑɚtɚ] *n.* [*usual. pl.*] [dames] jarretière *f*; [messieurs] support(s)-chaussette *m*(*pl*); [Hist.] (*Knight of*) *the Garter*, (Chevalier *m* de) l'Ordre *m* de la Jarretière.
gas [gæs] *n.* **1.** gaz *m*: *natural* ~, gaz naturel; ~ *company*, ~ *bill*, la compagnie, la note/du gaz; ~ *meter*, ~ *stove*, compteur *m*, fourneau *m*/à gaz; ~ *mask*, masque *m* à gaz; ~ *pipe*, conduite *f* de gaz; ~ *works*, usine *f* à gaz. **2.** [= GASOLINE] essence *f*; © *abus.* gaz *m*: ~ *station*, poste *m* d'essence, pompe *f.* || *v. tr.* **[-ss-]** asphyxier.
gash [gæʃ] *n.* entaille *f*, balafre *f.*
gasket [ˈgæskət] *n.* [Techn.] joint *m.*
gaso|line, -lene [ˌgæsəˈlijn] *n.* essence *f*, © *abus.* gazoline *f*, gaz *m.*
gasp [gæsp] *n.* hoquet *m*; sursaut *m* (de frayeur, &c.): *the last* ~, le dernier soupir. || *v. intr.* haleter, hoqueter: *to* ~ *for breath*, respirer avec difficulté.
gate [gejt] *n.* porte *f*; [metal] grille *f.* || **gateway** [-ˌwej] *n.* passage *m*; [grande porte] portail *m.*
gather [ˈgæðɚ] *v. tr.* [souvent employé avec *together*] amasser (de l'argent); rassembler, réunir (des personnes dispersées, ses forces); recueillir (des renseignements), cueillir (des fruits), percevoir (des taxes, &c.); prendre (de la vitesse): *Farmers* ~ *their crops*, Les fermiers rentrent leur moisson; [Fig.] *I gathered as much* → Je m'en doutais; *From what I could* ~, D'après ce que j'ai pu comprendre. || *v. intr.* [persons] se rassembler, se réunir. || **gathering** [-ɪŋ] *n.* **1.** [of people] rassemblement *m*, assemblée *f*, réunion *f*: *family* ~, réunion de famille. **2.** récolte *f* (de céréales, &c.), cueillette *f* (de fruits), perception *f* (des taxes).
gaudy [ˈgɔdɪ] *adj.* criard, aux couleurs voyantes.
gauge [gejʤ] *n.* mesure *f*; [Tech.] jauge *f*; calibre *m*: *steam* ~, manomètre *m*; *oil* ~, niveau *m* d'huile. || *v. tr.* jauger, mesurer, calibrer; [Fig.] juger, se faire une opinion sur/une personne.
Gaul [gɔl] *n.* [Hist.] la Gaule.
gaunt [gɔnt] *adj.* efflanqué, maigre.
gave [gejv] cf. GIVE.
gay [gej] *adj.* gai, joyeux; [colour] pimpant, vif. || **gayety** [ˈgejətɪ] *n.* cf. GAIETY.
gaze [gejz] *v. intr. to* ~ (*at so., sth.*), regarder (qqun, qqch.) fixement; fixer, contempler. || *n.* regard *m* (fixe).
gear [gijɚ] *n.* **1.** [on a wheel] dent *f*, rouage *m.* **2.** [Mech.] engrenage *m*, roue *f* dentée; commande *f*; appareil *m*, dispositif *m*: *set of gears*, système *m* d'engrenages; *landing* ~, train *m* d'atterrissage. **3.** [Auto.] transmission *f*; vitesse *f*: (*in*) *low,/second, high*/ ~, (en) première /deuxième, troisième/vitesse; *to change /shift/gears*, changer de vitesse; *in* ~, embrayé; *out of* ~, débrayé. **4.** [equipment] effets *mpl*, affaires *fpl*; attirail *m*, équipement *m* (de pêche). || *v. tr.* engrener (qqch. avec qqch.): *to* ~ *up, down*, multiplier, démultiplier; changer de vitesse. || **gearbox** [-ˌbɑks] *n.* carter *m*, boîte *f* de vitesses. || **gear shift** (lever) [-ˌʃɪft] (levier *m* de) changement *m* de vitesse.
geese [gijs] *n.* cf. GOOSE.
gem [ʤɛm] *n.* pierre *f* précieuse; [Fig.] bijou *m*, perle *f.*
gender [ˈʤɛndɚ] *n.* genre *m* (grammatical).
general [ˈʤɛnɹəl] *adj.* général, universel, commun: *in* ~, en général; *a* ~ *idea*, une idée/générale, d'ensemble/; *the* ~ *opinion*, l'opinion *f* de tout le monde; *general store* © magasin *m* général; épicerie *f* de village. || *n.* [Mil.] général *m*: *General X*, le général X. || **generally** [-ɪ] *adv.* généralement, en général, ordinairement. || **generality** [ˌʤɛnɚˈælɪtɪ] *n.* généralité *f.* || **generalize** [-ajz] *v. intr.* généraliser; parler en généralités.
generate [ˈʤɛnɚˌejt] *v. tr.* engendrer; produire (de l'électricité, &c.). || **generation** [ˌʤɛnɚˈejʃən] *n.* génération *f*; production

f. || **generator** [ˈʤɛnəˌejtə] *n.* [Tech.] génératrice *f*, dynamo *f.*

generosity [ˌʤɛnəˈɑsətɪ] *n.* générosité *f*, magnanimité *f*; libéralité *f.* || **generous** [ˈʤɛnəəs] *adj.* généreux, magnanime; libéral: *a ~ helping*, une portion abondante, une ample portion. || **generously** [ˈʤɛnəəslɪ] *adv.* généreusement; abon damment, amplement.

genial [ˈʤijnjḷ] *adj.* [×] affable, cordial. || **genius** [ˈʤijnjəs] *n.* [pers.] génie *m*; [talent] génie *m*, talent *m.*

genteel [ˌʤɛnˈtijl] *adj.* comme il faut *invar.*

gentle [ˈʤɛntḷ] *adj.* **1.** doux; léger; faible: *a ~ disposition*, un caractère doux; *a ~ tap*, une tape légère; *the ~ sex*, le sexe faible. **2.** noble, bien né: *the ~ art of . . .*, le noble art de . . .; *of ~ birth*, bien né, de bonne naissance. || **gentleman** [-mən] *pl.* **gentlemen** [-mən] *n.* monsieur *m*; [Fig.] homme *m* bien élevé, gentilhomme *m*: *He is a (real) ~*, C'est un homme/comme il faut, bien élevé/, C'est qqun de très bien; *Gentlemen!*, Messieurs!; *Ladies and Gentlemen*, Mesdames (et) Messieurs [☞ avoid *Hommes*, which is pejorative]. || **gentleness** [-nəs] *n.* gentillesse *f*, douceur *f.* || **gently** [ˈʤɛntlɪ] *adv.* doucement, poliment, délicatement: *Gently (now)!*, (Allez-y) doucement!

gentry [ˈʤɛntɹɪ] *n.* petite noblesse *f*; [Fig. & Pej.] individus *mpl.*

genuflect [ˈʤɛnjəflɛkt] *v. intr.* faire/une, la/génuflexion, s'agenouiller. || **genuflection** [ˌʤɛnjəˈflɛkʃən] *n.* génuflexion *f.*

genuine [ˈʤɛnjəwən] *adj.* [émotion] sincère; [objet] authentique, véritable.

geographical [ˌʤɪəˈgɹæfəkḷ] *adj.* géographique. || **geography** [ˌʤɪˈɑgɹəfɪ] *n.* géographie *f.*

geological [ˌʤɪəˈlɑʤəkḷ] *adj.* géologique. || **geology** [ˌʤɪˈɑləʤɪ] *n.* géologie *f.*

geometrical [ˌʤɪəˈmɛtɹəkḷ] *adj.* géométrique. || **geometry** [ˌʤɪˈɑmətɹɪ] *n.* géométrie *f.*

George [ʤɔəʤ] *n.* = Georges *m.*

Georgia [ˈʤɔəʤə] *n.* Géorgie *f*: *in, to ~*, en, dans l'état de/Géorgie.

germ [ʤəm] *n.* germe *m*, microbe *m*; [seed] germe *m.*

German [ˈʤəmən] *adj.* allemand; d'allemand; d'Allemagne: *a ~ car*, une voiture allemande; *a ~ teacher*, [nationality] un professeur allemand; [of the language] un professeur d'allemand; *~ history*, l'histoire d'Allemagne. || *n.* [pers.] Allemand *m*, -e *f*; [language] allemand *m.* || **german**, *adj.* (cousin) germain. || **Germany** [-ɪ] *n.* l'Allemagne *f*: *in, to/West(ern) ~*, en Allemagne de l'Ouest; *He comes from ~*, Il vient d'Allemagne.

gerrymander [ˈʤɛəɪˌmændə] *v. tr.* manipuler (un texte), tripatouiller; remanier les circonscriptions électorales.

gesticulate [ʤəsˈtɪkjəˌlejt] *v. intr.* gesticuler, faire de grands gestes. || **gesture** [ˈʤɛstʃə] *n.* geste *m*; [Fig.] geste *m*, symbole *m.* || *v. intr.* faire signe (à qqun de . . .), faire des gestes.

get [gɛt] **got, got** [gɑt] *v. intr.* **1.** [~ + *adj.*] devenir; se faire [☞ or use reflex. verb]: *She is getting (more and more) beautiful*, Elle devient (de plus en plus) belle; *It is getting late*, Il se fait tard; *to ~ old*, vieillir; *to ~ rich*, s'enrichir; *to ~ narrower*, se rétrécir cf. SICK, BETTER, &c. **2.** [~ + past part.] devenir; se faire [or use refl. verb or passive construction]: *You'll ~ killed!*, Vous allez vous faire tuer!; *He got shaved*, Il s'est rasé, Il s'est fait raser; *How did you ~ finished so fast?*, Comment avez-vous fait pour finir si vite? **3.** [~ + pr. part.] se mettre à, commencer à: *Once he gets talking . . .*, Dès qu'il se met à parler . . . **4.** [~ + *to*] se mettre à, commencer à; [succeed] arriver à: *I got to thinking about it*, Je me suis mis à y réfléchir; *You will ~ to see him later*, Vous pourrez le voir plus tard. cf. KNOW. **5.** [~ + expression of position] arriver, aller, aboutir, se mettre: *He got there on time*, Il (y) arriva à l'heure; *How do you ~ there?* Comment fait-on pour y aller?; *Where did you ~ to?*, [book, &c.] Où en êtes-vous?, [disappearance] Que vous est-il arrivé?; *What time did you ~ to work?* A quelle heure/êtes-vous arrivé à votre travail?/, [begin] . . . vous êtes-vous mis au travail?; *to ~ to bed*, aller se coucher. || *v. tr.* **1.** [obtain] se procurer, trouver; obtenir, acheter; acquérir: *Where did you ~ that?* Où avez-vous trouvé cela?, Où vous êtes-vous procuré ça?; *I must ~ (myself) a new coat*, Il faut que je m'achète un nouveau manteau; *to ~ results*, obtenir des résultats. **2.** [receive] recevoir, avoir; gagner; *He got the prize*, Il a reçu, remporté/le prix; *How much does your father ~ ?* Combien gagne votre père?. **3.** [catch] attraper, prendre, avoir; [Fig.] comprendre, saisir: *to ~/a cold, the measles/*, attraper/un rhume, la rougeole/; *The police will ~ you*, La police vous attrapera; *He got me this time*, Il m'a eu cette fois; [Fam.] *I don't ~/you, it/*, Je ne (vous) comprends pas. **4.** [fetch] aller chercher, aller prendre: *(Go and) ~ it* *for me*, Allez me le chercher; *I'll come and ~ you at four*, Je viendrai vous/chercher, prendre/à quatre heures. **5.** [~ + adj.] rendre; [~ + a verb]; réussir: *to get s.o. sick*, rendre qqun malade; *I got the window open*, J'ai réussi à ouvrir la fenêtre. **6.** [~ + p.p.] faire; finir; *He got the house painted*, Il a fait peindre la maison; *He got his hair cut*, Il s'est fait couper les cheveux; *Get your work done!*, Finissez votre travail! **7.** [~ + inf.] faire; persuader, décider; réussir: *She got him to come*, Elle l'a fait venir, Elle l'a persuadé de venir. **8.** [~ + expression of position] faire [and/or verb of motion]: *~ him here at once*, Faites-le venir (ici) tout de suite; *~ your bicycle inside*, Rentre ta bicyclette. **9.** *have got* [☞ s'emploie aux temps composés seulement, mais se traduit par des temps simples] avoir; falloir; devoir, avoir besoin (de): *Have you got your key?* Avez-vous votre clef?; *I've got a lot of work to do*, J'ai (beaucoup de travail) à faire; *I've got to leave*, Il faut que je parte. || **get about** *v. intr.* [person, news] circuler; [sick person] sortir. || **get above** *v. tr.* se mettre au-dessus de; surpasser. || **get across** *v. intr.* (réussir à) traverser (une rue), passer (une rivière). || *v. tr.* (réussir à) faire/traverser, passer; faire comprendre (qqch. à qqun). || **get along** *v. intr.* partir, s'en aller; (s')avancer, faire des progrès: *It's a hard street to ~*, C'est une rue où on (s')avance difficilement; *How are you getting along (with your work)?* Alors, ça marche, (le travail)?, Où en êtes-vous de votre travail?; *She can't ~ with him*, Elle ne peut pas s'entendre avec lui; *I can ~ without your help*, Je pourrai m'en tirer sans votre aide, Je pourrai me passer de votre aide. || **get around** *v. intr.* (réussir à) tourner (un obstacle); faire le tour (de qqch.); contourner (la loi); s'occuper de; sortir; [rumour] circuler: *I'll ~ to it in a moment*, Je m'en occuperai dans un instant; *She doesn't ~ much any more*, Elle ne sort plus guère; *He gets around*, → On le voit partout. || **get at** *v. intr.* atteindre, attraper: *I can't ~ it*, Je n'arrive pas jusque là, Je ne peux pas/l'atteindre, l'attraper/; *easy to ~*, facile à atteindre, accessible; *What are you getting at?*, Où voulez-vous en venir?; *Get at it!* (Mettez-vous) au travail!, Allez-y! || **get away** *v. intr.* partir; s'échapper, s'évader: *We got away early*, Nous sommes partis de bonne heure; *Get away (with you)!*, Allez-vous-en!, [Fig.] Vous n'êtes pas sérieux!; *He got away/from prison, from the police/*, Il s'est évadé de prison, Il a échappé à la police; [Fam.] *You won't ~ with it*, Ça ne se passera pas comme ça; [Fam.] *There's no getting away from it*, Il n'y a pas à sortir de là. || *v. tr.* éloigner. || **getaway** *n.* fuite *f*, évasion *f*; démarrage *m*: *He made a fast ~*, → Il s'est enfui rapidement; *This car has a fast ~*, Cette voiture a un démarrage rapide. || **get back** *v. intr.* reculer; être de retour, retourner, revenir, rentrer; re- [as prefix of verb of motion]: *When will you ~?* Quand serez-vous de retour?; *to ~ upstairs*, remonter (en haut); *to ~ at s.o.*, se venger de qqun. || *v. tr.* (se) faire rendre (qqch.); faire revenir (qqun); recouvrer (la santé, un objet perdu); regagner (la faveur); remettre, re- [as prefix of trans. verb of motion]: *to get sth. back downstairs*, redescendre qqch. en bas. || **get by** *v. intr.* passer; [Fig.] (arriver à) joindre les deux bouts. || *v. tr.* faire passer (qqch.) inaperçu. || **get down** *v. intr.* descendre; se mettre (à genoux, par terre, au travail, &c.): [Fig.] *to ~ to the facts*, en venir aux faits essentiels. || *v. tr.* descendre; noter; [swallow] avaler. || **get in** *v. intr.* entrer; s'introduire; [train, &c.] arriver; [election] être élu; monter (dans une voiture). || *v. tr.* rentrer; faire venir (qqun); acheter; placer (un mot). || **get into** *v. intr.* entrer, s'introduire, dans (qqch.); monter dans (une voiture); mettre (un vêtement); prendre (une habitude): *What am I getting into?*, Dans quoi est-ce que je m'engage?; *What has got into him?* Qu'est-ce qui lui prend? || *v. tr.* faire entrer, introduire, mettre (qqch.) dans (qqch.). || **get off** *v. intr.* descendre (de qqch.); [escape] s'en tirer: *to ~ with a fine*, en être quitte pour une amende; *to ~ to a good start*, faire un bon départ; *to ~ on the/left, wrong/foot*, partir du pied gauche. || *v. tr.* enlever, ôter; expédier (du courrier); tirer (un accusé) d'affaire: *to get sth. off one's hands*, se débarrasser de qqch. || **get on** *v. intr.* monter sur (qqch.), dans (un train, autobus); avancer, faire des progrès; continuer: *to ~ with/it, the job/*, continuer le travail. cf. GET ALONG; *He is getting on (in years)*, Il se fait vieux; *He is getting on (in his profession)*, Il fait son chemin (dans sa profession); *It is getting on for . . .*, Il n'est pas loin de. . . . || *v. tr.* mettre (un vêtement). || **get out** *v. intr.* sortir (de); s'échapper (de); se tirer (d'un embarras); descendre (d'une voiture); éviter (de faire qqch.); perdre (une habitude): *Let's ~ of here!* Sauvons-nous!; *If it ever gets out that . . .*, Si jamais on apprend que . . . || *v. tr.* sortir (une voiture, un livre); [pull] tirer, retirer, arracher; enlever (une tache); faire sortir (qqun); tirer (qqun) d'embarras. || **get over** *v. intr.* passer par-dessus, surmonter (un obstacle); se remettre (d'une maladie, catastrophe); revenir (d'une surprise): *I can't ~ it (that . . .)*, Je n'en reviens pas (que + subjunc.). || *v. tr.* faire passer (qqch.) par-dessus; en finir; faire comprendre, faire accepter: *Let's get it over (with)!*, Finissons-en! || **get round** cf. GET AROUND. || **get through** *v. intr.* passer (par une porte, à travers un bois); finir (du travail); être reçu (à un examen); arriver (jusqu'à qqch., qqun): *What time did you ~ ?* A quelle heure avez-vous fini? || *v. tr.* faire passer; faire réussir (un élève). || **get together** *v. tr. & intr.* (se) réunir; se mettre d'accord. || *n.* réunion *f.* || **get under** *v. intr.* passer par-dessous (qqch.); se mettre sous (qqch.). || **get up** *v. intr.* se mettre debout, se lever (du lit, d'une chaise); monter (l'escalier, &c.); [reach] arriver (à); *Get up!*, Debout!/Levez-vous!/; *Don't ~ !*, → Restez assis(e)! || *v. tr.* (réussir à) monter (qqch.), faire monter (qqun); lever; faire lever (qqun du lit); organiser, monter (une fête); préparer (un cours); habiller, déguiser (*as*, en): *nicely got-up (article)*, (article *m*) bien présenté. || **get-up** *n.* costume *m.*

Ghana ['gɑnə] *n.* le Ghana.

ghastly ['gæstlɪ] *adj.* affreux, horrible; [teint] livide.

ghost [gowst] **1.** spectre *m*, fantôme *m*, revenant *m*: *~ story*, histoire *f* de revenants; [Fam.] *not the ~ of a chance*, pas la moindre chance. **2.** esprit *m*, âme *f*: [Rel.] *the Holy Ghost*, le Saint-Esprit; *to give up the ~*, rendre l'âme. || **ghostly** [-lɪ] *adj.* spectral, fantômatique.

giant ['dʒjaənt] *n.* géant *m.* || *adj.* géant, énorme. cf. GIGANTIC.

gibberish ['dʒɪbərɪʃ] *n.* baragouin *m.*

giddy ['gɪdɪ] *adj.* étourdi; [height] vertigineux: *It makes me (feel) ~*, → Cela me donne le vertige.

gift [gɪft] *n.* **1.** [present] cadeau *m*, présent *m*, don *m*: *He gave me a ~*, Il m'a donné un/cadeau, présent/; *He gave me a book (as a ~)*, Il m'a fait/cadeau, présent, don/ d'un livre; *Christmas ~*, cadeau de Noël; [Fr.] *New Year's ~*, étrennes *fpl.* **2.** don *m*, talent *m*: *He has/the ~ of, a ~ for/languages*, Il a/le don des, du talent pour les/langues. || **gifted** [-əd] *adj.* doué (*with*, de; *in*, pour): *a ~ musician*, un musicien/bien doué, de talent.

gigantic [ˌdʒaj'gæntɪk] *adj.* gigantesque.

giggle ['gɪgl̩] *v. intr.* pouffer (de rire); ricaner (bêtement).

gild [gɪld] *v. tr.* dorer: || **gilding** *n.* ['gɪldɪŋ] dorure *f.*

Giles [dʒajlz] *n.* = Gilles.

gilt [gɪlt] *n.* dorure *f*: *~-edged (book)*, (livre) doré sur tranches; *~-edged securities*, valeurs *fpl* de père de famille. || *adj.* doré.

gimmick ['gɪmɪk] *n.* truc *m.*

ginger ['dʒɪndʒər] *n.* gingembre *m*: *~ bread*, pain *m* d'épices; *~-ale* [Fr.] bière *f* de gingembre, © ginger-ale *m.*

gingerly [-lɪ] *adv.* doucement, avec précaution.

gingham ['gɪŋəm] *n.* guingan *m.*

gipsy ['dʒɪpsɪ] cf. GYPSY.

giraffe [dʒər'æf] *n.* girafe *f.*

gird [gərd], **girt (girded)** [gərt] *v. tr.* ceindre, ceinturer (la taille); se préparer (à qqch.); attacher: *to ~ (up) one's loins*, se ceindre (les reins). || **girdle** [gərdl] *n.* [garment] gaine *f*; [gen.] ceinture *f*; [Fig.] enceinte *f.* || *v. tr.* [US, Fig.] ceindre, ceinturer; entourer (une ville de remparts): *to ~ the globe*, faire le tour du monde.

girl [gərl] *n.* jeune fille *f*; [opposed to *garçon*, *fils*] fille *f*; [opposed to *petit garçon*] petite fille *f*; [opposed to *jeune homme*] jeune fille *f*, †demoiselle *f*: *girls' school*, école *f* de filles; *girl (-student)*, [Br.] *schoolgirl*, élève *f*, écolière *f*, [University] étudiante *f*; *teen-age ~*, adolescente *f*; *~ friend*, © blonde. [Fr.] petite amie: *when I was a ~* → quand j'étais/petite, jeune/; *a Canadian ~*, → une jeune Canadienne; *chorus ~*, girl *f*; *sales ~*, vendeuse *f* [and other feminine forms]. || ©, [Br.] **girl guide,** [US] **girl scout** *n.* éclaireuse *f*, guide *f.* || **girlhood,** *n.* jeunesse *f.* || **girlish** *adj.* de jeune fille, jeune.

girt [gərt] cf. GIRD.

give [gɪv], **gave** [gejv], **given** [gɪvn̩] *v. tr.* [☞ Usually translated by *donner*; for **give** + noun, look up under noun, or substitute, e.g. *to give ground* under GROUND]. **1.** donner, offrir, faire cadeau de (qqch. à qqun): *I'm giving it to you*, Je vous le donne, Je vous en fais cadeau. **2.** donner, payer: *I'd give a lot to have that*, Je donnerais beaucoup pour avoir cela. **3.** donner, passer: *Please ~ me the* *salt*, Passez-moi le sel, s'il vous plaît; *He gave me his cold*, Il m'a/donné, passé/ son rhume. **4.** donner, remettre, transmettre: ~ *me your essay by Thursday*, Donnez-moi, Remettez-moi/votre dissertation jeudi au plus tard. **5.** donner, consacrer: *He gave much time to his studies*, Il a consacré beaucoup de temps à ses études. **6.** donner, fournir: *He will ~ me the information*, Il me fournira les renseignements. **7.** faire: *to ~ a /speech, lecture, class/*, faire/un discours, une conférence, un cours/; ~ *a/smile, jump, an answer/*, faire/un sourire, un saut, une réponse/, → sourire, (sur)sauter, répondre. **8.** pousser; *to ~ a/cry, sigh/*, pousser un/cri, soupir/; [Fam.] *I don't ~ two hoots*, Je m'en moque pas mal. ‖ *v. intr.* **1.** donner [→ être généreux]; fléchir cf. GIVE AWAY. ‖ *n.* élasticité *f*; [or use a verb]: *This support has too much ~*, Ce support a/trop d'élasticité, une trop grande tendance à fléchir. ‖ **give away** *v. tr.* **1.** donner, distribuer: *They are giving away free samples*, On /donne, distribue/des échantillons gratuits. **2.** trahir, donner, dénoncer; *His accent gave him away*, Son accent l'a trahi. **3.** *To ~ the bride*, Conduire la mariée à l'autel. ‖ **give again** *v. tr.* redonner; [give back] rendre. ‖ **give back** *v. tr.* rendre (qqch. à qqun). ‖ **give forth** *v. tr.* produire, émettre (un son); [smell, heat → cf. GIVE OFF]. ‖ **give in** *v. tr.* [hand in] remettre (un devoir). ‖ *v. intr.* céder, lâcher pied, se soumettre: *He had to give in (on this point)*, Il a dû céder (sur ce point-là); [Fig.] s'abandonner à ses émotions; céder à la tentation; se laisser emporter par la colère. ‖ **give off** *v. tr.* dégager, répandre: *This product gives off an unpleasant smell*, Ce produit/dégage, répand/une odeur désagréable. ‖ **give out** *v. tr.* [= give off] distribuer, annoncer, publier. ‖ *v. intr.* être à bout, arriver au bout de qqch.; s'épuiser: *Our supplies gave out*, Nos provisions se sont épuisées, → Nous sommes arrivés au bout de nos provisions. ‖ **give up** *v. tr.* **1.** renoncer à, abandonner: *He gave up smoking*, Il a renoncé au tabac; *He was given up for lost*, On le considérait comme perdu. **2.** rendre, livrer; *He gave himself up to the police*, Il s'est/rendu, livré/à la police. **3.** donner, se priver de; *His parents gave up many things to send him to university*, Ses parents se sont privés de bien des choses pour (pouvoir) l'envoyer à l'université. ‖ *v. intr.* abandonner, renoncer; *I give up!* J'abandonne! Je, J'y/renonce! ‖ **give way** *v. intr.* [break] céder; [collapse] s'effondrer; [sag] fléchir; *The roof gave way (a little) under the snow*, Le toit a fléchi (un peu) sous la neige; [Fig.] s'abandonner, céder, se laisser emporter [cf. GIVE IN]; céder la place à. ‖ **give-and-take** *n. & adj.*: *a give-and-take affair*, C'est donnant donnant. ‖ **given** *adj.* **1.** donné, fixé: ~ *name*, prénom *m*; *at a ~ moment*, à un moment donné; *at the ~ time*, à l'heure/fixée, dite; ~ *that A equals B*, Soit A égale B. **2.** [Fig.] *to be ~ to*, avoir tendance à (boire, &c.), être porté sur (l'alcool, &c.).

giver [-ɚ] *n.* (celui) qui donne; donateur *m* (d'un prix). ‖ **giving** ['gɪvɪŋ] *n.* **1.** [Gerund of GIVE, ☞ often better translated by some other form of the verb]: *without my ~ it to him*, Sans que je le lui donne. **2.** don *m*; ~ *away*, distribution *f* (des prix, etc.); trahison *f* (de qqun); révélation *f* (de qqch.); ~ *back*, restitution *f*; ~ *forth*, émission *m* (d'un son); ~ *in*, remise *f* (d'une composition, etc.), abandon *m* (d'une lutte), résignation *f*; ~ *off*, dégagement *m* (d'une odeur); ~ *out*, distribution *f*, publication *f*, épuisement *m* (de provisions); ~ *up*, abandon *m* (d'une lutte, d'une habitude), résignation *f*; ~ *way*, effondrement *m* (d'un plancher), fléchissement *m* (de la volonté), remplacement *m* (de qqch. par qqch.).

glacier ['glejsɪɚ] *n.* glacier *m*.

glad [glæd] *adj.* content, heureux (*at, of*, de; *to* + *infin.*, de + infin.; *that . . .*, que + subjunc.): *Glad to meet you*, Enchanté de faire votre connaissance; *He would be only too ~ to . . .*, Il ne demande pas mieux que de . . . . ‖ **gladden** [-n̩] *v. tr.* réjouir; rendre content, heureux: *It gladdens my heart to . . .*, Cela me réjouit le cœur de. . . .

glade [glejd] *n.* clairière *f*, éclaircie *f*.

gladly ['glædlɪ] *adv.* avec plaisir, volontiers: *I would ~ help*, → Je ne demande pas mieux que d'aider. ‖ **gladness** [-nəs] *n.* joie *f*, contentement *m*.

glamorous ['glæmərəs] *adj.* charmant, attrayant, ravissant. ‖ **glamour** ['glæmɚ] *n.* attrait (d'un spectacle), charme *m*, éclat *m* (d'une beauté).

glance [glæns] *n.* **1.** coup *m* d'œil, regard (rapide) *m*; *at a ~*, d'un seul coup d'œil; *at first ~*, à première vue. **2.** trait *m* de lumière, éclat *m* rapide. ‖ *v. intr.* **1.** jeter un regard (*at*, sur): *to ~ through a book*, feuilleter un livre; *to ~ up*, lever les yeux. **2.** *to ~ off*, dévier, ricocher/de: *a glancing blow*, un coup oblique. **3.** étinceler.

glare [glɛɚ] *n.* **1.** lumière *f* éblouissante, éclat *m*: réverbération *f* (du soleil). **2.** regard *m* irrité, méchant. || *v. intr.* **1.** briller (d'un grand éclat). **2.** *to ~ at s.o.*, foudroyer qqun du regard. || **glaring** [-ɪŋ] *adj.* évident: *a ~ mistake*, une faute/ évidente, qui saute aux yeux/.

glass, -es [glæs] [-əz] *n.* **1.** [material, utensil] verre *m*; [~ ware] verrerie *f*; [pane] vitre *f*, [mirror] miroir *m*, glace *f*; [lens] lentille *f*; *stained ~*, vitraux *mpl*; baromètre *m*; télescope *m*, longue-vue *f*; [hour ~] sablier *m*: *plate ~*, glace *f*; *cut ~*, cristal *m* taillé; *a wine ~*, un verre à vin; *a ~ of wine*, un verre de vin; *a piece of ~*, un éclat de verre; *a ~ bottle*, une bouteille/de, en/ verre; *a ~ door*, une porte vitrée; *~ eye*, œil *m*/artificiel, de verre/. **2.** [pl.] glasses: [spectacles] lunettes *fpl*; [field ~] jumelles *fpl*; *sun glasses*, lunettes noires. || **glassy** ['glæsɪ] *adj.* vitreux; transparent, limpide; [smooth] lisse.

glaze [glejz] *v. tr.* vernir, lustrer (une surface); vitrer (une maison, une fenêtre): [Fig.] *to ~ over sth.*, masquer qqch.

gleam [glijm] *n.* lueur *f* pâle. || *v. intr.* luire faiblement, luire d'une lueur pâle.

glean [glijn] *v. tr.* glaner; grappiller (du raisin).

glee [glij] *n.* **1.** allégresse *f*, gaîté *f*, joie *f*. **2.** [Mus.] chanson *f* à plusieurs voix (sans accompagnement): *glee club*, orphéon *m*.

glib [glɪb] *adj.* [**-bb-**] [tongue] déliée, bien pendue; [excuse] facile.

glide [glajd] *v. intr.* [Aviat.] planer; [Fig.] (se) glisser, s'insinuer (dans, *into*). || *n.* glissement *m*; [Aviat.] vol *m* plané; [singing] port *m* de voix; [Phon.] son *m* transitoire. || **glider** [-ɚ] *n.* [Aviat.] planeur *m*.

glimmer ['glɪmɚ] *n.* lueur *f* faible, tremblotante. || *v. intr.* luire d'une lueur faible ou tremblotante.

glimpse [glɪmps] *n.* coup *m* d'œil, aperçu *m*: *to/catch, get/a ~ of*, → entrevoir. || *v. tr.* voir (qqch.); entrevoir (qqch.).

glint [glɪnt] *n.* reflet *m* sur une surface sombre. || *v. intr.* jeter un reflet, luire doucement.

glisten [glɪsn̩] *v. intr.* luire (d'un éclat mouillé): *glistening sidewalks*, trottoirs luisants de pluie.

glitter ['glɪtɚ] *n.* scintillement *m*. || *v. intr.* briller, luire d'un éclat métallique. || **glittering** [-ɪŋ] *adj.* scintillant, rutilant, resplendissant; [Fam.] mirobolant.

gloat [glowt] *v. intr.* prendre un malin plaisir (*over*, à).

globe [glowb] *n.* [shape] globe *m*, sphère *f*; [world] (la) terre *f*: [Sch.] globe *m* terrestre: *to circle the ~*, faire le tour du monde.

gloom [gluwm] *n.* obscurité *f*; [Fig.] tristesse *f*. || **gloomy** [-ɪ] *adj.* sombre, triste: *It's a ~ day*, Il fait (un temps) sombre; *~ thoughts*, pensées *fpl* noires.

glorify ['glɔɚɪˌfaj] *v. tr.* glorifier.

glorious ['glɔɚɪəs] *adj.* [persons] glorieux, illustre; [things] splendide, resplendissant: *What a ~ day!*, Quelle journée superbe! || **gloriously** [-lɪ] *adv.* glorieusement; de façon splendide, superbe.

glory ['glɔɚɪ] *n.* gloire *f*; célébrité *f*; splendeur *f*. || *v. intr.* *to ~ in sth.*, se glorifier de, être fier de.

gloss[1] [glɑs] *n.* glose *f*, commentaire *m* (d'un texte). || *v. intr.* gloser, disserter (*upon sth.*, sur qqch.).

gloss[2] *n.* lustre *m* (d'une étoffe, &c.), brillant (du parquet): *to put a ~ on*, lustrer, faire briller; *to take the ~ off*, délustrer, ternir. || *v. tr.* lustrer, polir, cirer: [Fig.] *to ~ over the facts*, maquiller les faits.

glossary ['glɑsɚɪ] *n.* glossaire *m*.

glossy [-ɪ] *adj.* lustré, luisant, brillant.

glove [glʌv] *n.* [usual. pl.] gant(s) *m(pl)*: *boxing gloves*, (des) gants de boxe; [Fig.] *to handle with kid gloves* traiter (qqun) avec douceur, mettre des gants blancs. || *v. tr.* ganter.

glow [glow] *n.* rougeoiment *m*: *~ -worm*, ver *m* luisant. || *v. intr.* rougeoyer, être incandescent.

glower ['glawɚ] *v. intr.* avoir l'air renfrogné: *to ~ at s.o.*, regarder qqun de travers.

glowing [-ɪŋ] *adj.* **1.** rougeoyant, incandescent. **2.** [Fig.] favorable, enthousiaste.

glue [gluw] *n.* colle *f*. || *v. tr.* coller.

glum [glʌm] *adj.* [**-mm-**] maussade.

glut [glʌt] *n.* encombrement *m*, pléthore *f*, surabondance *f*. || *v. tr.* [**-tt-**] [food] rassasier; [market] inonder. || **glutton** [-n̩] *n.* glouton *m*, goinfre *m*. || **gluttonous** [-nəs] *adj.* glouton, gourmand.

gm. [= GRAMME(S)].

G-man ['ʤijˌmæn] agent *m* du F.B.I.

GMT [= Greenwich Mean Time], **G.M.T.** [also called T.M.G. = temps moyen de Greenwich, or T.U., = temps universel].

gnarled ['nɑɚld] *adj.* [wood] noueux; [Fig.] rabougri.

gnash ['næʃ] *v. tr.*: *to ~ one's teeth,* grincer des dents.
gnat ['næt] [Br.] *n.* moustique *m,* © maringouin *m.* || **gnat catcher** *n.* gobe-mouches.
gnaw [nɔ] *v. tr.* ronger (un os, &c.).
go [gow] **went** [wεnt] **gone** [gɔn] *v. intr.* **1.** aller; [a position] se mettre; [a more precise verb of movement] monter, descendre, &c.: *to ~ from Toronto to Montreal,* aller de Toronto à Montréal; *The dog went under the table,* Le chien s'est mis sous la table; *Go to your room!,* Va dans ta chambre!; *I am going to the dentist,* Je vais chez le dentiste; [if a place is understood, use 'y', except in fut. & condit.] *Did you ~ last night?,* Y êtes-vous allé hier soir?; *She went to her teacher,* Elle est allée trouver son professeur; *She went (downtown) to buy a hat* [but didn't], Elle est allée (en ville) pour s'acheter un chapeau; [and did] Elle est allée en ville s'acheter un chapeau; *She went (downtown) and bought a hat,* Elle est allée (en ville) s'acheter un chapeau. **2.** [immediate future] aller; avoir l'intention de, compter: *Are you going to come tonight?,* Allez-vous venir ce soir?; [usual. omitted in subjunc. clauses] *I don't think he is going to come,* Je ne pense pas qu'il vienne; *I was going to be through by nine, but . . . ,* Je comptais bien finir avant neuf heures, mais . . .; *Do it right now!, I'm not going to!* Faites-le tout de suite!, Je ne veux pas! **3.** [leave] partir, s'en aller: *It's time I was going,* Il est temps que/je parte, je m'en aille/; *Are, Have/they all gone?* Sont-ils tous partis? **4.** [cover a distance] faire: *to ~ ten miles (on foot),* faire dix milles (à pied); *He was going 60 miles an hour,* Il faisait/60 milles à l'heure, [Fam.] du soixante à l'heure/. **5.** [disappear] disparaître, partir: *I turned around, and my hat was gone,* Je me suis retourné, et mon chapeau avait disparu; *His money is all gone,* → Il n'a plus un sou; *Where did it go (to)?* Par où est-il passé? **6.** [function] marcher: *My watch won't ~ ,* Ma montre ne marche pas; *to be going,* être en marche; *to start sth. going,* mettre qqch. en marche; [Fig.] faire démarrer (une affaire, une conversation). **7.** [work out] aller, marcher: *How are things going?* Comment ça va?, [Com.] Comment vont les affaires?; *Everything went well,* Tout a bien marché; *How did the game ~ ?,* → Quel a été le résultat du match? **8.** [become] devenir; [a special verb]: *to ~ mad,* devenir fou; *to ~ /red, pale/,* pâlir, rougir. **9.** [noise, or action] faire: *Ducks ~ quack-quack,* Les canards font coin-coin; *Just ~ like me,* Faites simplement comme moi. **10.** [ring, strike] sonner: *The bell has just gone,* La cloche vient de sonner. **11.** [of song]: *How do the words ~ ?* Quelles sont les paroles? **12.** [place, order] *Where does this ~ ?* → Où met-on cela?; *He went first,* → Il a commencé, Il est passé le premier; *Who goes next?* → A qui le tour? **13.** [of time] passer, s'écouler. **14.** recevoir: *The first prize went to him,* → Il a reçu le premier prix. **15.** être connu: *He went under a false name,* Il était connu sous un faux nom. **16.** se vendre: *Hats are going well this year,* Les chapeaux se vendent bien cette année; *Going! Going! Gone!* Une fois! Deux fois! Adjugé! **17.** contribuer, servir, (*à*): *His acting went a long way to(ward) making the play a success,* Son jeu a contribué pour beaucoup au succès de la pièce; *That just goes to prove what I was saying,* Cela ne sert qu'à prouver ce que je disais. **18.** mourir. **19.** casser, céder, tomber, &c. **20.** [special uses]: *There goes /the bus, the bell/,* Voilà l'autobus qui s'en va, Voilà la sonnerie; *Here we ~ again!,* → Nous y revoilà!; Ça y est!, Ça recommence!; *Now you've gone and done it!* → Vous en avez fait, du joli!; *Well, here goes!,* → Eh bien, puisqu'il le faut . . . ; *What I say, goes!,* → C'est moi qui commande ici; *That goes without saying,* Cela va sans dire, Cela va de soi; *Two to ~ !* Encore deux!; *He went it alone,* Il l'a/fait, subi/ tout seul. || go *n. To have a ~ (at sth.),* essayer (de faire qqch.); *to be on the ~ ,* être en mouvement; *at a (single) ~ ,* d'un seul coup; [Fam.] *It's all the ~ ,* C'est le dernier cri, C'est très à la mode; *It's no ~!* Ça ne/marche, prend/pas! || **go about** *v. intr.* aller (ça et là, partout); [story] circuler; s'occuper de (son travail); se prendre à (une besogne): *How do you ~ it?* Comment s'y prend-on?; *Go about your business,* Occupez-vous de vos affaires. || **go across** *v. intr.* traverser. || **go after** *v. intr.* suivre; poursuivre, courir après, (qqun); attaquer (qqun). || **go against** *v. intr.* contrarier (qqun); être contraire à; [luck] tourner contre; être contre l'intérêt de qqun: *It will ~ you,* → Cela se retournera contre vous; *It goes against my better judgment,* → C'est à contrecœur que je fais cela; *He went against his word,* Il est revenu sur sa parole. || **go ahead** *v. intr.* aller de l'avant; avancer: *to ~ of s.o.,* précéder, [pass] dépasser/

qqun; *Go ahead!* Allez-y! || **go-ahead** *adj.* entreprenant. || *n.* ambition *f*; permission *f.* || **go along** *v. intr.* **1.** s'en aller; passer (par une rue); longer (un mur, une rivière, &c.). **2.** *to ~ with,* accompagner: *I'll ~ with you* (*on that*), Je suis d'accord avec vous (sur ce point). || **go around** *v. intr.* tourner (autour de qqch., qqun); [story] circuler; faire le tour (de qqch.); faire un détour; (y) en avoir assez (pour tout le monde); sortir (avec qqun). || **go at** *v. intr.* s'attaquer à (qqch., qqun); se mettre à (un travail). || **go away** *v. intr.* partir, s'en aller: *to ~ with sth.,* /emporter, enlever/qqch. || **go back** *v. intr.* **1.** retourner; [home] rentrer; [back up] reculer; [date back] remonter: *to ~ on one's word,* revenir sur sa parole; *to ~ to doing sth.,* se remettre à faire qqch. || **go before** *v. intr.* précéder (qqch., qqun). || **go-between** [-bəˌtwijn] *n.* intermédiaire *m/f.* médiat|eur *m,* -rice *f,* [Pej.] entremett|eur *m,* -euse *f.* || **go beyond** *v. intr.* aller au-delà de, dépasser (qqch.). || **go by** *v. intr.* **1.** passer: *He goes by* (*our school*) *every day,* Il passe (devant notre école) tous les jours; *An hour went by,* Une heure/passa, s'écoula/. **2.** [be guided] se régler sur; juger d'après; suivre: *to have nothing to ~,* ne rien avoir pour se guider. **3.** être connu sous le nom de. || **go-cart** *n.* poussette *f* (pour enfants). || **go down** *v. intr.* descendre; [sun] se coucher; [ship] sombrer; [price, temperature] baisser; [curtain] tomber: *He went down* (*the street*), Il est/descendu, allé/en bas de la rue/Il a descendu la rue; *That will ~ in history,* Cela passera/à la postérité, dans l'histoire; *He went down for the third time,* Il/est tombé, [Boxe] est allé au tapis,/pour la troisième fois/; Il s'est noyé; *The dessert went down well,* Le dessert a été bien reçu. || **go for** *v. intr.* [fetch] aller chercher; attaquer. || **go forth** *v. intr.* sortir. || **go forward** *v. intr.* avancer. || [Fam.] **go-getter** [-ˌgɛtər] *n.* homme *m* entreprenant; [pej.] arriviste *m.* || **go in** *v. intr.* entrer (dans); [one's own house, &c.] rentrer (dans); [sun] se cacher; [fit] tenir, entrer, (dans): *It won't ~ the drawer,* Cela ne tient pas dans le tiroir; *to ~ for/sport, teaching, maths/,* faire du sport, se consacrer/à l'enseignement, aux maths; *to ~ for a race,* participer à une course. || **go into** *v. intr.* entrer, [again] rentrer, dans; étudier, examiner (qqch.): *I'll ~ it,* Je vais m'en occuper; *How many times does 3 ~ 15? It goes* (*into it*) *5 times,* En quinze combien de fois trois? (Il y va) cinq fois. || **go off** *v. intr.* [leave] partir, s'en aller; [move away] s'éloigner; [gun] partir, se décharger; [bomb] partir, exploser; [affair] (bien, mal) marcher: *to ~ the road,* quitter, s'écarter de, la route; *to ~ with sth.,* emporter qqch. || **go on** *v. intr.* aller plus loin, reprendre son chemin, son travail, &c.; continuer (qqch., à faire qqch.); [happen] se passer; [Theat.] entrer (en scène): *What is going on here?,* Qu'est-ce qui se passe ici?; *to ~ to sth. else,* passer à autre chose; *to ~ at s.o.,* faire une scène à qqun; *These skates won't ~* (*me*), Ces patins ne me vont pas; *We haven't much to ~,* Nous n'avons pas grand'chose pour nous/guider, aider; *Go on* (*with you*)*!,* Allons, voyons! || **go out** *v. intr.* sortir (de la pièce, &c.); [socially] aller dans le monde, sortir (avec qqun); [light] s'éteindre; [tide] descendre; disparaître, se terminer. || **go over** *v. intr.* passer (la mer, un pont, à l'ennemi), traverser (la rue); [examine] parcourir (un livre, un bâtiment, &c.); [review] repasser (ses notes, qqch. dans son esprit). || **go round** cf. GO AROUND. || **go through** *v. intr.* passer par (une porte), traverser (une ville); [undergo] subir, souffrir; [examine] parcourir (un livre, un bâtiment); faire exécuter (un plan); dépenser (de l'argent); [law] passer; fouiller (les poches de qqun): *You'll have to ~ it,* Il faudra passer par là; *You'll have to ~ with it,* Il faudra/aller jusqu'au bout, le mener à bien. || **go up** *v. intr.* monter; [curtain] se lever; [shout] s'élever; [prices] augmenter. || **go with** *v. intr.* aller avec, accompagner (qqun, qqch.). || **go without** *v. intr.* se passer de (qqch.): *You'll have to ~,* Il faudra vous en passer.

goal [gowl] *n.* [Sport] but *m*; [Fig.] but, objectif *m*: *to score a ~,* marquer un but; *to play ~,* être gardien. || **goal-keeper** [-kijpər], **goalie** [-ɪ] *n.* gardien *m* de but.

goat [gowt] *n.* chèvre *f*: *he-goat, male ~,* bouc *m*; [Fig.] bouc *m* émissaire: *Rocky Mountain ~,* © chèvre des montagnes; [Fig.] *to get s.o.'s ~,* exaspérer, faire enrager qqun. || **goatee** [ˌgow'tij] *n.* barbiche *f*, bouc *m.*

gobble [gɑbl̩] *v. tr.*: *to ~ up one's food,* engloutir sa nourriture. || *v. intr.* [turkey] glouglouter. || **gobbler** [-ər] *n.* dindon *m.*

God [gɑd] *n.* Dieu *m.* [speaking of God, often] le bon Dieu: *God bless you!,* (Que le bon) Dieu vous bénisse!; [Myth.] *the gods,* les dieux. || **godchild** [-ˌtʃajld] *pl.*

godchildren, *n.* filleul *m*, -e *f.* || **goddaughter** [-ˌdɔtɚ] *n.* filleule *f.* || **goddess** [-əs] *n.* déesse *f.* || **godfather** [-ˌfɑðɚ] *n.* parrain *m*; *to stand* ~, être/parrain, © compère/. || **godless** [-ləs] *adj.* athée, impie. || **godlike** [-ˌlajk] *adj.* divin. || **godliness** [-lɪnəs] *n.* piété *f*, dévotion *f.* || **godly** [-lɪ] *adj.* pieux, dévot, divin. || **godmother** [-ˌmʌðɚ] *n.* marraine *f*: *to stand* ~, être/marraine, © commère/. || **godparents** [-ˌpɛɚənts] *n.pl.* les parrains *mpl.*, les parrain et marraine. || **godsend** [-ˌsɛnd] *n.*: *This is indeed a* ~, → C'est vraiment providentiel.

goggle [gɑgḷ] *v. intr.* rouler de gros yeux, écarquiller les yeux. || **goggles** [-z] *n.* lunettes *fpl.* (protectrices) (de chauffeur, de mécanicien).

going [ˈgowɪŋ] *adj.* qui marche; qui soit: *It's a* ~ *concern*, C'est une affaire qui marche; *It's the best* ~, C'est le meilleur qui soit. || *n.* départ *m*; progrès *m*: *Good* ~ *!* Bien joué!

gold [gowld] *n.* or *m*: ~ *standard*, étalon *m* or; *solid* ~, or massif; [Fig.] or, fortune *f*; *a* ~ *watch*, une montre en or; *a heart of* ~, un cœur d'or; ~ *mine*, mine *f* d'or. || **golden** [-ṇ] *adj.* d'or, en or; [gilded] doré: *the* ~ *mean*, le juste milieu. || **gold(en) eye** [-ˌaj] © *n.* [fish in Lake Winnipeg] garrot *m.* || **goldfinch** [-ˌfɪntʃ] *n.* chardonneret *m.* || **gold-fish** [-ˌfɪʃ] *n.* poisson *m* rouge.

golf [gɔlf] *n.* golf *m*: *to play* ~, jouer au golf; ~ *course*, terrain *m* de golf; ~ *club*, club *m*, canne *f* de golf; [society] club *m* de golf.

gondola [ˈgɑndələ] *n.* [Venice] gondole *f*; [airship] nacelle *f*; [Rail.] ~ *car*, wagon *m* ouvert.

gone [gɑn] cf. GO.

good [gud] *adj.* [**better, best**]. **1.** bon; bien; valide; gentil; fort; sage; brave; compétent: *Very* ~ *!*, Très bien!; *That's* ~, C'est bien, voilà qui est bien; [taste] C'est bon!; *It is* ~ *to be back*, C'est bon d'être de retour; [gen. statement] *It is* ~ *to have friends*, Il est bon d'avoir des amis; *It is* ~ *that you came*, Je suis content que vous soyez venu; [a veiled threat] Il est bon que vous soyez venu (sinon . . .); *It is* ~ *for you*, Cela vous fait du bien; ~ *for you!*, Bien joué!; *This ticket is* ~ *for three months*, Ce billet est valable trois mois; *It is* ~ *for nothing*, Ça ne vaut rien, Ce n'est bon à rien; *He is* ~ *to children*, Il est/bon, gentil/pour les enfants; *Would you be* ~ *enough to. . . ?*, Auriez-vous/l'obligeance, la bonté/de. . . ; *It is very* ~ *of you* (*to*) . . . , C'est très gentil à vous (de) . . . ; *He is* ~ *at French*, Il est/fort, bon/en français; *Be a* ~ */boy, girl/*, Sois sage; *He is a* ~ *man*, (a) [nice fellow], C'est un brave homme, (b) [morally ~], un homme de bien, (c) [at his job] un homme compétent; *the Good Book*, la Bible; *Good Friday*, Vendredi Saint; *as* ~ *as gold*, sage comme une image; *He is as* ~ *as dead*, Autant dire qu'il est mort; *as* ~ *as new*, comme neuf. **2.** [emphatic] bien; au moins: *a* ~ *deal, a* ~ *many*, beaucoup; *a* ~ 10 *years ago*, il y a/au moins, bien/dix ans; *He was* ~ *and hungry*, Il avait bien faim; ~ *and hot*, bien chaud. **3.** *to make* ~ : compenser, réparer (qqch.); indemniser (qqun de qqch.); tenir (promesse); effectuer (entreprise); réussir. || **good** *n.* bien *m*: *He works for the common* ~, Il travaille pour le bien commun; *That will do you* ~, Cela vous fera du bien; *It is no* ~, → Cela ne vaut rien; *It's no* ~, *I can't finish it*, → J'ai beau faire, je ne peux pas le finir; *It's no* ~ *just standing there*, → Cela ne sert à rien, Il est inutile/de rester là; *What's the* ~ *of/that, doing that/?*, A quoi bon (faire cela)?; *He is gone for* ~, Il est parti pour de bon. || **good afternoon** *interj.* [on meeting] [Fr.] © bonjour, [when parting] © bonjour, [Fr.] au revoir. || **good-by(e)** [ˌgud|ˈbaj] *interj.* au revoir; © bonjour; [farewell] adieu: ~ *till tomorrow*, à demain; *to say* ~, faire ses adieux (à qqun); [leave] prendre congé (de qqun). || **good-hearted** [-ˈhɑrtəd] *adj.* [pers.] qui a bon cœur. || **Good Hope (Cape of)**, (le Cap de) Bonne-Espérance. || **good-looking** [-ˈlʊkɪŋ] *adj.* [boy] beau; [girl] joli. || **goodly** [-lɪ] *adj.* **1.** [pers.] bon; beau. **2.** considérable. || **good morning** [-ˈmɔɚnɪŋ] *interj.* Bonjour. || **good-nature** [-ˈnejtʃɚ] bon naturel, gentillesse *f*: ~ *-natured*, d'un bon naturel, gentil. || **goodness** [-nəs] *n.* bonté *f*, bienveillance *f*: *My goodness!* [euphemism], Bonté divine!, Mon Dieu!; *For Goodness' sake!*, Pour l'amour de Dieu! || **good night** [-ˈnajt] *interj.* [when parting] bonsoir, au revoir; [when a person is going to bed] bonne nuit. || **goods** pl. biens *mpl* (personnels, de consommation); marchandises *fpl.*, articles *mpl.* [Br.] cf. FREIGHT: *dry* ~, nouveautés *fpl*; *manufactured* ~, produits *mpl* manufacturés. || **good-tempered** [-ˈtɛmpɚd], *adj.* de bon caractère, d'humeur égale, facile. || **good will** [-ˈwɪl] *n.* [pers.] bonne volonté *f.*; bienveillance *f*; considération *f* (envers qqun); [Com.] achalandage *m.* || **goody**

[-ɪ] *n.* **1.** sucrerie *f*, friandise *f*. **2.** [interj.] chic!

goose [guws] *pl.* **geese** [gijs] *n.* oie *f*; [Fig.] sot *m*, sotte *f*: *Canada* ~ (*grey* ~), bernache *f* canadienne; *a wild* ~ *chase*, un pas de clerc, un geste inutile.

gooseberry [ˈguwsˌbɛɚɪ] *n.* groseille *f* (à maquereau): ~ *bush*, groseillier *m* (cultivé).

gopher [ˈgowfɚ] citelle *m*, © gaufre *m*: *pocket* ~, gaufre gris, rat *m* des sables.

†**gore** [gɔɚ] *n.* sang *m.* caillé, coagulé; [poet.] sang versé. || *v. tr.* [bull, &c.] percer . . . d'un coup de corne, donner un coup de corne à . . . .

gorge [gɔɚʤ] *n.* [between mountains] gorge *f*, couloir *m*. 2. †*It makes my* ~ *rise*, Cela me soulève le cœur. || *v. tr.* gorger (qqun de nourriture). *to* ~ *o.s.*, s'empiffrer.

gorgeous [ˈgɔɚʤəs] *adj.* magnifique; [luxurious] fastueux.

gorilla [gəˈɹɪlə] *n.* gorille *m.*

†**gory** [ˈgɔɚɪ] *adj.* couvert de sang, sanglant, ensanglanté.

gospel [ˈgɑspl̩] *n.* [Rel.] Évangile *m*: ~ *truth*, parole *f* d'Évangile.

gossip [ˈgɑsɪp] *v. intr.* bavarder, [Fam.] potiner. || *n.* [pers.] bavard *m*; commère *f*; [stories] potin(s) *m*(*pl.*), commérages *mpl.*

got, gotten [gɑt] [-n̩] cf. GET [☞ *gotten* est moins fréquent que *got*].

gouge [gawʤ] *n.* gouge *f*. || *v. tr.* gouger: *to* ~ *out s.o.'s eyes*, arracher les yeux à qqun.

gout [gawt] *n.* goutte *f*.

govern [ˈgʌvɚn] *v. tr.* gouverner (un état); diriger (une administration); [Fig.] *motives which* ~ *my decision*, les motifs/qui commandent ma décision, → qui m'ont poussé à agir/. || **government** [-mənt] *n.* **1.** [state] gouvernement *m*, État *m* [qualified with adjective], régime *m*: *the Batista* ~, le régime B.; [City] conseil municipal. **2.** *adj.* d'État, administratif: ~ *offices*, l'administration *f*. || **governor** [-ɚ] *n.* gouverneur *m.*: *Governor-General*, Gouverneur-général, © *Lieutenant-Governor*, Lieutenant-gouverneur *m.*

gown [gawn] *n.* robe *f* (de soirée, de professeur, &c.): *dressing* ~, robe *f* de chambre.

grab [gɹæb] *v. tr.* [-bb-] empoigner; saisir. || *n.* prise *f*.

grace [gɹejs] *n.* grâce *f*: *to be in s.o.'s good graces*, être dans les bonnes grâces de qqun; *the* ~ *of God*, la grâce de Dieu; *3 days* ~, trois jours de grâce; *to say* ~, [before the meal] dire le bénédicité, [after the meal] dire les grâces. || **graceful** [-fl̩] *adj.* gracieux, élégant. || **gracefulness** [-fl̩nəs] *n.* grâce *f*, élégance *f*.

gracious [ˈgɹejʃəs] *adj.* gracieux.

grade [gɹejd] *n.* **1.** [Sch.] année *f*, classe *f*, cours *m*: *What* ~ *are you in?*, En quelle/classe, année/êtes-vous?; [esp. US] *grade*(*d*) *school*, école *f* primaire. **2.** degré *m*, rang *m*, échelon *m*; qualité *f*: *grade A milk*, lait *m*/de première qualité, supérieur/. **3.** rampe *f* (de chemin de fer), pente *f*: [Fig.] *to make the* ~, réussir, surmonter l'obstacle; ~ *crossing*, passage *m à* niveau. || **grade** *v. tr.* classer, trier (des objets); graduer [= faire graduellement]; niveler (un terrain). || **gradual** [ˈgɹæʤuwl̩] *adj.* graduel, progressif. || **gradually** [-ɪ] *adv.* peu à peu, petit à petit; par degrés, graduellement.

graduate [ˈgɹæʤuwət] *n.* diplômé *m*, -e *f* © gradué *m*, -e *f*; ancien(ne) élève: *He is a* ~ *of McGill* (*University*), → Il sort de McGill; *He is a high school* ~, → Il a obtenu son diplôme secondaire; *a university* ~, [Fr.] un(e) licencié(e). || *adj.* diplômé, © gradué: *a* ~ *student*, un(e) diplômé(e); *Graduate Reading Room*, Salle de lecture réservée aux Diplômés; (*post-*) ~ *studies*, études *fpl* supérieures. || **graduate** [ˈgɹæʤuw|ˌejt] *v. intr.*: *to* ~ *from a school*, /sortir, © graduer/d'une école, prendre ses diplômes: *When did you* ~ *?* En quelle année avez-vous reçu votre diplôme?; *the graduate class*, la classe sortante. || *v. tr.* graduer (un thermomètre, &c.): [Sch.] *This college graduated* 1000 *students last year*, Cette université a décerné des diplômes à mille étudiants l'année passée. || **graduation** [ˌgɹæʤuwˈejʃən] *n.* **1.** [marking] graduation *f*. **2.** [Sch.] collation *f*/des grades, des diplômes: *After* ~, *he* . . . , → Après avoir reçu son diplôme, il . . . cf. COMMENCEMENT.

graft [gɹæft] *n.* **1.** corruption *f* (de fonctionnaires, &c.); [money received] pot-de-vin *m.* **2.** greffe *f* (d'un arbre). || *v. tr.* greffer.

grain [gɹejn] **1.** *n.* grain *m.* (de blé, &c.); [Coll.] grains, *mpl* céréales *fpl.* [surtout le blé]: ~ *elevator*, élévateur *m.* à grains. **2.** grain *m.* (du bois); [Troy weight] grain: [Fig.] *It goes against the* ~, → Je le fais/à contre-cœur, en rechignant.

gram [gɹæm] cf. GRAMME.

grammar [ˈgɹæmɚ] *n.* grammaire *f*: ~ *school*, [US] école *f* primaire, [UK] école *f* secondaire, © collège *m* (classique). || **grammatical** [gɹəˈmætɪkl̩] *adj.* grammatical, correct.

gramme [gɹæm] *n.* [Meas.] gramme *m.*

granary [ˈgɹænɚɪ] *n.* grenier *m.*

grand [gɹænd] *adj.* [× surtout au figuré: *grandiose*, et dans des expressions figées] grandiose, magnifique: *a ~ old man*, une grande figure (politique, &c.); *~ piano*, piano *m* à queue. [Fam.] *Isn't it ~ !*, C'est/formidable!, superbe!, magnifique! &c./. ‖ **grandchild** [-ˌtʃajld] *pl.* **grandchildren** [-ˌtʃɪldɹən] *n.* petit-fils *m*, petite-fille *f*, petits-enfants *mpl.* ‖ **gran(d-)dad** [ˈgræn ˌdæd] cf. GRANDPA. ‖ **granddaughter** [-ˌdɔtɚ] *n.* petite-fille *f.* ‖ **grandeur** [ˈgɹændʒɚ] *n.* grandeur *f*, magnificence *f.* ‖ **grandfather** [-ˌfɑðɚ] *n.* grand-père *m.* ‖ **grandiose** [ˈgɹændɪˌows] *adj.* grandiose, magnifique. ‖ **grandma** [ˈgɹænˌmɑ], [Fam.] **granny** [ˈgɹænɪ] *n.* [Fam.] bonne-maman *f*, mémé *f*, grand-maman *f.* ‖ **grandmother** [-ˌmʌðɚ] *n.* grand-mère *f.* ‖ **grandpa** [ˈgɹænˌpa] *n.* [Fam.] bon-papa *m*, pépé *m*, grand-papa *m.* ‖ **grandparent** [-ˌpɛɚənt] *n.* grand-parent *m*, aïeul *m.* ‖ **grandson** [-ˌsʌn] *n.* petit-fils *m.* ‖ **grandstand** [-ˌstænd] *n.* tribune *f* (d'honneur).

grange [gɹejndʒ] *n.* [US] © association agricole; [Br.] manoir *m.*

granite [gɹænɪt] *n.* granit *m.*

granny [ˈgɹænɪ] cf. GRANDMA.

grant [gɹænt] *n.* concession *f*; [statutory] allocation *f*; [state] subvention *f.* ‖ *v. tr.* **1.** accorder, octroyer (qqch. à qqun). **2.** accorder, concéder (qqch.): *I ~ you that . . .*, Je vous/accorde, concède/ que . . .; *to take for granted*, poser en principe; admettre/au départ, sans discussion; *to take s.o. for granted*, traiter qqun en quantité négligeable; ne tenir aucun compte de qqun; *Granted!*, Entendu!, Je vous le concède!

grape [gɹejp] *n.* grain *m* de raisin, *pl.* raisins *mpl*, [used in a collective sense] le raisin: *a bunch of grapes*, une grappe de raisin; *Sour grapes!*, → Ils sont trop verts! ‖ **grapefruit** [ˈgɹejpˌfɹuwt] *n.* pamplemousse *m.*

graph [gɹæf] *n.* graphique *m*, diagramme *m*, courbe *f.* ‖ **graphic** [-ɪk] *adj.* graphique; [Fig.] pittoresque, vivant: *a ~ account*, un compte-rendu vivant, animé.

grapple [ˈgɹæpl̩] *v. tr.* (s')accrocher (à), (s')agripper (à); [Fig.] *to ~ with a problem*,/s'attaquer à, aborder résolument/une question.

grasp [gɹæsp] *n.* étreinte *f*, prise *f*; [Fig.] compréhension *f* (d'un problème), connaissance *f* (d'un sujet): *a strong ~*, une forte poigne; *He lost his ~*, Il a lâché prise; [Fig.] *It is within my ~*, C'est à ma portée; *to have a good ~ of one's subject*, → bien connaître son sujet. ‖ **grasp** *v. tr.* saisir, empoigner; [Fig.] saisir, comprendre: *He grasped my hand*, Il m'a serré la main. ‖ *v. intr. to ~ at sth.*, tâcher de saisir qqch.

grasping [ˈgɹæspɪŋ] *adj.* âpre au gain.

grass [gɹæs] *n.* herbe *f* (des champs); [lawn] gazon *m*: *~ plot*, pelouse *f*; *a blade of ~*, brin *m* d'herbe: *Keep off the ~*, → Défense de marcher sur la pelouse. ‖ **grasshopper** [ˈgɹæsˌhɑpɚ] *n.* sauterelle *f.* ‖ **grassland** [-ˌlænd] *n.* prairie *f.* ‖ **grassy** [gɹæsɪ] *adj.* herbeux, herbu.

grate[1] [gɹejt] *n.* grille *f*; [hearth] foyer *m.* ‖ **grating**[1] [-ɪŋ] *n.* grillage *m* (d'une porte, d'une fenêtre).

grate[2] *v. intr.* [door] grincer; [cheese] râper; [Fig.] irriter: *to ~ on one's/ears, nerves/*, écorcher les/oreilles, nerfs/de qqun. ‖ **grating**[2] *n.* grincement *m* (métallique, déplaisant). ‖ *adj.* grinçant, désagréable.

grateful [-fl̩] *adj.* reconnaissant (*to s.o. for sth.*) (à, envers/qqun de qqch.): *I should be very ~ to you if you would . . .*, Je vous serais infiniment reconnaissant de . . ., Je vous saurais infiniment gré de . . . ‖ **gratefully** [-fl̩ɪ] *adv.* avec reconnaissance.

gratify [ˈgɹætɪˌfaj] *v. tr.* faire plaisir à (qqun); satisfaire (qqun, aux désirs de qqun), contenter (le désir de qqun): *a gratifying feeling*, → un sentiment de satisfaction; *It is gratifying to know . . .*, Il est très agréable de savoir . . .; *I was much gratified to learn . . .*, J'ai été enchanté d'apprendre . . .

grating cf. GRATE[1, 2].

gratitude [ˈgɹætɪˌtjuwd] *n.* gratitude *f*, reconnaissance *f.*

gratuitous [gɹəˈtjuw/ɪtəs] *adj.* [free] gratuit; [without reason] arbitraire: *~ insult*, insulte *f* gratuite. ‖ **gratuity** [-ətɪ] *n.* [tip] pourboire *m*; [gift of money] gratification *f.*

grave[1] [gɹejv] (-r, -st) *adj.* [event] grave; important; sérieux; solennel: *~ accent*, accent *m* grave.

grave[2] *n.* tombe *f*; [monument] tombeau *m*, monument *m.*: *to carry s.o. to the ~*, porter qqun en terre.

gravel [ˈgɹævl̩] gravier *m*, © gravelle *f*; [Med.] gravelle *f*: *n. ~ road*, route *f* de terre, © route de gravier.

gravestone [ˈgɹəjvˌstown] *n.* pierre *f* tombale. ‖ **graveyard** [-ˌjɑɚd] *n.* cimetière *m.*

gravity [ˈgɹævɪtɪ] *n.* [weight] pesanteur *f*; [Phys.] gravité *f*, gravitation *f*; [Fig.]

gravité *f*, importance *f* (d'un événement): *the law of* ~, la loi de gravité; *the force of* ~, la force de la gravitation; *the centre of* ~, le centre de gravité; *specific* ~, poids *m* spécifique.

gravy ['gɹejvɪ] *n.* jus *m* (d'un rôti); sauce *f* au jus.

gray [gɹej] *adj.* gris: *to go, to turn/* ~, grisonner. || *n.* gris *m.* || *v. tr. & intr.* [of hair] grisonner. || **grayish** [-ɪʃ] *adj.* grisâtre, [hair] grisonnant.

graze [gɹejz] *v. tr.* **1.** brouter (l'herbe). **2.** faire paître (des moutons, &c.). **3.** [Fig.] raser, effleurer; [deep] écorcher (la peau, &c.), érafler. || *v. intr.* paître, brouter.

grease [gɹijs] *n.* graisse *f.* || *v. tr.* graisser. || **greasy** [-ɪ] *adj.* **1.** [hair, clothes] graisseux; [food] gras *m*, grasse *f*; [rag, skin] huileux; [road] glissant. **2.** [Pej.] [person, manner] onctueux, gluant.

great [gɹejt] *adj.* **1.** [size, quantity] grand, énorme, considérable: *a* ~ *deal (of)*, beaucoup (de). **2.** [importance, worth] [Fig.] *He was a* ~ *man*, C'était un/grand homme, homme célèbre/, *She was a* ~ *woman*, C'était une femme incomparable [× grande femme = *tall woman*]. **3.** [distinction, superiority] splendide, magnifique: *That's* ~ *!*, → [Fam.] formidable!, [iron.] On est gâté! **4.** arrière-; grand-; petit-: ~ *-grandfather*, ~ *-grandmother*, arrière-grand-père *m*, bisaïeul *m*, arrière-grand-mère *f*, bisaïeule *f*; ~ - ~ *-grand|father, -mother*, trisaïeul *m*, -e *f*; (~ -) ~ *-grandson, -daughter*, (arrière-) arrière-petit-fils *m*, -petite-fille *f*; ~ *-uncle, -aunt*, grand-oncle *m*, grand-tante *f*; ~ - ~ *-uncle, -aunt*, arrière grand-oncle, arrière-grand-tante; ~ *-nephew, -niece*, petit-neveu *m*, petite-nièce *f*; ~ - ~ *-nephew, -niece*, arrière-petit-neveu *m*, arrière-petite-nièce *f*. || **great-coat** [-ˌkowt] *n.* †cf. OVERCOAT; [Mil.] capote *f.* || **Greater Montreal**, l'agglomération montréalaise, le Grand Montréal. || **greatly** [-lɪ] *adv.* grandement, considérablement, (de) beaucoup; [Fig.] splendidement, magnifiquement, avec grandeur. || **greatness** [-nəs] *n.* grandeur *f*, énormité *f*; [vastness] étendue *f*; [Fig.] importance *f*; grandeur *f*.

Grecian ['gɹijʃən] *adj.* grec *m.* || **Greece** [gɹijs] *n.* la Grèce: *in, to/* ~, en Grèce.

greed [gɹijd] *n.* [gen. quality] avidité [usual. qualified]; [desire] cupidité *f*; [covetousness] convoitise *f* [food] gourmandise *f*; *the* ~ *with which he accepts everything*, l'avidité avec laquelle il accepte tout; ~ *for money, &c.*, soif *f* immodérée des richesses, &c. || **greedily** [-ɪlɪ] *adv.* avidement, avec gourmandise. || **greediness** [-ɪnəs] cf. GREED. || **greedy** [-ɪ] *adj.* avide, cupide; [food] gourmand.

Greek [gɹijk] *adj.* grec *m*, grecque *f*.

green [gɹijn] *adj.* **1.** vert: *to grow, turn/* ~, verdir; ~ *light*, feu *m* vert; [Fig.] *He has the* ~ *light*, → La route est libre, Il a la permission de.... **2.** [Fig.] nouveau; naïf; inexpérimenté. || *n.* vert *m*; [grass] gazon *m*; [trees] verdure *f*; *greens*, légumes *mpl* (verts). || **greenback** [-ˌbæk] [Fam.] *n.* dollar *m*, © tomate *f*. || **greenery** [-ərɪ] *n.* verdure *f*, espace *m* vert. || **green-grocer** [-ˌgɹowsər] *n.* [Br.] marchand *m* de légumes, fruitier *m.* || **greenhouse** [-ˌhaws] *n.* serre *f.* || **greenish** [-ɪʃ] *adj.* verdâtre.

Greenland [-ˌlænd] *n.* Groënland *m*: *in, to/* ~, au Groënland. || **Greenlander** *n.* Groënlandais *m.*

greenness ['gɹijnnəs] *n.* verdure *f*, vert *m*; [Fig.] verdeur *f* (d'un vieillard); inexpérience *f*.

greet [gɹijt] *v. tr.* saluer (qqun); [receive] accueillir (qqun, qqch.). || **greeting** [-ɪŋ] *n.* salutation *f*, salut *m*; *pl.* compliments *mpl*: *Greetings!*, Salut!; *(The) Season's Greetings*, Meilleurs/souhaits, vœux/(de joyeux Noël et) de nouvel An.

gregarious [gɹɛ'gɛərɪəs] *adj.* grégaire; qui aime la foule.

Gregory ['gɹɛgərɪ] *n.* = Grégoire.

grew [gɹuw] cf. GROW.

grey [gɹej] cf. GRAY. || **greyhound** [-ˌhawnd] *n.* lévrier *m.*

griddle ['gɹɪdl] *n.* plaque *f* chauffante. || **griddle-cake** [-ˌkejk] *n.* crêpe *f.*

gridiron ['gɹɪdˌajərn] *n.* gril *m*; [US, Fam.] terrain *m* de football.

grief [gɹijf] *n.* peine *f*, chagrin *m*, douleur *f*: *to cause s.o.* ~, faire/du chagrin, de la peine/à qqun; *to come to* ~ [pers.] finir mal, [plan] échouer. || **grieve** [gɹijv] *v. tr.* chagriner, peiner/qqun. || *v. intr.* se chagriner, s'affliger (*over sth.*, à cause de qqch.). || **grievous** [-əs] *adj.* [pain] grave, cruel; [cry] douloureux, [wound] grave. || **grievously** [-lɪ] *adv.* gravement, cruellement: ~ *wounded*, grièvement blessé.

grill [gɹɪl] *n.* **1.** [cooking] gril *m*: *mixed* ~, grillades *fpl.* **2.** © grill *m*, café *m* dansant. || *v. tr.* [cooking] faire griller; [Fam., Police] cuisiner qqun.

grim [gɹɪm] *adj.* [-mm-] [stern] farouche; [not yielding] implacable; [fierce] sinistre, menaçant; [ghastly] macabre; [smile] sardonique.

grimace [gɹə'mejs] *n.* grimace *f.* || *v. intr.* grimacer. [plus fort que GRIN].

grime [gɹajm] *n.* crasse *f*, saleté *f*. || **grimy** [-ɪ] *adj.* crasseux, sale.

grin [gɹɪn] *n.* large sourire *m*; grimace *f*. || *v. intr.* [-nn-] sourire (à qqun), avoir un large sourire (pour qqun); faire des grimaces à qqun: *~ and bear it*, Faites-le avec le sourire.

grind [gɹajnd] **ground, ground** [gɹawnd] *v. tr.* moudre (la farine); broyer (les aliments); hacher (la viande); aiguiser (un couteau); grincer (des dents); [Auto.] roder (les soupapes); jouer (d'un orgue de Barbarie). || *v. intr.* [noise] grincer; [Fam.] *to ~ away at* (*French, maths*), bûcher (le français, les maths). || **grind** *n.* café *m* moulu, © mouture *f*; [Fam.] boulot *m*: *the daily ~*, le train-train quotidien. || **grinder** [-ɚ] *n.* [man] repasseur *m*, [Fr.] rémouleur *m* [de couteaux, &c.]; [machine] broyeur *m*, moulin *m* (à café), hachoir *m* à viande. || **grinding** [-ɪŋ] *n.* broyage *m* (des aliments); grincement *m* (des dents, d'une roue); [Auto.] rodage *m* (des soupapes). || **grindstone** [-ˌstown] *n.* meule *f*.

grip [gɹɪp] *n.* **1.** prise *f*, [arms] étreinte *f*: *to come to grips*, en venir aux prises; *to lose one's ~*, lâcher prise; *He has a strong ~*, Il a une bonne poigne. **2.** [bag] valise *f*; sac *m* de voyage; [handle] poignée *f*. || **grip** *v. tr.* **[-pp-]** empoigner, saisir fortement, serrer (dans la main).

gripe [gɹajp] [Fam.] *v. intr.* ronchonner.

grippe [gɹɪp] also **grip** *n.* [Med.] grippe *f*.

grisly [gɹɪslɪ] *adj.* terrifiant, horrible; macabre.

grit [gɹɪt] *n.* grès *m*; [loose] gravier *m*; [Fig.] courage *m*: *to show ~*, avoir du cran. || *v. tr.* [-tt-] grincer (des dents).

grizzly [ˈgɹɪzlɪ] *adj.* grisâtre: *~ (bear)*, grizzly *m*, ours *m* gris d'Amérique.

groan [gɹown] *n.* gémissement *m*; [animal] grognement: *to give a ~*, pousser un gémissement. || *v. intr.* gémir: [Fig.] grogner, murmurer (*at*, contre; *in*, *with*, de).

grocer [ˈgɹowsɚ] *n.* épicier *m*. || **groceries** [-ɪz] *n.pl.* articles *mpl* d'épicerie, denrées *fpl*, provisions *fpl*; [budget item] nourriture *f*. || **grocery** [-ɪ] *n.* épicerie *f*, © marché *m*: *at, to/the grocer's*, à l'épicerie, chez l'épicier. || **groceteria** [ˌgɹowsəˈtijəɹə] *n.* épicerie *f* libre-service.

groin [gɹojn] *n.* [Med.] aine *f*.

groove [gɹuwv] *n.* rainure *f* (dans le bois): [Fam.] *to be in a ~*, devenir routinier. || *v. tr.* creuser; faire une rainure (dans le bois).

grope [gɹowp] *v. tr.* tâtonner: *to ~ for* (*sth.*), chercher (qqch.) à tâtons. || **gropingly** [-ɪŋlɪ] *adv.* à tâtons.

gross [gɹows] *adj.* [ignorance, mistake] grossier; [injustice] criant; [thick] épais; [weight, profit] (poids, bénéfice) brut, total. || *n.* [Meas.] grosse *f*. || **grossly** [-lɪ] *adv.* grossièrement; outre mesure.

grotto [ˈgɹɑtow] *n.* grotte *f*.

grouch [gɹawtʃ] [Fam.] *n.* [pers.] grognon *m*; [mood] humeur *f* grognon: *Don't be such a ~!*, Ne sois pas aussi grognon!; *I've got a ~ (against him)*, [Fam.] Je suis en rogne (après lui), Je lui en veux. || *v. intr.* grogner, ronchonner, être d'humeur maussade. || **grouchy** [-ɪ] *adj.* [character, disposition] maussade, [person] grognon. [*grognon* has no *fem.* form].

ground[1] [gɹawnd] *n.* **1.** terre *f*, [tract of land] terrain *m*; [soil] sol *m*: *to fall on the ~*, tomber/à terre, par terre/; *down to the ~, from the ~ up*, de fond en comble, [Fig.] à merveille; [Loc.] *to cover ~*, faire du chemin; *to gain ~*, gagner du terrain; *to give ~*, lâcher pied; *to stand one's ~*, tenir/bon, ferme/, → ne pas lâcher pied; *~ floor*, le rez-de-chaussée *m inv.*; [Aviat.] *~ crew*, équipe *f* au sol. **2.** [Fig. usual. *pl.*] fondement *m* (d'une théorie), base *f* (d'un accord); motif *m*, cause *f* (d'un jugement): *to have ~ for*, avoir matière à . . .; *There are grounds for (believing)*, Il y a lieu de (croire); **3.** [Electr.] terre *f*, masse *f*: *~ wire*, fil *m* de terre. **4.** *pl.* parc *m* (d'une propriété); terrain *m* (d'une université). **5.** *pl.* marc *m* (de café). || **ground** *v. tr.* fonder, baser; appuyer (qqch. sur qqch.); enseigner (qqch. à qqun) à fond; [Naut.] échouer (un bateau); [Aviat.] garder (un avion) au sol; [Elec.] mettre (qqch.) à la terre: *to be well grounded in . . .*, avoir de solides notions de . . .: *His suspicions are/well, ill/grounded*, Ses soupçons sont /bien, mal/fondés.

ground[2] [gɹawnd] cf. GRIND.

grounding [-ɪŋ] *n.* connaissance *f* de base: *He has a good ~ in history*, Il a de solides notions d'histoire. || **groundless** [-ləs] *adj.* sans fondement, injustifié.

group [gɹuwp] *n.* groupe *m*; [Mil.] *~ captain*, colonel *m* (d'aviation), © capitaine *m* de groupe. || *v. tr. to ~ (together)*, grouper.

grouse [gɹaws] *n.*: *Canada ~*, © perdrix *f*, tétras *m* (des savanes).

grow [gɹow], **grew** [gɹuw], **grown** [gɹown] *v. intr.* croître; [plants] pousser; [seeds] germer; [pers.] grandir, devenir grand; [increase] s'accroître; [become] devenir [or a special verb or expression]: *to ~ /big(ger), worried, dark, &c./*, grandir /s'inquiéter, faire nuit &c. [cf. adj.]; [Fig.] *It grows upon you*, Cela devient une habitude. || *v. tr.* cultiver, faire pousser; laisser pousser (sa barbe). || **grow out of** *v. intr. He will ~ it*, [clothes] Il sera bientôt trop grand; [habitude] Cela lui passera. || **grow up** *v. intr.* grandir, devenir grand: *to ~ into a man*, devenir homme. || **grower** [-ɚ] *n.* cultivateur *m.* || **growing** [-ɪŋ] *n.* croissance *f*; [cultivation] culture *f*: *~ pains*, douleurs *fpl* de croissance. || *adj.* croissant, qui pousse; [pers.] grandissant; de plus en plus . . . : *a ~ tendency to . . .*, une tendance de plus en plus marquée à . . .

growl [gɹawl] *v. intr.* grommeler, grogner.

grown [gɹown] *adj.*: *full-~*, grand, adulte. || **grown-up** [-ˌʌp] *n.* grande personne *f*, adulte *m.*

growth [gɹowθ] *n.* [increase] accroissement *m*; [persons, plants] croissance *f*, [Fig.] progrès *m*; [produce] produit *m*; [tumour] excroissance *f*, grosseur *f*.

grub [gɹʌb] *v. tr.* [-ff-] défricher (un terrain). || *v. intr.* creuser (en fouillant), fouiller. || *n.* [worm] asticot *m*; [Arg.] boustifaille *f*, mangeaille *f*.

grudge [gɹʌʤ] *n.* rancune *f*, haine *f* (tenace): *to/have, nurse/a ~ against s.o.*,/garder rancune à, en vouloir à, *to/keep, hold/a ~*, être rancunier. || *v. tr.* donner à contre-cœur. || **grudgingly** [-ɪŋlɪ] *adv.* à contre-cœur.

gruelling ['gɹuwlɪŋ] *adj.* pénible.

gruesome [gɹuwsəm] *adj.* macabre.

gruff [gɹʌf] *adj.* bourru, brusque. || **gruffly** [-lɪ] *adv.* d'une manière bourrue.

grumble [gɹʌmbl] *n.* grognement *m* (sourd). || *v. intr.* [animal] grogner; [person] grommeler (*at*, contre).

grumpy [gɹʌmpɪ] *adj.* [person, character] grognon, maussade, bourru.

grunt [gɹʌnt] *n.* grognement *m.* || *v. intr.* grogner.

guarantee ['gæɚəntɪ] *n.* garantie *f* (*against*, contre), caution *f*; [pers.] garant *m*, répondant *m.* || *v. tr.* garantir (qqch.); [sth. to s.o.] répondre à qqun de qqch.

guard [gɑɚd] *n.* garde *f*; protection *f*; [pers.] garde *m*, [prison] gardien *m*; [rail] garde-fou *m*; [subway, Br. railways] chef *m* de train: *on ~ !*, en garde!; *to be on one's ~ (against)*, être sur ses gardes (contre); *to be caught off (one's) ~*, être pris au dépourvu; [sentinel] *to be on ~*, être de garde; *to mount ~ (over)*, monter la garde (sur); *under ~*, sous bonne garde, sous surveillance. || **guard** *v. tr.* garder, protéger, défendre (*against*, contre). || *v. intr. to ~ against*, se garder de. || **guardedly** [-ədlɪ] *adv.* avec circonspection, prudemment. || **guardhouse** [-ˌhaws] *n.* corps-de-garde *m inv.* || **guardian** [-ɪən] *n.* gardien *m*, -ne *f*; [of child] tuteur *m*, tutrice *f*: *~ angel*, ange *m* gardien. || **guards|man** [-zmən] *n.* (*pl.* **-men**) garde *m.*

guerilla [gɚ'ɪlə] *n.* **1.** guérilla *f*: *~ warfare*, guerre *f* de partisans. **2.** partisan *m.*

guess [gɛs] *v. tr. & intr.* **1.** deviner: *~ who?* Qui est là? **2.** Supposer, penser: *It was my mistake, I ~*, → Je suppose que c'était de ma faute. || *n.* conjecture *f*, supposition *f*: *at a ~*, au jugé. || **guesswork** [-ˌwɚk] *n.* supposition *f*: *It's mere ~*, Ce ne sont que des suppositions.

guest [gɛst] *n.* hôte *m*, -esse *f* [qui est reçu], convive *m/f*, invité *m*, -e *f*: *~ room*, [-ɹuwm] chambre *f* d'amis; *~ house*, [-ˌhaws] pension *f* (de famille); *paying ~*, pensionnaire *m*; *~ speaker* [-ˌspijkɚ] orateur *m*/invité, de circonstance/.

guidance ['gajdəns] *n.* conduite *f*, direction *f*; [Psych.] orientation *f*. || **guide** [gajd] *v. tr.* guider, conduire; gouverner: *guided missile*, projectile *m*, engin *m*/téléguidé. || *n.* guide *m*; [girl ~] éclaireuse *f*; [book] guide *m.* || **guidebook** [-ˌbuk] *n.* guide *m.* || **guidepost** [-ˌpowst] poteau *m* indicateur (de route).

guile [gajl] *n.* ruse *f*, astuce *f*, artifice *m.*

guilt [gɪlt] *n.* culpabilité *f*; faute *f*; crime *m.* || **guiltless** [-ləs] *adj.* innocent. || **guilty** [-ɪ] *adj.* coupable: *to be found ~*, être reconnu coupable, *to plead ~*, s'avouer, plaider/coupable; *not ~*, → innocent.

guinea[1] ['gɪnɪ] *n.* [money] guinée *f*. || **Guinea**[2] ['gɪnɪ] *n.* Guinée *f*: *in, to/ ~*, en Guinée. || **guinea-fowl** [-ˌfawl], **guinea-hen** [-ˌhɛn] *n.* pintade *f*. || **guinea-pig** [-ˌpɪg] *n.* cobaye *m.*

guise [gajz] *n.* dehors *mpl*, aspect *m*; déguisement *m*: *in the ~ of (sth., s.o.)*, [person] déguisé en, sous le déguisement de, sous les apparences de (qqch., qqun): *under the ~ of friendship*, sous un semblant d'amitié.

guitar [gə'tɑɚ] *n.* guitare *f*.

gulch [gʌltʃ] *n.* ravin *m.*

gulf [gʌlf] *n.* golfe *m*; gouffre *m*, [Fig.] abîme *m*, séparation *f* profonde: *the Gulf Stream*, le Gulfstream; *the Gulf of St. Lawrence*, le golfe Saint-Laurent.

gull [gʌl] *n.* mouette *f*, goéland *m* (also *sea gull*).

gullible [ˌgʌlɪbḷ] *adj.* [pers.] crédule, naïf.
gully [ˈgʌlɪ] *n.* ravin *m.*
gulp [gʌlp] *v. tr.* gober, avaler (sa nourriture) (à grandes bouchées) [also ~ *down*]; dire (qqch.) d'une voix étranglée. || *n.* gorgée *f* (de liquide); bouchée (de nourriture): *He swallowed it at a* ~, Il l'avala d'un trait, d'un seul coup.
gum[1] [gʌm] *n.* gomme *f*: (*chewing*) ~, © la gomme *f* (à mâcher), (Fr.) le chewing (-gum). || *v. tr.* [-mm-] gommer [Tech.] gommer (un moteur): *gummed up*, encrassé.
gum[2] *n.* [usual. *pl.*] gencive *f.*
gun [gʌn] *n.* [artillery] canon *m*; [rifle] fusil *m*; [revolver] revolver *m*; [paint] pistolet *m*: *machine* ~, mitrailleuse *f*; *submachine* ~, mitraillette *f*; [Fig.] *to stick to one's guns*, suivre son idée. || **gunfire** [-ˌfajɚ] *n.* canonnade *f*; coups *mpl* de feu. || **gunman** [-mən] *n.* bandit *m,* malfaiteur *m* (armé): [Fr.] gangster *m.* || **gunner** [-ɚ] *n.* artilleur *m*; canonnier *m,* [Aviat.] mitrailleur *m.* || **gunpowder** [-ˌpawdɚ] *n.* poudre *f* à canon. || **gunshot** [-ˌʃɑt] *n.* coup *m*/de feu, de fusil, de canon: *within* ~, à portée de/ fusil, canon/; ~ *wound*, (il a reçu un) coup de fusil.
gurgle [ˈgɚgḷ] *n.* glouglou *m*, gargouillement *m* (de l'eau, &c.). || *v. intr.* [water] gargouiller.
gush [gʌʃ] *n.* [spring] jaillissement *m* (de l'eau). || *v. intr.* [blood, water] jaillir (à flots, à gros bouillons).
gust [gʌst] *n.* coup *m* de vent, rafale *f*; [Fig.] accès *m* (de colère, &c.). || **gusty** [ˈgʌstɪ] *adj.* [day] de grand vent, [weather] venteux.
gut [gʌt] *n.* boyau *m*, intestin *m*, tripe *f*: [Arg.] *guts*, cran *m*; || *v. tr.* [-tt-] vider (un poisson); [Fig.] [fire] raser (un édifice à l'intérieur).
gutter [ˈgʌtɚ] *n.* ruisseau *m* [dans la rue], caniveau *m* [sur une route]; gouttière *f* [sur le toit d'une maison].
guy[1] [gaj] *n.* hauban *m* (de mât), tendeur *m* (de tente, &c.).
guy[2] *n.* [Sl.] type *m*, gars *m.*
gym [ʤɪm] [abr. = GYMNASIUM].
gymnasium [ˌʤɪmˈnejzɪəm] *n.* gymnase *m.* || **gymnastics** [-ˈnæstɪks] *n.* gymnastique *f.*
gyp [ʤɪp] *v. tr.* [Fam.] entauler, refaire.
gypsy *adj.*, **Gypsy** *n.* [ˈʤɪpsɪ] gitan *m*, -e.

H

H, h [ejtʃ] *pl.* H's, h's *n.* la lettre H, le H.
Hab [hæb] *pl.* Habs [surnom, surtout journalistique, donné aux Canadiens français] cf. HABITANT.
Habana [həˈbɑnə], also **Havana** *n.* La Havane.
haberdasher [ˈhæbɚˌdæʃɚ] chemisier *m* (pour hommes); [Fr.] mercier *m.* || **haberdashery** [-ɪ] *n.* lingerie *f* (pour hommes), chemiserie *f*; [Br.] mercerie *f.* cf. NOTIONS.
habit [ˈhæbɪt] *n.* **1.** habitude *f*; coutume *f*: ~ *of mind*, tournure *f* d'esprit; *to/get, grow/into the* ~ *of* . . . /prendre, contracter/l'habitude de . . . . **2.** [religious] habit *m*; [riding] amazone *f.*
habitant [ˈhæbɪˌtɑnt] *n.* habitant *m*, cf. INHABITANT; © l'Habitant *m*; cultivateur *m.*
habitat [ˈhæbɪˌtæt] *n.* habitat *m.*
habitual [həˈbɪtʃuwəl] *adj.* habituel, assidu: *an* ~ *sight*, un spectacle habituel; *an* ~ *reader*, un lecteur assidu. || **habituate** [həˈbɪtʃuwejt] *v. tr.* habituer: *to* ~ *o.s. to*, s'habituer à.
hack [hæk] *v. tr.* tailler à coups de hache; hacher (*to pieces*, en morceaux): ~ *saw*, scie *f* à métaux.
hackmatack [ˈhækməˌtæk] *n.* [Bot.] © épinette *f* rouge.
hackneyed [ˈhækˌnijd] *adj.* [trite] banal, rebattu.
had [hæd] cf. HAVE.
haddock [ˈhædək] *n.* [pl. *-s* ou coll. invar.] aiglefin *m*; © goberge *f*, poisson de Saint-Pierre.
hæmorrhage [ˈhɛmɹəʤ] *n.* hémorragie *f.*

haft [hæft] *n.* [knife] manche *m*; poignée *f*; [sword] garde *f*.

hag [hæg] *n.* femme *f* vieille et laide: *old* ~, vieille sorcière.

haggard [ˈhægɚd] *adj.* [look] farouche, hâve.

haggle [ˈhægḷ] *v. intr.* [article, goods] marchander; découper maladroitement.

hail[1] [hejl] *v. tr.* saluer; [taxi] héler. || *n.* **1.** salut *m*; salutation *f*: *Hail Mary*, Salutation *f* angélique; Ave Maria *m*. **2.** appel *m*: *within* ~, à portée de la voix.

hail[2] *n.* grêle *f*. || *v. intr.* grêler. || **hailstone** [-ˌstown] *n.* grêlon *m*. || **hailstorm** [-ˌstɔɚm] *n.* tempête *f* de grêle, grêle *f*.

hair [hɛɚ] *n.* **1.** [human head] cheveu *m*; [elsewhere & animals] poil *m*; [horse] crin *m*: *to a* ~, exactement, [Vulg.] à un poil près; *to have a hairbreadth escape*, l'échapper belle; [Fig.] *to split hairs*, couper les cheveux en quatre. **2.** [coll. invar., cf. §1] cheveux *mpl*, chevelure *f*, poils *mpl*, crins *mpl*, [hog, &c.] soies *fpl*: ~ *cream*, cosmétique *m*; *to do one's* ~, se coiffer; *to comb one's* ~, se peigner; *to have one's* ~ *cut* (ou *to get a haircut*), se faire couper les cheveux. || **haircut** [-ˌkʌt] *n.* coupe *f* (de cheveux). || **hairdo** [-ˌduw] *n.* coiffure *f*. || **hairdresser** [-ˌdɹɛsɚ] *n.* coiffeur *m* pour dames; coiffeuse *f*. || **hairless** [-ləs] *adj.* chauve; sans poil. || **hairnet** [-ˌnɛt] *n.* résille *f*. || **hairpin** [-ˌpɪn] *n.* épingle *f* à cheveux: ~ *turn*, virage *m* en épingle à cheveux. || **hair-raising** [-ˌɹejzɪŋ] *adj.* à faire dresser les cheveux sur la tête. || **hairy** [-ɪ] *adj.* chevelu, poilu, velu.

Haiti [ˈhejtɪ] *n.* Haïti [no article]. || **Haitian** [-n] *adj.* & *n.* Haïtien

hale [hejl] *adj.* vigoureux, robuste; en bonne santé. || ~ *and hearty*, vigoureux.

half [hæf] **halves** [hævz] *n.* **1.** moitié *f*; demi *m*, -e *f*; [Sport] mi-temps *f*: *I read* ~ (*of*) *the book*, J'ai lu la moitié du livre; *I want* (*a*) ~, J'en veux la moitié; *one and a* ~ *days, a day and a* ~, un jour et demi; *three and a* ~ *oranges*, trois oranges et demie; *to cut sth. in* ~, couper qqch. en deux; *by* ~, de moitié; [Fig.] *to do sth. by halves*, (ne) faire qqch. (qu')à/moitié, demi/; *my better* ~, ma moitié. || *adj.* demi-; une moitié de: ~ *a day, a* ~ *day*, une demi-journée, la moitié d'une journée; ~ *an apple*, une moitié de pomme, la moitié d'une pomme; *at* ~ *-tide*, à mi-marée *f*; [Fig.] ~ *one thing and* ~ *another*, mi-figue, mi-raisin. || *adv.* moitié; à moitié, à demi; de moitié; mi-: *He is* ~ *English*, ~ *French*, Il est moitié anglais moitié français; *He is* ~ *as tall as I am*, Il est moitié aussi grand que moi; ~ *as much*, la moitié autant; ~ *as tall again*, plus grand de moitié; ~ *as much again*, moitié plus; ~ *dead*, à/moitié, demi/mort; *to* ~ *open sth.*, entr'ouvrir qqch.; ~ *loud*, à mi-voix; ~ *past/three, twelve/*, trois heures et demie; midi, minuit/et demi; *at* ~ *-past*, à la demie; *not* ~ (*bad, &c.*), assez (bon, &c.).

half-and-half [-n̩ˈhæf] *adj.* & *adv.* moitié l'un moitié l'autre; en parties égales.

halfback [-ˌbæk] *n.* demi(-arrière) *m*. || **halfbreed** [-ˌbɹijd] *n.* sang-mêlé *m*; métis *m*. || **halfbrother** [-ˌbɹʌðɚ] *n.* demi-frère *m*. || **half-closed** [-ˌklowzd] *adj.* entr'ouvert. || **half-hearted** [-ˌhɑɚtəd] *adj.* sans entrain. || **half hour** [-ˌəwɚ] *n.* demi-heure *f*: *at the* ~, à la demie. || **half-open** [-ˌowpən] *adj.* entr'ouvert, mi-ouvert. || **half pay** [-ˈpej] *n.* demi-solde *f*; *on* ~, en demi-solde; en disponibilité. || **half price** [-ˈpɹajs] *adv.* à moitié prix. || **halfsister** [-ˌsɪstɚ] *n.* demi-sœur *f*. || **half-way** [-ˈwej] *adv.* à moitié chemin, à mi-chemin: ~ *to Montreal*, à mi-chemin de Montréal; ~ *up*, à mi-hauteur; à mi-chemin du sommet, à mi-pente. || **halfwit** [-ˌwɪt] *n.* idiot *m*. || **half-witted** [-ˌwɪtəd] *adj.* faible d'esprit. || **half year** [-ˈjijɚ] *n.* semestre *m*.

halibut [ˈhælɪbət] *n.* flétan *m*.

Haligonian [ˌhælɪˈgownɪən] © *adj.* & *n.* habitant *m* d'Halifax (N.-É.).

hall [hɔl] *n.* **1.** [large building] hall *m* d'entrée; [private lounge] entrée *f*, vestibule *m*; salle *f* (de banquet); [Univ.] réfectoire *m*. **2.** édifice *m* public: *town* ~, hôtel *m* de ville; bâtiment *m* (d'école), pavillon *m* (d'université); *music-* ~, café *m* concert.

hallo cf. HELLO.

hallow [ˈhælow] *v. tr.* [consecrate] sanctifier, consacrer: *Hallowed be Thy name*, Que votre nom soit sanctifié; *All Hallows*, la Toussaint. || **Hallowe'en** [-ˈijn] *n.* [veille *f* de la Toussaint] © halloween *f*.

halltree [ˈhɔlˌtɹij] *n.* patère *f*; vestiaire *m*.

hallucination [həˌluwsɪˈnejʃən] *n.* hallucination *f*; méprise *f*.

hallway [ˈhɔlˌwej] *n.* vestibule *m*.

halo [ˈhejlow] *n.* halo *m*; [saint] auréole *f*; [Fig.] gloire *f* (de légende *f*).

halt[1] [hɔlt] *n.* halte; pause *f*: *to call a* ~, faire halte; [Mil.] *Halt !*, Halte! || *v. intr.* s'arrêter.

halt[2] *v. intr.* hésiter; †boiter. || †*adj.* estropié, boiteux. || **halting** [-ɪŋ] *adj.* hésitant;

boiteux, éclopé: *a ~ tone*, un ton hésitant.
halter [-ɚ] *n.* licou *m.*
halve [hæv] *v. tr.* diviser, partager/en deux; réduire de moitié.
ham [hæm] *n.* **1.** jambon *m*; © fesse *f* de porc: *~ and eggs*, œufs *mpl* au jambon. **2.** [Sl.] mauvais acteur *m* (de théâtre); (opérateur *m* de radio) amateur.
hamburger [-ˌbɚgɚ] *n.* © hamburger *m*: *~ steak*, biftek *m* haché, © steak *m* haché.
hamlet [ˈhæmlət] *n.* hameau *m.*
hammer [ˈhæmɚ] *n.* marteau *m*; [gun] chien *m*, percuteur *m*; [piano] marteau *m.* || *v. tr.*: *to ~ sth. into shape*, façonner qqch. à coups de marteau; [Fig.] *to ~ away at*, travailler d'arrache-pied à. || **hammering** [-ɪŋ] *n.* martelage *m*; martèlement *m.*
hammock [ˈhæmək] *n.* hamac *m.*
hamper[1] [ˈhæmpɚ] *n.* panier *m*, manne *f.*
hamper[2] *v. tr.* gêner, entraver.
hand[1] [hænd] *n.* **1.** main *f*: *second ~*, d'occasion [cf. USED]; *on, at/ ~*, sous, à portée de/la main; proche; *by ~*, (ouvrage fait) à la main [cf. HANDMADE]; *in ~*, (situation) bien en main; *cash in ~*, espèces *fpl* en caisse, argent *m* liquide; *My fate is in your hands*, Mon sort est entre vos mains; *on the one ~ . . . on the other ~*, d'une part . . . d'autre part; *~ to ~ combat*, lutte *f* corps à corps; *to give a ~ (to s.o.)*, aider, donner un coup de main à/qqun; *to change hands*, [property] changer/ de mains, de propriétaire; *to get out of ~*, s'émanciper; *to go ~ in ~ with*, aller de pair avec; *He had no ~ in the matter*, Il n'y était pour rien; *to lay hands on s.o.*, porter la main sur qqun; *to lay hands on*, mettre la main sur (qqch.); arrêter (un voleur); imposer les mains à qqun; *to live from ~ to mouth*, vivre au jour le jour; *to take in ~*, se charger (d'une affaire), prendre (une affaire) en main, se rendre maître (d'une situation); *to take sth. off one's hands*, se décharger de qqch.; *to turn one's ~ to*, se mettre à (faire qqch.); *to wash one's hands of*, s'en laver les mains. **2.** aiguille *f* (d'une montre): *the minute ~*, l'aiguille des minutes, la grande aiguille; *the hour ~*, l'aiguille des heures, la petite aiguille. **3.** ouvrier *m*, ouvrière *f*; manœuvre *m*; [Naut.] *pl.* l'équipage *m*: *All hands on deck!*, Tous les hommes sur le pont! **4.** côté *m*: *on the left ~ side*, sur le côté gauche; à main gauche; *At her left ~ stood two men*, Deux hommes se tenaient à sa gauche. **5.** écriture *f*, signature *f*: *to write a neat ~*, avoir une belle écriture; *in (a) small ~*, en petits caractères; *to set one's ~ to (a document)*, apposer sa signature à. **6.** applaudissements *mpl*: *The crowd gave the winner a big ~*, La foule applaudit chaleureusement le vainqueur. **7.** [Cards] jeu *m*; main *f*, tour *m*; joueur *m*: *to show one's ~*, montrer son jeu; abattre ses cartes; *to throw in one's ~*, quitter la partie; s'avouer vaincu.
hand[2] *v. tr.* passer, donner, remettre (qqch. à qqun): *Please, ~ me the salt*, Passez-moi le sel, s'il vous plaît. || **hand down** *v. tr.* léguer, donner (qqch. à qqun); [Fam.] passer à (qqun). || **hand in** *v. tr.* remettre (une lettre, &c.) à qqun. || **hand on** *v. tr.* transmettre (une nouvelle). || **hand out** *v. tr.* distribuer. || **hand over** *v. tr.* donner, remettre, transmettre (qqch. à qqun).
handbill [ˈhænd|bɪl] *n.* prospectus *m.*
handbook [ˈhændˌbʊk] *n.* manuel *m.*
hand brake [-ˌbɹejk] *n.* frein *m* à main.
handcuff [-ˌkʌf] *n.* menotte *f.* || *v. tr.* mettre les menottes à (qqun).
handful [-ˌful] *n.* une poignée *f* de . . . , quelques . . . : *a ~ of beans*, une poignée de fèves; [Fig.] *There was only a ~ of men*, Il n'y avait là que quelques hommes.
handicap [ˈhændɪ|ˌkæp] *n.* handicap *m.* || *v. tr.* **[-pp-]** handicaper.
handicraft [-ˌkɹæft] *n.* artisanat *m*; métier *m.*
handily [ˈhændɪlɪ] *adv.* commodément; adroitement.
handiwork [-ˌwɚk] *n.* ouvrage *m* manuel; œuvre *f*, ouvrage *m.*
handkerchief [ˈhæŋkɚˌtʃɪf] *n.* mouchoir *m*; [silk] foulard *m.*
handle [ˈhændl̩] *n.* [bicycle, door] poignée *f*; [knife] manche *m*; [wheelbarrow] brancard *m*; [frying-pan] queue *f*; [basket] anse *f*; [Mech.] manivelle *f*, manette *f*: *~ bar(s)*, guidon (de bicyclette). || *v. tr.* **1.** manier, manipuler (qqch.); palper, tâter (des mains): *~ with care*, → fragile. **2.** [Fig.] [vehicle] conduire; [men] manier; traiter; [ship, boat] manœuvrer, gouverner: *to ~ roughly*, malmener, maltraiter, rudoyer.
handmade [ˈhændˈmejd] *adj.* fait, fabriqué/ à la main; [Com. sewing] tout main *invar.*
handout [ˈhænd|ˌawt] *n.* **1.** notes *fpl* (distribuées à un cours); documentation *f* (polycopiée). **2.** secours *m*; soupe *f* (distribuée aux chômeurs, &c.).
handrail [-ɹejl] *n.* [stairs] rampe *f* (d'escalier); garde-fou *m.*
handshake [-ˌʃejk] *n.* poignée *f* de main.
handsome [ˈhænsəm] *adj.* **1.** beau, bel *m*;

belle *f*; élégant; joli [gén. réservé au sexe masculin; pour les dames ou les jeunes filles, dire *pretty*, *beautiful*]: *He's a ~ man*, C'est un bel homme. **2.** [Fig.] beau, considérable: *Ten thousand dollars is a ~ sum of money*, Dix mille dollars constituent une somme d'argent considérable. **3.** noble; généreux. || **handsomely** [-lɪ] *adv.* joliment, élégamment; [Fig.] généreusement. || **handsomeness** [-nəs] *n.* beauté *f*, grâce *f*, élégance *f*; [Fig.] générosité *f*.

handwheel [ˈhænd|ˌwijl] *n.* manivelle *f*.

handwriting [-ˌɹajtɪŋ] *n.* écriture *f* [cf. HAND 5.].

handy [-ɪ] *adj.* adroit, habile (de ses mains); commode, tout exprès: *This will come in ~*, → Cela pourra servir. || **handyman** [-ˌmæn] *n.* homme *m* à tout faire.

hang [hæŋ] **hung, hung** [hʌŋ] *v. tr.* **1.** pendre; [from above without other support] suspendre; [on nail, hook, &c.] accrocher (all three: *from*, *on*, à); garnir (de rideaux); coller (du papier à tapisser); baisser (la tête); *to ~ fire*, traîner (en longueur). **2.** pendre (un assassin) [☞ Dans le style soigné et dans certaines expressions, le prét. et le part. passé est *hanged*]: [Fam.] *Hang it (all)!*, Zut alors!; *(I'll be) hanged if . . .*, Que le diable m'emporte si . . . || *v. intr.* pendre; [from above without other support] être suspendu; [on nail, hook, &c.] être accroché (all three: *from*, *on*, à); [criminal] être pendu; [Fig.] dépendre (*on*, de); planer, peser (*on*, de); planer, peser (*over*, sur); *to ~ loose*, flotter, pendiller; *to ~ in the balance*, rester incertain; *to ~ by a thread*, ne tenir qu'à un fil; *Time hangs heavy on my hands*, Le temps me pèse. || **hang** *n.* tombée *f* (d'un costume) drapé *m* (d'une robe): [Fam.] *to get the ~ (of sth.)*, saisir le truc; [Fam.] *I don't care a ~!*, Je m'en moque (pas mal)! || **hang about, around** [-əˌbawt] [-əˌɹawnd] *v. intr.* flâner (devant, dans, &c.); [thief] rôder (autour de). || **hang back** [-ˈbæk] *v. intr.* **1.** rester en arrière. **2.** hésiter; montrer peu d'empressement (à faire qqch.). || **hang down** [-ˈdawn] *v. intr.* pendre. || **hang on** [-ˈɑn] *v. intr.* se cramponner, s'accrocher (à qqch.); [Fig.] tenir bon. || **hang out** [-ˈawt] *v. tr.* pendre (qqch.) au dehors. || *v. intr.* se pencher (par la fenêtre); [Arg.] habiter, percher: *His shirt was hanging out*, → On voyait le pan de sa chemise; *His tongue was hanging out*, → Il tirait la langue. || **hang over** [-ˈowvɚ] *v. intr.* surplomber (qqch.); [Fig.] peser, planer/sur; menacer. || **hangover** [-ˌowvɚ] *n.* survivance *f*; [morning after] [Arg.] gueule *f* de bois. || **hang together** [-təˈgɛðɚ] *v. intr.* être, rester/unis. || **hang up** [-ˌʌp] *v. tr.* accrocher, pendre (son chapeau); raccrocher (le récepteur du téléphone). || *v. intr.* [Tel.] raccrocher.

hangar [ˈhæŋɚ] *n.* [aviation] hangar *m*.

hanger [ˈhæŋɚ] *n.* crochet *m*, [hook] croc *m*: *coat ~*, cintre *m*. || **hanging** [-ɪŋ] *n.* **1.** pendaison *f* (d'un homme). **2.** tentures *fpl.* || **hangman** [-mən] *n.* exécuteur *m* des hautes œuvres, bourreau *m*.

hanker [ˈhæŋkɚ] *v. tr.* désirer passionnément: *to ~ (after)* soupirer (après).

Hansard [ˈhænsɚd] *n.* Journal *m* officiel; © le Hansard.

haphazard [ˌhæpˈhæzɚd] *adj.* imprévu, au petit bonheur. || **haphazardly** [-lɪ] *adv.* au hasard, d'une façon imprévue.

hapless [ˈhæpləs] *adj.* malchanceux, malheureux. || †**haply** *adv.* par hasard.

happen [ˈhæpn̩] *v. intr.* arriver (à, *to*): *What (has) happened?*, Qu'est il arrivé?; [by chance] survenir; être justement en train de . . . : *I happened to . . .*, Je venais justement de . . . ; *as if nothing had happened*, comme si de rien n'était; *Whatever happens*, Quoi qu'il advienne; *Happen what may!*, Advienne que pourra!; *How does it ~ that . . . ?*, Comment se fait-il que . . . ?, D'où vient-il que . . . ?; *It so happened that . . .*, Le hasard a voulu que . . . ; *As it happens . . .*, Justement . . . ; *to ~ on*, tomber sur (qqun, qqch.), /trouver, rencontrer/par hasard. || **happening** [-ɪŋ] *n.* événement *m*.

happily [ˈhæpɪlɪ] *adv.* heureusement; par bonheur. || **happiness** [ˈhæpɪnəs] *n.* bonheur *m*. || **happy** [ˈhæpɪ] *adj.* heureux; [glad] content: *by a ~ chance*, par un heureux hasard; *in a ~ hour*, à un moment propice; *He's perfectly ~*, → Il nage dans la joie; *to be trigger-~*, avoir/la détente, le revolver/facile.

harangue [həˈræŋ] *n.* harangue *f*. || *v. intr.* prononcer un discours. || *v. tr.* haranguer.

harass [ˈhærəs] *v. tr.* harasser, lasser; harceler, tourmenter.

harbour [ˈhɑɚbɚ] *n.* [Naut.] port *m*; havre *m*, asile *m*, refuge *m*. || *v. tr.* donner asile à (qqun); [Fig.] garder (rancune à qqun); entretenir (des doutes); nourrir (des soupçons). || *v. intr.* s'abriter.

hard [hɑɚd] *adj.* dur; difficile (à + infin.) [cf. IT]; [rough] rude; [Pers.] difficile, sévère, impitoyable (*on s.o.*, pour qqun); [blow, drinker] grand; [drink] boisson *f* alcoolique; [frost, rain] fort; [fact] brutal; [winter] rigoureux; [water] calcaire; [cash] espèces *fpl* sonnantes (*in*, en); [work] assidu; difficile, pénible; [labour] (travaux) forcés; [luck] malchance *f*: *as ~ as rock*, dur comme la pierre; *to get ~*, durcir; *to get harder*, s'endurcir; *to find it ~ to*, avoir du mal à; *to have a ~ time of it*, en voir de dures, passer des moments difficiles: *It was a ~ blow*, C'était un coup dur; *to try ~*, faire un effort; *to try one's hardest*, faire de son mieux; *~ of hearing*, dur d'oreille; *~ and fast*, absolu, rigoureux. || **hard** *adv.* [work, hit, freeze] dur, [sleep] profond; [blow, rain] fort; (réfléchir) bien, (penser) profondément; [drink] sec; [breathe] avec peine; [look] fixement; [treat] rudement; de toutes ses forces: *~ by*, tout près (de qqch.); *to be ~ at sth.*, être très occupé à faire qqch.; *It will go ~ with him*, Il aura des ennuis; *to be ~ put to it* (*to*), avoir bien du mal (à); *to be ~ up* (*for*), être à court (d'argent, d'excuses, &c.); [Naut.] *~ astern!*, en arrière toute! || **harden** [-n̩] *v. tr. & intr.* durcir; solidifier; [metal] *tr.* tremper, *intr.* se raidir; (s')endurcir, [Fig.] (s')aguerrir (qqun à, contre qqch.); [heart] (s')endurcir. || **hardening** [-n̩ɪŋ] *n.* durcissement *m*; [Pers.] endurcissement *m*; [metal] trempe *f*.

hardly [-lɪ] *adv.* à peine [a restricted affirmative, or = no sooner]; ne . . . guère [a softened negative, or = not very often]; presque [used before a negative word]: *He is ~ 21*, Il a à peine 21 ans; *We ~ had time to catch the train*, Nous avons eu tout juste le temps d'attraper le train; *Hardly had he arrived when*, A peine (était-il) arrivé (que); *I ~ (ever) go there*, Je n'y vais/guère, presque jamais/; *He will ~ come now*, Il ne viendra probablement pas maintenant; *I ~ know (why)*, Je ne sais trop (pourquoi); *Hardly!*, Sûrement pas!

hardness [-nəs] *n.* dureté *f*; difficulté *f*; sévérité *f*; brutalité *f*. || **hardship** [-ˌʃɪp] *n.* privation *f*; fatigue *f*; (dure) épreuve *f*; souffrance *f*. || **hardware** [-ˌwɛɚ] *n.* quincaillerie *f*: *~ store*, quincaillerie *f*, chez le quincaillier, © ferronnerie *f*, © marchand *m* de fer; [for paints, Fr.] le marchand de couleurs. || **hardy** [-ɪ] *adj.* hardi, audacieux, intrépide; robuste, résistant: *~ plants*, plantes qui supportent bien le froid.

hare [hɛɚ] *n.* lièvre *m*: [Fig.] *~ -brained*, étourdi, hurluberlu. || **harelip** [-lɪp] *n.* bec-de-lièvre *m*.

harm [hɑɚm] *n.* mal *m*; tort *m*: *It will do more ~ than good*, Cela fera plus de mal que de bien. || *v. tr.* faire du/mal, tort/à, porter préjudice à. || **harmful** [-ˌfl̩] *adj.* malfaisant; [pests] nuisible; [Med.] nocif. || **harmless** [-ləs] *adj.* inoffensif; [animal, man] pas méchant; [man] sans malice; [pastime] innocent; [medicine] anodin.

harmonic [ˌhɑɚ|ˈmɑnɪk] *n.* harmonique *f*. || *adj.* harmonique, musical.

harmonica [ˌhɑɚˈmɑnɪkə] *n.* [Mus.] harmonica *m*, © [Fam.] ruine-babines *f*, musique *f* à bouche.

harmonious [-ˈmownɪəs] *adj.* [feeling] harmonieux; mélodieux. || **harmonize** [ˈhɑɚməˌnajz] *v. intr.* s'harmoniser, être d'accord. || *v. tr.* harmoniser (un air); [Fig.] faire vivre en bonne intelligence.

harmony [ˈhɑɚmənɪ] *n.* harmonie *f*.

harness [ˈhɑɚnəs] *n.* harnais *m*, © attelage *m*: *~ race*, course *f* de trotteurs; [Fig.] harnachement *m*: *to get back into ~*, se remettre au travail, reprendre le collier. || *v. tr.* atteler (un cheval); [Fig.] équiper; [power] capter (l'énergie hydroélectrique, &c.).

harp [hɑɚp] *n.* harpe *f*. || *v. intr.* jouer de la harpe: [Fig.] *to ~ on*, rabâcher.

harpoon [ˌhɑɚˈpuwn] *n.* harpon *m*. || *v. tr.* harponner.

harrow [ˈhæɚow] *n.* herse *f*. || *v. tr.* herser; [Fig.] tourmenter. || **harrowing** [-ɪŋ] *adj.* [Fig.] torturant, déchirant.

harry [ˈhæɚɪ] *v. tr.* harceler (qqun); [city, &c.] piller, dévaster (une ville, &c.); *a harried expression*, une expression *f* tourmentée.

harsh [hɑɚʃ] *adj.* [touch] rude; [taste] âpre; [sight] criard; [hearing] discordant; [Fig.] sévère, dur. || **harshness** [-nəs] *n.* rudesse *f*; âpreté *f*; rigueur *f*.

harvest [ˈhɑɚvəst] *n.* [wheat, oats] moisson *f*; [vegetables] récolte *f*; [fruit] cueillette *f*; [hay] fenaison *f*; [grapes] vendange(s) *f* [usual. pl.]; © le temps des foins. || *v. tr.* [wheat] moissonner; [vegetables] récolter; [fruit] cueillir, faire la cueillette.

has [hæz] cf. TO HAVE || **hasn't** [= has not].

hash [hæʃ] *n.* hachis *m*, émincé *m*; [Fig.] gâchis *m*. || *v. tr.* hacher; [mess] gâcher.

haste [hejst] *n.* hâte *f*, précipitation *f*: *to make ~*, se hâter, se dépêcher; *in ~*, à la hâte, en hâte; [rashly] à la légère. || **hasten** [-n̩] *v. tr.* presser; *to ~ off*, pousser. || *v. intr.* se hâter; se dépêcher, s'empresser (de, *to*). || **hastily** [-ɪlɪ] *adv.* précipitamment, à la hâte; [rashly] à la légère. || **hasty** [-ɪ] *adj.* hâtif, rapide: *a ~ departure*, un départ *m* précipité; [rash] *~ deci-*

sions, décisions/irréfléchies, inconsidérées; [quick-tempered] emporté, violent: *Don't be ~ !*, → Gardez votre calme!

hat [hæt] *n.* chapeau *m*; coiffure *f*: *top ~*, (chapeau) haut *m* de forme; *felt ~*, chapeau mou; *to/put on, take off/one's ~*, mettre, enlever/son chapeau; [Fig.] *We take off our hats to X*, Chapeaux bas devant X; *to keep . . . under one's ~*, garder . . . pour soi; *to talk through one's ~*, parler à tort et à travers. ‖ **hatbox** [-ˌbɒks] *n.* carton *m* à chapeau.

hatch[1] [hætʃ] *v. tr.* couver (des œufs); [Fig.] manigancer (une action secrète). ‖ *v. intr.* éclore.

hatch[2] *v. intr.* hachurer. ‖ **hatching** [-ɪŋ] *n.* hachures *fpl.*

hatch[3] *n.* [Naut.] écoutille *f.*

hatchet [ˈhætʃət] *n.* hachette *f*: [Fig.] *to bury the ~*, faire la paix.

hate [hejt] *n.* haine *f*; aversion *f.* ‖ *v. tr.* haïr; [dislike] détester, avoir/qqun, qqch./ en horreur. ‖ **hateful** [-fl̩] *adj.* haïssable cf. HAÏR; odieux; détestable. ‖ **hatred** [-ɹəd] *n.* haine *f*; aversion *f.*

hatstand [ˈhæt|ˌstænd] *n.* patère *f*; porte-manteau *m.* ‖ **hatter** [-ɚ] *n.* chapelier *m.*

haughtily [ˈhɔtɪ|lɪ] *adv.* avec hauteur *f.* ‖ **haughtiness** [-nəs] *n.* arrogance *f.* ‖ **haughty** *adj.* fier, hautain, arrogant.

haul [hɔl] *v. tr.* [drag] haler, traîner, remorquer; [goods] transporter. ‖ *n.* remorquage *m*; transport *m*; [cargo] chargement *m*; [Fig.] coup *m* de filet, butin *m.*

haunch [hɔntʃ] *n.* hanche *f*; [Culin.] cuissot *m*, quartier *m* (de bœuf, de veau, de mouton); © fesse *f* de veau, &c.

haunt [hɔnt] *n.* rendez-vous *m*, [Pej.] repaire *m.* ‖ *v. tr.* hanter; [Fig.] fréquenter; [thoughts] obséder.

have [hæv], **had, had** [hæd] *v. tr.* [3e pers. sing. prés.: has [hæz]] **1.** avoir; posséder: Do you ~, Have you/a brother?, Avez-vous un frère?; *Don't you ~, Haven't you/a letter to write?*, N'avez-vous pas une lettre à écrire?; *I ~ it!*, J'y suis!; *Rumour has it that . . .*, Le bruit court que . . .; [Fam.] *He's had it!*, Il est fichu, Il en a assez, C'est trop tard; *He has it in for me*, Il m'en veut; *I had it out with him*, Je me suis expliqué avec lui; *That has nothing on our car*, Cela n'est pas mieux que notre voiture; *You ~ me there*, Je ne sais que/dire, faire/; [Fam.] I've been had!, On m'a eu!, J'ai été possédé! **2.** prendre (un repas, de la nourriture): *What will you ~ ?*, Qu'est-ce que vous prenez?; *Will you ~ a cup of coffee?*, Voulez-vous une tasse de café?; *to ~/dinner, a bath, a swim/*, dîner, prendre un bain, (aller) nager. [cf. also nouns]. **3.** obtenir; recevoir; avoir: *Where is that to be had?*, Où peut-on/trouver, obtenir, se procurer/ cela?; *I had a new bicycle for Christmas*, J'ai/reçu, eu/une bicyclette pour Noël. **4.** [put up with] supporter; tolérer: *We can't ~ such goings-on*, Nous ne pouvons pas tolérer ces agissements; *I won't ~ you coming in late*, Je ne supporterai pas que vous arriviez tard. **5.** [causative construction] faire + active infin.: *I had him come*, Je l'ai fait venir; *I had it done*, Je l'ai fait faire; *I had it done by him, I had him do it*, Je le lui ai fait faire; *I had my hair cut*, Je me suis fait couper les cheveux; *I had my arm broken in the accident*, Je me suis cassé le bras dans l'accident; *I'd like to have you win*, Je voudrais bien/vous voir gagner, que vous gagniez/. **6.** to ~ to + infin. [pos.]: devoir, falloir; [neg.] avoir besoin de: *I ~ to do it*, Je dois le faire, Il faut que je le fasse; *I don't ~ to do it*, Je n'ai pas besoin de le faire. **7.** *to let (s.o.) ~ (sth.)*; donner, laisser: *Let me ~ five dollars till Tuesday*, Donnez-moi, Prêtez-moi/5 dollars jusqu'à mardi; *He let me ~ it for a song*, Il me l'a /laissé, vendu/pour presque rien; *Let me ~ your address*, Donnez-moi votre adresse; [Fam.] *I let him ~ it*, [hit] Je lui ai flanqué une râclée, [scold] Je lui ai dit ses quatre vérités. ‖ **have** *v. aux.* [*to have* s'emploie devant un part. passé pour former les différents temps composés du passé]: avoir, être, + past part. [× French compound tenses are formed with *avoir* for all transitive verbs except reflexive and most intr. verbs except a small number taking être: cf. such verbs in the French part. Do not confuse with HAVE, 5.]: *I ~ come down*, Je suis descendu; *I ~ brought it down*, Je l'ai descendu; *I have washed (myself)*, Je me suis lavé; *I thought I had finished it*, Je croyais l'avoir fini. ‖ **have on,** porter, mettre (un vêtement): *He had his old coat on*, Il avait mis son vieux manteau; *What ~ you on for to-night?*, Qu'avez-vous en vue pour ce soir?

haven [ˈhejvn̩] *n.* [Naut.] havre *m*, abri *m*; [shelter] lieu *m* sûr.

haversack [ˈhævɚˌsæk] *n.* musette *f* [× havresac].

havoc [ˈhævək] *n.* dégât *m* considérable: *to play ~ with*, détruire; gaspiller (sa fortune).

Havre [ˈhɑvɹə] *n.* Le Havre (France): *in, to*/~, au Havre.
Hawaii [həˈwajɪ] *n.* (les îles) Hawaii: *in, to* ~, à Hawaii. || **Hawaiian** [-n] *adj.* & *n.* Hawaiien.
hawk[1] [hɔk] *n.* faucon *m*: *red-tailed* ~, buse *f*; *sparrow-* ~, épervier *m.*
hawk[2] *v. tr.* colporter. || **hawker** [-ɚ] *n.* colporteur *m.*
hawthorn [ˈhɔˌθɔɚn] *n.* aubépine *f*; © cenellier *m.*
hay [hej] *n.* foin *m*: *to make* ~, faire les foins. || **hay fever** [-ˌfijvɚ] *n.* fièvre *f*, rhume *m*/des foins. || **haymaking** [-ˌmejkɪŋ] *n.* fenaison *f.* || **haystack** [-ˌstæk] *n.* meule *f* (de foin).
haywire [ˈhejˌwajɚ] *n.* fil *m* de fer à lier le foin. || *adj.* [Fam.] en pagaille: *to go* ~, se mettre en pagaille; perdre la boussole.
hazard [ˈhæzɚd] *n.* **1.** risque *m*, danger *m.* **2.** obstacle *m*, accident *m* (de terrain, au golf). || *v. tr.* hasarder, risquer. || *v. intr.* se risquer, s'aventurer. || **hazardous** [-əs] *adj.* risqué, hasardé; dangereux.
haze [hejz] *n.* brume *f* (légère); [Fig.] obscurité *f* (de l'esprit).
hazel [ˈhejzl̩] *n.* noisetier *m.* || *adj.* [yeux] (couleur) noisette; brun clair; ~ *-nut*, noisette *f.*
hazy [ˈhejzɪ] *adj.* brumeux; [Fig.] confus; ~ *recollection*, vague souvenir *m.*
HBC [ˌejtʃˌbijˈsij] = © *Hudson's Bay Company*, Compagnie de la Baie d'Hudson.
H-bomb [ˈejtʃˌbɑm] *n.* bombe *f* à hydrogène, bombe-H *f.*
he [hij] *pron. pers.* il; ce; lui; celui; le: *What is* ~ *doing?*, Qu'est-ce qu'il fait, Que fait-il?; *He is clever*, Il est intelligent; *He is a doctor*, Il est médecin; *He is a famous actor*, C'est un acteur célèbre; *He is my father*, C'est mon père; *It is* ~ (*who is coming*), C'est lui (qui va venir); *He alone can do it*, Lui seul peut le faire; *Who is coming?—He is*, Qui vient?—Lui; *I am older than* ~ (*is*), Je suis plus âgé que lui; ~ *who . . .*, celui qui . . . ; *Here* ~ *is*, Le voici. || *n. It's a* ~, C'est un/homme, garçon/[animal] mâle: *a* ~ *-man*, un homme viril; *a* ~ *-*(*elephant*), un (éléphant) mâle.
head [hɛd] *n.* **1.** tête *f* (d'une personne, d'un animal); [pin, hammer, procession, &c.] tête; [lettuce] pied *m*; [arrow] pointe *f*; [axe, spear] fer *m*; [cane] pomme *f*; [barrel] fond *m*; [ship] avant *m*; [page, stairs] le haut; [bed] chevet *m*; [lake, table], le (haut) bout; [stream] source *f*; [coin] face *f*, effigie *f*; [motor] culasse *f*; [war ~] cône *m* (de charge); [beer] mousse *f*, © collet *m* (sur la bière): (*with one's*) ~/*up, down*/, la tête/haute, baissée/; ~ *down*(*wards*), la tête en bas; ~ *first*, la tête la première; *from* ~ *to* /*foot, toe*/, des pieds à la tête, de la tête aux pieds; *to stand on one's* ~, faire les pieds au mur; *turn* ~ *over heels*, faire la culbute; [Fig.] ~ *over heels in love* (*with*), éperdument amoureux (de); *over one's* ~, sans tenir compte de (qqun), hors de la portée de (qqun); *to have a good* ~, avoir du bon sens; *to have a good* ~ *for sth.*; s'entendre à qqch.; *to get into one's* ~ *to . . .*, se mettre en tête de . . . ; *to do it in one's* ~, le faire de tête; *to make it* (*up*) *out of one's* ~, imaginer qqch.; *Use your* ~ *!*, Réfléchissez!; *to*/*keep, lose*/*one's* ~, garder son sang-froid, perdre la tête; *to keep one's* ~ *above water*, se tenir à flot; *to bury one's* ~ *in the sand*, faire l'autruche; *to put one's heads together*, discuter d'une question ensemble; *I can't make* ~ *or tail of it*, Je n'y comprends rien; *Heads!*, Face! **2.** chef *m*; directeur *m* (d'une entreprise); principal *m* (d'une école): *to be at the* ~ *of*, être à la tête de, venir en tête de (liste). **3.** phase *f* critique; conclusion *f.* **4.** *inv. a hundred* ~ *of cattle*, (un troupeau) de cent têtes de bétail; *ten head of oxen*, → dix bœufs. || *attrib.* [leading] de tête, d'avant-garde; [wind] (vent) debout; [chief] principal, premier, . . . en chef: ~ *waiter*, maître *m* d'hôtel; ~ *cook*, chef *m* cuisinier; ~ *office*, siège *m* social. || **head** *v. tr.* conduire, mener (un cortège, une procession); être à la tête (d'une organisation, de sa classe); venir en tête (aux élections); diriger (qqch. vers . . .); mettre (un titre) en tête (qqch. vers . . .). || *v. intr.*: *to* ~ *for a place*, se diriger vers un endroit; [Naut.] mettre le cap sur un endroit; *We'd better* ~ *for home*, Nous ferions bien de rentrer à la maison. || **headache** [-ˌejk] *n.* mal *m* de tête: *to have a* (*terrible*) ~, avoir (terriblement) mal à la tête, avoir un (terrible) mal de tête; *to have a sick* ~, avoir la migraine. || **head cheese** [-ˌtʃijz] *n.* [Cul.] fromage *m* de tête, © tête *f* en fromage. || **head-dress** [-ˌdɹɛs] *n.* coiffure *f.* || **heading** [-ɪŋ] *n.* en-tête *m* (d'une lettre); titre *m* (d'un chapitre); rubrique *f* (d'un article): *under the* ~ *of*, sous la rubrique de; *to come under a* ~, tomber dans une catégorie. || **headlight** [-ˌlajt] *m.* phare *m* (d'auto). || **headline** [-lajn] *n.* manchette *f* (d'un journal); titre *m*, sous-titre *m*

(d'une rubrique, d'un article). || **headlong** [-ˌlaŋ] *adv. to fall* ~ , tomber la tête la première; *to rush* ~ *into*, se jeter tête baissée dans; [Fig.] courir impétueusement à (sa perte). || *adj.* la tête la première; précipité; [Pers.] irréfléchi. || **headmaster** [-ˌmæstɚ] *m.* directeur *m*, principal *m* (d'une école); [Fr.] proviseur *m* (d'un lycée). || **headmistress** [-ˌmɪstɹəs] *n.* directrice *f* (d'une école). || **headmost** [-ˌmowst] *adj.* au premier rang; le plus en avant. || **head-on** [-an] *adj.* & *adv.* de front. || **headphone** [-ˌfown] *n.* écouteur *m*. || **headquarters** [-ˌkwɔɚtɚz] *n.* quartier *m* général (de l'armée, de la police); poste *m* de commandement; siège *m* (social) (d'une entreprise). || **headstrong** [-ˌstɹaŋ] *adj.* obstiné, entêté; [animals] vicieux. || **headway** [-ˌwej] *n.* progrès *m*; marche *f* avant: *to make* ~ , avancer; progresser; aller de l'avant. **headwork** [-ˌwɚk] *n.* travail *m* mental. || **heady** [-ɪ] *adj.* **1.** (caractère) emporté. **2.** (vin) capiteux.

heal [hijl] *v. tr.* guérir (qqun, une blessure). || *v. intr.* guérir (d'une maladie); [wound] se cicatriser, se refermer. || **healing** [-ɪŋ] *adj.* onguent *m* cicatrisant; [wound] plaie qui/se ferme, se cicatrise; [Fig.] apaisant, salutaire. || *n.* guérison *f* (d'une maladie); cicatrisation *f* (d'une plaie).

health [hɛlθ] *n.* santé *f*; [sanitary condition] hygiène *f*: *to be in good* ~ , se bien porter; être/bien portant, en bonne santé; *to be in/bad, poor/* ~ , se mal porter; être mal portant; *to drink a* ~ *to*, boire à la santé de, porter un toast à; © *Department of National Health and Welfare*, Ministère de la Santé nationale et du Bien-être social. || **healthful** [-fḷ] *adj.* [air] salubre; [climate] sain; [Fig.] salutaire. || **healthy** [-ɪ] *adj.* bien portant; en bonne santé; [Fam.] [air] salubre; [climate] sain.

heap [hijp] *n.* tas *m*; [Fig. Fam.] tas *m*, foule *f* (de gens). || (~ **up**) *v. tr.* amasser, entasser.

hear [hijɚ] **heard, heard** [hɚd] *v. tr.* **1.** entendre; entendre dire (que); apprendre (une nouvelle): *I could* ~ *her* (*singing*), Je l'ai entendue/chanter, qui chantait/; *I heard her singing a song*, Je l'ai entendue chanter une chanson, Je lui ai entendu chanter une chanson; *I heard her singing it*, Je la lui ai entendu chanter, Je l'ai entendue qui la chantait; [×] *I have heard that . . .* , J'ai entendu dire, J'ai appris/que . . . ; *I* ~ *he is in town*, Il paraît qu'il est en ville. **2.** écouter (une explication, une plainte); [Jur.] entendre (une cause); [R.C.] assister (à la messe). || *v. intr.* **1.** entendre: *He can't* ~ *well*, Il n'entend pas bien; *to pretend not to* ~ , faire la sourde oreille; [Br.] *Hear! Hear!*, Très bien!, Bravo! **2.** *to* ~ *from s.o.*, avoir, recevoir/des nouvelles de qqun: *You'll* ~ *from me!*, [also threat] Vous aurez de mes nouvelles!; *Let me* ~ *from you*, Donnez-moi de vos nouvelles, Ecrivez-moi (un mot). **3.** *to* ~ *of sth., s.o.*, apprendre qqch., entendre parler de/qqch., qqun/: *I never heard of such a thing!*, C'est inouï!; *The teacher won't* ~ *of it*, Le professeur ne veut pas en entendre parler.

heard [hɚd] cf. HEAR.

hearer [-ɚ] *n.* audit|eur *m*, **-rice** *f*. || **hearing** [-ɪŋ] *n.* [sense] l'ouïe *f*; audition *f* (d'une chanson, d'un chanteur); [Jur.] audience *f*, audition *f* (de témoins): *within* ~ , à portée de la voix; (*with*)*in my* ~ , devant moi; *out of* ~ , hors de portée de la voix; *hard of* ~ , dur d'oreille; [Jur.] *The* ~ *is tomorrow*, L'audience est pour demain.

hearsay [-ˌsej] *n.* ouï-dire *m* (*by, from*, par; *on*, d'): *It is mere* ~ (*evidence*), Ce sont de simples ouï-dire.

hearse [hɚs] *n.* corbillard *m*.

heart [haɚt] *n.* cœur *m*; [Fig.] courage *m*, cœur *m*; [innermost part] cœur *m*, fond *m*, centre *m* cf. CORE: *to have a weak* ~ , être cardiaque; ~ *attack*, crise *f* cardiaque; [Loc. Fig.] *to have a kind* ~ , avoir bon cœur; *to take* ~ , prendre courage; *to set one's* ~ *upon*, avoir à cœur (de); *to lose* ~ , perdre courage; *to know by* ~ , savoir par cœur; *to have sth. at* ~ , avoir qqch. à cœur; *to/eat, drink/to one's heart's content*, manger, boire/tout son soûl. || **heartache** [-ˌejk] *n.* peine *f*, chagrin *m*. || **heartbeat** [-ˌbijt] *n.* battement *m* de cœur. || **heartbroken** [-ˌbɹowkn̩] *adj.* navré, chagriné. || **heartburn** [-ˌbɚn] *n.* point *m* au cœur. || **hearten** [-n̩] *v. tr.* encourager. || **heartfelt** [-ˌfɛlt] *adj.* sincère, authentique.

hearth [haɚθ] *n.* âtre *m*; [home] foyer *m*.

heartily [ˈhaɚtɪlɪ] *adv.* cordialement, de bon cœur. || **heartless** [-ləs] *adj.* sans cœur, insensible. || **heart-rending** [-ˌɹɛndɪŋ] *adj.* angoissant, déchirant. || **hearts** [-s] *n.pl.* [cards] cœur *m*; [flower] *bleeding-* ~ , dicentre *m* remarquable; © cœurs-saignants *mpl.* || **hearty** [-ɪ] *adj.* cordial; sincère; [strong] vigoureux; robuste: ~ *laugh*, rire sonore; *a* ~ *meal*, un repas/substantiel, copieux. || †*n.* gars *m* (de la marine): *my hearties*, les gaillards.

heat [hijt] *n.* [Phys.] chaleur *f*; [Fig.] chaleur *f*, colère *f*, vivacité *f*; [Sport] éliminatoire *f*; manche *f*: *dead* ~, course *f* nulle; [Sl.] troisième degré *m*, passage *m* à tabac. || *v. tr.* chauffer; [cold food] rechauffer: *to* ~ *up*, faire (ré)chauffer; [Fig.] enflammer. || *v. intr.* s'échauffer; [Fig.] s'enflammer. || **heater** [-ər] *n.* [stove] réchaud *m*; [Auto.] © chaufferette *f*: *space-*~, radiateur *m*; *water-*~, chauffe-eau *m*.

heathen [ˈhijðən] *n. & adj.* païen (*m*); [Fig.] barbare, sauvage.

heating [ˈhijtɪŋ] *n.* chauffage *m*: *central* ~, chauffage *m* central.

heave [hijv] **hove** [howv] **heaved** [hijvd] *v. tr.* **1.** hisser, soulever (une lourde caisse, un fardeau, &c.). **2.** haler (un câble): *to* ~ (*up*) *the anchor*, déraper, lever/l'ancre; *to* ~ *in sight*. /paraître, poindre/à l'horizon; [Naut.] *to* ~ *to*, mettre/en panne, à la cape/; [Fig.] [sigh] pousser (un soupir). || *v. intr.* se gonfler; s'enfler.

heaven [ˈhɛvən] *n.* **1.** le paradis; le ciel: *to go to* ~, aller au ciel. **2.** *Heaven*, Dieu *m*; la Providence *f*: [Fig.] *to be in* ~, être aux anges; être au septième ciel. || †**heavens** [-z] firmament *m*; les cieux *mpl*. || **heavenly** [-lɪ] *adj.* céleste, divin; [Fig.] délicieux.

heavily [ˈhɛvɪ|lɪ] *adv.* pesamment, lourdement. || **heaviness** [-nəs] *n.* pesanteur *f*; [Fig.] abattement *m*, tristesse *f*. || **heavy** *adj.* **1.** [hard to lift] lourd, pesant; [metal] massif. **2.** [Fig.] [sea] fort, gros; [sleep] pesant; [meal] copieux; [rain] battant: ~ *smoker*, un gros fumeur *m*; *to be a* ~ *sleeper*, → avoir le sommeil dur. **3.** [hard to bear] ~ *taxes* de lourds impôts *m*; ~ *weather*, temps *m* orageux; ~ *with sleep*, accablé de sommeil. **4.** [Phys.] ~ *water*, eau *f* lourde; [Sport] ~ *-weight*, poids *m* lourd.

Hebrew [ˈhijˌbɹuw] *n.* Hébreu; [Ling.] l'hébreu. || *adj.* hébreu *m*, hébraïque *f*; ☞ le peuple *m* hébreu, la langue *f* hébraïque.

heckle [ˈhɛkl̩] *v. tr.* harceler de questions.

hectic [ˈhɛktɪk] *adj.* fiévreux; [Fig.] trépidant.

he'd [hijd] = he had, cf. HAVE. || = he would, cf. WILL.

hedge [hɛʤ] *n.* haie *f*; clôture *f*. || *v. tr.* clôturer; enclore (un jardin d'une haie, &c.). || *v. intr.* chercher des échappatoires. || *v. tr.*: *to* ~ *a question*, éluder une question; *to* ~ *in*, entourer de tous côtés.

hedgehog [-ˌhɑg] *n.* © porc-épic *m*; [Fr.] hérisson *m*.

heed [hijd] *n.* attention *f*, précaution *f*: *to take* ~, prendre garde. || *v. intr.* faire attention à, observer. || **heedful** [-fl̩] *adj.* attentif, vigilant. || **heedless** [-ləs] *adj.* inattentif, distrait.

heel [hijl] *n.* **1.** talon *m*. **2.** [bread] quignon *m* (de pain); [Naut.] bande *f*, gîte *m* (d'un navire). **3.** [Fam.] salopard *m*: *down at the heels*, être/minable, [Sl.] dans la dèche/; *to take to one's heels*, prendre ses jambes à son cou.

heifer [ˈhɛfər] *n.* génisse *f*.

height [hajt] *n.* hauteur *f*; [mountain] altitude *f*: *heights*, les hauts *mpl*; ~ *of land*, /faîte *m*, ligne *f* de partage/des eaux; [Fig.] sommet *m*; faîte *m*; *at the* ~ *of his fame*, à l'apogée de sa gloire; *at the* ~ *of the storm*, au plus fort de l'orage; *at the* ~ *of her beauty*, dans tout l'éclat de sa beauté; *the* ~ *of folly*, le comble de la folie. || **heighten** [-n̩] *v. tr.* **1.** relever; rehausser. **2.** accroître (un plaisir); aggraver (un mal); faire ressortir (un contraste); rehausser (une qualité).

heinous [ˈhejnəs] *adj.* [crime] odieux.

heir [ɛər] *n.* héritier *m*. || **heiress** [-əs] *n.* héritière *f*. || **heirloom** [-ˌluwm] *n.* bijou *m*, souvenir *m*/de famille.

held [hɛld] cf. HOLD.

Helen [ˈhɛlən] *n.* = Hélène *f*.

helicopter [ˈhɛlɪˌkɑptər] *n.* hélicoptère *m*. || **heliport** [ˈhɛlɪˌpɔərt] *n.* [Aero.] héligare *f*, héliport *m*.

hell [hɛl] *n.* l'enfer *m*; [Fig.] ~ *on earth*, un véritable enfer; [Myth.] les Enfers *mpl*, cf. INFERNO; *to ride* ~ *for leather*, galoper/à bride abattue, ventre à terre/; [Vulg.] *a* ~ *of* (*a racket*), (un bruit) infernal; *to work like* ~, travailler d'arrache-pied; *what the* ~ . . . , que /diable, diantre/. . . .

he'll [hijl] = he will cf. WILL. || = he shall cf. SHALL.

hellish [ˈhelɪʃ] *adj.* diabolique, infernal.

hello [həˈlow] *interj.* [shout] Holà!, Hé, là-bas!; [surprise] Tiens! (c'est toi?); [phone] Allô!, Allô?; Oui!.

helm [hɛlm] *n.* gouvernail *m*, barre *f*; [Fig.] direction *f*.

helmet [ˈhɛlmət] *n.* casque *m*.

help [hɛlp] *n.* aide *f*, secours *m*, assistance *f*; remède *m*; [Pers.] domestique *m*/*f*: *with the* ~ *of*, avec l'aide de (qqun),/à l'aide, au moyen/de qqch.; *I need* ~, J'ai besoin d'aide; *to come to s.o.'s* ~, venir au secours de qqun; *There's no* ~ *for it*, Il n'y a rien à faire. || *v. tr. & intr.* aider, secourir, assister (qqun); faciliter (la digestion); soulager (un rhume); [food] servir: *to* ~ *s.o.* (*to do sth.*), aider qqun (à faire qqch.); *Help!*, Au secours!; *It can't be helped, You can't ~ it*, On n'y peut rien; *I couldn't ~ falling*, Je n'ai pas pu m'empêcher de tomber; *Help yourself* (*to more*), Servez-vous, (Re)prenez-en; *to ~ s.o. to meat*, servir de la viande à qqun. ‖ **help up, down, in, out, &c.** *v. tr.* aider (qqun) à monter, descendre, entrer, sortir, &c.: [Fig.] *to ~* (*s.o.*) *out*, donner un coup de main à qqun. ‖ **helper** [-ɚ] *n.* aide *m/f*; assistant *m*, -e *f.* ‖ **helpful** [-fl̩] *adj.* [Pers.] serviable, secourable; [thing] utile. ‖ **helping** [-ɪŋ] *n.* [food] portion *f.* ‖ **helpless** [-ləs] *adj.* faible, impuissant; sans initiative; abandonné, sans ressource, sans appui: *I'm ~*, Je n'y peux rien.

hem[1] [hɛm] *n.* **1.** bord *m* (d'un vêtement); ourlet *m.* **2.** limite *f.* ‖ *v. intr.* ourler: *to ~ in*, enfermer, entourer. ‖ **hem**[2] *interj.* Hem!, Hum!, [to attract attention] Hep!

hemisphere ['hɛmɪˌsfijɚ] *n.* hémisphère *m*: *northern ~*, hémisphère/nord, boréal; *southern ~*, hémisphère/sud, austral; *western ~*, le Nouveau Monde, l'Amérique *f.*

hemlock ['hɛmˌlɑk] *n.* **1.** [evergreen] © pruche *f*: *ground-~*, if *m* du Canada; © buis *m.* **2.** [plant] ciguë *f*: *water ~*, © carotte *f* à Moreau.

hemorrhage ['hɛməɹɪdʒ] *n.* hémorragie *f.*

hemp [hɛmp] *n.* chanvre *m* (cultivé).

hen [hɛn] *n.* poule *f*; [female of birds, e.g. hen-pheasant. ☞ Use feminine forms, e.g. faisan *m*, faisanne *f*, &c.]: *~ coop*, cage *f* à poules; *~ house*, poulailler *m.*

hence [hɛns] *adv.* **1.** [result] d'où, de là, par conséquent. **2.** [from now] désormais, dorénavant, à partir d'aujourd'hui. **3.** [from here] (à partir) d'ici. ‖ **henceforth** [-ˌfɔɚθ] *adv.* dorénavant, désormais, à l'avenir.

hench|man ['hɛntʃmən] *pl.* **-men** *n.* [Pej.] acolyte *m*, complice *m.*

henpecked ['hɛnˌpɛkt] *adj.* (mari *m*) mené par le bout du nez.

Henry ['hɛnɹɪ] *n.* = Henri *m.* ‖ **Henrietta** [-ˌɛtə] *n.* = Henriette *f.*

hep [hɛp] *adj.* [Sl.] à la page, à la coule: *to be ~ to . . .*, être au courant de. . . .

her [hɚ] *pron. pers.* **1.** [dir. obj.] la, [l' + vowel or mute h]: *I see ~*, Je la vois; *I saw ~*, Je l'ai vue. **2.** [indir. obj.] lui: *I gave/ ~ the book, the book to ~ /*, Je lui ai donné le livre; *I gave it to ~*, Je le lui ai donné; (*Don't*) *give it to ~*, Donnez-le-lui, Ne le lui donnez pas. **3.** [after prep.] elle: *I came with ~*, Je suis venu avec elle. **4.** [double obj.] elle: *I saw you and ~*, Je vous ai vues, vous et elle; *I told you and ~*, Je vous l'ai dit, à vous et à elle. **5.** [stressed] elle; à elle: *I know ~*, Je la connais,/elle, [Pej.] celle-là/; *Give it to ~ !*, Donnez-le-lui. à elle!; *I came with ~*, C'est avec elle que je suis venu. **6.** [Fam.] *It's ~*, C'est elle; *That's ~*, La voilà; *older than ~*, plus âgé qu'elle. ‖ **her** *adj. poss.* [☞ *her* désigne toujours un possesseur du genre féminin] son *m.sing.*, sa *f.sing.*, ses *m/f.pl.* [☞ The Fr. adj. agrees with the pers. or thing possessed in gender and number and NOT with the possessor; *son* replaces *sa* directly before a word beginning with a vowel or mute h: son livre *m*, sa jupe *f*, son école *f*, son autre jupe, ses gants *mpl*, ses (autres) robes *fpl*]: *~ father and mother*, son père et sa mère; *She raised ~ hand*, Elle a levé la main; [external action] *I washed ~ face*, Je lui ai lavé la figure; *She brushed ~ teeth*, Elle s'est brossé les dents; *Her hair is long*, Elle a/de longs cheveux, les cheveux longs); [stressed] *~ book*, son livre à elle.

herald ['hɛɚəld] *n.* héraut *m*; messager *m*; [Fig.] (signe) avant-coureur *m.* ‖ *v. tr.* donner des nouvelles de: [Fig.] annoncer.

heraldry [-ɹɪ] *n.* **1.** héraldique *f.* **2.** armoiries *fpl*, blason *m.*

herb [hɚb] *n. usual. pl.* [Cooking] fines herbes; [Med.] herbe *f* (médicinale); simples *mpl.* cf. GRASS, WEED.

herd [hɚd] *n.* troupeau *m* (de bêtes): *~ of horses*, troupe *f* de chevaux; [Fig.] foule *f* (de gens); [Pej.] populace *f* [×] ‖ *v. tr.* garder, soigner (un troupeau, des animaux). ‖ *v. intr.* [together] s'assembler en troupeau; [Fig.] s'associer (*with*, à). ‖ **herds|man** [-zmən] *pl.* **-men** *n.* gardien *m* de troupeau. cf. SHEPHERD.

here [hijɚ] *adv.* ici; voici; -ci [☞ L'anglais ajoute souvent à la notion de *here* des précisions que le français indique par un verbe de mouvement ou qu'il ne traduit pas: *up ~*, *down ~*, *out ~*, *in ~*, *over ~*, *back ~*, *&c.*, ici]: *up, down/to ~*, jusqu'ici; *around ~*, par ici; *~ below*, ici-bas; *from ~ to there*, d'ici là; *from ~ to Quebec*, d'ici à Québec; *~ and there*, çà et là, par-ci par-là, par endroits; *~, there and everywhere*, (un peu) partout; *That's neither ~ nor there*, Ça ne fait ni chaud ni froid; [no connection] Ça n'a rien à voir (à l'affaire), Ce n'est pas de cela qu'il s'agit; *Here/I am, he is/*, Me, Le/voici; *Here he comes*, Le voici qui arrive; *Here we are,* Nous voici (arrivés): *Here (you are),* Tenez, (voici pour vous); *my brother* ~, mon frère que voici; *this one* ~, celui-ci; *Here lies . . .*, Ci-gît . . .

hereabout [-əˌbawt] *adv.* dans les environs *mpl,* près d'ici. || **hereafter** [ˌhijə˞'æftə˞] *adv.* ci-après, ci-dessous; désormais, à l'avenir. || *n.*: *in the* ~, dans l'autre monde. || **hereby** ['hijə˞ˌbaj] *adv.* **1.** par ceci, par là, par ce moyen. **2.** [Jur.] par les présentes.

hereditary [hə˞'ɛdɪ|ˌtɛə˞ɪ] *adj.* héréditaire. || **heredity** [-tɪ] *n.* hérédité *f.*

herein ['hijə˞ɪn] *adv.* ci-inclus; sur ce point.

heresy ['hɛə˞ə|sɪ] *n.* hérésie *f.* || **heretic** [-tɪk] *n. & adj.* hérétique.

heretofore [ˌhijə˞|ˌtuw'tɔə˞] *adv.* jusqu'à présent. || **hereupon** [-ə'pɑn] *adv.* là-dessus, sur ces entrefaites. || **herewith** [-'wɪð] *adv.* avec ceci, ci-joint; de cette façon.

heritage ['hɛə˞ɪtədʒ] *n.* héritage *m;* [inheritance] patrimoine *m.*

hermit ['hə˞mət] *n.* ermite *m.*

hernia ['hə˞nɪə] *n.* hernie *f.*

hero ['hijə˞ow] *n.* héros *m.* || **heroic(al)** [hə'ɹowɪk(l̩)] *adj.* héroïque, brave, sublime, très grand. || **heroine** ['hɛə˞owˌɪn] *n.* héroïne *f.* || **heroism** ['hɛə˞owˌɪsm] *n.* héroïsme *m.*

heron ['hɛə˞ən] *n.* héron *m.*

herring ['hɛə˞ɪŋ] *n.* hareng *m;* [Gaspé] poisson *m* frais: *red* ~, hareng *m* saur; [Fig.] *a red* ~, échappatoire *m;* faux-fuyant *m.* || **herring choker** [-ˌtʃowkə˞] © [Fam.] *n.* Néo-Écossais *m,* Néo-Écossaise *f.*

hers [hə˞z] *pron. poss.* [☞ cf. note sur HER] le sien *m.sing.,* la sienne *f.sing.,* les siens *mpl,* les siennes *fpl.* [☞ The Fr. pron. agrees in gender and number with the noun it replaces.]; [predicate of *to be*] à elle: *Is this book* ~ ?, [ownership] Ce livre est-il/à elle, le sien/?, [authorship] Ce livre est-il d'elle?; *Hers is on the table,* Le sien est sur la table; *My bicycle and* ~, Ma bicyclette et la sienne; *A friend of* ~, Un(e) de ses ami(e)s, Un(e) ami(e) à elle.

herself [hə˞'sɛlf] *pron. refl.* [reinforcing subject], elle-même; [refl. obj. dir. & indir.] se, elle-même: *She came* ~, Elle est venue/elle-même, en personne/; *She did it* ~, Elle l'a fait/elle-même, toute seule/; *She washed* ~, Elle s'est lavée.

he's [hijz] [☞ Ne confondez pas avec HIS.] = he is, cf. BE. || = he has, cf. HAVE.

hesitate ['hɛzɪˌtejt] *v. intr.* hésiter; être/hésitant, indécis. || *v. tr.* [speech] balbutier. || **hesitating** [-ɪŋ] *adj.* hésitant, incertain. || **hesitatingly** [-ɪŋlɪ] *adv.* d'une manière indécise, en hésitant. || **hesitation** [hɛzɪ'tejʃən] *n.* hésitation *f;* doute *m;* indécision *f.*

hew [hjuw] *v. tr.* abattre, couper (un arbre avec une hache); tailler (une pierre); équarrir (une poutre): *rough-hewn,* taillé à coup de serpe, [Fig.] ébauché, dégrossi: *to* ~ *one's way,* se frayer un passage (à coups d'épée, &c.).

hexagon ['hɛksəˌgɑn] hexagone *m.*

hey [hej] *interj.* [to attract attention] Eh!, Hep!, Dites donc!; [surprise] Eh bien!

hi [haj] *interj.* [Fam.] salut! © hello!; [= How are you?] Ça va?

hiatus [ˌhaj'ejtəs] *n.* hiatus *m.*

hibernate ['hajbə˞ˌnejt] *v. intr.* hiberner.

hiccup ['hɪkʌp] *n.* hoquet *m.* || *v. intr.* avoir le hoquet.

hickory ['hɪkə˞ɪ] *n.* [wood] hickory; [tree] caryer *m.*

hid [hɪd] cf. HIDE.

hidden [-n̩] *adj.* caché, secret.

hide[1] [hajd] **hid** [hɪd] **hid(den)** [-n̩] *v. tr.* cacher; [in the ground] enfouir; [cover up] masquer; couvrir; voiler; [Fig.] dissimuler (ses sentiments, &c.): *to play* ~ *-and-seek,* jouer à cache-cache. || *v. intr.* se cacher, se dissimuler.

hide[2] *n.* peau *f* (d'animal); [thick hide] cuir *m.* || **hidebound** [-bawnd] *adj.* très maigre; [Fig.] à l'esprit/étroit, obstiné/.

hideous ['hɪdɪəs] *adj.* hideux, très laid.

hide-out ['hajdˌawt] *n.* repaire *m,* cachette *f.*

hiding[1] ['hajdɪŋ] *n.*: *to be in* ~, se cacher; ~ *-place,* cachette *f.* || **hiding**[2] *n.* [Fam.] râclée *f;* volée *f.*

hierarchy ['hajə˞ˌɑə˞kɪ] *n.* hiérarchie *f.*

Hi Fi, HiFi ['haj'faj] [= HIGH FIDELITY (SYSTEM)] (à) haute fidélité *f.*

high [haj] *adj.* [hill, office, official, tension, treason, &c.] haut; [price, rate, temperature, opinion] élevé; [speed, leap] grand; [proportion, fever, wind] fort; [noon] plein; [sea] gros; [explosive] puissant; [meat] avancé; [Fam.] ivre: *How* ~ *is . . . ?,* Quelle est/la hauteur de . . . , l'altitude d'(une montagne)/?; *It is 100 feet* ~, Il est haut de 100 pieds, Il a une hauteur de 100 pieds, Il a 100 pieds de haut(eur); ~ *and mighty attitude,* des airs prétentieux; *on the* ~ *seas,* en pleine mer; *in a* ~ *voice,* d'une voix /élevée, perçante/; *It is* ~ *time,* Il est grand temps de (+ infin., que + subjunc.); *the* ~ *table,* la table/des professeurs, d'honneur/; *higher/education, mathematics, &c./,*

l'enseignement supérieur, les mathématiques supérieures, &c./; *highest speed*, vitesse *f* maximum; *the Most High*, Le Tout-Puissant; ~ *and dry*, à sec; [Fig.] *to be left* ~ *and dry*, être laissé le bec dans l'eau. || **high** *adv.* haut *inv.*; à une grande /hauteur, altitude/; à un/point, degré/ élevé: *on* ~ , en haut, dans le ciel; *to fly* ~ , voler haut; *to run* ~ , [quarrel] s'échauffer; *to play* ~ , jouer gros jeu; *to go/* ~ , *higher/*, monter (plus) haut; *higher up*, plus/haut, loin/; *to search* ~ *and low*, chercher/partout, de la cave au grenier/.

high altar [-'oltə˞] *n.* [Rel.] maître-autel *m.* || **high-born** [-'bɔə˞n] *adj.* de naissance noble, de haute naissance. || **highchair** [-ˌtʃɛə˞] *n.* chaise *f* d'enfant, de bébé; © chaise haute. || **High Church** [-'tʃə˞tʃ] [Rel.] [Anglican] l'Église *f* haute. || [Fam.] **highfalutin(g)** [-fəˌluwtn̩] *adj.* (style *m*) pompeux, ampoulé: ~ *ideas*, idées *fpl* prétentieuses. || **high-handed** [-'hændəd] *adj.* [action] arbitraire; despotique. || **high-heeled** [-'hijld] *adj.* à talons hauts. || **highland** [-lənd] *n.* pays *m*/de montagnes, montagneux/: *the Highlands*, la Haute Écosse. || **highlight** [-ˌlajt] *n.* trait *m* /caractéristique, principal/: *the* ~ *of the evening*, le clou, le moment/de la soirée; *news highlights*, les manchettes *fpl.* || *v. tr.* mettre en relief, faire ressortir (une différence, un trait). || **highly** [-lɪ] *adv.* largement; fortement; fort; très: ~ *amusing*, fort divertissant; ~ *paid*, largement payé; *to/think, speak/* ~ *of s.o.*, avoir une haute opinion de qqun, parler en termes élogieux de qqun. || **High Mass** [-'mæs] *n.* [Rel.] grand-messe *f.*

highness [-nəs] *n.* hauteur *f*, altitude *f*; [Royalty] *Highness*, Altesse *f.* || **high-powered** [-'powə˞d] *adj.* à grande puissance; [Fig.] débordant d'activité, dynamique. || **high-priced** [-'pɹajst] *adj.* d'un grand prix, cher. || **highroad** [-'ɹowd] *n.* †**1.** grand-route *f*, route *f* nationale. **2.** [Fig.] *to be on the* ~ *to success*, avoir le vent dans les voiles. || **high school** [-ˌskuwl] *n.* école *f*/supérieure, secondaire; [Fr.] lycée *m*, collège *m*; © école supérieure; ~ *teacher*, professeur *m/f*; ~ *student*, élève *m/f* d'école secondaire; [Fr.] collégien *m*, -ne *f*, lycéen *m*, -ne *f*. || **high-sounding** [-'sawndɪŋ] *adj.* pompeux, prétentieux: ~ *sentences*, phrases ronflantes. || **highway** [-ˌwej] **1.** *n.* route *f* nationale; route de grande communication; *a* ~ *map*, une carte routière: *the Trans-Canada* ~ , la route transcanadienne; *express* ~ , autoroute *f*. **2** grand-route *f*, grand chemin *m*; *highwayman*, voleur *m* de grand chemin.

hike [hajk] *v. tr.* donner une secousse à [prices] hausser (les prix). || *v. intr.* faire une/randonnée, excursion/(à pied); vagabonder. || *n.* excursion *f* à pied.

hilarious [hɪ'lɛə˞əs] *adj.* hilare.

hill [hɪl] *n.* colline *f*; [incline] côte *f*; [large] mont *m*, montagne *f*; [small] coteau *m*: †*up* ~ *and down dale*, par monts et par vaux. || **hillock** [-ək] *n.* éminence *f*, butte *f*. || **hillside** [-ˌsajd] *n.* (flanc de) coteau *m.* || **hilltop** [-ˌtɑp] *n.* **1.** hauteur *f*, éminence *f*. **2.** /sommet *m*, haut *m*/de la côte, de la colline. || **hilly** [-ɪ] *adj.* (pays) montagneux; (chemin) montueux; (terrain) accidenté.

hilt [hɪlt] *n.* [sword] garde *f*: [Fig.] *up to the* ~, à fond.

him [hɪm] *pron. pers.* **1.** [dir. obj.] le, l' [+ vowel or mute h]: *I see* ~ , Je le vois; *I saw* ~ , Je l'ai vu; *(Don't) watch* ~ , Regardez-le, Ne le regardez pas. **2.** [indir. obj.] lui: *I gave/* ~ *the book, the book to* ~ / , Je lui ai donné le livre; *I gave it to* ~ , Je le lui ai donné. **3.** [after prep.] lui: *I came with* ~ , Je suis venu avec lui. **4.** [double obj.] lui: *I saw you and* ~ , Je vous ai vus, vous et lui; *I told you and* ~ , Je vous l'ai dit, à vous et à lui. **5** [stressed] lui; à lui: *I know* ~ , Je le connais,/lui, [Pej.] celui-là/; *I gave it to* ~ , Je le lui ai donné, à lui; *I came with* ~ , C'est avec lui que je suis venu. **6.** (celui) qui: *All things come to* ~ *who waits*, Tout vient à point à qui sait attendre. [☞ Le pron. *him* rendu par le pron. rel. fr. *qui*, précédé ou non par le dém. *celui*, s'emploie seulement dans les tournures adverbiales; dans la conversation courante, on lui préférera toujours la tournure: *the one who*: *I'll give a reward to the one who gets a good mark*, Je récompenserai celui qui aura une bonne note.] 7. [Fam.] *It's* ~ , C'est lui; *That's* ~ , Le voilà; *older than* ~ , plus âgé que lui.

Himalayas, the [hɪmə'lejəs] *n.* l'Himalaya *m.*

himself [ˌhɪm'sɛlf] *pron. refl.* [reinforcing subj.] lui-même; [reflexive obj., dir. & indir.] se; lui-même: *He came* ~ , Il est venu/lui-même, en personne/; *He did it* ~ , Il l'a fait/lui-même, tout seul/; *He washed* ~ , Il s'est lavé.

hind[1] [hajnd] *adj.* de derrière, postérieur.

hind[2] *n.* biche *f.*

hinder ['hɪndə˞] *v. tr.* gêner; empêcher (de); retarder.

hindmost [ˈhajndˌmowst] *adj.* dernier; au dernier rang.
hindrance [ˈhɪndɹəns] *n.* obstacle *m*; entrave *f*; empêchement *m.*
hindsight [ˈhajndˌsajt] *n.* hausse *f* (de fusil); [Fam.] clairvoyance *f* après coup.
Hindu, Hindoo [ˈhɪnduw] *pl.* **-s** *adj. & n.* Indien *m* (de l'Inde); Hindou *m*, -e *f.*
hinge [hɪndʒ] *n.* [door] gond *m*, [box] charnière *f*; [Fig.] pivot *m*, point *m* critique. ‖ *v. tr.* poser/des gonds, des charnières. ‖ *v. intr.* tourner sur des gonds; [Fig.] *to ~ on*, dépendre de.
hint [hɪnt] *n.* **1.** allusion *f*, insinuation *f*: *to drop a ~* , insinuer. **2.** [sign] signe *m*; indication *f*: *to give a ~* , annoncer; *to take a ~* , comprendre/à demi-mot, à mots couverts.
hip [hɪp] *n.* hanche *f*: *~ -pocket*, poche-revolver *f.*
hippo [ˈhɪpow] *pl.* **-s, hippopotamus** [ˌhɪpəˈpɑtəməs] *pl.* **-es** *n.* hippopotame *m.*
hire [hajɚ] *v. tr.* louer (une voiture, les services de qqun); engager (une bonne): *for ~* , à louer; *to ~ out*, louer les services. ‖ **hire-purchase** [-ˌpɚtʃəs] *n.* [Br.] location-vente *f*, vente *f* à tempérament. ‖ **hired** [-d] *adj.* de louage; [person] à gages: *~ waiter*, extra *m.*
his [hɪz] *adj. poss.* [☞ *his* désigne toujours un possesseur du genre masculin] son *m.s.*, sa *f.s.*, ses *m/f.pl.* [☞ The Fr. adj. agrees with the person or thing possessed in gender and number and NOT with the possessor: son livre *m*, sa voiture *f*, ses pieds *mpl*, ses chemises *fpl*]: *~ brother and sister*, son frère et sa sœur; *He raised ~ hand*, Il a levé la main; [external action] *I washed ~ face*, Je lui ai lavé la figure; *He brushed ~ teeth*, Il s'est brossé les dents; *~ feet are big*, Il a de grands pieds; [stressed] *~ book*, son livre à lui.
his *pron. poss.* [☞ cf. note sur HIS, adj.] le sien *m.s.*, la sienne *f.s.*, les siens *mpl*, les siennes *fpl.* [☞ The Fr. pron. agrees in gender and number with the noun it replaces]; [predicate of *to be*] à lui: *Is this book ~ ?*, [ownership] Ce livre est-il/à lui, le sien/; [authorship] Ce livre est-il de lui?; *~ is on the table*, Le sien est sur la table; *my car and ~* , ma voiture et la sienne; *a pupil of ~* , un(e) de ses élèves, un(e) élève à lui.
hiss [hɪs] *n.* sifflement *m* (de la vapeur, d'un serpent); [Theatre] huées *fpl.* ‖ *v. intr.* siffler; [Theatre] siffler, huer.
historian [hɪˈstɔɚɪ|ən] *n.* historien *m.* ‖ **historic(al)** [-k(l̩)] *adj.* de l'histoire, historique.
history [ˈhɪstəɪ] *n.* récit *m*, compte rendu *m*; historique *m* (d'un fait): *medical ~* , fiche *f* de santé; [science] l'histoire *f*; [past events] le passé *m*: *Canadian ~* , l'histoire du Canada.
hit [hɪt] *n.* **1.** coup *m*; impact *m*; choc *m*: *direct ~* , coup/au but, direct/; *~ or miss*, à tout hasard, [at any cost] vaille que vaille. **2.** sarcasme *m*; coup de patte: [baseball] coup de batte; frappe *f*; [fencing] touche *f.* **3.** [Fig.] succès *m*, [lucky] trouvaille *f*: *song ~* , chanson *f*/à succès, du jour/; *It was a (great) ~* , Ce fut un succès (fou). ‖ **hit, hit, hit, hitting** [-ɪŋ] *v. tr.* frapper, donner un coup; [bump] cogner, heurter; [reach] trouver, tomber sur; atteindre, arriver à; critiquer, attaquer: *He ~ me on the nose (with his fist)*, Il m'a frappé au nez, Il m'a donné un coup de poing sur le nez; *He ~ his head (on the pipe)*, Il s'est/cogné, heurté/la tête (contre le tuyau); *He ~ the mark*, Il a atteint le but [also Fig.]; *He ~ (on) the right answer*, Il/a trouvé, est tombé sur/la réponse juste, la solution; *You've ~ it!*, Vous y êtes; [Fam.] *to ~ the road*, se mettre en route; *to be hard ~ by sth.*, être gravement atteint par qqch.; *That hits my fancy*, C'est à mon goût, Ça me plaît. ‖ *v. intr.* frapper; (se) cogner; heurter: *He hits hard*, Il/frappe, cogne/dur. ‖ **hit back** [-ˈbæk] *v. intr.* rendre coup pour coup; riposter (contre). ‖ **hit it off** [-ɪtˌɑf] *v. tr.* s'entendre, s'accorder/(avec qqun). ‖ **hit out** [-ˈawt] (at s.o.) *v. intr.* décocher un coup (à qqun); [Fig.] attaquer violemment (ses critiques).
hitch [hɪtʃ] *n.* **1.** coup *m* sec (sur une corde). **2.** embarras *m*, difficulté *f*; accroc *m*, empêchement *m.* ‖ *v. tr.* accrocher (à), s'accrocher (à, *to*); boitiller; [Fam.] *to ~ a ride*, cf. HITCHHIKE.
hitchhike [-ˌhajk] *v. intr.* [Sport] faire de l'autostop; © faire du pouce, voyager sur le pouce. ‖ **hitchhiker** [-ˌhajkɚ] *n.* autostoppeur *m*, © pouceur *m.*
†hither [ˈhɪðɚ] *adv.* [mouvement vers] par ici, y: *~ and thither*, çà et là; *†Come ~ !*, Venez çà! ‖ **hitherto** [-ˌtuw] *adv.* jusqu'ici; jusqu'à/maintenant, présent.
hive [hajv] *n.* ruche *f*; [swarm] essaim *m.* ‖ **hives** [Med.] éruption *f*, urticaire *m.*
H.M. [ˈejtʃˈɛm] [= */His, Her/Majesty*] Sa Majesté.
HMCS [ˌejtʃˌɛmˈsijˌɛs] © [= Her Majesty's Canadian Ship] ☞ ne se traduit pas en français.
H.M.S. [ˈejtʃˈɛmˈɛs] [= */His, Her/Majesty's*

Service] Service *m* de Sa Majesté; [Br.] = /*His, Her/Majesty's Ship* ☞ne se traduit pas en français.

†**hoar** [hɔɚ] *adj.* blanc cf. HOARY: ~ *-frost,* gelée *f* blanche.

hoard [hɔɚd] *n.* tas *m*; [money] trésor *m*; [Pej.] magot *m.* ‖ *v. tr. & intr.*: *to* ~ *up,* amasser, [money] thésauriser.

hoarse [hɔɚs] *adj.* [voice] enroué, rauque. ‖ **hoarseness** [-nəs] *n.* enrouement *m,* raucité *f.*

hoary [hɔɚı] *adj.* blanc; [hair] †chenu.

hoax [howks] *n.* mystification *f*; [Fam.] blague *f.* ‖ *v. tr.* attraper, mystifier.

hob [hɑb] *n.* [fireplace] étagère *f,* plaque *f*; [play] galoche *f.*

hobble [ˈhɑbḷ] *v. intr.* boitiller, clopiner. ‖ *v. tr.* [horse] entraver. ‖ *n.* entrave *f.*

hobby [ˈhɑbı] *n.* [hobbyhorse] dada *m*; [Fig.] violon *m* d'Ingres; passe-temps *m,* distraction *f*; [Pej.] marotte *f.*

hobnob [ˈhɑbˌnɑb] *v. intr.* fréquenter, être à tu et à toi (*with,* avec).

hobo [ˈhowˌbow] *n.* chemineau *m*; vagabond *m,* clochard *m.*

hock [hɑk] *n.* [animals] jarret *m.* ‖ *v. tr.* couper les jarrets; [US, ©, Sl.] mettre en gage, engager.

hockey [ˈhɑkı] *n.* hockey *m*: ~ *player,* joueur *m* de hockey; © †gouret *m*; ~ *-stick,* crosse *f* de hockey.

hodgepodge [ˈhɑʤˌpɑʤ] *n.* salmigondis *m,* macédoine *f.*

hoe [how] *n.* houe *f.* ‖ *v. tr.* sarcler.

hog[1] [hɑg] *n.* porc *m*; [often pej.] cochon *m,* pourceau *m*: [Fam.] *to go the whole* ~, aller jusqu'au bout; risquer le tout pour le tout; *to* ~ *the road,* accaparer toute la route.

hog[2] *n.* [harbour porpoise] © pourcil *m*; *herring* ~ , marsoin *m* commun.

hoist [hojst] *n.* grue *f*; monte-charge *m* [invar.] ‖ *v. tr.* lever; [yard, sail] hisser; [flag] arborer.

hold [howld] *n.* prise *f*; (point *m* d') appui *m*; [ship] cale *f* (*in,* à fond de): *to have* ~ *of,* tenir; *to/catch, take, lay/* ~ *of,* saisir, empoigner, mettre la main sur; *to get* ~ *of,* se procurer (qqch.), découvrir (un secret); *to keep* ~ *of,* ne pas lâcher; *to release one's* ~ , lâcher prise. ‖ **hold, held, held** [hɛld] *v. tr.* **1.** tenir (qqch. à la main; une réunion, une promesse, &c.); retenir (son haleine, l'attention); arrêter, empêcher (qqun); contenir (une quantité de, l'ennemi); avoir, posséder (un emploi); occuper (un poste); défendre (une forteresse): *to* ~ *tight,* serrer . . . dans ses bras; *to* ~ *fast* (*to*), se cramponner (à); *to* ~ *hands,* se tenir par la main; *to* ~ *one's sides* (*with laughter*), se tenir les côtes (de rire); [Fam.] *to be left holding the baby,* [Fam.] être le dindon de la farce; *to* ~ *a conversation with s.o.,* s'entretenir avec qqun; *to* ~ *o.s. ready,* se tenir prêt; *to* ~ *s.o. to his word,* obliger qqun à tenir sa promesse; *Hold it!,* Arrêtez(-vous), Ne bougeons plus!; [Fig.] *Hold the fort!,* Restez là!; *to* ~ *one's tongue,* se taire; *to* ~ *one's ground,* tenir bon, ne pas lâcher pied; *to* ~ *one's own,* se défendre, [Fam.] tenir le coup (contre); *This car holds* 8, Cette voiture a huit places; *to* ~ *water,* être étanche; [Fig.] *Your story does not* ~ *water,* Votre histoire ne tient pas debout. **2.** avoir (une opinion); considérer . . . comme, tenir . . . pour: *He holds that* . . . , Il/est d'avis, estime, croit/que . . . ; *to* ~ *s.o./to be simple, for a simpleton/,* tenir qqun pour naïf; *to be held to be* . . . , passer pour . . . ‖ *v. intr.* **1.** *to hold fast,* tenir (bon), résister. **2.** continuer; durer; persister: *The weather held* (*warm*), Le temps s'est maintenu (au beau). **3.** *to* ~*/good, true,* être vrai, valable. ‖ **hold back** [-ˈbæk] *v. tr.* retenir; cacher, taire: *There was no holding him back,* pas moyen/de le retenir, de l'arrêter. ‖ *v. intr.* hésiter (à faire qqch.); se retenir (de faire qqch.); rester au second plan. ‖ **hold down** [-ˈdawn] *v. tr.* maintenir à terre, opprimer.

holder [-ɚ] *n.* **1.** teneur *m,* possesseur *m*; détenteur *m* (de titres); porteur *m* (d'un effet de commerce); propriétaire *m/f* (d'une terre); titulaire *m/f* (d'un droit, d'un poste). **2.** support *m,* monture *f*: *pen-* ~ , porte-plume *m, cigarette-* ~ , fume-cigarette *m*; *pot-* ~ , poignée *f.* ‖ **hold forth** [-ˈfɔɚθ] *v. intr.* discourir, pérorer. ‖ **hold in** [-ˈın] *v. tr.* retenir, maîtriser (une passion); réprimer (un désir). ‖ **hold off** [-ˈɑf] *v. tr.* tenir/éloigné, à distance/. ‖ *v. intr.* s'abstenir de; se tenir à distance. ‖ **hold on** [-ˈɑn] *v. intr.* se cramponner (à), ne pas lâcher; ne pas abandonner; continuer (à faire qqch.), tenir bon: *Hold on!,* [Tel.] Ne quittez pas!; Tenez-vous bien!; Pas si vite!, Minute! ‖ **hold out** [-ˈawt] *v. tr.* tendre (la main); offrir. ‖ *v. intr.* tenir; résister (*against,* à). ‖ **hold over** [-ˈowvɚ] *v. tr.* remettre à plus tard, différer, ajourner (une décision). ‖ **hold-over** [-ˌowvɚ] *n.* restant *m,* survivance *f.* ‖ **hold up** [-ˈʌp]. **1.** [support] soutenir; [lift] soulever, [raise] lever (la main); exposer (au ridicule); offrir, proposer (comme modèle); arrêter (un train); gêner (la circulation); retenir, retarder (qqun); attaquer (qqun) à main armée. || *v. intr.* durer; résister (à l'usage); [story] tenir debout. || **holdup** [-ˌʌp] *n.* arrêt *m*, suspension *f* (de la circulation); attaque *f*, vol *m* à main armée: *What's the ~ ?*, Qu'est-ce qu'on attend? || **hold with** [-ˌwɪð] être du parti de qqun; être du même avis que (qqun).

hole [howl] *n.* **1.** trou *m*; [hollow] creux *m*, cavité *f*; [rabbit] terrier *m*; [wolf, fox] tanière *f*; [mouse] trou *m*. **2.** [hovel] taudis *m*; bicoque *f*: *What a ~ !*, Quel trou!; *a rotten ~* , une sale boîte; *to find o.s. in a ~* , être dans/l'embarras, le pétrin; *to get s.o. out of a ~*, tirer qqun d'un mauvais pas; *to pick holes in an argument*, démolir, démontrer les points faibles d'/un argument.

holiday ['hɑlɪˌdej] *n.* **1.** (jour *m* de) fête; jour férié. **2.** (jour de)/congé *m*, sortie *f*: *to take a ~* , prendre un congé. || **holidays** [-z] *npl* [Br.] les vacances *fpl*: *to be on (one's) ~* , être en/vacances, congé; *the summer ~*, les vacances d'été, les grandes vacances. cf. VACATION.

holiness ['howlɪnəs] *n.* **1.** sainteté *f*. **2.** [R.C.] *His Holiness*, Sa Sainteté; *His Holiness the Pope*, le Saint-Père.

Holland ['hɑlənd] *n.* Hollande *f*: *in, to ~* , en Hollande. cf. NETHERLANDS, DUTCH.

hollow ['hɑlow] *adj.* creux; vide: *~ cheeks*, joues *fpl* creuses; *~ eyes*, yeux *mpl* enfoncés; [sound] sourd; [voice] caverneuse; [Fig.] trompeur: *a ~ joy*, une fausse joie; *a ~ promise*, une vaine promesse; *to feel ~* , avoir faim.

holly ['hɑlɪ] *n.* houx *m*.

holster ['howlstər] *n.* étui *m* (de revolver); [saddle] fonte *f*.

holy ['howlɪ] *adj.* saint; bénit: *The Holy Ghost*, le Saint-Esprit; *the Holy Father*, le Saint-Père; *Holy Writ*, l'Ecriture (Sainte); les Ecritures saintes; *~ bread*, pain *m* bénit; *~ water*, eau *f* bénite; *Holy Communion*, la sainte Communion *f*; *Holy City*, ville *f* sainte, la Jérusalem céleste, le Ciel; *~ day*, fête *f* religieuse; *Holy Grail*, le Saint Graal; *Holy Land*, Terre Sainte; Palestine *f*; *~ orders*, le sacrement *m* de l'ordre, les ordres *mpl*; *Holy See*, le Saint Siège; *Holy smoke!*, Sapristi!, © Viande à chien!, Sacrifice!

homage ['hɑmədʒ] *n.* hommage *m*.

home [howm] *n.* **1.** [idée d'un endroit où on est chez soi] foyer *m*, chez-soi *m*, [official] domicile *m*; [lodgings] logis *m*; [house] maison *f*: *the White(s') ~* , la maison des White; *Where do you make your ~ ?*, Où demeurez-vous?; *to have no ~* , être sans feu ni lieu; *to leave ~* , partir (de chez soi), quitter sa famille; *Is he at ~ ?*, Est-il/à la maison, chez lui/?; *away from ~* , absent; *to feel at ~ with s.o.*, se sentir à l'aise avec qqun; *Make yourself at ~* , Faites comme chez vous. **2.** [idée d'appartenance] patrie *f*, pays *m* natal, terre *f* natale: *~ country*, pays d'origine, © le vieux pays; *~ town*, ville *f* natale; *~ cooking*, cuisine bourgeoise; *back ~* , chez nous. **3.** habitat *m*: *Alaska is the ~ of seals*, l'A. est l'habitat du phoque. **4.** foyer *m*, asile *m*, hospice *m* (de vieillards, &c.). **5.** [Sport] le but; [races] l'arrivée *f*. || **home** *adj.*: *~ trip*, voyage *m* de retour; *~ address*, adresse *f* personnelle; *~ ground*, terrain *m* du club; *~ trade*, commerce *m* intérieur; *~ products*, produits *mpl* du pays; [baseball] *~ run*, © (coup *m* de) circuit. || *adv.* **1.** à la maison; chez soi; dans son pays (d'origine): *to/go, come/ ~* , rentrer (à la maison, chez soi, dans/sa famille, son pays); *to be ~* , être de retour/à la maison, chez soi/; *to send s.o. ~ (from abroad)*, rapatrier qqun; *to see s.o. ~* , raccompagner qqun (jusqu'à chez lui). **2.** *to strike ~* , atteindre le but, frapper juste, faire mouche; *The insult went ~* , L'insulte porta. **3.** *to drive ~* , *push ~* , *press ~* , enfoncer, pousser, &c. (qqch.) à fond. **4.** [Fig.] *It came ~ to me*, Je m'en suis rendu compte; *to bring sth. ~ to s.o.*, faire comprendre qqch. à qqun. || *v. intr.* se diriger par radioguidage (vers): *home-and-school club*, École *f* des Parents; Association *f* de parents d'élèves. || *v. intr.* revenir/à sa base, [pigeon] à son pigeonnier. || **homecoming** [-ˌkʌmɪŋ] *n.* retour *m* au foyer, à la maison; [Univ.] journée *f*, semaine *f*/des anciens. || **home economics** [-ˌɛkn̩'ɑmɪks] économie *f* domestique, enseignement *m* ménager.|| **Home Guard** [-'gɑərd] *n.* [Br.] garde *f* territoriale; [US] garde *f* civile. || **homeless** [-ləs] *adj.* sans foyer; sans feu ni lieu; [stateless] apatride. || **homelike** [-ˌlajk] *adj.* intime. || **homely** [-lɪ] *adj.* **1.** simple, ordinaire; [habits, tastes] bourgeois. **2.** [Pej.] sans beauté, sans élégance: *She has a ~ face*, Elle a un visage sans charme. || **homemade** [-ˌmejd] *adj.* de fabrication domestique, fait à la maison: *~ bread*, pain *m* de ménage; *~ pie*, tarte *f* grand'mère. || **homemaker** [-ˌmejkər] *n.* maîtresse *f* de maison; ménagère *f*. || **home-owner** [-ˌownər] *n.* propriétaire *m* (de maison). || **home plate** [-'plejt] *n.* [Sport] © le marbre. || **homer**

[-ɚ] *n.* [Sport] © (coup *m* de) circuit. || **homesick** [-ˌsɪk] *adj.* nostalgique: *to be* ~, avoir le mal du pays. || **homesickness** [-ˌsɪknəs] *n.* mal du pays, nostalgie *f.* || **homespun** [-ˌspʌn] *n.* tissu *m*/indigène, domestique/. || *adj.* filé à la maison; [Fig.] simple, sans prétention. || **homestead** [-ˌstɛd] *n.* propriété (rurale); ferme *f*; © concession *f.* || **homeward** [-wɚd] *adj.* & *adv.* (vers) chez soi; vers, dans/son pays: ~ /*trip, voyage*/, voyage *m* de retour. || **homework** [-wɚk] *n.* [Sch.] devoir(s) (du soir); [Ind.] travail *m* à domicile.

homicidal [ˈhowmɪsajdl̩] *adj.* homicide, meurtrier. || **homicide** [ˈhowmɪˌsajd] *n.* **1.** homicide *m.* **2.** [person] meurtrier *m.*

homing [ˈhowmɪŋ] *n.* (vol de) rentrée *f*, retour *m*: [Aviat.] ~ *mechanism*, radiogoniomètre *m*; ~ *pigeon*, pigeon *m* voyageur.

homogeneous [ˌhowməˈʤijnjəs] *adj.* homogène. || **homogenize** [həˈmɑʤəˌnajz] *v. tr.* homogénéiser: *homogenized milk*, lait *m* non écrémé.

hone [hown] *n.* pierre *f* à aiguiser [rasoir]. || *v. tr.* [razor] aiguiser.

honest [ˈɑnəst] *adj.* honnête; sincère, loyal; [profits] honnête; [work] consciencieux. || **honestly** [-lɪ] *adv.* honnêtement; sincèrement; loyalement. || **honesty** [-ɪ] *n.* honnêteté *f*, probité *f*; [truthfulness] droiture *f*: *in all* ~, en toute franchise *f.*

honey [ˈhʌnɪ] *n.* miel *m*; [Fig.] mon, ma/chéri, -e. || **honeycomb** [-ˈkowm] *n.* rayon *m* de miel; [Fig.] cavité *f.* || **honeycombed** [-ˈkowmd] *adj.* criblé (*with*, de). || **honeyed** [-d] *adj.* mielleux. || **honeymoon** [-ˌmuwn] *n.* lune *f* de miel. || *v. intr.* /être en, passer en/lune de miel. || **honeysuckle** [-sʌkl̩] *n.* chèvrefeuille *m.*

honorary [ˈɑnɚ|ˌɛəɪ] *adj.* honorifique, bénévole, non rétribué; honoraire.

honour [ˈɑnɚ] *n.* honneur *m*: *to be an* ~ *to*, faire /honneur à, l'orgueil de/; *word of* ~, parole *f* d'honneur; [dignity] distinction *f*, privilège *m*; [esteem] *person held in great* ~, personne/à qui l'on témoigne beaucoup de respect, que l'on tient en haute considération; [title] *His Honour, Mayor X . . .*, Son Honneur le maire X . . . ; *Your Honour*, votre Honneur; [Jur.] *Your Honour*, Votre Honneur, Monsieur le juge, [Fr.] Monsieur le président. || *v. tr.* honorer, respecter; [Com.] ~ *a debt*, faire honneur à une créance. || **honourable** [-əbl̩] *adj.* honorable; intègre; respectable; [Pol.] *the Honourable . . .*, l'honorable . . . ; *the Right Honourable X, Prime Minister of Canada . . .*, le très honorable X, premier ministre du Canada. . . . || **honoured** [-d] *adj.* valable; accepté; [Fr.] honoré: *Credit cards are* ~ *here*, Nous acceptons les cartes d'achat; *time-* ~, consacré par l'usage. || **honours** [-z] *n.pl.* [Scol.] mention *f*; distinction *f* honorifique; *academic* ~, distinctions académiques; ~ *list*, palmarès *m.*

hood [hʊd] *n.* capuchon *m*, [Auto.] capot *m*; [Photo.] parasoleil *m.* || **hoodwink** [-wɪŋk] *v. tr.* tromper, abuser/qqun.

hoof [huwf] [hʊf] *pl.* **hooves** *n.* sabot *m*, pied *m*/(de cheval, &c.).

hook [hʊk] *n.* crochet *m*; [boxing] *right* ~, crochet *m* du droit; [fish] hameçon *m.* || *v. tr.* accrocher, agrafer; [fish] prendre . . . (à l'hameçon), ferrer: [Fam.] *to* ~ *it*, filer, décamper; *to* ~ *up*, agrafer, assembler (les pièces/d'un appareil de radio, d'un téléphone, &c.); [connect] brancher.

hooky [-ɪ] *n.* [Sl.]: *to play* ~, [skip school] faire l'école buissonnière.

hooligan [ˌhuwlɪgən] *n.* voyou *m*; mauvais garçon *m.*

hoop [huwp] *n.* cerceau *m*; [skirt] crinoline *f.* || *v. tr.* cercler, entourer.

hoot [huwt] *n.* hululement *m*, cri *m* de la chouette; [Fig.] huées *fpl.*; [Fam.] *I don't care a* ~, Je m'en moque pas mal. || *v. intr.* [owl] hululer; [Fig.] huer; conspuer.

hooves [huwvz] cf. HOOF.

hop[1] [hɑp] *v. intr.* **[-pp-]** sauter à cloche-pied; [bird] sautiller: [Fam.] *Hop it!*, Fichez-moi le camp!; Filez!; *Hop in!*, Montez!, [Fam.] © Embarquez! || *n.* saut *m*; [dance] sauterie *f.*

hop[2] *n.* houblon *m.*

hope [howp] *n.* espoir *m*; espérance *f*: *in the* ~ *of . . .*, dans l'espoir de . . . ; dans l'attente de . . . || *v. tr.* espérer (*to*, + infin.); mettre son espoir en, mettre sa confiance en: *to* ~ *against* ~, ne pas désespérer; *to* ~ *for the best*, garder bon espoir. || **hopeful** [-fl̩] *adj.* **1.** plein d'espoir. **2.** prometteur. || **hopeless** [-ləs] *adj.* sans espoir; qui/ne permet, ne laisse/aucun espoir; [maladie] incurable; [situation] désespéré, sans issue. || **hopelessness** [-ləsnəs] *n.* désespoir *m.*

horde [hɔɚd] *n.* horde *f.*

horizon [həˈɹajzən] *n.* horizon *m*: *on the* ~, à l'horizon. || **horizontal** [ˌhɔɚˈzɑntəl] *adj.* horizontal.

horn [hɔɚn] *n.* **1.** [cow, &c.] corne *f*; [stag] bois *mpl*; [insect] antennes *fpl.* **2.** [Mus.] cor *m*: *hunting* ~, cor *m* de chasse; *French* ~ , cor *m* d'harmonie; *English* ~ , cor *m* anglais; [car] avertisseur *m*; †klaxon *m*; © criard *m*. || *adj*. de, en/corne.

hornet ['hɔɚnət] *n*. frelon *m*.

horrible [ˌhɔɚɪbl̩] *adj*. horrible, atroce: *How* ~ *!*, Quelle horreur! || **horribly** [-ɪ] *adv*. horriblement, atrocement.

horrid ['hɔɚɪd] *adj*. affreux, effrayant; [Fam.] désagréable.

horrify ['hɔɚɪˌfaj] *v. tr*. horrifier; [Fam.] surprendre désagréablement. || **horror** ['hɔɚɚ] *n*. horreur *f*.

horse [hɔɚs] *n*. cheval *m*; [breed] étalon *m*; [Mil.] (hommes de) cavalerie *f*; [Gymn.] cheval de bois: *to ride a* ~ , aller, monter/ à cheval; *draught* ~ , cheval de trait; *pack* ~ , cheval/de bât, de somme/; *saddle* ~ , cheval de selle; ~ *race*, course *f* de chevaux; ~ *show*, concours *m* hippique; [Fam.] ~ *sense*, gros bon sens *m*. || **horseback** [-ˌbæk] *n*.: *on* ~ , à cheval; *to go* ~ *-riding*, aller, monter/à cheval, faire de l'équitation. || **horseflesh** [-ˌflɛʃ] *n*. viande *f* de cheval. || **horsefly** [-ˌflaj] *n*. taon *m*. || **horsehair** [-ˌhɛɚ] *n*. crin *m*. || **horse|man,** *pl*. **-men** [-mən] *n*. cavalier *m*. || **horsemanship** [-mənˌʃɪp] *n*. équitation *f*. || **horseplay** [-ˌplej] *n*. grosse farce *f*; [Sch.] chahut *m*. || **horsepower** [-ˌpawɚ] cheval-vapeur *m*. || **horseradish** [-ˌɹædɪʃ] *n*. raifort *m*. || **horsewhip** [-ˌwɪp] *n*. cravache *f*. || *v. tr*. cravacher. || **horse|woman** [-ˌwʊmən] *pl*. **-women** [-ˌwɪmən] *n*. amazone *f*, cavalière *f*.

horticulture ['hɔɚtɪˌkʌltʃɚ] *n*. horticulture *f*.

hose [howz] *n*. **1.** [Com.] bas *mpl*; [men's] chaussettes *fpl*. **2.** tuyau *m* (d'arrosage, &c.).

†**hosiery** ['howʒɚɪ] *n*. bas *mpl*; [socks] chaussettes *fpl*.

hospitable [ˌhɑs'pɪtəbl̩] *adj*. hospitalier, accueillant.

hospital ['hɑspɪtl̩] *n*. hôpital *m*: [patient] *in* ~ , hospitalisé; ~ *train*, train *m* sanitaire; *mental* ~ , asile *m* d'aliénés. || **hospitality** [ˌhɑspɪ'tælətɪ] *n*. hospitalité *f*. || **hospitalize** ['hɑspɪtəˌlajz] *v. tr*. hospitaliser.

host[1] [howst] *n*. hôte *m* [☞ which also means "guest"]. || *v. tr*. recevoir: [Sport] *The Club will* ~ *the Canadians this week*, Le Club recevra les Canadiens cette semaine. || **host**[2] *n*. armée *f*, légion *f*. || **host**[3] *n*. [Rel.] *the Host*, l'Hostie *f*.

hostage ['hɑstədʒ] *n*. otage *m*; [Fig.] gage *m*.

hostel ['hɑstl̩] *n*. hôtellerie *f*: *Youth* ~ , Auberge *f* de la Jeunesse.

hostess ['howstəs] *n*. **1.** hôtesse *f*. **2.** hôtelière *f*.

hostile ['hɑstajl] *adj*. ennemi: ~ *forces*, les forces/ennemies, de l'ennemi; [Fig.] hostile, contraire. || **hostilities** [-z] *n.pl*. hostilités *fpl*, état *m* de guerre. || **hostility** [hɑs'tɪlətɪ] *n*. hostilité *f*, animosité *f*.

hot [hɑt] *adj*. [-tt-] **1.** chaud: *It is* ~ , [thing] C'est chaud, [weather] Il fait chaud; *I am* ~ , J'ai chaud; *boiling-* ~ , bouillant; *burning* ~ , brûlant; *piping* ~ , très chaud, sortant du four; *white* ~ , chauffé à blanc. **2.** [pepper] cuisant; [mustard] piquant; [Fig.] violent; acharné; [Nucl. Phys.] fortement radioactif: *to have a* ~ *temper*, → s'emporter facilement. **3.** [Loc.]: *in* ~ *pursuit*, serrer (qqun) de près; [Fig.] *in* ~ *water*, dans le pétrin; ~ *plate*, plaque *f* chauffante. || **hotbed** [-ˌbɛd] *n*. pépinière *f*, serre *f*; [Fig.] foyer *m*.

hotel ['howˌtɛl] *n*. hôtel *m*. || **hotel-keeper** [-ˌkijpɚ] *n*. hôtelier *m*, hôtelière *f*.

hothead ['hɑtˌhɛd] *n*. caractère *m* violent.

hothouse ['hɑtˌhaws] *n*. serre *f*.

hotly ['hɑtlɪ] *adv*. vivement; avec chaleur.

hound [hawnd] *n*. chien *m* de chasse: *pack of hounds*, meute *f* de chiens; [Fig.] butor *m*. || *v. tr*. chasser; [bother] être sur le dos de (qqun).

hour [awɚ] *n*. heure *f*; moment *m*; période *f*: *at any* ~ , à toute heure; *by the* ~ , à l'heure; *every* ~ *on the* ~ , toutes les heures à l'heure juste; *at the eleventh* ~ , à la onzième heure, au dernier moment; *man of the* ~ , l'homme *m* du moment; *question of the* ~ , question *f* d'une actualité brûlante; *his* ~ *of glory*, son moment *m* de gloire; [Sch.] *the music* ~ , la période de musique; *to keep/good, late/hours*, rentrer, se coucher/de bonne heure, tard/; *till the small hours* (*of the morning*), jusqu'à une heure avancée de la nuit; *office hours*, heures d'ouverture, [for individual] de bureau. || **hour hand** [-ˌhænd] *n*. aiguille *f* des heures. || **hourly** [-lɪ] *adj*. (rendement *m*, salaire *m*) à l'heure, horaire; de toutes les heures, de chaque instant. || *adv*. toutes les heures; d'heure en heure; d'un moment, d'un instant/à l'autre; incessamment.

house [haws] *n*. maison; © la Chambre (des communes); théâtre *m*, salle *f*; dynastie *f*, maison *f*: *at,/in, to/s.o.'s* ~ , chez qqun; *to set up* ~ , se mettre en ménage; *to keep* ~ (*for*), tenir la maison (de); *to clean* ~ , faire le nettoyage (de la maison); [Fig.] faire le nettoyage par le vide; *to put one's* ~ *in order*, mettre de l'ordre/dans la maison, [Fig.] dans ses affaires; *to bring down the* ~ , faire crouler la salle sous les applaudissements; *a full* ~ , une salle comble, [poker] main pleine; *It's on the* ~ , C'est aux frais/du patron, de la maison/. || **house** [hawz] *v. tr.* loger (qqun); mettre qqch. à l'abri. || **household** [ˈhawsˈhowld] *n.* **1.** famille *f*; ménage *m*; maisonnée *f*; maison *f*: *the whole* ~ , toute la maisonnée; ~ *expenses*, frais *mpl* de ménage; ~ *word*, mot *m* d'usage courant. **2.** *the Household*, la Maison du roi. || **householder** [-ˌhowldɚ] *n.* maître *m*, maîtresse *f* de maison; chef *m* de famille. || **housekeeper** [-ˌkijpɚ] *n.* femme *f* de charge, gouvernante *f*; © ménagère *f.* || **housekeeping** [-ˌkijpɪŋ] *n.* **1.** ménage *m*; les soins *mpl* du ménage: ~ *money*, argent *m* du ménage; *good* ~ , bonne tenue de la maison. **2.** économie *f* domestique. || **housewi|fe** [-ˌwajf] *pl.* **-ves** [-ˌwajvz]. **1.** maîtresse *f* de maison; ménagère *f.* [Fr. official documents] → sans profession. || **housework** [-ˌwɚk] *n.* le ménage, les soins *mpl* du ménage: *to do the* ~ , faire le ménage. || **housing** [hawzɪŋ] logement *m*, habitation *f*; [Mec.] carter *m*: ~ *development*, lotissement *m.*

hove [howv] cf. HEAVE.

hovel [hʌvl̩] *n.* [Pej.] bicoque *f*, cabane *f*; [Tech.] hangar *m.*

hover [ˈhʌvɚ] *v. intr.* voltiger; [bird, plane] planer; [stay near] rôder (*about, around*, autour de); [waver] être/indécis, en suspens: *to* ~ *between*, tenir le milieu entre; *to* ~ *over*, menacer.

how [haw] *adv. interrog.* **1.** comment, de quelle/manière, façon/: *How did you persuade him?*, Comment, De quelle façon, manière/l'avez-vous persuadé?; *Tell me* ~ *you persuaded him*, Dites-moi/comment, de quelle façon, manière/vous l'avez persuadé; *How is that?*, Qu'en dites-vous?; *How so*, Comment ça?; *I see* ~ *it is*, Je vois ce que c'est; *And* ~ *!*, Et comment!; *Show me* ~ *to do it*, Montrez-moi comment (le) faire. cf. KNOW; *How to (draw, &c.) in 5 lessons*, Le dessin en 5 leçons. **2.** [~ + adj. or adv.] *How old are you?*, Quel âge avez-vous?; *How wide is the street?*, Quelle est la largeur de la rue?; *How far is it to town?*, A quelle distance se trouve la ville?; *How sick is he?*, Est-il bien malade?; *How fast can you run?*, A quelle vitesse pouvez-vous courir?; cf. HOW MANY, HOW MUCH, HOW LONG. || *adv. exclam.* que, comme; [indir.] combien: *How beautiful it is!*, Que, Comme/c'est beau!, [weather] Qu'il, Comme il/fait beau!; *How beautiful a morning!*, Quelle belle matinée; *How stupid can you get!*, Jusqu'à quel point peut-on être bête!; *He told me* ~ *tired he was*, Il m'a dit combien il était fatigué; *Look* ~ *he is running!*, Regardez comme il court!; *and* ~ *!*, et comment! || **how long** *loc. adv.* **1.** [space] ~ *is the table?*, Quelle est la longueur de la table? **2.** [time] ~ *have you been waiting?*,/[since what time] Depuis quand, [for what length of time] Depuis combien de temps/ attendez-vous?, ~ *did you stay there?*, (Pendant) combien de temps y êtes-vous resté? || **how many, how much** *loc. adv.* combien (de): *How many (books) have you read?*, Combien/de livres avez-vous lus, avez-vous lu de livres?, Combien en avez-vous lu?; *How much (money) do you have?*, Combien/d'argent avez-vous, avez-vous d'argent?, Combien en avez-vous?; *He asked how/much, many/I had*, Il a demandé combien j'en avais.

however [ˌhawˈɛvɚ] *conj.* cependant; pourtant; toutefois; tout de même. || *adv.* **1.** *Do it* ~ *you want*, Faites-le comme vous voudrez; *However that may be*, Quoi qu'il en soit. **2.** *However tired they may be, they . . .*, Quelque fatigués qu'ils soient, ils . . . ; ~ *little*, si peu que ce soit.

howl [howl] *v. intr.* hurler; pousser des hurlements (après, *at*; de, *with*). || *n.* hurlement *m* (des loups); mugissement *m* (du vent).

HP [also: H.P., hp, h.p.] [ˈejtʃˈpij] [= *horsepower*] *n.* cheval-vapeur *m* (C.V.).

H.Q. [= HEADQUARTERS], [quartier général] Q.G.; [poste de commandement] P.C.

hr., *pl.* **hrs.** [= HOUR], h. [=heure].

hub [hʌb] *n.* [Tech.] moyeu *m*, [Fig.] centre *m*, cœur *m.*

hubbub [ˈhʌbʌb] *n.* tumulte *m*, vacarme *m.*

huckster [ˈhʌkstɚ] *n.* [peddler] regrattier *m*, revendeur *m*; [advertising] publicitaire *m.*

huddle [hʌdl] *v. intr.* s'entasser, se serrer les uns contre les autres. || *n.* entassement *m*; fouillis *m.*

hue[1] [hjuw] *n.* couleur *f*; [shade of colour] nuance *f.* || **hue[2]** *n.* clameur *f*: *with* ~ *and cry*, à cor et à cri.

huff [hʌf] *n.* accès *m* de colère: *in a* ~ , vexé, en colère. || *v. tr.* **1.** exciter, exaspérer. **2.** [draughts] souffler: *to/feel, be/huffed*, s'offusquer.

hug [hʌg] *v. tr.* [-gg-] embrasser, presser contre son cœur; [opinion] s'accrocher à. || *n.* **1.** étreinte *f*, embrassade *f.* **2.** [wrestling] prise *f.*

huge [hjuwʤ] *adj.* énorme; colossal. || **hugely** [-lɪ] *adv.* énormément; extrêmement.
hulk [hʌlk] *n.* †ponton *m*; [Fig.] grosse masse *f.*
hull [hʌl] *n.* **1.** balle *f* (d'avoine). **2.** écales *fpl* (de noix), cosse *f* (de pois). **3.** enveloppe *f.* **4.** [ship] coque *f*; [planes] fuselage *m.* || *v. tr.* décortiquer, écaler (des noix, des amandes); écosser (des petits pois); vanner (du grain).
hullo [hə'low] cf. HELLO.
hum [hʌm] *v. intr.* [-mm-] bourdonner; vrombir. || *v. tr.* [tune] fredonner: *to make things* ~, faire aller l'affaire rondement. || *interj.* Hem!, Hum!
human ['hjuwmən] *adj.* humain: ~ *being*, être *m* humain. || *n.* être *m* humain.
humane [ˌhjuw'mejn] *adj.* humain, compatissant. || **humanitarian** [ˌhjuwmænɪ'tɛərɪən] *adj.* humanitaire.
humanities [ˌhjuw'mænətɪz] *n.pl.* humanités *fpl.* || **humanity** *n.* humanité *f.*
humble ['hʌmbḷ] *adj.* **1.** humble: *in my* ~ *opinion*, à mon humble avis. **2.** modeste. || **humbleness** [-nəs] *n.* humilité *f*, modestie *f.* || **humbly** [-ɪ] *adv.* **1.** humblement; avec humilité. **2.** modestement.
humbug ['hʌmˌbʌg] *n.* **1.** farce *f*, blague *f.* **2.** farceur *m*, blagueur *m.* **3.** [candy] berlingot *m.*
humid ['hjuwmɪd] *adj.* humide (et chaud). || **humidity** [-ətɪ] *n.* humidité *f.*
humiliate [ˌhjuw'mɪlɪ|ˌejt] *v. tr.* humilier. || **humiliation** [ˌhjuwmɪlɪ'ejʃən] *n.* humiliation *f.* || **humility** [-tɪ] *n.* humilité *f.*
hummingbird ['hʌmɪŋˌbərd] *n.* colibri *m*; oiseau-mouche *m.*
humorist ['hjuwmərɪst] *n.* humoriste *m.*
humorous [hjuwmərəs] *adj.* **1.** humoristique. **2.** drôle, facétieux. || **humour** [hjuwmər] *n.* **1.** comique *m*, côté *m* plaisant (d'une situation, &c.). **2.** humour *m*: *He has no sense of* ~, Il n'a pas le sens de l'humour. **3.** humeur *f*; disposition *f*: *to be in/good, bad/humour*, être de/bonne, mauvaise/ humeur.
hump [hʌmp] *n.* bosse *f*, monticule *m.* || *v. intr.* faire une bosse: *Cats* ~ *their backs*, Les chats font le gros dos.
hunch [hʌntʃ] *n.* **1.** bosse *f*; [hunk] tranche *f* épaisse, gros morceau *m*; [Fig. Fam.] idée *f*, pressentiment *m*: *I have a* ~ *that . . .*, J'ai idée que . . .; soupçon *m.* || *v. tr.* **1.** arrondir, voûter (le dos). **2.** pousser (du coude). || **hunchback** [-ˌbæk] *n.* bossu *m.*
hundred ['hʌndɹəd] *n. num.* **1.** cent (*m*): *a* ~ *and ten*, cent dix; *two* ~ *men*, deux cents hommes; *five* ~ *and one pages*, cinq cent une pages; *a* ~ *per cent*, cent pour cent; *a* ~ *eggs*, un cent d'œufs; *It happened in eighteen* ~, C'est arrivé/en mil huit cent, en dix-huit cent. **2.** centaine *f*: *about a* ~ *people*, une centaine de personnes; *They came in hundreds, in hundreds of thousands*, Ils arrivaient par centaines, par centaines de mille. || **hundredth** [-θ] *adj.* & *n.* (le) centième.
hundredweight [-ˌwejt] *n.* [= cwt = about 50 kg.] quint|al *m*, *pl.* -aux.
hung [hʌŋ] cf. HANG.
Hungarian [ˌhʌŋ'gæərɪən] *n.* & *adj.* hongrois. || **Hungary** ['hʌŋgərɪ] *n.* Hongrie *f*: *in, to* ~, en Hongrie.
hunger ['hʌŋgər] *n.* **1.** faim *f*: *to suffer from* ~, souffrir de la faim; *to die of* ~, mourir de faim. **2.** [Fig.] ardent désir *m*, soif *f* (de qqch.).
hungrily ['hʌŋgɹəlɪ] *adv.* avidement, voracement.
hungry ['hʌŋgɹɪ] *adj.* affamé: *to be* ~, avoir faim; [Fig.] *a* ~ *look*, un regard avide.
hunk [hʌŋk] [Fam.] *n.* gros morceau *m* (de).
hunt [hʌnt] *v. tr.* chasser (le canard, l'orignal, &c.); parcourir, battre (le terrain); poursuivre, traquer (une bête); rechercher (un indice, une indication). || *v. intr.* chasser: *to go hunting*, aller à la chasse; *to* ~ *for sth.*, chercher qqch.; *to* ~ *down*, traquer, [~ *& find*] dénicher; *to* ~ *up*, rechercher; déterrer (des faits). || *n.* chasse *f*; chasse *f* à courre; [Fig.] recherche *f*: *to be on the* ~ *for*, chercher, être à la recherche de. || **hunter** [-ər] *n.* chasseur *m.* || **hunting** [-ɪŋ] *n.* chasse *f*: *big-game* ~, la chasse aux grands fauves. || **hunts|man, -men** [-smən] *n.* [Br.] chasseur *m.*
hurdle ['hərdḷ] *n.* [Sport] obstacle *m*, haie *f*: ~ *race*, course *f* de haies. || *v. tr.* franchir un obstacle; [Fig.] surmonter (un obstacle).
hurl [hərl] *v. tr.* lancer (avec force); © garrocher.
hurly-burly ['hərlɪˌbərlɪ] *n.* tumulte *m*, brouhaha *m.*
Huron ['hjuwərən] *n.* & *adj.* Huron *m*, -ne *f*: *Lake* ~, lac Huron.
hurrah, also **hurray** [hər'ɹej] *interj.* Hourra!, Bravo!: *Hurrah for . . . !*, Vive/le, la/. . . !
hurricane ['hərɪkən] *n.* ouragan *m.*
hurried ['hərɪd] *adj.* précipité, pressé, (fait) à la hâte: *a* ~ *note*, un billet écrit à la hâte. || **hurriedly** [-lɪ] *adv.* en, avec/ hâte.
hurry ['hərɪ] *v. intr.* se/hâter, presser, dépê-

cher/: *Don't* ∼ , Ne vous pressez pas, → Prenez votre temps; *to* ∼ *up*, se dépêcher; © [Fam.] se garrocher. || *v. tr. to hurry o.s.*, se/hâter, dépêcher/; *to* ∼ *s.o.*, presser qqun. || *n.* hâte *f*, précipitation *f*: *to be in a* ∼ , être pressé; *to be in no* ∼ , avoir (tout) le temps; *There is no* ∼ , Il n'y a rien qui presse. || **hurrying** [-ɪŋ] *adj.* pressé, qui se dépêche.

hurt [hɚt], **hurt**, **hurt** *v. tr.* blesser, faire mal à; [cause pain] faire ma. à, [Fig.] faire de la peine à, blesser; [harm] nuire à, faire du mal à: *to* ∼ *o.s.*, se blesser; *to* ∼ *o.'s hand*, se blesser à la main; *to get* ∼ , être blessé, recevoir une blessure; [Fig.] *to* ∼ *s.o.'s feelings*, blesser, froisser, faire de la peine à, peiner/qqun: *to* ∼ *s.o.'s chances*, nuire aux chances de qqun; *It wouldn't* ∼ *to be more careful*, Cela ne (vous) ferait pas de mal de faire attention. || *v. intr.* faire mal; avoir mal: *Where does it* ∼ *?*, Où est-ce que ça fait mal ?; *My arm hurts*, J'ai mal au bras, Mon bras me fait mal; *Give till it hurts*, Donnez jusqu'à votre dernier sou. || **hurtful** ['hɚtfl̩] *adj.* nuisible.

husband ['hʌzbənd] *n.* mari *m*, époux *m*. || *v. tr.* ménager (ses forces), économiser (son argent).

husbandry [-ɹɪ] *n.* **1.** agriculture *f*, économie *f* rurale. **2.** administration *f*, gestion *f* (de ses propres affaires).

hush [hʌʃ] *v. tr.* faire taire, calmer. || *v. intr.* se taire: *to* ∼ *up*, étouffer (une rumeur). || *interj.* Chut! || *n.* silence *m*: ∼ *money*, le prix du silence.

husk [hʌsk] *n.* [grain] balle *f* (d'avoine); [corn] enveloppe *f*; gousse *f* (de légumineuse); écale *f* (de noix); peau *f*, pelure *f*. || *v. tr.* [grain] vanner; [peas] écosser; [vegetable] éplucher; [nuts] écaler.

husky ['hʌskɪ] *adj.* [voice] voilé, enroué; [Fam.] costaud.

Husky ['hʌskɪ] *n.* chien *m* esquimau; Esquimau *m*, Esquimaude *f*.

hustle ['hʌsl̩] *n.* hâte *f*, bousculade *f*; [Fam.] énergie *f*. || *v. intr.* se dépêcher: *to* ∼ *off*, s'en aller précipitamment. || *v. tr.* presser, (se) bousculer.

hustler ['hʌstlɚ] *n.* personne *f* qui mène une affaire tambour battant.

hut [hʌt] *n.* hutte *f*, cabane *f*; [Mil.] baraquement *m*.

hyacinth ['hajəˌsɪnθ] *n.* [Bot.] jacinthe *f*.

hydrant ['hajdɹənt] *n.* prise *f* d'eau; bouche *f* d'incendie.

hydraulic [ˌhaj'dɹɑlɪk] *adj.*: ∼ *brake*, frein *m* hydraulique.

hydro [ˌhajdɹow] *adj.* [forme abrégée de *hydro-electric*; e.g. Hydro-Québec, Ontario Hydro] hydro-électrique. || *n.* l'électricité *f*.

hydroplane [-ˌplejn] *n.* hydravion *m*; hydroglisseur *m*.

hygiene [ˌhaj'dʒijn] *n.* hygiène *f*.

hymn [hɪm] *n.* hymne *m*; [Fig.] louange *f*.

hyphen ['hajfən] *n.* trait *m* d'union.

hyphenated [ˌhajfən'ejtəd] *adj.* allongé/d'un surnom, d'un qualificatif/; à particule; [Pej., name] à rallonge.

hypocrisy [hɪ'pɑkɹəsɪ] *n.* hypocrisie *f*. || **hypocrite** ['hɪpəˌkɹɪt] *n.* hypocrite *m*/*f*.

hypothecate [ˌhaj'pɑθə,kejt] *v. tr.* hypothéquer. cf. MORTGAGE.

hypothesis [ˌhaj'pɑθəˌsɪs] *n.* hypothèse *f*: *to propose, propound/a* ∼ , émettre une hypothèse.

hysteria [hɪ'stɛɚ|ɪə] *n.* hystérie *f*. || **hysterical** [-ɪkl] *adj.* hystérique. || **hysterics** [-ɪks] *n.* hystérie *f*, [Fig.] crise *f* de nerfs.

I

I, i [aj] **I's, i's** [ajz] I, i *m*; la lettre i.

I [aj] *pron. pers.* je, j' [+ vowel or mute h]; [stressed] moi: *I'm coming*, Je viens, J'arrive; *I'm here*, Moi, je suis ici; *I'll do it*, C'est moi qui vais le faire; *you and* ∼ , vous et moi; †*It is* ∼ , C'est moi; *So/am, have, do, &c./* ∼ , Moi aussi; *older than* ∼ *(am)*, plus âgé que moi.

Iberia [ˌaj'bijɚɪə] **Iberian Peninsula** *n.* péninsule *f*, ibérique.

ibis [ˈajbɪs] *n.* ibis *m*: *wood* ~ , cigogne *f* américaine.

ice [ajs] *n.* glace *f*: [Fig.] *to break the* ~ , rompre la glace; *to be* (*skating*) *on thin* ~ , s'engager sur un terrain dangereux; [Fam.] *That cuts no* ~ *with me*, Ça ne prend pas avec moi. || *v. tr.* (con)geler; [cake] glacer; [tea, coffee] glacer; [champagne] frapper. || **ice-age** [-ˌejʤ] *n.* époque *f* glaciaire. || **ice-axe** [-ˌæks] *n.* piolet *m.* || **iceberg** [-ˌbɚg] *n.* iceberg *m.* || **ice-bound** [-ˌbawnd] *adj.* [Naut.] pris dans les glaces. || **ice-box** [-ˌbɑks] *n.* glacière *f*; [electric] réfrigérateur *m*, [Fr.] frigidaire *m*: [Fam.] *to raid the* ~ , faire une descente sur le frigidaire. || **ice-breaker** [-ˌbɹejkɚ] *n.* [Naut.] brise-glace(s) *m.* || **ice cold** [-ˈkowld] *adj.* glacé; glacial. || **ice cream** [-ˈkɹijm] *n.* glace *f*, crème *f* glacée; © crème à la glace. || **ice field** [-ˌfijld] *n.* champ *m* de glace. || **ice-floe** [-ˌflow] *n.* banquise *f*; [piece] glaçon *m.* || **ice-house** [-ˌhaws] *n.* glacière *f.* || **ice-jam** [-ˌʤæm] *n.* embâcle *m.*

Iceland [ˈajsˌlænd] *n.* (l')Islande *f.* || **Icelander** [-ɚ] *n.* Islandais, -e. || **Icelandic** [-ɪk] *adj.* islandais.

ice|man [-ˌmæn] *pl.* **-men** [-ˌmɛn] *n.* marchand *m* de glace. || **ice-pack** [-ˌpæk] *n.* banquise *f*; embâcle *m* (sur un fleuve, une rivière). || **ice-pail** [-ˌpejl] *n.* seau *m* à glace. || **ice-pick** [-ˌpɪk] *n.* piolet *m* d'alpiniste; [utensil] © pic *m* à glace. || **ice water** [-ˌwɔtɚ] *n.* eau *f* glacée.

icicle [ˈajsɪkḷ] *n.* glaçon *m.* || **icy** [ˈajsɪ] *adj.* [water, &c.] glacé; [air, &c.] glacial. || **icily** [ˈajsɪlɪ] *adv.* [Fig.] [welcome] (avec) une froideur glaciale.

icing [ˈajsɪŋ] *n.* [cake] glaçage *m.*

I'd [ajd] = **1.** I had. cf. HAVE. **2.** I would. cf. WILL: *I'd rather not*, Je préfère que non.

idea [ˌajˈdijə] *n.* idée *f*: *with the* ~ *of*, dans l'idée de; *I have an* ~ *that* . . . , J'ai l'impression que . . . ; *I have no* ~ (*why* . . .), Je n'en sais rien; Je ne sais pas du tout pourquoi . . . ; *I haven't the faintest* ~ (*why* . . .), Je n'en ai pas la moindre idée; Je ne sais absolument pas pourquoi . . . ; *I had no* ~ *that* . . . , J'étais loin de me douter que . . . ; *You have no* ~ *how much* . . . , Vous n'avez pas idée combien . . . ; *The* (*very*) ~ *!*, (Ça,) par exemple!; *What's the* ~ *?*, Où voulez-vous en venir?; [Fam.] *What's the* (*big*) ~ *?*, Qu'est-ce qui vous prend?

ideal [ˌajˈdijl] *adj.* idéal. || *n.* idéal *m.* || **idealism** [-ɪsm] *n.* idéalisme *m.* || **idealist** [-ɪst] *n.* idéaliste *m.* || **idealistic** [-ɪstɪk] *adj.* idéaliste.

identical [ˌajˈdɛntɪkḷ] *adj.* identique (à, *to*); (le, la) même. || **identification** [ˌajdɛntɪfɪˈkejʃən] *n.* identification *f*; identité *f*: ~ *card*, carte *f* d'identité. || **identify** [ˌajˈdɛntɪˌfaj] *v. tr.* [recognize] identifier (qqun, qqch.); vérifier l'identité (de qqun). || **identity** [ˌajˈdɛntɪtɪ] *n.* identité *f*: [Adm.] *proof of* ~ , pièce *f* justificative.

ideology [ˌajdɪˈɑləʤɪ] *n.* idéologie *f.*

idiocy [ˈɪdɪəˌsɪ] *n.* idiotie *f.*

idiom [ˈɪdɪəm] *n.* **1.** idiotisme *m*; *French* ~ , gallicisme *m.* **2.** langue *f*, parler *m*, idiome *m*; [Fig.] langue *f*, style *m*: *the Canadian idiom*, la langue canadienne. **3.** génie *m* de la langue. || **idiomatic** [ˌɪdɪəˈmætɪk] *adj.* idiomatique [s'applique à l'anglais ou au français selon la circonstance]; conforme au génie de la langue.

idiosyncrasy [ˌɪdɪəˈsɪŋkɹəsɪ] *n.* particularité *f* individuelle, caractéristique *f*; [Tech.] idiosyncrasie *f.*

idiot [ˈɪdɪət] *n.* idiot *m*, -e *f.* || **idiotic** [ɪdɪˈɑtɪk] *adj.* (d')idiot.

idle [ajdḷ] *adj.* [person] oisif, inoccupé, désœuvré, [Pej.] paresseux; [Fig.] futile, frivole, inutile: *to/be, stand/* ~ , rester inactif, chômer; [funds] *to lie* ~ , dormir. || *v. intr.* fainéanter, paresser: *to* ~ *about*, flâner (dans les rues, &c.); [motor] tourner/au ralenti, à vide/. || *v. tr.* *to* ~ *one's time away*, perdre son temps. || **idleness** [-nəs] *n.* oisiveté *f*, désœuvrement *m*, [Pej.] paresse *f*, fainéantise *f*; [threat, words, &c.] futilité *f.* || **idler** [ˈajdl|ɚ] *n.* **1.** oisif *m*, flâneur *m.* **2.** [Pej.] fainéant *m.* || **idly** [-ɪ] *adv.* **1.** dans l'oisiveté. **2.** inutilement.

idol [ˈajdḷ] *n.* idole *f.* || **idolatrous** [ˌajˈdɑlə|tɹəs] *adj.* [admiration, &c.] idolâtre. || **idolatry** [-tɹɪ] *n.* idolâtrie *f.* || **idolize** [ˈajdḷˌajz] *v. tr.* [Fig.] [worship] idolâtrer (qqun, qqch.).

idyll [ˈajdḷ] *n.* [romance] idylle *f.*

i.e. [ˈajˈij] *Abbr.* [Lat. *id est* = that is (to say)] c'est-à-dire [abbr. *c-à-d.*].

if [ɪf] *conj.* **1.** si, s' [+ il(s)]: *If he/is, was/ late, it/is, was/his fault*, S'il/est, était, a été/en retard, c'est, c'était, ç'a été/sa faute; . . . ~ *there ever was one*, s'il y en a jamais eu; *If he/is, should be/late, he will be sorry*, S'il arrive en retard, il le regrettera; *If he/was, were to be/, should be/late, he would be sorry*, S'il venait en retard, il le regretterait; *If he had been late, he would have been sorry*, S'il avait été en retard, il l'aurait regretté; ~ *I were you*, si j'étais/de vous, à votre place/; ~ *necessary*, si nécessaire, s'il/le faut, le fallait/; ~ *so*, s'il en est ainsi, dans ce cas, auquel cas; ~ *not*, sinon. cf. AS, EVEN. **2.** [whether] si; que [+ subjunc.]: *He asked ~ I knew*, Il a demandé si je (le) savais; *I doubt ~ he is coming*, Je doute qu'il vienne. **3.** [although] si [+ indic.]; bien que [+ subjunc.]. ‖ *n.* si *inv.*

igloo [ɪg'luw] *n.* igloo *m.*

ignite [ɪg'najt] *v. tr.* allumer (qqch.), mettre le feu à (qqch.). ‖ *v. intr.* [substance] s'enflammer, prendre feu. ‖ **igniter** [-ɚ] *n.* [thing] allumeur *m*, dispositif *m* d'allumage. ‖ **ignition** [ɪg'nɪʃən] *n.* [motor] allumage *m*: ~ *switch*, [car] bouton *m* de contact.

ignoble [ɪg'nowbḷ] *adj.* [base] ignoble; [mean] vil, bas.

ignominious [ɪgnə'mɪnɪəs] *adj.* ignominieux. ‖ **ignominy** ['ɪgnəˌmɪnɪ] *n.* ignominie *f.*

ignorance ['ɪgnɚ|əns] *n.* ignorance *f.* ‖ **ignorant** [-ənt] *adj.* **1.** [without knowledge] ignorant. **2.** [unaware]: *to be ~ of a fact*, → ignorer un fait. ‖ **ignore** [ɪg'nɔɚ] *v. tr.* prétendre, vouloir, feindre d'/ignorer (qqun, qqch.); passer outre à (une défense, recommandation), [advice, &c.] ne pas tenir compte de; [circumstance, facts] méconnaître; [request] rejeter. [×] IGNORER.

ilex ['ajlɛks] *n.* [Bot.] yeuse *f.*

I'll [ajl] **1.** = I will. **2.** = I shall.

ill [ɪl] *adj.* **worse, worst** [q.v.] mauvais; [sick] malade, souffrant: *It's an ~ wind that blows nobody good*, A qqch. malheur est bon. ‖ *adv.* **worse, worst** [q.v.] mal. ‖ *n.* mal *m*: *to speak ~ of*, dire du mal de. ‖ **ill-advised** [-əd'vajzd] *adj.* [action] peu judicieux; [Pers.] mal avisé. ‖ **ill-bred** [-'bɹɛd] *adj.* mal élevé. ‖ **ill-fated** [-'fejtəd] *adj.* fatal; [Pers.] malheureux. ‖ **ill-favoured** [-'fejvɚd] *adj.* déshérité; [Pej.] déplaisant. ‖ **ill-founded** [-'fawndəd] *adj.* sans fondement. ‖ **ill-gotten** [-'gɑtṇ] *adj.* mal acquis. ‖ **ill-mannered** [-ˌmænɚd] *adj.* mal élevé, grossier. ‖ **ill-natured** [-'nejtʃɚd] also **ill-tempered** [-'tɛmpɚd] *adj.* désagréable, qui a mauvais caractère. ‖ **ill-timed** [-'tajmd] *adj.* intempestif, malencontreux. ‖ **ill-treat** [-'tɹijt] *v. tr.* rudoyer; maltraiter. ‖ **ill-will** [-'wɪl] *n.* rancune *f*; malveillance *f.*

illegal [ɪ'lijgḷ] *adj.* [Law] illégal; [morality] illicite. ‖ **illegality** [ɪlɪ'gælɪtɪ] *n.* illégalité *f.*

illegible [ɪ'lɛdʒɪbḷ] *adj.* [text] illisible.

illegitimate [ɪlə'dʒɪtɪmət] *adj.* [child] naturel, illégitime; [Pej.] bâtard. ‖ **illicit** [ɪ'lɪsɪt] *adj.* illicite. ‖ **illiteracy** [ɪ'lɪtɚəsi] *n.* manque *m* d'instruction; analphabétisme *m.* ‖ **illiterate** [ɪ'lɪtɚət] *n.* & *adj.* illettré (*m*), [unable to read] analphabète (*m*).

illness ['ɪlnəs] *n.* maladie *f.*

illogical [ɪ'lɑdʒɪkḷ] *adj.* illogique.

illuminate [ɪ'luwmɪˌnejt] *v. tr.* **1.** illuminer, éclairer. **2.** enluminer (de, *with*). ‖ **illuminating** [-ɪŋ] *adj.* [also Fig.] lumineux; [lecture, talk] instructif, révélateur. ‖ **illumination** [ɪˌluwmɪ'nejʃən] *n.* **1.** illumination *f*, éclairage *m.* **2.** [book] enluminure *f.*

illusion [ɪ'luwʒən] *n.* illusion *f.* ‖ **illusive** [ɪ'luw|sɪv] *adj.* illusoire; [hope] fallacieux. ‖ **illusory** [-sɚɪ] *adj.* illusoire.

illustrate ['ɪləsˌtɹejt] *v. tr.* [book] illustrer; [Fig.] expliquer (par des exemples). ‖ **illustration** [ɪləs'tɹejʃən] *n.* illustration *f*; gravure *f*; [Fig.] explication *f.* ‖ **illustrative** [ɪ'lʌstɹətɪv] *adj.* explicatif, qui sert à la démonstration. ‖ **illustrator** ['ɪləsˌtɹejtɚ] *n.* illustrateur *m.* ‖ **illustrious** [ɪ'lʌstɹɪəs] *adj.* illustre, célèbre, éminent.

I'm [ajm] [= I am] cf. BE.

im- [*il-*, *in-*, *ir-*] [☞ préfixes négatifs; le rapport radical/préfixe, moins net que pour *un-*, n'a pas été indiqué. cf. UN-].

image ['ɪmədʒ] *n.* image *f*; portrait *m*; [Fig.] symbole *m.* ‖ **imagery** [-ɹɪ] *n.* [style] images *fpl.*

imaginable [ɪ'mædʒɪnəbḷ] *adj.* imaginable. ‖ **imaginary** [ɪ'mædʒɪˌnɛɚɪ] *adj.* imaginaire. ‖ **imagination** [ɪˌmædʒɪ'nejʃən] *n.* imagination *f*; [fancy] fantaisie *f.* ‖ **imaginative** [ɪ'mædʒɪnətɪv] *adj.* imaginatif. ‖ **imagine** [ɪ'mædʒṇ] *v. tr.* (s')imaginer, se figurer, supposer: *to ~ things*, se faire des/ idées, imaginations: *Imagine meeting you here!*, Quelle surprise de vous trouver ici!

imbecile ['ɪmbəˌsajl] *adj.* & *n.* faible (*m/f*) d'esprit.

imbibe [ɪm'bajb] *v. intr.* [proper and Fig.] s'imbiber (de), absorber (de l'alcool, des idées), aspirer (de l'air). ‖ *v. intr.* boire.

imbue [ɪm'bjuw] *v. tr.* tremper, imprégner; [Fig.] pénétrer (de, *with*).

imitate ['ɪmɪˌtejt] *v. tr.* imiter; [Fig.] suivre l'exemple de (qqun); [Lit.] pasticher (un texte); prendre (l'accent de qqun). ‖ **imitation** [ˌɪmɪ'tejʃən] *n.* imitation *f*, copie *f*; [Com.] contrefaçon *f*; [Lit.] pastiche *m*: ~ *leather*, similicuir *m.* ‖ **imitator** ['ɪmɪˌtejtɚ] *n.* imitateur *m.*

immaculate [ɪ'mækjələt] *adj.* [clean; pure] immaculé; [spotless] sans tache; [dress] impeccable; [R.C.] ~ *Conception*, l'Immaculée Conception *f.*

immaterial [ɪmə'tijɚɪəl] *adj.* **1.** immatériel;

spirituel. **2.** [without consequence] sans importance, insignifiant: *This is ~ to me*, Ça m'est égal. || **immature** [ɪmə'tjuwɚ] *adj.* [fruit, &c.] pas mûr; [Fig.] prématuré. || **immeasurable** [ɪ'mɛʒɚəbl] *adj.* infini; [Fig.] incommensurable.

immediate [ɪ'mijdɪət] *adj.* immédiat, [cause] direct; [future, aim, &c.] prochain, le plus proche; [without delay] pressé, urgent. || **immediately** [-lɪ] *adv.* immédiatement, tout de suite, sans délai: *~ upon his arrival*, dès son arrivée.

immense [ɪ'mɛns] *adj.* immense; énorme. || **immensely** [-lɪ] *adv.* immensément; énormément. || **immensity** [ɪ'mɛnsɪtɪ] *n.* immensité *f*, énormité *f*.

immerse [ɪ'mɚs] *v. tr.* immerger; plonger (dans, *in*). || **immersion** [ɪ'mɚʒən] immersion *f*.

immigrant ['ɪmɪ|gɹənt] *n.* immigrant *m.* || **immigrate** [-ˌgɹejt] *v. intr.* immigrer. || **immigration** [ɪmə'gɹejʃən] *n.* immigration *f*: [at port of entry] formalités *fpl* de passeport, contrôle *m* des passeports.

imminent ['ɪmənənt] *adj.* imminent.

immobile [ɪ'mowˌbajl] *adj.* immobile. || **immobility** [ɪˌmow'bɪlɪtɪ] *n.* immobilité *f*. || **immobilize** [ɪ'mowbɪlˌajz] *v. tr.* immobiliser. || **immoderate** [ɪ'mɑdɚət] *adj.* immodéré; excessif. || **immodest** [ɪ'mɑdəst] *adj.* immodeste; indécent. || **immoral** [ɪ'mɔɚəl] *adj.* immoral; licencieux. || **immorality** [ɪˌmɔɚ'ælɪtɪ] *n.* immoralité *f*; licence *f*. || **immortal** [ɪ'mɔɚtl̩] *n.* & *adj.* immortel (*m*). || **immortality** [ɪˌmɔɚ'tælɪtɪ] *n.* immortalité *f*. || **immovable** [ɪ'muwvəbl̩] *adj.* fixe; [Fig.] [faith] inébranlable, [heart] insensible. || *n.pl.* [Jur.] immeubles *mpl.*

immune [ɪ'mjuwn] *adj.* dispensé (de, *from*); exempt (de, *from*); [Med.] immunisé (contre, *from*). || **immunity** [-ɪtɪ] *n.* immunité *f* (contre, *from*); dispense *f* (d'une obligation, &c.). || **immunize** ['ɪmjəˌnajz] *v. tr.* [Med.] immuniser.

imp [ɪmp] *n.* lutin *m*; [Fig.] petit diable *m.*

impact [ɪm'pækt] *n.* choc *m*; [Tech.] impact *m.*

impair [ɪm'pɛɚ] *v. tr.* endommager, altérer; [mental faculties] diminuer, affaiblir: *driving in an impaired condition*, → n'être pas en état de conduire; *impaired digestion*, estomac *m* délabré. || **impairment** [-mənt] *n.* altération *f*; [health, conditions, &c.] détérioration *f*.

impart [ɪm'pɑɚt] *v. tr.* donner; [information] faire part de (qqch.), [news] annoncer, faire savoir; [enthusiasm, knowledge] communiquer.

impartial [ɪm'pɑɚʃəl] *adj.* impartial; désintéressé. || **impartiality** [ɪmˌpɑɚʃɪ'ælɪtɪ] *n.* impartialité *f*; désintéressement *m.* || **impassable** [ɪm'pæsəbl̩] *adj.* [mountain range] infranchissable; [road] impraticable.

impassioned [ɪm'pæʃənd] *adj.* [feeling, &c.] passionné; [speech] véhément.

impassive [ɪm'pæsɪv] *adj.* [features, look] impassible, [heart] insensible.

impatience [ɪm'pej|ʃəns] *n.* impatience *f*. || **impatient** [-ʃənt] *adj.* impatient: *to get ~*, s'impatienter; [Fig.] emporté (contre, *with*). || **impatiently** [-lɪ] *adv.* impatiemment, → avec impatience.

impeach [ɪm'pijtʃ] *v. tr.* accuser (qqun) faussement; [Jur.] récuser (un témoin); mettre en accusation; [Fig.] attaquer.

impeccable [ɪm'pɛkəbl̩] *adj.* impeccable.

impede [ɪm'pijd] *v. tr.* [hinder] empêcher, entraver (une action, qqun). || **impediment** [ɪm'pɛdɪmənt] *n.* [hindrance] empêchement *m*, obstacle *m.*

impel [ɪm'pɛl] *v. tr.* **[-ll-]** forcer, pousser (à, *to*).

impend [ɪm'pɛnd] *v. intr.* [danger] menacer, [event] être imminent. || **impending** [-ɪŋ] *adj.* menaçant, imminent.

imperative [ɪm'pɛɚətɪv] *adj.* [voice] impératif; [need] urgent, impérieux: *It is ~ to*, → Il faut absolument que [+ subjunc.]. || *n.* [Gram.] impératif *m.*

imperceptible [ɪmpɚ'sɛptɪbl̩] *adj.* [sound, &c.] imperceptible. || **imperfect** [ɪm'pɚfəkt] *adj.* [reasoning, form] imparfait. || *n.* [Gram.] imparfait *m.* || **imperfectly** [-lɪ] *adv.* imparfaitement.

imperial [ɪm'pijɚɪəl] *adj.* [rule, &c.] impérial: *~ gallon*, © gallon *m* impérial [$= 1\frac{1}{5}$ US gallons]. || **imperialism** [-izm] *n.* [Pol., ambition] impérialisme *m.*

imperil [ɪm'pɛɚɪl] *v. tr.* **[-ll-]** mettre (qqun, qqch.) en danger; risquer (sa vie).

imperious [ɪm'pijɚɪəs] *adj.* impérieux.

impermeable [ɪm'pɚmɪəbl̩] *adj.* [mind] imperméable; [water-tight] étanche. || **impersonal** [ɪm'pɚsn̩|əl] *adj.* impersonnel. || **impersonate** [-ˌejt] *v. tr.* personnifier, imiter (qqun). || **impersonation** [ɪmˌpɚsn̩'ejʃən] *n.* [quality] personnification *f*; imitation *f* (d'un rôle, personnage); [Jur.] substitution *f* de personnes, usurpation *f* d'état civil.

impertinence ['ɪmpɚtnəns] *n.* impertinence *f*, insolence *f*. || **impertinent** [ɪm'pɚtn̩|ənt] *adj.* impertinent, insolent.

impervious [ɪm'pɚvɪəs] *adj.* [mind, &c.] impénétrable, [not allowing passage] imperméable, fermé (à, *to*).

impetuous [ɪmˈpɛtjuwəs] *adj.* impétueux. || **impetuously** [-lɪ] *adv.* impétueusement, avec impétuosité *f.*
impetus [ˈɪmpətəs] *n. inv.* impulsion *f*; [Fig.] élan *m*; [Tech.] vitesse *f* acquise.
impinge [ɪmˈpɪnʤ] *v. intr.* frapper.
impious [ˈɪmpɪəs] *adj.* [action] impie.
impish [ˈɪmpɪʃ] *adj.* [child] espiègle. cf. IMP.
implacable [ɪmˈplækəbl̩] *adj.* [hatred, enemy] implacable, acharné.
implant [ɪmˈplænt] *v.* implanter; [Fig.] imprimer, inculquer.
implement [ˈɪmpləmənt] *n.* outil *m*, instrument *m*; [utensil] ustensile *m*: *agricultural* ~, machine *f* agricole. || *v. tr.* outiller; [Fig.] exécuter, mettre en œuvre, réaliser (un projet). || **implementation** [ˌɪmpləmənˈtejʃən] *n.* exécution *f*, réalisation *f* (d'un projet, plan).
implicate [ˈɪmpləˌkejt] *v. tr.* [involve] impliquer (qqun dans un crime). || **implication** [ˌɪmpləˈkejʃən] sous-entendu *m*; [Pej.] insinuation *f*: *the full* ~ *of a statement*, la portée d'une affirmation; *by* ~, implicitement.
implicit [ɪmˈplɪsɪt] *adj.* implicite.
implore [ɪmˈplɔə˞] *v. tr.* implorer, supplier (qqun de faire qqch.).
imply [ɪmˈplaj] *v. tr.* **1.** [indicate] sous-entendre (qqch.), insinuer. **2.** [signify] signifier, vouloir dire; [involve] impliquer, comporter.
impolite [ɪmpəˈlajt] *adj.* impoli.
import [ˈɪmpɔə˞t] *n.* **1.** [Com.] importation *f.* **2.** [Fig.] importance *f* (d'une question, d'une décision); signification *f*, portée *f* (d'une remarque). || *v. tr.* [ɪmˈpɔə˞t] **1.** [goods] importer (qqch.). **2.** [statement, &c.] signifier, [mean] vouloir dire.
importance [ɪmˈpɔə˞t|əns] *n.* importance *f*: *of* ~, important; *of no* ~, sans importance; *It is of no* ~, Cela n'a pas d'importance. || **important** [-ənt] *adj.* [matter, look, &c.] important.
importation [ɪmˌpɔə˞ˈtejʃən] *n.* importation *f.* || **importer** [-ə˞] *n.* [Com.] importateur *m.*
importunate [ɪmˈpɔə˞tjənət] *adj.* importun. || **importune** [ˌɪmpə˞ˈtjuwn] *v. tr.* importuner, harceler (qqun).
impose [ɪmˈpowz] *v. tr.* imposer (son autorité, &c.). || *v. intr. to* ~ *(up)on*, en imposer à, [Pej.] abuser (de qqun), tromper. || **imposing** [-ɪŋ] *adj.* [look, &c.] imposant, [quantity, deed, &c.] impressionnant. || **imposition** [ɪmpəˈzɪʃən] *n.* [tax] imposition *f*; [Sch.] devoir *m* supplémentaire; [fraud] imposture *f*, abus *m* de confiance: *I trust this isn't (too much of) an* ~, J'espère que cela ne vous dérange pas.
impossibility [ɪmˌpɑsɪbɪlɪtɪ] *n.* impossibilité *f.* || **impossible** [ɪmˈpɑsɪbl̩] *adj.* impossible: *to find it* ~ *to*, → se trouver dans l'impossibilité de; [rumour] incroyable; [pers.] difficile (à vivre), ridicule.
impostor [ɪmˈpɑst|ə˞] *n.* [deceiver] imposteur *m.* || **imposture** [-ʃə˞] *n.* [deceit, cheating] imposture *f*, tromperie *f.*
impotence [ˈɪmpətəns] *n.* impuissance *f.* || **impotent** [ɪmˈpowtn̩t] *adj.* impuissant.
impound [ɪmˈpawnd] *v. tr.* [Jur.] confisquer, saisir (des biens, &c.); [Com.] *to* ~ *goods*, faire arrêt sur des marchandises; [car] mettre en fourrière.
impoverish [ɪmˈpɑvə˞ɪʃ] *v. tr.* appauvrir.
impracticable [ɪmˈpɹæktɪkəbl̩] *adj.* impossible, inexécutable.
impregnable [ɪmˈpɹɛg|nəbl̩] *adj.* [stronghold] imprenable; [Fig.] inébranlable. || **impregnate** [-nejt] *v. tr.* [imbue] imprégner (de, *with*); [fertilize, make pregnant] féconder.
impress [ɪmˈpɹɛ|s] *v. tr.* [movement, mark, &c.] imprimer; [notion, &c.] bien faire comprendre (qqch. à qqun, *sth. on s.o.*); impressionner (qqun). || [ˈɪmpɹɛs] *n.* [mark] impression *f*, [finger, mind] empreinte *f*, [Fig.] [imprint] cachet *m.* || **impression** [-ʃən] *n.* [marking, stamping, influence] impression *f*, [track, feet, &c.] empreinte *f*; [book, edition] tirage *m*: *to be under the* ~ *that*, → avoir l'impression que. || **impressionable** [-əbl̩] *adj.* impressionnable. || **impressive** [-sɪv] *adj.* [imposing] impressionnant.
imprint [ɪmˈpɹɪnt] *v. tr.* imprimer (une marque; une idée, une influence); marquer (qqch.), laisser une/empreinte, marque/sur (qqch.). || *n.* [ˈɪmˌpɹɪnt] empreinte *f*; [publishers] marque *f*, griffe *f.*
imprison [ɪmˈpɹɪzn̩] *v. tr.* emprisonner, mettre (qqun) en prison *f.* || **imprisonment** [-mənt] *n.* emprisonnement *m*; [sentence] mois *m* de prison.
improbable [ɪmˈpɹɑbəbl̩] *adj.* peu probable, improbable; invraisemblable. || **improbability** [ɪmˌpɹɑbəˈbɪlɪtɪ] *n.* improbabilité *f.*
impromptu [ɪmˈpɹɑmpˌtjuw] *adj.* improvisé, impromptu *invar.* || *adv.* à l'improviste. || *n.* impromptu *m.*
improper [ɪmˈpɹɑpə˞] *adj.* [not suitable] impropre (à, *for*); [not decent] inconvenant; [not correct] qui n'est pas convenable. || **improperly** [-lɪ] *adv.* improprement; d'une manière inconvenante.
improve [ɪmˈpɹuwv] *v. tr.* améliorer (qqch.),

rendre (qqun) meilleur; perfectionner (une machine, ses connaissances); cultiver (son esprit); profiter de (l'occasion); faire valoir (un terrain). || *v. intr.* [Pers., thing] s'améliorer, [Pers.] devenir meilleur, s'amender, faire/du, des/progrès, [health] aller mieux: *Things are improving*, La situation s'améliore, [Fam.] Ça va mieux. || **improved** [-d] *adj.* amélioré, [behaviour, &c.] amendé; [thing] perfectionné. || **improvement** [-mənt] *n.* amélioration *f*, [conduct, soil] amendement *m*; perfectionnement *m*.

improvidence [ɪm'pɹɑvɪ|dəns] *n.* imprévoyance *f*, prodigalité *f*. || **improvident** [-dənt] *adj.* imprévoyant; prodigue.

improvise ['ɪmpɹəˌvajz] *v. tr. & intr.* [speech, &c.] improviser.

imprudent [ɪm'pɹuwdənt] *adj.* imprudent. || **imprudently** [-lɪ] *adv.* imprudemment.

impudence ['ɪmpjə|dəns] *n.* impudence *f*, effronterie *f*. || **impudent** [-dənt] *adj.* impudent, effronté.

impulse ['ɪmˌpʌls] *n.* impulsion *f*, poussée *f*: *on (a sudden)* ~, par/impulsion, coup *m* de tête. || **impulsion** [ˌɪm'pʌlʃən] *n.* impulsion *f*; élan *m*. || **impulsive** [-sɪv] *adj.* impulsif, irréfléchi.

impunity [ɪm'pjuwnɪtɪ] *n.* impunité *f*: *with* ~, → impunément.

impure [ɪm'pjuwɚ] *adj.* [also Fig.] impur; [physical] malpropre, sale. || **impurity** [-ɪtɪ] *n.* [also Fig.] impureté *f*; [usual. pl.] saleté *f*.

imputation [ɪmˌpjuw'tejʃən] *n.* imputation *f*. || **impute** [ɪm'pjuwt] *v. tr.* imputer (*to*, à).

in[1] [ɪn] *prep.* **1.** dans; à; en [☞ Many uses of *in* depend on the noun it precedes (q.v.) or the verb, adj., or expression it follows (q.v.); other predictable uses are shown below. *Dans* has the basic meaning of *inside of*, and often replaces *à* or *en* when set expressions are modified; *à* indicates simple location [= at]; *en* appears in set expressions and constructions]: ~/*a box, the house, my room, &c.*/, dans/une boîte, la maison, ma chambre, &c./; *in/school, church, bed, &c.*, à l'école, à l'église, au lit, &c.; ~/*a, our/school*, ~ *the schools*, dans une école/dans, à notre école/dans les écoles/; ~ /*prison, a prison*/, en prison/dans une prison/; *Look* ~ *it*, Regardez-y, Regardez dedans; ~ *there*, là-dedans; ~ *which*, dans lequel/où. **2.** [geographical location] à [with names of towns]; en, à + def. art., dans + def. art. [with names of continents, countries, provinces, states, q.v.]: ~ *Montreal*, à Montréal; ~ *le Havre*, au Havre; ~ *France*, en France; ~ *Canada*, au Canada; ~ *the United States*, aux États-Unis; ~ *Newfoundland*, à Terre-Neuve [island]; ~ *Wyoming*, dans le Wyoming; ~ *Central Asia*, dans l'Asie centrale; *He lives* ~ (*side*) *Toronto*, Il habite dans (la ville de) Toronto; *the man* ~ *the street*, l'homme de la rue. **3.** [time expressions] dans; à; en; or no translation: *In the evening(s), I stay at home*, Le soir, je reste chez moi; *In (the course of) the evening I finished the book*, Dans la soirée, j'ai fini le livre; *at seven (o'clock)* ~ *the evening*, à sept heures du soir; ~ (*the month of*) *May*, en mai/au mois de mai/; ~ *spring/summer, fall, winter*, au printemps, en/été, automne, hiver/; ~ 1960, en 1960; *I'll do it* ~ *an hour*, Je le ferai/[after] dans une heure, [duration] en une heure/. **4.** [after superlative or equivalent] de: *the cleverest student* ~ *the class*, l'élève le plus intelligent de la classe; *The only/first, last/tree* ~ *the park*, Le seul/premier, dernier/arbre du parc. **5.** [before a pres. part.] en: *In reading the book, I . . .*, En lisant le livre, je. . . . **6.** [names of languages] en: ~ / *French, Spanish, &c.*/, en/français, espagnol/; ~ *perfect French*, dans un français impeccable. **7.** [vehicles] en: *He came* ~ *a car*, Il est venu en voiture; *He sat* ~ *the car*, Il restait (assis) dans la voiture. **8.** [ratio] sur: *one* ~ *ten*, un sur dix. **9.** [parts of the body] à; dans: *I have an ache* ~ *my leg*, J'ai mal à la jambe; *Don't put it* ~ *your mouth*, Ne le mettez pas à la bouche; *to hold sth.* ~ *o.'s hand*, tenir qqch. à la main; *What have I got* ~ *my hand?*, Qu'est-ce que j'ai dans ma main?; ~ *his hands*, dans ses mains/[Fig.] entre ses mains. **10.** [clothing] en: ~ *evening dress*, en tenue de soirée; *a woman* ~ *a green dress*, une femme en robe verte; *the woman* ~ *the green dress*, la femme à la robe verte. **11.** [pers., Fig.] en; chez, dans: *He has found his match* ~ *her*, En elle, il a trouvé son égal; *There are many good qualities* ~ *him*, Il y a de nombreuses qualités/en, chez/lui; *In Molière, we find . . .*, Dans/chez/Molière, on trouve. **12.** [expressions] ~ *that* (*no one is here*), en ce que/vu que/étant donné que/puisque/(personne n'est ici); *There's nothing* ~ *it*, Cela n'a pas de sens; *It is not dangerous* ~ *itself*, Ce n'est pas dangereux/en, par/soi-même. || *adv.* **1.** [As a verbal directive after verbs of motion and others, q.v.] entrer: *To/go, come/* ~, entrer; *to/run, walk/*

~, entrer/en courant, (à pied)/; *to fall* ~, tomber dans (l'eau); *to ask* ~, inviter à entrer (qqun)/rentrer qqch., &c./. **2.** [with verb *to be*] [pers.] être à la maison; [things] être rentré (dans la maison); [train] être arrivé (en gare); [political party] être au pouvoir: *Is your hand still* ~ *?*, Avez-vous toujours la main (pour le faire)?; *My luck is* ~, Je suis en veine; *We're* ~ *for/it, trouble/!*, Nous allons avoir des ennuis; *day* ~ *day out*, jour après jour. || *n.* [us. *pl.*] *The ins*, Le parti (politique) au pouvoir; *to know the ins and outs of a problem*, connaître un problème sous tous ses aspects. || **in-going,** *adj.* qui entre; entrant; [tenant] nouveau locataire. || **in-patient** *n.* (malade *m*) hospitalisé.

in.[2] *n.* [= inch, inches] pouce *m* [= po.].

in-[3] [préf. nég., cf. IM-].

inability [ɪnə'bɪlɪtɪ] *n.* **1.** impuissance *f* (à, *to*): *to regret one's* ~ *to*, regretter de ne pouvoir . . . cf. ABLE. **2.** incapacité *f* (de, *to*).

inaccessible [ɪnək'sɛsɪbl̩] *adj.* [mountain, place, &c.] inaccessible, [person] inabordable. || **inaccuracy** [ɪn'ækjɚ|əsɪ] *n.* inexactitude *f.* || **inaccurate** [-ət] *adj.* [answer, &c.] inexact. || **inactive** [ɪn'æktɪv] *adj.* [Pers.] inactif; [thing] inerte. || **inactivity** [ɪnæk'tɪvɪtɪ] *n.* inactivité *f*, inertie *f.* || **inadequate** [ɪn'ædəkwət] *adj.* [system, &c.] inadéquat; [help, &c.] insuffisant. || **inadvertently** [ɪnəd'vɚtəntlɪ] *adv.* par/inadvertance, mégarde/. || **inanimate** [ɪn'ænɪmət] *adj.* inanimé.

inappropriate [ˌɪnə'pɹowpɹɪət] *adj.* inapproprié.

inarticulate [ɪnˌɑɚ'tɪkjələt] *adj.* **1.** inarticulé. **2.** qui s'exprime difficilement.

inasmuch as [ɪnəz'mʌtʃˌæz] *conj.* dans la mesure où; [Legal] attendu que, vu que.

inattention [ɪnə'tɛn|ʃən] *n.* [mind, student] inattention *f*; négligence *f.* || **inattentive** [-tɪv] *adj.* inattentif; négligent. || **inaudible** [ɪn'ɔdɪbl̩] *adj.* imperceptible; [Tech.] inaudible.

inaugural [ɪn'ɔgɚl̩] *adj.* inaugural. || **inaugurate** [ɪn'ɔgɚˌejt] *v. tr.* inaugurer (une exposition, &c.); installer (un président). || **inauguration** [ɪnˌɔgɚ'ejʃən] *n.* [opening] inauguration *f.*

inborn ['ɪnbɔɚn] *adj.* [talent] inné, [science, knowledge] infus. || **inbred** [ɪn'bɹɛd] *adj.* inné, naturel.

inc. [= INCORPORATED].

incalculable [ɪn'kælkjələbl̩] *adj.* incalculable.

incapable [ɪn'kejpəbl̩] *adj.* [unable] incapable (de, *of*); inaccessible (à une émotion): *to be* ~ *of*, [+ -ing] → ne pas/pouvoir, être en mesure de/(+ inf.) cf. ABLE. || **incapacitate** [ɪnkə'pæsɪ|tejt] *v. tr.* [Jur.] incapaciter (qqun), rendre (qqun) incapable (*from*, de). || **incapacity** [-tɪ] *n.* incapacité *f.*

incarcerate [ɪn'kɑɚsɚˌejt] *v. tr.* incarcérer.

incarnate [ɪn'kɑɚnət] *adj.* incarné cf. INGROWING. || [ɪn'kɑɚnejt] *v. tr.* incarner. || **incarnation** [ɪnˌkɑɚ'nejʃən] *n.* incarnation *f.*

incendiary [ɪn'sɛndʒɚɪ] *adj.* & *n.* [bomb, &c.] incendiaire (*m*).

incense[1] ['ɪnsɛns] *n.* encens *m*: [Rel.] ~ *-bearer*, thuriféraire *m.*

incense[2] [ɪn'sɛns] *v. tr.* irriter: *to become incensed*, s'irriter (*at*, contre).

incentive [ɪn'sɛntɪv] *n.* stimulant *m*, motif *m* (déterminant) (pour, *to*), mobile *m* (de, *to*). || *adj.* stimulant, provoquant.

inception [ɪn'sɛpʃən] *n.* début *m*; [Med.] absorption *f.*

incessant [ɪn'sɛsənt] *adj.* incessant; continuel. || **incessantly** [-lɪ] *adv.* [×] sans cesse.

inch [ɪntʃ] *n.* pouce *m*; [Fig.] pouce *m*, parcelle *f*: *within an* ~ *of* [+ -ing], à deux doigts de [+ inf.]; *not to give way an* ~, ne pas reculer d'une semelle; ~ *by* ~, *by inches*, peu à peu, petit à petit. || *v. intr.*: *to* ~ *(o.'s way) forward, along, &c.*, avancer, se déplacer/lentement, imperceptiblement.

incident ['ɪnsɪdənt] *n.* [event] incident *m.* || *n.pl.* [story, &c.] péripéties *fpl.* || *adj.* [accessory] incident: ~ *to*, particulier, propre/à . . . , qui accompagne . . . || **incidental** [ɪnsɪ'dɛntl] *adj.* **1.** [circumstance] fortuit; [secondary] secondaire, accessoire: ~ *expenses*, faux frais *mpl*; ~ *to*, cf. INCIDENT. || **incidentally** [-ɪ] *adv.* **1.** incidemment: *Incidentally, what time is it?*, À propos, quelle heure est-il? **2.** accidentellement, à l'improviste.

incinerate [ɪn'sɪnɚˌejt] *v. tr.* incinérer (des déchets, &c.). || **incinerator** [-ɚ] *n.* [refuse] © incinérateur *m.*

incipient [ɪn'sɪpɪənt] *adj.* naissant, débutant, commençant.

incision [ɪn'sɪʒən] *n.* [cut] incision *f.* || **incisive** [ɪn'sajsɪv] *adj.* [Fig.] pénétrant, incisif. || **incisor** [ɪn'sajzɚ] *n.* [tooth] incisive *f.*

incite [ɪn'sajt] *v. tr.* inciter, pousser (à, *to*); monter la tête de qqun (contre qqun). || **incitement** [-mənt] *n.* motif *m*, raison *f* (d'agir); [Pej.] excitation *f* (à, *to*).

inclement ['ɪnkləmənt] *adj.* inclément.

inclination [ɪnklə'nejʃən] *n.* inclination *f*,

[slope] inclinaison *f*; [Fig.] [liking] penchant *m*, goût *m*, tendance *f* (à, *to*). || **incline** [ɪn'klajn] *n.* inclinaison *f*, [field, &c.] déclivité *f*, pente *f*. || *v. tr.* incliner, pencher (qqch.); [Fig.] porter (qqun à, *s.o. to*). || *v. intr.* (s')incliner, pencher; [Fig.] incliner (à), être enclin (à, *to*); avoir un penchant (pour), avoir une tendance (à): *I am inclined to think*, Je suis porté à croire . . .

include [ɪn'kluwd] *v. tr.* [contain] comprendre, [enclose] renfermer: *Does this ~ tips?, Is the tip included?*, Le service est-il compris? || **including** [-ɪŋ] (y) compris; [Loc.; inv. before *n.*, agrees following *n.*]: *~ myself*, moi compris, y compris moi (-même). || **inclusive** [ɪn'kluwsɪv] *adj.* [sum, &c.] global; *inclusive of*, qui comprend . . . , . . . inclusivement; [absol.] tout compris. || **inclusively** [-lɪ] *adv.* inclusivement.

incoherent [ɪn'kowhijɚənt] *adj.* incohérent.

income ['ɪnkʌm] *n.* [Fin.] revenu(s) *m* (*pl*): *~ -tax*, impôt *m* sur le revenu. || **incoming** [-ɪŋ] *adj.* qui (r)entre; nouveau.

incommensurate [ɪnkə'mɛnsɚət] *adj.* disproportionné (à, *with*), sans commune mesure (avec, *with*). || **incommunicative** [ɪnkə'mjuwnɪkətɪv] *adj.* [character, Pers.] renfermé, peu communicatif. || **incomparable** [ɪn'kɑmpɚəbl̩] *adj.* incomparable. || **incompatible** [ɪnkəm'pætɪbl̩] *adj.* incompatible (avec, *with*). || **incompetence** [ɪn'kɑmpə|təns] *n.* incompétence *f*. || **incompetent** [-tənt] *adj.* incompétent; [not qualified] non compétent.

incomplete [ɪnkəm'plijt] *adj.* incomplet; [unfinished] inachevé. || **incompleteness** [-nəs] *n.* état d'inachèvement. || **incomprehensible** [ɪn,kɑmpɹɪ'hɛnsibl̩] *adj.* incompréhensible. || **inconceivable** [ɪnkən'sijvəbl̩] *adj.* inconcevable, impensable. || **inconclusive** [ɪnkən'kluwsɪv] *adj.* non concluant. || **incongruous** [ɪn'kɑŋ,gɹuwəs] *adj.* [out of keeping] incongru; [not consistent] sans rapport. || **inconsiderate** [ɪnkən'sɪdɚət] *adj.* inconsidéré; irréfléchi [pers.] qui manque d'égards (envers). || **inconsistency** [ɪnkən'sɪs|tənsɪ] *n.* [lack of agreement] inconséquence *f*; [thing] contradiction *f*. || **inconsistent** [-tənt] *adj.* [at variance] incompatible (avec, *with*); [not adhering to principles] inconséquent (avec soi-même), contradictoire. || **inconspicuous** [ɪnkən'spɪk,juwəs] *adj.* peu visible; [Fig.] modeste, discret. || **inconstancy** [ɪn'kɔn|stənsɪ] *n.* inconstance *f*. || **inconstant** [-stənt] *adj.* inconstant, × versatile; [fickle] volage.

incontestable [,ɪnkən'tɛstɪbl̩] *adj.* incontestable.

inconvenience [ɪnkən'vijn|jəns] *n.* [bother] inconvénient *m*, ennui *m*, [hindrance] gêne *f*, dérangement *m*, [lack of comfort] incommodité *f*: *to put s.o. to ~*, → déranger, incommoder qqun. || *v. tr.* gêner, déranger (qqun, qqch.), [annoy] incommoder (qqun). || **inconvenient** [-jənt] *adj.* [situation, &c.] gênant, [installation, &c.] incommode; [time] inopportun.

incorporate [ɪn'kɔɚpɚ,ejt] *v. tr.* incorporer; [Com., Fin.] former en société; s'incorporer. || **incorporated** [-əd] *adj.* incorporé.

incorrect [ɪnkɚ'ɛkt] *adj.* [wrong] inexact; [not proper] incorrect.

incorrigible [ɪn'kɔɚɪʤɪbl̩] *adj.* incorrigible.

incorruptible [,ɪnkɚ'ʌptɪbl̩] *adj.* incorruptible.

increase ['ɪnkɹijs] *n.* augmentation *f* (des prix, taxes, &c.); [knowledge, &c.] accroissement *m*, gain *m*: *on the ~*, en voie *f* d'accroissement, à la hausse. || *v. tr.* [ɪn'kɹijs] [prices, &c.] augmenter, [interest, &c.] accroître; [Fig.] accentuer. || *v. intr.* [prices, &c.] augmenter, [population, &c.] s'accroître; [Fig.] s'accentuer. || **increasing** [-ɪŋ] *adj.* croissant. || **increasingly** [-ɪŋlɪ] *adv.* d'une façon croissante: *it becomes ~ difficult to*, → il devient de plus en plus difficile de . . .

incredible [ɪn'kɹɛdɪbl̩] *adj.* incroyable. || **incredulity** [ɪnkɹə'duwlɪtɪ] *n.* incrédulité *f*. || **incredulous** [ɪn'kɹɛdjələs] *adj.* [Pers.] incrédule.

increment ['ɪnkɹəmənt] *n.* augmentation *f*.

incriminate [ɪn'kɹɪmɪ,nejt] *v. tr.* incriminer.

incubate ['ɪnkjuw,bejt] *v. tr.* couver, incuber. || *v. intr.* couver. || **incubation** [,ɪŋkjə'bejʃən] *n.* incubation *f*. || **incubator** [-ɚ] *n.* couveuse *f*.

inculcate ['ɪnkəl,kejt] *v. tr.* inculquer.

incumbent [ɪn'kʌmbənt] *n.* titulaire *m*. || *adj.* *~ on*, imposé à, qui incombe à.

incur [ɪn'kɚ] *v. tr.* [-rr-] [debts] contracter, [punishment, expenses] encourir; [loss] subir; [risk] courir; [anger] s'attirer.

incurable [ɪn'kjuwɚəbl̩] *adj.* [sickness, habit, &c.] incurable. || *n.* incurable *m/f*. || **incurably** [-ɪ] *adv.* incurablement, sans espoir de guérison.

indebted [ɪn'dɛtəd] *adj.* endetté; [Fig.] redevable de, *for*): *to feel ~ to . . . for . . .*, savoir gré à . . . de . . .

indecent [ɪn'dijsənt] *adj.* [improper] inacceptable; [in bad taste] grossier; [obscene] indécent.

indeed [ɪn'dijd] *adv.* en effet; vraiment; très, bien; même; mais . . . : *It was ~ a* *lucky find*, C'était /en effet, en vérité/une trouvaille; *It may ~ be that . . .* , Il se peut/bien, même/que . . . ; *I am very happy ~* , Je suis/très, très/parfaitement/heureux; *Thank you very much ~* , Merci infiniment; *I am happy, ~ delighted*, Je suis heureux, ravi même; *Yes ~ !*, Mais bien sûr (que oui!); *Indeed?*, Vraiment?

indefatigable [ˌɪndəˈfætɪgəbḷ] *adj.* infatigable, inlassable.

indefensible [ɪndəˈfɛnsɪbḷ] *adj.* [stronghold] indéfendable; [opinion, &c.] insoutenable.

indefinable [ɪndəˈfajnəbḷ] *adj.* indéfinissable.

indefinite [ɪnˈdɛfɪnɪt] *adj.* indéfini; vague. || **indefinitely** [-lɪ] *adv.* indéfiniment; *~ postponed*, ajourné sine die.

indelible [ɪnˈdɛlɪbḷ] *adj.* indélébile.

indelicacy [ɪnˈdɛlɪ|kəsɪ] *n.* [Pers.] indélicatesse *f*, manque *m* de délicatesse, [manners] grossièreté *f*, inconvenance *f*. || **indelicate** [-kət] *adj.* [Pers.] indélicat, [manners] grossier, inconvenant.

indemnify [ɪnˈdɛmnɪfaj] *v. tr.* indemniser, dédommager (*for*, de). || **indemnity** [ɪnˈdɛmnɪtɪ] indemnité *f*, dédommagement *m*: *sessional ~* , indemnité *f* parlementaire.

indent [ɪnˈdɛnt] *v. tr.* **1.** denteler (qqch.); [paragraph] renfoncer. **2.** [goods] passer une commande (à qqun pour qqch., *on s.o. for sth.*). || **indentation** [ˌɪndɛnˈtejʃən] *n.* [action] dentelure *f*; [result] entaille *f*, échancrure *f*.

independence [ɪndəˈpɛndən|s] *n.* [financial, personal] indépendance *f*. || **independent** [-t] *adj. & n.* indépendant (*m*); [thinking] original, personnel. || **independently** [-tlɪ] *adv.* indépendamment; [act] avec indépendance.

indescribable [ɪndəˈskɹajbəbḷ] *adj.* indescriptible. || **indescribably** [-lɪ] *adv.* indiciblement, → d'une façon/indescriptible, indicible/.

ind|ex [ˈɪndɛks] *pl.* **-exes, [-ices]** *n.* **1.** [finger, list] index *m*; [scale] aiguille *f*; [book]/table *f*, répertoire *m* alphabétique: *card ~* , boîte *f* à fiches [*pl.* **indexes**]. **2.** [Math.] exposant *m*; [Phys.] indice *m pl.* **indices** || **index** *v. tr.* [names, items, &c.] dresser la/liste, table/alphabétique de (qqch.).

India [ˈɪndɪə] *n.* l'Inde *f*; [Hist.] les Indes *fpl*: *in, to ~* , en Inde, [Hist.] aux Indes; *~ ink*, encre *f* de Chine; *~ rubber*, caoutchouc *m*. || **Indian** [-n] *adj. & n.* **1.** [from India] indien (*m*): *~ Ocean*, Océan Indien. **2.** indien (*m*) (d'Amérique): *the Red Indians*, les Peaux-Rouges *mpl*; [language, customs, &c.] amérindien: *~ agent*, © agent *m* des /Indiens, sauvages; *~ corn*, maïs *m*, © blé *m* d'Inde; *~ reservation*, réserve indienne; *~ summer*, été *m*/de la Saint-Martin, © des sauvages/; *in ~ file*, en file indienne.

indicate [ˈɪndɪˌkejt] *v. tr.* indiquer, [point out] montrer, [show] dénoter: *Reports reaching here ~ that . . .* → D'après/nos informations, des informations reçues ici/ . . . || **indication** [ɪndəˈkejʃən] *n.* indication *f*; [sign.] indice *m*, signe *m*. || **indicative** [ɪnˈdɪkətɪv] *adj.* indicatif (*of*, de); [Gram.] indicatif *m*. || **indicator** [ˈɪndəˌkejtər] *n.* indicateur *m*.

indices, cf. INDEX.

indict [ɪnˈdajt] *v. tr.* poursuivre (en justice); inculper (pour crime de, *for*). || **indictment** [-mənt] *n.* inculpation *f*; mise *f* en accusation.

Indies [ˈɪndɪz] *n.pl.*: *the East ~* , les Indes Orientales; *the West ~* , les Antilles *fpl*.

indifference [ɪnˈdɪfərən|s] *n.* indifférence *f* (*to*, pour); manque *m* d'importance. || **indifferent** [ɪnˈdɪfərənt] *adj.* indifférent; [neutral] ni bon ni mauvais; [health] médiocre, mauvais. || **indifferently** [-lɪ] *adv.* [×] avec indifférence; [poorly] tant bien que mal.

indigenous [ɪnˈdɪdʒənəs] *adj.* indigène.

indigent [ˈɪndɪdʒənt] *adj.* indigent.

indigestible [ɪndɪˈdʒɛs|tɪbḷ] *adj.* indigeste. || **indigestion** [-tʃən] *n.* indigestion *f*: *to suffer from ~* , souffrir d'indigestion.

indignant [ɪnˈdɪgnənt] *adj.* indigné (de, *at*). || **indignantly** [-lɪ] *adv.* avec indignation. || **indignity** [ɪnˈdɪgnɪtɪ] *n.* indignité *f*.

indirect [ˌɪndɪˈɹɛkt] *adj.* indirect.

indiscreet [ɪndɪˈskɹijt] *adj.* [Pers.] indiscret; [action] imprudent. || **indiscretion** [ɪndɪˈskɹɛʃən] *n.* indiscrétion *f*, [action] imprudence *f*.

indiscriminately [ˌɪndɪˈskɹɪmɪnətlɪ] *adv.* sans distinction, au hasard.

indispensable [ɪndɪˈspɛnsəbḷ] *adj.* indispensable, → absolument nécessaire (à, *to*).

indispose [ɪndɪˈspowz] *v. tr.* [make reluctant; sicken] indisposer (contre qqun, qqch., *towards s.o., sth.*): *to feel indisposed*, être/indisposé, souffrant. || **indisposition** [ɪndɪspəˈzɪʃən] *n.* [sickness; reluctance] indisposition *f*, [sickness] malaise *m*. || **indistinct** [ɪndɪˈstɪŋkt] *adj.* [object, &c.] indistinct, [sight, pronunciation, &c.] confus; [Fig.] vague. || **indistinctness** [-nəs] *n.* indistinction *f*, confusion *f*; [Fig.] vague *m*.

indistinguishable [ˌɪndɪ'stɪŋgwɪʃəbl̩] *adj.* indiscernable: *They are* ~, → On ne peut pas les distinguer.

individual [ɪndɪ'vɪdjuwl̩] *n.* individu *m*, personne *f*, un particulier. || *adj.* [dish, &c.] individuel; personnel; particulier. || **individuality** [ˌɪndɪvɪdjuw'ælɪtɪ] *n.* individualité *f*; personnalité *f*; particularité *f*. || **individually** [ˌɪndɪ'vɪdjuwəlɪ] *adv.* individuellement, un à un; [people] personnellement.

indivisible [ɪn'dɪvɪzəbl̩] *adj.* indivisible.

indoctrinate [ɪnˌdɑktɹɪn'ejt] *v. tr.* endoctriner.

Indo-European [ˌɪndowˌjuwər'pɪən] *adj.* indo-européen.

indolence ['ɪndələn|s] *n.* indolence *f*. || **indolent** [-t] *adj.* indolent.

indomitable [ɪn'dɑmɪtəbl̩] *adj.* [courage, &c.] indomptable.

Indonesia [ɪndə'nijʒə] *n.* (République *f* d') Indonésie *f*.

indoor ['ɪndɔər] *adj.* [game, &c.] d'intérieur, de maison, de société; [tennis] couvert; [pool] fermé. || **indoors** [-z] *adv.* à l'intérieur, à la maison, dans la maison.

indorse [ɪn'dɔərs] *v. tr.* cf. ENDORSE.

induce [ɪn'djuws] *v. tr.* [conclude] induire (que . . . , *that* . . .); décider, porter (qqun à faire qqch., *s.o. to do sth.*); occasionner, produire (qqch.). || **inducement** [-mənt] *n.* provocation *f*, encouragement *m* (à qqch., *to sth.*).

induct [ɪn'dʌk|t] *v. tr.* initier (à, *to*); [Jur.] installer; [Mil.] incorporer. || **induction** [-ʃən] *n.* énumération *f* (de faits); [Jur., Eccl.] installation *f*; [Mil.] incorporation *f*; [Tech.] admission *f*; [Phil., Elect.] induction *f*.

indulge [ɪn'dʌldʒ] *v. tr.* favoriser, avoir trop d'indulgence pour (qqun); [child] gâter: *to* ~ *o.s.*, s'écouter. || *v. intr.* [habit] se livrer, s'adonner (à qqch., *in sth.*); [hope, dream] caresser. || **indulgence** [-əns] *n.* **1.** indulgence *f*. **2.** [confort, &c.] abandon (à, *in*); douceur *f*. **3.** [R.C.] indulgence *f*. || **indulgent** [-ənt] *adj.* **1.** [Pers.] indulgent; **2.** complaisant, accommodant. || **indulgently** [-əntlɪ] *adv.* avec indulgence.

industrial [ɪn'dʌstɹɪ|əl] *adj.* industriel. || **industrialize** [-ˌajz] *v. tr.* industrialiser. || **industrialization** [ɪnˌdʌstɹɪəlˌaj'zejʃən] *n.* industrialisation *f*. || **industrious** [-əs] *adj.* [student, &c.] assidu, zélé (à l'étude), travailleur, © travaillant. || **industry** ['ɪndəstɹɪ] *n.* **1.** industrie *f*. **2.** [Fig.] /assiduité *f*, application *f*/au travail.

ineffective [ɪnɪ'fɛktɪv] *adj.* inefficace, sans effet, [efforts] vain. || **ineffectively** [-lɪ] *adv.* sans effet, en vain. || **ineffectual** [ɪnɪ'fɛktjuwl̩] *adj.* cf. INEFFECTIVF. || **ineffectually** [-ɪ] *adv.* cf. INEFFECTIVELY. || **inefficiency** [ɪnɪ'fɪʃɪn|sɪ] *n.* [system, organization] inefficacité *f*; [Pers.] incapacité *f*, impuissance *f*. || **inefficient** [-t] *adj.* inefficace; [Pers.] incapable, impuissant.

ineligible [ɪn'ɛlɪdʒɪbl̩] *adj.* inéligible; qui n'a pas les qualités requises.

inept [ɪn'ɛpt] *adj.* **1.** [not suitable] → peu à propos. **2.** [foolish] inepte, sot.

ineptitude [ɪn'ɛptɪˌtjuwd] *n.* ineptie *f*.

inequality [ɪnɪ'kwɑlɪtɪ] *n.* inégalité *f*.

inert [ɪn'ərt] *adj.* [mass, matter, &c.] inerte. || **inertia** [ɪn'ərʃə] *n.* inertie *f*.

inestimable [ɪn'ɛstɪməbl̩] *adj.* inestimable, inappréciable. || **inevitable** [ɪn'ɛvɪtəbl̩] *adj.* inévitable. || **inexhaustible** [ɪnəks'ɔstɪbl̩] *adj.* [energy, &c.] inépuisable. || **inexpedient** [ɪnəks'pijdɪənt] *adj.* qui n'est pas à recommander; inopportun. || **inexpensive** [ɪnək'spɛnsɪv] *adj.* pas cher, bon marché; économique: *It is* ~, Cela ne coûte pas cher. || **inexperience** [ɪnək'spijərɪəns] *n.* inexpérience *f*, manque *m* d'expérience. || **inexperienced** [-t] *adj.* [Pers.] inexpérimenté, sans expérience. || **inexplicable** [ɪnək'splɪkəbl̩] *adj.* [situation, &c.] inexplicable. || **inexpressible** [ɪnək'spɹɛsɪbl̩] *adj.* [happiness, &c.] inexprimable, [suffering, &c.] indicible.

infallible [ɪn'fælɪbl̩] *adj.* infaillible; [necessary] immanquable.

infamous ['ɪnfəməs] *adj.* [behaviour, &c.] infâme. || **infamy** ['ɪnfəmɪ] *n.* infamie *f*.

infancy ['ɪnfən|sɪ] *n.* [child's] première enfance *f* [Fig.] *in its* ~, à ses débuts. || **infant** [-t] *n.* nourrisson *m*, bébé *m*, enfant *m* en bas âge. || *adj.* d'enfant, d'enfance; naissant. || **infantile** [-ˌtajl] *adj.* [reaction, behaviour] enfantin; [Med.] infantile, d'enfant.

infantry ['ɪnfəntɹɪ] *n.* [Mil.] infanterie *f*: ~ *soldier*, fantassin *m*.

infatuate [ɪn'fætjuwejt] *v. tr.* enticher (qqun de/qqun, qqch., *with/sth., s.o.*). || **infatuated** [-əd] *adj.* entiché (de, *with*): *She is* ~ *with him*, [Fam.] Elle a un béguin pour lui. || **infatuation** [ɪnˌfætʃuw'ejʃən] *n.* engouement *m*; [Fam.] toquade *f*; [Fig.] folie *f*.

infect [ɪn'fɛk|t] *v. tr.* infecter (une plaie, &c.), vicier (l'atmosphère, &c.); [Med.] contaminer (une personne). || **infection** [-ʃən] *n.* [also Fig.] infection *f*, contagion *f*; [Med.] contamination *f*. || **infectious** [-ʃəs] *adj.* [disease] infectieux, [atmosphere] vicié; [also Fig.] contagieux.

infer [ɪn'fər] *v. tr.* **[-rr-]** déduire, inférer (de, *from*); conclure. || **inference** ['ɪnfəəns] *n.* conclusion *f*, déduction *f*: *to/draw, make/ an* ~ (*from sth.*), tirer une conclusion (de qqch.).

inferior [ɪn'fijəɪə] *adj.* & *n.* inférieur (*m*). || **inferiority** [ɪnˌfijəɪ'əəɪtɪ] *n.* infériorité *f*: [Psychol.] ~ *complex*, /complexe *m*, sentiment *m*/d'infériorité.

infernal [ɪn'fən|ḷ] *adj.* infernal: [Fam.] ~ *noise*, un train *m* d'enfer. || **inferno** [-ow] *pl.* -s, *n.* [Fig.] un (véritable) enfer, cf. HELL.

infest [ɪn'fɛst] *v. tr.* infester.

infidel ['ɪnfɪdəl] *adj.* & *n.* [Rel.] infidèle (*m*), incroyant (*m*). || **infidelity** [ˌɪnfə'dɛlɪtɪ] *n.* infidélité *f*, déloyauté *f*, [Rel.] incrédulité *f*, incroyance *f*.

infiltrate ['ɪnfɪlˌtɹejt] *v. tr.* s'infiltrer dans.

infinite ['ɪnfɪnɪt] *adj.* infini. || **infinitely** [-lɪ] *adv.* infiniment.

infinitive [ɪn'fɪnɪtɪ|v] *n.* & *adj.* [Gram.] infinitif (*m*).

infinity [ɪn'fɪnɪtɪ] *n.* infinité *f*: *to*~, à l'infini; [Math.] infini *m*.

infirm [ɪn'fəm] *adj.* infirme, maladif. || **infirmary** [-əɪ] *n.* infirmerie *f*. || **infirmity** [-ɪtɪ] *n.* infirmité *f*, faiblesse *f*.

inflame [ɪn'flejm] *v. tr.* enflammer. || **inflammable** [ɪn'flæməbḷ] *adj.* inflammable. || **inflammation** [ɪnflə'mejʃən] *n.* inflammation *f*.

inflate [ɪn'flej|t] *v. tr.* gonfler. || **inflated** [-təd] *adj.* gonflé; [swollen] enflé; [price] exagéré; [currency] déprécié; [style] enflé. || **inflation** [-ʃən] *n.* gonflement *m*; [swelling] enflure *f*; [tire] gonflage *m*; [Fin.] inflation *f*.

inflection [ɪn'flɛkʃən] *n.* cf. INFLEXION.

inflict [ɪn'flɪkt] *v. tr.* [punishment, &c.] infliger (qqch. à qqun, *sth. on s.o.*); [wound] faire.

inflow ['ɪnflow] *n.* afflux *m*. cf. INFLUX; [Fig.] [immigration] courant *m*.

influence ['ɪnfluwəns] *n.* influence *f*: *He is a person of* ~ , C'est une personne influente. || *v. tr.* influencer (qqun); [thing] influer sur (qqch.). || **influential** [ɪnˌfluw'ɛnʃəl] *adj.* influent, qui a de l'influence (sur).

influenza [ɪnfluw'ɛnzə] *n.* grippe *f*, influenza *m*.

influx ['ɪnflʌks] *n.* afflux *m*; [Fig.] affluence *f*; invasion *f*.

inform [ɪn'fəəm] *v. tr.* informer (qqun de qqch., *s.o. of sth.*), renseigner (qqun au sujet de qqch., *s.o. of sth.*); [denounce s.o.] avertir (les autorités, la police); [against s.o.] dénoncer (qqun): *Please keep me informed of further developments*, Veuillez me/faire part, tenir au courant/ des futurs événements.

informal [-ḷ] *adj.* **1.** [Tech.] informe, irrégulier. **2.** [meeting, &c.] non officiel, [agreement] officieux, [interview, conversation, &c.] privé, particulier: ~ *gathering*, petit comité. **3.** → sans/cérémonie, façon; en toute simplicité: *an* ~ *dinner*, un repas/sans cérémonie, intime/. || **informality** [ɪnfə'mælɪtɪ] *n.* **1.** [Jur.] vice *m* de forme. **2.** [meeting, interview, &c.] caractère *m* non officiel (d'un acte, &c.). **3.** simplicité *f*, → manque *m*/ d'apparat, de cérémonie/.

informant [ɪn'fəəmənt] *n.* [Ling.] informat|eur *m*, -rice *f*. || **information** [ɪnfə'mejʃən] *n.* [Collect.] renseignements *mpl*: *a piece of* ~ , un renseignement; [knowledge] informations *fpl*; [against s.o.] délation *f*. || **informative** [-ətɪv] *adj.* instructif, formateur. || **informer** [ɪn'fəəmə] *n.* délateur *m*, [Fam.] mouchard *m*.

infraction [ɪn'fɹækʃən] *n.* infraction *f*, violation *f*.

infrequent [ɪn'fɹijkwənt] *adj.* → peu fréquent; rare.

infringe [ɪn'fɹɪnʤ] *v. tr.* enfreindre (une loi, un règlement), violer (un droit), transgresser (une loi, &c.). || *v. intr.* empiéter (*on*, sur). || **infringement** [-mənt] *n.* infraction *f* (à une loi, *of a law*), transgression *f* (d'une loi, d'un règlement, &c.), violation *f* (d'un droit): [Jur.] ~ *of a patent*, contrefaçon *f* d'un brevet.

infuriate [ɪn'fjuwəɪˌejt] *v. tr.* rendre (qqun) furieux.

infuse [ɪn'fjuw|z] *v. tr.* infuser; [Fig.] inspirer (qqch. à qqun, *sth. into s.o.*). || **infusion** [-ʒən] *n.* infusion *f*; [Fig.] inspiration *f*.

ingenious [ɪn'ʤijnjəs] *adj.* [talented, clever] ingénieux, [mind] inventif. || **ingeniousness** [-nəs] *n.* [talent] ingéniosité *f*, [cleverness, skill] génie *m*, esprit *m* d'invention. || **ingenuity** [ɪnʤə'nuwɪtɪ] *n.* cf. INGENIOUSNESS. || **ingenuous** [ɪn'ʤɛnjuwəs] *adj.* [person] naïf, ingénu. || **ingenuousness** [-nəs] *n.* naïveté *f*, ingénuité *f*.

ingest [ɪn'ʤɛst] *v. tr.* [Med.] ingérer.

ingot ['ɪngət] *n.* [gold, &c.] lingot *m*.

ingrained [ɪn'gɹejnd] *adj.* [habit, &c.] invétéré; [prejudice] enraciné.

ingrate ['ɪngɹejt] *n.* & *adj.* [ungrateful] ingrat. || **ingratiate** [ɪn'gɹejʃɪˌejt] *v. intr.*: *to* ~ *o.s. with*, [Fam.] se mettre bien avec; s'insinuer dans les bonnes grâces de . . .

ingratitude [ɪn'gɹætɪˌtjuwd] *n.* ingratitude *f*.

ingredient [ɪn′gɹijdɪənt] *n.* ingrédient *m.*
ingrowing [′ɪngɹowɪŋ] *adj.* (ongle) incarné.
inhabit [ɪn′hæbɪt] *v. tr.* habiter. ‖ **inhabitant** [-ənt] *n.* habitant [this is the usual word for "dweller"; for ©, see HABITANT]. ‖ **inhabited** [-əd] *adj.* [×] habité. cf. UNINHABITED.
inhale [ɪn′hejl] *v. tr.* [Med.] inhaler; aspirer, avaler (la fumée).
inherent [ɪn′hijɚənt] *adj.* inhérent (à, *to/in*); [inborn] inné. ‖ **inherit** [ɪn′hɛɚɪt] *v. tr.* hériter de; [Fig.] tenir . . . de (son père, sa mère). ‖ **inheritance** [-əns] *n.* héritage *m*: ~ *tax*, droit *m* de succession.
inhibit [ɪn′hɪbɪt] *v. tr.* empêcher (de, *from*); interdire (à . . . de . . .). cf. PROHIBITED. ‖ **inhibition** [ˌɪnhɪ′bɪʃən] *n.* interdiction *f*; [Med.] inhibition *f*; [Rel.] interdit *m.*
inhospitable [ɪnˌhɑs′pɪtəbl̩] *adj.* [Pers., country] inhospitalier.
inhuman [ɪn′hjuwmən] *adj.* [treatment, &c.] inhumain. ‖ **inhumane** [ɪn′hjuwˌmejn] *adj.* [Pers.] inhumain, brutal. ‖ **inhumanity** [ɪnˌhju′mænɪtɪ] *n.* inhumanité *f.*
inimical [ɪn′ɪmɪkl̩] *adj.* [feeling, &c.] ennemi (*to*, de), hostile (*to*, à).
inimitable [ɪn′ɪmɪtəbl̩] *adj.* inimitable.
iniquitous [ɪn′ɪkwɪ|təs] *adj.* [action] inique. ‖ **iniquity** [-tɪ] *n.* iniquité *f.*
initial[1] *n.* [Letter] initiale *f. npl.* parafe *m*, initiales *fpl.* ‖ *v. tr.* parafer, apposer ses initiales à (un document).
initial[2] [ɪ′nɪʃəl] *adj.* initial, premier. ‖ **initially** [-ɪ] *adv.* en premier lieu, à l'époque.
initiate [ɪ′nɪʃɪˌejt] *v. tr.* **1.** commencer (qqch.); [measure, &c.] prendre l'initiative de (qqch.). **2.** initier (qqun à qqch., *s.o. into sth.*). ‖ **initiation** [ɪˌnɪʃɪ′ejʃən] *n.* **1.** commencement *m* (d'une œuvre). **2.** initiation *f* (à qqch., *into sth.*). ‖ **initiative** [ɪ′nɪʃətɪv] *n.* initiative *f*, décision *f.*
inject [ɪn′ʤɛk|t] *v. tr.* [liquid, &c.] injecter. ‖ **injection** [-ʃən] *n.* [Med.] injection *f*; [rectal] lavement *m*; [hypodermic] piqûre *f.*
injunction [ɪn′ʤʌŋkʃən] *n.* injonction *f*, recommandation *f* formelle; [Jur.]: *to give an* ~, mettre en demeure (de).
injure [′ɪnʤɚ] *v. tr.* nuire à (qqun, qqch.), [rights, reputation] léser, faire tort à (qqun, qqch.); [wound] blesser (qqun). ‖ **injured** [-d] *adj.* blessé; offensé: *seriously injured*, grièvement blessé ; *the* ~ *party*, l'offensé. ‖ *n.* blessé *m*, -e *f.* ‖ **injurious** [ɪn′ʤuwɚɪəs] *adj.* nuisible, dommageable, préjudiciable. ‖ **injury** [′ɪnʤɚɪ] *n.* tort *m*, dommage *m*, préjudice *m* (à la réputation); [body] lésion *f*, blessure *f*: *to do* ~ (*to s.o.*), porter préjudice (à qqun); *to the* ~ *of* (*s.o.*), au détriment de (qqun); *without* ~ *to*, sans nuire à.
injustice [ɪn′ʤʌstɪs] *n.* injustice *f*, tort *m.*
ink [ɪŋk] *n.* encre *f.* ‖ *v. tr.* encrer; [blot] tacher (un cahier, &c.) d'encre; [Fig.] signer (un contrat).
inkling [-lɪŋ] *n.* soupçon *m*: *I didn't have the least* ~ *of it*, Je n'ai pas eu le moindre vent de cela/J'étais à cent lieues de me douter de cela.
inkstand [-ˌstænd], **inkwell** [-ˌwɛl] *n.* encrier *m.* ‖ **inky** [-ɪ] *adj.* [blotted] taché d'encre; [colour] noir comme de l'encre.
inlaid [′ɪnlejd] *adj.* incrusté (*with*, de).
inland [′ɪnlænd] *n.* intérieur *m* des terres. ‖ *adj.* [sea, &c.] intérieur, de l'intérieur; ~ *trade*, commerce *m* d'intérieur. ‖ *adv.* à l'intérieur (des terres).
in-law [′ɪnlɔ] *n.* [Fam.] parent *m*, -e *f* par alliance: *the in-laws*, la belle-famille.
inlay [ɪn′lej], **inlaid, inlaid** [-d] *v. tr.* [matter] incruster (du bois, &c.). ‖ *n.* incrustation *f* (dans le bois, dans le marbre &c.).
inlet [′ɪnlət] *n.* **1.** bras *m* de mer, fjord *m*; © inlet *m.* **2.** [air] prise *f*, [steam, fuel, &c.] admission *f*, arrivée *f.*
inmate [′ɪnmejt] *n.* [hospital, &c.] habitant *m*, -e *f* (d'une institution, maison, &c.).
inmost [′ɪnmowst] *adj.* [feeling, &c.] le plus /profond, secret/.
inn [ɪn] *n.* auberge *f*: *innkeeper*, aubergiste *m.*
innate [ɪ′nejt] *adj.* inné. cf. INBORN, INBRED.
inner [ɪnɚ] *adj.* [side, &c.] intérieur, interne; [Fig.] intime, secret: ~ *tube*, chambre *f* à air.
innermost [-ˌmowst] *adj.* cf. INMOST.
inning [′ɪnɪŋ] *n.* [sports, esp. baseball] manche *f.*
innocence [′ɪnəsən|s] *n.* innocence *f.* ‖ **innocent** [-t] ‖ *adj.* innocent (de, *of*). *n.* innocent *m.*
innocuous [ɪ′nɑkjuwəs] *adj.* [drug, person] inoffensif.
innovate [′ɪnowˌvejt] *v. intr.* innover. ‖ **innovation** [ɪnə′vejʃən] *n.* innovation *f.* ‖ **innovator** [-ɚ] *n.* novat|eur *m*, -trice *f.*
innuendo [ɪnˌjuw′ɛndow] *pl.* **-es** *n.* insinuation *f* (malveillante), sous-entendu *m.*
innumerable [ɪ′njuwmɚəbl̩] *adj.* innombrable.
inoculate [ɪn′ɑkjəlejt] *v. tr.* inoculer. ‖ **inoculation** [ɪnˌɑkjə′lejʃən] *n.* inoculation *f.*
inoffensive [ɪnə′fɛnsɪv] *adj.* inoffensif; [unobjectionable] anodin. ‖ **inoperative** [ɪn′ɑpɚətɪv] *adj.* sans effet. ‖ **inopportune** [ɪnˌɑpɚ′tjuwn] *adj.* inopportun; (moment) mal choisi, fâcheux.

inorganic [ɪnˌɔɚ'gænɪk] *adj.* inorganique.
input ['ɪnput] *n.* **1.** [Electr.] prise *f*, entrée *f* (sur un appareil de radio, &c.). **2.** [machine] consommation *f*.
inquest ['ɪnˌkwɛst] *n.* enquête *f* [en cas de mort violente].
inquire [ɪn'kwajɚ] *v. intr.* s'enquérir (de qqch., *about sth.*), se renseigner (/à propos de, sur/ qqch., *about sth.*); [case, &c.] faire des recherches (sur qqch., *into sth.*), demander (qqun, *for s.o.*). || *v. tr.* s'informer de (qqch.). || **inquiringly** [-ɪŋlɪ] *adv.* [observe, &c.] d'un air interrogateur. || **inquiry** [-ɪ] *n.* demande *f* (de renseignements); enquête *f* (au sujet de, *about*); [judicial] instruction *f*. || **inquisition** [ɪnkwɪ'zɪʃən] *n.* recherche *f*; [Rel.] Inquisition *f*; [Jur.] enquête *f*; perquisition *f*. || **inquisitive** [ɪn'kwɪzɪtɪv] *adj.* [look, &c.] curieux, chercheur.
inroad ['ɪnɹowd] *n.* [attack] incursion *f*; [encroachment] empiétement *m* (sur qqch., *upon sth.*).
inrush ['ɪnɹʌʃ] *n.* [people, water, &c.] irruption *f*.
insane [ɪn'sejn] *adj.* fou, dément. || **insanity** [ɪn'sænɪtɪ] *n.* folie *f*, démence *f*.
insatiable [ɪn'sejʃəbl̩] *adj.* insatiable.
inscribe [ɪn'skɹajb] *v. tr.* [name, &c.] inscrire; [Litt.] dédier (un livre). || **inscription** [ɪn'skɹɪpʃən] *n.* [name, titles] inscription *f*; [Litt.] dédicace *f*.
inscrutable [ɪn'skɹuwtəbl̩] *adj.* inscrutable.
insect ['ɪnsɛkt] *n.* insecte *m*: ~ *-powder*, insecticide *m*, poudre *f* insecticide.
insecure [ɪnsə'kjuwɚ] *adj.* peu sûr, incertain; inquiet; exposé.
insensible [ɪn'sɛnsɪbl̩] *adj.* [imperceptible] insensible, [person] inconscient, sans connaissance: *to become* ~ , tomber sans connaissance, s'évanouir. || **insensibly** [-ɪ] *adv.* insensiblement, imperceptiblement, peu à peu.
insensitive [ɪn'sɛnsɪtɪv] *adj.* [skin] insensible, peu sensible.
inseparable [ɪn'sɛpɚəbl̩] *adj.* inséparable.
insert [ɪn'sɚ|t] *v. tr.* insérer, introduire (qqch). (*in, into*, dans). || **insertion** [-ʃən] *n.* insertion *f*.
inside [ɪn'sajd] *adv.* (en) dedans, à l'intérieur: ~ *and out*, au-dedans et au-dehors. || *prep.* dans, en dedans de, à l'intérieur de. || *n.* (le) dedans *m*, (l')intérieur *m*: ~ *out*, complètement; *to turn* (*a place*) ~ *out*, mettre (une pièce) sens dessus dessous. || *attrib.* intérieur, d'intérieur.
insidious [ɪn'sɪdɪəs] *adj.* insidieux, traître.
insight ['ɪnsajt] *n.* [mind] pénétration *f*, perspicacité *f*; aperçu *m*, connaissance *f* (de qqch., *into sth.*).
insignificance [ɪnsɪg'nɪfɪ|kəns] *n.* peu d'importance, futilité *f*. || **insignificant** [-kənt] *adj.* insignifiant;/sans, dénué d'/ importance, futile.
insincere [ˌɪnsɪn|'sijɚ] *adj.* → qui manque de sincérité; [ext.] simulé, traître. || **insincerity** [-'sɛɚɪtɪ] *n.* dissimulation *f*, traîtrise *f*.
insinuate [ɪn'sɪnjuwejt] *v. tr.* [hint] insinuer, sous-entendre; [ingratiate] s'insinuer (dans les bonnes grâces *fpl* de . . .). || **insinuation** [-juw'ejʃən] *n.* insinuation *f*.
insipid [ɪn'sɪpɪd] *adj.* insipide, fade.
insist [ɪn'sɪst] *v. intr.* insister (*on sth.*, sur qqch.); tenir (absolument) (à qqch.): *He insisted/on it, on doing it, on my doing it/*, Il a insisté/là-dessus, pour le faire, pour que je le fasse/, Il a tenu absolument/à le faire, à ce que je le fasse/. || **insistence** [-əns] *n.* insistance *f*. || **insistent** [-ənt] *adj.* persistant; [pressing] pressant, sans répit.
insolation [ˌɪnsə'lejʃən] *n.* insolation *f*; [Med.] coup *m* de soleil.
insolence ['ɪnsəˌləns] *n.* insolence *f*. || **insolent** ['ɪnsələnt] *adj.* insolent, effronté. || **insolently** [-lɪ] *adv.* avec insolence, insolemment.
insoluble [ɪn'sɑljəbl̩] *adj.* insoluble.
insolvency [ɪnˌsɑlv|ənsɪ] *n.* insolvabilité *f*; [bankrupt] faillite *f*. || **insolvent** [-ənt] *adj.* insolvable; [bankrupt] en faillite: *to become* ~ , faire faillite.
insomnia [ɪn'sɑmnɪə] *n.* insomnie *f*.
insomuch [ɪnˌsow'mʌtʃ] *adv.*: ~ *that*, à tel point que, au point que.
inspect [ɪn'spɛk|t] *v. tr.* [work, &c.] inspecter, faire l'inspection (des troupes, &c.), passer (un regiment) en revue; vérifier (qqch.). || **inspection** [-ʃən] *n.* inspection *f*, contrôle *m*, [Mil. &c.] revue *f* (des troupes, &c.); vérification *f*. || **inspector** [-tɚ] *n.* [school] inspecteur *m*, © visiteur *m*; [Tech.] contrôleur *m*.
inspiration [ɪnspɚ'ejʃən] *n.* inspiration *f*; [Fig.] *X was an* ~ *to all of us*, X a toujours été un exemple pour nous tous. || **inspire** [ɪn'spajɚ] *v. tr.* inspirer (de, *with*): *to* ~ *s.o. with . . .*, inspirer (de la, du, des . . .) à qqun; suggérer, faire courir (un faux bruit); [breath] inspirer, respirer profondément.
install [ɪn'stɔl] *v. tr. & intr.* (s')installer; [fixture] poser. || **installation** [ˌɪnstə'lejʃən] *n.* installation *f*: *industrial* ~ , établissement *m* industriel. || **instalment**[1] [-mənt] *n.* installation *f*. || **instalment**[2] *n.* **1.** [Comm.] acompte *m*; versement *m* (partiel);

tranche *f* (d'un paiement): ~ *selling*, vente *f* à/tempérament, crédit/; *the first* ~, le premier versement; ~ *plan*, facilités *fpl* de paiement; *on the* ~ *plan*, à crédit. **2.** [serial story] (publié) par tranches; feuilleton *m*.

instance ['ɪnstən|s] *n*. **1.** exemple *m*, cas *m*; occasion *f*, circonstance *f*; *for* ~, par exemple; *in this particular* ~, → dans ce cas en particulier .... **2.** [Jur.] instance *f*; [request] requête *f*.

instant[1] [-t] *n*. instant *m*, moment *m*: *the* ~ *he* ..., dès qu'il ..., au moment où il ...; *this* ~ *!*, tout de suite! || **instant**[2] *adj*. [need, &c.] urgent, pressant; [coffee, &c.] instantané, soluble: [Comm.] *the 15th inst*(*ant*), le 15 courant. || **instantaneous** [ɪnstən'tejnɪəs] *adj*. instantané. || **instantly** ['ɪnstəntlɪ] *adv*. à l'instant, immédiatement.

instead [ɪn'stɛd] *adv*. au lieu de cela, plutôt: *I'll go* ~, J'irai à votre place. || **instead of** [-ˌʌv] *prep*. au lieu de; à la place de: *He'll come* ~ *me*, Il viendra à ma place, Il me remplacera; ~ *that*, *give me* ..., A la place (de cela), donnez-moi ... ; ~ *talking keep quiet*, Au lieu de parler, taisez-vous.

instep ['ɪnstɛp] *n*. cou-de-pied *m*.

instigate ['ɪnstɪˌgejt] *v. tr*. pousser (qqun à), provoquer (une révolte). || **instigation** [ˌɪnstɪ'gejʃən] *n*. instigation *f*.

instil [ɪn'stɪl] *v. tr*. [pour slowly] instiller; [Fig.] inspirer, faire naître (un sentiment).

instinct ['ɪnstɪŋkt] *n*. instinct *m*: *by*, *from*/ ~, /par, d'/instinct, instinctivement. || **instinctive** [-ɪv] *adj*. instinctif, [reaction] inné. || **instinctively** [-lɪ] *adv*. instinctivement; [Fam.] machinalement.

institute ['ɪnstɪˌtjuwt] *n*. institut *m*, école *f*, centre *m*. || *v. tr*. instituer, fonder; [inquiry] ouvrir. || **institution** [ˌɪnstɪ'tjuwʃən] *n*. [social, charitable, educational] institution *f*; [setting up] fondation *f*, création *f*; [by ext.] tradition *f*: *to become an* ~, passer dans les/mœurs, habitudes *fpl*/.

instruct [ɪn'stɹʌk|t] *v. tr*. enseigner (qqch. à qqun, *s.o. in sth.*); [inform] instruire (qqun de qqch., *s.o. of sth.*); [give directions to] charger (qqun de, *s.o. to*), donner des instructions (à qqun pour). || **instruction** [-ʃən] *n*. **1.** instruction *f*. **2.** [education] enseignement *m*. || *n.pl. to leave instructions with*, donner des/instructions, ordres *mpl*/ à. cf. DIRECTIONS. || **instructional** [-ʃənḷ] *adj*. ~ *material*, matériel *m* d'enseignement. || **instructive** [-tɪv] *adj*. instructif. || **instructor** [-tɚ] *n*. [Mil., physical education, trades, &c.] instruct|eur *m*, -rice *f*; [Sch.] répétit|eur *m*, -rice *f*: *Summer-Session* ~, professeur *m* au cours de vacances; [Univ.] chargé *m* de cours.

instrument ['ɪnstɹəmənt] *n*. [gen.] instrument *m*; [Tech.] instrument *m*, appareil *m*: ~ *panel*, tableau *m* de bord; [Mus.] instrument *m* (de musique); [Fig.] agent *m*. || **instrumental** [ɪnstɹə'mɛntḷ] *adj*. [Mus.] instrumental: [Fig.] *to be* ~ *in*, → contribuer à. || **instrumentalist** [-ɪst] *n*. instrumentiste *m*.

insubordination [ɪnsəˌbɔɚdɪ'nejʃən] *n*. insubordination *f*; refus *m* d'obéissance.

insufferable [ɪn'sʌfɚəbḷ] *adj*. insupportable, intolérable.

insufficiency [ɪnsə'fɪʃən|sɪ] *n*. insuffisance *f*. || **insufficient** [-t] *adj*. insuffisant. || **insufficiently** [-tlɪ] *adv*. insuffisamment.

insular ['ɪnsəlɚ] *adj*. insulaire.

insulate ['ɪnsəˌlejt] *v. tr*. isoler; [against cold] calorifuger. || **insulation** [ɪnsə'lejʃən] *n*. isolement *m*; calorifugeage *m*. || **insulator** [ˌɪnsə'lejtɚ] *n*. isolateur *m*.

insulin ['ɪnsəlɪn] *n*. insuline *f*.

insult ['ɪnsʌlt] *n*. insulte *f*. *v. tr*. [ɪn'sʌlt] insulter. || **insulting** [-ɪŋ] *adj*. [words] injurieux, grossier; [behaviour, &c.] offensant.

insuperable [ɪn'suwpɚəbḷ] *adj*. insurmontable.

insurance [ɪn'sjɚ|əns] *n*. assurance *f*: *life* ~, assurance-vie *f*, assurance *f* sur la vie; *to take out an* ~, s'assurer; *unemployment* ~, assurance-chômage *f*; *social* ~, assurances *fpl* sociales, prévoyance *f* sociale; *sickness* ~, assurance-maladie *f*. || **insure** *v. tr*. **1.** [against fire, accident, &c.] s'assurer (contre l'incendie, sur la vie, &c.). **2.** [= ensure] (s')assurer (de l'exactitude, &c. de qqch.): ~ *against*, se garantir contre....

insurgent [ɪn'sɚdʒənt] *n*. & *adj*. insurgé, rebelle (*m*).

insurmountable [ˌɪnsɚ'mawntəbḷ] *adj*. insurmontable; infranchissable.

insurrection [ɪnsɚ'ɛkʃən] *n*. insurrection *f*, rebellion *f*, soulèvement *m*.

intact [ɪn'tækt] *adj*. intact; [uninjured] indemne.

intangible [ɪn'tændʒɪbḷ] *adj*. imperceptible, impalpable: *the intangibles*, les impondérables *mpl*.

integer ['ɪntədʒɚ] *n*. nombre *m* entier.

integral ['ɪntəgɹəl] *adj*. intégral; [part] intégrant; *n*. intégrale *f*.

integrate ['ɪntəˌgɹejt] *v. tr*. intégrer (à, *in*): || **integrated** [-əd] *adj*. complet, harmonieux.

|| **integrity** [ɪn'tɛgɹɪtɪ] *n.* intégrité *f*, droiture *f*.
intellect ['ɪntəˌlɛkt] *n.* intelligence *f*; [Phil.] intellect *m*: *a man of* ~, un penseur *m*. || **intellectual** [ɪntə'lɛktjuwəl] *adj.* & *n.* intellectuel (*m*). || **intelligence** [ɪn'tɛlɪʤən|s] *n.* **1.** [mental ability] intelligence *f*; esprit *m*. **2.** [news] nouvelle(s) *f*(*pl*); renseignements *mpl* (secrets) [Br.] *Intelligence Service*, Service secret, [Fr.] Deuxième bureau *m*. || **intelligent** [-t] *adj.* intelligent, réfléchi. || **intelligentsia** [ɪnˌtɛlɪ'ʤɛnʃə] *n.* [souvent péjoratif] l'élite *f* (intellectuelle). || **intelligible** [ɪn'tɛlɪʤəbl̩] *adj.* intelligible.
intemperance [ɪn'tɛmpɚ|əns] *n.* intempérance *f*; [liquor] alcoolisme *m*. || **intemperate** [-ət] *adj.* immodéré, excessif; [liquor] intempérant, alcoolique; [language] peu mesuré. || **intemperately** [-ətlɪ] *adv.* immodérément, avec excès.
intend [ɪn'tɛnd] *v. tr.* avoir l'intention, projeter (de, *to*); destiner (*sth. for s.o.*, qqch. à qqun). || **intended** [-əd] *adj.* projeté, [meant] intentionnel; [prospective] futur: [Fam.] /*his, her*/ ~, son futur, sa future.
intense [ɪn'tɛns] *adj.* intense; [pain] vif, fort. || **intensely** [-lɪ] *adv.* intensément, vivement. || **intensify** [-ɪˌfaj] *v. tr.* intensifier, renforcer. || **intensity** [-ɪtɪ] *n.* intensité *f*; force *f*. || **intensive** [-ɪv] *adj.* intensi|f, -ve; [study] approfondi.
intent[1] [ɪn'tɛn|t] *n.* intention *f*; [purpose] but *m*: *to all intents and purposes*, en fait; pratiquement.
intent[2] *adj.* attenti|f, -ve (*on*, à): ~ *on* [+ *ing*], appliqué à . . . [+ inf.]. || **intention** [-ʃən] *n.* intention *f*, but *m*. || **intentional** [-ʃənl̩] *adj.* [intended] intentionnel, [deliberate] (de propos) délibéré. || **intentionally** [-ʃənl̩ɪ] *adv.* intentionnellement; délibérément, exprès.
inter[1] [ɪn'tɚ] *v. tr.* enterrer.
inter-[2] [préfixe exprimant la réciprocité]: **interact** [ɪntɚ'ækt], *v. intr.* agir réciproquement, avoir une/interaction, influence/ réciproque.
intercede [ˌɪntɚ|'sijd] *v. intr.* intercéder (*with*, auprès de; *for*, en faveur de). || **intercept** [-'sɛpt] *v. tr.* intercepter. || **intercession** [-'sɛʃən] *n.* intercession *f* (*for*, en faveur de). || **interchange** ['ɪntɚˌʧejnʤ] *n.* échange *m*; réciprocité *f*. || ~ *v. tr.* [ˌɪntɚ|'ʧejnʤ] échanger; [place] changer de place (avec qqun); [Admin.] permuter. || **intercom** ['ɪntɚˌkɑm] *n.* téléphone *m* intérieur. || **intercourse** ['ɪntɚkɔɚs] *n.* relations *fpl*, rapports *mpl*. || **interdenominational** [ˌɪntɚ|dɪˌnɑmɪ'nejʃənl̩] *adj.* conjoint. || **interdependence** [-'dɪpɛndəns] *n.* dépendance *f* mutuelle.
interdict [-'dɪkt] *n.* interdit *m*. || *v. tr.* interdire.
interest ['ɪntɹəst] *v. tr.* intéresser (*in*, à) *to be interested in*, s'intéresser à, s'occuper de; [Com.] être intéressé dans (une entreprise). || *n.* intérêt *m*: *to take an* ~ *in sth.*, s'intéresser à qqch.; *to have an* ~ *in sth.*, s'intéresser à qqch., [share] participer à, avoir un intérêt dans/qqch.; *It is to your* ~ *to do it*, → Vous avez intérêt à, Il est de votre intérêt de/le faire; *in the* ~ *(s) of clarity*, dans l'intérêt de la clarté; *in his own* ~, dans son propre intérêt; *to bear* ~, porter intérêt; *compound* ~, intérêts composés; *to pay back with* ~, rendre avec usure; *the financial interests*, les financiers. || **interesting** [-ɪŋ] *adj.* intéressant: *very* ~, passionnant.
interfere [ˌɪntɚ'fijɚ] *v. intr.* **1.** intervenir (*in*, dans); [Pol.] s'ingérer (dans). **2.** se mêler (*with*, de); [hinder] entraver, gêner (*with sth.*, qqch.); [Pers.] importuner, © achaler, (*with s.o.*, qqun); [meddle] toucher (*with*, à): *Don't* ~ *!*, → Mêlez-vous de vos affaires! || **interference** [-əns] *n.* [person] intervention *f*, ingérence *f* (*in*, dans); [radio] interférence *f*, [waves] brouillage *m* (des ondes).
interim ['ɪntɚɪm] *n.* intérim *m*: *in the* ~, entre temps; *ad* ~, par intérim, intérimaire.
interior [ɪn'tijɚɪɚ] *adj.* & *n.* intérieur (*m*).
interject [ɪntɚ'ʤɛkt] *v. tr.* [questions] lancer. || *v. intr.* interrompre. || **interjection** [ɪntɚ'ʤɛkʃən] *n.* [Gram.] interjection *f*.
interlace [ˌɪntɚ'lejs] *v. tr.* entrelacer; entremêler.
interlock [ˌɪntɚ'lɑk] *v. tr.* engrener. || *v. intr.* s'engrener.
interloper ['ɪntɚˌlowpɚ] *n.* intrus *m*.
interlude ['ɪntɚˌluwd] *n.* intermède *m*; interlude *m*.
intermediary [ɪntɚ'mijdɪˌɛɚɪ] *adj.* & *n.* intermédiaire (*m*). || **intermediate** [ɪntɚ'mijdɪət] *adj.* & *n.* intermédiaire. || **interment** [ɪn'tɚmənt] *n.* enterrement *m*, sépulture *f*. || **interminable** [ɪn'tɚmɪnəbl̩] *adj.* interminable, sans fin. || **intermingle** [ɪntɚ'mɪŋgl̩] *v. tr.* & *intr.* (s')entremêler; se mêler à.
intermission [ɪntɚ'mɪ|ʃən] *n.* relâche *f*, temps *m* d'arrêt; [temporary] interruption *f*; [Théâtre, &c.] entr'acte *m*; intermède *m*; [Sports] pause *f*; [school] récréation *f*. || **intermittent** [-tənt] *adj.* intermittent.
intern [ɪn'tɚn] *v. tr.* interner. || **intern**(e)

['ɪntɚn] *n.* [Med.] interne *m.* || **internal** [ɪn'tɚnḷ] *adj.* [inner] interne: [domestic] intérieur.

international [ˌɪntɚ'næʃənḷ] *adj.* international: ~ *law*, droit *m*/international, des gens/. || *n.* [Hist., Polit.] Internationale *f.* || **-ly** [-lɪ] *adv.* internationalement.

internment [ɪn'tɚnmənt] *n.* internement *m*: *internment camp*, camp *m* de concentration.

interpolate [ɪn'tɚpəˌlejt] *v. tr.* interpoler.

interpose [ˌɪntɚ'powz] *v. tr. & intr.* (s')interposer (*in*, dans; *between*, entre).

interpret [ɪn'tɚpɹət] *v. tr.* interpréter, expliquer (un rêve, &c.), interpréter (un rôle, un discours). || **interpretation** [ɪntɚpɹə'tejʃən] *n.* interprétation *f*; explication *f.* || **interpreter** [ɪn'tɚpɹətɚ] *n.* interprète *m*/*f*: *simultaneous* ~ , interprète de conférence.

interrogate [ɪn'tɛɚəˌgejt] *v. tr.* interroger. || **interrogation** [ɪnˌtɛɚə'gejʃən] *n.* interrogation *f*; [of witness] interrogatoire *m.* || **interrogative** [ɪntɚ'ɑgətɪv] *adj.* interrogatif; [look] interrogateur.

interrupt [ɪntɚ'ʌp|t] *v. tr. & intr.* interrompre; [break in] déranger (qqun dans son travail). || **interruption** [-ʃən] *n.* interruption *f*: *without* ~ , d'arrache-pied.

intersect [ɪntɚ'sɛkt] *v. tr.* (entre)couper. || *v. intr.* s'entrecouper, se croiser. || **intersection** ['ɪntɚˌsɛkʃən] *n.* intersection *f*, [roads] croisement *m*, carrefour *m*; [highway] *cloverleaf* ~ , saut *m* de mouton.

intersperse [ɪntɚ'spɚs] *v. tr.* [mix] entremêler, parsemer (qqch. de, *sth. with*).

interval ['ɪntɚvḷ] *n.* [space, time, music] intervalle *m*: *at intervals*, par intervalles; *at long intervals*, de loin en loin; [weather] *bright intervals*, éclaircies *f.* || **intervene** [ˌɪntɚ|'vijn] *v. intr.* venir, s'interposer/ entre; [time] s'écouler; [Fig.] intervenir (dans un conflit). || **intervening** [-'vijnɪŋ] *adj.* (qui joue le rôle d')intermédiaire. || **intervention** [-'vɛnʃən] *n.* intervention *f.*

interview ['ɪntɚˌvjuw] *n.* [radio, TV, &c.] interview *m*/*f*; [contact] entrevue *f*, [inquiry] interrogatoire *m.* || *v. tr.* interviewer (qqun); avoir un entretien avec (qqun).

intestine [ɪn'tɛstɪn] *n.* intestin *m*, [Fam.] boyau *m.* || *adj.* intérieur, intestin.

intimacy ['ɪntɪmə|sɪ] *n.* intimité *f.* || **intimate** [-t] *adj.* intime, lié; [knowledge] de première main. || *v. tr.* ['ɪntəˌmejt] donner à entendre (qqch. à qqun, *sth. to s.o.*); [notify] intimer (à qqun de faire . . . , *to*). || **intimately** ['ɪntəmətlɪ] *adv.* intimement. || **intimation** [ɪntɪ'mejʃən] *n.* annonce *f*; suggestion *f*; signification *f*; indication *f.*

intimidate [ɪn'tɪmɪˌdejt] *v. tr.* intimider. || **intimidation** [ɪntɪmɪ'dejʃən] *n.* intimidation *f.*

into ['ɪntuw; before cons. 'ɪntə] *prep.* [s'emploie après les verbes de mouvement, q.v.] [use the same prep. as with a verb of rest; *à* becomes *dans*; cf. also under verb of motion] dans, en: *to*/*go, come*/ ~ *a house*, entrer dans une maison; *to go* ~ /*the school, the church*/, entrer dans/ l'école, l'église/; *to get* ~ /*bed, the bed*/, se mettre/au lit, dans le lit/; *to translate* ~ *French*, traduire en français.

intolerable [ɪn'tɑlɚ|əbḷ] *adj.* intolérable. || **intolerance** [-əns] *n.* intolérance *f.* || **intolerant** [-ənt] *adj.* intolérant, dogmatique.

intonation [ɪntə'nejʃən] *n.* intonation *f*; [Rel.] psalmodie *f*; [Mus.] justesse *f*; [Fig.] timbre *m.* || **intone** [ɪn'town] *v. tr.* entonner (un air); [Rel.] psalmodier.

intoxicant [ɪn'tɑksɪ|kənt] [×] *n.* boisson *f* alcoolique. || **intoxicate** [-kejt] *v. tr.* enivrer (de, *with*): *to get intoxicated*, s'enivrer. || **intoxication** [ɪnˌtɑksɪ'kejʃən] *n.* ivresse *f*; [Med.] intoxication *f*, empoisonnement *m.*

intractable [ɪn'tɹæktəbḷ] *adj.* [Pers.] intraitable; [pupil] insoumis.

intransitive [ɪn'tɹænsɪtɪv] *adj.* [Gram.] intransitif.

intrench [ɪn'tɹɛntʃ] *v. intr.* se retrancher; [Fig.] *to* ~ *on*, empiéter sur. || **intrenchment** [-mənt] *n.* retranchement *m.*

intrepid [ɪn'tɹɛpɪd] *adj.* intrépide, brave.

intricacy ['ɪntɹɪkə|sɪ] *n.* complexité *f*, [Fig.] dédale *m.* || **intricate** [-t] *adj.* compliqué; complexe; [Pej.] embrouillé.

intrigue ['ɪntɹijg] *n.* intrigue *f*; [plot] complot *m.* || *v. tr.* [ɪn'tɹijg] intriguer; comploter. || **intriguer** [-ɚ] *n.* intrigant *m.* || **intriguing** [-ɪŋ] *adj.* intrigant, qui intrigue; attirant (par sa nouveauté).

intrinsic [ɪn'tɹɪnsɪk] *adj.* intrinsèque.

introduce [ɪntɹə|'djuws] *v. tr.* [bring in] introduire . . . (dans), faire/entrer, pénétrer/ . . . (dans); [make known] présenter (*to*, à); [bring up] amener (une question). || **introduction** [-'dʌkʃən] *n.* introduction *f*, [book] avant-propos *m*; [person] présentation *f*; lettre *f* de recommandation; [Sch.] manuel *m* élémentaire. || **introductory** [ɪntɹə'dʌktɚɪ] *adj.* [notion] préliminaire; [text] liminaire; [speech, letter] d'introduction, de présentation.

introspection [ˌɪntɹə'spɛk|ʃən] *n.* introspection *f.* || **introspective** [-tɪv] *adj.* introspectif.

introvert ['ɪntɹəˌvɚt] *adj. & n.* introverti, -e.

intrude [ɪn'tɹuwd] *v. intr.* se mêler à, s'immiscer dans; [Fig.] se mêler de (ce qui ne nous regarde pas); *to ~ on s.o.*, déranger qqun: *I hope I'm not intruding!*, J'espère que je ne vous dérange pas! || **intruder** [-ɚ] *n.* intrus *m*, -e *f*; importun *m.* || **intruding** [-ɪŋ] *adj.* intrus, -e, importun, -e. || **intrusion** [ɪn'tɹuw|ʒən] *n.* intrusion *f*; dérangement *m.* || **intrusive** [-sɪv] cf. INTRUDING.

intuition [ɪnˌtuw'ɪʃən] *n.* intuition *f.* || **intuitive** [ɪn'tjuwɪtɪv] *adj.* intuitif.

inundate ['ɪnʌnˌdejt] *v. tr.* inonder (*with*, de). || **inundation** [ɪnˌʌn'dejʃən] *n.* inondation *f*, débordement *m.*

inure [ɪn'juwɚ] *v. tr.* habituer, endurcir, aguerrir (*to*, à).

invade [ɪn'vejd] *v. tr.* envahir; [encroach upon] outrepasser ses droits. || **invader** [-ɚ] *n.* envahisseur *m.*

invalid [ɪn'vælɪd] *adj.* non valide. || *adj. & n.* ['ɪnvəlɪd] invalide (*m*), malade (*m*). || *v. tr.* [Mil.]: *to ~ (out)*, réformer. || **invalidate** [ɪn'vælɪdejt] *v. tr.* invalider.

invaluable [ɪn'væljəbl̩] *adj.* inestimable, sans prix.

invariable [ɪn'væɚɪəbl̩] *adj.* invariable.

invasion [ɪn'vejʒən] *n.* invasion *f*; [encroachment] envahissement.

invective [ɪn'vɛktɪv] *n.* invectives *fpl.*

inveigle [ɪn'vijgl̩] *v. tr.* séduire, leurrer; enjôler.

invent [ɪn'vɛn|t] *v. tr.* inventer, [make up] forger. || **invention** [-ʃən] *n.* invention *f.* || **inventive** [ɪn'vɛntɪv] *adj.* inventif, ingénieux. || **inventor** *n.* inventeur *m.* || **inventory** ['ɪnvənˌtɔɚɪ] *n.* [Com.] inventaire *m*; stock *m.*

inverse [ɪn'vɚ|s] *adj.* inverse. *n.* contraire *m.* || **inversion** [ɪn'vɚʒən] *n.* interversion *f*; [Gram., Math.] inversion *f*; [Mus.] renversement *m.* || **invert** [-t] *v. tr.* inverser, intervertir: *inverted commas*, guillemets *mpl.*

invest [ɪn'vɛst] *v. tr.* [money] placer, investir (des capitaux dans); [authority] investir (*with*, de); [besiege] investir, assiéger.

investigate [-ɪˌgejt] *v. tr.* [police] faire une enquête sur (un crime, &c.); [cause] rechercher (qqch.); [matter] examiner (qqch.). || **investigation** [ɪnˌvɛstɪ'gejʃən] *n.* enquête *f* (de police, &c.), recherches *fpl* (scientifiques, &c.); [question, case] examen *m*; [philosophy] investigation *f.* || **investigator** [ɪn'vɛstɪˌgejtɚ] *n.* investigat|eur, -rice.

investment [ɪn'vɛst|mənt] *n.* [money] placement *m*, mise *f* (de fonds): [Mil.] investissement *m.* || **investor** [-ɚ] *n.* actionnaire *m.*

inveterate [ɪn'vɛtɚət] *adj.* invétéré.

invidious [ɪn'vɪdɪəs] *adj.* odieux. || **invidiousness** [-nəs] *n.* odieux *m.*

invigilate [ɪn'vɪʤɪlˌejt] *v. tr.* surveiller (un examen, des candidats à un examen). || **invigilator** [-ɚ] *n.* surveillant *m*, -e *f.*

invigorate [ɪn'vɪgɚˌejt] *v. tr.* fortifier.

invincible [ɪn'vɪnsɪbl̩] *adj.* invincible.

invisible [ɪn'vɪzɪbl̩] *adj.* invisible; caché, secret.

invitation [ɪnvɪ'tejʃən] *n.* invitation *f.* || **invite** [ɪn'vajt] *v. tr.* inviter (*to*, à); [attract] donner envie de. || **inviting** [-ɪŋ] *adj.* invitant, accueillant. [food] appétissant, tentant. || **invitingly** [-ɪŋlɪ] *adv.* d'une manière/attrayante, appétissante/.

invocation [ˌɪnvə'kejʃən] *n.* invocation *f.*

invoice ['ɪnvojs] *n.* [Com.] facture *f.*

invoke [ɪn'vowk] *v. tr.* invoquer.

involuntarily [ɪn'vɑləntɛɚɪ|lɪ] *adv.* involontairement. || **involuntary** *adj.* involontaire, machinal.

involve [ɪn'vɑlv] *v. tr.* [also Fig.] envelopper; [imply] impliquer, comporter, entraîner: *It would ~ leaving your position*, Cela vous obligerait à quitter votre emploi; *to get involved in*, se laisser entraîner dans, être mêlé à; *the persons involved*, les personnes en cause; *Don't be so ~ !* → Soyez précis!; *an ~ story*, une histoire embrouillée. || **involved** [ɪn'vɑlvd] *adj.* **1.** impliqué, compromis (*in*, dans), mêlé (*in*, à). **2.** [style] confus, embarrassé.

invulnerable [ɪn'vʌlnɚəbl̩] *adj.* invulnérable.

inward ['ɪnwɚd] *adj.* intérieur; [face, &c.] interne. || **-ly** [-lɪ] *adv.* en dedans; intérieurement. || **inwards** [-z] *adv.* intérieurement, vers l'intérieur, en dedans.

iodin(e) ['ajəˌdajn] *n.* iode *f.*

I.O.U. [ˌajˌow'juw] [= I owe you] *n.* reconnaissance *f* de dette.

I.Q. ['aj'kjuw] *n.* [= intelligence quotient] quotient *m* intellectuel.

Iran [ɪ'ɹæn] *n.* l'Iran *m*: *in, to/ ~*, en Iran. || **Iranian** [ɪ'ɹejnɪən] *adj. & n.* iranien, -ne.

Iraq [ɪ'ɹæk] *n.* l'Irak *m*: *in, to/ ~*, en Irak. || **Iraqi** [-ɪ] *adj. & n.* irakien, -ne, d'Irak.

irascible [ɪɚ'æsəbl̩] *adj.* irascible.

irate [aj'ɹejt] *adj.* irrité, courroucé.

ire ['ajɚ] *n.* courroux *m.*

Ireland ['ajɚlənd] *n.* l'Irlande *f*: *in, to/ ~*, en Irlande; *Northern ~*, l'Irlande du Nord.

iridescent [ˌijɚ'dɛsənt] *adj.* irisé, iridescent.

Irish ['ajɚɪʃ] *adj.* [nationality] irlandais, [thing, produce] d'Irlande. || *n.* **1.** [language] l'irlandais. **2.** *the ~*, [nationality] les Irlandais *mpl.* || **Irish|man, -woman** [-mən] [-ˌwumən] *n.* Irlandais *m*, -e *f.*

irk [ɚk] *v. tr.* [annoy] fâcher, peiner; [disgust] répugner (à); [trouble] ennuyer. ‖ **irksome** [ˈɚksəm] *adj.* [person] ennuyeux, [task] fastidieux.

iron [ajɚn] *n.* fer *m*: [electric] *flat* ~, fer *m* à repasser; *pig* ~, gueuse *f*; ~ *-clad*, [chest, &c.] blindé, cuirassé; [Fig.] [contract] infrangible; *scrap* ~, ferraille *f*; *wrought* ~, fer forgé. ‖ *attrib.* ~ *curtain*, rideau *m* de fer; ~ *ore*, minerai *m* de fer; ~ *-work*, ferrure *f*. ‖ *v. tr.* repasser (un pantalon): *to* ~ *out* (*sth.*), faire disparaître (un pli) au fer chaud; [Fig.] aplanir (une difficulté), résoudre (un problème).

ironical [ajˈɹɑnɪkl̩] *adj.* ironique.

ironing [ˈajənɪŋ] *n.* repassage *m*: ~ *board*, planche *f* à repasser.

irony [ˈajɹənɪ] *n.* ironie *f*.

Iroquois [ˈijɚəˌkwɑ] *n.* & *adj.* [American Indian] Iroquois, -se.

irradiate [ɪˈɹejdɪˌejt] *v. tr.* irradier. ‖ *v. intr.* s'irradier. ‖ **irradiation** [ɪˌɹejdɪˈejʃən] *n.* irradiation *f*.

irrational [ɪˈɹæʃənl̩] *adj.* déraisonnable; [Math.] irrationnel.

irreconcilable [ɪˌɹɛkənˈsajləbl̩] *adj.* irréconciliable, incompatible (*with*, avec).

irredeemable [ɪɚɹəˈdijməbl̩] *adj.* irrémédiable, irréparable; [Fin., bonds, &c.] non/remboursable, rachetable/. ‖ **irredeemably** [-ɪ] *adv.* d'une façon/irrémédiable, irréparable/.

irregular [ɪˈɹɛgjələ˞] *adj.* [shape; conduct; procedure] irrégulier. ‖ **irregularity** [ɪˌɹɛgjəˈlæɚiti] *n.* irrégularité *f*.

irrelevant [ɪˈɹɛləvənt] *adj.* hors de propos; [detail, information] inapplicable, non pertinent (*to*, à).

irreligious [ɪɹəˈlɪʤəs] *adj.* irréligieux.

irremediable [ɪɚəˈmijdɪəbl̩] *adj.* irrémédiable. ‖ **irremovable** [ɪɚəˈmuwvəbl̩] *adj.* inamovible. ‖ **irreparable** [ɪˈɹɛpɚəbl̩] *adj.* irréparable. ‖ **irreplaceable** [ɪɚəˈplejsəbl̩] *adj.* irremplaçable. ‖ **irreproachable** [ɪɚəˈpɹowʧəbl̩] *adj.* irréprochable. ‖ **irresolute** [ɪˈɹɛzəˌluwt] *adj.* irrésolu. ‖ **irrespective of** [ɪɚəˈspɛktɪv əv] *adv.* sans tenir compte de, sans égard pour. ‖ **irresponsible** [ɪɚəˈspɑnsɪbl̩] *adj.* irresponsable. ‖ **irretrievable** [ɪɚəˈtɹijvəbl̩] *adj.* [Fig.] irréparable. ‖ **irreverent** [ɪˈɹɛvɚənt] *adj.* irrévérent. ‖ **irreversible** [ɪɚəˈvɚsɪbl̩] *adj.* ‖ **irrevocable** [ɪˈɹɛvəkəbl̩] *adj.* irrévocable.

irrigate [ˈɪɚəˌgejt] *v. tr.* irriguer. ‖ **irrigation** [ˌijɚˈgejʃən] *n.* irrigation *f*.

irritable [ˈɪɚɪt|əbl̩] *adj.* irritable. ‖ **irritant** [ˈɪɹətənt] *adj.* & *n.* irritant (*m*). ‖ **irritate** [-ˌejt] *v. tr.* irriter. ‖ **irritating** [ɪɹəˈtejtɪŋ] *adj.* irritant. ‖ **irritation** [ˌɪɚɪˈtejʃən] *n.* irritation *f*.

is[1] [ɪz] cf. BE: *as is*, tel quel. ‖ **is.**[2], **Is.** [= Island(s), Isle(s)].

-ish [-ɪʃ] [☞ suffixe dénotant une caractérisation; s'emploie régulièrement dans *Turkish* (Turc), *whitish* (blanchâtre, blanc sale); et pour indiquer une approximation *seven-ish* (vers les 7 heures)].

Islam [ˈɪsləm] *n.* [Rel.] l'Islam *m*. ‖ **Islamic** [ɪsˈlæmɪk] *adj.* [creed, customs; studies] islamique. ‖ **Islamism** [ˈɪsləmˌɪsm] *n.* l'islamisme *m*, l'Islam *m*.

island [ˈajlənd] *n.* île *f*: *safety* ~, refuge *m* (pour piétons); *small* ~, îlot *m*. ‖ **islander** [-ɚ] *n.* insulaire *m*: [Fr.] îlien *m*.

isle [ajl] *n.* île *f*: *the British Isles*, les îles Britanniques. ‖ **islet** [-ət] *n.* îlot *m*.

isn't [ɪzn̩t] = is not cf. BE: ~ *it?*, N'est-ce pas?.

isolate [ˈajsəˌlejt] *v. tr.* isoler; faire le vide (autour de). ‖ **isolation** [ˌajsəˈlejʃən] *n.* isolement *m*.

isosceles [ajˈsɑsəˌlɪz] *adj.* [triangle] isocèle.

Israel [ˈɪzɹɪəl] *n.* Israel [☞ No definite article]. ‖ **Israeli, -s** [ɪzˈɹejlɪ(s)] *n.* Israélien *m*, -ne *f*. ‖ **Israelite** [ˈɪzɹɪəˌlajt] *n.* Israélite *m* & *f*.

issue [ɪʃuw] *n.* **1.** [way out] issue *f*, sortie *f* [also Fig.]; embouchure *f* (d'un cours d'eau). **2.** [outcome] issue *f*, résultat *m*, dénouement *m*. **3.** [coming out] épanchement *m*, écoulement *m* (d'un liquide); [Fin.] émission *f* (de papier-monnaie); lancement *m* d'obligations, &c.; [book, &c.] parution *f*, publication *f*; délivrance *f* (d'un passeport); [Mil.] distribution *f* (d'équipement). **4.** [output] édition *f* (d'un livre); numéro *m* (d'un périodique). **5.** [problem] question *f*: *to take* ~ (*with s.o.*), être en désaccord (avec qqun); *at* ~, contesté; dont il s'agit; en jeu. ‖ *v. intr.* sortir, provenir (de, *from*). ‖ *v. tr.* [Fin.] émettre (des obligations, &c.), mettre (qqch.) en circulation; publier (un numéro de revue, journal); distribuer, donner (des ordres, &c.).

isthmus [ˈɪsməs] *n.* isthme *m*.

it [ɪt] *pron. pers.* [☞ S'emploie pour représenter les noms de choses, de bêtes, tout ce dont le sexe n'est pas évident, et aussi comme mot passe-partout représentant des idées vagues.] [☞ There is no neuter in Fr.: use m. or f. pronouns to represent a noun in Fr. Exceptions and other cases are indicated below.] A. [precise reference] **1.** [subject] il *m*, elle *f*: *It has disappeared*, Il [= livre *m*], Elle [= clef *f*] a disparu; *Here* ~ *is*, Le, La/voici. **2.**

[dir. obj.] le *m*, la *f*; l' *m/f* [before vowel or mute h]: *I see* ~, Je/le [= livre *m*], la [= clef *f*]/vois; *I saw* ~, Je l'ai vu(e). **3.** [indir. obj.] lui *m/f*: *I gave* ~ *some milk*, Je lui ai donné du lait. **4.** [after a prep. ☞ The pron. referring to a thing is usual. not expressed after a prep. in Fr.: preps. of precise position are rendered by the pron. adv. *y*, although three have spec. forms: dedans, dessus, dessous; *about, from, of, &c.*, translated by Fr. *de* become *en*; some, such as *down, through, up*, are best rendered by the accompanying verb; the others are translated by the prep. minus the pron. and any linking *de*]: *Look in(to)* ~, Regardez-y, Regardez dedans; *Think of* ~, Pensez-y; *What do you think of* ~ *?*, Qu'en pensez-vous?; *I know a lot about* ~, J'en sais beaucoup; *He walked across* ~, Il l'a traversé (à pied); *He went/behind, round, under/* ~, Il est allé/derrière, autour, en dessous/; *for, with, without/* ~, pour, avec, sans/ cela. **B.** [general references] **1.** [preceding idea] ce: *It* [= the whole scene] *is beautiful*, C'est beau; *It is easy to do*, C'est facile à faire. **2.** [a following idea] ce; il; cela; no translation: *Who is* ~*?, It is my father*, Qui est-ce? C'est mon père; *It is easy to do that*, Il est facile de faire cela; *It surprises me to learn that . . .*, Cela m'étonne d'apprendre que . . . ; *I find it hard to believe that . . .*, Je trouve difficile de croire que . . . ; *It is said that*, On dit que . . . ; *It appears that . . .*, Il paraît que. . . . **3.** [impers.] il: *It is raining*, Il pleut; *It's a nice day*, Il fait beau; *It's late*, Il est tard; *It is 3 o'clock*, Il est 3 heures; *It is the 3rd today*, C'est aujourd'hui le trois. **4.** [emphatic construction] ce + être + / qui, que, dont, &c./: *It was he who told me*, C'est lui qui me l'a dit; *It was then I knew*, C'est alors que j'ai su. **5.** [special uses] *He thinks he is* ~, Il se croit sorti de la cuisse de Jupiter; *This is* ~, Nous y/sommes, voilà/; *That is really* ~, C'est vraiment qqch.; *That's it!*, C'est ça!; [tag] *Who's* ~ *?*, A qui est-ce?; *The strange thing about* ~ *is that . . .*, Ce qu'il y a d'étrange/là-dedans, dans l'affaire/, c'est que . . .

Italian [ɪ'tæljən] *adj.* italien; [produce, &c.] d'Italie. || *n.* **1.** [nationality] Italien *m*, -ne *f.* **2.** [Ling.] l'italien *m.* || **italics** [ɪ'tælɪks] *n.pl.* italiques *mpl.* || **italicize** [ɪ'tælɪˌsajz] *v. tr.* mettre, imprimer (un texte, des lettres) en italiques. || **Italy** ['ɪtəlɪ] *n.* (l')Italie *f*: *in, to* ~, en Italie.

itch [ɪtʃ] *n.* démangeaison *f.* || *v. intr.* démanger.

it'd ['ɪtəd] = **1.** it would, cf. WOULD. **2.** it had, cf. BE.

item ['ajtm] *n.* article *m*; point *m* (d'une énumération); [= piece of news] nouvelle *f.*

itinerary [aj'tɪnəˌɛərɪ] *n.* itinéraire *m.*

it'll [ɪtl] [=it will]. cf. WILL.

its [ɪtz] *adj. poss. neutre* [☞ L'adj. anglais s'accorde en genre avec le possesseur; voir aussi la note à IT] son *m*, sa *f*, ses *m/fpl.* [☞ The Fr. adj. agrees in gender and number with the noun it modifies, and NOT the possessor; *sa* is replaced by *son* before a following word beginning with a vowel or mute *h*: *son frère, sa sœur, son autre sœur, son histoire, ses parents*]: *The dog hurt* ~ *paw*, Le chien s'est fait mal à la patte; *We saw the boat, but couldn't make out* ~ *nationality*, Nous aperçûmes le navire, mais ne pûmes en déterminer la nationalité; *Its smoke was visible on the horizon*, La fumée en était visible à l'horizon. || *pron. poss. neutre* [☞ Le pron. anglais s'accorde en genre avec le possesseur; voir aussi la note à IT] le sien *m*, la sienne *f*, les siens *mpl*, les siennes *fpl* [☞ The Fr. adj. agrees in gender and number with the noun it replaces, and NOT the possessor]. || **itself** [ɪt'self] *pron.* [voir note à IT]. **1.** [reinforcing a noun] lui-même *m*, elle-même *f*; même: [☞ The Fr. pron. takes its gender from the noun it reinforces]; *The child did it* ~, L'enfant l'a fait/lui-même, tout seul/; *She was kindness* ~, Elle était la bonté même. **2.** [reflexive obj.] se: *The cat washed* ~, Le chat s'est lavé. **3.** [after a prep.] lui(-même) *m*, elle(-même) *f*, [voir **1.**]; [impers. construction] soi: *The dog kept it for* ~, Le chien l'a gardé pour lui (-même); *Love is in* ~ *. . .*, L'amour est en soi . . . ; *by* ~, à part; *by, of/* ~, tout(e) seul(e).

I've [ajv] = I have, cf. TO HAVE: [Br.] *I've got* [= I have] J'ai . . .

ivory ['ajvərɪ] *n.* ivoire *f.* || *adj.* d'ivoire, en ivoire.

ivy ['ajvɪ] *n.* lierre *m*: *poison* ~, sumac *m* /vénéneux, toxique/, © herbe *f* à la puce.

J, j [ʤej] [dixième lettre de l'alphabet] J, j cf. A.

jab [ʤæb] *v. tr.* piquer, donner un coup sec à. || *n.* coup *m* (de canif, de coude); [poke] coup sec.

jabber ['ʤæbər] *n.* [chattering] papotage *m*, jabotage *m*; [mumbling] bredouillage *m*, baragouinage *m.* || *v. tr.* & *intr.* papoter, jaboter; [mumble] bredouiller, baragouiner.

jack [ʤæk] *n.* [nom familier donné aux hommes, particulièrement aux marins] type *m*, [sailor] marin *m*; [cards] valet *m*; [auto] cric *m*; [flag] pavillon *m*: [Fig.] *~ of all trades*, factotum *m*, Maître *m* Jacques; *~ fish*, brochet *m* (commun) cf. PIKE. || *v. tr.* [auto] soulever (avec un cric); *to ~ up (prices, &c.)*, hausser brusquement.

jackal ['ʤækḷ] *n.* chacal *m.*

jackass ['ʤækˌæs] *n.* âne *m*; [Fig.] sot *m*, imbécile *m.*

jacket ['ʤækət] *n.* [man's] veston *m*; [sailor's] vareuse *f*; [Mil.] tunique *f*, blouson *m*; *leather jackets*, © vestes *fpl.* de cuir, [Fr.] blousons *mpl.* noirs; [book] liseuse *f*, jaquette *f*; *life ~*, ceinture *f* de sauvetage.

jack-knife, *pl.* **-ves** ['ʤækˌnaj|f, -vz] *n.* couteau *m* de poche. || **jack-pot** [-ˌpɑt] *n.*: [Fam.] *to hit the ~*, gagner le gros lot, décrocher la timbale.

jag [ʤæg] *n.* pointe *f*, dent *f.* || **jagged** [-əd] *adj.* dentelé, ébréché.

jaguar ['ʤægˌwər] *n.* jaguar *m.*

jail [ʤejl] *n.* prison *f*: */to, in/ ~*, en prison; *to break (out of) ~*, s'évader (de prison); *~ bird*, gibier *m* de potence. || *v. tr.* emprisonner. || **jailer, jailor** [-ər] *n.* gardien *m* de prison.

jalopy [ʤə'lɑpɪ] *n.* vieux clou *m.*

jam¹ [ʤæm] *n.* [people] foule *f*; [traffic] embouteillage *m*: *ice ~*, embâcle *m*; *log ~*, © prise *f* de billes; cf. JAMMING: [Loc. Fam.] *to be in a ~*, être dans le pétrin. || *v. tr.* & *intr.* [-mm-] presser (plusieurs choses l'une contre l'autre); [parts of mach.] (se) coincer, (se) bloquer; [radio signals] brouiller.

jam² *n.* confiture *f*: *strawberry ~*, confiture/de, aux/fraises; *~ jar*, pot *m* à confitures.

Jamaica [ʤə'mejkə] *n.* la Jamaïque: *to, in/~*, à la Jamaïque.

jamboree ['ʤæmbərɪ] *n.* [scouts] jamboree *m.*

James [ʤejmz] *n.* = Jacques *m.*

jamming ['ʤæmɪŋ] *n.* [parts of mach.] enrayage *m*, bloquage *m*; [radio signals] brouillage *m.*

Ja(n). [= JANUARY].

Jane [ʤejn] *n.* = Jeanne *f.*

jangle [ʤæŋgḷ] *n.* bruit *m* discordant; [quarrel] criaillerie(s) *f(pl)*; prise *f* de bec. || *v. tr.* & *intr.* faire un bruit de ferraille; [quarrel] criailler.

janitor ['ʤænɪtər] © *n.* concierge *m/f*; gardien, -ne *m/f*, cf. CARETAKER.

January ['ʤænjuwˌɛərɪ] *n.* janvier *m*, cf. APRIL.

Japan [ʤə'pæn] *n.* le Japon: */to, in/ ~*, au Japon. || **japan** *n.* laque *f*, vernis *m.* || *v. tr.* [-nn-] laquer, vernir. || **Japanese** [ˌʤæpə'nijz] *adj.* japonais. || *n.* Japonais.

jar¹ [ʤɑər] *n.* [pot] © jarre *f*, pot *m*; [wine] cruche *f*; [Pharm.] bocal *m.*

jar² *n.* secousse *f*; son *m* discordant; [Fig.] querelle *f.* || *v. intr.* [-rr-] s'entrechoquer; [sound] grincer (désagréablement): [Fig.] *to ~ on (s.o.'s nerves)*, taper sur les nerfs de qqun. || *v. tr.* choquer, heurter. || **jarring** [-ɪŋ] *adj.* discordant; désagréable.

jargon ['ʤɑərgən] *n.* jargon *m.*

jasmin(e) ['ʤæzmən], *also* **jessamine** ['ʤɛsəmɪn] *n.* jasmin *m.*

jaundice ['ʤɔndəs] *n.* jaunisse *f.* || **jaundiced** [-t] *adj.* [Fig.] prévenu (contre qqun), ayant des préjugés *m* défavorables: *with a jaundiced eye*, d'un œil désapprobateur.

jaunt [ʤɔnt] *n.* excursion *f*, [Fam.] balade *f.* || **jauntily** [-ɪlɪ] *adv.* d'une manière/enjouée, désinvolte/. || **jauntiness** [-ɪnəs] *n.* désinvolture *f.* || **jaunty** [-ɪ] *adj.* vif, enjoué; [smart] chic, gracieux.

Javel (water) [ʤə'vɛlˌwɔtər] *n.* eau *f* de Javel.

jaw [ʤɔ] *n.* mâchoire *f*; [animal] gueule *f*: *~ bone*, mâchoire *f*, maxillaire *m*; [Fam. gossip] caquet *m.* || *v. tr.* [Fam.] © achaler, [Fr.] gronder, grogner. || *v. intr.* bavarder.

jay [ʤej] *n.* geai *m.*

jaywalk [-ˌwɔk] *v. intr.* s'aventurer sur la chaussée, traverser étourdiment la rue. || **jaywalker** [-ˌwɔkər] *n.* piéton *m*/distrait, imprudent/.

jazz [ʤæz] *n.* le jazz: *~ band*, orchestre *m* de jazz.

Je. [= June].

jealous ['ʤɛləs] *adj.* jaloux. || **jealously** [-lɪ] *adv.* jalousement, avec jalousie. || **jealousy** [-ɪ] *n.* jalousie *f.*

Jean [ʤijn] *n.* = Jeanne *f.*

jeans [ʤijnz] *n.*: *blue ~*, pantalon *m* (de coutil).

jeep [ʤijp] *n.* [Auto.] jeep *f*, © *m.*

jeer [ʤijər] *n.* raillerie *f.* || *v. intr.*: *to ~ at*, se moquer de (qqun, qqch.), railler (qqun).

Jehovah [ʤə'howvə] *n.* [Rel.] Jahvé; [sect] *~'s Witnesses,* Témoins *mpl* de Jéhovah.

jell [ʤɛl] *v. intr.* prendre, se solidifier; [Fig.] réussir.

jelly ['ʤɛlɪ] *n.* gelée *f.* || *v. tr.* mettre en gelée; [Fig.] fixer. || *v. intr.* prendre en gelée; se congeler; [Fig.] se fixer. || **jelly-fish** [-ˌfɪʃ] *n.* méduse *f*; [Fig.] *~ policy,* politique *f* de demi-mesures.

jeopardize ['ʤɛpɚˌ|dajz] *v. tr.* mettre en /danger, péril/; exposer, risquer; compromettre. || **jeopardy** [-dɪ] *n.* danger *m,* risque *m*, péril *m.*

jerk [ʤɚk] *n.* saccade *f,* secousse *f*: *by jerks,* par saccades; [Arg.] nigaud *m*; *Jerkville,* Fouilly-les-Oies. || *v. tr.* donner une secousse, tirer brusquement. || **jerky** [-ɪ] brusque, saccadé.

jersey ['ʤɚzɪ] *n.* maillot *m*, [lady's] jersey *m.*

Jerusalem [ʤɚ'uwsələm] *n.* Jérusalem *f*: *~ artichoke,* topinambour *m.*

jessamine. cf. JASMIN.

jest [ʤɛst] *n.* plaisanterie *f* : *in ~* , en plaisantant. || *v. intr.* plaisanter (*with,* de qqch., avec qqun; *at,* sur); [deride] railler (*at,* -). || **jester** [-ɚ] *n.* bouffon *m.*

Jesus (Christ) ['ʤijzəs (ˌkrajst)] *n.* Jésus (Christ) *m.*

jet[1] [ʤɛt] *n.* [water, gas] jet *m* (d'eau, de gaz); moteur *m* à réaction, turbo-réacteur *m*; *~ airplane,* avion *m* à réaction, réacté *m* ; *~ pilot,* pilote *m*/de réacté, de chasse/; *~ liner,* © aérobus *m*, avion/à réaction.

jet[2] *n. & adj.* (de) jais *m*: *~ -black,* noir de jais.

jetsam ['ʤɛtsəm] *n.* marchandise *f* jetée à la mer (pour délester un bateau); [Fig.] de rebut: *flotsam and ~* , épaves *fpl*; choses *fpl* de flot et de mer.

jettison ['ʤɛtɪsən] *v. tr.* délester (un navire, avion); jeter (une cargaison) à la mer; [Fig.] jeter du lest.

jetty[1] ['ʤɛtɪ] *n.* [pier] appontement *m*; [breakwater] jetée *f.*

jetty[2] *adj.* noir/comme du, de/jais. cf. JET.

Jew [ʤuw] *n.* Juif *m*; [Rel.] Israélite *mf*; cf. HARP.

jewel ['ʤuwəl] *n.* †joyau *m*, bijou *m*; *jewels,* bijoux *m*, pierreries *fpl*; [Horlogerie] rubis *m*; *~ case,* écrin *m.* || **jeweller** [-ɚ] *n.* bijoutier *m*, joaillier *m.* || **jewelry, jewellery** [-ɹɪ] *n.* [*coll.*] bijoux *mpl*; joaillerie *f*, bijouterie *f.*

Jewess ['ʤuw/ɛs] *n.* Juive *f.* || **Jewish** [-ɪʃ] *adj.* juif *m*, juive *f*; [Rel.] judaïque.

jiffy [ʤɪfɪ] *n.*: *in a ~* , en un clin d'œil.

jig [ʤɪg] *n.* **1.** danse *f*, gigue *f*: *The ~ is up,* [Fam.] C'est tout cuit. **2.** [Tech.] crible *m*; jig *m.*

jig-saw ['ʤɪgˌsɔ] *n.* scie *f* à découper: *~ puzzle,* © casse-tête *m* (chinois), [Fr.] puzzle *m.*

jilt [ʤɪlt] *v. tr.* [Fam.] lâcher (un amoureux, &c.).

jingle [ʤɪngl̩] *n.* [bells] tintement *m*, grelot *m*; [Com.] rimette *f*, réclame *f* chantée. || *v. intr.* tinter, sonner.

jitters ['ʤɪtɚ|z] *n.pl.* [Fam.] frousse *f*: *to get the ~* , avoir la frousse; *to give the ~* , flanquer la frousse (*to,* à). || **jittery** [-ɪ] *adj.* [Fam.] froussard.

Joan [ʤown] *n.* = Jeanne *f.*

job [ʤɑb] *n.* **1.** [Fam. for *position*] travail *m*, emploi *m*, †place *f*: *a soft ~* , sinécure *f*, [Fam.] fromage *m*: *to be out of a ~* , → chômer, être en chômage; *to be on the ~* , être attentif, sérieux. **2.** [piece of work] tâche *f*, besogne *f*: *by the ~* , (travail) à la pièce; *odd- ~ man,* homme *m* à tout faire; *to do odd jobs,* bricoler; *to make a/good, bad/ ~ of . . . ,* /bien, mal/ faire;/bien, mal/travailler; [Fig.] *a/good, bad/ ~* , une/bonne, mauvaise/affaire; *It's a good ~ that . . . ,* Il est bon que . . . [+ subjunc.]; *I had a ~ finishing in time,* J'ai eu du mal à finir à temps.

jobber ['ʤɑbɚ] *n.* **1.** [Com.] grossiste *m.* **2.** [Fam.] tripoteur *m.* **3.** tâcheron *m.*

jockey ['ʤɑkɪ] *n.* jockey *m*: *disc ~* , présentateur *m* (de disques).

jocular ['ʤɑkjələ] *adj.* plaisant, facétieux.

jog [ʤɔg] *n.* secousse *f*, saccade *f*; coup *m* de coude; [carriage] cahot *m*; [horse] petit trot; [Fam., routine] train-train *m. inv.* || *v. tr. & intr.* [-gg-] donner des /secousses, saccades/; [carriage] cahoter; [horse, *on, along*] aller au petit trot; donner un coup de coude; [routine] aller/tout doucement, son petit bonhomme de chemin/.

John [ʤɑn] *n.* = Jean: *~ Bull* [= personnification légendaire de l'Anglais]; *~ Doe* [nom passe-partout. cf. © Jos. La Trémouille; [Fr.] Durand, Dupont].

join [ʤɔjn] *v. tr.* **1.** [put together] joindre (deux choses); unir (des personnes); (re)joindre, (ré)unir, (qqch. à qqch.): *to ~ hands,* joindre les mains. **2.** [connect] relier: *The bridge joins the suburbs to the city,* Le pont relie la banlieue à la ville. **3.** [become a member]: entrer dans (une société); adhérer à, devenir membre d', (un club); s'associer à (un mouvement): *to ~ the army,* s'engager (dans l'armée). **4.** [unite with] s'unir, se joindre, à: *The stream joins the river*, Le ruisseau se jette dans la rivière; *My wife joins me in . . .* , Ma femme se joint à moi pour . . . **5.** [meet] rejoindre: *I'll ~ you later*, Je vous rejoins dans un moment; *to ~ one's ship*, rejoindre son navire. || *v. intr.* se (re)joindre, s'unir: *The two rivers ~ here*, Les deux rivières se/rejoignent, rencontrent/ici; *to ~ in (a song)*,/participer, se joindre/au chœur; *to ~ up*, s'engager (dans l'armée).

joint[1] [ʤojnt] *n.* [Tech.] joint *m*, raccord *m*; [finger, &c.] articulation *f*, jointure *f*; [meat] rôti *m* (de bœuf): *out of ~*, disloqué.

joint[2] *adj.* réuni, commun; co-: *our ~ efforts*, nos communs efforts; *~ owner*, co-propriétaire *m*.

joint[3] *n.* [Fam.] boîte *f*, bistrot *m*: *gambling ~*, tripot *m*, © barbotte *f*; [house, place] baraque *f*.

jointed [-əd] *adj.* articulé. cf. JOINT[1]. || **jointly** [-lɪ] *adv.* conjointement, de concert.

joke [ʤowk] *n.* bon mot *m*, plaisanterie *f*, [Fam.] blague *f*; [practical] attrape *f*: *off-colour ~*, © farce *f* plate; [Fr.] plaisanterie *f* déplacée; *That's no ~*, → Il n'y a pas de quoi rire. || *v. intr.* plaisanter (*at*, de): *joking apart*, blague à part; *You're joking!*, Vous voulez rire! || **joker** [-ɚ] [person] (mauvais) plaisant *m*, farceur *m*; [Law] échappatoire *f*; [cards] joker *m*; [Arg.] type *m*, individu *m*. || **jokingly** [-ɪŋlɪ] *adv.* en plaisantant, pour rire.

jolly [ˈʤɑlɪ] *adj.* jovial, enjoué: *~ fellow*, (gai) luron *m*. || *adv.* [esp. Br., Fam.] rudement; fameusement, joliment.

jolt [ʤowlt] *n.* secousse *f*; choc *m*; [road] cahot *m*. || *v. tr.* secouer; cahoter. || *v. intr.* [of a cart] cahoter.

Jordan [ˈʤɔɚdən] *n.* la Jordanie: *in, to*/~, en Jordanie; [river] le Jourdain.

jostle [ˈʤɑsl̩] *n.* cohue *f*, bousculade *f*. || *v. tr.* coudoyer, bousculer (qqun).

jot [ʤɑt] *v. tr.* [-tt-] prendre note de: *to ~ down*, griffonner (qqch.), prendre rapidement note (de). || **jottings** [ˈʤɑtɪŋz] *n.pl.* notes *fpl.* rapides.

journal [ˈʤɚnl̩] *n.* [daily record, register] journal *m*, cf. DIARY; [newspaper] journal; [periodical] revue *f*, périodique *m*. || **journalese** [-ˌijz] *n.* sabir *m*, charabia *m*/(de journal). || **journalism** [-ɪsm] *n.* journalisme *m*. || **journalist** [-ɪst] *n.* journaliste *m/f*.

journey [ˈʤɚnɪ] *n.* voyage *m*; [distance] trajet *m*: *to go on a ~*,/partir en, faire un/voyage. || *v. intr.* voyager: *to ~ through a country*, parcourir un pays.

journey|man, *pl.* **-men** [-mən] *n.* compagnon *m*: *~ carpenter*, compagnon charpentier.

jovial [ˈʤowvɪl] *adj.* jovial, joyeux.

joy [ʤoj] *n.* joie *f*:/*with, for*/ ~, de joie; *the joys of*..., les charmes *mpl.* de...; *I take great ~ in* [+ . . .], J'ai l'immense plaisir de [+ inf.]. || **joyful** [-fl̩] *adj.* joyeux. || **joyfully** [-fl̩ɪ] *adv.* joyeusement. || **joyless** [-ləs] *adj.* triste. || **joyous** [-əs] *adj.* joyeux.

J.P. [ˈʤejˈpij] [= Justice of the Peace] juge *m* de paix.

Jr., jr. [= Junior].

jubilant [ˈʤuwbɪ|lənt] *adj.* → dans la jubilation, triomphant: *to be ~*, → jubiler. || **jubilee** [-ˌlij] *n.* jubilé *m*.

Judea [ˌʤuwˈdijə] *n.* la Judée: *to, in ~* en Judée.

judge [ʤʌʤ] *n.* [Law] juge *m*; [Fig.] arbitre *m*, juge *m*: *to be a good ~ of*, → s'y connaître en . . . ; *You be the ~*, → A vous d'en juger; *the judges*, le jury (d'un concours agricole, &c.). || *v. tr.* juger; [Fig.] décider, apprécier (les mérites de . . .): *judging by . . .* , à en juger par . . . || **judgment** [-mənt] *n.* [Law] jugement *m*, arrêt *m*: *Judgment day*, le jugement dernier; [Fig.] opinion *f*; [faculty] jugement *m*: *to pass ~ on*, porter un jugement sur.

judicial [ˌʤuwˈdɪ|ʃəl] *adj.* [proceeding] judiciaire; [enforced by court] juridique. || **judicious** [-ʃəs] *adj.* [sensible] judicieux.

judo [ˈʤuwˌdow] *n.* [Sport.] judo *m* [forme particulière du jiu-jitsu].

jug [ʤʌg] *n.* [metal] broc *m*, [pot] cruche *f*, pot *m*; [Arg. = JAIL] violon *m*.

juggle [ˈʤʌgl̩] *n.* jonglerie *f*, tour *m* de passe-passe. || *v. tr. & intr.* jongler; ~ (*away*), escamoter. || **juggler** [ˈʤʌglɚ] *n.* jongleur *m*.

Jugo-slavia [ˌjuwgowˈslævɪə] cf. YUGOSLAVIA.

juice [ʤuws] *n.* jus *m*; [sap] suc *m*: *tomato ~*, jus de tomate; [Arg. = gas] essence *f*; [Electr.] [Sl.] jus *m*. || **juiciness** [-ɪnəs] *n.* succulence *f*. || **juicy** [-ɪ] *adj.* juteux, succulent; [Fig.] savoureux.

jukebox [ˈʤuwˌbɑks] *n.* tourne-disques *m. invar.* automatique.

Jul. [= JULY.] || **July** [ʤəˈlaj] *n.* juillet *m*. cf. APRIL.

Julia [ˈʤuwljə] *n.* = Julie *f*.

Juliet [ˌʤuwlɪˈɛt] *n.* = Juliette *f*.

jumble [ˈʤʌmbl̩] *n.* mélange *m*, embrouillamini *m.* || *v. tr.* jeter pêle-mêle, embrouiller.

jump [ʤʌmp] *v. tr. & intr.* sauter, bondir (*over*, par-dessus): [Fig.] *Prices jumped*, Les prix ont fait un bond; [Rail.] *to ~ the track*, dérailler; *to ~ at*, saisir l'occasion de . . . ; *to ~/down, out of/*, sauter à bas de; *~ in!*, Montez vite!; [Fam.] *to ~ on*, tomber sur qqun; *to ~ on a horse, bicycle*, enfourcher un cheval, son vélo; *to ~ (over) a passage*, sauter un passage; *to ~ to conclusions*, en juger sans réfléchir. || **jump** *n.* saut *m*; [jerk] bond *m*: [Sport] *high ~*, saut en hauteur; *long ~*, saut en longueur; *ski ~*, saut à skis. || **jumper** [-ɚ] *n.* **1.** sauteur *m.* **2.** [jacket] jumper *m.* || **jumping-rope** [-ɪŋ-ˌɹowp] *n.* corde *f* à sauter.

jumpy [ˈʤʌmpɪ] *adj.* nerveux.

Jun. [= JUNE, †JUNIOR.]

Junc. [= JUNCTION.]

junction [ˈʤʌŋkʃən] *n.* jonction *f*, point *m* de rencontre; [Tech.] raccord *m*; [rivers] confluent *m*; [Rail.] embranchement *m.* || **juncture** [ˈʤʌŋkʧɚ] *n.* [joint] jointure *f*; [crisis] conjoncture *f*: *at this ~*, en cette occasion, dans cette situation.

June [ʤuwn] *n.* juin *m.* cf. APRIL.

jungle [ˈʤʌngl̩] *n.* jungle *f.*

junior [ˈʤuwnjɚ] *abbr.* **Jr.** *adj.* jeune; cadet *m*, cadette *f*: *Smith Jr.*, le jeune Smith, [Com.] Smith fils; *~ partner*, second (associé), associé *m* en second; *~ commander*, officier *m* subalterne; [Univ.] *He is in his ~ year*, Il est en troisième année. || *n.* cadet *m*; [Univ.] étudiant *m* (-e *f*) de troisième année: *He is 5 years my ~*, Il est plus jeune que moi de cinq ans.

juniper [ˈʤuwnɪpɚ] *n.* genévrier *m*; [berry] genièvre *m.*

junk [ʤʌŋk] *n.* matériaux *mpl* de rebut; [Fam.] camelote *f*, bric à brac *m.*

junket [ˈʤʌnkət] *n.* [Cul.] lait *m* caillé; [trip] excursion *f*; [US, Fam.] voyage *m* officiel/payé par le gouvernement, [Fam.] aux frais de la princesse/.

junkman [-ˌmæn] *n.* chiffonnier *m.*

jurisdiction [ˌʤuwɚɪsˈdɪkʃən] *n.* [Law] juridiction *f*; [Fig.] ressort *m*, compétence *f*: *within one's ~*, du ressort de. || **juror** [ˈʤuwɚɚ] *n.* juré *m.* || **jury** [ˈʤuwɚɪ] *n.* jury *m*: *to be on the ~*, faire partie du jury.

just [ʤʌst] *adj.* juste; [lawful] équitable; [true] exact. || *adv.* **1.** [exactly] juste, exactement: *~ in time*, juste à temps: *~ one pound*, exactement une livre, une livre juste; [barely] *It ~ missed the target*, → Il a manqué la cible de peu; *only ~*, à peine. **2.** [time] justement, à l'instant [or use VENIR DE]: *~ now*, à l'instant (même); *~ then*, juste alors; *~ as . . .*, à l'instant où . . . ; *He has ~ gone*, → Il vient (justement) de sortir; *I was ~ writing to you*, J'étais justement en train de vous écrire; *I was ~ leaving*, J'étais sur le point de partir; [book] *Just out*, Vient de paraître. **3.** [= ONLY] ne . . . que, seulement: *He is ~ a boy*, Ce n'est encore qu'un enfant; *~ a line to tell you . . .*, Un mot seulement pour vous annoncer . . . ; *Just listen!*, Écoutez donc (un peu)!; *Just take the white of one egg, &c.*,/Prenez simplement, On n'a qu'à prendre/un blanc d'œuf, &c. **4.** [Loc.] *I'd ~ as soon . . .*, Cela m'est égal de . . . ; *~ right*, parfait. || **justice** [ˈʤʌstɪs] *n.* **1.** bien-fondé *m*, justice *f*: *High Court of ~*, Cour *f* suprême: [Fig.] *to do ~ to*, rendre justice à, [to a good dinner] faire honneur à; *the ~ of a cause*, le bien-fondé d'une cause. **2.** [person] juge *m*: *Mr. Justice Smith*, le juge Smith; *~ of the (US) Supreme Court*, juge de la Cour suprême (des États-Unis); *~ of the peace*, juge *m* de paix. || **justifiable** [ˌʤʌstɪˈfajəbl̩] *adj.* justifiable. || **justifiably** [-ɪ] *adv.* d'une façon justifiable, à juste titre. || **justification** [ˌʤʌstɪfɪˈkejʃən] *n.* justification *f* || **justify** [ˈʤʌstɪˌfaj] *v. tr.* justifier, autoriser: *to be justified in thinking that . . .*, être fondé à croire que . . . ; *to ~ o.s.*, se justifier. || **justly** [ˈʤʌstlɪ] *adv.* justement; à juste titre; à bon droit.

jut [ʤʌt] *v. intr.* [-tt-]: *to ~ out*, faire saillie.

juvenile [ˈʤuwvəˌnajl] *adj.* [youthful] jeune, juvénile: [×] [person] d'enfants, de (la) jeunesse: *~ court*, tribunal *m* pour enfants. || *n.* jeune *m/f*, garçonnet *m*, fillette *f.*

Jy. [= JULY].

K, k [kej] *n.* K, k.

Kan(s) [= KANSAS]. || **Kansas** *n.* le Kansas: *to, in/* ~ , dans le Kansas.

kangaroo [ˌkæŋgə'uw] *n.* kangourou *m.*

Kashmir [ˌkæʃ'mijə] *n.* le Cachemire: *to, in/* ~ , au Cachemire.

kayak[1] ['kajæk] *n.* [Eskimo boat] kayak *m*: *in a* ~ , en kayak.

kayak[2] *n.* © gasparot *m,* faux hareng *m.* cf. ALEWIFE.

K.C.[1] ['kej'sij] [= King's Counsel], C.R. = [Conseiller *m.* du Roi] || **K.C.**[2] [= Knights of Columbus], C.C. [= Chevaliers *m* de Colomb].

keel [kijl] *n.* quille *f.* || *v. tr.*: *to* ~ *over,* faire chavirer. || *v. intr.*: *to* ~ *over,* chavirer; [Fig., pers.] s'écrouler, s'évanouir.

keen [kijn] *adj.* [sharp] aiguisé, affilé; [Fig., things] [mind] perçant, [satire] mordant, [interest, competition] vif; [mind] pénétrant, perspicace; [Pers.] ardent, enthousiaste: *to be* ~*/about, on/* . . . , désirer ardemment. || **keenly** [-lɪ] *adv.* vivement; [harshly] rudement. || **keenness** [-nəs] *n.* **1.** tranchant *m* (d'une arme). **2.** [Fig.] [eagerness] ardeur *f*; rigueur *f* (du froid); [Pej.] amertume *f,* acrimonie *f*; subtilité *f* (de l'air); acuité *f.* (visuelle); finesse *f* (de l'ouie).

keep [kijp] **kept, kept** [kɛpt] *v. tr.* **1.** [retain] garder, conserver: *You may* ~ *it,* Vous pouvez le garder; *to* ~ *a secret,* garder un secret; *to* ~ *sth. to o.s.,* garder qqch. pour soi, taire qqch.; ~ *him in sight,* → Ne le perdez pas de vue; ~ *it in mind,* Pensez-y, Ne l'oubliez pas. **2.** [+ adj. or p.p.] tenir: *to* ~ *sth. clean,* tenir qqch. propre; *to* ~ *sth./cool, warm/,* tenir qqch./au frais, au chaud/; *to* ~ *s.o. interested,* maintenir l'intérêt de qqun; *to* ~ *s.o. quiet,* faire taire qqun; *to* ~ *s.o. busy,* occuper qqun [cf. also under adjs. and verbs]. **3.** [+ pr.p.] faire; laisser: *to* ~ *s.o. waiting,* faire attendre qqun; *to* ~ *the motor running,* laisser marcher le moteur; *to* ~ *s.o. guessing,* laisser qqun deviner. **4.** [detain] retenir: *I hope I'm not keeping you,* J'espère que je ne vous retiens pas; *to* ~ *s.o. in jail,* tenir qqun en prison. **5.** [prevent] empêcher, retenir: *to* ~ *s.o. from doing sth.,* empêcher, retenir/qqun de faire qqch. **6.** [observe] tenir (sa parole, une promesse); observer (une loi): *to* ~ *Lent,* observer le Carême; *to* ~ *Christmas,* fêter la Noël; *to* ~ *an appointment,* ne pas manquer à un rendez-vous. **7.** [look after] avoir, élever (des animaux); avoir à sa charge, entretenir (des parents); tenir (un établissement): *to* ~ *house,* tenir maison; *to* ~ (the) books, tenir la comptabilité; *to* ~ *o.s.,* gagner sa vie. **8.** [protect] garder, protéger, préserver (de). || *v. intr.* **1.** rester; continuer à, → continuellement, constamment, sans cesse: ~ *near the house,* Restez près de la maison; *How are you keeping?,* Comment va votre santé?; ~ *working,* Continuez à travailler; *He keeps interrupting me,* Il m'interrompt constamment; ~ *going!,* Continuez (à marcher, à faire cela, &c.). **2.** se conserver, se garder: *Canned food keeps well,* Les conserves se gardent longtemps; *It'll* ~ , → Ça peut attendre, Ça ne perdra rien pour attendre. **3.** tenir; garder; s'en tenir (à): *to* ~ *to/the road, the right/,* tenir/la route, la droite/; *to* ~ *to one's room,* garder la chambre; *to* ~ *to facts,* s'en tenir aux faits. || **keep** *n.* entretien *m*: *to earn one's* ~ , gagner/sa nourriture, son entretien/; *for keeps,* pour de bon, à (tout) jamais; [Fig.] *to play for keeps,* jouer le tout pour le tout.

keep away [-ə'wej] *v. tr. & intr.* (s')éloigner, (se) tenir éloigné: ~ *from heat,* → tenir au frais; ~ *(from me)!,* → Ne m'approchez pas! || **keep back** [-'bæk] *v. intr.* se retenir, rester en arrière: *Keep back!,* → N'avancez pas! || *v. tr.* retenir, retarder. || **keep down** [-'dawn] *v. intr.* rester à l'abri; [prices] rester bas. || **keep** (*s.o., sth.*) **down** *v. tr.* empêcher de monter, &c.; [head] baisser la tête; [voice] baisser, ne pas élever (la voix); [feelings] modérer (ses sentiments); [prices] maintenir bas. || **keep in** [-'ɪn] *v. intr.* ne pas sortir, garder la chambre; rester bien (avec qqun). || *v. tr.* tenir (qqun) enfermé; [secret] cacher (qqch.); entretenir (un feu); contenir (sa colère); [Sch.] mettre, garder (un élève) en retenue. || **keep off** [-'ɔf] *v. intr.* s'éloigner, ne pas approcher. || *v. tr.* éloigner qqun; détourner, empêcher/qqun (*from,* de + inf.); (se) protéger (de qqch.); éviter (un sujet). || **keep on** [-'ɑn] *v. intr.* continuer (sans cesse) [+ *ing,* à, de/ + inf.]: *keep straight on,* Continuez tout droit. || *v. tr.* garder (un employé): ~ *your hat on,* → Restez couvert. || **keep out** [-'awt] *v. intr.* se tenir éloigné, ne pas se mêler/de: *You* ~ *of this!,* Mêlez-vous de ce qui vous regarde!; *Keep out!,* Défense d'entrer! || *v. tr.* tenir (qqun) éloigné, empêcher d'entrer; (se) protéger (de qqch.). || **keep up** [-'ʌp] *v. intr.* veiller, [with] aller de pair avec: *I can't ~ with you,* Je ne peux pas vous suivre [also Fig.]. || *v. tr.* [spirits] ne pas se laisser abattre; [fire] entretenir; [attitude] continuer, conserver la même attitude; soutenir, ne pas laisser tomber; maintenir (en bon état): *Keep it up!,* → Ne flanchez pas!, Continuez! || **keeper** [-ɚ] *n.* [prison] gardien *m*; [guard] garde *m,* surveillant *m*; [museum] conservateur *m*; [Fig.] dépositaire (d'un secret, &c.). || **keeping** [-ɪŋ] **1.** garde *f,* surveillance *f. in safe ~,* sous bonne garde. **2.** [observance] célébration *f*; [Loc.] *in ~ with,* en rapport avec. || **keepsake** [-ˌsejk] *n.* souvenir *m,* gage *m* d'amitié.

keg [kɛg] *n.* petit fût *m.*

ken [kɛn] *n.* vue *f,* savoir *m*: *It's beyond my ~,* Cela dépasse mon entendement.

kennel ['kɛnl̩] *n.* chenil *m*; [pack] meute *f.*

Kentucky [kən'tʌkɪ] le Kentucky: *to, in/ ~,* dans le Kentucky.

kept [kɛpt] cf. KEEP.

kernel ['kɚnl̩] *n.* fruit *m*; [seed] graine *f*; [stone] noyau *m*; [nut] amande *f*; [Fig.] partie *f* centrale, cœur *m* (d'un problème).

kerosene ['kɛɚəˌsijn] pétrole *m* (lampant) kérosène *f,* © huile *f* de charbon.

ketchup ['kɛtʃəp] *n.* cf. CATSUP.

kettle ['kɛtl̩] *n.* bouilloire *f,* © canard *m,* bombe *f*; [for cooking] chaudron *m*: [Loc.] *Here is a/pretty, nice/kettle of fish!,* C'est du propre!, Nous voilà propres!

key[1] [kij] **1.** clé *f* (also spelt *clef*); [piano, typewriter] touche *f*; [Mus.] ton *m*; [Tech.] cheville *f,* clavette *f*; [watch] remontoir *m*: *master ~,* passe-partout *m*; *under lock and ~,* sous clef. **2.** [Fig.] clé *f* (d'un problème), solution *f* (d'une énigme); livre *m* du maître; [map] légende *f*; [Com.] *a ~ position,* un poste-clef, une position stratégique; *~ man,* cheville *f* ouvrière, poste *m* de commande. || **key** *v. tr. to ~ up (a piano),* accorder (un piano); [Fig.] *to be (all) keyed up,* être/surexcité, tendu, nerveux/.

key[2] [Geog. = a low island, esp. in place-names, e.g. *Key West, Fla.*] caye *f.*

keyboard [-ˌbɔɚd] *n.* clavier *m* (de piano, &c.). || **keyhole** [-ˌhowl] *n.* trou *m* de la serrure. || **keynote** [-ˌnowt] *n.* [Mus.] tonique *f*; [Fig.] idée *f* dominante. || **keystone** [-ˌstown] *n.* clef *f* de voûte. || **key-word** ['kijˌwɚd] *n.* mot clé *m.*

khaki ['kɑɚkɪ] *n. & adj. inv.* kaki.

kibitz ['kɪbətz] [Sl.] *v. intr.* se mêler de ce qui ne vous regarde pas, faire la mouche du coche. || **kibitzer** *n.* casse-pieds *m*; © écornifleur *m.*

kick [kɪk] *n.* coup *m* de pied; [horse] ruade *f*; [gun] recul *m*; [Sl.] effet *m*; plainte *f.* || *v. tr.* donner un coup de pied à qqch., qqun; [Fam. & ©] botter (un ballon); *to ~ at,* regimber, se rebiffer/contre; [Fam.] *to kick the bucket,* casser sa pipe; [Fam.] *to ~ one's heels,* poireauter. || *v. intr.* donner des coups de pied; [horse] ruer; [gun] reculer. || **kick back** [-'bæk] *v.* [Fam.] **1.** [motor] donner des retours en arrière. **2.** rendre (un objet emprunté); restituer (un objet volé); rembourser (un emprunt) à son propriétaire. **3.** rembourser une partie des/honoraires, cachets, droits, &c./ || **kick in** [-'ɪn] *v. tr.* enfoncer à coups de pied; [Argot.] mourir; casser sa pipe; payer un dû. || **kick off** [-ˌɔf] *v. intr.* **1.** [football] donner le coup d'envoi. **2.** [Argot.] casser sa pipe. || **kick up** *v. tr.* [Argot.] provoquer; commencer. lancer.

kid [kɪd] *n.* chevreau *m,* chevrette *f*: *~ gloves,* gants *mpl* (en peau) de chevreau; [Fam.] mioche *m,* gosse *m,* enfant *m.* || *v. tr.* [Fam.] taquiner. || *v. intr.* [Fam.] blaguer, faire marcher: *no kidding?,* sans blague?

kidnap [ˌnæp] *v. tr.* [-pp-] enlever, kidnapper. || **kidnapper** [-ˌnæpɚ] *n.* ravisseur *m.* || **kidnapping** [-ˌnæpɪŋ] *n.* enlèvement *m,* rapt *m.*

kidney ['kɪdnɪ] *n.* [man] rein *m*; [animals] rognon *m*: *~ bean,* haricot *m*; [Fig.] humeur *f,* disposition *f*; sorte *f*: *of his ~,* de son acabit.

kill [kɪl] *v. tr.* **1.** tuer; [abattoir] abattre; [weeds] détruire: *He killed himself,* Il s'est tué (volontairement); *He was killed,* Il s'est tué (accidentellement); [Fig.] éliminer. **2.** faire échouer (un projet); mettre son veto à (une proposition, un projet de loi, &c.). || **killer** [-ɚ] *n.* tueur *m,* assassin *m.* || **-killer** [in compounds] -icide: *insect, vermin/-killer,* insecticide *m.*

kiln [kɪl] *n.* four *m* à chaux.

kilogram(me) ['kɪləˌgɹæm] *n.* kilo-(gramme) *m* [= 2.2046 lbs. Note that the abbr. *kilo* is only used when referring to weight]. || **kilometre** [kɪ'lɑmətɚ] *n.* kilomètre *m* [= 3,280 ft.]. || **kilowatt** ['kɪləˌwɑt] *n.* kilowatt *m.*

kilter ['kɪltɚ] *also* **kelter** ['kɛltɚ] *n.* [Fam.] en bon état, en bonne santé: *out of ~* en mauvais état, détraqué.

kin [kɪn] *n.* parenté *f,* les parents *mpl.*:

of ~, apparenté; *next of* ~, le(s) plus proche(s) parent(s).

kind[1] [kajnd] *n.* **1.** espèce *f*, classe *f*: *the human* ~, le genre humain. **2.** sorte *f*, genre *m*: *of the* ~, de la sorte; *of a* ~, de même nature, semblable; *of a* ~ *to* . . ., de nature à . . . ; *sth. of the* ~, qqch./du genre, comme cela/; *nothing of the* ~, rien de semblable; *I'll do nothing of the* ~, Je n'en ferai rien. **3.** [Loc.] *difference in* ~, différence *f* spécifique; *payment in* ~, paiement *m* en nature; [Fig.] *to repay s.o. in* ~, payer qqun de la même monnaie. || **kind of** [-əv] *loc. adv.* [Fam.] plutôt, en quelque sorte: *I feel* ~ *tired*, Je me sens plutôt fatigué; *It's* ~ *a nice thing to do*, C'est plutôt gentil à faire; *He* ~ *bent over*, Il s'est en quelque sorte penché en avant; *in a* ~ *a way*, en quelque façon, d'une certaine façon.

kind[2] *adj.* bon, aimable; [doing good] bienveillant, charitable: *to be* ~ *to s.o.*, être bon pour qqun; *It is* ~ *of you to* . . ., C'est aimable à vous de . . . ; *Be so* ~ *as to* . . ., Veuillez (avoir l'amabilité de) . . . ; *Kind(est) regards*, Amitiés *fpl.*

kindergarten ['kɪndɚ,gɑɚtn̩] *n.* jardin *m* /d'enfants, © de l'enfance/; école *f* maternelle.

kindle ['kɪndl̩] *v. tr.* **1.** allumer, enflammer [also Fig.] || *v. intr.* s'enflammer. || **kindling wood** [-ɪŋ,wʊd] *n.* petit bois; bois *m* d'allumage.

kindly ['kajnd|lɪ] *adj.* doux, bienveillant. cf. KIND.[2] || *adv.* avec/bonté, bienveillance/; aimablement, gracieusement: *Kindly come this way*, Veuillez (vous donner la peine de) me suivre; ~ *sit down*, Asseyez-vous, je vous en prie; *Will you* ~ . . ., Voulez-vous avoir/la bonté, l'obligeance/de, Je vous prie de bien vouloir . . . ; *If you would* ~ . . ., Si vous vouliez bien . . . ; *to take sth.* ~, prendre qqch. en bonne part; *to take* ~ *to s.o.*, prendre qqun en amitié. || **kindness** [-nəs] *n.* bonté *f* (pour qqun), obligeance *f*; [favour] service *m*: *Will you have the* ~ *to* . . . ?, Veuillez, Voulez-vous/ avoir/la bonté, l'obligeance/ de . . . ?; *to do s.o. a* ~, rendre service à qqun.

kindred ['kɪndɹəd] *n.* famille *f*, parenté *f*; [Fig.] ressemblance *f*. || *adj.* apparenté; allié, de même nature.

† **kine** + [kajn] *pl.* of cow.

king [kɪŋ] *n.* **1.** roi *m*: *H.M. the King*, S.M. le Roi; *King's Counsel*, Conseiller *m* du Roi; *King's Bench*, © Cour *f* du Banc du Roi; [Rel.] *the three Kings*, les (trois Rois) Mages *mpl.* **2.** [Fig.] magnat *m* (de la finance), roi (du pétrole, &c.). **3.** [chess, cards] roi *m*; [checkers] dame *f*. || *attrib. adj.*: ~ *-size*, géant, grand format. || **kingdom** [-dəm] *n.* royaume *m*; [Fig.] domaine *m*; champ *m*; [nature] règne *m*: *the animal* ~, le règne animal.

kingfisher [-,fɪʃɚ] *n.* martin-pêcheur *m.*

kingly [-lɪ] *adj. & adv.* royal, noble. || *adv.* de, en/roi.

kink [kɪŋk] *n.* [string] nœud *m*; [wire] faux pli; [Fig.] point *m* faible. || *v. tr. & intr.* (se) nouer, (se) tortiller; faire une coque à (un cordage).

kinkajou [-ə,ʤuw] *n.* © carcajou *m*; [Fr.] kinkajou *m.*

kinky [-ɪ] *adj.* noué; [hair] crépu.

kin(s)folk ['kin(z),fowk] *n.* les parents, © la parenté. || **kinship** [-,ʃɪp] *n.* parenté *f*; [Fig.] ressemblance *f*. || **kins|man'** [-mən] **-woman** [-,wʊmən] *n.* parent(e) *m/f.*

kiss [kɪs] *n.* baiser *m*; embrassade *f*; [Fig.] caresse *f*, frôlement *m*. || *v. tr.* **1.** donner un baiser (à qqun); cf. EMBRASSER; *to* ~ *each other*, s'embrasser; *to* ~ *s.o.'s cheek*, embrasser qqun sur la joue; *to* ~ *s.o.'s hand*, baiser la main de qqun. **2.** [Fig.] effleurer, frôler; caresser.

kit [kɪt] *n.* **1.** [soldier] équipement *m*, fourniment *m*. **2.** trousse *f* (de voyage). **3.** [tools] nécessaire *m* de réparations. **4.** [Fam.] (*the whole*) ~ *and caboodle*, le tout, toute la boutique. || **kitbag** [-,bæg] [Mil.] musette *f.*

kitchen ['kɪtʃən] *n.* cuisine *f*: ~ *garden*, jardin *m* potager; ~ *ware*, ustensiles *mpl* de cuisine. || **kitchenette** [-,ɛt] *n.* cuisinette *f.*

kite [kajt] *n.* cerf-volant *m*; [bird] milan *m.*

kitten ['kɪtn̩] *n.* petit(e) chat(te) *m(f)*, chaton *m.*

kleptomania [,klɛptow'mejnɪ|ə] *n.* kleptomanie *f*. || **kleptomaniac** [-,æk] *n.* kleptomane *m/f.*

Klondike ['klɑn,dajk] *n.* le Klondike: *to, in*/~, au Klondike.

knack [næk] **1.** dextérité *f*, facilité *f* (à faire qqch.). **2.** truc *m*, habitude *f* (de faire qqch.).

knapsack ['næp,sæk] *n.* [soldiers, scouts] sac *m* à dos, havresac *m.*

knave [nejv] *n.* coquin *m*, canaille *f*; [cards] valet *m.*

knead [nijd] *v. tr.* pétrir (la pâte); [Fig.] masser.

knee [nij] *n.* genou *m*; [Tech.] coude *m*, joint *m* articulé: *on one's knees*, à genoux; *to get* (*down*) *on one's knees*, se mettre à genoux, s'agenouiller. || **kneecap** [-,kæp] *n.*

rotule *f.* || **kneel** [-l] **knelt, knelt** [nɛlt] *v. intr.*: *to ~ (down)*, s'agenouiller, se mettre à genoux; *kneeling*, à genoux.

knell [nɛl] *n.* [bell] glas *m*; [Fig.] mauvais présage. || *v. tr.* sonner le glas.

knelt [nɛlt] cf. KNEEL.

knew [njuw] cf. KNOW.

knick(k)nack [ˈnɪkˌnæk] *n.* [Fam.] babiole *f*, colifichet *m*.

knife [najf] *pl.* **knives** [najvz] *n.* couteau *m*; [pocket] canif *m*; [Tech.] couteau *m*; [blade] lame *f*; [surgeon] bistouri *m*. || *v. tr.* donner un coup de couteau, poignarder.

knight [najt] *n.* chevalier *m*; [chess] cavalier *m*; [Fig.] chevalier servant. || *v. tr.* décorer (qqun); créer (qqun) chevalier. || **knighthood** [-hud] *n.* chevalerie *f*.

knit [nɪt] *v. tr.* [-tt-] tricoter; joindre; [Fig.] lier: *to ~ one's brows*, froncer les sourcils. || *v. intr.* tricoter; [bones] se (res)souder. || **knitting** [-ɪŋ] *n.* tricot *m*: *~ needle*, aiguille *f* à tricoter.

knives cf. KNIFE.

knob [nɑb] [door]/bouton *m*, poignée *f*/ de porte, de tiroir; [radio] bouton; [bump] bosse *f*.

knock [nɑk] *n.* **1.** coup *m*; heurt *m*; choc *m*: *There was a ~ at the door*, On frappa à la porte; *~, ~!*, toc, toc!, pan, pan!; *He got a ~ on the head*, Il a reçu un coup sur la tête. **2.** [Mec.] cognement *m* du moteur. || **knock** *v. tr.* **1.** frapper, donner un coup à; heurter, cogner: *to ~ one's head/on, against/sth.*, se heurter/se cogner/ la tête contre qqch. **2.** faire tomber: *He knocked it out of my hand*, Il l'a fait/ tomber, sauter/de ma main. **3.** [Fam.] dénigrer. || *v. intr.* frapper; [bump into] se heurter, se cogner (contre); [motor] cogner: *to ~/on, at/the door*, frapper à la porte; *His knees knocked (together)*, Ses genoux s'entrechoquaient. || **knock about** [-əˈbawt] *v. tr.* bousculer, maltraiter. || *v. intr.* parcourir le monde; flâner. || **knock down** [-ˈdawn] *v. tr.* renverser (d'un coup de poing, d'un mouvement brusque); démolir (un bâtiment); [take apart] démonter; baisser (un prix), faire baisser le prix (à qqun). || **knock in** [-ˈɪn] *v. tr.* enfoncer (un clou, une porte). || **knock off** [-ˈɔf] *v. tr.* faire/ sauter, tomber; expédier (une besogne); faire rapidement; cesser (le travail): *to knock sth. off (the price)*, rabattre qqch. du prix. || *v. intr.* finir; cesser (le travail), faire la pause. || **knock out** [-ˈɑwt] *v. tr.* faire sortir (d'un coup de marteau, &c.); secouer (une pipe); assommer (qqun), [boxing] mettre (qqun) knock-out, knockouter (qqun): [Fam.] *to knock o.s. out . . . -ing*, s'esquinter à . . . || **knock over** [-ˈowvɚ] *v. tr.* renverser. || **knock together** [-təˈgɛðɚ] *v. tr.* frapper (des choses) l'une contre l'autre; faire à la hâte. || *v. intr.* s'entrechoquer. || **knocker** [-ɚ] *n.* [Pers.] frappeur *m*; [door] marteau *m*.

knoll [nowl] *n.* (petite) colline *f* arrondie, mamelon *m*.

knot [nɑt] *n.* nœud *m* (de ruban); [in wood] [Naut.] nœud: *to/tie, untie/a ~*, faire, défaire/un nœud. || *v. tr.* [-tt-] nouer; faire un nœud, des nœuds; [tangle] emmêler, embrouiller. || **knotty** [-ɪ] *adj.* noueux; [Fig.] difficile: *a ~ problem*, un problème épineux.

know [now] **knew** [njuw] **known** [nown] *v. intr.* **1.** savoir, être au courant: *Now I ~*, Maintenant je/sais, suis au courant/; *As you ~*, Comme vous (le) savez; *He has already left, you ~*, Il est déjà parti, vous savez; *I don't ~*, Je ne sais pas, Je l'ignore; *As far as I ~*, Autant que je sache; *I wouldn't ~*, Je ne saurais dire; *Not that I ~ (of)*, Pas que je sache; *I didn't ~ /of, about/that*, Je ne savais pas cela, Je n'étais pas au courant; *Let me ~ when you are ready*, /Faites-moi savoir, Dites-moi/quand vous serez prêt(e). || *v. tr.* **1.** [be acquainted with] connaître (qqun, qqch.): *to ~ a subject*, connaître un sujet; × *to ~ a poem (by heart)*, savoir un poème (par cœur); *to ~ a language*, /connaître, savoir parler/ une langue: [Fig.] *He has never known hunger*, Il n'a jamais connu la faim; *to get to ~ s.o.*, en arriver à connaître qqun; *Do you ~ (of) a good mechanic?*, Connaissez-vous un bon mécanicien?; *to make sth. known*, faire connaître qqch. **2.** [to learn] savoir, apprendre (qqch.): *to ~ one's lesson (by heart)*, savoir sa leçon (par cœur); *I already ~ that*, Je le sais déjà; *He knew that we were there*, Il savait que nous étions là; *I don't ~ why (I did it)*, /Je ne sais pas, J'ignore/pourquoi (je l'ai fait); *I was glad to ~ that . . .*, J'ai été content d'apprendre que . . . ; *He let us ~ what he thought*, Il nous a fait savoir ce qu'il en pensait; *Do you ~ how to play bridge?*, Savez-vous jouer au bridge?; *I don't ~ how to begin*, Je ne sais pas comment m'y prendre. **3.** [to recognize] reconnaître: *I didn't ~ you in your new dress*, Je ne vous ai pas reconnue dans votre robe neuve. **4.** [distinguish] distinguer: *He didn't ~ one from the other*, Il ne pouvait pas les distinguer (l'un(e) de l'autre). **5.** [Loc.] *to ~ better*, être/assez, trop/ raisonnable pour faire qqch.; se garder bien de faire qqch.; *to ~ best*, être le meilleur juge. || **know** (now] *n.*: *to be in the ~*, être au courant, avoir le mot de l'affaire. || **know-how** [-ˌhaw] *n.* tour *m* de main; technique *f* (de fabrication); connaissances *fpl* techniques; [Fam.] truc *m*, © tour *m*. || **knowing** ['nowɪŋ] *adj.* **1.** avisé. **2.** bien informé. **3.** conscient. || **knowingly** [-ɪŋlɪ] *adv.* sciemment, à bon escient. || **knowledge** ['nɑlədʒ] *n. invar.* **1.** connaissance *f*; science *f*; connaissances *fpl*: *the advance of ~*, les progrès *mpl* de la science; *useful ~*, connaissances utiles; *to have a thorough ~ of*, posséder une connaissance approfondie de . . ., → connaître . . . à fond. **2.** nouvelle *f* (d'un événement, &c.); perception *f*, compréhension *f*: *to get ~ of sth.*, apprendre qqch.; *lack of ~*, ignorance *f*; *to the ~ of everyone, to everyone's ~*, au su de tout le monde; *without my ~*, à mon insu; *to* (*the best of*) *my ~*, à ma connaissance, autant que je sache; *not to my ~*, pas que je sache.

known [nown] cf. KNOW.

knuckle ['nʌkḷ] *n.* jointure *f* (du doigt); articulation *f*; [Culin.] jarret *m* (de veau, de porc, &c.). || *v. intr.*: *to ~ down*, se soumettre; [Fam.] s'y mettre sérieusement; *to ~ under*, se soumettre, baisser pavillon.

k.o., K.O. ['kejˌow] [= KNOCKOUT] *n.* knock-out *m.* || *v. tr.* mettre (qqun) K.O.

komatik [kow'mætɪk] © *n.* cométique *m.*

Koran [ˌkɔɚ'æn] *n.* [Rel.] Coran *m.*

Korea [ˌkɔɚ'ijə] *n.* la Corée: *North, South/ ~*, la Corée/du Nord, du Sud/; *to, in/ ~*, en Corée. || **Korean** [-n] *adj.* coréen: *the ~ war*, la guerre de Corée.

kosher ['kowʃɚ] *adj.* [Jewish] *cachère.

kowtow, kotow ['kaw'taw] *v. intr.* saluer (à la façon des Chinois); [Fig.] se prosterner, se montrer obséquieux.

kudos ['kjuwdɑz] *n.* gloire *f*, éloges *mpl*, flatteries *fpl.*

kw. [= KILOWATT].

Ky. [= KENTUCKY].

L

L, l [ɛl] *pl.* **L's, l's** [douzième lettre de l'alphabet] L *m*, l *m*; la lettre l.

La. [= LOUISIANA].

lab [kæb] *n.* labo *m.*

label ['lejbḷ] *n.* étiquette *f*; [Com.] marque *f.* || *v. tr.* [**-ll-**] étiqueter (un produit); [Rail.] enregistrer (des bagages pour X).

labor cf. LABOUR.

laboratory ['læbɚəˌtɔɚɪ] *n.* laboratoire *m.*

laborious [lə'bɔɚɪəs] *adj.* [hard-working] laborieux; [hard] pénible.

labour ['lejbɚ] *n.* travail *m*; [toil] labeur *m*, peine *f*; [Fam.] main-d'œuvre *f*, le monde ouvrier; [woman's] couches *fpl*, travail *m*: [Fig.] *~ of love*, travail *m* de Bénédictin; *~ relations*, relations industrielles; *the Labour Party*, le parti travailliste; © *Department of Labour*, Ministère *m* du Travail; *hard ~* [punishment] travaux *mpl* forcés; *organized ~*, les syndicats, le syndicalisme. || **labour** *v. intr.* travailler dur, [up a hill] gravir (une colline), [toil] peiner: *to ~ under a misconception*, être victime d'une erreur. || **labourer** [-ɚ] *n.* travailleur *m* (manuel); [Indus.] manœuvre *m.*

Labrador ['læbɹəˌdɔɚ] *n.* le Labrador: © *~ tea*, thé *m* du Labrador, bois *m* de savane.

labyrinth ['læbɚˌɪnθ] *n.* labyrinthe *m.*

lace [lejs] *n.* lacet *m* (de soulier); [shoe] cordon *m*; dentelle *f*; [uniform] broderies *fpl.* || *v. tr.* lacer (ses souliers), entrelacer; garnir, border (de dentelle, &c.).

lacerate ['læsɚˌejt] *v. tr.* lacérer; [Fig.] déchirer.

lack [læk] *n.* manque *m*, défaut *m* (*of*, de), absence *f*, besoin *m*: *for ~ of.* faute de. || *v. tr.* manquer (de qqch.), être dépourvu (*in*, de).

lackadaisical [ˌlækə'dejzɪkḷ] *adj.* languissant; apathique.

lacking [-ɪŋ] *adj.* manquant, dénué, dépourvu (*in*, de).

laconic [lə'kɑnɪk] *adj.* [answer, &c.] laconique.

lacquer ['lækər] *n.* [varnish] laque *f.* || *v. tr.* laquer (un meuble, &c.).

lacrosse [lə'kɹɑs] © (jeu de) crosse *f.*

lad [læd] *n.* jeune homme *m*, garçon *m*; [Fam.] gaillard *m.*

ladder [lædər] *n.* échelle *f.*

lade[1] [lejd] *n.* [R.C.] *the* ~, la crèche (de Noël).

lade[2] [lejd], **laded** [-əd], **laden** [-n̩] *v. tr.* [ship, &c.] charger. || **laden** *adj.* [ship, &c.] chargé.

ladies [lejdɪz] cf. LADY.

lading ['lejdɪŋ] cf. LADE[2]; [Com.] *bill of* ~, connaissement *m.*

ladle ['lejdl̩] *n.* louche *f.* || *v. tr.* servir (le potage).

lady ['lejdɪ] *n.* dame *f*; [Br.] Lady; [when addressing person] Madame; [Fam.] femme *f*: *young* ~, demoiselle *f*, jeune personne *f*; *Ladies & Gentlemen*, Mesdames & Messieurs; [R.C.] *Our Lady*, Notre Dame. || **lady-bug** [ˌbʌg] *n.* coccinelle *f*, [Fam.] bête *f* à bon Dieu.

lag [læg] *n.* retard *m.* || *v. intr.* [-gg-] rester en arrière, traîner. || *v. tr.* [machine] revêtir, envelopper.

lager ['lɑgər] *n.* [beer] bière *f* blonde.

laggard ['lægərd] *n.* traînard *m.*

lagoon [lə'guwn] *n.* lagune *f.*

laic ['lejɪk] *adj.* [as opposed to clerics] laïc. cf. LAYMAN.

laid cf. LAY. || **laid up**, *adj.* malade, alité.

lain [lejn] cf. LIE.

†**lair** ['lejər] *n.* [lion's, &c.] tanière *f*; [Fig.] repaire *m.*

laity ['lejɪtɪ] *n.* les laïques *mpl.*

lake [lejk] *n.* lac *m*: *The Great Lakes*, Les Grands Lacs; © [Geo.] *Lakehead*, Fond du Lac.

lama ['læmə] *n.* [Rel.] [Tibetan] lama *m*: *the Grand Lama*, le grand lama.

lamb [læm] *n.* agneau *m.*

lambskin ['læmˌskɪn] *n.* peau *f* d'agneau, agneau *m.*

lame [lejm] *adj.* boiteux, [maimed] estropié; [US] † ~ *duck Congress*, la Chambre sortante. || *v. tr.* rendre (qqun) boiteux, [cripple] estropier.

lament [lə'mɛnt] *n.* lamentation *f.* || *v. tr.* pleurer, (se) lamenter sur (qqch.): *the lamented X*, le regretté X. || **lamentable** ['læməntəbl̩] *adj.* lamentable.

laminate [ˌlæmɪ'nejt] *v. tr.* laminer (un métal). || **laminated** ['læmɪˌnejtəd] *adj.* laminé.

lamp [læmp] *n.* lampe *f*; ampoule *f* (électrique): *ceiling* ~, plafonnier *m*; *wall* ~, applique *f.*

lampoon [ˌlæm'puwn] *n.* pasquinade *f.*

lance [læns] *n.* lance *f*: ~ *-corporal*, [Br.] soldat *m* de première classe; [Fig.] *to break a* ~ *with* (*s.o.*), croiser le fer avec (qqun). || *v. tr.* percer (d'un coup de lance); [Surg.] donner un coup de/lancette, bistouri/à (un abcès). || **lancet** ['lænsət] *n.* [Surg.] lancette *f*, bistouri *m.*

land [lænd] *n.* terre *f*: *piece of* ~, terrain *m*; [country] pays *m*: *native* ~, patrie *f*; [Pol.] ~ *reform*, réforme *f* agraire. || *v. tr.* décharger (des marchandises), mettre (qqch.) à terre; [troops, &c.] débarquer (qqun, qqch.). || *v. intr.* [plane] atterrir, /débarquer, descendre/(à terre); [on sea] amerrir; [passengers from ship, train] débarquer, descendre/à terre; [on the moon] alunir. || **landholder** [-ˌhowldər] *n.* propriétaire *m* foncier.

landing [-ɪŋ] *n.* **1.** [Naut.] débarquement *m*; atterrissage *m* (d'un avion), amerrissage *m* (d'un hydravion): ~ *-ground*, terrain *m* d'atterrissage. **2.** arrivée *f* (d'un groupe de voyageurs). **3.** palier *m* (d'un escalier).

landlady [-ˌlejdɪ] *n.* propriétaire *f*, logeuse *f.* || **landlord** [-ˌlɔərd] *n.* [land, house] propriétaire *m.* || **landmark** [-ˌmɑərk] *n.* repère *m*, événement *m* (marquant), [Naut.] amer *m.* || **landowner** [-ˌownər] *n.* propriétaire *m* (foncier). || **landscape** [-ˌskejp] *n.* paysage *m*; [sight] coup *m* d'œil. || *v. tr.* dessiner (un parc, un jardin): *The palace grounds were landscaped by Lenôtre*, Lenôtre a dessiné les jardins du palais. || **landslide** [-ˌslajd] *n.* éboulement *m* (de terrain); éboulis *m*; [Fig.] victoire *f* écrasante.

lane [lejn] *n.* [country] (petit) chemin *m*; [city] ruelle *f*; [Mil.] haie *f* (de troupes): *four-* ~ *highway*, route *f* à quatre voies; *shipping* ~, route *f* de navigation.

language ['læŋgwədʒ] *n.* [tongue] langue *f*; [speech] langage *m*; ~ *lab*, laboratoire *m* d'écoute.

languid ['læŋgwɪd] *adj.* languissant. || **languish** ['læŋgwɪʃ] *v. intr.* languir. || **languor** ['læŋgər] *n.* langueur *f.*

lank [læŋk] *adj.* [Pers.] maigre, sec; (cheveux) plats.

lanky ['læŋkɪ] *adj.* grand et maigre.

lantern ['læntərn] *n.* lanterne *f*: [Br.] *Chinese*, [US] *Japanese* ~, lanterne vénitienne.

lap [læp] *n.* genoux *mpl*, giron *m*; pan *m* (d'un vêtement); [Sport] tour *m* (de piste), circuit *m*; gorgée *f* (d'un liquide); [sound]

clapotis *m*, clapotement *m* (des vagues). || *v. tr.* [-pp-] rabattre, recouvrir; [dog, cat] laper (un liquide). || *v. intr.* [wave, water] clapoter.

lapel [lə'pɛl] *n.* revers *m* (de veston).

lapse [læps] *n.* **1.** faute *f*, erreur *f*. **2.** cours *m*, marche *f* (du temps). || *v. tr. & intr.* déchoir, [Jur.] tomber en désuétude.

larboard ['lɑɚˌbɔɚd] *n.* [Naut.] bâbord *m.*

larceny ['lɑɚsənɪ] *n.* larcin *m.*

larch [lɑɚtʃ] *n.* [Bot.] mélèze *m*, © épinette *f* rouge, tamarac *m.*

lard [lɑɚd] *n.* saindoux *m.* || *v. tr.* larder. || **larder** [-ɚ] *n.* garde-manger *m.inv.*

large [lɑɚdʒ] *adj.* [in general] grand: *on a ~ scale*, sur une grande échelle; [thing] volumineux, gros; [ideas, influence] large, considérable; [power] étendu: *the public at ~*, le grand public. || **largely** [-lɪ] *adv.* en majorité, pour une grande part, en grande partie; [enough] amplement. || **largeness** [-nəs] *n.* grandeur *f*; grosseur *f*; [power, &c.] étendue *f*. || **largess** ['lɑɚdʒɛs] *n.* [generosity] libéralité *f*, largesse *f*.

lariat ['læɚɪət] *n.* lasso *m.*

lark [lɑɚk] *n.* **1.** [*sky ~*] alouette *f*: *meadow ~*, alouette des champs. **2.** [Br.] farce *f*, blague *f*.

larva ['lɑɚv|ə] *pl.* **larvae** [-ɪ] *n.* larve *f*.

larynx ['læɚɪŋks] *n.* larynx *m.*

lascivious [ˌlæ'sɪvɪəs] *adj.* lascif.

lash [læʃ] *n.* coup *m* de fouet; mèche *f* (d'un fouet); [eye ~] cil *m.* || *v. tr.* **1.** fouetter, cingler (un cheval), flageller (un homme); [lion] se battre les flancs (avec sa queue); [Fig.] cingler (un adversaire), faire une déclaration cinglante. **2.** [pack] attacher, assujettir; [boat] amarrer.

lass [læs] *n.* jeune fille.

lassitude ['læsɪˌtjuwd] *n.* lassitude *f*.

lasso [ˌlæ'suw] *n.* lasso *m.*

last [læst] *adj.* dernier: *~ Tuesday*, mardi dernier; *~ week*, la semaine dernière; *~ /evening, night/*, hier (au) soir/la nuit dernière/; *the evening before ~*, avant-hier soir; *the same day ~ year*, l'année dernière à pareil jour; *the ~ three days*, les trois derniers jours; *the ~ year of his life*, la dernière année de sa vie; *the ~ but one*, l'avant-dernier; *That's the ~ thing I'd do*, C'est la dernière des choses que je ferais; *He was the ~ to arrive*, Il est arrivé le dernier/Il a été le dernier à arriver; *It's the last word*, C'est le dernier cri. || *adv.* en dernier, à la fin: *to arrive ~*, être le dernier à arriver/arriver le dernier/; *to speak ~*, parler en dernier; *When ~ I did that/, I did that ~*, Quand j'ai fait cela pour la dernière fois/La dernière fois que j'ai fait cela. || *n.* fin *f*, bout *m*: *to the ~*, jusqu'au bout; *We haven't heard the ~ of it*, Nous n'avons pas fini d'en entendre parler; *That was the ~ I saw of them*, C'est la dernière fois que je les ai vus; *I think I've seen the ~ of it*, Je crois m'en être enfin débarrassé; *at ~*, enfin; *At ~ he understood*, Il a fini par comprendre. || *v. intr.* durer; [hold out] tenir: *This suit has to ~ me another year*, Ce costume doit me/faire, durer/encore une année. || **to ~ out** *v. tr.* survivre à (qqun); durer jusqu'au bout de, aussi longtemps que. || **lasting** [-ɪŋ] *adj.* durable. || **lastly** [-lɪ] *adv.* pour finir, en dernier lieu.

latch [lætʃ] *n.* [door] serrure *f* de sûreté, loquet *m.*

late [lejt] *adj.* **1.** [pers.] en retard; [plant] tardif; [art] de la dernière époque: *I was (3 hours) ~*, J'ai été en retard (de 3 heures); *The train was ~*, Le train/était en retard, avait du retard/; *The train was 3 hours ~*, Le train avait 3 heures de retard; *to make s.o. ~*, retarder qqun, mettre qqun en retard; *It is ~*, Il est tard; *It is getting ~*, Il se fait tard; *Is it/Am I/too ~ to . . . ?*, Est-il trop tard pour . . . ?; *in the ~ winter*, vers la fin de l'hiver; *Better ~ than never*, Mieux vaut tard que jamais. **2.** récent, dernier: *Late events have shown that . . .*, Les événements récents/Les derniers événements/ont montré que . . . ; *of ~*, récemment, dernièrement. **3.** [deceased] feu: *The ~ king*, feu le roi; *my ~ mother*, feu ma mère. **4.** [former] ancien, ex-: *The ~ champion*, L'ancien/ex-/champion. || *adv.* en retard; tard: *He came (2 hours) ~*, Il arriva en retard de 2 heures [cf. TRAIN under adj.]; *He came ~ (in the day)*, Il arriva tard (dans la journée) *~ in the winter*, vers la fin de l'hiver; *~ in life*, sur le tard; *as ~ as today*, aujourd'hui encore/pas plus tard qu'aujourd'hui; *~ of . . .*, anciennement de . . . . || **lately** [-lɪ] *adv.* dernièrement, récemment. || **later** [-ɚ] *adj. comp.* [cf. LATE] [Pers.] plus en retard; [time] plus tard; [date] postérieur (à, *than*). || *adv. comp.* [cf. LATE] plus tard: *(I'll) see you ~*, à plus tard/à tout à l'heure. || **latest** [-əst] *adj. superl.* [Pers.] le plus en retard; [time] le plus tard; le plus récent; [news] les dernières (nouvelles); [fashion] dernier cri; [date] (délai) de rigueur: *his ~ novel*, son dernier roman/roman le plus

récent/; *at the (very)* ~, au plus tard; *What is the* ~ *(from)?*, Quelles sont les dernières nouvelles (de)?
latent ['lejtn̩t] *adj.* latent, caché.
lateral ['lætɚəl] *adj.* latéral.
latest, cf. LATE.
lath [læθ] *pl.* **-s** *n.* latte *f.*
lathe [lejð] *n.* tour *m*: *turning-* ~, tour *m.*
lather ['læðɚ] *n.* mousse *f* (de savon), écume *f* (de cheval). || *v. tr.* savonner.
Latin ['lætn̩] *adj.* latin: ~ *America*, l'Amérique latine. || *n.* [language] le latin.
latitude ['lætɪˌtjuwd] *n.* latitude *f.*
latter ['lætɚ] *adj.* dernier, récent: *the* ~, [of two], ce dernier, celui-ci; [Rel.] *Latter-Day Saints*, Mormons *mpl.*
lattice ['lætɪs] *n.* treillis *m*, treillage *m.*
laud [lɔd] *v. tr.* [praise] louer, louanger (qqun, qqch.).
lauds *n.* [R.C.] laudes *fpl.*
laugh [læf] *n.* rire *m*; [mocking] risée *f.* || *v. intr.* rire, se moquer (de, *at*): *to* ~ *on the/wrong side of one's mouth, other side of one's face/*, rire/jaune, du bout des lèvres. || **laughable** [-əbl̩] *adj.* risible, ridicule. || **laughing** [-ɪŋ] *adj.* [Pers.] rieur. || *n.* rire(s) *m(pl)*: [Pers.] ~ *-stock*, risée *f.* || **laughter** [-tɚ] *n.* rire(s) *m(pl)*: *burst o,* ~, éclat *m* de rire.
launch [lɔntʃ] *n.* chaloupe *f.* || *v. tr.* lancer, [Mil.] déclencher (une offensive).
launder ['lɔnd|ɚ] *v. tr.* blanchir, laver (le linge). || *v. intr.* résister (au lavage): *not* ~ *proof,* → déteint au lessivage. || **laundress** [-ɹəs], **laundrywoman** [-ɹɪˌwumən] *n.* blanchisseuse *f.* || **laundry** [-ɹɪ] *n.* blanchisserie *f*, © buanderie *f*; [room] buanderie *f*: *self-service* ~, lavomat *m*; *Chinese* ~, © [Fam.] le Chinois; ~ *man*, blanchisseur *m.*
laurel [lɔɚəl] *n.* laurier *m.* || **laurelled** [-d] *adj.* [hero] couronné de lauriers.
Laurentian [ˌlɔɚ'ɛnʃən] *adj.* laurentien; *the* ~ *Mountains*, les Laurentides *fpl.* || *n.pl. the Laurentians*, les Laurentides *fpl.*
lava ['lævə] *n.* [volcano] lave *f.*
lavatory ['lævəˌtɔɚɪ] *n.* lavabo *m*, cabinet *m* de toilette.
lavender ['lævəndɚ] *n.* [Bot.] lavande *f.*
lavish ['lævɪʃ] *adj.* **1.** [Pers.] prodigue (de, *in, of*). **2.** [reception, &c.] somptueux, magnifique. || *v. tr.* [favours, &c.] prodiguer. || **lavishly** [-lɪ] *adv.* avec prodigalité, à profusion.
law [lɔ] *n.* **1.** [rule, regulation, &c.] loi *f*: ~ *court*, cour *f* de justice. **2.** [legislation] la loi, le droit: *civil* ~, le droit civil; *criminal* ~, le code criminel; *common* ~, [Br.] la common law; le droit coutumier; [by ext.] le droit civil; *to go to* ~ *(with s.o.)*, intenter un procès (à qqun), poursuivre (qqun) en justice; *man of* ~, homme *m* de loi, juriste *m*; ~ *-clerk*, greffier *m*, clerc *m*/de notaire, d'avoué; © légiste *m* [aux Communes]; ~ *-student*, étudiant *m* en droit.
law-abiding [-əˌbajdɪŋ] *adj.* [Pers., citizen] soumis aux lois, règlements; respectueux des/lois, règlements/. || **lawbreaker** [-ˌbɹejkɚ] *n.* transgresseur *m* (de la loi, des lois). || **lawful** [-fl̩] *adj.* [currency, &c.] légal, [action, &c.] licite, [child, &c.] légitime, [deed] valide. || **lawfully** [-fəlɪ] *adv.* légalement; licitement; légitimement. || **lawgiver** [-ˌgɪvɚ] *n.* législateur *m.* || **lawless** [-ləs] *adj.* [Pers., country] sans loi, [country, organization] anarchique; [system, &c.] désordonné, [proper, Fig.] déréglé. || **lawlessness** [-ləsnəs] *n.* anarchie *f*; [Fig.] désordre *m*, dérèglement *m.* || **lawmaker** [-ˌmejkɚ] *n.* législateur *m.* || **lawmaking** [-ˌmejkɪŋ] *n* législation *f.*
lawn [lɔn] *n.* gazon *m*, pelouse *f*: ~ *-mower*, tondeuse *f* (à gazon).
Lawrence ['lɔɚəns] *n.* = Laurent *m.*
lawsuit ['lɔˌsuwt] *n.* procès *m.* || **lawyer** ['lojɚ] *n.* homme *m* de loi, avocat *m.*
lax [læks] *adj.* [behaviour, &c.] relâché, [Pers.] négligent. || **laxative** [-ɪtəv] *adj. & n.* [Med.] laxatif (*m*). || **laxity** [-ɪtɪ] *n.* relâchement *m* (des mœurs, &c.); [language, &c.] imprécision *f.*
lay[1] [lej], **laid** [lejd], **laid** [lejd] || *v. tr.* étendre, coucher (par terre); abattre (la poussière); dissiper (les craintes); mettre, poser, (qqch. sur qqch.); mettre (la table, le couvert); poser (la première pierre); ranger (des briques); [hen] pondre (un œuf); [Fig.] présenter (les faits à); porter (plainte, une accusation, contre); infliger (une amende à); faire (un pari); miser (une somme sur); tendre (un piège à); faire (le siège d'une ville); [hold] mettre la main sur: *to* ~ *low*, abattre/ [sickness] terrasser; *The story is laid in*, L'histoire se passe (à). || *v. intr.* [hen] pondre: *to* ~ *about one*, frapper de tous côtés; [Fam.] *He really laid into me*, Il m'a vraiment sauté dessus. || **lay aside** [ˌlejə'sajd] *v. tr.* abandonner; mettre de côté. || **lay away, by** [-ə'wej] *v. tr.* mettre de côté. || **lay down** [-ˌdawn] *v. tr.* poser; déposer (les armes); [ship] mettre en chantier; [Fig.] stipuler (que . . .); poser (qqch.) en principe; établir (un règlement); abandonner (ses fonctions): *to* ~ *down*

the law to s.o., expliquer la loi à qqun/ [Fam.] rappeler qqun à l'ordre. || **lay in** [-ɪn] *v. tr.* faire (des provisions); faire provision de (qqch.). || **lay off** [-'ɑf] *v. tr.* congédier (des ouvriers). || *v. intr.* [Arg.] *Lay off (me), will you?,* Tu veux bien me laisser tranquille? || *n.* congédiement *m*, mise *f* à pied (d'employés). || **lay on** [-'ɑn] *v. tr.* appliquer; [Rel.] imposer (les mains): [Fam.] *to lay it on thick*, exagérer; *Everything was laid on*, Tout était arrangé/pourvu/. || **lay out** [-'awt] *v. tr.* arranger, disposer; étaler (des marchandises); tracer (un plan, une route); aménager (un jardin); étendre, abattre (qqun); débourser (de l'argent). || *n.* [goods] étalage *m*; [things] disposition *f*; dessin *m*, plan *m*; [Tech.] (schéma *m* de) montage *m*: [Fam.] *It's a nice ~ you have here*, Vous avez ici une belle installation. || **lay up** [-'ʌp] *v. tr.* amasser (des réserves de); désarmer (un navire); aliter (qqun).

lay² [lej] cf. LIE.

lay³ *adj.* [as opposed to religious, sacred] laïc, profane.

layer ['lejɚ] *n.* **1.** [person] poseur *m* (de tuiles, briques, &c.); [gunner] pointeur *m*. **2.** couche *f* (de vernis, &c.): *~ cake*, gâteau *m*. **3.** [hen] pondeuse *f*.

layette [ˌlej'ɛt] *n.* [infant] layette *f*.

layman [-mən] *n.* **1.** [R.C.] laïc *m*. **2.** [Fig.] profane *m*.

lazily ['lejzɪ|lɪ] *adv.* paresseusement. || **laziness** [-nəs] *n.* paresse *f*. || **lazy** *adj.* paresseux.

lead¹ [lɛd] *n.* [metal; rifle] plomb *m*; [pencil] mine *f* de plomb: *~ -work*, les plombs *mpl* (d'un vitrail). || *adj.* /en, de/ plomb.

lead² [lijd], **led, led** [lɛd] *v. tr.* [people, group, &c.] conduire, mener; être à la tête de (la classe); commander (un groupe), diriger (un parti); passer, mener (sa vie, son existence): [Fig.] *to ~ a dog's life*, mener une vie de/chien, galérien/. || *v. intr.* [street] conduire, mener, aboutir (à, *to*); donner accès à (un endroit); [Fig.] *~ to results, &c.*, produire des résultats, &c.. || **lead** *n.* [direction] conduite *f*; [passage] piste *f*, voie *f*; [cards] tour *m* (d'un joueur), main *f*; [Thea.] rang *m* de vedette, premier rôle; [Sport] avance *f* (sur qqun, *on s.o.*); initiative *f*: *to take the ~ (over s.o.)*, prendre le pas (sur qqun).

leaden ['lɛdn̩] *adj.* /en, de/plomb.

leader [lijdɚ] *n.* chef *m* (d'un groupe; d'un parti politique); conducteur *m*, guide *m*; [Journ.] article *m* de fond, éditorial *m*. || **leadership** [-ʃɪp] *n.* habileté *f* à diriger, direction *f*, conduite *f*; [Pol.] leadership: *to assume ~ of*, prendre la/direction, tête/de (qqch.). || **leading** ['lijdɪŋ] *adj.* [Pers., part, &c.] principal, premier, grand: [Mus.] *~ note*, note *f* sensible.

leaf [lijf] *pl.* **leaves** [lijvz] *n.* [tree] feuille *f*; [book] feuillet *m*; [table] rallonge *f*; [door] battant *m*: [Fig.] *to turn over a new ~*, rentrer dans le droit chemin, changer de conduite. || *v. intr.*: *to ~ (out)*, [tree] pousser des feuilles, †feuiller. || **leafless** ['lijf|ləs] *adj.* [plant, tree] sans feuilles, effeuillé. || **leaflet** [-lət] *n.* [paper] feuillet *m*; [Pub.] papillon *m*. || **leafy** [-ɪ] *adj.* feuillu, touffu.

league [lijg] *n.* **1.** [group] ligue *f*: [Hist.] *the League of Nations*, la Société des Nations; [Sport] © *the National Hockey League*, la Ligue nationale de hockey. **2.** lieue *f* [= 3 miles]. || *v. intr.* se liguer (contre, *against*).

leak [lijk] *n.* [liquid] fuite *f*, perte *f*; [in a ship] voie *f* d'eau: *~ -proof*, [tank, &c.] étanche. || *v. intr.* [container, &c.] couler, fuir, avoir/une fuite, des fuites/; [ship] faire eau: [Fig.] *to ~ out*, [information] transpirer. || **leakage** [-əʤ] *n.* [liquid, gas, news, &c.] fuite *f*. || **leaky** [-ɪ] *adj.* [tank, &c.] qui coule, qui a des fuites; [ship] qui fait eau.

lean¹ [lijn] *n.* [meat] maigre *m*. || *adj.* [Pers., &c.] maigre, décharné.

lean² [lijn], **leaned** [-d], **leaned or leant** [lɛnt] *v. intr.* s'appuyer (sur qqun, qqch., *on s.o., sth.*), s'incliner (en avant, *forward*), [thing] pencher, incliner: *Do not ~ out of the window*, Ne vous penchez pas à la fenêtre. || *v. tr.* appuyer (qqch. contre qqch., *sth. against sth.*), incliner, faire pencher (qqch.). || **leaning** [lijnɪŋ] *n.* inclinaison *f* (d'un édifice, &c.); [Fig.] inclination *f*, penchant *m* (vers, pour, *towards*). || *adj.* [thing] penchant, penché.

leanness [lijnnəs] *n.* maigreur *f*.

leant cf. LEAN. || **lean-to** ['lijnˌtuw] *n.* appentis *m*.

leap [lijp], **leapt** [lɛpt] **or leaped** [lijpt] *v. intr.* sauter, bondir: *to ~ up*, sursauter. || *n.* saut *m*, bond *m*: *~ year*, année *f* bissextile.

leapt [lɛpt] cf. LEAP.

learn [lɚn], **learned** [-d] **or learnt** [-t], **learnt** *v. intr.* apprendre, s'instruire. || *v. tr.* [lesson, subject, &c.] apprendre, étudier. || **learned** ['lɚn|əd] *adj.* instruit; [scholarly] savant, érudit, lettré: *learned society*, société *f* savante. || **learner** [-ɚ] *n.* débutant *m*, -e *f*, élève *m*/*f*. || **learning** [-ɪŋ] *n.* savoir *m*, science *f*, érudition *f*. || **learnt** [-t] cf LEARN.

lease [lijs] *n*. bail *m*. || *v. tr*. [landlord] donner (un appartement, une maison) à bail; [lessee] prendre (un appartement, une maison) à bail; [landlord, lessee] louer (un appartement, une maison).

leash [lijʃ] *n*. laisse *f*. || *v. tr*. [dog, &c.] tenir en laisse.

least [lijst] *adj. superl*. [cf. LITTLE] le, la/moindre; le, la plus petit(e): *the ~ detail*, le moindre/le plus petit/détail; *the ~ distance*, la distance la plus courte; *He is not the ~ bit/in the ~/tired*, Il n'est pas le moins du monde fatigué; *That was not the ~ of his talents*, Ce n'était pas le moindre de ses talents; *That is the ~ you could expect*, C'est la moindre des choses (auxquelles on pourrait s'attendre); *to say the ~*, → pour ne pas dire plus; *at ~*, du moins . . . /au moins/; *at the very ~*, tout au moins; *at ~ as . . . as*, pour le moins aussi . . . que . . . || *adv. superl*. [cf. LITTLE] le moins: *the ~ happy*, le/la moins heureux(-se); *the ~ sincerely*, le moins sincèrement; *(the) ~ of all*, moins que personne/que tou(te)s les autres/.

leather [ˈlɛðər] *n*. cuir *m*: *morocco ~*, maroquin *m*; *fancy ~ goods*, maroquinerie *f*. || *adj*./de, en/cuir: *~ bottle*, outre *f*, gourde *f*. || **leatherette** [-ˌɛt] *n*. simili-cuir *m*. || **leathern** [-n] *adj*. /de, en/cuir. || **leathery** [-ɪ] *adj*. comme du cuir; [Fig.] [food] coriace.

leave [lijv], **left** [lɛft], **left** *v. tr*. **1.** [go without taking; let remain] laisser: *He left his/book, brother/at home*, Il a laissé son /livre, frère/à la maison; *Take it or ~ it*, C'est à prendre ou à laisser; *~ me alone*, Laissez-moi/seul, tranquille/; *~ that alone*, Laissez ça (tranquille); *~ the door shut*, Laissez la porte fermée; *He left it lying on the table*, Il l'a laissé sur la table; *I ~ it to you to . . .*, Je vous laisse le soin de . . . ; *~ it to me*, Laissez-moi faire; *~ him to me*, Je m'occuperai de lui. cf. LEFT¹. **2.** laisser, léguer (des biens, une fortune). **3.** [go/away, out/from] quitter (un endroit, qqun), partir, sortir/(d'un endroit): *I must ~ you here*, Il faut que je vous quitte ici; *to ~ town*, quitter la, partir de la/ville; *to ~ the table*, se lever de table; *May I ~ the table/*, Est-ce que je peux/sortir, sortir de table/? **4.** abandonner, quitter (sa femme, le domicile conjugal). || *v. intr*. [go away] partir, s'en aller (d'un endroit); [go out] sortir (d'un endroit); quitter. [☞ *quitter* is transitive, and must be followed by a direct object]: *I have to ~ at 4*, Il faut que je /parte, m'en aille, vous quitte/à 4 heures; *Close the door as you ~*, Fermez la porte en sortant; *He has left for France*, Il est parti pour la France. || *n*. **1.** permission *f*, autorisation *f*: *He has my ~ to . . .*, Il a ma permission de . . . ; *with your ~*, avec votre permission. **2.** [long absence] congé *m* (*on*, en); [Mil.] permission *f* (*on*, en). **3.** [farewell] congé *m*: *to take one's ~*, prendre congé, faire ses adieux; *to take ~ of s.o.*, prendre congé de, faire ses adieux à/qqun; *to take French ~*, filer à l'anglaise; *to take ~ of one's senses*, perdre la raison. || **leave about** [-əˈbawt] *v. tr*. laisser traîner (des objets). || **leave behind** [-bɪˈhajnd] *v. tr*. laisser; distancer, [Fam.] semer (qqun). || **leave off** [-ˈɔf] *v. tr*. cesser (qqch., de faire qqch.); renoncer à (qqch., faire qqch.); ne pas mettre (un vêtement). || *v. intr*. cesser: *Where did we ~ ?*, Où en sommes-nous (restés)? || **leave out** [-ˈawt] *v. tr*. exclure (qqun); omettre, supprimer/(qqch.); [skip] sauter (un mot, &c.). || **leave over** [-ˈowvər] *v. tr*. **1.** remettre (qqch.) à plus tard. **2.** rester: *Was anything left over?*, Est-il resté qqch.?

leaven [ˈlɛvn̩] *n*. levain *m*; [Fig.] ferment *m*. || *v. tr*. **1.** [dough] faire lever. **2.** affecter, infecter.

leaves¹ [lijvz] *cf*. LEAF. || **leaves**² cf. LEAVE.

Lebanon [ˈlɛbəˌ|nɑn] *n*. le Liban. || **Lebanese** [-nɪz] *adj*. & *n*. Libanais.

lecherous [ˈlɛtʃərəs] *adj*. lubrique, libertin. || **lecherousness** [-nəs] *n*. cf. LECHERY. || **lechery** [ˈlɛtʃərɪ] *n*. luxure *f*, lubricité *f*.

lectern [ˈlɛktərn] *n*. [church] lutrin *m*.

lecture [ˈlɛktʃər] *n*. [Sch., &c.] conférence *f* (sur, *on*); leçon *f* (de, *on*); cours *m* (de français, &c.). || *v. intr*. donner une conférence (sur, *on*), [Sch.] /faire, donner/ un cours (de français, &c., *on French*, &c.); [Fig.] faire la morale à (qqun), sermonner (un élève). || **lecturer** [-ər] *n*. conférencier; [Univ.] maître *m* de conférences.

led [lɛd] cf. LEAD².

ledge [lɛdʒ] *n*. rebord *m*, saillie *f* (dans le roc).

ledger [-ər] *n*. [accounting] grand livre *m*.

leech [lijtʃ] *n*. sangsue *f*.

leek [lijk] *n*. poireau *m*.

leer [lijər] *n*. œillade *f*; regard *m* du coin de l'œil. || *v. intr*. regarder/en coin, de travers/.

left¹ [lɛft] cf. LEAVE. || *adj*. de surplus qui reste: *There are none ~*, Il n'en reste plus, Il n'y en a plus; *Nothing was ~ (to me, for me to do) but to . . .*, Il ne (me) restait plus qu'à . . .; *~ -off*, de rebut; *~ -over*, de surplus.

left[2] [lɛft] *adj.* gauche: *on/the, your/~ hand*, à (votre) gauche. || *adv.* à gauche: [Auto.] *Turn ~ at . . .*, Prenez à gauche à . . . || *n.* [direction] gauche *f*; [boxing] gauche *m*; [Pol.] *the Left*, la gauche. || **left-hand** [-'hænd] *adj.* de gauche: [Tech.] *~ /drive, screw/*, direction *f*, filet *m*/à gauche. || **left-handed** [-əd] *adj.* gaucher: [Fig.] *~ compliment*, compliment *m*/douteux, peu flatteur/. || *adv.* de la main gauche. || **leftist** [-ɪst] [Pol.] homme *m* de gauche; © gauchiste *m*.

leg [lɛg] *n.* [human being; trousers] jambe *f*; [animal] patte *f*, [of lamb] gigot *m*; [furniture] pied *m* (de tabouret, &c.); [US] © étape *f* (d'une randonnée): [Fig.] *to be on one's last legs*, être à bout de souffle; tirer vers sa fin; [Fam.] *to pull s.o.'s ~*, se payer la tête de qqun.

legacy ['lɛgəsɪ] *n.* legs *m*: *~ -duty*, droit *m* de succession.

legal ['lijgḷ] *adj.* [status, holiday, &c.] légal, [procedures, expenses, &c.] judiciaire; [reputation, language, framework, &c.] juridique: *~ adviser*, conseiller *m* juridique, © [abus.] aviseur *m* légal; *~ expert*, expert juriste *m*; [Fin.] *~ value*, valeur *f* numéraire; *~ holiday*, © fête *f* légale. || **legalize** [-ˌajz] *v. tr.* légaliser, légitimer, sanctionner (un acte, &c.). || **legally** [-ɪ] *adv.* légalement.

legate ['lɛgət] *n.* **1.** ambassadeur *m*, envoyé *m*. **2.** [R.C.] légat *m* (pontifical). || **legatee** [-ɪ] *n.* légataire *m*. || **legation** [lə'gejʃən] *n.* légation *f*.

legend ['lɛʤənd] *n.* **1.** [story, caption] légende *f*. **2.** [coins] inscription *f*. || **legendary** [-ˌɛəɪ] *adj.* légendaire.

legerdemain [ˌlɛʒɚdə'mæn] *n.* escamotage *m*, tours *mpl* de passe-passe.

leggings ['lɛgɪŋz] *n.pl.* guêtres *fpl*.

legibility [ˌlɛʤɪ'bɪlɪtɪ] *n.* lisibilité *f*. || **legible** ['lɛʤɪbḷ] *adj.* [text] lisible.

legion ['lijʤən] *n.* [soldiers] légion *f*; [Fig.] grand nombre *m*; [Fr.] Association *f* d'anciens combattants: © *the Canadian Legion*, la Légion canadienne.

legislate ['lɛʤɪsˌlejt] *v. intr.* légiférer. || **legislation** [ˌlɛʤɪs'lejʃən] *n.* législation *f*, ensemble *m* de lois; loi *f*. || **legislative** ['lɛʤɪsˌlejtɪv] *adj.* législatif: [provincial] *~ assembly*, © Assemblée *f* législative; *~ Council* ©, Conseil *m* législatif. || **legislator** [-ɚ] *n.* législateur *m*. || **legislature** ['lɛʤɪsˌlejtʃɚ] *n.* législature *f*: *provincial ~*, [Pol.] © assemblée législative (provinciale), législature *f* provinciale.

legitimacy [lə'ʤɪtɪ|məsɪ] *n.* légitimité *f*. || **legitimate** [-mət] *adj.* **1.** [birth, &c.] légitime. **2.** régulier, en règle. **3.** pertinent, permis. **4.** logique.

leisure ['lɛʒɚ] *n.* loisir *m*: *at ~*, à loisir; *in ~ moments*, à temps *m* perdu. || **leisurely** [-lɪ] *adv.* lentement, sans se presser. || *adj.* [fashion, pace] tranquille.

lemon ['lɛmən] *n.* **1.** [fruit, colour] citron *m*; *~ -tree*, citronnier *m*: *~ -squash*, citron pressé. **2.** [US, Sl.] [car] clou *m*, rossignol *m*; © citron *m*. || **lemonade** [-ˌejd] *n.* limonade *f*.

lend [lɛnd], **lent** [lɛnt], **lent** *v. tr.* prêter (qqch. à qqun). || **lendable** [lɛnd|əbḷ] *adj.* [funds] prêtable. || **lender** [-ɚ] *n.* prêteu|r *m*, -se *f*. || **lending** [-ɪŋ] *adj.* prêteur, qui prête. || *n.* prêt *m*, [Fin.] prestation *f*. *~ -library*, bibliothèque *f* /de prêts, circulante/.

length [lɛŋkθ] *n.* longueur *f*; [speech, &c.] durée *f*; [material, stuff] bout *m*, pièce *f*, morceau *m*: *It is three feet in ~*, Il est long de trois pieds, Il a trois pieds de long(ueur); *~ of time*, temps *m*; *at ~*, (parler) longuement; [finally] enfin, à la fin, finalement; *to go to the ~ of . . .*, aller jusqu'à (faire qqch.); *to go to great lengths to . . .*, se donner bien du mal pour . . . ; *to go to any lengths to . . .*, ne reculer devant rien pour . . . || **lengthen** [-ən] *v. tr.* allonger, rallonger. || *v. intr.* (s')allonger. || **lengthwise** [-ˌwajz] *adv.* en longueur, dans le sens de la longueur, en long. || **lengthy** [-ɪ] *adj.* long; [speech] trop long.

leniency ['lijnjən|sɪ] *n.* [drug, &c.] douceur *f*; [Pers.] indulgence *f*, clémence *f*. || **lenient** [-t] *adj.* [drug, &c.] doux; [Pers.] indulgent, clément.

lens [lɛnz] *n.* **1.** [Phot.] lentille *f*; objectif *m*. **2.** verre *m* (de lunettes).

Lent[1] [lɛnt] *n.* [Rel.] carême *m*. || **Lenten** [-ən] *adj.* [liturgy, &c.] de carême.

lent[2] [lɛnt] cf. LEND.

lentil ['lɛntḷ] *n.* [vegetable] lentille *f*.

leopard ['lɛpɚd] *n.* léopard *m*.

leper ['lɛpɚ] *n.* lépreux. || **leprosy** ['lɛpɹəs|ɪ] *n.* [Med.] lèpre *f*. || **leprous** *adj.* lépreux.

lesion ['lijʒən] *n.* [injury] lésion *f*.

less [lɛs] *adj. compar.* [cf. LITTLE] **1.** moindre; inférieur (à, *than*): *of ~ importance*, de moindre importance; *of ~ value*, de valeur inférieure; *to/become, grow/ ~*, s'amoindrir. **2.** moins: *He has ~ than I do*, Il en a moins que moi;

I have ~ than six, J'en ai moins de six; *so much the ~ (because),* d'autant moins (que); *nothing ~ than,* (ne) . . . rien moins que/moins de + numeral. || *adv. compar.* [cf. LITTLE] moins: *I like it ~* , Cela me plaît moins; *It is ~ expensive than the other,* C'est moins cher que l'autre; *~ and ~* , de moins en moins; *not ~ than twice,* pas moins de deux fois; *none the ~* , néanmoins; *I admire him none the ~ for it,* Je ne l'en admire pas moins. || *prep.* moins: *seven ~ five,* sept moins cinq. || **no less**: *~ a person than . . .* , rien moins que . . . lui-même; *I am ~ surprised to learn that . . .* , Je ne suis pas moins surpris d'apprendre que . . . ; *It was ~ than a shock,* Ce n'était rien moins qu'un choc/Cela n'en a pas moins été un choc/; *It's an outrage, ~ !,* C'est un outrage, pas moins/Ce n'est ni plus ni moins qu'un outrage; [ironical] *Now he's a hero, ~ !,* Maintenant, c'est un héros, ni plus ni moins/s'il vous plaît/! || **lessen** [-ṇ] *v. tr.* [influence, &c.] amoindrir (qqch.), diminuer: *to ~ the damage,* atténuer les dégâts; *to ~ the burden,* alléger le fardeau. || *v. intr.* diminuer, s'amoindrir, (se) rapetisser. || **lessening** [-ṇıŋ] *n.* réduction *f,* diminution *f*; atténuation *f.* || **lesser** [-ɚ] *adj. compar.* cf. LITTLE: [of two] petit; [importance, &c.] moindre: *To choose the ~ evil,* De deux maux choisir le moindre.

-less [-ləs] [in compounds] *adverbial suffix* sans . . . , dénué de . . . : *lifeless,* sans vie, inanimé.

lessee [ˌlɛ'sij] *n.* locataire *m* (à bail); [gas station, &c.] concessionnaire *m.*

lessen [lɛsṇ] cf. LESS.

lesser [lɛsɚ] cf. LESS.

lesson ['lɛsṇ] *n.* leçon: *music ~* , leçon *f* de musique.

lest [lɛst] *conj.* [☞ Suivi du subjonc. ou de *should*] de/peur, crainte/que . . . ne [+ subjunc.]; afin que, pour que/ . . . ne [+ subjunc.] pas; [after v. of fearing] que . . . ne [+ subjunc.]: *He hid ~ he (should) be caught,* Il se cacha de peur /d'être pris, qu'on ne le prenne/; *He was afraid ~ they arrest him,* Il avait peur qu'on ne/l'arrêtât, [Fam.] l'arrête/, → de se faire arrêter.

let[1] [lɛt] **let, let** *v. tr.* **1.** laisser; permettre (à qqun de faire qqch.); *He ~ himself be killed,* Il s'est laissé tuer; *He was ~ do it,* On l'a laissé faire/On lui a permis de le faire; *I ~ him sit down,* Je l'ai laissé s'asseoir; *I ~ him read it,* Je le lui ai laissé lire/Je l'ai laissé le lire; *to ~ s.o. in the house,* laisser entrer qqun dans la maison; *Let me see it,* Donnez-le-moi; *Let me see (it),* Faites(-le) voir; *Let me go,* Lâchez-moi/Laissez-moi partir/; *Let go (of me),* Lâchez-le/Lâchez-moi/; *Let me know,* Faites(-le)-moi savoir; *Let it stand,* N'y changez rien; *Let me be/Let me alone/,* Laissez-moi tranquille/Laissez-moi faire/; *~ alone . . .* , sans parler de; *Let well enough alone,* Le mieux est souvent ennemi du bien. **2.** louer (une maison): *(House) to ~* , (Maison) à louer. **3.** *to ~ blood,* saigner qqun. || *v. aux.* [☞ s'emploie avec l'infin. sans *to* pour former les 1ère et 3e personnes de l'impératif]. [☞ Do not confuse with *let* = allow: *Let him come in,* Laissez-le entrer; but Qu'il entre/Faites-le entrer/.] *Let's/Let us/think,* Réfléchissons; *Don't let's/Let's not/get excited,* Ne nous énervons pas; *Just ~ me catch you (at it) again,* Que je vous y reprenne!; *Let me see,* Voyons; *Let him/them/keep quiet,* Qu'il(s) se taise(nt). || **let down** [ˌlɛt'dawn] *v. tr.* baisser; descendre (qqun); allonger (une robe); défaire (ses cheveux); [Fig.] décevoir (qqun); laisser (qqun) en panne: *I won't let you down,* → Vous pouvez compter sur moi. || **let-down** ['lɛtˌdawn] *n.* déception *f.* || **let in** [ˌlɛt'ın] *v. tr.* laisser, faire entrer; ouvrir la porte à: *to let s.o. in on a secret,* mettre qqun dans le secret; *What am I letting myself in for?,* A quoi est-ce que je m'engage? || **let off** [-'ɑf] *v. tr.* faire partir (un canon); laisser échapper (de la vapeur); pardonner (qqch. à qqun): *I'll let you off this time,* Je vous pardonnerai cette fois; *I'll let you off it,* Je vous en dispenserai, fais grâce/; *to be ~ with a reprimand,* en être quitte pour une réprimande. || **let on** [-'ɑn] *v. tr.* [Fam.] *Don't ~ (about it)/Don't ~ that you know/,* Ne vendez pas la mèche/Ne dites pas que vous savez. || **let out** [-'awt] *v. tr.* laisser sortir (qqun); laisser s'échapper (un prisonnier, un secret, un cri); louer (un appartement); élargir (une robe): *to be ~ on bail,* être relâché sous caution. || **let up** [-'ʌp] *v. intr.* s'arrêter; diminuer.

let[2] [lɛt] *n.* location *f* (d'une maison). || **let, let, let** *v. tr.* louer (un appartement, &c.). || *v. intr.* [house, &c.] se louer.

lethal ['lijθəl] *adj.* [dose, &c.] mortel. || **lethargy** ['lɛθɚdʒı] *n.* léthargie *f.*

let's [lɛts] = let us: *~ go,* Allons(-y)!

letter ['lɛtɚ] *n.* [alphabet, message] lettre *f,* missive *f*; caractère *m* (d'écriture): *men of letters,* gens *mpl* de lettres; *night-~* , lettre *f* de nuit, lettre-nuit *f*; *~ -box,* boîte *f* aux lettres, © [in rural areas]

boîte postale; ~ *carrier*, facteur *m*, © postillon *m*.
lettuce ['lɛtəs] *n*. laitue *f*, © salade *f*.
let-up ['lɛtˌʌp] *n*. accalmie *f*; halte *f*, pause *f*: [Fam.] *without* ~, sans souffler, © sans dérougir.
level [lɛvḷ] *n*. niveau *m*, surface *f*/plane, unie; égalité avec (qqch.): [Rail.] [Br.] © ~ *crossing*, passage *m* à niveau, © traverse *f* de chemin de fer. ‖ *adj*. /au, de/ niveau avec (qqch.); [country, &c.] plat, uni; [surface] horizontal, égal: ~ *-headed*; [Fig.] [Pers.] équilibré; ~ *tract of land*, terrain *m*/plat, © planche *f*. ‖ *v. tr*. [-ll-] niveler, mettre (qqch.) de niveau (avec qqch.), aplanir; égaliser; viser, ajuster; braquer (une arme sur qqun, qqch.): *to* ~ (*sth*.) *up*, [surface, &c.] égaliser.
lever ['lijvɚ] *n*. **1.** levier *m*. **2.** bras *m*. ‖ **leverage** ['lijvɹədʒ] *n*. puissance *f* d'un levier; pesée *f*; [Fig.] surcroît *m* de puissance.
levity ['lɛvɪtɪ] *n*. légèreté *f*, ton *m* badin.
levy ['lɛvɪ] *n*. [troops, tax] levée *f*; [Fin.] impôt *m*. ‖ *v. tr*. lever (des troupes), imposer (des taxes).
lewd [luwd] *adj*. licencieux, impudique.
Lewis [luwɪs] *n*. = Louis *m*.
lexicography [ˌlɛksɪ'kɑgɹəfɪ] *n*. lexicographie *f*.
liability [ˌlajə'bɪlətɪ] *n*. **1.** risque *m*, danger *m* (*to*, de). **2.** [dette] obligation *f*, responsabilité *f*. ‖ *pl*. **liabilities** [-z] obligations *fpl*, engagements *mpl*, dette *f*; [accounting] passif *m*. ‖ **liable** ['lajbḷ] *adj*. [fine, &c.] passible (de, *to*); [Pers.] sujet (à, *to*); [thing] susceptible (de, *to*); [Pers.] responsable (de, *to*).
liaison [lijejzɑn] *n*. liaison *f*.
liar [lajɚ] *n*. menteur *m*, menteuse *f*.
libel ['lajbḷ] *n*. libelle *m*; diffamation *f* (par écrit). ‖ *v. tr*. [-ll-] diffamer, calomnier (qqun).
libellous ['lajbələs] *adj*. infamant.
liberal ['lɪbɚəl] *adj*. [Pers.] libéral, généreux; [share, &c.] copieux, abondant; large (d'idées): [Pol.] *the Liberal Party*, les libéraux *mpl*, le parti libéral. ‖ *n*. [Pol.] *Liberal*, libéral *m*, membre *m* du parti libéral.
liberality [ˌlɪbɚ'ælətɪ] *n*. **1.** générosité *f*, largesses *fpl*, don *m*. **2.** largeur *f* (de vues).
liberate ['lɪbɚˌejt] *v. tr*. [free] libérer (qqun, qqch.), délivrer (de contraintes), débarrasser d'obstacles). ‖ **liberation** [ˌlɪbɚ'ejʃən] *n*. libération *f*, [slave] affranchissement *m*; décharge *f* (d'une dette). ‖ **liberator** ['lɪbɚˌejtɚ] *n*. libérateur *m*.
libertine ['lɪbɚˌtijn] *adj*. libertin, débauché, licencieux. ‖ *n*. **1.** libertin *m*, [Argot.] affranchi *m*. **2.** libre-penseur *m*.
liberty ['lɪbɚtɪ] *n*. liberté *f*; franchise *f*, privilège(s) *m*(*pl*): *I take the* ~ *of* [+ *ing*], Je me permets de [+ *inf*.]; *at* ~, en liberté; *at* ~ *to*, libre de.
librarian [ˌlaj'bɹɛɚɪən] *n*. bibliothécaire *m*/*f*. ‖ **library** ['lajbɹɛɚɪ] *n*. [×] bibliothèque *f*; *classroom* ~, bibliothèque *f* de classe; *lending*- ~, bibliothèque *f* /circulante, de prêts/; cabinet *m* de lecture; *record* ~, discothèque *f*.
lice [lajs] *n.pl*. cf. LOUSE.
licence ['lajsəns] *n*. **1.** autorisation *f*; [patent] licence *f*, brevet *m*; [driving, &c.] permis *m*; ~ *plate*, numéro *m*, plaque *f*/ d'immatriculation; [Sch.] *teacher's* ~, certificat *m* d'aptitude au professorat; © brevet *m* d'enseignement; *marriage* ~, certificat *m* de mariage; dispense *f* de bans. **2.** [Pej.] licence *f*.
license ['lajsəns] *v. tr*. autoriser (qqun), /accorder, donner/un permis à (qqun). ‖ **licensed** [-t] *adj*. [Com.] autorisé, [merchant] patenté; [driver, pilot] breveté; ~ *premises*, (restaurant, hôtel) qui sert/du vin, de l'alcool; © permis *m* de la Commission.
licentious [ˌlaj'sɛnʃəs] *adj*. [talk] licencieux, [life, &c.] immoral, déréglé.
lichen ['lajkən] *n*. [Bot.] lichen *m*.
lick [lɪk] *v. tr*. **1.** lécher: *to* ~ *one's fingers*, se lécher les doigts. **2.** [dogs] *to* ~ (*sth*.) *up*, laper. **3.** [Fam.] battre, défaire (qqun). *n*. coup *m* de langue; [bit] brin *m*: *to give a* ~, lécher.
lid [lɪd] *n*. couvercle *m* (d'une marmite, &c.); [eye-] paupière *f*.
lie[1] [laj] **lay** [lej] **lain** [lejn] **lying** ['lajɪŋ] *v. intr*. **1.** être couché, étendu (à plat, sur le côté, &c.). **2.** [often not rendered directly in Fr. *Here lies* . . . , Ci-gît . . .] être, se trouver, rester: *to* ~ *awake, still*, rester éveillé, tranquille; *to* ~ *in ruins*/*open*/, être en ruines/ouvert/; *the town lies on the plain*, La ville se trouve /est située/sur la plaine; *to* ~ *heavy upon*, peser sur qqch., à qqun; *to* ~ *low*, rester/caché, tapi/. **3.** [Fig.] résider; [responsibility] incomber à: *The difference lies in* . . . , La différence réside en; *It lies*/*upon, with*/*him, to*, Il lui incombe de. **4.** [road] a verb of motion, esp. passer: *Our*/*roadway*/*lay through the valley*/*down the mountain*, Notre chemin passait par la vallée/descendait la montagne. ‖ *n*. disposition *f* (du terrain): *to get the* ~ *of the land*, s'orienter. ‖ **lie about, around**

v. intr. traîner (partout). || **lie back** [ˌlaj'bæk] *v. intr.* se mettre à plat. || **lie down** [-'dawn] *v. intr.* se coucher (dans un lit, par terre); s'étendre (sur un lit, par terre); se reposer: [to dog] *(Go)* ~ *!*, (Va) coucher!; *to take sth. lying down*, se laisser faire, ne pas réagir (contre); *to* ~ *on the job*, [Sl.] s'endormir sur le rôti. || **lie off** [-'ɑf] *v. intr.* cesser le travail; chômer. || **lie over** [-'owvɚ] *v. intr.* être remis, reporté (à plus tard). || **lie to** [-'tuw] *v. intr.* [ship] être à la cape.

lie[2] [laj] *n.* mensonge *m*, [Fam.] menterie *f.* || **lie** [laj], **lied** [-d], **lied** *v. intr.* mentir, raconter des mensonges.

lieutenant [ˌlɛf'tɛnənt] *n.* [army, navy] © [Pol.] lieutenant *m*: *Lieutenant-Governor*, lieutenant-gouverneur *m.*

life [lajf] *pl.* **lives** [lajvz] *n.* **1.** vie *f*, existence *f*; [life time] vie *f*, vivant *m*; [thing] durée *f*; [book] biographie *f*, vie *f*; [animation] vie *f*, animation *f*; [energy] entrain *m*; vivacité *f* (des traits, d'un visage): *to/take, save/s.o.'s* ~, tuer, sauver la vie à/qqun; *to/risk, lose/one's* ~, risquer/sa peau, la mort/; perdre la vie, périr; *for* ~, à/vie, perpétuité/; *Run for your* ~ *!*, Sauve qui peut!; *for dear* ~, tant qu'il peut; *Not on your* ~ *!*, *Never in my* ~ . . . , Jamais de la vie . . . ; *during his* ~ *(time)*, de son vivant; *at my time of* ~, à mon âge; *in his early* ~ , dans/son enfance, sa jeunesse/; *way of* ~ , manière *f* de vivre; *Such is* ~, C'est la vie; ~ *insurance*, assurance *f* sur la vie.

lifebelt ['lajf|ˌbɛlt] cf. JACKET. || **lifeboat** [-ˌbowt] *n.* canot *m* de sauvetage. || **lifebuoy** [-ˌboj] *n.* bouée *f* de sauvetage. || **lifeguard** [-ˌgaɚd] *n.* [swimming] sauveteur *m.* || **lifeless** [-ləs] *adj.* sans vie, mort; [Fig.] inanimé. || **lifelike** [-ˌlajk] *adj.* [picture, portrait] vivant, ressemblant. || **life-long** [-ˌlɑŋ] *adj.* [feeling, &c.] /de, pour/toute la vie. || **life-saver** [-ˌsejvɚ] *n.* [Pers.] sauveteur *m.* || **life-size** [-ˌsajz] *adj.* [object] grandeur nature. || **lifetime** [-ˌtajm] *n.* (toute une) vie: *in his* ~, de son vivant.

lift [lɪft] *n.* **1.** haussement *m*, levée *f*; [Br.] ascenseur *m.* **2.** aide *f*; promenade (gratuite) en voiture. || *v. tr.* lever, soulever (qqch. de lourd, &c.); dérober, subtiliser (un objet): *to* ~ *(sth.) down (from)*, descendre (qqch. de). || *v. intr.* [darkness, &c.] se dissiper, s'en aller.

light[1] [lajt] *n.* **1.** lumière *f*; jour *m*; [dim] lueur *f*: [diffused] clarté *f*, [room, &c.] éclairage *m*; [smokers] du feu: *switch/on, off/the* ~, allumer, éteindre (la lumière); *Give me a* ~, Donnez-moi du feu; *turn /on, off/the* ~, → allumer, éteindre (la lumière); *It will soon be* ~, Il fera bientôt jour; *against the* ~ , à contre-jour. **2.** [proper & Fig.] jour, [*pl.*] lumières *fpl*, intelligence *f*; connaissance *f* (d'un sujet): *to be seen in a new* ~ , → se révéler sous un jour nouveau; *to see the* ~ , voir le jour; *to bring (sth.) to* ~ , [reveal] mettre (qqch.) en lumière. **3.** phare *m*, feu *m*, lumière *f*: [= traffic ~] feu *m* (de circulation); *to cross on the green* ~ , traverser au feu vert; [Fig.] *to give s.o. the green* ~, donner à qqun carte blanche; [Auto.] *tail-lights*, feux (d')arrière; *headlight* ['hɛdˌlaɪt] phare *m*; *night-* ~, veilleuse *f*; *driving lights*, phares-code *mpl*; *Leave the lights on*, Laissez/les lumières, la lumière/ allumée(s); *flashlight* ['flæʃˌlajt] lampe *f* de poche. **4.** *northern lights*, aurore *f* boréale, © clairons *mpl.* || *adj.* clair: ~ *blue*, bleu clair [no agreement with the noun]: *a* ~ *blue dress*, une robe bleu clair.

light[2] [lajt] *adj.* léger: *He is a* ~ *sleeper*, Il a le sommeil léger; ~ *-headed*, [Pers.] écervelé, étourdi; *to make* ~ *of*, traiter à la légère.

light[3] [lajt], **lighted** [-ed], **lighted** or **lit** [lɪt], **lit** *v. tr.* allumer (un feu, une bougie, &c.); [Elect.] éclairer, illuminer (une pièce, &c.): *He lit a cigarette*, Il alluma une cigarette. || *v. intr.* s'allumer; [proper and Fig.] s'éclairer, s'illuminer; allumer (les lampes); [Fig.] [face, &c.] *to* ~ *up*, s'éclairer.

light[4] [lajt], **lit** [lɪt], **lit** or **lighted** ['lajtəd], **lighted** *v. intr* [bird] se poser (sur une branche); [object] tomber, s'abattre.

lighten[1] [laɪtn] *v. tr.* **1.** éclairer, illuminer (qqch.). || *v. intr.* faire des éclairs, éclairer; briller.

lighten[2] [lajtn] *v. tr.* alléger (qqch.); soulager (qqun).

lighter[1] [-ɚ] *n.* [Pers.] allumeu|r *m*, -se *f*; [tool] briquet *m*, allumoir *m.*

lighter[2] [-ɚ] *n.* [Naut.] péniche *f.* || **lighter**[3] cf. LIGHT[3]. || **light-hearted** [ˌlajt'haɚtəd] *adj.* [Pers.] allègre, joyeux, au cœur léger *inv.*

lighthouse ['lajtˌhaws] *n.* [Naut.] phare *m.* || **lighting** ['lajt|ɪŋ] *n.* éclairage *m* (au gaz, &c.), illumination *f.*

lightly [-lɪ] *adv.* légèrement, facilement; agilement; gaîment; à la légère, négligemment: *to get off* ~, s'en tirer à bon compte; *to speak* ~ *of sth.*, parler de qqch. à la légère.

lightness [-nəs] *n.* **1.** clarté *f* (du ciel); [complexion, &c.] pâleur *f*, blancheur *f.* **2.**

légèreté *f*, [movement] agilité *f*; **3.** [character] enjouement *m*, gaîté *f*. **4.** [Fig.] frivolité, humeur *f* volage. ‖ **lightning** [-nɪŋ] *n.* la foudre, (les) éclairs *mpl*: *a flash of* ~, un éclair: ~ *rod*, (tige *f* de) paratonnerre *m*. ‖ **light-weight** [-ˌwejt] *adj.* léger. ‖ *n.* [boxing] poids *m* léger.

lik(e)able [-əbḷ] *adj.* agréable, apprécié; [Pers.] sympathique, populaire.

like[1] [lajk] *v. tr.* aimer, avoir du goût pour/(qqch.); aimer bien, avoir de la sympathie pour/(qqun); → plaire; trouver/bon, bien/; vouloir: *I* ~ *him*, Je l'aime (assez) bien, Il me plaît, Je le trouve sympathique, J'ai de la sympathie pour lui; *I don't* ~ *him*, Je ne l'aime pas, Il me déplaît, Je le trouve antipathique, [Fam.] Je ne peux pas le/ voir, sentir/; *I* ~ *that*, J'aime cela, Cela me plaît, Je trouve ça bien, [food] bon; [Iron.] Ça, par exemple!; *He won't* ~ *it if* . . . , Il ne sera pas content si . . . ; *How do you* ~ */it, him/?*, Comment le trouvez-vous?; *He likes/this place, it here/*, Il se plaît ici; *Whether they* ~ *it or not*, Qu'ils le veuillent ou non; *I* ~ *to go out in the evening*, J'aime (bien) (à) sortir le soir; *I don't* ~ */him to do that, his doing that/*, Je n'aime pas, Je ne trouve pas/bien, bon/qu'il fasse cela; *I'd* ~ *to see him*, J'aimerais, Je voudrais/(bien) le voir; *I'd* ~ *to have seen him, I'd have liked to see him*, J'aurais/bien voulu, aimé/le voir; *I'd* ~ *him to* . . . , J'aimerais qu'il [+ subjunc.]; *Would you* ~ *another* (*one*)*?*, En voulez-vous encore un?, *Or would you* ~ *the other* (*one*)*?*, Ou/préfér(eri)ez-vous, aimeriez-vous mieux/l'autre?; *as, what/you* ~, comme, ce que/vous voudrez. ‖ *n.* sympathie *f*, penchant *m*, goût *m* (pour qqch., *for sth.*). [d'ordinaire au plur.].

like[2] *prep.* comme, de la même façon que; en; pareil, semblable, à: *He thinks* ~ *me*, Il pense comme moi; *He does it* ~ *me*, Il le fait/comme, de la même façon que/moi; *You'll have to work*, ~ *me*, Vous devrez travailler,/comme, de même que/moi; *He behaved* ~ *a little gentleman*, Il s'est conduit/ comme un, en/vrai gentleman; *I am getting ready* ~ *a soldier on the eve of a battle*, Je me prépare /comme un, tel le/soldat à la veille d'une bataille; ~ *father*, ~ *son*, tel père, tel fils; *What is it* ~ *?*, Comment est-ce?, A quoi cela ressemble-t-il?; *It's* ~ *a box*, C'est comme, C'est pareil à, Cela ressemble à/une boîte; *It's* ~ *watching a movie*, C'est comme si on regardait un film; [Iron.] *That's just* ~*/a woman, you!/*, Voilà bien les femmes, C'est bien de vous!; *I have seen one* ~ */it, that/*, J'en ai vu un/pareil, comme cela/; *You mustn't talk* ~ *that*, Il ne faut pas parler/comme cela, ainsi/; *sth., anything, nothing/* ~ *it*, qqch., n'importe quoi, rien/de pareil; *sth.* ~ *twenty*, environ vingt; *nothing* ~ *as* . . . , certainement pas aussi . . . ; *There's nothing* ~ *a swim to* . . . , Il n'y a rien de meilleur/qu'un bain, que d'aller se baigner/pour . . . cf. FEEL, LOOK. ‖ *adj.* pareil, semblable, même: ~ *causes*, des causes/pareilles, semblables, de même nature/; ... *and the* ~, et d'autres/semblables, de même nature/; *its, his/* ~, son pareil; *I never heard the* ~ *of it*, Je n'ai jamais entendu chose pareille. ‖ **likelihood** [-lɪˌhud] *n.* probabilité *f*, vraisemblance *f*. ‖ **likeliness** [-lɪnəs] *n.* cf. LIKELIHOOD. ‖ **likely** [-lɪ] *adj.* probable, vraisemblable: *He is* ~ *to come tomorrow*, Il est probable qu'il viendra demain; *a* ~ *story!*, une histoire de brigands!; *the candidate most* ~ *to be elected*, le candidat qui a le plus de chances d'être élu. ‖ *adv.* probablement, vraisemblablement.

liken [-ṇ] *v. tr.* comparer (à); assimiler (à). ‖ **likeness** [-nəs] *n.* **1.** ressemblance *f*; air *m* (de famille). **2.** apparence *f*: *in the* ~ *of*, sous l'apparence de. **3.** portrait *m*; *to be a good* ~ *of s.o.*, être ressemblant, ressembler bien à qqun. ‖ **likewise** [-ˌwajz] *adv.* également, pareillement, aussi, de même: *to do* ~, en faire autant. ‖ **liking** [-ɪŋ] *n.* penchant *m*, préférence *f*: *to take a* ~ *to*, prendre goût à; *She had a great* ~ *for old things*, Elle avait la manie des vieilleries; (*not much*) *to his* ~, (peu) à son goût.

lilac [ˈlajlək] *n.* [Bot., colour] lilas *m*. ‖ *adj.* lilas *inv*.

lilt [lɪlt] *n.* [verse, song] cadence *f*. ‖ *v. tr. & intr.* chanter/gaiement, en cadence/.

lily [lɪlɪ] *n.* [Bot.] lis *m*: ~ *-of-the-valley*, muguet *m*; *water* ~, nénuphar *m*.

limb [lɪm] *n.* membre *m*; [tree] (grosse) branche *f*.

limber [-bɚ] *adj.* souple, flexible. ‖ *v. tr.* (s')assouplir.

limbo [-bow] *n.* [Rel.] les limbes *mpl*.

lime[1] [lajm] *n.* [Bot.] lime *f*: ~ *juice*, jus *m* de limon.

lime[2] *n.* [Chem.]: *quick* ~, chaux *f* vive. ‖ **limelight** [-ˌlajt] *n.* [Theat.] projecteur *m*: [Fig.] *in the* ~, très en vue, en vedette *f*. ‖ **limestone** [-ˌstown] *n.* calcaire *m*, pierre *f* à chaux.

limit [ˈlɪmɪt] *n.* limite *f*, borne *f*; [Fig.]

restriction *f.* || *v. tr.* limiter, [ambition, &c.] borner, restreindre. || **limitation** [ˌlɪmɪ'tejʃən] *n.* limite *f*, restriction *f.* || **limited** ['lɪmɪtəd] *adj.* **1.** limité, borné, restreint. **2.** [Com.] (société) à responsabilité limitée, anonyme; © (compagnie) limitée.

limp [lɪmp] *n.* claudication *f.* || *v. intr.* boiter: *to ~ off*, s'en aller en clopinant. || *adj.* mou, flasque, [cover] souple.

limpid [-ɪd] *adj.* [water, &c.] limpide, transparent.

linden ['lɪndən] *n.* ~ *-tree*, tilleul *m* (glabre), [Pop.] bois *m* blanc.

line [lajn] *n.* **1.** [cord] ligne *f* (de pêche, &c.); corde *f* (à linge, &c.), [wire] ligne, fil *m* (télégraphique, téléphonique): [Tel.] *on the ~*, au bout du fil; *Hold the ~*, Ne quittez pas (l'écoute). **2.** [narrow mark] ligne *f*; [dash] trait *m*; [bar] barre *f*; [streak of colour] raie *f*; [wrinkle on face] ride *f*; [equator] la ligne (équatoriale): *in a straight ~*, en ligne droite; *dotted ~*, pointillé *m*; *to draw a ~*, tracer une ligne, [Fig.] établir une distinction (très nette entre deux choses); *That's where I draw the ~*, Après cela, je tire l'échelle; *to toe the ~*, se mettre au pas, suivre la consigne; [Fam.] *to get a ~ on/s.o., sth./*, apprendre qqch. sur (qqun, qqch.). **3.** [Print.] ligne *f* (d'un texte), vers *m* (d'un poème), [letter, note] mot *m*: (*Begin on the*) *next ~*, A la ligne; *Drop me a ~*, Envoyez-moi un mot; [Theat.] *to learn one's lines*, apprendre son rôle. **4.** *pl.* [shape] contours *mpl*; ligne(s) *f(pl)*: *That has fine lines*, Cela a/de la ligne, une ligne élégante/; [Fig.] *the broad lines of a book*, les grandes lignes d'un livre; *on, along/traditional lines*, d'une manière, à la manière/ traditionnelle. **5.** [row] ligne *f*, rangée *f*; [Mil.] rang *m*; [file of persons] file *f*, [waiting] queue *f*: *in a ~*, [row] en ligne, aligné, [file] à la file; *to stand in a ~*, [waiting] faire la queue; *to get into ~*, s'aligner [also Fig.], se mettre à la queue; [car] prendre la file; [Fig.] se mettre au pas; *to fall out of ~*, se désaligner [also Fig.], [Mil.] quitter les rangs; [Pol.] *to follow the party ~*, suivre la ligne du parti; [Mil.] *the front ~*, le front; *behind the enemy lines*, derrière les lignes ennemies; *ship of the ~*, vaisseau *m* de ligne. **6.** [transportation] ligne *f*, compagnie *f*, (maritime, aérienne, &c.); [Rail.] ligne, [track] voie *f*: *main ~*, grande ligne. **7.** [genealogy] lignée *f* (généalogique); ligne *f* (d'ancêtres). **8.** [course of action] ligne (de conduite); suite (d'idées): *What ~ did he take at the meeting?*, Quelle position *f* a-t-il prise à la réunion? **9.** [specialty] métier *m*; [wares] article *m*, modèle *m*: *What's his ~?*, *What ~ is he in?*, Dans quel genre/d'affaires, de métier/ travaille-t-il?, Quelle est son occupation?; *a complete ~ of British woollens*, un assortiment complet, une collection complète/de lainages anglais; *We do not carry that ~*, Nous ne tenons pas cet article; [Fam.] *That's not in my ~*, Ce n'est pas de/mon ressort, [Fam.] mon rayon/; *or sth. in that ~*, ou qqch. dans ce genre. || **line** *v. tr.* ligner (un cahier, &c.); rider (un visage); doubler (un costume de qqch.): *The street was lined with/trees, people/*, La rue était bordée d'arbres, La foule s'était alignée le long de la rue. || **line up** [-'ʌp] *v. tr.* aligner; [Fam.] obtenir. || *v. intr.* s'aligner, se mettre en ligne; [waiting] faire la queue. || **lineage** ['lɪnɪəʤ] *n.* lignée *f*; [History] généalogie *f.* || **linear** ['lɪnɪə˞] *adj.* linéaire.

linen [lɪnən] *n.* toile *f* (de lin); [clothes] linge *m*; *~ -room*, lingerie *f* || *attrib.* de, en/toile; *pure ~*, de/en fil, pur fil: *all-~ sheets*, des draps pur fil.

liner ['lajnə˞] *n.* [Naut.] paquebot *m*, transatlantique *m*, [air] avion *m*/de ligne, long-courrier *m*, © aérobus *m*; [Sch.] guide-âne *m*.

line-up ['lajnˌʌp] *n.* [people] file *f*, queue *f* (à la porte d'un établissement, &c.).

linger ['lɪŋgə˞] *v. intr.* s'attarder (dans un endroit), flâner; persister, subsister.

lingerie ['lɑnʒəɪ] *n.* lingerie *f* (pour dames).

lingo ['lɪŋgow] *n.* [Pej.] jargon *m*.

linguist ['lɪŋgwɪst] *n.* polyglotte *m*: *scientific ~*, [souvent abrégé en *linguist*] linguiste *m*. || **linguistic** [-ɪk] *adj.* linguistique. || **linguistics** [-s] *n.* linguistique *f*.

lining ['lajnɪŋ] *n.* **1.** [garment] doublure *f* (d'un manteau); [box] garniture *f* intérieure; [shoe] ailette *f.* **2.** revêtement *m* (intérieur).

link [lɪŋk] *n.* **1.** [chain] anneau *m*, maillon *m*. **2** jointure *f*, lien *m*. **3.** [Fig.] enchaînement *m*, suite *f*. **4.** [survey] © chaînon *m* [= 7·92 pouces]. **5.** *pl.* boutons *mpl* de manchette. || *v. tr.* lier, enchaîner, joindre; se raccorder.

links [lɪŋks] *n.pl.* [golf] terrain *m*.

linoleum [lɪn'owlɪəm] *n.* linoléum *m*; © [abus.] prélart *m*.

linotype ['lajnəˌtajp] *n.* [Typ.] linotype *f*.

linseed ['lɪnˌsijd] *n.* graine *f* de lin; *~ oil*, huile *f* de lin.

lint [lɪnt] *n.* filasse *f*, [Surg.] charpie *f*.

lion ['lajən] *n.* lion *m*: *mountain ~*, cougouar *m*, puma *m*, © lion de montagne; ~ *cub*, lionceau *m*. || **lioness** [-əs] *n*. lionne *f*.

lip [lɪp] *n*. lèvre *f*; bord *m*, rebord *m*, bec *m* [d'objets ayant un bord aigu, bien marqué]; [Fig.] insolence *f*: *to pay ~ -service to (s.o., sth.)*, louanger hypocritement. || **lipstick** [-ˌstɪk] *n*. rouge *m* à lèvres.

liqueur [lɪ'kjuwɚ] *n*. [×] liqueur *f*.

liquid ['lɪkwəd] *n*. & *adj*. liquide (*m*).

liquidate [-ejt] *v. tr*. **1**. [money] liquider, solder. **2**. fixer (le montant d'un compte). [Fam.] liquider, se débarrasser de. || **liquidation** [lɪkwə'dejʃən] *n*. liquidation *f*; solde *m*.

liquor ['lɪkɚ] *n*. spiritueux *m*; [Fam.] *hard ~*, boisson *f* (forte); © ~ *Commission*, Commission *f* des liqueurs; Régie *f* des Alcools.

liquorice ['lɪkɚəs] *n*. réglisse *f*.

lisp [lɪsp] *n*. zézayement *m*. || *v. intr*. zézayer, balbutier.

list [lɪst] *n*. **1**. [names, &c.] liste *f*, rôle *m*; [things] série *f*: ~ *of wines*, carte *f* des vins; *mailing ~*, liste *f* d'abonnés, fichier *m* d'adresses, répertoire *m*: *price ~*, barême *m*, prix *m* courant. **2**. [Naut.] bande *f*. 3. *pl*. [Sport.] lice *f*: *to enter the lists*, entrer en lice.

list *v. tr*. [names, &c.] enregistrer, [items, &c.] cataloguer. || *v. intr*. [ship] donner de la bande; [Mil.] †s'enrôler.

listen ['lɪsn̩] *v. tr*. écouter (qqun, *to s.o.*); prêter l'oreille (aux paroles de . . .). || *v. intr*. écouter: *(say) ~ !*, Écoute(z) donc!; *to ~ in*, écouter (la radio). || **listener** [-ɚ] *n*. audit|eur *m*, -rice *f*.

listing ['lɪst|ɪŋ] *n*. inscription *f* (dans un annuaire, &c.).

listless [-ləs] *adj*. apathique, inattentif. || **listlessness** [-ləsnəs] indifférence *f*, apathie *f*.

lit cf. LIGHT 1, 3.

literacy ['lɪtɚəsɪ] *n*. le fait de savoir lire et écrire.

literal ['lɪtɚəl] *adj*. [translation, &c.] littéral, mot-à-mot *inv*. || **literally** [-ɪ] *adv*. littéralement, mot-à-mot, à la lettre: *~ speaking . . .*, à proprement parler. || **literary** ['lɪtɚ|ˌɛɚɪ] *adj*. littéraire, [man, profession] de(s) lettres. || **literate** [-ət] *adj*. [Pers.] sachant lire et écrire. || **literature** [ətʃɚ] *n*. [writing] littérature *f*; publications *fpl*, documentation *f* (sur une question); [pamphlets] brochures *fpl*, tracts *mpl*: *trade ~*, imprimés *mpl* publicitaires.

litigation [ˌlɪtɪ'gejʃən] *n*. litige *m*; [coll.] litiges *mpl* contentieux.

litre ['lijtɚ] *n*. litre *m* [= 1.0567 qt. liquid measure, or .908 qt. dry measure].

litter ['lɪtɚ] *n*. [conveyance] litière *f*; [stretcher] civière *f*; [young] portée *f*; [Fig.] fouillis *m*, désordre *m*. || *v. intr*. **1**. mettre bas, avoir une portée. **2**. laisser traîner (des objets): *The floor was littered with butts*, Le parquet était/jonché, couvert/de mégots.

little [lɪtl̩] *adj*. **smaller** ['smɔlɚ], **smallest** ['smɔləst] [q.v.] †**less** [lɛs] **least** [lijst] [q.v.] **1**. petit; minime; [mean] mesquin: *a ~ boy*, un/petit garçon, garçonnet/. **2**. peu: *He has ~ (money)*, Il a peu d'argent, Il en a peu; *ever so ~* , un petit peu (de). || **little** [lɪtl̩] *n*. peu *m*; peu de chose, pas grand-chose: *He has a ~ (money)*, Il a un peu d'argent, Il en a un peu; *after a ~ (while)*, après un petit moment; *He is a ~ wiser now*, Il est un peu plus raisonnable maintenant; *He eats ~* , Il mange peu (de chose); *He knows very ~* , Il sait très peu de chose, Il ne sait pas grand-chose; *the, what/ ~ he knows*, le peu qu'il sait; *~ by ~* , peu à peu, petit à petit. || **little** *adv*. **less, least** [q.v.] peu; ne . . . guère: *~ known*, peu connu; *He ~ thinks that . . .*, Il ne se doute guère que . . . ; *He is ~ wiser than before*, Il n'est guère plus sage qu'avant.

liturgy ['lɪtɚdʒɪ] *n*. liturgie *f*.

live[1] [lajv] *adj*. **1**. vivant, en vie. **2**. vif, actif. 3. [Tech.]: *~ wire*, fil sous tension; [Rail.] rail *m* conducteur; *~ -oak*, chêne vert.

live[2] [lɪv] *v. intr*. vivre: *to ~ on vegetables*, se nourrir de légumes; *as long as I ~* , tant que je vivrai; *We ~ and learn*, Qui vivra verra. **2**. demeurer, habiter: *Where do you ~ ?*, Où demeurez-vous?; *I ~ in Montreal*, J'habite Montréal. || *v. tr*. mener, passer: *to ~ a happy life*, passer une vie tranquille. || **live down** [-'dawn] *v. tr*. faire oublier (un scandale, &c.). || **live in** [-'ɪn] *v. intr*. être logé et nourri (sur le lieu de son travail). || **livelihood** ['lajvlɪhud] *n*. moyens *mpl* d'existence: *to make a ~* , gagner sa vie. || **liveliness** [-nəs] *n*. animation *f*, entrain *m*. || **lively** [-lɪ] *adj*. vif, plein d'entrain, enjoué: *to take a ~ interest in*, s'intéresser vivement à.

liven [-n̩] *v. tr*. (up) animer (qqun, qqch.). || *v. intr*. (up) s'animer.

liver ['lɪvɚ] *n*. foie *m*.

livery [-ɪ] *n*. **1**. livrée *f*, uniforme *m*: [Fig.] couleurs *fpl*. **2**. *~ horse*, cheval *m* de louage.

lives cf. LIFE & TO LIVE.

livestock ['lajvˌstɑk] *n.* (le) bétail *m,* les bestiaux *mpl*; cheptel *m.*

liveyer ['lɪvjɚ] © *n.* [Newfoundland] habitant *m* du Labrador.

livid ['lɪvɪd] *adj.* [colour, face] livide.

living ['lɪvɪŋ] *adj.* vivant, en vie; †vif, en existence. ‖ *n.* vie *f*, existence *f*: *to/earn, make/one's* ~ (*at*), gagner sa vie (à); *to make a* (*bare*) ~ , gagner (tout juste) de quoi vivre; *the cost of* ~ , le coût de la vie; *standard of* ~ , conditions *fpl* d'existence, niveau *m* de vie; ~ *-room,* salon *m*, salle *f* de séjour, © vivoir *m.*

lizard ['lɪzɚd] *n.* lézard *m.*

load [lowd] *n.* charge *f* (d'un véhicule, d'un fusil); fardeau *m,* poids *m*; chargement *m* (de sable, &c.); [Naut.] cargaison *f.* ‖ *v. tr.* charger (un véhicule, une arme à feu); combler (qqun de compliments, &c.), accabler (qqun de reproches). ‖ *v. intr.* [Naut.] faire la cargaison; [truck]: *to* ~ *up,* prendre un chargement.

loaf[1] [lowf] *pl.* **loaves** [preceded by a numeral adj.] pain *m,* miche *f* (de pain).

loaf[2] *v. intr.* flâner, fainéanter. ‖ **loafer** [-ɚ] *n.* badaud *m,* fainéant *m.*

loam [lowm] *n.* glaise *f.*

loan [lown] *n.* [money] prêt *m,* avance *f*; [Fin.] emprunt *m*: ~ *on mortgage,* /prêt, emprunt/hypothécaire; ~ *on overdraft,* prêt à découvert. ‖ *v. tr.* prêter (de l'argent).

loath [lowθ] *adj.* peu enclin à, ayant de la répugnance pour: *nothing* ~ , enclin (à), porté (vers.) ‖ **loathe** [lowð] *v. tr.* détester (qqun, qqch.), avoir (qqun, qqch.) en horreur. ‖ **loathsome** [-səm] *adj.* dégoûtant, odieux.

loaves [lowvz] cf. LOAF[1].

lobby ['lɑbɪ] *n.* couloir *m,* antichambre *f*; foyer *m* (d'un théâtre); hall *m* d'hôtel. ‖ **lobbying** [-ŋ] *n.* [US, Pol.]/menées *fpl,* intrigues *fpl*/de couloir, cabale *f.* ‖ **lobbyist** ['lɑbɪɪst] *n.* intrigant *m* de couloir.

lobster ['lɑbstɚ] *n.* homard *m*: *rock-lobster,* → *n.* langouste *f.*

local ['lowkḷ] *adj.* local, d'intérêt local, régional: ~ *train,* train *m* omnibus, d'intérêt local/, [Pop.] tortillard *m*; © ~ *parliament,* parlement provincial. ‖ *n.* habitant(e) du lieu; [Rail.] train *m* omnibus; succursale *f* (de syndicat, &c.); poste *m* téléphonique. ‖ **locality** [low'kælɪtɪ] *n.* [place] localité *f*, emplacement *m,* lieu *m*; scène *f* (d'un événement); [town, village] endroit *m,* [Fam.] patelin *m.* ‖ **localize** ['lowkḷˌajz] *v. tr.* **1.** [Med.] localiser. **2.** fixer (dans un endroit). ‖ **locally** [-ɪ] *adv.* localement, sur place, dans/le pays, la région/.

locate [low'kejt] *v. intr.* se fixer, s'établir. ‖ *v. tr.* trouver, localiser; repérer (un objectif); situer (une ville sur la carte). ‖ **location** [low'kejʃən] *n.* endroit *m.* situation *f* (d'une ville, chose, &c.).

lock[1] [lɑk] *n.* [Naut.] écluse *f.*

lock[2] *n.* [hair] boucle *f*, mèche *f.*

lock[3] *n.* [door] serrure *f*; [bolt] verrou(s) *m*(*pl*): *under* ~ *and key,* sous clef; ~ , *stock and barrel,* [Fam.] tout le/fourbi, tremblement, bataclan/. ‖ *v. tr.* verrouiller, © barrer (une porte), fermer (une porte, &c.) à clef; mettre (qqun, qqch.) sous clef (*s.o., sth. in*). ‖ *v. intr.* se fermer à clef; [wheel] se bloquer. ‖ **locker** [-ɚ] *n.* [in stations and public buildings] compartiment *m* individuel; vestiaire *m*/individuel, métallique/; coffre *m* (de sûreté). ‖ **lock in** [-'ɪn] *v. tr.* enfermer à clef. ‖ **lock out** [-'awt] *v. tr.* fermer la porte (à clef) sur qqun: *I am locked out,* → Je ne peux pas rentrer, la porte est fermée à clef. ‖ **locksmith** [-ˌsmɪθ] *n.* serrurier *m.* ‖ **lock up** [-'ʌp] *v. tr.* mettre (qqun) sous les verrous; serrer (qqch.) sous clef; fermer (une maison) à clef.

locomotive [ˌlowkə'mowtɪv] *n.* [Rail.] locomotive *f*: ~ *engineer,* mécanicien *m.*

locust ['lowkəst] *n.* **1.** [insect] locuste *f*, sauterelle *f.* **2.** [tree] caroube *f.*

lodge [lɑdʒ] *n.* cabane *f*, hutte *f*; [hotel] relais *m,* hostellerie *f*; [Freemasons] loge *f*; [beaver] tanière *f.* ‖ *v. intr.* habiter (chez qqun), se loger. ‖ *v. tr.* loger, héberger (qqun chez . . .); loger (une balle); [Fig.] *to* ~ *a complaint with . . .* , porter plainte auprès de . . . ‖ **lodger** [-ɚ] *n.* locataire *m,* pensionnaire *m.* ‖ **lodging** [-ɪŋ] *n.* logement *m,* appartement *m*; abri *m,* gîte *m*: *board and* ~ , chambre *f* et pension *f*; *with board and* ~ , logé et nourri; *lodgings,* logement *m*; appartement *m* meublé, chambre *f* meublée, meublé *m.*

loft [lɔft] *n.* **1.** grenier *m,* soupente *f.* **2.** tribune *f* (d'une église). ‖ **lofty** [-ɪ] *adj.* **1.** très haut; [Fig.] exalté, élevé. **2.** [Pers., character] hautain.

log [lɔg] *n.* **1.** [wood, timber] bûche *f*, rondin *m,* billot *m,* tronc *m* d'arbre: *to/shoot, drive/logs,* © faire la drave; ~ *cabin,* cabane *f* de/rondins, troncs d'arbres, © en bois ronds/; ~ *-jam,* embâcle *m* de/bois flotté, billes/; ~ *-rolling,* [timber]/roulage *m,* débardage *m*/des grumes; [US, Pol.] trafic *m* de votes; [literature, &c.] entr'aide *f* intéressée; [Fig.] *to sleep like a* ~ , dormir à poings fermés. **2.** [ship] journal *m* de bord, livre *m* de loch; [car] carnet *m* de route; [flight] livre de vol. || *v. tr.* [event] /inscrire, porter/(qqch.) au journal. || *v. intr.* couper des/rondins, bûches/, scier des troncs d'arbres.

logic ['lɑʤɪk] *n.* (la) logique *f.* || **logical** [-l̩] *adj.* logique.

loin(s) [lojn(z)] *n.* [Pers.] reins *mpl*; [animals] aloyau *m* (de bœuf), longe *f* (de veau).

loiter ['lojtɚ] *v. intr.* flâner, s'attarder (en chemin); [stand and watch] faire le badaud: *No loitering!*, Circulez! [sign] Défense de stationner. || *v. tr.* [away] perdre (son temps) avec insouciance.

loll [lɑl] *v. intr.* **1.** s'étendre à son aise. **2.** [tongue] pendre.

lollipop ['lɑlɪˌpɑp] *n.* © sucre *m* d'orge; [Fr.] sucette *f.*

London ['lʌndən] *n.* [UK] Londres; [Ont.] London. || *adj.* de Londres, londonien. || **Londoner** [-ɚ] *n.* Londonien, -ne.

lone [lown] *adj.* **1.** seul, solitaire: ~ *survivor*, seul survivant; isolé, esseulé. **2.** [humorous] célibataire, veuf. || **loneliness** [-lɪnəs] *n.* solitude *f*, sentiment *m* d'isolement. || **lonely** [-lɪ] *adv.* solitaire; isolé. || **lonesome** [-səm] *adj.* [Pers.] solitaire, seul.

long[1] [lɔŋ] *adj.* **1.** [space] long: *How ~ is the road?*, Quelle est la longueur de la route?; *It is 6 miles ~*, Elle a 6 milles de long(ueur), Elle est longue de 6 milles; *~ measure*, mesure *f* de longueur; *~ jump*, saut *m* en longueur; *to make sth. longer*, (r)allonger qqch.; *to make a ~ face*, faire/la grimace, triste figure/; *to have ~ arms*, avoir les bras longs; [Fig.] *to have a ~ arm*, avoir le bras long; *in the ~ run*, à la longue, en fin de compte; *It's as broad as it is ~*, C'est bonnet blanc et blanc bonnet. **2.** [time] long; prolongé: *How ~ /is, are/. . .?*, Quelle est la durée de . . . ?; *It won't be ~ (/before, till/ . . .)*, Ce ne sera pas long (d'ici que + subjunc.); *I won't be ~*, Je n'en ai pas pour longtemps; *I won't be ~ (in) doing it*, Je ne serai pas longtemps à le faire; *It is a (very) ~ time since I saw him*, Il y a, Voilà/(bien) longtemps que je ne l'ai vu; *Is it ~ since . . . ?*, Y a-t-il longtemps que . . . ?; *I haven't seen him for a ~ time*, Je ne l'ai pas vu depuis longtemps; *He lived there for a ~ time*, Il y a demeuré (pendant) longtemps; *He won't do that for a ~ time*, Il ne recommencera pas de/sitôt, longtemps/, Il n'est pas près de recommencer; ***at the (very) longest***, (tout) au plus; [Fam.] *So ~ !*, A bientôt! **3.** [syllable] (une) longue: *before ~*, avant (qu'il soit) peu; *for ~*, pendant, depuis, pour/longtemps; cf. FOR; *I haven't ~ (to do it)*, Je n'ai pas beaucoup de temps (pour le faire); *It won't take ~ (to do it)*, Cela ne prendra pas longtemps, Il ne faudra pas longtemps pour le faire; *~ enough to . . .*, le temps nécessaire pour . . . || *adv.* longtemps: *Have you been here ~ ?*, Y a-t-il longtemps que vous êtes ici?; *I have ~ wondered*, Je me le demande depuis longtemps; *How ~ have you been waiting?*, Depuis/quand, combien de temps/attendez-vous?; *How ~ /did, will/ he live here?*, (Pendant) combien de temps/a-t-il demeuré, demeurera-t-il/ici?; *(not) ~ ago*, il y a/longtemps, peu de temps/; *~ /before, after/*, longtemps/avant, après/; *all day ~*, tout le long du jour, toute la journée; *Long live the Queen!*, Vive la Reine! || **as long as**: *He stayed ~ I did*, Il y est resté aussi longtemps que moi; *~ I am here*, tant que je serai ici; *~ you don't make a noise*, Pourvu que vous ne fassiez pas de bruit.

long[2] *v. intr.* désirer ardemment (qqch., *for sth.*), avoir la nostalgie (de la patrie): *to ~ to see s.o.*,/être impatient, brûler du désir/de voir qqun.

longboat [-ˌbowt] *n.* chaloupe *f.* || **long-distance** [-'dɪstəns] *adj.* à longue distance; [runner] de fond; [Tel. call] (appel) interurbain *m*: *to call s.o. ~*, appeler qqun à l'inter(urbain).

longer [-ɚ] *adj. compar.* cf. LONG[1]. || *adv. compar.* plus longtemps; plus; encore: *I can't wait any ~*, Je ne peux pas attendre plus longtemps; *That/is no, isn't any/ ~ possible*, Cela n'est plus possible; *How much ~ . . . ?*, Combien de temps encore . . . ?; *one month ~*, un mois/de plus, encore/.

longevity [lɑn'ʤɛvɪtɪ] *n.* longévité. *f.*

longhand ['lɔŋˌhænd] *n.* écriture *f* ordinaire: *in ~*, à la main.

longing [lɔŋɪŋ] *n.* désir *m* ardent, envie *f* impatiente, souhait *m* vif. || **longing** *adj.* [look] plein d'envie.

longitude ['lɑnʤɪˌtuwd] *n.* longitude *f*; [Fig.] longueur *f.*

long-lived [-lɪvd] *adj.* [Pers.] qui a la vie longue; [Fig.] vivace. || **long-range** [-'ɹejnʤ] *adj.* à longue portée. || **longshore|-man, -men** [-ˌʃɔɚmən] *n.* docker *m*, débardeur *m.* || **long-sighted** [-'sajtəd] *adj.* [Pers.] presbyte; [Fig.] clairvoyant, prévoyant. || **long-suffering** [-'sʌfɚɪŋ] *adj.* [Pers.] patient, †longanime. || *n.* patience *f*; †longanimité *f*. || **long-winded** [-'wɪndəd] *adj.* [speech, &c.] sans fin, interminable; [Pers.] intarissable.

look [lʊk] *n.* **1.** regard *m*, coup *m* d'œil: *to give s.o. a* ~ , *to/take, have/a* ~ *at s.o.*, regarder qqun, jeter un coup d'œil sur qqun; *to give s.o. an angry* ~ , lancer un regard furieux à qqun; *I'll/take, have/a* ~ *around*, Je vais/inspecter les lieux, faire le tour/. **2.** air *m*, aspect *m*, apparence *f*; mine *f*: *He has a strange* ~ , [expression] Il a une drôle de mine, [gen.] Il a l'air étrange; *It has a foreign* ~ , Cela a/l'air étranger, une apparence étrangère/; *I don't like the* ~ *of it*, Je n'aime pas l'aspect de l'affaire, Ça me paraît suspect; *by the/* ~ , *looks/of it*, d'après l'apparence, à ce qu'il paraît. **3.** *pl.* belle apparence *f*, beauté *f* [usual.] *good looks.* || **look** *v. tr.* & *intr.* **1.** regarder: ~ *before you leap*, Regardez à deux fois avant de sauter; ~ *here!*, Dites donc, Voyons! **2.** [seem] avoir l'air, paraître, sembler: *She looks happy*, Elle/a l'air, semble/heureuse; *She looks happy*, Elle/a l'air heureux, paraît (être) heureuse/; *She returned, looking happy*, Elle revint, l'air heureux; *She doesn't* ~ *her age*, Elle ne/porte, paraît/pas son âge; *She looked* (*like*) *it*, Elle en avait l'air; *He looks* (*like*) *the part*, Il a le physique de l'emploi; *He looks/well, ill/*, Il a/bonne, mauvaise/mine; *It looks well* (*on you*), Cela/vous va (bien), fait bien, bon effet/(sur vous); *It looks bad*, Ça/va mal, ne va pas (bien); *How do I* ~ *?*, *What do I look like?*, De quoi est-ce que j'ai l'air, Comment me trouvez-vous?; *He looks* (*to me*) *like a policeman*, Il m'a l'air d'un agent (de police); *It looks like rain*, On dirait qu'il va pleuvoir; *He looked* (*to me*)*/as if, as though/he were going to jump*, Il avait l'air de vouloir, Il me semblait qu'il allait/sauter; *It looks* (*to me*) *as if we can't go*, Il/me semble, semble(rait)/que nous ne pourrons pas y aller. || **look about** [-ə'bawt] *v. intr.* regarder autour de soi: *to* ~ *for s.o.*, chercher qqun des yeux. || **look after** [-'æftər] *v. intr.* soigner, s'occuper de, avoir, prendre soin de: *to* ~ *o.s.*, se soigner, se débrouiller tout seul. || **look around** [-ə'ɹawnd] *v. intr.* tourner la tête. cf. LOOK ABOUT. || **look at** [-ˌæt] *v. intr.* regarder (qqun, qqch.); voir; [Fig.] considérer, envisager, voir: *to* ~ *one's watch*, regarder à sa montre (pour voir l'heure); *to* ~ *him, one would say . . .*, à le voir, on dirait . . . ; *way of looking at things*, façon *f* de voir les choses. || **look away** [-ə'wej] *v. intr.* détourner les yeux. || **look back** [-'bæk] *v. intr.* regarder en arrière; se retourner; [Fig.] se reporter (à, *upon*); se rappeler (qqch.). || **look down** [-'dawn] *v. intr.* regarder en bas; baisser les yeux: *to* ~ *upon*, dominer, [Fig.] mépriser, regarder (qqun) de haut en bas. || **look for** [-ˌfɔər] *v. intr.* chercher (qqun, qqch.); [expect] s'attendre à: *looking for . . .*, à la recherche de. . . . || **look forward (to)** [-'fɔərwərd] *v. intr.* envisager, attendre . . . avec plaisir, impatience; [expect] s'attendre à: *I am looking forward to seeing him again*, C'est avec plaisir que je le reverrai. || **look in** [-ˌɪn] *v. intr.* passer voir (qqun); ne faire qu'entrer et sortir; [TV] regarder/la télévision, un programme/. || **look into** [-'ɪntuw] *v. intr.* examiner, étudier; s'occuper de. || **look on** [-'ɑn] *v. intr.* considérer . . . (comme); être spectateur, regarder. || **look out** [-'awt] *v. intr.* regarder au dehors; [room] donner, avoir vue (*on, on to*, sur); faire attention (à): *to* ~ *of the window*, regarder par la fenêtre; *to* ~ *for sth.*, être à la recherche de, essayer de trouver/qqch.; ~ *!*, Attention!; ~ *for the traffic*, Faites attention à la circulation; ~ *for him*, Méfiez-vous de lui. || **look over** [-'owvər] *v. intr.* examiner, revoir, relire (qqch.); visiter (une maison); parcourir (qqch. des yeux). || **look through** [-'θɹuw] *v. intr.* regarder par (une fenêtre), dans (un télescope); parcourir, feuilleter/(un livre, &c.); examiner (rapidement). || **look to** [-'tuw] *v. intr.* s'occuper de, veiller à/(qqch.); envisager (l'avenir); avoir recours à, compter sur. || **look up** [-'ʌp] *v. intr.* regarder en haut, lever les yeux, relever la tête; chercher (un mot); aller, venir/voir (qqun): *Things are looking up*, Les choses vont mieux, Les affaires reprennent. || **look upon** [-ə'pɑn] *v. intr.* considérer . . . comme; voir, envisager/(qqch. comme).

loom[1] [luwm] *n.* [weaving] métier *m*.

loom[2] *v. intr.* [usual. + **up**) apparaître, se dessiner; [Fig.] apparaître, être imminent (d'une façon imprécise et menaçante).

loon [luwn] *n.* [bird] plongeon *m*; © huard *m*. || **loony** [-ɪ] *adj.* loufoque, [Arg.] timbré.

loop [luwp] *n.* **1.** [shape] boucle *f*. **2.** [button hole] bride *f*. **3.** [Auto.] courbe *f*. || *v. tr.* courber, boucler. || **loophole** [-ˌhowl] *n.* **1.** [Fortif.] meurtrière *f*. **2.** [Fig.] échappatoire *f*, faux-fuyant *m*.

loose [luws] *adj.* **1.** mal assujetti, branlant;

[page] détaché; [knot] défait; [lace] défait, délié; [screw] desserré; [tooth] qui remue; [end] pendant; [rope] détendu; [dress] large, ample; [change] petite (monnaie); [earth] meuble; [dog, &c.] déchaîné, échappé. **2.** [Fig.] [style] décousu, vague; [morale] relâché; [Pej., habits, Pers.] débauché, dissolu: *to come, work*/ ~, se défaire, se délier, se desserrer, se détacher; *to get* ~ , s'échapper; *to break* ~ , [prisoner] s'évader, [war] éclater, [Fig.] se déchaîner; *to go, run*/ ~ , être en liberté; *to be on the* ~ , courir la prétentaine; *to be at a* ~ *end*, être, se trouver/sans rien à faire; *to let* ~ , lâcher (un chien, &c.), donner libre cours à (sa colère). || *v. tr.* délier, détacher; dénouer (un nœud). || **loose-leaf** [-ˌlijf] *adj.*: à feuilles mobiles. || **loosely** [-lɪ] *adv.* d'une façon lâche, détendue; vaguement, abusivement. || **loosen** [-n̩] *v. tr. & intr.* (se) relâcher, (se) desserrer, (se) détendre. || **looseness** [-nəs] *n.* relâchement *m*; ampleur *f*; [mécanique] jeu *m*; [Fig.] vague *m*, imprécision *f*.

loot [luwt] *n.* [war, &c.] butin *m*, pillage *m*. || *v. tr.* piller, saccager (une ville &c.).

lop [lɑp] *v. tr.* **1.** [off] couper; [trees] émonder, élaguer. **2.** laisser pendre.

loquacious [ˌlow'kwejʃəs] *adj.* loquace, bavard.

lord [lɔɚd] *n.* [master, ruler] seigneur *m*; [Br.] lord *m*; [Rel.] *Our Lord*, Notre-Seigneur; [Br.] *the Lord Mayor (of London)*, le lord maire (de Londres); [Rel.] *the Lord's Prayer*, l'oraison dominicale, le Pater; [Br. Parliament] *the House of Lords*, la Chambre des Lords. || **lordly** [-lɪ] *adj.* [look, attitude] noble; [Pej.] hautain. || **lordship** [-ˌʃɪp] *n.* seigneurie *f*, pouvoir *m*, autorité *f* (sur, *over*); propriété *f* (de, *over sth.*): *Your* ~ , Votre Seigneurie, [Rel.] Monseigneur, Excellence.

lore [lɔɚ] *n.* savoir *m*, doctrine *f*: [Anthr.] *folk* ~ , folklore.

lorry ['lɔɚɪ] *n.* [Br.] cf. TRUCK.

lose [luwz] **lost, lost** [lɔst] *v. tr.* **1.** perdre, égarer: *to* ~ *one's temper*, perdre patience, s'emporter; *to* ~ *one's way*, s'égarer, se perdre; *to* ~ *sight of*, perdre de vue; *to* ~ *touch*, perdre le contact; *to* ~ *o.s.*, s'absorber (*in*, dans). **2.** perdre, gaspiller: *to* ~ *one's life*, perdre la vie; *to* ~ *time*, gaspiller son temps; [watch] retarder de (5 minutes, &c.). || *v. intr.* perdre; [watch] retarder; [Loc.] *to get lost*, se perdre, s'égarer.

loser ['luwzɚ] *n.* perdant *m*, -e *f*.

loss [lɔs] *n.* [time, &c.] perte *f*, [article] égarement *m*: *to be quite at a* ~ *(to . . .)*, être bien embarrassé (pour . . .); [Com.] *dead* ~ , perte *f* sèche.

lost [lɔst] cf. LOSE. || *adj.* perdu, égaré: *to get* ~ , s'égarer, © s'écarter.

lot [lɑt] *n.* **1.** lot *m*; sort *m*: *to draw lots for sth.*, tirer qqch. au sort; *It fell to my* ~ *to . . .*, Le sort voulut que je (+ subjonct.). **2.** [land] terrain *m*, lot *m*. **3.** [Com.] partie *f*: *in lots*, par parties; *in a* ~ , en bloc. **4.** [Fam.] *He is, They are/a bad* ~ , C'est de la mauvaise graine; *That's the* ~ , C'est tout. **5.** [Fam.] *a* ~ *(of)*, beaucoup, un tas/(de); [adv.] beaucoup, souvent: *what a* ~ *of . . .*, que de . . .; *such a* ~ *of*, tellement de; *quite a* ~ , beaucoup, une quantité considérable (de): *lots of people*, des tas de gens.

lotion ['lowʃən] *n.* lotion *f*.

lottery ['lɑtɚɪ] *n.* loterie *f*.

loud [lawd] *adj.* [noise, cry] grand; [voice] haut, fort; [laugh, &c.] bruyant; [colour] criard, tapageur; [cheers] (applaudissements *mpl*) nourri(s): *in a* ~ *voice*, à haute voix. || *adv.* fort, (tout) haut, à haute voix: *out* ~ , à haute voix, tout haut; *Louder!*, Plus fort! || **loudly** [-lɪ] *adv.* à haute voix, tout haut; bruyamment, avec grand bruit: *to dress* ~ , porter des couleurs criardes. || **loudspeaker** [-'spijkɚ] *n.* haut-parleur *m*.

lounge [lawndʒ] *n.* [hotel] salon *m*, © vivoir *m*: *cocktail* ~ , salon-bar *m*, salon de dégustation; ~ *chair*, chaise *f* longue; ~ *suit*, complet veston *m*. || *v. intr.* flâner, se vautrer (dans un fauteuil).

louse [laws] *pl.* **lice** [lajs] *n.* [insect] pou *m*.

louse-wort ['lawsˌwɔɚt] *n.* [Bot.] pédiculaire *f*, © herbe *f* à poux.

lousy ['lawzɪ] *adj.* pouilleux; [Arg.] moche.

lovable ['lʌv|əbl̩] *adj.* aimable, digne/d'amour, d'affection/; [likeable] sympathique. || **love** [lʌv] *n.* amour *m* (pour qqun, de qqch.); [motherly] tendresse *f* (pour); affection *f* (pour); [friendship] amitié *f* (pour); [act] charité *f* (envers); [Pers.] (mon) amour; [tennis] zéro *m*: *to/be, fall/in* ~ *with s.o.*, être, tomber/amoureux de qqun; × *to make* ~ *to s.o.*, faire la cour à qqun; *for* ~ *nor money*, pour rien au monde; *(Give) my* ~ *to all*, (Faites) mes amitiés à tous. || *v. tr.* aimer (d'amour), adorer: *I* ~ *fishing*, J'adore la pêche; *to* ~ *to do sth.*, aimer, adorer/faire qqch.; *I'd* ~ *to!*, Avec le plus grand plaisir! || **loveliness** [-lɪnəs] *n.* beauté *f*, charme *m*. || **lovely** [-lɪ] *adj.* beau; charmant, ravissant; un amour de . . . || **lover** [-ɚ] *n.* **1.** amoureux *m*, amoureuse *f*: [Fam.] *lover*, mon chéri. **2.** amateur *m* (de): *music* ~, amateur de (belle) musique, mélomane *m*. || **loving** [-ɪŋ] *adj.* [Pers., feeling] *adj.* aimant, affectueux, [Pers.] affectionné. || **lovingly** [-ɪŋlɪ] *adv.* affectueusement, avec/tendresse, affection/.

low[1] [low] *n.* meuglement *m* (d'une vache). || *v. intr.* meugler.

low[2] [low] *adj.* [height] bas, peu élevé; [bow] profond; [dress] décolleté; [price] bas, faible, modique; [number] faible, restreint; [speed] petit, faible; [gear] (en) première (vitesse); [language] bas; [condition] humble, modeste; [Pers., character] vil, ignoble; [trick] sale (coup); [opinion] mauvais; [note] bas, grave; [light] faible, en veilleuse; [fever] lent; *to get, run/* ~, baisser, s'épuiser; *to bring* ~, humilier; *to lie* ~, se cacher, rester caché; *to lay* ~, étendre (qqun) (mort); [sickness] terrasser: *to feel (in)* ~ *(spirits)*, se sentir déprimé; *in a* ~ *voice*, à voix basse; [Rel.] ~ *mass*, messe *f* basse; *the Low Countries*, les Pays-Bas *mpl* (*in, to*, aux); *at the lowest*, au bas mot, au minimum. || *adv.* bas; [bow] profondément, [speak, sing] à voix basse. || **lowbrow** [-ˌbɹaw] *n. & adj.* (personne *f*) peu intellectuel(le). || **low-down** [-ˌdawn] *adj.* bas; vil, ignoble; [Fam.] sale: [Sl.] *to give s.o. the* ~ *on sth.*, mettre qqun au courant de qqch. || **lower** [-ɚ] *adj.* inférieur, d'en bas; → bas: *the* ~ *classes*, les basses classes; *the* ~ *town*, la basse ville; *Lower Canada*, le Bas Canada; [Typ.] ~ *case*, bas *m* de casse. || *v. intr.* [sun] baisser, descendre. || *v. tr.* baisser, abaisser (un drapeau, &c.); (faire) descendre (qqch.); [boat] mettre à/l'eau, la mer/; [Fig.] réduire, diminuer (qqch.); amoindrir (qqch.). || **lowering** [-ɪŋ] *n.* abaissement *m*, diminution *f*. || **low-grade** [-gɹejd] *adj.* de qualité inférieure.

lowland [-'lænd] *adj.* de la plaine, situé dans un terrain bas. || *n.* basse terre *f*, (la) plaine [par opposition à la montagne, dans un même pays]: *the Lowlands*, la Basse-Écosse. || **lowliness** [-lɪnəs] *n.* **1.** humilité *f*, modestie *f*. **2.** petitesse *f*, manque *m* de dignité. || **lowly** [-lɪ] *adj.* [rank] bas; [condition] humble. || *adv.* humblement; bassement, vilement. || **lowness** [-nəs] *n.* humilité *f*, médiocrité *f* (de condition); étroitesse *f* (d'esprit); vulgarité *f*; [sounds] gravité *f* (du son); [prices] modicité *f* (des prix).

loyal ['lojəl] *adj.* loyal (envers qqun, *to s.o.*); fidèle (à qqun).

lozenge ['lɑzəndʒ] *n.* [shape] losange *m*; [cough] pastille *f* (pour le rhume, &c.).

lubricant ['luwbɹɪ|kənt] *n.* lubrifiant *m*. || **lubricate** [-ˌkejt] *v. tr.* [car, &c.] lubrifier (qqch.). || **lubrication** ['luwbɹɪ'kejʃən] *n.* [car, machine] graissage *m*.

lucid ['luwsɪd] *adj.* **1.** [understanding] clair, limpide; [stream] clair, limpide. **2.** [Pers.] lucide. **3** brillant, éclatant.

luck [lʌk] *n.* hasard *m*, chance *f*; fortune *f*: *good* ~, bonheur *m*, bonne chance; *ill* ~, *bad* ~, malchance *f*, [Fam.] déveine *f*, guigne *f*; *Hard* ~ *!*, Pas de chance!; *a bit/stroke/of luck*, un coup de veine. || **luckily** [-ɪlɪ] *adv.* heureusement, par bonheur. || **lucky** [-ɪ] *adj.* heureux, → qui a de la chance: *How* ~ *(that)* . . ., Quelle chance (que + subj.); *It is* ~ *that* . . ., C'est une chance que [+ subj.]; [Fam.] veinard; [thing] porte-bonheur *invar.*

lucrative ['luwkɹətɪv] *adj.* [occupation, &c.] lucratif.

ludicrous ['luwdɪkɹəs] *adj.* comique, drôle, ridicule.

lug [lʌg] *v. tr.* **[-gg-]** traîner, tirer (de force). || *n.* anse *f*, oreille *f*; crampon *m*; [worm] limace *f*.

luggage ['lʌgədʒ] *n. coll.* bagages *mpl*; valises *fpl*, &c.: ~ *-store*, magasin *m* de bagages; ~ *-rack*, filet *m* aux bagages; [Auto.] ~ *-carrier*, porte-bagages *m. inv.* cf. BAGGAGE. [☞ In Canada, *luggage* is one's personal property (suitcases, bags, &c.) small enough to be carried by the individual. It becomes *baggage* when given to a public carrier or too big to be handled personally: *baggage car, baggage ticket, baggage room*, &c.]: ~ *ticket*, bulletin *m* de bagages; ~ *van*, fourgon *m* (de bagages).

lukewarm ['luwk,woɚm] *adj.* [proper and Fig.] tiède; [Fig.] froid, indifférent, sans enthousiasme.

lull [lʌl] *n.* accalmie *f*, [Naut. & Fig.] /moment *m*, instant *m*/de calme, de répit. || *v. tr.* [s.o. to sleep] bercer, endormir (qqun); calmer (la douleur). || *v. intr.* s'apaiser, se calmer. || **lullaby** [-əˌbaj] *n.* [Mus.] berceuse *f*.

lumber ['lʌmbɚ] *n.* **1.** bois *m* (de/construction, charpente/) [often *bois* is enough; cf. TIMBER]: ~ *mill*, scierie *f*. ~ *camp*, © chantier *m*; camp *m* de bûcherons. **2.** fatras *m*, vieilleries *fpl*, bric-à-brac *m*: ~ *-room*, chambre *f*, réduit *m*/de débarras. || *v. intr.* se traîner /avec difficulté, lourdement/. || *v. tr.* [up]

entasser (des objets, &c.) pêle-mêle. || **lumberer** [-ɚ] *n.* **1.** marchand *m* de bois; concessionnaire *m* de coupe; exploitant forestier. || **lumbering** [-ɚɪŋ] *adj.* [pace] pesant, lourd. || **lumberjack** [-ˌdʒæk] *n.* bûcheron *m* (de forêt). || **lumberman** [-ˌmæn] *n.* **1.** © [US] exploitant, propriétaire/forestier. cf. LUMBER[1]. **2.** [Br.] bûcheron *m.* **3.** contremaître *m* de bûcherons.

luminous [ˈluwmɪnəs] *adj.* [idea, &c.] lumineux, brillant, éclatant.

lump [lʌmp] *n.* [sugar, &c.] morceau *m* (assez gros), masse *f*, [ice] bloc *m*; motte *f* (de terre); [money] total *m*; bosse *f* (à la tête, au front); [sauce, &c.] grumeau *m*: ~ *sum*, somme/globale, payée en un seul versement; *in a* ~, en bloc. || *v. tr.* [together] réunir, mettre en commun; prendre en bloc: *If you don't like it, you can* ~ *it!* Si vous n'êtes pas content, allez le dire à Rome! || **lumper** [-ɚ] *n.* [Br.] débardeur *m*, docker *m.* cf. LONGSHOREMAN. || **lumpy** [-ɪ] *adj.* [porridge, &c.] grumeleux; [human body] couvert de bosses, de protubérances; [ocean] clapoteux.

lunacy [ˈluwnə|sɪ] *n.* aliénation *f* mentale, folie *f.* || **lunatic** [-tɪk] *adj.* **1.** [eccentric] extravagant. **2.** fou, folle; d'aliéné, de fous: ~ *asylum*, maison *f* de fous, asile *m* d'aliénés. cf. MENTAL. || *n.* fou *m*, folle *f*; aliéné *m.*

lunch [lʌntʃ] *n.* **1.** [Fr.] déjeuner *m*, © dîner *m*, lunch *m*: *business(men's)* ~, © dîner *m* d'affaires. **2.** [snack] casse-croûte *m*, goûter *m*, © lunch. || *v. intr.* [Fr.] déjeuner, © dîner: *to* ~ *out*, dîner en ville. || **luncheon** [-ən] cf. LUNCH.

lung [lʌŋ] *n.* **1.** poumon *m.* **2.** mou (de veau) *m.* || **lungwort** [-ˌwɔɚt] *n.* [Bot.] pulmonaire *f.*

lurch [lɚtʃ] *n.* [car, ship, cart] embardée *f*; [Fig.] embarras *m*: *to leave (s.o.) in the* ~, laisser (qqun) en plan, tenir (qqun) le bec dans l'eau. || *v. intr.* [car, ship, cart] faire une embardée.

lure [luwɚ] *n.* **1.** attrait *m*: [Fig.] *the* ~ *of the mountains*, l'appel *m* des cimes. **2.** appât *m*, [bait] leurre *m.* || *v. tr.* attirer, séduire, leurrer (qqun).

lurid [ˈluwɚɪd] *adj.* **1.** [light] blafard. **2.** [crime, &c.] terrible.

lurk [lɚk] *v. intr.* **1.** être aux aguets. **2.** se cacher, se tapir.

luscious [ˈlʌʃəs] *adj.* délicieux, succulent, agréable au goût.

lush [lʌʃ] *adj.* luxuriant.

lust [lʌst] *n.* **1.** désir *m* ardent; convoitise *f*; soif *f* (du pouvoir). **2.** goûts *mpl* dépravés, luxure *f.* || *v. intr.*: *to* ~ *after*, désirer ardemment, convoiter; soupirer après (qqun).

lustful [-fl̩] *adj.* [Pers.] luxurieux.

lustre [-ɚ] *n.* **1.** lustre *m*, éclat *m.* **2.** gloire *f*, renommée *f.* || **lustrous** [-ɹəs] *adj.* lustré, brillant.

lusty [-ɪ] *adj.* [Pers., fellow] fort, robuste, vigoureux.

lute [luwt] *n.* [Mus.] luth *m*: ~ *-maker*, luthier *m.*

Lutheran [ˈluwθɚən] *adj.* & *n.* [Rel.] luthérien (*m*, -ne *f*).

Luxemburg [ˈlʌksəmˌbɚg] *n.* [Geog.] le Luxembourg.

luxuriant [ˌlʌkˈʒuwɚɪ|ənt] *adj.* [vegetation] luxuriant; [Fig.] riche.

luxurious [-əs] *adj.* [×] **1.** [Pers.] adonné au luxe. **2.** [pleasures] voluptueux, [house, &c.] confortable; somptueux, luxueux.

luxury [ˈlʌkʃɚɪ] *n.* **1.** luxe *m.* **2.** objet *m* de luxe.

lye [laj] *n.* lessive *f.*

lying cf. LIE[1]. || *adj.* menteur. || *n.* le mensonge.

lymphatic [ˌlɪmˈfætɪk] *adj.* d'un tempérament lymphatique.

lynch [lɪntʃ] *v. tr.* lyncher (qqun).

lynx [lɪŋks] *n.* lynx *m.*

Lyons [ˈlajənz] *n.* [Geog.] Lyon.

lyric [ˈlɪrɪ|k] *adj.* lyrique. || *n.* (poème *m*) lyrique *m*; [*pl.*] poésie *f* lyrique; [Fam.] paroles *fpl* (d'une chanson). || **lyricism** [-sɪzm̩] *n.* lyrisme *m.*

M, m [ɛm] *pl.* **M's, m's,** [letter] M, m *m.*

M.A. ['ɛm'ej] [= Master of Arts] *n.* [degree] maîtrise *f* ès Arts; [Pers.] Maître *m* ès Arts [no fem.].

macabre [mə'kɑbɹə] *adj.* macabre.

macadam [mə'kædəm] *n.* macadam *m.*

macaroni [ˌmækə'ownı] *n.* macaroni *m.*

macaroon [ˌmækə'uwn] *n.* macaron *m.*

machine [mə'ʃijn] *n.* [mechanism, instrument, organization] machine *f*: *dishwashing* ~, laveuse *f* de vaisselle. || *v. tr.* usiner, façonner (une pièce). || **machinery** [-əɹ] machinerie *f*, [Fam.] les machines *fpl*; mécanisme *m.* || **machinist** [mə'ʃijnıst] *n.* mécanicien *m*; [skilled worker] machiniste *m.*

mackerel ['mækəəl] *n.* maquereau *m.*

mackinaw ['mækınɔ] © *n.* [clothing] mackinaw *m.*

mackintosh ['mækınˌtɑʃ] *n.* [Br.] imperméable *m*, caoutchouc *m.*

mad [mæd] *adj.* [Pers., &c.]. **1.** fou, insensé; furieux, enragé (contre, *with*): *to drive* ~, rendre fou; *to go* ~, devenir fou; *stark, raving*/ ~, complètement fou; *as* ~ *as a hatter*, fou à lier; [Loc.] *like* ~, [work] comme un perdu, [strive] désespérément; *to be* ~ *about sth.*, être fou de qqch.; *to be* ~ *about bridge*, être un joueur de bridge enragé. **2.** [Fam.] furieux (*at*, contre).

Madam(e) ['mædəm] [polite, to a lady] Madame.

madcap ['mæd|ˌkæp] *adj.* fou, folle; écervelé; étourdi.

madden [-n̩] *v. tr.* rendre (qqun) fou, affoler (une personne, une bête); faire enrager (qqun). || *v. intr.* devenir fou.

made cf. MAKE. || *adj.* fait, fabriqué: ~ *in Canada*, [produce] → (de) fabrication canadienne, produit canadien; ~ *-up*, [face] maquillé; [story, &c.] inventé; [argument, &c.] factice.

madly ['mædlı] *adv.* follement; comme un fou. || **madman** [-ˌmæn] *n.* fou *m*, dément *m.* || **madness** [-nəs] *n.* folie *f*, aliénation *f* mentale, démence *f*; rage *f*, fureur *f.*

magazine [ˌmægə'zıjn] *n.* magazine *m*, revue *f.*

Maggie ['mægı] *n.* [dim. de Margaret] = Margot.

maggot ['mægət] *n.* asticot *m.* || **maggoty** [-ı] *adj.* véreux, grouillant de vers.

magic ['mædʒık] *adj.* magique. || *n.* magie *f*: *as if by* ~, comme par enchantement. || **magical** [l̩] *adj.* magique, enchanté. || **magically** [-l̩ı] *adv.* magiquement, par magie. || **magician** [mə'dʒıʃən] *n.* magicien *m*, prestidigitateur *m.*

magistracy ['mædʒıstɹ|əsı] *n.* [Jur.] magistrature *f.* || **magistrate** [-ejt] *n.* magistrat *m.*

magnanimous [mæg'nænıməs] *adj.* magnanime.

magnate ['mægˌnejt] *n.* magnat *m*: ~ *of industry*, potentat *m*, magnat *m*/de l'industrie.

magnesia [mæg'nijʒə] *n.* magnésie *f*: [Pharm.] *milk of* ~, lait *m* de magnésie.

magnet ['mægnət] *n.* aimant *m.* || **magnetic** [mæg'nɛtık] *adj.* magnétique; aimanté. || **magnetism** ['mægnə|tısm] *n.* magnétisme *m*; [Fig.] (pouvoir *m* d') attraction. || **magnetize** [-ˌtajz] *v. tr.* magnétiser; [needle] aimanter.

magnificence [mæg'nıfı|səns] *n.* magnificence *f*, splendeur *f.* || **magnificent** [-sənt] *adj.* magnifique, splendide. || **magnify** ['mægnıˌfaj] *v. tr.* amplifier (un son, &c.); grossir (qqch.): *magnifying glass*, loupe *f.*

magnitude ['mægnıˌtuwd] *n.* grandeur *f*; [astronomie] magnitude *f.*

magpie ['mægˌpaj] *n.* [bird] pie *f.*

mahogany [mə'hɑgənı] *n.* acajou *m.* || *adj.* d'acajou; en acajou.

maid [mejd] *n.* **1.** †jeune fille *f*, demoiselle *f*, †vierge *f*: *The Maid* (*of Orleans*), la Pucelle (d'Orléans); © ~ *of honour*, [wedding] demoiselle *f* d'honneur. **2.** servante *f*, bonne *f.* || **maiden** [-n̩] *n.* cf. MAID. || *adj.* de jeune fille, virginal; [Fig.] neuf, frais, premier: ~ *aunt*, tante *f* non mariée; ~ *name*, nom *m* de jeune fille; ~ *voyage*, [ship] premier voyage *m*, voyage inaugural. || **maidenlike** [-ˌlajk] *adj.* cf. MAIDENLY. || **maidenly** [-l̩ı] *adj.* de jeune fille, virginal; pudique. || *adv.* avec pudeur, virginalement.

mail[1] [mejl] *n.* courrier *m*, © malle *f*; [service] la poste, les postes *fpl*: *air* ~, la poste aérienne, [on a letter] par avion; ~ *bag*, sac *m*/à dépêches, de poste/; *item of* ~, envoi *m* postal; ~ *order*, commande *f*/postale, par correspondance/ vente *f* sur catalogue. || **mail** *v. tr.* mettre (une lettre, un colis) à la poste, poster, © maller (une lettre, &c.).

mail[2] *n.* [chain-] maille *f*: [Hist.] *coat of* ~, cotte *f* de mailles.

mail box [-ˌbɑks] *n.* boîte *f* postale, boîte aux lettres. || **mail car** [-ˌkɑə] *n.* poste *f* ambulante, wagon-poste *m.* || **mailman** [-ˌmæn] facteur *m.*

maim [mejm] *v. tr.* mutiler; [Fig.] tronquer.

main [mejn] *adj.* [street, &c.] principal, essentiel: [Rail.] ~ *lines*, les grandes lignes; *The ~ thing is to . . .*, L'essentiel est de . . . || *n.* [water, gas, &c.] égout *m* collecteur, conduite *f* principale; [Electr.] (le) courant (de la maison): *in the ~*, en général, pour la plupart. || **mainland** [-ˌlænd] *n.* terre *f* ferme. || **mainly** [-lɪ] *adv.* surtout, principalement. || **mainmast** [-ˌmæst] *n.* [Naut.] grand mât. || **mainsail** [-ˌsejl] *n.* [Naut.] grand'voile *f.* || **mainspring** [ˈmejnˌspɹɪŋ] *n.* ressort *m* moteur; [Fig.] principe *m* (d'une action). || **mainstay** [ˈmejnˌstej] *n.* [Naut.] étai *m* de grand mât; [Fig.] point *m* d'appui.

maintain [mejnˈtejn] *v. tr.* maintenir (l'ordre); entretenir (des relations); observer (le silence); faire subsister (une famille): *I ~ that*, Je/maintiens, prétends/que . . . || **maintenance** [ˈmejntənəns] *n.* maintenance *f*, soutien *m*, [subsistence] entretien *m*; [Adm.] service(s) *m(pl)* d'entretien.

maize [mejz] [Br.] *n.* maïs *m*; © blé *m* d'Inde. cf. CORN.

majestic(al) [məˈʤɛstɪk(l̩)] *adj.* majestueux. || **majesty** [ˈmæʤəstɪ] *n.* majesté *f*: *Her Majesty (the Queen)*, Sa Majesté (la Reine).

major [ˈmejʤɚ] *adj.* majeur; principal, plus important: *the ~ part*, la majeure partie. || *n.* **1.** [Mil.] commandant *m*, © major *m*. **2.** [Sch.] [US] spécialisation *f.* || *v. intr.* [Sch.] se spécialiser (dans une matière). || **majority** [məˈʤɔɚɪtɪ] *n.* [number, age] majorité *f*: *to attain one's ~*, atteindre sa majorité.

make [mejk] *n.* marque *f*; fabrication *f.* || **make, made, made** [mejd] *v. tr.* **1.** faire; gagner (de l'argent); causer (des ennuis): *It is made of wood*, C'est en bois: *They made a hero of him*, Ils ont fait de lui un héros; *They made him their leader*, Ils l'ont nommé chef, Ils l'ont pris pour leur chef; *What do you ~ of it ?*, Qu'en pensez-vous?; *I can ~ nothing of it*, Je n'y comprends rien; *He made a table/ out of, with/it*, Il en a fait une table; *He made the attic into a study*, Il a transformé le grenier en studio. **2.** faire (faire qqch. à qqun), obliger, forcer qqun (à faire qqch.): *He made the class laugh*, Il a fait rire les élèves; *He was made to do it*, Il a été forcé de le faire, On le lui a fait faire, On l'y a obligé; *What made you do that?*, Pourquoi avez-vous fait cela?, Qu'est-ce qui vous a poussé, incité, à le faire?; *He made do with what he had*, Il s'est tiré d'affaire avec, Il a tiré le meilleur parti de/ce qu'il avait. **3.** [+ *adj.* or past part.] rendre: faire: *to ~ s.o. sad*, rendre qqun triste; *to ~ s.o./angry, worried, tired/*, fâcher/inquiéter, fatiguer/ qqun; *to ~ sth. understood*, faire comprendre qqch.; *to ~ o.s. understood*, se faire comprendre. **4.** faire, couvrir (une distance); arriver à (un endroit); [Fig.] réussir (qqch.): *I knew he'd ~ it*, Je savais bien qu'il y/arriverait, réussirait/; [bridge] *to ~ a/trick, contract/*, faire un pli, réussir un contrat. || *v. intr.* **1.** se diriger (*for*, vers), se mettre en route (*for*, pour); [ship] mettre le cap (*for*, sur); se précipiter (*at*, sur). **2.** *to ~ for*, favoriser, contribuer à. **3.** [Elec.] *to ~ and break*, s'interrompre et se rétablir. || **make away** (*with sth.*) [-əˈwej] *v. intr.* faire disparaître (qqun, qqch.); enlever (qqch.); [money] subtiliser. || **make off** (with) [-ˈaf] *v. intr.* filer (avec). || **make out** [-ˈawt] *v. tr.* [decipher] comprendre (qqch.); distinguer; prouver (qqch.); [claim] prétendre; [list, &c.] rédiger, établir; [Fam.] se débrouiller. || **make up** [-ˈʌp] *v. tr.* [complete] parfaire (qqch.); composer (qqch.); [story, &c.] inventer (qqch. de toutes pièces); [explanation, &c.] forger; [arrange] composer, aménager (qqch.); [face] se maquiller: *to ~ one's mind*, se décider; *to ~ for sth.*, remplacer (qqch.), dédommager (qqun de qqch.). || *v. intr.* se réconcilier. || **make-believe** [-bɪˌlijv] *v. intr.* faire semblant, feindre (de). || *n.* (faux-) semblant *m*, feinte *f*: [Litt.] *the land of ~*, le Pays des Merveilles. || *attrib.* simulé, imaginaire. || **maker** [-ɚ] *n.* fabricant *m* (d'un produit, &c.); créateur *m* (d'un modèle); auteur *m* (d'une œuvre artistique, &c.): *cabinet-~*, ébéniste *m*; [Rel.] *The Maker*, le Créateur. || **makeshift** [-ˌʃɪft] *n.* expédient *m*, pis-aller *m*: *a ~ installation*, une installation de fortune. || **make-up** [ˈmejkˌʌp] *n.* [face] maquillage *m*; [arrangement] confection *f*, aménagement *m*; [story] invention *f*; [pers.] nature *f.* || **making** [-ɪŋ] *n.* **1.** fabrication *f*, création *f*; *pl.* [money] recettes *fpl.* **2.** formation *f*, croissance *f*; étapes *fpl*, stade *m*: *the ~ of English*, les étapes de la langue anglaise; *a country in the ~*, un pays en plein essor, en voie d'édification. **3.** composition *f*, éléments constitutifs, constitution *f*, l'étoffe *f*: *He has the makings of a writer*, Il a l'étoffe d'un écrivain; © *pl.* [US] nécessaire *m* d'un fumeur. **4.** [suit, fashion] façon *f.*

maladjusted [ˌmæləˈʤʌstəd] *adj.* inadapté. || **maladjustment** [ˌmæləˈʤʌstmənt] *n.* inadaptation *f.*

malady [ˈmælədɪ] *n.* maladie *f.*
malaria [məˈlɛəɪə] *n.* malaria *f* (fièvre *f* paludéenne), paludisme *m.*
Malay [məˈlej] *adj. & n.* Malais, -e. || *n.* [Ling.] le malais. || **Malaya** [məˈlejə] *n.* la Malaisie. || **Malayan** [-n] *adj.* malais.
malcontent [ˈmælkən,tɛnt] *n. & adj.* mécontent (*with*, de).
male [mejl] *adj.* [animal] mâle; [Pers.] (de sexe) masculin: [cock] © ∼ *bird*, (le) mâle. || *n.* mâle *m.*
malefactor [ˈmælə,fæktər] *n.* malfaiteur *m.*
malevolence [məˈlɛvələn|s] *n.* malveillance *f.* || **malevolent** [-t] *adj.* malveillant.
malice [ˈmælɪs] *n.* malice *f*; méchanceté *f*: *to bear s.o.* ∼, vouloir du mal, garder rancune/à qqun. || **malicious** [məˈlɪʃəs] *adj.* malicieux; méchant.
malign [məˈlajn] *adj.* mali|n, -gne. || *v. tr.* diffamer; calomnier; [Fig.] noircir. || **malignant** [məˈlɪgnənt] *adj.* malin; méchant, malfaisant: ∼ *growth*, tumeur maligne. || **malinger** [məˈlɪŋgər] *v. intr.* faire le malade, tirer au flanc.
mallard [ˈmælərd] *n.* [bird] canard *m* (malard).
mallet [ˈmælət] *n.* maillet *m.*
malnutrition [mæl,njuwˈtɪɪʃən] *n.* sous-alimentation *f.*
malpractice [mælˈpɪæktɪs] *n.* **1.** [Med.] pratique *f*, contraire aux règles établies. **2.** chose *f* illicite; conduite *f* illégale.
malt [mɔlt] *n.* malt *m.*
malted [ˈmɔltəd] *adj.*: ∼ *milk*, farine *f* lactée.
maltreat [mælˈtɪijt] *v. tr.* maltraiter; malmener.
maltreatment [,mælˈtɪijtmənt] *n.* mauvais traitement *m.*
mammal [ˈmæməl] *n.* mammifère *m.*
mammoth [ˈmæməθ] *n.* mammouth *m.* || *adj.* [Fig.] énorme, colossal.
mammy [ˈmæmɪ] *n.* [Fam.] nounou *f.*
man [mæn] *pl.* **men** [mɛn] *n.* homme *m*; [coll.] l'humanité *f*, le genre humain; soldat *m*, employé *m*, domestique *m*; [chess] pièce *f*; [chequers] pion *m*: *to speak (as)* ∼ *to* ∼, parler d'homme à homme; *to fight* ∼ *to* ∼, se battre homme à homme; *to/be, act like/a* ∼, agir en homme; être courageux; ∼ *and wife*, mari et femme; *Man proposes and God disposes*, L'homme propose et Dieu dispose; [☞ *On*, or a Fr. adj. in the masc. is often sufficient]; *Where can a* ∼ *go?*, Où peut-on aller?; *A rich* ∼, Un (homme) riche; *an old* ∼, un/vieux, vieillard/; . . . , *old* ∼ *!*, . . . , mon vieux!; *to the last* ∼, jusqu'au dernier; *No* ∼ *can do that*, Personne ne peut faire cela; *No* ∼*'s land*, no-man's-land *m.* || *v. tr.* [-nn-] équiper (un navire); garnir (une forteresse); armer (un canon, les pompes).
manacle [ˈmænəkḷ] *v. tr.* mettre les menottes à (qqun). || *n.pl.* menottes *fpl.*
manage [ˈmænəʤ] *v. tr.* conduire, gouverner, diriger (une affaire), gérer (une entreprise, &c.); arranger (une situation). || *v. intr.* s'arranger (pour + inf., pour que + subjunc.), se débrouiller; réussir à (accomplir une tâche), trouver moyen (de): *How did you* ∼ *to . . . ?*, Comment avez-vous fait pour . . . ?; *He managed to convince me*, Il a su me persuader; *I managed to get there on time*, J'ai pu (y) arriver à l'heure; *I managed all right*, Je me suis débrouillé, J'ai pu me débrouiller; *At last he managed to . . .*, → Il a fini par . . . || **manageable** [-əbḷ] *adj.* facile (à diriger); maniable. || **management** [-mənt] *n.* direction *f* (d'une entreprise commerciale, d'un magasin); administration *f* (d'une société); gérance *f* (d'une banque, d'un bureau). || **manager** [-ər] *n.* [company] directeur *m*; [hotel, &c.] gérant *m*; [newspaper, &c.] administrateur *m*, [stage] régisseur *m*; [boxing] manager *m*: *business* ∼, directeur *m* commercial; *department* ∼, chef *m* de service. || **managing** [-ɪŋ] *adj.* [executive] gérant; [Pers.] débrouillard, entreprenant: ∼ *director*; directeur-gérant *m*, administrateur *m* délégué.
mandarin [ˈmændərɪn] *n.* **1.** [Chinese] mandarin *m.* **2.** [orange] mandarine *f.* || **mandarine** *n.* cf. MANDARIN.
mandate [ˈmæn,dejt] *n.* **1.** commandement *m*, ordre *m.* **2.** [Law] mandat *m.* || *v. tr.* placer (un territoire, &c.) sous le mandat de: *mandated territory*, territoire *m* sous mandat.
mandatory [ˈmændə,tɔɔɪ] *adj.* impératif, obligatoire.
mane [mejn] *n.* [lion's, &c.] crinière *f.*
man-eater [ˈmæn,ijtər] *n.* cannibale *m*, anthropophage *m.*
manful [ˈmænfḷ] *adj.* hardi, brave, courageux; viril.
mange [mejnʤ] *n.* gale *f.*
manger [ˈmejnʤər] *n.* mangeoire *f*; [crib] crèche *f.*
mangle [ˈmæŋgəl] *n.* calandre *f.* || *v. tr.* **1.** lacérer, déchirer (en coupant); [Fam.] charcuter. **2.** mutiler, abîmer, © maganer. **3.** [pressing] calandrer.
mangy [ˈmejnʤɪ] *adj.* galeux.

manhandle [ˈmænˌhændl̩] *v. tr.* malmener.
manhole [ˈmænˌhowl] *n.* bouche *f* d'égout.
manhood [ˈmænˌhʊd] *n.* virilité *f*; âge *m* adulte; [Fig.] courage *m*.
mania [ˈmejnɪ|ə] *n.* manie *f* [au sens fort]. || **maniac** [-æk] *adj. & n.* fou *m*, folle *f*.
manifest [ˈmænɪˌfɛst] *n.* [Naut.] déclaration *f* d'expédition.
manifestation [ˌmænɪfəˈstejʃən] *n.* manifestation *f*.
manifesto [ˌmænɪˈfɛstow] *n.* manifeste *m*.
manifold [ˈmænɪˌfowld] *adj.* multiple. || *v. tr.* polycopier.
manipulate [məˈnɪpjəˌlejt] *v. tr.* manipuler (un objet); manœuvrer (une machine); [Pej.] tripoter (des comptes).
Manitoba [mænɪˈtowbə] *n.* le Manitoba. || **Manitoban** [-n] *adj. & n.* Manitobain, -e, habitant du Manitoba.
manitou [ˈmænɪˌtuw] *n.* manitou *m*.
mankind [ˈmænˌkajnd] *n.* l'humanité *f*, le genre humain. || **manlike** [-ˌlajk] *adj.* [manners, strength] viril, d'homme. || **manly** [ˈmænlɪ] *adj.* viril, mâle.
manna [ˈmænə] *n.* [Bibl.] (la) manne *f*.
mannequin [ˈmænəkɪŋ] *n.* mannequin *m*.
manner [ˈmænɚ] *n.* **1.** manière *f*, façon *f*: *in this* ~, de cette manière; *the* ~ *in which*, la manière dont; *in such a* ~ *that* . . . , de (telle)/manière, façon/que [result: + indic., purpose: + subjunc.]; *in a* ~ *(of speaking)*, en quelque sorte, pour ainsi dire; *in the French* ~ , à la (manière) française. **2.** air *m*, attitude *f*. **3.** espèce *f*, sorte *f*, genre *m*: *What* ~ *of?*, Quel genre, Quelle espèce/de?; *all* ~ *of*, toute(s) sorte(s) de. **4.** *pl.* mœurs *fpl*, usages *mpl*: *a comedy of manners*, une comédie de mœurs. **5.** *pl.* savoir-vivre *m*: *good, bad/manners*, bonnes, mauvaises/ manières: *to teach s.o. manners*, apprendre à qqun à vivre; *It's bad manners to*, C'est mal élevé de.
mannerism [ˈmænɚɪzm̩] *n.* tic *m*, affectation *f*.
mannish [ˈmænɪʃ] *adj.* [Fig.] masculin; [Péj.] hommasse.
manœuvre [məˈnuwvɚ] *n.* **1.** [Army] manœuvre *f*. **2.** conduite *f*, direction *f*/ adroite, habile. || *v. tr.* faire manœuvrer (des troupes); [handle] manier; pousser (qqun dans un coin). || *v. intr.* manœuvrer, conduire avec adresse.
man-of-war [mænəvˈwɔɚ] *n.* [Naut.] navire *m* de guerre.
manpower [ˈmænˌpawɚ] *n.* main-d'œuvre *f. inv.*
manse [mæns] *n.* maison *f* du pasteur.
mansion [ˈmænʃən] *n.* **1.** résidence *f*, hôtel particulier; [Br.] [country] château *m*. **2.** maison *f* de rapport.
manslaughter [ˈmænˌslɔtɚ] *n.* [Jur.] homicide *m* involontaire.
mantel, mantelpiece [ˈmæntl̩] [-ˌpijs] *n.* manteau *m* de cheminée: *on the* ~ sur la cheminée.
mantle [ˈmæntl̩] *n.* manteau *m*, mante *f*.
manual[1] [ˈmænjuwl̩] *adj.* [training, work] manuel.
manual[2] *n.* [book] manuel *m*.
manufacture [ˌmænjəˈfæktʃɚ] *n.* manufacture *f*, fabrication *f* (en série); usine *f*, fabrique *f*. || *v. tr.* fabriquer (des articles en série); [produce] manufacturer.
manure [məˈnuwɚ] *n.* fumier *m*, engrais *m*.
manuscript [ˈmænjəˌskɹɪpt] *n.* manuscrit *m*.
many [ˈmɛnɪ] *adj.* **1.** [MORE, MOST, q.v.] [s'emploie devant un substantif au pluriel, sauf dans l'expression *many a* . . .]. beaucoup (de + noun); bien (du, de la, de l', des, + noun); de nombreux, -ses . . . ; un grand nombre (de); une quantité (de); [Fam.] un tas (de); †maint: *(Very) Many (people) have seen it*, Beaucoup (de gens), Bien des gens, De (très) nombreuses gens, Un (très) grand nombre de personnes/l'ont vu; *I have seen* ~ , J'en ai vu/beaucoup, un grand nombre, de nombreux/; *His faults are* ~ *(and various)*, Ses défauts sont nombreux et variés; †*Many a critic says that*, De nombreux, Maints/critiques le disent; [with *fois*, *cas*, *années*, use *bien des*]; *in* ~ *ways*, de nombreuses façons; *of* ~ *kinds*, de toutes sortes. **2.** *How* ~ *are you?*, Combien êtes-vous?; *How* ~ *(people) did you see?*, Combien/en avez-vous vu, avez-vous vu de personnes/?; *I saw as* ~ *(as you)*, J'en ai vu autant (que vous); *as* ~ *again*, deux fois autant; *He did it as* ~ *as five times in a row*, Il l'a fait jusqu'à cinq fois de suite; *I don't have/ as, so/* ~ , Je n'en ai pas (au)tant; *They behaved like so* ~ *little boys*, Ils se sont conduits comme autant de petits garçons; *There are so* ~ *books to read*, Il y a tant de livres à lire; *There are too* ~ *(of them)*, Il y en a trop; *There are 5 too* ~ , Il y en a 5 de trop; *A/great, good/* ~ *(of)*, un/ grand, assez grand/nombre (de); *He has read a/great, good/* ~ *(of them)*, Il en a lu/beaucoup, pas mal/; *The* ~ , la multitude, la foule. [See also under MUCH.]
map [mæp] *n.* carte *f* (géographique). || *v. tr.* faire/la, une/carte (d'une ville, &c.).
maple [ˈmejpl̩] *n.* [~ -tree] érable *m*: ©

~ *sugar*, sucre *m* d'érable; © ~ *taffy*, tire *f* d'érable.

mar [mɑɚ] *v. tr.* [-rr-] gâter (le plaisir, &c.).

maraud [məˈɹɔd] *v. intr.* marauder. || *v. tr.* piller. || **marauder** [-ɚ] *n.* malandrin *m.*

marble [ˈmɑɚbl̩] *n.* [substance] marbre *m*; [toy] bille *f.* || *adj.* en, de/marbre. || *v. tr.* [decorate] marbrer (qqch.); [edge of book] jasper.

March [mɑɚtʃ] *n.* (le mois de) mars *m*, cf. APRIL.

march *n.* marche *f* (militaire, funèbre, &c.); [Hist., events] progrès *m*, cours *m*: ~ *past*, défilé *m.* || *v. intr.* marcher, avancer: *to* ~ *past*, défiler; *to* ~ */in, out/*, entrer, sortir. || *v. tr.* faire marcher; *to* ~ *s.o. away*, emmener qqun.

marchioness [ˈmɑɚʃɪnəs] *n.* [Hist.] marquise *f.*

mare [mɛɚ] *n.* jument *f.*

Margaret [ˈmɑɚgəət] *n.* = Marguerite *f.*

margarine [ˈmɑɚdʒəɪn] *n.* margarine *f.*

margin [ˈmɑɚdʒɪn] *n.* **1.** bord *m*, marge *f* (d'une page). **2.** profit *m*, marge *f* (bénéficiante): *in the* ~ , en marge. || **marginal** [-l̩] *adj.* marginal.

Maria [məˈɹajə] *n.* Maria *f*: [Br.] *Black* ~ , le panier à salade.

marigold [ˈmæəɪˌgowld] *n.* [Bot.] souci *m.*

marine [ˈməˈijn] *adj.* marin, maritime. || *n.* [Naut.] **1.** marine *f*, flotte (marchande). **2.** [US] fusilier *m* marin; *the Marines*, l'infanterie *f* de marine: [Fig.] *Tell that to the Marines*, A d'autres! || **mariner** [ˈmæəɪ|nɚ] *n.* marin *m*, matelot *m*: ~ *'s card*, rose des vents. || **maritime** [ˈmæəɪˌtəjm] *adj.* © *the Maritime Provinces*, les Provinces Maritimes. || *n.pl.* © *(the) Maritimes*, (les) Provinces *fpl* maritimes. || **Maritimer** [-ˌtajmɚ] © *n.* habitant *m*, -e *f* des Provinces maritimes.

marjoram [ˌmɑɚˈdʒoɚəm] *n.* [Bot.] marjolaine *f.*

mark [mɑɚk] *n.* marque *f*, signe *m*, trace *f*, empreinte *f*: [Sch.] point *m*, note *f*; [target] but *m*, cible *f*: [Fig.] *to make o.'s* ~ , se faire un nom; *punctuation* ~, signe *m* de ponctuation; [Sch.] *to get/ a good* ~ , *good marks/on, at/an exam(ination)*, recevoir une bonne note à un examen, être bon élève; *This question is worth 20 marks*, Cette question vaut 20 points; [Fig.] *to come up to the* ~ , répondre à l'attente; laisser à désirer; *(not) to feel up to the* ~ , (ne pas) se sentir dans son assiette; *as a* ~ *of*, en témoignage de; *to hit, miss/the* ~ , atteindre, manquer/le but [also Fig.]; [Fig.] *to overshoot the* ~ , dépasser la mesure; *I don't think I'm far from the* ~ , Je ne crois pas me tromper de beaucoup; †*a man of* ~ , un homme marquant; [Sport] *On /the, your/* ~ *!*, A vos places! || **mark down** [dawn] *v. tr.* noter (qqch.); baisser (un prix); donner une mauvaise note à (un élève). || **mark off** [ɔf] *v. tr.* distinguer, séparer (de). || **mark up** [ʌp] *v. tr.* augmenter, hausser/(un prix).

Mark *n.* = Marc *m.*

market [ˈmɑɚkət] *n.* marché *m*: *to* ~ , *in the* ~ , au marché; [Fr.] [covered] halle(s) *f(pl)*; [Com.] débouché *m*: ~ *place*, place *f* du marché. || *v. tr.* [produce] vendre (qqch.) au marché, lancer (un produit) sur le marché. || *v. intr.* aller au, faire son/marché. || **marketable** [-əbl̩] *adj.* [Com.] (valeur) marchand(e). || **marketability** [ˌmɑɚkətɪˈbɪlɪtɪ] *n.* valeur marchande. || **marketing** [ˈmɑɚkətɪŋ] *n.* commercialisation *f*, distribution *f* (des produits) cf. MERCHANDISE.

marking [ˈmɑɚkɪŋ] *n.* marquage *m*; *pl.* marques *fpl.*

marksman [-mən] *n.* tireur *m* d'élite.

mark-up [-ˌʌp] *n.* [Com.] majoration *f*, bénéfice *m.* || *v. tr.* [price, value] *to mark up*, augmenter.

marmalade [ˈmɑɚməˌlejd] *n.* confiture *f* d'orange. © marmelade *f.*

maroon [məˈɹuwn] *adj.* & *n.* [colour] lie *f* de vin. || *v. tr.* abandonner (qqun) dans un lieu éloigné; [Fig.] laisser (qqun) à son triste sort.

marquee [ˌmɑɚˈkij] *n.* marquise *f*; [Br.] grande tente *f.*

marquis [ˈmɑɚkwɪs] *n.* marquis *m.*

marriage [ˈmæəɪdʒ] *n.* mariage *m*; vie *f* conjugale; [ceremony] noce *f*, bénédiction *f* nuptiale; [match] alliance *f*; [Fig.] union *f* (d'intérêts); *by* ~ , par alliance. || **marriageable** [-əbl̩] *adj.* [Pers.] nubile: *to be of* ~ *age*, être en âge de se marier.

married [ˈmæəɪd] *adj.* marié (à qqun): ~ *life*, la vie conjugale; *to get* ~ , se marier.

marrow [ˈmæəow] *n.* moelle *f*: *spinal* ~, moelle *f* épinière.

marry [ˈmæəɪ] *v. tr.* **1.** épouser (qqun), se marier avec (qqun); marier, unir (une personne à une autre): *They married each other*, Ils se sont épousés; *to* ~ *off o.'s daughter*, marier sa fille. **2.** [priest] donner la bénédiction nuptiale à (un couple de fiancés). || *v. intr.* se marier.

marsh [mɑɚʃ] *n.* marais *m*, marécage *m.*

marshal [-əl] *n.* **1.** officier *m* de police, [Am.] sheriff *m.* **2.** [Army] maréchal *m.*

|| *v. tr.* [-ll-] **1.** ranger, distribuer: [Rail.] *marshalling yard*, gare *f* de triage. **2.** conduire (en grandes pompes).

marshmallow [-ˌmɛlow] *n.* guimauve *f.*

marshy [-ɪ] *adj.* marécageux, humide, fangeux.

mart [mɑɚt] *n.* marché *m*, foire *f.*

marten [-n̩] *n.* [animal] martre *f.*

Martha [ˈmɑɚθə] *n.* = Marthe *f.*

martial [ˈmɑɚʃəl] *adj.* **1.** martial: ~ *law*, état *m* de siège; *a* ~ *music*, une musique guerrière. **2.** brave.

martin [ˈmɑɚtɪn] *n.* [bird] martinet *m.*

martinet [ˌmɑɚtɪnˈɛt] *n.* personne *f* stricte sur la discipline.

martyr [ˈmɑɚtɚ] *n.* **1.** martyr *m*: *to die a* ~ *to*, mourir martyr de. **2.** souffre-douleur *m.* || *v. tr.* martyriser, torturer. || **martyrdom** [-dəm] *n.* martyre *m*: *to suffer* ~, souffrir le martyre, être torturé. || **martyrology** [mɑɚtəˈɑlədʒɪ] *n.* [R.C.] le martyrologe *m.*

marvel [ˈmɑɚvl̩] *n.* merveille *f*, prodige *m.* || *v. intr.* [-ll-] s'étonner, s'émerveiller (*at*, de). || **marvel(l)ous** [-əs] *adj.* **1.** merveilleux, extraordinaire. **2.** peu probable, incroyable.

Mary [ˈmɛəɪ] *n.* = Marie *f.*

mascot [ˈmæskɑt] *n.* mascotte *f*; porte-bonheur *m* (au jeu).

masculine [ˈmæskjəlɪn] *adj.* **1.** masculin, mâle. **2.** fort, vigoureux, viril: [Gram.] *in the* ~, au masculin.

mash [mæʃ] *v. tr.* **1.** mélanger, mêler. **2.** écraser: *mashed potatoes*, purée *f* (de pommes de terre); © [Fam.] patates *fpl* pilées.

mask [mæsk] *n.* **1.** masque *m*: *gas* ~, masque à gaz. **2.** [Fig.] voile *m*, subterfuge *m*: *to pull off one's* ~, se démasquer. || *v. tr.* masquer, couvrir (un/visage, paysage, fait); déguiser.

masochism [ˈmæsowˌkɪ|zm] *n.* masochisme *m.* || **masochist** [-st] *n.* masochiste *m/f.*

mason [ˈmejsən] *n.* **1.** maçon *m.* **2.** franc-maçon *m.* || **masonic** [məˈsɑnɪk] *adj.* [lodge] maçonnique. || **masonry** [ˈmejsn̩.ɪ] *n.* [trade] maçonnerie *f*: [secret society] *free-* ~, franc-maçonnerie *f.*

masquerade [ˈmæskɚˌejd] *n.* mascarade *f*, bal *m* masqué, déguisement *m.* || *v. intr.* se déguiser (*as*, en); se faire passer (*as*, pour).

Mass. [= Massachusetts (US)] le Massachusetts, l'État *m* de Massachusetts.

mass[1] [mæs] *n.* masse *f*; multitude *f*, foule *f*; amas *m*: *the masses*, les masses *fpl*, les classes *fpl* ouvrières: ~ *media*, techniques *fpl* de diffusion de la pensée; ~ *meeting*, © assemblée *f* monstre, [Fr.] meeting *m* monstre, rassemblement *m*; ~ *produced*, fabriqué/sur une grande échelle, en série/; ~ *production*, fabrication *f* en série; ~ *transportation*, transport *m* en commun. || *v. tr.* masser (des troupes, &c.).

mass[2] *n.* [R.C.] (la) messe *f*: *to say* ~, dire, célébrer/la messe; *to/hear, attend/* ~ assister à la messe; *high* ~, grand-messe *f*; *low* ~, messe basse, © basse-messe; ~ *-book*, livre *m* de messe, missel *m.*

massacre [ˈmæsəkɚ] *n.* massacre *m.* || *v. tr.* massacrer.

massage [məˈsɑdʒ] *n.* massage *m.* || *v. tr.* masser (qqun), donner un massage à qqun.

massive [ˈmæsɪv] *adj.* massif, gros; imposant.

mast[1] [mæst] *n.* [oak] gland *m*, [beech] faine *f.*

mast[2] [mæst] *n.* mât *m*: [Fam.] *the* ~, la mâture *f*: *to fly a flag at half* ~, mettre un drapeau en berne; *to serve before the* ~, servir comme simple matelot. || **masted** [-əd] *adj.* qui a un (ou plusieurs) mât: *a two-* ~ *ship*, un deux-mâts.

master [ˈmæstɚ] *n.* **1.** maître *m*, chef *m*, directeur *m*, patron *m*; [ship] commandant. **2.** *The Master*, Jésus-Christ. **3.** [Sch.] [École primaire] maître, [École secondaire] professeur *m*: ~ *key*, passe-partout *m*; ~ *mind*, esprit *m* supérieur; ~ *of Ceremonies*, maître de cérémonies [= M.C.]; animateur (à la T.V., &c.); ~ *stroke*, coup *m* de maître; *Master of Arts*, Maître ès Arts [= M.A.]. || **master** *v. tr.* maîtriser (un animal); [difficulty] vaincre; [subject] connaître à fond, posséder. || **masterful** [-ɚfl̩] *adj.* impérieux, en maître. || **masterly** [-lɪ] *adj.* magistral, de maître. || **masterpiece** [-ˌpijs] *n.* chef-d'œuvre *m.* || **mastery** [-ɚɪ] *n.* maîtrise *f* (*of*, de).

mastiff [ˈmæstɪf] *n.* mâtin *m*, dogue *m.*

mat [mæt] *n.* natte *f*; [burlap] paillasson *m*; dessous *m* de plat: *door* ~, paillasson. || *v. tr.* [-tt-] emmêler (les cheveux), enchevêtrer (qqch.).

match[1] [mætʃ] *n.* allumette *f*: *to strike a* ~, frotter une allumette; *safety* ~, allumette de sûreté.

match[2] *n.* **1.** égal *m*, -e *f* (de qqun): [Fig.] *to meet one's* ~, trouver à qui parler; *to be a* ~ *for s.o.*, être de la force de qqun; *to be more than a* ~ *for s.o.*, être trop fort pour qqun. **2.** [mating] alliance *f* (de personnes); [pers.] parti *m*; assortiment *m* (de couleurs, &c.). **3.** [Sport.] match *m* (de football, &c.). ‖ *v. tr.* égaler (qqun); assortir (des objets); [people] marier (deux personnes). ‖ *v. intr.* [things, Pers.] s'assortir. ‖ **matching** [-ɪŋ] *n.* [colours, &c.] assortiment *m* (d'objets). ‖ *adj.* assorti. ‖ **matchless** [-ləs] *adj.* incomparable, sans/égal, pareil/.

mate [mejt] *n.* **1.** camarade *m/f*; compagnon *m*, compagne *f*; [animals, esp. birds] mâle *m*, femelle *f.* **2.** [Naut., officer] second maître *m*; [cook] aide *m.* ‖ *v. tr.* [people] marier (*s.o. with*, qqun à); [birds] accoupler. ‖ *v. intr.* [people] épouser (qqun, *with s.o.*); [birds] s'accoupler.

material [mə'tijərəl] *adj.* **1.** matériel. **2.** essentiel, important; pertinent. ‖ *n.* [×] matière *f*, substance *f*; [cloth] tissu *m*; [building] matériau(x) *m(pl)*, élément(s) *m(pl)* de base: [building] *insulation* ~, matériel *m* isolant.

materialism [mə'tijərəl|ɪzm] *n.* matérialisme *m.* ‖ **materialist** [-ɪst] *adj.* & *n.* matérialiste (*m/f*). ‖ **materialize** [-ajz] *v. tr.* matérialiser. ‖ *v. intr.* se réaliser, aboutir.

maternal [mə'tən|əl] *adj.* [care, &c.] maternel. ‖ **maternity** [-ɪtɪ] *n.* maternité *f.*

mathematical [mæθ'mætɪk|] *adj.* mathématique. ‖ **mathematician** [mæθmə'tɪʃən] *n.* mathématicien *m*, -ne *f.* ‖ **mathematics** [mæθ'mætɪks] *n.* les mathématiques *fpl.*

matinée [mætn̩'ej] *n.* [Thea.] matinée *f.*

mating ['mejtɪŋ] *n.* [Pers.] union *f*, [Zool.] accouplement *m.*

matriarchy ['mejtɹɪˌɑəkɪ] *n.* matriarcat *m.*

matriculate [mə'tɹɪkjəˌlejt] *v. tr.* immatriculer (un étudiant) ‖ *v. intr.* [Sch.] s'inscrire à l'université, passer l'examen d'entrée. ‖ **matriculation** [məˌtɹɪkjə'lejʃən] *n.* [Sch.] © immatriculation *f*; examen *m* d'entrée (à l'université); [Ontario] examen de fin d'études secondaires.

matrimony ['mætɹɪˌmownɪ] *n.* le mariage *m*; la vie conjugale.

matrix ['mætɹɪks] *n.* **1.** matrice *f*, moule *m.* **2.** sein *m* (maternel).

matron ['mejtɹən] *n.* **1.** matrone *f.* **2.** directrice *f* (d'un hôpital); surveillante *f* (d'une école de filles).

matter ['mætər] *n.* **1.** matière *f*, substance *f*; [Med.] pus *m*: *printed* ~, imprimé *m.* **2.** sujet *m*, matière *f*: *a* ~ *for complaint*, un sujet de plainte; *in matters of*, en matière de. **3.** chose *f*; affaire *f*; question *f*: *That's a small* ~, C'est peu de chose; *That's a different* ~, C'est différent/ C'est autre chose/; *As matters stand*, Au point où en sont les choses; *In this* ~, Dans cette/affaire, circonstance/; *for that* ~, à ce compte-là; *It is a* ~ *of opinion*, C'est une question d'opinion; *It's a* ~ *of life and death*, Il y va de la vie, C'est une question de vie ou de mort; *It is a* ~ *of finishing in time*, Il s'agit de finir à temps; *It is a* ~ *of a few/dollars, days*, C'est l'affaire de quelques/dollars, jours; *in a* ~ *of days*, en quelques jours seulement; *What is the* ~ *?*, Qu'y a-t-il?, De quoi s'agit-il?; *What is the* ~ *with you?*, Qu'avez-vous?; *Sth. is the* ~, Il y a qqch. (qui ne va pas); *There is sth. the* ~ *with/him, his eye/*, Il a qqch. (à l'œil); *What's the* ~ *with the TV?*, Qu'est-ce qu'elle a, la télévision?; *no* ~ *who*, quel que soit celui qui, peu importe qui . . . ; *no* ~ *when*, quel que soit le moment où, peu importe quand; *No* ~ */what he does, when he comes/*, Quoi qu'il/fasse, Où qu'il aille; *It is a* ~ *of course*, Cela va de soi; *as a* ~ *of course*, comme de raison; *as a* ~ *of fact*, en effet, effectivement, en réalité, au fait. ‖ *v. intr.* importer: *It doesn't* ~, Qu'importe!, Cela ne fait rien, Cela n'a pas d'importance; *What does it* ~ *to you?*, Qu'est-ce que cela vous fait?; *It doesn't* ~ *(to me) whether he comes or not*, Peu (m') importe qu'il vienne ou non.

Matthew ['mæθuw] *n.* = Mathieu *m.*

mattock ['mætək] *n.* pioche *f.*

mattress ['mætɹəs] *n.* matelas *m.*

mature [mə'tjuwər] *adj.* mûr, mûri: *to grow* ~, mûrir, *a* ~ *maiden*, une jeune fille faite; ~ *deliberation*, mûre réflexion; [Fin.] échu. ‖ *v. intr.* **1.** mûrir. **2.** [business] échoir. ‖ **maturity** [-ɪtɪ] *n.* **1.** maturité *f.* **2.** [business] échéance *f.*

maudlin ['mɔdlɪn] *adj.* d'une sentimentalité larmoyante.

maul [mɔl] *n.* masse *f*, maillet *m.* ‖ *v. tr.* **1.** frapper à coups de maillet. **2.** malmener; mutiler.

maverick ['mævərɪk] *n.* [US] bovin *m* non marqué; [Fig.] indépendant *m.*

mawkish ['mɔkɪʃ] *adj.* [flavour] fade.

maxillary ['mæksɪˌlɛərɪ] *adj.* [bone] maxillaire.

maxim ['mækzɪm] *n.* maxime *f*; proverbe *m.*

maximum ['mæksɪməm] *n.* maximum *m.* ‖ *adj.* le plus grand, maximum.

may [mej] *prét.* **might** [majt] *v. aux.* [☞ Cet auxiliaire défectif n'a que deux formes suivies de l'infin. sans *to*: *may*, présent, et *might*, prétérit et imparfait du subjonctif. Notez la 3e pers. du prés.: *he* *may.*] **1.** [possibility] pouvoir, se pouvoir: *He/may, might/come,* Il se/peut, pourrait qu'il vienne; *He/may, might/still come,* Il/peut, pourrait/toujours venir; *It /may, might/(well) be that . . . ,* Il se/peut, pourrait/bien que . . . ; *He may have found it,* Il a pu le trouver, Peut-être qu'il l'a trouvé, Il l'aura peut-être trouvé, Il se peut qu'il l'ait trouvé; *He might have found it,* Il/aurait, a/pu le trouver, Il se pourrait qu'il l'ait trouvé; [indirect discourse] *I thought (that) he might/be, have been/sick,* Je croyais qu'il/pouvait bien, aurait bien pu/être malade. †**2.** [permission: ☞ se remplace de plus en plus par *can*, sauf dans le style soutenu, et certaines expressions figées] pouvoir: *May I come in?,* Est-ce que je peux entrer?; *May I?,* Vous permettez?; *May I have the salt, please?,* Voulez-vous me passer le sel, s'il vous plaît?; *May, Might/I ask who?,* Peut-on, Pourrait-on/, Est-il permis de, Serait-il permis de/demander qui?; *if I ~ say so,* si j'ose dire; [indirect discourse] *I said (that) he might come in,* J'ai dit qu'il pouvait entrer. †**3.** [subjunctive aux.]: *I write that you may know my plans,* J'écris pour que vous sachiez mes projets; *I was afraid (that) he might be late,* J'avais peur qu'il ne/fût, [Fam.] soit/en retard; *May God bless you!,* (Que) Dieu vous bénisse!; *May/I, you, he/be very happy!,* Puissé-je, Puissiez-vous, Puisse-t-il/être très heureux! **4.** [special uses]: *I/ may, might/as well stay,* Autant (vaut, vaudrait) rester; *You might listen when I'm talking to you,* Vous pourriez bien m'écouter quand je vous parle; *Be that as it may,* Quoi qu'il en soit; *Search as he might, he couldn't find it,* Il a eu beau chercher, il n'a pas pu le trouver; *What might you be doing?,* Et peut-on savoir ce que vous faites là?; *It might be well to tell him,* On ferait peut-être bien de le lui dire. ‖ **maybe** [ˈmejbɪ] *adv.* [☞ Ne confondez pas avec *may be*, cf. MAY, 1]: peut-être: *Maybe you're right,* Peut-être /que vous avez, avez-vous/raison, Vous avez peut-être raison, Il se peut que vous ayez raison.

May [mej] *n.* (le mois de) mai *m.* ‖ **May-day** [-ˌdej] *n.* le Ier mai.

mayflower [-ˌflәwәr] *n.* épigée *f* rampante; [Fam.] fleur *f* de mai.

mayor [mejәr] *n.* maire *m* (d'une ville, d'un village). ‖ **mayoress** [-ˌɛs] *n.* **1.** femme *f* du maire. **2.** mairesse *f.*

maze [mejz] *n.* **1.** dédale *m,* labyrinthe *m.* **2.** brouillamini *m,* méli-mélo *m.* **3.** [Fig.] perplexité *f,* incertitude *f.*

McIntosh [ˈmækɪnˌtɑʃ] © *n.* [apple] la (pomme) McIntosh *f.*

M.D. [= doctor of medicine] docteur *m* en médecine.

me [mij] *pron. pers.* me; moi [*me* becomes *m'* before a vowel or a mute *h*]. **1.** *He /hates, likes/ ~ ,* Il/me déteste, m'aime; *Help ~ ,* Aidez-moi; [indir. obj.] *He tells ~ everything,* Il me dit tout; *Give ~ the book,* Donnez-moi le livre; *Give ~ some,* Donnez-m'en; [obj. of prep.] *Come with ~ ,* Venez avec moi; *He gave it to ~ ,* Il me l'a donné; *Give it to ~ ,* Donnez-le-moi. **2.** [stressed] moi: [dir. obj.] *He hates me?,* Il me déteste, moi?; *He chose me,* C'est moi qu'il a choisi; [indir. obj.] *He tells me everything,* Il me dit tout, à moi, C'est à moi qu'il dit tout; [obj. of prep.] *Come with me,* C'est avec moi qu'il faut venir. **3.** [double subj.] moi: [dir. obj.] *He saw you and ~ ,* Il nous a vus, vous et moi; [indir. obj.] *He gave you and ~ the book,* Il nous a donné le livre, à vous et à moi; [obj. of prep.] *between you and ~ ,* entre vous et moi, [Fig.] entre nous. **4.** [Fam.] moi: *It's ~ ,* C'est moi; *He is taller than ~ ,* Il est plus grand que moi.

meadow [ˈmɛdow] *n.* prairie *f,* pré *m.* ‖ **meadowlark** [-ˌlɑәrk] *n.* [bird] sturnelle *f* des prés; © alouette *f.*

meagre [ˈmijgәr] *adj.* maigre; [Fig.] pauvre, succinct.

meal[1] [mijl] *n.* repas *m*: *mealtime,* heure *f* du repas; *at mealtimes,* aux heures des repas.

meal[2] *n.* farine *f* (d'avoine, de maïs, &c.). ‖ **mealy** [-ɪ] *adj.* farineux: [Pers.] *~ -mouthed,* mielleux.

mean[1] [mijn], **meant, meant** [mɛnt] *v. tr.* **1.** [intend] avoir l'intention de, compter, vouloir, (faire qqch.): *I didn't ~ to (do it),* Je ne l'ai pas fait exprès; *without meaning to,* sans le vouloir; *He meant well,* Il croyait bien faire; *to ~ well by s.o.,* vouloir du bien à qqun; *He means to have his way,* Il/veut absolument, entend/ faire à sa guise. **2.** [destine] destiner (*for,* à). **3.** [signify] signifier, vouloir dire: *What do you ~ ?,* Que voulez-vous dire?; *What does that ~ ?,* Que veut dire cela, Que signifie cela?; *That means nothing,* Cela/ne signifie rien, n'a aucun sens/; *I ~ by that . . . ,* J'entends par là; *What do you ~ by coming in late?,* → Qu'est-ce que c'est que ces façons d'arriver en retard!; *Tuesday, no, I ~ Wednesday,* Mardi, non, je veux dire mercredi; *The world's most famous acrobat, I ~ my old friend X,* L'acrobate le plus célèbre, je veux parler de mon vieil ami X; *You don't ~ it?,* Vous ne parlez pas sérieusement, Vous n'êtes pas sérieux?; *Poverty means nothing (to him),* La pauvreté est sans importance (pour lui); *Marriage means responsibility,* Le mariage entraîne des responsabilités.

mean[2] *adj.* **1.** [average] moyen: *Greenwich Mean Time* [= GMT], Heure moyenne de G. **2.** [lowly] bas, misérable, humble; [ignoble] bas, mesquin, méprisable; [stingy] mesquin, avare, chiche: *That was no ~ trick,* C'était un tour de force; *That is a ~ trick,* Voilà un vilain tour. || *n.* milieu *m*: *the happy ~,* le juste milieu; [Math.] moyenne *f* arithmétique.

meander [mɪ'ændɚ] *v. intr.* faire des méandres.

meaning [-ɪŋ] *n.* **1.** signification *f,* sens *m* (d'un mot): *What is the ~ of . . . ?,* Que signifie . . . ? **2.** [Pers.] intention *f;* la pensée (de qqun). || **meaningful** [-ɪŋfl̩] *adj.* significatif, chargé de sens. || **meaningless** [-ɪŋləs] *adj.* sans signification, dénué de sens.

meanness [-nəs] *n.* **1.** médiocrité *f.* **2.** manque *m* de mérite. **3.** bassesse *f* d'esprit, lâcheté *f.* **4.** mesquinerie *f.*

means [-z] *n. s. & pl.* **1.** moyen(s) *m(pl)*: *by ~ of,* au moyen de, à l'aide de, grâce à; *Is there a ~ of . . . ?,* Y a-t-il moyen de . . . ?; *There is no ~ of . . . ,* Il n'y a pas moyen de . . . ; *by all ~,* par tous les moyens, [strong affirmative] Mais/oui, certainement/, Je vous en prie; *by no ~,* en aucune façon, nullement, pas du tout; *by this ~,* par ce moyen, de cette façon (-ci); *by fair ~,* loyalement. **2.** *n.pl.* [wealth] moyens *mpl;* ressources *fpl,* fortune *f.*

meant cf. MEAN[1].

meantime [-ˌtajm] *n.* intervalle *m* (de temps): *in the ~,* dans l'intervalle, sur ces entrefaites, entre-temps; en attendant, cependant. || **meanwhile** [-ˌwajl] *adv.*: (*in the*) *~,* dans l'intervalle, cf. MEANTIME.

measles ['mijzəlz] *n.* rougeole *f.*

measurable ['mɛʒɚ|əbl̩] *adj.* mesurable. || **measured** [-d] *adj.* **1.** [pace] uniforme, mesuré. **2.** en mesure, rythmé. || **measure** *n.* mesure *f* (musicale; de surface, &c.); dimension *f;* [law] projet *m* de loi; [step] mesure *f,* démarche *f*: *made to ~,* fait sur mesure; *in a ~,* dans une certaine mesure, jusqu'à un certain point; *in a large ~,* en grande partie; *to take measures to,* prendre des mesures pour; *to take extreme measures,* employer les grands moyens. || *v. tr.* mesurer (qqch.), prendre la mesure, les dimensions (de qqch.). || *v. intr.* mesurer. || **measurement** [-mənt] *n.* [action] mesurage *m; pl.* dimensions *fpl*: *to take s.o.'s measurements,* prendre les mesures de qqun.

meat [mijt] *n.* **1.** viande *f; pl. Meats,* Boucherie *f.* **2.** nourriture *f,* aliment *m.*

meatless ['mijtləs] *adj.* sans viande; [Rel.] maigre.

mechanic [mə'kænɪk] *n.* mécanicien *m.* || **mechanical** [-l̩] *adj.* [Tech.] mécanique; automatique, machinal. || **mechanically** [-l̩ɪ] *adv.* [operate] mécaniquement; [act] automatiquement, machinalement. || **mechanics** [-s] *n.pl.* [ordinairement suivi d'un verbe au plur.]. **1.** (la) mécanique *f.* **2.** mécanisme *m.* || **mechanism** ['mɛkən|-ɪzm̩] *n.* mécanisme *m,* mécanique *f;* dispositif *m.* || **mechanize** [-ajz] *v. tr.* mécaniser (le travail).

medal ['mɛdl̩] *n.* médaille *f.*

meddle ['mɛdl̩] *v. intr.* se mêler (*with,* de); s'ingérer, s'immiscer (*with,* dans). || **meddler** [-ɚ] *n.* intrigant *m;* fâcheux *m,* © [Fam.] écornifleux *m.* || **meddlesome** [-səm] *adj.* intrigant; © [Fam.] écornifleux.

meddling ['mɛdlɪŋ] *adj.* indiscret. || *n.* ingérence *f,* immixtion *f.*

mediæval [mɛdɪ'ijvl̩] *adj.* [Hist.] médiéval; du Moyen-Âge.

median ['mijdɪɪən] *adj.* du milieu; central; [Math.] médian. || *n.* [Highway] platebande *f.*

mediate [-ˌejt] *v. tr.* procurer par sa médiation, son entremise; négocier. || *v. intr.* servir d'arbitre. || **mediation** [ˌmijdɪ'ejʃən] *n.* médiation *f;* intercession *f;* [labour] arbitrage *m.* || **mediator** ['mijdɪˌejtɚ] *n.* médiateur *m,* arbitre *m.*

medical ['mɛdɪkl̩] *adj.* [care] médical: *~ student,* étudiant *m* en médecine. || **medically** [-ɪ] *adv.* médicalement; du point de vue médical. || **medicine** ['mɛdɪsɪn] *n.* [profession; drug] médecine; *f;* médicament *m,* remède *m.*

mediocre [ˌmijdɪ'owkɚ] *adj.* médiocre, moyen, ordinaire. || **mediocrity** [ˌmijdɪ-ɑkɹɪtɪ] *n.* médiocrité *f.*

meditate ['mɛdɪtejt] *v. intr.* méditer (*on, upon*/, sur); se recueillir. || **meditation** [mɛdɪ'tejʃən] *n.* méditation *f;* recueillement *m.*

Mediterranean [ˌmɛdɪtə'ejnɪən] *adj.*

[climate, country] méditerranéen. || *n.* [sea] (la) Méditerranée.

medium [ˈmijdɪə|m] *pl.* **mediums** [-z], **media** *n.* **1.** milieu *m*; [Pers., &c.] intermédiaire *m*; moyen *m* (de publicité, &c.); [newspaper, &c.] organe *m* de diffusion: *through the ~ of,* par l'intermédiaire de; *the happy ~*, le juste milieu. **2.** [occultisme] médium *m.* || *adj.* moyen.

medley [ˈmɛdlɪ] *n.* bariolage *m,* mélange *m*; [Mus.] pot-pourri *m.*

meek [mijk] *adj.* humble, dou|x, -ce. || **meekly** [-lɪ] *adv.* humblement. || **meekness** [-nəs] *n.* humilité *f,* douceur *f* de caractère.

meet[1] [mijt], **met, met** [mɛt] *v. tr.* rencontrer (qqun); [by arrangement] trouver, retrouver, rejoindre, (qqun); faire la connaissance de (qqun); croiser (qqun) (dans/la rue, un escalier/); satisfaire à (un besoin); se conformer à (des exigences); faire face à (un problème); honorer (ses dettes); trouver (la mort): *I'll ~ you in front of the school, at the exit,* Je vous retrouverai devant l'école, Je vous rejoindrai à la sortie; *I went to ~ him,* Je suis allé à sa rencontre, Je suis allé le/trouver, prendre, chercher/(à la gare, &c.); *We/arranged, agreed/to ~ at 3 o'clock,* Nous avons pris rendez-vous pour trois heures; *Where did you ~ your wife?,* Où avez-vous connu votre femme?; *Glad to ~ you,* Très heureux, Enchanté (de faire votre connaissance); *Meet my wife,* Je vous présente ma femme; *We were met by a strange sight,* Une scène bizarre s'offrait à nos yeux; *There is more in it than meets the eye,* Il y a quelque anguille sous roche. || *v. intr.* **1.** se rencontrer: [by arrangement] se retrouver; [organization] se réunir; [things] se rencontrer, se joindre, se toucher; [rivers] confluer: *to make (both) ends ~*, joindre les deux bouts; *Our eyes met,* Nos regards se sont croisés. **2.** *to ~ with,* rencontrer (qqun), se rencontrer avec (qqun); rencontrer, trouver (qqch.); éprouver (des difficultés); subir (un échec); essuyer (un refus); avoir, être victime d'/un accident. || **meet**[2] *n.* réunion *f,* assemblée *f* (de sportifs, &c.).

†**meet**[3] *adj.* [seemly] séant; digne (*for,* de): *It is ~ that . . . ,* Il convient que + subjunct.

meeting [-ɪŋ] *n.* assemblée *f,* réunion *f*; rencontre *f* [Fr., Pol.] meeting *m.*

megalomania [ˌmɛgələˈmejn|jə] *n.* mégalomanie *f.* || **megalomaniac** [-ɪæk] *adj. & n.* mégalomane (*m/f*).

melancholic [mɛlənˈkɑlɪk] *adj.* mélancolique. || **melancholy** [ˈmɛlənˌkɑlɪ] *n.* mélancolie *f.* || *adj.* mélancolique, triste.

mellow [ˈmɛlow] *adj.* doux; [wine] moelleux. || *v. intr.* mûrir, adoucir; devenir moelleux.

melodrama [ˈmɛləˌdɹæmə] *n.* mélodrame *m.* || **melodramatic** [ˌmɛlədɹəˈmætɪk] *adj.* mélodramatique.

melodious [məˈlowdɪəs] *adj.* mélodieux.

melody [ˈmɛlədɪ] *n.* mélodie *f,* air *m.*

melon [ˈmɛlən] *n.* melon *m*; *water ~*, pastèque *f,* © melon d'eau.

melt [mɛlt], **melted, melted** [-əd] *v. tr.* fondre, faire fondre (du métal, &c.); dissoudre (du sucre, &c.). || *v. intr.* [ice, metal, &c.] fondre, se fondre; [sugar, &c.] se dissoudre: [Fig.] s'attendrir; *to ~ away,* se dissiper, s'évanouir.

member [ˈmɛmbɚ] *n.* membre *m*: *~ of Parliament,* député *m*: *the ~ for Pembroke,* le député de Pembroke; *the honourable ~*, l'honorable député. || **membership** [-ˌʃɪp] *n.* nombre *m*/de membres, d'abonnés/, les membres *mpl*: *~ fee,* cotisation *f* de membre.

membrane [ˈmɛmˌbɹajn] *n.* membrane *f.*

memento [məˈmɛntow] *n.* aide-mémoire *m*; rappel *m.* || **memo** [ˈmɛmow] *n.* note *f* (de service); rappel *m.* cf. MEMORANDUM.

memoir [ˈmɛmwɑɚ] *n.* **1.** biographie *f.* **2.** mémoire *m.* || **memorable** [ˈmɛmɚəbḷ] *adj.* remarquable, mémorable, signalé. || **memoran|dum** [mɛmɚˈændəm] *n. pl.* **-dums, -da,** mémo(randum) *m,* aide-mémoire *m*: *~ book,* calepin *m*; *~ pad,* bloc-notes *m.* || **memorial** [məˈmoɚɪəl] *adj.* [monument] commémoratif. || *n.* [document] mémorial *m*; monument *m* (aux morts). || **memorize** [ˈmɛmɚ|ˌajz] *v. tr.* apprendre (une leçon) par cœur. || **memory** [-ɪ] *n.* [faculty] mémoire *f*; [remembrance] souvenir *m*: *to have a good ~*, avoir bonne mémoire; *to lose o.'s ~*, perdre la mémoire; *in ~ of,* en souvenir de, à la mémoire de.

men [mɛn] *n.pl.* cf. MAN: [Litt.] *~ of letters,* gens *mpl* de lettres.

menace [ˈmɛnəs] *n.* menace *f.* || *v. tr.* menacer (qqun de qqch.).

mend [mɛnd] *n.* [stocking, &c.] raccommodage *m,* reprise *f*; [Fig.] amélioration *f* (de l'état de santé, &c.): *to be on the ~*, être en voie de guérison, [Com.] reprendre. || **mend** *v. tr.* raccommoder (un vêtement), repriser (des chaussettes); [Fig.] améliorer, corriger (une situation), réparer (un tort), rectifier (une erreur): [Prov.] *Least said soonest mended,* Trop parler nuit, trop gratter cuit. || *v. intr.* [people] s'amender; [health] s'améliorer, se rétablir. || **mending** [-ɪŋ] *n.* cf. MEND.

†**menial** ['mijnɪəl] *n.* **1.** domestique *m* & *f*, valet *m.* **2.** [Fig.] valet *m.* || *adj.* **1.** domestique. **2.** [Fig.] servile; bas, vil.

menstruate ['mɛnstɹuw,ejt] *v. intr.* [Med.] avoir ses règles.

mensuration [,mɛnsə'ejʃən] *n.* **1.** mensuration *f*, mesure *f.* **2.** mesurage *m.*

mental ['mɛntḷ] *adj.* mental: ~ *clinic*, clinique *f* psychiâtrique, asile *m* d'aliénés: ~ *reservation*, arrière-pensée *f.* || **mentality** [mɛn'tælɪtɪ] *n.* mentalité *f*; état *m* d'esprit.

mention ['mɛnʃən] *n.* mention *f.* || *v. tr.* citer, mentionner (qqch.), faire mention (de qqch.): [after thanking] *Don't ~ it!*, Il n'y a pas de quoi!, De rien!; *not to ~ . . .*, sans parler de . . .

menu ['mɛnjuw] *n.* [restaurant] menu *m*; carte *f.*

mercantile ['mərkən,tajl] *adj.* commercial, commerçant, marchand: *a ~ establishment*, une maison de commerce.

mercenary ['mərsə,nεəri] *n.* mercenaire *m.*

mercerize ['mərsər,ajz] *v. tr.* merceriser (du coton, &c.).

merchandise ['mərtʃən,dajz] *n. coll.* marchandise(s) *f(pl)*, produits *mpl.* || *v. tr.* vendre, mettre en vente: [Com.] *merchandising*, techniques marchandes *fpl*, présentation *f* des produits. || **merchant** ['mərtʃənt] *n.* marchand *m*, commerçant *m*; négociant *m.* || *adj.* marchand.

merciful ['mərsɪ|fḷ] *adj.* miséricordieux. || **merciless** [-ləs] *adj.* impitoyable, sans /merci, pitié/.

mercurial [mər'kjuwəriəl] *adj.* mercuriel; [Fig.] inconstant.

mercury ['mərkjərɪ] *n.* [Chem.] mercure *m*; [Fam.] le baromètre. || **Mercury** [Rel.] Mercure; [Astr.] Mercure.

mercy ['mərsɪ] *n.* pitié *f*, miséricorde *f*, †merci *f*; charité *f*: *to have ~ on s.o.*, avoir pitié de qqun; *to be at s.o.'s ~*, être à la merci de qqun.

mere[1] [mijər] *n.* étang *m.*

mere[2] *adj.* simple, seul: *a ~ chance*, un pur hasard; *a ~ spectator*, un simple spectateur; *He's a ~ child*, C'est encore un enfant. || **merely** [-lɪ] *adv.* simplement, seulement, rien que: *He ~ nodded*, → Il se contenta de faire oui de la tête; *You have ~ to*, Vous n'avez qu'à, cf. ONLY.

merge [mərʤ] *v. tr.* se fondre (dans qqch.), s'amalgamer; [Fig.] fusionner (deux sociétés).

merger ['mərʤər] *n.* fusion *f*, amalgame *m.*

meridian [mə'rɪdɪən] *n.* **1.** méridien *m.* **2.** [Fig.] apogée *f*, midi *m* (de la vie): *the ~ of life*, la force de l'âge. || *adj.* méridien: ~ *day*, plein jour; ~ *heat*, chaleur de midi.

merit ['mərɪt] *n.* mérite *m*: *to discuss a question on its merits*, étudier le fond de la question. || *v. tr.* mériter (une récompense, &c.).

meritorious [mεərɪ'toərəs] *adj.* [Pers.] méritant; [deed] méritoire.

mermaid ['mər,mejd] *n.* sirène *f.*

merrily ['mεərɪlɪ] *adv.* gaîment, gaiement. || **merriment** [-mənt] *n.* gaîté *f*, réjouissance *f.* || **merry** ['mεərɪ] *adj.* gai, légèrement gris (sous l'effet de l'alcool); [Fam.] pompette: *to make ~*, se divertir, se réjouir; *Merry Christmas*, Joyeux Noël. || **merry-go-round** [-gow,ɹawnd] *n.* chevaux *mpl* de bois, carrousel *m.* || **merry-maker** [-,mejkər] *n.* [Pers.] boute-en-train *m.* || **merry-making** [-,mejkɪŋ] *n.* réjouissances *fpl*, partie *f* de plaisir.

mesh [mɛʃ] *n.* **1.** maille *f* (d'un filet): *a ~ work*, un réseau *m.* **2.** *in ~*, engrené, enclanché. || *v. tr.* **1.** prendre au filet. **2.** engrener.

mesmerize ['mɛzmər,ajz] *v. tr.* hypnotiser (qqun).

mess [mɛs] *n.* **1.** gâchis *m*, saleté *f*, bric-à-brac *m*: *to make a ~ of*, [dirty] salir, [untidy] laisser en désordre. **2.** [Fig.] difficulté *f*, embarras *m*: *to be in a ~*, être dans de beaux draps; *to make a ~ of sth.*, gâcher (un travail, &c.); *What a ~!*, Quel gâchis! **3.** [Mil.] mess *m*; mets *m*: [Bibl.] *a ~ of pottage*, un plat de lentilles. || *v. tr.* **1.** mettre en désordre. **2.** gâcher, salir: [Fig.] *to ~ (sth.) up*, embrouiller. || *v. intr.* manger au mess: *to ~ /around, about*, gaspiller son temps, flâner; [potter] bricoler.

message ['mɛsəʤ] *n.* message *m*, commission *f*: *I'll give him the ~*, Je lui ferai la commission. || **messenger** ['mɛsn̩ʤər] *n.* messager *m*, commissionnaire *m/f.*

Messiah [mə'sajə] *n.* [Bibl.] Messie *m.*

messy ['mɛsɪ] *adj.* en désordre; sale, salissant.

met cf. MEET[1].

metal [mɛtḷ] *n.* **1.** métal *m*: *sheet ~*, tôle *f.* **2.** [road] empierrement *m.* || *adj.* /de, en/métal. || **metallic** [mə'tælɪk] *adj.* métallique. || **metallurgist** ['mɛtḷ,ərʤɪ|st] *n.* métallurgiste *m.* || **metallurgy** *n.* métallurgie *f.*

metamorphosis [,mɛtə'moərfəsɪs] *n.* métamorphose *f.*

metaphor [ˈmɛtəˌfɔɚ] *n.* métaphore *f,* image *f.*
metaphysical [mɛtəˈfɪzɪkḷ] *adj.* métaphysique. || **metaphysics** [ˌmɛtəˈfɪzɪk|s] *n.* métaphysique *f.*
mete [mijt] *v. tr.* [gén. suivi de *out*] allouer.
meteor [ˈmijtɪɚ] *n.* météore *m.* || **meteorological** [ˌmijtɪɚ|əˈlɑdʒɪkḷ] *adj.* météorologique. || **meteorology** [-ˈɑləʤɪ] *n.* météorologie *f.*
meter [ˈmijtɚ] cf. METRE.
method [ˈmɛθəd] *n.* méthode *f*; ordre *m.* || **methodical** [məˈθɑdɪkḷ] *adj.* méthodique, ordonné.
meticulous [məˈtɪkjələs] *adj.* méticuleux, scrupuleux.
Metis [ˈmejˈtij] © *n.* Métis *m.* || **Metiss** [ˈmejˈtijs] © *n.* cf. METIS.
metre [ˈmijtɚ] *n.* **1.** [Meas.] mètre *m* [= 39.37 inches]. **2.** [Poet., Ling.] métrique *f,* vers *m,* mesure *f.* **3.** compteur *m* (de courant électrique, de gaz): *postage* ~, affranchisseuse *f* à compteur; *parking* ~, compteur *m* de stationnement, © [abus.] parcomètre *m.* || **metric** [ˈmɛtɹɪk] *adj.* [system] métrique.
metropolis [məˈtɹɑpəlɪs] *n.* métropole *f*; ville *f* importante. || **metropolitan** [ˌmɛtɹəˈpɑlətn̩] *n.* **1.** citadin *m* d'une grande ville. **2.** [Rel.] métropolitain *m.* || *adj.* d'une grande ville, métropolitain: *Metropolitan Toronto,* l'agglomération *f* torontoise.
mettle [ˈmɛtḷ] *n.* courage *m,* fougue *f,* ardeur *f*: *Private operators will be on their* ~, Les compagnies privées vont se piquer au jeu.
mew[1] [mjuw] *n.* miaulement *m.* || *v. intr.* [cat] miauler.
mew[2] *n.* [Orn.] mouette *f.* cf. (SEA)GULL.
Mexican [ˈmɛksɪkən] *n.* Mexicain *m.* || *adj.* mexicain. || **Mexico** [ˈmɛksɪkow] *n.* le Mexique: ~ *City,* (la ville de) Mexico.
mezzanine [mɛzəˈnijn] *n.* mezzanine *f,* entresol *m.*
mfg. [= MANUFACTURING].
mgr. [= MANAGER].
mica [ˈmajkə] *n.* mica *m.*
mice [majs] cf. MOUSE.
Michael [ˈmajkḷ] *pr. n.* = Michel *m.*
mickey [ˈmɪkɪ] *n.* boisson *f* droguée.
microbe [ˈmajkɹowb] *n.* microbe *m.*
microphone [ˈmajkɹə|ˌfown] *n.* [Electr.] microphone *m*: *Please speak* (*clearly*) *into the* ~, Parlez (distinctement) dans l'appareil, s'il vous plaît.
microscope [-ˌskowp] *n.* microscope *m.* || **microscopic** [ˌmajkɹəˈskɑpɪk] *adj.* **1.** microscopique, minuscule. **2.** perçant, vif: *a* ~ *eye,* l'œil *m* américain.
mid- [mɪd-] *adj.* mi-, du milieu (de), en plein(e) . . . : *in* ~ *-June,* à la mi-juin; *in* ~ *-ocean,* en plein océan.
midday [-ˌdej] *n.* midi *m.* || *adj.* [sun, &c.] de midi.
middle [ˈmɪdḷ] *adj.* du milieu; [size, &c.] moyen; intermédiaire, central: *in the* ~ (*of*), au milieu (de); *in the* ~ *of June,* à la mi-juin; *in the* ~ *of the night,* en pleine nuit; *to be in the* ~ *of doing sth.,* être en train de faire qqch.; [Hist.] (*the*) *Middle Ages,* (le) moyen âge; ~ *class,* classe *f* moyenne, petite bourgeoisie *f*; ~ *-aged,* d'âge moyen, d'un certain âge. || **middleman** [-ˌmæn] *n.* [Com.] intermédiaire *m.* || **middle-sized** [-ˌsajzd] *adj.* de/grandeur, taille/moyenne.
middling [-ɪŋ] *adj.* passable. || *adv.* passablement, couci-couça.
middy [ˈmɪdɪ] *n.* [Fam.] aspirant *m* (de marine).
midge [mɪʤ] *n.* **1.** cousin *m.* **2.** [Fig.] moucheron *m*; moustique *m,* minus *m.*
midget [ˈmɪʤət] *n.* nain *m.*
midnight [ˈmɪd|ˌnajt] *n.* minuit *m.* || *adj.* [sun] de minuit.
midriff [-ɹɪf] *n.* [body] diaphragme *m.*
midship [-ˌʃɪp] *n.* [Naut.] milieu *m* du vaisseau. || **midshipman** [-ˌʃɪpmən] *n.* [Naut.] aspirant *m.*
midst [mɪdst] †*n.* milieu *m,* centre *m,* cf. MIDDLE]. || *adv.* au milieu de, parmi, en plein; au cœur de: *in the* ~ *of all this,* sur ces entrefaites *fpl*; *Be welcomed to our* ~, Soyez le bienvenu parmi nous.
midsummer [ˈmɪd|ˈsʌmɚ] *n.* plein été *m* (vers le 21 juin). || **midtown** [-ˌtawn] *n.* centre de la ville. || **midway** [-ˌwej] *adj. & adv.* à mi-chemin. || *n.* foire *f,* fête *f* foraine. || **Midwest** [-ˈwɛst] also **Middle West,** *n.* [US] le centre des États-Unis.
midwife [-ˌwajf] *n.* [Med.] sage-femme *f.* || **midwifery** [-ˌwajfɚɪ] *n.* obstétrique *f.* || **midwinter** [-ˈwɪntɚ] *n.* plein hiver *m* [vers le 21 décembre]. || **midyear** [-ˌjijɚ] *n.* mi-année *f*: ~ *exam,* examen *m* de fin de semestre [≠ de fin d'année].
mien [mijn] *n.* mine *f,* contenance *f* (d'un visage); aspect *m,* allure *f.*
might[1] cf. MAY. || **might**[2] [majt] *n.* puissance *f*; force *f,* pouvoir *m*; *with all one's* ~, de/toute sa force, toutes ses forces/. || **mighty** [-ɪ] *adj.* **1.** vigoureux, fort, puissant. **2.** grand: *a* ~ *famine,* une grande famine. **3.** retentissant: *a* ~ *tempest,* une violente tempête. || *adv.* [Fam.] beaucoup, à un haut degré; furieusement.

migrant ['majgɹənt] *n.* nomade *m/f*, émigrant *m.* || **migrate** *v. intr.* émigrer. || **migration** [ˌmaj'gɹejʃən] *n.* migration *f.* || **migratory** ['majgɹəˌtɔəɪ] *adj.* migrateur.

mike [majk] *n.* [Fam.] micro *m* cf. MICROPHONE.

Mike [majk] *pr. n.* [Fam.] [= Michael] = Michel *m*: [Fam.] *For the love of Mike!*, Sapristi!, © Pour l'amour!

mild [majld] *adj.* **1.** [person, &c.] doux, paisible. **2.** [climate, &c.] doux, peu rigoureux, tempéré; [harmless] bénin.

mildew ['mɪldjuw] *n.* [plants] nielle *f*; [paper] tache *f* d'humidité, piqûre *f*.

mildly ['majldlɪ] *adv.* doucement, avec douceur; avec modération. || **mildness** [-nəs] *n.* douceur *f*; [person] caractère *m* paisible; [drug] bénignité *f*.

mile [majl] *n.* [measure] mille *m* [= 1609.432]; ~ *post*, borne *f* milliaire, [Fr.] borne *f* kilométrique: *nautical* ~, mille marin [2025 yards] [= 1853^{m}]; *square* ~, mille *m* carré. || **mileage** [-əʤ] *n.* **1.** © millage *m*; [Fr.] kilométrage *m.* **2.** distance *f* en milles (entre deux points de la carte): ~ *chart*, table *f* des distances. **3.** tarif *m* au mille, [Fr.] au kilomètre. || **milestone** [-ˌstown] *n.* borne/routière, milliaire/; [Fr.] borne *f* kilométrique; [Fig.] jalon *m.*

militant ['mɪlɪtənt] *n.* militant *m.* || **militarism** ['mɪlɪtəɪzm] *n.* militarisme *m.* || **military** ['mɪlɪtˌɛəɪ] *adj.* militaire: ~ *man*, un militaire.

militia [mɪ'lɪʃə] *n.* milice *f*.

milk [mɪlk] *n.* lait *m*: ~ *bar*, crémerie *f*; [Fr.] milk-bar *m*; ~ *-can*, boîte *f* à lait; ~ *-tooth*, dent *f* de lait; ~ *-white*, blanc comme du lait, [complexion] d'un blanc laiteux; ~ *diet*, régime *m* lacté. || *v. tr.* traire (une vache). || **milking** [-ɪŋ] *n.* traite *f* (des vaches). || **milkmaid** [-ˌmejd] *n.* laitière *f*. || **milkman** [-ˌmæn] *n.* [person] laitier *m*, [Fr.] crémier *m.* || **milksop** [-ˌsɑp] *n.* [person] [Fig.] poule *f* mouillée. || **milky** [-ɪ] *adj.* laiteux; [Astr.] *the Milky Way*, la Voie Lactée.

mill [mɪl] *n.* **1.** moulin *m*: *wind* ~, moulin *m* à vent; *water* ~, moulin *m* à eau; *coffee* ~, moulin *m* à café; *saw* ~, scierie *f*. **2.** broyeur *m*, concasseur *m.* **3.** usine *f*; manufacture *f*; © moulin *m*: *paper* ~, fabrique *f* de papier; *sugar* ~, sucrerie *f*. || *v. tr.* moudre, broyer; [Fig.] piétiner (sur place): *the milling crowd*, les remous de la foule. || **miller** [-əɪ] *n.* meuni|er *m*, -ère *f*.

milli- ['mɪlɪ-] *préf.* milli-: *milligramme*, milligramme *m*; *millimetre*, millimètre *m*: &c.

milliner ['mɪlɪ|nəɪ] *n.* modiste *f*. || **millinery** [-ˌnɛəɪ] *n.* modes *fpl.*

million ['mɪljən] *n.* million *m*: [NB]: *Canada has a population of eighteen* ~, Le Canada compte dix-huit millions d'habitants: *millions of years ago*, il y a des millions d'années. || **millionaire** [ˌmɪljə'nɛəɪ] *n.* millionnaire *m.* || **millionth** ['mɪljənθ] *n. & adj.* millionnième.

millstone ['mɪlˌstown] *n.* **1.** meule *f*. **2.** [Fig.] fardeau *m.*

mime [majm] *n.* mime *m.* || *v. tr. & intr.* mimer.

mimeograph ['mɪmɪəˌgɹæf] *v. tr.* [Fr.] ronéotyper (des documents), polycopier, © miméographer.

mimic ['mɪmɪk] *n.* imitateur *m*, mime *m.* || *v. tr.* imiter, singer, (se) moquer. || *adj.* mimique, imitateur. || **mimicry** [-ɹɪ] *n.* bouffonnerie *f*, imitation *f*.

mince [mɪns] *v. tr.* [meat] hacher menu. || **mincemeat** [-ˌmijt] *n.* [Cul.] mincemeat *m*: *to make* ~ *of* (*s.o., sth.*), hacher (qqch.) menu comme chair à pâté; réduire, mettre/(qqun) en charpie. || **mincer** [-əɪ] *n.* hache-viande *m. inv.* || **mincing** [-ɪŋ] *adj.* [look, attitude] minaudier.

mind [majnd] *n.* esprit *m*, intelligence *f*; raison *f*: [soul] âme *f*; avis *m*, opinion *f*; souvenir *m*: *presence of* ~, présence *f* d'esprit, sang-froid *m*; *state of* ~, état *m* d'âme; *peace of* ~, tranquillité *f* d'esprit; *to have sth. on one's* ~, avoir qqch. qui vous préoccupe; *That's a weight off my* ~, Voilà qui me soulage (l'esprit); *It takes one's* ~ *off one's troubles*, Cela vous distrait de vos ennuis; *I'm losing my* ~, Je perds la raison, je deviens fou; *to be out of one's* ~, avoir perdu la raison; *Out of sight, out of* ~, Loin des yeux, loin du cœur; *to make up one's* ~, se décider (à faire qqch.); *to change one's* ~, changer d'avis, se raviser; *to my* ~, à mon/avis, idée/; *to know one's* ~, savoir ce qu'on veut; *to give s.o. a piece of one's* ~, dire/son fait, ses vérités/à qqun; *I have/a good, half a/* ~ *to* . . ., J'ai/bien, presque/envie de . . .; *to set one's* ~ *on* . . ., être résolu à (faire qqch), avoir (qqch.) à cœur; *to keep sth. in* ~, se souvenir de, tenir compte de, (qqch.); *to bring to* ~, rappeler (qqch. à qqun); *to drive out of s.o.'s* ~, faire oublier (qqch. à qqun). || *v. tr.* faire attention (à qqun, qqch.); obéir à (ses parents); garder (des enfants, une maison); s'inquiéter de (qqch.): *Mind your* *manners*, Fais attention à tes manières; *Mind you don't slip!*, Faites attention de ne pas, Prenez garde de/glisser; *Mind the step*, Prenez garde à la marche; ~ *your own business!*, Occupez-vous de vos affaires!; *Never* ~ *!*, N'importe!, Ça ne fait rien!, Ne vous inquiétez pas!; *Never* ~ */him, that/*, Ne vous/occupez, inquiétez/pas de/lui, cela/, Ne faites pas attention à/lui, cela/; *If you don't* ~ , Si cela/ne vous fait rien, vous est égal/. ‖ **minded** [-əd] *adj.* [Pers.] enclin (à), à l'esprit . . . ; narrow- ~ , [Pers.] à l'esprit étroit. ‖ **mindedness** [-ədnəs] *compound*: *absent-* ~ , distraction *f*; *narrow-* ~ , étroitesse *f* de vues. ‖ **mindful** [-fl̩] *adj.* attentif, (*of*, à); soigneux (*of*, de): *to be* ~ *of*, se souvenir de. ‖ **mindless** [-ləs] *adj.* insouciant (*of*, de); oublieux (*of*, de).

mine[1] [majn] *n.* [coal, &c.] mine *f*: ~ *-shaft*, puits *m* de mine. ‖ *v. tr.* [field, sea, &c.] miner.

mine[2] *pron. poss. 1ère pers. sing.* le mien, la mienne, les miens *mpl*, les miennes *fpl*: *This is* ~ , C'est/le mien, la mienne/; C'est à moi; Ceci m'appartient; [by me] C'est de moi; *a friend of* ~ , un de mes amis.

miner [-ɚ] *n.* mineur *m.*

mineral [ˈmɪnɚəl] *n.* minéral *m.* ‖ *adj.* minéral: *the* ~ *kingdom*, le règne *m* minéral. ‖ **mineralogy** [ˌmɪnɚˈɑlədʒɪ] *n.* minéralogie *f.*

mingle [ˈmɪŋgl̩] *v. tr.* mêler, mélanger. ‖ *v. intr.* se mêler, se mélanger.

miniature [ˈmɪnɪətʃɚ] *n.* **1.** chose *f* de petite dimension, modèle *m* réduit: *in* ~ , en miniature. **2.** [painting] miniature *f.* ‖ *adj.* miniature, minuscule; sur une petite échelle.

minimize [ˈmɪnɪ|ˌmajz] *v. tr.* minimiser; réduire au minimum, diminuer l'importance de. ‖ **minimum** [-məm] *n.* minimum *m.* ‖ *adj.* minimum; le plus bas, le moindre.

mining [ˈmajnɪŋ] *adj.* minier: ~ *district*, région minière; ~ *engineer*, ingénieur des mines. ‖ *n.* exploitation *f* des mines.

minister [ˈmɪnɪst|ɚ] *n.* **1.** ministre *m*: © *prime* ~ , premier ministre (fédéral). **2.** [Rel.] ministre *m* (du culte); [especially protestant] pasteur *m* (luthérien, &c.). ‖ **ministry** [-ɹɪ] *n.* ministère *m*, cf. DEPARTMENT.

mink [mɪŋk] *n.* **1.** vison *m* (d'Amérique du Nord). **2.** fourrure *f* de vison: *a* ~ *coat*, un manteau de vison.

minnow [ˈmɪnow] *n.* vairon *m*; © méné *m.*

minor [ˈmajnɚ] *n.* [age] mineur *m.* ‖ *adj.* **1.** mineur; moindre, sans importance. **2.** petit, menu: ~ *detail*, menu détail; ~ *fault*, faute légère. ‖ **minority** [mɪˈnɔɚɪtɪ] *n.* **1.** [age] minorité *f.* **2.** [number] minorité *f*: *large* ~ , forte minorité.

minstrel [ˈmɪnstɹəl] *n.* ménestrel *m*, chanteur *m.*

mint [mɪnt] *n.* menthe *f*: *peppermint*, menthe poivrée.

minuet [ˌmɪnjuwˈɛt] *n.* [Mus.] menuet *m.*

minus [ˈmajnəs] *adj.* moins; négatif. ‖ *n.* **1.** (signe *m*) moins; moins *m.* **2.** déficit *m*, perte *f.* ‖ *prép.* moins; sans: *He went off* ~ *his money*, Il partit sans son argent.

minute[1] [ˈmɪnət] *n.* **1.** [time, legal deed] minute *f*, instant *m*: ~ *hand*, grande aiguille *f*; */on, to/the* ~ , ponctuel: *five minutes after two*, deux heures cinq; *Just a* ~*!*, Un instant!; *at any* ~ , d'un instant à l'autre; *in a* ~ , dans un instant; *in a few minutes*, *minutes later*, quelques minutes plus tard, dans quelques minutes. **2.** *pl.* [meeting, &c.] procès-verbal *m*, compte rendu *m.*

minute[2] [mɪnˈjuwt] *adj.* **1.** [pieces, &c.] menu, minuscule. **2.** [description] minutieux, circonstancié. ‖ **-ly** [-lɪ] *adv.* minutieusement, en détail.

miracle [ˈmɪɚəkl̩] *n.* miracle *m.* ‖ **miraculous** [mɚˈækjələs] *adj.* [healing, &c.] miraculeux.

mirage [mɪˈɹæʒ] *n.* mirage *m*; illusion *f.*

mire [majɚ] *n.* **1.** fange *f*, boue *f.* **2.** bourbier *m.* ‖ *v. tr. & intr.* (s')embourber.

mirror [ˈmijɚɚ] *n.* miroir *m*, glace *f*: [car] *driving* ~ , rétroviseur *m.* ‖ *v. tr.* refléter.

mirth [mɚθ] *n.* joie *f*, allégresse *f.* ‖ **mirthful** [-fl̩] *adj.* joyeux, gai, enjoué.

miry [ˈmajɚɪ] *adj.* bourbeux, fangeux.

mis- [mɪs-] préfixe négatif. ‖ **misadventure** [mɪsədˈvɛntʃɚ] *n.* mésaventure *f.* ‖ **misapply** [mɪsəˈplaj] *v. tr.* **1.** mal appliquer. **2.** [funds] détourner. ‖ **misbehave** [mɪs|-bɪˈhejv] *v. intr.* se conduire mal. ‖ **misbelief** [-bɪˈlijf] *n.* /opinion *f*, croyance *f*/erronée. ‖ **misbelieve** [-bɪˌlijv] *v. tr.* croire par erreur, avoir une opinion erronée; douter de. ‖ **miscalculate** [-ˈkælkjəˌlejt] *v. tr. & intr.* mal calculer; faire une erreur de calcul (sur, *about*). ‖ **miscarriage** [ˈmɪs-kæɚɪdʒ] *n.* **1.** [Med.] fausse couche *f.* **2.** insuccès *m.* ‖ **miscarry** [mɪsˈkæɚɪ] *v. intr.* **1.** [Med.] faire une fausse couche, avorter. **2.** [goods, letters] s'égarer; [Fig.] échouer.

miscellaneous [mɪsəˈlejnɪəs] *adj.* mêlé, mélangé; divers.

miscellany [ˈmɪsl̩ˌejnɪ] *n.* mélange *m*, variété *f.*

mischance [mɪs'ʧæns] *n.* malchance *f*, mésaventure *f*; [Pop.] guigne *f*.

mischief ['mɪsʧə|f] *n.* méchanceté *f*; mal *m*, tort *m*; espièglerie *f*. || **mischievous** [-vəs] *adj.* [conduct] méchant; [child] espiègle; [harmful] nuisible.

misconception [ˌmɪskən'sɛpʃən] *n.* conception *f* erronée.

misconduct [mɪs'kɑndʌkt] *n.* **1.** [moral] inconduite *f*. **2.** [Com.] mauvaise administration *f*. || *v. tr.* [mɪskən'dʌkt] **1.** *to ~ o.s.* se conduire mal. **2.** [business] mal administrer.

misconstrue [ˌmɪskən'stɹuw] *v. tr.* mal interpréter, se méprendre (sur le sens de qqch.).

miscount [mɪs'kawnt] *v. tr. & intr.* mal compter.

misdeed [mɪs|'dijd] *n.* méfait *m*. || **misdemeanour** [-də'mijnər] *n.* **1.** [Jur.] délit *m*, contravention *f*. **2.** mauvaise conduite *f*. || **misdirect** [-'dajɹɛkt] *v. tr.* [people] mal diriger, mal renseigner; [letter] mal adresser.

miser ['majzər] *n.* avare *m*.

miserable ['mɪzərəbl̩] *adj.* misérable; [weather, &c.] triste, [Pers., feeling] malheureux. || **miserably** [-ɪ] *adv.* misérablement, tristement; malheureusement.

miserly ['majzərlɪ] *adj.* sordide, avare.

misery ['mɪzəɹɪ] *n.* souffrance(s) *f(pl)*; misère *f*; [moral] détresse *f*.

misfire ['mɪs'fajər] *n.* coup *m*/raté, manqué/. || [mɪs'fajər] *v. tr.* manquer (son coup, sa cible); [Auto] rater. || **misfit** ['mɪsˌfɪt] *n.* habit *m*, vêtement *m*/manqué; [Fig.] [person] laissé-pour-compte *m inv.* || **misfortune** [mɪs|'fɔərtjən] *n.* infortune *f*, malheur *m*. || **misgiving** [-'gɪvɪŋ] *n.* crainte *f*, doute *m*; pressentiment *m*. || **misgovern** [-'gʌvərn] *v. tr.* mal/gouverner, administrer/. || **misguide** [-'gajd] *v. tr.* mal guider, fourvoyer (qqun). || **misguided** [-'gajdəd] *adj.* [person] égaré; [action, &c.] inopportun. || **mishap** ['mɪsˌhæp] *n.* contretemps *m*, mésaventure *f*, malheur *m*. || **misinform** [ˌmɪsɪn'fɔərm] *v. tr.* donner de faux renseignements à (qqun); mal renseigner (qqun); [Fig.] fourvoyer. || **misinformed** [-əd] *adj.* [person] mal renseigné. || **mislaid** cf. MISLAY. || **mislay** [mɪs'lej], **mislaid, mislaid** [-d] *v. tr.* égarer, perdre. || **mislead** [-'lijd], **misled, misled** [-'lɛd] *v. tr.* induire (qqun) en erreur, tromper; corrompre. || **misleading** [-'lijdɪŋ] *adj.* [answer, &c.] fallacieux. || **misled** cf. MISLEAD. || **misnomer** [-'nowmər] *n.* faux nom *m*; fausse appellation *f* © [Fam.] trompe *f*. || **misplace** [-'plejs] *v. tr.* **1.** mal placer. **2.** [Fam.] ranger (qqch. sans pouvoir retrouver). || **misprint** ['mɪsˌpɹɪnt] *n.* [Typ.] faute *f* d'impression, coquille *f*. || **mispronounce** [ˌmɪs|pɹə'nawns] *v. tr.* mal prononcer. || **misread** [-'ɹijd] *v. tr.* lire/mal, incorrectement/. || **misrepresent** [-ˌɹɛpɹə'zɛnt] *v. tr.* représenter sous un faux jour; dénaturer (les faits).

miss[1] [mɪs] *v. tr.* manquer, rater; [occasion] laisser échapper: *I have missed you*, → Vous m'avez manqué, J'ai regretté votre absence; *I (just) missed falling*, J'ai failli tomber; *to ~ o.'s way*, se tromper de route. || *n.* coup *m* manqué; manque *m* à toucher.

miss[2] *pl.* **misses** [-ɪz] *n.* [young lady] demoiselle *f*; [form of address] mademoiselle *f*: *Dear Miss X.*, Mademoiselle.

missal [mɪsl̩] *n.* [R.C.] missel *m*.

missile ['mɪsˌajl] *n.* projectile *m*; fusée *f*: *guided ~*, projectile *m* téléguidé.

missing ['mɪsɪŋ] *adj.* [person] disparu, absent; [thing] manquant: *the ~ link*, l'être *m* intermédiaire, le pithécanthrope *m*.

mission ['mɪʃən] *n.* mission *f*.

missionary [-ˌɛərɪ] *adj.* de mission, missionnaire. || *n.* **1.** missionnaire *m*. **2.** zélateur *m*.

misspell [mɪs'spɛl], **misspelt, misspelt** [-t] *v. tr. & intr.* épeler, écrire/mal. || **misspelling** [-ɪŋ] *n.* faute *f* d'orthographe.

mist [mɪst] *n.* brume *f*; brouillard *m*. || *v. tr.* couvrir (qqch.) de buée. || *v. intr.*: *to ~ over*, se couvrir de/brume, [window] buée.

mistake [mɪs|'tejk], **mistook** [-'tʊk], **mistaken** [-'tejkn̩] *v. tr.* se méprendre sur (qqun, qqch.); se tromper de (route, numéro, &c.); confondre (*for s.o., sth.*, avec qqun, qqch.); *to be mistaken*, être dans l'erreur, se tromper (*about*, sur); *If I am not mistaken*, Si je ne m'abuse, sauf erreur; *to be mistaken for*, être pris pour (qqun d'autre). || **mistake** *n.* [grammar, &c.] faute *f*; [judgment] erreur *f*: *to make a ~*, se tromper (mistake), faire une faute, commettre une erreur; *to make the ~ of . . .*, avoir le tort de . . . ; *Make no ~ (about it)*, Que l'on ne s'y trompe pas; *There can be no ~ about it*, Il n'y a pas à s'y/tromper, méprendre; *by ~*, par/erreur, méprise.

mister ['mɪstər] [☞ Employé sans nom de famille, signe de familiarité le plus souvent de mauvais goût.] cf. MR.

mistletoe ['mɪsl̩ˌtow] *n.* gui *m*.

mistook cf. MISTAKE.

mistreat [mɪs'tɹijt] *v. tr.* maltraiter.
mistress ['mɪstɹəs] *n.* **1.** cf. MRS. **2.** maîtresse *f* de maison; [Sch.] maîtresse *f* (d'école).
mistrust [mɪs'trʌst] *n.* méfiance *f.* || *v. tr.* se méfier de (qqun, qqch.). || **mistrustful** [-fḷ] *adj.* méfiant, défiant.
misty ['mɪstɪ] *adj.* brumeux, nuageux; sombre.
misunderstand [mɪsˈʌndɚ|'stænd], **misunderstood, misunderstood** [-'stʊd] *v. tr.* mal comprendre; [Fig.] mal interpréter, se méprendre sur (qqch.). || **misunderstanding** [-ɪŋ] *n.* malentendu *m*; [discord] mésentente *f.* || **misuse** [mɪs'juws] *n.* abus *m*, mauvais/usage *m*, emploi *m*; mauvais traitement *m.* || [mɪs'juwz] *v. tr.* abuser de (qqch.), mal employer (qqch.); [person] maltraiter (qqun).
mite [majt] *n.* **1.** bestiole *f.* **2.** [Fig.] rien *m*, bagatelle *f.*
mitigate ['mɪtɪˌgejt] *v. tr.* (s')adoucir; [Fig.] alléger (la souffrance).
mitre ['majtɚ] *n.* [Rel.] mitre *f.*
mitt [mɪt] *n.* [Fam.] poing *m.*
mitten ['mɪtn̩] *n.* mitaine *f.* || *pl.* moufles *fpl*; © mitaines *fpl.*
mix [mɪks] *v. tr.* mêler; [prepare] mélanger (*with*, à); [cement] malaxer: [Fig.] *to* ~ *up*, confondre (*with*, avec); embrouiller (qqch.). || *v. intr.* se mêler, se mélanger; s'allier (*with*, à, avec); [people] fréquenter (qqun), frayer (avec qqun). || **mixed** [-t] *adj.* mêlé, mélangé; [group, &c.] mixte; [number] fractionnaire: *He is all* ~ *up*, Il a les idées embrouillées. || **mixer** [-ɚ] *n.* **1.** personne *f* sociable. **2.** [cement, kitchen] malaxeur *m.* || **mixing** [-ɪŋ] *n.* mélange *m*; [cement, &c.] malaxage *m*; [Pej.] confusion *f* (d'idées, &c.); [contacts] relations *fpl* (avec les gens, *with people*). || **mixture** [-tʃɚ] *n.* mélange *m*; [Pharm., drink, &c.] mixture *f.*
mm. [= millimetre(s)] mm. [= millimètre(s)].
moan [mown] *n.* gémissement *m.* || *v. intr.* gémir; pousser des gémissements.
moat [mowt] *n.* fossé *m* (de rempart).
mob [mɑb] *n.* **1.** foule *f.* **2.** peuple *m*, populace *f*: *to raise a* ~, attrouper, ameuter le peuple. || *v. intr.* s'attrouper. || *v. tr.* **1.** *to* ~ *s.o.*, entourer qqun. **2.** houspiller; attaquer.
mobile ['mowˌbajl] *adj.* mobile: ~ *trailer*, remorque *f*, unité *f* mobile. || **mobilization** [mowbɪlaj'zejʃən] *n.* mobilisation *f.* || **mobilize** ['mowbɪlˌajz] *v. tr.* **1.** [soldiers] mobiliser (des troupes). **2.** mettre en valeur, exploiter.

moccasin ['mɑkəsɪn] *n.* **1.** mocassin *m.* **2.** serpent *m* (de Caroline).
mock [mɑk] *adj.* simulé, faux; dérisoire: ~ *trial*, simulacre *m* de procès. || *n.* **1.** moquerie *f*; (objet *m* de) risée *f*, dérision *f*/: *to make a* ~ *of* (*s.o.*), tourner (qqun) en ridicule. **2.** imitation *f.* || *v. tr. & intr.* se moquer (de qqun, qqch., *s.o., sth., at s.o., sth.*). || *v. tr.* railler (qqun); singer, contrefaire (qqun, qqch.); tromper (qqun). || **mockery** [-ɚɪ] *n.* **1.** raillerie *f*, risée *f.* **2.** jouet *m*, sujet *m* de la risée: *to make a* ~ *of*, se moquer de. **3.** semblant *m*, simulaire *m* (de qqch.). || **mockingbird** [-ɪŋˌbɚd] *n.* oiseau *m* moqueur, moqueur *m* polyglotte.
mode [mowd] *n.* manière *f*, mode *m* (de faire qqch.); [vogue] mode *f*, usage *m*; [Gram.] mode *m.* || **model** [mɑdḷ] *n.* modèle *m*; [mock-up, dummy] maquette *f.* || *adj.* modèle. || *v. tr.* [-ll-] modeler (qqch. sur, *sth./after, upon/*).
moderate ['mɑdɚət] *adj.* [person] modéré, sobre; [dimension] moyen; [price] modique. || *v. tr.* ['mɑdɚˌejt] modérer. || **moderately** ['mɑdɚət|lɪ] *adv.* modérément, avec modération. || **moderateness** [-nəs] *n.* modération *f*; [taste, &c.] sobriété *f*; [price] modicité *f.* || **moderation** [ˌmɑdɚ'ɛjʃən] *n.* modération *f*; [taste] sobriété *f.* cf. MODERATENESS. || **moderator** ['mɑdɚˌejtɚ] *n.* modérat|eur *m*, -rice *f.*
modern ['mɑdɚn] *adj.* moderne: ~ *languages*, langues *fpl* vivantes. || **modernity** [mɑ'dɚnɪtɪ] *n.* les temps *mpl* modernes, modernité *f.* || **modernize** ['mɑdɚnajz] *v. tr.* moderniser, rénover.
modest ['mɑdəst] *adj.* modeste; [chaste] pudique; [reasonable] simple, sans prétention(s). || **-ly** [-lɪ] *adv.* modestement; pudiquement; sans prétention(s). || **modesty** [-ɪ] *n.* modestie *f*; [life, means] simplicité *f.*
modification [ˌmɑdɪfɪ'kejʃən] *n.* modification *f*; adoucissement *m.* || **modify** ['mɑdɪˌfaj] *v. tr.* **1.** modifier, changer. **2.** adoucir, atténuer.
modiste [mow'dijst] *n.* [dress] couturière *f*; [hats] modiste *f.*
modulate ['mɑdjəˌlejt] *v. tr.* **1.** régulariser; ajuster; varier. **2.** [voice, Mus.] moduler; [Electr.] moduler.
Mohammedan [mow'hæmədən] *adj. & n.* Mahométan *m.*
moist [mojst] *adj.* humide (et tiède), mouillé (de rosée, &c.); [skin, &c.] moite. || **moisten** ['mojsn̩] *v. tr.* humecter (du linge, &c.), mouiller (qqch.). || *v. intr.*

se mouiller, s'humecter. || **moistness** ['mojs|tnəs] *n.* humidité *f,* moiteur *f.* || **moisture** [-tʃɚ] *n.* humidité *f* (légère).

molar ['mowlɚ] *n. & adj.* molaire (*f*).

molasses [mə'læsəz] *n.pl.* mélasse *f.*

mold, cf. MOULD.

mole [mowl] *n.* **1.** grain *m* de beauté. **2.** môle *m,* jetée *f.* **3.** taupe *f*: *hairy-tailed* ~, taupe *f* du Canada.

molecule ['mɑləˌkjuwl] *n.* molécule *f.*

molest [mə'lɛst] *v. tr.* molester (qqun).

mollify ['mɑlɪˌfaj] *v. tr.* adoucir, attendrir (qqch.); calmer, apaiser (la douleur, la colère); apaiser, adoucir (qqun).

molten ['mowltn̩] *adj.* fondu: ~ *steel,* acier *m* en fusion.

moment ['mowmən|t] *n.* **1.** moment *m*; instant *m*: *One* ~, *please!,* Ne quittez pas!; *at the* ~, pour le moment; *at every* ~, à chaque instant ; *at any* ~, d'un instant à l'autre; *just this* ~, à l'instant (même); *the* ~ *I see him,* dès que je le vois; *at/this, that/* ~, en ce moment, à ce moment-là; *I'll be with you in a* ~, Je suis à vous dans un instant. **2.** importance *f.* || **momentarily** [ˌmowmən'tɛɚɪlɪ] *adv.* momentanément. || **momentary** [-ˌtɛɚɪ] *adj.* momentané.

momentous [mow'mɛntəs] *adj.* [decision, &c.] important, d'importance.

momentum [mow'mɛntəm] *n.* [Phys.] moment *m*; impulsion *f,* élan *m.*

monarch ['mɑnɑɚk] *n.* monarque *m,* souverain *m,* -e *f.* || **monarchy** ['mɑnɚkɪ] *n.* monarchie *f*; [country] royaume *m.*

monastery ['mɑnəsˌtɛɚɪ] *n.* monastère *m*; [nuns] couvent *m*; prieuré *m*; abbaye *f.*

monastic [mə'næstɪk] *adj.* monastique; monacal.

Monday ['mʌndej] *n.* lundi *m*: *on* ~, lundi (prochain), le lundi; *he is coming on* ~, il vient lundi; *he works on Mondays,* il travaille le lundi; *every* ~, tous les lundis, le lundi; *Monday, July 18, 1961,* (le) lundi 18 juillet 1961.

monetary ['mɑnəˌtɛɚɪ] *adj.* monétaire; en espèce: *a* ~ *reward,* un prix en argent.

money ['mʌnɪ] *n.* argent *m*; [currency, coin] monnaie *f*: ~ *bag,* sacoche *f*; ~ *box,* tirelire *f*; ~ *market,* marché *m* monétaire, bourse *f*; ~ *order,* mandat *m*; *counterfeit* ~, fausse monnaie; *ready* ~, argent/comptant, liquide; *to get one's money's worth,* en avoir pour son argent. || **moneyed** [-d] *adj.* [person] fortuné, riche.

Mongolia [ˌmɑn'gowlɪə] *n.* Mongolie *f*: *Outer* ~, la Mongolie extérieure.

mongrel ['mʌŋgɹəl] *adj.* métissé, croisé || *n.* [animals, plants] métis *m.*

Monica ['mɑnɪkə] *n.* = Monique *f.*

monitor ['mɑnɪtɚ] *n.* monit|eur *m,* -rice *f.*

monk [mʌŋk] *n.* [Rel.] moine *m.*

monkey [-ɪ] *n.* singe *m*: *female, she-/* ~, guenon *f*; ~ *tricks,* singeries *fpl,* espièglerìes *fpl*; ~ *wrench,* clef *f* anglaise.

monogamy [mə'nɑgəmɪ] *n.* monogamie *f.*

monogram ['mɑnəˌgɹæm] *n.* monogramme *m.*

monologue ['mɑnəˌlɔg] *n.* monologue *m*; soliloque *m*; [Thea.] tirade *f.*

monopolize [mə'nɑpə|ˌlajz] *v. tr.* monopoliser. || **monopoly** [-lɪ] *n.* monopole *m,* privilège *m* exclusif.

monotonous [mən'ɑtən|əs] *adj.* monotone. || **monotony** [-ɪ] *n.* monotonie *f.*

monsoon [mɑn'suwn] *n.* mousson *f.*

monster ['mɑnstɚ] *adj.* énorme. || *n.* monstre *m.* || **monstrosity** [mɑn'stɹɑsətɪ] *n.* monstruosité *f.* || **monstrous** ['mɑnstɹəs] *adj.* monstrueux, prodigieux, horrible.

month [mʌnθ] *n.* mois: *once a* ~, une fois par mois; [Fam.] *a* ~ *of Sundays,* une éternité. || **monthly** [-lɪ] *adj.* mensuel: ~ *instalment,* mensualité *f.*

monument ['mɑnjəmənt] *n.* monument *m.* || **monumental** [mɑnjə'mɛntl̩] *adj.* **1.** monumental. **2.** commémoratif.

moo [muw] *n.* meuh! || *v. intr.* beugler, meugler.

mood [muwd] *n.* **1.** humeur *f,* inclination *f,* disposition *f* (d'esprit): *to be in the* ~ *to* (*do*), être disposé à (faire); *to be in a /good, bad/* ~, être de/bonne, mauvaise/ humeur; *He has his moods,* Il a des accès *m* de mauvaise humeur. **2.** [Gram.] mode *m.* || **moody** [-ɪ] *adj.* irritable, chagrin; morose, d'humeur changeante.

moon [muwn] *n.* lune *f*; [Fig.] un mois *m*: *new* ~, nouvelle lune; *full* ~, pleine lune; [Fig.] *once in a blue* ~, la semaine des 4 jeudis tous les 36 du mois. || *adj.* de (la) lune. || *v. intr. to* ~ *about,* muser. || **moonlight** [-ˌlajt] *n.* clair *m* de lune. || **moonshine** [-ˌʃajn] *n.* **1.** cf. MOONLIGHT. **2.** [alcohol] mauvaise boisson *f,* © robine *f.* || **moonshiner** [-ˌʃajnɚ] *n.* © robineux *m.*

moor[1] [muwɚ] *v. tr.* [boat] amarrer. || *v. intr.* s'amarrer.

moor[2] *n.* [Br.] lande *f,* bruyère *f.*

Moor [muwɚ] *n.* Maure *m.* || **Moorish** [-ɪʃ] *adj.* Mauresque.

moorage [-ədʒ] *n.* [boat] amarrage *m.* || **mooring** [-ɪŋ] *n.* amarrage *m*: *moorings,* amarres *fpl.*

moose [muws] *n.* élan *m* d'Amérique; © orignal *m*: ~ *-caller* bourgot *m*.

moot [muwt] *v. tr.* soulever (une question), mettre sur le tapis. || **mooted** *adj.* controversé.

mop [mɑp] *n.* **1.** [cleaning] vadrouille *f.*; [dry] balai *m* à franges; O'cédar *m*, mop *m*, © mop *f.* **2.** [hair] tignasse *f.* || **mop up** *v. tr.* **[-pp-]** nettoyer; [also Fig.] éponger, essuyer.

mope [mowp] *v. intr.* **1.** être/hébété, stupide, triste, découragé/. **2.** s'ennuyer.

moral [ˈmɔɚəl] *adj.* moral. || *n.* [tale, story] morale *f*, moralité *f.* || **morale** [mɔɚˈæl] *n.* moral *m* (des troupes). || **moralist** [ˈmɔɚəlɪst] *n.* moraliste *m.* || **morality** [mɔɚˈælɪtɪ] *n.* moralité *f*; [ethics] la morale. || **moralize** [ˈmɔɚə|ˌlajz] *v. tr.* **1.** moraliser. **2.** donner un sens moral à (une action, &c.). || **morally** [-lɪ] *adv.* moralement, au moral. || **morals** [-lz] *pl.* la morale *f*; les mœurs *fpl*: *person without* ~, personne *f* immorale.

morass [məˈɹæs] *n.* marais *m*, bourbier *m.*

morbid [ˈmɔɚbɪd] *adj.* **1.** [disease] morbide. **2.** malsain; aux idées/malsaines, morbides.

more [mɔɚ] *adj. compar.* [cf. MUCH, MANY] plus; davantage; encore: *He has* ~ *money than you* (*think*), Il a plus d'argent que vous (ne croyez); *Does he have* ~ (*of it*)?, En a-t-il/davantage, plus/?; *He has* ~ *than five*, Il en a plus de cinq; *Do you want* (*some*) ~ (*tea*)?, En voulez-vous encore/Voulez-vous encore du thé?; *He wants/a little, a few, a lot, many/* ~, Il en veut encore/un peu, quelques-uns, beaucoup/; *I don't want* (*any*) ~ *dessert*, Je ne veux plus de dessert; *He has nothing* ~, Il n'a plus rien; *He has no* ~ (*of it*), Il n'en a plus; *He doesn't have any* ~, *He has no* ~ (*than you*), Il n'en a pas plus (que vous), Il n'en a pas davantage; *He has one* ~ (*than you*), Il en a un de plus (que vous); *What* ~ *can you ask?*, Qu'est-ce que vous voulez de plus? *I can't do* ~, Je ne peux pas faire/plus, davantage/; *That's* ~ *than enough*, C'est plus qu'il n'en faut; *and what is* ~ . . . , et qui plus est . . . ; *He knows* ~ *about it than you*, Il en sait plus long que vous. || *adv.* [cf. MUCH]. **1.** plus, davantage; plutôt: *That hurts* ~ (*than before*), Ça fait plus mal (qu'avant); *He is as rich, if not* ~ (*so*), Il est aussi riche, sinon davantage; *He is clever, but you are* ~ *so*, Il est intelligent, mais vous l'êtes davantage; *It was* ~ (*like*) *a rout than a retreat*, C'était plutôt une déroute qu'une retraite; ~ (*or less*) *rapid*(*ly*), plus (ou moins) rapide(ment); *His condition is* ~ *and* ~ *serious*, Sa condition/est de plus en plus grave, s'aggrave de plus en plus/; *It is all the* ~ *beautiful since* . . . , C'est d'autant plus beau que . . . ; *He is no* ~, Il/n'est, n'existe/plus; *He will return no* ~, *He won't come back any* ~, Il ne reviendra (jamais) plus; *He spoke no* ~ *distinctly* (*than you*), Il n'a pas parlé plus distinctement (que vous).

moreover [-ˈowvɚ] *adv.* d'ailleurs, de plus.

morgue [mɔɚg] *n.* morgue *f.*

morning [ˈmɔɚnɪŋ] *n.* **1.** matin *m*: *in the* ~(*s*), le matin; *the* ~ */after, before/*, le lendemain matin, la veille au matin; *three* (*o'clock*) *in the* ~, trois heures du matin; *from* ~ *to night*, du matin au soir; *Good* ~*!*, Bonjour!; [Bot.] ~ *-glory*, gloire *f* du matin. **2.** matinée *f*: *a beautiful* ~, une belle matinée; *during the* ~, dans la matinée; *the whole* ~, toute la matinée; *to spend the* ~ *doing sth.*, passer la matinée à faire qqch.

Moroccan [məˈrɑkən] *n. & adj.* Marocain *m*, **-e** *f.* || **Morocco** [məˈrɑkow] *n.* Maroc *m.* || **morocco** *n.* [leather] maroquin *m*: ~ *goods*, maroquinerie *f.*

moron [ˈmɔɚɑn] *n.* faible d'esprit, minus habens *m.*

morose [məˈɹows] *adj.* morose.

morphia [ˈmɔɚfɪə] *n.* [drugs] morphine *f.*

†morrow [ˈmɔɚow] *n.* **1.** lendemain *m.* **2.** demain *m.* **3.** †matin *m.*

morsel [ˈmɔɚsəl] *n.* morceau *m*, bouchée *f*; [little bit] brin *m.*

mortal [ˈmɔɚtəl] *adj.* mortel; fatal. || *n.* mortel *m*; être *m* humain. || **mortality** [mɔɚˈtælɪtɪ] *n.* mortalité *f.* || **mortally** [ˈmɔɚtəlɪ] *adv.* mortellement; (blessé) à mort.

mortar [ˈmɔɚtɚ] *n.* **1.** [construction] mortier *m.* **2.** [bowl] mortier *m.* **3.** [Artil.] mortier *m.*

mortgage [ˈmɔɚgəʤ] *n.* [Jur.] hypothèque *f.* || *v. tr.* hypothéquer.

mortician [mɔɚˈtɪʃən] *n.* entrepreneur *m* de pompes funèbres.

mortification [ˌmɔɚtɪfɪˈkejʃən] *n.* mortification *f*; [Fig.] humiliation *f.* || **mortify** [ˈmɔɚtɪˌfaj] *v. tr.* **1.** humilier (qqun); abaisser, blesser (qqun). **2.** (se) mortifier. **3.** [Méd.] gangrener.

mortuary [ˈmɔɚtʃuwˌɛɚɪ] *adj.* mortuaire. || *n.* morgue *f.*

Moscow [ˈmɑskaw] *n.* Moscou *m.* || *adj.* moscovite; [Pej.] moscoutaire.

Moses [ˈmowzəs] *pr. n.* [Bibl.] Moïse *m.*

Moslem ['mɑzləm] *adj. & n.* musulman (*m*), -e (*f*).
mosquito [mə'skijtow] *n.* moustique *m*, © maringouin *m*.
moss [mɑs] *n.* mousse *f.* || **mossy** *adj.* mousseux: *a ~ green*, un vert (de) mousse.
most [mowst] *adj. superl.* cf. MUCH, MANY. **1.** le plus (de): *Who has (the) ~ money?*, Qui est-ce qui a le plus d'argent?; *at the (very) ~*, tout au plus, au maximum; *to make the ~ of sth.*, tirer le meilleur parti (possible) de, [show off] faire valoir, [save] économiser, ménager/qqch. **2.** la plupart (de): *~ (people) say that . . .*, la plupart (des gens) disent que . . . ; *~ of the spectators*, la plupart des spectateurs; *~ of the electorate*, la plus grande, la majeure/partie, la majorité, du corps électoral; la plupart des votants; *~ of the time*, la plupart du temps; *for the ~ part*, pour la plupart, la plupart du temps. || *adv.* **1.** [with a verb] le plus: *He is the one I hate (the) ~*, C'est lui que je déteste le plus. **2.** [with an adj.] le, la, les, plus . . . : *They are the ~ respected teachers in the school*, Ce sont les professeurs les plus respectés de l'école; *the ~ beautiful women (in the world)*, les plus belles femmes (du monde). **3.** [with an adv.] le plus: *He spoke (the) ~ distinctly*, Il a parlé le plus distinctement. **4.** [emphatic] très, bien, fort [cf. VERY, note]; extrêmement: *a ~ beautiful day*, une très belle journée, une journée extrêmement belle, une journée des plus belles; *It was ~ unlikely (that)*, Il était peu probable (que). || **mostly** [-lı] *adv.* pour la plupart, principalement; (pour) la plupart du temps, le plus souvent.
mote [mowt] *n.* grain *m* de poussière, [Bibl.] paille *f* (dans l'œil).
motel [mow'tɛl] *n.* © motel *m*.
moth [mɔθ] *n.* [insect] mite *f*: *~ balls*, boules *fpl*/ © à mites, [Fr.] de naphtaline/; *~ -eaten*, mité.
mother ['mʌðɚ] *n.* mère *f*: *~ tongue*, langue *f* maternelle. || *v. tr.* [child] servir de mère à (qqun); [coddle] dorloter. || **motherhood** [-ˌhʊd] *n.* maternité *f.* || **motherless** [-ləs] *adj.* sans mère, orphelin de mère. || **motherly** [-lı] *adj.* [affection] maternelle, de mère. || **mother-in-law** [-ınˌlɔ] *n.* belle-mère *f.*
motion ['mowʃən] *n.* **1.** mouvement *m*; signe *m*, geste *m*: *to set (sth.) in ~*, mettre (qqch.) en/mouvement, marche/. **2.** [Polit.] motion *f*, proposition *f.* || **motionless** ['mowʃənləs] *adj.* sans mouvement, immobile.
motivation [ˌmowtı'vejʃən] *n.* raison *f* (d'agir), mobile *m*; [Psych.] motivation *f.* || **motive** ['mowtıv] *adj.* mot|eur, -rice: *~ power*, force *f* motrice. || *n.* motif *m*; stimulant *m*; [Fig.] aiguillon *m*.
motley ['mɑtlı] *adj.* **1.** bigarré, moucheté. **2.** varié. || *n.* mélange *m*.
motor ['mowtɚ] *n.* [Mech.] moteur *m*; [Br.] automobile *f.* || *adj.* mobile, mot|eur *m*, -rice *f.* || *attrib.* automobile: *~ vehicle*, véhicule *m* automobile; *~ show* salon *m* de l'automobile. || *v. intr.* aller en voiture. || **motorboat** [-ˌbowt] *n.* canot *m* automobile. || **motorcar** [-ˌkɑɚ] *n.* auto(mobile) *f*, voiture *f*; © [Fam.] char *m*. || **motorcoach** [-ˌkowtʃ] *n.* autocar *m*; © autobus *m*. || **motorcycle** [-ˌsajkl̩] *n.* motocyclette *f.*; [Fam.] moto *f.* || **motorcyclist** [-ˌsajklıst] *n.* motocycliste *m/f.* || **motorist** [-ıst] *n.* automobiliste *m*, conducteur *m* (d'automobile). || **motorize** [-ˌajz] *v. tr.* **1.** équiper (qqch.) d'un moteur. **2.** [army] motoriser. || **motorman** [-mən] *n.* conducteur *m* (de train, tramway), wattman *m*, © garde-moteur *m*.
mottle ['mɑtl̩] *v. tr.* marbrer. || **mottled** [-d] *adj.* marbré, tacheté.
motto ['mɑtow] *n.* devise *f.*
mould[1] [mowld] *n.* [earth] terreau *m*; [fungus] moisi *m*. || *v. intr.* moisir.
mould[2] *n.* **1.** moule *m*, modèle *m*, matrice *f.* **2.** caractère *m*, trempe *f.* || *v. tr.* mouler. || **moulder** [-ɚ] *v. intr.* tomber, (se) réduire en poussière. || **moulding** [-ıŋ] *n.* [Arch.] moulure *f*; [Sculp.] moulage *m*. || **mouldy** [-ı] *adj.* moisi.
moult [mowlt] *v. intr.* muer. || *n.* mue *f.*
mound [mawnd] *n.* monticule *m*; [earth] butte *f*; [funeral] tertre *m*, tumulus *m*.
mount [mawnt] *n.* mont *m*; [climbing] montée *f*; [horse] monture *f*; [picture] encadrement *m*: © *Mount Royal*, le Mont Royal. || *v. tr.* monter (un cheval, une pièce de théâtre, &c.); encadrer (des photos, &c.). || *v. intr.* monter (à cheval, &c.); [prices] s'élever. || **mountain** ['mawtn̩] *n.* montagne *f*; [Fig.] monceau *m* (de détritus): *~ ash*, sorbier *m*; *~ goat*, chèvre *f* des montagnes; *~ sheep*, mouflon *m* des Rocheuses; *~ range*, chaîne *f* de montagnes; *~ pass*, col *m*, défilé *m*. || **mountaineer** [ˌmawntn̩'ijɚ] *n.* **1.** montagnard *m*. **2.** [Sport.] alpiniste *m/f.* || **mountaineering** [-ıŋ] *n.* alpinisme *m*. || **mountainous** ['mawntn̩əs] *adj.* montagneu|x, -se, de(s) montagne(s).
Mountie ['mawntı] *n.* © [= ROYAL CANADIAN MOUNTED POLICE]. gendarme *m* à cheval, © police *f* montée.

mounting [-ŋ] *n.* monture *f,* garniture *f.*

Mounty cf. MOUNTIE.

mourn [mɔə̃n] *v. tr.* pleurer (qqun), déplorer (un malheur), [death] s'affliger (de qqch.). || *v. intr.* pleurer, se lamenter; être en deuil (de qqun, *for s.o.*). || **mournful** [-fl̩] *adj.* lugubre, funèbre. || **mourning** [-ɪŋ] *n.* deuil *m,* lamentation *f,* affliction *f*: *to be in* ~ *for s.o.,* porter le deuil de qqun.

mouse [maws] *pl.* **mice** [majs] *n.* souris *f*: ~ *trap,* piège *m,* tapette *f* à souris, souricière *f.* || *v. intr.* [cat] chasser les souris. || **mousy** ['mawsɪ] *adj.* de souris; [Fig.] effacé, timide.

moustache [mə'stæʃ] *n.* moustache *f.*

mouth [mawθ] *pl.* **mouths** [mawðz] *n.* bouche *f*; [wolf; gun, &c.] gueule *f*; [river] embouchure *f*; [tunnel, &c.] orifice *m*; [bottle] goulot *m*: ~ *organ,* harmonica *m*; *to be down in the* ~ , être/abattu, déprimé, découragé/. || *v. tr.* attraper, happer/avec la bouche; [speech, &c.] déclamer. || **mouthful** ['mawθ|ˌfʊl] *n.* bouchée *f.* || **mouthpiece** [-ˌpijs] *n.* **1.** [Mus.] embouchure *f* (d'instrument). **2.** [Fig.] [person] porte-parole *m.*

movable ['muwvəbl̩] *adj.* **1.** mobile: *a* ~ *holiday,* une fête mobile. || *n.* meuble *m.* || **movables** [-z] biens *mpl* meubles, denrées *fpl.*

move [muwv] *n.* **1.** mouvement *m,* déplacement *m*: *on the* ~ , en mouvement; [Fam.] *to get a* ~ *on,* se remuer. **2.** [politesse, &c.] manœuvre *f,* démarche *f,* décision *f,* action *f.* **3.** [chess, &c.] coup *m,* tour *m*: *It's your* ~ , A vous, C'est à votre tour/de jouer. **4.** déménagement *m.* || *v. tr.* **1.** déplacer, changer de place, transporter; remuer, bouger (la main, le pied, &c.); mettre en mouvement, en marche; faire marcher, actionner (un mécanisme). **2.** toucher, émouvoir (qqun); faire changer d'avis; pousser, inciter/(qqun) (à faire qqch.): *to* ~ *s.o. to/pity, tears, anger/,* exciter la pitié de qqun, attendrir qqun au point de le faire pleurer; provoquer la colère de qqun. **3.** proposer (une résolution, que + subjunc.). || *v. intr.* **1.** se déplacer [traffic, crowd] circuler. **2.** remuer; [esp. with neg.] bouger; faire un mouvement; [things] marcher: *Don't* ~ , Ne bougez pas. **3.** aller, venir, se diriger (and other verbs of motion). **4.** agir. **5.** [household] déménager. || **move about** [-ə'bawt] *v. tr.* déplacer, changer de place. || *v. intr.* se déplacer; [crowd] circuler; aller et venir. || **move away** [-ə'wej] *v. tr.* éloigner, écarter. || *v. intr.* s'en aller, s'éloigner; déménager. || **move back** [-'bæk] *v. tr.* reculer (qqch.), faire reculer (qqun); ramener (qqch.) en arrière. || *v. intr.* reculer; revenir en arrière. || **move forward** [-'fɔə̃wə̃d] *v. tr.* avancer (qqch.), faire avancer (qqun). || *v. intr.* avancer. || **move in** [-'ɪn] *v. tr.* emménager. || *v. intr.* entrer; emménager. || **move off** [-'ɑf] *v. tr.* éloigner; écarter. || *v. intr.* s'éloigner; se mettre en route; [train] se mettre en marche. || **move on** [-'ɑn] *v. tr. & intr.* (faire) circuler. || **move out** [-'awt] *v. tr.* sortir (qqch.); faire sortir (qqun); déménager. || *v. intr.* sortir; déménager. || **move over** [-'owvə̃] *v. tr.* déplacer (vers le côté), pousser. || *v. intr.* se ranger, s'écarter: *Move over!,* Poussez-vous!

movement [-mənt] *n.* mouvement *m,* déplacement *m*; geste *m*; [Pol.] mouvement *m*; mécanisme *m.* || **mover** [-ə̃] *n.* **1.** déménageur *m.* **2.** auteur *m* d'une motion, motionnaire *m.* || **movie** [-ɪ] *n.* film *m,* cinéma *m*: *a first-run* ~ , un film en exclusivité; *to go to the movies,* aller/au cinéma, © aux vues/. || **moving** [-ɪŋ] *adj.* mouvant; [Fig.] émouvant, touchant. || **movingly** [-ɪŋlɪ] *adv.* en termes émus, d'une manière touchante.

mow [mow], **mowed** [-d], **mown** [-n] *v. tr.* **1.** faucher, moissonner. **2.** tondre (le gazon). || **mower** [-ə̃] *n.* faucheu|r, -se: *lawn-* ~ , tondeuse *f* à gazon.

mown cf. MOW.

M.P. ['ɛm'pij] [= Member of Parliament] membre *m* du Parlement. || **M.P.P.** ['ɛm'pij'pij] membre *m* de l'Assemblée législative; député *m.*

Mr. ['mɪstə̃] [= MISTER] [☞ Toujours suivi du nom de famille]: *Mr. Brown,* Monsieur Lebrun, M. Lebrun.

Mrs. ['mɪsɪz] *n.* [autrefois *Mistress*; ☞ toujours suivi du nom de famille]: *Mrs. Brown,* Madame Brown, Mme Brown.

M.S., M.Sc. ['ɛmˌɛs('sij)] [= Master of Science] maître *m* ès sciences.

much [mʌtʃ] *adj.* [MORE, MOST] [s'emploie devant un substantif collectif] beaucoup (de + noun); bien (du, de la, de l', des + noun); un(e) grand(e) (+ noun): *I don't have* ~ *time,* Je n'ai pas beaucoup de temps; *with* ~ *trouble,* avec bien/du mal, de la peine/; *It is with* ~ *surprise that . . .,* C'est avec une grande surprise que . . . ; *Much (of it) was wasted,* Une bonne partie a été gaspillée; *I didn't use* ~ *(of it),* Je n'en ai pas employé beaucoup; *He is not* ~ *of a bridge-player,* Il ne vaut pas grand-chose comme joueur de bridge, Il ne joue au bridge que rarement; *I don't/ think, make/* ~ *of it,* Cela ne me dit, Je n'y comprends/pas grand-chose; *to make* ~ *of,* faire grand cas de; *Much happened while you were away,* Bien des choses se sont passées, [better] Il s'est passé/bien des, beaucoup de/choses en votre absence; *Nothing, Not/* ~ *happened,* Il ne s'est pas passé grand-chose; *It's all* ~ *of a muchness,* C'est bonnet blanc et blanc bonnet. || *adv.* **1.** [with a verb] beaucoup; souvent: *Did he complain (very)* ~ *?,* S'est-il beaucoup plaint?; *I don't see him (very)* ~, Je ne le vois/pas (très) souvent, guère; *Thank you very* ~, Merci/bien, beaucoup/; *He is* ~ *to be pitied,* Il est très à plaindre. **2.** [with a past part.] très, bien; †fort [cf. VERY, note]: *I am (very)* ~ *surprised (to . . .),* Je suis/très, bien, fort/étonné, Cela m'étonne beaucoup (de . . .). **3.** [with a comparative] bien, beaucoup; de beaucoup: *He is* ~ *cleverer (than his brother),* Il est/beaucoup, bien/plus intelligent, Il est plus intelligent de beaucoup (que son frère); *He works* ~ *better than you,* Il travaille/bien, beaucoup/mieux que vous; ~ *worse,* bien/pire, pis/; *He* ~ *outshines his rivals,* Il surpasse de beaucoup ses concurrents. **4.** [with a superlative] de beaucoup: *He is (by)* ~ *the cleverest,* Il est de beaucoup le plus intelligent. **5.** [before a phrase] ~ *to my surprise,* à ma grande surprise; *and* ~ *less,* et encore moins; *It is* ~ *the same (thing),* C'est à peu près la même chose; *Much as, However* ~ */I want to,* Pour autant que je le veuille. || **as much (as)** [æz'mʌtʃˌæz], autant (que): *Has he* ~ *money (as I)?,* A-t-il autant d'argent (que moi)?, *Give me* ~ *again,* Donnez-m'en encore autant; *Do you like it* ~ *(as the other)?,* Est-ce que cela vous plaît autant, L'aimez-vous aussi bien que l'autre?; *He did* ~ *for me,* Il en a fait autant pour moi; *I thought* ~, Je m'en doutais bien; *It's* ~ *as I can do to . . . ,* C'est tout juste si j'arrive à . . . || **how much** combien (de): ~ *money do you have?,* Combien d'argent avez-vous, Combien avez-vous d'argent?; ~ *do you want?,* Combien en voulez-vous?; ~ *is it?,* C'est combien?; *You don't know* ~ *I hate it,* Vous ne savez pas/combien, à quel point/je le déteste. || **so much** tant (que); tellement: *He has* ~ *money (that),* Il a/tant, [Fam.] tellement/d'argent (que); *He works* ~ *(that),* Il travaille/tant, tellement/(que); ~ *overworked (that),* si, tellement/surmené (que); ~ *the/better, worse/,* tant/mieux, pis/; *at* ~ *a pound,* à tant la livre; †*So much did he suffer (that),* Tant il a souffert (que); ~ *the more as . . . ,* d'autant plus que . . . ; *He has not grown/so, as/much as you,* Il n'a pas grandi (au)tant que vous; *He didn't* ~ *as look at me,* Il ne m'a pas même regardé; ~ *for that,* Voilà pour cela. **too much** trop (de): *He eats* ~ *(meat),* Il mange trop (de viande); *He sleeps* ~, Il dort trop; *He goes out* ~, Il sort trop souvent; *six pounds* ~, six livres de trop; *It's* ~ *of a good thing,* Voilà qui est trop fort.

muck [mʌk] *n.* boue *f,* fumier *m*; [Fam.] saleté *f.*

mud [mʌd] *n.* boue *f,* vase *f,* †fange *f*: ~ *guard,* garde-boue *m.*

muddle ['mʌdl̩] *n.* confusion *f,* fouillis *m*; [Fam.] pagaille *f*: ~ *-headed,* brouillon, à l'esprit confus. || *v. tr.* embrouiller; brouiller l'esprit à.

muddy ['mʌdɪ] *adj.* boueux; [clothes, &c.] crotté, /taché, couvert/de boue.

muff[1] [mʌf] *n.* manchon *m.*

muff[2] [mʌf] *n.* [Fam.] coup *m* raté, loupage *m.* || *v. tr.* [Fam.] louper, rater.

muffin ['mʌfɪn] *n.* gâteau *m,* © brioche *f.*

muffle ['mʌfl̩] *v. tr.* assourdir (un son): *to* ~ *o.s. up,* s'emmitoufler. || **muffler** ['mʌflər] *n.* [car] silencieux *m,* pot *m* d'échappement.

mufti ['mʌftɪ] *n.* vêtement/ordinaire, civil/: *in* ~, en/pékin, civil/.

mug [mʌg] *n.* **1.** gobelet *m,* pot *m* (à bière). **2.** [Sl.] gueule *f,* bobine *f,* fraise *f.*

muggy ['mʌgɪ] *adj.* [weather] lourd; chaud et humide.

mulatto [mə'lætow] *n* mulâtre *m.*

mulberry ['mʌlˌbərɪ] *n.* mûrier *m*

mule [mjuwl] *n.* mule *f*; [he- ~] mulet *m*; [she - ~] mule *f.*

mulish ['mjuwlɪʃ] *adj.* [Fig.] têtu (comme une mule), entêté.

mull [mʌl] *v. intr.* [Fam.]: *to* ~ *over sth.,* ressasser qqch.

multiple ['mʌltɪpl̩] *adj. & n.* multiple (*m*).

multiplication [ˌmʌltɪplɪ'kejʃən] *n.* multiplication *f*; accroissement *m.* || **multiply** ['mʌltɪˌplaj] *v. tr.* multiplier, accroître. || *v. intr.* [people, &c.] se multiplier, s'accroître. || **multitude** ['mʌltɪtuwd] *n.* multitude *f*; [people] foule *f.*

mum [mʌm] *adj.* silencieux, muet: *to be* ~, ne souffler mot.

mumble [-bl̩] *n.* murmure *m.* || *v. tr. & intr.* murmurer, marmotter.

mummy ['mʌmɪ] *n.* **1.** [Hist.] momie *f.* **2.** [Fam.] maman *f.*

mumps [mʌmps] *n.* [Med.] oreillons *mpl.*
munch [mʌntʃ] *v. tr.* mâchouiller (qqch.); [cigar, &c.] mâchonner.
mundane [ˌmʌn'dejn] *adj.* mondain, terrestre.
municipal [ˌmjuwnɪsɪpḷ] *adj.* [council, &c.] municipal. || **municipality** [ˌmjuwnɪsɪ'pælɪtɪ] *n.* municipalité *f.*
munition [mjuw'nɪʃən] *n.* munitions *fpl*: *~ plant*, usine *f* de guerre.
mural ['mjuwɚḷ] *adj.* mural, de mur. || *n.* peinture *f* murale.
murder ['mɚdɚ] *n.* meurtre *m*, assassinat *m.* || *v. tr.* tuer, assassiner (qqun); [Fig.] massacrer (une langue). || **murderer** [-ɚ] *n.* meurtrier *m*, assassin *m.* || **murderess** [-əs] *n.* meurtrière *f.* || **murderous** [-əs] *adj.* meurtrier; de meurtre.
murky ['mɚkɪ] *adj.* sombre, obscur.
murmur ['mɚmɚ] *n.* murmure *m* (des vagues). || *v. tr. & intr.* murmurer.
muscle ['mʌsḷ] *n.* muscle *m*; [Fig.] force *f.* || **muscular** ['mʌskjəlɚ] *adj.* **1.** musculaire. **2.** musculeux; musclé, fort.
muse [mjuwz] *n.* **1.** muse *f*: *the nine Muses*, les neuf Muses. **2.** rêverie *f.* || *v. intr.* méditer, être rêveur.
museum [-ɪəm] *n.* [Art] musée *m*; [Science] muséum *m.*
mush [mʌʃ] *n.* bouillie *f*; [US] bouillie/de maïs, de céréale/; [Fam.] sensiblerie *f*, niaiserie *f* sentimentale.
mushroom ['mʌʃˌɹuwm] *n.* champignon *m.*
mushy ['mʌʃɪ] *adj.* détrempé, spongieux.
music ['mjuwzɪk] *n.* musique *f*: *~-lover*, mélomane *m/f.* || **musical** [-ḷ] *adj.* musical; [word, verse, &c.] harmonieux: instrument. instrument *m* de musique. || **musician** [ˌmjuw'zɪʃən] *n.* musicien *m*, -ne *f.*
musk [mʌsk] *n.* musc *m.*
muskeg ['mʌskɛg] *n.* © fondrière *f* (de mousse), muskeg *m.* || **muskeg-moss** [ˌmʌskɛg'mɑs] *n.* sphaigne *f.*
muskellunge ['mʌskəˌlʌndʒ] *n.* © [fish] maskinongé *m.*
musket ['mʌskət] *n.* mousquet *m.* || **musketeer** [mʌskə'tijɚ] *n.* [Hist.] mousquetaire *m.*
muskox ['mʌskɑks] *n.* bœuf *m* musqué.
muskrat ['mʌskˌɹæt] *n.* rat *m* musqué.
muslin ['mʌzlɪn] *n.* mousseline *f.*
muss (up) [mʌs] *v. tr.* froisser, mettre en désordre. || *n.* désordre *m.*
mussel ['mʌsḷ] *n.* [mollusk] moule *f.*
Mussulman ['mʌzḷmən] *n. pl.* -s Musulman, -e. || *adv.* musulman.
must[1] [mʌst] *v. aux.* [défectif: *must* s'emploie à toutes les personnes pour former le présent, et parfois dans le discours indirect comme temps passé.] **1.** [obligation] falloir; devoir: *You ~ do it*, Il faut (absolument)/le faire, que vous le fassiez/, Vous devez le faire; [with future meaning] Il faudra . . . , Vous devrez . . . ; *You ~ hurry*, Il faut vous dépêcher; *You/ ~ not, mustn't/be late*, Il ne faut pas/être, que vous soyez/en retard; *I ~ say* . . . , Je dois dire . . . , Il faut avouer . . . ; *He said he ~ see me*, Il a dit qu'il/devait, lui fallait/me voir. **2.** [conjecture] devoir: *He ~ be sick*, Il doit être malade; *He ~ have been sick*, Il a dû être malade; *I saw that he ~ be sick*, J'ai compris qu'il devait être malade, *I knew that he ~ have been sick*, Je savais qu'il avait dû être malade. || *n.* This is a ~, → c'est une nécessité absolue; se faut absolument.
must[2] *n.* moisissure *f*, moisi *m.*
mustache [mə'stæʃ] *n.* cf. MOUSTACHE.
mustard ['mʌstɚd] *n.* moutarde *f*: *~ plaster*, sinapisme *m.*
muster ['mʌstɚ] *n.* **1.** réunion *f.* **2.** rassemblement *m*, revue *f*: *to pass ~*, être porté à l'appel, [Fig.] être acceptable; *~ books*, états *mpl*, contrôles *mpl* (de l'effectif militaire). || *v. tr.* rassembler (des troupes); [Fig.] *to ~ up courage*, prendre son courage à deux mains.
mustn't ['mʌsṇt] = MUST NOT.
musty ['mʌstɪ] *adj.* moisi, aigre; [Fig.] désuet.
mute [mjuwt] *adj.* muet, silencieux: *a ~ grief*, une douleur muette. || *n.* **1.** muet *m.* **2.** [Mus.] sourdine *f.* **3.** [Phon.] lettre *f* muette. || *v. intr.* mettre une sourdine. || **muteness** [-nəs] *n.* silence *m*, mutisme *m.*
mutilate ['mjuwtɪˌlejt] *v. tr.* mutiler, estropier; tronquer (une histoire). || **mutilation** [ˌmjuwtɪ'lejʃən] *n.* mutilation *f.*
mutiny ['mjuwtɪnɪ] *n.* mutinerie *f*, insurrection *f.* || *v. intr.* se mutiner, se révolter.
mutter ['mʌtɚ] *n.* marmottage *m*, murmure *m* (entre les dents). || *v. tr. & intr.* marmotter. || **muttering** [-ɪŋ] *n.* cf. MUTTER.
mutton ['mʌtṇ] *n.* [Cul.] mouton *m*: *leg of ~*, gigot *m.*
mutual ['mjuwtʃuwəl] *adj.* mutuel, réciproque; [friend] commun: *by ~ consent*, d'un commun accord.
muzzle ['mʌzḷ] *n.* **1.** [horse, &c.] museau *m.* **2.** [dog] muselière *f*; [Fig.] bâillon *m.* || *v. tr.* [dog] museler; [Fig.] bâillonner (qqun).
my [maj] *pr. poss.* mon *m*, ma *f*, mes *m/f pl.* cf. HIS, HER.
myopia [maj'owpɪə] *n.* myopie *f.*
myriad ['mijɚɪəd] *n.* dix mille; [Fig.] myriade *f*, grand nombre.
myrtle ['mɚtḷ] *n.* [Bot.] myrte *m.*

myself [maj'sɛlf] *pr. pers.* moi, moi-même: *all by* ~, (à) moi tout(e) seul(e). cf. HIMSELF, HERSELF.

mysterious [mɪ'stijəɪəs] *adj.* [secret] mystérieux. || **-ly** [-lɪ] *adv.* mystérieusement || **mystery** ['mɪstəɪ] *n.* mystère *m*; secret *m* (d'un art, &c.).

mystic ['mɪstɪk] *adj.* **1.** mystérieux. **2.** mystique. || *n.* mystique *m.* || **mystical** [-l̩] *adj.* **1.** mystérieux. **2.** mystique. || **mysticism** ['mɪstɪˌsɪzm] *n.* mysticisme *m.* || **mystification** [mɪstɪfɪ'kejʃən] *n.* [puzzlement] mystification *f.*

myth [mɪθ] *n.* **1.** mythe *m.* **2.** légende *f*, fable. *f.* || **mythical** [-ɪkl̩] *adj.* mythique; fabuleux. || **mythological** [mɪθə'lɑʤɪkl̩] *adj.* mythologique. || **mythology** [mɪ'θɑləʤɪ] *n.* mythologie *f.*

N

N, n [ɛn] pl. N's, n's. [quatorzième lettre de l'alphabet N *m*, n *m*, la lettre n.]

'n, 'n' [n̩] [abr. encore non reconnue mais fréquente de **and**]: *rock 'n' roll.*

nab [næb] [Fam.] *v. tr.* **[-bb-]** attraper, saisir, arrêter.

nag [næg] *n.* **1.** [Fam., horse] canasson *m*, © picouille *f.* **2.** [quarrel] dispute *f*, chamaillerie *f.* || *v. tr.* **[-gg-]** disputer, bousculer. || *v. intr.* se disputer, se chamailler.

nail [nejl] *n.* **1.** clou *m*: *to drive (in) a* ~, planter, enfoncer/un clou (à coups de marteau); *You hit the* ~ *on the head,* Vous avez mis le doigt dessus. **2.** ongle *m* (des doigts): *to cut one's nails*, se couper, se faire les ongles (avec des ciseaux); ~ *polish*, vernis *m* à ongles. || *v. tr.* clouer (une planche, &c.); clouter (un soulier).

naive, également **naïve** [ˌnaj'ijv] *adj.* naï/f *m*, -ve *f*; inexpérimenté, sans préjugés.

naked ['nejkəd] *adj.* **1.** (tout) nu; [used in predicate] à nu: *stark* ~, tout nu; *with the* ~ *eye*, à l'œil nu; *the* ~ *truth*, la vérité toute nue. **2.** [room] dégarni; [town] sans défense; exposé (aux regards, au froid, &c.).

name [nejm] *n.* **1.** nom *m*: *What's your* ~ *?* → Comment vous appelez-vous?; *My* ~ *is John,* → Je m'appelle Jean; [Fam.] *What's the* ~ *again?*, Comment est-ce que vous vous appelez déjà?; *in the* ~ *of*, au nom de; *in your* ~, en votre nom; *by* ~, de nom; *by the* ~ *of*, du nom de; *He went/by, under/the* ~ *of*, → Il était connu sous le nom de; *maiden* ~, nom *m* de jeune fille; *first* ~, *given* ~, *Christian* ~, petit nom, nom de baptême, prénom; *family* ~, *last* ~, *surname*, nom de famille; *assumed* ~ pseudonyme *m.* **2.** réputation *f.* || **name** *v. tr.* nommer, appeler, mentionner; désigner (une date): ~ *the day,* → choisissez le jour qui vous conviendra; *I* ~ *Mr. X for president*, je propose la nomination de M. X à la présidence; *to* ~*/after, for*, nommer qqun d'après (son père, &c.). || **nameless** [-ləs] *adj.* anonyme, sans nom. || **namely** [-lɪ] *adv.* à savoir, c'est-à-dire. || **namesake** [-ˌsejk] *n.* homonyme *m.*

nanny ['nænɪ] *n.* [Fam.] nounou *f.*

nap [næp] *n.* somme *m*, sieste *f*: *to take a* ~, faire la sieste, un somme. || *v. intr.* **[-pp-]** sommeiller, faire la sieste; [Fig.] *to be caught napping*, être pris au dépourvu.

nape (of the neck) [nejp] *n.* nuque *f.*

napkin ['næpkɪn] *n.* serviette *f* (de table); [Br.] couche *f* (de bébé).

narrate [ˌnæ'ɹej|t] *v. tr.* raconter, narrer. || **narration** [-ʃən] *n.* narration *f*, récit *m.* || **narrative** ['næɹətɪv] *n.* récit *m*, narration *f*, exposé *m.* || *adj.* narratif.

narrow ['næɹow] *adj.* **(-er, -est) 1.** étroit: *The valley was getting narrower (and narrower)*, La vallée allait en se rétrécissant; ~ *gauge railway*, chemin *m* de fer à voie étroite. **2.** limité; [majority] faible: [Fig.] ~ *mind*, esprit *m* borné; ~ *-minded*, à l'esprit borné; *to have a* ~ *escape*, l'échapper belle. || *n.pl* [Geog.] détroit *m*, passe *f.* || *v. tr. & intr. to narrow (down)*, (se) rétrécir; [limit] (se) borner. || **narrowly** [-lɪ] *adv.* étroitement;

scrupuleusement, de près: *He ~/escaped, missed/being killed,* → Il faillit se faire tuer.

nasal [ˈnejzḷ] *adj.* nasal. || *n.* [Phon.] nasale *f.*

nasty [ˈnæstɪ] *adj.* vilain, méchant; sale, malpropre; [Fig.] grossier, obscène: *~ weather,* vilain, sale/temps *m*; *~ boy,* vilain, méchant/garçon; *~ smell,* une mauvaise odeur *f*; *a ~ mind,* un esprit *m* grossier.

natal [ˈnejtḷ] *adj.* natal; de naissance.

nation [ˈnejʃən] *n.* **1.** nation *f,* peuple *m*: *the English ~* , la nation britannique, les Anglais; [→ Traduisez par le nom du peuple en question]: *What this ~ needs . . .*, ce dont le Canada a besoin . . . ; *The League of Nations,* la Société des Nations, la SDN; *the United Nations,* les Nations Unies, l'ONU. **2.** [Ethn.] tribu *f,* ethnie *f*: *the Eskimo ~* , les Esquimaux. || **national** [ˈnæʃənḷ] *adj.* national, public, intérieur, de l'État: *~ laws,* législation intérieure; *~ ownership,* étatisme; [*US*] *~ bank,* banque *f* à charte. || *n.* ressortissant *m* national *m.* || **nationalism** [-ɪsm] *n.* nationalisme *m*; sentiment national; patriotisme *m.* || **nationality** [ˌnæʃəˈnælɪtɪ] *n.* nationalité *f.* || **nationalize** [ˈnæʃənḷ|ˌajz] *v. tr.* nationaliser, étatiser. || **nationally** [-ɪ] *adv. ~ known,* connu dans tout le pays. || **nationhood** [ˈnejʃənˌhud] *n.*: *The colony attained ~* , La colonie fut élevée au rang de nation. || **nationwide** [ˈnejʃənˌwajd] *adj.* national, intéressant toute la nation.

native [ˈnejtɪv] *adj.* originaire (d'un pays); naturel, indigène: *~ country,* pays *m* natal, patrie *f*; *~ tongue,* langue *f* maternelle; *a ~ speaker of English,* → qui parle anglais de naissance; *~ copper,* cuivre (à l'état) natif. || *n.* habitant *m*; indigène *m*; autochtone *m. A ~ of . . .*, originaire de . . . ; *A ~ of* (*Canada*), → (Canadien), (Canadienne) de naissance.

nativity [nəˈtɪvɪtɪ] *n.* [Rel.] Nativité *f.*

NATO [ˈnejˈtow] [= North Atlantic Treaty Organization] l'OTAN *f* [= Organisation du Traité de l'Atlantique Nord].

natty [ˈnætɪ] *adj.* élégant, coquet; [skilful] habile.

natural [ˈnætʃ(ə)ɹəl] *adj.* naturel; [Fig.] simple, naturel: *~ gas,* le gaz naturel; *~ resources,* ressources *f* naturelles; *~ history,* histoire *f* naturelle; *It is ~ that,* il est naturel que + subjonc. || *n.* [Mus.] bécarre *m.* || **naturalize** [-ˌajz] *v. tr.* naturaliser; accorder (à qqun) la citoyenneté (canadienne, &c.). || **naturally** [-ɪ] *adv.* naturellement; d'une manière naturelle. || **nature** [ˈnejtʃɚ] *n.* **1.** nature *f,* Nature *f*: *the laws of ~* , les lois de la Nature; *by ~* , par nature; **2.** nature *f* naturel *m*: *good ~* , bon naturel; *ill ~* , mauvais naturel; *good-natured,* d'un bon naturel. cf. GOOD, ILL, &c.

naught [nɔt] *n.* **1.** rien: *to come to ~* , n'aboutir à rien. **2.** zéro *m,* cf. ZÉRO.

naughty [ˈnɔtɪ] *adj.* **1.** polisson, → pas sage. **2.** vilain; [story] risqué.

nausea [ˈnɔzɪ|ə] *n.* nausée *f*: *to have a feeling of ~* , avoir la nausée, → avoir mal au cœur. || **nauseate** [-ˌejt] *v. tr.* donner mal au cœur (à qqun); [Fig.] dégoûter, écœurer, (qqun): *to be nauseated* (*by sth.*), avoir mal au cœur; être écœuré (par qqch.). || **nauseating** [-ˌejt,ŋ] *adj.* écœurant. || **nauseous** [-əs] *adj.* nauséabond.

nautical [ˈnɔtɪkḷ] *adj.* nautique; naval; marin, maritime: *~ mile,* mille *m* marin (= 6,080 pi.).

naval [ˈnejvḷ] *adj.* **1.** naval, de mer: *~ school,* école *f* navale; *~ station,* port *m* de guerre; *~ forces,* forces *f* navales. **2.** de marine, marin: *~ officer,* officier *m* de marine; *~ gunner,* canonnier *m* marin; *~ construction,* génie *m* maritime; *~ service,* la marine.

nave [nejv] *n.* nef *f.*

navel [ˈnejvḷ] *n.* nombril *m.*

navigable [ˈnævɪ|gəbḷ] *adj.* navigable. || **navigate** [-ˌgejt] *v. intr.* naviguer, se diriger vers. || *v. tr.* naviguer sur (un fleuve, &c.); piloter (un avion): *to ~ a ship,* gouverner un navire. || **navigation** [ˌnævɪˈgejʃən] *n.* navigation *f* (maritime, aérienne, &c.): *~ laws,* code *m* maritime. || **navigator** [ˈnævɪˌgejtɚ] *n.* navigateur *m* (surtout à bord des avions).

navy [ˈnejvɪ] *n.* marine *f* (de guerre); [fleet] flotte *f*: [*US*] *~ Department,* ministère *m* de la marine [Br. Admiralty]; *navy-yard,* arsenal *m* (maritime); *~ blue,* bleu *m* marine.

nay [nej] *pl.* **nays** [-z] *n.* © [Polit.] vote *m* négatif [Br. *no*(*es*)].

Nazarene [ˌnæzɚˈijn] *adj.* nazaréen; de Nazareth.

N.B. [ˈɛnˈbij] *Abr.* **1.** [= NOTA BENE] n.b. **2.** [= NEW BRUNSWICK].

N.C. [ˈɛnˈsij] [= NORTH CAROLINA].

N.D(ak). [= NORTH DAKOTA].

NE [= NORTH-EAST].

near [nijɚ] *adj.* proche; direct; [friend] intime, cher: *a ~ relation,* un proche parent; *the Near East,* le Proche Orient;

the nearest village, le village le plus proche; *by the nearest road*, par le chemin le plus/court, direct; *in the ~ future*, dans un avenir proche/prochain; (*to estimate sth.*) *to the nearest thousand*, (estimer qqch.) à un millier près; *It was a ~ thing*, On l'a échappé belle. || **near** *adv.* **1.** [place] (tout) près; [time] tout proche: *The school is quite ~* , L'école est tout près (d'ici), à deux pas; *to get, come, draw/near(er)* (*to*), s'approcher (de), se rapprocher (de); *~ at hand*, tout près, à portée de la main; *~ to*, près de. **2.** [Fam.] presque, à peu près cf. NEARLY. || *prep.* près de: *stand ~ me*, mettez-vous près de moi; *He was ~ /success, succeeding*, Il était/près de, sur le point de/réussir; *to come ~ s.o., sth.*, s'approcher de qqun, qqch.; *to put sth. ~ s.o., sth.*, approcher qqch. de qqun, qqch.; *You aren't anywhere ~/it, the answer/*, Vous n'y êtes pas du tout. || *v. intr.* s'approcher de: *to ~ land*, s'approcher des côtes; *This book is nearing completion*, → Ce livre est presque terminé. || **nearby** [ˌnijəʳˈbaj] *adj.* voisin, du voisinage. || *adv.* dans le voisinage. || **nearly** [ˈnijəʳ|lɪ] *adv.* presque, à peu près, près de; → faillir: *I'm ~ finished*, J'ai presque fini, Je suis sur le point de finir; *~ the same thing*, à peu près la même chose; *He was ~ (run over, &c.)*, → Il a failli (être écrasé, &c.). || **nearness** [-nəs] *n.* proximité *f.* || **near-sighted** [ˈnijəʳˌsajtəd] *adj.* myope; [Fig.] dénué d'imagination.

neat [nijt] *adj.* **1.** [Pers.] (net et) ordonné, propre; [room] en ordre; [work] net; [place, book, clothes] bien tenu; [dress] correct; [well dressed] bien mis. **2.** [action] adroit, habile: *a ~ trick*, un bon tour; **3.** [esp. Br.] pur, nature: *to take, drink/one's whisky ~* , boire son whisky sec. cf. STRAIGHT. || **neatly** [-lɪ] *adv.* avec ordre, avec soin, proprement; adroitement: *~ dressed*, bien vêtu. || **neatness** [-nəs] *n.* ordre *m*, propreté *f*; simplicité *f.*

Neb(r). [= NEBRASKA]. || **Nebraska** [nəˈbræskə] *n.* le Nébraska: *in, to/~* , dans le Nébraska.

nebulous [ˈnɛbjələs] *adj.* nébuleux; [Fig.] flou, vague.

necessarily [ˌnɛsəˈsɛəʳlɪ] *adv.* nécessairement; obligatoirement: *not ~* , pas /forcément, nécessairement. || **necessary** [ˈnɛsəˌsɛəʳɪ] *adj.* nécessaire (*to, for/sth., s.o.*, à qqch., qqun); *to* + infin., de + infin.): *It is ~ for me to go* [= must] Il faut que j'y aille, je dois y aller; [= need] Il est nécessaire que j'y aille, J'ai besoin d'y aller; [×] *It isn't ~ for me to do that*, Je n'ai pas besoin de faire cela, Il n'est pas nécessaire que je fasse cela [il ne faut pas = one must not]; *if ~*, s'il le faut; au besoin; *to take the ~ steps to . . .* , *to do what is ~ to . . .* , faire le nécessaire pour. || **necessity** [nəˈsɛsɪtɪ] *n.* **1.** nécessité *f*: *from ~* , par nécessité; *of ~* , nécessairement, inévitablement, forcément. **2.** [poverty] besoin *m*: *to be in great ~* , être dans le besoin.

neck [nɛk] *n.* cou *m* (de l'homme); goulot *m* (d'une bouteille); langue *f* (de terre): *to break one's ~* , se casser le cou; *to have a stiff ~* , avoir le torticolis; *~ and ~* , à égalité, en même temps. || **neckerchief** [-əʳˌtʃɪf] *n.* foulard *m.* || **necking** [ˈnɛkɪŋ] *n.* [Fam.] pelotage *m.* || **necklace** [-ləs] *n.* collier *m*, parure *f.* || **necktie** [-ˌtaj] *n.* cravate *f.* [= © tie].

née, nee [nej] *adj.* [= born]: *Mrs Smith, née Jones* = Mme Smith née Jones.

need [nijd] *n.* **1.** besoin *m*: *to be in* (*great*) *~ of*, avoir (grand) besoin de; *what ~ is there/to* [+ infin.], *of* [+ pres. part.], A quoi bon [+ infin.]; *there is no ~ to . . . , of . . .* , (Il est) inutile de . . . ; *to have ~ to*, avoir besoin de; *if ~ be*, s'il le faut; au besoin; *to meet the needs of*, satisfaire les besoins de. **2.** [poverty] besoin *m*, misère *f*; malheur *m*: *He is in* (*great*) *~* , Il est dans la (plus grande) misère; *A friend in ~ is a friend indeed*, C'est dans le malheur qu'on reconnaît ses amis. **3.** [lack] manque *m*: *for ~ of*, faute de. || **need** *v. tr.* avoir besoin de; [require] demander: *to ~ money*, avoir besoin d'argent; *What do you ~ ?*, Qu'est-ce qu'il vous faut?; De quoi avez-vous besoin?; *What do you ~ to do?*, Qu'avez-vous besoin de faire?; [Fam.] *What do you ~ me to do?*, Qu'avez-vous besoin que je fasse?; *All you ~ to do is to . . .* , Vous n'avez qu'à . . . ; *That needs thought*, Cela demande de la réflexion. || **need** *v. aux.* [employé comme auxiliaire de nécessité, ne prend pas d's à la 3e pers. sg. et est suivi d'un infinitif sans **to**; une deuxième construction, plus familière, est indiquée entre parenthèses, cf. NEED *v. tr.* Le passé simple 'need' est rare]. avoir besoin de; [absolute necessity] falloir, devoir: *He ~ not come* (*He does not/need to, have to/come*), Il n'a pas besoin de venir [× il ne faut pas qu'il . . . = *he must not . . .*]; *~ we go?* (= *Do we need to go?*), Avons-nous besoin d'y aller, Est-il nécessaire que nous y allions?

needle ['nijdḷ] *n.* aiguille *f* (à coudre, à tricoter, de phono, de seringue). || *v. tr.* [Fam.] agacer (qqun); pousser (qqun à).

needless ['nijdləs] *adj.* inutile: ~ *to say that*, inutile d'ajouter que . . . .

needlewoman ['nijdḷ|ˌwumən] *n.* couturière *f.* || **needlework** [-ˌwɚk] *n.* ouvrage *m* à l'aiguille; la couture.

†**needs** [nijdz] *adv.* nécessairement.

needy ['nijdɪ] *adj.* indigent, dans le besoin.

negate [nə'gejt] *v. tr.* nier.

negation [nə'gejʃən] *n.* négation *f.* ||**negative** ['nɛgətɪv] *n.* négative *f*: *He replied in the* ~ , Il répondit par la négative; (photo) négatif *m.* || *adj.* négatif.

neglect [nə'glɛkt] *n.* négligence *f*; oubli *m*; abandon *m.* || *v. tr.* négliger (son travail), manquer à (son devoir); négliger, oublier de [+ infin.]: *Don't* ~ *to* . . . , N'oubliez pas de . . . . || **neglectful** [-fḷ] *adj.* négligent, oublieux. || **negligence** ['nɛglɪʤ|əns] *n.* négligence *f*, oubli *m.* || **negligent** [-ənt] *adj.* négligent; oublieux. || **negligible** ['nɛglɪʤəbḷ] *adj.* négligeable.

negotiable [nə'gowʃəbl] *adj.* [Fin.] négociable; [road] praticable.

negotiate [nə'gowʃɪˌejt] *v. tr.* **1.** négocier, conclure, (un traité); négocier (des valeurs). **2.** [Fig.] tourner, franchir (un obstacle), prendre/un virage, un tournant (en auto); régler une affaire; venir à bout d'(une difficulté). || *v. intr. to* ~ *with s.o. for*, entreprendre des pourparlers de . . . avec qqun. || **negotiation** [nəˌgowʃɪ'ejʃən] *n.* négociation *f*; *negociations*, pourparlers *mpl.*

Negress ['nijgɹəs] *n.* négresse *f*, noire *f* cf. NEGRO. || **Negro** ['nijgɹow] **1.** *n.* nègre *m*, noir *m* [the tendency is to avoid *nègre* and use *noir* or *Africain*]. || **2.** *adj.* nègre; négroïde.

neigh [nej] *n.* hennissement *m.* || *v. intr.* hennir.

neighbour ['nejbɚ] *n.* voisin *m*, voisine *f*; [Bib.] prochain *m.* || **neighbourhood** [-ˌhud] *n.* **1.** [proximity] voisinage *m*, environs *mpl.*: [Fig.] *In the* ~ *of $100*, dans les cent dollars. **2.** [district] quartier *m*, voisinage *m*: *in our* ~ , dans notre quartier; *the* ~ *drug store*, la pharmacie du quartier. || **neighbouring** [-ɪŋ] *adj.* avoisinant, voisin. || **neighbourly** [-lɪ] *adv.* aimable: *He is quite* ~ , Il est (très) bon voisin; [Fam.] *That is downright* ~ *of you*, C'est très aimable de votre part.

neither [najðɚ, nijðɚ] *conj.* ni (. . . ni . . . ne); ne (. . . ni . . . ne); (ni) . . . non plus: ~ *you nor I* (*will go*), Ni vous ni moi (n'irons); *He can* ~ *read nor write*, Il ne sait ni lire ni écrire; *He* ~ *drinks nor smokes*, Il ne boit ni ne fume; ~ *do/will &c./I*, (ni) moi non plus; *Are you tired or sick?* (*I am*) ~ , Êtes-vous fatigué ou malade?—(Je ne suis) ni l'un ni l'autre. || *adj.* aucun des deux [+ ne before verb, if any]: ~ *answer is correct*, Aucune des (deux) réponses n'est juste; *He went to* ~ *country*, Il n'est allé /dans aucun des deux pays, ni dans un pays ni dans l'autre. || *pron.* ni l'un(e) ni l'autre; aucun(e) des deux; [+ ne before verb, if any]: ~ (*of them*) *came*, Ils ne sont venus ni l'un ni l'autre.

nephew ['nɛfjuw] *n.* neveu *m.*

nepotism ['nijpəˌtɪzm] *n.* népotisme *m.*

nerve [nɚv] *n.* **1.** nerf *m*: *A* ~ *case*, malade nerveux, névropathe *mf*; ~ *cell*, neurone *m*; *to get on s.o.'s nerves*, taper sur les nerfs à qqun. **2.** [leaf] nervure *f.* **3.** [Fig.] sang-froid *m*; [Fam. = impudence] toupet *m.* || **nervous** [-əs] *adj.* nerveux; timide, craintif; *the* ~ *system*, le système nerveux; ~ *breakdown*, dépression *f* nerveuse. || **nervousness** [-əsnəs] *n.* nervosité *f*, inquiétude *f.*

nervy ['nɚvɪ] *adj.* [Fig.] énervé, agacé; nerveux; [Fam.] culotté; cf. NERVE.

nest [nɛst] *n.* nid *m*; [Fig.] repaire (de voleurs): ~ *egg*, une poire pour la soif; ~ *of tables*, table *f* gigogne. || *v. intr.* nicher (dans un arbre, &c.); faire son nid. || **nestle** ['nɛsḷ] *v. tr. & intr.* [Fig.] (se) nicher; (s')installer (confortablement dans): *A village nestling in the valley*, Un village blotti dans la vallée.

net[1] *adj.* net: ~ *profit*, bénéfice *m* net. || *v. tr.* [-tt-] [Com.] rapporter net (par an) gagner, faire un profit net, &c.

net[2] [nɛt] *n.* filet *m* (de pêche, de tennis); résille *f* (pour les cheveux); réseau *m* (d'espionnage). || *v. tr.* [-tt-] prendre au filet.

Netherlands (the) ['nɛðɚləndz] *n.* les Pays-Bas *mpl*; la Hollande: *to, in* ~ , aux Pays-Bas, en Hollande.

netting ['nɛtɪŋ] *n.* grillage *m*, moustiquaire *f.*

nettle ['nɛtḷ] *n.* ortie *f.* || *v. tr.* [Fig.] irriter, piquer.

network ['nɛtˌwɚk] *n.* réseau *m* (de chemin de fer, &c.): [TV, Radio] *The Dominion* ~ , le réseau national; *radio* ~ , réseau radiophonique; chaîne *f* (de postes de radio).

neurology [ˌnjuwɚ|'ɑləʤɪ] *n.* neurologie *f.*

neuros|is [-'owsɪs] *pl.* **-es** [-'owsijz] *n.* névrose *f.* || **neurotic** [-'ɑtɪk] *adj.* névrosé.

neuter ['njuwtər] *n.* & *adj.* [Gram.] neutre (*m*). || **neutral** ['njuwtɹəl] *n.* & *adj.* [country] neutre *m*; [auto] point *m* mort (*in, to,* au). || **neutrality** [ˌnjuw'tɹælətɪ] *n.* neutralité *f.* || **neutralize** ['njuwtɹəlˌajz] *v. tr.* neutraliser.

Nev. [= NEVADA].

Nevada [nə'vædə] *n.* le Névada: *to, in/~* , dans le Névada.

never ['nɛvər] *adv.* jamais [+ ne before verb, if any]; [Fam. emphatic] ne . . . pas; [not again] ne . . . plus: *He has ~ gone there,* Il n'y est jamais allé; *I ~ did it!,* Je n'ai pas fait ça (moi)!; *~ do that (again)!,* Ne recommencez plus!; *~ again, ~ more,* jamais plus; *~ in my life,* jamais de la vie; *~ mind!,* n'importe!, tant pis!; *~ fear!,* soyez tranquille!; *Well I ~ !,* Ça par exemple!, Pas possible! || **nevertheless** [-ðəˌlɛs] *adv.* néanmoins, quand même.

new [njuw, nuw] *adj.* [unused] neuf; [latest or stressed] nouveau [usual. follows noun]; [additional, different; or unstressed] nouveau [before noun]: *brand ~* , flambant neuf; *to make sth as good as ~* , remettre qqch. à neuf; *I bought a ~ hat,* Je me suis acheté un chapeau neuf; *I want to read his ~ book,* Je veux lire son livre nouveau; *We are using a ~ book this year,* Nous nous servons d'un nouveau (autre) livre cette année; *He is ~ to/at/his work,* → Il n'a pas l'habitude de ce genre de travail; *What's ~ ?,* Quoi de nouveau?, [Fam.] de neuf?; *the New Year,* le nouvel an; cf. YEAR; *the ~ moon,* la nouvelle lune; *a ~ laid egg,* un œuf du jour. || **new-born** [-'bɔən] *adj.* nouveau-né *m.* || **New Brunswick** [ˌnjuw'bɹʌnzwɪk] *n.* Nouveau-Brunswick *m*: *to, in/ ~* , au N.-B. || **New Caledonia** [-ˌkælə'downɪəl] *n.* la Nouvelle-Calédonie *f*: *to, in/ ~* , en N.-C. || **New Canadian** [-kə'nejdɪən] *n.* © Néo-Canadien *m,* -ne *f.* || **New England** [-'Iŋglənd] la Nouvelle-Angleterre *f*: *to, in ~* , dans la N.-A.

Newfoundland ['njuwfəndˌlænd] *n.* Terre-Neuve *f*; [dog] un terre-neuve: *to, in ~* , à T.-N. || **Newfoundlander** [-ər] *n.* Terreneuvien *m,* -ne *f.* || **New Guinea** [ˌnjuw'gɪnɪ] *n.* la Nouvelle-Guinée *f.* || **New Hebrides** [ˌnjuw'hɛbɹədɪz] *n.* les Nouvelles-Hébrides *fpl.* || **newly** ['njuwlɪ] *adv.* nouvellement, récemment: *~ wed(s),* jeune(s) marié(s). || **New Mexico** [ˌnjuw'mɛksɪkow] *n.* le Nouveau-Mexique: *to, in/~* , au N.-M. || **New Orleans** [ˌnjuw'ɔərlɪəns] *n.* la Nouvelle-Orléans: *to, in/ ~* , à la N.-O.

news [njuwz, nuws] *n.* [Coll.] nouvelle *f,* nouvelles *fpl.*: *A/piece, bit/of ~* , une nouvelle; *~ bulletin,* bulletin *m* de nouvelles; *to break the ~* , annoncer, dire/une nouvelle (à qqun); *What's (the) news?,* → Quoi de neuf? Quelles nouvelles? || **news agency** [-ˌejdʒənsɪ] *n.* agence *f* de nouvelles; agence *f* de presse. || **news agent** [-ˌejdʒənt] *n.* marchand *m* de journauxl || **news boy** [-ˌboj] *n.* crieur *m* de journaux.

newscast [-ˌkæst] *n.* [TV] téléjournal *m*; [Rad.] les nouvelles *fpl,* les informations *fpl,* [Fr.] le journal parlé.

newsdealer [-ˌdijlər] *n.* vendeur *m* de journaux, cf. NEWS AGENT, dépositaire *m.* || **newsletter** [-ˌlɛtər] *n.* bulletin *m* (d'une Société); bulletin intérieur; circulaire *f.* || **newsman** [-ˌmæn] also **newspaperman** [-ˌpejpərˌmæn] *n.* journaliste *m.* || **newspaper** [-ˌpejpər] *n.* journal *m.* || **newsprint** [-ˌpɹɪnt] *n.* papier-journal *m.* || **newsreel** [-ˌɹijl] *n.* (film *m* d') actualités *fpl.* || **newsstand** [-ˌstænd] *n.* kiosque *m* à journaux. || **news vendor** [-ˌvɛndər] *n.* marchand *m* de journaux.

newsy [njuwzɪ] *adj.* [Fam.] (journal) à potins. || *n.* crieur (vendeur) de journaux; camelot *m.*

New Testament ['njuwˌtɛstəmənt] *n.* [Rel.] le Nouveau Testament *m*; l'Évangile *m* (≠ Ancien Testament). || **New World** ['njuwˌwərld] *n.* le Nouveau Monde, l'hémisphère occidental: *to, in/the ~* , dans le Nouveau Monde. || *adj. new-world,* du Nouveau Monde. || **New Year** [ˌnjuw'jijə] *n.* le nouvel an: *New Year's Day,* le jour de l'an, le Nouvel An; *New Year's Eve,* la Saint-Sylvestre; *Happy ~ !,* Bonne année! || **New York** ['njuw'jɔərk] *n.* l'État *m* de New-York (*to, in,* dans): *New York (City),* New-York (*to, in,* à). || **New Yorker** [-ər] *n.* (un) New-Yorkais.

New Zealand [ˌnjuw'zijlənd] *n.* la Nouvelle-Zélande: *to/in/ ~* , en N.-Z. || **New Zealander** *n.* (un) Néo-Zélandais.

next [nɛkst] *adj.* **1.** [place] le plus proche, voisin: *Where is the ~ town?,* Où est la ville la plus proche?; *the ~ house,* la maison/voisine, d'à côté; *the ~ house but/one, two,* la deuxième (troisième) maison d'ici; *the house ~ to the church,* la maison à côté de l'église; [Fig.] next to [+ neg.] presque, pour ainsi dire. **2.** [time] prochain [follows the noun in expressions referring to the future];

suivant [used in expressions referring to the past]: *I'll see you ~/Thursday, month, week, year/*, Je vous (re)verrai jeudi/le mois/prochain; . . . la semaine, l'année/prochaine; *He came back the ~ /day, month, week, year*, Il est revenu/le lendemain, le mois suivant/la semaine, l'année suivante; *the ~ time*, cf. §3; *the next few days*, [Fut.] les jours qui viennent; [Past] les jours qui suivirent. **3.** [order] suivant; prochain [before noun]; *Next!*, Au suivant!; *Take the ~ train*, Prenez le train suivant; *in the ~ issue*, au prochain numéro; *It's the ~ (street) on the right*, C'est la prochaine (rue) à droite; *the ~ time*, la prochaine fois; *What ~ !*, [in a store], Et ensuite?; [surprise] Ça, par exemple!; *The ~ thing is/was/to* → Maintenant, il faut/Ensuite, il fallait; ‖ **next** *adv.* ensuite, puis; après: *Next, we must . . .*, Ensuite, Maintenant/il faut . . . ; *and ~, I . . .*, et puis, et ensuite, et après/je . . . ; *What did you do ~ ?* Qu'avez-vous fait/ensuite, après (cela)?; *Who comes ~ ?*, A qui le tour?; *What comes ~ ?*, Qu'est-ce qui/suit, vient après? ‖ *prép.* à côté de. ‖ **next door** [ˌnɛkst'dɔɚ] *adv.* à côté: *He lives ~ (to the school)*, Il habite à côté (de l'école); [Fig.] *That is ~ to (the same thing)*, C'est/presque, à peu près/la même chose (que). ‖ **next-door** *adj.* d'à côté. ‖ **next of kin** ['nɛkst əv ˌkɪn] *n.* la famille, les plus proches parents *mpl.*

Nfld. [= NEWFOUNDLAND].

nib [nɪb] *n.* pointe *f*, bec *m* (d'une plume).

nibble ['nɪbḷ] *n.* grignotement *m*: [fishing] *I've got a ~ !*, J'ai une touche! ‖ *v. tr.* mordiller, grignoter; [Fig.] manger du bout des lèvres.

nice [najs] *adj.* **1.** [terme général d'approbation, dont la traduction varie suivant le contexte] charmant, agréable, bon, gentil. cf. FINE, GOOD: *A ~ face*, une physionomie agréable; *How ~ !* (que c'est) charmant! **2.** †*a ~ distinction*, une distinction subtile. ‖ **nicely** [-lɪ] *adv.* bien, agréablement, gentiment. ‖ **nice (-looking)** [-ˌlukɪŋ] *adj.* gentil, charmant; © fin: *Isn't she ~ ?*, Comme elle a l'air fin! cf. GOOD-LOOKING.

nicety ['najsətɪ] *n.* précision *f*, exactitude *f*; subtilité *f.* ‖ *pl.* minuties *fpl*; [Pej.] détails *mpl* insignifiants.

niche [nɪtʃ] *n.* [Arch.] niche *f.*

nick [nɪk] *n.* entaille *f*, encoche *f*; [on blade] brèche *f*: [Fig.] *in the ~ of time*, à point nommé, [Fam.] à pic. ‖ *v. tr.* entailler, encocher; [blade] ébrécher; [Fam.] pincer (un voleur).

nickel ['nɪkḷ] *n.* **1.** [metal] nickel *m*: *to ~ -plate*, nickeler. **2.** [= a 5¢ piece] © un cinq-sous, [Fr.] une pièce de cinq cents.

nickname ['nɪkˌnejm] *n.* sobriquet *m*; surnom *m.* ‖ *v. tr.* surnommer.

niece [nijs] *n.* nièce *f.*

niggard ['nɪgɚd] *n. & adj.* grippe-sous *m*, avare *m.* ‖ **niggardly** [-lɪ] *adj.* avare; [mean] mesquin. ‖ *adv.* avec avarice *f*, chichement.

nigger ['nɪgɚ] [à éviter] *n.* nègre *m*; moricaud *m*: *There's a ~ in the woodpile*, Il y a anguille *f* sous roche. cf. NEGRO

night [najt] *n.* **1.** nuit *f*; [evening, before retiring] soir *m*: *last ~* , hier (au) soir; [after retiring] la nuit dernière, cette nuit; *tonight*, ce soir; cette nuit; *tomorrow ~*, demain soir; *the ~ before*, la veille (au soir): *good ~ !*, bonsoir!, [upon retiring] bonne nuit!; [exclam.] mon Dieu!; *at ~* , la nuit; *ten o'clock at ~* , dix heures du soir; *by ~* , de nuit, pendant la nuit; *during, in/the ~* , (pendant) la nuit; *during the ~ of the 15th*, dans la nuit du 15 (au 16); *He works nights*, Il travaille de nuit; *I couldn't sleep last ~*, → Je n'ai pas fermé l'œil de la nuit; J'ai passé/une nuit blanche, © la nuit sur la corde à linge; *It is ~* , Il fait nuit. **2.** [occasion] soirée *f*: *Parents' Night*, Soirée des familles. **3.** *adj.* du soir; de nuit; nocturne: *~ school*, cours *mpl* du soir; *~ train*, le train de nuit; *~ bird*, oiseau *m* nocturne, de nuit. ‖ **night club** [-ˌklʌb] *n.* boîte *f* de nuit. ‖ **nightfall** [-ˌfɔl] *n.* (à la) tombée de la nuit, © (à la) brunante. ‖ **night gown,** †**night shirt** [-ˌgawn], [-ˌʃɚt] *n.* chemise *f* de nuit, © jaquette *f.*

nighthawk [-ˌhɔk] *n.* engoulevent *m*, © mange-maringouins *m*; [Fig.] oiseau *m* de nuit. ‖ **nightingale** [-ŋˌgejl] *n.* rossignol *m.*

night letter [-ˌlɛtɚ] *n.* © lettre *f* de nuit. ‖ **nightlong** [-ˌlɑŋ] *adv.* qui dure toute la nuit, nocturne. ‖ **nightly** [-lɪ] *adj.* nocturne, de nuit. ‖ *adv.* la nuit, de nuit; [shows] tous les soirs, en soirée. ‖ **nightmare** [-ˌmɛɚ] *n.* cauchemar *m.* ‖ **night stick** [-ˌstɪk] *n.* bâton *m* (d'agent), matraque *f.* ‖ **(at) night time** [-ˌtajm] *n.* la nuit [s'opposant à JOURNÉE]. ‖ **night watchman** [-'wɑtʃmən] *n.* veilleur *m* de nuit.

nihilism ['nɪhɪlˌɪ|zm] *n.* nihilisme *m.* ‖ **nihilist** [-st] *n.* nihiliste *m.*

nimble ['nɪmbḷ] *adj.* agile, leste; [mind] vif, prompt.

nincompoop [ˈnɪŋkəmˌpuwp] *n.* [Fam.] crétin *m.*

nine [najn] *adj. & n.* neuf (*m*). || **nineteen** [-ˈtijn], [najnˈtijn] *adj. & n.* dix-neuf (*m*). || **nineteenth** [-ˈtijnθ] *adj. & n.* dix-neuvième (*m*): le dix-neuf (mai, &c.). || **ninetieth** [-tɪəθ] *adj. & n.* quatre-vingt-dixième (*m*). || **ninety** [ˈnajntɪ] *adj. & n.* quatre-vingt-dix (*m*): ~*-one*, quatre-vingt-onze, &c. || **ninth** [najnθ] *adj.* neuvième. || *n.* le neuvième; le neuf (+ mai, juin, &c.).

nip [nɪp] *v. tr.* [-pp-] pincer; couper [en parlant de ciseaux, tenailles, &c.]; [cold wind] mordre, brûler (les oreilles, &c.); [by dog] mordiller. || *n.* pincement *m*, morsure *f.*

nipple [ˈnɪpḷ] *n.* [breast] mamelon *m*, bout *m* de sein; [bottle] tétine *f*, © suce *f*; [Tech.] raccord *m.*

nippy [ˈnɪpɪ] *adj.* leste, rapide; [cold] vif, piquant.

Nisei [ˈnijˈsej] *pl. unchanged* [A native-born Can. or US citizen of Japanese descent] Nisei *m.*

nitre [ˈnajtɚ] *n.* [Chem.] nitre *m*, salpêtre *m.*

nitrogen [ˈnajtɹəʤən] *n.* azote *m.*

nitwit [ˈnɪtˌwɪt] *n.* [Fam.] idiot *m*, crétin *m.*

no, pl. **noes** [now] *n.* non *m.* || *adv.* **1.** non! [Polite refusal] non, merci; [☞ Simplify such answers as *No, I haven't*: *No, I don't &c.* and add "Monsieur," &c. when talking to an older person or a stranger] → non; mais non; pas du tout (Monsieur): *When I asked him, he said no,* [question] Quand je lui ai demandé, il a dit non; [invitation] Quand je l'ai invité, il a dit que non; [Fam.] *No, sir!* Ça non, alors! **2.** [not any] ne . . . pas: *It is ~ smaller than I thought,* Ce n'est pas plus petit que je (le) croyais; cf. LESS, LONGER, MORE, SOONER. || *adj.* **1.** [not any] (ne) . . . pas (de); (ne) . . . aucun(e): [☞ the neg. depends on the affirmative construction in French.] *I have no/luck, friends,* Je n'ai pas /de chance, d'amis; *I have no time* (*to*), Je n'ai pas le temps (de); *I have no need to . . .*, Je n'ai pas besoin de . . . ; *I had no opportunity to . . .*, Je n'ai pas eu l'occasion de . . . ; *No Smoking!*, Défense de fumer! **2.** [not a] ne . . . pas (un): *He is ~ musician,* Il n'est pas musicien. **3.** [not one] aucun(e) . . . ne: *No Canadian would* (*ever*) *do that,* Aucun Canadien ne ferait cela. **4.** [not] *Train or ~ train, I must get there by tomorrow,* Qu'il y ait un train ou non (peu m'importe), il faut que j'y arrive demain. **5.** [not any way of] *There was ~ stopping him,* Il n'y avait pas moyen de l'arrêter.

No(s). [= NUMBER(S)].

Nobel prize [ˈnowbɛlˌpɹajz] *n.* le prix Nobel *m.*

nobility [ˌnowˈbɪlətɪ] *n.* noblesse *f.* || **noble** [ˈnowbḷ] *adj.* noble [= membre de la noblesse]. aristocrate: noble, généreux. || **noble**; **noble|man** (**-men**) [-mən], **noble|woman** (**-women**) [ˈwumən, ˈwɪmən] noble *m/f.* || **nobly** [-ɪ] *adv.* noblement, avec noblesse.

nobody [ˈnowˌbʌdɪ] *pron. indéf.* (ne) . . . personne [with masc. agreement]: nul . . . ne [1st word in elevated or official style]: ~ *came*, Personne, Nul/n'est venu; *Who knows? ~!*, Qui le sait? Personne!; *I know ~ (who is) richer than he (is),* Je ne connais personne de plus riche que lui/ . . . personne qui soit plus riche que lui; ~ [*stressed*] *is . . .* → Il n'y a personne qui soit . . . || *n.* nullité *f*, zéro *m*: *He is a mere ~*, C'est un zéro, une nullité, → Il ne compte pas.

nocturnal [ˌnɑkˈtɚnəl] *adj.* nocturne.

nod [nɑd] *v. tr. & intr.* [-dd-] *To ~ (one's head/one's approval),* faire oui de la tête, opiner (de la tête). || *n.* signe *m* de tête: *to give a ~*, faire un signe de tête.

noise [nojz] *n.* bruit *m*; [burst] éclat *m*; [ringing] tintement *m*; [buzzing] bourdonnement *m*; [uproar] vacarme *m*; [din] tapage *m*: [Fam.] *a big ~*, une grosse légume; *to make a ~*, faire un bruit, &c. || **noise about** [-əˌbawt] *v. intr.* répandre, publier (une nouvelle): *It is being noised about that . . .*, Le bruit court que . . . || **noiseless** [-ləs] *adj.* sans bruit, silencieux. || **noiselessly** [-ləslɪ] *adv.* silencieusement, sans bruit. || **noisily** [-ɪlɪ] *adv.* avec bruit, bruyamment. || **noisy** [-ɪ] *adj.* bruyant.

nominal [ˈnɑmɪnəl] *adj.* nominal, de nom: [Fig.] *For a ~ fee,* pour une somme minime; → pour presque rien. || **nominate** [ˈnɑmɪnˌejt] *v. tr.* présenter un candidat, mettre qqun en candidature; nommer (un candidat à un poste). || **nomination** [ˌnɑmɪnˈejʃən] *n.* choix *m*, proposition *f*, présentation *f* (d'un candidat); nomination *f* (de qqun à un poste). || **nominee** [ˌnɑmɪˈnij] *n.* candidat *m* (agréé, officiel), candidate *f* (agréée, officielle).

non- [nɑn-] [Préfixe négatif, écrit avec ou sans trait d'union. Se rend souvent par un tour négatif avec **ne** . . . **pas**]: *non-smoker*, qui ne fume pas, qui n'est pas fumeur; *a motion of non-confidence*, une motion de censure. [Some other compounds in *non-*]: *non-combatant*, non-combattant *m*; *non conformist*, non-conformiste *m*; *nonfiction* [This concept does not exist in French, use → histoire *f*, biographie *f*, critique *f*, &c.]; *non-sectarian* (school), neutre, laïque.

nonchalance ['nɑntʃələn|s] *n.* indifférence *f*; nonchaloir *m.* ‖ **nonchalant** [-t] *adj.* indifférent; nonchalant.

nonconformist [ˌnɑnkən'fɔɚmɪst] *adj. & n.* [Rel.] non-conformiste.

nondescript ['nɑndəˌskɹɪpt] *adj.* indéfinissable, indescriptible; [Pej.] quelconque.

none [nʌn] *pron. indéf.* **1.** [not any] (ne) . . . pas de, n'en . . . pas; rien: *We have ~ of the paper left*, Il ne nous reste/pas, plus/ de papier; *How much is left? ~ !*, Combien en reste-t-il?—Rien!; *~ but*, cf. ONLY. **2.** [not one] (ne) . . . aucun(e): *~ of these books is/are/really satisfactory*, Aucun de ces livres n'est vraiment satisfaisant; *~ (of them) will do*, Aucun ne fera mon affaire; *~ (at all)?*, Aucun? ‖ *adv.* ne . . . pas; [with comparatives] n'en . . . pas: *He is ~ too intelligent*, Il n'est pas trop intelligent; *He was ~ the happier (for it)*, Il n'en était pas plus heureux (pour ça).

nonentity [ˌnɑn'ɛntɪtɪ] *n.* néant *m*; [Pej.] nullité *f*.

nonplus ['nɑnplʌs] *v. tr.* **[-ss-]** déconcerter, dérouter.

nonsense ['nɑnsəns] *n.* sottise *f*, absurdité *f*: *No ~ !*, Pas d'histoires!; *~ !*, C'est absurde!; [Fam.] Des blagues! ‖ **nonsensical** ['nɑn'sɛnsɪkḷ] *adj.* absurde, qui n'a pas le sens commun, © qui n'a pas de bon sens.

non-stop ['nɑn'stɑp] *adj. & adv.* sans arrêt; [plane] sans escale, continu, ininterrompu.

noodle ['nuwdḷ] *n.* nouille *f*: *~ soup*, soupe *f* aux nouilles; [fool] nigaud *m*, nouille *f*; [Arg., = head] tête *f*; [Sl.] citron *m*.

nook [nʊk] *n.* coin *m*, recoin *m*.

noon [nuwn] *n.* midi *m*: *Twelve ~* , midi (juste); *at ~* , à midi, sur le coup de midi; *before ~* , avant midi, dans la matinée, © dans l'avant-midi. ‖ **noonday** [-ˌdej] *n. & adj.* midi *m*; de midi.

no one ['nowˌwʌn] cf. NOBODY.

noose [nuws] *n.* nœud coulant *m*, lacet *m.* ‖ *v. tr.* nouer (qqch.); prendre . . . au lacet.

nor ['nɔɚ, nɚ] *conj.* **1.** [précédé de NEITHER] (ne . . . ni . . .) ni; (ne . . .) ni . . . ne. **2.** [= and not, or other neg.] et . . . [+ neg.] ni; ni . . . non plus: *~ was that all*, Et ce n'était pas tout; *He has no friends ~ enemies*, Il n'a pas d'amis ni d'ennemis; †*I will not stay, ~ he either/ ~ will he (either)*, Je ne veux pas rester, ni lui non plus.

norm [nɔɚm] *n.* norme *f*.

normal ['nɔɚml] *adj.* normal; habituel: © *Normal School* [= Teachers College], École *f* normale. ‖ **normally** [-ɪ] *adv.* normalement; en principe.

Norman ['nɔɚmən] *adj. & n.* normand. ‖ **Normandy** [-dɪ] La Normandie: *to, in/~* , en N.

north [noɚθ] *n.* nord *m* (d'un pays); le Grand Nord: *on, to/the ~* , au nord; *in the ~* , dans le nord. ‖ *adj.* nord *invar.*; (pays, vent) du nord; (étoile) polaire: *the ~ / side, coast, &c.*, le côté/ la côte, &c./nord; *North Toronto*, Toronto-Nord; *the North Country*, le Grand Nord. [Br.] le nord de l'Angleterre. ‖ *adv.* au nord; vers le nord: *~ of Boston*, au nord de Boston; *He went (up) ~* , Il est parti dans le nord, © Il est allé dans le nord. ‖ **North Africa** [-'æfɹɪkə] *n.* l'Afrique *f* du Nord: *to, in ~* , en A. du N. ‖ **North-African** [-'æfɹɪkən] *adj. & n.* nord-africain. ‖ **North America** [-ə'mæɚɪkə] *n.* l'Amérique *f* du Nord: *to, in/~* , en/dans l'/A. du N. ‖ **North-American** [-ə'mæɚɪkən] *adj. & n.* nord-américain. ‖ **North Cape** [-'kejp] *n.* le Cap nord. ‖ **North Carolina** [-ˌkæɚə'lajnə] *n.* la Caroline du Nord. ‖ **North Dakota** [-də'kowtə] *n.* le Dakota-Nord.

north-east [ˌnɔɚθ'ijst] [for constructions, cf. NORTH] *n.* nord-est *m.* ‖ *adj.* nord-est *invar.*; du nord-est: *the ~ wind*, norêt *m.* ‖ *adv.* au, vers le, nord-est. ‖ **north-easter** [-ɚ] *n.* norêt *m.* ‖ **north-easterly** [-ɚlɪ] *adj.* (du) nord-est cf. NORTH: *in a ~ direction*, vers le nord-est. ‖ *adv.* vers le nord-est. ‖ **north-eastern** [-ɚn] *adj.* (du) nord-est cf. NORTH. ‖ **north-eastward** [-wɚd] *adj.* au, du, vers le, nord-est. ‖ *adv.* vers le nord-est. ‖ **northerly** ['nɔɚθɚ|-lɪ] *adj.* nord *invar.*; (pays) du nord, septentrional: *in a ~ direction*, vers le nord. ‖ *adv.* vers le nord. ‖ **northern** [-n] *adj.* (du) nord, septentrional; boréal: *Northern France*, → Le nord de la France; *~ hemisphere*, → l'hémisphère *m* nord; *Northern Ireland*, l'Irlande *f* du Nord; *~ lights*, aurore *f* boréale, © clairons *mpl.* ‖ **northerner** [-nɚ] *adj. & n.* nordique; habitant *m* du Nord; [US] Nordiste *m/f*. ‖ **northland** [-ˌlænd] *n.* le nord. ‖ **North Sea (the)** [-'sij] *n.* la mer du Nord. ‖ **northward** [-wɚd] *adj.* au, du, vers, le nord. ‖ **northward(s)** [-wɚdz] *adv.* vers le, au, nord.

north-west [ˌnɔɚθˈwɛst] [for constructions, cf. NORTH] *n.* nord-ouest *m*: [US] *the North West*, le Nord-ouest américain. || *adj.* nord-ouest *invar.*; du nord-ouest: *the ~ wind*, noroit *m.* || *adv.* au, vers le, nord-ouest. || **North-West Territories (the)** [-ˈtɛɚɪtɔɚɪz] *n.pl.* les Territoires *mpl* du Nord-Ouest. || **north-wester** [-ɚ] *n.* noroit *m.* || **north-westerly** [-ɚlɪ] *adj.* (du) nord-ouest cf. NORTH: *in a ~ direction*, vers le nord-ouest. || *adv.* vers le nord-ouest. || **north-western** [-ɚn] *adj.* (du) nord-ouest cf. NORTH. || **north-westward** [-wɚd] *adj.* au, du, vers le, nord-ouest. || **north-westwards** [-wɚdz] *adv.* vers le nord-ouest.

Norway [ˈnɔɚwej] *n.* la Norvège: *to/in/ ~*, en N. || **Norwegian** [ˌnɔɚˈwijʤən] *adj.* & *n.* Norvégien (*m*).

nose [nowz] *n.* nez *m* (d'une personne); museau *m* (d'un cheval, &c.); avant *m* (d'un avion): *to blow one's ~*, → se moucher; [Fig.] *to pay through the ~*, payer un prix exorbitant, se faire écorcher; *under one's ~*, → sous ses yeux; *to turn up, to look down/one's ~ at sth.*, dédaigner, faire fi de/qqch. || *v. tr. to ~ around*, fureter, fouiner; *to ~ in*, s'insinuer; *to ~ out*, dénicher, dépister. || **nosebleed** [ˈnowzˌblijd] *n.* saignement *m* de nez: *to have a ~*, → saigner du nez. || **nose dive** [-ˌdajv] [Aviat.] *n.* (vol) *m* piqué.

nostalgia [ˌnɑsˈtælʤ|ə] *n.* nostalgie *f.* || **nostalgic** [-ɪk] *adj.* nostalgique.

nostril [ˌnɑstɹil] *n.* [humans] narine *f*; [animals] naseau *m.*

nosy, nosey [-ɪ] [Fam.] *adj.* indiscret, fureteur: *~ Parker*, curieux comme une vieille fille.

not [nɑt] *adv.* **1.** [dans le style fam., souvent abrégé en *-n'*] (ne) . . . pas, †point ne pas; non (pas): *I/have ~, haven't/ given him any*, Je ne lui en ai pas donné; *I asked you ~ to go*, Je vous ai demandé de ne pas y aller; *I am sorry I did ~ / didn't/go*, Je regrette de ne pas y être allé; *Not having any money on me, I . . .*, N'ayant pas d'argent sur moi, je . . . ; *Who did it? Not I/Ididn't*, Qui l'a fait? Pas moi; *They were tired, but I was ~*, Ils étaient fatigués, moi/non, pas; *I hope/ think/ ~*, J'espère, Je crois/que non; *If ~, we . . .*, Sinon, nous . . . ; *Whether he wants to or ~*, Qu'il le veuille ou non; *It was a beaver, ~ a muskrat*, C'était un castor,/(et) non, [Fam.] pas/un rat musqué. **2.** [linked with EVER, or the compounds of ANY-] ne . . . jamais, rien, personne, &c. **3.** †[in set phrases with cesser, oser, pouvoir, savoir, &c.] ne: *I don't dare do it*, Je n'ose le faire; *I couldn't say*, Je ne saurais dire; &c. **4.** [sometimes rendered by an affirmative word or expression]: *Not guilty!* → Innocent!; *I didn't remember his name*, → Son nom m'échappait, &c. **5.** *Not that*, non (pas) que + Subjunc.: (*It's*) *~ that I don't want to . . .*, Ce n'est pas que/ non (pas) que/je ne veuille pas . . . ; *Not that* [= *as far as*] *I know*, pas que, pas autant que/je sache.

notable [ˈnowtəbl̩] *adj.* remarquable, notable: *a ~ event*, un fait/événement *m*/ remarquable, saillant. || *n.* notable *m.* || **notably** [-ɪ] *adv.* notablement; [namely] notamment.

notary [ˈnowtɚɪ] *n.* notaire *m*: *notary public*, notaire.

notation [ˌnowˈteiʃən] *n.* notation *f.*

notch [nɑʧ] *n.* encoche *f*, entaille *f* (sur un bâton); [Geog.] col *m*, © passe *f.* || *v. tr.* entailler, cocher.

note [nowt] *n.* **1.** note *f*; [short letter] mot *m*; billet *m*: *to make a ~ of*, prendre (bonne) note de; *to take notes at a lecture*, prendre des notes au cours. **2.** [Bank] billet *m*, coupure *f.* **3.** marque *f*, signe *m*: *~ of interrogation*, point *m* d'interrogation. **4.** remarque *f*: *of ~*, d'importance, digne de remarque. **5.** [Mus.] note *f*, ton *m*: *a ~ of anxiety* (*in s.o.'s voice*), un ton anxieux. || **note** *v. tr.* prendre note de, noter; remarquer, constater. || **notebook** [-ˌbʊk] *n.* carnet *m* (de notes); agenda *m*; [Sch.] cahier *m.* || **noted** [-əd] *adj.* célèbre, bien connu: *He was ~ for . . .*, Il était célèbre par . . . || **notepaper** [-ˌpejpɚ] *n.* papier *m* à lettres. || **noteworthy** [-ˌwɚðɪ] *adj.* remarquable, digne de remarque.

nothing [ˈnʌθɪŋ] *pron. indéf.* (ne) . . . rien: *I saw ~ (at all)*, Je n'ai rien vu (du tout); *I can do ~ about it*, Je n'y peux rien; *~ much*, (ne) . . . pas grand-chose; *to do ~ but*, ne faire que; *There's ~ for it but to . . .*, Nous n'avons qu'à . . . ; *There's ~ to thank me for*, Il n'y a pas de quoi (me remercier); *to say ~ of . . .*, sans parler de . . . ; *There's ~ to it*, C'est tout ce qu'il y a de plus simple, Cela n'a pas d'importance; *Think ~ of it*, Ne vous en faites pas; *Do ~ of the /kind, sort/!*, N'en faites rien!, Gardez-vous-en bien!; *Nothing doing!*, Rien à faire! || *n.* rien *m*: *a mere ~*, un petit rien, une bagatelle. || *adv.* en rien, nullement.

notice [ˈnowtɪs] *n.* **1.** attention *f*, connaissance *f*: *This came to my ~*, On a porté à ma connaissance . . . ; *to take ~ of*, faire attention à, remarquer; *to attract ~*, se faire remarquer. **2.** délai *m*, préavis *m*: *at short ~*, à bref délai: *after three months' ~*, moyennant un préavis de trois mois; *without ~*, sans avertissement (préalable). **3.** avis *m*, affiche *f*; avis *m*, congé *m*: *Until further ~*, Jusqu'à avis contraire; *to give ~*, donner congé (à qqun); prévenir (qqun que . . .). ‖ **notice** *v. tr.* remarquer, s'apercevoir (de qqch.). ‖ *v. intr.* remarquer, s'en apercevoir, (y) faire attention. ‖ **noticeable** [-əbḷ] *adj.* perceptible; remarquable. ‖ **notice board** [-ˌbɔɚd] *n.* tableau *m* d'affichage. ‖ **notify** ['nowtɪˌfaj] *v. tr.* faire savoir (qqch. à qqun), aviser (qqun de qqch.): *I was notified of . . .*, On m'a/fait savoir que . . . /avisé de . . . .

notion ['nowʃən] *n.* **1.** notion *f*, idée *f*, opinion *f*: *I haven't the slightest ~*, Je n'en ai pas la moindre idée. **2.** caprice *m*, fantaisie *f*; intention *f*: *to take/a, the/ ~ to*, s'aviser de, se mettre, en tête de. ‖ **notions** [-z] *n.pl.* [esp. US] mercerie *f*, passementerie *f*; [menus objets] bimbeloterie *f*.

notoriety [ˌnowtɚ'ajətɪ] *n.* **1.** [Pej.] scandale *m*, mauvaise réputation *f*. **2.** notoriété *f*. ‖ **notorious** [ˌnow'tɔɚɪəs] *adj.* **1.** [Pej.] de mauvaise réputation, d'une triste notoriété; (quartier) mal famé. **2.** [× a well-known fact] notoire.

notwithstanding [ˌnɑtwɪð'stændɪŋ] *prép.* en dépit de. ‖ *conj.* en dépit du fait que + indic.; quoique + subjunc. ‖ *adv.* cependant, malgré tout, quand même.

nought [nɔt] cf. NAUGHT.

noun [nawn] *n.* [Gram.] nom *m*, substantif *m*: *a ~ clause*, une proposition substantive.

nourish ['nɚɪʃ] *v. tr.* nourrir, alimenter (un enfant, &c.); [Fig.] entretenir (un espoir, &c.). ‖ **nourishing** [-ɪŋ] *adj.* nourrissant. ‖ **nourishment** [-mənt] *n.* nourriture *f*, alimentation *f*.

Nov. [= NOVEMBER].

Nova Scotia ['nowvə'skowʃə] *n.* la Nouvelle-Écosse: *to, in/ ~*, en Nouvelle-Écosse. ‖ **Nova Scotian** [-n] *adj. & n.* © néo-écossais (*m*).

novel ['nɑvḷ] *adj.* **1.** nouveau, récent: *of a ~ kind*, d'un nouveau genre. **2.** inusité, original: *a ~ sensation*, une sensation originale. ‖ *n.* roman *m*. ‖ **novelist** [-ɪst] *n.* romancier *m*. ‖ **novelty** [-tɪ] *n.* nouveauté *f*: [Com.] *novelties*, articles *mpl* de nouveautés, bimbeloterie *f*.

November [ˌnow'vɛmbɚ] *n.* novembre *m*. cf. APRIL.

novice ['nɑvɪs] *n.* novice *m*; [Rel.] novice *m/f*.

now [naw] *adv.* **1.** maintenant, en ce moment; à présent, actuellement, à l'heure actuelle; [by this time] déjà; [at once] tout de suite; [in such circumstances] dans ces conditions: (*It's*) *~* (*or never*)! C'est le moment (ou jamais)!; [no longer] *He is not sad ~*, Il n'est plus triste; *Not ~! Later*, Pas maintenant! Plus tard; *He will have finished by ~*, Il aura déjà fini; *Before, Up to, Till/ ~*, Jusqu'ici; *two days from ~*, d'ici deux jours; *between ~ and then*, d'ici là; *I saw him* (*every*) *~ and/then, again*, Je l'ai revu de temps/en temps, à autre/; *right ~*, tout de suite; *Do it ~!*, Faites ça tout de suite! → Ne remettez pas à demain; *I saw him just ~*, Je l'ai vu il y a un instant, [a while ago] tout à l'heure, © tantôt; *~ here, ~ there*, tantôt ici, tantôt là; *as of ~/from ~ on*, dès maintenant, à partir de maintenant. **2.** [introd. or explan.] alors; or: *~, as I was saying . . .*, Alors, comme je disais . . . ; *~, if such be the case, then . . .*, Or, s'il en est ainsi, . . . donc . . . ; *~ it so happened that . . .*, Or, il se trouva que . . . . **3.** [Exclam.] *Well ~!*, Eh bien (alors)!; *Come,* (*come,*) *~!*, Allons donc!; *Now, now!* Voyons, voyons!; *~ then, as you were saying*, Alors, (comme) vous disiez . . . ; *~ then,* (*do*) *be careful*, Faites donc attention (, voyons). ‖ *conj.* maintenant que; depuis que; puisque: *Now* (*that*) *I am here, I . . .*, Maintenant, Puisque/je suis là, je . . . ; *I feel better ~* (*that*) *it's all over*, Je me sens mieux, / maintenant que, depuis que/c'est fini. ‖ **nowadays** [-əˌdejz] *adv.* aujourd'hui, de nos jours, à l'heure actuelle.

nowhere ['nowˌwɛɚ] *adv.* (ne) . . . nulle part: *I had seen it ~*, Je ne l'avais vu nulle part; *He came out of ~*, Il est sorti d'on ne sait où; [Fig.] *I am getting ~*, Je n'arrive à rien; [Loc.] *~ near*, pas à beaucoup près. ‖ *n.* © voyage *m* surprise.

nowise ['noˌwajz] *adv.* [= in no way] nullement, en aucune façon.

noxious ['nɑkʃəs] *adj.* nocif, malsain: *~ fumes*, émanations *fpl* nocives.

nozzle ['nɑzḷ] *n.* bec *m*; [hose] lance *f*; [Med.] canule *f*.

N.S. [= NOVA SCOTIA].

-n't [nt] [= NOT]. [☞ Les formes en *-n't* sont généralement employées dans la langue parlée pour éviter la mise en relief qui résulterait de l'accentuation de *not*; à éviter dans la prose soutenue].

nt. wt. [= NET WEIGHT] poids *m* net.

nub [nʌb] *n.* petit morceau *m*: [Fig.] *the ~ of the matter,* le/nœud, fond/du problème.

nuclear ['nuwklɪ|ɚ] *adj.* nucléaire: *~ physics,* physique *f* nucléaire. || **nucleus** [-əs] *pl.* **nuclei** [-ˌaj] *n.* [Phys., Biol.] noyau *m*, nucléus *m.*

nude [njuwd] *adj.* nu [☞ usual.: tout nu] *n.* nu *m*, nue *f*: *in the ~*, tout(e) nu(e).

nudge [nʌʤ] *n.* coup *m* de coude. || *v. tr.* pousser (qqun) du coude, donner un coup de coude (à qqun).

nudism ['nuwdɪ|zm] *n.* nudisme *m.* || **nudist** [-st] *n.* nudiste *m/f.*

nugget ['nʌgət] *n.* pépite *f* (d'or).

nuisance ['njuwsəns] *n.* [no single equivalent in Fr.] **1.** ennui *m*, désagrément *m*; [Jur.] atteinte *f* portée aux droits du public; [Fig.] plaie *f*, fléau *m*: *What a ~ !*, → Comme c'est ennuyeux; *He's a ~*, → Il gêne tout le monde, Il est assommant, [Sl.] C'est un casse-pieds. **2.** © *~ ground,* dépotoir *m* (d'ordures); cf. GARBAGE.

null [nʌl] *adj.* **1.** [not binding] nul: *~ and void,* nul et non avenu. **2.** inutile, sans valeur. || **nullify** [-ɪˌfaj] *v. tr.* annuler.

numb [nʌm] *adj.* engourdi. *~ with cold,* engourdi de froid. || *v. tr.* engourdir.

number ['nʌmbɚ] *n.* **1.** nombre *m*; quantité *f*: *even, odd / numbers,* nombres / pairs, impairs; *ten in ~*, au nombre de dix; [indef.] *a ~ of,* plusieurs, une foule de (gens); *a/great, large/ ~ of . . .*, un grand nombre de, → de nombreu|x, -ses . . . , *a/good, fair/ ~ of,* bon nombre de. **2.** [numeral] chiffre *m*; numéro *m* (des maisons, de téléphone, &c.); [serial] matricule *m*: *Wrong ~ !* → Vous vous trompez de numéro. **3.** numéro *m*, livraison *f* (d'une revue); [performance] numéro *m.* **4.** [Gram.] nombre *m.* || *v. tr.* compter, se monter à; [give a number] numéroter: *The crew numbered eight men,* L'équipage/se montait à, comptait/huit hommes; *Number!* Numérotez-vous! || **numberless** [-ləs] *adj.* innombrable.

numbskull ['nʌmˌskʌl] [Fam.] *n.* idiot *m*, crétin *m.*

numeral ['nuwmɚəl] *n.* chiffre *m*: *Arabic/ Roman/ ~*, chiffre/arabe, romain. || *adj.* numéral. || **numerical** [ˌnuw'mɛɚɪkḷ] *adj.* numérique. || **numerous** ['nuwmɚəs] *adj.* nombreux.

nun [nʌn] *n.* [R.C.] religieuse *f*, nonne *f*, [Fam.] bonne sœur *f*, © sœur *f.*

nuncio ['nʌnsɪˌow] *n.* [R.C.] nonce *m.*

nuptial ['nʌpʧəl] *adj.* [wedding] nuptial; [marriage] conjugal: *~ blessing,* bénédiction *f* nuptiale. || **nuptials** [-z] *n.pl.* noce(s) *f* (*pl*). cf. MARRIAGE, WEDDING.

nurse [nɚs] *n.* **1.** nourrice *f*, bonne *f* d'enfants. **2.** infirmière *f*, garde-malade *f*, © *abus.* garde *f*: *male ~*, infirmier *m.* || *v. tr.* nourrir, élever (un enfant); soigner, garder (un malade); [Fig.] nourrir (un sentiment): *to ~ a grudge,* garder rancune. || **nursery** [-ɚɪ] *n.* chambre *f* des enfants; [hospital] pouponnière *f*; [Hort.] pépinière *f.*

nursing ['nɚsɪŋ] *n.* allaitement *m* (d'un enfant), soins *mpl*; cours *m* d'infirmière, © nursing *m*; [Fig.] entretien *m.*

nurture ['nɚʧɚ] *v. tr.* élever (un enfant). †nourrir (un enfant, un malade). || *n*; éducation *f*; †nourriture *f.*

nut [nʌt] *n.* noix *f*, noisette *f*; [Tech.] écrou *m.* || **nut-cracker** [-ˌkɹækɚ] *n.* casse-noisette *m. inv.* || **nuts** *n.* [as a class] noix *fpl*; [Fr.] mendiants *mpl.* || [Arg.] *adj.* cinglé, détraqué: *to be ~*, être cinglé; *to be ~ about* (*sth.*), être entiché (de qqch.); [renforcement de la négation] *He can't sing for ~*, Il est incapable de chanter. || *Interj.* zut! || **nutshell** [-ˌʃɛl] *n.* coquille *f* de noix: *in a ~*, en un mot.

nutriment ['nuwtɹɪmənt] *n.* éléments *mpl* nutritifs.

nutrition [ˌnjuw'tɹɪʃ|ən] *n.* nourriture *f*; [Tech.] nutrition *f.* || **nutritious** [-əs] *adj.* nourrissant. || **nutritive** ['njuwtɹɪtəv] *adj.* nutritif.

nutty ['nʌtɪ] *adj.* (à goût) de noisette; [Fig.] savoureux; [Fam.] cinglé, toqué.

NW [= NORTH-WEST].

N.W.T. [= NORTH-WEST TERRITORIES].

N.Y. ['ɛn'waj] [= NEW YORK STATE].

N.Y.C. [ˌɛnˌwaj'sij] [= NEW YORK CITY].

nylon ['najˌlɑn] *n.* nylon *m*: nylons, *n.pl.* bas *mpl* nylon.

nymph [nɪmf] *n.* nymphe *f.*

N.Z. ['ɛn'zɛd] [= NEW ZEALAND].

O, o [ow] *pl.* **O's, o's** [-z] *n.* [letter] O, o *m.*
o' [ə] [= of] [dans des locutions figées: *five o'clock*, cinq heures].
oaf [owf] *n.* lourdaud *m*, nigaud *m.* || **oafish** [-ɪʃ] *adj.* stupide.
oak [owk] *n.* chêne *m.* || *adj.* /de, en/ chêne. || **oaken** [-ən] *adj.* /de, en/chêne.
oar [ɔɚ] *n.* rame *f*, [Tech.] aviron *m*: [Fig.] *to put o.'s ~ in*, se mêler de (ce qui ne vous regarde pas). || *v. intr.* ramer. || **oarsman** [-zmən] *n.* rameur *m.*
oasis [ow'ej|sɪs] *pl.* **oases** [-sijz] *n.* oasis *f.*
oath [owθ] *pl.* **oaths** [owðz] *n.* serment *m*; [curse] juron *m*: *to take the ~*, prêter serment; *~ of office*, serment d'office; *to utter an ~*, proférer un juron.
oats [owts] *n.pl.* avoine *f*: *oatmeal*, farine *f* d'avoine; *to feel o.'s ~*, se sentir plein d'ardeur; *to sow o.'s wild ~*, avoir une jeunesse aventureuse.
obdurate ['ɑbdjɚət] *adj.* obstiné, entêté; invétéré.
O.B.E. [= Order of the British Empire]. Ordre *m* de l'Empire Britannique.
obedience [ow'bijdɪən|s] *n.* obéissance *f*, soumission *f.* || **obedient** [-t] *adj.* obéissant; [submissive] soumis.
obesity [ow'bijsɪtɪ] *n.* obésité *f.*
obey [ow'bej] *v. tr. & intr.* obéir: *to ~/s.o., an order*, obéir/à qqun, à un ordre.
obituary [ˌow'bɪtjuwɚɪ] *adj.* nécrologique: *~ column*, nécrologie *f.*
object[1] ['ɑbdʒəkt] *n.* **1.** objet *m*, chose *f*: *~ lesson*, leçon *f* de choses; [Fig.] exemple *m.* **2.** but *m*, objet *m*: *The ~ of . . . is to . . .* → . . . a pour objet de . . . ; *with the ~ of . . .*, dans le but de . . . ; [Gram.] régime *m*, complément *m.*
object[2] [əb'dʒɛkt] *v. intr.*: *to ~ (to sth.)*, s'opposer (à qqch.), désapprouver (qqch.), ne pas aimer (qqch.): *I ~ !*, Je proteste! || *v. tr.* objecter, rétorquer (que). || **objection** [-ʃən] *n.* objection *f*; opposition *f*: *to raise an ~*, soulever une objection; *I have/no, a strong/ ~ to*, /Je ne vois aucun inconvénient, Je m'oppose catégoriquement/à ce que [+ subjunc.]. || **objectionable** [-ʃənəbl̩] *adj.* (conduite) répréhensible; désagréable, répugnant.
objective [-tɪv] *adj.* objectif: [Gram.] *~ case*, cas *m* régime. || *n.* objectif *m*, but *m.* || **objectivity** [ˌɑbdʒɛk'tɪvɪtɪ] *n.* objectivité *f.* || **objector** [əb'dʒɛktɚ] *n.* objecteur *m.*
obligate ['ɑblɪˌgejt] *v. tr.* imposer à (qqun) l'obligation (de faire qqch.); *to be obligated*, avoir l'obligation (de faire qqch.). || **obligation** [ˌɑblɪ'gejʃən] *n.* obligation *f*; [Com.] engagement *m*: *to/be, put s.o./under an ~ to . . .*, /être, mettre qqun/dans l'obligation de . . . ; *to meet o.'s obligations*, faire honneur à ses engagements. || **obligatory** [ə'blɪgəˌtɔɚɪ] *adj.* obligatoire.
oblige [ə'blajdʒ] *v. tr.* obliger, forcer (qqun à faire qqch.); rendre service, faire plaisir (à qqun): *to be obliged to do sth.*, être/ obligé, forcé/de faire qqch.; *I'd like to ~*, J'aimerais faire ça pour vous; *I am much obliged to you (for + -ing)*, je vous suis (infiniment) reconnaissant (d'avoir + p.p.). || **obliging** [-ɪŋ] *adj.* obligeant.
oblique [ow'blijk] *adj.* oblique, de biais.
obliterate [ə'blɪtɚejt] *v. tr.* effacer, oblitérer, rayer. || **obliteration** [əˌblɪtɚ'ejʃən] *n.* oblitération *f.*
oblivion [ə'blɪvɪ|ən] *n.* oubli *m.* || **oblivious** [-əs] *adj.* oublieux (*of*, de).
oblong [ˌɑb'lɔŋ] *adj.* oblong *m*, -ue *f.*
obnoxious [əb'nɑkʃəs] *adj.* odieux; [offensive] désagréable.
oboe ['owbow] *n.* hautbois *m.*
obs. [= OBSOLETE].
obscene [əb'sijn] *adj.* obscène. || **obscenity** [əb'sɛnɪtɪ] *n.* obscénité *f*, grossièreté *f.*
obscure [əb'skjuwɚ] *adj.* obscur; [dim] sombre; [hidden] caché: *to become ~*, s'obscurcir. || *v. tr.* obscurcir. || **obscurity** [-ɪtɪ] *n.* obscurité *f.*
obsequious [əb'sijkwɪəs] *adj.* obséquieux.
observable [əb'zɚv|əbl̩] *adj.* observable. || **observance** [-əns] *n.* observance *f* (d'une fête religieuse, &c.); pratique *f* (religieuse). || **observant** [-ənt] *adj.* [quick to notice] observateur; [of rules] respectueux; [watchful] attentif. || **observation** [ˌɑbzɚ'vejʃən] *n.* observation *f*: *to be (placed) under ~*, être (mis) en observation; *to escape ~*, → éviter de se faire remarquer; *~ car*, wagon *m* d'observation. || **observatory** [əb'zɚv|ətɔɚɪ] *n.* observatoire *m.* || **observe** [ɑb'zɚv] *v. tr.* **1.** observer; apercevoir, noter (qqch.); [celebrate] célébrer (une fête), observer (le carême, &c.), suivre (une règle). **2.** faire remarquer, faire observer (que); dire: . . . , *he observed*, . . . , dit-il. || **observer** [-ɚ] *n.* observateur *m.*
obsess [əb'sɛs] *v. tr.* obséder (*with*, par): *to be obsessed by sth.*, → vivre dans la hantise de qqch. || **obsession** [əb'sɛʃən] *n.* obsession *f.* || **obsessive** [-ɪv] *adj.* obsessif.
obsolescent [ˌɑbsə'lɛsənt] *adj.* vieillissant, (déjà) vieilli, (modèle) dépassé. || **obsolete**

['absə,lijt] *adj.* vieilli; (mot) désuet, (modèle) suranné: *to have become* ~, avoir vieilli.

obstacle ['abstkl̩] *n.* obstacle *m*; [Fig.] obstacle, empêchement *m.*

obstetrical [,ab'stɛtɹɪk|l̩] *adj.* [Med.] obstétrique. ‖ **obstetrics** [-s] *n.* obstétrique *f.*

obstinacy ['abstɪnə|sɪ] *n.* obstination *f*, entêtement *m*; [persistence] opiniâtreté *f*, ténacité *f.* ‖ **obstinate** [-t] *adj.* [stubborn] obstiné, entêté; [persistent] opiniâtre, tenace: *to be* ~, s'obstiner, s'entêter à.

obstreperous [,ab'stɹɛpərəs] *adj.* turbulent, bruyant; [quarrelsome] rouspéteur.

obstruct [əb'stɹʌk|t] *v. tr.* bloquer, encombrer/ (le chemin); gêner (la vue, la circulation, qqun, &c.); [Pol.] s'opposer systématiquement à, entraver (les débats), faire de l'obstruction. ‖ **obstruction** [-ʃən] *n.* **1.** obstacle *m.* **2.** obstruction *f*; [Pol.] opposition/factieuse, systématique;/tactique *f*, moyen *m*/dilatoire.

obtain [əb'tejn] *v. tr.* **1.** se procurer, obtenir; [☞ In current speech, avoid *obtenir* which expresses effort.] cf. OBTAINABLE; [prize] gagner; [without effort] avoir, trouver. ‖ *v. intr.* [rules] être en vigueur; [conditions] prévaloir, être la règle. ‖ **obtainable** [-əbl̩] *adj.* [on sale] en vente (chez . . ., à . . .); [that you can get] → qu'on peut se procurer.

obtrusive [əb'tɹuwsɪv] *adj.* importun.

obtuse [ab'tjuws] *adj.* [angle] obtus; [stupid] obtus, stupide.

obviate ['abvɪ,ejt] *v. tr.* obvier à (une difficulté, &c.).

obvious ['abvɪəs] *adj.* évident, manifeste; qui saute aux yeux: *Don't be so* ~, → Inutile de mettre les points sur les i. ‖ **obviously** [-lɪ] *adv.* évidemment.

occasion [ow'kejʒən] *n.* **1.** [time] occasion *f*, circonstance *f*: *on the* ~ *of*, à l'occasion de: *on/one, another/* ~,/une, une autre/ fois; *on several occasions*, à plusieurs reprises; *on such an* ~, dans de telles circonstances, en pareille circonstance; *on* ~, à l'occasion; *as the* ~ *demands*, au besoin; *for the* ~, pour la circonstance; */suitable to, made for/the* ~, de circonstance. **2.** [event] occasion *f*: *This is quite an* ~, C'est/une occasion importante, une grande affaire/; *a state* ~, une réception officielle. **3.** [cause] cause *f*, raison *f*: *to have* ~ *to*, être appelé à; *to have no* ~ *to*, ne pas avoir lieu de. **4.** [chance] occasion *f* (de, *to*). ‖ **occasion** *v. tr.* déterminer, provoquer. ‖ **occasional** [-l̩] *adj.* [by chance] fortuit [once in a while] → de temps à autre; [for an occasion] de circonstance: *He made/the, an/* ~ *comment*, Il faisait une observation de temps à autre. ‖ **occasionally** [-lɪ] *adv.* à l'occasion, parfois, de temps à autre.

Occident ['aksɪdənt] *n.* l'occident *m*; [Geog.] l'ouest *m*: *to, in/the* ~, à l'occident, dans l'ouest. ‖ **occidental** [-l̩] *n.* & *adj.* occidental.

occult ['akʌlt] *adj.* occulte.

occupancy ['akjəpən|sɪ] *n.* [Law] prise *f* de possession; occupation *f.* ‖ **occupant** [-t] *n.* occupant *m*; [country] habitant *m*; [house] propriétaire *m/f*; [tenant] locataire; [post] titulaire. ‖ **occupation** [,akjə'pejʃən] *n.* [employment] emploi *m*, profession *f*; [Mil.] occupation *f* (d'un pays); [holding] possession *f*: *during the* ~, sous l'occupation. ‖ **occupy** ['akjə,paj] *v. tr.* occuper, employer (à, *in, with*) employer; [live in] habiter: *to* ~ *o.s. with*, se consacrer à.

occur [ə'kər] *v. intr.* **[-rr-]** [happen] avoir lieu, arriver, se produire; [come to mind] venir à l'esprit, se présenter: *It occurred to me that* . . ., → L'idée m'est venue que . . . ‖ **occurrence** [-əns] *n.* occurrence *f*; [event] événement *m.*

ocean ['owʃən] *n.* océan *m*: ~ *(-going) liner*, transatlantique *m*, © océanique *m.* ‖ **Oceania** [,owʃɪ'ænjə] *n.* l'Océanie *f*: */to, in/* ~, en Océanie.

o'clock [ə'klak] [☞ sert à indiquer l'heure]: *(It is) five* ~, (Il est) cinq heures.

octane ['ak,tejn] *n.* [Chem.] octane *m*: ~ *number*, indice *m* d'octane.

October [ak'towbər] *n.* octobre *m.* cf. APRIL.

ocular ['akjə|lər] *adj.* oculaire. ‖ *n.* oculaire *m.* ‖ **oculist** [-lɪst] *n.* (médecin) oculiste *m.*

odd [ad] *adj.* (nombre) impair; (objet) dépareillé [i.e. one of a pair]; [queer] étrange, bizarre, original, [Fam.] drôle; [occasional] divers: ~ *moments*, moments perdus, *at* ~ *times*, à diverses reprises; *six hundred* ~ *horses*, six cents chevaux et quelques, quelque six cents chevaux. cf. ODDS. ‖ **oddity** [-ɪtɪ] *n.* bizarrerie *f.* ‖ **oddly** [-lɪ] *adv.* bizarrement, étrangement: ~ *enough*, chose *f* étrange. ‖ **odds** [-z] *n.pl.* **1.** chances *fpl*: *The* ~ *are in his favour*, Les chances sont pour lui. **2.** [games] enjeu *m*: *to lay* ~, parier. **3.** brouille *f*, querelle *f*: *to be at* ~ *with*, se disputer avec. **4.** ~ *and ends*, débris *mpl* petits bouts *mpl* (de . . .).

ode [owd] *n.* ode *f.*

odious ['owdɪəs] *adj.* odieux.

odor cf. ODOUR. ‖ **odorous** [-əs] *adj.* odorant, parfumé. || **odour** ['owdɚ] *n.* odeur *f*: [fragrance] parfum *m.*

of [ʌv] *prep.* **1.** de [Other idiomatic translations not listed here are to be looked up under the construction to which they belong.] **2.** à: *to ask sth. ~ s.o.*, demander qqch. à qqun; *It is nice ~ you to . . .*, C'est gentil/à vous, de votre part/de . . . ; *a friend ~ mine*, un ami à moi, un de mes amis; *to think ~ sth.*, /penser, réfléchir/ à qqch. **3.** en: *It is made ~ brick*, C'est en brique; *a house ~ stone*, une maison en pierre; *a doctor ~ medicine*, un docteur en médecine; *a bachelor ~ arts*, un bachelier ès arts; *He makes use ~ /it, them/*[things], Il s'en sert. **4.** entre; d'entre: *he ~ all people*, lui entre tous; *some ~ /them, you/*, certains d'entre/eux, vous/. **5.** par: *~ itself*, /par, de/soi-même; tout seul; *~ necessity*, par nécessité. **6.** no translation: *the tenth ~ April*, le dix avril; *I often see him ~ a morning*, Je le vois souvent le matin; *It is a quarter ~ three*, Il est trois heures moins le quart; *It smells ~ fish*, Ça sent le poisson.

off [ɔf] *adv.* **1.** loin: *far ~*, au loin; *farther ~*, plus loin; *ten miles ~*, à (une distance de) dix milles. **2.** parti: *They're ~ !*, Les voilà partis; *I'm ~ !*, Je pars!; *Off with him!*, Emmenez-le! **3.** enlevé; [light] éteint; [tap, radio] fermé: *Hats ~ (to . . .)*, Chapeau bas (devant . . .); [Fig.] *The deal is ~*, L'affaire ne marche plus. **4.** [Loc.] *to be/well, badly/ ~*, être dans/l'aisance, la misère/; *to be /better, worse/ ~*, se trouver en/meilleure, plus mauvaise/posture; *~ and on*, de temps en temps; *right ~*, tout de suite; *to get a day ~*, obtenir une journée de congé; *Wednesday is my day ~*, Mercredi, c'est mon jour de congé; *I have evenings ~*, J'ai les soirées libres. || **off** *prép.* de; éloigné de; [Naut.] au large de: *to fall ~ the table*, tomber de la table; *to take sth. ~ the table*, prendre qqch. sur la table; *~ the highway*, /éloigné, écarté/de la grand-route; [Fig.] *to be ~ the track*, → ne plus être dans la bonne voie; *to be ~ o.'s food*, → ne plus avoir d'appétit; [Sport.] *to be ~ side*, être hors jeu; *~ Halifax*, au large d'Halifax; *~ the coast*, au large. || **off** *adj.* *the ~ side*, le côté extérieur, l'autre côté, [Br.] le côté droit (d'un véhicule); *~ day*, journée *f* libre; une mauvaise journée; *~ season*, la morte-saison, *~ street*, rue *f* transversale.

offence [ow'fɛn|s] *n.* offense *f* (contre, *against*); [Jur.] infraction *f* (au règlement), contravention *f*: *to give ~ to s.o.*, offenser, froisser/qqun; *to take ~ at . . .*, s'offusquer, s'offenser/de. . . . || **offend** [-d] *v. tr.*; [displease] froisser: *to ~ against*, enfreindre (un règlement, &c.). || **offender** [-dɚ] *n.* délinquant *m/f*, coupable *m/f.* || **offense** cf. OFFENCE. || **offensive** [-sɪv] *adj.* offensant, blessant; [Mil.] offensif.

offer ['ɑfɚ] *v. tr. & intr.* offrir (qqch. à qqun): *to ~ one's best wishes*, adresser, présenter/ses meilleurs vœux; *this is what we have to ~*, voici ce que nous proposons; *to ~ to do sth.*, s'offrir à faire qqch.; *The property is offered for sale*, La propriété est mise en vente. || *n.* offre *f*; proposition *f.* || **offering** [-ɪŋ] *n.* offrande *f.* || **Offertory** [-ˌtɔɚɪ] *n.* [Rel.] Offertoire *m.*

offhand [ɑf'hænd] *adv.* sur-le-champ; au pied levé. || *adj.* improvisé, impromptu; [casual] sans gêne.

office¹ ['ɑfɪs] *n.* [general term] bureau *m*; [lawyer, notary] étude *f*; [agent] agence *f*: *company head ~*, siège *m* social.

office² *n.* [duty] office *m*; [task] fonction *f*, charge *f*; [Rel.] office *m* (religieux); [Fig.] *pl. through the good offices of . . .*, grâce aux bons offices de . . . ; *the government in ~*, le gouvernement/en fonction, au pouvoir/; *the highest elective ~ in Canada*, le plus haut poste électif au Canada; [Polit.] *to run for ~*, se présenter aux élections. || **office-holder** [-ˌhowldɚ] *n.* employé *m* de l'État; fonctionnaire *m/f* [Br. public servant; © civil servant]. || **officer** [-ɚ] *n.* **1.** [executive] administrateur *m*; dirigeant *m*; la direction *f* (d'une affaire); [as a group] les cadres *mpl*, les responsables, les chefs; [charity, &c.] le comité *m* (de la campagne, &c.); [of a company] le bureau *m*, les dirigeants *mpl* (de la société). **2.** [Mil.] officier *m*; [police] agent *m* (de police), officier *m* de police: *non-commissioned ~*, sous-officier *m*; *~ of the day*, officier de service. || **official** [ow'fɪʃəl] *adj.* officiel; [duties] public; [stationery] réglementaire. || *n.* employé *m*, fonctionnaire *m*: *higher officials*, les hauts fonctionnaires. || **officialdom** [-dəm] *n.* **1.** l'administration *f*; le fonctionnarisme *m.* **2.** bureaucratie *f*, chinoiseries *fpl* de l'administration. || **officiate** [ow'fɪʃɪˌejt] *v. intr.* (of a priest) officier (à une cérémonie religieuse). || **officious** [ow'fɪʃəs] *adj.* trop zélé, empressé.

offing ['ɑfɪŋ] *n.*: *in the ~*, au large *m*; [Fig.] en perspective.

offset [′ɔfˌsɛt] *n.* **1.** rejeton *m.* **2.** [typogr.] offset *m.* ‖ **off|set, -set, -set** *v. tr.* [ɔf′sɛt] compenser, contrebalancer (des pertes); désaxer, décentrer.

offshoot [′ɔfˌʃuwt] *n.* [Bot.; also Fig.] rejeton *m.*

offspring [′ɔfˌspɹɪŋ] *n.* **1.** progéniture *f*; descendance *f.* **2.** conséquence *f*, résultat *m.*

often [ɔfn̩] *adv.* souvent, fréquemment: *how ~ ?*, combien de fois?, [= at what intervals] tous les combien?; *once too ~*, une fois de trop; *every so ~*, de temps en temps; *I don't see him very ~ now*, Je ne le vois plus/guère, très souvent/.

ogre [′owgɚ] *n.* ogre *m.*

oil [ojl] *n.* huile *f*: *crude ~*, pétrole *m* brut; [*fuel ~*] mazout *m*: [Fig.] *to burn, the midnight ~*, travailler tard dans la nuit; *to pour ~ on troubled waters*, apaiser les esprits. *adj.*: *oilcloth*, toile *f* cirée; *~ share*, valeur *f* pétrolifère; *~ tanker*, pétrolier *m*; *~ well*, puits *m* de pétrole. ‖ *v. tr.* huiler, graisser; lubrifier. ‖ **oily** [-ɪ] *adj.* huileux, graisseux; [of manner] onctueux.

ointment [′ojntmənt] *n.* onguent *m*, pommade *f.*

OK, O.K. [′ow′kej] *pl.* **OK's, O.K.'s** [-z] *n.* approbation *f.* ‖ **OK, OK'd** [-d] **OK'ing** [ɪŋ] *v. tr.* approuver. ‖ *adj.* en bon état, en bonne condition. ‖ *adv.* [Com.] vu; bon pour livraison; vérifié; [Printing] O.K. = bon à tirer. ‖ *interj.* d'accord!, parfait!; [Fam.] ça va!., O.K.

old [owld] *adj.* cf. ELDER, ELDEST aîné. **1.** [aged] vieux, vieil *m*, vieille *f*, âgé: *to /grow, get/ ~*, vieillir; *an ~ man*, un vieillard, [Fam.] un vieux, *an ~ woman*, une vieille; *~ /folk, people/*, les vieux; [Fam.] *Hello, ~ /man, fellow/!*, Bonjour, mon vieux; [Fam.] *There goes ~ Jones*, Voilà le père Jones; *~ age*, vieillesse *f*; *~ -age pension*, retraite *f* des vieux: *an ~ maid*, une vieille fille: *~ /French, English/*, l'ancien français, le vieil anglais. **2.** [expressions of age] *How ~ are you?*, Quel âge avez-vous?; *I am 15 (years ~)*, J'ai 15 ans; *He is 3 years older than I (am)*, Il a 3 ans de plus que moi, Il est plus âgé que moi de 3 ans; *a 50-year- ~ man, a man 50 years ~*, un homme (âgé) de 50 ans; *to be ~ enough to . . .*, être/en âge de . . ., assez grand pour . . . /. **3.** [former] ancien [placed before its noun] *the Old Testament*, l'Ancien Testament; [Sch.] *~ boy*, ancien élève. **4.** [pour remplacer une expression indéfinie] n'importe . . . quelconque: *any ~ /time, place/*, n'importe/quand, où/; *any ~ book*, un livre quelconque. **5.** [Pej.] *you and your ~ car!*, toi et ta (vieille) guimbarde! **6.** [Loc.] *of ~*, [after v.] jadis; [after n.] de jadis. ‖ **old-fashioned** [ˌowld′fæʃənd] *adj.* démodé; [Pej.] vieux jeu; d'autrefois; de l'ancien temps. ‖ **old-time** [′owld′tajm] *adj.* d'autrefois, d'antan. ‖ **old-timer** [-ɚ] *n.* vieux routier *m*; [Fam.] vieux copain *m.* ‖ **old-world** [′owld′wɚld] *adj.* d'autrefois, suranné: *Old World* l'ancien continent, © les vieux pays.

olive [′ɑlɪv] *n.* olive *f*: *~ oil*, huile *f* d'olive. ‖ *adj.* olivâtre, verdâtre. ‖ **olive tree** [-ˌtɹij] *n.* olivier *m.*

Oliver [-ɚ] *n.* = Olivier *m.* ‖ **Olivia** *n.* = Olive *f.*

Olympia [ow′lɪmpɪə] *n.* [Geo.] Olympe *f.* ‖ **Olympian** [-n] *adj.* olympien, -ne; [Fig.] supérieur. ‖ **Olympic games,** also **the Olympics** les jeux *mpl* olympiques.

omelet(te) [′ɑmlət] *n.* [Cul.] omelette *f.*

omen [′owmən] *n.* présage *m*, augure *m.* ‖ *v. tr.* présager, augurer: *ill-omened*, de mauvais augure. ‖ **ominous** [′ɑmɪnəs] *adj.* menaçant, de mauvais présage.

omission [ow′mɪʃən] *n.* omission *f*; oubli *m*; négligence *f.*

omit [ow′mɪt] *v. tr.* [-tt-] [leave out] omettre; [neglect] [+ ing] omettre de, négliger de.

omnipotent [ɑm′nɪpətənt] *adj.* omnipotent, tout-puissant: *The Omnipotent*, Le Tout-Puissant.

on [ɑn] *adv.* **1.** *to put one's hat ~*, mettre son chapeau; *to have one's hat ~*, avoir son chapeau sur la tête, être couvert. **2.** [continuity] continuer à: *to walk ~*, continuer sa promenade; *to talk ~*, continuer à parler; *to sleep ~ and ~*, dormir sans arrêt; *and so ~*, et ainsi de suite; *~ and off*, par intervalles. **3.** [light, radio] allumé; [tap] ouvert; [machine] en marche; [appliance] branché. **4.** [Theat.] *What is ~ ?*, Qu'est-ce qu'on joue?, Qu'y a-t-il au programme?; [Fig.] *I have nothing ~ (for) tonight*, Je suis libre ce soir; [cue] *You're ~ !*, C'est à vous!. En scène! **5.** [time] *From that day ~*, A partir de ce jour-là; *from now ~*, désormais; *well ~ in the night*, à une heure avancée de la nuit. **6.** [agreement] *You're ~ !*, C'est d'accord!; [job] Vous êtes engagé! **7.** *to be ~ to sth.*, avoir/compris, découvert/ qqch.; *to be ~ to s.o.*, avoir deviné le secret de qqun. ‖ *prép.* **1.** sur; dessus; y: *The book (is) ~ the table*, Le livre (est) sur la table; *What is there ~ it?*, Qu'y a-t-il dessus?; *There is the shelf. Put the book ~ it*, Voilà l'étagère. Mettez-y le livre; [Fig.] *Have you any money ~ you?*, Avez-vous de l'argent sur vous? **2.** à: *~ the ceiling*, au plafond; *~ the wall*, [inside] au mur, [outside] sur le mur; *~ the/head, leg/*, à la/ tête, jambe/; *He lives ~ the 3rd floor*, il habite au 3e (étage); *~ my arrival*, à mon arrivée; *~ the/right, left/*, /à droite, à gauche/; *to be ~ the telephone*, avoir le téléphone chez soi, être en train de parler au téléphone. **3.** en: *A house ~ fire*, une maison en feu; */~ my arrival, ~ arriving/*, en arrivant; *work ~ hand*, travail en cours; *~ sale here*, en vente ici. **4.** dans: *~ /the bus, the train/*, dans /l'autobus, le train/; *He came ~ the/bus, train/*, Il est venu par/l'autobus, le train/; *~ a farm*, dans une ferme; *~ the jury*, dans le jury; *~ the island*, dans l'île; *~ the street*, dans la rue; *He lives ~ Laurier St.*, Il habite (dans la) rue Laurier. **5.** de: *to live ~ bread and water*, vivre de pain et d'eau; *~ the one hand . . . ~ the other hand*, d'une part . . . d'autre part. **6.** au sujet de, sur: *To speak ~ gardening*, faire une conférence sur le jardinage. **7.** [no translation] *~ Monday*, lundi (prochain); *~ Mondays*, le lundi, tous les lundis; *~ Jan. 1st*, le 1er janvier. **8.** [Loc.] *~ or after the 15th of August*, à partir du quinze août; *~ or about the 30th of June*, aux environs du 30 juin; *This round is ~ me*, C'est ma tournée; *It is ~ the house*, C'est la tournée du patron; *He has nothing ~ me*, (1) Il ne me surpasse en rien; (2) Il ne peut rien trouver contre moi.

once [wʌns] *adv.* **1.** [one time] une fois: *~ /again, more/*, encore une fois, une fois de plus; *never ~* , pas un instant; *~ in a while*, (une fois) de temps en temps. **2.** [formerly] autrefois: *He was a rich man ~* , Il était riche autrefois; *~ upon a time there was . . .*, Il était une fois . . . **3.** Une fois (que); dès que: *(If) ~ you see it, (then) . . .*, Une fois que vous l'aurez vu . . . , Dès que vous le verrez . . . ; *~ convinced, he . . .*, Une fois convaincu, il . . . . **4.** *at ~* , immédiatement, tout de suite, aussitôt, &c.; [at the same time] à la fois; *~ and for all*, une fois pour toutes. ‖ *conj.* cf. ONCE, *adv.* §3. ‖ **once-over** *n.* [Sl.] *to give . . . the ~* , jeter un coup d'œil à.

one [wʌn] *n.* un *m*: *the number ~*, le un, le numéro un; *~ two, ~ two*, une deux, une deux; *two in ~* , deux dans un; *last but ~* , avant-dernier; *It must be ~ of two things, ~ (thing) or the other*, De deux choses l'une; *~ thirty*, une heure trente, un dollar trente (sous); *to do sth. as ~* , faire qqch./en harmonie, comme un seul homme/; *to be at ~ (with)*, être d'accord (avec). ‖ *adj.* **1.** un, une: *twenty- ~* , vingt et un(e); *seventy- ~* , soixante-et-onze; *eighty- ~* , quatre-vingt-un(e); *ninety- ~* , quatre-vingt-onze; *~ hundred (and ~)*, cent (un, une); *~ thousand (and ~)*, mille (et/un, une); *~ million (and ~)*, un million (et/un, une). **2.** [only] seul: *My ~ objection is . . .* , Ma seule objection c'est . . . ; *as ~ man*, comme un seul homme; *~ and only*, seul et unique. **3.** [same] même: *They all came ~ way*, Ils ont tous pris le même chemin; *all in ~ place*, tout dans un même endroit; *on ~ and the same day*, dans une (seule et) même journée. **4.** [some] un, une: *~ day when . . .*, un jour que . . . . **5.** certain: *~ John Brown*, un certain Jean Durand. ‖ *pron.* un(e): *I haven't got ~* , Je n'en ai pas; *Will you show me ~ ?*, Voulez-vous m'en montrer un(e)?; *~ of my friends*, un(e) de mes ami(e)s, un(e) ami(e) à moi; *~ of my French friends*, un(e) Français(e) de mes ami(e)s; *~ of them*, l'un(e) d'(entre)/eux, elles; *(The) ~ was talking, the other was listening*, L'un parlait, l'autre écoutait; *They helped ~ another*, Ils s'aidaient/les uns les autres, (l'un l'autre), mutuellement/; *~ by ~* , un(e)/à, par/un(e); *I am not (the) ~ to . . .*, Ce n'est pas moi qui . . . ; *I, for ~ . . .*, /pour ma part, pour moi, quant à moi/je . . . . **2.** */this, that/ ~* , celui-ci, celle-ci/celui-là, celle-là; */these, those/ ones*, ceux-ci, celles-ci/ceux-là, celles-là. [× the forms in -ci, -là are not used when 'de' or a rel. pron. follows]; *Which ~ (s) do you want?*, Le(s)quel(s) désirez-vous?; *I'll take the ~ on the table*, Je prendrai celui qui est sur la table; *He is the ~ I am looking for*, C'est lui que je cherche. **3.** [usual. no translation] *He always takes the big piece(s) and leaves me the small ~ (s)*, Il prend toujours le(s) grand(s) morceau(x) et me laisse le(s) petit(s): *His lecture was an interesting ~* , Sa conférence était intéressante; *Yes, we have red ones*, Certainement, nous en avons des rouges. **4.** on; vous; soi; [or impers. construction]: *~ should always be polite*, On devrait toujours être poli; *~ must always look both ways before* *crossing the street*, Il faut toujours regarder des deux côtés avant de traverser la rue; *Yes, that helps* ~ , Oui, cela (vous) aide; *Everything is against* ~ , Tout est contre vous; ~ *has tradition against* ~ , On a la tradition contre soi; cf. also ONE's. || **one-legged** [-ˌlɛgəd] *adj.* ~ *man*, → unijambiste *m.* || **oneness** [-nəs] *n.* unité *f*, identité *f*; accord *m.* || **one's** [-z] *pron. poss.* son, sa, ses, se [or impers. construction]: *One must take* ~ *hat off in the theatre*, /Il faut, on doit/enlever son chapeau au théâtre; *to get* ~ *hair cut*, se faire couper les cheveux; *to lose* ~ *breath*, perdre le souffle. || **onesel|f** [ˌwʌn'sɛlf] *pl.* **-ves** [-'sɛlvz] *pron.* se; soi, soi-même, *to cut* ~ , se couper; *to think of* ~ , penser à soi; *to have confidence in* ~ , avoir confiance en soi-même. || **one-sided** [ˌwʌn'sajdəd] *adj.* à un côté, à une face; [Fig.] partial; unilatéral. || **one-way** ['wʌn'wej] *adj.* ~ *ticket*, billet *m* simple; ~ *street*, rue *f* à sens unique.

onion ['ʌnjən] *n.* oignon *m.*

onlooker ['ɑnˌlʊkɚ] *n.* spectat|eur, -rice, [Pej.] badaud *m.*

only ['ownlɪ] *adj.* seul, unique: *one and* ~ , seul et unique; *an* ~ *child*, un enfant unique; *She is the* ~ *one who knows about it*, Elle est la seule à le savoir, Il n'y a qu'elle qui le sait. || *adv.* seulement; ne . . . que, rien que; seul: *Open on Wednesday(s)* ~ , Ouvert le mercredi seulement; *if* ~ . . . , si seulement . . . ; *not* ~ . . . *but also*, non seulement . . . /mais aussi, mais encore/; *I've read* ~ *two pages*, Je n'ai lu que deux pages; ~ *two?*,/rien que deux, deux seulement/?; *I have* ~ *to* . . . , Je n'ai qu'à . . . ; *He* ~ *repeated the same thing*, Il n'a fait que répéter la même chose; ~ *a miracle can save him*, Seul un miracle pourra le sauver; ~ *his courage saved him*, Son seul courage le sauva; ~ *the fact that* . . . , Le seul fait que . . . ; ~ *he can do it*, Lui seul sait le faire; *I saw him* ~ *last week*, Je l'ai vu (pas plus tard que) la semaine dernière; *I'd be* ~ *too happy to*, Je ne serais que trop heureux de . . . ; *Staff* ~ , Réservé au personnel.

onomatopœic [ˌɑnəmətə'pɪjɪk] *adj.* onomatopéique.

onrush ['ɑnˌɹʌʃ] *n.* ruée *f.*

onset ['ɑnˌsɛt] *n.* assaut *m*; attaque *f*: *At the (first)* ~ , Au premier abord.

onslaught ['ɑnˌslɔt] *n.* assaut *m.*

Ont. [= ONTARIO]. || **Ontarian** [ɑn'tɛɚɪən] *n.* habitant *m/f* de l'Ontario, Ontarien *m*, -ne *f.* || **Ontario** [ɑn'tɛɚɪow] *n.* l'Ontario *m*: /*in, to*/ ~ , /en, dans l'/Ontario; *Lake* ~ , le lac Ontario; *the* ~ *government*, le gouvernement de l'Ontario.

onto ['ɑntuw; before consonant: 'ɑntə] cf. ON [exprime le mouvement vers qqch. ou qqun]. [Use the same French prep. as in an equivalent expression of rest.]

onus ['ownəs] *n.* [Jur., also Fig.] charge *f*, fardeau *m.*

onward ['ɑnwɚd] *adv.* en avant: *to go* ~ , avancer, aller de l'avant; *from this day* ~ , désormais. || *adj.* en avant; progressif.

ooze [uwz] *v. intr.* suinter, dégoutter: *to* ~ *out*, sourdre, s'écouler. || *n.* vase *f*, limon *m*; suintement *m.*

opaque [ow'pejk] *adj.* opaque.

open ['owpn̩] *adj.* **1.** ouvert: *half-* ~ , entr'ouvert; *wide-* ~ , grand ouvert; [Fig.] sans foi ni loi; déréglé, immoral; *in the* ~ *air*, cf. OPEN AIR; *in the* ~ *country*, en rase campagne; *on the* ~ *sea(s)*, en pleine mer. **2.** découvert; exposé (à); *an* ~ *car*, une automobile découverte; ~ *to attack*, exposé aux attaques; [Fig.] ~ *to temptation*, exposé à la tentation; ~ *to doubt*, douteux. **3.** libre, vacant: *Is your evening* ~ *?*, Êtes-vous libre ce soir?; *Is the job still* ~ *?*, Le poste est-il encore vacant? **4.** évident; public: *an* ~ *truth*, une vérité évidente; *the* ~ *market*, le marché public. **5.** franc, sincère. **6.** non déterminé: *an* ~ *question*, une question discutable, indécise; *to keep an* ~ *mind (on sth.)*, /être, rester/sans préjugés (au sujet de qqch.). [Sport] = accessible à tous: *the Canadian Open Golf Championship*, Championnat *m* international de golf du Canada. || *v. tr.* **1.** ouvrir; déboucher (une bouteille); dépouiller (le courrier), [in a car] baisser (une glace); percer (un trou): *to half-* ~ , entr'ouvrir; *to* ~ *wide*, ouvrir tout grand. **2.** découvrir; révéler. **3.** commencer; inaugurer. || *v. intr.* s'ouvrir; [store, &c.] ouvrir; commencer. || **open air** [-'ɛɚ] *n.* (le) plein air *m*: *in the* ~ *air*, au grand air, en plein air. || **open-air** *adj.* [of plays] de plein air. || **opening** [-ɪŋ] *n.* [porte, fenêtre, &c.] ouverture *f*; [clearing] éclaircie *f*; [Fig.] inauguration *f*; poste *m* libre; [Com., outlet] débouché *m*; [Fig.] occasion *f* (favorable). || *adj.* d'ouverture, d'inauguration; débutant; premier. || **openly** [-lɪ] *adv.* ouvertement; publiquement. || **open-minded** [-ˌmajndəd] *adj.* libéral, à l'esprit large; sans préjugé, non prévenu.

opera ['ɑpɚə] *n.* opéra *m*: ~ *glasses*, jumelles *fpl* de théâtre; ~ *hat*, chapeauclaque, gibus *m*; *grand* ~, grand opéra; *comic* ~, opéra-bouffe; *light* ~, opérette *f*.

operate [ˈɑpɚˌejt] *v. intr.* [Med.] opérer. **2.** agir, produire de l'effet, fonctionner. || *v. tr.* opérer, effectuer (un changement); actionner, faire marcher (une machine); gérer, diriger, exploiter (une affaire): *operated* (*by*), exploité, dirigé (par). || **operation** [ˌɑpɚˈejʃən] *n.* opération *f*, fonctionnement *m*: *to be in* ~, être en vigueur, en activité, en action; [machine] être en marche; [Mil.] *landing* ~ *s*, opérations de débarquement; *combined* ~, opération *f* combinée. || **operative** [ˈɑpɚətɪv] *adj.* opératif, actif: *This decree is* ~ *forthwith*, Ce décret/entre en vigueur, prend effet/immédiatement. || *n.* ouvrier *m*; agent *m*. || **operator** [ˈɑpɚˌejtɚ] *n.* opérateur *m*, -trice *f*; exploitant *m*, agent *m*; [Auto] conducteur *m*, chauffeur *m*; [Radio] le radio : *to dial* ~, appelez la standardiste, © l'opératrice *f*.

operetta [ˌɑpɚˈɛtə] *n.* opérette *f*.

opinion [owˈpɪnjən] *n.* opinion *f*; avis *m*: *in my* ~, à mon avis; *to be of the* ~ *that*, être d'avis que; *to have a high* ~ *of someone*, avoir bonne opinion de qqun; *public* ~ l'opinion publique; [Jur.] *It is the* ~ *of the Court that* . . . , Le jugement du Tribunal est que . . . . || **opinionated, opinionative** [-ˌejtəd] [-ˌejtɪv] *adj.* obstiné, têtu.

opium [ˈowpɪəm] *n.* opium *m*.

opossum [owˈpɑsəm] *n.* opossum *m*.

opponent [owˈpownənt] *n.* adversaire *m*/*f*; antagoniste *m*/*f*.

opportune [ˌɑpɚˈtjuwn] *adj.* opportun, convenable. || **opportuneness** [-nəs] *n.* opportunité *f*; l'à-propos *m*. || **opportunity** [-ɪtɪ] *n.* occasion *f*: *a great* ~ *to* . . . , une belle occasion de; *I'd like to take this* ~ *to* . . . , Je tiens à profiter de cette occasion pour . . . .

oppose [owˈpowz] *v. tr.* opposer (un argument), combattre; mettre en opposition; s'opposer à (qqun, qqch.), mettre obstacle (à qqch.). || **opposing** *adj.* opposé: *the* ~ *team*, l'adversaire *m*. || **opposite** [ˈɑpəzɪt] *adj.* opposé, contraire (à, *to*), d'en face: ~ *to*, en face de. || *n.* contraire *m*, opposé *m*. || *adv.* en face. || *prép.* en face de, vis-à-vis de. || **opposition** [ˌɑpəˈzɪʃən] *n.* opposition *f*: *the leader of the* ~, © le chef de l'opposition.

oppress [owˈpɹɛ|s] *v. tr.* opprimer (un peuple); [burden] accabler; [Med.] oppresser. || **oppression** [-ʃən] *n.* oppression *f*. || **oppressive** [-sɪv] *adj.* opprimant, oppressif; [mentally] accablant; [weather] étouffant, lourd. || **oppressively** [-sɪvlɪ] *adv.* tyranniquement; de façon accablante, étouffante: *The evening was* ~ *warm*, → La soirée était d'une chaleur accablante. || **oppressor** [-sɚ] *n.* oppresseur *m*.

opprobrious [əˈpɹowbɹɪəs] *adj.* infamant, injurieux.

optic [ˈɑptɪk] *adj.* optique. || **optical** [-l̩] *adj.* optique. || **optician** [ɑpˈtɪʃən] *n.* opticien *m*. || **optics** [ˈɑptɪks] *n.pl.* optique *f*.

optimism [ˈɑptɪmɪ|zm] *n.* optimisme *m*. || **optimist** [-st] *n.* optimiste *m*/*f*. || **optimistic** [ˌɑptɪˈmɪstɪk] *adj.* optimiste *m*/*f*.

option [ˈɑpʃən] *n.* option *f*, choix *m*; faculté *f*: *To sign a lease with* ~ *of purchase*, Signer un bail avec faculté d'achat. || **optional** [-l̩] *adj.* facultatif, -ve.

optometrist [ɑpˈtɑmətɹ|ɪst] *n.* oculiste *m*, © optométriste *m*/*f*. || **optometry** [-ɪ] © optométrie *f*.

opulence [ˈɑpjəl|əns] *n.* opulence *f*; richesse *f*. || **opulent** [-ənt] *adj.* riche, opulent.

or [ɔɚ] *conj.* **1.** [×] ou, ou bien; [either . . . or . . .] soit . . . soit . . . ; ~ *else*, autrement, ou bien, [menace] sinon cf. EITHER. **2.** [explanation] ou, ou mieux.

oracle [ˈɔɚək]] *n.* oracle *m*.

oral [ˈɔɚəl] *adj.* oral. *n.* (examen) oral *m*. || **orally** [-ɪ] *adv.* oralement: [Med.] *taken* ~, → par voie buccale.

orange [ˈɔɚəndʒ] *n.* orange *f*; [colour] orangé *m*, orange *m*. || *adj.* orangé; orange. || **orangeade** [-ˈejd] *n.* orangeade *f*. || **Orangeman** [-mən] *n.* Orangiste *m*.

oration [ɔˈɹejʃən] *n.* oraison *f*, discours *m*; [Fam.] laïus *m*. || **orator** [ˈɔɚətɚ] *n.* orateur *m*, -trice *f*. || **oratory** [ˈɔɚəˌtɔɚ] *n.* **1.** oratoire *m*: *St. Joseph's* ~, l'Oratoire Saint-Joseph. **2.** éloquence *f*, art *m* oratoire.

orb [ɔɚb] *n.* orbe *m*; sphère *f*; globe *m*. || **orbit** [ˈɔɚbɪt] *n.* orbite *f*: *in* ~, sur orbite.

orchard [ˈɔɚtʃɚd] *n.* verger *m*.

orchestra [ˈɔɚkəstɹ|ə] *n.* orchestre *m*: ~ *seat*, fauteuil *m* d'orchestre. || **orchestrate** [-ejt] *v. tr.* orchestrer.

orchid [ˈɔɚkɪd] *n.* orchidée *f*: *orchids for X*, compliments, félicitations à/Monsieur X, la maison X, &c.

ordain [ɔɚˈdejn] *v. tr.* [Rel.] ordonner (un prêtre, un ministre); destiner (à); décréter (que): *it was ordained that* . . . , le sort a voulu que . . . .

ordeal [ˌɔɚˈdijl] *n.* épreuve *f*; jugement *m* de Dieu.

order [ˈɔɚdɚ] *n.* **1.** [command] ordre *m*, commandement *m*; [Mil.] consigne *f*: *to give orders/to s.o. to do sth., for sth. to be done*, donner l'ordre à qqun de faire qqch./ qu'on fasse qqch.; *Orders are orders*, La consigne, c'est la consigne; *to/obey, follow/orders*, suivre/les ordres, la consigne/; *His orders are to . . ., /He has orders to . . .*, Il a reçu l'ordre de . . . ; *until further orders*, jusqu'à nouvel ordre; *by* ~ (*of*), d'ordre (de); ~ *-in-council*, décret *m* (du Conseil), arrêté en conseil; ~ *of the day*, ordre *m* du jour; [cheque] *to the* ~ *of*, à l'ordre de; *Bravery was the* ~ *of the day*, La bravoure était de mise. **2.** [condition, nature] ordre *m*: *the old* ~ (*of things*), l'ancien régime; *It is in the natural* ~ *of things*, C'est dans l'ordre des choses; *to be in* ~, être/en règle, en bon état de marche; *to put sth. in* ~, mettre qqch. en règle, mettre de l'ordre dans qqch.; *in apple-pie* ~, en ordre parfait; *to be out of* ~, /être déréglé, être en panne, ne pas être en état de marche; *Out of* ~, /en dérangement, en panne/ → ne fonctionne pas; *His remarks are* (*not*) *in* ~, Ses remarques (ne) sont (pas) pertinentes; *Congratulations are in* ~, *are not out of* ~, Les félicitations ne seraient pas hors de propos. **3.** [discipline] ordre *m*; *to/keep, restore/* ~, maintenir/ l'ordre, la discipline/; *law and* ~, l'ordre public; [Parl.] *point of* ~, rappel *m*/à l'ordre, au règlement/; *Order!, Order!*, à l'ordre! **4.** [class, society] classe *f*, ordre *m*: *of the first* ~, de premier ordre; *religious orders*, ordres *mpl* religieux; *the Order of the Garter*, l'Ordre de la Jarretière. **5.** [rank] ordre *m*, rang *m*: *in alphabetical* ~, par ordre alphabétique; *out of* (*the normal*) ~, en dehors de l'ordre établi; ~ *of battle*, ordre de bataille. **6.** [purchase] commande *f*; *to give an* ~, donner, passer/une commande; *It is on* ~, C'est commandé; *made to* ~, fait sur commande; (*by*) *postal money* ~, (par) mandat-poste *m*; [Restaurant] *short orders*, buffet *m*. **7.** [costume] tenue *f*: [Mil.] *in marching* ~, en tenue de route; *in review* ~, en grande tenue. **8.** [Mil.] (*Arms*) *at the* ~, l'arme au pied. **9.** *In* ~ *to*, afin de, pour/+ inf.; *in* ~ *that*, afin que, pour que/+ subj. ‖ *v. tr.* **1.** donner l'ordre, ordonner (*s.o. to do sth.*, à qqun de faire qqch.); *He was ordered to . . .*, Il a reçu l'ordre de . . . ; *The doctor ordered a complete rest*, Le médecin lui a ordonné un repos complet. **2.** [purchase] commander (qqch. à qqun, *sth. from s.o.*). **3.** arranger, mettre de l'ordre dans. **4.** [Mil.] reposer l'arme: *Order arms!*, Reposez armes!. ‖ **orderly** [-lɪ] *adj.* ordonné; discipliné: *in* ~ *fashion*, en (bon) ordre. ‖ *n.* [Mil.] ordonnance *f*; planton *m*; [hospital] infirmier *m*. ‖ **ordinal** [ˈɔɚdɪnl̩] *adj.* ordinal: ~ *number*, nombre ordinal. ‖ **ordinance** [ˈɔɚdɪnəns] *n.* ordonnance *f*, décret *m*, arrêté *m*. ‖ **ordinarily** [ˌɔɚdn̩ˈɛɚɪlɪ] *adv.* ordinairement, d'ordinaire, habituellement, normalement. ‖ **ordinary** [ˈɔɚdn̩ˌɛɚɪ] *adj.* ordinaire, commun, habituel; [Pej.] quelconque. ‖ *n.* ordinaire *m*: *it is out of the* ~, cela sort de l'ordinaire. ‖ **ordinate** [ˈɔɚdn̩ˌejt] *n.* [Math.] ordonnée *f*. ‖ **ordination** [ˌɔɚdn̩ˈejʃən] *n.* [Rel.] ordination *f* (d'un prêtre, d'un ministre): *candidate for* ~, ordinand *m*.

ordnance [ˈɔɚdn̩əns] *n.* artillerie *f*; [Mil.] service *m* du matériel: ~ *map*, carte *f* d'état-major; ~ *survey*, cadastre *m*.

ore [ɔɚ] *n.* minerai *m* (de fer, cuivre, &c.) *iron* ~, minerai de fer.

Oregon [ˈɔɚəˌgɑn] *n.* l'Orégon *m*: /*in, to*/ ~, dans l'Orégon.

organ [ˈɔɚgən] *n.* organe *m*; [Mus.] orgue *m*, orgues *fpl*: *house* ~, journal *m* d'entreprise, revue *f* (publiée par la firme X): *This paper is the official* ~ *of the Party*, Ce journal est l'organe officiel du Parti. ‖ **organic** [ɔɚˈgænɪk] *adj.* organique. ‖ **organism** [ˈɔɚgən|ɪsm] *n.* organisme *m*. ‖ **organist** [-ɪst] *n.* organiste *m/f*. ‖ **organization** [ˌɔɚgənɪˈzejʃən] *n.* organisation *f*, aménagement *m*; [Pol.] organisme *m*. ‖ **organize** [ˈɔɚgənajz] *v. tr.* organiser, agencer, arranger. ‖ **organized** [-d] *adj.* organisé, agencé, arrangé: ~ *labour*, les syndicats *mpl*, les centrales *fpl* ouvrières. ‖ **organizer**[-ɚ] *n.* organisateur *m*, -trice *f*.

orgy [ˈɔɚʤɪ] *n.* orgie *f*.

Orient [ˈɔɚɪənt] *n.* Orient *m*: *in, to/the* ~, en Orient. ‖ **orient** *v. tr.* orienter. ‖ **oriental** *adj.* oriental. ‖ **orientate** [-ejt] *v. tr.* orienter. ‖ **orientation** [ˌɔɚɪənˈtejʃən] *n.* orientation *f*.

orifice [ˈɔɚəfɪs] *n.* orifice *m*, ouverture *f*.

origin [ˈɔɚɪʤɪn] *n.* origine *f*, extraction *f*; [Com.] provenance *f*. ‖ **original** [əˈɹɪʤɪnl̩] *adj.* original; [earliest] primitif; [first] premier ‖ *n.* original *m*. ‖ **originality** [əˌɹɪʤɪˈnælɪtɪ] *n.* originalité *f*. ‖ **originally** [-ɪ] *adv.* originalement; originairement, à l'origine. ‖ **originate** [əˈɹɪʤɪˌnejt] *v. tr.* faire naître, créer, instituer. ‖ *v. intr.* prendre naissance; provenir, émaner (de, *from*). ‖ **origination** [əˌɹɪʤɪˈnejʃən] *n.*

source *f*, provenance *f*; création *f* (d'un projet). || **originator** [ə'ɹɪʤɪnˌejtɚ] *n.* auteur *m*; créa|teur *m*, -trice *f*; fonda|teur *m*, -trice *f*.

oriole ['ɔɚɪəl] *n.* loriot *m*; © oriole *m.*

Orleans [ɔɚ'lijnz] *n.* Orléans *m/f*: *New* ~, la Nouvelle-Orléans.

ornament ['ɔɚnəmənt] *n.* ornement *m*, garniture *f*, décoration *f*. || *v. tr.* ornementer, orner, décorer; agrémenter (une robe). || **ornamental** [ˌɔɚnə'mɛntl̩] *adj.* ornemental, décoratif. || **ornate** [ɔɚ'nejt] *adj.* orné, ornementé; [style] fleuri.

orphan ['ɔɚfən] *n.* & *adj.* orphelin *m*, -e *f*. || **orphanage** [-əʤ] *n.* orphelinat *m*.

orthodox ['ɔɚθəˌdɑks] *adj.* [Rel.] orthodoxe; bien pensant: ~ *Church*, l'Eglise *f* Orthodoxe.

orthography [ɔɚ'θɑgɹəfɪ] *n.* orthographe *f*. || **orthop(a)edics** [ˌɔɚθə'pijdɪks] *n. inv.* orthopédie *f*.

oscar ['ɑskɚ] *n.* oscar *m*, grand prix *m*.

oscillate ['ɑsɪˌlejt] *v. intr.* osciller; [Fig.] balancer, hésiter. || **oscillation** [ˌɑsɪ'lejʃən] *n.* oscillation *f*.

ossify ['ɑsɪˌfaj] *v. intr.* s'ossifier.

ostensible [ɑs'tɛnsɪbl̩] *adj.* ostensible; apparent. || **ostentation** [ˌɑstən'tej|ʃən] *n.* ostentation *f*. || **ostentatious** [-ʃəs] *adj.* ostentatoire, pompeux.

ostracize ['ɑstɹəˌsajz] *v. tr.* frapper (qqun) d'ostracisme.

ostrich ['ɑstɹɪʧ] *n.* autruche *f*.

OT, O.T. [= OLD TESTAMENT].

other [ʌðɚ] *adj.* autre: *the* ~ *day*, l'autre jour; *better than any* ~ *car*, mieux que toute autre voiture; *Have you read any* ~ *book(s)?*, Avez-vous lu un autre livre, d'autres livres?; *He has no* ~ *friend(s)*, Il n'a pas d'autres amis; *every* ~ *day*, tous les deux jours; *He ate the* ~ *five candies*, Il a mangé les cinq autres bonbons; *any solution* ~ *than that one*, toute solution autre que celle-là; *Skiing and* ~ *winter sports*, Le ski et autres sports d'hiver. || *pron.* autre; autrui: *Some were talking, the others were listening*, Les uns parlaient, les autres écoutaient; *Some were standing, others were sitting*, Certains se tenaient debout, d'autres étaient assis; *one on top of the* ~, l'un(e) sur l'autre; *they hate each* ~, *one another*, Ils se détestent l'un l'autre, les uns les autres; *I want three others*, [the same] J'en veux encore trois, [different] J'en veux trois autres; *I read in some book or* ~, Je l'ai lu dans un livre quelconque; *the faults of others* [= *other people*], les défauts d'autrui; *It was no* ~ *than John*, C'était Jean/lui-même, en personne/. || *adv.* autrement.

otherwise ['ʌðɚˌwajz] *adv.* autrement; à part cela: *I could not do* ~, Je ne saurais faire autrement; *He is noisy, but* ~ *a nice boy*, Il fait beaucoup de bruit, mais à part cela, c'est un gentil garçon. || *conj.* sinon; sans cela: *Come at once,* ~ *it will be too late*, Venez tout de suite, sinon il sera trop tard; *Thanks,* ~ *I'd have forgotten*, Merci, sans cela j'aurais oublié.

Ottawa ['ɑtəˌwɑ] *n.* [city] Ottawa, la ville d'Ottawa; [river] l'Outaouais *m*, la rivière Ottawa.

otter ['ɑtɚ] *n.* loutre *f*.

ought [ɔt] *v. aux.* **1.** [obligation] devoir; falloir: [gen. statement] *You* ~ *to study*, /Vous devez, on doit, il faut/étudier; [qualified statement] *I* ~ *to go (but . . .)*, Je devrais y aller (mais . . .); *I* ~ *not to have done this (but . . .)*, Je n'aurais pas dû faire cela (mais . . .). **2.** [advisability] devoir, falloir: [strong assertion] *You really* ~ *to see it*, Il faut vraiment que vous le voyiez; *You really* ~ *to have seen it*, /Il aurait vraiment fallu, Vous auriez vraiment dû/le voir; [weak assertion] *Perhaps you* ~ *to go and see him*, /Vous devriez peut-être aller, Il faudrait peut-être que vous alliez/le voir; *Perhaps you* ~ *to have asked him*, /Vous auriez peut-être dû, Il aurait peut-être fallu/le lui demander. **3.** [probability] devoir: *That* ~ *to do the trick*, /Cela devrait faire l'affaire, Je pense que cela fera l'affaire/.

ounce [awns] [*abr.* oz] *n.* once *f*: ~ *troy*, once *f* troy; *fluid* ~, once *f* liquide.

our [awɚ] *adj. poss.* notre, *pl.* nos. || **ours** *pron. poss.* (le, la) nôtre, (les) nôtres: *it is* ~, c'est/le, la/nôtre; [ownership] c'est à nous; [authorship] c'est de nous; *He is a friend of* ~, C'est un de nos amis, c'est un ami à nous. || †**ourself** [terme du style noble] *pron. sg.* nous (-même). || **ourselves** [awɚ'sɛlvz] *pron. ref.* nous-mêmes: **1.** [Emphasis] *We did it (by)* ~, Nous l'avons fait /nous-mêmes, tout seuls. **2.** *obj. ref.* nous: *We washed* ~, Nous nous sommes lavés; *We told* ~ *the truth*, Nous nous sommes dit la vérité.

oust [awst] *v. tr.* expulser; évincer (qqun).

out[1] [awt] *adv.* **1.** [with a verb of motion] dehors; sortir: *to rush* ~, se précipiter dehors; *to/go, come/* ~, sortir; *to run* ~, sortir en courant. [see also under such verbs]. **2.** [with a verb of activity] dehors, &c.: *to kick s.o.* ~, mettre qqun/dehors, à la porte/, /chasser, faire sortir/ qqun à coups de pieds; *to lean* ~ , se pencher au dehors; *to dine* ~ , dîner/dehors, au restaurant, &c./; *to hear s.o.* ~ , écouter qqun jusqu'au bout; *to be all talked* ~ , ne plus avoir la force de parler; *to speak* ~, parler clairement. [see also under such verbs]. **3.** [with 'to be']: . . . *is* ~ , [pers.] est sorti; [K.O.] est sans connaissance; [baseball] est hors jeu; [worker] est en grève; [political party] n'est plus au pouvoir; [tide] (la marée) est basse; [sun] il fait (du)soleil; [flower] est en fleur; [secret] est/connu, exposé/; [light, fire] est éteint; [book] vient de paraître; [school] est fini; *It is his day* ~ , C'est son jour de sortie; *He is $5* ~ , Il s'est trompé de cinq dollars, Il a perdu $5 (dans l'affaire); *That is* ~ *!*, C'est hors de question; *When school is* ~ , après l'école. **4.** [used alone]: *Out!*, Dehors!; *Out with it!*, Allez, dites-le!; *Out for lunch*, Parti déjeuner. **5.** cf. OUT OF. **6.** [other uses]: ~ *there*, là-bas; *He lives (a long) way* ~ *(in the suburbs)*, Il habite très loin (dans la banlieue); ~ *West*, dans l'ouest; *to go all* ~ , aller à toute vitesse; [Fig.] mettre tout en œuvre; *He is* ~ */after, for/sth.*, Il est à la recherche de qqch.; *That is* ~ *and away the best*, C'est de loin le meilleur; ~ *and* ~ , complètement. || *prép.* par: ~ *the/door, window/*, par la/porte, fenêtre. || *n.* excuse *f*, moyen *m* d'en sortir. || **out-and-out** [-n'awt] *adj.* vrai, intégral. || **out of** [-əv] *prep.* **1.** [with a verb of motion] de, &c.: *to/go, come/* ~ *the house*, sortir de la maison; *to take sth.* ~ *one's pocket*, sortir qqch. de sa poche, prendre qqch. dans sa poche; ~ *the/window, door*, par la /fenêtre, porte/; *to drink* ~ *a/glass, bottle*, boire/dans un verre, à (même) la bouteille. **2.** [beyond] hors de: ~ */danger, reach, sight, &c.*, hors de/danger, portée, vue, &c.; *to be* ~ *it*, en être sorti; être laissé à l'écart. [cf. also under nouns]. **3.** [because of] par; de: ~ *curiosity*, par curiosité; *He wept* ~ *joy*, Il pleura de joie. **4.** [among] sur; parmi: *two* ~ *(every) six*, deux sur six. **5.** de, en: *made* ~ *an old box*, fait d'une vieille boîte; *made* ~ *brick*, (fait)/de, en/briques. **6.** [without]: *to be (all)* ~ *sugar*, /ne plus avoir, manquer, être à court/de sucre. || **out-of-date** [-əv'dejt] *adj.* démodé, suranné, désuet. || **out-of-door** [-əv'dɔɚ] *adj.* cf. OUTDOOR. || **out of gear** [-əv'gijɚ] *adj.* [Auto., Mech.] débrayé; [Fig.] détraqué, dérangé, hors d'action. || **out-of-the-way** [-əvðə'wej] *adj.* isolé, écarté; peu commun, insolite.

out-[2] *prép.* indique **1.** l'éloignement: *outgoing*, sortant; **2.** un lieu éloigné: *outskirts*, lisière *f* (d'une forêt), faubourgs *mpl* (d'une ville); **3.** une augmentation ou une amélioration: *outsail*, *v. tr.* dépasser (à la voile). [☞ Dans ce dernier cas, où *out-* est un préfixe vivant, nous avons indiqué ce rapport entre préfixe et radical par une barre verticale. cf. UN-.]

out|balance [awt'bæləns] *v. tr.* [Fig.] l'emporter sur (qqch.).

outbid [ˌɑwt'bɪd], **outbid, outbid, outbidden** *v. tr.* surenchérir; [Fig.] renchérir sur.

outboard ['awtˌbɚd] *adj.* [Naut.] (moteur *m*) hors-bord *m.* || *adv.* [Naut.] hors bord, par-dessus bord.

outbreak [-ˌbɹejk] *n.* début *m*, commencement *m*; éruption *f* (volcanique); déchaînement *m*, explosion *f.*

outburst [-ˌbɚst] *n.* explosion *f*, éruption *f*; élan *m.*

outcast [-ˌkæst] *adj.* exclu, proscrit, déchu, banni. || *n.* hors-caste *m inv.*, paria *m*, proscrit *m.*

outclass [ˌɑwt'klæs] *v. tr.* surclasser.

outcome [-ˌkʌm] *n.* résultat *m*, dénouement *m*, issue *f*, conséquence *f.*

outcry [-ˌkɹaj] *n.* clameur *f.*

out|do [awt'duw], **outdid** [-'dɪd], **outdone** [-'dʌn] *v. tr.* surpasser (qqun); l'emporter (sur qqun).

outdoor ['awtˌdɔɚ] *adj.* (d') extérieur; (sport, jeu) de plein air. || **out|doors** [-z] *adv.* en plein air, (au) dehors. || *prép.*: ~ *of*, en dehors de. || *adj.* extérieur, du dehors; [Fam.] le plus haut, le plus large. || *n.* extérieur *m*, dehors *m*: *in the* ~ , à l'extérieur.

outer ['awtɚ] *adj.* du dehors, extérieur, externe. || **outermost** [-ˌmowst] *adj.* extérieur, le plus à l'extérieur; extrême.

outfit ['awtˌfɪt] *n.* équipement *m*, attirail *m*; trousse *f* (d'outils); [clothes] effets *mpl*; [Mil.] unité *f.* || *v. tr.* [-tt-] équiper.

outflow ['awtˌflow] *n.* écoulement *m* (d'un liquide, &c.).

outgoing ['awtˌgowɪŋ] *adj.* (train) en partance; [official] sortant. || **out|grow** [awt'|gɹow]. || **outgrew** [-'gɹuw]. || **outgrown** [-'gɹown] *v. tr.* devenir plus grand que (qqun, qqch.); dépasser en croissance; se défaire de (qqch.) avec le temps. || **outgrowth** ['awtˌgɹowθ] *n.* excroissance *f*; [Fig.] conséquence *f*, résultat *m.*

outing [-ɪŋ] *n.* excursion *f*, sortie *f*, promenade *f*: *to go for an* ~ , faire une sortie.

outlandish [ˌɑwt'lændɪʃ] *adj.* étrange; bizarre.
out|last [awt'læst] *v. tr.* survivre à.
outlaw ['awtˌlɔ] *n.* hors la loi *m*, proscrit *m.* || *v. tr.* mettre hors la loi, proscrire.
outlay [-ˌlej] *n.* débours *mpl*, dépenses *fpl.* || *v. tr.* **outlay, outlaid, outlaid** [ˌlejd] débourser, dépenser.
outlet [-ˌlɛt] *n.* sortie *f*, issue *f*; [Com.] débouché *m*; [Elec.] prise *f*; [liquor] débit *m.*
outline [-ˈlajn] *n.* contour *m*, silhouette *f*, profil *m*; [sketch] esquisse *f*, tracé *m*; sommaire *m*, aperçu *m*; [Fig.] les grandes lignes *fpl* (d'un plan, &c.). || *v. tr.* esquisser, tracer; ébaucher.
out|live [-'lɪv] *v. tr.* survivre à (qqun, qqch.).
outlook [-ˌlʊk] *n.* perspective *f*; [Fig.] point *m* de vue; vues *fpl.*
out|lying [-ˌlajɪŋ] *adj.* éloigné, écarté, isolé.
out|manœuvre [ˌawtmə'nuwvɚ] *v. tr.* déjouer (les plans de qqun). || **out|number** [ˌawt'nʌmbɚ] *v. tr.* l'emporter sur, surpasser en nombre; être plus nombreux que. || **out-of-date** ['awtəv'dejt] *adj.* suranné, dépassé, démodé.
outpost ['awtˌpowst] *n.* avant-poste *m.*
outpouring [ˌɑwt'pɔɚɪŋ] *n.* débordement *m*; [abuse] flot *m*; [heart] épanchement *m.*
output [-ˌpʊt] *n.* rendement *m*, débit *m*; énergie *f* produite; [Techn.] sortie *f* (sur un appareil de radio, &c.).
outrage [-ˌɹejʤ] *n.* outrage *m.* || *v. tr.* outrager, faire outrage à. || **outrageous** [ˌawt|'ɹejʤəs] *adj.* outrageux, outrageant, révoltant.
out|ran cf. OUTRUN. || **out|rank** [-'ɹæŋk] *v. tr.* dépasser . . . en grade; [Fig.] avoir priorité sur.
outright ['awtˌɹajt] *adj.* [manner] franc, direct; pur (et simple). || *adv.* sur le coup; franchement; [Com.] comptant.
out|run [ˌawt|'ɹʌn] **outran** [-'ɹæn] **outrun,** *v. tr.* dépasser (qqun) à la course, distancer (qqun).
out|sell [-'sɛl] *v. tr.* (se) vendre en plus grande quantité que; (se) vendre plus cher que (qqch.).
outset ['awtˌsɛt] *n.* commencement *m*, début *m*: *from the* ~, dès le début.
out|shine [awt|'ʃajn] **outshone** [-'ʃɑn], **outshone** *v. tr.* surpasser en éclat, éclipser.
outside [-'sajd] *adv.* dehors, à l'extérieur. || **outsider** [-'sajdɚ] *n.* étranger *m*; [arts] profane *m*; [Sport.] outsider *m.*
outskirts ['awtˌskɚts] *n.pl.* faubourgs *mpl*, périphérie *f*, approches *fpl* (d'une ville); lisière *f* (d'un bois).
out|smart [awt|'smɑɚt] *v. tr.* surpasser en finesse; être plus malin que (qqun).
outspoken [-'spowkn̩] *adj.* franc, explicite: *an* ~ *critic*, un critique indépendant, qui a son franc-parler. || **outspread** [-ˌspɹɛd] *adj.* étalé, déployé.
outstanding [-'stændɪŋ] *adj.* saillant, marquant; hors-pair *inv.*, excellent; [Com.] compte non réglé, impayé; en suspens.
outstretched [-ˌstɹɛtʃt] *adj.* étendu, déployé; [main] tendue.
outward ['awtwɚd] *adj.* en dehors, extérieur; [Fig.] apparent, -e. || **outward bound** [-ˌbawnd] [Naut.] en partance. || **outwardly** [-lɪ] *adv.* extérieurement, en apparence. || **outwards** [-z] *adv.* au dehors, vers le dehors.
out|wear [awt|'wɛɚ] **outwore** [-'wɔɚ] **outworn** [-'wɔɚn] || *v. tr.* user (qqch.). || *v. intr.* [of a thing] durer plus longtemps que (qqch.).
out|weigh [-'wej] *v. tr.* peser plus que (qqch., qqun) l'emporter en poids, valeur sur (qqch.).
out|wit [-'wɪt] *v. tr.* [-tt-] être plus malin que, damer le pion à (qqun); duper (qqun).
oval ['owvl̩] *n. & adj.* ovale *m.*
ovation [ow'vejʃən] *n.* ovation *f.*
oven ['ʌvən] *n.* four *m*; © fourneau *m.*
over[1] ['owvɚ] *prép.* **1.** [above] au-dessus de; [with motion] par-dessus: *There was a light* ~ *the door*, Il y avait une lumière au-dessus de la porte; *a door with a light* ~ *it*, une porte avec une lumière au-dessus; *Only the president was* ~ *him*, Il n'y avait que le président (qui était) au-dessus de lui; *He jumped* ~ *the fence*, Il a sauté par-dessus la barrière; *He pulled his shirt* ~ *his head*, Il tira sa chemise par-dessus la tête. **2.** [on top of] sur, par-dessus: *She laid the sheet* ~ *the bed*, Elle étendit le drap sur le lit; *He wore a sweater* ~ *his shirt*, Il portait un chandail/sur, par-dessus/sa chemise; *They painted* ~ *the varnish*, Ils ont peint par-dessus le vernis. **3.** [on the other side of] de l'autre côté de: ~ *the street*, de l'autre côté (de la rue), en face. **4.** [more than] au-dessus de; plus de: ~ *15 (years of age)*, au-dessus de 15 ans; *It cost* ~ *10 dollars*, Cela a coûté plus de 10 dollars. **5.** [during] pendant; depuis; *It happened* ~ *a 10-week period*, Cela s'est produit/pendant, au cours d'/une période de 10 semaines; *It has improved* ~ *the last 3 months*, Cela s'est

amélioré/depuis, au cours des/trois derniers mois. **6.** [all through] partout + *prep.*; *prep.* + tout: (*all*) ~ *Europe,* partout en, dans toute l'/Europe. **7.** [concerning] à propos de; au sujet de; sur, &c.: *to/laugh, cry, quarrel/* ~ *sth.,/* rire de, pleurer sur, se quereller au sujet de/qqch. **8.** ~ *the radio,* à la radio; ~ *the telephone,* au téléphone; *a bridge* ~ *the river,* un pont sur la rivière; *to be* ~ *an illness,* s'être remis d'une maladie; *to talk* ~ *coffee,* parler en prenant le café; ~ *and above a certain amount,* en plus d'un montant donné. || *adv.* **1.** fini: *The play is* ~ , La pièce est finie; *after winter is* ~ , après la fin de l'hiver. **2.** *How much is* ~ *?,* Combien en reste-t-il?; [Arith.] *and two* ~ , je retiens deux, [remainder] et il en reste deux. **3.** au-dessus: *Those 14 and* ~ , Tous ceux qui ont 14 ans et au-dessus. **4.** [with other words]: *all* ~ , partout; ~ (*again*), de nouveau; *twenty times* ~ , vingt fois de suite; ~ *and* ~ (*again*), mille fois, à coups répétés; *to turn sth.* ~ *and* ~ , tourner et retourner qqch.; ~ *against,* en face de; [Fig.]/comparé, à, auprès de/; ~ *there,* là-bas; *I'll be right* ~ , J'arrive tout de suite; *to have friends* ~ , inviter du monde; [Radio] *Over!,* A vous!; *Over and out!,* Terminé!

over [2] *pref.* [indique **1.** un excès: *overfull,* trop plein; **2.** une quantité ajoutée: *overtime,* heures *fpl* supplémentaires; **3.** un état de supériorité: *overlord,* suzerain *m*; *overpass,* un passage au-dessus: *overseas,* outre-mer.] ☞ *over-* est un préfixe vivant qui forme un grand nombre de mots nouveaux. Pour les mots où le rapport direct est senti entre le radical et le préfixe, on a séparé *over* par une barre verticale. cf. UN-.

overact [ˌowvɚ'ækt] *v. intr.* [Theat.] charger.

over-all ['owvɚˌɔl] *adj.* cf. OVERALL: ~ *measurements,* dimensions *fpl* hors tout; [Fig.] ~ *impression,* impression *f* générale. || **overalls** ['owvɚˌɔlz] *n.pl.* salopette *f,* tablier-blouse *m.* || **overbalance** [ˌowvɚ'bæləns] *v. tr.* peser plus que (qqch.), l'emporter sur (qqch.). || *v. intr.* [of a person] perdre l'équilibre; [of a thing] tomber, basculer. || **overbearing** [-'bɛərɪŋ] *adj.* arrogant, autoritaire, arbitraire.

overboard ['owvɚˌbɔɚd] *adv.* par-dessus bord: *Man* ~ *!,* Un homme à la mer!

overcame cf. OVERCOME.

overcast ['owvɚˌkæst] *adj.* [of weather] nuageux; (temps) couvert, sombre. || [prét. & pp. **overcast**] *v. tr.* obscurcir, couvrir (le ciel) de nuages, assombrir.

over|charge [-'ʧɑɚʤ] *n.* surcharge *f*; majoration *f* (des prix). || *v. tr. & intr.* **1.** surcharger (*with,* de). **2.** demander un prix excessif; faire payer trop cher; [Fam.] écorcher.

overcoat [-ˌkowt] *n.* pardessus *m*; [Mil.] capote *f.*

overcome [-'kʌm] **overcame** [-'kejm] **overcome** *v. tr.* triompher de, surmonter (ses craintes); vaincre (un obstacle); [Fig.] accablé (de soucis): ~ *with emotion,* étouffé d'émotion.

over|confidence [ˌowvɚ|'kɑnfɪdəns] *n.* témérité *f.* || **over|crowd** [-'kɹawd] *v. tr.* surcharger (un véhicule, un espace); surpeupler (une région). || **over|crowded** [-əd] *adj.* [espace] bondé; [pays] surpeuplé. || **over|do** [-'duw] **overdid** [-'dɪd] **overdone** [-'dʌn] *v. tr.* exagérer (un rapport, &c.); (faire) trop cuire (une viande): *to* ~ *o.s.,* se surmener. || **overdraught** ['owvɚˌdɹæft] *n.* [Bank] découvert *m*; solde *m* débiteur. || **over|draw** [ˌowvɚ'dɹɔ] **overdrew** [-'dɹuw] **overdrawn** [-'dɹɔn] *v. tr.* [Bank] tirer un chèque sans provision.

over|drive [-'dɹajv] **overdrove** [-'dɹowv] **overdriven** *v. tr.* surmener; [Fam.] éreinter (une bête). || *n.* [Auto.] surmultiplication *f.* || **over|due** [-'djuw] *adj.* en retard; [Com.] échu; arriéré, en souffrance. || **over|eat** [-'ijt], **overate** [-'ejt], **overeaten** [-'ijtn̩] *v. intr.* trop manger; ~ *o.s.,* faire des excès de table. || **over|-estimate** [-'ɛstɪmejt] *v. tr.* surestimer. || **over|feed** [-'fijd], **overfed, overfed** [-'fɛd] *v. tr.* suralimenter. || *v. tr. & pron.* trop manger.

overflow ['owvɚˌflow] *n.* trop-plein *m*; inondation *f*; débordement *m.* || *v. intr.* [-'flow] déborder; surabonder (*with,* de/en). || *v. tr.* inonder.

over|grow [ˌowvɚ'gɹow] **overgrew** [-'gɹuw] **overgrown** [-'gɹown] *v. tr.* [of moss, plants] recouvrir (une muraille); [of weeds] envahir (un jardin): *to* ~ *o.s.,* grandir trop vite. || **over|grown** *adj.* couvert (*with,* de); démesuré, énorme. || **over|growth** ['owvɚˌgɹowθ] *n.* croissance *f*/trop rapide, excessive/.

overhang [-ˌhæŋ] *n.* saillie *f,* surplomb *m,* porte-à-faux *m inv.* || *v. tr.* **overhang** [ˌowvɚ|'hæŋ], **overhung** [-hʌŋ] surplomber (qqch.), faire saillie sur; [Fig.] menacer, planer sur. || **overhanging** [-'hæŋɪŋ] *adj.* surplombant, en porte-à-faux.

overhaul [ˈowvɚˌhɔl] *n.* remise *f* en état (d'un mécanisme): *a complete* ~, une révision complète. ‖ *v. tr.* [ˌowvɚˈhɔl] remettre (un mécanisme) en état; [Naut.] rattraper; [Fig.] réexaminer (des idées, des opinions).

overhead [ˈowvɚˌhɛd] *n.* frais *mpl* généraux. ‖ *adj.* (au-dessus, en haut), élevé; aérien, surélevé: ~ *railway*, métro *m* aérien. ‖ *adv.* en haut, en l'air, au-dessus de la tête.

overhear [ˌowvɚˈhijɚ], **overheard, overheard** *v. tr.* surprendre (une conversation), entendre par hasard.

over|heat [-ˈhijt] *v. tr.* surchauffer.

overhung cf. OVERHANG.

overjoy [ˌowvɚˈʤoj] *v. tr.* remplir (qqun) de joie.

overland [ˈowvɚˌlænd] *adj.* & *adv.* par voie de terre.

overlap [ˌowvɚ|ˈlæp] *v. intr.* & *tr.* **[-pp-]** chevaucher (qqch.), recouvrir (qqch.) en partie; dépasser, empiéter sur (qqch.) ‖ *n.* chevauchement *m*, recouvrement *m*, empiètement *m*. ‖ **overlay** [-ˈlej], **overlaid, overlaid** [-ˈlejd] *v. tr.* (re)couvrir (*with*, de). ‖ *n.* couche *f*, placage *m*.

overleaf [-ˈlijf] *adv.* (voir) au verso; TSVP.

over|load [-ˈlowd] *n.* surcharge *f*. ‖ *v. tr.* surcharger; surmener (une machine).

overlook [-ˈluk] *v. tr.* oublier, négliger; laisser passer, fermer les yeux sur (qqch.); donner sur, avoir vue sur.

over|much [ˈowvɚˈmʌʧ] *adj.* excessif, trop de. *adv.* à l'excès, outre-mesure.

overnight [ˈowvɚˈnajt] *adj.* de la veille: *an* ~ *bag*, un sac de nuit; *an* ~ *triumph*, un triomphe du jour ..u lendemain. ‖ *adv.* la veille (au soir); pendant la nuit: *to stay* ~, passer la nuit.

overpass [ˈowvɚˌpæs] *n.* voie *f* surélevée; passage *m* en dessus; pont-route *m*.

overpower [ˌowvɚˈpawɚ] *v. tr.* subjuguer, maîtriser (qqun, qqch.). ‖ **overran** cf. OVERRUN. ‖ **over|rate** [-ˈɹejt] *v. tr.* estimer trop haut; [Pej.] surfaire; [taxes] surtaxer. ‖ **over|reach** [-ˈɹijʧ] *v. intr.* s'étendre jusqu'à; dépasser ses limites. ‖ *v. tr.* [Fig.] tromper. ‖ **override** [-ˈɹajd], **overrode** [-ˈɹowd], **overridden** [-ˈɹɪdn̩] piétiner; surmener; [Fig., objections] passer outre à, ne pas tenir compte de. ‖ **overrule** [-ˈɹuwl] *v. tr.* **1.** †gouverner. **2.** rejeter (une demande), annuler (un texte de loi).

overrun [-ˈɹʌn], **overran** [-ˈɹæn], **overrun** *v. tr.* envahir: *Vines had* ~ *the old walls*, Les vignes vierges avaient envahi les vieux murs; [mostly of liquids] inonder, se répandre; dépasser (la limite). ‖ *v. intr.* [of liquids] déborder.

oversea(s) [ˈowvɚˌsijz] *adv.* outre-mer; → [give name of continent implied]: en Afrique, &c. ‖ *adj.* d'outre-mer.

oversee [ˌowvɚˈsij], **oversaw** [-ˈsɔ], **overseen** [-ˈsijn] *v. tr.* surveiller. ‖ **overseer** [ˈowvɚˌsijɚ] *n.* surveillant *m*, inspecleur *m*, -trice *f*.

overshoe(s) [ˈowvɚˌʃuwz] *npl.* snow-boots *mpl*, couvre-chaussure(s) *mpl*; © pardessus *mpl*. ‖ **oversight** [ˈowvɚˌsajt] *n.* **1.** oubli *m*, omission *f*. **2.** surveillance *f*. ‖ **over|stay** [ˌowvɚ|ˈstej] *v. intr.* & *tr.* prolonger son séjour: *to* ~ *one's welcome*, s'imposer au-delà des limites de l'hospitalité. ‖ **over|step** [-ˈstɛp] **[-pp-]** *v. tr.* dépasser; *to* ~ *the mark*, /passer, outrepasser/les bornes.

overt [ˈowvɚt] *adj.* évident, manifeste, → non déguisé.

overtake [-ˈtejk], **overtook**, [-tuk], **overtaken** [-ˈtejkn̩] *v. tr.* rattraper, rejoindre; doubler (une auto); [misfortune] atteindre.

overthrow [ˈowvɚˌθɹow] *n.* renversement *m*; ruine *f*. ‖ **overthrow** [ˌowvɚ|ˈθɹow], **overthrew** [-ˈθɹuw], **overthrown** [-ˈθɹown] *v. tr.* renverser, ruiner, abattre (un régime politique, un tyran).

overtime [ˈowvɚ|ˌtajm] *n.* heures *fpl* supplémentaires. ‖ *adv. to work* ~, faire des heures supplémentaires. ‖ **overtook** cf. OVERTAKE. ‖ **overtone** [-ˌtown] *n.* [Mus.] harmonique *m*.

overture [ˈowvɚʧɚ] *n.* ouverture *f*.

overturn [ˌowvɚˈtɚn] *v. tr.* renverser, faire chavirer. ‖ *v. intr.* se renverser; [Naut.] chavirer.

over|weight [ˈowvɚˌwejt] *n.* excédent *m* de poids. ‖ *adj.* trop lourd, au-dessus du poids normal. ‖ *v. tr.* surcharger.

overwhelm [ˌowvɚ|ˈwɛlm] *v. tr.* submerger, écraser; [Fig.] accabler (de, *with*, *by*). ‖ **overwhelming** [-ˈwɛlmɪŋ] *adj.* accablant, irrésistible: *an* ~ *majority*, une majorité écrasante.

over|work [-ˈwɚk] *v. tr.* surmener, surcharger (qqun) de travail.

owe [ow] *v. tr.* devoir, être redevable de (qqch. à qqun, *sth. to s.o.*): *How much do I* ~ *you?*, Combien vous dois-je? ‖*v.intr.* avoir des dettes, devoir de l'argent: *this is owing*, cette somme est due. ‖ **owing to** [ˈowɪŋˌtuw] *prep. loc.* grâce à, [pej.] à cause de, en raison de.

owl [awl] *n.* hibou *m*, chouette *f*.

own[1] [own] *v. tr.* **1.** posséder (qqch.), avoir

(qqch.) à soi; avoir/la propriété, la possession/de (qqch.). **2.** reconnaître (qqch. comme sien); avouer (sa culpabilité); réclamer (un droit).

own² *adj.* à soi, propre [☞ or simply a poss. *adj.*]: *his ~ family . . .*, sa propre famille, même sa famille . . . ; *my ~ car*, ma propre voiture, ma voiture à moi; *at his ~ expense*, à ses frais; *He makes his ~ wine*, Il fait son vin lui-même. || *n.* à moi, à toi, à soi, &c.; le mien, le tien, le sien, &c.: *This is my ~*, C'est à moi, C'est le mien; *to make . . . one's ~*, faire (une théorie) sienne, faire (un argument) sien; *to hold one's ~*, maintenir ses positions; *to come into one's ~*, rentrer en possession de ses biens; [Fam.] *to be on one's ~*, se débrouiller tout seul.

owner ['ownər] *n.* propriétaire *m*, possesseur *m.* || **ownership** [-ʃɪp] *n.* propriété *f*, possession *f.*

ox [ɑks] *pl.* **oxen** [-ŋ] *n.* bœuf *m.*

oxfords ['ɑksfərdz] *n.* [shoes] (chaussures) richelieus *mpl.*

oxide ['ɑksajd] *n.* [Chem.] oxyde *m.* || **oxidize** ['ɑksɪˌdajz] *v. tr.* oxyder.

Oxonian [ˌɑks'ownɪən] *adj.* d'Oxford.

oxygen ['ɑksɪʤən] *n.* [Chem.] oxygène *m.*

oyster ['ojstər] *n.* huître *f*: © *~ party*, partie *f* d'huîtres; *~ bed*, banc *m* d'huîtres; *~ shell*, coquille *f* d'huître.

oysterplant [-ˌplænt] *n.* salsifis *m.*

oz. *pl.* **ozs.** [= ounces] onces avoirdupoids.

P

P, p [pij] *pl.* **P's p,'s** [letter] (le) P *m.*

Pa. [ˌpij'ej] [= Pennsylvania].

pace [pejs] *n.* pas *m*; [speed] allure *f*, train *m.* || *v. intr.* aller au pas; [of a horse] aller l'amble: *to quicken one's ~*, allonger le pas, doubler le pas; *to keep ~ with sth. or s.o.*, marcher du même pas que qqun, marcher de pair avec qqun. || *v. tr.*: *to ~ up and down*, arpenter (une pièce).

pacific [pə'sɪfɪk] *adj.* pacifique, paisible. || **Pacific** *n.* le Pacifique, l'Océan *m* Pacifique. || **pacification** [ˌpæsɪfɪ'kejʃən] *n.* pacification *f*; apaisement *m* (des esprits). || **pacify** ['pæsɪˌfaj] *v. tr.* pacifier (un pays); apaiser (l'opinion), calmer (qqun).

pack [pæk] *n.* paquet *m*; [Mil.] sac *m*, paquetage *m*; ballot *m*; [Naut.] flotte *f* (de sous-marins); meute *f* (de loups, de chiens); jeu *m* (de cartes); banquise *f*: *~ horse*, bête *f* de somme. || *v. tr.* empaqueter, emballer (de la marchandise); faire (une valise, une malle) remplir; bâter (une bête de somme): *the room was packed*, la salle était comble. || *v. intr.* faire ses bagages: *to ~ up and leave*, plier bagages; *to send s.o. packing*, envoyer promener qqun. || **package** [-əʤ] *n.* [US] paquet *m*; colis *m.* cf. (Br., Can.) parcel; *~ deal*, forfait *m*; → tout compris; *~ tour*, excursion *f* (accompagnée). || **packer** [-ər] *n.* emballeur *m*; *meat packers*, conserverie *f.*

packet [-ət] *n.* paquet *m*; [Naut.] paquebot *m.* || **packing** [-ɪŋ] *n.* empaquetage *m*; emballage *m*; rembourrage *m*: *~ case n.* caisse *f* d'emballage.

pact [pækt] *n.* pacte *m*; contrat *m*; accord *m*; convention *f.*

pad [pæd] *n.* bloc *m*, bloc-notes *m*; bourrelet *m*; [wad] tampon *m.* || *v. tr.* **[-dd-]** rembourrer; matelasser; ouater. || **padded** [-əd] *adj.* rembourré; matelassé; ouaté. || **padding** [-ɪŋ] *n.* rembourrage *m*; bourre *f*; [style] remplissage *m.*

paddle ['pædl] *n.* pagaie *f*; aube *f* (d'une roue); palette *f.* || *v. intr.* pagayer; ramer; [wade] patauger. || *v. tr.*: *to ~ one's own canoe*, conduire sa barque, arriver par soi-même. || **paddle steamer** [-ˌstijmər] *n.* [Naut.] vapeur *m*/à roues, à aubes/.

paddock ['pædək] *n.* [at races] paddock *m*, pesage *m*; [pasture] enclos *m.*

padlock ['pædˌlɑk] *n.* cadenas *m.* || *v. tr.* cadenasser.

Padre ['pædɹej] *n.* [Rel.] aumônier *m* militaire, © Padre *m.*

pagan ['pejgən] *n. & adj.* païen. || **paganism** [-ɪzm] *n.* paganisme *m.*

page[1] [pejʤ] *n.* page *f*: © *the yellow pages* (*Telephone Directory*), les pages jaunes, cf. [Fr.] le Bottin. ‖ *v. tr.* paginer (un document).

page[2] *n.* page *m*; chasseur *m* (d'hôtel). ‖ *v. tr.* envoyer chercher (qqun) par un chasseur.

pageant [ˈpæʤənt] *n.* parade *f*; spectacle *m*; manifestation *f*, revue *f* (historique). ‖ **pageantry** [-ɹɪ] *n.* pompe *f*; faste(s) *m* (*pl*).

paid cf. PAY.

pail [pejl] *n.* seau *m*.

pain [pejn] *n.* douleur *f*, souffrance *f*; mal *m* (physique); [mental, punishment] peine *f*: *to be in* ~, → souffrir; *on* (*or under*) ~ *of* (*death, &c.*), sous peine de (mort, &c.); *for one's pains*, pour ses frais, pour sa peine; *to be at pains, to take pains to do sth.*, se donner du mal pour faire qqch., mettre un soin infini à faire qqch. ‖ *v. tr.* [physical] faire souffrir, faire mal à; [mental] faire de la peine à: *It pains me to . . .*, Il m'en coûte de . . . ‖ **painful** [-fḷ] *adj.* douloureu|x, -se; pénible; laborieu|x, -se. ‖ **painfully** [-fḷɪ] *adv.* douloureusement; péniblement; laborieusement. ‖ **painless** [-ləs] *adj.* indolore, sans douleur; [mental] sans peine. ‖ **painstaking** [-ˌztejkɪŋ] *adj.* [of a person] [Fig.] appliqué; laborieux; qui se donne de la peine; [work] soigné.

paint [pejnt] *n.* peinture *f*; *pl.* couleurs *fpl*: the paintwork [coll.], les peintures (d'une maison, &c.); *Wet* ~, → Attention à la peinture. ‖ *v. tr.* peindre; © peinturer, badigeonner (un mur). ‖ **painter** [-ɚ] *n.* peintre *m*. ‖ **painting** [-ɪŋ] *n.* [Art.] peinture *f*.

pair [pɛɚ] *n.* paire *f*; couple *m*. ‖ *v. tr.*: *to* ~ *off*, assortir (des personnes); [Fig.] marier (des personnes). ‖ *v. intr.* s'accoupler; s'apparier.

pajamas [pəˈʤæməs] *n.* pyjama *m*.

Pakistan [ˈpækɪˌstæn] *n.* le Pakistan. ‖ **Pakistani** [-ɪ] *adj.* pakistanais, du Pakistan.

pal [pæl] *n.* copain *m*, copine *f*.

palace [ˈpæləs] *n.* palais *m*.

palatable [ˈpælətəbḷ] *adj.* savoureux. ‖ **palate** [ˈpælət] *n.* palais *m*.

pale[1] [pejl] *adj.* pâle; blême; [of light] blafard, -e. ‖ *v. intr.* pâlir. ‖ *v. tr.* pâlir; faire pâlir: *He went* ~ *as death*, Il devint pâle comme un mort.

pale[2] *n.* pieu *m*; enceinte *f*; limites *fpl*; [punishment] pal *m*; *to be beyond the* ~, être au ban de la société.

paleness [-nəs] *n.* pâleur *f*.

Palestine [ˈpæləsˌtajn] *n.* la Palestine.

palisade [ˈpælɪˌsejd] *n.* palissade *f*.

pall[1] [pɔl] *n.* poêle *m*, drap *m* (mortuaire); [Fig.] voile *m* (épais); [R.C.] pale *f*.

pall[2] *v. intr.* devenir fade (*on*, pour), s'affadir: *It palls on one*, → On s'en dégoûte.

pallid [ˈpælɪd] *adj.* pâle; [face] blême; [light] blafard. ‖ **pallor** [ˈpælɚ] *n.* pâleur *f*.

palm[1] [pɑm] *n.* [branch] palme *f*; [tree] palmier *m*: *Palm Sunday*, dimanche *m* des Rameaux: *to bear the* ~, remporter la palme.

palm[2] *n.* paume *f* (de la main). ‖ *v. tr.* escamoter (une carte): *to* ~ *off* (*a bad coin, &c.*) *on* (*s.o.*), refiler (une fausse pièce) à (qqun). ‖ **palmy** [-ɪ] *adj.* glorieu|x, -se; heureu|x, -se: ~ *days*, jours *mpl* heureux.

palpable [ˈpælpəbḷ] *adj.* palpable; [Fig.] évident, manifeste.

palpitate [ˈpælpɪˌtejt] *v. intr.* palpiter. ‖ **palpitation** [ˌpælpɪˈtejʃən] *n.* palpitation *f*.

palsied [ˈpɔlzɪd] *adj.* paralytique, atteint(e) de paralysie.

palsy [ˈpɔlzɪ] *n.* paralysie *f*. cf. PARALYSIS.

paltry [ˈpɔltɹɪ] *adj.* pauvre, mesquin; [Pers.] chétif, un gringalet; [excuse] faible: *Let's not argue about a* ~ *five cents*, Ne discutons pas pour cinq malheureux cents.

pamper [ˈpæmpɚ] *v. tr.* choyer, gâter, flatter (la vanité).

pamphlet [ˈpæmflət] *n.* [×] brochure *f*; [tract] pamphlet *m*.

pan [pæn] *n.* casserole *f*; cuvette *f*: *frying* ~, poêle *f*.

panacea [ˌpænəˈsijə] *n.* panacée *f*.

Panama [ˈpænəˌmɑ] *n.* Panama *m*: *in, to*/~, au P.; ~ *city*, Panama; *the* ~ *canal*, le canal de Panama.

Pan-American [ˌpænəˈmɛəɪkən] *adj.* panaméricain: ~ *Union*, l'Union *f* panaméricaine.

pancake [ˈpænˌkejk] *n.* [Cul.] crêpe *f*.

pander [ˈpændɚ] *v. intr.*: *to* ~ *to*, se prêter à.

pane [pejn] *n.* carreau *m*; vitre *f*.

panel [ˈpænḷ] *n.* panneau *m*; lambris *m*; tableau *m*; liste *f* (de noms, de personnes); groupe *m* de discussion. ‖ *v. tr.* [-ll-] diviser (un mur, &c.) en panneaux; lambrisser (une pièce).

pang [pæŋ] *n.* angoisse *f*, vive douleur *f*.

panhandle [ˈpænˌhændḷ] *v. intr.* mendier. ‖ **panhandler** [-ɚ] *n.* mendigot *m*, vagabond *m*.

panic [ˈpænɪk] *n.* panique *f*; terreur *f* (folle): ~ *-stricken*, frappé de panique, terrifié. || **panicky** [-ɪ] *adj.* affolé, qui s'affole facilement; [report] alarmiste.

panorama [ˌpænə'ɹæmə] *n.* panorama *m.*

pansy ['pænzɪ] *n.* [Bot.] pensée *f.*

pant [pænt] *v. intr.* panteler, haleter: *to ~ for sth.*, aspirer à, soupirer après/qqch.

panther ['pænθɚ] *n.* [Zool.] panthère *f.*

panting ['pæntɪŋ] *n.* palpitation *f* (du cœur); essoufflement *m.* || *adj.* pantelant; palpitant.

pantry ['pæntɹɪ] *n.* © paneterie *f*; [Fr.] office *m*, dépense *f.*

pants [pænts] *n.pl.* [Fam.] pantalon *m*; [Br.] caleçon *m.*

papa ['pɑpə] *n.* papa *m.*

papacy ['pejpɪəsɪ] *n.* [Rel.] papauté *f.* || **papal** [-l̩] *adj.* papal.

paper ['pejpɚ] *n.* papier *m*; document *m*; article *m*; [news] journal *m*; [assignment] devoir *m*; [learned] communication *f*, mémoire *m*: *~ clip*, trombone *m*; *~ work*, [Pej.] paperasserie *f*, paperasse *f.* || *v. tr.* garnir (qqch) de papier; tapisser (un mur). || **paper mill** [-ˌmɪl] *n.* papeterie *f.*

par [pɑɚ] *n.* pair *m*, égalité *f*; [average] moyenne *f*: *at ~*, au pair, à égalité; *His generosity is on a ~ with his willingness*, Sa générosité n'a d'égal que sa bonne volonté; *His performance was below ~*, Son rendement était médiocre, au-dessous de la moyenne; *to feel below ~*, ne pas être/en train, dans son assiette/.

parable ['pæɚəbl̩] *n.* parabole *f.*

parabola [pɚ'æbələ] *n.* parabole *f.*

parachute ['pæɚəˌʃuwt] *n.* parachute *m.* || *v. intr.* sauter en parachute. || *v. tr.* parachuter (des vivres, &c.). || **parachutist** [-ɪst] *n.* parachutiste *m/f.*

parade [pɚ'ejd] *n.* parade *f*; procession *f*; cortège *m*; défilé *m*: *~ ground*, place *f* d'armes; *ceremonial ~*, prise *f* d'armes. || *v. intr.* parader, défiler. || *v. tr.* faire parade de (qqch.): [Mil.] faire l'inspection de troupes, faire défiler des troupes.

paradise ['pæɚəˌdajs] *n.* paradis *m.*

paradox ['pæɚəˌdɑks] *n.* paradoxe *m.*

paraffin ['pæɚəfɪn] *n.* [Chem.] pétrole *m*; [Med.] paraffine *f.*

paragon ['pæɚəˌgɑn] *n.* parangon *m* (de vertu), modèle *m.*

paragraph ['pæɚəˌgɹæf] *n.* paragraphe *m*; [law] alinéa *m.* || *v. tr.* diviser (un texte) en paragraphes.

Paraguay ['pæɚəˌgwej] *n.* le Paraguay *m*: *~ tea*, thé du Paraguay, maté *m.*

parallel ['pæɚəˌlɛl] *adj.* parallèle; pareil, -le; semblable (à, *with*): *to run ~ with*, être parallèle à. || *n.* parallèle *m/f*, ligne *f* parallèle; [Fig.] comparaison *f*; équivalent *m*: *This situation is without ~ in recent history*, → Cet état de choses n'a jamais eu son pareil dans l'histoire contemporaine. || *v. tr.* [-ll-] mettre (qqun, qqch.) en parallèle (avec qqun, qqch., *with s.o., sth.*); comparer (qqun, qqch.) à (qqun, qqch.). || *v. intr.* être semblable (à qqun, qqch., *with s.o., sth.*).

paralyse ['pæɚəˌlajz] *v. tr.* paralyser. || **paralysis** [pə'ɹæləsɪs] *n.* paralysie *f.*

paramount ['pæɚəˌmawnt] *adj.* capital; suprême; vital: *of ~ importance*, d'une importance capitale.

paraphernalia [ˌpæɚəfə'nejljə] *n.pl.* attirail *m*, [Fam.] barda *m.*

paraphrase [ˌpæɚə'fɹejz] *n.* paraphrase *f.* || *v. tr.* paraphraser.

parasite ['pæɚəˌsajt] *n.* parasite *m*; [of pers.] pique-assiette *m.*

parasol ['pæɚəˌsɑl] *n.* parasol *m* ombrelle *f.*

paratrooper [ˌpæɚə'tɹuwpɚ] *n.* [Mil.] para(chutiste) *m.*

parcel ['pɑɚsl̩] *n.* colis *m*; [lot] lot *m*, parcelle *f*; portion *f*: *postal ~*, colis postal; *~ post*, service *m* des colis postaux; *~ of land*, parcelle *f* de terrain. || *v. tr.* [-ll-] morceler (un terrain); diviser, séparer en portions; répartir.

parch [pɑɚtʃ] *v. tr.* dessécher; [cereals] griller: *to be parched (with thirst)*, mourir de soif.

parchment [-mənt] *n.* parchemin *m.*

pardon ['pɑɚdn̩] *n.* pardon *m*; [criminal] grâce *f*: *to/give, grant/ ~ (for sins)*, donner l'absolution; *I beg your ~!*, (Je vous demande) pardon!, [question] Plaît-il?, Pardon? || *v. tr.* pardonner (qqch.) à (qqun); gracier.

pare [pɛɚ] *v. tr.* rogner; [apples] peler; [books] ébarber: *to ~ down expenses*, réduire les frais.

parent ['pɛɚənt] *n.* père *m*; mère *f*; *pl.* parents *mpl* [au sens étroit]: *~ -teacher association*, association de parents et maîtres. || *adj.* -mère: *~ language*, langue-mère *f.* || **parentage** [-ədʒ] *n.* extraction *f*; origine *f*; naissance *f*; famille *f.* || **parental** [pɚ'ɛntl̩] *adj.* des parents; du père; de la mère; paternel, maternel.

parenthes|is [pɚ'ɛnθəs|ɪs] *pl.* **-es** [-ijz] *n.* parenthèse *f.*

parish ['pæɚɪʃ] [Rel.] *n.* paroisse *f*; [Admin.] commune *f*: *~ school*, école *f* paroissiale. || **parishioner** [pɚ'ɪʃənɚ] *n.* paroissien *m*, -ne *f.*

Parisian [pə'ɹɪʒən] *adj.* parisien, -ne; de

Paris. *n.* Parisien, -ne; [Arg.] Parigot *m.*

parity ['pæərɪtɪ] *n.* égalité *f*; [Fin.] parité *f.*

park [pɑək] *n.* parc *m.* ‖ *v. tr.* parquer; garer (une auto); stationner; enclore (un troupeau). ‖ *v. intr.* stationner. ‖ **parking** [-ɪŋ] *n.* stationnement *m*, parcage *m*: *~ place*, parc *m*, aire *f*/de stationnement; *no ~*, stationnement interdit; *~ meter*, compteur *m* de stationnement, © parcomètre *m.* ‖ **parkway** [-ˌwej] *n.* autoroute *f*, route *f* panoramique.

parley ['pɑəlɪ] *n.* pourparlers *mpl*, conférence *f.* ‖ *v. tr.* engager des pourparlers, des négociations; parlementer (avec qqun).

parliament ['pɑəlɪmənt] *n.* parlement *m*: *the Houses of Parliament*, le Parlement, les Chambres *fpl*; © *~ Hill*, (la) colline parlementaire. ‖ **parliamentarian** [ˌpɑəlɪ|mən'tɛəɪən] *n.* membre *m* du parlement, parlementaire *m*, homme *m* politique. ‖ **parliamentary** [-'mɛntəɪ] *adj.* parlementaire.

parlour ['pɑələ] *n.* (petit) salon *m*, parloir *m* (de couvent, collège): *beauty ~*, salon *m* de coiffure; *~ games*, jeux *mpl* de société; *~ car*, wagon-salon *m.*

parochial [pə'ɹowkɪəl] *adj.* paroissial; communal; [Pej.] provincial: *~ school*, école/paroissiale, séparée.

parody ['pæərədɪ] *n.* parodie *f*; [artistic] pastiche *m.* [Fig.] travestissement *m* (de justice). ‖ *v. tr.* parodier, pasticher.

parole [pə'ɹowl] *n.* parole *f* (d'honneur): *to be put on ~*, être libéré/sous surveillance, conditionnellement/. ‖ *v. tr.* libérer conditionnellement.

parrot ['pæərət] *n.* perroquet *m.* ‖ *v. tr.* [-tt-] répéter (qqch.) comme un perroquet; rabâcher (une histoire).

parry ['pæəɪ] *n.* parade *f* (d'escrime, de boxe). ‖ *v. tr.* parer, éviter, détourner: [Fig.] *to ~ a question*, éluder une question.

parsimonious [ˌpɑəsɪ'mownɪəs] *adj.* parcimonieux; [Fam.] regardant.

parsley ['pɑəslɪ] *n.* persil *m.*

parsnip ['pɑəsnɪp] *n.* panais *m.*

parson ['pɑəsən] *n.* [R.C.] curé *m*; [Prot.] pasteur *m.* ‖ **parsonage** [-əʤ] *n.* [Prot.] presbytère *m.*

part [pɑət] *n.* **1.** partie *f*: *the parts of speech*, les parties du discours; *in ~ (s)*, en partie; par endroits; *to/be, form/ ~ of*, faire partie (intégrante) de; *in great ~*, en grande partie; *the greater ~ of*, la/plus grande, majeure/partie de. **2.** [Share] part *f*: *for my ~*, pour ma part; *on the ~ of*, de la part de. **3.** [Theat.] rôle *m*: *to play a ~ in*, jouer un rôle dans [also Fig.]; *to have no ~ in*, n'y être pour rien; *to take ~ (in)*, prendre part (à). **4.** [side] parti *m*: *to take s.o.'s ~*, prendre parti pour qqun. **5.** région *f*: *What ~ of Canada are you from?*, De quelle région du Canada êtes-vous?; *in these parts*, dans ces parages; *in all parts of Canada*, partout au Canada; *all parts of the world*, tous les/pays, coins/du monde. **6.** [Tech.] pièce *f*: *spare ~*, pièce/détachée, de rechange. **7.** [hair] raie *f.* ‖ *v. tr.* séparer, diviser (en, *in*; de, *from*); [hair] se faire une raie: *to ~ company (with s.o.)*, se séparer (de qqun). ‖ *v. intr.* [things] se diviser, se séparer; [pers.] se quitter, se séparer; [road] diverger; [rope] rompre: *to ~ from s.o.*, quitter, se séparer de/qqun; *to ~ with sth.*, se défaire de qqch.

partake [ˌpɑə|'tejk], **partook** [-'tʊk], **partaken** [-'tejkn̩] *v. intr.* partager (qqch., *of sth.*); prendre part, participer (à qqch., *in*, *of sth.*); tenir (à la fois) de; [eating] prendre (qqch., un repas).

partial ['pɑəʃəl] *adj.* partiel, partial; qui a un penchant (pour, *to*, *towards*); injuste (envers, *to*, *towards*). ‖ **partiality** [ˌpɑəʃɪ'ælɪtɪ] *n.* partialité *f*; penchant *m* (pour, *to*, *towards*). ‖ **partially** ['pɑəʃɪlɪ] *adv.* partiellement, en partie; partialement, avec partialité.

participant [ˌpɑə'tɪsɪ|pənt] *n.* & *adj.* participant (*m*). ‖ **participate** [-ˌpejt] *v. intr.* participer, s'associer, (*in*, à). ‖ **participation** [ˌpɑətɪsɪ'pejʃən] *n.* participation *f.* ‖ **participle** ['pɑətɪsɪpl̩] *n.* participe *m.*

particle ['pɑətɪkəl] *n.* particule *f*; parcelle *f.*

particular [pə'tɪkjələ] *adj.* particuli|er, -ère; spécial; [of a person] difficile, méticuleu|x, -se. ‖ *n.pl.* détails *mpl*; particularités *fpl.* ‖ **in particular** *loc.* en particulier, particulièrement. ‖ **particularly** [-lɪ] *adv.* particulièrement, en particulier; spécialement; surtout.

parting [pɑətɪŋ] *n.* séparation *f*; raie *f* (des cheveux).

partisan ['pɑətɪ|ˌzæn] *n.* & *adj.* partisan *m* (en faveur) de; (par ext.) membre d'un parti; soutien, ami, appui. ‖ **partisanship** [-zənˌʃɪp] *n.* partialité *f.*

partition [ˌpɑə'tɪʃən] *n.* partage *m*, morcellement *m* (d'un pays, héritage, &c.); [wall] cloison *f*, séparation *f.* ‖ *v. tr.* morceler, partager: *to ~ off*, séparer par des cloisons.

partly ['pɑətlɪ] *adv.* partiellement, en partie.

partner ['pɑətnə] *n.* partenaire *m*/*f* (aux cartes, &c.); associé *m*; collègue *m*; [in a party, dance] cavalier *m* (d'une jeune fille).

partook cf. PARTAKE.

partridge ['pɑɚtɪɪʤ] *n.* perdrix *f.*

party ['pɑɚtɪ] *n.* réunion *f*; soirée *f*; (→ déjeuner *m*, dîner *m*, goûter *m*, &c.); réception *f*: *evening* ~, © veillée *f*; *dinner* ~, dîner *m*; *to go to, give a* ~, se rendre, prendre part à une/réunion, soirée, réception; [Mil.] groupe *m* (de personnes); détachement *m* (militaire): [Br.] *firing* ~, peloton *m* d'exécution; [Jur.] partie *f*; individu *m*: *to be a* ~ *to*, être complice de; [Jur.] signer (un contrat); [Pol.] parti *m.*

pass [pæs] *n.* permis *m*; [Rail.] carte *f* de circulation; [police] laissez-passer *m*; [Mil.] permission *f* (*on*, en); [Theat.] billet *m* de faveur; [Sport, &c.] passe *f*; [Sch.] ~ *mark*, la moyenne *f*; ~ *degree*, diplôme *m* sans mention; [Geog.] col *m*: ‖ *v. intr.* passer; [time] passer, s'écouler; [Sch.] être reçu, réussir (aux examens); [Fig.] disparaître; [feelings] passer: *to* ~ *by the name of*, être connu sous le nom de; *He passes for an expert*, Il passe pour un expert; [bridge] *I* ~ *!*, Je passe!. ‖ *v. tr.* passer (le pain, un ballon, le temps, la frontière); passer devant, près d'(un endroit); croiser (qqun allant en sens contraire); dépasser (une voiture); être reçu, réussir, à (un examen); passer, voter (un projet de loi); faire (la critique de, des remarques sur qqch.); [Fam.] *to* ~ *the buck*, mettre l'affaire sur le dos d'un autre; *to* ~ *the time of day*, faire un brin de causette avec qqun; *to* ~ *o's time doing sth.*, passer son temps à faire qqch. ‖ **pass across** [-ə'kɹɑs] *v. intr.* traverser (la rue). ‖ **pass along** [-ə'lɔŋ] *v. intr.* passer par (la rue). ‖ *v. tr.* faire passer: *Pass it along*, Faites passer. ‖ **pass around** [-ə'ɹawnd] *v. intr.* contourner (un obstacle); circuler. ‖ *v. tr.* faire circuler. ‖ **pass away** [-ə'wej] *v. intr.* passer, disparaître; [die] s'éteindre, rendre le dernier soupir, trépasser. ‖ **pass by** [-'baj] *v. intr.* passer (devant, près de, qqch.). ‖ *v. tr.* passer (qqch.) sous silence; pardonner (qqch. à qqun). ‖ **pass down** [-'dawn] *v. tr. & intr.* descendre. ‖ **pass off** [-'af] *v. intr.* passer, disparaître; [happen] se passer. ‖ *v. tr.* repasser; [Sl.] refiler (qqch. à qqun); se faire passer (pour qqch.). ‖ **pass out** [-'awt] *v. intr.* sortir; s'évanouir. ‖ *v. tr.* sortir, distribuer. ‖ **pass over** [-'owvɚ] *v. intr.* franchir (un obstacle); traverser; passer sous silence, excuser; se dissiper. ‖ *v. tr.* donner, transmettre; passer sur le dos à (qqun). ‖ **pass through** [-'θɹuw] *v. intr.* passer par; traverser (une crise). ‖ **pass up** [-'ʌp] *v. tr.* monter; laisser passer, refuser. ‖ **passable** [-əbl̩] *adj.* (route, gué, pont) passable, praticable, carrossable, franchissable; (rivière, fleuve, cours d'eau) navigable; [quality] passable, assez bon. ‖ **passage** [-əʤ] *n.* [passing, text] passage *m*; trajet *m*; [hall] couloir *m*; [ocean trip] traversée *f*; [Pol.] adoption *f* (d'un projet de loi).

passbook ['pæsbʊk] *n.* carnet *m* de banque.

passenger ['pæsn̩ʤɚ] *n.* [land] voyageur *m*; [sea, air] passager *m*: ~ *train*, convoi *m*/train *m*/de voyageurs; ~ *car*, voiture *f*/wagon *m*/de voyageurs; ~ *ship*, navire *m* à passagers.

passer-by ['pæsɚ'baj] *n.* passant *m*, -e *f.*

passing[1] ['pæsɪŋ] *n.* passage *m*; [Fig.] trépas *m*; [Pol.] adoption *f* (d'un projet de loi). ‖ **passing**[2] *adj.* passager, éphémère, fugitif; [Fig.] éminent, extrême. ‖ † **passing**[3] *adv.* extrêmement; [before an adjective] au plus haut point.

passion ['pæʃən] *n.* passion *f*; emportement *m*; fureur *f*; [Rel.] (la) Passion *f* (du Christ). ‖ **passionate** [-ət] *adj.* passionné, emporté.

passive ['pæsɪv] *adj.* passi|f, -ve. ‖ *n.* [Gram.] (le) passif *m.*

passkey ['pæskij] *n.* passe-partout *m.*

Passover ['pæsˌowvɚ] *n.* [Rel.] la Pâque (juive).

passport ['pæsˌpɔɚt] *n.* passeport *m*: [Fig.] ~ *to success*, la porte ouverte au succès.

password [-ˌwɚd] *n.* mot *m*/de passe, d'ordre/.

past [pæst] *adj.* passé: *the* ~ *week, the week just* ~, la semaine/dernière, passée/: *the* ~ *3 weeks*, les 3 dernières semaines; ~ *tense*, [Gram.] (le temps) passé *m*; ~ *master*, passé maître (dans l'art de . . .). ‖ *n.* (le) passé *m*: *in the* ~, dans le passé, autrefois; [Gram.] au passé. ‖ *prép.* après, plus loin que; au-delà de; [Pop.] dépassé: *to/go, come/* ~ *sth.*, passer/devant, près de/qqch.; *to/run, ride/* ~, passer/en courant, en voiture/; *It is 20* ~ *6 (o'clock)*, Il est 6 heures 20; *It's a quarter* ~ *eight*, Il est huit heures un quart; *It's* ~ *4 (o'clock)*, Il est 4 heures passées; *He is* ~ *20*, Il a plus de 20 ans; *I am* ~ */hoping, working/*, Je n'espère plus, J'ai passé l'âge de travailler.

paste [pejst] *n.* pâte *f*; [glue] colle *f*. ‖ *v. tr.* coller. ‖ **pasteboard** [-ˌbɔɚd] *n.* carton (-pâte) *m.*

pasteurize [ˈpæstjɚˌajz] *v. tr.* pasteuriser.
pastime [ˈpæsˌtajm] *n.* passe-temps *m,* distraction *f.*
pastor [ˈpæstɚ] *n.* pasteur *m*; ecclésiastique *m*; [R.C.] curé *m.* ‖ **pastoral** [-əl] *adj.* pastoral: ~ *staff,* bâton *m* pastoral. ‖ *n.* pastorale *f.*
pastry [ˈpejstɹɪ] *n.* pâtisserie *f*: ~ *shop,* pâtisserie *f.*
pasture [ˈpæstʃɚ] *n.* pâturage *m*; pâture *f*; [Fig.] nourriture *f.* ‖ *v. intr.* paître. ‖ *v. tr.* (faire) paître.
pat [pæt] *n.* petite tape *f,* caresse *f*: *to give s.o. a* ~ *on the back,* complimenter qqun. ‖ *v. tr.* [-tt-]: ~ *s.o. on the back,* taper sur l'épaule de qqun. ‖ *adj.* à propos; [Fam.] (réponse) bien tapée; [excuse] toute prête. ‖ *adv.* à propos; (savoir) par cœur: *to stand* ~, ne pas en démordre, refuser de bouger.
patch [pætʃ] *n.* pièce *f*; plaque *f*; tache *f*; morceau *m* (de terrain); emplâtre *m*: [Fig.] *not to be a* ~ *on s.o.,* n'être pas de taille avec qqun. ‖ *v. tr.* rapiécer; arranger. ‖ **patchwork** [-ˌwɚk] *n.* mosaïque *f.*
paten [ˈpætn̩] *n.* [R.C.] patène *f.*
patent [ˈpætn̩t] *n.* brevet *m* (d'invention): ~ *leather,* cuir *m* verni; ~ *-leather shoes,* chaussures *fpl* vernies, ~ */medicine, food,* spécialité *f*/pharmaceutique, alimentaire. ‖ [ˈpejtn̩t] *adj.* [fact] manifeste, évident: *letters* ~, lettres *fpl* patentes. ‖ *v. tr.* (faire) breveter, patenter.
pater [ˈpejtɚ] *n.* [R.C.] (le) Pater *m.*
paternal [pəˈtɚnəl] *adj.* paternel. ‖ **paternalism** [-ɪzm] *n.* tutelle *f* de l'État; paternalisme *m.* ‖ **paternity** [pəˈtɚnɪtɪ] *n.* paternité *f*; filiation *f.*
path [pæθ] *n.* sentier *m*; chemin *m*; piste *f* (d'une course); [Elect.] circuit *m*; trajectoire *f* (d'une balle, &c.); allée *f* (d'un jardin): *follow the primrose* ~, être (ou jouer) sur le velours.
pathetic [pəˈθɛtɪk] *adj.* pathétique; lamen table.
pathological [ˌpæθəˈlɑʤɪkl̩] *adj.* pathologique. ‖ **pathology** [pəˈθɑləʤɪ] *n.* pathologie *f.*
pathos [ˈpejθɑs] *n.* [×] pathétique *m,* émotion *f.*
pathway [ˈpæθˌwej] *n.* sentier *m*; [Fig.] voie *f.*
patience [ˈpejʃən|s] *n.* patience *f.* ‖ **patient** [-t] *adj.* patient, -e. ‖ *n.* patient *m,* malade *m*/*f.* ‖ **patiently** [-tlɪ] *adv.* patiemment.
patriarch [ˈpejtɹɪɑɚk] *n.* patriarche *m.*
Patrick [ˈpætɹɪk] *n.* = Patrice *m.*
patrimony [ˈpætɹɪˌmownɪ] *n.* patrimoine *m.*
patriot [ˈpejtɹɪət] *n.* patriote *m*/*f.* ‖ **patriotic** [ˌpejtɹɪˈɑtɪk] *adj.* [of a pageant, ceremony, &c.] patriotique; [of a person] patriote. ‖ **patriotism** [-ˈɑtɪzm] *n.* patriotisme *m.*
patrol [pəˈtɹowl] *n.* patrouille *f*; ronde *f*; ~ *car,* voiture *f* de police; ~ *wagon,* voiture *f* cellulaire, [Fam.] panier *m* à salade. ‖ *v. intr.* patrouiller; aller en patrouille; faire une ronde. ‖ **patrolman** [-mən] *pl.* **patrolmen** [US] *n.* agent *m* (de police); © [abus.] constable *m.*
patron [ˈpejtɹən] *n.* patron *m*; protecteur *m*; [Com.] client *m.* ‖ **patronage** [-əʤ] [×] encouragement *m,* protection *f,* favoritisme *m*; [Fig.] clientèle *f.* ‖ **patroness** [-əs] *n.* protectrice *f*; (dame) patronnesse *f* (d'œuvres de charité). ‖ **patronize** [-ˌajz] *v, tr.* [Art] protéger, patronner (qqun, qqch.); traiter (qqun) avec condescendance; acheter chez, © encourager/(un commerçant). ‖ **patronizing** [-ˌajzɪŋ] *adj.* protecteur, condescendant.
patter [ˈpætɚ] *v. intr.* **1.** trottiner, marcher à petits pas *m* rapides; [rain] tapoter. **2.** parler rapidement sans penser, marmotter. ‖ *n.* **1.** léger bruit *m* de pas; [rain] bruit de la pluie, crépitement *m.* **2.** [magician, announcer] boniment *m,* bavardage *m.*
pattern [-n] *n.* modèle *m*; [dress] patron *m*; [drawing] dessin *m*; [sample] échantillon *m*; exemple *m.* ‖ *v. tr.* modeler (qqch. d'après qqch., *sth. after sth.*); copier; suivre l'exemple de.
paunch [pɔntʃ] *n.* panse *f*; [Fam.] bedaine *f,* bedon *m.*
pauper [ˈpɔpɚ] *n.* indigent *m,* économiquement faible *m.* ‖ **pauperize** [ˌpɔpɚˈajz] *v. tr.* réduire à l'indigence.
pause [pɔz] *n.* pause *f,* silence *m*; [Mus.] point *m* d'orgue. ‖ *v. intr.* s'arrêter; faire une pause.
pave [pejv] *v. tr.* paver (une rue, un sentier). ‖ **pavement** [-mənt] *n.* pavé *m*; [inside] dallage *m,* (les) dalles *fpl* (d'une église); [roadway] chaussée *f,* [Br.] trottoir *m* cf. SIDEWALK.
pavilion [pəˈvɪljən] *n.* pavillon *m.*
paving [ˈpejvɪŋ] *n.* pavage *m.*
paw [pɔ] *n.* patte *f* (d'un chat, &c.). ‖ *v. tr.* caresser (un chien, &c.); [Pej.] tripoter. ‖ *v. intr.* [of a horse] piaffer.
pawn [-n] *n.* **1.** gage *m,* objet *m* déposé en garantie. **2.** [chess] pion *m*; [Fig.] jouet *m.* ‖ *v. tr.* engager, mettre au mont-de-piété: [Fam.] *He pawned it off on me,* Il me l'a refilé; *He pawned it off as genuine,* Il l'a fait passer pour authentique.
pawnbroker [ˈpɔn|ˌbɹowkɚ] *n.* prêteur *m* sur gages. ‖ **pawnshop** [-ˌʃɑp] *n.* [Fr.]

mont-de-piété *m*, crédit *m* municipal, © boutique *f* de prêteur sur gages.

pay [pej] *n.* paie *f*; [employee, worker] salaire *m*; [civil servant] traitement *m*; [servant] gages *mpl*; [soldier] prêt *m*; [officer] solde *f*: *in the ~ of*, aux gages, à la solde/de; *holiday with ~*, congé payé; *~ day*, jour *m* de paie. || *v. tr.* **pay, paid, paid** [pejd] payer (qqun, une dette): *to ~ (s.o.) for sth.*, payer qqch. (à qqun); *to ~ 2 dollars (to s.o.) for sth.*, payer qqch. 2 dollars (à qqun); *to ~ s.o. to do sth.*, payer qqun pour faire qqch.; *to ~ for s.o.*, payer/pour, à la place de/qqun, [treat] offrir qqch. à qqun; *He paid dearly for it*, Il l'a payé cher [also Fig.]: *to ~ the piper*, payer les pots cassés; *to ~ through the nose*, payer le prix fort; *There'll be the devil to ~ !*, Ça va barder! || *v. intr.* [business] rapporter: *It pays (one) to . . .*, On y gagne à . . . || **pay back** [-ˈbæk] *v. tr.* rendre (de l'argent); rembourser (qqun): *to pay s.o. back (in his own coin)*, rendre la pareille à qqun. || **pay down** [-ˈdawn] *v. tr.* verser (de l'argent): *to pay sth. down*, faire un premier versement. || **pay in** [-ˈın] *v. tr.* verser. || **pay off** [-ˈɔf] *v. tr.* acquitter (une dette), finir de payer (une hypothèque). || *v. intr. It pays off to . . .*, On y gagne à . . . . || **pay out** [-ˈawt] *v. tr.* payer, débourser; [cable] filer. || **pay up** [-ˈʌp] *v. tr. & intr.* payer (ses dettes). || **payable** [-əbļ] *adj.* [Fin.] payable, dû, due. || **paying** [-ıŋ] *adj.* payant; rémunérateur, lucrati|f, -ve: *a ~ guest*, un(e) pensionnaire; *a ~ business*, une entreprise rémunératrice; *a ~ proposition*, une affaire. || **payment** [-mənt] *n.* paiement *m*; versement *m* (d'une somme d'argent); [instalment] versement *m*, [monthly] mensualité *f*. || **payroll** [-ˌɹowl] *n.* feuille *f* de paie des salaires; [Adm.] feuille d'émargement; [Mil.] état *m* de solde: *to put s.o. on the ~*, engager qqun: *He is on the ~*, Il émerge au budget; [Fig.] *He never had to meet a ~*, Il n'a jamais eu à calculer un prix de revient.

pd. [abbr. = paid] payé. || **P.D.** [= Police Department].

pea [pij] *n.* pois *m*: *~ soup*, soupe aux pois.

peace [pijs] *n.* paix *f*; tranquillité *f*; quiétude *f*: *~ -pipe*, calumet *m* de (la) paix; *in, at/~*, en paix; *to keep the ~*, ne pas troubler l'ordre public; *to disturb the ~*, troubler l'ordre public; *to give s.o. no ~*, ne laisser ni paix ni trève à qqun; *to hold o.'s ~*, se taire; *Justice of the Peace*, Juge *m* de paix; *Peace River*, La Rivière de la Paix. || **peaceful** [-fļ] *adj.* paisible; tranquille; [usually of a person] pacifique.

peach [pitʃ] *n.* pêche *f*: *~ -tree*, pêcher *m*.

peacock [ˈpijˌ|kɑk] *n.* paon *m*. || **peahen** [-ˌhɛn] *n.* paonne *f*.

peak [pijk] *n.* pic *m*, sommet *m*; cime *f*; pointe *f*; visière *f* (d'une casquette); [Tech.] pointe *f*, crête *f*; *~ hour*, heure *f* de pointe; *off-peak hour*, heure *f* creuse; *~ load*, charge *f* maximum.

peal [pijl] *n.* carillon *m*; fracas *m* (du tonnerre); éclat *m* (de rire), cf. BURST. || *v. intr.* [of bells] résonner, carillonner; [of thunder] gronder, retentir. || *v. tr.* faire sonner (les cloches); faire retentir (un grand bruit).

peanut [ˈpijˌnʌt] *n.* arachide *f*, [Fr.] cacahuète *f*, © [Fam.] pinotte *f*.

pear [pɛɚ] *n.* poire *f*: *pear tree*, poirier *m*.

pearl [pɚl] *n.* perle *f*: *to cast pearls before swine*, jeter des perles aux pourceaux. || **pearly** [-ı] *adj.* perlé, nacré.

peasant [ˈpɛzənt] *n.* paysan *m*, -ne *f*; campagnard *m*, -e *f*. || *adj.* paysan, -ne, → de la campagne. || **peasantry** [-ɹı] *n.* paysannat *m*; paysannerie *f*.

peasoup(er) [ˌpijˈsuwp(ɚ)] © *n.* "soupe aux pois," Canadien *m.* français.

peat [pijt] *n.* tourbe *f*.

pebble [ˈpɛbļ] *n.* caillou *m*; galet *m* (sur une plage).

pecan [ˈpijkən] *n.* pécan *m*.

peck[1] [pɛk] *n.* [Meas.] boisseau *m*, © minot *m* (de pommes, &c.); (grand) tas *m*.

peck[2] *n.* coup *m* de bec (d'une poule, &c.). || *v. tr.* [of a hen, &c.] becqueter; picorer; picoter.

peculiar [pəˈkjuwljɚ] *adj.* particuli|er, -ère; propre; singuli|er, -ère; bizarre. || **peculiarity** [pəˌkjuwlıˈæɚətı] *n.* particularité *f*; singularité *f*; bizarrerie *f*; individualité *f*; signe *m*, trait *m* distinctif. || **peculiarly** [pəˈkjuwljɚlı] *adv.* particulièrement; singulièrement; personnellement.

pedagogue [ˈpɛdəˌgɑ|g] *n.* pédagogue *m*. || **pedagogy** [-dʒı] *n.* pédagogie *f*.

pedal [ˈpɛdļ] *n.* pédale *f* (de bicyclette, de piano). || *v. intr.* [-ll-] pédaler.

pedant [ˈpɛdņt] *n.* pédant *m*. || **pedantic** [pəˈdæntık] *adj.* pédantesque.

peddle [ˈpɛdļ] *v. tr.* colporter (des produits). || **peddler** [-ɚ] *n.* colporteur *m*.

pedestal [ˈpɛdəstļ] *n.* piédestal *m*.

pedestrian [pəˈdɛstɹıən] *n.* piéton *m*. || *adj.* pédestre.

pedigree [ˈpɛdıˌgɹij] *n.* [dog] pedigree *m*;

généalogie *f*; ascendance *f*: ~ *dog*, chien *m* de race.

pedlar [ˈpɛdlər] cf. PEDDLER.

peek [pijk] *v. intr.* regarder furtivement. ‖ *n.* coup *m* d'œil: *to take a* ~, jeter un coup d'œil; *No peeking!*, Ne trichez pas!

peel [pijl] *n.* pelure *f* (d'un fruit, légume); peau *f* (d'une pêche); zeste *m* (d'un citron); pelure *f* (d'une orange). ‖ *v. tr.* peler (des légumes); éplucher; décortiquer: *to* ~ *off o.'s clothes*, ôter (un, ses) vêtements, se débarrasser de (ses) vêtements; se déshabiller. ‖ *v. intr.* [paint] s'écailler.

peep [pijp] *n.* coup *m* d'œil furtif. ‖ *v. intr.* épier, observer en cachette; *to* ~ *through the window*, regarder à la dérobée par la fenêtre: [Fig.] [day, character] *to* ~ *out*, se laisser entrevoir.

peer[1] *v. intr.* regarder (qqun, qqch., *at s.o., sth.*) avec attention; scruter (qqch., *at sth.*).

peer[2] [pijər] *n.* pair *m*; égal *m*; [Hist.] pair *m*, noble *m.* ‖ **peerage** [-əʤ] *n.* pairie *f.* ‖ **peerless** [-ləs] *adj.* sans égal, incomparable.

peeve [pijv] *v. tr.* irriter, agacer, fâcher (qqun). ‖ **peevish** [-ɪʃ] *adj.* maussade, irritable, acariâtre.

peg [pɛg] *n.* cheville *f* (en bois); [hat] patère *f*; [tent] piquet *m*; [clothes] pince *f* (à linge). ‖ *v. tr.* [-gg-] cheviller: *to take (a person) down a* ~, remettre (qqun) à sa place, rabattre le caquet (à qqun); [Fam.] *to* ~ *out*, passer l'arme à gauche; *to* ~ *away*, persévérer. ‖ **pegging** [-ɪŋ] *adj.* ~ *prices*, stabilisation *f* des prix.

P.E.I. [ˌpijˌijˈɑj] *abr.* [= Prince Edward Island] I.P.E.

pejorative [pəˈʤɔərɪtəv] *adj.* péjoratif.

Pekinese [pijkɪˈnijz] *n.* Pékinois *m.*

Peking [pijˈkɪŋ] *n.* Pékin *m* [also Peiping].

pelican [ˈpɛlɪkən] *n.* pélican *m.*

pellet [ˈpɛlət] *n.* boulette *f*, [Pharm.] pastille *f*, pilule *f*; [shotgun] grain *m* de plomb.

pell-mell [ˈpɛlˈmɛl] *n.* pêle-mêle *m*, désordre *m.* ‖ *adj.* pêle-mêle, en désordre. ‖ *adv.* pêle-mêle, en confusion, à la débandade.

pelt[1] [pɛlt] *n.* peau *f*, fourrure *f*/non tannée, brute/.

pelt[2] [pɛlt] *v. tr.* cribler (*with*, de). ‖ *v. intr.* tomber à verse: *pelting rain*, pluie *f* battante.

pen[1] [pɛn] *n.* plume *f*; *fountain-pen*, stylo *m*; [ball-point] stylo à bille. ‖ *v. tr.* [-nn-] écrire.

pen[2] *n.* enclos *m*, parc *m* (à moutons); [chickens] poulailler *m*; © soue *f* (à cochons); [Sl. = penitentiary] prison *f*, [Sl.] taule *f*, violon *m.* ‖ *v. tr.* [-nn-] parquer (des moutons, etc.).

penal [ˈpijnḷ] *adj.* pénal: ~ *Code*, code *m* criminel. ‖ **penalize** [-ajz] *v. tr.* infliger une pénalité à; [Sport] pénaliser. ‖ **penalty** [ˈpɛnḷtɪ] *n.* pénalité *f*; punition *f*; sanction *f*; [Fig.] conséquences *fpl*: *under* ~ *of*, sous peine de.

penance [ˈpɛnəns] *n.* pénitence *f*: *to impose a* ~, imposer/donner/une pénitence.

pencil [ˈpɛnsḷ] *n.* crayon *m*; [automatic] porte-mine *m. inv.*: *in* ~, au crayon. ‖ *v. tr.* [-ll-] marquer (qqch.) au crayon: ~ *sharpener*, taille-crayon *m.*

pendant [ˈpɛndənt] *n.* **1.** [Jewelry] [on necklace] pendentif *m*, [on bracelet] breloque *f.* **2.** [ornament] pendeloque *f.* ‖ **pending** [ˈpɛndɪŋ] *adj.* en cours, pendant. ‖ *prép.* en attendant.

pendulum [ˈpɛnʤələm] *n.* pendule *m*, balancier *m.*

penetrate [ˈpɛnəˌtɹejt] *v. tr. & intr.* pénétrer, percer. ‖ **penetrating** [ˈpɛnəˌtɹejtɪŋ] *adj.* pénétrant: ~ *eyes*, yeux perçants; [mind] clairvoyant, perspicace. ‖ **penetration** [ˌpɛnəˈtɹejʃən] *n.* pénétration *f*; [mind] perspicacité *f*; [of water] infiltration *f.*

penguin [ˈpɛŋgwɪn] *n.* pingouin *m.*

peninsula [pəˈnɪnsələ] *n.* péninsule *f*, presqu'île *f.*

penitence [ˈpɛnɪtən|s] *n.* pénitence *f*; repentir *m.* ‖ **penitent** [-t] *adj.* contrit, repentant. ‖ *n.* pénitent. ‖ **penitentiary** [ˌpɛnɪˈtɛnʃərɪ] *adj.* pénitentiaire. ‖ *n.* pénitencier *m.*

penknife [ˈpɛn|ˌnajf] *n.* canif *m.*

penmanship [-mənˌʃɪp] *n.* calligraphie *f.*

Penn., Penna. [= Pennsylvania].

pennant [ˈpɛnənt] *n.* banderole *f*; [Mil.] fanion *m.*

penniless [ˈpɛnɪˌləs] *adj.* sans le sou, indigent.

Pennsylvania [ˌpɛnsɪlˈvejnjə] *n.* la Pensylvanie, la Pennsylvanie.

penny [ˈpɛnɪ] [*pl.* **pennies**; sens collectif [Br.] **pence**] *n.* penny *m*, sou *m*; ~ *bank*, caisse *f* d'épargne. ‖ **pennyworth** [-ˌwərθ] *adj.* (pour) un penny, deux sous (de).

pension [ˈpɛnʃən] *n.* pension *f* (de retraite), retraite *f*: *Old Age Pension*, pension de vieillesse. ‖ *v. tr.* mettre (qqun) à la retraite; pensionner (un fonctionnaire).

pensive [ˈpɛnsɪv] *adj.* pensif, songeur. ‖ **pensively** [-lɪ] *adv.* → d'un air/pensif, songeur.

pent [pɛnt] *adj.* : ~ *in, up*, enclos, **-e**; renfermé; [Fig.] réprimé, refoulé: ~ *-up* *emotions*, sentiments, émotions / contenu(e)s, réprimé(e)s.

pentagon [ˈpɛntəˌgɑn] *n. & adj.* pentagone (*m*): [US] *the Pentagon*, le Pentagone.

penthouse [ˈpɛntˌhaws] *n.* appentis *m*; auvent *m*; [on roof] appartement *m* avec terrasse.

penury [ˈpɛnjəɪ] *n.* pénurie *f*, disette *f*.

people [ˈpijpḷ] *pl.* **people, peoples** *n.* peuple *m*, nation *f*; (les) gens *mpl* [NB dans cette dernière acception, *people* fonctionne comme un pluriel, mais ne prend pas l's]: *good, clean, honest* ~, braves gens; *society* ~, gens du monde; ~ *say that*..., on dit que ... ; *How many* ~ ?, Combien de personnes?; *a lot of* ~, beaucoup de monde. || *v. tr.* peupler (une région).

pep [pɛp] *n.* [Fam.] allant *m*, © pep *m*.

pepper [ˈpɛpər] *n.* poivre *m*. || *v. tr.* poivrer.

peppermint [ˈpɛpərˌmɪnt] *n.* menthe *f* poivrée.

per [pər] *prép.* pour; par: ~ *cent*(*um*) cf. PER CENT; ~ *year*, ~ *annum*, par année.

perceive [pərˈsijv] *v. tr.* percevoir; apercevoir; s'apercevoir de (qqch.).

per cent [pərˈsɛnt] *n.* pour cent: *five* ~, cinq pour cent. || **percentage** [-ədʒ] *n.* pourcentage *m*, proportion *f*: *He gets a* ~ *on sales*, Il a/tant pour cent, un pourcentage sur les ventes.

perceptible [pərˈsɛp|tɪbḷ] *adj.* perceptible. || **perception** [-ʃən] *n.* perception *f*; *lack of* ~, manque *m* de discernement. || **perceptive** [-tɪv] *adj.* perceptif.

perch[1] [pərtʃ] *v. intr.* se percher, se poser (*on*, sur).

perch[2] [pərtʃ] *n.*: *pike* ~, doré *m*, cf. PIKE; *trout* ~, (*or sand roller*), perche-truite *f*; *yellow* ~, *American* ~, perche *f*, © perchaude *f*.

†**perchance** [pərˈtʃæns] *adv.* par hasard, peut-être; †d'aventure.

percolate [ˈpərkəˌlejt] *v. tr. & intr.* [coffee] passer, filtrer; [Fig.] filtrer, s'infiltrer. || **percolator** [-ər] *n.* filtre *m*; [café] percolateur *m*.

perdition [pərˈdɪʃən] *n.* perdition *f*; [downfall] perte *f*; [place] enfer *m*.

perennial [pərˈɛnɪəl] *adj.* perpétuel, éternel; [Bot.] vivace.

perfect [ˈpərfəkt] *adj.* parfait; accompli; achevé. || *n.* [Gram.] parfait *m*: *pluperfect*, plus-que-parfait. || *v. tr.* [pərˈfɛk|t] parfaire; perfectionner; améliorer; mettre (un procédé, &c.) au point; parachever (une tâche). || **perfection** [-ʃən] *n.* perfection *f*; perfectionnement *m*; (par-) achèvement *m*. || **perfectly** [ˈpərfəktlɪ] *adv.* parfaitement.

perfidious [pərˈfɪdɪəs] *adj.* perfide, traître. || **perfidy** [ˈpərfɪdɪ] *n.* perfidie *f*.

perforate [ˈpərfəˌejt] *v. tr.* perforer, percer.

perform [pərˈfɔərm] *v. tr.* représenter (une pièce); accomplir (un devoir); remplir (une tâche); faire (une opération). || **performance** [-əns] *n.* représentation *f* (théâtrale, artistique); rendement *m* (d'une machine); fonctionnement *m* (d'un mécanisme); performance *f* (sportive). || **performer** [-ər] *n.* [Mus.] exécutant *m*, musicien, -ne; [Theat., Cin.] act|eur, -rice; comédien, -ne.

perfume [ˈpərfjuwm] *n.* parfum *m*. || *v. tr.* [pərˈfjuwm] parfumer. || **perfumer** [-ər] *n.* parfumeur *m*. || **perfumery** [-ərɪ] *n.* parfumerie *f*.

perfunctory [pərˈfʌŋktərɪ] *adj.* superficiel, → pour la forme.

perhaps [pərˈhæps, ˈpɹæps] *adv.* peut-être: ~ *not*, peut-être que non; ~ *he won't come*, Peut-être ne viendra-t-il pas, Il ne viendra peut-être pas, Peut-être qu'il ne viendra pas.

peril [ˈpɛərɪl] *n.* péril *m*, danger *m*: *in* ~ (*of*), en danger (de), *at your* ~, à vos risques et périls. || *v. tr.* mettre en péril, en danger. || **perilous** [-əs] *adj.* périlleux, dangereux.

perimeter [pərˈɪmətər] *n.* périmètre *m*.

period [ˈpijərɪəd] *n.* période *f*, époque *f*; durée *f*; [Punctuation] point *m*; [Sch.] cours *m*; [at end of sentence] *Period!* Un point, c'est tout [also Fig.]. || **periodic** [pɪərɪˈɑdɪk] *adj.* périodique. || **periodical** [-ḷ] *n.* revue *f*, publication *f* périodique. || *adj.* périodique.

peripheral [pərˈɪfərḷ] *adj.* périphérique.

periscope [ˈpɛərɪˌskowp] *n.* [Naut.] périscope *m*.

perish [ˈpɛərɪʃ] *v. intr.* périr, mourir; [things, food, &c.] se gâter. || **perishable** [-əbḷ] *adj.* (matière *f*) périssable.

perjure [ˈpərdʒər] (o.s.) *v. tr.* se parjurer; [Jur.] porter un faux témoignage. || **perjury** [-ɪ] *n.* parjure *m*, faux témoignage.

perk [pərk] *v. intr.*: *to* ~ *up*, se ranimer, se ragaillardir. || **perky** [-ɪ] *adj.* éveillé; [Pej.] effronté.

permanence [ˈpərmənən|s] *n.* permanence *f*; stabilité *f*; durée *f*. || **permanent** [-t] *adj.* permanent, immuable; durable; stable: ~ *wave kit*, nécessaire *m* à permanente. || *n.* permanente *f*. || **permanently** [-tlɪ] *adv.* en permanence; de façon durable.

permeate [ˈpərmɪˌejt] *v. tr.* pénétrer; imprégner.

permissible [pərˈmɪ|sɪbḷ] *adj.* permis, -e; admissible; faisable. || **permission** [-ʃən] *n.*

permission *f*; autorisation *f*. || **permit** ['pɚmɪt] *n*. permis *m*; laissez-passer *m*; autorisation *f*; [clearance] congé *m*. || *v. tr.* [-tt-] [pɚ'mɪt] permettre (qqch. à qqun, à qqun de + inf.); autoriser (qqun à + inf.).

pernicious [pɚ'nɪʃəs] *adj*. pernicieu|x, -se.

pernickety [pɚ'nɪkətɪ] *adj*. méticuleux, embêtant, mauvais coucheur; pointilleux, chatouilleux; qui cherche la petite bête, minutieux, tâtillon; [task] minutieux, délicat.

perpendicular [ˌpɚpən'dɪkjələr] *adj*. perpendiculaire.

perpetrate ['pɚpəˌtɹejt] *v. tr*. perpétrer, commettre/(un crime).

perpetual [pɚ'pɛtʃuw|əl] *adj*. perpétuel. || **perpetuate** [-ˌejt] *v. tr*. perpétuer.

perplex [pɚ'plɛks] *v. tr*. embarrasser; confondre (qqun). || **perplexed** [-t] *adj*. perplexe; embarrassé; confus. || **perplexity** [-sɪtɪ] *n*. embarras *m*; confusion *f*.

persecute ['pɚsəˌkjuwt] *v. tr*. persécuter. || **persecution** [ˌpɚsə'kjuwʃən] *n*. persécution *f*.

perseverance [ˌpɚsə'vijɚ|əns] *n*. persévérance *f*. || **persevere** *v. intr*. persévérer, persister (à, dans, *in*).

Persia ['pɚʒə] *n*. [Hist.] Perse *f*: *in, to*/~, en P. || **Persian** [-n] *adj. & n*. [Hist.] perse; [modern, cat] persan; [carpet] de Perse. || **Persian Gulf** ['pɚʒən'gʌlf] *n*. le golfe Persique.

persist [pɚ'sɪst] *v. intr*. persister, s'obstiner (à, dans, *in*). || **persistence** [-əns] *n*. persistance *f*; persévérance *f*. || **persistent** [-ənt] *adj*. persistant, persévérant; tenace.

person ['pɚsən] *n*. personne *f*; type *m*; individu *m*. || **personable** [-əbḷ] *adj*. de bonne mine, de grand air, beau; [Jur.] capable d'ester en justice. || **personage** [-ədʒ] *n*. personnage *m*; [important pers.] personnalité *f*. || **personal** ['pɚsənḷ] *adj*. personnel, -le; (liberté) individuelle; [private] particulier: [Theat.] ~ *appearances by X, Y, Z (at a show)*, → avec X, Y, Z en personne; *This is not a ~ remark*, → Il ne s'agit pas de vous, N'y voyez là aucune critique à votre égard. || **personality** [ˌpɚsən'æləti] *n*. personnalité *f*; personnage *m*. || **personally** ['pɚsənəlɪ] *adv*. personnellement, en personne; pour ma part, pour moi. || **personnel** [ˌpɚsən'ɛl] *n*. [Adm.] personnel *m*, employés *mpl*.

perspective [pɚ'spɛktɪv] *n*. [drawing] perspective *f*; [prospect] *in* ~, en perspective.

perspiration [ˌpɚspɚ'ejʃən] *n*. transpiration *f*, sueur *f*. || **perspire** [pɚ'spajɚ] *v. intr*. transpirer.

persuade [pɚ'swej|d] *v. tr*. persuader (*s.o. of sth*., qqun de qqch., qqch. à qqun; *s.o. to do sth*., à qqun de faire qqch.). || **persuasion** [-ʒən] *n*. persuasion *f*; croyance *f*. || **persuasive** [-sɪv] *adj*. [discours, &c.) persuasi|f, -ve; convaincant, -e.

pert [pɚt] *adj*. effronté; insolent; impertinent.

pertain [pɚ'tejn] *v. intr*. appartenir (à, *to*).

pertinent ['pɚtṇənt] *adj*. pertinent; opportun.

perturb [pɚ'tɚb] *v. tr*. troubler (l'ordre, la paix, &c.); [Techn.] perturber (l'atmosphère, &c.). || **perturbation** [pɚtɚ'bejʃən] *n*. perturbation *f*, [moral] inquiétude *f*; [social] trouble *m*.

Peru [pɚ'uw] *n*. le Pérou: *in, to*/~, au P.

peruse [pɚ'uwz] *v. tr*. examiner (un document); lire attentivement.

pervade [pɚ'vejd] *v. tr*. traverser; pénétrer; se répandre dans (qqch.); [Fig.] régner dans (qqch.).

perverse [pɚ'vɚ|s] *adj*. pervers; méchant. || **pervert** [-t] *v. tr*. pervertir: dénaturer; fausser. || ['pɚvɚt] *n*. perverti *m*; pervers *m*.

pessimism ['pɛsɪmɪ|zm] *n*. pessimisme *m*. || **pessimist** [-st] *n*. pessimiste. || **pessimistic** [ˌpɛsɪ'mɪstɪk] *adj*. (attitude) pessimiste.

pest [pɛst] *n*. peste *f*; insecte *m* nuisible; [Fig.] fléau *m*: *What a ~ !*, Quel poison! || **pester** [-ɚ] *v. tr*. importuner, tourmenter, harceler; [Fam.] embêter.

pestilence [-ɪləns] *n*. pestilence *f*, peste *f*.

pet [pɛt] *adj*. [pers., animal] favori; [thing] préféré: ~ *hate*, bête *f* noire. || *n*. animal *m*/familier, favori; [pers.] favori *m*; [name] chouchou *m*. || *v. tr*. [-tt-] → choyer, dorloter; caresser.

petal ['pɛtḷ] *n*. pétale *m*.

petard [pə'tɑɚd] *n*. pétard *m*: *He is hoist with his own ~*, Il s'est pris à son propre piège.

Peter ['pijtɚ] *n*. Pierre.

peter out ['pijtɚˌawt] *v. intr*. mourir; s'épuiser; disparaître; s'éteindre; [of a plan, project] avorter, tomber à l'eau. *The light petered out*, → La lumière vacilla, puis s'éteignit.

petition [pə'tɪʃən] *n*. pétition *f*, requête *f*; ~ *for mercy*, recours *m* en grâce; ~ *for a divorce*, demande *f* en divorce. || *v. tr*. présenter une pétition, une requête.

petrify ['pɛtɹɪˌfaj] *v. tr. & intr*. (se) pétrifier.

petrol ['pɛtɹəl] *n*. [Br.] essence *f* cf. GASOLINE. || **petroleum** [pə'tɹowlɪəm] *n*. pétrole *m.* || **petroliferous** [ˌpɛtɹə'lɪfɚəs] *adj.* pétrolifère.

petticoat ['pɛtɪˌkowt] *n.* jupon *m.*

petty ['pɛtɪ] *adj.* petit, insignifiant; *~ cash*, menue monnaie *f*, petite caisse *f*; [navy] *~ officer*, maître *m*; *chief ~ officer*, premier maître *m.*

petulance ['pɛtjələn|s] *n.* [×] irritabilité *f.* || **petulant** [-t] *adj.* [×] irritable.

pew [pjuw] *n.* banc *m* (d'église).

P.Ex. ['pij'ɛks, = Post Exchange] *n.* [US] cantine *f.*

Pfc. [ˌpijˌɛf'sij] [US = Private first class], *n.* soldat *m* de 1ère classe.

phantom ['fæntəm] *n.* fantôme *m.*

pharmacist ['fɑɚməsɪ|st] *n.* pharmacien *m*, -ne *f.* || **pharmacy** *n.* pharmacie *f.*

phase [fejz] *n.* phase *f*; aspect *m*: *out of ~*, (moteur) décalé, déphasé; [Fig. of a person] en désaccord (avec son temps, *with o.'s time*).

Ph.D. [ˌpijˌejtʃ'dij] [= Doctor of Philosophy] *n.* D.Ph. [= Doctor Philosophiæ].

pheasant ['fɛzənt] *n.* faisan *m.*

phenomenal [fə'nɑmənəl] *adj.* phénoménal [also Fig.]; prodigieux. || **phenomen|on**, *pl.* **-a** [fə'nɑməˌnɑ|n] *n.* phénomène *m.*

phial [fajl] *n.* ampoule *f*, fiole *f.*

Phila. [Philadelphia] *n.* Philadelphie *f.*

philanthropy [fɪ'lænθɹəˌpɪ] *n.* philanthropie *f.*

Philip ['fɪlɪp] *n.* = Philippe *m.*

Philippines (the), the Philippine Islands ['fɪlɪˌpijnz] *n.* les Philippines *fpl*: *in, to/the ~*, aux P.

philology [fɪ'lɑlədʒɪ] *n.* philologie *f.*

philosopher [fɪ'lɑsəfɚ] *n.* philosophe *m.* || **philosophical** [ˌfɪlə'sɑfɪkḷ] *adj.* philosophique; [of pers.] philosophe. || **philosophy** [fɪ'lɑsəfɪ] *n.* philosophie *f*; opinion *f*; attitude *f*; point *m* de vue.

phlegmatic [ˌflɛg'mætɪk] *adj.* flegmatique.

phone [fown] *n.* [Fam.] téléphone *m.* || *v. tr.* téléphoner à (qqun) cf. TELEPHONE.

phoneme ['fownijm] *n.* phonème *m.* || **phonemics** [fə'nijmɪks] *n.* phonologie *f.*

phonetics [fə'nɛtɪks] *n.* phonétique *f.*

phoney ['fownɪ] *adj.* [Fam.] faux, truqué.

phonograph ['fownəˌgɹæf] *n.* phonographe *m*; [electric] tourne-disque *m*, électrophone *m.*

phosphate ['fɑsˌfejt] *n.* phosphate *m.* || **phosphorus** ['fɑsˌfɚəs] *n.* phosphore *m.*

photo ['fowtow] *n.* photo *f.* || **photoflood** [-ˌflʌd] *n.* lampe *f* survoltée. || **photograph** ['fowtəˌgɹæf] *n.* photographie *f*, photo *f.* || *v. tr.* photographier. || **photographer** [fə'tɑgɹəfɚ] *n.* photographe *m.* || **photographic** [ˌfowtə'gɹæfɪk] *adj.* photographique. || **photography** [fə'tɑgɹəfɪ] *n.* [of an act and technique] (la) photographie *f.*

phrase [fɹejz] *n.* expression *f*; locution *f.* || *v. tr.* exprimer (une idée, une théorie); formuler; rédiger (une lettre).

physic ['fɪzɪk] *n.* purge *f*; laxatif *m*; purgatif *m*; médecine *f*; médicament *m.* || *v. tr.* [coll.] purger; droguer (qqun). || **physical** [-ḷ] *adj.* physique. || **physician** [fɪ'zɪʃən] *n.* médecin *m*; [Fam.] docteur *m.* || **physicist** ['fɪzɪsɪst] *n.* physicien *m.* || **physics** ['fɪsɪks] *n.* physique *f.*

physiological [ˌfɪzɪə'lɑdʒɪkḷ] *adj.* physiologique. || **physiology** [fɪzɪ'ɑlədʒɪ] *n.* physiologie *f.*

physique [fɪ'zijk] *n.* physique *m.*

pianist ['pijənɪst] *n.* pianiste *m/f.* || **piano** [pɪ'ænow] *n.* piano *m*: *to play the ~* jouer du piano; *grand ~*, piano *m* à queue; *upright ~*, piano droit.

picayune [ˌpɪkə'juwn] *n.* [US] picaillon *m*; [Fig.] chose de peu de valeur. || *adj.* petit, mesquin, méprisable.

piccolo ['pɪkəlow] *n.* piccolo *m*, petite flûte *f.*

pick [pɪk] *n.* [tool] pioche *f*, pic *m*; choix *m*: *Take your ~*, Faites votre choix; *the ~ of the crop*, le dessus du panier. || *v. tr.* cueillir (des fleurs, &c.); piocher (le sol); crocheter (une serrure); ronger (un os); se curer (les dents); choisir: *to ~ a quarrel with s.o.*, chercher querelle à qqun; *to have a bone to ~ with s.o.*, avoir maille à partir avec qqun; *to ~ pockets*, voler à la tire; *to ~ o.'s way*, marcher avec précaution; *to ~ and choose*, faire le difficile; [Fig.] *to ~ holes in an argument*, déchirer un argument; *to ~ at o.'s food*, pignocher (sa nourriture). || **pick off** *v. tr.* enlever, arracher; [snipe] abattre, descendre/(un à un). || **pick out** *v. tr.* choisir; [distinguish] repérer. || **pick over** *v. tr.* trier. || **pick up** *v. tr.* ramasser; [lift] soulever; apprendre (une langue sans effort); cf. PICTURE.

pickaxe ['pɪkˌæks] *n.* pioche *f.*

pickerel ['pɪkɚəl] *n.* brochet *m* maillé; petit brochet.

picket [pɪkət] *n.* piquet *m*, pieu *m*: (*strike*) *pickets*, piquets (de grève). || *v. tr.* [horse] mettre, attacher, au piquet; [strike] faire le piquet.

pickle ['pɪkḷ] *n.* marinade *f*; [brine] saumure *f*; *pl.* conserves au vinaigre: *to be in a pretty ~*, être dans le pétrin, être dans de beaux draps. || *v. tr.* mariner (des cornichons).

pickpocket ['pɪkˌpɑkət] *n.* pickpocket *m*, voleur *m* à la tire.

pickup [ˈpɪkˌʌp] *n.* [Com.] reprise *f* des affaires, redressement *m*; [Mus.] pick-up *m*; ~ *truck*, camionnette *f*.

picnic [ˈpɪkˌnɪk] *n.* pique-nique *m.* ‖ *v. intr.* **[-ked]** pique-niquer.

pictorial [ˌpɪkˈtɔəɪl̩] *adj.* pittoresque; [periodical] illustré; en images.

picture [ˈpɪktʃɚ] *n.* [book] image *f*, gravure *f*; portrait *m*; tableau *m*; peinture *f*; [Cinema] film *m*: *to pick up, receive the* ~, capter l'image; [Fig.] *He is not in the* ~, Il n'est pas dans le coup. ‖ *v. tr.* représenter; décrire; peindre; [Fig.] s'imaginer (qqun, qqch.). ‖ **picture gallery** **[-ˌgæləɪ]** *n.* musée *m* de peinture. ‖ **picturesque** [-ˌɛsk] *adj.* pittoresque.

pie [paj] *n.* [meat] pâté *m*; [fruit] tarte *f*, tartelette *f*; [Fr.] tourte *f*: *to have a finger in the* ~, être mêlé à l'affaire, tremper dans le complot; *to eat humble* ~, s'humilier (devant qqun), présenter d'humbles excuses, faire amende honorable.

piebald [ˈpajˌbɔld] *adj.* (cheval) pie.

piece [pijs] *n.* **1.** [bit] morceau *m*; [odd piece] bout *m*, coupon *m* (de tissu, &c.); [broken piece] éclat *m*, fragment *m*; [unit, cannon, coin] pièce *f*; [music] morceau *m*; [chess] pièce *f*; [land] parcelle *f*: *to/break, fall/into pieces*, mettre, s'en aller/en morceaux; *to go to pieces*, [things] se désagréger/[pers.] perdre son sang-froid, s'effondrer/; *to fly into pieces*, voler en éclats; *to/tear, pull, pick/to pieces*, déchirer, [Fig.] démolir; *to take sth. to pieces*, démonter qqch.; *(by) the* ~, à la pièce. **2.** [not translated: use indef. art.] *a* ~ *of/advice, furniture, luck, news, &c./*, un conseil, un meuble, une chance, une nouvelle, &c. ‖ *v. tr.* rapiécer: *to* ~ *sth. together*, joindre, coordonner (des faits); rassembler (des morceaux).

piecemeal [ˈpijsˌmijl] *adv.* pièce à pièce, par morceaux, en plusieurs fois.

pier [pijɚ] *n.* jetée *f*; pile *f* (de pont); pilier *m*; pilastre *m*.

pierce [pijɚs] *v. tr.* percer, transpercer. ‖ **piercing** [-ɪŋ] *adj.* perçant; [sharp] aigu.

piety [ˈpajətɪ] *n.* piété *f*.

pig [pɪg] *n.* cochon *m*, porc *m*; †pourceau *m.* ‖ **pig iron** [-ˌajɚŋ] *n.* gueuse *f* de fonte; fonte *f*.

pigeon [ˈpɪdʒən] *n.* pigeon *m*: *homing* ~, pigeon voyageur. ‖ **pigeonhole** [-ˌhowl] case *f*, casier *m*, classeur *m*; oubliettes *fpl*; [Fig.] ~ *-holed*, classé, enterré; mis aux oubliettes, au rancart.

piggish [ˈpɪgɪʃ] *adj.* malpropre; [greedy] goinfre. ‖ **piggishness** [-nəs] *n.* saleté *f*, malpropreté *f*; goinfrerie *f*. ‖ **pig-headed** [-ˌhɛdəd] *adj.* entêté, têtu.

pigment [ˈpɪgmənt] *n.* pigment *m*, colorant *m*, couleur *f*.

pigskin [ˈpɪgˌskɪn] *n.* peau *f* de porc.

pike[1] [pajk] *n.* brochet *m*; © *wall-eyed* ~, *yellow* ~, doré *m*.

pike[2] *n.* pique *f*; [Geol.] pic *m*.

pile [pajl] *n.* pile *f*; tas *m*; amas *m*; monceau *m*, pieu *m*, pilot *m*, pilotis *m*; [Text.] poil *m* (d'un tapis): *atomic* ~, pile *f* atomique. ‖ *n. pl.* hémorroïdes *fpl.* ‖ *v. tr.* empiler, accumuler, entasser, amasser; soutenir (qqch.) avec des pilotis.

pilfer [ˈpɪlfɚ] *v. tr.* chiper; chaparder.

pilgrim [ˈpɪlgɹəm] *n.* pèlerin *m.* ‖ **pilgrimage** [-ədʒ] *n.* pèlerinage *m*.

pill [pɪl] *n.* pilule *f*; [tablet] comprimé *m*.

pillar [ˈpɪlɚ] *n.* pilier *m*; colonne *f*: *to drive (s.o.) from* ~ *to post*, renvoyer (qqun) de Caïphe à Pilate. ‖ **pillarbox** [-ˌbɑks] *n.* [Br.] boîte *f* aux lettres.

pillory [ˈpɪləɪ] *n.* pilori *m.* ‖ *v. tr.* clouer au pilori.

pillow [ˈpɪlow] *n.* oreiller *m*: *pillowslip*, taie *f* d'oreiller.

pilot [ˈpajlət] *n.* pilote *m*; [Fig.] guide *m*: ~ *project*, coup *m* d'essai, avant-projet *m.* ‖ *v. tr.* piloter; guider; conduire: ~ *a bill*, défendre un projet de loi, l'expliquer, en diriger la discussion. ‖ **pilot boat** [-ˌbowt] *n.* [Naut.] bateau *m* pilote. ‖ **pilot flame** [-ˌflejm] *n.* veilleuse *f*. ‖ **pilot lamp** [-ˌlæmp] *n.* lampe *f* témoin.

pimple [ˈpɪmpl̩] *n.* bouton *m* (dans la figure).

pin [pɪn] *n.* épingle *f*; cheville *f*; goupille *f*; boulon *m*: *king-* ~, pivot *m.* ‖ *v. tr.* **[-nn-]** épingler; clouer; goupiller: *to* ~ *down*, lier, [Fig.] mettre le doigt (sur un défaut); *to* ~ *up*, épingler (les cheveux); accrocher au mur.

pinball [ˈpɪnˌbɔl] *n.* * billard *m* américain.

pincers [ˈpɪnsɚz] *n.pl.* pinces *fpl*; pincettes *fpl*.

pinch [pɪntʃ] *n.* pincée *f*; pincement *m*; prise *f* (de tabac); [Fig.] gêne *f*: *at a* ~, à la rigueur. ‖ *v. tr.* pincer; serrer; [Fam., = steal] chiper; [Fam., = arrest] pincer: *This shoe pinches me*, Cette chaussure me blesse.

pine[1] [pajn] *n.* pin *m*: *jack* ~, pin gris; *white* ~, pin blanc; *red* ~, pin rouge; ~ *cone*, pomme *f* de pin.

pine[2] *v. intr.* languir; dépérir: *to* ~ *for (s.o., sth.)*, soupirer après (qqun, qqch.); aspirer à (qqch.).

pineapple [-ˌæpl̩] *n.* ananas *m*.

ping-pong [ˈpɪŋˌpɑŋ] *n.* ping-pong *m*.

pink [pɪŋk] *n.* œillet *m.* || *adj.* [colour] rose: [Fig.] *to be in the* ~, se porter comme un charme, se porter à merveille.
pinnacle ['pɪnəkl̩] *n.* pinacle *m*, faîte *m*; tourelle *f*.
pint [pajnt] *n.* [×] © chopine *f*; [Fr.] demi-litre *m*, pinte *f*.
pintail ['pɪn,tejl] *n.* canard pilet *m*.
pin-up ['pɪn,ʌp] *n.* [Fam.] jolie fille, pin-up *f*.
pioneer [,pajə'nijɚ] *n.* pionnier *m*; fondateur *m*; précurseur *m*. || *v. tr.* promouvoir; explorer. || *v. intr.* faire œuvre de pionnier.
pious ['pajəs] *adj.* pieu|x, -se.
pipe [pajp] *n.* **1.** tuyau *m*, conduit *m*, conduite *f* (d'eau), cf. MAIN: *pipeline*, pipeline *m*, oléoduc *m* [pour le pétrole]; *windpipe*, trachée-artère *f*. **2.** pipe *f*: *to smoke a* ~, → fumer la pipe [= to be a pipe-smoker]; *clay* ~, pipe en terre; *the* ~ *of peace*, le calumet de paix. **3.** tuyau *m* (d'orgue), pipeau *m*, sifflet *m*. || **piping** [-ɪŋ] *n.* tuyauterie *f*, tubulure *f*. || *adv.* ~ *hot*, bouillant, très chaud.
pippin ['pɪpɪn] *n.* pomme *f* de reinette.
piquant ['pijkənt] *adj.* piquant.
pique [pijk] *n.* pique *f*, ressentiment *m*. || *v. tr.* piquer, vexer: *to* ~ *o.s.* (*about sth.*), se piquer, être fier/de qqch.
piracy ['pajɚəsɪ] *n.* piraterie *f*; [Fig.] plagiat *m*. || **pirate** ['pajɚət] *n.* pirate *m*; [Fig.] plagiaire *m/f*. || *v. intr.* exercer la piraterie; [Fig.] plagier. || *v. tr.* piller (un auteur); contrefaire (une preuve).
pistol ['pɪstl̩] *n.* pistolet *m*.
piston ['pɪstən] *n.* piston *m*: ~ *ring*, segment *m* de piston.
pit [pɪt] *n.* trou *m*, puits *m* (de mine); fosse *f*. || *v. tr.* trouer: *to* ~ *o.s. against s.o.*, se mesurer contre qqun.
pitch[1] [pɪʧ] *n.* poix *f*; bitume *m*. || *v. tr.* enduire (qqch.) de poix; bitumer.
pitch[2] *n.* jet *m*, lancement *m* (d'un projectile; [Fig.] point *m*, degré *m*; [propeller] pas *m* de vis; pente *f*; [Mus.] diapason *m*, ton *m*; [Naut.] tangage *m*. || *v. tr.* lancer (une balle); [away] jeter; établir; fixer; dresser (une tente); [Mus.] donner le ton (d'un chant, d'une chanson). || *v. intr.* [Naut.] tanguer: *pitched battle*, bataille *f* rangée. || **pitcher** [-ɚ] *n.* lanceur *m* (au baseball); pichet *m*, cruche *f*.
pitchfork [-,fɔɚk] *n.* fourche *f* (à foin). || *v. tr.* [Fam.] *to* ~ *s.o. into a job*, bombarder qqun (à un poste).
pitchpine [-,pajn] *n.* pitchpin *m*; bois *m* blanc.
piteous ['pɪtɪəs] *adj.* piteux, pitoyable.
pitfall ['pɪt,fɔl] *n.* piège *m*.
pith [pɪθ] *n.* moelle *f* (de sureau, &c.); [Fig.] substance *f*; l'essentiel *m*; [vigour] vigueur *f*, énergie *f*. || **pithy** [-ɪ] *adj.* substantiel; concis; savoureux.
pitiful ['pɪtɪ|fl̩] *adj.* pitoyable, lamentable. || **pitiless** [-ləs] *adj.* impitoyable.
pittance ['pɪtəns] *n.* †pitance *f*: [Fig.] *a mere* ~, la portion congrue.
pity *n.* pitié *f*, compassion *f*; dommage *m*: *to/have, take/* ~ *on*, prendre pitié de; *to feel* ~ *for*, avoir pitié de; *It's a* ~ *!*, C'est bien dommage!, © C'est de valeur! || *v. tr.* avoir pitié de, plaindre (qqun).
Pius ['pajəs] *n.* = Pie *m*.
pivot ['pɪvət] *n.* pivot *m*, axe *m*. || *v. tr. & intr.* (faire) pivoter.
pkg., pkgs. [= package, packages].
placard ['plækɚd] *n.* écriteau *m*, placard *m*; pancarte *f*. || *v. tr.* placarder (un mur, une annonce, &c.).
place [plejs] *n.* [spot] endroit *m*; [area] lieu *m*; [seat, situation, square] place *f*; localité *f*; [rank] rang *m*; [job] poste *m*, emploi *m*, place *f*: *from* ~ *to* ~, de-ci de-là; *all over the* ~, partout, de tous côtés; ~*/of business, in the country/*, maison *f*/de commerce, de campagne/; *at my* ~, chez moi; *to take* ~, avoir lieu; *to take s.o.'s* ~, remplacer qqun; *to win first* ~, remporter la première place; *Everything in its* ~, Chaque chose à sa place; *to put s.o. in his* ~, remettre qqun à sa place; *to change places*, changer de place; *in your* ~, à votre place; ~*-name*, nom *m* de lieu. || *v. tr.* placer, mettre; [set down] poser; [recall] remettre (qqun).
placid ['plæsɪd] *adj.* placide, calme.
plagiarism ['plejʤɚ|,izm] *n.* plagiat *m*. || **plagiarize** [-,ajz] *v. tr.* plagier.
plague [plejg] *n.* peste *f*; [calamity] fléau *m*. || *v. tr.* tourmenter, harceler, [Fam.] raser, embêter.
plaid [plæd] *n.* plaid *m*, couverture *f* de voyage.
plain [plejn] *adj.* clair, évident; simple; [truth, answer] franc; [colour] uni; [cooking] bourgeois; [pers.] sans attraits; plat, uni: *It is/as* ~ *as can be, as* ~ *as the nose on your face/*, C'est clair comme le jour, Cela saute aux yeux; *in* ~ *language*, en clair; *in* ~ *clothes*, en bourgeois; ~ *omelette*, omelette *f* nature. || *n.* plaine *f*. || *adv.* cf. PLAINLY. || **plainly** [-lɪ] *adv.* clairement; simplement; carrément; franchement.
plaintiff ['plejntɪf] *n.* demandeur *m*, plaignant *m*. || **plaintive** ['plejntɪv] *adj.*

plaintif. || **plaintively** [-lı] *adv.* d'une voix plaintive.

plan [plæn] *n.* plan *m*, projet *m*; dessein *m*; système *m*: *to change o.'s plans*, changer d'idée. || *v. tr.* [-nn-] tracer; dessiner; projeter; décider.

plane[1] [plejn] *n.* [tool] rabot *m.* || *v. tr.* raboter; [Fig.] aplanir.

plane[2] *n.* [tree] platane *m*; © plaine *f.*

plane[3] *adj.* plan, plat: ~ *geometry*, géométrie plane. || *n.* [Géom.] plan *m*; [Aviat.] avion *m*; [Fig.] plan *m* (*on*, sur), niveau *m* (*on*, à).

planet [ˈplænət] *n.* planète *f.*

plank [plæŋk] *n.* planche *f*; madrier *m*; [Pol.] cheval *m* de bataille, programme *m* électoral; [Naut.] bordage *m.* || *v. tr.* planchéier; [Naut.] border.

planning [ˈplænıŋ] *n.* planification *f*; élaboration *f* de plans: *town* ~, urbanisme *m.*

plant [plænt] *n.* **1.** plante *f*; plant *m.* **2.** outillage *m*; usine *f.* || *v. tr.* planter, ensemencer; implanter (une idée). || **plantation** [ˌplænˈtejʃən] *n.* plantation *f.* || **planter** [ˈplæntɚ] *n.* planteur *m.*

plash [plæʃ] *n.* flaque *f* d'eau, mare *f*: ~ *of the weir*, bruit *m* du barrage. || *v. tr.* éclabousser, entrelacer.

plasma [ˈplæzmə] *n.* plasma *m.*

plaster [ˈplæstɚ] *n.* plâtre *m*; [Med.] emplâtre *m.* || *v. tr.* plâtrer (qqch.); mettre, poser un emplâtre à (qqun); [Arg., = drunk] *plastered*, noir.

plastic [ˈplæstık] *n. & adj.* plastique (*m*).

Plata [ˈplætə] *also* the Plate (River) [river in S. America], le Rio de la Plata.

plate [plejt] *n.* assiette *f*; vaisselle *f* (d'argent); plaque *f* (de métal; de photographie); [Typ.] planche *f*: *to have too much on one's* ~, avoir du travail par-dessus la tête; *hot* ~, poêle *f* électrique. || *v. tr.* plaquer (qqch. d'argent, *sth. with silver*); argenter (de la vaisselle); étamer (un miroir).

plateau [plæˈtow] *n.* [Geog.] plateau *m.*

plateful [ˈplejtˌfʊl] *n.* assiettée *f*, [Fam.] platée *f.*

platform [ˈplætˌfoɚm] *n.* plate-forme *f*; [hall] estrade *f*; [Rail.] quai *m*; programme *m* politique.

platinum [ˈplætn̩əm] *n.* platine *m.*

platitude [ˈplætıˌtjuwd] *n.* platitude *f*, banalité *f.*

platter [ˈplætɚ] *n.* plat *m* (de service); [Fam.] disque *m.*

plausible [ˈplɔsıbl̩] *adj.* vraisemblable, plausible; [Pej.] spécieux.

play [plej] *n.* [fun] jeu *m*, amusement *m*; [game] partie *f*; jeu *m*; [looseness] jeu *m*; [light] jeu *m*; [Theat.] pièce *f* (de théâtre): *at* ~, en train de jouer, [Sch.] en récréation/; *in* ~, pour rire; ~ *on words*, jeu de mots, calembour *m*; *to bring, come/ into* ~, mettre, entrer/en jeu; *to give full* ~ *to . . .*, donner libre cours à . . . ; *to put on a* ~, représenter une pièce; *to go to a* ~, aller au théâtre. || *v. intr.* jouer (*at*, à + def. art.; *with*, avec; *on*, sur): *to* ~ *on s.o.'s feelings*, jouer sur les sentiments de qqun. || *v. tr.* jouer (à un sport, jeu; d'un instrument de musique); jouer (une carte, un rôle); diriger (*on*, sur); [trick] jouer (un tour à qqun); épuiser (un poisson): *to* ~ */football, the piano*, jouer/au football, du piano; *to* ~ *a game of* (*chess with s.o.*), faire une partie d'(échecs avec qqun); *to* ~ *with s.o.* (*at sth.*), faire une partie (de qqch.) avec qqun; *to* ~ *the fool*, faire l'imbécile. || **play down** [-ˈdawn] *v. tr.* diminuer. || **play off** [-ˈɔf] *v. intr.* [Sport.] se rencontrer en finale. || *n.* finale *f.* || **play out** [-ˈawt] *v. tr.* jouer jusqu'au bout: *to be* (*all*) *played out*, être (complètement) /démodé, épuisé. || **play up** [-ˈʌp] *v. tr.* accentuer, exploiter: [Fam.] *to* ~ *to s.o.*, flatter qqun. || **player** [-ɚ] *n.* joueur *m*; acteur *m*; musicien, -ne; [records] tourne-disque *m.* || **playground** [-ˌgɹawnd] *n.* terrain *m* de jeux; région *f*, lieux *mpl*/de plaisance. || **playpen** [-ˌpɛn] *n.* parc *m* (d'enfants, à jouer). || **playroom** [-ˌɹuwm] *n.* salle *f* de jeux. || **plaything** [-ˌθıŋ] *n.* jouet *m.* || **playwright** [-ˌɹajt] *n.* auteur *m* dramatique, †dramaturge *m.*

plea [plij] *n.* **1.** [Jur.] requête *f*, demande *f*: *to present a* ~ *of not guilty*, plaider non coupable. **2.** excuse *f*, prétexte *m*: *on the* ~ *of*, sous prétexte de.

plead [plijd] *v. tr. & intr.* plaider; alléguer; se défendre; arguer.

pleasant [ˈplɛzənt] *adj.* agréable; [pers.] aimable, sympathique; [in wishes] bon, bons, bonne (voyage, rêves, soirée, &c.). || **please** [plijz] *v. tr.* plaire (à qqun), faire plaisir à: (*if you*) ~, s'il vous plaît; *as you* ~, comme vous/voulez, voudrez. || **pleasing** [ˈplijzıŋ] *adj.* agréable; charmant, aimable. || **pleasure** [ˈplɛʒɚ] *n.* plaisir *m*: *with* ~, avec plaisir, volontiers; *to take* ~ *in*, éprouver du plaisir à; *at the* ~ *of*, au/gré, bon plaisir/de.

pleat [plijt] *n.* pli *m.* || *v. tr.* plisser.

pledge [plɛʤ] *n.* **1.** gage *m*, garantie *f*: *He gave his word as a* ~, Il a donné sa parole en garantie. **2.** promesse *f*: *He has taken the* ~, Il a fait la promesse de s'abstenir d'alcool. || *v. tr.* mettre en gage: *I ~ my word that . . .*, Je vous donne ma parole que . . . .

plentiful [ˈplɛntɪ|fl̩] *adj.* abondant, copieux; généreux. || **plenty** *n.* abondance *f*, profusion *f*. || *adv.* beaucoup (*of*, de).

pliable [ˈplajə|bl̩] *adj.* pliable, flexible; (caractère) souple, accommodant. || **pliant** [-nt] *adj.* cf. PLIABLE.

pliers [ˈplajɚz] *n.pl.* pinces *fpl*.

plight [plajt] *n.* **1.** condition *f*, situation *f*, position *f*: *What a ~ (to be in)!*, Quelle triste situation!; *in a sorry ~*, en fâcheuse position. †**2.** promesse *f*, engagement *m*. || †*v. tr.*: *to ~ one's troth*, promettre fidélité.

plod [plɑd] *v. intr.* **[-dd-]** marcher lourdement, péniblement: [Fig.] *to ~ on*, persévérer. || **plodder** [-ɚ] *n.* [Fam.] bûcheur *m*, piocheur *m*.

plot [plɑt] *n.* complot *m*, conspiration *f*; plan *m*, intrigue *f* (d'une pièce de théâtre, &c.); lopin *m* (de terre): *the ~ thickens*, l'action se complique. || *v. tr.* **[-tt-]** comploter; faire le plan de (qqch.); tracer (une courbe, &c.). || **plotter** [-ɚ] *n.* conspirateur *m*; [Tech.] traceur *m* de route.

plough [plaw] *n.* charrue *f*: *to put o.'s hand to the ~*, mettre la main à la charrue. || *v. tr.* labourer (la terre). || **ploughshare**, soc *m* (d'une charrue).

plow cf. PLOUGH.

pluck [plʌk] *n.* cran *m*, courage *m*; [Fig.] cœur *m*. || *v. tr.* cueillir (une fleur); arracher (des poils); plumer (une volaille); pincer (les cordes d'une guitare). || **plucky** [-ɪ] *adj.* courageux.

plug [plʌg] *n.* tampon *m*, bouchon *m*; [Elect.] prise *f* de courant; [prongs] fiche *f*; [Auto] bougie *f*. || *v. tr.* **[-gg-]** boucher; *~ in*, brancher (un appareil). || **plugugly** [-ˌʌglɪ] *n.* [US] dur *m*, brute *f*.

plum [plʌm] *n.* prune *f*: *dried ~*, pruneau *m*; *~-tree*, prunier *m*.

plumage [ˈpluwmədʒ] *n.* plumage *m*.

plumb [plʌm] *n.* plomb *m*; aplomb *m*: *~ line*, fil *m* à plomb; *out of ~*, hors d'aplomb. || *v. tr.* sonder (un lac); éclaircir (un mystère). || *adj.* droit, vertical, d'aplomb; [Fam.] pur. || *adv.* droit, d'aplomb; [Fam.] juste; tout à fait. || **plumber** [-ɚ] *n.* plombier *m*. || **plumbing** [-ɪŋ] *n.* [trade] plomberie *f*; [pipes] tuyauterie *f*, tuyaux *mpl*.

plume [pluwm] *n.* plume *f*; plumet *m*; panache *m*: *borrowed plumes*, se parer des plumes du paon. || *v. tr.* plumer (une volaille); empanacher (un chapeau).

plump[1] [plʌmp] *adj.* potelé; gras *m*, -se *f*. || *v. intr.* gonfler, engraisser.

plump[2] *v. intr.* tomber lourdement. || *adv.* en plein, d'aplomb; tout droit.

plunder [ˈplʌndɚ] *n.* pillage *m* (d'une ville, &c.); butin *m*. || *v. tr.* piller, dépouiller.

plunge [plʌndʒ] *n.* plongeon *m*. || *v. intr.* plonger, se plonger, s'enfoncer; [of a horse] se cabrer. || *v. tr.* plonger, enfoncer.

pluperfect [ˈpluwˌpɚfəkt] *n.* plus-que-parfait *m*.

plural [ˈpluwɚəl] *adj.* pluriel. || *n.* [Gram.] pluriel *m*. || **plurality** [-ɪtɪ] *n.* majorité *f*; cumul *m* (de fonctions).

plus [plʌs] *n.* [Math. Typ.] plus *m*: *2 ~ 2 equals 4*, 2 plus 2 font 4.

plush [plʌʃ] *n.* peluche *f*.

plutocrat [ˈpluwtəˌkɹæt] *n.* ploutocrate *m*.

ply [plaj] *v. tr.* **1.** manier (un instrument): *to ~ the needle*, tirer l'aiguille, coudre. **2.** faire: *to ~ a trade*, faire, exercer/un métier. **3.** presser: *to ~ s.o. with questions*, presser qqun de questions; *to ~ s.o. with drink(s)*, pousser qqun à boire (beaucoup). || *v. intr.* faire le service (entre A et B). || **plywood** [-ˌwʊd] *n.* (panneau) contre-plaqué *m*.

P.M.[1] [ˈPijˈɛm] [= Prime Minister; Postmaster].

P.M.[2] also **p.m.** [= post meridiem] © P.M.; [Fr.] de l'après-midi, du soir [☞ In France, hours are counted from 0 to 24: *at two P.M.*, à deux heures de l'après-midi, à 14 heures; *at 10 P.M.*, à 10 heures du soir, à 22 heures.]

pneumatic [ˌnjuwˈmætɪk] *adj.* pneumatique, à air *m* comprimé. || **pneumonia** [ˌnjuwˈmownjə] *n.* pneumonie *f*.

P.O. [= Post Office].

poach [powtʃ] *v. tr.* pocher (des œufs). || *v. intr.* braconner. || **poacher** [-ɚ] *n.* braconnier *m*.

pocket [ˈpɑkət] *n.* poche *f*; cavité *f*; blouse *f* (d'une table de billard): *to put o.'s hands in o.'s pockets*, mettre les mains dans les poches. || *v. tr.* empocher; [Fig.] encaisser, avaler (des injures). || **pocketbook** [-ˌbʊk] *n.* livre *m* de poche; [notes] calepin *m*; [wallet] portefeuille *m*. || **pocketknife** [-ˌnajf] *n.* couteau *m* de poche, canif *m*.

pod [pɑd] *n.* cosse *f*; gousse *f* (de pois).

poem [ˈpowəm] *n.* poème *m*, poésie *f*. || **poet** [ˈpowət] *n.* poète *m/f*. || **poetic** [powˈɛtɪk] *adj.* poétique. || **poetics** [-s] *n.pl.* poétique *f*, art *m* poétique. || **poetry** [ˈpowətɹɪ] *n.* poésie *f*: *a piece of ~*, une poésie; *to write ~*, faire des vers.

poignant [ˈpojnjənt] *adj.* poignant; émouvant.

point [pojnt] *n.* [tip] pointe *f*; promontoire *m*, pointe *f*; [spot, dot, score, punctuation, stocks, printing] point *m*; [compass] aire *f* de vent; quart *m*; [Fig.] point *m*, détail *m*; question *f*; *pl.* [auto] pointes *fpl* (d'allumage); [Rail.] aiguillage *m*: *boiling* ~, point *m* d'ébullition; *from the economic* ~ *of view*, au, du/point de vue économique; *10.5* (*ten* ~ *five*), 10,5 (dix virgule cinq); *What is the* ~ (*of that*)?, À quoi bon (cela), À quoi cela sert-il?; *There is no* ~ *in doing that*, Il ne sert à rien de faire cela; *I don't see the* ~ *of that*, Je ne comprends rien à cela; *Here is the* ~, Voici de quoi il s'agit; *That is not the* ~, Ce n'est pas là la question; *On this* ~, A ce propos; *That is off the* ~, Cela sort de la question; *His answer was to the* ~, Sa réponse ne manquait pas d'à propos; *Let's stick to the* ~, Parlons peu mais parlons bien; *He/carried, made/his* ~, Il a fait valoir son point de vue; *He made a* ~ *of being impartial*, Il se faisait un devoir d'être impartial. || *v. tr.* braquer (un fusil, &c., sur qqun), diriger (qqch. vers qqun); indiquer (le chemin), montrer (du doigt); tailler (un crayon); aiguiser (un outil). || *v. intr.* indiquer; montrer (du doigt); se diriger (vers); [Fig.] indiquer. || **point blank** [-ˌblæŋk] *adv.*: *to fire* ~, tirer à bout portant; *to ask* ~, demander de but en blanc; *to refuse* ~, refuser catégoriquement. || **pointer** [-ɚ] *n.* aiguille *f*, index *m*; [Hunt] chien *m* d'arrêt; [Sch.] baguette *f*. || **pointless** [-ləs] *adj.* sans pointe, émoussé; [Fig.] inutile, gratuit; [joke] sans sel. || **point out** [-ˈawt] *v. tr.* montrer (du doigt), signaler (qqch. à qqun); [Fig.] attirer l'attention (de qqun) sur (qqch.); faire observer (à qqun que). || **point up** [-ˈʌp] *v. tr.* faire remarquer, souligner (qqch.).

poise [pojz] *n.* équilibre *m*, aplomb *m* [also Fig.]. || *v. tr.* tenir, porter/en équilibre.

poison [ˈpojzn̩] *n.* poison *m*. || *v. tr.* empoisonner, intoxiquer. || *adj.* ~ *ivy*, sumac vénéneux, © herbe à la puce. || **poisonous** [-əs] *adj.* empoisonné; [of a gas, or drink] toxique; [of a plant] vénéneu|x, -se; [of a snake, &c.] venimeu|x, -se.

poke [powk] *v. tr.* pousser; [thrust into] fourrer dans; [fire] tisonner; *to* ~ *about*, fourgonner; *to* ~ *fun at*, se moquer de. || *n.* poussée *f*, coup *m*. || **poker** [-ɚ] *n.* tisonnier *m*; [cards] poker *m*.

Poland [ˈpowlənd] *n.* la Pologne *f*: *in, to*/~, en P.

polar [ˈpowlɚ] *adj.* polaire: ~ *bear*, ours *m* blanc, © polaire. || **Polaris** [ˌpowˈlaɚıs] *n.* l'étoile *f* polaire.

pole[1] [powl] *n.* **1.** pôle *m*; *poles apart*, diamétralement opposé. **2.** poteau *m*; mât *m*; gaule *f*, perche *f*.

Pole[2] *n.* Polonais, -e.

police [pəˈlijs] *n.* police *f*; [mounted] gendarmerie *f*; ~ *station*, poste *m* de police, [Fr.] commissariat *m*. || **policeman** [-mən] *pl.* **policemen** [-mən] *n.* agent *m* (de police), © [abus.] constable *m*, [abus.] police *f*.

policy [ˈpɑlısı] *n.* politique *f*; ligne *f* de conduite; [Insurance] police *f* d'assurance.

polish[1] [ˈpɑlıʃ] *n.* poli *m*, lustre *m* (d'une surface); [shoe-] cirage *m*, crème *f* (à chaussures); [floor] cire *f* (à parquet); encaustique *f* (à meubles); [nail-] vernis *m* (pour ongles); [metal-] brillant *m* à métaux; [Fig.] vernis, politesse *f*. || *v. tr.* polir; [wax] cirer (les chaussures, le parquet); vernir (les ongles). || **polish off** [ˈɔf] *v. tr.* expédier (du travail); régler le compte de (qqun). || **polish up** [ˈʌp] *v. tr.* faire reluire; dérouiller (son français, &c.); relimer (son style).

Polish[2] [ˈpowlıʃ] *adj.* polonais.

polite [pəˈlajt] *adj.* poli, courtois. || **politely** [-lı] *adv.* poliment. || **politeness** [-nəs] *n.* politesse *f*, courtoisie *f*.

politic [ˈpɑlıtık] *adj.* adroit, habile; [of pers.] avisé, rusé. || **political** [pəˈlıtıkl] *adj.* politique. || **politically** [-lı] *adv.* politiquement. || **politician** [ˌpɑlıˈtıʃən] *n.* homme *m* politique; homme public, homme d'État. || **politics** [ˈpɑlıˌtıks] *n.* politique *f*; opinions *fpl* politiques.

poll [powl] *n.* **1.** liste *f* électorale; élection *f*, scrutin *m*; sondage *m* d'opinion. **2.** bureau *m* de vote, [également *polling-booth*]: *to go to the polls*, aller aux urnes, voter. || *v. tr.* voter; obtenir (un certain nombre de voix); exprimer (un vote).

pollute [pəˈluwt] *v. tr.* polluer, corrompre.

polygamy [pəˈlıgəmı] *n.* polygamie *f*.

Polynesia [ˌpɑlıˈnijʒə] *n.* la Polynésie *f*: *in, to*/~, en P.

pomade [pɑmˈejd] *n.* pommade *f*.

pomegranate [ˈpɑməˌgɹænıt] *n.* grenade *f*.

pomp [pɑmp] *n.* pompe *f*, faste *m*, apparat *m*. || **pompous** [-əs] *adj.* fastueux [style, person] pompeux.

pond [pɑnd] *n.* étang *m*, mare *f*.

ponder [pɑndɚ] *v. tr.* peser, réfléchir sur/(une question). || **ponderous** [ˈpɑndɹəs] *adj.* pesant, massif.

Pontiff [ˈpɑntıf] *n.* [R.C.] pontife *m*: *to*

elect a new ~, élire un nouveau pape. || **pontifical** [ˌpɑn'tɪfɪkl̩] *adj.* [Rel.] pontifical.

pontoon [ˌpɑn'tuwn] *n.* ponton *m*, bac *m*; flotteur *m* (d'hydravion): ~ *bridge*, pont *m* de bateaux.

pony ['pownɪ] *pl.* **ponies** [-z] *n.* poney *m.*

poodle ['puwdl̩] *n.* caniche *m.*

pool [puwl] *n.* étang *m*; bassin *m*; [Com.] fonds commun: *swimming* ~, piscine *f*; ~ *room*, salle *f* de billard; ~ *train*, train commun (à deux réseaux).

poor [puwɚ] *adj.* pauvre, indigent; [Fig.] médiocre, piètre, mauvais: *the* ~, les pauvres *mpl*, les indigents *mpl.*

poorly [-lɪ] *adj.* souffrant, en mauvaise santé: *to feel* ~, → ne pas se sentir bien. || *adv.* pauvrement, médiocrement.

pop [pɑp] *n.* explosion *f*, détonation *f* (d'une bouteille qu'on débouche), saut *m* (d'un bouchon); [drink] limonade *f.* || *v. intr.* [-pp-] exploser, détoner, sauter (avec un petit bruit sec): *to* ~ *in, out*, entrer, sortir/brusquement. || *v. tr.* tirer, faire sauter (un bouchon); faire griller (du maïs); soulever (une question) à brûle-pourpoint; crever (un ballon).

Pope[1] [powp] *n.* [R.C.] le Pape *m*; le Saint-Père *m.* || **pope**[2] *n.* [Rel.] pope *m* (de l'Église orthodoxe).

poplar ['pɑplɚ] *n.* peuplier *m.*

poppy ['pɑpɪ] *n.* coquelicot *m.*

poppycock [-ˌkɑk] *n.* baliverne *f*, boniment *m*, inepties *fpl*, foutaises *fpl*, fadaises *fpl*, bouillie *f* pour les chats.

populace ['pɑpjə|ləs] *n.* foule *f*; [Pej.] populace *f.* || **popular** [-lɚ] *adj.* populaire, en vogue. || **popularity** [ˌpɑpjə'læɚɪtɪ] *n.* popularité *f* (d'une personne); vogue *f* (d'une chose). || **popularly** ['pɑpjə|lɚlɪ] *adv.* populairement de, par tout le monde, communément: *It is* ~ *supposed that*, → Les gens se figurent que. || **populate** [-ˌlejt] *v. tr.* peupler. || **population** [ˌpɑpjə'lejʃən] *n.* population *f.*

porcelain ['pɔɚsələn] *n.* porcelaine *f.*

porch [pɔɚtʃ] *n.* porche *m* (d'une église); portique *m* (d'une maison), © galerie *f.*

porcupine ['pɔɚkjəˌpajn] *n.* porc-épic *m.*

pore [pɔɚ] *n.* pore *m.* || *v. tr.*: *to* ~ *over*, examiner avec attention; dévorer (un livre).

pork [pɔɚk] *n.* (viande *f* de) porc *m*: ~ *chop*, côtelette *f* de porc.

porous [pɔɚəs] *adj.* poreux, perméable.

porridge ['pɔɚɪdʒ] *n.* gruau *m*, bouillie *f* (d'avoine).

port[1] [pɔɚt] *n.* port *m*; †havre *m*: ~ *of call*, port d'escale; *home* ~, port d'attache; ~ *of entry*, poste *m* de douane; ~ *warden*, capitaine *m*, maître *m*/ de port.

port[2] *n.* [Naut. = porthole] hublot *m*; bâbord *m*; ~ *and starboard*, bâbord et tribord.

port[3] *n.* [wine] porto *m.*

portable [-əbl̩] *adj.* portati|f, -ve. || **portage** ['pɔɚtɪdʒ] *n.* © portage *m.* || *v. tr.* © portager.

portend [ˌpɔɚ'tɛnd] *v. tr.* présager, augurer.

portent ['pɔɚtɛnt] *n.* mauvais présage *m.* || **portentous** [pɔɚ'tɛnʃəs] *adj.* de mauvais augure *m*; extraordinaire.

porter ['pɔɚtɚ] *n.* portier *m*, concierge *m*; portefaix *m*; porteur *m* (dans une gare); chasseur *m* (d'hôtel).

portfolio [ˌpɔɚt'fowlɪow] *n.* portefeuille *m*; serviette *f* (à documents).

portion ['pɔɚʃən] *n.* portion *f*, part *f*; [dowry] dot *f.* || *v. tr.* partager, répartir; doter.

portly [-lɪ] *adj.* corpulent, fort.

portrait ['pɔɚtɹejt] *n.* portrait *m.* || **portray** [pɔɚ'tɹej] *v. tr.* peindre; dépeindre, décrire, faire le portrait de (qqun). || **portrayal** [-l] *n.* portrait *m*, représentation *f.*

Portugal ['pɔɚtʃəg|əl] *n.* le Portugal: *in, to*/~, au P. || **Portuguese** [-ɪz] *n. & adj.* portugais, -e.

pose [powz] *n.* pose *f*; affectation *f.* || *v. tr.* poser. || *v. intr.* **1.** poser, prendre une pose. **2.** affecter une attitude, être poseur: *to* ~ *as*, se faire passer pour.

position [pə'zɪʃən] *n.* position *f*, attitude *f*; [location] situation *f*, place *f*; [situation] état *m*, situation; [job] poste *m*, situation; [rank] rang *m*, condition *f*; [window] guichet *m*, comptoir *m*; [Mil.] position, [ship] lieu *m* (du navire); point *m* de vue: *in, out of*/~, en place, déplacé; *in a high* ~, haut placé; *in your* ~, à votre place; *to be in a* ~ *to*, être/en état, à même/de; [Fig.] *to take up, adopt*/*a* ~, prendre position. || *v. tr.* mettre en position, situer.

positive ['pɑzɪtɪv] *adj.* positif; [convinced] sûr, certain; affirmatif; [proof, statement] formel: *It's a* ~ *scandal*, C'est un vrai scandale.

posse ['pɑsɪ] *n.* détachement *m* (de police).

possess [pə'zɛs] *v. tr.* posséder. || **possession** [pə'zɛʃən] *n.* possession *f.* || **possessive** [pə'zɛsɪv] *adj.* possessif. || *n.* [Gram.] possessif *m.* || **possessor** [pə'zɛzɚ] *n.* possesseur *m.*

possibility [pɑsɪ'bɪlɪtɪ] *n.* possibilité *f*; éventualité *f*: *if by any* ~, si par hasard; *within the bounds of* ~, dans la mesure du **possible.** || **possible** [ˈpɑsɪbl̩] *adj.* possible. || **possibly** [-ɪ] *adv.* possiblement, peut-être, sans doute.

post [powst] *n.* **1.** [wooden, metal] poteau *m*; [bed] colonne *f*: *lamppost*, réverbère *m*; *signpost*, poteau *m* indicateur. **2.** [mail] poste *f*; [Br.] courrier *m*: *by* ~, par la poste; *by parcel* ~, par colis postal; *to receive sth. in the* ~, recevoir qqch. par la poste/dans le courrier/. **3.** [station] poste *m* (de sentinelle); [job] poste *m*; [trading] factorerie *f*. **4.** [Mil.] sonnerie *f*: *the last* ~, la retraite (du soir); [Fr.] aux champs, © la sonnerie aux morts. || *v. tr.* **1.** placarder (une affiche); afficher (un avis, un nom): *Post no bills*, Défense d'afficher. **2.** mettre à la poste, à la boîte, poster; envoyer, expédier par la poste: [Com.] *to* ~ *an item in the ledger*, porter un article au grand livre; *to keep s.o. posted*, tenir qqun au courant. **3.** mettre (une sentinelle) en faction; affecter (à une unité militaire). || **postage** [-ədʒ] *n.* port *m*, affranchissement *m*, taxe *f*, droit *m*: ~ *stamp*, timbre-poste *m*; ~ *due*, port dû; *free* ~, franchise postale; ~ *paid*, port payé, franco. || **postal** [-l̩] *adj.* postal: ~ *box*, boîte *f* postale, case *f* postale; ~ *station*, bureau *m* de poste; succursale *f*; ~ *employee/clerk/*, posti|er, -ère. || **postcard** [-kɑɚd] *n.* carte *f* postale.

poster [-ɚ] *n.* affiche *f*.

posterior [ˌpɑsˈtijɚɪɚ] *adj.* & *n.* postérieur (*m*). || **posterity** [pɑsˈtɛɚɪtɪ] *n.* postérité *f*.

post-free [ˈpowstˌfɹij] *adj.* [Br.] franco (de port).

post-graduate [ˌpowstˈgɹædjuwət] *n.* & *adj.* © post-gradué; [Fr.] universitaire, avancé.

posthumous [ˈpɑstuwməs] *adj.* posthume.

postman [ˈpowstmən] *n.* facteur *m*, © postillon *m*. || **postmark** [-ˌmɑɚk] *n.* timbre *m* d'oblitération. || *v. tr.* timbrer. || **postmaster** [-ˌmæstɚ] *n.* maître de poste: ~ *General*, ministre *m* des Postes. || **post office** [-ˌɑfɪs] *n.* bureau *m* de poste.

postpone [powsˈpown] *v. tr.* remettre (qqch. à plus tard), différer (une action), ajourner (une réunion). || **postponement** [-mənt] *n.* ajournement *m*.

postscript [-ˌskɹɪpt] *n.* post-scriptum *m*.

postulate [ˈpɑstjəˌlejt] *v. tr.* postuler: *Let us* ~ *that . . .*, Admettons que . . . [+ subjunc.].

posture [ˈpɑstʃɚ] *n.* posture *f*, position *f* [also Fig.]. || *v. tr.* & *intr.* cf. POSE.

pot [pɑt] *n.* pot *m*; vase *m*; marmite *f*: *pots and pans*, batterie *f* de cuisine; ~*-holder*, poignée *f*; *to keep the* ~ *boiling*, pourvoir aux besoins du ménage; *to take* ~ *luck with s.o.*, manger chez qqun à la fortune du pot; [Fam.] *a big* ~, une grosse légume, un gros bonnet; *to go to* ~, s'en aller à vau-l'eau, aller à la ruine; *The* ~ *calling the kettle black*, La pelle se moque du fourgon.

potash [-ˌæʃ] *n.* potasse *f*. || **potassium** [pəˈtæsɪəm] *n.* potassium *m*.

potato [pəˈtejtow] *pl.* **potatoes** [-z] *n.* pomme *f* de terre, © patate *f*; *sweet* ~, [Fr.] patate *f*, © patate douce.

potency [ˈpowtən|sɪ] *n.* [power] puissance *f*; [strength] force *f*; efficacité *f*. || **potent** [-t] *adj.* puissant; fort; efficace. || **potential** [pəˈtɛnʃəl] *adj.* potentiel; [possible] en puissance. || *n.* potentiel *m*.

pot-hole [ˈpɑtˌhowl] *n.* [road] nid *m* de poule.

potter[1] [ˈpɑtɚ] *v. intr.* cf. PUTTER.

potter[2] *n.* potier *m*. || **pottery** [-ɪ] *n.* poterie *f*.

pouch [pawtʃ] *n.* poche *f*, petit sac *m*, bourse *f*: *tobacco* ~, blague *f* à tabac.

poultice [ˈpowltɪs] *n.* [Med.] cataplasme *m*.

poultry [ˈpowltɹɪ] *n.* volaille *f*: ~ *yard*, basse-cour *f*.

pounce [pawns] *v. intr.* se précipiter (sur), fondre (sur); saisir: [Fig.] *He skilfully pounced on a fact which almost everyone else overlooked*, Il souligna habilement un fait qui avait échappé à la plupart.

pound [pawnd] *n.* [weight, money] livre *f*; [dogs, cars] fourrière *f*. || *v. tr.* broyer, concasser; piler, pilonner; taper sur (qqun). || *v. intr.* cogner, frapper.

pour [pɔɚ] *v. tr.* verser (de la crème), répandre (un liquide). || *v. intr.* pleuvoir à verse; [of a liquid] couler à flots: *pouring rain*, pluie *f*/torrentielle, battante.

pout [pawt] *v. intr.* faire la moue, bouder.

poverty [ˈpɑvɚtɪ] *n.* pauvreté *f*, indigence *f*; pénurie *f*.

POW [ˌPijˌowˈdʌbl̩juw] *pl.* **POW'S** [= Prisoner of War], P.G. [= prisonnier *m* de guerre].

powder [ˈpawdɚ] *n.* poudre *f*: *gunpowder*, poudre à canon; *face* ~, poudre *f*, poudre de riz; *body* ~, poudre *f* de toilette, talc *m*; ~ *room*, boudoir *m*, salle *f* de toilette; lavabos *mpl* (pour dames); ~ *puff*, houppe *f*; [Arg.] *to take a* ~, prendre la poudre d'escampette. || **powdered** [-d] *adj.* pulvérisé, en poudre (sucre, &c.); saupoudré. || **powdery** [-ɪ] *adj.* poudreu|x, -se; friable.

power [ˈpawɚ] *n.* **1.** [authority] pouvoir *m*, autorité *f*: *the powers that be*, les autorités (constituées); *legislative, judicial*/~, le pouvoir/législatif, judiciaire/; *to be, come to*/~, être, arriver/au pouvoir; *to grant full powers*, accorder les pleins pouvoirs; *with full powers*, de pleine autorité; *to fall into s.o.'s* ~, tomber au pouvoir de qqun; *to have s.o. in o.'s* ~, avoir qqun sous sa coupe; *to have* ~ *over*, avoir autorité sur; *to do all in o.'s* ~, faire tout ce qui est en son pouvoir; ~ *of pardon*, droit *m* de grâce. **2.** [strength] puissance *f*, force *f*; [nation, Math.] puissance; [energy] énergie *f*, force; [Elect.] électricité *f*, énergie électrique; [capacity] faculté *f*, talent *m*: *mental powers*, facultés intellectuelles; ~ *of attorney*, procuration *f*; *with* ~ *to*, avec faculté de; ~ *-brakes*, servo-freins *mpl*; ~ *-/house, station/*, centrale *f* électrique. || *v. tr.* actionner. || **powerful** [-fḷ] *adj.* puissant. || **powerless** [-ləs] *adj.* impuissant; inefficace.

practicable ['pɹæktɪ|kəbḷ] *adj.* praticable, faisable; [road, river] praticable. || **practical** [-kḷ] *adj.* pratique; réel; positif. || **practically** [-kḷɪ] *adv.* pratiquement; en pratique; presque. || **practice** [-tɪs] *n.* pratique *f*; [custom] usage *m*; [Med.] clientèle *f*: *to put into* ~, mettre en pratique; *to be in* ~, être/en forme, bien entraîné; *to be out of* ~, être rouillé. || **practise** [-tɪs] *v. tr.* pratiquer, exercer/(une profession); s'exercer à (qqch.); étudier, travailler/(le violon, &c.). || **practitioner** ['pɹæktɪʃənə˞] *n.* praticien *m*: *general* ~, médecin *m* de médecine générale.

pragmatic [ˌpɹæg'mætɪ|k] *adj.* pragmatique. || **pragmatism** [-zm] *n.* réalisme *m*, dogmatisme *m*, [Phil.] pragmatisme *m*.

prairie ['pɹɛəɪ] *n.* prairie *f*, savane *f*: *Prairie Provinces*, Provinces *fpl* des Prairies.

praise [pɹejs] *n.* louange *f*, éloge *m*: *in* ~ *of*, à la louange de. || *v. tr.* louer, louanger, vanter (qqun, qqch.): *to* ~ *s.o. for sth.*, faire l'éloge de qqun pour qqch.

prance [pɹæns] *v. intr.* [horse] caracoler; [pers.] se pavaner, plastronner.

prank [pɹæŋk] *n.* escapade *f*, frasque *f*, espièglerie *f*: *to play pranks* (*on s.o.*), /faire des niches, jouer des tours/(à qqun).

prattle ['pɹætḷ] *n.* [enfants] babillage *m*; [pers.] bavardage *m*, papotage *m*. || *v. intr.* [child] babiller: [pers.] bavarder, papoter.

pray [pɹej] *v. tr. & intr.* prier, faire une prière: *to* ~ *to God*, prier Dieu. || **prayer** [pɹɛə˞] *n.* prière *f*; supplication *f*: *to say a* ~, faire une prière; *to address a fervent* ~ *to God*, adresser à Dieu une fervente prière; *the first prayers*, les prières au bas de l'autel; *praystool*, prie-Dieu *m inv.*

preach [pɹijtʃ] *v. tr.* prêcher (un sermon, &c.). || **preacher** [-ə˞] *n.* prédicateur *m*. || **preaching** [ɪŋ] *n.* prédication *f*; sermon *m*.

preamble [ˌpɹɪ'æmbḷ] *n.* préambule *m*; remarque *f* préliminaire.

precarious [pɹɪ'kɛəɹəs] *adj.* précaire, incertain.

precaution [pɹɪ'kɔʃən] *n.* précaution *f*.

precede [pɹɪ'sijd] *v. tr.* précéder, devancer; faire précéder de; avoir la préséance sur. || **precedence** ['pɹɛsədən|s] *n.* préséance *f*, priorité *f*: *To take* ~ *over*, Avoir le pas sur. || **precedent** [-t] *n.* précédent *m*. || **preceding** [pɹɪ'sijdɪŋ] *adj.* précédent, -e: *the* ~ *day*, la veille.

precept ['pɹɪˌsɛpt] *n.* précepte *m*.

precious ['pɹɛʃəs] *adj.* précieu|x, -se, de valeur.

precipice ['pɹɛsɪpəs] *n.* précipice *m*. || **precipitate** [pɹə'sɪpɪˌtejt] *n.* [Chim.] précipité *m*. || *v. tr.* précipiter; [events] accélérer, hâter. || *adj.* [actions] précipité; [Pers.] trop pressé. || **precipitation** [pɹəˌsɪpɪ'tejʃən] *n.* précipitation *f*. || **precipitous** [pɹə'sɪpɪtəs] *adj.* escarpé, abrupt.

precise [pɹɪ'sajs] *adj.* précis, exact. || **precision** [pɹɪ'sɪʒən] *n.* précision *f*, exactitude *f*.

preclude [pɹɪ'kluwd] *v. tr.* empêcher, prévenir, exclure; empêcher (de + inf.).

precocious [pɹɪ'kowʃəs] *adj.* précoce.

preconception [ˌpɹɪkən'sɛpʃən] *n.* idée *f* préconçue.

predecessor [pɹɪdɪ'sɛsə˞] *n.* prédécesseur *m*.

predicament [pɹɪ'dɪkəmənt] *n.* situation *f* difficile, [Fam.] embêtement *m*.

predicate ['pɹɛdɪkət] *n.* [Gram.] prédicat *m*, [le verbe et son attribut ou ses compléments]. || *v. tr.* ['pɹɛdɪkejt] affirmer; [Fig.] fonder sur.

predict [pɹɪ'dɪk|t] *v. tr.* prédire; [Fig.] prophétiser. || **prediction** [-ʃən] *n.* prédiction *f*.

predilection [ˌpɹɪdɪ'lɛkʃən] *n.* prédilection *f* (*for*, pour).

predispose [ˌpɹɪdɪ'spowz] *v. tr.* prédisposer.

predominance [pɹɪ'dɑmɪn|ən|s] *n.* prédominance *f*. || **predominant** [-ənt] *adj.* prédominant, prévalent. || **predominate** [-ˌejt] *v. intr.* prédominer, prévaloir.

prefab ['pɹijˌfæb] [= prefabricated] *adj.* préfabriqué.

preface ['pɹɛfəs] *n.* préface *f* (d'un livre, &c.). || *v. tr.* préfacer (un livre, &c.).

prefer [pɹɪ'fɚ] *v. tr.* [-rr-] préférer; aimer mieux; [Jur.] déposer (une plainte contre qqun, *a charge against s.o.*): *to ~ sth. to sth.*, préférer qqch. à qqch., aimer mieux qqch. que qqch.; *to ~ to stay rather than leave*, préférer rester plutôt que de partir. || **preferable** ['pɹɛfɚ|əbl̩] *adj.* préférable. || **preferably** [-əblɪ] *adv.* de préférence. || **preference** [-əns] *n.* préférence *f.*

prefix ['pɹij,fɪks] *n.* [Ling.] préfixe *m.* || *v. tr.* préfixer.

pregnant ['pɹɛgnənt] *adj.* enceinte; [animal] pleine; [Fig.] fertile: *(a situation) ~ with possibilities*, fertile en possibilités.

prejudice ['pɹɛʤədɪs] *n.* préjugé *m*, parti *m* pris; préventions *fpl*; [Jur.] préjudice *m*; détriment *m* (contre qqun, *against s.o.*): *to the ~ of*, au préjudice de; *without ~ to*, sans préjudice de. || *v. tr.* inspirer des préventions à (qqun), donner des préjugés à (qqun); [Jur.] causer du préjudice à (qqun); agir au détriment de (qqun). || **prejudicial** [,pɹɛʤə'dɪʃəl] *adj.* préjudiciable (*to*, à).

prelate ['pɹɛlət] *n.* prélat *m.*

preliminary [pɹɪ'lɪmɪnɛɚɪ] *n.* préliminaire *m*: *preliminaries* (*of peace, &c.*), préliminaires (de paix, &c.). || *adj.* préliminaire, préalable.

prelude ['pɹɛljuwd] *n.* prélude *m.* || *v. intr.* préluder (à).

premature [,pɹɪmə'tjuwɚ] *adj.* prématuré; [child] né avant terme.

premeditated [pɹɪ'mɛdɪ,tejtəd] *adj.* prémédité.

premier ['pɹijmjɚ] *n.* premier ministre *m*, [Fr.] président *m* du Conseil. || *adj.* principal. || **premiership** [-ʃɪp] *n.* poste *m* de premier ministre.

premise ['pɹɛmɪs] *n.* **1.** prémisse *f.* **2.** *pl.* locaux *mpl*, lieux *mpl*, immeuble *m.*

premium ['pɹijmjəm] *n.* prime *f*; récompense *f.*

premonition [,pɹɪmə'nɪʃən] *n.* prémonition *f*, pressentiment *m.*

preoccupation [pɹɪ,ɑkjə'pejʃən] *n.* préoccupation *f*, souci *m.* || **preoccupied** [pɹɪ'ɑkjə,paj|d] *adj.* préoccupé, inqui|et, -ète: *to be ~*, avoir l'esprit ailleurs. || **preoccupy** *v. tr.* préoccuper; prévenir.

prepaid ['pɹɪ'pejd] *adj.* affranchi, franc de port. || *adv.* franco.

preparation [,pɹɛpɚ'ejʃən] *n.* préparation *f*; *pl.* préparatifs *mpl.* || **preparatory** [pɹə'pɛɚ|ɪ,tɔɚɪ] *adj.* préparatoire, préalable. || *adv.* *~ to*: en vue de, préalablement à.

prepare [pɹɪ'pɛɚ] *v. tr.* préparer, apprêter (*for, to*, à). || *v. intr.* se préparer (*for, to*, à). || **preparedness** [-ədnəs] *n.* état *m* de préparation.

prepay ['pɹij'pej] *v. tr.* [Post.] affranchir (qqch.), payer (qqch.) d'avance: *prepaid parcel*, colis affranchi. || **prepayment** [-mənt] *n.* [Post.] affranchissement *m* (d'un colis).

preponderant [pɹɪ'pɑndɚənt] *adj.* prépondérant.

preposition [,pɹɛpə'zɪʃən] *n.* [Gram.] préposition *f.*

prepossessing [,pɹɪpə'zɛsɪŋ] *adj.* aimable, avenant.

preposterous [pɹɪ'pɑstɚəs] *adj.* absurde.

prerequisite [pɹɪ'ɹɛkwɪzɪt] *adj.* requis, -e. || *n.* exigence *f* préalable, nécessité *f* préalable, condition *f* préalable.

prerogative [pɹɪ'ɹɑgətɪv] *n.* prérogative *f*, privilège *m.*

†**presage** ['pɹɛsəʤ] *n.* présage *m*, augure *m.* || [pɹɪ'sejʤ] *v. tr.* présager, prédire, augurer.

Presbyterian [,pɹɛzbɪ'tɛɚɪən] *n.* & *adj.* [Rel.] presbytérien, -ne.

prescribe [pɹɪ'skɹajb] *v. tr.* prescrire, ordonner. || **prescription** [pɹɪ'skɹɪpʃən] *n.* [Jur., Fig.] prescription *f*; [Med.] ordonnance *f*; prescription (énoncé du traitement médical): *to fill prescriptions*, exécuter des ordonnances.

presence ['pɹɛzənt|s] *n.* présence *f*: *in ~ of*, en présence de. || **present** ['pɹɛzənt] *adj.* présent; [~ -day] actuel; [month] courant; présent, en question: *to be ~ at*, être présent à, assister à; *at the ~ time*, à présent, à l'heure actuelle; *in the ~ case*, dans le cas/présent, qui nous occupe. || *n.* [gift] cadeau *m*, présent *m*; [time, Gram.] présent *m*: *at ~*, à présent; *for the ~*, pour le moment; *to make a ~ of sth. to s.o.*, faire cadeau de, offrir/qqch. à qqun. || [pɹə'zɛnt] *v. tr.* présenter; offrir: *to ~ s.o. with sth.*, offrir, donner/(qqch.) à qqun; *to ~ one's compliments and best wishes*, présenter/ses vœux, ses souhaits/. || **presentation** [,pɹɛzn̩'tejʃən] *n.* présentation *f*: *to make a ~*, faire un cadeau.

presentiment [pɹɪ'sɛntɪmənt] *n.* pressentiment *m.*

presently ['pɹɛzəntlɪ] *adv.* **1.** [×] Dans quelques instants, tout à l'heure, bientôt. **2.** présentement, à l'heure actuelle.

preservation [,pɹɛzɚ'vejʃən] *n.* préservation *f* (de qqch.); conservation *f*; maintien *m* (de la paix), salut *m.* || **preserve** [pɹɪ'zɚv] *n.* [game] chasse *f* gardée; *pl.* conserves *fpl*, confiture *f.* || *v. tr.* préserver (de); protéger (contre); mettre (qqch.) en conserve, conserver; [Fig.] garder, conserver; maintenir (la paix).

preside [pɹɪ'zajd] *v. intr.* présider (à, *at*). || **presidency** ['pɹɛzɪdəntsɪ] *n.* présidence *f.* || **president** ['pɹɛzɪdənt] *n.* président *m.* || **presidential** [ˌpɹɛzɪ'dɛnʃəl] *adj.* présidentiel, de président.

press [pɹɛs] *n.* [action] pression *f*; [machine] presse *f*; [wine] pressoir *m*; [Fig.] presse *f*; la foule *f*; urgence *f* (des affaires); [pants] coup *m* de fer: *to go to* ~, mettre sous presse; *to have a good* ~, avoir bonne presse; *to give one's pants a* ~, donner un coup de fer à son pantalon. || *v. tr.* presser (du citron, l'ennemi); appuyer sur (un bouton, &c.); donner un coup de fer à (un pantalon); serrer (qqun, la main à qqun); presser (qqun de faire qqch.); insister sur (une question, une demande); réclamer (une dette, une réponse) à qqun; forcer (qqun) à accepter (qqch.); poursuivre (un avantage): *to* ~ */s.o., sth./into service*, enrôler qqun, réquisitionner qqch.; *to be pressed for time*, être pressé. || *v. intr.* [time] presser; [pers.] se serrer (contre qqun); appuyer (sur qqch.); demander (qqch.) avec insistance. || **press back** [-'bæk] *v. tr.* refouler. || **press down** [-'dawn] *v. tr.* appuyer sur (qqch.). || **press on** [-'ɑn] *v. intr.* se dépêcher; aller (toujours) de l'avant. || **press out** [-'awt] *v. tr.* exprimer (du jus). || **pressing** [-ɪŋ] *adj.* pressant, urgent. || *n.* [clothes] repassage *m.*

pressure ['pɹɛʃɚ] *n.* **1.** pression *f*: *high, low/* ~, haute, basse/pression. **2.** [Fig.] pression *f*, urgence *f* (des événements): *to bring* ~ *(to bear) on s.o.*, faire pression sur qqun; *under the* ~ *of events*, sous la pression des circonstances; *to act on* ~, agir par contrainte.

prestige [ˌpɹɛs'tijʒ] *n.* prestige *m.*

presumable [pɹɪ'zuwm|əbl] *adj.* probable. || **presumably** [-ɪ] *adv.* probablement, selon toute évidence. || **presume** [pɹɪ'zuwm] *v. tr.* présumer, supposer. || *v. intr.* présumer (de); abuser (*on*, de); se permettre (*to*, de). || **presumption** [pɹɪ'zʌmp|ʃən] *n.* présomption *f*; supposition *f*; prétention *f*. || **presumptuous** [-tjuwəs] *adj.* présomptueu|x, -se; prétentieu|x, -se.

presuppose [ˌpɹɪsə'powz] *v. tr.* présupposer.

pretence [pɹɪ'tɛn|s] (also) **pretense** *n.* prétexte *m*; [claim] prétention *f*; feinte *f*, faux-semblant *m*: *under (the)* ~ *of*, sous prétexte de; *to make a* ~ *of*, faire semblant de; *under false pretences*, par des moyens frauduleux; *to make* ~ *to*, avoir des prétentions à. || **pretend** [-d] *v. tr.* & *intr.* feindre (qqch., de + inf.), faire semblant (de + inf.); [claim] prétendre (qqch., + inf.): *to* ~ *to be sick*, faire le malade; *to* ~ *to sth.*, prétendre à qqch. || **pretension** [-ʃən] *n.* prétention *f.* || **pretentious** [-ʃəs] *adj.* prétentieu|x, -se, présomptueu|x, -se.

preterite ['pɹɛtɚɪt] *n.* [Gram.] prétérit *m.*

pretext ['pɹijˌtɛkst] *n.* prétexte *m*: *under* ~ *of*, sous prétexte de.

prettily ['pɹɪtɪ|lɪ] *adv.* joliment; gentiment. || **prettiness** [-nəs] *n.* gentillesse *f*, †joliesse *f.* || **pretty** *adj.* joli; gentil, -le. || *adv.* assez; presque.

prevail [pɹɪ'vejl] *v. intr.* prévaloir (*against*, contre; *over*, sur); l'emporter (*over*, sur); décider, déterminer (*upon s.o. to*, qqun à); (pré)dominer; réussir. || **prevailing** [-ɪŋ] *adj.* dominant, prédominant: ~ *opinion*, opinion/courante, régnante/. || **prevalent** ['pɹɛvələnt] cf. PREVAILING.

prevent [pɹɪ'vɛn|t] *v. tr.* empêcher (de, *from*); [avert] prévenir (un malheur). || **prevention** [-ʃən] *n.* prévention *f*; précautions *fpl*, lutte *f*, mesures *fpl* préventives (contre); empêchement *m.* || **preventive** [-tɪv] *adj.* préventi|f, -ve.

preview ['pɹijˌvjuw] *n.* avant-première *f.*

previous ['pɹijvjəs] *adj.* précédent, antérieur; préalable (*to*, à).

prey [pɹej] *n.* proie *f*: [Fig.] *to fall, be/a* ~ *to*, tomber, être/la proie de. || *v. intr.* faire sa proie (de, *on*): [Fig.] *to be preyed on by*, être/en proie à, tourmenté par.

price [pɹajs] *n.* prix *m*; coût *m*: ~ *list*, prix *m* courant; barème *m*; tarif *m.* || *v. tr.* tarifier, coter, évaluer. || **priceless** [-ləs] *adj.* sans prix; [Fam.] absurde.

prick [pɹɪk] *n.* piqûre *f.* || *v. tr.* piquer: *His conscience pricked him*, Sa conscience lui a fait éprouver du remords; [Fig.] *to* ~ *up o.'s ears*, dresser l'oreille. || **prickly** [-lɪ] *adj.* piquant, épineux.

pride [pɹajd] *n.* [vice] orgueil *m*; [good quality] fierté *f*: *to take* ~ *from*, tirer vanité de; *to take a* ~ *in*, être fier de. || *v. tr. to* ~ *o.s. on*, s'enorgueillir de, être fier de.

priest [pɹijst] *n.* prêtre *m.* || **priestess** [-əs] *n.* prêtresse *f.* || **priesthood** [-ˌhʊd] *n.* [Rel.] prêtrise *f*, sacerdoce *m*: *steps to the* ~, les Ordres *mpl.*

prig [pɹɪg] *n.* poseur *m.* || **priggish** [-ɪʃ] *adj.* poseur, pédant; collet monté.

prim [pɹɪm] *adj.* compassé, guindé; [smile] pincé.

primarily [pɹaj'mɛɚlɪ] *adv.* à l'origine, primitivement; principalement. || **primary**

[ˈpɹajmɚ] *adj.* primaire, [cours] élémentaire, premier; principal; primitif. || **prime** [pɹajm] *adj.* premi|er, -ère; excellent; principal: (*to be*) *of* ~ *importance*, (être) de toute première importance; *to buy the* ~ *cuts*, acheter les meilleurs morceaux; *Prime Minister*, premier ministre, [Fr.] Président *m* du Conseil; ~ *number*, nombre premier. || *n.* origine *f*, commencement *m*; [Fig.] printemps *m*: (*the*) ~ *of youth*, fleur *f* de la jeunesse, de l'âge; (*to be*) *in one's* ~, (être) dans la force de l'âge. || *v. tr.* [pump] amorcer; instruire, styler (qqun); [paint] appliquer une couche de fond.

primer[1] [ˈpɹɪmɚ] *n.* manuel *m* élémentaire.

primer[2] [ˈpɹaɪmɚ] *n.* couche *f* de fond.

primeval [ˌpɹajmˈijvl̩] *adj.* primitif.

primitive [ˈpɹɪmɪtɪv] *adj.* & *n.* primitif.

primness [ˈpɹɪmnəs] *n.* afféterie *f*, air *m* collet-monté.

primrose [ˈpɹɪmˌɹowz] *n.* primevère *f*.

prince [pɹɪns] *n.* prince *m.* || **princely** [-lɪ] *adj.* princi|er, -ère, somptueu|x, -se. || **princess** [-ɛs] *n.* princesse *f.* || **Prince Edward Island** [ˌpɹɪntzˈɛdwɚdˌajlənd] *n.* l'Ile *f* du Prince-Édouard: *in, to*/~, dans l'Ile du P.-É.

principal [ˈpɹɪnsɪpl̩] *adj.* principal; premier. || *n.* principal *m* (d'école), [Fr.] proviseur *m* (d'un lycée); [Fin.] principal *m.*

principle [pɹɪnsɪpl̩] *n.* principe *m*; base *f*; fondement *m*: *as a matter of* ~, par principe.

print [pɹɪnt] *n.* [mark] empreinte *f*; [type] caractère *m*, impression *f*; [art] estampe *f*; [cloth] indienne *f*: *out of* ~, (livre) épuisé. || *v. tr.* imprimer; tirer (un négatif): *printed matter*, imprimés *mpl.* || **printer** [-ɚ] *n.* imprimeur *m*: *Queen's* (*King's*) *Printer*, Imprimeur *m* de la Reine (du Roi). || **printing** [-ɪŋ] *n.* impression *f*.

prior [ˈpɹajɚ] *adj.* antérieur (à, *to*); préalable. || *adv.* ~ (*to*), antérieurement (à). || *n.* [R.C.] prieur *m* (d'une abbaye).

priority [ˌpɹajˈɔɚɪtɪ] *n.* antériorité *f*; priorité *f* (*over*, sur).

prison [pɹɪsn̩] *n.* prison *f* (*in*, en). || *v. tr.* emprisonner, incarcérer. || **prisoner** [-ɚ] *n.* prisonni|er, -ère, détenu *m.*

privacy [ˈpɹajvə|sɪ] *n.* intimité *f*; solitude *f*; retraite *f.* || **private** [-t] *adj.* privé; particulier; personnel, confidentiel, intime; secret; réservé, isolé: ~ *secretary*, secrétaire particuli|er, -ère; ~ *eye*, détective *m* privé; ~ [on a door], → Défense d'entrer. || *n.* simple soldat *m*; soldat *m* de deuxième classe.

privation [ˌpɹajˈvejʃən] *n.* privation *f*.

privilege [ˈpɹɪvlədʒ] *n.* privilège *m.* || **privileged** [-d] *adj.* privilégié.

privy [ˈpɹɪvɪ] *adj.* privé: ~ *Council*, © Conseil *m* privé; ~ *Seal*, © le petit Sceau *m.*

prize [pɹajz] *n.* prix *m*; [ship] prise *f*, capture *f*; récompense *f.* || *v. tr.* estimer; tenir à (qqun, qqch.).

pro[1] [pɹow] *adv.* pour, en faveur de. || *n.* pour *m*, argument *m* qui milite en faveur de: *the pros and cons*, le pour et le contre.

pro[2] *pl.* **pros** *n.* [Fam.] professionnel *m* (du football, &c.).

probability [pɹɑbəˈbɪlɪtɪ] *n.* probabilité *f*. || **probable** [ˈpɹɑbəbl̩] *adj.* probable. || **probably** [-ɪ] *adv.* probablement.

probate [ˈpɹowˌbejt] *n.* homologation *f* (d'un testament). || *v. tr.* homologuer (un testament).

probe [pɹowb] *v. tr.* approfondir, sonder (un problème). || *n.* [Med.] sonde *f*; [Journ.] enquête *f*.

problem [ˈpɹɑbləm] *n.* problème *m*: *to examine, to look into*/*a* ~, examiner un problème.

procedure [ˌpɹowˈsijdʒɚ] *n.* **1.** [Tech.] procédé *m.* **2.** [Jur.] procédure *f*; [association]: *rules of* ~, règlement *m* intérieur.

proceed [ˌpɹowˈsijd] *v. intr.* [act] procéder; continuer; [begin] se mettre à; avancer; se rendre (à quelque part), aller. || **proceedings** [-ɪŋz] *n.* procédé *m*; procédure *f*; démarches *fpl*: © *votes and* ~ (*House of Commons*), Procès-verbaux *mpl* de la Chambre des Communes; [Jur.] procès *m.* || **proceeds** [-z] *n.pl.* produit *m*, bénéfices *mpl.*

process [ˈpɹowsɛs] *n.* procédé *m*, processus *m*; méthode *f*, opération *f*; [Jur.] procédure *f* (légale). || *v. tr.* soumettre (qqch.) à un procédé.

procession [ˌpɹowˈsɛʃən] *n.* procession *f*, cortège *m.*

proclaim [ˌpɹowˈklejm, prəˈklejm] *v. tr.* proclamer, annoncer (qqch.). || **proclamation** [pɹɑkləˈmejʃən] *n.* proclamation *f*, déclaration *f*.

procrastinate [pɹəˈkɹæstɪnˌejt] *v. intr.* temporiser, atermoyer, remettre au lendemain. || **procrastination** [pɹəˌkɹæstɪnˈejʃən] *n.* temporisation *f*, remise *f* au lendemain.

procure [ˌpɹowˈkjuwɚ] *v. tr.* procurer (*sth. for s.o.*, qqch. à qqun); se procurer, obtenir: *To* ~ *a visa* (*for o.s.*), /Se procurer, obtenir/un visa. || **procurement** [-mənt] *n.* obtention *f*, acquisition *f*.

prod [pɹɑd] *n.* coup *m* [donné par un objet pointu]. || *v. tr.* & *intr.* pousser, presser; [Fig.] aiguillonner.

prodigal ['pɹɑdɪgəl] *adj.* prodigue: *The Prodigal Son,* L'Enfant Prodigue.

prodigious [pɹə'dɪʤəs] *adj.* prodigieu|x, -se. ‖ **prodigy** ['pɹɑdɪʤɪ] *n.* prodige *m*: (*a*) *child* ~, (un) enfant *m* prodige.

produce ['pɹɑdjuws] *n.* produit *m*; [food] denrées *fpl.* ‖ *v. tr.* [pɹow'djuws] produire; fabriquer (un objet); exhiber. ‖ **producer** [-ɚ] *n.* [Rad., TV] réalisateur *m,* producteur *m.*

product ['pɹɑdʌkt] *n.* produit *m,* denrée *f* (alimentaire, &c.). ‖ **production** [pɹə'dʌk|ʃən] *n.* production *f,* fabrication *f.* ‖ **productive** [-tɪv] *adj.* productif.

Prof. [= Professor] ☞ avoid this abbreviation in French.

profanation [ˌpɹowfə'nejʃən] *n.* profanation *f.* ‖ **profane** [ˌpɹow'fejn] *v. tr.* profaner. ‖ *adj.* profane; [rite, language] impie, blasphématoire. ‖ **profanity** [ˌpɹow'fænɪtɪ] *n.* caractère *m* profane; [oath] juron *m,* blasphème *m.*

profess [ˌpɹow'fɛ|s] *v. tr.* professer; déclarer. ‖ **profession** [-ʃən] *n.* profession *f*; [trade] métier *m*; [job] emploi *m.* ‖ **professional** [-ʃənl̩] *adj.* professionnel, -le. ‖ *n.* membre *m* d'une profession libérale, © professionnel *m.*

professor [-sɚ] *n.* professeur *m*; maître *m.*

proffer ['pɹɑfɚ] *n.* offre *f.* ‖ *v. tr.* offrir, présenter (qqch. à qqun).

proficiency [ˌpɹow'fɪʃənt|sɪ] *n.* compétence *f,* capacité *f.* ‖ **proficient** *adj.* compétent, capable: ~ *in,* expert, versé/en, dans.

profile ['pɹowˌfajl] *n.* profil *m* (*in,* de); [outline] contour *m,* silhouette *f*; [Fig.] courte biographie. ‖ *v. tr.* profiler: *to be profiled against,* se profiler sur.

profit ['pɹɑfɪt] *n* profit *m,* avantage *m*; [Com.] bénéfice *m*; utilité *f*; rapport *m.* ‖ *v. tr.* profiter à (qqun), avantager (qqun). ‖ *v. intr.* profiter (de qqch., *by sth.*); servir à qqch. ‖ **profitable** [-əbl̩] *adj.* profitable, avantageux. ‖ **profiteer** [ˌpɹɑfɪ'tijɚ] *n.* profiteur *m,* mercanti *m.* ‖ *v. intr.* faire des bénéfices excessifs.

profligate ['pɹɑflɪgət] *adj. & n,* débauché; prodigue.

profound [ˌpɹow'fawnd] *adj.* profond; [study] approfondi.

profuse [ˌpɹow'fjuws] *adj.* abondant, excessif; [usual. pers.] prodigue (*in, with,* de). ‖ **profusion** [ˌpɹow'fjuwʒən] *n.* profusion *f,* abondance *f*; [lavishness] libéralité *f.*

progeny ['pɹɑʤənɪ] *n.* descendants *mpl,* lignée *f.*

prognosticate [ˌpɹɑg'nɑstɪˌkejt] *v. tr.* pronostiquer.

programme ['pɹowˌgræm] *n.* programme *m*; plan *m*: (for a meeting), ordre *m* du jour (d'une assemblée).

progress ['pɹowgɹɛs] *n.* progrès *m*; avancement *m*; cours *m* (des événements); †voyage *m*: *to make* ~, faire des progrès; *in* ~, en cours. ‖ *v. intr.* [pɹow'gɹɛs] progresser, faire des progrès; avancer. ‖ **progression** [ˌpɹow'gɹɛ|ʃən] *n.* progression *f.* ‖ **progressive** [-sɪv] *adj.* progressi|f, -ve; [Pol.] progressiste.

prohibit [ˌpɹow'hɪbɪt] *v. tr.* prohiber, défendre, interdire: *strictly prohibited,* formellement interdit. ‖ **prohibition** [ˌpɹowə'bɪʃən] *n.* prohibition *f*; interdiction *f.* ‖ **prohibitive** [ˌpɹow'hɪbɪtɪv] *adj.* prohibitif.

project ['pɹowˌʤɛkt] *n.* projet *m*; dessein *m,* intention *f.* ‖ **project** [pɹə'ʤɛkt] *v. tr.* projeter, lancer (qqch.). ‖ *v. intr.* faire saillie, s'avancer. ‖ **projectile** [-ˌajl] *n.* projectile *m.* ‖ **projection** [-ʃən] *n.* projection *f.*

proletarian [ˌpɹowlə'tɛəɪ|ən] *n.* prolétaire. ‖ *adj.* prolétaire, prolétarien. ‖ **proletariat** [-ət] *n.* prolétariat *m.*

prolific [ˌpɹow'lɪfɪk] *adj.* prolifique.

prolong [ˌpɹow'lɔŋ] *v. tr.* prolonger: *to* ~ *the due date of a note,* proroger l'échéance d'un billet. ‖ **prolongation** [ˌpɹowlɔŋ'gejʃən] *n.* prolongation *f.*

prom [pɹɑm] [US, © Fam.] *n.* bal *m.*

prominence ['pɹɑmɪnən|s] *n.* [in a physical sense] proéminence *f*; [Fig.] prééminence *f,* excellence *f,* distinction *f.* ‖ **prominent** [-t] *adj.* **1.** [protuberant] protubérant, proéminent. **2.** [conspicuous] saillant, remarquable. **3.** [outstanding] (pro-)éminent, important.

promise ['pɹɑmɪs] *n.* promesse *f.* [pers.] *of* ~, → qui promet. ‖ *v. tr. & intr.* promettre (de + inf.). ‖ **promising** [-ɪŋ] *adj.* prometteur, d'avenir. ‖ **promissory** [-ɛəɪ] *adj.*: ~ *note,* billet *m* à ordre.

promontory ['pɹɑmən,tɔəɪ] *n.* promontoire *m.*

promote [pɹə'mow|t] *v. tr.* **1.** donner de l'avancement à (qqun): *to be promoted* (*to corporal*), être promu (caporal); *to be promoted to the next class,* passer à la classe supérieure. **2.** encourager, favoriser (les arts, &c.); lancer, faire de la réclame pour (un produit). ‖ **promoter** [-tɚ] *n.* instigateur (d'un projet); organisateur *m*; [Pej.] monteur *m,* lanceur/(d'affaires). ‖ **promotion** [-ʃən] *n.* avancement *m,* promotion *f*; [Com.] vente-réclame *f*; stimulation *f* de la vente.

prompt [pɹɑmpt] *adj.* prompt, rapide;

empressé; immédiat; ponctuel. || *v. tr.* inciter; suggérer; [Theat.] souffler. || **promptly** [-lɪ] *adv.* promptement, immédiatement, ponctuellement. || **promptness** [-nəs] *n.* promptitude *f*, ponctualité *f*, empressement *m.*

promulgate [ˈpɹɑməlˌgej|t] *v. tr.* promulguer; répandre (une idée, une nouvelle). || **promulgation** [-ʃən] *n.* promulgation *f.*

prone [pɹown] *adj.* à plat ventre; [Fig.] enclin (à), qui a tendance (à): *in a ~ position,* à plat ventre; *accident-~*, sujet, prédisposé/aux accidents.

prong [pɹɑŋ] *n.* dent *f* de fourche, de fourchette; pointe *f.*

pronoun [ˈpɹowˌnawn] *n.* [Gram.] pronom *m.*

pronounce [pɹəˈnawns] *v. tr.* prononcer; déclarer. || **pronounced** [-t] *adj.* prononcé: *This letter can be ~ in two ways,* → Cette lettre se prononce de deux façons. || **pronunciation** [pɹəˌnʌnsɪˈejʃən] *n.* prononciation *f.*

proof [pɹuwf] *pl.* **proofs** [-s] *n.* preuve *f*; [Photo, printing] épreuve *f*; justification *f*: *to/supply, furnish/ ~*, fournir des preuves; *to establish a ~*, établir une preuve; *The ~ of the pudding is in the eating,* À l'œuvre on connaît l'artisan. || **proof,** *adj.* à l'épreuve de; *waterproof* [ˈwɔtɚˌpɹuwf] imperméable. || **proofread** [ˈpɹuwfˌɹijd] *v. tr.* [cf. READ] corriger les épreuves (d'un livre, &c.).

prop [pɹɑp] *n.* **1.** support *m*, soutien *m*; [plants] tuteur *m.* **2.** *usual. pl.* [Theat.] accessoires *mpl*: *~ man,* accessoiriste *m.* **3.** [Fam.] *abr.* [= propeller]. || *v. tr.* **[-pp-]** [usual. *to ~ up*] soutenir, étayer.

propaganda [ˌpɹɑpəˈgændə] *n.* propagande *f.*

propagate [ˈpɹɑpəˌgejt] *v. tr.* propager. || **propagation** [ˌpɹɑpəˈgejʃən] *n.* propagation *f.*

propel [pɹəˈpɛl] *v. tr.* **[-ll-]** propulser. || **propeller** [-ɚ] *n.* hélice *f.*

propensity [ˌpɹowˈpɛnsɪtɪ] *n.* tendance *f*, propension *f* (*for,* à).

proper [ˈpɹɑpɚ] *adj.* propre, particulier (à); [appropriate] convenable, à propos; [in order] bon, régulier; exact, juste; compétent: *at the ~ time,* en temps voulu; *in ~ shape,* en bon état; *The ~ authority to issue this document is the bank,* Il incombe à la banque d'établir ce document. || **properly** [-lɪ] *adv.* convenablement, régulièrement; comme il faut.

property [ˈpɹɑpɚtɪ] *n.* propriété *f*; possession *f*; biens *mpl*; qualité *f*; [Theat.] accessoire *m.*

prophecy [ˈpɹɑfə|sɪ] *n.* prophétie *f.* || **prophesy** [-ˌsaj] *v. tr.* prophétiser, prédire. || **prophet** [-t] *n.* prophète *m.* || **prophetic** [pɹəˈfɛtɪk] *adj.* prophétique.

propitious [ˌpɹowˈpɪʃəs] *adj.* propice (*for,* à).

proportion [pɹəˈpoɚʃən] *n.* proportion *f.* || *v. tr.* proportionner.

proposal [pɹəˈpowz|l̩] *n.* proposition *f*; demande *f* en mariage. || **propose** *v. tr.* proposer; offrir. || *v. intr. to ~ to s.o.,* demander (qqun) en mariage. || **proposition** [pɹɑpəˈzɪʃən] *n.* proposition *f*; [Fam.] affaire *f*; *It's a different ~.* → C'est une autre affaire.

proprietary [pɹəˈpɹajətɚɪ] *adj.* de propriétaire; [class] possédant. || *n.* propriété *f*; droit *m* de propriété *f.* || **proprietor** [pɹəˈpɹajət|ɚ] *n.* propriétaire *m/f.* || **propriety** [-ɪ] *n.* propriété *f*; exactitude *f* (d'un terme); [moral] bienséance *f.*

prorogation [ˌpɹowɹəˈgejʃən] *n.* prorogation *f.*

prosaic [ˌpɹowˈzejɪk] *adj.* prosaïque. || **prose** [pɹowz] *n.* prose *f* (*in,* en).

prosecute [ˈpɹɑsəˌkjuwt] *v. tr.* poursuivre (qqun); traduire (qqun) en justice; revendiquer (des droits); [Jur.] intenter une action à (qqun); [Fig.] poursuivre. || **prosecution** [ˌpɹɑsəˈkjuwʃən] *n.* poursuites *fpl* judiciaires: *the ~*, accusation *f.* || **prosecutor** [ˈpɹɑsəˌkjuwtɚ] *n.* [Jur.] procureur *m*; [plaintiff] plaignant *m.*

prospect [ˈpɹɑspɛkt] *n.* perspective *f*, vue *f* [also Fig.] panorama *m*; avenir *m* [pers.] client *m* éventuel, [marriage] parti *m.* || *v. tr.* prospecter, explorer. || **prospective** [prɑsˈpɛktɪv] *adj.* futur, à venir, en perspective. || **prospector** [ˈpɹɑspɛktɚ] *n.* prospecteur *m*, chercheur *m* (d'or, &c.).

prosper [ˈpɹɑspɚ] *v. intr.* prospérer, réussir. || **prosperity** [pɹɑsˈpɛɚɪtɪ] *n.* prospérité *f.* || **prosperous** [ˈpɹɑspɚəs] *adj.* prospère, florissant.

prostitute [ˈpɹɑstɪˌtjuwt] *n.* prostituée *f.* || *v. tr.* prostituer.

prostrate [ˈpɹɑstɹejt] *v. tr.* abattre, étendre (à terre): *to ~ o.s.,* se prosterner: *to be prostrated by an illness,* être terrassé par une maladie. || *adj.* prosterné, prostré; [Fig.] abattu, accablé. || **prostration** [ˈpɹɑsˈtɹejʃən] *n.* abattement *m*; [Med.] prostration *f*, accablement *m.*

protect [pɹowˈtɛk|t] *v. tr.* protéger; défendre: *to ~ o.s. from the cold,* se protéger du froid. || **protection** [-ʃən] *n.* protection *f*; défense *f*; sauvegarde *f.* || **protective** [-tɪv] *adj.* protect|eur, -trice. || **protector** [-tɚ] *n.* protectuer *m*; [arts] mécène *m*, patron *m.* || **protectorate** [-tɚət] *n.* protectorat *m.*

protégé ['pɹowtəˌʒej] *n.* protégé *m,* protégée *f.*
protein ['pɹowtijn] *n.* protéine *f.*
protest ['pɹowtɛst] *n.* protestation *f*; [Com.] protêt *m*: *under ~*, à son corps défendant. || *v. intr.* [pɹə'tɛst] protester (contre une décision; de son innocence). || **protestant** ['pɹɑtəstənt] *n.* Protestant, -e. || *adj.* protestant, -e. || **protestation** [pɹɑtɛs-tejʃən] *n.* protestation *f.*
protrude [pɹow'tɹuwd] *v. intr.* faire saillie, dépasser.
proud [pɹawd] *adj.* [vain] orgueilleu|x, -se, vaniteu|x, -se; [noble, pleased] fier *m,* fière *f*; [stately] imposant: *to be ~ of,* être fier de, s'enorgueillir de. || **proudly** [-lɪ] *adv.* orgueilleusement; fièrement.
prove [pɹuwv], **proved** [-d]; **proved** ou **proven** [-n̩] *v. tr.* prouver, démontrer; éprouver; se montrer.
proverb ['pɹɑvɚb] *n.* proverbe *m*; maxime *f.* || **proverbial** [pro'vɚbjəl] *adj.* proverbial.
provide [pɹə'vajd] *v. tr.* (*s.o. with sth.*), fournir (qqch. à qqun), munir (qqun de qqch.), pourvoir (qqun de qqch.). || *v. intr.* pourvoir (*for sth.*, à qqch.); se prémunir (*against*, contre); prévoir (*for*, —); *to ~ for o.s.*, se suffire. || **provided** [-əd] *conj.* pourvu que, à condition que (+ subj.).
providence ['pɹɑvɪdən|s] *n.* providence *f*; prévoyance *f.* || **provident** [-t] *adj.* prévoyant; de prévoyance: *~ fund*, caisse de prévoyance. || **providential** [pɹɑvɪ'dɛnʃəl] *adj.* providentiel. || **providentially** [-ɪ] *adv.* providentiellement; d'une manière providentielle.
province ['pɹɑvɪns] *n.* province *f*; [Fig.] ressort *m,* compétence *f*; [sphere] domaine *m*. *This falls within our ~*, Ceci relève de notre compétence; *Canada is made up of ten provinces,* Le Canada se compose de dix provinces. || **provincial** [pɹə'vɪnʃəl] *adj.* provincial: *the ~ Government* [*as opposed to Federal*], le gouvernement *m*/provincial, de la Province/; *~ police,* police *f*, sûreté *f*/provinciale.
provision [pɹə'vɪʒən] *n.* stipulation *f*, clause *f*; mesure *f*; *pl.* provisions *fpl*: *to make ~ for*, pourvoir à. || *v. tr.* approvisionner (un bateau).
provisional [pɹə'vɪʒən|l̩] *adj.* provisoire, temporaire. || **provisionally** [-əlɪ] *adv.* provisoirement, à titre/provisoire, temporaire/.
proviso [pɹə'vajzow] *pl.* **provisos** ou **provisoes** [-s] *n.* condition *f*, clause *f*: *with the ~ that*, à condition que . . .
provocation [ˌpɹɑvə'kejʃən] *n.* provocation *f*; [anger] accès *m* de colère; [Fig.] agacerie *f.* || **provoke** [pɹə'vowk] *v. tr.* **1.** provoquer, inciter (qqun à faire qqch.); mettre en colère, irriter, agacer. **2.** causer, susciter, faire naître. || **provoking** [-ɪŋ] *adj.* contrariant, énervant; [Pej.] fâcheux.
provost ['pɹowˌvow] *n.* [Univ.] principal *m,* doyen *m*; [Mil.] prévôt *m.*
prow [pɹaw] *n.* proue *f.*
prowess [-əs] *n.* prouesse *f.*
prowl [-l] *v. intr.* rôder. || *n.*: *to be on the ~*, rôder.
proximity [ˌpɹɑks'ɪmɪtɪ] *n.* proximité *f*: *in the ~ of*, à proximité de.
proxy ['pɹɑksɪ] *n.* [person] mandataire *m*; [document] procuration *f.*
prude [pɹuwd] *n.* prude *f*, mijaurée *f.*
prudence ['pɹuwdən|s] *n.* prudence *f*, sagesse *f.* || **prudent** [-t] *adj.* prudent, sage.
prudery ['pɹuwd|əɹ] *n.* pruderie *f.* || **prudish** [-ɪʃ] *adj.* prude, [Fam.] bégueule.
prune [pɹuwn] *n.* pruneau *m.* || *v. tr.* émonder, élaguer (une frondaison).
Prussia ['pɹʌʃə] *n.* la Prusse *f.*
pry [praj] *n.* levier *m.* || *v. tr.* soulever (qqch.) avec un levier.
psalm [sɑm] *n.* psaume *m.*
pseudonym ['suwdn̩ɪm] *n.* pseudonyme *m.*
PST [= Pacific Standard Time] heure *f* normale du Pacifique.
psychiatrist [sə'kajətɹɪ|st] *n.* psychiatre *m.* || **psychiatry** *n.* psychiatrie *f.* || **psychological** [ˌsajkə'lɑdʒɪkl̩] *adj.* psychologique. || **psychologist** [ˌsaj'kɑlədʒɪ|st] *n.* psychologue *m.* || **psychology** *n.* psychologie *f.*
Pte [© = Private] *n.* simple soldat *m.*
public ['pʌblɪk] *n.* public *m* (*in*, en); les gens *mpl.* || *adj.* publi|c, -que: *~ school*, école *f* primaire, [Br.] école privée; *~ library*, bibliothèque *f* municipale; *~ holiday*, fête *f* légale; *~ Works*, Travaux publics. || **publican** [-ən] *n.* [Bible] publicain *m*; [Br.] cabaretier *m*, patron *m* (d'un café). || **publication** [ˌpʌblɪ'kejʃən] *n.* publication *f*: *~ of/banns, bans/*, publication *f* des bans. || **publicity** [ˌpʌb'lɪsɪtɪ] *n.* publicité *f.* || **publicly** ['pʌblɪklɪ] *adv.* publiquement, → en public.
publish ['pʌblɪʃ] *v. tr.* publier, éditer (une revue, un livre). || **publisher** [-ɚ] *n.* éditeur *m.*
puck [pʌk] *n.* © [Hockey] (la) rondelle, (le) disque.
pucker [-ɚ] *v. tr.* plisser, froncer. || *v. intr.* [usual. to ~ up] froncer: *His mouth puckered up*, Sa bouche se crispa.
pudding ['pʊdɪŋ] *n.* pudding *m*: *blood-~*, boudin *m.*
puddle ['pʌdl̩] *n.* flaque *f*, mare *f.* || *v. intr.* patauger.

pudgy ['pʌdʒɪ] *adj.* bouffi; [Fam.] rondouillard.
Puerto Rico [ˌpɚtə'ɹijkow] *n.* Porto Rico.
puff [pʌf] *n.* souffle *m*; [smoke] bouffée *f*; [powder] houppe *f*; [swelling] bouffissure *f*; [comforter] courtepointe *f*. ‖ *v. tr.* souffler, gonfler. ‖ *v. intr.* souffler, bouffir, se gonfler: *to ~ at (one's cigar)*, tirer des bouffées (de son cigare). ‖ **puffy** [-ɪ] *adj.* [face] bouffi; [sleeve] bouffant; [pers.] poussif.
pugilist ['pjuwdʒɪˌlɪst] *n.* pugiliste *m.*
pugnacious [ˌpʌg'nejʃəs] *adj.* batailleur.
pull [pʊl] *n.* coup *m* (pour tirer qqch.); [jerk] secousse *f*; effort *m*; traction *f*; [handle] poignée *f*: *to give a ~ on sth.*, tirer (sur) qqch.; [Fam.] *to have a ~ at/the bottle, o.'s pipe/*, boire un coup à la bouteille, tirer une bouffée de sa pipe; [Fam.] *to have ~*, avoir du piston; *It was a long ~*, Il a fallu (fournir) un grand effort (pour) . . . ‖ *v. intr.* tirer. ‖ *v. tr.* tirer; [drag] traîner; [trigger] appuyer sur (la gâchette); [trick] jouer (un tour à qqun): *to ~ s.o.'s leg*, se payer la tête de qqun; [Slang] *You can't ~ that on me*, Avec moi, ça ne prend pas. ‖ **pull about** [-ə'bawt] *v. tr.* tirailler; malmener (qqun). ‖ **pull away** [-ə'wej] *v. tr.* arracher; entraîner (qqun). ‖ **pull back** ['-bæk] *v. tr.* tirer en arrière; (faire) reculer; [troops] retirer. ‖ *v. intr.* [troops] se replier. ‖ **pull down** [-'dawn] *v. tr.* baisser (un store), rabattre (son chapeau sur les yeux); démolir (une maison); [Fig.] abattre (qqun). ‖ **pull in** [-'ɪn] *v. tr.* rentrer. ‖ *v. intr.* arriver; [train] entrer en gare. ‖ **pull off** [-'ɔf] *v. tr.* enlever; [Fig.] *He pulled it off*, Il a réussi (son coup). ‖ **pull on** [-'ɑn] *v. tr.* mettre (un vêtement). ‖ **pull out** [-'awt] *v. tr.* sortir; (re)tirer; arracher (une dent). ‖ *v. intr.* [train] sortir de la gare; [car] sortir de la file (pour doubler). ‖ **pull over** ['-owvɚ] *v. tr.* renverser; tirer à soi. ‖ *v. intr.* se ranger. ‖ **pull through** [-'θɹuw] *v. tr. & intr.* (se) tirer d'affaire. ‖ **pull together** [-tə'gɛðɚ] *v. tr.* to pull o.s. together, se ressaisir. ‖ *v. intr.* s'accorder. ‖ **pull up** [-'ʌp] *v. tr.* lever; [hoist] hisser; remonter (des chaussettes); arrêter. ‖ *v. intr.* s'arrêter.
pullet [-ət] *n.* poulette *f.*
pulley [-ɪ] *n.* poulie *f.*
Pullman ['pʊlmən] *n. & attrib.* pullman (*m*); wagon-lit (*m*).
pulp [pʌlp] *n.* **1.** pulpe *f.* **2.** pâte *f* (à papier), © [abus.] pulpe *f*: [Journ.] *~ magazine*, feuille *f* à sensation.
pulpit ['pʊlpɪt] *n.* [in the church] chaire *f.*
pulpwood ['pʌlpˌwʊd] *n.* bois *m* de pâte; © [abus.] bois de pulpe.
pulsate ['pʌlsejt] *v. intr.* palpiter, vibrer; [heart] battre. ‖ **pulsation** [ˌpʌl'sejʃən] *n.* pulsation *f.* ‖ **pulse** [pʌls] *n.* pouls *m.*
pulverize ['pʌlvɚˌajz] *v. tr.* pulvériser, broyer.
pumice ['pʌmɪs] *n.* pierre *f* ponce. ‖ *v. tr.* poncer.
pump [pʌmp] *n.* pompe *f.* ‖ *v. tr.* pomper; [Fam.] tirer les vers du nez à (qqun): *to ~ up*, gonfler (un pneu).
pumpkin ['pʌmkɪn] *n.* citrouille *f.*
pun [pʌn] *n.* jeu *m* de mots, calembour *m.* ‖ *v. intr.* **[-nn-]** faire des calembours, des jeux de mots.
punch [-tʃ] *n.* **1.** poinçon *m*, perforateur *m*, poinçonneuse *f.* **2.** coup *m* de poing; [Fig.] force *f*, énergie *f*: *~ line*, le mot de la fin. **3.** [drink] punch *m.* ‖ *v. tr.* **1.** percer, poinçonner, perforer. **2.** donner un coup de poing à (qqun).
punctilious [ˌpʌŋk'tɪlɪəs] *adj.* pointilleux; [Pej.] formaliste, → à cheval sur l'étiquette.
punctual ['pʌŋktʃuwəl] *adj.* ponctuel, exact. ‖ **punctuality** [ˌpʌŋktʃuw'ælɪtɪ] *n.* ponctualité *f*; exactitude *f.* ‖ **punctually** ['pʌŋktʃuwəlɪ] *adv.* ponctuellement, exactement.
punctuation [ˌpʌŋktʃuw'ejʃən] *n.* ponctuation *f*: *~ mark*, signe *m* de ponctuation.
puncture ['pʌŋktʃɚ] *v. tr.* crever, perforer. ‖ *n.* [sens général] trou *m*; [pneu, &c.] crevaison *f*; [action] perforation *f.*
pungent ['pʌndʒənt] *adj.* [smell] piquant, âcre; [taste] relevé; [pain] aigu, déchirant; [remark] caustique.
punish ['pʌnɪʃ] *v. tr.* punir, châtier. ‖ **punishment** [-mənt] *n.* punition *f*, châtiment *m*; [Jur.] peine *f*, sanction *f.*
puny ['pjuwnɪ] *adj.* chétif, malingre, menu: *a ~ excuse*, une excuse/faible, mesquine.
pup [pʌp] *n.* jeune chien *m*, chiot *m*; [Fig.] freluquet *m.*
pupil[1] ['pjuwpl̩] *n.* élève *m/f.*
pupil[2] *n.* pupille *f*, prunelle *f* (des yeux).
puppet ['pʌpət] *n.* marionnette *f*; [Fig.] fantoche *m.*
puppy ['pʌpɪ] cf. PUP.
purchase ['pɚtʃəs] *n.* **1.** achat *m*, emplette *f.* **2.** [hold] prise *f*, point *m* d'appui. ‖ *v. tr.* acheter, acquérir (qqch.). ‖ **purchaser** [-ɚ] *n.* acheteur *m.*
pure ['pjuwɚ] *adj.* pur, propre. ‖ **purely** [-lɪ] *adv.* purement, proprement.
purgative ['pɚgət|ɪv] *n.* purge *f*, purgatif *m.* ‖ *adj.* purgatif. ‖ **purgatory** [-ɔɚɪ] *n.*

purgatoire *m.* || **purge** [pɚdʒ] *n.* [Med.] purge *f*; épuration *f* (gouvernement, administration). || *v. tr.* [Med.] purger; assainir, épurer, nettoyer.

purify [ˈpjuwɚı|ˌfaj] *v. tr.* purifier (l'atmosphère); dépurer (le sang); clarifier (un liquide). || **purity** [-tı] *n.* pureté *f*; propreté *f*.

purple [ˈpɚpl̩] *n. & adj.* [×] violet, rouge violacé; [Fig.] pourpre *f*.

purport [pɚˈpoɚt] *n.* sens *m*, teneur *f*. || *v. tr.* être censé: *The document/purporting, (which is) purported/to be official*, Le document (qui est) censé être officiel.

purpose [ˈpɚpəs] *n.* but *m*, objet *m*, fin *f*; intention *f*, dessein *m*, résolution *f*; utilité *f*: *on* ~, exprès; *for the* ~ *of*, dans le dessein de, [Fam.] dans le but de; *to serve the* ~, faire l'affaire; *What is the* ~ *of . . . ?*, Quel est le but de . . . ?, À quoi sert . . . ?, À quoi bon . . . ?; *for all* ~, (à) tous usages; pratiquement; *to no* ~, vainement; *to some* ~, utilement. || **purposeful** [-fl̩] *adj.* réfléchi; pondéré.

purr [pɚ] *n.* ronron *m*. || *v. intr.* ronronner.

purse [pɚs] *n.* bourse *f*; [wallet] porte-monnaie *m inv.*; [handbag] sac *m* (à main). || *v. tr.* pincer (les lèvres). || **purser** [ˈpɚsɚ] *n.* [ship] commissaire *m*.

pursue [pɚˈsuw] *v. tr.* poursuivre; exercer (une activité). || **pursuit** [-t] *n.* poursuite *f*, recherche *f*: *to set out in pursuit of s.o.*, se lancer à la poursuite de qqun.

push [puʃ] *n.* poussée *f*; [Fig.] initiative *f*. || *v. tr.* pousser, presser, inciter (à); ~ *down* (*sth.*), renverser (qqch.): *He pushed the door open*, → Il poussa la porte. || *v. intr.* pousser; bousculer: *to* ~ */on, forward*, avancer, pousser (jusqu'à). || **pushing** [-ıŋ] *adj.* [of a person] entreprenant.

puss [pus] *n.* minet *m*, chat *m*: ~ *in boots*, le chat botté. || **pussy** [-ı] *n.* minet *m*, chat: ~ *willow*, chaton *m* (de saule, &c.).

put [put], **put, put, putting** [-ıŋ] *v. tr.* mettre, placer; [down] poser; poser (une question à qqun); dire, exprimer (qqch.); faire faire (qqch. à qqun); lancer (le poids): *to stay* ~, rester en place, ne plus changer/; *Put it there*, Touchez là; *to* ~ *it bluntly*, pour parler franc; *to* ~ *it differently*, pour m'exprimer autrement; *I don't know how to* ~ *it*, Je ne sais comment dire; *I* ~ *it to him* (*that . . .*), Je lui ai/demandé, proposé/(que . . .); *I* ~ *him to doing it*, Je l'ai mis à le faire; *I don't want to* ~ *you to any trouble*, Je ne voudrais pas vous déranger. || **put about** [-əˈbawt] *v. intr.* [ship] virer (de bord). || **put across** [-əˈkɹɑs] *v. tr.* passer; faire accepter, faire comprendre. || **put aside** [-əˈsajd] *v. tr.* mettre de côté. || **put away** [-əˈwej] *v. tr.* ranger (des livres); [save] mettre de côté; mettre en prison; chasser (une idée). || **put back** [-ˈbæk] *v. tr.* remettre (à sa place); retarder. || *v. intr.* revenir (au port). || **put by** [-ˈbaj] *v. tr.* mettre de côté. || **put down** [-ˈdawn] *v. tr.* poser, déposer; baisser (un store); noter, inscrire (un nom); réprimer (une révolte); attribuer (qqch. à qqch.): *Put it down!*, Laissez cela! || **put forth** [-ˈfoɚθ] *v. tr.* déployer (sa force); fournir (un effort); avancer (une théorie); publier (une brochure); pousser (des bourgeons). || **put forward** [-ˈfoɚwɚd] *v. tr.* avancer (une montre, une théorie). || **put in** [-ˈın] *v. tr.* mettre (dans, en, à, &c.); introduire (une clef); placer (un mot); (faire) installer (le gaz); passer (le temps à faire qqch.): *to* ~ *an appearance*, faire acte de présence. || *v. intr.* entrer (dans un port); poser sa candidature (*for*, à). || **put off** [-ˈɔf] *v. tr.* remettre (qqch.), différer (qqch., de faire qqch.); renvoyer (qqun avec une excuse); dérouter (qqun); dégoûter, décourager (qqun de qqch.). || **put on** [-ˈɑn] *v. tr.* mettre (des vêtements); mettre (qqch.) à chauffer; serrer (le frein); mettre (une pièce de théâtre) en scène; avancer (une montre); prendre (du poids, un air de . . .); allumer (la lumière, le fourneau); [inform] mettre au courant (*to*, de): *to put sth. on*, faire du genre, faire/le malin, l'important, le snob, &c. || **put out** [-ˈawt] *v. tr.* tendre (la main); tirer (la langue); [outside] mettre dehors; éteindre (un feu, une lumière); embarrasser, contrarier (qqun); publier (un livre); crever (les yeux): *He is quite* ~ *about it*, Il en est très contrarié. || *v. intr.* prendre/la mer, le large. || **put over** [-ˈowvɚ] *v. tr.* passer, faire accepter; faire comprendre. || **put through** [-ˈθɹuw] *v. tr.* voter (un projet de loi); faire subir (qqch. à qqun); [Tel.] *Put me through to . . .*, Passez-moi . . . || **put to** [-ˈtuw] *v. tr. to be hard* ~ *it* (*to . . .*), avoir bien du mal (à) . . . || **put together** [-təˈgɛðɚ] *v. tr.* mettre ensemble, réunir; rassembler (ses idées); monter (une machine); additionner; rapprocher (deux idées): *to put two and two together*, en tirer ses propres conclusions. || **put up** [-ˈʌp] *v. tr.* lever; ouvrir (un parapluie); relever (son col, les cheveux); accrocher (un tableau); afficher (un avis); (faire) construire (une maison); dresser (une tente); augmenter (le prix); fournir (des fonds); **présenter** (un candidat); loger (qqun); mettre (qqch.) en vente; offrir (une résistance): *to put up with/sth., s.o./*, supporter, s'accommoder de/qqch., qqun; *to put s.o. up to sth.*, pousser qqun à faire qqch. || **put upon** [-ə'pɑn] *v. tr.* en imposer à qqun.

putrefy ['pjuwtɹ|ə,faj] *v. tr.* putréfier, pourrir. || *v. intr.* se putréfier, (se) pourrir. || **putrid** [-ɪd] *adj.* putride, pourri; corrompu.

putter ['pʌt|ɚ] *v. intr.* bricoler, toucher à tout.

putty [-ɪ] *n.* mastic *m.* || *v. tr.* mastiquer.

puzzle ['pʌzḷ] *n.* énigme *f*; casse-tête *m* (chinois): *crossword* ~, mots-croisés *mpl.* || *v. tr.* embarrasser, intriguer (qqun), embrouiller les esprits de (qqun). || **puzzling** [-ɪŋ] *adj.* embarrassant.

Pvt. [US] [= private] simple soldat *m.*

pyjamas [pə'dʒæməz] also **pajamas** *n.* pyjama *m.*

pylon ['pajlɑn] *n.* pylône *m.*

pyramid ['pijɚəmɪd] *n.* pyramide *f.*

Pyrenees (The) ['pijɚənɪz] *n.* Les Pyrénées *fpl.*

Q

Q, q [kjuw] *n.* Q, q. [cf. **A**]; *Q Department*, © Services du Q.M.G. [=Quartier-maître général].

Q.C. *abbr.* [=Queen's Counsel], C.R. [= Conseiller de la Reine].

qt(s). [= QUART(s)].

quack [kwæk] *n.* **1.** ~ *(doctor)*, charlatan *m.* **2.** [duck] *to go* ~, faire couin-couin.

quadrangle ['kwad,ɹæŋgḷ] *n.* quadrilatère *m*; [Arch.] cour *f* d'honneur.

quadrilateral [,kwadɹɪ'lætɚəl] *adj. & n.* quadrilatère *m.* || **quadruped** ['kwadɹuw|-,pɛd] *adj. & n.* quadrupède *m.* || **quadruple** [-pḷ] *adj. & n.* quadruple *m.* || **quadruplet** [-plət] *adj. & n.* quadruplet *m.* || **quadruplex** [-,plɛks] *n.* © duplex *m* double.

quail [kwejl] *pl.* **-s** [or *inv.* collectively] *n.* caille *f*; © perdrix *f.*

quaint [kwejnt] *adj.* bizarre, singulier, curieux; pittoresque, exotique: ~ *customs*, des coutumes bizarres/singulières/; *how* ~ *!*, comme c'est curieux!; *a* ~ *little cottage*, une maisonnette pittoresque. || **quaintness** [-nəs] *n.* cachet *m* d'exotisme; singularité *f*; pittoresque *m.*

quake [kwejk] *v. intr.* trembler (de peur), frémir (d'horreur). || *n.* *(earth)* ~, tremblement *m* de terre. || **Quaker** [-ɚ] *n.* Quaker *m*; *Quakers*, la Société des Amis.

qualification [,kwɑlɪfɪ'kejʃən] *n. usual. pl.* **1.** [×] [ability] compétence *f* (pour faire qqch.), aptitude *f* (à faire qqch.); [training] qualités *fpl*, formation *f*; [degrees] titres *mpl*, diplômes *mpl*; [documents] papiers *mpl*: *to have the necessary qualifications for a job*, avoir les qualités requises pour un poste. cf. QUALIFIED 1. **2.** [limitation] restriction *f*: *a statement made without any* ~, déclaration *f* catégorique. cf. QUALIFIED 2. || **qualified** [-d] *adj.* **1.** [competent] compétent, capable; [expert] qualifié: *to be* ~ *for* → avoir qualité *f* pour . . . , être apte à . . . . **2.** [modified]: *a* ~ *statement*, une déclaration nuancée. || **qualify** ['kwɑlɪfaj] *v. tr.* **1.** [make competent] acquérir/les titres/les qualités voulues/: *to* ~ *o.s. (for a job)*, se préparer à . . . , se rendre apte (au poste de . . .). **2.** [modify] modérer, nuancer (une déclaration); [Gram.] qualifier. || *v. intr.* [be competent] avoir les titres/les qualités/la formation/nécessaire(s). || **qualitative** ['kwɑlɪtejtɪv] *adj.* qualitatif. || **quality** ['kwɑlɪtɪ] *n.* **1.** [attribute] qualité *f*, caractère *m* spécifique: [excellence] qualité *f*: *This is a good* ~ *of merchandise*, C'est une marchandise de bonne qualité; *She has many/good/fine qualities, and few bad ones*, Elle a de nombreuses qualités et peu de défauts. **2.** [Fig.] qualité *f*: *in (my)* ~ *of* . . . , en (ma) qualité de . . . , en tant que . . . .

qualm [kwɔm] *n.* nausée(s) *f(pl).* || *n.pl.*

[Fig.] [misgiving] scrupules *mpl*, remords *mpl*: *to feel qualms at* [+ -ing], avoir des remords de . . . [+ inf.]; *to have no qualms about* . . . , ne pas hésiter à (faire . . .), ne pas avoir d'inquiétudes sur (qqch.).

quandary ['kwɑndərɪ] *n.* impasse *f*, dilemme *m*.

quantitative ['kwɑntɪ|ˌtejtəv] *adj.* quantitatif. || **quantity** [-tɪ] *n.* **1.** quantité *f*, somme *f*: *large quantities of* . . . , de grandes quantités de . . . ; [Math.] *unknown* ~ , inconnue *f*. **2.** quantité *f*, volume *m*: *to buy* . . . *in* ~ , acheter . . . / en gros/en quantité/; [Fig.] *any* ~ *of* . . . , en masse, à foison.

quarantine ['kwɔərn̩ˌtijn] *n.* quarantaine *f*., || *v. tr.* mettre en quarantaine.

quarrel ['kwɔərəl] *n.* querelle *f*; sujet *m* de querelle: *to pick a* ~ *with s.o.*, chercher querelle à qqun, → se disputer avec qqun; *I have no* ~ *with that*, Je n'ai rien à redire à cela. || *v. intr.* [-ll-]. **1.** se quereller, se disputer (*with s.o.*, avec qqun). **2.** [find fault with] réprimander/blâmer/ qqun (de faire qqch.); trouver à redire à (qqch.). || **quarrelsome** [-səm] *adj.* querelleur, irascible.

quarry[1] ['kwɔərɪ] *n.* carrière *f* (de marbre, &c.). || *v. tr.* exploiter une carrière; extraire (du marbre, &c.).

quarry[2] *n.* proie *f*.

quart [kwɔərt] *n.* [Meas.] © pinte *f* (= 2 pints).

quarter ['kwɔərtər] *n.* **1.** quart *m* (¼): *a* ~ *of an hour*, un quart d'heure; *a* ~ *to four*, quatre heures moins/un, le/quart; *a* ~ *past four*, quatre heures et quart; *You can have three quarters of it*, Je vous en laisse les trois quarts. **2.** quartier *m*: *the Latin* ~ , le Quartier Latin (à Paris), [moon] quartier; [globe] partie *f*, région *f*: *from that* ~ , de ce côté-là [☞ voir plus bas, QUARTERS. **3.** [3 months] trimestre *m* cf. QUARTERLY; [rent] terme *m*. **4.** [coin] = pièce *f* de 25 cents © un trente sous. **5.** [Fig.] quartier *m*, pitié *f*: *to give no* ~ , ne point faire quartier; (*the motorist*) *can expect no* ~ *from his own kind*, (l'automobiliste) n'a aucune pitié à attendre de ses semblables. || **quarter** *v. tr.* **1.** diviser/en quatre/en quartiers; écarteler (qqun). **2.** [Mil.] cantonner, loger (des troupes). || **quarterback** [-ˌbæk] *n.* [Sport] © quart-arrière *m*. || **quarterly** [-lɪ] *adj.* trimestriel. || *adv.* par trimestre. || *n.* /revue *f*, publication *f*/trimestrielle.

quarters [-z] *n.pl.* **1.** logement *m* (d'employés); [Mil.] quartier *m*, cantonnement *m*. **2.** [Proper station] poste *m*: *to take up one's* ~ , s'installer, prendre son poste; *in high* ~ , en haut lieu; *head* ~ , quartier *m* général (d'une armée, [Fig.] d'une association), siège *m* social (d'un organisme). **3.** [Loc.] *at close* ~ , de tout près, à se toucher. || **quartet(te)** [ˌkwɔər'tɛt] *n.* [Mus.] quatuor *m*: *wind/string/* ~ , quatuor/à vent, à cordes.

quaver ['kwejvər] *n.* tremblement *m* (de la voix); [Mus.] trémolo *m* (dans la voix); [note] croche *f*. || *v. intr.* [voix qui tremble] trembloter, chevroter.

quay [kij] *n.* [Naut.] quai *m*.

Que. [= Quebec] ☞ The preferred abbr. in French is P.Q. [= Province de Québec].

queasy ['kwijzɪ] *adj.* [food] répugnant, → qui soulève le cœur; [Pers.] dégoûté.

Quebec [kwə'bɛk] *n.* **1.** [City] Québec *f*, la ville de Québec: *to/in* ~ , à Québec; *the* ~ *Winter Carnival*, le Carnaval d'hiver de Québec. **2.** [Province] la Province de Québec, le Québec *m*: *to/ in* ~ , au Québec; *the* ~ *Government*, le gouvernement du Québec. || **Quebec(k)er** [-ər] *adj. & n.* québécois; natif *m* de Québec.

queen [kwijn] *n.* reine *f*; *the Queen*, la Reine; *the Queen Mother*, la Reine Mère; *the Queen's Printer*, l'Imprimeur *m* de la Reine; [cards] dame *f* (de cœur, &c.), [chess] dame *f*; [Fig.] *the Queen City*, la Ville-Reine [= Toronto]; *Queen Charlotte Islands*, l'archipel *m* de la Reine-Charlotte.

queer [kwijər] *adj.* bizarre, étrange, curieux; [peculiar] drôle: *I feel* ~ , je me sens tout drôle, je ne me sens pas bien; *a* ~ *fellow*, un drôle de type. || *n.* excentrique *m*, perverti *m*. || *v. tr.* faire échouer (les plans de qqun).

quell [kwɛl] *v. tr.* réprimer, étouffer (une révolte, &c.); calmer (ses sentiments).

quench [kwɛntʃ] *v. tr.* éteindre (un feu); [Fig.] étancher (sa soif); étouffer (une rébellion).

querulous ['kwɛərələs] *adj.* grognon, [Fam.] rouspéteur.

query ['kwijərɪ] *n.* question *f*; interrogation *f*; [Gram.] point *m* d'interrogation. cf. QUESTION. || *v. tr.* questionner; mettre (qqch.) en doute: *to* ~ *whether* . . . , (se) demander si . . .

†**quest** [kwɛst] *n.* recherche *f*: *to set out in* ~ *of* . . . , se mettre/en quête, à la recherche/de . . . .

question ['kwɛstʃən] *n.* **1.** question *f*; [Parliam.] interpellation *f*: *to ask* (*s.o.*) *a* ~ , poser une question (à qqun); *list of questions*, questionnaire *m*; ~ *mark*, point *m* d'interrogation. **2.** [controversy] doute *m*: *beyond/without/* ~, sans aucun doute. **3.** [problem] problème *m*, question *f*: *the* ~ *is to . . . , It's a* ~ *of . . .* → il s'agit (ici) de . . . ; *the man in* ~, l'homme/dont il s'agit/en question; *beside the* ~, à côté de la question; *out of the* ~, impossible, impensable. || *v. tr.* **1.** questionner, interroger (qqun). **2.** douter de (qqch.); contester; se demander si (qqch. est vrai, &c.). || **questionable** [-əbḷ] *adj.* discutable, contestable: *it seems very* ~, ça me paraît fort discutable. || **questioning** [-ɪŋ] *n.* interrogatoire *m.* || *adj.* [look, &c.] interrogateur.

question-mark [-ˌmɑɚk] *n.* point *m* d'interrogation.

queue [kjuw] [Esp. Br.] *n.* queue *f*, file *f* d'attente, cf. LINE. || *v. intr. to* ~ *up (for the bus)* → attendre l'autobus; [in Paris] prendre son numéro, faire la queue.

quibble ['kwɪbḷ] *n.* chicane *f*; argutie *f*; subtilité *f*: *I have no* ~ *with that*, Je n'y trouve rien à redire. || *v. intr.* chicaner; ergoter.

quick [kwɪk] *adj.* rapide, prompt, agile; (esprit) vif; (oreille) fin(e); [temper] (tempérament) emporté: *(as)* ~ *as lightning*, prompt comme l'éclair; *(Be)* ~ *(about it)!*, (Faites) vite!; *He was* ~ *to answer*, Il se dépêcha de répondre; *He is* ~ */to reply/in replying*, Il est prompt à répondre. || *adv.* vite, rapidement: *Come here* ~ *!* Viens vite! cf. QUICKLY. || *n.* vif *m*: *cut/stung/to the* ~, piqué au vif. || **quicken** [-ən] *v. tr.* accélérer (le pas); [Fig.] enflammer (l'imagination). || **quickly** [-lɪ] *adv.* vite, rapidement: *Come quickly!*, Venez vite!; [soon] promptement, (bien)-tôt: *Do it as* ~ *as possible*, Faites-le aussitôt que possible; *He* ~ *sat down*, → Il se dépêcha de s'asseoir. || **quickness** [-nəs] *n.* rapidité *f*, promptitude *f*; [Fig.] vivacité *f* (d'esprit); acuité *f* (des sens). || **quicksand** [-ˌsænd] *n.* sable *m* mouvant. || **quicksilver** [-ˌsɪlvɚ] *n.* vif-argent *m*, mercure *m.* || **quick-tempered** [-ˌtɛmpɚd] *adj.* emporté, de caractère vif. || **quick-witted** [-ˌwɪtəd] *adj.* à l'esprit vif.

quiescent [kwɪ'ɛsənt] *adj.* inactif, tranquille.

quiet ['kwajət] *adj.* **1** [still] tranquille, calme: *Be* ~ *!*, Silence!, Tenez-vous tranquille!, Taisez-vous!; *a* ~ *neighbourhood*, un quartier tranquille; *to be* ~, se taire, rester tranquille; *He/became, fell, kept/* ~, Il se tut. **2.** [undisturbed] doux, paisible, tranquille: ~ *manners*, des manières douces; *a* ~ *conscience*, une conscience paisible; *to lead a* ~ *life*, mener une vie tranquille. **3.** [colours] doux, reposant. || *n.* tranquillité *f*, calme *m*; paix *f*, quiétude *f.*: [Fam.] *on the* ~, en douce. || *v. tr.* tranquilliser, apaiser, calmer; faire taire. || *v. intr. to* ~ *down*, se tranquilliser. || **quietly** [-lɪ] *adv.* tranquillement, calmement; en silence. || **quietness** [-nəs] *n.* tranquillité *f*; [peace] calme *m*, recueillement *m*; [absence of noise] silence *m.*

quilt [kwɪlt] *n.* couvre-pieds *m*, édredon *m*, piqué *m.*

quintet(te) [ˌkwɪn'tɛt] *n.* [Mus.] quintette *m*: *string* ~, quintette à cordes. || **quintuplet** [kwɪn'tʌplət] *adj.* & *n.* quintuplé, -e.

quip [kwɪp] *n.* raillerie *f*, quolibet *m.* || *v. intr.* **[-pp-]** railler.

quirk [kwɚk] *n.* **1.** raillerie *f*; échappatoire *f.* **2.** [handwriting] fioriture *f*, paraphe *m.*

quit [kwɪt] **quit** or **quitted** [-əd] *v. tr.* **1.** s'arrêter (de faire qqch.); [Fig.] abandonner, démissionner: [Fam.] *Quit it!*, Assez!; *to* ~ *work*, cesser le travail. **2.** quitter (une pièce), sortir. || *v. intr.* abandonner: *I* ~ *!*, J'abandonne!, J'en ai assez! || *adj.* quitte, libéré: *to be* ~ *of sth.*, être débarrassé de qqch.

quite [kwajt] *adv.* **1.** [completely] tout à fait, complètement, entièrement; absolument, parfaitement: *I haven't* ~ *finished*, Je n'ai pas tout à fait fini; *I* ~ *agree*, Je suis entièrement d'accord; *You are* ~ *right*, Vous avez/absolument, parfaitement/raison; *Quite (so)!*, Parfaitement!; ~ *another*, un(e) tout autre. **2.** [Fam.] [rather] bien, assez; [very; just] tout: *We were* ~ *tired*, Nous étions bien fatigués; *She was* ~ *glad to . . .*, Elle était /toute contente/tout heureuse/de . . . ; ~ *as (clever, &c.) as*, tout aussi (intelligent, &c.) que; ~ *as/much, many/*, tout autant; ~ *a lot/number/(of)*, un (assez) grand nombre (de); ~ *a few of*, pas mal (de): ~ *enough*, bien assez. **3.** [really] tout, véritable: *It's* ~ *a story!*, C'est toute une histoire!; *It was* ~ *a disaster*, Ce fut une véritable catastrophe.

quits [kwɪt|z] *adj. inv.*: *I am* ~ *with/him, you/*; *We are* ~, Nous sommes quittes. || **quitter** [-ɚ] *n.* [Fam.] défaitiste *m*, lâcheur *m.*

quiver ['kwɪvɚ] *v. intr.* trembler, frissonner (de froid, &c.); [Fig.] [voice] vibrer; [heart] palpiter. || *n.* tremblement *m*, frisson *m*, palpitation *f.*

quiz [kwɪz] *n.* devinette *f*; [Sch.] test *m*, questionnaire *m*; [Rad., TV] ~ *-show*, © émission-questionnaire *f.* || *v. tr.* **[-zz-]**

questionner, examiner (un elève, une personne); railler, se moquer de.
quorum ['kwɔɚəm] *n.* **1.** chambre *f*, section *f* (d'un tribunal); bureau *m* d'appel. **2.** groupe *m* choisi. **3.** quorum *m*.
quota ['kwowtə] *n.* [share] quote-part *f*, quota *m*; [immigration] contingent *m*, quota *m*: ~ *system*, contingentement *m*: *to do one's* ~, faire sa part.
quotation [ˌkwow'tejʃən] *n.* citation *f* (d'un texte); [Stock Exchange] cote *f*, cours *m*; ~ *marks*, guillemets *mpl*. ‖ **quote** [kwowt] *v. tr.* citer (des paroles; un passage d'un livre); [Prices] coter; [Gram.] mettre (des mots) entre guillemets. ‖ *n.* [Fam.] citation *f*; guillemet *m*: *in quotes*, entre guillemets, cf. QUOTATION.
quotient ['kwowʃənt] *n.* [Math.] quotient *m*: *intelligence* ~ [*abr.* I.Q.], quotient *m* intellectuel.
q.v. [ˌkjuw'vij] [= Lat. quod vide, *which see*] voir, V.

R

R, r [ɑɚ] *pl.* **R's, r's** [letter] R *m*, r *m*.
rabbi ['ɹæbaj] *n.* [Rel.] rabbin *m*.
rabbit ['ɹæbɪt] *n.* lapin *m*, lapine *f*.
rabble ['ɹæb|] *n.* populace *f*, (la) foule; (la) canaille *f*.
rabid ['ɹæbɪd] *adj.* furieux, enragé. ‖ **rabies** ['ɹejbɪz] *n.* [dog, &c.] rage *f*.
raccoon [ɹæ'kuwn] *n.* raton *m* laveur, © chat *m* sauvage.
race[1] ['ɹejs] *n.* race *f*; [family] lignée *f*: *the human* ~, le genre humain. [Pej.] engeance *f*. ‖ **racial** ['ɹejʃəl] *adj.* racial, ethnique.
race[2] *n.* course *f*; [water] courant *m*; [Fig.] carrière *f*; [Mec.] affolement *m* (d'un moteur): ~ *horse*, cheval *m* de course; ~ *track*, piste *f*, champ *m* de courses. ‖ *v. intr.* courir, faire une course; [of a motor] s'emballer. ‖ *v. tr.* faire courir (un cheval); lutter de vitesse avec (qqun); emballer (un moteur). ‖ **racer** ['ɹejsɚ] *n.* [Pers.] coureur *m*; cheval *m*, /auto *f*, bicyclette *f*, avion *m*, bateau *m*/de course.
racing [-ɪŋ] *n.* courses *fpl*; [engine] emballement *m*.
rack[1] [ɹæk] *n.*: *to go to* ~ *and ruin*, tomber en ruine; aller à vau-l'eau.
rack[2] *n.* râtelier *m* (dans une grange); [old instrument of torture] chevalet *m*; [Rail.] filet *m*, porte-bagages *m*; *hat-* ~, porte-chapeau *m*; *towel-* ~, porte-serviette *m*; [Fig.] *He was on the* ~, Il était sur des charbons ardents. ‖ *v. tr.* mettre (une victime)/à la torture, sur la roue/; distendre (des membres, &c.); arracher violemment, extorquer (qqch.); [Fig.] tourmenter: *to* ~ *one's brains*, se creuser la tête, se fatiguer les méninges; *to be racked with fever*, brûler de fièvre; *to be racked with troubles*, être mangé de soucis; *to have a racking headache*, avoir un mal de tête/fou, terrible/.
racket[1] [-ət] *n.* raquette *f* (de tennis).
racket[2] *n.* **1.** [Fam.] racket *m*, [Pop.] combine *f*. **2.** [noise] vacarme *m*: *to make a* ~, faire/du tapage, [Fam.] du chahut. ‖ *v. intr.* mener le vacarme. ‖ **racketeer** [ɹækə'tijɚ] *n.* **1.** escroc *m*, combinard *m*. **2.** tapageur *m*. ‖ *v. intr.* escroquer, pratiquer l'escroquerie; exercer un métier louche.
racy [-ɪ] *adj.* [animal] de (bonne) race; [Fig., style] vigoureux; [Pers.] plein de verve.
radar ['ɹejdɑɚ] *n.* radar *m*.
radiance ['ɹejdɪ|əns] *n.* rayonnement *m*; éclat *m*. ‖ **radiant** [-ənt] *adj.* [permanent] radieux; [passing] rayonnant. ‖ **radiate** [-ˌejt] *v. intr.* irradier; rayonner. ‖ *v. tr.* [radio] irradier (des ondes). ‖ **radiation** [ɹejdɪ'ejʃən] *n.* [atomic, &c.] radiation *f*; rayonnement *m*. ‖ **radiator** ['ɹejdɪˌejtɚ] *n.* [car] radiateur *m*.
radical ['ɹædɪk|] *adj.* radical, [judgment, &c.] absolu, [measure] draconien.
radio ['ɹejdɪow] *pl.* **radios** *n.* radio *f*, T.S.F. *f*: ~ *set*, poste *m* de/radio, T.S.F., récepteur *m*; ~ *station*, /poste *m* émetteur,

station *f* (radiophonique); ~ *tube*, lampe *f*: *to turn/on, off/the* ~, allumer, fermer/le poste. || *v. tr.* radiodiffuser (un programme); radio-télégraphier, émettre (un message), transmettre par radio. || **radioactive** [-ˌæktɪv] *adj.* radio-actif. || **radioactivity** [-ˌæktɪvɪtɪ] *n.* [Phys.] radioactivité *f.* || **radiologist** [ɹejdɪ'ɔləʤ|-ɪst] *n.* [Med.] radiologiste *m.* || **radiology** [-ɪ] *n.* [Phys.] radiologie *f.* || **radioscopy** [ɹejdɪ'ɔskəpɪ] *n.* radioscopie *f.* || **radio|-telegraphy** [-tə'lɛgrəfɪ] *n.*, **-telephony** [-tə'lɛfənɪ] *n.* radio|télégraphie *f*, -téléphonie *f.*

radish ['ɹædɪʃ] *pl.* **radishes** radis *m*: *horse* ~, raifort *m.*

radium ['ɹejdɪəm] *n.* [Chem.] radium *m.*

radius [ɹejdɪəs] *n. pl.* **radii** ['ɹejdɪˌaj], **radiuses** [-əz] rayon *m* (de cercle, &c.).

radix ['ɹejdɪ|ks] *pl.* **radices** [-ˌsijz] *n.* [Math., &c.] racine *f*, base *f.*

raffle ['ɹæfḷ] *n.* [charities] loterie *f*, tombola *f.* || *v. tr.* mettre (qqch.) en/tombola, loterie/.

raft [ɹæft] *n.* radeau *m*; tas *m*, amas *m*: *lumber* ~, train *m* de flottage.

rafter [-ɚ] *n.* [building] chevron *m.*

rafts|man [-smən] *pl.* **-men** flotteur *m* (de bois), © raftsman *m.*

rag[1] [ɹæg] *n.* guenille *f*, chiffon *m*; ~ *-book* [children] livre *m* d'images imprimé sur toile; haillon *m*; ~ *-and-bone man*, ~ *-picker*, chiffonnier *m*, © guenillou *m.*

rag[2] *n.* chahut *m.* || *v. tr. & intr.* **[-gg-]** chahuter.

ragamuffin [-əˌmʌfɪn] *n.* gueux *m*, misérable *m.*

rage [rejʤ] *n.* **1.** rage *f*; fureur *f*, furie *f.* **2.** toquade *f* (pour qqch., *for sth.*): *to be in a* ~, être furieux; *to fly into a* ~, devenir furieux; *It's all the* ~, Cela fait fureur, c'est le dernier cri. || *v. intr.* rager, être/en fureur, déchaîné/.

ragged ['ɹægəd] *adj.* [Pers.] déguenillé; [torn] déchiqueté, en lambeaux; [rough] hérissé, raboteux.

raging ['rejʤɪŋ] *adj. & n.* furieux. || *n.* cf. RAGE *n.* **1.**

ragman ['ɹægmæn] *n.* chiffonnier *m*, © guenillou *m.*

raid [ɹejd] *n.* [air, &c.] raid *m*; [plunder] razzia *f*; [police] descente *f*: *air* ~, alerte *f.* || *v. tr.* faire une/descente, rafle/ dans (un lieu); [ransack] razzier (une ville, &c.); [attack] effectuer un raid dans.

rail [ɹejl] *n.* [Rail.] rail *m*; barre *f*; rampe *f* (d'escalier); barreau *m*; barrière *f*; balustrade *f*: *by* ~, par (chemin de) fer. || **railhead** [-ˌhɛd] *n.* terminus *m* (ferroviaire). || **railing** [-ɪŋ] *n.* balustrade *f*; grille *f*; garde-fou *m.* || **railroad** [-ˌɹowd] [esp. US] *n.* chemin *m* de fer; [track] voie *f* ferrée: ~ *station*, gare *f*; *by* ~, en, par/ chemin de fer; ~ *crossing*, passage *m* à niveau. || **railway** [-ˌwej] [esp. Br.] *n.* chemin de fer. cf. RAILROAD. || **railway|man** [-ˌwejmən] *pl.* **-men** *n.* cheminot *m*, employé *m* de chemin de fer.

rain [ɹejn] *n.* pluie *f*: *in the* ~, sous la pluie. || *v. intr.* pleuvoir: *It is raining cats and dogs*, Il pleut à/seaux, boire debout, torrents, verse/; *It never rains but it pours*, Un malheur n'arrive jamais seul; *rained-out/game, meeting/*, partie/ remise, contremandée/à cause de la pluie. || **rainbow** [-ˌbow] *n.* arc-en-ciel *m.* || **raincoat** [-ˌkowt] *n.* imperméable *m.* || **raindrop** [-ˌdɹɑp] *n.* goutte *f* de pluie. || **rainfall** [-ˌfɔl] *n.* averse *f*; [Coll.] les pluies *fpl*, le régime des pluies. || **rain gauge** [-ˌgejʤ] *n.* pluviomètre *m.* || **rain-proof** [-ˌpɹuwf] *adj.* imperméable, à l'épreuve de l'eau. || **rainwater** [-ˌwɔtɚ] *n.* eau *f* de pluie. || **rainy** [-ɪ] *adj.* pluvieux: [Fig.] *a nest egg for a* ~ *day*, une poire pour la soif.

raise [ɹejz] © [US] *n.* augmentation *f*, hausse *f* (de salaire). || **raise** *v. tr.* lever, relever; [lift up] soulever; [voice] élever; soulever (une objection); [head] hausser; pousser (un cri, un hurlement); provoquer (les rires); évoquer (un revenant, &c.); ressusciter (un mort); se procurer (des fonds); [Fin.] émettre (une obligation); augmenter (les prix): *to* ~ *Cain*, faire un scandale, en faire une affaire d'État; [Fig.] *to* ~ *the wind*, se procurer de l'argent.

raisin ['ɹejzɪn] *n.* raisin *m* (sec).

rake[1] [ɹejk] *n.* râteau *m.* || *v. tr.* râteler (un jardin), ratisser (une pelouse), racler (qqch.): *to* ~ *up* (*the fire*), attiser (le feu).

rake[2] *n.* [mast] inclinaison *f.* || *v. intr.* [mast] être en pente, incliner.

rakish [-ɪʃ] *adj.* [behaviour] dissolu, débauché.

rally ['ɹælɪ] *n.* ralliement *m*, rassemblement *m.* || *v. tr.* rallier; rassembler (des adhérents, &c.). || *v. intr.* [gather] se rallier, se rassembler; se reprendre, reprendre des forces.

ram [ɹæm] *n.* bélier *m.* || **[-mm-]** *v. intr.* enfoncer, bourrer. || *v. tr.* enfoncer; éperonner (un navire), tamponner (une voiture).

ramble ['ɹæmbḷ] *v. intr.* **rôder, se promener.** || *n.* **longue/promenade, excursion/.**

|| **rambler** [-ɚ] *n.* promeneu|r *m*, -se *f*; rôdeu|r *m*, -se *f*. || **rambling** [-ɪŋ] *adj.* [Pers.] qui va à l'aventure, [mind] vagabond.

ramify [ˈɹæmɪˌfaj] *v. intr.* ramifier.

ramp [ɹæmp] *n.* rampe *f*, [slope] pente *f*.

rampage [ˈɹæmˌpejʤ] *n.* rage *f*, tempête *f*. || *v. intr.* tempêter, se mettre en rage.

rampant [ˈɹæmpənt] *adj.* [Herald.] rampant; [Pers.] colérique, rageur.

rampart [ˈɹæmpɑɚt] *n.* rempart *m*; [Fig.] protection *f*.

ramrod [ˈɹæmˌɹɑd] *n.* baguette *f* de fusil.

ramshackle [ˈɹæmˌʃækl̩] *adj.* croulant, délabré.

ran cf. RUN.

ranch [ɹæntʃ] *n.* ranch *m*, élevage *m*: *dude* ~, ranch *m*/d'opérette, pour touristes/. || **rancher** [-ɚ] *n.* propriétaire *m* d'un ranch, éleveur *m*.

rancid [ˈɹænsɪd] *adj.* [butter, oil] rance.

rancour [ˈɹæŋkɚ] *n.* rancune *f*, ressentiment *m*; [bitterness] rancœur *f*.

random [ˈɹændəm] *adj.* fortuit. || *n.* hasard *m*: *at* ~, *adv. loc.* au hasard; à tort et à travers.

rang cf. RING[1].

range [ɹejnʤ] *n.* rangée *f*, rang *m*; [mountain] chaîne *f*; étendue *f*, distance *f*; domaine *m*, champ *m* (d'activité, visuel, &c.); alignement *m*; direction *f*; portée *f* (d'une arme), champ *m* de tir; [gas, Electr.] fourneau *m*, © poêle *m*/de cuisine: *within* ~, à portée (de la voix, de tir); *a wide* ~ *of*, une grande variété de. || *v. tr.* ranger; arranger; franchir, parcourir, aligner. || *v. intr.* se ranger; s'aligner: *to* ~ *from* . . ., varier entre, de . . . jusqu'à, ➡ s'échelonner sur une gamme, un éventail.

rank[1] [ɹæŋk] *n.* rang *m*; ordre *m*; [Mil.] grade *m*; classe *f*; ~ *and file*, la troupe; *risen from the ranks*, sorti du rang. || *v. tr.* ranger, classer, disposer; mettre (qqun, qqch.) au rang de. || *v. intr.* [Br.] occuper un rang; se ranger; *to* ~ *with*, avoir le même grade que; *to* ~ *first*, être à la tête de la classe, occuper le premier rang (parmi) . . .

rank[2] *adj.* [odour] fort, rance; [richness, &c.] extrême.

rankle [ˈɹæŋkl̩] *v. intr.* laisser une rancœur; [Fam.] rester sur le cœur.

ransack [ˈɹænˌsæk] *v. tr.* **1.** fouiller (de fond en comble). **2.** piller, saccager.

ransom [ˈɹænsəm] *n.* rançon *f*. || *v. tr.* rançonner (qqun); [redeem] racheter (qqch.).

rant [ɹænt] *n.* [speech] divagation *f*, discours *m* extravagant. || *v. intr.* divaguer; [Pej.] déclamer; *to* ~ *and rave*, tempêter.

rap [ɹæp] *n.* **1.** tape *f*; coup *m* léger (sur une porte, &c.). **2.** blâme *m*, pénalité *f*. || *v. tr.* **[-pp-]** frapper (d'un coup sec); [Fig.] *to* ~ *s.o.'s knuckles*, blâmer, critiquer, tancer (qqun).

rapacious [ɹəˈpejʃəs] *adj.* [Pers.] pillard; violent; rapace.

rape [ɹejp] *n.* enlèvement *m*; viol *m*. || *v. tr.* enlever de force; violer.

rapid [ˈɹæpɪd] *adj.* rapide, prompt. || *n. pl.* rapides *mpl*. || **rapidity** [ɹəˈpɪdɪtɪ] *n.* rapidité *f*, promptitude *f*. || **rapidly** [ˈɹæpɪdlɪ] *adv.* rapidement, promptement.

rapt [ɹæp|t] *adj.* [ecstatic] ravi (*by*, par); absorbé (*in*, dans). || **rapture** [-tʃɚ] *n.* [Fig.] ivresse *f*, extase *f*; ravissement *m*; transport *m* (de joie).

rare[1] [ɹɛɚ] *adj.* [Cul.] saignant; mal cuit.

rare[2] *adj.* rare; incomparable. || **rarely** [-lɪ] *adv.* rarement; extraordinairement; incomparablement. || **rarity** [-ɪtɪ] *n.* rareté *f*; curiosité *f*.

rascal [ˈɹæskəl] *n.* coquin *m*, gredin *m*.

rash[1] [ɹæʃ] *n.* [Med.] éruption *f*, [skin] irritation *f*.

rash[2] *adj.* [decision] irréfléchi; téméraire; imprudent; impétueux. || **rashness** [-nəs] *n.* témérité *f*; imprudence *f*; irréflexion *f*.

rasp [ɹæsp] *n.* **1.** grattement *m*, raclement *m*. **2.** [tool] râpe *f*, lime *f*. || *v. tr.* **1.** râper, racler. **2.** [speech] aboyer (un ordre). **3.** [nerves] exciter, mettre les nerfs/à vif, à fleur de peau/. **4.** gratter.

raspberry [ˈɹæzˌbɛəɹɪ] *n.* framboise *f*: ~ *bush*, framboisier *m*.

rat [ɹæt] *n.* rat *m*; [Fig.] renégat *m*; [Fam.] lâcheur *m*, faux-frère *m*: ~ *poison*, mort *f* aux rats; ~ *trap*, ratière *f*; [Fig.] *to smell a* ~, soupçonner anguille sous roche. || *v. tr.* **[-tt-]** dératiser (un immeuble). || *v. intr.* [Fig.] trahir.

rate [ɹejt] *n.* taux *m*, pourcentage *m*; régime *m*; vitesse *f*, allure *f*; [Fin.] cours *m* (du change); taxe *f*, impôt *m*: *birth-*~, (taux de) natalité *f*; *subscription rates*, tarif *m* des abonnements; *air mail rates*, tarif de la poste aérienne; *freight rates*, tarif-marchandises *m*; © ~ *-payer*, contribuable *m*; *at a great* ~, à grande/vitesse, allure; *at that* ~, [speed] à ce train-là, [case] dans ces conditions(-là); *at the* ~ *of*, à la vitesse de, [price] à raison de; *at any* ~, en tout cas; *first-* ~, de premier ordre. || **rate** *v. tr.* **1.** taxer (qqun), [goods, &c.] tarifer; évaluer (qqun, qqch.): *He rated a large office* *on the tenth floor*, Il avait droit à un grand bureau au dixième. **2.** gronder (qqun).

rather ['ɹæðɚ] *adv.* plutôt; assez; passablement; de préférence: ~ *than*, plutôt que (de + inf., + subjunc.).

ratify ['ɹætɪˌfaj] *v. tr.* ratifier, confirmer, approuver; homologuer.

rating ['ɹejtɪŋ] *n.* cote *f*, évaluation *f*; répartition *f* (des taxes); valeur *f*, classement *m*, rang *m*; [Navy] matelot *m*.

ratio ['ɹejʃow] *n.* rapport *m*; proportion *f*; *in the* ~ *of*, dans le rapport de; *in/direct, inverse/* ~ *to*, en raison/directe, inverse/ de.

ration ['ɹæʃən] *n.* ration *f*. ‖ *v. tr.* rationner (qqun, qqch.), mettre (qqun) à la ration. ‖ **rational** ['ɹæʃə|nəl] *adj.* rationnel; raisonné; raisonnable; logique. ‖ **rationing** [-ɪŋ] *n.* rationnement *m*.

rattle ['ɹætḷ] *n.* [metal] cliquetis *m*; bruit *m* de ferraille; hochet *m* (de bébé); crécelle *f*: (*the*) *rattle of a cab*, (le) roulement d'un fiacre; *death-* ~, râle *m*. ‖ *v. intr.* cliqueter. ‖ *v. tr.* agiter; [Fig.] agacer, affoler: *He rattled his sabre*, Il agita son sabre. ‖ **rattlesnake** [-ˌsnejk] *n.* serpent *m* à sonnettes.

raucous ['ɹɔkəs] *adj.* [voice] rauque.

ravage ['ɹævəʤ] *n.* ravage *m*; pillage *m*; ruine *f*. ‖ *v. tr.* ravager; piller.

rave [ɹejv] *v. intr.* **1.** [to be mad] divaguer, délirer. **2.** souffler en tempête, être déchaîné. **3.** être en extase (*on*, devant), ne pas tarir (*on*, sur).

ravel ['ræv!] *v. intr.* & *tr.* [**-ll-**] (s')embrouiller, (s')enchevêtrer.

raven ['ɹejvən] *n.* [bird] corbeau *m*. ‖ *v. intr.* [beast] chercher sa proie. ‖ *v. tr.* [beast] dévorer (une proie). ‖ **ravenous** ['ɹævənəs] *adj.* [hunger] vorace; [animal, &c.] rapace: *to be* ~, avoir une faim de loup.

ravine [ɹə'vijn] *n.* ravin *m*, ravine *f*.

raving ['ɹejvɪŋ] *n.* [madness] divagation *f*, délire *m*: ~ *mad*, fou furieux.

ravish ['ɹævɪʃ] *v. tr.* ravir, enlever; charmer, enchanter (qqun). ‖ **ravishing** [-ɪŋ] *adj.* ravissant, charmant, [site] enchanteur. ‖ **ravishment** [-mənt] *n.* **1.** [joy] ravissement *m*. **2.** rapt *m*, enlèvement *m*.

raw [ɹɔ] *adj.* [meat] cru, [material] brut; [weather] aigre, © cru, [air] vif; [silk] grège; [wound] à vif; [Pers.] novice; ~ *materials*, matières *fpl* premières; ‖ *n.* [Fam.] (point) sensible, névralgique. ‖ **rawness** [-nəs] *n.* crudité *f*; [weather] humidité *f* (froide); [Pers., Fig.] inexpérience *f*.

ray [ɹej] *n.* rayon *m*, radiation *f*.

rayon ['ɹejɑn] *n.* [textile] rayonne *f*, soie *f* artificielle.

raze [ɹejz] *v. tr.* raser; effacer; rayer. ‖ **razor** ['ɹejzɚ] *n.* rasoir *m*: ~ *blade*, lame *f* de rasoir; *electric* ~ [souvent electric SHAVER] rasoir *m* électrique; *safety* ~, rasoir de sûreté.

RCAF [= Royal Canadian Air Force] Aviation *f* Royale Canadienne (ARC).

RCMP © [= Royal Canadian Mounted Police] Gendarmerie Royale du Canada.

re- [ˌɹij-] *prefix* [☞ signifiant "de nouveau". cf. Fr. *re-* (*refaire*, &c.).

reach [ɹijtʃ] *n.* atteinte *f*; portée *f*; étendue *f*: (*with*)*in* ~, à portée de; *out of* ~, hors de portée de; *beyond* ~, hors d'atteinte. ‖ *v. tr.* atteindre, rejoindre; tendre, étendre; arriver, parvenir à; donner, passer à: *to* ~ (*out*) *for* (*sth.*), s'efforcer d'atteindre (qqch.). ‖ *v. intr.* s'étendre: *as far as the eye can* ~, à perte de vue.

react [ɹɪ'æk|t] *v. intr.* réagir (*against*, contre; *on*, sur). ‖ **reaction** [-ʃən] *n.* [nuclear, &c.] réaction *f*. ‖ **reactionary** [-ʃənˌɛəɪ] *n.* & *adj.* [Pol., &c.] réactionnaire (*m*/*f*).

reactor [ɹɪ'æktɚ] *n.* réacteur *m*.

read[1] [ɹijd], **read**, **read** [ɹɛd] *v. tr.* lire: *to* ~ *over*, parcourir (un livre, des documents); *to* ~ *out* (*sth.*), lire (qqch.)/tout haut, à haute voix/; *to* ~ *up*, étudier (un sujet). ‖ *v. intr.* [novel, description, &c.] se lire: *the thermometer reads zero*, le thermomètre marque zéro.

read[2] [ɹɛd] cf. READ[1]: *to be well* ~, avoir beaucoup lu. ‖ **readable** ['ɹijd|əbḷ] *adj.* lisible, qui se lit bien. ‖ **reader** [-ɚ] *n.* **1.** lecteur *m*, lectrice *f*; [Typ.] *proof-* ~, correcteur *m* d'épreuves. **2.** livre *m* de lecture, morceaux *mpl* choisis.

readily ['ɹɛdɪ|lɪ] *adv.* promptement, volontiers.

readiness [-nəs] *n.* promptitude *f*; empressement *m*; [mind, reaction] vivacité *f*; bonne volonté *f*; degré *m* de préparation.

reading ['ɹijdɪŋ] *n.* lecture *f* (d'un texte, testament, projet de loi); indication *f*; relevé *m* (de données, &c.); ~ *desk*, pupitre *m*; ~ *-room*, cabinet *m*, salle *f*/de lecture; discussion *f* (d'un bill).

readjust [ˌɹijə'ʤʌst] *v. tr.* rajuster (qqch.), réadapter (qqun), remanier, retoucher (qqch.). ‖ *v. intr.* se réadapter. ‖ **readjustment** [-mənt] *n.* rajustement *m*, réadaptation *f*, mise *f* au point.

ready ['ɹɛdɪ] *adj.* prêt, disposé (*to*, à); [mind] vif, prompt; (argent) comptant: ~ *-made*, [clothes] de confection, prêt à

porter. || *v. tr.*: *to get* ~, préparer (qqch.). || *v. intr.* [Pers.] se préparer, se disposer/à.
reagent [ɹɪ'ejʤənt] *n.* [Chem.] réactif *m.*
real [ɹijl] *adj.* réel, vrai, véritable; [concrete] matériel: ~ *estate*, immeuble *m*, propriété immobilière; *He is a* ~ *fool*, C'est un fieffé imbécile. || **realism** [-ɪzm] *n.* réalisme *m.* || **realist** [-ɪst] *n.* réaliste *m.* || **realistic** [ˌɹɪə'lɪstɪk] *adj.* réaliste. || **reality** [ɹɪ'ælɪtɪ] *n.* réalité *f*; (le) réel *m*: *in* ~, en/réalité, fait, réellement. || **realization** [ɹɪəˌlaj'zejʃən] *n.* réalisation *f*; [understanding] conception *f* nette. || **realize** ['ɹijəˌlajz] *v. tr.* se rendre compte de (qqch.), réaliser; [imagine] concevoir; saisir, comprendre; [achieve, perform] réaliser (un but). || **really** ['ɹijlɪ] *adv.* réellement, vraiment; en vérité, véritablement: *Really!*, Vraiment!
realm [ɹɛlm] *n.* royaume *m*; [Fig.] domaine *m.*
realtor ['ɹijəlt|ɚ] *n.* agent *m* d'immeubles. || **realty** [-ɪ] *n.* immeubles *mpl*; agence *f* immobilière.
ream [ɹijm] *n.* [paper] rame *f.*
reap [ɹijp] *v. tr.* moissonner; [Fig.] recueillir. || **reaper** [-ɚ] *n.* moissonneur *m*; [machine] moissonneuse *f.* || **reaping** [-ɪŋ] *n.* moisson *f.*
reappear [ˌɹijə'pijɚ] *v. intr.* réapparaître, [book] reparaître. || **reappearance** [-əns] *n.* réapparition *f.*
rear [ɹijɚ] *n.* arrière *m*, derrière *m*, [person's] postérieur *m*, [end] queue *f*: *in the* ~, à l'arrière; *to the* ~, en arrière; *at the* ~ *of*, derrière, à l'arrière de; [Naut.] ~ *-admiral*, contre-amiral *m*; [Mil.] ~ *-guard*, arrière-garde *f*; [car] *rear view mirror*, miroir *m* rétroviseur. || *adj.* ~ *door*, porte *f* de derrière; ~ *seat*, banquette *f* arrière. || *v. tr.* élever (un enfant, bâtiment). || *v. intr.* [horse] se cabrer.
rearm [ɪɪ'ɑɚm] *v. intr.* réarmer. || **rearmament** [-əmənt] *n.* réarmement *m.*
rearrange [ˌɹijə'ɹejnʤ] *v. tr.* arranger (qqch.) de nouveau.
reason [ɹijzən] *n.* raison *f* (*for sth.*, de qqch.): *the* ~ *why . . .*, la raison pour laquelle . . . ; *for good* ~, pour cause; *for the same* ~, au même titre; *He has* (*every*) ~ *to*, Il a (tout) lieu de (+ *infin.*); *within* ~, dans des limites raisonnables; *by* ~ *of* . . . , à cause de . . . ; *to listen to* ~, entendre raison; *It stands to* ~, Cela va/de soi, sans dire/. || *v. intr.* raisonner. || **reasonable** [-əbl̩] *adj.* raisonnable, rationnel. || **reasonably** [-əblɪ] *adv.* raisonnablement; modérément; passablement.
reasoning [-ɪŋ] *n.* raisonnement *m.*
reassure [ˌɹij'æʃuwɚ] *v. tr.* **1.** rassurer. **2.** réassurer.
rebate ['ɹijbejt] *n.* rabais *m*, escompte *m*; [refund] remboursement *m.* || *v. tr.* faire un rabais (sur qqch.); rabaisser; rembourser: *to* ~ *s.o.'s pride*, rabattre l'orgueil (de qqun).
rebel ['ɹɛbəl] *n.* rebelle *m.* || *v. intr.* **[-ll-]** [ɹɪ'bɛl] [people] se révolter, se soulever. || **rebellion** [-jən] *n.* rébellion *f*, soulèvement *m.* || **rebellious** [-jəs] *adj.* rebelle.
rebound ['ɹijˌbawnd] *n.* rebondissement *m*, contre-coup *m.* || [ɹɪ'bawnd] *v. intr.* rebondir. || *v. tr.* faire rebondir.
rebuff [ɹɪ'bʌf] *n.* rebuffade *f*, refus *m*, résistance *f* (à une offre); échec *m.* || *v. tr.* mal accueillir, refuser, décliner (une demande).
rebuild [ɹɪ'bɪl|d], **rebuilt** [-t], **rebuilt** *v. tr.* (faire) rebâtir, reconstruire.
rebuke [ɹɪ'bjuwk] *n.* réprimande *f.* || *v. tr.* réprimander.
rebut [ɹɪ'bʌt] *v. tr.* **[-tt-]** rejeter (une prétention); repousser (qqun). || **rebuttal** [-əl] *n.* rejet *m* (d'une prétention); refus *m.*
recall [ɹɪ'kɔl] *n.* rappel *m*: *beyond* ~, irrévocablement. || *v. tr.* [remind; annul, revoke] rappeler; [remember] se rappeler (qqch.); *to try to* ~, faire un effort de réflexion.
recant [ɹɪ'kænt] *v. intr.* se rétracter. || *v. tr.* reviser (une opinion).
recapitulate [ˌɹɪkə'pɪtjəˌlejt] *v. tr.* récapituler.
recede [ɹɪ'sijd] *v. intr.* reculer, s'éloigner, se rétracter: *a receding chin*, un menton fuyant.
receipt [ɹɪ'sijt] *n.* [Com.] reçu *m*, récépissé *m*; réception *f*; facture *f*; quittance *f*; *pl.* recettes *fpl*: *to acknowledge* ~ *of*, accuser réception de; *on* ~ *of*, au reçu de; *I am in* ~ *of*, J'ai bien reçu. || *v. tr.* acquitter (une facture, &c.).
receive [ɹɪ'sijv] *v. tr.* **1.** recevoir (qqun, qqch.) accueillir (qqun); accepter (qqch.); [Radio] capter (un poste). **2.** recéler (qqch.). || **receiver** [-ɚ] *n.* **1.** [letter, message] destinataire *m/f*; [phone] récepteur *m*; [Fin.] receveur *m*; © *Receiver General of Canada*, Receveur général du Canada. **2.** [Pers.] recéleur.
recent ['ɹijsənt] *adj.* récent, tout nouveau. || **recently** [-lɪ] *adv.* récemment, dernièrement.
receptacle [ɹɪ'sɛptəkl̩] *n.* réceptacle *m*; récipient *m.*
reception [ɹɪ'sɛpʃən] *n.* réception *f*; accueil

m: [hotel] ~ *desk*, réception *f*, bureau *m*. || **receptionist** [-ɪst] *n*. réceptionniste *f*.

recess [ˈɹijˌsɛs] *n*. [hiding place] (re)coin *m*; [Sch.] récréation *f*; [Jur., Pol.] vacances *fpl*. || **recession** [ɹɪˈsɛʃən] *n*. [Econ., &c.] régression *f*, recul *m*; ralentissement *m* des affaires, © la récession.

recipe [ˈɹɛsɪpɪ] *n*. [Cul.] recette *f*. de cuisine.

recipient [ɹəˈsɪpɪənt] *adj*. qui reçoit, accueillant. || *n*. [Pers.] récipiendaire *m*; [objet] récipient *m*, destinataire *m* (d'une lettre), bénéficiaire *m* (d'un chèque).

reciprocal [ɹəˈsɪpɹək|l̩] *adj*. réciproque, mutuel. || **reciprocate** [-ejt] *v. tr*. échanger, faire échange de; répondre à: *to* ~ *a blow*, rendre un coup. || *v. tr*. retourner (un compliment); en faire autant. || **reciprocity** [ɹɛsɪˈpɹɔsɪtɪ] *n*. réciprocité *f*, échange *m*.

recital [ɹɪˈsajtl̩] *n*. **1.** exposé *m*, description *f* (des faits). **2.** récit *m*, narration *f*. **3.** [Mus.] récital *m*. || **recitation** [ɹɛsɪˈtejʃən] *n*. **1.** récitation *f*. **2.** répétition *f* de mémoire. || **recite** [ɹɪˈsajt] *v. tr*. [poem, &c.] réciter, [story] narrer.

reckless [ˈɹɛkləs] *adj*. insouciant (*of*, de); imprudent, téméraire; [obstination, &c.] insensé. || **recklessly** [-lɪ] *adv*. avec insouciance, témérairement; de/façon, manière/ insensée. || **recklessness** [-nəs] *n*. témérité *f*, manque *m* de soin, négligence *f*.

reckon [ˈɹɛkən] *v. tr. & intr*. **1.** calculer (un prix). **2.** juger: *He is reckoned a poor fellow*, On le considère comme un pauvre type. **3.** [Fam.] supposer, (s')imaginer: *to* ~ *with*, tenir compte de; *to* ~ *on sth*., compter sur qqch.; [Fam.] *I* ~ *you're right*, J'ai comme l'impression que vous avez raison. || **reckoning** [-ɪŋ] *n*. **1.** calcul *m*. **2.** facture *f* [restaurant] addition *f*. **3.** [navy] estime *f*: *by dead* ~, à l'estime.

reclaim [ɹɪˈklejm] *v. tr*. **1.** corriger, réformer, redresser. **2.** réclamer, revendiquer; défricher (du terrain), récupérer (un sous-produit).

reclassify [ˌɹijˈklæsɪfaj] *v. tr*. reclasser.

recline [ɹɪˈklajn] *v. tr*. appuyer, reposer (sur), faire pencher (qqch.). || *v. intr*. s'appuyer (sur); se reposer, s'étendre. || **reclining** [-ɪŋ] *adj*. incliné, penché, appuyé: [car] ~ *seat*, siège *m* inclinable.

recluse [ɹɪˈkluws] *adj*. [Pers.] séquestré, reclus, retiré du monde. || *n*. [Fig.] ermite *m*.

recognition [ˌɹɛkəg|ˈnɪʃən] *n*. reconnaissance *f*; identification *f*. || **recognize** [-ˈnajz] *v. tr*. reconnaître, identifier (qqun, qqch.).

recoil [ˈɹijˌkojl] *n*. recul *m* (d'une arme); répugnance *f*, horreur *f*. || *v. intr*. [ɹɪˈkojl] **1.** reculer (d'horreur), bondir en arrière; [gun] reculer. **2.** [Fig.] rejaillir (*on*, sur).

recollect [ˌɹɛkəˈlɛk|t] *v. tr*. se rappeler (qqch.). || **recollection** [-ʃən] *n*. souvenir *m*.

recommend [ˌɹɛkəˈmɛnd] *v. tr*. recommander, conseiller. || **recommendation** [ˌɹɛkəmɛnˈdejʃən] *n*. recommandation *f*.

recompense [ˈɹɛkəmˌpɛns] *n*. récompense *f* (*for*, de); indemnité *f*, dédommagement *m* (*for*, de). || *v. tr*. **1.** payer (qqun), récompenser (qqun de qqch.). **2.** dédommager (qqun de qqch.).

reconcile [ˈɹɛkənˌsajl] *v. tr*. **1.** réconcilier. **2.** [quarrel] régler (une dispute). **3.** mettre d'accord (deux personnes). **4.** donner satisfaction (à qqun): *to become reconciled to*, accepter (qqch.), se résigner à (faire qqch.). || **reconciliation** [ˌɹɛkənˌsɪlɪˈejʃən] *n*. réconciliation *f*, conciliation *f*.

recondition [ˌɹɪkənˈdɪʃən] *v. tr*. reconditionner, remettre à neuf.

reconnaissance [ɹəˈkɑnəsəns] *n*. [Mil.] reconnaissance *f*. || **reconnoitre** [ˌɹɛkəˈnojtɚ] *v. tr*. [Mil.] reconnaître (un pays, une armée ennemie).

reconsider [ˌɹijkənˈsɪdɚ] *v. tr*. réexaminer (une question), revenir sur (une décision). || *v. intr*. changer d'avis.

re|construct [ˌɹijkənstɹʌk|t] *v. tr*. reconstruire. || **re|construction** [-ʃən] *n*. reconstruction *f*.

reconvene [ˌɹijkənˈvijn] *v. intr*. se réunir à nouveau: *when Parliament reconvenes*, → à la rentrée du Parlement.

record [ˈɹɛkɚd] *n*. **1.** enregistrement *m* (d'un fait); note *f*, procès-verbal *m*; registre *m*, [Jur.] dossier *m*, casier *m* judiciaire; archives *fpl*, copie *f* (d'un acte, document): *to have a good* ~, avoir bonne réputation, être bien noté; *to have a* (*criminal*) ~, avoir un casier judiciaire chargé; *on the* ~, officiellement; *off the* ~, officieusement, [Fam.] entre nous. **2.** [Mus., &c.] disque *m*. **3.** [Sport.] record *m*: *to break the* ~, battre le record (de . . .). || *adj*. [dominant] record. || **record** [ɹɪˈkɔɚd] *v. tr*. [words, Mus., &c.] enregistrer; prendre/note, acte/de (qqch.): *to* ~ *a vote*, voter. || **recorder**[1] [-ɚ] *n*. **1.** [Jur.] greffier *m*: © *the Court of the Recorder*, © la Cour du Recorder. **2.** [device] enregistreur *m*: *tape* ~, magnétophone *m*.

recorder[2] *n*. [Mus.] flûte *f*/à bec, douce/.

recording [-ɪŋ] *n*. [facts] consignation *f*; enregistrement *m* (de disques, de programmes radiophoniques, &c.).

recount [ˈɹijˌkawnt] *n.* [election] nouvelle addition *f* de voix; © recomptage *m* (de votes). ‖ *v. tr.* [ɹɪˈkawnt] recompter (des chiffres); raconter (ce qui s'est passé).

recoup [ɹɪˈkuwp] *v. tr.* dédommager (qqun): *to ~ o.'s losses*, rentrer dans ses fonds, se rattraper.

recourse [ɹɪˈkɔɚs] *n.* **1.** [help] recours *m* (à): *to have ~ to*, avoir recours à, recourir à. **2.** [Pers.] aide *f*, assistance *f*, soutien *m*.

recover[1] [ˌɹijˈkʌvɚ] *v. tr.* recouvrer, retrouver; récupérer. ‖ [ɹɪˈkʌvɚ] *v. intr.* se rétablir, revenir à la santé, se remettre (de, *from*).

recover[2] *v. tr.* recouvrir (d'une étoffe, &c.).

recovery [-ɪ] *n.* **1.** [money] recouvrement *m*. **2.** [health] guérison *f*, rétablissement *m*. **3.** reprise *f* (économique). **4.** récupération *f* (d'un produit).

re-create [ˌɹijkɹɪˈejt] *v. tr.* [= to create again] recréer [see following entry].

recreate [ˈɹɛkɹɪˌejt] *v. tr.* récréer, divertir, distraire. ‖ **recreation** [ˌɹɛkɹɪˈejʃən] *n.* récréation *f*, divertissement *m*, distraction(s) *f. usual. pl.* ‖ **recreative** [ˈɹɛkɹɪˌejtɪv] *adj.* récréatif, divertissant, amusant, distrayant.

recrimination [ɹɪˌkɹɪmɪˈnejʃən] *n.* récrimination *f*.

recruit [ɹɪˈkɹuwt] *n.* [soldier] recrue *f*, [Fam.] bleu *m*; novice *m*, nouveau *m* (à l'école). ‖ *v. tr.* [army] recruter, lever (des hommes), refaire (une armée); se procurer (de l'aide).

rectangle [ˈɹɛktæŋgl̩] *n.* rectangle *m*. ‖**rectangular** [ˌɹɛkˈtæŋgjələ] *adj.* rectangulaire, à angle droit.

rectify [ˈɹɛktɪˌfaj] *v. tr.* **1.** rectifier, corriger. **2.** [Elect.] redresser. **3.** [Chem.] raffiner, purifier.

rector [ˈɹɛktɚ] *n.* **1.** [R.C.] curé *m* (d'une paroisse). **2.** © [Scol.] recteur *m* (d'un collège secondaire, d'une université). ‖ **rectory** [-ɪ] *n.* **1.** cure *f*. **2.** presbytère *m*.

rectum [ˈɹɛktəm] *n.* rectum *m*.

recuperate [ɹɪˈkuwpɚˌejt] *v. tr.* [recover] récupérer, recouvrer (ses forces).

recur [ɹɪˈkɚ] *v. intr.* [-rr-] **1.** revenir, se produire de nouveau: *That will never ~*, Cela ne se représentera plus jamais. **2.** revenir (à l'esprit). ‖ **recurrence** [-əns] *n.* retour *m*, renouvellement *m* (d'un fait). ‖ **recurrent** [-ənt] *adj.* intermittent, périodique; [Med.] récurrent.

red [ɹɛd] *adj.* rouge; roux; [Pol.] radical, communiste: *to turn ~*, rougir, [sky] rougeoyer; *to see ~*, voir rouge. [Hist.] *~ -coat*, soldat anglais; *the Red Cross*, la Croix-rouge; [Rail.] *~ cap*, porteur *m*; *~ deer*, cerf *m*; *~ bird*, cardinal *m*; [Pers.] *~ -blooded*, brave, fort, puissant; *red-head*, une rousse; [traffic] *~ light*, feu *m* rouge; [Fig.] signal *m* d'alarme; [Fin.] *~ tape*, paperasserie *f*, bureaucratie *f*, formalités *fpl* (administratives): [Fig.] *It's like a ~ rag to a bull!*, Ça me fait bondir!; *~ -hot*, chauffé au rouge; © *Red River*, (la) rivière Rouge. ‖ **redden** [-n̩] *v. tr. & intr.* rougir. ‖ **reddish** [-ɪʃ] *adj.* rougeâtre, roussâtre.

redeem [ɹɪˈdijm] *v. tr.* **1.** racheter; [pawn] dégager. **2.** [pay off] libérer (des obligations), acquitter. **3.** remplir (une promesse). **4.** délivrer (du péché). ‖ **redeemer** [-ɚ] *n.* **1.** sauveur *m*, libérateur *m*. **2.** [Jesus-Christ] Le Rédempteur *m*. ‖ **redemption** [ɹɪˈdɛmpʃən] *n.* **1.** rachat *m*, libération *f* (d'un bien hypothéqué). **2.** [Theol.] Rédemption *f*.

red-head [ˈɹɛdˌhɛd] *n.* roux *m*, rousse *f*; [Pej.] rouquin *m*, -e *f*.

redness [ˈɹɛdnəs] *n.* rougeur *f*, rouge *m*.

redolent [ˈɹɛdələnt] *adj.* parfumé, odorant: *~ of*, exhalant une senteur de.

redouble [rɪˈdʌbl̩] *v. tr.* **1.** redoubler. **2.** doubler, augmenter beaucoup; [Bridge] surcontrer.

redoubt [ɹɪˈdawt] *n.* [fortifications] redoute *f*.

redress [ɹɪˈdɹɛs] *n.* redressement *m*, réparation *f*: *to seek ~*, demander justice. ‖ *v. tr.* redresser, réparer (un tort, &c.).

redskin [ˈɹɛdˌskɪn] *n.* Peau-Rouge *m*.

reduce [ɹɪˈdjuws] *v. tr.* réduire, diminuer: *to be reduced to . . .*, en être réduit à . . . ‖ *v. intr.* maigrir. ‖ **reduction** [ɹɪˈdʌkʃən] *n.* réduction *f*; diminution *f*.

redundant [ɹɪˈdʌndənt] *adj.* redondant, superflu.

redwood [ˈɹɛdˌwʊd] *n.* [Bot.] séquoia *m*.

reed [ɹijd] *n.* **1.** roseau *m*. **2.** [Mus.] anche *f* (d'instrument à vent).

reef [ɹijf] *n.* récif *m*; atoll *m*; [hidden, & Fig.] écueil *m*.

reek [ɹijk] *n.* fumée *f*; [Pej.] relent *m*. ‖ *v. intr.* fumer; empester (*of*, de qqch.). ‖ **reeky** [-ɪ] *adj.* enfumé.

reel [ɹijl] *n.* **1.** rouleau *m*, bande *f* (de film, &c.); [sewing, tape recorder] bobine *f*; [fishing rod] moulinet *m*: *feed ~*, bobine pleine; *take-up ~*, bobine vide. **2.** [Scottish] danse *f* écossaise, © reel *m*. ‖ *v. tr.* [thread] bobiner, [spindle] dévider. ‖ *v. intr.* [Pers.] tituber.

re-elect [ˌɹijəˈlɛkt] *v. tr.* [candidate] réélire.

re-enter [ˌɹij'ɛntɚ] *v. intr.* rentrer.
re-establish [ɹijə'stæblɪʃ] *v. tr.* rétablir.
reeve [ɹijv] © *n.* préfet *m* de comté.
refectory [ɹɪ'fɛktɚɪ] *n.* réfectoire *m.*
refer [ɹɪ'fɚ] *v. tr.* [-rr-] référer (à, *to*); [cause, fact, &c.] rapporter, imputer, faire remonter (qqch. à qqch.); [Jur.] déférer, soumettre, transmettre (une question), renvoyer (qqch.) à. || *v. intr.* se référer, s'en référer, en référer, s'en remettre (à qqun, *to s.o.*): *referring to* (*your letter . . .*), comme suite à (votre lettre . . .); *to* ~ *to sth.*, faire allusion à qqch.
referee [ˌɹɛfɚ'ij] *n.* [Sport., Jur.] arbitre *m.* || *v. tr. & intr.* [Sport.] arbitrer (un match de baseball, une joute de hockey, &c.).
reference ['ɹɛfɚəns] *n.* référence *f*; mention *f*, allusion *f*; [for application] recommandation *f*; [Pers.] répondant *m*; [in book] renvoi *m*: *to have* ~ *to* (*sth.*), avoir rapport à (qqch.), se rapporter (à qqch.); *with* ~ *to . . .*, à propos de . . . , en ce qui concerne . . . ; ~ *-book*, livre *m*, ouvrage *m*/de référence.
referral [ɹɪ'fɚl] *n.* [question] renvoi *m* (pour étude), proposition *f.*
refill ['ɹijfɪl] *n.* mine *f*, pile *f*, feuillets *mpl*/de rechange; cartouche *f* (de stylobille). || [ɹɪ'fɪl] *v. tr.* remplir (à nouveau), réapprovisionner.
refine [ɹɪ'fajn] *v. tr.* raffiner (du sucre, son style), épurer, polir (sa langue), purifier (les mœurs). || **refined** [-d] *adj.* raffiné; poli, bien élevé; distingué. || **refinement** [-mənt] *n.* **1.** raffinement *m* (de manière, de langage). **2.** raffinage *m* (du pétrole, du sucre). **3.** amélioration *f.* || **refinery** [-ɚɪ] *n.* [Indus.] raffinerie *f.*
reflect [ɹɪ'flɛk|t] *v. tr.* réfléchir, refléter (qqch.); [mirror] renvoyer. || *v. intr.* réfléchir (à qqch., *upon sth.*); [Pej.] donner une mauvaise idée de. || **reflection** [-ʃən] *n.* réflexion *f*; [light, &c.] reflet *m*; [Pej.] blâme *m*, remarque désobligeante. || **reflector** [-tɚ] *n.* réflecteur *m* (de lumière, de son).
reflex ['ɹijflɛks] *adj.* réfléchi, réflexe. || *n.* **1.** réflexe *m.* **2.** réflexion *f*, reflet *m*, image *f.* || **reflexive** [ɹɪ'flɛksɪv] *adj.* [Gram.] verbe *m*/réfléchi, pronominal.
reform [ɹɪ'fɔɚm] *n.* réforme *f.* || *v. tr.* réformer. || **reformation** [ˌɹɛfɚ'mejʃən] *n.* **1.** réforme *f*, réformation *f.* **2.** [Hist.] *Reformation*, la Réforme.
reformatory [ɹɪ'fɔɚməˌtɔɚɪ] *adj.* réformat|eur *m*, -rice *f.* || *n.* maison *f*/de correction, de redressement/. || **reformer** [ɹɪ'fɔɚmɚ] *n.* réformat|eur *m*, -rice *f.*
refraction [ɹɪ'fɹæk|ʃən] *n.* [Phys.] réfraction *f* (de la lumière).
refractory [-tɚɪ] *adj.* **1.** réfractaire, obstiné. **2.** [disease] récalcitrant, résistant.
refrain[1] [ɹɪ'fɹejn] *n.* [Mus.] refrain *m.*
refrain[2] *v. intr.* s'abstenir (de, *from*).
refresh [ɹɪ'fɹɛʃ] *v. tr.* rafraîchir, [Fig.] détendre, reposer (qqun); [apartment, &c.] restaurer, rénover. || **refresher** [-ɚ] *n.* [drink] rafraîchissement *m*;/ce, celui·celle/qui rafraîchit: [US] © ~ *course*, [Sch.] cours *m* de/perfectionnement, révision/. || **refreshing** [-ɪŋ] *adj.* rafraîchissant; [Fig.] délassant. || **refreshment** [-mənt] *n.* rafraîchissement *m*, [rest] délassement *m*; *refreshments*, (léger) goûter *m*, rafraîchissements *mpl.*
refrigerate [ɹɪ'fɹɪʤɚˌejt] *v. tr.* réfrigérer; frigorifier (des denrées alimentaires); frapper (un vin). || **refrigeration** [ɹɪˌfɹɪʤɚ'ejʃən] *n.* réfrigération *f.* || **refrigerator** [ɹɪ'fɹɪʤɚˌejtɚ] *n.* réfrigérateur *m*; frigidaire *m*, armoire *f* frigorifique.
refuel ['ɹij'fjuw|l] *v. intr.* [-ll-] [Naut.] se ravitailler en combustible; [Aero.] faire le plein d'essence.
refuge ['ɹɛfjuwʤ] *n.* refuge *m*; asile *m.* || **refugee** [ˌɹɛfjuw'ʤij] *n.* réfugié, -e.
refund ['ɹijfʌnd] *n.* remboursement *m.* || *v. tr.* [ɹɪ'fʌnd] [money] rembourser. || **refunding** [-ɪŋ] *n.* remboursement *m.*
refusal [ɹɪ'fjuwz|əl] *n.* refus *m.*
refuse[1] *v. tr.* refuser (qqch., qqun; de faire qqch.); [reject] repousser; se refuser (à faire qqch., *to do sth.*).
refuse[2] ['ɹɛfjuws] *n.* rebut *m*, ordures *fpl.*
refute [ɹɪ'fjuwt] *v. tr.* réfuter (un argument).
regain [ɹɪ'gejn] *v. tr.* regagner, récupérer (qqch.).
regal ['ɹɪgəl] *adj.* [authority] royal.
regale [ɹə'gejl] *v. tr.* **1.** régaler, divertir agréablement. **2.** offrir un bon repas, un banquet (à qqun).
regalia [ɹə'gæljə] *n.* insignes *mpl* (de la royauté, d'un ordre, d'une fonction).
regard [ɹɪ'gɑɚd] *n.* égard *m*; respect *m*; estime *f*; considération *f*: *with* ~ *to*, quant à, à l'égard de; *in* ~ *to*, en ce qui concerne; *to pay* ~ *to*, faire attention à; *to have* (*no*) ~ *for*, avoir de l'estime pour, ne faire aucun cas de; *without* ~ *for*, sans égard pour; *out of* ~ *for*, par égard pour; (*Best*) *regards*, (Meilleures) amitiés *fpl.*; *Give my best regards to your mother*, *&c.*, (Faites) mes/compliments, amitiés/à Madame votre mère, &c. || *v. tr.* †regarder, [deem] considérer, estimer; concerner (qqun, qqch.): *He*

regards himself (*as*) *lucky*, Il s'estime heureux; *He is regarded as the best student*, Il passe pour être le meilleur étudiant; *as regards*, en ce qui concerne. || **regarding** [-ɪŋ] *prep.* concernant, touchant, par rapport à, quant à, à l'égard de. || **regardless** [-ləs] *adj.* sans égard (pour, *of*); [Pers.] négligent, inattentif. || *adv.* sans tenir compte de.

regent [ˈɹijʤənt] *n.* régent *m*; régisseur *m*, administrateur *m*.

regime [ɹəˈʒijm] *n.* [Govt.] régime *m*; [living] mode *m* (de vie), régime (alimentaire).

regiment [ˈɹɛʤɪmənt] *n.* [Mil.] régiment *m*. || **regimentation** [ˌɹɛʤɪmənˈtejʃən] *n.* enrégimentation *f*, [propre & Fig.] enrégimentement *m*; [Fig.] dictature *f*.

region [ˈɹijʤən] *n.* région *f*.

register [ˈɹɛʤɪst|ɚ] *v. tr.* enregistrer (qqun, qqch.), [Sch., &c.] immatriculer, inscrire; [letter] recommander. || *v. intr.* [Sch., &c.] s'enregistrer (à, *for*), [university] s'inscrire. || *n.* registre *m*. || **registrar** [-ɹɑɚ] *n.* [Sch.] secrétaire *m*; [Jur.] greffier *m*; © *Registrar General of Canada*, Registraire général du Canada. || **registration** [ˌɹɛʤɪˈstɹejʃən] *n.* enregistrement *m*; [Sch., &c.] inscription *f*, immatriculation *f*; [letter] recommandation *f*: [Sch.] ~ *fee*, frais *mpl* d'inscription; ~ *number*, numéro *m* matricule.

registry [ˈɹɛʤɪstɹɪ] *n.* inscription *f*, enregistrement *m*: [Naut.] *port of* ~, port *m* d'attache.

regret [ɹɪˈgɹɛt] *n.* regret *m*. || *v. tr.* regretter (qqch., de faire qqch.; que + subjunc.). || **regrettable** [-əbl] *adj.* regrettable.

regular [ˈɹɛgjəlɚ] *adj.* régulier; [proper] normal, en règle; [Mil.] permanent; accoutumé; assidu; [intensive] vrai: ~ *customer*, client habituel; *He's a* ~ *fellow*, [Fam.] C'est un chic type. || **regularity** [ˌɹɛgjəˈlæɚɪtɪ] *n.* régularité *f*. || **regularly** [ˈɹɛgjə|ˌlɚlɪ] *adv.* régulièrement; dans les règles. || **regulate** [-ˌlejt] *v. tr.* **1.** former, discipliner (des élèves). **2.** régler (la température, une montre). **3.** régulariser (la digestion). || **regulation** [ˌɹɛgjəˈlejʃən] *n.* règlement *m*, ordonnance *f*, précepte *m*, loi *f*: *traffic* ~, règlement de la circulation; *against regulations*, contre le règlement. || *attrib.* réglementaire.

rehabilitate [ˌɹijhəˈbɪlɪˌtejt] *v. tr.* × réhabiliter (qqun); [thing] remettre en état; [Fig.] relever, rétablir, régénérer. || **rehabilitation** [ˌɹijhəˌbɪlɪˈtejʃən] *n.* [Pers.] réhabilitation *f*; [thing] mise *f* en état de service; [Fig.] régénération *f*, [moral] rééducation *f*, réadaptation *f*.

rehearsal [ɹɪˈhɚs|əl] *n.* **1.** répétition *f* (d'une pièce de théâtre, d'une représentation): *dress* ~, répétition générale. **2.** [drill] entraînement *m*, exercice *m* préliminaire. **3.** [story] récitation *f*, narration *f*. || **rehearse** *v. tr.* **1.** répéter (une pièce). **2.** exercer, entraîner (qqun). **3.** raconter (une histoire).

reign [ɹejn] *n.* [monarch's] règne *m*. || *v. intr.* régner (sur, *over*).

reimburse [ˌɹijɪmˈbɚs] *v. tr.* rembourser (qqun, qqch.). || **reimbursement** [-mənt] *n.* [money] remboursement *m*.

rein [ɹejn] *n.* rêne *f*; [Fig.] *reins*, rênes *fpl*, direction *f*; *to take the* ~, prendre les rênes en main; *to keep a tight* ~ *over*, tenir la bride serrée à (qqun). || *v. tr.* mener, guider, contenir.

reindeer [-ˌdijɚ] *n.* renne *m*.

reinforce [ˌɹijɪnˈfɔɚs] *v. tr.* renforcer (une armée, un argument). || **reinforcement** [-mənt] *n.* renforcement *m*. *pl.* **reinforcements,** renforts *mpl* (de troupes).

reinstate [ˈɹijɪnˌstejt] *v. tr.* rétablir (*in*, dans).

reiterate [ˌɹijˈɪtɚejt] *v. tr.* [repeat] réitérer (qqch.).

reject [ɹɪˈʤɛkt] *v. tr.* rejeter (qqun, qqch.); repousser (une offre); refuser (un candidat). || *n.* rejet *m*.; *pl.* **rejects,** rebuts *mpl*, déchets *mpl*; [Pers.] laissés-pour-compte *mpl*.

rejection [ɹɪˈʤɛkʃən] *n.* rejet *m*; [offer] refus *m*; *pl.* rebuts *mpl*. cf. REJECT.

rejoice [ɹɪˈʤojs] *v. tr.* réjouir (qqun): †*to be rejoiced*|*at, by*|*sth.*, se réjouir de qqch. || *v. intr.* se réjouir (*at, over*, de). || **rejoicing** [-ɪŋ] *n.* réjouissance *f*; joie *f*.

rejoin [ɹɪˈʤojn] *v. tr.* **1.** réunir (après séparation). **2.** rejoindre. || *v. intr.* [retort] répliquer.

rejoinder [ɹɪˈʤojndɚ] *n.* réplique *f*, riposte *f*, répartie *f*.

rejuvenate [ɹɪˈʤuwvəˌnejt] *v. tr.* rajeunir (qqch., qqun).

relapse [ɹɪˈlæps] *n.* [illness] rechute *f*, retour *m* (au silence). || *v. intr.* **1.** retomber; [illness] faire une rechute. **2.** [criminal] récidiver.

relate [ɹɪˈlejt] *v. tr.* relater; raconter. || *v. intr.* se rapporter (à, *to*). || **related** [-əd] *adj.* apparenté, allié; en relation (avec), ayant rapport (à, *to*): *We're* ~, Nous sommes parents. || **relating (to)** [-ɪŋ], relatif (à).

relation [ɹɪˈlejʃən] *n.* **1.** [report] rapport *m*, récit *m*, †relation *f*. **2.** [Pers.] parent *m*,

-e *f*; [relationship] parenté *f*. **3.** [social, business] rapport *m*, relation *f*: *public relations*, relations *fpl* extérieures; [logic] *to bear* ~ *to*, avoir un rapport (quelconque) avec. || **relationship** [ɹɪ'lejʃən,ʃɪp] *n.* **1.** relation *f*, rapport *m* (avec, *with*). **2.** [blood] affinité *f*, parenté *f*. || **relative** ['ɹɛlətɪv] *adj.* relatif: ~ *to*, relativement à. || *n.* parent *m*.

relativity [,ɹɛlə'tɪvɪtɪ] *n.* relativité *f*.

relax [ɹɪ'læks] *v. intr.* se détendre, se *décontracter. || *v. tr.* relâcher. || **relaxation** [ɹɪ,læks'ejʃən] *n.* relaxation *f*, détente *f*, délassement *m*, relâchement *m*.

relay ['ɹijlej] *n.* **1.** [supply] nouvelle équipe *f* (d'hommes), nouvel équipage *m* (de chevaux). **2.** [race] course *f* de relais. **3.** [Electr.] relais *m*. || [ɹɪ'lej] *v. intr.* **1.** porter plus loin. **2.** [Elect.] relayer. **3.** [lay again] replacer.

release [ɹɪ'lijs] *n.* [prisoner] élargissement *m*; délivrance *f*; [Jur.] mise *f* en liberté (sous caution, *on bail*): *news* ~, communiqué *m* (de presse). || *v. tr.* relâcher, délivrer; libérer (un prisonnier); dégager (de, *from*), mettre en circulation, rendre public.

relegate ['ɹɛlɛ,gejt] *v. intr.* **1.** reléguer (*to*, dans). **2.** [task] passer; [communication] transmettre.

relent [ɹɪ'lɛnt] *v. intr.* [Pers.] s'adoucir, se laisser fléchir; [storm] s'apaiser. || **relentless** [-ləs] *adj.* [Pers., hatred] implacable. || **relentlessness** [-ləsnəs] *n.* implacabilité *f*.

relevance ['ɹɛləvən|s] *n.* pertinence *f*, rapport *m* (avec, *to*). || **relevancy** [-sɪ] *n.* cf. RELEVANCE. || **relevant** [-t] *adj.* [fact] pertinent, dans la note; utile, relatif (à, *to*).

reliability [ɹɪ,lajə'bɪlɪtɪ] *n.* [Pers., thing] sûreté *f*, [Pers.] honnêteté *f*, confiance *f* qu'on inspire. || **reliable** [ɹɪ,lajəbl̩] *adj.* digne de confiance, sûr; [data, &c.] exact; © fiable. || **reliably** [ɹɪ'lajəbl̩|ɪ] *adv.* [know] de source sûre. || **reliance** [ɹɪ'lajəns] *n.* confiance *f* (*on*, en).

relic ['ɹɛlɪk] *n.* **1.** relique *f*. **2.** reliques *fpl* (d'un saint). **3.** souvenir *m*. **4.** *relics*, ruines *fpl*, restes *mpl*.

relief[1] [ɹə'lijf] *n.* relief *m*: *to bring out in* ~, mettre en/relief, valeur/; ~ *map*, carte *f* en relief.

relief[2] *n.* **1.** [help] aide *f*, secours *m*: ~ *fund*, caisse *f* de secours. **2.** [comfort] soulagement *m*. || **relieve** [-v] *v. tr.* soulager; secourir: *to feel relieved*, se sentir soulagé.

religion [ɹə'lɪʤ|ən] *n.* religion *f*. || **religious** [-əs] *adj.* religieux, [Pers.] dévot.

relinquish [ɹɪ'lɪŋkwɪʃ] *v. tr.* abandonner (qqch.), renoncer à (qqch.).

relish ['ɹɛlɪʃ] *n.* **1.** [Cul.] goût *m*, saveur *f*; [seasoning] condiment *m*, assaisonnement *m*; [Fig.] penchant *m* (*for*, pour): *to do sth. with* ~, faire qqch. avec un plaisir évident. || *v. tr.* goûter; [enjoy] apprécier; [Cul.] assaisonner.

relive ['ɹij'lɪv] *v. tr.* revivre.

reluctance [ɹɪ'lʌktən|s] *n.* répugnance *f*; aversion *f*: *with* ~, à contre-cœur. || **reluctant** [-t] *adj.* opposé, hésitant: *a* ~ *obedience*, une obéissance forcée; *to be* ~ *to do sth.* faire qqch. à contre-cœur.

rely [ɹɪ'laj] *v. intr.* faire confiance (à qqun, *on s.o.*); se reposer, compter (sur qqun pour faire qqch.).

remain [ɹɪ'mejn] *v. intr.* rester; demeurer: *That remains to be seen*, On verra bien; *It remains to be seen whether* . . . , Reste à savoir si . . . ; *Nothing remains*, Il n'en reste rien; *Nothing remains but to* . . . , Il ne reste qu'à . . . || **remainder** [-dɚ] *n.* **1.** reste *m*, restant *m*; les autres. **2.** [account] reliquat *m*. || **remaining** [-ɪŋ] *adj.* restant, de reste: *There are 10* ~, Il en reste 10; *the* ~ *ten*, les dix autres; *the* ~ *books*, les autres livres. || **remains** [-z] *n.pl.* **1.** débris *mpl*. **2.** [corpse] restes *mpl* (mortels).

re|make [,ɹij'mejk] *v. tr.* refaire.

remark [ɹɪ'mɑɚk] *n.* remarque *f*; observation *f*; note *f*. || *v. tr.* faire remarquer. || **remarkable** [-əbl̩] *adj* remarquable.

remedial [ɹə'mijdɪl̩] *adj.* réparat|eur, -rice: ~ *course*, cours *m* de perfectionnement.

remedy ['ɹɛmədɪ] *n.* remède *m*. || *v. tr.* remédier à (une situation, &c.); réparer, guérir.

remember [ɹɪ'mɛmb|ɚ] *v. tr.* se rappeler (qqch.), se souvenir de (qqun, qqch.); retenir (une leçon): *Remember me* (*kindly*) *to* . . . , Rappelez-moi au bon souvenir de . . . || **remembrance** [-ɹəns] *n.* souvenir *m*; mémoire *f*: *Remembrance Day*, © (le) Jour du Souvenir; *in* ~ *of*, en/souvenir, mémoire/de.

remind [ɹɪ'majnd] *v. tr.* remémorer, rappeler (qqch. à qqun, *s.o. of sth.*); faire penser/à qqch., à faire qqch. || **reminder** [-ɚ] *n.* mémento *m*, aide-mémoire *m* [*pl inv.*]; rappel *m* (d'une obligation, &c.).

reminiscence [,ɹɛmɪ'nɪsəns] *n.* réminiscence *f*. || **reminiscent** [,ɹɛmɪ'nɪsənt] *adj.* qui se souvient vaguement de: ~ *of*, qui fait penser à.

remiss [ɹɪ'mɪs] *adj.* [Pers.] négligent.

remission [ɹɪ'mɪʃən] *n.* rémission *f*; [Jur.] remise *f*; [sins] absolution *f*.

remit [ɹɪ'mɪt] *v. tr.* **[-tt-]** remettre; [slacken]

relâcher; [sins] pardonner. || **remittal** [-l̩] *n.* remise *f* (de dette). || **remittance** [-əns] *n.* remise *f*; envoi *m*, versement *m* (de fonds); © ~ *man*, émigré *m* entretenu par sa famille.

remnant ['ɹɛmnənt] *n.* reste *m*; résidu *m*; *pl.* [Text.] coupons *mpl*, soldes *mpl*.

remodel ['ɹij'mɑdl̩] *v. tr.* [-ll-] remanier, refondre; [Tech.] remodeler; [hat, &c.] (re)mettre/à la mode, au goût du jour/.

remonstrate [ˌɹɛmən'stɹejt] *v. tr.* [×] faire /observer, remarquer/. || *v. intr.* protester (*against*, contre); faire des remontrances (*upon*, au sujet de).

remorse [ɹɪ'mɔɚs] *n.* remords *m*: *to feel* ~, avoir des remords. || **remorseless** [-ləs] *adj.* [Fig.] sans remords; impitoyable.

remote [ɹɪ'mowt] *adj.* éloigné; [time] reculé; vague, léger: *not the remotest idea*, pas la moindre idée. || **remotely** [ɹə'mowtlɪ] *adv.* [distance] loin, au loin; [related] de loin; [Fig.] vaguement.

removal [ɹɪ'muwv|əl] *n.* enlèvement *m*; déménagement *m*; déplacement *m*. || **remove** *v. tr.* enlever; éliminer; supprimer (qqch.). || *v. intr.* [move out] déménager.

remunerate [ɹɪ'mjuwnɚˌejt] *v. tr.* rémunérer. || **remuneration** [ɹɪˌmjuwnɚ'ejʃən] *n.* rémunération *f*.

renaissance ['ɹɛnəsɑns] *n.* renaissance *f*; [Hist.] *the Renaissance*, la Renaissance.

renascence [ɹə'nejsəns] *n.* renaissance *f*.

rend [ɹɛnd] *v. intr.* se déchirer, se fendre (en deux). || *v. tr.* fendre (en deux); [Fig.] déchirer.

render[1] [-ɚ] *v. tr.* donner en retour; rendre (service, &c.); fournir, donner (un rapport); interpréter (un morceau de musique); rendre, traduire (un texte d'une langue à l'autre).

render[2] *v. tr.* faire fondre (de la graisse); extraire (l'huile &c.).

rendering [-ɪŋ] *n.* interprétation *f*; [translation] traduction *f*, version *f*.

renegade ['ɹɛnəˌgejd] *n.* renégat *m*.

renege [ɹə'nejg] *v. intr.* [Fam.] renoncer (à), revenir sur sa parole.

renew [ɹɪ'njuw] *v. tr.* renouveler; rénover. || *v. intr.* se renouveler; rajeunir. || **renewal** [-l̩] *n.* renouvellement *m*.

renounce [ɹɪ'nawns] *v. tr.* renoncer (à); répudier, renier.

renovate ['ɹɛnəˌvejt] *v. tr.* rénover, renouveler.

renown [ɹɪ'nawn] *n.* renom *m*, renommée *f*, grande réputation *f*.

rent[1] cf. REND.

†**rent**[2] *n.* [ɹɛnt] [clothes] accroc *m*, déchirure *f*; [rock] fissure *f*.

rent[3] *n.* loyer *m*. || *v. tr.* louer (une maison): *We ~ typewriters*, → location *f* de machines à écrire; *~-a-car service*, → location *f* (de voitures) sans chauffeur; [thing] *to* ~, à louer. || **rental** [-l̩] *n.* loyer *m*.

renunciation [ɹɪˌnʌnsɪ'ejʃən] *n.* reniement *m* (*of*, de); renonciation *f* (*of*, à).

re|open [ˌɹij'opn̩] *v. tr.* rouvrir. || **reopening** [-ɪŋ] *n.* réouverture *f*; [Sch., Theat.] rentrée *f*.

reorganization [ɹɪˌɔɚgn̩ˌajz'ejʃən] *n.* réorganisation *f*. || **reorganize** [ɹɪ'ɔɚgn̩ˌajz] *v. tr. & intr.* (se) réorganiser.

repair [ɹɪ'pɛɚ] *n.* réparation *f* (*under*, en): *to keep in good* ~, maintenir en bon état. || *v. tr.* réparer (qqch.). || **reparation** [ˌɹɛpɚ'ejʃən] *n.* réparation *f*; dédommagement *m*, satisfaction *f* (pour un dommage).

repartee [ˌɹɛpɑɚ'tij] *n.* répartie *f*, réplique *f*.

repay [ɹɪ'pej] *v. tr.* **1.** rembourser (qqun de qqch.), récompenser (qqun de qqch.). **2.** [Fig.] rendre. || **repayment** [-mənt] *n.* remboursement *m*; récompense *f*.

repeal [ɹɪ'pijl] *n.* abrogation *f*, révocation *f*, annulation *f*. || *v. tr.* révoquer, rapporter, annuler.

repeat [ɹɪ'pijt] *v. tr.* répéter, réitérer; réciter (une leçon). || *n.* répétition *f*. || **repeated** [-əd] *adj.* répété; réitéré; [efforts, &c.] redoublé. || **repeatedly** [-ədlɪ] *adv.* à plusieurs reprises; souvent. || **repeater** [-ɚ] *n.* **1.** [US] arme *f*/à répétition, automatique/. **2.** [US], © [élections] télégraphe *m*. **3.** répétiteur *m*.

repel [ɹɪ'pɛl] *v. tr.* [-ll-] **1.** repousser. **2.** se repousser (l'un l'autre). **3.** dégoûter (qqun).

repellent [ɹə'pɛlənt] *adj.* répulsif; [Fig.] répugnant. || *n.* → produit *m* qui chasse (les insectes, &c.), → anti-(insectes, requins, &c.).

repent [ɹɪ'pɛnt] *v. tr. & intr.* se repentir (de qqch.); regretter (un choix). || **repentance** [-əns] *n.* repentir *m*, regret *m*. || **repentant** [-ənt] *adj.* repentant: ~ *tears*, des larmes de repentir.

repercussion [ˌɹɪpɚ'kʌʃən] *n.* répercussion *f*.

repetition [ˌɹɛpə'tɪʃən] *n.* **1.** répétition *f*, réitération *f*; récitation *f*: *grown wearisome from constant* ~, → qui finit par lasser à force d'être répété.

repetitive [ɹɛ'pɛtɪtɪv] *adj.* plein de répétitions, redondant.

replace [ɹɪ'plejs] *v. tr.* **1.** remplacer (*with*, *by*, par). **2.** [put back] replacer, remettre en place. || **replaceable** [-əbl̩] *adj.* remplaçable. || **replacement** [-mənt] *n.* remise *f* en place; remplacement *m.*

replenish [ɹɪ'plɛnɪʃ] *v. tr.* remplir, garnir (*with*, de). || **replenishment** [-mənt] *n.* remplissage *m.* || **replete** [ɹɪ'plijt] *adj.* plein, rempli (*with*, de).

replica ['ɹɛplɪkə] *n.* reproduction *f*; [painting] copie *f*, réplique *f*.

reply [ɹɪ'plaj] *n.* réponse *f* (à qqch.); [retort] réplique *f*: [Com.] ~ *-coupon*, coupon-réponse *m.* || *v. tr. & intr.* répondre (à qqch.); [retort] répliquer.

report [ɹɪ'pɔɚt] *v. tr.* rapporter (qqch.), faire un rapport sur (qqun, qqch.); rendre compte de (qqch.); [point out] signaler; dénoncer (qqun, qqch.]: *It is reported that* . . . , Le bruit court que . . . , On dit que . . . || *v. intr.* se présenter (qq. part), donner de ses nouvelles; / donner, faire/un compte rendu, un rapport: *to ~ for duty*, se présenter au travail, prendre son service; *Please ~ to the airport 20 minutes prior to flight departure*, Veuillez vous présenter à l'aéroport au moins vingt minutes avant l'heure prévue (pour le départ); *Report to me at the end of the term*, Revenez me voir à la fin du trimestre; *the chairman will ~ on*, le président fera (un) rapport sur, relatif à . . . || *n.* rapport *m*, compte rendu *m*; exposé *m*; nouvelle *f*; bulletin *m* (météorologique); [Sch.] bulletin *m* scolaire; [noise] détonation *f.* || **reporter** [-ɚ] *n.* reporter *m.* || **reporting** [-ɪŋ] *n.* reportage *m.*

repose [ɹɪ'powz] *n.* **1.** repos *m*, sommeil *m.* **2.** tranquillité *f*, quiétude *f.* || *v. intr.* **1.** se reposer, se détendre. **2.** *to ~ in*, faire confiance à (qqun). || **repository** [ɹə'pɑsɪtɚɪ] *n.* [R.C.] **1.** reposoir *m.* **2.** custode *f.*

reprehend [ˌɹɛpɹɪ'hɛn|d] *v. tr.* blâmer; réprimander. || **reprehensible** [-sɪbḷ] *adj.* [action] répréhensible. || **reprehension** [-ʃən] *n.* blâme *m.*

represent [ˌɹɛpɹɪ'zɛnt] *v. tr.* représenter. || **representation** [ɹɛpɹɪˌzɛn'tejʃən] *n.* **1.** représentation *f.* **2.** exposé *m* (de faits). || **representative** [ˌɹɛpɹɪ'zɛntətɪv] *n.* représentant *m*, -e *f.* || *adj.* [typical] représentatif.

repress [ɹɪ'pɹɛ|s] *v. tr.* réprimer, contenir (ses réactions, &c.). || **repression** [-ʃən] *n.* répression *f.*

reprieve [ɹɪ'pɹijv] *v. tr.* accorder un sursis à (qqun); [death sentence] gracier (qqun). || *n.* [Jur.] sursis *m.*

reprimand ['ɹɛpɹɪˌmænd] *n.* réprimande *f.* || *v. tr.* réprimander, [Fam.] chapitrer.

reprint ['ɹijˌpɹɪnt] *n.* **1.** réimpression *f.* **2.** [article] tirage *m* à part. || *v. tr.* [ɹɪ'pɹɪnt] réimprimer.

reprisals [ɹɪ'pɹajzəlz] *n.pl.* représailles *fpl*, revanche *f.*

reproach [ɹɪ'pɹowtʃ] *v. tr.* faire des reproches à (qqun); blâmer (qqun, qqch.): *to ~ s.o. with sth.*, reprocher qqch. à qqun; *to ~ s.o./with, for/having done sth.*, reprocher à qqun d'avoir fait qqch. || *n.* reproche *m.* || **reproachful** [-fḷ] *adj.* [look] réprobateur, plein de reproche, chargé de blâme.

reprobate ['ɹɛpɹəˌbejt] *v. tr.* [Rel.] réprouver. || *adj. & n.* [Rel.] réprouvé (*m*); [Fam.] dépravé (*m*).

reproduce [ɹɪ'pɹowdjuws] *v. tr.* [copy] reproduire (un objet, document). || *v. intr.* se reproduire. || **reproduction** [ˌɹijpɹə'dʌkʃən] *n.* reproduction *f*, [copy] réplique *f*, copie *f.*

reproof [ɹɪ'pɹuw|f] *n.* reproche *m.* || **reprove** [-v] *v. tr.* blâmer: *to ~ s.o. for laziness*, reprocher à qqun sa paresse.

reptile ['ɹɛptajl] *n.* reptile *m.*

republic [ɹɪ'pʌblɪk] *n.* [Pol.] république *f.* || **republican** [-ən] *adj. & n.* républicain, -e.

repudiate [ɹɪ'pjuwdɪˌejt] *v. tr.* **1.** repousser (une idée), répudier (une doctrine). **2.** [debt] refuser; [son] désavouer; [wife] répudier.

repugnance [ɹɪ'pʌgnən|s] *n.* répugnance *f*, aversion *f.* || **repugnant** [-t] *adj.* contraire, opposé, répugnant (*to*, à): *It is ~ to him to*, → Il lui répugne de.

repulse [ɹɪ'pʌls] *n.* **1.** refoulement *m*, échec *m.* **2.** refus *m.* || *v. tr.* repousser; refuser, rejeter. || **repulsive** [-ɪv] *adj.* repoussant, rebutant.

reputable ['ɹɛpjətəbḷ] *adj.* estimé, honorable; de bonne réputation. || **reputation** [ˌɹɛpjə'tejʃən] *n.* réputation *f*; renommée *f.* || **repute** [ɹɪ'pjuwt] *n.* réputation *f*; bonne réputation. || *v. tr. & intr.* tenir (qqun) pour, considérer (qqun) comme; *to be reputed as*, passer pour.

request [ɹɪ'kwɛst] *n.* demande *f*; requête *f*; pétition *f*: *at the ~ of*, à la demande de; *on ~*, sur demande; *in (great) ~*, (très) recherché, en vogue. [Br.] *~ stop*, arrêt facultatif. || *v. tr.* [ask] demander (*sth. of s.o.*, qqch. à qqun; *s.o. to do sth.*, à qqun de faire qqch.); [as a favour] prier (qqun de faire qqch.); [require politely] inviter (qqun à faire qqch.).

Requiem ['ɹɛkwɪəm] *n.* [Rel.] requiem *m*: [R.C.] *~ Mass*, messe *f* des morts.

require [ɹɪ'kwajɚ] *v. tr.* [demand] exiger, †requérir (qqch. de qqun); [need] demander, [stronger] exiger; avoir besoin de, [must] falloir: *That requires thought*, Cela demande réflexion; *It required two men to . . .*, Il a fallu deux hommes pour . . . ; *He required help*, Il avait besoin d'aide. || **required** [-d] *adj.* voulu, nécessaire, requis. || **requirement** [-mənt] *n.* exigence *f*; qualité *f*, condition *f*/ (requise). || **requisite** [ˈɹɛkwɪzɪt] *adj.* nécessaire, indispensable (*for*, à). || *n.* condition *f* (requise); chose *f* nécessaire. || **requisition** [ɹɛkwɪˈzɪʃən] *n.* demande *f* (surtout par écrit); [Mil.] réquisition *f*. || *v. tr.* réquisitionner.

resale [ˈɹijˌsejl] *n.* revente *f*.

rescind [ɹɪˈsɪnd] *v. tr.* [Jur.] révoquer (un décret), abroger (une loi), casser (un jugement).

rescue [ˈɹɛskjuw] *n.* sauvetage *m*, délivrance *f*; *to come to the ~ of s.o.*, venir au secours de qqun. || *v. tr.* secourir; venir à la rescousse de (qqun); sauver, délivrer (qqun de qqch.).

research [ɹɪˈsɚtʃ] *n.* recherche(s) *f(pl)*, investigations *fpl.*: *to do ~ on*, faire des recherches sur; © *National Research Council*, Conseil national de recherches. || *v. tr.* rechercher (qqch.); faire des recherches, enquêter/sur (qqch.).

resemblance [ɹɪˈzɛmb|ləns] *n.* ressemblance *f*. || **resemble** [-l̩] *v. tr.* ressembler à (qqch., qqun).

resent [ɹɪˈzɛnt] *v. tr.* s'offenser de, être sensible à (un affront, une injure): *I ~ that!*, Je proteste! || **resentful** [-fl̩] *adj.* plein de ressentiment, rancunier; [Fig.] froissé, blessé. || **resentment** [-mənt] *n.* ressentiment *m*, indignation *f*.

reservation [ˌɹɛzɚˈvejʃən] *n.* **1.** [hotel] réservation *f*, [train] réservation *f* (de compartiment); demande *f* de location, place retenue. **2.** [US] réserve *f*. (indienne). **3.** arrière-pensée *f*.

reserve [ɹɪˈzɚv] *n.* réserve *f*; restriction *f*; discrétion *f*; © réserve *f* (indienne). || *v. tr.* réserver (qqch.); louer (une place), retenir (une chambre). || **reserved** [ɹɪˈzɚvd] *adj.* réservé; [seat] loué; [Fig.] réservé. || **reservist** [-ɪst] *n.* [Mil.] réserviste *m*.

reservoir [ˈɹɛzɚˌvwɑɚ] *n.* **1.** réservoir *m* d'eau. **2.** [store] réserve *f*.

reset [ˈɹijˌsɛt], **reset, reset, resetting** *v. tr.* replacer, remettre en place; [limb] remettre; [watch] remettre à l'heure; [diamond] remonter; [printing] recomposer.

reshuffle [ˌɹijˈʃʌfl̩] *v. tr.* [cards] rebattre; [Fig.] remanier (une administration). || **reshuffling** [-ɪŋ] [positions] *n.* remaniement *m*.

reside [ɹɪˈzajd] *v. tr.* résider, demeurer, séjourner. || **residence** [ˈɹɛsɪdən|s] *n.* **1.** résidence *f*; habitation *f*, domicile *m*. **2.** séjour *m* (dans un pays). **3.** [Univ.] internat *m*; foyer *m*, maison *f* (des étudiants). || **resident** [-t] *n.* résident *m*. || **residential** [ˌɹɛsɪˈdɛnʃəl] *adj.* [part of town, &c.] de résidence, bourgeois, d'habitation, résidentiel: [Sch.] *~ student*, (élève *m/f*) interne *m/f*.

residual [ɹɪˈzɪdʒuwl] *adj.* restant; [Tech.] résiduel. || *n.* résidu *m*; [Math.] reste *m*.

residue [ˌɹɛzɪˈdjuw] *n.* résidu *m*, reste *m*; [Acct.] reliquat *m*.

resign [ɹɪˈzajn] *v. tr.* [position] démissionner de; céder (qqch.). *v. intr.* **1.** se résigner, se soumettre. **2.** démissionner, donner sa démission, se démettre (d'un emploi, d'une fonction). || **resignation** [ˌɹɛsɪgˈnejʃən] *n.* démission *f*; résignation *f*: *to tender one's ~*, remettre sa démission.

resilience [ɹɪˈzɪljəns] *n.* élasticité *f*; [Fig.] ressort *m* moral; [action] rebondissement *m*.

resin [ˈɹɛzn̩] *n.* résine *f*.

resist [ɹɪˈzɪst] *v. tr.* résister à (qqun, qqch., *s.o.*, *sth.*); s'opposer à (qqun, qqch.). || *v. intr.* résister. || **resistance** [-əns] *n.* résistance *f*. || **resistant** [-ənt] *adj.* résistant.

resolute [ˈɹɛzəˌluwt] *adj.* résolu, déterminé, décidé. || **resolution** [ˌɹɛzəˈluwʃən] *n.* **1.** résolution *f*. **2.** [Pol.] /projet *m*, proposition *f*/de résolution.

resolve [ɹɪˈzɑlv] *v. tr.* résoudre. || **resolvent** [-ənt] *n.* **1.** dissolvant *m*. **2.** [Med.] résolutif *m*.

resonance [ˈɹɛzənən|s] *n.* résonance *f*. || **resonant** [-t] *adj.* résonnant; sonore.

resort [ɹɪˈzɔɚt] *n.* **1.** station *f* thermale, balnéaire: *seaside ~*, plage *f*. cf. BEACH, WATERING. **2.** ressource *f*, recours *m*: *to have ~ to*, avoir recours à (qqch.); *in the last ~*, en dernier ressort; *the court of last resort*, le tribunal de dernière instance, la cour des cas désespérés. || *v. intr. to ~ to*, recourir à, avoir recours à.

resound [ɹɪˈzawnd] *v. intr.* **1.** résonner, retentir, faire écho. **2.** retentir: *His fame resounds everywhere*, Son nom retentit partout.

resource [ɹɪˈzɔɚs] *n.* ressource *f*. || **resourceful** [ɹɪˈzɔɚsfl̩] *adj.* → plein de ressources, → jamais pris au dépourvu; [Fam.] débrouillard.

respect [ɹɪˈspɛkt] *n.* respect *m*, estime *f*, considération *f* (pour, envers/qqun);

rapport *m*, égard *m*; *pl.* hommages *mpl*: *with* ~ *to*, en ce qui concerne, quant à; *in many respects*, à bien des égards; *in this* ~, sous ce rapport, à cet égard; *to pay o.'s respects*, présenter ses/hommages, respects. ‖ *v. tr.* respecter. ‖ **respectability** [ɹɪˌspɛktəˈbɪlɪtɪ] *n.* honorabilité *f*, air *m* respectable. ‖ **respectable** [ɹɪˈspɛkt|əbḷ] *adj.* respectable, honorable, comme il faut; [number] considérable; [Fam.] passable: *a* ~ *speech*, un discours passable. ‖ **respectful** [-fḷ] *adj.* respectueux. ‖ **respecting** [-ɪŋ] *prép.* à l'égard de, par rapport à. ‖ **respective** [-tɪv] *adj.* respectif, particulier, relatif: *Go to your* ~ *rooms*, Allez chacun à votre chambre. ‖ **respectively** [-tɪvlɪ] *adv.* respectivement.

respiration [ˌɹɛspəˈejʃən] *n.* respiration *f*: *want of* ~, asphyxie *f*.

respite [ˈɹɛspɪt] *n.* **1.** repos *m*, répit *m*; pause *f*, relâche *f*. **2.** [law] sursis *m*, délai *m*.

resplendent [ɹɪˈsplɛndənt] *adj.* resplendissant.

respond [ɹɪˈspɑn|d] *v. intr.* répondre (à), réagir (contre). ‖ **response** [-s] *n.* **1.** réponse *f*; [physiological, &c.] réaction *f*. **2.** [R.C.] répons *m*. ‖ **responsibility** [ɹɪˌspɑnsɪˈbɪlɪtɪ] *n.* responsabilité *f*; [Fin.] solvabilité *f*. ‖ **responsible** [ɹɪˈspɑnsɪbḷ] *adj.* **1.** responsable (*for*, de; *to s.o.*, envers qqun); digne de confiance: *to be* ~ *for*, répondre de; *a* ~ *position*, poste qui comporte des responsabilités. **2.** [Fin.] solvable.

responsive [ɹɪˈspɑnsɪv] *adj.* sensible; [public] vibrant, enthousiaste.

rest[1] [ɹɛst] *n.* repos *m*; support *m*; [Mus.] pause *f*: ~ *room*, © toilettes, [Fr.] W.C. ‖ *v. intr.* (se) reposer; s'appuyer (sur, *on*); dépendre (de qqun, qqch. *on s.o., sth.*): *to* ~/*on one's laurels, on one's oars*, s'endormir sur ses lauriers; *to* ~ *with* (*s.o.*), incomber à (qqun); *to* ~ *up*, se remettre de ses fatigues. ‖ *v. tr.* reposer, appuyer; [Fig.] baser (sur).

rest[2] *v. intr.* rester. ‖ *n.* reste *m*; restant *m*; les autres.

restaurant [-əˌɑnt] *n.* restaurant *m*.

restful [-fḷ] *adj.* paisible, calme, tranquille.

restitution [ˌɹɛstɪˈtjuwʃən] *n.* **1.** restitution *f*: *to make* ~, restituer (qqch.). **2.** [damage] réparation *f*.

restive [ˈɹɛst|ɪv] *adj.* rétif; inquiet.

restless [-ləs] *adj.* agité; turbulent: *to become* ~, s'agiter, s'impatienter. ‖ **restlessness** [-ləsnəs] *n.* agitation *f*; turbulence *f*.

restoration [ˌɹɛstəˈejʃən] *n.* restauration *f*; [health] rétablissement *m*: [return] restitution *f*. ‖ **restorative** [ɹɪˈstoə|ətɪv] *n.* cordial *m*. ‖ **restore** *v. tr.* restaurer; [health] rétablir; rendre, restituer (qqch.); [put back] remettre, réintégrer; ramener (la confiance, la paix).

restrain [ɹɪˈstɹejn] *v. tr.* retenir; contenir. ‖ **restraint** [-t] *n.* **1.** contrainte *f*, empêchement *m*, frein *m*, obstacle *m*: *to be under* ~, → ne pas avoir la liberté de ses mouvements. **2.** restriction *f*, limitation *f*: *to stand in the restraints* (*of*), rester dans les limites (de); ~ *of trade*, les entraves *fpl* au commerce.

restrict [ɹɪˈstɹɪk|t] *v. tr.* restreindre; limiter. ‖ **restricted** [-təd] *adj.* restreint; officiel; privé. [≠ for general distribution]. ‖ **restriction** [-ʃən] *n.* **1.** restriction *f*; contrainte *f*; limitation *f*. ‖ **restrictive** [ɹɪˈstɹɪktɪv] *adj.* restrictif; [clause] limitatif.

result [ɹɪˈzʌlt] *n.* résultat *m*; [after effect] suite *f*: *the* ~ *is that*, → il en résulte que. ‖ *v. intr.* résulter (de, *from*); aboutir (à, *in*): *to* ~ *in*/*sth.*, + *-ing*, avoir pour résultat/qqch., que.

resume [ɹɪˈzjuwm] *v. tr.* reprendre (les cours, le travail); se remettre à (la tâche); récapituler. ‖ **résumé** [ˈɹɛzjuwˌmej] *n.* résumé *m*; abrégé *m*: *in* ~, en résumé.

resumption [ɹɪˈzʌmpʃən] *n.* reprise *f*.

resurrect [ˌɹɛzəˈɛk|t] *v. intr. & tr.* ressusciter. ‖ **resurrection** [-ʃən] *n.* résurrection *f*.

resuscitate [ɹɪˈsʌsɪˌtejt] *v. intr.* ressusciter; [Fig.] se réveiller. ‖ *v. tr.* ressusciter; [Fig.] ranimer (qqun).

retail [ˈɹijtejl] *n.* [Com.] (vente *f* au) détail *m*. ‖ *v. tr.* [Com.] détailler, vendre (qqch.) au détail. ‖ **retailer** [-ə] *n.* [Com.] détaillant *m*. ‖ **retailing** [-ɪŋ] *n.* commerce *m* de détail.

retain [ɹɪˈtejn] *v. tr.* retenir; [keep] conserver. ‖ **retainer** [-ə] *n.* [Fin.] honoraire *m* préalable, avance *f*, arrhes *fpl*; [Hist.] serviteur *m*; *pl.* gens *mpl*. ‖ **retaining** [-ɪŋ] *adj.* qui retient: ~ *dam*, barrage *m*/de retenue, d'emmagasinage/.

retaliate [ɹɪˈtælɪˌejt] *v. intr.* rendre la pareille (à qqun); user de représailles (envers qqun, *upon s.o.*). ‖ **retaliation** [ɹɪˌtælɪˈejʃən] *n.* représailles *fpl*; [Hist.] talion *m*: *law of* ~, la loi du talion.

retard [ɹɪˈtɑəd] *n.* **1.** retard *m*. **2.** [dam] barrage *m*. ‖ *v. tr.* retarder; [slow] ralentir, entraver. ‖ **retarded** [ɹɪˈtɑədəd] *adj.* retardé; [Med.] arriéré.

retch [ɹɛtʃ] *v. intr.* avoir des haut-le-cœur, avoir envie de vomir.

retentive [ɹɪ'tɛntɪv] *adj.* → qui retient, [memory] fidèle.

reticence ['ɹɛtɪsən|s] *n.* réticence *f.* || **reticent** [-t] *adj.* réticent.

retinue ['ɹɛtɪnjuw] *n.* cortège *m,* suite *f* (d'un prince).

retire [ɹɪ'tajɚ] *v. intr.* prendre sa retraite *f,* se retirer (des affaires); [withdraw, go to bed] se retirer. || **retired** [-d] *adj.* retraité, en retraite; [merchant] retiré des affaires. || **retirement** [-mənt] *n.* retraite *f.* || **retiring** [-ɪŋ] *adj.* [room] → où l'on se retire, particulier; [chairman, &c.] sortant; [pension] → qui prend sa retraite; [Fig.] effacé, modeste.

retort [ɹɪ'tɔɚt] *v. intr.* riposter, [words] rétorquer. || *n.* riposte *f,* [words] réplique *f;* [Chem.] cornue *f.*

retouch [ɹɪ'tʌtʃ] *v. tr.* retoucher (qqch.). || *n.* retouche *f.*

retrace [ɹɪ'tɹejs] *v. tr.* remonter à la source de (qqch.); [o.'s steps] revenir sur (ses pas).

retract [ɹɪ'tɹækt] *v. tr.* **1.** rentrer, tirer en arrière. **2.** rétracter, retirer, désavouer (une opinion).

retreat [ɹɪ'tɹijt] *v. intr.* battre en retraite; se retirer. || *n.* retraite *f;* refuge *m.;* [lair] repaire *m.*

retrench [ɹɪ'tɹɛntʃ] *v. tr.* [expenses, &c.] réduire. || **retrenchment** [-mənt] *n.* suppression *f,* retranchement *m,* diminution *f.*

retribution [ˌɹɛtɹɪ'bjuwʃən] *n.* [×] châtiment *m;* [reward] récompense *f.*

retrieve [ɹɪ'tɹijv] *v. tr.* **1.** retrouver, recouvrer; [dog] rapporter; [Com.] récupérer. **2.** relever, rétablir: *to ~ one's affairs,* rétablir ses affaires; *to ~ a loss,* réparer une perte.

retroactive [ˌɹɛtɹow|'æktɪv] *adj.* rétroactif.

retrogression [-'gɹɛʃən] *n.* recul *m,* retour *m* en arrière; rétrogradation *f.*

retrospect ['ɹɛtɹəˌspɛkt] *n.* (vue) rétrospective *f.*

return [ɹɪ'tɚn] *v. intr.* [come back] revenir; [go back to] retourner; rentrer (chez soi); [to owner] retourner, revenir (*to,* à). || *v. tr.* **1.** [bring back] rapporter, rendre (*to,* à); [send back] retourner (*to,* à). **2.** rendre (une visite, répondre (à un sentiment). **3.** [Tech.] élire (un député); rendre (une sentence): *to ~ o.'s income to,* faire sa déclaration (d'impôts) à. || *n.* **1.** retour *m*: *on/his, her/ ~,* à, dès/son retour; *~ ticket,* (billet *m* d')aller et retour. **2.** retour *m,* renvoi *m,* restitution *f;* [Com.] rendu *m.* **3.** [Com.] bénéfice *m,* profit *m;* *pl.* recettes *fpl;* [Tech.] rendement *m;* [taxes] déclaration *f* (d'impôts). **4.** [élections] résultat *m;* [census] recensement *m;* statistiques *fpl.*

reunion [ɹɪ'juwnjən] *n.* réunion *f.* || **reunite** [ɹɪˌjuw'najt] *v. tr.* réunir. || *v. intr.* se réunir, se rassembler.

reveal [ɹɪ'vijl] *v. tr.* [identity] révéler, dévoiler.

revel ['ɹɛvl̩] *n.* réjouissances *fpl,* plaisirs *mpl,* fêtes *fpl;* ébats *mpl*: *the revels of the King,* les menus-plaisirs du roi. || *v. intr.* [-ll-] **1.** se réjouir bruyamment. **2.** banqueter, festoyer: *to ~ in doing sth.,* se délecter à faire qqch.

revelation [ˌɹɛvl̩'ejʃən] *n.* révélation *f;* [Rel.] la Révélation *f* (par les Prophètes); [Rel.] Apocalypse *f.*

reveller ['ɹɛvl̩|ɚ] *n.* [Pers.] noceur *m.* || **revelry** [-ɹɪ] *n.* réjouissance(s) *f(pl);* [Pej.] orgie *f.*

revenge [ɹɪ'vɛndʒ] *n.* vengeance *f;* [in fun] revanche *f*: *to take ~ on s.o. for sth.,* se venger de qqch. sur qqun. || *v. tr.* se venger (*on s.o., for sth.,* de qqun, pour qqch., de qqch. sur qqun).

revenue ['ɹɛvənˌjuw] *n.* **1.** revenu *m.* **2.** [Govt.] trésor *m,* fisc *m,* revenu national: *~ officer,* percepteur *m;* employé *m* des douanes; *public ~,* revenus de l'État: *Department of National Revenue,* ministère *m* du Revenu national.

reverberate [ɹɪ'vɚbɚˌejt] *v. tr.* [heat, light] réfléchir; [sound] renvoyer. || *v. intr.* [heat, light] réverbérer; [sound] résonner.

revere [ɹɪ'vijɚ] *v. tr.* révérer (qqun). || **reverence** ['ɹɛvɚən|s] *n.* **1.** vénération *f*: *to pay ~,* rendre hommage; *with ~,* sauf votre respect. **2.** †révérence *f.* **3.** [Rel.] *His Reverence,* Révérend Père. || **reverend** [-d] *adj.* [Rel.] révérend; vénérable: *the (Very/Right) Reverend . . . ,* le (Très) Révérend (Père). || **reverent** [-t] *adj.* [Pers.] révérencieux.

reverie ['ɹɛvɚɪ] *n.* rêverie *f,* rêves *mpl.*

reversal [ɹɪ'vɚs|əl] *n.* [ideas, &c.] renversement *m,* revirement *m;* [Jur.] annulation *f.* || **reverse** [ɹɪ'vɚs] *adj.* contraire, opposé (*to,* à). || *n.* contraire *m,* opposé *m;* [medal] revers *m;* [printed page] verso *m;* [Auto.] marche *f* arrière. || *v. tr.* renverser, retourner; [Auto.] faire marche arrière; [engine] faire machine arrière; [Jur.] *to ~ a decision,* casser, annuler/un jugement. || *v. intr.* faire / marche, machine/ arrière. || **reversible** [-ɪbl̩] *adj.* [Jur., &c.] annulable, révocable; [either side] réversible. || **reversion** [ɹɪ'vɚ|ʒən] *n.* **1.** [Biol.] réversion *f;* retour *m* (à une ancienne/pratique, politique, croyance).

|| **revert** [-t] *v. tr.* retourner, tourner en sens contraire, renverser, revenir (à un état ancien).
revery ['ɹɛvɚɪ] *n.* rêverie *f.*
review [ɹɪ'vjuw] *n.* [Mil., journal] revue *f*; critique *f*, compte rendu *m* (d'un livre); [Jur.] revision *f*; [Sch.] révision *f*: *to pass in* ~, passer en revue. || *v. tr.* [Jur.] réviser; [Mil.] passer en revue; [book] faire la critique de. || **reviewer** [ɹɪ'vjuwɚ] *n.* [Pers.] critique *m.*
revile [ɹɪ'vajl] *v. tr.* injurier, outrager, insulter.
revise [ɹɪ'vajz] *v. tr.* réviser, revoir; vérifier. || **revision** [ɹɪ'vɪʒn̩] *n.* révision *f*, vérification *f.*
revival [ɹɪ'vajvəl] *n.* renaissance *f*; reprise *f.*
revive [ɹɪ'vajv] *v. tr.* ressusciter; ranimer; [pep up] remonter, ravigoter; faire revivre (des coutumes); réveiller (un souvenir). || *v. intr.* revivre; ressusciter; se ranimer; se raviver.
revocation [ˌɹɛvə'kejʃən] *n.* révocation *f*, annulation *f* (d'un/décret, testament/). || **revoke** [ɹɪ'vowk] *v. tr.* **1.** révoquer, annuler, abroger (une loi). **2.** [cards] ne pas fournir (la couleur).
revolt [ɹɪ'vowlt] *n.* révolte *f*; rébellion *f*; soulèvement *m.* || *v. intr.* se révolter; se soulever; s'indigner. || **revolution** [ˌɹɛvə'luwʃən] *n.* révolution *f*; [Mec.] rotation *f*, [turn] tour *m.* || **revolutionary** [-ˌɛɚɪ] *n.* révolutionnaire. || *adj.* révolutionnaire: [US] *Revolutionary War*, la guerre d'Indépendance. || **revolutionist** [-ɪst] *n.* révolutionnaire *m.*
revolve [ɹɪ'vɑlv] *v. intr.* **1.** tourner (en rond). **2.** [planets] accomplir sa révolution. **3.** tourner (sur soi-même): [Fig.] retourner (une question dans son esprit).
revolver [-ɚ] *n.* revolver *m.*
revulsion [ɹɪ'vʌlʃən] *n.* [Med.] révulsion *f*; [Fig.] volte-face *f.*
reward [ɹɪ'wɔɚd] *n.* **1.** récompense *f*; gratification *f*; dédommagement *m.* **2.** || *v. tr.* récompenser.
rewarding [ɹɪ'wɔɚdɪŋ] *adj.* rémunérat|eur *m*, -rice *f*; [experience] → qui en vaut la peine, enrichissant.
rewrite [ɹɪ'ɹajt], **rewrote** [ɹɪ'ɹowt], **rewritten** [ɹɪ'ɹɪtn̩] *v. tr.* écrire de nouveau, récrire: remanier (un article).
Rheims [ɹɛmz] *n.* (la ville de) Reims.
rhetoric ['ɹɛtɚɪk] [US] *n.* rhétorique *f*; éloquence *f*; [Schol.] composition *f.*
rheumatism ['ɹuwmətɪzm] *n.* [Med.] rhumatisme *m.*
Rhine [ɹajn] *n.* (le) Rhin *m*: ~ *wine*, vin *m* du Rhin. || **Rhineland** [-ˌlænd] *n.* Rhénanie *f.*
rhinoceros [ˌɹaj'nɑsɚəs] *n.* rhinocéros *m.*
Rhodesia [ˌɹow'dijʒə] *n.* la Rhodésie *f.*
Rhone [ɹown] *n.* (le) Rhône *m.*
rhubarb ['ɹuwbɑɚb] *n.* rhubarbe *f.*
rhyme [ɹajm] *n.* [Poet.] rime *f*, vers *m.* || *v. tr. & intr.* rimer
rhythm ['ɹɪðəm] *n.* rythme *m.* || **rhythmic(al)** ['ɹɪðmɪkl̩] *adj.* rythmique.
rib [ɹɪb] *n.* [Anat.] côte *f*; baleine *f* (de parapluie); [Tech.] nervure *f*; [boat] membrure *f.*
ribald ['ɹɪbəld] *adj.* [Pej.] ordurier, grossier. || *n.* grossier personnage *m.*
ribbon ['ɹɪbən] *n.* ruban *m*; bande *f.* || *v. tr.* enrubanner (une boîte, &c.).
rice [ɹajs] *n.* riz *m*: ~ *field*, rizière *f.*
rich [ɹɪtʃ] *adj.* [Pers.] riche, opulent; [soil] fertile, fécond; [food] gras; [meal] succulent; [wine] généreux; [colour, &c.] vif: [Pers.] *to become* ~, s'enrichir; ~ *in*, riche, abondant/en. || **riches** [-əz] *n.* richesse *f*; fortune *f.* || **richness** [-nəs] *n.* richesse *f*; fécondité *f*; opulence *f*; abondance *f*; fertilité *f*; chaleur *f* (d'un coloris).
rick [ɹɪk] *n.* meule *f* de foin.
rickets [-əts] *n.pl.* [Med.] rachitisme *m.* || **rickety** [-ətɪ] *adj.* rachitique; [chair, &c.] boiteux, branlant: *a* ~ *old house*, une vieille maison délabrée.
rickshaw [-ˌʃɔ] *n.* pousse-pousse *m.*
rid [ɹɪd], **rid** or **ridded** *v. tr.* défaire, débarrasser (*of*, de): *to get* ~ *of*, se débarrasser de, [employee] renvoyer. || **riddance** [-əns] *n.* débarras *m.*
ridded cf. RID.
ridden cf. RIDE.
riddle[1] ['ɹɪdl̩] *n.* énigme *f*; [game] devinette *f.*
riddle[2] *n.* crible *m.* || *v. tr.* cribler (de, *with*), passer qqch. au/crible, tamis/.
ride [ɹajd], **rode** [ɹowd], **ridden** ['ɹɪdn̩] *v. tr.* monter (à cheval, à bicyclette); [Fig.] dominer, opprimer: *ridden by fear*, hanté par la peur; *priest-ridden*, dans la main du clergé. || *v. intr.* [Sport] faire du cheval, monter (à cheval); [stroll] faire une promenade à cheval: *He rode back home*, → Il rentra chez lui/à cheval, à bicyclette/; [Naut.] *to* ~ *at anchor*, être/mouillé, à l'ancre/; [Fam.] *Let it* ~, Laissez courir. [☞ Dans le cas de postposition, on pourra souvent ne pas traduire *ride*]: *to* ~ *along*, → continuer son chemin; *to* ~ *away*, → partir, disparaître à l'horizon; *to* ~ *by*, passer (par là); *to* ~/*in, out*/, → entrer, sortir (à

cheval); *to ~ on*, continuer sa route, &c. || *n.* promenade *f* (à cheval, à bicyclette, en auto); [distance] trajet *m*, voyage *m*; [Fam.] *to take s.o. for a ~*, [murder] descendre qqun; [dupe] faire marcher qqun; *Thanks for the ~*, Merci de m'avoir emmené(e) avec vous.

rider ['ɹajdɚ] *n.* cavalier *m*; [Jur.] codicille *m*, [document] annexe *f*.

ridge [ɹɪʤ] *n.* [mountain] crête *f*, [top] faîte *m* (d'un toit).

ridicule ['ɹɪdɪˌkjuwl] *n.* raillerie *f*, moquerie *f*. || *v. tr.* ridiculiser, se moquer de/qqun. || **ridiculous** [ɹɪ'dɪkjələs] *adj.* risible, un peu ridicule.

riding ['ɹajdɪŋ] cf. RIDE. || *n.* promenade *f* à cheval; [horse] équitation *f*; [Pol.] arrondissement *m*, circonscription *f* (électorale).

rife [ɹajf] *adj.* répandu, → qui/sévit, court/.

riff-raff ['ɹɪfˌɹæf] *n.* canaille *f*.

rifle[1] [ɹajfḷ] *n.* fusil *m*, carabine *f*. || *v. tr.* fusiller.

rifle[2] *v. tr.* piller, dévaliser, faire une razzia dans (un endroit).

rift [ɹɪft] *n.* fente *f*, crevasse *f*.

rig [ɹɪg] *n.* [Naut.] gréement *m*; [Fig.] accoutrement *m*; [Tech.] montage *m*, équipement *m*. || *v. tr.* [-gg-] équiper; accoutrer; [prices] faire/monter, descendre/(les prix): *to ~ out s.o. in old clothes*, affubler (qqun) de vieux habits; *to ~ (sth.) up*, [temporarily] installer. || **rigging** [-ɪŋ] *n.* cf. RIG *n.*

right [ɹajt] *adj.* [hand, angle] droit; [statement] exact; [answer, &c.] juste; [name, &c.] vrai; direct; [time, &c.] bon: *It is all ~ !*, C'est (très) bien!, [Fam.] Ça va! || **right** *n.* also **rights** [-s] droit *m*; équité *f*: *by ~*, de droit; *by rights*, à la rigueur, en toute justice; *in one's own ~*, de (plein) droit; *~ of way*, droit *m* de passage, priorité *f*; *to have the ~ to*, avoir le droit de, avoir des droits à; *to be within one's rights*, être dans son droit; *to set to rights*, arranger, redresser une affaire. || **right** *n.* **1.** raison *f*, justice *f*, droiture *f*; (→ adjectives): *to be in the ~* (≠ *in the wrong*), avoir raison (≠ avoir tort); (*How*) *~ you are* → (comme) c'est juste; (c'est) très juste; †*to be ~ -hearted*, avoir le cœur droit; *to be ~ -minded*, être, avoir un esprit droit. cf. RIGHTEOUS. **2.** bien *m*, intérêt *m*: *right and wrong*, le bien et le mal; *to do ~*, faire ce qui est bien. cf. RIGHTFUL, RIGHTLY. **3.** la droite, le côté droit: *turn to the ~*, tournez, prenez à droite; *on the ~*, à droite [sans mouvement] ≠LEFT. || **right** *v. tr.* faire droit à, rendre justice à. || *v. intr.* se redresser, redresser. || *adv.* droit; directement; comme il faut; tout à fait. || **righteous** ['ɹajtʃəs] *adj.* [Pers., action] droit, juste. || **righteousness** [-nəs] *n.* (esprit de) droiture; justice *f*. || **rightful** ['ɹajt|fḷ] *adj.* légitime, véritable: (*the*) *~ owner*, (le) possesseur légitime. || **rightfully** [-fḷɪ] *adv.* légitimement. || **right-hand** ['ɹajt'hænd] *adj.* de droite, à droite. || **right-handed** [-əd] *adj.* droitier. || **rightly** [-lɪ] *adv.* à juste titre, à bon droit (i.e. doing the right thing).

rigid ['ɹɪʤɪd] *adj.* **1.** raide, rigide. **2.** [Fig.] sévère, austère, strict: *a ~ rule*, une règle rigoureuse. || **rigidity** [ɹɪ'ʤɪdɪtɪ] *n.* **1.** raideur *f*, [corpse, &c.] rigidité *f*. **2.** [Fig.] rigidité *f*, sévérité *f*.

rigmarole ['ɹɪgmɚˌowl] *n.* [Pej.] galimatias *m*; [long speech] propos *mpl* incohérents.

rigour ['ɹɪgɚ] *n.* **1.** sévérité *f*, austérité *f*; rigueur *f* (de l'hiver). **2.** raideur *f*. || **rigorous** [-əs] *adj.* rigoureux; [science] exact.

rile [ɹajl] *v. tr.* agacer, exaspérer.

rim [ɹɪm] *n.* **1.** [hat] bord *m*, rebord *m*. **2.** [bicycle] jante *f*.

rime [ɹajm] *n.* [hour] gelée *f* blanche.

rind [ɹajnd] *n.* [potato] pelure *f*, [banana] peau *f*, [orange] écorce *f*.

ring [ɹɪŋ], **rang** [ɹæŋ], **rung** [ɹʌŋ] *v. tr.* (faire) sonner (une cloche, &c.); [Fig.] *It rings a bell somewhere*, Cela me dit quelque chose, J'ai déjà vu ça quelque part. || *v. intr.* sonner; résonner; tinter.

ring [ɹɪŋ] *n.* coup *m* de sonnette, son *m* de/timbre, cloche/, [voice, &c.] timbre *m*, tintement *m*; coup *m* de téléphone.

ringleader ['ɹɪŋˌliidɚ] *n.* meneur *m*.

ringlet [-lət] *n.* **1.** petit anneau *m*. **2.** [hair] boucle *f*.

rink [ɹɪŋk] *n. skating ~*, patinoire *f*.

rinse [ɹɪns] *n.* rinçage *m* (de cheveux). || *v. tr.* /rincer, nettoyer/à l'eau claire.

riot ['ɹajət] *n.* émeute *f*; sédition *f*. || *v. intr.* faire une émeute.

rip [ɹɪp] *n.* déchirure *f*. || *v. tr.* [-pp-] déchirer, fendre, [tear open] éventrer; *to ~ away*, *off*, arracher, déchirer (brusquement, d'un coup sec); *to ~ up*, découdre, éventrer. || *v. intr.* (away) se déchirer, se fendre; [Fam.] *Let her ~ !* [Auto.] Fonce!

ripe [ɹajp] *adj.* mûr. || **ripen** [-ən] *v. tr.* & *intr.* mûrir. || *v. tr.* [Fig.] amener à la perfection. || **ripeness** [-nəs] *n.* [fruit] maturité *f*.

ripple ['ɹɪpḷ] *n.* [water] ride *f*. || *v. intr.* [water] se rider.

rise [ɹajz] *n.* ascension *f*; montée *f*; [tide]

flux *m*; élévation *f* (de terrain); [prices] hausse *f*, [salary] augmentation *f*; [Fig.] croissance *f*; [river] *to take its ~ (in)*, prendre sa source (dans). || **rise** [ɹajz], **rose** [ɹowz], **risen** [ɹɪzən] *v. intr.* se lever; s'élever; monter; [river] prendre sa source; [Fig.] grandir; progresser: *This mountain rises to 6,000 feet*, Cette montagne s'élève à © 6,000 pieds, [Fr.] 2,000 mètres. || **riser** ['ɹajzɚ] *n.* **1.** celui, celle/qui se lève: *I am not an early ~*, Je ne suis pas matinal(e). **2.** marche *f* (d'escalier). || **rising** [-ɪŋ] *adj.* [sun, &c.] levant, qui se lève; ascendant, qui monte, à la hausse. || *n.* **1.** hausse *f*, lever *m* (de rideau, &c.); [upheaval] soulèvement *m*. **2.** [Rel.] résurrection *f* (des morts, *from the dead*).

risk [ɹɪsk] *n.* risque *m*, péril *m*: *to run a ~*, courir un risque; *at your own ~*, à vos risques et périls; [Ins.] risques *mpl.* || *v. tr.* risquer, hasarder: *to ~ it*, courir le risque, tenter le coup. || **risky** *adj.* risqué, aléatoire; dangereux.

rite [ɹajt] *n.* rite *m*; cérémonie *f*; [Rel.] *to administer the last rites*, administrer les derniers sacrements. || **ritual** ['ɹɪtʃuwḷ] *adj.* rituel. || *n.* [Rel.] rituel *m*.

rival ['ɹajvəl] *adj. & n.* rival, concurrent *m*. || *v. intr.* **[-ll-]** rivaliser (with, *avec*). || **rivalry** [-ɹɪ] *n.* rivalité *f*.

river ['ɹɪvɚ] *n.* rivière *f*; fleuve *m* [☞ In Fr., a *rivière* flows into a *fleuve*, which flows into the sea. This distinction does not always hold in Canada]: *(the) Saskatchewan River*, la (rivière) Saskatchewan; *(the) St. Lawrence River*, le (fleuve) Saint-Laurent; *up the ~*, en amont; *down the ~*, en aval; [Fam.] *to sell s.o. down the ~*, trahir (qqun).

Riviera, (the) [ɹɪvɪ'ɛɚə] (la) Riviéra, (la) Côte d'Azur.

rivulet ['ɹɪvjələt] *n.* ruisselet *m*.

road [ɹowd] *n.* chemin *m*, voie *f*, itinéraire *m*, route *f*: *Côte des Neiges Road*, © Chemin de la Côte des Neiges (Montréal), [Fr.] Route de la Porte d'Ivry (Paris); *rural ~*, route *f* de campagne, [Fr.] chemin/vicinal, communal/; [car] *~ holding*, tenue *f* de route; *winding ~*, route *f* en lacets, virages *mpl* (sur × Km.). || **roadside** [-ˌsajd] *n.* bas-côté *m*, bord *m* de la route. || **roadway** [-wej] *n.* chaussée *f*, voie *f* carrossable.

roam [ɹowm] *v. intr.* rôder, errer.

roar [ɹɔɚ] *n.* [crowd] hurlement *m*, clameur *f*; [laughter] éclat *m* (de rire); [bull] mugissement *m*; [lion] rugissement *m*; [engine, fire] grondement *m*. || *v. tr.* hurler, vociférer; [bull] mugir; [lion] rugir; [engine, fire] gronder: *to ~ with laughter*, rire aux éclats. || *v. tr.*: *to ~ an order*, hurler un commandement.

roast [ɹowst] *adj.* rôti; *~ beef*, rosbif *m*. || *n.* rôti *m*. || *v. tr.* (faire) rôtir; [coffee] torréfier; [Fig.] se griller (au soleil). || **roaster** [-ɚ] *n.* rôtissoire *f*; [coffee] brûloir *m*; [fowl] volaille *f* à rôtir.

rob [ɹɑb] *v. tr.* **[-bb-]** voler (qqch. à qqun, *s.o. of sth.*); dérober (un objet); cambrioler (une banque). || **robber** [-ɚ] *n.* voleur *m*. || **robbery** [-ɚɪ] *n.* vol *m*, cambriolage *m*: *armed ~*, vol *m* à main armée.

robe [ɹowb] *n.* robe *f*; [Sch.] toge *f*.

robin ['ɹɑbɪn] *n.* [bird] rouge-gorge *m*, © grive *f*.

robust ['ɹowbʌst] *adj.* robuste; [health] vigoureux.

rock[1] [ɹɑk] *n.* roc *m*; [Fam.] pierre *f*, caillou *m*: *the ~ of Gibraltar*, le rocher de G.; [Fam.] *to be on the rocks*, être /fauché, à sec/; *whisky on the rocks*, whisky sur glace.

rock[2] *n.* balancement *m*. || *v. tr.* [shake] faire osciller, ébranler; [child] bercer. || *v. intr.* se bercer, se balancer; [shake] osciller, trembler (sur ses bases): [crowd] *to ~ with laughter*, se tordre de rire.

rocker ['ɹɑkɚ] *n.* fauteuil *m* à bascule, © chaise *f* berçante: *to go off one's ~*, devenir fou, © sortir de son caractère.

rocket ['ɹɑkət] *n.* fusée *f*.

Rockies (the) ['ɹɑkɪz] © *n.pl.* les (montagnes) Rocheuses *fpl.*

rocking ['ɹɑkɪ|ŋ] *n.* bercement *m*; balancement *m*: *~ chair*, cf. ROCKER.

rocky[1] *adj.* rocailleux; rocheux: *the Rocky Mountains*, les Montagnes Rocheuses.

rocky[2] *adj.* branlant; chancelant.

rod [ɹɑd] *n.* [metal] baguette *f*, tige *f*; [curtain] tringle *f*; [connecting] bielle *f*; [fishing] canne *f* (à pêche); [Meas.] perche *f*; [Sport.] *~ and gun*, la chasse et la pêche; [Fig.] *~ of iron*, une main de fer; *Spare the ~ and spoil the child*, Qui aime bien châtie bien.

rode cf. RIDE.

Rogations [ˌɹow'gejʃəns] *n.pl.* [R.C.] (les) Rogations *fpl.*

rogue [ɹowg] *n.* **1.** coquin *m*, -e *f*; fripon *m*, -ne *f*. **2.** [animals] isolé, solitaire *m*. || **roguish** [-ɪʃ] *adj.* fripon; espiègle.

rôle [ɹowl] *n.* [Theat.] rôle *m*; [Fig.] rôle (politique).

roll [ɹowl] *n.* **1.** [paper] rouleau *m*; [thunder, music] roulement *m*; [ship] roulis *m*; [bread] petit pain *m*; [Tech.] rouleau *m*, cylindre *m*. **2.** [-call] appel *m*. || *v. intr.*

rouler; [thunder] gronder; [walk] se balancer, rouler des hanches. || *v. tr.* rouler (la pâte, une cigarette, des yeux): *to ~ into a ball*, rouler en boule. || **roll about** *v. tr. & intr.* (se) rouler çà et là. || **roll along** *v. tr. & intr.* rouler (le long de). || **roll away** *v. tr. & intr.* (s')éloigner. || **roll down** *v. tr.* rouler (qqch.) de haut en bas. || *v. intr.* descendre (en boule); [tears] couler. || **roll in** *v. tr.* faire entrer (en roulant). || *v. intr.* [Fig.] entrer lourdement; [Fam.] *Money is rolling in*, L'argent arrive à flots. || **roll on** *v. intr.* continuer de/rouler, s'écouler/. || **roll out** *v. intr.* sortir en titubant. || *v. tr.* faire sortir (en roulant). || **roll over** *v. intr. & tr.* (se) retourner. || **roll up** *v. tr.* enrouler; [sleeves] retrousser. || *v. intr.* se rouler en boule.

roller ['ɹowlɚ] *n.* rouleau *m*: *steam ~*, rouleau compresseur; *~ skate*, patin *m* à roulettes; *~ bearing*, coussinet *m* à rouleaux; *~ coaster*, montagnes *fpl* russes.

rolling ['ɹowlɪŋ] *adj.* roulant; qui ondule: *~ land*, ondulations *fpl* de terrain; *~ country*, pays *m* montueux. || **rolling pin** [-ˌpɪn] *n.* rouleau *m* (à pâtisserie), © rouleau *m* à pâte.

Roman ['ɹowmən] *adj. & n.* romain, -e: [Prov.] *When in Rome, do as the Romans do*, Il faut hurler avec les loups.

romance [ɹow'mæns] *adj.* roman: *~ languages*, les langues romanes. || *n.* affaire *f* de cœur, aventure *f*.

romanesque [ˌɹowmən'ɛsk] *adj.* romanesque; [Arch.] (style) roman.

romantic [ɹow'mæntɪ|k] *adj.* romantique; [story] romanesque; rêveur. || **romanticism** [-sɪzm] *n.* [Litt.] romantisme *m.* || **romanticist** [-sɪst] *n.* [Litt.] romantique *m.*

Rome [ɹowm] *n.* Rome *f*; la Ville Éternelle.

romp [ɹɑmp] *n.* **1.** jeu *m*, gambades *fpl.* **2.** [girl] garçon *m* manqué; [boy] casse-cou *m.* || *v. intr.* s'ébattre, prendre ses ébats; © se tirailler; jouer rudement. || **rompers** [-ɚz] *n.* barboteuse *f.*

roof [ɹuwf] *n.* toit *m*; [large] toiture *f*; [mouth] palais *m.*

rook [ɹʊk] *n.* corneille *f*, freux *m.* || **rookie** [-ɪ] *n.* [Fam., Mil.] bleu *m.*

room [ɹuwm] *n.* **1.** [apartment] pièce *f*, salle *f*: *dining ~*, salle à manger; *bedroom*, chambre *f* (à coucher); *work-~* cabinet *m* (de travail); *dark ~*, chambre noire; [address] *Room 303*, porte, bureau/ 303. **2.** [space] place *f*, espace *m*: *There's plenty of ~*, Il y a beaucoup de place; [Fig.] *There is no ~ for* [+ ing], Il n'y a pas lieu de [+ infin.]; *to make ~ for*, faire place à. || **roomer** [-ɚ] *n.* locataire *m/f*, © chambreu|r *m*, -se *f*.

roomette [ɹuwm|'ɛt] *n.* [Rail.] compartiment *m* de wagon-lit. || **rooming house** [-ɪŋ haws] *n.* maison *f*/garnie, meublée. || **roommate** [-mejt] *n.* camarade *m* de chambre. || **roomy** [-ɪ] *adj.* spacieux, vaste.

roost [ɹuwst] *n.* **1.** perchoir *m*; [Fig., Pop.] *to go to ~*, aller se coucher. **2.** [US] logis *m*, demeure *f*; [Fam.] *rule the ~* faire la loi. || *v. intr.* **1.** [birds] se percher. **2.** [Fam.] percher, se nicher. || **rooster** [-ɚ] *n.* coq *m.*

root [ɹuwt] *n.* racine *f*; source *f*: *to take ~*, prendre racine; [Fig.] *to get at the ~ of the matter*, approfondir la chose. || *v. intr.* s'enraciner; prendre racine. || *v. tr. to ~ out*, déraciner (une plante, &c.); [Fig.] extirper (une mauvaise habitude). || **rooted** [-əd] *adj.* enraciné; [Fig.] [habit] invétéré.

rope [ɹowp] *n.* corde *f*; câble *m*: [Fig.] *to know the ropes*, connaître son affaire; *to be at the end of o.'s ~*, être au bout de son rouleau. *Give him enough ~*, Laissez-le faire. || *v. tr.* (en)corder (qqch.); lier (qqch.); prendre (au lasso): *to ~ s.o. in*, entraîner (qqun) dans un projet, associer (qqun) à une entreprise.

rosary ['ɹowsəɪ] *n.* [R.C.] rosaire *m.*

rose[1] [ɹowz] *n.* rose *f*: *~ bush*, rosier *m.*

rose[2] cf. RISE.

rosin ['ɹɑzɪn] *n.* colophane *f.* || *v. tr.* enduire, frotter de colophane.

roster ['ɹɑstɚ] *n.* [Naut.] rôle *m* (d'un équipage); [Mil.] tableau *m* de service, liste *f*. *to call the ~*, faire l'appel.

rostrum ['ɹɑstɹəm] *n.* tribune *f*, estrade *f.*

rosy ['ɹowzɪ] *adj.* rose, rosé.

rot [ɹɑt] *n.* pourriture *f*, putréfaction *f*; carie *f*; [Fam.] bêtises *fpl*; de la blague. || *v. intr.* [-tt-] pourrir; [teeth] se carier; [fruit, eggs] se gâter. || *v. tr.* (faire) pourrir; carier (les dents); [Fig.] corrompre (le cœur).

rotary ['ɹowtəɪ] *adj.* [movement] rotatif, rotatoire. || *n.* sens *m* giratoire. || **rotate** [ɹow'tej|t] *v. intr.* tourner; pivoter. || **rotation** [-ʃən] *n.* **1.** rotation *f.* **2.** roulement *m*: *in ~*, à tour de rôle.

rote [ɹowt] *n.* **1.** [Mus.] vielle *f.* **2.** routine *f*: *by ~*, par cœur.

rotten ['ɹɑtn̩] *adj.* pourri; [teeth] carié; [fruit, eggs] gâté; [Pers.] véreux, corrompu.

rouge [ɹuwʤ] *n.* rouge *m*, fard *m.* || *v. tr.* farder (ses joues), mettre du rouge à.

rough [ɹʌf] *adj.* [Pers., &c.] rude; [manners] grossier; [material, &c.] brut; [weather] orageux; [road] raboteux, accidenté; [sea] agité, gros, houleux; [glass] dépoli; [game] brutal; [surface] rugueux, raboteux; [guess] approximatif: *the ~ work*, les brouillons *mpl*, l'ébauche *f*; [Fig.] *He is a ~ diamond*, C'est un homme excellent sous des dehors un peu frustes. || **roughen** [ˈɹʌf|ən] *v. tr.* rendre/rude, rugueux/. || *v. intr.* devenir/rude, rugueux/; rudoyer (qqun). || **roughly** [-lɪ] *adv.* **1.** brusquement, brutalement; [guess] approximativement; [Fam.] à vue de nez.

roughneck [ˈɹʌfˌnɛk] *n.* [Fam.] dur *m.*

roughness [-nəs] *n.* aspérité *f*; [touch] rugosité *f*, aspérité *f*; [Fig.] brusquerie *f*; [Naut.] mauvais état (de la mer).

round[1] [ɹawnd] *n.* rond *m*, cercle *m*; [series] série *f*, cycle *m*; [circuit] tour *m*, tournée *f* (d'inspection); [drinks] tournée *f*; [ammunition] coup *m*, [or more precisely] cartouche *f* [for rifle], obus *m* [for a gun, &c.]; [policeman] ronde *f*; [cheers, &c.] salve *f*; [boxing] round *m*; [Culin.] gîte *f* à la noix, © ronde *f.*

round[2] *adj.* rond, circulaire: *in ~ numbers*, en chiffres ronds; [shoulders] arrondi, voûté; [pace] vif: *~ -eyed*, → d'un œil rond, abasourdi; *~ -table conference*, conférence *f* paritaire, table *f* ronde. *~ trip*, voyage *m*/aller et retour, circulaire/. || *adv. & prep.* [☞ *around* a plutôt le sens de "çà et là" et *round* "autour, d'une façon circulaire"; mais ces deux mots sont souvent interchangeables] tout autour; *~ about*, aux alentours; *five feet ~*, cinq pieds de/tour, circonférence/; *to pass sth. ~*, faire circuler qqch.; *to look ~*, faire un tour, jeter un coup d'œil. || *prep.* autour de: *A wall was built ~ the garden*, Un mur était bâti (tout) autour du jardin, → le jardin était entouré d'un mur; *Go ~ the corner*, Tournez le coin (à droite, à gauche). || *v. intr.* s'arrondir. || *v. tr.* [a corner] prendre (un tournant); [Naut.] doubler (un cap). || **round off, out** [-ˈɔf/awt] *v. tr.* achever (un ouvrage). || **round up** [-ˈʌp] *v. tr.* rassembler (un troupeau); [Fam.] faire une rafle.

roundabout [-əˌbawt] *adj.* [way] détourné; [Fig., answer] indirect, vague. || *n.* carrousel *m*; manège *m*; détour *m.*

roundhead [-hɛd] *n.* [Fig.] tête dure, homme entêté, fanatique *m.*

roundly [ˈɹawndlɪ] *adv.* [Fig.] rondement, carrément.

roundup [-ˌʌp] *n.* [cattle] rassemblement *m*, battue *f.*

rouse [ɹawz] *v. tr.* réveiller, éveiller (qqun de son sommeil); [indignation] soulever; [indifference] secouer; [admiration] susciter; [feeling] exciter, stimuler: *to ~ to action*, inciter à agir. || **rousing** [-ɪŋ] *adj.* → qui/éveille, stimule, excite/; [feeling] chaleureux, émouvant: *~ cheers*, applaudissements *mpl* frénétiques.

rout [ɹawt] *v. tr.* mettre en déroute. || *n.* [Mil.] déroute *f*; [crowd] débandade *f.*

route [ɹuwt] *n.* itinéraire *m*; [bus] ligne *f*, parcours *m.*

routine [ɹuwˈtijn] *n.* [×] les affaires *fpl* courantes; cours *m* habituel des événements. || *adj.* routinier; courant; habituel.

routing [ˈɹuwtɪŋ] *n.* acheminement *m*, tracé *m* de la voie, routage *m.*

rove [ɹowv] *v. intr.* errer, rôder, vagabonder. || **rover** [-ɚ] *n.* vagabond *m*; © [scouting] routier *m.*

row[1] [ɹow] *n.* rang *m*; [several objects in row] rangée *f*: *in a ~*, en rang; *in rows*, par rangs; [cars] file *f.*

row[2] *n.* promenade *f* en barque: *~ boat*, bateau *m* à rames, © chaloupe *f.* || *v. tr. to ~ . . . across*, faire passer/l'eau, le fleuve/à . . . || *v. intr.* ramer; [Mar.] nager.

row[3] [ɹaw] *n.* dispute *f*, altercation *f*; [Fam.] boucan *m*, © train *m*: *to kick up a ~*, faire du/boucan, train/.

rowdy [ˈɹawdɪ] *adj.* bruyant, tapageur; grossier.

rower [ˈɹowɚ] *n.* [Sport.] rameur *m.*

royal [ˈɹojəl] *adj.* royal: (*the*) *Royal Canadian Mounted Police*, (la) Gendarmerie royale du Canada. || **royalist** [-ɪst] *n.* royaliste *m.* || **royalty** [-tɪ] *n.* **1.** royauté *f.* **2.** la famille royale. *pl.* [Jur.] droit *m*/d'auteur, d'inventeur/.

r.p.m. [ˌɑɚˌpijˈɛm] [= × revolutions per minute] × tours à la minute.

R.S.V.P. [ˌɑɚˌɛsˌvijˈpij] [= Répondez, s'il vous plaît] R.S.V.P.

rub [ɹʌb] *v. tr.* [-bb-] frotter (*on*, sur; *against*, contre); [Med.] frictionner: [Fam.] *to ~ s.o. the wrong way*, prendre qqun à rebrousse-poil. || *v. intr.* se frotter; [Med.] se frictionner. || **rub down** *v. tr.* frotter, frictionner; [horse] bouchonner, panser. || **rub in** *v. tr.* faire pénétrer en frottant; [Fig.] *to ~ it in*, retourner le fer dans la plaie: *You don't have to ~ it in*, Ça va; Inutile d'insister. || **rub out** *v. tr.* effacer; [Sl.] descendre, liquider (qqun).

rub-a-dub [ˈɹʌbəˌdʌb] *n.* [drum] rataplan *m.*

rubber [ˈɹʌbɚ] *n.* **1.** caoutchouc *m.* **2.**

gomme *f* à effacer; © efface *f*. **3.** frotteur *m*; frottoir *m*. **4.** [Bridge] robre *m*: ~ *band*, élastique *m*; ~ *boots*, bottes *fpl* de caoutchouc; ~ *gloves*, gants *mpl* en caoutchouc; ~ *tree*, arbre *m* à gomme. || **rubberize** [-ajz] *v. tr.* caoutchouter. || **rubbers** [-z] *n.pl.* caoutchoucs *mpl*; © claques *fpl*.

rubbish [ˈɹʌbɪʃ] *n.* détritus *mpl*, ordures *fpl*; camelote *f*; [Fig.] sottises *fpl*, blague *f*.

rubble [ˈɹʌbl̩] *n.* **1.** moellon *m*. **2.** décombres *mpl*.

ruby [ˈɹuwbɪ] *n.* [stone] rubis *m*.

rucksack [ˈɹʌkˌsæk] *n.* sac-à-dos *m*.

rudder [ˈɹʌdəɹ] *n.* [Naut.] gouvernail *m*.

ruddy [ˈɹʌdɪ] *adj.* [face] vermeil, rouge.

rude [ɹuwd] *adj.* [words] grossier; [Pers.] impoli; [look] rébarbatif; [crude] rudimentaire, grossier, primitif. || **rudely** [-lɪ] *adv.* rudement; grossièrement; brusquement (réveillé). || **rudeness** [-nəs] *n.* grossièreté *f*; impolitesse *f*; rigueur (du climat).

rudiment [ˈɹuwdɪmənt] *n.* rudiment *m*; éléments *mpl*. || **rudimentary** [ˌɹuwdɪ-ˈmɛntəɹɪ] *adj.* rudimentaire.

rue [ɹuw] *v. tr.* regretter (qqch.) amèrement, se repentir de (qqch.).

rueful [ˈɹuwfl̩] *adj.* malheureux: *a ~ sight*, un triste spectacle.

ruffian [ˈɹʌfɪən] *n.* bandit *m*, brigand *m*.

ruffle [ˈrʌfl̩] *v. intr.* [feathers] se hérisser; [hair] s'ébouriffer; [water] se rider. || *v. tr.* ébouriffer; [water] agiter, rider; [crease] froisser, chiffonner; [Fig.] froisser, contrarier.

rug [ɹʌg] *n.* tapis *m*; [motor, &c.] couverture *f*.

rugby [ˈɹʌgbɪ] *n.* [Sport.] rugby *m*.

rugged [ˈɹʌgəd] *adj.* **1.** rude, raboteux. **2.** difficile, rude, âpre, sévère: ~ *weather*, un froid sévère; ~ *Canadian operating conditions*, dures/circonstances, conditions/de fonctionnement au Canada. **3.** résistant, à toute épreuve.

rugger [ˈɹʌgəɹ] [Br.] cf. RUGBY.

ruin [ˈɹuwɪn] *n.* ruine *f*; destruction *f*: [Fig.] *Everything is going to rack and ~*, Tout marche de travers. || *v. tr.* ruiner; détruire; abîmer: *to ~ o.'s eyes*, s'abîmer la vue.

ruinous [ˈɹuwɪnəs] *adj.* délabré, tombant en ruines; [Fig.] ruineux, désastreux.

rule [ɹuwl] *n.* règle *f*, autorité *f*, pouvoir *m*; [tool] mètre *m*, © pied *m*: *a hard and fast ~*, une règle/absolue, immuable; *as a (general) rule*, en général; *to make it a ~ to*, se faire une règle de; *rules and regulations*, statuts *mpl* et règlements *mpl*; *against the rules*, contre/les règles, le règlement; *under French ~*, © sous le régime français; *by ~ of thumb*, empiriquement, à vue de nez. || *v. tr.* régler; gouverner; réglementer; décider, déclarer (que); régler (du papier): *to ~ over a country*, régner sur une nation. || **ruler** [-əɹ] *n.* [drawing, writing] règle *f*; dirigeant *m*, chef *m*. || **ruling** [-ɪŋ] *n.* [law] jurisprudence *f*, décision *f*, jugement *m*. || *adj.* dominant, prédominant, maître: *the ruling classes*, les classes *fpl* dirigeantes.

rum [ɹʌm] *n.* rhum *m*.

Rumania [ɹuwˈmejnjə] *n.* la Roumanie. || **Rumanian** [-n] *adj.* & *n.* roumain *m*, -e *f*.

rumble [ˈɹʌmbl̩] *n.* [thunder] grondement *m*; [vehicle] roulement *m*: ~ *seat*, siège *m* de derrière. || *v. intr.* [thunder, &c.] gronder, [vehicle, &c.] rouler. || **rumbling** [-ɪŋ] cf. RUMBLE, *n.*

ruminate [ˈɹuwmɪnˌejt] *v. intr.* ruminer; [Fig.] méditer, réfléchir.

rummage [ˈɹʌmədʒ] *n.* remue-ménage *m*, fouille(s) *f(pl)*; [junk] antiquités *fpl*: ~ *sale*, vente *f* de charité. || *v. tr.* fouiller (une pièce). || *v. intr.* [about] fouiller, fureter.

rumour [ˈɹuwməɹ] *n.* rumeur *f*, on-dit *m*: ~ *has it that . . .*, le bruit court que. || *v. tr.* faire courir le bruit (que . . .).

rump [ɹʌmp] *n.* [horse, &c.] croupe *f*; [fowl] croupion *m*; [Fam.] [person's] postérieur *m*; [Cul.] ~ *steak*, rumsteck *m*.

rumple [ˈɹʌmpl̩] *n.* [material]/mauvais, faux/pli. || *v. tr.* chiffonner, froisser: *rumpled skin*, peau toute ridée.

rumpus [ˈɹʌmpəs] *n.* tapage *m*, chahut *m*: *to kick up a ~*, faire du chahut.

run [ɹʌn], **ran** [ɹæn], **run** *v. intr.* courir; se sauver; [liquid] fuir; [water] couler; [rumour] circuler; [news] s'étendre, se répandre; [machinery] marcher, fonctionner; [writing] être conçu, s'exprimer; [Sch.] être candidat, se présenter (à un examen, *for an examination*); [time] passer, s'écouler. || *v. tr.* diriger (une affaire, des hommes); exploiter (un commerce); [stocking] se démailler.

runaway [ˈɹʌn|əˌwej] *n.* fuyard *m*, fugitif *m*. || **rundown** [-ˌdawn] *n.* reportage *m*; compte rendu *m*, récit *m*.

rung[1] cf. RING[1].

rung[2] [ɹʌŋ] *n.* [chair] barreau *m*, [ladder] échelon *m*.

runnel [ˈɹʌnl̩] *n.* rigole *f*.

runner [ˈɹʌnəɹ] *n.* **1.** [Pers.] coureur *m*. **2.**

patin *m* de traîneau: *runner-up*, bon second *m*.
running ['ɹʌnɪŋ] *n*. [water] écoulement *m*; [train] circulation *f*, course *f*; [machine] marche *f*, fonctionnement *m*.
runt [ɹʌnt] *n*. avorton *m*.
runway ['ɹʌn,wej] *n*. **1.** glissière *f*, coulisse *f*, rainure *f*, sillon *m*. **2.** [track] piste *f* d'un animal. **3.** [enclosed place] enclos *m*. **4.** [planes] piste *f* (d'atterrissage).
Rupert ['ɹuwpɚt] *n*. © ~'*s Land*, la Terre de Rupert.
rupture ['ɹʌptʃɚ] *n*. rupture *f*, brouille *f*; [Med.] hernie *f*. ‖ *v. intr*. **1.** (se) briser, éclater, (s')ouvrir. **2.** avoir une hernie.
rural ['ɹuwɚl] *adj*. [county, &c.] rural, [customs, &c.] rustique.
ruse [ɹuwz] *n*. ruse *f*, stratagème *m*, fraude *f*.
rush[1] [ɹʌʃ] *n*. jonc *m*.
rush[2] *n*. ruée *f*, course *f* précipitée: *the gold* ~, la ruée vers l'or; *to make a* ~ *at s.o.*, s'élancer sur qqun; *to be in a* ~ *to*, être pressé de; ~ *hours*, heures *fpl* d'affluence; ~ *order*, commande *f* urgente. ‖ *v. tr*. pousser, faire aller vite: *He was rushed to hospital*, On le transporta d'urgence à l'hôpital. ‖ *v. intr*. se précipiter, se ruer (at, *sur*); [on letters, &c.] *Rush*, Urgent. ‖ **to rush about** [-ə'bawt] *v. intr*. courir, se précipiter /çà et là, de tous côtés/. ‖ **to rush into** [-ɪn'tuw] *v. intr*. faire irruption (dans); [Fig.] se précipiter tête baissée (dans). ‖ **to rush out** [-'awt] *v. intr*. sortir précipitamment (de). ‖ **to rush through** [-'θɹuw] *v. tr*. [a book, &c.] lire (un livre) à la hâte; [a town] visiter (une ville) au pas de course; [work] expédier. ‖ **rushed** [-t] *adj*. [Pers.] débordé (de travail); [thing] expédié en toute hâte, par les voies les plus rapides; [Péj.] bâclé. ‖ **rushing** [-ɪŋ] *adj*. [water] impétueux, bondissant.
russet ['ɹʌsət] *adj*. [colour] roussâtre, brun rouge.
Russia ['ɹʌʃə] *n*. la Russie. ‖ **Russian** [-n] *n*. Russe *m/f*. ‖ *adj*. russe, de Russie.
rust [ɹʌst] *n*. rouille *f*. ‖ *v. intr*. se rouiller.
rustic [-ɪk] *adj*. **1.** rustique; rural; campagnard. **2.** simple, net, clair. **3.** grossier, rude, © habitant. ‖ *n*. paysan *m*; villageois *m*; habitant *m*.
rustle ['ɹʌsl̩] *n*. [leaves] bruissement *m*; frôlement *m*. ‖ *v. intr*. [leaves] bruire; [US, Sl.] mener une affaire rondement. ‖ *v. tr*. faire bruire; voler [du bétail].
rustproof ['ɹʌst|,pɹuwf] *adj*. antirouille, [steel, &c.] inoxydable. ‖ **rusty** [-ɪ] *adj*. rouillé; [metal] oxydé.
rut [ɹʌt] *n*. **1.** ornière *f*. **2.** routine *f*. ‖ *v. intr*. [-tt-] faire des ornières; [Fig.] tracer une ligne (de conduite).
ruthless ['ɹuwθləs] *adj*. cruel, impitoyable, barbare. ‖ **ruthlessness** [-nəs] *n*. cruauté *f*, insensibilité *f*.
rye [ɹaj] *n*. seigle *m*: ~ *bread*, pain *m* de seigle; ~ *whiskey*, © rye *m*.

S

S, s [ɛs] *pl*. **S's, s's** *n*. [letter] S, s *m*.
's[1] [-z] [☞ signe du possessif singulier, par opposition à *s'* pour le pluriel]: *My father's house*, La maison de mon père; *the boys' room*, la chambre des enfants; *CPR's chiefs*, les dirigeants du Pacifique Canadien; *France's Dupont*, M. Dupont,/délégué, représentant/de la France.
's[2] *abr*. [= is] cf. BE.
sabbath ['sæbəθ] *n*. **1.** sabbat *m*. **2.** [Rel.] dimanche *m*.
sable [sejbl̩] *n*. zibeline *f*: *Alaska* ~, mouffette *f* cf. SKUNK; *American* ~, martre *m* d'Amérique.
sabotage ['sæbə,tæʒ] *n*. sabotage *m*. ‖ *v. tr*. saboter (un ouvrage, &c.).
sabre ['sejbɚ] *n*. sabre *m*.
sack [sæk] *n*. **1.** sac *m* (en papier, en toile). **2.** [loot] pillage *m* (d'une ville, &c.). **3.** [Fam. Br.] *To give s.o. the* ~, renvoyer qqun; *to get the* ~, se faire renvoyer. ‖ *v. tr*. **1.** ensacher (du grain), mettre (qqch.) dans un sac. **2.** mettre (qqch.) à sac, piller, saccager (une ville, &c.).

3. [Fam. Br.] renvoyer (qqun), mettre qqun à la porte.

sacrament [ˈsækɹəmənt] *n.* sacrement *m.* || **sacramental** [ˌsækɹəˈmentḷ] *n.* [rite] sacramentel.

sacred [ˈsejkɹəd] *adj.* sacré: ~ *history*, histoire *f* sainte; [dedicated] ~ *to*, consacré à. || **sacredly** [-lɪ] *adv.* religieusement; avec piété. || **sacredness** [-nəs] *n.* sainteté *f*, caractère *m* sacré.

sacrifice [ˈsækɹɪˌfajs] *n.* sacrifice *m* (*to*, à); [Fig.] victime *f* (*to*, de). || *v. tr.* [victim, &c.] sacrifier (*to*, à); [Fig.] renoncer à (ses idées, principes, &c.). || **sacrificial** [ˌsækɹɪˈfɪʃəl] *adj.* sacrificatoire.

sacrilege [ˈsækɹɪlədʒ] *n.* sacrilège *m.* || **sacrilegious** [ˌsækɹɪˈlɪdʒəs] *adj.* sacrilège.

sacristan [ˈsækɹɪst|ən] *n.* [Rel.] [sexton] sacristain *m.* || **sacristy** [-ɪ] *n.* [Rel.] sacristie *f.*

sad [sæd] *adj.* [feeling] triste, malheureux; mélancolique; [situation] déplorable; [loss] cruel: [Arg.] ~ *sack*, souffre-douleur *m.* || **sadden** [-ṇ] *v. tr.* attrister (qqun), rendre qqun triste. || *v. intr.* s'attrister.

saddle [-ḷ] *n.* selle *f*: ~ *bag*, sacoche *f*; ~ *horse*, cheval de selle. || *v. tr.* [up] seller (un cheval); bâter (un âne); charger (une bête de somme); [Fig.] accabler, charger (qqun d'un fardeau).

sadism [ˈsædɪzm] *n.* sadisme *m.*

sadist [ˈsejdɪst] *n.* sadique *m.* || **sadistic** [səˈdɪstɪk] *adj.* sadique.

sadly [ˈsæd|lɪ] *adv.* tristement; [very much] beaucoup, de façon déplorable: *to be* ~ *wanting in* . . . , → laisser beaucoup à désirer en matière de . . . || **sadness** [-nəs] *n.* tristesse *f*, mélancolie *f.*

safe[1] [sejf] *adj.* [unhurt] (sain et) sauf; [place] sûr; [person] en sûreté, hors de danger; [person, thing] à l'abri (de, *from*): *It is not* ~ *to*, → Il est dangereux de . . . , Il y a du danger à . . .

safe[2] *n.* coffre-fort *m* cf. VAULT; [meat] garde-manger *m.* || **safeguard** [-ˌgɑɚd] *n.* sauvegarde *f.* || *v. tr.* protéger (contre); sauvegarder. || **safely** [-lɪ] *adv.* [manner] sain et sauf, à bon port; [in a safe place] en lieu sûr, en sécurité; [without risk] sans danger. || **safeness** [-nəs] *n.* sécurité *f*, sûreté *f.* || **safety** [-tɪ] *n.* sûreté *f*, sécurité *f*; [preservation] salut *m*: ~ *first!*, → Prudence est mère de sûreté!, Soyez, Soyons/prudents! || *attrib.* ~ *pin*, épingle /de sûreté, à nourrice/; ~ *valve*, soupape *f* de sûreté. || **safety razor** [ˈsejftɪˌrejzɚ] *n.* rasoir *m* de sûreté.

sag [sæg] *n.* fléchissement *m.* || *v. intr.* [-gg-] céder, fléchir, s'affaisser.

sagacious [səˈgejʃəs] *adj.* sagace, intelligent. || **sagacity** [səˈgæsɪtɪ] *n.* sagacité *f*, pénétration *f.*

sage[1] [sejdʒ] *adj.* sage, prudent. || *n.* sage *m*, philosophe *m.*

sage[2] *n.* sauge *f.*

Saguenay [ˈsægəˌnej] *n.* © [river] le Saguenay; [district] le (royaume du) S.

Sahara [səˈhæɚə] *n.* Sahara *m.*

said cf. SAY. || *adj. the* ~ *Mr. Brown*, ledit M. Lebrun. || *pp*: *It isn't* ~, → Cela ne se dit pas; *It is* ~ (that . . .), On dit, on raconte (que) . . .

sail [sejl] *n.* **1.** [Naut.] voile *f*, [coll.] voilure *f.* **2.** aile *f* (d'un moulin): *to go for a* ~, faire de la voile, faire une promenade à la voile; *to get under* ~, *to set* ~, †faire voile; appareiller. || *v. intr.* †faire voile, voguer; [steamer] naviguer: *The ship sails from Halifax*, Le navire part de H.; *to* ~ */up, down/the river*, remonter, descendre/la rivière. || **sailboat** [-ˌbowt] *n.* bateau *m* à voiles. || **sailing** [-ɪŋ] *n.* **1.** [Sport] voile *f*: ~ *vessel*, voilier *m.* **2.** navigation *f*: *point of* ~, port *m* de départ *m.* || **sailor** [-ɚ] *n.* marin *m*: matelot *m*; [Fig.] *to be a good* ~, avoir le pied marin.

saint [sejnt] *adj.* saint *m*, sainte *f* [abbr. *St.* = St, Ste: *St. John*, Saint-Jean, St-Jean]. || *n.* saint *m*, -e *f*: *saint's day*, fête *f* (de saint); *All Saints Day*, la Toussaint. || **saintly** [-lɪ] *adj.* [manners, deeds, &c.] saint, → de saint.

sake [sejk] *n.* **1.** pour, pour l'amour de, par égard pour: *for your* ~, pour vous; *for mercy's* ~, par pitié. **2.** pour, en vue de: *art for art's* ~, l'art pour l'art

salable [ˈsejləbḷ] *adj.* vendable, → qui peut se vendre.

salad [ˈsæləd] *n.* salade *f*: © laitue *f*: ~ *oil*, huile *f* de table; *fruit* ~, salade de fruits; ~ *bowl*, saladier *m*; [Fr.] ~ *dressing*, vinaigrette *f.*

salary [ˈsælɚɪ] *n.* [civil servants] traitement *m*; [employees] appointements *mpl*; [workers & Fig.] salaire *m*: *to draw a* ~, toucher un traitement, cf. FEE, WAGE, PAY.

sale [sejl] *n.* **1.** vente *f*: *on* ~, en vente; *for* ~, mise *f* en vente, à vendre; *auction* ~, vente aux enchères; *cash, credit/* ~, vente/au comptant, à terme/; ~ *price*, prix de vente; ~ *value*, valeur *f* marchande; *white* ~, exposition *f* de blanc. **2.** [bargain] grande vente, occasions *fpl*: [goods] soldes *mpl.* || **salesclerk** [-zˌklɚk] *n.* commis *m*, vendeur *m.* || **salesgirl** [-zˌgɚl] *n.* vendeuse *f.* || **sales|man, -men** [-zmən] *n.* [de magasin] commis *m*, vendeur *m*; [commerçant] marchand *m*: *travelling* ~, commis voyageur *m*, voyageur *m* de commerce. || **salesmanship** [-ʃɪp] *n.* art *m* de la vente.

salient [ˈsejljənt] *adj.* †jaillissant, [angle] saillant, en saillie; [Fig.] (argument) frappant, (fait, caractéristique) saillant.

saline [ˈsejlajn] *adj.* [lac, source] salé: (marais) salant. || *n.* saline *f*; [Med.] sel *m* purgatif.

saliva [səˈlajvə] *n.* salive *f.*

sallow [ˈsælow] *adj.* & *n.* [teint] blême, blafard; [or] jaune. || *v. intr.* jaunir, pâlir.

sally [ˈsælɪ] *n.* sortie *f*, excursion *f*; [Mil.] sortie *f*; [Fig.] [émotion] sursaut *m*, élan *m*; [d'esprit] saillie *f*, boutade *f.* || **sally forth** [-ˈfɔɚθ] *v. intr.* partir en promenade. || **sally out** [-ˈawt] *v. intr.* [Mil.] faire une sortie.

salmon [ˈsæmən] *n.* saumon *m*: *Atlantic* ~, saumon atlantique; *sockeye* ~, saumon /sockeye, du Fraser/; ~ *trout*, truite *f* saumonée. || *adj.* saumon.

saloon [səˈluwn] *n.* bar *m*, bistrot *m*; [Br.] salle *f* de café; [Naut.] salon *m*; [Auto. Br.] conduite *f* intérieure, cf. SEDAN.

salsify [ˈsælsɪ,faj] *n.* salsifis *m.*

salt [sɔlt] *n.* sel *m*: *sea* ~, sel *m* marin; *rock* ~, sel gemme; *table* ~, sel/fin, de table/; *kitchen* ~, sel de cuisine, gros sel; [preserve] *in* ~, salé; ~ *marsh*, marais *m* salant; *salt-shaker*, salière *f.* || *v. tr.* saler; [Fam.] *to* ~ *away*, économiser (de l'argent).

saltpetre [-ˌpijtɚ] *n.* salpêtre *m.*

salt water [-ˌwɔtɚ] *n.* eau *f* salée: ~ *fish*, poisson de mer.

salty [ˈsɑltɪ] *adj.* salé, saumâtre.

salubrious [səˈluwbɹɪəs] *adj.* salubre.

salutary [ˈsæljəˌtɛɚɪ] *adj.* salutaire.

salutation [ˌsæljəˈtejʃən] *n.* salutation *f*, cf. GREETING: *Angelic* ~, salutation angélique, (l')Ave Maria. || **salute** [səˈluwt] *n.* salut *m*, salutation *f*; [canons] salve *f.* || *v. tr.* saluer, faire un salut (à); accueillir (qqun).

salvage [ˈsælvəʤ] *n.* [action] sauvetage *m*; [things] effets *mpl*, biens sauvés: ~ *plant*, appareil *m* de renflouage. || **salvation** [ˌsælˈvejʃən] *n.* salut *m*, préservation *f*; [economic] relèvement *m*; [Rel.] salut *m*: *Salvation Army*, l'Armée *f* du Salut.

salve [sæv] *n.* [Med.] baume *m*; onguent *m*, pommade *f*; [Fig.] baume *m*, apaisement *m.* || *v. tr.* **1.** appliquer un onguent sur. **2.** [sælv] [Mar.] sauver (un navire, du matériel).

salvo [ˈsælvow] *n.* **1.** [Mil.] salve *f.* **2.** restriction *f* (mentale); réserve *f*, excuse *f*, faux-fuyant *m.*

same [sejm] *adj.* même: *at the* ~ *time*, au même/instant, moment/; [Fig.] par la même occasion cf. TIME: *at the* (*very*) ~ *time as*, au même moment que, au moment même où, en même temps que; *one and the* ~ *thing*, *the very* ~ *thing*, une seule et même chose; *That amounts to the* ~ *thing*, Cela revient au même; *in the* ~ *way*, de même. || *pron. the* ~, le, la/même; les mêmes: la même chose: *all the* ~, tout de même, néanmoins; *It's all the* ~ *to me*, Ça m'est égal; *You look the* ~, → Vous n'avez pas changé; *The* ~ *to you*, À vous de même, Pareillement; *to do the* ~, faire de même, en faire autant. || **sameness** [-nəs] *n.* ressemblance *f*; [Péj.] monotonie *f.*

sample [ˈsæmpḷ] *n.* [fabric] échantillon *m*; [wine] essai *m*; [ore, Med.] prélèvement *m*; spécimen *m*: ~ *card*, carte *f* d'échantillon; ~*-post*, échantillon *m* sans valeur. || *v. tr.* échantillonner; [food, drink] déguster, goûter.

sanatori|um [ˌsænəˈtɔɚɪəm] *pl.* **-a** *n.* sanatorium *m.*

sanctify [ˈsæŋktɪˌfaj] *v. tr.* & *intr.* sanctifier.

sanctimonious [ˌsæŋtɪˈmownɪəs] *adj.* [Péj.] bigot, papelard.

sanction [ˈsæŋkʃən] *n.* sanction *f*, approbation *f*; [assent] consentement *m*; [punishment] sanction *f*; [Jur.] ordonnance *f*, décret *m.* || *v. tr.* sanctionner, approuver, consentir (à); accompagner de sanctions; [Jur.] sanctionner, décréter: *sanctioned by usage*, consacré par l'usage.

sanctity [ˈsæŋktɪtɪ] *n.* sainteté *f*; [Fig.] [promesse, serment] caractère *m* sacré.

sanctuary [ˈsæŋʧəˌɛɚɪ] *n.* sanctuaire *m*, temple *m*; [Fig.] asile *m*, refuge *m*: *bird* ~, refuge *m* (d'oiseaux).

sand [sænd] *n.* sable *m*; grain *m* de sable.

sandal [ˈsændḷ] *n.* [shoe] sandale *f*; [strap] barrette *f.* || *v. tr.* chausser de sandales.

sandbag [-ˌbæg] *n.* sac *m* à terre. || **sand dune** [-ˌdjuwn] *n.* dune *f.* || **sandglass** [-ˌglæs] *n.* sablier *m.* || **sandpaper** [-ˌpejpɚ] *n.* papier *m*/émeri, de verre/. || **sandstone** [-ˌstown] *n.* grès *m.* || **sandstorm** [-ˌstɔɚm] *n.* tempête *f* de sable, [Africa] simoun *m.*

sandwich [ˈsændwɪʧ] *pl.* **-es** *n.* sandwich *m.* || *v. tr.* serrer, intercaler, coincer (*between*, entre).

sandy [ˈsændɪ] *adj.* sablonneux; (fond) de sable; (sentier) sablé; (cheveux) blond roux *inv.*

sane [sejn] *adj.* [Med.] sain d'esprit, bien équilibré; [Fig.] raisonnable: *to be* ~, avoir toute sa raison.
sang cf. SING.
sanguine [ˈsæŋgwɪn] *adj.* de sang; (tempérament) sanguin; (teint) rubicond, congestionné, rouge; [Fig.] confiant: *to be* ~ *about*, envisager avec optimisme. ‖ *v. tr.* teinter, couvrir/de sang, ensanglanter.
sanitarium [ˌsænɪˈtɛɚɪəm] cf. SANATORIUM.
sanitary [ˈsænɪˌtɛɚɪ] *adj.* sanitaire; hygiénique: ~ *engineering*, matériel *m* sanitaire. ‖ **sanitation** [ˌsænɪˈtejʃən] *n.* [science] hygiène *f*; [town planning] aménagements *mpl* sanitaires, tout à l'égout *m*.
sanity [ˈsænɪtɪ] *n.* santé *f* mentale; [Fig.] rectitude *f* (du jugement), bon sens *m*.
sank cf. SINK.
sap[1] [sæp] *n.* sape *f*. ‖ *v. intr.* [-pp-] saper. ‖ *v. tr.* [Mil.] saper, miner; [Fig.] miner, affaiblir (la santé); ébranler, [plus fort] miner, saper (la foi).
sap[2] *n.* [Fam., stupid person] ballot *m*, gourde *f*.
sap[3] *n.* sève *f*. ‖ **sapling** [-lɪŋ] *n.* jeune arbre *m*.
sapphire [ˈsæfajɚ] *n.* saphir *m*; [Zool.] colibri *m*.
sarcasm [ˈsɑɚkæzm] *n.* sarcasme *m*; moquerie *f*, raillerie *f*. ‖ **sarcastic** [ˌsɑɚˈkæstɪk] *adj.* sarcastique: ~ *spirit*, esprit *m*/sarcastique, mordant/.
sash[1] [sæʃ] *n.* (large) ceinture *f* nouée: © *arrow* ~, ceinture fléchée; [officiel; Mil.] écharpe *f*.
sash[2] *n.* châssis *m* (d'une fenêtre): ~ *cord*, cordon *m* de châssis; ~ *window*, fenêtre *f* à guillotine.
sat cf. SIT.
satchel [ˈsætʃəl] *n.* carton *m*, cartable *m* (d'écolier); sacoche *f* (de selle); [hunting] gibecière *f*.
sate [sejt] *v. tr.* [also Fig.] assouvir (son appétit); [Péj.] blaser.
satiate [ˈsejʃɪˌejt] *adj.* rassasié. ‖ *v. tr.* rassasier, assouvir; [Fig.] gorger, blaser/ (*with*, de).
satire [ˈsætajɚ] *n.* [literature] satire *f*; [Fig.] raillerie *f*, ironie *f*. ‖ **satirical** [səˈtijɚɪ|kḷ] *adj.* satirique; [Fig.] sarcastique, railleur. ‖ **satirist** [-st] *n.* esprit/ mordant, railleur/. ‖ **satirize** [ˈsætɚˌajz] *v. tr.* railler, faire la satire de.
satisfaction [ˌsætɪsˈfæk|ʃən] *n.* satisfaction *f*, plaisir *m* (*at*, *with*, de); [insult, &c.] réparation *f*; [of damage] dédommagement *m*: *to give* ~ *to*, rendre raison à; [desire, curiosity] apaisement *m*; [appetite] assouvissement *m*; [Com.]règlement *m*, liquidation *f* (de dette); [creditor] désintéressement *m*; [promise] exécution *f*; [obligation] accomplissement *m*. ‖ **satisfactory** [-tɚɪ] *adj.* qui donne satisfaction; [thing] satisfaisant: *to bring . . . to a* ~ *conclusion*, mener . . . à bien; *This is far from being* ~, cela laisse beaucoup à désirer. ‖ **satisfy** [ˈsætɪsˌfaj] *v. tr.* satisfaire, contenter (qqun); [desire] apaiser; [hatred] assouvir: *to be satisfied to*, se contenter de; [Com.] payer, régler/ une dette; désintéresser, satisfaire (un créditeur); convaincre: *to* ~ *o.s. that*, s'assurer que.
saturate [ˈsætʃɚˌejt] *v. tr.* saturer, imprégner, imbiber (*with*, de). ‖ *adj.* saturé.
Saturday [ˈsætɚˌdej] *n.* samedi *m*.
sauce [sɔs] *n.* assaisonnement *m*, condiment *m*; [× distinguer entre *stock* (bouillon), *gravy* (jus de rôti) et *sauce* (condiment)]: *tomato* ~, sauce *f* tomate; *apple* ~, compote *f* de pommes; [Fig.] insolence *f*, effronterie *f*; [Fam.] *apple* ~, des boniments *mpl*, de la fichaise *f*. ‖ **saucepan** [ˈsɔspən] *n.* casserole *f*; poêlon *m*. ‖ **saucer** [-ɚ] *n.* soucoupe *f*; [painting] godet *m*; [Aéro.] *flying* ~ soucoupe volante.
saucy [ˈsɔsɪ] *adj.* effronté, impertinent; [hat, &c.] chic, pimpant.
saunter [ˈsɔntɚ] *v. intr.* flâner; déambuler.
sausage [ˈsɔsədʒ] *n.* saucisse *f*; [dry] saucisson *m*.
savage [ˈsævədʒ] *adj.* sauvage, de sauvage; brutal, cruel, furieux; [animal] féroce. ‖ *n.* [native] sauvage *m*. ‖ **savagely** [-lɪ] *adv.* en sauvage; sauvagement; brutalement, furieusement. ‖ **savagery** [-ɚɪ] *n.* sauvagerie *f*; brutalité *f*, fureur *f*; [uncivilized state] état *m* sauvage.
save[1] [sejv] *v. tr.* **1.** [rescue] sauver (*from*, de); empêcher (de faire qqch.); [preserve] préserver (*from*, de), garantir (*from*, contre); [Rel.] sauver: *to be saved*, être sauvé, faire son salut; [Loc.] *God save the/King, Queen*, Dieu protège/le Roi, la Reine. **2.** [avoid waste] épargner, économiser: *to* ~ *money*, → faire des économies, mettre de l'argent de côté; [labour] économiser (du temps, des forces, &c.) collectionner (des timbres, &c.). ‖ *v. intr.* économiser, faire des économies.
save[2] [prep.] sauf, excepté, à l'exception de. ‖ *conj.* ~ *that*, sauf que; sinon que [+ indic.]; à moins que (ne) [+ subjunc.].
saver [-ɚ] *n.* sauveur *m*. ‖ **saving** [-ɪŋ] *n.* sauvetage *m*; [labour] économie *f*. ‖ *pl.*

économies *fpl*: *savings bank*, caisse *f*, © banque *f*/d'épargne. || *adj.* économe: *labour-*~ (*device*), pratique; qui économise/le travail, la main-d'œuvre/. || **saviour** [-jər] *n.* [Rel.] le Sauveur.

savour ['sejvər] *n.* saveur *f*, goût *m*; [Fig.] arrière-goût *m* (de), soupçon *m* (de). || *v. tr.* savourer, goûter: *to* ~ *of*, avoir un goût de, © goûter. || **savourless** [-ləs] *adj.* insipide, sans saveur. || **savoury** [-ɪ] *adj.* savoureux, succulent; [Cul.] ~ *herbs*, plantes *fpl* aromatiques.

saw[1] cf. SEE.

saw[2] [sɔ] *n.* diction *m*; proverbe *m*, cf. SAYING.

saw[3] *n.* scie *f*: *handsaw*, scie *f* à main, égoïne *f*; *hacksaw*, scie à métaux; *power* ~, *chain* ~, scie *f* mécanique; *lumberman's* ~, © godendard *m*; *table* ~ scie d'établi. || *v. tr.* scier; débiter. || **sawdust** [-ˌdʌst] *n.* sciure *f*. || **sawhorse** [-ˌhɔərs] *n.* chevalet *m*. || **sawmill** [-ˌmɪl] *n.* scierie *f*; © (abus.) moulin *m* à scie.

say [sej], **said** [sɛd], **said** [N.B. **says** [sɛz]] *v. tr.* & *intr.* dire; [again] répéter, redire; [lesson] réciter; [opinion] dire, affirmer; [Loc.] *to* ~ *nothing*, → se taire; *to* ~ *nothing of*, sans parler de; *to* ~ *the least*, (c'est) le moins qu'on puisse dire; *there's much to be said for it*, → Ce (projet, &c.) présente des avantages certains; *I say!*, Dites donc!; *You don't say!*, Pas possible!; ~ *no more*, n'en dites pas davantage; *to* ~ *the word*, faire signe, donner le signal: *I should* ~ *so!*, Je crois bien!; *I should* ~ *not!*, Absolument pas!; [Fam.] *You said it!*, Et comment!, [Fam.] Tu parles!; *Let's* ~ *Monday*, Disons lundi; *Let's* ~ *you don't know me*, Mettons que vous ne me connaissez pas; *that is to* ~, c'est-à-dire; *That goes without saying*, Cela va sans dire. || *n.* mot *m*: *to have a* ~ *in the matter*, avoir son mot à dire, avoir voix au chapitre. || **saying** ['sejɪŋ] *n.* **1.** proverbe, cf. †SAW. **2.** *there is no* ~ (*but that*) . . . , impossible de dire (si).

scab [skæb] *n.* **1,** [Med.] croûte *f*. **2.** [Fam.] jaune *m*, briseur de grève. || *v. intr.* **[-bb-]** former une croûte; remplacer un gréviste.

scaffold ['skæfəld] *n.* **1.** échafaudage *m*. **2.** [executioner's] échafaud *m*. || **scaffolding** [-ɪŋ] *n.* échafaudage *m*.

scald [skɑld] *v. tr.* ébouillanter, échauder; [Cul.] blanchir, échauder.

scale[1] [skejl] *n.* échelle *f*; [thermometer] échelle *f* graduée, graduation *f*. [salaries] échelle, barème *m*; [map] échelle; [Mus.] gamme *f*: [Fig.] échelle: étendue *f* (d'un désordre); *on a/small, large/* ~, sur une/petite, grande/échelle; en petit, en grand. || *v. tr.* [mur] escalader; [mountain] faire l'ascension de; [thermometer] graduer.

scale[2] *n.* [fish] écaille *f*; [nuts, &c.] écale *f*; [skin] squame *f*; [teeth, rust] tartre *m*; écaille *f*. || *v. tr.* [fish] écailler; [nut] écaler; [skin] se desquamer; [teeth] détartrer; [rust] désincruster.

scale[3] *n.* [balance] plateau *m*; [track] bascule *f*.: *to turn the* ~, faire pencher la balance. || [pl.] balance *f*; [letters] pèse-lettres *m*. || *v. tr.* peser.

scallop ['skɑləp] *n.* [Zool.] coquille *f* Saint-Jacques; © pétoncle *f*; [Cul.] coquille au gratin; [art] dentelure *f*, feston *m*. || *v. tr.* **[-pp-]** faire gratiner en coquilles; découper; denteler.

scalp [skæld] *n.* cuir *m* chevelu; [Hist.] scalp *m*: ~ *-hunter*, chasseur *m* de têtes, [Fig., critic] éreinteur *m*. || *v. tr.* scalper; [Fam.] éreinter.

scan [skæn] *n.* regard *m* scrutateur. || *v. tr.* **[-nn-]** [a face] examiner, scruter; [TV] explorer; [Fig.] sonder: [Pej.] *to* ~ *s.o.* (up and down), toiser qqun.

scandal ['skændl̩] *n.* **1.** scandale *m*; honte *f*: *to create a* ~, faire un esclandre. **2.** [gossip] cancans *mpl*: *to talk* ~ *about* . . . , cancaner sur le compte de . . . ; [Jur.] diffamation *f*: ~ *-monger*, mauvaise langue. || **scandalize** [-ˌajz] *v. tr.* scandaliser: *to be scandalized* (*by*), se scandaliser (de). || **scandalous** [-əs] *adj.* [action, fait] scandaleux, honteux: *It's* ~, → C'est une honte; [Jur.] diffamatoire.

Scandinavia [ˌskændɪ'nejvjə] *n.* la Scandinavie. || **Scandinavian** [-n] *adj.* & *n.* scandinave.

scant [-t] *adj.* [attire] sommaire; [Meas., weight] juste; [vegetation] maigre, pauvre; [success] maigre: *a* ~ *amount*, une somme à peine suffisante; [Med.] ~ *of breath*, hors d'haleine, essoufflé. || **scanty** [-tɪ] *adj.* restreint, peu abondant; [vegetation] rare: *a* ~ *meal*, un maigre repas.

scapegoat ['skejpˌgowt] *n.* bouc *m* émissaire.

scar [skɑər] *n.* cicatrice *f*; [on the face] balafre *f*: ~ *-face*, balafré. || *v. tr.* **[-rr-]** laisser une cicatrice; balafrer (le visage).

scarce [skɛər s] *adj.* rare, peu abondant: *to become* ~, se faire rare; *to be* ~ *of*, manquer, être à court/de: [Fam.] *to make o.s.* ~, se défiler, s'éclipser. || **scarcely** [-lɪ] *adv.* **1.** presque pas, à peine; ~ *ever*, presque jamais; *to be* ~ *able to*, avoir peine à. **2.** certainement pas: *He can* ~ *have done that*, C'est impossible/qu'il ait, que ce soit lui qui ait/fait cela. || **scarceness, scarcity** [-nəs] [-ɪtɪ] *n.* rareté *f*, disette *f*, pénurie *f*, manque *m* (*of*, de).

scare [skɛɚ] *n.* panique *f*, peur *f* irraisonnée: *to give s.o. a* ~, faire une peur terrible à qqun. || *v. tr.* épouvanter, effrayer; [away] faire peur à, chasser; [Fig.] *to* ~ . . . *to death*, faire mourir . . . de peur. || *v. intr.* s'effaroucher, prendre peur. || **scarecrow** [-ˌkɹow] *n.* épouvantail *m.* || **scared** [-d] *adj.* épouvanté, effrayé. || **scaremonger** [ˌmɔŋgɚ] *n.* alarmiste *m.*

scarf [skɑɚf] *pl.* **scarfs, scarves** [skɑɚvz] *n.* écharpe *f*; †fichu *m*; cache-col *m*, cache-nez *m*; [silk] foulard *m.*

scarlet ['skɑɚlət] *n.* [colour] écarlate *f*; [cloth] étoffe *f*, tissu *m*/écarlate: ~ *fever*, (fièvre *f*) scarlatine. || *adj.* écarlate.

scathing ['skejðɪŋ] *adj.* [comment] cinglant, mordant; [criticism] virulent, âpre.

scatter ['skætɚ] *v. tr.* [things] éparpiller, disséminer, joncher (*with*, de); [troops, rioters, &c.] disperser, mettre en déroute; [clouds] dissiper. || *v. intr.* s'éparpiller; se disperser. || **scatter-brain** [-ˌbɹejn] *n.* étourdi, -e. || **scatter-brained** [-ˌbɹejnd] *adj.* étourdi, écervelé.

scavenger ['skævŋʤ|ɚ] *n.* boueur *m.* boueux [Fam.] *m*; [sewers] égoutier *m.*

scene [sijn] *n.* **1.** [part of a drama; location of/a drama, an event/; spectacle] scène *f*; [Fig., quarrel] scène *f.* **2.** [sight] spectacle; paysage *m*, vue *f*; [Theat.] décor *m*: *behind the scenes*, dans les coulisses; ~*-shifter*, machiniste *m.*

scenery ['sijnəɹ] *n.* paysage *m*, [Theat.] décors *mpl.* || **scenic** ['sijnɪk] *adj.* [Theat.] théâtral, scénique; [Fig.] spectaculaire; ~ *railway*, montagnes *fpl* russes.

scent [sɛnt] *n.* **1.** parfum *m*, [smell] odeur *f*: **2.** [Sport] fumet *m*, piste *f*: [Fig.] *to be on the* (*right*) ~, être sur la (bonne) piste; *to get* ~ *of*, avoir vent de; *to lose* ~ *of*, perdre la trace; *to throw s.o. off the* ~, dérouter, faire perdre la piste. || *v. tr.* **1.** [exhale] parfumer; [strong scent; Péj.] imprégner (*with*, de). **2.** [man] renifler (une odeur, &c.); [dog] sentir, flairer.

sceptic ['skɛptɪ|k] *n.* sceptique. || **sceptical** [-kl̩] *adj.* sceptique. || **scepticism** [-ˌsɪzm] *n.* scepticisme *m.*

sceptre ['sɛptɚ] *n.* sceptre *m.*

schedule ['skɛʤuwl, 'ʃɛdjuwl] *n.* liste *f*; [timetable] horaire *m* (des chemins de fer, &c.); inventaire *m*; [prices] barème *m*; *working* ~ , calendrier *m*, plan *m* (de travail): *Everything worked according to* ~, Tout s'est déroulé selon les prévisions. || *v. tr.* dresser/une liste, un plan; inscrire (un match, &c.) au programme: *scheduled for 2 pm, &c.*), prévu pour (2 h., &c.).

scheme [skijm] *n.* plan *m*, projet *m* (*for*, de; *to*, destiné à, tendant à); combinaison *f*, système *m*: *colour* ~ , harmonie *f* de couleurs; [Pej.] machination *f*, complot *m.* || *v. intr.* [Pej.] comploter, intriguer. || *v. tr.* combiner, machiner (un plan, &c.). || **schemer** ['skijmɚ] *n.* intrigant *m*, -e *f*; bâtisseur *m* de projets.

schism ['sɪzm] *n.* [Rel.] schisme.

scholar ['skɑlɚ] *n.* **1.** [learner] élève *m*/*f*, écoli|er, -ère; disciple *m*; [bursar] boursi|er, -ère. **2.** [learned person] savant *m*, érudit *m*: *a fine* ~ , un fin lettré. || **scholarly** [-lɪ] *adj.* savant, érudit. || **scholarship** [-ʃɪp] *n.* **1.** savoir *m*, érudition *f.* **2.** bourse *f* (d'études).

scholastic [skə'læstɪk] *adj.* [Phil.] scolastique; [Sch.] scolaire.

school[1] [skuwl] *n.* [of fish] banc *m* (de poissons).

school[2] *n.* **1.** école *f.* [☞ For various names of schools, cf. ÉCOLE]: *high* ~ , école secondaire; *public* ~, [US] école publique, [Br.] collège *m*; *to go to* ~ , aller/à l'école, en classe/. **2.** *evening* ~ , cours *mpl* du soir ; © *separate* ~ , école séparée; *summer* ~ , cours de/ vacances, d'été/; [Prot.] *Sunday* ~ , école du dimanche, *Trade* ~ , école professionnelle. **3.** *Dancing* ~ , Académie *f* de danse; *Music* ~ , Conservatoire *m* (de musique); [Auto.] *driving* ~, auto-école *f*; [manner] *the French, Italian*/ ~ , l'école française, italienne/ (de peinture, &c.). || **school book** [-ˌbuk] *n.* livre/scolaire, de classe/. || **schoolboy** [-ˌboj] *n.* élève *m*, écolier *m.* || **school fellow** [-ˌfɛlow] *n.* condisciple *m*; camarade *m*, compagne *f*/de classe. || **school girl** [-ˌgɚl] *n.* élève *f*, écolière *f.* || **school house** [-ˌhaws] *n.* école *f.* || **schooling** [-ɪŋ] *n.* études *fpl*; instruction *f*; éducation *f*; frais *mpl* de scolarité. || **school|man,** *pl.* **-men** [-mɑn] [-mɛn] *n.* enseignant *m*; [Phil.] scolastique *m.* || **school-marm** [-ˌmɑɚm] *n.* [Fam.] la maîtresse *f* (d'école). || **schoolmaster** [-'mæstɚ] *n.* instituteur *m*, maître *m* d'école; [US] professeur *m.* || **schoolmistress** [-ˌmɪstɹəs] *n.* institutrice *f*, maîtresse *f* d'école. || **schoolroom** [-ˌɹuwm] *n.* salle *f* de classe. || **schoolteacher** ['skuwlˌtijtʃɚ] *n.* maître *m* d'école, maîtresse *f* d'école.

science ['sajəns] *n.* [knowledge] savoir *m*, connaissances *fpl*; [branch of knowledge] science *f.* || **scientific** [ˌsajən'tɪfɪk] *adj.*

scientifique; [instruments] de précision. || **scientist** ['sajəntɪst] *n.* savant *m*; homme *m* de science; scientifique *m.*

scintillate ['sɪntɪˌlejt] *v. intr.* scintiller, étinceler.

scissors ['sɪzɚz] *n.pl.* ciseaux *mpl.*

scoff [skɑf] *n.* sarcasme *m,* raillerie *f.* || *v. intr.* se moquer (*at,* de): *to ~ at danger,* mépriser le danger.

scold [skowld] *v. tr.* gronder, morigéner. || *v. intr.* gronder, criailler. || **scolding** [-ɪŋ] *n.* gronderie *f,* réprimande *f.*

scoop [skuwp] *n.* **1.** [tool] pelle *f* à main; [ladle] louche *f*; [coal] seau *m* (à charbon); [Naut.] écope *f.* **2.** [news] primeur *f* (d'une nouvelle), nouvelle *f* sensationnelle; coup *m.* || *v. tr.*: *to ~ out,* excaver (à la pelle); écoper (de l'eau); gouger (le bois).

scoot [skuwt] *v. intr.* détaler. || **scooter** [-ɚ] *n.* [child's] trottinette *f*; [Mech.] scooter *m.*

scope [skowp] *n.* [space] étendue *f*; [distance] portée *f*; [undertaking] envergure *f*; [field] domaine *m,* compétence *f*: *to give free ~ to,* donner libre carrière à; *to have full ~*, avoir ses coudées franches; *beyond s.o.'s ~*, hors de la compétence de qqun; *within s.o.'s ~*, du/ressort *m,* domaine *m*/de qqun.

scorch [skɔɚtʃ] *n.* brûlure *f* (superficielle). || *v. tr.* brûler (superficiellement).

score [skɔɚ] *n.* **1.** [cut, mark] entaille *f,* coche *f*; trait *m* de repère; [Mus.] partition *f*; [Fig.] point *m,* marque *f*; compte *m,* total *m*/des points: *to keep the ~*, compter, marquer/les points; *What's the score?,* Quelle est la marque?, Où en est le jeu?; *on that ~*, à cet égard; [Fam.] *to know the ~*, en tâter un bout. **2.** †[= 20] vingt; une vingtaine: [invar.] *fourscore and seven years ago . . .*, voici quatre-vingt-sept ans que . . . ; **3.** *scores of . . .*, un grand nombre de . . ., de grandes quantités de . . . || *v. tr.* entailler, cocher (une pièce de bois); [Sport] marquer (un but), compter (un point). || *v. intr.* [Sport] marquer © compter; [win] gagner. || **scoring** [-ɪŋ] *n.* incision *f*; [Mus.] orchestration *f*; arrangement *m* (*for,* pour); [Sport] marque *f.*

scorn [skɔɚn] *n.* dédain *m,* mépris *m.* || *v. tr.* dédaigner, mépriser. || **scornful** [-fl̩] *adj.* dédaigneux, méprisant. || **scornfully** [-fəlɪ] *adv.* dédaigneusement, → avec dédain, d'un air méprisant.

Scot [skɑt] *n.* Écossais *m,* -e *f*; [Fam.] *Scots,* les Écossais; *Mary, Queen of Scots,* Marie Stuart. || **Scotch** [skɑtʃ] *adj.* écossais, d'Écosse: *~ tape,* ruban *m* cellulosique; [Fr.] du "Scotch". || *n. the ~*, les Écossais; [whisky] scotch *m.* || **Scotch|man, -men** [-mən] *n.* cf. SCOTSMAN. || **Scotland** ['skɑt|lənd] *n.* l'Écosse *f.* || **Scots.** || **Scots|man, -men** [-smən]; **-woman, -women** [-ˌwʊmən, -ˌwɪmən] *n.* Écossais *m,* Écossaise *f.* || **Scottish** [-ɪʃ] *adj.* écossais.

scoundrel ['skawndɹəl] *n.* scélérat *m,* misérable *m*; [Fam.] canaille *f.*

scour [skawɚ] *v. tr.* [floor] nettoyer; [pan] récurer; [metal] fourbir. || *n.* nettoyage *m,* récurage *m.*

scourge [skɚdʒ] *n.* fouet *m*; [Fig.] fléau *m.* || *v. tr.* fouetter; [Fig.] opprimer.

scout [skawt] *n.* **1.** [Mil.] éclaireur *m*; [ship] vedette *f.* **2.** [boy] scout *m*: *~ -master,* chef-scout *m*; *~ -mistress,* cheftaine *f.* || *v. intr.* [person] aller, partir/en éclaireur; faire une reconnaissance. || **scouting** [-ɪŋ] *n.* reconnaissance *f*; [Boy Scouts] scoutisme *m.*

scowl [skawl] *n.* air *m* maussade, mine *f* renfrognée. || *v. intr.* prendre un air maussade, se renfrogner: *to ~ at s.o.*, regarder qqun de travers.

scram [skɹæm] *v. intr.* **[-mm-]** [Sl.] décamper, filer.

scramble ['skɹæmbl̩] *v. tr.* brouiller: *scrambled eggs,* oeufs *mpl* brouillés. || *v. intr.* avancer péniblement; [up a hill] escalader en rampant: *to ~ for sth.*, se battre pour avoir qqch. || *n.* escalade *f*; bousculade *f*; [Sport] mêlée *f.*

scrap[1] [skɹæp] *n.* fragment *m,* petit morceau *m*; [iron] ferraille *f*; [food] bribe *f* (de nourriture); [paper] bout *m* de papier; coupure *f* (de journal). || **scraps** [-s] [food] les restes *mpl.* || *v. tr.* **[-pp-]** mettre . . . au rebut; [metal] envoyer . . . à la ferraille; [Fig.] renoncer à (un projet).

scrap[2] *n.* [Fam.] dispute *f*; [brawl] bagarre *f.* || *v. intr.* **[-pp-]** se battre, se bagarrer.

scrapbook [-ˌbʊk] *n.* album *m* (à coller). cf. SCRAP.[1]

scrape [skɹejp] *v. tr.* gratter; [hide] racler; [erase] raturer: *to ~ /away, off/*, enlever en/grattant, raclant; [Fig.] *to ~ together $100,* amasser 100 dollars sou par sou. || *v. intr.* frotter (*against,* contre): *to ~ along,* tirer le diable par la queue; [Fig.] *to ~ through,* passer de justesse. || *n.* grattage *m*; [noise] grincement *m*; [Fam.] mauvais pas *m.*

scratch [skɹætʃ] *n.* raie *f,* éraflure *f*; [sound] bruit *m* grinçant, grincement *m*; [on skin] égratignure *f*; [Fam.]: *to come up to* ∼ , être à la hauteur des événements; *to start from* ∼ , partir/de rien, à zéro. ‖ *v. tr. & intr.* **1.** rayer, érafler; [skin] égratigner; [write] griffonner: *to* ∼ *out*, biffer, rayer (un mot). **2.** se gratter (le nez, &c.). ‖ *adj.* [Pej.] hétéroclite; [hasty] improvisé. ‖ **scratch pad** [-ˌpæd] *n.* bloc-notes *m. inv.*

scream [skɹijm] *n.* **1.** [fright] cri *m* perçant; [pain] hurlement *m* (de douleur). **2.** [Fam.] type *m*/tordant, marrant. ‖ *v. intr.* pousser/un, des/cri(s) perçant(s); hurler (de douleur): *to* ∼ *with laughter*, rire aux larmes. ‖ **screaming** [ɪŋ] *adj.* [Pers.] criard; [sound] perçant; [Fig.] ∼ *colours*, couleurs/qui jurent, qui hurlent, voyantes.

screen [skɹijn] *n.* écran *m*; [partition] paravent *m*; [windows] grillage *m.*: *fire* ∼ , pare-feu *m*; [Mil.] rideau *m*; [Auto.] pare-brise *m.* ‖ *v. tr.*: *to* ∼ *off*, cacher, abriter/derrière un paravent; [Fig.] *to* ∼ *from*, soustraire à; [candidates] trier, effectuer un choix; *carefully screened*, triés sur le volet; *screening committee*, jury *m.*

screw [skɹuw] *n.* vis *f*; [Naut., Aviat.] hélice *f*; [Fam.] *to have a* ∼ *loose*, être toqué; ∼ *-driver*, tourne-vis *m.* ‖ *v. tr.* *to* ∼ */on, off/*, visser, dévisser; *to* ∼ *tight*, visser à bloc; *to* ∼ *up*, revisser, [Fig.] rassembler (son courage). ‖ *v. intr.* se visser.

screwball [ˈskɹuwˌbɔl] *adj. & n.* [Pej., Fam.] détraqué, toqué.

scribble [skɹɪbl̩] *v. tr.* griffonner; [Pej.] gribouiller: *scribbling pad*, bloc-notes *m.* ‖ **scribbler** [-ɚ] *n.* [Pej.] gribouilleur *m*, gratte-papier *m*; cahier *m.*

scribe [skɹajb] *n.* scribe *m.*

script [skɹɪpt] *n.* manuscrit *m* (d'un livre); scénario *m* (d'un film); [handwriting] écriture *f* script, script *m.* ‖ **script girl** [-ˌgɚl] *n.* [TV] assistante *f*, script-girl *f.* ‖ **script-writer** [-ˌɹajtɚ] *n.* scénariste *m.*

Scripture [ˈskɹɪptʃɚ] **the (Holy) Scriptures** *n.* l'Écriture *f* (Sainte), les Saintes Écritures *fpl.*

scrub [skɹʌb] *n.* [Bot.] arbuste *m* rabougri, buisson *m*; brousse *f*; [beard] barbe courte; [scour] nettoyage *m* à la brosse. ‖ *adj.* rabougri, malingre. ‖ *v. tr.* **[-bb-]** frotter (un parquet, &c.) à la brosse; récurer (une casserole). ‖ **scrubbing** [-ɪŋ] *n.* nettoyage *m* (à la brosse); récurage *m* (d'une casserole, &c.). ‖ **scrubby** [-ɪ] *adj.* rabougri, chétif; [beard] dru, court; [Bot.] broussailleux.

scruff [skɹʌf] *n.* nuque *f*: [Fig.] *to take by the* ∼ (*of the neck*), prendre au collet.

scruple [ˈskɹuwp|l̩] *n.* scrupule *m*; [weight = 20 grains] scrupule; [Fig.] grain *m.* ‖ *v. intr.* se faire scrupule de. ‖ **scrupulous** [-jələs] *adj.* scrupuleux; [careful] méticuleux. ‖ **scrupulously** [-jələslɪ] *adv.* scrupuleusement, méticuleusement.

scrutinize [ˈskɹuwtɪn|ˌajz] *v. tr.* scruter; examiner à fond; [a person] dévisager avec insistance. ‖ **scrutiny** [-ɪ] *n.* examen *m*/minutieux, attentif/.

scuffle [skʌfl̩] *n.* mêlée *f*, bagarre *f.* ‖ *v. intr.* se bagarrer (avec, *with*).

scull [skʌl] *n.* aviron *m*, godille *f.* ‖ *v. intr.* aller à la godille.

sculptor [ˈskʌlp|tɚ] *n.* sculpteur *m.* ‖ ∼ , also **sculptress** [-tɹəs] *n.* femme *f* sculpteur. ‖ **sculpture** [-tʃɚ] *n.* sculpture *f.* ‖ *v. tr.* sculpter (dans, *in, out of*). ‖ *v. intr.* faire de la sculpture.

scum [skʌm] *n.* écume *f*; [Metall.] scories *fpl*; [Fig.] lie *f*, rebut *m* (de la société).

scythe [sajð] *n.* faux *f.*

sea [sij] *n.* **1.** mer *f*: *the North Sea*, la mer du Nord: *at* ∼ , en mer; *to put to* ∼ , prendre le large; *to go to* ∼ , se faire marin; *by the* ∼ , au bord de la mer; [Fig.] *to be* (*all*) *at* ∼ , être perdu, désorienté. **2.** (grosse) lame *f*, paquet *m* de mer. **3.** *heavy* ∼ , houle *f*, grosse mer; ∼ *air*, air *m* marin; ∼ *captain*, capitaine *m*/de navire, au long cours/; ∼ *fish*, poisson *m* de mer. ‖ **seaboard** [-ˌbɔɚd] *n.* littoral *m*, bord *m* (de la mer): *Atlantic* ∼ , la côte de l'Atlantique. ‖ **seafaring** [-ˌfɛɚɪŋ] *adj.* navigant, → de mer. ‖ **seafood** [-ˌfuwd] *n.* poisson *m*, fruits *mpl* de mer; [Fr.] rocaille *f.* ‖ **seagoing** [-ˌgowɪŋ] *adj.* [Pers.] marin, navigant; [ship] de long cours, de haute mer. ‖ **seagull** [-ˌgʌl] *n.* mouette *f.* ‖ **seawards** [-wɚdz] *adv.* vers/la mer, le large/, au large ‖ **seaweed** [-wijd] *n.* algue *f* (marine), varech *m.*

seal[1] [sijl] *n.* phoque *m*, veau *m* marin.

seal[2] *n.* [document] sceau *m*, enveloppe *f*, cachet *m*; [Jur.] scellés *mpl*; [Com.] cachet; [bottle] capsule *f*; [customs] plomb *m*; [Fig.] empreinte *f*; [genius] sceau *m*; [love] preuve *f.* ‖ *v. tr.* [document] sceller; [Jur.] apposer/un sceau, les scellés/sur; [envelope] cacheter; [customs] plomber; [leak] boucher: [bargain] confirmer; [Fig.] *to* ∼ *s.o.'s fate*, régler le sort de qqun.

seam [sijm] *n.* couture *f*: *French* ∼ , couture/double, anglaise/; [metal] joint *m*; [rock] fissure *f*; [mine] couche *f*, veine *f*, filon *m*; [face] balafre *f*. || *v. tr.* coudre: *to ~ up*, réunir par une couture; [rock] fissurer; [welding] agrafer; [Med., face] couturer, balafrer.

sea|man, -men [ˈsijmən] *n.* matelot *m*, marin *m*. || **seamanship** [-ˌʃɪp] [Naut.] manœuvre *f*.

seamstress [ˈsijmstɹəs] *n.* couturière *f*.

seaplane [ˈsijˌplejn] *n.* [Aviat.] hydravion *m*.

seaport [ˈsijˌpɑət] *n.* port *m* de mer.

sear [sijɚ] *v. tr.* [plants, also Fig.] dessécher, faner; [brand] marquer au fer rouge. || *v. intr.* se dessécher, se faner.

search [sɚtʃ] *n.* recherche *f*; [prisoner, &c.] fouille *f* : *in ~ of*, à la recherche, en quête/de; *to make a ~*, faire des recherches; [Jur.] perquisition *f*, fouille domiciliaire; *~ warrant*, mandat *m* de perquisition. || *v. tr.* fouiller (un prisonnier, un meuble); visiter (des bagages); faire une perquisition (domiciliaire); [Med., a wound] sonder; [Fig.] [one's heart] sonder; [one's memory] scruter. || *v. intr.* faire/des recherches, des fouilles/. || **search/after, for/** [-aftɚ|-ˈfɔɚ] *v. intr.* chercher. || **searching** [-ɪŋ] *adj.* attentif, minutieux; [look] pénétrant; [examen] approfondi. || *n.* enquête *f*, visite *f* (de bagages); fouille *f* (d'un prisonnier). || **searchingly** [-ɪŋlɪ] *adv.* minutieusement. || **searchlight** [-ˌlajt] *n.* projecteur *m*.

seasick [ˈsijˌsɪk] *adj.*: *to be ~*, → avoir le mal de mer. || **seasickness** [-nəs] *n.* mal *m* de mer.

seaside [ˈsijˌsajd] *n.* bord *m* de la mer: [resort] *at the ~*, à la mer; *~ resort*, station *f* balnéaire.

season [ˈsijzn̩] *n.* **1.** [of the year] saison *f*, époque *f*: *late ~*, arrière-saison *f*. **2.** [time] époque, temps *m*: *At what ~?*, En quelle saison?, À quelle époque?; *in due ~*, en temps voulu; [Theat.] saison théâtrale; [Com.] *dull ~*, morte-saison *f*; [Agric.] *in ~*, en saison; [Sport] *open ~*, saison de la/chasse, pêche/; [Fig., Loc.] *in ~*, à propos, opportun; *out of ~*, déplacé, inopportun. || *v. tr.* acclimater; [with spices, &c.] assaisonner; [Fig.] atténuer (un jugement). || *v. intr.* [Mil.] s'aguerrir; [Pers.] s'acclimater; [bois] sécher; [vin] se faire. || **seasonable** [-əbl̩] *adj.* de saison; [Fig.] à propos, opportun. || **seasonableness** [-əbl̩nəs] *n.* l'à-propos (d'une remarque, &c.). || **seasonably** [-blɪ] *adv.* à propos; opportunément. || **seasonal** [-əl] *adj.* [job] saisonnier. || **seasoning** [-ɪŋ] *n.* [wine] maturation *f*; [wood] séchage *m*; [Cul.] assaisonnement *m*; [Fig.] acclimatement *m*; modération *f*. || **season ticket** [-ˌtɪkət] *n.* carte *f* d'abonnement.

seat [sijt] *n.* **1.** siège *m*; [armchair] fauteuil *m*; [chair] chaise *f*; [Auto.] siège, banquette *f*: *to take a ~*, prendre un siège, s'asseoir; *Keep your ~*, Restez assis. **2.** [Govt.] siège; [Member of Assembly] siège; [of learning] centre *m*, maison *f*; [Tech.] assiette *f*. **3.** place *f*: *This ~ taken?* → Cette place est-elle libre? || *v. tr.* (faire) asseoir: *to ~ o.s.*, s'asseoir; [Fig.] fonder; [Theat., Auto.] contenir (... spectateurs, places). || *v. intr.* s'asseoir; être assis: *Please be seated.* Veuillez vous asseoir. || **seating** [-ɪŋ] *n.*: [capacity of a room, &c.] nombre *m* de places assises.

seaway [ˈsijˌwej] *n.* voie *f* maritime; canal *m*.

secede [səˈsijd] *v. intr.* se séparer (*from*, de); [Rel.] faire scission. || **secession** [səˈsɛʃən] *n.* sécession *f*; scission *f*; [Rel., Pol.] dissidence *f*.

seclude [sɪˈkluw|d] *v. tr.* tenir/éloigné, écarté/du monde: *to ~ o.s.*, vivre à l'écart (*from*, de). || **seclusion** [-ʒən] *n.* retraite *f*, isolement *m*: *in ~*, retiré, solitaire.

second [ˈsɛkənd] *adj.* **1.** second, deuxième: *the Second Assembly*, la deuxième Assemblée; *in the ~ place*, en second lieu, secondo; *on the ~ floor*, [Fr.] au premier (étage), © au deuxième (étage); *every ~ day*, tous les deux jours. **2.** autre; inférieur: *on ~ thoughts*, à la réflexion, réflexion faite; *to be ~ to none*, ne le céder en rien à personne; *~-hand*, d'occasion, © usagé; *~-rate*, de second ordre; de qualité inférieure. || *n.* **1.** second, deuxième; [duel] témoin *m*; [boxing] second *m*; [Com.] marchandise *f* de deuxième qualité. **2.** [watch] seconde *f*: *~ hand*, aiguille *f* des secondes, trotteuse *f*; *Just a ~!*, Un instant! || *v. tr.* seconder, soutenir; [motion] appuyer [Adm.] [səˈkɑnd] détacher (un fonctionnaire).

secondary [ˈsɛkn̩ˌdɛəɪ] *adj.* secondaire; [meaning] dérivé.

secondly [-lɪ] *adv.* deuxièmement.

secrecy [ˈsijkɹə|sɪ] *n.* secret *m*; discrétion *f*. || **secret** [-t] *n.* secret *m*; confidence *f*. || *adj.* secret; retiré; [Fig.] peu communicatif, renfermé.

secretary [ˈsɛkɹəˌtɛəɪ] *n.* secrétaire *m/f*; [desk] secrétaire *m*: *Honorary ~*, Secrétaire [d'une société]; *~ of State*, © Secrétaire d'État, [US] Ministre *m* des Affaires étrangères.

secrete [sɪˈkɹij|t] *v. tr.* soustraire à la vue

(*from*, de); [Med.] sécréter. || **secretion** [-ʃən] *n.* [Med.] sécrétion *f*; [Jur.] recel *m.* || **secretive** ['sijkɹətɪv] *adj.* [Fig.] renfermé, cachottier.

sect [sɛkt] *n.* secte *f.* || **sectarian** [sɛk'tɛərɪən] *adj.* & *n.* membre d'une secte; [Pej.] sectaire.

section ['sɛkʃən] *n.* section *f*; [part] partie *f*, division *f*; [town] quartier *m*; [Tech.] profil *m*, coupe *f*; [newspaper] rubrique *f*, page *f*; [Mil.] escouade *f.* || *v. tr.* sectionner, trancher. || **sectional** [-l] *adj.* [Tech.] **1.** en coupe, en profil. **2.** de section, démontable; [Fig.] → d'une catégorie, d'un groupe.

sector ['sɛktə˞] *n.* secteur *m.*

secular ['sɛkjələ˞] *adj.* [ancient] séculaire; [temporal] séculier; [education] laïque. || **secularize** [-ˌajz] *v. tr.* laïciser; [Rel.] séculariser.

secure [sɪ'kjuwə˞] *adj.* tranquille, en sûreté, en paix; [firmly fastened] ferme, solide; [Fig.] assuré, certain: ~ *from*, à l'abri de. || *v. tr.* **1.** mettre/en sûreté, en lieu sûr, à l'abri/. **2.** [obtain] se procurer, acquérir; [seat] réserver. **3.** [Tech.] attacher, fixer/ solidement; immobiliser. || **security** [-ɪtɪ] *n.* sécurité *f*, sûreté *f*; [against] protection *f*, garantie *f* (contre); [Fin., usual. pl.] valeur *f*, titre *m*; [pledge] garantie *f*; [Pers.] garant *m*; ~ *police*, sûreté *f*; *Security Council*, Conseil *m* de sécurité: *to be* ~ *for*, se porter garant de.

sedan [sə'dæn] *n.* conduite *f* intérieure, limousine *f*: © sedan *m*: [Hist.] ~ *chair*, chaise *f* à porteurs.

sedate [sə'dejt] *adj.* calme, discret; [Pers.] calme, posé. || **sedative** ['sɛdətɪv] *adj.* & *n.* sédatif *m.*

sedentary ['sɛdn̩ˌtɛərɪ] *adj.* sédentaire.

sediment ['sɛdɪmənt] *n.* sédiment *m*; [wine] lie *f*; [Chem.] résidu *m.* || **sedimentary** [ˌsɛdɪ'mɛntərɪ] *adj.* sédimentaire, d'alluvions.

sedition [sədɪʃ|ən] *n.* sédition *f.* || **seditious** [-əʃ] *adj.* séditieux.

seduce [sə'djuws] *v. tr.* corrompre; [a woman] séduire. || **seducer** [-ə˞] *n.* corrupteur *m*, corruptrice *f*; séducteur *m*, séductrice *f.* || **seduction** [sə'dʌk|ʃən] *n.* **1.** [Pej.] corruption *f*, séduction *f*. **2,** charme *m*; attrait *m.* || **seductive** [-tɪv] *adj.* [not Pej.] séduisant, attrayant; alléchant.

see[1] [sij], **saw** [sɔ], **seen** [sijn] *v. tr.* **1.** voir, apercevoir; distinguer; consulter: *I can't* ~ *it*, Je ne le vois pas; *I saw him/do, doing/it*, Je l'ai vu/(le) faire, qui le faisait/; *not fit to be seen*, pas présentable; *You should* ~ *a lawyer*, Vous devriez consulter un avocat; *I'll* ~ *you/soon, on Tuesday/*; A/bientôt, mardi/; *He can't* ~ *you now*, Il ne peut pas vous recevoir en ce moment; *Let me, Let's/* ~ *your new knife*, Faites(-moi) voir votre nouveau canif. **2.** [understand] voir, comprendre, saisir; [notice] s'apercevoir: *Do you* ~ *what I mean?*, Vous/voyez, comprenez, saisissez/ce que je veux dire?; *I saw that he was disappointed*, J'ai vu, Je me suis aperçu/qu'il était déçu; *That remains to be seen*, Cela reste à savoir, On verra bien. **3.** veiller, s'assurer: *See (to it) that he finishes it*, Veillez à ce que, Faites (attention), Assurez-vous/ qu'il le finisse; *See that you don't do it again*, Faites attention de ne plus recommencer. || *v. intr.* **1.** voir: *Dogs don't* ~ *well*, Les chiens/ne voient pas bien, ont la vue faible/; *Let me* ~, *Let's* ~, [show] Faites voir, [wait] Voyons, Attendez/(un peu); *See here!*, Dites donc, Voyons! **2.** [Fig.] voir, comprendre: *I* ~ *!*, Je comprends!, Je vois ce que c'est!; . . . *you* ~ . . . , . . . voyez-vous . . . ; *See?*, Vous comprenez? || **see about** [-ə'bawt] *v. intr.* s'occuper de: *We'll* ~ *that*, C'est ce que nous allons voir. || **seeing (that)** [-ɪŋ] *conj.* étant donné que, vu que, puisque. || **see off** [-'ɔf] *v. tr.* accompagner (qqun jusqu'à la gare, &c.); reconduire (jusqu'à la porte). || **see through** [-'θɹuw] *v. tr.* participer, assister/à (qqch.) jusqu'au bout: *I'll see it through*, Je tiendrai jusqu'au bout. || *v. intr.* voir à travers (qqch.); [Fig.] voir clair dans, pénétrer/(qqch.). || **see to** [-'tuw] *v. intr.* s'occuper de (qqun, qqch.), veiller/sur (qqun), à (qqch.)/: *I'll* ~ *it*, Je m'en occupe(rai). cf. see *intr.* §3.

see[2] *n.* archevêché *m*, siège *m* épiscopal: *Holy* ~, Saint-Siège *m.*

seed [sijd] *n.* graine *f*; semence *f*, semences *fpl*; pépin *m*; [Fig.] progéniture *f.* || *v. tr.* semer, ensemencer. || *v. intr.* monter en graine [= to go to seed].

seek [sijk] *v. tr.* [after, for] chercher, s'efforcer de trouver; [aim] poursuivre; [favour] briguer. || *v. intr.* se livrer à des recherches. || **seek to** [-'tuw] *v. intr.* essayer, tenter/de.

seem [sijm] *v. intr.* [external evidence] paraître, [Fam.] avoir l'air; [belief] sembler; [sensation] avoir l'impression: *She seems happy*, Elle/paraît, a l'air, [but may not] semble/heureuse; *He seems to understand*, Il/paraît, a l'air de, [but may not] semble/comprendre; *He seems sick to me*, Il me/paraît, semble/ malade; *It seems that he is rich*, [gossip]

Il paraît qu'il est riche, [qualified statement] Il semble qu'il soit riche; *so it seems*, à ce qu'il paraît; *It seems to me that . . .* , Il me semble que + indic. [☞ + subjunct., if neg. or interrog.]; *I seemed to be falling, It seemed to me/that I was, as if I were, as though I were/falling*, Il me semblait/tomber, que je tombais/, J'avais l'impression/de tomber, que je tombais/; *It seemed like a dream*, On aurait dit un rêve. || **seeming** [-ɪŋ] *adj. a ~ advantage*, un avantage apparent. || *n.* apparence *f*, ressemblance *f.* || **seemingly** [-ɪŋlɪ] *adv.* en apparence. || **seemly** [-lɪ] *adj.* gracieux; [proper] bienséant, convenable.

seen cf. SEE[1].

seep [sijp] *v. intr.* suinter; *~ in*, s'infiltrer.

seer [sijɚ] *n.* [Fig.] prophète *m.*

seesaw ['sij,sɔ] *n.* bascule *f*, balançoire *f*, © balancigne *f.*

seethe [sijð] *v. intr.* [also Fig.] bouillonner, s'agiter. || **seething** [-ɪŋ] *adj.* bouillonnant, agité; [Fig.] en ébullition, en effervescence.

segment ['sɛgmənt] *n.* segment *m.* || *v. tr. & intr.* (se) segmenter.

segregate ['sɛgɹə,gejt] *v. tr.* isoler, mettre à part. || *v. intr.* se disssocier (*from*, de). || **segregation** [,sɛgɹə'gejʃən] *n.* ségrégation *f.*

seize ['sij|z] *v. tr.* saisir; s'emparer de, se saisir de; [Jur.] saisir (qqch.), arrêter (qqun); [Fig.] saisir, comprendre. || *v. intr.* se saisir (*upon*, de); [bearing] gripper, coincer. || **seizure** [-ʒɚ] *n.* prise *f*; capture *f*; [Jur.] arrestation *f* (d'une personne); saisie *f* (d'un bien); [Med.] attaque *f* cf. FIT.

seldom ['sɛldəm] *adv.* rarement, peu souvent.

select [sɪ'lɛk|t] *v. tr.* choisir (*from*, parmi); faire choix de; [Com.] sélectionner, trier. || *adj.* choisi, de (premier) choix, d'élite; chic. || **selection** [-ʃən] *n.* [anthology] recueil *m* (de morceaux choisis); [Mus.] extrait *m.* || **selective** [-tɪv] *adj.* sélectif.

self [sɛl|f] *pl.* **selves** [-z] *n.* **1.** individualité *f*, personnalité *f.* **2.** égoïsme *m*, intérêt *m* personnel; [Phil.] moi *m*, ego *m*: *o.'s better ~*, notre bon côté; *my other ~*, un autre moi-même, cf. SHADOW. || **self-adjusting** [,sɛlf|ə'ʤʌstɪŋ] *adj.* à réglage, automatique. || **self-centred** [-'sɛntɚd] *adj.* égocentrique. || **self-command** [-kə'mænd] *n.* maîtrise *f* de soi. || **self-confidence** [,sɛlf|'kɑnfɪdəns] *n.* confiance *f* en soi. || **self-confident** [-'kɑnfɪdənt] *adj.* sûr de soi. || **self-conscious** [-'kɑnʃəs] *adj.* gêné, embarrassé. || **self-consciousness** [-nəs] *n.* gêne *f*, embarras *m*, respect *m* humain. || **self-criticism** [-'kɹɪtɪ,sɪzm] *n.* autocritique *f.* || **self-defence** [-də,fɛns] *n.* instinct *m* de conservation: *in ~*, en légitime défense *f.* || **self-esteem** [-ə'stijm] *n.* amour-propre *m.* || **self-examination** [-ɪg,zæmɪ'nejʃən] *n.* examen *m* de conscience. || **self-explanatory** [-ks'plænətɔɚɪ] *adj.* → qui s'explique de soi-même, évident. || **self-governing** [-'gʌvɚnɪŋ] *adj.* autonome. || **selfish** ['sɛlfɪʃ] *adj.* égoïste; [motive] personnel. || **selfishness** [-nəs] *n.* égoïsme *m.* || **self-made** [-'mejd] *adj.* autodidacte: *~ man*, fils *m* de ses œuvres. || **self-possessed** [-pə'zɛst] *adj.* maître *m* de soi, de sang-froid. || **self-preservation** [-,pɹɛzɚ'vejʃən] *n.* (instinct *m* de) conservation *f.* || **self-respect** [,sɛlf|ɹɪs'pɛkt] *n.* dignité *f* personnelle, respect *m* de soi. || **self-satisfied** [-'sætɪs,fajd] *adj.* [Fig.] content de soi, suffisant. || **self-service** [-'sɚvɪs] *n.* auto-service *m.* || **self-suggestion** [-səg'ʤɛstʃən] *n.* autosuggestion *f.* || **self-supporting** [-sə'pɔɚtɪŋ] *adj.* [venture] qui couvre ses frais; [Pers.] qui subvient à ses propres besoins, indépendant financièrement. || **self-taught** [-'tɔt] *adj.* autodidacte. || **self-winding** [-'wajndɪŋ] *adj.* à remontage automatique.

sell [sɛll] *v. tr.* vendre (de la marchandise, &c.); [Fig.] faire accepter (une idée), persuader, convaincre (qqun de faire qqch.): *He was sold on that idea*, On l'avait/persuadé, convaincu/. || *v. intr.* [object, &c.] se vendre: *This article is selling well this year*, Cet article se vend bien cette année. || **seller** ['sɛlɚ] *n.* vendeur *m*, marchand *m*; [Com.] *best- ~*, succès *m* de librairie: *a good ~*, article *m* /qui se vend bien, qui se vend tout seul/. || **sell out** *v. intr.* vendre (tout ce qu'on a): *to be sold out*, jouer à/ bureaux, guichets/fermés; [book trade] (édition) épuisé.

semantics [sə'mæntɪks] *n.sing.* sémantique *f*; [Tech.] vocabulaire *m* spécialisé.

semblance ['sɛmbləns] *n.* air *m*, apparence *f.*

semester [sə'mɛstɚ] *n.* semestre *m.*

semicolon ['sɛmɪ,kowlən] *n.* point-virgule *m.* || **semi-detached** *adj.* accolé, jumelé.

seminary ['sɛmɪ,nɛɚɪ] *n.* [Rel.] séminaire *m*; [Sch.] © collège *m.*

senate ['sɛnət] *n.* sénat *m.* || **senator** [-ɚ] *n.* sénateur *m.*

send [sɛnd], **sent** [sɛnt], **sent** *v. tr.* envoyer, expédier (une lettre, un colis); lancer (une balle, &c.); [cause] faire [+ inf.]: *to ~*

s.o. running, faire sauver qqun; *to ~ s.o. crazy*, rendre qqun fou. || *v. intr.*: *to ~ after s.o.*, envoyer chercher qqun; *to ~ for a doctor*, aller chercher le médecin; *to ~ forth* (*light*, *&c.*), émettre (des rayons, &c.) exhaler, dégager (une odeur). || **send away** [sɛnd|ə'wej] [servant] congédier, chasser; [parcel] expédier. || **send down** [-'dawn] faire descendre; [Br., Sch.] renvoyer (un élève). || **send in** [-'ɪn] faire entrer (qqun); [resignation] remettre (sa démission). || **send off** [-'ɔf] renvoyer; [colis] expédier; accompagner (qqun) à la gare, &c. || *n.* fête *f* d'adieu.

sender [-ɚ] *n.* expéditeur *m.*

senile ['sɛnajl] *adj.* sénile. || **senility** [sə'nɪlɪtɪ] *n.* sénilité *f.*

senior ['sijnjɚ] *adj.* **1.** [age] aîné. **2.** [rank] supérieur: *~ staff*, personnel hors classe: *Mr. Smith Senior*, M. Smith père; *~ year*, dernière année (d'études). || *n.* [Sch.] élève *m*, étudiant *m*/de dernière année: *He is two years my ~*, Il est mon aîné de deux ans. || **seniority** [sɪn'jɔɚɪtɪ] *n.* [age] aînesse *f*; [rank] ancienneté *f.*

sensation [sɛn'sejʃən] *n.* **1.** [physical] sensation *f*, impression *f.* **2.** sentiment *m.* **3.** [Fig.] sensation *f*: *to make a ~*, faire sensation. || **sensational** [ˌsɛn'sejʃənl̩] *adj.* sensationnel, → à sensation. || **sensationalism** [-ɪzm] *n.* recherche *f* du sensationnel.

sense [sɛns] *n.* [body, logical] sens *m*; [awareness] sentiment *m*; [feeling] impression *f*; [opinion] avis *m*; [good] bon sens, sens commun: *It does not make ~*, Cela n'a pas de (bon) sens, C'est insensé; [word] sens *m*, acception *f*, signification *f*; [Med., *pl.*] connaissance *f*: *in a ~*, dans un (certain) sens; *in the literal sense*, au sens propre; *in the ~ that*, en ce sens que. || **senseless** [-ləs] *adj.* **1.** [body, thing] insensible, inanimé. **2.** [Pers.] insensé. || **sensibility** [ˌsɛnsɪ'bɪlɪtɪ] *n.* sensibilité *f*; finesse *f* de perception; *sensibilities pl.* susceptibilité *f.* || **sensible** ['sɛnsɪ|bl̩] [Pers. statement] sensé, raisonnable, doué de bon sens. || **sensibly** [-bl̩ɪ] *adv.* [augment] perceptiblement, sensiblement; raisonnablement, avec bon sens. || **sensitive** [-tɪv] *adj.* [skin, &c.] sensible; [Pers.] sensible, sensitif, impressionnable; [Fig., Pers.] susceptible. || **sensitivity** [ˌsɛnsɪ'tɪvɪtɪ] *n.* [body] sensibilité *f* (à, *to*); [character] sensibilité *f*, susceptibilité *f.* || **sensual** ['sɛnʃuwəl] *adj.* sensuel; voluptueux. || **sensuality** [ˌsɛnʃuw'ælɪtɪ] *n.* sensualité *f.* || **sensuous** ['sɛnʃuwəs] *adj.* voluptueux; [style] sensuel.

sent cf. SEND.

sentence ['sɛntəns] *n.* **1.** phrase *f.* **2.** [Jur.] jugement *m*, sentence *f* (de mort). || *v. tr.* [law] condamner (qqun): *to be sentenced to death*, être condamné à mort; [judge] prononcer une sentence, un jugement, un arrêt (contre qqun).

sentiment ['sɛntɪmənt] *n.* [opinion, advice] sentiment *m*, opinion *f*, avis *m.* || **sentimental** [ˌsɛntɪ'mɛntl̩] *adj.* **1.** sentimental. **2.** impressionnable, émotif. **3.** sensible. || **sentimentality** [ˌsɛntɪmɛn'tælɪtɪ] *n.* **1.** sentimentalité *f.* **2.** sensiblerie *f.* || **sentimentalize** [ˌsɛntɪ'mɛntl̩'ajz] *v. intr.* faire du sentiment.

sentinel ['sɛntɪnl̩] *n.* sentinelle *f*: *to stand ~*, monter la garde.

sentry ['sɛntɹɪ] *n.* **1.** sentinelle *f.* **2.** garde *m*: *to stand ~* (*over*), monter la garde (auprès de): *~ -box*, guérite *f.*

separable ['sɛpɚəbl̩] séparable (*from*, de). || **separate** ['sɛpɚət] *adj.* séparé; distinct; à part, à l'écart; isolé; privé: © *~ school*, © école *f* séparée. || *v. tr.* ['sɛpɚˌejt] séparer, désunir (des amis, &c.), détacher (de, *from*). || *v. intr.* se séparer, se désunir, se détacher (de, *from*), se quitter. || **separately** ['sɛpɚətlɪ] *adv.* séparément, à part, individuellement. || **separation** [sɛpɚ'ejʃən] *n.* séparation *f*, désunion *f*, [US] démobilisation *f.* || **separatism** ['sɛpɚətɪzm] *n.* séparatisme *m.*

September [səp'tɛmbɚ] *n.* (le mois de) septembre *m.*

septic ['sɛptɪk] *adj.* septique.

sepulchre ['sɛpl̩kɚ] *n.* sépulcre *m*, tombeau *m.*

sepulture ['sɛpl̩tʃɚ] *n.* sépulture *f.*

sequel ['sijkwəl] *n.* **1.** suite *f.* **2.** résultat *m*, conséquence *f.* **3.** suite *f* (d'une histoire, d'un discours).

sequence ['sijkwəns] *n.* **1.** succession *f* (des faits). **2.** ordre *m* (de succession) [cards, Cin.] séquence *f*; [Gram.] *the ~ of tenses*, concordance *f* des temps.

sequester [sɪ'kwɛstɚ] *v. tr.* isoler: *a sequestered life*, une vie retirée; *the sequestered pool*, l'étang mystérieux. || *v. intr.* [Pers.] se séquestrer. © se renfermer. || **sequestration** [sɪˌkwɛs'tɹejʃən] *n.* **1.** [Law] séquestre *m*, saisie *f.* **2.** séquestration *f* (d'une personne).

serenade [sɚə'nejd] *n.* [song] sérénade *f.* || *v. tr.* donner une sérénade à.

serene [sɚ'ijn] *adj.* **1.** paisible, calme: *a ~ smile*, un sourire serein. **2.** [weather] clair. || **serenity** [sɚ'ɛnɪtɪ] *n.* **1.** paix *f*, tranquillité *f*, calme *m*, sérénité *f.* **2.** clarté *f* (du ciel).

serfdom ['sɚfdəm] *n.* servage *m.*
sergeant ['sɑɚdʒənt] *n.* [army] sergent *m*; [Fr. cavalry, artillery] maréchal *m* des logis; [policeman] [Fr.] brigadier *m.* || **sergeant-at-arms** [-ət,ɑɚmz] *n.* [Parliament] © sergent *m* d'armes, [Fr.] commandant *m* militaire (du Parlement). || **sergeant-major** [-mejdʒɚ] *n.* sergent major *m.*
serial ['sijɚɪəl] *adj.* de série: ~ *number*- matricule *m*, numéro *m*/d'ordre, d'im, matriculation/. || roman-feuilleton *m.*
series ['sijɚɪz] *n.* série *f* (*in*, en); suite *f*: [US, Sport]: *the World Series*, (les parties *fpl* du) championnat mondial.
serious ['sijɚɪəs] *adj.* [earnest] sérieux, [illness, &c.] grave: *Be* ~ , → Ne plaisantez pas. **seriously** [-lɪ] *adv.* sérieusement; gravement: *to take* ~, prendre au sérieux. || **seriousness** [-nəs] *n.* sérieux *m*; gravité *f.*
sermon ['sɚmən] *n.* [Rel.] sermon *m* [also Fig.]; [R.C.] prône *m*, [Prot.] prêche *m.*
serpent ['sɚpənt] *n.* serpent *m*; [Fig., Pers.] renard *m*, filou *m.*
serrated [sɛɚ'ejtəd] *adj.* en dents de scie.
serum ['sijɚəm] *n.* sérum *m.*
servant ['sɚvənt] *n.* **1.** domestique *m*; serviteur *m*, servante *f*; **servants,** †gens *mpl* de maison; [hotel] personnel *m.* **2.** employé(e) *m*(*f*): *civil* ~ , fonctionnaire *m.*
serve [sɚv] *v. tr.* servir, être au service de (qqun); rendre service, être utile à (qqun); [food] servir (un repas, qqun); [transportation] desservir (une ville); [Jur.] subir (une peine); [subpœna] signifier (une assignation à qqun); [Fig.] répondre à (un besoin); satisfaire, suffire à/(qqun); [tennis] servir (la balle): *to* ~ *the purpose*, servir, faire l'affaire; *to* ~ *the purpose of*, remplacer, tenir lieu de, jouer le rôle de; *to* ~ *3 years in prison*, faire 3 ans de prison; *It serves you right*, C'est bien fait (pour vous); *It serves you right for . . .* , Ça vous apprendra à . . . || *v. intr.* servir, être utile, rendre service; [Mil.] servir: *It will* ~ , Cela/servira, fera l'affaire/; *to* ~ *as*, servir de, tenir lieu de: *That will* ~ *to convince him*, Cela servira à le persuader; *to* ~ *on a committee*, être (membre) d'un comité. || *n.* [tennis] service *m*: *Your* ~ , À vous de servir. || **serve out** [-'awt] *v. intr.* se venger de, rendre la pareille à; distribuer. || **server** ['sɚv|ɚ] *n.* serveu|r, -se; [R.C.] servant *m* (de messe), acolyte *m.*
service ['sɚv|ɪs] *n.* **1.** [Adm.] service *m*, bureau *m*: *civil* ~ , fonctionnariat *m*, administration *f*; © [abus.] le service civil. **2.** service *m*; utilité *f*, aide *f*: *to be of* ~ *to*, rendre service à, se rendre utile à; *at your* ~ , à votre service; [Com.] service *m*, pourboire *m.* **3.** [Mil.] *the services*, l'armée *f*, l'aviation *f* et la marine; *national, compulsory/* ~ , service militaire (obligatoire). || **serviceable** [-ɪsabl̩] *adj.* **1.** utile, profitable, avantageux, solide. **2.** [Pers.] serviable: *They are* ~ *to you*, Ils vous rendent service. || **service-station** [-ɪs'stejʃn̩] *n.* station-service *f*, pompe *f* (à essence).
serviette [,sɚɪ'ɛt] *n.* serviette *f* (de table).
servile ['sɚv|ajl] *adj.* **1.** servile, bas. **2.** asservi.
serving [-ɪŋ] *n.* service *m*; [dish] portion *f*; [tennis] service *m*; [Jur.] signification *f.* || *pres. p.*: ~ *two cities*, au service de deux villes.
servitude [-ɪ,tjuwd] *n.* **1.** esclavage *m*, servitude *f.* **2.** *penal* ~ , travaux *mpl* forcés.
session ['sɛʃən] *n.* **1.** séance *f* (de la cour, du conseil, de délibération). **2.** réunion *f*, assemblée *f.* **3.** [Parliament] session *f*: *to be in* ~ , siéger. **4.** [US] période *f* d'étude, trimestre *m.* || **sessional** [-l̩] *adj.* de session; [Pol.] [indemnity] parlementaire.
set [sɛt] *n.* **1.** jeu *m* (d'outils, de pièces); série *f* (de billets, de casseroles); service *m* (de porcelaine); batterie *f* (de cuisine); série, collection *f* (complète) (de livres); garniture *f* (de cheminée, bureau); parure *f* (de pierres précieuses); corps *m*, ensemble *m* (de doctrines): *a dressing table* ~ , garniture *f* de toilette; ~ *of furniture*, mobilier *m*; *construction* ~ , jeu *m* de construction. **2.** [Radio, TV] poste *m*; © [radio receiver] appareil *m* (de radio). **3.** [social] groupe *m*; société *f*; [Pej.] coterie *f*; bande *f* (de voleurs): *the smart* ~, le monde élégant; *in their* ~ , dans leur milieu. **4.** [tennis] set *m.* **5.** conformation *f*; attitude *f*; disposition *f*; arrangement *m* (d'un groupe d'objets); assiette *f* (d'un appareil, objet, bâtiment); tournure *f* (d'une robe, d'un manteau, chapeau). **6.** [Cin.] plateau *m*, décor *m*, mise *f* en scène (d'une pièce). || **set** *adj.* [time] fixé; [price] fixe; [rule] établi; [purpose] ferme (intention): [phrase] (expression) consacrée, (locution) figee; [task] assigné; [smile] figé; [face] immobile, impassible: *He is* ~ *in his ways*, Il a ses habitudes à lui: *to be* (*all*) ~ /*to, for*/ *. . .* , être (tout) prêt à . . . ; *to be* ~ *on . . .* , être résolu à . . . || **set, set, set,**

setting [-ɪŋ] *v. tr.* **1.** [place] mettre, placer; [put down] poser, déposer; [table] mettre le couvert, © mettre la table; monter (une pierre précieuse); planter (des graines, un pieu); faire couver (une poule); dresser, tendre (un piège à); [type] composer (une page); mettre (des paroles en musique); [Fig., rank] ranger (parmi): *to have one's heart ~ (on)*, avoir (qqch.) à cœur, avoir à cœur (de faire qqch.); *a ring ~ with diamonds*, une bague sertie de diamants; *The scene is ~ in . . .*, La scène se passe à . . . **2.** [fix] fixer (un prix, un dernier délai, une date); assigner (une valeur à, un certain temps pour, des limites à/qqch.); régler (une montre sur); mettre (une montre) à l'heure; régler (des commandes); ajuster (des pièces); remettre (un membre cassé); faire prendre (la gelée); serrer (les dents); donner l'exemple, un problème à résoudre); composer, rédiger (un examen): *to ~ great store by sth.*, attacher un grand prix à qqch. **3.** [start] mettre (qqun à faire qqch.), faire (faire qqch. à qqun), donner (qqch. à faire à qqun); lancer (une mode); *to ~ going*, mettre (une machine) en marche, mettre (des pourparlers) en train; déclencher (un mécanisme, une conversation); *to ~ s.o. on the/right, wrong/track*, diriger qqun sur la/bonne, mauvaise/piste; *to ~ /a dog, the police/ on(to), after/s.o.*, lancer un chien, mettre la police/ aux trousses de qqun; [Fig.] *to ~ the/stone, ball/rolling*, mettre une affaire en branle; *to ~ s.o.'s teeth on edge*, agacer qqun. || *v. intr.* [sun] se coucher; [hen] couver; [jelly] prendre; [bone] se ressouder; [cement] durcir; [expression] se figer; [character] se former; [dress] (bien, mal) tomber; [current] porter: *to ~ to work*, se mettre au travail. || **set about** [ə'bawt] *v. intr.* commencer, se mettre à: *to ~ it*, s'y prendre. || **set against** [-ə'gɛnst] *v. tr.* prévenir, indisposer (qqun) contre (qqun); comparer (qqch.) à (qqch.). || **set apart** [-ə'pɑɚt] *v. tr.* mettre (qqch.) à part, réserver (qqch.); isoler (qqun). || **set aside** [-ə'sajd] *v. tr.* mettre d'un côté; [Fig.] mettre (de l'argent) de côté, réserver; écarter (ses préjugés); rejeter, annuler (un jugement). || **set back** [-'bæk] *v.tr.* retarder (une montre, le progrès). || **set-back** [-ˌbæk] *n.* échec *m*; recul *m* (dans les affaires); [sickness] rechute *f*: *to have a ~* , subir un échec, faire une rechute. || **set down** [-'dawn] *v. tr.* poser, déposer; mettre (qqch.) par écrit, inscrire (un nom); attribuer (qqch.) à. || **set forth** [-'fɔɚθ] *v. intr.* se mettre en route, partir. || *v. tr.* énoncer (une proposition); exposer (des motifs), avancer (une théorie); proposer (une explication). || **set forward** [-'fɔɚwɚd] *v. tr.* avancer. || **set in** [-'ɪn] *v. intr.* commencer; s'annoncer, se déclarer. || **set off** [-'ɔf] *v. intr.* se mettre en route. || *v. tr.* faire ressortir, rehausser, relever (des charmes); exploser, faire partir. || **set out** [-'awt] *v. intr.* partir, se mettre en route. || *v. tr.* disposer, étaler (des marchandises); exposer (des raisons). || **set square** [-ˌskwɛɚ] *n.* équerre *f* (à dessin). || **setting** [-ɪŋ] *n.* **1.** cadre *m* (d'un récit); [Theat.] mise *f* en scène; [jewellery] monture *f* (d'une pierre précieuse); [Mus.] arrangement *m* (pour un instrument). **2.** disposition *f*, arrangement *m* (de qqch.); réglage *m* (d'une montre, d'une horloge); ajustage *m* (d'un mécanisme). **3.** coucher *m* (du soleil). **4.** imposition *f* (d'une tâche); fixation *f* (d'une date). **5.** recollement *m* (d'un os); prise *f* (du ciment). **6.** [poultry] couvée *f*. || **set to** [-'tuw] *v. intr.* se mettre au travail, s'y mettre. || **set-to** [-ˌtuw] *n.*: *to have a ~* , en venir aux/coups, injures/, avoir une violente discussion. || **set up** [-'ʌp] *v. tr.* monter, élever, dresser; fonder (une société); établir (une école); instaurer (un règne); causer; pousser (une clameur); [health] remettre (d'aplomb); proposer (comme modèle): *to set o.s. up as*, s'ériger en . . . || *v. intr.* s'établir (dans le commerce). || **set-up** [-ˌʌp] *n.* installation *f*; arrangement *m*: [Sl.] *It's a ~ !*, C'est du tout cuit.

settle ['sɛtl̩] *v. tr.* décider, déterminer, convaincre; calmer, apaiser; fixer (une date); résoudre (un problème); régler (une affaire, une facture, une dette); établir, installer/(qqun quelque part); coloniser (une région), assigner (un héritage): *Settled!*, Entendu! || *v. intr.* s'établir, s'installer; se calmer, s'apaiser; [sediment] déposer; [bird] se poser; [house] se tasser; [Com.] régler une note, &c.: *to get settled*, s'organiser, s'installer /dans une nouvelle demeure/; *to ~ in Vancouver*, (aller) se fixer à V.; *to ~ on sth.*, se décider pour qqch. || **settle down** *v. intr.* s'établir (quelque part); [be less wild] se ranger: *to ~ to a job*, s'appliquer à une tâche. || **settlement** [-mənt] *n.* **1.** établissement *m*, colonie *f*; localité *f*. **2.** [arrangement] règlement *m*; [debt] liquidation *f*; [Jur.] rente *f*, pension *f*: *marriage ~* , contrat *m* de mariage.
settler [-ɚ] *n.* colon *m*.

seven ['sɛvn̩] *adj. & n.* sept (*m*): *the ~ Seas,* les mers du globe. || **seventeen** [ˌsɛvn̩'tijn] *adj. & n.* (*m*) dix-sept. || **seventeenth** [ˌsɛvn̩'tijnθ] *adj. & n.* dix-septième (*m*); [date] le dix-sept. || **seventh** ['sevn̩|θ] *adj. & n.* septième (*m*). || **seventieth** [-tɪəθ] *adj. & n.* soixante-dixième (*m*). || **seventy** [-tɪ] *adj. & n.* soixante-dix (*m*).

sever ['sɛvɚ] *v. tr.* séparer, couper; détacher (*from,* de); [Fig.] rompre.

several ['sɛvɚl̩] *adj.* **1.** plusieurs. **2.** distinct, séparé: *on two ~ occasions,* à deux reprises. || *pron.* plusieurs. || **severally** [-lɪ] *adv.* séparément, individuellement.

severance [-əns] *n.* séparation *f*; interruption *f* (de rapports), rupture *f.*

severe [sə'vijɚ] *adj.* **1.** sévère; [penalty] rigoureux. **2.** violent; [illness] grave; [pain] aigu; [climate] rigoureux; [criticism] mordant. || **severely** [-lɪ] **1.** sévèrement, avec sévérité. **2.** violemment; [Med.] gravement malade: *~ wounded,* grièvement blessé. || **severity** [sə'vɛəɪtɪ] *n.* sévérité *f*; [penalty, climate] rigueur *f*; [Med.] gravité *f,* [pain] acuité *f.*

sew [sow], **sewed** [-d], **sewed** or **sewn** [-n] *v. tr.* coudre: *to ~ on a button,* coudre un bouton; *to ~ up,* coudre, raccommoder; [livre] brocher. || *v. intr.* coudre, faire de la couture.

sewage ['suwədʒ] *n.* eaux *fpl* d'égouts: *~ -farm,* champs *mpl* d'épandage. || **sewer** ['suwɚ] *n.* égout *m.* || **sewerage** [-ədʒ] cf. SEWAGE.

sewing ['sowɪŋ] *n.* couture *f.*: *~ -machine,* machine *f* à coudre.

sex [sɛks] *n.* sexe *m.* || **sexual** [-juwl̩] *adj.* sexuel. || **sexy** [-ɪ] *adj.* [Fam.] excitant: *to be ~,* avoir du sex-appeal.

shabbily ['ʃæb|ɪlɪ] *adv.* [behaviour] mesquinement; *~ dressed,* mal mis, mal habillé. || **shabbiness** [-ɪnəs] *n.* pauvreté *f,* délabrement *m* (d'une maison, &c.); [clothes] râpé, → en piteux état; [behaviour] mesquinerie *f,* petitesse *f.* || **shabby** [-ɪ] *adj.* [clothes] râpé, élimé; [Pers.] mal/mis, vêtu/; [mean] mesquin, petit; [house] pauvre, misérable, délabré.

shack [ʃæk] *n.* cabane *f,* hutte *f.*

shackle ['ʃækl̩] *n.* boucle *f*; *pl.* [prisoner] fers *mpl,* [horse, &c.] entraves *fpl.* || *v. tr.* mettre les fers à; entraver.

shade [ʃejd] *n.* **1.** ombre *f*: *in the ~,* à l'ombre; [pl.] ombres *fpl,* ténèbres *fpl*; [classics] les Enfers *mpl*; fantôme *m,* ombre *f*: [Fam.] *to put s.o. in the ~,* éclipser qqun. **2.** [small quantity] un soupçon *m* (de lait, &c.); nuance *f*: *a ~ too long,* un/peu, rien/trop long. **3.** [screen] écran *m*; [lamp] abat-jour *m.* || *v. tr.* ombrager; [light] voiler, atténuer; [paint] estomper; [Fig.] nuancer. || *v. intr.* se fondre (*into,* en). || **shaded** ['ʃejdəd] *adj.* ombragé: *a garden ~ by two majestic oaks,* un jardin qu'ombragent deux chênes majestueux.

shadow ['ʃædow] *n.* **1.** ombre *f*: *The lamp-post casts a ~ across the road,* Le réverbère projette son ombre sur la chaussée; *He hid in the ~ of the barn,* Il se dissimula dans l'ombre de la grange; [Fig.] *There is not the ~ of a doubt,* Il n'y a pas l'ombre d'un doute; [Fig.] *He is afraid of his own ~,* Il a peur de son ombre; *He is a mere ~ of his former self,* Il n'est plus que l'ombre de lui-même. **2.** [ghost] ombre, fantôme *m.* **3.** [Fig.] *He is his brother's ~,* Il est le compagnon inséparable de son frère. **4.** silhouette *f* indécise; [microscopy] image *f* imprécise; [photo, X-rays] noir *m*: *He was too much in the ~,* Il se trouvait trop dans le noir; [radar] tache *f*; *~ region,* zone *f* de silence; *to have shadows under o.'s eyes,* avoir les yeux cernés. **5.** [Fig.] *His arrival cast a ~ of gloom over the assembled company,* Son arrivée jeta un voile de tristesse sur l'assemblée. **6.** [*pl.*] *the shadows,* le crépuscule. || **shadow** *v. tr.* [detective] filer, pister (qqun). || **shadowy** [-ɪ] *adj.* [Fig.] *He led a ~ existence,* Il menait une existence obscure.

shady ['ʃejdɪ] *adj.* **1.** vague, indécis, imprécis: *He could make out ~ forms in the darkness,* Il arrivait à distinguer dans l'obscurité des formes indécises. **2.** ombreux, ombragé: *~ nook* (*of a garden, &c.*), coin *m* ombreux (dans un jardin, &c.); *~ walk,* allée *f* couverte. **3.** louche, douteux: *~ dealings,* activités louches; *~ character,* louche individu.

shaft [ʃæft] *n.* **1.** flèche *f,* lance *f,* [Fig.] trait *m*; [of a spear] hampe *f,* bois *m*; [of an arrow] bois *m*; [Arch.] tige *f,* fût *m* (d'une colonne); [Bot., stem; feather] tige *f*; [flag] mât *m*; [golf club] manche *m.* **2.** [of a horse-drawn vehicle] brancard *m,* limon *m.* **3.** [mine, elevator] puits *m* (de mine, d'ascenseur). **4.** [Mech.] *drive ~,* arbre *m* de transmission; *crankshaft,* arbre-manivelle *m,* arbre coudé, [Auto] vilebrequin *m*; *propeller-shaft,* arbre de l'hélice. **5.** [light, sunlight] rayon *m* (de lumière, de soleil): *a ~ of lightning,* un éclair.

shaggy ['ʃægɪ] *adj.* **1.** velu, poilu, touffu; à poils longs: *a ~ dog,* barbet *m.* **2.** hérissé; raboteux, inégal.

shagreen [ʃə'gɹijn] *n.* [leather] peau *f* de chagrin.

shake [ʃejk], **shook** [ʃʊk], **shaken** [ʃejkn̩] *v. tr.* **1.** [child, rug, tree, &c.] secouer: *to ~ one's head,* hocher la tête; *Montana was shaken by an earthquake,* Un tremblement de terre secoua le M.; *to ~ hands with s.o.,* serrer la main à qqun; [Fam.] *~ a leg!,* Grouillez-vous un peu! **2.** [liquids in containers] agiter; [thermometer] secouer: *to ~ sth. loose,* dégager qqch.; *She shook herself loose from his grasp,* Elle se/dégagea, libéra/de son étreinte; [on bottles] *Shake well before using,* Agitez/le flacon, la bouteille/. **3.** [buildings, pieces of furniture, opinions, faith] ébranler; [Fig.] *His novel shook the English-speaking world,* Son roman troubla le public de langue anglaise; *She was utterly shaken by her experience,* Elle était toute bouleversée par son aventure; *Roman society was shaken to its very foundations,* La société romaine fut atteinte jusque dans ses assises. || *v. intr.* **1.** trembler: *His hand was shaking,* La main lui tremblait. **2.** [voice] chevroter, trembloter: *His voice shook,* Sa voix s'altéra (sous le coup de l'émotion); *Her voice was shaking with emotion,* Sa voix vibrait d'émotion; *He is shaking with cold,* Il grelotte de froid; [Fig.] *His courage began to be shaken,* Son courage commença à chanceler; *to ~ with laughter,* → se tenir les côtes. || *n.* secousse *f*; ébranlement *m*, tremblement *m*; [Mus.] trille *m*; [Fam.] *in two shakes,* in deux temps trois mouvements; *no great shakes,* sans grande importance, ordinaire. || **shake down** ['dawn] *v. tr.* faire tomber en secouant; [thermometer] secouer; [Fam.] faire cracher (de l'argent à qqun). || **shake off** [-'ɑʃ] *v. tr.* secouer: *to shake the snow off (o.'s garments),* secouer la neige (de ses vêtements); *to ~ o.'s pursuers,* semer, se débarrasser de/ ses poursuivants; *to ~ a cold,* se débarrasser d'un rhume. || **shake up** [-'ʌp] *v. tr.* [bottle] agiter; secouer (qqch., qqun) énergiquement; [Fig.] ébranler, agacer (les nerfs de qqun): *He was quite shaken up over the affair,* L'affaire l'a/bouleversé, fortement secoué.

shaken cf. SHAKE.

shaky ['ʃejkɪ] *adj.* tremblant, branlant; [voice] tremblotant; [writing] tremblé; [health] chancelant.

shall [ʃæl] *v. aux.* [☞ S'emploie selon l'usage le plus strict à la 1ère pers. pour indiquer la simple futurité, et aux 2e et 3e pers. pour le commandement, l'obligation, la promesse, la menace, &c. Cette distinction a plus ou moins disparu dans le langage parlé qui remplace *I, we/shall* par *I'll, we'll, I, we/shall not* par *I, we/ won't* ou *I'll, we'll/not,* et *Shall I, we/ not* par *Won't/I, we/*; *shall* s'emploie surtout aux 1ère et 3e pers. de l'interrogatif à l'affirmatif pour solliciter l'avis de l'interlocuteur. cf. WILL.] **1.** [simple future] *I ~ , I'll/tell him/at once, tomorrow/,* Je vais le lui dire tout de suite, Je le lui dirai demain/; *Shall I see you again before you leave?,* Est-ce que je vous reverrai avant votre départ?; *If I see him, I ~ , I'll/tell him,* Si je le vois, je le lui dirai. **2.** [future anterior] *I ~ , I'll/have/ finished, come, got up/before you,* J'aurai fini, Je serai arrivé, Je me serai levé/avant vous. **3.** [advice] vouloir; devoir: *Shall I help you?,* Voulez-vous que je vous aide?; *When ~ /I, he/come?,* A quelle heure/ dois-je, doit-il/arriver?; *Let's go to the movies, ~ we?,* Allons, Si nous allions/au cinéma, (voulez-vous)? **4.** [order, obligation] devoir: *This door ~ remain closed,* Cette porte/doit, devra/rester fermée; *You shall listen to me!,* J'exige que vous m'écoutiez! **5.** [promise, threat] *You ~ rue the day when . . . ,* Vous regretterez (amèrement) le jour où, *You ~ have a new one for Christmas,* Vous en aurez un nouveau pour Noël (c'est promis).

shallot [ʃə'lɑt] *n.* échalote *f.*

shallow ['ʃælow] *adj.* [water] peu profond; [dish] plat: *~ waters,* haut-fond *m*; [mind] superficiel, borné, léger. écueil *m.* || **shallowness** [-nəs] *n.* [water] peu *m* de profondeur; [mind] légèreté *f*, frivolité *f.*

sham [ʃæm] *n.* **1.** feinte *f*, simulacre *m*; comédie *f*, [person] imposteur *m.* **2.** imitation *f.* || *adj.* imité, feint, contrefait: *a ~ quarrel,* une fausse chicane.

shamble ['ʃæmbl̩] *v. intr.* marcher/lourdement, en traînant les pieds. || **shambles** [-z] *n.* abattoir *m*; boucherie *f*; [Fig.] pétaudière *f.*

shame [ʃejm] *n.* honte *f*; [self-respect] pudeur *f*: *Shame on you!, For ~ !,* Quelle honte!; *to put s.o. to ~ ,* faire honte à qqun; *What a ~ !,* Quelle honte!, [pity] Quel dommage!; *It is a ~ to do that,* Il est honteux de faire cela; [pity] *It is a ~ he can't be here,* C'est dommage qu'il ne puisse (pas) être ici. || *v. tr.* déshonorer, faire honte à (qqun). || **shamefaced** [-ˌfejst] *adj.* [Pers.] penaud. || **shameful** [-fl̩] *adj.* [Pers., action] honteux, [action] déshonorant. || **shameless** [-ləs] *adj.* éhonté, sans vergogne. || **shamelessness** [-ləsnəs] *n.* impudeur *f*, effronterie *f*.

shampoo [ˌʃæm'puw] *n.* **1.** shampooing *m.* **2.** massage *m.* || *v. tr.* **1.** faire un shampooing. **2.** masser.

shamrock ['ʃæmˌɹɑk] *n.* **1.** trèfle *m* rampant. **2.** luzerne *f.* **3.** [Irish emblem] trèfle *m.*

shank [ʃæŋk] *n.* [leg] tibia *m*, jambe *f*; [horse's leg] canon *m*; tuyau *m* (de pipe); tige *f* (d'une clé): [Fig.] *to go on Shank's /mare, pony/*, prendre le train onze.

shan't [ʃænt] [= SHALL NOT.]

shanty ['ʃæntɪ] *n.* cabane *f*; © [lumbering] chantier *m* [also *chanty*]: *~ -town*, bidonville *m.*

shape [ʃejp] *n.* forme *f*, figure *f*; [person's] taille *f*; [clothes] façon *f*, coupe *f*: *in the ~ of*, sous forme de; *to get out of ~*, se déformer; *to lick sth. into shape*, polir, fignoler, mettre qqch. au point; [Sport] *to be/in, out of ~/*, être/en forme, mal en point/; *to take ~*, prendre forme. || *v. tr.* former (l'esprit, &c.), façonner (un objet). || **shapeless** [-ləs] *adj.* informe, sans forme. || **shapely** ['ʃejplɪ] *adj.* beau; bien fait de sa personne; bien proportionné.

share [ʃɛɚ] *v. tr. & intr.* partager (qqch.), prendre part à (qqch.): *to ~ in a manifestation*, participer à une manifestation. || *n.* part *f.* (de profit, &c.); portion *f* (de nourriture); [Fin., Com.] valeur *f*, action *f.* || **shareholder** [-ˌhowldɚ] *n.* [company] actionnaire *m/f*, sociétaire *m/f.* || **shares** [-z] *npl.* cf. STOCK.

shark [ʃɑɚk] *n.* **1.** [fish] requin *m*; *cod ~*, aiguillot *m*, chien *m* de mer. **2.** [pers.] escroc *m.*

sharp [ʃɑɚp] *adj.* [angle, sound] aigu, [flavour, taste] acide, âcre; [curve] raide, brusque; [knife] pointu, tranchant, affilé; [sight, mind] perçant, pénétrant; [corner, angle] saillant, [feature] accentué, net; [Pers., mind] fin, malin, vif; [wind] piquant; [Mus.] dièse. || *n.* [Mus.] dièse *m.* || *adv.* exactement: *I'll be there at eight o'clock ~*, J'y serai à huit heures/précises, exactement/; vivement; [look] attentivement, de près. cf. SHARPLY. || **sharpen** [-n̩] *v. tr.* aiguiser, affiler (un couteau, une lame), repasser (des ciseaux, un rasoir); tailler (un crayon). || **sharpener** [-n̩ɚ] *n.* [pencil] taille-crayon *m. inv.*; © [abus.] aiguisoir *m.*

sharper [-ɚ] *n.* [Sl.] escroc *m*, filou *m*, tricheur *m.*

sharply [-lɪ] *adv.* [distinctly] nettement; vivement; [look, observe] attentivement; [hit] rudement. || **sharpness** [-nəs] *n.* acuité *f* (de vision, d'un angle); finesse (de l'ouïe, d'esprit); acidité *f*, âpreté *f* (d'une saveur, &c.).

shatter ['ʃætɚ] *v. tr.* briser (en éclats), fracasser; ébranler (les nerfs); détraquer (la santé), briser (des espérances). || *v. intr.* se fracasser; se briser.

shave [ʃejv] *v. tr.* **1.** [hair, beard] raser, faire la barbe à (qqun); [Fig.] effleurer (qqch., qqun). **2.** [Com.] baisser, réduire (légèrement le prix). || *v. intr.* se raser, se faire la barbe. || *n.* action *f* de se raser: *It was/a close thing, a close ~ /*, Il l'a échappé belle, Il était moins cinq, Il l'a évité de justesse. || **shaver** [-ɚ] *n.* barbier *m*: *electric ~*, rasoir *m* électrique; [Fam.] *a little ~*, un petit gamin. || **shaving** [-ɪŋ] *n.* **1.** action de (se) raser, tonte *f*: *~ -brush*, blaireau *m*; *~ -cream*, © crème *f* à barbe. **2.** [wood] copeau *m.*

shawl [ʃɔl] *n.* châle *m*, fichu *m.*

she [ʃij] *pron. pers.* [subject] elle *f*: [female of animals] *~ -cat*, chatte *f.* || *n.* femelle *f.*

sheaf [ʃijf] *n. pl.* **sheaves** [ʃijvz] [wheat] gerbe *f*; [weapons] faisceau *m.* || *v. tr.* mettre en gerbes, javeler.

shear [ʃijɚ], **sheared** [-d], **sheared** or **shorn** [ʃɔɚn] *v. tr.* tondre (un mouton); corroyer (de l'acier). || **shearer** ['ʃijɚɚ] *n.* **1.** tondeur *m.* **2.** †moissonneur *m.* || **shears** [ʃijɚz] *n.pl.* ciseaux *mpl*; cisailles *fpl.*

sheath [ʃijθ] *n.* **1.** [sword] fourreau *m*; étui *m*, [knife] gaine *f.* **2.** [Bot.] enveloppe *f.* || **sheathe** [ʃijð] *v. tr.* **1.** remettre (une épée) dans son fourreau, rengainer (un couteau). **2.** envelopper.

sheaves cf. SHEAF.

shed [ʃɛd], **shed**, **shed** *v. tr.* **[-dd-]** répandre, verser (le sang, des larmes, &c.); [tree] perdre (ses feuilles). || *n.* [big] hangar *m*, remise *f.*

sheen [ʃijn] *n.* lustre *m*, brillant *m.*

sheep [ʃijp] *pl.* **sheep** *n.* mouton *m*: *~ dog*, chien *m* de berger; [Fig.] *a black ~*, une brebis galeuse. || **sheepish** [-ɪʃ] *adj.* [look, &c.] timide; honteux, penaud; [Pej.] bébête. || **sheepskin** [-ˌskɪn] *n.* basane *f*; peau *f* de mouton; [diploma] diplôme *m*, peau *f* d'âne.

sheer [ʃijɚ] *adj.* **1.** [lie, &c.] pur, complet; [strength] vif: *by ~ force*, de vive force; *in ~ desperation*, en désespoir de cause. **2.** transparent, clair, [material] léger; [stocking] extra-fin. **3.** perpendiculaire, à pic.

sheet [ʃijt] *n.* [bed] drap *m*; feuille *f* (de

papier); nappe *f* (d'eau): ~ *anchor*, planche *f* de salut; ~ *lightning*, éclair *m* de chaleur; ~ *-metal*, tôle *f*.

shelf [ʃɛlf] *n.pl.* **shelves** [ʃɛlvz] **1.** [book] rayon *m* (de bibliothèque), casier *m* (à documents); *pl.* étagère *f*. **2.** [seal] récif *m*, écueil *m*: *continental* ~, plateau *m* continental.

shell [ʃɛl] *n.* coquille *f* (d'œuf); coquille *f*, écale *f* (de noix); cosse *f* (de pois); écaille *f* (d'huître, de poisson), *shell-fish*, mollusque *m*, coquillage *m*: *to take oysters out of their shells*, écailler des huîtres; carapace *f* (de homard); [hard] enveloppe *f*, coque *f*, écorce *f* (terrestre, &c.); [projectile] obus *m*. ‖ **shell** *v. tr.* écailler (une huître, un poisson); écaler (des noix); écosser (des pois); [Mil.] bombarder, pilonner (une place forte, &c.).

shellac [ʃə'læk] *n.* vernis *m*; gomme *f* laque. ‖ *v. tr.* laquer; [Arg.] tabasser (qqun).

shellfish ['ʃɛlfɪʃ] *n.* coquillage *m*; fruit *m* de mer.

shelling ['ʃɛlɪŋ] *n.* **1.** écossage *m* (des pois). **2.** [Mil.] *a severe* ~, un bombardement (d'obus) intense.

shelter ['ʃɛltə˞] *n.* abri *m*, refuge *m*, asile *m*; [Fig.] protection *f*: *under* ~, à l'abri; *to take* ~, se mettre à l'abri, s'abriter. ‖ *v. tr.* abriter, mettre (qqun, qqch.) à l'abri; protéger. ‖ *v. intr.* s'abriter; [Fig.] se protéger (*contre*, from).

shelve[1] [ʃɛlv] *v. tr.* **1.** ranger (sur une étagère, un rayon); entreposer, mettre de côté. **2.** garnir de/planches, tablettes, rayons/. **3.** [Fig.] enterrer, mettre sur une voie de garage. ‖ **shelved** [-d] [notes, papers] documents, [Fig., affaire] classé.

shelve[2] *v. intr.* s'incliner (*vers*, to).

shelves, cf. SHELF, SHELVE.

shelving[1] [-ɪŋ] rayons *mpl*, rayonnage *m*.

shelving[2] *adj.* incliné.

shepherd ['ʃɛpə˞d] *n.* berger *m*; [Fig.] pasteur *m*: ~ *('s) pie*, hachis *m* (parmentier). ‖ **shepherdess** [-əs] *n.* bergère *f*.

sherbet ['ʃə˞bət] *n.* sorbet *m*.

sheriff ['ʃɛə˞ɪf] [US] *n.* shérif *m*: [Jur.] ~ *'s officer*, huissier *m*; ~ *sale*, vente *f* par autorité de justice.

sherry ['ʃɛə˞ɪ] *n.* [wine] xérès *m*.

Shetland ['ʃɛtlənd] *n.* [Islands] les (îles) Shetland *fpl*.

shew, shewn cf. SHOW, SHOWN.

shield [ʃijld] *n.* [Mil.] bouclier *m*; [Her.] écu *m*, écusson *m*; [animal] carapace *f*: © *the Laurentian shield*, le bouclier/canadien, laurentien. ‖ *v. tr.* protéger (qqun, qqch. contre qqun, *s.o.*, *sth./against*, *from*); [Fig.] défendre (qqun, qqch.); [Elec.] blinder.

shift[1] [ʃift] *n.* **1.** [place, speed] changement *m*; [wind] saute *f*; [tide] renverse *f*. **2.** [workmen] équipe *f*. **3.** [Fig.] expédient *m*, échappatoire *f*; ressource *f*: *to make* ~ *with sth.*, s'arranger, s'accommoder/de qqch.

shift[2] *v. tr.* [place, speed, &c.] changer (qqch.); [from one place to the other] déplacer, transférer (qqun, qqch.); [move] bouger: *to* ~ *gears*, changer de vitesse; *to* ~ *the blame onto s.o.*, rejeter le blâme sur qqun. ‖ *v. intr.* [move] changer (de position), dévier; bouger, se déplacer: *to* ~ *for o.s.*, se débrouiller (tout seul). ‖ **shifter** [-ə˞] *n.* **1.** [Theat.] *scene-* ~, machiniste *m*. **2.** [Fig., shuffler] biaiseur *m*, biaiseuse *f*. ‖ **shiftless** [-ləs] *adj.* paresseux; inactif, inefficace.

shilling ['ʃɪlɪŋ] [Br.] *n.* [coin] shilling *m*, chelin *m*.

shimmer ['ʃɪmə˞] *v. intr.* chatoyer; [moonlight on water] luire faiblement. ‖ *n.* chatoiement *m*, lueur *f* pâle.

shin [ʃɪn] *n.* [leg] devant *m* du tibia; [meat] jarret *m*; ~ *-bone*, tibia *m*.

shine [ʃajn], **shined, shone; shined, shone** [-d], [ʃɑn] *v. intr.* luire, reluire; [sun, moon] briller: *The sun is shining*, Il fait du soleil; [Fig.] resplendir; [wit] briller, être brillant. ‖ *v. tr.* faire/reluire, briller/; [shoes] cirer. ‖ **shiner** [-ə˞] *n.* cireur *m* (de bottes); [Fam.] œil *m*/poché, au beurre noir/.

shingle ['ʃɪŋgəl] *n.* [building] bardeau *m*.

shingles [-z] *n.pl.* [Med.] zona *m*.

shining ['ʃajnɪ|ŋ] *adj.* brillant, resplendissant; [Fig.] illustre. ‖ *n.* éclat *m*; lustre *m*. ‖ **shiny** *adj.* [stuff] luisant; [shoe, clothes] lustré; [Fam.] bien astiqué; reluisant.

ship [ʃɪp] *n.* navire *m*, vaisseau *m*, [Navy] bâtiment *m*; [Aero.] appareil *m*: [Naut.] *on board* ~, à bord. ‖ *v. tr.* expédier (de la marchandise) par/bateau, train. ‖ **shipbuilding** [-ˌbɪldɪŋ] *n.* construction *f* /de navires, navale/. ‖ **shipment** [-mənt] *n.* [goods] expédition *f* par bateau, train/; transport *m* (de marchandises); [on a ship, train] chargement *m*. ‖ **shipowner** [-ˌownə˞] *n.* armateur *m*. ‖ **shipper** [-ə˞] *n.* **1.** [goods] expéditeur *m*, chargeur *m*, expéditionnaire *m*. **2.** agence *f* maritime. ‖ **shipping** [-ɪŋ] **1.** (la) navigation *f*: /*inshore*, *coastal*/ ~, cabotage *m*. **2.** [train, ship] expédition *f*; [Naut.] transport *m* maritime: ~ *agent*, agent *m* maritime, expéditeur *m*; ~ *bill*, connaisscment *m*; ~ *charges*, frais *mpl* de/chargement, mise à bord; frais d'envoi (d'un paquet, &c.); ~ *company*, compagnie *f* de navigation; ~ *trade*, commerce *m* maritime, exportations *fpl*; ~ *department*, service *m* des expéditions; ~ *ticket*, fiche *f*, bulletin *m*/d'expédition. || **shipwreck** [-ˌɹɛk] *n.* naufrage *m.* || *v. tr.* faire naufrager: *to be shipwrecked*, faire naufrage. || **shipyard** [-ˌjɑɚd] *n.* [Naut.] chantier *m* de construction (navale).

shire [ʃajɚ] [Br.] *n.* [ne s'emploie qu'au pluriel ou en composition] comté *m.*

shirk [ʃɚk] *v. tr.* éviter, esquiver, manquer à (un cours, son travail). || *v. intr.* [Fam.] tirer au flanc. || **shirker** [-ɚ] *n.* insoumis *m*, paresseux *m*; [Sl.] flemmard *m*, lâcheur *m.*

shirt [ʃɚt] *n.* chemise *f* (d'homme, d'enfant); chemisier *m* (de femme): *sport* ~, chemise sport; *nightshirt*, chemise de nuit. || **shirt collar** [-ˌkɑlɚ] *n.* col *m* (de chemise). || **shirt sleeves** [-ˌslijvz] *n.pl.* manches *fpl* de chemise: *to be in o.'s* ~, être en bras de chemise.

shiver[1] [ˈʃɪvɚ] *n.* [piece] éclat *m.* || *v. tr. & intr.* (se) fracasser, (se) briser en/miettes, morceaux/.

shiver[2] *n.* frisson *m*; tremblement *m.* || *v. intr.* frissonner, grelotter; [building] s'ébranler, être ébranlé. || **shivering** [-ɪŋ] *adj.* frissonnant; tremblant. || *n.* frissons *mpl.*

shoal [ʃowl] *n.* [fish] banc *m*; [shallow] haut-fond *m*; banc *m* (de sable).

shock [ʃɑk] *n.* **1.** choc *m* (de deux corps, des idées); [emotional] secousse *f*, commotion *f*: [Med.] traumatisme *m*, choc *m*; [Elec.] choc *m*; [earth] séisme *m*: *It gave me* (*quite*) *a* ~, Cela m'a donné un coup; ~ *troops*, troupes *fpl* de choc; [car] ~ *-absorber*, amortisseur *m.* **2.** [hair] tignasse *f* (de cheveux).

shock *v. tr.* choquer (qqun, qqch.), heurter (qqun, qqch.); [Fig.] offenser, scandaliser (qqun). || **shocker** [-ɚ] *n.* film *m*, roman *m* à sensation. || **shocking** [-ɪŋ] *adj.* **1.** choquant, blessant. **2.** repoussant. **3.** [Fam.] très mal, affreux, terrible.

shod cf. SHOE.

shoddy [ˈʃɑdɪ] *adj.* **1.** [wool] bourre *f.* **2.** pacotille *f*; camelote *f.*

shoe [ʃuw] *n.* chaussure *f*, soulier *m*: *a pair of shoes*, une paire de chaussures; ~ *polish*, cirage *m* de chaussures; *wooden shoes*, sabots *mpl*; *horseshoe*, fer *m* (à cheval); [Fig.] *That is where the* ~ *pinches*, C'est là que le bât le blesse; *This is another pair of shoes*, C'est une autre paire de manches; *What size shoe*(*s*) *do you take?*, → Quelle est votre pointure?; *to set up in business on a shoestring*, s'établir avec de minces capitaux; *in your shoes*, à votre place; *to step into s.o.'s shoes*, prendre la place de qqun; *to put on one's shoes*, se chausser, mettre ses chaussures; *to take off one's shoes*, se déchausser, ôter ses chaussures. || **shoe, shod** [ʃɑd], **shod** *v. tr.* chausser, ferrer (un cheval): *He crossed the stream dry-shod*, Il traversa le ruisseau à pied sec. || **shoeblack** [-ˌblæk] *n.m.* [Br.] cireur *m* de chaussures, décrotteur. || **shoeing** [-ɪŋ] cf. SHOE. || **shoe lace** [-ˌlejs] lacet *m* de soulier. || **shoe-maker** [-ˌmejkɚ] *n.* cordonnier *m.* || **shoe-shine** [-ˌʃajn] *n.* cireur *m* de bottes; cirage *m.*

shone cf. SHINE.

shook cf. SHAKE.

shoot [ʃuwt] *n.* [Sport] bond *m*; [Bot.] rejeton *m*, pousse *f.* || **shoot** [ʃuwt], **shot** [ʃɑt], **shot** *v. tr.* [bullet] tirer (une balle); décocher (une flèche); [game] chasser (le gibier) au fusil; atteindre (qqun) d'une balle; [execute] fusiller (qqun); sauter (les rapides); [Cinema] tourner (un film): *to* ~ *at* (*s.o.*), faire feu sur (qqun); *shooting star*, étoile *f* filante; [Fig.] *to* ~ *one's last bolt*, brûler sa dernière cartouche, vider son carquois. || *v. intr.* s'élancer, se lancer: *to* ~ *ahead*, s'élancer en avant; [Mil.] tirer; [Sport] shooter.

shop [ʃɑp] *n.* magasin *m* (de nouveautés, &c.); atelier *m* (de réparations); boutique *f* (de coiffeur): [Fig.] *like a bull in a china* ~, (arriver) comme un chien dans un jeu de quilles; ~ *assistant*, [Br.] vendeu|r, -se; ~ *window*, vitrine *f* (d'un magasin); étalage *m* de/marchandises, nouveautés/: *to talk* ~, parler/affaires, boutique; *to keep* ~, tenir boutique; *to shut up* ~, fermer boutique; *machine* ~, atelier *m* d'usinage; *sweat* ~, exploitation *f* de la main-d'œuvre. || **shop** *v. intr.* **[-pp-]** faire/les, des/emplettes, courir les magasins, faire des courses, © magasiner; [groceries] faire le marché. || **shopkeeper** [-ˌkijpɚ] *n.* boutiquier *m.* || **shopkeeping** [-ˌkijpɪŋ] *n.* [small] commerce *m.* || **shoplifter** [ˈʃɑp|ˌlɪftɚ] *n.* voleur *m* à l'étalage. || **shopper** [-ɚ] *n.* acheteu|r, -se. || **shopping** [-ɪŋ] *n.* achats *mpl*, emplettes *fpl*; ~ *bag*, filet *m* à provisions; ~ *centre*, centre *m* commercial, © centre d'achats.

shore [ʃɔɚ] *n.* [sea] rivage *m*, littoral *m*; bord *m* (d'un lac), rive *f* (d'un fleuve, d'une rivière): *off* ~ , au large; *in* ~ , près de la côte; *on* ~ , à terre.

shorn cf. SHEAR.

short [ʃɔət] *adj.* [size] court; [pers.] petit; [while] bref; [temper] brusque: *to grow* ~ , se raccourcir; *to be* ~ *of* (*sth.*), être à court de (qqch.); *He is ten cents* ~ , Il lui manque dix cents; [Electr.] ~ *-circuit*, court-circuit *m*: *to fall* ~ *of what is necessary*, être insuffisant; *to fall* ~ *of one's duty*, manquer à son devoir; *to/make*, *cut/ a long story* ~ , pour abréger; *a* ~ *cut*, un raccourci; *to take a* ~ *cut*, prendre au plus court; ~ *story*, conte *m*, [longer] nouvelle *f*, ~ *sight*, myopie *f*. || **shortage** [-ədʒ] *n.* manque *m*; disette *f*, pénurie *f*. || **shortcoming** [-ˌkʌmɪŋ] *n.* **1.** faute *f*, défaut *m*. **2.** manquement *m* (au devoir). || **shorten** [-n̩] *v. tr.* raccourcir, abréger. || **shortening** [-n̩ɪŋ] *n.* **1.** saindoux *m*; matière *f* grasse. **2.** raccourcissement *m*. || **shorthand** [-ˌhænd] *n.* sténographie *f*; [Fam.] sténo *f*: *to take* (*down*) *in* ~ , sténographier (un discours, &c.). || **short-handed** [ˌʃɔət'hændəd] *adj.* à court de /personnel, main-d'œuvre/. || **shortly** [-lɪ] *adv.* **1.** bientôt. **2.** brièvement. **3.** rudement, sèchement. || **shortness** [-nəs] *n.* brièveté *f*; concision *f* (d'un discours); [size] petitesse *f*; insuffisance *f*. || **shorts** [-z] *n.pl.* [men's] caleçon *m*; [Sport] short *m*. || **short-sighted** [-'sajtəd] *adj.* myope; [Fig.] à courte vue. || **short-tempered** [-tɛmpərd] *adj.* coléreux, emporté.

shot[1] cf. SHOOT.

shot[2] [ʃɑt] *n.* [rifle] coup *m* de feu; boulet *m* (de canon); [penicillin, &c.] piqûre *f*; [pistol] tireur *m*, [pellet] plomb *m*, [photo] prise *f* (de vue); [Cin.] plan *m*: *a long* ~ , une chance sur mille; *by a long* ~ , à beaucoup près; *at the first* ~ , du premier coup; *to be off like a* ~ , partir comme une flèche; *to have a* ~ *at*, essayer. || *adj.* [Fam.] fichu. || **shotgun** [-ˌgʌn] *n.* fusil *m* de chasse; [paint, &c.] pistolet *m*.

should [ʃud] *v. aux.* [☞ Seule autre forme du verbe défectif SHALL. Selon l'usage le plus strict, *should* s'emploie pour former la 1ère pers. du conditionnel, dont les autres pers. se construisent avec WOULD. Cette distinction a plus ou moins disparu dans le langage parlé qui remplace *I*, *we/ should* par *I'd*, *we'd*, *I*, *we/should not* par *I*, *we/wouldn't*, et *Should I*, *we/not* par *Wouldn't/I*, *we/*. Ailleurs, *should* s'emploie à toutes les pers. pour indiquer l'obligation, l'opinion, la surprise, ou pour former le subjonctif d'autres verbes.] **1.** [conditional uses.—Do not confuse with *should* used to indicate obligation]: Condit. tenses: *If it were so/I* ~ , *I'd/be glad*, S'il en était ainsi, je serais content; *If it had been so/I* ~ , *I'd/have been glad*, S'il en avait été ainsi, j'aurais été content; *I* ~ , *I'd/like to come*, Je voudrais (bien) venir; *I told him/I* ~ , *I'd/come*, Je lui ai dit que je viendrais. **2.** [obligation] devoir: *I* ~ *come*, (*but . . .*), Je devrais venir, mais . . . ; *You* ~ *have come*, (*but . . .*), Vous auriez dû venir, (mais . . .). **3.** [probability] *He* ~ *have finished by now*, Il devrait en avoir déjà fini, Je crois qu'il en aura déjà fini; *That* ~ *be enough*, Je crois que cela/suffit, suffira/; *I* ~ *think so!*, Je crois bien!; *I asked him when I* ~ *come*, Je lui ai demandé à quelle heure je devrais venir; *He asked me if he* ~ *come*, Il m'a demandé/s'il devait venir, si je voulais qu'il vienne/; *How* ~ *I know?*, Comment voulez-vous que je sache cela? **4.** [after, or replacing *if*] *If it* ~ *rain*, *Should it rain/*, *bring in the washing*, S'il pleut, rentrez le linge; *If it* ~ *rain*, *Should it rain/it would be a catastrophe*, S'il pleuvait, ce serait la catastrophe. **5.** [English subjunc.] *It is surprising that he* ~ *come now*, Il est étonnant qu'il vienne maintenant; *It is only natural that he* ~ *have come*, Il n'est que naturel qu'il soit venu; *I suggested that he* ~ *leave*, J'ai suggéré qu'il parte; *No matter what* ~ *happen*, *don't worry*, Quoi qu'il arrive, ne vous en faites pas. **6.** [surprise] . . . *and what* ~ *I find but my own watch!*, et quelle ne fut pas ma surprise de trouver ma montre!

shoulder ['ʃowldər] *n.* épaule *f*: *shoulder blade*, omoplate *f*; [road] *soft* ~ , berme *f*, accotement *m*; [Fig.] *to give a person the cold* ~ , faire grise mine, tourner le dos/à qqun; *straight from the* ~ , tout net. || *v. tr.* pousser (qqun)/de, avec/l'épaule; porter (qqch.) sur les épaules; [gun] mettre (son fusil) sur l'épaule.

shouldn't ['ʃudnt] [= SHOULD NOT].

shout [ʃawt] *v. intr.* crier (de joie, &c.); pousser des cris: *to* ~ *for s.o.*, appeler qqun à grands cris; *to* ~ *at s.o.*, s'adresser à qqun en criant, élever la voix en parlant à qqun; *Don't* ~ *at me!*, Ne criez pas (comme ça). || *v. tr.* crier (des injures, &c. à qqun): *to* ~ *s.o. down*, huer qqun, faire taire qqun sous les huées. || *n.* [joy, &c.] cri *m*, [laughter] éclat *m*; [coll.] acclamation *f*, clameur *f*.

shove [ʃʌv] *v. tr.* pousser (brusquement),

bousculer. || *v. intr.*: *to* ~ *through*, se frayer un chemin à travers (la foule); [Fam.] *to* ~ *along*, filer, décamper. || *n.* [Fam.] poussée *f*.

shovel ['ʃʌvḷ] *n.* pelle *f*. || *v. tr.* **[-ll-]** pelleter (de la neige, du charbon, &c.): *to* ~ (*snow, &c.*) *away*, enlever (la neige, &c.) à la pelle.

show [ʃow], **showed** [ʃowd], **shown** [ʃown] or **showed** *v. tr.* montrer, faire voir (qqch.); indiquer (le chemin); [produce, &c.] exposer, étaler; présenter (sa carte d'identité); faire preuve (de courage, d'intelligence); témoigner (de la reconnaissance); révéler (une émotion); [prove] démontrer, montrer; [Cin.] projeter (un film): *to* ~ *s.o. how to do sth.*, montrer, expliquer/à qqun comment faire qqch., apprendre à qqun à faire qqch.; *to* ~ *s.o. to/his, her/room*, conduire qqun à sa chambre; [Fig.] *to* ~ *o.'s face somewhere*, se montrer quelque part, montrer le bout du nez quelque part; *to* ~ *the cloven hoof*, se montrer sans fard; *to* ~ *o.'s hand*, jouer cartes sur table; [☞ avec postpositions] *to* ~ (*s.o.*) *down*, reconduire (un visiteur) en bas; *to* ~ (*s.o.*) *in*, faire entrer (qqun); *to* ~ (*s.o.*) *out*, reconduire (un visiteur); *to* ~ (*s.o.*) *up*, faire monter (un visiteur); [Fig.] démasquer, dénoncer. || *v. intr.* se montrer, paraître, se voir; [garment] dépasser; [prove] faire voir, montrer: *to* ~ *through*, transparaître; *to* ~ *off*, étaler (son savoir), faire parade de (ses connaissances); [to child] *Don't* ~ *off!*, Ne fais pas l'intéressant(e); *to* ~ *up*, faire son apparition, faire acte de présence: *He never showed up*, Il ne s'est jamais présenté, On ne l'a jamais vu; *to* ~ *up against* (*the sky*), se silhouetter, se détacher/sur le ciel. || *n.* [look] apparence *f*, simulacre *m*; [fashion] défilé *m* (de mode); [shop] étalage *m*; [theatre] spectacle *m*; [fair] concours *m* (agricole); [automobile] salon *m* (de l'automobile); [horse ~] concours *m* hippique; *to make a* ~ *of*, faire/mine, semblant/de; *to run the* ~ , mener/l'affaire, la barque; *Good* ~ *!*, Bravo!; *a* ~ *of hands*, vote *m* à main levée; *on* ~ , exposé, [Com.] à l'étalage, en vitrine. || **show-bill** ['ʃowˌbɪl] *n.* [theatre] affiche *f*. || **show-card** [-ˌkɑɚd] *n.* affiche *f*, pancarte *f*. || **show-case** [-ˌkejs] *n.* vitrine *f*, †montre *f*; armoire *f* vitrée; [Fig.] *Switzerland is a* ~ *for democracy*, la Suisse est/une démocratie-témoin, une démocratie-modèle. || **show-down** [-ˌdawn] *n.* [Fig.] moment *m* /critique, décisif/: *to come to a* ~ (*with s.o.*), mettre (qqun) au pied du mur, en venir au fait. || **show-girl** [-ˌgɚl] *n.* figurante *f*, girl *f*. || **show-place** [-ˌplejs] *n.* lieu *m*/célèbre, touristique. || **show-room** [-ˌruwm] *n.* salon *m*/d'exposition, de démonstration.

shower ['ʃawɚ] *n.* **1.** [copious] averse *f*; [slight] ondée *f*; [Fig.] pluie *f*, grêle *f* (d'injures, de coups, &c.). **2.** [bath] douche *f*. **3.** [party] © shower *m*. || *v. tr.* arroser (un endroit); [Fig.] faire pleuvoir (les injures, les coups). || *v. intr.* pleuvoir à verse.

showman ['ʃow|mən] *n.* directeur *m* de spectacle. || **shown** cf. SHOW. || **showy** [-ɪ] *adj.* [colour] voyant, criard; [Pers., Fig.] prétentieux.

shrank cf. SHRINK.

shrapnel ['ʃɹæpnəl] *n.* shrapnel *m*; [Fam.] éclat *m* d'obus.

shred [ʃɹɛd] *n.* morceau *m*; bout *m* (d'étoffe), bande *f* (de cuir); fragment *m*, particule *f*, miette *f*: *to tear to shreds*, mettre en lambeaux, déchiqueter; [Fig.] *not a* ~ *of*, pas l'ombre de. || *v. tr.* **[-dd-]** réduire (qqch.) en fragments, effilocher. || **shreddy** [-ɪ] *adj.* composé de pièces, disparate.

shrew [ʃɹuw] *n.* **1.** femme *f* acariâtre: [Litt.] *The Taming of the Shrew*, la Mégère apprivoisée. **2.** musaraigne *f*. || **shrewd** [-d] *adj.* **1.** clairvoyant, sagace, adroit. **2.** subtil, fin. || **shrewdly** [-dlɪ] *adv.* adroitement, finement. || **shrewdness** [-dnəs] *n.* discernement *m*, adresse *f*; malice *f*. || **shrewish** [-ɪʃ] *adj.* acariâtre.

shriek [ʃɹijk] *n.* cri *m*/perçant, aigu/. || *v. intr.* pousser un cri perçant. || *v. tr.*: *to* ~ *out*, crier.

shrift [ʃɹɪft] *n.* absolution *f*: [Fig.] *to give s.o. short* ~ , expédier vite son homme, renvoyer (qqun) avec pertes et fracas.

shrike [ʃɹajk] *n.* [Orn.] pie-grièche *f*.

shrill [ʃɹɪl] *adj.* aigu, perçant: ~ *-voiced*, à la voix perçante.

shrimp [ʃɹɪmp] *n.* **1.** crevette *f*. **2.** [Fig.] gringalet *m*.

shrine [ʃɹajn] *n.* **1.** [casket] châsse *f*, reliquaire *m*. **2.** [tomb] autel *m* (de saint). **3.** temple *m*, sanctuaire *m*.

shrink [ʃɹɪŋk], **shrank** [ʃɹæŋk], **shrunk** [ʃɹʌŋk] *v. intr.* (se) rétrécir, (se) resserrer; [Fig.] diminuer: *Does this material* ~ *?*, Est-ce que ce tissu rétrécit?; *My shirt shrank*, Ma chemise s'est rétrécie; *to* ~ *back*, se dérober (*from*, à). || *v. tr.* (faire) rétrécir, contracter. || **shrinkage** ['ʃɹɪŋk|ədʒ] *n.* rétrécissement *m*, raccourcissement *m*. [Chem.] diminution *f*, retrait *m*.

|| **shrinking** [-ɪŋ] *adj.* qui rétrécit; [Fig.] qui diminue; timide, retiré.

†**shrive** [ʃɹajv] *v. tr.* confesser (qqun), absoudre (qqun).

shrivel [ˈʃɹɪvl̩] *v. tr. & intr.* **[-ll-]** [up] (se) dessécher, (se) ratatiner, (se) plisser, (se) recroqueviller.

shroud [ʃɹawd] *n.* **1.** linceul *m*, suaire *m*. **2.** [Fig.] voile *m*, couvert *m*, abri *m*. || **shrouds** [-z] *n.* hauban *m*. || *v. tr.* **1.** ensevelir (un mort). **2.** [Fig.] cacher, voiler.

Shrovetide [ˈʃɹowvˌtajd] *n.* jours *mpl* gras. || **Shrove Tuesday** [-ˌtjuwsdej] *n.* mardi *m* gras.

shrub [ʃɹʌb] *n.* [bush] arbuste *m*, [hawthorn] arbrisseau *m*.

shrug [ʃɹʌg] *v. tr.* **[-gg-]** hausser (les épaules): [Fig.] *He merely shrugged off the challenge*, Il n'a même pas relevé le défi. || *n.* haussement *m* d'épaules.

shrunk cf. SHRINK.

shudder [ˈʃʌdɚ] *n.* frisson *m*, frémissement *m* (de frayeur). || *v. intr.* frémir, frissonner (de peur, &c.).

shuffle [ˈʃʌfl̩] *n.* **1.** [shoes] traînement *m* (des pieds). **2.** paperasse *f*; mélange *m* (des cartes). **3.** tour *m*, ruse *f*; [Fam.] truc *m*; échappatoire *f*. || *v. intr.* **1.** [feet] traîner les pieds; marcher péniblement, [Fam.] tirer la patte. **2.** battre (les cartes). **3.** biaiser, tergiverser, se tirer d'affaire. **4.** ~ *off*, rejeter (une faute sur qqun d'autre).

shun [ʃʌn] *v. tr.* **[-nn-]** éviter (qqun, qqch., de faire qqch.); fuir, éluder.

shunt [ʃʌnt] *n.* dérivation *f*; [Rail.] voie *f* /d'évitement, de garage/. || *v. tr. & intr.* (se) garer; [Electr.] shunter: *a shunting yard*, gare *f* de manœuvre.

shut [ʃʌt] **shut**, **shut** *v. tr.* fermer (la porte, sa bouche); [lid] rabattre; [trade] fermer (un établissement). || **shut in** *v. tr.* enfermer (qqch.). || **shut off** [-ˈɔf] *v. tr.* [steam] intercepter; couper (l'électricité, le courant). || **shut out** [ˈawt] *v. tr.* exclure (qqun de qqch., *s.o. from sth.*). || **shut up** [-ˈʌp] *v. tr.* enfermer, emprisonner (qqun): [Vulg.] ~ !, Ferme-la!, La ferme!

shutter [-ɚ] *n.* volet *m*, persienne *f*; [photo] obturateur *m*.

shuttle [ˈʃʌtl̩] *n.* [weaving] navette *f*; [train] navette. || *v. intr.* faire/le va et vient, la navette/.

shy [ʃaj] *adj.* [Pers.] timide, sauvage; [horse] ombrageux: *to be ~ of sth.*, se défier, se méfier de qqch.; *to fight ~ of sth.*, éviter qqch. || **shyness** [-nəs] *n.* timidité *f*; réserve *f*, retenue *f*.

shyster [ˈʃajstɚ] *n.* [Sl.] avocat *m* malhonnête, sans scrupules, [Fr.] marron, homme *m* d'affaires véreux.

Siam [sajˈæm] *n.* le Siam, cf. THAILAND. || **Siamese** [-ˌmijz] *adj.* siamois: ~ *twins*, frères *mpl* siamois, sœurs *fpl* siamoises.

Siberia [sajˈbijɚɪə] *n.* (la) Sibérie *f*.

sibyl [ˈsɪbl̩] *n.* **1.** [Hist.] sibylle *f*. **2.** sorcière *f*, tireuse *f* de cartes, voyante *f*. || **sibyllic** [sɪˈbɪlɪk] cf. SIBYLLINE. || **sibylline** [ˈsɪblˌijn] *adj.* [Fig., mysterious and prophetic] sibyllin.

Sicily [ˈsɪsɪlɪ] *n.* (la) Sicile *f*: *in, to/Sicily*, en S.

sick [sɪk] *adj.* [Pers.] malade, souffrant (*with*, de); [Br. *ill*, e.g. *he was ill*, but *a sick man*]: *to fall ~*, tomber malade; *to be ~ (to, at/o.'s stomach)*, vomir, rendre; [Fig.] *I am ~ of*, J'en ai assez (de); [Fig.] *~ as a/cat, dog/*, être malade comme un chien; *the ~*, les malades *mpl.*; *~ leave*, congé *m* de maladie: *sickroom*, *n.* chambre *f* de malade. || **sicken** [-n̩] *v. intr.* tomber malade. || *v. tr.* rendre (qqun) malade. || **sickening** [-n̩ɪŋ] *adj.* → qui rend malade; [surtout Fig.] répugnant, dégoûtant.

sickle [-l̩] *n.* faucille *f*.

sickly [-lɪ] *adj.* **1.** maladif, malingre. **2.** [plants] étiolé. **3.** malsain, insalubre. || **sickness** [-nəs] *n.* **1.** maladie *f*. **2.** nausée *f*.

side [sajd] *n.* côté *m*; bord *m*; versant *m* (d'une colline); [Sport] camp *m*; [Pol.] parti *m*: *on, to, from/the other side*, de l'autre côté; *on, from/all sides*, de tous côtés; *from ~ to ~*, d'un côté à l'autre, © [Fam.] d'un bord à l'autre; *wrong ~ out*, à l'envers; *~ by ~*, côte à côte; *on its ~*, couché; *This Side Up*, Haut; *to take sides*, prendre parti; *to take s.o.'s side*, prendre le parti de qqun, *to hear both sides*, entendre les deux parties; *the blind ~ of s.o.*, le côté faible de qqun; *He has got out of bed on the wrong side*, Il s'est levé du pied gauche. || *v. intr.* prendre parti (*with*, pour; *against*, contre). || **side-altar** [-ˌɔltɚ] *n.* [Rel.] autel *m* latéral. || **side-arm** [-ˌɑɚm] *n.* [Mil.] arme *f* blanche, épée *f*, baïonnette *f*. || **sideboard** [-ˌbɔɚd] *n.* buffet *m*; desserte *f*. || **side-door** [-ˌdɔɚ] *n.* porte *f* de service; porte latérale. || **side-entrance** [-ˌɛntɹəns] *n.* entrée *f* latérale. || **side-glance** [-ˌglæns] *n.* coup *m* d'œil oblique, regard *m* de côté. || **side-issue** [-ˌɪʃuw] *n.* question *f* secondaire. || **side-kick** [-ˌkɪk] *n.* [Fam.] copain *m*. || **side-light** [-ˌlajt] *n.* éclairage *m*/indirect, de côté; [Fig.] aperçu/ nouveau, inattendu. || **side-line** [-ˌlajn] *n.*

voie *f* secondaire; [Fig.] occupation *f* secondaire; [hobby] violon *m* d'Ingres. || **sidelong** [-ˌlɑŋ] *adj.* oblique, de côté; [glance] du coin de l'œil. || *adv.* obliquement, de côté. || **side-rail** [-ˌrejl] *n.* garde-fou *m*; main *f* courante. || **side-road** [-ɹowd] *n.* chemin *m* de traverse. || **side-show** [-ˌʃow] *n.* baraque *f*, numéro *m*/de fête foraine, de music-hall. || **side-slip** [-slɪp] *n.* [Auto.] dérapage *m.* || *v. intr.* déraper. || **side-splitting** [-ˌsplɪtɪŋ] *adj.* [Fam.] tordant, désopilant, [Fam.] crevant. || **side-step** [-ˌstɛp] *n.* écart *m.* || *v. tr. & intr.* faire un pas de côté; [Fig.] esquiver (une difficulté). || **side-track** [-ˌtɹæk] *n.* [Railway] voie *f*/de garage, d'évitement; [Fig.] question *f* d'intérêt secondaire. || *v. tr.* [Railway] diriger sur une voie de garage; [Fig.] éviter (un problème), s'écarter du sujet. || **side-view** [-ˌvjuw] *n.* vue *f* de profil. || **sidewalk** [-ˌwɔk] *n.* trottoir *m.* || **sideways** [-ˌwejz] *adv.* [to go] de côté, latéralement. || *adj.* latéral. || **siding** [-ɪŋ] *n.* [Rail.] voie *f* d'évitement, embranchement *m.* || **sidle** [-l̩] *v. intr.* avancer de biais; se ranger à côté de: *to ~ up to s.o.*, s'approcher de qqun/avec hésitation, timidement.

siege [sijʤ] *n.* [Mil.] siège *m* (d'une ville, place forte): *to lay ~ to*, assiéger.

sieve [sɪv] *n.* tamis *m*, crible *m*; [tea] passoire *f.*

sift [sɪft] *v. tr.* [flour] passer/au crible, au tamis/, tamiser (de la farine); [news] censurer, examiner soigneusement.

sigh [saj] *n.* soupir *m.* || *v. intr.* soupirer.

sight [sajt] *n.* [eye] vue *f*; vision *f* (d'un spectacle); mire *f* (d'une arme à feu); *short ~*, myopie *f*: *within ~*, (objet, &c.) en vue; *to be in ~ of*, pouvoir apercevoir; *to come into ~*, apparaître; *to go out of ~*, disparaître; *by ~*, de vue; *at ~*, à vue, à livre ouvert; *at first ~*, *on ~*, à première vue; *love at first ~*, coup *m* de foudre; *to catch ~ of*, apercevoir; *to see the sights*, visiter (une ville); *to make a ~ of o.s.*, se donner en spectacle. || *v. tr.* apercevoir (qqun, qqch.). || **sightseeing** [-ˌsijɪŋ] *n.* visite *f* touristique (d'une ville, &c.). || **sightseer** [-ˌsijɚ] *n.* excursionniste *m*, touriste *m*, visiteur *m.*

sign [sajn] *n.* **1.** signe *m*; symbole *m*; [smoke, tracks] indice *m*, trace *f*: *to give signs of*, donner des signes de, annoncer; *to give s.o. a ~ (to)*, faire signe à qqun (de); *to make the ~ of the Cross*, se signer. **2.** [shop] enseigne *f*: *traffic ~*, panneau *m* de signalisation; *road signs*, signalisation *f* routière. || *v. tr.* marquer (qqch.) d'un signe; signer (un document): [Fig.] *to ~ on the dotted line*, obéir à la lettre. || *v. intr.* signer; [signal] faire un signe, donner un signal.

signal [ˈsɪgnl̩] *n.* signal *m* (du départ, dans les sports); [bell] avertisseur *m*; [station] sémaphore *m*: *~ board*, tableau *m* des sonneries. || *adj.* [service] signalé; [heroism] insigne. || *v. tr.* [-ll-] signaler (qqch.); donner le signal (du départ). || *v. intr.* faire des signaux, donner un signal. || **signal flashers** [-ˌflæʃɚz] *n.pl.* [Auto.] clignotants *mpl.* || **signalize** [-ajz] *v. tr.* signaler; faire ressortir (qqch.). || **signalling** [-ɪŋ] *n.* signalisation *f.*

signature [ˈsɪgnətʃɚ] *n.* signature *f.*

signboard [ˈsajn|ˌbɔɚd] *n.* panneau *m* (d'affichage); enseigne *f.*

signet [ˈsɪgnət] *n.* sceau *m* (du souverain); [ring] chevalière *f.*

significance [sɪgˈnɪfɪkən|s] *n.* **1.** importance *f.* **2.** [meaning] signification *f.* **3.** énergie *f*, force *f*, impression *f.* || **significant** [-t] *adj.* important, significatif. || **signification** [-ˈkejʃən] *n.* **1.** sens *m*, signification *f.* **2.** communication *f.* || **signify** [ˈsɪgnɪˌfaj] *v. tr.* **1.** signifier, dénoter. **2.** importer. || *v. intr.* avoir du sens.

signpost [-ˌpowst] *n.* poteau *m* indicateur.

silence [ˈsajlən|s] *n.* silence *m.* || *v. tr.* réduire (qqun) au silence; fermer la bouche à (qqun, qqch.); amortir (un bruit). || **silent** [-t] *adj.* silencieux, taciturne : *Keep ~ !*, Taisez-vous!; *He fell ~*, Il s'est tu; *He remained ~*, Il se taisait; [thing, matter] insonore; [Com.] *~ partner*, commanditaire *m.* || **silently** [-tlɪ] *adv.* silencieusement.

silex [ˈsajlɛks] *n.* **1.** silice *f.* **2.** [coffee] © silex *m.*

silhouette [ˌsɪluwˈɛt] *n.* silhouette *f.* || *v. tr.* faire ressortir: *to be silhouetted against*, se dessiner sur, se silhouetter sur.

silk [sɪlk] *n.* soie *f*: *~ stockings*, bas *mpl* de soie; *~ -hat*, haut-de-forme *m.* || **silken** [-n̩] *adj.* soyeux. || **silkworm** [-ˌwɚm] *n.* ver *m* à soie. || **silky** [-ɪ] *adj.* [stuff] soyeux.

sill [sɪl] *n.* **1.** [door] seuil *m*; [window] rebord *m.* **2.** [walls] semelle *f.*

silly [-ɪ] *adj.* [Pers.] sot; [answer, &c.] idiot; ridicule.

silo [ˈsajlow] *n.* silo *m.*

silt [sɪlt] *n.* vase *f*, limon *m*; alluvion *f.* || *v. tr.* [up] obstruer (par de la vase). || *v. intr.*: *to ~ up*, s'ensabler, s'envaser.

silver [ˈsɪlvɚ] *n.* [metal] argent *m*; [coll.] argenterie *f*; [change] petite monnaie *f*: *~ plate*, argenterie *f.* || *v. tr.* argenter (qqch.); étamer (une glace). || **silversmith** [-ˌsmɪθ] *n.* orfèvre *m.* || **silverware** [-ˌwɛɚ] *n.* argenterie *f.* || **silvery** [-ɪ] *adj.* [moon] argenté, d'argent; [son] argentin.

similar [ˈsɪmɪlɚ] *adj.* semblable, [situation] analogue, identique. || **similarity** [sɪmɪˈlærɪtɪ] *n.* similitude *f*, ressemblance *f*, analogie *f*, identité *f* (entre, *between*)

simile [ˈsɪmɪlɪ] *n.* comparaison *f.*

simmer [ˈsɪmɚ] *v. intr.* **1.** bouillir/doucement, à feu doux/, mijoter. **2.** [Fig.] [anger] monter, gronder: [Fam.] *to ∼ down*, (s')apaiser.

simper [ˈsɪmpɚ] *n.* sourire *m*/niais, affecté. || *v. intr.* **1.** sourire bêtement. **2.** exprimer (qqch.) avec un sourire niais, minauder.

simple [ˈsɪmpḷ] *adj.* simple; [unaffected] naturel, tout simple; [gullible] naïf; simple (d'esprit); *∼ words*, quelques paroles sans prétentions; *∼ -hearted*, franc, ingénu; *∼ -minded*, candide, naïf. || **simpleness** [-nəs] *n.* simplicité *f*; [often pej.] naïveté *f*, candeur *f.* || **simpleton** [ˈsɪmpḷtən] *n.* nigaud *m*; faible *m* d'esprit. || **simplicity** [sɪmˈplɪsɪtɪ] *n.* [problem, Pers.] simplicité *f*; [Pers.] naïveté *f*, candeur *f.* || **simplification** [ˌsɪmplɪfɪˈkejʃən] *n.* simplification *f.* || **simplify** [ˈsɪmplɪˌfaj] *v. tr.* simplifier. || **simply** [ˈsɪmplɪ] *adv.* simplement; [superl.] absolument, tout simplement, purement et simplement.

simulate [ˈsɪmjəˌlejt] *v. tr.* **1.** simuler; faire semblant; feindre. **2.** imiter (qqun); ressembler à (qqun, qqch.).

simultaneous [ˌsajməlˈtejnɪəs] *adj.* [event] simultané.

sin [sɪn] *n.* péché *m*: *to commit a ∼* , commettre un péché, *to fall into ∼* , tomber dans le péché; *to forgive sins*, remettre les péchés; [R.C.] *to confess, tell/sins to a priest*, confesser, dire/ses péchés à un prêtre. || *v. intr.* [-nn-] pécher: *to ∼ against*, enfreindre (une règle); manquer à (un devoir).

since [sɪns] *adv.* depuis: *Have you seen him ∼ ?*, L'avez-vous revu depuis?; *He has been doing it ever ∼* , Depuis (lors),/il l'a toujours fait, il continue à le faire; *long ∼* , il y a longtemps. || *prep.* depuis: *I haven't seen him ∼ Tuesday*, Je ne l'ai pas (re)vu depuis mardi; *He has been doing it ∼ that time*, Il le fait depuis lors; *∼ doing it*, depuis que je l'ai fait, (je, &c.). || *conj.* [time] depuis que; [because] puisque: *Since you left*, . . . Depuis votre départ, Depuis que vous êtes parti . . . ; *Since that's the way it is*, Puisqu'il en est ainsi.

sincere [sɪnˈsijɚ] *adj.* sincère, de bonne foi. || **sincerely** [-lɪ] *adv.* sincèrement, avec sincérité, de bonne foi: *Yours sincerely*, Veuillez agréer l'expression de mes salutations distinguées.

sincerity [sɪnˈsɛɚɪtɪ] *n.* sincérité *f*, bonne foi *f.*

sinecure [ˈsajnəˌkjuwɚ] *n.* sinécure *f*; [Fam.] planque *f.*

sinew [ˈsɪnjuw] *n.* **1.** tendon *m.* **2.** [Fig.] force *f*; énergie *f*; *the sinews of war*, le nerf de la guerre. || **sinewless** [-ləs] *adj.* sans/force *f*, énergie *f*/. || **sinewy** [-ɪ] *adj.* nerveux; énergique; [stringy] tendineux.

sinful [ˈsɪnfḷ] *adj.* coupable, criminel: *a ∼ person*, un pécheur, une pécheresse.

sing [sɪŋ], **sang** [sæŋ], **sung** [sʌŋ] *v. tr. & intr.* chanter: [Fig.] *to ∼ a different tune* changer de/disque, refrain/; *to ∼ of sth.*, chanter qqch.; *to ∼ s.o. to sleep*, bercer, endormir/en chantant.

singe [sɪndʒ] *v. tr.* [*p.pr.* **singeing**] brûler (légèrement), flamber (ses cheveux, &c.); roussir (ses vêtements).

singer [ˈsɪŋɚ] *n.* chanteu|r *m*, -se *f*, [classical] cantatrice *f.*

single [ˈsɪŋgəl] *adj.* seul, unique; [person, heart] simple, honnête: *a ∼ bed*, un lit à une place; *a ∼ room*, une chambre à une personne; [Railway] *∼ track*, voie *f* unique; *∼ (ticket)*, billet *m* simple, aller *m* simple; *He is ∼* , C'est un célibataire, il est célibataire. || *v. tr.*: *to ∼ out (s.o., sth.)*, distinguer, choisir (qqun, qqch.). || **single-handed** [-ˈhændəd] *adj.* **1.** [tool, &c.] qui se manie/d'une, avec une/(seule) main. **2.** [Fig., Pers.] (tout) seul, sans aide.

singly [ˈsɪŋglɪ] *adv.* seulement, uniquement; simplement; [working, &c.] séparément, un à un; sans aide.

singsong [ˈsɪŋˌsɔŋ] *n.* rengaine *f*, mélopée *f.* || *adj.* chantonnant; [Fig.] monotone.

singular [ˈsɪŋgjəlɚ] *n.* [number] singulier *m.* || *adj.* [thing] singulier, surprenant; [beauty, show] extraordinaire; [behaviour] bizarre.

sinister [ˈsɪnɪstɚ] *adj.* **1.** de mauvais augure; sombre; menaçant. **2.** mauvais, malhonnête. **3.** désastreux; malheureux.

sink [sɪŋk], **sank** [sæŋk], **sunk** [sʌŋk] *v. intr.* [ship] sombrer, couler; [earth, house] s'affaisser; [voice] faiblir; [heart] se serrer; [Fig.] [strength, courage] décliner, défaillir; [Pers.] s'enfoncer, s'embourber (dans le vice, &c.); [on a sofa, into an armchair] s'affaler (sur); [sun] baisser, se coucher; [value, &c.] diminuer, s'amoindrir: *∼ or swim*, advienne que pourra, (var. *California or bust!*)

[US, Hist.] La Californie ou la mort! || *v. tr.* [ship] couler, faire sombrer; [pole, &c.] enfoncer; [well] creuser; amortir, éteindre (une dette). || *n.* évier *m*; [drain] égout *m*.

sinner ['sɪnɚ] *n.* péche|ur *m*, -resse *f*.

sinuous ['sɪnjuwəs] *adj.* **1.** sinueux. **2.** [Fig.] tortueux.

sinus ['sajnəs], *pl.* -es *n.* **1.** [Anat.] sinus *m*: *~ trouble, ~ infection*, sinusite *f*. **2.** creux *m*, cavité *f*.

sip [sɪp] *n.* petite gorgée *f*. || *v. tr.* **[-pp-]** siroter, déguster (à petites gorgées).

siphon ['sajfən] *n.* siphon *m*. || *v. tr.* siphonner.

sir [sɚ] *n.* **1.** [titre de politesse, employé sans prénom ni nom de famille] monsieur *m*: *Yes, ~*, Oui, monsieur. **2.** [Mil.: s'emploie quand on s'adresse à un officier de rang supérieur] *Yes, ~*, Oui, [Army] mon lieutenant/[Navy] lieutenant; *Sir!* Présent! **3.** [titre de noblesse qui doit toujours être accompagné par le prénom en présence du porteur du titre, ou du prénom et, au besoin, du nom de famille en son absence] Sir *m* Frederick (Banting). **4.** [au commencement d'une lettre] (*Dear*) *Sir*/*Sirs*/, Monsieur/Messieurs/.

sire [sajɚ] *n.* **1.** [Poet.] père *m*; aïeux *mpl*. **2.** [animals] père *m*. mâle *m*. **3.** [king] Sire *m*.

siren ['sajɚən] *n.* **1.** [Myth.] sirène *f*. **2.** séductrice *f*. enjôleuse *f*. **3.** [alarm] sirène *f*.

sirloin ['sɚlojn] *n.* aloyau *m*; [beef] surlonge *f*.

sirup cf. SYRUP.

sissy ['sɪsɪ] *n.* [Péj.] poule *f* mouillée.

sister ['sɪstɚ] *n.* sœur *f*; [Rel.] sœur *f*, religieuse *f*: [☞ when addressing a sister] ma sœur: *~ -in-law*. belle-sœur *f*.

sit [sɪt], **sat** [sæt], **sat** *v. intr.* **1.** [verb of motion] s'asseoir; se mettre [bird] se percher: *~ on the floor*, Asseyez-vous par terre; *~ beside me*, Mettez-vous à côté de moi. **2.** [verb of rest] être, rester/assis; [bird] percher; [hen] couver (des œufs); poser (pour un portrait); [Parliament, judge] siéger; [clothes] (bien, mal/) tomber: *I was sitting in the living-room reading*, J'étais (assis) dans le salon en train de lire; *to ~ at home*, rester chez soi; *to ~ on a committee*, être du comité; [Fig.] *to ~ on s.o.*, remettre qqun à sa place; *to ~ over sth.*, rester longtemps à faire qqch.: *to ~ tight*, ne pas bouger, rester sur ses positions; *to ~ heavy by s.o.*, peser à qqun; *to ~ on the fence*, regarder d'où vient le vent, ne pas prendre position; *to ~ with s.o.*, tenir compagnie à qqun; *to ~ for s.o.*, garder un enfant pour qqun. || *v. tr.* asseoir (un bébé sur ses genoux): *to ~ a horse well*, se tenir bien à cheval. || **sit back** [-'bæk] *v. intr.* se renverser (dans son fauteuil). || **sit down** [-'dawn] *v. intr.* s'asseoir; se mettre, prendre place/(à table). || **sit-down** [strike]: *to stage a ~*, faire la grève *f*/d'occupation, sur le tas/. || **sit out** [-'awt] *v. tr.* rester assis pendant une danse; rester jusqu'au bout: *I think I'll sit this one out*, Je ne crois pas que je danserai cette fois-ci, [Fig.] Je préfère ne pas en être pour cette fois. || **sit through** [-'θɹuw] *v. intr.* rester jusqu'au bout de . . . || **sit up** [-'ʌp] *v. intr.* se redresser; se tenir droit; [in bed] se mettre sur son séant; [at night] veiller tard: *~ straight*, Tenez-vous droit; [Fig.] *That made him ~*, Cela a attiré son attention, [Fam.] Cela l'a épaté; *to ~ for s.o.*, (rester debout à) attendre qqun; *to ~ with s.o.*, veiller, garder/qqun.

site [sajt] *n.* [town, camp, &c.] [×] emplacement *m*, siège *m*.

sitter ['sɪt|ɚ] *n.* modèle *m*/*f* (qui pose); (poule) couveuse *f*; *baby ~*, gardien, -ne d'enfants.

sitting [-ɪŋ] *adj.* assis. || *n.* séance *f*, session *f*; *~ -up*, veillée *f*. || **sitting-room** [-ɪŋ-ˌɹuwm] *n.* salon *m*, © vivoir *m*.

situated ['sɪtʃuwˌejtəd] *adj.* **1.** situé; [Law] sis. **2.** [Pers.] placé. || **situation** [ˌsɪtʃuw'ejʃən] [location; events] situation *f*; position *f* (d'un objet); [site] emplacement *m* (d'une maison); [events] circonstances *fpl*; [job] emploi *m*.

six [sɪks] *num. adj.* six *m*. || **sixteen** [-'tijn] *num. adj.* seize. || **sixteenth** [-'tijnθ] *num. adj.* seizième; cf. FIRST. || **sixth** [-θ] *num. adj.* sixième; cf. FIRST. || **sixthly** [-θlɪ] sixièmement, en sixième lieu. || **sixtieth** [-tɪəθ] *adj.* soixantième. || **sixty** [-tɪ] *adj.* soixante.

size [sajz] *n.* [body] dimension(s) *f*(*pl*) (d'un corps, d'un objet); grandeur *f* (d'un parc, d'un champ); pointure *f* (d'un soulier, d'un chapeau); taille *f* (d'une robe; d'une personne); format *m* (d'une boîte, d'un livre); étendue *f* (d'un lac); [Com., ribbon, &c.] numéro *m* (d'une marchandise). || *v. tr.* **1.** classer (des objets) par dimensions. **2.** [paint] (en)-coller (un mur, du bois, &c.). **3.** *to ~ up* (*a person, a situation*), juger (une personne, une situation); [Fig.] toiser (qqun).

sizzle ['sɪzḷ] *v. intr.* grésiller; [Fam.] avoir très chaud.

skate[1] [skejt] *n.* raie *f*.

skate² *n.* [ice ~, roller ~] patin *m.* || *v. intr.* patiner: [Fig.] *to ~ on thin ice,* s'engager sur un terrain brûlant. || **skater** [-ɚ] *n.* patineur. || **skating** [-ɪŋ] *n.* patinage *m*; *~ rink,* patinoire *f.*

skeletal [skɛlə|təl] *adj.* squelettique, décharné. || **skeleton** [-tən] *n.* [Pers.] squelette *m*; [general] charpente *f.*

skeptic ['skɛptɪk] cf. SCEPTIC.

sketch [skɛtʃ] *n.* esquisse *f,* croquis *m*; [Fig.] aperçu *m,* exposé *m* sommaire. || *v. tr. & intr.* esquisser; dessiner.

skewer ['skjuwɚ] *n.* [cooking] brochette *f.*

ski [skij] *n.* [Sport] ski *m*: *~ pole,* bâton *m* de ski; *~ -jump,* saut *m* à skis; *~ tow,* monte-pente *m. inv.* || *v. intr.* faire du ski, skier; aller/en ski, à skis.

skid [skɪd] *n.* **1.** [Auto.] dérapage *m.* **2.** frein *m,* sabot *m*; [plane] patin *m,* [tail] béquille *f.* **3.** défense *f.* || *v. intr.* [-dd-] déraper. || **skidding** [-ɪŋ] *n.* dérapage *m.*

skidrow [-'ɹow] *n.* [Sl.] quartier *m* mal famé: [Fr.] [Sl.] *~ joint,* boui-boui *m.*

skiff [skɪf] *n.* petite barque *f*; [Poet.] esquif *m.*

skill [skɪl] *n.* [physical] habileté *f,* adresse *f,* dextérité *f*; [mental] art *m,* talent *m*; [job] métier *m.* || **skilled** [-d] *adj.* habile, adroit, expérimenté (en, *in*), spécialisé. || **skillful** [-fḷ] *adj.* adroit, expert, habile; ingénieux. || **skillfully** [-fḷɪ] *adv.* avec habileté, habilement, adroitement.

skillet [-ət] *n.* casserole *f*; [frying pan] poêle *f.*

skim [skɪm] *v. tr.* [-mm-] écrémer (le lait); écumer (un métal en fusion); [Fig.] [airplane] raser (le sol). || *v. intr.*: *to ~ over,* glisser, passer légèrement (sur).

skimp [skɪmp] *v. intr.* lésiner (*on,* sur); [Fam.] bâcler (un travail).

skimpy ['skɪmpɪ] *adj.* maigre, insuffisant; [garment] étriqué.

skin [skɪn] *n.* [man, animal] peau *f*; [grape, milk] pellicule *f*; pelure *f* (d'un fruit): *wet to the ~,* trempé jusqu'aux os; *by the ~ of o.'s teeth,* par un cheveu. || *v. tr.* écorcher (qqun, un animal); peler (une banane, &c.); éplucher (un légume, une volaille). || *v. intr.* [-nn-] [wound] se cicatriser. || **skinner** [-ɚ] *n.* pelletier *m*; peaussier *m.* || **skinny** [-ɪ] *adj.* maigre, maigrichon, décharné; comme la peau.

skip [skɪp] *v. tr. & intr.* [-pp-] sauter; [hop] sautiller, gambader: *to ~ rope,* sauter à la corde; [Fig.] omettre, négliger, sauter (un passage); [Fig., Fam.] *~ it!,* Laisse tomber!, Ça suffit!; *to ~ /off, out,* filer.

skipper [-ɚ] *n.* capitaine *m,* patron *m* (de bateau); [Fig.] patron *m.*

skirmish ['skɚmɪʃ] *n.* escarmouche *f*: *~ of wit,* assaut *m* d'esprit.

skirt [skɚrt] *n.* **1.** jupe *f*; pan *m* (d'un habit, d'un manteau). **2.** lisière *f* (de la forêt), bord *m* (d'un champ). || *v. tr.* border, longer (une forêt, &c.).

skit [skɪt] *n.* satire *f*; sketch *m.*

skittish [-ɪʃ] *adj.* **1.** fantasque, capricieux; [horse] ombrageux. **2.** timide.

skulduggery [ˌskʌl'dʌgəɪ] [US] *n.* fourberie, *f,* ruse *f.*

skulk [skʌlk] *v. intr.* se cacher; [Fam.] se planquer; [prowl] rôder.

skull [skʌl] *n.* crâne *m.* || **skullcap** [-ˌkæp] *n.* [headgear] calotte *f.*

skunk [skʌŋk] *n.* putois *m* (d'Amérique), mouffette *f,* © bête *f* puante; [Fig.] chameau *m,* salaud *m.*

sky [skaj] *pl.* **skies** [-z] *n.* ciel *m*; *skies,* le ciel, les cieux; [Fig.] climat *m.* || **skylark** [-ˌlaɚk] *n.* alouette *f* (des champs). || **skyscraper** [-ˌskɹejpɚ] *n.* gratte-ciel *m. inv.*

slab [slæb] *n.* [stone] dalle *f,* plaque *f*; [metal] feuille *f*; [meat] tranche *f* épaisse.

slack [slæk] **1.** lâche; mou: *The rope is ~,* La corde/a du mou, est lâche; *~ hours,* heures *fpl* creuses; *~ season,* morte-saison *f.* **2.** négligent, lent. || *v. tr.* détendre, relâcher. || *v. intr.* prendre du/lâche, jeu, mou; *to ~ off,* se relâcher. || **slacken** [-ən] *v. tr. & intr.* (se) ralentir, (se) relâcher. || **slacker** [-ɚ] *n.* [Fam.] paresseux *m*; tire-au-flanc *m.* || **slacks** [-s] *n.* pantalon *m.*

slain cf. SLAY.

slam [slæm] *n.* **1.** claquement *m* (de porte, de portière). **2.** critique *f*; [cards] chelem *m.* || *v. tr.* [-mm-] [door] claquer, pousser violemment; [Fig.] critiquer vertement.

slander ['slændɚ] *n.* médisance *f,* faux bruit *m*; calomnie *f,* diffamation *f.* || *v. tr.* médire (de qqun); calomnier, diffamer. || **slanderer** [-ɚ] *n.* médisant *m,* calomniateur *m,* diffamateur *m.* || **slanderous** [-ɔs] *adj.* médisant, calomnieux, diffamatoire.

slang [slæŋ] *adj.* argotique. || *n.* [Ling.] argot *m.*

slant [slænt] *adj.* oblique, incliné. || *n.* pente *f*; *on a ~,* en pente; [Fig.] point *m* de vue. || *v. tr.* rendre oblique; incliner. || **slanting** [-ɪŋ] *adj.* **1.** oblique, de travers. **2.** en pente, incliné.

slap [slæp] *n.* gifle *f,* tape *f.* || *v. tr.* [-pp-] *to ~ s.o. in the face,* gifler qqun.

slash [slæʃ] *n.* entaille *f,* balafre *f*; coup *m* de fouet. || *v. intr.* taillader (d'un coup de couteau); fouetter (durement); [Fig.] réduire beaucoup; [text] couper (dans le texte), élaguer. || **slashing** [-ɪŋ] *n.* **1.** [timbering] défrichage, abattage. **2.** [timbering] *pl.* déchets *mpl* d'abattage.

slat [slæt] *n.* [wood] latte *f.*

slate [slejt] *n.* ardoise *f*; [Pol., Adm.] liste *f* (des candidats): *A new ~ of officers was elected,* On procéda à l'élection du nouveau bureau; [Fig.] *He has a ~ missing,* Il lui manque/ © un bardeau, [Fr.] une case/.

slaughter [ˈslɔtɚ] *n.* boucherie *f*, massacre *m*, carnage *m*: *~ -house,* abattoir *m.* || *v. tr.* abattre (une bête, un animal, du bétail); massacrer (des gens).

Slav [slæv] *adj. & n.* [nationality] slave *m/f.* || **Slav(on)ic** [sləˈvɑnɪk] *adj.* slave.

slave [slejv] *n.* esclave *m/f.* || *v. intr.* travailler comme un/nègre, esclave/, trimer. || **slaver** [-ɚ] *n.* négrier *m*; bâtiment *m* négrier. || **slavery** [-ɚɪ] *n.* esclavage *m.* || **slavish** [-ɪʃ] *adj.* servile.

slaw [slɔ] *n.* cf. COLE-SLAW.

slay [slej], **slew** [sluw], **slain** [slejn] *v. tr.* tuer, massacrer. || **slaying** [ˈslejɪŋ] *n.* massacre *m*, [Fig.] boucherie *f.* cf. SLAUGHTER.

sleazy [ˈslijzɪ] *adj.* [cloth] mince, râpé.

sled [slɛd] **sledge** [slɛʤ] *n.* traîneau; © catherine *f*, carriole *f.*

sleek [slijk] *adj.* lisse, luisant; [Fig.] mielleux, onctueux. || *v. tr.* [hair] lisser.

sleep [slijp], **slept** [slɛpt], **slept** *v. intr.* dormir; [place] passer la nuit, coucher: *to ~ like a top,* dormir à poings fermés; *to go to ~ ,* s'endormir; *Go to ~ !,* Dors!; *to ~ late,* faire la grasse matinée; *to ~ off one's wine,* cuver son vin. || *n.* sommeil *m.* || **sleeper** [ˈslijp|ɚ] *n.* **1.** dormeu|r *m*, -se *f.* **2.** [Rail.] wagon-lit *m*, voiture-couchette *f*; [tie] traverse *f.* || **sleepiness** [-ɪnəs] *n.* [feeling] somnolence *f*; assoupissement *m.* || **sleeping** [-ɪŋ] *adj.* dormant, endormi. || *n.* sommeil *m*: *~ bag,* sac *m* de couchage. || **sleeping-car,** cf. SLEEPER. || **sleeping room,** *n.* dortoir *m.* || **sleepless** [-ləs] *adj.* [night] sans sommeil, (nuit *f*) blanche. || **sleeplessness** [-ləsnəs] *n.* insomnie *f.* || **sleepy** [-ɪ] *adj.* [Pers.] endormi, assoupi; [Fig., tune] soporifique; [look] indolent: *to/be, feel/ ~ ,* avoir sommeil.

sleet [slijt] *n.* [ice] grésil *m*; [Br.] neige *f* fondue.

sleeve [slijv] *n.* **1.** manche *f.* **2.** [Tech.] [-coupling] manchon *m*, douille *f* (d'accouplement); *to have sth. up o.'s ~ ,* avoir un atout en réserve; *to laugh up o.'s ~ ,* rire sous cape. || **sleeveless**]-ləs] *adj.* sans manches.

sleigh [slej] *n.* traîneau *m* cf. SLED. || *v. intr.* aller en traîneau.

sleight [slajt] *n.* adresse *f*, dextérité *f*; *~ of hand,* prestidigitation *f.*

slender [ˈslɛndɚ] *adj.* [Pers.] mince, [body, waist] svelte; [argument, proof] faible, fragile; [resources] maigre.

slept cf. SLEEP.

sleuth [sluwθ] *n.* limier *m*, détective *m.*

slew[1] cf. SLAY.

slew[2] [sluw] © *n.* marais *m*, étang *m*; cf. SLOUGH.

slew[3] *v. tr. & intr.* (faire) pivoter.

slice [slajs] *n.* tranche *f* (de pain, de viande). || *v. tr.* trancher (du pain, de la viande), couper (qqch.) en tranches.

slick [slɪk] *adj.* lisse; [road] glissant; [Fig.] rusé, adroit: *a ~ talker,* un beau parleur; [appearance] élégant. || *n.* tache *f* (d'huile).

slicker [-ɚ] *n.* imperméable *m*; [Fig.] roublard *m.*

slid cf. SLIDE. || **slide** [slajd], **slid, slid** [slɪd] *v. tr. & intr.* glisser, coulisser; se glisser. || *n.* **1.** glissade *f*, (sur la glace, &c.) glissement *m*; coulisse *f*: *~ rule,* règle *f* à calcul; *~ trombone,* trombone *m* à coulisse. **2.** [projection] diapositive *f.* || **sliding** [ˈslajdɪŋ] *adj.* glissant, coulant, [~ door] à coulisse. || *n.* glissement *m*, glissade *f.*

slight [slajt] *adj.* [trifle] léger; [figure] mince, menu; [Fig.] [effort, &c.] faible; [unimportant] insignifiant: *I haven't the slightest idea,* Je n'en ai pas la moindre idée. || *v. tr.* dédaigner (qqun, qqch.); manquer d'égards envers (qqun). || **slightly** [-lɪ] *adv.* légèrement, faiblement; un peu.

slim [slɪm] *adj.* **[-mm-] 1.** svelte, élancé, mince. **2.** [Fig.] mince: *a ~ chance,* une faible chance. || *v. intr.* maigrir, s'amincir.

slime [slajm] *n.* limon *m*, vase *f*; [fish, slugs, &c.] bave *f*; [Fig.] fange *f.*

sling [slɪŋ] *n.* fronde *f*; [strap] bretelle *f* (de fusil), bandoulière *f*; [Med.] écharpe *f.* || **sling, slung** [slʌŋ], **slung** *v. tr.* lancer (qqch.) avec une fronde; passer en bandoulière; [Fig.] jeter (qqch. à la tête de qqun); [Fam., = toss] lancer, envoyer.

slink [slɪŋk], **slunk** [slʌŋk], **slunk** *v. intr.*: *to ~ away,* s'esquiver.

slip [slɪp] *v. intr.* **[-pp-]** (se) glisser; [car] patiner; faire un faux-pas; *to ~ /away, off/,* s'échapper, se dérober, s'esquiver; *time slips/away, by,* le temps s'enfuit, s'écoule; *to ~ into,* se glisser (furtivement) dans; *to ~ out,* sortir à la dérobée (d'une maison), *to let ~ ,* laisser échapper. || *v. tr.* (faire) glisser; perdre, lâcher; s'échapper: *to ~ into one's* *clothes*, enfiler ses vêtements à la hâte [= *to ~ one's coat, &c. on*]; *It slipped my mind*, Cela m'est sorti de l'esprit. || **slip** *n.* **1.** [landslide] glissement *m* (de terrain), éboulement *m*; glissade *f*, [Fig.] faux-pas *m*, méprise *f*, gaffe *f*: *a ~ of the tongue*, un lapsus. **2.** combinaison *f*; *~ cover*, housse *f* (d'auto, &c.). **3.** brin *m*; bouture *f* [Bot.]; [Naut.] cale *f*, [card] fiche *f*. || **slipper(s)** [-ɚ] *n.* (*pl.*) pantoufle(s) *f*(*pl*). || **slippery** [-ɚɪ] *adj.* **1.** [roads] glissant: *Slippery when wet*, Chaussée glissante par temps humide. **2.** [Fig.] fuyant, rusé. || **slipshod** [-ˌʃɑd] *adj.* négligé, bâclé.

slit [slɪt] *n.* fente *f*, fissure *f*. || **slit, slit, slit** *v. tr. & intr.* (se) fendre; inciser; [pages] couper: *to ~ s.o.'s throat*, égorger qqun.

slither [ˈslɪðɚ] *v. intr.* glisser; [snakes, &c.] ramper.

sliver [ˈslɪvɚ] *n.* tranche *f* mince; [wood, glass] éclat *m*; [in finger] écharde *f*.

slobber [ˈslɑbɚ] *n.* bave *f*, salive *f*; [Fig.] sentimentalité *f*; [Pej.] sensiblerie *f*. || *v. intr.* baver; [Fig.] larmoyer.

sloe [slow] *n.* prunelle *f*: *~ gin*, liqueur *f* de prunelle.

slogan [ˈslowgən] *n.* mot *m* d'ordre; [Com.] devise *f*, slogan *m*.

slop [slɑp] *n.* **1.** [clothing] blouse *f*, hardes *fpl.* **2.** liquide *m* répandu; [Pej.] rinçure *f*, eau *f* sale; *~ basin*, vide-tasse *m inv.* || *v. tr.* [-pp-] [liquids] répandre; *to ~ paint on sth.*, peinturlurer, barbouiller qqch.; *to ~ over*, déborder; [Fig.] déborder de sensiblerie.

slope [slowp] *n.* [hill] pente *f*; [angle] inclinaison *f*; [Rail.] talus *m*; [road] côte *f*: *~ of stream*,/pente *f*, © pied *m*/du courant. || *v. intr.* [road, &c.] être en pente; [thing] pencher, incliner: *to ~ up, down*, monter, descendre.

sloppy [ˈslɑpɪ] *adj.* mouillé, [Fig.] négligé, débraillé; [work] bâclé.

slot [slɑt] *n.* entaille *f*; [metres, distributors, &c.] fente *f*: *~ machine*, distributeur automatique. || *v. tr.* [-tt-] entailler, faire une fente dans qqch.

sloth [slɑθ] *n.* paresse *f*, indolence *f*. *n.* [animal] paresseux *m*. || **slothful** [-fl] *adj.* paresseux, fainéant, indolent.

slouch [slawtʃ] *n.* lourdaud *m*; [Fam.]: *He's no ~*, Il n'est pas empoté; [gait] démarche *f*/allure *f*/lourde. || *v. intr.* [tenue, démarche] se laisser aller, ne pas se tenir droit; *to ~ along*, traîner le pas, le dos courbé.

slough[1] [slaw] *n.* marais *m*, fondrière *f*.

slough[2] [slʌf] *n.* **1.** mue *f*, dépouille *f* (d'un serpent, d'une couleuvre). **2.** croûte *f* (sur une plaie). || *v. tr.* se dépouiller (d'un vêtement, &c.). || *v. intr.* [serpent] muer.

Slovakia [ˌslowˈvækɪə] *n.* (la) Slovaquie *f*.

sloven [ˈslʌvən] *n.* souillon *f*, personne *f* négligée. || **slovenliness** [-lɪnəs] *n.* négligence *f* de tenue; malpropreté *f*. || **slovenly** [-lɪ] *adj.* négligé, sans soin; [Pers.] négligent, mal tenu: *~ appearance*, tenue *f* débraillée.

slow [slow] *adj.* [move] lent, [mind] borné; [dull] terne; [late] en retard: *My watch is 5 minutes ~*, Ma montre retarde de 5 minutes. || *v. tr.* [up] ralentir (un mouvement): *Slow, Children*, Ralentir École. || *v. intr.*: *to ~ down*, ralentir. || **slow-motion** [-ˈmowʃən] *n.* ralenti *m*. || **slowly** [-lɪ] *adv.* lentement; tardivement. || **slowness** [-nəs] *n.* lenteur *f*, retard *m*; [Fig.] lenteur *f*, lourdeur *f*.

sludge [slʌdʒ] *n.* boue *f*; vase *f*.

slug [slʌg] *n.* **1.** limace *f*. **2.** [metal] jeton *m*, projectile *m*. || **sluggard** [-ɚd] *n.* paresseux *m*, fainéant *m*. || **sluggish** [-ɪʃ] *adj.* paresseux, traînard.

sluice [sluws] *n.* écluse *f*: *~ gate*, vanne *f*. || *v. tr.* rincer (à grande eau).

slum [slʌm] *n.* bas quartier *m*; [dwelling] taudis *m*. || *v. intr.* [-mm-] aller visiter les taudis.

slumber [-bɚ] *n.* sommeil *m*, assoupissement *m*. || *v. intr.* sommeiller, être assoupi.

slump [-p] *n.* affaissement *m*; [business] crise *f*, baisse *f*, marasme *m*. || *v. intr.* s'affaisser, tomber lourdement; [prices] dégringoler, s'effondrer.

slung cf. SLING.

slunk cf. SLINK.

slur [slɚ] *n* affront *m*, flétrissure *f*; [reputation] atteinte *f* (à). || *v. tr.* [-rr-] [speech] bredouiller: *to ~ over an incident*, passer/glisser/sur un incident; [Mus.] lier des notes; [reputation] flétrir, porter atteinte (à).

slush [slʌʃ] *n.* neige *f* à moitié fondue; boue *f*, © sloche *f*; boue *f*; sentimentalité *f* larmoyante. || **slushy** [-ɪ] *adj.* trempé de neige, de boue; [Fig.] bêtement sentimental.

sly [slaj] *adj.* rusé, sournois: *on the ~*, en cachette, furtivement; *a ~ question*, une question insidieuse; *a ~ wink*, un clin d'œil/espiègle, malicieux/. || **slyness** [-nəs] *n.* ruse *f*. espièglerie *f*.

smack [smæk] *n.* claquement *m* (des lèvres, &c.); tape *f*; gifle *f*; [kiss] bécot *m*, © bec *m*. || *v. intr.* claquer; [kiss] retentir. || **smacking** *adj.* qui/claque, retentit/; [Fig.] vigoureux.

small [smɔl] *adj.* **1.** petit: *a ~ house*, une petite maison; [time] de courte durée, petit; *~ letters*, minuscules *fpl.* **2.** [Fig.] [income] modique; [question] insignifiante; [numbers] petit, peu nombreux; [people] petites gens, gens de condition humble; [petty] mesquin. **3.** [Loc.] *~ change*, (petite) monnaie *f*; *~ wonder!*, (Ce n'est) pas étonnant!; *to look ~*, avoir l'air penaud; *~ hours (of the morning)*, le petit matin; *~ talk*, ragots *mpl*, papotage *m.* || **smallish** [-ɪʃ] *adj.* plutôt petit. || **smallness** [-nəs] *n.* petitesse *f*: [dimensions of a room, &c.] exiguïté *f*; [Fig.] mesquinerie *f.* || **smallpox** [-ˌpɑks] *n.* variole *f*, © [Fam.] picote *f.* || **smalltime** [-ˌtajm] *adj.* [Pej.] de troisième ordre. || **smallwares** [-ˌwɛəˑz] *n.pl.* mercerie *f.* cf. NOTIONS.

smart [smɑəˑt] *adj.* **1.** [person] éveillé, vif; intelligent. **2.** [person, clothes] chic, élégant, bien mis. **3.** [pain] cuisant. **4.** impertinent. || *v. intr.* [pain, sore] cuire. || **smartness** [-nəs] *n.* [mind] intelligence *f*; vivacité *f*; [Pej.] habileté; [appearance] élégance *f*, chic *m.*

smash [smæʃ] *v. tr.* [car] fracasser (qqch.); écraser, [Fam.] écrabouiller (qqun, qqch.); briser (qqch. en morceaux); [enemy] écraser, démolir; [tennis] smasher. || *v. tr.* s'écraser; se fracasser; *to ~ into sth.*, s'écraser contre qqch. || *n.* fracassement *m*, écrasement *m*; accident *m* (de chemin de fer); [Fin.] débâcle *f*, [Com.] faillite *f.*

smattering [ˈsmætəˑɪŋ] *n.* notion *f*, connaissance *f*/superficielle (*of*, sur).

smear [smijəˑ] *n.* tache *f*, souillure *f*; [Med.] frottis *m.* || *v. tr.* barbouiller, enduire (with, *de*); maculer, salir (une réputation).

smell [smɛl] *n.* odeur *f*, senteur *f*; (faculté de l')odorat *m*; [dog] flair *m.* || **smell, smelt** [-t], **smelt** *v. tr. & intr.* sentir (qqch.); [dog] flairer: *to ~ of tobacco*, sentir le tabac; *to ~ /good, bad*, sentir/bon, mauvais.

smelt[1] cf. SMELL.

smelt[2] *n.* [fish] éperlan *m.*

smelt[3] *v. tr.* [Metall.] fondre (le fer). || **smeltery** [-əˑɪ] *n.* fonderie *f.* || **smelting** [-ɪŋ] *n.* fonte *f.*

smile [smajl] *v. intr. & tr.* sourire (*at, on*, à). || *n.* sourire *m.* || **smiling** [-ɪŋ] *adj.* souriant; [face] avenant, ouvert. || **smilingly** [-ɪŋlɪ] *adv.* en souriant, avec/un, le/sourire.

smirch [sməˑtʃ] *v. tr.* souiller (qqun, qqch.).

smirk [sməˑk] *n.* minauderie *f.* || *v. intr.* minauder.

smite [smajt], **smote** [smowt], **smitten** [smɪtn̩] frapper (qqun, qqch.); [Fig.] *to be smitten with*, être frappé (de terreur); avoir (du remords); être épris de (qqun).

smith [smɪθ] *n.* forgeron *m*: *goldsmith*, orfèvre *m*; *tinsmith*, ferblantier *m.*

smithy [smɪθɪ] *n.* forge *f.*

smitten cf. SMITE.

smock [smɑk] *n.* blouse *f* (de travail), tablier *m*; © [abus.] froc *m.*

smoke [smowk] *n.* fumée *f*, © [Fam.] boucane *f*; [Fig.] cigarette *f*, cigare *m*: [Br.] *Have a ~ ?*, Cigarette?, → Vous fumez?; *He went out for a ~*, Il est sorti fumer une cigarette; *~ bomb*, bombe *f* fumigène. || *v. tr.* fumer: *He smokes cigars*, Il fume le cigare; *smoked glasses*, conserves *fpl*, verres *mpl* fumés; [Cul.] fumer; [Hist.] boucaner. || *v. intr.* fumer. || **smoker** [-əˑ] *n.* fumeur *m*; [Br.] compartiment *m* de fumeurs. || **smokestack** [-ˌstæk] *n.* [train, steamship, factory] cheminée *f.* || **smoking** [-ɪŋ] *adj.* fumant. || *n.* action de fumer: *No ~*, Défense de fumer; [Rail.] *~ car*, (voiture *f* de) fumeurs; *~ room*, fumoir *m.* || **smoky** [-ɪ] *adj.* fumeux; enfumé.

smooth [smuwð] *adj.* lisse, [au toucher] doux, moelleux; [Fig.] doux, régulier; [sea] calme; [voice] onctueux; [life] paisible; [caractère] facile; *~ -shaven*, rasé de près; [Pej.] *~ -spoken*, onctueux, enjôleur. || **smoothe** *v. tr.* lisser; [wood] aplanir; [wrinkles] effacer; *to ~ away*, apaiser, calmer; *to ~ out*, défroisser, aplanir; *to ~ down*, se calmer, s'apaiser. || **smoothly** [-lɪ] *adv.* doucement, sans heurts. || **smoothness** [-nəs] *n.* douceur *f*; calme *m*; [langue] style *m*/coulant, sans heurts/.

smother [ˈsmʌðəˑ] *v. tr.* [Pers.] suffoquer; étouffer (*s.o., sth.*) qqun, qqch.; recouvrir (de crème, de sauce, &c.).

smoulder [ˈsmowldəˑ] *v. intr.* brûler sans flamme *f*, brûler lentement; [fire, anger, passion] couver.

smudge [smʌdʒ] *n.* **1.** tache *f.* **2.** fumée *f* épaisse: *~ pot*, pot *m* à fumée; appareil *m* fumigène. || *v. tr.* tacher, noircir.

smug [smʌg] *adj.* vaniteux; (air, attitude) suffisant(e).

smuggle [-l̩] *v. tr. & intr.* passer en contrebande, faire de la contrebande. || **smuggler** [-ləˑ] *n.* contrebandier *m.* || **smuggling** [-lɪŋ] *n.* contrebande *f*, fraude *f.*

smut [smʌt] *n.* parcelle *f* de suie, tache *f* noire, de suie; [Fig.] langage *m* indécent, grivoiserie *f.* || *v. tr.* [-tt-] noircir, salir. || **smutty** [-ɪ] *adj.* noirci, sali; [Fig.] malpropre, ordurier.

snack [snæk] *n.* casse-croûte *m. inv.*: ~ *bar*, buffet *m.*

snag [snæg] *n.* souche *f* à fleur d'eau; [Fig.]: *to hit a* ~, rencontrer, se heurter à un obstacle. || *v. tr.* [-gg-] accrocher.

snail [snejl] *n.* escargot *m*: *at a snail's pace*, à pas de tortue.

snake [snejk] *n.* serpent *m.* || *v. intr.* serpenter.

snap [snæp] *v. tr.* **[-pp-]** casser net, briser; [up] happer, saisir; [Photo.] prendre un instantané de. || *v. intr.* [pistol] partir; [whip] claquer: *to* ~ *at s.o.*, parler à qqun d'un ton sec, rembarrer qqun. || *n.* cassure *f*, brisure *f* soudaine; bruit *m* sec; [fingers] chiquenaude *f*; bouton-pression *m*, pression *f*; *a cold* ~, une vague de froid; [Arg.] *It's a* ~, C'est du tout cuit! || *adj.* imprévu, à l'improviste. || **snappy** [-ɪ] *adj.* énergique, plein d'allant; vif: [Fam.] *Make it* ~ *!*, Grouillez-vous! || **snapshot** [-ˌʃɑt] *n.* [Phot.] instantané *m.*

snare [snɛɚ] *n.* piège *m*, collet *m.* || *v. tr.* prendre au collet, au piège; attraper.

snarl [snɑɚl] *v. intr.* grogner, gronder. || *v. tr.* emmêler, enchevêtrer.

snatch [snætʃ] *n.* courte période; fragment *m*: *snatches of conversation*, bribes *fpl* de conversation. || *v. tr.* saisir, empoigner, enlever: *to* ~ *up*, ramasser vivement; *to* ~ (*away*) *from*, arracher à.

sneak [snijk] *v. intr.* [out] se sauver, sortir/ furtivement; [in] se glisser, se faufiler/ furtivement dans/. || *v . tr.* chiper, chaparder. || *v. intr.* rapporter, moucharder. || *n.* pleutre *m*; [Fam.] mouchard *m.* || **sneakers** [-ɚz] *n.pl.* chaussures *fpl* de tennis; souliers *mpl* de toile.

sneer [snijɚ] *v. intr.* sourire/en se moquant, d'un air méprisant/, ricaner. || *n.* ricanement *m.*

sneeze [snijz] *v. intr.* éternuer: *It's not to be sneezed at*, Il ne faut pas cracher dessus. || *n.* éternuement *m.*

sniff [snɪf] *v. tr.* renifler; [smell] flairer, humer. || *n.* reniflement *m*; [of air] bouffée *f.*

sniffle [ˈsnɪfl̩] *n.* reniflement *m*: *to have the sniffles*, être enchifrené. || *v. intr.* renifler.

snip [snɪp] *n.* [paper, fabric, &c.] petit morceau *m*, bout *m*; coup *m* de ciseaux *mpl*; [*pl.*] cisailles *fpl.* || *v. tr.* **[-pp-]** couper (d'un coup de ciseaux *mpl*); *to* ~ *off*, enlever, détacher (d'un coup de ciseaux).

snipe [snajp] *n.* [Zool.] bécassine *f.* || *v. tr.*: [Mil.] *to* ~ *at*, canarder, tirer sur. || **sniper** [-ɚ] *n.* [Mil.] tireur *m* embusqué.

snitch [snɪtʃ] *v. tr.* [Fam.] chiper, escamoter. || *v. intr.* [Fam.] moucharder.

snivel [ˈsnɪvl̩] *n.* reniflement *m*, pleurnicherie *f.* || *v. intr.* **[-ll-]** avoir le nez qui coule; larmoyer, pleurnicher.

snob [snɑb] *n.* snob *m*, poseur *m.* || **snobbishness** [-ɪʃnəs] *n.* snobisme *m.*

snoop [snuwp] *v. intr.* fureter, fouiller (en cachette): *to* ~ *around*, fouiner partout. || *n.* curieux *m*: *to be a* ~, fouiller partout.

snooze [snuwz] *n.* petit somme *m*, sieste *f.* || *v. intr.* faire un (petit) somme *m.*

snore [snɔɚ] *n.* ronflement *m.* || *v. intr.* ronfler.

snort [snɔɚt] *n.* reniflement *m*; [horse] ébrouement *m.* || *v. intr.* renifler fortement: *to* ~ *at sth.*, dédaigner qqch.; *to* ~ *with anger*, grogner.

snout [snawt] *m.* museau *m*; [pig] groin *m.*

snow [snow] *n.* neige *f*: ~ *-ball*, boule *f* de neige; ~ *-bound*, enneigé, bloqué par la neige; ~ *-drift*, congère *f*, © banc *m* de neige; ~ *-fall*, chute *f* de neige; © bordée *f* de neige; ~ *-flake* flocon *m* de neige; ~ *-man*, bonhomme *m* de neige; ~ *-plough*, chasse-neige *m*; ~ *-shoe*, raquette *f*; ~ *storm*, tempête *f* de neige; © poudrerie *f.* || *v. intr.* neiger; tomber de la neige; *It is snowing*, Il neige, La neige tombe; [Fam.] *to be snowed under* (*with work*), être/écrasé sous le travail, débordé de travail || **snowy** [-ɪ] *adj.* neigeux, de neige.

snub [snʌb] *n.* rebuffade *f*, [stronger] affront *m.* || *v. tr.* **[-bb-]** rabrouer; traiter (qqun) avec froideur. || *adj.* [nose] retroussé.

snuff [snʌf] *n.* tabac *m* à priser: ~ *snuffbox*, tabatière *f.* || *v. intr.* priser. || *v. tr.* [candle, life] *to* ~ *out*, éteindre.

snuffle [-fl̩] cf. SNIFFLE.

snug [snʌg] *adj.* **[-gg-]** confortable; [clothes] bien ajusté.

snuggle [ˈsnʌgl̩] *v. tr.* serrer (qqun) dans ses bras, dorloter. || *v. intr.* se serrer, se pelotonner (*up to*, tout près de).

so [sow] *adv.* **1.** [in such a way] ainsi, de cette/façon, manière/, [Fam.] comme ça: *You mustn't shout* ~ *!*, Il ne faut pas crier/ainsi, comme ça/; *If* (*it were*) ~, S'il en était ainsi; ~ *to/say, speak/*, pour ainsi dire; †*So it was that* . . ., C'est ainsi que . . . ; *It was* ~ *arranged as to* . . ., C'était arrangé de/façon, manière/à . . . ; *He* ~ *explained the lesson that we understood*, Il a expliqué la leçon de telle façon que nous avons compris; *You must* ~ *invest your money that you will have a regular income*, Il faut placer votre argent de (telle) façon que vous ayez un revenu régulier; *It ~ happens that . . .* , Il se trouve que . . . [+ indic.] **2.** [to such a degree] si, tellement; aussi: *He is ~ clever*, Il est/si, tellement/intelligent; *He is not ~ clever*, Il n'est pas/tellement intelligent, si intelligent que ça/; *I'm not ~ well*, Je ne vais pas très bien; *He is not ~ clever as you*, Il n'est pas aussi intelligent que vous; *~ interesting a book (as that one)*, un livre aussi intéressant (que celui-là); *~ large a country*, un si grand pays; *Would you be ~ kind as to . . . ?*, Auriez-vous la/bonté, gentillesse/de., Seriez-vous assez gentil pour . . . ?, *He is (not) ~ absent-minded that he . . .* , Il est/si, tellement/distrait qu'il [+ indic.], Il n'est pas/si, tellement/distrait qu'il ne [+ subjunc.] **3.** *~ much, ~ many*, (au)tant (de), [Fam.] tellement (de): *He has ~ many friends (that . . .)*, Il a tant d'amis (que . . .); *He has ~ much (of it)*, Il en a tant; *You exaggerate ~ (much)*, Vous exagérez/tellement, tant/; *not ~ /much, many/as . . .* , pas autant (de . . .) que . . . ; *~ many a week*, tant (de . . .) par semaine; *They behaved like ~ many monkeys*, Ils se sont conduits comme autant de singes. **4.** [substitute] le; cela; ainsi: *I think ~* , Je le crois, Je crois que oui; *I hope ~* , Je l'espère bien; *I told you ~ !*, Je vous l'avais bien dit!; *How ~ ?*, Comment cela?; *So it is*, Il en est ainsi, C'est juste; *Quite ~ !*,Très juste!; *Is that ~ ?*, Vraiment?; *So/you are, he did, &c./!*, En effet, c'est vrai!; *So/am I, did you, &c./*, /Moi, Vous/aussi. **5.** *~ that*, [Fam.] ~: [purpose] *He shouted ~ that I could hear him*, Il a crié pour que je puisse l'entendre; [result] Il a crié de telle sorte que j'ai pu l'entendre. **6.** *~ as to*: *He hurried ~ as not to be late*, Il s'est dépêché pour ne pas être en retard; *He pulled his hat down ~ as to hide his face*, Il a rabattu son chapeau de façon à cacher son visage. **7.** [special uses] *all the more ~ (because)*, d'autant plus (que); *so so*, comme ci comme ça; *He likes it just ~* , Il a des idées arrêtées là-dessus. || *conj.* alors; ainsi; donc, aussi [+ inversion]; par conséquent: *It is slippery, ~ be careful*, Les routes sont glissantes, alors faites attention; *It is too late, ~ I'm not going*, Il est trop tard,/alors, par conséquent/je n'y vais pas; *He was late (and) ~ we thought he wasn't coming*, Il était en retard,/aussi avons-nous cru, de sorte que nous avons cru/qu'il ne venait pas; *. . . and ~ I said to him . . .* , alors je lui ai dit . . .; *And ~ this is your brother?*, Voici donc votre frère? *So!*, Ça, par exemple!, Alors, (je vous y prends) !|| **so-and-so** [-n̩ˌsow] *n.* un(e) tel(le): *Mr. So-and-so*, Monsieur/un tel, Chose/; [Fam.] *He is an old ~* , C'est un vieux gredin. || **so-called** [-ˌkɔld] *adj.* prétendu [before n.]; [self-styled] soi-disant, prétendu [both before n.].

soak [sowk] *v. tr.* tremper, imbiber. || *v. intr.* baigner, tremper; [through] s'infiltrer, pénétrer; [up] s'imbiber, se détremper. || **soaking** [-ɪŋ] *adj.* détrempé; [Pers.] trempé: *~ wet*, trempé jusqu'aux os.

soap [sowp] *n.* savon *m*: *a cake of ~* , un pain de savon; *~ suds*, eau *f* de savon, lessive *f*; *~ flakes*, savon en paillettes; *~ bubble*, bulle *f* de savon; *shaving ~* , savon pour la barbe; *soft ~* , savon noir; [Fig.] (basse) flatterie *f*; *~ box*, caisse *f* à savon; [Fam.] *~ opera*, mélo radio-diffusé. || *v. tr.* savonner. || **soap ball** [-ˌbɔl] *n.* savonnette *f*. || **soapstone** [-ˌstown] *n.* stéatite *f*. || **soapy** [-ɪ] *adj.* savonneux, savonné.

soar [sɔɚ] *v. intr.* prendre son essor, s'élever (dans les airs); [prices] monter, augmenter; [ambition] planer. || **soaring** [-ɪŋ] *n.* essor *m*; [prices] hausse *f*.

sob [sɑb] *n.* sanglot *m.* || *v. intr.* **[-bb-]** sangloter.

sober [ˈsowbɚ] *adj.* **1.** qui n'a pas bu, à jeun [× SOBRE]. **2.** modéré, raisonnable. || *v. tr.* [down] dégriser; calmer (qqun); [opinion] réfléchi; [fact] réel; [truth] simple; [expression] grave. || **soberly** [-lɪ] *adv.* sobrement; avec modération, sagement. || **soberness** [-nəs] *n.* **1.** sobriété *f*. **2.** modération *f*; sérieux *m*. || **sobriety** [sowˈbɹajətɪ] *n.* sobriété *f*, tempérance *f*.

sociable [ˈsowʃəbl̩] *adj.* sociable; affable. || **sociableness** [-nəs] *n.* sociabilité *f*. || **social** [ˈsowʃəl] *adj.* **1.** [work, science, &c.] social, de société: *Social Credit*, le Crédit Social; *~ worker*, travailleur *m* social, assistante *f* sociale. **2.** [reception, gathering] mondain: *Social Register (of Canada)* = le bottin mondain. || **socialism** [-ˌɪzm] *n.* socialisme *m*. || **socialist** [-ɪst] *n.* socialiste *m/f*. || **socialistic** [-ˌɪstɪk] *adj.* socialiste. || **socially** [-ɪ] *adv.* socialement; en société; en compagnie.

society [səˈsajətɪ] *n.* **1.** société *f*: *the Royal Society of Canada*, la Société royale du Canada. **2.** association *f*: [R.C.] *The Society of Jesus*, la Compagnie de Jésus, les Jésuites. **3.** la (haute) société, le monde (chic, savant, &c.).

sociology [ˌsowsɪˈɔləʤɪ] *n.* sociologie *f*.

sock [sɑk] *n.* chaussette *f*: *a pair of socks*, une paire de chaussettes; © chausson *m.* cf. HOSE.

socket ['sɑkət] *n.* [Electr.] douille *f*; alvéole *m* (d'une dent); trou *m*, cavité *f*; orbite *f* (de l'œil).

Socred ['sɑk,ɹɛd] [= Social Credit Party] cf. SOCIAL.

sod [sɑd] *n.* (motte *f* de) gazon: [Fig.] *to turn the ~*, donner le premier coup de pioche. || *v. tr.* [-dd-] couvrir (un terrain) de gazon, gazonner.

soda ['sowdə] *n.* soude *f*; *baking ~*, bicarbonate *m* de soude; *~ water*, eau *f*/de seltz, gazeuse/; soda *m*; *~ fountain*, buffet-comptoir *m*; *washing ~*, cristaux *mpl* de soude.

sodden [-n̩] *adj.* [soil] détrempé.

sodium ['sowdɪəm] *n.* [Chem.] sodium *m.*

sofa ['sowfə] *n.* canapé *m*; sofa *m*, divan *m.*

soft [sɔft] *adj.* doux, tendre; [bed] moelleux; [rock] tendre; [coal] gras; [hat] mou; [hair] doux, flou; [leather] souple; [water] douce; [drink] non alcoolisé, © doux; [sound] sourd; [Fig.] délicat; mou; [Pej.] faible, efféminé: *~ -hearted*, au cœur tendre: [Fig.] *~ job*, fromage *m*, filon *m*; *to go ~*, [body] ramollir, [Fig.] perdre la boule; [Phon.] *~ palate*, le palais mou, le voile du palais. || *adv.* cf. SOFTLY. || **soften** ['sɔfn̩] *v. tr.* adoucir; (r)amollir; [Fig.] attendrir, affaiblir, efféminer. || *v. intr.* **1.** s'adoucir; s'amollir, se ramollir; s'attendrir. **2.** s'affaiblir. **3.** se calmer. || **softly** ['sɔft|lɪ] *adv.* doucement; tendrement; délicatement; mollement. || **softness** [-nəs] *n.* douceur *f*; mollesse *f*; [Fig.] faiblesse *f*; [Pers.] niaiserie *f.*

soggy ['sɑgɪ] *adj.* saturé (d'eau), détrempé.

soil[1] [sojl] *n.* saleté *f*; ordure *f*; [stain] tache *f.* || *v. tr.* salir, tacher, souiller; [Fig.] profaner (un temple); fumer (une terre).

soil[2] *n.* **1.** sol *m*, terrain *m.* **2.** pays *m*, territoire *m.*

sojourn ['sowʤən] *n.* séjour *m.* || *v. intr.* séjourner.

solace ['sowləs] *n.* consolation *f*, soulagement *m.* || *v. tr.* consoler; soulager; réconforter.

solar ['sowlər] *adj.* solaire.

sold [sowld] *adj.* vendu; [Fig.] *~ on* (*an idea*), persuadé (d'une idée), imbu (de, *on*).

solder ['sɑdər] *n.* soudure *f.* || *v. tr.* souder.

soldier ['sowlʤər] *n.* soldat *m.*

sole[1] [sowl] *adj.* **1.** seul, unique; (droit) exclusif. **2.** [Jur.] *~ legatee*, légataire *m* universel.

sole[2] *n.* **1.** semelle *f.* **2.** plante *f* des pieds. || *v. tr.* ressemeler (une chaussure).

sole[3] *n.* [fish] sole *f.*

solely [-lɪ] *adv.* seulement, uniquement.

solemn ['sɑləm] *adj.* solennel; grave; sérieux; [look] majestueux. || **solemnity** [sə'lɛmnɪtɪ] *n.* solennité *f*; gravité *f*; sérieux *m*; majesté *f.* || **solemnize** [-,najz] *v. tr.* solenniser; célébrer (un mariage). || **solemnly** ['sɑləm|lɪ] *adv.* solennellement; majestueusement; avec/sérieux, gravité/.

solicit [sə'lɪsɪt] *v. tr.* solliciter. || **solicitation** [sə,lɪsɪ'tejʃən] *n.* sollicitation *f.* || **solicitor** [sə'lɪsɪt|ər] *n.* [Jur.] avocat *m* avoué *m.* chef *m* du contentieux (d'une société commerciale); *the Solicitor General*, avocat général, © solliciteur général. || **solicitous** [-əs] *adj.* soucieux, préoccupé (about, *de*): *to be ~ of sth.*, avoir le souci de, désirer/qqch. || **solicitude** [-juwd] *n.* sollicitude *f.*

solid ['sɑlɪd] *adj.* [gold, silver] massif, plein; [colour] uni; [Fig.] digne de confiance; [vote] unanime: *~ line*, trait *m* plein. || **solidarity** [,sɑlɪ'dæərɪtɪ] *n.* solidarité *f.* || **solidify** [sə'lɪdɪ|,faj] *v. intr. & tr.* (se) solidifier, (se) figer. || **solidity** [-tɪ] *n.* solidité *f.* || **solidly** ['sɑlɪdlɪ] *adv.* massivement; [Fig.] [voter] à l'unanimité.

soliloquy [sə'lɪləkwɪ] *n.* soliloque *m.*

solitary ['sɑlɪ|,tɛərɪ] *n. & adj.* solitaire *m/f.* || **solitude** [-,tjuwd] *n.* solitude *f*, isolement *m.*

solo ['sowlow] *n. & adj.* solo (*m*): *to play ~*, jouer en solo. || **soloist** [-ɪst] *n.* soliste *m/f.*

soluble ['sɑljəbl̩] *adj.* soluble; [Fig.] résoluble. || **solution** [sə'luwʃən] *n.* solution *f*; dissolution *f*; [Fig.] résolution *f* (d'un problème). || **solve** [sɑlv] *v. tr.* résoudre (un problème). || **solvency** [-ənsɪ] *n.* solvabilité *f.* || **solvent** [-ənt] *adj.* **1.** [Fin.] solvable. **2.** dissolvant. || *n.* dissolvant *m.*

sombre ['sɑmbər] *adj.* sombre, morne. || **sombrely** [-lɪ] *adv.* sombrement, d'un air *m* morne.

some [sʌm] [Pour l'interrogatif de SOME et des composés, cf. ANY et pour le négatif cf. NOT ANY, NO] *adj.* **1.** quelque, certain: *~ day*, un de ces jours; *~ other day*, quelque autre jour. **2.** [indéfini] du, de l', de la, des; quelques: *~ people think*, → Il y a des gens qui pensent (que . . .); *~ time ago*, il y a quelque temps; *~ distance away*, à quelques/arpents, milles/ de là, → assez loin de là. **3.** [Emphatic] [Fam.] *~ city!*, Hein, quelle ville!, © c'est tout une ville!; [Fam.] . . . , *and then ~*, j'en passe et des meilleurs; pour ne citer que/ceux-là, celles-là/; ~

such, de la sorte. || *adv.* quelque: ~ *fifty people*, quelque cinquante personnes, cinquante personnes environ. || *pron. indéf.* **1.** [quantity] un peu de, une partie de: *Would you like* ~ *tea?*, Voulez-vous/un peu de, du/thé?; *Do you want* ~ *?*, En voulez-vous? **2.** [nombre] quelques-uns (de), quelques-unes (de); les uns, les unes; certains, certaines: ~ *of them came early*, quelques-uns arrivèrent en avance; ~ *like it hot*, Il y en a qui la/prennent, préfèrent/chaud.

somebody [ˈsʌmˌbʌdɪ] *pron. ind.* quelqu'un; on: ~ *go and tell him*, → Il faudrait qu'on le prévienne. || **somehow** [-haw] *adv.*: ~ *or other*, d'une/manière, façon/ou d'une autre; tant bien que mal. || **someone** [-ˌwʌn] *pron. ind.* quelqu'un. *cf.* SOMEBODY.

somersault [ˈsʌmɚˈsɔlt] *n.* saut *m* périlleux, culbute *f*: *to turn a* ~ , faire le saut périlleux. || *v. intr.* [Pers.] culbuter; [Auto.] capoter, faire la culbute; [Gymn.] faire un saut périlleux.

something [ˈsʌmθɪŋ] *pron. indef.* quelque chose; ~ *else*, autre chose: ~ *or other*, je ne sais (trop) quoi; [Fam.] *That's quite* ~ , C'est toute une affaire; ~ *of*, un/semblant, soupçon/de. || *adv.* un peu, dans une certaine mesure: ~ *like it*, quelque chose comme ça. || **sometime** [-ˌtajm] *adv.* **1.** [past] jadis, autrefois. **2.** [future] un jour, un de ces jours. || **sometimes** [-ˌtajmz] *adv.* quelquefois; parfois: ~ *this one*, ~ *that one*, tantôt celui-ci, tantôt celui-là. || **somewhat** [-ˌwɑt] *adv.* quelque peu, un peu, assez: ~ *cold*, assez froid. || *pron.*: ~ *of a* (*snob*, *&c.*), un peu (snob, &c.). || **somewhere** [-ˌwɛɚ] *adv.* quelque part; ~ *else*, quelque part ailleurs; ~ *or other*, je ne sais/plus, trop/où.

somnolent [ˈsɑmnələnt] *adj.* somnolent.

son [sʌn] *n.* fils *m*: ~ *-in-law*, gendre *m*; *step-* ~ , beau-fils *m.*

sonata [səˈnætə] *n.* sonate *f.*

song [sɔŋ] *n.* [act, birds] chant *m*; [Music] chanson *f*; [Rel.] cantique *m*: [Fig.] *I bought it for a* ~ , Je l'ai/eu, acheté/pour une bouchée de pain.

sonnet [ˈsɑnət] *n.* sonnet *m.*

sonority [səˈnɔɚɪtɪ] *n.* sonorité *f.* || **sonorous** [ˈsɑnɚəs] *adj.* sonore.

Soo [suw], **the** *n.* © [Fam.] = Sault-Sainte-Marie.

soon [suwn] *adv.* bientôt, sous peu: *so* ~ , *too* ~ , si tôt, trop tôt; *as* ~ *as*, aussitôt que, dès que: *He will do it as* ~ *as he is ready*, Il le fera/aussitôt, dès/qu'il sera prêt; *how* ~ *?*, quand?; *He* ~ *realized that . . .* , → Il ne tarda pas à se rendre compte que . . . ; *I'd just as* ~ *not do it*, J'aimerais/autant, mieux/ne pas le faire; *Come back* ~ *!*, Revenez vite! || **sooner** [-ɚ] *adv.* plus tôt; *no* ~ , à peine, pas plus tôt (*than*, que): *I'd* ~ *wait*, Je préfère, J'aime mieux/attendre; ~ *or later* tôt ou tard.

soot [sʊt] *n.* suie *f.*

soothe [suwð] *v. tr.* calmer, apaiser; [mind] tranquilliser. || **soothing** [-ɪŋ] *adj.* calmant, apaisant.

soothsayer [ˈsuwθˌsejɚ] *n.* devin *m*, devineresse *f.*

sooty [ˈsʊtɪ] *adj.* [couleur] de suie; couvert de suie.

sop [sɑp] *v. tr.* [-pp-] tremper, imbiber (qqch.). || *v. intr.*: *to* ~ *up*, éponger. || *n.* trempette *f*: [Fig.] *a* ~ *to Cerberus*, un don propitiatoire.

sophism [ˈsɑfɪzm] *n.* sophisme *m.* || **sophistic** [səˈfɪstɪ|k] *adj.* sophistique. || **sophisticated** [səˈfɪstɪˌkejtəd] *adj.* [Pers., taste, &c.] artificiel, blasé, trop/compliqué, raffiné/. || **sophistication** [səˌfɪstɪˈkejʃən] *n.* attitude *f* blasée.

sophomore [ˈsɑfəˌmɔɚ] *n.* [School] étudiant, -e de deuxième année (dans un collège), © rhétoricien, -ne.

soporific [ˌsowpɚˈɪfɪk] *adj.* &*n.* soporifique; [Méd.] somnifère.

sopping, soppy [sɑp|ɪŋ], [-ɪ] *adj.* trempé, détrempé: ~ *wet*, trempé jusqu'aux os.

sorcerer [ˈsɔɚsɚ|ɚ] *n.* sorcier *m*, magicien *m.* || **sorceress** [-əs] *n.* sorcière *f*, magicienne *f.* || **sorcery** [-ɪ] *n.* sorcellerie *f*, magie *f.*

sordid [ˈsɔɚdɪd] *adj.* sordide, vil, bas. || **sordidly** [-lɪ] *adv.* sordidement, bassement.

sore [sɔɚ] *adj.* **1.** [limb] endolori, douloureux; irrité: *to have* ~ *eyes*, avoir mal aux yeux. **2.** [Pers.] fâché. || *n.* plaie *f*; écorchure *f.* || **sorely** [-lɪ] *adv.* **1.** douloureusement. **2.** †[Fig.] extrêmement.

sorrow [-ow] *n.* chagrin *m*; peine *f*; affliction *f.* || *v. intr.* s'affliger; avoir/de la peine, du chagrin/(de qqch., *at*, *about*, *over sth.*). || **sorrowful** [-owfl̩] *adj.* pénible; affligeant; peiné. || **sorrowfully** [-owfl̩ɪ] *adv.* avec affliction, avec douleur. || **sorry** [-ɪ] *adj.* [Pers.] chagriné; désolé; fâché: *I am* ~ , Veuillez m'excuser, Je regrette; *to be* ~ *about*, regretter; *to feel* ~ *for s.o.*, plaindre qqun; *She feels* ~ *for herself*, Elle se croit très malheureuse, elle se plaint tout le temps; [Fig.] triste, piteux: *to be in a* ~ *plight*, se trouver dans une triste situation.

sort [sɔɚt] *n.* **1.** sorte *f*; [plant] espèce *f*;

[car] marque *f*. **2.** manière *f*: *Out of sorts*, mal en train. || *v. tr.* assortir (des couleurs); classer (des documents): *of all sorts*, de toutes sortes; *in a ~*, en quelque sorte; *Nothing of the ~*, Il n'en est rien; [Fam.] *to ~ of feel*, avoir comme une idée (*that*, que). || **sorter** [-ər] *n.* [Pers., device] classeu|r, -se, trieu|r, -se.
SOS [ˌɛsˌow'ɛs] S.O.S. *m* [= au secours].
sot [sɑt] *n.* alcoolique *m.*
sought cf. SEEK.
soul [sowl] *n.* âme *f*: *not a ~*, pas un chat, pas âme qui vive; *to/render, surrender/ one's ~ to God*, rendre son âme à Dieu.
soulful ['sowlfl̩] *adj.* sentimental; [eyes] expressif.
sound¹ [sawnd] *n.* son *m*; bruit *m*: *~ -absorbing*, amortisseur de son. || *v. intr.* [voice] résonner, retentir; sembler; *to ~ off*, donner bruyamment son avis; [Fig.] *to ~ strange*, sembler étrange. || *v. tr.* faire résonner (une consonne); [Fig.] [opinion] exprimer (qqch.) à haute voix; *sounding brass*, des paroles ronflantes; *~ -proofing*, isolation phonique; *~ -effects*, bruitage *m*; *~ barrier*, la barrière du son; *~ -track*, bande *f* sonore; *~ -wave*, onde *f* sonore.
sound² *adj.* sain, solide, en bon état; [proof, argument] bien fondé; [health] robuste; [sleep] profond; [Jur., title] valide, légal, en règle: *to be as ~ as a bell*, se porter/comme un charme, à ravir/.
sound³ *n.* sonde *f*. || *v. tr.* [depth] sonder (une profondeur); [Med.] ausculter (un patient); [Fig.] pressentir (qqun).
sound⁴ *n.* [Geog.] détroit *m*, goulet *m.*
sounding ['sawnd|ɪŋ] *n.* [Naut.] sondage *m.*
soundly [-lɪ] *adv.* [sleep] profondément, [argue] sainement, judicieusement: [Fam.] *to thrash ~*, donner une/bonne vigoureuse/correction.
soundness ['sawndnəs] *n.* [Pers.] état *m* sain; solidité *f* (d'une affaire, d'un jugement): *~ of mind*, équilibre *m* mental.
soundproof ['sawndpruwf] *adj.* insonore. || *v. tr.* insonoriser.
soup [suwp] *n.* soupe *f* (au riz, &c.); [course] potage *m*; [stock] consommé *m* (de bœuf): [Fig.] *to be in the ~*, être dans /le bain, de beaux draps/; *~ tureen*, soupière *f*; *~ -plate*, assiette *f* creuse; *~ -ladle*, louche *f*.
sour [sawər] *adj.* **1.** [smell] aigre; [taste] acide, sur, [milk] tourné. **2.** [Fig.] [temper] acariâtre: [Fig.] *~ grapes!*, Ils sont trop verts! || *v. intr.* s'aigrir. || *v. tr.* [also *turn ~*] [Chem.] acidifier (un liquide); [Fig.] aigrir (un caractère).
source [sɔərs] *n.* source *f*; [Fig.] origine *f*; début *m.*
sourish ['sawər|ɪʃ] *adj.* aigrelet. || **sourness** [-nəs] *n.* acidité *f*, [Fig.] aigreur *f*, acrimonie *f*.
south [sawθ] *n.* sud *m*, midi *m*. || *adj.* du sud, méridional. || *adv.* vers le sud. || **southeast** [-'ijst] *n.* sud-est *m*. || *adv.* vers le sud-est. || **southeastern** [-'ijstərn] *adj.* du sud-est. || **southerly** ['sʌðər|lɪ] *adj.* du sud. || **southern** [-n] *adj.* du sud, méridional. || **southerner** [-nər] *n.* [Pers.] habitant *m* du sud, [Fr.] méridional *m*. || **southward**(s) ['sawθ|wərdz] *adv.* vers le sud. || **southwest** [-'wɛst] *n.* sud-ouest. || *adv.* vers le sud-ouest. || **southwestern** [-'wɛstərn] *adj.* du sud-ouest.
souvenir [ˌsuwvə'nijər] *n.* (objet-) souvenir *m.*
sovereign ['sɑvɹən] *n. & adj.* souverain *m.* || **sovereignty** [-tɪ] *n.* souveraineté *f*.
Soviet ['sowvɪət] *n.* Soviet *m*. || *adj.* soviétique: *the ~ Union*, l'Union *f* Soviétique.
sow¹ [saw] *n.* truie *f*; [female wild boar] laie *f*.
sow² [sow], **sowed [-d], sowed or sown [-n]** *v. tr.* semer (le blé, &c.); ensemencer (un champ de . . . , *a field with . . .*); répandre (qqch.): [Fig.] *to ~ one's wild oats*, jeter sa gourme. || **sower** [-ər] semeur. || **sowing** [-ɪŋ] *n.* semailles *fpl*: *~ -machine*, semoir *f*.
sown cf. sow².
soya ['sojə] *n.* (bean) soya *m*, © fève *f* soya *inv.*
spa [spɑ] *n.* ville *f* d'eaux, station *f* thermale.
space [spejs] *n.* espace *m*, [land] surface *f*: *office ~*, [Fam.] bureaux *mpl*; locaux *mpl* commerciaux: *to take up ~*, prendre de la place; *outer ~*, espace interplanétaire; *~ ship*, engin *m* interplanétaire, *~ of time*, intervalle *m*, espace de temps; *short ~*, court laps *m* de temps. || *v. tr.* espacer, écarter (des objets). || **space-man** [-ˌmæn] *n.* astronaute *f*. || **spacing** [-ɪŋ] *n.* espacement *m*, écartement *m.*
spacious ['spejʃəs] *adj.* spacieux, vaste.
spade [spejd] *n.* **1.** [garden] bêche *f*. **2.** [cards] pique *m*. || *v. tr.* bêcher (le jardin).
spaghetti [spə'gɛtɪ] *n.* [Cul.] spaghetti *mpl.*
Spain [spejn] *n.* (l')Espagne *f*: *in, to/ ~*, en E.
span [spæn] *n.* [Meas.] empan *m*, écartement *m* de la main; [wing] envergure *f*; [bridge] travée *f*, arche *f*; [length] portée *f*; [Fig.] durée *f*, moment *m*. || *v. tr.* **[-nn-]** mesurer; [bridge] enjamber, traverser.
spangle ['spæŋgəl] *n.* [glitter] paillette *f*. || *v. tr.* [cover with] pailleter (une robe,

&c.): [US] (*the*) *Star-spangled Banner*, (le) drapeau étoilé.

Spaniard ['spænjɚd] *n.* Espagnol, -e.

spaniel ['spænjəl] *n.* [dog] épagneul *m.*

Spanish ['spænɪʃ] *adj.* espagnol. || *n.* [language] l'espagnol.

spank [spæŋk] *v. tr.* fesser, donner une fessée (à qqun). || *v. intr.*: *to ~ along*, aller à vive allure. || **spanking** [-ɪŋ] *n.* fessée *f.* || **spanking** *adj.* de premier ordre *m*; [Fam.] épatant: *at a ~ pace*, à toute vitesse *f*: *~ new*, flambant neuf.

spanner ['spænɚ] [Br.] *n.* clé *f* anglaise. cf. WRENCH.

spar[1] [spɑɚ] *n.* combat *m* d'entraînement. || *v. intr.* **[-rr-]** se battre, s'entraîner (à la boxe).

spar[2] *n.* [Naut.] bout *m* de mât, espar *m*; [Aero.] longeron *m.*

spare [spɛɚ] *v. tr.* épargner, économiser; faire grâce à (qqun); [energy] ménager (ses efforts); se passer de (qqch.); [time, moment, money] disposer de. || *adj.* **1.** [time] disponible, libre. **2.** de rechange; *~ room*, chambre *f* d'ami; [Auto.] *~ parts*, pièces *fpl* de rechange; *~ wheel*, roue *f* de secours. **3.** maigre, sec. || *n.* pièce *f* de rechange. || **spare time** [-ˌtajm], **spare moments** [-ˌmowmənts] loisirs, *mpl*, heures *fpl* libres: *to do sth. in one's spare time*, faire qqch. dans ses/moments perdus, moments de liberté, loisirs/; *a spare-time writer*, un écrivain amateur (≠ professionnel). || **sparing** [-ɪŋ] *adj.* économe; parcimonieux; frugal, sobre. || **sparingly** [-ɪŋlɪ] *adv.* avec parcimonie, frugalement.

spark [spɑɚk] *n.* étincelle *f*; [Fig.] lueur *f* (d'intelligence); [wit] trait *m* (d'esprit): [Auto.] *~ plug*, bougie *f* (d'allumage). || *v. tr.* allumer (un moteur). || *v. intr.* jeter des étincelles. || **sparkle** [spɑɚkl] *n.* étincellement *m*, éclat *m*; [gems] feux *mpl.* || *v. intr.* étinceler, scintiller [wine, wit] pétiller. || **sparkling** [-ɪŋ] *adj.* étincelant, brillant: *~ wine*, vin *m* mousseux.

sparrow ['spæɚow] *n.* moineau *m*, passereau *m*: *English house/ ~*, moineau *m* domestique; *~ -hawk*, épervier *m.*

sparse [spɑɚs] *adj.* clairsemé; [hair] rare; [things] éparpillé; [population] peu dense, dispersé.

spasm ['spæzəm] *n.* spasme *m.*

spasmodic [ˌspæz'mɑdɪk] *adj.* [Med.] spasmodique, convulsif; [Fig.] → fait par à-coups. || **spasmodically** [-lɪ] *adv.* spasmodiquement, convulsivement; [Fig.] par à-coups.

spat, cf. SPIT.

spats [spætz] *n.* guêtres *fpl.*

spatter ['spætɚ] *n.* éclaboussure *f.* || *v. tr.* & *intr.* éclabousser.

spawn [spɔn] *n.* [fish] frai *m*, œufs *mpl*; [Fig.] progéniture *f.* || *v. intr.* [fish] frayer; [Fig.] *to ~ from*, naître de, provenir de.

speak [spijk], **spoke** [spowk], **spoken** [-n̩] *v. intr.* parler (*to*, à; *of*, *about*, de); causer, s'entretenir/(avec qqun, *with s.o.*) adresser la parole à qqun: *He never speaks to me*, Il ne m'adresse jamais la parole; prendre la parole: *so to ~*, pour ainsi dire; [Fig.] *to ~ by the card*, parler d'autorité; *to/ ~ with, have/one's tongue in one's cheek*, parler à mots couverts; [Loc.] *to ~ back to*, répondre à (qqun); *to ~ out*, parler franc; *to ~ up*, parler/fort, à voix haute; *to ~ well for*, dire du bien de; *so to ~*, pour ainsi dire. || *v. tr.* parler (une langue); dire, prononcer/(une parole): *to ~ one's mind*, exprimer (ses pensées); *English spoken here*, Ici on parle anglais. || **speaker** [-ɚ] *n.* **1.** personne *f* qui parle, orateur *m*, conférencier *m*: *He is an excellent French-speaker*, Il parle admirablement le français. **2.** © [Pol.] (l')orateur (de la Chambre des communes), (le) président. **3.** [radio] haut-parleur *m.*

spear [spijɚ] *n.* **1.** lance *f*; [hunting] épieu *m.* **2.** brin *m*, pousse *f* (d'herbe). || *v. tr.* percer (qqun) d'un coup de lance.

special ['spɛʃəl] *adj.* spécial, [permission] exprès, [detail, &c.] particulier, extraordinaire: *~ delivery*, [US] © (postage) envoi *m* par exprès, exprès *m.*: [Com.] *to be on ~*, être en réclame. || **specialist** [-ɪst] *n.* [art, science] spécialiste *m*, [skill] technicien *m* (de qqch., *in sth.*). || **specialize** [-ˌajz] *v. tr.* se spécialiser (en); être spécialisé (en). || **specially** [-ɪ] *adv.* spécialement, particulièrement; [on purpose] exprès. || **specialty** [-tɪ] *n.* spécialité *f.*

species ['spijsɪs] *n. inv.* espèce *f* (animale), [kind] genre *m*, sorte *f.*

specific [spə'sɪfɪk] *adj.* [quality] spécifique, [detail] caractéristique; [aim] déterminé, précis: *a ~ project* un projet/en particulier, distinct. || *n.* [remedy] spécifique *m*; spécialité *f* (médicale). || **specifically** [-əlɪ] *adv.* spécifiquement; précisément. || **specification** [-'ejʃən] *n.* spécification *f.* || *pl.* [Com.] cahier *m* des charges. || **specify** ['spɛsɪ|ˌfaj] *v. tr.* spécifier, préciser.

specimen [-mən] *n.* spécimen *m*, échantillon *m.*

specious ['spijʃəs] *adj.* spécieux, trompeur.

speck [spɛk] *n.* point *m*; [dust] grain *m*; [colour] petite tache *f*, touche *f.* || *v. tr.* tacheter; moucheter.

speckle ['spɛkḷ] *n.* petite tache *f*, moucheture *f*. || *v. tr.* tacheter, moucheter. || **speckled** [-d] *adj.* tacheté, moucheté: ~ *trout*, truite *f* mouchetée.

spectacle ['spɛktəkḷ] *n.* spectacle; *spectacles*, lunettes *fpl*. || **spectacular** [ˌspɛk'tækjələ˞] *adj.* spectaculaire. || **spectator** ['spɛkˌtejtə˞] *n.* spectat|eur *m*, -rice *f*.

spectre ['spɛktə˞] *n.* spectre *m*, fantôme *m*. || **spectrum** [-tɹəm] *n.* spectre *m*.

speculate ['spɛkjəˌlejt] *v. intr.* spéculer, réfléchir sur qqch.; [Fin.] spéculer (sur, *in*). || **speculation** [ˌspɛkjə'lejʃən] *n.* spéculation *f*, conjecture *f*. || **speculative** ['spɛkjə|lətɪv] *adj.* spéculatif, conjectural, théorique. || **speculator** [-ˌlejtə˞] *n.* spéculateur *m*.

sped, cf. SPEED.

speech [spijtʃ] *n.* **1.** [in gen.] parole *f*; discours *m*, allocution *f* (de bienvenue): *to lose one's (power of)* ~, perdre l'usage de la parole; © [Pol.] ~ *from the throne*, discours du trône; ~ *-defect*, difficulté *f* d'élocution. **2.** [language] langue *f*, parler *m*; [Gram.] discours *m*: *figure of* ~, figure *f* de rhétorique; *part of* ~, partie *f* du discours. || **speechless** [-ləs] *adj.* sans parole, muet; [Fig.] stupéfié, sidéré.

speed [spijd] *n.* **1.** vitesse *f*: *at full* ~, à toute vitesse; [boat, train] à toute vapeur; [sailing boat] à toutes voiles, toutes voiles dehors; [horse] à toutes jambes; à bride abattue; ~ */limit, law/*, limite *f* de vitesse; *maximum* ~ *limit*, maximum *m* légal de vitesse. **2.** rapidité *f*, hâte *f*, promptitude *f*: *with all possible* ~ au plus vite, dans les meilleurs délais. **3.** [Fig.] bon succès *m*, bonne chance *f*: *I wish you God-* ~, Je vous souhaite/bon succès, bonne chance/. || **speed, speeded** [-əd], **speeded** or **sped** [spɛd] *v. tr.* expédier, hâter, accélérer. || *v. intr.* se hâter, se dépêcher; réussir, prospérer. || **speedboat** [-ˌbowt] *n.* hydroglisseur *m*. || **speedily** ['spijdɪ|lɪ] *adv.* rapidement, promptement. || **speedometer** [spij'dɑmɪtə˞] *n.* indicateur *m* de vitesse. || **speedway** [-ˌwej] *n.* [racing] piste *f*; [road] autoroute *f*. || **speedy** *adj.* rapide, prompt.

spell[1] [spɛl] *n.* sortilège *m*, [magic] sort *m*, charme *m*: *to cast a* ~ *over s.o.*, jeter un sort sur qqun.

spell[2] *n.* période *f*, temps *m* (de froid, de chaleur, &c.).

spell[3], **spelled** [-d], **spelled** or **spelt** [spɛlt] *v. tr.* **1.** [orally] épeler (un mot); [in writing] orthographier, écrire. **2.** signifier; [out] dire (qqch.) en toutes lettres. || **speller** ['spɛlə˞] *n.* [book] syllabaire *m*, abécédaire *m*; [Pers.]: *to be a/good, bad/* ~, → savoir, ne pas savoir/l'orthographe. || **spelling** ['spɛlɪŋ] *n.* [oral] épellation *f*, [writing] orthographe *f*. || **spelt**, cf. SPELL[3].

spend [spɛnd], **spent** [spɛnt], **spent** *v. tr.* dépenser (de l'argent); consumer (ses énergies); épuiser (des réserves); consacrer (du temps à); passer (le temps): *He spends his time in reading*, Il passe son temps à lire. || **spendthrift** ['spɛndˌθɹɪft] *adj.* dépensier, dilapidateur. || *n.* dépensier *m*, prodigue *m*; [Fam.] panier percé *m*.

spent, cf. SPEND.

spew [spjuw] *v. tr. & intr.* vomir, rejeter.

sphere [sfijə˞] *n.* sphère *f*; [Fig.] domaine *m* (d'activité), rayon *m* (d'action).

spice [spajs] *n.* [food] épice *f*; [perfume] aromate *m*; [Fig.] piment *m*. || *v. tr.* épicer; [Fig.] pimenter.

spick and span ['spɪkṇ'spæn] *loc. adj.* brillant comme un sou neuf, tiré à quatre épingles.

spicy ['spajsɪ] *adj.* [food] épicé; [conversation] salé.

spider ['spajdə˞] *n.* araignée *f*: *spider's web*, toile *f* d'araignée.

spigot ['spɪgət] *n.* robinet *m*, [barrel] cannelle *f*, fausset *m*.

spike [spajk] *n.* [metal] pointe *f*; clou *m*; [barbed wire] piquant *m*; [plant] épi *m*: ~ *heel*, talon *m*/pointu, aiguille. || *v. tr.* clouer (qqch.); [shoes] garnir de pointes; [Fig.] *to* ~ *a person's gun*, priver qqun de ses moyens d'action, mettre qqun dans l'impossibilité de nuire, damer le pion à (qqun). || **spiked** [-t] *n.* [shoes] à pointes, [fence] barbelé: *ladies'* ~ *heels*, talons *mpl* à pointes.

spill [spɪl], **spilled** [-d] or **spilt** [spɪlt], **spilled** or **spilt** *v. tr.* **1.** renverser (un liquide) [out of a bucket], répandre (du sable); [blood] verser. **2.** [Fig., Fam.] *to* ~ *the beans*, vendre la mèche. || *v. intr.* [liquid] se répandre, s'écouler. || **spilt**, cf. SPILL.

spin [spɪn], **spun** [spʌn], **spun** *v. tr.* [-nn-] [wool, &c.] filer; [partner] faire tourner; [object] faire pivoter; [coin] jouer à pile ou face: [Fig.] *to* ~ *a yarn*, raconter une histoire; *to* ~ *out*, faire traîner en longueur. || *v. intr.* [wool, &c.] filer; [top] tournoyer, ronfler; *to* ~ *along*, filer à toute vitesse: *My head is spinning*, La tête me tourne. || *n.* rotation *f*, [Phys.] spin *m*, [billiards] effet *m*.

spinach ['spɪnətʃ] *n.* épinards *mpl*.

spinal ['spajnəl] *adj.* spinal: ~ *column*, épine *f* dorsale, colonne *f* vertébrale.

spindle ['spɪndḷ] *n.* fuseau *m*; [Mec.] essieu *m*, axe *m*.

spine [spajn] *n.* épine *f* dorsale, colonne *f* vertébrale; [Bot.] épine *f.*

spinner ['spɪnər] *n.* [Pers.] filateur *m*, fileur *m*; machine *f* à filer. || **spinning** [-ɪŋ] *n.* filature *f*; tournoiement *m*, rotation *f*: ~ *-wheel*, rouet *m.*

spinster ['spɪnstər] *n.* fille *f* (non mariée), célibataire *f*; [Fam.] vieille fille *f.*

spiral ['spajər|əl] *n.* spirale *f*: ~ *staircase*, escalier *m* en/spirale, colimaçon/. || *v. intr.* se déplacer, tourner, monter, descendre en spirale.

spire *n.* flèche *f* (d'église); spirale *f*, spire *f.*

spirit ['spijər|t] *n.* esprit *m*: [Rel.] *the Holy Spirit*, le Saint Esprit. || *pl.* alcool *m*, spiritueux *mpl.* || *v. tr.* animer, encourager: *to ~ away*, faire disparaître comme par enchantement.

spirited [-təd] *adj.* vif, animé; [horse] fougueux. || **spiritual** [-tʃuwəl] *n.*: *negro ~*, spiritual *m*, chant *m* religieux nègre. || *adj.* de l'esprit, spirituel. || **spiritualism** [-tʃuwəlˌɪzm] *n.* spiritisme *m.* || **spirituality** [ˌspɪjərɪtʃuw'ælɪtɪ] *n.* spiritualité *f.* || **spirituous** ['spijərɪtʃuwəs] *adj.* alcoolique, spiritueux.

spirt, cf. SPURT.

spit[1] [spɪt], **spat** [spæt], **spat** *v. intr. & tr.* [-tt-] cracher. || *n.* crachat *m*, salive *f.*

spit[2] *n.* [kitchen utensil] broche *f.*

spite [spajt] *n.* dépit *m*; rancune *f*, malveillance *f* (envers qqun, *against s.o.*); *in ~ of*, en dépit de, malgré; *in ~ of the fact that*, bien que, quoique/[+ subjunc.]. || *v. tr.* dépiter, contrarier (qqun).

spiteful ['spajtf|l] *adj.* rancunier, vindicatif; [remark] venimeux, méchant. || **spitefully** [-əlɪ] *adv.* par/rancune, dépit/. || **spitefulness** *n.* rancune *f*; méchanceté *f.*

spittle ['spɪtl̩] *n.* salive *f*, crachat *m.*

splake [splejk] © *n.* moulac *f*, truite *f* mouchetée.

splash [splæʃ] *n.* [liquid, slush] éclaboussure *f*; [act] éclaboussement *m*; clapotis *m* (des vagues); tache *f* (de couleur); [Fig.] *to make a ~*, faire sensation. || *v. tr.* éclabousser (de boue, &c., *with mud, &c.*). || *v. intr.* [liquid] éclabousser, rejaillir (en éclaboussures); [spurt] cracher (l'eau, &c.); [waves] clapoter: *to ~ about in the puddles of water*, patauger dans les flaques d'eau. || **splasher** [-ər] *n.* éclabousseur *m.* || **splashy** [-ɪ] *adj.* bourbeux; [Fig.] voyant, tapageur.

splatter ['splætər] *v. tr.* éclabousser (*with*, de).

spleen [splijn] *n.* rate *f*; [Fig.] mauvaise humeur *f*, spleen *m.*

splendid ['splɛndɪd] *n.* [opportunity] splendide; [beauty, &c.] superbe. || **splendidly** [-lɪ] *adv.* splendidement, superbement.

splendour ['splɛndər] *n.* splendeur *f*, magnificence *f.*

splice [splajs] *n.* [rope] épissure *f*; ligature *f*; [films] point *m* de collure, raccord *m.* || *v. tr.* épisser; [film] raccorder, coller; [Fam.] *to get spliced*, se marier.

splint [splɪnt] *n.* éclisse *f*, attelle *f.* || *v. tr.* éclisser. || **splinter** [-ər] *n.* éclat *m*; [under the skin] écharde *f*; [bone] esquille *f*; [Fig.] ~ *group*, groupe *m*/sécessionniste, schismatique. || *v. tr. & intr.* briser en éclats, (faire) voler en éclats.

split [splɪt] *v. tr.* [-tt-] fendre (du bois, &c.); partager, diviser (un fruit, &c.); rompre (l'unité), fractionner (un groupe): [Fig.] *to ~ hairs*, couper les cheveux en quatre; *to ~ the difference*, couper la poire en deux; *to ~ o.'s sides* (*laughing*), se tenir les côtes (de rire). || *v. intr.* [things] se fendre, se briser (en deux, &c.); [skin] se gercer. || *n.* fente *f* (dans le bois); fissure *f* (dans une muraille, &c.); crevasse *f* (dans le rocher); déchirure *f* (dans une étoffe); [Fig.] [people] scission *f* (dans un groupe); rupture *f* (entre personnes); division *f.*

splurge [splərdʒ] *v. intr.* éclabousser, battre l'eau; [Fig.] jeter (son argent par les fenêtres; [Fam.] épater.

splutter ['splʌtər] *v. tr.* [out] bredouiller. || *v. intr.* crachoter (en parlant); [grease, candle] grésiller.

spoil [spojl], **spoiled** [-d] or **spoilt** [-t], **spoiled** or **spoilt** *v. tr.* [fruit, child] gâter; gâcher, détruire, avarier/(qqch.); dépouiller, spolier/(qqun de qqch., *s.o. of sth.*), piller (qqun, qqch.). || *v. intr.* [goods] se gâter, s'avarier, s'abîmer. || **spoils** [-z] *n.pl.* [loot] dèpouilles *fpl*, butin *m.* || **spoilt**, cf. SPOIL.

spoke[1], cf. SPEAK.

spoke[2] [spowk] *n.* rayon *m* (d'une roue): [Fig.] *to put a ~ in a person's wheel*, mettre des bâtons dans les roues à qqun.

spoken, cf. SPEAK.

spokesman ['spowksmən] *n.* porte-parole *m. inv.*

spoliation [ˌspowlɪ'ejʃən] *n.* spoliation *f*, pillage *m.*

sponge, [spʌndʒ] *n.* éponge *f*; coup *m* d'éponge; [Cul.] ~ *cake*, gâteau *m* mousseline *inv.* || *v. tr.* [liquid] éponger (qqch.); nettoyer (qqch.) avec une éponge, [face, &c.] passer l'éponge sur (qqch.). || *v. intr.* écornifler: *to ~ on s.o.*, vivre aux crochets de qqun.

sponsor ['spɑnsər] *n.* [Jur.] répondant *m*,

garant *m*; [baptême, club] parrain *m*; [TV, radio] commanditaire *m*. || *v. tr.* se porter garant de, être le garant de; répondre pour; commanditer.

spontaneity [ˌspɑntəˈnɪətɪ] *n.* spontanéité *f.* || **spontaneous** [ˌspɑnˈtejnɪəs] *adj.* spontané.

spook [spuwk] *n.* spectre *m*, fantôme *m*, revenant *m*.

spool [spuwl] *n.* [thread, wire] bobine *f*, canette *f* (de fil). || *v. tr.* bobiner (du fil).

spoon [spuwn] *n.* cuiller, cuillère *f*: *to be born with a silver ~ in one's mouth*, être élevé sur les genoux d'une duchesse. || **spoonfeed** [-ˌfijd], **spoonfed, spoonfed** [-ˌfɛd] *v. tr.* faire manger à la cuillère; [Fig.] mâcher la besogne (à qqun): *~ -fed*, parasite, parasitaire, subventionné; *~ -feeding*, paternalisme *m*, tutelle *f* de l'État. || *v. tr.*: *to ~ (up) one's soup*, manger sa soupe à la cuiller. || **spoonful** [-fʊl] *n.* cuillerée *f*.

sport [spɔɚt] *n.* **1.** sport *m*; jeu *m*; amusement *m*. **2.** [US] [Pers.] bon copain *m*. || *v. intr.* se divertir, jouer. || **sporting** [-ɪŋ] *adj.* [spirit] sportif, de sport. || *n.* [hunting, fishing] (le) sport *m*. || **sports-car** [-ˌkɑɚ] *n.* voiture *f* de sport. || **sports-jacket** [-ˌʤækət] *n.* veste *f* de sport. || **sportsman** [-mən] *pl.* **sportsmen** [-mən] sportif *m*, sportsman *m*; [hunter, fisherman, &c.] amateur *m* de sport.

spot [spɑt] *n.* **1.** tache *f* (sur un habit); [Fig.] souillure *f*. **2.** endroit *m*, [Fam.] coin *m*; lieu *m*: *It's a beauty/scenic ~*, C'est un site admirable; *to be on the ~*, être très embarrassé; *on the ~*, sur le champ. || *v. tr.* [-tt-] **1.** tacher (une nappe); [colour] tacheter, moucheter; [Fig.] souiller (une réputation); tacheter (qqch.). **2.** repérer (qqch., qqun). || **spotlessly** [-ləslɪ] *adv.*: *~ clean*, → d'une propreté immaculée.

spotlight [ˈspɑtˌlajt] *n.* [Theat.] projecteur *m*. || *v. tr.* [Theat.] diriger les projecteurs sur; [Fig.] mettre (qqch., qqun) en /vedette, évidence/.

spotted [-əd] *adj.* [leaf] tacheté, [fabric, stuff] moucheté; [skin] tigré.

spotty [ˈspɑtɪ] *adj.* tacheté; couvert de taches.

spouse [spaws] *n.* époux *m*, épouse *f*; conjoint, -e.

spout [spawt] *n.* bec (d'une cruche); [house] gouttière *f*; goulot *m* (d'un récipient); [Fig., clothes, watch] *up the ~*, en gage, au clou. || *v. intr.* [liquid] (re)-jaillir; gicler; [Fam.] déclamer.

sprain [spɹejn] *n.* foulure *f* (au poignet), entorse *f* (au pied). || *v. tr.* se fouler (le poignet), se faire une entorse (au pied).

sprang, cf. SPRING.

sprat [spɹæt] *n.* [fish] sprat *m*: [Fig.] *to throw out a ~ to catch a mackerel*, donner un œuf pour avoir un bœuf.

sprawl [spɹɔl] *v. intr.* s'étendre, s'étaler (largement); [Pej.] se vautrer/par terre, de tout son long/.

spray [spɹej] *n.* **1.** brin *m*, brindille *f* (d'herbe); [small] branche *f* (d'arbre). **2.** pulvérisation *f*; pulvérisateur *m*; [sea] embruns *n.pl.* || *v. tr.* vaporiser (un insecticide); pulvériser (qqch.). || **sprayer** [-ɚ] *n.* vaporisateur *m*. || **spray-gun** [-ˌgʌn] *n.* pistolet *m* (à peinture).

spread [spɹɛd] *v. tr.* étendre (du beurre, &c.), étaler (qqch.); propager (une maladie), répandre (une nouvelle); [bread] tartiner, étaler; [bird] déployer (ses ailes); [Naut.] tendre (une voile); dresser (une tente). || *v. intr.* [water, &c.] s'étendre, s'étaler; [news, epidemics] se propager, se répandre; [wings] se déployer: *to ~ out*, se développer, prendre de l'extension; *The news ~ like wildfire*, La nouvelle se répandit comme une traînée de poudre. || *n.* étendue *f*; développement *m*; [wing] envergure *f*; [wages] éventail *m* (des salaires), [ideas] diffusion *f*; [sandwich] pâte *f* (d'anchois, &c.), margarine *f*. || *adj.* étendu, écarté; ouvert.

spree [spɹij] *n.* partie *f* de plaisir; [Fam.] bombe *f*: *to go on a ~*, faire la bombe; *to go on a spending ~*, (aller) faire une orgie de dépense.

sprig [spɹɪg] *n.* brin *m*, petite branche *f*: *a ~ of an illustrious family*, un rejeton d'une famille illustre.

sprightly [ˈspɹajtlɪ] *adj.* vif, enjoué.

spring [spɹɪŋ], **sprang** [spɹæng], **sprung** [spɹʌng] *v. intr.* [people, animal] bondir, sauter, s'élancer; [liquid] jaillir; [suddenly] surgir; [plants] pousser; [Mec., &c.] se détendre. || **spring** [spɹɪŋ] *n.* **1.** bond *m*, saut *m*. **2.** [metal] ressort *m*; suspension *f* (d'auto). **3.** [season] printemps *m* (*in*, au). **4** source *f* (d'eau); [Fig.] [beginning] source *f*, origine *f*. || *adj.* **1.** à ressort. **2.** printanier, de printemps. || **springboard** [-ˌbɔɚd] *n.* tremplin *m*. || **spring-cleaning** [-ˌklijnɪŋ] *n.* grand nettoyage *m* du printemps, © le grand ménage. || **springtime** [-ˌtajm] *n.* printemps *m*. || **springy** [-ɪ] *adj.* élastique.

sprinkle [ˈspɹiŋkl] *v. tr.* [water] asperger, arroser (qqun, qqch. de); [salt, sugar] saupoudrer (qqun, qqch. de); parsemer (qqch. de). || *n.* **1.** [pinch] pincée *f* (de sel, sucre). **2.** pluie *f* fine. || **sprinkler** [-ɚ] *n.* **1.** [R.C.] goupillon *m.* **2.** gicleur *m* (à incendie). || **sprinkling** [-ɪŋ] *n.* arrosage *m*: [of water] aspersion *f* d'eau bénite. || **sprinkling can** [US] *n.* arrosoir *m.*

sprint [spɹɪnt] *n.* course *f* de vitesse, sprint *m.* || *v. intr.* faire une course de vitesse, courir à toute vitesse. || **sprinter** [-ɚ] *n.* sprinter.

sprout [spɹawt] *n.* pousse *f,* rejeton *m*; *bean* ~, germe *m* de haricot; *Brussels* ~, chou *m* de Bruxelles. || *v. intr.* pointer, pousser, germer.

spruce [spɹuws] *n.* © épinette *f,* [Fr.] sapin *m.*

sprung, cf. SPRING.

spry [spɹaj] *adj.* vif, alerte; [old man] vert, [spruce] pimpant.

spun, cf. SPIN.

spur [spɚ] *n.* éperon *m*; [Fig.] stimulant *m*: *on the ~ of the moment,* sous l'impulsion *f* du moment; [rooster] ergot *m*; [Rail.] embranchement *m.* || *v. tr.* **[-rr-]** éperonner; [Fig.] stimuler.

spurious ['spjuwɚɪəs] *adj.* faux; [money] contrefait; [writings] apocryphe.

spurn [spɚn] *v. tr.* repousser (du pied); [Fig.] faire fi (d'une offre), rejeter (avec mépris): *a spurned suitor,* un prétendant repoussé (avec dédain, mépris).

spurt [spɚt] *n.* jaillissement *m,* giclée *f,* jet *m*; [Fig.] effort *m* soudain: *a ~ of enthusiasm,* un élan *m* d'enthousiasme; *the final* ~, le coup *m* de collier final. || **spurt out** [-'awt] *v. intr.* gicler; [Fig.] s'emballer. ||**spurt up** [-'ʌp] *v. intr.* jaillir.

sputnik ['spʊtnɪk] *n.* spoutnik *m.*

sputter ['spʌtɚ] *n.* bafouillage *m,* bredouillement *m*; [candle, fire] grésillement *m,* pétillement *m*; [feu] crachement *m.* || *v. tr.* bafouiller, bredouiller; grésiller, pétiller; [feu] cracher.

spy [spaj] *n.* espion *m,* -ne *f.* || *v. tr.* espionner, épier/(qqun): *to ~ out,* explorer (qqch.), *to ~ into* (*sth.*), scruter (qqch.). || **spyglass** [-ˌglæs] *n.* longue-vue *f,* lunette *f* d'approche. || **spying** [-ɪŋ] *n.* espionnage *m.*

sq. [= square].

squabble [skwɑbḷ] *n.* querelle *f,* chamaillerie *f.* || *v. intr.* se quereller, se chamailler.

squad [skwɑd] *n.* escouade *f,* équipe *f*: *the firing* ~, le peleton d'exécution; [police] brigade *f*: *morality, vice/* ~, la brigade des mœurs.

squadron [-ɹən] *n.* [Mil.] escadron *m*; [navy] escadre *f*; [Aero.] escadrille *f*: ~ *leader,* commandant *m* d'escadrille.

squalid [skwɑlɪd] *adj.* misérable, sordide, crasseux.

squall [skwɔl] *n.* **1.** braillement *m,* cri *m.* **2.** bourrasque *f,* rafale *f*; [sea] grain *m.* || *v. intr.* **1.** crier, brailler. **2.** souffler en /rafale, bourrasque.

squalor ['skwɔlɚ] *n.* saleté *f,* crasse *f*; → (caractère) sordide (de).

squander ['skwɑndɚ] *v. tr.* gaspiller, dilapider (une fortune).

square [skwɛɚ] *n.* **1.** carré *m*; carreau *m* (de verre); [town] place *f,* © carré *m*; [garden] square *m.* **2.** [measuring] équerre *f.* || *adj.* [thing] carré; [meal] vrai, véritable; franc (jeu); [deal] loyal, équitable: ~ *dance,* quadrille *m,* © danse carrée; *to give s.o. a/* ~, *fair and* ~ */deal,* agir loyalement envers qqun; *to feel like a ~ peg in a round hole,* se sentir comme un poisson hors de l'eau; *four* ~, solidement établi; *It is all* ~, C'est à égalité; *We'll call it* ~, Nous sommes quittes. || *v. tr.* équarrir (du bois); mesurer (qqch.); [Fin.] balancer (les comptes), payer (une dette); [Math.] élever (une quantité) au carré; [Fig.] se concilier (qqun). || *v. intr.* [things] être en conformité (avec): *to ~ (up) with s.o.,* s'accorder, être d'accord/ avec qqun; régler ses comptes avec qqun.

squash [skwɑʃ] *n.* **1.** écrasement *m,* aplatissement *m*; pulpe *f*: *lemon* ~, citron pressé; **2.** courge *f.* || *v. tr.* écraser, aplatir, presser (un citron); [Fig.] *to ~ a rumour,* étouffer une rumeur; *to ~ s.o.,* remettre qqun à sa place.

squat [skwɑt] *v. intr.* **[-tt-]** s'accroupir, se blottir; [US] occuper (un lieu) sans titre, abusivement. || *n.* position *f* accroupie. || *adj.* accroupi, blotti. || **squatter** [-ɚ] *n.* colon *m,* occupant *m* (sans titre), squatter *m.*

squaw [skwɔ] *n.* © sauvagesse *f,* indienne *f*; [Fam., Pej.] femme *f.*

squawk [skwɔk] *n.* cri *m* rauque; [Fam.] protestation *f.* || *v. intr.* crier d'une voix rauque; protester.

squeak [skwijk] *n.* grincement *m,* cri *m* aigu. || *v. intr.* grincer; [deer, mouse] pousser un cri aigu. || **squeaking** [-ɪŋ] *n.* grincement *m* (d'une porte, d'un levier de pompe).

squeal [skwijl] *n.* cri/aigu, perçant/. || *v. intr.* [pigs, children] crier, pousser des cris perçants; [Fam.] *to ~ on* (*s.o.*), dénoncer, [Pop.] moucharder/(qqun).

squeamish ['skwijmɪʃ] *adj.* sujet aux nausées; difficile; prude; [Fam.] qui fait le dégoûté.

squeeze [skwijz] *v. tr.* [hand] serrer; [orange] presser; [in a crowd] comprimer, serrer; [in arms] étreindre; [Fig.] exercer une pression sur: *to ~ money from s.o.*, extorquer de l'argent à qqun; [avec postpositions] *to ~ into*, faire entrer de force (dans); *to ~ out (from)*, faire sortir de force (de); [money] soutirer. [avec postpositions] *to ~ into*, s'introduire de force dans; *to ~ through*, se frayer un passage (à travers la foule, &c.). || *n.* [arms] étreinte *f*, [hands] pression *f*; [crowd] cohue *f*; [Fig.] extortion *f* (d'argent); passage *m* difficile.

squelch [skwɛltʃ] *v. tr.* écraser (qqch.); étouffer, réprimer/(une révolte). || *n.* remarque/méprisante, écrasante/.

squint [skwɪnt] *n.* strabisme *m*; coup *m* d'œil (furtif). || *v. intr.* loucher; regarder, jeter un coup d'œil à qqch. (furtivement).

squire [skwajər] *n.* écuyer *m*; propriétaire *m* terrien; [lady's escort] chevalier *m* servant. || *v. tr.* escorter, être le cavalier de.

squirm [skwərm] *v. intr.* se tortiller, se tordre (de douleur).

squirrel ['skwərəl] *n.* écureuil *m*.

squirt [skwərt] *n.* jet *m*, giclée *f*; seringue *f*: *~ gun*, pistolet *m* à eau. || *v. tr.* faire gicler, lancer en jet. || *v. intr.* jaillir, gicler.

St. *abr.* [= Saint] St-, Ste-. [*N.B.* Avoid French abbreviation except for street names; in Canada, *St-* and *Ste-* are often used in place-names: *the St. Lawrence*, le Saint-Laurent; *St. Anne's*, Sainte-Anne, Ste-Anne].

stab [stæb] *n.* coup *m* de poignard. || *v. tr.* [-bb-] poignarder (qqun).

stability [stə'bɪlɪtɪ] *n.* stabilité *f*, solidité *f*. || **stabilize** ['stejbəˌlajz] *v. tr.* stabiliser.

stable[1] ['stejbḷ] *adj.* stable, constant, fidèle, ferme, solide.

stable[2] *n.* [cattle] étable *f*; [horses] écurie *f*.

stack [stæk] *n.* **1.** meule *f* (de foin); pile *f* (de livres); tas *m* (de charbon), corde *f* (de bois). **2.** cheminée *f*; souche *f* (de cheminée). **3.** faisceau *m* (d'armes): [bibliothèque] *library stacks*, (la) réserve. || *v. tr.* **1.** mettre (du foin) en meule; empiler (des livres, du bois, des journaux). **2.** [Mil.] mettre (des armes) en faisceau.

stadium ['stejdɪəm] *n.* stade *m*.

staff[1] [stæf] *n.* **1.** personnel *m*, corps *m*: *teaching ~*, personnel, corps/enseignant; [Mil.] état-major *m*; [Journ.] *editorial ~*, (la) rédaction. **2.** bâton *m*; mât *m*; gaule *f*; hampe *f* (d'un drapeau). **3.** [Fig.] appui *m*, soutien *m*; tuteur *m*: *pilgrim's ~*, bâton *m* de pèlerin.

staff[2] *n. pl.* staves [stejvz] [Mus.] portée *f*.

stag [stæg] *n.* cerf *m*.

stage [stejdʒ] *v. tr.* [Theat.] monter (une pièce), mettre (une pièce) à la scène; monter, organiser (une démonstration). || *v. intr.* [Fig.] avancer, progresser par étapes. || *n.* **1.** estrade *f*; scène *f* (de théâtre), [Fig.] les planches *fpl*; plateforme *f*; tréteaux *mpl*; échafaudage *m*. **2.** étape *f* (d'un voyage); relais *m*; phase *f* (d'une expérience); degré *m*, stade *m*: *at this ~*, à ce stade, à ce moment (d'une opération). || **stagecoach** [-ˌkowtʃ] *n.* diligence *f*. || **stage door** [-'dɔər] *n.* entrée *f* des artistes. || **stage folk** [-ˌfowk] gens *mpl* de théâtre. || **stage fright** [-ˌfɹajt] trac *m*. || **stage hand** [-ˌhænd] *n.* machiniste *m*. || **stage player** [-ˌplejə] *n.* comédien *m*, comédienne *f*.

stagger ['stægər] *v. intr.* chanceler, tituber; [Fig.] hésiter, fléchir. || *v. tr.* **1.** faire/chanceler, tituber/(qqun); [Fig.] renverser, ébranler (une conviction, &c.). **2.** disposer (des objets) en zigzag; [Fig.] échelonner, décaler (des tâches). || *n.* **1.** étourdissement *m*, vertige *m*. **2.** échelonnement *m* (des tâches, &c.); [Aviat.] décalage *m* (des ailes). || **staggering** [-ɪŋ] *n.* **1.** chancellement *m*; [Fig.] hésitation *f*. **2.** échelonnage *m*, échelonnement *m*; étalement *m*. || *adj.* [step] chancelant; [Pers.] hésitant; [blow] foudroyant; [news] atterrant, bouleversant. || **staggeringly** [-ɪŋlɪ] *adv.* en chancelant; [Fig.] avec hésitation.

staging ['stejdʒɪŋ] *n.* [Theat.] mise *f* en scène; [Arch.] échafaudage *m*.

stagnant ['stægnənt] *adj.* stagnant; [Fig.] inactif, dormant.

stagnate ['stægˌnejt] *v. intr.* [water] croupir; [Fig.] stagner; piétiner, → ne pas avancer.

staid [stejd] *adj.* posé, sérieux.

stain [stejn] *n.* **1.** [blot] tache *f*. **2.** [product] teinte *f*. || *v. tr.* **1.** tacher, souiller, salir; [Fig.] ternir (le nom, la réputation d'une personne), **2.** colorier; teindre: *stained glass window*, vitrail *m*; vitraux *mpl*. || **stainless** [-ləs] *adj.* sans souillure, immaculé; [steel] inoxydable.

stair [stɛər] *n.* **1.** marche *f* (d'escalier). **2.** *pl.* escalier *m*: *three flights of stairs*, trois étages *mpl*. || **staircase** [-ˌkejs] *n.* [Br.] cf. STAIRWAY. || **stairway** [-ˌwej] [US] © *n.* escalier *m*.

stake [stejk] *n.* pieu *m*, poteau *m*; bûcher *m*; [bet] enjeu *m*: *to die at the ~*, mourir sur le bûcher. || *v. tr.* **1.** garnir, enclore (un champ) de pieux. **2.** [Fig.] hasarder, parier, miser (une somme au jeu): *to ~ one's reputation*, mettre sa réputation en jeu, jouer son honneur.

stale [stejl] *adj.* [bread] rassis; [beverage] éventé; [air] vicié; [joke] vieux, rebattu, défraîchi; [cheque] périmé. || *v. tr. & intr.* rendre/banal, insipide; s'éventer, perdre son intérêt.

stalemate ['stejlˌmejt] *n.* [chess] pat *m*; [Fig.] impasse *f.*

stalk [stɔk] *n.* **1.** [plant] tige *f*; [fruit] queue *f*; [cabbage] trognon *m.* **2.** démarche *f* majestueuse, marche *f* à grands pas. || *v. tr.* suivre/furtivement, en se dissimulant/; traquer. || **stalk along** [-ə'lɔŋ] *v. intr.* marcher/fièrement, à grandes enjambées.

stall [stɔl] *n.* **1.** stalle *f* (du chœur). **2.** stalle *f*, écurie *f.* **3.** [Com.] stand *m*, étal *m*; kiosque *m*; étalage *m* (de livres, &c.). **4.** blocage *m* (d'un moteur) de vitesse. || *v. tr.* **1.** mettre (un cheval) à l'écurie. **2.** [car] caler (un moteur). || *v. intr.* [of engine] se bloquer: *to* ~ (*for time*), temporiser; *Quit stalling!*, Au fait!; *to* ~ *off*, écarter, éviter. || **stalling** [-ɪŋ] [car] calage *m*, blocage *m* (du moteur).

stallion ['stæljən] *n.* [horse] étalon *m.*

stalwart ['stɔlwɚt] *adj.* vigoureux, solide: *my* ~ *friend*, mon vaillant ami.

stamina ['stæmɪnə] *n.* vigueur *f*, résistance *f*, force *f* vitale.

stammer ['stæmɚ] *v. intr.* bégayer; [Fig.] bredouiller, balbutier. || *v. tr.*: *to* ~ *out* (*words*), bredouiller (des paroles). || *n.* **1.** bégaiement *m.* **2.** balbutiement *m.* || **stammerer** [-ɚ] bègue *n. m/f.* || **stammering** [-ɚɪŋ] *n.* **1.** bégaiement *m.* **2.** balbutiement *m.* || *adj.* bègue.

stamp [stæmp] *n.* **1.** timbre *m*; vignette *f*; [postmark] cachet *m*; [imprint] estampille *f*; empreinte *f*, marque *f*: *postage* ~, timbre-poste *m*; ~ *-issuing machine*, distributeur *m* automatique de timbres-poste; *date* ~, timbre à date; *rubber* ~, timbre/en caoutchouc, humide/; [Fig.] *rubber-* ~ *executive*, homme *m* de paille. **2.** trépignement *m*, piétinement *m.* || **stamp** *v. tr.* **1.** [letter] apposer un timbre à, affranchir; [acte notarié, document] estampiller; [metal] estamper; [ore] broyer; [leather] estamper; [médaille, monnaie] frapper. **2.** *to* ~ *one's feet*, trépigner, piétiner. || *v. intr.* trépigner, piétiner. || **stamped** [-t] *adj.* timbré: ~ *paper*, papier *m* timbré [France]. || **stamp out** [-'awt] *v. tr.* éteindre (un feu de camp en le piétinant); [Fig.] étouffer (une révolte, &c.).

stampede [ˌstæm'pijd] © *n.* **1.** [animals] rodéo *m.* || **2.** déroute *f*, panique *f*, ruée *f.*

stamping ['stæmpɪŋ] *n.* **1.** [postage] timbrage *m*, affranchissement *m* (d'une lettre). **2.** trépignement *m*, piétinement *m.*

stanch [stɔntʃ], cf. STAUNCH.

stand [stænd] *n.* façon *f* de se tenir (debout); arrêt *m*, halte *f*; résistance *f*; position *f*; [grandstand] tribune *f*; [platform] estrade *f*; [Jur.] barre *f* des témoins; poste *m*, station *f* de taxis; [news stand] kiosque *m* (à journaux); [at exhibition] stand *m*; socle *m* (d'un buste); support *m* (de lampe); pied (d'un vase); [umbrella ~] porte-parapluie *m*; [music ~] pupitre *m*: *to take a* ~, prendre position; *to make a* ~ *against* . . . , s'opposer à . . . ; *to make a last* ~ , résister jusqu'au dernier homme, → opposer une résistance désespérée. || **stand, stood** [stʊd], **stood** *v. intr.* se tenir (debout), rester, être/debout; [☞ Fr. usual. remains vague as to sitting or standing positions, unless contrast is intended; use être, se trouver, rester, se mettre, &c.]; [measure] mesurer; [last] durer, rester; [resist, stay in force] tenir; se présenter (comme candidat); venir (en premier rang), être (le premier de sa classe); [tea] infuser: *I had to* ~ *all evening*, J'ai dû rester debout toute la soirée; *He was standing by the door*, Il se /tenait, trouvait/près de la porte; *Stand over here!*, Venez vous mettre ici!; *Where shall I* ~ *?*, Où faut-il me mettre?; *Don't just* ~ *there!* Ne restez pas là (à ne rien faire)!; *He, His story/hasn't a leg to* ~ *on*, Son histoire ne tient pas debout; *It made my hair* ~ *on end*, Cela m'a fait dresser les cheveux sur la tête; *The house stands at the corner*, La maison/se trouve, est située/au coin; *to* ~ *fast*, tenir bon; *The agreement stands*, L'accord/tient, reste en vigueur, reste tel quel/; *He stands to/win, lose/a fortune*, Il/a la possibilité de gagner, court le risque de perdre/une fortune; *Where do we* ~ *?*, Où en sommes-nous?; *as matters* ~, au point où en sont les choses; *to* ~ *well with s.o.*, être en faveur auprès de, [Fam.] être bien avec/qqun/. || *v. tr.* mettre, placer; [put down] poser; [endure] supporter, soutenir, [things] résister à; payer (à boire, une tournée, un dîner) à qqun: ~ *it/in the corner, against the wall, on its end/*; Mettez-, Posez-/le dans le coin, Mettez-, Appuyez-/ le contre le mur, Mettez-le debout; *to* ~ *one's ground*, tenir bon; *I can't* ~ *him*, Je ne peux pas le souffrir. || **stand aside** [-ə'sajd] *v. intr.* se ranger, s'écarter, s'effacer; [Fig.] se désister. || **stand back** [-'bæk] *v. intr.* reculer; se ranger. || **stand by** [-'baj] *v. intr.* **1.** regarder faire; se tenir à côté, près de/(qqun); se tenir prêt; [Naut.] se tenir paré; *Stand by!*, [Theat., Cin.] Tout le monde en place! [Radio] Ne quittez pas l'écoute! **2.** défendre la cause de (qqun); demeurer, rester fidèle à (sa parole, &c.). || **stand-by** [-ˌbaj] *n.* [Pers.] appui *m*; ressource *f*; signal *m* de se tenir prêt: *as a* ~ , en réserve; *an old* ~ , une vieille excuse. || *attrib.* de réserve. || **stand down** [-'dawn] *v. intr.* [of witness] quitter la barre. || **stand for** [-'fɔɚ] tolérer, supporter/(qqch.); se déclarer/pour, en faveur de/(qqch.); tenir lieu (de qqch.), remplacer (qqun); signifier, représenter/(qqch.). || **stand in** [-'ɪn] (*for s.o.*) *v. intr.* remplacer (qqun). || **stand-in** [-ˌɪn] *n.* remplaçant *m*. || **stand off** [-'ɔf] *v. intr.* se tenir à l'écart. || **stand-offish** [-'ofɪʃ] *adj.* distant. || **stand out** [-'awt] *v. intr.* faire saillie; se détacher (sur qqch.); contraster (avec qqch.). || **stand over** [-'owvɚ] *v. intr.* être (laissé) en suspens, être remis (à plus tard); se pencher sur (qqun), [Fig.] surveiller qqun de près. || **stand up** [-'ʌp] *v. intr.* se lever, se mettre debout; se tenir (debout). cf. STAND: *to* ~ *against* (*s.o., sth.*), s'appuyer sur, résister à/(qqun, qqch.); *to* ~ *for* (*s.o., sth.*), défendre, soutenir/(qqun, qqch.); *to* ~ *to* (*s.o., sth.*), affronter; tenir tête, résister à/(qqun, qqch.).

standard[1] ['stændɚd] *n.* **1.** étalon *m* [poids, mesures]; *the gold* ~ , l'étalon or. **2.** type *m*, degré *m*, modèle *m*: *a high* ~ *of . . .*, un haut degré de . . . ; ~ *of living*, niveau *m* de vie, [Fr.] standing *m*, standard *m*/de vie. **3.** étendard *m*, pavillon *m*: *The Queen's* ~ , l'étendard de la reine. || *adj.* qui sert/de modèle, de type, d'étalon/; standard, classique: ~ *English*, le bon anglais, l'anglais courant; (*Eastern*) *Standard Time*, heure *f* officielle (de l'Est). || **standardization** [ˌstændɚdaj'zejʃən] *n.* standardisation *f*, normalisation *f*; [Meas.] étalonnement *m*, étalonnage *m*; [Chem.] titrage *m*. || **standardize** ['stændɚˌdajz] *v. tr.* standardiser, uniformiser.

standing [-ɪŋ] *n.* station *f* debout [time] durée *f*; [rank, position] place *f*, rang *m*; réputation *f*; position *f*, importance *f*. || *adj.* debout, stationnant; [army, committee] permanent: ~ *water*, eau *f* stagnante; ~ *rule*, règle *f*/fixe, permanente/: *to have a* ~ *invitation* (*in*), avoir ses entrées (dans); ~ *price*, prix fixe; ~ *expenses*, frais courants; ~ *room only*, places *fpl* debout seulement.

standpoint ['stænd|ˌpojnt] *n.* point *m* de vue.

standstill [-ˌstɪl] *n.* arrêt *m*, immobilisation *f*: *to come to a* ~ , s'arrêter; s'arrêter court, ne plus pouvoir avancer: *The industry is at a* ~ , L'industrie est au point mort.

stank, cf. STINK.

stanza ['stænzə] *n.* [Poet.] stance *f*.

staple[1] ['stejpl̩] *n.* crampon *m*; [book binding] agrafe *f*, broche *f*. || *v. tr.* brocher, attacher, agrafer (des feuilles).

staple[2] *adj.* [food, &c.] de base, principal.

stapler [-ɚ] *n.* agrafeuse *f*, © brocheuse *f*.

star [stɑɚ] *n.* **1.** étoile *f*; [Fig.] [actress] étoile *f*, vedette *f*, star *f*. **2.** [Typo.] astérisque *m*: *shooting* ~ , étoile filante; *His* ~ *is rising*, Son étoile grandit. || *v. tr.* [-rr-] étoiler (qqch.), couvrir, consteller (qqch.) d'étoiles. || *v. intr.* être une vedette (dans une revue, un film), être la vedette (d'une revue, d'un film).

starboard [-ˌbɚd] *n.* [Naut.] tribord *m* (*on the*, à).

starch [stɑɚtʃ] *n.* empois *m*; [corn] fécule *f*; amidon *m*. || *v. tr.* empeser (une chemise); amidonner. || **starched** [-t] *adj.* empesé, raide, apprêté; [manners] cérémonieux, affecté, guindé. || **starchy** [-ɪ] *adj.* pâteux, empesé; cérémonieux; affecté.

stare [stɛɚ] *v. intr.* regarder/fixement, effrontément/(qqun, *at s.o.*); dévisager (qqun). || *n.* regard *m*/fixe, effronté/: *He does not like being stared at*, Il n'aime pas qu'on le dévisage. || **staring** [-ɪŋ] *adj.* fixe, grand ouvert.

stark [stɑɚk] *adj.* raide, rigide; rigoureux: ~ *nonsense*, pure bêtise *f*; ~ *disaster*, désastre/complet, entier/. || *adv.* entièrement: ~ *raving mad*, complètement fou.

starlight ['stɑɚˌlajt] *n.* lumière *f*, clarté *f*/des étoiles.

starling ['stɑɚlɪŋ] *n.* étourneau *m*, sansonnet *m*, cf. BLACKBIRD.

starry ['stɑɚɪ] *adj.* [sky] étoilé.

start [stɑɚt] *v. intr.* [of a car] partir, démarrer; commencer, débuter; [surprise] sauter, sursauter. || *v. tr.* commencer, se mettre à (faire qqch.); faire partir (une auto, &c.), faire démarrer (un projet, un travail); entamer (une discussion); réveiller, exciter (qqun); faire lever (le gibier). || **to start anew** [-ə'njuw], **afresh** [-ə'fɹɛʃ] *v. intr.* repartir, recommencer/à neuf, à zéro/. || **to start off** [-'ɔf] *v. intr.* démarrer, se mettre en marche; [pers.] se mettre en route. || **to start out** [-'awt] *v. intr.* se mettre en route. || **to start (all) over** [-'owvɚ] (**again**) *v. intr.* repartir, recommencer à neuf, à zéro. || **to start up** [-'ʌp] (*from one's sleep*) *v. intr.* se réveiller en sursaut. || *v. tr.* mettre en marche, faire démarrer; [Pers.] se lever brusquement. || *n.* départ *m*, démarrage *m*; début *m*; élan *m*; haut-le-corps *m*: *by starts*, par accès, par saccades; *by fits and starts*, à bâtons rompus. || **starter** [-ɚ] *n.* **1.** [Auto.] démarreur *m*. **2.** [Sport] [races] starter *m*. **3.** initiateur *m* (d'un mouvement). || **starting** [-ɪŋ] *n.* **1.** démarrage *m*; mise *f* en marche. **2.** départ *m*, début *m*; point *m* de départ.

startle [-l̩] *v. tr.* faire tressaillir, frémir; [qqun] effrayer (qqun). || **startling** [-lɪŋ] *adj.* [news, event, &c.] saisissant; sensationnel.

starvation [ˌstɑɚ'vejʃən] *n.* famine *f*. || **starve** [stɑɚv] *v. intr.* être réduit à, souffrir de/la famine; mourir de faim. || *v. tr.* affamer, faire mourir (qqun) de faim. || **starving** [-ɪŋ] *adj.* famélique, affamé.

state [stejt] *n.* **1.** [Polit., &c.] état *m*; condition *f*: ~ *ownership*, étatisation *f*, nationalisation *f* (d'une industrie, &c.); *The United States* (*of America*), Les États-Unis d'Amérique. **2.** [ceremony] apparat *m*. || *v. tr.* affirmer, dire, spécifier (qqch.). || **stateless** [-ləs] *adj.* apatride; [Pej.] sans patrie. || **stately** [-lɪ] *adj.* majestueux, imposant, plein de dignité. || *adv.* majestueusement, d'un air noble. || **statement** ['stejtmənt] *n.* déclaration *f*, affirmation *f*; [official] rapport *m*, compte rendu *m*; [Com.] relevé *m* (de compte). || **stateroom** [-ˌɹuwm] *n.* [boat] cabine *f*. || **statesman** [-smən] *pl.* **statesmen** [-smən] *n.* homme *m*/d'État, politique/.

static ['stætɪk] *adj.* statique; stationnaire. || *n.* [radio] parasites *mpl*.

station ['stejʃən] *n.* **1.** station *f*; gare *f* (de chemin de fer); poste *m* (de police, de secours); rang *m*; place *f*; condition *f*: *service, gas* ~, [Auto.] poste *m* d'essence; (*the*) *Stations of the Cross*, (le) chemin *m* de Croix; ~ *master*, chef de gare; ~ *wagon*, canadienne *f*, fermière *f*, familiale *f*. || *v. tr.* placer; ranger (qqch.); [Mil.] poster (qqun).

stationary [-ˌɛɚɪ] *adj.* stationnaire, fixe.

stationer [-ɚ] *n.* **1.** papetier *m*. **2.** †imprimeur *m* du Roi, de la Reine (en Angleterre). || **stationery** [-ɚɪ] *n.* papeterie *f*; papier *m* à lettres; fournitures *fpl* de bureau: *on official* ~, sur du papier à en-tête.

statistics [stə'tɪstɪks] *n.* statistique *f*.

statuary ['stætʃuwˌɛɚɪ] *n.* statuaire *m/f*.

statue ['stætʃ|uw] *n.* statue *f*.

stature [-ɚ] *n.* [height] stature *f*, taille *f*.

status ['stætəs, stejtəs] *n.* position *f*, rang *m* (dans une organisation); statut *m* (de fonctionnaire); qualité *f*, titre *m*, état *m* civil: *marital* ~, état *m* civil.

statute ['stætʃuwt] *n.* [Polit.] loi *f*, © statut *m*. || *adj.* légal, © [grant, &c.] statutaire.

staunch [stɔntʃ] *v. tr.* étancher (de l'eau, du sang). || *adj.* [water-tight] étanche; [Fig.] ferme, solide; vrai.

stave [stejv] *n.* **1.** [Mus.] portée *f*; couplet *m*, strophe *f* (d'une chanson). **2.** douve *f* (d'un tonneau). || *v. intr.*: *to* ~ *in* (*a barrel*), défoncer (un baril).

stay [stej] *n.* **1.** séjour *m*. **2.** [Jur.] sursis *m*; support *m*; suspension *f*. **3.** étai *m*. || *v. intr.* **1.** séjourner; demeurer; rester. **2.** s'arrêter. || *v. tr.* **1.** apaiser (sa faim, *one's stomach*). **2.** arrêter, mettre (qqch.) en échec. **3.** étayer; soutenir; [Jur.] différer (un jugement). || **to stay away** [-ə'wej] (*from s.o., sth.*) se tenir éloigné (de qqun, qqch.); s'absenter (de la maison). || **to stay up** [-'ʌp] *v. intr.* veiller. || **stay-at-home** [-ətˌhowm] *adj.* & *n.* [person] casani|er, -ère. || **stay-on strike** [-ɑnˌstɹajk] *n.* grève sur le tas, occupation *f* illégale (d'une usine, d'un magasin).

stead [stɛd] *n.* place *f*: *This will stand you in good* ~, Ceci vous sera fort utile. || **steadfast** [-ˌfæst] *adj.* ferme, stable, constant. || **steadily** [-ɪlɪ] *adv.* fermement; constamment; [time] régulièrement. || **steadiness** [-ɪnəs] *n.* fermeté *f*, stabilité *f*, persévérance *f*.

steady ['stɛdɪ] *adj.* [object] ferme, solide; [movement] régulier, continu; [worker] régulier, persévérant; [friend] attitré. || *v. tr.* affermir; régulariser. || *v. intr.* s'affermir, se régulariser.

steak [stejk] *n.* [Cul.] **1.** bifteck *m*. **2.** tranche *f* (de bœuf, &c.).

steal [stijl], **stole** [stowl], **stolen** [-n̩] *v. tr.* voler (*from*, à); dérober (qqch.): *to* ~ *a march on s.o.*, prendre les devants; devancer qqun. || *v. intr.* voler; [Fig.] aller, venir à la dérobée. || **to steal away** [-ə'wej] *v. intr.* se dérober; s'esquiver (*from*, de). || **stealth** [stɛlθ] *n.*; *by* ~ : **1.** à la dérobée, furtivement. **2.** par des moyens détournés. || **stealthily** [-ɪlɪ] *adv.* à la dérobée; furtivement. || **stealthy** [-ɪ] *adj.* furtif, secret.

steam [stijm] *n.* vapeur *f*; [on window] buée *f*: ~ *boiler*, chaudière *f* à vapeur; ~ *steamroller*, rouleau *m* compresseur; ~ *shovel*, pelle *f* à vapeur; ~ *engine*, machine *f* à vapeur. || *v. intr.* **1.** fumer; dégager, jeter/de la vapeur. **2.** s'évaporer. || *v. tr.* passer (qqch.) à la vapeur; cuire (un aliment) à/la vapeur, l'étuvée/.

‖ **steamboat** [-ˌbowt], **steamer** [-ɚ] *n.* cf. STEAMSHIP. ‖ **steamship** [-ˌʃɪp] *n.* (bateau *m* à) vapeur *m.* ‖ **steamy** [-ɪ] *adj.* plein de /buée, vapeur/.

steed [stijd] *n.* coursier *m*, monture *f.*

steel [stijl] *n.* **1.** acier *m.* **2.** [sword] fer *m.* **3.** fusil *m* (à aiguiser les couteaux). ‖ *v. tr.* **1.** aciérer (du fer). **2.** [Fig.] endurcir; cuirasser, aguerrir (qqun contre, *s.o. against*). ‖ **steel wool** [-ˌwʊl] *n.* laine *f* d'acier, paille *f* de fer. ‖ **steely** [ˈstijlɪ] *adj.* d'acier; [Fig.] dur (comme l'acier).

steep[1] [stijp] *adj.* [cliff, &c.] à pic; escarpé; [steps] raide. ‖ *n.* escarpement *m* (d'une falaise); pente *f* rapide.

steep[2] *v. tr.* tremper; (faire) infuser (du thé, de la camomille, &c.).

steeple [ˈstijpl̩] *n.* clocher *m*, flèche *f.*

steer[1] [stijɚ] *v. tr.* **1.** conduire (un véhicule); [Fig.] diriger (qqun, qqch.). **2.** [Naut.] gouverner (une embarcation); piloter (un navire). ‖ *v. intr.* [ship] se gouverner; se diriger: *to* ~ *clear* (*of sth.*), éviter (qqch.), s'écarter (de qqch.).

steer[2] *n.* bouvillon *m.*

steering [-ɪŋ] *n.* direction *f*; action *f* de gouverner; pilotage *m* (d'un navire): [car] *power* ~, servo-direction *f*; ~ *wheel*, volant *m* (de direction), roue *f* de gouvernail.

stem [stɛm] *n.* **1.** tige *f* (d'une fleur). **2.** [Naut.] étrave *f.* **3.** tuyau *m* (d'une pipe), pied *m* (d'un verre). ‖ *v. tr.* [-mm-] **1.** arrêter (un écoulement); endiguer, refouler/(un courant, la marée); aller contre, remonter/(la marée). **2.** [Fig.] lutter contre (qqch.); s'opposer à (qqch.); résister (à qqun, qqch.). ‖ **stem from** [-ˌfɹʌm] *v. intr.* [Pers.] descendre de (qqun); [things] provenir, dériver/de (qqch.).

stench [stɛntʃ] *n.* puanteur *f.*

stencil [ˈstɛnsɪl] *n.* stencil *m*; pochoir *m*; patron *m* à jour, à calquer. ‖ *v. tr.* polycopier.

stenographer [stəˈnɑgɹəf|ɚ] *n.* sténographe *f/m.* ‖ **stenography** [-ɪ] *n.* sténographie *f.*

step [stɛp] *n.* **1.** pas *m*; degré *m*; marche *f* (d'escalier); [Fig.] démarche *f.* **2.** échelon *m* (d'une échelle); marchepied *m* (d'une voiture). **3.** *pl.* échelle *f*; perron *m*: [Fig.] *to be out of* ~ *with*, ne pas être au pas, ne pas être en sympathie avec; ne pas bien s'entendre avec; ~ *by* ~, pas *m* à pas; *to retrace o.'s steps*, revenir sur ses pas. ‖ *v. intr.* [-pp-] faire un pas; marcher (pas à pas); avancer. ‖ **step aside** [-əˈsajd] *v. intr.* s'écarter. ‖ **step back** [-ˈbæk] *v. intr.* rebrousser chemin; revenir sur ses pas; reculer (d'un pas). ‖ **step in** [-ˈɪn] *v. intr.* entrer. ‖ **step off** [-ˈɔf] *v. tr.* [a distance, &c.] arpenter, mesurer (une distance).

stepchild [-ˌtʃajld] *n.* beau-fils *m*, belle-fille *f.* ‖ **stepdaughter** [-ˌdɔtɚ] *n.* belle-fille *f.* ‖ **stepfather** [ˈstɛp|ˌfɑðɚ] *n.* beau-père *m.*

step-ladder [-ˌlædr] *n.* escabeau *m.*

stepmother [-ˌmʌðɚ] *n.* belle-mère *f.*

steps [stɛps] *n.pl.* escalier *m*: [Fig.] *to take* ~, prendre des /dispositions, mesures *fpl*/.

stepsister [ˈstɛpˌsɪstɚ] *n.* demi-sœur. ‖ **stepson** [-ˌsʌn] *n.* beau-fils.

stereo(phony) [ˈstɛəɪəˌfownɪ] *n.* stéréophonie *f.* ‖ **stereotype** [ˈstɛəɪəˌtajp] *n.* stéréotype *m*, cliché *m.*

sterile [ˈstɛɚajl] *adj.* stérile. ‖ **sterility** [stəˈɹɪlɪtɪ] *n.* stérilité *f.* ‖ **sterilize** [ˈstɛəɪ-ˌlajz] *v.* stériliser.

sterling [ˈstɚlɪŋ] *n.* sterling *m.* ‖ *adj.* **1.** [money] de bon aloi; qui a cours légal. **2.** [Fig.] authentique, vrai: *pound* ~, livre *f* sterling.

stern[1] [stɚn] *adj.* [Pers.] sévère, austère; rigoureux; [look, &c.] rébarbatif.

stern[2] *n.* [Naut.] arrière *m*; poupe *f*: *from stem to* ~, de l'avant à l'arrière.

sternness [-nəs] *n.* sévérité *f*, austérité *f*, rigueur *f.*

stethoscope [ˈstɛθəˌskowp] *n.* stéthoscope *m.*

stevedore [ˈstijvəˌdɔɚ] *n.* débardeur *m.*

stew [stjuw] *n.* [Culin.] ragoût *m*, fricassée *f*; civet *m* (de lapin, &c.); *Irish* ~, ragoût. ‖ *v. tr.* mettre (une viande) en ragoût; apprêter (une viande) en fricassée, civet; fricasser; cuire à l'étouffée: *stewed apples*, compote *f* de pommes.

steward [ˈstjuwɚd] *n.* régisseur *m*, intendant *m*; [club] maître d'hôtel *m*; [Naut.] commis aux vivres; [liner] garçon *m* (de cabine, de table). ‖ **stewardess** [-əs] *n.* [Naut.] femme *f* de chambre; [aviation] stewardess *f*, hôtesse *f* (de l'air).

stick [stɪk], **stuck** [stʌk], **stuck** *v. tr.* **1.** piquer (une fleur dans ses cheveux, à son corsage); enfoncer (un pieu, &c.); planter (un poignard, &c.); coller (une étiquette); tuer (un porc), saigner (un mouton): *Stick them up!*, Haut les mains! **2.** [Fig.] déconcerter, confondre (qqun). ‖ *v. intr.* adhérer; (se) coller: *to get stuck*, s'enliser; s'empêtrer; être en panne; [Fig.] se cramponner (à ses habitudes, à une opinion), *to* ~ *to one's habits*, *to* ~ *to one's guns*, → défendre ses positions, ne pas vouloir en démordre. ‖ *n.* baguette *f*; tige *f*; [Culin.] *fish* ~, croquette *f* de poisson. || **stick out** [-'awt] *v. tr.* faire saillir, dépasser (qqch.); tirer (la langue); [Fig.] endurer, souffrir (qqch.): *He stuck it out to the end,* Il a tenu le coup jusqu'au bout. || *v. intr.* saillir, dépasser. || **sticker** [-ɚ] *n.* colleur *m*; étiquette *f*; tueur *m* (de porcs). || **stickiness** [-ɪnəs] *n.* viscosité *f*, adhésivité *f*. || **sticky** [-ɪ] *adj.* collant, adhésif; visqueux; [Fam.] ardu, malaisé, épineux.

stiff [stɪf] *adj.* [neck] raide, dur; [corps] rigide; [arm, leg] ankylosé; [Fig.] [style] guindé; [Pers.] inflexible, obstiné; [task] difficile. || **stiffen** [-n̩] *v. tr.* raidir, rendre rigide, renforcer: *to ~ one's attitude,* raffermir son attitude; *to ~ a drink,* corser une boisson. || *v. intr.* se raidir. || **stiffly** [-lɪ] *adv.* avec raideur; obstinément. || **stiffness** [-nəs] *n.* raideur *f*; rigidité *f*; consistance *f* (d'un liquide, de la colle); [Fig.] gêne *f*, contrainte *f*; [Pers.] obstination *f*; difficulté *f* (d'un travail); affectation *f* (du style).

stifle ['stajfl̩] *v. tr.* étouffer; [emotion, impulse, &c.] réprimer, maintenir. || *v. intr.* suffoquer, étouffer.

stigma ['stɪgmə] *n.* stigmate *m*, flétrissure *f*, tache *f*, marque *f*.

still[1] [stɪl] *adj.* calme, tranquille; [Pers.] silencieux; paisible; immobile: *~ life,* nature morte; *~ -born* (*child*), (enfant) mort-né. || *n.* calme *m*, silence *m*. || *v. tr.* calmer, apaiser; faire taire.

still[2] *adv.* **1.** encore; [≠always] toujours: **2.** cependant, pourtant, néanmoins: *situation ~ critical,* la situation reste critique.

still[3] *n.* **1.** alambic *m*. **2.** distillerie *f*. || *v. tr.* distiller (une liqueur).

stillness [-nəs] *n.* calme *m* (de la nature), tranquillité *f* (d'une personne, d'un lieu); paix *f* (d'un lieu); immobilité *f* (de l'eau, de l'atmosphère, d'un animal).

stilt [stɪlt] *n.* échasse *f*. || **stilted** [-əd] *adj.* monté sur des échasses, surhaussé; [style] guindé.

stimulant ['stɪmjə|lənt] *n. & adj.* stimulant *m*, tonique *m*. || **stimulate** [-ˌlejt] *v. tr.* stimuler, aiguillonner, encourager (qqun à faire qqch.). || **stimulation** [ˌstɪmjə'lejʃən] *n.* stimulation *f*, encouragement *m*. || **stimulus** ['stɪmjələs] *pl.* **-i** [-aj] *n.* stimulant *m*, aiguillon *m*, encouragement *m*.

sting [stɪŋ] *n.* [insect, &c.] aiguillon *m*; [wasp] dard *m*; piqûre *f*; [Fig.] pointe *f*. || **sting** [stɪŋ], **stung** [stʌŋ], **stung** *v. tr.* [insect] piquer; [Fig.] mortifier, irriter (qqun). || *v. intr.* cuire, picoter.

stinginess ['stɪndʒɪnəs] *n.* avarice *f*, mesquinerie *f*. || **stingy** ['stɪndʒɪ] *adj.* ladre, pingre.

stink [stɪŋk], **stank** [stæŋk], **stunk** [stʌŋk] *v. intr.* puer. || **stinker** [-ɚ] *n.* sale individu; [Fam.] salaud: *the translation was a ~*, la version était vache. || **stinking** ['stɪŋk|ɪŋ] *adj.* puant, nauséabond, infect.

stint [stɪnt] *v. tr.* rationner, économiser, limiter; [money, expense] lésiner sur, être chiche de. || *n.* restriction *f*, limite *f*; tâche *f*, besogne *f*: *after a ~ in the army,* après un stage dans l'armée.

stipend ['stajpɛnd] *n.* honoraires *mpl.* (d'un médecin, avocat); traitement *m* (d'un juge, fonctionnaire).

stipulate ['stɪpjəˌlejt] *v. tr. & intr.* stipuler, préciser. || **stipulation** [ˌstɪpjə'lejʃən] *n.* stipulation *f*, clause *f*.

stir [stɚ] *v. tr.* [-rr-] remuer (qqch.), agiter (un liquide &c.); bouger (les doigts, &c.); [Fig.] irriter, exciter (qqun), troubler (les esprits); émouvoir (l'opinion). || *v. intr.* (se) renuer, bouger. || **stir up** [-'ʌp] *v. tr.* renuer (qqch.); [Fig.] exciter, pousser (qqun à qqch., *s.o. to sth.*), encourager, susciter, provoquer (qqch.). || *n.* **1.** mouvement *m*, remuement *m*, agitation *f*, renueménage *m*. **2.** [Fig.] émotion *f*, émoi *m*. **3.** [Sl.] prison *f*, violon *m*, taule *f*. || **stirring** [-ɪŋ] *adj.* [Pers.] remuant; [activities] mouvementé; [Fig.] [example, speech] entraînant, stimulant; [scene] émouvant; intéressant.

stirrup ['stɚəp] *n.* étrier *m*; *~ cup,* coup de l'étrier.

stitch [stɪtʃ], **stitches** [-z] *n.* [sewing] point *m* (de couture); [knitting] maille *f*; [Surg.] point *m* de suture. || *v. tr.* piquer, coudre (une étoffe), brocher (un livre); [Surg.] faire un point de suture (à une blessure).

St. John ['sn̩|'dʒɑn] *n.* © [Nfld.] Saint-Jean (de Terre-Neuve); Saint-Jean (N.-B.); [P.Q.] Saint-Jean.

St. Lawrence (River) ['sn̩t-'lɔɚəns] *n.* le (fleuve) Saint-Laurent: *The St. Lawrence Seaway Authority,* l'Administration de la voie maritime du Saint-Laurent.

St. Martin's [Summer) [-'mɑɚtn̩z] *n.* [Fr.] été de la Saint-Martin; © été des Sauvages.

stoat [stowt] *n.* hermine *f* (d'été).

stock[1] [stɑk] *n.* souche *f* (d'un arbre, d'une famille); bûche *f*, tronc *m*, bloc *m* (d'arbre); lignée *f* (d'ancêtres), famille *f*, race *f*; provisions *fpl*, approvisionnement *m*, stock *m* (d'un magasin); [Fin. US] valeurs *fpl*, actions *fpl*, rentes *fpl*, capital *m*, fonds *m*; [Hort.] ente *f*; *pl.*

[Naut.] chantier *m*, cale *f* (de construction navale); [Culin.] consommé; [US] wagon *m* à bestiaux; *Stock Exchange*, (la) Bourse *f* des valeurs; ~ *raising*, élevage *m*/du, de/bétail. *v. tr.* approvisionner (un magasin), monter (qqch. en), outiller, meubler (une ferme); peupler (une forêt, un lac).

stock[2] *n.* oeillet *m*.

stockade [stɑ'kejd] *n.* **1.** palissade *f*, estacade *f*. **2.** prison *f* (militaire), camp *m* de détention.

stockbroker [-ˌbɹowkɚ] *n.* agent *m* de change.

stock-car [-ˌkɑɚ] *n.* stock-car *m*.

stockholder [-ˌhowldɚ] *n.* [US] actionnaire *m*/*f*.

stocking ['stɑkɪŋ] *n.* bas *m(pl)*: *a pair of nylon stockings*, une paire de bas nylon. cf. HOSE.

stock-in-trade [Fig.] bagage *m*, répertoire *m*.

stock-market [Fin.] marché *m*.

stockroom [-ˌɹuwm] *n.* magasin *m*.

stocky [-ɪ] *adj.* trapu.

stockyard [-ˌjaɚd] *n.* **1.** parc *m* à bétail. **2.** parc *m* à matériaux.

stodgy ['stɑdʒɪ] *adj.* indigeste, lourd.

stoic ['stowɪ|k] *n. & adj.* [Phil.] stoïcien, -ne; stoïque *m*/*f*. || **stoicism** [-ˌsizm] *n.* stoïcisme *m*.

stoke [stowk] *v. tr.* [furnace] charger, alimenter, entretenir/le feu. || **stoker** [-ɚ] *n.* chauffeur *m*.

stole[1] [stowl] *n.* [fur; also R.C.] étole *f*: *diagonal* ~ , sautoir *m*.

stole[2], **stolen**, cf. STEAL.

stolid ['stɑlɪd] *adj.* lourd, lent.

stomach ['stʌmək] *n.* estomac *m*; [polite form for belly] ventre *m*. || *v. tr.* digérer, [Fig.] supporter: *I cannot* ~ *him*, Je ne peux pas le sentir. || **stomach ache** [-ˌejk] *n.* mal *m*, douleur *f*/d'estomac; [Fam.] mal de ventre.

stone [stown] *n.* pierre *f*; noyau *m* (d'un fruit); [Med.] calcul *m* (biliaire): ~ *deaf*, [Fig.] sourd comme un pot; ~ *dead*, raide mort. || *adj.* de, en/pierre. || *v. tr.* [Fig.] lapider (qqun); revêtir (un mur, une maison) de pierres; enlever le noyau, les pépins (des fruits, d'un fruit): [Fig.] *a rolling* ~ , un roule-sa-bosse. || **stony** [-ɪ] *adj.* pierreux, de pierre; [Fig.] [heart] endurci.

stood, cf. STAND.

stooge [stuwdʒ] *n.* [Sl.] complice *m*, compère *m*.

stool [stuwl] *n.* [Piano] tabouret *m*; escabeau *m*: [Fig.] *to go to* ~ , aller à la selle; [Sl.] ~ *pigeon*, mouchard *m*; [Bot.] plante *f* mère; *campstool*, pliant *m*.

stoop[1] [stuwp] *v. intr.* **1.** se pencher, se baisser; [Fig.] s'incliner, s'abaisser (*to*, jusqu'à): *She stoops to conquer*, Elle s'abaisse pour mieux vaincre. **2.** se tenir/ courbé, voûté, le dos rond/: *Don't* ~ *!* Tiens-toi droit!; *stooping from old age*, courbé sous le poids des ans. **3.** [birds of prey] fondre (*on*, sur). || *v. tr.* pencher, courber. || *n.* inclinaison *f*; [Pers.]→ le dos rond, voûté.

stoop[2] *n.* [R.C.] bénitier *m*.

stop [stɑp] *v. intr.* [-pp-] [moving beings] (s')arrêter, cesser: *to* ~ *talking*, s'arrêter de parler; [pipe, &c.] se bloquer, se boucher. || *v. tr.* arrêter (un mouvement, une auto), cesser (son activité); obstruer, bloquer, boucher (un tuyau, un conduit); empêcher (qqun de faire qqch.); [Loc.] ~ *it!*, Finissez!; ~ *thief!*, Au voleur!; [autobus, tramways] *Cars* ~ *here*, Arrêt *m* obligatoire; *Cars* ~ *here on request*, Arrêt *m* facultatif; [Rail.] *flag* ~ , halte *f*; *whistle* ~ , [Rail.] petite station, halte; [US Pol.] arrêt bref. || **stop** *n.* arrêt *m* (d'un mouvement, de l'autobus); empêchement *m*, obstacle *m*; station *f* (de chemin de fer); [Mus.] jeu *m* (d'orgue). || **stop by, in** [-'baj] [-'ɪn] *v. intr.* faire une (brève) visite à, passer chez. || **stop over** [-'owvɚ] *v. intr.* interrompre (momentanément) un voyage. || *n.* [travel] arrêt en cours de route; étape *f* (d'un voyage). || **stoppage** [-ədʒ] *n.* arrêt *m*; obstacle *m*; suspension *f* (de la circulation, de paiements). || **stopper** [-ɚ] *n.* bouchon *m*; capsule *f*; obturateur *m*. || **stopping place** [-ɪŋˌplejs] *n.* halte *f*, arrêt *m*; escale *f*, cf. STOPOVER; refuge *m*, auberge *f*, relais *m*. || **stop watch** [-ˌwɑtʃ] *n.* compte-secondes; chronomètre à déclic.

storage ['stɔɚədʒ] *n.* entreposage *m*; emmagasinage *m* (de marchandises). || **storage battery** [-ˌbætɚɪ] *n.* (batterie *f* d')accumulateurs.

store [stɔɚ] *n.* magasin *m* (de nouveautés); boutique *f* (d'épicier, &c.); entrepôt *m*, dépôt (de vivres); abondance *f*; approvisionnement *m*: *Department stores*, les grands magasins; *pl.* matériel *m*; vivres *mpl*; [Mil.] munitions *fpl*. || *v. tr.* emmagasiner (des provisions); mettre (qqch.) en dépôt; approvisionner; fournir (qqch. de, *sth. with*). || **storehouse** [-ˌhaws] *n.* magasin *m*, entrepôt *m*, dépôt *m* (de vivres, munitions). || **storeroom** [-ˌɹuwm]

n. **1.** [home] dépense *f*, office *m*. **2.** [Naut.] soute *f* aux provisions.
storey [-ɪ] *n.* cf. STORY².
storied [-ɪd] *adj.* **1.** [Arch.] historié; célébré dans l'histoire, la légende. **2.** [building] à (un, deux, trois, &c.) étage(s).
stork [stɔɚk] *n.* cigogne *f*: © *They had a visit from the* ~, Les sauvages ont passé (chez eux), [Fr.] La cigogne a passé (chez eux).
storm [stɔɚm] *n.* [rain] orage *m*; [wind] tempête *f*; [Mil.] assaut *m* (d'une place forte): ~ *window*, double fenêtre. ‖ *v. tr.* [Mil.] emporter, prendre (une forteresse, &c.) d'assaut. ‖ *v. intr.* **1.** [weather] faire de l'orage; [wind, rain] faire rage; [Fig. Pers.] tempêter. **2.** [Mil.] [troops] monter à l'assaut. ‖ **stormy** [-ɪ] *adj.* [weather] orageux, d'orage; [wind] tempêtueux, violent; [Fig.] [temper] déchaîné.
story¹ [stɔɚɪ] *n.* [tale] histoire *f*, conte *m*; récit *m*; [Fig.] mensonge: *the* ~ *so far*, → résumé des chapitres précédents; *as the* ~ *goes*, d'après ce que l'on/raconte, dit/. ‖ **story-teller** [-ˌtɛlɚ] *n.* conteur *m*, -se *f*; [Fig.] menteu|r *m*, -se *f*.
story² *n.* étage *m*.
stoup [stuwp] cf. STOOP².
stout [stawt] *adj.* corpulent, gros [polite form] fort; [Fig.] courageux, énergique. ‖ *n.* bière forte (anglaise), stout *m*. ‖ **stoutly** [-lɪ] *adv.* solidement; énergiquement, résolument.
stove [stowv] *n.* [heating] poêle *m*; [cooking] fourneau *m* (de cuisine); [Fr.] cuisinière *f*, © [abus.] poêle *m*.
stow [stow] *v. tr.* installer, mettre en place; ranger, serrer (dans une malle): *to* ~ *away* (*on a ship*), embarquer clandestinement; [Naut.] arrimer. ‖ **stowage** [-əʤ] *n.* [Naut.] arrimage *m*; frais *mpl* d'arrimage. ‖ **stowaway** [ˈstowəˌwej] *n.* passager *m* (passagère *f*) clandestin(e).
straddle [ˈstɹædl̩] *v. tr.* enfourcher (un cheval, une bicyclette), chevaucher (un mur); se mettre à califourchon sur: [Mil.] *to* ~ *a target*, encadrer une cible; [Fig.] biaiser, éviter de prendre parti. ‖ *n.* écartement *m*, chevauchement *m*.
strafe [stɹejf] *v. tr.* mitrailler, bombarder.
straggle [ˈstɹægl̩] *v. intr.* traîner, rester en arrière: *to* ~ *along*, marcher sans ordre, suivre en débandade. ‖ **straggler** [-ɚ] *n.* traînard *m*, rôdeur *m*. ‖ **straggling** [-ɪŋ] *adj.* épars, sans ordre.
straight [stɹejt] *adj.* **1.** droit, direct, en ordre; [Pers.] loyal, honnête, juste. **2.** [liquor] sec. ‖ *adv.* (tout) droit, directement; [Fig.] loyalement, honnêtement: ~ *away*, sur-le-champ, tout de suite, immédiatement. ‖ **straighten** [n̩] *v. tr.* rectifier, redresser (qqch.); [Fig.] (ar)ranger, mettre (qqch.) en ordre. ‖ **straightforward** [-ˌfɔɚwɚd] *adj. & adv.* franc, direct, droit, sans détour. ‖ **straightness** [-nəs] *n.* rectitude *f*; [Fig.] droiture *f*. ‖ **straightway** [-ˌwej] *adv.* tout de suite; immédiatement.
strain¹ [stɹejn] *v. tr.* **1.** tendre (une corde), serrer (qqun, qqch.); se fouler (une épaule, une cheville); forcer (qqch.). **2.** filtrer, passer (un liquide). **3.** contraindre (qqun, qqch.); surmener (qqun): *to* ~ *one's eyes*, s'abîmer les yeux, se fatiguer la vue. ‖ *v. intr.* faire un (grand) effort; [liquid] suinter. ‖ *n.* tension *f* (physique ou morale); surmenage *m*; effort *m*; foulure *f*, entorse *f*.
strain² *n.* **1.** héritage *m* (moral); lignée *f*. **2.** [Fig.] veine *f*, ton *m* (d'un discours, d'une pièce littéraire).
strainer [-ɚ] *n.* filtre *m* (pour les liquides); tamis *m*, passoire *f*.
strait [stɹejt] *adj.* étroit, serré; [Fig.] strict, rigoureux. ‖ *n.* détroit *m*: *the* ~ *of Davis*, le détroit de D.; *the Straits of Dover*, le Pas de Calais.
strand¹ [stɹænd] *n.* grève *f*, côte *f* basse; estran *m*; © batture *f*. ‖ *v. tr.* (s')échouer; [Fig.] *to be stranded*, être/abandonné, en panne/.
strand² *n.*: ~ *of pearls*, collier *m* de perles.
stranded [ˈstɹændəd] *adj.* [Naut.] échoué; [Fam.] égaré, en plan.
strange [stɹejnʤ] *adj.* **1.** étrange; bizarre; inhabituel, singulier: *to feel* ~, se sentir dépaysé. **2.** [Pers.] inconnu. ‖ **strangely** [-lɪ] *adv.* étrangement, singulièrement. ‖ **strangeness** [-nəs] *n.* étrangeté *f*; singularité *f*; froideur *f*. ‖ **stranger** [-ɚ] *n.* étrang|er *m*, -ère *f*; cf. FOREIGNER, ALIEN; inconnu, -e; [new to] novice *m* (*to*, dans): *You're quite a* ~ *now!*, → On ne vous voit plus!
strangle [ˈstɹæŋg|l̩] *v. tr.* étrangler, étouffer. ‖ **stranglehold** [ˈstɹæŋl̩ˌhowld] *n.* prise à la gorge; [Fig.] étau *m*. ‖ **strangulate** [-jəˌlejt] *v. tr.* [Med.] étrangler. ‖ **strangulation** [ˌstɹæŋgjeˈlejʃən] *n.* strangulation *f*, étranglement *m*.
strap [stɹæp] *n.* courroie *f* (de cuir), lanière *f*; sangle *f*; bande *f* (de fer). ‖ *v. tr.* **[-pp-]** attacher (avec une courroie), sangler.
strapping [ˈstɹæpɪŋ] *adj.* [Fam.] bien découplé.
stratagem [ˈstɹætəʤəm] *n.* stratagème *m*, ruse *f*.

strategic [stɹə'tijʤɪk] *adj.* stratégique. || **strategy** ['stɹætəʤɪ] *n.* stratégie *f.*

stratosphere ['stɹætəsˌfijɚ] *n.* stratosphère *f.*

straw [stɹɔ] *n.* paille *f*; †chalumeau *m*: [Loc.] *It's the last* ~, Il ne manquait plus que cela! || *adj.* de, en/paille: ~ *hat*, chapeau de paille.

strawberry [-ˌbɛɚɪ] *n.* fraise *f.*

stray [stɹej] *n.* [animal] égaré, vagabond. || *v. intr.* s'égarer, s'écarter de. || *adj.* égaré, errant: *a* ~ *bullet*, une balle perdue.

streak [stɹijk] *n.* rayure *f*, raie *f*, bande *f*: *a* ~ *of light*, un filet de lumière; [Fig.] *He has a mean* ~, Il y a de la méchanceté en lui. || *v. tr.* rayer, strier: *The sky (was) streaked with lightning*, Le ciel (était) sillonné d'éclairs.

stream [stɹijm] *n.* [small] ruisseau *m*; [large] fleuve *m*; rivière *f*; [mountain] torrent *m*; [water] courant *m*; [Fig.] flot *m.* || *v. intr.* [water] couler, [blood] ruisseler; [light] jaillir; [flag] flotter: *to* ~ *out*, [water, blood] couler, sortir à flots. || **streamer** [-ɚ] *n.* banderole *f*; flamme *f.* || **streamlined** [-ˌlajnd] *adj.* [car] aérodynamique; [Fig.] abrégé, concis.

street [stɹijt] *n.* **1.** rue *f*: *back* ~, passage *m*, © ruelle *f*, *main* ~, grand'rue, © rue principale; artère *f* principale; *one way* ~, rue *f* à sens/unique, interdit/. **2.** [= PAVEMENT] chaussée *f*, rue. **3.** [= SIDEWALKS] trottoir *m*, rue: *I met him on the street*, Je l'ai rencontré dans la rue. || **street door** [-ˌdɔɚ] porte *f* d'entrée. || **streetcar** [-ˌkɑɚ] *n.* tram(way) *m.* || **streetwalker** [-ˌwɔkɚ] *n.* → qui fait le trottoir, prostituée *f.*

strength ['stɹɛŋθ] *n.* **1.** [Pers.] force *f*; [affection] intensité *f.* **2.** effectif *m* [militaire]. || **strengthen** [-n̩] *v. tr.* fortifier (son corps); (r) affermir (ses muscles), renforcer (un régiment); consolider (ses positions); resserrer (des liens). || *v. intr.* [of person] prendre des forces; se fortifier; s'affermir, se raffermir.

strenuous ['stɹɛnjuwəs] *adj.* [Pers.] actif, zélé; énergique; [task, work] ardu; [effort] acharné: *a* ~ *objection (to)*, une objection vigoureuse (à). || **strenuously** [-lɪ] *adv.* énergiquement.

stress [stɹɛs] *n.* **1.** force *f*: *under the* ~ *of circumstance(s)*, par la force des choses. **2.** [emphasis] insistance *f* (*on*, sur): *to lay* ~ *on*, insister sur. **3.** [Ling.] accent *m* (tonique). **4.** [Tech.] effort *m*, stress *m*; tension *f*: *in/under/* ~, sous tension. **5.** [Fig.] tension *f*: *He works well under* ~, Il travaille bien sous/tension, pression/; *The* ~ *of the daily routine*, Les tensions (et les fatigues) du train-train quotidien; *in time(s) of* ~, en période troublée. || *v. tr.* insister/appuyer/sur; accentuer (une syllabe), || *v. intr.* faire ressortir (que...).

stretch [stɹɛtʃ] *v. tr.* tendre, étendre, étirer, déployer: *to* ~ *a point*, faire une concession. || *v. intr.* se tendre, s'étendre, s'étirer, se déployer. || *n.* extension *f*, tension *f*; portée *f* (du bras); allongement *m*; section *f* (de route).

stretcher ['stɹɛtʃɚ] *n.* [trousers] tendeur *m*; [shoes] forme *f*; [Med.] civière *f*: ~ *-bearer*, brancardier *m.*

strew [stɹuw], **strewed** [-d], **strewed** or **strewn** [-n] *v. tr.* semer, éparpiller (sur le sol); [Pej.] joncher. || **strewn** cf. STREW.

stricken, cf. STRIKE. || *adj.* frappé; atteint (de maladie, &c.).

strict [stɹɪkt] *adj.* [ordres] strict; [discipline] sévère; rigoureux; [meaning, fact] exact, précis. || **strictly** [-lɪ] *adv.* strictement; sévèrement; [forbidden] formellement. || **strictness** [-nəs] *n.* rigueur *f*, sévérité *f*; [Fig.] exactitude *f.*

stridden, cf. STRIDE.

stride [stɹajd] *n.* (grand) pas *m*, enjambée *f*; [progress] pas *m* de géant: *to take sth. in one's* ~, faire, s'accommoder de/qqch. sans difficulté; *to hit one's* ~, trouver/son allure, sa cadence/. || **stride, strode** [stɹowd], **stridden** ['stɹɪdn̩] aller à/grands pas, grandes enjambées/: *to* ~ *along*, marcher, avancer/à grands pas; *to* ~ *over*, enjamber. || **strider** ['stɹajdɚ] *n.*: *water* ~, © patineur *m.*

strife [stɹajf] *n.* [Fig.] lutte *f.*

strike [stɹajk] *n.* coup *m*; [labour] grève *f.* || **strike, struck, struck** [stɹʌk] *v. tr.* frapper (qqch.), cogner (qqun, qqch.); donner un coup à (qqun, qqch.); [bell] sonner (une cloche), frotter (une allumette); conclure (un marché); [colours, flag] baisser (pavillon); heurter, donner contre (un écueil); frapper (une pièce de monnaie): *to* ~ *oil*, trouver du pétrole; [Fig.] *to* ~ *it rich*, trouver le filon, réussir un beau coup. || *v. intr.* faire la grève. || **strike down** ['stɹajk|'dawn] *v. tr.* abattre. || **strike off** [-'ɔf] *v. tr.* effacer, biffer (un mot, &c.). **strike on** [-'ɑn] *v. intr.* [Mar.] donner contre (un récif), se heurter sur. || **strike out** [-'awt] *v. tr.* rayer (un mot); se frayer (une voie nouvelle). || **strike up** [-'ʌp] *v. intr.* [Mus.] attaquer (un morceau), entonner (une chanson); *to* ~ *an acquaintance with*, faire la connaissance de, lier connaissance avec. || **striker** [-ɚ] *n.* gréviste *m*; [Sport] © frappeur *m.* || **striking** [-ɪŋ] *adj.* frappant, saisissant; [feature] saillant; [proof] éclatant.

string [stɹɪŋ] *n.* ficelle *f*, corde *f*; [hat, apron] cordon *m*; [group of things] série *f*; chapelet *m* (d'oignons, d'injures); [barges] train *m* (de péniches); [Mus.] corde *f*: *the strings*, les instruments à corde; [Fig.] *to pull strings*, tirer les ficelles, avoir de l'influence; *with no ~ attached*, sans restrictions; *to have the world on a ~*, commander/mener/le monde; *~ of medals*, brochette de décorations. || *v. tr.* **string, strung** [stɹʌŋ], **strung** mettre une ficelle, une corde (à qqch.); garnir de cordes; [Mus.] accorder; [beads] enfiler: *to ~ along*, aller à la file, suivre; *to ~ up*, pendre haut et court; *to ~ out*, prolonger; *strung out along the road*, dispersés, égaillés/le long de la route. || **string-bag** ['stɹɪŋˌbæg] *n.* filet *m* à provisions; *~ bean*, haricot *m* vert.

stringent ['stɹɪndʒənt] *adj.* rigoureux.

strip [stɹɪp] *n.* bande *f* (d'étoffe); ruban *m* (de papier); lambeau *m* (d'écorce); [Aero.] piste *f*. || *v. tr.* dépouiller; mettre à nu; déshabiller (qqun); [tree] écorcer; [Fig.] dévaliser.

stripe [stɹajp] *n.* raie *f*; rayure *f* (sur une étoffe); barre *f*; bande *f* (de couleur); [US] *Stars and Stripes*, la bannière étoilée; [whip] marque *f* (d'un coup de fouet); [Mil.] chevron *m*, galon *m*. || *v. tr.* rayer, barrer. || **striped** [-t] *adj.* [fabric] à rayures, rayé.

stripling ['stɹɪplɪŋ] *n.* adolescent(e).

strive [stɹajv], **strove** [stɹowv], **striven** ['stɹɪvən] *v. intr.* s'efforcer (*to*, de); [struggle] lutter (*against*, contre).

striven, cf. STRIVE.

strode [stɹowd], cf. STRIDE.

stroke[1] [stɹowk] *n.* coup *m* (de pinceau, de cloche); trait *m* (de plume); [heart] attaque *f* (d'une maladie): *sun ~*, coup *m* de soleil, insolation *f*.

stroke[2] *v. tr.* [animal] caresser.

stroll [stɹowl] *v. intr.* flâner, se promener, déambuler. || *n.* (petite) promenade, flânerie *f*: *to go for a ~*, aller faire un tour. || **stroller** [-ɚ] *n.* promeneur, flâneur; *baby ~*, poussette *f*.

strong [stɹɔŋ] *adj.* [Pers.] fort; énergique; [thing] solide; [will] ferme: *~ -willed*, volontaire, qui a une volonté de fer; [health, &c.] *to be getting stronger*, (re)prendre/de la force, des forces/. cf. STRENGTH. || **stronghold** [-ˌhowld] *n.* forteresse *f*, place *f* forte. || **strongly** [-lɪ] *adv.* énergiquement, fortement; [Fig.] fortement; fermement; [tied] solidement.

strop [stɹɑp] *n.* cuir *m* (à rasoir). || *v. tr.* [-pp-] aiguiser, affiler, repasser (un rasoir sur le cuir).

strove, cf. STRIVE.

struck, cf. STRIKE.

structural ['stɹʌktʃɚ|l̩] *adj.* structural. || **structure** *n.* structure *f* (d'acier, &c.), [pattern] construction *f* (d'une phrase); [building] bâtiment *m*, édifice *m*, © bâtisse *f*; [Fig.] armature *f* (sociale).

struggle ['stɹʌgl̩] *n.* combat *m*; effort *m*; lutte *f* (des classes, &c.). || *v. intr.* combattre, lutter; se débattre (dans, au milieu de, *in*): *to ~ /along, on, up/*, → avancer, monter/péniblement.

strung, cf. STRING.

strut [stɹʌt] *n.* démarche *f* fière, orgueilleuse; [construction] étai *m*, support *m*. || *v. intr.* se pavaner [along, in, out] marcher, entrer, sortir d'un air important. || *v. tr.* étayer, soutenir.

stub [stʌb] *n.* souche *f*, tronçon *m*; [pencil] bout *m*; [cigarette] mégot *m*, bout *m*; [cheque] souche *f*, talon *m*. || *v. tr.* [up] extraire; [out] essoucher: *to ~ one's toe*, se cogner le bout du pied (contre qqch.).

stubble [-l̩] *n.* chaume *m*; [Fig.] barbe *f*/rude, de quelques jours/.

stubborn [-ɚn] *adj.* [Pers.] têtu, entêté, opiniâtre; [horse, donkey] rétif; [metals] réfractaire: *a ~ soil*, un sol ingrat. || **stubbornness** [-ɚnəs] *n.* entêtement *m*, obstination *f*; opiniâtreté *f*.

stubby [-ɪ] *adj.* [beard] hirsute; [Pers.] trapu.

stucco ['stʌkow] *n.* stuc *m*. || *v. tr.* enduire, couvrir/de stuc.

stuck, cf. STICK. || **stuck-up** ['stʌkˌʌp] *adj.* [Fam.] prétentieux, poseur.

stud[1] [stʌd] *n.* clou *m* à grosse tête; [chemise d'homme] bouton *m*; [boots] crampon *m*: *~ -hole*, boutonnière *f*. || *v. tr.* clouter; [boot] ferrer; [Fig.] *studded with*, jonché de.

stud[2] *n.* [Sport] écurie *f* (de courses): *~ -farm*, haras *m*; *~-horse*, étalon *m*.

student ['stjuwdənt] *n.* [Univ.] étudiant *m*, -e *f*: *university ~*, © carabin *m*, poutchinette *f*; [Sch.] élève *m/f*: *medical students*, (les) étudiants *mpl* en médecine; *Students' Residence*, pavillon *m* (d'une Cité universitaire); maison *f* (des étudiants), © habitation *f*. || **studied** ['stʌdɪd] *adj.* [in] versé (dans); [Pej.] étudié, apprêté. || **studio** ['stjuwdɪ|ˌow] *n.* [artist] atelier *m*; [broadcast] studio *m*. || **studious** [-əs] *adj.* (élève) studieux; [Pers.] empressé (de, *of*); diligent. || **study** ['stʌdɪ] *n.* étude *f*; [room] bureau *m*, cabinet *m* de travail; †[worry] préoccupation *f*: [Fig.] (*a*) *brown* ~ , (une) rêverie *f*. || *v. tr.* étudier (les mathématiques, une question, &c.). || *v. intr.* faire/des, ses/études: *to* ~ *for*, préparer (un examen); *to* ~ *under X.*, être l'élève de X.

stuff [stʌf] *n.* étoffe *f*, tissu *m*; matière(s) *f(pl)*, matériau(x), *m(pl)*: *It's all* ~ *and nonsense*, balivernes! *fpl*: *That's the* ~ *to give/him, her, them/*, C'est comme ça qu'il faut/le, la, les/traiter; Ça/lui, leur/apprendra. || *v. tr.* rembourrer (un meuble); empailler (un oiseau), bourrer (qqch.); farcir (une volaille); boucher (un trou). || **stuffiness** [-ɪnəs] *n.* manque *m* d'air; [Fig.] esprit *m* étroit. || **stuffing** [-ɪŋ] *n.* rembourrage *m*, empaillage *m*, bourre *f*; [food] farce *f*: *to knock the* ~ *out of s.o.*, donner une correction à qqun, remettre qqun à sa place. || **stuffy** [-ɪ] *adj.* [air] lourd, étouffant; [room] qui sent le renfermé, mal ventilé; [Fig.] → à l'esprit étroit; [Sl.] maussade, en rogne.

stumble ['stʌmbl̩] *v. intr.* trébucher, faire un faux pas; se heurter (*against*, contre); tomber (*upon*, sur); [speech] bafouiller, hésiter.

stumbling block ['stʌmblɪŋˌblɑk] *n.* [Fig.] pierre *f* d'achoppement.

stump [stʌmp] *n.* souche *f*, tronçon *m* (d'arbre), chicot *m* (d'une dent); moignon *m* (d'une jambe, d'un bras); trognon *m* (de chou); [cigarette] mégot *m*; [US, hustings] estrade *f* (d'assemblées publiques). || *v. tr.* (d)essoucher. || *v. intr.* marcher lourdement; [Fig.] *to be stumped*, [Fam.] sécher (*on*, sur une question). [US] faire une campagne électorale. || **stumping** [-ɪŋ] *n.* essouchement *m*. || **stumpy** [-ɪ] *adj.* [person] trapu; [field] plein de souches.

stun [stʌn] *v. tr.* **-nn-** assommer, étourdir; [Fig.] abasourdir.

stung, cf. STING.

stunk, cf. STINK.

stunning ['stʌnɪŋ] *adj.* [blow] étourdissant, accablant; [appearance] élégant, épatant.

stunt [stʌnt] *n.* tour *m* de force, acrobatie *f*: *a publicity* ~ , un canard publicitaire. || *v. tr.* rabougrir, arrêter la croissance (de qqun, qqch.). || *v. intr.* faire des tours de force, des acrobaties. || **stunted** [-əd] *adj.* rabougri.

stupefaction [ˌstjuwpə'fækʃən] *n.* stupéfaction *f*, ahurissement *m*. || **stupefy** ['stjuwpəˌfaj] *v. tr.* [Med.] engourdir; stupéfier, hébéter, abrutir; [surprise] frapper de stupeur, abasourdir.

stupendous [ˌstjuw'pɛndəs] *adj.* prodigieux, formidable.

stupid [ˌstjuwpɪd] *adj.* [Pers.] stupide, sot, bête. || **stupidity** [stjuw'pɪdɪtɪ] *n.* stupidité *f*, bêtise *f*. || **stupidly** ['stjuwpɪdlɪ] *adv.* stupidement, bêtement.

stupor ['stjuwpɚ] *n.* stupeur *f*: *He drank himself into a* ~, Il a bu jusqu'à l'engourdissement.

sturdily ['stɚdɪlɪ] *adv.* → avec robustesse; [Fig.] résolument, fermement. || **sturdy** ['stɚdɪ] *adj.* robuste, vigoureux; solide, ferme: ~ *chap*, luron *m*.

sturgeon ['stɚdʒən] *n.* esturgeon *m*.

stutter ['stʌtɚ] *v.* bégayer, bredouiller. || *n.* bégaiement *m*. || **stutterer** [-ɚ] *n.* bègue *m/f*. || **stuttering** [-ɚɪŋ] *n.* bégaiement *m*.

sty [staj] *n.* **1.** porcherie *f*, étable *f* à porcs; © soue *f*. **2.** [Med.] orgelet *m*.

style [stajl] *n.* style *m*; genre *m*; type *m*; manière *f*; [fashion] mode *f*; [instrument] style(t) *m*: [Fig.] *to do things in* ~ , bien faire les choses; *to have* ~ , avoir /du cachet, du chic. || *v. tr.* désigner, nommer (qqch. d'après, *sth. after*); *to* ~ *o.s.*, s'intituler. || **stylish** [-ɪʃ] *adj.* élégant, à la mode, chic.

stylist ['stajlɪst] *n.* styliste *m*. || **stylistic** [ˌstajl'ɪstɪk] *adj.* de style. || **stylistics** [-s] *n. sing.* stylistique *f*.

suave [swɑv] *adj.* suave; [Pers.] affable, souriant; [Pej.] doucereux.

sub [sʌb] *abr.* [= SUBMARINE].

subaltern ['sʌbl̩tɚn] *n.* subalterne *m*, subordonné *m*; [Mil.] sous-lieutenant *m*; lieutenant *m*.

subcommittee ['sʌbkəˌmɪtɪ] *n.* sous-comité *m*.

subconscious [ˌsʌb'kɑnʃəs] *n.* subconscient *m*. || **subconsciously** [-lɪ] *adv.* inconsciemment, de façon subconsciente. || **subconsciousness** [-nəs] *n.* subconscient *m*.

subdeacon ['sʌbˌdijkən] *n.* [Rel.] sous-diacre. || **subdeaconship** [-ʃɪp] *n.* [Rel.] sous-diaconat *m*.

subdivision ['sʌbdɪˌvɪʒən] *n.* subdivision *f*.

subdue [səb'djuw] *v. tr.* subjuguer, soumettre; [fire, feelings, &c.] maîtriser, dompter; [light, pain] adoucir, atténuer; [voice] assourdir. || **subdued** [-d] *adj.* vaincu, subjugué; [Pers.] déprimé, triste: ~ *light*, demi-jour.

subject [səb'dʒɛkt] *v. tr.* assujettir, soumettre (qqun, qqch./à, *s.o.*, *sth./to*); exposer (qqun, qqch. à, *s.o.*, *sth. to*). || *n.* ['sʌbdʒəkt] [citizen, matter] sujet *m*; personne *f*, individu *m*; question *f*: *Let's change the* ~ , Parlons d'autre chose. || *adj.* sujet, assujetti, soumis, subordonné

(à, *to*); [inclined] porté (à, *to*). || **subject to** [səb'dʒɛkt'tuw] *loc. prép.* [condition] sous réserve de, sous toute réserve. || **subjection** [səb'dʒɛk|ʃən] *n.* sujétion *f*, soumission *f*: *to bring into* ~, soumettre, conquérir.
subjective [-tɪv] *adj.* subjectif.
subjugate ['sʌbdʒəˌgejt] *v. tr.* subjuguer, asservir, dompter.
subjunctive [səb'dʒʌŋktɪv] *n.* subjonctif *m.*
sublet [ˌsʌb'lɛt] *v. tr.* [apartments] sous-louer (un appartement).
sublimate ['sʌblɪˌmejt] *adj.* [Tech.] sublimé; [Fig.] sublimisé, idéalisé. || *n.* [Chem.] sublimé *m.* || *v. tr.* sublimer; [Fig.] sublimiser, idéaliser. || **sublimation** [ˌsʌblɪ-'mejʃən] *n.* sublimation *f.*
sublime [sə'blajm] *adj.* sublime; [scene] imposant, majestueux.
submachine gun [ˌsʌbmə'ʃijnˌgʌn] *n.* mitraillette *f.*
submarine [ˌsʌbmər'ijn] *n.* & *adj.* sous-marin (*m*), submersible (*m*).
submerge [səb'mərdʒ] *v. tr.* submerger, inonder. || *v. intr.* plonger.
submission [səb'mɪ|ʃən] *n.* soumission *f* (*to*, à); docilité *f*, résignation *f*. || **submissive** [-siv] *adj.* soumis, docile.
submit [səb'mɪt] *v. tr.* soumettre (*to*, à); prétendre, soutenir (*that*, que). || *v. intr.* [Pers.] se soumettre (à, *to*).
subnormal [ˌsʌb'nɔərməl] *adj.* au-dessous de, inférieur à/la normale.
subordinate [sə'bɔərdɪnət] *n.* subordonné *m*, -e *f*, sous-ordre *m.* || *v. tr.* [sə'bɔərdɪn-ˌejt] subordonner (*to*, à). || *adj.* subalterne, subordonné: ~ *clause*, proposition *f* subordonnée.
subpoena [sə'pijnə] *n.* citation *f*, assignation *f* (en justice). || *v. tr.* citer, assigner (qqun à comparaître).
sub rosa [ˌsʌb'ɹowzə] *loc. adv.* secrètement; sous le manteau; sub rosa.
subscribe [səb'skɹajb] *v. tr.* **1.** apposer (son nom; *to*, au bas de), signer. **2.** [sum of money] souscrire, verser. || *v. intr.* souscrire, donner son assentiment (*to*, à); [society] verser une cotisation (*to*, à); [book] souscrire, [periodical] s'abonner (*to*, à). || **subscription** [səb'skɹɪpʃən] *n.* souscription *f*; cotisation *f*: *to take up a* ~, se cotiser; [newspaper, magazine] abonnement *m*; [Fig.] adhésion (à une doctrine).
sub-section ['sʌbˌsɛkʃən] *n.* paragraphe *m* (d'une loi).
subsequent ['sʌbsəkwənt] *adj.* subséquent, ultérieur, qui suit: ~ *to*, consécutif à. || **subsequently** [-lɪ] *adv.* subséquemment, → par la suite.
subservient [səb'sərvɪənt] *adj.* utile; subordonné; [Pej.] servile.
subside [səb'sajd] *v. intr.* [building] s'affaisser, s'enfoncer; [liquid] déposer; [flood] baisser; [storm, anger] s'apaiser, se calmer. || **subsidence** ['sʌbsɪdəns] *n.* affaissement *m*; baisse *f*; apaisement *m.*
subsidiary [səb'sɪdʒərɪ] *adj.* subsidiaire. || *n.* auxiliaire *m.*
subsidize ['sʌbsɪ|ˌdajz] *v. tr.* subventionner. || **subsidy** [-dɪ] *n.* subside *m*, subvention *f.*
subsist [səb'sɪst] *v. intr.* subsister, vivre.
subsistence [səb'sɪstən|s] *n.* subsistance *f*; moyens *mpl* d'existence. || **subsistent** [-t] *adj.* subsistant.
substance ['sʌbstəns] *n.* [chemical, &c.] substance *f*, matière *f*; [content] fond *m*; (l')essentiel *m* (de la question); [riches] avoir *m.* || **substantial** [səb'stæn|ʃəl] *adj.* substantiel, réel: *a* ~ *amount of money*, une somme considérable; [business] important, solide, sérieux; [cloth] résistant.
substantiate [səb'stænʃjejt] *v. tr.* établir (une accusation), apporter des preuves à (une théorie).
substantive ['sʌbstəntɪv] *n.* [Gram.] substantif *m.* || *adj.* [Gram.] substantif; réel, explicite.
substitute ['sʌbstəˌtjuwt] *v. tr.* substituer (qqun, qqch. à, *s.o.*, *sth. for*). || *n.* [person] substitut *m*, remplaçant *m*, suppléant *m*, [thing] succédané *m.* || **substitution** [ˌsʌbstɪ'tjuwʃən] *n.* substitution *f.*
subterfuge ['sʌbtərˌfjuwdʒ] *n.* subterfuge *m.*
subterranean [ˌsʌbtər'ejnɪən] *adj.* souterrain.
subtle ['sʌtḷ] *adj.* subtil; fin, raffiné: *a* ~ *mind*, un esprit ingénieux; [Pej.] *a* ~ *scheme*, un projet astucieux. || **subtlety** [-tɪ] *n.* subtilité *f*; finesse *f*; [Pej.] ruse *f*, astuce *f.*
subtract [səb'tɹæk|t] *v. tr.* soustraire, retrancher (*from*, de). || **subtraction** [-ʃən] *n.* [number] soustraction *f.*
suburb ['sʌbərb] *n.* [town, city] banlieue *f*, faubourg *m.* || **suburban** [sə'bərbən] *adj.* suburbain, de banlieue. || **suburbanite** [-ajt] *n.* [Fam.] banlieusard *m.*
subvention [səb'vɛnʃən] *n.* subvention *f.*
subversion [səb'vərʒən] *n.* subversion *f.* || **subversive** [səb'vərsɪv] *adj.* subversif.
subway ['sʌbˌwej] *n.* **1.** [Rail.] métro *m.* **2.** [surtout Br.] passage souterrain [= UNDERPASS].
succeed [sək'sijd] *v. intr.* réussir (à, *in*), parvenir (à); succéder (à); © arracher. || **success** [sək'sɛs] *n.* succès *m*, réussite *f*: *to be a* ~ , avoir du succès, réussir; *to score a* ~ , remporter un succès.

|| **successful** [-fḷ] *adj.* → qui réussit, couronné de succès; [Pers.] heureux (en affaires, &c.); [exam] ~ *candidates*, les candidats reçus. || **successfully** [-fḷɪ] *adv.* avec succès; [issue] heureusement.

succession [sək'sɛ|ʃən] *n.* succession *f*, suite *f*, série *f*; [Jur.] succession *f*; héritage *m.* || **successive** [-sɪv] *adj.* successif, consécutif. || **successor** [-ɚ] *n.* successeur *m* (*to, of*, de).

succour ['sʌkɚ] *n.* secours *m*, aide *f.* || *v. tr.* secourir, venir en aide à. || **succourer** [-ɚ] *n.* secouriste *m*/*f.*

succulent ['sʌkjələnt] *adj.* succulent.

succumb [sə'kʌm] *v. intr.* succomber, céder (*to*, à); mourir (*to*, de).

such [sʌtʃ] *adj.* **1.** tel, -le: *He was in ~ a state that . . .*, Il se trouvait dans/un tel état, une telle détresse, [stronger] une détresse telle/que . . . ; ~ *a man*, un tel homme. **2.** pareil, -le; semblable: *I never saw ~ a thing* (*in my life*), Jamais je n'ai vu chose pareille; *In ~ a case, use a small brush*, Dans un cas semblable, employez un petit pinceau. **3.** [extreme] si, tellement: *He is ~ a nice man!*, Il est si charmant!; *He is ~ a bore*, Il est tellement ennuyeux. **4.** [Loc.] ~ *as*, comme, telle que; ceux, celles/qui . . . ; ~ *that*, tel(le) que, si [+ *adj.*] que . . . ; *all* ~ , tous ceux-là (qui), toutes celles-là (qui); *as* ~ , comme tel. || **suchlike** [-lajk] *adj.* de ce genre.

suck [sʌk] *v. tr.* [general] sucer (qqch.); [infant] téter (du lait); [in] absorber, [pump] aspirer (l'air, &c.). || *v. intr.* sucer; [infant] téter. || **sucker** [-ɚ] *n.* **1.** suceur *m*: *carp* ~ , brème *f.* **2.** *chub, sweet*/ ~ , sucette *f*; [Sl.] gogo *m*, poire *f.*

suckle [-ḷ] *v. tr.* [mother] allaiter (un bébé), donner le sein à (un bébé), nourrir (son enfant). || **suckling** [-lɪŋ] *n.* **1.** allaitement *m.* **2.** nourrisson *m.*

suction [-ʃən] *n.* succion *f*, aspiration *f*; ~ *cup*, ventouse *f.*

Sudan, the [suw'dæn] *n.* le Soudan *m.*

sudden ['sʌdṇ] *adj.* [move] soudain; [decision] prompt; [development] imprévu; [change] brusque: *all of a* ~ , tout à coup, brusquement. || **suddenly** [-lɪ] *adv.* brusquement, soudainement. || **suddenness** [-nəs] *n.* soudaineté *f*, précipitation *f.*

suds [sʌdz] *n.pl.* [soap] savonnage *m*, eau savonneuse, eau *f* de savon.

sue [suw] *v. tr.* poursuivre, traduire/qqun en justice: *I'll ~ you!*, Je vous intenterai un procès!; *to ~ for pardon*, solliciter un pardon, une amnistie.

suet ['suwət] *n.* graisse *f* de bœuf, suif *m.*

suffer ['sʌfɚ] *v. tr.* souffrir [que + subj.] [Fig.] supporter (des insultes), subir (des conséquences): *to ~ losses*, essuyer des pertes. || *v. intr.* souffrir (de qqch., *from sth.*); éprouver de la souffrance. || **sufferer** [-ɚ] *n.* patient *m*, malade *m.* || **suffering** [-ɪŋ] *n.* souffrance *f*, douleur *f.* || *adj.* [Pers.] souffrant.

suffice [sə'fajs] *v. intr.* & *tr.* suffire. || **sufficiency** [sə'fɪʃɪn|sɪ] *n.* suffisance *f.* **sufficient** [-t] *adj.* suffisant. || **sufficiently** [-tlɪ] *adv.* suffisamment.

suffocate ['sʌfə,kejt] *v. tr.* & *intr.* étouffer, suffoquer, asphyxier. || **suffocating** [-ɪŋ] *adj.* suffoquant, étouffant. || **suffocation** [ˌsʌfə'kejʃən] *n.* suffocation *f*, asphyxie *f.*

suffrage ['sʌfɹədʒ] *n.* suffrage *m*, vote *m.*

suffuse [sə'fjuwz] *v. tr.* inonder, se répandre sur: *to be suffused with*, baigner dans.

sugar [ʃʊgɚ] *n.* sucre *m*: ~ *bowl*, sucrier *m*; ~ *beet*, betterave *f* sucrière; ~ *bush*, © érablière *f*; sucrerie *f*; ~ *maple*, érable *m* à sucre; *maple* ~ , sucre *m* du pays: *sugaring-off* (*party*), © partie *f* de sucre; *sugaring-off time*, le temps des sucres. || *v. tr.* sucrer.

suggest [sə'dʒɛst] *v. tr.* suggérer (une idée), proposer (une mesure); inspirer (une pensée). || **suggestion** [sə'dʒɛstʃən] *n.* suggestion *f*; proposition *f*; idée *f.* || **suggestive** [sə'dʒɛstɪv] *adj.* suggestif.

suicide ['suwəˌsaid] *n.* suicide *m*: *to commit* ~ , se suicider.

suit [suwt] *n.* [women] (costume) tailleur *m*; [men] complet *m*; [law] poursuite *f*, procès *m.* || *v. intr.* s'adapter, convenir (*to*, à): *That suits me just fine*, Cela me va à merveille; [people] *They ~ one another perfectly*, Ils, elles s'accordent très bien. || **suitable** ['suwtəbḷ] *adj.* [thing] convenable, propre (à, *to*); adapté (à, *to*); [Pers.] (qui vient) à propos. || **suitably** ['suwtəblɪ] *adv.* convenablement, comme il convient.

suitcase [-ˌkejs] *n.* [for clothes, travelling] valise *f*, mallette *f.*

suite [swijt] *n.* suite *f*, escorte *f*; [rooms] appartement *m*: ~ *of furniture*, meubles *mpl.* mobilier *m.*

suitor ['suwtɚ] *n.* prétendant *m*, soupirant *m*; [Jur.] plaideu|r *m*, -se *f.*

sulk [sʌlk] *v. intr.* bouder; [Fam.] faire la tête. || *n.*: *to have the sulks*, bouder; bouderie. || **sulky** [-ɪ] *adj.* boudeur, maussade.

sullen ['sʌlən] *adj.* [pers.] maussade, morose, renfrogné; [thing] lugubre; [silence] obstiné; [weather] menaçant. || **sullenly** [-lɪ] *adv.* → d'un air/maussade, renfrogné. || **sullenness** [-nəs] *n.* → humeur *f*/maussade, sombre.

sully [ˈsʌlɪ] *v. tr.* souiller, salir; [reputation] flétrir, tacher.

sulphate [ˈsʌlf|ejt] *n.* sulfate *m.* || **sulphide** [-ajd] *n.* sulfure *m.* || **sulphur** [-ɚ] *n.* soufre *m.* || **sulphuric** [ˌsʌlˈfjuwɚɪk] *adj.* [acid] sulfurique. || **sulphurous** [ˈsʌlfɚəs, sʌlˈfjuwɚəs] *adj.* sulfureux.

sultan [ˈsʌltən] *n.* sultan *m.* || **sultana** [sʌlˈtænə] *n.* sultane *f.*

sultry [ˈsʌltɹɪ] *adj.* étouffant, chaud et humide, orageux.

sum [sʌm] *n.* somme *f* (d'argent); [numbers] somme *f*, total *m*: *lump* ~, prix *m* forfaitaire. || **sum up** [-ˈʌp] *v. tr.* [-mm-] additionner; récapituler (des affirmations, &c.): *to sum up*, en résumé.

summarily [ˈsʌməɹɪlɪ] *adv.* sommairement.

summarize [ˈsʌmɚ|ˌajz] *v. tr.* résumer. || **summary** [-ɪ] *n.* sommaire *m*, résumé *m*; *news* ~, récapitulation *f* des nouvelles. || *adj.* sommaire, succinct.

summer [-ɚ] *n.* été *m.* || *adj.* [season, weather] estival, d'été; [Br.] ~ *time*, cf. DAYLIGHT; ~ *cottage*, maison *f* de campagne, © camp *m.*

summit [ˈsʌmɪt] *n.* sommet *m*: *the* ~ *Conference*, la Conférence au sommet, [mountain, also Fig.] faîte *m*, cime *f.*

summon [ˈsʌmən] *v. tr.* convoquer (qqun, le Parlement); sommer (qqun de, *s.o. to*); [law] assigner (qqun). || **summons** [ˈsʌmənz] *n.pl.* [Jur.] sommation *f* (de comparaître), citation *f* (à comparaître); [ticket] procès-verbal *m*, *pl.* procès-verbaux; [Govt., management] convocation *f* urgente.

sump [sʌmp] *n.* puisard *m*; [Auto] carter *m.*

sumptuary [-tjuwɚɪ] *adj.* somptuaire. || **sumptuous** [-tjuwəs] *adj.* somptueux, fastueux. || **sumptuously** [-tjuwəslɪ] *adv* somptueusement.

sun [sʌn] *n.* soleil *m*: ~ *-dial*, cadran *m* solaire; ~ *-glasses*, lunettes *fpl* de soleil; ~ *-helmet*, casque *m* colonial; ~ *-spot*, tache *f* solaire; ~ *-up*, lever *m* du soleil. || [-nn-] *v. intr.*: *to* ~ *o.s.*, s'exposer au soleil. || **sunbeam** [-ˌbijm] *n.* rayon *m* de soleil. || **sunburn** [-ˌbɚn] *n.* [skin] coup *m* de soleil, hâle *m.* || **sunburnt** [-ˌbɚnt] *adj.* [complexion] hâlé, basané.

sundae [-dɪ] *n.*: *caramel* ~, glace *f* au caramel.

Sunday [-dej] *n.* dimanche *m*: ~ *school*, patronage *m*; [Prot.] école *f* du dimanche.

sundown [-ˌdawn] *n.* [US] © coucher *m* du soleil, soleil *m* couchant.

sundries [ˈsʌndɹɪ|z] *n.* articles *mpl* divers; [accounts] frais *mpl* divers, faux-frais *mpl.* || **sundry** *adj.* divers, varié: *all and* ~, tout le monde, tout un chacun.

sung, cf. SING.

sunk, cf. SINK.

sunken [ˈsʌŋkən] *adj.* coulé, submergé; [Fig., road] creux, encaissé; [eyes] cave.

sunlight [ˈsʌn|ˌlajt] *n.* lumière *f*/solaire, du soleil/. || **sunlit** [-ˌlɪt] *adj.* ensoleillé. || **sunny** [-ɪ] *adj.* [sky] ensoleillé; [smile] radieux. || **sunrise** [-ˌɹajz] *n.* lever *m* du soleil. || **sunset** [-ˌsɛt] *n.* coucher *m* du soleil. || **sunshine** [-ˌʃajn] *n.* soleil *m*, clarté *f* du soleil. || **sunstroke** [-ˌstɹowk] *n.* coup *m* de soleil; [Med.] insolation *f.* || **sunup** [-ˈʌp] cf. SUNRISE. || **sun visor** [-ˌvajzɚ] *n.* [Auto.] pare-soleil *inv. m.*

super [ˈsuwpɚ] *n.* [Theat.] figurant, -e.

superabundant [ˌsuwpɚ|əˈbʌndənt] *adj.* surabondant.

superannuated [-ˈænjuwˌejtəd] *adj.* suranné, démodé; [retirement] en retraite.

superb [səˈpɚb, suw-] *adj.* superbe, magnifique, somptueux.

supercargo [ˈsuwpɚ|ˌkɑɚgow] *n.* subrécargue *m.*

supercharger [-ˌtʃɑɚdʒɚ] *n.* compresseur *m*, supercompresseur *m.*

supercilious [ˌsuwpɚ|ˈsɪlɪəs] *adj.* sourcilleux, hautain, dédaigneux. || **superciliously** [-lɪ] *adv.* avec hauteur, dédaigneusement.

superficial [-ˈfɪʃəl] *adj.* superficiel; en surface. || **superficially** [-ɪ] *adv.* superficiellement.

superfluity [-ˈfluwɪtɪ] *n.* superflu *m*, superfluité *f*, excédent *m.* || **superfluous** [səˈpɚfluwəs] *adj.* superflu.

superhighway [ˈsuwpɚ|ˈhajˌwej] *n.* autoroute *f.*

superhuman [-ˈhjuwmən] *adj.* surhumain.

superintend [ˌsuwpɚɪnˈtɛnd] *v. tr.* surveiller, diriger. || **superintendence** [-əns] *n.* surintendance *f*, surveillance *f*, contrôle *m.* || **superintendent** [-ənt] *n.* surintendant *m*, direct|eur *m*, -rice *f*, chef *m.*

superior [səˈpijɚɪɚ] *adj.* supérieur (à, *to*). || *n.* supérieur: *Lake Superior*, (le) lac Supérieur. || **superiority** [səˌpijɚɪˈɔɚɪtɪ] *n.* supériorité *f.*

superlative [səˈpɚlətɪv] *n.* superlatif *m.* || *adj.* superlatif, suprême.

superman [ˈsuwpɚˌmæn] *n.* surhomme *m.*

supermarket [ˈsuwpɚˌmɑɚkət] *n.* centre *m* commercial.

supernatural [ˌsuwpɚ|ˈnætʃɚəl] *adj.* surnaturel: [R.C.] (*the*) ~ *life*, (la) vie surnaturelle. || **supernaturally** [-ɪ] *adv.* surnaturellement.

supernumerary [-'nuwmərɪ] *adj.* & *n.* surnuméraire (*m*/*f*).

supersede [-'sijd] *v. tr.* remplacer, supplanter; [Jur.] surseoir (à).

superstition [-'stɪʃən] *n.* superstition *f.* || **superstitious** [-'stɪʃes] *adj.* superstitieux.

superstructure ['suwpər|ˌstɹʌktjər] *n.* superstructure *f*; [bridge] tablier *m.*

supervise [-ˌvajz] *v. tr.* [playground] surveiller; [Tech.] contrôler, diriger. || **supervision** [ˌsuwpər|'viʒṇ] *n.* surveillance *f* (d'examens, &c.); inspection *f* (de travaux); direction *f*, contrôle *m.* || **supervisor** ['suwpərˌvajzər] *n.* surveillant *m*, -e *f*; contrôleu|r *m*, -se *f.* || **supervisory** [ˌsuwpər'vajzərɪ] *adj.*: ~ *authority*, autorité *f* de surveillance.

supine ['suwpajn] *n.* [Gram.] supin *m.* || *adj.* couché, étendu/(sur le dos); [Pej.] indolent, inerte. || **supinely** [-lɪ] *adv.* sur le dos; [Fig.] avec/indolence, mollesse.

supper ['sʌpər] *n.* souper *m*, [Fr.] dîner *m*; [Rel.] *the Last Supper*, la Cène.

supplant [sə'plænt] *v. tr.* supplanter, prendre la place de, remplacer.

supple ['sʌpḷ] *adj.* souple, flexible, [Fig.] docile, [Pej.] obséquieux, complaisant.

supplement ['sʌpləmənt] *n.* supplément *m*, appendice *m.* || *v. tr.* ajouter à, compléter, augmenter. || **supplementary** [ˌsʌplə'mɛntərɪ] *adj.* supplémentaire. || **suppleness** ['sʌpḷnəs] *n.* souplesse *f*; [Pej.] servilité *f.*

suppliant ['sʌplɪənt] *n.* & *adj.* suppliant *m*, -e *f.*

supplicate ['sʌplɪk|ejt] *v. tr.* supplier (*to*, de). || **supplication** [ˌsʌplɪ'kejʃən] *n.* supplication *f*; supplique *f.*

supplier [sə'plajər] *n.* fournisseur *m.* || **supply** [sə'plaj] *n.* ravitaillement *m*; [trade, &c.] fournitures *fpl*: *the law of ~ and demand*, la loi de l'offre et de la demande. || **supplies** [-z] *n.pl.* approvisionnements *mpl* (en vivres); fournitures *fpl.* || *v. tr.* ravitailler (une population), approvisionner (une armée, &c.); [Fig.] fournir; [loss] compenser; [need] subvenir à; [proof] fournir.

support [sə'pɔərt] *v. tr.* [×] soutenir (qqun, une cause), appuyer (un groupe); entretenir, faire vivre/(une famille). || *n.* [to a party, &c.] appui *m*; entretien *m* (d'une famille); adhésion *f* (à une croyance). || **supporter** [-ər] *n.* [Pers.] partisan *m*, adhérent *m*, défenseur *m* (d'une cause, d'une opinion); soutien *m*, support *m.*

suppose [sə'powz] *v. tr.* supposer, croire/(qqch.), s'imaginer (que, *that*). || *v. intr.* supposer. || **supposed** [-d] *adj.* supposé, présumé, prétendu: *to be ~ to*, être censé [+ infin.]; *You're not ~ to . . .*, Vous ne devriez pas . . . , Il est défendu de . . . || **supposition** [ˌsʌpə'zɪʃən] *n.* supposition *f*, hypothèse *f.*

suppository [sə'pɑzɪˌtɔərɪ] *n.* suppositoire *m.*

suppress [sə'pɹɛ|s] *v. tr.* supprimer; réprimer (une rébellion); faire disparaître, dissimuler (un abus); étouffer (la voix, un scandale). || **suppression** [-ʃən] *n.* suppression *f*; répression *f*; dissimulation *f.*

supremacy [sə'pɹɛməsɪ] *n.* suprématie *f* (*over*, sur).

supreme [sə'pɹijm] *adj.* [degree] suprême, [power] souverain; [law] *Supreme Court*, © la Cour suprême. || **supremely** [-lɪ] *adv.* suprêmement.

sure [ʃuwər] *adj.* sûr, [means] assuré; [thing] certain; [friendship] solide, stable: *to make ~ of*, s'assurer de; *Be ~ to come*, Venez sans faute; *She is ~ to come*, Il est certain qu'elle viendra, Elle viendra sans faute; *She is not ~ of coming*, Elle n'est pas sûre de venir; *to be ~ -footed*, avoir le pied sûr; [Fam.] *That's for ~* , Pour sûr, © Certain. || *adv.* Bien sûr, Sûrement. || **surely** [-lɪ] *adv.* sûrement, certainement; [statement] assurément; [I shall come] sans faute. || **surety** [-ɪtɪ] *n.* sûreté *f*, certitude *f*; [Jur.] caution *f.*

surf [sərf] *n.* ressac *m*, barre *f* (de plage); brisants *mpl.*

surface ['sərfəs] *n.* surface *f*; [Meas.] superficie *f*; [Fig.] extérieur *m*, apparence *f*: *on the ~* , en surface, superficiellement. || *v. tr.* [paint, plaster] revêtir (un mur). || *v. intr.* [submarine] remonter, revenir/à la surface.

surfeit ['sərfət] *n.* surabondance *f*, excès *m*; satiété *f*: *to have a ~ of food*, être rassasié; dégoût *m*; nausée *f.* || *v. intr.* se gorger, faire un excès/de. || *v. tr.* gorger, rassasier; écœurer, dégoûter.

surge [sərʤ] *n.* lame *f*, vague *f.* || *v. intr.* [sea] être houleux, se soulever, bondir; [ship] monter sur la vague; [Fig.] déborder, monter: *to ~ back*, refluer: *The blood surged to her head*, Le sang lui reflua à la tête.

surgeon ['sərʤ|ən] *n.* chirurgien *m*, -ne *f*; [Mil., Naut.] médecin *m.* || **surgery** [-ərɪ] *n.* chirurgie *f*; [hospital] dispensaire *m*, clinique *f.* || **surgical** [-ɪkḷ] *adj.* chirurgical.

surliness ['sərlɪnəs] *n.* maussaderie *f*, → caractère *m* hargneux. || **surly** ['sərlɪ] *adj.* maussade, hargneux.

surmise [sər'majz] *n.* conjecture *f*, supposition *f.* || *v. tr.* soupçonner, supposer, conjecturer: *I surmised he was wrong*, Je me doutais, Je devinais/qu'il avait tort.

surmount [sɚ'mawnt] *v. tr.* surmonter; vaincre, triompher d'(une difficulté, un obstacle).

surname ['sɚˌnejm] *n.* [×] nom *m* de famille: *name and* ~, nom et prénom(s).

surpass [sɚ'pæs] *v. tr.* surpasser (*in*, en), l'emporter sur: *to* ~ *o.s.*, se surpasser. || **surpassing** [-ɪŋ] *adj.* excellent, incomparable, sans pareil.

surplice ['sɚplɪs] *n.* [Rel.] surplis *m.*

surplus ['sɚpləs] *n.* surplus *m*, excédent *m.* || *adj.* excédentaire: ~ *stock*, solde *m.*

surprise [sə'pɹajz] *n.* [good, bad] surprise *f*; étonnement *m*: *much to my* ~, à mon grand étonnement; *to give s.o. a* ~, faire une surprise à qqun; *He was taken by* ~, Il a été pris au dépourvu. || *v. tr.* surprendre (qqun); étonner (qqun); prendre au dépourvu: *to be surprised at*, s'étonner de, être surpris de. || **surprising** [-ɪŋ] [news, event] surprenant, étonnant. || **surprisingly** [-ɪŋlɪ] *adv.* étonnamment; considérablement.

surrender [sə'ɹɛndɚ] *v. tr.* rendre, livrer (une ville à l'ennemi); céder (des droits). || *v. intr.* [of soldiers, stronghold] se rendre, capituler; [prisoners] se livrer (à, *to*); [Fig.] s'abandonner (à une tentation, une mauvaise habitude). || *n.* [war] reddition *f*, capitulation *f*: [war] *unconditional* ~, capitulation sans condition; abandon *m* (de ses droits).

surreptitious [sɚˌɛp'tɪʃəs] *adj.* subreptice. || **surreptitiously** [-lɪ] *adv.* subrepticement.

surround [sə'ɹawnd] *v. tr.* entourer (qqun, qqch.); [war] cerner (une place forte). || **surrounding** [-ɪŋ] *adj.* [place] environnant. || **surroundings** [-ɪŋz] [atmosphere] ambiance *f* (d'un lieu), l'entourage *m* (d'une personne); [town, &c.] alentours *mpl.*

surveillance [sɚ'vejləns] *n.* [Jur., Med.] surveillance *f.*

survey ['sɚvej] *n.* [facts] examen *m* (soigneux et attentif), étude *f* (approfondie de qqch., *of sth.*), enquête *f* (sérieuse sur qqch., *of sth.*); [land] arpentage *m* (d'un terrain, territoire); [building] relevé *m*, levé *m* de plans (d'une construction, &c.); inspection *f.* || [sɚ'vej] *v. tr.* [facts, situation] examiner (avec soin); [land] arpenter (un terrain); [building] lever le plan (d'une construction); [Fig.] inspecter (un endroit). || **surveying** [-ɪŋ] *n.* relevé *m* de plans, expertise *f.* || **surveyor** [-ɚ] *n.* [land] arpenteur *m* (géomètre), ingénieur *m* topographe.

survival [sɚ'vajv|l̩] *n.* survivance *f*; survie *f.* || **survive** *v. intr.* survivre. || **survivor** [-ɚ] *n.* survivant *m*, rescapé *m.*

Susan ['suwzən] *n.* = Suzanne *f.*

susceptibility [səˌsɛptɪ'bɪlɪtɪ] *n.* susceptibilité *f.* || **susceptible** [sə'sɛptɪbl̩] *adj.* susceptible; sensible (à, *to*); accessible (*of*, à); capable: ~ *to the cold*, frileux.

suspect ['sʌspɛkt] *n.* suspect *m.* || *v. tr.* [sə'spɛkt] soupçonner; s'imaginer, se douter de; suspecter (*s.o. of*, qqun de). || *v. intr.* soupçonner, s'en douter.

suspend [sə'spɛnd] *v. tr.* suspendre; [Jur.] surseoir à; [activity] interrompre.

suspenders [-ɚz] *n.pl.* [US] © bretelles *fpl*; [Br.] fixe-chaussettes *mpl.*

suspense [sə'spɛn|s] *n.* suspens *m*; doute *m*; indécision *f*; [Lit.] suspense *m.* || **suspension** [-ʃən] *n.* [Mech.] suspension *f*; [Jur.] surséance *f.*

suspicion [sə'spɪʃ|ən] *n.* soupçon *m*; doute *m*, suspicion *f.* || **suspicious** [-əs] *adj.* [person] soupçonneux; [things] suspect; équivoque. || **suspiciously** [-əslɪ] *adv.* avec méfiance; d'une/façon, manière/suspecte.

sustain [sə'stejn] *v. tr.* soutenir; [loss, injury] éprouver, subir, souffrir; [Jur.] *to* ~ *an objection*, accepter, admettre/une objection. || **sustenance** ['sʌstənəns] *n.* subsistance *f*; nourriture *f*: *to partake of* ~, se restaurer.

suture ['suwtʃɚ] *n.* suture *f.*

swab [swɑb] *n.* [Naut.] écouvillon *m*; torchon *m*; tampon *m* d'ouate. || *v. tr.* [Naut.] écouvillonner (le pont); [ext.] nettoyer (à grande eau).

swagger ['swægɚ] *v. intr.* crâner, fanfaronner, poser.

†**swain** [swejn] *n.* [courtship] prétendant *m*, galant *m.*

swallow[1] ['swɑlow] *n.* hirondelle *f.*

swallow[2] *v. tr.* avaler; [Fig.] endurer. || *n.* gorgée *f.*

swam, cf. SWIM.

swamp [swɑmp] *n.* marécage *m*, marais *m*, fondrière *f.* || *v. tr. & intr.* (s')embourber (dans un marécage); [boat] embarquer (de l'eau), couler; [Fig.]: *to be swamped with work*, être débordé de travail. || **swampland** [-ˌlænd] *n.* terrain *m* marécageux. || **swampy** [-ɪ] *adj.* marécageux.

swan [swɑn] *n.* cygne *m*: *trumpeter* ~, cygne trompette; *whistling* ~, cygne siffleur. || **swan-neck** [-ˌnɛk] *n.* col *m* de cygne.

swap [swɑp] *n.* troc *m.* || *v. tr.* troquer, échanger (des articles).

sward [swɔɚd] *n.* gazon *m.*

swarm [swɔɚ|m] *n.* essaim *m* (d'abeilles);

ribambelle *f* (d'enfants); nuée *f* (de sauterelles). || *v. intr.* essaimer; fourmiller.

swarthy [-ðɪ] *adj.* basané, bronzé.

†swash [swɑʃ] *n.* clapotis *m* (des vagues). || *v. intr.* [waves] clapoter. || *v. tr.* agiter (l'eau).

swashbuckler [-ˌbʌklɚ] *adj.* bretteur *m*, fanfaron *m.*

swat [swɑt] *n.* coup *m.* || *v. tr.* [-tt-] frapper, écraser (une mouche).

swathe [swejð] *n.* maillot *m.* || *v. tr.* emmailloter, envelopper (*in*, de).

sway [swej] *v. tr.* ballotter; balancer; brandir; gouverner; régir; influencer. || *v. intr.* se balancer; incliner (d'un côté et de l'autre); se pencher; osciller. || *n.* balancement *m*; influence *f*; [power] empire *m* (*over*, sur).

swear [swɛɚ], **swore** [swɔɚ], **sworn** [-n] *v. tr.* [in] faire prêter serment à (un témoin). || *v. intr.* prêter serment; jurer; *to ~ in*, assermenter; *to ~ at* (*s.o., sth.*), maudire (qqun, qqch.); *to ~ to*, déclarer sous serment (que). || **swearing** ['swɛɚɪŋ] *n.* serments *mpl*; jurons *mpl*: [Jur.] *~ in, n.* assermentation *f* (d'un magistrat); prestation *f* de serment.

sweat [swɛt] *n.* sueur *f*; transpiration *f*; [Fig.] fatigue *f*, lassitude *f*. || *v. intr.* transpirer, suer. || *v. tr.* faire suer. || **sweater** [-ɚ] *n.* chandail *m*; [Fam.] exploiteur *m.* || **sweating** [-ɪŋ] *n. & adj.* sueur *f*; fatigue *f*; en sueur, couvert de sueur; [Fig.] exploitation *f* (des ouvriers). || **sweaty** [-ɪ] *adj.* suant, pénible.

swede [swijd] *n.* [Bot.] rutabaga *m.*

Swede [swijd] *n.* Suédois, -e. || **Sweden** [-n̩] *n.* (la) Suède *f*: *in, to*/ ~ , en S. || **Swedish** [-ɪʃ] *adj.* suédois, -e.

sweep [swijp], **swept** [swɛpt], **swept** *v. tr.* balayer; ramoner (une cheminée); draguer (des mines); *to ~ clean*, nettoyer à fond, balayer avec soin; *to ~ s.o. along*, entraîner, emporter/qqun. || *v. intr.* balayer; [landscape] s'étendre; [movement] avancer majestueusement. || *n.* balayage *m*; balayeur *m*; ramoneur *m*: *to make a clean ~ of*, faire/maison nette, table rase/. || **sweeper** ['swijp|ɚ] *n.* balayeur *m*; ramoneur *m.* || **sweeping** [-ɪŋ] *adj.* qui balaie; [gesture] vigoureux, large; [statement] catégorique, absolu. || *n.* balayage *m.* || **sweepings** [-z] *n.pl.* balayures *fpl*; [Fig.] rebut *m*, lie *f* (de la société).

sweepstake [-ˌstejk] *n.* loterie *f*; poule *f*.

sweet [swijt] *adj.* [food] doux, sucré; [milk] frais; [air] parfumé; [Fig.] gentil; charmant; [Mus.] mélodieux: *to have a ~ tooth*, être amateur de friandises. || *n.* [Cul.] sucrerie *f*, bonbon *m*; [Br.] dessert *m*; entremets *m.* || **sweetbread** [-ˌbɹɛd] *n.* [Cul.] ris *m* de veau. **sweetbrier** [-ˌbɹajɚ] *n.* églantier *m.* || **sweet by-an-by** [-ˌbajn̩-d ˌbaj] dans un avenir problématique, [Fam.] à la Saint-Glinglin. || **sweeten** [-n̩] *v. tr.* **1.** sucrer; [Fig.] adoucir; parfumer. **2.** assainir, purifier (l'atmosphère d'une pièce). || **sweetheart** [-ˌhɑɚt] *n.* (petite) amie, [vocative] chérie. || **sweetly** [-lɪ] *adv.* doucement, avec douceur; mélodieusement. || **sweetness** [-nəs] *n.* douceur *f*; [Fig.] charme *m*; gentillesse *f*. || **sweet pea** [-ˌpij] *n.* pois *m* de senteur. || **sweet potato** [-pə'tejtow] *n.* patate *f*, © patate douce. || **sweetshop** [-ˌʃɑp] *n.* confiserie *f*.

swell [swɛl] *n.* **1.** gonflement *m*, enflure *f*, boursouflure *f*. **2.** houle *f* (de la mer); renflement *m* (d'un son); [Mus.] récit *m* (d'un orgue). || *adj.* [Sl.] **1.** élégant, bien mis. **2.** épatant, chic. || **swell** [swɛl], **swelled** [-d], **swollen** ['swolən] *v. intr.* (s')enfler, (se) gonfler, se tuméfier, se boursoufler; [waves] se soulever: *to ~ with pride*, être gonflé d'orgueil; *to ~ (up)*, augmenter, croître, grossir. || *v. tr.* **1.** enfler, gonfler, boursoufler; augmenter, grossir. **2.** aggraver. || **swelling** ['swɛlɪŋ] *n.* enflure *f*, boursouflure *f*; protubérance *f*; crue *f* (d'un fleuve).

swelter ['swɛltɚ] *v. intr.* étouffer de chaleur; être en nage.

swept, cf. SWEEP.

swerve [swɚv] *n.* écart *m*, déviation *f*; [Auto.] embardée *f*; [horse] incartade *f*. || *v. intr.* faire/une embardée, un écart; [horse] se dérober.

swift [swɪft] *adj.* rapide, prompt, [Fig.] vif (d'esprit, de répartie). || *adv.* rapidement, vite. || **swiftly** [-lɪ] *adv.* vite, rapidement. || **swiftness** [-nəs] *n.* rapidité *f*, promptitude *f*.

swim [swɪm], **swam** [swæm], **swum** [swʌm] *v. intr.* nager: *to ~ across the lake*, traverser le lac à la nage; *to go swimming*, se baigner. || *v. tr.* faire nager; [a river] traverser (une rivière) à la nage. || *n.* nage *f*; [Fam.] *to be in the ~* , être dans le train. || **swimmer** ['swɪm|ɚ] *n.* nageu|r, -se. || **swimming** [-ɪŋ] *n.* natation *f*, nage *f*: *~ -pool*, piscine *f*. || **swimsuit** [-ˌsuwt] *n.* maillot *m* de bain.

swindle ['swɪndl̩] *n.* escroquerie *f*. || *v. tr.* escroquer (qqun; qqch. à qqun, *s.o. out of sth.*). || **swindler** [-ɚ] *n.* escroc *m.*

swine [swajn] *pl.* **swine** *n.* porc *m*, cochon

m. || **swineherd** [-ˌhɚd] *n.* porcher *m*, gardien *m* de porcs.

swing [swɪŋ] *n.* **1.** balancement *m*, branle *m*, va-et-vient *m*; oscillation *f.* **2.** [Fig.] entrain *m*, envol *m*, (libre) essor *m*. 3. balançoire *f*, escarpolette *f*: ~ *-door*, porte *f* va-et-vient; *to be in full* ~, battre son plein, être en pleine activité, fonctionner à plein rendement. || **swing, swung** [swʌŋ], **swung** *v. intr.* [arms] se balancer; [bell] branler; [door] pivoter (*on*, sur); être suspendu; [pendulum] osciller: *to* ~ *round*, faire volte-face. || *v. tr.* (faire) balancer (qqch.); agiter (un bâton); brandir (une épée); branler; faire tourner, pivoter; pendre, accrocher (qqch.).

swinish [ˈswajnɪʃ] *adj.* de pourceau; bestial, grossier, sale. || **swinishly** [-lɪ] *adv.* salement, comme un pourceau.

swipe [swajp] *n.* coup *m* violent, à toute volée. || *v. tr. & intr.* frapper à toute volée, cogner avec violence; [Fam.] rafler, barboter.

swirl [swɚl] *n.* remous *m* (de l'eau); tourbillon *m* (de poussière). || *v. intr.* [of water, dust] tournoyer, tourbillonner.

swish [swɪʃ] *v. intr.* [whip, cane] siffler, claquer; [wind, water] bruire, susurrer. || *n.* sifflement *m* (d'une baguette, d'un fouet); bruit *m* cinglant, claquement *m* (d'une verge, d'un fouet); susurrement *m* (de l'eau, du vent).

Swiss [swɪs] *adj.* suisse. || *n.* Suisse *m*, Suissesse *f.*

switch [swɪʧ] *n.* **1.** [Electr.] commutateur *m*, interrupteur *m*; [Rail.] aiguille *f.* **2.** badine *f.* || *v. tr.* [Rail.] aiguiller (un train); donner un coup de/badine, baguette/à (qqun): *to* ~ *off*, couper le courant (électrique); *to* ~ *on*, mettre le contact, donner le courant. || **switchback** [-ˌbæk] *n.* **1.** lacet *m* (de la route): *The road made a number of switchbacks*, La route faisait de nombreux lacets. **2.** [Rail.] montagnes *fpl* russes. || **switchboard** [ˈswɪʧˌbɔɚd] *n.* [Tel.] standard *m* (téléphonique); [Elect.] tableau *m* de distribution: ~ *operator*, standardiste *f*; → demoiselle *f* du téléphone. || **switch-rail** [-ˌɹejl] *n.* rail *m* mobile.

Switzerland [ˈswɪtzɚlənd] (la) Suisse *f*, la Confédération *f* suisse: *in, to*/ ~, en S.

swivel [ˈswɪvl̩] *v. tr.* [-ll-] pivoter: *She swivelled her chair*, Elle fit pivoter sa chaise: ~ *-seat*, fauteuil *m* tournant.

swollen, cf. SWELL.

swoon [swuwn] *n.* évanouissement *m*, syncope *f.* || *v. intr.* défaillir, s'évanouir, avoir une syncope.

swoop [swuwp] *n.* attaque *f* brusque, chute *f* brutale sur, ruée *f* (sur): *at one fell* ~, d'un seul coup. || *v. intr.* foncer, s'abattre, fondre/(*on*, sur).

sword [sɔɚd] *n.* épée *f*, [cutting, drawn] sabre *m*; †glaive *m*: [Fig.] *to cross, measure/swords with s.o.*, croiser le fer avec qqun, se mesurer contre qqun; [Hist.] *the* ~ *of Damocles*, l'épée de Damoclès; *to put* (*s.o.*) *to the* ~, passer (qqun) au fil de l'épée. || **sword-fish** [-ˌfɪʃ] *n.* espadon *m.* || **swords|man,** *pl.* **-men** [-mən], *n.* tireur *m*; [Fig.] lame *f.*

swore, cf. SWEAR. || **sworn,** cf. SWEAR.

swum, cf. SWIM.

swung, cf. SWING.

syllable [ˈsɪləbl̩] *n.* syllabe *f.*

syllogism [ˈsɪləʤizm̩] *n.* syllogisme.

symbol [ˈsɪmbl̩] *n.* symbole *m*; signe *m.* || **symbolic** [sɪmˈbɑlɪk] *adj.* symbolique.

symbolize [ˈsɪmbl̩ˌajz] *v. tr.* symboliser, représenter (symboliquement).

symmetrical [sɪˈmɛtɹɪkl̩] *adj.* symétrique. || **symmetry** [ˈsɪmətɹɪ] *n.* symétrie *f.*

sympathetic [ˌsɪmpəˈθɛtɪk] *adj.* **1.** sympathisant. **2.** compatissant (envers qqun, *towards s.o.*). || **sympathetically** [-lɪ] *adv.* **1.** sympathiquement; avec sympathie. **2.** par sympathie. || **sympathize** [ˈsɪmpə|ˌθajz] *v. intr.* sympathiser (avec qqun, *with s.o.*); compatir (à qqch., *with sth.*). || **sympathy** [-θɪ] *n.* **1.** sympathie *f*; préférence *f* (pour/qqun, qqch., *towards s.o., to sth.*). **2.** compassion *f* (envers qqun, *towards s.o.*): *to offer one's sincere sympathy*, présenter ses sincères condoléances.

symphony [ˈsɪmfənɪ] *n.* [Mus.] symphonie *f.*

symposium [sɪmˈpowzɪəm] *n.* colloque *m*; [Acad.] recueil *m* (d'articles scientifiques ou littéraires).

symptom [ˈsɪmptəm] *n.* symptôme *m*, indice *m.* || **symptomatic** [ˌsɪmptəˈmætɪk] *adj.* symptomatique.

synagogue [ˈsɪnəˌgɑg] *n.* synagogue *f.*

synchronize [ˈsɪŋkɹə|ˌnajz] *v. tr. & intr.* synchroniser, être/synchronique, simultané/. || **synchronizer** [-ˌnajzɚ] *n.* synchroniseur *m.* || **synchronous** [-nəs] *adj.* synchrone.

syncope [ˈsijŋkəˌpij] *n.* syncope *f.*

syndicate [ˈsɪndəkət] *n.* syndicat *m*; consortium *m.* || *v. tr.* [ˈsɪndəˌkejt] syndiquer (des ouvriers, travailleurs). || *v. intr.* [of people] se syndiquer.

synonym [ˈsɪnənɪm] *n.* synonyme *m.*

|| **synonymous** [sɪ'nɑnəməs] *adj.* synonyme (de, *with*).

synops|is [sɪ'nɑpsɪs] *pl.* **-es** *n.* tableau *m* synoptique; [Sch.] résumé *m*, aide-mémoire *m*; [Cin.] synopsis *m*.

syntax ['sɪntæks] *n.* [Gram.] syntaxe *f.*

synthesis ['sɪnθə|sɪs] *n.* synthèse *f.* || **synthesize** [-ˌsajz] *v. tr.* synthétiser.

synthetic [sɪn'θɛtɪk] *adj.* synthétique: ~ *rubber*, caoutchouc *m* synthétique.

Syria ['sijərɪə] *n.* la Syrie: *in, to/* ~, en S.

syringe [sə'rɪndʒ] *n.* seringue *f.*

syrup ['sijərəp] *n.* sirop *m*: © *maple* ~, sirop *m* d'érable.

system ['sɪstəm] *n.* **1.** système *m*; régime *m*. **2.** méthode *f.* **3.** dispositif *m* (électrique); [Rail.] réseau *m* (de chemins de fer). || **systematic** [sɪstə'mætɪk] *adj.* **1.** systématique. **2.** méthodique; [list] raisonnée.

T

T, t [tij] *n. pl.* **T, t's** [letter] T, t: *to fit to a T*, aller comme un gant; *to cross one's t's*, mettre les points sur les i; *to a T*, exactement, à la perfection; *That suits me to a T*, Cela me va à merveille; *T-shaped*, en T, en potence.

t. [= TON], t. [= tonne].

tab [tæb] *n.* [piece, flap, strap, &c.] patte *f*, languette *f*: *index* ~, signet *m*, onglet *f*; [clothing] pan *m*; [loop] ganse *f*; [tag, label, &c.] étiquette *f*: [Fig.] *to keep tab on s.o.*, garder à l'œil.

tabernacle [-ərˌnækl̩] *n.* tabernacle *m.*

table ['tejbl̩] *n.* **1.** table *f*; [Rel.] *the Lord's Table, the Communion Table*, la Sainte Table; [Bibl.] *the Tables of the Law*, les Tables de la Loi: *to lay the* ~, mettre /la table, le couvert; *to clear the* ~, desservir. **2.** table *f*; tableau *m*; ~ *of contents*, table des matières; ~ *of weights and measures*, table des poids et mesures; *multiplication* ~, table *f* de multiplication. **3.** plaque *f* (de métal); tablette *f* (de marbre, de pierre, &c.). **4.** [land] plateau *m*. || *v. tr.* déposer: *to* ~ *a report*, déposer un rapport (pour qu'on en fasse l'étude), [US] ajourner la discussion d'un rapport; classer un rapport. || **tablecloth** [-ˌklɑθ] *n.* nappe *f.* || **table-d'hote (dinner)** *n.* (repas à) prix fixe. || **tablespoon** [-ˌspuwn] *n.* cuiller *f* à soupe, © cuiller à table.

tabletalk ['tejblˌtɔk] *n.* conversation *f*, propos *mpl* de table. || **table tennis** [-ˌtɛnɪs] *n.* ping-pong *m*, © tennis *m* de table.

tablet ['tæblət] *n.* **1.** [pad] tablette *f*; [inscription] plaque *f*, ex-voto *m*. **2.** [Med.] comprimé *m*, pastille *f*, cachet *m*, capsule *f*, tablette *f*, pilule *f.*

tabloid ['tæbˌlojd] *n.* **1.** [Med.] tablette *f*, pastille *f.* **2.** journal *m* à sensation.

taboo [ˌtæ'buw] *n.* tabou *m*. || *v. tr.* déclarer (qqch.) tabou, proscrire.

tabular [-jələr] *adj.* **1.** [list] tabulaire. **2.** [shape] tabulaire. || **tabulate** [-jəˌlejt] *v. tr.* mettre sous forme de tableau; disposer (des chiffres en forme de table(s).

tachometer [tə'kɑmətər] *n.* tachymètre *m.*

tacit ['tæsɪt] *adj.* **1.** [Pers.] taciturne. **2.** [meaning] implicite, tacite.

taciturn [-ərn] *adj.* taciturne, morose.

tack [tæk] *n.* [nail] semence *f*, broquette *f*; [sewing] faufilure *f*: *to get down to brass tacks*, en venir aux faits; arriver/à la réalité, aux faits/. || *v. tr.* clouer; [sewing] faufiler: *to* ~ *sth. to sth.*, attacher qqch. à qqch.

tackle [-l̩] *n.* **1.** [lifting] poulie *f*, moufle *f*, palan *m*; treuil *m*; [fishing] engins *mpl* de pêche. **2.** [seize] prise *f*, action *f* de saisir un adversaire. || *v. tr.* **1.** empoigner, saisir: [Fig.] *to* ~ *the job*, attaquer l'ouvrage; *to* ~ *a problem*, chercher à résoudre un problème; [Sport.] plaquer (un joueur au football).

tact [tækt] *n.* tact *m*, savoir-faire *m*, entregent *m*. || **tactful** [-fl̩] *adj.*: *a* ~ *man*, un homme/de tact, délicat/; *to be* ~, avoir du tact. || **tactfully** [-fl̩ɪ] *adv.* avec tact.

tactical [-ɪkḷ] *adj.* [Mil.] tactique; [Fig.] adroit, bien combiné, ingénieux. || **tactics** [-ɪks] *n.* [Mil.] tactique *f*; [Fig.] manœuvre *f*; [Fam.] combine *f*.

tactile [-ˌajḷ] *adj.* **1.** tactile. **2.** tangible.

tactless [ˈtæktləs] *adj.* sans tact.

tadpole [ˈtædˌpowl] *n.* têtard *m*.

taffeta [ˈtæfətə] *n.* taffetas *m*.

taffy [ˈtæfɪ] *n.* © tire *f*: ~ *-on-the-snow*, tire sur la neige.

tag [tæg] *n.* **1.** étiquette *f* (sur les bagages, habits, &c.); *baggage claim* ~, reçu *m* de bagage. **2.** morceau *m* (d'étoffe) qui pend. **3.** ferret *m* (de lacet). **4.** citation *f* banale, cliché: *one of his favourite tags*, une de ses expressions favorites; *old* ~, vieille rengaine; *moral* ~, devise *f* morale. **5.** refrain *m* (d'une chanson, d'un poème). || **tag day** [-ˌdej] *n.* jour *m* de collecte publique; quête *f* (en faveur de...).

tail [tejl] *n.* [animal, kite, airplane, Fig.] queue *f*; [shirt] pan *m* (de chemise); *the* ~ *of a plane*, l'empennage *m*; [car] l'arrière *m*; [hair] queue *f*, natte *f*: *to turn* ~, s'enfuir; tourner les talons; tails *pl.* (of a coin), pile *f*, revers *m* (d'une pièce de monnaie); *heads or* ~, pile ou face; [= tail-coat] *to wear* ~, porter l'habit. || *v. tr.* [Fam.] suivre (qqun). || *v. intr.* marcher sur les talons (*after*, de). || **tail end** [-ˈɛnd] *n.* queue *f*, bout *m*; || **tail light** [-ˌlajt] *n.* [Auto] feu *m* arrière.

tailor [ˈtejlɚ] *n.* tailleur *m*: *custom* ~, tailleur *m* sur mesures. || **tailor-made** [-ˌmejd] *adj.* tailleur; [US, Fam.] fait sur commande.

taint [tejnt] *n.* tache *f*, souillure *f*; [Fig.] infection *f*. || *v. tr.* corrompre, gâter, souiller. || *v. intr.* se corrompre, se gâter, s'infecter.

take [tejk] **took** [tʊk] **taken** [-ṇ] *v. tr.* **1.** [transport, lead] porter qqch.; conduire, mener/qqun: *Take it to/him, his house/*, (Ap)portez-le-lui, portez-le chez lui; *Take it with you*, Prenez-le, Emportez-le/avec vous; *Take him/home, with you/*, (A)menez-le, (Re)conduisez-le, (R)accompagnez-le/chez lui, Emmenez-le avec vous. **2.** [remove] [from sth]. prendre [+ prep. of position]; sortir, enlever, retirer/(de); [from s.o.] prendre, enlever (à qqun); emprunter (un/mot, passage/à qqun, un livre); [subtract] soustraire, enlever, ôter (qqch. de qqch.): *He took it/from, out of/the drawer*, Il l'a pris dans le tiroir, Il l'a/sorti, retiré/du tiroir; *He took it/from, off/the table*, Il l'a pris sur la table, Il l'a/enlevé, retiré/de la table; *S.o. had taken his coat*, Qqun lui avait pris son manteau; *Take it from him*, Enlevez-le-lui. **3.** [grasp] prendre, saisir, empoigner; s'emparer de; [Fig.] profiter d'(une occasion): *He took/my hand, me by the hand/*, Il m'a pris/la main, par la main/; *He took me by the throat*, Il m'a saisi à la gorge. **4.** [catch, capture] prendre, attraper, capturer; prendre (du poisson, des notes, qqch. en dictée, la température de qqun, une photo, la photo de qqun); prendre, attraper/(froid); [Bridge] faire, prendre/(un pli): *to* ~ *s.o. prisoner*, faire qqun prisonnier; *to be taken ill*, tomber malade; *to* ~ *s.o.'s eye*, attirer les regards de qqun; [Fig.] *to be taken with/s.o., sth./*, être attiré par/qqun, qqch./; *I am not taken by/it, him/*, Cela, Il/ne me plaît pas; *to have one's picture taken*, se faire photographier. **5.** [occupy] prendre, occuper/(une place); [reserve] prendre, retenir, louer/(une place, des billets, une chambre); [rent] prendre, louer/(une chambre): *Please* ~ *a seat*, Veuillez prendre un siège; *This seat is taken*, Cette place est /prise, occupée/; *That takes a lot of room*, Cela/prend, occupe/beaucoup de place. **6.** [direction] prendre; emprunter (un passage); suivre (un chemin): *Take the next/street, turn/to the right*, Prenez/la prochaine (rue, route) à droite, [in car] à droite à la prochaine (rue)/; *He took the turn on two wheels*, Il a pris le virage sur deux roues. **7.** [accept, receive] prendre, accepter, recevoir; prendre (des pensionnaires); [advice] prendre (l'avis de qqun), suivre (le conseil de qqun); accepter, prendre/(de l'argent, un cadeau), recevoir (le premier prix); acheter, être abonné à/(un journal); prendre (de la nourriture, un repas): *Go ahead,* ~ *it*, Allez-y, prenez-le; *How much will you* ~ *for it?*, Combien en voulez-vous?; *How much did he* ~ *for it?*, Combien l'a-t-il vendu?; *taking all in all*, → dans l'ensemble, à tout prendre; *Take it from me*, *Take my word for it*, Croyez-m'en; *to* ~ *sth. to/eat, drink/*, manger, boire/qqch.; [Fig.] *to* ~ *sth./seriously, literally/*, prendre qqch./au sérieux, au mot/; *Take that!*, Attrape! **8.** [contain, absorb] tenir, contenir, avoir de la place pour; supporter: *How many people will this room* ~ *?*, Combien de personnes/peuvent tenir dans cette pièce, cette pièce peut-elle contenir/?; *Will this garment* ~ *much washing?*, Est-ce que ce vêtement supportera d'être lavé souvent?; *He took* *the blow without flinching,* Il a/pris, [Fam.] encaissé/le coup sans broncher; [Fam.] *He can ~ it,* [Fam.] Il tient bien le coup. **9.** [undergo] prendre (des leçons); suivre, s'inscrire à/(un cours); passer, subir/(un examen). **10.** [require] avoir besoin de, falloir; demander; prendre, mettre, falloir/(du temps); [size] prendre; [Gram.] prendre, être suivi de: *It will ~ courage,* Vous aurez besoin de, Il faudra, Cela demandera/du courage; *That will ~ some finding,* Il faudra chercher bien longtemps avant de trouver cela; *He took his time,* Il a pris son temps; *That will ~ /three hours, a long time/,* Cela prendra/3 heures, longtemps/; *He took* 3 *hours to do it,* Il a mis, Il lui a fallu, Cela lui a pris/3 heures pour le faire; *What size do you ~ ?,* Quelle est votre pointure? cf. SIZE; *I take size 8,* Je/prends, [shoes] chausse/du 8; *This verb does not ~ an object,* Ce verbe ne/prend, demande/pas de complément d'objet. **11.** [assume] prendre; supposer; croire: *I ~ it that . . . ,* Je suppose que . . . ; *Do you ~ that to be important?* Croyez-vous que ce soit important, Tenez-vous cela pour important?; *What do you ~ me for?,* Pour qui me prenez-vous? **12.** [consider] prendre (comme exemple), regarder, considérer. **13.** [spec. uses: for ~ + noun, see also under noun] prendre (un bain), faire (son choix, une promenade, un voyage, une somme), prêter (serment), &c.; prendre (la place de qqun): *Prof. X is taking the class to-day,* Le professeur X fait la classe aujourd'hui cf. *9.* || *v. intr.* [fire, vaccination, &c.] prendre; [plant] prendre racine, commencer à pousser; [idea, book, &c.] avoir du succès, réussir: *Her paleness takes from her beauty,* La pâleur de son teint/diminue, atténue/sa beauté; *to ~ sick,* tomber malade. || *n.* prise *f* (de poisson), pêche *f*; [money] recette *f* (de la journée); [film] prise *f* de vues: *give and ~ ,* concessions *fpl* mutuelles, donnant donnant. || **take after** [-'æftɚ] *v. intr.* [resemble] tenir de, ressembler à/(qqun); [Fam.] se lancer à la poursuite de (qqun). || **take away** [-ɔ'wej] *v. tr.* [carry] emporter (qqch.); [lead] emmener (qqun); [remove] enlever, ôter, (qqch. de qqch., qqch. à qqun); [subtract] enlever, ôter, soustraire: *to take s.o. away from his work,* déranger qqun de, enlever qqun à/son travail. || *v. intr.* [detract from] diminuer, atténuer. || **take back** [-'bæk] *v. tr.* reporter, rapporter/(qqch. à qqun); reprendre (un cadeau, &c.); ramener, reconduire, raccompagner/(qqun chez lui); remmener qqun (en prison); retirer, revenir sur/(sa parole), revenir sur (sa promesse): *That takes me back to when . . . ,* Cela me ramène à l'époque où . . . ; *I take it all back,* Mettons que je n'aie rien dit. || **take down** [-'dawn] *v. tr.* descendre (qqch.); [unhook] décrocher; démolir (une maison); prendre (par écrit, des notes), noter (qqch.): [Fam.] *to take s.o. down a/peg, notch/,* rabattre le caquet à qqun. || **take in** [-'ɪn] *v. tr.* faire entrer (qqun); prendre, recevoir, loger/(des pensionnaires); prendre (du blanchissage) à faire à la maison; rentrer (qqch. dans la maison, la moisson); [include] comprendre, embrasser; [understand] comprendre, se rendre compte de; [deceive] duper, tromper; reprendre (les coutures d'une robe). || **take off** [-'ɔf] *v. tr.* enlever, ôter, retirer/(qqch.); [clothes: also] se déshabiller; rabattre (qqch.) (sur le prix); détourner (l'attention de qqun de qqch.); caricaturer; [Fam.] singer (qqun); [= TAKE AWAY]: *to take o.s. off,* s'en aller, [Fam.] filer; *to take sth. off s.o.'s hands,* débarrasser qqun de qqch.; *to take a day off,* prendre un jour de congé. || *v. intr.* [Aviat.] décoller; [Sl.] filer. || **take-off** [-ˌɔf] *n.* [Aviat.] décollage *m*; caricature *f*, charge *f*; *to do a ~ of s.o.,* faire la charge de qqun. || **take on** [-'ɑn] *v. tr.* [load] charger; [ship] embarquer; entreprendre (un travail); accepter (un défi, un pari); [game] faire une partie de . . . (avec qqun); engager, embaucher/(des ouvriers); porter, miner, transporter jusqu'à; prendre (un air, &c.). || *v. intr.* [Pers.] s'affliger, faire une scène; [be successful] réussir, prendre. || **take out** [-'awt] *v. tr.* sortir (qqch., le chien); faire sortir (qqun); [invite] → sortir avec (qqun); [remove] enlever (qqch.), emmener (qqun); arracher (une dent); extraire (qqch.); prendre, obtenir/(un permis, brevet): *He is taking me out to dinner,* Il m'emmène dîner/en ville, chez des amis/; *Take it out of this $10 bill,* Prenez-le sur ce billet de 10 dollars; [Fam.] *It takes it out of you,* Ça vous esquinte; *I'll take it out of/him, his hide/,* Je me payerai sa peau; *Don't take it out on me,* Ne vous en prenez pas à moi; (coffee, &c.) *to ~ ,* (café, &c.) à emporter). || **take over** [-'owvɚ] *v. tr.* (ap)porter (qqch.), (a)mener (qqun) jusqu'à; prendre la succession de, succéder à, remplacer; prendre (des dettes) à sa charge. || *v. intr.* [from s.o.] remplacer, succéder à, relever/(qqun); prendre la succession (d'un poste). || **taker** [ɚ] *n.* preneu|r *m*, -se *f*. || **take to** [-ˈtuw] *v. intr.* se réfugier (quelque part), prendre (la fuite, le maquis, &c.); prendre (une mauvaise habitude), s'adonner à (la boisson, &c.); se mettre à (faire qqch.); s'accoutumer à (qqch.); [like] prendre (qqun) en amitié, trouver (qqun) sympathique, [negative] prendre (qqun) en grippe, trouver (qqun) antipathique; prendre goût à (qqch.). || **take up** [-ˈʌp] *v. tr.* [pick up] ramasser; [lift] (re)lever; [carry up] monter; [lead up] faire monter; [remove] enlever; [a stitch] relever (une maille); [shorten] raccourcir (une robe); rattraper (du jeu dans un mécanisme); relever (un défi), tenir (un pari); épouser (une querelle); adopter (une idée, une méthode); aborder (une question, l'étude de qqch.); s'occuper de (qqch.); se mettre à (faire qqch.), embrasser (une carrière); occuper (le temps, de la place), absorber (de l'eau, des choses); [contradict] reprendre (qqun de qqch.): [Fam.] *to ~ with s.o.*, se lier avec qqun. || **taking** [-ɪŋ] *adj.* attrayant, séduisant; contagieux. || *n.* prise *f*: *takings*, recette *f* (de la journée).

talcum [ˈtælkəm] *n.* talc *m*.

tale [tejl] *n.* **1.** conte *m*, récit *m*, histoire *f*. **2.** [Pej.] histoire *f*, racontar *m*. **3.** nombre *m*, quantité *f*: *to tell tales*, rapporter, [Fam.] cafarder; *It/is, sounds, reads/like a fairy ~*, On dirait un conte de fées; C'est une histoire à dormir debout.

talent [ˈtælənt] *n.* **1.** aptitude *f*, talent *m*: *He has ~ for painting*, Il a du talent pour la peinture. **2.** [coll.] gens *mpl* de talent. **3.** [monnaie] *golden, silver/ ~*, talent *m*/d'or, d'argent/.

talented [ˈtæln̩təd] *adj.* doué, → qui a du talent.

talk [tɔk] *v. tr.* **1.** parler: *to ~ French*, parler français; *to ~ sense*, parler raison; *to ~ nonsense*, dire des bêtises. **2.** discuter, s'entretenir, causer/de: *to ~ business*, discuter d'affaires, parler affaires. || *v. intr.* **1.** parler (*to*, à; *about*, de); [converse] causer, s'entretenir (*with*, avec): *to ~ in riddles*, parler par énigmes. **2.** jaser, bavarder; [Fam.] *to ~ to s.o.*, passer un savon à qqun; *to ~ through one's hat*, débiter des sottises. || **talk back**, [-ˈbæk] *v. intr.* répliquer; répondre (d'une manière impertinente). || **talk down** [-ˈdawn] *v. tr.* réduire (qqun) au silence [en parlant plus haut et plus longuement]; faire taire (qqun). || **talk over** [-ˈowvɚ] *v. tr.* discuter, débattre (une question). || **talk (s.o.) over**, persuader, convaincre/ qqun. || *n.* **1.** paroles *fpl*; propos *mpl*; conversation *f*: *idle ~*, paroles en l'air; *to indulge in small ~*, parler de la pluie et du beau temps; *to have plenty of small ~*, avoir de la conversation. **2.** entretien *m*, causerie *f*: *to have a ~ with s.o.*, s'entretenir avec qqun. **3.** conférence *f*, consultation *f*. **4.** bruit *m*; dires *mpl*; racontars *mpl*: *She is the ~ of the town*, On ne parle que d'elle.

talkative [ˈtɔkətɪv] *adj.* bavard.

tall [tɔl] *adj.* **1.** haut, élevé: *a ~ building*, un édifice élevé; *How ~ is that tree?*, Quelle est la hauteur de cet arbre? **2.** [Pers.] grand, de haute taille: *How ~ are you?*, Quelle est votre taille?; *I am taller than you*, Je suis plus grand que vous. **3.** [Fam.] trop élevé; extravagant, exorbitant: *a ~ price*, un prix exorbitant. **4.** [Fam.] incroyable, invraisemblable: *a ~ tale*, une histoire/incroyable, marseillaise.

tallow [ˈtælow] *n.* suif *m*: *~ candle*, chandelle *f* de suif. || *v. tr.* suiffer. || **tallowy** [-ɪ] *adj.* suiffeux, graisseux.

tally [tælɪ] *n.* [stick] taille *f*; [label] étiquette *f*; [counterpart] *~ of*, pendant *m* de; [Jur.] contrepartie *f*. || *v. tr.* marquer, contrôler, ajuster. || *v. intr.*: *to ~ with*, s'accorder, cadrer/avec.

tamarack [ˈtæmɚˌæk] *n.* mélèze *m* d'Amérique.

tame [tejm] *adj.* **1.** [mostly for large, wild animals] dompté; [mostly for small, domestic animals] apprivoisé: *a ~ lion*, un lion dompté; *a ~ fox*, un renard apprivoisé. **2.** peu farouche. **3.** [Fig.] (un style) fade, terne, monotone; [histoire] insipide, ennuyeux. || *v. tr.* **1.** domestiquer (une bête sauvage); dompter (un lion, un cheval); apprivoiser (une souris, un renard). **2.** [Fig.] brider (l'ardeur, le courage de qqun). || *v. intr.* **1.** s'apprivoiser. **2.** [Fig., story, &c.] tomber dans le banal; devenir insipide.

tam o'shanter [ˈtæməˌʃæntɚ] *n.* béret *m*.

tamper [ˈtæmpɚ] *v. intr.* [to practise secretly] machiner. **2.** *to ~ with sth.*, jouer avec, falsifier, déranger/qqch. **3.** *to ~ with a witness*, suborner un témoin.

tan [tæn] *v. tr.* **[-nn-] 1.** tanner (des peaux). **2.** hâler, bronzer (la peau d'une personne). || *v. intr.* [complexion] se hâler, se basaner: [Fig.] *to ~ s.o.'s hide*, tanner le cuir à qqun, étriller qqun. || *n.* **1.** [colour]

tanné *m*; couleur *f* du tan. **2.** [complexion] hâle *m*. **3.** [Tech.] tan *m*.

tandem [-dəm] *adj*. [chevaux] en flèche, en tandem: ~ *drive*, propulsion *f* arrière double. || *adv*. en tandem, en flèche. || *n*. tandem *m*.

tang [tæŋ] *n*. saveur *f*, goût *m*.

tangent ['tændʒənt] *adj*. tangent, tangentiel (à): ~ *screw*, vis *f*/tangentielle, sans fin/. || *n*. tangente *f*; [Math.] *the* ~ *of an angle*, la tangente d'un angle; [Fig.] *to go off at a* ~, s'échapper par la tangente.

tangerine [ˌtændʒə'ijn] *n*. mandarine *f*.

tangible ['tændʒɪbḷ] *adj*. tangible, palpable; [Fig.] clair, réel, tangible.

tangle ['tæŋgḷ] *n*. embrouillement *m*; emmêlement *m* (des cheveux); *to get into a* ~, s'embrouiller, [Fig.] se mettre dans le pétrin; *to be in a* ~, ne plus savoir où on en est; *It's a hopeless* ~, [Fam.] C'est le pot au noir. || *v. tr. & intr*. (s')embrouiller, (s')enchevêtrer, (s')entortiller.

tank [tæŋk] *n*. **1.** réservoir *m*; *water* ~, réservoir *m* à eau, citerne *f*; *gas* ~, réservoir à essence. **2.** [Mil.] char *m* /d'assaut, de combat. || **tanker** [ə] *n*. [Mar.] bateau-citerne *m*, pétrolier *m*.

tanner ['tænə] *n*. tanneur *m*. || **tannery** [-ɪ] *n*. tannerie *f*. || **tanning** [-ɪŋ] *n*. tannage *m*.

tantalize ['tæntə,lajz] *v. tr*. torturer, tenter

tantrum ['tæntɹəm] *n*. accès *m* de colère; mauvaise humeur *f*.

tap[1] [tæp] *n*. robinet *m*, cf. FAUCET; [Electr.] branchement *m*: *on* ~, en perce; [Fig.] disponible; disposé à. || *v. tr*. [-pp-] [cask] mettre en perce [wine] tirer; [Electr.] brancher sur; [Phone] écouter, passer à la table d'écoute; [Fig.] drainer (des ressources).

tap[2] *n*. petit coup *m*: *There was a* ~ *at the door*, On frappa doucement à la porte. || *v. intr*. frapper légèrement; tapoter: *to* ~ *on the door*, frapper doucement à la porte. || **tap dance** [-ˌdæns] *n*. danse à claquettes.

tape [tejp] *n*. ruban *m* (de fil, de coton), ganse *f*; [Electr.] ruban isolant, [Fr.] chatterton *m*: *paper* ~, ruban de papier gommé; *scotch* ~, ruban cellulosique; *ticker* ~, bande *f* (du téléscripteur): *surveyor's* ~, © roulette *f* d'arpenteur; ~ *-measure*, mètre-ruban *m*; *magnetic* ~, bande magnétique; ~ *recorder*, magnétophone *m*.

taper ['tejpə] *n*. petite bougie *f*, cierge *m*. || *v. tr*. effiler, tailler en pointe. || *v. intr*. se terminer en pointe.

tapestry ['tæpəstɹɪ] *n*. tapisserie *f*: ~ *-maker*, tapissier *m*. || *v. tr*. tapisser.

tapioca [ˌtæpɪ'owkə] *n*. tapioca *m*.

tappet ['tæpət] *n*. taquet *m*, heurtoir *m*; [Auto] culbuteur *m*: ~ *rod*, tige-poussoir *f*.

taproom [-ˌɹuwm] *n*. bar *m*, buvette *f*.

tar [taə] *n*. goudron *m*: *wood* ~, goudron végétal. || *v. tr*. [-rr-] goudronner (une route, un cordage, &c.).

tardily [-dɪ|lɪ] *adv*. lentement, à contrecœur. || **tardy** *adj*. lent, nonchalant; en retard.

tare [tɛə] *n*. **1.** ivraie *f*. **2.** [Com.] tare *f*. || *v. tr*. faire la tare.

target ['taəgət] *n*. cible *f*; but *m*; objectif *m*: *to be the* ~ *for*, être en butte (aux sarcasmes de qqun).

tariff ['tæəɪf] *n*. tarif *m*: *customs* ~, tarif douanier.

tarnish ['taənɪʃ] *n*. ternissure *f*. || *v. tr*. ternir; [Fig.] flétrir, souiller. || *v. intr*. se ternir.

tarpaulin [ˌtaə'pɔlɪn] *n*. bâche *f*; [Naut.] prélart *m*.

tarry[1] [taəɪ] *adj*. goudronné.

†**tarry**[2] ['tæəɪ] *v. intr*. **1.** rester, demeurer. **2.** tarder, différer: *to* ~ *for* (*s.o.*, *sth.*), attendre (qqun, qqch.).

tart [taət] *adj*. **1.** au goût âcre; aigrelet. **2.** [Fig.] *a* ~ *reply*, une réponse mordante. || *n*. tartelette *f*.

tartan ['taətn] *n*. tartan *m*; [fabric] écossais *m*.

task [tæsk] *n*. tâche *f*, travail *m*, ouvrage *m*: *a Sisyphian* ~, le rocher de Sisyphe; *to take s.o. to* ~ *for sth*., réprimander, morigéner/qqun pour avoir fait qqch.; prendre qqun à partie pour avoir fait qqch. || *v. tr*. **1.** imposer, assigner/une tâche à qqun. **2.** charger; faire violence à; forcer; surmener.

tassel ['tæsḷ] *n*. gland *m*, houppe *f*; [book] signet *m*; [Arch.] tasseau *m*. || **tasselled** [-d] *adj*. orné de glands.

taste [tejst] *n*. goût *m*: ~ *bud*, papille *f* gustative. || *v. tr*. goûter (qqch., à qqch.). || *v. intr*. [pers.] goûter; [thing, food] avoir un goût: *It tastes good*, Cela a bon goût, © [abus.] Cela goûte bon; *to* ~ *of sth*., avoir goût de qqch. || **tasteless** [-ləs] *adj*. sans goût, insipide.

tatter ['tætə] *n*. lambeau *m*, haillon *m*, guenille *f*. || *v. tr*. déchirer. || **tattered** [-d] *adj*. en loques, déguenillé.

tattle ['tætl] *n*. bavardage *m*; [gossip] commérage *m*, cancans *mpl*. || *v. intr*. commérer, jaser; [child] rapporter. || **tattler** [-ə] *n*. bavard, cancanier; [child] rapporteur *m*.

tattoo [ˌtæˈtuw] *n.* tatouage *m*; [Mil.] retraite *f*. ‖ *v. tr.* tatouer. ‖ **tattooing** [-ɪŋ] *n.* tatouage *m*.

taught, cf. TEACH.

taunt [tɔnt] *n.* injure *f*, sarcasme *m*; raillerie *f*. ‖ *v. tr.* railler, outrager, injurier. ‖ **tauntingly** [-ɪŋlɪ] *adv.* injurieusement, d'un ton méprisant.

taut [tɔt] *adj.* [rope] tendu; [Fig.] tendu, crispé.

tavern [ˈtævɚn] *n.* †taverne *f*; [saloon] © taverne *f*; [Fr.] cabaret *m*, bar *m*.

tawdry [ˈtɔwdɹɪ] *adj.* voyant, criard.

tax [tæks] *n.* [Fin.] impôt *m*; taxe *f*: *income* ~, impôt sur le revenu; *sales* ~, taxe de vente, [Fr.] T.V. ‖ *v. tr.* imposer, taxer. ‖ **taxable** [-əbl̩] *adj.* imposable, taxable. ‖ **taxation** [tæksˈejʃən] *n.* taxation *f*; impôts *mpl*, taxes *fpl*, charges *fpl* fiscales. ‖ **tax-collector** *n.* percepteur *m*. ‖ **tax-free** [-ˌfrij] *adj.* net d'impôts, en franchise.

taxi [ˈtæksɪ] *n.* taxi *m*.

taxpayer [ˈtæksˌpejɚ] *n.* contribuable *m*.

TCA [ˌtijˌsijˈej] [= Trans-Canada Air Lines], Air Canada *m*.

tea [tij] *n.* thé *m*; [afternoon] thé *m*, goûter *m*: *a cup of* ~, une tasse de thé.

teach [tijʧ] **taught** [tɔt] **taught** *v. tr.* instruire (qqun): *to* ~ *s.o. sth.*, *to* ~ *sth. to s.o.*, enseigner, apprendre/qqch. à qqun; *to* ~ *French*, enseigner le français. ‖ *v. intr.* enseigner, être professeur. ‖ **teacher** [ˈtijʧɚ] *n.* professeur *m*, [primary school] institut|eur *m*, -rice *f*. ‖ **teaching** [ˈtijʧɪŋ] *n.* enseignement *m*.

tea-cup [ˈtijˌkʌp] *n.* tasse *f* à thé.

team [tijm] *n.* [horses] attelage *m*; [Sport, &c.] équipe *f*: *teamwork*, coordination *f* des efforts, collaboration *f*; travail *m* en équipe, jeu *m* d'ensemble; *a scratch*/ ~, *crew*/, une équipe improvisée; ~ *spirit*, esprit *m* d'équipe.

tea-pot [ˈtijˌpɑt] *n.* théière *f*.

tear[1] [tɛɚ] **tore** [tɔɚ] **torn** [-n] *v. tr.* [off, out, up] déchirer, mettre en pièces; arracher (*from*, de): *She tore her dress*, Elle a déchiré sa robe; *She tore up the letter*, Elle a déchiré la lettre; *She tore off the ticket*, Elle arracha l'étiquette; *She tore out a page of her notebook*, Elle a/déchiré, arraché/une page de son carnet. ‖ *v. intr.* se déchirer; [Fig.] *to* ~ *along*, filer, se hâter. ‖ *n.* déchirure *f*, accroc *m*; trou *m*.

tear[2] [tijɚ] *n.* larme *f*; [with sobbing] *pl.* pleurs *mpl.*: *to burst into tears*, fondre en larmes: *crocodile tears*, des larmes de crocodile. ‖ **tearful** [-fl̩] *adj.* tout en larmes, éploré; [Pej.] larmoyant. ‖ **tearless** [-ləs] *adj.* sans larmes, sec.

tea-room [ˈtijˌruwm] *n.* salon *m* de thé.

tease [tijz] *v. tr.* **1.** taquiner, © agacer. **2.** [Tech.] carder (de la laine).

teaspoon [ˈtijˌspuwn] *n.* cuiller *f* à thé; [Meas.] cuillerée *f* à thé [also *teaspoonful*].

teat [tijt] *n.* mamelon *m*, tétine *f*; [cow] trayon *m*; [animals] tette *f*.

technical [ˈtɛknɪkl̩] *adj.* [Sch., &c.] technique. ‖ **technicality** [ˌtɛknɪˈkælɪtɪ] *n.* technicité *f*, question *f* de forme, point *m* de droit: **technicalities,** subtilités *fpl* (de la loi, d'un règlement). ‖ **technician** [ˌtɛkˈnɪʃən] *n.* technicien *m*.

technique [ˌtɛkˈnijk] *n.* technique *f*.

technological [ˌtɛknɪˈlɑʤɪkl̩] *adj.* technologique. ‖ **technology** [ˌtɛkˈnɑləʤɪ] *n.* technologie *f*.

tedious [ˈtijdɪəs] *adj.* fatigant, ennuyeux, fastidieux. ‖ **tediously** [-lɪ] *adv.* d'une façon/ennuyeuse, fastidieusement. ‖ **tediousness** [-nəs] *n.* ennui *m*, lenteur *f* fastidieuse.

teem [tijm] *v. intr.* **1.** †enfanter. **2.**: *to* ~ (*with*), regorger (de), fourmiller (de), abonder (en). ‖ **teeming** [-ɪŋ] *adj.* grouillant; [room] bondé; [rain] torrentiel.

teen-age [ˈtijnˌejʤ] *adj.* [Com.] (pour) adolescents. ‖ **teenager** [-ɚ] *n.* adolescent *m*. ‖ **teens** [tijnz] *npl.* années *fpl* de l'adolescence, adolescence *f*: *He is in his* ~, C'est un adolescent.

teetertotter [ˈtijtɚˌtɑtɚ] *n.* [seesaw] balançoire *f*; © balancigne *f*.

teeth cf. TOOTH. ‖ **teethe** [tijð] *v. intr.*: *to* ~, *to be teething*, faire ses dents.

telecast [ˈtɛlə|ˌkæst] *n.* [TV] émission *f* télévisée. ‖ *v. tr. & intr.* téléviser.

telegram [-ˌgɹæm] *n.* télégramme *m*. ‖ **telegraph** [-ˌgɹæf] *v. tr.* télégraphier (un message, une nouvelle/à qqun). ‖ *n.* télégraphe *m*. ‖ **telegrapher,** [Br.] **telegraphist** [təˈlɛgrəf/ɚ, -ɪst] *n.* télégraphiste. ‖ **telegraphy** [təˈlɛgɹəfɪ] *n.* télégraphie *f*: *wireless* ~, télégraphie sans fil (T.S.F.).

telephone [ˈtɛlə|ˌfown] *n.* téléphone *m*. ~ *booth*, cabine *f* téléphonique; ~ *call*, appel *m* téléphonique; ~ *exchange*, central *m* téléphonique. ‖ *v. tr.* téléphoner (une nouvelle à qqun). ‖ *v. intr.* téléphoner.

telephoto lens [-ˌfowtow ˌlɛnz] *n.* téléobjectif *m*.

telescope [ˌskowp] *n.* longue-vue *f*, [astronomy] télescope *m*. ‖ **telescopic** [ˌtɛləˈskɑpɪk] *adj.* télescopique: ~ *lens*, téléobjectif *m*; ~ *tripod*, trépied *m* à coulisse; [Fig.] ~ *view*, résumé *m*.

television ['tɛləˌvɪʒən] *n.* télévision *f.*
tell [tɛll], **told** [towld], **told** *v. tr.* dire (qqch. à qqun, à qqun de faire qqch.); raconter (une histoire); montrer (le chemin); [distinguish] distinguer, voir (la différence), savoir; reconnaître (*by*, à); †compter: *He told his brother the story*, [avec insistance sur le complément d'objet direct] *He told the story to his brother*, Il a raconté cette histoire à son frère; *I told you so!*, Je vous l'avais bien dit!; *Do ~ !*, Vraiment!; *You're telling me!* À qui le dites-vous!, → Vous ne m'apprenez rien, [Fam.] Tu parles!; *Tell me another!*, À d'autres!; . . . , *I ~ you!*, . . . , je vous assure!; *to ~ s.o. about sth.*, parler de qqch. à qqun, [story] raconter qqch. à qqun; *all told*, en tout, tout compris, tout compte fait; *to ~ o.'s beads*, dire son chapelet; *You can never ~* , On ne sait jamais; *How can you ~ ?*, Comment le savez-vous?; *to ~ the time* [Pers.] dire l'heure, [clock] marquer l'heure; *Time will ~* , Qui vivra, verra; *I'm going to ~ Mom on you*, Je m'en vais le dire à maman; *to ~ s.o. off*, dire à qqun sa façon de penser. || *v. intr.* produire un effet, [blow] porter; se faire sentir; influer (*on*, sur). || **teller** ['tɛlɚ] *n.* **1.** *story- ~* , (ra)conteur *m*; narrateur *m* (d'histoires, &c.). **2.** [bank] caissier *m.* || **telling** [-ɪŋ] *n.* récit *m*, narration *f* (d'une histoire, d'un événement). || *adj.* [effect] puissant; [blow] qui porte; [result] efficace. || **telltale** [-ˌtejl] *n.* rapporteur *m*; [Mach.] compteur *m*; [Naut.] axiomètre *m.* || *adj.* bavard; [choses] révélat|eur, -rice.
temerity [tə'mɛɚɪtɪ] *n.* témérité *f.*
temper[1] ['tɛmpɚ] *n.* [Pers.] tempérament *m*, humeur *f* (habituelle), caractère *m*; *She lost her ~* , Elle s'est/mise en colère, emportée/; *to be in a bad ~* , être de mauvaise humeur.
temper[2] *n.* [metal] trempe *f* (du fer).
temperament ['tɛmpɹəmənt] *n.* tempérament *m*, humeur *f.* || **temperamental** [ˌtɛmpɹə'mɛntl̩] *adj.* capricieux, instable, fantasque.
temperance ['tɛmpɚə|ns] *n.* tempérance *f*, sobriété *f*, modération *f*: *~ society*, société *f* de tempérance. || **temperate** [-ət] *adj.* [climate] tempéré; [Pers.] modéré, sobre, tempérant.
temperature ['tɛmpɹətʃɚ] *n.* température *f*: *to run a ~* , faire de la température.
tempest ['tɛmpəst] *n.* tempête *f*, orage *m*: *a ~ in a teacup*, une tempête dans un verre d'eau. || **tempestuous** [ˌtɛm'pɛstjuwəs] *adj.* tempétueux, orageux.

temple ['tɛmpl̩] *n.* **1.** temple *m.* **2.** [Pers.] tempe *f.*
temporal ['tɛmpɚl̩] *adj.* temporel; [Anat.] temporal || **temporarily** [ˌtɛmpɚ'ɛɚɪlɪ] *adv.* temporairement, provisoirement. || **temporary** ['tɛmpɚ|ɛɚɪ] *adj.* [measure, &c.] temporaire. || **temporize** [-ˌajz] *v. intr.* **1.** temporiser, différer. **2.** [adapt o.s.] s'accommoder à. **3.** [compromise] transiger avec.
tempt [tɛmpt] *v. tr.* tenter (qqun), allécher. || **temptation** [ˌtɛmp'tejʃən] *n.* tentation *f*: *to lead (s.o.) into ~* , induire (qqun) en tentation. || **tempter** ['tɛmpt|ɚ] *n.* tentateur *m*, -trice *f.* || **tempting** [-ɪŋ] *adj.* tentant, séduisant.
ten [tɛn] *n.* dix *m.*
tenable [-əbl̩] *adj.* tenable, soutenable.
tenacious [-'ejʃəs] *adj.* tenace, obstiné: *~ of*, qui tient à, qui est attaché à; *to be ~ of life*, avoir la vie dure. || **tenacity** [-'æsɪtɪ] *n.* ténacité *f.*
tenant [-ənt] *n.* locataire *m*: *~ for life*, usufruitier *m*; *joint ~* , co-locataire *m.*
tench [-tʃ] *n.* tanche *f.*
tend[1] [tɛnd] *v. tr.* [Pers., animal] prendre soin de, [wound, wounded person] soigner, panser; [sheep, goal] garder, surveiller; [garden, machine, &c.] s'occuper de. || *v. intr. to ~ to one's business*, vaquer, veiller/à ses affaires.
tend[2] *v. intr.* tendre (à, *to*)
tendency [-ənsɪ] *n.* tendance *f*, propension *f* (à, *to*).
tender[1] [-ɚ] *n.* garde *m*; [Naut., Rail.] tender *m.*
tender[2] *adj.* tendre; [painful] sensible; [subject] délicat. || *n.* offre *f*; [Jur.] soumission *f*: *to put in a ~ on sth.*, soumissionner (pour) qqch.; *legal ~* , cours *m* légal; *to be legal ~* avoir cours. || *v. tr.* offrir. || **tenderfoot** [-ɚˌfʊt] *n.* blanc-bec *m*, novice *m*, débutant *m*; [Fr.] bleu *m.* || **tenderloin** [-ˌlojn] *n.* filet *m.* || **tenderly** [-ɚlɪ] *adv.* tendrement. || **tenderness** [-ɚnəs] *n.* [person's] tendresse *f.*
tendon [-ən] *n.* tendon *m.*
tendril [-ɹɪl] *n.* [Bot.] vrille *f.*
tenement ['tɛnəmənt] *n.* **1.** maison *f* d'habitation, logement *m.* **2.** domaine *m*, fief *m*, propriété *f* foncière; *~ house*, maison *f* de rapport.
tennis ['tɛnɪs] *n.* tennis *m*: *to play ~* , jouer au tennis; *~ court*, court *m* de tennis.
tenor ['tɛnɚ] *n.* **1.** [Mus.] ténor *m*; [instrument) ténor, alto. **2.** [Fig.] teneur *f* (d'un discours); cours *m*: *the even ~ of his life*, le cours paisible de sa vie.

tense [tɛns] *adj.* tendu, raide. || *n.* [Gram.] temps *m.*
tensile [-ˌajl] *adj.* extensible. || **tension** [ˈtɛnʃən] *n.* extension *f*, tension *f*.
tent [tɛnt] *n.* tente *f*: *to pitch* ~, dresser une tente, © tenter. || *v. intr.* camper, vivre sous la tente.
tentative [-ətɪv] *adj.* provisoire, expérimental, d'essai; [Pers.] timide, hésitant.
tenterhook [ɚˌhʊk] *n.* clou *m* à crochet: [Fig.] *to be on tenterhooks*, être sur des charbons ardents.
tenth [tɛnθ] *adj.* & *n.* dixième (*m*).
tenuous [ˈtɛnjuwəs] *adj.* ténu, menu, mince; [Fig.] subtil.
tenure [ˈtɛnjɚ] *n.* possession *f*; [of office] occupation *f*.
tepid [ˈtɛpɪd] *adj.* tiède.
term [tɚm] *n.* **1.** terme *m*: ~ *of office*, durée *f* des fonctions, mandat *m*, années *fpl* d'exercice. **2.** [Sch.] trimestre *m*, semestre *m*: ~ *paper*, dissertation *f*; composition *f*. **3.** [Gram.] mot *m*, terme *m*: *in technical terms*, en termes techniques, en langage technique. **4.** [Math.] terme *m*: *in terms of*, en fonction de; *the terms of a problem*, l'énoncé d'un problème. **5.** [relationship] *pl.* termes *mpl*, rapports *mpl*, relations *fpl*: *to be on /good, bad/terms with s.o.*, être/bien, mal/ avec qqun. **6.** [Com.] conditions *fpl*, prix *m*; termes *mpl*, clauses *fpl* (d'un contrat): *What are your terms?*, Quelles sont vos conditions?; *Easy terms*, Facilités *fpl* de paiement; *by the terms of . . .*, aux termes de . . . ; *to come to terms*, en venir à un accommodement, [enemy] capituler.
terminal [-ɪnḷ] *n.* [bus, Rail.] terminus *m.* || **terminate** [ˈtɚmɪ|ˌnejt] *v. tr.* terminer, achever. || *v. intr.* se terminer, être achevé. || **termination** [ˌtɚmɪˈnejʃən] *n.* limite *f*, extrémité *f*, fin *f*, conclusion *f*, résultat *m*; [Gram.] désinence *f*, terminaison *f*. || **terminus** [-nəs] *n.* [Br.] cf. TERMINAL.
terrace [ˈtɛɚəs] *n.* terrasse *f*; esplanade *f*.
terrain [tɚˈɹejn] *n.* [Mil.] terrain *m.*
terrapin [ˈtɛɚəˌpɪn] *n.* tortue *f* aquatique, © terrapène *f*.
terrestrial [tɚˈɹɛstɹɪəl] *adj.* terrestre.
terrible [ˈtɛɚɪbḷ] *adj.* terrible. || **terribly** [-ɪ] *adv.* terriblement.
terrier [ˈtɛɚɪɚ] *n.* [Zool.] terrier *m.*
terrific [tɚˈɹɪfɪk] *adj.* terrifiant; [Fam.] formidable, mirobolant; *You are* ~ *!*, Vous êtes/formidable, épatant/! || **terrify** [ˈtɛɚɪˌfaj] *v. tr.* terrifier.
territory [ˈtɛɚɪˌtɔɚɪ] *n.* territoire *m.*
terror [ˈtɛɚɚ] *n.* terreur *f*.
terse [tɚs] *adj.* concis, succinct. || **tersely** [-lɪ] *adv.* avec concision, succinctement.
test [tɛst] *n.* **1.** [trial] épreuve *f*; [Fig.] critère *m*: *the acid* ~, la pierre de touche. **2.** [Tech., Scol.] test *m*, essai *m*: *I.Q.* ~, épreuve *f* du quotient intellectuel; *intelligence* ~, test d'intelligence; *driving* ~, examen *m* du permis de conduire; ~ *pilot*, pilote *m* d'essai. || *v. tr.* expérimenter, éprouver; [try out] éprouver, mettre à l'épreuve.
testament [ˈtɛst|əmənt] *n.* testament *m.* || **testator** [-ejtɚ] *n.* testateur *m.*
testify [-ɪˌfaj] *v. tr.* [Jur.] déclarer, attester, affirmer; [Fig.] témoigner de. || **testimonial** [tɛstɪˈmownɪəl] *n.* attestation *f*, certificat *m.* || **testimony** [ˈtɛstɪˌmownɪ] *n.* témoignage *m*: *tables of* ~, Tables de la Loi.
testy [ˈtɛstɪ] *adj.* susceptible, irritable.
tetanus [ˈtɛtnəs] *n.* tétanos *m.*
tether [ˈtɛðɚ] *n.* attache *f*: *to come to the end of one's* ~, être à bout de ressources.
text [tɛkst] *n.* texte *m.* || **textbook** [-ˌbʊk] *n.* [chemistry, physics, &c.] manuel *m* scolaire.
textile [ˈtɛksˌtajl] *n.* [fabrics] textile *m*, tissu *m.* || *adj.* [industry] textile.
texture [ˈtɛkstʃɚ] *n.* tissu *m*; texture *f*.
Thames [tɛmz] *n.* la Tamise *f*.
than [ðæn] *conj.* [unit les deux termes d'une comparaison] que.
thank [θæŋk] *v. tr.* remercier (*s.o. for sth.* qqun de qqch.): *Thank you* (*for the book*), Merci (du livre); *to* ~ *o.'s* (*lucky*) *stars*, bénir le ciel, remercier sa bonne étoile. || **thankful** [-fḷ] *adj.* reconnaissant (*to*, à; *for*, de). || **thankless** [θæŋkləs] *adj.* [person, task] ingrat. || **thanks** [-s] *npl.* remerciements *mpl*, merci *m*; grâces *fpl*; *Thanks!*, Merci!; *thanks to*, grâce à. || **thanksgiving** [ˌθæŋksˈgɪvɪŋ] *n.* action *f* de grâce(s): ~ *Day*, (le) jour d'action de grâces.
that [ðæt] *adj. dém.* [*pl.* **those**] **1.** ce *m. sing.*, cette *f.sing.*, ces *m/f.pl.* [☞ *ce* is replaced by *cet* before a vowel or a mute h; for contrast or emphasis, *-là* is added to the following noun]: ~ *knife and* (~) *fork*, ce couteau et cette fourchette; *this knife and* ~ *fork*, ce couteau-ci et cette fourchette-là; *No, I want* **that** *book!*, Non, je veux ce livre-là; *Do you get* ~ *tired feeling?*, Éprouvez-vous une sensation de fatigue?; [Fam.] *How is* ~ *youngster of yours?*, Alors, ce petit, comment va-t-il, Comment va votre petit? **2.** *That one*, *pl. those* (*ones*), celui-là *m.sing.*, celle-là *f.sing.*, ceux-là *mpl*, celles-là *fpl*: *I'll take* ~ *one*, Je

prendrai celui-là. || *pron. dém. pl.* **those** **1.** [indef. with the verb *to be*] cela [Fam.] ça; ce; *What/is ~, are those/?*, Qu'est-ce (que c'est) que/cela, ça/?; *That is an antenna,* (Cela,) c'est une antenne; *Those are my glasses,* Ce sont mes lunettes; *Is ~ the city-hall?*, Est-ce (bien) là la mairie?; *That is what he told me,* Voilà ce qu'il m'a dit; *That is very interesting,* Cela, Voilà qui/est très intéressant; *That's all,* C'est, Voilà/tout; . . . *~ is,* . . . c'est-à-dire . . . ; *That's ~*, Ça y est, (c'est fini), Voilà une bonne chose de faite. **2.** [indef. with constructions other than *to be*] cela, [Fam.] ça; là: *That surprises me,* Cela m'étonne; *Did you see ~ ?*, Avez-vous vu cela?; *and* (. . .) *at ~ . . .*, et encore, et pourtant; *What do you mean by ~ ?*, Qu'entendez-vous par là?; *We haven't come to ~ yet,* Nous n'en sommes pas encore (arrivés) là; *in, on, under/ ~*, là-dedans, là-dessus, là-dessous; †*~ which . . .*, ce qui, ce que, &c. **3.** [referring to def. noun] *pl.* **those** celui (-là) *m.sing.*, celle (-là) *f.sing.*, ceux (-là) *mpl*, celles (-là) *fpl*: *I'll take/ ~ (one), those/*, Je prendrai/celui-là, ceux-là/; *Those/who, which/ . . .*, ceux, celles/ qui, que, &c. || *adv. dém. I didn't know it was ~ hard,* Je ne savais pas que c'était/ aussi difficile que cela; si, tellement, difficile/. || *pron.rel.* qui, que, auquel, avec lequel, &c.: [subj. of Fr. clause] *The book ~ is on the table,* Le livre qui est sur la table; [dir. object of Fr. clause] *The film (~) we saw yesterday,* Le film que nous avons vu hier; [obj. of a prep. coming at end of English clause]: *the man (~) I was speaking/of, to, with/*, l'homme/dont, auquel, avec lequel/je parlais; [after expression of time]: *the/ day, time/ (~) he saw us,* le jour, la fois/où il nous a vus; *every time (~) he did it,* chaque fois qu'il le faisait. || *conj.* que [☞ the construction preceding *que* may require the subj. in French]: *He said (~) he was coming,* Il a dit qu'il venait; *I don't think he is coming,* Je ne crois pas qu'il vienne; †*O ~ it might be so!*, Plût au ciel qu'il en fût ainsi!

thatch [θætʃ] *n.* chaume *m.* || *v. tr.* couvrir de chaume: *thatched cottage,* chaumière *f.*

thaw [θɔ], *v. intr.* fondre, dégeler. || *v. tr.* faire dégeler. || *n.* dégel *m*; fonte *f.*

the [ðə], preceding a vowel or for emphasis [ðij] *art.déf.* **1.** le *m.sing.*; la *f.sing.*, les *m/fpl.* [☞ *le, la,* become *l'* before a vowel or mute h; *le, les,* combine with the prepositions *à, de,* to become *au, aux*; *du, des.*]: *~ brother and (~) sister,* le frère et la sœur; *~ 4th and 5th of July,* les 4 et 5 juillet; *George the Sixth,* Georges VI. **2.** ce *m.sing.*, cette *f.sing.*, ces *m/fpl.* [☞ *ce* is replaced by *cet* before a vowel or mute h]: *Are ~ ladies ready?*, Et ces dames, sont-elles prêtes?; *How's the garden?*, Et ce jardin, (il pousse)?; *at ~ time,* à cette époque-là; *He is away at ~ moment,* Il est parti en ce moment. **3.** [stressed] ***the** car,* la voiture entre toutes; ***the** Dr. Smith,* le/célèbre, grand/ docteur Smith. || *adv.* [précède un adj. ou adv. comparatif] plus, moins; d'autant plus: *The richer he becomes, ~ less happy he is,* Plus il devient riche, (et) moins il est heureux; *He will be (all) ~ happier for it,* Il en sera d'autant plus heureux; *all ~ more (so) . . . because,* d'autant plus . . . que; *The sooner, ~ better,* Le plus tôt sera le mieux; *The less said about it, ~ better,* Moins on en parlera, mieux cela vaudra; *so much ~ /better, worse/(for you)*, tant/mieux, pis/(pour vous).

theatre [ˈθijətər] *n.* **1.** théâtre *m.* **2.** © cinéma *m.* || **theatrical** [ˌθijˈætɹɪkl] *adj.* théâtral, de théâtre; [art] scénique, dramatique.

†**thee** [ðij] *pron. pers.* te, toi. cf. THOU.

theft [θɛft] *n.* [robbery] vol *m.*

their [ðɛər] *adj. poss.* leur, *pl.* leurs *m/f.* || **theirs** [-z] *pron. poss.* le leur, la leur, les leurs; à eux, à elles.

them [ðɛm] *pron. pers.* **1.** [dir. obj. of Fr. verb] les: *I saw ~*, Je les ai vu(e)s; *Bring ~ (to me),* Apportez-les(-moi). **2.** [indir. obj. of Fr. verb] leur: *He showed ~ the house,* Il leur a montré la maison; *Give ~ some,* Donnez-leur-en. **3.** eux *mpl,* elles *fpl.* [after Fr. prep.] *with ~*, avec/eux, elles/; [double obj.] *He saw you and ~*, Il vous a vus, vous et eux; [after compar.] *He watched us longer than ~*, Il nous a regardés plus longtemps qu'eux; [Fam.] *It's ~*, Ce sont eux, Les voilà.

theme [θijm] *n.* thème *m,* sujet *m*; [Schol.] composition *f*: *~ song,* indicatif *m.*

themselves [ðəmˈsɛlvz] *pron. pers. réfl.* **1.** eux-mêmes *mpl,* elles-mêmes *fpl*: *They saw it ~*, Ils l'ont vu eux-mêmes; *They did it ~*, Ils l'ont fait/eux-mêmes, tout seuls/. **2.** [refl. obj.] se: *They washed ~*, Ils se sont lavés; *They gave ~ a raise,* Ils se sont donné une augmentation.

then [ðɛn] *adv.* [at that time] alors, à ce moment-(là), à cette époque(-là); [therefore] donc, par conséquent; [in that case] alors, dans ce cas, donc; [next] puis, ensuite; [moreover] (et) puis; et, mais /aussi/; d'ailleurs: (every) *now and* ~, de temps/en temps, à autre/; *now this,* ~ *that*, tantôt ceci, tantôt cela; *before, after/* ~/, avant, après/cela, cette époque(-là), ce moment-(là)/; *by* ~, déjà, d'ici là; *between now and* ~, d'ici là; *till* ~, jusque-là, jusqu'alors; *since* ~, dès lors, depuis cette époque(-là). || †**thence** [-s] *adv.* [place] de là; [time] dès lors; [conclusion] par conséquent.

theology [ˌθij'ɑlədʒɪ] *n.* théologie *f.*

theorem ['θijərəm] *n* [Math.] théorème *m.*

theoretical [θijə'ɛtɪkl̩] *adj.* théorique. || **theory** ['θijərɪ] *n.* théorie *f*: *to/ propose, propound/a* ~, émettre une hypothèse.

there [ðɛər] *adv.* **1.** là [☞ used for emphasis or when no def. place has yet been mentioned]: *There one finds . . .*, Là on trouve . . . ; *Who is* ~ *?*, Qui est là?; *I left them* ~ *(on the table)*, Je les ai laissés là (sur la table); *Put it (over)* ~, Posez-le là (-bas); *Hand me that knife* ~, Passez-moi ce couteau-là; *You* ~ *!*, Vous là-bas!; *There I can't agree*, (C'est) là (que) je ne suis pas d'accord; [Fam.] *You've got me* ~, Ça, je n'en sais rien; ~ *and then*, séance tenante; *a ticket* ~ *and back*, un billet aller et retour; *He's, He isn't/all* ~, Il (n')a (pas) sa tête à lui. cf. HERE. **2.** [pointing out s.o., sth.] voilà: *There is the book*, Voilà le livre; *There/it, he/is*, Le voilà; *There he goes!*, Le voilà qui s'en va; *There it goes again!*, Voilà que ça recommence!; *There goes the bell!*, Voilà la cloche qui sonne; *There's sth. new*; En voilà du nouveau!; *There's a good fellow!*, Tu seras bien gentil; *Just add water, and* ~ *you are!*, Ajoutez simplement de l'eau, et ça y est! **3.** [referring to a place just mentioned] y: *Yes, I'm going* ~, Oui, j'y vais; *Yes, put them* ~, Oui, mettez-les-y. **4.** [introducing an inverted subject + verb] Il (y a, est, &c.): *There is one book, There are two books/on the table*, Il y a/un livre, deux livres/sur la table; *There/was, will be/not one*, Il n'y en/avait, aura/pas un (seul); *There must be (some)*, Il doit y en avoir; *There/exist, remain/only two*; Il n'en/existe, reste/que deux; *There are three coming*, Il en vient trois. **5.** [after a prep.] *down* ~, *over* ~, là-bas; *in* ~, là-dedans; *on* ~, là-dessus; *under* ~, là-dessous; *from* ~, de là; *I've just come from* ~, j'en (re)viens. || *interj. There, I told you so!*, Là, vous voyez/, je vous l'avais bien dit!; *There, take it*, Tenez, prenez-le; *There there, There now/, don't cry*, Allons, allons, il ne faut pas pleurer; *There now, it's all over/, I've forgotten again*, Ça y est, C'est fini/, j'ai encore oublié; *I will go, so* ~ *!*, J'irai (et) voilà (tout).

thereabouts ['ðɛərəˌbawts] *adv.* aux environs de, près de là; à peu près, environ. || **thereafter** [ˌðɛər'æftər] *adv.* par la suite. || **thereby** ['ðɛərˌbaj] *adv.* de cette manière; de ce fait; par là. || **therefore** ['ðɛərˌfɔər] *adv.* par conséquent, donc. || **therein** [ˌðɛər'ɪn] *adv.* dedans, là-dedans; †à ce sujet, à cet égard. || **thereof** [ˌðɛər|'ʌv] *adv.* de cela, en. || **thereon** [-'ɑn] *adv.* dessus, là-dessus. || **thereupon** ['ðɛər|əˌpɑn] *adv.* sur ce, là-dessus, sur quoi. || **therewith** [-ˌwɪð] *adv.* †avec cela, en outre; [Fam.] par-dessus le marché.

Theresa [tər'ijsə] *n.* = Thérèse *f.*

thermal ['θərməl] *adj.* [units] thermal, thermique.

thermometer [θər'mɑmətər] [θə-] *n.* thermomètre *m.*

thermos *n.* thermos *m.*

thermostat ['θərməs|tæt] *n.* thermostat *m.*

these [ðijz] *adj.* ces (. . . -ci) cf. THIS. || *pron.* ceux-ci *mpl*, celles-ci *fpl* cf. THIS.

thesis ['θijsɪs] *n.* thèse *f.*

thews [θjuwz] *n.pl.* nerfs *mpl*, muscles *mpl*; [Fig.] force *f*, énergie *f.*

they [ðej] *pron. pers.* **1.** [subj. of Fr. verb] ils *mpl*, elles *fpl*: *They came*, Ils, Elles/sont venu(e)s/. **2.** [stressed] eux *mpl*, elles *fpl*: *It is* ~ *(who . . .)*, Ce sont eux (qui . . .); *They alone can . . .*, Eux seuls peuvent . . . ; *more than* ~, plus qu'eux; *You and they can . . .*, Vous et eux pouvez . . . **3.** [indef.] on; ceux *mpl*, celles *fpl*, (qui . .): *They say that . . .*, On dit que . . . ; *They who can . . .*, Ceux, Celles/qui peuvent. . . . || **they'd** [-d] **1.** they would, cf. WILL. **2.** they had, cf. HAVE. || **they'll** [-l̩] they will, cf. WILL. || **they're** [-ər] they are, cf. TO BE [ne pas confondre avec *their* pron. poss. et *there* adv.]. || **they've** [-v] they have, cf. TO HAVE.

thick [θɪk] *adj.* épais; [Pers.] gras; [liquid] consistant; [matter] dense; dru; [woods] touffu. || *n.* [flesh] gras *m*; milieu *m*: *in the* ~ *of*, au milieu de, en plein(e) . . . ; au fort de . . . ; *to go through* ~ *and thin for s.o.*, aller contre vents et marées pour qqun; *It's a bit* ~ *!*, C'est trop fort!, Ça par exemple! || *adv.* dru, épais; en couche épaisse: *to lay it on* ~, ne pas y aller avec le dos de la cuiller. || **thicken** [-n̩] *v. tr.* [liquid] épaissir. || *v. intr.* [sauce] s'épaissir; [darkness] s'obscurcir.

thicket [-ət] *n.* fourré *m*, bosquet *m*.

thickly [-lɪ] *adv.* abondamment; rapidement. || **thickness** [-nəs] *n.* épaisseur *f*; densité *f*; grosseur *f*; consistance *f*.

thief [θij|f] *pl.* **thieves** [-vz] *n.* voleur *m*, †larron *m*: *honour among thieves*, les loups ne se mangent pas entre eux. || **thieve** [-v] *v. tr.* voler, dérober (qqch.).

thigh [θaj] *n.* cuisse *f*.

thimble ['θɪmbl̩] *n.* dé *m* (à coudre).

thin [θɪn] *adj.* [Pers., body] maigre, mince; [delicate] fin; [thread, &c.] tenu; [voice] faible: *to grow thin(ner)*, maigrir, amincir. || *v. tr.* [**-nn-**] amincir, amaigrir, éclaircir.

†thine [ðajn] *pron. poss.* le tien, la tienne, les tiens, les tiennes, cf. THOU.

thing [θɪŋ] *n.* chose *f*, objet *m*, affaire *f*; [Pers.] être *m*; *pl.* [clothes] effets *mpl*; *One ~ or the other*, De deux choses l'une; *to know a ~ or two*, [Fam.] être à la coule; *How are things?*, Comment ça va?; *as things are*, dans l'état actuel des choses; *for one ~* , tout d'abord, en premier lieu; *for another ~* , d'autre part; *That's the very ~* , Voilà ce qu'il me faut; *It would be a good ~ to*, Il serait bon de; *The main ~ is to*, L'essentiel est de; *The strange ~ is that . . .* , Ce qu'il y a d'étrange, c'est que . . . ; *The ~ is to . . .* , Le tout, Le difficile/est de. . . .

think [θɪŋk], **thought, thought** [θɔt] *v. intr.* penser, réfléchir, songer: *He can ~ clearly*, Il sait penser clairement; *~ before you answer*, Réfléchissez avant de répondre; *~ again!*, Réfléchissez(-y) encore!; *to ~ twice before . . .* , y regarder à deux fois avant de . . . ; *let me ~* , voyons . . . ; *Just ~ !*, Songez y!; *to ~ /of, about/sth., s.o.*, penser à /qqun, qqch./; *Now that I ~ of it*, Maintenant que j'y pense; *I wouldn't ~ of it!*, Il n'en est pas question!; *I can't ~ of the date*, Je ne peux pas me rappeler la date; *I hadn't thought of leaving before tomorrow*, Je n'avais pas/pensé, songé/à, Je n'avais pas l'intention de partir/avant demain; *I didn't ~ to find you here*, Je ne pensais pas, Je ne m'attendais pas à/vous trouver ici. || *v. tr.* **1.** penser; croire, trouver; s'imaginer: *I ~ so*, Je le/crois, pense/, Je/crois, pense/que oui; *I don't ~ so*, Je ne crois pas, Je crois que non; *I should ~ so!*, Je/crois, pense/bien; *I thought as much*, Je m'y attendais; *I ~ I am right*, Je crois avoir raison; *I ~ (that) he is coming*, Je crois qu'il vient; *Do you ~ he is coming?*, Croyez-vous qu'il vienne?; *I don't ~ he is coming*, Je ne crois pas qu'il vienne; *I ~ he is honest*, Je le crois honnête; *I ~ he is better*, Je le trouve mieux; *I ~ it useless to insist*, Je trouve inutile d'insister; *I ~ it's unfair*, Je trouve que c'est injuste; *I ~ we should go*, Il me semble que nous devrions partir; *It is not what you ~* , Ce n'est pas ce que vous croyez; *What he means I can't ~* , Je ne peux pas m'imaginer ce qu'il veut dire; *Do what you ~ best*, Faites ce que bon vous semblera; *He thought (it) best to . . .* , Il jugea bon de . . .; *What do you ~ of it?*, Qu'en pensez-vous; *to ~ /well, ill/of s.o.*, penser du/bien, mal/de qqun; *He thought better of it*, Il s'est ravisé; *I ~ the world of him*, J'ai une excellente opinion de lui; *Think nothing of it*, Ce n'est rien. || **think out** [-'awt] *v. tr.* imaginer; combiner (un plan); trouver la solution à (qqch.): *well thought out*, bien/imaginé, pensé/. || **think over** [-'owvɚ] *v. tr.* réfléchir, méditer/sur (qqch.): *Think it over!*, Réfléchissez-y (bien)!; *After thinking it over . . .* , après (mûre) réflexion. || **think up** [-'ʌp] *v. tr.* imaginer, inventer (qqch.).

thinker [-ɚ] *n.* penseur *m*.

thinly [-lɪ] *adv.* maigrement; légèrement (couvert), de façon clairsemée. || **thinness** [-nəs] *n.* minceur *f*, maigreur *f*; légèreté *f*; rareté *f*; ténuité *f*.

third [θɚd] *adj. num. ord.* (le, la) troisième.

thirst [θɚst] *n.* soif *f*. || *v. intr.* avoir soif (*for*, de) [Fig.] être assoiffé, avide (de qqch., *for sth.*). || **thirsty** [-ɪ] *adj.* assoiffé; (gosier) altéré: *I am ~* , J'ai soif.

thirteen [θɚ'tijn] *adj. num. card.* treize (*m*). || **thirteenth** [-θ] *adj.* (le, la) treizième. || **thirtieth** ['θɚtɪ|əθ] *adj. num. ord.* (le, la, les) trentième(s). || **thirty** *adj. num.* trente.

this [ðɪs] *adj. dém. pl.* **these 1.** ce *m.sing.*, cette *f.sing.*, ces *m/fpl.* [☞ ce is replaced by *cet* before a vowel or a mute h; for contrast or emphasis, -ci is added to the following noun]: *~ knife and (~) fork*, ce couteau et cette fourchette; *~ knife and that fork*, ce couteau-ci et cette fourchette-là; *No, I want* **this** *book!*, Non, je veux ce livre-ci!; *~ /morning, afternoon, evening, &c./*, ce matin, cet après-midi, ce soir, &c.; *~ text is intended for . . .* , Le présent manuel s'adresse à . . . ; *these (last) two years*, voilà deux ans que . . . ; *these days*, de nos jours; *by ~ time*, déjà. **2.** *this one, pl. these (ones)*, celui-ci *m.sing.*, celle-ci *f.sing.*, ceux-ci *mpl*, celles-là *fpl*: *I'll take ~ one*, Je prendrai celle-ci. || *pron.dém.*

[*pl.* **these**] **1.** [indef. with the verb *to be*] ceci; ce; voici: *What/is this, are those/?*, Qu'est-ce (que c'est) que ceci?; *This is a new model*, C'est un nouveau modèle; *These are my glasses*, Ce sont mes lunettes; *Is ~ the city-hall?*, Est-ce (bien) ici la mairie?; *This is what he told me*, Voici ce qu'il m'a dit; *This is very interesting*, Ceci, C', Voici qui/est très intéressant; *~ is where . . .*, voici où . . . . **2.** [indef. with constructions other than *to be*] ceci: *This will interest you*, Ceci vous intéressera; *Have you seen ~ ?*, Avez-vous vu ceci?; *before ~* , déjà; *after ~* , désormais: *This may reach you before I arrive*, Il se peut que ce mot vous parvienne avant mon arrivée. **3.** [referring to def. noun] [*pl.* **these**] celui-ci *m.sing.*, celle-ci *f.sing.*, ceux-ci *mpl*, celles-ci *fpl*: *I'll take/ ~ (one), these/*, Je prendrai/celui-ci, ceux-ci/. || *adv. dém. I didn't know it was ~ hard*, Je ne savais pas que c'était/aussi difficile que ceci; si, tellement difficile/.

thistle ['θɪsl̩] *n.* chardon *m.*

†thither [ðɪðɚ] *adv.* †là: *hither and ~* , çà et là.

thong [θɔŋ] *n.* courroie *f*, lanière *f.*

thorn [θɔɚn] *n.* épine *f*; buisson *m* d'épines: *a ~ in the flesh*, une épine au pied. || **thorny** [-ɪ] *adj.* épineux.

thorough ['θɚə] *adj.* parfait, entier, complet; [study] consciencieux: *a ~ examination*, un examen approfondi.

thoroughbred ['θɚəˌbɹɛd] *adj.* [horse] pur sang; [dog] de race pure; [Pers.] racé. || *n.* [horse] pur-sang *m*; [animal] animal *m* de race; [Pers.] personne *f* racée.

thoroughfare ['θɚəˌfɛɚ] *n.* artère *f*, voie *f* de communication; grande rue *f*: *no ~* , rue *f* barrée; entrée *f* interdite.

thoroughgoing ['θɚəˌgowɪŋ] *adj.* parfait.

thoroughly [-lɪ] *adv.* entièrement, complètement, totalement: *to study ~* , approfondir ses connaissances.

those [ðowz] cf. THAT.

†thou [ðaw] *pr. pers.* [☞ archaïsme employé en poésie et dans la langue religieuse] [subject] tu; [predicate] toi.

though [ðow] *conj.* **1.** quoique, bien que [+ subjunc.]: *Though he is clever, Clever ~ he (may) be*, Quoiqu'il soit intelligent, Si intelligent qu'il soit; *even ~* , quand bien même, même si; *as ~* , cf. AS. **2.** [after a statement] cependant, vraiment.

thought[1] [θɔt] *n.* pensée *f*; idée *f*; réflexion *f*. *to have one's thoughts elsewhere*, avoir l'esprit ailleurs; *the mere ~ of it*, rien que d'y penser; *on second ~* , tout bien réfléchi, toute réflexion faite; *I didn't give it a second ~* , Je n'y ai plus repensé; *with the ~ of*, dans le dessein de; *My one ~ is to . . .* , → Je ne pense qu'à . . .

thought[2] cf. THINK.

thoughtful ['θɔtfl̩] *adj.* [Pers.] pensif; réfléchi, soucieux; attentif; [book] profond.

thoughtless ['θɑtˌləs] *adj.* étourdi, irréfléchi; sans prévenance (*of*, de).

thousand ['θawzənd] *adj. num. card.* mille: *thousands of people*, des milliers *mpl* de/gens, personnes/: *Thousand-Islands River*, (la) Rivière des Mille-Îles. || **thousandth** [-θ] *adj.* (le, la) millième.

thrash [θɹæʃ] *v. tr.* **1.** rosser (qqun), donner une volée à (qqun). **2.** [Fig.] débattre, passer au crible: *to ~ out problems* débattre, étudier à fond/des problèmes.

thread [θɹɛd] *n.* [cotton, silk, &c.] fil *m*; [screw] filet *m* (d'une vis); [plant] filament *m* (d'une plante). || *v. tr.* enfiler (une aiguille): *to/lose, break/the ~* , perdre le fil (de ses idées); *to pick up the threads of a story*, rassembler les fils d'un discours. || **threadbare** [-ˌbɛɚ] *adj.* élimé, râpé.

threat [θɹɛt] *n.* menace *f.* || **threaten** [-n̩] *v. tr.* menacer (qqun, qqch.).

three [θɹij] *adj. num. card.* trois: *Three Rivers*, Trois-Rivières *fpl.*

thresh [θrɛʃ] *v. tr.* [Agric.] battre (le grain). || **thresher** [-ɚ] *n.* batteuse *f.* || **threshing** [-ɪŋ] *n.* battage *m*: *~ floor*, aire *f*; *~ machine*, batteuse *f.*

threshold ['θɹɛʃˌhowld] *n.* seuil *m.*

thrice [θɹajs] *adv.* trois fois.

thrift [θɹɪft] *n.* économie *f*, épargne *f.* || **thrifty** [-ɪ] *adj.* économe, ménager.

thrill [θɹɪl] *v. intr.* frémir, frissonner. || *v. tr.* émouvoir, bouleverser; faire frémir. || *n.* frisson *m*, frémissement *m.*

thriller ['θɹɪlɚ] *n.* roman *m*, spectacle *m*/à sensation.

thrive [θɹajv], **thrived** [θɹajvd], **thrived** or **throve** [θɹowv], **thriven** ['θɹɪvən] *v. intr.* [industry, business] croître, réussir, prospérer.

throat [θɹowt] *n.* gorge *f*; [gullet] gosier *m*: *I have a sore ~* , J'ai mal à la gorge, J'ai un mal de gorge: *~ wash*, gargarisme *m.*

throb [θɹɑb] *v. intr.* [-**bb**-] battre, palpiter; [infection] élancer; [engine] vrombir. || *n.* battement *m*; palpitation *f*; élancement *m.*

throe [θɹow] *n.* douleurs *fpl*; affres *fpl*; [Fig.] tourments *mpl*: *the throes of death*, les affres de la mort, l'agonie; *in the last throes*, à l'agonie.

throne [θɹown] *n.* [king's] trône *m.*

throng [θɹɑŋ] *n.* foule *f*; cohue *f.* || *v. intr.* affluer, accourir en foule; se bousculer.

throttle ['θɹɑtl̩] *n.* gosier *m*; [Tech.] soupape *f* de réglage; [Auto.] commande *f* des gaz. || *v. tr.* étrangler; [Fig.] juguler.

through [θɹuw] *prép.* **1.** [via] par; [~ an obstacle] à travers: *to go, come/ ~ /the door, a town/*, entrer, passer/par une porte; passer par, traverser/une ville; *He walked ~ the crowd,* Il marcha à travers la foule; *to drive ~ a forest*, traverser, passer à travers/une forêt en voiture; *to get ~ /a book, one's work/*, finir/un livre, son travail/; *He has been ~ a lot,* Il a passé par beaucoup d'épreuves; *Monday ~ Friday*, de lundi en vendredi, [repeated] du lundi au vendredi. **2.** d'un bout à l'autre de: *The children had slept ~ the storm*, Les enfants avaient dormi pendant tout l'orage; *all ~ Canada*, dans tout le Canada. **3.** grâce à, au moyen de, par (l'intermédiaire de): *I got to know her ~ my cousin*, J'ai fait sa connaissance grâce à mon cousin; *He did it ~ loyalty*, Il l'a fait par fidélité; *It happened ~ a mistake*, C'est arrivé par (suite d'une) erreur. || *adv.* **1.** à travers [cf. accompanying verbs]: *Is it ~ (to the other side)?*, Est-ce que ça a traversé?; *~ and ~* , de part en part, complètement. **2.** fini; *Are you ~ (with it)?*, (L')avez-vous fini?; *I'm ~ with you*, J'en ai fini avec vous; [of career] *He is (all) ~* , Il est fini. **3.** jusqu'au bout: *to hear s.o. ~* , écouter qqun jusqu'au bout; *You have to go ~ with it*, Il faut aller jusqu'au bout. **4.** directement: *~ to Vancouver*, directement/à, pour/Vancouver; *I can't get ~ to him*, Je ne peux pas l'avoir (au téléphone, &c.). || *adj.* [train, &c.] direct: *~ street*, rue *f* à circulation prioritaire; *~ traffic*, circulation *f* prioritaire. || **throughout** [-'awt] *adv.* d'un bout à l'autre, entièrement. || *prép.* d'un bout à l'autre de, partout (dans, à, &c.).

throughway ['θɹuwˌwej] *n.* route *f* à péage; autoroute *f.*

throw [θɹow], **threw** [θɹuw], **thrown** [θɹown] *v. tr.* jeter, lancer (des pierres, &c.); © [Fam.] garrocher; [toss] envoyer; [Fig.] lancer, plonger, mettre: *to ~ the blame on*, rejeter la responsabilité (de qqch.) sur; *to ~ open*, ouvrir brusquement, ouvrir toute grande (la porte): [Fam.] *to ~ a party*, lancer une invitation, inviter . . . (à un thé, un coquetel, &c.). || **throw** *n.* jet *m*; [sport] lancement *m*; [pêche] lancer *m*; [scarf] châle *m*, écharpe *f.* || **throw away** [ə'wej] *v. tr.* jeter (qqch. qui ne sert plus); perdre (son temps). || **throw back** [-'bæk] *v. tr.* renvoyer (une balle); renvoyer, réfléchir (un rayon). || *v. intr.* retourner au type primitif (de): *to be thrown back on*, se rabattre sur. || **throw-back** [-ˌbæk] *n.* régression *f*, recul *m.* || **throw down** [-'dawn] *v. tr.* abattre, faire tomber (un mur, &c.); démolir (une maison); jeter (du haut de . . .). || **throw in** [-'ɪn] *v. tr.* [Fig.] placer (un mot); ajouter par-dessus le marché. || **throw off** [-'ɔf] *v. tr.* se débarrasser (de qqun); [clothes] se déshabiller (à la hâte); jeter (le masque). || **throw on** [-'ɑn] *v. tr.* [clothes] s'habiller (à la hâte), enfiler (ses vêtements). || **throw out** [-'awt] *v. tr.* rejeter; expulser, mettre (qqun) à la porte; bomber (le torse). || *v. intr.* [plant] pousser (des tiges, &c.). || **throw-out** [-ˌawt] *n.* rejet *m*, rebut *m.* || **throw up** [-'ʌp] *v. tr.* abandonner, renoncer à; [hands] lever. || *v. intr.* vomir. || **thrower** [-ɚ] *n.* [sport] lanceur *m*; [dice] joueur *m.*

thrush [θɹʌʃ] *n.* grive *f.*

thrust [θɹʌst], **thrust**, **thrust** *v. tr.* enfoncer (un pieu, une dague, &c.), pousser (une pointe dans . . .). || *v. intr.* porter, donner/un coup (à qqun, *at s.o.*). || *n.* coup *m* (de bâton, lance, &c.); [fencing] botte *f*; poussée *f* (en pointe): [Fig.] *to ~ sth. down a person's throat*, forcer qqun à accepter qqch., imposer (son opinion) à qqun.

thud [θʌd] *n.* bruit *m* sourd.

thug [θʌg] *n.* bandit *m*; séide *m.*

thumb [θʌm] *n.* pouce *m*; *to be under s.o.'s ~* , être sous la coupe de qqun. || *v. tr.* feuilleter (un livre, &c.); [Fig.] tripoter (qqch.). || **thumbtack** [-ˌtæk] *n.* punaise *f.*

thump [θʌmp] *v. tr.* cogner, marteler; frapper. || *n.* coup violent. || **thumping** [-ɪŋ] *adj.* [Fam.] énorme.

thunder ['θʌndɚ] *n.* tonnerre *m*; [Fig.] foudre *f*: *(a) clap of ~* , (un) coup de tonnerre: *to steal a person's ~* , couper l'herbe sous le pied de qqun. || *v. intr.* tonner, gronder; [Fig.] fulminer. || **thunderclap** [-ˌklæp] *n.* cf. THUNDER. || **thunderstorm** [-ˌstɔɚm] *n.* orage *m.*

Thursday ['θɚzdej] *n.* jeudi *m*: *Come (next) ~* , Venez jeudi (prochain); *Maundy, Holy/ ~* , Jeudi-Saint.

thus [ðʌs] *adv.* ainsi, donc, de cette/façon, manière/; *~ far*, jusqu' ici.

thwart [θwɔɚt] *v. tr.* contrarier. || *adj.* transversal.

†**thy** [ðaj] *adj.* ton, ta, tes. cf. THOU. || †**thyself** [-ˌsɛlf] toi-même, te.

tiara [tɪ'æɹə] *n.* tiare *f.*

Tiber (the) ['tajbɚ] *n.* [river] (le) Tibre.

tibia ['tɪbɪə] *n.* tibia *m.*

tick [tɪk] *n.* **1.** coutil *m.* **2.** tic-tac *m* (d'une horloge). **3.** [check] marque *f*: [Fam.] *on* ~, à crédit. || *v. tr.*: *to* ~ *(an item) off*, pointer, marquer/(un article): [Fam.] *to* ~ *a person off*, parler crûment à qqun. || *v. intr.* [clock, &c.] faire tic-tac.

ticket [-ət] *n.* [bus] ticket *m*, [rail, intercity bus] billet *m*; bulletin *m* (de consigne); [Rail., Theat.] billet *m*; [boat] passage *m*, [US. Pol.] liste *f* (électorale); [infraction] contravention *f*, procès-verbal *m*: *to get a* ~, recevoir une contravention; *to give s.o. a* ~, verbaliser: *Ticketed passengers check here*, → Entrée des voyageurs munis de (leurs) billets; [Fam.] *That's the* ~ *!*, Voilà qui fera l'affaire! A la bonne heure!, C'est bien ça!

tickle [-l̩] *v. tr. & intr.* chatouiller. || *n.* chatouillement *m.* || **ticklish** [-l̩ɪʃ] *adj.* **1.** [Pers., &c.] chatouilleux. **2.** [Pers.] susceptible. **3.** [subject] délicat.

tidal ['tajdl̩] *adj.* de marée: ~ *wave*, raz de marée. || **tide** [tajd] *n.* **1.** marée *f*; [Fig.] courant *m.* **2.** temps *m*, saison *f*, époque *f*: *Yule* ~, (l') époque de, © le temps de /Noël. || *v. tr.*: *This will* ~ *you over till Tuesday*, Ceci vous permettra de tenir le coup jusqu' à mardi.

tidiness ['tajdɪnəs] *n.* ordre *m*; netteté *f*, propreté *f.*

†**tidings** ['tajdɪŋz] *n.* nouvelles *fpl*: *I bring you/good, glad/* ~, Je suis porteur de bonnes nouvelles.

tidy ['tajdɪ] *adj.* [Pers.] propre, net; [room, &c.] en ordre.

tie [taj] *n.* lien *m*; nœud *m*; [Fig.] attache *f*, entrave *f*; [Mus.] liaison *f*; [Rail.] traverse *f*; [Sport] match *m* nul, match de championnat: *neck* ~, cravate *f*; ~ *-up*, embouteillage *m* (de la circulation). || *v. tr.* lier, attacher (qqun, qqch.); nouer (qqch.): *to* ~ *down (s.o. to sth.)*, assujettir, astreindre (qqun à qqch.); *to* ~ *up*, attacher (un chien, &c.); emballer, envelopper (des marchandises); ficeler (un paquet); ligoter (un prisonnier); panser, bander (une blessure); [Fin.] bloquer (des capitaux). || *v. intr.* se lier; s'attacher, se nouer.

tier [tijɚ] *n.* étage *m*; [stadium] gradin *m.*

tiff [tɪf] *n.* [Fam.] chamaillerie *f*, brouille *f.*

tiger ['tajgɚ] *n.* tigre *m.*

tight [tajt] *adj.* serré; [rope] raide, tendu; [compartment] étanche; [clothes] étroit; [Pers.] [Fam.] chiche; [Sl. = drunk] rond, noir: *water-* ~, imperméable à l'eau. || *adv.* fortement, fermement; hermétiquement. || **tighten** [-n̩] *v. tr.* serrer (qqch.), tendre (une corde); [Fig.] [friendship] resserrer (des liens). || **tightly** [-lɪ] *adv.* [cf. TIGHT adv.]. || **tights** [-s] *n.* collants *mpl.*

tightwad ['tajtˌwɑd] *n.* [Fam.] grippe-sou *m.*

tigress ['tajgɹəs] *n.* tigresse *f.*

tile [tajl] *n.* tuile *f* (de toit); carreau *m* (de plancher, &c.): [Fam.] *He has a* ~ *missing*, © Il lui manque un bardeau, Il est/toqué, timbré/. || *v. tr.* couvrir (un toit, &c.)/de, en/tuiles; carreler (un plancher, &c.). || **tiling** [-ɪŋ] *n.* **1.** pose *f* des tuiles. **2.** carrelage *m*, carreaux *n.pl.*

till[1] [tɪl] cf. UNTIL.

till[2] *n.* tiroir-caisse *m*, caisse *f.*

till[3] *v. tr.* cultiver, labourer.

tiller [-ɚ] *n.* [Naut.] barre *f.*

tilt [tɪlt] *n.* **1.** pente *f*, inclinaison *f.* **2.** bâche *f.* **3.** © balançoire *f*: [Fig.] *at full* ~, à/tête baissée, bride abattue/. || *v. tr.* **1.** incliner; [wagon] faire pencher (qqch.). **2.** couvrir (un camion, chariot) d'une bâche.

timber ['tɪmbɚ] *n.* bois *m* de construction [rafter, &c.] poutre *f*, madrier *m*; forêt(s) *fpl*: ~ *licence*, permis de coupe (de bois); ~ *floating*, flottage *m* (du bois). || *v. tr.* charpenter.

time[1] [tajm] *n.* **1.** [duration] temps *m*: *Time flies*, Le temps passe vite; *a race against* ~, une course contre la montre; *for the* ~ *being*, pour le moment; *in (the course of)* ~, avec le temps; *in due* ~, en temps et lieu; *to play for* ~, chercher à gagner du temps; *to save, waste/* ~, gagner, perdre/du temps/; *We've got plenty of* ~, Nous avons/bien, tout/le temps; *to have* ~ *on o.'s hands*, avoir du temps de reste; *There is no* ~ *to do that*, On n'a pas le temps de faire cela; *to take o.'s* ~ *(in) doing sth.*, mettre le temps à faire qqch.; *Take your* ~ *!*, Prenez votre temps!; [Fam.] *to do* ~, faire de la prison. **2.** [period of time] temps *m*; délai *m*, époque *f*: *for/a, some/* ~, pendant quelque temps; *for some* ~ *past*, depuis quelque temps; *for a/long, short/* ~ *(past)*, depuis/longtemps, peu de temps/; *a short* ~ *after*, après peu (de temps); *to take a long* ~ *to do sth.*, mettre bien du temps à faire qqch.; cf. 1.; *in no* ~, en moins de rien; *in the shortest possible* ~, dans le plus bref délai; *the good old times*, le bon vieux temps; *Times are hard*, Les temps sont durs; *to be/ahead of*, *behind/the times*, être en/avance, retard/ (sur son époque); *in/my, my father's/* ~, de mon temps, du temps de mon père; *to have a good* ~, bien s'amuser; *to have a/hard, rough/* ~ *(of it)*, en voir de dures, passer un mauvais quart d'heure. **3.** [point in time] moment *m*; heure *f*; époque *f*: *on* ~, à l'heure; *in (the nick of)* ~ *(to)*, à temps (pour); *at/the, that/* ~, alors à ce moment (-là), à cette époque(-là); *at this* ~, à cette occasion; *(at) this* ~ *last year*, l'année passée à pareille époque; *at the present* ~, à l'heure actuelle, à présent; *at one* ~, autrefois; *at any* ~, d'un moment à l'autre; *if at any* ~, si jamais; *at all times*, en tout temps; *at times*, parfois; *at no* ~, (ne) . . . jamais; *from* ~ *to* ~, de temps/en temps, à autre/; *at the same* ~ *(as)*, en même temps (que); [contrast] mais, par ailleurs, d'autre part, cf. 5; *dinner-* ~, l'heure *f* du dîner; *It is* ~ *to . . .*, C'est/l'heure, le moment/de . . ., Il faut . . . maintenant; *It is* ~ *we told him, Now is the* ~ *(for us) to tell him*, Il est temps que nous le lui disions; *The* ~ *has come when . . .* Le moment est venu de . . . ; *This is no* ~ *to*, Ce n'est pas le moment de . . . . **4.** [telling time] heure *f*: *What* ~ *is it?*, Quelle heure est-il?; *The* ~ *is 3 o'clock*, Il est 3 heures; *day-light-saving* ~, heure *f* d'été; *standard* ~, heure *f* normale; *Greenwich Mean Time*, Heure (moyenne) de Greenwich, cf. G.M.T. **5.** [series of occasions] fois *f*; reprise *f*: *the/first, last, &c./* ~, la/ première, dernière, &c./fois; *this* ~, cette fois(-ci); *several times*, à plusieurs reprises; ~ *and* ~ *again*, ~ *after* ~, maintes et maintes fois, mille fois; *at times*, parfois; *between times*, entre-temps. **6.** [Mus.] mesure *f*: *to beat* ~, battre la mesure; *to keep* ~, jouer, chanter/en mesure. **7.** [Mil.] pas *m*: *to mark* ~, marquer le pas; *in quick* ~, au pas accéléré.

time² *v. tr.* mesurer, calculer (la durée d'un phénomène); régler (un mécanisme); [Sport.] chronométrer. || *v. intr.* calculer; [Fig.] choisir son moment (pour).

time-keeper ['tajm|ˌkijpɚ] *n.* [Pers.] pointeur *m*, chronométreur *m*; [watch] chronomètre *m* de précision. || **timeless** [-ləs] *adj.* éternel, sans fin. || **timeliness** [-lɪnəs] *n.* opportunité *f*; bon moment *m*. || **timely** [-lɪ] *adv.* [remark, step] opportun, à propos; (qui arrive) à temps, à point; de saison. || **timer** [-ɚ] *n.* chronométreur *m*; [Photo.] *self* ~, retardateur *m*.

timid ['tɪmɪd] *adj.* timide; craintif. || **timidity** [tɪ'mɪdɪtɪ] *n.* timidité *f*.

timing ['tajmɪŋ] *n.* réglage *m*; [Sports] chronométrage *m*.

timorous ['tɪməəs] *adj.* timoré, craintif, peureux.

tin [tɪn] *n.* **1.** étain *m*, fer-blanc *m*. **2.**: ~ *can*, boîte *f*, récipient *m*, bidon *m*/en fer-blanc: ~ *ware*, (de la) ferblanterie [also ~ *work*], articles *mpl*, objets *mpl*/en fer-blanc. || *v. tr.* [-nn-] **1.** étamer (du fer, du cuivre). **2.** mettre (des légumes, &c. en boîte(s).

tincture['tɪŋktʃɚ] *n.* couleur *f*, teinte *f*; [Fig.] teinture *f*.

tinder ['tɪndɚ] *n.* amadou *m*.

tinfoil ['tɪnˌfojl] *n.* papier *m* d'argent; [Tech.] feuille *f* d'étain.

tinge [tɪndʒ] *n.* teinte *f*, nuance *f*. || *v. tr.* teinter, nuancer, colorer.

tingle ['tɪŋgl̩] *n.* [membres] fourmillement *m*; [oreilles] bourdonnement *m*. || *v. intr.* fourmiller; [oreilles] bourdonner; [peau] cuire.

tinkle [tɪnkl̩] *v. intr.* tinter. || *n.* tintement *m*.

tinned ['tɪnd] *adj.* **1.** [iron, &c.] étamé. **2.** ~ *food*, conserves *fpl*.

tinsel ['tɪnsl̩] *n.* lamé *m*, clinquant *m*, paillettes *fpl*. || *adj.* clinquant, voyant, faux.

tint [tɪnt] *n.* teinte *f*, nuance *f*. || *v. tr.* teinter.

tiny ['tajnɪ] *adj.* minuscule, très, tout/petit.

tip¹ [tɪp] *n.* bout *m* (de la langue, &c.); [toes] pointe *f* (des pieds, &c.); [land, &c.] extrémité *f*. || *v. tr.* [-pp-] [cane, &c.] mettre un bout à (qqch.), embouter (qqch.).

tip² *n.* **1.** [slant] inclinaison *f*; [slope] pente *f*. **2.** tape *f* (légère). **3.** pourboire *m*. **4.** [Fam.] [advice] tuyau *m*: *a straight* ~, un tuyau sûr. || *v. tr.* [-pp-] **1.** basculer, culbuter, faire pencher. **2.** donner, payer/un pourboire à (qqun). || **tip off** [-'ɑf] *v. tr.* faire tomber; [Fam.] tuyauter. || **tip out** [-'awt] *v. tr.* verser, déverser. || **tip over** [-'owvɚ] *v. tr. & intr.* (se) renverser.

tipsiness ['tɪpsɪ|nəs] *n.* (légère) ivresse *f*. || **tipsy** *adj.* [Fam.] éméché.

tiptoe [-ˌtow] *n.* pointe *f*, bout *m*/des pieds: *to stand on* ~, se hausser sur la pointe des pieds: [Fig.] *to be on* ~, être sur le qui-vive, être sur ses gardes. || *v. intr.* marcher sur la pointe des pieds: *to* ~ *down (to)*, descendre sur la pointe des pieds.

tip up [-'ʌp] *v. tr. & intr.* (faire) basculer.

tirade ['tajˌɹejd] *n.* tirade *f*.

tire[1] [tajɚ] *v. tr.* fatiguer, épuiser (qqun), lasser (la patience de qqun). ‖ *v. intr.* se fatiguer, se lasser (*of*, de); s'épuiser.

tire[2] *n.* [car] pneu *m.*

tired [-d] *adj.* fatigué, las (de qqch., qqun, *of sth.*, *s.o.*): *to be dog-* ~ , *dead-* ~ , être/éreinté, rendu, claqué/, dormir debout; *to get over being* ~ , se remettre de ses fatigues.

tiresome [ˈtajɚsəm] *adj.* [tiring] fatigant, épuisant; [boring] agaçant, ennuyeux; [Fam.] assommant.

†'tis [tɪz] = it is, cf. TO BE.

tissue [ˈtɪʃuw] *n.* **1.** tissu *m.* **2.** [s'applique à des articles en papier] papier *m* de soie: *toilet* ~ , papier hygiénique; ~ *napkin*, serviette *f* en papier; *facial* ~ , serviette *f* à démaquiller; ~ *paper*, papier-mouchoir *m*; ~ *handkerchief*, mouchoir *m* à jeter. ‖ **tissues** [-z] *n.* [collectif pour mouchoirs et serviettes en papier] papier-tissu *m.*

tit [tɪt] *n.* cf. TITMOUSE. ‖ ~ *for tat*, à bon chat, bon rat.

titbit [ˈtɪdˌbɪt] *n.* bon morceau *m*, friandise *f.*

tithe [tajð] *n.* dîme *f.* ‖ *v. tr.* soumettre à la dîme.

title [ˈtajtl̩] *n.* titre *m*; [deed] droit *m*, titre *m*; [Fig.] [right] qualification *f.* ‖ *v. tr.* intituler (un ouvrage, un article, &c.); donner un titre à (qqch.).

titmouse [ˈtɪt|ˌmaws] *pl.* **titmice** [-ˌmajs] *n.* [bird] mésange *f.*

to [tuw] *prép.* **1.** [after a verb of motion] à, en, dans, &c. [☞ Fr. uses the same prep. as after a verb of rest]: *He is going* ~ */Halifax, Ireland, Canada, my house, &c./*, Il va/à H., en Irlande, au C., chez moi, &c./; *Go up* ~ *your room*, Monte dans ta chambre. **2.** [coupled with *from*] de . . . à; de . . . en; depuis . . . jusqu'à: *from London* ~ *Paris*, de Londres à Paris; *from six* (*o'clock*) ~ *eight*, de six (heures) à huit heures; *from door* ~ *door*, de porte en porte; *from head* ~ *foot*, de la tête aux pieds, depuis les pieds jusqu'à la tête. **3.** de [☞ between nouns, a more precise prep. often is replaced by *de* if the meaning remains the same]: *the/road, way/train/* ~ *Winnipeg*, la route, le chemin, le train/de Winnipeg; *secretary* ~ *the president*, secrétaire *m/f* du président. **4.** [towards] vers; à; [Fig.] envers, pour: *turn* ~ *the/north, right/*, tourner/vers le nord, à droite/; "*To the Trains*", Accès aux quais; [Fig.] *good, kind/* ~ *s.o.*, bon, gentil, aimable/envers, pour/qqun. **5.** [as far as, until] jusqu'à: ~ *this day*, jusqu'à ce jour; *to count* ~ *100*, compter jusqu'à 100; *I'll see you* ~ *the door*, Je vous accompagne(rai) jusqu'à la porte. **6.** à . . . près: ~ (*within*) *a day*, à un jour près. **7.** [ratio] contre; par; pour: *five* ~ *one*, [betting, &c.] cinq contre un, [Sport.] cinq à un; *one teaspoon*(*ful*) ~ (*every*) *two cups*, une cuillerée par deux tasses; *one third vinegar* ~ *two thirds oil*, un tiers de vinaigre pour deux tiers d'huile. **8.** [English prep. expanded in Fr.] *The shortest way* ~ *school*, Le chemin le plus court pour aller à l'école; *to wear a raincoat* ~ *school*, mettre un imperméable pour aller à l'école; *That's nothing* ~ *what I saw*, Cela n'est rien/comparé à, à côté de/ce que j'ai vu (moi-même); *to drink* ~ *s.o.*, boire à la santé de qqun. **9.** [special uses: cf. also under other words calling for the use of *to*]: *a quarter* ~ *ten*, dix heures moins le quart; *It's a quarter* ~ , Il est moins le quart; *back* ~ *back*, dos à dos; [letter] *To*, Destinataire; ~ *my great surprise*, à ma grande surprise; ~ (*the best of*) *my knowledge*, à ma connaissance, autant que je sache; *That's all there is* ~ *it*, Voilà tout (ce qu'il y a à dire); *Is that all there is* ~ *it?*, C'est tout?; *There's nothing* ~ *it*, C'est peu de chose, Ce n'est rien; *to have, keep/sth.* ~ *o.s.*, avoir, garder/qqch. pour soi (tout seul). **10.** [devant un substantif ou pronom pour indiquer le compl. ind. du verbe] [ind. obj.] à; me, te, se, nous, vous, lui, leur: *I spoke* ~ *him*, Je lui ai parlé; *The boy I was talking* ~ , Le garçon à qui je parlais; *Give it* ~ *them*, Donnez-le-leur; *He told it* ~ *my brother*, Il l'a raconté à mon frère; × *I listened* ~ *the teacher*, J'ai écouté le professeur; *I paid attention* ~ *him*, J'ai fait attention à lui; *I went* (*up*) ~ *him*, Je suis allé à lui. ‖ [sign of inf. mood] **1.** [simple inf.] [no dir. translation; the inf. alone, or preceded by *à, de, par*]: *To be or not* ~ *be*, être ou ne pas être; *He came* ~ *see me*, Il est venu me voir; *He/prefers, hates/* ~ *do that*, Il/préfère, déteste/faire cela. [☞ Verbs of movement and liking are usual. followed directly by the Fr. inf., as are various other verbs; still others as well as adjectives and nouns take various prepositions before a following inf.: cf. these constructions elsewhere in the English and French parts. ☞ Note that in Fr. a clause must translate an English inf.] *He wants me* ~ *come*, Il veut que je vienne. **2.** [to = in order to] pour, afin de: *He shouted* ~ *attract my attention*, Il a crié pour attirer mon attention; *To succeed, one must work,* Pour, Afin de/réussir, il faut travailler.

to and fro [-n̩'fɹow] *adv.* de long en large: *to go* ~, aller et venir, aller de long en large.

toad [towd] *n.* crapaud *m.*

toast [towst] *n.* **1.** [drink] toast *m*; [bread] rôtie *f*: (*a*) *piece of* ~, (un) toast *m.* **2.** *French* ~, pain perdu, © pain doré. || *v. tr.* **1.** porter un toast à (qqun, qqch.). **2.** (faire) rôtir, griller (du pain). || **toaster** [-ɚ] *n.* grille-pain *m.*

tobacco [tə'bæk|ow] *n.* tabac *m*: ~ *pouch,* blague *f* (à tabac). || **tobacconist** [-əˌnɪst] *n.* © marchand *m* de tabac, [Fr.] buraliste *m/f*; débit *m* de tabac.

toboggan [tə'bɑgən] *n.* toboggan *m,* © traîne *f* sauvage.

today [tə'dej] *adv.* aujourd'hui; [nowadays] de nos jours, à l'heure actuelle, à l'époque actuelle: *What is* ~ *?,* Quel jour est-ce aujourd'hui?, Quel jour sommes-nous?; *Today is Monday,* C'est, Nous sommes/ aujourd'hui lundi; *a week ago* ~, il y aujourd'hui huit jours; *a week (from)* ~, (d') aujourd'hui en huit.

toe [tow] *n.* orteil *m,* doigt *m* de pied: *to walk on s.o.'s toes,* marcher sur le pied à qqun; [Fam.] *to turn up one's toes,* casser sa pipe, passer l'arme à gauche; [Fig.] *to stand on one's toes,* être sur le qui-vive, être sur ses gardes.

toehold ['towˌhowld] *n.* [Sport] prise *f*; [Fig.] prise *f* de possession: *to get a* ~ *on,* prendre pied sur.

together [tə'gɛðɚ] *adv.* ensemble, à la fois, en même temps: *all* ~, tous, toutes/ensemble: *to speak all* ~, parler tous à la fois.

toil [tojl] *n.* [very hard work] peine *f,* (du) labeur *m.* || *v. intr.* peiner, [Fr.] trimer, travailler dur: *The loaded truck toiled up the hill,* → Le camion, (lourdement) chargé, gravissait péniblement la colline.

toilet ['tojlət] *n.* **1.** toilette *f.* **2.** [lady's] costume *m.* **3.** [WC] cabinet *m*: ~ */paper, tissue, roll/,* papier *m* hygiénique, © papier *m* de toilette.

token ['towkən] *n.* **1.** marque *f* (d'affection, &c.); gage *m,* témoignage *m* (matériel), preuve *f,* symbole *m*: *as a* ~ *of,* en témoignage de; *by the same* ~, de plus . . . . **2.** [coin] jeton *m.* || *adj.* symbolique: *a* ~ *contribution,* un/versement, une contribution/symbolique.

told cf. TELL.: *Were you* ~ *to wait for him?,* → Vous a-t-on dit de l'attendre?

tolerable ['tɑlɚ|əbl̩] *adj.* tolérable, supportable; passable, assez bon; [Fam.] potable. || **tolerance** [-əns] *n.* tolérance *f,* patience *f*; endurance *f,* résistance *f.* || **tolerant** [-ənt] *adj.* tolérant, patient; résistant. || **tolerate** [-ˌejt] *v. tr.* admettre, tolérer, supporter, souffrir, endurer. || **toleration** [ˌtɑlɚ'ejʃən] *n.* tolérance *f.*

toll [towl] *n.* péage *m*: *toll road,* route *f* à péage.

Tom [tɑm] Thomas: ~, *Dick and Harry,* le premier venu; Pierre, Jean, Jacques.

tomahawk ['tɑməˌhɔk] *n.* tomahawk *m,* hache *f* de guerre.

tomato [tə'mejtow] *n.* tomate *f*: ~ *soup,* soupe *f* aux tomates; ~ *sauce,* sauce *f* tomate.

tomb [tuwm] *n.* tombe *f*; tombeau *m.* || **tombstone** [-ˌstown] *n.* pierre *f* tombale.

tomcat ['tɑmˌkæt] *n.* matou *m.*

tomorrow [tə'mɑɚow] *adv.* demain: (*the*) *day after* ~, après-demain. || *n.* (le) lendemain *m.*

ton [tʌn] *n.* tonne *f*: *short* ~, tonne courte; *long* ~, tonne forte; *metric* ~, tonne métrique.

tone [town] *n.* ton *m* (d'une note, &c.), son *m* (de la voix, &c.); tonalité *f* (d'un instrument de musique, d'une peinture); [general appearance] allure *f,* caractère *m*; [tenor] accent *m,* style *m* (d'un discours, d'une allocution); [colour] teinte *f,* nuance *f,* éclat *m*: *Listen for the dial* ~, Attendez la tonalité d'appel. || *v. tr.* [music] accorder (une guitare, &c.). || *v. intr.* [decoration, colour]: *to* ~ *in* (*with sth.*), s'harmoniser (avec qqch.). || **tone down** [-'dawn] *v. tr.* baisser, adoucir (la voix, Fam. le ton, &c.) atténuer (un effet, &c.). || *v. intr.* [Pers.] s'adoucir, se radoucir. || **tone up** [-'ʌp] *v. tr.* renforcir, tonifier (des muscles, une constitution); rafraîchir (des couleurs), renforcer (des sons). || *v. intr.* [Pers.] se remettre (d'une maladie).

tongs [tɑŋz] *n.pl.* pincettes *fpl*; pinces *fpl,* tenailles *fpl.*

tongue [tʌŋ] *n.* [mouth, language] langue *f*; [wagon] flèche *f*: *to hold one's* ~, garder le silence, se taire.

tonic ['tɑnɪk] *n.* [Med.] tonique *m*: ~ *water,* eau *f* gazeuse; [Mus.] tonique *f.* || **tonicity** [tow'nɪsɪtɪ] *n.* tonicité *f.*

tonight [tə'najt] *adv.* **1.** ce soir. **2.** cette nuit.

tonnage ['tʌnəʤ] *n.* tonnage *m.*

tonsil ['tɑnsɪ|l] *n.* amygdale *f.* || **tonsillitis** [-ˌlajtəs] *n.* amygdalite *f,* angine *f.*

tonsure ['tɑnʃɚ] *n.* [R.C.] tonsure *f.*

too [tuw] *adv.* **1.** trop: ~ *little* (*money*), trop peu (d'argent); cf. MUCH, MANY; [☞ *trop* is sometimes sufficient to translate *too* + adv.] ~ *well known*, trop connu; *to work* ~ *hard*, travailler trop; *to drink* ~ *heavily*, boire trop; *That's going* ~ *far*, C'en est trop; *You are* ~ *kind*, Vous êtes trop aimable; *It was* ~ (~) *charming!* C'était tellement (tellement) ravissant! **2.** aussi, également: *I want some* ~, J'en veux aussi; *He* ~ *was there*, Lui aussi était là; [Fam.] *Me* ~, Moi aussi; *My father*, ~, Mon père /aussi, également/. **3.** [moreover] d'ailleurs; de plus et qui plus est: . . . *and I was hungry* ~, . . . et d'ailleurs, j'avais faim; *and without her knowing* ~, et/de plus, qui plus est/à son insu! **4.** [Fam., emphatic]: *I did* ~ *!*, Mais si!

took [tʊk] cf. TAKE.

tool [tuwl] *n.* outil *m*, ustensile *m*;[Fig.] instrument *m* (de propagande, &c.): || *v. tr.* usiner (une pièce de métal); dorer (la tranche d'un livre); repousser, ciseler (le cuir): *tooled leather*, cuir repoussé.

toot [tuwt] *n.* son *m* du cor; [Auto.] coup *m* de klaxon. || *v. intr.* [Auto.] klaxonner; [Mus.] sonner du cor.

tooth [tuwθ] *pl.* **teeth** [tijθ] *n.* **1.** dent *f*; *back* ~, molaire *f*; *eye* ~, canine *f*; *first teeth*, dents de lait; *false teeth*, fausses dents, *fpl.* © dentier *m*; appareil *m* (de prothèse dentaire); ~ (*of a saw*), dent de scie; *wisdom* ~, dent de sagesse; *to have a* ~ *out*, se faire arracher une dent; *to brush one's teeth*, se brosser les dents; *to cast sth. in the teeth of s.o.*, jeter/à la face, en pleine figure/de qqun, (reprocher violemment à qqun); *to fight* ~ *and nail*, se battre comme un enragé; *to have a sweet* ~, aimer/les douceurs, le sucre, les sucreries/; *to get one's teeth into*, mordre sérieusement à qqch.; se mettre pour de bon à l'ouvrage. || **toothache** [-ˌejk] *n.* mal *m* de dents, rage *f* de dents: *to have a* ~, avoir mal aux dents. || **tooth brush** [-ˌbɹʌʃ] *n.* brosse *f* à dents. || **tooth paste** [-ˌpejst] *n.* pâte *f*/dentifrice, © à dents/. || **tooth pick** [-ˌpɪk] *n.* cure-dents *m.* || **tooth powder** [-ˌpawdɚ] *n.* poudre *f* dentifrice.

top[1] [tɑp] *n.* toupie *f*: *to sleep like a* ~, dormir/comme un loir, à poings fermés/.

top[2] *n.* sommet *m* (d'une montagne); faîte *m* (d'un toit); (le) haut *m*, (le) dessus; couvercle *m*; (la) tête; [Fig.] (le) comble *m*; capote *f* (d'une auto): *at the* ~ *of*, au/haut, sommet/de; *on* ~, sur le dessus; *to come out on* ~, avoir le dessus; *on* ~ *of it all*, pour comble, par-dessus le marché; *from* ~ *to bottom*, de haut en bas, de fond en comble; *from* ~ *to toe*, de la tête aux pieds. || *v. tr.* surmonter; [Fig.] couronner, dominer (qqch.). || *adj.* premier; [Fig.] principal, de première classe; [high] extrême, supérieur, du haut, d'en haut, du dessus.

topic [ˈtɑpɪk] *n.* sujet *m*, [subject] matière *f.*

topical [ˈtɑpɪkḷ] *adj.* d'actualité, d'intérêt courant; → qui se rapporte au sujet.

topple [tɑpḷ] *v. intr.* culbuter, tomber; dégringoler. || *v. tr.* faire tomber, renverser.

topsy-turvy [ˈtɑpsɪˌtɚvɪ] *adv.*: *to turn* ~, tout mettre sens dessus dessous.

torch [tɔɚtʃ] *n.* torche *f.*

tore [tɔɚ] cf. TEAR.

torment [ˈtɔɚmɛnt] *n.* supplice *m*, torture *f.* || *v. tr.* [ˌtɔɚˈmɛnt] torturer, tourmenter.

torn cf. TEAR. || *adj.* déchiré.

tornado [tɔɚˈnejdow] *n.* tornade *f.*

Toronto [təˈɹɑntow] *n.* Toronto. || **Torontonian** [ˌtɔɚɑnˈtownɪən] *n.* Torontois, -e.

torpedo [ˌtɔɚˈpijdow] *n.* torpille *f*: ~ *boat*, torpilleur *m.*

torpid [ˈtɔɚpɪd] *adj.* engourdi; [Fam.] endormi.

torpor [ˈtɔɚpɚ] *n.* torpeur *f.*

torrent [ˈtɔɚənt] *n.* torrent *m.*

tortoise [ˈtɔɚtɪs] *n.* tortue *f*: ~ *shell*, écaille *f.*

tortuous [ˈtɔɚtʃuwəs] *adj.* tortueux.

torture [ˈtowɚtʃɚ] *n.* torture *f*, supplice *m*, tourment *m.* || *v. tr.* torturer, supplicier, tourmenter (qqun).

toss [tɔs] *v. tr.* lancer, jeter négligemment, jeter (une pièce de monnaie, &c.) en l'air; cahoter, ballotter, secouer (violemment): *to* ~ *up a coin*, jouer à pile ou face.

tot [tɑt] *n.* bambin *m*; *pl.* les tout petits.

total [ˈtowtḷ] *n.* total *m*, somme *f*, montant *m.* || *adj.* total, entier, complet. || *v. intr.* atteindre le total de, [amount] s'élever à. || *v. tr.* [column of figures, &c.] faire le total de, additionner. || **totality** [ˌtowˈtælɪtɪ] *n.* totalité *f.* || **totalizator** [ˈtowtḷ|ɪˌzejtɚ] [Sport.] totalisateur *m.* || **totalize** [-ˌajz] *v. tr.* totaliser. || **totally** [-ɪ] *adv.* totalement, entièrement, complètement.

totem [ˈtowtṃ] *n.* totem *m.*

totter [ˈtɑtɚ] *v. intr.* chanceler; tituber.

touch [tʌtʃ] *v. tr.* toucher; [reach] atteindre: [Fig.] émouvoir, remuer, toucher (qqun); concerner, affecter (qqun): *to* ~ *off*, déclencher; *to* ~ *up*, retoucher (une photo). || *v. intr.* se toucher; [ship] toucher, faire escale (*at*, à): *to* ~ *on a subject*, toucher à, effleurer/un sujet. || *n.* touche *f*, attouchement *m*: (le) toucher *m*, (le) tact *m*; contact *m*; [a bit of sth.] pointe *f*, soupçon *m* (de qqch.): *to be in* ~

(*with s.o.*), être en/relations, contact/(avec qqun); *to get in ~ with*, se mettre en rapport, prendre contact/avec qqun; [Fig.] *It was ~ and go!*, Il était moins cinq!

touchdown [ˈtʌtʃˌdawn] *n.* [Sport] but *m.*

touchy [ˈtʌtʃɪ] *adj.* susceptible, chatouilleux; irritable, emporté.

tough [tʌf] *adj.* [Pers., thing] dur; [meat] coriace, [Pers.] résistant, tenace; [task] difficile; [Fam.] *~ luck*, déveine *f.*

tour [tuwɚ] *n.* tour *m,* [trip] tournée *f,* voyage *m* (de tourisme); excursion *f*: *all-expense ~*, voyage à forfait. || *v. tr.* voyager dans, visiter (un pays). || **tourist** [-ɪst] *n.* touriste *m/f.*

tournament [ˈtɚnəmənt] *n.* tournoi *m.*

tow¹ [tow] *v. tr.* remorquer (un navire, un véhicule).

tow² [taw] *n.* [textile] filasse *f,* fibres *fpl* discontinues.

toward(s) [təˈwɔɚd(z)] *prép.* [direction] vers; [Fig.] envers, à l'égard de.

towel [ˈtawl̩] *n.* **1.** serviette *f,* essuie-mains *m.* **2.** [R.C.] manuterge *m.*

tower [ˈtawɚ] *n.* [building] tour *f*; [electric] pylône *m.* || *v. intr.* [Fig.] dominer (qqun, qqch., *above s.o., sth.*), s'élever (au-dessus de, *above*). || **towering** [-ɪŋ] *adj.* très/haut, grand, élevé/; [Fig.] géant, illimité.

town [tawn] *n.* ville *f*; cité *f*: *to be/in, out of/ ~*, être/à la ville; en voyage, à la campagne. || **town hall** [-ˌhɔl] *n.* hôtel *m* de ville, mairie *f.* || **town planning** [-ˈplænɪŋ] *n.* urbanisme *m.* || **township** [-ˌʃɪp] *n.* [Fr.] commune *f,* © canton *m*: (*the*) *Eastern Townships*, (les) Cantons *mpl* de l'Est, *l'Estrie *f.*

toxic [ˈtɑksɪ|k] *n. & adj.* toxique. || **toxin** [-n] *n.* toxine *f.*

toy [toj] *n.* jouet *m.* || *v. intr.* jouer (avec qqch.), manier (qqch.): [Fig.] *to ~ with one's food*, manger du bout des lèvres.

trace [tɹejs] *n.* trace *f,* empreinte *f*; [drawing] tracé *m*; piste *f.* cf. TRACK. || *v. tr.* tracer (une ligne); calquer (un plan, &c.).

trachea [ˈtɹækɪə] *n.* trachée-artère *f.*

track [tɹæk] *n.* piste *f* (d'un animal), © passes *fpl*; route *f* (tracée), chemin *m* (à suivre), [ship] sillage *m*; [Rail.] voie *f*: [Fig.] *to be on the wrong ~*, faire fausse route: *to be on the right ~*, être sur la bonne voie; *to/lose, keep/ ~ of sth.*, perdre, ne pas perdre/qqch. de vue. || *v. tr.* pister, suivre (un animal) à la/piste, (trace); [Fig.] traquer (qqun).

tract [tɹækt] *n.* tract *m*; opuscule *m*; [Méd.] appareil *m*; voies *fpl.*

tractable [-əbl̩] *adj.* [Pers.] docile, traitable; maniable.

traction [ˈtɹækʃən] *n.* traction *f.* || *adj.* moteur. || **tractor** [ˈtɹæktɚ] *n.* [Agric.] tracteur *m.*

trade [tɹejd] *n.* commerce *m*; métier *m* (manuel); [gen.] occupation *f,* état *m*: *inshore, coastal/ ~*, cabotage *m.* || *v. intr.* commercer; faire le commerce (de qqch., *in sth.*). || *v. tr.* échanger, troquer/(qqch. contre qqch., *sth. for sth.*); [Fig.] faire trafic de (qqch.): *to ~ in on sth.*, donner en reprise contre qqch. || **trade-in** [-ˌɪn] *n.* [Com.] reprise *f.* || **trader** [-ɚ] *n.* commerçant *m.* négociant *m,* traiteur *m.* || **tradesman** [-zmən] *pl.* **tradesmen** *n.* commerçant *m,* boutiquier *m.* || **trade union** [ˌjuwnjən] *n.* syndicat *m.* || **trade winds** [-ˌwɪndz] *n.pl.* (vents *mpl*) alizés. || **trading French** [-ˈfɪɛntʃ] *n.* petit-nègre *m,* sabir *m.*

tradition [tɹəˈdɪʃən] *n.* tradition *f.*

traditional [tɹəˈdɪʃənl̩] *adj.* traditionnel.

traffic [ˈtɹæfɪk] *n.* **1.** [Com.] trafic *m,* commerce *m.* **2.** [street, highway] circulation *f*: *inshore, coastal ~*, cabotage *m* (≠ navigation *f* hauturière; long cours); *~ circle*, rond-point *m,* sens *m* giratoire; *~ lights* [street] feux *mpl* de signalisation. || *v. intr.* trafiquer (*in*, de).

tragedy [ˈtɹædʒ|ədɪ] *n.* tragédie *f.* || **tragic** [-ɪk] *adj.* tragique (*in*, de).

trail [tɹejl] *n.* trace *f* (dans la forêt), piste *f* (de pas). || *v. tr.* suivre (qqun, qqch.) à la piste; [drag] traîner: [Fig.] *to ~ one's coat*, chercher noise à qqun. || *v. intr.* traîner. || **trailer** [-ɚ] *n.* [truck, baggage] remorque *f*; [house] roulotte *f* (de plaisance), caravane *f*; [Cinema] film-annonce *m.*

train¹ [tɹejn] *n.* train *m* (de voyageurs, &c.); traînée *f* (de poudre); escorte *f,* cortège *m,* traîne *f* (d'une robe): (*the*) *express ~*, l'express *m,* le rapide; *local ~*, omnibus *m*; *train (running) to . . .*, train *m* à destination de . . .

train² *v. tr.* [recruit] entraîner (qqun), dresser, dompter (un animal); instruire, former (de nouvelles recrues); exercer, entraîner (un athlète, &c.). || *v. intr.* [soldier] s'entraîner, s'exercer (à), cf. DRILL.

trainer [ˈtɹejnɚ] *n.* [animals] dresseur *m*; [Sport] entraîneur *m.*

training [-ɪŋ] *n.* entraînement *m* (sportif), instruction *f* (d'une recrue), éducation *f* (physique); dressage *m* (d'un chien, &c.).

trait [tɹejt] *n.* trait *m.*

traitor [ˈtɹejtɚ] *n.* traître *m.* || **traitorous** [-əs]

adj. traître *m*, -sse *f*. ‖ **traitress** [ˈtɹejtɹəs] *n.* traîtresse *f*.
trajectory [tɹəˈdʒɛktəɹ] *n.* trajectoire *f*.
tram [tɹæm] *n.* trame *f*.
tramp [-p] *v. intr.* marcher lourdement. ‖ *n.* bruit *m* de pas lourds; [Fam.] chemineau *m*, vagabond *m*.
trample [ˈtɹæmpḷ] *v. tr.* fouler (qqch.) aux pieds, piétiner: *the trampled grass*, l'herbe piétinée.
trance [tɹæns] *n.* transe *f* (*in a*, en); [Fig.] extase *f*.
tranquil [ˈtɹæŋkwɪl] *adj.* tranquille. ‖ **tranquillity** [ˌtɹæŋˈkwɪlɪtɪ] *n.* tranquillité *f*.
transact [ˌtɹænzˈæk|t] *v. tr. & intr.*: *to ~ business*, faire des affaires, traiter une /affaire, opération; négocier, conclure des affaires (avec, *with*). ‖ **transaction** [-ʃən] *n.* opérations *fpl*, négociations *fpl*, conduite *f* des affaires, opération *f* commerciale; *pl.* actes *mpl*, mémoires *mpl* (d'une société).
transalpine [ˌtɹænz|ˈælpajn] *adj.* transalpin. ‖ **transamerican** [-əˈmɛəɹɪkən] *adj.* © transaméricain. ‖ **transatlantic** [-ətˈlæntɪk] *adj.* transatlantique. ‖ **Trans-Canada Airlines,** cf. T.C.A. ‖ **Trans-Canada Highway** [-ˈkænədəˈhajˌwej] la route transcanadienne.
transcend [ˌtɹænˈsɛnd] *v. tr.* transcender, dépasser; surpasser.
transcribe [tɹænˈskɹajb] *v. tr.* transcrire. ‖ **transcript** [ˈtɹænˌskɹɪpt] *n.* texte *m* in extenso (d'un discours), procès-verbal *m* (d'une déclaration); copie *f* (d'un texte écrit); [Univ.] relevé *m* de notes, carnet *m* scolaire. ‖ **transcription** [tɹænˈskɹɪpʃən] *n.* transcription *f*; reproduction *f* (mécanique).
transept [ˈtɹænsɛpt] *n.* [church] transept *m*.
transfer [ˈtɹænsfəɹ] *n.* [of job] changement *m*, déplacement *m*, mutation *f*; [railway, transit] (billet *m* de) correspondance *f*; transport *m*. ‖ *v. tr.* **[-rr-]** [tɹænsˈfəɹ] transférer (qqch.), permuter (des emplois); transporter (qqch.). ‖ *v. intr.* [railway, transit] changer, correspondre: *to ~ trains*, changer de train, changer.
transform [ˌtɹænsˈfɔəɹm] *v. tr.* convertir; transformer (*into*, en). ‖ **transformation** [ˌtɹænsfəɹˈmejʃən] *n.* conversion *f*; transformation *f*; métamorphose *f*; transmutation *f*; changement *m*. ‖ **transformer** [ˌtɹænsˈfɔəɹməɹ] *n.* [Electr.] transformateur *m*.
transfusion [ˌtɹænsˈfjuwʒən] *n.* transvasement *m*; [Méd.] transfusion *f*.
transgress [ˌtɹænsˈgɹɛ|s] *v. tr.* transgresser. *v. intr.* pécher, violer la loi. ‖ **transgression** [-ʃən] *n.* transgression *f*; violation *f* de la loi. ‖ **transgressor** [-səɹ] *n.* violateur *m*.
transient [ˈtɹænzɪənt] *adj.* éphémère, passager, transitoire.
transit [ˈtɹænzɪt] *n.* transit *m* (*in*, en); passage *m*: *sea ~*, parcours *m* maritime.
transition [ˌtræn'zɪʃən] *n.* transition *f*. ‖ **transitory** [ˈtɹænzɪtɔəɹɪ] *adj.* transitoire.
translate [ˌtɹænsˈlej|t] *v. tr.* traduire (*in*, en; *as*, par): *Do not ~*, Ne pas traduire; [religion] transférer (un évêque). ‖ **translation** [-ʃən] *n.* traduction *f*; [religion] translation *f* (d'un évêque). ‖ **translator** [-təɹ] *n.* traducı|eur *m*, -rice *f*.
translucent [ˌtɹænsˈluwsənt] *adj.* diaphane, translucide.
transmission [ˌtɹænsˈmɪ|ʃən] *n.* [Auto., &c.] transmission *f*, boîte *f* de vitesse; émission *f* (radiophonique). ‖ **transmit** [-t] *v. tr.* [-tt-] transmettre (à, *to*). ‖ *v. intr.* [radio] émettre. ‖ **transmitter** [-təɹ] *n.* transmetteur *m*; [radio] émetteur *m*, station *f* émettrice.
transom [ˈtɹænsəm] *n.* linteau *m*; [window] imposte *f*, vasistas *m*.
transparent [ˌtɹænsˈpɛəɹənt] *adj.* transparent; limpide.
transpire [ˌtɹænˈspajəɹ] *v. intr.* transpirer; [Fam.] se produire; se passer.
transplant [tɹænsˈplænt] *v. tr.* [Méd.] greffer; [Bot.] transplanter.
transport [ˈtɹænspɔəɹt] *n.* **1.** transport *m*; moyen *m* de transport. **2.** enthousiasme *m*, élan *m* (de joie). ‖ *v. tr.* [tɹænsˈpowəɹt] transporter (qqch.). ‖ **transportation** [ˌtɹænzpəɹˈtejʃən] *n.* transport *m*: *public ~*, le transport en commun.
transpose [ˌtɹæns|ˈpowz] *v. tr.* transposer. ‖ **transposition** [-pəˈzɪʃən] *n.* transposition *f*.
trap [tɹæp] *v. tr.* **[-pp-]** [game, &c.] attraper, prendre (qqun, qqch.) au piège. ‖ *n.* [door] trappe *f*; piège *m*; [also Fig.] traquenard *m*.
trapeze [tɹəˈpijz] *n.* trapèze *m*.
trapper [-əɹ] *n.* trappeur *m*, © coureur *m* des bois.
trappings [ˈtɹæpɪŋz] *n.* harnachement *m*; [Fig.] atours *mpl*.
trash [tɹæʃ] *n.* rebus *m*; débris *m*, déchets *mpl*; camelote *f*.
trashy [ˈtɹæʃɪ] *adj.* → de camelote, sans valeur.
travel [ˈtɹævḷ] *n.* [employé très rarement au sing., sauf au sens collectif dans les expressions d'aspect duratif: *a six days' ~*, un voyage de six jours, un trajet qui dure six jours] voyage *m*; parcours *m*: *~ bureau*, agence *f* de voyage(s). ‖ **travel**

[**-ll-**] *v. intr.* voyager; faire un trajet. || **traveller** [-ɚ] *n.* voyageu|r, -se: *traveller's cheque,* chèque *m* de voyage. || **travelling** [-ɪŋ] *adj.* [Pers.] ambulant; [thing] mobile. || *n.* voyage(s) *m/pl*: [sac, dépenses, &c.] de voyage.

traverse ['tɹəvɚs] *n.* traversée *f*; [Arch.] traverse *f*. || *v. tr.* [tɹæ'vɚs] traverser; parcourir.

travesty ['tɹævəstɪ] *v. tr.* travestir, parodier. || *n.* travestissement *m.*

tray [tɹej] *n.* [food] plateau *m*; [Photo.] cuvette *f* (pour développement): *ash* ~, cendrier *m*; *letter* ~, boîte *f*, corbeille *f* à correspondance.

treacherous ['tɹɛtʃɚ|əs] *adj.* déloyal; traître, perfide. || **treachery** [-ɪ] *n.* trahison *f.*

treacle ['tɹijkḷ] *n.* [Br.] mélasse *f.*

tread [tɹɛd], **trod** [tɹɑd], **trodden** [tɹɑdṇ] *v. tr.* marcher sur, fouler/(qqch.) (aux pieds); piétiner (le sol, &c.); écraser (qqch.). || *v. intr.* marcher; avancer. || *n.* piétinement *m*, pas *m.*

treason ['tɹijzṇ] *n.* trahison *f.*

treasure ['tɹɛʒɚ] *n.* trésor *m.* || *v. tr.* conserver/soigneusement, précieusement/ (qqch.); tenir beaucoup à (qqch.): *to* ~ (*money*), thésauriser (l'argent). || **treasurer** [-ɚ] *n.* [business] trésorier *m.* || **Treasury** [-ɪ] *n.* (le) Trésor *m*, trésorerie *f*: ~ *Board,* (le) Conseil *m* du Trésor.

treat [tɹijt] *v. intr.* traiter (d'une question, &c., *of a question, &c.*); négocier (avec qqun, *with s.o.*). || *v. tr.* **1.** considérer (qqun, qqch./comme, *s.o., sth./as*). **2.** [Fam.] payer (un verre à qqun). **3.** traiter (une maladie, un malade). || *n.* [drink] tournée *f*; régal *m.* || **treatise** [-ɪs] *n.* traité *m.* || **treatment** [-mənt] *n.* traitement *m*, [Med.] cure *f.* || **treaty** [-ɪ] *n.* [Pol.] traité *m* (de paix, &c.); [agreement, alliance] pacte *m.*

treble ['tɹɛbḷ] *adj.* triple. || *n.* [Mus.] soprano *f.* || *v. tr.* tripler.

tree [tɹij] *n.* **1.** arbre *m.* **2.** [Fig., Rel.] croix *f.* **3.** [boots] embauchoir *m.*

tremble ['tɹɛmbḷ] *v. intr.* trembler (de peur, de froid, *with fear, with cold*).

tremendous [tɹə'mɛndəs] *adj.* [intense] terrible, formidable, épouvantable. || **tremendously** [-lɪ] *adv.* [emphasis] terriblement, extraordinairement.

tremor ['tɹɛm|ɚ] *n.* tremblement *m*, frisson *m*, frémissement *m*: *earth* ~, tremblement de terre. || **tremulous** [-jələs] *adj.* fébrile, fiévreux; tremblant, hésitant.

trench [tɹɛntʃ] *n.* tranchée *f*; [in a field] rigole *f*; [ditch] fossé *m.*

trend [tɹɛnd] *n.* tendance *f*, direction *f*: *the* ~ *of employment,* l'évolution *f* du marché du travail. || *v. intr.* [opinions, &c.] tendre, se diriger vers.

trepidation [ˌtɹɛpɪ'dejʃən] *n.* trépidation *f*; [Fig.] agitation *f*, trac *m.*

trespass ['tɹɛspæs] *v. intr.* **1.** [against] empiéter, enfreindre, offenser. **2.** entrer sans permission. || *n.* [Jur.] délit *m.* || **trespasser** [-ɚ] *n.* intrus *m*; [Jur.] délinquant: *Trespassers will be prosecuted,* → Défense *f* d'entrer sous peine d'amende.

trial ['tɹajl] *n.* essai *m*, tentative *f*; épreuve *f*; [law] procès *m*, jugement *m*: *article sold on a* ~ *basis,* article *m* vendu à titre d'essai.

triangle ['tɹajˌæŋgḷ] *n.* triangle *m.* || **triangular** [ˌtɹaj'æŋgjəlɚ] *adj.* triangulaire.

tribe [tɹajb] *n.* tribu *f.*

tribunal [ˌtɹaj'bjuwnəl] *n.* tribunal *m.*

tributary ['tɹɪbjəˌtɛɚɪ] *adj.* & *n.* tributaire (*m*); [river] affluent *m.*

tribute ['tɹɪbjuwt] *n.* tribut *m*: [Fig.] *to pay* ~ *to,* rendre hommage à.

trice [tɹajs] *n.* bref instant *m*: *in a* ~, en un clin d'œil, en une seconde.

trick [tɹɪk] *n.* **1.** truc *m*, [skill] tour *m*; blague *f*, farce *f.* **2.** ruse *f*; artifice *m*; [cards] levée *f*: *to play a* ~ *on s.o.,* jouer un tour à qqun; *He is up to his old tricks,* Il fait encore des siennes; *a card* ~, un tour de cartes. || *v. tr.* duper (qqun): *to* ~ *s.o. out of his money,* escroquer de l'argent à qqun. || **trickery** [-ɚɪ] *n.* tromperie *f*: *piece of* ~, supercherie *f.*

trickle [tɹɪkḷ] *v. intr.* dégoutter, couler goutte à goutte; [truth] se faire jour, transpirer: *to* ~ *in,* s'infiltrer, pénétrer peu à peu.

tricky [-ɪ] *adj.* [Pers.] rusé, astucieux; (problème) compliqué, (travail) délicat.

tried [tɹajd] cf. TRY.

trifle ['tɹajfḷ] *n.* bagatelle *f*, vétille *f*; petite somme. || *v. tr. to* ~ *away,* gaspiller. || *v. intr.* badiner; agir avec légèreté.

trifler ['tɹajfl|ɚ] *n.* marivaudeur *m*; → (qui n'est) pas sérieux. || **trifling** [-ɪŋ] *adj.* [Pers.] léger, frivole, → pas sérieux; [thing] insignifiant, négligeable. || *n.* légèreté *f*, frivolité *f.*

trigger ['tɹɪgɚ] *n.* [gun] gâchette *f*, détente *f*; déclenchement *m*, déclic *m.*

trill [tɹɪl] *v. intr.* faire des trilles. || *n.* trille *m.*

trim [tɹɪm] *v. tr.* [**-mm-**] arranger (qqch.); tailler (une haie), émonder (un arbre), orner (un arbre de Noël); rafraîchir (les cheveux); battre, corriger (qqun); rogner (un livre). || *n.* (bon) ordre *m*; ornement *m*; attirail *m*: *in perfect* ~ , en parfait état; *in fighting* ~ , prêt pour le combat. || *adj*. ordonné, coquet, soigné. || **trimming** [-ɪŋ] *n*. arrangement *m*, mise *f* en ordre; [haie] taille *f*; [dress, &c.] garniture *f*.

trimonthly [ˌtɹaj'mʌnθlɪ] *adj*. trois fois/le mois, par mois/.

trinket ['tɹɪŋkət] *n*. [trifle] babiole *f*, [jewellery] colifichet *m*.

trip [tɹɪp] *n*. **1.** trajet *m*; voyage *m*. **2.** faux-pas, croc-en-jambe *m*. || *v. intr*. [-pp-] trébucher. || *v. tr*. *to* ~ *up* (*s.o.*), donner un croc-en-jambe à (qqun).

triple ['tɹɪpḷ] *adj*. triple; [Mus.] à trois temps. || *v. tr. & intr*. tripler.

tripod ['tɹajpɑd] *n*. trépied *m*.

trite [tɹajt] *adj*. banal, rebattu.

triumph ['tɹajəmf] *n*. triomphe *m*. || *v. intr*. triompher. || **triumphal** [ˌtɹaj'ʌmf|ḷ] *adj*. triomphant: ~ *arch*, arc *m* de triomphe. || **triumphant** [-ənt] *adj*. triomphant. || **triumphantly** [-əntlɪ] *adv*. triomphalement.

trivial ['tɹɪvɪəl] *adj*. banal, ordinaire, monotone; frivole, léger; insignifiant, sans importance.

trod [tɹɑd] cf. TREAD.

trolley ['tɹɑlɪ] *n*. chariot *m*; diable *m*; petite voiture *f*. || **trolleybus** [-ˌbʌs] *n*. électrobus, *m*, trolleybus *m*.

trombone [ˌtɹɑm'bown] *n*. trombone *m*.

troop [tɹuwp] *n*. troupe *f*, bande *f* (de gens): (*the*) *troops*, (l')armée *f*, (les) troupes *fpl*. || *v. intr*.: [people] *to* ~ *together*, s'attrouper. || **trooper** [-ɚ] *n*. [army] cavalier *m*.

trophy ['tɹowfɪ] *n*. trophée *m*; panoplie *f*.

tropic ['tɹɑpɪk] *n*. tropique *m*. || *adj*. tropical. || **tropical** [-ḷ] *adj*. [climate, plant] tropical.

trot [tɹɑt] *v. intr*. trotter. || *n*. trot *m*.

trouble ['tɹʌbl] *n*. **1.** [bother] dérangement *m*, peine *f*: *to take the* ~ (*to*), se donner la peine (de); *to go to a lot of* ~ (*to*), se donner bien/du mal, de la peine/(pour); *It isn't worth the* ~ (*to*), Ce n'est, Cela ne vaut/pas la peine (de); *It's no* ~ *at all*, Ce n'est rien. **2.** [difficulty] difficulté *f*, ennui *m*: *The* ~ *is that* . . . , L'ennui, la difficulté/c'est que; *What's the* ~ ?, Qu'est-ce qu'il y a?, Qu'est-ce qui ne va pas?; *to get*/*into, out of*/ ~ , s'attirer des ennuis, se tirer d'affaire; *to be in* ~ , avoir des ennuis; *to have* ~ *with s.o*., avoir des désagréments avec qqun; *to make* ~ (*for*), créer des ennuis (à); *to look for* ~ , se préparer des ennuis. **3.** [distress] peine *f*, chagrin *m*; malheur *m*; *Tell me* (*about*) *your troubles*, Racontez-moi vos chagrins; *love trouble*(*s*), chagrins d'amour; *to be in* ~ , être dans l'adversité *f*; *money troubles*, soucis *m* d'argent. **4.** [disorder] dérangement *m*, trouble *m*, mal *m*: *to have heart* ~ , être malade du cœur; souffrir du cœur; *eye* ~ , troubles de vision; [Auto.] *motor* ~ , panne *f* de moteur; *political* ~ , troubles, désordres/politiques. || *v. tr*. **1.** [bother] déranger, importuner/(*with*, avec): *May I* ~ *you for the* . . . , Voudriez-vous me passer le . . . **2.** [pain] affliger, tourmenter, chagriner; [worry] s'inquiéter, se soucier: *to be troubled about sth*., se tourmenter au sujet de qqch.; *Don't* ~ /*yourself*, [Fam.] *your head*/*about that*, Ne vous/inquiétez, [Fam.] tracassez/pas de cela. || *v. intr*. se déranger; s'inquiéter: *Don't* ~*!*, Ne vous dérangez pas; *Don't* ~ *to do it*, Ne vous donnez pas la peine de le faire.

troubled [-d] *adj*. [water] trouble, agité; [Pers.] inquiet. || **troublesome** [-səm] *adj*. [Pers.] ennuyeux, gênant, importun; [event] fâcheux; [circumstance] incommode.

trough [tɹɔf] *n*. abreuvoir *m*; auge *f*: [wave] creux *m*.

trounce [tɹawns] *v. tr*. [Fam.] rosser (qqun), donner une raclée (à qqun).

trousers ['tɹawzɚz] *n.pl*. pantalon *m* [in French Canada, *une paire de pantalons, des pantalons*, is preferred].

trousseau [ˌtɹuw'sow] *n*. trousseau *m*.

trout [tɹawt] *pl*. **trout** *n*. truite *f*: *speckled* ~ , truite *f* mouchetée; *rainbow* ~ , truite *f* arc-en-ciel.

trowel ['tɹawəl] *n*. truelle *f*.

truancy ['tɹuwən|sɪ] *n*. école *f* buissonnière. || **truant** [-t] *n. & adj*. truand, vagabond: *to play* ~ , faire l'école buissonnière.

truce [tɹuws] *n*. trêve *f*.

truck [tɹʌk] *n*. camion *m*. || *v. tr*. camionner (qqch.), transporter (de la marchandise) par camion.

trudge [tɹʌʤ] *v. intr*. cheminer, traîner la jambe. || *v. tr*. parcourir en se traînant.

true [tɹuw] *adj*. vrai; exact; véritable; [heart] sincère, droit, fidèle; [copy] conforme, authentique: *to come* ~ , se réaliser. || **truly** [-lɪ] *adv*. vraiment, réellement; franchement, loyalement, sincèrement; *Yours* ~ , [at the end of a letter] Sincèrement vôtre, Bien à vous, [formal] Veuillez agréer, /Monsieur, Madame/, (l'assurance de) mes salutations distinguées.

trump[1] [tɹʌmp] *v. tr*. [~ *up*] inventer, forger/(une excuse, &c.).

trump[2] *n*.: *a* ~ *card*, un atout: *no-* ~ , sans atout. || *v. tr. & intr*. couper.

trumpet [ˈtɹʌmpət] *n.* trompette *f*; [musician] trompette *m*.

truncheon [ˈtɹʌnʃən] *n.* [police] bâton *m*, matraque *f*.

trunk [tɹʌŋk] *n.* **1.** tronc *m* (d'arbre): *a tree* ~, un tronc d'arbre; *the* ~ *of a tree*, le tronc d'un arbre. **2.** [luggage] (grosse) malle *f*. **3.** trompe *f* (d'éléphant). **4.** [Rail.] ~ *line*, grande ligne *f*; [Telephone] ligne interurbaine.

trust [tɹʌst] *n.* confiance *f* (*in*, en); [hope] espoir *m*, espérance *f*; [duty] charge *f*, responsabilité *f*; [safekeeping] garde *f*, dépôt *m*; [Jur.] fiducie *f*; [Com.] crédit *m* (*on*, à); [Ind.] trust *m*: ~ *company*, société *f* de fiducie. ‖ *v. tr.* avoir confiance en, se fier à; confier (*s.o. with sth.*, qqch. à qqun); [hope] espérer: *Don't* ~ *him out of your sight*, Ne le perdez pas de vue. ‖ *v. intr.* avoir confiance (*in*, en), se fier (*in*, à); compter (*in*, sur); se fier, se confier, faire confiance, s'en remettre (*to*, à); espérer. ‖ **trusted** [-əd] *adj.* [Pers., thing] de confiance. ‖ **trustee** [ˌtɹʌstˈij] *n.* [heritage, &c.] dépositaire *m* (de qqch., *for sth.*); administrateur *m* (d'une société); [in a bankruptcy, &c.] syndic *m*. ‖ **trustworthy** [ˈtɹʌst|ˌwəðɪ] *adj.* [Pers.] digne de confiance; [thing] sûr, © fiable. ‖ **trusty** [-ɪ] *adj.* [Pers.] (digne) de confiance, loyal, sûr.

truth [tɹuwθ] *n.* vérité *f*: *to tell the* ~, dire la vérité, . . . à vrai dire . . . ; *There is some* ~ *in that*, Il y a du vrai là-dedans. ‖ **truthful** [-fḷ] *adj.* vrai, véridique; [Pers.] sincère. ‖ **truthfulness** [-fḷnəs] *n.* véracité *f* (d'un récit, &c.).

try [traj] *n.* essai *m*, tentative *f*/(*to*, de): *to have a* ~ *at* (*doing*) *sth.*, essayer (de faire) qqch.; *at the first* ~, au premier essai, du premier coup. ‖ *v. tr.* [also Fig.] essayer, éprouver, mettre à l'épreuve; tenter, faire, (une expérience); [Jur.] juger (qqun): *to* ~ *o.'s*/*best, hardest*/(*to*), faire/tous ses efforts, tout son possible/(pour); *to* ~ *o.'s luck*, tenter sa chance; *to* ~ *o.'s hand at sth.*, s'essayer à qqch. ‖ *v. intr.* essayer, tâcher/(*to*, de); chercher (*to*, à): *to* ~ *for sth.*, tâcher d'avoir qqch. ‖ **try on** *v. tr.* essayer. ‖ **try out** *v. tr.* faire l'essai de, essayer à fond, mettre à l'épreuve. ‖ **trying** *adj.* pénible, difficile; contrariant, ennuyeux.

T-shirt [ˈtijˌʃət] *n.* © maillot *m*.

tub [tʌb] *n.* cuve *f*, baquet *m*; [bath] baignoire *f*.

tube [tjuwb] *n.* tube *m*; conduit *m*, tuyau *m*; [Br.] métro *m*; lampe *f*, tube *m* (de radio); [Auto.] chambre *f* à air.

tubercular [tjuwˈbəkjələ] *adj.* tuberculeux. ‖ **tubercule** [ˈtjuwbək|ḷ] *n.* tubercule *m*. ‖ **tuberculosis** [tjuwˌbəkjəˈlowsɪs] *n.* tuberculose *f*.

tuck [tʌk] *n.* **1.** pli *m*. **2.** sucreries *fpl*: ~ *-shop*, confiserie *f*; cantine *f*. ‖ *v. tr.* plisser; enfoncer (*in*, dans): *to* ~ *s.o. in* (*bed*), border; *to* ~ *up*, border (qqun), retrousser (ses manches).

Tuesday [ˈtjuwzdɪ] [-dej] *n.* mardi *m*.

tuft [tʌft] *n.* touffe *f* (de cheveux); [bird] huppe *f*.

tug [tʌg] *v. tr.* & *intr.* [-gg-] tirer (fort) (*at*, sur); [Fig.] tirailler; [Nau.] remorquer (un bateau). ‖ *n.* tiraillement *m*; effort *m* de traction; ~ *of war*, lutte *f*, © souque *f* à la corde; *tugboat*, remorqueur *m*.

tugboat [ˈtʌgˌbowt] *n.* remorqueur *m*.

tuition [ˌtjuwˈɪʃən] *n.* **1.** enseignement *m*; cours *n.pl.* [surtout Br.], instruction *f*. **2.** frais *mpl* scolaires: ~ *fees*, frais *mpl* de scolarité.

tulip [ˈtjuwlɪp] *n.* tulipe *f*.

tumble [ˈtʌmbḷ] *v. intr.* **1.** tomber, dégringoler: *to* ~ *down*, débouler, culbuter; *to* ~ *over*, faire la culbute. ‖ *n.* chute *f*, dégringolade *f*, culbute *f*. ‖ **tumble-down** [-ˌdawn] *adj.* croulant, délabré.

tumbler [ˈtʌmblə] *n.* gobelet *m*, verre *m*; [Tech.] culbuteur *m*.

tumefy [ˈtjuwm|əˌfaj] *v. tr.* tuméfier. ‖ **tumour** [-ə] *n.* tumeur *f*.

tumult [ˈtjuwmʌlt] *n.* tumulte *m*; émoi *m*, agitation *f*. ‖ **tumultuous** [tjuwˈmʌltʃuwəs] *adj.* tumultueux.

tuna [tjuwnə] *n.* [fish] thon *m*.

tune [tjuwn] *n.* **1.** air *m* (de musique), mélodie *f*; [speech] ton *m*; accord *m* (de piano, &c.), harmonie *f*: *to sing out of* ~, chanter faux. *This instrument is in* ~, Cet instrument est/d'accord, juste. **2.** [motor] ~ *up*, réglage *m*. ‖ *v. tr.* accorder (un piano, &c.): *to* ~ *in to a* (*radio*) *station*, prendre, capter, syntoniser/un poste (de radio); *to* ~ (*up*) *a motor*, *&c.*, régler, (re)mettre/un moteur, &c. au point. ‖ *v. intr.* [Fam.]: *to* ~ (*up*) *with s.o.*, *sth.*, s'accorder, être en harmonie/avec qqun, qqch.

tunic [ˈtjuwnɪk] *n.* tunique *f*.

tuning [ˈtjuwnɪŋ] *n.* [Mus.] accordage *m*; [Radio] réglage *m*, syntonisation *f*: ~ *fork*, diapason *m*.

tunnel [ˈtʌnḷ] *n.* tunnel *m*. ‖ *v. tr.* [-ll-] [mountain, &c.] percer un tunnel dans (qqch.).

tuque [tuwk] © *n.* © tuque *f*.

turbine [ˈtəbajn] [-bɪn] *n.* turbine *f*.

turbulent [ˈtəbjələnt] *adj.* agité, indiscipliné.

turf [tɚf] *n.* gazon *m*; motte *f*; tourbe *f*.
Turk [tɚk] *n.* turc, -que. || **Turkey** [-ɪ] *n.* Turquie *f*: *in, to*/ ~, en T. || **turkey** [-ɪ] *n.* [fowl] dinde *f*, dindon *m*. || **Turkish** [-ɪʃ] *n. & adj.* turc.
turmoil [ˈtɚmojl] *n.* agitation *f*; effervescence *f*; trouble *m*, remous *m*.
turn [tɚn] *n.* **1.** tour *m* (de roue, &c.): (*done*) *to a* ~, (cuit) à point. **2.** [change of direction] changement *m* (de la marée, &c.); [Auto.] virage *m*; [road] tournant *m*; [Fig.] tournure *f*: *to take a* ~ (*to the right*), prendre un virage; tourner, prendre/à droite; *the next* ~ *to the right*, le prochain tournant, la prochaine rue à droite; *No left* ~, Virage à gauche interdit; [Fig.] *to take a* ~ *for the better*, s'améliorer, changer pour le mieux; *Matters have taken a new* ~, Les choses ont pris une nouvelle tournure; [Fig.] *at every* ~, à tout/propos, bout de champ/. [place in order] tour *m*: *It is my* ~ (*to do it*), C'est mon tour, C'est à moi (de le faire); *by turns*, tour à tour, *in* ~, à tour de rôle; *out of* ~, avant/son, votre, &c./ tour; *to take turns*, faire qqch. à tour de rôle. **4.** [deed] action *f*: *to do s.o. a/good, bad/* ~, rendre un service, jouer un mauvais tour/à qqun. **5.** [stroll] tour *m*: *to/go for, take/a* ~ *in*, (aller) faire un tour dans. **6.** [Fam.] choc *m*, coup *m*: *It gave me quite a* ~, Cela m'a donné un coup. **7.** [style] tournure *f* (d'une phrase, d'esprit). || **turn** *v. tr.* **1.** [rotate] tourner; [= ~ /around, over] retourner: [Fig.] *Success turned his head*, Le succès lui a tourné la tête; [Fig.] *without turning a hair*, sans/broncher, sourciller/. **2.** [direct] diriger ses pas vers, tourner (ses pensées vers): *to* ~ *o.'s attention to*, diriger son attention vers, attirer l'attention de qqun sur; *to* ~ *o.'s attention from*, détourner l'attention de; *to* ~ *s.o. from*, détourner qqun de; [Fig.] *to* ~ *sth. to good use*, mettre qqch. à profit; [Fig.] *to* ~ *a deaf ear* (*to*), faire la sourde oreille (à). **3.** [transform] changer, transformer (en, *into*). **4.** [make, become] rendre + adj., (faire +) spec. verb: *to* ~ *s.o. sick*, rendre qqun malade; *to* ~ */sth., s.o./red*, faire rougir qqch., faire tourner qqch. au rouge, faire rougir qqun; *to* ~ *the milk* (*sour*), faire tourner le lait; *to* ~ *s.o.'s stomach*, soulever le cœur à qqun. **5.** [go past] tourner (un coin): *He has just turned eighteen*, Il vient d'atteindre ses dix-huit ans; *It has already turned eleven* (*o'clock*), Il est déjà onze heures passées. **6.** [make] tourner: *to* ~ *on a lathe*, tourner qqch., faire qqch. au tour; [Fig.] *a well-turned phrase*, une expression bien tournée. **7.** [blunt] émousser. || *v. intr.* **1.** [rotate] [things] tourner, [Pers.] se tourner; [~ around, over], (se) retourner: [Fig.] *The outcome turned on his answer*, Le résultat dépendait de sa réponse. **2.** [change direction] tourner; changer; tourner, prendre (à droite, à gauche); se diriger (vers); [Fig.] avoir recours à; passer (à un autre sujet); porter l'attention (sur): *The/wind, tide/turned*, /Le vent, La marée/a changé (de direction); [Fig.] *The tide turned*, Le courant a changé; [Fig.] *He didn't know which way to* ~, Il ne savait pas où donner de la tête; *Even a worm will* ~, La patience a des limites. **3.** [change] se changer, se transformer (en, */to, into/*). **4.** [become] devenir + adj., spec. verb: *to* ~ *red*, devenir rouge, rougir; *The milk turned* (*sour*), Le lait a tourné; *The leaves were turning* (*yellow*), Les feuilles jaunissaient. || **turn about, around** [-əˈbawt|əˈɹawnd] *v. tr.* (re)-tourner; faire faire demi-tour (à qqun). || *v. intr.* se (re)tourner; faire demi-tour: [Mil.] *About turn!*, Demi-tour!; *Turn around!*, Retournez-vous!; *Turn around a bit*, Tournez-vous un peu! || **to turn aside** [-əˈsajd] *v. tr. & intr.* (se) détourner, (s')écarter. || **to turn away** [-əˈwej] *v. tr.* [head, eyes] détourner; écarter (la colère de qqun); congédier (qqun); refuser (du monde). || *v. intr.* [person] se détourner: [Fig.] *He turned away from her*, Il l'a délaissée. || **turn back** [-ˈbæk] *v. tr.* faire revenir (qqun) sur ses pas; repousser (une attaque, l'ennemi). || *v. intr.* revenir sur ses pas, rebrousser chemin. || **turn down** [-ˈdawn] *v. tr.* rabattre (un col); baisser (les lumières); refuser (une offre, un candidat). || **turn in** [-ˈɪn] *v. tr.* rentrer, replier; rendre, restituer. || *v. intr.* s'engager dans; (aller) se coucher. || **turn off** [-ˈɔf] *v. tr.* fermer (l'eau, le gaz), éteindre (la lumière, la radio); quitter (la route). || **turn on** [-ˈɑn] *v. tr.* ouvrir (le robinet); faire couler (l'eau); allumer (le gaz, la lumière, la radio); /attaquer, se retourner contre/(qqun). || **turn out** [-ˈawt] *v. tr.* **1.** mettre dehors, à la porte; renverser (le gouvernement); vider (un bureau). **2.** produire, fabriquer: [Pers.] *well turned out*, bien/mis, habillé/. **3.** éteindre (le gaz, la lumière, &c.). || *v. intr.* **1.** sortir; assister (à): *The whole class turned out*, Toute la classe y a assisté. **2.** finir: */He, It/turned out/well, badly/*, Il a/bien, mal/tourné; *The weather*

turned out fine, Le temps a tourné au beau. **3.** arriver, se trouver: *It turns out that . . . ,* Il se trouve que . . . . || **turn over** [-'owvɚ] *v. tr.* **1.** retourner; tourner (une page): *to turn sth. over (and over) in o.'s mind,* tourner et retourner qqch. dans son esprit. **2.** transférer, remettre (qqch. à qqun). || *v. intr.* [Pers.] se retourner (dans son lit); [car, plane] capoter; [boat] chavirer. || **turn round** cf. TURN AROUND. || **turn up** [-'ʌp] *v. tr.* relever (son col); retrousser (ses manches); donner un peu plus de (lumière, [radio] son); retourner (le sol, une carte); déterrer; découvrir: [Fig.] *to ~ o'.s nose at sth.,* dédaigner qqch. || *v. intr.* venir, arriver, se présenter; [card] sortir.

turncoat [-ˌkowt] *n.* renégat *m,* [Rel.] apostat *m*; [traitor] transfuge *m.* || **turning** [-ɪŋ] *n.* [Tech.] tournage *m.* || **turning point** [-ɪŋˌpojnt] *n.* le moment/décisif, critique/, le tournant (de, *of*).

turnip ['tɚnɪp] *n.* navet *m.*

turnout [-ˌawt] *n.* assistance *f*; [output] rendement *m* (d'une usine): *a/good, poor/ ~ ,* une assistance/nombreuse, peu nombreuse/; *Let's have a good ~ !,* Venez nombreux!

turnover [-'owvɚ] *n.* renversement *m*; [Com.] chiffre *m* d'affaires: *apple ~ ,* chausson *m* aux pommes.

turnpike ['tɚnˌpajk] *n.* †barrière *f* de péage; [Auto.] autoroute *f* à péage.

turntable [-ˌtejbḷ] *n.* plaque *f* tournante.

turpentine ['tɚpənˌtajn] *n.* térébenthine *f.*

turtle ['tɚtḷ] *n.* tortue *f*: *~ dove,* tourterelle *f.*

tutor ['tjuwtɚ] *n.* précepteur *m,* répétiteur *m.* || *v. tr.* [Jur.] être tuteur de.

tuxedo [tʌk'sijdow] *n.* veston *m* de demi-cérémonie; smoking *m.*

TV ['tijˌvij] [= television] © la T.V., [Fr.] la télé: *~ viewer,* téléspectat|eur, -rice.

twang [twæŋ] *v. intr.* [strings] vibrer, résonner; [speech] nasiller, parler du nez. || *v. tr.* [Mus.] gratter de (la guitare).

†'twas [twʌz] = it was. || **†'twere** [twɚ] it were. cf. TO BE.

tweed [twijd] *n.* tweed *m.*

tweezers ['twijzɚs] *n.pl.* pince *f.*

twelfth [twɛlfθ] *adj. num. ord.* (le, la, les) douzième(s): *~ Night,* La Nuit des Rois, les Rois. || **twelve** [twɛlv] *adj. num. card.* douze.

twentieth ['twɛntɪ|əθ] *adj. num. ord.* (le, la, les) vingtième(s). || **twenty** *adj. num. card.* vingt.

twice [twajs] *adv.* deux fois.

twiddle ['twɪdḷ] *v. tr.* tourner (qqch. entre ses doigts): *to ~ one's thumbs,* se tourner les pouces.

twig [twɪg] *n.* [Bot.] brindille *f.*

twilight ['twajˌlajt] *n.* crépuscule *m.*

twin [twɪn] *adj. & n.* jumeau *m,* jumelle *f*: *~ -engine,* bi-moteur *m.*

twine [twajn] *n.* ficelle *f.* || *v. tr.* enrouler (du fil, &c.). || *v. intr.* [thread, &c.] s'enrouler.

twinge [twɪndʒ] *v. intr.* élancer, cf. THROB; lanciner, tourmenter. || *n.* élancement *m*; brûlure *f* (de remords).

twinkle ['twɪŋkḷ] *v. intr.* scintiller, étinceler. || *n.* scintillement *m*; cliquement *m,* clignotement *m.* || **twinkling** [-ɪŋ] *n.*: *in the ~ of an eye,* en un clin d'œil.

twirl [twɚl] *v. intr.* tournoyer. || *n.* tournoiement *m*; fioriture *f.*

twist [twɪst] *n.* [strand] cordon *m* (de soie, &c.); (con)torsion *f,* tortillement *m*; [sharp] détour *m*; [moral] prédisposition *f* (à). || *v. tr.* tordre, enrouler, entrelacer (des fils, &c.). || *v. intr.* se tortiller, s'enrouler, s'entrelacer. || **twister** [-ɚ] *n.* cyclone *m,* tornade *f*; © sorcière *f,* tourniquet *m.*

twitch [twɪtʃ] *n.* saccade *f*; crispation *f.* || *v. intr.* se crisper, se contracter; [nose] remuer.

twitter ['twɪtɚ] *n* gazouillement *m*, [Fam.] agitation *f.* || *v. intr.* gazouiller.

two [tuw] *adj. num. card.* deux *m*: *~ by ~ ,* deux à deux; *~ -door sedan,* coach *m*; *~ -faced,* homme/à double face, à deux visages/. || **twofold** [-ˌfowld] *adj.* double.

tycoon [ˌtaj'|kuwn] *n.* potentat *m,* magnat *m* de l'industrie.

tying [-ɪŋ] cf. TIE.

tympan ['tɪmpən] *n.* tympan *m.*

type [tajp] *n.* [Pers., thing] type *m*; individu *m*; caractère *m* (d'imprimerie); [kind] type, genre *m.* || *v. tr.* cf. TYPEWRITE. || **typesetter** [-ˌsɛtɚ] *n.* typographe *m.* || **typewrite** [-ˌɹajt], **typewrote** [-ˌɹowt], **typewritten** [[-ɹɪtṇ] *v. tr.* dactylographier (un document), taper (qqch.) à la machine. || **typewriter** [-ˌɹajtɚ] *n.* machine *f* à écrire, © clavigraphe *m.* || **typewritten** [-ˌɹɪtṇ] *adj.* (document, acte) dactylographié.

typhoid ['tajˌfojd] *n.* typhoïde *f.*

typhoon [taj'fuwn] *n.* typhon *m.*

typhus ['tajfəs] *n.* typhus *m.*

typical ['tɪpɪkḷ] *adj.* [detail, feature] typique, caractéristique.

typify ['tɪpɪˌfaj] représenter, symboliser. **typist** ['tajpɪst] *n.* dactylo *m/f.* **tyrannical** [tɪ'ɹænɪkl̩] *adj.* tyrannique. || **tyranny** ['tijərənɪ] *n.* tyrannie *f.* || **tyrant** ['tajərənt] *n.* tyran *m.* **tyre** [tajər] *n.* [Br.] cf. TIRE.[2]

U

U, u [juw] *n.* U, u *m*: *U-boat,* sous-marin *m* (allemand); *U-turn,* virage *m* sur place.

U.E.L. [juwij'ɛl] *abr.* = © *United Empire Loyalists,* les Loyalistes *m, fpl* de l'Empire Uni.

ugliness ['ʌglinəs] *n.* laideur *f.* || **ugly** ['ʌglɪ] *adj.* laid; [Fig.] mauvais, dangereux: *in an ~ mood,* d'une humeur dangereuse.

U.K. ['juw'kej] *abr.* = *United Kingdom,* R.-U. = Royaume-Uni *m*: *to, in / the ~,* dans le Royaume-Uni.

ulcer ['ʌlsər] *n.* ulcère *m.*

ulterior [ʌl'tijərjər] *adj.* ultérieur; secret.

ultimate ['ʌltimət] *adj.* final [*mpl*: finals]; définitif. || **ultimately** ['ʌltimətli] *adv.* finalement; en définitive, en dernière analyse.

ultimatum [ˌʌltɪ'mejtəm] *n.* ultimatum *m.*

umbrella [ʌm'bɹɛlə] *n.* parapluie *m*; [sunshade] ombrelle *f.*

umpire ['ʌmpajər] *n.* arbitre *m.* || *v. tr.* arbitrer.

UN, U.N. ['juw'ɛn] [autrefois *U.N.O.*] *abr.* = *United Nations* (*Organization*), l'ONU *f.* [lɔ'ny] = les Nations Unies, l'Organisation des Nations Unies.

un- [ˌʌn-] Préfixe négatif, correspondant souvent au français *il-, im-, in-, ir-, dé-, non-, mal-,* ainsi qu'à des constructions avec *pas, peu, mal,* &c. **1.** ☞ *Orthographe*: Normalement, le préfixe *un-* se colle sans aucun trait d'union au radical qu'il modifie. Cependant, pour distinguer ici les mots préfixés de *un-* des autres mots commençant par UN-, on a utilisé ici la barre simple verticale; cette barre indique, par la même occasion, que le radical simple existe séparément, ex. **un|able** (V. ABLE) différent de **unanimous.** **2.** ☞ *Ordre alphabétique*: Le nombre des mots "négativés" par *un-* est considérable. On a indiqué ici les principaux, dans leur ordre alphabétique. Ils sont tous considérés comme rentrant dans une rubrique unique; celle-ci peut être coupée par des mots commençant par UN, qui constituent alors des articles séparés. **3.** ☞ For further help in distinguishing between Fr. equivalents of words in *un-*, students should consult the affirmative form of the word. **4.** ☞ Used predicatively, adjs. in *un-* may often be translated by a Fr. verb in the neg. (this must be done in the case of Fr. translations formed by placing 'non' before an affirmative adj.): *I am unafraid,* → Je n'ai pas peur; *an unfurnished room,* une chambre non meublée; *This room is unfurnished,* → Cette chambre n'est pas meublée.

un|able [ˌʌn'ejbl̩] *adj.* incapable de, [powerless] impuissant à (faire qqch.): *I was ~ to come,* Je n'ai pas pu / J'ai été empêché de, J'ai été dans l'impossibilité de / venir; *He was ~ to answer,* Il n'a pas/pu, su/répondre, Il a été incapable de répondre. || **un|acceptable** [ˌʌnək'sɛptəbl̩] *adj.* inacceptable. || **un|accompanied** [ˌʌnə'kʌmpənɪd] *adj.* seul; non accompagné (de); [Mus.] sans accompagnement, a capella. || **un|accountable** [ˌʌnə'kawntəbl̩] *adj.* inexplicable, étrange, bizarre. || **unaccountably** [-lɪ] *adv.* d'une manière étrange, inexplicable; sans raison apparente, sans qu'on sache pourquoi. || **un|accounted for** [ˌʌnə'kawntədˌfɔər] *adj.* **1.** inexpliqué, inexplicable: *There still remain things ~,* Beaucoup de choses demeurent encore inexpliquées / inexplicables/. **2.** [missing] dont on ne saurait expliquer la disparition; [person] qui manque à l'appel, [Mil.] porté disparu: *Two guests from the hotel that burnt down are still ~,* Deux clients de l'hôtel ravagé par les flammes manquent toujours à l'appel; *There were* 30 *dollars* ~, Il manquait 30 dollars. || **un|accustomed** [ˌʌnəˈkʌstəmd] *adj.* inhabituel, inaccoutumé, inusité: *to be ~ to,* être inaccoutumé à, ne pas avoir l'habitude de. || **un|acknowledged** [ˌʌnəkˈnɑləʤd] *adj.* non reconnu; (lettre) sans réponse. || **un|acquainted** [ˌʌnəˈkwejntəd] *adj. to be ~ with,* être peu familier avec (les coutumes du pays), être peu versé dans (les arts), ignorer (qqch.), ne pas connaître (qqun) || **un|affected** [ˌʌnəˈfɛktəd] *adj.* simple, naïf, naturel; impassible: ~ *by,* [person] insensible à, [thing] qui résiste à, qui n'est pas affecté par. || **un|afraid** [ˌʌnəˈfɹejd] *adj.* sans peur: *He is ~,* → Il n'a pas peur. || **un|aided** [ˌʌnˈejdəd] *adj.* tout seul, sans aide; → par ses propres moyens. || **un|alloyed** [ˌʌnˈælojd] *adj.* pur, sans alliage; [Fig.] pur, sans mélange. || **un|alterable** [ˌʌnˈɑltɚ|əbl̩] *adj.* [×] immuable. || **un|altered** [-d] *adj.* inchangé, sans changement.

unanimity [ˌjʊnəˈnɪmətɪ] *n.* unanimité *f.* || **unanimous** [jʊˈnænɪməs] *adj.* unanime. || **unanimously** *adv.* à l'unanimité, unanimement: *carried ~,* voté à l'unanimité.

un|answerable [ˌʌnˈænsɚəbl̩] *adj.* incontestable, sans réplique; → auquel on ne saurait répliquer, &c. || **un|appreciated** [ˌʌnəˈpɹɪʃɪˌejtəd] *adj.* inapprécié; incompris. || **un|approachable** [ˌʌnəˈpɹowtʃəbl̩] *adj.* [place] inaccessible; [person] inabordable; [Fig.] incomparable. || **un|armed** [ˌʌnˈɑɚmd] *adj.* sans armes; désarmé. || **un|asked** [ˌʌnˈæskt] *adj.* spontanément; → sans (y) être invité. || **un|assuming** [ˌʌnəˈsjuwmɪŋ] *adj.* sans prétention; modeste. || **un|attainable** [ˌʌnəˈtejnəbl̩] *adj.* inaccessible; hors de portée, impossible. || **un|attractive** [ˌʌnəˈtɹæktəv] *adj.* sans attrait, peu attrayant; peu sympathique. || **un|authorized** [ˌʌnˈɔθɚˌajzd] *adj.* sans autorisation, → non pourvu d'une autorisation; défendu, illicite. || **un|available** [ˌʌnəˈvejləbl̩] *adj.* non disponible, → que l'on ne peut se procurer; (article) épuisé. || **unavailing** [ˌʌnəˈvejlɪŋ] *adj.* inutile. || **un|avoidable** [ˌʌnəˈvojdəbl̩] *adj.* inévitable. || **unavoidably** *adv.* inévitablement, à coup sûr. || **un|aware** [ˌʌnəˈwɛɚ] *adj.*: *to be ~ of,* ignorer, → qui n'est pas au courant de: *I am not ~ that,* Je n'ignore pas que. || **unawares** [ˌʌnəˈwɛəz] *adv.* à l'improviste; à l'insu de qqun, à mon/son/insu, *to be caught/taken/ ~,* être pris au dépourvu. || **un|balanced** [ˌʌnˈbælənst] *adj.* non équilibré; [mind] déséquilibré; [bank account] non soldé. || **un|bearable** [ˌʌnˈbɛɚabl̩] *adj.* insupportable; [situation] intolérable. || **un|beatable** [ˌʌnˈbijtəbl̩] *adj.* imbattable, invincible. || **un|beaten** [ˌʌnˈbijtn̩] *adj.* invaincu. || **un|becoming** [ˌʌnbɪˈkʌmɪŋ] *adj.* → qui ne sied pas, → qui ne convient pas (à); inconvenant, déplacé. || **un|believable** [ˌʌnbɪˈlijvəbl̩] *adj.* incroyable. || **un|believer** [ˌʌnbɪˈlijvɚ] *n.* incroyant *m,* -e *f.* || **un|believing** [ˌʌnbɪˈlijvɪŋ] *adj.* incrédule, sceptique. || **un|bend** [ˌʌnˈbɛnd] **unbent, unbent** [ˌʌnˈbɛnt] *v. tr.* [straighten] rendre droit, redresser; [relax] détendre, relâcher; [Fig.] délasser (le corps, l'esprit). || *v. intr.* se détendre; se laisser fléchir. || **un|bending** [ˌʌnˈbɛndɪŋ] *adj.* inflexible, intransigeant. || **un|biased** [ˌʌnˈbajəst] *adj.* sans préjugé, impartial. || **un|bind** [ˌʌnˈbajnd] **unbound, unbound** [ˌʌnˈbawnd] *v. tr.* délier, desserrer (des liens, des noeuds), défaire (des noeuds), détacher. || **un|bounded** [ˌʌnˈbawndəd] *adj.* infini, sans limite(s), illimité; sans bornes, démesuré. || **un|breakable** [ˌʌnˈbɹejkəbl̩] *adj.* incassable. || **un|broken** [ˌʌnˈbɹowkn̩] *adj.* intact; ininterrompu, continu; [Fig.] indomptable, indompté. || **un|button** [ˌʌnˈbʌtn̩] *v. tr.* déboutonner. || **un|called-for** [ˌʌnˈkɔldˌfɔə] *adj.* [remark] déplacé, [insult] gratuit; inutile, non mérité, → que rien ne justifie. || **un|canny** [ˌʌnˈkænɪ] *adj.* étrange, mystérieux; surnaturel. || **unceasing** [ˌʌnˈsijsɪŋ] *adj.* incessant, → sans cesse. || **unceasingly** *adv.* sans cesse, sans arrêt. || **un|certain** [ˌʌnˈsɚtn̩] *adj.* incertain, peu sûr (de qqch., de soi-même); hésitant, mal assuré: *to be ~,* → ne pas savoir. || **un|certainty** [ˌʌnˈsɚtəntɪ] *n.* incertitude *f.*, l'incertain *m.* || **un|chain** [ˌʌnˈtʃejn] *v. tr.* déchaîner. || **un|changeable** [ˌʌnˌtʃejnʤəbl̩] *adj.* inaltérable, immuable. || **un|changed** [ˌʌnˈtʃejnʤd] *adj.* invariable, inchangé; → toujours/le, la/même. || **un|changing** [ˌʌnˈtʃejnʤɪŋ] *adj.* → qui ne change pas, qui demeure; constant, invariable. || **un|charitable** [ˌʌnˈtʃæɚətəbl] *adj.* peu charitable. || **un|chartered** [ˌʌnˈtʃɑɚtəd] *adj.* inexploré; non porté sur la carte. || **un|civilized** [ˌʌnˈsɪvl̩ˌajzd] *adj.* incivilisé; [Pej.] barbare.

uncle [ˈʌnkl̩] *n.* oncle *m* [Fam., Fr.] tonton *m*: *Uncle Sam,* l'Oncle Sam.

un|clean [ˌʌnˈklijn] *adj.* malpropre, sale; [Fig.] impur. || **un|cleanliness** [ˌʌnˈklɛnlɪnəs] *n.* malpropreté *f,* saleté *f*; [Fig.] impureté *f.* ||**un| comfortable** [ˌʌnˈkʌmfɚtəbl̩] *adj.* [things] peu confortable, incommode; [persons] mal à l'aise, mal à son aise; [Fig.] [sensations] désagréable; [persons] gêné, inquiet. || **un|comfortably** *adv.* peu confortablement, incommodément; mal à aise; désagréablement. || **un|common** [ˌʌn'kɑmən] *adj.* peu commun, peu ordinaire, → sortant de l'ordinaire; rare, extraordinaire. || **un|commonly** *adv.* rarement; singulièrement, extrêmement. || **un|completed** [ˌʌnkəm'plijtəd] *adj.* inachevé, incomplet. || **un|complimentary** [ˌʌnˌkamplə'mɛnt(ɚ)ɹɪ] *adj.* peu flatteur *m.* || **un|compromising** [ˌʌn'kɑmpɹəˌmajzɪŋ] *adj.* intransigeant. || **un|concerned** [ˌʌnkən'sɚnd] *adj.* indifférent, imperturbable, → sans broncher. || **un|concernedly** [ˌʌnkən'sɚnədlɪ] *adv.* avec indifférence, sans paraître s'apercevoir de . . . || **un|conditional** [ˌʌnkən'dɪʃənl̩] *adj.* sans conditions. || **un|congenial** [ˌʌnkən'ʤijnjl̩] *adj.* peu agréable, désagréable; [person] peu sympathique. || **un|conquered** [ˌʌn'kɑŋkɚd] *adj.* inconquis; indompté. || **un|conscious** [ˌʌn'kɑnʃəs] *adj.* **1.** inconscient, sans connaissance. **2.** ignorant, n'ayant pas conscience de. || **un|consciously** [ˌʌn'kɑnʃəslɪ] *adv.* à mon/ton, son/insu; sans le savoir, inconsciemment. || **un|consciousness** [ˌʌn'kɑnʃəsnəs] *n.* inconscience *f*, ignorance *f*; évanouissement *m*; insensibilité *f*: *to lapse into* ~, perdre connaissance. || **un|controllable** [ˌʌnkən'tɹowləbl̩] *adj.* irrésistible; (rire) inextinguible, cf. CONTROL. || **un|controlled** [ˌʌnkən'tɹowld] *adj.* indépendant; [feelings] indompté. || **un|conventional** [ˌʌnkən'vɛnʃənl̩] *adj.* non conformiste, original; → qui ne se soumet pas aux conventions. || **uncouth** [ˌʌn'kuwθ] *adj.* [coarse] grossier; [awkward] gauche. || **un|cover** [ˌʌn'kʌvɚ] *v. tr.* découvrir, exposer aux regards: *to* ~ (*o.s., one's head*), se découvrir. || **un|critical** [ˌʌn'kɹɪtɪkl̩] *adj.* → dépourvu de sens critique; → peu porté à critiquer.

unction ['ʌnkʃən] *n.* onction *f*: [Rel.] *Extreme Unction*, l'Extrême-Onction.

unctuous [ˌʌŋkʃəs] *adj.* onctueux; [Pej.] mielleux.

un|cultivated [ˌʌn'kʌltəˌvejtəd] *adj.* inculte, en friche, non cultivé; [person] sans culture. || **un|cultured** [ʌń'kʌlʧɚd] *adj.* [land] inculte; [person] sans culture. || **un|damaged** [ʌn'dæməʤd] *adj.* non endommagé, intact. || **un|decided** [ˌʌndə'sajdəd] *adj.* [person] irrésolu, incertain, indécis; [question, &c.] non décidé, en suspens: *He is* ~ *about going*, Il est indécis au sujet de son départ, Il ne peut (pas) décider s'il y va (ou non). || **un|delivered** [ˌʌndə'lɪvɚd] *adj.* non livré, non distribué: *If* ~ *please return to* . . . , En cas de non-remise, prière de retourner à . . . || **un|deniable** [ˌʌndə'najəbl̩] *adj.* incontestable, irréfutable; évident, → qui saute aux yeux. || **un|deniably** *adv.* incontestablement, de toute évidence.

under ['ʌndɚ] *prép.* **1.** [= underneath] sous, dessous, en dessous, par-dessous: *to be, go*/ ~ *sth.*, être, aller/sous qqch.; (*come out*) *from* ~ *sth.*, (sortir) de sous qqch.; (*to go*) ~ *it* [and stay there], (aller, se mettre) (en) dessous; [and out the other side] (passer) par-dessous; *put sth.* ~ *that*, Mettez-/le, la, les/là-dessous; (*to come out*) *from* ~ *it*, (sortir) d'en dessous; *It isn't on the table, it's* ~ *it*, Ce n'est pas sur la table, c'est en dessous. **2.** [= below] au-dessous (de), moins de: *the apartment* ~ *us*, l'appartement au-dessous de nous; *boys* ~ *15* (*years of age*), les garçons de moins de 15 ans; *He is* ~ *15* (*years old*), Il a moins de 15 ans. **3.** [loc.] ~ *penalty of*, sous peine de; ~ *our very eyes*, sous nos propres yeux; ~ *George XI*, sous (le règne de) Georges VI; ~ *construction*, ~ *repair*, ~ *observation*, ~ *treatment*, en construction, en réparation, en observation, en traitement; ~ *these, those*/*circumstances*, dans ces conditions; *to look* ~ *the word X*, voir le mot X . . . , chercher au mot X . . . ; ~ (*the terms of*) *the agreement*, aux termes de/en vertu de, d'après/l'accord; *to be* ~ *the impression that* . . . , avoir l'impression que . . . || *adv.* au-dessous: *boys 15 years and* ~ , les garçons de 15 ans et au-dessous.

under- [ʌndɚ-] [Préfixe entrant en composition, pour rendre l'idée de *sous-*, *sub-*, *moins*, *peu*, *inférieur*, *subalterne*]. || **underbrush** ['ʌndɚˌbɹʌʃ] *n.* broussailles *fpl*, sous-bois *m.* || **underclothes** [ˌʌndɚˌklowðz], **underclothing** *n.* sous-vêtement(s) *m.* (*pl.*), linge *m.* || **underdone** [ˌʌndɚ'dʌn] *adj.* [meat] saignant, cf. RARE; pas assez cuit. || **underestimate** [ˌʌndɚ'ɛstəˌmejt] *v. tr.* sous-estimer. || **underfed** [ˌʌndɚ'fɛd] *adj.* sous-alimenté. || **underfoot** [ˌʌndɚ'fʊt] *adv.* *to trample sth.* ~ , fouler qqch. aux pieds. || **undergarment** ['ʌndɚˌgɑɚmənt] *n.* sous-vêtement *m.* || **undergo** [ˌʌndɚ'gow], **underwent** [ˌʌndɚ'wɛnt], **undergone** [ˌʌndɚ'gɔn] *v. tr.* subir (une opération, un changement); supporter, endurer (une épreuve).

undergraduate [ˌʌndɚ'gɹæʤuɪt] *n.* †collégien *m*, élève *m* (des grandes classes); [Universités de langue anglaise] étudiant *m*, -e *f* de B.A. || *adj.* d'étudiant, estudiantin, universitaire: ∼ *activities*, vie *f* estudiantine; ∼ *course*, cours *m* collégial [qui mène au B.A.]; ∼ *days*, années *fpl* d'étudiant. || **underground** ['ʌndɚˌgɹawnd] *adj.* souterrain; [World War II] clandestin. || *n.* [World War II] résistance *f*, maquis *m*; [Br.] ∼ (*railway*), métro *m* [cf. SUBWAY]. || *adv. to go* ∼, [World War II] entrer dans la clandestinité, prendre le maquis; *to work* ∼, travailler sous (la) terre. || **underhand** ['ʌndɚˌhænd] *adv.* [Sport] par en dessous. || *adj.* par en dessous; [Fig.] [ˌʌndɚ'hænd] secret, sournois. || **underline** ['ʌndɚˌlajn] *v. tr.* souligner. || **underlying** [ˌʌndɚ'lajɪŋ] *adj.* sous-jacent, caché. || **undermine** [ˌʌndɚ'majn] *v. tr.* miner, saper. || **undermost** ['ʌndɚˌmowst] *adj.* le plus bas *m*, la plus basse *f*; inférieur, -e.

underneath [ˌʌndɚ'nijθ] *prép.* sous, dessous, en dessous, par-dessous [cf. UNDER §1]. || *adv.* (en) dessous, par-dessous: *to go* ∼ [and stay there], aller se mettre (en) dessous, [and out the other side] passer par-dessous; *to come out from* ∼, sortir d'en dessous; *It isn't on the table, it's* ∼, Ce n'est pas sur la table, c'est dessous. || *n.* dessous *m*: *the* ∼ *of the table*, le dessous de la table; *The table is not varnished on the* ∼, La table n'est pas vernie en dessous. || *adj.* de dessous: *the* ∼ *part*, la partie d'en dessous.

underpass ['ʌndɚˌpæs] *n.* [pedestrian] passage *m* souterrain; [road] passage *m* en dessous. || **underrate** [ˌʌndɚ'ɹejt] *v. tr.* sous-estimer; mésestimer (un adversaire). || **under-secretary** [ˌʌndɚ'sɛkɹəˌtɛɚɪ] *n.* sous-secrétaire *m* (d'un ministère, &c.). || **undersell** [ˌʌndɚ'sɛl] **undersold, undersold** [ˌʌndɚ'sowld] *v. tr.* vendre à meilleur marché/moins cher/que . . .; solder (des marchandises). || **undershirt** ['ʌndɚˌʃɚt] *n.* gilet *m* de dessous; chemisette *f*; maillot *m* de corps. || **undersized** [ˌʌndɚ'sajzd] *adj.* de/d'une/ taille inférieure à la moyenne; (trop) petit. || **underskirt** ['ʌndɚˌskɪɚt] *n.* jupon *m*.

understand [ˌʌndɚ'stænd], **understood, understood** [ˌʌndɚ'stʊd] *v. intr.* comprendre: *Now I* ∼ *!*, Je comprends !, J'y suis !; *You are, I* ∼, *the young man in question*, C'est vous, si je comprends bien, le jeune homme en question? || *v. tr.* **1.** comprendre, comprendre à: *I don't* ∼ *Chinese*, Je ne comprends pas le chinois; *I don't* ∼ *a thing*, Je n'y comprends rien; *He understands his job well*, Il/comprend, connaît bien/son travail. **2.** apprendre, (entendre) dire, comprendre, (sous-)entendre: *I* ∼ *you were late*, On me dit/J'ai entendu dire, J'apprends, Il paraît/que vous êtes arrivé en retard; *I gave him to* ∼ *that . . .*, Je lui ai donné à entendre que . . ., Je lui ai fait comprendre que . . . ; *Let it be clearly understood that . . .*, Qu'il soit bien entendu que . . . ; *The verb is* (*to be*) *understood*, Le verbe est sous-entendu. || **understandable** [ˌʌndɚ'stændəbl̩] *adj.* compréhensible, intelligible: *That is* ∼, Cela se comprend. || **understanding** [ˌʌndɚ'stændɪŋ] *n.* **1.** intelligence *f*, esprit *m*, jugement *m*: *to show* ∼, faire preuve d'intelligence. **2.** compréhension *f* (d'un texte, &c.). **3.** accord *m*, entente *f*: *to come to an* ∼ *with*, s'entendre avec (qqun); *to reach a* (*friendly*) ∼, parvenir à un accord, à une entente (cordiale); *on the* ∼ *that . . .*, à condition que . . . .

understate [ˌʌndɚ'stejt] *v. tr.* minimiser (les faits). || **understatement** [ˌʌndɚ'stejtmənt] *n.* amoindrissement *m* (des faits). || **undertake** [ˌʌndɚ'tejk], **undertook** [ˌʌndɚˌtʊk], **undertaken** [ˌʌndɚ'tejkn̩] *v. tr.* entreprendre, commencer (un travail); se charger (d'un travail), promettre (de faire un travail); assumer (une responsabilité. || **undertaker** ['ʌndɚˌtejkɚ] *n.* © directeur *m* de funérailles; entrepreneur *m* de pompes funèbres. || **undertaking** [ˌʌndɚ'tejkɪŋ] *n.* entreprise *f*; engagement *m*, promesse *f*. || **undertone** [ˌʌndɚˌtown] *n. In an* ∼, bas, à mi-voix, à voix basse. || **underwear** ['ʌndɚˌwɛɚ] *n.* sous-vêtements *mpl*; lingerie *f* (pour dame). || **underworld** ['ʌndɚˌwɚld] *n.* bas-fonds *mpl* (de la société); [Fam.] pègre *f*.

underwrite ['ʌndɚˌɹajt] *v. tr.* souscrire (une police). || **underwriter** [-ɚ] *n.* assureur *m*.

un|deserved [ˌʌndə'zɚvd] *adj.* injuste, immérité. || **un|deservedly** *adv.* à tort, injustement. || **un|desirable** [ˌʌndə'zajɚəbl̩] *adj.* peu désirable, inopportun, peu judicieux. || *n.* indésirable *m*, sujet *m* dangereux. || **un|determined** [ˌʌndə'tɚmənd] *adj.* indéterminé, vague; [person] irrésolu, hésitant. || **un|dignified** [ˌʌn'dɪgnəˌfajd] *adj.* sans dignité: *to be* ∼, manquer de dignité. || **un|disguised** [ˌʌndəs'gajzd] *adj.* non déguisé, non dissimulé; franc, sincère. || **un|disputed** [ˌʌndə'spjuwtəd] *adj.* incontesté. || **un|disturbed** [ˌʌndə'stɚbd] *adj.* tranquille, calme; → sans être dérangé. || **un|do**

[ˌʌn'duw] **undid** [ˌʌn'dɪd] **undone** [ˌʌn'dʌn *v. tr.* défaire; [Fig.] ruiner (une personne), détruire (le bon travail): *to come undone*, se défaire; se délacer [en parlant d'un soulier]; *to leave sth. undone*, ne pas faire qqch.; *to leave nothing undone* (*to*), ne rien négliger (pour); *What's done cannot be undone*, Ce qui est fait est fait. || **un|doing** [ˌʌn'duwɪŋ] *n.* perte *f*: *to be s.o.'s* ~, perdre qqun. || **un|doubted** [ˌʌn'dawtəd] *adj.* indiscutable, incontestable. || **undoubtedly** [ˌʌn'dawtədlɪ] *adv.* sans aucun doute, incontestablement. || **un|dreamt of** [ˌʌn'dɹɛmt'ʌv] *adj.* inattendu; insoupçonné; → qui passe l'imagination. || **un|dress** [ˌʌn'dɹɛs] *v. tr. & intr.* (se) déshabiller: *to get undressed*, se déshabiller. || **un|drinkable** [ˌʌn'dɹɪŋkəbl̩] *adj.* imbuvable. || **un|due** [ˌʌn'djuw] *adj.* **1.** injustifié, non justifié, injuste. **2.** excessif, exagéré. || **un|duly** *adv.* indûment, à tort; à l'excès, exagérément. || **un|dying** [ˌʌn'dajɪŋ] *adj.* immortel; éternel. || **unearth** [ˌʌn'ɚθ] *v. tr.* déterrer; [Fig.] découvrir, mettre à jour. || **un|earthly** *adj.* surnaturel; étrange, bizarre; [hour] indu. || **un|easily** [ˌʌn'ijzəlɪ] *adv.* mal à l'aise, mal à son (&c.) aise; avec gêne, difficilement. || **un|easiness** [ˌʌn'ijzɪnəs] *n.* malaise *m*; gêne *f*; inquiétude *f.* || **un|easy** [ˌʌn'ijzɪ] *adj.* [uncomfortable] mal à l'aise; [worried] inquiet; [embarrassed] gêné: *to feel* ~ *about sth.*, s'inquiéter de qqch. || **un|eatable** [ˌʌn'ijtəbl̩] *adj.* immangeable. || **un|educated** [ʌn'ɛʤəˌkejtəd] *adj.* ignorant; sans instruction, inculte. || **un|employed** [ˌʌnəm'plojd] *adj.* inoccupé, inactif; en chômage: *the* ~, les sans-travail *mpl*, les chômeurs *mpl.* || **un|employment** [ˌʌnəm'plojmənt] *n.* chômage *m*: *Unemployment Insurance Commission*, Commission *f* d'assurance-chômage.

un|ending [ˌʌn'ɛndɪŋ] *adj.* interminable; → sans fin. || **un|equal** [ˌʌn'ijkwəl] *adj.* inégal; disproportionné, variable: ~ *to the task*, pas à la hauteur de la tâche. || **un|equalled** *adj.* sans égal, → qui n'a pas son égal. || **un|equally** *adv.* inégalement.

UNESCO [ˌjuw'nɛskow] *n. abr.* = *United Nations Educational, Scientific and Cultural Organization*, l'Unesco *m* [lynɛs'ko] = Organisation *f* des Nations Unies pour l'éducation, la science et la culture.

un|even [ˌʌn'ijvən] *adj.* (terrain) inégal; (combat, &c.) disproportionné: ~ *number*, nombre *m* impair. || **un|evenly** *adv.* inégalement. || **un|evenness** *n.* inégalité *f.* || **un|eventful** [ˌʌnə'vɛntfəl] *adj.* sans accidents. || **un|expected** [ʌnək'spɛktəd] *adj.* inattendu, imprévu. || *n.* imprévu *m.* || **unexpectedly** *adv.* inopinément, → alors qu'on ne s'y attend(ait) pas: *to come* ~, arriver à l'improviste. || **un|explained** [ˌʌnək'splejnd] *adj.* inexpliqué. || **un|fair** [ˌʌn'fɛɚ] *adj.* injuste; déloyal, → de mauvaise foi: *That's* ~ *!*, Ce n'est pas juste! || **un|fairly** *adv.* injustement, déloyalement. || **un|fairness** *n.* injustice *f*, déloyauté *f*, mauvaise foi *f.* || **un|faithful** [ˌʌn'fejθfl̩] *adj.* infidèle; (récit) inexact. || **un|faithfulness** *n.* infidélité *f.* || **un|familiar** [ˌʌnfə'mɪljɚ] *adj.* étrange, inaccoutumé, nouveau, → peu familier (avec), qui n'est pas au courant (*with*, de). || **un|familiarity** *n.* manque *m* de familiarité (avec); nouveauté *f.* || **un|fashionable** [ˌʌn'fæʃənɪbəl] *adj.* démodé; peu élégant → qui n'est pas à la mode. || **un|fasten** [ˌʌn'fæsn̩] *v. tr.* relâcher, desserrer (une prise); détacher, défaire (des liens, des nœuds); ouvrir (une porte). || **un|favourable** [ʌn'fejvɚɪbl̩] *adj.* défavorable, peu favorable. || **un|favourably** *adv.* défavorablement. || **un|finished** [ˌʌn'fɪnɪʃt] *adj.* inachevé, incomplet. || **un|fit** [ˌʌn'fɪt] *adj.* impropre, peu propre (*for*, à); (physiquement) inapte (à), incapable (de): ~ *for consumption*, impropre à la consommation. || **un|fitness** *n.* inaptitude *f* (à), incapacité *f* (de). || **un|fold** [ˌʌn'fowld] *v. tr.* déplier (un papier), déployer (un tissu), ouvrir; [Fig.] révéler; exposer (des plans, des théories). || *v. intr.* se révéler, s'ouvrir; [events] se dérouler. || **un|foreseen** [ˌʌnfɚ'sijn] *adj.* imprévu: *due to* ~ *circumstances*, en raison de circonstances imprévues. || **un|forgettable** [ˌʌnfɚ'gɛtəbl̩] *adj.* inoubliable, → qui ne s'oublie pas. || **un|forgivable** [ˌʌnfɚ'gɪvəbl̩] *adj.* impardonnable. || **un|forgiving** *adj.* implacable, rancunier. || **un|fortunate** [ʌn'fɔɚʧənət] *adj.* malheureux, †infortuné; fâcheux, regrettable. || **un|fortunately** *adv.* malheureusement. || **un|friendly** [ˌʌn'fɹɛndlɪ] *adj.* peu amical, peu obligeant; hostile. || **un|furnished** [ʌn'fɚnɪʃt] *adj.* non meublé. || **un|gainly** [ˌʌn'gejnlɪ] *adj.* gauche, disgracieux.

un|grateful [ˌʌn'gɹejtfl̩] *adj.* ingrat (envers qqun): *to be* ~ (*to s.o.*) *for sth.*, être peu reconnaissant (envers qqun) de qqch. || **un|grudgingly** [ˌʌn'gɹʌʤɪŋlɪ] *adv.* de bon cœur; libéralement. || **un|happily** [ˌʌn'hæpəlɪ] *adv.* malheureusement. || **un|happiness** [ˌʌn'hæpɪnəs] *n.* malheur *m*, tristesse *f.* || **un|happy** [ˌʌn'hæpɪ] *adj.* malheureux, triste; [expression] peu heureux. || **un|healthy** [ˌʌnˈhɛlθɪ] *adj.* malsain, (climat) insalubre: *an ~ child,* un enfant maladif, → en mauvaise santé. || **un|heard-of** [ˌʌnˈhɚdˌʌv] *adj.* inouï, extraordinaire: *~ event,* événement extraordinaire; *It's ~ !,* C'est inouï! || **un|hesitating(ly)** [ˌʌnˈhɛzəˌtejtɪŋ(lɪ)] *adj. & adv.* sans hésiter, hésitation. || **un|hindered** [ʌnˈhɪndɚd] *adj.* sans empêchement; librement. || **un|hoped-for** [ˌʌnˈhowptˌfɔɚ] *adj.* inespéré. || **un|hurt** [ˌʌnˈhɚt] *adj.* sain et sauf; sans blessure.

unicorn [ˈjuwnəˌkɔɚn] *n.* licorne *f.*

uniform [ˈjuwnəˌfɔɚm] *n.* uniforme *m* (de), tenue *f* (de); costume *m* (de): *in (the) ~ (of an admiral),* en uniforme (d'amiral). || *adj.* uniforme, → de même taille, de même forme; régulier. || **uniformity** [ˌjuwnɪˈfɔɚmətɪ] *n.* uniformité *f.* || **uniformly** *adv.* uniformément. || **unify** [ˈjuwnəˌfaj] *v. tr. & intr.* (s') unifier.

un|imaginable [ʌnəˈmæʤənəbḷ] *adj.* inimaginable, inconcevable. || **un|impaired** [ˌʌnɪmˈpɛɚd] *adj.* intact; non détérioré, non diminué. || **un|important** [ˌʌnɪmˈpɔɚtənt] *adj.* peu important, insignifiant; → sans importance: *It's ~ ,* C'est peu de chose, Cela ne fait rien. || **un|informed** [ˌʌnɪnˈfɔɚmd] *adj.* non informé, non averti; [Pej.] ignorant. || **un|inhabited** [ˌʌnɪnˈhæbɪtəd] *adj.* inhabité, désert. || **un|inspired** [ˌʌnɪnˈspajɚd] *adj.* terne, sans inspiration, terre à terre. || **un|intelligible** [ˌʌnɪnˈtɛləʤəbḷ] *adj.* inintelligible; incompréhensible. || **un|intentional** [ˌʌnɪnˈtɛnʃənl] *adj.* involontaire; fait sans intention. || **un|interested** [ˌʌnˈɪntɹɛstəd] *adj.* indifférent: *to be ~ in,* ne prendre aucun intérêt à. || **un|interesting** [ˌʌnˈɪntɹɛstɪŋ] *adj.* peu intéressant; sans intérêt. || **un|interrupted** [ˌʌnɪntɚˈɹʌptəd] *adj.* ininterrompu, continu. || **un|inviting** [ˌʌnɪnˈvaijtɪŋ] *adj.* peu attrayant; [food] peu appétissant.

union [ˈjuwnjən] *n.* **1.** union *f*: *the Union Jack,* le pavillon britannique; *the French Union,* l'Union française (→ La Communauté française); *Union of South Africa,* l'Union sud-africaine; [US] *the Union,* les États-Unis; [US] *the State o, the Union message,* le discours sur l'état de l'Union; *the Soviet Union,* l'Union soviétique [USSR]; [Rail.] *Union Station,* Gare *f* centrale. **2.** mariage *m* (avec). **3.** syndicat *m*: *labour ~ ,* syndicat ouvrier; *~ rate,* tarif *m* syndical; *~ shop,* atelier *m* syndical.

unique [ˌjuwˈnijk] *adj.* unique; → comme on n'en voit pas. || **uniquely** *adv.* → d'une manière unique. || **uniqueness** *n.* → le caractère unique (de).

unit [ˈjuwnət] *n.* **1.** unité *f* (de longueur); [Mil.] unité, formation *f.* **2.** élément *m*, appareil *m*; section *f* (d'un motel); service *m* (d'une administration); groupe *m* (de maisons).

unite [ˌjuwˈnajt] *v. tr.* (ré)unir (à, avec), joindre (à). || *v. intr.* s'unir, se réunir, se joindre: *to ~ against,* faire bloc contre; *to ~ to do sth.,* s'associer pour faire qqch. || **united** *adj.* (ré)uni: *a ~ family,* une famille unie; *~ efforts,* des efforts réunis; *United we stand, divided we fall,* L'union fait la force; *the United Church (of Canada),* l'Église *f* Unie (du Canada); *the United Kingdom, the U.K.,* le Royaume-Uni; *the United Nations, the U.N.,* les Nations Unies *fpl,* l'O.N.U. *f*; *the United States (of America), the U.S.,* les États-Unis *mpl* (d'Amérique), © les É.-U., [Fr.] les U.S.A.; [Fam.] © les États.

unity [ˈjuwnətɪ] *n.* unité *f,* union *f,* concorde *f*: *national ~ ,* l'unité nationale; *to live in ~ ,* vivre dans la concorde, en harmonie; *the (dramatic) unities of time, place, and action,* les unités dramatiques de temps, de lieu et d'action; *Unity is strength,* l'union fait la force.

universal [ˌjuwnəˈvɚsḷ] *adj.* universel; de l'univers; [Mec.] *universal joint,* joint *m* de cardan. || **universally** *adv.* universellement; à l'échelle mondiale.

universe [ˌjuwnəˈvɚs] *n.* univers *m.*

university [ˌjuwnəˈvɚsətɪ] *n.* université *f*: *the University of Montreal,* l'Université de Montréal; *Laval University,* l'Université Laval; *Where did you go to ~ ?,* Où avez-vous fait vos études/supérieures, universitaires/? || *adj.* universitaire: *~ degree,* grade *m* universitaire; *~ professor,* professeur *m* (de faculté); *~ student,* étudiant *m,* -e *f*; *to have a ~ education,* être allé à l'université, avoir fait les études supérieures.

un|just [ˌʌnˈʤʌst] *adj.* injuste, inique. || **un|justifiable** [ˌʌnˌʤʌstəˈfajəbl] *adj.* injustifiable, inexcusable. || **un|justified** [ˌʌnˈʤʌstəˌfajd] *adj.* injustifié; → non justifié, sans justification. || **un|justly** *adv.* injustement. || **un|kind** [ˌʌnˈkajnd] *adj.* [*-er, -est*] peu aimable, désobligeant; cruel, méchant: *It's ~ of him (to),* C'est mal à lui (de) . . . || **un|kindly** *adv.* sans bienveillance; cruellement: *to take sth. ~ ,* prendre qqch. en mauvaise part. || **un|kindness** *n.* désobligeance *f*; cruauté *f.* || **un|knowingly** [ˌʌnˈnowɪŋlɪ] *adv.* inconsciemment; sans le savoir. || **un|known**

[ˌʌn'nown] *adj.* inconnu; étrange: ~ *to s.o., me, him, &c.*, à l'insu de qqun, à mon insu, à son insu, &c. ‖ **un|lawful** [ˌʌn'lɔfl̩] *adj.* illégal; illicite.

unless [ˌʌn'lɛs] *conj.* à moins que . . . (ne) [+ *subjonc.*]; si . . . ne . . . [+ *ind.*] . . . pas: *Unless you ask him specifically, he will not come,* A moins que vous (ne) le lui demandiez expressément, il ne viendra pas [*Ne* may be omitted, but is still preferred. When the subjects of both clauses are the same, an infinitive may be used], à moins de [+ *inf.*]: *Unless you hurry, you will miss your train,* A moins de vous dépêcher, vous manquerez votre train.

un|like [ˌʌn'lajk] *adj.* différent (de), → qui ne ressemble pas (à): *The two brothers are quite* ~ , Les deux frères sont très différents, → ne se ressemblent en rien. ‖ *prép.* différemment (de), à la différence (de), contrairement (à). ‖ **unlikely** *adv.* improbable, peu probable; invraisemblable: *He is the most* ~ *man for the job,* → C'est le dernier homme auquel on aurait pensé pour ce travail. ‖ **un|limited** [ˌʌn'lɪmətəd] *adj.* illimité, → sans limites, sans bornes. ‖ **un|load** [ˌʌn'lowd] *v. tr.* décharger (des marchandises, un navire); désarmer (un fusil). ‖ **un|lock** [ˌʌn'lɑk] *v. tr.* ouvrir (une porte fermée à clef); [Fig.] découvrir, révéler (ses sentiments, &c.). ‖ **un|looked-for** [ˌʌn'lʊktˌfɔɚ] *adj.* inattendu, imprévu. ‖ **un|lovely** [ˌʌn'lʌvlɪ] *adj.* sans charme; laid. ‖ **un|lucky** [ˌʌn'lʌkɪ] *adj.* malheureux, †infortuné, malchanceux, → qui n'a pas de chance: *to be* ~ , → ne pas avoir de chance; *That's* ~ , Cela porte malheur. ‖ **un|manageable** [ˌʌn'mænədʒəbl̩] *adj.* difficile [person] à diriger, [thing] à manier. ‖ **un|married** [ˌʌn'mæɚɪd] *adj.* célibataire, → qui n'est pas marié. ‖ **un|mask** [ˌʌn'mæsk] *v. tr. & intr.* (se) démasquer. ‖ **un|matched** [ˌʌn'mætʃt] *adj.* [set] dépareillé; [Fig.] sans égal, sans pareil. ‖ **un|mentionable** [ˌʌn'mɛnʃənəbl̩] *adj.* → dont on ne parle pas. ‖ **un|mindful** (of) [ˌʌn'majndfl̩] *adj.* oublieux (de), inattentif (à); peu soucieux (de), → sans penser à. ‖ **un|mistakable** [ˌʌnmə'stejkəbl̩] *adj.* évident, → qui saute aux yeux, qui ne saurait tromper; facilement reconnaissable. ‖ **un|moved** [ˌʌn'muwvd] *adj.* immobile; impassible, insensible, indifférent. ‖ **un|natural** [ʌn'nætʃɚəl] *adj.* contre nature; anormal, artificiel; dénaturé. ‖ **un|necessary** [ˌʌn'nɛsəˌsɛɚɪ] *adj.* inutile, peu nécessaire. ‖ **un|neighbourly** [ˌʌn'nejbɚlɪ] *adj.* peu obligeant: *to be* ~ , être un voisin peu obligeant. ‖ **un|noticed** [ˌʌn'nowtəst] *adj.* inaperçu. ‖ **un|obtainable** [ˌʌnəb'tejnəbl̩] *adj.* impossible à trouver. ‖ **un|occupied** [ˌʌn'ɑkjuwˌpajd] *adj.* [person] inoccupé; [chair] libre; [house] inhabité. ‖ **un|offending** [ˌʌnə'fɛndɪŋ] *adj.* innocent, pacifique. ‖ **un|official** [ˌʌnə'fɪʃəl] *adj.* non officiel; [news] officieux, non confirmé. ‖ **un|opened** [ˌʌn'owpn̩d] *adj.* fermé, non ouvert; [letter] non décacheté. ‖ **un|opposed** [ˌʌnə'powzd] *adj.* sans opposition. ‖ **un|pack** [ˌʌn'pæk] *v. tr.* défaire (ses bagages), ouvrir ses valises; déballer (des marchandises). ‖ **un|paid** [ˌʌn'pejd] *adj.* non payé, impayé; [bill, debt] non acquitté; [letters, &c.] non affranchi: *unpaid-for services,* services *mpl* gratuits, bénévoles. ‖ **un|palatable** [ˌʌn'pælɪtəbl̩] *adj.* désagréable (au goût); [Fig.] désagréable, difficile à avaler, (à accepter). ‖ **un|paralleled** [ˌʌn'pæɚəˌlɛld] *adj.* sans pareil; sans précédent; inouï. ‖ **un|pardonable** [ˌʌn'paɚdənəbl̩] *adj.* impardonnable, inexcusable: *It is* ~ *of you to . . . ,* Vous êtes impardonnable de . . . ‖ **un|pleasant** [ˌʌn'plɛzənt] *adj.* [*-er, -est*] désagréable, fâcheux. ‖ **un|pleasantness** *n.* désagrément *m*; attitude *f* désagréable, incident *m* fâcheux. ‖ **un|popular** [ˌʌn'pɑpjəlɚ] *adj.* impopulaire; → qui n'a pas de succès (*with,* auprès de), mal vu, mal accueilli (de). ‖ **un|precedented** [ˌʌn'pɹɛsɪˌdɛntəd] *adj.* sans précédent, sans exemple.

unprejudiced [ˌʌn'pɹɛdʒədɪst] *adj.* sans préjugé, impartial. ‖ **un|prepared** [ˌʌnpɹə'pɛɚd] *adj.* sans préparation, improvisé: *to be* (*taken*) ~ (*for*), être pris au dépourvu (par). ‖ **un|profitable** [ˌʌn'pɹɑfɪtəbl̩] *adj.* improfitable; inutile. ‖ **un|promising** [ˌʌn'pɹɑməsɪŋ] *adj.* → qui ne promet pas; qui s'annonce mal. ‖ **un|published** [ˌʌn'pʌblɪʃt] *adj.* inédit. ‖ **un|qualified** [ˌʌn'kwɑləˌfajd] *adj.* incompétent (à), incapable (de, *for*); [of statement] absolu, catégorique. ‖ **un|questionable** [ˌʌn'kwɛstʃənəbl̩] *adj.* incontestable, indiscutable. ‖ **un|questionably** *adv.* incontestablement, sans le moindre doute. ‖ **un|quote** [ˌʌn'kwowt] fin *f* de la citation cf. QUOTE. ‖ **un|readable** [ˌʌn'ɹijdəbl̩] *adj.* illisible. ‖ **un|real** [ˌʌn'ɹijl] *adj.* irréel, sans réalité; chimérique, imaginaire. ‖ **un|reasonable** [ˌʌn'ɹijzn̩əbl̩] *adj.* déraisonnable; excessif, extravagant; [hour] indu. ‖ **un|recognizable** [ˌʌnɹɛkəg'najzəbl̩] *adj.* méconnaissable. ‖ **un|reliable** [ˌʌnɹə'lajəbl̩] *adj.* peu sûr, douteux; → sur qui/quoi/on ne peut pas compter. || **un|rest** [ˌʌn'ɹɛst] *n.* inquiétude *f*; [social] troubles *mpl*, émeutes *fpl*, agitation *f*. || **un|roll** [ˌʌn'ɹowl] *v. tr. & intr.* (se) dérouler. || **un|ruly** [ˌʌn'ɹuwlɪ] *adj.* indiscipliné; [feelings] déréglé. || **un|safe** [ˌʌn'sejf] *adj.* peu sûr, dangereux, hasardeux. || **un|satisfactory** [ˌʌnˌsætɪs'fæktərɪ] *adj.* peu satisfaisant; [school work] insuffisant. || **un|screw** [ˌʌn'skɹuw] *v. tr.* dévisser. || **un|scrupulous** [ˌʌn'skɹuwpjələs] *adj.* sans scrupule(s). || **un|seen** [ˌʌn'sijn] *adj.* sans être/aperçu, vu/; invisible. || **un|selfish** [ˌʌn'sɛlfɪʃ] *adj.* désintéressé; altruiste, → qui pense aux autres. || **un|selfishness** *n.* désintéressement *m*. || **un|settled** [ˌʌn'sɛtl̩d] *adj.* [Fig.] instable; indécis; [weather] variable; [question] en suspens; [region] inhabité, non colonisé. || **un|sightly** [ˌʌn'sajtlɪ] *adj.* désagréable (à voir); laid. || **un|skilful** [ˌʌn'skɪlfl̩] *adj.* maladroit. || **un|skilled** [ˌʌnskɪld] *adj.* inexpérimenté; (ouvrier) non spécialisé. || **un|sound** [ˌʌn'sawnd] *adj.* en mauvais état, malsain; [mind] dérangé; [opinions] faux. || **un|speakable** [ˌʌn'spijkəbl̩] *adj.* [joy] indicible; [pain] inexprimable; [showing disgust] sans nom. || **un|stable** [ˌʌn'stejbl̩] *adj.* instable; [character] inconstant. || **un|steadily** [ˌʌn'stɛdɪlɪ] *adv.* d'une façon/chancelante, tremblante, mal assurée, variable, irrégulière/. || **un|steady** [ˌʌn'stɛdɪ] *adj.* [thing] peu solide; [shaky] chancelant; [voice, hand, light] tremblant; variable, irrégulier. || **un|successful** [ˌʌnsək'sɛsfl̩] *adj.* non réussi, sans succès; [person] qui n'a pas réussi: *to be* ~, ne pas réussir; ~ *candidate*, candidat *m* refusé. || **un|suitable (for)** [ʌn'suwtəbl̩] *adj.* → qui ne convient pas (à); [person] peu fait (pour); [thing, expression] impropre (à), [time] inopportun (pour). || **un|suited (for)** [ˌʌn'suwtəd] *adj.* peu convenable (pour); impropre (à); mal approprié (à). || **un|surpassed** [ˌunsər'pæst] *adj.* sans égal. || **un|suspected** [ˌʌnsə'spɛktəd] *adj.* insoupçonné; [person] non suspect. || **un|suspecting** [ˌʌnsə'spɛktɪŋ] *adj.* confiant; → qui ne se doute de rien. || **un|tamed** [ˌʌn'tejmd] *adj.* indompté; [animal] sauvage. || **un|thankful** [ˌʌn'θæŋkfl̩] *adj.* peu reconnaissant, ingrat. || **un|thinkable** [ˌʌn'θɪŋkəbl̩] *adj.* inconcevable. || **un|thinking** [ˌʌn'θɪŋkɪŋ] *adj.* irréfléchi, étourdi. || **un|tidiness** [ˌʌn'tajdɪnəs] *n.* désordre *m*; manque *m* de soin. || **un|tidy** [ˌʌn'tajdɪ] *adj.* [thing] en désordre; [person] sans soin, peu soigneux. || **un|tie** [ˌʌn'taj] *v. tr.* défaire (un nœud, un paquet); détacher (qqun).

until [ən'tɪl] *prép.* **1.** jusqu'à, en attendant: *He stayed* ~ *nine o'clock*, Il est resté jusqu'à neuf heures; *She kept quiet* ~ *the end of the class*, Elle s'est tue en attendant la fin de la classe; ~ *now*, jusqu'ici, jusqu'à maintenant, jusqu'à présent; ~ *then*, ~ *that time*, jusqu'alors; ~ *after dinner*, jusqu'après le dîner; (*goodbye*) ~ *tomorrow*, à demain. **2.** [×] *not* ~, pas avant, ne . . . que, jusqu'à: [×] *Don't leave* ~ *nine*, Ne partez pas avant neuf heures; [×] *He didn't leave* ~ *nine*, Il n'est parti qu'à neuf heures; [×] *Don't go* ~ *after nine*, Ne partez qu'après neuf heures, Ne partez pas avant neuf heures passées; *Don't stay* ~ *9 o'clock*, Ne restez pas jusqu'à neuf heures. || *conj.* **1.** [likely possibility in future and past events] jusqu'à ce que [+ *subjunc.*], jusqu'au moment où [+ *ind.*]: [affirmative] *I'll stay* ~ *he gets back*, Je resterai jusqu'à ce qu'il revienne, jusqu'au moment où il reviendra, jusqu'à son retour; *I stayed* ~ *he came back*, Je suis resté/jusqu'à ce qu'il soit revenu, jusqu'au moment où il est revenu, jusqu'à son retour; [negative] jusqu'à ce que [+ *subjunc.*], jusqu'au moment où [+ *ind.*]; avant que [+ *subjunc.*], ne . . . que, lorsque [+ *ind.*]: *I don't want to stay* ~ *he gets back*, Je ne veux pas rester jusqu'à ce qu'il revienne, jusqu'au moment où il reviendra, jusqu'à son retour; [×] *I won't leave* ~ *(after) he gets back*, Je ne partirai pas avant qu'il revienne/avant son retour/; Je ne partirai que lorsqu'il reviendra/qu'après son retour/; [×] *He didn't leave* ~ *(after) he had finished*, Il n'est parti/que lorsqu'il a eu fini, qu'après avoir fini/. **2.** [unlikely possibility in future] jusqu'à ce que [+ *subjunc.*]: *Are you going to do that* ~ *I lose my patience?*, Allez-vous continuer jusqu'à ce que je perde patience/jusqu'à me faire perdre patience/? **3.** [= until such time as] jusqu'à ce que [+ *subjunc.*], en attendant que [+ *subjonc.*], tant que . . . ne . . . pas [+ *ind.*]: *Until (such time as) you have finished, stay there, don't go away*, Jusqu'à ce que/ En attendant que/ vous ayez fini, restez là; Tant que vous n'aurez pas fini, ne vous en allez pas. **4.** [degree] jusqu'à ce que [+ *subjunc.*], jusqu'au point où [+ *ind.*]: *He often eats* ~ *he makes himself sick*, Il mange souvent jusqu'à ce qu'il se rende malade, jusqu'à s'en rendre malade. **5.** [×] *to wait* ~, attendre que [+ *subjunc.*].

un|timely [ˌʌnˈtajmlɪ] *adj.* prématuré; inopportun. ‖ **un|tiring** [ˌʌnˈtajɚɪŋ] *adj.* infatigable, inlassable. ‖ **un|told** [ˌʌnˈtowld] *adj.* [joy] indicible; [suffering] inouï; [loss] incalculable; [years] innombrable; [story] passé sous silence. ‖ **un|touched** [ˌʌnˈtʌtʃd] *adj.* non manié; intact; [Fig.] insensible. ‖ **un|trained** [ˌʌnˈtɹejnd] *adj.* inexpérimenté; indiscipliné; [animals] non dressé. ‖ **un|troubled** [ˌʌnˈtɹʌbl̩d] *adj.* calme; [water] non troublé. ‖ **un|true** [ˌʌnˈtɹuw] *adj.* inexact, erroné, faux; infidèle. ‖ **un|truth** [ˌʌnˈtɹuwθ] *n.* inexactitude *f*, mensonge *m*, fausseté *f*. ‖ **un|used** [ˌʌnˈjuwzd] *adj.* peu employé, inutilisé; [building] désaffecté; [word] inusité. ‖ **unused to** [ˌʌnˈjuwstˌtuw] *adj.* peu accoutumé à: *to be* ~, ne pas être accoutumé à; *to get* ~, perdre l'habitude de. ‖ **un|usual** [ˌʌnˈjuwʒ(w)əl] *adj.* insolite, extraordinaire, rare, peu habituel; [word] peu usité. ‖ **un|veil** [ˌʌnˈvejl] *v. tr.* dévoiler; inaugurer (un monument). ‖ **un|warranted** [ˌʌnˈwɔɚəntəd] *adj.* injustifié; injustifiable; [Com.] sans garantie. ‖ **un|wary** [ˌʌnˈwɛɚɪ] *adj.* imprudent; irréfléchi. ‖ **un|welcome** [ˌʌnˈwɛlkəm] *adj.* mal accueilli, importun; [news] désagréable. ‖ **un|well** [ˌʌnˈwɛl] *adj.* indisposé, souffrant. ‖ **un|willing** [ˌʌnˈwɪlɪŋ] *adj.* peu disposé (*to*, à): *to be* ~, → ne pas vouloir, se refuser à (faire qqch.). ‖ **un|willingly** *adv.* à contre-cœur, de mauvaise grâce. ‖ **un|willingness** *n.* mauvaise volonté *f*. ‖ **un|wind** [ˌʌnˈwajnd] **un|wound, un|wound** [ˌʌnˌwawnd] *v. tr. & intr.* (se) dérouler, (se) détordre. ‖ **un|wise** [ˌʌnˈwajz] *adj.* malavisé, imprudent. ‖ **un|wisely** *adv.* imprudemment. ‖ **un|wittingly** [ˌʌnˈwɪtɪŋlɪ] *adv.* inconsciemment; sans le savoir, vouloir. ‖ **un|worthy** [ˌʌnˈwɚðɪ] *adj.* indigne. ‖ **un|wrap** [ˌʌnˈɹæp] *v. tr.* [-pp-] défaire (un paquet). ‖ **un|written** [ˌʌnˈɹɪtən] *adj.* non écrit; [tradition] oral: ~ *law*, droit *m* coutumier, [Fig.] habitude *f*, tradition *f*/ reconnue. ‖ **un|yielding** [ˌʌnˈjijldɪŋ] *adj.* ferme, solide; [Fig.] inébranlable.

up [ʌp] [☞ **[-pp-]** Cet article traite principalement de *up* après *to be* et en combinaison avec diverses constructions non verbales: pour *up* après d'autres verbes, voir ces mots et cf. UP *adv.* 1. et *prép.*] [☞ This entry includes for the most part only *up* used with the verb *to be* and in conjunction with various non-verbal constructions; for *up* with other verbs, see under the verb and UP *adv.* 1. and *prép.*] *adv.* **1.** [after verbs of motion]: *to go, come*/ ~, monter [aux, *être*]; *to walk/run, ride, drive*/ ~, monter à pied, en courant, à cheval/à bicyclette/ en auto, &c.; *to take, bring, carry/sth.* ~, monter qqch. [aux. *avoir*]. **2.** [with adverbial phrases]: ~ *there*, là-haut; ~ *here*, ici (en haut), par ici; ~ *above*, en haut; ~ *ahead*, en avant; ~ *north*, dans le nord; *high* ~, (très) haut; 100 *feet* ~, à une hauteur de cent pieds; *half-way* ~, à mi-hauteur; *all the way* ~, tout en haut; *to go all the way* ~, monter jusqu'au haut, jusqu'en haut; *farther* ~, plus haut, plus loin (dans la rue); *This Side Up* → Haut; *Other Side Up* → Bas; *One dollar and* ~, *from one dollar* ~, à partir d'un dollar; [Sport] *one* ~, un partout; *Their team is one goal* ~, Leur équipe mène par un but. **3.** [with following prep.]: ~ *above sth.*, au-dessus de qqch.; ~ *against the wall*, contre le mur, appuyé au mur; *to be* ~ *against a dangerous opponent*, avoir affaire à un adversaire dangereux; *to be* ~ *against it*, avoir de la malchance, connaître la misère; ~ *at the cottage*, © au camp, [Fr.] à la maison d'été; (*right*) ~ *beside sth.*, tout près de qqch.; ~ *in Sudbury*, à Sudbury; ~ *in my room* (en haut) dans ma chambre; *to be* ~ *in arms* (*against*), être en révolte, se révolter, protester (contre); *to be well* ~ (*in a subject*), être fort en; ~ *to now*, ~ *to then*, jusqu'ici, jusqu'alors; (*right*) ~ *to the door*, jusqu'à/jusque devant/la porte; ~ *to* (*the age of*) *20, the 3rd of May*, jusqu'à (l'âge de) 20 ans, jusqu'au 3 mai; *to come/go/* ~ *to s.o.*, s'approcher de qqun; *He is not* ~ *to this work*, Il n'est pas à la hauteur de ce travail; *It's not* ~ *to much*, Cela ne vaut pas grand'chose; *He is* ~ *to us*, Il a découvert notre secret; Il nous a rattrapés; *He is* ~ *to sth.*, Il a qqch. en tête; *What are you* ~ *to?*, Qu'est-ce que vous fabriquez?; Où en êtes-vous (dans le livre)?; *It's* ~ *to you!* A vous de jouer/de faire mieux/; C'est votre affaire!; *It's* ~ *to you to do it*, C'est à vous de le faire, C'est vous qui devez le faire. **4.** [alone, or alone after *to be*]: *Up!*, Debout!, Levez-vous!; *The red side was* ~, Le côté rouge était en dessus; *I was* ~ *late last night*, Je me suis couché tard hier soir; *I was* ~ *late this morning*, Je me suis levé tard ce matin; *My friend was* ~ *for a week*, Mon ami est venu passer une semaine chez nous; *He is* ~ *and about now*, Il est sur pied maintenant; *What's* ~ *?*, Qu'est-ce qui se passe?; *The sun is* ~, Le soleil est levé; *The window is* ~, La fenêtre est ouverte; *The new building is* ~, Le nouveau bâtiment est fini; (*Your*) *time is* ~, C'est l'heure; *When the hour is* ~ . . ., Quand l'heure sera finie, A la fin de l'heure . . . ; *The game is* ~, C'en est fait (de moi, lui); *Prices are* ~, Les prix ont augmenté; ‖ *prép. The house* ~ *the street*, La maison plus loin dans la rue; *The town* ~ *the river*, La ville en amont; *to go, come*/ ~ *the street, the stairs, the hill, &c.*, monter [aux. *avoir*] la rue, l'escalier, la côte, &c.; *to go, come*/ ~ *the river*, remonter [aux. *avoir*] la rivière, le fleuve. ‖ *n. ups and downs*, des hauts *mpl.* et des bas *mpl.*, des vicissitudes *fpl*; [Loc.] *Everything is on the* ~ *and* ~, Tout est parfaitement honorable, Il n'y a rien de louche. ‖ **up [-ped]** *v.* augmenter, améliorer. ‖ **up-and-coming** [ˌʌpn̩ˈkʌmɪŋ] *adj.* **1.** débrouillard, entreprenant, alerte, énergique, qui promet. **2.** arriviste, ambitieux. ‖ **up and down** [ˌʌpn̩ˈdawn] *adv. & prép.*: *to go* ~ (*the stairs*), monter et descendre (un escalier); *to walk* ~ (*the room*), se promener de long en large (dans la pièce), arpenter la pièce; *He walked* ~ (*the street*) *in front of the house*, Il a fait les cent pas (dans la rue) devant la maison; *He ran* ~ (*the streets*) *looking for his dog*, Il a parcouru les rues (dans tous les sens) en cherchant son chien.

upbraid [ˌʌpˈbɹejd] *v. tr.* réprimander: *to* ~ *s.o. for sth.*, reprocher vivement qqch. à qqun.

upbringing [ˈʌpˌbɹɪŋɪŋ] *n.* éducation *f.*

upheaval [ˌʌpˈhijvl̩] *n.* soulèvement *m.*

uphill [ʌpˈhɪl] *adv. to go* ~, monter (la côte), (vers le haut de . . .). ‖ [ˈʌpˌhɪl] *adj.* montant, [Fig.] pénible, difficile.

uphold [ˌʌpˈhowld], **upheld, upheld** [ʌpˈhɛld] *v. tr.* soutenir, maintenir.

upholster [ˌʌpˈhowlstɚ] *v. tr.* (re)couvrir, tapisser. ‖ **upholstery** [ʌpˈhowlstɹɪ] *n.* tapisserie *f.*

upkeep [ˈʌpˌkijp] *n.* entretien *m*: *low* ~, frais *m* d'entretien minimum, entretien *m* économique.

upland [ˈʌpˌlænd] *n.* terrain *m* élevé; région *f* montagneuse.

uplift [ˌʌpˈlɪft) *v. tr.* soulever, élever. ‖ [ˈʌpˌlɪft] *n.* [Fig.] élévation *f*, effort *m* de relèvement.

upon [əˈpɑn] *prep.* sur [équivalent de ON].

upper [ˈʌpɚ] *adj.* [Do not use comparative form in French] supérieur; haut [of two levels]: ~ *lip*, la lèvre supérieure; *the* ~ *part*/*side*/, le dessus; *Upper Canada*, le Haut-Canada; *the Upper House*, la Chambre haute, © le Sénat; [Rail.] ~ *berth*, couchette *f* du haut; [Sch. and socially] ~ *classes*, les hautes classes; *the* ~ 10 *percent*, les premiers dix pour cent; *to keep the* ~ *hand*, garder la haute main; *to get the* ~ *hand of*, l'emporter sur. ‖ **uppermost** [also †**upmost**] [ˈʌpɚˌmowst] *adj.* le plus élevé; [Fig.] le plus fort: *to be* ~, être en dessus, [Fig.] prédominer, occuper la première place. ‖ *adv.* en dessus.

upright [ˈʌpˌɹajt] *adj.* droit, debout; vertical; [Fig.] honnête, intègre. ‖ *adv.* [also *uprightly*] (tout) droit, verticalement. ‖ **uprightness** *n.* rectitude *f*, droiture *f* (morale).

uprising [ˈʌpˌɹajzɪŋ] *n.* soulèvement *m*, insurrection *f.*

uproar [ˈʌpˌɹoɚ] *n.* tumulte *m*, vacarme *m*: *to be in an* ~, être en tumulte.

uproot [ˌʌpˈɹuwt] *v. tr.* déraciner, arracher; [Fig.] extirper.

upset, upset, upset [ˌʌpˈsɛt] **[-tt-]** *v. tr.* renverser, faire chavirer (une barque); [Fig.] bouleverser (des plans, qqun), rendre malade: *to* ~ *the applecart*, tout flanquer par terre. ‖ *v. intr.* se renverser, [boat] chavirer. ‖ *adj.* renversé; malade; [emotionally] bouleversé; [stomach] dérangé. ‖ *n.* bouleversement *m.*

upshot [ˈʌpˌʃɑt] *n.* résultat *m.*

upside down [ˌʌpsajdˈdawn] *adv.* sens dessus dessous, la tête en bas: *to turn* ~, renverser; [Fig.] bouleverser.

upstairs [ʌpˈstɛɚz] *adv.* en haut; à l'étage supérieur: *to go* ~, monter, monter l'escalier. ‖ *adj.* d'en haut; → à l'étage supérieur. ‖ *n.* l'étage *m*, les étages, supérieur(s).

upstanding [ˌʌpˈstændɪŋ] *adj.* debout, droit; [hair] hérissé, qui se dresse.

upstart [ˈʌpˌstɑɚt] *n.* parvenu *m*, nouveau riche *m.*

upstream [ˌʌpˈstɹijm] *adv.* en amont. ‖ *adj.* [ˈʌpˌstɹijm] d'amont.

up-to-date [ˌʌptəˈdejt] *adj.* tout nouveau, (le plus) moderne; [person] à la page; [fashions] dernier cri; [car] dernier modèle; [account] mis à jour.

upturn [ˌʌpˈtɚn] *v. tr.* lever (les yeux); [soil] retourner.

upward [ˈʌpwɚd] *adj.* (dirigé) vers le haut, montant. ‖ *adv.* [also **upwards**] en haut, vers le haut, en montant: ~ *of*, plus de.

uranium [jəˈɹejnɪəm] *n.* uranium *m.*

urban [ˈɚbən] *adj.* urbain.

urbane [ɚˈbejn] *adj.* [×] courtois. ‖ **urbanely** [-lɪ] *adv.* avec urbanité. ‖ **urbanity** [ɚˈbænɪtɪ] *n.* urbanité *f.*

urchin ['ɚtʃɪn] *n.* gamin *m*, gamine *f*; gosse *m/f*; [Pej.] garnement *m*.

urge [ɚdʒ] *v. tr.* pousser, exhorter (qqun à faire qqch.); recommander (que + subjunc.): *to ~ s.o. on*, encourager, presser qqun. || *n.* impulsion *f*, incitation *f*, mobile *m*. || **urgency** ['ɚdʒənsɪ] *n.* urgence *f*. || **urgent** [ɚdʒənt] *adj.* urgent, pressant. || **urgently** *adv.* [speedily] d'urgence; [insistently] avec insistance.

urn [ɚn] *n.* urne *f*; [tea] samovar *m*.

Uruguay [ˌjɚə'gwej] *n.* [Géog.] l'Uruguay *m*: *in/to/ ~*, en Uruguay.

U.S. [ˌjuw'ɛs] *abr.* = *the United States* [également **U.S.A.** [ˌjuwɛs'ej] = *the United States of America*], © les É.-U., [Fr.] les U.S.A. [yɛs'a] = les États-Unis *mpl* (d'Amérique): *to/in/the U.S.(A.)*, aux É.-U., aux U.S.A.; *the ~ Consulate*, le consulat des États-Unis.

us [əs ou ʌs] *pron.* **1.** [dir. or ind. obj. of a verb] nous: *He sees ~*, Il nous voit; *He gives ~ the money*, Il nous donne l'argent; *He gives it to ~*, Il nous le donne; *Give it to ~*, Donnez-le-nous. **2.** [after a prep. or *to be*] nous: *Come with ~*, Venez avec nous; *It's ~ !*, C'est nous! **3.** [emphatic] nous, nous autres: *He wants* US, Il nous veut, nous (autres), C'est nous (autres) qu'il veut; *He likes ~ Canadians*, Il nous aime, nous autres Canadiens. **4.** [in imperative] -ons: *Let ~ begin*, *Let's* [lɛts] *begin*, Commençons; [×] *Let ~ finish* [= allow us to], Laissez-nous finir; *Let's see (it)*, Faites (-le) voir, Montrez-le-nous, Montrez!

usable ['juwzəbḷ] *adj.* utilisable. || **usage** ['juwsədʒ] *n.* **1.** usage *m*, coutume *f*. **2.** traitement *m*. **3.** [Ling.] usage *m*. || **use** [juws] *n.* **1.** usage *m*, emploi *m*: *to make (good) ~ of*, faire (bon) usage de; *to put into ~*, mettre en usage; *to put sth. to ~*, utiliser, profiter de/qqch.; *to find a ~ for sth.*, trouver un moyen d'utiliser qqch.; *to have many uses*, servir à de nombreux usages; *to be in ~*, [machine] être en service; [word] être usité; [place] être occupé; *to be out of ~*, [machine] être hors d'usage, hors de service; [word] être inusité; *to be ready for ~*, être prêt à servir; *for the ~ of*, à l'usage de; *with ~*, à l'usage; *For ~ in case of fire*, A employer en cas d'incendie; *Directions for ~*, Mode *m* d'emploi. **2.** utilité *f*, avantage *m*: *to be of ~ (as)*, être utile (à qqch.); servir (à qqch.); *to be of no ~*, être inutile, ne servir à rien; *(of) what ~ is it (to)?*, à quoi sert-il (de)?; *It's no ~ shouting*, (Il est) inutile de crier; *It's no ~ (your) trying, you won't do it*, Vous avez beau essayer, vous n'y arriverez pas; *What's the ~ of trying?*, *What ~ is it to try?*, A quoi bon essayer? A quoi sert-il d'essayer?; *I have no ~ for him*, Il ne m'intéresse pas, Il me déplaît; *I have no (more) ~ for it*, Je n'en ai pas besoin, Je n'en ai plus besoin. || **use** [juwz] *v. tr.* **1.** se servir de, employer, utiliser, faire usage de: *to be used for doing sth.*, servir à faire qqch.; *to be used (by s.o.) as sth.*, servir (à qqun) de qqch.; *Use your hands*, Servez-vous de vos mains; *Use your head*, Réfléchissez; *Use the back-door*, Entrez par la porte de derrière; *Our furnace uses a lot of fuel*, Notre chaudière consomme beaucoup de combustible. **2.** use to, cf. USED. || **to ~ up** *v. tr.* utiliser, épuiser: *to ~ the left-overs*, utiliser les restes; *to ~ one's patience, &c.*, épuiser sa patience, &c.; *It's all used* [juwzd] *up*, Il n'en reste plus. || **used** [juwzd] *adj.* **1.** usité, employé. **2.** d'occasion, usagé; → qui a servi: *~ car*, voiture *f* d'occasion, © *abus.* char *m.* usagé. || **used to** ['juwsˌtuw] *adj.* habitué, accoutumé (à qqch., à faire qqch.): *I am not ~ it*, Je n'y suis pas habitué, Je n'en ai pas l'habitude; *to get ~ (doing) sth.*, s'habituer, s'accoutumer à (faire) qqch.; *You'll get ~ it*, Vous vous y habituerez, Vous vous y ferez. || *aux.* [pour indiquer une série d'événements dans le passé] avoir l'habitude, →autrefois, [→ or use Fr. imperfect]: *I ~ go there every day*, J'avais l'habitude d'y aller/J'y allais (autrefois)/tous les jours; *You are taller than you ~ be*, Vous êtes plus grand qu'autrefois. || **useful** ['juwsfḷ] *adj.* utile, pratique. || **usefulness** *n.* utilité *f*. || **useless** ['juwsləs] *adj.* inutile, vain; → qui ne peut servir à rien, (qui n'est) bon à rien: *It's ~ to shout, he can't hear you*, (Il est) inutile de crier/Vous avez beau crier/ il ne vous entend pas. || **uselessness** ['juwsləsnəs] *n.* inutilité *f*. || **user** ['juwzɚ] *n.* usager *m* [no feminine].

usher ['ʌʃɚ] *n.* huissier *m*.

U.S.S.R. [ˌjuwˌɛsˌɛs'ɑɚ] *abr.* = *Union of Soviet Socialist Republics*, l'U.R.S.S. [lyʀs] = l'Union des Républiques Socialistes Soviétiques: *to/in/the ~*, en U.R.S.S.

usual ['juwʒ(w)əl] *adj.* habituel [= the same]; [common] courant; [traditional] d'usage: *his ~ smile*, son sourire habituel; *It is the ~ practice (to)*, C'est la pratique courante (de); *the ~ speeches*, les discours d'usage; *it is ~ to*, il est d'usage de; *as* ~, comme d'habitude; *more* (. . .) *than* ~, plus (. . .) que d'habitude; *in the* ~ *manner*, à l'ordinaire. || **usually** ['juwʒ(w)əlɪ] *adv.* d'habitude, d'ordinaire, en général, habituellement, généralement, normalement, ordinairement.

usurer ['juwzjɚɚ] *n.* usurier *m.*

usurp [ˌjuw'zɚp] *v. tr.* usurper. || *v. intr.*: *to* ~ *upon*, empiéter sur. || **usurper** [-ɚ] *n.* usurpat|eur *m*, -rice *f.*

Ut. *abr.* = Utah ['juwtɔ] l'Utah *m.*

utensil [ˌjuw'tɛnsl̩] *n.* ustensile *m.*

utilitarian [juwˌtɪlɪ'tɛɚɪən] *adj.* utilitaire.

utility [ˌjuw'tɪlətɪ] *n.* **1.** utilité *f* [USEFULNESS]: ~ *kit*, trousse *f*, nécessaire *m* (de toilette). **2.** [US] (*public*) *utilities*, entreprises *fpl* de service public [chemins de fer, autobus, gaz, électricité].

utilize ['juwtəˌlajz] *v. tr.* utiliser.

utmost ['ʌtˌmowst] (also †**uttermost**) *adj.* extrême; le plus grand, le plus élevé, le plus éloigné. || *n.* l'extrême *m*; le comble *m* (de): *at the* (*very*) ~, tout au plus; *to the* ~, (jusqu') au dernier point, degré; *to do one's* ~ (*to*), faire tout son possible (pour).

utopia [ˌjuw'towpɪ|ə] *n.* utopie *f.* || **utopian** [-ən] *adj.* utopique.

utter[1] ['ʌtɚ] *v. tr.* pousser (un cri), prononcer (des paroles).

utter[2] ['ʌtɚ] *adj.* total, complet, absolu; le plus grand: *to my* ~ *surprise*, à ma grande surprise.

utterance ['ʌtɚəns] *n.* expression *f*; déclaration *f*, propos *m*; [Ling.] énoncé *m*: *to give* ~ *to*, exprimer.

utterly ['ʌtɚlɪ] *adv.* tout à fait, totalement, complètement.

V

V, v [vij] *pl.* **V's, v's** [vijz] *n.* V, v *m*; *V-shaped*, en forme de V.

v. *abr.* cf. VERSUS.

Va. *abr.* cf. VIRGINIA.

vacancy ['vejkənsɪ] *n.* **1.** vacance *f*, poste *m* libre: *There is a* ~ *in our firm*, Il y a une vacance/un poste libre/dans notre maison; [motel] *Do you have a* ~?, Avez-vous une cabine (de) libre?; *No Vacancy*, Complet. **2.** vide *m* (de l'expression, de l'esprit). || **vacant** ['vejkənt] *adj.* **1.** vacant; libre: ~ *house*, maison vacante, inoccupée; ~ *seat*, siège vacant, libre; *The* ~ *lot* (*next door*), Le terrain vague (à côté). **2.** [Fig.] vide; distrait: ~ *smile*, sourire *m* vide (d'expression); ~ *look*, air distrait, ahuri.

vacate [ˌvej'kejt] *v. tr.* quitter (un lieu, un poste); vider (les lieux); laisser (un siège) libre.

vacation [və'kejʃən) *n.* vacances *fpl*: *He's* (*away*) *on* ~, Il est (parti) en vacances. || *v. intr.* prendre des vacances.

vaccinate ['væksəˌnejt] *v. tr.* vacciner. || **vaccination** *n.* vaccination *f.* || **vaccine** ['vækˌsijŋ] *n.* vaccin *m.*

vacillate ['væsɪˌlejt] *v. intr.* vaciller, fluctuer. || **vacillating** [-ɪŋ] *adj.* vacillant; [Fig.] irrésolu. || **vacillation** [ˌvæsɪ'lejʃən] *n.* vacillation *f*, hésitation *f.*

vacuum ['vækjʊm] *pl.* **vacuums, vacua,** *n.* vide *m*: *Nature abhors a* ~, La nature a horreur du vide. || *v. tr. & intr.* passer l'aspirateur. || **vacuum cleaner** *n.* aspirateur *m.*

vagabond ['vægəˌbɑnd] *n.* vagabond *m.* || *adj.* vagabond, -e.

vagrancy ['vejgɹən|sɪ] *n.* vagabondage *m.* || **vagrant** [-t] *adj.* & *n.* vagabond *m*, itinérant *m.*

vague [vejg] *adj.* vague, imprécis: *I haven't the vaguest idea*, Je n'en ai pas la moindre idée. || **vaguely** ['vejglɪ] *adv.* vaguement.

vain [vejn] *adj.* **1.** vain, inutile: *in* ~, en vain, vainement, inutilement. **2.** vaniteux. || **vainly** *adv.* en vain, vainement.

valentine ['væln̩ˌtajn] *n.* **1.** [personne] Valentin *m*: (*Saint*) *Valentine's Day*, La Saint-Valentin. **2.** carte *f* ou lettre *f* (de la Saint-Valentin), © Valentin *m.*

valet ['vælət] *n.* valet *m*: ~ *service*, nettoyage et repassage.

valiant ['væljənt] *adj.* vaillant, valeureux, brave.

valid ['væləd] *adj.* **1.** valide: *This passport is no longer* ~, Ce passeport n'est plus valide, → Ce passeport est périmé. **2.** valable: *This ticket is* ~ *for a month*, Ce billet est valable un mois; ~ *excuse*, excuse valable.

validity [və'lɪdɪtɪ] *n.* [argument] valeur *f*, justesse *f*; [document] validité *f*.

valley ['vælɪ] *n.* vallée *f*, vallon *m*; [Geog.] vallée *f*, bassin *m*: *the St. Lawrence* ~, la vallée du St-Laurent; *the Mississipi* ~, le bassin du Mississipi.

valorous ['vælərəs] *adj.* valeureux; vaillant, brave. ‖ **valour** ['vælər] *n.* valeur *f*; vaillance *f*.

valuable ['væljəbl̩] *adj.* [s.o., sth.] précieux, de (grande) valeur, [sth.] de (grand) prix: *a* ~ *contribution* (*to a cause*), une importante contribution (à une cause); *It proved very* ~, Cela nous a rendu de grands services. ‖ **valuables** *n. pl.* objets *mpl* de valeur. ‖ **value** ['væljuw] *n.* **1.** valeur *f*, prix *m*: *to be of* ~, avoir de la valeur; *to be of great* ~ (*to*), être de grande valeur (pour); *of little* ~, de peu de valeur, → sans (grande) valeur; *of no* ~, sans (aucune) valeur; *to set a* ~ *on sth.*, estimer, évaluer qqch.; *What is the* ~ *of . . .?*, Quel est le prix de . . .? **2.** [Com.] occasion *f*, © aubaine *f*: *Values!*, Aubaines! Des prix!. ‖ **value** *v. tr.* **1.** évaluer, estimer (un objet). **2.** attacher/du prix, de la valeur/à: *to* ~ *sth. highly*, attacher beaucoup de prix à qqch.; *If you* ~ *your life*, Si vous tenez à la vie. ‖ **valued** *adj.* de valeur; de (grand) prix. ‖ **valueless** ['væljuwləs] *adj.* sans valeur.

valve [vælv] *n.* soupape *f*: *safety* ~, soupape de sûreté.

van (væn] *n.* **1.** camion *m* (couvert); [Br.] fourgon *m*: *moving* ~, camion, fourgon, voiture *f* de déménagement; *delivery* ~, camionnette *f* de livraison. **2.** avant-garde *f* (d'une armée, &c.): *in the* ~, à l'avant-garde.

Vancouver Island [ˌVæŋ'kuwvər 'ajlənd] *n.* [Geog.] l'île *f* de Vancouver. ‖ **Vancouverite** [ˌVæŋ'kuwvərˌəjt] © *n.* habitant *m*, -e *f*, de Vancouver.

vandal ['vændl̩] *n.* vandale *m.* ‖ **vandalism** [-ɪzm] *n.* vandalisme *m.*

vanguard [væŋˌgɑərd] *n.* avant-garde *f*.

vanilla [və'nɪlə] *n.* vanille *f*: ~ *ice cream*, glace *f* à la vanille.

vanish ['vænɪʃ] *v. intr.* disparaître, s'évanouir.

vanity ['vænətɪ] *n.* **1.** vanité *f*: ~ *bag*, sac *m* de dame, de soirée; ~ *case*, poudrier *m* de sac. **2.** coiffeuse *f*.

vanquish ['væŋkwɪʃ] *v. tr. & intr.* vaincre.

vantage ['væntəʤ] *n.* avantage *m*: *point of* ~, position *f* avantageuse.

vapor cf. VAPOUR.

vapour ['vejpər] *n.* vapeur *f* (d'eau, de produit chimique); brume *f* (de marais).

variable ['væərɪəbl̩] *adj.* variable; changeant, incertain; (fête) mobile. ‖ **variability** [ˌværɪə'bɪlətɪ] *n.* variabilité *f*; caractère *m* changeant. ‖ **variably** ['væərɪəblɪ] *adv.* d'une manière variable, changeante.

variant ['væərɪənt] *adj. & n(f)* → variante.

variation [ˌvæərɪ'ejʃən] *n.* variation *f*. ‖ **varied** ['væərɪd] *adj.* varié, divers; diversifié; [style] nuancé.

variety [və'ɹajətɪ] *n.* variété *f*; assortiment *m*: *He showed me a* ~ *of products*, Il m'a montré tout un assortiment de marchandises; ~ *show*, music-hall *m*; variétés *fpl*.

various ['væərɪəs] *adj.* divers, différent: *on* ~ *occasions*, en diverses occasions; ~ *tools*, différentes sortes d'outils. ‖ **variously** *adv.* de plusieurs façons.

varnish [vɑərnɪʃ] *n.* vernis *m.*‖ *v. tr.* **1.** vernir, passer au vernis; vernisser (des poteries, &c.). **2.** [Fig.] farder (la vérité).

varsity ('vɑərsətɪ] *n.* [abr. de UNIVERSITY].

vary [væərɪ] *v. intr.* **1.** varier; s'écarter (d'une route, d'un précédent). **2.** ne pas être du même avis, être d'avis contraire: *Opinions* ~, → Les avis sont partagés; *It varies*, Cela dépend. ‖ *v. tr.* varier, diversifier; apporter des variations à.

vase [vejz] [vɑz] *n.* vase *m.*

vaseline [ˌvæsə'lijn] *n.* vaseline *f* [in French, a common noun, not a trade mark].

vast [væst] *adj.* vaste, immense (étendue, &c.); énorme (quantité); (projet) grandiose. ‖ **vastly** *adv.* immensément; énormément; extrêmement. ‖ **vastness** ['væstnəs] *n.* vaste étendue *f*, vastes dimensions *fpl*, immensité *f*; énormité (d'une quantité, &c.); grandeur *f* (d'un projet).

vat [væt] *n.* cuve *f*, bac *m.*

Vatican (the) ['vætɪkən] *n.* le Vatican *m*; *the Vatican City*, la Cité du Vatican.

vault [vɔlt] *n.* **1.** [Arch.] voûte *f*. **2.** chambre *f* forte, caveau *m*: *the vaults of the Bank of Montreal*, les caveaux de la Banque de Montréal. 3. saut *m*: *pole* ~, saut *m* à la perche. ‖ **vault** *v. tr. & intr.* sauter.

V.C. ['vij'sij] *abr.* = *Victoria Cross* [médaille militaire pour bravoure insigne]; également abr. de *Vice-Chairman*, *Vice-Chancellor*.

veal [vijl] *n.* (la viande de) veau *m*: ~ *cutlet*, côtelette *f* de veau.
vegetable ['vɛdʒ(ə)təbl̩] *n.* légume *m.* || *adj.* végétal: ~ *kingdom*, règne *m* végétal; ~ *garden*, jardin *m* potager; ~ *soup*, potage *m* aux légumes. || **vegetation** [ˌvɛdʒə'tejʃən] *n.* végétation *f.*
vehemence ['vijəmən|s] *n.* véhémence *f*, violence *f.* || **vehement** [-t] *adj.* véhément, violent; [love] ardent.
vehicle ['vijəkl] *n.* véhicule *m*: *motor* ~, véhicule automobile; [Fig. = medium] véhicule, moyen *m* (de propagation).
veil [vejl] *n.* [full] voile *m*; [half] voilette *f*; [Fig.] apparence *f*, prétexte *m.* || *v. tr.* voiler, mettre un voile sur; dissimuler, masquer (son visage, la vérité, &c.): *veiled threat*, menace *f* voilée.
vein [vejn] *n.* veine *f*: *in the same* ~, de la même nature; *of/in/(a) humorous* ~, d'un genre humoristique.
velocity [və'lɑsətɪ] *n.* **1.** [Tech.] vitesse *f.* †**2.** vélocité *f.*
velvet ['vɛlvət] *n.* velours *m.* || *adj.* [clothes] de, en/velours; velouté; [également velvety].
venal ['vijnl̩] *adj.* vénal. || **venality** [vɪ'nælɪtɪ] *n.* vénalité *f.*
vend [vɛnd] *v. tr.* vendre. || *v. intr.* (se) vendre.
vendor ['vɛndɚ], also **vender,** *n.* **1.** marchand *m* ambulant: *peanut* ~, marchand de cacahuètes. **2.** distributeur *m* automatique.
veneer [və'nijɚ] *n.* **1.** plaque *f* [pour le revêtement de la surface de certains ouvrages de menuiserie, d'ébéniste, etc.]: *to have a* ~ *of oak*, être (contre-)plaqué de chêne *m.* **2.** || vernis *m*: [Fig.] ~ *of elegance*, vernis d'élégance. || **veneer** *v. tr.* plaquer.
venerable ['vɛnɚ|əbl̩] *adj.* vénérable. || **veneration** [-ejʃən] *n.* vénération *f.*
Venetian [və'nijʃən] *n.* Vénitien, -ne. || *adj.* vénitien, -ne: ~ *blind*, © store *m* vénitien.
Venezuela [ˌvɛnəz'wejlə] *n.* le Venezuela: *to, in* ~, au Venezuela. || **Venezuelan** [ˌvɛnəz'wejlən] *adj.* vénézuélien, -enne.
vengeance ['vɛndʒəns] *n.* **1.** vengeance *f*: *to take* ~ *for sth.*, se venger de qqch. **2.** (Loc.) *with a* ~ → (a) [= more than expected] à outrance, de plus belle: *He started to work with a* ~, Il s'est mis à travailler/de plus belle, à outrance; (b) [to the utmost limit] tant que ça peut: *It's raining with a* ~, Il pleut tant que ça peut.
vengeful ['vɛndʒfl̩] *adj.* vindicatif; vengeur *m*, vengeresse *f.*
venial ['vijnɪəl] *adj.* léger, excusable; [sin] véniel.
Venice ['vɛnəs] *n.* [Geog.] Venise *f*; cf. VENETIAN.
venom ['vɛnəm] *n.* venin *m* (de serpent, &c.) [also Fig.]. || **venomous** ['vɛnəməs] *adj.* [serpent *m*, araignée *f*, &c.] venimeux.
vent [vɛnt] *n.* **1.** orifice *m*; fente *f*; évent *m*; trou *m* (d'une flûte); lumière *f* (d'une arme à feu); [breathing hole] soupirail *m.* **2.** [Fig.] (libre) cours *m*: *to give* ~ *to*, [one's anger] donner libre cours à, [sigh, cry of pain] laisser échapper. || **vent** *v. tr.* [anger, indignation, &c.] donner libre cours *m* à; exhaler, décharger: *He vented his anger on his horse*, Il déchargeait sa colère sur son cheval. || **ventilate** ['vɛntəˌlejt] *v. tr.* ventiler, aérer (une pièce). || **ventilation** [ˌvɛntə'lejʃən] *n.* ventilation *f*, aération *f.*
venture ['vɛntʃɚ] *n.* aventure *f*; tentative *f*, entreprise *f*, initiative *f*; risque *m*: *a worthwhile* ~, une initiative qui en vaut la peine; *a useless* ~, une tentative inutile; *a risky* ~, une entreprise pleine de risques. || **venture** *v. tr.* hasarder (une opinion, une hypothèse, sa vie, son argent). || *v. intr.* s'aventurer: *to* ~ (*to do sth.*), oser (faire qqch.); *to* ~ *out/into, too far/*, s'aventurer dehors/dans, trop loin/. || **venturesome** ['vɛntʃɚsəm] *adj.* aventureux, audacieux.
veranda [vɚ'ændə] *n.* véranda *f.*
verb [vɚb] *n.* verbe *m.* || **verbal** ['vɚbl̩] *adj.* verbal, -e: *a* ~ *agreement*, un accord verbal. || **verbatim** [vɚ'bejtəm] *adv.* & *adj.* in extenso, (au) complet.
verbose [vɚ'bows] *adj.* verbeux, prolixe.
verdict ['vɚdɪkt] *n.* verdict *m*; [Fig.] jugement *m*; décision *f*; opinion *f*; *to bring in a* ~, (*of guilty, not guilty*), rendre un verdict (de coupable, non-coupable).
verge [vɚdʒ] *n.* 1. bord *m* (d'un précipice); limite *f*, confins *mpl* (de la folie, &c.): *on the* ~ *of*, sur le point de (faire faillite, éclater en larmes), sur le penchant (de la ruine).
verger ['vɚdʒɚ] *n.* [R.C.] sacristain *m.*
verification [ˌvɛɚɪfə'keiʃən] *n.* vérification *f*; confirmation *f.* || **verify** ['vɛɚəˌfaj] *v. tr.* [check] vérifier; confirmer.
†**verily** ['vɚəlɪ] *adv.* [surtout biblique] en vérité. || **veritable** ['vɚɪtəbl̩] *adj.* vrai, véritable.
vermin ['vɚmɪn] *n.* vermine *f*; [coll.] bêtes *fpl*, insectes *mpl*/nuisibles.
Vermont [vɚ'mɑnt] *n.* le Vermont *m.*
vernacular [vɚ'nækjəlɚ] *adj.* & *n.* vernaculaire: ~ *language*, langue *f*/locale, vernaculaire/.

virtual [ˈvərtʃuwl̩] *adj.* virtuel, → qui équivaut à; vrai, de fait. || **virtually** [-ɪ] *adv.* au fait, effectivement; virtuellement.
virtue [ˈvərtʃuw] *n.* vertu *f*; [Fig.] mérite *m*, avantage *m*; qualité *f* (intrinsèque): *by, in/ ~ of,* en vertu de, en raison de; *It has the ~ of being cheap,* Cela a l'avantage d'être bon marché; [Loc.] *to make a ~ of necessity,* faire contre mauvaise fortune bon cœur. || **virtuous** [ˈvərtʃuwəs] *adj.* vertueux; méritoire. || **virtuously** *adv.* vertueusement.
virulence [ˈvijərələn|s] *n.* virulence *f.* || **virulent** [-t] *adj.* virulent, violent.
virus [ˈvajərəs] *n.* virus *m.*
visa [ˈvijzə] *n.* visa *m.* || **visa** *v. tr.* viser (un passeport).
visage [ˈvɪzədʒ] *n.* visage *m.*
vise cf. VICE 2.
visibility [ˌvɪzəˈbɪlətɪ] *n.* visibilité *f.* || **visible** [ˈvɪzəbl̩] *adj.* visible; évident, manifeste. || **visibly** [ˈvɪzəblɪ] *adv.* visiblement, de toute évidence; à vue d'œil.
vision [ˈvɪʒən] *n.* vision *f*; [= sight] vue *f*: *field of ~,* champ visuel; *man of (great) ~,* homme qui a une (large) vision de l'avenir.
visionary [ˈvɪzɪˌnɛərɪ] *adj.* visionnaire; [idea] chimérique, imaginaire. || *n.* visionnaire *m/f.*
visit [ˈvɪzət] *n.* visite *f*; [stay] séjour *m*: *to pay a ~ (to s.o.)* → rendre visite (à qqun); *a ~ to the country,* un séjour à la campagne; *to be (away) on a ~ to friends,* être en visite chez des amis. || **visit** *v. tr.* visiter (qqch.); aller voir, venir voir (qqun, qqch.), rendre visite (à); séjourner (dans un pays). || *v. intr.*: *to go visiting,* faire des visites; aller visiter (les pauvres); *to be visiting,* être en visite. || **visiting** *adj. the ~ team,* les visiteurs; *~ professor,* professeur invité; *~ card,* carte *f* de visite. || **visitor** [ˈvɪzətər] *n.* visiteur *m.*
visor [ˈvajzər] *n.* visière *f* (de casquette, &c.); [Auto] pare-soleil *m.*
visual [ˈvɪʒuwəl] *adj.* visuel; optique: *~ aids,* (enseignement) par l'image. || **visualize** [ˈvɪʒuwəlˌajz] *v. intr.* se représenter qqch., se faire une image (mentale) de qqch., qqun.
vital (ˈvajtl̩] *adj.* [organs, force, question] vital; indispensable: *Hard work is ~ to success,* Le travail assidu est indispensable au succès. || **vitality** [ˌvajˈtælətɪ] *n.* vitalité *f*, vigueur *f.* || **vitals** *n. pl.* les organes *mpl* /vitaux, essentiels/, les parties *fpl* vitales.
vitamin [ˈvajtəmən] *n.* vitamine *f*; *~ A, B, C, &c.,* vitamine A, B, C, &c.; *~ deficiency,* avitaminose *f.*

vituperation [vɪˌtuwpərˈejʃən] *n.* [coll.] injures *fpl.*
vivacious [vɪˈvejʃəs] *adj.* vif; éveillé, enjoué. || **vivacity** [vɪˈvæsətɪ] *n.* vivacité *f* (d'esprit, de caractère), verve *f.*
vivid [ˈvɪvəd] *adj.* [colour] frappant, vif; [description] frappant; [souvenir] vivace. || **vividly** *adv.* d'une manière frappante.
viz. [vɪz] or [ˈnejmlɪ] *abr. videlicet* [mot latin, mais on prononce *namely*] (à) savoir; c'est-à-dire, c.-à-d.
vocabulary [vəˈkæbjəˌlɛərɪ] *n.* vocabulaire *m*: *~ entry,* article *m* (de dictionnaire).
vocal [ˈvowkl̩] *adj.* vocal; oral; doué de (la) voix; [Fig.] *to be ~ about,* revenir à la charge à propos de . . . || **vocalist** [ˈvowkl̩ɪst] *n.* chanteur *m*, cantatrice *f.*
vocation [ˌvowˈkejʃən] *n.* vocation *f*, profession *f*, métier *m*: *to have a/sacerdotal, priestly/~,* avoir la vocation sacerdotale. || **vocational** [ˌvowˈkejʃənəl] *adj.* professionnelle: *~ guidance,* orientation *f* professionnelle; *~ school,* école *f* professionnelle.
vociferous [vəˈsɪfərəs] *adj.* criard, vociférant.
vogue [vowg] *n.* vogue *f*, mode *f*: *to be in ~,* avoir de la vogue, être à la mode.
voice [vojs] *n.* voix *f*; opinion *f*; [Gram.] voix (active, passive): *in a/loud, low/~,* à haute voix, à voix basse; *in, with/a soft ~,* d'une voix douce; *at the top of his ~,* à tue-tête; *with one ~,* unanimement, à l'unanimité; [Radio] *The Voice of America,* La voix de l'Amérique. || **voice** *v. tr.* exprimer. || **voiced** [vojst] *adj.* [Phon.] voisé, sonore: *loud-voiced,* à la voix forte. || **voiceless** [ˈvojsləs] *adj.* **1.** sans voix, muet, silencieux. **2.** [Phon.] sourd.
void [vojd] *adj.* vide; nul, annulé: *~ of,* dénué de. || *n.* vide *m*; espace *m* libre. || *v. tr.* vider; annuler, rendre nul: *to ~ (a cheque, &c.),* annuler (un chèque, &c.).
volatile [ˈvɑləˌtajl] *adj.* **1.** volatil. **2.** [Fig.] (personne) volage.
volcanic [vɑlˈkænɪk] *adj.* volcanique. || **volcano** [vɑlˈkejnow] *n.* volcan *m.*
volley [ˈvɑlɪ] *n.* salve *f*, volée *f* (de coups de canon); décharge *f*, rafale *f* (de mitraille); bordée *f* (d'injures); [tennis] volée *f.* || **volley** *v. tr.* tirer une salve; lancer/une volée, une décharge/. || **volleyball** [ˈvɑlɪˌbɔl] *n.* [Sport] volley ball *m*, © ballon *m* volant.
volt [vowlt] *n.* volt *m.* || **voltage** [ˈvowltədʒ] *n.* voltage *m*: *high ~ wire,* fil à haute tension.
voluble [ˈvɑljəbl̩] *adj.* [Pers.] volubile; [speech] facile.

volume ['vɑljəm] *n.* **1.** volume *m*, quantité *f*; [*pl.*] nuages *m* (de fumée). **2.** volume *m* [= livre]; tome *m*: *a 20-volume encyclopædia*, une encyclopédie en vingt volumes; [Fig.] *to speak volumes for*, en dire long sur. ‖ **voluminous** [və'luwmɪnəs] *adj.* volumineux, encombrant.

voluntarily [ˌvɑlən'tɛə̃əlɪ] *adv.* volontairement, librement, de soi-même, spontanément. ‖ **voluntary** ['vɑlənˌtɛə̃ɪ] *adj.* volontaire, spontané, libre. ‖ **volunteer** [ˌvɑlən'tijə̃] *n.* volontaire *m.* ‖ *v. intr.* s'engager comme volontaire; offrir (spontanément) ses services comme/en qualité de/, s'offrir.

voluptuous [və'lʌptʃuwəs] *adj.* voluptueux.

vomit ['vɑmət] *v. tr. & intr.* vomir, [Fam.] rendre.

voracious [ˌvɔə̃'ejʃəs] *adj.* vorace.

votary ['vowtə̃ɪ] *n.* adorat|eur *m*, -rice *f*; fidèle *m*, partisan *m.*

vote [vowt] *n.* vote *m*, voix *f*; [= ballot] scrutin *m*: *to have a* ~, avoir le droit de vote; *to pass a* ~ *of thanks*, voter des remerciements (à), *to put a motion to the* ~, mettre une proposition aux voix. ‖ *v. intr.* voter (*for*, pour; *against*, contre). ‖ *v. tr.* élire qqun. ‖ **voter** *n.* votant *m*, électeur *m.* ‖ **voting** *n.* vote *m*; © votation *f.*

vouch [vɑwtʃ] *v. intr. to* ~ *for*, garantir, répondre de. ‖ **voucher** ['vɑwtʃə̃] *n.* récépissé *m*, talon *m*; pièce *f* justificative. ‖ **vouchsafe** [vɑwtʃ'sejf] *v. tr.* accorder [*to*, à], daigner (faire qqch.).

vow (vaw] *n.* vœu *m*; serment *m*: *marriage vows*, serments de mariage; *to make a* ~ (*to do sth.*), faire un vœu, faire vœu (de faire qqch.); *to take one's vows*, entrer en religion; *to take a* ~ *of poverty*, faire vœu de pauvreté. ‖ *v. tr.* [dedicate] vouer; [swear] jurer.

vowel ['vawəl] *n.* voyelle *f.*

voyage ['vojəʤ] *n.* [×] voyage *m* (par mer), parcours *m* maritime; traversée *f*; *Bon Voyage!*, Bon voyage!; *We had a pleasant* ~ (*across the Atlantic*), Nous avons fait une traversée agréable (de l'Atlantique). ‖ *v. intr.* traverser la mer; parcourir les mers. ‖ **voyager** ['vojəʤə̃] *n.* voyag|eur *m*, -euse *f*; [on a boat] passag|er *m*, -ère *f.*

vs. ['vəsəs] *abr.* cf. VERSUS.

Vt. [və'mɑnt] *abr.* cf. VERMONT.

vulgar ['vʌlgə̃] *adj.* [common] vulgaire, [coarse] grossier: *Vulgar Latin*, le bas-latin, le latin vulgaire. ‖ **vulgarity** [vʌl'gæə̃ətɪ] *n.* vulgarité *f*; grossièreté *f.* ‖ **vulgarize** ['vʌlgə̃ajz] *v. tr.* vulgariser, populariser (une théorie, &c.). ‖ **Vulgate** (the) ['vʌlˌgejl̩] *n.* [R.C.] la Vulgate *f.*

vulnerable ['vʌlnɔə̃bl] *adj.* vulnérable.

vulture ['vʌltʃə̃] *n.* vautour *m*

vying [-ɪŋ] cf. VIE.

W

W, w ['dʌbəljuw] *n.* **1.** W, w *m.* **2.** w. *abr.* cf. WATT. **3.** W. *abr.* cf. WEST, WESTERN.

wacky ['wækɪ] *adj.* [Fam.] cinglé.

wad [wɑd] *n.* **1.** [pad] tampon *m* (d'ouate, &c.) **2.** [firearms] bourre *f.* **3.** [Fam.] paquet *m*, liasse *f* (de billets de banque). ‖ *v. tr.* bourrer.

waddle ['wɑdl̩] *v. intr.* se dandiner, marcher en canard.

wade [wejd] *v. intr.* **1.** marcher (dans l'eau), patauger (dans la mer, la boue); [through an obstacle] se frayer un chemin. **2.** [Fig.] *to* ~ *through a book*, avancer péniblement dans la lecture d'un livre. ‖ *v. tr.* traverser (une rivière) à gué. ‖ **wader** ['wejdə̃] *n.* [Ornith.] échassier *m.*

wafer ['wejfə̃] *n.* **1.** gaufrette *f.* **2.** [R.C.] hostie *f.*

waffle ['wɑfl̩] *n.* gaufre *f*: ~ *iron*, gaufrier *m.*

waft [wɑft] *v. tr.* [smell, &c.] porter; [kiss] envoyer. ‖ *v. intr.* [smell, &c.] flotter; [breeze] souffler; s'exhaler (*from*, de).

wag [wæg] *v. tr.* [-gg-] [dog] agiter, remuer (la queue); [bird] hocher (la queue): *to* ~ *o.'s head*, hocher la tête. ‖ *v. intr.* [tail] remuer, s'agiter; [tête] branler. ‖ *n.*

hochement *m*, frétillement *m* (de la queue).

wage [wejʤ] *v. tr.* mener (une lutte): *to ~ war* (*on s.o., against sth.*), faire la guerre à (qqun, qqch.). || *n.* [généralement au pl.] **1.** salaire *m*; paye *f* (d'ouvrier); gages *mpl* (de domestique). **2.** [Fig.] récompense *f*, prix *m*. || **wage-earner** [ˈwejʤˌɚnɚ] *n.* salarié *m*.

wager [ˈwejʤɚ] *n.* pari *m*, [esp. ©] gageure *f*. || *v. tr.* parier [esp. ©] gager.

wagon [ˈwægən] *n.* voiture *f* (à quatre roues); charrette *f* (à foin); chariot *m* (à bœufs); [plaything] chariot *m*.

waif [wejf] *n.* enfant *m* abandonné; [Fig.] épave *f*.

wail [wejl] *v. intr.* se lamenter, gémir. || *n.* lamentation *f*, plainte *f*.

waist [wejst] *n.* taille *f*; [belt] ceinture *f*: *to strip to the ~*, se mettre torse nu. || **waistcoat** [ˈwejstˌkowt] *n.* gilet *m* [N.B. in French Canada, *gilet* often means *coat*].

wait [wejt] *v. intr.* attendre: *to keep s.o. waiting*, faire attendre qqun; *Wait a minute!*, Attendez(-moi)/une minute, un instant/; *I'll ~/till, until/he comes*, J'attendrai qu'il vienne; *He is waiting to be told*, Il attend qu'on le lui dise; *He didn't ~ to be told twice*, → Il ne se l'est pas fait dire deux fois; *~ and see*, voir venir. || *~* **for** (*s.o., sth.*) attendre (qqun, qqch.): *He waited for me to write to him*, Il a attendu que je lui écrive. || *~* **(up)on s.o.** (at table) servir qqun (à table). || *~* **up** (*for s.o.*) rester debout à attendre qqun: *Don't wait up* (*for me*), → Ne m'attendez pas (pour vous coucher). || **wait** [wejt] *n.* attente *f*; [stop] arrêt *m*: *He had a long ~*, → Il a dû attendre longtemps; *to lie in ~* (*for s.o.*), guetter l'arrivée/le passage/de qqun; [ambush] se tenir en embuscade, dresser un guet-apens à qqun. || **waiter** [ˈwejtɚ] *n.* garçon *m* (de café, de restaurant): *head ~*, maître *m* d'hôtel. || **waiting** [ˈwejtɪŋ] *n.* attente *f* [or some form of *attendre*]: *~ room*, salle d'attente; *It's no use* (*your*) *~*, → Inutile d'attendre. || **waitress** [ˈwejtɹəs] *n.* serveuse *f* (de restaurant, de café), fille *f* de salle: *Waitress!*, Mademoiselle!

waive [wejv] *v. tr.* renoncer à, abandonner (un droit, &c.); ne pas exiger (une prime), ne pas insister sur (un point de règlement). || **waiver** [-ɚ] *n.* renonciation *f*, désistement *m*; dérogation *f* (à un règlement).

wake[1] [wejk], **woke** [wowk], **waked** [wejkt] [moins souvent: *waked, woken*; dans le language courant, on emploie dans les sens 1 et intr.: *to wake up.*] *v. tr.* **1.** réveiller. **2.** [arouse] éveiller (une émotion, un soupçon, &c.). || *v. tr.* se réveiller. || **wake**[2] [wejk] *n.* sillage *m* [d'un navire]; [Fig.] *in the ~ of*, à la suite de, à la remorque de.

waken [ˈwejkən] *v. tr.* éveiller, [habitual] réveiller (qqun). || *v. intr.* [habitual] se réveiller.

walk [wɔk] *n.* **1.** marche *f*: *at a ~*, au pas, lentement; *It's an hour's walk from here*, C'est à une heure de marche d'ici. **2.** promenade *f* (à pied): *to go for a ~, to take a ~*, (aller) faire une promenade (à pied), se promener; *to take for a ~*, emmener (qqun) en promenade; promener (le chien). **3.** démarche *f*: *I know him by his ~*, Je le reconnais à sa démarche. **4.** allée *f* (de jardin, &c.). **5.** *~ of life*, [class] milieu *m*, [calling] métier *m*. || **walk** [wɔk] *v. intr.* **1.** [activity] marcher: *He can't ~*, (*his leg is broken*), Il ne peut pas marcher, (sa jambe est cassée). **2.** [from one place to another] aller/venir, &c./à pied: *He walked here*, Il est venu ici à pied; *They walked five miles*, Ils ont fait cinq milles à pied. || *v. tr.* **1.** promener (un cheval) au pas; promener (un chien, &c.). **2.** [the floor] marcher de long en large; [the deck] arpenter le pont; [the streets] parcourir les rues. || *~* **away/back, down, in(to), off, out, (a)round, through, up/** [use a verb of motion + *à pied* if necessary—for ordinary uses, see GO, COME, &c.; for special uses, see below.] || *~* **along, on, up and down/**, cf. ALONG, ON, UP/. || *~* **about** se promener. || *~* **off with** gagner (un prix), obtenir (les meilleures notes); décamper avec (un objet volé). || [Fam.] *~* **out 1.** se retirer: *to ~ out on s.o.*, laisser tomber qqun. **2.** [strike] se mettre en grève. || **walking** [ˈwɔkɪŋ) *n.* marche *f*: *Walking is good for you*, La marche vous fait du bien; *It is within* (*5 minutes'*) *~ distance*, On peut s'y rendre à pied (en 5 minutes). || **walking stick** [ˈwɔkɪŋˌstɪk] *n.* canne *f*.

wall [wɔl] *n.* mur *m* (d'une maison, d'une chambre); [fortification] muraille *f*; [partition] cloison *f*; paroi *f* (de cylindre, d'un tunnel, &c.): *on the ~*, [inside] au mur, [outside] sur le mur, au mur. || *adj.* mural: *~ map*, carte *f* murale. || **wall** [wɔl] *v. tr.* entourer (une ville, un jardin) de murs; murer (une fenêtre).

wallet [ˈwɔlət] *n.* portefeuille *m*.

wallflower [ˈwɔlˌflawɚ] *n.* [Bot.] ravenelle *f*; [Fig.] → (personne qui fait) tapisserie.

wallop ['wɔləp] *n.* [Fam.] coup *m*, [Sl.] gnon *m*: [Fig.] *with a* ~, à grand fracas.

wallow ['wɔlow] *v. intr.* se vautrer (*in*, dans): *to* ~ *in money*, être cousu d'or.

wallpaper ['wɔl,pejpɚ] *n.* papier *m* peint, tapisserie *f*.

walnut ['wɔl,nʌt] *n.* [nut] noix *f*; [tree] noyer *m*; (bois *m* de) noyer *m*: ~ *dresser*, commode *f* en noyer.

walrus ['wɔlɹəs] *n.* morse *m*, cheval *m* marin.

waltz [wɑltz] *n.* valse *f*.

wan [wɑn] *adj.* [complexion] blême, livide, [sky] blafard; [smile] pâle.

wander ['wɑndɚ] *v. intr.* errer, se promener au hasard; [thoughts] s'égarer: *to* ~ *off the subject*, digresser; *His mind must be wandering*, Il doit divaguer.

wane [wejn] *v. intr.* [moon, &c.] décroître; [Fig.] décliner. || *n.* déclin *m*.

wangle ['wæŋgḷ] *v. intr.* [Fam.] se débrouiller. || *v. tr.* se débrouiller pour avoir; [Fam.] resquiller.

want [wɑnt] *v. tr.* **1.** vouloir [→ the present tense conveys the idea of determination; politeness often requires *je voudrais, &c.*]; [less intense] désirer; demander: *Do you* ~ *another helping?*, En voulez-vous encore (une portion); *He wanted to come* [*but didn't*], Il voulait venir; [*and did*], Il a voulu venir; *I* ~ *you to do this*, Je veux que vous fassiez ceci; *I* ~ *it done properly*, Je veux que ce soit fait comme il faut; *He wants his hair cut*, Il veut se faire couper les cheveux; *The wanted man*, L'homme recherché (par la police); *You are wanted on the phone*, On vous demande à l'appareil; *How much do you* ~ *for it?*, Combien en demandez-vous?; /*What do you* ~ /*from*/*of*/ *with*/ *me?*/ Que me voulez-vous?, Que voulez-vous de moi?; *The cat wants in*/*out*/, Le chat veut rentrer/sortir/. **2.** [need] avoir besoin (de), falloir: *The baby wants his mother*, Le bébé a besoin de sa maman; *I have all I* ~, J'ai tout ce qu'il me faut. **3.** †[−LACK]. || *v. intr.* **1.** être dans le besoin. **2.** [ord. à la forme progressive] manquer: *Several books are wanting*, Il y a plusieurs livres qui manquent; *He is not wanting in self-confidence*, Il ne manque pas d'assurance, → Ce n'est pas l'assurance qui lui manque. || **want** *n.* **1.** besoin *m*; désir *m*: *His wants are few*, Ses besoins sont peu nombreux. **2.** manque *m*: *for* ~ *of*, faute de, à défaut de; *to be in* ~ *of sth.*, avoir besoin de qqch. **3.** misère *f*, besoin *m*: *to be* (*living*) *in* (*great*) ~, être/vivre/dans la misère/dans le besoin/. || **wanted** ['wɑnt|əd] *adj.* demandé; → on demande; [police] recherché (par la police).

wanton ['wɑntən] *adj.* [child] espiègle; [love] déréglé; [women] impudique.

wapiti ['wɔpətı] *n.* [Zool.] cerf *m* du Canada.

war [wɔɚ] *n.* **1.** guerre *f*: *at* ~, en (état de) guerre; *to go to* ~, déclarer la guerre, se mettre en guerre, [soldier] aller à la guerre; *the American Civil War* [also: *The War between the States*], la guerre de Sécession; *the First*/*Second*/ *World War*, la première/deuxième/guerre mondiale; *the Korean War*, la guerre de Corée. **2.** [fight] combat *m*, lutte *f* (contre la maladie). || **war** [wɔɚ] *v. intr.* **[-rr-]** faire la guerre (contre).

warble ['wɔɚbḷ] *v. intr.* gazouiller. || *n.* gazouillement *m*; [Fam.] gazouillis *m*.

warbler ['wɔɚblɚ] *n.* [Ornith.] fauvette *f*; bec-fin *m*.

ward [wɔɚd] *n.* **1.** quartier *m* (d'une ville), [in Paris] arrondissement *m*. **2.** salle *f* (d'hôpital). **3.** pupille *m, f*.

warden [wɔɚdṇ] *n.* **1.** gardien *m*, surveillant *m*; geôlier *m*. **2.** directeur *m* (d'une prison, d'une institution). **3.** © préfet *m* [à la tête d'un comité].

-ward(s) [-wɚd(z)] [suf. marque un mouvement *vers*] vers: *northward(s)* vers le nord.

wardrobe ['wɔɚd,ɹowb] *n.* garde-robe *f*.

ware(s) [wɛɚ(z)] *n.* [souvent *pl*] marchandise(s) *f* (pl); porcelaine *f*. || **warehouse** ['wɛɚ,haws] *n.* entrepôt *m*, magasin *m*: *furniture* ~, garde-meuble *m*.

warfare ['wɔɚ,fɛɚ] *n.* guerre *f*.

warlike ['wɔɚ,lajk] *adj.* guerrier, martial.

warm [wɔɚm] *adj.* **[-er, -est] 1.** chaud; [lukewarm] tiède: *to be* ~, [things] être chaud(e), [persons] avoir chaud, [weather] faire chaud; *to get* ~, [persons] se réchauffer, [things] commencer à chauffer, [weather] commencer à faire chaud]; [game] *You're getting* ~ *!*, Vous brûlez!; *to keep* ~, se tenir au chaud, tenir qqch. chaud, au chaud. **2.** [Fig.] [welcome, thanks, friend, &c.] chaleureux; [heart] généreux; [admirer] ardent; [temper] vif; [discussion] animé; [tone, colour] chaud: *to make things* ~ *for a person*, en faire voir de dures à qqun. || **warm** [wɔɚm] *v. intr.* chauffer: *The milk is warming on the stove*, Le lait chauffe sur le fourneau; *My heart warmed to him*, → Il m'est devenu (plus) sympathique. || *v. tr.* (se) chauffer: *I am warming myself*/*my hands*/*at the fire*, Je me chauffe (les mains) au feu; *I'll ~ some milk*, Je vais faire chauffer du lait. || **~ up** *v. tr.* faire chauffer (du lait, une salle, &c.); réchauffer (un repas, des restes, &c.). || *v. intr.* [liquid] chauffer; [person, weather] se réchauffer; [speaker] s'échauffer; [discussion] s'animer; [audience] s'intéresser; [company] devenir plus cordial. || **warmly** ['wɔɚmlɪ] *adv.* (s'habiller, applaudir) chaudement; (accueillir, remercier) chaleureusement; (répliquer) avec chaleur, vivement.

war-monger ['wɔɚˌmɑŋɚ] *n.* fauteur *m* de guerre.

warmth [wɔɚmθ] *n.* chaleur *f*; [Fig.] ardeur *f*, ferveur *f*; [speech] feu *m.*

warn [wɔɚn] *v. tr.* [inform] avertir; [forewarn] prévenir: *to ~ s.o. of sth.*, avertir qqun de qqch.; *to ~ s.o. against sth.*, mettre qqun en garde contre qqch.; *She was warned against beginning again, She was warned not to begin again*, → On lui a conseillé de ne pas recommencer. || **warning** ['wɔɚnɪŋ] *n.* avertissement *m*: *without ~*, sans avis préalable; *without the slightest ~*, sans donner la moindre indication de ses intentions.

warp [wɔɚp] *v. intr.* gauchir, dévier; [wheel] voiler. || **warped** [wɔɚpt] *adj.* gauchi, voilé; [Fig.] faussé.

warrant ['wɔɚənt] *n.* [Com.] autorisation *f*, garantie *f*; [Jur.] mandat *m* (d'amener): *search ~*, mandat de perquisition. || *v. tr.* garantir, certifier; [Fig.] justifier, autoriser.

warranty ['wɔɚəntɪ] *n.* autorisation *f*; [Jur.] garantie *f.*

warrior ['wɔɚɪɚ] *n.* guerrier *m*; soldat *m.*

warship ['wɔɚˌʃɪp] *n.* navire *m* de guerre.

wart [wɑɚt] *n.* verrue *f.*

wartime ['wɔɚˌtajm] *n. in ~*, en temps de guerre. || *adj.* de temps de guerre.

wary ['wæəɪ] *adj.* circonspect, avisé, prudent: *to be ~ of*, → se méfier de.

was [wʌz] cf. BE; voir *Introduction grammaticale.*

wash [wɑʃ] *n.* **1.** lavage *m*, toilette *f*: *to have a ~, to give o.s. a ~*, se laver; *Your hands need a good ~*, Tes mains ont grand besoin d'être lavées; *That will come out in the ~*, Cela s'en ira au lavage. **2.** blanchissage *m*: *My shirt got lost in the ~*, Ma chemise s'est perdue au blanchissage. **3.** sillage *m* (d'un bateau); bruit *m* (de l'eau). **4.** *mouth-~, throat-~*, gargarisme *m.* || **wash** *v. tr.* **1.** se laver: *Go (and) ~ (yourself)*, Va te laver. **2.** laver (le plancher, la table, un enfant, &c.); [dishes] faire la vaisselle; [laundry] faire la lessive; blanchir, laver (le linge). **3.** [sea, river, lake] baigner (une côte); *to be washed ashore*, être rejeté sur le rivage; *to be washed overboard*, être emporté par une vague. || *v. intr.* **1.** se laver: *This material washes (well)*, Cette étoffe se lave bien, est lavable. **2.** faire la lessive: *She washes on Mondays*, Elle fait la lessive le lundi. || **~ away**, enlever (une tache); emporter (un pont); ronger (une rive). || **~ down** laver, lessiver (les murs); arroser (un repas); [river] emporter, déposer. || **~ off** enlever: *That will ~ off*, Cela partira au lavage. || **~ out** nettoyer (une tasse, &c.); enlever (une tache): [Fig.] *I feel washed out*, Je me sens à plat. || **~ up** se laver; faire la vaisselle; rejeter (sur le rivage). || **washable** [wɑʃəbḷ] *adj.* lavable. || **washbasin, ~ bowl** ['wɑʃˌbejsṇ, -bowl] *n.* [bathroom fixture] lavabo *m*; [basin on table] cuvette *f.* || **washday** ['wɑʃˌdej] *n.* jour *m* de lessive, © de lavage. || **washer** ['wɑʃɚ] *n.* **1.** [Mec.] rondelle *f.* **2.** lessiveuse *f.* || **washerwoman** ['wɑʃɚˌwʊmən] *n.* blanchisseuse *f.* || **washing** [wɑʃɪŋ] *n.* **1.** lavage *m* cf. LAVER: *My shirt needs ~*, Ma chemise a besoin d'être lavée, → d'aller au lavage. **2.** lessive *f*, linge *m.*: *to do the ~*, faire la lessive, *to hang out the ~*, étendre le linge dehors. || **washing machine** *n.* machine *f* à laver, lessiveuse *f.* || **washrag** ['wɑʃˌɹæg] *n.* **1.** [dishes] lavette *f.* **2.** [face] © débarbouillette *f.* || **washroom** ['wɑʃˌɹuwm] *n.* [Fr.] lavabo *m*, © toilette *f* cf. LAVATORY. || **washstand** ['wɑʃˌstænd] *n.* table *f* de toilette.

wasn't ['wʌzṇt] = was not [BE].

wasp [wɑsp] *n.* guêpe *f.* || **wasps' nest** ['wɑspsˌnɛst] *n.* guêpier *m.*

waste [wejst] *n.* **1.** gaspillage *m*; perte *f* (de temps): *to go to ~*, se perdre; *What a ~ of energy!*, Que d'efforts pour rien! **2.** déchets *mpl*: *cotton ~*, déchets de coton. **3.** région *f* inculte, désert *m.* || *adj.* **1.** superflu, inutilisé; de rebut: *~ matter*, matière *f* de rebut. **2.** inculte; désertique. **3.** *to lay ~*, dévaster, ravager. || **waste** *v. tr.* **1.** gaspiller (l'argent, la nourriture, sa vie); perdre (le temps, une occasion): *Don't ~ your time doing that*, Ne perdez pas votre temps à faire cela; *Don't ~ your energy*, Ne vous fatiguez pas pour rien. **2.** dévaster, ravager (un pays). || *v. intr. to ~ away*, dépérir; perdre des forces; maigrir. || **wastebasket** ['wejstˌbæskət], **wastepaper basket** ['wejspejpɚˌbæskət] *n.* corbeille *f* à papier. || **wasteful**

['wejstf!] *adj.* ruineux; [persons only] gaspilleur. || **wastefulness** ['wejstf!nəs] *n.* prodigalité *f*: gaspillage *m.*

wasting [-ɪŋ] *adj.* dévastat|eur *m*, -rice *f*; [patient] → qui dépérit. || *n.* dévastation *f*; [illness] dépérissement *m.*

watch [wɑtʃ] *v. tr.* **1.** regarder, observer: *I watched him coming closer,* Je l'ai regardé s'approcher, Je l'ai regardé qui s'approchait; *We are being watched,* On nous observe; *to* ~ *TV,* regarder la télévision; *to* ~ *s.o. on TV,* regarder qqun à la télévision. **2.** surveiller, faire attention à: *You must* ~ *your spending,* Vous devrez surveiller vos dépenses; [Fam.] *Watch it!, Watch your step!,* (Faites) attention (où vous marchez)!; *Watch (me) closely!,* Faites bien attention! **3.** surveiller, garder: *I watched him closely,* Je l'ai surveillé de (très) près; *I have to* ~ *my sister this afternoon,* Je dois surveiller/garder/ma sœur cet après-midi. **4.** guetter: *He watched his opportunity,* Il a guetté l'occasion. || *v. intr.* **1.** veiller: *to* ~ *by s.o.,* veiller auprès de qqun; *to* ~ *after/over/,* veiller sur, surveiller. **2.** *to* ~ *for,* attendre, guetter (l'occasion de): *Watch for next year's model,* → Ne manquez pas la sortie du modèle de l'année prochaine. **3.** *to* ~ *out (for),* faire attention à: *Watch out!,* (Faites) attention!. || **watch** [wɑtʃ] *n.* **1** garde *f*: *to be on the* ~ , ouvrir l'œil; *to be on the* ~ *for,* attendre, guetter; *to keep* ~ , monter la garde; *to keep a (close)* ~ *on s.o.,* surveiller qqun (de près). **2.** [Naut.] quart *m*: *to be on* ~ , être de quart. **3.** montre *f*: *pocket* ~ , montre de poche: *wrist* ~ , [Fr.] bracelet-montre *m*, © montre-bracelet *f*; *by my* ~ , à ma montre. || **watchdog** ['wɑtʃ,dɔg] *n.* chien *m* de garde. || **watchful** ['wɑtʃfl] *adj.* vigilant. || **watchfully** *adv.* avec vigilance. || **watchfulness** *n.* vigilance *f.* || **watch-maker** ['wɑtʃ,mejkər] *n.* horloger *m.* || **watchman** ['wɑtʃmən] *n.* gardien *m*, garde *m*: *night* ~ , veilleur *m* de nuit.

water ['wɔtər] *n.* **1.** eau *f*: *fresh* ~ , eau douce; *salt* ~ , eau salée; *soft* ~ , eau douce, eau non calcaire; *hard* ~ , eau dure, eau calcaire; *sea-* ~ , eau de mer, eau salée; *spring* ~ , eau de source; *drinking* ~ , eau potable; [Rel.] *Holy Water,* eau bénite; *high* ~ , marée *f* haute; *low* ~ , marée basse; *below* ~ , submergé, au-dessous de la surface (de l'eau); *above* ~ , à la surface, au-dessus de la surface (de l'eau); *javel* ~ , eau de Javel; [Fig.] *of the first* ~ , de premier ordre; *to be in hot* ~ , être dans le pétrin. **2.** mer *f*, océan *m*, eau *f*: *on land and* ~ , sur terre et sur mer; *by* ~ , par mer, par bateau; *on this/on the other/side of the* ~ , de ce côté-ci, de l'autre côté/de l'océan; *territorial waters,* eaux territoriales. || **water** *v. tr.* arroser (des plantes, &c.); abreuver (un cheval); diluer, couper d'eau (le vin, &c.). || *v. intr. My eyes are watering,* Mes yeux se mouillent; *That makes my mouth* ~ , Cela me fait venir l'eau à la bouche. || ~ **down** *v. tr.* couper d'eau (le vin, &c.); [Fig.] atténuer. || **watercolour** ['wɔtər,kʌlər] *n.* aquarelle *f*, peinture *f* à l'aquarelle: || **watercolours,** couleurs *fpl* pour l'aquarelle. || **waterfall** ['wɔtər,fɔl] *n.* chute *f* (d'eau); cataracte *f.* || **waterfowl** ['wɔtər,fɑwl] *n.* oiseau *m* aquatique. || **waterfront** ['wɔtər,fɹʌnt] *n.* les quais *mpl*; les docks: *on the* ~ , chez les dockers. || **water-hen** ['wɔtər,hɛn] *n.* poule *f* d'eau. || **watering** ['wɔtərɪŋ] *n.* arrosage *m*; irrigation *f* (des terres). || **watering-can** ['wɔtərɪŋ,kæn] *n.* arrosoir *m.* || **waterlily** ['wɔtər,lɪlɪ] *n.* nénuphar *m.* || **watermelon** ['wɔtər,mɛlən] *n.* pastèque *f*; © melon *m* d'eau. || **water pipe** ['wɔtər,-pajp] *n.* tuyau *m* d'eau; conduite *f* d'eau. || **water power** ['wɔtə,pawər] *n.* houille *f* blanche, force *f* hydraulique. || **waterproof** ['wɔtər,pɹuwf] *adj.* imperméable, à l'épreuve de l'eau. *v. tr.* imperméabiliser. || **water rate** ['wɔtər,rejt] *n.* taxe *f* d'eau. || **watershed** ['wɔtər,ʃɛd] *n.* ligne *f* de partage des eaux. || **water-supply** ['wɔtər-sə,plaj] *n.* le service *m* (municipal) des eaux; les eaux (de la ville). || **water tank** ['wɔtər,tæŋk] *n.* [in the ground] citerne *f*; [above ground] réservoir *m* d'eau. || **watertight** ['wɔtər,tajt] *adj.* étanche; [clothes] imperméable; [Fig.] inattaquable. || **waterway** ['wɔtər,wej] *n.* voie *f* navigable, voie fluviale; canal *m.* || **waterworks** ['wɔtər,-wərks] *n.* usine *f* de distribution des eaux. || **watery** [wɔtərɪ] *adj.* aqueux; humide; plein d'eau; [eyes] larmoyant; [weather] pluvieux.

watt [wɑt] *n.* [Elect.] watt *m.*

wave [wejv] *n.* **1.** vague *f*: *heat* ~ , *cold* ~ , vague de chaleur, vague de froid. **2.** [Tech.] onde *f* (sonore, lumineuse): *short* ~ , onde courte; ~ *length,* longueur *f* d'onde. **3.** ondulation *f*: *a permanent* (~), une (ondulation) permanente. **4.** signe *m* (de la main). || **wave** *v. intr.* **1.** s'agiter; flotter (au vent). **2.** faire signe à qqun (de la main, avec qqch.). **3.** [cheveux] onduler. || *v. tr.* **1.** agiter (le bras, un mouchoir, &c.). **2.** faire signe à qqun:

He waved us goodbye, Il nous a fait un signe d'adieu; *I waved him/on, back, away, &c./*, Je lui ai fait signe (de la main)/de s'approcher, de reculer, de s'écarter, &c./. **3.** onduler, se faire onduler (les cheveux).

waver ['wejvɚ] *v. intr.* vaciller, trembler; [flame] trembler; [courage] chanceler; [hesitate] hésiter, balancer.

wavy ['wejvɪ] *adj.* ondulé.

wax [wæks] *n.* cire *f*: *sealing* ~ , cire à cacheter. || *adj.* [made of] de cire, [waxed] ciré. || *v. tr.* cirer. || **waxing** ['wæksɪŋ] *n.* cirage *m.*

waxwing ['wæks,wɪŋ] *n.* [Ornith.] *cedar* ~ , jaseur *m* du cèdre; © récollet *m.*

way [wej] *n.* **1.** [route, road] chemin *m*: *Which is the* ~ *to . . . ?*, Quel est le chemin de . . . , pour aller à . . . ?; *You are going the right* ~ , Vous êtes dans le bon chemin; *You are going the wrong* ~ , Vous vous êtes trompé de chemin; *He/lost, ound/his* ~ , Il a perdu, (re)trouvé son chemin; *on the* ~ , chemin faisant; *on the* ~ *to . . .* , en route pour . . . , en allant à . . . ; *on the* ~ *back/here, home, &c./*, en retournant, en venant (ici), en rentrant, &c.; *to go one's* ~ , aller son chemin; *out of the* ~ , égaré, *to go out of one's* ~ , faire un détour, [Fig.] se déranger; *to find one's* ~ *towards*, se diriger vers; *to stand in the* ~ *of*, barrer le chemin (à qqun), [Fig.] faire obstacle à qqch.; *(Get) out of the* ~ *!* Ôtez-vous de là!; *to get out of the* ~ *of*, s'ôter du chemin de; *to make* ~ *for s.o.*, s'écarter pour laisser passer qqun; *to keep out of s.o.'s* ~ , se tenir à l'écart de qqun; ~ *in*, entrée *f*; ~ *out*, sortie *f*; ~ *up*, montée *f*; ~ *down*, descente *f*; ~ *through*, passage *m*, &c. **2.** [direction] côté *m*; sens *m*: *Which* ~ *are you going?*, De quel côté allez-vous?; *this* ~ , *that* ~ !, (C'est) par ici!, par là!; *this* ~ *and that*, de tous côtés; *Are you coming my* ~ *?*, Venez-vous de mon côté?; *He was going the same* ~ *as I was*, Il allait du même côté/dans le même sens/que moi; *You are holding it the wrong* ~ *(up)*, Vous le tenez dans le mauvais sens. **3.** [distance] distance *f*: *a little* ~ *away*, à peu de distance, pas trop loin; *to go a little* ~ */ part (of the)* ~ */with s.o.*, faire un bout de chemin/une partie du chemin/avec qqun; [Fig.] *I've come a long* ~ , Je viens de loin; *He will go a long* ~ , Il ira loin. **4.** [manner] façon *f*, manière *f*: *(in) this* ~ , de cette façon; *in no* ~ , en aucune façon; *the* ~ *(that, in which)*, la façon dont; *in such a* ~ *as to*, de façon à; *the right/wrong/* ~ *of doing sth.*, la bonne/mauvaise/façon de faire qqch.; *to do sth. the right* ~ , faire qqch. comme il faut; *in my (own)* ~ , à ma façon; *in the French* ~ , à la française; ~ *of life*, vie *f*, manière *f*/de vivre/: *the American* ~ *of life*, la vie américaine, la vie des Américains. **5.** [means] moyen *m*: *Is there a* ~ *to do it?*, Y a-t-il moyen de le faire?; *There is no* ~ , Il n'y a pas moyen; *I know a* ~ , Moi, je connais un moyen. **6.** [respect] égard *m*: *in some ways*, à certains égards; *in many ways*, à bien des égards; *in every* ~ , à tous les égards; *in a* ~ , en un certain sens. **7.** [state] *to be in a/good, bad/* ~ , aller/bien, mal/. **8.** [wish, will] *to have/get/one's (own)* ~ , (pouvoir) faire ce qu'on veut; *If I had my* ~ *. . .* , Si ce n'était que de moi . . . ; *Have it your own* ~ *!*, (Faites) comme vous voudrez! **9.** [habit, custom] manière *f*, habitude *f*, usage *m*: *He has a* ~ *of looking at you which I don't like*, Il a une manière (à lui) de vous regarder qui ne me plaît pas; *She has a* ~ *with her class*, Elle sait se faire aimer de ses élèves; *He has pleasing ways*, Il a des manières sympathiques. **10.** [motion] *to be under* ~ , [ship] être en marche, [Fig.] être en cours. **11.** *by the* ~ , à propos, en passant. **12.** *by* ~ *of*, par; comme: *He came by* ~ *of Halifax*, Il est venu par Halifax; *What can I give you by* ~ *of dessert?*, Qu'est-ce que je peux vous offrir comme dessert?

waylay [,wej'lej], **waylaid, waylaid** *v. tr.* attirer (qqun) dans/une embuscade, un guet-apens).

wayside ['wejsajd] *n.* bord *m* de la route, du chemin.

wayward ['wej,wərd] *adj.* capricieux, fantasque; [stubborn] entêté.

we [wij] *pron.* **1.** [unstressed] nous; [Fam. when verbal idea is uppermost] on: *We went out together*, Nous sommes sortis ensemble; *What'll* ~ *do to-night?*, Qu'est-ce qu'on fait ce soir? **2.** [stressed] nous, nous autres: *What'll* WE *do to-night?*, Qu'est-ce que nous allons faire ce soir, nous (autres)?; *We Canadians are proud to . . .* , Nous autres Canadiens (nous) sommes fiers de . . . ; *We of the class of '62 wish to . . .* , Nous, les élèves de la promotion de (mil neuf cent) soixante-deux, désirons . . . ; *We of to-day . . .* , Nous les hommes d'aujourd'hui . . . . **3.** [editorial *we*] nous [followed by a pl. v. and adj. agreement in the sing.]: *We are convinced our readers will agree*, Nous sommes persuadé que nos lecteurs en conviendront.

weak [wijk] *adj.* faible; [in health] débile: *to grow* ~, s'affaiblir. || **weaken** ['wijkən] *v. tr.* affaiblir. || *v. intr.* faiblir; [grow weak] s'affaiblir. || **weakling** ['wijklıŋ] *n.* un (être, homme, &c.) faible. || **weakly** ['wijklı] *adv.* faiblement, d'une manière faible. || **weakness** ['wijknəs] *n.* faiblesse *f*: *to have a* ~ *for*, avoir un faible pour.

wealth [wɛlθ] *n.* richesse(s) *f*, opulence *f*; prospérité *f*; abondance *f* (de détails, &c.). || **wealthy** ['wɛlθı] *adj.* riche, opulent; abondant (en).

wean [wijn] *v. tr.* sevrer.

weapon ['wɛpən] *n.* arme *f.*

wear [wɛə˞] *n.* **1.** usage *m*: *hard* ~ *fabrics*, tissus d'(un bon) usage; *These shoes still have* ~ *in them*, Ces souliers ont encore de l'usage, sont encore mettables. **2.** vêtement *m*: *ladies'* ~, articles *mpl* pour dames; *men's* ~, vêtements pour hommes; *evening* ~, tenue *f* de soirée; *spring* ~, vêtements de printemps; *footwear*, chaussures *fpl*. **3.** usure *f*, fatigue *f*: *His clothes show signs of* ~, Ses vêtements montrent des signes d'usure, paraissent usés; ~ *and tear*, détérioration *f*; *fair* ~ *and tear*, usure normale; *to be the worse for* ~, [things] être usé, [persons] las; *little the worse for* ~, qui n'a pas souffert. || **wear** [wɛə˞] **wore** [wɔə˞] **worn** [wɔə˞n] *v. tr.* **1.** porter (un vêtement, &c.); [put on] mettre: *What shall I* ~ ?, Qu'est-ce que je dois mettre?; *I have nothing to* ~, Je n'ai rien à mettre, à me mettre sur le dos. **2.** [Fig.] *to* ~ *a sad expression*, avoir un air de tristesse, avoir l'air triste. **3.** user: *to* ~ *sth. threadbare*, user qqch. jusqu'à la corde; *to* ~ *a hole*, faire un trou. || *v. intr.* **1.** *to* ~ *well*, durer (longtemps). **2.** s'user: *This cloth wears quickly*, Cette étoffe s'use vite. || ~ **away** *v. tr.* user; effacer. || *v. intr.* s'user; s'effacer; [pain, time] passer (peu à peu). || ~ **down** *v. tr.* user [exhaust] épuiser. || *v. intr.* s'user; s'épuiser. || ~ **off** *v. tr.* faire disparaître. || *v. intr.* disparaître; passer. || ~ **on** *v. intr.* s'avancer. || ~ **out** *v. tr.* user; épuiser (la patience, &c.): *I'm worn out*, Je suis épuisé. || *v. intr.* s'user; s'épuiser. || **wearable** ['wɛə˞əbl̩] *adj.* mettable. || **wearing** ['wɛə˞ıŋ] *adj.* fatigant, épuisant. || *part.* portant (un vêtement); coiffé (d'un chapeau); chaussé (de souliers, &c.).

weary ['wijə˞ı] *adj.* las, -se (*with, of*, de). || **weary** *v. tr.* lasser, fatiguer; [bore] ennuyer (qqun). || *v. intr.* se fatiguer, se lasser, s'ennuyer (*of*, de). || **wearily** ['wijə˞əlı] *adv.* avec lassitude. || **weariness** ['wijə˞ınəs] *n.* lassitude *f.* || **wearisome** ['wijə˞ısəm] *adj.* ennuyeux.

weasel ['wijzl̩] *n.* belette *f.*

weather ['wɛðə˞] *n.* temps *m*: *in warm* ~, par (un) temps chaud; *in such* ~, par un temps pareil, par le temps qu'il fait; *The* ~ *is fine*, Il fait beau (temps), Le temps est beau; *What's the* ~ *(like)?*, Quel temps fait-il?; *The* ~ *is bad/cold, hot, cool, warm, mild, sunny, windy, &c./*, Il fait mauvais temps/Il fait (un temps) froid, très chaud, frais, chaud, doux, Il fait (du) soleil, du vent, &c./; [Fig.] *to be, feel, under the* ~, ne pas se sentir bien. || *adj.* météorologique: *Weather Office*, bureau *m* météorologique; ~ *map, station*, carte *f*, station *f*/météorologique; ~ *forecast*, bulletin *m* météorologique, (les prévisions de) la météo; ~ *conditions*, conditions atmosphériques. || **weather** *v. tr.*: *to* ~ *(out) a storm, &c.*, survivre à, résister à, une tempête, [Fig.] se tirer d'affaire.

weave [wijv] **wove** [wowv] **woven** ['wowvn̩] *v. tr.* **1.** tisser (une étoffe); tresser (un panier). **2.** [Fig.] tramer (un complot). **3.** *to* ~ *together*, combiner (en un tout). || *v. intr.* tisser: [Fig.] *to* ~ *(one's way) through*, se faufiler à travers. || **weaver** ['wijvə˞] *n.* tisserand *m*, -e *f.* || **weaving** ['wijvıŋ] *n.* tissage *m.*

web [wɛb] *n.* [material] tissu *m*; rouleau *m* (de papier, &c.); [spider] toile *f*; [duck, &c.] palme *f*; [Fig.] trame *f*: ~ *-footed*, palmipède, aux pieds palmés.

wed [wɛd] *v. tr.* [-dd-] épouser. || *v. intr.* épouser, s'unir à.

we'd [wijd] **1.** = we had [TO HAVE]. **2.** = we would [WILL]. **3.** = we should [SHALL].

wedding ['wɛdıŋ] *n.* mariage *m*, noce(s) *f(pl)*/ *The* ~ *will take place tomorrow*, Le mariage aura lieu demain; *I'm going to a* ~, Je vais à un mariage, à une noce. || *adj.* nuptial: ~ *march*, marche *f* nuptiale; ~ *anniversary*, anniversaire de mariage; ~ *dress*, robe *f* de mariée; ~ *trip*, voyage *m* de noces; ~ *ring*, alliance *f.*

wedge [wɛʤ] *n.* coin *m* (en bois, &c.); [pour les voitures] cale *f*; [Fig.] *the thin end of the* ~, le commencement de la fin. || **wedge** *v. tr.* coincer; [one thing against the other] serrer. || ~ **through** pénétrer comme un coin.

wedlock ['wɛdˌlɑk] *n.* mariage *m*, vie *f* conjugale: *born in* ~, (enfant) légitime.

Wednesday ['wɛnzdej] *n.* mercredi *m*: *Ash* ~, mercredi des Cendres [MONDAY].

weed [wijd] *n.* herbe *f* folle; [in garden] mauvaise herbe *f.* || **weed** *v. tr. & intr.* **1.** arracher les mauvaises herbes (d'un jardin); sarcler (un champ, un jardin). **2.** [Fig.] *to ~ out*, éliminer.

week [wijk] *n.* semaine *f*: *a ~ from today*, d'aujourd'hui en huit; *a ~ ago yesterday*, il y a eu une semaine hier; *during the ~* [not the weekend], en semaine [cf. NEXT, LAST]; *Holy Week*, la semaine sainte. || **weekday** ['wijkˌdej] *n.* jour *m* de semaine: *on weekdays*, en semaine. || **weekend** ['wijk'ɛnd] *n.* © fin *f* de semaine; [Fr.] week-end *m*: *at the ~*, en fin de semaine. || **weekly** ['wijklɪ] *adj.* hebdomadaire. || *n.* hebdomadaire *m.* || *adv.* par semaine.

weep [wijp] **wept, wept** [wɛpt] *v. tr. & intr.* pleurer: *to ~ for joy*, pleurer de joie; *weeping willow*, saule *m* pleureur; *to ~ one's heart, one's eyes, out*, pleurer à chaudes larmes; *to ~ for s.o.*, pleurer (sur les malheurs, &c., de) qqun.

weigh [wej] *v. tr.* **1.** peser (un colis, un bébé, &c.): *to ~ sth. in one's hand*, soupeser qqch. **2.** [Fig.] considérer; calculer (les conséquences); peser (ses paroles, le pour et le contre). **3.** [Naut.] lever (l'ancre). **4.** *to ~ down*, faire pencher, faire plier, [Fig.] accabler (de). || *v. intr.* peser: *He, It, weighs a lot, 100 lb.*, Il pèse lourd, cent livres; *The idea weighed on his mind*, L'idée lui pesait, le tourmentait; *That will ~ heavily with the jury*, Cela aura du poids auprès du jury. || **weight** [wejt] *n.* **1.** poids *m*: *to gain, lose, ~*, prendre, perdre, du poids; *to pull one's ~*, y mettre du sien, faire sa part de . . . ; *It is worth its ~ in gold*, Cela vaut son pesant d'or. **2.** [burden] fardeau *m*, poids *m*: [Fig.] *the ~ of years*, le fardeau, le poids, des ans. **3.** importance *f*: *His opinion carries ~*, Son opinion a de l'importance; *He is throwing his ~ around*, Il fait l'important. || **weight** *v. tr.* alourdir, charger: *to ~ a (fishing) line (with a sinker)*, alourdir un fil (de pêche) (avec un plomb); *to ~ with chains*, charger de chaînes. || **weightiness** ['wejtɪnəs] *n.* pesanteur *f*, poids *m*; importance *f* (d'une décision, &c.). || **weighty** ['wejtɪ] *adj.* pesant, lourd; [Fig.] important.

weird [wijɚd] *adj.* surnaturel; étrange.

welcome ['wɛlkəm] *n.* bienvenue *f*; (bon) accueil *m*: *to give s.o. a hearty ~*, faire un accueil chaleureux à qqun; *He bid her ~*, Il lui a souhaité la bienvenue. || *adj.* **1.** bienvenu: *He is a ~ guest in my house*, Il est le bienvenu chez moi; *Make her ~!*, Faites-lui bon accueil!. **2.** agréable, libre: *a ~ change*, un changement agréable; *You are ~ to try*, Vous êtes libre d'essayer; *Thank you! You are ~ !*, Merci! Je vous en prie! || **welcome** *v. tr.* accueillir (qqun ou qqch.) avec plaisir: *We ~ the news*, Nous accueillons la nouvelle avec plaisir; *The mayor welcomed the delegation*, Le maire a accueilli, a souhaité la bienvenue à, la délégation.

weld [wɛld] *v. tr.* souder. || *v. intr.* se souder.

welfare ['wɛlˌfɛɚ] *n.* bien-être *m*: *social ~*, sécurité *f* sociale; *~ work*, assistance *f* sociale; œuvres *fpl* sociales; © *Department of National Health and Welfare*, le Ministère de la Santé nationale et du Bien-être social.

well[1] [wɛl] *n.* puits *m*; cage *f* (d'un escalier): *oil ~*, puits de pétrole; *to drill, dig, a ~*, forer, creuser, un puits. || **well** *v. intr. to ~ (up, forth, out)*, [liquid, tears] jaillir, [spring] sourdre.

well[2] [wɛl] *adv.* [cf. BETTER, BEST] bien: *. . . and my friend as ~*, . . . et mon ami aussi; *as ~ as*, aussi bien que; *As ~ he might (be expected to)*, Comme on s'y attendait, comme il convenait; *I can just as ~ come with you*, Je peux aussi bien venir avec vous; *I might (just) as ~ stay at home*, Je ferais (tout) aussi bien de rester, Autant rester chez moi; *You would do ~ to pay attention*, Vous feriez bien de faire attention; *He will do ~*, Il ira loin; *Well done!*, Voilà qui est bien!, Bravo!, Bien joué, chanté, &c.!; *He did ~ by me*, Il a bien agi envers moi; *I did as ~ as I could*, J'ai fait de mon mieux; *I know only too ~ that . . .*, Je ne sais que trop bien que . . . ; *As is ~ known . . .*, Comme on, chacun, le sait . . . ; *~ on in the night, life, years*, à une heure avancée (de la nuit), à un âge avancé; *to be ~ up in*, être fort en; *That's pretty ~ everything*, Voilà à peu près tout; *Very ~ !*, C'est bien! || *adj.* [cf. BETTER, BEST]: *He is ~*, Il va bien; *I'm feeling ~*, Je me sens bien; *You look ~*, Vous avez bonne mine; *He is (feeling) ~ again*, Il est remis; *He is going to get ~ (again)*, Il va guérir, se remettre; *It would be (just as) ~ (for you) not to go there again*, Il serait bon de ne pas y retourner, que vous n'y retourniez pas; *It is ~ (for you) that I got here in time*, Il est heureux, vous avez de la chance, que je sois arrivé à temps; *All's ~ !*, Tout va bien!; *All's ~ that ends ~*, Tout est bien qui finit bien;

That's all very ~, *but . . .*, Tout cela est très bien, mais . . . ; *It's all very* ~ *(for you) to say that, but . . .*, C'est bien gentil (à vous) de dire cela, mais . . . || *interj.* eh bien: [questions] *Well, what do you say?*, Eh bien, qu'en dites-vous?; [orders] *Well, go ahead*, Eh bien, allez-y; [indignation] *Well, if that's the way it is . . .*, Eh bien (mon vieux), si c'est comme ça . . . ; *Well!*, Ça alors!; [hesitating] *Well, hardly ever*, C'est-à-dire, presque jamais; [resuming] *Well, as I was saying . . .*, Enfin, comme je disais . . . ; *Well anyway . . .*, Enfin . . . ; *Well then . . .*, Eh bien alors . . . ; [surprise] *Well,* ~, *fancy meeting you here!*, Tiens, tiens! comme on se retrouve!; [impatience] *Well,* ~, *this will never do!*, Ah non alors, ça ne peut pas marcher! || *n.* bien *m*: *to wish s.o.* ~, vouloir du bien à qqun; *to say, think,* ~ *of s.o.*, dire, penser, du bien de qqun. || **well-being** [ˈwɛlˈbijɪŋ] *n.* bien-être *m.* || **well-bred** [ˈwɛlˈbɹɛd] *adj.* bien élevé. || **well-built** [ˈwɛlˈbɪlt] *adj.* [of a man] bien bâti. || **well-informed** [ˌwɛlɪn-ˈfɔɚmd] *adj.* bien renseigné; [educated] instruit: *to keep (o.s.)* ~, se tenir au courant. || **well-known** [ˈwɛlˈnown] *adj.* bien connu, célèbre: *a* ~ *novelist*, un romancier bien connu; *This painter is* ~ *abroad*, Ce peintre est très connu à l'étranger; *It is (a)* ~ *(fact) that . . .*, Il est/bien connu, notoire/que. . . . || **well-meaning** [ˈwɛlˈmijnɪŋ] *adj.* [of a person] bien intentionné. || **well-meant** [ˈwɛlˈmɛnt] *adj.* [of an action] fait avec une bonne intention. || **well-off** [ˈwɛlˈɔf] *adj.* aisé, riche: *to be* ~ *for*, être bien pourvu de; *He doesn't know when he is* ~, Il ne connaît pas sa chance. || **well-read** [ˈwɛlˈɹɛd] *adj.* cultivé, qui a beaucoup lu. || **well-to-do** [ˈwɛltəˈduw] *adj.* aisé, riche.

we'll [wijl] = we will.

welt [wɛlt] *n.* cicatrice *f*, zébrure *f*; [Tech.] bordure *f.*

wench [wɛntʃ] *n.* [Pej.] fille *f.*

wend [wɛnd] *v. tr.*: *to* ~ *o.'s way*, diriger ses pas (vers).

went [wɛnt] cf. GO.

wept [wɛpt] cf. WEEP.

were [wɚ] cf. BE.

we're [wɪɚ] = we are [ne pas confondre avec *were*, forme du passé de BE].

weren't [wɚnt] = were not [BE].

west [wɛst] *n.* ouest *m*, occident *m*: *the West*, [Canada] l'Ouest, [Western powers, civilization] Occident; *the Far West*, le far-west; *on, to, the* ~ *of*, à l'ouest de; *in the* ~ *(of)*, à l'ouest (de). || *adj.* ouest *invar.*; (pays, &c.) de l'ouest, occidental; (vent) d'ouest: *the West Coast of Italy*, la côte occidentale de l'Italie; *the West Coast*, la côte occidentale, de l'ouest, © la côte du Pacifique; *the* ~ *side, &c.*, le côté ouest, &c.; *West Vancouver*, Vancouver-Ouest. || *adv.* à l'ouest, à l'occident; vers l'ouest: ~ *of here*, à l'ouest (d'ici); *He went (out)* ~, Il est parti pour l'ouest, Il s'en est allé dans l'ouest; *He drove (due)* ~, Il a conduit (droit) vers l'ouest. || **western** [ˈwɛstɚn] *adj.* occidental, de l'ouest. || **westerner** [ˈwɛstɚnɚ] *n.* habitant *m*, -e *f*, de l'ouest (du pays); Occidental *m*, -e *f.* || **westward** [ˈwɛstwɚd] *adj.* à, de, vers, l'ouest. || **westward(s)** *adv.* vers, à, l'ouest.

wet [wɛt] *adj.* **[-tt-] 1.** mouillé: *to get (one's feet)* ~, se mouiller (les pieds); *to be / dripping, wringing, soaking, sopping/* ~, *to be* ~ *through*, ~ *to the skin*, être trempé (jusqu'aux os); *Wet Paint*, → Attention à la peinture. **2.** (climat temps) pluvieux; (temps, jour) de pluie; (saison) des pluies. || **wet** *n.* pluie *f*: *You can't go out in the* ~, Tu ne peux pas sortir sous la pluie, quand tout est mouillé. || **wet** *v. tr.* **[-tt-]** mouiller (le linge); humecter (les lèvres); arroser (le jardin, les fleurs).

we've [wijv] = we have cf. HAVE.

whale [wejl] *n.* baleine *f.*

wharf [wɔɚf] *pl.* **wharves** or **wharfs** *n.* [Naut.] appontement *m*, débarcadère *m.*

what [wɑt] *pron. interrog.* **1.** [subj. in Fr.] qu'est-ce qui: *What happened?*, Qu'est-ce qui s'est passé?; *What is funny?*, Qu'est-ce qui est drôle? [ind.] ce qui: *I know/* ~ *happened*, ~ *is funny/*, Je sais/ce qui s'est passé, ce qui est drôle/. **2.** [obj. in Fr.] (a) [dir.] que, [Fam.] qu'est-ce que: *What are you doing?*, Que faites-vous, Qu'est-ce que vous faites?; *What am I to/do, think/?*, Que/faire, penser/?; (b) [ind.] ce que: *He asked me* ~ *I was doing*, Il m'a demandé ce que je faisais; *He didn't know* ~ *(he was) to/do, say/*, Il ne savait que/faire, dire/. **3.** [after prep. in Fr.] [dir.] quoi: *What are you complaining about?*, De quoi vous plaignez-vous?; *What are you thinking about?*, À quoi pensez-vous?; [ind.] quoi; [less often] ce dont, ce à quoi, ce sur quoi, &c.: *He wanted to know/* ~ *you were complaining about*, ~ *you were thinking about*, ~ *you were counting on, &c./*, Il voulait savoir/de quoi vous vous plaigniez, (ce) à quoi vous pensiez, (ce) sur quoi vous comptiez, &c./; [Loc.] *What about you?*, Et vous?; *What is that for?*, À quoi ça sert? **4.** [as predicate of "to be," "to become," &c.] [definition or indignation] (a) [dir.] que, qu'est-ce que: *What is it?*, Qu'est-ce que c'est?; *What is/that, that box, &c./?*, Qu'est-ce (que c'est) que/ça, cette boîte, &c./?; [Loc.] *What!*, Comment!; *What next!*, Ça, par exemple! [ind.] ce que; *They wondered ~ it was*, Ils se sont demandé ce que c'était; *She understands ~/that, that thing/is*, Elle comprend ce que c'est que/cela, cette chose/; *I know ~ it is to . . .*, Je sais ce que c'est que de . . . [persons] (b) [dir.] que, qu'est-ce que: *What do you want to do now?*, Que voulez-vous faire maintenant?; *What did they become?*, Que sont-ils devenus? (b) [ind.] ce que: *I asked him ~ he wants to do*, Je lui ai demandé ce qu'il voulait faire. **5.** [distinction] (a) [dir.] quel *m*, quelle *f*: *What is/your address, your favourite colour/?*, Quelle est/votre adresse, votre couleur préférée/? (b) [ind.] quel *m*, quelle *f* [☞ **what** is often not translated]: *He said ~ his name was*, → Il a dit son nom; *I asked him ~ the time was*, Je lui ai demandé l'heure (qu'il était); *He explained ~ his intentions were*, Il a expliqué/ses intentions, quelles étaient ses intentions/. [Loc.] *What is it?* [= *What do you want?*] Qu'est-ce qu'il y a?, Qu'est-ce que c'est?; *What is your father?*, Que fait votre père?; *What is that to me?*, → Qu'est-ce que ça peut bien me faire?; *What is the French for . . . ?*, → Comment dit-on . . . en français?; *What became of them?*, → Que sont-ils devenus? [cf. also GOOD, LIKE, MATTER, MORE, NEW, TIME, USE.] [= how much] combien (a) [dir.] combien: *What are 3 and 5?*, *What do 3 and 5 make?*, Combien font 3 et 5?; *What are your oranges today?*, Combien sont vos oranges aujourd'hui?; *What do I owe you?*, Combien vous dois-je? (b) [ind.] combien: *He doesn't even know ~ 3 and 5 are*, Il ne sait même pas combien font 3 et 5. [= that which; subject of Fr. clause] ce qui: *I'll take ~ costs least*, Je prendrai ce qui coûte le moins cher; *What worries me is . . .*, Ce qui m'inquiète, c'est . . . ; *He will use ~ is (to be found) here*, Il se servira de ce qui se trouve ici. [object of Fr. clause] ce que: *He gave me ~ I wanted*, Il m'a donné ce que je voulais; *What I mean is . . .*, Ce que je veux dire, c'est . . . ; *I am counting on ~ you can do*, Je compte sur ce que vous pourrez faire. [the verbal construction in the Fr. clause is completed by **de**] ce dont: *She bought me ~ I needed*, Elle m'a acheté ce dont j'avais besoin; *What I want is . . .*, Ce dont j'ai envie, c'est . . . ; *I have an idea of ~ he is afraid of*, J'ai une idée de ce dont il a peur. [the verbal construction in the Fr. clause is completed by a prep. other than **de**]: ce à quoi, ce sur quoi, &c.: *She brought ~ I was counting on*, Elle m'a apporté ce sur quoi je comptais; *What you do with it is . . .*, Ce avec quoi vous le faites c'est . . . [prep. uses] [Loc.] *What if I don't pass?*, Et si je ne suis pas reçu?; *What now?*, Quoi encore; *What of it*, *So ~ ?*, Et alors?, Et puis après?; (*Listen*), *I'll tell you ~ . . .* (Écoutez), je vais vous dire . . . [see also COME] *What ever, What on earth/are we going to do?*, Qu'est-ce que nous pourrions bien faire?; *What I have let myself in for*, Ce à quoi je me suis engagé. [with Fr. impers. verbs] ce que: *He sent me ~ I needed*, Il m'a envoyé ce qu'il me fallait. ‖ **what** *adj. interrog.* (a) [dir.] quel *m*, quelle *f*: *What class are you in?*, Dans quelle classe êtes-vous?; *What day are you leaving?*, Quel jour partez-vous?; *What colour is your car?*, De quelle couleur est votre voiture? (b) [ind.] [☞ ind.; note that **what** is often not translated]: *He asked ~ flavour I preferred*, Il a demandé quel parfum je préférais; *He told me/ ~ films he had seen, ~ day he was leaving, ~ time it was*; → Il m'a dit/les films qu'il avait vus, le jour de son départ, l'heure qu'il était/. [see also DAY, GOOD, NEWS, PLACE, USE. ‖ **what** *adj. exclam.* **1.** [quality] (a) [dir.] quel *m*, quelle *f*: *What a (beautiful) day!*, Quelle (belle) journée!; *What (strange) people!*, Quelles gens étranges!; *What a beautiful opportunity to . . . !*, La belle occasion de . . . !; *What luck you had!*, La chance que tu as eue! (b) [ind.] *He said ~ a beautiful day it was, ~ luck he had had*, Il a parlé de la belle journée qu'il faisait, de la chance qu'il avait eue. **2.** [quantity] (a) [dir.] que de: *What a lot of people!*, Que de gens!, Que de monde!; *What a (lot of) fuss for nothing!*, Que de bruit pour rien!; *What troubles he gets himself into!*, Que d'ennuis il s'attire! (b) [ind.] *He said ~ a lot of people were there, ~ a fuss there had been for nothing*, Il s'est exclamé sur le grand nombre de gens qui étaient là, sur le grand bruit qu'on avait fait pour rien. ‖ **what,** *adj. rel.*: *I'll give ~ (little)* *sugar I have left,* Je donnerai/ce qui me reste de sucre, le (peu de) sucre qui me reste/.

whatever [wɑt′ɛvɚ] *pron. indef.* [ne pas confondre avec *what ever*] **1.** [introducing a noun clause = anything that] tout ce qui, tout ce que, &c.: *He always understands* (a) *~ happens* (*to me*), (b) *~ we do,* (c) *~ you talk about,* (d) *~ I am referring to,* Il comprend toujours (*a*) tout ce qui (m′) arrive, (*b*) tout ce que nous faisons, (*c*) tout ce dont on parle, (*d*) tout ce à quoi je fais allusion; *Tell him ~ you like,* Dites-lui (tout) ce que vous voudrez/n'importe quoi/. **2.** [introducing a concessive adv. clause = no matter what] quoi que + *subjonc.*; quelle que soit la chose qui/dont, &c./ + *indic.* [☞ ne pas confondre avec *quoique,* although]: *He always understands* (a) *~ may happen* (*to me*), (b) *~ is/may be/ on your mind,* (c) *~ we* (*may*) *do,* (d) *~ you* (*may*) *talk about,* (e) *~ I may refer to,* Il comprend toujours (*a*) quoi qu'il (m′) arrive, (*b*) quelle que soit la chose qui vous préoccupe, (*c*) quoi que vous fassiez, (*d*) quelle que soit la chose dont on parle, (*e*) quelle que soit la chose à laquelle je fais allusion. || *adj.* **1.** [introducing a noun clause = any . . . that] tout (le) . . . qui/que, dont, auquel, &c./: *I need* (a) *~ friends are willing to help,* (b) *~ help you can give me,* J'ai besoin (*a*) de tous les amis qui voudront bien m'aider, (*b*) de toute l'aide que vous pourrez me donner. **2.** [introducing a concessive adv. clause = no matter what] quelque . . . que + *subjunc.*; quel(le) que soit . . . qui/dont, auquel, &c./ + *indic.*: *I don't believe you, ~ reasons you* (*may*) *give,* Je ne vous crois pas, quelques raisons que vous donniez; *Whatever book you* (*may*) *use, read it thoroughly,* Quel que soit le livre dont vous vous servez, lisez-le attentivement. **3.** [after n. or pron. for emphasis] le moindre: *Is there any hope ~ ?,* Y a-t-il le moindre espoir/un espoir quelconque/?; [neg.] pas du tout; aucun: *He hasn't any money/friends/ ~ ,* Il n'a pas d'argent/d'amis/du tout; *I have no intention ~ of . . . ,* Je n'ai pas du tout l'intention de . . .

wheat [wijt] *n.* blé *m,* [more specifically] froment *m*: *~ field,* champ *m* de blé.

wheel [wijl] *n.* **1.** roue *f*; [Auto] [steering] volant *m*: *~ alignment,* alignement *m* des roues. **2.** [Fam.] vélo *m.* || **wheel** *v. tr.* tourner, faire pivoter (qqch.); pousser, rouler (qqch.): *to ~ around,* faire demi-tour. || **wheelbarrow** [′wijlˌbæɚow] *n.* brouette *f.* || **wheelchair** [′wijlˌtʃɛɚ] *n.* fauteuil roulant.

when [wɛn] *adv. interrog.* [direct & indirect] quand, à quel moment: *When will he come?,* Quand viendra-t-il?; *I don't know ~ I'll go,* J'ignore quand je partirai. || *conj.* **1.** quand, lorsque: *When it rains, you must wear your raincoat,* Quand/Lorsqu'/il pleut, il faut mettre votre imperméable; *When you have finished, you may leave the table,* Quand tu auras fini, tu pourras sortir de table. **2.** au moment où, à l'époque où, date à laquelle: *When Toronto was still a small town . . . ,* A l'époque où Toronto était encore une petite ville . . . ; *That goes back to ~ . . . ,* Cela remonte à l'époque où . . . ; *When crossing the street, look both ways,* En traversant la chaussée, regardez des deux côtés; *When* (*he was*) *a child . . . ,* Dans son enfance . . . ; *Books are renewed ~ worn out,* Les livres sont renouvelés quand ils sont usés. **3.** au moment de, à l'époque de, au temps de, lors de: *When he left . . . ,* Au moment de son départ . . . ; *When sunshades were in fashion,* A l'époque des ombrelles; *When the King was crowned . . . ,* Lors du couronnement du roi . . . ; *It reminds me of ~ I was a student,* Cela me rappelle le temps de mes études. || *rel.* **1.** où, que: *the day ~ . . . ,* le jour où . . . ; *one day ~ . . . ,* un jour que . . . ; *at/a, the/time ~ . . . ,* à un moment où . . . , au moment où . . . , à une époque où . . . , à l'époque où . . . ; *now is ~ . . . ,* c'est maintenant que. . . . **2.** [= at which time]: *Back in 1919, ~ the treaty was signed,* En 1919, époque à laquelle le traité a été signé; *On the 30th April, ~ taxes are due . . . ,* Le 30 avril, date à laquelle il faut payer ses impôts . . . ; *There will be a ceremony on Saturday, ~ the mayor will be sworn in,* On a prévu pour samedi une cérémonie, au cours de laquelle le maire prêtera serment; *The Queen will arrive on Tuesday ~ she will open the new Seaway,* La Reine arrivera mardi pour l'inauguration de la nouvelle Voie maritime.

whence [wɛns] *adv. & pron.* d'où?

whenever [wɛn′ɛvɚ] *conj.* **1.** [= every time that] chaque fois que, toutes les fois que: *Whenever I go there, he is out,* Chaque fois, Toutes les fois/ que j'y vais, il est sorti; *Whenever I/he, &c./can,* Aussi souvent que possible [see also WHEN 1. 1st example]. **2.** [= no matter when] quand; quelle que soit l'heure à laquelle/la date où, l'époque où/: *Whenever you (may) need me, I'll come,* Quelle que soit l'heure à laquelle vous aurez besoin de moi, je viendrai; *You can do it ~ you have time,* Vous pourrez le faire quand vous aurez le temps; *Whenever you like . . . ,* Quand vous voudrez . . . .

where [wɛɚ] *adv. interrog.* [direct & indirect] où: *Where am I?,* Où suis-je?; *Where on earth have you been?,* (Mais) où donc étiez-vous?; *Where are we (in the book)?,* Où en sommes-nous (dans le livre)?; *Where are you going (to)?,* Où allez-vous?; *Where do you come from?,* D'où venez-vous?; *He told me ~ he was going,* Il m'a dit où il allait; *I don't know ~ to put it,* Je ne sais pas où le mettre. || *conj.* **1.** où: *The country ~ he lives,* Le pays où/dans lequel/il habite; *That is ~ I left it,* Voilà où/C'est là que/je l'ai laissé. **2.** [contains its antecedent] là où, à l'endroit où: *I left it ~ you'd find it,* Je l'ai laissé là où vous le trouveriez; *We walked to ~ he had left the car,* Nous avons marché jusqu'à l'endroit où il avait laissé la voiture; *He went back (to) ~ he came from,* Il est retourné (à l'endroit) d'où il était venu.

whereabouts [ˈwɛəˌbawts] *adv.* Où donc?, En quel endroit? || *n.* endroit *m* où l'on se trouve.

whereas [ˈwɛɚˌæz] *conj.* tandis que, alors que (au contraire), [Jur.] attendu que, étant donné que. || **wherein** [ˈwɛɚˌɪn] *adv.* d'où; en quoi, dans lequel. || **whereof** [ˈwɛɚˌʌv] *adv.* dont; de quoi, duquel. || **whereto** [ˈwɛɚˌtuw] *adv.* à quoi, auquel. || **whereupon** [ˈwɛəˌpɑn] *adv.* sur quoi. || *conj.* sur quoi, sur lequel; sur ce.

wherever [wɛɚˈɛvɚ] *conj.* **1.** [= everywhere that] partout où: *Wherever I go, I keep seeing him,* Partout où je vais, je continue à le voir. **2.** [= no matter where] où que + subjonc.: *Wherever you are, may be, this will be of use,* Où que vous soyez, ceci vous sera utile; *Put it ~ you want,* Posez-le n'importe où.

wherewithal [ˈwɛɚˌwɪðˈɔl] *n.* ressources *fpl,* moyens *mpl.*

whet [wɛt] *v. tr.* aiguiser, affûter (des couteaux, des ciseaux, &c.); [Fig.] aiguiser, stimuler (l'appétit, &c.).

whether [ˈwɛðɚ] *conj.* **1.** [introducing a reported question] si: *I don't know ~ she'll come or not,* Je ne sais pas si elle viendra ou non; *It is doubtful ~ he can finish in time,* Il est douteux qu'il puisse finir à temps. **2.** [introducing alternative conditions] que: *Whether rich or (~) poor, he . . . ,* (Qu'il soit) riche ou (qu'il soit) pauvre, il . . . ; *Whether he likes it or not . . . ,* Que cela lui plaise ou non . . . .

which [wɪtʃ] *adj. interrog.* quel *m,* quelle *f*: (*a*) [direct] *Which film did you see?,* Quel film avez-vous vu?; *Which school do you go to?,* A quelle école allez-vous? (*b*) [indirect] quel *m,* quelle *f* [or sometimes not translated]: *He asked me ~ film I had seen,* Il m'a demandé quel film j'avais vu; *He told me ~ book he had read,* Il m'a dit le livre qu'il avait lu. || *adj. rel.* [us. no direct translation]: *He explained his desire to buy a helicopter, ~ idea seemed strange to me,* Il a expliqué son désir de s'acheter un hélicoptère, idée qui m'a parue bizarre; *I was told to come at three thirty, at ~ time I would learn further details of the plan,* On m'a dit de venir à 15 heures 30, heure à laquelle j'aurais d'autres détails du plan. || *pron. interrog.* [direct & indirect] lequel *m,* laquelle *f* [see LEQUEL for other forms and contractions]: *Which (one) did you buy?,* Lequel avez-vous acheté?; *Which of you wants to come?,* Lequel/Laquelle/ d'entre vous veut venir?; *Which of the students were you talking to?,* Auquel des élèves parliez-vous?; *Tell me ~ one you bought,* Dites-moi lequel vous avez acheté; *He wondered ~ of the students I was talking about,* Il se demandait de quel élève je parlais. || **which** *pron. rel.* (*a*) [with a n. or pron. as antecedent] qui, que, dont, duquel, auquel, sur lequel, &c. [see LEQUEL for other forms and contractions]: **1.** [subject of Fr. clause] qui: *The book (~ is) on the table,* Le livre qui est sur la table. **2.** [object of Fr. clause] que: *The book (~) I see on the table,* Le livre que je vois sur la table. **3.** [the construction in the Fr. clause is completed with *dont*]: *The book (~)/I am talking about, (~) I need/,* Le livre dont je parle, dont j'ai besoin. **4.** [= whose; see also 3] dont: *The book, of ~ the cover/the cover of ~/is torn,* Le livre dont la couverture est déchirée; *The book/the title of ~ I forget, of ~ I forget the title/,* Le livre dont j'oublie le titre. **5.** [= *whose* after a prep. in Fr.] duquel, &c.: *The book, on the cover of ~ there is an ink blot,* Le livre, sur la couverture duquel il y a une tache d'encre; *The book, the author of ~ I was telling you about,* Le livre, de l'auteur duquel je vous parlais. **6.** [the construction in the Fr. clause is completed with a prep. other than *de*;

see also 7] auquel, sur lequel, &c.: *The book* (~) *I am thinking about,* Le livre auquel je pense; *The book* (~) *he wrote his name on,* Le livre sur lequel il a écrit son nom. **7.** *The street* (~) *he lives on,* La rue/où, dans laquelle/il habite; *The town* (~) *he is going to,* La ville/où, à laquelle/il va; *The town* (~) *he comes from,* La ville/d'où, de laquelle/il vient; *He asked for a sheet of paper on* ~ *to write his address,* Il m'a demandé une feuille de papier sur laquelle il pourrait écrire son adresse; *He has nothing with* ~ *to pay for his dinner,* Il n'a pas de quoi payer son dîner, cf. QUOI. [☞ (*b*) The antecedent in English is a general idea] *ce*, or a word such as *chose, idée, fait,* &c. + the suitable rel. pron., qui, que, &c. **1.** [subject of a Fr. clause] ce qui: *He smiled,* ~ *surprised me,* Il a souri, ce qui m'a surpris. **2.** [object of Fr. clause] ce que: *He ran away,* ~ (*was what*) *I wanted to do too,* Il s'est sauvé, ce que je voulais faire aussi. **3.** [with Fr. impers. verbs] ce que: *He taught me to pronounce well,* ~ (*was what*) *I needed to be understood,* Il m'a appris à bien prononcer, ce qu'il me fallait pour me faire comprendre. **4.** [as predicate of *être* and other linking verbs] ce que: *He thought he was a good driver,* ~ *he was,* → Il trouvait qu'il conduisait bien, et c'était vrai. **5.** [the construction in the Fr. clause is completed by *de*] ce dont: *At least I can swim,* ~ (*is what*) *I need to be allowed out in a boat,* Enfin, je sais nager, ce dont j'ai besoin avant de pouvoir sortir dans un canot. **6.** [the construction in the Fr. clause is completed by another prep., than *de*] (ce) à quoi, (ce) quoi, [illegible], sur quoi, après quoi; *He was annoyed,* ~ *I expected,* Il se vexa, ce à quoi je m'attendais; *He protested, in* ~ *he was right, and to* ~ *I replied . . .,* Il a protesté, (ce) en quoi il avait raison, et à quoi j'ai répondu . . .; *Upon* ~, *At* ~/*everyone laughed,* Sur quoi, tout le monde a ri; *After* ~ *he laughed too,* Après quoi, il a ri lui aussi. || **whichever** [wɪtʃ'ɛvɚ] *pron. rel.* **1.** [= the one which] celui/qui, que, dont, &c./[see CELUI for other forms]: *Send me* ~ *you don't need,* Envoyez-moi/celui, &c./dont vous n'avez pas besoin. **2.** [= no matter which]: *Whichever* (*one*/*ones*) *you* (*may*) *use, it's all the same to me,* Quel que soit celui que vous employez, Quels que soient ceux que vous employez/cela m'est égal. || *adj. rel.* **1.** [= the . . . which] le, la, les . . ., qui, que: *Take* ~ *book you like best,* Prenez le livre que vous préférez. **2.** [= no matter which]: *Whichever book you* (*may*) *take, I am sure you will like it,* Quel que soit le livre que vous choisissiez, je suis sûr qu'il vous plaira.

while [wajl] *conj.* **1.** [during the time that] pendant que, tandis que: *While I was talking, he listened,* Pendant que je parlais, il écoutait; [subject of both clauses is the same] *While* (*you are*) *in town, you ought to see the Exhibition,* Pendant que vous êtes en ville, vous devriez visiter l'Exposition; *He tripped* ~ *going down the stairs,* Il a trébuché en descendant l'escalier; *While listening, he went on with his work,* Tout en écoutant, il continuait à faire son travail; *While this was going on . . .,* Pendant ce temps-là . . . . **2.** [as long as] tant que; *While there is life, there is hope,* Tant qu'il y a de la vie, il y a de l'espoir. **3.** [= whereas] tandis que: *He is clever,* ~ *his brother is stupid,* Lui est intelligent, tandis que son frère est bête. **4.** [= although] quoique, bien que: *While you may be right, I am still not convinced,* Quoique vous ayez peut-être raison, je n'en suis toujours pas persuadé; [the subjects of the clauses are the same] *While I like coffee, I don't have it with every meal,* Tout en aimant bien le café, je n'en prends pas a tous les repas. || *n.* **1.** temps *m*; moment *m*: *a good* ~, un bon moment, assez longtemps; *quite a* ~, pas mal de temps; *He has been ill* (*for*) *a long* ~, Il est malade depuis longtemps; *He stayed* (*for*) *a little* ~, Il est resté un (petit) moment; *I saw him a* (*little*) ~ *ago,* Je l'ai vu/tout à l'heure, il y a peu de temps/; *I'll see you in a* (*little*) ~, Je vous reverrai/tout à l'heure, avant peu, sous peu/; *He came back after a* (*little*) ~, Il est revenu/peu de temps après, quelque temps après/. **2.** [WORTH].

whilst [wajlst] cf. WHILE.

whim [wɪm] *n.* caprice *m*, lubie *f*.

whimper [wɪmpɚ] *v. intr.* pleurnicher, gémir. || *n.* pleurnicherie *f*, ton *m* geignard.

whimsical ['wɪmzɪkḷ] *adj.* capricieux, fantasque; [thing] bizarre, étrange. || **whimsically** [-ɪ] *adv.* capricieusement; bizarrement.

whine [wajn] *v. intr.* pleurnicher, geindre; [dog] gémir, © onigner. || *n.* pleurnicherie *f*; gémissement *m*.

whip [wɪp] *n.* fouet *m*; coup *m* de fouet: © [Polit.] *party* ~, chef *m* de file. || **whip [-pp-]** *v. tr. & intr.* **1.** fouetter (un cheval, une personne, des œufs, &c.). **2.** (faire qqch.) vivement, brusquement: *He whipped a knife out (of his pocket)*, Il sortit brusquement un couteau (de sa poche). || *v. tr.* [Fam.] vaincre, battre qqun.

whip-poor-will [ˈwɪpɚˌwɪl] *n.* engoulevent *m*, © bois-pourri *m.*

whirl [wɚl] *n.* **1.** tourbillon *m*; [slower] tournoiement *m.* **2.** [Fig.] confusion *f* (des idées): *My head is in a* ~, La tête me tourne. || **whirl** *v. tr. & intr.* (faire) tourner, (faire) tournoyer, (faire) tourbillonner (qqch.); *whirling snow*, © neige *f* poudrante, poudrerie *f.*

whirlpool [ˈwɚlˌpuwl] *n.* [water] tourbillon *m*, remous *m.* || **whirlwind** [-ˌwɪnd] *n.* [wind] tourbillon *m*, remous *m.*

whiskers [ˈwɪskɚz] *n. pl.* [side whiskers] favoris *mpl*; [animals] moustaches *fpl.*

whisky [ˈwɪskɪ] *n.* whisky *m.*

whisper [ˈwɪspɚ] *v. intr.* **1.** chuchoter, murmurer; parler bas, à voix basse. **2.** souffler, dire qqch. (à l'oreille de qqun). || *n.* **1.** chuchotement *m*, murmure *m*: *in a* ~, à voix basse. **2.** bruit *m*, rumeur *f.*

whistle [ˈwɪsl̩] *n.* sifflement *m*; [instrument] sifflet *m*: *to give a* ~, *to blow a* ~, donner un coup de sifflet. || **whistle** *v. tr. & intr.* siffler (un air): *to* ~ *for one's dog*, siffler son chien. || **whistle-stop** [ˈwɪsl̩stɑp] *n.* arrêt facultatif.

white [wajt] *adj.* **1.** blanc *m*, blanche *f*; pâle, blême: *to turn/go, get/*~, blanchir, [person] pâlir, blêmir; *as* ~ *as (the driven) snow*, blanc comme neige; *as* ~ *as a ghost*, pâle comme la mort; ~ *with rage*, blême de rage; *a* ~ *man*, un blanc; ~ *hot*, chauffé à blanc; [PAINT]. **2.** pur, innocent; [spotless] sans tache. || *n.* **1.** blanc *m*, couleur *f* blanche: *dressed in* ~, habillé/de, en/blanc. **2.** [Misc.] blanc *m* (de l'œil, d'œuf); *a* ~ *sale*, vente *f* de blanc; *whites*, pantalon *m* de flanelle blanche. || **white-collar** [ˈwajtˈkɑlɚ] *adj.* ~ *worker*, employé(e) de bureau, © collet *m* blanc. || **whitefish** [ˈwajtˌfɪʃ] *n.* corégone *m*, poisson *m* blanc. || **white-haired** [ˌwajtˈhɛɚd] *adj.* aux cheveux blancs. || **white-headed** [ˌwajtˈhɛdəd] *adj.* à la tête blanche; aux cheveux blancs. || **whiten** [wajtn̩] *v. tr. & intr.* **1.** blanchir [WHITEWASH]. **2.** [person] pâlir, blêmir. || **whiteness** [ˈwajtnəs] *n.* blancheur *f*; pâleur *f.* || **whitewash** [ˈwajtˌwɑʃ] *n.* blanc *m* de chaux; ~ *brush*, badigeon *m.* || *v. tr* **1.** badigeonner en blanc; blanchir à. la chaux. **2.** [Fig.] blanchir (qqun). || **whitewashing** [ˈwajtˌwɑʃɪŋ] *n.* peinture *f* à la chaux; badigeonnage *m* en blanc.

whiting [ˈwajtɪŋ] *n.* merlan *m.*

Whitsun(tide) [ˈwɪtsənˌtajd] *n.* [Rel.] la Pentecôte.

whittle [ˈwɪtl̩] *v. tr.* tailler au couteau, © gosser: *to* ~ */away, down/*, amenuiser.

whiz(z) [wɪz] *n.* sifflement *m* (d'une balle, &c.). || *v. intr.* siffler: *to* ~ *past*, passer en sifflant, siffler aux oreilles; [motor cycle, &c.] passer à toute vitesse.

who [huw] *pron. interrog.* **1.** [direct] qui, quel: *Who is coming?*, Qui vient?; *Who is it?*, Qui est-ce?; *Who is there?*, Qui est là?; *Who is that lady?*, Qui est cette dame? [C'est Mme Dupont], ☞ Quelle est cette dame? [C'est la femme de ménage]; *Who are the ones you saw?*, Quels sont ceux que vous avez vus?; *Who is there to help me now?*, Qui va m'aider maintenant?; [indirect] *He asked* ~ *was coming*, Il m'a demandé qui venait; *He asked* ~ *it was*, Il m'a demandé qui c'était. **2.** [Fam.] = †WHOM || **who** *pron. rel.* **1.** qui: *My father,* ~ *is leaving on a trip* . . ., Mon père, qui part en voyage. . . . **2.** [= the one who] celui qui, &c.: *If it's* ~ *I think it is* . . ., Si c'est celui que je crois . . .; *(He)* ~ *wants to eat must work*, (Celui) qui veut manger doit travailler. **3.** [Fam.] = †WHOM. || **whoever** [huwˈɛvɚ] *pron. indef.* [do not confuse with *who ever*, see WHO 1]. **1.** [= the one who] celui qui, quiconque, qui: *Whoever gets the highest mark will win the prize*, Celui qui aura la meilleure note recevra un prix; *You can give it to* ~ *wants it*, Vous pourrez le donner/à (celui) qui, à quiconque/le voudra. **2.** [= no matter who] qui que [+ subjunc.]: *Whoever you/are, may be/, you can't go in there*, Qui que vous soyez, vous ne pouvez pas entrer; [as subject of other verb] *Whoever is doing that, tell him to stop*, Qui que ce soit qui fait cela, dites-lui de s'arrêter.

whole [howl] *adj.* **1.** tout/toute, tous/toutes; entier/entière, entiers/entières; [emphatic] tout entier, tout entière: *He ate the* ~ *pie*, Il a mangé toute la tarte, Il a mangé la tarte (tout) entière; *He ate a* ~ *pie* [all of it], Il a mangé toute une tarte, [one ~ pie] Il a mangé une tarte entière; *He ate two* ~ *pies*, Il a mangé deux tartes entières; *the* ~ *world*, le monde entier; *The* ~ *thing/affair/is ridiculous*, → La chose est complètement ridicule; *The* ~ *thing is to* . . ., Le tout est de . . .; *I didn't sleep the* ~ *night*, Je n'ai pas fermé l'œil de toute la nuit. **2.** complet *m*, complète *f*: *She bought a ~ (new) outfit*, Elle a acheté un trousseau complet; *~ -wheat bread*, pain *m* complet. **3.** [person] sain et sauf *m*, saine et sauve *f*; [thing] intact. || *n.* tout *m*; totalité *f*; ensemble *m*: *The ~ will cost two dollars*, Le tout coûtera deux dollars; *The ~ of our class*, Toute notre classe, Notre classe tout entière, La totalité de notre classe; *The ~ of the nation*, L'ensemble de la nation; *(taken) as a ~, on the ~*, dans l'ensemble.

wholesale [ˈhowlˌsejl] *n.* [Com.] gros *m.* || *adj.* de gros, en gros: *~ trade*, commerce de gros; *~ dealer*, commerçant *m* en gros, grossiste *m*; [Fig.] *~ slaughter*, une tuerie en masse, un massacre. || *adv. to sell, buy/~*, vendre, acheter/en gros; *I can get it ~*, Je peux me le procurer au prix de gros.

wholesome [ˈhowlsəm] *adj.* sain; [climate] salubre; [advice] salutaire.

wholly [ˈhowlɪ] *adv.* tout à fait; entièrement, complètement; en tout: *This is ~ satisfactory*, Ceci est/entièrement, tout à fait/satisfaisant; *He is ~ reliable*, On peut se fier à lui en tout.

†**whom** [huwm] *pron. interrog.* [direct & indirect] qui: *Whom did he visit?*, [Fam.] *Who did he go and see?*, Qui est-il allé voir? Qui est-ce qu'il est allé voir?; *To ~ do you wish to speak?*, [Fam.] *Who do you want to talk to?*, A qui voulez-vous parler? *He wondered ~* [Fam. who] *(he was going) to take to the dance*, Il se demandait qui il allait amener au bal; *He enquired to ~ he should apply*, [Fam.] *He asked who to apply to*, Il a demandé à qui (il devait) s'adresser. || *pron. rel.* **1.** [direct object of Fr. clause] que: *The student ~* [Fam.: omettez] *they congratulated . . .*, L'élève qu'ils ont félicité . . . ? [the verbal construction in the Fr. clause is completed by *de*] dont: *The man of ~ he was speaking*, *The man he was talking about*, L'homme dont il parlait. **3.** [The verbal construction in the Fr. clause is completed by a prep. other than *de*] qui: *The man to ~ I gave the money*, *The man I gave the money to*, L'homme à qui j'ai donné l'argent; [after *entre*, *parmi*: lesquel(le)s]; *The two boys between ~ I was seated . . .*, *The two boys I was sitting between*, Les deux garçons entre lesquels j'étais assis . . . . **4.** [Loc.] *both of ~*, qui . . . tous les deux, que . . . tous les deux.

who's [huwz] = who is [TO BE]: *Who's Who*, Bottin *m* mondain, le Who's Who; *~ there?*, Qui est là? Qui va là?

whose [huwz] *pron. interrog.* **1.** [direct] à qui; de qui; quel *m*, quelle *f*: [ownership] *Whose book is this?*, A qui/est, appartient/ce livre?; [otherwise] *Whose sister is she?*, De qui est-elle la sœur?; *Whose car did you come in?*, Dans quelle auto, Dans l'auto de qui/êtes-vous venu? **2.** [indirect]: *He wanted to know ~ book that was*, Il voulait savoir à qui était/appartenait/ce livre; *He wondered ~ sister she was, ~ car we had come in*, Il s'est demandé de qui elle était la sœur, dans quelle auto nous étions venus. || *pron. rel.* **1.** dont [if it modifies the subject, object, or a predicate noun in the Fr. clause; note the word order]: *The man ~ friend is coming*, L'homme dont l'ami vient; *The man ~ friend I saw*, l'homme dont j'ai vu l'ami; *The man ~ friend he is*, L'homme dont il est l'ami. **2.** de qui [if the Fr. clause is introduced by a prep.: note the word order]: *The man ~ friend I went with*, L'homme avec l'ami de qui j'y suis allé.

why [waj] *adv. interrog.* pourquoi: *Why did you do that?*, Pourquoi avez-vous fait cela?; *Why didn't you say so (right away)?*, → Il fallait le dire (tout de suite)!; *Why not?*, Pourquoi pas?; [indirect] *He asked ~ (I did it)*, Il a demandé pourquoi (je l'avais fait). || *conj. rel.* pourquoi: *That is (the reason) ~ I did it*, Voilà pourquoi/Voilà la raison pour laquelle, C'est pour cela que, C'est pourcette raison que/je l'ai fait. || *n.* [*us. pl.*] pourquoi *m*: *He always wants to know the why(s and wherefores) of everything I tell him*, Il veut toujours connaître le pourquoi de tout ce que je lui dis. || *exclam. Why yes! Why no! Why, of course (not)!*, Mais oui!, Mais non!, Mais bien sûr que oui!, Mais bien sûr que non!; *Why, it's you!*, Tiens, c'est vous!; *Why, what a nice surprise!*, Tiens, quelle belle surprise!; *Why, I must confess . . .*, Franchement, il faut avouer que . . .; *Why then . . .*, Eh bien alors . . . .

wicked [ˈwɪkəd] *adj.* [sinful] méchant; [mischievous] malicieux, malin; [Fam.] affreux. || **wickedly** [ˈwɪkədlɪ] *adv.* méchamment; malicieusement; affreusement. || **wickedness** [ˈwɪkədnəs] *n.* [quality] méchanceté *f*; [deed] mauvaise action *f*; [mischief] malice *f*.

wicker [ˈwɪkɚ] *n.* osier *m.*

wicket [ˈwɪkət] *n.* [door] guichet *m.*

wide [wajd] **wider** [wajdɚ] **widest** [wajdəst] *adj.* **1.** large; *to make wider*, élargir; *to grow/get/wider*, s'élargir; *This room is 10* *feet* ~ , Cette pièce/est/large de 10 pieds, a une largeur de 10 pieds/a 10 pieds de largeur/; *How* ~ *is* . . . ?, Quelle est la largeur de . . . ?. **2.** [difference, margin, experience] grand, large: *to a* ~ *extent*, dans une large mesure; [culture, connaissances, influence] étendu, vaste [☞ *vaste* precedes the *n.*]: *a* ~ *expanse*, une vaste étendue; *to go forth into the* ~ *world*, parcourir le (vaste) monde; *in the widest sense*, au sens le plus large; ~ *of the mark*, loin du but. || *adv. far and* ~ , loin, partout, de tous côtés; ~ *apart*, espacé; ~ *open* (*eyes*), (des yeux) grand(s) ouvert(s); *to open* (*the door*) ~ , ouvrir (la porte) tout(e) grand(e); *to open one's eyes* ~ , ouvrir de grands yeux; [dentist] *Open* ~ *!*, Ouvrez bien la bouche!. || **wide-awake** ['wajdə'wejk] *adj.* bien éveillé; [Fig.] (à l'esprit) éveillé, alerte. || **widely** ['wajdlɪ] *adv.* très, beaucoup: ~ *known*, très connu; *to be* ~ *read*, [book] être très lu, [person] avoir beaucoup lu, [author] avoir un public très étendu; *to differ* ~ , différer grandement, être très différent. || **widen** ['wajdn̩] *v. tr. & intr.* (s')élargir; [Fig.] ('s')étendre. || **widespread** ['wajd'spɹɛd] *adj.* étendu; [Fig.] répandu; universel; général.

widow ['wɪdow] *n.* veuve *f.* || **widower** ['wɪdowɚ] *n.* veuf *m.*

width [wɪdθ] *n.* largeur *f*: *The room is 10 feet in* ~ , La pièce a une largeur de 10 pieds [WIDE 1]; *The* ~ *between* . . . , La distance entre.

wield [wijld] *v. tr.* manier (une arme); exercer (le pouvoir).

wife [wajf] *pl.* **wives** [wajvz] *n.* femme *f*, épouse *f* [☞ many occupations have a fem. form: *the farmer's* ~ , la fermière, &c.].

wig [wɪg] *n.* perruque *f.*

wiggle ['wɪgl̩] *v. intr.* se dandiner.

wigwam ['wɪgˌwɑm] *n.* wigwam *m.*

wild [wajld] *adj.* **1.** [natural state] (homme, bête, plante, pays) sauvage: *to grow* ~ , pousser librement, à l'état naturel. **2.** [fierce] farouche. **3.** [wind, action] furieux, violent; [torrent, night] tumultueux. **4.** [life] déréglé; [person] dissipé; [room, hair] en désordre: *to run* ~ , se dissiper, courir les rues. **5.** [idea, plan] insensé, extravagant. **6.** [frenzied] *a* ~ *look*, un regard/air/affolé; ~ *applause*, des applaudissements frénétiques; ~ *with fear*, fou de peur; *to be* ~ *about sth.*, [anger] être furieux de qqch., [joy] aimer qqch. follement; *It drives me* ~ , Cela me rend fou.

wildcat ['wajldˌkæt] *adj.* risqué, extravagant: ~ *strike*, grève *f* illégale.

wilderness ['wɪldɚnəs] *n.* désert *m.* || **wildly** ['wajldlɪ] *adv.* [talk, act] d'une façon extravagante, comme un fou; [react, blow, &c.] violemment; [clap] frénétiquement; [live] d'une façon dissolue. || **wildness** ['wajldnəs] *n.* état *m* sauvage (d'un pays, d'un animal, &c.); violence *f* (du vent, d'une action) dérèglement *m* (de mœurs); extravagance *f*, folie *f* (d'idées). || **wilds** [wajldz] *n. pl.* région *f* sauvage, brousse *f.*

wilful ['wɪlfl̩] *adj.* [intentional] voulu, prémédité; [stubborn] entêté.

will [wɪl] *aux.* Formes nég.: *will not*, [Fam.] *won't*, *'ll not*. [☞ défectif: passé cf. WOULD. Suivi de l'inf. sans *to*, s'emploie selon l'usage le plus strict pour former les 2e et 3e pers. (s. et pl.) du futur simple et antérieur pour exprimer la simple futurité, et à la 1ère pers. (s. et pl.) pour exprimer la volonté du locuteur; à l'interrog., cet auxiliaire exprime la simple futurité aux 1ère et 3e pers., tandis qu'à la 2e pers., il sollicite un engagement de la part de l'interlocuteur. Ailleurs, il faudrait employer SHALL, mais étant donné que les formes affirmatives de *will* et de *shall* se réduisent dans la langue courante à *I'll*, *you'll*, *&c.*, la distinction traditionnelle entre *shall* et *will* a de plus en plus tendance à disparaître: on emploie *will* partout pour signaler la simple futurité et *shall* pour indiquer l'engagement de la volonté.] [☞ Distinguish between aux. *will* expressing simple future and volition.] **1.** [Futurity; use Fr. "futur" or "futur antérieur"]: (*I am sure*) *he* ~ *do it some day*, (Je suis sûr qu') il le fera un jour; (*I know*) *he* ~ *have finished it* (*by*) *tomorrow*, (Je sais qu') il l'aura fini (pour) demain; *Will we get there in time?*, Y arriverons-nous à temps? **2.** [immediate future; use present tense of aller + inf.]: *What* ~ *he do now?*, Que va-t-il faire maintenant?; *I'll tell him right away*, Je vais le lui dire tout de suite [☞ *I'll tell him to-morrow*, Je le lui dirai demain]; *I'll be back in an hour*, Je vais revenir dans une heure. **3.** [general statement: use Fr. present tense]: *Yes, that* ~ *often happen*, Oui, cela arrive souvent; *When teased, our dog* ~ *usually starts to bark*, Si on le taquine, notre chien se met généralement à aboyer. **4.** [orders: use *veuillez* + inf. or imperative]: *You* ~ *kindly keep quiet*, Veuillez vous taire; *You* ~ *all be back at three*, Soyez/Veuillez être/tous de retour ici à trois heures. **5.** [conjecture: use Fr. present tense]: *This* ~ *be your school,* (*I suppose*), C'est là (sans doute) ton école? **6.** [volition] vouloir: *Will you pass the salt, please?*, Voulez-vous passer le sel, s'il vous plaît?, [more formally] Voudriez-vous, &c.; [very formal] *Will you* (*kindly*) *follow me?*, Veuillez (vous donner la peine de) me suivre; [Fam.] *Will you be quiet!*, Veux-tu te taire!; *No, I* ~ *not/I won't/*, Non, je ne veux pas; *Give me a hand,* ~ *you?*, Donne-moi un coup de main, veux-tu?; *Try as I* ~ , J'ai beau essayer; (*Do*) *as you* ~, (Faites) comme vous voudrez. **7.** [☞ The Fr. subordinate clause may require the subjunc. mood]: *I don't think he* ~ *come,* Je ne crois pas qu'il vienne; *Although you won't have finished it . . . ,* Bien que vous ne l'ayez pas fini . . . . ‖ *v. tr.* **willed, willed** [wɪld] **1.** vouloir: *The law wills* (*it*) *that all shall be equal,* La loi veut que tous soient égaux. **2.** léguer: *He willed his money to the university,* Il a légué son argent à l'université. ‖ **will** *n.* **1.** [= will-power] volonté *f*: *to have a strong* ~/*an iron* ~ , *the* ~ *to do sth./*, avoir/la volonté forte, une volonté de fer, la volonté de faire qqch./; [Loc.] *Where there's a* ~ , *there's a way,* Vouloir, c'est pouvoir; [Phil.] *free* ~ , le libre arbitre; (*to work*) *with a* ~ , (travailler) de bon cœur. **2.** volonté *f*: *Thy* ~ *be done,* Que votre volonté soit faite; *It is his* ~ *that . . . ,* Il veut que + subjonc.; *At* ~ , à volonté; *of one's own* (*free*) ~ , de bon gré, de (son) plein gré; *against one's* ~ , à contre-cœur. **3.** testament *m.* ‖ **willing** [ˈwɪlɪŋ] *adj.* de bonne volonté, serviable: ~ *helpers,* des assistants de bonne volonté; *a* ~ *servant,* un(e) domestique serviable; *to be* ~ *to do sth.,* → vouloir bien, être prêt à/faire qqch.; ~ *or not,* bon gré mal gré. ‖ **willingly** [ˈwɪlɪŋlɪ] *adv.* **1.** spontanément; de plein gré. **2.** volontiers; de bon cœur. ‖ **willingness** [ˈwɪlɪŋnəs] *n.* bonne volonté *f*; consentement *m.*

willow [ˈwɪlow] *n.* saule *m*: *pussy* ~ , **chaton** *m*; *weeping* ~ , saule pleureur.

wilt [wɪlt] *v. intr.* se flétrir.

wily [ˈwajlɪ] *adj.* [often Pej.] rusé, astucieux.

win [wɪn], **won, won** [wʌn] **[-nn-]** *v. intr.* gagner; l'emporter: *He won hands down,* Il a gagné dans un fauteuil; *He always wins at cards,* Il gagne toujours aux cartes; *He won easily* (*over his opponents*), Il l'a emporté facilement (sur ses adversaires). ‖ *v. tr.* **1.** remporter (une victoire, un prix); gagner (un concours, de l'argent à qqun): [Sport] *to* ~ *the title,* gagner le championnat; *to* ~ *the toss,* gagner (à pile ou face). **2.** gagner (des amis, l'amitié); acquérir (une réputation); atteindre (la gloire): *This essay won him first prize,* → Cette dissertation lui a valu le premier prix. **3.** parvenir à. ‖ **win back** *v. tr.* regagner; reconquérir. ‖ **win over** *v. tr.* gagner, convaincre qqun: *to win s.o. over to one's side,* gagner qqun à son parti; convaincre qqun de son opinion. ‖ **win** *n.* [rephrase using *v.*, or] victoire *f.*

wince [wɪns] *v. intr.* broncher: *without wincing,* sans/broncher, sourciller/.

wind[1] [wɪnd] *n.* **1.** vent *m*: *The* ~ *is blowing,* Le vent souffle, Il fait du vent; *A high* ~ *is blowing,* Il fait grand vent; *There's quite a* ~ *outside,* Il fait un vent (très) fort dehors; *Which way is the* ~ *blowing?*, De quel côté vient le vent?; [Loc.] *There's sth. in the* ~, Il y a quelque anguille sous roche; *to get* ~ *of,* avoir vent de; *to take the* ~ *out of s.o.'s sails,* couper l'herbe sous le pied de qqun. **2.** coup *m* de vent; grand vent. **3.** souffle *m*: *to have a good* ~, avoir du souffle; *to get one's* (*second*) ~ , reprendre haleine. ‖ *adj.* ~ *instrument,* instrument *m* à vent.

wind[2] [wajnd] **wound, wound** [wawnd] *v. intr.* tourner; [road] faire des détours; [path, river] serpenter; [staircase] monter en colimaçon; [plant] s'enrouler. ‖ *v. tr.* **1.** enrouler (du fil, de la laine, &c.); [wrap] envelopper; entourer (de ses bras). **2.** remonter (une montre, &c.). ‖ **wind off** *v. tr.* dérouler. ‖ **wind up** *v. tr.* **1.** enrouler (une corde, &c.); remonter (un ressort, une horloge). **2.** terminer; régler. ‖ **winding** [ˈwajndɪŋ] *adj.* [road, river] sinueux; [mountain road] en lacet; [street] tortueux; [stairs] tournant: *Winding Road,* Virages *mpl* (sur *x* milles). ‖ *n.* [Fr. usually pl.] virage *m* (sur une route), détour *m* (d'un chemin); méandre *m* (d'une rivière).

windmill [ˈwɪndˌmɪl] *n.* moulin *m* à vent.

window [ˈwɪndow] *n.* **1.** fenêtre *f*: *to look out* (*of*) *the* ~ , *in* (*at*) *the* ~ , regarder par la fenêtre, à la fenêtre; *stained-glass* ~ , vitrail *m* [pl. *vitraux*]. **2.** [pane] vitre *f,* carreau *m*: *to break the windows,* casser les vitres; *to clean the windows,* nettoyer les carreaux. **3.** [Com.] vitrine *f*: *in the* ~ , en vitrine. **4.** [Rail., vehicle] glace *f*: *to lower, open/the* ~ , baisser la glace; *to raise, close/the* ~ , remonter la glace. **5.** [wicket] guichet *m* (de banque, des billets, &c.). ‖ **window blind** [ˈwɪndow ˌblajnd] *n.* store *m.* ‖ **window display**

[ˌwɪndowˌdɪsplej] *n.* étalage *m.* || **window-frame** [ˈwɪndowˌtɹejm] *n.* châssis *m* de fenêtre. || **windowledge** [ˈwɪndowˌlɛʤ] *n.* rebord *m* de fenêtre. || **windowpane** [ˈwɪndowˌpejn] *n.* carreau *m,* vitre *f.* || **window shop** [ˈwɪndowˌʃɑp] *v. intr.* **[-pp-]** regarder les vitrines, [Slang] lécher les vitrines, faire du lèche-vitrines. || **windowsill** [ˈwɪndowˌsɪl] *n.* appui *m,* tablette *f,* de fenêtre.

windshield [ˈwɪndˌʃijld] *n.* [Auto] pare-brise *m invar.*: ~ *wiper,* essuie-glace *m.* || **windstorm** [ˈwɪndˌstɔɚm] *n.* tempête *f* (de vent).

Windward Islands [ˈwɪndwɚdˈajləndz] *n.* [Geog.] les îles *fpl* du Vent.

windy [wɪndɪ] *adj.* **1.** venteux: ~ *weather,* temps *m* venteux; *It is very* ~ , → Il fait beaucoup de vent. **2.** [place] exposé aux quatre vents; balayé par le vent. **3.** [Fig.] verbeux.

wine [wajn] *n.* vin *m*: *the Bread and Wine,* le pain et le vin; *dry, sweet,* ~ , vin sec, doux. || *adj.* ~ *bottle,* bouteille *f* à vin; ~ *cellar,* cave *f*; ~ *country,* pays *m* de vignobles; ~ *glass,* verre *m* à vin; ~ *grower,* viticulteur *m,* vigneron *m*; ~ *growing,* viniculture *f,* viticulture *f*; ~ *list,* carte *f* des vins; ~ *vinegar,* vinaigre *m* de vin; ~ *steward,* sommelier *m.*

wing [wɪŋ] *n.* [bird, plane, building, army, team] aile *f*; [hospital] pavillon *m*; [player] ailier *m*: *to be on the* ~, voler; *to take* ~ , s'envoler; [Pol.] *the Right/Left/Wing,* la droite, la gauche; [Theat.] *in the wings,* dans les coulisses; [Aviation] *to win one's wings,* gagner ses ailes de pilote. || **wing** *v. tr.* **1.** [bird] *to* ~ *(its way) towards the south,* voler vers le sud. **2.** frapper, blesser (un oiseau) à l'aile: *I have winged him,* Je lui ai mis du plomb dans l'aile. || **wing-commander** [ˈwɪŋkəˌmændɚ] *n.* [Aviation] © commandant *m* d'escadre; [Fr.] lieutenant-colonel *m.*

wink [wɪŋk] *n.* clin *m,* clignement *m,* d'œil: *to give s.o. a* ~ , faire signe de l'œil à qqun; *with a* ~ , en clignant de l'œil; *to have forty winks,* faire un (petit) somme; *I didn't sleep a* ~ *all night,* Je n'ai pas fermé l'œil de la nuit. || **wink** *v. intr.* **1.** cligner les yeux: *to* ~ *at s.o.,* faire signe de l'œil à qqun; *to* ~ *at sth.,* fermer les yeux sur qqch. **2.** [light] vaciller; clignoter.

winner [ˈwɪnɚ] *n.* gagnant *m,* -e *f,* vainqueur *m* [for both sexes]. || **winning** [ˈwɪnɪŋ] *adj.* **1.** gagnant: ~ *number,* numéro *m* gagnant, [lottery] numéro sortant; ~ *stroke,* coup *m* décisif. **2.** [manners] séduisant; [smile] engageant. || **winnings** *npl* gains *mpl* (au jeu).

winter [ˈwɪntɚ] *n.* **1.** hiver *m*: *in* ~ , en hiver; *a severe* ~ , un hiver rigoureux. **2.** [Fig.] soir *m* (de la vie); (période de) solitude *f,* d'adversité *f.* || *adj.* (saison, sports, &c.) d'hiver: ~ *resort,* station *f* hivernale. || *v. tr.* hiverner. || © **winter-green** [ˈwɪntɚˈgɹijn] *n.* © gaulthérie *f* couchée; [Fam.] thé *m* des bois. || **wintry** [wɪntɹɪ] *adj.* hivernal, d'hiver; [Fig.] glacial.

wipe [wajp] *n. to give sth. a* ~ , essuyer qqch., donner un coup de torchon à qqch. || *v. tr.* **1.** essuyer; frotter. **2.** effacer; enlever; faire disparaître; *to* ~ *one's feet,* s'essuyer les pieds; *to* ~ *the blackboard,* essuyer/effacer, nettoyer/le tableau noir; *to* ~ *sth. dry,* → bien essuyer qqch. || **wipe off** *v. tr.* essuyer, enlever. || **wipe out** *v. tr.* essuyer (un bol, &c.); effacer (un souvenir, &c.); liquider (une dette); exprimer, anéantir (un groupe), détruire (la récolte, &c.). || **wipe up** *v. tr.* nettoyer.

wire [wajɚ] *n.* **1.** fil *m* de fer, de cuivre, métallique, électrique, télégraphique, téléphonique, &c.: *ordinary* ~, fil de fer; © broche *f*; *barbed* ~ , fil (de fer) barbelé; [Fig.] *to pull wires,* tirer des ficelles; *to get (in) under the* ~, terminer juste à temps. **2.** télégramme *m*: *Reply by* ~, Réponse télégraphique; *He sent me a* ~ , Il m'a envoyé un télégramme. || *adj.* (fait) en fil (de fer, &c.): ~ *fence,* clôture *f* en fil de fer. || **wire** *v. tr.* **1.** attacher qqch. avec du fil de fer. **2.** [Elect.] canaliser (une maison). **3.** [or *intr.*] télégraphier (qqch). à qqun. || **wireless** [ˈwəjɚləs] *n.* T.S.F. [Br. pour RADIO]. || **wiring** [ˈwajɚɪŋ] *n.* **1.** [Elect.] canalisation *f* (électrique) (d'une maison). **2.** [Radio] montage *m*: ~ *diagram,* schéma *m* de montage.

wiry [ˈwajɹɪ] *adj.* raide; [Fig.] nerveux, sec.

Wisconsin [wɪsˈkɑnsən] *n.* [Geog.] le Wisconsin: *to/in/*~ , dans le Wisconsin.

wisdom [ˈwɪzdəm] *n.* **1.** [learning] sagesse *f,* érudition *f*: ~ *tooth,* dent *f* de sagesse. **2.** [judiciousness] sagesse *f,* prudence *f* (d'une action). || **wise** [wajz] *adj.* **1.** [learned] sage: *a* ~ *man,* un (homme) sage; *the three Wise Men,* les (Rois) Mages *mpl.* **2.** [judicious] sage, prudent: ~ *advice,* des conseils *mpl* sages; *It, You/would be* ~ *to say nothing about it,* Il serait sage/prudent/de ne rien dire à ce sujet, que vous ne disiez rien à ce sujet. **3.** [informed] *a* ~ *look,* un air entendu; *I am none the wiser,* Je n'en sais pas plus long; *with anyone being the wiser,* à l'insu de tout le monde; *to put s.o.* ~, avertir qqun. || **wisely** ['wajzlɪ] *adv.* sagement, prudemment.

wish [wɪʃ] *v. tr.* **1.** souhaiter, vouloir: *to ~ s.o. (a) happy New Year, a merry Christmas, a pleasant trip*, souhaiter la bonne année, un joyeux Noël, bon voyage; *to ~ s.o./well, ill/*, vouloir/du bien, du mal/à qqun. **2.** désirer, souhaiter: *He wished for a good harvest*, Il souhaitait une bonne récolte, &c.; *He wished for the weather to improve*, Il a souhaité qu'il fasse meilleur temps. **3.** [polite form of *want*) désirer, vouloir, tenir à: *What do you ~ for your birthday?*, Que voudriez-vous pour votre/fête, anniversaire/?; *I ~ to speak to Mr. So-and-So*, Je désire, voudrais/parler à M. Untel; *I ~ to take this opportunity to ....* Je tiens à profiter de cette occasion pour . . . . **4.** vouloir (bien), souhaiter, regretter + inf., [or if subjects different] + subjunc.; *I ~ he would do it*, Je voudrais bien qu'il le fasse; *I am beginning to ~ I could do it*, Je commence à souhaiter (de) pouvoir le faire; *I ~ I knew*, Je voudrais bien le savoir; *He said he wished he knew*, Il a dit qu'il voudrait bien le savoir; *I ~ I had known*, J'aurais bien voulu le savoir, Je regrette de ne pas l'avoir su; || **wish** *n.* désir *m*, vœu *m*, souhait *m*: *to make a ~*, faire un vœu; *You will get your ~*, Votre vœu, désir/sera réalisé; *to express the ~ to . . .*, exprimer le désir de . . . ; *I have no ~ to . . .*, Je n'ai aucune envie de . . . ; according to the wish(es) of . . ., selon le(s) désir(s) de . . . ; *against my wishes*, à l'encontre de mon désir; *Best wishes*, Souhaits, Meilleurs vœux (de bonne année, &c.), [letter] Amitiés. || **wishful** ['wɪʃfl] *adj.* désireux (*of*, de); [look] → d'envie: *~ thinking*, → qui prend ses désirs pour des réalités.

wistful ['wɪstfl] *adj.* → d'envie, de convoitise; [dreamy] pensif, [sad] désenchanté.

wit [wɪt] *n.* **1.** (vivacité d') esprit *m*: *to have a/slow, quick/~*, avoir un esprit /lent, vif/; *to have/to keep/one's wits about one*, avoir, conserver/toute sa présence d'esprit. **2.** intelligence *f*: *to live by one's wits*, vivre d'expédients; [Fig.] *to be at one's wits' end*, ne plus savoir de quel côté se tourner, à quel saint se vouer. **3.** homme *m*, femme *f*/d'esprit: *He's a real ~*, C'est (vraiment) un homme d'esprit; *Sacha Guitry was a famous ~*, → Sacha Guitry était célèbre pour son esprit.

witch [wɪtʃ] *n.* sorcière *f*: *~-doctor*, sorcier *m* (guérisseur); [Fam.] mégère *f.* || **witchcraft** [-ˌkɹæft] *n.* sorcellerie *f*; [charm] sortilège *m.*

with [wɪð, wɪθ] *prép.* [☞ Many uses in English and Fr. are determined by the words around *with*.] **1.** [along with] avec: *Come ~ me*, Venez avec moi [cf. 3]; *He was arrested (along) ~ his accomplices*, Il fut arrêté avec ses complices; *I'll be ~ you in a moment*, Je suis à vous dans un instant. **2.** [instrument] avec: *Don't eat ~ your fingers*, Ne mange pas avec tes doigts; *He loosened it ~ (the aid of) a monkey wrench*, Il l'a desserré/avec, à l'aide d'/une clé anglaise. **3.** [at the place of] chez: *He lives ~ his uncle*, Il habite chez son oncle. **4.** [+ abstract noun] avec [the partitive is dropped before unqualified noun]: *~ pleasure*, avec plaisir; *~ uninterrupted interest*, avec un intérêt soutenu. **5.** [with following neg.] sans: *~ no difficulty (at all)*, sans (aucune) difficulté: *He stayed home ~ nobody to talk to*, Il est resté chez lui sans personne à qui parler. **6.** [after many verbs and adjectives] de: *to be satisfied ~*, être satisfait de; *to fill ~*, remplir de; &c. **7.** [from, because of] de: *to dance ~ joy*, danser de joie. **8.** [manner] de, à: *~ all his strength*, de toutes ses forces; *~ a trembling voice*, d'une voix tremblante; *~ open arms*, à bras ouverts; *~ the naked eye*, à l'œil nu. [Other idiomatic expressions of this sort should be looked for under the noun.] **9.** [a distinguishing feature, after a noun] à: *The man ~ a big nose and (the) white hair*, L'homme au grand nez et aux cheveux blancs; [when speaking generally, one may omit the definite article] *In the suburbs, one finds houses ~ red roofs and green shutters*, Dans la banlieue, on trouve des maisons au toit rouge et à volets verts. **10.** [Culin.] à: *coffee ~ milk*, café *m* au lait; &c. **11.** [an attendant circumstance, modifying the verb, and involving part of the body and/or one's possessions] → no translation: *He stood there ~ his hands in his pockets*, Il se tenait là, les mains dans les poches. **12.** [in the case of] avec, chez, pour: *With many people, tact is wasted*, Avec bien des gens, le tact ne sert à rien; *With him, it's different*, Chez lui, c' différent; *With me, it's all the same*, Pour moi c'est parfaitement égal. **13.** [progressively] avec: *His health will improve ~ time*, Sa santé s'améliorera avec le temps. **14.** [at the same time as] à: *With every step, he grew weaker*, A chaque pas, il s'affaiblissait; *With these words, he turned his back on me*, A ces mots, il me tourna le dos. **15.** [on the same side as] avec: *I'm ~ you*, Je suis avec vous. **16.** [in spite of] *With all his faults, he is still a friend of mine*, Malgré tous ses défauts, il est toujours de mes amis.

withdraw [wɪð'dɹɔ], **withdrew** [wɪð'dɹuw], **withdrawn** [wɪð'dɹɔn] *v. tr. & intr.* (se) retirer. || **withdrawal** [wɪð'dɹɔl] *n.* retrait *m* (d'argent d'une banque, d'une accusation); repli *m* (de troupes); désistement *n.* (d'un candidat).

wither ['wɪðɚ] *v. intr.* se flétrir, se faner.

withhold [wɪð'howld], **withheld, withheld** [wɪð'hɛld] *v. tr.* cacher (la vérité); refuser (son consentement); retenir (de l'argent).

within [wɪð'ɪn] †*adv.* à l'intérieur: *to go ~*, entrer; *from ~*, de l'intérieur, [Fig.] de l'âme. || *prép.* **1.** [inside] à l'intérieur de, dans (qqch.); [Fig.] au sein de, en (qqun): *Is your house ~ the city limits?*, Est-ce que votre maison se trouve dans la ville (même)?; *A quarrel broke out ~ the family*, Une querelle a éclaté au sein de la famille; *a voice ~ me*, une voix intérieure. **2.** [from inside] de l'intérieur; [Fig.] du sein de: *The cry came from ~ the house*, Le cri est venu de l'intérieur de la maison; *An attack (coming) from ~ the party*, Une attaque venant du sein du parti. **3.** [not beyond] dans: *He remained ~ the law*, Il est resté dans la légalité; *That is not ~ my power*, Cela n'est pas dans mon pouvoir; *~ the bounds of possibility*, dans le domaine du possible; *~ reason*, dans des limites raisonnables. **4.** [range] à, à (la) portée de: *~ 10 feet of us*, à (moins de) 10 pieds de nous; *to stop ~ 60 feet*, s'arrêter en moins de 60 pieds; *~ (my) reach*, à (ma) portée; *~ sight*, en vue; *~ calling distance*, à portée de la voix; *~ range*, à portée de tir; *~ (a radius of) 30 feet*, dans un rayon de 30 pieds [ACE]. **5.** [length of time] en (moins de); [future] d'ici: *I'll be through ~ an hour, &c.*, J'aurai fini/en (moins d') une heure, d'ici une heure/, &c.; *Within an hour of leaving*, (Moins d') une heure /avant, après/le départ. **6.** [time limit] dans (un délai de), dans le . . . qui suit; [future] d'ici: *I'll be through ~ the (next) week*, J'aurai fini d'ici une semaine, dans la semaine qui suit; *Be here ~ (the next) 24 hours*, Soyez ici dans les 24 heures. **7.** [almost] à . . . près: *His guess was ~ minutes of being right*, Il a deviné juste à deux minutes près.

without [wɪð'awt] *prép.* **1.** sans [+ n. or inf.]; sans que [+ subjunc.]: *He came ~ his book*, Il est venu sans son livre; [The partitive is dropped after ~, and neg. forms are used.] *Without (any) money, hope, or friends*, Sans argent, espoir ni amis; *~ any difficulty (at all)*, sans aucune difficulté; *He left ~ telling anyone*, Il est parti sans le dire à personne; *I'll never finish ~ your help(ing me)*, Je ne finirai jamais sans votre aide, sans que vous m'aidiez; *to be ~ sth.*, manquer de qqch.; *to go, do/~ sth.*, se passer de qqch. **2.** †à l'extérieur de; en dehors de. || *adv.* †à l'extérieur; au dehors.

withstand [wɪð'stænd], **withstood, withstood** [wɪð'stud] *v. tr.* résister à (une pression extérieure), s'opposer à.

witness ['wɪtnəs] *n.* **1.** témoin *m*: *eye ~*, témoin oculaire; *~ for the/defense, prosecution/*, témoin/à décharge, à charge/; *to call s.o. as ~*, citer qqun comme témoin; *The ~ may step down*, Le témoin peut se retirer; *~ to a document*, témoin à un acte. **2.** témoignage *m*: *to bear ~ to sth.*, rendre, porter/témoignage de qqch., témoigner de qqch. **3.** *~ -box, ~ -stand*, barre *f* des témoins. || **witness** *v. tr.* **1.** [see] être témoin de, spectateur de; assister à (un accident, crime, &c.). **2.** signer (un accord, contrat). **3.** témoigner, attester.

wittily ['wɪtəlɪ] *adv.* spirituellement: avec esprit. || **witty** ['wɪtɪ] *adj.* spirituel.

wives cf. WIFE.

wizard ['wɪzɚd] *n.* [also Fig.] magicien *m.* sorcier *m.* || **wizardry** [-ɚɪ] *n.* sorcellerie *f.*

wk., wks. *abr.*, cf. WEEK.

wobble ['wɑbl̩] *v. intr.* trembler (sur ses jambes); [table] branler; [car] zigzaguer; [Fig.] hésiter, vaciller. || *n.* tremblement *m*; [Fig.] hésitation *f*, tergiversation *f.*

woe [wow] *n.* malheur *m.* || **woeful** [-fl̩] *adj.* [Pers.] désolé, navré; [event] lamentable, triste. || **woefully** [-ɪ] *adv.* tristement, lamentablement, douloureusement.

woke, woken cf. WAKE.

wolf [wulf] *pl.* **wolves** [wulvz] *n.* **1.** loup *m*: *she-~*, louve *f*; *~-cub*, louveteau *m*; *prairie ~*, coyote *m*; *timber ~*, loup gris; *I'm as hungry as a ~*, J'ai une faim de loup; *to keep the ~ from the door*, joindre les deux bouts; *A ~ in sheep's clothing*, Un loup déguisé en brebis. **2.** [Fam.] galant *m*; don juan *m.* || **wolf** *v. tr.* dévorer, engloutir: *Don't ~ your food!* → Mange plus lentement!

Wolfe's Cove, © [Geog.] l'Anse-au-Foulon *f.*

wolverine, wolverene ['wulvəɹijn] © *n.* glouton *m*, [Fam.] carcajou *m.*

woman [ˈwʊmən] *pl.* **women** [ˈwɪmən] *n.* femme *f* [☞ with reference to one woman in particular, use *dame*: *That ~ over there*, Cette dame là-bas]. ‖ **womanly** [ˈwʊmənlɪ] *adj.* de femme, féminin.

womb [wuwm] *n.* [Med.] utérus *m*, matrice *f*; sein *m.*

won cf. WIN.

wonder [ˈwʌndə˞] *n.* **1.** merveille *f*; prodige *m*; miracle *m*: *the Garden of Wonders* (Montreal), le Jardin des Merveilles; *to work wonders*, faire merveille; *It's a ~ you didn't drown*, Il est étonnant que vous ne vous soyez pas noyé; *Little ~/No ~/ you were afraid*, (Il n'est) pas étonnant que vous ayez eu peur. **2.** étonnement *m*, surprise *f*, émerveillement *m*: *I stared at him in ~*, Je l'ai regardé longuement avec étonnement, → d'un air/étonné, émerveillé/. ‖ **wonder** *v. intr.* s'émerveiller de, s'étonner (*at*, de): *There's nothing to ~ at!*, Il n'y a pas de quoi s'étonner!; *I shouldn't ~ if he were right*, Cela ne m'étonnerait pas qu'il ait raison. ‖ *v. tr.* se demander, vouloir savoir (*if/whether*, si): *I ~ what his name is*, Je me demande comment il s'appelle; *I ~ !*, Je me le demande!, C'est ce que je me demande!; *I ~ why?*, Je voudrais bien savoir pourquoi!; *One wonders*, Sait-on jamais? ‖ **wonderful** [ˈwʌndə˞fl̩] *adj.* merveilleux, étonnant: *a ~ new invention*, une merveilleuse invention nouvelle; *a ~ experience*, une aventure étonnante; *We had a ~ time*, → Nous nous sommes vraiment bien amusés. ‖ **wonderfully** [ˈwʌndə˞flɪ] *adv.* merveilleusement, à merveille: *This radio works ~ (well)*, Ce poste marche merveilleusement (bien),/à merveille/. *It was ~ interesting*, C'était extrêmement intéressant.

won't [wownt] = will not: *No, I ~ !*, Certainement pas!, Non, non, non! cf. WILL.

woo [wuw] *v. tr.* courtiser, faire la cour à; [Fig., danger] rechercher.

wood [wʊd] *n.* **1.** [trees] bois *m*: *in the woods*, dans le(s) bois, dans la forêt; [Fig.] *You can't see the ~ for the trees*, Vous vous perdez dans les détails; *out of the woods*, tiré d'affaire, hors de danger. **2.** [material] bois *m*: *hard ~*, bois dur; *soft ~*, bois blanc, © bois mou; [Fam.] *Touch ~ !*, Je touche du bois. ‖ *adj.* (fait) de bois, en bois. ‖ **wood-carving** [ˈwʊd ˌkɑə˞vɪŋ] *n.* sculpture *f* sur bois. ‖ **wooded** [ˈwʊdəd] *adj.* boisé. ‖ **wooden** [ˈwʊdn̩] *adj.* de bois, en bois; [Fig., gait, manners] guindé, compassé. ‖ **woodland** [ˈwʊdˌlænd] *n.* forêt *f*; pays *m* boisé; © le(s) bois *m(pl)*. ‖ **woodman** [ˈwʊdmən] *n.* bûcheron *m.* ‖ **woodpecker** [ˈwʊdˌpɛkə˞] *n.* pic *m*, pivert *m*; © pic-bois *m.* ‖ **woodwinds** [ˈwʊdˌwɪndz] *n. pl.* [Mus.] les bois *mpl.* ‖ **woodwork** [ˈwʊdˌwə˞k] *n.* boiserie *f.* ‖ **woody** [ˈwʊdɪ] *adj.* boisé; planté d'arbres.

wool [wʊl] *n.* laine *f.* ‖ **wool-gathering** [ˈwʊlˌgæðə˞ɪŋ] *n.* rêvasserie *f*, musardise *f.* ‖ **woollen** [wʊln̩] *adj.* de laine, en laine. ‖ *n.* [généralement pl.] lainages *mpl* ‖ **woolly** [ˈwʊlɪ] *adj.* de laine, en laine; [hair] cheveux crépus.

word [wə˞d] *n.* **1.** mot *m*, terme *m*; parole *f*: *in a ~ , in one ~* , en un mot; *in other words*, autrement dit; *~ for ~* , mot pour mot; *What were his last words?*, Quelles furent ses dernières paroles?; *the words of a song*, les paroles d'une chanson; *in the words of*, selon l'expression de; *in your own words*, en vos propres termes; *He said only a few words*, Il n'a dit que quelques mots; *I couldn't get a ~ in (edgewise)*, Je n'arrivais pas à placer un mot; *I'll put in a (good) ~ for him*, Je dirai un mot en sa faveur; *He left without (saying) a ~* , Il est parti sans mot dire, sans dire un mot; *You have taken the words (right) out of my mouth*, C'est précisément ce que j'allais dire; *His room is beyond words*, L'état de sa chambre n'a pas de nom; *I'll have a ~ with him about it*, Je lui en toucherai un mot; *to have words (with s.o.)*, se disputer (avec qqun); *to suit the action to the ~* , joindre le geste à la parole; *by ~ of mouth*, verbalement. **2.** [promise] parole *f*: *to give/keep, break/ one's ~*, donner, tenir, manquer à/sa parole; *You may take my word for it*, Vous pouvez m'en croire sur parole. **3.** [message] nouvelle *f*; → prévenir: *to send ~ (to s.o. about sth.)*, prévenir (qqun de qqch.); *to receive ~* , être prévenu, *to leave ~ to, that . . .* , faire dire (à qqun) de, que . . . . **4.** [order] ordre *m*: *to give the ~ to*, donner l'ordre de. **5.** [Rel.] *The Word (of God)*, le Verbe; la (sainte) Bible. **6.** *(Upon) my ~ !*, ça alors!; *Upon my ~ !*, parole d'honneur! ‖ **word** *v. tr.* exprimer (une idée), formuler (un document, une pensée), rédiger (un télégramme); énoncer (un problème): *thus worded*, ainsi conçu. ‖ **wording** [ˈwə˞dɪŋ] *n.* expression *f*, formulation *f*; rédaction *f*; énoncé *m.*

wordy [ˈwə˞dɪ] *adj.* verbeux, prolixe.

wore [wɔə˞] cf. WEAR.

work [wə˞k] *n.* **1.** [activity] travail *m*,

ouvrage *m*: *to be at* ~, être au travail, à l'ouvrage, [machine] en marche; *hard at* ~, en plein travail; *to set/get/to* ~, se mettre au travail, à l'ouvrage, [machine] mettre en marche; *After much hard* ~, *I succeeded,* Après bien des efforts, j'ai réussi. **2.** [task] travail *m*; besogne *f*, tâche *f*: *I have some* ~ *to do,* J'ai (du travail) à faire; *It will be (a) hard (bit of)* ~, Ce sera un travail dur, une rude besogne, une tâche difficile. **3.** [output] travail *m*, rendement *m*: *The* ~ *done by this machine has doubled recently,* Le rendement de cette machine a doublé dernièrement. **4.** [product] ouvrage *m*, œuvre *f*: *She brought her* ~ *with her,* Elle a apporté son ouvrage avec elle; *a* ~ *of art,* une œuvre d'art; *the complete works of . . .,* l(es) œuvre(s) complète(s) de . . . . **5.** [doings] œuvre *f*: *works of charity,* œuvres de charité. **6.** [job] travail *m*, emploi *m*; occupation *f*: *to find* ~, trouver du travail, un emploi; *to be out of* ~, être sans travail, en chômage; *What is your* ~ ?, Quelle est votre occupation? **7.** *pl.* travaux *mpl*: *Works Department,* Service *m* des Travaux publics. **8.** *pl.* usine *f*: *gas-works,* l'usine à gaz. **9.** *pl.* mécanisme *m*; mouvement *m* (de montre). || **work** *v. intr.* **1.** travailler: *to* ~ *hard,* travailler dur, ferme [not: *fort*]; *to* ~ *on a book,* travailler à, écrire/un livre/; travailler sur, étudier/un livre: *to* ~ *on a newspaper,* collaborer à, écrire dans/un journal; *to* ~ *on s.o.,* persuader qqun, influencer qqun; *to* ~ *for . . .,* être employé par . . . . **2.** [machine, system, &c.] marcher, fonctionner: *It didn't* ~, ça n'a pas/marché, réussi/; *Does this pill really* ~ ?, Est-ce que cette pilule fait vraiment de l'effet? **3.** *To* ~ *loose,* se desserrer, se détacher. || *v. tr.* **1.** faire travailler (qqun): *to* ~ *o.s. /too hard, to death/,* se surmener, se tuer au travail. **2.** faire marcher, faire fonctionner: *Can you* ~ *a tape recorder?,* Savez-vous faire marcher un magnétophone? **3.** travailler (le bois, le fer). **4.** [difficult action] faire: [Fig.] *He worked himself into a rage,* Il a fini par se mettre en colère; *His keys worked a hole in his pocket,* Ses clés ont fini par faire un trou dans ses poches; *I worked my way through the crowd,* Je me suis frayé un chemin à travers la foule; *I worked my way through college,* J'ai travaillé pour payer mes études; *to* ~ *a miracle,* faire un miracle. || **work down** *v. tr. & intr.* (faire) descendre (peu à peu): *to work one's way down,* descendre avec peine. || **work in** *v. tr. & intr.* (faire) entrer (peu à peu): *to work one's way in,* entrer avec peine. || **work off** *v. tr.* se débarrasser de (qqch.) (en travaillant). || **work out** *v. tr.* faire, élaborer (un projet), faire (un calcul); calculer (un prix); résoudre (un problème). || *v. intr.* **1.** faire aboutir: *How will things work out?,* A quoi tout cela aboutira-t-il? **2.** s'élever: *How much does it work out to?,* A combien est-ce que cela s'élève? **3.** [Sport] s'entraîner: *He works out every morning,* Il s'entraîne tous les matins. || **work up** *v. tr.* préparer (un cours): [Fig.] *to get worked up,* se monter la tête. || *v. intr.* remonter (peu à peu); [Fig.] *What are you working up to?,* A quoi voulez-vous en venir? || **worker** ['wɚkɚ] *n.* **1.** travaill|eur *m*, -euse *f*: *He's a hard* ~, C'est un gros travailleur. **2.** ouvr|ier *m*, -ière *f*: *The workers are (out) on strike,* Les ouvriers sont en grève. || **working** ['wɚkɪŋ] *adj.* **1.** ouvrier, → qui travaille: *the* ~ *classes,* les classes *fpl* ouvrières; ~ *man,* ~ *woman,* ouvrier *m*, ouvrière *f*. **2.** de travail: ~ *clothes,* vêtements *mpl* de travail; ~ *party,* équipe *f* de travail; ~ *hours,* heures *fpl* de travail. **3.** de service: *a machine in* ~ *order,* une machine en (état de) service; *Is everything in* ~ *order?,* Est-ce que tout va bien?, Tout est-il en bon état? **4.** *a* ~ *agreement,* modus *m* vivendi; *a* ~ *majority,* une majorité suffisante. || *n.* travail *m* (de l'esprit); exploitation *f* (d'une mine); fonctionnement *m* (d'une machine). || **workman** ['wɚkmən] *n.* ouvrier *m*. || **workmanship** ['wɚkmən,ʃɪp] *n.* travail *m*, habileté *f* professionnelle; facture *f*. || **workshop** ['wɚk,ʃɑp] *n.* atelier *m*; cercle *m* d'étude.

world [wɚld] *n.* **1.** monde *m*: *the New World,* le Nouveau Monde; *to go around the* ~, faire le tour du monde; *in the next* ~, dans l'autre monde; *all over the* ~, (un peu) partout dans le monde. **2.** [Fig.] [special group, section] *the fashion, business,* ~, le monde de la haute couture, des affaires. **3.** [all people] monde *m*, le Tout Montréal, le Tout Paris; *to laugh at the* ~, se moquer du monde; *The whole* ~ *knows it,* Tout le monde le sait. **4.** [Loc.] *a* ~ *of, the* ~ *of,* énormément, infiniment, *The rest did him a* ~ *of good,* Le repos lui a fait énormément de bien; *to think the* ~ *of s.o.,* estimer qqun énormément. **5.** [Loc.] *I wouldn't do it for all the* ~, Je ne le ferais pour rien au monde; *The stone looked for all the* ~

like a real diamond, La pierre ressemblait exactement à un véritable diamant; *What in the ~ are you doing?,* (Mais) qu'est-ce que tu fais donc? || *adj.* mondial, universel: *World War II,* la deuxième guerre mondiale; *~ record,* record *m* mondial; *~ language,* langage universel. || **world-famous** ['wɚld,fejməs] *adj.* de renommée mondiale. || **worldliness** ['wɚldlınəs] *n.* mondanité *f.* || **worldly** ['wɚldlı] *adj.* **1.** [attitude] mondain, -e. **2.** de ce monde, d'ici-bas: *~ wealth,* richesses *fpl* d'ici-bas. || **world-wide** ['wɚld,wajd] *adj.* mondial, universel.

worm [wɚm] *n.* **1.** ver *m*: *earthworm,* ver de terre; *to fish with worms,* pêcher au(x) ver(s). **2.** [Fig.] [person] pauvre type *m.* || *v. tr.* **1.** se glisser, se faufiler (dans, *into*). **2.** [Fig.] soutirer (de l'argent, un secret) à qqun; s'insinuer dans les bonnes grâces de qqun: *I'll ~ it out of him,* Je vais lui tirer les vers du nez. || **worm-eaten** ['wɚm,ijtn̩] *adj.* rongé des vers; [wood] vermoulu.

worn cf. WEAR. || **worn-out** ['woɹn,awt] *adj.* [vêtement, outil, sujet, &c.] usé; [personne] épuisé; usé (par l'âge); [animal] éreinté.

worry [,wɚı] *n.* souci *m*; [Fam.] tracas *m*; [when in danger] inquiétude *f*; [large, long-lasting] tourment *m*: *That's the least of my worries,* C'est/le moindre, le cadet/ de mes soucis; *the worries of life,* les tracas de la vie; *to have worries as to one's safety,* avoir des inquiétudes au sujet de sa propre sécurité. || **worry** *v. tr.* **1.** [health, danger] inquiéter; [serious] tourmenter; *His cough worries me,* Sa toux m'inquiète; **2.** [bother] tracasser, importuner: *Don't ~ me with so many questions,* Ne me tracasse pas avec tant de questions. || *v. intr.* [serious] se tourmenter; [health, danger] s'inquiéter, se faire des soucis; [small] se tracasser; [Fam.] s'en faire: *Don't ~ (about it),* Ne vous tourmentez pas, Ne vous faites pas de souci, Ne vous en faites pas; *Don't ~ about me,* [Fam.] Ne vous en faites pas pour moi. || **worrying** ['wʌɚııŋ] *adj.* inquiétant.

worse [wɚs] *adj. compar.* cf. BAD **1.** plus mauvais, pire, †pis [☞ *pire* has the idea of harmful or morally bad, and is used in set phrases]: *Coffee is ~ than tea* [for one's health], Le café est pire que le thé; *The coffee here is ~ than tea.* Le café qu'on sert ici est plus mauvais que le thé; *There is nothing ~,* Il n'y a rien de/pire, plus mauvais, †pis/; *There is ~ to come,* Il y a pire, †pis; *to make ~,* empirer, aggraver; *to get ~,* empirer, s'aggraver; *and to make matters ~ . . . ,* et par surcroît de malheur . . . ; *a little the ~ for . . . ,* quelque peu (fatigué, usé); *none the ~,* sans aucun mal, pas plus mal. **2.** plus mal, †pis [*pis* only in set phrases]: *He feels ~ to-day,* Il se sent plus mal aujourd'hui; *from bad to ~, ~ and ~,* de mal en pis; *so much the ~,* tant pis; *and what's ~ . . . ,* et ce qui est pis . . . || *adv. compar.* plus mal: *He sings ~ than I do,* Il chante plus mal que moi; *~ than before,* plus (mal) qu'auparavant; *~ than ever,* de plus en plus mal, [more than ever] de plus belle. || *n.* pire, †pis: *I've been through ~ (than that),* Je suis passé par pire que cela; *Worse was yet to come,* → Le pire était encore à venir; *His health has changed for the ~,* Son état (de santé) a empiré. || **worsen** ['wɚsn̩] *v. tr.* empirer; aggraver. || *v. intr* empirer; s'aggraver; aller plus mal.

worship ['wɚʃıp] *n.* **1.** culte *m*: *hero ~,* le culte des héros; *hours of ~,* heures des offices. **2.** [Fig.] adoration *f*: *to be an object of ~,* être un objet d'adoration. **3.** [title] *Yes, Your Worship,* Oui, Monsieur le maire, Monsieur le juge, © Oui, votre Honneur; *His Worship the Mayor,* Son Honneur le maire. || **worship** *v. tr.* [-pp-] **1.** adorer (Dieu), rendre un culte à, vénérer (un saint). **2.** [Fig.] adorer, aimer follement.

worst [wɚst] *adj. superl.* cf. BAD (le) plus mauvais, (le) pire [*pire* is used in set phrases] ☞ or use a more precise adj.: *The ~ tennis player I know,* Le plus mauvais joueur de tennis, Le joueur de tennis le plus maladroit/que je connaisse; *his ~ enemy,* son pire ennemi, son ennemi le plus dangereux; *of the ~ kind,* de la pire espèce. || *adv.* (le) plus mal [☞ or use a more precise adv.]: *She sang (the) ~ of all,* Elle a chanté/le plus mal, le moins bien/de toutes; *Which one was hurt the ~?,* Lequel a été le plus (gravement) atteint? || *n.* le pire: *to fear the ~,* craindre le pire; *at the (very) ~, if the ~ comes to the ~,* au pire; *to get the ~ of it,* avoir le dessous; *He did his ~ at yesterday's examination,* Il n'a jamais aussi mal travaillé qu'à l'examen d'hier; [Loc.] *Go ahead! Do your ~!,* Allez-y! Faites ce que vous voudrez!

worth [wɚθ] *n.* valeur *f*; mérite *m*, utilité *f*, importance *f*; prix *m*: *of (great/little) ~,* de (grande/peu de) valeur; *of no ~ (at all),* sans (aucune) valeur; *I bought a dollar's*

~ *of paper*, J'ai acheté pour un dollar de papier; *I got my money's* ~, J'en ai eu pour mon argent; *Fifty dollars'* ~ *of athletic equipment has disappeared*, → De l'équipement sportif d'une valeur de cinquante dollars a disparu. || *adj.* **1.** valant; → valoir (la peine de), mériter: *a book* ~ *two dollars*, un livre valant deux dollars; *to be* ~ (*sth.*), valoir qqch.; *That watch is* ~ *$80*, Cette montre vaut $80; *It's not* ~ *much*, Cela ne vaut pas grand-chose; *It isn't* ~ *the trouble*, Cela n'en vaut pas la peine; *Is it* ~ *seeing that film?*, Est-ce la peine d'aller voir ce film?; *Yes, it's a film* ~ *seeing*, Oui, c'est un film qui vaut la peine (d'être vu), qui mérite d'être vu; *No, it isn't* ~ *your going there*, Non, cela ne vaut pas le déplacement. **2.** riche; évalué (à): *He is* ~ *millions*, Il est riche à millions; *He is* ~ *35 millions*, Il est riche de 35 millions; *A fortune* ~ *35 millions*, Une fortune évaluée à 35 millions; *He isn't* ~ *his salt*, Il ne vaut pas le pain qu'il mange. || **worthless** ['wɚθləs] *adj.* sans valeur, inutile; [person] bon à rien, indigne. || **worth-while** ['wɚθˌwajl] *adj.* utile, → qui vaut la peine. || **worthy** ['wɚðɪ] *adj.* digne, brave; [things] utile, méritoire: *to be* ~ *of*, être digne de, mériter; *the* ~ *fellow*, le brave homme.

would [wʊd] *aux.* [☞ passé du verbe défectif, cf. WILL. Suivi de l'inf. sans *to*, il s'emploie selon l'usage le plus strict, pour former les 2ᵉ et 3 pers. (s. et pl.) du conditionnel simple et antérieur, et à la 1ère pers. (s. et pl.) pour exprimer la volonté du locuteur; à l'interrog., cet aux. sert à former les temps du conditionnel aux 1ère et aux 3ᵉ pers., tandis qu'à la 2ᵉ pers. il sollicite un engagement de la part de l'interlocuteur. Formes nég.: *would not*, [Fam.] *wouldn't*, *'d not*. Ailleurs, il faudrait employer *should*, mais étant donné que pour les formes affirmatives la langue courante emploie régulièrement les contractions *I'd*, *you'd*, *&c.*, la distinction entre *should/would* a de plus en plus tendance à disparaître; on la remplace par *would* partout pour signaler le conditionnel et *should* pour indiquer l'obligation] [☞ Distinguish between aux. *would* expressing the conditional, volition, and habitual action]. **1.** [conditional] ☞ Fr. cond. or cond. anterior tenses: *I'd be glad to come*, Je serais content de venir; *If he were still alive, he* ~ *be 100 years old*, S'il vivait encore, il aurait cent ans; *If he had lived, he* ~ *have been rich*, S'il avait vécu, il aurait été riche; *He said he* ~ *come at 10 o'clock*, Il a dit qu'il viendrait à 10 heures; *He said he* ~ *have finished before we got there*, Il a dit qu'il aurait fini avant notre arrivée; *So! you* ~, ~ *you?*, Ah! vous oseriez? **2.** [habitual action] ☞ Fr. imperfect tense: *Every afternoon, he* ~ *go fishing*, Tous les après-midi, il allait à la pêche. **3.** [volition] vouloir: *He wouldn't do it*, Il n'a pas voulu le faire; *Would you help us, please?*, Voudriez-vous nous aider, s'il vous plaît?; *Try as I* ~, *the car just wouldn't start*, J'ai eu beau essayer, la voiture n'a pas voulu démarrer; *He* ~*!*, C'est bien de lui! **4.** †[wish] vouloir: *Would I were dead!*, Je voudrais être mort!; *Would to heaven I could be there!*, Le Ciel fasse que je sois là! **5.** [☞ The Fr. subordinate clause may require the subjunc. mood]: *I was afraid he* ~ *come*, J'avais peur qu'il ne vienne [†vînt]; *I doubt that they* ~ *have been able to finish it in time*, Je doute qu'ils aient [†eussent] pu le finir à temps.

wound[1] [wawnd] cf. WIND.

wound[2] [wuwnd] *n.* blessure *f*; [with infection] plaie *f*: *knife* ~, blessure faite par un couteau; [Fig.] blessure (d'amour-propre). || **wound** *v. tr.* **1.** blesser (*in*, à); [to hurt] faire une blessure à qqun. **2.** [Fig.] blesser, [weaker] froisser/qqun/.

wove, woven cf. WEAVE.

wrangle ['ɹæŋ̍l] *v. intr.* se quereller, se disputer. || *n.* querelle *f*, dispute *f*.

wrap [ɹæp] *v. tr.* **[-pp-] 1.** [also *wrap up*] envelopper; [solidly] emballer, empaqueter: *to* ~ *a parcel*, envelopper un paquet, [for mailing] emballer, empaqueter un colis; *Wrap yourself up* (*warmly*)*!*, Couvrez-vous bien!; [Fig.] *to be wrapped in thought*, être plongé dans ses pensées; *to be wrapped up in one's work*, être absorbé par son travail. **2.** [around] enrouler; [without regularity] entortiller; *Wrap the blanket around you*, Enroulez-vous dans la couverture. || **wrap** *n.* couverture *f* (de voyage); châle *m*; cache-nez *m*: *evening* ~, manteau *m* du soir. || **wrapper** ['ɹæpɚ] *n.* **1.** [person] emballeur *m.* **2.** papier *m* (d'emballage), bande *f* (de journal). || **wrapping** ['ɹæpɪŋ] *n.* papier *m* (d'emballage) emballage *m.*

wrath [ɹæθ] *n.* colère *f*, courroux *m.*

wreak [ɹijk] *v. tr.* [vengeance] assouvir: *to* ~ *vengeance upon*: se venger de.

wreath [ɹijθ] *pl.* **-s** *n.* couronne *f* (mortuaire); [smoke] panache *m.* || **wreathe** [ɹijð] *v. tr.* enguirlander; enrouler, entrelacer. || *v. intr.* s'enrouler (*round*, autour de); [smoke] s'élever, tourbillonner.

wreck [ɹɛk] [event] *n.* **1.** naufrage *m* (d'un navire), déraillement *m* (d'un train), écrasement *m* (d'un avion), accident *m* (d'auto). **2.** [remains] débris *mpl*; épave *f* (d'un bateau). || *v. tr.* faire dérailler (un train), causer le naufrage (d'un bateau), démolir; [Fig.] ruiner (la santé de qqun), faire échouer (un plan).

wreckage [ˈɹɛkəʤ] *n.* décombres *mpl.*

wren [ɹɛn] [Zool.] *n.* roitelet *m.*

wrench [ɹɛnʧ] *n.* **1.** clef *f*; *monkey* ~ , clef anglaise. **2.** effort *m* violent (de torsion).

wrest [ɹɛst] *v. tr.* arracher violemment (*from*, à).

wrestle [ˈɹɛsl̩] *v. tr.* lutter (avec), combattre (contre); être aux prises (avec un problème). || *n.* lutte *f.* || **wrestling** [ˈɹɛslɪŋ] *n.* [Sport] la lutte, [Fr.] le catch.

wretch [ɹɛʧ] *n.* malheureux *m*, infortuné *m*; [Pej.] misérable *m.* || **wretched** [-d] *adj.* malheureux, infortuné; [Pej.] misérable, détestable.

wriggle [ˈɹɪgl̩] *v. tr.* se tortiller, frétiller; [Fig.] s'insinuer (*into*, dans). || *v. tr. & intr.* tortiller, agiter. || *n.* tortillement *m*, frétillement *m.*

wring [ɹɪŋ], **wrung, wrung** [ɹʌŋ] *v. tr.* **1.** [by hand] tordre, [by machine] essorer (le linge); serrer fortement (la main de qqun); tordre (le cou à une volaille, [Fam.] à qqun); se tordre (les mains de désespoir); faire sortir (un liquide de qqch.). **2.** [Fig.] torturer, déchirer (le cœur); arracher (un renseignement, un secret, à qqun). || **wringer** [ˈɹɪŋər] *n.* essoreuse *f* (à linge).

wrinkle [ˈɹɪŋkl̩] *n.* [skin] ride *f*; [in a dress, &c.] (faux) pli *m.* || **wrinkle** *v. tr.* froncer (les sourcils), plisser (le front). || *v. intr.* [skin] se rider, se plisser, se gercer; [clothes] faire des (faux) plis.

wrist [ɹɪst] *n.* poignet *m.* || **wrist watch** [ˈɹɪstˌwɑʧ] *n.* © montre-bracelet *f*, [Fr.] bracelet-montre *m.*

writ [ɹɪt] *n.* [Jur.] acte *m* judiciaire; ordonnance *f*; [Rel.] écriture *f.*

write [ɹajt] **wrote** [ɹowt] **written** [ˈɹɪtn̩] *v. tr.* **1.** écrire; inscrire (un nom sur une formule, un registre); faire (un chèque); rédiger (un article); écrire, composer (un poème). **2.** [Fig.] *Honesty was written on his face*, L'honnêteté se lisait sur son visage. || *v. intr.* **1.** [letter, card, &c.] écrire (à qqun): *Be sure to ~ (to John)*, Ne manquez pas d'écrire (à Jean). **2.** [for a paper] écrire dans un journal, faire du journalisme, collaborer à un journal; être/faire profession d'/écrivain: *Her ambition is to* ~ , Son ambition est de devenir écrivain. || **write down** *v. tr.* prendre (une dictée); noter (des idées, ses dépenses); écrire (son nom). || **to ~ for** (sth.) *v. tr.* commander, faire venir (qqch.). || **write in** *v. tr. & intr.* insérer (une correction); écrire à (un poste de radio, &c.). || **write off** *v. tr.* [Com.] passer qqch. aux profits et pertes; [Fig.] *He wrote it off to experience*, Ça lui a servi de leçon. || **write out** *v. tr.* faire (un devoir) en entier; [in full] écrire qqch. en toutes lettres; rédiger (un document); transcrire, copier (une lettre, &c.) au propre; faire (un chèque). || **write up** [event] rédiger, faire la description de; [Press] faire un papier sur; [book] donner un compte rendu de; [Com.] mettre à jour (les livres de qqun). || **write-up** [ˈɹajtʌp] *n.* [event] rédaction *f*, description *f* (par écrit); [Press] un papier sur; [book, article] compte rendu *m.* || **writer** [ˈɹajtər] *n.* écrivain *m*, auteur *m*; [hack] écrivassier *m*; [as a living] homme *m* de lettres. || **writing** [ˈɹajtɪŋ] *n.* **1.** [hand] écriture *f.* **2.** rédaction *f* (d'un devoir, d'une page, d'une lettre): [Press] *At the time of* ~ , → Au moment où (cet article) fut rédigé; *the art of* ~ , l'art d'écrire. **3.** écrit *m*, œuvre *f* (littéraire): *the writings of Victor Hugo*, les œuvres, les écrits/ de Victor Hugo; *Put that in* ~ , Mettez ça par écrit, → Ecrivez-le; *agreement in* ~ , convention par écrit. || **written** [ˈɹɪtn̩] *adj.* écrit, par écrit: *to give a ~ statement*, faire un rapport écrit; *a ~ consent*, consentement *m* par écrit.

wrong [ɹɔŋ] *adj.* **1.** [immoral] mal; → avoir tort: *It is ~ (of you) to lie*, C'est mal (à vous) de mentir; *You are ~ to do that*, Vous avez tort de faire cela. **2.** [incorrect] faux; [inaccurate] inexact: *Your answer is* ~ , Votre réponse est fausse; *What you say is* ~ , Ce que vous dites est inexact; *The clock is* ~ , La pendule n'est pas à l'heure. **3.** [mistaken] avoir tort, se tromper [of persons]: *You are (quite)* ~ , Vous avez tort, Vous vous trompez. **4.** [unsuitable] mauvais; [→ *neg.* + . . . qu'il faut]: *He waited at the ~ place*, Il a attendu au mauvais endroit, Il n'a pas attendu à l'endroit qu'il fallait; *on the ~ side*, du mauvais côté; *to get out of bed on the ~ side*, se lever du pied gauche; (*the*) *~ side out*, à l'envers; (*the*) *~ side up*, sens dessus dessous; *You have used the ~ word*, Vous avez employé un terme impropre; *You're doing it the ~ way*, Vous vous y prenez de la mauvaise manière; *to swallow the ~ way*, avaler de travers. **5.** [to do sth. by mistake] mauvais, → se tromper de: *You have (got) the ~ number*, Vous avez le mauvais numéro, Vous vous êtes trompé de numéro; *He took the ~ road, He went the ~ way*, Il a pris le mauvais chemin, Il s'est trompé de chemin. **6.** [amiss] → qui ne va pas: *What's ~ (with you)?*, Qu'est-ce qui ne va pas?, Qu'est-ce qu'il y a?, Qu'est-ce que vous avez?; *Sth. is ~ (with his back)*, Il a qqch. (au dos); *There's sth. ~ with the TV (set)*, Il y a qqch. qui ne marche pas dans le poste de télévision; *Nothing's ~*, Il n'y a rien, Tout va bien; *Everything's ~*, Tout va mal. || *adv.* mal, → se tromper: *He got my name ~*, Il a mal écrit mon nom, Il a mal compris mon nom; *He guessed ~*, Il s'est trompé; [Fam.] *You've got me ~*, Vous avez mal compris; *I did ~ in inviting him*, J'ai eu tort de l'inviter; *Everything is going ~*, Tout va mal; *Where did I go ~?*, Où est-ce que je me suis trompé; *What went ~?*, Qu'est-ce qui n'a pas marché?; *Sth. has gone ~ with the radio*, Il y a qqch. qui ne marche pas dans le poste. || *n.* **1.** [evil] mal *m*: *right and ~*, le bien et le mal. **2.** tort *m*, injustice *f*: *This accusation does him (great) ~*, Cette accusation lui fait (grand) tort; *He has suffered many wrongs*, Il a souffert de nombreuses injustices; *I am in the ~*, Je suis dans mon tort, J'ai tort. || **wrong** *v. tr.* [harm] faire (du) tort (à qqun); être injuste envers: *He forgave those who had wronged him*, Il pardonna à ceux qui l'avaient injustement traité. || **wrong-doer** [ˈɹɔŋˌduwɚ] *n.* auteur *m* d'une injustice; délinquant *m*, malfaiteur *m*. || **wrong-doing** [ˈɹɔŋˌduwɪŋ] *n.* mal *m*, délinquance *f*; mauvaise action *f*. || **wrongly** [ˈɹɔŋlɪ] *adv.* **1.** [unjustly] à tort. **2.** mal: *That's my name, ~ spelled as usual*, Voilà mon nom, mal écrit comme toujours.

wrote cf. WRITE.

wrung cf. WRING.

wry [ɹaj] *adj.* tordu: *to pull a ~ face*, faire une grimace.

Wyoming [wajˈowmɪŋ] *n.* [Geog.] le Wyoming *m*.

X

X, x [ɛks] *pl.* **X's, x's** [ˈɛksəz] *n.* X, x *m*.

xenophobia [zɛnəˈfowbɪjə] *n.* xénophobie *f*.

Xmas [ˈɛksməs] *abr.* = CHRISTMAS.

X-ray [ˈɛksˈɹej] *n.* **1.** [généralement au pluriel] rayons *pl m* X. **2.** radiographie *f*: *to have an ~*, passer à la radio(graphie), se faire radiographier; *to take an ~*, prendre une radiographie. || **X-ray** *v. tr.* radiographier. || *adj.* radiographique; *~ treament*, radiothérapie; *~ examination*, examen *m* radioscopique.

xylophone [ˈzajləˌfown] *n.* [Mus.] xylophone *m*.

Y

Y, y [waj] *pl.* **Y's, y's** [wajz] *n.* Y, y *m.*

yacht [jɔt] *n.* yacht *m*, bateau *m* de plaisance.

Yahweh [ˈjɔwɛ] [also Yahwe, Jahve, Jahveh] *n.* [Bibl.] Yahvé *m* [Yahweh, Jahvé, Iahvé].

Yank, Yankee [jæŋk, ˈjæŋkɪ] *n.* **1.** Américain *m*, Américaine *f*; Yankee *m.* **2.** Nordiste *m, f.* || *adj.* américain; nordiste; yankee.

yard¹ [jɑɚd] *n.* **1.** cour *f*: *back yard*, cour, jardin *m* (de derrière). **2.** chantier *m*; gare *f*: *lumber* ~ , chantier de bois (de construction); [Rail.] *marshalling* ~ , gare de triage.

yard² [jɑɚd] *n.* [mesure de longueur] [Fr.] yard *m*, [approx.] mètre *m*; © verge *f*: *This material is sold by the* ~ , Ce tissu se vend/à la verge, au yard/ → au mètre/. || **yardstick** [-stɪk] *n.* © verge *f*; [Fig.] mesure *f*, unité *f* de comparaison, †aune *f.*

yarn [jɑɚn] *n.* **1.** fil *m* (de coton, de lin, &c.). **2.** [Fig.; généralement péjoratif] histoire *f.*

yawn [jɔn] *n.* bâillement *m.* || *v. intr.* bâiller; [Fig.] s'ouvrir (tout grand). || **yawning** [-ɪŋ] *adj.* béant, grand ouvert; qui bâille.

yd. *pl.* **yds.** [jɑɚd(z)] *abr.* cf. YARD².

†yea [jej] *adv.* †vraiment, en vérité; voire. || *n.* vote *m* affirmatif; votant *m* affirmatif.

yeah [jæ] [Arg.] *adv.* oui: (*Oh*) ~ *!*, Ouais!; tu parles!

year [jijɚ] *n.* **1.** an *m*, année *f* [Usually *année* when used with ordinal and non-numerical determinatives: *cette, chaque, quelques, toute(s), plusieurs, bonne, scolaire, intéressante, nouvelle, bissextile,* &c.; Usually *an* with cardinal adjectives and *tous.* With *prochain, dernier, passé,* either can be used]: *New Year's Day*, le jour de l'an [NEW YEAR]; *three times a* ~ , trois fois/l'an, par an, par année/; ~ *in and* ~ *out*, bon an mal an; *years* (*and years*) *ago*, il y a des années (et des années); *in my* ~ (*at school*), dans/mon année, ma classe, ma promotion/(à l'école); *in second* ~ , en deuxième (année). **2.** *pl.* âge *m*: *From my earliest years,* Dès mon plus jeune âge; *He is getting on in years,* Il avance en âge, est d'un âge avancé; *He is twenty* (*years old*), Il a vingt ans. || **yearbook** [ˈjijɚˌbʊk] *n.* **1.** annuaire *m*: *The Canada* ~ , l'Annuaire du Canada. **2.** album *m*: *Blue and Gold* ~ , l'album Bleu et Or. || **yearly** [ˈjijɚlɪ] *adj.* annuel, chaque année, par an: *His* ~ *salary is $6000,* Son traitement annuel est de $6000, Il gagne $6000 par an. || *adv.* chaque année, par an, annuellement: *I see him* ~ , *twice* ~ , Je le vois chaque année, deux fois par an. || **year-old** [ˈjijɚˌowld] *n.* bébé *m*, enfant *m*, âgé d'un an. || *adj.* d'un an; [ou indiquer l'âge]: *a seventeen -* ~ *girl,* une jeune fille de dix-sept ans.

yearn (for) [jɚn] *v. intr.* désirer ardemment qqch., soupirer après qqch. || **yearning** [-ɪŋ] *n.* désir *m* (profond, intense); aspiration *f*, élan *m.*

yeast [jijst] *n.* levure *f*; ferment *m*: *baker's* ~ , *brewer's* ~ , levure de boulanger, levure de bière; *natural yeasts,* les ferments naturels.

yell [jɛl] *n.* **1.** cri *m*, hurlement *m* (de douleur, de rage, &c.). **2.** [Sch.] le "boum" universitaire, le cri de ralliement (de l'école). || **yell** *v. tr.* crier, hurler/qqch. (à qqun). || *v. intr.* pousser un grand cri, un hurlement: *to* ~ *at s.o.*, hurler à qqun; *to* ~ (*out*)/*with pain, in anger*/, crier, hurler/de douleur, de rage.

yellow [ˈjɛlow] *adj.* jaune: *to turn, become, get* ~ , jaunir; [Fig.] *to turn* ~ , avoir la frousse. || *n.* le jaune. || **yellow** *v. tr. & intr.* jaunir: *paper yellowed with age,* papier jauni (par l'âge). || **yellowish** [-ɪʃ] *adj.* jaunâtre.

yelp [jɛlp] *v. intr.* [dog] japper; [fox] glapir. || *n.* jappement *m.*

yep [jɛp] [Fam.] *adv.* oui.

yes [jɛs] *adv.* **1.** oui: *I asked him and he said* ~ , Je lui ai demandé et il a/dit oui, répondu que oui/; Je l'ai invité et il a dit oui. [Simplify such answers as *Yes, I have; Yes, I do,* &c., and add *Monsieur,* &c., when talking to an older person or stranger: *Oui; Mais oui; Mais certainement,* (*Monsieur*)]. **2.** [Fr.] si [in reply to a negative statement]: *You don't like this? Yes, I do!*, Tu n'aimes pas ça? (Mais) si! **3.** [questioningly] Vraiment?; [clerk in a store] Vous désirez? **4.** [= I'm coming] Voilà! J'arrive!

yesterday [ˈjɛstədej] *n.* hier *m*: *all day* ~ , toute la journée d'hier; *yesterday's paper,* le journal d'hier; *Yesterday was the second of January,* C'était, Nous étions/hier le deux janvier. || *adv.* hier: *the day before* ~ , avant-hier; ~ *morning,* hier matin; ~ *evening,* hier (au) soir; *I wasn't born* ~ , Je ne suis pas né(e) d'hier.

yet [jɛt] *adv.* **1.** encore, déjà: *not* ~ , pas

encore; *Is he up ~ ?*, Est-il (déjà) levé?; *I have ~ to find a better one*, Je n'en ai pas encore trouvé de meilleur. **2.** [with future] un de ces jours; → finir (bien) par: *I'll win ~* , Je finirai bien par gagner. **3.** *as ~* , jusqu'ici, jusqu'à présent. || *conj.* cependant, pourtant: *He did not mention it and ~ I am sure he knew*, Il n'en a pas parlé, et cependant je suis sûr qu'il était au courant.

yield [jijld] *n.* [produce] produit *m*; [output] rendement *m*; [return on investment] rapport *m.* || **yield** *v. tr.* **1.** donner, produire; rendre; rapporter: *This tree yields a great deal of fruit*, [in terms of produce] Cet arbre/donne. produit/beaucoup de fruit, [in terms of output] Cet arbre (fruitier) rend bien, [in terms of returns on investment] Cet arbre (fruitier) rapporte bien, beaucoup. **2.** céder (qqch. à qqun): *The enemy yielded ground*, L'ennemi a cédé du terrain; *He yielded the point*, Il a cédé le point. || *v. intr.* [surrender] se rendre; céder [cf. GIVE WAY]: *The enemy yielded*, L'ennemi s'est rendu; *He yielded /to reason, to temptation, to force/*, Il a cédé/à la raison, à la tentation, à la force/; *We ~ to nobody in intelligence*, Nous ne le cédons à personne en intelligence; [traffic sign] *Yield (right o, way)*, Priorité/à droite, à gauche/.

Y.M.C.A. [ˌwajɛm'sij'ej] *[abr. = Young Men's Christian Association]*, © le Y.M.C.A. || **Y.M.Y.W.H.A.** *[abr. = Young Men's & Young Women's Hebrew Association]*.

yoke [jowk] *n.* [also Fig.] joug *m.*

yolk [jowk] *n.* jaune *m* (d'œuf).

†yonder, yon ['jɔndɚ] *adv.* là-bas, au loin; là. || *adj.* ce, &c., . . . -là; là-bas: *~ hills*, ces collines lointaines, ces collines là-bas.

you ['juw, jə] *pron. pers.* [General Remarks]: [(1) Addressing one person respectfully: one's elders, superiors, acquaintances, strangers] vous; [(2) addressing one person familiarly: parents, relatives, good friends, children, animals] tu, te, toi [note that (1) replaces (2) to denote estrangement; (2) replaces (1) to denote increased friendship or contempt]; [(3) addressing more than one person familiarly or respectfully] vous; © vous autres. [Numbers in brackets throughout this entry refer to the above remarks.] **1.** [subj.] *You came*, (1) Vous êtes venu(e), (2) Tu es venu(e), (3) Vous êtes venu(e)s; [obj.] *I saw ~* , (1) Je vous ai vu(e), (2) Je t'ai vu(e), (3) Je vous ai vu(e)s; [obj. of prep.] *I'll go with ~* , J'irai (1, 3) avec vous, (2) avec toi; [after *to be*] *Is it ~ ?*, Est-ce (1, 3) vous?, (2) toi? **2.** [emphatic uses] [subj.] (1) vous, (2) toi, (3) vous, vous autres: YOU *will come, won't ~ ?*, (1) Vous, vous viendrez/, (2) Toi, tu viendras/, (3) Vous (autres), vous viendrez/, n'est-ce pas?; *Did* YOU *do it?*, *Was it* YOU *who did it?*, (1) Est-ce vous qui l'avez fait?, (2) Est-ce toi qui l'as fait?, (3) Est-ce vous (autres) qui l'avez fait?; [obj.] *He wouldn't harm* YOU, *would he?*, Il ne vous ferait pas de mal (1) à vous, (3) à vous (autres)/; Il ne te ferait pas de mal (2) à toi/, n'est-ce pas?; *I wasn't expecting ~* , (1) Je ne vous attendais pas, vous, (2) Je ne t'attendais pas, toi, (3) Je ne vous attendais pas, vous (autres); Ce n'était pas (1) vous, (2) toi, (3) vous (autres) que j'attendais; [after prep.] *I want to come with* YOU, C'est avec (1) vous, (2) toi, (3) vous (autres), que je veux venir; [after *to be*] YOU'*re the expert*, C'est (1) vous, (2) toi, l'expert. **3.** [with imperat.] *You, stand over there*, (1) Vous, (3) vous (autres), mettez-vous là-bas; (2) toi, mets-toi là-bas; *Now ~ do it*, (1, 3) A votre tour, (2) A ton tour/de le faire; *Don't ~ do that!*, Surtout (1, 3) ne faites pas ça, (2) ne fais pas ça! **4.** [indef. subject] on; [indef. object, dir. or indir.] vous; [object of prep.] soi, [→ impersonal construction]: *The older ~ get, the more ~ have to work*, Plus on grandit, plus il faut travailler; *The less it amuses ~ , the harder it is to go on*, Moins cela vous amuse, plus il (vous) est difficile de continuer; *You should always bring your books with ~ !*, Il faut toujours porter ses livres avec soi, (voyons)! **5.** [misc. uses]: ~ [suj. indéf.]; *people, fellows, girls, &c.*, vous autres; *You Canadians . . .* , Vous autres (les) Canadiens . . . ; *If I were ~* , Si j'étais à votre/ta/place; *Between ~ and me*, Entre vous/toi/et moi; → Entre nous; *He likes ~ and me*, Il nous aime, vous/toi/et moi; *You birdbrain, &c., ~ !* (Espèce de) cervelle d'oiseau, va!; *Oh ~/nice, bad/little fellow!*, Ah, le/gentil, méchant/petit bonhomme!; *Now, there's a car for ~ !*, [approving] Ça, c'est une voiture!, [iron.] En voilà une voiture!

you'd [juwd] **1.** = you had [TO HAVE]. **2.** = you would [WILL].

you'll [juwl] = you will [WILL].

young [jʌŋ] *adj.* **[-er, -est]** jeune, petit; [Fig.] inexpérimenté, à ses débuts: *a ~ boy*, un petit garçon, un garçonnet [3-10], un jeune garçon [10-14]; *a ~ girl*, une petite fille [3-10], une fillette [10-14]; *a ~ man*, un jeune homme [16-30]; *a ~ lady*, [married] une jeune femme, [unmarried] une jeune fille [15-24], †une jeune personne [18-30]; *a ~ woman*, une jeune femme [25-35], †une jeune personne [18-30]; [×] *~ men*, jeunes gens; *~ people*, des jeunes, des jeunes gens et des jeunes filles, la jeunesse; *Canada is still a ~ country*, Le Canada est encore un pays jeune; *~ Mr. X*, le fils X, le jeune X; *The night is still ~*, → La nuit commence à peine; *to make/grow/ ~ again*, rajeunir; [animal] *a ~, one*, un petit. ‖ *n.pl.* les jeunes, [Fam.] la jeunesse; les petits (d'un animal): *with ~*, [en parlant d'un animal], être pleine; *the old and the ~*, les grands et les petits; *the ~ at heart/in mind/*, les jeunes de cœur/d'esprit/. ‖ **younger** ['jʌŋgɚ] *adj. compar.* plus jeunes; cadet: *my ~ sister*, ma sœur cadette; *He is (5 years) ~ than I*, Il est plus jeune que moi (de 5 ans), Il est mon cadet (de 5 ans); *He is 5 years ~ (than I)*, Il a 5 ans de moins (que moi); *He is the ~ of the two*, C'est le plus jeune des deux, [if brothers] C'est le cadet; *Pitt the Younger*, Pitt le jeune; *In my young(er) days*, Dans ma jeunesse. ‖ **youngest** ['jʌŋgəst] *adj. super.* le plus jeune, le benjamin: *She is the ~ (person) in her family/in the class/*, C'est la plus jeune/la benjamine/de sa famille, de la classe. ‖ **youngster** ['jʌŋstɚ] *n.* **1.** enfant *m, f*: *How is your ~ ?*, Comment va votre enfant? **2.** jeune homme *m*, jeune fille *f*; *pl* jeunes (gens), adolescents: *They are just youngsters*, Ce ne sont que des adolescents, Ils sont encore des adolescents; *She is a plucky ~*, C'est une (jeune) fille courageuse.

your [jɚ] *adj. poss.* **1.** (1) votre, vos; (2) ton, ta, tes; (3) votre, vos [for distinction between (1, 2, 3), see YOU]: *Is this ~ book?*, Est-ce (1, 3) votre, (2) ton, livre?, (1, 3) Ce livre vous appartient-il?, (2) C'est à toi, ce livre?; *Where are ~ mother and father?*, Où sont (1, 3) (†Monsieur) votre père et (†Madame) votre mère? **2.** [emphatic] (1, 3) votre, vos . . . à vous, (2) ton, ta, tes . . . à toi: *Bring* YOUR *friend*, (1, 3) Amenez votre ami(e) à vous, (2) Amène ton ami(e) à toi. **3.** [before a dir. obj. when subj. is *you*] (*a*) [natural action of the body] le, la, les: *Raise ~ hand*, (1) Levez la main; (2) Lève la main; (3) *Raise ~ hands*, Levez la main [one hand each]. (*b*) [external action upon the body] (1, 3) vous, (2) te . . . le, la, les: *Wash ~ hands*, (1, 3) Lavez-vous, (2) Lave-toi les mains [both hands each]. **4.** [= one's] son, sa, ses: *You must always watch ~ language*, On doit toujours surveiller son langage. **5.** [ethical] [affectif] le, la, les: *There's ~ modern girl for you*, Voilà bien les jeunes filles modernes! **6.** [jeux, &c.] *Your turn!*, à vous, à toi!

you're [jɚ] = you are [TO BE] [ne pas confondre avec *your* adj. poss.].

yours [jɚz] *pron. poss.* [employé comme attribut, ou du moins sans nom exprimé]. **1.** (1) le vôtre, la vôtre, les vôtres; (2) le tien, la tienne, les tien(ne)s; (3) le/la/vôtre, les vôtres [for distinction between (1, 2, 3) see YOU]: *I lost my book and ~ too*, J'ai perdu mon livre et (1) le vôtre, (2) le tien, (3) le(s) vôtre(s)/aussi; *Our friends and ~ are coming*, Nos ami(e)s et (1, 3) les vôtres, (2) les tien(ne)s/vont venir; *This isn't my book, This book isn't mine; is it ~ ?*, Ce n'est pas mon livre, Ce livre n'est pas le mien; est-ce (1, 3) le vôtre/(2) le tien? [see also 2, next]. **2.** [after the verb être, when the idea of possession is uppermost] (1) à vous, (2) à toi, (3) à vous: *This isn't my book, This book isn't mine; is it ~ ?*, Ce livre n'est pas à moi; est-il (1, 3) à vous/(2) à toi? **3.** [= by you] (1) de vous, (2) de toi, (3) de vous: *Is this idea ~ ?*, Cette idée est-elle de (1, 3) vous/(2) toi? **4.** *A friend of ~*, Un de (1, 3) vos amis, (2) un de tes amis; un ami à (1, 3) vous/(2) toi; *A French friend of ~*, Un Français de vos amis, Un de vos amis français. **5.** *Yours truly, Yours sincerely, &c.* [formule de courtoisie à la fin d'une lettre], Veuillez agréer, Monsieur/Madame/cher(s) ami(s)/, &c., (l'expression de) mes salutations distinguées.

yourself [jɚ'sɛlf] *pl.* **yourselves** [jɚ'sɛlvz] *pron. réfl.* **1.** [renforcement de *you*; emphasizes *you*] (1) vous-même, (2) toi-même, (3) vous-mêmes; (1, 3) vous, (2) toi; soi-même [for distinction between (1, 2, 3), see YOU]: *You said so ~, You ~ said so*, (1) Vous l'avez dit vous-même, C'est vous(-même) qui l'avez dit, (2) Tu l'as dit toi-même, C'est toi(-même) qui l'as dit; *Are you pleased with yourselves?*, Êtes-vous content(e)s de vous(-mêmes)?; *You should always do it ~*, On devrait toujours le faire soi-même. **2.** [compl. dir. ou indir.; dir. or indir. obj.] (1, 3) vous, (2) te: *You must wash ~*, Il faut (1) vous, (2) te, laver; *Did you buy yourselves anything?*, (3) Vous êtes-vous acheté qqch.?

3. [recip.] entre vous: *You can settle it between/among/yourselves,* Vous pouvez régler cela entre vous. **4.** *by yourself,/-ves/ Were you at home* (*all*) *by* ~ *?*, (1) Étiez-vous/(2) Étais-tu/(tout) seul à la maison ?; *Can you finish it by yourselves?*, (3) Pourrez-vous l'achever/tout(es) seul(es), vous-mêmes/? **5.** *You aren't* ~ *today,* Vous n'êtes pas dans votre assiette aujourd'hui.

youth [juwθ] *n.* **1.** jeunesse *f*; adolescence *f* [approx. 14-18]. **2.** jeune homme *m* [approx. 14-25]; adolescent *m* [approx. 14-18]. **3.** les jeunes *m, fpl,* les jeunes gens *mpl*; la jeunesse *f.* || *adj.* de la jeunesse: ~ *movement, hostel,* mouvement, auberge de la jeunesse. || **youthful** [ˈjuwθfḷ] *adj.* jeune; juvénile, de jeunesse: *He looks* ~, Il a l'air jeune; *a* ~ *enthusiasm,* un enthousiasme juvénile, de jeunesse. || **youthfully** [ˈjuwθfəlɪ] *adv.* (se conduire) en, comme un(e), jeune (homme, fille).

you've [juwv] = you have [HAVE].

yowl [jawl] *v. intr.* hurler. || *n.* hurlement *m.*

Yugoslavia [ˌjuwgowˈslævɪə] [Geog.] la Yougoslavie *f.*

Yukon [ˈjuwkɔn] *n.* [Geog.] le Yukon *m.* || **Yukoner** © *n.* habitant *m* du Yukon.

Y.W.C.A. [*abr.* = *Young Women's Christian Association*].

Z

Z, z [zɛd] *pl.* **Z's, z's** *n.* Z, z *m.*

zeal [zijl] *n.* zèle *m,* ardeur *f*; dévouement *m,* enthousiasme *m*: *He feels full of* ~, Il se sent plein de zèle/d'ardeur/; *He went at the problem with* (*great*) ~, Il a attaqué le problème avec (beaucoup de) zèle/ardeur/; *His* ~ *for lost causes is well known,* Son dévouement aux causes perdues est bien connu. || **zealous** [ˈzɛləs] *adj.* zélé, enthousiaste, dévoué: *That young man is overly* ~, Ce jeune homme veut faire du zèle. || **zealously** [ˈzɛləslɪ] *adv.* avec zèle.

zebra [ˈzɛbɹə] *n.* zèbre *m.*

zenith [ˈzɛnɪθ] *n.* zénith *m*; [Fig.] comble *m.*

zero [ˈzijɚow] *n.* zéro *m*: *It's twenty* (*degrees*)/*below, above*/~, Il fait vingt (degrés)/au-dessous, au-dessus/de zéro; ~ *hour,* → l'heure H.

zest [zɛst] *n.* zeste *m*; [Fig.] piquant *m*; goût *m* (*for,* pour).

zigzag [ˈzɪgˌzæg] *n.* zigzag *m.* || *adj. & adv.* (marcher) en zigzag, (chemin) en lacet. || *v. intr. & tr.* [-gg-] zigzaguer, faire des zigzags, aller en zigzag; [éclair] sillonner: *The car zigzagged* (*back and forth*) *along the road,* L'auto s'en allait en zigzaguant.

zinc [zɪŋk] *n.* zinc *m.*

Zion (Mount) [ˈzajən] *n.* [Geog.] Sion (la colline de).

zipper [ˌzɪpɚ] [également **zip fastener**] *n.* fermeture *f* éclair: *a* ~ *bag,* un sac à fermeture éclair. || *adj.* de à/à/fermeture éclair: *a* ~ *bag,* un sac à fermeture éclair; *a* ~ *factory,* une manufacture de fermetures éclair.

zodiac [ˈzowdɪˌæk] *n.* zodiaque *m.*

zone [zown] *n.* zone *f,* district *m*: (*Quiet*) *Hospital* ~, → Hôpital, silence.

zoo [zuw] *abr.* [= *zoological gardens*] *n.* zoo *m*; jardin *m* zoologique. || **zoologist** [ˌzowˈɔlədʒəst] *n.* zoologiste *m.* || **zoology** [ˌzowˈɔlədʒɪ] *n.* zoologie *f.*

PRINTED AND BOUND IN ENGLAND BY
HAZELL WATSON AND VINEY LTD
AYLESBURY AND SLOUGH

TABLEAU DES SYMBOLES

I. VOYELLES

N	S	M/C	
1	ɪ	[fɪl]	fill
2	ɛ	[fɛl]	fell
3	æ	['fælow]	fallow
4	ɑ	['fɑlow]	follow
5	ɔ	[fɔl]	fall
6	ʊ	[fʊl]	full
7	ʌ	['ʌðɚ]	other
8	ə	['sowfə]	sofa
9	ɚ	['ɛvɚ]	ever

II. DIPHTONGUES

N	S	M/C	
10	ij	[fijl]	feel
11	ej	[fejl]	fail
12	aj	[fajl]	file
13	oj	[fojl]	foil
14	uw	[fuwl]	fool
15	aw	[fawl]	foul
16	ow	[fowl]	foal
17	ɛɚ	[fɛɚ]	fare
18	ɑɚ	[fɑɚ]	far
19	ɔɚ	[ə'kɔɚd]	accord

III. CONSONNES SYLLABIQUES

N	S	M/C	
20	l̩	['kændl̩]	candle
21	n̩	['sevn̩]	seven

N = Numéro du mot-clef

S = Symbole

M/C = Mots-clefs

PHONÉTIQUES ANGLAIS

IV. CONSONNES

N	S	M/C	
22	p	[pɪl]	pill
23	b	[bɪl]	bill
24	t	[tɪl]	till
25	d	[dɪl]	dill
26	k	[kɪl]	kill
27	g	[gɪld]	gild
28	s	[sɪl]	sill
29	z	[zɪjl]	zeal
30	f	[fɪl]	fill
31	v	[vijl]	veal
32	ʃ	[ʃɛl]	shell
33	ʒ	['mɛʒɚ]	measure
34	tʃ	[tʃɪl]	chill
35	dʒ	[dʒɪl]	Jill
36	θ	[θɪk]	thick
37	ð	[ðow]	though
38	l	[lɪt]	lit
39	m	[mɪl]	mill
40	n	[nɪl]	nil
41	ŋ	[sɪŋ]	sing
42	h	[hɪl]	hill
43	w	[wɪl]	will
44	j	[jɛl]	yell
45	ɹ	[ɹɪl]	rill

V. AUTRES SYMBOLES

46	ʹ	Indique l'accent principal qui tombe sur la syllabe: [ə'gɛn], *again*.
47	ˌ	Indique l'accent secondaire: ['tɚmɪˌnejt], *terminate*.